CRITICAL VALUES OF *t*

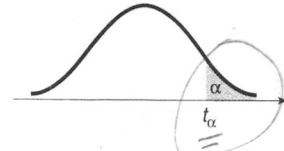

DEGREES OF FREEDOM	$t_{.100}$	$t_{.050}$ 90%	$t_{.025}$ 95%	$t_{.010}$	$t_{.005}$ 99%
1	3.078	6.314	12.706	31.821	63.657
2	1.886	2.920	4.303	6.965	9.925
3	1.638	2.353	3.182	4.541	5.841
4	1.533	2.132	2.776	3.747	4.604
5	1.476	2.015	2.571	3.365	4.032
6	1.440	1.943	2.447	3.143	3.707
7	1.415	1.895	2.365	2.998	3.499
8	1.397	1.860	2.306	2.896	3.355
9	1.383	1.833	2.262	2.821	3.250
10	1.372	1.812	2.228	2.764	3.169
11	1.363	1.796	2.201	2.718	3.106
12	1.356	1.782	2.179	2.681	3.055
13	1.350	1.771	2.160	2.650	3.012
14	1.345	1.761	2.145	2.624	2.977
15	1.341	1.753	2.131	2.602	2.947
16	1.337	1.746	2.120	2.583	2.921
17	1.333	1.740	2.110	2.567	2.898
18	1.330	1.734	2.101	2.552	2.878
19	1.328	1.729	2.093	2.539	2.861
20	1.325	1.725	2.086	2.528	2.845
21	1.323	1.721	2.080	2.518	2.831
22	1.321	1.717	2.074	2.508	2.819
23	1.319	1.714	2.069	2.500	2.808
24	1.318	1.711	2.064	2.492	2.797
25	1.316	1.708	2.060	2.485	2.787
26	1.315	1.706	2.056	2.479	2.779
27	1.314	1.703	2.052	2.473	2.771
28	1.313	1.701	2.048	2.467	2.763
29	1.311	1.699	2.045	2.462	2.756
30	1.310	1.697	2.042	2.457	2.750
35	1.306	1.690	2.030	2.438	2.724
40	1.303	1.684	2.021	2.423	2.704
50	1.299	1.676	2.009	2.403	2.678
60	1.296	1.671	2.000	2.390	2.660
120	1.289	1.658	1.980	2.358	2.617
∞	1.282	1.645	1.960	2.326	2.576

From M. Merrington, "Table of Percentage Points of the *t*-Distribution," *Biometrika*, 1941, 32, 300.
Reproduced by permission of the *Biometrika* trustees.

5TH EDITION

INTRODUCTION TO BUSINESS STATISTICS

A COMPUTER INTEGRATED, DATA ANALYSIS APPROACH

ALAN H. KVANLI

ROBERT J. PAVUR

C. STEPHEN GUYNES

UNIVERSITY OF NORTH TEXAS

South-Western College Publishing
Thomson Learning

Australia • Canada • Denmark • Japan • Mexico • New Zealand • Philippines
Puerto Rico • Singapore • South Africa • Spain • United Kingdom • United States

Introduction to Business Statistics: A Computer Integrated, Data Analysis Approach, 5e,
by Alan H. Kvanli, Robert J. Pavur, and C. Stephen Guynes

Publisher: Dave Shaut
Acquisitions Editor: Charles McCormick, Jr.
Developmental Editor: Atietie O. Tonwe
Marketing Manager: Joseph A. Sabatino
Production Editor: Kara ZumBahlen
Manufacturing Coordinator: Dana Began Schwartz
Internal Design: Jennifer Martin-Lambert
Cover Design: Michael H. Stratton
Cover Photo: FPG International LLC
Photography Manager: Cary Benbow
Production House: Shepherd, Inc.
Compositor: Shepherd, Inc.
Printer: WestGroup

Printed in the United States of America
3 4 5 02 01 00

For more information contact South-Western College Publishing, 5101 Madison Road,
Cincinnati, Ohio, 45227 or find us on the Internet at http://www.swcollege.com

For permission to use material from this text or product, contact us by
• **telephone: 1-800-730-2214**
• **fax: 1-800-730-2215**
• **web: http://www.thomsonrights.com**

Library of Congress Cataloging-in-Publication Data

Kvanli, Alan H.
   Introduction to business statistics : a computer integrated
approach / Alan H. Kvanli, Robert J. Pavur, C. Stephen Guynes. —
5th ed.
      p.   cm.
   Includes index.
   ISBN 0–324–01207–1 (package)
   ISBN 0–324–01308–6 (text only)
   ISBN 0–324–01309–4 (CD only)
   1. Commercial statistics—Data processing. 2. Statistics—Data
processing. I. Pavur, Robert J. II. Guynes, C. Stephen (Carl Stephen)
III. Title.
HF1017.K83   2000   99-24430
519.5'0285—dc21

ABOUT THE AUTHORS

ALAN H. KVANLI

Dr. Alan H. Kvanli is Associate Professor of Management Science. His research is primarily in the areas of statistical auditing, operations research techniques applied to multi-year financial planning, and product pricing/cost analysis. His current research examines issues resulting from highly skewed audit populations. For the past ten years he has served as statistical consultant for the audit staff within the Department of Health and Human Services (Washington, D. C.). While employed in industry, Dr. Kvanli was a systems analyst at Rockwell International and was involved in the analysis of a mainframe computer system. He also held a staff position in corporate financial planning within Texas Instruments, Inc. He has a doctorate in Mathematical Statistics from Southern Methodist University and a Master's degree in Mathematics from the University of Kansas.

ROBERT J. PAVUR

Dr. Robert J. Pavur is Full Professor of Management Science. His specializations are multiple regression analysis and experimental design. Research interests include alternate test procedures in multivariate analysis of variance designs when standard assumptions do not hold. His current research project is investigating the behavior of multivariate discriminant analysis procedures. He has served as the President of the Southwest Decision Sciences Institute. He received a doctorate degree in Mathematical and Applied Statistics and a Master of Science degree from Texas Tech University.

C. STEPHEN GUYNES

Dr. C. Stephen Guynes is Full Professor of Business Computer Information Systems. His prior research topics included an empirical investigation of computer security practices and an investigation of privacy issues in a computer-based environment. His most recent research efforts have been directed in the areas of data administration and database management. He has consulted with many of the largest banks in the country in the area of trust performance systems. He is currently consulting with the Internal Revenue Service in the areas of information systems training and software evaluation. He received a doctorate in Quantitative Analysis from Texas Tech University.

BRIEF CONTENTS

CONTENTS

PREFACE

In the previous edition of this textbook, our goal was to make the text more data interactive with additional emphasis placed on the interpretation of data and statistical graphs. With this edition, we are reacting to the increased emphasis of late on the use of spreadsheet statistics. We approached this concept rather hesitantly at first (after all, a spreadsheet package, such as Microsoft® Excel, is *not* a statistical package) but as the project began to take form, we became quite enthusiastic about the ability to truly teach the application of statistics using such an approach. We were able to overcome any statistical shortcomings of Microsoft Excel by constructing a number of Excel macros that allow the user to perform a complex statistical task on a very large set of data with the click of a mouse button. What we did *not* want was a textbook that contained an endless stream of Enter this in cell . . . , Drag this cell down through cell . . . , Enter this formula in cell. . . . In short, we wanted this textbook to provide an understanding of statistics, not serve as an Excel manual.

With the textbook is an accompanying CD containing this set of Excel macros, some 150 data sets, and the two databases at the end of the text. The flavor of the previous edition was maintained in the chapter exercises, whereby students could first learn the mechanics of a new technique, see their application, and finally apply this procedure to several large data sets using the revised set of computer exercises. We have kept the Minitab statistical package in this edition but the within-chapter illustrations are now carried out using Excel and the steps necessary to carry out a windows-based Minitab analysis are explained at the end of each chapter.

As mentioned in the preface to the earlier editions, we feel that a statistics text that *fully* integrates the use of computers with statistics is a necessity in today's marketplace. This edition has retained the "non-intimidating" approach to describing the concepts and applications of statistics while giving students the opportunity to observe and actually carry out computer-generated solutions using a spreadsheet or statistical package. The text has once again been designed so that those requiring or desiring a more traditional calculator-based approach will find an abundance of exercises and examples that can be solved in this manner.

The text is intended to be an undergraduate or M.B.A. introduction to basic statistics. We assume that the student has a good understanding of basic algebra. Reference is made on a few occasions to calculus applications, but no calculus background is required to read the material. The reading level is interesting and easy-to-understand without sacrificing any credibility in the descriptive material. It is a non-mathematical, but not a "black box," approach to teaching the appreciation and application of statistics. We've included a large number of new examples to better guide the student to an understanding of statistical concepts and applications. These examples include more realistic illustrations, many taken from the process/quality improvement area.

TO THE INSTRUCTOR

This text can be used for either a one- or two-semester introduction to business statistics. Suggested material to be covered in the first semester would be chapters 1 through 8, in order, which concludes with an introduction to hypothesis testing. Chapters 9 and 10 could be included in a second-semester course, along with those remaining chapters that you feel are particularly relevant and of interest to your students. We have found that the chapter on Quality Improvement (Chapter 12) and the chapter on time series decomposition and index numbers (Chapter 16) can be included in either the first or second semester since they are largely descriptive in nature.

The text has intentionally been written in somewhat of a conversational style to make it less intimidating to the student. Our intent was for the student to read the text; not just use it as a source of homework exercises.

The text fully integrates the use of Microsoft Excel (a spreadsheet package) and Minitab (an easy to use, but very powerful statistical package). The featured package throughout all of the chapter examples and many of the exercises is Excel and corresponding Minitab descriptions are contained at the ends of chapters—a feature unique to this text. We have fully integrated Excel and Minitab throughout the text, making it possible for you to include computer usage as part of your course without having to spend a great deal of time explaining the mechanics of either package. For instructors who wish to avoid computer usage, the text allows for a calculator-based approach—most of the exercises do not require a computer package and contain reasonably sized data sets.

OTHER FEATURES OF THE TEXT INCLUDE

- **An introductory case study at the start of each chapter.** The intent here is to describe an actual situation explaining WHAT type of problem this chapter addresses and WHY this chapter is important. The case study questions at the end of each chapter return to the case study scenario and ask in-depth questions that require an understanding beyond the number crunching level. All case studies have been revised in this edition.

- **A Look Back/Introduction at the start of each chapter to tie the chapter to the relevant material from the preceding chapters.** Each chapter closes with a summary section containing the key words (in bold-face print) introduced in the chapter and a summary of the formulas.

- **An abundance of exercises (over 1,300) using realistic business situations.** The exercises within each section are split into UNDERSTANDING THE MECHANICS, APPLYING THE NEW CONCEPTS (using actual applications in a business setting), and USING THE COMPUTER (using data sets from the accompanying CD).

- **A full treatment of the use of p-values to make statistical decisions.** These are derived and discussed throughout the entire text.

- **Three continuous distributions** (normal, uniform, and exponential), along with four discrete distributions (uniform, binomial, hypergeometric, and Poisson).

- **Various sampling procedures** (including stratified and cluster sampling), along with corresponding sample estimators and confidence intervals, as separate sections in two of the earlier chapters. In this way, you are able to cover this often-neglected material without having to spend the time to cover an entire chapter.

- **Separate chapters for inference regarding normal parameters (μ, σ) and inference on a binomial parameter (p).** Chapters 7, 8, and 9 are strictly devoted to normal inference, both one population (Chapters 7 and 8) and two populations (Chapter 9). Binomial inference (one and two populations) is covered in Chapter 10.

- **An entire chapter devoted to forecasting using time series data (Chapter 17).** It includes several exponential smoothing models and discusses the pros and cons of using multiple regression versus time series modeling techniques for such data. The Excel macros supplied on the accompanying CD make time series decomposition (Chapter 16) and time series forecasting astonishingly simple while at the same time providing a great deal of numerical and graphical output.

- **An entire chapter on statistical decision theory.** This chapter is placed near the end of the text (Chapter 18) but can be covered at any time, including the first semester, if desired.

- **A revised database** (1,140 observations) containing data on family income, family size, total indebtedness, monthly utility expenditures, and other variables. There is also a second database containing 1,000 observations selected from companies listed in the Moody's Investor Service Industrial Manual. Both data sets are contained in the accompanying CD.
- **Appendices that provide an introduction to Microsoft Excel and Minitab.**

NEW TO THE 5TH EDITION ARE

- **The use of Microsoft Excel as the featured package within each chapter.**
- **An extensive library of Excel add-ins (macros)** that perform *every* analytical technique discussed in the text. Microsoft's Excel's built-in toolbox and function set provide many standard statistical functions/procedures and so the add-in macros were intended to complement and enhance the standard Excel tools.
- **Larger emphasis on data and graphical interpretation within the chapter examples, exercises, and case studies.**
- **Examples within each chapter that allow the student to see how Excel can be used to analyze a problem and not merely crunch numbers that summarize the data.** These chapter examples contain the Excel output and discussion, but more importantly, the instructor and/or student can run this example using the data contained on the accompanying CD.
- **A discussion in Chapter 7 on constructing a confidence interval for a population mean using a bootstrap procedure.** An Excel macro was also written to carry out the rather extensive calculations using this procedure.
- **The chapter on Quality Improvement has been updated considerably,** including the revised scoring system for the Malcolm Baldrige National Quality Award and a discussion of ISO 9000 registration.
- **The construction of a regression line through the medians.** This alternative to the least squares linear regression line is included in the chapter on Nonparametric Statistics (Chapter 19).
- **All new case studies,** designed to develop an international perspective, and provide the student with more in-depth applications in the quality improvement area.
- **Finding areas under any probability curve using Microsoft Excel and Minitab.** This can easily eliminate the use of tables for homework assignments and allows for exact calculation of p-values.

ANCILLARY TEACHING AND LEARNING MATERIALS

Prepared by Wilke English, the *Study Guide* (ISBN 0–324–01313–2) will provide the student with important supplementary study and review materials. It contains self-testing questions and answers and will guide the student through applications of the chapter material. To order, please contact your local bookstore or contact Thomson Learning directly at 800–347–7707.

The *Instructor's Resource CD-ROM* (ISBN 0–324–01311–6) is available to adopters from the Thomson Learning Academic Resource Center at 800–423–0663 or through www.swcollege.com. The *Instructor's Resource CD-ROM* includes:

- **Instructor's Manual**—The Instructor's Manual contains solutions to all exercises and case studies presented within the text.
- **PowerPoint Presentation Slides**—The PowerPoint slides contain the important concepts introduced within each chapter and are designed to assist instructors in creating even more visually stimulating lectures.
- **Test Bank and Thomson Learning Testing Tools™**—The test bank includes true/false, completion exercises, and additional application problems. Thomson Learning Testing Tools™ is an easy-to-use test creation software compatible with Microsoft® Windows. Instructors can add, edit, store, and print materials. Instructors can also create and administer tests online—using the Internet, a local-area network (LAN), or a wide-area network (WAN).

We certainly hope that this text will meet your classroom needs. If you care to offer comments and suggestions, we would like to hear from you. Address any correspondence to Al Kvanli, College of Business Administration, University of North Texas, Denton, Texas 76203 (email: *kvanli@unt.edu*).

TO THE STUDENT

We believe you will find this text to be a readable, easily understood treatment of business statistics. This textbook allows you to learn the application of statistics by letting the computer carry out the heavy number crunching, using either Microsoft Excel (a popular spreadsheet package) or Minitab (a windows-based and easy-to-use statistical package). Our intent is to carefully explain the various statistical concepts and strategies without getting bogged down in unnecessary mathematics. We have also provided you with a set of Excel add-in macros on the accompanying CD that you can easily store and use in your home or office version of Excel. These click-and-go procedures make using Excel to carry out statistical analyses extremely simple and maybe, even fun!

We have included many examples and Excel illustrations within each chapter that allow you to see how each procedure works. Each chapter opener will consist of an actual application of the chapter material illustrating what you'll be able to accomplish upon completion of the chapter and hopefully stimulating your interest a bit. Also at the beginning of each chapter you will find a Look Back/Introduction section which will set up the chapter and tie it in with the previous chapters. At the end of each chapter is a summary containing all of the key definitions and concepts introduced within the chapter, along with a summary of the formulas. At the end of the book you will find introductions to both Microsoft Excel and Minitab. There is a CD accompanying the textbook containing the set of Excel add-in macros, over 150 data sets, and two large databases listed at the end of the text (Appendices E and F).

As the old adage goes, "practice makes perfect," and mastering statistics is no exception. To this end, we have included a large number of exercises to help you along the road to perfection. Data entry for large data sets is never an enjoyable experience, so we have included all of the data sets for those exercises requiring a computer on the accompanying CD. Also, you will find the solutions to the odd-numbered exercises at the end of the text. A study guide, which contains additional examples along with their solutions, has also been prepared. These solutions take you step-by-step through the applications of the various statistical techniques with many blanks where you supply the missing number or word.

ACKNOWLEDGMENTS

We are very much indebted to the people who helped in the production and preparation of this text. Ms. Kellie Keeling was extremely helpful in the preparation of the Excel macros and we would not have completed this project without her wonderful assistance. Mr. Ben Moore lent his expertise in the preparation and solution of many of the chapter exercises containing a quoted source (the real world exercises) and coming up with potential topics for the introductory and closing case studies. Beverly Kenney has once again done a superb job of putting her word processing skills to work on the *Instructor's Manual*.

Wilke English has once again authored a very helpful and entertaining study guide to accompany the text. We feel that his study guide has been (and will continue to be) a big plus for the textbook and we are most appreciative for having his time and talent. Many thanks to George Neimanis who put together a very complete (and accurate) test bank. George is a new member of the team and was a real pleasure to work with. We would have been unable to complete this project without the timely and highly professional help of Wade Jackson who prepared the set of PowerPoint presentations that accompany the textbook.

In this edition, we received exceptional editorial support from the folks at South-Western College Publishing. Charles McCormick was very instrumental in encouraging, guiding, and assembling this entire project. Atietie Tonwe was most helpful in keeping track of the million and one details and lining up top-notch people to assist in our efforts. Kara ZumBahlen kept this (at times overwhelming) project on course and helped the authors keep a positive attitude as time and energy were dwindling.

Last, but certainly not least, we would like to thank the reviewers who had a multitude of excellent suggestions for this edition. We took every suggestion very seriously and we hope that you can see your contributions in this latest edition. The following list contains the names and affiliations of these individuals:

Stuart Warnock
University of Southern Colorado

Robert Carver
Stonehill College

Lee McClain
Western Washington University

Alan Humphrey
University of Rhode Island

Barbara McKiney
Western Michigan University

Richard McGowan
Boston College

Steve Yourstone
University of New Mexico

Jeff Jarrett
University of Rhode Island

John Charalambakis
Ashbury College

Don Gren
Salt Lake Community College

David Pentico
Duquesne University

David Tufte
University of New Orleans

Virginia Fisher
Albuquerque TVI Community College

Kenneth Lawrence
New Jersey Institute of Technology

DEDICATION

Elaine and Justin
(A. H. K.)

Gail, Robert, Michael, and Gregory
(R. J. P.)

Elana, Holly, Stephen, and Darin
(C. S. G.)

A First Look at Statistics and Data Collection

Statistics in Action: Why So Many Polls?

Every functional area of business needs to collect data to gain insight into projections for the future or information for decision making. In accounting, a survey could provide an estimate of the proportion of overstatements on balance sheets; in marketing, a survey could reveal how people respond to an advertisement; in finance, a poll could reveal how retirement-age adults are allocating their money in IRAs; in information systems, a survey could give insight into the types of database software that users find to be the most user-friendly; and in operations management, a survey could explain how workers feel about being empowered to make decisions regarding the manufacturing of a product.

Polls are conducted frequently by major newspapers. For example, the *Wall Street Journal* wrote the following on how one of its recent polls was conducted for its newspaper: "The *Wall Street Journal*/NBC News poll was based on nationwide telephone interviews of 2,006 adults. The sample was drawn from 520 randomly selected geographic points in the continental U.S. Each region was represented in proportion to its population. Households were selected by a method that gave all telephone numbers, listed and unlisted, an equal chance of being included."

In the summer of 1998, the Metro Poll conducted by Virginia Commonwealth University (VCU) asked a randomly selected sample of 1,206 residents of Richmond, Henrico, Chesterfield, and Hanover counties how serious they believed crime to be. The poll was conducted by telephone over a three-week period.

"There have been some rather significant changes in residents' opinion about crime in their jurisdictions over the last 12 months," said Michael D. Pratt, professor of economics and director of VCU's Center for Urban Development. A year ago, 77 percent of the Chesterfield residents polled felt crime in their neighborhoods was not very serious or not serious at all, compared with 83 percent who feel that way this year. Along with residents feeling less threatened by crime, the poll showed that resi-

dents generally feel good about the job their police departments are doing to meet neighborhood needs.

Polls such as the Metro Poll and the *Wall Street Journal* poll give decision makers quick feedback on how a general population responds to current happenings. The data collected from these surveys can be analyzed using a variety of statistical techniques. The statistical analysis allows managers and officials to make conclusions that can have local or national implications.

When you have completed this chapter, you will be able to examine the results of a poll and discuss such questions as

- What is the **population** of interest?
- Was a **random sample** used in the poll?
- What type of data were obtained?
- How "strong" are the data?

A First Look at Statistics

Many people probably think a statistician is someone who figures batting averages during a baseball game broadcast. You might wonder how we can devote an entire textbook to compiling numbers and making simple calculations. Surely it cannot be that complicated!

Statistics is the science comprising rules and procedures for collecting, describing, analyzing, and interpreting numerical data. The applications of statistics are evident everywhere. Hardly a day goes by in which we are not bombarded by such statements as:

> Results show that Crest toothpaste helps prevent tooth decay.

> The chance of rain tomorrow is 30%.

> The state court has ruled that the XYZ Company is guilty of age discrimination in its termination procedure.

> Smoking causes lung cancer, heart disease, emphysema, and may complicate pregnancy.

Or how about:

> American companies are continuing to place more emphasis on quality improvement in an attempt to offer better products that can be delivered on time at less cost.

Besides using statistics to inform the public, statisticians help businesses make forecasts for planning and decision making.

The use of statistics began as early as the first century A.D., when governments used a census of land and properties for tax purposes. Census taking was gradually extended to include such local events as births, deaths, and marriages. The *science* of statistics, which uses a sample to predict or estimate some characteristics of a population, began its development during the nineteenth century.

Use of statistical methods has undergone a dramatic change as computers and powerful calculators have entered the research environment. Companies can store and manipulate large collections of data, and once-formidable statistical calculations are reduced to a few keystrokes. Sophisticated computer software allows users merely to specify the type of analysis desired and input the necessary data. This textbook concentrates on two of these software packages: Excel (a spreadsheet package developed by Microsoft) and MINITAB (a statistical computer package originally designed at Penn State University specifically for students).

Although most statistical functions are performed by professional statisticians, it may be your job to draw a valid conclusion from a statistical report. In addition, you may be asked to perform a statistical analysis. Although you may elect to obtain outside assistance, you will need to know when to consult a statistician and how to tell him or her what you need.

So welcome to the world of uncertainty. Statistical methods offer you a way of evaluating an uncertain future by using limited information to assess the likelihood of future events occurring. But despite the best intent of statistical measurements, it's important to remember that an event with a high chance of occurring may, in fact, not occur at all. Anyone who has changed plans because of a 90% chance of rainy weather only to sit home on a sunny day can attest to this fact.

1.1 USES OF STATISTICS IN BUSINESS

Modern businesses have more need to predict future operations than did those of the past, when businesses were smaller. Small-business managers often can solve problems simply through personal contact. Managers in large corporations, however, must try to summarize and analyze the various data available to them. They do this by using modern statistical methods.

Areas of business that rely on statistical information and techniques include:

1. *Quality control.* Statistical quality-control procedures assure high product quality and enhance productivity.
2. *Product planning.* Statistical methods are used to analyze economic factors and business trends and to prepare detailed sales budgets, inventory-control systems, and realistic sales quotas.
3. *Forecasting.* Statistics are used to predict sales, productivity, and employment trends.
4. *Yearly reports.* Annual reports for stockholders are based on statistical treatment of the many cost and revenue factors analyzed by the business comptroller.
5. *Personnel management.* Statistical procedures are used in such areas as age- and sex-discrimination lawsuits, performance appraisals, and workforce-size planning.
6. *Market research.* Corporations that develop and market products or services use sophisticated statistical procedures to describe and analyze consumer purchasing behavior.

1.2 SOME BASIC DEFINITIONS

Statistics has specialized definitions for terms crucial to statistical reasoning. In **descriptive statistics,** you collect and describe data. If you analyze the data and make decisions or estimates based on information obtained from the data, you are using **inferential statistics.**

Descriptive statistics are used to describe a large set of data. For example, you can reduce the set of data values to one or more single numbers, such as the average of 150 test scores, or you can construct a graph that represents some feature of the data.

You use inferential statistics to form conclusions about a large group—a population—by collecting a portion of it—a sample. Thus, a **population** is the set of all possible measurements (generally pertaining to a group of people or objects) that is of interest. A **sample** is the portion of the population from which information is gathered.

Another way to distinguish between a population and a sample is to view a population as the set of values you would obtain if you observed a particular **variable** indefinitely. For example, this variable could be the total of two dice, and the *population* would consist of the dice totals when the two dice are rolled time and time again. To gain insight into this population, you could observe this variable, say, 100 times; that is, roll the dice 100 times and record the resulting totals. This set of **observations** of the corresponding variable (total of two dice) results in a *sample*. Consequently, you can view a sample as a set of values obtained by observing a variable of interest a finite number of times. Such variables are actually called **random variables** and will be explored further in Chapters 5 and 6.

The analyst decides what the population is. Typically, the population is so large that it would be nearly impossible to obtain information about every item in it. Instead, we obtain information about selected population members and attempt to draw a conclusion about all members. In other words, we attempt to infer something about the population using information about only some of the members of this population.

To make an early prediction of the election results for governor of California, for example, analysts could use a sample of voters leaving the voting booths, as illustrated in Figure 1.1. The population is all the votes cast in the election. To make a valid statistical inference using a sample, it is crucial that the sample **represent** the population; that is, the values in the sample must be representative (typical) of values in the population. One way to make sure the sample is representative is to collect a sample of size *n*, where each set of *n* people has the same chance of being selected for the sample. This is a **simple random sample** (Figure 1.1). It is akin to drawing names out of a hat; each name in the hat

FIGURE 1.1
Population versus a sample.

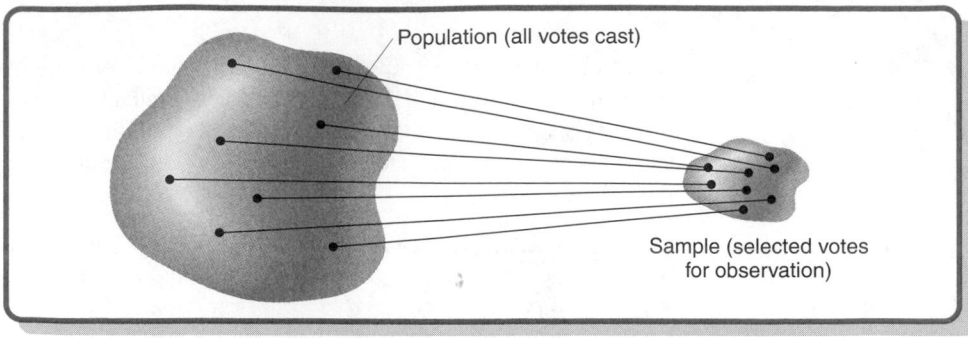

has the same chance of being pulled out. Thus, if our population is all votes cast on the day of the gubernatorial election, a sample of votes cast in only one city would not be representative, because we would have no guarantee that these votes would represent the votes of the entire state. A random sample obtained across the entire state would better represent this population.

As another illustration, assume that Calcatron, a producer of electronic calculators, orders 50,000 components from GLC. Calcatron instructs GLC that they will accept the shipment if an outside laboratory that randomly selects 100 components from the batch finds that fewer than three are defective. Calcatron relies on inferential statistics; they infer that the population of components is of satisfactory quality if the sample is satisfactory. Note that it is possible that the sample could contain fewer than three defective components even if the population contains, say, 80% defective parts. Whenever we attempt to infer something about a population from a sample, there is always a chance of drawing an incorrect conclusion. The only way of being 100% sure is to list the entire population. Such a sample is called a **census.**

In the Calcatron example, there are two proportions of interest. The first proportion, the proportion of defective components in the *population,* is referred to as a **parameter.** The second proportion, the proportion of defective components in the *sample,* is referred to as a **statistic.** In general, any value describing a population (such as the average or a particular proportion) is a parameter. Parameters typically are unknown and are estimated using the corresponding statistic derived from a statistical sample. In the chapters to follow we will examine a number of sample statistics and their corresponding population parameters.

1.3 DISCRETE AND CONTINUOUS NUMERICAL DATA

Proper use of numerical data can be a great aid in making a critical decision. However, using an improper technique or "bad data" can lead you down the wrong path. Generally, the technique we use to analyze data in statistics depends on the nature of the data. We can distinguish between two types of numerical data.

How do the following two sets of numbers differ?

3, 5, 2, 1, 4, 4, 3, 5, 5, 1, 2, 4
4.31, 11.62, 5.37, 1.55, 3.71, 6.88, 7.23, 9.52, 2.36, 7.42, 6.11, 4.85

The primary difference is that the values in the first data set consist of *counting numbers,* or *integers.* Such data are **discrete.** For example, these data may be the coded responses from 12 people who answered a particular question in a marketing survey where 1 = strongly agree, 2 = agree, 3 = uncertain, 4 = disagree, and 5 = strongly disagree. Note that discrete data may contain a decimal point. Nevertheless, discrete data have *gaps in* their possible values. For example, if you throw a single die twice and record the average of the two throws, the possible values are 1, 1.5, 2, 2.5, 3, 3.5, 4, 4.5, 5, 5.5, and 6. If you repeatedly averaged two throws of the die, you would obtain discrete data.

Examples of discrete data that have integer values are the number of automobiles that arrive at a drive-up window over a 5-minute period, the number of children in your family, and the total of the two numbers appearing on a throw of two dice. Note that although the first two have infinite (theoretically, at least) possible values, the data are discrete. Your family cannot have 2.5 children.

Now consider the second data set. These data might represent the weights of 12 parcels received at a post office. A list of all the possible values of package weights would be long—if our scale were completely accurate, the list would be infinite and any value would be possible. Such data are **continuous:** *any value* over some particular range is possible. There are no gaps in possible values for continuous data. For example, although we may say Sandra is 5.5 feet tall, we mean her height is about 5.5 feet. In fact, it might be 5.50372 feet. Height data are continuous. Or consider the contents of a coffee cup filled by a vending machine. Will the machine release exactly 6 ounces every time? Certainly not. In fact, if you were to observe the machine fill five such cups and measure the contents to the nearest .001 ounce, you might observe values of 6.031, 5.932, 5.871, 6.353, and 5.612 ounces. Here again, any value between, say, 5.5 ounces and 6.5 ounces is possible: these are continuous data. *Data such as weights, heights, age (actual), and time are generally continuous data and will be used in the examples in the chapters to follow.*

It is important to remember that *discrete data* can be the result of observing a *continuous variable.* For example, actual age is a continuous variable, but if a recorded age is the age at the last birthday, the data will be discrete. Very often, measurements on a continuous variable (such as height in inches) result in discrete data. However, discrete data can also be the result of observing a discrete variable, such as the number of traffic tickets a person has received during the past three years.

1.4 LEVEL OF MEASUREMENT FOR NUMERICAL DATA

In addition to classifying numerical data as discrete or continuous, we can also classify these data according to their level of measurement. We will discuss them in order of strength, beginning with the weakest. **Nominal data** are really not numerical at all but are merely labels or assigned values. Examples include: gender (1 = male, 2 = female), manufacturer of automobile (1 = General Motors, 2 = Ford, 3 = Chrysler), or color of eyes (1 = blue, 2 = green, 3 = brown). Assigning a numerical code to such data is merely a convenience so that, for example, one can store the information in a computer. Therefore, it makes no sense to perform calculations with such numbers, such as finding their average. What would it mean to claim that "the average eye color is 2.73"? This statement is meaningless. Generally, we are interested in the **proportion** of such data in each category. Consider Calcatron's shipment, in which each component is either defective or not defective. We could assign the code 1 = defective, 0 = not defective. The parameter of interest here is p, where p = proportion of defective components in the population of 50,000 components. If Calcatron believes p is too large, they will not accept the shipment. We will consider what is "too large" in Chapter 10.

Ordinal data can be arranged in order such as worst to best or F to A (grades on an exam). A classic example of ordinal data is the result of a cross-country race, where ten people compete and 1 = the fastest (the winner), 2 = the runner-up, and so on, with 10 = the slowest. Here, the *order* of the values is important (3 finished before 4) but the *difference* of the values is not. For example, $2 - 1 = 1$ and $10 - 9 = 1$, but this does not imply that 1 and 2 were just as close in the final results as were 9 and 10.

The difference between values of **interval data** *does* have meaning. It is meaningful to add and average such data. The classic example is *temperature,* where it is true that the difference in heat between 60°F and 61°F is the same as that between 80°F and 81°F. Many of the techniques used to analyze data in statistics require data that are at least of this strength.

Ratio data differ from interval data in that there is a definite *zero point,* which indicates that nothing exists for the variable being measured. To decide if your data are interval or ratio, ask yourself whether twice the value is twice the strength. For example, is

TABLE 1.1   Summary of data levels of measurement.

| | LEVEL OF MEASUREMENT | | | |
Property	Nominal	Ordinal	Interval	Ratio
Order of data is meaningful	N	Y	Y	Y
Difference between data values is meaningful	N	N	Y	Y
Zero point represents total absence	N	N	N	Y

NOIR

100°F twice as hot as 50°F? The answer is no, so these data are interval. Is a 4-acre field twice as large as a 2-acre field? The answer is yes, so these are ratio data. Here the zero point is a field of 0 acres. An important distinction between interval and ratio data is that for interval data, a value of zero (such as 0°F) is an arbitrary point and does not reflect an absence of the characteristic of interest (such as temperature). Typically, data consisting of areas, counts, volumes, and weights are ratio data. These four levels of measurement are summarized in Table 1.1.

COMMENTS

1. When deciding whether data are interval or ratio, the good news is that techniques used in statistics generally do not distinguish between these two data types; that is, these techniques can be used on interval *or* ratio data.
2. Interval and ratio data are often referred to as **quantitative data,** since such data consist of values that naturally take on numerical (quantitative) values (such as age or weight).

3. Nominal and ordinal data can be grouped together under the heading **qualitative data,** since they consist essentially of labels that are either unordered (nominal data) or ordered (ordinal data).

A summary of the various data classifications is shown in Figure 1.2. Notice that discrete data can result from any of the four levels of measurement, whereas continuous data can be only interval or ratio.

EXERCISES 1.1–1.6

1.1 Give an example of a population of interest to a business manager. Do you believe that a business manager would prefer to select a sample from this population or take a census? Why?

1.2 What differentiates ratio data from data that is only interval?

1.3 To generalize the results of a statistical study, what type of statistics are more useful—descriptive statistics or inferential statistics?

1.4 Many businesses are concerned about the amount of sleep their employees get. The National Sleep Foundation of Washington asked 1,000 Americans in a recent survey about the total number of hours that they typically sleep at night. The nonprofit group found that men average 6.7 hours a night and women 6.8 hours. In this survey, the respondents were asked their total number of hours of sleep per night. What if the question were asked so that the respondent had to check one of four boxes: (1) Less than 4 hours, (2) Between 4 hours and 6 hours, (3) Between 6 hours and 8 hours, (4) More than 8 hours?

   a. For each of these formats, decide whether the level of measurement is nominal, ordinal, interval, or ratio.

   b. Which of these formats do you believe the respondents would find easier to answer?

   c. Which of these formats would yield a more accurate measure of the number of hours of sleep that the respondents obtain per night?

   d. Which of these formats do you believe would yield a higher response rate?

(Source: *The Washington Times,* "Shut Eye Statistics." Aug. 25, 1997, p. 4.)

1.5 Classify each of the following variables as being either a qualitative or quantitative and as having nominal, ordinal, interval, or ratio level of measurements:

   a. The time that a Chief Executive Officer spends at work
   b. The ordered preference that investors have for different investment funds for retirement purposes
   c. The state where an individual was born
   d. The average temperature for the summer months in Chicago
   e. The ranking of computer stores with respect to their competitors, based on sales

FIGURE 1.2

Classifications of numerical data.

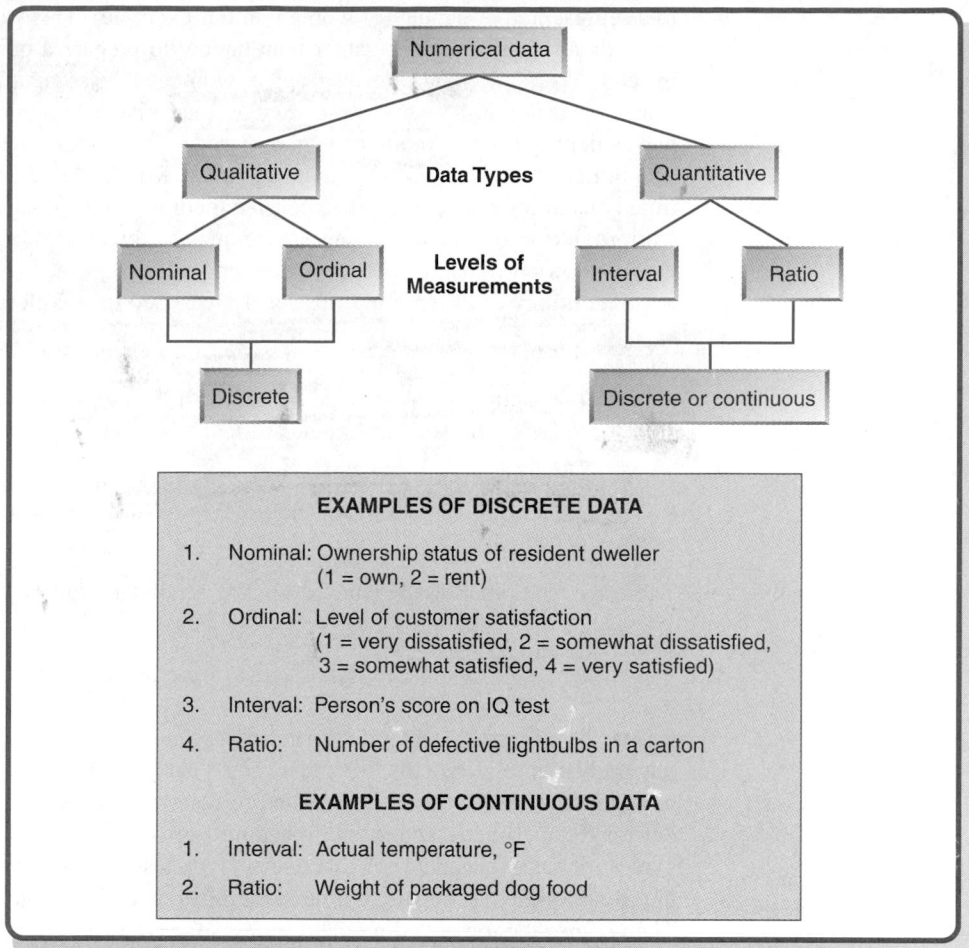

EXAMPLES OF DISCRETE DATA

1. Nominal: Ownership status of resident dweller
   (1 = own, 2 = rent)

2. Ordinal: Level of customer satisfaction
   (1 = very dissatisfied, 2 = somewhat dissatisfied,
   3 = somewhat satisfied, 4 = very satisfied)

3. Interval: Person's score on IQ test

4. Ratio: Number of defective lightbulbs in a carton

EXAMPLES OF CONTINUOUS DATA

1. Interval: Actual temperature, °F

2. Ratio: Weight of packaged dog food

1.6 Motor Industry Association executive director Perry Kerr wished to determine the proportion of used import automobiles with odometers showing less than their recorded reading in Japan. A random sample of Japanese imported automobiles revealed that 24% of the odometers had readings that were less than that recorded before being shipped to the United States.

a. What is the population of interest?

b. What is the difference between numerical facts and statistics? What does the value of 24% represent?

c. What type of data is the value of the odometer setting?

d. Why would a sample be used in this study? Explain.

(Source: *Waikato Times*, "Odometers Still Wound Back: Survey." Dec. 2, 1997, p. 2.)

1.5 SOURCES OF DATA

Without the availability of data, the science of statistics would cease to exist. Information obtained from sample data is typically used to gain insight into a much larger population. The reliability of conclusions drawn from sample data depends to a great extent on the *quality* of the data. Are they accurate? Do the data really represent the population of interest? Was the sample obtained properly? Before we can answer such questions, we first examine where you look for such data, that is, the source of the data.

PRIMARY AND SECONDARY DATA

Data sources can be categorized as being *primary* or *secondary* sources. **Primary data** come from an original (primary) source and are collected with a specific research question in mind, such as, "Are single women more likely to encounter sexual harassment in the workplace?" Very often, you may wish to design a questionnaire that addresses your research question and then to collect the data yourself by administering the questionnaire to a representative sample (of women, in our example). This would be an example of primary data. In our example, rather than having to prepare a questionnaire, you may elect instead to personally interview a group of women at the company where you are employed. The latter sample, a *convenience sample,* may give you some valuable insight into the harassment question. Another method of collecting primary data that is gaining momentum in manufacturing-based industries is the use of *designed experiments.* This is rather a time consuming and seemingly expensive method of data collection, but in the long run it can provide information that saves a company a great deal of money and, more importantly, allows it to build a product of better quality.

Secondary data represent previously recorded data collected for another purpose or as part of a regularly scheduled data collection procedure (such as an annual report released by the U.S. Department of Transportation). Such data are considerably easier and cheaper to obtain than primary data, but may not adequately address your research question. Here are some other advantages of secondary data.

- Secondary data can cover many years of operation.
- Secondary data may exist for many geographical regions (including foreign facilities and workers).

There are also other disadvantages of using secondary data:

- The data may be out of date.
- There is no way to verify that the data were obtained properly.

PRIMARY DATA SOURCES.   Obtaining primary data generally requires more effort, but has the huge advantage of specifically addressing your particular research question, such as the harassment question mentioned earlier, or determining cause-and-effect relationships in a designed experiment. The usual procedure for obtaining primary data involves designing a questionnaire that addresses this question, pretesting this instrument several times, refining it each time, and finally administering it to a sample from the population of interest. Then comes the job of coding the responses for computer input, analyzing the results, and coming to a conclusion on the research question. There are many things to consider and to watch out for when designing a questionnaire; these will be explored further in section 1.7.

The statistical and management worlds of *quality improvement* are getting a great deal of attention these days. As you get further into this area, you will begin to view business operations as a collection of *processes* that can be monitored, measured, and improved. This applies to processes within manufacturing companies, service industries, city and government organizations, and educational institutions. The use of statistics enters in since, if we intend to improve a process, we first need to measure a quality characteristic associated with this process (such as the number of rejected parts in a manufacturing process) so that we are able to determine if, in fact, the quality has been improved.

Consider a situation where the local fire department is attempting to improve the response time to a fire call. They have gone to a great deal of effort and expense to improve this process, including computerizing the dispatch operation and improving the "state of readiness" for workers on duty. Suppose that you were asked to offer your opinion prior to implementation of this quality improvement effort as to whether response time is improved as a result of these changes. One possibility would be to obtain a sample of times before the changes were made and another sample afterwards. This is another example of *primary data,* since you obtain the data first-hand for a specific purpose. The intent would be to determine whether the average response time after the quality improvement effort was less than the average time before the effort—a question we will deal with in Chapter 9.

To recap, primary data are obtained using a "hands-on" procedure, such as designing and administering a questionnaire that addresses a particular research question or observing and measuring a characteristic of interest within a particular business process. Very often this is the only data source available if there are no other published data (secondary data) that address the question or process of interest. As you delve into very specific research topics, or "hot" topics (such as harassment or abortion), you will need current data that address these issues; designing a procedure to collect primary data is your only alternative, despite the fact that such a method can be very time-consuming and costly.

SECONDARY DATA SOURCES.   Once you begin to search out sources of secondary data, you will soon discover that there is an overwhelming amount of data stored up in (1) government reports, (2) industry financial statements, (3) business periodicals (magazines), and (4) sites available through the World Wide Web. Often the difficulty is finding data that meet your needs, appear to be current, and were obtained in a proper manner (*yes:* a random sample of industrywide computer programmers; and *no:* a haphazard sample of programmers within a particular department at Texas Instruments).

It would be impossible in this short space to discuss all sources of secondary data. However, here are several sources that provide a large volume of data on a very wide assortment of variables.

- U.S. Bureau of the Census, *Statistical Abstracts of the United States,* published by the U.S. Government Printing Office.* This book contains summary statistics on the political, social, industrial, and economic climate in the United States. It contains data from over 200 authoritative sources summarized in over 1500 tables. Very often, if specific detailed data are not presented, the source notes for these tables in the attached bibliography are useful guides for further research.
- *Canadian Business and Current Affairs.* This provides indexing to more than 200,000 articles per year appearing in 200 Canadian periodicals, nearly 300 popular magazines, and 10 newspapers. This data source is updated monthly.
- *United Nations Statistical Publications and Documents.* This is an annual publication containing data on a variety of topics gathered *worldwide.* There are summary statistics on international trade, industry and construction, demographic and housing, and international price comparisons.
- *Census of the Population,* published by the U.S. Government every 10 years, the next to appear after the census in the year 2000. This is a very powerful data source in which the U.S. population is categorized according to income level, ethnicity, geographic location, and occupation.
- Business periodicals, including the *Wall Street Journal* and *Fortune* magazine. Periodicals offer a good method of retrieving current (perhaps daily) information. Three very comprehensive business periodical indexes are the *Reader's Guide to Periodical Literature* (references to over 1500 magazines, including *Newsweek, Fortune, Business Week*), *Business Periodicals Index* (references to 1500 business and economic periodicals, allowing the researcher to target a specific type of business), and *Periodical Abstracts* (contains indexing and abstracting to significant articles appearing in top general and academic periodicals as well as full text from more than 600 journals).
- Many libraries now have a business index called *ABI/INFORM* available on CD-ROM that offers a *very* extensive database of business-related information and articles. You merely specify the company, journal, author, geographical area, or key words (such as BANKRUPTCY AND DELAWARE) for which you need information, and ABI/INFORM will identify the corresponding source(s) stored in the database. ABI/INFORM is also available on shared resources networks, which can be accessed in some locations. Check your local public or university library for availability.
- The latest (and largest) source of secondary data is the World Wide Web. Using the Web, you have access to periodical abstracts, DIALOG (a collection of more than 470 databases with more than 200 billion pages of text and images), Uncover (a database of current article information taken from multidisciplinary journals with brief description information for more than seven million articles), and electronic journals (complete electronic versions of more than 260 journals).

---

* An easier-to-read version with larger type size is available through Bernan Press, Lanham, Maryland.

DESIGNING AN EXPERIMENT.   In the previous discussion, it was pointed out that one advantage of collecting primary data is that you have direct control over the data collection. In this way, you are able to get data obtained for a specific purpose that will generally be of high quality due to the "hands-on" nature of this procedure. Designing an industrial experiment is another source of primary data—one that at first glance appears to be a very elaborate and costly method of collecting sample data. But as many industrial testimonials in the literature have made clear, experimental designs provide an extremely effective way of studying an industrial process. Data collected from such an experiment can help design better quality into a product so that, long-range, such a procedure *is* very cost effective.

One of the key advantages to collecting data from a designed experiment is that you are able to study the effect of changes to a process. For example, Acme Brick produces brick for residential construction. One of the key decisions in the production process is the oven firing temperature, since this can affect the strength of the brick. A quality engineer at Acme decides to test the brick strength at oven temperatures of 150° C, 175° C, and 200° C. Fifteen bricks are randomly selected and randomly assigned to one of the three temperatures. Using a test device, the strength of the bricks is measured, with the following results.

150°	175°	200°
110	145	103
106	132	110
118	151	105
122	148	112
114	144	126

At first glance, it would appear that 175° produces the strongest brick. (The analysis for such a design will be discussed in Chapter 11, where it could be shown that this conclusion is supported.)

This chapter will demonstrate that data collected from designed experiments allow you to determine what variables (such as oven temperature) affect the process and in what manner these variables are related to each other.

RANDOM SAMPLING VERSUS NONRANDOM SAMPLING

When it comes time to obtain (primary) sample data, a key decision you will need to make is whether to gather data that are obtained in a random manner or are obtained using a more deliberate selection procedure. Samples generated using the latter method are **nonrandom samples** and are often referred to as **nonprobability samples.** There are many situations, such as an exploratory study, where you simply want to gain insight into a population of interest rather than make a statistical estimate. When using nonrandom sampling methods, you can use a variety of procedures for obtaining a sample with little or no attention paid to randomization. For example, you may wish to restrict your sample to hand-picked individuals who satisfy a certain requirement, such as individuals over age 50 who have recently been laid off from their jobs. This section will consider three nonrandom sampling strategies: convenience sampling, judgment sampling, and quota sampling.

Convenience Sampling. A convenience sample is obtained just as the name implies—in a convenient manner. You may elect to use a group of friends, fellow students in your marketing class, shoppers at a local mall, and so on. Individuals for such a sample are selected based on their presumed resemblance to the population of interest (potential customers of your new product or service) and their ready availability. Such a sample can be extremely valuable in gaining insight into a new idea or the sentiment of a much larger population. If a convenience sample of 20 coworkers indicates that 19 of these 20 people think your idea is not a good one, it's probably time to go back to the drawing board. On the positive side, many a good idea has been born by obtaining information through a convenience sample.

Consider a situation in which a company's records are being audited. If the audit is merely exploratory, a convenience sample may be in order. Typically, no effort is made to locate missing items, records that are in storage, or records that are at another location. It is important to realize that these missing records may be "missing" because the auditee does not want them to be reviewed. However, if the purpose of the audit is to determine a total amount owed to another party (such as an insurance carrier's improper Medicare charges owed to the federal government), then a simple random sample* is essential. For this situation, you will need to outline your sampling procedure carefully and to use a method that will hold up in court should this result be appealed.

Judgment Sampling. For situations where you want to handpick individuals who satisfy certain requirements or who you believe have expertise regarding the population, a judgment sample often works very well. The earlier illustration of laid-off workers over age 50 is an example of a judgment sample, and this group of people may provide excellent insight into problems facing middle-aged employees. Other examples of judgment samples would include divorced individuals or voting districts likely to represent the opinions of the entire state or nation. A certain city may be selected to test market a new product since it is believed that potential customers within this city have buying behaviors that are typical of a much larger population.

When using a judgment sample, you take the risk that your sample is not representative of the associated population. Generally, there is no attempt to cover the entire spectrum of key population characteristics, such as age and income. The judgment sample may include mostly middle-age and middle-income individuals. But if your interest is to gain insight into the population rather than represent them as a whole, a pilot study conducted using a judgment sample can be very valuable.

Quota Sampling. Quota sampling is a form of nonrandom sampling that is a bit more deliberate in an attempt to obtain a sample that is representative of the entire population. To illustrate this technique, if you know that 60% of the registered voters in a particular community are women, you may, in a sample of 100 voters, restrict your sample to 60 women and 40 men. In this way, your sample is a "miniature" of the population.

Very often in a quota sample, the researcher restricts the sample according to more than one criteria, such as age level, religious affiliation, race, or smoking status. Such criteria are believed by the researcher to have an effect on the response of the person being interviewed. Certainly, one's religious affiliation could have an effect on his or her view of a proposed ordinance forbidding the sale of alcoholic beverages. Consequently, a quota sample would attempt to duplicate the proportions of each religious category present in the community where the ordinance would take effect. Oftentimes, these proportions are estimated (or known) from prior surveys or government census results.

Once the criteria have been determined, a judgment sampling technique can then be used to make the sample selection. The sample may in fact not represent the population if care is not taken in obtaining a representative cross section of people satisfying the sample criteria. Despite this defect of quota sampling, it remains a very popular technique among opinion pollsters, market researchers, and other researchers since it is usually less expensive than obtaining a random sample and takes less time.

RANDOM SAMPLING.   When using a **simple random sample** (usually referred to as a *random sample*), you will need to make sure that every sample of size n has the same chance of being selected. One method of doing this is to use a computer to generate random numbers between 1 and N, where N is the size of the population. For example, you may want to select a set of six numbers between 1 and 50 for a lottery ticket. Here, n is 6, and N is 50. We will illustrate this procedure in the next section. The main advantage of using a random sample is that the sample results can be extended to estimating something of interest in the population. Furthermore, you can measure and control how reliable this estimate is. **The use of simple random samples will be the primary focus of the chapters to follow.**

---

* Other types of sampling besides simple random sampling that are also legally defensible, and often preferred, are discussed in Chapter 7. These include *stratified* sampling and *cluster* sampling.

ADVANTAGES AND DISADVANTAGES OF RANDOM SAMPLING. As just discussed, the main advantage of random sampling is you can generalize beyond the sample itself. A result derived from such a sample (such as a recovery amount estimated from an audit) is legally defensible in a court of law. Just the opposite holds for the results of a nonrandom sample—you cannot safely generalize to the entire population, and the results are *not* legally defensible. The main advantages behind the use of nonrandom sampling are: (1) data are more easily obtained, (2) such data may provide you with enough information to make a decision with much less expense, and (3) data from a nonrandom sample can be used as an informal base of knowledge in preparation for a later sample based on random sampling.

GENERATING A SET OF RANDOM NUMBERS

When obtaining a simple random sample, you will need to generate your sample using a set of random values. One option is to use a table of randomly generated numbers, such as Table A.13 (page A–33) at the end of this textbook. A much simpler method is to utilize a computer-generated list of random digits to determine your sample elements.

To illustrate the process of generating a set of random numbers, consider a situation in which an auditor is responsible for obtaining a random sample of 50 hospital records from a list of 1000 records, numbered sequentially from 1 to 1000. For this procedure to work, it is vital that you be able to list sequentially all of the population elements from 1 to 1000. Here is one way you could use the table of random numbers (Table A.13).

a. Start in any arbitrary position, such as row 5 of column 3.
b. Select a list of 50 random numbers by reading either across or down the table.
c. For each five-digit number selected, place a decimal between the third and fourth digits and round this value to the nearest counting number (integer); for example, 24127 would become 241.27, which is then rounded to 241. One of the sample elements will be the population element in location 241.

Excel provides a simple method of generating a computerized list of random numbers. A set of random numbers can be obtained using Excel's Analysis ToolPack by: (1) selecting the Tools menu from the menu bar, (2) choosing Data Analysis, and (3) clicking on Random Number Generation and then on OK. The random number generation dialog window will appear, and the values should be filled in as illustrated in Figure 1.3. This set of

FIGURE 1.3
Excel input screen for generating 50 random numbers between 1 and 1000.

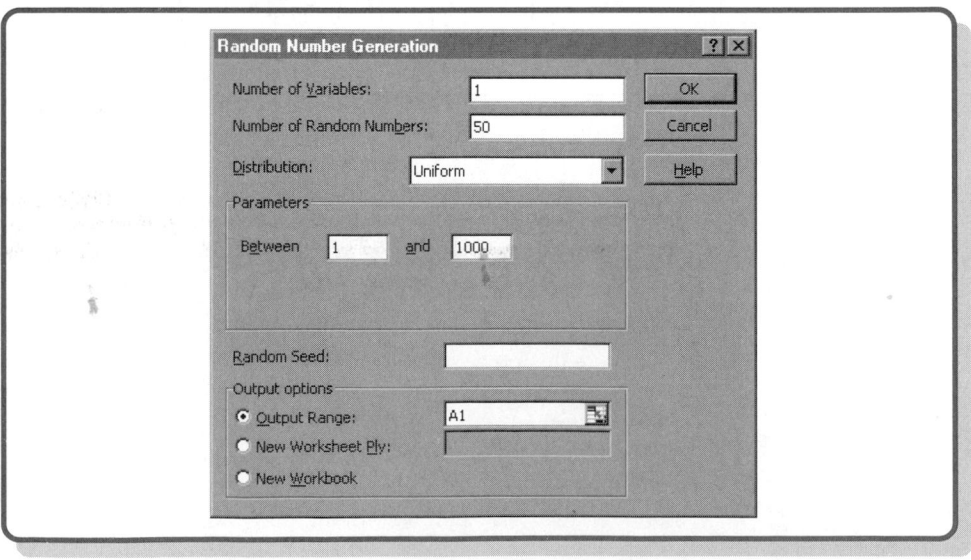

FIGURE 1.4

Excel spreadsheet containing first 17 random numbers arranged in ascending order.

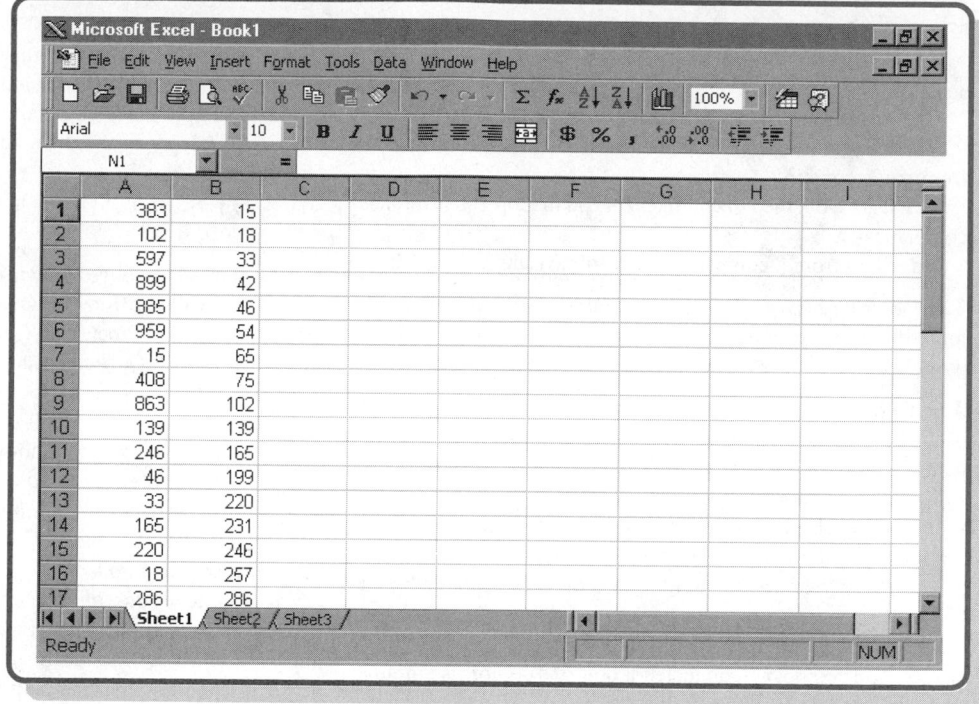

input values will result in column A of Figure 1.4 and consists of a list of 50 numbers randomly selected from the values 1 through 1000.

To obtain integer values (no decimal places) in column A, you must: (1) highlight column A by clicking on the column A heading (the letter "A" at the top of this column) and (2) click on the Decrease Decimal icon ( ) the same number of times as the number of decimal places that appear. For example, if the values in column A have four decimal places (such as 467.2931), then click on this icon four times. Column A now should contain a list of 50 integers between 1 and 1000. The first 17 values from one such execution of this procedure are shown in Figure 1.4.

Column B in Figure 1.4 contains the values in column A arranged in ascending order. To obtain this column (and still retain column A) you must first copy column A into column B by: (1) highlighting column A by clicking on the column A heading, (2) placing the mouse pointer on the right-hand boundary of this column until its shape becomes a white arrow, (3) while holding the Ctrl key (you should observe a small plus sign alongside the white arrow), pressing and holding the left mouse button while dragging column A onto column B, and finally (4) releasing the mouse button and then releasing the Ctrl key. Column B should now contain the same values as column A. To arrange the column B values in ascending order, highlight column B by clicking on the column B heading and then click on the Sort Ascending icon ( ).

The values in column A of Figure 1.4 are arranged in the *original* order. The main advantage of obtaining your sample elements in this order is that the auditor maintains the randomness of the sample. At any interim point, if there is sufficient evidence, the auditor can terminate sampling. When using the sorted values in column B of Figure 1.4, the sample elements can be located in *sequential* order. The advantage of obtaining the sample values in this order is that oftentimes it becomes much easier to locate each value, particularly if the sample elements are selected from a hard-copy format (computer listing, files in a drawer, boxes in a storage area). On the other hand, when selecting the sample using the sequential order, the sample results cannot be generalized to the population unless the entire sample is examined; otherwise you would be ignoring a section of the population.

EXERCISES 1.7-1.11

1.7 Classify each of the following data sources as primary or secondary:

a. Data from the *World Almanac* and *Book of Facts*

b. Data from telephone interviews of graduating seniors from the accounting department

c. Data from the *Forbes* magazine on the top 100 insurance companies

d. Data from a company survey to measure productivity

1.8 Describe how an experiment could be designed to determine if the day, evening, and night shift differ in their productivity? How would random samples be obtained?

1.9 To obtain information, primary or secondary sources are used. For each of the following statements, indicate the company's most likely source of information.

a. "The majority of the employees of our company are willing to work in self-directed work teams to achieve a 10% reduction in administrative cost."

b. "Last year, the 4.2 million tons of steel imported by the United States had a significant impact on the earnings of all American steel companies, including our own."

c. "Our company conducted a poll of 1000 of its employees. The poll indicates that the company's president enjoys increasing popularity among all employees of the company."

d. "The Value Line Survey has recently given our company the highest ranking for price appreciation."

1.10 According to a public opinion poll, about 53% of Poles who bought mass privatization units have already sold them on the secondary market. Would this sample be considered a convenience sample or a simple random sample? How do you think a random sample could be obtained for this population? Would a listing of telephone numbers be useful in drawing a random sample?

(Source: *The Financial Times Limited,* "Poles Sell Privatization Units." Jan. 24, 1997.)

1.11 Colgate-Palmolive Co. will spend $100 million on advertising for its Colgate Total toothpaste in a bid to steal U.S. customers from rival Procter & Gamble Co.'s Crest toothpaste. According to an A.C. Nielsen survey, during the past year, Colgate's market share rose to 36.3% from 21.5%, while Proctor and Gambles market share fell to 27.3% from 35%. Typically, surveys of this type will randomly select various localities and then random sample from that locality. Suppose that a particular locality is selected and 500 homeowners are listed.

a. Explain how Table A.13 can be used to choose 20 numbers between 1 and 500.

b. In Excel click on **Tools > Data Analysis > Random Number Generation.** Then type 1 variable and 20 random numbers. Choose the uniform distribution with numbers between 1 and 500. Put the output in column A. Then click on **Format > Cells > Number > Custom** and select 0. This will display the numbers as integers. Do you prefer generating random numbers in this fashion or using Table A.13?

(Source: *The Baltimore Sun,* "Colgate Plans Big Ad Push for Toothpaste." Dec. 30, 1997, p. 2C.)

1.6 BUSINESS RESEARCH QUESTIONS IN PRACTICE (OPTIONAL)

Why study statistics in the first place? After all, how likely is it that someone will come to your office some day with a bucketful of numbers to analyze? We would argue that this is much more likely to occur than you might expect.

Statistics is the science of answering questions. To answer questions such as those that follow, you will need to gather evidence, that is, a sample. Based on the results of this sample, you will be able to arrive at a conclusion regarding the question of interest.

Statistics often appears to be a very abstract subject, filled with probability and Greek letters. Though statistical theory can appear that way, statistics in practice is filled with useful applications. To give you an idea as to the types of research questions you are likely to encounter (and hopefully to spark your interest a bit), we have included applications from the areas of marketing, management, finance, accounting, and information systems. For each scenario, we discuss the possible sources of sample data to answer the research question and the level of measurement for the data.

MARKETING

Companies spend billions of dollars each year on spokespeople to represent their companies. Attempting to increase market share, many companies have targeted a growing minority population.

Research question: Does the use of minority spokespeople increase product preference among minority consumers?

Variable of interest: Relative preference for one product over another.

Level of measurement for data collected on this variable: Ordinal

Possible sources of data:
> Primary—focus groups, marketing experiments
> Secondary—sales records that have been tabulated by an information service that buys its data from retail outlets

MANAGEMENT

In current efforts to downsize corporations, many companies are reducing salaries. Since older workers tend to earn higher salaries than younger workers, they may be overrepresented in any terminations. An important part of managing downsizing is ensuring that no group of workers suffers disproportionately; frequently, unequal employment practices result in contentious litigation leading to large settlements.

Research question: Is the average age of terminated workers greater than that of retained workers?
Variable of interest: Ages of terminated workers
Level of measurement for data collected on this variable: Ratio
Possible sources of data:
> Primary—personnel records
> Secondary—data provided by state or federal agencies

FINANCE

Initial public offerings (IPOs) offer financiers a quick way to raise capital for expansion of a company. If the subscription price (the original price at which the stock is offered for sale to the public) of an IPO is too low, the price of a share of the stock will rise above the IPO level, meaning that the company did not receive full value for its stock.

Research question: Are IPOs on the New York Stock Exchange (NYSE) more likely to be underpriced than those on the American Stock Exchange (AMEX)?
Variable of interest: Prices of shares of stocks during the period following an IPO
Level of measurement for data collected on this variable: Ratio
Possible sources of data:
> Primary—NYSE and AMEX financial data files
> Secondary—Company reports, magazine or newspaper articles

ACCOUNTING

With a limited (though it may not seem so!) number of agents, the IRS finds it impractical to audit every account of large taxpayers. With sampling theory, a small percentage of accounts can be used to estimate the tax liability of the firms.

Research question: Has a firm significantly understated tax liabilities of certain accounts?
Variable of interest: Total value of understated accounts minus total value of overstated accounts
Level of measurement for data collected on this variable: Ratio
Possible sources of data:
> Primary—auditing of primary records (e.g., invoices)
> Secondary—records kept and administered by an external accounting firm

INFORMATION SYSTEMS

Outsourcing (the employment of an outside company to perform Information System functions) is another means taken by some companies to reduce cost. One fear regarding outsourcing is a lessened productivity by outside programmers who are unfamiliar with a company's business goals and information strategies. One common (although frequently questioned) measure of productivity is "thousands of lines of code" (kloc) that a programmer generates in a measurement period.

> *Research question:* Is the productivity of outsourced programmers, as measured in kloc's, lower than that of the in-house staff?
> *Variable of interest:* Thousands of lines of code generated by each programmer
> *Level of measurement for data collected on this variable:* Ratio
> *Possible sources of data:*
>> Primary—physical counts of codes from ongoing projects
>> Secondary—published reports relating relative counts of code based on the information provided by outsourcing firms

A Final Look: Primary Versus Secondary Data

Since the quality of secondary data depends on knowledge about its collection, it is recommended that primary sources be used when possible. Primary sources are reports that originate from the agency that actually collected the data. On the other hand, secondary sources are compilations, abstracts, summaries, or reports that take their information from either a primary or another secondary source. The primary source is almost always preferred to a secondary source, since it is more likely to detail the limitations of the data collection process and to be free of errors resulting from transcription mistakes.

An analogous situation is in a court of law, where every effort is made to guarantee the authenticity of any data presented as evidence. The actual spoken word of the person on the witness stand (primary data) is much preferred to secondary information consisting of what someone heard someone else say. If there is no way to support this secondary information with testimony from the primary source (perhaps the victim), this information is treated as hearsay evidence and is often taken very lightly.

It is important to understand that business decisions made through the use of statistics can only be as sound as the data used in those statistics. Primary data, data collected for the express purpose of analyzing a particular research question, are frequently difficult and expensive to collect. Business researchers often use secondary data, data that have been collected for another purpose but applied to a new research question. Although secondary data are usually easier to obtain than primary data, their use frequently entails both the employment of older data as well as a lack of knowledge about the limitations of the data collection process. Thus, the decision about the use of primary or secondary data in a statistical analysis balances the reliability and freshness of primary data against the availability and convenience of secondary data.

1.7 Designing and Coding a Questionnaire (Optional)

Questionnaires as statistical tools began nearly 100 years ago when an early research pioneer, Francis Galton, realized that these instruments were an excellent device for studying behavior that could not be observed or experimented on directly. They provide a very versatile and relatively inexpensive method of collecting primary data. When it comes to studying and predicting human behavior, questionnaires very often are the only practical method of acquiring information. For example, if a sporting goods manufacturer is interested in consumer preferences in camping equipment, it would be much easier for the company to construct a questionnaire and to poll a sample of potential buyers than to design an experiment to detect differences in consumer preference. In this way, they can explore customer expectations and obtain current, in-depth responses to a variety of questions.

A key factor in the success of conclusions drawn from questionnaire data is the care taken in designing a set of questions that are relevant, nonthreatening, easy to understand, and not so numerous that respondents would refuse to answer them. This section will provide some pointers to consider when constructing a questionnaire. The last part of this discussion will assist you in getting the responses in suitable form for computer input, referred to as *data coding.*

FIVE STEPS IN QUESTIONNAIRE DESIGN

The key steps in designing a reliable questionnaire include deciding the types of questions to use, the sequence of questions, questionnaire directions and length, pretesting and revising, and, finally, ensuring a good response rate. Each of these topics will be looked at more closely in the discussion to follow.

STEP 1. DECIDE WHAT TYPES OF QUESTIONS TO USE. In general, it is best to restrict a questionnaire to a single issue. Otherwise, the intent of the instrument is unclear and the questionnaire length can be excessive. Be sure to investigate and determine whether another questionnaire exists that suits your needs. If you are the first person to investigate this issue, you will need to start from scratch, although you may be able to use individual questions (or blocks of questions) from previously designed instruments.

A key decision for each question is whether to make it *open-ended* or *closed-ended*. An open-ended question requires a written response, such as "How do you feel about the President's plan to reduce the defense budget?" A closed-ended "question" is actually a statement (not a question) that typically asks the individual to select a response from a list. An example of a closed-ended question would be:

	Strongly disagree	Disagree	Undecided	Agree	Strongly agree
The President's plan to reduce the defense budget is a good one.	_____	_____	_____	_____	_____

The main advantage of open-ended questions is that they are excellent for in-depth exploration of a new topic. On the other hand, such questions require more time from the respondent. And if there is an excessive number of such questions, the response rate (percentage of filled-out questionnaires returned) is likely to drop. Closed-ended questions provide data that are easy to quantify but suffer from their inherent lack of flexibility, since the respondent is forced to select from a specified list of items.

Here are some types of closed-ended questions.

- *Likert-scale questions:* The just-displayed question involving five possible responses is an example of a *five-point* Likert-scale question, since the five responses consist of five ordered categories. A classic debate with Likert data is whether they should be treated as *ordinal* or *interval* data. By our earlier definitions, we could make a very strong argument in favor of Likert data being considered ordinal, since, for example, the distance between "Agree" and "Strongly Disagree" is not necessarily the same as that between "Disagree" and "Undecided." However, a great deal of research has supported the contention that treating this type of data as interval data does not have a serious effect on the research conclusions. Generally, five- or seven-category Likert data is recommended. Be sure that each category has a label, such as "Strongly Agree" or "Very Strongly Disagree."
- *Yes/no or true/false questions:* Such questions are usually not recommended, since the responses provide very limited information.
- *Multiple choice questions:* You have undoubtedly encountered such questions on college exams. The *Peanuts* comic strip some years ago described such questions as "offering a menu to a starving person." However, such responses are easy to code for computer input, convey a great deal of information and, like all closed-ended questions, allow you to compare the responses from one group of people to another.
- *"Rank in order" questions:* With these questions, you give the respondent a list of choices and ask him or her to rank the choices in order, from most important (should receive a "1") to least important, most preferred to least preferred, and so on. Such questions can confuse respondents, meaning the order gets reversed (least important receives the "1") or the respondent only lists the top two or three choices. For such questions, the corresponding list should never contain more than 10 items.

STEP 2. WRITE THE QUESTIONS.   Here are some key things to keep in mind at this stage.

- *Reading level:* Be sure the wording isn't overly complex and that you have not used an acronym that many people will fail to recognize (such as mentioning "NAFTA" rather than "North American Free Trade Agreement").
- *Leading questions:* Avoid questions that lead the respondent to answer in a certain way, for example, "Countless millions of U.S. tax dollars are being drained each year by illegal immigrants for social and medical benefits. Do you think the United States should enact tougher immigration laws?"
- *Questions with loaded terms:* Avoid the use of such phrases as *dangerous* drugs, *noisy* trucks, and *excessive* government spending. These adjectives could be considered leading, since they invite a negative response.
- *Questions that ask too much.* In an effort to reduce the number of questions, a common trap is to include questions that really contain two questions, such as "Are you in favor of allowing liquor sales on Sundays and holidays?" Respondents may be confused here, since they feel one way about Sundays and another about holidays.
- *Measuring the middle position:* When using a Likert scale (such as "Strongly Disagree," "Disagree," etc.), it is important to include a middle category, such as "Undecided" or "Don't Know." Such an alternative guards against a false appearance of opinion one way or the other and respects the respondent's right to have neutral feelings on a subject. Along these lines, a response of "Not Applicable (NA)" should also be included, to reduce respondent frustration over questions that are not relevant.

STEP 3. DECIDE ON THE QUESTION SEQUENCE AND QUESTIONNAIRE LENGTH.   One of the surest ways to guarantee a poor response rate is to give little thought to the order of your questions and to end up with a questionnaire that gives the potential respondent a headache when it is first examined. With this in mind, we have compiled a short list of things to keep in mind when putting together your list of questions.

- *Include introductory and closing statements.* At the top of the questionnaire, you should identify yourself (or whatever group is conducting the survey) and provide a brief description of the purpose of the instrument. This paragraph should also contain general instructions, along with more specific instructions for questions needing additional explanation. For example, if you are trying to measure customer perceptions, you might wish to caution the respondent to check the first response that comes to mind rather than dwelling on the response. At the end of the questionnaire, include a section for additional comments or suggestions and for thanking the respondents for their time and effort.
- *Deciding on the questionnaire length.* A general rule is that the shorter the questionnaire, the better. This becomes a delicate matter, since if the questionnaire is too short you may fail to get the information you need. On the other hand, if it is too long the response rate may be very low, since potential respondents will not take the effort to fill it out. For a very long questionnaire, your respondent sample may contain only people that have a great deal of time on their hands (retired or unemployed individuals, for instance), which may distort your findings since the sample may poorly represent the intended population.
- *Pay close attention to the question sequence.* Begin with factual, nonthreatening questions. In this way, you establish a good relationship with the respondent. More detailed, thought-provoking, or sensitive questions should appear later in the instrument, after the respondent feels comfortable answering your questions. A generally recommended procedure is to use general, open-ended questions at the beginning, followed by more specific, closed-ended items.

For mildly sensitive questions, such as age or income, rather than using

Age _____

consider using

Age: under 20	_____	41 to 50	_____
21 to 30	_____	51 to 60	_____
31 to 40	_____	61 or over	_____

In this manner, you obtain *ordinal* data. The person's actual age would be considered *ratio* data, which is "stronger" than ordinal data; however, if age is a sensitive issue, the ordinal response may be much more reliable.

The questionnaire should maintain a logical order that is understandable to the respondent. Questions addressing a specific topic should be grouped together so that the respondent does not feel "bounced around" by questions that do not allow him or her to maintain a constant stream of thought.

STEP 4. PRETEST AND REVISE. It is important that you review carefully the first draft of your questionnaire. Despite your best efforts, there will be some words that are difficult or unclear and some questions that are confusing. Such self-administered instruments allow no opportunity by the researcher to clarify the meaning of obscure terms. You should attempt to identify all poorly worded questions, and don't be offended by criticism of certain questions during the pretest phase. In fact, during this stage you need to encourage respondents not only to answer the questions but also to comment on their wording and clarity.

Most often, a convenience sample (a group of students or customers) is used to pretest a questionnaire. Once you are satisfied that the problems have been identified, revise the instrument accordingly. Many researchers suggest pretesting and revising an additional time before the questionnaire is ready for final use.

STEP 5. ENSURE A HIGH RESPONSE RATE. A high response rate to your questionnaire helps reduce the bias introduced when your sample fails to represent the nonrespondents in the population. There are many things you can do to increase the percentage of people that complete and return the mailed questionnaire. These include getting prior commitment to participate, writing an effective cover letter, including an incentive to participate, and following up after the initial mailing.

- *Prior commitment to participate*: If you intend to get a large block of respondents from a particular company (or government organization, school, etc.), it is important to obtain commitment from someone in the organization to use this group as participants in the study. This person may lend support to the survey if you are able to convince him or her that the results will benefit the company.
- *An effective cover letter:* Your cover letter is where you sell the importance of your research study to the potential respondent. It also should spell out who you want to fill out the questionnaire, if it is likely to be completed by someone other than the person to whom the instrument was mailed. Be brief and to the point, but be emphatic about the benefits of your project and the importance of this person's input.*
- *Incentives:* An *incentive* refers to something you include along with the questionnaire that encourages someone to take the time and effort to complete it. Not long ago, a quarter was attached to the cover letter as an incentive (some would say "guilt motivator" should they not fill it out). Inflation has made it more difficult to come up with incentives with much impact, and it is not uncommon for market research studies to include a dollar bill. Other common incentives include pens, pins, coupons, calendars, and other small items that may be of interest to the targeted population. For many individuals (such as corporate executives), any "trinket" of this nature will have marginal effect, and the best incentive is to offer to share the research results upon completion of the study.
- *The final packet:* Now that you have designed your questionnaire, pretested and revised it, and done the necessary front-end work (including getting prior commitment from people holding key positions within companies selected for sample participation), it's time to put together the final packet. The essential ingredients to include are (1) the cover letter, (2) the questionnaire, (3) any incentive, and (4) a self-addressed, stamped envelope

---

* For more information on developing a clear, concise cover letter, consult any of the following: Chapter 8 in *Basic Business Communication,* 7th ed., by R. V. Lesikar, J. D. Pettit, Jr., and M. E. Flatley (New York: McGraw-Hill, 1995); Chapter 11 in *Business Communications,* 11th ed., by W. C. Himstreet, W. M. Baty, and C. M. Lehman (Cincinnati, OH: South-Western, 1996); *Business Communications Today,* 4th ed., by C. L. Bovée and J. V. Thill (Upper Saddle River, NJ: Prentice Hall, 1997).

(SASE). The SASE obviously increases the cost of conducting your study, but is essential for mail-in questionnaires, to increase the response rate. Using first-class mail is recommended so that the post office will return the undelivered questionnaires and so that delivered packets are more likely to get the attention of the potential respondents.

- *Follow ups:* A follow up consists of a letter or phone call that thanks the individual for returning the completed questionnaire or reminding others to complete it and mail it in. Typically, the first follow up arrives one week after the initial contact. Additional follow ups will result in added returns, so the persistent researcher can achieve a higher response rate—but at a much higher cost. The value of the additional information must be weighed against the added cost of the follow ups.

If there is no response to the initial follow up, a second letter should be sent to those who are known not to have responded. This letter should include another copy of the questionnaire and a restatement of the study's impact and the importance of receiving their input.

CODING QUESTIONNAIRE DATA

Data coding refers to the process of converting questionnaire responses into a form suitable for storing in a computer file. Interval and ratio data (such as age and weight) are in a form that may be used as is. Nominal data (such as color of eyes) are most easily handled by first converting such data into a numerical form, such as 1 = blue, 2 = green, 3 = brown, 4 = hazel, 5 = other. Use of the "other" category is recommended whenever you expect to encounter a relatively few "unusual" responses. Ordinal data (such as Likert data) should also be coded numerically, such as 1 = strongly disagree, 2 = disagree, 3 = undecided, 4 = agree, 5 = strongly agree.

To illustrate the coding procedure, take a look at Appendix F at the end of the text, page A–64. This is a database containing a sample of 1000 companies listed in the Moody's Investor Service Industrial Manual, with nine variables recorded for each company. Notice that the data are aligned in columns. This *fixed-format* presentation is recommended for data recording and data display. Using this presentation, it is easier to edit the values and detect unusual values (referred to as *outliers*). The nine variables and data type are presented in Table 1.2.

For data entry, we suggest you use a computer spreadsheet package, such as Microsoft® Excel or Lotus or the data editor contained in MINITAB. With such programs, you will not need to worry about aligning your columns (referred to as *fields*) because the computer will do this for you. Such programs also can provide summary information (various *statistics*) for each column in your spreadsheet. These statistics will be described in Chapter 3.

TABLE 1.2   Description and data type for variables in Appendix F.

Variable	Description	Data Type
	Observation number (1, 2, . . .)	Nominal
1	Bond rating (Aaa–A is 1, Baa–B is 2, Caa–C is 3)	Ordinal
2	Region of United States where main office is located (NE is 1, SE is 2, SW is 3, NW is 4)	Nominal
3	Number of employees	Ratio
4	Gross sales (thousands of dollars)	Ratio
5	Cost of sales (thousands of dollars)	Ratio
6	Net income	Ratio
7	Current assets	Ratio
8	Current liabilities	Ratio
9	Total assets	Ratio

Data from Appendix F are shown using an Excel worksheet in Figure 1.5 (first 17 rows and all nine variables) and a MINITAB data window in Figure 1.6 (first 14 rows and all nine variables). Notice that the fields are clearly separated and right aligned. Referring to Table 1.2, the first company in this sample has a bond rating between A and Aaa, and their main office is located in the northeastern United States.

	A	B	C	D	E	F	G	H	I	J
1	1	1	1	11600	1204236	932014	38378	355606	167371	650812
2	2	2	1	23000	2303731	1713703	-107331	947651	662653	1989945
3	3	3	1	4000	911002	692227	3116	389884	196724	511393
4	4	1	4	15592	9259100	6705200	310000	2617400	1424600	5282000
5	5	3	1	6100	1268580	991863	40723	221308	112590	407926
6	6	2	1	37481	3516289	3237018	-229627	20296124	1509417	4974267
7	7	1	1	8300	701059	460513	31215	279361	114844	469184
8	8	3	1	5320	413668	266110	34905	244063	76659	409064
9	9	1	1	51300	11113000	8332000	732000	4569000	2808000	12242000
10	10	1	1	141268	27148000	15129000	1538000	8960000	5636000	26733000
11	11	1	1	6200	1155711	857101	19088	321878	196566	4.01E+08
12	12	3	1	13200	901890	613606	48844	413346	144692	685750
13	13	1	3	60700	4952900	3208100	408900	2432300	867200	3769000
14	14	1	1	34173	2094300	1407900	-10200	930800	581200	1856700
15	15	3	2	11082	635076	461671	25611	113650	67696	248067
16	16	3	1	7000	239352	119407	1798	84052	43298	114079
17	17	1	1	1401	100094161	200072391	20000360	60369060	181676	739445

FIGURE 1.5
Excel spreadsheet containing the first 17 rows of Appendix F.

↓	C1	C2	C3	C4	C5	C6	C7	C8	C9	C10
1	1	1	1	11600	1204236	932014	38378	355606	167371	650812
2	2	2	1	23000	2303731	1713703	-107331	947651	662653	1989945
3	3	3	1	4000	911002	692227	3116	389884	196724	511393
4	4	1	4	15592	9259100	6705200	310000	2617400	1424600	5282000
5	5	3	1	6100	1268580	991863	40723	221308	112590	407926
6	6	2	1	37481	3516289	3237018	-229627	20296124	1509417	4974267
7	7	1	1	8300	701059	460513	31215	279361	114844	469184
8	8	3	1	5320	413668	266110	34905	244063	76659	409064
9	9	1	1	51300	11113000	8332000	732000	4569000	2808000	12242000
10	10	1	1	141268	27148000	15129000	1538000	8960000	5636000	26733000
11	11	1	1	6200	1155711	857101	19088	321878	196566	401135257
12	12	3	1	13200	901890	613606	48844	413346	144692	685750
13	13	1	3	60700	4952900	3208100	408900	2432300	867200	3769000
14	14	1	1	34173	2094300	1407900	-10200	930800	581200	1856700

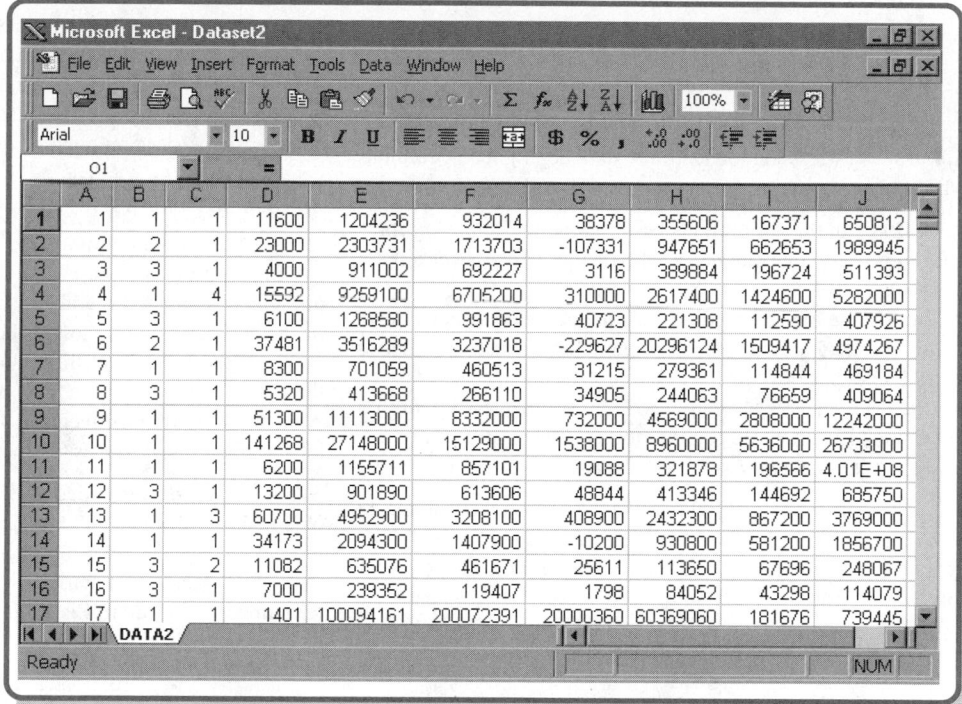

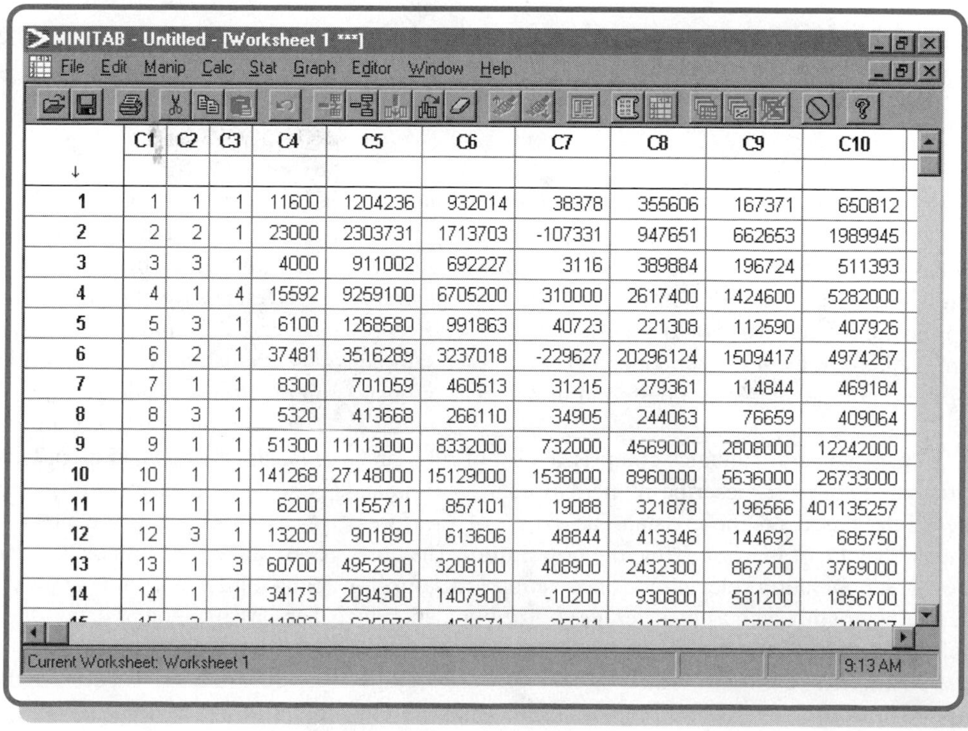

FIGURE 1.6
MINITAB data window containing the first 14 rows of Appendix F.

EXERCISES 1.12–1.20

1.12 What advantage do closed-ended questions have for a questionnaire in comparison to open-ended questions?

1.13 Rather than asking someone his or her exact income on a questionnaire, how might a question of this type be phrased to make the respondent feel more comfortable in answering the question?

1.14 What is the importance of pretesting a questionnaire?

1.15 What should be included in the introductory and closing statements of a questionnaire?

1.16 Why is it recommended that data be aligned in columns when converting the data into coding format?

1.17 Explain the appropriateness of using the following three questions on a questionnaire. How might you reword these questions?

   a. "Some experts predict a decline in the educational level of high school graduates. Do you believe teachers' salaries should be raised?"

   b. "Have you ever seen 'The Nightly Business Report' on television? List three of your favorite television programs."

   c. "Which country is larger, Canada or Australia?"

1.18 A University of Michigan study tracked the careers of 1226 physicians trained at the Michigan Medical School. Ten years after graduation, it was found that 26% of the male doctors were married to full-time working spouses, compared to 88% of the women.

(Source: *Washington Post*, June 15, 1993, p. Z5, "Women Doctors Lag in Status and Pay," by Don Colburn.)

   a. Is this sample a random sample or a convenience sample?

   b. Write two qualitative and two quantitative questions that would be appropriate in a questionnaire administered to the physicians 10 years after graduation.

   c. To encourage the physicians to participate in the survey, what are some statements you might include in the cover letter?

1.19 The wording of questions in a survey can be critical to the response. A *USA Today* article made this comment on polls conducted to determine the support of the public for the North American Free Trade Agreement (NAFTA): "For one thing, polls show the public either split on the issue or solidly opposed, depending on how the questions are phrased."

(Source: *USA Today*, Sept. 3, 1993, p. 8A, "Opposition Building to Free Trade Agreement," by Richard Wolf.)

   a. What is the relevant population?

   b. Suppose you were asked to formulate a few specific questions and a few general questions for the poll. What would be the appropriate order to ask these questions?

   c. Is the wording of the following question appropriate for the poll? "Since American jobs may be lost due to the North American Free Trade Agreement, do you think that it is in the best interest of the United States to have Congress pass the trade pact?"

1.20 The following coded statements represent information obtained from applicants for a car loan. The data correspond to these items: (a) number of years employed at current job; (b) annual salary; (c) marital status; (d) monthly payments; (e) number of children. List four entries in which you suspect an error:

$$
\begin{array}{ccccc}
10 & 50321 & 1 & 1435 & 15 \\
6 & 41871 & 0 & 1563 & 4 \\
2 & 34390 & 8 & 9000 & 1 \\
60 & 45200 & 1 & 850 & 2 \\
\end{array}
$$

SUMMARY

Decision making using statistical procedures continues to grow in popularity, since calculators and computers make it easy to avoid "seat-of-the-pants" decisions by analyzing sample results in a scientific manner. Contemporary applications (such as, should a particular company accept an outside shipment of components based upon a sample of these components?) can be found in a variety of business disciplines.

The science of statistics comprises a set of rules and procedures used to describe numerical data or to make decisions based on these data. The group of measurements that are of interest define the **population.** The portion of a population selected for observation is a **sample.** A characteristic (such as the average) of the population is referred to as a **parameter,** and the corresponding sample characteristic is a **statistic.** For example, the average age of a sample of 100 people passing the most recent CPA exam is a statistic. The average age of *all* people passing this exam is a parameter. A sample that contains the entire population is a **census.**

Descriptive statistics is concerned only with collecting and describing data. **Inferential statistics** is used when tentative conclusions about a population are drawn on the basis of data contained in a representative sample. The question of whether to accept the shipment of components (the population) based on the sample of 100 components is an example of inferential statistics.

Numerical data are either discrete or continuous. **Discrete data** have limited, specific possible values. **Continuous data** can assume any value over some range. A further classification of data is their level of measurement. At the lowest level, **nominal data** are categorical data that are assigned numeric codes. **Ordinal data** are ranked—the order of the data values is meaningful. In **interval data,** both the order of the data and the difference between any two data values have meaning. Finally, **ratio data** have all the properties of interval data and also contain a definite zero point. Nominal and ordinal data make up the category of **qualitative data,** while **quantitative data** consist of interval and ratio data. Most statistical techniques do not distinguish between interval and ratio data but do require that the data have at least an interval level of measurement; that is, the sample consists of quantitative data.

To obtain information (a sample), data can be obtained from primary or secondary sources. **Primary data** come from an original (primary) source, and are meant to gain insight into a specific research question. Sources of primary data include mail-in questionnaires, personal interviews, and designed experiments. **Secondary data** consist of previously recorded data, such as information contained in government reports, industry financial statements, and business periodicals.

Most statistical methods assume that a **simple random sample** of size n has been collected such that each set of n measurements has the same chance of being selected for the sample. Such a sample allows you to generalize information from the sample to the entire population. An easy way of producing random numbers is via a computerized random number generator.

Nonrandom samples are samples selected in a convenient or deliberate manner with little or no attention paid to randomization. The three nonrandom sampling strategies discussed in this chapter were convenience sampling, judgment sampling, and quota sampling. A sample selected on the accessibility of the sample subjects is a **convenience sample.** Such a sample may consist of close friends, a classroom of students, shoppers haphazardly selected at a local mall, and so on. A **judgment sample** is one where sample subjects are deliberately selected because they are believed to have expertise regarding the population of interest. Data collected from a city intentionally selected to test market a new product would also be an example of a judgment sample. A sample that matches proportions for one or more key characteristics of the population is a **quota sample.**

Questionnaires can provide you with a large amount of data that address a specific question (or topic) of interest. Care must be taken when designing a questionnaire to avoid such things as leading questions, too many questions, and questions that fail to follow a logical pattern. The five steps involved in constructing such an instrument are: (1) deciding what types of questions to use, (2) writing the questions, (3) deciding on the question sequence and questionnaire length, (4) pretesting and revising the questionnaire, and (5) ensuring a high response rate.

Preparing questionnaire data for computer input is referred to as **data coding.** Qualitative data consisting of nominal data (such as male/female) and interval data (such as Likert-scale responses) are generally converted to numerical form for easier computer input and manipulation.

REVIEW EXERCISES 1.21–1.30

1.21 An operations manager at a semiconductor company is interested in the satisfaction level of the firms that buy computer chips from the company. Approximately 1000 firms buys chips from this company. The manager has developed a satisfaction scale from 1 to 100 for the respondents to mark their level of satisfaction with the company's products. This scale is to be included on a survey to a sample of 100 firms that buy from this firm.

  a. What is the population of interest?
  b. How can a random sample be selected?
  c. What is the parameter of the population that is of interest?
  d. What is the statistic corresponding to the parameter requested in part (c)?

1.22 Classify each of the following data sources as primary or secondary.

  a. Data collected during a manufacturing process to determine the proportion of defective items produced
  b. Data published by the U.S. Bureau of Census in their document *Statistical Abstracts of the United States*
  c. Data collected by management to determine the acceptability of a new policy by its employees
  d. Data published in *Standard and Poors* on the financial liabilities of energy service companies

1.23 Rikkyo University's Institute of Industrial Relations, commissioned by the National Institute for Research Advancement, conducted a survey in summer 1996 on labor-management relations in Japanese companies operating in China. Questionnaires were sent to 837 Japanese companies doing business in China with 50 or more employees, of which 266 responded.

a. What is the population of interest?

b. How might a random sample of the Japanese companies be obtained?

c. How might a convenience sample be obtained? Which would be more appropriate for statistical analysis?

1.24 Nihon Keizai Shimbun, Inc., conducted its annual survey in Japan on growth potential and the thinking of executives at entrepreneurial companies on Sept. 1, 1997. Of the 1302 subject companies, all established in the 1970s and later, 553, or 42.4%, returned valid replies. From these respondents, 214 companies plan to issue public shares within five years.

a. Explain how descriptive statistics could be used to show the yearly results of the survey with respect to the number of companies indicating that their company is planning on issuing public shares.

b. Could inferential statistics be used to draw conclusions about the population of interest?

(Source: *The Nikkei Weekly*, "Poll Finds Great Interest in Getting to Market." Nov. 24, 1997, p. 11.)

1.25 State which each of the following groups of people or objects represents, a population or a sample.

a. A list of 500 employees of General Motors (*Hint:* Could this be either a sample or a population? Explain.)

b. Forty students who were randomly stopped and questioned on a university campus

c. Two hundred people who were selected randomly from a telephone book to receive a marketing questionnaire

d. The list of all possible choices of 2 cards from a deck of 52 cards

e. A batch of electronic parts ready for inspection

1.26 Typically after live presidential candidate debates on network television, there appears a phone number for viewers to call and state which candidate performed the best. Would this be considered a simple random sample? a convenience sample? Why?

1.27 Questionnaires are often sent to employees to determine their overall job satisfaction and to determine how certain groups of individuals perceive the work environment. For example, psychologist Barbara Ilardi conducted a study of 117 employees at a New York shoe factory. She administered a questionnaire to determine the self-esteem, health, and personal initiative of employees. Suppose she had collected the following information on two employees:

	Employee 1	Employee 2
Own home	Yes	No
Number of promotions in the past seven years	3	2
Medical expenses last year	$1830	$250
Enjoy current job (always, sometimes, usually not, never)	Always	Usually Not
Expect a promotion in the next two years	Yes	No
Date of birth	April 22, 1955	Aug. 18, 1958
Annual salary	$71,000	$56,000
Years married	13	8

(Source: *Washington Post*, July 11, 1993, p. H2, "Odd Jobs," by Sherwood Ross)

a. What type of data and which level of measurement would you classify each response?

b. Set up a spreadsheet (with column labels) and enter the data from these two employees.

1.28 "A lot of new wealth has been created this year [1997], and a lot of people are wanting to splurge," says John Macht, president of the Macht Group, retail and marketing consultants in Boston. According to a Dom Perignon survey of chief executives at Fortune 1,000 companies, 70% will hand out year-end bonuses. In New England, 81% planned to give cash rewards. Suppose that the following data were requested of employees in the New England area to determine the demand for retail buying. Classify each of the requested data items as either qualitative or quantitative and give the appropriate level of measurement:

a. How many people in your family?

b. Rank the three most desirable gifts you would like to receive during this holiday season.

c. What was the price of the most expensive gift that you have purchased this year?

d. What was the name of the store where you bought the most expensive gift purchased this year?

e. What is your age?

f. What is your gender?

(Source: *The Boston Herald*, "Luxury Retailers See Brisk Gift Sales." Dec. 16, 1997, p. 36.)

1.29 The Marketing Research Institute conducted a survey showing that Americans boosted their retirement savings by 2% in 1997, to $203 a month, from $199 in 1996. It was the third straight annual increase, not counting pension benefits and Social Security, after the figure fell to $148 a month in 1994. Suppose you are working for the Marketing Research Institute and are asked to conduct a sample survey on how the working class is saving for retirement.

a. What is population of interest?

b. Describe a procedure to select a random sample.

c. Write five questions to determine how much workers have been saving over the years, how satisfied they are with their savings, and how and when they plan to retire.

d. What incentive might be appropriate to encourage customers to complete the survey?

e. What follow-up action might achieve a higher response rate?

(Source: *The Baltimore Sun,* "Americans' Savings for Retirement Grew by 2%." Dec. 9, 1997, p. 2D.)

1.30 Marketing researchers often use a list for drawing simple random samples of consumers to assess a new product. To illustrate one way of selecting a random sample from a list of members, perform the following procedure. In Excel, type a 1 in A1 and a 2 in A2. Highlight both A1 and A2. Now drag the handle on the highlighted region down to row 100. Think of the 100 numbers as representing 100 consumers on a list. Click on **Tools ➤ Data Analysis ➤ Sampling.** Now select the 100 numbers in the first column for input (A1: A200) and click on Random and type in 10. Select an output cell (say, B1). Then click OK. Note that the 10 numbers displayed represent a random sample from the population of 100 members.

COMPUTER EXERCISES USING THE DATABASES

EXERCISE 1 — APPENDIX E

For each of the variables defined in the database of household financial variables, determine if the corresponding data would be classified as discrete or continuous.

EXERCISE 2 — APPENDIX E

For each of the variables in the database of household financial variables, what is the highest level of measurement for the corresponding data?

EXERCISE 3 — APPENDIX E

Would you classify the data in this database as primary or secondary?

EXERCISE 4 — APPENDIX E

For each of the variables defined in the database of household variables, would you classify the corresponding data as qualitative or quantitative?

EXERCISE 5 — APPENDIX F

Answer exercises 1 through 4 for each variable defined in the database using the financial variables on companies.

INSIGHTS FROM STATISTICS IN ACTION: WHY SO MANY POLLS?

The introductory case study in Statistics in Action mentioned that a poll (be it nationwide or local) is actually a *sample* taken from a much larger *population.* Data obtained from polls vary in type (discrete/continuous) and strength (nominal/ordinal/interval/ratio). For example, yes/no responses would be discrete data with a nominal level of measurement, whereas incomes would be continuous/ratio data. Using the concepts introduced in this chapter, answer the following questions.

1. The *Wall Street Journal* examines politics and the economy as well as changes in society brought about by technology and the introduction of new products. What are some types of data that might have been collected? Can you think of data from several of the functional areas of business: accounting, finance, marketing, management, and information systems?

2. In the Metro Poll, what do you believe is the population of interest? Do you believe that descriptive statistics may have been used to illustrate some of the findings of Metro Poll? Give an example of how the results of this poll for the different local areas might have been presented.

3. Here are some questions that a *Wall Street Journal* poll might use in a survey. Which level of measurement would you classify each response?

   a. Are you a voting citizen?
   b. What is your mortgage payment?
   c. How much money have you saved in a Roth IRA?
   d. How long have you owned your home?
   e. Would you say that your confidence in the present government administration is: (1) Very high, (2) Somewhat high, (3) Low, or (4) Very low?
   f. List your favorite three TV commercials.
   g. Rank your favorite three TV commercials in order of creativity.

4. Think of a way that names can be selected from a phone directory that would make the list easy to construct and yet still essentially a random sample.

Sources: *The Wall Street Journal,* "How This Poll Was Conducted." June 25, 1998, p. A24.

The Richmond Times Dispatch, "Area Poll Finds Less Worry about Crime." July 10, 1998, p. B1.

CHAPTER 1 APPENDIX: DATA ANALYSIS WITH MINITAB

OPENING EXCEL DATA FILES IN MINITAB

To open a worksheet in Minitab, click on File ➤ Open Worksheet and select a file. In the Files of Type box, select Excel. The user form will look like the one shown here.

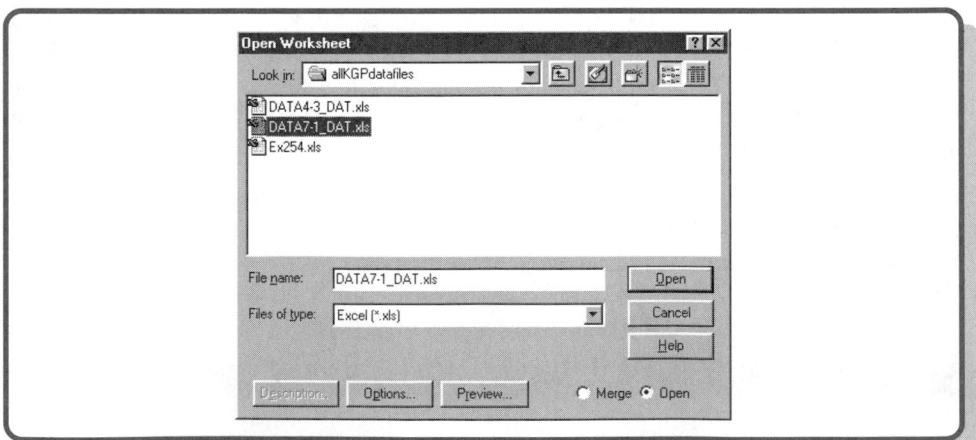

Click on the Options button to specify whether the columns have headings. The user form below will appear. Select the None option if there are no variable names listed in the first row; otherwise select Automatic. Note that a row number can be selected to read in the data (see the Use Row option). The period is selected in this example as the decimal separator in numeric data.

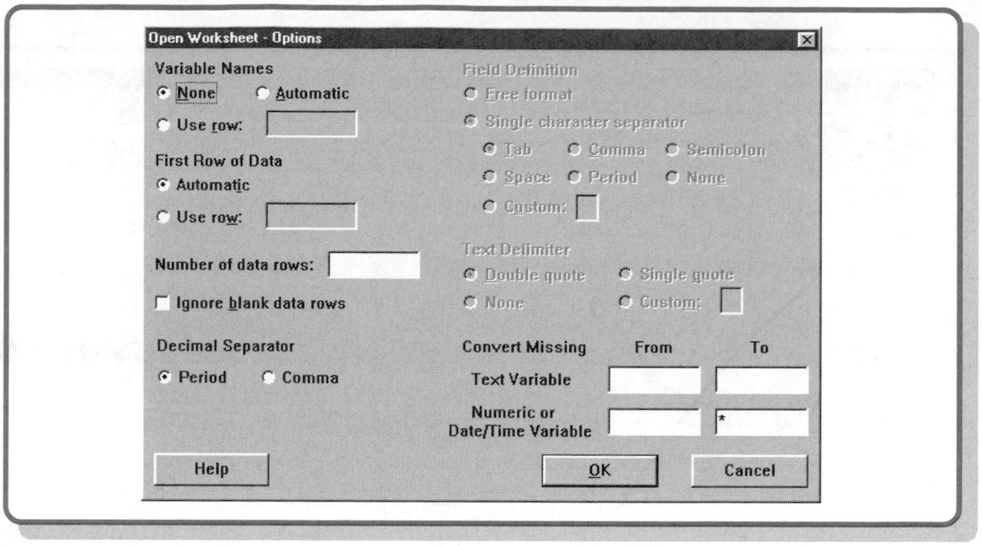

RANDOMLY GENERATING UNIFORM OBSERVATIONS

To illustrate the process of generating random observations in MINITAB, two examples are provided. In the first example, real numbers between two specified values are randomly generated. In the second example, only integer numbers are randomly generated. In these examples, twenty numbers will be generated in three columns of MINITAB. The numbers generated are between 0 and 1000.

Open MINITAB so that both a session and a data window are opened (both visible). Click on the blank cell above the first row and below the column label C1. Type in X. Likewise, label columns C2 and C3 as Y and Z. Now click on Calc ➤ Random Data ➤ Uniform. In the form that appears, type 20 for the number of observations to generate. Press the return key, and the labels of the columns X, Y, and Z will appear. Highlight these three columns and click on the select button, or alternatively, type X-Z in the Store in Columns(s) box. Type in 0 for the lower endpoint and 1000 for the upper endpoint. Note that the X, Y, and Z need to be in contiguous columns if the notation X-Z is used. If the columns of output are not contiguous, then each column name needs to be inputted separately. The column names C1-C3 could also have been used in this example in lieu of the column names. The MINITAB diagram below shows the user form with the necessary information for generating 20 random observations between 0 and 1000 for this example.

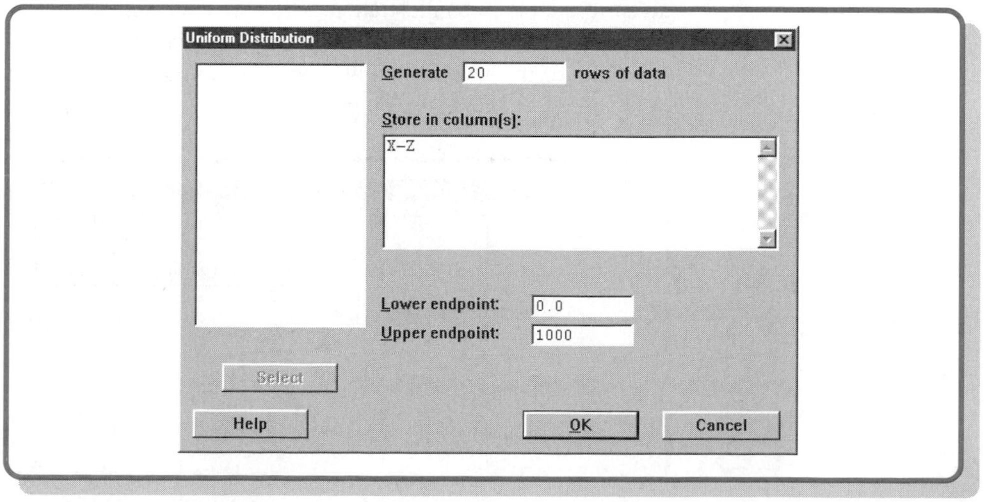

The randomly generated observations appear in the data sheet illustrated here. Note that the MINITAB code for this example is automatically typed in the session window. This code could be used as command language to generate the random observations rather than using the pull-down menus. Under the Editor pull-down menu, an option is available so that command language can be either enabled or disabled.

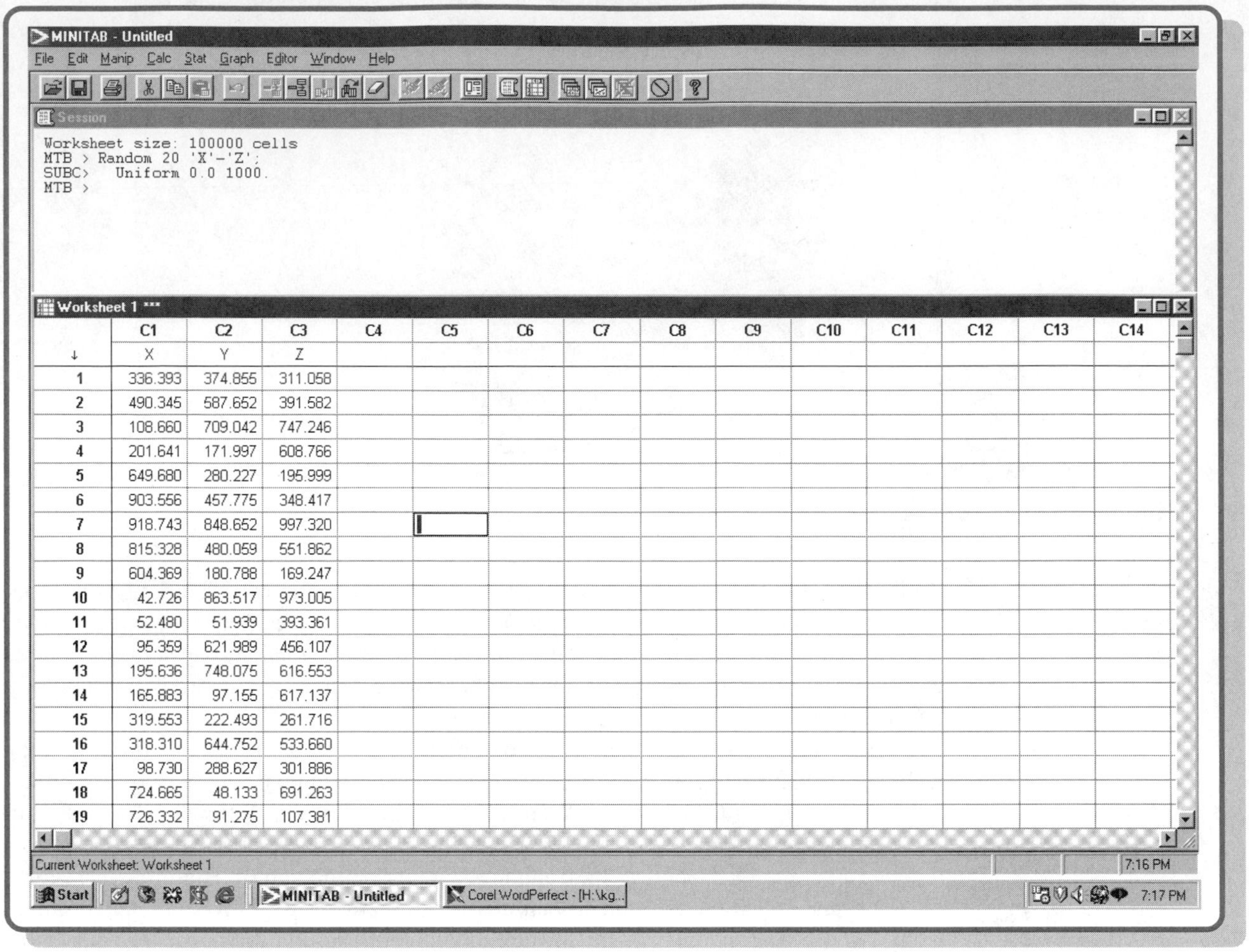

MINITAB - Untitled
File Edit Manip Calc Stat Graph Editor Window Help
Session
Worksheet size: 100000 cells
MTB > Random 20 'X'-'Z';
SUBC> Uniform 0.0 1000.
MTB >
Worksheet 1 ***
C1 C2 C3 C4 C5 C6 C7 C8 C9 C10 C11 C12 C13 C14
X Y Z
1 336.393 374.855 311.058
2 490.345 587.652 391.582
3 108.660 709.042 747.246
4 201.641 171.997 608.766
5 649.680 280.227 195.999
6 903.556 457.775 348.417
7 918.743 848.652 997.320
8 815.328 480.059 551.862
9 604.369 180.788 169.247
10 42.726 863.517 973.005
11 52.480 51.939 393.361
12 95.359 621.989 456.107
13 195.636 748.075 616.553
14 165.883 97.155 617.137
15 319.553 222.493 261.716
16 318.310 644.752 533.660
17 98.730 288.627 301.886
18 724.665 48.133 691.263
19 726.332 91.275 107.381
Current Worksheet: Worksheet 1
7:16 PM
Start
MINITAB - Untitled
Corel WordPerfect - [H:\kg...]
7:17 PM

RANDOMLY GENERATING INTEGER OBSERVATIONS

Open MINITAB so that both a session and a data window are opened (both visible). As in the previous illustration, label columns C1, C2, and C3 as X, Y, and Z. Now click on **Calc ➤ Random Data ➤ Integer.** Notice that the user form for this example is identical to that given in the previous illustration. The only exception is that the title of the user form says Integer Distribution rather than Uniform Distribution. This user form is presented below. The execution of this user form will produce results similar to that in the data window presented in the previous MINITAB output, except there will be no decimal part in these numbers.

Integer Distribution
Generate 20 rows of data
Store in column(s):
X-Z
Minimum value: 0
Maximum value: 1000
Select
Help
OK
Cancel

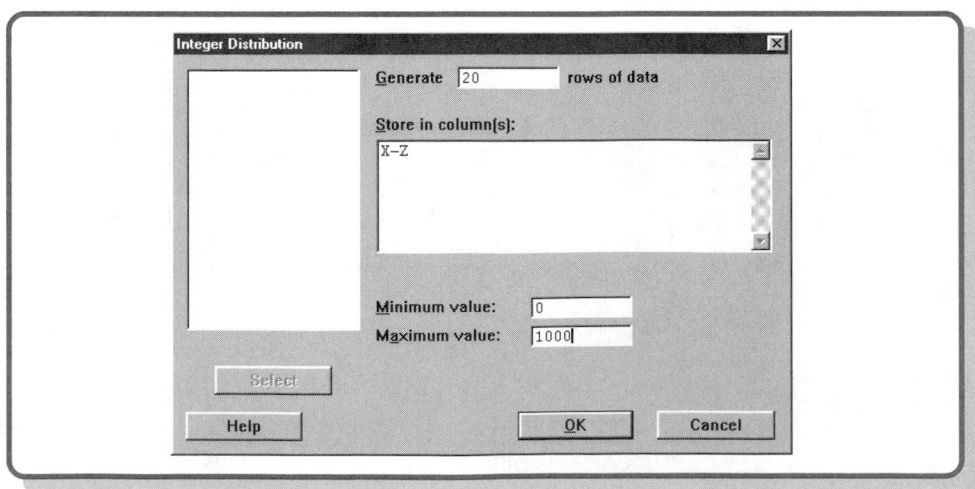

CHAPTER 2
DATA PRESENTATION USING DESCRIPTIVE GRAPHS

STATISTICS IN ACTION: HOW WELL RUN ARE THE TOP 100 GLOBAL COMPANIES?

Top executives of large companies reap millions from running their companies successfully. But with the economies of many countries being interdependent, are companies in the United States still able to maintain their profit momentum among so many global competitors? Corporate America is willing to handsomely compensate its executives for overcoming barriers and obstacles to increased marketshare and profits in an increasingly global marketplace. Do these compensation packages squander resources that could be used by the company to become more competitive?

The norm in corporate America is to pay top management in the form of thousands—sometimes millions—of dollars in stock options. The idea behind this thinking is that top executives will be motivated to drive up their stock by skillfully managing their companies. "The trend today is incentive compensation," says Alfred Fiore, general manager of Manhattan-based HSM&R Consulting.

While many consultants and company officials defend the millions being offered in executive pay packages, many financial analysts and working-class citizens are wondering if these amounts can be justified. A growing national debate about how much is too much is causing middle America to examine U.S. companies on a comparative basis with global companies. Not only increases in revenue but also the changes in profits are examined. Should these companies share the wealth with their employees as opposed to rewarding top management so heavily? Are the top companies in the U.S. really showing much better performance than companies across the world? Alfred Fiore believes that when you consider the total pay package and when you consider the size of many companies, the hurdles are not being set high enough for the compensation that CEOs are receiving.

Unlike salaries and bonuses, stock options are not considered an expense to the company on its income statement and help show that senior management is looking after shareholder interests, Fiore said. A recent study revealed that newly granted options at 100 of the largest public companies in the United States were worth an average of $8.933 million, which was up 33% from the previous year. Overall, a booming stock market that has increased the value of option grants by hefty numbers for some companies. The notion of exercising options has long been accepted as part of top management's compensation. In a bull market, these numbers look high. However, there is no guarantee what options, in general, will be worth when top management is allowed to exercise them.

This chapter will enable you to

- Discuss the differences in performance of the largest global companies;
- Construct various graphs that describe the sales and profits of the top 100 global companies;

- Use these graphs to form conclusions about the performance of these companies; and
- Compare the performance of companies in the U.S. with Japanese companies.

A LOOK BACK/INTRODUCTION

Chapter I introduced you to some of the basic terms used in statistics. One of the key concepts was the idea of acquiring data using a sample from a population. It was also emphasized that the proper use of statistics depends on the nature of the data involved. Are the data discrete or continuous? Are the values nominal, ordinal, interval, or ratio?

Once the data have been gathered, the problem becomes learning whatever we can from them. One method is to describe the data by means of a graph. A graph allows us to discuss intelligently the "shape" of the data.

Everyone has heard the expression that a picture is worth a thousand words (or, more appropriate here, a thousand numbers). This is especially true in statistics, where it may be vital to reduce a large set of numbers to a graph (or picture) that illustrates the structure underlying the data. For example, in a business meeting a quick glance at a graph demonstrates a point much more easily than does a page filled with numbers and words.

Let's illustrate why you may want to describe a data set by using a graph. Suppose that the student affairs director at Bellaire College (a fictitious, small private college in California) has compiled the starting salaries of the 50 graduating business majors. Bellaire offers business degrees in accounting, information systems, and marketing. The salaries, along with the number of campus interviews for each person, are shown in Table 2.1.

How can you summarize and present these data in a form that is easily understood? There are many graphical methods that can be used, depending on the nature of the data and what you are trying to demonstrate about them. When presenting data graphically, the first step usually is to combine the data values into a frequency distribution.

TABLE 2.1

Starting salaries (thousands of dollars) and number of campus interviews for graduating business majors at Bellaire College.

Major	No. of Graduating Students	Starting Salary/No. of Interviews						
Accounting	26	36.5	34.4	35.9	30.9	32.4	34.5	35.3
		15	19	5	7	14	12	11
		34.3	36.6	31.6	36.1	30.7	38.7	32.0
		6	7	5	12	13	7	6
		36.3	35.6	33.0	37.4	30.7	36.4	34.2
		7	10	16	5	11	21	4
		31.8	34.3	38.8	33.5	38.0		
		19	21	5	16	19		
Information systems	10	31.3	30.6	31.2	33.1	29.8	33.1	30.7
		15	14	10	16	5	16	21
		31.5	34.5	32.9				
		8	14	14				
Marketing	14	29.3	31.8	28.8	30.0	32.8	33.7	32.2
		11	13	7	12	5	17	9
		27.8	33.2	32.0	34.7	33.8	30.2	31.2
		8	20	16	19	8	20	8

2.1 FREQUENCY DISTRIBUTIONS

We need to reduce a large set of data to a much smaller set of numbers that can be more easily comprehended. If you have recorded the population sizes of 500 randomly selected cities, there is no easy way to examine these 500 numbers visually and learn anything. It would be easier to examine a condensed version of this set of data, such as that presented in Table 2.2.

This type of summary, called a **frequency distribution,** consists of *classes* (such as "10,000 and under 15,000") and *frequencies* (the number of data values within each class). What do you gain using this procedure? You reduce 500 numbers to ten classes and frequencies. You can study the frequency distribution in Table 2.2 and learn a great deal about the shape of this data set. For example, approximately 50% of the cities in your sample have a population between 20,000 and 35,000. Also, only 1% of the cities contain 50,000 people or more.

FREQUENCY DISTRIBUTION FOR CONTINUOUS DATA

A frequency distribution is typically condensed from data having an interval or ratio level of measurement. When you construct a frequency distribution for continuous data, you need to decide how many classes to use (10 in Table 2.2) and the class width (5000 in Table 2.2).

There is no "correct" **number of classes** (K) to use in a frequency distribution. However, you can best condense a set of data by using between 5 and 20 classes. The usual procedure is to choose what you think would be an adequate number of classes and to construct the resulting frequency distribution. A quick look at this distribution will tell you if you have reduced the data too much (not enough classes; K is too small) or not enough (too many classes; K is too large). One indication that K is too small is that a large portion of your data (say, nearly 50%) lies in one class. If you observe a number of empty classes, or many classes with a frequency of 1 or 2, this may indicate that K is too large. If you have a very large set of data, you can use a larger number of classes than you would for a smaller data set. Whenever you construct frequency distributions using a computer, select several different values of K and look at the effects of the different choices.

Having chosen a value for K, the next step is to examine

$$\frac{\text{range}}{\text{number of classes}} = \frac{H - L}{K}$$

where H = the highest value in your data and L = the lowest value in your data. Round the result to a value that provides an easy-to-interpret frequency distribution. This is the **class width (CW).** The width of each class should be the same. Later we will discuss possible exceptions to this rule for the first and last classes.

TABLE 2.2

Frequency distribution of the population of 500 cities.

Class Number	Size of City	Frequency
1	Under 10,000	4
2	10,000 and under 15,000	51
3	15,000 and under 20,000	77
4	20,000 and under 25,000	105
5	25,000 and under 30,000	84
6	30,000 and under 35,000	60
7	35,000 and under 40,000	45
8	40,000 and under 45,000	38
9	45,000 and under 50,000	31
10	50,000 and over	5
		500

DEFINITION

Class width (CW) = the value of $\dfrac{H-L}{K}$ rounded (up or down) to a value that is easy to interpret

Suppose that, for a particular set of data, you have elected to use $K = 10$ classes in your frequency distribution and that $H = 106$ and $L = 10$. Then

$$\frac{H-L}{K} = \frac{106-10}{10} = 9.6$$

The desirable class width to use here is CW = 10.

Here are some additional examples of rounding to determine the class width:

$\dfrac{H-L}{K}$	Rounded Value (the CW)
89.6	100
1.38	1.5
48.2	50
12.4	10

Now let us use the 50 salaries in Table 2.1 to construct a frequency distribution of the salaries, using six classes. Our first step should be to arrange the data from smallest to largest. This arrangement is called an **ordered array.** Both the original data and the ordered data are **raw data,** since they are not grouped into classes. The ordered salaries are listed in Table 2.3. Using the ordered data, $H = 38.8$ and $L = 27.8$. Since $K = 6$, we compute CW:

$$\frac{38.8-27.8}{6} = 1.83$$

The best choice for CW is CW = 2.

There are two rules to remember in selecting the first class: this class must contain L, your lowest data value, and it should begin with a value that makes the frequency distribution easy to interpret. Because $L = 27.8$, our first class should begin with 27, that is, $27,000. The resulting frequency distribution is shown in Table 2.4, which also shows each **relative frequency,** where

---

TABLE **2.3**   Fifty starting salaries for business majors at Bellaire College, presented as original data and as an ordered array.

Original Data					Ordered Array				
36.5	34.4	35.9	30.9	32.4	27.8	28.8	29.3	29.8	30.0
34.5	35.3	34.3	36.6	31.6	30.2	30.6	30.7	30.7	30.7
36.1	30.7	38.7	32.0	36.3	30.9	31.2	31.2	31.3	31.5
35.6	33.0	37.4	30.7	36.4	31.6	31.8	31.8	32.0	32.0
34.2	31.8	34.3	38.8	33.5	32.2	32.4	32.8	32.9	33.0
38.0	31.3	30.6	31.2	33.1	33.1	33.1	33.2	33.5	33.7
29.8	33.1	30.7	31.5	34.5	33.8	34.2	34.3	34.3	34.4
32.9	29.3	31.8	28.8	30.0	34.5	34.5	34.7	35.3	35.6
32.8	33.7	32.2	27.8	33.2	35.9	36.1	36.3	36.4	36.5
32.0	34.7	33.8	30.2	31.2	36.6	37.4	38.0	38.7	38.8

TABLE 2.4

Frequency distribution of starting salaries using six classes. This format is used for *continuous* data.

Class Number	Class	Frequency	Relative Frequency
1	27 and under 29	2	.04
2	29 and under 31	9	.18
3	31 and under 33	13	.26
4	33 and under 35	14	.28
5	35 and under 37	8	.16
6	37 and under 39	4	.08
		50	1.00

TABLE 2.5

Frequency distribution of starting salaries using CW = 1.

Class Number	Class	Frequency	Relative Frequency
1	27 and under 28	1	.02
2	28 and under 29	1	.02
3	29 and under 30	2	.04
4	30 and under 31	7	.14
5	31 and under 32	7	.14
6	32 and under 33	6	.12
7	33 and under 34	7	.14
8	34 and under 35	7	.14
9	35 and under 36	3	.06
10	36 and under 37	5	.10
11	37 and under 38	1	.02
12	38 and under 39	3	.06
		50	1.00

$$\text{relative frequency} = \frac{\text{frequency}}{\text{total number of values in data set}}$$

For example, in class 2 the relative frequency is .18; this class contains 9 of the 50 values. The advantage of using relative frequencies is that the reader can tell immediately what percentage of the data values lies in each class.

COMMENTS

Often a set of data contains one or two very small or very large numbers quite unlike the remaining data values. Such values are called **outliers.** It is generally better to include these values in one or two **open-ended classes.** The distribution in Table 2.2 contains two open-ended classes: class 1 (under 10,000) and class 10 (50,000 and over). *You may need an open-ended class if your data set includes one or more outliers or your present frequency distribution has too many empty classes on the low or high end.*

Another alternative for the salary data is to use CW = 1, to provide more detail in the frequency distribution. This would produce 12 classes, as shown in Table 2.5. We could argue that 12 classes are too many, consid-

ering that the data set has only 50 values. Many classes contain only one or two data values. Another alternative would be to use open-ended classes on each end of the distribution, such as "under 29" and "37 and over."

The highest and lowest values describing a class are the **class limits.** For example, in Table 2.4, the lower class limit of class 2 is 29, and the upper class limit is 31. The **class midpoints** are those values in the center of the class.* Each midpoint in a sense "represents" its class. These values often are used in a statistical graph as well as for calculations performed on the information contained within a frequency distribution. The midpoint of class 2 in Table 2.4 is (29 + 31)/2 = 30.

---

* Class midpoints are often referred to as *class marks*.

CONSTRUCTING A FREQUENCY DISTRIBUTION

1. Gather the sample data.
2. Arrange the data in an ordered array.
3. Select the number of classes to be used.
4. Determine the class width.
5. Determine the class limits for each class; begin by assigning to the first class a lower class limit that will make the frequency distribution easy to interpret.
6. Count the number of data values in each class (the class frequencies).
7. Summarize the class frequencies in a frequency distribution table.

FREQUENCY DISTRIBUTION FOR DISCRETE DATA

When your data are discrete, the procedure is almost the same as when they are continuous, except (1) we define the class width CW to be the difference between the lower class limits and not the difference between an upper and lower limit (this also will work for continuous data) and (2) the description of each class is slightly different because we no longer use the "and under" definition of each class. Thus, if CW = 5, and *the data are continuous,* our classes might be 5 and under 10, 10 and under 15, and 15 and under 20. *If the data are discrete,* they might be 5 to 9, 10 to 14, and 15 to 19. Note that for the continuous data, the class midpoints are 7.5, 12.5, and 17.5. For the discrete data, however, the midpoints are 7, 12, and 17.

Using the data in Table 2.1, we can construct a frequency distribution using six classes for the number of campus interviews for each student. First we develop an ordered array:

4	5	5	5	5	5	5	6	6	7	7
7	7	7	8	8	8	8	9	10	10	11
11	11	12	12	12	13	13	14	14	14	14
15	15	16	16	16	16	16	17	19	19	19
19	20	20	21	21	21					

So, $H = 21$ and $L = 4$. Since

$$\frac{H - L}{K} = \frac{21 - 4}{6} = 2.83$$

we use CW = 3. The resulting frequency and relative frequency distributions are shown in Table 2.6.

TABLE 2.6

Frequency distribution of the number of interviews. This format is used for discrete data.

Class Number	Class	Frequency	Relative Frequency
1	4–6	9	.18
2	7–9	10	.20
3	10–12	8	.16
4	13–15	8	.16
5	16–18	6	.12
6	19–21	9	.18
		50	1.00

EXERCISES 2.1–2.7

UNDERSTANDING THE MECHANICS

2.1 A frequency table is displayed below indicating the number of individuals with a minimum balance in their check book at a local bank.

Minimum Balance in Dollars	Frequency
0 and under 1000	1200
1000 and under 2000	1500
2000 and under 3000	2500
3000 and under 4000	2300
4000 and under 5000	500
5000 and under 6000	50
6000 and under 7000	10
7000 and under 8000	2

a. What is the class width?
b. What are the class limits?
c. Calculate the group relative frequencies of each group.

2.2 Milk cartons with expired dates typically are discarded. The number of milk cartons with expired dates at EZ Shop for each day of January are presented below.

3	5	6	0	1	3	4	9	12	15
21	10	15	18	5	8	11	16	8	1
5	2	3	9	19	15	12	7	6	11

a. Convert the original data into an ordered array.
b. What number of classes would you use?
c. Are the data discrete or continuous?
d. Construct a frequency distribution.

2.3 A random sample of two-bedroom condominium apartments at Vera Beach, Florida, revealed that the asking price of units on the market varied from $111,000 to $224,000. A frequency distribution of the asking price of the condominiums is needed.
a. Set up class limits if 5 classes are desired.
b. Set up class limits if 6 classes are desired.
c. Set up class limits if 12 classes are desired.

APPLYING THE NEW CONCEPTS

2.4 The percentage of increase in the property tax of 26 randomly selected homes in a certain subdivision of Memphis, Tenn., are as follows.

5.10	7.35	13.34	18.19	9.12
9.89	10.45	12.89	17.91	.51
3.42	8.34	11.12	14.51	7.25
12.35	11.89	14.10	29.1	14.91
11.89	17.89	15.30	26.1	19.80
18.45				

a. Construct a relative frequency distribution with 6 classes.
b. From the relative frequency distribution, determine what proportion of homes had an increase of more than 15% in property tax.
c. What interpretation can you give to the shape of the distribution?

2.5 The United States Office of Employment Projections conducted a population survey to determine the characteristics about the work force. In its survey, a tabulation was performed to state the number of multiple job holders (in thousands) and their respective weekly earnings. The results are presented below.

Weekly Earnings	Number of Multiple Job Holders
$0 and under $211	1462
$211 and under $334	1295
$334 and under $493	1354
$493 and under $730	1297
$730 and higher	1288

a. What do you achieve by tabulating the data in the form of a frequency distribution?
b. Form a relative frequency distribution.
c. What proportion of the multiple job holders were making $493 or more per week?

2.6 Corporate Resources Group conducted a study of several cities across the United States to compare cost of living. More than 200 items were used to compile an index measuring the cost of living. These items included housing, food, clothing, cars, drink, and entertainment. The cities selected and their rating are presented below.

City	Cost-of-Living Rating
Atlanta	72
Boston	82
Chicago	88
Cleveland	70
Detroit	81
Honolulu	87
Houston	85
Lexington, KY	71
Los Angeles	88
San Francisco	86
St. Louis	79
Miami	89
Minneapolis	74
Pittsburgh	74
Portland, OR	67
New York	100
Seattle	74
Washington	83
White Plains, NY	86
Winston-Salem	70

(Source: *Star-Telegram,* "Survey says Tokyo is priciest city in the world," Aug 6, 1997, p. 2C.)

a. Summarize the data by forming a frequency distribution with 7 classes.
b. Describe the shape of the relative frequency distribution.
c. Is it easier to make conclusions about the number of cities with cost of living ratings using the raw data or using the frequency distribution?

2.7 The following are the unemployment rates (percent of available labor) for the year 1984 for selected northern cities in the United States:

6.8, 2.6, 4.6, 5.4, 6.8, 4.3, 17.1, 6.7, 6.2, 6.4, 4.7, 5.1, 2.7, 16.8, 3.4, 2.2, 4.1, 9.8, 10.4, 11.5

a. Calculate the class width for a frequency distribution of the data.

b. What would you hope to achieve by tabulating the data in the form of a frequency distribution?

c. Prepare a frequency distribution table.

2.2 HISTOGRAMS AND STEM-AND-LEAF DIAGRAMS

HISTOGRAMS

After you complete a frequency distribution, your next step will be to construct a "picture" of these data values using a histogram. A **histogram** is a graphical representation of a frequency distribution. It describes the shape of the data. You can use it to answer quickly such questions as, are the data symmetric? and where do most of the data values lie? For the frequency distribution in Table 2.4, the corresponding histogram is illustrated in Figure 2.1. The height of each bar represents the frequency of that particular class, and the bars must be adjoining (no gaps).

Avoid constructing a "squashed" histogram by using the vertical axis wisely. The top of this axis (15 in Figure 2.1) should be a value close to your largest class frequency (14). Notice also that, for this example, you obtain a more concise picture by starting the horizontal axis at 27 rather than at zero and putting a scale break (⌄) before the 27 mark.

A histogram can be constructed using the relative frequencies rather than the frequencies. A **relative frequency histogram** of the salary distribution in Table 2.4 is shown in Figure 2.2. Notice that the shape of a frequency histogram (Figure 2.1) and its corresponding relative frequency histogram (Figure 2.2) are the same. One advantage of using a relative frequency histogram is that the units on the vertical axis are always between zero and one, so the reader can tell at a glance what percentage of the data lies in each class.

Most standard statistical packages will construct a histogram from your data. Using the Excel macro provided with this textbook,* or using MINITAB, you can control the number of classes and the class width in your histogram. Constructing a MINITAB histogram is discussed in the end-of-chapter appendix. We will illustrate the Excel procedure using the salary data in Table 2.3. The data must first be entered into column A of your Excel spreadsheet. The first 17 values (out of 50) are shown in Figure 2.4. To use the Excel macro provided with this textbook, click on **KGP Data Analysis ➤ Quantitative Data Charts/Tables ➤ Histogram/Freq. Charts.** You will then see the input form shown in Figure 2.3. Fill in the input range (A1:A50—that is, cells A1 through A50) and the output range (B1—this is the upper left cell of the output section). Also click on the checkbox alongside **Frequencies** in the **Table** section and **Frequency Histogram** in the **Chart Output Options** section and finally click on "OK." The result of this is the frequency distribution

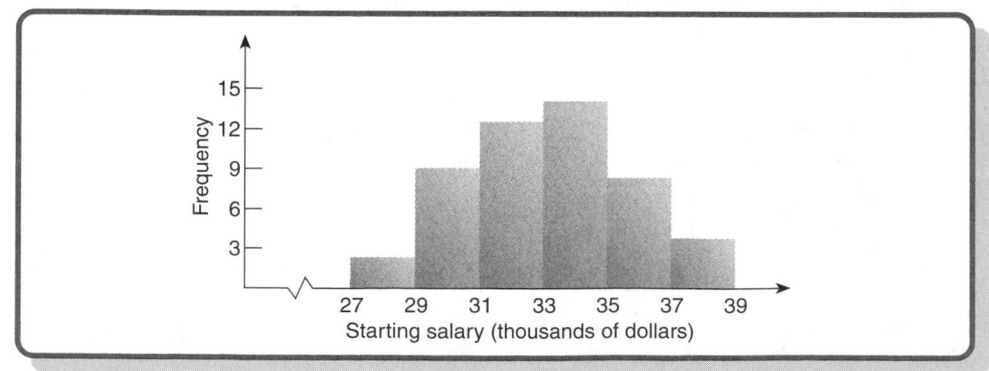

FIGURE 2.1

Frequency histogram for the frequency distribution shown in Table 2.4. Twenty-seven (out of 50) salaries were between $31,000 and $35,000, with 12 people receiving $35,000 or more.

---

* An Excel macro is a set of instructions that greatly simplifies an Excel graph or statistical procedure. These macros will be invisible to you but are available whenever you click on **KGP Data Analysis** in the menu bar at the top of your Excel screen.

FIGURE 2.2

Relative frequency histogram for the frequency distribution in Table 2.4. This histogram shows that 54% (26% plus 28%) of the salaries were between $31,000 and $35,000. 24% (16% plus 8%) of the people received $35,000 or more.

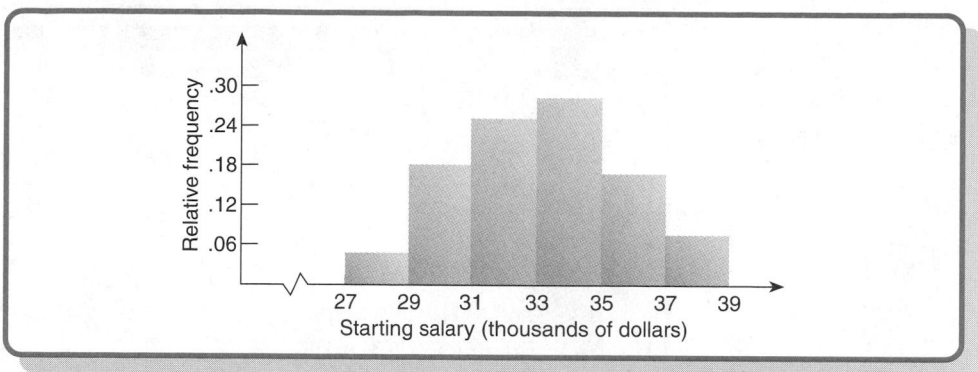

FIGURE 2.3

Input form for the Excel KGP Data Analysis macro. Click on **KGP Data Analysis ➤ Quantitative Data Charts/Tables ➤ Histogram/Freq. Charts.**

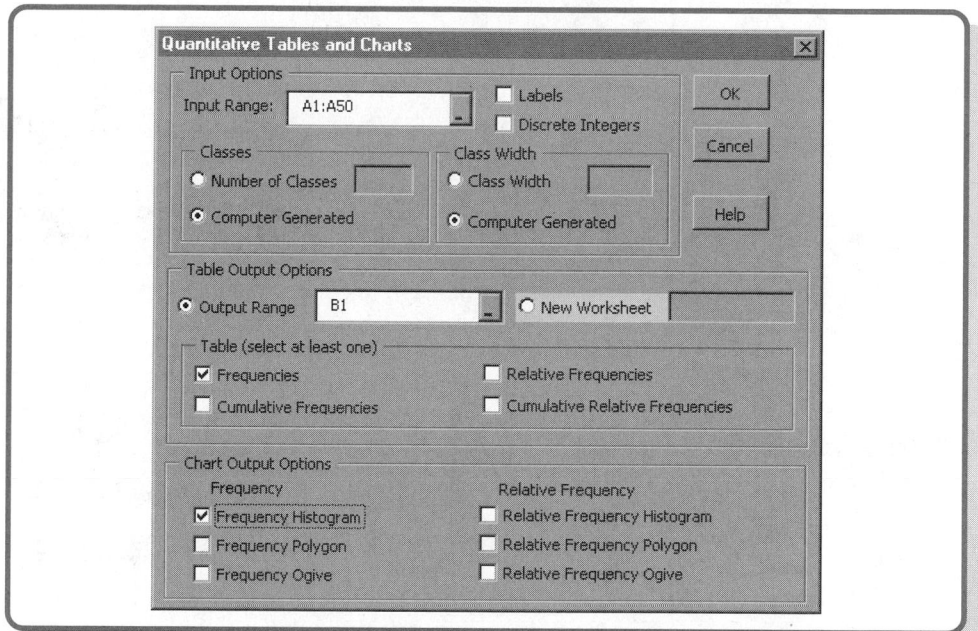

FIGURE 2.4

Excel spreadsheet created by KGP Data Analysis procedure.

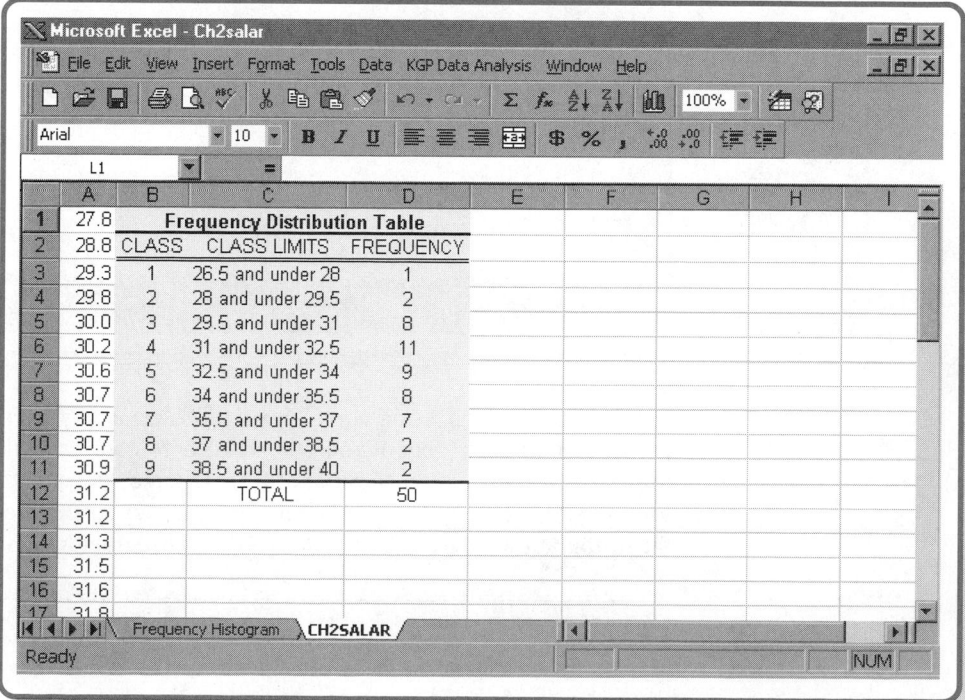

FIGURE 2.5
Histogram created by KGP
Data Analysis (frequency
distribution in Figure 2.4).

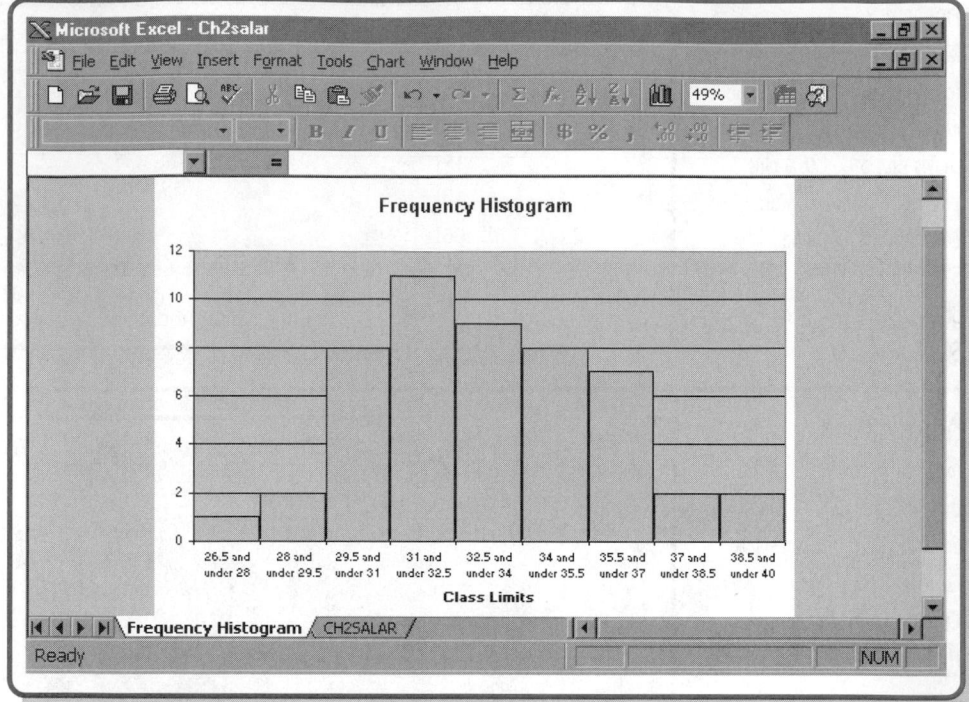

FIGURE 2.6
Excel spreadsheet created by
KGP Data Analysis procedure
where number of classes is 6
and class width is 2 (refer to
Figure 2.3).

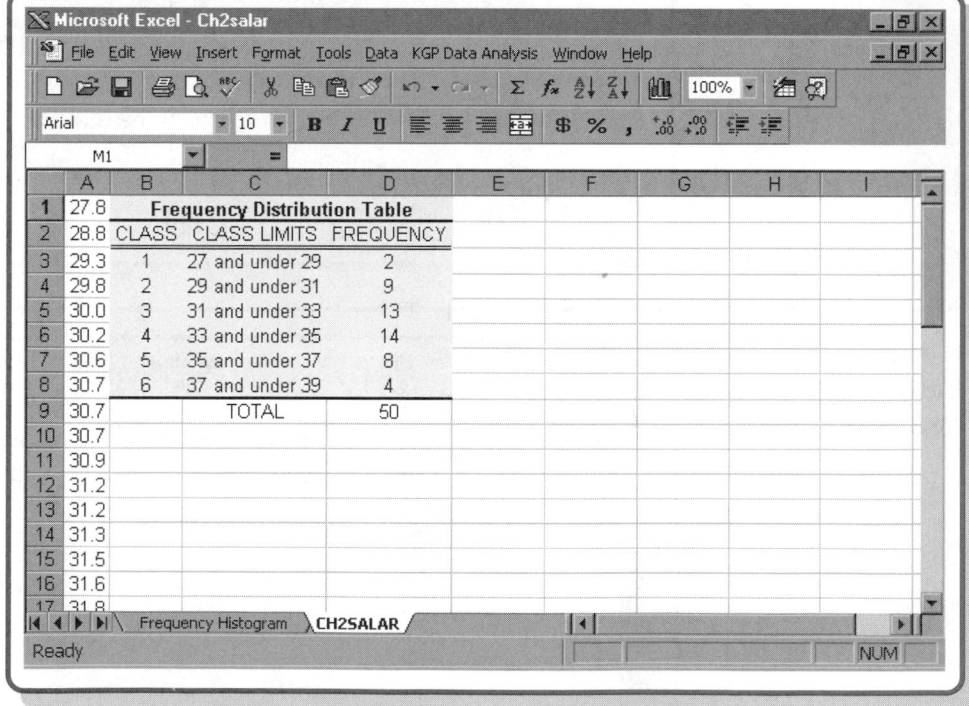

in Figure 2.4 and the histogram in Figure 2.5, obtained by clicking on the **Frequency Histogram** tab at the bottom of your spreadsheet. To obtain the histogram in Figure 2.1, refer to Figure 2.3 and click on **Number of Classes** (enter "6") and **Class Width** (enter "2"), followed by "OK." You should now see the frequency distribution shown in Figure 2.6, and the histogram will be an Excel version of the histogram in Figure 2.1.*

---

* The Excel frequency distribution and histogram provided by the KGP Data Analysis procedure attempts to derive an easy-to-interpret table and graph, as stressed in the chapter discussion. As a result, a lot of rounding to "nice numbers" takes place, and the final frequency distribution and histogram may contain slightly more (or less) classes than you specified. If you specified a class width, it will not be changed.

FIGURE 2.7

Histogram for discrete data from Table 2.6.

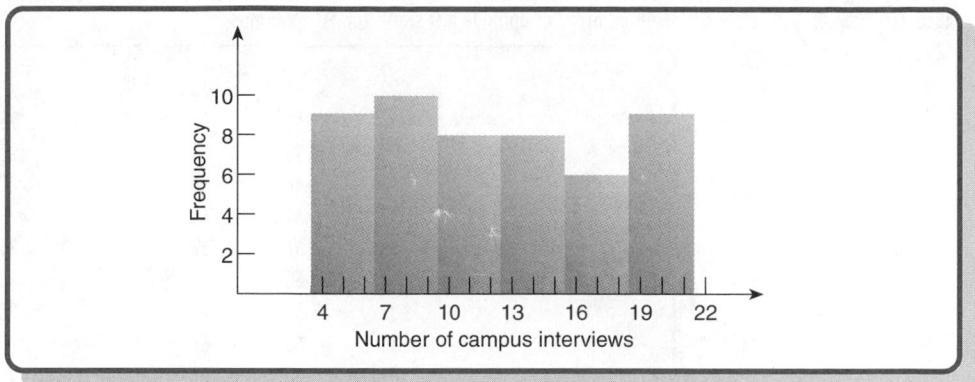

FIGURE 2.8

Stem-and-leaf diagram for after-tax profits.

Stem	Leaf (unit = .1)
2	3 4 7
3	4 4 6 8
4	1 5 7
5	1 9

When constructing a histogram for discrete data, the boxes should be constructed so there are no gaps between them. This can best be accomplished by extending each upper and lower class limit to a value midway between this limit and the adjoining limit (in a sense, "stretching" each class). For example, a histogram of Table 2.6 will contain a bar between 3.5 and 6.5 (height of 9), the next bar between 6.5 and 9.5 (height of 10), and so forth. The final bar (height of 9) will extend from 18.5 to 21.5. In this way, the histogram takes on the appearance of a continuous-data histogram, with no space between successive boxes. This is illustrated in Figure 2.7.

STEM-AND-LEAF DIAGRAMS

Stem-and-leaf diagrams were originally developed by John Tukey (pronounced Too'key) of Princeton University. They are extremely useful in summarizing reasonably sized data sets (under 150 values as a general rule) and, unlike histograms, result in no loss of information. By this we mean that it is possible to retrieve the original data set from a stem-and-leaf diagram, which is not the case when using a histogram—some of the information in the original data is lost when a histogram is constructed. Nevertheless, histograms provide the best alternative when attempting to summarize a large set of sample data.

To illustrate the construction of a stem-and-leaf diagram, suppose that a study reports the after-tax profits of 12 selected companies. The profits (recorded as cents per dollar of revenue) are as follows:

3.4   4.5   2.3   2.7   3.8   5.9   3.4   4.7   2.4   4.1   3.6   5.1

The stem-and-leaf diagram for these data is shown in Figure 2.8. Each observation is represented by a **stem** to the left of the vertical line and a **leaf** to the right of the vertical line. For example, the stems and leaves for the first and last observation would be:

Stem	Leaf (unit = .1)		Stem	Leaf (unit = .1)
3	4		5	1

In a stem-and-leaf diagram, the stems are put *in order* to the left of the vertical line. The leaf for each observation is generally the last digit (or possibly the last two digits) of the data value, with the stem consisting of the remaining first digits. The leaf values are generally arranged in ascending order. The value 562 could be represented as 5 | 62 or as 56 | 2 in a stem-and-leaf diagram, depending on the range of the sample data. If the

TABLE 2.7   Ordered array of aptitude test scores for 50 applicants.

22	44	56	68	78
25	44	57	68	78
28	46	59	69	80
31	48	60	71	82
34	49	61	72	83
35	51	63	72	85
39	53	63	74	88
39	53	63	75	90
40	55	65	75	92
42	55	66	76	96

FIGURE 2.9

Stem-and-leaf diagram for aptitude test scores.

Stem	Leaf (unit = 1)
2	2 5 8
3	1 4 5 9 9
4	0 2 4 4 6 8 9
5	1 3 3 5 5 6 7 9
6	0 1 3 3 3 5 6 8 8 9
7	1 2 2 4 5 5 6 8 8
8	0 2 3 5 8
9	0 2 6

FIGURE 2.10

Stem-and-leaf diagram for aptitude test scores using repeated stems.

Stem	Leaf (unit = 1)
2	2
2	5 8
3	1 4
3	5 9 9
4	0 2 4 4
4	6 8 9
5	1 3 3
5	5 5 6 7 9
6	0 1 3 3 3
6	5 6 8 8 9
7	1 2 2 4
7	5 5 6 8 8
8	0 2 3
8	5 8
9	0 2
9	6

diagram is rotated counterclockwise, it has the appearance of a histogram and clearly describes the shape of the sample data.

To illustrate this diagram, suppose that the personnel manager at Texas Industries has administered an aptitude test to 50 applicants. The ordered data are shown in Table 2.7; the corresponding stem-and-leaf diagram is shown in Figure 2.9. From this diagram we observe that the minimum score is 22, the maximum score is 96, and the largest group of scores is between 60 and 69. Also, the 5 leaves in stem row 3 indicate that 5 people scored at least 30 but less than 40. The 3 leaves in stem row 9 tell us at a glance that 3 people scored 90 or better.

For larger data sets, you may want to consider spreading out the stem column by repeating the stem value two or three times. To illustrate, the same 50 test scores are used to construct another stem-and-leaf diagram in Figure 2.10, where each stem value is repeated twice. The first stem value contains leaves between 0 and 4, the second stem contains leaves between 5 and 9.

FIGURE 2.11

Excel spreadsheet obtained using **KGP Data Analysis ➤ Quantitative Data Charts/Tables ➤ Stem and Leaf Plot.**

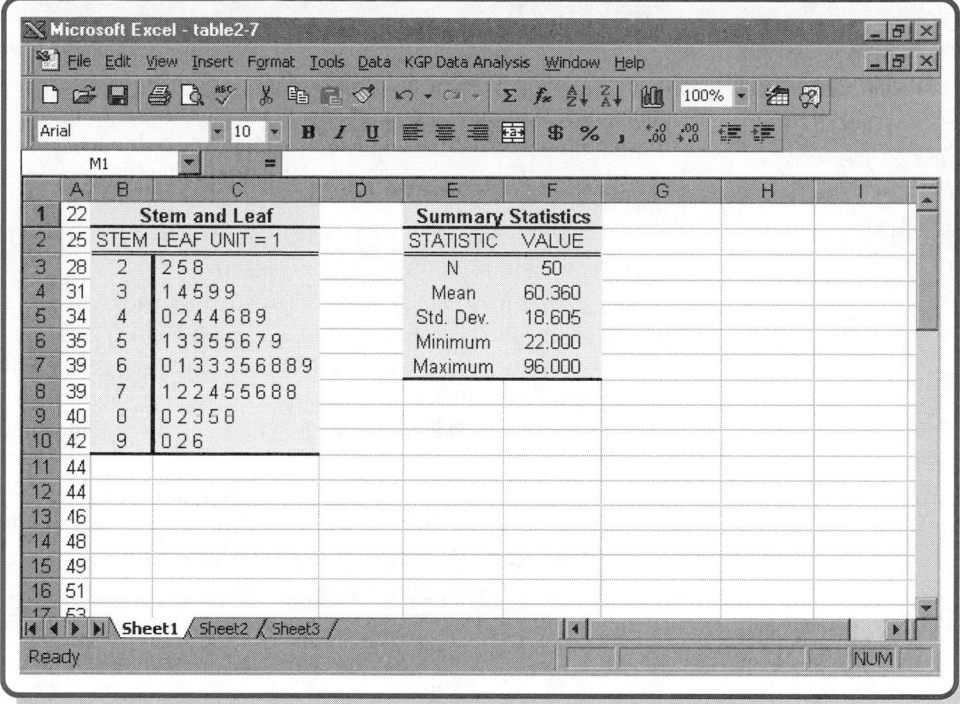

FIGURE 2.12

Stem-and-leaf diagram for production amounts (leaf unit = 1).

Stem	Leaf (unit = 1)					
5	21	36	50	72		
6	33	47	55	62	71	
7	11	21	31	40	57	62	83
8	16	35	44	92		

FIGURE 2.13

Stem-and-leaf diagram for production amounts (leaf unit = 10).

Stem	Leaf (unit = 10)					
5	2	3	5	7		
6	3	4	5	6	7	
7	1	2	3	4	5	6	8
8	1	3	4	9		

Although there is no built-in Excel procedure to construct a stem-and-leaf plot, you can use the stem-and-leaf macro contained under **KGP Data Analysis** to construct such a graph. To illustrate this procedure, first enter the 50 values from Table 2.7 into column A (refer to Figure 2.11). Next, click on **KGP Data Analysis ➤ Quantitative Data Charts/Tables ➤ Stem and Leaf Plot** and enter A1:A50 as the input range and B1 as the output range . The resulting output in columns B, C, E, and F is shown in Figure 2.11. The stem-and-leaf plot in columns B and C is identical to the one in Figure 2.9, again illustrating that the largest group of scores is in the 60 to 69 range.

In many situations, the leaves in your diagram may consist of a *pair* of digits. In Figure 2.12, the tons of chemical produced by Sarhad Industries are illustrated for 20 randomly selected days. The amounts range from 521 pounds to 892 pounds. Here each stem consists of a single digit and each leaf represents the last two digits of the production amount. An alternative would be to use a single digit in each leaf by dropping the right-hand digit in each data value. The leaf unit would then be 10 pounds; the resulting stem-and-leaf diagram is shown in Figure 2.13. Notice that we cannot *exactly* reproduce the sample from this diagram. To illustrate, the first value in this figure is $52 \times 10 = 520$, which means that the actual value is between 520 and 529.

MICROSOFT® EXCEL APPLICATION   USE DATA2-1

EXAMPLE 2.1
Using Excel to Construct a Histogram and a Stem-and-Leaf Diagram

In a production process, certain requirements referred to as *specification limits* are often imposed on the product. For example, the inside diameter of a certain machined part must be between 10.1 millimeters and 10.3 millimeters. The value 10.1 is the lower specification (spec) limit, and 10.3 is the upper spec limit. These spec limits can be written as $10.2 \pm .1$ millimeters. Any part with an inside diameter outside these limits is called *nonconforming* and is considered unacceptable.

By gathering a sample and constructing a histogram and stem-and-leaf diagram, production personnel can learn a great deal about a process, in particular, whether the process is capable of meeting these specifications. The Boston plant of Allied Manufacturing produces these parts. As an Allied employee, you have obtained a sample of 100 machine part diameters, contained in column A1. What can you conclude about this production process?

SOLUTION

Begin by clicking on the open icon ( ) and opening file **DATA2-1.** The first 16 values can be seen in Figure 2.14. Click on **KGP Data Analysis ➤ Quantitative Data Charts/Tables ➤ Histogram/Freq. Charts.** Using the input screen (shown in Figure 2.3) enter A1:A100 in the **Input Range** box and B1 in the **Output Range** box. Click on the checkboxes alongside **Frequencies** in the **Table** section and **Frequency Histogram** in the **Chart Output Options** section. The resulting frequency distribution is shown in Figure 2.14 and the histogram in Figure 2.15. To obtain the stem-and-leaf plot in Figure 2.14, click on **KGP Data Analysis ➤ Quantitative Data Charts/Tables ➤ Stem and Leaf Plot** and enter A1:A100 as the input range and E1 as the output range.

Since any part with a diameter over 10.3 is nonconforming, both the histogram and the stem-and-leaf plot make it clear that the process is struggling to meet specifications and is shifted too far to the right. The stem-and-leaf plot is especially useful here since you actually are able to see the 17 values (underlined) that are exceeding the upper spec limit—not possible using a histogram, where the data are condensed into classes.

A suggestion would be for Allied to try shifting the process to the left by whatever means are available, such as making a machine adjustment or changing raw material. With such a change, the process will be more capable of meeting the required specifications.

FIGURE 2.14
Excel frequency distribution and stem-and-leaf plot for Example 2.1.

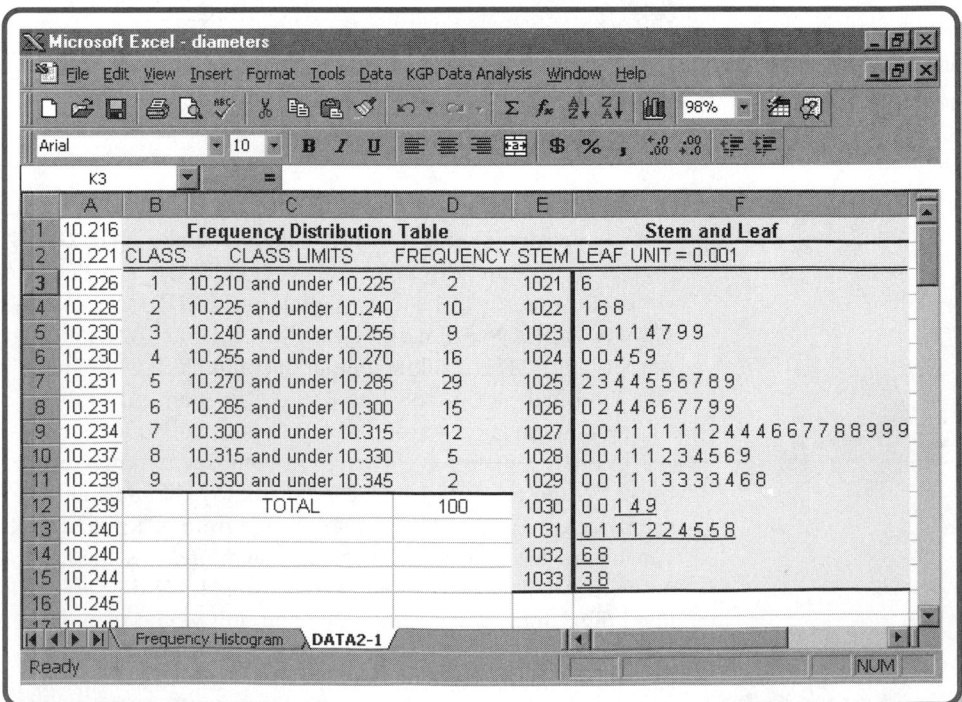

FIGURE 2.15

Excel histogram of 100 inside diameters (Example 2.1).

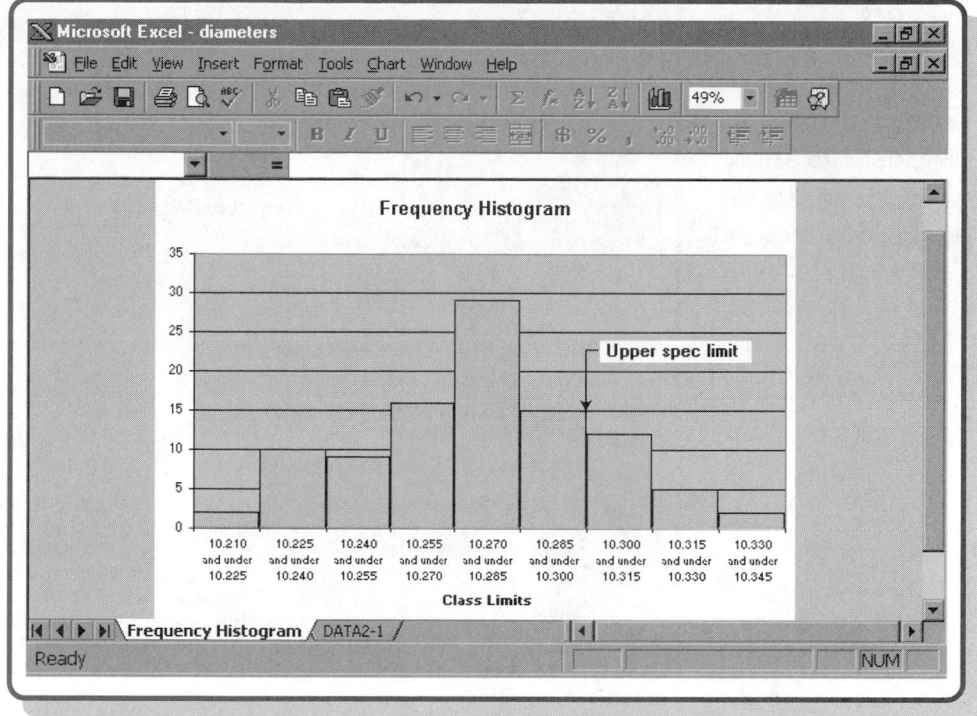

Histograms and stem-and-leaf diagrams are very simple yet powerful tools for analyzing and improving product quality. (Additional graphical and measurement techniques will be discussed in Chapter 12, "Quality Improvement.")

2.3 FREQUENCY POLYGONS

Although a histogram does demonstrate the shape of the data, perhaps the shape can be more clearly illustrated by using a **frequency polygon.** Here, you merely connect the centers of the tops of the histogram bars (located at the class midpoints) with a series of straight lines. The resulting multisided figure is a frequency polygon. Figure 2.16 is an example that uses the frequency distribution of salaries in Table 2.4.

To obtain the Excel generated frequency polygon in Figure 2.16, begin by entering the 50 salaries into column A of the spreadsheet. Next, click on **KGP Data Analysis ➤ Quantitative Data Charts/Tables ➤ Histogram/Freq. Charts.** Fill in the input screen as shown in Figure 2.3, except set the number of classes equal to 6 and the class width equal to 2 in the **Classes** section. Finally, click on the checkbox alongside **Frequency Polygon.**

COMMENTS

The polygon can also be constructed from the relative frequency histogram. The shape will not change, but the units on the vertical axis will now represent relative frequencies.

The polygon must begin and end at zero frequency (as in Figure 2.16). To accomplish this, imagine a class at each end of the corresponding histogram that is empty (contains no data values). Begin and end the polygon with the class midpoints of these imaginary classes. Thus, your vertical axis *must* begin at zero. This need not be true for the horizontal axis.

How do you handle an open-ended class? The easiest way is to construct a frequency polygon of the closed classes and place a footnote at each open-ended class location indicating the frequency of that particular class. Figure 2.17 demonstrates this, using the city size data from Table 2.2.

Frequency polygons are usually better than histograms for comparing the shape of two (or more) different frequency distributions. For example, Figure 2.18 demonstrates at a glance that salaries at Texcom Electronics are higher (for the most part) for management personnel who have a college degree.

FIGURE 2.16

Excel frequency polygon using KGP Data Analysis and Table 2.4. Twenty-seven (out of 50) salaries are between $31,000 and $35,000, with 12 people receiving $35,000 or more.

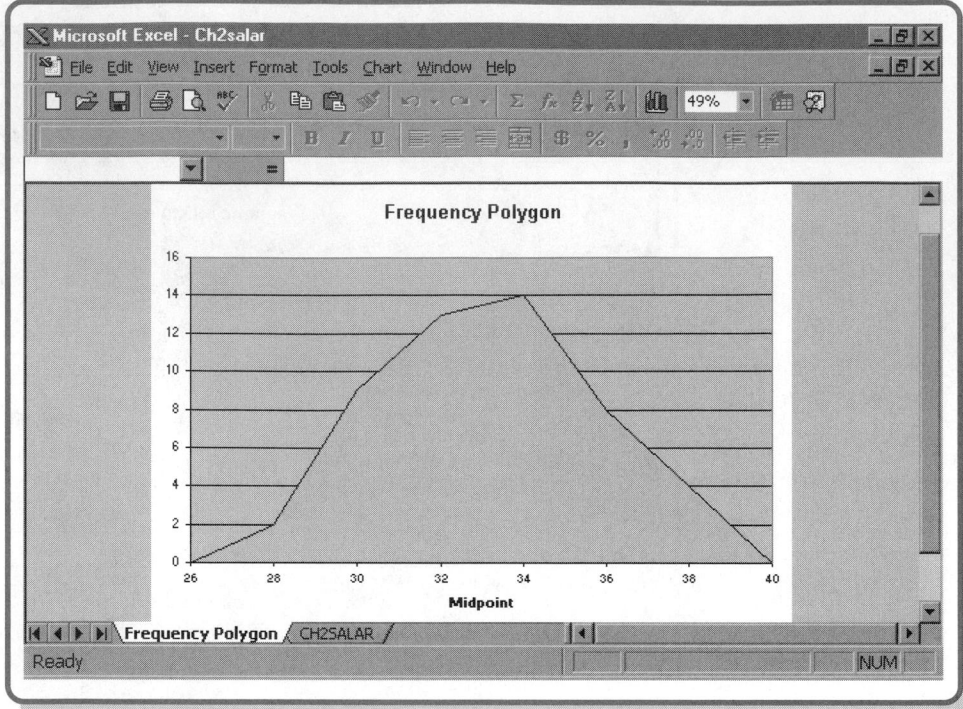

FIGURE 2.17

Frequency polygon using footnotes to handle open-ended classes. The data are from Table 2.2.

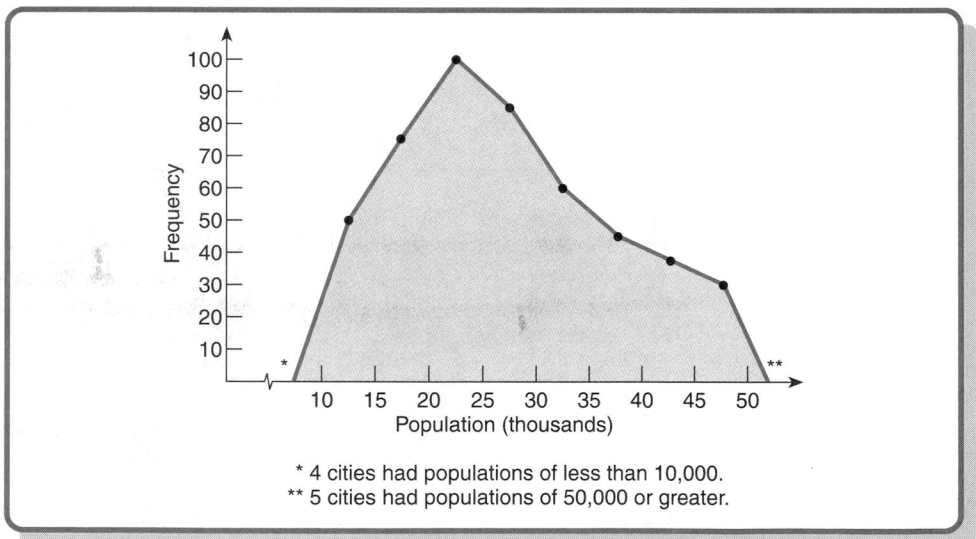

* 4 cities had populations of less than 10,000.
** 5 cities had populations of 50,000 or greater.

FIGURE 2.18

Frequency polygon showing annual salaries for Texcom Electronics management personnel. Higher salaries are observed in the college degree sample.

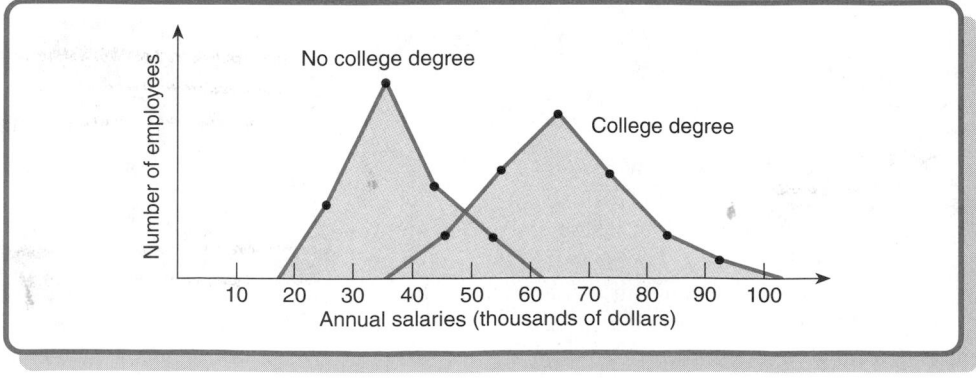

Both histograms and frequency polygons represent the actual number of data values in each class. Suppose that your annual salary is one of the values contained in a sample of 250 salaries. One question of interest might be, what fraction of the people in the sample have a salary *less than* mine? Such information can be displayed using a statistical graph called an *ogive*.

2.4 CUMULATIVE FREQUENCIES (OGIVES)

Another method of examining a frequency distribution is to list the number of observations (data values) that are *less than* each of the class limits rather than how many are *in* each of the classes. You are then determining **cumulative frequencies.** Table 2.8 shows the cumulative frequencies for the frequency distribution in Table 2.4. Notice that you can determine cumulative frequencies (column 4) or cumulative relative frequencies (column 6). The results in Table 2.8 can be summarized more easily in a simple graph called an **ogive** (pronounced oh'-jive). The ogive is useful whenever you want to determine what percentage of your data lies *below* a certain value. Figure 2.19 is constructed by noting that

2 values (2/50 = .04) are less than $29,000

2 + 9 = 11 values (11/50 = .22) are less than $31,000

11 + 13 = 24 values (24/50 = .48) are less than $33,000, and so on.

The ogive allows you to make such statements as "Twenty-two percent of the salaries were less than $31,000," and "Fifty percent of the salaries were under $33,100."

You always begin at the lower limit of the first class (27 here). The cumulative relative frequency at that point is always 0, because the number of data values less than this number is 0. You always end at the upper limit of the last class (39 here). The cumulative relative frequency at the upper limit is always 1, because all the data values are less than this upper limit. This ogive value would be n = the number of data values ($n = 50$ here) if you are constructing a frequency ogive rather than a relative frequency ogive. *However, the shape of the ogive is the same for both procedures.*

To obtain the Excel generated ogive in Figure 2.19, begin by entering the 50 salaries into column A of the spreadsheet. Next, click on **KGP Data Analysis ➤ Quantitative Data Charts/Tables ➤ Histogram/Freq. Charts.** Fill in the input screen as shown in Figure 2.3, except set the number of classes equal to 6 and the class width equal to 2 in the **Classes** section. Finally, click on the checkbox alongside **Relative Frequency Ogive.**

TABLE 2.8   Summary of starting salaries from Table 2.3, including the cumulative frequencies and cumulative relative frequencies.

Class Number	Class	Frequency	Cumulative Frequency	Relative Frequency	Cumulative Relative Frequency
1	27 and under 29	2	2	.04	.04
2	29 and under 31	9	11	.18	.22
3	31 and under 33	13	24	.26	.48
4	33 and under 35	14	38	.28	.76
5	35 and under 37	8	46	.16	.92
6	37 and under 39	4	50	.08	1.00
		50		1.00	

FIGURE 2.19

Excel ogive (cumulative relative frequencies) using KGP Data Analysis and Table 2.8. One half of the graduates received a salary less than $33,100; 22% of the salaries were less than $31,000.

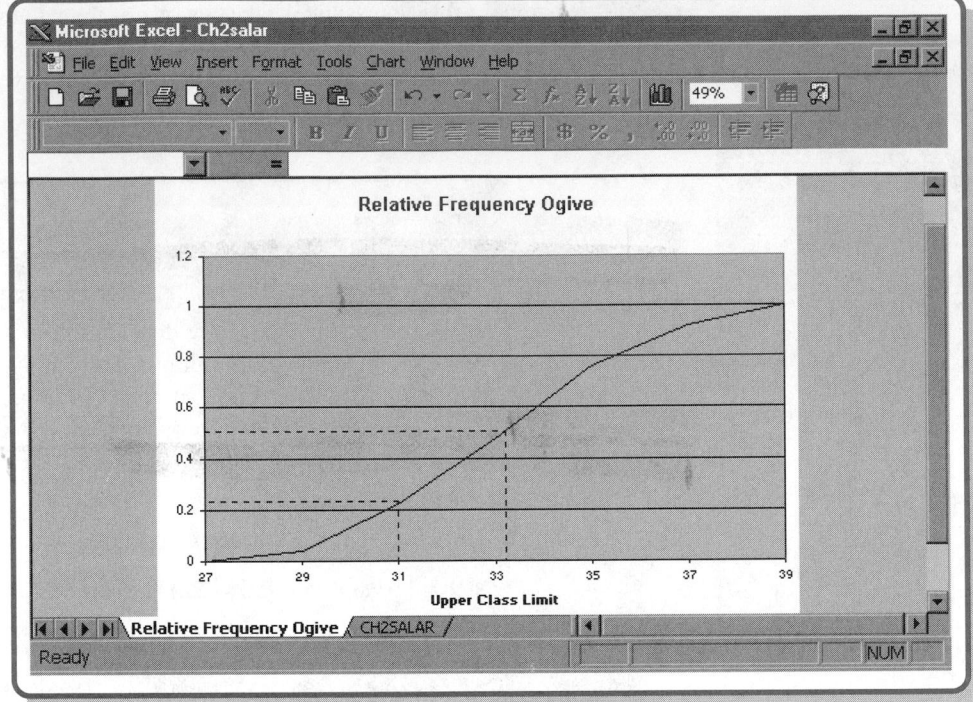

EXERCISES 2.8–2.26

UNDERSTANDING THE MECHANICS

2.8 The number of hours worked by 50 randomly selected employees during the first week of February are as follows.

Hours Worked	Number of Employees
20 and under 25	3
25 and under 30	8
30 and under 35	10
35 and under 40	13
40 and under 45	15
45 and under 50	1

a. Calculate the relative frequencies and the cumulative relative frequencies.
b. Draw a relative frequency histogram.
c. Draw a relative frequency polygon.

2.9 The number of vacant seats on a sample of 40 flights is as follows.

Number of Vacant Seats	Number of Flights with Vacant Seats
0–4	15
5–9	10
10–14	8
15–19	5
20–24	2

a. Construct a frequency histogram.
b. Describe the shape of the histogram.
c. Construct a cumulative frequency distribution.
d. Construct a frequency polygon.
e. Construct an ogive.

2.10 The monthly repair costs for Video Cassette Recorders (VCR) returned within the past 3 years for malfunction problems are as follows, in dollars.

73.20	99.60	72.80	102.97	87.45	92.45
89.75	63.70	112.60	68.40	96.75	68.70
80.57	93.80	115.90	89.98	77.93	82.50
84.67	99.75	103.65	63.71	74.39	110.90
69.45	88.70	107.40	86.90	82.25	74.80
88.69	113.30	67.50	87.50	92.57	94.45

a. Convert the data into an ordered array using six classes.
b. Construct a relative frequency distribution. Start the first class at $60.00.
c. Construct a relative frequency histogram.
d. Construct a cumulative frequency distribution.
e. Draw a stem-and-leaf diagram.

2.11 The response times to emergency maintenance problems at an assembly plant for 27 randomly selected emergency calls are as follows, in hours.

1.21	1.87	2.35	4.16	1.50	1.30	2.78	3.71	2.80
1.80	2.60	3.30	4.30	3.10	1.80	3.07	2.19	1.67
2.89	4.25	1.10	2.25	3.94	4.22	1.73	2.54	3.27

a. Arrange the observations in increasing order of magnitude.
b. Present the data in the form of a frequency distribution. Use seven classes.
c. Construct a cumulative frequency distribution.
d. Construct an ogive.
e. Draw a stem-and-leaf diagram.

2.12 Construct the cumulative frequency distribution for the frequency distribution in Exercise 2.1. Draw the corresponding ogive.

2.13 Draw a frequency histogram and a frequency polygon for the data in Exercise 2.2.

2.14 Bonuses for 40 midlevel managers at a manufacturing plant are as follows, in units of $1,000.

4.5	4.8	5.3	5.9	4.6	4.8	4.9	5.2	4.1	5.8
4.6	4.9	5.1	5.3	3.8	3.9	2.8	6.4	4.7	7.1
7.8	7.3	2.9	3.2	4.9	5.2	4.5	6.2	5.7	4.3

  a. List the stem possibilities.
  b. Form a stem-and-leaf display.
  c. Comment on the shape of the distribution of the data.

APPLYING THE NEW CONCEPTS

2.15 The price of an alternator for a Buick LeSabre was priced at various auto parts outlet stores throughout the Dallas and Ft. Worth Metroplex. The resulting prices are as follows, in dollars.

95	86	89	105	89	99	78	110	113	87
77	96	115	103	86	95	94	106	99	99
83	76	99	94	102	99	104	93	101	94

Use a stem-and-leaf diagram to describe the distribution of the data. What is the most commonly quoted price?

2.16 A quality-control engineer has been gathering a sample of cylinders that have completed the manufacturing process. The cylinders must be manufactured such that the inside diameter is between 10.6 centimeters and 11 centimeters. These two limits are called the specification limits. Any cylinder with an inside diameter outside of these limits is called nonconforming and is considered a defective cylinder.

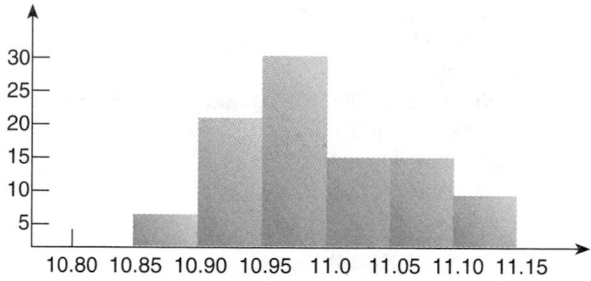

The engineer can make a machine adjustment to shift the process to the right or left. How far and in what direction should the process be shifted to minimize the number of nonconforming cylinders?

2.17 A county library's records show the following information regarding the number of patrons who used the library during the past 30 days.

  100, 87, 44, 53, 17, 34, 88, 67, 31, 40, 98, 77, 55, 41, 73, 62, 88, 28, 70, 51, 82, 44, 32, 50, 33, 49, 59, 67, 79, 84

  a. Construct a cumulative frequency distribution.
  b. Convert the cumulative frequency distribution in part (a) into an ogive graph.
  c. The number of patrons attending the library was less than what value 80% of the time?

2.18 The following is a frequency distribution of the number of daily automobile accidents reported for a month in Newark, N.J.

Accidents Per Day	Frequency
0–3	12
4–7	10
8–11	7
12–15	1
16–19	1

  a. Construct a cumulative relative frequency distribution for the data.
  b. What percentage of the time do 8 or more daily accidents occur?
  c. Construct a cumulative frequency distribution for the data.
  d. Compare the shape of the distributions in parts (a) and (c).

2.19 The number of Web users for March 1998 are listed below for 20 Web search engines. Frequencies are listed in millions of users.

	Search Engine	Number of Users
1	altavista.digital.com	7.5
2	amazon.com	4.9
3	angelfire.com	4.5
4	aol.com	17.7
5	cnn.com	4.2
6	excite.com	16.4
7	fourll.com	4.8
8	geocitres.com	14.7
9	hotbot.com	4.6
10	hotmail.com	6.6
11	infoseek.com	13.5
12	lycos.com	11.5
13	microsoft.com	17.9
14	msn.com	8.7
15	netscape.com	23.4
16	real.com	5.2
17	tripod.com	6.1
18	webcrawler.com	6.3
19	yahoo.com	31.8
20	zdnet.com	6.4

(Source: *USA Today*, "Top Web Domains for March," April 15, 1998, p. 5D.)

  a. Construct a frequency histogram.
  b. Draw a stem-and-leaf diagram.
  c. What can you say about the frequency with which a search engine is used?

2.20 The Gabelli Asset Fund invests in various sectors of the economy. Listed next are the cost and final value of investments made during the second quarter of 1993. The investments selected were from the portion of the portfolio that invested in companies associated with automotive parts and accessories. Units are in millions.

Company	Cost	Value
The Allen Group	.61	2.02
Chrysler Corp.	1.02	1.81
Echlin, Inc.	4.80	9.66
Federal-Mogul Corp.	3.65	4.09
Ford Motor Corp.	1.06	1.23
General Motors Corp.	11.26	14.31

Company	Cost	Value
Genuine Parts Company	4.78	5.19
Handy & Harman	2.12	2.58
Johnson Controls, Inc.	3.18	5.91
Kollmorgen Corp.	1.89	1.14
Modine Manufacturing Company	1.38	3.14
Myers Industries, Inc.	.14	.63
Navistar International Corp.	5.16	4.75
Pep Boys	.87	1.58
Quaker State Corp.	1.64	1.41
Republic Automotive Parts, Inc.	.34	.60
SPX Corp.	.29	.24
Standard Motor Products, Inc.	.69	1.91
Superior Industries International, Inc.	.08	.49
Wynn's International, Inc.	.35	.47

(Adapted from the semiannual report of the Gabelli Asset Fund, 1993.)

a. Construct a frequency histogram of the costs for the investments in the automotive sector of the portfolio. Use five classes and a class width of 1.5.

b. Do part (a) with the value of the investments at the end of the quarter.

c. Compare the histograms in parts (a) and (b). Comment on the differences.

2.21 The *Toronto Star* ("Native Jobless Rate 2½ Times Canada's," Sept. 21, 1993, p. A12) reported that among all adults of the Indian community, 13% had no income in 1990 while only 5% earned $40,000 or more. Suppose that a random sample of 40 native adults living in Toronto yielded the following annual salaries. Construct a relative frequency distribution, and comment on whether the distribution is consistent with the percentages reported in the *Toronto Star.* Units are in dollars. Use six classes.

21,000	32.000	500	0	48,000
6,000	10,000	11,000	30,000	14,000
200	19,000	28,000	32,000	8,000
12,000	15,000	21,000	15,000	5,000
42,000	53,000	22,000	13,500	6,000
31,000	17,000	9,000	27,000	34,000
4,000	14,000	20,500	29,000	33,000
44,000	31,000	24,000	26,000	18,000

2.22 A survey of households in a certain metropolitan district revealed the number of consumers that have purchased camping equipment and also the number that have purchased exercise equipment. The following table displays the age groups and number of consumers purchasing these products.

Age Group (in Years)	Camping Equipment	Exercise Equipment
15 and under 20	37	4
20 and under 25	30	10
25 and under 30	29	12
30 and under 35	20	13
35 and under 40	19	20
40 and under 45	20	24
45 and under 50	22	21
50 and under 55	12	30
55 and under 60	8	28
60 and under 65	6	31
65 and under 70	5	35

a. Construct a relative frequency distribution for the consumers purchasing camping equipment.

b. Construct a relative frequency distribution for the consumers purchasing exercise equipment.

c. Comment on the differences in the relative frequency distributions in parts (a) and (b).

2.23 Metro Power manufactures a high-powered copper coil to be used in giant power transformers. Tensile strength (given in thousands of pounds per square inch) is of critical importance in the manufacture of the copper coil. The following data are from a sample of copper coils tested for tensile strength:

5, 8, 12, 10, 15, 18, 21, 24, 7, 26, 7, 18, 10, 6, 4, 11, 15, 9, 22, 10

a. Construct an ogive.

b. Find an appropriate value, X, in units of pounds per square inch, such that more than one-half of the coils sampled have tensile strengths greater than X.

2.24 [DATA SET EX2-24] *Variable description:*

Phone Time: Total daily times spent on the telephone by an employee (in hours).

The manager of a marketing firm wished to determine the distribution of the total daily time that the firm's 50 employees spend on the telephone. Data were collected for a randomly selected day.

a. Use the command **KGP ➤ Quantitative ➤ Histogram** to construct a histogram of the data.

b. Select a class width of 1 hour. What happens to the shape of the frequency distribution?

2.25 [DATA SET EX2-25] *Variable description:*

Insurance Amt: Amount of life insurance elected by each employee.

Data from 100 employees were collected to determine the distribution of the amount of insurance elected by employees of a manufacturing plant.

a. Use the command **KGP ➤ Quantitative ➤ Stem-and-Leaf** to construct a stem-and-leaf diagram.

b. Comment on the shape of the distribution.

c. Comment on what an unusually large amount of insurance coverage might be.

2.26 [DATA SET EX2-26] *Variable description:*

Shift 1:   Time for first shift to complete production tasks
Shift 2:   Time for second shift to complete production tasks
Shift 3:   Time for third shift to complete production tasks.

To determine the time (in hours) that it takes each shift to complete a certain production task, a manager records the completion times for 100 identical production tasks assigned to each of three shifts in a manufacturing assembly plant.

a. Use the command **KGP ➤ Quantitative ➤ Stacked Histogram** to examine the distribution of times for each of the three work shifts.

b. Compare the histograms in part (a). Does it appear that the times for one shift are smaller than the times for one of the other two shifts?

2.5 BAR CHARTS

Histograms, frequency polygons, and ogives are used for data having an interval or ratio level of measurement. For data having a **nominal** level, we use a bar chart. For situations producing a sample of **ordinal** level data with a reasonable set of possible values (such as 1 = strongly agree, 2 = agree, . . . , 5 = strongly disagree), a bar chart can be used to summarize the sample. A bar chart is similar to a histogram, in that the height of each bar is proportional to the frequency of that class. Such a graph is most helpful when you have many categories to represent.

Consider the data in Table 2.1. If you are interested in the number of business graduates in each of the three disciplines (accounting, information systems, and marketing), a bar chart will do a good job of summarizing this information (Figure 2.20). Notice that a gap is inserted between each of the bars in a bar chart. The data here are nominal, so the length of this gap is arbitrary.

Figure 2.21 is an example of a bar chart in which the bars are constructed horizontally rather than vertically. This form enables you to label each category *within* the bar.

FIGURE 2.20

Bar chart showing the number of this year's graduating business majors at Bellaire College in each of the three disciplines. Twenty-six were accounting majors; the smallest group consisting of the information systems majors (20%).

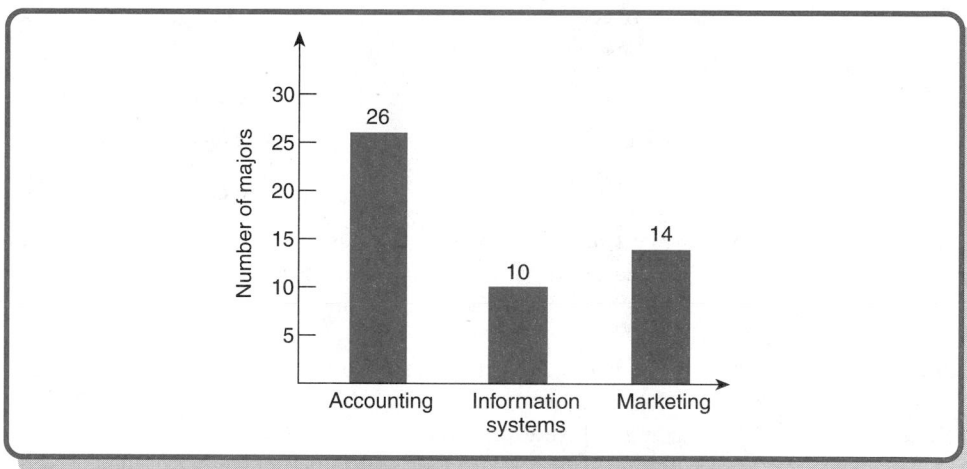

FIGURE 2.21

Bar chart drawn horizontally; note that it is easy to place labels within the boxes.

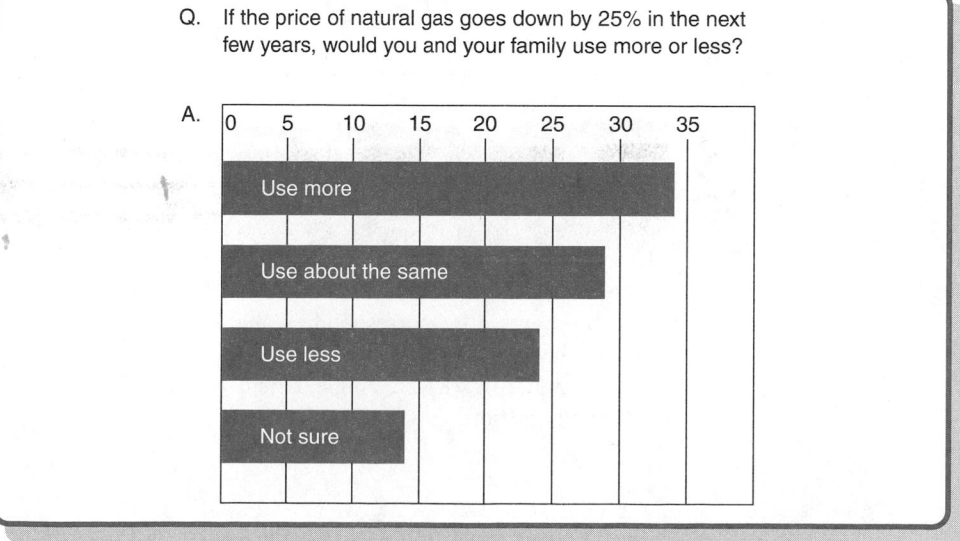

FIGURE 2.22
Bar chart of quality costs for
Microtech (Example 2.2).

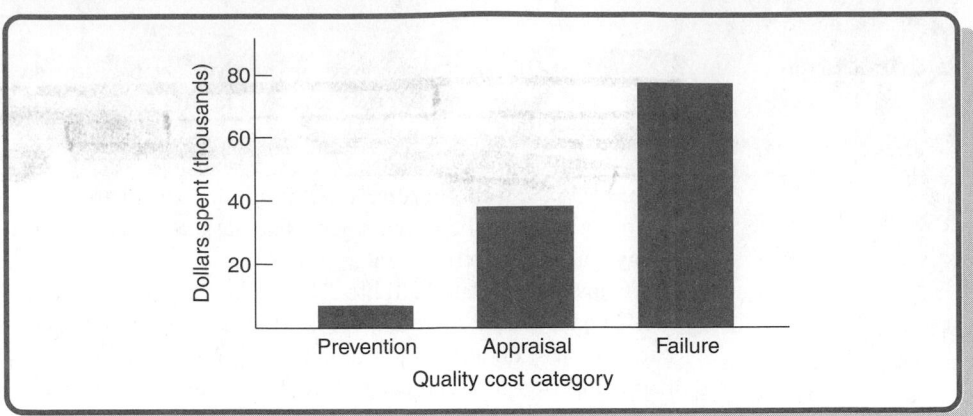

EXAMPLE 2.2

The head of Quality Assurance at Microtech (a fictional company) has categorized company costs related to quality improvement into three categories: prevention, appraisal, and failure. These three costs for the past fiscal year were:

Prevention costs: $ 3,600

Appraisal costs: $38,400

Failure costs: $78,000

She wants to demonstrate at a glance the small amount spent on prevention measures and the large amount spent on failure costs (largely due to warranty claims but also due to having to rework defective components). Construct a bar chart to illustrate this information.

SOLUTION

The bar chart consists of three boxes (bars), where the height of each box represents the dollar amount for that category. It is shown in Figure 2.22. This bar chart is a rather dramatic illustration that many more dollars are being spent in the failure cost category than in the other two categories—in particular, for prevention costs. Such a chart can have a tremendous impact in a business presentation.

2.6 PIE CHARTS

An alternative to the bar chart for nominal or ordinal data is the **pie chart.** This graph is used to split a particular quantity into its component pieces, typically at some specified point in time or over a specified time span. It is a convenient way of representing percentages or relative frequencies (rather than frequencies). Figure 2.23 shows a pie chart of the major discipline for the 50 graduates in Table 2.1. To construct a pie chart, draw a line from the center of the circle to the outer edge. Then construct the various pieces of the pie chart by drawing the corresponding angles. For example, the accounting majors represent 52% of the total number of business graduates (26 out of 50), so angle A in Figure 2.23 is 52% of 360°, or 187.2°. Angle B is 20% of 360°, or 72°, and angle C represents the remaining portion.

FIGURE 2.23

Pie chart showing the percentage of this year's graduating business majors at Bellaire College in each of the three disciplines. Fifty-two percent were accounting majors, with the smallest percentage being the information systems majors (20%).

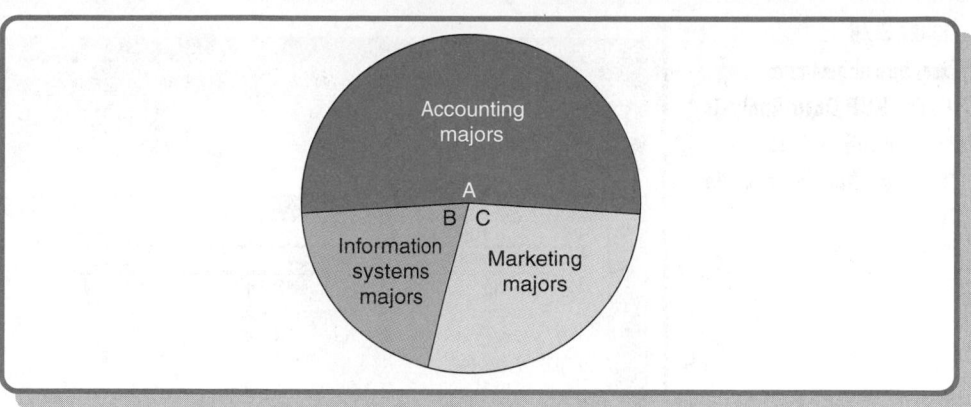

MICROSOFT® EXCEL APPLICATION   USE DATA2-3

EXAMPLE 2.3

Using Excel to Construct a Bar Chart and Pie Chart

The manager of Freedman Furniture Store has compiled a list of the types of written customer complaints during the past three months. The complaints have been categorized as follows:

Type	Coded Value
Error in billing	1
Rudeness by store personnel	2
Late delivery	3
Question not answered during telephone inquiry	4
Other	5

The total complaints for the three months is 75 and the coded values (1s, 2s, . . . , 5s) are contained in a column in DATA2-3. Using Excel, construct the corresponding bar chart and pie chart and discuss the results.

SOLUTION

Click on the Open icon ( ) and open the file DATA2-3. You should see 75 integers, 1 through 5. You can see the first 17 values in column A of Figure 2.24. Next, click on **KGP Data Analysis ➤ Qualitative Data Charts ➤ Bar Chart.** For the input range enter A1:A75, and for the output range enter B1. You should then see the bar chart table in Figure 2.24 (columns B and C) and the bar chart in Figure 2.25. Repeat this sequence and use **Pie Chart** in place of **Bar Chart,** entering D1 for the output range. This produces the pie chart table in Figure 2.24 (columns D and E) and the corresponding pie chart in Figure 2.25. To make the output easier to interpret, replace the integers 1 through 5 using the labels "Billing," "Rudeness," "Late," "Not Answered," and "Other" in cells B3 through B7 and cells D3 through D7 as shown in Figure 2.24. By doing this, you also change the labels on the graphs to the ones shown in Figure 2.25.*

Both charts make it very clear that the bulk of the customer complaints during this three-month period (42 out of 75) are related to billing errors, with rudeness by store personnel a distant second (14 out of 45). The quality of service at Freedman would be greatly improved if the billing department would make a serious effort to eliminate the billing errors.

---

* When you clicked on **KGP Data Analysis ➤ Qualitative Data Charts,** you may have noticed another option called **Pareto Chart.** This particular graph modifies the bar chart to distinguish the few important categories (one, in this example) from the categories with low relative frequencies. They will be illustrated in the exercises at the end of this section.

FIGURE 2.24

Excel spreadsheet after running **KGP Data Analysis ➤ Qualitative Data Charts ➤ Bar Chart** or **Pie Chart.**

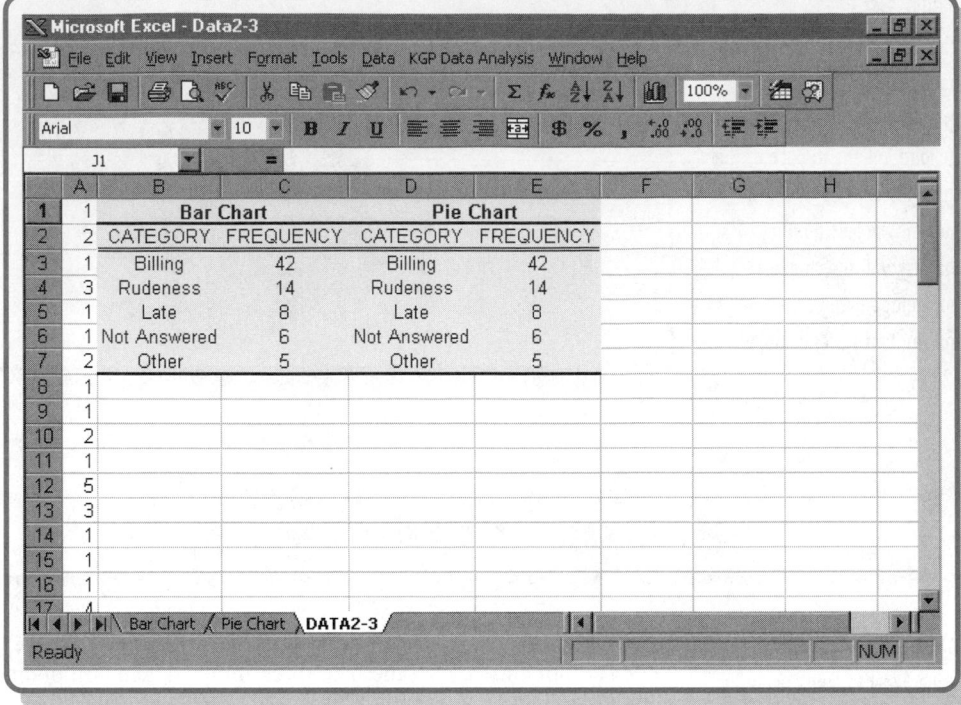

FIGURE 2.25

Excel bar chart and pie chart created by KGP Data Analysis (Example 2.3).

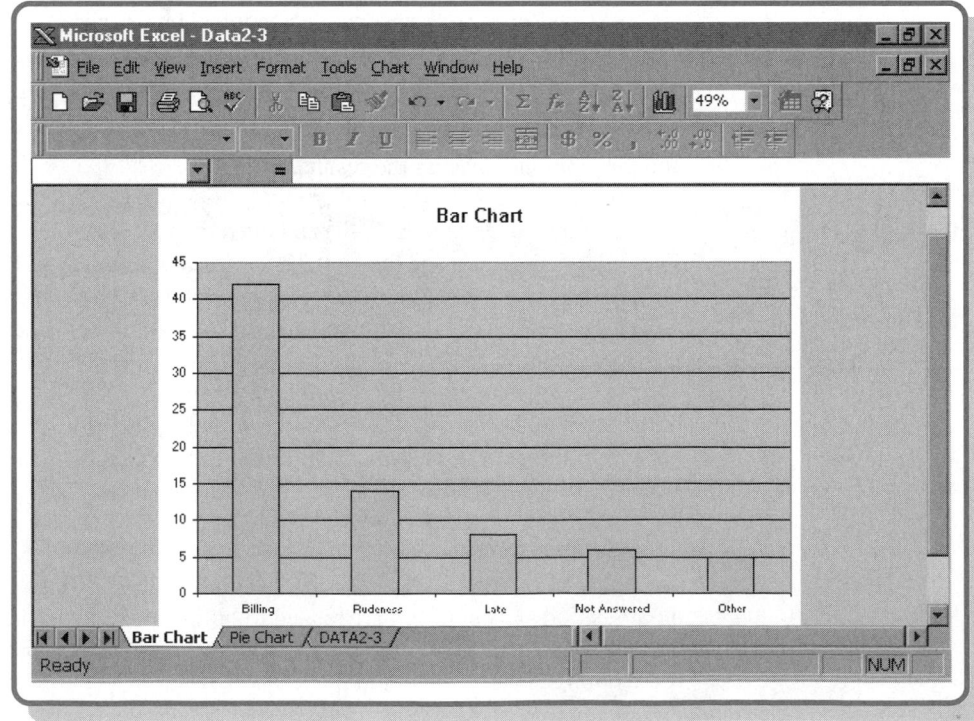

FIGURE 2.25
(continued)

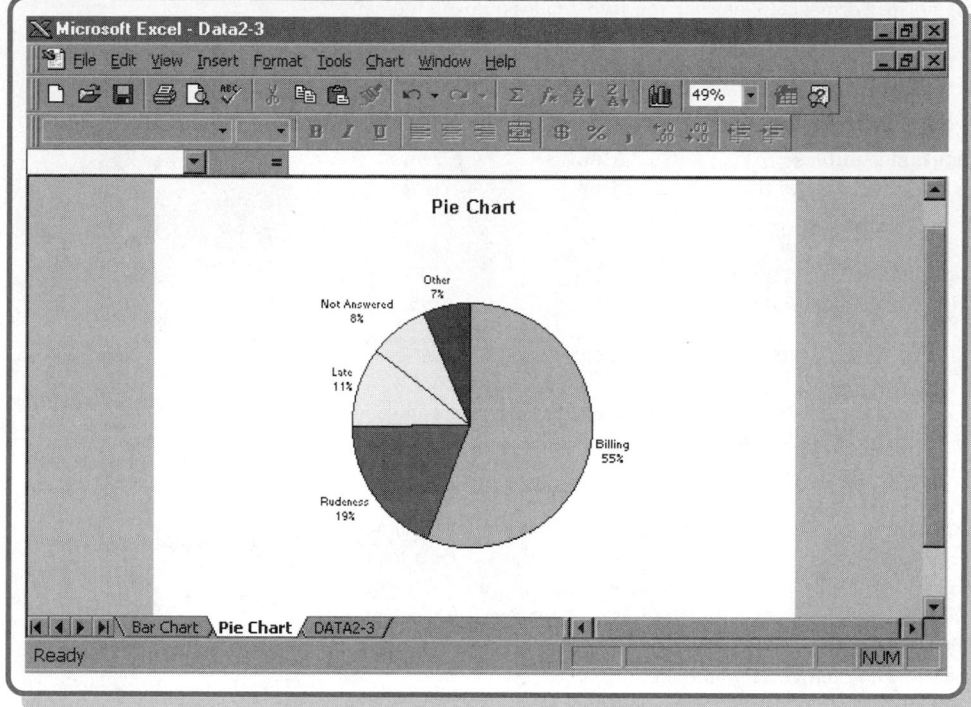

EXERCISES 2.27–2.50

UNDERSTANDING THE MECHANICS

2.27 Four brands of the same product are sold at a department store. The number of times each brand is sold is listed below. Construct a bar chart and a pie chart to represent these data.

Brand	Frequency
A	10
B	40
C	50
D	10

2.28 An electronics firm has the following percentages of its employees with different educational backgrounds. Construct a pie chart to display the data.

Highest Educational Degree	Percentage of Employees
High school degree	5
Associate degree	20
College degree	50
Masters degree	15
Doctorate degree	10

2.29 A survey of 200 households revealed the following results on how residential homeowners feel about a proposed increase in property tax.

Category	Number of Households
Strongly Agree	23
Agree	30
Neutral	10
Disagree	90
Strongly Disagree	27
Not Sure	20

a. Draw a bar graph.

b. Change the numbers to relative percentages and construct a bar graph.

c. Draw a pie chart.

2.30 Summarize the information in Exercise 2.1 in the form of a pie chart.

APPLYING THE NEW CONCEPTS

2.31 The top 10 motion pictures to dominate the box office in 1997 are presented below with respect to box office sales in millions of dollars.

Movie Picture	Box Office Sales
Men in Black	249.5
Lost World: Jurassic Park	229.0
Liar Liar	181.4
Air Force One	171.7
Star Wars	138.2
My Best Friend's Wedding	126.7
Face/Off	112.3
Batman & Robin	107.3
George of the Jungle	105.2
Con Air	100.9

(Source: *USA Today*, "Big and Splashy Pictures Ruled Box Office in '97," Dec. 31, 1997, p. 1D.)

a. Summarize the data in the form of a pie chart.

b. Omit the movies *Men in Black* and *Lost World: Jurassic Park* from the list and construct a pie chart.

c. Describe your findings in parts (a) and (b).

2.32 Small-company stocks funds are prone to periodic bursts of hot performance. Consider the five small-company mutual funds and their performance as listed below.

Small-Company Mutual Fund	Performance Over the Past 12 Months	Performance Over the Past 5 Years
Babson Enterprises II	31.8%	119%
Eclipse Equity	33.8%	131%
Fasciano	25.3%	133%
Gabelli Small Cap Growth	36.8%	123%
Nicholas Limited Edition	30.0%	119%

(Source: *USA Today,* "Hot Small-Company Funds," Feb. 20, 1998, p. 4B.)

Construct a bar chart for the 12-month performance and another bar chart for the 5-year performance. Comment on the differences in the two charts.

2.33 Many developing countries receive loans or loan guarantees from the United States Export-Import Bank. These loans help some of these countries to have economies that are growing faster than that of the United States. Ten important recipients of large loans from the Export-Import Bank are listed below with their current amount borrowed.

Country	Amount (In Billions of Dollars)
Brazil	3.9
Russia	1.5
Indonesia	3.5
Argentina	2.3
Phillipines	2.2
Turkey	2.0
Mexico	5.4
China	4.1
India	1.5

(Source: *The Wall Street Journal,* "U.S. Ex-Im Bank is Beating the Drum in China," June 20, 1997, p. A12.)

To analyze this data, a Pareto diagram is used. A Pareto diagram summarizes the findings of categorical responses so that the few important categories are distinguished from the numerous categories with low-relative frequencies. A Pareto diagram is a vertical bar chart with the categories placed in descending rank order of their bar heights. A cumulative graph is plotted with the bar chart. The scale on the right-hand side displays the cumulative percentages. The left-hand axis shows the amount of loans borrowed by a country. The 100% figure on the right-hand axis corresponds to the total amount of loans borrowed by all the countries.

   a. What conclusions can be drawn from the Pareto diagram?

   b. What information is available through a Pareto diagram that is not available from a bar chart or pie chart?

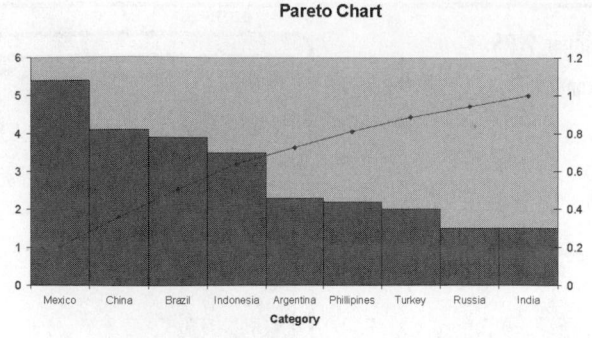

Pareto Chart

2.34 A senior manager at Four-Mile-Island Utility Company collected various complaints from customers during the past 6 months. The following table shows the types of complaints and the frequency of each.

Type of Complaint	Number of Customers with this Complaint
A. Customer's check was lost	10
B. Customer's bill was mailed late	80
C. The serviceman was rude to the customer	20
D. The meter was read incorrectly	60
E. The electric utility service was mistakenly disconnected	5
F. Other	25

   a. Draw a Pareto diagram (see Exercise 2.33) to summarize the data.

   b. Draw a pie diagram to summarize the data.

   c. What course of action does the Pareto diagram suggest that the senior manager take?

2.35 A successful businessperson receives the following yearly incomes (in dollars) from seven business partnerships.

Business Partnership	Yearly Income
A	23,160
B	30,070
C	32,732
D	35,900
E	37,304
F	43,608
G	60,014
Total	262,788

Express the yearly incomes from each partnership as a percentage of the businessperson's total income, and summarize this information using a pie chart.

2.36 Several brands of mobile PCs have made major inroads into the U.S. corporate market with portable computers. A Gallup interview of various corporations found the following frequencies of responses for the brands listed below.

Brand	Frequency of Response for Using This Brand
IBM	108
Toshiba	104
Compaq	100
Dell	50

Brand	Frequency of Response for Using This Brand
NEC	28
Hewlett-Packard	22
Acer/TI	18
Gateway	12
AST	10
Apple	10

(Source: Adapted from *Dallas Morning News,* "TECHBITS," by Jennifer Files, Aug. 4, 1997, p. D2.)

Present the data in the form of a bar graph. In your opinion, which brands appear to dominate the mobile PC market for the corporations surveyed?

2.37 The numbers of models of light trucks and also of cars for the years 1978 and 1993 are as follows. Choose a graphical technique to compare the number of models for the two years. Why did you select this technique?

	1978	**1993**
Car models	135	174
Light truck models	33	65

(Adapted from "Light Trucks Outpace Cars," *USA Today,* Oct. 1, 1993, p. 1E.)

2.38 A study by the U.S. Office of Employment Projections revealed the employment distribution of adult workers, age 25 through 64. The results below present the percentage of adult workers in each of the specified occupational groups.

Occupational Group	Percentage of Adult Workers
Administrative support occupations, including clerical	15.9
Professional specialty occupations	13.9
Precision production, craft, and repair occupations	13.6
Executive, administrative, and managerial occupations	11.6
Service occupations	11.0
Sales occupations	10.3
Machine operators, assemblers, and inspectors	9.7
Transportation and material moving occupations	4.7
Handlers, equipment cleaners, helper, and laborers	3.5
Farming, forestry, and fishing occupations	3.1
Technicians and related support occupations	2.7

(Source: *Occupational Outlook Quarterly,* "Employment Distribution of All Adults and Young Adults," U.S. Dept of Labor, Winter 1996–97, Vol. 40, No. 4, p. 27.)

a. Display these data using a bar chart and a pie chart.
b. Which chart do you prefer to display these data. Why?

2.39 The amount of time it takes to order a special automotive part from the manufacturer is of great concern to a local automotive dealer. The following data are the average delivery times (in days) from nine different stores for parts that were special-ordered.

Store	1	2	3	4	5	6	7	8	9
Average Delivery Time	2.5	4.5	3.0	6.0	3.0	7.0	4.0	3.5	4.0

a. Draw a bar chart, then describe the shape of the chart.
b. How does a bar chart differ from a histogram?

2.40 A random sample of one-bedroom apartments in Middletown, U.S.A., revealed the following monthly rentals. Forty units were sampled.

249	180	190	230	349	299	300	175	305	205
225	160	195	395	245	275	155	225	360	180
205	239	305	260	155	255	310	230	305	210
320	168	309	380	190	225	365	302	285	395

a. Order the data. Determine the class intervals if 5 class intervals are desired for a frequency distribution.
b. Construct a cumulative frequency distribution.
c. What proportion of the apartments is priced over $299 per month?

2.41 Thirty-year fixed-rate mortgages vary according to the financial institution. A sample of 40 banks and financial institutions in the Chicago area yielded the following 30-year fixed mortgage rates.

7.20	6.51	7.80	7.65	7.01	6.90	7.35	7.10	7.80	6.80
7.05	6.90	7.25	7.35	7.95	6.80	7.15	7.35	7.20	7.55
7.65	7.75	7.15	7.25	7.05	6.70	7.35	7.65	7.80	7.05
7.10	7.25	7.60	7.35	7.45	7.65	7.20	6.80	7.30	7.10

a. Present a stem-and-leaf display of the data.
b. Construct a relative frequency distribution for these data using class intervals of width .25.
c. Which 30-year fixed-rate mortgages are most common?

2.42 Various occupational groups are employed by a textile apparel manufacturer. The following table lists the number of employees in each occupation for the years 1990 and 1993.

Occupation	1990	1993
Professional researchers	120	290
Managers	200	130
Technicians	530	740
Salespersons	210	220
Clerical workers	175	120
Unskilled workers	250	350

a. Construct a bar chart for each of the years 1990 and 1993.
b. Construct a pie chart for each of the years 1990 and 1993.
c. Explain what changes have occurred in the company from 1990 to 1993. Which chart do you think provides the easiest means of comparison?

2.43 The manager of a production workshop monitored daily the number of incoming work orders and the number of work orders completed for 60 days. The following table illustrates the frequency distribution of daily incoming and completed work orders.

Number of Work Orders	Days with Incoming Work Orders	Days with Completed Work Orders
5–9	3	20
10–14	10	15
15–19	12	12
20–24	20	9
25–29	10	3
30–31	5	1

a. Construct a cumulative relative frequency distribution for the incoming work orders. Do the same for the completed work orders.

b. What percent of the time do 20 or more work orders come into the production workshop? What percent of the time are 20 or more work orders completed by the production workshop? What recommendation might you make to the manager based on the cumulative relative frequency distributions?

2.44 A mutual fund has its assets spread over seven sectors of the economy. The following data are the total value (in millions of dollars) of the stocks in which the fund is invested for each sector.

Stock	Value
Electronics and electrical equipment	2.116
Aerospace and defense	10.375
Food and beverage	4.864
Utilities	2.713
Insurance and finance	6.538
Health care	3.675
Oil and gas	1.532

a. Express the amount invested in each sector of the economy as a percent.

b. Summarize the list in a pie chart.

2.45 A survey of 12th graders across Europe and the United States was conducted to access their mathematical and science aptitude. The results of the International Mathematical and Science Study (TIMSS) are presented below. A score of 500 is considered average.

Country	Score
Austria	519
Czech Republic	476
Denmark	528
France	505
Germany	496
Italy	475
Norway	536
Russian Federation	476
United States	471

(Source: *USA Today*, "Global Report Card," Feb. 25, 1998, p. 2D.)

Present the data collected from TIMSS using a bar chart.

2.46 An independent oil firm recently hired 10 engineers, 5 geologists, 3 accountants, 1 statistician, 4 computer scientists, and 1 chemist. Present these data in the form of a pie chart.

2.47 The price for a one-day admission cost at Disney World is presented below for 1993 to 1998.

Year	Cost for an Adult	Cost for a Child
1993	34.00	27.00
1994	36.00	29.00
1995	37.00	30.00
1996	40.81	32.86
1997	42.14	33.92
1998	44.52	36.04

(Source: *USA Today*, "The Price of Fun," Apr. 13, 1998, p. 8B.)

a. Draw a bar chart for an adult's cost.

b. Draw a bar chart for a child's cost.

c. Compare the two bar charts.

2.48 The ages (in years) of the 20 loan officers, 4 vice presidents, and the president of American Bank are

47, 52, 55, 65, 42, 37, 29, 52, 47, 36, 60, 50, 48, 42, 45, 35, 38, 45, 57, 43, 39, 41, 33, 58, 60

a. Construct a frequency distribution.

b. Construct a cumulative frequency distribution.

c. Write a summary statement about the distribution of the ages of the loan officers.

2.49 A Pareto diagram (See Exercise 2.33) is useful for showing that only a few categories account for a large percentage of the observed frequencies. Consider the following data, illustrating a breakdown of all Federal income taxes paid in 1995.

Income Level	Total Income	Percentage of All Federal Income Taxes Paid
Top 1 percent	Above $209,105 a year	30.2%
Top 5 percent	Above $96,104 a year	48.8%
Top 10 percent	Above $72,092 a year	60.5%
Bottom 50 percent	Below $22,361 a year	4.6%

(Source: *The Washington Times*, "Who Pays What in Taxes?" Apr. 15, 1998, p. A10.)

Explain how income categories can be created so that a Pareto diagram would illustrate that only a few categories contribute to a very large percentage of all Federal income taxes paid. The last category listed on the horizontal scale is sometimes listed as an "other" category even if its frequency is not the smallest (see Exercise 2.33).

2.50 A survey was conducted to examine how job applicants view what happens after their résumé is submitted. The categories from which they could respond are presented below for a sample of 500 applications.

Response Category	Number Responding to This Category
Needs attention-grabbing tactic to be read	125
Goes into big pile with other résumés	115
Sender has no control over fate	100
Company will call immediately	60
Must send résumé again to be noticed	40
Position filled; ad is just a formality	35
Don't know	25

(Source: *USA Today*, "What Happens to That Resume?" Feb. 19, 1998, p. 1B.)

Use the data above to construct a Pareto diagram. What insight do you gain from the cumulative relative frequency graph in the Pareto diagram? (See Exercise 2.33.)

2.7 DECEPTIVE GRAPHS

You might be tempted to be creative in your graphical displays by using, for example, a three-dimensional figure. Such originality is commendable, but does your graph accurately represent the situation? Consider Figure 2.26, which someone drew in an attempt to demonstrate that there are twice as many men as women in management positions. The artist constructed a box for the category "men" twice as high—but also twice as deep—as that for the category "women." The result is a rectangular solid for men that is, in fact, four times the volume of the one for women. The illustration is misleading—it appears that there are four times as many men as women in management.

When data values correspond to specific time periods—such as monthly sales or annual expenditures—the resulting data collection is a **time series.** A time series is represented graphically by using the horizontal axis for the time increments. For example, Figure 2.27 contains a return-on-investment time series for two mutual funds, plotted over a six-year period. A glance at this figure might lead you to believe that mutual fund A is performing nearly twice as well as mutual fund B. A closer look, however, reveals that *the vertical axis does not start at zero;* such a construction can seriously distort the information contained in such a graph. The 1998 return for fund A appears to be roughly twice that for fund B. However, the actual returns are 15.8% for fund A and 14.5% for fund B. Granted, fund A is outperforming fund B, but not nearly as dramatically as Figure 2.27 seems to indicate. Also, fund B is not as "unstable" as Figure 2.27 would indicate, since the return only fluctuates between 14% and 15%.

Such examples, and many others, are contained in an entertaining and enlightening book by Darrell Huff entitled *How to Lie with Statistics.** Other deceptive graphs described by Huff include bar charts similar to those in Figure 2.28. Here, you may be tempted to conclude that there is a significant difference in bar heights, either because the vertical axis does not begin at zero (left side) or because the bars are chopped in the middle without a corresponding adjustment of the vertical axis (right side). *As an observer, beware of such trickery. As an illustrator, do not intentionally mislead your reader by disguising the results through the use of a misleading graph.* This practice tends to give statisticians a bad name!

FIGURE 2.26

The illustrator wished to show that there are twice as many men as women in management positions. However, box B is twice the height and twice the depth of box A and thus is four times the volume.

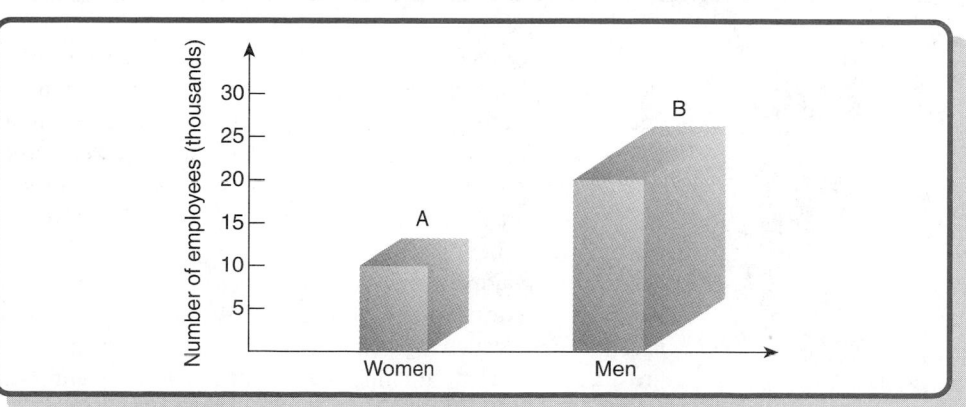

* Darrell Huff, *How to Lie with Statistics* (New York: Norton, 1954 [and 1982 by Darrell Huff with Irving Geis, illustrator]). More recent discussions are included in *Statistics: Concepts and Controversies* by David S. Moore, 4th ed. (New York: Freeman, 1996) and "How to Display Data Badly" by Howard Wainer, *The American Statistician,* May 1984.

FIGURE 2.27

Time-series graph of the performance of two mutual funds. The graph is misleading because the vertical axis does not start at zero.

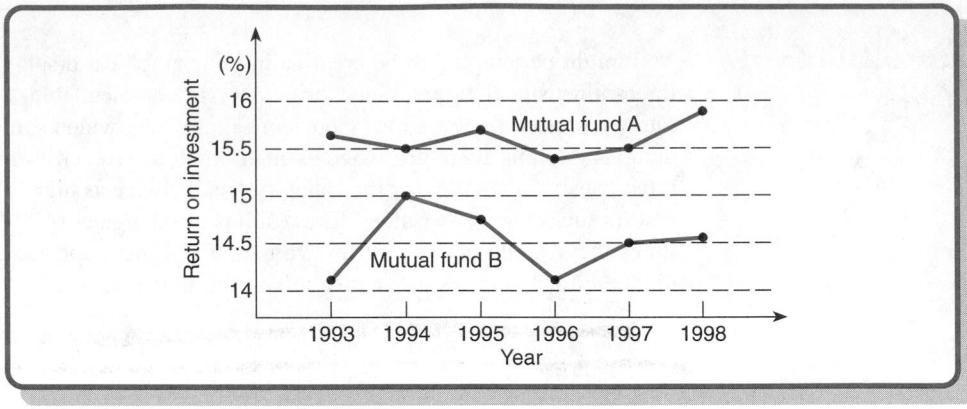

Instructor
likes these

FIGURE 2.28

Two misleading bar charts. The vertical axis of the left-hand chart does not begin at zero, and the bars in the right-hand chart are chopped without a corresponding adjustment in the vertical axis.

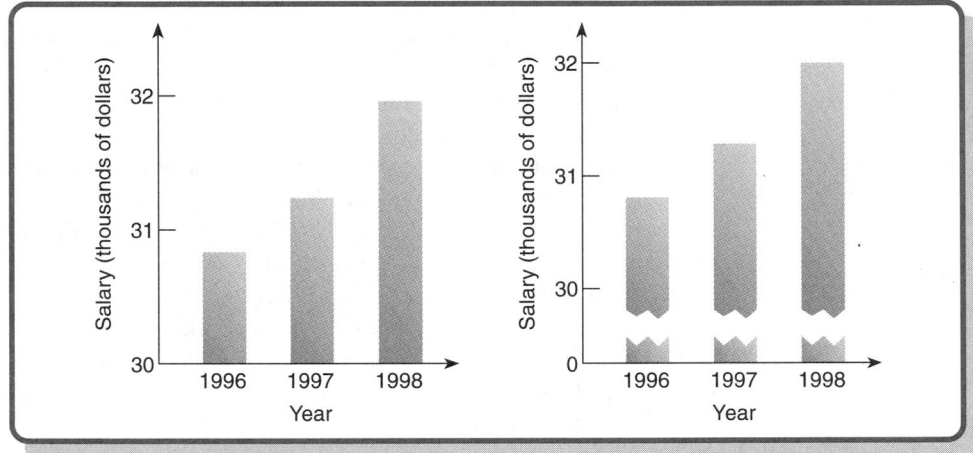

2.8 USING COMPUTER GRAPHICS

With the fairly recent introduction of powerful graphics available on the microcomputer, sales of graph paper and protractors have taken a heavy hit! A large number of PC packages allow you to construct a variety of multicolored and multidimensional bar charts, pie charts, and histograms. These are available in most word processing (e.g., Word Perfect), spreadsheet (e.g., Excel), and statistical (e.g., Minitab) software.

Minitab graphics will be illustrated in the end-of-chapter appendix. Excel gives you the option of obtaining three-dimensional graphs. The bar chart in Figure 2.29 is a summary of the majors of the 50 individuals in Table 2.1 and is a three-dimensional representation of the bar chart in Figure 2.20. Excel's three-dimensional pie chart in Figure 2.30 uses the same data and is a more colorful and interesting version of the pie chart in Figure 2.23. When constructing a graph using **KGP Data Analysis ➤ Qualitative Data Charts,** you will have the option of selecting either a two-dimensional or a three-dimensional graph. There are many other PC graphics packages available that can be used for statistical graphics presentations. Two of the more popular ones are MS PowerPoint and WP Presentations.

If you think you will have to create graphical summaries, try to gain access to a computer package with easy-to-use graphics capabilities, such as Excel or MINITAB. One thing the authors picked up in their industrial experience is that no presentation or report is complete without at least one of the graphs discussed in this chapter!

FIGURE 2.29

Illustration of Excel's three-dimensional bar chart (see two-dimensional chart in Figure 2.20).

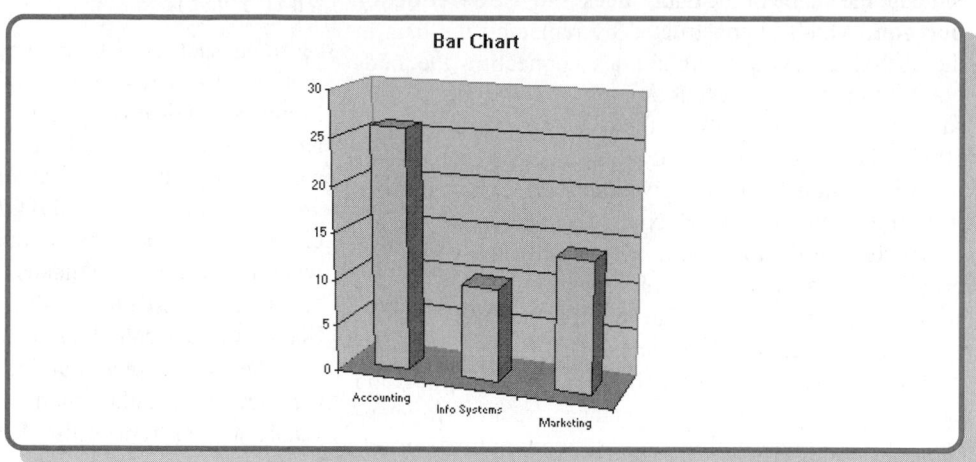

FIGURE 2.30

Illustration of Excel's three-dimensional pie chart.

Instructor Doesn't like pie charts. Fancy but not practical

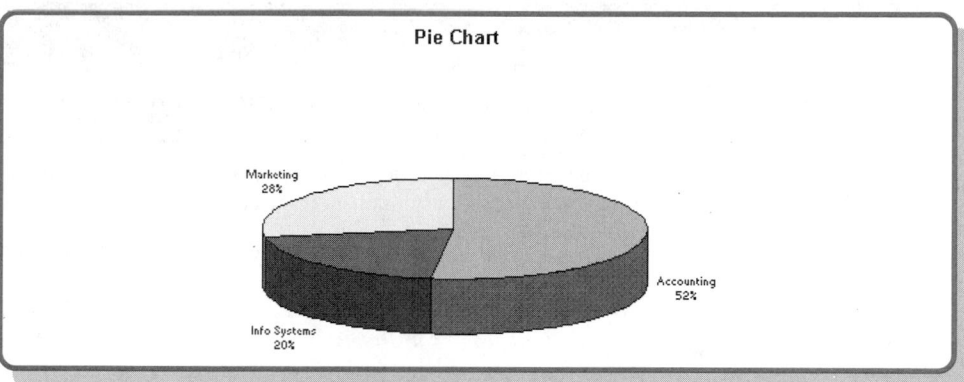

SUMMARY

This chapter examined methods of summarizing and presenting a large set of data using a graph. You begin by placing the sample data in order, from smallest to largest (an **ordered array**). The next step is to summarize the data in a **frequency distribution,** which consists of a number of classes (such as "150 and under 250") and corresponding frequencies.

The data summary can then be displayed using an appropriate graph. We discussed five kinds of graphs.

1. A **histogram,** or **frequency polygon,** is a graphical view of a frequency distribution that summarizes a sample by placing the values into groups (classes).
2. A **stem-and-leaf diagram** is a graphical representation of an *entire* sample.
3. An **ogive** allows you to illustrate cumulative or "less-than" percentages of frequencies.
4. A **bar chart** summarizes categorical (nominal) or ordinal data.
5. A **pie chart** presents a percentage breakdown of a particular quantity.

A frequency distribution provides a summary of the data by placing them into groups called **classes.** The number of values in each class is the **class frequency.** For example, there may be ten values in the class "150 and under 250." The numbers 150 and 250 here are the **class limits,** and the difference between consecutive lower class limits is the **class width.** The center of this class $[(150 + 250)/2 = 200]$ is the **class midpoint.** All classes should have the same width, except possibly the first and last class, which may be open-ended if you have a few outliers. For comparisons, the same data can be summarized using **relative frequencies,** which indicate the fraction of data values in each class rather than actual counts (**frequencies**).

Histograms and **stem-and-leaf diagrams** are graphical representations of a frequency distribution and are generally used for data having an interval or ratio level of measurement. A **stem-and-leaf diagram** does not condense the sample data into classes, but rather represents *each* value in an easy-to-read graph. An excellent way to indicate the shape of the data values is to use a **frequency polygon,** which is constructed by replacing the bars in the histogram with straight lines connecting the midpoints at the top of each bar. An **ogive** allows you to make such statements as "40% of the data values are less than 500." Like a frequency polygon, an ogive consists of many straight lines; in an ogive, the lines always increase from 0 to 1 on the vertical axis.

When the data are nominal or ordinal, a **bar chart** provides an excellent graphical summary. When constructing a bar chart, gaps are inserted between the bars because of the nature of this data type. A **pie chart** is also useful for nominal or ordinal data. This circular graph can be used to represent percentages (relative frequencies) at some point in time or over a certain time period.

WHAT'S NEXT?

A graph such as a frequency polygon is an excellent method of describing a set of data, but it does have its limitations. For example, we might look at Figure 2.16 and ask where the middle (center) of the data is. One person might argue that it is somewhere around $33,000, whereas someone else might decide that it is some value closer to $34,000. The point is that we need to define what the word *middle* means and define some method of calculating this value, so that we all get the *same* result. Such a value is called a *numerical measure.*

The next chapter examines a variety of such numerical measures. Rather than reducing a set of data to a graph, we will reduce the data to one or more *numbers* that give us some information about the data.

REVIEW EXERCISES 2.51–2.61

2.51 The ten top theater movies for the week of April 14, 1998, are listed below. The box office revenue listed in millions of dollars is included.

Theater Movie	Box Office Revenue
1. *City of Angels*	15.4
2. *Lost in Space*	13.4
3. *Titanic*	8.6
4. *Species 2*	7.3
5. *The Players Club*	5.9
6. *Mercury Rising*	5.5
7. *The Odd Couple II*	4.8
8. *My Giant*	3.1
9. *Grease*	2.5
10. *Primary Colors*	2.4

(Source: *USA Today,* "Angels' Soars to Top," Apr. 14, 1996, p. D1.)

   a. Form a stem-and-leaf display. Do any outliers appear?
   b. Form a frequency distribution, starting with the class 0 and under 5.
   c. Interpret the shape of the distribution.

2.52 Many of the phone companies offer their customers Internet access over existing copper telephone lines using ADSL—asymmetrics digital subscribe line technology. Suppose that a marketing director at GTE believes that the range of fees for installation is from $60 to $140. Assume that 100 telephone users who have had this service installed are randomly sampled.

(Source: *The Baltimore Sun,* "GTE to Offer High-Speed Links to Internet," Apr. 14, 1998, p. 3C.)

   a. Would you use a frequency distribution for discrete data or continuous data?
   b. Set up class limits such that the class width is 15.
   c. Suppose that only four classes were desired. What class limits would you choose?

2.53 A survey by the University of Iowa queried 249 employers on their hiring practices. Employers rated sources from 1 to 5 on both the extent that the source was used and the usefulness of the source. A 5 indicated that the source was used a great deal and a 1 indicated that the source was not used at all. Results are shown below.

Source	Extent Used	Usefulness
Newspaper advertisements	3.70	3.45
Informal referrals	3.66	3.72
Direct applications	3.49	3.14

Source	Extent Used	Usefulness
Formal referrals	3.03	3.14
College placement offices	2.94	2.80
Private search firms	2.76	3.20
Professional association ads	2.65	2.78
Temporary employment agencies	2.43	2.61
Online employment exchanges	1.88	1.92

(Source: *Occupational Outlook Quarterly,* "Experienced Job Seekers Benefit Most From Want Ads?" U.S. Dept of Labor, Winter 1996–97, Vol. 40, No. 4, p. 31.)

Construct a bar chart for the Extent Used column of data and for the Usefulness column of data. Compare the two charts.

2.54 When money is allowed to grow in a tax-deferred retirement account, the results can be impressive when the money is allowed to grow for several decades. Consider the results below.

Starting Age	Investment Value at Age 65 When Investing $500 Annually
20	$221,238
30	$ 96,216
40	$ 39,890

Starting Age	Investment Value at Age 65 When Investing $1000 Annually
20	$442,475
30	$192,431
40	$ 79,781

Construct a bar chart for the investment values at age 65 for the case where an investor saves $500 annually and for the case where an investor saves $1000 annually. Compare the two charts. How will an investor who saves $1000 annually starting at age 30 fare against an investor who starts at age 20 and saves $500 annually?

(Source: *Stages: The Fidelity Investments Magazine of Personal Finance,* "A Little Can Go a Long Way," Winter 1998, p. 22–23.)

2.55 Many car rental companies offer special weekly rates on economy cars. A sample of Hertz's weekly economy rate at 18 locations (3 of which are in Canada) is presented below.

City	Weekly Economy Rate (in Dollars)
Miami	137
Orlando	144
Tampa	145
Los Angeles	169
San Francisco	190
Las Vegas	120
Seattle	179
Denver	131
Atlanta	207
Detroit	191
Dallas/Fort Worth	169
Boston	194
Chicago	184
Honolulu	142
Puerto Rico	170
Toronto	190
Calgary	133
Vancouver	137

(Source: *USA Today,* "Plan Ahead and Save Rates," Apr. 14, 1998, p. 9A.)

a. Construct a stem-and-leaf diagram using the last digit as the leaf.
b. Construct a frequency histogram with nine class intervals.
c. Compare the shapes of the stem-and-leaf diagram in part (a) and the histogram in part (b).

2.56 Seven day annualized yields for the 15 biggest money market mutual funds open to investors immediately follow.

Money Market Fund (Listed in Order of Fund Asset Size)	Week of Feb. 20 1998 (in %)	Six Months Ago (in %)
Merrill Lynch CMA Money Fund	5.11	5.12
Smith Barney Cash Port/Class A	5.07	5.08
Vanguard MMR/Prime Port/Rt 1	5.33	5.33
Fidelity Cash Reserves	5.28	5.28
Schwab Money Market Fund	4.98	4.99
Schwab Value Advantage	5.32	5.34
Centennial Money Market Trust	5.03	5.08
Dean Witter/Liquid Asset Fund	5.15	5.13
Merrill Lynch Retirement Reserves	5.24	5.25
Dean Witter/Active Assets	5.25	5.26
Paine Webber RMA MF/MM Port	5.11	5.10
Fidelity Spartan	5.30	5.31
Prudential/Command Money	5.18	5.17
Merrill Lynch Ready Assets	5.09	5.10
Prudential Money Mart Assets	5.05	5.10

(Source: *USA Today*, "Savers' Scoreboard," Feb. 20, 1988, p. 4B.)

a. Construct a relative frequency distribution for the money market yields on February 20, 1998.

b. Repeat part (a) for six months ago.

c. Comment on the similarities or differences in parts (a) and (b).

2.57 For the week of April 13, 1998, $1.954 billion of initial public stock offerings was sold on the United States stock exchange. The companies and their market values are presented below.

Companies	Market Value (Millions of dollars)
American Dental Partners	96
ARM Holdings	346
Brightstar Information	88
Broadcom	475
Conecel	389
Cunningham Graphics	58
DA Consulting Group	78
Horizon Medical Products	180
Nanogen	197
Prima Group International	47

(Source: *USA Today*, "At Issue: IPOs this Week," Apr. 13, 1998, p. 6B.)

a. Draw a Pareto diagram (see Exercise 2.33) to summarize the data.

b. What percent of the market value do the companies ARM Holdings, Broadcom, and Conecel constitute? What conclusions can you make from viewing this diagram?

2.58 **[DATA SET EX2-58]** *Variable description:*

OrderTime: Time that a customer needs to wait in a queue before receiving service for renting an automobile.

On-Time Rent-A-Car wishes to determine how long its customers wait in a busy airport before being serviced by an attendant. The length of time (in minutes) is recorded for 200 randomly sampled customers.

a. Use the command **KGP ➤ Quantitative ➤ Histogram** to examine a relative frequency histogram of the data.

b. Write a brief report on the distribution of the length of time that a customer waits before being served.

2.59 **[DATA SET EX2-59]** *Variable description:*

Mileage V6:   Gas mileage with a V6 engine
Mileage V8:   Gas mileage with a V8 engine

The marketing director of Robertson Chevrolet wishes to determine the gas mileage that customers can expect from its best selling van for the V6 engine (standard) and for the V8 engine (optional).

a. Use the **KGP ➤ Quantitative ➤ Stacked Histogram** option to examine the distribution of gas mileage for the van with a V6 engine and for a van with a V8 engine.

b. Compare the two histograms in part (a). What differences do you notice?

2.60 A manufacturing process has produced 25 ball bearings during one shift. The spec limits for the ball bearings are 39.8 to 40.2 cm. A histogram of the data follows. What interpretation can you give to the pattern observed? Would a shift in the process help reduce the number of nonconforming ball bearings?

39.86	39.86	40.23	40.19	39.97
39.91	40.13	39.81	40.04	40.06
39.96	40.34	40.24	39.87	40.23
40.04	40.17	39.96	40.22	39.86
40.08	40.24	40.07	40.14	40.16

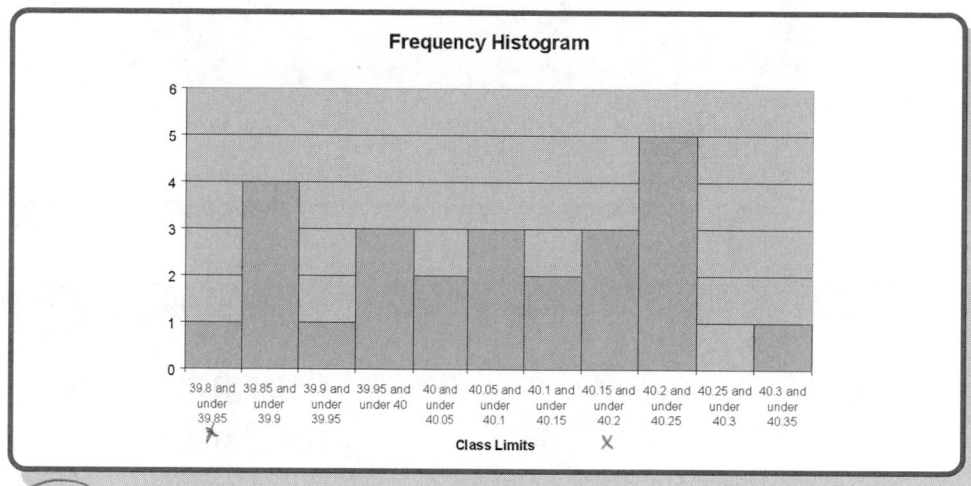

2.61 The travel department of a marketing research firm wishes to determine the distribution of the number of frequent-flyer miles that their 110 salespeople have accumulated over a 2-year period. In the table below are the frequent-flyer miles, in thousands of miles. A histogram with 10 classes is presented. Another histogram with 4 classes is presented. Describe the shape of each of these histograms. What interpretations can be concluded from the first histogram but not in the second?

30.1	14.1	27.3	22.4	19.1	18.4	19.7	20.1	20.1	18.7	36.7
10.2	20.5	14.3	33.3	17.7	18.8	19.3	19.9	23.5	19.5	40.3
16.7	11.3	33.7	23.8	19.9	23.9	25.1	19.7	21.7	21.5	44.1
34.7	14.5	27.9	31.8	20.0	18.7	19.6	19.3	21.2	18.6	29.1
26.3	16.1	16.5	48.3	20.2	18.2	19.8	19.7	20	19.2	28.6
32.7	30.7	17.5	27.2	19.6	20.6	21.5	20.3	21	22.1	38.7
29.9	26.8	26.3	47.7	17.7	19.7	22.9	23.0	21.4	19.1	38.2
15.6	10.6	21.1	32.1	18.7	19	20.2	19.6	19.1	19.6	20.1
33.7	25.5	34.5	10.7	21.9	21.2	16.6	21.2	21.2	21.9	21.5
49.5	16.5	31.7	12.7	21.6	20.5	20.0	19.0	21.3	20.7	19.7

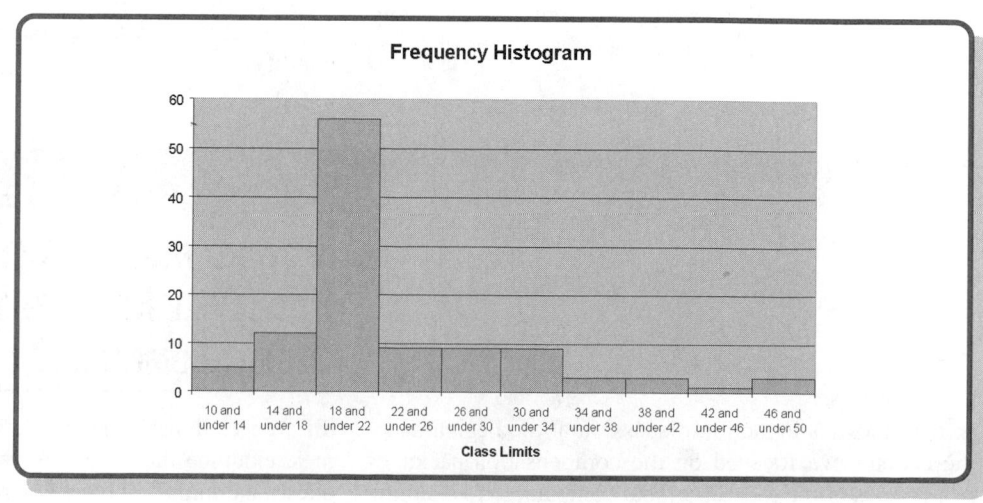

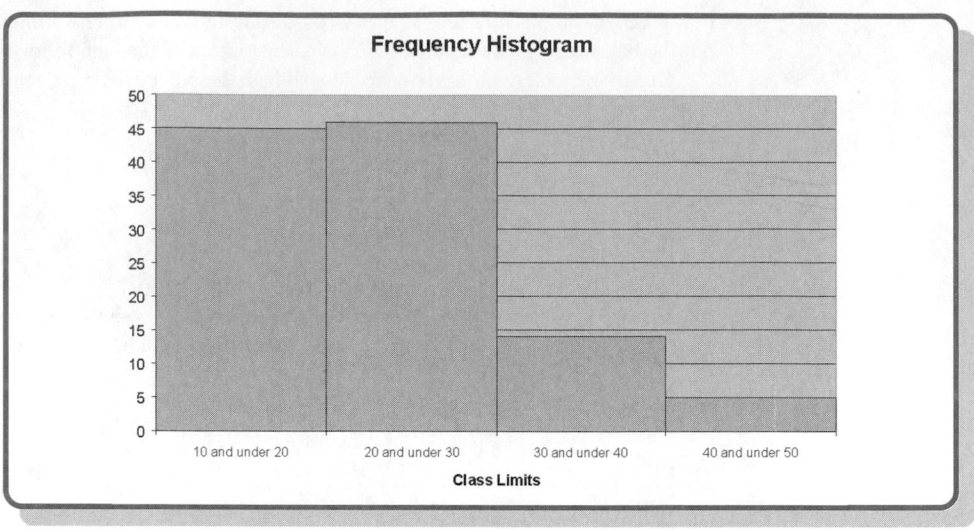

Frequency Histogram

COMPUTER EXERCISES USING THE DATABASES

EXERCISE 1—APPENDIX E

Select 50 observations at random from the database. Using a convenient statistical package, construct a frequency histogram and a stem-and-leaf diagram on the variable HPAYRENT (house payment or house/apartment rent). Using this same set of observations, construct separate frequency histograms and stem-and-leaf diagrams on the variable HPAYRENT for those who own their residence and for those who rent their residence. Comment on the shapes of the frequency histograms. Note: If using MINITAB, you can easily obtain the random sample with the following statement: MTB > SAMPLE 50 OBSERVATIONS FROM C1-C9, PUT INTO C11-C19

EXERCISE 2—APPENDIX E

Choose at random 30 observations from families living in the NE sector and then choose another 30 observations at random from families living in the SW sector. Using a convenient statistical computer package, construct frequency histograms and stem-and-leaf diagrams on the variable INCOME1 (income of principal wage earner) for each group of 30 observations, and comment on the frequency distribution of each.

EXERCISE 3—APPENDIX F

Select 100 observations at random from the database. Construct a frequency distribution and a histogram of the values of the variable ASSETS (current assets). Construct a stem-and-leaf diagram. What do you observe from these two graphs?

EXERCISE 4—APPENDIX F

Repeat Exercise 3 using the variable LIABIL (current liability).

INSIGHTS FROM STATISTICS IN ACTION: HOW WELL RUN ARE THE TOP 100 GLOBAL COMPANIES?

In the Statistics in Action discussion at the beginning of the chapter, we focused on the compensation packages from CEOs of the top 100 global companies. To examine differences in performance for the largest global companies, examine the following set of data and answer the questions immediately following.

THE WORLD'S 100 LARGEST PUBLIC COMPANIES

1997 Rank	1996 Rank	Company (Country)	Market Value (m$)	Fiscal 1996 Sales (m$)	Percent Change from 1995	Fiscal 1996 Profit (m$)	Percent Change from 1995
1	1	General Electric (U.S.)	214,454	79,179	13	7,280	11
2	2	Royal Dutch/Shell (Netherlands/U.K.)	177,537	131,020	21	9,434	39
3	3	Coca-Cola (U.S.)	167,334	18,546	3	3,492	17
4	4	Nippon Telegraph and Telephone (Japan)	152,784	54,749	2	1,544	−16
5	5	Exxon (U.S.)	152,706	134,357	8	7,510	16
6	12	Microsoft (U.S.)	151,438	11,358	31	3,454	57
7	10	Merck (U.S.)	124,936	19,829	19	3,881	16
8	14	Intel (U.S.)	116,144	20,847	29	5,157	45
9	7	Toyota Motor (Japan)	111,924	105,927	14	3,319	50
10	8	Phillip Morris (U.S.)	107,778	69,204	5	6,303	16
11	34/52	Novartis (Switzerland)	99,031	26,986	1	1,716	−45
12	15	Procter & Gamble (U.S.)	95,677	35,764	1	6,415	12
13	6	Bank of Tokyo-Mitsubishi (Japan)	93,712	752,318	N.A.	352	N.A.
14	16	International Business Machines (U.S.)	89,570	75,947	6	5,429	30
15	13	Johnson & Johnson (U.S.)	85,740	21,620	15	2,887	20
16	11	Roche Holding (Switzerland)	85,403	11,891	8	2,904	16
17	31	Bristol-Myers Squibb (U.S.)	80,989	15,065	9	2,850	57
18	29	Pfizer (U.S.)	77,152	11,306	13	1,929	23
19	19	Wal-Mart Stores (U.S.)	76,603	106,146	12	3,056	12
20	25	Glaxo Wellcome (U.K.)	73,574	14,274	9	3,417	17
21	26	DuPont (U.S.)	70,983	43,810	4	3,636	10
22	22	British Petroleum (U.K.)	70,710	76,548	37	3,679	18
23	30	American International Group (U.S.)	70,139	28,205	9	2,897	15
24	—	Deutsche Telekom (Germany)	66,041	40,946	6	1,038	−70
25	59	Eli Lilly (U.S.)	60,710	7,347	9	1,524	−34
26	28	Hewlett-Packard (U.S.)	58,218	38,420	22	2,586	6
27	—	Berkshire Hathaway (U.S.)	58,162	100,500	37	2,489	198
28	24	PepsiCo (U.S.)	57,901	31,645	4	1,149	−28
29	40	Unilever (Netherlands/U.K.)	57,160	108,120	10	5,173	13
30	9	AT&T (U.S.)	56,968	52,184	3	5,908	7
31	64	SBC Communications (U.S.)	56,444	13,898	10	2,101	N.A.
32	38	Citicorp (U.S.)	55,846	277,563	10	3,788	9
33	70	Lloyds TSB Group (U.K.)	55,251	252,303	0	2,697	64
34	32	Mobil (U.S.)	54,976	80,782	7	2,964	25
35	39	Walt Disney (U.S.)	54,176	18,739	54	1,214	−12
36	33	HSBC Holdings (U.K.)	54,093	405,037	4	5,330	26
37	27	Nestle (Switzerland)	53,159	45,053	7	2,533	17
38	69	Gillette (U.S.)	52,789	9,868	10	949	−11
39	50	Abbott Laboratories (U.S.)	51,632	11,013	10	1,882	11
40	17	Sumitomo Bank (Japan)	51,552	513,781	8	294	−10
41	66	Smithkline Beecham Group (U.K.)	50,827	13,562	13	1,922	21
42	47	American Home Products (U.S.)	49,245	14,088	5	1,883	12
43	35	Allianz Holding (Germany)	48,396	41,899	6	1,428	45
44	42	Chevron (U.S.)	48,315	43,893	18	2,607	180
45	—	DDI (Japan)	48,220	8,738	52	−225	N.A.
46	48	British Telecom (U.K.)	47,273	25,558	3	3,554	5
47	78	NationsBank (U.S.)	47,085	184,936	−1	2,375	22
48	49	Fannie Mae (U.S.)	46,286	350,496	11	2,725	26
49	91	Lucent Technologies (U.S.)	46,114	23,286	9	224	−77
50	36	BellSouth (U.S.)	46,030	19,040	6	2,863	N.A.
51	67	BankAmerica (U.S.)	45,785	247,892	8	2,873	8
52	46	Eni (Italy)	45,425	37,915	1	2,927	3
53	58	Motorola (U.S.)	45,165	27,973	3	1,154	−35
54	41	Ford Motor (U.S.)	44,911	146,991	7	4,446	7
55	—	Muenchener Ruckversicherungs (Germany)	44,747	17,701	2	327	81
56	56	Cisco Systems (U.S.)	44,547	6,440	57	1,049	15

1997 Rank	1996 Rank	Company (Country)	Market Value (m$)	Fiscal 1996 Sales (m$)	Percent Change from 1995	Fiscal 1996 Profit (m$)	Percent Change from 1995
57	18	Fuji Bank (Japan)	43,509	474,371	4	942	N.A.
58	23	Sanwa Bank (Japan)	43,061	470,336	5	223	N.A.
59	55	Amoco (U.S.)	42,961	36,078	16	2,834	52
60	45	Matsushita Electric Industrial (Japan)	42,575	66,013	13	1,186	N.A.
61	20	Dai-Ichi Kangyo Bank (Japan)	42,500	476,696	1	−1,531	N.A.
62	72	Minnesota Mining & Mfg. (U.S.)	42,456	14,236	6	1,526	56
63	71	Daimler-Benz (Germany)	42,446	29,003	3	1,817	N.A.
64	37	GTE (U.S.)	41,898	21,339	7	2,798	N.A.
65	63	Chase Manhattan (U.S.)	41,845	336,099	11	2,461	−17
66	44	General Motors (U.S.)	40,602	164,069	2	4,953	−28
67	—	Travelers Group (U.S.)	40,446	148,997	33	2,331	27
68	21	Industrial Bank of Japan (Japan)	39,464	399,509	16	110	N.A.
69	61	Boeing (U.S.)	38,247	22,681	16	1,095	179
70	—	Ericson (Sweden)	38,043	18,205	26	1,050	32
71	60	Ameritech (U.S.)	37,302	14,917	11	2,134	6
72	62	Hitachi (Japan)	37,298	73,299	5	760	−38
73	93	ING Group (Netherlands)	36,208	277,941	13	1,908	16
74	—	American Express (U.S.)	35,233	107,402	1	1,901	22
75	—	Schering-Plough (U.S.)	35,030	5,656	11	1,212	37
76	—	Warner-Lambert (U.S.)	33,718	7,231	3	787	6
77	90	Sony (Japan)	33,677	48,703	23	1,199	157
78	87	Home Depot (U.S.)	33,479	19,535	26	938	28
79	65	Siemens (Germany)	33,371	61,113	6	1,801	50
80	57	McDonald's (U.S.)	33,327	10,687	9	1,573	10
81	77	Bell Atlantic (U.S.)	33,215	13,081	−3	1,882	1
82	74	Oracle (U.S.)	32,916	5,684	35	821	36
83	—	Allstate (U.S.)	32,188	24,299	7	2,079	9
84	73	Seven-Eleven (Japan)	31,484	22,627	10	502	9
85	—	Zeneca Group (U.K.)	31,373	9,178	9	1,100	91
86	—	Hutchison Whampoa (Hong Kong)	31,290	4,740	5	1,554	26
87	—	Schlumberger (U.S.)	30,856	8,956	18	851	31
88	80	Astra (Sweden)	30,370	5,712	9	1,376	8
89	—	Barclays (U.K.)	30,142	318,551	10	2,807	20
90	—	Elf Aquitaine (France)	29,430	47,571	2	1,344	39
91	92	Honda Motor (Japan)	29,345	45,522	24	1,902	212
92	83	Deutsche Bank (Germany)	29,307	575,693	23	1,441	4
93	76	Broken Hill Proprietary (Australia)	29,178	17,729	13	326	−61
94	97	Sun Hung Kai Properties (Hong Kong)	28,765	2,921	14	1,426	6
95	98	Texaco (U.S.)	28,670	45,500	24	2,018	232
96	—	L'Oreal (France)	28,466	11,611	13	673	11
97	53	Tokyo Electric Power (Japan)	28,463	43,334	0	702	58
98	43	Singapore Telecommunications (Singapore)	28,153	3,160	11	1,065	12
99	89	Bayer (Germany)	28,052	31,542	9	1,769	14
100	—	Carrefour (France)	27,922	29,847	8	649	−4

1. You would like to include descriptive graphics with a report discussing market value of the world's largest public companies. What type(s) of graphs would be appropriate? What type of information does each graph best convey?

2. Construct a histogram for the market value of the 100 companies. Comment on the shape of that histogram. What does the shape indicate?

3. Repeat Question 2 for the 1996 fiscal profit of those 100 companies. What does this histogram tell you about the profitability of the 100 companies?

4. For each of the countries—Japan, UK, Germany, and the United States—calculate the proportion of companies, wholly in the corresponding country, that have a percent change in profit that is larger than a percent change in sales? Present these results in the form of a bar chart, showing the results for the four countries.

5. For companies based in the United States, categorize each company that you can as being primarily manufacturing, automotive, chemical/pharmaceutical, retail (or other) sales, banking, and so on. Determine the frequency of each category and present this information using a Pareto diagram.

6. In your opinion, what type of graph(s) would be useful in comparing the United States and Japan in terms of the number of different types of companies?

7. Can you think of any other financial variables in which these companies could be compared?

Sources: *The Wall Street Journal,* "Top 100 Largest Public Companies," September, 18, 1997, p. R25. Reprinted by permission of Dow Jones, Inc., via Copyright Clearance Center, Inc., © 1997, Dow Jones and Company, Inc. All Rights Reserved Worldwide.

Newsday (New York), "Top 100 Companies/Executive Pay/Top Dollars for Top-Flight Execs/Is It Time to Deflate Golden Parachutes?" June 15, 1998, p. C8.

CHAPTER 2 APPENDIX: DATA ANALYSIS WITH **MINITAB**

HISTOGRAMS

The MINITAB procedure to construct a histogram will be illustrated with the salary data in Table 2.3. Observations that fall on interval boundaries are placed into the interval to the right. However, observations that fall on the far-right boundary are placed in the last interval. Missing data are automatically omitted. To construct a histogram using MINITAB, click on **Graph ➤ Histogram.** On the histogram user form, select **Salary** as a graph variable. Also select **Bar** under the **Display** box and **Graph** using the **For each** box.

On the histogram user form, click on **Options.** Under **Type of Histogram** on the options userform, click on the **Frequency** button to obtain a frequency histogram. The midpoint and cutpoint options are available to allow the user to have the tic mark on the histogram graph at either the midpoint of the interval or at the interval limits, respectively. For this example, the cutpoint option is selected. The endpoints or midpoints can be input under the **Midpoint/Cutpoint Positions** box. For this example, the number of intervals selected is 6 and no other box is selected under **Definitions of Intervals.** MINITAB will select the endpoints for the 6 intervals. The user forms illustrate the selections made for this histogram.

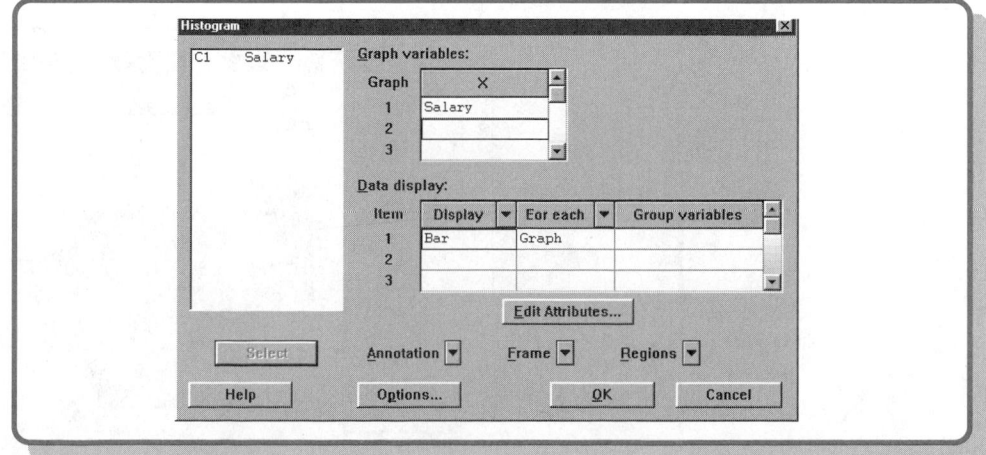

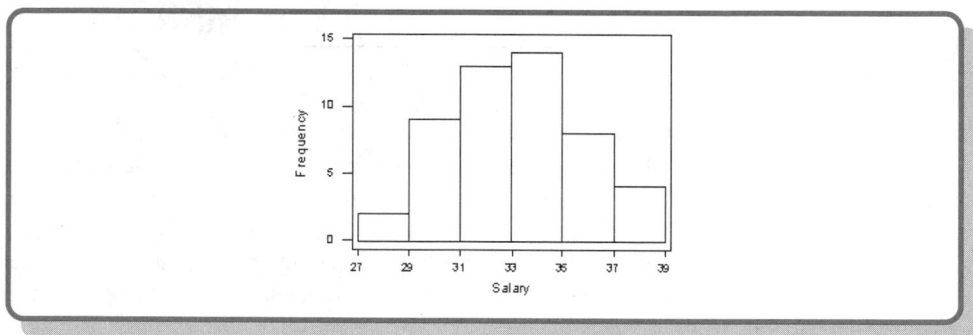

To execute the histogram command click on the OK button on both of these user forms. The following histogram will appear.

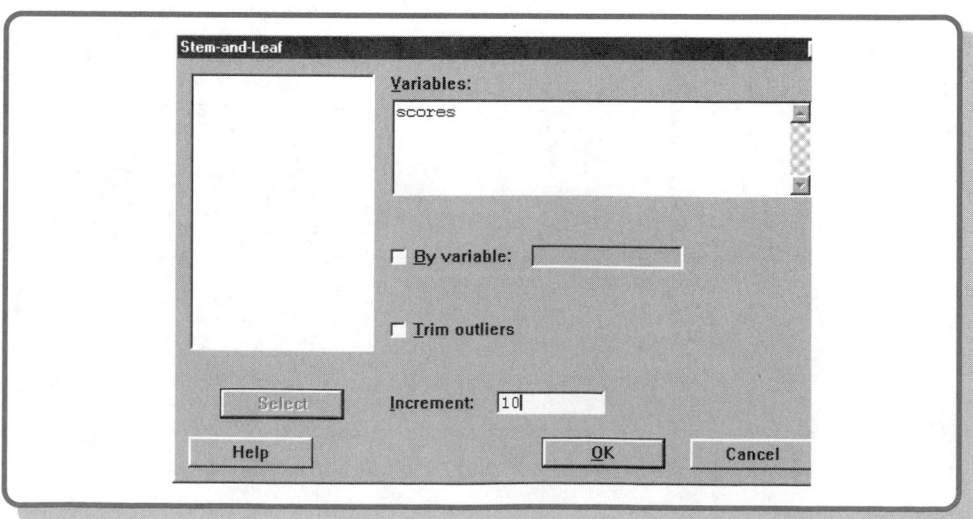

STEM-AND-LEAF PLOT

To illustrate how to construct a stem-and-leaf plot in MINITAB, the test scores data in Table 2.7 are used. With the data in column C1 (test scores), click on **Graph ➤ Stem-and-Leaf.** On the user form select C1 and select 10 for the increment option. The increment is the distance in data units between two lines of display. The display will have the 20s on one line, the 30s on the next line, and so on. The trim outliers option can be used if there are outliers in the data that, once eliminated, will allow for an expanded display of the central portion of the data. The following user form illustrates the options. The output is displayed in the next screen.

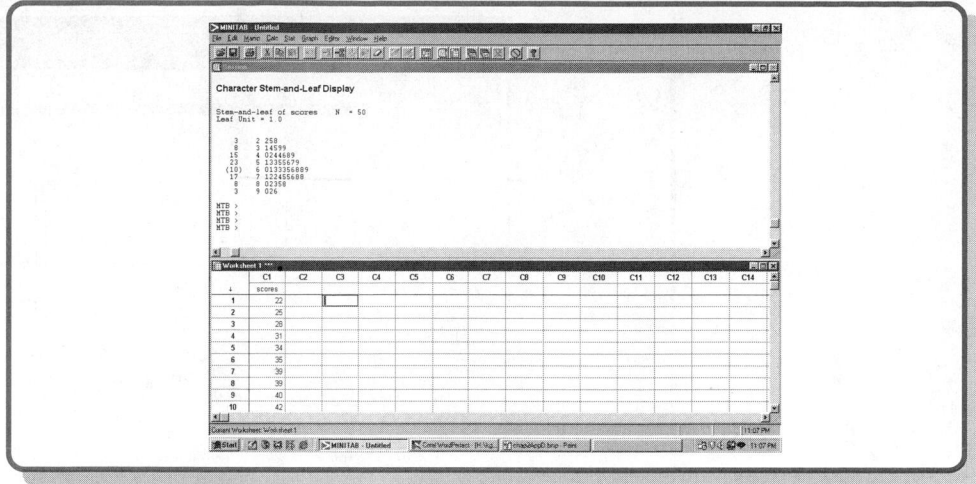

FREQUENCY POLYGON

The frequencies for the salaries data in the frequency distribution presented in Figure 2.6 will be used to illustrate the construction of a frequency polygon in MINITAB. The midpoints of each interval, including the midpoint of the interval before the first one and after the last one, are listed in C1, and the corresponding frequencies in C2. Click on **Graph ➤ Plot.** Then select frequencies for Y and salaries for X. Under the **Display** box, select **Connect** and under the graph box, select **Graph.** The user form using these options is presented below. The resulting output follows. An ogive also can be constructed in a similar manner. Simply list the endpoints of the intervals and the corresponding cumulative frequencies in columns C1 and C2, respectively, and select the same plot options.

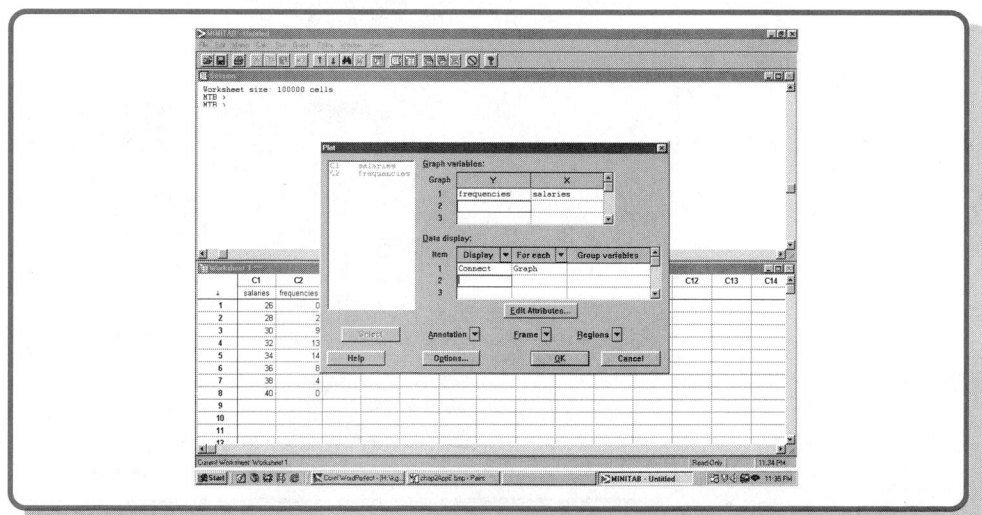

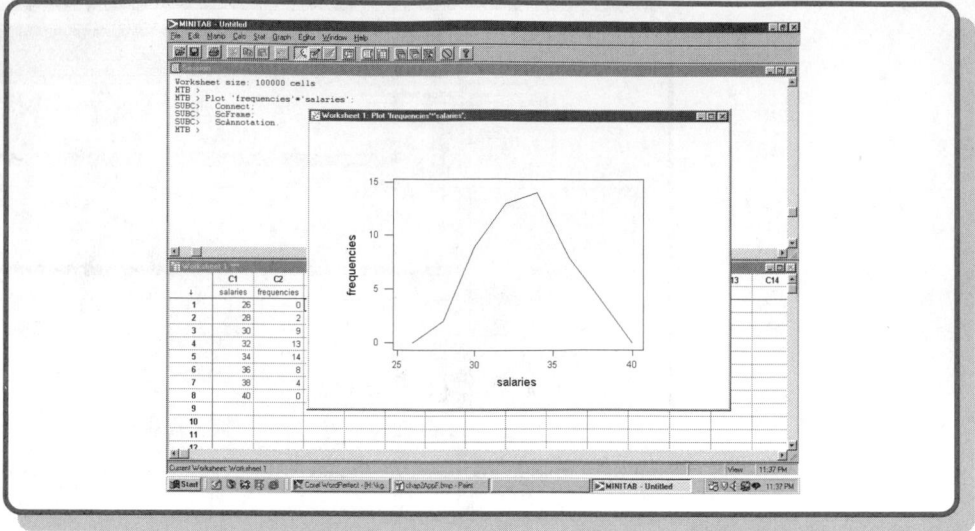

BAR CHARTS AND PIE CHARTS

To illustrate the process of constructing bar charts and pie charts, the data consisting of the frequency of complaints in Figure 2.24 (using data set DATA2-3) are used. The categories are coded 1 through 5. Click on **Graphs ➤ Plots.** Select **Frequency** for the Y variable and **Category** for the X variable. Under the **Display** box choose **Bar** and select **Graph** under the **For each** box. The following user form shows these options. The output follows in the next screen.

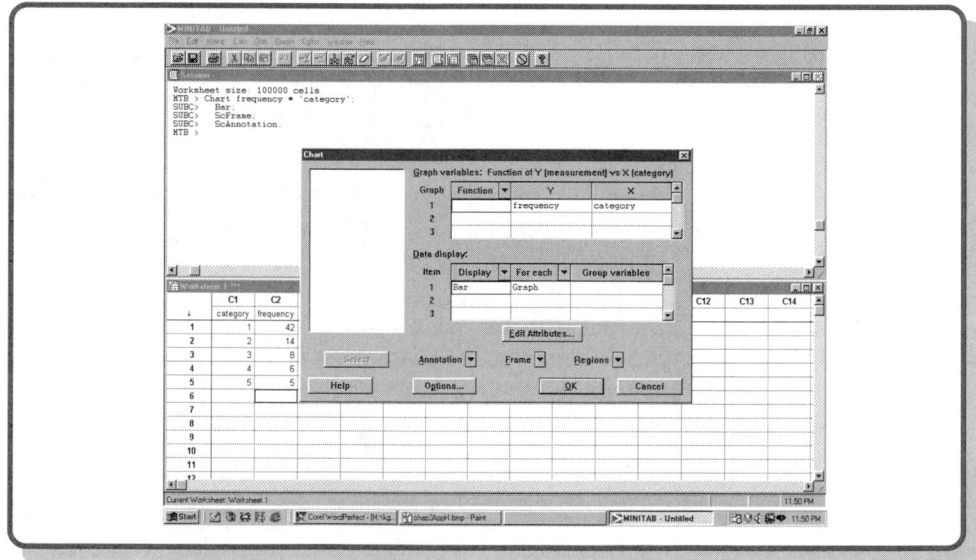

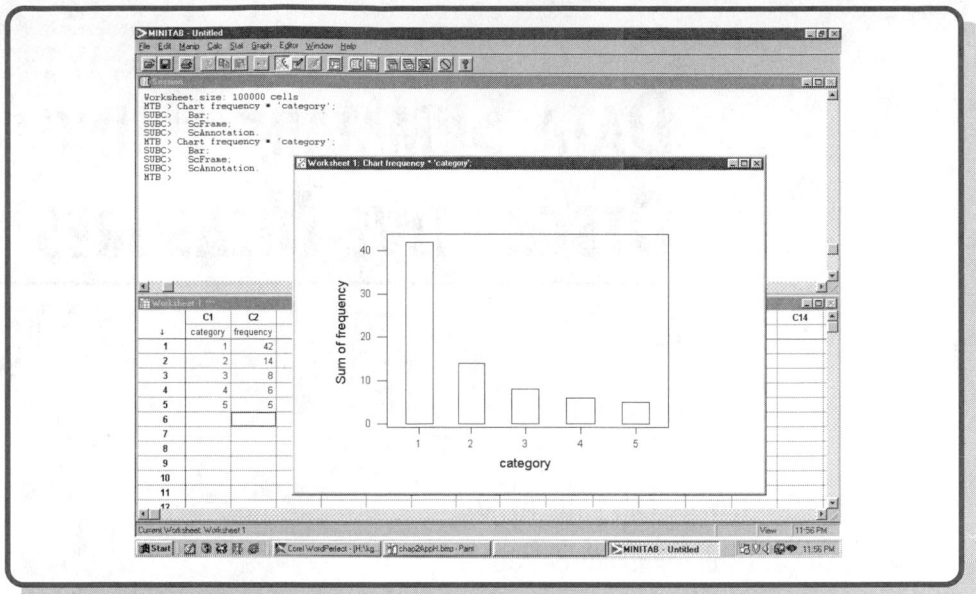

To illustrate the construction of a pie chart, the data contained in DATA2-3 are listed in C1 with the label complaints. Click on **Graph ➤ Pie Chart.** Then click on the button that says **Chart data in** and use column C1 (complaints). This user form has an option to move a slice of the pie away from the center of pie. To illustrate this, complaint 2 is selected as a pie slice to "explode." A title is given to this chart, but this is optional. If the title is left blank, the title will be Pie Chart of Complaints. The following two screens illustrate these options and the output.

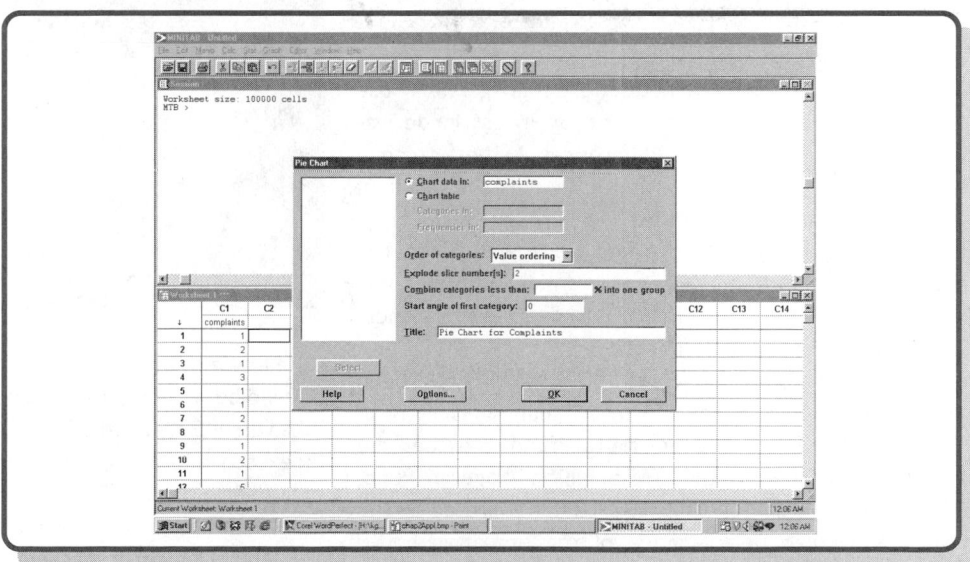

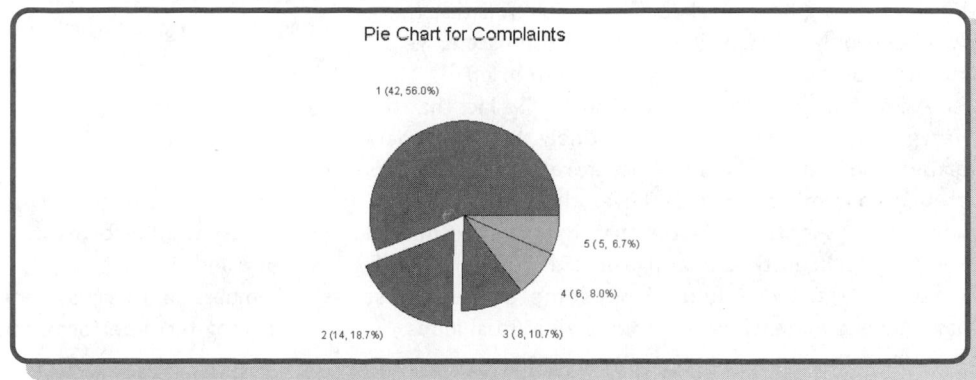

DATA SUMMARY USING DESCRIPTIVE MEASURES

STATISTICS IN ACTION: WHY CAN'T THE AVERAGE MUTUAL FUND BEAT THE STANDARD & POOR'S 500 INDEX?

Active mutual fund managers have the toughest time beating or even matching one of the mostly followed financial indexes: the Standard & Poor's 500 Index (S&P 500). Many funds have turned to indexing since the average mutual fund often cannot perform as well as this index. Indexing is a strategy that aims to match the market by investing in securities in the same proportion as they are represented in a market benchmark.

Index funds are generally successful in mimicking the returns of their target markets. These managers may use sophisticated computer programs or invest in derivatives. Usually, if there are differences in performance between one index fund and another, it is the result of different fees and expenses. In the past few years, large company stocks have performed very well. Since the average mutual fund typically favors small companies, it is not surprising that the S&P 500 is able to easily outperform the average mutual fund.

The Vanguard Index Trust-500 Portfolio has been immensely popular, garnering more than $64 billion in assets in 1998. The only other mutual fund to exceed the assets of this fund is the $71.5 billion Magellan Fund. Many active mutual fund managers are humiliated by the consistently high performance of the unmanaged S&P 500 Index. Some of these managers claim that they earn their pay during bear markets. The problem is that there have been only a few bear markets in the past 15 years, and most of the bear markets have been brief.

A few managers have caught on to the fact that the average mutual fund almost routinely has underperformed the S&P 500 Index. Therefore, these managers attempt to mimic the S&P 500 even though they are not index funds. Another reason that the average mutual fund has a difficult time beating the S&P 500 Index funds is because the index funds have some of the lowest management-expense ratios among all mutual funds.

How much has the average equity fund lagged the S&P 500 index? In 1996, the average equity mutual fund gained 20% versus 23% for the S&P 500. But in 1997, the S&P 500 Index soared 33.4%, while the average equity fund was only able to rise 24.4%. Of course, many mutual funds have money invested in stock markets around the world as well. The Asian stock markets took a tumble at the end of 1997. Still, most mutual fund managers use the S&P 500 as a benchmark against which to evaluate performance.

After completing this chapter, you will be able to

- Compare various fund categories (growth, capital appreciation, balanced, international fund, and so on);
- Determine the *average* performance for these mutual fund categories;
- Discuss the performance *variation* within each category; and
- Compare and discuss short-term performance versus long-term performance.

A LOOK BACK/INTRODUCTION

The first two chapters focused on different types of numerical sample data and methods of summarizing and presenting data. A frequency distribution is used to condense data from a sample into groups (called classes). Different types of statistical graphs can be used to illustrate sample data in different ways. The types of graphs we have discussed so far include the histogram, stem-and-leaf diagram, bar chart, ogive, frequency polygon, and pie chart. The purpose of these graphs is to convey information at a glance about the distribution of the values in your sample.

Every sample data set is a small part of a much larger population. Even if we don't always mention the word *population,* it is always there, since the sample values were selected from this group of interest. Every population has properties (called parameters) that describe it. By collecting a set of sample data, we can then estimate these properties by computing statistics and making graphs.

We have seen how to reduce a set of sample data to a graph. It also is helpful to reduce data to one or more numbers (such as an average). Such a number is called a descriptive measure. Because this number is derived from a sample, it also can be called a sample statistic. In this chapter we discuss the commonly used descriptive measures and explain what you can expect to learn from each one. In later chapters we discuss how you can use many of these sample statistics to estimate the corresponding population parameters.

3.1 VARIOUS TYPES OF DESCRIPTIVE MEASURES

A **descriptive measure** is a *single* number computed from the sample data that provides information about the data. The class of descriptive measures described here consists of four types. Which one you select depends on what you want to measure. These types are:

1. **Measures of central tendency.** These answer the questions, where is the "middle" of my data? and, which data value occurs most often?
2. **Measures of variation.** These answer the questions, how spread out are my data values? and, how much do the data values jump around?
3. **Measures of position.** These answer the questions, how does my value (score on an exam, for example) compare with all the others? and, which data value was exceeded by 75% of the data values? by 50%? by 25%?
4. **Measures of shape.** These answer the questions, are my data values symmetric? and, if not symmetric, just how nonsymmetric (skewed) are the data?

3.2 MEASURES OF CENTRAL TENDENCY

The purpose of a **measure of central tendency** is to determine the "center" of your data values or possibly the "most typical" data value. *Some measures of central tendency are the mean, median, midrange, and mode.* We will illustrate each of these measures using as data the number of accidents (monthly) reported over a particular five-month period:

accident data: 6, 9, 7, 23, 5

THE MEAN

The **mean** is the most popular measure of central tendency. It is merely the average of the data. The mean is easy to compute and explain, and it has several mathematical properties that make it more advantageous to use than the other three measures of central tendency.

Business managers often use a mean to represent a set of values. They select one value as typical of the whole set of values, such as average sales, average price, average salary, or average production per hour. In economics, the term *per capita* is a measure of central tendency. The income per capita of a certain district, the number of clothes washers per capita, and the number of televisions per capita are all examples of a mean.

The *sample mean*, $\bar{x}$ (read "x bar"), is equal to the sum of the data values divided by the number of data values. For the accident data set,

$$\bar{x} = \frac{6+9+7+23+5}{5} = 10.0$$

In general, let an arbitrary data set be represented as

$$x_1, x_2, x_3, \ldots, x_n$$

where n is the number of data values. (In the accident data set, $x_1 = 6$, $x_2 = 9$, $x_3 = 7$, $x_4 = 23$, $x_5 = 5$, and n is 5.) Then,

$$\bar{x} = \frac{x_1 + x_2 + \cdots + x_n}{n} = \frac{\sum x}{n} \qquad (3.1)$$

The symbol $\sum$ (sigma) means "the sum of." In this case, the sample mean, $\bar{x}$, is the sum of the x values divided by n.* When dealing with discrete data, the sample mean is very often *not* an integer (such as 10, here) and should *not* be rounded to an integer. For example, remove the last value (5) from the accident data set. The sample mean is now

$$\bar{x} = \frac{6+9+7+23}{4} = 11.25$$

In subsequent chapters, we will be concerned with the mean of the *population*. The symbol of the population mean is μ (mu). For a population consisting of N elements, denoted by

$$x_1, x_2, x_3, \ldots, x_N$$

the *population mean* is defined to be

$$\mu = \frac{x_1 + x_2 + \cdots + x_N}{N} = \frac{\sum x}{N} \qquad (3.2)$$

Population: $x_1, x_2, \ldots, x_N$

Population mean $= \mu = \dfrac{x_1 + x_2 + \cdots + x_N}{N} = \dfrac{\sum x}{N}$

Sample values (selected from the population): $x_1, x_2, \ldots, x_n$, where $n \leq N$

Sample mean $= \bar{x} = \dfrac{x_1 + x_2 + \cdots + x_n}{n} = \dfrac{\sum x}{n}$

---

* In another application of this symbol, we square each of the sample values and sum these values. For the accident data, this operation would be written as

$$\sum x^2 = 5^2 + 6^2 + 7^2 + 9^2 + 23^2$$
$$= 25 + 36 + 49 + 81 + 529$$
$$= 720$$

For these data, then, $\sum x = 50$ and $\sum x^2 = 720$.

THE MEDIAN

The **median** of a set of data is the value in the center of the data values when they are arranged from smallest to largest. Consequently, it is in the center of the ordered array.

Using the accident data set, the median, **Md,** is found by first constructing an ordered array:

In the middle

5, 6, ⑦, 9, 23

The value that has an equal number of items to the right and the left is the median. Thus, Md = 7.

In general, if n is *odd,* Md is the center data value of the ordered set:

$$Md = \left(\frac{n+1}{2}\right) \text{ st ordered value}$$

Number in set

Here, the median is the $(5 + 1)/2 = 3$rd value in the ordered array. Note that for these data, the *position* of the median is 3, and the *value* of the median is 7. If n is *even,* Md is the average of the two center values of the ordered set. Thus, the median of the array, 3, 8, 12, 14 is $(8 + 12)/2 = 10.0$.

In our accident data set, one of the five values (23) is much larger than the remaining values—it is an outlier. Notice that the median (Md = 7) was much less affected by this value than was the mean ($\bar{x} = 10$). *When dealing with data that are likely to contain outliers (for example, personal incomes or prices of residential housing), the median usually is preferred to the mean as a measure of central tendency, since the median provides a more "typical" or "representative" value for these situations.*

i.e. housing prices

Finally, note that newspaper and magazine articles often refer to the mean and the median as an "average" value. Care must be taken not to always interpret this word as representing the sample mean unless this is specified in the discussion.

THE MIDRANGE   *middle of the range*

Although less popular than the mean and median, the **midrange (Mr)** provides an easy-to-grasp measure of central tendency. Notice that it also is severely affected (even more than $\bar{x}$) by the presence of an outlier in the data. In general:

(sample mean)

$$Mr = \frac{L+H}{2} \tag{3.3}$$

where L = smallest (lowest) value in the sample and H = largest (highest) value in the sample. Using the accident data set, $L = 5$, $H = 23$, and

$$Mr = \frac{5+23}{2} = 14.0$$

Compare this to $\bar{x} = 10$ and Md = 7.

THE MODE

The **mode (Mo)** of a data set is the value that occurs more than once and the most often. The mode is not always a measure of central tendency; this value need not occur in the "center" of your data. One situation in which the mode is the value of interest is the manufacturing of clothing. The *most common* hat size is what you would like to know, not the *average* hat size. Can you think of other applications where the mode would provide useful information? Consider situations where your sample consists of nominal data.

Note that there is no mode for our accident data set because all values occur only once. Instead, consider the data set

4, 8, 7, 6, 9, 8, 10, 5, 8

Mo = 8 (occurs three times).

There may be more than one mode if several numbers occur the same (and the largest) number of times. This is the only exception to our earlier statement that a descriptive measure consists of a *single* number.

EXAMPLE 3.1

A sample of ten was taken to determine the typical completion time (in months) for the construction of a particular model of Brockwood Homes:

4.1, 3.2, 2.8, 2.6, 3.7, 3.1, 9.4, 2.5, 3.5, 3.8

We find the mean completion time as follows:

$$\bar{x} = \frac{4.1 + 3.2 + \cdots + 3.8}{10} = \frac{38.7}{10} = 3.87 \text{ months}$$

Notice that there is an outlier in the data, namely, 9.4 months. To be safe, you should double-check this figure to make sure that it is, in fact, correct, that is, that there was no mistake in recording or transcribing this value. In the presence of one or two outliers, the median generally provides a more reliable measure of central tendency, so we construct an ordered array:

2.5, 2.6, 2.8, 3.1, **3.2, 3.5,** 3.7, 3.8, 4.1, 9.4

Consequently, since n is even

$$Md = \frac{3.2 + 3.5}{2} = 3.35 \text{ months}$$

Also, the midrange is given by

$$Mr = \frac{2.5 + 9.4}{2} = 5.95 \text{ months}$$

This value is severely affected by the presence of the outlier; the midrange value of nearly 6 months is a poor measure of central tendency for this application.

Finally, no mode exists because there are no repeats in the data values. These results are summarized in the graph in Figure 3.1, a **dot plot.** Each data value is represented as a dot on the horizontal line. The outlier of 9.4 is very obvious when the data are displayed in this type of plot.

FIGURE 3.1

Dot plot, along with several measures of central tendency for a sample of ten housing construction times. See text for application.

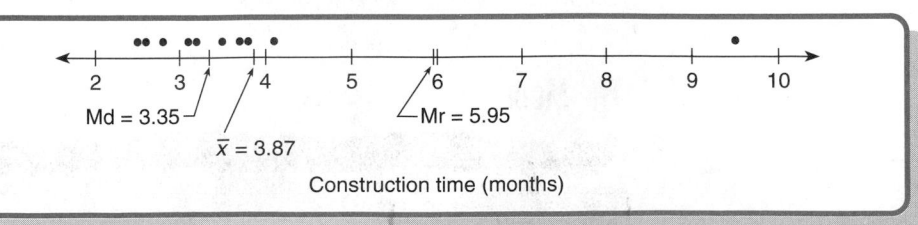

MICROSOFT® EXCEL APPLICATION   USE DATA3-2

EXAMPLE 3.2
Using Excel to Compute Measures of Central Tendency

In Chapter 2, we examined the starting salaries of the 50 business majors at Bellaire College. The data are presented in Tables 2.1 and 2.3. Dataset DATA3-2 contains these 50 sorted salaries, stored in a single column (column A in Figure 3.3) and also by type of major (columns B, C, and D). After opening this file, you should see columns A through D in Figure 3.3. Determine the mean, median, and midrange for the entire class of graduating business majors and for each of the three disciplines (accounting, information systems, and marketing). What can you conclude about the "typical" starting salaries for these three groups at Bellaire?

SOLUTION

To obtain the various statistics in Figure 3.3, use the Excel Descriptive Statistics command. To obtain this command, click on **Tools ➤ Data Analysis ➤ Descriptive Statistics ➤ OK.** You should see the input screen in Figure 3.2. Fill in the values as shown and be sure to click on the box for **Labels in First Row** and the box for **Summary Statistics.** After clicking on "OK" you obtain the statistics in Figure 3.3 describing all 50 individuals in the sample. You will need to widen column E by placing the cursor on the cell boundary alongside "E" and dragging it to the right until all the titles in this column are visible. **You can ignore the shaded cells for now; they'll be covered later in the chapter.** To obtain the midrange, type "Midrange" in cell E16 and type "=(F12+F13)/2" in cell F16. This uses Excel's formula capability and merely averages the minimum and maximum values in cells F12 and F13.

To derive the same set of statistics for the three disciplines, refer to Figure 3.2; for the input range, type "B1:D27" and for the output range, type "G1". This results in columns G through L shown in Figure 3.4. The midranges can be obtained by: (1) highlighting cells E16 and F16 by dragging the mouse across these two cells, (2) finding the fill handle in cell F16 (the small square in the lower right corner) and placing the cursor over the fill handle (you should see a black "+"), and (3) dragging the fill handle through L16. You should now see the midrange label and the corresponding value for each of the three majors.

FIGURE 3.2

Excel input screen for **Tools ➤ Data Analysis ➤ Descriptive Statistics.**

Descriptive Statistics	? X
Input	
Input Range: `A1:A51`	OK
Grouped By: ⦿ Columns ○ Rows	Cancel
☑ Labels in First Row	Help
Output options	
⦿ Output Range: `E1`	
○ New Worksheet Ply:	
○ New Workbook	
☑ Summary statistics	
☐ Confidence Level for Mean: `95` %	
☐ Kth Largest: `1`	
☐ Kth Smallest: `1`	

FIGURE 3.3

File DATA3-2 and the four measures of central tendency using Excel's descriptive statistics (midrange added).

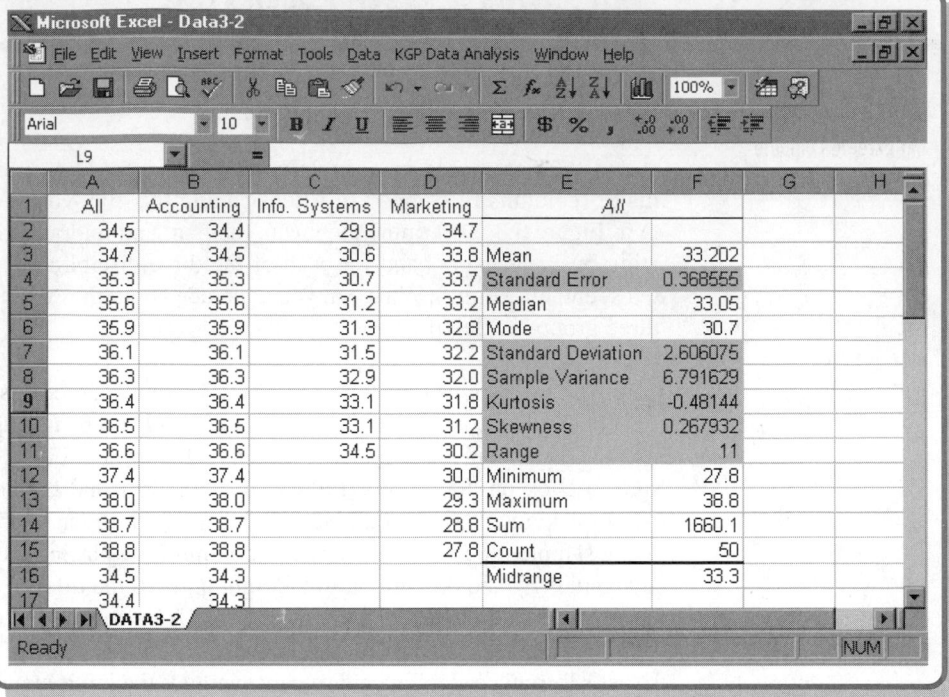

FIGURE 3.4

The four measures of central tendency using descriptive statistics on the three samples (midrange added).

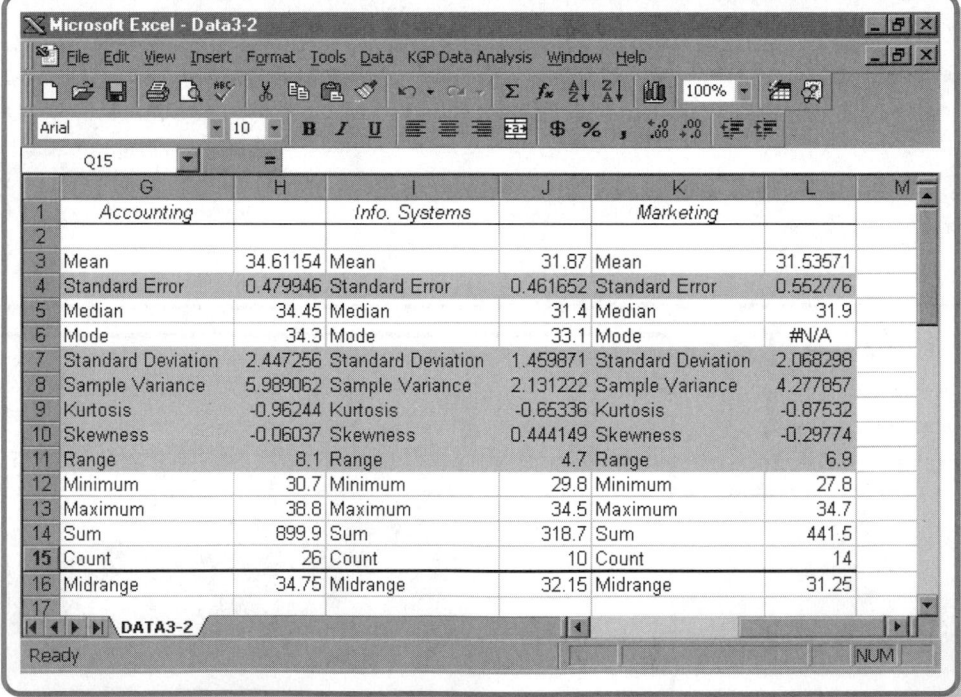

SUMMARY.   Since there appear to be no unusual values (outliers)* in each of the three sets of salaries, we will examine the means. The mean average starting salary for these 50 business graduates is $33,202. The accounting graduates had the largest mean starting salary ($34,612), followed by the information systems graduates ($31,870) and the marketing graduates ($31,536). For this graduating class at Bellaire, on the average, accounting graduates received a starting salary approximately $3000 higher than for the other two disciplines.

---

* The subject of outliers will be discussed in more detail in Section 3.8.

TABLE 3.1   Summary of levels of measurement and appropriate measure of central tendency. A "Y" indicates this measure can be used with the corresponding level of measurement.

Measure of Central Tendency	LEVEL OF MEASUREMENT			
	Nominal	Ordinal	Interval	Ratio
Mean			Y	Y
Median		Y	Y	Y
Midrange			Y	Y
Mode	Y	Y	Y	Y

Often the choice of which measure of central tendency to use is affected by the level of measurement (nominal, ordinal, interval, ratio) of the sample data. For interval/ratio data, you can use any of these four measures. For ordinal data, the difference between data values has no meaning and so only the mode and median are appropriate. For nominal data (such as hair color), the sample mode is the only measure of central tendency that should be used. These comments are summarized in Table 3.1.

EXERCISES 3.1–3.11

UNDERSTANDING THE MECHANICS

3.1 For each of the following data sets, find the mean, median, and midrange.
    a. 10 20 30
    b. 3 5 6 8 9
    c. 10 8 7 1 3 9 14 2 7 2

3.2 Determine the mean, mode, median, and midrange for each of the following sets of numbers. Specify the units. Convert numbers to an appropriate scale if necessary.

    a.

4 cubic meters	8 cubic meters	13 cubic meters
7 cubic meters	14 cubic meters	18 cubic meters
13 cubic meters	10 cubic meters	6 cubic meters

    b.

14 feet	28 feet	10 yards	4 yards
30 feet	16 feet	20 feet	3 yards

    c.

.10	.11	.08	.20	.25
16%	30%	14%	15%	10%
13%	15%	25%	10%	15%
14%	9%	21%	7%	22%

APPLYING THE NEW CONCEPTS

3.3 Select five different values between 1 and 20 such that
    a. The mean is smaller than the median.
    b. The mean is larger than the median.

3.4 The number of automobiles that are serviced daily by EZ Service Stations are recorded as follows for 30 days.

50	45	50	51	42	49	80	42	52	49
48	50	88	49	42	50	50	48	50	46
50	51	52	49	49	50	51	40	50	42

    a. Calculate the mean, median, mode, and midrange.
    b. Interpret each statistic in part (a). Which measure of central tendency appears to be most appropriate? Why?

3.5 Several years ago, the office occupancy costs, which include rents, real estate taxes, and operating expenses, were sky-high in Japan. Recently, the costs have fallen. The average occupancy costs have slid from $130 to $95 in Tokyo. Interpret this information. Does this imply that the median occupancy costs have decreased by this amount?

(Source: *Business Week*, "Less of a Gulf in Office Rents," June 16, 1997, p. 28.)

3.6 A traveling salesperson in Canada records the number of kilometers his Ford Taurus can drive on a full tank of gas. The following data give the kilometers traveled on a full tank of gas until the gas gauge indicated "empty."

640	620	640	521	655	605	638	678	630	650
420	595	670	633	628	660	595	670	640	630

    a. Calculate the mean, median, and mode.
    b. Which value appears to be more appropriate as a measure of central tendency?
    c. Recalculate the mean, median, and mode with the value of 420 kilometers omitted. Compare your answers to part (a).

3.7 The National Safety Board has investigated ship fires that have occurred on the open seas. In the past 19 years, seven of the 15 major cruise ship fires in U.S. waters occurred on older ships. A listing of major ship fires and their damage in millions of dollars is presented below.

Ship	Damage (in Millions)
Vistafjord	.68
Universe Explorer	1.50
Celebration	4.00
Regal Empress	.25
Song of America	.29
Britanis	.08
Sovereign of the Seas	.50
Regent Star	.02

Ship	Damage (in Millions)
Song of America	.35
Scandinavian Star	3.50
Emerald Seas	.30
Scandinavian Sea	16.00
Boheme	2.00
Angelina Lauro	26.30

(Source: *USA Today*, "Poor Fire Protection Sends Ships Cruising into Danger," May 5, 1998, p. 12A.)

Compute the mean and median for the data set above. Which observation affects the value of the mean the most if it is omitted? How is the median affected if this observation is omitted?

3.8 The number of slight imperfections noted in manufacturing a sheet of aluminum is recorded below for 10 sheets of aluminum manufactured from each of two different processes.

Process 1					Process 2				
13	11	13	15	12	13	19	13	14	13
14	12	15	11	13	20	12	13	15	10

a. Calculate the mean, median, mode, and midrange for each process.

b. Explain to the production manager what the statistics in part (a) mean.

3.9 The North Atlantic Treaty Organization (NATO) has taken on new meaning with the end of the Cold War. Cooperation between eastern European countries and NATO should bring both economic and military stability to Europe. However, a large number of active troops remain part of NATO. Below is a list of NATO members and their number of troops.

Country	Number of Active Military Personnel (Units in Thousands)
Belgium	46.3
Canada	70.5
Denmark	32.9
France	398.9
Germany	358.4
Greece	168.3
Italy	325.2
Luxembourg	.8
Netherlands	63.1
Norway	30.0
Portugal	54.2
Spain	206.8
Turkey	639.0
United Kingdom	226.0
USA	1400.0

(Source: *USA Today*, "NATO Founded During the Cold War," May 1, 1998, p. 6A.)

a. For the number of military personnel from each country, compute the mean, median, and midrange. Would you expect these statistics to be much different from each other?

b. Compute the mean, median, and midrange with the USA removed. Which statistics changed the most?

3.10 [DATA SET EX3-10] *Variable description:*

Waittime: Time that airline completely unloads luggage

Passengers have complained to airport authorities at Baltimore/Washington International (BWI) airport that the waiting time to pick up baggage from a particular flight from Mexico to BWI was excessive. After monitoring the wait time, management implemented a system that should on average take no more than 25 minutes to completely unload the plane. A sample of 50 flights yielded wait times for each flight.

a. Use the histogram command to view the waittime data. Does it appear that management is successful in having the wait time be no more than 25 minutes?

b. What is the mean and median of wait time? (Excel: Use the **Paste Function ➤ Statistical.**) What can you say about the new procedure with respect to the target of having passengers wait no more than 25 minutes?

3.11 [DATA SET EX3-11] *Variable description:*

Iowatest: Standardized scores from a national intelligence test

An educational researcher was interested in describing the distribution of test scores from the Iowatest for a local high school. The Iowatest data is a collection of 150 test scores from students in their junior year of school.

a. Plot the histogram of the Iowatest data. (Excel: Use **KGP Data Analysis ➤ Quantitative Data Charts/Tables ➤ Histogram/Freq. Charts.**) What is the mean and median of the Iowatest data? (Excel: Use the **Paste Function ➤ Statistical.**)

b. Give a brief description of the distribution of the Iowatest data from using the shape of the histogram.

c. To convert the standardized scores to nonstandardized scores, multiply the standardized scores by 4.5 and add 50. Can you guess what the new mean and median will be for the nonstandardized data?

d. Transform the data to nonstandardized data and find the mean and median. Compare the computed values to your values in part (c).

3.3 MEASURES OF VARIATION

Measures of central tendency, such as the mean, are certainly useful. However, the use of any single statistic to describe a complete distribution fails to reveal important facts.

Homogeneity refers to the degree of similarity within a set of data values. For example, the values in data set 1 (sunrise times for 10 randomly selected days in May) are much more homogeneous than the values in data set 2 (current batting averages for the starting lineup of the Minnesota Twins).

Data set 1:   6:20, 6:20, 6:20, 6:21, 6:21, 6:22, 6:22, 6:24, 6:26, 6:27

Data set 2:   .163, .186, .220, .250, .278, .283, .294, .318, .334

The more homogeneous a set of data is, the better the mean will represent a typical value. **Variation** is the tendency of data values to scatter about the mean, $\bar{x}$. If all the data values in a sample are identical, then the mean provides perfect information, the variation is zero, and the data are perfectly homogeneous. This is rarely the case, however, so we need a measure of this variation that will increase as the scatter of the data values about $\bar{x}$ increases.

Knowledge of variation can sometimes be used to control the future variability of your data values. Industrial production operations maintain quality control by observing and measuring the variation of the units produced. If there is too much variation in the production process, the causes are determined and corrected using an inspection control procedure.

Commonly used measures of dispersion are the **range, variance, standard deviation, and coefficient of variation.** Such measures are meaningful only when computed from *interval* or *ratio* data. To illustrate the various dispersion measures, we will use the accident data from the previous section: 6, 9, 7, 23, 5.

THE RANGE.   The simplest measure of variation is the **range** of the data, which is the numerical difference between the largest value (H) and the smallest value (L). For the accident data,

$$\text{range} = H - L = 23 - 5 = 18$$

The range is a rather crude measure of variation, but it is an easy number to calculate and contains valuable information for many situations. Stock reports generally give prices in terms of their ranges, citing the high and low prices of the day. The value of the range is strongly influenced by an outlier in the sample data.

THE VARIANCE AND STANDARD DEVIATION

By far the most commonly used measures of variation are the **variance** and **standard deviation.** Both measures describe the variation of the sample values about the sample mean, $\bar{x}$. Using the accident data, the sample mean is $\bar{x} = 10$. To calculate the sample variance, you begin by finding (1) the distance from each sample value to the mean, (2) the square of these distances, and (3) the sum of the squared distances. The closer the sample values are to $\bar{x} = 10$, the smaller this sum will be. Figure 3.5 illustrates the distance from the second sample value (6) to the mean, $\bar{x}$. The calculations necessary to compute the variance are as follows.

Data Value (x)	$(x - \bar{x})$	$(x - \bar{x})^2$
5	−5	25
6	−4	16
7	−3	9
9	−1	1
23	13	169
	$\Sigma (x - \bar{x}) = 0$	$\Sigma (x - \bar{x})^2 = 220$

So, $\Sigma (x - \bar{x})^2 = 220$.

The obvious thing to do next would be to find the average of these squared deviations:

$$\frac{\Sigma (x - \bar{x})^2}{n}$$

FIGURE 3.5

This presentation of the accident data shows their variation.

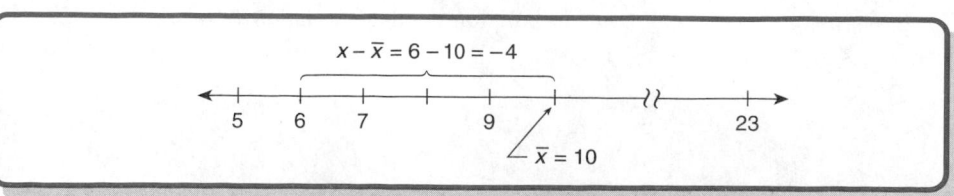

One use of this particular statistic in subsequent chapters is an *estimator*. In particular, we will need to estimate the variation within an entire population, using sample data collected from the population. However, a better estimator is obtained by dividing the sum of the squared deviations by $n - 1$ rather than by n. This leads to the **sample variance, s^2.** In general,

DEFINITION

$$s^2 = \frac{\sum (x - \bar{x})^2}{n - 1} \tag{3.4}$$

Using the accident data,

$$s^2 = \frac{220}{5 - 1} = \frac{220}{4} = 55.0$$

The square root of the variance is referred to as the **sample standard deviation, s.** In general,

$$s = \sqrt{\frac{\sum (x - \bar{x})^2}{n - 1}} \tag{3.5}$$

Using the accident data,

$$s = \sqrt{55.0} = 7.416$$

As previously mentioned, the sample variance s^2, is used to estimate the variance of the entire population. The symbol for the population variance is σ^2 (read as sigma squared). For a population consisting of N elements,

$$x_1, x_2, x_3, \ldots, x_n$$

the population variance is defined to be

$$\sigma^2 = \frac{\sum (x - \mu)^2}{N} \tag{3.6}$$

where μ is the population mean, defined in equation 3.2.

As we saw, the *population* variance can be obtained by dividing the sum of the squared deviations about μ by the population size N. The *sample* variance is calculated by dividing the sum of the squared deviations about $\bar{x}$ by the sample size (n) minus one. Had we chosen to divide by n rather than by $n - 1$, the resulting estimator would (on the average) underestimate σ^2. For this reason, we use $n - 1$ in the denominator of s^2.

- Population: $x_1, x_2, \ldots, x_N$

- Population variance $= \sigma^2 = \dfrac{(x_1 - \mu)^2 + \cdots + (x_N - \mu)^2}{N}$

  $= \dfrac{\sum (x - \mu)^2}{N}$

- Population standard deviation $= \sigma = \sqrt{\dfrac{\sum (x - \mu)^2}{N}}$

- Sample values (selected from the population): $x_1, x_2, \ldots, x_n$, where $n \leq N$

- Sample variance $= s^2 = \dfrac{(x_1 - \bar{x})^2 + \cdots + (x_n - \bar{x})^2}{n-1}$

  $= \dfrac{\Sigma(x - \bar{x})^2}{n-1}$

- Sample standard deviation $= s = \sqrt{\dfrac{\Sigma(x - \bar{x})^2}{n-1}}$

Now consider what the units of measurement are for s and s^2. The units of s are the same as the units on the data. If the data are measured in pounds, the units of s are pounds. Consequently, the units of the variance, s^2, would be (pounds)^2—a rather difficult unit to grasp at best. For the accident data, $s = 7.416$ accidents and $s^2 = 55$ (accidents)^2.

COMMENTS

The units of measurement for s are the same as the units of measurement on the mean ($\bar{x}$)—namely, the units of measurement for the sample values. As a result we are able to combine the sample standard deviation and the sample mean and ask questions such as, "How many of the sample values are less than $\bar{x} + s$?" or "How many of the sample values lie between $\bar{x} - s$ and $\bar{x} + s$?". Such questions will be discussed in Section 3.6.

There is another way to compute the sample variance. Using equation 3.4 to compute the value of s^2 may have appeared easy enough, but the computation was helped in part by the fact that the sample mean, $\bar{x}$, was an integer (10). When $\bar{x}$ is not an integer, it is easier to find s^2 using

COMPUTING FORMULA FOR s^2 (variance of sample)

$$s^2 = \frac{\Sigma x^2 - (\Sigma x)^2/n}{n-1} \tag{3.7}$$

As before, the standard deviation is the square root of the variance. To illustrate the use of equation 3.7, consider the accident data:

x	x^2
5	25
6	36
7	49
9	81
23	529
50	720

S is Sample Std. Deviation

S² is Sample Variance

So, $n = 5$, $\Sigma x = 50$, and $\Sigma x^2 = 720$. Consequently, using equation 3.7

$$s^2 = \frac{720 - (50)^2/5}{5-1}$$

$$= \frac{720 - 500}{4} = 55.0 \qquad \text{(as before)}$$

Also

$$s = \sqrt{55.0} = 7.416 \qquad \text{(as before)}$$

Finally, you may wish to interpret the magnitude of the value of s or s^2—that is, whether your value of s (or s^2) is large. This is difficult to determine because the values of

s and s^2 depend on the magnitude of the data values. In other words, large data values generally lead to large values of s. For example, which of the following two data sets exhibits more variation?

Data set 1:   5, 6, 7, 9, 23   (accident reports)

Data set 2:   5000, 6000, 7000, 9000, 23,000   (seating capacity of five football stadiums)

As we have already seen, for data set 1, $\bar{x} = 10.0$ and $s = 7.416$. For data set 2, the mean and standard deviation are $\bar{x} = 10,000$ and $s = 7416$.

Do these results mean that data set 2 has a great deal more variation, given that its standard deviation is 1000 times that of data set 1? Another look at the values reveals that the large value of s for data set 2 is due to the large values within this set. In fact, considering the size of the numbers within each data set, the *relative* variation within each group of values is the same. So comparing the standard deviations or variations of two data sets is not a good idea unless you know that their mean values ($\bar{x}$) are approximately equal. The next section deals with another statistical measure that will allow you to compare the relative variation within two data sets.

THE COEFFICIENT OF VARIATION

Consider again our two data sets, which appear to have the same variation (relative to the size of the data values) yet have vastly different standard deviations:

Data set 1:   5, 6, 7, 9, 23   ($\bar{x} = 10$, $s = 7.416$)

Data set 2:   5000, 6000, 7000, 9000, 23,000   ($\bar{x} = 10,000$, $s = 7416$)

To compare their variation, we need a measure of variation that will produce the same value for both of them. The solution here is to measure the standard deviation in terms of the mean; that is, what percentage of $\bar{x}$ is s? This measure of variation is the **coefficient of variation, CV.** In general, for samples containing nonnegative values,

$$CV = \frac{s}{\bar{x}} \cdot 100 \qquad \qquad (3.8)$$

For our example data sets:

Data set 1: $CV = \dfrac{7.416}{10} \cdot 100 = 74.16$

Data set 2: $CV = \dfrac{7,416}{10,000} \cdot 100 = 74.16$

So our conclusion here is that both data sets exhibit the same relative variation; s is 74.16% of the mean for both sets. As a final word here, we must point out that for data sets with *extreme* variation, it is possible to obtain a coefficient of variation larger than 100%.

EXAMPLE 3.3

To review the various measures of variation, let's use the data on housing construction time in Example 3.1.

Completion time: 4.1, 3.2, 2.8, 2.6, 3.7, 3.1, 9.4, 2.5, 3.5, 3.8 (months)

First, compute the range:

$$H - L = 9.4 - 2.5 = 6.9 \text{ months}$$

To find the variance and the standard deviation, first determine

$$\Sigma x = 4.1 + 3.2 + \cdots + 3.8 = 38.7$$

and

$$\sum x^2 = (4.1)^2 + (3.2)^2 + \cdots + (3.8)^2 = 186.25$$

Hence,

$$s^2 = \frac{186.25 - (38.7)^2/10}{10-1}$$

$$= \frac{186.25 - 149.77}{9} = 4.05 \text{ (months)}^2$$

and

$$s = \sqrt{4.05} = 2.01 \text{ months}$$

To calculate the coefficient of variation, use the previously obtained values of s and $\bar{x}$, where

$$CV = \frac{2.01}{3.87} \cdot 100 = 51.9$$

The standard deviation is 51.9% of the sample mean.

MICROSOFT® EXCEL APPLICATION   USE DATA3-4

EXAMPLE 3.4
Using Excel to Compute Various Sample Statistics

Example 2.1 introduced a sample of inside diameters for 100 machined parts produced at the Boston facility of Allied Manufacturing. This sample is also contained in Excel file DATA3-4. The machined part is supposed to have an inside diameter of 10.2 millimeters, with specification (spec) limits of 10.1 to 10.3 millimeters. Prior to examining this sample, you received word that the Toronto facility of Allied obtained a random sample of their parts, which have the same specs. Their sample produced a mean of 10.191 millimeters and a standard deviation of .0448 millimeter. Determine the sample mean, range, standard deviation, and coefficient of variation of the Boston sample. Comment on this sample—in particular, do these parts appear to be better than the Toronto parts?

SOLUTION

The Excel output using the descriptive statistics command is shown in Figure 3.6. To obtain this output, refer to Figure 3.2 and enter A1:A101 for the input range and B1 for the output range. Be sure to click on the checkboxes for **Labels in First Row** and **Summary Statistics** (as illustrated in Figure 3.2). The coefficient of variation in cells B16 and C16 is not part of the initial output but can be easily obtained by typing "Coeff. of Variation" in cell B16 and "=(C7/C3)*100" in cell C16.

The smallest sample value is 10.216, the largest value is 10.338, and the range is 10.338 − 10.216 = .122 millimeter. This machined part is supposed to have an inside diameter of 10.2 millimeters. The specification limits were from 10.1 to 10.3 millimeters; that is, these parts are of acceptable quality only if the diameter is between these two values. The sample mean of 10.275 is much larger than 10.2 millimeters and so the conclusion here would be the same as in Example 2.1: The process is off center and needs adjustment. The standard deviation for the Boston sample is .0267, and the coefficient of variation is .260. Consequently, the sample standard deviation is .26% of the sample mean.

To compare the Boston and Toronto samples, consider the following summary information:

	$\bar{x}$	s
Boston	10.275	.0267
Toronto	10.191	.0448

FIGURE 3.6

Descriptive statistics for 100
machined parts (inside
diameters) (coefficient of
variation added).

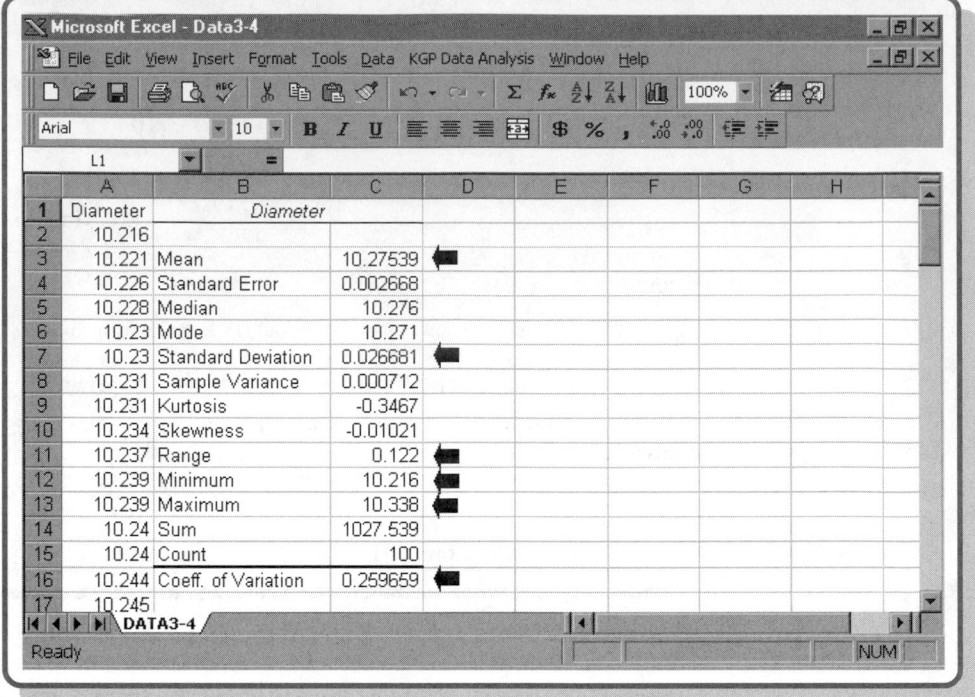

Based on this information, is the Boston process better or worse than the Toronto process? The answer is *both*! The Boston process is worse based on the value of $\bar{x}$, since this indicates that this process is .075 (10.275 − 10.2) millimeter off-center, whereas for the Toronto sample, the production process is .009 (10.2 − 10.191) millimeter off center. However, the Boston process is more consistent, since the standard deviation (s = .0267 millimeter) is much smaller than for the Toronto sample (s = .0448 millimeter). So you have mixed results here—the Boston process has less variation but is producing parts having inside diameters that are too large, on the average.

So far, you can reduce a set of sample data to a number that indicates a typical or average value (a measure of central tendency) or one that describes the amount of variation within the data values (a measure of variation). The next section examines yet another set of statistics—measures of position.

EXERCISES 3.12–3.21

UNDERSTANDING THE MECHANICS

3.12 From 50 collected data points, the statistics Σx and Σx^2 are calculated to be 20 and 33, respectively. Compute the sample mean, sample variance, sample standard deviation, and coefficient of variation.

3.13 Calculate the range, variance, standard deviation, and coefficient of variation for each of the following random samples.

    a. 3 5 8 2 4
    b. 10 15 18 21 22 13 19 20 17 16
    c. 3.2 4.5 3.6 4.7 2.1 4.7 5.3 3.8 4.1 3.5
        4.2 5.3 3.2 4.2 2.8 3.6 4.7 4.8 5.1 3.0

3.14 The values of the difference between the data values and the sample mean are −5, 1, −3, 2, 3, and 2.

    a. Do these values add to 0? Should they?
    b. What is the variance of the data?
    c. What is the standard deviation?

APPLYING THE NEW CONCEPTS

3.15 Airlines in the United States will pay $3 billion more in aviation taxes over the next five years, thanks to new airline ticket taxes imposed by Congress. Below is listed the amount of taxes the major airlines are expected to pay.

Airline	Taxes (in Millions)
American	$140
Alaska	$12
America West	$7
Continental	$48
Delta	$73
Northwest	$71
Southwest	$27
TWA	$16
United	$102
US Airways	$11

(Source: *USA Today*, "Ticket Tax: A Bittersweet Victory for Big Airlines," July 31, 1997, p. 5B.)

a. Consider two groups (large and small carriers) of Airlines: (1) American, Delta, Northwest, and United; and (2) Alaska, America West, Continental, TWA, and US Airways. Which group do you believe has a larger variability in taxes?

b. Calculate the standard deviation for the taxes of each group. Are these values consistent with your response in part (a)?

3.16 The prices of two stocks are shown to vary over a 12-month period. Describe the variability of the stocks. Which stock appears to be more stable? Why?

Month	Stock A	Stock B
Jan	10	30
Feb	11	33
Mar	12	36
Apr	11	32
May	15	45
June	18	49
Jul	13	37
Aug	16	48
Sept	11	33
Oct	10	30
Nov	9	33
Dec	13	39

3.17 Show that

$$s^2 = \frac{\sum(x - \bar{x})^2}{n-1}$$

is equivalent to

$$s^2 = \frac{\sum x^2 - (\sum x)^2 / n}{n-1}$$

3.18 a. Name an advantage and a disadvantage of using either the range or the standard deviation as a measure of variation.

b. What is the smallest value for either the range or the standard deviation?

c. If either the range or standard deviation is equal to zero, what can you say about each value of the sample?

3.19 The Hyatt Regency advertises get-away vacation packages. Listed below are the costs for four nights at various popular resorts.

Hotel Location	Cost for Four Nights
Hyatt Regency Grand Cypress (Orlando, FL)	$205
Hyatt Regency Hill Country (San Antonio, TX)	$209
Hyatt Grand Champions (Indian Wells, CA)	$125

Hotel Location	Cost for Four Nights
Hyatt Key West	$235
Hyatt Regency Pier 66 (Ft. Lauderdale, FL)	$159
Hyatt Regency Lake Tahoe	$205
Hyatt Regency Waikiki	$230

(Source: *USA Today*, "Hyatt Resorts' Summer Sale," May 6, 1988, p. 2A.)

a. What would you guess is the mean and the standard deviation?

b. Calculate the mean and the standard deviation.

c. Remove the largest and smallest observations. What would you guess is the mean and the standard deviation?

d. Calculate the mean and the standard deviation with the largest and smallest observations removed.

e. Compare the calculated mean and standard deviation with the values that you guessed. What characteristics about the data give you a clue as to what the mean and standard deviation might be?

3.20 [DATA SET EX3-20] *Variable description:*

Refundgov: Amount of tax refund to government employees for those receiving refunds
Refundpriv: Amount of tax refund to private sector employees for those receiving refunds

A financial planner was interested in the variability of tax refunds from workers employed by the government and workers employed by the private sector. The financial planner believes that tax laws tend to be more complicated for employees working for the private sector. Thus, she believes that there is more variability in the amount of tax refund for the private sector than for employees.

a. Plot the histogram for the Refundgov and Refundpriv data. Which variable appears to have more variability? (Excel: Use **KGP Data Analysis ➤ Quantitative Data Charts/Tables ➤ Histogram/Freq. Charts.**)

b. Find the mean and standard deviation for Refundgov and Refundpriv. (Excel: Use the **Paste Function ➤ Statistical.**) Which variable has a larger mean? Larger standard deviation? Relate this answer to part (b).

3.21 [DATA SET EX3-21] *Variable description:*

TimeTV: Total daily time in minutes spent watching TV

Marketing managers are interested in TV viewership to attract company advertising. Viewers are customers for many products. To justify the millions of dollars spent on advertising, marketing departments must assess the percentage of the population that TV advertisement will reach as well as the likelihood of a viewer seeing the advertisement. One hundred adult viewers were sampled, and their total daily time in minutes spent watching TV for that day was recorded.

a. Find the mean and standard deviation of TimeTV. (Excel: Use the **Paste Function ➤ Statistical.**) Compute the coefficient of variation and variance from these values.

b. Convert the values of TimeTV to hours by dividing by 60. How do you think the mean, standard deviation, and variance will change?

c. Compute the mean, standard deviation, and variance of the values of TimeTV in units of hours. Compare these results to your answer in part (b). Is this what you expected?

TABLE 3.2

Ordered array of aptitude test scores for 50 applicants ($\bar{x} = 60.36$, $s = 18.61$).

must put data in order

22	44	56	68	78
25	44	57	68	78
28	46	59	69	80
31	48	60	71	82
34	49	61	72	83
35	51	63	72	85
39	53	63	74	88
39	53	63	75	90
40	55	65	75	92
42	55 *20th position*	66	76	96

40th Percentile = The 20 must be behind you - so go to 55.5

3.4 MEASURES OF POSITION

Suppose that you think you are drastically underpaid compared with other people with similar experience and performance. One way to attack the problem is to obtain the salaries of these other employees and demonstrate that *comparatively* you are way down the list. To evaluate your salary compared with the entire group, you would use a measure of position. *Measures of position* are indicators of how a particular value fits in with all the other data values. Two commonly used measures of position are (1) a percentile (and quartile), and (2) a *z*-score.

To illustrate these measures, we suppose that the personnel manager of Texon Industries has administered an aptitude test to 50 applicants. The ordered data are shown in Table 3.2. The mean of the data is $\bar{x} = 60.36$, and the standard deviation is $s = 18.61$. Ms. Jenson received the score of 83. She wishes to measure her performance in relation to all the applicant scores. We will return to this illustration in Example 3.5.

PERCENTILES

A **percentile** is the most common measure of position. The value of, for example, the 35th percentile is essentially the value that exceeds 35% of all the data values. More precisely, the 35th percentile is that value (say, P_{35}) such that at most 35% of the data values are less than P_{35} and at most 65% of the data values are greater than P_{35}. We will use the Texon Industries applicant data to determine the 35th percentile. Which data value is located 35% of the way between the first and last locations? Here the number of data values is $n = 50$ and the percentile is $P = 35$. We define the *position* of the 35th percentile as follows:

$$n \cdot \frac{P}{100} = 50 \cdot .35 = 17.5$$

To satisfy the more precise definition of a percentile, whenever $n \cdot P/100$ is *not* a counting number, it should be rounded *up* to the next counting number. So, 17.5 is rounded up to 18, and the 35th percentile is the 18th value *of the ordered values*. Referring to Table 3.2, the 35th percentile is $P_{35} = 53$.

In general, to find the **location** of the Pth percentile, determine $n \cdot P/100$ and use one of the following two location rules.

Location rule 1. If $n \cdot P/100$ is *not* a counting number, round it *up*, and the Pth percentile will be the value in this position of the ordered data.

Location rule 2. If $n \cdot P/100$ *is* a counting number, the Pth percentile is the average of the number in this location (of the ordered data) and the number in the next largest location.

Now we can use the applicant data to determine the 40th percentile. Here $n \cdot P/100 = (50)(.4) = 20$. Then, using the second rule, *(There must be 20 behind you.)*

(position 20)

$$P_{40} = \text{40th percentile} = \frac{(\text{20th value}) + (\text{21st value})}{2}$$

50 data points

$$= \frac{55 + 56}{2} = 55.5$$

Notice here that the 40th percentile is *not* one of the data values but is an average of two of them. Now work out the 50th percentile yourself. What measure of the central tendency uses the same procedure? From our previous discussion, you should realize that *the 50th percentile is the median.*

EXAMPLE 3.5

Recall that Ms. Jenson received a score of 83. What is her percentile value?

SOLUTION

Her value is the 45th largest value (out of a total of 50). An initial guess of her percentile would be:

$$P = \frac{45}{50} \cdot 100 = 90$$

However, due to the percentile rules used here, this guess may be slightly incorrect. Your next step should be to examine this value of P, along with the next two smaller values. The following calculations of $P = 88$, $P = 89$, and $P = 90$ reveal that Ms. Jenson's score is the 89th percentile.

must go a step (.5) further to assure you have that many behind you for Percentile #.

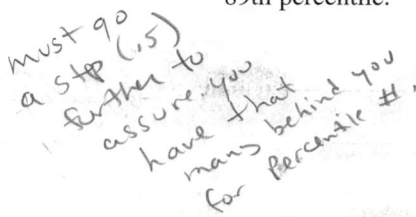

P	$\dfrac{n \cdot P}{100}$	**Pth Percentile**
88	$50 \cdot .88 = 44$	$(82 + 83)/2 = 82.5$
89	$50 \cdot .89 = 44.5$	45th value = 83
90	$50 \cdot .90 = 45$	$(83 + 85)/2 = 84$

Note: Other books + Calculators may give other answers.

EXAMPLE 3.6

What is the 50th percentile for the applicant data in Table 3.2?

SOLUTION

Here, $n \cdot P/100 = 50 \cdot .5 = 25$. The 50th percentile is an average of the 25th and 26th ordered data values:

$$P_{50} = \text{50th percentile} = \frac{61 + 63}{2} = 62$$

QUARTILES

Quartiles are merely particular percentiles that divide the data into quarters, namely:

Q_1 = 1st quartile = 25th percentile (P_{25})

Q_2 = 2nd quartile = 50th percentile = median (P_{50})

Q_3 = 3rd quartile = 75th percentile (P_{75})

They are used as benchmarks, much like the use of A, B, C, D, and F on examination grades. Using the applicant data in Table 3.2, we can determine the first quartile by first calculating:

$$n \cdot \frac{P_{\text{Percentile}}}{100} = (50)(.25) = 12.5$$

 # in set

This result is rounded up to 13, and Q_1 = 13th ordered value = 46.

$$Q_2 = \text{median} = 62$$

from Example 3.6. Finally, for Q_3,

$$n \cdot \frac{P}{100} = (50)(.75) = 37.5$$

This is rounded up to 38, and Q_3 = 38th ordered value = 75.

Another measure, commonly used in conjunction with quartiles is the **interquartile range (IQR),** defined as

$$\text{IQR} = Q_3 - Q_1$$

In the applicant data, the interquartile range is

$$\text{IQR} = 75 - 46 = 29$$

Consequently, the middle 50% of the data are between 46 and 75.

Strictly speaking, the interquartile range is a measure of variation, since it can be expected to increase as the data become more spread out. It is not a commonly used measure of variation, although it is certainly easy to compute (much like the range of a sample data set). Its primary disadvantage is that it measures the spread within the middle of the data, not within the entire data set. The interquartile range can be illustrated in a simple graph called a box plot, discussed in Section 3.8.

Z-Scores

Another measure of position is a sample z-score, which is based on the mean ($\bar{x}$) and standard deviation of the data set. Like a percentile, a z-score determines the relative position of any particular data value x; it is expressed in terms of the number of standard deviations above or below the mean. The z-score of x is defined as

$$z = \frac{x - \bar{x}}{s} \tag{3.9}$$

Recall from Example 3.5 that Ms. Jenson had a score of 83 on the test. For this data set, $\bar{x} = 60.36$ and $s = 18.61$. Her score of 83 is in the 89th percentile. The corresponding z-score is

$$z = \frac{83 - 60.36}{18.61} = 1.22$$

This z-score means that Ms. Jenson's score of 83 is 1.22 standard deviations to the *right* of the mean, or above the group's average. Thus, if z is positive, it indicates how many standard deviations x is to the right of the mean.

A negative z-score implies that x is to the *left* of the mean. Again referring to Table 3.2, what is the z-score for the individual who obtained a total of 35 on the aptitude examination?

$$z = \frac{35 - 60.36}{18.61} = -1.36$$

This individual's score is 1.36 standard deviations to the left of the mean, or below the group's average.

The process of subtracting the mean and dividing by the standard deviation is referred to as **standardizing** the sample data, and the corresponding z-value is the **standardized** value. So Ms. Jensen's raw score is 83, and her standardized score is 1.22 indicating that her raw score is 1.22 standard deviations to the right of the mean. For a "typical" sample, you can expect nearly all of the standardized values to lie between –3 and 3 (the z-scores range from –3 to 3). This will be discussed further in Section 3.6.

EXAMPLE 3.7

Example 3.4 contained data listing 100 measurements for the inside diameter of a certain machined part. The specification limits for this part are 10.1 millimeters (the lower spec limit, or LSL) and 10.3 millimeters (the upper spec limit, or USL). Any part falling outside this range is said to be nonconforming and is not of acceptable quality. Of interest here is the following question: What is the z-score for both the LSL and the USL and which z-score has the smaller absolute value?

SOLUTION

The z-score for each of these limits is found by subtracting the sample mean and dividing by the standard deviation. In Example 3.4, the sample mean was found to be $\bar{x} = 10.275$ and the sample standard deviation was $s = .0267$. The z-score for the USL (10.3) is

$$\frac{10.3 - 10.275}{.0267} = .94$$

and the z-score for the LSL is

$$\frac{10.1 - 10.275}{.0267} = -6.55$$

The absolute values of these two z-scores are .94 and 6.55. The minimum of these two absolute values is .94, indicating that the nearer spec limit is the upper spec limit and that the sample mean is .94 standard deviations away from this limit. *A very general rule here is that to consistently produce products of acceptable quality, the minimum absolute value of these two z-scores should be at least 3.* In this case, the product is not capable of meeting these specifications—a result consistent with Examples 2.1 and 3.4.

3.5 MEASURES OF SHAPE

A basic question in many applications is whether your data exhibit a **symmetric** pattern. **Measures of shape** include measures of skewness and kurtosis.

SKEWNESS

The histogram in Figure 3.7 demonstrates a perfectly symmetric distribution. When the data are symmetric, the sample mean, $\bar{x}$, and the sample median, Md, are the same. As the data tend toward a nonsymmetric distribution, referred to as skewed, the mean and median drift apart. The easiest method of determining the degree of skewness present in

FIGURE 3.7

Histogram constructed with symmetric data. The mean, median, and mode are equal.

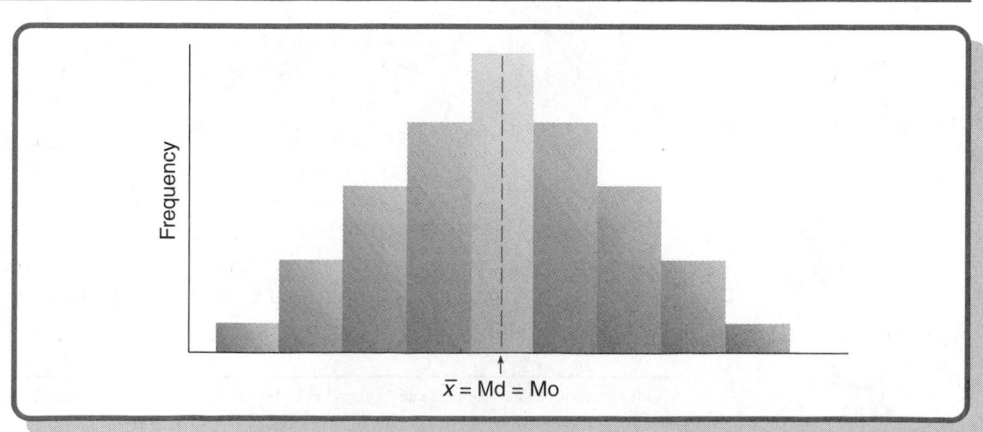

FIGURE 3.8

Histogram showing right (positive) skew.

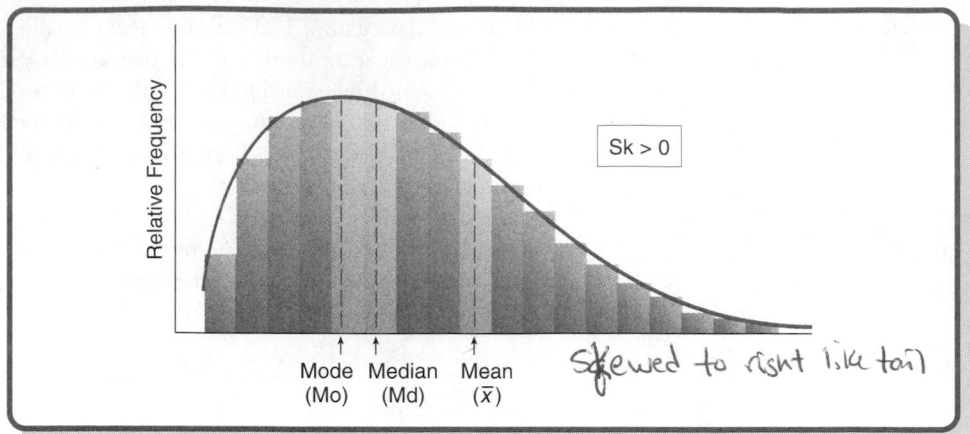

your sample data is to calculate a measure referred to as the **Pearsonian coefficient of skewness, Sk.** Its value is given by:

$$Sk = \frac{3(\bar{x} - Md)}{s} \qquad (3.10)$$

where s is the standard deviation of the sample data.

The value of Sk ranges from -3 to 3.* If the data are perfectly symmetric (a rare event), Sk = 0, because $\bar{x}$ = Md. For Figure 3.7, Sk is zero. If the mean is larger than the median, then Sk is positive, and we say that the data are *skewed right*. Consequently, for data that are skewed right, *values above the mean occur less frequently than values below the mean.* This merely means the data exhibit a pattern with a right tail, as illustrated in Figure 3.8. We know the mean is affected by extreme values, so we would expect the mean to move toward the right tail, above the median, resulting in a positive value of Sk. Similarly, if the mean is smaller than the median, then Sk is negative and the data are *skewed left.* As a result, in a negatively skewed sample, *values above the mean occur more frequently than values below the mean.* Figure 3.9 shows a data distribution exhibiting a left tail and negative skew.

Excel and MINITAB both use a slightly more complicated measure of skewness. This involves finding the z-score for each data value, cubing each z-score, and then summing the results (that is, (z-score)$_1^3$ + (z-score)$_2^3$ + (z-score)$_3^3$ + . . .). Where Excel and MINITAB differ is what to multiply this sum by to determine the measure of skewness. The two formulas are given below, where Sk(E) is the Excel measure of skewness and Sk(M) is the corresponding value using MINITAB.

$$Sk(E) = \frac{n}{(n-1)(n-2)} \sum \left(\frac{x - \bar{x}}{s} \right)^3 = \frac{n}{(n-1)(n-2)} \sum (z\text{-}score)^3 \qquad (3.11)$$

$$Sk(M) = \frac{1}{n} \sum \left(\frac{x - \bar{x}}{s} \right)^3 = \frac{1}{n} \sum (z\text{-}score)^3 \qquad (3.12)$$

The Excel and MINITAB skewness measures will be very close and are nearly identical for large values of n. Similar to the Pearsonian skewness measure, both measures will be positive for samples that are skewed right (Figure 3.8) and negative for samples that are skewed left (Figure 3.9).

---

* A recent proof of this statement can be found in Colm Art O'Cinneide, "The Mean is Within One Standard Deviation of Any Median," *The American Statistician* 44, no. 4 (1990), p. 292.

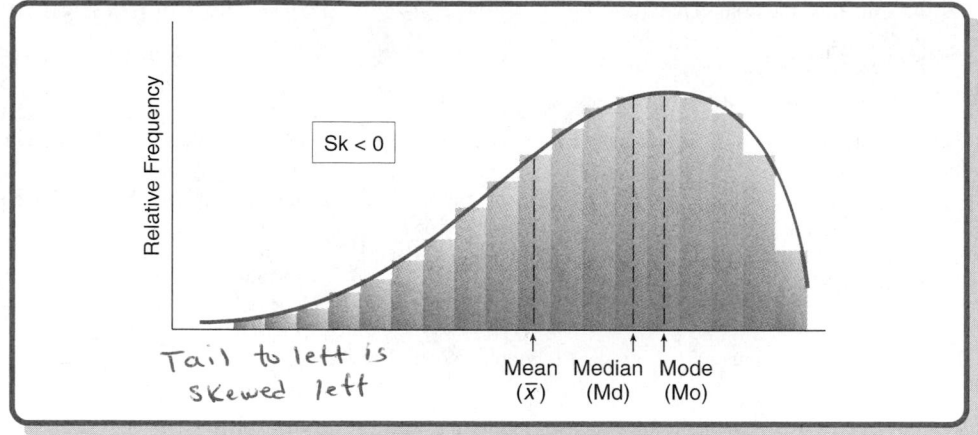

FIGURE 3.9
Histogram showing left (negative) skew.

Examples 3.4 and 3.7 were concerned with the inside diameters of 100 machined parts. To examine the symmetry of the data, we can use the various statistics in Figure 3.6. The Pearsonian measure of skewness is

$$Sk = \frac{3(10.27539 - 10.276)}{.02668} = -.069$$

This is nearly zero and we conclude that the data are nearly symmetric and a histogram of these 100 values would resemble the one in Figure 3.7. According to Figure 3.6, the Excel measure of skewness is $Sk(E) = -.0102$ (in cell C10). It easy to show that

$$Sk(M) = \left(1 - \frac{1}{n}\right)\left(1 - \frac{2}{n}\right)Sk(E) \tag{3.13}$$

and so $Sk(M) = (1 - 1/100)(1 - 2/100)(-.0102) = -.0099$.* Since both measures are nearly zero, we again conclude that the data are nearly symmetric.

KURTOSIS

Sk measures the tendency of a distribution to stretch out in a particular direction. Another measure of shape, referred to as the **kurtosis,** measures the *peakedness* of your distribution. The calculation of this measure is a bit cumbersome, and the kurtosis value is not needed in the remaining text material.† Briefly, this value is large if there is a high frequency of observations near the mean and in the tails of the distribution.

EXERCISES 3.22-3.33

UNDERSTANDING THE MECHANICS

3.22 The number of defects in 10 rolls of carpets are

3 2 6 0 1 3 2 1 0 4

  a. What are the 75th percentile and the 50th percentile?
  b. What are the mean and standard deviation?
  c. What is the coefficient of skewness?

3.23 Assume that the sum of 10 observations is 10, that the sum of the squares of 10 observations is 20, and that the median is 1.5. What is the coefficient of skewness?

3.24 The percentage of unemployed workers in each of 20 randomly selected cities are as follows.

3.1 4.5 8.2 1.4 6.3 1.8 2.4 8.8 1.9 2.4
5.4 3.8 7.2 3.8 4.6 7.2 2.5 4.8 3.7 4.2

---

* See the end-of-chapter MINITAB discussion for the procedure used to obtain MINITABs measure of skewness.
† Using Excel, you can click on **Help ➤ Contents and Index,** and type "kurtosis." The formula used by Excel is in this discussion.

a. Calculate the 20th percentile.
b. Calculate the 40th percentile.
c. Calculate the 60th percentile.
d. Calculate the 80th percentile.
e. Calculate the interquartile range.

3.25 From a random sample, the mean is 50 and the sample standard deviation is 5.
   a. What is the z-score if an observation's value is 40?
   b. What is the z-score if an observation's value is 65?
   c. What is the value of an observation with a z-score of 1?
   d. What is the value of an observation with a z-score of -2.5?

3.26 The time (in minutes) that it takes 20 people to complete a task follows.

30 35 51 65 22 35 44 55 30 50 40 60 64 38 52 68 38 53 62 49

   a. Find the interquartile range.
   b. Find the mean of the data.
   c. Find the standard deviation of the data.
   d. Find the coefficient of skewness.

APPLYING THE NEW CONCEPTS

3.27 The following data were obtained from a survey requesting 30 different families to list their weekly expenditure on food.

105	85	72	59	130	120	95	83	78	91
64	106	86	87	78	108	145	102	86	74
72	103	94	63	73	89	75	88	107	101

   a. Calculate the 20th percentile.
   b. Calculate the 80th percentile.
   c. Calculate the interquartile range.
   d. Calculate the mean, median, standard deviation, and coefficient of skewness.
   e. Write up a brief description of the survey's results, and interpret each of the values of the statistics.

3.28 Consider the following grades recorded on an aptitude test.

70	15	42	21	73	45	22	71	20	74
74	53	74	86	52	19	77	84	73	54
87	90	71	53	21	71	75	72	12	47

   a. Calculate each of the quartiles and the coefficient of skewness to describe the distribution of the data.
   b. What observations would you consider to be unusually low or high? Why?
   c. How would you evaluate a student who scored 75 on the exam?

3.29 Select five numbers between 0 and 10.
   a. Calculate the standard deviation of these five numbers.
   b. Form the z-scores for these five numbers.
   c. What do you think is the standard deviation of the z-scores? Calculate the standard deviation of the z-scores.

3.30 The prices (in dollars) for unleaded gas at 10 service stations in Boyston and in Farmersville are as follows. Describe the distribution of the price of unlead gas using the mean, standard deviation, and coefficient of skewness.

Boyston: 1.20 1.17 1.20 1.25 1.24 1.35 1.18 1.20 1.40 1.18
Farmersville: 1.19 1.25 1.14 1.20 1.30 1.25 1.33 1.25 1.20 1.24

3.31 Promising treatments of eradicating cancer, companies involved in scientific research to develop cancer drugs have attracted many speculative investors. Often, these companies face large challenges before they become profitable companies. The following companies, betting on a cure for cancer, are listed with their market capitalization.

Company	Market Capitalization (in Millions of Dollars)
Genetech	8,620
Agouron	1,110
Imclone Systems	264
Vical Pharmaceuticals	252
Sugen	236
Maganin	153
Onyx Pharmaceuticals	116
Ribozyme Pharmaceuticals	47
Targeted Genetics	47

(Source: *The Wall Street Journal*, "Investors Hunt for Small Stocks with Cancer Projects in the Lab," May 7, 1998, p. C1.)

   a. Calculate the mean, median, variance, standard deviation, coefficient of skewness, and interquartile range for the market capitalization data.
   b. Remove the companies Genetech and Agouron from the list. How do you think the coefficient of skewness will change?
   c. Calculate the coefficient of skewness with Genetech and Agouron removed. Compare your answer in part (b) to this calculated value.

3.32 [DATA SET EX3-32] *Variable description:*

Checkfee: Fee that financial institution charges for a checking account with no minimum

Bank and financial institutions have been steadily increasing checking fees for no-minimum checking accounts. A sample of 75 banks and financial institutions that offer checking accounts with no minumum balance required was selected in the Toronto metropolitan area. Data are presented in units of Canadian dollars.
   a. What are the mean, median, and standard deviation, coefficient of skewness, and the interquartile range? How would you interpret these statistics?
   b. Convert the data to U.S. dollars. Use the conversion 1 Canadian dollar equals .70 U.S. dollars. Calculate the statistics in part (a). How do these values change?

3.33 [DATA SET EX3-33] *Variable description:*

RentalCost: The cost of renting a compact car for a weekend

Many rental car agencies offer special rates for the weekend. These rates vary by locality. A random sample of 50 rental car agencies across the United States was taken to obtain information on the distribution of the total cost of a compact car on the weekend.
   a. Use the KGP menu to obtain a histogram of the data. Would you conclude that the data are skewed?
   b. Use the mean, median, and standard deviation functions in Excel and compute the coefficient of skewness.
   c. Delete the five most extreme values. Recompute the coefficient of skewness. Did you think that the coefficient of skewness would change by that much?

3.6 INTERPRETING $\bar{x}$ AND s

Now that you have gone through several pencils determining the sample mean and standard deviation, what can you learn from these values? The type of question that you can answer is, how many of the data values are within two standard deviations of the mean?

Take a look at the aptitude test scores in Table 3.2. Here $\bar{x} = 60.36$ and $s = 18.61$, and so we obtain

$$\bar{x} - s\ = 60.36 - 18.61 \qquad\qquad \bar{x} + s\ = 60.36 + 18.61$$
$$= 41.75 \qquad\qquad\qquad\qquad = 78.97$$

$$\bar{x} - 2s = 60.36 - 37.22 \qquad\qquad \bar{x} + 2s = 60.36 + 37.22$$
$$= 23.14 \qquad\qquad\qquad\qquad = 97.58$$

$$\bar{x} - 3s = 60.36 - 55.83 \qquad\qquad \bar{x} + 3s = 60.36 + 55.83$$
$$= 4.53 \qquad\qquad\qquad\qquad = 116.19$$

Examine these data and observe that (1) 33 out of the 50 values (66%) lie between $\bar{x} - s$ and $\bar{x} + s$; (2) 49 out of the 50 values (98%) lie between $\bar{x} - 2s$ and $\bar{x} + 2s$; and (3) 50 out of the 50 values (100%) lie between $\bar{x} - 3s$ and $\bar{x} + 3s$. Or, put another way: (1) 66% of the data values have a z-score between -1 and 1; (2) 98% have a z-score between -2 and 2, and (3) 100% have a z-score between -3 and 3.

What can we say in general for any data set? There are two types of statements we can make. One of these, *Chebyshev's inequality,* is usually conservative but makes *no assumption* about the population from which you obtained your data. Following are the components of Chebyshev's inequality.

CHEBYSHEV'S INEQUALITY

For any data set:
1. At least 75% of the data values are between $\bar{x} - 2s$ and $\bar{x} + 2s$.
   At least 75% of the data values have a z-score between -2 and 2.
2. At least 89% of the data values are between $\bar{x} - 3s$ and $\bar{x} + 3s$.
   At least 89% of the data values have a z-score between -3 and 3.
3. In general, at least $(1 - 1/k^2) \times 100\%$ of your data values lie between $\bar{x} - ks$ and $\bar{x} + ks$ (have z-scores between $-k$ and k) for any $k > 1$.

Note that if $k = 1$, $1 - 1/k^2 = 0$; so Chebyshev's inequality provides no information on the number of data values to expect between $\bar{x} - s$ and $\bar{x} + s$.

The other type of statement is called the **empirical rule.** We make a key assumption here, namely, that the population from which you obtain your sample has a *bell-shaped distribution;* that is, it is symmetric and tapers off smoothly into each tail. Such a population is called a **normal population** and is illustrated in Figure 3.10. Thus, the data set should have a skewness measure, Sk, near zero and a histogram similar to that in Figure 3.7. The empirical rule has three components.

EMPIRICAL RULE

Under the assumption of a bell-shaped population:*
1. Approximately 68% (roughly two-thirds) of the data values lie between $\bar{x} - s$ and $\bar{x} + s$ (have z-scores between -1 and 1).
2. Approximately 95% (19 out of 20) of the data values lie between $\bar{x} - 2s$ and $\bar{x} + 2s$ (have z-scores between -2 and 2).
3. Approximately 99.7% (nearly all) of the data values lie between $\bar{x} - 3s$ and $\bar{x} + 3s$ (have z-scores between -3 and 3).

---

* Strictly speaking, the empirical rule applies to population values (substituting μ for $\bar{x}$ and σ for s). However, this rule works very well for large samples having an approximate bell-shaped histogram.

FIGURE 3.10

A bell-shaped (normal) population.

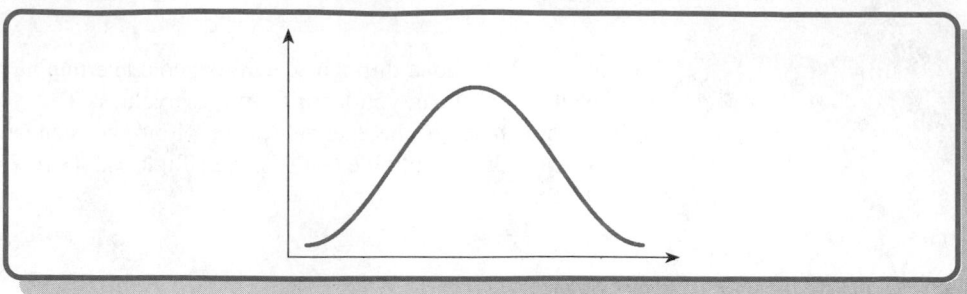

TABLE 3.3

Summary of percentages of sample values by interval, using data from Table 3.2.

Between	Actual Percentage	Chebyshev's Inequality Percentage	Empirical Rule Percentage
$\bar{x} - s$ and $\bar{x} + s$	66% (33 out of 50)	—	≈68%
$\bar{x} - 2s$ and $\bar{x} + 2s$	98% (49 out of 50)	≥75%	≈95%
$\bar{x} - 3s$ and $\bar{x} + 3s$	100% (50 out of 50)	≥89%	≈100%

Returning to Table 3.2, we can summarize our previous results along with the information provided by Chebyshev's inequality and the empirical rule. The actual percentages of the sample values in each interval, as well as the percentages specified using each of the two rules, are shown in Table 3.3.

As you can see, Chebyshev's inequality is very conservative, but it always works. The empirical rule predicted results close to what was observed. For these data, the median is $Md = 62$ (see Example 3.6), and so the Pearsonian measure of skewness is

$$Sk = \frac{3(60.36 - 62)}{18.61} = -.26$$

Recalling that this measure ranges from –3 to 3, we could call this skewness measure "close to zero," and so it is not surprising that the empirical rule was quite accurate, since we are dealing with a nearly symmetric set of data.

EXAMPLE 3.8

In a random sample of 200 automobile insurance claims obtained from Landmark Insurance Company, $\bar{x} = \$615$ and $s = \$135$.

1. What statement can you make using Chebyshev's inequality?
2. If you have reason to believe that the population of all insurance claims is bell-shaped (normal), what does the empirical rule say about these 200 values?

SOLUTION 1

Chebyshev's inequality provides information regarding the number of sample values within a specified number of standard deviations of the mean. For $k = 2$, we have:

$$\bar{x} - 2s = 615 - 2(135) = \$345$$

$$\bar{x} + 2s = 615 + 2(135) = \$885$$

We conclude that at least 75% of the sample values lie between \$345 and \$885 and have z-scores between −2 and 2. Because $.75 \cdot 200 = 150$, this implies that at least 150 of the claims are between \$345 and \$885.

For $k = 3$,

$$\bar{x} - 3s = 615 - 3(135) = \$210$$

$$\bar{x} + 3s = 615 + 3(135) = \$1020$$

and we conclude that at least 8/9 (89%) of the data values are between \$210 and \$1020. Here, $8/9 \cdot 200 = 177.8$, and so at least 178 of the claims are between \$210 and \$1020.

SOLUTION 2

If the distribution of automotive claims at Landmark Insurance Company is believed to be bell-shaped, the empirical rule allows us to draw stronger conclusions. In particular, for $k = 1$, we have

$$\bar{x} - s = 615 - 135 = \$480$$

$$\bar{x} + s = 615 + 135 = \$750$$

and we conclude that approximately 68% of the data values ($.68 \cdot 200 = 136$) are between \$480 and \$750 and have z-scores between −1 and 1.

For $k = 2$,

$$\bar{x} - 2s = \$345$$

$$\bar{x} + 2s = \$885$$

and we conclude that approximately 95% of the data values ($.95 \cdot 200 = 190$) will lie between \$345 and \$885.

EXAMPLE 3.9

Examples 2.1 and 3.4 examined the 100 inside diameters produced at the Boston plant of Allied Manufacturing. Based on the histogram of these diameters in Figure 2.15 (page 43), do you think the empirical rule is applicable? What does this rule tell you about the number of data values with corresponding z-scores between −2 and 2? Examining the data in Example 3.4, does this appear to be a correct statement?

SOLUTION

The histogram in Figure 2.15 has an approximate bell-shaped (normal) appearance. The shape is not perfectly symmetric with tails that taper off smoothly; but in practice, histograms based on sample data from bell-shaped populations rarely are perfectly bell-shaped in appearance. As a result, use of the empirical rule is appropriate here.

The number of sample values with z-scores between −2 and 2 is the same as the number of data values within two standard deviations of the mean, that is, the number of data values between $\bar{x} - 2s$ and $\bar{x} + 2s$. Here, $\bar{x} - 2s = 10.275 - 2(.0267) = 10.2216$ and $\bar{x} + 2s = 10.275 + 2(.0267) = 10.3284$. Referring to the ordered data in Example 3.4, the only values that are *not* between 10.2216 and 10.3284 are 10.216 and 10.221 on the low end and 10.333 and 10.338 on the upper end. As a result, 96 out of 100 (96%) of the data values have z-scores between −2 and 2, a result consistent with the empirical rule, which states that this percentage should be approximately 95%.

EXERCISES 3.34–3.45

UNDERSTANDING THE MECHANICS

3.34 A random sample of observations has a sample mean of 20 and a standard deviation of 5. Use Chebyshev's inequality to find the following intervals:

    a. An interval that has at least 75% of the data within it.

    b. An interval that has at least 89% of the data within it.

3.35 A random sample from a bell-shaped population yields a mean of 100 and a standard deviation of 20. Calculate the following intervals:

    a. An interval that has approximately 68% of the data values within it.

    b. An interval that has approximately 99.7% of the data values within it.

APPLYING THE NEW CONCEPTS

3.36 A manager notices that the mean weight of a bag of grain from a recent shipment is 50 pounds with a standard deviation of 3. At least what percentage of values can the manager say will lie within 4 standard deviations of the mean?

3.37 The following random sample of annual salaries was recorded. Units are in thousands of dollars.

    50 52 48 46 32 51 47 20 53 49

    a. Calculate the mean and standard deviation.

    b. Using Chebyshev's inequality, between what two bounds will at least 75% of the data lie?

    c. Using Chebyshev's inequality, between what two bounds will at least 89% of the data values lie?

    d. Are the percentage of values within the bounds in parts (b) and (c) from these data consistent with Chebyshev's inequality?

3.38 The sample mean is 120 and the standard deviation is 30 for a random sample of 300 observations.

    a. At least how many observations are expected to lie between 60 and 180?

    b. Under the assumption that the data are from a bell-shaped population, how many observations are expected to lie between 60 and 180?

3.39 Refer to the data in Exercise 3.4 on the number of automobiles serviced daily by EZ Service Station. Calculate the percentage of observations between 1, 2, and 3 standard deviations of the mean. Could these data be considered to have been collected from a normal population?

3.40 An increasing number of foreign carriers are allowing their cockpit crews to take short, planned naps on long-haul flights. These planned naps are intended to counteract the effects of fatigue. Currently, the Federal Aviation Administration does not allow domestic carriers to nap, even on overseas flights. Suppose that it is known that on approximately 95% of the flights between Tokyo and Sydney, pilots nap between 30 minutes and 1 hour, with the average being 45 minutes. Assuming that the empirical rule can be used, what is the standard deviation of the time spent napping by the pilots?

(Source: Adapted from *The Wall Street Journal*, "Nap Time," May 8, 1998, p. W6.)

3.41 Refer to the data in the weekly expenditure on food by various families in Exercise 3.27. Between what two values would you expect at least 75% of the data to fall? How many observations actually lie within this interval?

3.42 Approximately how many standard deviations from the mean will at least 55% of the data values lie for any population. Note that this number is not an integer value.

3.43 How-to-get-rich books have been very appealing to the general public and several have made the bestseller list. The weekly sales of several of the best-selling financial success books are presented below.

Financial Book	Sales Index
The Millionaire Next Door	34
Nine Steps to Financial Freedom	31
7 Habits of Highly Successful Investing	22
How to Retire Rich	20
Don't Worry, Make Money	12
Reach for the Summit	11
Motley Fool . . . Guide	9
The Roaring 2000's	8
What Color . . . Parachute?	8
Investing for Dummies	7
Success Is a Choice	6
Die Broke	6
Wall Street Money Machine	6
One Minute Manager	6
Motley Fool . . . Workbook	5

(Source: *Wall Street Journal*, "Best Selling Books," May 8, 1998, p. W10.)

    a. How many observations lie within 2 standard deviations of the mean of the sales indexes for the data above? How many lie within 3 standard deviations?

    b. How do your answers in part (a) compare to what Chebyshev's inequality provides?

3.44 **[DATA SET EX3-44]** *Variable description:*

Servtime: Amount of time that it takes to be served the main course at Anthony's Restaurant

The manager of Anthony's restaurant is interested in examining the total wait time that customers spend in the restaurant before being served their main course. A random sample of 75 parties was observed and their total wait time in minutes was recorded.

    a. Plot a histogram of the data. Would you conclude that the data appear to be bell-shaped?

    b. Use the mean and standard deviation functions to compute intervals such that the mean is in the center of the interval and the distance from the mean to either endpoint is two standard deviations. Use an appropriate rule to approximate the percentage of data values within this interval.

3.45 **[DATA SET EX3-45]** *Variable description:*

MMbal: Balance in money market fund

A local bank offers a money market fund that pays above average interest rates provided the investor maintains a minimum balance of $10,000. A vice president of the bank has a random sample of 200 accounts examined and their balances were recorded.

    a. Find the mean and standard deviation of MMbal. Compute ranges in which at least 75% and 89% of the data will lie.

    b. Sort the data. (Excel: Use **Data ➤ Sort**.) Determine how many observations actually fall outside the ranges computed in part (a). Compare these to the minimum numbers expected by Chebyshev's inequality.

3.7 GROUPED DATA

Sometimes we may have to work with data in the form of a frequency distribution, called **grouped data,** when the raw data are not available. This situation can arise when a magazine or newspaper article displays a histogram or frequency distribution but does not include the actual raw data used to construct the histogram. We do not have the data values used to make up this frequency distribution, so we are forced to approximate the sample statistics, in particular the mean and standard deviation.

APPROXIMATING THE SAMPLE MEAN, $\bar{x}$

Assume we obtain the frequency distribution shown in Table 3.4, which contains the ages of 36 individuals who recently passed a CPA examination. The 36 data values are not available, so we cannot add them up. A procedure that works well for estimating $\bar{x}$ is simply to pretend that the 36 data values are equal to their respective class midpoints. Consequently, there are

$$5 \text{ values at } (20 + 30)/2 = 25$$
$$14 \text{ values at } (30 + 40)/2 = 35$$
$$\cdot$$
$$\cdot$$
$$\cdot$$
$$2 \text{ values at } (60 + 70)/2 = 65$$

We can then estimate the value of $\bar{x}$ ($\cong$ means "is approximately equal to"):

$$\bar{x} \cong \frac{(25 + 25 + 25 + 25 + 25) + \cdots + (65 + 65)}{36}$$

$$= \frac{(5)(25) + (14)(35) + (9)(45) + (6)(55) + (2)(65)}{36}$$

$$= \frac{1480}{36} = 41.1$$

Our estimate of the average age of these 36 individuals is

$$\bar{x} \cong 41.1 \text{ years}$$

In general,

$$\bar{x} \cong \frac{\sum f \cdot m}{n} \tag{3.11}$$

where n = sample size, f = frequency of each class, and m = midpoint each class.

TABLE 3.4 Age of 36 individuals who recently passed a CPA examination.

Class Number	Class (Age in Years)	Frequency
1	20 and under 30	5
2	30 and under 40	14
3	40 and under 50	9
4	50 and under 60	6
5	60 and under 70	2
		36

APPROXIMATING THE SAMPLE STANDARD DEVIATION, s

Using the same fictitious data set at the various class midpoints, the variance, s^2, can be found in the usual way, using equation 3.7.

$$s^2 = \frac{\sum (\text{each data value})^2 - [\sum (\text{each data value})]^2/n}{n-1}$$

$$\sum (\text{each data value})^2 = (\overbrace{25^2 + 25^2 + \cdots + 25^2}^{5 \text{ times}})$$

$$+ (\overbrace{35^2 + 35^2 + \cdots + 35^2}^{14 \text{ times}}) + \cdots$$

$$+ (65^2 + 65^2)$$

$$= (5)(25^2) + (14)(35^2) + (9)(45^2) + (6)(55^2) + (2)(65^2)$$

$$= 65,100$$

Also, $\sum (\text{each data value}) = 1480$, as we determined previously when approximating $\bar{x}$.

$$s^2 \cong \frac{65,100 - (1480)^2/36}{35} = \frac{4255.56}{35} = 121.59$$

and

$$s \cong \sqrt{121.59} = 11.03$$

In general,

$$s^2 \cong \frac{\sum f \cdot m^2 - (\sum f \cdot m)^2/n}{n-1} \qquad (3.12)$$

where f, m, and n are as defined in equation 3.11.

The calculations necessary to estimate $\bar{x}$ and s are performed more easily using a table similar to Table 3.5. An even simpler procedure is use Excel or MINITAB (for a MINITAB solution, see the end-of-chapter appendix). To use Excel on the Table 2.4 values, refer to Figure 3.11 and begin by placing 25 in cell A1. Click on the fill handle in the lower right corner of cell A1 and drag it down through cell A5. You should now have five values of 25 in cells A1 through A5. Next, enter 35 in cell A6 and drag this cell down through cell A19. At this point, you have five values of 25 and 14 values of 35. Repeat this by entering 45 in cell A20 and dragging through cell A28, entering 55 in cell A29 and dragging through cell A34, and finally entering 65 in cells A35 and A36. Finally, type "=AVERAGE(A1:A36)" in cell B1, "=STDEV(A1:A36)" in cell B2, "Mean" in cell C1, and "St. Dev." in cell C2. Referring to Figure 3.11, cell B1 will contain the mean of the grouped data (41.11), and cell B2 will contain the standard deviation (11.03).

TABLE 3.5   Summary of calculations for grouped data.

Class Number	Class	f	m	$f \cdot m$	$f \cdot m^2$
1	20 and under 30	5	25	125	3,125
2	30 and under 40	14	35	490	17,150
3	40 and under 50	9	45	405	18,225
4	50 and under 60	6	55	330	18,150
5	60 and under 70	2	65	130	8,450
		36		$\sum f \cdot m = 1,480$	$\sum f \cdot m^2 = 65,100$

FIGURE 3.11
Using Excel to determine the
mean and standard deviation
for grouped data.

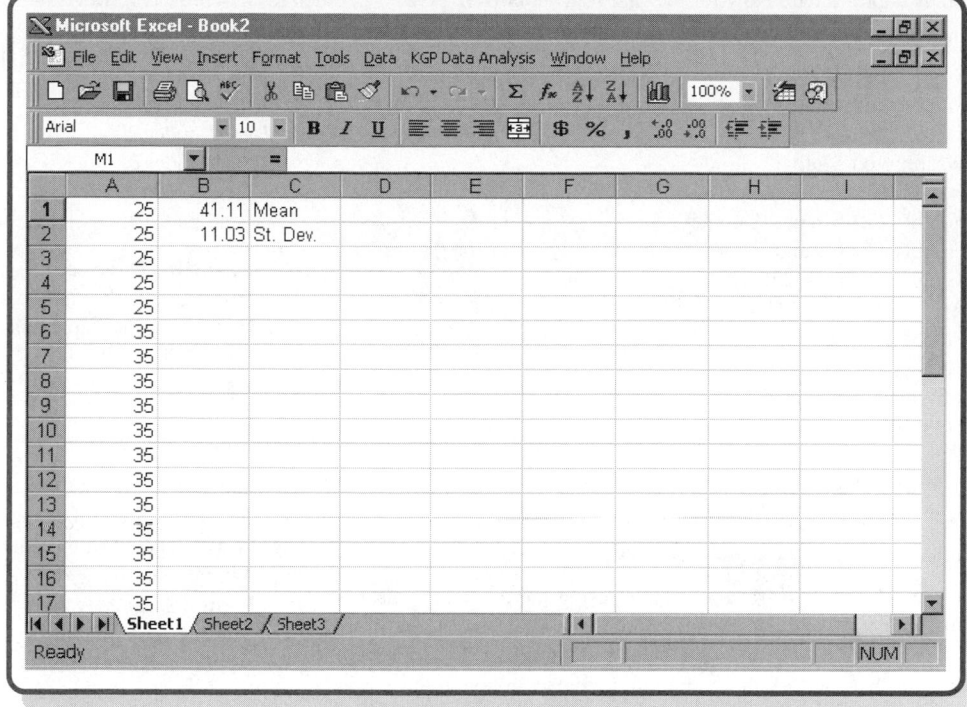

	A	B	C
1	25	41.11	Mean
2	25	11.03	St. Dev.
3	25		
4	25		
5	25		
6	35		
7	35		
8	35		
9	35		
10	35		
11	35		
12	35		
13	35		
14	35		
15	35		
16	35		
17	35		

Remember that these procedures for approximating the sample statistics are used only when the raw data are not available and your only information is a frequency distribution or corresponding histogram. *If the actual data values are available, these statistics can be determined exactly, and the approximation procedures described in this section should not be used.*

EXERCISES 3.46–3.52

UNDERSTANDING THE MECHANICS

3.46

Class	Midpoint	Frequency
0 and under 10	5	4
10 and under 20	15	7
20 and under 30	25	5
30 and under 40	35	4

a. Approximate the sample mean.
b. Approximate the sample standard deviation.

3.47 A set of grouped continuous data has five classes. Each class has a frequency of 10. The midpoints are:

$$10 \quad 20 \quad 30 \quad 40 \quad 50$$

a. Approximate the sample mean.
b. Approximate the sample variance.
c. Approximate the sample standard deviation.

APPLYING THE NEW CONCEPTS

3.48 Advertising expenditures constitute one of the important components of the cost of goods sold. From the following data giving the advertising expenditures (in millions of dollars) of 50 companies, approximate the mean advertising expenditure.

Advertising Expenditure	Number of Companies
25 and under 35	5
35 and under 45	11
45 and under 55	18
55 and under 65	6
65 and under 75	10
	50

3.49 The cost for an overnight stay in the center of one of the major cities across the United States has been rising over the years. Listed below is a frequency table of the total cost of an overnight stay in the center of one of 22 cities. Find the approximate mean and standard deviation of the cost of an overnight stay at these cities.

	Frequency Distribution Table Total Costs of an	
Class	Overnight Stay	Frequency
1	100 and under 130	2
2	130 and under 160	12
3	160 and under 190	4
4	190 and under 220	1
5	220 and under 250	2
6	250 and under 280	1
	TOTAL	22

(Source: *The Wall Street Journal*, "The Dow Jones Travel Index," May 8, 1998, p. W6.)

3.50 The year-to-date performance of the 15 largest stock funds is presented below for the first four months of 1998.

Stock Mutual Fund	Year-to-Date Performance (in Percentage)
Fidelity Magellan	14.0
Vanguard Index 500 Port	13.4
Washington Mutual	11.1
Investment Co of America	11.8
Fidelity Growth and Income	11.3
Fidelity Contrafund	11.9
Vanguard Windsor II	13.4
Amer. Century 20 Ultra	15.7
Fidelity Puritan	7.8
Fidelity Equity Income	10.4
Vanguard Wellington	8.4
Fidelity Adv. Growth Oppty	9.2
Vanguard Windsor	14.2
Income Fund of America	6.6
Janus Fund	15.7

(Source: *USA Today*, "15 Largest Stock Funds," May 8, 1998, p. 3B.)

a. Construct a frequency table, using the class intervals 6 and under 9, 9 and under 12, 12 and under 15, 15 and under 18.

b. Find the approximate mean and standard deviation of the performance of these mutual funds from the frequency table.

c. Calculate the mean and standard deviation from the data and compare your answer to that obtained in part (b).

3.51 A summary of the price paid for dinner at the Green Garden restaurant is as follows, in dollars.

Dinner Cost	Number of Customers
5 and under 10	5
10 and under 15	15
15 and under 20	31
20 and under 25	30
25 and under 30	16
30 and under 35	3

a. Approximate the sample mean.

b. Approximate the sample standard deviation.

c. Is the mean an appropriate summary statistic for these data?

3.52 [DATA SET EX3-52] *Variable description:*

OilServTime: Service time for oil change

The manager of Express Oil Change is interested in examining the service times for an oil change. A random sample of 200 oil changes was selected and the time to perform an oil change was recorded in minutes.

a. Form a frequency table of the data. Use intervals of width 5 starting at 10 minutes.

b. Approximate the mean and standard deviation of the data set from the frequency table.

c. To understand how accurate these approximations are, find the mean and standard deviation of the OilServTime data. Compare the computed mean and standard deviation from the data to that obtained in part (a).

3.8 Box Plots

Exploratory data analysis (EDA) is a recently developed set of tools for providing easy-to-construct pictures that summarize and describe a sample. Two popular diagrams that fall under this category are *stem-and-leaf diagrams* (introduced in Chapter 2) and *box plots*. Section 2.2 gave several illustrations of stem-and-leaf diagrams. These graphs provide a representation of the *entire* sample and, unlike histograms, do not condense the data into classes. This section discusses box plots that are graphical illustrations of the quartile measures of position discussed in Section 3.4.

A **box plot** is a graphical representation of a set of sample data that illustrates the lowest data value (L), the first quartile (Q_1), the median (Q_2, Md), the third quartile (Q_3), the interquartile range (IQR), and the highest data value (H).

In Section 3.4, the following values were determined for the aptitude test scores in Table 3.2:

$$L = 22 \qquad\qquad Q_3 = 75$$

$$Q_1 = 46 \qquad\qquad IQR = 75 - 46 = 29$$

$$Q_2 = Md = 62 \qquad\qquad H = 96$$

A box plot of these values is shown in Figure 3.12. The ends of the box are located at the first and third quartiles, with a vertical bar inserted at the median. Consequently, the length of the box is the interquartile range. If the data are symmetric, the median bar should be located at the center of the box. *Consequently, the bar location indicates the skewness of the data: If located in the left half of the box, the data are skewed right; and if located in the right half, the data are skewed left.*

Box plots provide a very easy method of detecting outliers in a set of sample data. First, we define the two *inner fences*. The lower inner fence is the first quartile minus 1.5

FIGURE 3.12

Box plot for 50 aptitude
test scores (data in
Table 3.2).

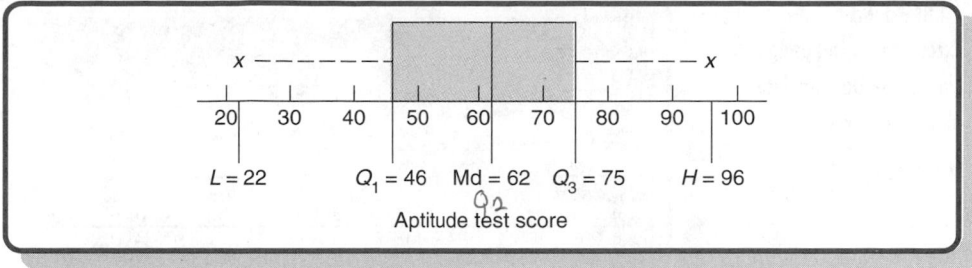

times the interquartile range, and the upper inner fence is the third quartile plus 1.5 times
the interquartile range.

$$\text{lower inner fence} = Q_1 - 1.5 \cdot \text{IQR} \qquad\qquad (3.13)$$

$$\text{upper inner fence} = Q_3 + 1.5 \cdot \text{IQR} \qquad\qquad (3.14)$$

Any value smaller than the lower inner fence or larger than the upper inner fence will be
classified as an outlier. Using the aptitude test scores in Table 3.2, we get

lower inner fence $= 46 - (1.5)(29) = 2.5$

upper inner fence $= 75 + (1.5)(29) = 118.5$

Since none of the data values are less than 2.5 or larger than 118.5, we conclude that this
sample contains no outliers.

Extreme outliers are identified by defining *outer fences:*

$$\text{lower outer fence} = Q_1 - 3 \cdot \text{IQR} \qquad\qquad (3.15)$$

$$\text{upper outer fence} = Q_3 + 3 \cdot \text{IQR} \qquad\qquad (3.16)$$

Any value less than the lower outer fence or greater than the upper outer fence are **extreme
outliers.** We expect *less than one-hundreth of 1%* of the sample values from a bell-shaped
population to lie outside the outer fence. Sample values that lie beyond an inner fence but
inside the outer fence are **mild outliers.** For a sample from a bell-shaped population, we
expect *less than 1%* of the values to lie outside the inner fences. The sample in Table 3.2
contains no values beyond the inner fences (mild outliers), and, as a result, contains no
extreme outliers.

We mentioned earlier that in a box plot, the ends of the box are the first and third quartiles. To be more precise, the left end of the box is defined to be the **lower hinge,** and the
right end of the box is the **upper hinge.** For n even, the lower hinge is the same as Q_1, and
the upper hinge is the same as Q_3, according to our quartile definitions. This is also true
for n odd, where $n - 1$ is evenly divisible by 4 (that is, $n = 5, 9, 13, 17, \ldots$). For the
remaining odd values of n (that is, $n = 3, 7, 11, 15, \ldots$), the lower hinge is defined to be
the average of Q_1 and the ordered data value to the *right* of Q_1, and the upper hinge is
defined to be the average of Q_3 and the ordered data value to the *left* of Q_3. To illustrate,
consider the following ordered sample of seven values:

Sample: 25, 31, 45, 52, 63, 87, 95

Here, Q_1 is the second value (31), the lower hinge is $(31 + 45)/2 = 38$, Q_3 is the sixth value
(87), and the upper hinge is $(63 + 87)/2 = 75$. Despite this slight discrepancy, we will continue to refer to the ends of the box as the first quartile (lower hinge) and third quartile
(upper hinge).

The dotted lines on a box plot, called the **whiskers,** connect the highest and lowest
data values *contained within the inner fences* to the ends of the box. Thus, approximately
25% of the data values will lie in each whisker and in each portion of the box.

FIGURE 3.13
Excel spreadsheet using box plot in KGP Data Analysis (data are 75 residential appraisals).

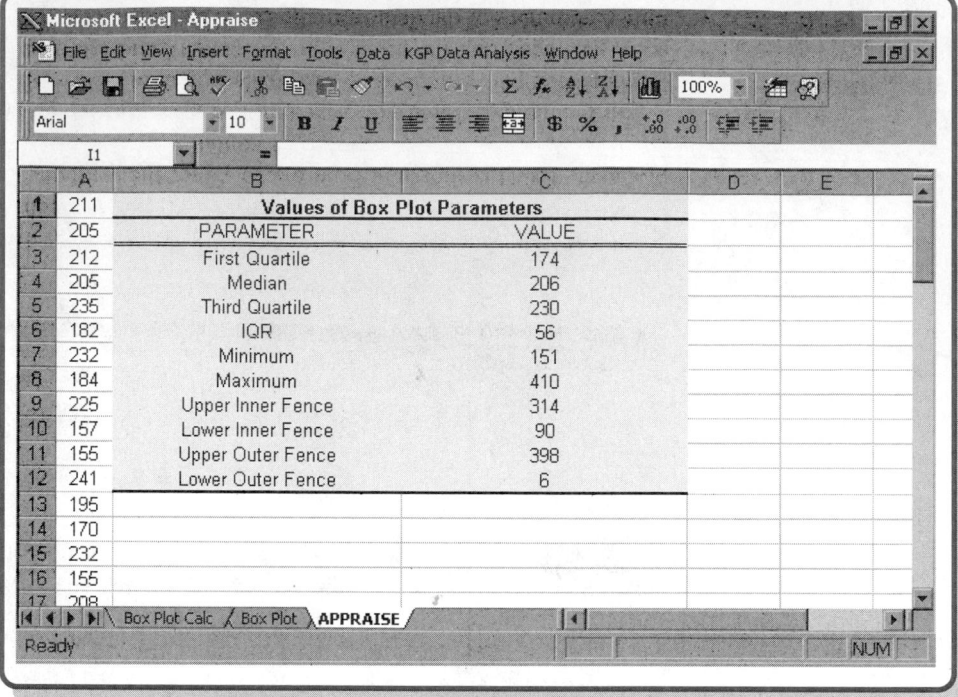

FIGURE 3.14
Excel box plot created using KGP Data Analysis (data are 75 residential appraisals).

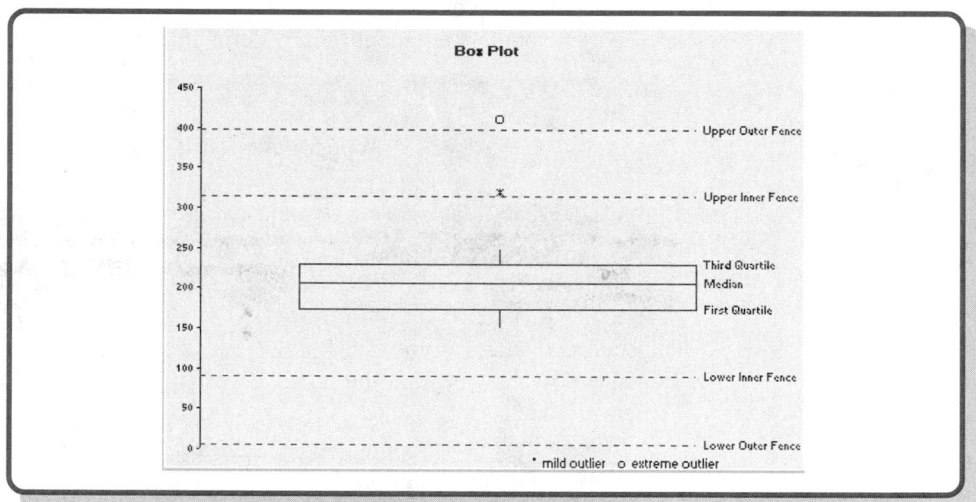

USING EXCEL TO CONSTRUCT A BOX PLOT

Excel does not have a data analysis tool to construct a box plot, but the set of KGP data analysis macros supplied with this textbook does have this feature. The spreadsheet in Figure 3.13 is a result of: (1) entering (loading) the data into column A, and (2) clicking on **KGP Data Analysis ➤ Quantitative Data Charts/Tables ➤ Box Plot.** In Figure 3.13, the data in column A consist of 75 residential appraisals (in thousands of dollars) having a median value of $206,000. After clicking on **Box Plot** you should see a small input screen. Enter "A1:A75" as the input range and enter "B1" in the output range box. The resulting box plot is shown in Figure 3.14 where the median value ($206,000) is represented by the line inside the box. Any mild outlier is represented by the symbol "✱," and extreme outliers are represented using the symbol "O". The sample of residential appraisals contains one mild outlier and one extreme outlier. A closer look at the data revealed one appraised value of $320,000 (the mild outlier) and one value of $410,000 (the extreme outlier). The extreme outlier is equal to the maximum value in cell C8, Figure 3.13.

FIGURE 3.15

Excel box plot created by KGP Data Analysis (data are aptitude test scores in Table 3.2).

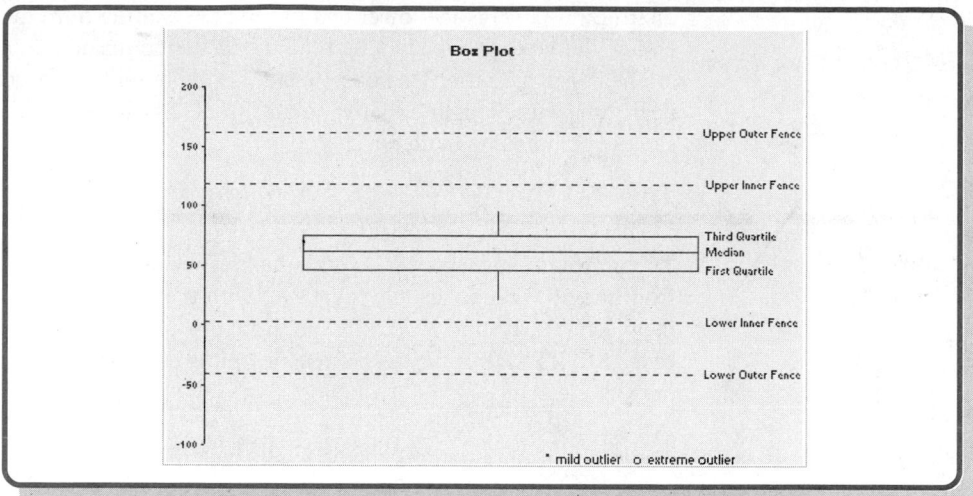

FIGURE 3.16

Excel summary and box plot using KGP Data Analysis (data are 100 machine part diameters from Example 3.4).

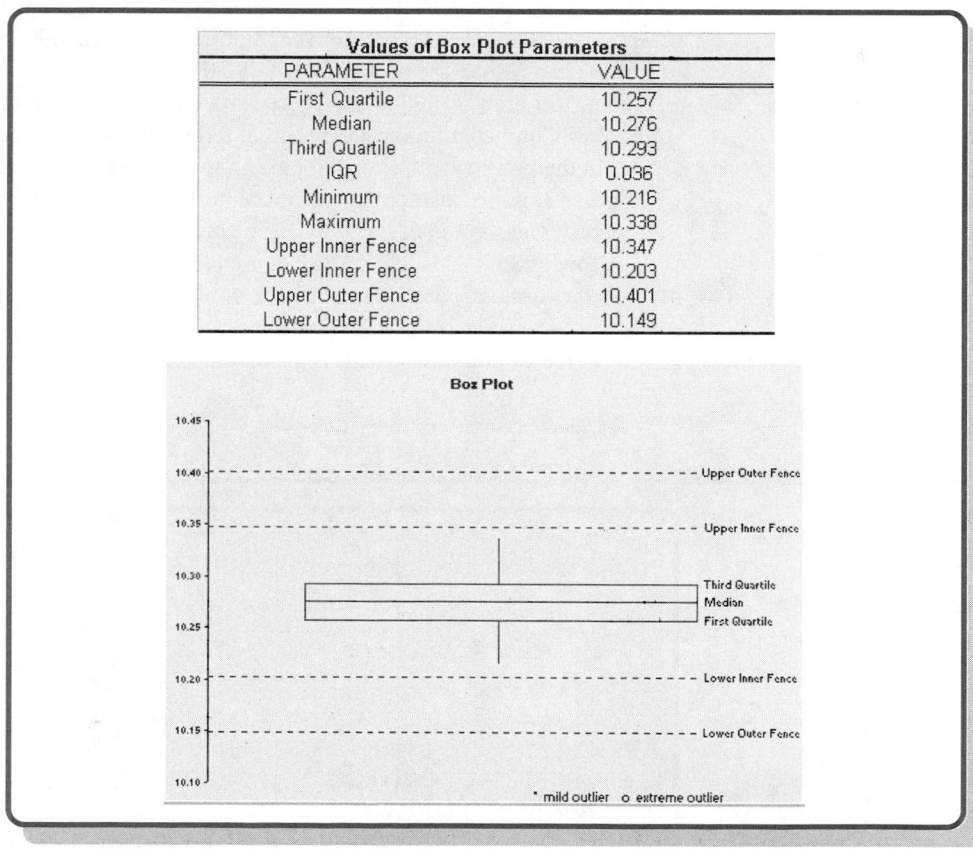

Values of Box Plot Parameters	
PARAMETER	VALUE
First Quartile	10.257
Median	10.276
Third Quartile	10.293
IQR	0.036
Minimum	10.216
Maximum	10.338
Upper Inner Fence	10.347
Lower Inner Fence	10.203
Upper Outer Fence	10.401
Lower Outer Fence	10.149

For the aptitude test scores, Figure 3.12 indicates that the data appear to have a very slight left skew, since the vertical line is slightly right of center in the box. This same box plot using Excel is shown in Figure 3.15. Since the symbols "✱" and "O" do not appear in the plot, we conclude that the sample contains no outliers.

In Examples 2.1 and 3.4, we examined a sample of 100 inside diameters of a particular machined part produced by the Boston plant of Allied Manufacturing. The conclusion so far has been that the process is "off center" and too near the upper spec limit of 10.3 mm. A summary of the data from the Excel spreadsheet and the corresponding box plot are shown in Figure 3.16. A large portion of the upper whisker is larger than 10.3, indicating that a large number of sample items have a diameter beyond the upper spec limit. The first quartile (10.257) is the lower end of the box, and the third quartile (10.293) is the upper end of the box. The median of 10.276 is centered inside the box, indicating that the data are nearly symmetric. This observation is supported by the fact that the two whiskers are nearly the same length. Finally, no "∗" or "O" symbols appear in the plot, indicating the sample contains no outliers.

EXAMPLE 3.10

The personnel manager of Texon Industries is interested in comparing the aptitude scores from the 50 job applicants (Table 3.2) with those of 100 people randomly selected from people currently employed at Texon. Both box plots are shown in Figure 3.17, which illustrates MINITAB's ability to put two box plots in the same graph. What conclusions can be drawn?

SOLUTION

A number of observations can be made, including:

1. The median of each group is represented by the line within the corresponding box. The median score of the job applicants [sample (1)] is roughly $62 - 50 = 12$ points higher than for the sample of 100 current employees [sample (2)].
2. The range for sample (1), using Table 3.2, is $96 - 22 = 74$ points. The range for sample (2) is $80 - 30 = 50$ points. The middle 50% for sample (1), as indicated by the ends of the box, covers a spread of roughly 30 points. The corresponding spread for sample (2) is 15 points. Conclusion: There is much more variation in the job applicant scores.
3. The job applicant scores have a slight left skew (the median line is slightly above center in the box), whereas for sample (2), the scores contain a heavy right skew, since the median line is considerably below center, and the right whisker is quite long. Consequently, the sample of current employees contains a higher concentration of scores at the low end.
4. After examining the box plots, we could conclude that, based on the aptitude test scores, there are some very good and some not-so-good applicants (a lot of variation in scores), but that overall this group outscored the sample of current employees.

FIGURE 3.17

MINITAB box plots of 50 job applicants (sample 1) and 100 current employees (sample 2).

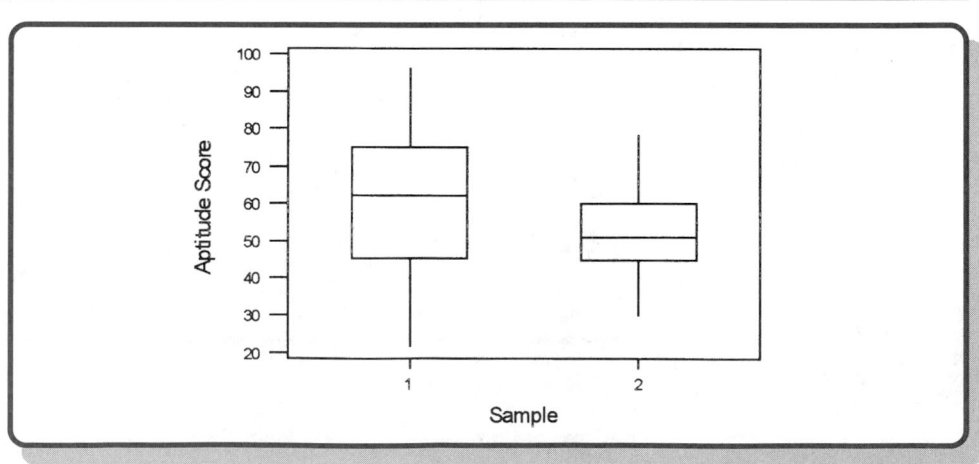

EXERCISES 3.53–3.60

UNDERSTANDING THE MECHANICS

3.53 Construct a box plot using only the following information about a data set with 30 observations.

First Quartile	=	25
Second Quartile	=	50
Third Quartile	=	75
Lowest Value	=	1
Largest Value	=	100

3.54 From the MINITAB box plot displayed below, approximate the following:

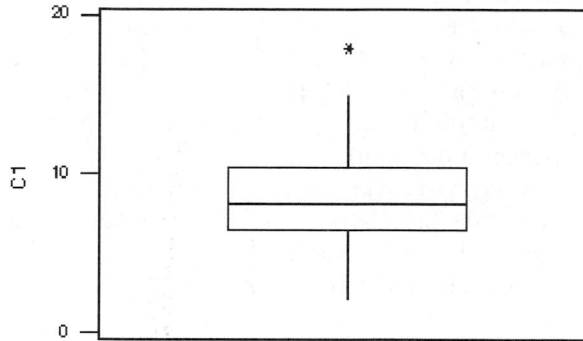

a. Lower hinge
b. Median
c. Upper hinge
d. Any mild outliers
e. Any extreme outliers

3.55 Using the information from the MINITAB output below, construct a box plot.

APPLYING THE NEW CONCEPTS

3.56 The manager of a small restaurant wished to determine how long the average customer had to wait to be served during the lunch hour. At the lunch hour on a particular "typical" day, 20 customers experienced the following waiting times (in minutes):

5.5, 10.3, 7.5, 8.1, 6.8, 11.0, 10.2, 9.0, 7.0, 5.8, 12.5, 7.5, 6.0, 13.7, 5.5, 14.0, 7.0, 6.9, 6.3, 7.4

a. Construct a box plot of the data.

b. Should the manager feel comfortable in advertising that if meals are not served in 10 minutes or less, the customer eats for free?

3.57 The number of unemployed workers in selected areas of California is presented below for February of 1997.

City/Locality	Number Unemployed (in Thousands)
Bakersfield	38.4
Fresno	66.4
Modesto	30.9
Oakland	52.2
Orange County	46.4
Riverside-San Bernardino	92.8
Sacramento	43.4
Salinas	30.9
San Diego	55.9
San Francisco	30.1
San Jose	30.2
Santa Barbara-Santa Maria-Lompoc	12.1
Santa Rosa	10.1
Stockton-Lodi	31.2
Vallejo-Fairfield-Napa	16.2
Ventura	23.6

(Source: *Employment and Earnings*, U.S. Department of Labor and Bureau of Labor Statistics, April 1997, p. 126.)

a. Construct a box plot of the unemployment data.

b. Describe this distribution in words. Are there any outliers? Extreme or mild?

3.58 Refer to the weekly expenditure on food by 30 different families in Exercise 3.27. Construct a box plot for these data. How many outliers would you expect if these data were from a normal population?

3.59 [DATA SET EX3-59] *Variable Description:*

Brakedist: Braking distance in feet for Buick LeSabre

A consumer research group was interested in the braking distance of a Buick LeSabre to confirm the manufacturers reports of a braking distance of 250 feet. A random sample of 100 Buick LeSabres was taken and each car was tested. The results are under the variable Brakedist. (Excel: Use **KGP Data Analysis ➤ Quantitative Data Charts/Tables ➤ Box Plot.**) Describe the distribution of the data.

MINITAB OUTPUT FOR EXERCISE 3.55

Descriptive Statistics

Variable	N	Mean	Median	TrMean	StDev	SE Mean
C1	20	94.4	82.0	89.7	51.9	11.6

Variable	Minimum	Maximum	Q1	Q3		
C1	22.0	250.0	65.5	115.2		

3.60 [DATA SET EX3-60] *Variable Description:*

OccRateNorth: Occupancy rate of Holiday Hotel North
OccRateSouth: Occupancy rate of Holiday Hotel South

To better manage two hotels in the north and south side of Atlanta, the managers decide to collect 60 days of data representing the occupancy rate in percentage. Staff and resources could be more proportionally divided between the two hotels based on projected occupancy rates.

    a. Construct box plots—one for each hotel's occupancy rate.

    b. Compare and contrast the distribution of each hotel. Which hotel has fewer outliers?

SUMMARY

The purpose of analyzing or describing sample data is to learn more about the population from which it was obtained. Every population has properties that describe it. These properties are referred to as **parameters.** We can estimate these parameters by obtaining a sample and deriving the corresponding sample statistic, which is a particular **descriptive measure.**

This chapter has introduced you to some of the more popular descriptive measures used to describe a set of sample values. **Measures of central tendency** are used to describe a typical value within the sample: the **mean** (the average of the sample data), the **median** (the value in the center of the ordered data), the **mode** (that data value occurring the most often), and the **midrange** (an average of the lowest and highest data values). To measure the variation within a set of sample data, we use **measures of variation:** the **range** (difference between the highest and lowest data values), the **variance** (sum of the squares of the deviations from the sample mean, divided by $n - 1$), the **standard deviation** (square root of the variance), and the **coefficient of variation** (standard deviation divided by the mean, times 100).

Percentiles and **quartiles** are **measures of position** and indicate the relative position of a particular value. The first quartile (Q_1) and the third quartile (Q_3) are the 25th and 75th percentiles, respectively. The second quartile (Q_2) is the 50th percentile, which is identical to the sample median. The difference between the first and third quartiles is the **interquartile range** (IQR), which is another measure of dispersion, since it measures the spread within the middle 50% of the data values. Another measure of position is the sample *z*-**score**, which is derived for a particular observation by subtracting the sample mean and dividing by the sample standard deviation.

Finally, the shape of a data set can be described using various **measures of shape.** Two such measures are the sample **skewness** (the degree of symmetry in the data) and **kurtosis** (the tendency of a distribution to stretch out in a particular direction).

The two most commonly used measures are the sample mean and standard deviation. These two statistics can be used together to describe the sample data by applying **Chebyshev's inequality** or the **empirical rule.** The latter procedure draws a stronger conclusion about the concentration of the data values but assumes that the population of interest is bell-shaped (normal).

We examined how to approximate the sample mean and standard deviation when the only information available is a frequency distribution, or **grouped data.**

Exploratory data analysis provides easy-to-construct, yet very powerful, graphs that summarize and describe a set of sample data. Chapter 2 introduced one such graph—the **stem-and-leaf diagram.** The **box plot** introduced in this chapter contains (1) the lowest and highest values within the portion of your sample not considered to be outliers, (2) the three quartiles, and (3) any sample values determined to be outliers. A sample value is considered to be an **extreme outlier** if it lies beyond either of the **outer fences,** and is considered a **mild outlier** if it lies beyond either of the **inner fences** but not beyond the corresponding outer fence. The left and right ends of the box are at the first and third quartiles (more accurately, the **lower** and **upper hinges**). A box plot can be used to detect sample skewness by observing the position of the median line inside the box.

[handwritten: Sample mean is $\bar{x}$]

SUMMARY OF FORMULAS

MEASURES OF CENTRAL TENDENCY

1. Sample mean

$$\bar{x} = \frac{\sum x}{n}$$

[handwritten: sum of data values / (numbers in set)]

2. Population mean

$$\mu = \frac{\sum x}{N}$$

[handwritten: sum of data values / numbers in set]

3. Midrange

$$Mr = \frac{L + H}{2}$$

[handwritten: Low, High]

MEASURES OF VARIATION

1. Range

$$range = H - L$$

2. Sample variance

$$s^2 = \frac{\sum(x - \bar{x})^2}{n - 1}$$

$$= \frac{\sum x^2 - (\sum x)^2/n}{n - 1}$$

3. Population variance

$$\sigma^2 = \frac{\sum(x - \mu)^2}{N}$$

4. Sample standard deviation

$$s = \sqrt{\frac{\sum(x - \bar{x})^2}{n - 1}}$$

$$= \sqrt{\frac{\sum x^2 - (\sum x)^2/n}{n - 1}}$$

5. Population standard deviation

$$\sigma = \sqrt{\frac{\sum(x - \mu)^2}{N}}$$

6. Coefficient of variation

$$CV = \frac{s}{\bar{x}} \cdot 100$$

MEASURES OF POSITION

1. Sample z-score

$$z = \frac{x - \bar{x}}{s}$$

MEASURES OF SHAPE

1. Pearsonian coefficient of skewness

$$Sk = \frac{3(\bar{x} - Md)}{s}$$

2. Excel coefficient of skewness

$$Sk(E) = \frac{n}{(n-1)(n-2)} \sum \left(\frac{x - \bar{x}}{s} \right)^3$$

$$= \frac{n}{(n-1)(n-2)} \sum (z\text{-}score)^3$$

3. MINITAB coefficient of skewness

$$Sk(M) = \frac{1}{n} \sum \left(\frac{x - \bar{x}}{s} \right)^3$$

$$= \frac{1}{n} \sum (z\text{-}score)^3$$

GROUPED DATA

1. Sample mean

$$\bar{x} \cong \frac{\sum f \cdot m}{n}$$

[handwritten: frequency of each class, midpoint of each class, sample size]

2. Sample variance

$$s^2 \cong \frac{\sum f \cdot m^2 - (\sum f \cdot m)^2/n}{n - 1}$$

BOX PLOTS

1. Interquartile range

$$IQR = Q_3 - Q_1$$

2. Lower inner fence

$$Q_1 - 1.5 \cdot IQR$$

3. Upper inner fence

$$Q_3 + 1.5 \cdot IQR$$

4. Lower outer fence

$$Q_1 - 3 \cdot IQR$$

5. Upper outer fence

$$Q_3 + 3 \cdot IQR$$

REVIEW EXERCISES 3.61–3.80

3.61 Internet stocks are hot. One measure of how hot they are is to look at the price-to-sales ratio. Since it is too early to measure earnings for many of these companies, price-to-earnings ratios are not meaningful. Therefore price/sales ratios are used to compare these companies. As the table below shows, some of the valuations are quite high.

Company	Price/Sales
Yahoo!	46.0
RealNetworks	16.0
CNET	11.3
Excite	11.0
Amazon.com	7.7
Onsale	3.9

(Source: *Forbes*, "The Net Grows to the Sky," April 20, 1998, p. 232.)

a. Compare the mean, median, and mode for the above data. Which measure would be most reasonable to use?

b. Interpret the coefficient of skewness for the price/sales data.

c. What is the z-score for Yahoo!? What is the z-score for RealNetworks? What does this say about the price/sales ratio for Yahoo!?

3.62 The consumer price index (CPI) for food expenditure by urban wage earners is listed below for several categories of food and beverage. This index is presented in its seasonally adjusted form.

Expenditure Category	Seasonally Adjusted CPI
Cereals and bakery products	176.0
Meats, poultry, fish, and eggs	147.9
Dairy products	146.0
Fruits and vegetables	186.7
Desserts and sweets	146.9
Nonalcoholic beverages	126.9
Alcoholic beverages	160.9

(Source: *U.S. Department of Labor and Bureau of Labor Statistics*, "CPI Detailed Report," Feb. 1997, p. 37.)

Calculate and interpret each of the statistics in parts (a) through (f).

a. Mean
b. Midrange
c. Standard deviation
d. Coefficient of variation
e. Fortieth percentile
f. Interquartile range

3.63 While software is becoming easier to use, computer users are demanding new features that make programs more complex. To deliver a satisfying experience, a software package must strike a balance between new features and ease of use. The software must also have the support behind it to get customers up and running. Satisfaction scores for telephone technical support with various database, spreadsheet, and word processor applications are presented below.

Databases/Spreadsheet/Word Processors	Satisfaction Score
dBase	7.3
Lotus Approach	7.1
Microsoft Access	6.7
Microsoft FoxPro	6.5
Paradox	7.5
Corel Quattro Pro	7.9
Lotus 1-2-3	7.5
Microsoft Excel	6.9
Ami Pro/Word Pro	7.4
Correl WordPerfect	8.0
Microsoft Word	6.8

(Source: *PC Magazine*, "Telephone Technical Support," July 1997, p. 206.)

a. Find the interval in which at least 75% of the data would be expected to lie.

b. Calculate the interquartile range. Is this value easily affected by an extreme observation? Calculate with 8.0 removed and compare.

3.64 Sea cruises have been a popular way to see Europe. Caribbean cruises typically cost more than European cruises by about $70 per person per day. The European Travel Commission expects a record 10.5 million Americans in 1998. Assume that a sample of 15 cruises is obtained and their average cost per person per day are recorded both for Caribbean cruises and European cruises. The data sampled are presented below in units of American dollars.

European	Caribbean
205	285
208	275
196	310
183	268
225	257
250	330
190	220
173	205
164	360
230	407
240	235
180	195
189	206
209	300
207	277

(Source: Adapted from *USA Today*, "Europe Ahoy!" May 8, 1998, p. D1.)

a. Find the mean, standard deviation, and coefficient of skewness for the cost of a European cruise.

b. Find the mean, standard deviation, and coefficient of skewness for the cost of a Caribbean cruise.

c. Compare and contrast the statistics in parts (a) and (b).

3.65 The following task completion times were recorded for a task presented to 15 teams of employees. Units are in hours.

1.8	2.7	3.4	2.6	2.7	4.4
6.9	3.4	4.1	3.0	2.1	2.4
3.1	4.7	3.0	3.5	4.2	3.8

a. Calculate the interquartile range and the standard deviation of these data.

b. Remove the observation with a value of 6.9. Recalculate the statistics in part (a). Which statistics are affected the most by omitting this observation?

3.66 The number of phone calls received daily by a secretary at a bank is recorded over a 30-day period.

18	30	10	16	34	25	13	21	19	29
24	17	34	40	20	16	18	22	17	28
31	24	26	18	32	23	20	31	21	27

a. Calculate the coefficient of skewness for this data set.

b. Calculate a z-score for each observation.

c. Interpret the statistics in parts (a) and (b). Which observations would you say are unusual?

3.67 The risk-adjusted performance of a mutual fund can be measured using the Sharpe measure. A fund's return, in excess of a riskless treasury bill investment, divided by its standard deviation is the Sharpe measure. For example, over the past 10 years the Sharpe measure for the Magellan Fund and the Janus funds are .87 and .99, respectively.

(Adapted from "Screening Equity Funds to Find Top Reward-to-Risk Investments," *Dallas Morning News*, March 23, 1993, p. 1D.)

a. Would a high or a low Sharpe measure indicate that you are being well paid for the risk you are taking? Which fund, Magellan or Janus, had a better risk-adjusted performance?

b. How is the Sharpe measure related to the coefficient of variation?

3.68 Consider a sample of observations:

10   15   30   25

Transform these values into z-scores. What is the mean and standard deviation of the z-scores? Show that the mean of any set of z-scores is always equal to zero.

3.69 Answer the questions below for the following data set:

2.0, 1.1, −1.5, .3, 1.9, −2.3, −1.2, .7, −.5, 3.1, −.2, 1.0, −.6, 1.3, −.9, −.1, .8, −1.1, 2.4, .9, −.1, −1.5

    a. Do the data appear to be bell-shaped?
    b. Calculate the coefficient of skewness.
    c. Using the empirical rule, estimate the range of values within which about 68% of the data values are expected to lie.

3.70 The distribution of annual births in the United States is illustrated by the following frequency distribution. Units of frequency are in thousands.

Age	Number of Births
15 and under 20	484
20 and under 25	1010
25 and under 30	1188
30 and under 35	795
35 and under 40	278
40 and under 45	44

(Adapted from "Cesarean Births," *The World Almanac and The Book of Facts,* 1993, p. 955.)

    a. Approximate the mean number of births from the given dates.
    b. If the actual data were available, would the mean of these data be identical to your answer in part (a)? Explain.

3.71 The mean rate charged by the CPAs in a certain city is about $75 per hour, with a standard deviation of $15. Assuming that the data came from a normal population, estimate the range of rates within which about 95% of the CPA's charges are expected to lie.

3.72 The z-score is −1.50, the mean is 45, and $x = 15$. What is the value of the variance?

3.73 A manufacturing plant requires one of its suppliers to provide aluminum sheets that have a special coating that is between 1.5 and 4.5 millimeters in depth. A shipment of 800 coated aluminum sheets was delivered to the plant. The supervisor at the plant was told that the mean depth of the coating was 3.0 millimeters, with a standard deviation of .5. If there are more than 100 aluminum sheets with a coating thickness outside of the range 1.5 to 4.5 millimeters, the plant supervisor will not accept the shipment. What decision should the supervisor make?

3.74 The mean GMAT score of the 65 applicants who were accepted into the MBA program of Xavier Business School was 520 with a standard deviation of 25. About how many applicants scored between 470 and 570 on the GMAT?

3.75 Owning a one-of-a-kind print work is a fleeting fantasy for the average art aficionado. Christie's Auction typically sells original fine-art prints by famous artists for mostly between $5,000 to $25,000. Occasionally, prints will go for six figures when the art market is sizzling. Assume that the following data are a sample of 30 fine-art prints auctioned at Christie's.

3,500	12,500	2,800	4,500	15,300	21,500	8,500	7,570	12,000	18,400
1,600	22,000	21,300	17,400	8,500	12,300	14,500	2,500	23,300	24,500
17,500	13,500	15,400	17,500	14,900	24,000	16,300	7,400	4,500	6,400

(Source: Adapted from *USA Today,* "Fine Artwork Prints Gaining in Popularity, Price," May 1, 1998, p. 3B.)

    a. Using the empirical rule, estimate the interval in which approximately 68% of the data will lie.
    b. Find the 25th, 50th, and 75th percentiles for the data above. Interpret these values.

USING THE COMPUTER

3.76 **[DATA SET EX3-76]** *Variable description:*

Product: Brand and flavor of ice cream
Calories: Number of calories in brand and flavor of ice cream
Fat: Fat in grams

Many marketing managers are promoting advertisements that encourage ice cream lovers to not give up ice cream but to switch to reduced-fat ice cream without abandoning their favorite brand. A listing of these types of ice creams, their calories, and their fat content in grams are recorded for 26 choices of ice cream.

(Source: *Shape*, "Inside Scoop," July 1997, p. 56.)

   a. Plot a histogram of the calories. Repeat this for the fat content.
   b. Which of the histograms in part (a) more closely resembles a bell-shaped curve?
   c. For the data corresponding to the histogram selected in part (a), find an interval in which you would expect 95% of the data to lie.
   d. Obtain the summary statistics for both variables. (Excel: Use **Tools ➤ Data Analysis ➤ Descriptive Statistics.**) Use these values to describe the data.

3.77 [DATA SET EX3-77] *Variable Description:*

JobArr: Number of job orders arriving at a manufacturing plant

A production facility manufactures air compressors for automobiles. The facility tries to accommodate special orders that arrive on a daily basis. Allowing capacity for the special orders is important to the planning process. For 120 working days, the number of job orders have been recorded.
   a. Plot a histogram and a box plot of the data.
   b. How would you describe the data?
   c. Find the mean and standard deviation of the data. From these values, compute the coefficient of skewness. Does the value of this measure appear to be consistent with your description in part (b)?

3.78 [DATA SET EX3-78] *Variable Description:*

MarketExp: Travel expenses for the marketing department
R&DExp: Travel expenses for the research and development department

The vice president of a semiconductor company wished to compare the distribution of travel expenses in two departments, the marketing department and the research and development department. The travel expenses of 120 persons from the marketing department and 150 persons from the research and development department are listed under MarketExp and R&DExp, respectively, in dollars.
   a. Form a box plot for the expenses of each department.
   b. Form a histogram for the expenses of each department.
   c. Do the data from either department appear to be bell shaped?
   d. Contrast the distributions of the two departments.

3.79 An accountant is interested in determining the distribution of the amounts overcharged to customers by a health clinic. A random sample of 50 accounts in which an overcharge occurred was examined (Excel: in columns A through E). Type in the formulas below the random sample of account overcharges.
   a. Give a description of the data based on these formulas.
   b. Determine the effects of eliminating the largest overcharge. Replace the largest overcharge by 0. What effect did this have on the descriptive statistics?
   c. Determine the effects of eliminating the four largest overcharges. Replace the four largest overcharges by 0. What effect did this have on the descriptive statistics?

31.56	25.88	26.34	24.34	30.45
26.43	21.55	29.32	24.98	19.89
26.49	32.12	21.62	21.56	24.98
25.12	29.67	19.21	22.65	25.98
29.65	22.89	25.54	34.42	22.67
23.15	28.34	24.98	27.99	24.67
22.56	30.93	31.99	12.78	26.45
10.21	27.45	32.88	24.89	27.67
16.43	21.05	19.64	12.12	30.89
15.09	30.92	28.34	21.44	25.43

mean	=AVERAGE(A1:E10)
median	=MEDIAN(A1:E10)
min	=MIN(A1:E10)
max	=MAX(A1:E10)
first Quartile	=PERCENTILE(A1:E10,0.25)
third Quartile	=PERCENTILE(A1:E10,0.75)

3.80 A TV cable company in Houston wanted to estimate the hours per week that households watch television. A random sample of 50 households was used to construct the box plot below. Write a brief summary of the characteristics of the data in a report to the management of the TV cable company based on this plot.

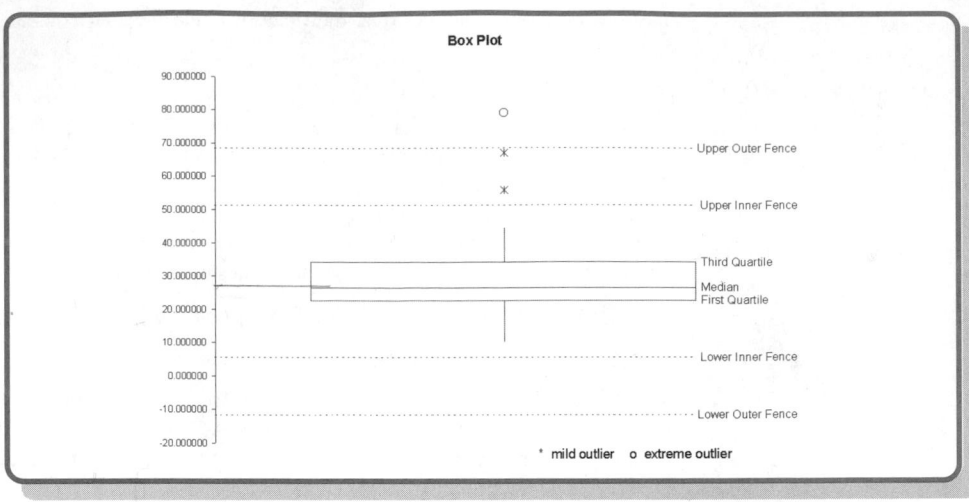

COMPUTER EXERCISES USING THE DATABASES

EXERCISE 1—APPENDIX E

Randomly select 100 observations of variable INCOME1 (income of principal wage earner) from the database.

a. Use a convenient statistical computer package to determine the various descriptive measures that describe the distribution of INCOME1.

b. What are the actual proportions of observations that are between ±2.0 and ±3.0 standard deviations of the mean of the data set? Are these proportions consistent with:
   (i) Chebyshev's inequality?
   (ii) the empirical rule?

c. Construct a box plot of this sample. What do you observe from this graph?

EXERCISE 2—APPENDIX F

Randomly select 100 observations of the variable SALES from the database.

a. Use a convenient statistical computer package to find the mean, median, range, variance, coefficient of variation, and coefficient of skewness for this variable.

b. Construct a box plot, and use this graph to describe your sample of SALES values.

INSIGHTS FROM STATISTICS IN ACTION: WHY CAN'T THE AVERAGE MUTUAL FUND BEAT THE STANDARD & POORS 500 INDEX?

The Statistics in Action section at the beginning of this chapter discussed the inability of many mutual funds to outperform the S&P 500 Index. Financial advisors are continually assessing whether the S&P Index funds are the best choice for the long run. Many mutual funds can outperform the S&P 500 Index for several quarters, but over a five-year period the S&P 500 is hard to beat. Consider the data listed below for several mutual funds with large asset size. The performance listed is for the first half of 1998, the second quarter of 1998, and for the 5-year period ending on July 1, 1998. In parentheses after each fund listed is the category abbreviated: G—Growth, CA—Capital Appreciation, GI—Growth and Income, B—Balanced, EI—Equity Income, IF—International Fund, and GL—Global. The funds are listed in the table by asset size.

Mutual Fund	1st Half 1998	2nd Qtr 1998	Past 5 Yrs
Fidelity Magellan Fund (G)	18.10%	3.40%	142%
Vanguard Index 500 (SP)	17.70%	3.30%	181%
Washington Mutual Invest (GI)	12.60%	0.30%	165%
Investment Co of America (GI)	13.10%	1.60%	145%
Fidelity Growth & Income (GI)	16.10%	3.00%	169%
Fidelity Contrafund (G)	17.30%	4.50%	153%
Vanguard Windsor II (GI)	14.80%	1.80%	174%
Amer Cent TC Ultra Inv (G)	24.00%	7.00%	147%
Fidelity Puritan (B)	10.80%	2.60%	107%
Fidelity Equity-Income (EI)	11.30%	−0.10%	151%
Vanguard Wellington Fund (B)	8.90%	1.00%	116%
Fidelity Adv Growth Opp T (G)	11.50%	1.20%	155%
Vanguard Windsor (GI)	10.30%	−2.30%	139%
Income Fund of America (EI)	6.40%	−0.50%	97%
Janus Fund (CA)	21.50%	6.10%	142%
EuroPacific Growth (IF)	13.40%	−0.20%	106%
Putnam Growth & Income A (GI)	9.80%	−1.00%	140%
New Perspective Fund (GL)	18.60%	2.60%	137%
Fidelity Equity-Inc II (EI)	16.00%	3.10%	143%
MSDW Div Growth B (GI)	13.60%	0.80%	134%
Putnam Growth & Income B (GI)	9.40%	−1.20%	131%
Fidelity Blue Chip (G)	18.80%	4.20%	171%
Templeton Foreign I (IF)	2.60%	−7.40%	74%
T Rowe Price Equity Income (EI)	6.30%	−2.40%	145%
Templeton Growth I (GL)	4.50%	−5.30%	109%
Growth Fund of America (G)	14.50%	2.40%	139%
Putnam Voyager A (CA)	16.80%	1.90%	168%
Janus Worldwide (GL)	24.80%	7.20%	188%
Fidelity Asset Manager (G)	8.10%	0.50%	84%
Fidelity Low-Price (G)	7.90%	−1.40%	157%
Fidelity Sprt US Eq Index (SP)	17.50%	3.20%	179%
Fundamental Investors (GI)	12.80%	1.60%	153%
Fidelity Growth Company (G)	14.60%	1.60%	133%
T Rowe Price Internat Stock (IF)	13.70%	0.10%	86%
American Mutual (GI)	8.30%	−1.00%	119%
Vanguard Primecap (G)	11.90%	1.30%	199%
IDS New Dimensions A (G)	16.70%	3.50%	158%
Merrill Glob Alloc B (GL)	5.00%	−2.90%	70%
Templeton World I (GL)	7.00%	−4.60%	126%
Putnam New Opportunity A (G)	18.60%	2.90%	193%
Smallcap World Fund (G)	6.40%	−4.30%	105%
Vanguard World US Growth (G)	23.90%	7.30%	194%
Oakmark Fund (G)	7.00%	−2.70%	169%
Capital Income Builder (EI)	7.80%	0.00%	109%
Lord Abbett Affiliated A (GI)	10.50%	−0.30%	142%
Mutual Shares Z (GI)	6.70%	0.70%	143%
Capital World Growth & Inc (GL)	11.80%	−1.00%	136%
Fidelity Value Fund (CA)	9.20%	−2.10%	134%
Scudder Growth & Income (GI)	9.90%	−2.70%	154%

1. Find the mean of the above mutual funds excluding the Vanguard Index 500 (SP) and the Fidelity Spartan US Eq Index (SP) for each of the three time periods. How do these averages compare to the Vanguard Index 500 (SP) and the Fidelity Spartan US Eq Index (SP)? What overall conclusion can you make? Why do you think that the performance of the Vanguard Index 500 (SP) and the Fidelity Spartan US Eq Index (SP) are not identical? (For example, do you think that the management fees charged by the funds are different?)

2. Find the median for all of the mutual funds excluding the two index funds for each time period. How do these figures compare to the means found in Question 1 for each of the three time periods?

3. Which of the categories, G or GI, would you expect to have the smallest amount of variation (standard deviation)? Why? Calculate the standard deviation for each of the three time periods for mutual funds in the G and GI categories. How do these numbers compare? What interpretation would you give them?

4. For each of the categories, G, GI, and CA, find the mean for each of the three time periods. How do these

compare? How many of each of these categories were able to outperform the Vanguard Index 500 (SP)?

5. Construct a bar chart to describe the results that you found in Question 4. Are these results convincing that investing in the S&P 500 Index is a very competitive option?

Sources: *Toronto Star,* "Index Funds Offer Consistency," June 24, 1998, p. 1, Business section.

USA Today, "S&P 500 Beats Stock Funds Again," Jan. 2, 1998, p. 1B. Copyright 1998, USA TODAY. Reprinted with permission.

USA Today, "How Largest Stock Funds Fared," July 6, 1998, p. 7B. Copyright 1998, USA TODAY. Reprinted with permission.

CHAPTER 3 APPENDIX: DATA ANALYSIS WITH **MINITAB**

DESCRIPTIVE STATISTICS

The MINITAB procedure to display descriptive statistics will be illustrated using the salary data in Table 2.3, discussed in Example 3.2. To obtain this command click on **Stat ➤ Basic Statistics ➤ Display Descriptive Statistics.** You will see the input screen below. Click on each of the input variables and then click on OK.

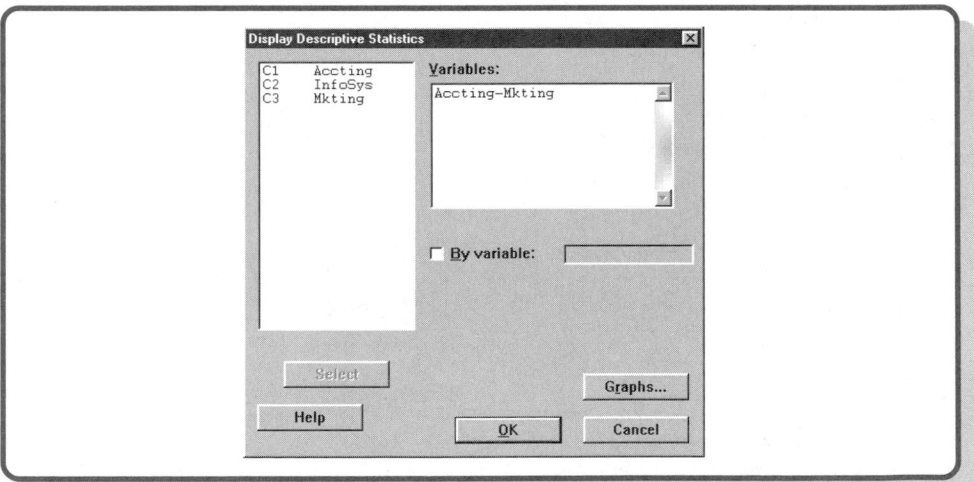

The output will appear in the session window as follows.

DESCRIPTIVE STATISTICS

Variable	N	Mean	Median	TrMean	StDev	SE Mean
InfoSys	10	31.870	31.400	31.800	1.460	0.462
Mkting	14	31.536	31.900	31.583	2.068	0.553
Accting	26	34.612	34.450	34.600	2.447	0.480

Variable	Minimum	Maximum	Q1	Q3
InfoSys	29.800	34.500	30.675	33.100
Mkting	27.800	34.700	29.825	33.325
Accting	30.700	38.800	32.300	36.425

To obtain one of the less common descriptive statistics, click on **Stat ➤ Basic Statistics ➤ Store Descriptive Statistics.** After selecting the variable on which you wish to obtain descriptive statistics, you will see a wide range of statistics from which to choose. In the screen displayed below, the skewness and the kurtosis coefficients are selected. Click OK on both screens and the skewness and kurtosis will be displayed in the data window. By typing "print" following by the cell labels in which the statistics are stored, the selected statistics will appear in the session window.* To obtain a statistic such as the coefficient of variation, click on standard deviation and the mean and if these values are stored in, say c10 and c11, respectively, simply type "let c12 = (c10/c11)*100" and the coefficient of variation will appear in column c12. As there are different expressions used to estimate the skewness coefficient, MINITAB and Excel's calculations will not agree. As the sample size gets large the difference becomes smaller.

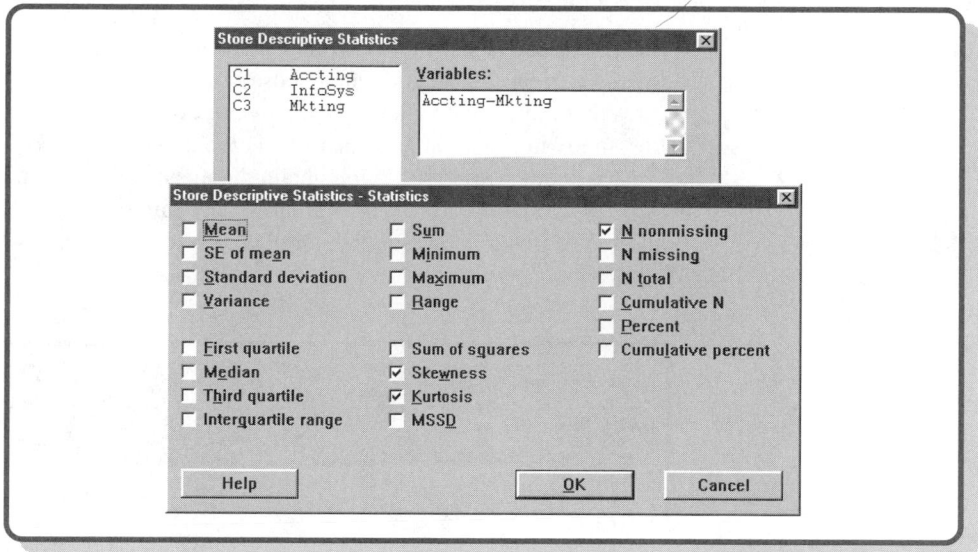

To obtain a box plot from the aptitude test scores of 50 applicants listed in Table 3.2, click on **Stat ➤ EDA ➤ Box Plot.** The **Display** box defines the way data points look on the graph. Your points on the box plot can be displayed in any combination of the following: CI Box, IQRange Box, Range Box, Median Connect, Individual Symbol, Median Symbol, and Outlier Symbol. See Displaying Data Overview. IQRange Box was selected for the box plot in this example. The output follows the box plot screen.

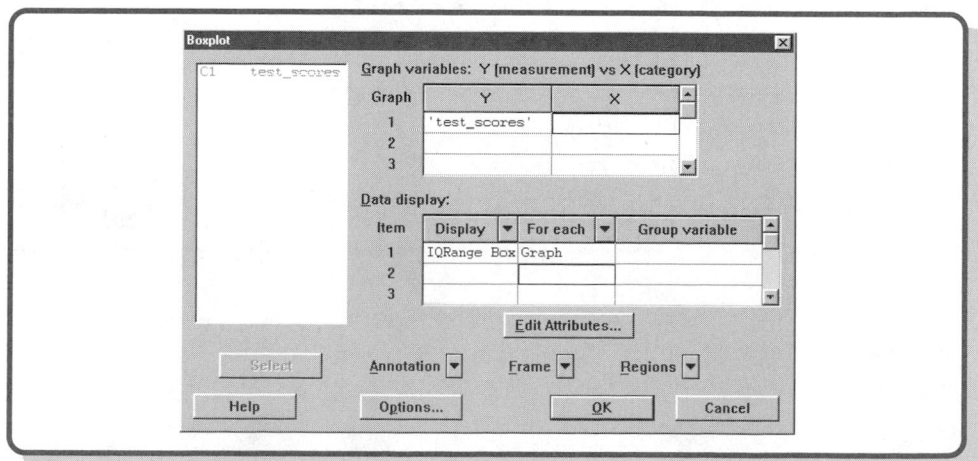

---

* An easier method of obtaining the skewness and kurtosis for these three columns is to type "%describe C1-C3"in the MINITAB command line, i.e. you should see "MTB > %describe C1-C3" in the command line. This output includes many of the descriptive statistics (including skewness and kurtosis) as well as a box plot of the data, a histogram of the data, and a bell-shaped curve that best fits the sample data constructed on top of the histogram.

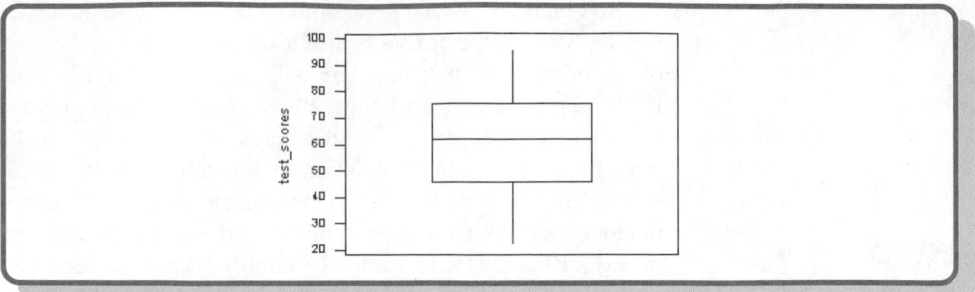

GROUPED DATA

MINITAB can be used to construct the "made up" data discussed in Section 3.7. In the following screen, the **set** command is used to enter data into column c1. The next line indicates that there are 5 values of 25, 14 values of 35, and so on, in c1. By typing **end** in the line following, you indicate that this is the end of the data. By typing "mean of c1" and "standard deviation of c1", you obtain the mean and standard deviation of the sample created by replicating the class midpoints. The same mean (41.111) and standard deviation (11.027) derived in Section 3.7 are obtained here.

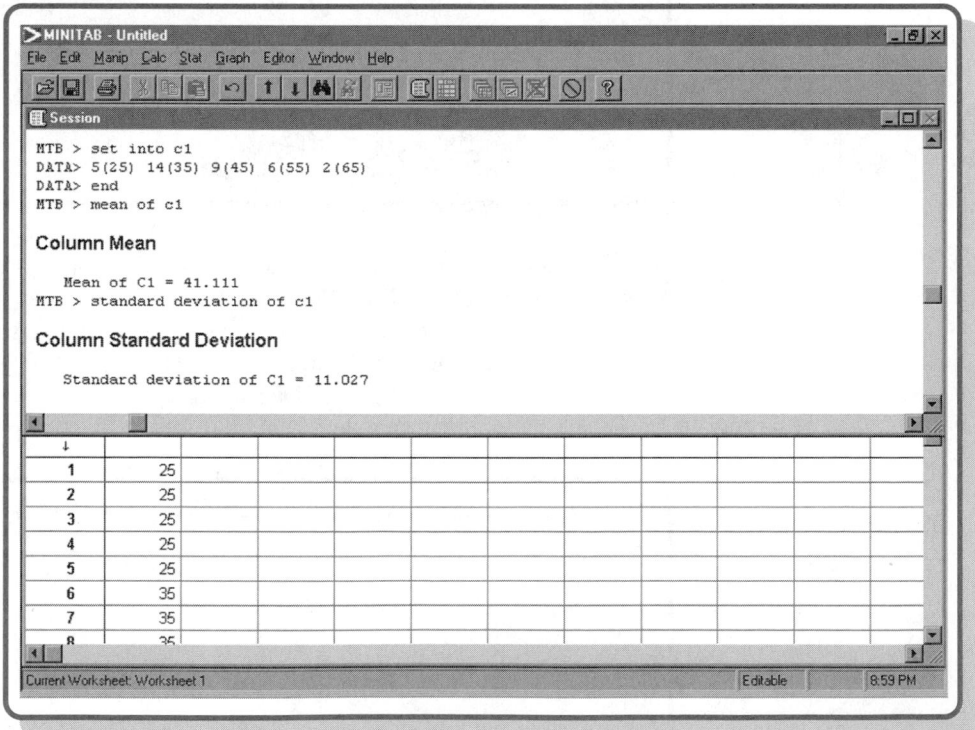

PROBABILITY CONCEPTS

STATISTICS IN ACTION: GAINING MARKET SHARE IN THE FRUIT JUICE INDUSTRY

PepsiCo, Inc., agreed to acquire Tropicana Products, Inc., for 3.3 billion dollars in 1998. Pepsi's brass had tough decisions to make in the areas of growth for the company. Adding Tropicana to PepsiCo's soft-drink and Frito-Lay snack lines hopefully would increase Pepsi's already impressive marketing clout with retailers. The deal put Pepsi on familiar turf, fighting Coca-Cola Co., who owns Tropicana's biggest rival, Minute Maid. The president of Minute Maid has vowed to become the "Coca-Cola Co. of the juice business worldwide." Both beverage companies are now determined to squeeze the most money out of the juice market.

Pepsi and Coca-Cola have been faced with many challenging decisions in their history. Statistics and probabilities have been widely used by marketing analysts for the companies to monitor and adjust to the changing climates of the consumer. For example, Coke and Pepsi both tried a novel "morning" soft drink. Marketing analysts remember the high-caffeine, low-carbonated Pepsi A.M. drink and Coca-Cola's "Coke in the morning" radio ad campaigns. But surveys of supermarket sales and trends in the proportion of consumers who have turned health conscious showed that the probability of consumers switching to these drinks to be rather low.

At most companies, subjective probabilities and probabilities estimated from survey data are used in the decision-making process of management. If these probabilities are not high enough to justify the investment, then the compelling logic of entering a new segment of the market may not be reasonable, considering the risk. Before acquiring Tropicana Products, PepsiCo needed to consider many probabilities. Some of these are as follows:

a. The probability that weather and futures prices for fruit will stay sufficiently stable to allow PepsiCo to realize a significant profit margin from the sale of a fruit drink product.

b. The probability that consumers will continue to gravitate toward "neutraceutical" drinks (industry jargon for energy drinks). Orange juice and other fruit juices are considered a "natural" drink with vitamins and therefore are considered neutraceutical drinks.

c. The probability that Tropicana and Pepsi could work together closely to develop and market "shelf-stable" juice drinks, which can be stored without refrigeration.

d. The probability that Tropicana will be a viable product to export internationally without cost overruns.

To improve their market share, both Tropicana and Minute Maid have advertised heavily to get juice buyers to purchase their brands. One Minute Maid ad shows a New Yorker traveling by subway to Florida orange groves, where he bites into a ripe orange and pronounces it to be as good as Minute Maid's. Tropicana has a series of advertisements with a bright orange river of juice, from which orange slices jump like dolphins. In one version, the sun comes up each time that a kid sucks the juice through a straw. Marketing analysts are continually surveying the supermarkets to determine if the proportions above have changed as a result of their advertising.

After completing this chapter, you will be able to

- Discuss market shares in terms of probabilities;
- Combine various market shares and discuss the results as probabilities; and
- Revise a probability when provided with additional information.

A LOOK BACK/INTRODUCTION

You use descriptive statistics to summarize or present data that consist of observations that have already occurred. If these data are drawn from a population, then you describe your sample in some way. If you wish to infer something about the population using the smaller sample, you must deal with uncertainty. To measure the chance that something will occur, you use its **probability.** The concepts of probability form the foundation of all decision making in statistics. By using probabilities, you are able to deal with uncertainty because you are able, at least, to measure it.

To illustrate this idea, suppose that a recent report contained the results of a random sample of 100 homes within a large metropolitan city and stated that the average electric bill was $185. However, the electric company claims that the average bill for all of its customers is $110. Is something wrong here? Do you believe that the *population* mean is $110 based on the fact that the *sample* mean is $185? Here we need a probability, in particular the probability of observing a sample mean at least this large (that is, $185 or more), assuming that the electric company is correct in their claim. If we decide that this probability is extremely small, we can infer that the *population* claim is incorrect, based on the *sample* results.

As mentioned in Chapter 1, there is always the possibility of arriving at the wrong decision (maybe the electric company *is* correct) when using sample results to infer something concerning a population. This particular type of question will be addressed in Chapter 8. We begin the journey into probability in this chapter by introducing some basic concepts and discussing various ways of determining probabilities.

4.1 EVENTS AND PROBABILITY

An activity for which the outcome is uncertain is an **experiment.** An experiment need not involve mixing chemicals in the laboratory; it could be as simple as throwing two dice and observing the total of the faces turned up. At the completion of an experiment, a measurement of some kind is obtained. An **event** consists of one or more possible outcomes of the experiment; it is usually denoted by a capital letter.* The following are examples of experiments and some corresponding events:

1. *Experiment:* Rolling two dice; *events:* A = rolling a total of 7, B = rolling a total greater than 8, C = rolling two 4s.
2. *Experiment:* Taking a CPA exam; *events:* A = pass, B = fail.
3. *Experiment:* Observing the number of arrivals at a drive-up window over, a 5-minute period; *events:* A_0 = no arrivals, A_1 = one arrival, A_2 = two arrivals, and so on.

---

* The set of all possible outcomes of an experiment is often referred to as the *sample space.*

When you estimate a probability, you are estimating the probability *of an event.* For example, when rolling two dice, the probability that you will roll a total of 7 (event A) is the probability that event A occurs. It is written **P(A).** The probability of any event is always between 0 and 1, inclusive.

NOTATION

$$P(A) = \text{probability that event } A \text{ occurs}$$

CLASSICAL DEFINITION OF PROBABILITY

Suppose a particular experiment has n possible outcomes and event A occurs in m of the n outcomes. The *classical definition* of the probability that event A will occur is

$$P(A) = m/n \tag{4.1}$$

This definition assumes that all n possible outcomes have the same chance for occurring. Such outcomes (events) are said to be **equally likely,** and each has probability $1/n$ of occurring. If this is not the case, the classical definition does not apply.

Consider the experiment of tossing a nickel and a dime into the air and observing how they fall. Event A is observing one head and one tail. The possible outcomes are (H = head, T = tail):

Nickel	Dime
H	H
H	T
T	H
T	T

Thus, there are two ($m = 2$) outcomes that constitute event A of the four possible outcomes ($n = 4$). These four outcomes are equally likely, so each occurs with probability 1/4. Consequently,

$$P(A) = 2/4 = .5$$

RELATIVE FREQUENCY APPROACH

Another method of estimating a probability is referred to as the **relative frequency** approach. It is based on observing the experiment n times and counting the number of times an event (say, A) occurs. If event A occurs m times, your estimate of the probability that A will occur in the future is

$$P(A) = m/n \tag{4.2}$$

Suppose that a particular production process has been in operation for 250 days; 220 days have been accident-free. Let A = a randomly chosen day in the future is free of accidents. Using the relative frequency definition, then

$$P(A) = 220/250 = .88$$

SUBJECTIVE PROBABILITY

Another type of probability is **subjective probability.** It is a measure (between 0 and 1) of your belief that a particular event will occur. A value of one indicates that you believe this event will occur with complete certainty.

Examples of situations requiring a subjective probability are:

The probability that the Dow Jones closing index will be below 3500 at some time during the next 6 months.

The probability that your newly introduced product will capture at least 10% of the market.

The probability that an audited voucher will contain an error.

The probability that your recently married cousin, divorced five times already, will once again go down alimony lane.

Although no two people may agree on a particular subjective probability, these probabilities are governed by the same rules of probability, which are developed later in the chapter.

4.2 Basic Concepts

Datacomp recently has conducted a survey of 200 selected purchasers of their newly introduced laptop computer to obtain a gender-and-age profile of their new customers. A summary by gender revealed

Class	Frequency
Male	120
Female	80
	200

and a summary by age resulted in the following frequency distribution (note that 30–45 includes the 30 and 45 year olds)

Class	Frequency
Under 30	100
30–45	50
Over 45	50
	200

These two categories (gender and age) can be summarized *together* in a **contingency, or cross-tab table,** shown in Table 4.1. The numbers within the table represent the frequency, or number of individuals, within each pair of subcategories, and so the contingency table allows you to see how these two categories interact.

There are 60 purchasers who are male *and* under 30; 10 purchasers are female *and* over 45. One person from the total group of 200 is to be selected at random to receive a free software package. We can define the following events:

M = a male is selected

F = a female is selected

U = the person selected is under 30

B = the person selected is between 30 and 45

O = the person selected is over 45

TABLE 4.1

Datacomp survey of microcomputer purchasers.

| Sex | AGE (YEARS) | | | Total |
	<30 (U)	30–45 (B)	>45 (O)	
Male (M)	60	20	40	120
Female (F)	40	30	10	80
Total	100	50	50	200

Because there are 200 people, there are 200 possible outcomes to this experiment. All 200 outcomes are equally likely (the person is randomly selected), so the classical definition proves an easy way of determining probabilities.

The probability of any one single event used to define the contingency table is a **marginal probability.** When you use a contingency table, you can obtain the marginal probabilities by merely counting. For example, of the 200 purchasers, 120 are males. So the probability of selecting a male is

$$P(M) = 120/200 = .6$$

Similarly,

$$P(F) = 80/200 = .4$$

$$P(U) = .5$$

$$P(B) = .25$$

$$P(O) = .25$$

Notice that $P(O) = 50/200 = .25$, which implies that (1) if you repeatedly selected a person at random from this group, 25% of the time the person selected would be over 45 years of age, and (2) 25% of the people in this group are over 45 years old. So a probability here is simply a **proportion.**

COMPLEMENT OF AN EVENT. The **complement** of an event A is the event that A does *not* occur. This event is denoted by $\overline{A}$. For example, A = it rains tomorrow, $\overline{A}$ = it does not rain tomorrow; or A = stock market rises tomorrow, $\overline{A}$ = stock market does not rise tomorrow.

In our Datacomp survey, $P(M) = .6$, and so

$$P(\overline{M}) = P(F) = .4$$

Notice that $P(M) + P(\overline{M}) = .6 + .4 = 1.0$. In general, for any event A, either A or $\overline{A}$ must occur. Consequently,

$$P(A) + P(\overline{A}) = 1$$

and so

$$P(\overline{A}) = 1 - P(A)$$

Written another way,

$$P(A) = 1 - P(\overline{A})$$

How can we determine what proportion of the purchasers are age 45 or younger?

$$P(\overline{O}) = 1 - P(O) = 1 - .25 = .75$$

JOINT PROBABILITY

What if we wish to know the probability of selecting a purchaser who is female *and* under age 30? Such a person is selected if events F and U occur. This probability is written $P(F$ and $U)$ and is referred to as a **joint probability.*** There are 40 purchasers who are female and under 30, so

$$P(F \text{ and } U) = 40/200 = .2$$

What proportion are males between 30 and 45? This is the same as

$$P(M \text{ and } B) = 20/200 = .1$$

because 20 out of 200 satisfy both requirements.

---

* The joint probability of events A and B is often written as $P(A \cap B)$, read as "the probability of A intersect B."

PROBABILITY OF *A* OR *B*

In addition to calculating joint probabilities involving two events, we can also determine the probability that *either* of the two events will occur. In our discussion, "either *A* or *B*" will refer to the event that *A* occurred, *B* occurred, or both occurred. This probability is written as

$$P(A \text{ or } B)$$

for any two events *A* and *B*.*

Now we will calculate the probability of selecting someone who is a male *or* under 30 years of age. This is $P(M \text{ or } U)$. How many people qualify? There are 120 males and there are 100 people under 30. Is the answer $(120 + 100)/200 = 1.1$? You should realize that this is not correct, because *a probability is never greater than 1*. What is the mistake here? The problem is that the 60 males under age 30 were counted *twice*. How many purchasers are male or under 30? The answer is the 120 males plus the 40 females under age 30. So

$$P(M \text{ or } U) = (120 + 40)/200 = .8$$

What is $P(F \text{ or } B)$? In Table 4.1, the 80 females and 20 of the males qualify. So,

$$P(F \text{ or } B) = (80 + 20)/200 = .5$$

CONDITIONAL PROBABILITY

Suppose that someone has some inside information about who has been selected from the group of 200 purchasers. This person informs you that the selected individual is under 30 years of age; that is, event *U* occurred. Armed with this information, we can calculate the probability that the selected person is a male. Given that event *U* occurred, we have immediately narrowed the number of possible outcomes from 200 to the 100 people under age 30. Each of these 100 people is equally likely to be chosen, and 60 of them are male. So the answer is $60/100 = .6$.

Whenever you are given information and are asked to find a probability based on this information, the result is a **conditional probability.** This probability is written as

$$P(A \mid B)$$

where *B* is the event that you know occurred and *A* is the uncertain event whose probability you need, given that event *B* has occurred. The vertical line indicates that the occurrence of event *B* is given, so the expression is read as the "probability of *A* given *B*." In the example, $P(M \mid U) = .6$.

Suppose that you were given *no information* about *U* and were asked to find the probability that a male is selected. This is a marginal probability. We earlier determined that $P(M) = .6$. For our example, note that

$$P(M) = P(M \mid U) = .6$$

This means that being given the information that the person selected is under 30 has *no effect* on the probability that a male is selected. In other words, whether *U* happens has no effect on whether *M* occurs. Such events are said to be independent. *Thus, events* A *and* B *are* **independent** *if the probability of event* A *is unaffected by the occurrence or nonoccurrence of event* B.

There are a number of ways to demonstrate that any two events *A* and *B* are independent.

DEFINITION

Events *A* and *B* are **independent** if and only if:

1. $P(A \mid B) = P(A)$ (assuming $P(B) \neq 0$), or   **(4.3)**
2. $P(B \mid A) = P(B)$ (assuming $P(A) \neq 0$), or   **(4.4)**
3. $P(A \text{ and } B) = P(A) \cdot P(B)$.   **(4.5)**

---

* The probability $P(A \text{ or } B)$ can be written as $P(A \cup B)$, read as "the probability of *A* union *B*."

You need not demonstrate all three conditions. If one of the equations is true, they are all true; if one is false, they are all false (in which case A and B are not independent). Events that are not independent are **dependent** events.

In our example, are events F and O independent? We previously showed that

$$P(O) = 50/200 = .25$$

Since $P(O \mid F) = 10/80 = .125$, then $P(O) \neq P(O \mid F)$, and these events are dependent. Put another way, if someone informs you that event F (a female) has occurred, this *does* have an effect on whether the person selected is over 45 years of age. If you are told that F occurred, the probability that the selected person is over 45 *drops* from .25 to .125. These events do affect each other and so are dependent events.

We could also approach this by showing that $P(F \mid O)$ is not the same as $P(F)$:

$$P(F \mid O) = 10/50 = .2$$
$$P(F) = 80/200 = .4$$

These are not the same values, so events F and O are not independent.

The final option is to show that $P(F \text{ and } O)$ is not the same as $P(F) \cdot P(O)$. This follows since

$$P(F \text{ and } O) = 10/200 = .05$$
$$P(F) \cdot P(O) = (.4)(.25) = .1$$

In our discussion of joint probabilities, we showed that

$$P(F \text{ and } U) = 40/200 = .2$$

Consequently, events F and U *can both occur* because their joint probability is not zero.

How would you calculate $P(F \text{ and } M)$? One cannot be both a male and a female, so $P(F \text{ and } M) = 0$. Because events M and F cannot both occur, these events are said to be mutually exclusive.

DEFINITION

Events A and B are **mutually exclusive** if A and B cannot both occur simultaneously. To demonstrate that two events A and B are mutually exclusive, you must show that their joint probability is zero: $P(A \text{ and } B) = 0$.

EXAMPLE 4.1

The quality-improvement department of Lectron has selected 10 devices for testing purposes. Which of these outcomes are mutually exclusive?

A = exactly one device is defective
B = more than two devices are defective
C = fewer than four devices are defective

SOLUTION

A and B are mutually exclusive events—they cannot both occur.
A and C are *not* mutually exclusive—if A occurs, so does event C.
B and C are *not* mutually exclusive—if three devices are defective, both events B and C will occur.

By "not mutually exclusive" we do not mean that both of these events *must* occur, only that both *could* occur. *Also, be sure to distinguish between the terms mutually exclusive and independent.* Loosely, mutually exclusive means that they cannot both occur and independent means that one event occurring has no effect on the other. For example, when drawing a single card from a deck of 52 playing cards, the events K = drawing a king and

H = drawing a heart are *not* mutually exclusive since they can both occur, namely when drawing the king of hearts. However, they *are* independent, since $P(K) = 4/52 = 1/13$ (there are four kings out of 52 cards), and $P(K \mid H) = 1/13$ (there are 13 hearts and one of them is a king). Consequently, knowing that a heart was selected has *no effect* on whether this card was a king, and so these events are independent.

SUMMARY OF PROBABILITY DEFINITIONS

1. **Experiment:** An experiment is any process that yields a measurement (observation).
2. **Outcome:** An outcome is any particular result of an experiment.
3. **Event:** An event consists of one or more possible outcomes of an experiment.
4. **Complement:** The complement of event A is the event that A does not occur. This is written $\overline{A}$.
5. **Mutually exclusive events:** Two events are mutually exclusive if they cannot both occur simultaneously.
6. **Independent events:** Two events are independent if the probability of one event occurring is unaffected by the occurrence or nonoccurrence of the other.
7. **Probability:** A probability is a measure of the likelihood that an event will occur when the experiment is performed.
8. **Marginal probability:** A marginal probability is the probability that any one single event used to define a contingency table will occur.
9. **Joint probability:** The joint probability of events A and B is the probability that both A and B will occur. This is written as $P(A$ and $B)$.
10. **Conditional probability:** The conditional probability of A given B is the probability that event A occurs given that event B occurs. This is written $P(A \mid B)$.

EXERCISES 4.1–4.15

UNDERSTANDING THE MECHANICS

4.1 Assume that there are only four distinct possible outcomes in an experiment: $A, B, C,$ and D. Explain what is incorrect about each of the following sets of assigned probabilities.
   a. $P(A) = .25$ $P(B) = 1.25$ $P(C) = .50$ $P(D) = .25$
   b. $P(A) = .15$ $P(B) = .01$ $P(C) = .01$ $P(D) = .01$
   c. $P(A) = .40$ $P(B) = .40$ $P(C) = .40$ $P(D) = .40$

4.2 Let Event A consist of the numbers 1, 2, and 3. Let Event B consist of the numbers 2, 3, and 4. Assume that each number is equally likely to occur.
   a. What is the probability of A?
   b. What is the probability of B?
   c. What is the probability of A and B?
   d. What is the probability of the complement of A?

4.3 Let A and B be two events such that $P(A$ or $B) = .60$, $P(A$ and $B) = .10$, $P(A \mid B) = .25$, $P(B \mid A) = .333$, $P(\overline{A}) = .70$, and $P(\overline{B}) = .60$.
   a. What is the joint probability of events A and B?
   b. What is the probability of event A conditioned on the occurrence of event B?
   c. What is the probability of either event A or event B occurring?
   d. What is the probability that event A does *not* occur?

4.4 Events A and B are independent. The probability of A occurring is .4, and the probability of B occurring is .6.
   a. What is the probability of both A and B occurring?
   b. What is the probability of A occurring if B is known to have occurred?
   c. What is the probability of B occurring if A is known to have occurred?

APPLYING THE NEW CONCEPTS

4.5 Let A represent freshmen and B represent both juniors and seniors at a community college with various undergraduate programs. Are A and B mutually exclusive? What is the complement of A? Are the complement of A and the complement of B mutually exclusive?

4.6 Four hundred randomly sampled automobile owners were asked whether they selected the particular make and model of their present car mainly because of its appearance or because of its performance. The results were as follows:

Owner	Appearance	Performance	Totals
Male	95	55	150
Female	85	165	250

   a. What is the probability that an automobile owner buys a car mainly for its appearance?
   b. What is the probability that an automobile owner buys a car mainly for its appearance and the automobile owner is a male?
   c. What is the probability that a female automobile owner purchases the car mainly because of its appearance?

4.7 A quality-control engineer summarized the frequency of the type of defect with the manufacturing of a certain motor. The following table shows which of three shifts was responsible for the type of defect.

	Type of Defect				
Shift	Misaligned Component	Missing Component	Measurement Outside of Specification Limits	Other	Total
1	23	13	12	14	62
2	15	15	18	12	60
3	5	11	10	2	28

a. What is the probability that a defective motor will have a measurement outside of its specification limits?

b. What is the probability that a defective motor was not produced by Shift 1?

c. What is the probability that a defective motor produced by Shift 3 does not have a misaligned component?

d. What is the probability that a defective motor has a misaligned component or was produced by Shift 1?

4.8 The employment center at a university wanted to know the proportion of students who worked and also the proportion of those who lived in the dorm. The following data were collected:

	Work Situation			
Living Arrangements	Full Time	Part Time	Do Not Work	Total
In dorm	19	22	20	61
Not in dorm	25	9	5	39
				100

a. What is the probability of selecting a student at random who works either full or part time?

b. What is the probability that a student who works lives in the dorm?

c. What is the probability that a student either works full time or does not live in the dorm?

d. Is the event that a student lives in the dorm independent of the event that a student works full time? Discuss what your answer means.

4.9 An investment newsletter writer wanted to know in which investment areas her subscribers were most interested. A questionnaire was sent to 331 randomly selected professional clients, with the following results:

	Investment Area					
Business	Stocks	Bonds	Commercial Paper	Commodities	Stock Options	Total
Doctors	30	25	15	2	0	72
Lawyers	29	34	12	0	5	80
Bankers	50	35	29	5	10	129
Others	21	14	10	3	2	50
						331

a. What is the probability that an investment client is neither a doctor nor a lawyer?

b. What is the probability that an investment client is a banker and that the investment client's main investment interest is in commodities?

c. If an investment client's main investment interest is commodities, what is the probability that he or she is a banker?

d. What is the probability that an investment client's main investment interest is not in stock options?

e. Let A be the event that an investment client is a lawyer. Let B be the event that an investment client's main investment interest is in commodities. Are the events A and B mutually exclusive?

4.10 If events A and B are mutually exclusive, is the occurrence of event A affected by the occurrence of event B? Can one say that if two events are mutually exclusive, they are not independent?

4.11 A random sample of Americans were asked the question, "Do you approve or disapprove of a new Federal tax code that applies one low tax rate to all Americans?" Assume that the results of 2,000 Americans are as follows.

Political Party	Approve	Disapprove	Don't Know
Democrat	576	313	111
Republican	656	251	93

(Source: *The Washington Times,* "Backing the Flat Tax," April 15, 1998, p. A10.)

Suppose that one of the 2,000 Americans in the survey is selected at random.

a. What is the probability that the participant is a Democrat and disapproves?

b. What is the probability that the participant is either a Republican or approves or doesn't know?

c. What is the probability that the participant either approves or disapproves and is a Democrat?

4.12 The table below lists the number of stocks on the most active list for May 13, 1998, on both the NYSE and the NASDAQ. Category A is used to represent a stock that has at least 15 million shares traded. Category B is used to represent a stock that has at least 10 million but less than 15 million shares traded. Category C is used to represent a stock that has at least 5 million but less than 10 million shares traded.

Category	NYSE	NASDAQ
A	1	4
B	2	4
C	8	5

(Adapted from *The Wall Street Journal,* "Most Active Issues," May 14, 1998, p. C2.)

a. Suppose that a stock is selected from one of the most actives listed in the table. What is the probability that the stock has at least 5 million but less than 10 million shares traded and is not listed on the NYSE?

b. What is the probability that a stock randomly selected from the table above is listed on the NASDAQ or has traded at least 15 million shares?

c. If a stock randomly selected from the table is listed on the NASDAQ, what is the probability that it has traded at least 10 million shares?

4.13 A listing of the top 21 companies in the world with respect to market value reveals a strong showing by American firms. The letter A is assigned to companies with a market value at least $150 billion. The letter B is assigned to companies with a market value at least $100 billion but less than $150 billion. And the letter C designates a company with a market value less than $100 billion.

Company	European/Asian/ American	Market Value Classification
General Electric	American	A
Coca-Cola	American	A
Royal Dutch/Shell	European	A
NTT	Asian	A
Microsoft	American	B
Exxon	American	B
Intel	American	B
Toyota Motor	Asian	B
Merck	American	B
Philip Morris	American	B
Novartis	European	C
Proctor & Gamble	American	C
IBM	American	C
Roche Holding	European	C
Bank of Tokyo-Mitsubishi	Asian	C
HSBC Holdings	European	C
Johnson & Johnson	American	C
Bristol-Myers Squibb	American	C
Glaxo Wellcome	European	C
Wal-Mart Stores	European	C
British Petroleum	European	C

(Adapted from *Business Week,* "The Top 100 Companies," July 7, 1997, p. 53.)

a. Construct a contingency table with the rows listed as European/Asian/American and the columns listed as A/B/C. Use the the KGP menu in Excel to form the contingency table by clicking on **KGP Data Analysis ➤ Qualitative Data Charts ➤ Contingency Table.**

b. Suppose one company is randomly selected from the list of 21 companies. What is the probability that the company is European or is classified as a B with respect to market value?

c. Let Event 1 be the event that a company selected at random is classified as a C and is American. Let Event 2 be the event that a company is selected at random is classified as a B and is either European or Asian. Are Event 1 and Event 2 mutually exclusive? Are the events independent?

4.14 If the probability that it is going to rain today is .3, what can you say about the probability that it is not going to rain today?

4.15 Give an example of two events that are mutually exclusive. Explain why they are mutually exclusive. Give an example of two events that are independent. Explain why they are independent.

4.3 Going Beyond the Contingency Table

Our Datacomp survey served as an intuitive introduction to probability definitions. The classical approach was used to derive probabilities by dividing the number of outcomes favorable to an event by the total number of (equally likely) outcomes. Not all probability problems, however, are concerned with randomly selecting an individual from a contingency table.

When dealing with two or more events in general, one approach is to illustrate these events by means of a **Venn diagram.** A Venn diagram representing any two events A and B is shown in Figure 4.1.

In a Venn diagram, the probability of an event occurring is its corresponding area. This may sound complicated, but it really is not. The Venn diagram for $P(A) = .4$ is shown in Figure 4.2. The area of the rectangle is 1; it represents all possible outcomes. The shaded area is the complement of A, namely, $\overline{A}$. Here, $P(\overline{A}) = 1 - P(A) = 1 - .4 = .6$. No effort is made to construct a circle with an area of .4; it is simply labeled .4. The shaded area then represents $\overline{A}$, and the corresponding area must be .6.

Figure 4.3 shows $P(A \text{ and } B)$, and Figure 4.4 shows $P(A \text{ or } B)$.

If A and B are mutually exclusive (they cannot both occur), then $P(A \text{ and } B) = 0$. For example, an auto dealer has data that indicate that 20% of all new cars ordered contain a red interior and 25% have a blue interior. Only one interior color is allowed. Let A be the

FIGURE 4.1

Venn diagram for events A and B. The rectangle represents all possible outcomes of an experiment.

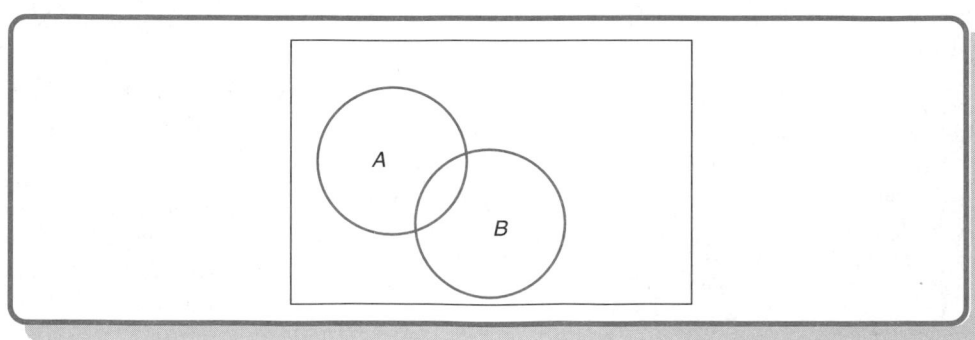

FIGURE 4.2

Venn diagram for $P(A) = .4$.

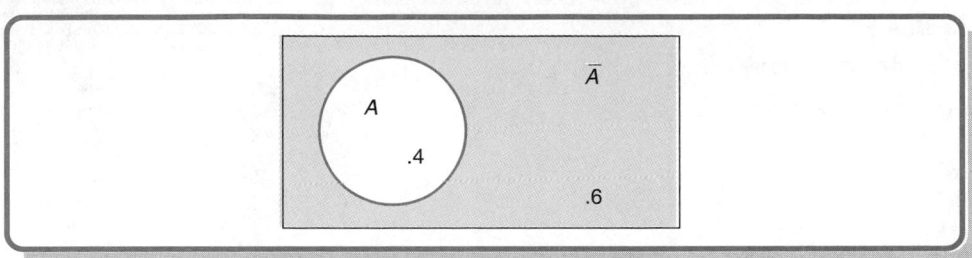

FIGURE 4.3

$P(A$ and $B)$. The points in the shaded area are in A and B.

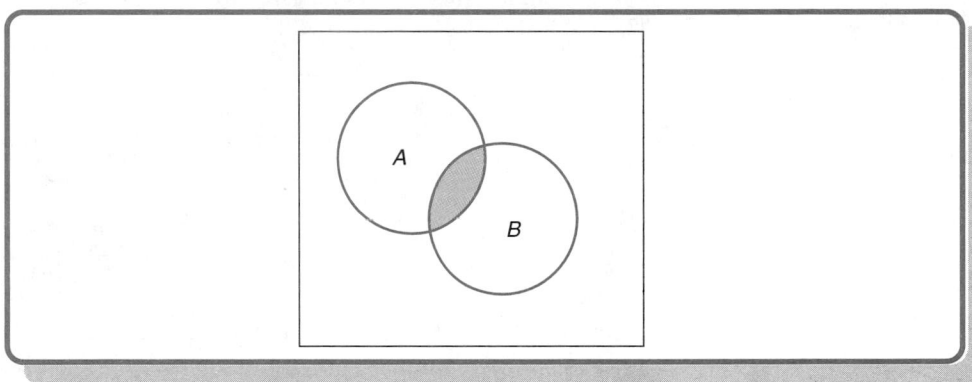

FIGURE 4.4

$P(A$ or $B)$. The points in the shaded area are in A or B.

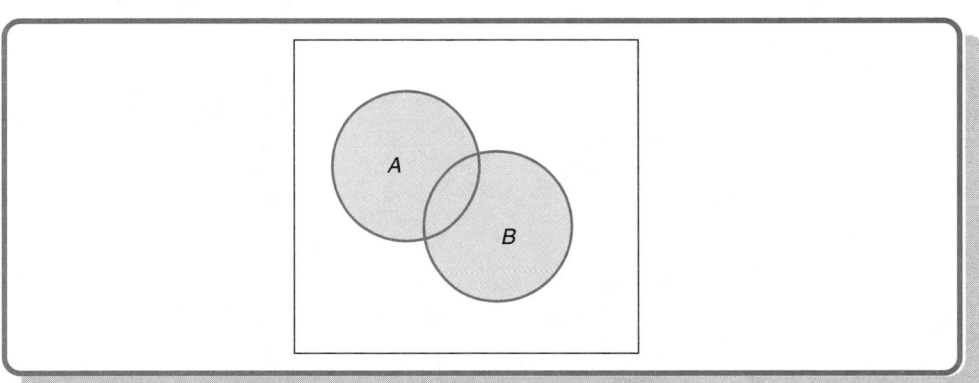

FIGURE 4.5

Venn diagram of mutually exclusive events.
$P(A$ and $B) = 0$.
$P(A$ or $B) = P(A) + P(B)$
$= .2 + .25 = .45$.

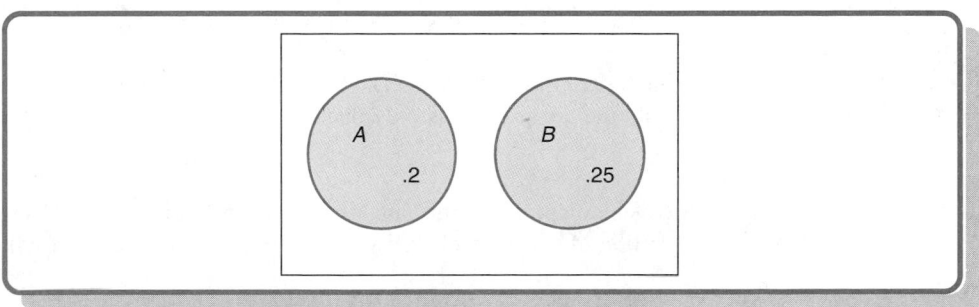

event that a red interior is selected and B be the event that a blue interior is selected. A Venn diagram for this situation is shown in Figure 4.5.

Each person can select only one color, so events A and B are mutually exclusive, and the resulting circles do not overlap in the Venn diagram. What is the probability that a person selects red *or* blue? This is $P(A$ or $B)$ and is represented by the shaded area in the circles in Figure 4.5. The Venn diagram allows us to see clearly that this shaded area is $P(A) + P(B) = .2 + .25 = .45$. In other words, 45% of the people will purchase either red or blue interiors. We thus have the following rule.

FIGURE 4.6
A Venn diagram illustrating
$P(A$ or $B)$ and $P(A$ and $B)$.

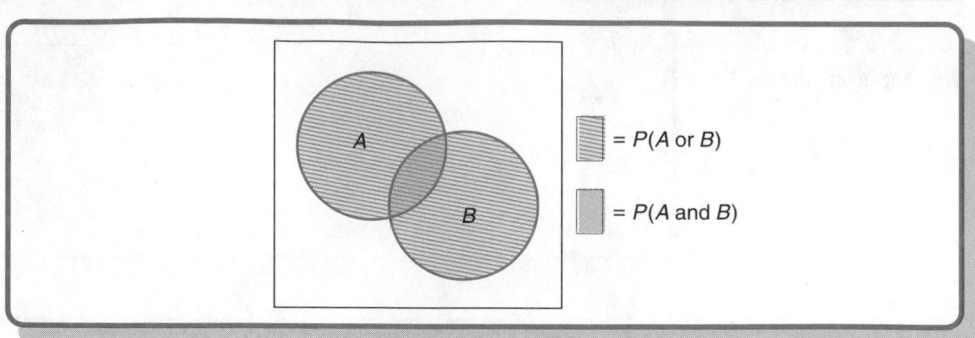

SPECIAL CASE

If events A and B are **mutually exclusive,** then

$$P(A \text{ or } B) = P(A) + P(B) \qquad \qquad \textbf{(4.6)}$$

This rule does *not* work when A and B can both occur, but there is an easy way to devise another solution. Look at the Venn diagram for this situation, shown in Figure 4.6. By adding $P(A) + P(B)$, we do not obtain $P(A$ or $B)$ because we have counted $P(A$ and $B)$ *twice.* So we need to subtract $P(A$ and $B)$ to obtain the actual area corresponding to $P(A$ or $B)$. This is the **additive rule of probability.**

ADDITIVE RULE

For **any** two events, A and $B,$

$$P(A \text{ or } B) = P(A) + P(B) - P(A \text{ and } B) \qquad \qquad \textbf{(4.7)}$$

Notice that if A and B are mutually exclusive, then $P(A$ and $B) = 0$, and we obtain the previous rule; namely, that $P(A$ or $B) = P(A) + P(B)$.

EXAMPLE 4.2

Draw a single card from a deck of 52 playing cards. Let Q be the event that the card is a queen and H be the event that the card is a heart. What is $P(Q$ or $H)$?

SOLUTION

First, determine $P(Q$ and $H)$. $P(Q$ and $H)$ is the probability of selecting a queen of hearts from the deck. There is only one such card, so

$$P(Q \text{ and } H) = 1/52$$

A Venn diagram for this situation is shown in Figure 4.7. Using the additive rule, the proportion of draws (probability) on which a queen *or* a heart will be selected from the deck is

$$P(Q \text{ or } H) = P(Q) + P(H) - P(Q \text{ and } H)$$

$$= 4/52 + 13/52 - 1/52$$

$$= 16/52$$

FIGURE 4.7

$P(Q) = 4/52$; $P(H) = 13/52$.

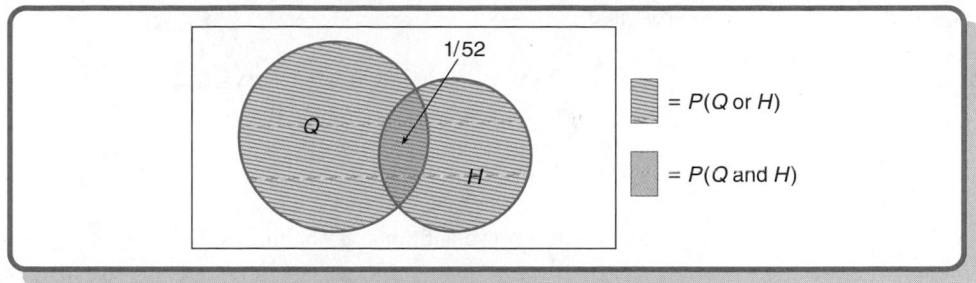

FIGURE 4.8

A Venn diagram illustrating a conditional probability.

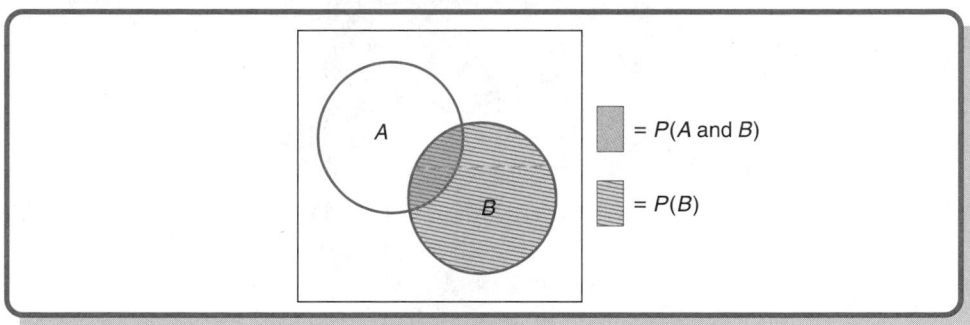

Refer back to the Datacomp survey data in Table 4.1. Does the additive rule work here also? It does—this rule works for *any* two events—but it certainly is a hard way to solve this problem. Suppose we want to find the probability (from our previous example) that the person selected is a male or is under age 30. By inspection, we previously found that

$$P(M \text{ or } U) = 160/200 = .8$$

Using the additive rule, we obtain the same result:

$$P(M \text{ or } U) = P(M) + P(U) - P(M \text{ and } U)$$

$$= 120/200 + 100/200 - 60/200$$

$$= 160/200 = .8$$

CONDITIONAL PROBABILITIES

Using the Datacomp survey data, we found that the probability the person selected is a male (M), given the information that the person selected is under 30 (U), was ($M \mid U$) = .6. Our reasoning here was: (1) There are 100 people under 30 years of age, (2) 60 of them are male, (3) each of these 100 people is equally likely to be selected, and so (4) the result is 60/100 = .6. Notice that

$$P(U) = 100/200 = .5$$

$$P(M \text{ and } U) = 60/200 = .3$$

$$P(M \mid U) = P(M \text{ and } U)/P(U) = .3/.5 = .6$$

This procedure for finding a conditional probability applies to *any* two events. Use the Venn diagram in Figure 4.8 to determine $P(A \mid B)$. Given the information that event B occurred, we are immediately restricted to the lined area (B). What is the probability that a point in B is also in A (that is, event A occurs)? A point is also in A if it lies in the shaded area, and

$$P(A \mid B) = \frac{\text{shaded area}}{\text{striped area}}$$

$$= \frac{P(A \text{ and } B)}{P(B)}$$

This is the rule for conditional probabilities.

RULE FOR CONDITIONAL PROBABILITIES

For any two events, A and B,

$$P(A \mid B) = \frac{P(A \text{ and } B)}{P(B)} \qquad (P(B) \neq 0) \qquad \textbf{(4.8)}$$

and

$$P(B \mid A) = \frac{P(A \text{ and } B)}{P(A)} \qquad (P(A) \neq 0) \qquad \textbf{(4.9)}$$

INDEPENDENT EVENTS

In the Datacomp example, equations 4.3, 4.4, and 4.5 provided a summary of how to demonstrate that two events are independent. *One need demonstrate only that one of these equations holds to verify independence.* These three methods of proving independence apply to *any two events,* not just to contingency table applications.

To summarize, events A and B are **independent** if any of the following statements can be verified:

$$P(A \mid B) = P(A)$$

$$P(B \mid A) = P(B)$$

$$P(A \text{ and } B) = P(A) \cdot P(B)$$

In many situations, it is unnecessary (or impossible) to prove independence of two events. However, one can often argue convincingly that two events are independent or dependent without resorting to a mathematical proof. Consider these events:

A = Procter and Gamble's new laundry detergent will capture at least 5% of the market next year

and

B = General Motors will introduce a new line of compact automobiles next year

Whether event B happens should have no effect on whether event A occurs. So $P(A \mid B) = P(A)$, and these events are independent. Next, change event A to: Toyota automobile sales will drop next year. Now whether event B occurs could very well have an effect on whether event A occurs. It is not safe to assume that $P(A \mid B) = P(A)$—it seems reasonable that $P(A \mid B)$ is *larger* than $P(A)$. Notice that we have not discussed the values of $P(A)$ and $P(A \mid B)$. The probability values are not necessary to show that the events are dependent. The important thing is that $P(A \mid B) \neq P(A)$, so these events are clearly dependent events.

JOINT PROBABILITIES

The rule for conditional probabilities in equations 4.8 and 4.9 can be rewritten as

MULTIPLICATIVE RULE

For any two events A and B,

$$P(A \text{ and } B) = P(A \mid B) \cdot P(B) \tag{4.10}$$

$$= P(B \mid A) \cdot P(A) \tag{4.11}$$

This is the **multiplicative rule of probability.** Using equation 4.5, we also have the following rule for two independent events.

SPECIAL CASE

For any two independent events A and B,

$$P(A \text{ and } B) = P(A) \cdot P(B) \tag{4.12}$$

You may be wondering how we can use the same equation to define the rule for $P(A \mid B)$ (equation 4.8) and the rule for $P(A \text{ and } B)$ (equation 4.10). This is not a bad question! It appears that we have used the same rule twice to make two different statements—and in fact we have. However, for any application you encounter, either $P(A \mid B)$ or $P(A \text{ and } B)$ must be provided or can be determined without resorting to formulas. We can clarify this using our card-drawing example:

$$Q = \text{select a queen}$$

$$H = \text{select a heart}$$

Here $P(Q \text{ and } H)$ (the probability of selecting a queen of hearts) is 1/52. No formulas were necessary to determine this, only a little head-scratching.

Now, what is $P(Q \mid H)$? Using equation 4.8,

$$P(Q \mid H) = P(Q \text{ and } H)/P(H)$$

$$= (1/52)/(13/52)$$

$$= 1/13$$

REPLACEMENT IN SAMPLING

Assume that you select a card from a deck, examine it, and then discard it. You then select another card. This procedure is called **sampling without replacement.** Let

$$A = \text{selecting a queen on the first draw}$$

$$B = \text{selecting a queen on the second draw}$$

What is the probability of drawing two queens [$P(A \text{ and } B)$]? If you selected a queen on the first draw, then, of the 51 cards remaining, three are queens. So $P(B \mid A) = 3/51$. Again, we used no formulas.

Next, we use the multiplicative rule, equation 4.11:

$$P(A \text{ and } B) = P(B \mid A) \cdot P(A)$$

$$= \left(\frac{3}{51} \right) \cdot \left(\frac{4}{52} \right) \cong .0045$$

Notice that $P(A) = 4/52$ because there are four queens available on the first draw. So you would expect to draw two queens from a card deck about 45 times out of 10,000, if you are drawing without replacement.

Now suppose you select a card from a deck but replace it before selecting the second card. This procedure is called **sampling with replacement.** What is $P(B \mid A)$? There are still 52 cards in the deck when you select your second card, and four of these are queens. So

$$P(B \mid A) = 4/52 = P(B)$$

If event A occurs, the probability of a queen on the second draw is unaffected. This probability is 4/52 *whether or not A* occurs; these events are now independent. For this situation,

$$P(A \text{ and } B) = P(A \mid B) \cdot P(B)$$

$$= P(A) \cdot P(B) \qquad \text{(since they are independent)}$$

$$= 4/52 \cdot 4/52 = .0059$$

The probability of getting two queens is higher when drawing cards with replacement— not a surprising result.

MICROSOFT® EXCEL APPLICATION   USE DATA4-3

EXAMPLE 4.3
Using Excel to Construct a Contingency Table

A quality engineer at Microtek obtained a random sample of 200 electrical components produced over a one-week period. Each component was inspected and classified as (1) OK, (2) OK after the component was reworked (repaired), or (3) scrap (unusable). The engineer also made note of which of the three Microtek plants produced the component: Memphis, Miami, or Pittsburgh. The sample information was stored in two columns in dataset DATA4-3, where

City = the city producing the component: 1 = Memphis
                                          2 = Miami
                                          3 = Pittsburgh

Quality = the component quality: 1 = OK
                                          2 = OK after rework
                                          3 = scrapped

Using Excel, construct a contingency table. (i) If a component is selected at random, determine the probability that this component is OK and produced in Miami. (ii) What percentage of the reworked components in the sample were produced in Memphis?

SOLUTION

To construct the contingency table using Excel, first open the Excel file DATA4-3 by clicking on the Open file icon and identifying the location of this file. You should then see the first two columns labeled "City" and "Quality" in Figure 4.9. The Excel Tool Pack does not contain a procedure for constructing a contingency table from these two columns; however, the KGP data analysis add-ins do allow you to do this. Click on **KGP Data Analysis ➤ Qualitative Data Charts ➤ Contingency Table.** It is important when using this procedure to make sure that the two columns of data contain labels in the top row ("City" and "Quality" here). Enter "A1:A201" in the top box. This is the input range for the row variable (City), and includes the label. Repeat this for the column variable (Quality) by typing "B1:B201" in the second box. Enter "A202" as the output range and click on "OK." You will obtain the output shown in Figure 4.9 by cutting and pasting the output in cells A202:E208 into cells C1:G7. To make this table easier to interpret, enter the city names in cells C4, C5, and C6 and the quality labels in cells D3, E3, and F3 (as in Figure 4.9).

FIGURE 4.9

Excel contingency table for Example 4.3.

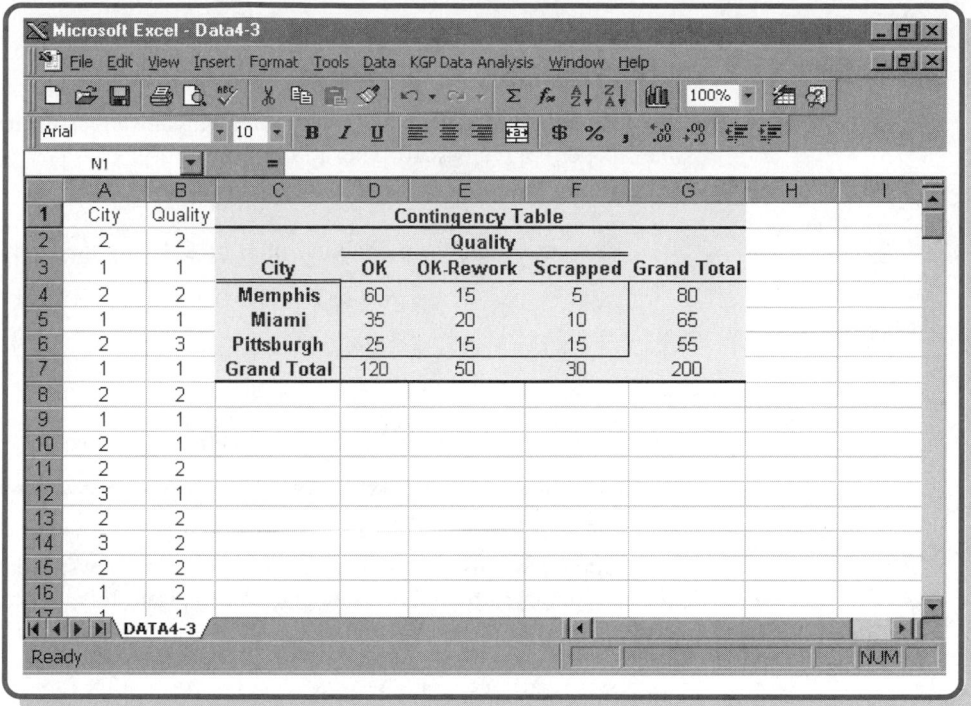

SOLUTION TO (i)

Thirty-five of the 200 components (in cell D5) are OK and produced in Miami, and so

$$P(\text{OK and Miami}) = 35/200 = .175$$

That is, 17.5% of the components are OK *and* produced in Miami.

SOLUTION TO (ii)

There are 50 reworked components in the sample, 15 of which were produced in Memphis. Consequently,

$$P(\text{Memphis} \mid \text{reworked}) = 15/50 = .3$$

That is, 30% of the reworked components were produced in Memphis.

4.4 APPLYING THE CONCEPTS

USING THE FORMULAS

EXAMPLE 4.4

In a particular city, 20% of the people subscribe to the morning newspaper, 30% subscribe to the evening newspaper, and 10% subscribe to both. Determine the probability that an individual from this city subscribes to the morning newspaper, the evening newspaper, or both.

SOLUTION

The most important step in solving a wordy probability problem is to set up the problem correctly. Your first step should always be to define the events clearly using capital letters. Your initial step should be to define

$$M = \text{person subscribes to the morning newspaper}$$

$$E = \text{person subscribes to the evening newspaper}$$

We do not need to define another event for a person subscribing to both newspapers, as we shall see.

We now have

$$P(M) = .2$$

$$P(E) = .3$$

The probability that a selected individual subscribes to the morning *and* the evening newspaper is given as .10. This a *joint* probability:

$$P(M \text{ and } E) = .1$$

We want to find the probability of *M* or *E*. Using the additive rule,

$$P(M \text{ or } E) = P(M) + P(E) - P(M \text{ and } E)$$

$$= .2 + .3 - .1$$

$$= .4$$

So 40% of the people in this city subscribe to at least one of the two newspapers.

Suppose we also know that 1/3 of the evening newspaper subscribers are also morning newspaper subscribers. How can you translate this statement into a probability? We can restate the preceding sentence as "Given that a randomly selected individual subscribes to the evening newspaper, the probability that this person also subscribes to the morning newspaper is 1/3." In other words, this is a *conditional* probability:

$$P(M \mid E) = 1/3$$

EXAMPLE 4.5

Referring to the subscription data in Example 4.4, what percentage of the evening subscribers do not subscribe to the morning newspaper?

SOLUTION 1

A Venn diagram for this problem is shown in Figure 4.10. Notice that *M* (the morning subscribers) is made up of two components: (1) those people in *E* (the evening subscribers) and (2) those not in *E*. Since $P(M \text{ and } E) = .1.$, the area of *M* that is striped is

$$P(M) - P(M \text{ and } E) = P(M \text{ and } \bar{E})$$

$$= .2 - .1 = .1$$

Similarly, the area of *E* that is striped is

$$P(E) - P(M \text{ and } E) = P(\bar{M} \text{ and } E)$$

$$= .3 - .1 = .2$$

FIGURE 4.10

Venn diagram for Example 4.5.

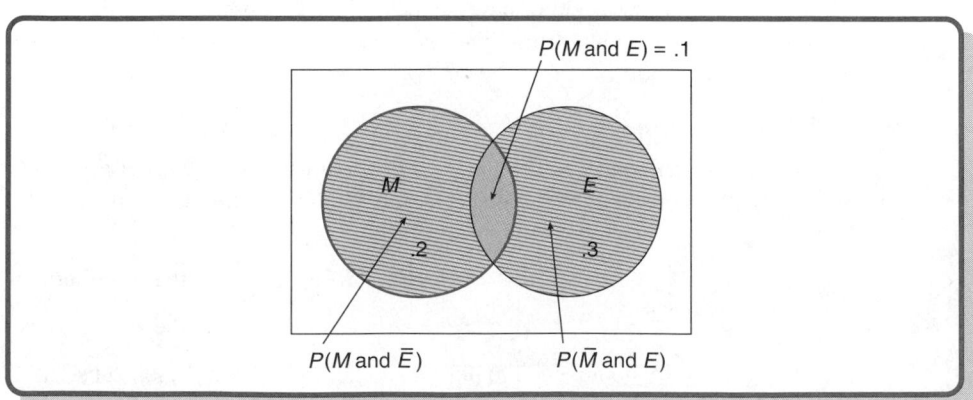

Our question could be stated, "Given that a person subscribes to the evening newspaper, what is the probability that this person does not subscribe to the morning newspaper?" This is the *conditional* probability

$$P(\bar{M} \mid E)$$

Look at the Venn diagram. You know that E occurred, so the outcome is in the E circle. What is the probability that the outcome is not in M? We know that the total area of E is .3 and that the area that is not in M but is in E is .2. So

$$P(\bar{M} \mid E) = .2/.3 = 2/3$$

Another approach here is to utilize the formulas in the section by noting that given event E has occurred, either event M occurs or it doesn't. Consequently,

$$P(\bar{M} \mid E) = 1 - P(M \mid E)$$

$$= 1 - [P(M \text{ and } E)]/P(E)$$

$$= 1 - (.1/.3) = 2/3$$

USING A CONTINGENCY TABLE

SOLUTION 2

Although Example 4.4 made no mention of a random sample, a useful device here is to imagine that a random sample of, say, $n = 100$ people is obtained (actually, any sample size (n) could be used). Next, construct a contingency table like the one in Section 4.2, by *assuming that the population percentages given in the problem apply to these 100 people.* In Example 4.4, we would assume that 20% of the sample (20 people) subscribe to the morning newspaper and 30% of the sample (30 people) subscribe to the evening newspaper. So far, the contingency table would be

	M	$\bar{M}$	
E			30
$\bar{E}$			
	20		100

Since the sample size is 100, the totals for $\bar{M}$ and $\bar{E}$ are 80 and 70, respectively, producing the following table:

	M	$\bar{M}$	
E			30
$\bar{E}$			70
	20	80	100

The final piece of information is that 10% of the people (10 people) subscribe to *both* newspapers. So 10 people are in the cell in the upper left corner, corresponding to E and M, and the table is now

	M	$\bar{M}$	
E	10		30
$\bar{E}$			70
	20	80	100

By using the row and column totals, the remaining cells can be filled in.*

	M	$\bar{M}$	
E	10	20	30
$\bar{E}$	10	60	70
	20	80	100

---

* This procedure is easier to apply and explain if the sample size (n) is chosen so that all numbers in the contingency table are counting numbers (integers).

Once the table is filled in, probabilities become very easy to derive via the approach used in Section 4.2. To illustrate, the solution to Example 4.4 is

$$P(M \text{ or } E) = \frac{10+10+20}{100} = \frac{40}{100} = .4$$

The conditional probability in Example 4.5 is

$$P(\overline{M} \mid E) = \frac{20}{30} = 2/3$$

since there are 30 people who subscribe to the evening newspaper (E), 20 of whom do not subscribe to the morning newspaper ($\overline{M}$).

HELPFUL HINTS FOR PROBABILITY APPLICATIONS

Using the Formulas
1. Define each event using capital letters.
2. Translate each statement into a probability. Does a particular statement tell you $P(A)$? $P(B)$? $P(A$ and $B)$? $P(A$ or $B)$? $P(A \mid B)$? $P(B \mid A)$?
3. Determine the answer by identifying the probability rule that applies and by using a Venn diagram. Using both allows you to check your logic and your arithmetic.

Using a Contingency Table
1. Select *any* sample size, say, $n = 100$ or 1000.
2. Using the information given, fill in the row and column totals.
3. Using the final piece of information given, fill in the appropriate cell and complete the contingency table.
4. Determine the answer by dividing the proper value by the appropriate total.

EXAMPLE 4.6

In a certain northeastern state that is going through financial difficulties, it is believed that 5% of the banks will fail. It is known that the deposits of 90% of the banks in this state are insured by the Federal Depository Insurance Company (FDIC). It is also believed, from past experience, that 3% of the banks protected by FDIC will fail. A bank examiner employed by the federal government would like to know:

1. What is the probability that, for a randomly chosen bank, the bank has deposits protected by FDIC and the bank will fail?
2. What is the probability that, for a randomly chosen bank, the bank has deposits covered by FDIC or the bank will fail?
3. What percentage of the banks that go under have deposits protected by FDIC?

USING THE FORMULAS

SOLUTION 1

The first step is to define appropriate events:

$$A = \text{bank has deposits protected by FDIC}$$

$$B = \text{bank will fail}$$

We now translate each of the statements into a probability. We have the following marginal probabilities:

$$P(A) = .90$$

$$P(B) = .05$$

The last statement in the problem can be written as "Given that a bank has accounts protected by FDIC, the probability that the bank will fail is .03." So this is a conditional probability, namely,

$$P(B \mid A) = .03$$

What does question 1 ask for? $P(A$ or $B)$? $P(A \mid B)$? $P(A$ and $B)$? The examiner wishes to know the probability that a bank is protected by FDIC *and* will fail. This is $P(A$ and $B)$. Using the multiplicative rule,

$$P(A \text{ and } B) = P(B \mid A) \cdot P(A)$$

$$= (.03)(.90) = .027$$

SOLUTION 2

For question 2, we wish to know the probability that A or B occurs. By the additive rule,

$$P(A \text{ or } B) = P(A) + P(B) - P(A \text{ and } B)$$

$$= .90 + .05 - .027 = .923$$

Thus, 92.3% of the banks are covered by the FDIC, will fail, or both.

SOLUTION 3

Question 3 can be phrased as, "Given that a bank has failed, what is the probability that this bank has deposits protected by FDIC?" This is $P(A \mid B)$.

$$P(A \mid B) = [P(A \text{ and } B)]/P(B) = .027/.05 = .54$$

Therefore, 54% of those banks that fail have deposits protected by FDIC.

USING A CONTINGENCY TABLE

To obtain a table containing all counting numbers, a sample size of $n = 1000$ is selected here. Remember that any sample size can be used with this approach. Five percent of the banks failed ($.05 \times 1000 = 50$ banks) and 90% of the banks are insured by FDIC ($.90 \times 1000 = 900$ banks). Filling in the remaining row and column totals, we get the following table:

	FDIC	$\overline{\text{FDIC}}$	
FAIL			50
$\overline{\text{FAIL}}$			950
	900	100	1000

Finally, 3% of the banks *protected by FDIC* failed. There are 900 banks protected by FDIC and so we find $.03 \times 900 = 27$ banks.* Thus, 27 of the banks are protected by FDIC and failed. This value goes into the upper left cell and the table is

	FDIC	$\overline{\text{FDIC}}$	
FAIL	27		50
$\overline{\text{FAIL}}$			950
	900	100	1000

Filling in the remaining cells, we get the following completed contingency table:

	FDIC	$\overline{\text{FDIC}}$	
FAIL	27	23	50
$\overline{\text{FAIL}}$	873	77	950
	900	100	1000

---

* A sample size of $n = 100$ would have produced a value of 2.7 here. The problem can still be solved using $n = 100$, but is easier to explain using counting numbers in each cell; hence, $n = 1000$ was selected.

SOLUTION 1
$$P(\text{FDIC and FAIL}) = 27/1000 = .027$$

SOLUTION 2
$$P(\text{FDIC or FAIL}) = \frac{27 + 873 + 23}{1000} = \frac{923}{1000} = .923$$

SOLUTION 3
$$P(\text{FDIC} \mid \text{FAIL}) = 27/50 = .54$$

since 50 of the banks failed, 27 of which are protected by FDIC.

EXERCISES 4.16–4.35

UNDERSTANDING THE MECHANICS

4.16 The probabilities of events A and B are .7 and .2, respectively. The probability of the intersection of A and B is .1.
   a. What is the probability of the union of A and B?
   b. What is the conditional probability of A given B?
   c. What is the conditional probability of B given A?

4.17 Let $A = \{1, 3, 5, 7, 9\}$ and $B = \{4, 5, 6\}$. An experiment results in any number between 1 and 10, inclusively, being randomly selected.
   a. Draw a Venn diagram.
   b. Find $P(A \text{ and } B)$.
   c. Find $P(\bar{A} \text{ and } \bar{B})$.
   d. Find $P(\bar{A} \mid B)$.

4.18 The probabilities of the independent events A and B are .3 and .6, respectively.
   a. What is the probability of A or B?
   b. What is the probability of A and B?
   c. What is the probability of A given B?
   d. What is the probability of B given A?
   e. What is the probability of neither A nor B occurring?

4.19 An experiment has the following outcomes and probabilities:

Outcome	Probability
2	.1
4	.2
6	.4
8	.2
10	.1

Let $A = \{2, 6, 8\}$ and $B = \{6, 8, 10\}$.
   a. Find the probability that either A or B occurs.
   b. Find the probability that B occurs if A occurs.
   c. Find the probability that A occurs and B does not occur.
   d. Find the probability that A occurs if B does not occur.

4.20 The probabilities of the independent events A and B are .4 and .5, respectively. Find the following probabilities.
   a. The probability of A and B occurring.
   b. The probability of A but not B occurring.
   c. The probability of A or B occurring.
   d. The probability of A or not B occurring.
   e. The probability of A occurring given that B has occurred.
   f. The probability of A occurring given that B has not occurred.

4.21 Assume that events A, B, C, and D are the only possible events to an experiment. Furthermore, assume that every pair of these events is mutually exclusive. The following probabilities are known:

$$P(A) = .20 \qquad P(B) = .30$$

Find the following probabilities.
   a. $P(A \text{ or } B)$
   b. $P(\bar{A})$
   c. $P(A \mid D)$
   d. $P(C \text{ or } D)$
   e. $P(C \text{ and } D)$
   f. $P(A \mid \bar{B})$
   g. $P(B \mid \bar{A})$

4.22 Let $P(A) = .6$, $P(B) = .2$, and $P(A \mid B) = .1$. Find the following probabilities.
   a. $P(A \text{ or } B)$
   b. $P(\bar{A} \text{ or } B)$
   c. $P(B \mid A)$
   d. $P(B \mid \bar{A})$
   e. $P(\bar{A} \text{ and } B)$
   f. $P(\bar{A} \text{ and } \bar{B})$
   g. $\overline{P(A \text{ or } B)}$
   h. $\overline{P(A \text{ and } B)}$

4.23 Do you have enough information to determine if A and B are mutually exclusive or are independent from the following: The probabilities of A and B are .7 and .5, respectively, and the probability of A or B occurring is .85? Why? (Hint: Can you find the probability of A and B?)

4.24 Define event A to consist of the even numbers from 1 to 20. Define B to consist of numbers that are multiples of 3 between 1 and 20. Assume that each number between 1 and 20 is equally likely to occur as the outcome to an experiment.
   a. Draw a Venn diagram representing the events.
   b. Find $P(A \text{ or } B)$.
   c. Find $P(A \mid B)$.
   d. Find $P(B \mid \bar{A})$.

APPLYING THE NEW CONCEPTS

4.25 A computer program generates integers randomly from 1 to 100. Even numbers therefore have the same probability of appearing as odd numbers. Assuming that the numbers generated are truly random and that the probability of one number appearing does not affect the probability of the next number generated, what is the probability that two generated numbers are even?

4.26 Two quality-control inspectors need to examine boxes of electrical components at random to determine if certain specifications are being met during the manufacturing process. Assume that the first inspector and the second inspector have a 90% and 60% chance, respectively, of noticing a flawed component if the component is truly flawed. Also, assume that the percentage of defective components in each box is 20%. The inspectors inspect only one component at random from each box.

a. If one of two inspectors is randomly selected to examine a box, what is the probability that a defective component will be noticed in that box?

b. If both inspectors inspect the same box, what is the probability that at least one will notice a defective component?

4.27 When high school teenagers were asked who has taught them the most about managing money, 73% percent said their parents. Suppose that 11% of the teenagers said that a relative other than their parents taught them the most about managing money. What is the probability that a high school teenager learned the most about money from someone other than the teenager's parents or relatives if it is known that the teenager did not learn the most about managing money from his/her parents?

(Source: *USA Today,* "Mom's the Money Teacher," May 8–10, 1998, p. 1A.)

4.28 At a certain university, 30% of the students major in mathematics. Of the students majoring in mathematics, 60% are males. Of all the students at the university, 70% are males.

a. What is the probability that a student selected at random in the university is a male majoring in mathematics?

b. What is the probability that a student selected at random in the university is a male or is majoring in mathematics?

c. What proportion of the males are majoring in mathematics?

4.29 At a semiconductor plant, 60% of the workers are skilled and 80% of the workers are full-time. Ninety percent of the skilled workers are full-time.

a. What is the probability that an employee selected at random is a skilled full-time employee?

b. What is the probability that an employee selected at random is a skilled worker or a full-time worker?

c. What percentage of the full-time workers are skilled?

4.30 An overwhelming number of video rental customers make the decision to rent a movie on the same day that they visit the store. This percentage is 84%. Of this group, 56% say that they make their decision on the spur of the moment.

(Adapted from *Dallas Morning News,* "Techbits," July 14, 1997, p. 2D.)

a. What is the probability that a video rental customer makes the decision to rent a movie on the same day as visiting the store but does not make a decision on the spur of the moment?

b. If a video rental customer does make the decision to rent a movie on the same day as visiting the store, what is the probability that the decision is not made on the spur of the moment?

4.31 For every person who visits the leasing office of an apartment community near a certain university, there is an 80% chance that the person will lease an apartment if the person is a student and a 50% chance that the person will lease an apartment if the person is not a student. If two people, one of whom is a student and the other of whom is not, enter the office, what are the chances of leasing an apartment to at least one of the two people? What assumption did you have to make here?

4.32 There has been a dramatic increase in the percentage of dual-income families working for corporate America. In 1996, 59.4% of the husbands worked full time for corporate America and 52% of the wives worked full time for corporate America. Assume that 94.7% of the married population has at least one spouse working for corporate America. What is the probability that a married couple in 1996 has both spouses working for corporate America?

(Adapted from *Forbes,* "On My Mind," July 7, 1997, p. 22.)

4.33 The Equal Employment Opportunity Commission documents discrimination charges with the most frequent being listed below.

Alleged Discrimination Charge	Number of Cases
Discharge	37760
Failure to provide reasonable accommodations	20447
Harassment	8718
Hiring	7095
Discipline	5676
Layoff	3407
Promotion	2827
Benefits	2807
Wages	2501
Rehire	2457
Suspension	1608
Miscellaneous	2500

(Adapted from *The Dallas Morning News,* "Disability Issues at Work," June 18, 1997, p. 10D.)

a. What is the probability of selecting a discrimination charge at random from the above list that is either for discharge or failure to provide reasonable accommodations?

b. What is the probability of selecting a discrimination charge at random from the above list that is not for promotion and not for discharge?

c. What is the probability of selecting a discrimination charge at random from the above list that is for failure to provide reasonable accommodations if the charge is selected from those that do not involve discharge?

4.34 [DATA SET EX4-34] *Variable description:*

Exper: Years of experience on the job
Productivity: Performance on a task designed to measure productivity

The manager of a manufacturing plant noticed that there was a somewhat high turnover by many of the company's skilled laborers. To assess the importance of years of experience on productivity of a laborer, the manager assigned a task to every laborer and measured their productivity. Scores of high, medium, and low were recorded as 1, 2, and 3, respectively. These measures of productivity are listed for 100 randomly selected employees.

a. Construct a contingency table with the variables Exper and Productivity. Use Exper as the row variable and Productivity as the column variable. (Excel: Use **KGP Data Analysis ➤ Qualitative Data Charts/Tables ➤ Contingency Table.**)

b. What is the probability that a laborer has at least 6 years of experience and has a score of low?

c. What is the probability that a laborer has between 3 and 6 years of experience, inclusively, or does not have a score of high?

d. What is the probability that a laborer with a score of medium or high has more than 5 years of experience?

4.35 [DATA SET EX4-35] *Variable description:*

Checkret: A yes or no answer to the question, "Are checks returned?"
ATMFee: Fee to use another bank's ATM

Data from the Bank Rate Monitor's survey of large banks and thrifts revealed the following list of banks and their policy on returning checks and the fees that they charge to use another bank's ATM.

Bank Account Name	Checks Returned?	Fee to Use Another Bank's ATM
First Union Personal Checking	Yes	1.25
American NationalSavings	No	.75
U.S. Trust Free Checking	Yes	0
Superior Bank Free Checking	Yes	1.00
Oak Hills S&L Noninterest Checking	Yes	0
Home Federal Savings Home Checking	Yes	.75
Bank United Free 2000 Checking	Yes	1.00
Commercial Bank Free Checking	No	1.50
First Federal Money Saver	Yes	.50
Bank United Free 2000 Checking	Yes	1.00

Bank Account Name	Checks Returned?	Fee to Use Another Bank's ATM
Commerce Bank of Kansas Checking	No	1.25
American Savings Bank Checking	No	1.25
Commerce Bank Regular Checking	Yes	1.00
First Financial Checking	No	1.00
InterBank Value Checking	No	0
Astoria Federal Bank Checking	No	1.00
Frankford Bank Key Checking	Yes	.50
First Arizona Savings Value	No	0
Bell Federal Savings Checking	No	.75
Heartland Savings Bank Checking	Yes	1.00
Union Bank Regular Checking	Yes	1.25
California Federal Checking	Yes	1.25
Cascade Free Checking	No	0
Beneficial Savings Checking	Yes	0
Independence Federal Economy	No	1.00

(Source: *Money*, "Where to Go in 25 Cities to Find Banking Bargains," May 1997, p. 127.)

a. Construct a contingency table using Checkret as the row variable and ATMFee as the column variable. (Excel: **Use KGP Data Analysis ➤ Qualitative Data Charts/Tables ➤ Contingency Table.**)

b. What is the probability that a banking account selected at random from this list charges less than $1.00 as a fee for using another bank's ATM and returns checks?

c. What is the probability that a banking account selected at random from this list returns checks if the banking account charges less than $1.00 as a fee for using another bank's ATM?

4.5 TREE DIAGRAMS

Another useful device for determining probabilities is a **tree diagram.** Notice in Example 4.6 that both marginal probabilities $P(\text{FDIC})$ and $P(\text{Fail})$ were known; that is, the percentage of banks protected by FDIC was known (90%) and the percentage of banks that would fail was known (5%). The contingency table approach illustrated in the previous section works well for this situation.

Suppose instead that one of the marginal probabilities is missing, say, $P(\text{Fail})$, but that we *do* know that

1. 90% of the banks are protected by FDIC (and 10% are not).
2. 3% of the banks protected by FDIC will fail.
3. 23% of the banks not protected by FDIC will fail.

So we can write

$$P(\text{FDIC}) = .90$$

$$P(\overline{\text{FDIC}}) = .10$$

$$P(\text{Fail} \mid \text{FDIC}) = .03$$

$$P(\text{Fail} \mid \overline{\text{FDIC}}) = .23$$

This information can be summarized in the following picture, which we refer to as a tree diagram.

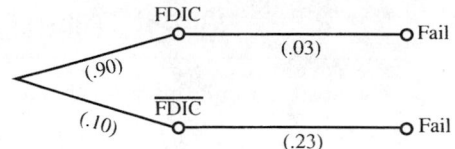

Each number in parentheses is the probability associated with that particular branch. For example, .03 is the probability of a bank failing *given* that it is protected by FDIC, and so this value is placed on the Fail branch corresponding to FDIC.

To find the remaining marginal probability, $P(\text{Fail})$, the following rule is used.

RULE #1 WHEN USING A TREE DIAGRAM

The probability of the event on the right side (say, event B) of the tree is equal to the sum of the paths; that is, all probabilities along a path leading to event B are multiplied, and then summed over *all* parts leading to B.

For the preceding tree diagram, Rule #1 states that

$$P(\text{Fail}) = (.90)(.03) + (.10)(.23)$$

$$= .027 + .023 = .05$$

Consequently, we conclude that 5% of the banks will fail, the same conclusion reached in Example 4.6.

Another question of interest might be, given that a bank fails, what is the probability it is protected by FDIC? Or put another way, what percentage of banks that fail are protected by FDIC? This can be written

$$P(\text{FDIC} \mid \text{Fail})$$

Recall that earlier we were given that $P(\text{FDIC}) = .90$; that is, 90% of the banks are protected by FDIC. For this probability we were given no conditions at all; it is referred to as a **prior probability.** Now we are asked to determine the probability of this event having been given some information, namely that the bank failed. The probability $P(\text{FDIC} \mid \text{Fail})$ is called a **posterior probability** and is always a conditional probability; in particular, we are given that the event on the right side of the tree diagram (Fail) did, in fact, occur. Since FDIC lies on the first branch and $\overline{\text{FDIC}}$ lies on the second branch, we are asked to determine the probability that we got to event Fail along the first path, given that event Fail occurred.

The tree diagram used in this example has two paths. In general, there can be any number of paths, as illustrated in Figure 4.11.

To determine a posterior probability, written as $P(E_i \mid B)$ for some i, we use the following rule, usually referred to as Bayes' rule (named after Thomas Bayes, an English Presbyterian minister and mathematician).

FIGURE 4.11

General form of a tree diagram.

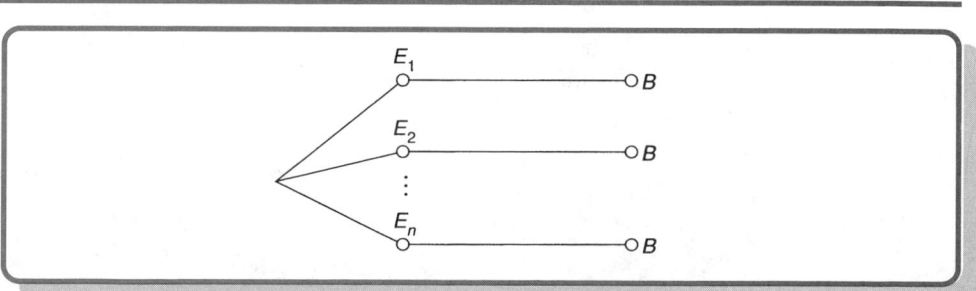

RULE #2 FOR TREE DIAGRAMS (BAYES' RULE)

The posterior probability for the ith path is

$$P(E_i \mid B) = \frac{i\text{th path}}{\text{sum of paths}}$$

where the "sum of paths" is found using Rule #1.

To illustrate:

$$P(\text{FDIC} \mid \text{Fail}) = \frac{1\text{st path}}{\text{sum of paths}}$$

since FDIC lies on the first path. By "1st path" we mean the product of all probabilities along this path. So

$$P(\text{FDIC} \mid \text{Fail}) = \frac{(.9)(.03)}{(.9)(.03) + (.1)(.23)}$$

$$= \frac{.027}{.05} = .54$$

Consequently, 54% of the banks that fail are protected by FDIC (the same result obtained in Example 4.6).

EXAMPLE 4.7

Zetadyne Corporation produces electrical components utilizing three nonoverlapping work shifts. It is known that 50% of the components are produced during shift 1, 20% during shift 2, and 30% during shift 3. A further look at product quality reveals that 6% of the components produced during shift 1 are defective. The corresponding percentage for shift 2 is 8%. Shift 3, the late-night shift, produces a relatively large percentage, 15%, of defective components. Determine

1. What percentage of all components is defective?
2. Given that a defective component is found, what is the probability that it was produced during shift 3?

SOLUTION 1

The tree diagram for this example is

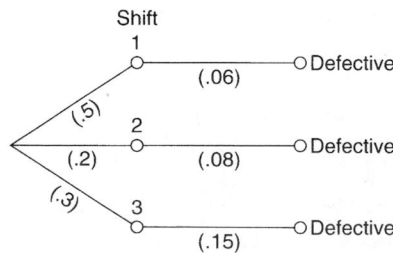

Using Rule #1, we find that

$$P(\text{Defective}) = \text{sum of paths}$$

$$= (.5)(.06) + (.2)(.08) + (.3)(.15)$$

$$= .030 + .016 + .045$$

$$= .091$$

Consequently, 9.1% of the components produced are defective.

SOLUTION 2   We know that P(shift 3) is .3; that is, 30% of the components produced are produced during shift 3. This is a *prior probability*. To determine the *posterior probability*, P(shift 3 | defective), we use Rule #2.

$$P(\text{shift 3} \mid \text{defective}) = \frac{\text{3d path}}{\text{sum of paths}}$$

$$= \frac{(.3)(.15)}{.091}$$

$$= \frac{.045}{.091} = .495$$

So approximately half of the defective components produced are produced during shift 3. This means that once a component is identified as defective, the probability that it came from shift 3 increases from .3 (the prior probability) to .495 (the posterior probability).

The tree diagram illustrated in Figure 4.11 is actually a simplified version of more elaborate decision trees that can be used for more complicated decision problems. A full treatment of decision trees and how they can be used to structure more complex types of decision analyses is provided in Chapter 18.

EXERCISES 4.36–4.43

UNDERSTANDING THE MECHANICS

4.36 Using the given probabilities, construct a tree diagram to find $P(B)$.
   a. $P(A) = .3$, $P(B \mid A) = .2$, $P(B \mid \overline{A}) = .1$
   b. $P(A) = .8$, $P(B \mid A) = .5$, $P(B \mid \overline{A}) = .5$

4.37 Using the given probabilities, construct a tree diagram to find $P(B)$.
   a. $P(E_1) = .4$, $P(E_2) = .1$, $P(E_3) = .5$, $P(B \mid E_1) = .2$, $P(B \mid E_2) = .6$, $P(B \mid E_3) = .4$
   b. $P(E_1) = .6$, $P(E_2) = .1$, $P(E_3) = .1$, $P(E_4) = .2$, $P(B \mid E_1) = .3$, $P(B \mid E_2) = .4$, $P(B \mid E_3) = .1$, $P(B \mid E_4) = .1$

4.38 Using the given probabilities, construct a tree diagram to find $P(E_1 \mid B)$.
   a. $P(E_1) = .4$, $P(E_2) = .6$, $P(B \mid E_1) = .5$, $P(B \mid E_2) = .3$
   b. $P(E_1) = .35$, $P(E_2) = .25$, $P(E_3) = .2$, $P(E_4) = .2$, $P(B \mid E_1) = .2$, $P(B \mid E_2) = .4$, $P(B \mid E_3) = .2$, $P(B \mid E_4) = .1$

APPLYING THE NEW CONCEPTS

4.39 Many organizations, including the military and defense-related companies, require their employees to be screened for drugs. Some employees are concerned that a "false positive" may be recorded from the screening; that is, employees who are not drug abusers may incorrectly test positive. Assume that 10% of a certain population are drug abusers. Suppose that the probability of a "false positive" is .5% and that the probability of a correct positive on someone who is under the influence of certain drugs is 99.9%. What is the probability that a person who tests positive is really a drug user?

4.40 Seventy percent of all Big Burger chain stores decided to advertise in their local newspapers. Of those chain stores that advertised in their local newspapers, 60% had an increase in sales. Of those chain stores that did not advertise in their local newspapers, 25% had an increase in sales. What is the proba-

bility that a randomly selected store with an increase in sales advertised in its local newspaper?

4.41 A large manufacturing company is in the process of training its personnel in quality-control procedures. At present, 40% of the assembly lines use control charts, 40% use inspection techniques, and 20% do not use any method for controlling quality. The assembly lines that use control charts have a 1% defective rate. The assembly lines that use inspection techniques have a 5% defective rate. The assembly lines that do not use any quality-control techniques have a 12% defective rate. What is the probability that an item produced by this company is defective?

4.42 The Social Security Advisory Council is considering several plans to keep Social Security healthy. If nothing changes, the Social Security System will run a deficit around 2030 because of the large number of retirees expected then and the relatively lower number of workers paying into the system. Of importance is the percentage of retirement income for which retirees depend on Social Security. For retirees between the ages of 55 and 64, approximately 10% feel dependent on Social Security. For retirees between the ages of 65 and 80, this increases to 35%. And for retirees over 80, it is approximately 50%. Suppose that the retirees between the ages of 55 and 64, between 65 and 80, and over 80 years of age are 30%, 45%, and 25% respectively.

(Adapted from *Consumers Digest,* "Money Watch," June 1997, p. 14–15.)

   a. What is the probability that a retiree selected at random feels dependent on Social Security?

   b. What is the probability that a retiree who feels dependent on Social Security is over 80 years old?

4.43 Materials for a food-processing plant are supplied by four companies. The following table lists the percentage of defective items from each company and the percentage of materials supplied by that company to the food-processing plant.

	Percentage of Materials Supplied	Percentage of Defective Materials
Supplier 1	40	2
Supplier 2	5	10
Supplier 3	20	8
Supplier 4	35	3

a. Determine the percentage of all materials that are defective.

b. Given that a material supplied to the plant is defective, what is the probability that it came from supplier 3?

4.6 PROBABILITIES FOR MORE THAN TWO EVENTS

We illustrate what happens when you encounter more than two events by considering three events, A, B, and C. The following rules can easily be extended to any finite number of events. In the applications of probability in the chapters that follow, we typically will be dealing with multiple events that are either mutually exclusive or independent.

MUTUALLY EXCLUSIVE EVENTS

Events A, B, and C are pairwise mutually exclusive if no two events can occur simultaneously. A Venn diagram of this situation is shown in Figure 4.12. When dealing with mutually exclusive events, we usually will be interested in the probability that *one* of these events will occur, that is, $P(A$ or B or $C)$. We can use a simple rule here:

> For mutually exclusive events, A, B, and C,
> $$P(A \text{ or } B \text{ or } C) = P(A) + P(B) + P(C) \qquad (4.13)$$

Thus, to determine "or" probabilities when the events are mutually exclusive, add the respective probabilities.

INDEPENDENT EVENTS

Events A, B, and C are independent if all the following are true:

$$P(A \text{ and } B) = P(A) \cdot P(B)$$

$$P(A \text{ and } C) = P(A) \cdot P(C)$$

$$P(B \text{ and } C) = P(B) \cdot P(C)$$

$$P(A \text{ and } B \text{ and } C) = P(A) \cdot P(B) \cdot P(C)$$

Thus the events are independent if the "and" probability for *any* subset of the events (including the set containing all the events) is equal to the corresponding product of marginal probabilities. When dealing with independent events, the probability of interest usually is that *all* of the events occur, that is, $P(A$ and B and $C)$. Using the fourth condition just given, we can make the following statement.

FIGURE 4.12
Three mutually exclusive events.

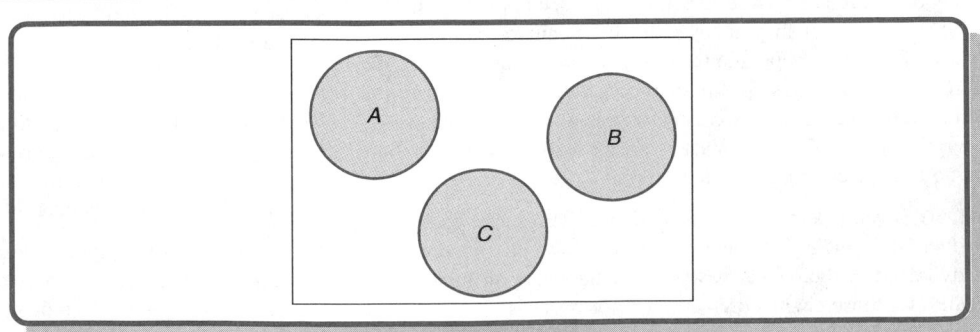

> For independent events, A, B, and C,
>
> $$P(A \text{ and } B \text{ and } C) = P(A) \cdot P(B) \cdot P(C) \qquad (4.14)$$

Thus, to determine "and" probabilities when the events are independent, multiply the respective probabilities.

EXAMPLE 4.8

Dellex Industries makes memory units for a microcomputer. Dellex customers have agreed to select three units randomly from a very large shipment and test them. If none of the units is defective, the customer will accept the shipment.

Usually, 2% of all Dellex units are defective. Determine the probability that the shipment will be accepted, that is, that all three units tested will be nondefective.

SOLUTION

Let

$$A = \text{first unit is nondefective}$$

$$B = \text{second unit is nondefective}$$

$$C = \text{third unit is nondefective}$$

We know that 2% of the units produced are defective, so 98% of them are not defective; consequently, $P(A) = P(B) = P(C) = .98$.

We want to find $P(A \text{ and } B \text{ and } C)$. Are the events independent? There is no need to use fancy formulas here. The answer is yes, simply because the units are selected randomly from the very large shipment. Therefore,

$$P(A \text{ and } B \text{ and } C) = P(A) \cdot P(B) \cdot P(C)$$

$$= .98 \cdot .98 \cdot .98 = .94$$

Consequently, there is a 94% chance that the customer will accept the shipment.

EXERCISES 4.44–4.51

UNDERSTANDING THE MECHANICS

4.44 Given $P(A) = .3$, $P(B) = .1$, $P(C) = .4$, find the following probabilities.

a. $P(A \text{ or } B \text{ or } C)$ assuming that A, B, and C are mutually exclusive

b. $P(A \text{ and } B \text{ and } C)$ assuming that A, B, and C are independent events

4.45 Let $P(A) = .2$, $P(B) = .5$, $P(C) = .1$.

a. Are events A, B, and C mutually exclusive if $P(A \text{ or } B \text{ or } C) = .72$?

b. Are events A, B, and C independent events if $P(A \text{ and } B \text{ and } C) = .01$?

APPLYING THE NEW CONCEPTS

4.46 Let A be the event that a new apartment rents for less than $450 per month, let B be the event that a new apartment rents for at least $550 but less than $650 per month, and let C be the event that a new apartment rents for $750 or more per month. Assume each event has a probability of .25.

a. Are the events A, B, and C mutually exclusive?

b. Find $P(A \text{ or } B \text{ or } C)$.

c. Find $P(A \text{ and } B \text{ and } C)$.

4.47 An engineer has a very large batch of electronic components that were produced when the machinery was malfunctioning. The engineer knows that half are defective and half are nondefective. The engineer suggests taking a sample of the components to place in certain test equipment. Assume that one component is randomly selected and then a second component is randomly selected. The events A, B, and C are defined as follows:

A is the event that the pair of sampled components is either (first component is nondefective, second component is nondefective) or (first component is nondefective, second component is defective).

B is the event that the pair of sampled components is either (first component is defective, second component is nondefective) or (first component is nondefective, second component is nondefective).

C is the event that the pair of sampled components is either (first component is defective, second component is nondefective) or (first component is nondefective, second component is defective).

a. Find $P(A)$, $P(B)$, and $P(C)$.

b. Find $P(A \text{ and } B)$, $P(A \text{ and } C)$, and $P(B \text{ and } C)$.

c. Find $P(A \text{ and } B \text{ and } C)$.

d. What can the engineer conclude about the independence of the events *A, B,* and *C?*

4.48 For NBC, the last series of *Seinfeld* was a big blowout, drawing viewers from 41.6% of U.S. TV households. Suppose that three TV households are randomly selected.

(Source: *USA Today,* "Even Show's Producer Embarrassed by the Hype," May 14, 1998, p. 2A.)

a. What is the probability that all three households have viewed the last series of *Seinfeld?*

b. What is the probability that none of the three households have viewed the last series of *Seinfeld?*

4.49 Three cards are picked with replacement from a deck of 52 playing cards. What is the probability that the first card will be a queen, the second a spade, and the third a king?

4.50 A special Newspoll revealed that South Australia's election would go down to the wire. The Newspoll surveyed a sample of 1700 voters from South Australia. The results are presented below for the 3 political parties. What is the probability that a person either prefers ALP, the Democrats or Others? Are these events mutually exclusive?

Political Party	Voters Preference (in Percentage)
Coalition	39
ALP	34
Democrats	18
Others	9

(Adapted from *The Weekend Australian,* "Margin Slashed in Surprise Poll Swing," Oct 11, 1997, p. 1.)

4.51 The percent of American adults who use personal computers at home or at work has dramatically increased in the past 10 years. Today, for the population 25 to 34 years of age, 48% use a PC. This compares to 58% of the population between 35 and 49 years of age who use a PC. For the population between 50 and 64 years of age, 36% of the population use a PC. Suppose that three adults, one from each of the age categories, are randomly selected. What is the probability that none of them use a PC?

(Adapted from *The Dallas Morning News,* "PC Use in America," March 31, 1997, p. 2D.)

4.7 COUNTING RULES (OPTIONAL)

Counting rules determine the number of possible outcomes that exist for a certain broad range of experiments. They can be extremely useful in determining probabilities. For instance, consider an experiment that has 200 possible outcomes, all of which are equally likely to occur. The probability of any one such outcome is $1/200 = .005$.

The question we wish to answer here is, for a particular experiment, how many possible outcomes are there? No set of rules applies to all situations, but we will consider three very popular counting procedures: (1) filling slots, (2) permutations (a special case of filling slots), and (3) combinations.

FILLING SLOTS

We use **counting rule 1** to fill *k* different slots. Let

n_1 = the number of ways of filling the first slot

n_2 = the number of ways of filling the second slot *after* the first slot is filled

n_3 = the number of ways of filling the third slot *after* the first two slots are filled

$\vdots$

n_k = the number of ways of filling the *k*th slot *after* filling slots 1 through $k - 1$

The number of ways of filling all the *k* slots is

$$n_1 \cdot n_2 \cdot n_3 \cdot \cdots \cdot n_k$$

EXAMPLE 4.9

When ordering a new car, you have a choice of eight interior colors, ten exterior colors, and four roof colors. How many possible color schemes are there?

SOLUTION

There are three slots to fill here, (eight) interior color, (ten) exterior color, and (four) roof color. To answer the question, you simply *multiply* the number of ways of filling each slot. So the answer is $8 \cdot 10 \cdot 4 = 320$ different color schemes.

The order in which you fill the slots is unimportant. So $n_2 = 10$, regardless of whether you have filled the first slot. For some applications, this is not the case. Consider the following example.

EXAMPLE 4.10

A local PTA group is selecting their officers for the current year. There are 15 individuals in the group, whom we label as $I_1, I_2, \ldots, I_{15}$. They need to select a president, vice president, secretary, and treasurer. How many possible groups of officers are there?

SOLUTION

We have four slots to fill here, president (n_1), vice president (n_2), secretary (n_3), and treasurer (n_4). We know that n_1 is 15. After a president is elected, only 14 people remain, so $n_2 = 14$. By a similar argument, $n_3 = 13$ and $n_4 = 12$. The answer is $15 \cdot 14 \cdot 13 \cdot 12 = 32,760$ different slates of officers.

PERMUTATIONS

Example 4.10 is a counting situation in which you select people *without replacement* since duplication is not allowed; that is, 4 different people must be selected. If a particular individual, say, I_3, is elected president, then I_3 is not available to fill the remaining slots. Another way of stating the result is that there are 32,760 ways of selecting 4 distinct people out of 15, where the **order of selection** is important. For example,

$$I_2 = \text{president}$$

$$I_6 = \text{vice president}$$

$$I_{12} = \text{secretary}$$

$$I_7 = \text{treasurer}$$

is not the same slate of officers as

$$I_7 = \text{president}$$

$$I_{12} = \text{vice president}$$

$$I_2 = \text{secretary}$$

$$I_6 = \text{treasurer}$$

even though the same four people are involved.

The number of ways of selecting k distinct objects (or people) from a group of n distinct objects, where the order of selection is important, is referred to as the number of permutations of n objects using k at a time. This is written

$$_nP_k$$

In Example 4.10, $_{15}P_4 = 32,760$. Determining the number of permutations is just a special case of counting rule 1; this is also a slot-filling application.

The symbol $n!$ is read as "*n* factorial." Its value is determined by multiplying n by all the positive integers smaller than n.

$$n! = (n)(n-1)(n-2) \cdots (2)(1) \qquad \textbf{(4.15)}$$

For example,

$$5! = (5)(4)(3)(2)(1) = 120$$

$$1! = 1$$

$$0! = 1 \text{ (by definition)}$$

Notice that $n!$ is the number of ways of filling n slots using n objects. There are n ways of filling the first slot, $(n-1)$ ways of filling the second slot, $(n-2)$ ways for the third slot, and so on.

In Example 4.10 the result was obtained by finding $15 \cdot 14 \cdot 13 \cdot 12 = 32,760$. This also can be written as

$$\frac{15 \cdot 14 \cdot 13 \cdot 12 \cdot \cancel{11} \cdot \cancel{10} \cdot 9 \cdot 8 \cdot 7 \cdot 6 \cdot 5 \cdot 4 \cdot 3 \cdot 2 \cdot 1}{\cancel{11} \cdot \cancel{10} \cdot 9 \cdot 8 \cdot 7 \cdot 6 \cdot 5 \cdot 4 \cdot 3 \cdot 2 \cdot 1} = 32,760$$

This is an application of **counting rule 2** where the order of selection *does* produce different arrangements (permutations). The number of **permutations** of n objects using k objects at a time is

$$_nP_k = \frac{n!}{(n-k)!} = (n)(n-1) \cdots (n-k+1) \qquad \textbf{(4.16)}$$

EXAMPLE 4.11

How many two-digit numbers can you construct using the digits, 1, 2, 3, and 4, without repeating any digit?

SOLUTION

The order of selection is certainly important here—the number 42 is not the same as 24. The answer is $_4P_2$, where

$$_4P_2 = \frac{4!}{(4-2)!} = \frac{(4)(3)(2!)}{2!} = 12$$

These 12 permutations are

12	21	31	41
13	23	32	42
14	24	34	43

COMBINATIONS

Take another look at Example 4.10, where we selected 4 people from a group of 15. This time, however, choose a committee of 4 people from a group of 15 where the order of selection does not matter. Each such committee is one *combination* of the 15 people, using four at a time. For example,

$$I_2 \quad I_6 \quad I_{12} \quad I_7 \quad \text{and} \quad I_7 \quad I_{12} \quad I_2 \quad I_6$$

are different permutations but the same combination. These two arrangements are made up of the same individuals; hence they form the same committee or combination.

Clearly, there are not as many combinations (using I_2, I_6, I_{12}, I_7) as there are permutations. The two preceding permutations form the same combination. There are now 24 possible permutations of this combination ($4 \cdot 3 \cdot 2 \cdot 1 = 24$).

Now we wish to determine how many possible committees (combinations) of 4 there are for the group of 15. This is written as

$$_{15}C_4$$

Each combination has 24 permutations, so

$$_{15}C_4 = \frac{_{15}P_4}{24} = \frac{32{,}760}{24} = 1365$$

There are 1365 possible committee combinations. Notice that 24 is the number of *permutations* of these four numbers (2, 6, 7, and 12); that is, $24 = {}_4P_4 = 4!$

Counting rule 3 is used to count the number of possible combinations where the order of selection *does not* produce different arrangements (combinations). The number of **combinations** of n objects using k at a time is

$$_nC_k = \frac{_nP_k}{k!} = \frac{n!}{k!(n-k)!} \qquad\qquad (4.17)$$

EXAMPLE 4.12

A company must select 5 employees from a department of 40 people to attend a national conference. How many possible delegations are there?

SOLUTION

The order of selection is not a factor here, so this is a combination problem rather than a permutation problem. The answer is

$$_{40}C_5 = \frac{40!}{5!35!}$$

$$= \frac{(40)(39)(38)(37)(36)(35!)}{(5!)(35!)} = \frac{(\overset{8}{40})(\overset{13}{39})(\overset{19}{38})(37)(\overset{9}{36})}{(5)(4)(3)(2)(1)} = 658{,}008$$

EXERCISES 4.52–4.67

UNDERSTANDING THE MECHANICS

4.52 Calculate each of the following.
  a. 5!
  b. $_3P_2$
  c. $_7P_6$
  d. $_5C_3$
  e. $_{10}C_8$

4.53 Suppose there is a pool of 10 applicants.
  a. What is the number of ways of selecting two applicants from this pool of applicants?
  b. What is the number of ways of ranking the applicants?
  c. What is the number of permutations of four applicants from this pool of applicants?

APPLYING THE NEW CONCEPTS

4.54 Identify whether it is permutations or combinations that need to be calculated in each of the following statements.
  a. The number of ways 1st, 2nd, and 3rd place can be selected by a judge in an art contest.
  b. The number of ways 3 cities can be selected from a group of cities used to test a new product.
  c. The number of ways of selecting 5 managers from the list of managers in a company to attend a conference being held in Hawaii.

  d. The number of ways of ordering 4 different pairs of shoes in a display window.

4.55 How many ways can a random sample (sampling without replacement) of size 5 be taken from a box of eight electronic switches?

4.56 How many ways can a quality-control inspector select 4 components from a batch of 20 components if the inspector samples without replacement?

4.57 How many ways can an advisory board of 10 members be chosen from a list of 15 executives?

4.58 How many different phone numbers are possible at a university with all 7-digit phone numbers starting with 565?

4.59 How many ways can five employees be assigned to three different shifts?

4.60 A builder has five different house styles and three lots on which to build. If each lot has a different style of house on it, how many sets of the five house styles are possible on these three lots?

4.61 A firm has 100 laborers, 20 salespersons, and 10 executives. If an employee is chosen from each of these categories, how many different sets of three employees are possible?

4.62 A company is automating the outsourcing of several of its logistics functions involving inventory transportation. If the company wishes to reduce its logistics staff from 25 to 20 personnel, how many ways can this be achieved?

4.63 An investor chooses 5 stocks for her portfolio. How many different arrangements are possible in which at least 3 stocks increase and the rest do not increase in value?

4.64 A company is trying to encourage women to fill executive positions. For the latest batch of executive trainees, it wishes to fill 7 vacancies with 5 women and 2 men. The company has 7 women and 8 men, making a total of 15 finalists for these seven vacancies.

    a. In how many ways can the 7 vacancies be filled if sex is disregarded?

    b. In how many ways can the 7 vacancies be filled if the company insists on 5 women and 2 men?

    c. What is the probability that the company gets the combination it wants if positions are filled randomly?

4.65 The Monetary Authority of Singapore has been busy examining bank mergers. Six of its largest banks in Singapore are Overseas Union Bank, OCBC Bank, United Overseas Bank, DBS Bank, Keppel Bank, and Tat Lee Bank. A merger typically achieves significant cost savings through elimination of duplicated functions and operations as well as through optimizing the deployment of human and capital resources.

(Adapted from *The Straits Time* (Singapore), "OUB to Merge with Wholly-Owned Unit IBS," March 21, 1998, p. 70.)

    a. How many ways can a merger occur among the six banks? List all combinations.

    b. Suppose that Keppel Bank and Tat Lee Bank merge. How many ways can a merger occur among the remaining four banks?

4.66 Mr. Pirate, a well-known computer programmer and a not-so-well-known user of copyrighted software that he did not purchase, has 20 software programs installed on his personal computer. He has 4 programs on his personal computer that are not authorized. An auditor will randomly check 5 programs for legitimate use of software.

    a. How many ways can the auditor choose 5 programs at random and not select one of the unauthorized programs.

    b. How many ways can the auditor choose 5 programs at random from the 20 installed programs?

    c. What is the probability that the auditor will not select one of the unauthorized programs from the installed programs on Mr. Pirate's personal computer?

4.67 List all the ways in which three different numbers can be selected without replacement from the set $\{1, 3, 5, 7, 8, 9\}$? What is the probability of selecting the numbers 7, 8, and 9?

4.8 SIMPLE RANDOM SAMPLES (OPTIONAL)

In later chapters, practically all the applications that use probabilities derived from sample results to make a decision concerning the population are based on the assumption of a simple random sample, or, more simply, a random sample.

We introduced this concept in Chapter 1. A sample of size *n*, selected from a population of size *N*, constitutes a *simple random sample* if every possible sample of size *n* has the same probability of being selected.

To obtain a representative sample when N is extremely large or unknown requires good judgment. Stopping the first 10 people you meet on the street is a very poor way of sampling your population.

You sometimes may be forced to select items for the sample in a nonrandom manner, realizing that a poorly gathered sample can easily lead to an incorrect decision having serious consequences. Accountants often encounter this problem when performing a statistical audit. However, when such a sample is *not* a random sample, it is not correct to use probability theory in your analysis.

In Example 4.12, we determined that there were 658,008 possible delegations when selecting 5 people from a group of 40. If we view this group as the population of interest, then $n = 5$ and $N = 40$. Our concern here is to determine the probability that any specified group of 5 individuals will be the designated delegation if simple random sampling is used.

Notice here that we do not allow any one person to be selected more than once (that is, all five members of the delegation are different people). In effect, we randomly select the first individual from the group of 40, randomly select the second individual from the remaining group of 39, randomly select the third individual from the remaining group of 38, and so on. Consequently, at each step we do *not* replace the people previously selected for the sample when selecting the next individual. In Section 4.3, this sampling procedure was referred to as **sampling without replacement.** This procedure can be simplified in practice by randomly selecting 5 different individuals *at one time* from the group of 40.

When the sample data are obtained one at a time by returning a person or object to the population prior to selection of the next sample value, this procedure is **sampling with**

replacement. Using this scheme, a particular person (or object) can be selected *more than once* in the sample. These sampling procedures will be discussed further in Chapter 7.

For this illustration there are $_{40}C_5 = 658,008$ possible delegations when selecting without replacement, and each has the same probability of being selected. Therefore, the probability that any one combination of people will be picked is $1/658,008 = .000002$.

In general, when employing a simple random sample of size n, selected without replacement from a population of size N, the total number of possible random samples is

$$_N C_n$$

Also, each of these samples has a probability of being selected equal to

$$\frac{1}{_N C_n}$$

EXAMPLE 4.13

Your task is to obtain a random sample of two individuals selected without replacement from a group of five employees ($E_1, E_2, E_3, E_4,$ and E_5). What is the probability that you select E_2 and E_5 as your sample?

SOLUTION

There are

$$_5 C_2 = \frac{5!}{2!3!} = 10$$

possible random samples. They are:

Sample Number	Sample	Sample Number	Sample	
1	E_1, E_2	6	E_2, E_4	
2	E_1, E_3	7	E_2, E_5	← contains E_2 and E_5
3	E_1, E_4	8	E_3, E_4	
4	E_1, E_5	9	E_3, E_5	
5	E_2, E_3	10	E_4, E_5	

Each random sample (including the one containing E_2 and E_5) has a probability of being selected of $1/10 = .1$.

EXAMPLE 4.14

In the Texas lottery, you select six *different* numbers between 1 and 50. To win the lottery, you must select all six numbers in any order. You buy one lottery ticket and select six numbers. What are the chances that your ticket is a winner?

SOLUTION

The order of the numbers does not matter, and all six numbers must be different; that is, the six numbers are selected *without replacement*. The question can then be stated, "How many combinations are there when selecting six numbers from a set of 50?" This is

$$_{50} C_6 = \frac{(50)(49)(48)(47)(46)(45)}{(6)(5)(4)(3)(2)(1)} = 15,890,700$$

Consequently, your chances of winning the lottery with one ticket are 1 in 15,890,700; that is, $\frac{1}{_{50} C_6} = .000000063$—not exactly astronomical odds.

EXERCISES 4.68–4.71

UNDERSTANDING THE MECHANICS

4.68 Calculate the following probabilities.

   a. The probability of selecting two particular objects from 5 objects when sampling 2 objects without replacement

   b. The probability of selecting 8 particular objects from 10 objects when sampling 8 objects without replacement

   c. The probability of selecting 15 particular objects from 20 objects when sampling 15 objects without replacement

APPLYING THE NEW CONCEPTS

4.69 An automotive company is considering 10 different locations for possible sites as distribution centers. Two of these sites are in Texas. What is the probability that these two sites will be chosen if the two sites are selected at random?

4.70 Explain how to select a simple random sample for a population of 100,000 using the computer-generated random numbers in Table A.13.

4.71 The school-newspaper photographer takes 10 different pictures of the homecoming queen at the school's football game. All 10 pictures are excellent, so the photographer chooses two at random to place in the school newspaper. What is the probability that the first two pictures taken will be selected?

SUMMARY

This chapter has examined methods of dealing with uncertainty by applying the concept of **probability.** An activity that results in an uncertain outcome is called an **experiment;** the possible outcomes are **events.** Uncertainty is measured in terms of the probabilities of events. To determine the value of a particular probability, we used the classical approach, the relative frequency method, and the subjective probability approach. The **classical** definition for the probability of event A occurring assumes that the experiment has n equally likely outcomes and event A occurs in m of the n outcomes with a resulting probability of occurring equal to m/n. When using the **relative frequency** approach, the experiment is observed n times. Letting m represent the number of times event A occurs out of the n times, then the resulting probability of event A occurring in the future is m/n. A **subjective probability** is a measure of your belief that a particular event will occur, and like all probabilities, ranges from zero to one, inclusive.

When examining more than one event, say A and B, several types of probabilities can be derived. The probability of A and B occurring is a **joint probability** and is written $P(A \text{ and } B)$. The **multiplicative rule** is a method of determining a joint probability. The probability of A or B (or both) occurring is written $P(A \text{ or } B)$ and can be obtained using the **additive rule.** When asked to find a probability given particular information about events, you determine a **conditional probability.** For example, the probability that B occurs given that A has occurred is a conditional probability, written $P(B \mid A)$. A variation of the multiplicative rule provides a method of determining a conditional probability. The probability of a single event, such as P(the person selected is a female) or P(an individual subscribes to the *Wall Street Journal*), is a **marginal probability.**

Two events are said to be **independent** if the occurrence of the one event has no effect on the probability that the other event occurs. Do not confuse "has no effect" with "will never occur simultaneously." If two events can never occur simultaneously, they are **mutually exclusive.** For example, these two events are certainly independent but are not mutually exclusive (since both events could occur): A, the stock market drops more than two points during a particular week, and B, your company's copying machine breaks down during the same week.

An effective method of determining a probability in complicated situations is to use a **Venn diagram.** When you represent the various events visually, you can often obtain a seemingly complex probability easily. Another useful device for structuring a decision problem is a **decision tree.** Using this approach, one or more **prior probabilities** are provided; they state the probability of these events occurring when no additional information is available. If such information is available, these probabilities can be revised, producing **posterior probabilities.** By using **Bayes' Rule,** these posterior probabilities are easily derived, once the decision tree is constructed.

We discussed various counting rules, including **permutations** and **combinations.** These rules are used to count the number of possible outcomes for experiments that select a certain number of people or objects (k) from a large group of n such objects. When determining the corresponding number of permutations (written $_nP_k$), the order of selection is considered. The number of combinations for this situation (written $_nC_k$) ignores the order of selection and counts only the number of groups that can be obtained.

We also discussed the number of random samples that exists when the population size is known, and we examined methods of obtaining such a sample. *In the chapters to follow, any results using a statistical sample assume that the sample is obtained randomly.*

Summary of Formulas

1. Additive rule

   $$P(A \text{ or } B) = P(A) + P(B) - P(A \text{ and } B)$$

   Special case: If A and B are *mutually exclusive,*

   $$P(A \text{ or } B) = P(A) + P(B)$$

2. Multiplicative rule

   $$P(A \text{ and } B) = P(A \mid B) \cdot P(B)$$

   $$= P(B \mid A) \cdot P(A)$$

   Special case: If A and B are independent,

   $$P(A \text{ and } B) = P(A) \cdot P(B)$$

3. Conditional probability

   $$P(A \mid B) = \frac{P(A \text{ and } B)}{P(B)}$$

4. Independence   Two events A and B are independent if one of the following can be shown:

   $$P(A \mid B) = P(A)$$

   $$P(B \mid A) = P(B)$$

   $$P(A \text{ and } B) = P(A) \cdot P(B)$$

5. Mutually exclusive   Two events A and B are mutually exclusive if $P(A \text{ and } B)$ is zero.

6. Posterior probability (Bayes' Rule)   For any event E_i, the posterior probability of event E_i, given that the final event B occurred is

   $$P(E_i \mid B) = \frac{i\text{th path}}{\text{sum of paths}}$$

   where the sum of paths is obtained by multiplying all probabilities along a path leading to event B and summing the results over all paths leading to event B.

7. Permutations and combinations   The number of permutations of n objects taking k objects at a time is

   $$_nP_k = \frac{n!}{(n-k)!}$$

   The number of combinations of n objects taking k objects at a time is

   $$_nC_k = \frac{n!}{k!(n-k)!}$$

Review Exercises 4.72–4.92

4.72 Let A denote the set of values 1, 2, and 3; let B denote the set of values 4 and 5; and let C denote the set of values 1, 3, and 5. Suppose that each value in the set of numbers from 1 to 5, inclusively, is equally likely to occur.
   a. Draw a Venn Diagram.
   b. What is the probability that A occurs?
   c. What is the probability that either A or B occurs?
   d. What is the probability that C occurs given that A occurs?

4.73 Define the events A, B, and C to have the probabilities $P(A) = .4$, $P(B) = .3$, $P(C) = .1$.
   a. Find $P(A \text{ and } B)$ if A and B are independent.
   b. Find $P(A \text{ or } B)$ if A and B are independent.
   c. Find $P(\bar{A} \text{ and } B)$ if A and B are mutually exclusive.
   d. Find $P(A \mid B)$ if A and B are mutually exclusive.
   e. Find $P(A \text{ and } B \text{ and } C)$ if A, B, and C are mutually exclusive.
   f. Find $P(\bar{A} \text{ or } \bar{C})$ if A and C are mutually exclusive.
   g. Find $P(A \text{ and } B \text{ and } C)$ if A, B, and C are independent.
   h. Find $P(A \text{ or } B \text{ or } C)$ if A, B, and C are mutually exclusive.

4.74 A study by Clayton/Curtis/Cottrell found significant numbers of consumers in the mood for breakfast foods at dinner. This may be because many adults are sufficiently awake to enjoy the eggs and bacon if they are eating them at 7:00 P.M. rather than at 7:00 A.M. Assume that the following table shows the results of a survey of teenagers, working adults, and retired adults and their likelihood of ordering breakfast-type meals at a restaurant for dinner.

	Very Likely	Somewhat Likely	Somewhat Unlikely	Not At All Likely
Teenager	12	20	15	53
Working Adults	10	25	20	45
Retired Adults	5	15	20	60

Consider the following events.
A: {A person is a working adult or a retired adult}
B: {A person is very likely or somewhat likely to order a breakfast-type meal at dinner time}
C: {A person is not a retired adult}
D: {A person is not at all likely to order a breakfast-type meal at dinner time}

(Adapted from *Adweek*, "A Toast to Consumers Who Want a Change of Pace," March 24, 1997, p. 21.)

   a. Find the probability of each event.
   b. Find $P(A \text{ and } B)$, $P(A \mid B)$, and $P(B \mid A)$.
   c. What is $P(A \text{ or } D)$ and $P(A \text{ and } D)$?
   d. Which events are mutually exclusive?

4.75 A marketing-research group conducted a survey to find out where people did their holiday shopping. Out of a group of 110 randomly selected shoppers, 70 said that they shopped exclusively at the local mall, 30 said that they shopped exclusively in the downtown area, and 10 said that they shopped both at the local mall and in the downtown area.
   a. What is the probability that a customer shops both at the local mall and in the downtown area?
   b. What proportion of customers who shop at the local mall also shop in the downtown area?
   c. What is the probability that a customer shops downtown but not at the local mall?

4.76 An electronics firm decides to market three different software packages for its personal computers. The marketing analyst gives each of the three packages an 80% chance of success. The outcomes for each of the software packages are independent.
   a. What is the probability that all three will be a success?
   b. What is the probability that only two of the packages will be a success?
   c. What is the probability that none will be successful?

4.77 A payroll record with an error in it is placed in a filing cabinet with six error-free payroll records. Two payroll records are randomly selected, without replacement, by an auditor.
   a. What is the probability of drawing the payroll record with the error on the first draw?
   b. What is the probability of drawing the payroll record with the error on the second draw?
   c. What is the probability of drawing the payroll record with the error on the first or second draw?
   d. What is the probability of drawing an error-free payroll record on the first or second draw?

4.78 The Texas Department of Insurance compares rates among companies that sell more than 80 percent of the auto liability insurance in the Dallas area. It also rates companies that have asked to be rated. One index that is compiled is the complaint index. A value of one is average. If the value is below one, the complaint index is labeled as L (for low); otherwise, the complaint index is labeled as H (for high). Also included below is the A.M. best rating.

Insurance Company Name	Complaint Classification	A.M. Best Rating
Allstate County Mutual Insurance Co.	L	A
Allstate Indemnity	L	A
Allstate Insurance Co.	H	A
Allstate Property & Casualty Insurance Co.	L	A
Beacon National Insurance Co.	L	C+
Colonial County	H	A+
Farmers Texas County	H	B++
First Preferred	L	C+
GEICO	H	A++
Liberty Mutual	H	A
Mid-Century Insurance	L	B++
Nationwide	L	A+
Petrolia Insurance Co.	L	C+
Potomac	H	A+

Insurance Company Name	Complaint Classification	A.M. Best Rating
Progressive County	H	A++
Prudential Property & Casualty	H	B++
Southern Farm Bureau	L	A++
State Farm County Mutual	L	A++
State Farm Mutual Auto Insurance Co.	L	A++
Teachers Insurance Co.	L	A
Texas Farm Bureau	H	B++
Texas Farmers Insurance Co.	L	B++
United Services Automobile Assoc.	L	A++

(Source: *Dallas Morning News,* "Automobile Insurance Rates for Dallas County," Aug 1, 1997.)

a. Form a contingency table with the rows listed as A++/A+/A/B++/C+ and the columns listed as H/L. (Excel: **Use KGP Data Analysis ➤ Qualitative Data Charts/Tables ➤ Contingency Table.**)

b. Suppose one company is randomly selected from the list of insurance companies listed above. What is the probability that the company has a low number of complaints or is classified as an A or higher by A.M. best rating?

c. Let Event 1 be the event that a company selected at random is classified as a company with high complaints and is rated as a B++ or C+. Let Event 2 be the event that a company selected at random is classified as having low complaints. Are Event 1 and Event 2 mutually exclusive? Are the events independent?

4.79 For a marketing survey, 200 customers were classified according to their age (in years) and their favorite type of donut.

Age of Customer	Glazed	Chocolate-covered	Creme-filled	Cake	
<21	3	25	10	7	
21–30	5	23	26	10	
31–45	15	12	3	20	
>45	29	5	1	6	
Total	52	65	40	43	(200)

a. What is the probability that a person prefers creme-filled donuts and is age 45 years or less?

b. What is the probability that a person's favorite donut is not glazed or that the person is less than 21 years of age?

c. What is the probability that a person is between 21 and 30 years of age if that person favors chocolate-covered donuts?

d. Are age and favorite donut independent variables?

4.80 "We've noticed a big increase in the number of Americans coming into our store," said Richard Montgomery, manager of Eaton's at Yorkdale Mall in Toronto. But the biggest change is the number of Canadian shoppers looking for deals at home instead of south of the border. "It's the Canadian consumer that's making the difference." Since the beginning of October 1997 to April 1998, the Canadian dollar has fallen from 73 cents per U.S. dollar to below 70 cents per U.S. dollar. Assume that the table below is from a sample of Americans and Canadians that shopped at Yorkdale Mall in Toronto.

(Adapted from *The Financial Post,* "Lower C$ Prompts U.S. Bargain Hunting," Jan. 2, 1998, p. 6.)

	Shopping at Mall Because of Weak Canadian Dollar	Shopping at Mall Because of Reasons Other Than the Weak Canadian Dollar
American	55	45
Canadian	60	140

a. What is the probability that a person selected at random from the sample is an American who is shopping at the mall for reasons other than the weak Canadian dollar?

b. What is the probability that a Canadian person selected at random from the sample is shopping at the mall because of the weak Canadian dollar?

4.81 If A and B are mutually exclusive and $P(A) + P(B) = 1$, then explain what the following two sets are equal to: $\bar{A}, \bar{B}$.

4.82 A busy executive has to meet with five production managers during the day. The executive needs to decide in which order to see the managers. How many different orderings can the executive choose? What is the probability of the executive's choosing any one ordering, if the choice is random?

4.83 A defective tape recorder is inspected by two service representatives. If one representative has a 50% chance of finding the defect, and the other has a 60% chance, what is the probability that at least one will find the defect if both check the tape recorder independently? What is the probability that neither will spot the defect?

4.84 A student forgot the combination for his bike lock. The combination consists of a sequence of three numbers and each number can range from 0 to 9. How many different sequences are possible?

4.85 The Investment Funds Institute of Canada is assessing the impact of regulations that restrict the foreign content of investments by Canadian institutions. The foreign content limit was approximately 10% in the early 1990s. Now, a report commissioned last year by Canada's mutual and pension funds suggested an increase to 30%, roughly the level most fund managers favor for their portfolios. Suppose that 75% of the Canadian mutual fund managers favor having 30% of their portfolio consisting of foreign investments. Suppose that four Canadian mutual fund managers were selected at random.

(Adapted from *Financial Times* (London), "Canada Investors Eye New Foreign Holdings," July 17, 1997, p. 6.)

a. What is the probability that all four managers favor having 30% of their portfolio consisting of foreign investments?

b. What is the probability that at least one of the four managers favors having 30% of their portfolio consisting of foreign investments?

c. What is the probability that either all four managers favor having 30% of their portfolio consisting of foreign investments or that none of the four managers favors having 30% of their portfolio consisting of foreign investments?

4.86 Many of Fidelity's Select mutual funds have yielded remarkable returns in the five-year period ending March 31, 1998, with the highest return being 330% from Fidelity Select Electronics. The Standard & Poor's 500 Index yielded 174.71% during this period. A breakdown of the performance is presented below.

Performance Level for Five-Year Period	Number of Select Mutual Funds
Less than 100%	11
At least 100% and less than 174.71%	12
At least 174.71%	14

(Source: *Fidelity Focus,* Summer 1998, pp. 33–34.)

a. Are the mutual fund performance categories mutually exclusive?

b. What is the probability that a Fidelity Select mutual fund does not perform better than the Standard & Poor's 500 Index?

c. Suppose that two Fidelity Select mutual funds are selected at random. What is the probability that at least one performs better than the Standard & Poor's 500 Index?

d. Suppose that three Fidelity Select mutual funds are selected at random. What is the probability that none of the funds yields a return less than 100%?

4.87 On May 19, 1998, 90% of the more than 44 million pager customers nationwide lost service when a communications satellite spun out of control, causing the largest and longest outage of its kind. Suppose that three persons (persons A, B, and C) are selected at random from the population of customers who own pagers.

(Source: *Los Angeles Times,* "Satellite Problem Cuts Service to 90% of Pagers," May 20, 1998, p. 1A.)

a. What is the probability that person A's pager is of out of service?

b. What is the probability that person A's pager or person B's pager is out of service?

c. What is the probability that person A's pager, person B's pager, and person C's pager are out of service?

4.88 Much controversy was stirred by Marilyn VosSavant's response to whether contestants on a game show should switch their random selection of a door with a possible prize behind it when the host gives additional information. The following is a basic description of the game as described in *Ask Marilyn:* "Suppose you're on a game show and you're given a choice of three doors. Behind one door is a car; behind the others are goats. You pick a door—say, Number 1—and the host, who knows what's behind each door, opens another door—say, Number 3—which has a goat behind it. He then says to you 'Do you want to keep door Number 1 or switch doors?' Is it to your advantage to switch your choice?" Marilyn's response is, "Yes, you should switch. The first door has a ⅓ chance of winning, but the second has a ⅔ chance." Marilyn received letters from numerous mathematicians that described her response as being absurd. In particular, one comment was: "I am in shock that after being corrected by at least three mathematicians, you still do not admit your mistake."

(Adapted from *Dallas Morning News*, "Ask Marilyn," by Marilyn VosSavant, February 17, 1991.)

   a. Pair up with another student and label three paper cups Number 1, Number 2, and Number 3. While one student (the contestant) is not looking, the other student (the host) generates a number between 1 and 3 using the following Excel commands:
   Put the numbers 1, 2, and 3 in cells A1, A2, and A3.
   Type =1/3 in cells B1, B2, and B3.
   Click on **Tools ➤ Data Analysis ➤ Random Number Generator.**
   Type into the user form:
      1 for the number of variables;
      1 for the number of random numbers;
      Discrete for distribution;
      A1:B3 for value and probability input range; and
      C1 for output range.
The host puts a key under the cup corresponding to the random integer generated. The contestant then randomly selects a cup using the same Excel commands. The host then lifts a losing cup. Let's say that the contestant never switches. Then the contestant lifts his or her cup. Keep a tally of the contestant's wins. Repeat this game 100 times.
   b. Perform the game in part (a), except have the contestant switch cups each time.
   c. Compare the number of wins in parts (a) and (b). Do you believe Marilyn's response is correct?
   d. Give a convincing argument that either supports Marilyn's response or supports the contention that there is no advantage in switching doors.

4.89 Political contributions from the Washington Education Association (WEA) dropped by 77 percent, even though the dues-paying membership of the teachers union actually grew by 7,000. Why? Because since 1992, under the state of Washington's law, prior written permission is required before a union can devote part of an employee's dues to political causes. This is known as Initiative 134. Now 30 states, through referendums and legislative efforts, either have or are considering enacting laws similar to Washington's.

(Source: *Legal Times*, "Last Gasp For Unions' Political Clout," May 18, 1998, p. S34.)

   a. What is the probability that a state in the United States, picked at random, is not considering and does not have laws similar to Initiative 134?
   b. What is the probability that two states in the United States, picked at random, are considering or already have laws similar to Initiative 134? (Note that one state is picked first, and then the second state is picked. The probability for the second state considering laws similar to Initiative 134 is different since there are only 50 states in the nation, with 30 states considering Initiative 134.)

4.90 The schematic diagram presented below denotes three components that operate in series. That is, if one component fails, the system does not work. Suppose that the probabilities of C1, C2, and C3 failing are .4, .1, and .1, respectively. What is the probability that the system operates without failure?

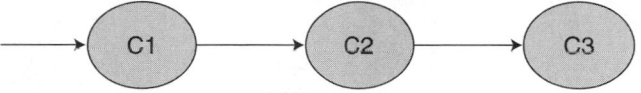

4.91 The schematic diagram presented below denotes four components such that C1 and C2 operate in parallel to C3 and C4. The system will not fail unless the system C1 and C2 fails and the system C3 and C4 fails. Note that C1 and C2 operate in series, and C3 and C4 operate in series. Suppose that the probabilities of C1, C2, C3, and C4 failing are .4, .1, .1, and .2, respectively. What is the probability that the system operates without failure?

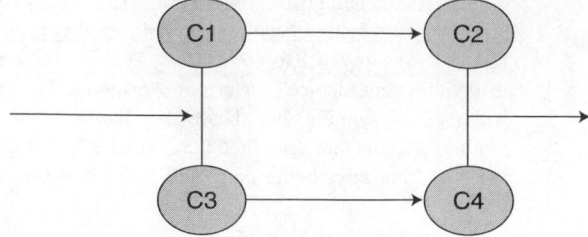

4.92 People are often amazed when they find someone who was born on the same day as themselves. To keep the solution simple, assume in this problem that leap years can be ignored and thus that all years have 365 days. Also, assume that the probability of being born on any day of the year is the same for all days of the year.

   a. If two persons are selected at random, what is the probability that these two persons were born on the same day?

   b. If three persons are selected at random, what is the probability that at least two of the three persons were born on the same day?

   c. In general, the probability that at least two of n people have the same birthday is given by the formula:

$$\text{Probability} = 1 - \left(\frac{365}{365}\right)\left(\frac{364}{365}\right)\cdots\left(\frac{365-n+1}{365}\right)$$

Use this formula to determine the probability that at least two people out of a class of 40 people have the same birthday.

   d. The following Excel commands simulate a group of 40 people with birthdays randomly selected between 1 and 365.

     Click on **Tools ➤ Data Analysis ➤ Random Number Generator.**

     Type into the user form:

        1 for the number of variables;

        40 for the number of random numbers;

        Uniform for distribution, between 1 and 365;

        4367 for the value of the random seed;

        A2 for the output range.

     (You should now see a column of random numbers starting in cell A2.)

     In cell B2 type in "round(A2,0)," hit return, and drag cell B2 to cell B41.

     In cell B1 type "birthdays"; in cell C1 type "tally."

     In cell C2 type "Person" and drag down to C41.

     Click on **KGP Data Analysis ➤ Qualitative Data Charts ➤ Contingency Table.**

        Type in B1:B41 for the row variable and type in C1:C41 for the column variable.

        Type in D2 for the output range.

The output is given on the next page. The number of times a birthday appears is given in the tally column. Does the output seem reasonable? Repeat with a different random seed.

	Birthday	Tally	Contingency Table		
159.8438	160	Person		Tally	
247.9917	248	Person	Birthday	Person	Grand Total
150.6014	151	Person	5	1	1
364.4779	364	Person	20	1	1
327.2525	327	Person	23	2	2
247.1918	247	Person	27	1	1
20.09592	20	Person	45	1	1
316.4437	316	Person	51	1	1
300.5471	301	Person	53	2	2
211.9771	212	Person	59	1	1
171.0414	171	Person	67	1	1
265.8767	266	Person	115	1	1
178.8731	179	Person	124	1	1
52.6223	53	Person	150	1	1
67.27473	67	Person	151	1	1
51.15595	51	Person	160	1	1
115.2978	115	Person	171	1	1
123.5183	124	Person	179	1	1
27.17219	27	Person	212	1	1
214.6655	215	Person	215	1	1
360.4676	360	Person	226	1	1
45.37941	45	Person	229	1	1
252.4685	252	Person	230	1	1
229.5289	230	Person	247	1	1
257.8007	258	Person	248	2	2
309.323	309	Person	250	1	1
247.5029	248	Person	252	2	2
287.5388	288	Person	258	1	1
23.40632	23	Person	259	1	1
258.7449	259	Person	266	1	1
5.121342	5	Person	288	1	1
334.962	335	Person	301	1	1
225.9964	226	Person	309	1	1
58.86541	59	Person	316	1	1
149.646	150	Person	327	1	1
53.23328	53	Person	335	1	1
252.4129	252	Person	360	1	1
249.7246	250	Person	364	1	1
229.129	229	Person	Grand Total	40	40
23.33967	23	Person			

COMPUTER EXERCISES USING THE DATABASES

EXERCISE 1—APPENDIX E

Select a random sample of 100 observations from the database. Using the relative frequency approach of finding a probability value, find the probability that a family owns its home.

EXERCISE 2—APPENDIX F

Generate 200 random numbers from a uniform distribution and use them to select 200 observations from the database. Using the relative frequency approach, find the probability that a company has an A bond rating. Also find the probability that a company has a B bond rating.

INSIGHTS FROM STATISTICS IN ACTION: GAINING MARKET SHARE IN THE FRUIT JUICE INDUSTRY

The Statistics in Action case study presented at the beginning of this chapter introduced the concept of viewing a market share as a probability. For example, if Company A has a 40% marketshare of Product X, then we can write

$$P(\text{Company A} \mid \text{Purchased Product X}) = .4$$

So each marketshare can be written as a conditional probability.

Before attempting to determine the four probabilities in the introductory case study (such as P(Tropicana and PepsiCo working together to develop and market a new product), a good starting point would be to look at the marketshares for two product lines: chilled juice and frozen concentrate. The following table contains proportions (marketshares) of consumers who buy juice from one of the following brands of chilled juices and frozen concentrate juices. Juices can be of any fruit variety.

Chilled Juice Market

Brand Name	Proportion of Consumers Buying This Brand
Tropicana	39.8%
Minute Maid	19.3%
Citrus World	8.7%
Private Label	22.5%
Other	9.7%

Frozen Concentrate

Tropicana	5.4%
Minute Maid	44.7%
Private Label	39.4%
Other	10.5%

1. What is the probability that a person will buy either the Tropicana or the Minute Maid brand when purchasing a chilled juice? Assume that these events are mutually exclusive.

2. If a person buys both chilled juice and buys frozen concentrate, what is the probability that the brand of the chilled juice is Tropicana or that the brand of the frozen concentrate is Minute Maid? Assume that these two events are independent.

3. While Minute Maid and Tropicana may consider each other to be archrivals, private label juice brand is not far behind. If a person buys both chilled juice and frozen concentrate, what is the probability that the brand of chilled juice is a private brand or that the brand of frozen juice is a private brand? As in Part 2, assume that these two events are independent.

4. Suppose that 40% of the buyers of chilled Tropicana juice buy other energy drinks that are vitamin enriched and that 25% of the purchasers of chilled juice other than Tropicana buy other energy drinks that are vitamin enriched. What is the probability that a consumer who purchases vitamin-enriched drinks that are not part of the chilled juice market also buys chilled Tropicana juice? Would you say that the purchasers of chilled juices would be likely customers for other energy drinks?

Source: *The Wall Street Journal,* "Storming the OJ Wars, Pepsi to Buy Tropicana," July 21, 1998, p. B1.

CHAPTER 4 APPENDIX: DATA ANALYSIS WITH MINITAB

CONTINGENCY TABLE

To construct a contingency table in MINITAB, a cross tabulation option is available in the menu to print one-way, two-way, and even three-way tables. In the case of a three-way table, separate two-way tables for each level of the third variable can be displayed. An example using the data file DATA4-3 used in Example 4.3 will illustrate the construction of a two-way contingency table. Click on **Stats ➤ Tables ➤ Cross tabulation.** After selecting **City** and **Quality** and the options of count, row percents, column percents, and total percents, the user form will look like that displayed below. The output will appear in the session window and follows the user form. Note that under each count in a cell, the percentages of the row sum, column sum, and total appear.

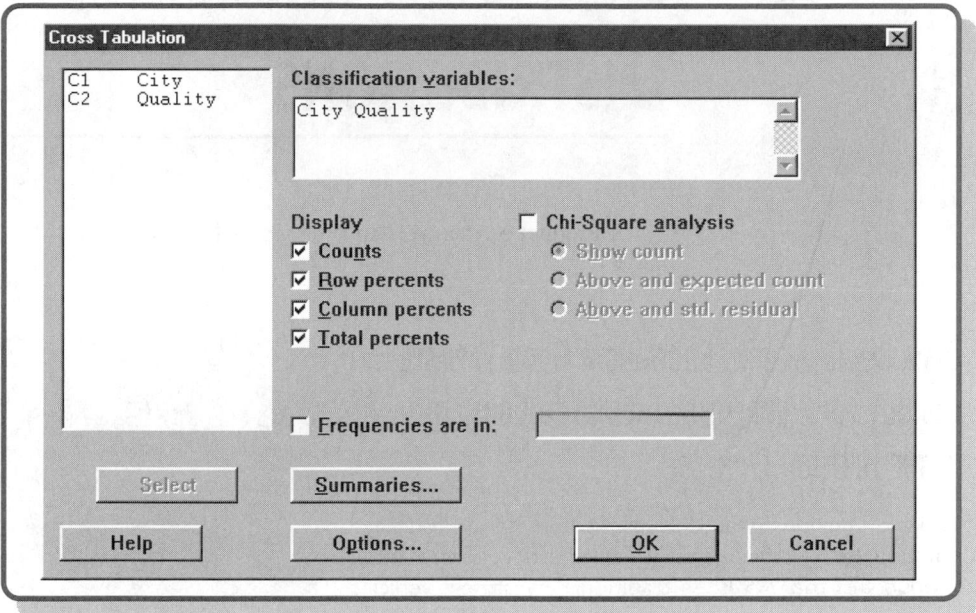

TABULATED STATISTICS

Rows: City   Columns: Quality

	1	2	3	All
1	60	15	5	80
	75.00	18.75	6.25	100.00
	50.00	30.00	16.67	40.00
	30.00	7.50	2.50	40.00
2	35	20	10	65
	53.85	30.77	15.38	100.00
	29.17	40.00	33.33	32.50
	17.50	10.00	5.00	32.50
3	25	15	15	55
	45.45	27.27	27.27	100.00
	20.83	30.00	50.00	27.50
	12.50	7.50	7.50	27.50
All	120	50	30	200
	60.00	25.00	15.00	100.00
	100.00	100.00	100.00	100.00
	60.00	25.00	15.00	100.00

Cell Contents--
        Count
        % of Row
        % of Col
        % of Tbl

CHAPTER 5

DISCRETE PROBABILITY DISTRIBUTIONS

STATISTICS IN ACTION: CHOOSING A GOOD VARIABLE ANNUITY FOR RETIREMENT: FACTORS TO CONSIDER IN THE DECISION PROCESS

Variable annuities, that is, investments with an insurance component, have been one of the fastest-growing financial products of the 1990s. As traditional investment vehicles for retirement continue to have limitations, variable annuities appear to be an attractive option for investors in the future. But not all annuities are alike. Financial analysts often warn investors from choosing an annuity at random.

Since the money invested in a variable annuity grows tax-deferred until it is withdrawn, many investors who have already contributed to their IRA or company tax-deferred plan are quick to consider variable annuities as an investment vehicle since there are no restrictions on the amount invested. Investors may be readily persuaded by advertisements from large insurance companies. To entice investors, many insurance companies have brought well-known fund managers to direct the funds. Furthermore, insurance companies vary in the number of options allowing investors to reallocate investments within their annuity without any tax consequence.

Money managers and financial advisors are often interested in the distribution of the insurance expenses and investment choices associated with annuities as investors often choose randomly from a vast array of annuity products on the market. While individual investors look up to financial wizards for recommendations on a variable annuity, these investors must understand some additional terminology that is not associated with non-retirement accounts. Not only should the benefits of tax deferral be a factor in choosing an annuity, but the payout benefits need to be examined.

Investors must first recognize that there is not only an annual insurance expense but also a mutual fund expense for management fees. The insurance expense gives the investor the death benefit feature of the policy. This benefit provides a guaranteed stream of income, based on the performance of the annuity's investments. Pay-out options can vary and can affect an investor's stream of income. Surrender fees also can affect invest-

ment return, should an emergency require an investor to withdraw his or her money. After wading through the jargon, all the investment choices may be confusing.

Very often, uncertain future events have a discrete number of possible outcomes, such as the number of times each individual at your company has been audited by the IRS during the past 10 years. The possible values for this situation are 0, 1, 2, . . . , 10. At the completion of this chapter, you will be able to

- Visualize such a number as a **discrete random variable;**
- Examine a list of insurance companies and discuss the probabilities of certain events using the values and probabilities of the corresponding random variable; and
- Identify certain classes of discrete random variables and determine if a particular random variable (such as the minimum initial purchase amount for a certain type of insurance policy) belongs to one of these classes.

A Look Back/Introduction

The early chapters were concerned with describing sample data that had been gathered from a previous experiment, a printed report, or some other source. The data were summarized using one or more numerical measures (for example, a sample mean, variance, or correlation) or using a statistical graph (such as a histogram, bar chart, or scatter diagram).

Chapter 4 introduced you to methods of dealing with uncertainty by using a probability to measure the chance of a particular event occurring. Rules were defined that enabled you to compute various probabilities of interest, such as a conditional or a joint probability. However, so far we have defined only the probability of a certain event happening.

Whenever an experiment results in a numerical outcome, such as the total value of two dice, we can represent the various possible outcomes and their corresponding probabilities much more conveniently by using a **random variable,** the topic of this chapter. Suppose that your company manufactures a product that is sometimes defective and is returned for repair during the warranty period in 10% of the cases. An excellent way of describing the chance that 3 of 20 products will be returned before the warranty runs out is to use the concept of a random variable.

Random variables can be classified into two categories: discrete and continuous. This chapter introduces both but concentrates on the discrete type. Several commonly used discrete random variables will be discussed, as will methods of describing and applying them.

Definition

random (not controlled

A **random variable** is a function that assigns a numerical value to each outcome of an experiment.

In Chapter 3 we used various statistics (numerical measures) to describe a set of sample data. For example, the sample mean and standard deviation provide measures of a "typical" value and variation within the sample, respectively. Similarly, we will use a random variable and its corresponding distribution of probabilities to describe a *population*. Just as a sample has a mean and standard deviation, so does the population from which the sample was obtained. We will use the basic concepts from Chapter 4 to derive probabilities related to a random variable.

5.1 Random Variables

Discrete Random Variables

The probability laws developed in the previous chapter provide a framework for the discussion of random variables. We will still be concerned about the probability of a particular event; often, however, some aspect of the experiment can be easily represented using a random variable. The result of a simple experiment can sometimes be summarized concisely by defining a discrete random variable to describe the possible outcomes.

Pg 148

Flip a coin three times. The possible outcomes for each flip are heads (H) and tails (T). According to counting rule 1 from Chapter 4, there are $2 \cdot 2 \cdot 2 = 8$ possible results. These are TTT, TTH, THT, HTT, HHT, HTH, THH, and HHH. Let

A = event of observing 0 heads in 3 flips (TTT)

B = event of observing 1 head in 3 flips (TTH, THT, HTT)

C = event of observing 2 heads in 3 flips (HHT, HTH, THH)

D = event of observing 3 heads in 3 flips (HHH)

We wish to find $P(A)$, $P(B)$, $P(C)$, and $P(D)$.

Consider one outcome, say, HTH. The coin flips are independent, so we use equation 4.14: $P(A \cdot B \cdot C) = P(A) \cdot P(B) \cdot P(C)$

$P(\text{HTH})$ = (probability of H on 1st flip) · (probability of T on 2nd flip) ·
(probability of H on 3rd flip)

$= (1/2) \cdot (1/2) \cdot (1/2) = 1/8$

This same argument applies to all eight outcomes. These outcomes are all equally likely, and each occurs with probability 1/8.

Event A occurs only if you observe TTT. It has the probability of occurring one time out of eight:

$$P(A) = 1/8$$

Event B will occur if you observe HTT, TTH, or THT. It would be impossible for HTT and TTH *both* to occur, so *P(HTT and TTH) = 0. This is true for any combination of these three outcomes so these three events are all mutually exclusive. Consequently, according to equation 4.13,*

$$P(B) = P(\text{HTT or TTH or THT})$$

$$= P(\text{HTT}) + P(\text{TTH}) + P(\text{THT})$$

$$= 1/8 + 1/8 + 1/8 = 3/8$$

By a similar argument,

$$P(C) = 3/8 \qquad (\text{using HHT, HTH, THH})$$

$$P(D) = 1/8 \qquad (\text{using HHH})$$

The variable of interest in this example is X, defined as

$$X = \text{number of heads out of three flips}$$

We defined all the possible outcomes of X by defining the four events A, B, C, and D. This method works but is cumbersome. Consider having to do this for 100 flips of a coin! A more convenient way to represent probabilities is to examine the value of X for each possible outcome.

Outcome	Value of X	
TTT	0	1 outcome
THT	1	
TTH	1	3 outcomes
HTT	1	
HHT	2	
HTH	2	3 outcomes
THH	2	
HHH	3	1 outcome

Each outcome has probability 1/8, so the probability that X will be 0 is 1/8, written:

$$P(X = 0) = P(0) = 1/8$$

The probability that X will be 1 is 3/8, written:

$$P(X = 1) = P(1) = 3/8$$

The probability that X will be 2 is 3/8, written:

$$P(X = 2) = P(2) = 3/8$$

The probability that X will be 3 is 1/8, written:

$$P(X = 3) = P(3) = 1/8$$

Notice that

$$P(X = 0) + P(X = 1) + P(X = 2) + P(X = 3) = 1/8 + 3/8 + 3/8 + 1/8 = 1$$

because 0, 1, 2, and 3 represent *all the possible values* of X.

The values and probabilities for this random variable can be summarized by listing each value and its probability of occurring.

$$X = \begin{cases} 0 & \text{with probability } 1/8 \\ 1 & \text{with probability } 3/8 \\ 2 & \text{with probability } 3/8 \\ 3 & \text{with probability } 1/8 \end{cases}$$

This list of possible values of X and the corresponding probabilities is a **probability distribution.**

In any such formulation of a problem, the variable X is a **random variable.** Its value is not known in advance, but there is a probability associated with each possible value of X. Whenever you have a random variable of the form

$$X = \begin{cases} x_1 & \text{with probability } p_1 \\ x_2 & \text{with probability } p_2 \\ x_3 & \text{with probability } p_3 \\ \vdots \\ x_n & \text{with probability } p_n \end{cases}$$

where $x_1, \ldots, x_n$ is the set of possible values of X, then X is a **discrete random variable.** In the coin-flipping example, $x_1 = 0$ and $p_1 = 1/8$; $x_2 = 1$ and $p_2 = 3/8$, $x_3 = 2$ and $p_3 = 3/8$, and $x_4 = 3$ and $p_4 = 1/8$.

Other examples of a discrete random variable include:

$X =$ the number of cars that drive up to a bank within a 5-minute period ($X = 0, 1, 2, 3, \ldots$).

$X =$ the number of people out of a group of 50 who will suffer a fatal accident within the next 10 years ($X = 0, 1, 2, \ldots, 50$).

$X =$ the number of people out of 200 who make an airline reservation and then fail to show up ($X = 0, 1, 2, \ldots, 200$).

$X =$ the number of calls arriving at a telephone switchboard over a two-minute period ($X = 0, 1, 2, 3, \ldots$).

Notice that, for each example, the discrete random variable is a count *of the number of people, calls, accidents, and so on that can occur.*

EXAMPLE 5.1

You roll two dice, a red die and a blue die. What is a possible random variable X for this situation? What are its possible values and corresponding probabilities? (*Hint:* Roll the dice and observe a particular number. This number is your value of the random variable, X. What observations are possible from the roll of two dice?)

SOLUTION

There are many possibilities here, including

X = total of the two dice

X = average of the two dice

X = the higher of the two numbers that appear (possible values: 1, 2, 3, 4, 5, 6)

X = the number of dice with 3 appearing (possible values: 0, 1, 2)

Suppose that the random variable X equals the total of the two dice. The next step is to determine the possible values of X and the corresponding probabilities. When you roll the two colored dice, there are $6 \cdot 6 = 36$ possible outcomes, using counting rule 1 from Chapter 4.

Outcome	Red Die	Blue Die	Value of X
1	1	1	2
2	1	2	3
3	1	3	4
4	1	4	5
5	1	5	6
6	1	6	7
7	2	1	3
8	2	2	4
9	2	3	5
⋮	⋮	⋮	⋮
34	6	4	10
35	6	5	11
36	6	6	12

$P(X = 3) = 2/36$

The 36 outcomes are equally likely because the number appearing on each die (1, 2, 3, 4, 5, or 6) has the same chance of appearing. Notice that we are *not* saying that each value of X is equally likely, as the following discussion will make clear. Each of the above 36 outcomes has probability 1/36 of occurring. If you write down all 36 outcomes and note what can happen to X, your random variable, you will observe:

Value of X	Number of Possible Outcomes	
2	1	(rolling a 1, 1)
3	2	(rolling a 1, 2, or 2, 1)
4	3	(rolling a 1, 3 or 3, 1 or 2, 2)
5	4	(and so on)
6	5	
7	6	
8	5	
9	4	
10	3	
11	2	
12	1	

Consequently,

$$X = \begin{cases} 2 \text{ with probability } 1/36 \\ 3 \text{ with probability } 2/36 \\ 4 \text{ with probability } 3/36 \\ 5 \text{ with probability } 4/36 \\ 6 \text{ with probability } 5/36 \\ 7 \text{ with probability } 6/36 \\ 8 \text{ with probability } 5/36 \\ 9 \text{ with probability } 4/36 \\ 10 \text{ with probability } 3/36 \\ 11 \text{ with probability } 2/36 \\ 12 \text{ with probability } \underline{1/36} \end{cases}$$

$$\text{Total } 1.0$$

Because 2 through 12 represent all possible values of X, the total of all probabilities is equal to 1.

Suppose instead X is defined to be the *average* of the two dice, rather than the total. Now the possible values of X are 1 (with probability 1/36), 1.5 (with probability 2/36), . . . , 5.5 (with probability 2/36), and 6 (with probability 1/36). Notice that X is still a discrete random variable, since there are gaps in the possible values (a value of 4.2 is not possible, for example). However, the possible values of X are *not* all counting numbers. In general, the possible values of a discrete random variable need not be positive integers but generally are since the discrete random variable typically counts the number of occurrences of a particular event.

CONTINUOUS RANDOM VARIABLES

The previous section introduced you to the discrete random variable, where the possible values of X can be listed along with corresponding probabilities. Characteristic of this type of random variable is the presence of *gaps* in the list of possible values. For example, when throwing two dice, a total of 8.5 cannot occur.

The other type of random variable is the **continuous random variable,** for which *any* value is possible over some continuous range of values. For a random variable of this type, there are no gaps in the set of possible values. As a simple example, consider two random variables: X is the number of days that it rained in Boston during any particular month, and Y is the amount of rainfall during this month. X is a *discrete* random variable, because it counts the number of days, and consequently there are gaps in the possible values (7.4, for example, is not possible). Y, on the other hand, is a *continuous* random variable because (at least in principle) the amount of rainfall could be any nonnegative value.

Suppose the heights of all adult males in the United States range from 3 feet to 7.5 feet. Your task is to describe these heights using such statements as:

15% of the heights are under 5.5 ft.

88% of the heights are between 5 ft and 6 ft.

We first define the random variable

X = height of a randomly selected adult male in the United States

Figure 5.1 shows the range of X.

We are unable to list all possible values of X, since *any* height is possible over this range. However, we can still discuss probabilities associated with X. For example, the two preceding statements can be described by using the probability statements

$$P(X < 5.5) = .15$$

$$P(X \text{ is between 5 ft and 6 ft}) = P(5 < X < 6) = .88$$

FIGURE 5.1

Example of a continuous random variable. X = height, in feet, of a randomly selected adult male in the United States.

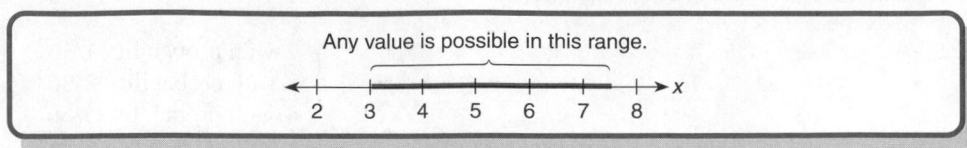

For this situation, X is a continuous random variable. Probabilities for continuous random variables can be found only for *intervals*. (Probabilities of exact values are meaningful only for discrete random variables.) **Determining probabilities for a continuous random variable is discussed in Chapter 6.**

The discussion in Chapter 1 on discrete and continuous data is directly related to our present topic. *When you observe a discrete random variable, you obtain discrete data. When you observe a continuous random variable (such as 100 heights), you obtain continuous data.*

EXERCISES 5.1–5.8

UNDERSTANDING THE MECHANICS

5.1 In a batch of circuit board there are two boards that need to be returned to the factory, three boards that need repair but do not need to be sent back to the factory, and three boards that are in good working condition.

a. What is the probability that a circuit board selected at random needs to be returned to the factory?

b. What is the probability that a circuit board is in good working condition?

5.2 A manager can either hire or not hire an applicant after an interview. Let H represent "hire" and N represent "not hire". Suppose that both outcomes are equally likely. Let X equal the number of of Ns after two interviews.

a. List all possible outcomes from two interviews. List these as pairs. Are each of these pairs of outcomes equally likely.

b. What is $P(X = 0)$? $P(X = 1)$? $P(X = 2)$?

5.3 A die is tossed.

a. List all possible outcomes.

b. Let X equal 0 if the die shows a value of 1 or 2; let X equal 1 if the die shows a value of 3; and let X equal 2 if the die shows a value greater than 3. What is $P(X = 0)$? $P(X = 1)$? $P(X = 2)$?

5.4 State the values that the following random variables can assume. Classify each random variable as either discrete or continuous.

a. The number of employees absent at a Texas Instruments plant.

b. The increase in spending by consumers at Christmas time.

c. The total return achieved by a municipal bond fund.

d. The number of cars recalled by an automaker next year.

e. The waiting time of a customer at a supermarket checkout counter.

5.5 Consider an experiment in which a coin is tossed and a die is rolled. Let X be the number observed from rolling the die. Let Y be the value 1 if a head appears and 0 if a tail appears. List the values that the random variables X and Y can have, along with the corresponding probabilities.

APPLYING THE NEW CONCEPTS

5.6 In the spring of 1998, the Federal Aviation Administration (FAA) ordered urgent inspections and repairs of 152 older Boeing 737s after Continental Airlines mechanics found fuel leaking into a conduit carrying wires through a fuel tank of one jet. The FAA ordered less-urgent inspections for missing or frayed fuel pump wire insulation on Boeing 747s and 767s. List examples of both discrete and continuous random variables that would be of interest to an inspector of Boeing 737s, 747s, and 767s. Classify each as being either a discrete or a continuous random variable.

(Source: Adapted from *USA Today,* "FAA Orders Urgent 737 Fixes," May 8–10, 1998, p. 1A.)

5.7 An IRS auditor only has time to audit two of three tax returns. Suppose two of the tax returns show a refund due to the taxpayer and one tax return shows that the taxpayer owes the IRS. Assume that the IRS auditor is to randomly select two of the returns. Define X to equal the number of tax returns among the two selected that show a refund due the taxpayer.

a. List all possible outcomes of this experiment.

b. Show the values that the random variable X can assume.

c. List the probabilities associated with the values in part (a).

5.8 Each day shift, engineer 1 and engineer 2 select a switch. Let $X1$ have a 0 outcome if engineer 1 selects a faulty switch and 1 if engineer 1 selects a switch that is not faulty. In a similar fashion, define $X2$ for engineer 2. Now assume that each engineer has a probability of .5 of selecting a faulty switch. Let Y be the sum of $X1$ and $X2$.

a. What do you guess is the probability that Y is equal to 0? 1? 2?

b. To confirm your answer in part (a), generate 500 random observations for $X1$ and $X2$. In Excel, first put the numbers 0 and 1 in cells D1 and D2. In E1 and E2, put the value .5. Now that the probabilities are listed for each of the values of the random variable in cells D1 through E2, click on **Tools ➤ Data Analysis ➤ Random Number.** Put "2" into the box **Number of Variables.** Type "500" in the **Number of Random Numbers** box. Select **Discrete** for the **Distribution** box. For the **Value and Probability Input Range** box, type in "D1:E2." Type "A1" in the **Output Range** box. After clicking on the "OK" button, the random numbers will appear in column A. These are the observations for X1 and X2. The user form alongside illustrates the necessary values for generating these random data.

c. To create the values for the Y variable, type "=A1 + B1" in cell C1. Then drag C1 down through C500.

d. Obtain a histogram of the random numbers for Y. In Excel, use **KGP Data Analysis ➤ Quantitative Data Charts/Tables ➤ Histogram/Freq. Charts.** Fill in the user form with the input being the cells C1:C500 and select three for the number of classes. Describe the shape of the histogram.

e. From the histogram in part (d), approximate the probabilities of Y equaling 0, 1, or 2. How do these numbers compare to your answer in part (a)?

Random Number Generation   ? X

Number of Variables:	2	OK
Number of Random Numbers:	500	Cancel
Distribution:	Discrete ▼	Help

Parameters

Value and Probability Input Range:

D1:E2

Random Seed:

Output options
- ⦿ Output Range: | A1 |
- ○ New Worksheet Ply:
- ○ New Workbook

5.2 REPRESENTING PROBABILITY DISTRIBUTIONS FOR DISCRETE RANDOM VARIABLES

There are three popular methods of describing the probabilities associated with a discrete random variable X. They are:

List each value of X and its corresponding probability.

Use a histogram to convey the probabilities corresponding to the various values of X.

Use a function that assigns a probability to each value of X.

Remember our coin-flipping example, in which X = number of heads in three flips of a coin. We can list each value and probability:

$$X = \begin{cases} 0 & \text{with probability } 1/8 \\ 1 & \text{with probability } 3/8 \\ 2 & \text{with probability } 3/8 \\ 3 & \text{with probability } 1/8 \end{cases}$$

This works well when there is only a small number of possible values for X; it would not work well for 100 flips of a coin.

Using a histogram also is a convenient way to represent the shape of a discrete distribution having a small number of possible values. For this situation, you construct a histogram in which the height of each bar is the probability of observing that value of X (Figure 5.2). It is easier to determine the shape of the probability distribution by using such a chart. The distribution in Figure 5.2 is clearly symmetric and concentrated in the middle values.

Using a function (that is, an algebraic formula) to assign probabilities is the most convenient method of describing the probability distribution for a discrete random variable. For any given application of such a random variable, however, this function may or may not be known. Later in the chapter we identify certain useful discrete random variables, each of which has a corresponding function that assigns these probabilities.

The function that assigns a probability to each value of X is called a **probability mass function (PMF)**. Denoting a particular value of X as x, this function is of the form

$$P(X = x) = \text{some expression (usually containing } x\text{)}$$
that produces the probability of observing x

$$= P(x)$$

FIGURE 5.2

A histogram representation of a discrete random variable, where X = number of heads in three coin flips.

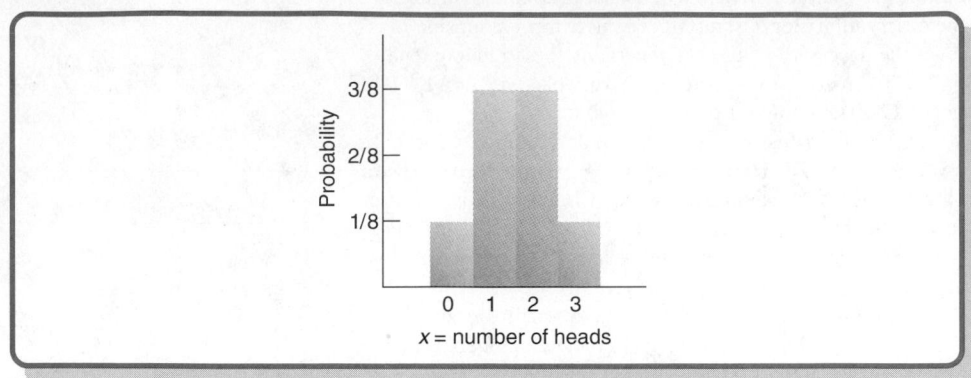

Not every function can serve as a PMF. The requirements for a PMF function are:

1. $P(x)$ is between 0 and 1 (inclusively) for each x
2. $\sum P(x) = 1$

EXAMPLE 5.2

Consider a random variable X having possible values of 1, 2, or 3. The corresponding probability for each value is:

$$X = \begin{cases} 1 \text{ with probability } 1/6 \\ 2 \text{ with probability } 1/3 \\ 3 \text{ with probability } 1/2 \end{cases}$$

Determine an expression for the PMF.

SOLUTION

Consider the function

$$P(X = x) = P(x) = x/6 \qquad \text{for } x = 1, 2, 3$$

This function provides the probabilities   *Probability is between 0 and 1*

$$P(X = 1) = P(1) = 1/6 \qquad \text{(OK)}$$

$$P(X = 2) = P(2) = 2/6 = 1/3 \qquad \text{(OK)}$$

$$P(X = 3) = P(3) = 3/6 = 1/2 \qquad \text{(OK)}$$

This function satisfies the requirements for a PMF: each probability is between 0 and 1, and $P(1) + P(2) + P(3) = 1/6 + 1/3 + 1/2 = 1$. Consequently, the function

$$P(x) = x/6 \qquad \text{for } x = 1, 2, 3 \qquad \text{(and zero elsewhere)}$$

is the PMF for this discrete random variable.

EXAMPLE 5.3

Consider Example 5.1, where X is the total of two dice. Determine the PMF for this discrete random variable.

SOLUTION

Consider the expression

$$P(x) = \frac{x-1}{36} \qquad \text{for } x = 2, 3, 4, \ldots, 12 \qquad \text{(and zero elsewhere)}$$

If this is the proper PMF, then, for example,

$$P(2) = P(X = 2) = \frac{2-1}{36} = 1/36$$

This does appear to be correct, so far. Also,

$$P(5) = P(X = 5) = \frac{5-1}{36} = 4/36$$

This also is correct. But now consider

$$P(10) = P(X = 10) = \frac{10-1}{36} = 9/36$$

According to our previous solution, we know that $P(10) = 3/36$, not 9/36. So this particular function is not the PMF for this random variable; the PMF must work for *all* values of X.

Consider the expression

$$P(x) = \frac{6 - |x - 7|}{36} \quad \text{for } x = 2, 3, \ldots, 12 \quad \text{(and zero elsewhere)}$$

where $|\ |$ represents the absolute value of a number. See if you can demonstrate that this function is a bona fide PMF for this example (it is). Do not worry about where this expression came from, but do verify that it works. The truth of the matter is that often PMFs are derived by trial and error.

Notice that a probability mass function provides a theoretical "model" of the population by describing the chance of observing any particular value of the random variable. *You can view the population as what you would obtain if you observed the corresponding random variable indefinitely.*

EXERCISES 5.9–5.19

UNDERSTANDING THE MECHANICS

5.9 Which of the following probability mass functions are valid? Why?

a. x	P(x)
-2	.4
-3	.4
4	.2

b. x	P(x)
10	-.1
20	.9
30	.2

c. x	P(x)
1	.1
2	.2
3	.3
4	.4

d. x	P(x)
0	.1
5	.6
7	.1
9	.1

e. x	P(x)
100	.3
120	.3
300	.3
500	.3

5.10 Let $P(X = x)$ be equal to .125 for x equal to 10, 20, 30, 40, 50, 60, 70, or 80 and zero elsewhere. Why is this function a probability mass function?

5.11 Is the following function a probability mass function? Why?

$P(X = x) = x/30$ for $x = 0, 10,$ and 20 (and zero elsewhere)

5.12 Is the following function a probability mass function? Why?

$$P(X = x) = \frac{3}{4(3-x)!x!} \quad \text{for } x = 0, 1, 2, 3$$

(and zero elsewhere)

5.13 Is the following function a probability mass function? Why?

$$P(X = x) = \frac{\sqrt{x}}{9} \quad \text{for } x = 4, 9, 16 \quad \text{(and zero elsewhere)}$$

APPLYING THE NEW CONCEPTS

5.14 There are 3 electrical components that a quality-control inspector needs to inspect. One of the components does not function. Suppose that the inspector only chooses two randomly and that the random variable X represents the number of components not working.

a. List all possible outcomes.
b. Find the probability mass function for X.

5.15 A loan officer knows that the monthly payments for loan A, loan B, and loan C are paid on time, with probabilities of .60, .80, and .95, respectively. Consider the payment of each loan to be independent of the payment of the other loans. Define X to be the number of loans from loans A, B, and C that are paid on time in a randomly selected month of the year.

a. List all possible outcomes.

b. List the probabilities of each outcome.

c. Find the probability mass function for X.

5.16 A real estate broker needs to advertise two townhouses, two duplexes, and two single-family homes. However, the broker decides to choose at random only one of the six properties for open house on a certain weekend. Let the random variable X take on the value 1 if a townhouse is chosen, 2 if a duplex is chosen, and 3 if a single-family home is chosen. Write the probability mass function of X.

5.17 Suppose that in Exercise 5.16, the random variable X is assigned the value of 2 if a townhouse is chosen, 4 if a duplex is chosen, and 6 if a single-family home is chosen. Write the probability mass function of X.

5.18 An investor has two investments, A and B. The investor believes that investment A is equally likely to increase by $1000 or to decrease by $1000 by the end of the year. The investor also believes that investment B is equally likely to increase by $2000 or decrease by $2000 by the end of the year. Let X represent the total amount of change in investments A and B. Assume that these investments perform independent of each other. Find the probability mass function of X.

5.19 A quality-control inspector is checking incoming lots of materials for excessive numbers of defective items. The inspector needs to choose at random one of six incoming lots, and then needs to inspect only that lot. Suppose one lot has zero defective items, two of the lots have three defective items, and the remaining three each have 10 defective items. Let the random variable X be equal to 1 if the lot with zero defective items is drawn, 2 if a lot with three defective items is drawn, and 3 if a lot with 10 defective items is drawn. Verify that the following function is the probability mass function of X.

$$P(X = x) = x/6 \qquad \text{if } x = 1, 2, 3 \qquad \text{(and zero elsewhere)}$$

5.3 MEAN AND VARIANCE OF DISCRETE RANDOM VARIABLES

MEAN OF DISCRETE RANDOM VARIABLES

Chapter 3 introduced you to the mean and variance of a set of sample data consisting of n values. Suppose that these values were obtained by observing a particular random variable n times. The sample mean, $\overline{X}$, represents the *average* value of the sample data. In this section, we determine a similar value, the **mean of a discrete random variable**, written as μ. The value of μ represents the average value of the random variable if you were to observe this variable over an indefinite period of time.

Reconsider our coin-flipping example, where X is the number of heads in three flips of a coin. Suppose you flip the coin three times, record the value of X, flip the coin three times again, record the value of X, and repeat this process 10 times. Now you have 10 observations of X. Suppose they are

$$2, 1, 1, 0, 2, 3, 2, 1, 1, 3$$

The mean of these data is the *statistic* $\overline{X}$, where

$$\overline{x} = \frac{2 + 1 + 1 + \cdots + 1 + 3}{10}$$

$$= 1.6 \text{ heads}$$

If you observed X *indefinitely*, what would X be on the average?

$$X = \begin{cases} 0 \text{ with probability } 1/8 \\ 1 \text{ with probability } 3/8 \\ 2 \text{ with probability } 3/8 \\ 3 \text{ with probability } 1/8 \end{cases}$$

So 1/8 of the time you should observe the value 0; 3/8 of the time, the value 1; 3/8 of the time, the value 2; and 1/8 of the time, the value 3. In a sense, each probability represents the *relative frequency* for that particular value of X. So the average value of X is

$$(0)(1/8) + (1)(3/8) + (2)(3/8) + (3)(1/8) = 1.5 \text{ heads}$$

Notice that X cannot be 1.5; this is merely the value of X on the average.

DEFINITION

The average value of the discrete random variable X (if observed indefinitely) is the mean of X. The symbol for this parameter is μ.

We found that $\mu = 1.5$ by multiplying each value of X by its corresponding probability and summing the results:

$$\mu = 1.5 = 0 \cdot P(0) + 1 \cdot P(1) + 2 \cdot P(2) + 3 \cdot P(3)$$

This procedure applies to any discrete random variable, and so we define*

$$\mu = \sum xP(x) \qquad\qquad (5.1)$$

EXAMPLE 5.4

A personnel manager in a large production facility is investigating the number of reported on-the-job accidents over a period of one month. We define the random variable

$$X = \text{number of reported accidents per month}$$

Based on past records, she has derived the following probability distribution for X:

$$X = \begin{cases} 0 & \text{with probability } .50 \\ 1 & \text{with probability } .25 \\ 2 & \text{with probability } .10 \\ 3 & \text{with probability } .10 \\ 4 & \text{with probability } \underline{.05} \\ & \qquad\qquad\quad 1.00 \end{cases}$$

During 50% of the months there were no reported accidents, 25% of the months had one accident, and so on. (Notice that deriving an algebraic expression for the PMF for this distribution would be extremely difficult. This poses no problem, however.)

What is the mean (average value) of X?

SOLUTION

Using equation 5.1,

$$\mu = (0)(.5) + (1)(.25) + (2)(.1) + (3)(.1) + (4)(.05)$$

$$= .95$$

There is .95 (nearly 1) accident reported on the average per month.

VARIANCE OF DISCRETE RANDOM VARIABLES

We previously considered 10 observations of the random variable that counted the number of heads in three flips of a coin. These data were 2, 1, 1, 0, 2, 3, 2, 1, 1, 3. We used the notation from Chapter 3 to define the mean of these data, and we obtained $\bar{x} = 1.6$. The variance of these data, using equation 3.8, is $s^2 = .933$. Since s^2 describes a sample, it is a statistic.

Once again, consider observing X indefinitely. For this situation, the average value of X is defined as the mean of X, μ. When we observe X indefinitely, this particular variance is defined to be the variance of the random variable, X, and is written σ^2 (read as "sigma squared").

$$\sigma^2 = \text{variance of the discrete random variable, } X$$

---

* μ is often referred to as the *expected* value of the random variable, X, and is written $\mu = E(X)$.

The **variance of a discrete random variable,** X, is a parameter describing the variation of the corresponding population. It is the average (expected) value of $(X - \mu)^2$ if X were observed indefinitely, and it can be obtained by using one of the following expressions, which are mathematically equivalent:*

$$\sigma^2 = \sum (x - \mu)^2 \cdot P(x) \qquad (5.2)$$

$$\sigma^2 = \sum x^2 P(x) - \mu^2 \qquad (5.3)$$

Equation 5.3 generally provides an easier method of determining the variance and will be used in all of the examples to follow. For the coin-flipping example,

$$\sigma^2 = \sum x^2 P(x) - \mu^2$$

$$= [(0)^2 \cdot (1/8) + (1)^2 \cdot (3/8) + (2)^2 \cdot (3/8) + (3)^2 \cdot (1/8)] - (1.5)^2$$

$$= 3 - 2.25 = .75$$

So our final results would be:

Using the Sample of 10 Observations		For the Random Variable, X (Indefinite Number of Observations)	
$\bar{x} = 1.6$	$s^2 = .933$	$\mu = 1.5$	$\sigma^2 = .75$
mean	variance	mean	variance
statistics		parameters	

In Chapter 3, the square root of the variance, s, was defined to be the standard deviation of the data. The same definition applies to a random variable. The **standard deviation of a discrete random variable,** X, is denoted σ, where:

$$\sigma = \sqrt{\sum (x - \mu)^2 \cdot P(x)} \qquad (5.4)$$

$$\sigma = \sqrt{\sum x^2 P(x) - \mu^2} \qquad (5.5)$$

EXAMPLE 5.5

Determine the variance and standard deviation of the random variable concerning on-the-job accidents in Example 5.4.

SOLUTION

A convenient method of determining both the mean and variance of a discrete random variable is to summarize the calculations in tabular form:

x	$P(x)$	$x \cdot P(x)$	$x^2 \cdot P(x)$
0	.5	0	0
1	.25	.25	.25
2	.1	.2	.4
3	.1	.3	.9
4	.05	.2	.8
	1.00	.95	2.35

So,

$$\mu = \sum x P(x) = .95 \text{ accident}$$

---

* Using the expectation notation, σ^2 is the expected value of $(X - \mu)^2$ and can be written $\sigma^2 = E(X - \mu)^2$ or $\sigma^2 = E(X^2) - [E(X)]^2$.

and

$$\sigma^2 = \sum x^2 P(x) - \mu^2 = 2.35 - (.95)^2$$

$$= 1.45 \quad \text{Variance}$$

Also

$$\sigma = \sqrt{1.45} = 1.20 \text{ accidents} \quad = \text{std Deviation}$$

EXAMPLE 5.6

Suppose that a computerized procedure generates integer values between 1 and 5 (that is, 1, 2, 3, 4, and 5) in such a way that each value has the same chance of selection. Let X represent a generated value. (i) Describe the probability distribution of X. (ii) What is the mean and variance of this random variable?

SOLUTION TO (i)

Since each value of X has the same chance of selection, namely, 1 chance in 5, the probability distribution of X is

$$X = \begin{cases} 1 \text{ with probability } 1/5 \\ 2 \text{ with probability } 1/5 \\ 3 \text{ with probability } 1/5 \\ 4 \text{ with probability } 1/5 \\ 5 \text{ with probability } 1/5 \end{cases}$$

The corresponding probability mass function is

$$P(X = x) = 1/5 \qquad \text{for } x = 1, 2, 3, 4, 5 \qquad \text{(and zero elsewhere)}$$

SOLUTION TO (ii)

The mean of X is

$$\mu = 1 \cdot \frac{1}{5} + 2 \cdot \frac{1}{5} + 3 \cdot \frac{1}{5} + 4 \cdot \frac{1}{5} + 5 \cdot \frac{1}{5} = \frac{15}{5} = 3$$

and the variance of X is

$$\sigma^2 = \sum x^2 P(x) - \mu^2$$

$$= \left[1 \cdot \frac{1}{5} + 4 \cdot \frac{1}{5} + 9 \cdot \frac{1}{5} + 16 \cdot \frac{1}{5} + 25 \cdot \frac{1}{5} \right] - (3)^2$$

$$= \frac{55}{5} - 9 = 2$$

Also, the standard deviation of X is $\sqrt{2} = 1.414$.

A discrete random variable X having the property that each value of X has the same probability of occurring is called a *discrete uniform random variable*. In general, for such a random variable, the possible values of X are all values between, say, a and b, that is, a, $a + 1$, $a + 2$, . . . , b. In Example 5.6, $a = 1$ and $b = 5$. Since each of the $(b - a) + 1$ values of X has the same probability of occurring, the probability mass function for the discrete uniform random variable is

$$P(X = x) = \frac{1}{(b-a)+1} \quad \text{for } x = a, a+1, a+2, \ldots, b \qquad \textbf{(5.6)}$$

(and zero elsewhere)

A nice feature of this type of random variable is that there is a shortcut method of determining the mean and variance of X. It can be shown that for the discrete uniform random variable,

$$\mu = \frac{a+b}{2} \tag{5.7}$$

$$\sigma^2 = \frac{(b-a)(b-a+2)}{12} \tag{5.8}$$

In Example 5.6, $a = 1$ and $b = 5$, so

$$\mu = \frac{1+5}{2} = 3 \qquad \text{(same as before)}$$

$$\sigma^2 = \frac{(5-1)(5-1+2)}{12} = \frac{24}{12} = 2 \qquad \text{(same as before)}$$

In the sections to follow, we will examine three other "special" discrete random variables. Each of these random variables will also have a shortcut formula for calculating the mean and variance.

EXAMPLE 5.7

Using Excel to Generate Values From a Discrete Uniform Distribution

Refer to Example 5.6. Generate 100 random integer values between 1 and 5, inclusively. What are the mean and variance of these values? Do they agree with the results of Example 5.6? If not, why not?

SOLUTION

To generate these values using Excel, follow the following sequence: (1) click on the **Paste Function** icon (f_*), (2) click on **Math & Trig** in the **Function** category list, (3) click on **RANDBETWEEN** in the **Function** name list, (4) set the bottom value equal to 1 and the top value equal to 5, and (5) click on OK. Assuming the spreadsheet is empty, this random value will appear in cell A1. Next, place the cursor on the small square in the lower right corner of this cell and drag it down through cell A100. You should now see 100 integers between one and five in column A. The first 17 values for one such run are shown in Figure 5.3.

To obtain the descriptive statistics, click on **Tools ➤ Data Analysis ➤ Descriptive Statistics.** For the input range, enter "A1:A100," and for the output range, enter "B1." Finally, click on the white square alongside **Summary Statistics.** These results are also shown in Figure 5.3.

The mean of the 100 values in the sample is $\bar{x} = 3.03$, and the sample variance is $s^2 = 2.05$. According to Exercise 5.6, the mean of the random variable is 3, and the variance is 2. What we have in the solution is 100 *observations* of the random variable—that is, a sample. The population here consists of the observations we would obtain if we were to observe this random variable *indefinitely*. The mean of this population is the mean of the random variable—that is, 3. Since we only observed the variable 100 times, it is not surprising that the sample mean of 3.03 is unequal to 3—although it is quite close. A similar argument applies to the variance since the *population* variance here is 2, and the *sample* variance obtained from the sample of 100 observations is 2.05.

This example illustrates once again the difference between a *population* (indefinite number of observations of a random variable) and a *sample* (a finite number of actual observations of this random variable).

FIGURE 5.3

Random sequence generated by Excel and descriptive statistics.

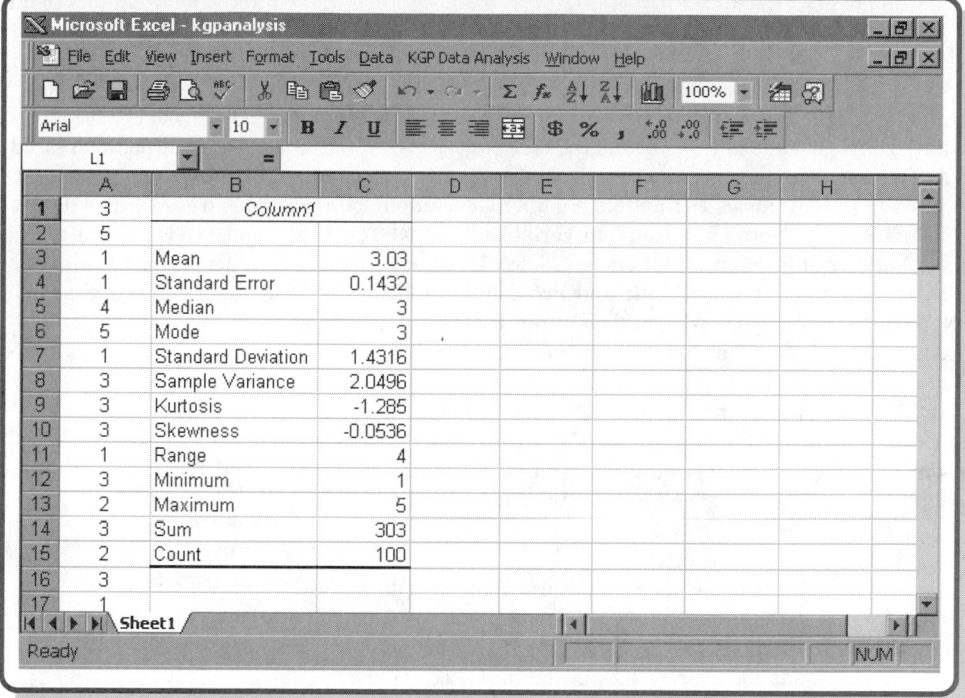

EXERCISES 5.20–5.27

UNDERSTANDING THE MECHANICS

5.20 Find the mean and standard deviation for the random variable X with the following distributions.

a. x	$P(x)$	b. x	$P(x)$	c. x	$P(x)$
0	.2	−3	.1	1	.1
1	.6	0	.3	2	.1
2	.2	3	.6	3	.4
				4	.3
				5	.1

5.21 For each of the following probability mass functions, determine the mean and standard deviation.
   a. $P(X = x) = x/60$ for $x = 20$ and 40 (and zero elsewhere)
   b. $P(X = x) = \sqrt{x}/11$ for $x = 4$, 16, and 25 (and zero elsewhere)

5.22 The random variable X has a discrete uniform distribution with an equal chance of the numbers 2, 3, 4, 5, and 6 occurring.
   a. What is the probability that X is greater than 4?
   b. What is the mean of X?
   c. What is the standard deviation of X?

APPLYING THE NEW CONCEPTS

5.23 Suppose that a coin is flipped three times. Define the random variable X to be equal to twice the number of heads that appear. Determine the mean and variance of X.

5.24 The discrete uniform random variable X has a positive probability for the values 5, 6, 7, 8, 9, and 10. Verify that the mean and variance of this random variable can be calculated using formulas 5.1 and 5.3 or formulas 5.7 and 5.8.

5.25 A Times Orange County poll sampled voters from Orange County, California, whether a commercial airport at El Toro should be built. Although voters countywide believed an airport would benefit the local economy, Orange County respondents remained deeply divided over building a county airport. The results of the poll were as follows:

	Percentage (%)
Favor building the airport	43
Undecided	13
Disfavor building the airport	44

(Source: *Los Angeles Times*, "EL TORO: Will it Fly?" May 24, 1998, p. 1A.)

   a. Let the random variable X represent the following values:

X	Category
1	Favor building the airport
0	Undecided
−1	Disfavor building the airport

What is the mean and the standard deviation of X?
   b. Let the random variable X represent the following values:

X	Category
3	Favor building the airport
2	Undecided
1	Disfavor building the airport

What is the mean and standard deviation of X?
   c. Compare the answers in part (a) to those in part (b). Do they appear to be what you would expect?

5.26 A discrete uniform random variable X has the following probability mass function:

$$P(X = x) = 1/4 \quad \text{if } x = 1, 2, 3, \text{ and } 4 \text{ (and zero elsewhere)}$$

a. Generate 400 random observations from this distribution. In Excel, first put the numbers 1 through 4 in cells B1 through B4. In column C, put .25 in cells C1 through C4. Now that the distribution is listed in the cells B1 through C4, click on **Tools ➤ Data Analysis ➤ Random Number Generation.** Put "1" into the box **Number of Random Variables.** Type "400" in the **Number of Random Numbers** box. Select **Discrete** for the **Distribution** box. For the **Value and Probability Input** box, type in "B1:C4." Type "A1" for the **Output Range** box. After clicking on the "OK" button, the random numbers will appear in column A.

b. Obtain a histogram of the random numbers in column A. In Excel, use **KGP Data Analysis ➤ Quantitative Data Charts/Tables ➤ Histogram/Freq. Charts.** Fill in the user form with the input being the cells A1:A400 and select 4 for the number of classes. Describe the shape of the histogram. Is this the shape that you would expect?

c. From observing the shape of the histogram, what do you think the mean of the random variable X might be? Does a standard deviation of 3.5 seem reasonable for this distribution?

d. Determine the exact values of the mean and standard deviation of the random variable X, and compare your answer to part (c).

5.27 A parent-educator group in Utah headed by the Alpine school district superintendent made a proposal to the Legislative Education Interim Committee. A request for $11 million to eliminate textbook fees in every school district in Utah got a cool reception from this committee. The committee requested that the parent-educator group compile additional information from all 40 of the state's school districts and make its presentation again. Suppose that the parent-educator group followed their advice and conducted a survey across the 40 school districts. The main question asked of both adults with children and adults without children was, "Do you support the elimination of textbook fees in school districts by having the Utah legislature appropriate $11 million for this cause?" Let the random variable X denote the ordered number of the response. The results of the survey and corresponding values of X follow.

Response	X Random Variable Value	Adults with Children (Percentage)	Adults without Children (Percentage)
Not supportive	1	10	25
Somewhat supportive	2	20	60
Supportive	3	56	10
Very supportive	4	14	5

(Adapted from *The Salt Lake Tribune*, "Textbook Funds Request Greeted Coolly," May 21, 1998, p. D6.)

a. Find the mean and standard deviation of the responses for adults with children.

b. Find the mean and standard deviation of the responses for adults without children.

c. Compare and interpret the statistics found in parts (a) and (b).

5.4 BINOMIAL RANDOM VARIABLES

The random variable X representing the number of heads in three flips of a coin is a special type of discrete random variable, a **binomial** random variable.

We next list the conditions for a binomial random variable in general and as applied to our coin-flipping example:

A Binomial Situation
1. Your experiment consists of n repetitions, called **trials.**
2. Each trial has two mutually exclusive possible outcomes, (or can be considered as having two outcomes), referred to as **success** and **failure.**
3. The n trials are *independent.*

4. The probability of a success for each trial is denoted p; the value of p remains the same for each trial.
5. The random variable X is the number of *successes* out of n trials.

For Example 5.1
1. $n = 3$ (flips of a coin)

2. Success = head, failure = tail (this is arbitrary)

3. The results on one coin flip do not affect the results on another flip.
4. p = the probability of flipping a head on a particular trial = 1/2
5. X = the number of heads out of three flips

You encounter a binomial random variable when a certain experiment is repeated many times (n trials), the trials are independent, and each experiment results in one of two mutually exclusive outcomes. For example, a randomly selected individual is either male or female, is on welfare or is not, will vote Republican or will not, and so on.

The two outcomes for each experiment are labeled as *success* or *failure.* A success need not be considered "good" or "desirable." Instead, it depends on what you are counting at the completion of the n trials. If, for example, the object of the experiment is to determine the probability that 3 people out of 20 randomly selected individuals *are* on welfare, then a success on each of the $n = 20$ trials is the event that the person selected on each trial *is* on welfare.

EXAMPLE 5.8

In Example 4.4, it was noted that 30% of the people in a particular city read the evening newspaper. Select four people at random from this city. Consider how many of these four people read the evening paper. Does this situation satisfy the requirements of a binomial situation? What is your random variable here?

SOLUTION

Refer to conditions 1 through 5 in our list for a binomial situation.

1.   There are $n = 4$ trials, where each trial consists of selecting one individual from this city.
2.   There are two outcomes for each trial. We are interested in counting the number of people, out of the four selected, who *do* read the evening paper, so define

$$\text{success} = \text{read the evening newspaper}$$

$$\text{failure} = \text{do not read the evening newspaper}$$

3.   The trials are independent since the people are selected randomly.
4. $p = $ probability of a success on each trial $= .3$.
5.   The random variable here is X, where

$$X = \text{number of successes in } n \text{ trials}$$

$$X = \text{number of people (out of four) who read the evening newspaper}$$

All the requirements are satisfied. Thus, X is a binomial random variable (it is also discrete).

COUNTING SUCCESSES FOR A BINOMIAL SITUATION

How many ways are there of getting two heads out of four flips of a coin? There are six: HHTT, HTHT, HTTH, THHT, THTH, and TTHH. How many ways can you select two people from a group of four people, where the order of selection is unimportant (say, you are selecting a two-person committee)? Label the individuals as I_1, I_2, I_3, and I_4. You want to find the number of combinations of four people using two at a time:

$$_4C_2 = \frac{4!}{2!2!} = 6$$

Put these results side by side. The scheme for matching the two results is to select I_1 if H appears on the first flip, select I_2 if H appears on the second flip, and so on.

Two Heads Out of Four Flips	Two People from a Group of Four
HHTT	I_1, I_2
HTHT	I_1, I_3
HTTH	I_1, I_4
THHT	I_2, I_3
THTH	I_2, I_4
TTHH	I_3, I_4

You should see a direct correspondence between the two solutions. Our conclusion is that the number of ways of getting two heads out of four flips of a coin is $_4C_2$. Extending this to any number of flips of a coin, the number of ways of getting k heads out of n flips of a coin is $_nC_k$. Finally, for any binomial situation, the number of ways of getting k successes out of n trials is $_nC_k$. We are thus able to determine the probability mass function (PMF) for any binomial random variable.

Once again, let X equal the number of heads out of three flips. Here X is a binomial random variable, with $p = .5$. Consider any value of X, say, $X = 1$. Then the probability of any one outcome where $X = 1$, such as HTT, is 1/8 and the number of ways of getting one head (success) out of three flips (trials) is $_3C_1 = 3$. Consequently, the probability that X will be 1 is:

$$P(1) = {_3C_1}(1/8) = 3/8$$

The resulting PMF for this situation can be written as

$$P(x) = {_3C_x} \cdot (1/8) \qquad \text{for } x = 0, 1, 2, 3 \qquad \text{(and zero elsewhere)}$$

Using this function, we obtain the same results as before:

$$P(0) = {_3C_0}(1/8) = 1 \cdot (1/8) = 1/8$$

$$P(1) = {_3C_1}(1/8) = 3 \cdot (1/8) = 3/8$$

$$P(2) = {_3C_2}(1/8) = 3 \cdot (1/8) = 3/8$$

$$P(3) = {_3C_3}(1/8) = 1 \cdot (1/8) = \underline{1/8}$$
$$1$$

EXAMPLE 5.9

In Example 5.8, the binomial random variable X is the number of people (out of four) who read the evening newspaper. Also, there are $n = 4$ trials (people) with $p = .3$ (30% of the people read the evening newspaper). Let S denote a success and F a failure. Then define:

$$S = \text{a person reads the evening newspaper}$$

$$F = \text{a person does not read the evening newspaper}$$

What is the probability that exactly two people (out of four) will read the evening paper?

SOLUTION

This is $P(X = 2)$, or $P(2)$. Consider any one result where $X = 2$, such as SFSF. The probability of this result, using equation 4.14, is

(probability of S on first trial) · (probability of F on second trial)
                    · (probability of S on third trial) · (probability of F on fourth trial)

which is

$$(.3)(.7)(.3)(.7) = (.3)^2(.7)^2$$

Also note that the probability of *each* result with two S's and two F's ($X = 2$) also is $(.3)^2(.7)^2 = p^2(1 - p)^2$. How many ways can we get two successes out of four trials? This is:

$$_4C_2 = \frac{4!}{2!2!} = 6$$

So the final result here is

$$P(2) = (\text{number of ways of getting } X = 2)(\text{probability of each one})$$

$$= {_4C_2}(.3)^2(.7)^2$$

$$= (6)(.09)(.49) = .265$$

So 26.5% of the time, exactly two people out of four will read the evening newspaper.

FIGURE 5.4
Probability mass function for
$n = 4$, $p = .3$.

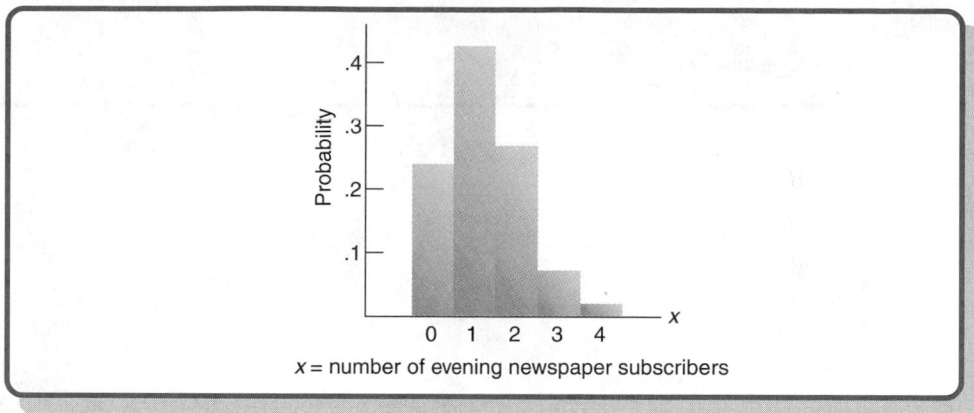

We can extend the results of Example 5.9 to obtain the PMF for a binomial random variable:

$$P(x) = {}_nC_x \, p^x(1-p)^{n-x} \quad \text{for } x = 0, 1, 2, \ldots, n \qquad \textbf{(5.9)}$$

(and zero elsewhere)

where n is the number of trials and p is the probability of a success for each trial.

For the newspaper example, $x = 2$, $n = 4$, and $p = .3$. The complete list of probabilities for this example is:

$$X = \begin{cases} 0 \text{ with probability } {}_4C_0 \,(.3)^0 \,(.7)^4 = & .240 \\ 1 \text{ with probability } {}_4C_1 \,(.3)^1 \,(.7)^3 = & .412 \\ 2 \text{ with probability } {}_4C_2 \,(.3)^2 \,(.7)^2 = & .265 \\ 3 \text{ with probability } {}_4C_3 \,(.3)^3 \,(.7)^1 = & .076 \\ 4 \text{ with probability } {}_4C_4 \,(.3)^4 \,(.7)^0 = & .008 \\ \hline & 1.001 \end{cases}$$

Note that the total value may be slightly greater or less than 1.0, because of rounding. A graphical representation of this PMF is shown in Figure 5.4.

USING THE BINOMIAL TABLE

The binomial PMFs have been tabulated in Table A.1 for various values of n and p. The maximum number of trials in this table is $n = 20$. For binomial situations where n > 20, we suggest the use of a computer package, such as Excel or MINITAB.

For the evening newspaper illustration in Example 5.9, $n = 4$ and $p = .3$. To find $P(2)$, locate $n = 4$ and $x = 2$. Go across the table to $p = .3$ and you will find the corresponding probability (after inserting the decimal in front of the number). This probability is .265. Similarly, $P(0) = .240$, $P(1) = .412$, $P(3) = .076$, and $P(4) = .008$, as before.

The probability that no more than two people will read the evening paper is written $P(X \le 2)$, where

$$P(X \le 2) = P(X = 0) + P(X = 1) + P(X = 2)$$

$$= P(0) + P(1) + P(2)$$

$$= .240 + .412 + .265$$

$$= .917$$

This is a **cumulative probability** and is obtained by summing $P(x)$ over the appropriate values of X.

FIGURE 5.5
Shape of the binomial distribution.

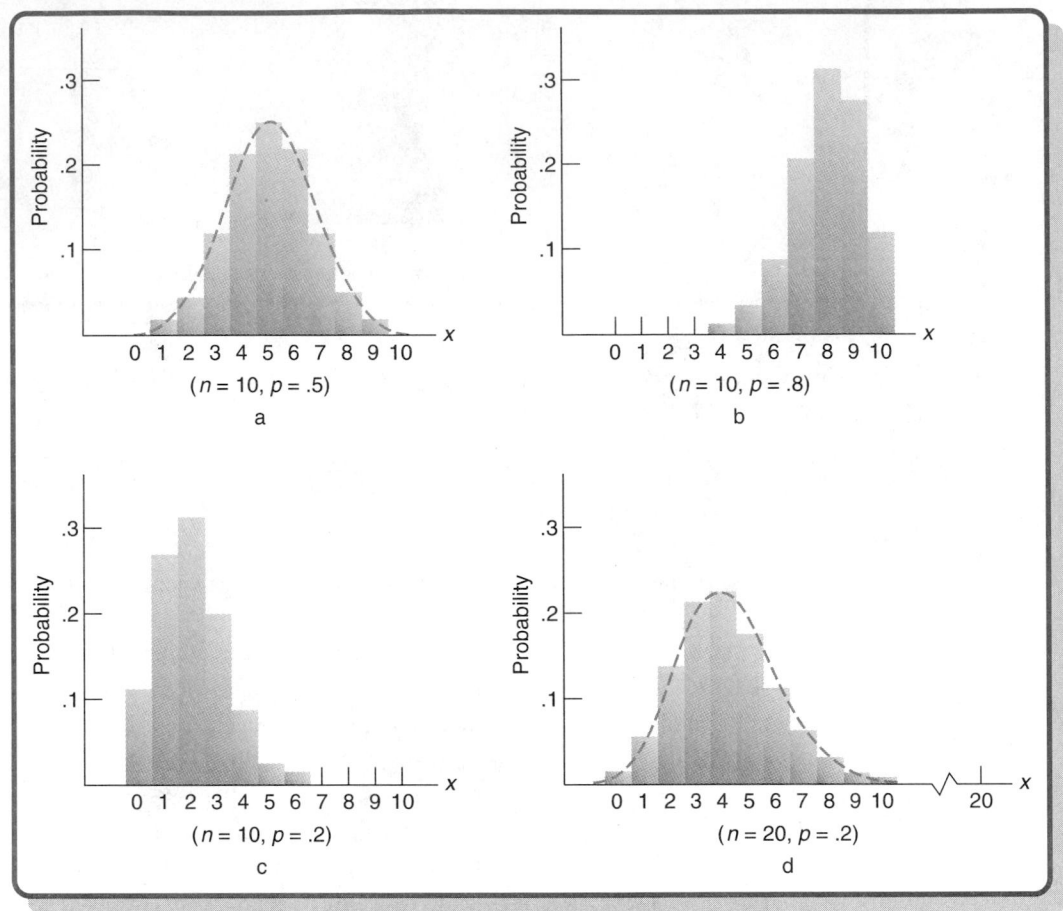

SHAPE OF THE BINOMIAL DISTRIBUTION

Figure 5.5 contains a graphical representation of four binomial distributions. In particular, notice that:

1. When $p = .5$, the shape is perfectly *symmetrical* and resembles a bell-shaped (normal) curve.
2. When $p = .2$, the distribution is *skewed right*. This skewness increases as p decreases.
3. For $p = .8$, the distribution is *skewed left*. As p approaches 1, the amount of skewness increases.

Compare Figure 5.5(c) and (d). Notice that, in both cases, p is .2; however, the number of trials increased from $n = 10$ in (c) to $n = 20$ in (d). For the larger value of n, the shape of this distribution is nearly bell-shaped, *despite the small value of p. This suggests that, regardless of the value of p, the shape of a binomial distribution approaches a bell-shaped distribution as the number of trials (n) increases.* We will use this fact in the next chapter, when we demonstrate an approximation to the binomial distribution using a bell-shaped (normal) curve for large samples.

In summary, the shape of a binomial distribution is:

1. Skewed left for $p > 1/2$ and small n.
2. Skewed right for $p < 1/2$ and small n.
3. Approximately bell-shaped (symmetric) if p is near $1/2$ or if the number of trials is large.

MEAN AND VARIANCE OF BINOMIAL RANDOM VARIABLES

In Example 5.9, we examined the binomial random variable X representing the number of people (out of four) who read the evening newspaper. If you select four people, observe X, select four more people, observe X, and repeat this procedure indefinitely, what will X be on the average? This is the mean of X, where, using equation 5.1,

$$\mu = \Sigma \, xP(x)$$

$$= (0)(.240) + (1)(.412) + (2)(.265) + (3)(.076) + (4)(.008)$$

$$= 1.2 \text{ people}$$

Also, using equation 5.3, the variance of X is

$$\sigma^2 = \Sigma \, x^2 P(x) - \mu^2$$

$$= [(0)^2(.240) + (1)^2(.412) + (2)^2(.265) + (3)^2(.076) + (4)^2(.008)] - (1.2)^2$$

$$= 2.28 - 1.44 = .84$$

and so σ = standard deviation of $X = \sqrt{.84} = .92$ people. (Watch the units.)

The good news is that there is a convenient shortcut for finding the mean and variance of a binomial random variable. For this situation, you need not use equations 5.1 and 5.3. Instead, for any binomial random variable,

$$\mu = np \qquad\qquad\qquad\qquad (5.10)$$

$$\sigma^2 = np(1 - p) \qquad\qquad\qquad\qquad (5.11)$$

How these expressions were derived is certainly not obvious, but let us verify that they work for Example 5.9. Here $n = 4$ and $p = .3$, so

$$\mu = (4)(.3) = 1.2 \qquad (\text{OK})$$

$$\sigma^2 = (4)(.3)(.7) = .84 \qquad (\text{OK})$$

EXAMPLE 5.10

If you repeat Example 5.9 using $n = 50$ people (rather than $n = 4$ people), how many evening newspaper readers will you observe on the average?

SOLUTION

Now, X is the number of people (out of 50) who read the evening paper. Consequently,

$$\mu = np = (50)(.3) = 15$$

So, on the average, X will be 15 people. For this situation, the variance of X is

$$\sigma^2 = np(1 - p) = (50)(.3)(.7) = 10.5$$

Also,

$$\sigma = \sqrt{10.5} = 3.24 \text{ people}$$

EXAMPLE 5.11

Airline overbooking is a common practice. Many people make reservations on several flights due to uncertain plans and then cancel at the last minute or simply fail to show up. Eagle Air is a small commuter airline. Their planes hold only 15 people. Past records indicate that 20% of the people making a reservation do not show up for the flight. We will assume that all reservations are independent; that is, each reservation is for one person and these reservations are made independent of one another.

Suppose that Eagle Air decides to book 18 people for each flight.

1. Determine the probability that on any given flight, at least one passenger holding a reservation will not have a seat.
2. What is the probability that there will be one or more empty seats for any one flight?
3. Determine the mean and standard deviation for this random variable.

SOLUTION 1

The binomial random variable for this situation is $X =$ the number of people (out of 18) who book a flight and actually do appear. For this binomial situation, $n = 18$ (18 reservations are made) and $p = 1 - .2 = .8$ (the probability that any one person will show up). At least one passenger will have no place to sit if X is 16 or more. Using Table A.1,

$$P(X \geq 16) = P(X = 16) + P(X = 17) + P(X = 18)$$

$$= .172 + .081 + .018 = .271$$

We see that if the airline follows this policy, 27% of the time one or more passengers will be deprived of a seat—not a good situation.

SOLUTION 2

We want to find the probability that the number of people who actually arrive (X) is 14 or less. Using Table A.1 (where $n = 18$, $p = .8$),

$$P(X \leq 14) = .215 + .151 + \cdots + .003 + .001 = .50$$

(Notice that the four remaining probabilities are nearly zero.) With this booking policy, the airline will have flights with one or more empty seats approximately one-half of the time.

SOLUTION 3

The mean of X is

$$\mu = np = (18)(.8) = 14.4 \text{ people}$$

which implies that the average number of people who book a flight and do appear is 14.4. The standard deviation of X is

$$\sigma = \sqrt{np(1-p)} = \sqrt{(18)(.8)(.2)} = 1.70 \text{ people}$$

EXAMPLE 5.12

It is estimated that one out of 10 vouchers examined by the audit staff employed by a branch of the Department of Health and Human Services will contain an error. Define X to be the number of vouchers in error out of 20 randomly selected vouchers.

1. What is the probability that at least three vouchers will contain an error?
2. What is the probability that no more than one contains an error?
3. Determine the mean and standard deviation of X.

SOLUTION 1

The random variable X satisfies the requirements for a binomial random variable with $n = 20$ and $p = .1$. For this situation, a "success" is defined to be that a voucher contains an error. The probability that at least three vouchers will contain an error is the probability that X is *3 or more*, which is

$$P(X \geq 3) = 1 - P(X < 3)$$

$$= 1 - P(X \leq 2)$$

$$= 1 - [P(0) + P(1) + P(2)]$$

$$= 1 - (.122 + .270 + .285)$$

$$= .323$$

Consequently, the probability that at least three vouchers will contain an error is .323.

SOLUTION 2

The chance that no more than one voucher is in error is the probability that X is *1 or less,* which is

$$P(X \leq 1) = P(0) + P(1) = .122 + .270 = .392$$

So this event will occur with probability .392.

SOLUTION 3

The mean of the random variable X is

$$\mu = np = (20)(.1) = 2 \text{ vouchers}$$

and the standard deviation of X is

$$\sigma = \sqrt{np(1-p)} = \sqrt{(20)(.1)(.9)} = 1.34 \text{ vouchers}$$

This implies that, on the average, the audit staff will encounter 2 vouchers containing an error (out of 20 randomly selected vouchers).

One situation that requires the use of a binomial random variable is **lot acceptance sampling,** in which you decide whether to accept or send back a lot (batch) of many electrical components, machine parts, or whatever.

USING EXCEL TO DETERMINE BINOMIAL PROBABILITIES

In an earlier section titled Using the Binomial Table, we mentioned that this table only contains values of $n \leq 20$. Excel offers a simple way of finding binomial probabilities for any sample size (n)—in particular, for values of n greater than 20. Excel can be used to calculate an individual probability [such as $P(X = 3)$] or a cumulative probability [such as $P(X \leq 3)$]. This will be illustrated in the next example.

EXAMPLE 5.13

A shipment of 2500 calculator chips arrives at Cassidy Electronics. The contract specifies that Cassidy will accept this lot if a sample size of 100 from the shipment has no more than one defective chip. What is the probability of accepting the lot if, in fact, 5% of the lot (125 chips) are defective?

SOLUTION

This is approximately a binomial situation where:

1. There are $n = 100$ trials.
2. Each trial has two outcomes:

$$\text{success} = \text{chip is defective}$$

$$\text{failure} = \text{chip is not defective}$$

(*Note:* Since the object is to count the number of *defective* chips in the shipment, a success on each trial (chip) will be that the chip is defective. As mentioned earlier, a success need not be a desirable event.)

3. $p = $ probability of a success $= .05^*$

---

* If the lot size is large (2500 here) and the sample size is relatively small (100 here), then the value of p is nearly, although not completely, unaffected by the previous trials. For example, if 5% of the chips are defective, then on the first trial, p is $125/2500 = .05$. On the second trial, p is either $125/2499 = .05002$ (if the first chip was nondefective) or $124/2499 = .04962$ (if the first chip was defective). We typically ignore this minor problem in lot sampling from large populations, but this is why at the start of the solution we mentioned that this is "approximately a binomial situation." Situations in which the value of p is severely affected by what occurred on previous trials will be dealt with in the next section, where we discuss the hypergeometric distribution. Refer to Example 5.16.

4. The random variable here is X = number of successes out of n trials = number of defective chips out of 100. Cassidy accepts the lot of chips if X is 0 or 1. The corresponding probability is a cumulative probability:

$$P(\text{accept}) = P(X \le 1)$$

$$= P(0) + P(1)$$

To determine binomial probabilities using Excel, click on the **Paste Function** icon (f_x), click on **Statistical** under **Function Category,** and click on **BINOMDIST** under **Function Name.** You should then see the input screen shown in Figure 5.6. Panel A of Figure 5.6 is what you would enter to determine $P(X = 0)$, and Panel B provides $P(X = 1)$. Notice that "false" was entered in the box labeled **Cumulative** since individual probabilities were desired. From Panels A and B, we also learn that $P(X \le 1) = P(X = 0) + P(X = 1)$ = .0059 + .0312 = .0371. Consequently, there is about a 4% chance that a sample of size 100 from this population will contain zero or one defective chip (the lot will be accepted).

The easiest way to find $P(X \le 1)$ is to use Panel C in Figure 5.6 where "true" was entered in the **Cumulative** box and the result .0371 (rounded) appears. To summarize: enter "false" in the **Cumulative** box for individual probabilities and "true" for cumulative probabilities.

FIGURE 5.6

Using Excel to find individual probabilities (panels A and B) or cumulative probabilities (panel C).

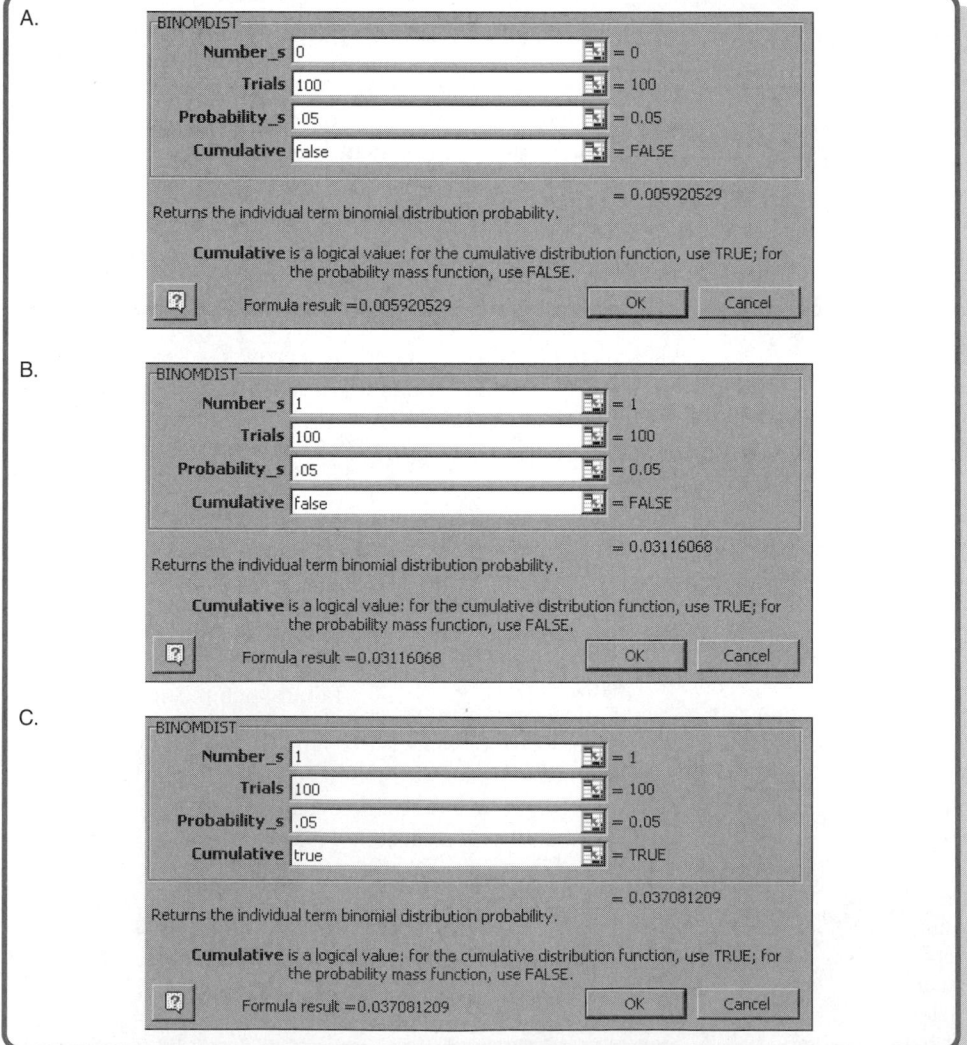

The concept of lot acceptance sampling was originally presented in Chapter 1 to illustrate the distinction between a population and a sample. It also serves as a brief introduction to the area of inferential statistics, discussed at length in Chapter 7. In Example 5.13, we inferred something about a population (the lot of 2500 chips) using a sample (the 100 chips selected for testing). The sample does not include all elements of the population, so there is a risk of making an incorrect decision, such as (1) accepting the lot of chips when in fact it should be rejected or (2) rejecting the lot of chips when in fact it was satisfactory. *Such possibilities for error* always *exist when a statistical sample is used as a basis for an assertion about a population.*

EXERCISES 5.28–5.41

UNDERSTANDING THE MECHANICS

5.28 Using the binomial probabilities in Table A.1, find the following probabilities for a binomial random variable X.
  a. $P(X = 2)$, $n = 4$, $p = .2$
  b. $P(X = 7)$, $n = 9$, $p = .8$
  c. $P(X = 4)$, $n = 10$, $p = .5$
  d. $P(X = 0)$, $n = 20$, $p = .1$

5.29 Using the binomial probabilities in Table A.1, find the probabilities of each of the following if $n = 12$ and $p = .4$.
  a. X is exactly equal to 6.
  b. X is no more than 2.
  c. X is at least 2.
  d. X is greater than 5.
  e. X is between 3 and 6, inclusively.

5.30 For a binomial random variable with $n = 5$ and $p = .25$, compute the following.
  a. $P(X = 1)$
  b. $P(X \geq 1)$
  c. $P(X \leq 3)$
  d. $P(1 \leq X \leq 3)$

5.31 What is the probability that a binomial random variable with $n = 21$ and $p = .1$ does not exceed 1?

APPLYING THE NEW CONCEPTS

5.32 A lawyer estimates that 40% of the cases in which she represented the defendant were won. If the lawyer is presently representing 10 defendants in different cases, what is the probability that at least 5 of the cases will be won? What are you assuming here?

5.33 A market-research firm has discovered that 30% of the people who earn between $25,000 and $50,000 per year have bought a new car within the past two years. In a sample of 12 people earning between $25,000 and $50,000 per year, what is the probability that between 4 and 10 people, inclusive, have bought a new car within the past two years?

5.34 Sweden is an unusual environment for car makers. Together, Volvo and Saab account for the country's five top-selling models, but 70% are sold as company cars because most Swedes can't afford to buy products that cost up to $44,000 (counting a 25% value-added tax). Suppose that 10 cars, all of which are either Volvos or Saabs, are randomly selected in Sweden. Let the random variable X represent the number of company cars from this sample of 10 cars.

(Source: *Fortune,* "Too Slow for the Fast Lane?" July 21, 1997, pp. 68–72.)

  a. Why is X a binomial random variable?
  b. What is the probability that X is more than 6? Would this be considered unusual?
  c. What is the mean and standard deviation of $X?$

5.35 According to the Consumer Aerosol Products Council, when adults were asked if it is true or false that aerosol cans may use CFC propellants (which eat the earth's ozone), approximately three in 10 adults knew that it was false. CFCs were banned in almost all sprays 20 years ago. However, 37% of the adults still believed the answer to be true.

(Source: *USA Today,* "Do Spray Cans Use CFCs?" Apr. 22, 1998, p. 1A.)

  a. For a random sample of 10 adults, what do you think the probability is that fewer than three adults know that the answer is false? Compute it.
  b. For a random sample of 10 adults, what do you think the probability is that fewer than three believe that the answer is true (the incorrect answer)? Compute it.
  c. What is the mean number of sampled adults that you would expect to say that the answer is false [part (a)] and to say that the answer is true [part (b)]?

5.36 Many foreign multinationals are scaling back their China ambitions. The market is not as big as China's population statistics imply. Only about 120 million urban Chinese can afford most of the goods that foreign companies hope to sell. What's more, they are hard to reach because they are so spread out. In a survey by Fiducia, Ltd., approximately sixty percent of the multinationals said that they overestimated the market potential of China.

(Adapted from *The Wall Street Journal,* "Reality Check," Apr. 30, 1998, p. R17.)

  a. From a sample of 10 multinationals, what is the mean and standard deviation of the number of multinationals that say they overestimated the market potential of China?
  b. What is the probability that less than three of the multinationals out of the 10 randomly selected say that they overestimated the market potential of China? Would this be considered an unusual event?

5.37 Let the random variable X represent the number of correct responses on a multiple choice test that has 15 questions. Each question has five multiple choice answers.
  a. What is the probability that the random variable X is greater than 8 if the person taking the test randomly guesses?
  b. What is the mean value of X if the person randomly guesses?

c. What is the standard deviation of X if the person randomly guesses?

d. Estimate the probability that X will fall within the limits $\mu \pm 2\sigma$.

5.38 The *Professional Technician* recommends stocks each month. If 40% of the stocks recommended advance at least 20%, what is the probability that of the five stocks most recently recommended, at least three will advance at least 20%?

5.39 The manager of a retail store knows that 10% of all checks written are "hot" checks. Of the next 25 checks written at the retail store, what is the probability that no more than 3 checks are hot?

5.40 Thousands of Web sites offer consumers medical information. In cyberspace, the doctor is always in. While a person should not be diagnosed with an illness through online sources, a cybersurfer can ask any question, under the cover of anonymity, no matter how embarrassing that question may be in real life. In a survey by IntelliQuest, Inc., approximately 50% of the Web users who queried about medical advice were looking for information about a personal medical problem.

(Adapted from *The Wall Street Journal*, "CybeRx: Getting Medical Advice and Moral Support on the Web," Apr. 30, 1998, p. B10.)

a. For a random sample of 80 users of the Web, who are seeking medical advice, let X represent the number of users who are looking for information about a personal medical problem. To find the probability that X is less than 50, use the Excel binomial function. (Use the **Paste Function ➤ Statistical ➤ Binomdist.**)

b. For the random variable X in part (b), find the probability that X is less than 30.

c. From parts (a) and (b), find the probability that X is greater than or equal to 30 and less than 50. Interpret this probability.

5.41 In a telephone survey, Dallas adults were asked whether Dallas police officers should be allowed to continue to use their discretion when exceeding the speed limit without their flashing lights and sirens when answering certain calls. Sixty-five percent said that the city should change its policy to require officers to activate flashing lights and sirens.

(Adapted from *The Dallas Morning News*, "Breakdown of Results," Apr. 25, 1998, p. 26A.)

a. From a random selection of 54 Dallas adults, how many would you expect to say that the city should change its policy to require officers to activate flashing lights and sirens?

b. Use the Excel function **Binomdist**(x, 54, .65, false) to obtain the probability of obtaining precisely your answer in part (a). If "false" is changed to "true" in the **Binomdist** function, what is the corresponding probability? How do you interpret this probability?

5.5 THE HYPERGEOMETRIC DISTRIBUTION

Another type of discrete random variable that fits many sampling situations is the **hypergeometric random variable.** It bears a strong resemblance to the binomial random variable since the experiment once again consists of n trials, with each trial having two possible outcomes (success or failure).

The conditions for a hypergeometric random variable are:

1. Population size $= N$. In this population, k members are S (successes) and $N - k$ are F (failures).
2. Sample size $= n$ trials, obtained *without replacement.*
3. $X =$ the number of successes out of n trials (a hypergeometric random variable).

The main distinction between a hypergeometric and a binomial situation is that the trials in the former *are not independent.* As a result, the probability of a success on each trial is affected by the results of the previous trials. This situation occurs when sampling *without replacement* from a *finite* population.

The situation surrounding a hypergeometric random variable is similar to the binomial situation in that you count "successes" in both cases. However, for the hypergeometric situation, you have a *finite* population (of size N) and you know the number of successes (k) and failures ($N - k$) that make up this population. For example, you might select a random sample of $n = 8$ from a group of $N = 30$ unionized workers, of which $k = 20$ are in favor of a strike and $N - k = 10$ are not. For this situation, the hypergeometric random variable is $X =$ the number of workers (of the 8) who favor the strike.

We can repeat Example 5.13 using 50 chips (instead of 2500), 10 of which are selected for testing. Suppose that 10% of these chips (5 chips) are defective. As before, define

$$S = \text{success} = \text{chip is defective}$$

$$F = \text{failure} = \text{chip is not defective}$$

Here, out of the 50 chips, 5 are defective. So

$$P(S \text{ on first trial}) = 5/50 = .10$$

The conditional probability of S on the second trial is:

$$5/49 = .102 \text{ if first chip was not defective}$$

$$4/49 = .082 \text{ if the first chip was defective}$$

The probability of a success on the second trial is affected by what occurred on the first trial; this is a hypergeometric situation.

The PMF for the hypergeometric random variable is:

$$P(x) = \frac{_kC_x \cdot _{N-k}C_{n-x}}{_NC_n} \tag{5.12}$$

for $x = a, a + 1, a + 2, \ldots, b$, where a is the maximum of 0 and $n + k - N$ and b is the minimum of k and n. The value of $P(x)$ is zero for all other values of X. Also, n is the sample size and N is the population size, k of which are successes.

EXAMPLE 5.14

Determine the probability of observing exactly 1 defective chip out of a sample of size 10.

SOLUTION

Imagine two containers (the population). One contains 5 S's and the other has 45 F's. The sample consists of 10 chips, randomly selected from these two containers. If x chips are selected from the success container, then $10 - x$ chips are selected from the failure container. For this situation, $N = 50$, $k = 5$, and $n = 10$. The possible values for X are from $a = $ maximum of 0 and -35 (0) to $b = $ minimum of 5 and 10 (5). The probability of obtaining one S and nine F's in your sample is

$$P(X = 1) = P(1) = \frac{_5C_1 \cdot _{45}C_9}{_{50}C_{10}}$$

As you will quickly see, the term $_NC_n$ gets very large—in fact, it becomes too large for many calculators. The only practical way to evaluate a hypergeometric probability, short of relying on a computer, is to cancel as many terms as possible in the expression.

The final result here is $P(1) = .431$; 43% of the time, you will obtain exactly 1 defective chip in your sample of size 10.

EXAMPLE 5.15

A local group of 30 unionized workers contains 20 people who are in favor of a strike and 10 who are not. Determine the probability that a random sample of 8 workers contains 5 individuals who favor the strike and 3 who are opposed.

SOLUTION

This situation fits the requirements for a hypergeometric random variable, where X is the number of workers (out of 8) who favor a strike, $n = 8$, $N = 30$, and $k = 20$. Consequently,

$$P(X = 5) = P(5) = \frac{_{20}C_5 \cdot _{10}C_3}{_{30}C_8}$$

$$= \frac{\dfrac{20!}{5!15!} \cdot \dfrac{10!}{3!7!}}{\dfrac{30!}{8!22!}}$$

$$= \frac{(15,504)(120)}{5,852,925} = .318$$

Approximately 32% of the time, in a sample of size 8 from this group, 5 people would favor a strike.

MEAN AND VARIANCE OF A HYPERGEOMETRIC RANDOM VARIABLE

As we did with the binomial random variable, we could use the definition of the mean and variance of a discrete random variable contained in equations 5.1 and 5.3. For example,

$$\mu = \sum xP(x)$$

where $P(x)$ is the PMF given in equation 5.12.

As in the binomial situation, simpler expressions exist for both the mean and the variance of the hypergeometric random variable. These are:

$$\mu = \sum xP(x) = \frac{nk}{N} \qquad (5.13)$$

and

$$\sigma^2 = \sum x^2 P(x) - \mu^2$$
$$= \frac{k(N-k)n(N-n)}{N^2(N-1)} = \left[n\left(\frac{k}{N}\right)\left(1 - \frac{k}{N}\right) \right]\left(\frac{N-n}{N-1}\right) \qquad (5.14)$$

For Example 5.14, $N = 50$, $k = 5$, $n = 10$. Consequently,

$$\mu = \frac{(10)(5)}{50} = 1 \text{ chip}$$

$$\sigma^2 = \frac{(5)(45)(10)(40)}{(50)^2(49)} = .735$$

and so

$$\sigma = \sqrt{.735} = .857 \text{ chip}$$

This means that if we observed this process of sampling 10 chips out of a batch of 50 indefinitely, we would obtain one ($= \mu$) defective chip on the average. Also, $\sigma = .857$ (or $\sigma^2 = .735$) is our measure of the variation in the observations of this random variable if we observe it over an indefinite period.

USING EXCEL TO DETERMINE HYPERGEOMETRIC PROBABILITIES AND THE BINOMIAL APPROXIMATION

As the earlier examples illustrate, calculating hypergeometric probabilities with paper and pencil gives new meaning to the expression "gruesome calculation." Excel offers a very simple method of determining these probabilities—nearly identical to the procedure used for finding binomial probabilities. To find a hypergeometric probability: click on the **Paste Function** icon (**fx**), click on **Statistical** under **Function Category,** and click on **HYPGEOMDIST** under **Function Name.** The input screen in Figure 5.7 contains the solution to Example 5.15. Notice that: (1) the first box contains the particular value of X (5, here), (2) the second box contains the sample size, n, (3) the third box contains the number of successes in the population, k, and (4) the fourth box contains the population size, N. The formula result is .318 and agrees with the solution in Example 5.15. This formula result also appears in your spreadsheet in the current active cell.

COMMENT

Excel does not offer a cumulative probability option for hypergeometric probabilities as was available for binomial probabilities.

FIGURE 5.7

Determining a hypergeometric probability using Excel.

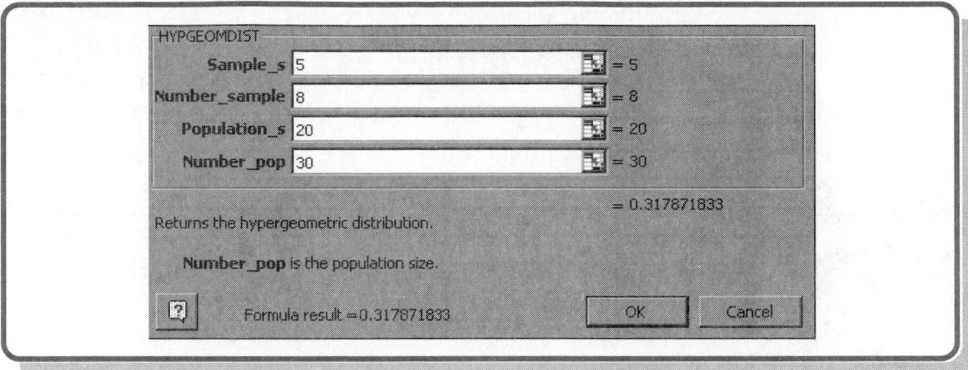

FIGURE 5.8

Determining hypergeometric probabilities for Example 5.16.

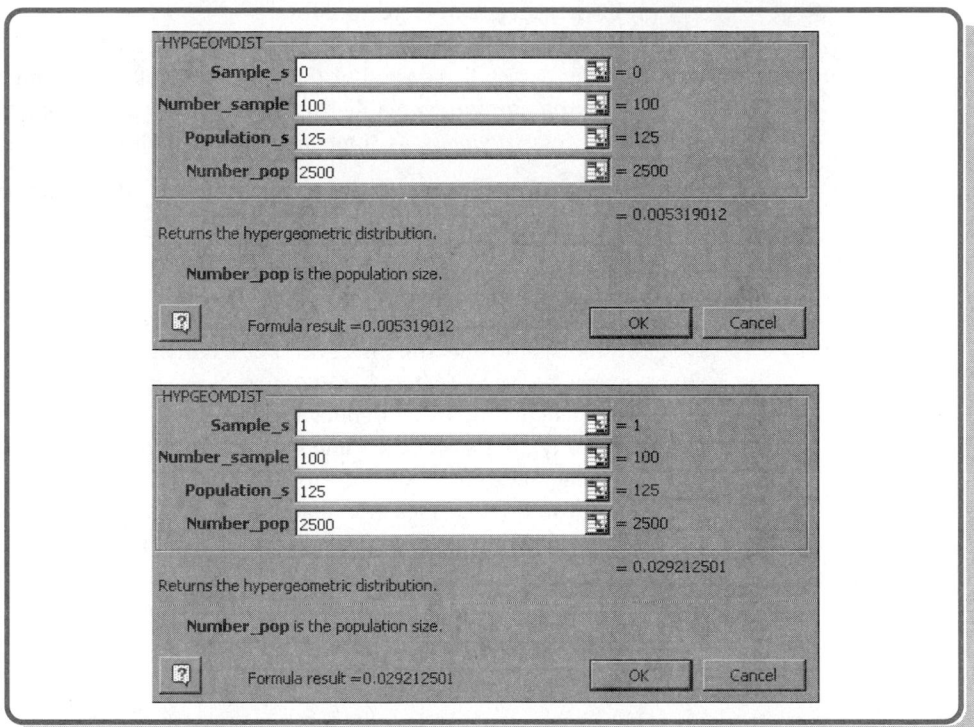

EXAMPLE 5.16

In Example 5.13 a sample of 100 chips was randomly selected from a lot of 2500 chips. It was assumed that 5% of the chips in the lot were defective—that is, the lot contained $k = 125$ defective chips and $N - k = 2375$ nondefective chips. The footnote in this example mentioned that this was an "approximate" binomial situation since the chances of selecting a defective chip on each draw was nearly the same, but not exactly. In fact, this example satisfies the requirements of a hypergeometric situation, and the important thing to remember is that whenever you select a random sample **without replacement** from a finite population, you are dealing with a hypergeometric situation.

The footnote explained that whenever the sample size (n) is small compared to the population size (N), treating the situation as binomial will work quite well. **A general rule is that you can treat such a situation as binomial provided n/N is < .05.** For that example, $n/N = 100/2500 = .04$, and so we would expect the final answer to be quite accurate. However, using Excel's ability to determine hypergeometric probabilities, we can easily determine the exact answer.

The problem is to find the chances of a sample of 100 chips containing one or fewer defective chips when sampling from a population of size 2500 containing 125 defective chips. In this case, the shipment of 2500 chips is accepted. Refer to Figure 5.8. The top panel is used to find $P(X = 0)$ for this situation, and the bottom panel contains $P(X = 1)$. Summing the results, we see that $P(X \leq 1) = P(X = 0) + P(X = 1) = .0053 + .0292 = .0345$, which is quite close to the binomial solution of .0371 in Example 5.13. To recap: the hypergeometric value of .0345 is the exact probability of accepting this shipment, and the binomial probability of .0371 offers an excellent approximation since n/N is less than .05.

5.6 THE POISSON DISTRIBUTION

The Poisson distribution, named after the French mathematician Simeon Poisson, is useful for counting the number of times a particular event occurs over a specified period of time. It also can be used for counting the number of times an event (such as a manufacturing defect) occurs over a specified area (such as a square yard of sheet metal) or in a specified volume. **We will restrict our discussion to counting over time, although any unit of measurement is permissible.**

The random variable X for this situation is the number of occurrences of a particular event over a specified period of time. The possible values are 0, 1, 2, 3, ... For X to be a **Poisson random variable** over a given interval of time, the occurrences of this event need to occur *randomly,* as summarized by the following three conditions:

1. The number of occurrences in one interval of time is unaffected (statistically independent of) the number of occurrences in any other nonoverlapping time interval. For example, what took place between 3:00 and 3:20 P.M. is unaffected by what took place between 9:00 and 10:00 A.M.
2. The expected (or average) number of occurrences over any time period is proportional to the size of this time interval. For example, we would expect half as many occurrences between 3:00 and 3:30 P.M. as between 3:00 and 4:00 P.M.

    This condition also implies that the probability of an occurrence must be constant over any intervals of the same length. A situation in which this is usually *not* true is at a restaurant from 12:00 noon to 12:10 P.M. and 2:00 to 2:10 P.M. Due to the differences in traffic flow for these two intervals, we would not expect the arrivals between, say, 11:30 A.M. and 2:30 P.M. to satisfy the requirements of a Poisson situation.
3. Events cannot occur exactly at the same time. More precisely, there is a unit of time sufficiently small (such as one second) that no more than one occurrence of an event is possible during this time.

Four situations that usually meet these conditions are:

The number of arrivals at a local bank over a five-minute interval.

The number of telephone calls arriving at a switchboard over a one-minute interval.

The number of daily accidents reported along a 20-mile stretch of an intercity toll road.

The number of trucks in a fleet that break down over a one-month period.

For each situation, the (discrete) random variable X is the number of occurrences over the time period T. If all the assumptions are satisfied, then X is a Poisson random variable. Define μ to be the expected (or average) number of occurrences over this period of time.* For any application, the value of μ must be specified or estimated in some manner. The Poisson PMF for X follows.

---

* The symbol λ (lambda) often is used to denote this parameter.

POISSON PROBABILITY MASS FUNCTION

X = number of occurrences over time period T.

$$P(x) = \frac{\mu^x e^{-\mu}}{x!} \qquad \text{for } x = 0, 1, 2, 3, \ldots \tag{5.15}$$

where μ = expected number of occurrences over T.

Equation 5.15 contains the number e, which is an interesting and useful number in mathematics and statistics. To get an idea how this number is derived, consider the following sequence:

$$(1 + 1/2)^2 = 2.25$$

$$(1 + 1/3)^3 = 2.37$$

$$(1 + 1/4)^4 = 2.44$$

$$(1 + 1/5)^5 = 2.49$$

$$\vdots$$

$$(1 + 1/100)^{100} = 2.705$$

$$\vdots$$

$$(1 + 1/1000)^{1000} = 2.717$$

$$\vdots$$

This sequence of numbers is approaching e. The actual value of e is

$$e = 2.71828 \ldots$$

One interesting application of the number e occurs when calculating compound interest. For example, if you invest \$100 at 12% compounded annually, then at the end of the year you will have \$112. However, if your interest is compounded not monthly, not daily, but continuously, the amount in your account will be $(100)(e^{.12}) = (100)(1.1275) = \$112.75$. The difference in these amounts is not as large as you might expect!

We will use e again in Chapter 6.

MEAN AND VARIANCE OF A POISSON RANDOM VARIABLE

Once again, we could use the definition of the mean and variance of a discrete random variable in equations 5.1 and 5.3. However, this is not necessary. It is fairly easy to show, using equation 5.15, that

$$\text{mean of } X = \sum xP(x)$$

$$= \mu$$

This is hardly a surprising result, given how μ was originally defined. Also,

$$\text{variance of } X = \sigma^2$$

$$= \sum x^2 P(x) - \mu^2$$

$$= \mu$$

So, *both the mean and the variance of the Poisson random variable X are equal to* μ. Recall that the Poisson random variable is the number of occurrences of a particular event (such as a traffic accident) over a given time period (such as an hour). If the time period is doubled to two hours, then the mean of the "new" Poisson random variable is twice the original mean; if the time period is halved to 30 minutes, the corresponding mean is halved, and so on. This is illustrated in the next two examples.

APPLICATIONS OF A POISSON RANDOM VARIABLE

EXAMPLE 5.17

Handy Home Center specializes in building materials for home improvements. They recently constructed an information booth in the center of the store. Define X to be the number of customers who arrive at the booth over a 5-minute period. Assume that the conditions for a Poisson situation are satisfied with

$$\mu = 4 \text{ customers over a 5-minute period}$$

A graph of the Poisson probabilities for $\mu = 4$ is contained in Figure 5.9.

1. What is the probability that over any 5-minute interval, exactly four people arrive at the information booth?
2. What is the probability that more than one person will arrive?
3. What is the probability that exactly six people arrive over a 10-minute period?

SOLUTION 1

First, this probability is not 1, because $\mu = 4$ is the *average* number of arrivals over this time period. The actual number of arrivals over some 5-minute period may be fewer than four, more than four, or exactly four. The fraction of time that you observe exactly four people is, using Table A.3,

$$P(4) = \frac{4^4 e^{-4}}{4!} = .1954$$

If you stand in the booth for many 5-minute periods, 19.5% of the time you will observe four people arrive.

SOLUTION 2

This is $P(X > 1) = P(X \geq 2)$. We could try

$$P(X \geq 2) = P(X = 2) + P(X = 3) + \cdots$$

$$= P(2) + P(3) + \cdots$$

$$= .1465 + .1954 + \cdots$$

There is an infinite number of terms here, however, so this is *not* the way to find this probability. A much better way is to use the fact that these probabilities sum to 1. Consequently,

$$P(X \geq 2) = 1 - P(X < 2)$$

$$= 1 - P(X \leq 1)$$

$$= 1 - [P(0) + P(1)]$$

$$= 1 - \left[\frac{4^0 e^{-4}}{0!} + \frac{4^1 e^{-4}}{1!} \right]$$

$$= 1 - [.0183 + .0733] = .9084$$

SOLUTION 3

For this time interval,

$$\mu = \text{expected (average) number of people over a 10-minute time period}$$

$$\mu = 8 \text{ (we expect four people over a 5-minute period)}$$

Therefore, the probability of observing six people over a 10-minute period is

$$\frac{8^6 e^{-8}}{6!} = .1221$$

using Table A.3.

FIGURE 5.9

Poisson probabilities for
$\mu = 4$.

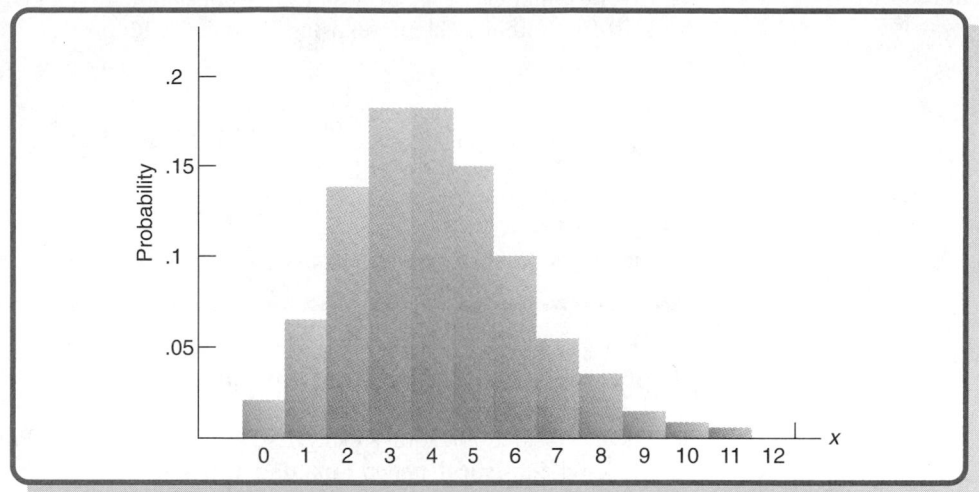

The Poisson distribution is widely used in the area of quality control for describing the number of nonconformities observed in a sampling unit. A *nonconformity* is defined as a failure to conform to a particular specification, such as "no scratches on a strip of sheet metal" or "no leaks in an automobile radiator." If a sampling unit is a square yard of sheet metal, then the number of nonconformities might be the number of observed scratches. Or if the sampling unit is a radiator, the number of nonconformities is the number of observed leaks. If the occurrences of a nonconformity are relatively rare (compared to the number that could occur if everything went wrong), then the Poisson distribution typically works well to describe the random variable X = number of nonconformities per sampling unit, as illustrated in the following example.

EXAMPLE 5.18

A certain process produces 100-foot long sheets of vinyl composed of a simulated wood grain top layer and a black bottom layer. A blemish (nonconformity) occurs when the black layer shows through or the wood grain pattern is not distinct. A 10-foot sample is obtained by trimming the end of a roll, at which point the number of blemishes is observed and recorded. It is believed that the number of blemishes per sample follows a Poisson distribution with an average of two blemishes per 10-foot sample. Determine the probability that:

1. There will be no blemishes observed in a 10-foot sample.
2. There will be more than eight blemishes observed if a 30-foot sample is used.

SOLUTION 1

The Poisson variable X for this situation is the number of observed blemishes. The average number of observed blemishes in a 10-foot sample is two, so

$$P(X = 0) = \frac{2^0 e^{-2}}{0!} = .1353$$

using Table A.3. This result means that 13.5% of the 10-foot samples will contain no blemishes.

SOLUTION 2

The average number of blemishes in a 30-foot sample is six, given that the average is two for a 10-foot sample. Therefore, using Table A.3 with $\mu = 6$,

$$P(X > 8) = 1 - P(X \leq 8)$$

$$= 1 - \left[\frac{6^0 e^{-6}}{0!} + \frac{6^1 e^{-6}}{1!} + \cdots + \frac{6^7 e^{-6}}{7!} + \frac{6^8 e^{-6}}{8!} \right]$$

$$= 1 - (.0025 + .0149 + \cdots + .1377 + .1033) = .153$$

We can expect more than eight blemishes in a 30-foot sample about 15% of the time.

USING EXCEL TO DETERMINE POISSON PROBABILITIES

To find a Poisson probability using Excel: (1) click on the **Paste Function** icon (f_x), (2) click on **Statistical** under **Function Category,** and (3) click on **POISSON** under **Function Name.** The Poisson probabilities in Example 5.18 are calculated using Excel in Figure 5.10. The top panel is used to find $P(X = 0)$, where the mean of X is 2. Notice that "false" is entered in the **Cumulative** box since an individual probability is desired. The formula result of .1353 will appear in the current active cell in the Excel spreadsheet and agrees with Solution 1 in Example 5.18.

The bottom panel of Figure 5.10 is used to determine $P(X > 8)$ for the situation posed in the second part of Example 5.18, where the mean of X is now 6. To find $P(X > 8)$, remember that $P(X > 8)$ is the same as $1 - P(X \leq 8)$. According to the Excel output, $P(X \leq 8)$ is .847, and so $P(X > 8)$ is $1 - .847 = .153$, which agrees with Solution 2 in Example 5.18. To find the cumulative probability $P(X \leq 8)$, enter "true" in the **Cumulative** box.

FIGURE 5.10

Using Excel to determine Poisson probabilities for Example 5.18.

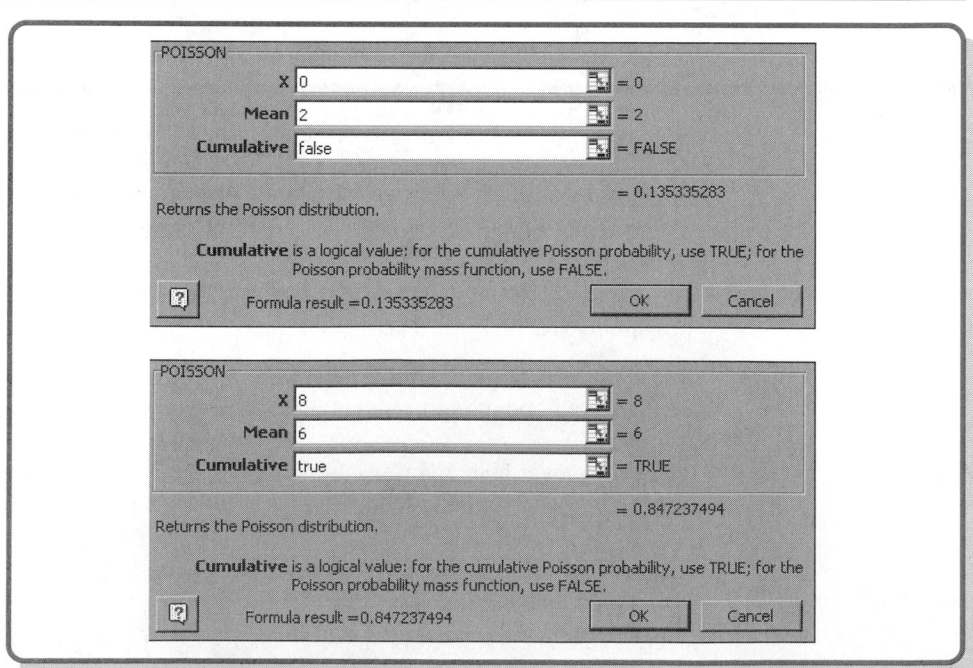

EXERCISES 5.42–5.56

UNDERSTANDING THE MECHANICS

5.42 Let X be a random variable with a hypergeometric distribution. Assume that $N = 10$ and $n = 5$.
  a. Find $P(X = 3)$ if $k = 3$.
  b. Find $P(X = 3)$ if $k = 6$.

5.43 Let X be a Poisson random variable with a mean of 5.
  a. What is the probability that X will be equal to 5?
  b. What is the probability that X will exceed 1?
  c. What is the probability that X will be at least 3 but no more than 6?

5.44 Find the mean and standard deviation of each of the following random variables.
  a. X is a hypergeometric random variable with $N = 6$, $k = 2$, $n = 3$.
  b. X is a hypergeometric random variable with $N = 100$, $k = 20$, $n = 40$.
  c. X is a Poisson random variable with expected number of occurrences equal to 9.

APPLYING THE NEW CONCEPTS

5.45 A batch of 350 resistors is to be shipped if a random sample of 15 resistors has 2 or fewer defective resistors. If it is known that there are 50 defective resistors in the batch, what is the probability that 2 or fewer of the sample of 15 resistors will be defective?

5.46 The Good Olde Boys used-car lot has 20 cars for sale. It is known that 8 of the cars get over 28 miles per gallon on the highway and 12 do not. Let X be the random variable equal to the number of cars out of the next five cars sold that get over 28 miles per gallon. Assume that each car is equally likely to sell.
  a. What is $P(X \leq 2)$?
  b. What is $P(1 \leq X \leq 3)$?
  c. Find the mean and variance of X.

5.47 In a sample of 10 men, it is found that 6 are physically fit. If 4 men are randomly selected from this sample of 10, what is the probability that no more than 3 are physically fit?

5.48 Despite increased emphasis on pensions and individual retirement accounts, many working adults are financially assisting their parents in household expenses, medical expenses, leisure, and rent or mortgage. This assistance can affect decisions by employees to relocate when asked by company managers. Assume that in a group of 20 employees that work for a small business firm, eight of the employees are assisting their parents financially. If five of the employees are selected at random to relocate to another state for the opening of a new store, what is the probability that no more than two are financially assisting their parents?

(Adapted from *USA Today*, "Helping Mom and Dad," May 21, 1998, p. 1B.)

5.49 Employees at many corporations are expected to travel for the company. According to a poll by Runzheimer International, 42% of all travelers receive corporate charge cards. Suppose that 30 accountants are employed by a corporation in which 12 of the accountants have corporate charge cards. Determine the probability that a random sample of seven accountants, selected from the 30 accountants to travel to a business seminar, contains three individuals who have corporate charge cards.

(Adapted from *USA Today*, "Who Gets Corporate Charge Cards," May 28, 1998, p. 1B.)

5.50 The Internal Revenue Service reviewed 1.1 million returns of taxpayers reporting adjusted gross income tax of $200,000 or more, and 1,137 did not owe any income tax. Perhaps several of these taxpayers have read Jeff Schnepper's book, *How To Pay Zero Taxes*. Suppose that an IRS employee randomly selects 1000 taxpayers to audit from the 1.1 million returns reviewed for audit purposes. The employee wishes to know what is the probability that five or less of the taxpayers did not owe income tax.

(Source: *Wall Street Journal*, "Affluent Taxpayers Find Way of Escape," Apr. 15, 1998, p. 3B.)

  a. What is the random variable of interest? Why can this random variable be considered a hypergeometric random variable?
  b. Can the binomial approximation to the hypergeometric distribution be used to find the probability that five or less of the taxpayers did not owe income tax? Why?
  c. Find the probability that five or less of the taxpayers from the IRS's random sample did not owe income tax.

5.51 Some analysts believe that the number of Internet surfers clicking on a Web site has a Poisson distribution. Suppose that the number of times that the University of North Texas's (UNT) home page is accessed over the noon hour has an average rate of 10 times per hour. The Web master of this home page wants to determine various probabilities. Assuming that the number of times this Web page is accessed during the noon hour is Poisson distributed, find the following probabilities.
  a. What is the probability that no more than 10 Internet users will access the UNT home page during the noon hour?
  b. What is the probability that the number of Internet users accessing the UNT home page will exceed 15 during the noon hour?

5.52 The number of parts per million of certain chemical compounds in air emissions is vital to the safety of the general population, according to the Environmental Protection Agency (EPA). Suppose that for a certain chemical, the average number of parts per million in a cubic unit of air emissions at Biochemical, Inc., is 5.
  a. Does it appear reasonable to suspect that the number of parts per million of the chemical in a cubic unit of air emissions has a Poisson distribution?
  b. What is the likelihood that a particular sample of air emissions at Biochemical, Inc., exceeds the EPA's limit of no more than 8 parts per million?

5.53 The auto parts department of an automotive dealership sends out an average of eight special orders daily. The number of special orders is assumed to follow a Poisson distribution.

    a. What is the probability that for any day, the number of special orders sent out will be more than four?

    b. What is the standard deviation of the number of special orders sent out daily?

5.54 Seattle coffee-retailer Starbucks currently has 56 Starbucks-style retail stores in Britain. One problem that Starbucks stores in Britain face is persuading Europeans, who generally regard American coffee as watery, that a U.S. company can brew a good cup. Suppose that at 45 of these stores, the coffee is brewed to taste more European than that served in the United States. If two of the Starbucks-style retail stores in Britain are selected at random, what is the probability that one will serve coffee brewed to taste more European than that served in the United States? Compare the binomial approximation to the actual value obtained using the hypergeometric distribution.

(Adapted from *Wall Street Journal,* "Starbucks Wafts Toward Europe," Apr. 30, 1998, p. A12.)

5.55 A certain manufacturer sells a machine that has numerous moving parts. A quality-control inspector counts the number of moving parts that are misaligned as the number of nonconformities for a particular machine. It is believed that the number of nonconformities per machine follows a Poisson distribution, with an average of three nonconformities per machine.

    a. Determine the probability that the quality-control inspector finds no more than one nonconformity on a particular machine selected at random.

    b. What is the standard deviation of the number of nonconformities per machine.

5.56 Airline travelers list lost luggage as the second most common travel problem behind canceled flights. Assume that over a 24-hour period, an average of 10 travelers complain of lost luggage at New Orleans International Airport. Assume that the conditions of a Poisson situation are satisfied.

(Adapted from *USA Today,* "Travel Travails," May 21, 1998, p. 1B.)

    a. What is the probability that over any 24-hour interval, exactly 10 travelers complain of lost luggage?

    b. What is the probability that no more than 10 travelers complain of lost luggage?

In a cell on an Excel spreadsheet, type in the following: "=Poisson(10, 10, true)." What happens if you use false instead of true in this statement?

SUMMARY

When an experiment results in a numerical outcome, a convenient way of representing the possible values and corresponding probabilities is to use a random variable. A **random variable** takes on a numerical value for each outcome of an experiment. If the possible values of this variable can be listed along with the probability for each value, this variable is said to be a **discrete random variable.** Conversely, if any value of this variable can occur over a specific range, then it is a **continuous random variable.** This chapter concentrated on the discrete type, whereas Chapter 6 discusses the continuous random variable.

For a discrete random variable, the set of possible values and corresponding probabilities is a **probability distribution.** There are several ways of representing such a distribution, including a list of each value and its probability, a histogram, or an expression called a **probability mass function (PMF),** which is a numerical function that assigns a probability to each value of the random variable.

If you could observe a random variable indefinitely, you would obtain the corresponding *population. A sample* then consists of a finite number of random variable observations. In Chapter 3, we introduced ways of describing a set of sample data using various statistics, including the sample mean and variance. Similarly, we can describe a random variable using its mean and variance. Since they describe the population, they are pa-

rameters. The **mean** of a discrete random variable, μ, is the average value of this variable if observed over an indefinite period. The mean is found by summing the product of each value and its probability of occurring. The **variance** of a discrete random variable, σ^2, is a measure of the variation for this variable. The **standard deviation,** σ, also measures this variation and is the square root of the variance.

Four popular discrete random variables used in a business setting are the discrete uniform, binomial, hypergeometric, and Poisson random variables. A **discrete uniform** random variable has possible values between two integers (say, a and b), where each integer in this interval has the same chance of occurring. A **binomial** random variable counts the number of successes out of n independent trials. When the trials are dependent and the population size (N) as well as the number of successes in the population (k) are known, the **hypergeometric** random variable can be used to describe the number of successes out of the n trials. The **Poisson** random variable is used for situations in which you observe the number of occurrences of a particular event over a specified period of time or space. The Poisson distribution is also used in the area of quality improvement to describe the number of nonconformities observed in a sampling unit, such as the number of surface flaws in a square yard of finished sheet metal.

SUMMARY OF FORMULAS

ANY DISCRETE RANDOM VARIABLE, X

1. Mean $= \mu = \sum xP(x)$
2. Variance $= \sigma^2 = \sum (x - \mu)^2 P(x) = \sum x^2 P(x) - \mu^2$
3. Standard deviation $= \sigma = \sqrt{\sum (x - \mu)^2 P(x)} = \sqrt{\sum x^2 P(x) - \mu^2}$

BINOMIAL DISTRIBUTION

1. $X =$ the number of successes out of n independent trials. Each trial results in a success (with probability p) or a failure (with probability $1 - p$).
2. PMF is $P(X = x) = P(x) = {}_nC_x p^x (1 - p)^{n-x}$ for $x = 0, 1, \ldots, n$
3. Mean $= \mu = np$
4. Variance $= \sigma^2 = np(1 - p)$ and standard deviation $= \sigma = \sqrt{np(1 - p)}$
5. Probabilities for the binomial random variable are provided in Table A.1.

HYPERGEOMETRIC DISTRIBUTION

1. $X =$ the number of successes in a sample of size n when selecting from a population of size N containing k successes and $N - k$ failures
2. PMF is $P(x) = ({}_kC_x \cdot {}_{N-k}C_{n-x})/{}_NC_n$ for $x = a, a + 1, \ldots, b$, where $a = $ maximum $\{0, n + k - N\}$ and $b = $ minimum $\{k, n\}$
3. Mean $= \mu = n(k/N)$
4. Variance $= \sigma^2 = [n(k/N)(1 - k/N)][(N - n)/(N - 1)]$

POISSON DISTRIBUTION

1. $X =$ the number of occurrences of a particular event over a certain unit of time, length, area, or volume
2. PMF is $P(x) = (\mu^x e^{-\mu})/(x!)$ for $x = 0, 1, 2, \ldots$
3. Mean $= \mu$
4. Variance $= \mu$
5. Probabilities for the Poisson random variable are provided in Table A.3.

REVIEW EXERCISES 5.57–5.78

5.57 Which of the following is a property of a discrete probability distribution?
  a. The probability for every value of a random variable is positive and not greater than .9.
  b. The sum of the probabilities for the values of a random variable is 1.
  c. The probabilities for any two different values of a random variable are different.
  d. At least one of the values of a random variable has a probability equal to .5.

5.58 Which of the following situations would be best described by a Poisson distribution, and which would be best described by a hypergeometric distribution? What assumptions do you have to make in each case?
  a. The number of students in your class that voted in a campus election.
  b. The number of accidents on interstate I-10 each month.
  c. The number of defects in a new automobile.
  d. The number of tires on your car that are underinflated.

5.59 A manager has four employees with 0, 1, 3, and 4 years of job experience. The manager will assign two of the employees at random to a team. Define X to be equal to the total number of years of job experience for the two selected employees.
  a. What values can X assume?
  b. What is the probability mass function of X?
  c. What is the mean of X?
  d. What is the standard deviation of X?

5.60 A realtor conducts a survey of 300 homeowners and finds that 30 have no mortgage on their homes.
  a. If a random sample of 10 homes from those surveyed is selected, what is the approximate probability that exactly one home has no mortgage.
  b. In part (a), what is the probability that more than one home has no mortgage?

5.61 A supervisor believes that a new worker installs the wrong electrical component 30% of the time. The supervisor randomly selects 20 components installed by the new worker. The supervisor finds one incorrectly installed component. Is this a likely occurrence if the supervisor's belief is correct? What assumptions are necessary?

5.62 Let the variable X be equal to -1 if stock XYZ declines, 0 if stock XYZ remains unchanged, and 1 if stock XYZ increases in price. If $P(X = x)$ is equal to $(x + 2)/6$, what are the mean and standard deviation of X?

5.63 A manager has 10 research projects to assign to either engineer 1 or engineer 2. If each research project is randomly assigned to either one of the two engineers, what is the probability that engineer 1 will be assigned no more than 5 research projects?

5.64 An average of five books per week are returned to a bookstore. Assume that the number of returned books is Poisson distributed.
   a. What is the probability that less than four books will be returned in one week?
   b. What is the standard deviation of the distribution of the number of books returned in one week?

5.65 The supervisor of the employees who solder resistors on certain electrical components would like to know what the average number of absentees is daily and also what the standard deviation is of the daily employee absentee rate. Find these two values from the following probability mass function, which was constructed from historical data of the company:

X: Number of Daily Absentees	$P(x)$
0	.50
1	.23
2	.12
3	.10
4	.02
5	.02
6	.01

5.66 Ten employees are being reviewed for promotion. Four of the employees are females. If each employee is equally likely to get promoted, what is the probability that two females and three males will be promoted, if a total of five promotions are given?

5.67 There are 90 drill bits in a box at a machine shop. Fifty of the drill bits are 3/8-inch diameter, and 40 are 7/16-inch diameter. If four drill bits are selected at random, what is the probability that two drill bits of 3/8-inch diameter and two drill bits of 7/16-inch diameter will be chosen?

5.68 A population consists of 15 employees, 6 of whom have less than two years experience. Let X equal the number of employees with less than two years experience from a sample of eight employees randomly drawn from this population.
   a. Find $P(X = 3)$.
   b. Find $P(X \leq 2)$.
   c. Find the average value of X.
   d. Find the standard deviation of X.

5.69 Blair's Moving Company loads an average of three boxes of damaged merchandise daily. What is the probability that exactly three boxes of damaged merchandise are shipped daily? What is the standard deviation of the number of boxes of damaged merchandise that are shipped daily? Assume a Poisson distribution.

5.70 For most investors, the only practical way to invest in China is through mutual funds. However, most mutual funds don't publicize the percentage that are based in China and, indeed, this percent can change over time. As of April 10, 1998, the following list displays mutual funds that have a concentration of their assets in China. If an investor chooses two of the following 13 mutual funds, what is the probability of the following.

Mutual Fund	Percent of Assets in China (in Percentage)
Greater China	59
Lexington Crosby Small Cap Asia Growth	31
Jardine Fleming China Region	30
U.S. Global Investors China Reg Opportunity	24

Mutual Fund	Percent of Assets in China (in Percentage)
Guinness Flight Asia Small Cap	23
Matthews Pacific Tiger I	23
Robertson Stephens Global Low-Priced	21
Matthews Asian Convertible Securities	17
Templeton China World	16
Merrill Lynch Emerging Tigers	16
Govett Asia	15
China Fund	12
Templeton Dragon	11

(Adapted from *Wall Street Journal,* "Getting In the Door," Apr. 30, 1998, p. R16.)

    a. Exactly one mutual fund having at least 20% of its assets invested in China.

    b. None of the mutual funds having at least 20% of their assets invested in China.

    c. Both of the mutual funds having at least 20% of their assets invested in China.

5.71 What binomial expression would you use to approximately evaluate the following expression?

$$(_{200}C_3 \cdot {}_{300}C_7)/_{500}C_{10}$$

5.72 After losing its luster—and market share—in 1997 to rivals Sega and Sony, the stalwart Japanese video game maker Nintendo is back in the race with its Nintendo 64 game player (N64). In April 1998, 70 percent of the video games in the U.S. were for N64.

(Adapted from *Business Week,* "Nintendo: At the Top of its Game," June 9, 1997, p. 72.)

    a. If 15 video game buyers were randomly selected, how many would you expect to have bought an N64?

    b. What is the standard deviation of the number of game buyers purchasing an N64 from a random sample of 15 video game buyers?

    c. What is the probability that the number of game buyers puchasing an N64 is less than five? Would this be unusual?

    d. What assumptions are you making in answering parts (a), (b), and (c)?

5.73 The most accurate golfing clubs reported to be sold by retailers are manufactured by Olimar, Callaway, Taylor Made, and Adams. Independent tests by golfing facilities demonstrated that Olimar manufactured the most accurate club. If a golfing professional were to randomly choose two of the four brands to recommend to golfers, what is the probability that at least one of the two recommended brands is an Olimar?

(Adapted from *USA Today,* "Oversize Is Overrated," June 12, 1998, p. 2B.)

5.74 The Acorn International mutual fund rose 18.2% in the first quarter of 1998. Five countries—Italy, UK, Netherlands, Finland, and Sweden—contributed more than 80% of the total gains for the three months. Suppose there were 10 countries in which this mutual fund primarily invested during this period.

(Adapted from First Quarter Report of Acorn, "Acorn International—In a Nutshell," March 31, 1998, p. 6.)

    a. If an individual investor randomly selected five countries from the 10 countries in which the Acorn International mutual fund was primarily invested at the beginning of 1998, what is the probability that the five countries selected by the individual investor contains at least two of the five countries that contributed more than 80% of the total gains for the first quarter of 1998?

    b. Using the **Paste Function ➤ Statistical ➤ Hypgeomdist** from Excel, do a "what if" analysis by comparing how the probability in part (a) would change if the number of countries in which this mutual fund primarily invested was changed to 12 instead of 10.

5.75 El Nino, a phenomenon that has cost states millions of dollars in environmental damage, is often debated by meteorologists as to how long it will affect the United States. In a poll of the American Meteorological Society, 53% of the members believed that El Nino would have a strong effect on the United States for the summer of 1998, while 34% disagreed. Thirteen percent of the members surveyed were undecided. Suppose that a separate random sample of 50 meteorologists from this society was independently obtained. Let X represent the number that believe that El Nino would have a strong effect on the United States for the summer of 1998, and let Y represent the number that disagree.

(Source: *USA Today,* "Will El Nino Take Summer Off," May 26, 1998, p. 1A.)

a. What is the probability that X is greater than 25? Do a "what if" analysis by clicking on the **Paste Function ➤ Statistical ➤ Binomdist** and changing the proportion of members that believe there will be a strong effect from .53 to .60.

b. What is the probability that Y is greater than 25? Do a "what if" analysis by clicking on the **Paste Function ➤ Statistical ➤ Binomdist** and changing the proportion of members that disagree from .34 to .40.

c. Interpret the probabilities in parts (a) and (b). Do these probabilities seem reasonable given the stated percentages of meteorologists that agree and disagree on the effects of El Nino?

5.76 Major brokerage houses recommend a blend of stocks, bonds, and cash for portfolios. According to Wishire Associates and Carpenter Analytical Services, of the 13 leading brokerage houses, only seven beat the blend of stocks, bonds, and cash recommended by a robot mix of these same investment vehicles for the one-year period ending March 31, 1998.

(Source: *The Wall Street Journal*, "The Wisdom of Wall Street Is Decidedly Short on Cash," Apr. 30, 1998, p. C1.)

a. Suppose that an investment advisor had four financial portfolios to create one year ago from this date. If this advisor randomly selected the recommendation of four different major brokerage houses, what is the probability that at least two of the portfolios would have had a mix of investments that would outperform that from the robot mix?

b. Do a "what if" analysis by clicking on the **Paste Function ➤ Statistical ➤ Hypgeomdist** to examine the probability if the number of financial portfolios changed to five, thus randomly selecting five different major brokerage houses. What happens if four is changed to six?

5.77 To obtain a better idea of what plots of binomial probabilities look like, consider two binomial distributions, both with $n = 20$ and one with $p = .2$, and the other with $p = .8$. In Excel, fill column A with numbers from 0 to 20. In B1, put "=Binomdist(A1,20,.2,0)" to obtain the probability of a binomial random variable being equal to 0 when $n = 20$ and $p = .2$. Now fill column B (down through B21) with the probabilities. Repeat this process in column C to obtain the probabilities for a binomial random variable with $n = 20$ and $p = .8$. Now select the scatter plot from chart wizard to obtain the plot below.

a. Comment on the shape of each binomial distribution. If the probabilities for a binomial distribution with $p = .2$ are known, how can the probabilities for a binomial distribution with $p = .8$ be easily found.

b. Plot other binomial distributions with the probability of a success being p and also being $1 - p$. Comment on the shape of the graphs.

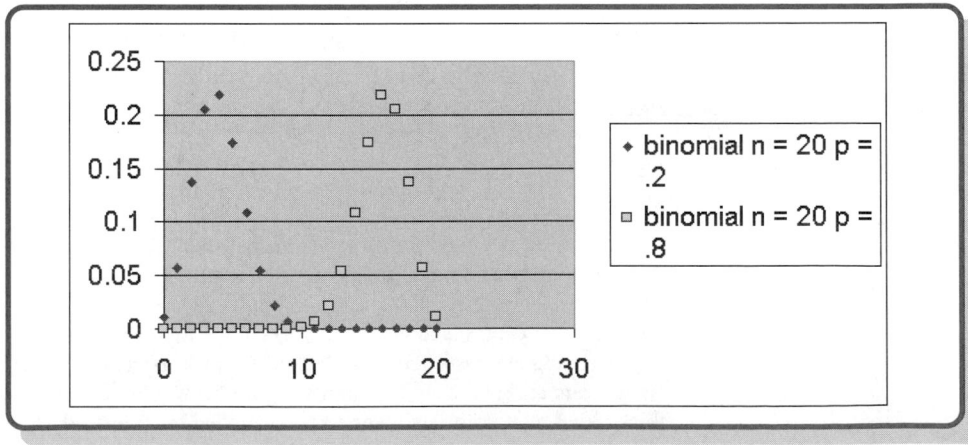

5.78 To obtain insight into how the shape of the Poisson distribution changes by varying the mean, consider four values for the mean of a Poisson distribution: 1, 4, 8, and 15. Starting in A2, fill column A with the numbers 0 through 25. Now in B1 put the value 1 (for the mean of the Poisson). In cell B2, put "=Poisson(A2,B$1,0)" and fill down to B26. Now put 4, 8, and 15 in cells C1, D1, and E1, respectively. Fill down through C26, D26, and E26, with the Poisson distribution just as for column B. Use the scatter plot from the chart wizard to obtain the graphs on the next page.

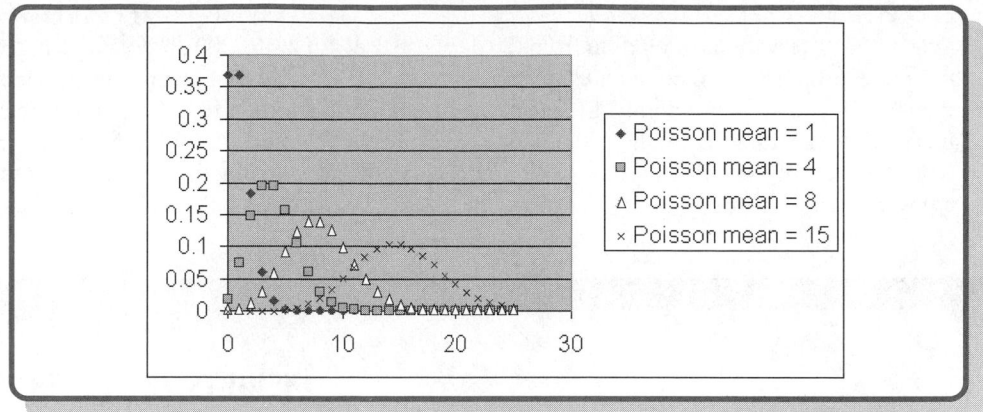

Comment on the shape of the Poisson distribution as the value of the mean changes. For which value of the mean would you say that the Poisson distribution appears to be most bell shaped? Repeat the plot of the graphs by assigning other values of the mean between 1 and 20. Simply change the values in B1, C1, D1, and E1, and watch the plots change shape.

COMPUTER EXERCISES USING THE DATABASES

EXERCISE 1—APPENDIX E

Generate 100 random numbers, and select a sample of 100 observations from the database. Consider the variable FAMLSIZE (family size). Let p represent the proportion of observations in your set of 100 observations in which the family size is no greater than 2. If you randomly select 10 observations (with replacement) from the 100 possible, what is $P[X \leq 5]$, where X is the number of observations (out of 10) in which the family size is no greater than 2? What type of random variable is X?

Note: The MINITAB procedure here is

MTB > SAMPLE 10 FROM Cxx, PUT INTO Cyy;

SUBC > REPLACE.

where the 100 values of FAMLSIZE are in column Cxx and the 10 selected values are in column Cyy.

EXERCISE 2—APPENDIX E

Repeat Exercise 1, where 10 observations are selected without replacement.

Note: The MINITAB procedure here is the same as in Exercise 1, except the subcommand is omitted.

EXERCISE 3—APPENDIX E

Referring to Exercise 2, if you were to obtain samples of size 10 indefinitely, what would X be on the average? What is the standard deviation of this random variable?

EXERCISE 4—APPENDIX E

Estimate the proportion of homeowners in a randomly selected set of 100 observations. From this set of 100 observations, select with replacement a random set of 10 observations. Can this be considered a binomial experiment with $n = 10$ and p equal to the proportion of homeowners in the set of 100 observations? Estimate the probability that the number of homeowners in the set of 10 observations is greater than or equal to 5.

EXERCISE 5—APPENDIX E

Randomly select 200 observations from the database. From this set, estimate the proportion of observations in which the location of residence is in one of the northern sectors. From this set of observations, randomly select without replacement 8 observations. Find the probability that, in this sample of size 8, the residences of 4 or fewer observations are in the northern sectors. Can the binomial approximation be used? Why?

EXERCISE 6—APPENDIX F

Select 200 observations at random from the database. Let p be the proportion of companies with a positive net income. If you were randomly to select (with replacement) 15 observations from the 200 possible, what would be the probability of selecting at least 9 companies with a positive net income?

EXERCISE 7—APPENDIX F

For the 200 observations in Exercise 6, let p equal the proportion of companies in which the number of employees exceeds 10,000. If you were randomly to select 15 observations (with replacement) from the 200 possible, what would be the probability of selecting at least 7 companies in which the number of employees exceeds 10,000?

INSIGHTS FROM STATISTICS IN ACTION: CHOOSING A GOOD VARIABLE ANNUITY FOR RETIREMENT

The Statistics in Action presentation at the beginning of this chapter discussed various factors to consider when choosing a good variable annuity for retirement. Such factors include management fees, pay-out options, and surrender fees.

Financial analysts would like to determine the probability of an individual selecting an annuity by simply choosing from a recommended list. Consider the list given below to be a popular recommended list of insurance companies that offer variable annuities with total insurance costs of 1% or less. This list can be considered a population of standard annuities companies/policies from which an investor can choose.

Insurance Company/Policy	Insurance Expense (in Percent)	Minimum Initial Purchase	Investment Choices	Mutual Fund Expense (in Percent)
Valic/Independence Plus	1.00	0	10	.50
American Step Acct 2	.70	0	16	.60
American Partners	1.00	2,000	12	.83
American Skandia/Choice 2000	.65	10,000	33	1.09
American Skandia/Impact	1.00	10,000	33	1.09
American Skandia/Galaxy	1.00	5,000	8	1.02
Ameritas	.75	2,000	10	1.03
Charter National	.70	2,500	8	.93
Fidelity Retirement Res.	.80	2,500	28	.94
First Invstrs Life/Fund A	.75	2,000	1	.86
First Invstrs Life/Fund C	1.00	2,000	9	.80
Fortis/Value Plus	.45	5,000	28	.95
Genl American	1.00	0	8	.50
Golden American	1.00	10,000	14	1.02
Great West	.85	5,000	25	.89
Guardian	1.00	500	14	.79
IDS Life Flexible	1.00	2,000	9	.73
J. Hancock/Accommodator	1.00	1,000	18	.77
J. Hancock/Declaration	1.00	500	11	.88
J. Hancock/Marketplace	1.00	500	18	.77
Lincoln National	1.00	3,000	14	.68
Manufacturers Life	1.00	1,000	8	.85
Minnesota Mutual	.95	25,000	20	.56
Mony Life	.90	0	7	.50
Nationwide Life	.95	15,000	39	.93

Insurance Company/Policy	Insurance Expense (in Percent)	Minimum Initial Purchase	Investment Choices	Mutual Fund Expense (in Percent)
Ohio National	.90	10,000	13	.89
PFL Life	.80	5,000	13	.63
Phoenix Home Life	1.00	1,000	10	1.18
Providian Life/Vanguard	.38	5,000	9	.33
Providian Life/Advisors	.65	5,000	15	.86
Providian Life/Prism	.80	5,000	12	1.14
Providian Life/Marquee	.80	5,000	12	.78
Security Benefit	.55	10,000	7	.82
United Investment	.90	5,000	11	.77
USAA	.75	1,000	9	.53
Western Res./Janus	.65	2,500	9	.76

1. List the possible minimum initial purchase amounts and the probability that each would occur if one of these insurance companies is picked at random.
2. If one of these insurance companies is picked at random, what is the probability that the minimum initial purchase amount is less than $7500?
3. For the random variable, minimum initial purchase amounts, find the mean and standard deviation of its distribution.
4. Suppose that Security Benefit offers three aggressive mutual fund choices and four conservative mutual fund choices. What is the probability that an investor will choose one aggressive and one conservative mutual fund if the investor randomly chooses two of the investment choices that Security Benefit offers?
5. What proportion of the insurance companies/policies have mutual fund expenses over 1.0%? Suppose that a financial advisor selected companies at random from the above list for 10 investors. What is the probability that at least two of the ten investors will own a policy that has mutual fund expenses over 1.0%?

Source: *USA Today,* "Annuities: Worth a Look—A Good, Hard Look," May 29, 1998, p. 3B. Copyright 1998, USA TODAY. Reprinted with permission.

CHAPTER 5 APPENDIX: DATA ANALYSIS WITH MINITAB

BINOMIAL PROBABILITIES

Probabilities, cumulative probabilities, and inverse cumulative probabilities can be calculated for a number of distributions in MINITAB. The inverse cumulative probability is the value of the random variable that corresponds to a specified value of the cumulative probability function of the random variable. The examples below will demonstrate how to find the probabilities for a specified value of a random variable. To obtain cumulative probabilities or inverse cumulative probabilities, one simply selects these options rather than the probability option. MINITAB currently does not have an option for displaying probabilities of the hypergeometric distribution.

To obtain binomial probabilities say for $n = 10$ and $p = .5$, first put 0 through 10 in a column, say column 1, named "X." Then click **Calc ➤ Probability Distributions ➤ Binomial.** Then type in number of trials to be 10 and probability of success to be .5. Select **Probability** and use X as the input column. The user form should look like the one following. The output will be displayed in the session window and follows the user form. To obtain only one probability for a specified value of the random variable, use the **Input constant** option.

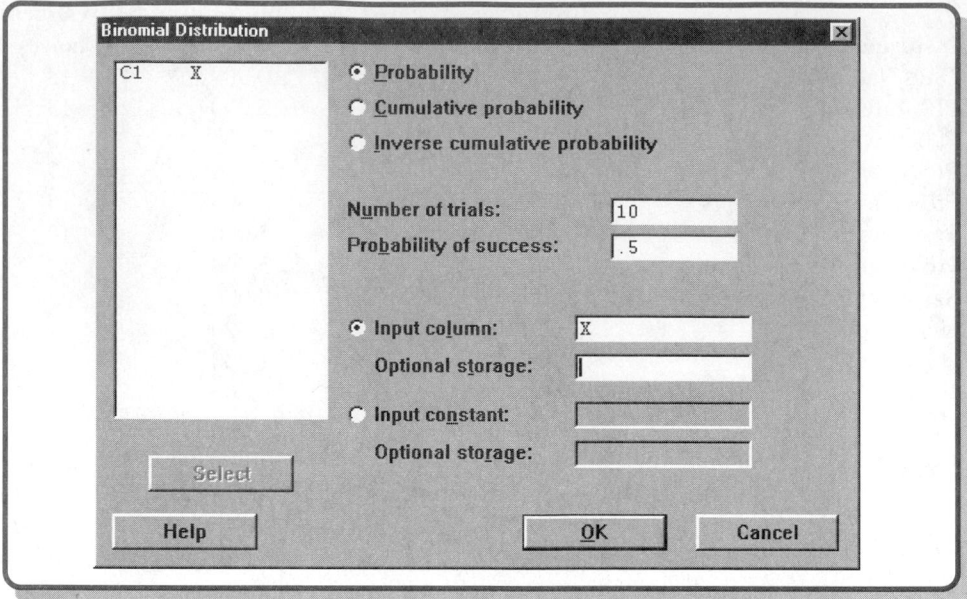

Probability Density Function

Binomial with n = 10 and p = 0.500000

x	P(X = x)
0.00	0.0010
1.00	0.0098
2.00	0.0439
3.00	0.1172
4.00	0.2051
5.00	0.2461
6.00	0.2051
7.00	0.1172
8.00	0.0439
9.00	0.0098
10.00	0.0010

POISSON PROBABILITIES

To obtain Poisson probabilities say for a Poisson random variable with a mean of 2, first put the values in a column, say column 1 (named "X"), for which you wish to obtain probabilities. Then click **Calc ➤ Probability Distributions ➤ Poisson.** Then type in the value of the mean to be 2. Select **Probability** and use X as the input column. The user form should look like the one following. The output will be displayed in the session window and follows the user form.

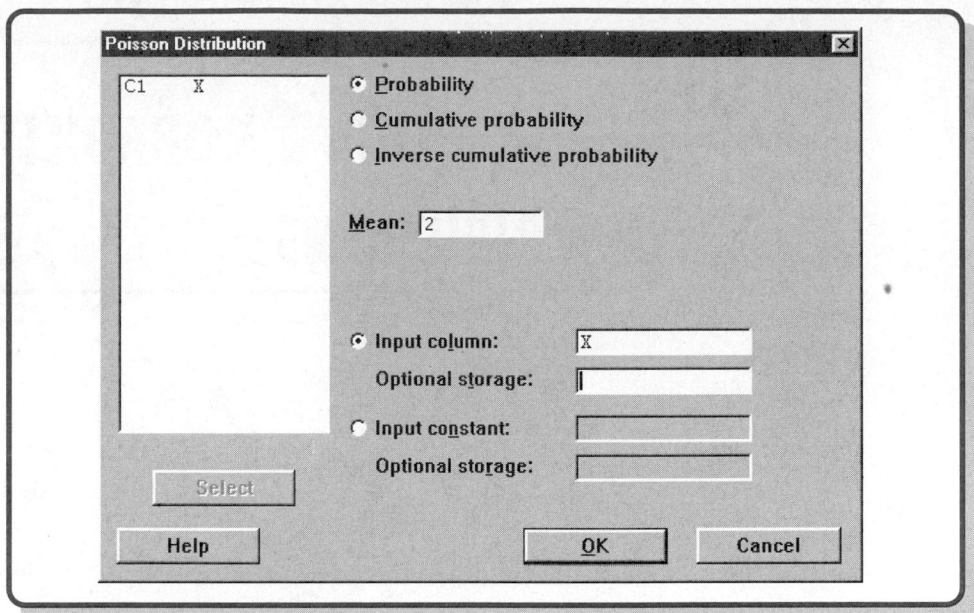

Probability Density Function

Poisson with mu = 2.00000

x	P(X = x)
0.00	0.1353
1.00	0.2707
2.00	0.2707
3.00	0.1804
4.00	0.0902
5.00	0.0361
6.00	0.0120
7.00	0.0034
8.00	0.0009
9.00	0.0002
10.00	0.0000

CONTINUOUS PROBABILITY DISTRIBUTIONS

STATISTICS IN ACTION: CHANGES IN THE SOCIAL SECURITY SYSTEM AND ITS EFFECT ON THE DISTRIBUTION OF RETIREMENT FUNDS FOR WORKING AMERICANS

With the United States Social Security Trust Funds projected to be exhausted by the year 2032, political and economics analysts are examining the distribution of older Americans in the United States and their sources of income. Virtually unaltered since it was created six decades ago, the Social Security system has triggered studies on the aging of the U.S. population. What is the distribution of retirement funds that the elderly have to rely on in case Social Security cannot provide much of one's income during retirement?

Some financial analysts are interested in the population distribution of the proportion of Social Security contributions that working citizens would be willing to invest in a private account if given a choice. While many solutions have been proposed, few politicians and working-class Americans agree on a solution. Americans reject the most common proposals: 85% oppose cutting benefits, 70% are against raising the retirement age to 70, and 62% oppose increasing taxes. Yet everyone agrees that a solution must be found.

Fortunately, many of today's workers have benefited from the explosive growth in the stock market through mutual funds or 401(k) retirement plans at work. Now they would like to see similar gains from Social Security. Interestingly, many young people believe that they will be taxed for the next 45 years to fund a system from which they will never see a penny. John Sweeney, president of the AFL-CIO, says, "A vocal minority is fixated on scrapping the Social Security system. It is time that the truth be told about the high costs of privatization that America's working families will be forced to pay."

In a poll, the following question was asked of voters: Who do you trust to take care of Social Security, and which party would do a better job of dealing with the Social Security system? While many voters are skeptical that anyone can take care of Social Security, 43% said that the Democrats would do a better job, and 36% said that Republicans would do a better job. Wendell Primus, a social

policy expert at the Center on Budget and Policy Priorities, says that it is hard to imagine a Social Security reform plan that does not include some type of private account.

Chapter 5 introduced you to discrete random variables. Such variables, when observed, produce discrete data. Many variables (such as height and weight) have possible values lying within a certain range (e.g., any height is possible between say, 3′ and 7.5′). These variables are called **continuous random variables.**

At the completion of this chapter, you will be able to

- Examine a group of people (say, under 30 years of age) and answer questions such as, "What percentage of this group would prefer more than half of their contributed Social Security payments to be put into a private fund?";
- Describe the meaning of a continuous random variable; and
- Describe the distribution (shape) of a continuous random variable—in particular, is it bell shaped?

A Look Back/Introduction

After we discussed the use of descriptive statistics, we introduced you to the area of uncertainty by using probability concepts and random variables. Random variables offer you a convenient method of describing the various outcomes of an experiment and their corresponding probabilities.

When each value of the random variable as well as its probability of occurring can be listed, the random variable is discrete. The other type of random variable, a continuous random variable, can assume any value over a particular range. Continuous random variables include such variables as X = height, X = weight, and X = time. For such variables it is impossible to list all values of X, yet you can still make probability statements regarding X if you can make certain assumptions about the type of population.

In statistics, making decisions from sample information is called **statistical inference.** In subsequent chapters, we will develop a formal set of rules to offer you as a guide in making statistical decisions. Making such a decision typically involves one or more assumptions about the population from which the sample was obtained. One such assumption, widely used in statistics, is that the data came from a normal population, which means that you are dealing with a normal random variable.

6.1 Continuous Random Variables

The concept of a continuous random variable was introduced in Chapter 5. What distinguishes a discrete random variable from one that is continuous is the presence of *gaps* in the possible values for a discrete random variable. To illustrate, X = total of two dice is a discrete random variable; there are many gaps over the range of possible values, and a value of 10.4, for example, is not possible. One can list the possible values of a discrete variable, along with the probability that each value will occur.

Determining probabilities for a continuous random variable is quite different. For such a variable, any value over a specific range is possible. Therefore we are unable to list all the possible values of this variable. Probability statements for a continuous random variable (such as X) are not concerned with specific values of X (such as the probability that X will equal 50) but rather deal with probabilities over a range of values, such as the probability that X is *between* 40 and 50, *greater than* 65, or *less than* 20, for example.

Such probabilities can be determined by first making an assumption regarding the nature of the population involved. We assume that the population can be described by a curve having a particular shape—such as normal, uniform, or exponential. Once this curve is specified, a probability can be determined by finding the corresponding area under this curve. As an illustration, Figure 6.1 shows a particular curve (called the normal curve) for which the probability of observing a value of X between 20 and 60 is the area under this curve between these two values. *The entire range of probability is covered using such a curve, since, for any continuous random variable, the total area under the curve is equal to 1.*

The following sections examine the normal, uniform, and exponential distributions, since these are the most widely encountered random variables in practice. The graphs and descriptive statistics discussed in the previous chapters can help determine if one of these random variables might be appropriate for a particular situation. If a histogram of the sample data appears nearly flat, the population might be represented by a uniform random variable. If the histogram is symmetric with decreasing tails at each end, a normal random variable may be in order. If the sample histogram steadily decreases from left to right, the

FIGURE 6.1

Finding a probability for a
continuous random variable.

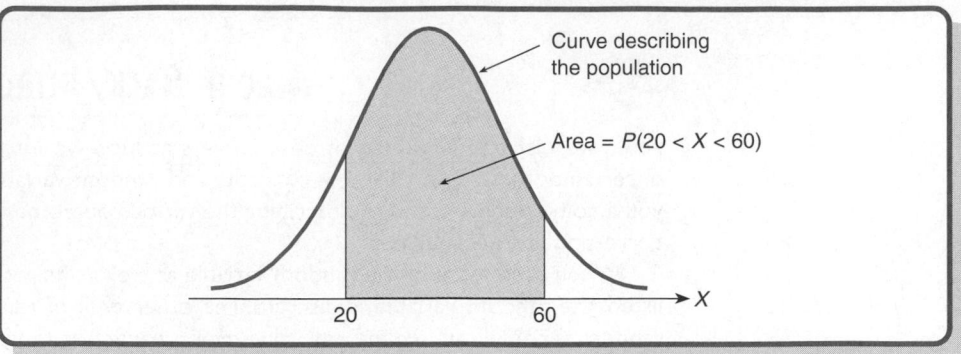

population of all possible values perhaps can be described using an exponential random
variable. In the first two cases, the mean and median should be nearly equal (the population is symmetric), providing a skewness measure near zero. For the exponential case, the
median should be less than the mean with a corresponding positive measure of skewness.

6.2 NORMAL RANDOM VARIABLES

The normal distribution is the most important of all the continuous distributions. You will
find that this distribution plays a key role in the application of many statistical techniques.
When attempting to make an assertion about a population, oftentimes a major assumption
(based on sample evidence) is that the population has a normal distribution.

When discussing measurements such as height, weight, thickness, or time, the resulting population of all measurements often can be assumed to have a probability distribution that is normal if evidence obtained from the sample supports this assumption.

A histogram constructed from a large *sample* of such measurements can help determine whether this assumption is realistic. Assume, for example, that data were collected
on the length of life of 200 Everglo light bulbs. Let *X* represent the length of life (in hours)
of an Everglo bulb. One thing we are interested in is the *shape* of the distribution of the
200 lifetimes. Where are they centered? Are they symmetric? The easiest way to approach
such questions is to construct a histogram of the 200 values, as illustrated in Figure 6.2.
This histogram indicates that the data are nearly symmetric and are centered at approximately 400.

The curve in Figure 6.2 is said to be a **normal curve** because of its shape. A normal
curve is characterized by a **symmetric, bell-shaped appearance,** with tails that "die out"
rather quickly. We use such curves to represent the **assumed population** of all possible
values. This example contained 200 values observed in a *sample*. Consequently:

1. A histogram represents the shape of the sample data.
2. A smooth curve represents the assumed shape (distribution) of the population.

If all possible values of a variable *X* follow an assumed normal curve, then *X* is said
to be a **normal random variable,** and the population is **normally distributed.**

When you assume that a particular population follows a normal distribution, you
assume that *X,* an observation randomly obtained from this population, is a normal random
variable. Based on the histogram in Figure 6.2, it appears to be a reasonable assumption
that the smooth curve describing the population of *all* Everglo bulbs can be approximated
using a normal curve centered at 400 hours. Therefore, we will assume that *X* is a normal
random variable, centered at 400 hours.

There are two numbers used to describe a normal curve (distribution); they tell where
the curve is centered and how wide it is. The **center** of a normal curve is called the *mean*
and is represented by the symbol μ (mu). The **width** of a normal curve can be described
using the *standard deviation,* which is represented by the symbol σ (sigma). These

FIGURE 6.2

Histogram of 200 Everglo light bulb lifetimes (in hours). The curve represents all possible values (population). The histogram represents the sample (200 values).

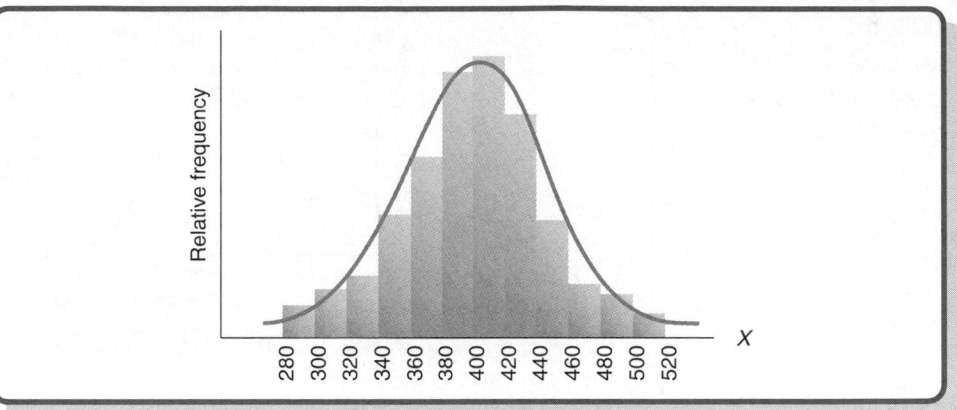

FIGURE 6.3

Distribution of the lifetime of Everglo bulbs showing the mean ($\mu = 400$), the standard deviation ($\sigma = 50$), and the inflection point (P).

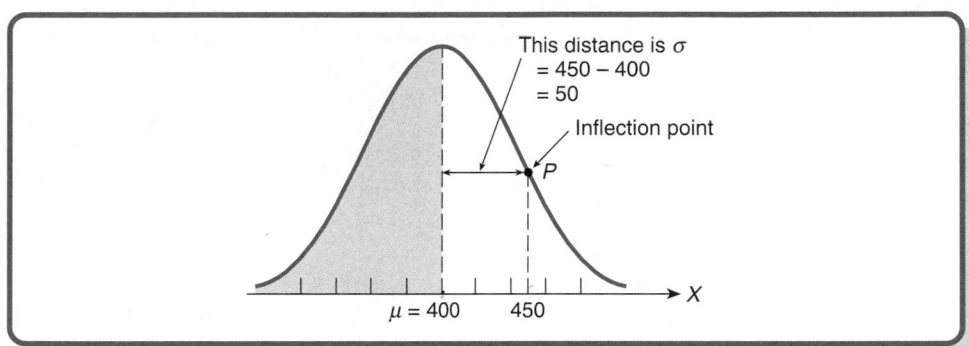

descriptions are illustrated in Figure 6.3, which shows the normal curve representing the lifetime of Everglo light bulbs. Another way of stating this situation is: X is a normal random variable with $\mu = 400$ hours and $\sigma = 50$ hours. Notice that the units of μ and σ are the same as the units of the data (hours).

In Figure 6.3, there is a point P on the normal curve. Above this point P, the curve resembles a bowl that is upside down, and below P the curve is "right side up." In calculus, this point is referred to as an **inflection point.** The distance between vertical lines through μ and P is the value of σ.

Because μ and σ represent the location and spread of the normal distribution, they are called **parameters.** The parameters are used to define the distribution completely. The values of μ and σ of a normal population are all you need to distinguish it from all other normal populations that have the same bell shape but different location and/or variability. The values of the parameters must be specified in order to make probability statements regarding X. As a result, there are infinitely many normal curves (populations), one for each pair of values of μ and σ.

In Chapter 5, we discussed the mean of (say) 10 observations of the random variable X, written as $\overline{X}$. If you were to observe X indefinitely, then you could obtain the mean of the population, μ. The same concept applies to continuous random variables; for the Everglo example, $\overline{X}$ represents the mean of the 200 bulbs (the sample) and μ is the mean of all Everglo bulbs (the population).

Mean		Standard Deviation	
Sample	**Population**	**Sample**	**Population**
$\overline{X}$	μ	s	σ
the average of the sample	the average of the population	the standard deviation of the sample	the standard deviation of the population

FIGURE 6.4

Two normal curves with unequal means and equal standard deviations.

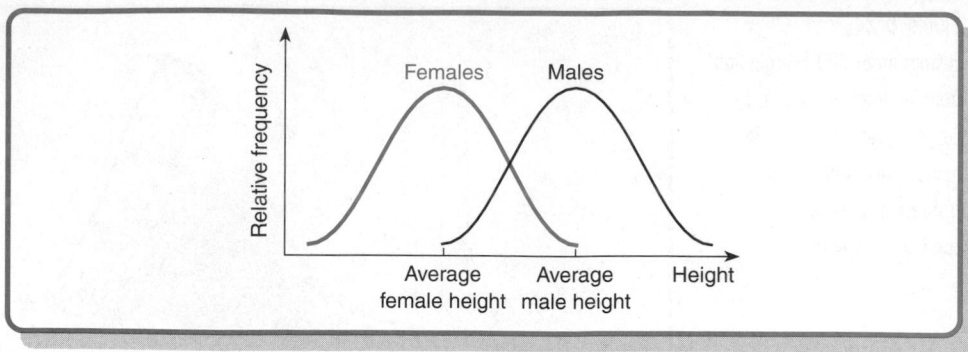

FIGURE 6.5

Two normal curves with equal means and unequal standard deviations.

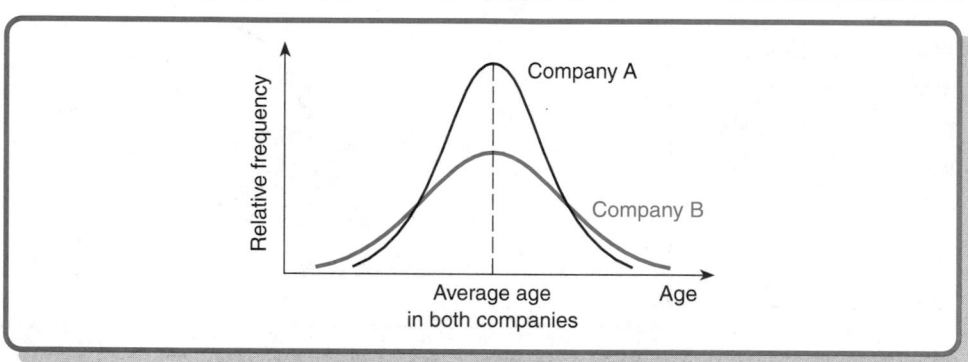

In our Everglo example, the average lifetime of all bulbs is *assumed* to be $\mu = 400$ hours. The standard deviation of the population, σ, just like s, is a measure of **variability.** The larger σ is, the more variation (jumping around) we would see if X were observed indefinitely. For both the sample and the population, the square of the standard deviation is referred to as the variance. It is another measure of the variability of X. The **variance** of a random variable, X, is represented by σ^2.

Consider whether the sample average ($\overline{X}$) of the 200 values in our example is the *same* as μ. It is not. Do not confuse the average lifetime of all light bulbs (μ) with the average lifetime of just 200 bulbs ($\overline{X}$). This is an important distinction in statistics. However, if our assumed normal distribution (with $\mu = 400$ and $\sigma = 50$) is correct, then $\overline{X}$ most often will be "close to" μ. We examine this again in Chapter 7.

The curve in Figure 6.3 is an illustration of a normal random variable with a mean of 400 hours and a standard deviation of 50 hours. We can compare normal curves that may differ in mean, standard deviation, or both. The normal curves in Figure 6.4 indicate that, on the average, males are taller than females. The mean of the male curve is to the right of the mean of the female curve. The male heights "jump around" about as much as female heights. In other words, there is about the same amount of *variation* in male and female heights because the standard deviation of each curve is the same; that is, each curve is equally wide.

In Figure 6.5, the two normal curves represent the ages of the employees at two large companies. It appears that:

1. The average age of employees for the two companies is the same.
2. The ages in Company B have more variability. This simply means that there are more old people and more young people in Company B than in Company A.

FIGURE 6.6

Area under a normal curve.

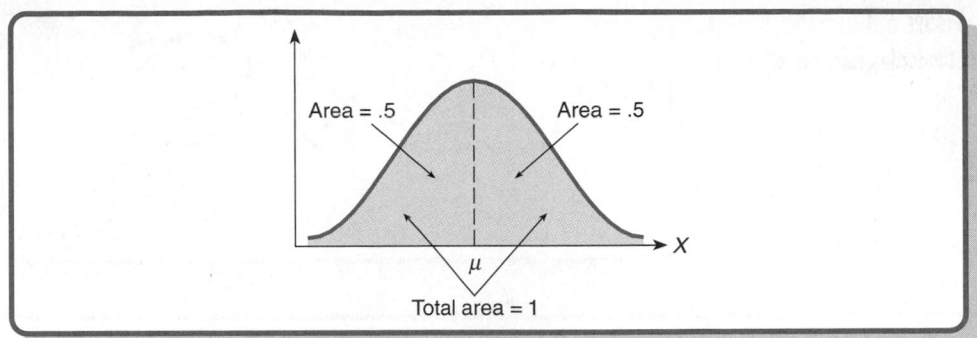

FIGURE 6.7

Normal curve for Everglo light bulbs showing $P(X < 360)$. The shaded area is the percentage of time that X will be less than 360. (X = lifetime of Everglo bulb.)

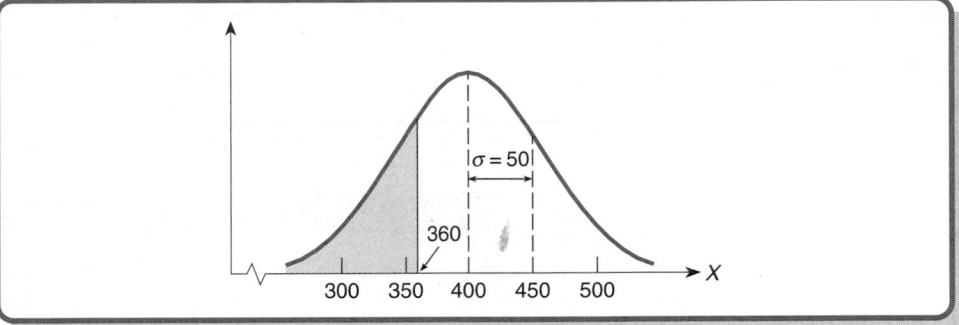

6.3 DETERMINING A PROBABILITY FOR A NORMAL RANDOM VARIABLE

So you have assumed that the lifetime of an Everglo light bulb is a normal random variable with $\mu = 400$ and $\sigma = 50$. Now what? This brings us back to the subject of probability. Before we describe probabilities for a normal random variable, consider one important property of *any* normal curve (or of any curve representing a continuous random variable, for that matter), namely, that the total area under the curve is 1 (see Figure 6.6). When we described the normal curve as bell-shaped, we also determined that it was symmetrical. If the halves are identical, then the probability above the mean (μ) is equal to .5 and is the same as the probability below the mean. Thus, in Figure 6.3 the shaded area is equal to the nonshaded area under the curve.

Returning to the Everglo bulb example, what percentage of the time will the burnout time, X, be less than 360? This probability is written as

$$P(X < 360)$$

We discuss how to determine this area (a simple procedure) later in the chapter, but for now, just remember that when dealing with a normal random variable, a **probability** is represented by an **area** under the corresponding normal curve. The value of $P(X < 360)$ is illustrated in Figure 6.7. It appears that roughly 20% of the total area has been shaded, so we can conclude that (1) roughly 20% of the Everglo bulbs will burn out in less than 360 hours, and (2) the probability that X is less than 360 is approximately .2.

6.4 FINDING AREAS UNDER A NORMAL CURVE

AREAS UNDER THE STANDARD NORMAL CURVE

We begin our discussion by finding the area under a special normal curve—namely, one that is centered at 0 ($\mu = 0$) and has a standard deviation of 1 ($\sigma = 1$). This random variable is typically represented by the letter Z and is referred to as the **standard normal random variable.** As Figure 6.8 demonstrates, Z is as likely to be negative as positive; that is, $P(Z \leq 0) = P(Z \geq 0) = .5$. Although you probably never will observe a random variable like Z in practice, it is a useful normal random variable. In fact, an area under *any* normal curve

FIGURE 6.8
Standard normal curve.

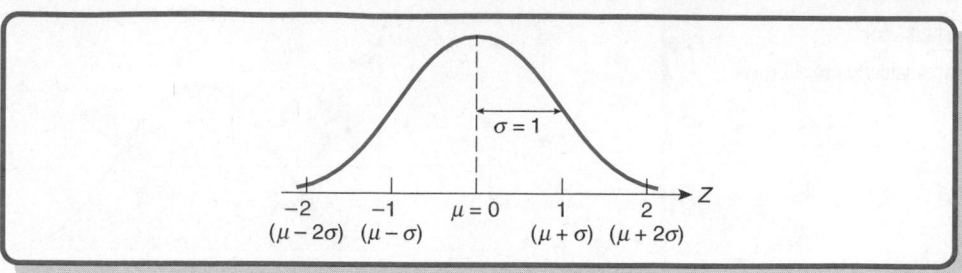

FIGURE 6.9
Shaded area = .4474, from
Table A.4.

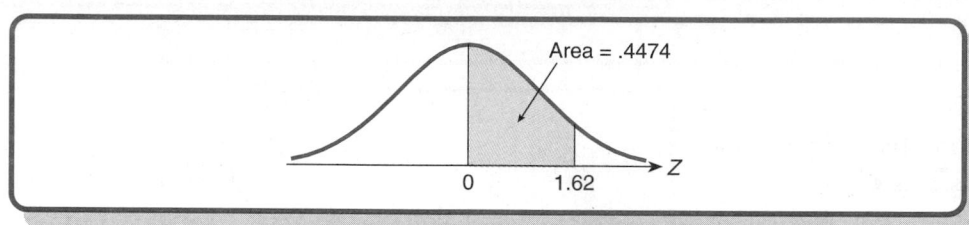

(as in Figure 6.7) can be determined by finding the corresponding area under the standard normal curve.

To derive the area under the standard normal curve requires the use of integral calculus. Unfortunately, the integral of the function describing the standard normal curve does not have a simple (closed form) expression. By using excellent approximations of this integral, however, we can tabulate these areas—see Table A.4 and Figure 6.9.

For example, suppose we want to determine the probability that a standard normal random variable will be between 0 and 1.62. This is written as

$$P(0 < Z < 1.62)$$

The value of this probability is obtained from Table A.4, which contains the area under the curve between the mean of zero and the particular value of Z. The far left column of Table A.4 identifies the first decimal place for Z, and you read across the table to obtain the second decimal place.

In our example, we find the intersection between 1.6 on the left and .02 on the top, because Z = 1.62. Look at Table A.4; the value .4474 is the *area* between 0 and 1.62. In other words, the probability that Z will lie between 0 and 1.62 is .4474.

You can begin to see why it is a good idea to sketch the curve and shade in the area when dealing with normal random variables. It gives you a clear picture of what the question is asking and cuts down on mistakes.

EXAMPLE 6.1   What is the probability that Z will be greater than 1.62?

SOLUTION   We wish to find P(Z > 1.62). Examine Figure 6.10. The area under the right half of the Z curve is .5, so, using our value from Table A.4, the desired area here is

$$.5 - .4474 = .0526$$

So the probability that Z will exceed 1.62 is .0526.

     What if we wish to know the probability that Z is equal to a particular value, such as P(Z = 1.62)? There is no area under the curve corresponding to Z = 1.62, so

$$P(Z = 1.62) = 0$$

FIGURE 6.10
The shaded area represents the probability that Z will be greater than 1.62 [$P(Z > 1.62)$].

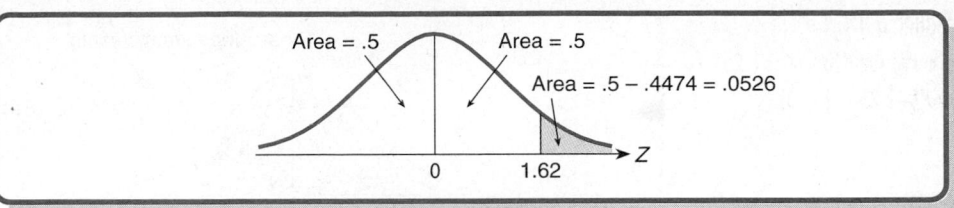

FIGURE 6.11
Area under the Z curve for $P(Z < 1.62)$.

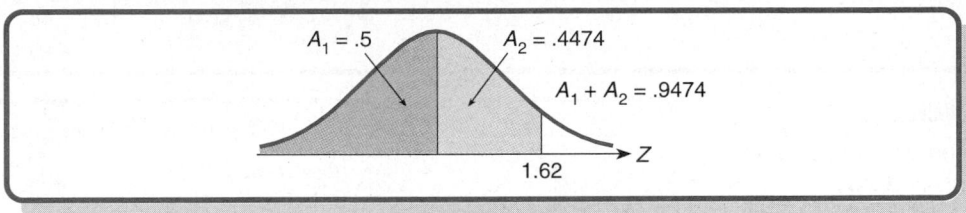

FIGURE 6.12
Area under the Z curve for $P(1.0 < Z < 2.0)$.

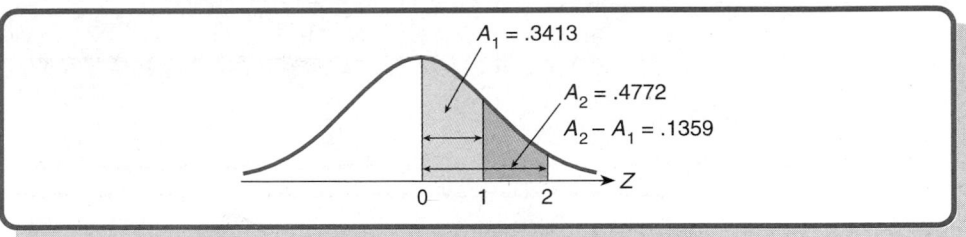

FIGURE 6.13
Area under the Z curve for $P(-1.25 < Z < 1.15)$.

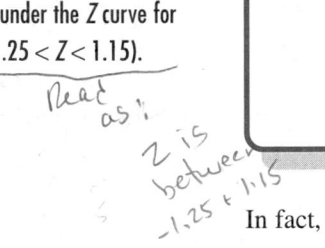

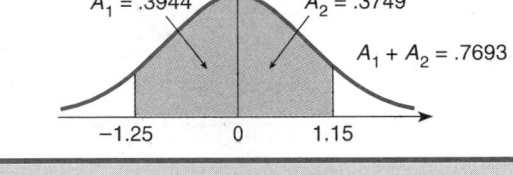

In fact,

$$P(Z = \text{any value}) = 0$$

One nice thing about this fact is that $P(Z \geq 1.62)$ is the *same* as $P(Z > 1.62)$ (that is, .0526). So putting the equal sign on the inequality ($\geq$ or $\leq$) has *no* effect on the resulting probability.

By looking at the Z curve in Figure 6.11, you can see that

$$P(Z < 1.62) = .5 + .4474 = .9474$$

As before, this also is $P(Z \leq 1.62)$.

Figure 6.12 shows $P(1.0 < Z < 2.0)$ (areas from Table A.4). We see that

$$P(1.0 < Z < 2.0) = P(0 < Z < 2.0) - P(0 < Z \leq 1.0)$$

$$= .4772 - .3413$$

$$= .1359$$

By subtracting the two areas, we find that the probability that Z will lie between 1.0 and 2.0 is .1359.

We use Figure 6.13 and Table A.4 to determine $P(-1.25 < Z < 1.15)$:

$$P(-1.25 < Z < 1.15) = P(-1.25 < Z < 0) + P(0 < Z < 1.15)$$

$$= A_1 + A_2$$

FIGURE 6.14

Z curve for $P(0 < Z < 1.25)$ $= P(-1.25 < Z < 0)$.

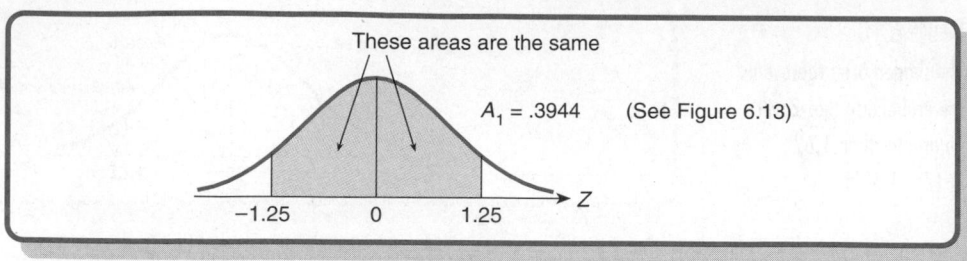

FIGURE 6.15

Area under the Z curve for $P(Z < -1.45)$.

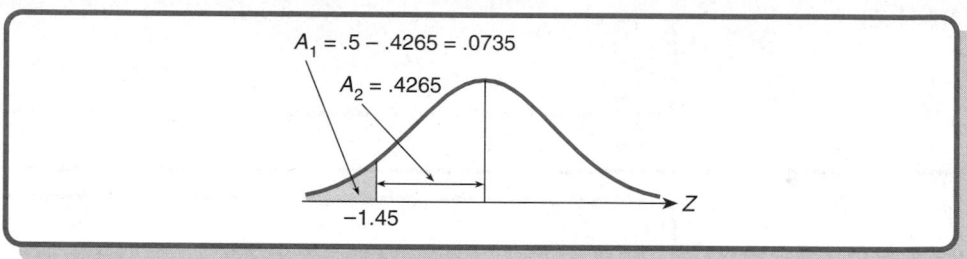

FIGURE 6.16

Value of Z having a right-tailed area of .03.

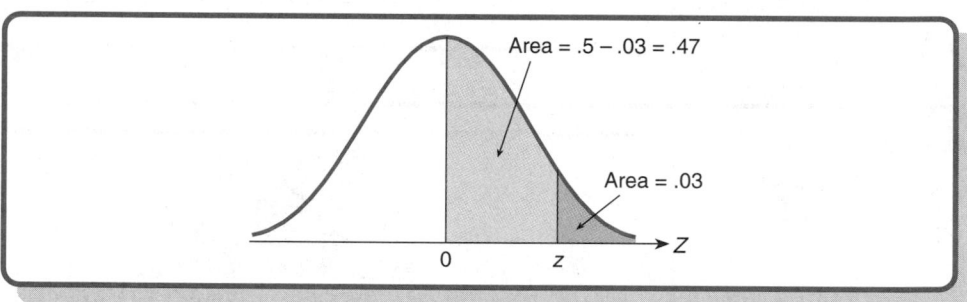

Using the symmetry of the Z curve and Figure 6.14, the area of A_1 is the same as $P(0 < Z < 1.25)$ and thus is .3944. The area of A_2, from Table A.4, is .3749. So we add A_1 and A_2:

$$.3944 + .3749 = .7693$$

Finally, we can determine $P(Z < -1.45)$ using Figure 6.15. This can be written as $P(Z < 0) - P(-1.45 < Z < 0)$, that is, $.5 - A_2$. Using the symmetry of the Z curve, the area between 0 and -1.45 is $A_2 = .4265$ (from Table A.4). As a result, Z will be less than (or equal to) -1.45 approximately 7.35% of the time.

FINDING THE Z VALUE FOR A SPECIFIED AREA. This is the reverse of what we have discussed so far. Here, you will be given the area and asked to determine the value of Z having this specified area. For example, for what value of Z (say, z) is the following statement true?

$$P(Z \geq z) = .03$$

The value of z is the one having a right-tailed area (due to the $\geq$ in this statement) of .03. This is illustrated in Figure 6.16. The value of z having a right tail of .03 is the value of z having a shaded area in Table A.4 of $.5 - .03 = .47$. By examining this table, we see that the value closest to .47 is .4699 (belonging to 1.88). Consequently, $z = 1.88$.

Another example: For what value of Z (say, z) is the following statement true?

$$P(Z \leq z) = .2$$

FIGURE 6.17

Value of Z having a left-tailed area of .2.

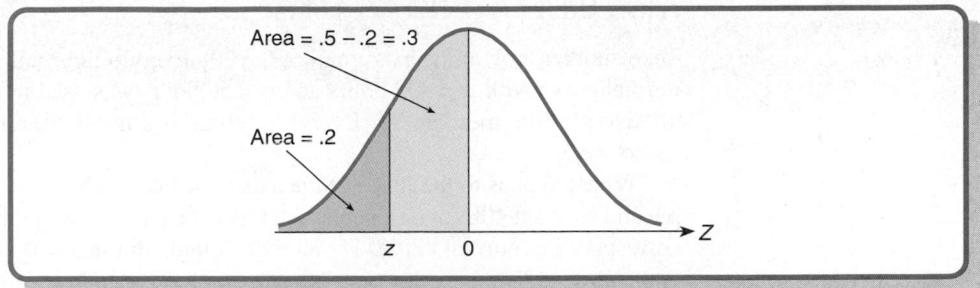

This is a left-tailed area of .2 due to the ≤ (see Figure 6.17). The z having this left-tailed area is the negative of the z having a shaded area in Table A.4 of $.5 - .2 = .3$. Examining this table, we see that the value closest to .3 is .2995, belonging to .84. We know that z is negative because it is to the left of zero, and so $z = -.84$.

EXERCISES 6.1–6.10

UNDERSTANDING THE MECHANICS

6.1 Draw a normal curve with the following values for μ and σ.
   a. $\mu = 0, \sigma = 1$
   b. $\mu = 4, \sigma = 1$
   c. $\mu = 4, \sigma = 3$
   d. $\mu = -4, \sigma = 3$

6.2 Find the area under the standard normal distribution between the following Z values.
   a. $Z = 0$ and $Z = 1$
   b. $Z = 0$ and $Z = 2$
   c. $Z = 0$ and $Z = .55$
   d. $Z = 0$ and $Z = -1.52$

6.3 For a random variable that has a standard normal distribution, find the following probabilities.
   a. The probability that the random variable is between –2 and 0.
   b. The probability that the random variable is between –1.66 and –1.00.
   c. The probability that the random variable is between –1.15 and 2.15.

6.4 Find the following probabilities. Sketch the corresponding area.
   a. $P(0 \leq Z \leq .5)$
   b. $P(Z \leq .5)$
   c. $P(Z \leq -.5)$
   d. $P(Z \geq .5)$
   e. $P(-.5 \leq Z \leq .5)$

6.5 For a standard normal random variable Z, what is the probability that:
   a. Z is less than 1.23.
   b. Z is less than or equal to 1.23.
   c. Z is at least –1.23.
   d. Z is between the mean and 1.96.
   e. Z is less than –1.5 or greater than .62.

6.6 Find the value of z for the following probability statements, and sketch the corresponding area.
   a. $P(0 \leq Z \leq z) = .4901$
   b. $P(z \leq Z \leq 0) = .2324$
   c. $P(Z \leq z) = .8888$
   d. $P(Z \geq z) = .2090$
   e. $P(Z \geq z) = .7910$

6.7 Find the value of z for the following probability statements, and sketch the corresponding area.
   a. $P(-1.0 \leq Z \leq z) = .6898$
   b. $P(1.0 \leq Z \leq z) = .0072$
   c. $P(-2.0 \leq Z \leq z) = .0164$
   d. $P(-2.0 \leq Z \leq z) = .9544$
   e. $P(z \leq Z \leq 2.0) = .9544$

APPLYING THE NEW CONCEPTS

6.8 An educational testing service administers a national test to measure the reading comprehension of third-grade students. Only standardized scores are reported. The scores are approximately normally distributed. The testing service classifies scores above the 90th percentile as outstanding, between the 70th and 90th percentile as above average, between the 30th percentile and 70th percentile as average, between the 10th percentile and the 30th percentile as below average, and below the 10th percentile as poor. Find the z-scores corresponding to the 90th, 70th, 30th, and 10th percentiles.

6.9 An instructor is interested in the Z value that corresponds to the 50th and 97th percentile. Find these Z values. In Excel, find the Z value for the 50th percentile by typing into a cell "=NORMINV(.5,0,1)". This command will find the value of z such that the probability Z is less than z is equal to .5. The values of 0 and 1 represent the mean of 0 and the standard deviation of 1 for a standard normal distribution. Likewise, find the Z value for the 97th percentile.

6.10 A production process is designed to produce a cylinder that has a diameter of 10 cm. Let Z be the difference between the diameter of the manufactured cylinder and 10 cm. Assume that Z is a standard normal random variable. The manager would like the deviation of the actual diameter to be no more than 1.67 from 10 cm. Find the probability that the absolute value of Z is less than 1.67. In Excel, this probability can be found by typing into a cell "=NORMSDIST(1.67) – NORMSDIST(–1.67)".

AREAS UNDER ANY NORMAL CURVE

Take another look at the histogram of the 200 Everglo light bulb lifetimes in Figure 6.2. A normal curve with $\mu = 400$ hours and $\sigma = 50$ hours was used to describe the population of *all* Everglo lifetimes. So X = Everglo lifetime is a normal random variable with $\mu = 400$ and $\sigma = 50$.

What happens to the shape of the data if we take each of the 200 lifetimes in this example and subtract 400 (that is, subtract μ)? As you can see in Figure 6.18, the histogram (and corresponding normal curve) is merely "shifted" to the left by 400. It resembles the normal curve for X, except the "new" mean is 0. The random variable defined by $Y = X - 400$:

1. is a normal random variable
2. has a mean equal to zero
3. has a standard deviation equal to that of X, that is, 50

Figure 6.19 shows what happens to the shape of 200 Y values if each of them is *divided* by 50 (that is, by σ). Notice the horizontal axis in the histogram and the corresponding normal curve. The resulting normal curve resembles a normal curve with a mean of 0 and a standard deviation equal to 1.

Thus, if X is a normal random variable with mean 400 and standard deviation 50, then the random variable defined by

$$Z = \frac{X - 400}{50}$$

1. is a normal random variable
2. has a mean equal to zero
3. has a standard deviation equal to 1

FIGURE 6.18

Histogram obtained by subtracting $\mu = 400$ (compare with Figure 6.2).

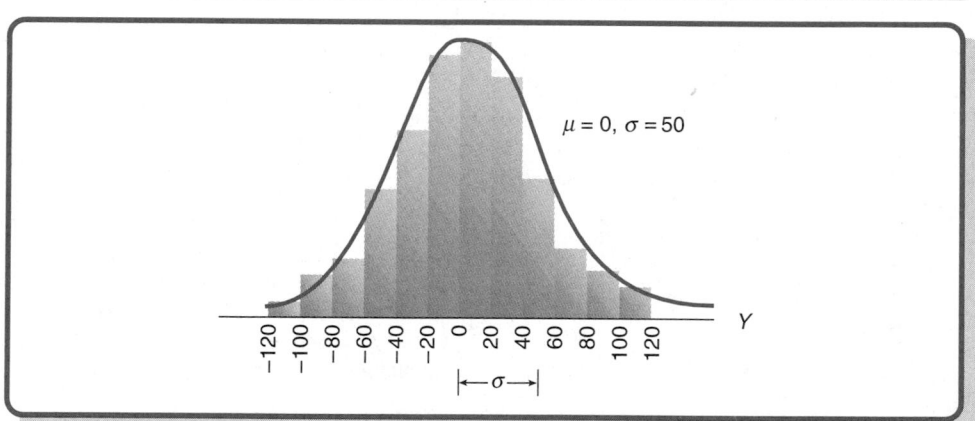

$\mu = 0, \ \sigma = 50$

FIGURE 6.19

Histogram obtained by subtracting μ and dividing by σ (compare with Figures 6.2 and 6.18).

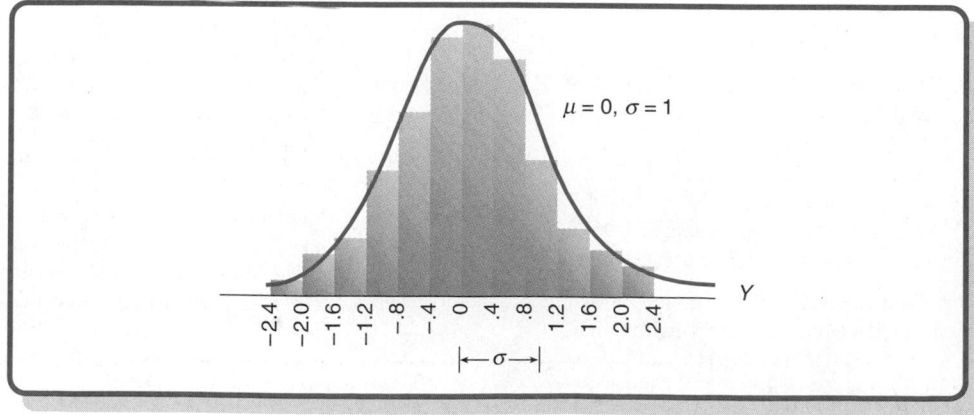

$\mu = 0, \ \sigma = 1$

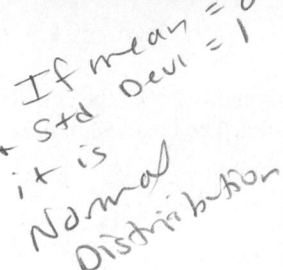

In general, for *any* normal random variable X,

$$Z = \frac{X - \mu}{\sigma}$$

is a **standard normal random variable.** This procedure of subtracting μ and dividing by σ is referred to as **standardizing** the normal random variable X. *It allows us to determine probabilities for any normal random variable by first standardizing it and then using Table A.4. So the standard normal distribution turns out to be much more important than you might have expected!*

EXAMPLE 6.2

The normal curve in Figure 6.7 represented the lifetime of all Everglo bulbs, with $\mu = 400$ hours and $\sigma = 50$ hours. What percentage of the bulbs will burn out in less than 360 hours? Or, put another way, what is the probability that any particular bulb will last less than 360 hours?

SOLUTION

This probability is written as

$$P(X < 360)$$

This random variable is continuous, so $P(X < 360) = P(X \le 360)$. To determine the probability, you need to standardize this variable:*

$$P(X < 360) = P\left(\frac{X - 400}{50} < \frac{360 - 400}{50}\right)$$

$$= P(Z < -.8)$$

where $Z = (X - 400)/50$ (Figure 6.20).

FIGURE 6.20

Compare the areas for (a) the X and (b) the Z normal curves to find $P(X < 360)$.

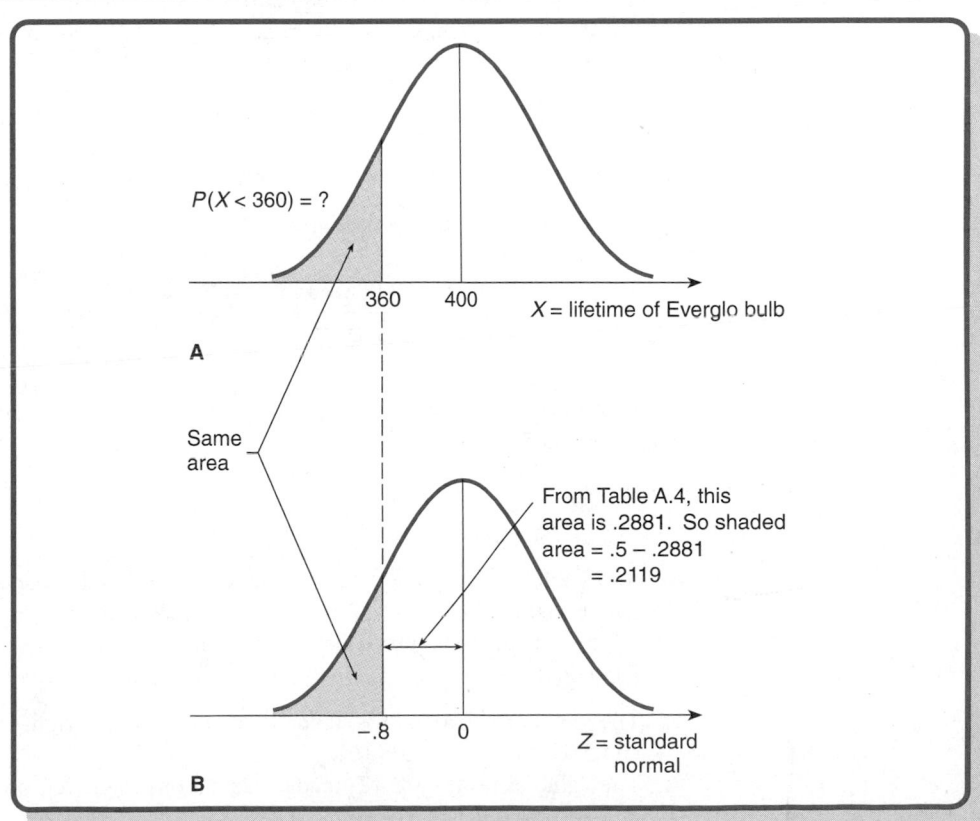

---

* Since 400 is subtracted from *both* sides of the inequality and *both* sides are divided by 50, the events described by the original inequality $P(X < 360)$ and the standardized inequality $P(Z < -.8)$ are the same.

Earlier, by examining Figure 6.7, we estimated this area to be roughly 20%. The actual area, from Figure 6.20, is .2119; that is, it is 21.19% of the total area. The conclusion here is that

$$P(X < 360) = .2119$$

and so 21% of all Everglo bulbs will have a lifetime of less than 360 hours.

INTERPRETING Z

 What does a Z value of $-.8$ imply in Example 6.2? It simply means that 360 is .8 standard deviations to the left of the mean (Z is negative). So

$$\mu - .8(\sigma) = 400 - .8(50) = 360$$

Recall that a z-score was defined in exactly the same way in Chapter 3 using a sample mean ($\overline{X}$) and standard deviation (s). In this chapter, we use the population mean (μ) and standard deviation (σ). In general:

1. A *positive* value of Z designates how many standard deviations (σ) X is to the *right* of the mean (μ).
2. A *negative* value of Z designates how many standard deviations X is to the *left* of the mean.

EXAMPLE 6.3

The funds dispensed daily by an automatic teller machine (ATM) in a Denver grocery store are believed to be normally distributed with a mean of $3700 and a standard deviation of $625. The machine is programmed to notify the store manager if the daily dollar volume is very low (less than or equal to $2000) or unusually high (greater than or equal to $5000). What percentage of the time will the daily dollar volume *not* be in either of these two conditions?

SOLUTION

This probability can be written as

$$P(2000 < X < 5000)$$

Using the standardization procedure:

$$P(2000 < X < 5000) = P\left(\frac{2000 - 3700}{625} < \frac{X - 3700}{625} < \frac{5000 - 3700}{625} \right)$$

$$= P(-2.72 < Z < 2.08)$$

where Z once again represents the *standardized* normal random variable, which for this example is defined by

$$Z = \frac{X - 3700}{625}$$

Refer to Table A.4 and Figure 6.21 and note that the shaded areas in Figure 6.21(a) and (b) are both equal to $.4967 + .4812 = .9779$. As a result, the manager can expect no notification of unusual activity approximately 98% of the time.
   Also note that:

1. The value of $5000 is 2.08 standard deviations to the right of the mean, since $Z = 2.08$ and $5000 = 3700 + (2.08)(625)$.
2. The value of $2000 is 2.72 standard deviations to the left of the mean, since $Z = -2.72$ and $2000 = 3700 - (2.72)(625)$.

FIGURE 6.21

(a) The probability that X is between $2000 and $5000.
(b) The probability that Z is between -2.72 and 2.08.

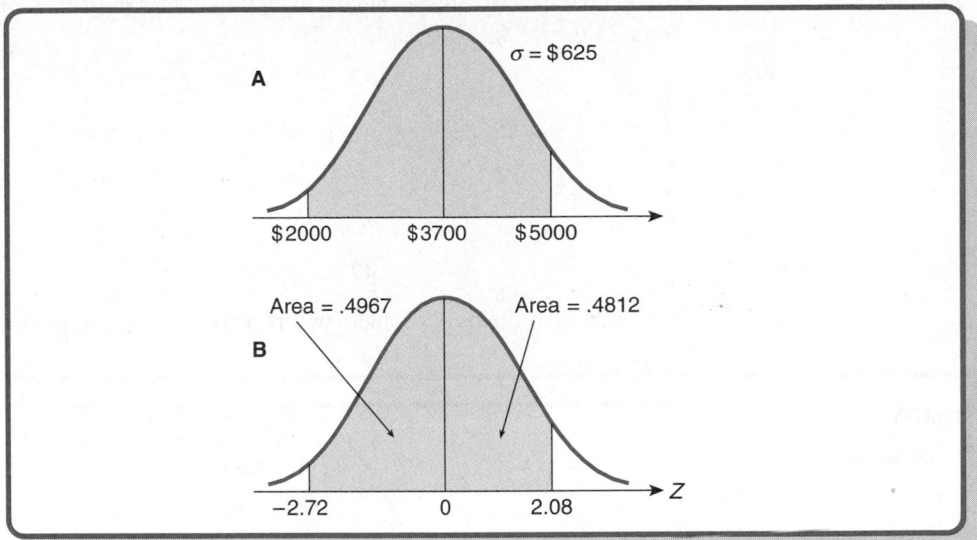

EXAMPLE 6.4

Actuarial scientists in an insurance company formulate insurance policies that will be both profitable and marketable. For a particular policy, the lifetimes of the policyholders follow a normal distribution with $\mu = 66.2$ years and $\sigma = 4.4$ years. One of the options with this policy is to receive a payment following the 65th birthday and a payment every five years thereafter.

1. What percentage of policyholders will receive at least one payment using this option?
2. What percentage will receive two or more payments?
3. What percentage will receive exactly two payments?

SOLUTION 1

The normal curve for the policyholder lifetimes is shown in Figure 6.22. To receive at least one payment, the policyholder must live beyond 65 years of age. So we need to determine (see Figure 6.23):

$$P(X > 65) = P[(X - 66.2)/4.4 > (65 - 66.2)/4.4]$$

$$= P(Z > -.27) = .1064 + .5$$

$$= .6064$$

So nearly 61% of the policyholders will receive at least one payment.

SOLUTION 2

Because the policyholder receives a payment every five years, he or she will receive two or more payments provided he or she lives to be older than 70 years of age. Thus the probability of two or more payments is determined by (see Figure 6.24):

$$P(X > 70) = P[(X - 66.2)/4.4 > (70 - 66.2)/4.4]$$

$$= P(Z > .86) = .5 - .3051$$

$$= .1949$$

Thus, 19.5% of the policyholders will survive long enough to collect two payments.

SOLUTION 3

To receive exactly two payments, the policyholder must live longer than 70 years and less than 75 years. This probability is

$$P(70 < X < 75)$$

Using the same standardization procedure (see Figure 6.25):

$$P(70 < X < 75) = P[(70 - 66.2)/4.4 < (X - 66.2)/4.4 < (75 - 66.2)/4.4]$$

$$= P(.86 < Z < 2.00)$$

$$= .4772 - .3051 = .1721$$

So 17.21% of the policyholders will receive exactly two payments.

FIGURE 6.22

The normal curve for policyholder lifetimes. X = age at death (in years).

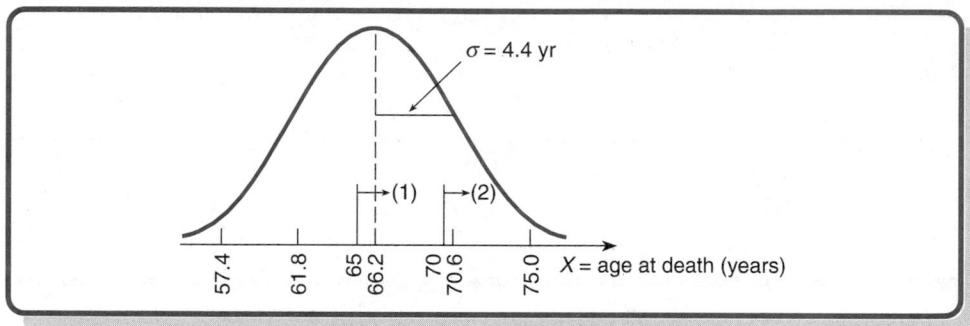

FIGURE 6.23

Z curve for $P(Z > -.27)$.

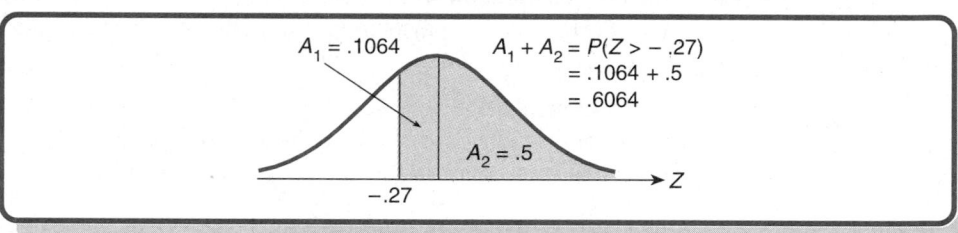

FIGURE 6.24

Z curve for $P(Z > .86)$.

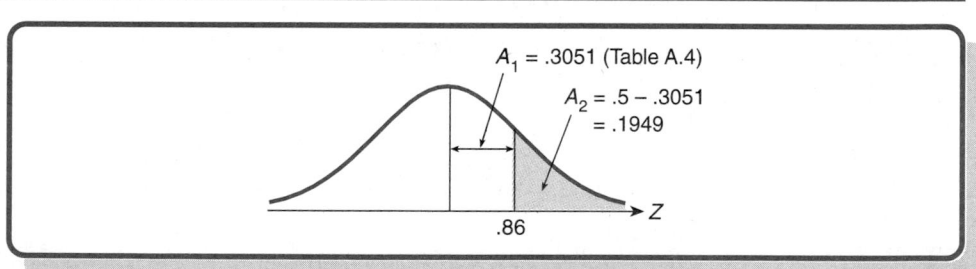

FIGURE 6.25

Z curve for $P(.86 < Z < 2.00)$.

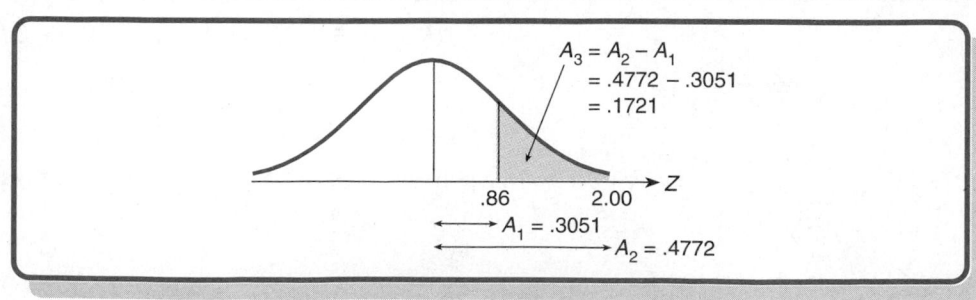

6.5 APPLICATIONS WHERE THE AREA UNDER A NORMAL CURVE IS PROVIDED

Another twist to dealing with normal random variables is a situation where you are given the area under the normal curve and asked to determine the corresponding value of the variable. This is a common application of a normal random variable. For example, the manufacturer of a product may want to determine a warranty period during which the product will be replaced if it becomes defective, so that at most 5% of the items are returned during this period. Or, in a grocery store on any given day, the demand for a freshly made food item may or may not exceed the supply. The owner may want to determine how much to supply each day, such that the demand (a normal random variable) will exceed this value 10% of the time (in other words, the customers will be disappointed no more than 10% of the time).

EXAMPLE 6.5

Referring to Example 6.2, after how many hours will 80% of the Everglo bulbs burn out? Recall that $\mu = 400$ and $\sigma = 50$.

SOLUTION

The first step here is to sketch this curve [Figure 6.26(a)] and estimate the value of X (say x_0) so that

$$P(X < x_0) = .8 \quad (80\%)$$

Because .8 is larger than .5, x_0 must lie to the *right* of 400.

Next, find the point on a standard normal (Z) curve such that the area to the left is also .8 [Figure 6.26(b)]. Using Table A.4, the area between 0 and .84 is .2995. This means that

$$P(Z < .84) = .5 + .2995$$

$$= .7995$$

$$= .8 \quad \text{(approximately)}$$

FIGURE 6.26
(a) $P(X < x_0) = .8$.
(b) $P(Z < .84) = .8$.

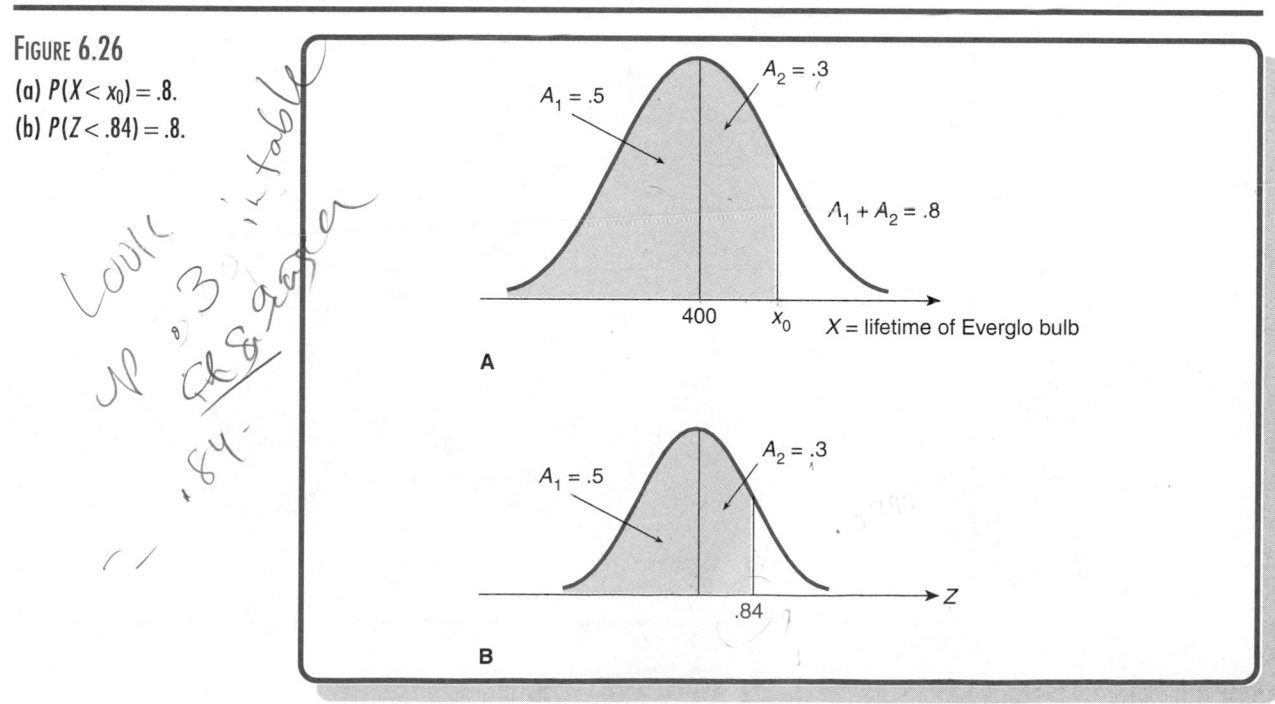

By standardizing X, we conclude that

$$\frac{x_0 - 400}{50} = .84$$

$$x_0 - 400 = (50)(.84) = 42$$

$$x_0 = 400 + 42 = 442$$

So 80% of the Everglo bulbs will burn out within 442 hours.

EXAMPLE 6.6

A bakery shop sells loaves of freshly made French bread. Any unsold loaves at the end of the day are either discarded or sold elsewhere at a loss. The demand for this bread has followed a normal distribution with $\mu = 35$ loaves and $\sigma = 8$ loaves.

How many loaves should the bakery make each day so that they can meet the demand 90% of the time?

SOLUTION

The normal random variable X here is the demand for French bread (measured in loaves) [Figure 6.27(a)]. To meet the demand 90% of the time, the bakery must determine an amount, say x_0 loaves, such that:

$$P(X \leq x_0) = .90$$

Proceeding as before, examine a Z curve and find the value having an area to the left equal to .90 [Figure 6.27(b)]. Using Table A.4:

$$P(0 \leq Z \leq 1.28) = .4 \qquad \text{(more accurately, .3997)}$$

which means that

$$P(Z \leq 1.28) = .4 + .5 = .9$$

FIGURE 6.27
(a) $P(X \leq x_0) = .90$.
(b) $P(Z \leq 1.28) = .90$.

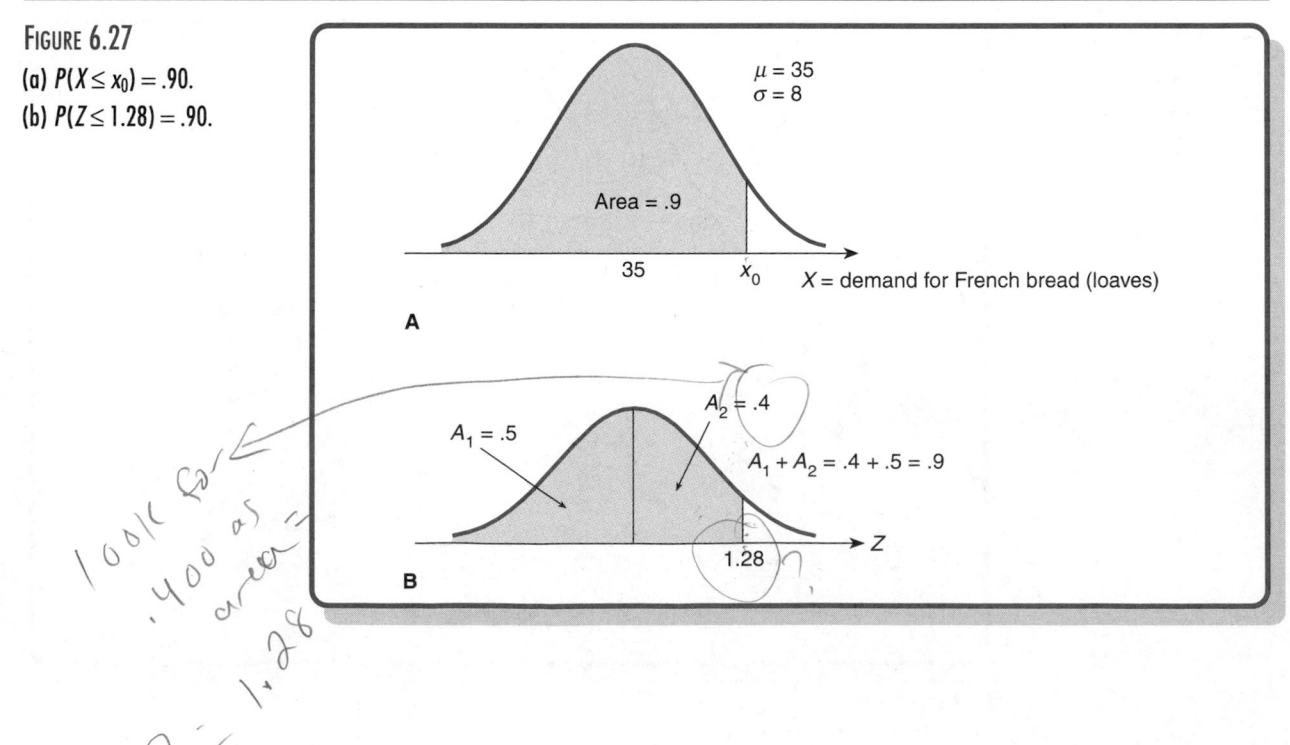

So

$$\frac{x_0 - 35}{8} = 1.28$$

and

$$x_0 = 35 + (1.28)(8) = 45.24$$

To be conservative, round this value up to 46 loaves. By stocking 46 loaves each day, the bakery will meet the demand for this product 90% of the time.

6.6 ANOTHER LOOK AT THE EMPIRICAL RULE

In Chapter 3, the empirical rule specified that when sampling from a bell-shaped distribution (which means a normal distribution):

1. Approximately 68% of the data values should lie between $\bar{X} - s$ and $\bar{X} + s$.
2. Approximately 95% of them should lie between $\bar{X} - 2s$ and $\bar{X} + 2s$.
3. Approximately 99.7% of them should lie between $\bar{X} - 3s$ and $\bar{X} + 3s$.

Nothing was said at that time about the origin of these numbers. They actually came directly from Table A.4. To see this, consider Figure 6.28, in which

$$P(-1 < Z < 1) = .68 \qquad \text{``Z is between} -1 \text{ al'}$$

This implies that, for any normal random variable X,

$$P[-1 < (X - \mu)/\sigma < 1] = .68$$

That is,

$$P[(\mu - \sigma) < X < (\mu + \sigma)] = .68$$

As a result, for a set of data from a normal population where $\bar{X}$ is the sample mean and s is the sample standard deviation, we would expect approximately 68% of the data to lie between $\bar{X} - s$ and $\bar{X} + s$.

Similarly, $P(-2 < Z < 2) = .4772 + .4772 = .9544$, so you can expect (approximately) 95% of the data points from a normal (bell-shaped) population to lie between $\bar{X} - 2s$ and $\bar{X} + 2s$.

Finally, $P(-3 < Z < 3) = .4987 + .4987 = .9974$, which leads to the third conclusion of the empirical rule.

FIGURE 6.28

Z curve for

$P(-1 < Z < 1) \cong .68$.

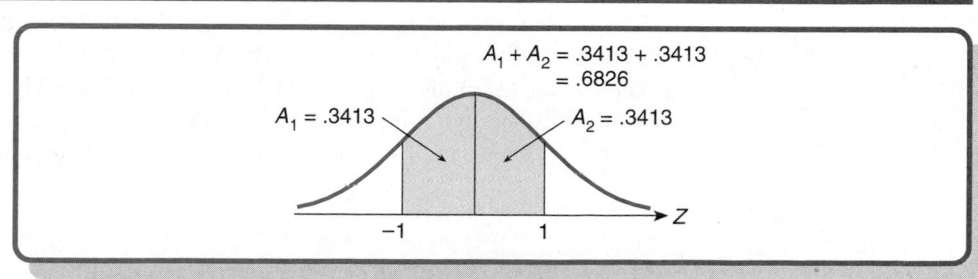

$A_1 + A_2 = .3413 + .3413$
$= .6826$

$A_1 = .3413$ $A_2 = .3413$

FIGURE 6.29
Illustration of Excel functions NORMDIST (Example 6.2) and NORMINV (Example 6.5).

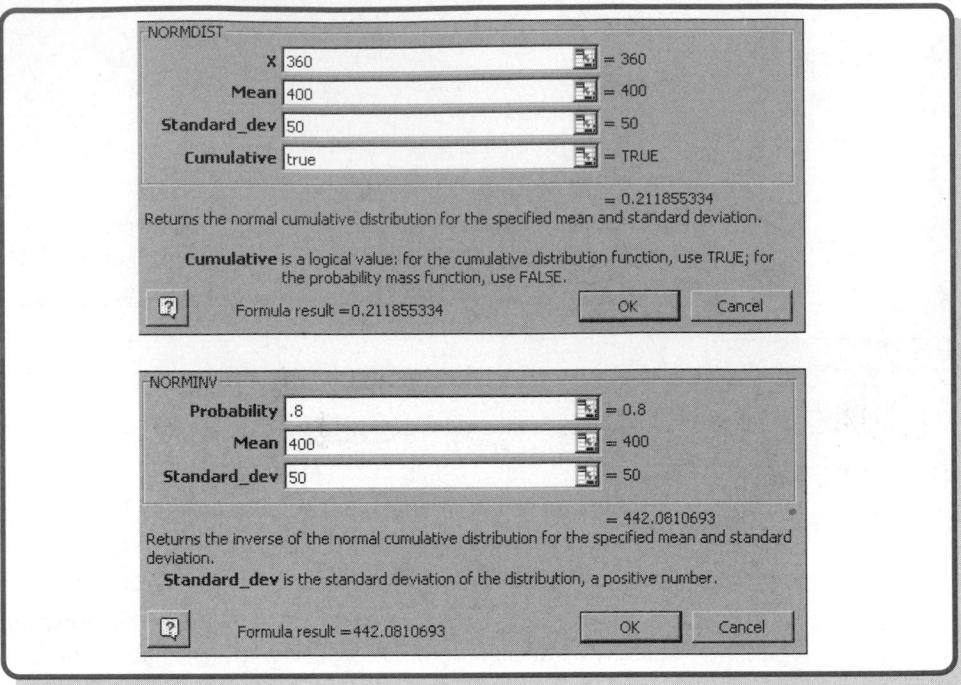

6.7 USING EXCEL TO DETERMINE AREAS AND VALUES HAVING A SPECIFIED AREA FOR NORMAL POPULATIONS

The calculations demonstrated in Sections 6.4 and 6.5 to determine areas under a normal curve or determine a value of a normal random variable having a specified area can be done very easily using Excel and MINITAB. In Example 6.2, the area to the left of 360 was determined for a normal curve with a mean of 400 and a standard deviation of 50. To find this area (probability) using Excel, click on the Paste Function icon (*fx*), click on **Statistical** under **Function Category** and click on **NORMDIST** under **Function Name.** Fill in the entries as in the top panel of Figure 6.29. Entering "true" in the last box indicates that you want the area to the *left* of 360, and you will always enter "true" in this box for all the applications in this textbook. The formula result is .2119 and agrees with Example 6.2.

COMMENT

Whenever you need to find $P(X > \text{some value})$, use Excel's NORMDIST function as described here and subtract the result from one. For example, the probability that the bulb lifetime (X) in Example 6.2 exceeds 360 hours is $1 - .2119 = .7881$. Remember, Excel always determines the area to the left of the specified value of X.

The bottom panel of Figure 6.29 illustrates Excel's NORMINV function and repeats the solution to Example 6.5. The NORMINV function finds the value of X having a specified area to the *left* of this value. Using the Excel solution in Figure 6.29, 80% of the Everglo bulbs will burn out within 442 hours—that is, $P(X \le 442) = .8$, where X if normally distributed with a mean of 400 hours and a standard deviation of 50 hours.

MICROSOFT® EXCEL APPLICATION   USE DATA6-7

EXAMPLE 6.7
Using Excel to Find Areas Under a Normal Curve

In chapter 3 (Example 3.4), we examined a sample of 100 inside diameters of a machined part produced at the Boston facility of Allied Manufacturing. It was concluded in Example 3.9 that the sample histogram was approximately bell shaped (normal). Consequently, an assumption of a normal population was reasonable, and the empirical rule

FIGURE 6.30
Partial listing of DATA6-7 and
results of descriptive statistics.

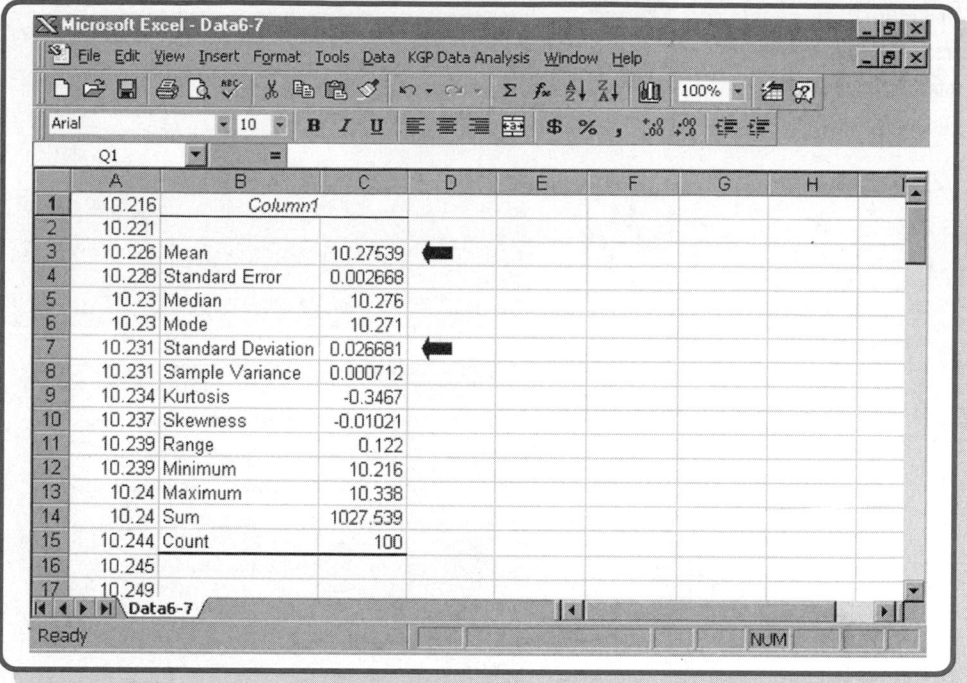

was applied. Earlier discussion of this sample in Chapter 2 (Example 2.1) mentioned that for this part to be acceptable, the diameter must be between 10.1 mm (the lower spec limit) and 10.3 mm (the upper spec limit). Any part outside these spec limits is said to be nonconforming. The targeted diameter is 10.2 mm.

This same data set is contained in DATA6-7. Determine the mean and standard deviation of this sample and compute the sample Z scores for the two spec limits. Assuming the population is normal, with mean $\bar{x}$ and standard deviation $s,$ what proportion of the population will lie outside the spec limits—that is, be nonconforming? What can you say about this process?

In Figure 6.30 you can see the first 17 of the 100 values in DATA6-7. By clicking on **Tools ➤ Data Analysis ➤ Descriptive Statistics** and (1) entering "A1:A1000" for the input range, (2) entering "B1" for the output range, and (3) clicking on the small box to the left of **Summary Statistics,** you will obtain the remaining portion of Figure 6.30. Notice that $\bar{x} = 10.27539$, and $s = .026681$.

Using Figure 6.31 and Excel's NORMDIST function, the area to the left of the lower spec limit of 10.1 mm is 2.46843E-11—that is, 2.46843 with the decimal point moved 11 places to the left. This number is nearly zero, so we will treat it as zero. The area to the left of the upper spec limit of 10.3 mm is .8218, and so the area to the right of this spec limit is $1 - .8218 = .1782$.

CONCLUSION

The total tail area outside the spec limits is $0 + .1782 = .1782$. For this population, we can expect 17.82% of the parts to be nonconforming. As a reminder, this percentage is approximate, since we have estimated the population parameters (μ and σ) using the corresponding sample statistics ($\bar{x}$ and s). It is interesting to note that in Example 2.1, it was determined that 17% of the 100 values in this sample were outside the spec limits. Our observations regarding this process remain the same as in earlier examples that examined the process: The z-score for the upper spec limit is $(10.3 - 10.27539)/.026681 = .922$, which indicates that this process is shifted too far to the right (both z-scores should be at least 3 in absolute value) and is producing parts that are too large in diameter. An adjustment to the process that shifts the mean toward the stated target of 10.2 mm will reduce the percentage of parts exceeding the upper spec limit (now an estimated 17.82%).

FIGURE 6.31
Areas to the left of the
standardized spec limits.

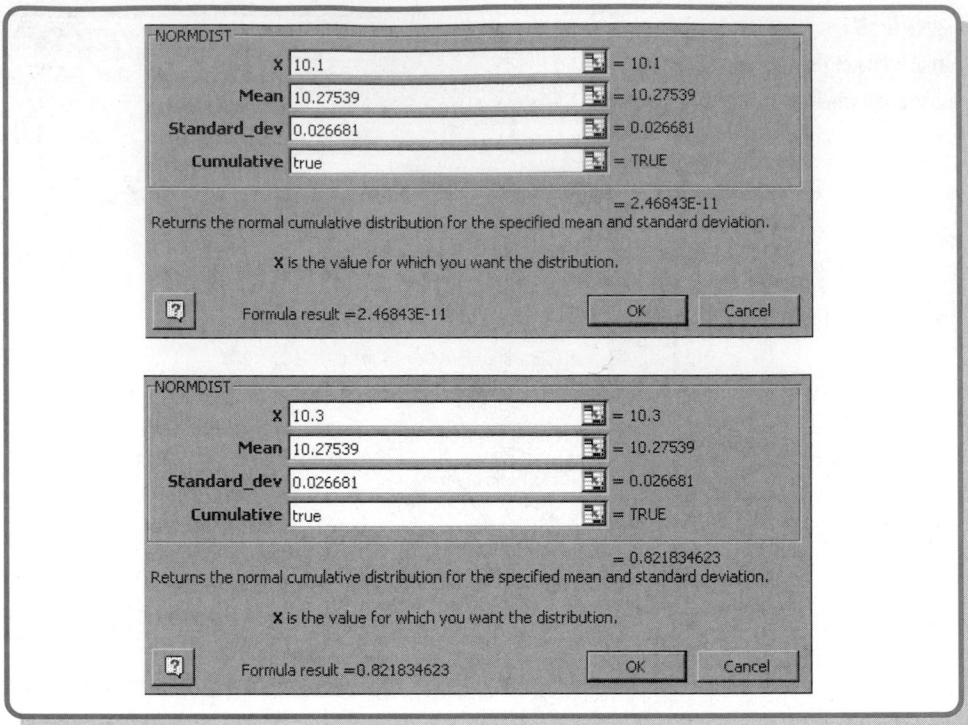

EXERCISES 6.11–6.25

UNDERSTANDING THE MECHANICS

6.11 Let X be a random variable with a normal distribution having a mean of 30 and a standard deviation of 20.

    a. What is the probability that X is less than 10?

    b. What is the probability that X is greater than 70?

    c. What is the probability that X is between 20 and 40?

6.12 Find the value of x if the random variable X is normally distributed with mean 50 and standard deviation 6.

    a. $P(X \geq x) = .0655$

    b. $P(X \leq x) = .8686$

    c. $P(40 \leq X \leq x) = .6715$

    d. $P(x \leq X \leq 50) = .3531$

APPLYING THE NEW CONCEPTS

6.13 High-Tech Inc., produces an electronic component, GX-7, that has an average life span of 4500 hours. The life span is normally distributed with a standard deviation of 500 hours. The company is considering a 3800 hours' warranty on GX-7. If this warranty policy is adopted, what proportion of GX-7 components should High-Tech expect to replace under warranty?

6.14 The estimated miles-per-gallon (on the highway) ratings of a class of trucks are normally distributed with a mean of 12.8 and a standard deviation of 3.2. What is the probability that one of these trucks selected at random would get

    a. between 13 and 15 miles per gallon?

    b. between 10 and 12 miles per gallon?

6.15 The yearly cost of dental claims for the employees of D. S. Inc. is normally distributed with a mean of $75 and a standard deviation of $30. At least what yearly cost would be expected for 40% of the employees?

6.16 How many ounces are there in a glass of wine at fine restaurants in Los Angeles? According to Steven Kolpan, a professor of wine studies at the Culinary Institute of America, the careful bartender always tries to eke approximately five glasses of wine out of each bottle. Some restaurants use a relatively small glass to create the illusion that the customer is getting his/her money's worth. Suppose that the mean number of ounces in a glass of wine is 5.5 with a standard deviation of .5. Assume that the amount of wine served in a glass is normally distributed.

(Adapted from *U.S. News & World Report*, "A Drop in the Wine Glass," June 8, 1998, p. 62.)

    a. What is the probability that a restaurant selected at random, serves a glass of wine with less than 5 ounces?

    b. At least what amount of wine would be expected to be served 60% of the time?

6.17 The inside diameter of a manufactured cylinder is believed to follow a normal distribution centered at 5.00 inches with a standard deviation of .03 inches. The diameter of the cylinder must be within 4.95 inches (the lower spec limit) and 5.07 inches (the upper spec limit). If the diameter is outside these two spec limits, then the cylinder is nonconforming? What proportion of the manufactured cylinders is nonconforming?

6.18 The thickness of a manufactured sheet of metal is believed to follow a normal distribution with a mean of .30 inches and a standard deviation of .02 inches. The lower spec limit is 2.5 standard deviations to the left of the mean. The upper spec limit is 3.0 standard deviations to the right of the mean. Nonconforming sheets of metal have thicknesses outside of these two spec limits. What proportion of the sheets of metal are nonconforming?

6.19 The *Truman Show,* starring Jim Carrey, brought into the box office an average of $13,625 per theater site during its opening week. The total revenue brought in by this movie was the third highest opening for the first 6 months of 1998. Suppose that the distribution of revenue per site was normally distributed with a standard deviation of $1000.

(Source: *USA Today,* "Truman Triumphs," June 9, 1998, p. D1.)

a. What is the probability that a randomly selected theater made between $12,000 and $15,000 during the opening week from showing the *Truman Show?*

b. What is the probability that a randomly selected theater made less than $10,500 during the opening week from showing the *Truman Show?* Would this be considered unusual?

6.20 The vice president of Offshore Oil and Gas, a consulting firm, notices that the average length of time that a consultant spends on the telephone with a client at any one time is 40 minutes with a standard deviation of 18 minutes. Assuming that the length of such conversations is normally distributed, what percent of the consultant's phone calls would take longer than 50 minutes?

6.21 A quality engineer has collected data that reveals a machine takes an average of 10 minutes to complete a task with a standard deviation of 1.5 minutes.

a. The engineer would like to know the probability that the task will take between 8 minutes and 11 minutes. Find this probability. In Excel, type in a cell "=NORMDIST (11,10,1.5,1) – NORMDIST(8,10,1.5,1)". Note that in the notation NORMDIST(11,10,1.5,1) represents the cumulative normal when the fourth component is 1.

b. The engineer would also like to know what the time is such that 40% of the task times are less than this value. Using Excel, find this time by typing "=NORMINV(.40,10,1.5)" in a cell.

6.22 A survey of New York hospital residents revealed that 80-hour weeks were still an acceptable average for a workweek. While 80 hours may seem like a large number of hours per week, residents at various hospitals throughout the country have reported as much as 136 hours per week. New York became the first state to limit the hours worked by doctors in training since studies indicate that the quality of patient care suffers after long shifts by doctors.

(Adapted from *USA Today,* "Hospitals Resist Reform, Work New Doctors Too Hard," May 28, 1998, p. 12A.)

a. Assume that the number of hours worked by a resident in New York City is normally distributed with a mean of 80 hours per week and a standard deviation of 6 hours per week. What is the probability that a resident selected at random from a New York hospital works more than 90 hours per week?

b. Between what two number of hours per week (symmetrical about the mean of 80 hours) would 80% of the residents work per week?

USING THE COMPUTER

6.23 **[DATA SET EX6-23]** *Variable description:*

Refunddamage: Amount of refund to customers who return damaged merchandise.

A store manager recorded the refund to customers on 100 returned items that were sold to the customer and found to be damaged. The manager knows that historically the average refund is $70 with a standard deviation of $20 on such merchandise.

a. The manager would like to know the probability of randomly receiving a refund that is at least as large as the amount in **Refunddamage.** For very small probabilities, the manager may suspect that customers have damaged very expensive goods and returned them. The manager treats these refunds as unusual. Find these probabilities. In Excel, put the values of **Refunddamage** in column A, starting in A1. Then type into cell B1 "=1-NORMDIST(A1,70,20,1)". Drag this cell down to B100.

b. How many of the probabilities obtained in part (a) are less than .01? Do you think that the manager should consider these refunds as unusual?

6.24 **[DATA SET EX6-24]** *Variable description:*

RentResident: Amount of monthly profit from residential rent homes
RentCommercial: Amount of monthly profit from rent paid on commercial buildings

A realtor owns numerous residential and commerical buildings and collects rent on these properties. The realtor selects 100 months over the past several years and lists the monthly profit in thousands of dollars for these properties. These values are listed in the variables **RentResident** and **RentCommercial,** in thousands of dollars.

a. Plot a histogram of the data in **RentResident** and also of the data in **RentCommercial.** Would you say that the data are approximately normally distributed? Find the mean and the variance for each of the variables.

b. What type of distribution do you believe the sum of **RentResident** and **RentCommercial** would have? What do you think the resulting mean and variance would be?

c. Plot a histogram of the sum of **RentResident** and **RentCommercial.** Does the distribution appear to be approximately normally distributed? Find the mean and variance. Compare these results to your answers in part (b). Is the variance of the sum equal to the sum of the variances?

6.25 The thickness of a certain manufactured sheet of metal must be between .95 and 1.05 inches. If the thickness of the manufactured sheets of metal is normally distributed with a mean of 1 and a standard deviation of .03, the probability of obtaining a nonconforming sheet of metal is

$$P(X < .95) + P(X > 1.05) = 2P(X < .95)$$

Now, $P(X < .95)$ can be found using Excel or MINITAB to be .0478. Hence, the probability of obtaining a nonconforming sheet of metal is .0956. Use Excel or MINITAB with different values for the standard deviation to find which values of the standard deviation yield a probability of obtaining a nonconforming sheet of metal of approximately .08, .05, and .01.

6.8 NORMAL APPROXIMATION TO THE BINOMIAL (OPTIONAL)

The binomial random variable was introduced in Chapter 5. It is a discrete random variable used to count the number of successes in a binomial situation.

CHARACTERISTICS OF A BINOMIAL SITUATION

1. You have n independent identical trials.
2. Each trial is a success (with probability p) or a failure (with probability $1 - p$).
3. The binomial random variable X is the number of successes out of n trials.
4. The mean of X is $\mu = np$, and the standard deviation of X is $\sigma = \sqrt{np(1-p)}$.

Examples included:

X = the number of heads (successes) out of three flips (trials) of a coin

X = the number of people who read the evening newspaper (successes) out of a sample of 50 people (trials)

X = The number of defectives (successes) out of a sample of 10 electrical components (trials)

Table A.1 contains values of n (the number of trials) up to only $n = 20$. One option here is to use the Poisson approximation to determine binomial probabilities for values of $n > 20$. In other words, we pretend that X is a Poisson random variable *having the same mean* as the actual binomial random variable. This is a good approximation, provided n is large (>20), p is small, and $np \le 7$.

Despite the fact that Table A.1 only contains values of $n \le 20$, many statistical and spreadsheet packages (including MINITAB and Excel) provide binomial probabilities for extremely large sample sizes (n). Using Excel to determine binomial probabilities was illustrated in Figure 5.6, and the MINITAB procedure was discussed in the end-of-chapter appendix for Chapter 5. A less-preferred alternative here is to use the **normal approximation** to the binomial random variable. Here we pretend that X is a normal random variable *having the same mean and standard deviation* as the actual binomial random variable. This approximation works well when p is near .5 and in general offers a good estimate when both $np > 5$ and $n(1 - p) > 5$.

APPROXIMATIONS TO THE BINOMIAL

- Poisson approximation: Use when $n > 20$ and $np \le 7$.
- Normal approximation: Use when $np > 5$ and $n(1 - p) > 5$.

Consider 12 flips of a coin. We want to determine (1) the probability of observing no more than 4 heads, and (2) the probability of observing more than 5 heads. First, notice that a normal approximation is not necessary here. This is a binomial situation with $n = 12$ and $p = .5$, and Table A.1 does contain probabilities for this set of values. We chose this illustration to compare the actual binomial probability to the approximated probability using the normal distribution. Look at Figure 6.32, which demonstrates how we estimate binomial probabilities using a normal curve.

To solve question 1, let X = the number of heads in 12 flips, so X is a binomial random variable. We want to determine $P(X \le 4)$. We can obtain an exact solution using Table A.1:

$$P(X \le 4) = P(0) + P(1) + P(2) + P(3) + P(4)$$

$$= 0 + .003 + .016 + .054 + .121$$

$$= .194$$

FIGURE 6.32

Approximating binomial probabilities using a normal curve.

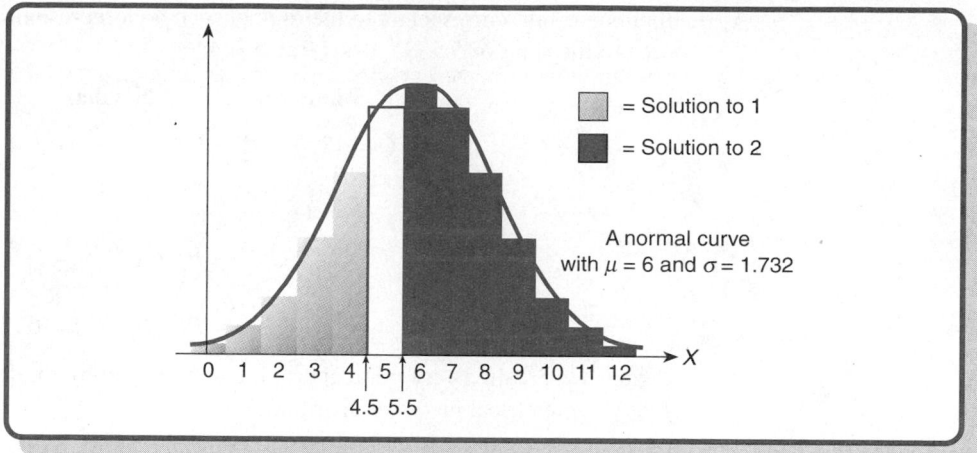

In Figure 6.32, this value is the sum of the areas of the boxes corresponding to $X = 0, 1, 2, 3,$ and 4. Note that the width of each box is 1, and so the height of the box (the probability) is the same as the area of the box. As a result, the total area of all the boxes is 1.

We can also obtain an approximate solution. For this binomial random variable,

$$\mu = np = (12)(.5) = 6$$

and

$$\sigma = \sqrt{np(1-p)}$$

$$= \sqrt{3} = 1.732$$

To obtain an approximation, treat X as a normal random variable with $\mu = 6$ and $\sigma = 1.732$, illustrated in Figure 6.32. Note that both the total area of the boxes and the total area under the normal curve are 1. The area under the normal curve that approximates $P(X \le 4)$ is the area to the left of 4.5. So we obtain a better approximation here if we find the area under the normal curve to the left of 4.5, not 4.0. This .5 adjustment is referred to as an **adjustment for continuity.** This adjustment is necessary whenever you approximate a *discrete* random variable (such as a binomial random variable) using a *continuous* distribution (such as the normal distribution). Remember that the discrete distribution has gaps, whereas the continuous does not, so we must assign a portion of the space (probability) between 4 and 5 when we use a continuous distribution to approximate a discrete one. Using Table A.4:

Binomial   **Normal**

$(n = 12, p = .5)$ $(\mu = 6, \sigma = 1.732)$

$P(X \le 4) \cong P(X \le 4.5)$

$$= P\left[Z \le \frac{4.5 - 6}{1.732}\right]$$

$$= P(Z \le -.87) = .1922$$

Notice that the approximate solution of .1922 is very close to the actual probability of .194. This is helped in part by the fact that $p = .5$ for this situation, which means that the binomial distribution is perfectly symmetric. *As the value of* p *moves away from .5, larger values of* n *are necessary to achieve an approximation this good.*

Now consider question 2, the probability of observing more than 5 heads in 12 flips, or $P(X > 5) = P(X \ge 6)$. Using Table A.1, we can obtain an *exact* solution:

$$P(X \ge 6) = P(6) + P(7) + \cdots + P(11) + P(12)$$

$$= .226 + .193 + \cdots + .003 + 0 = .613$$

We can also obtain an approximate solution. Using Figure 6.32, the area under the normal curve that corresponds to the dark shaded area representing the exact solution is the area to the right of 5.5. So, using Table A.4:

Binomial   **Normal**

$(n = 12, p = .5)$ $(\mu = 6, \sigma = 1.732)$

$P(X \geq 6) \cong P(X \geq 5.5)$

$$= P\left(Z \geq \frac{5.5 - 6}{1.732}\right)$$

$$= P(Z \geq -.29) = .6141$$

Again, we obtain a very good approximation, helped by the fact that we are using a perfectly symmetrical binomial distribution.

How to Adjust for Continuity

If X is a binomial random variable with n trials and probability of success $= p$, then:

1. $P(X \leq b) \cong P\left(Z \leq \dfrac{b + .5 - \mu}{\sigma}\right)$

2. $P(X \geq a) \cong P\left(Z \geq \dfrac{a - .5 - \mu}{\sigma}\right)$

3. $P(a \leq X \leq b) \cong P\left(\dfrac{a - .5 - \mu}{\sigma} \leq Z \leq \dfrac{b + .5 - \mu}{\sigma}\right)$

where $\mu = np$, $\sigma = \sqrt{np(1 - p)}$, and Z is a standard normal random variable.

4. Be sure to convert a < probability to a $\leq$, and to convert a > probability to a $\geq$ before switching to the normal approximation.

EXAMPLE 6.8

In Example 5.11, we discussed a binomial situation in which Eagle Air was intentionally overbooking their flights. On a particular flight from Dallas to El Paso, they use a much larger aircraft that holds 200 people. As in our previous example, 20% of the people who make reservations do not show up. Assume that all reservations are for one individual and are made independent of each other. If Eagle Air accepts 235 reservations, what is the probability that at least one passenger will end up without a seat on this flight?

SOLUTION

The binomial random variable X here is the number of people (out of 235) who show up for the flight. For this situation, $n = 235$, and $p = .8$ represents the probability that any one passenger *will* show up. The mean of this random variable is

$$\mu = (235)(.8) = 188$$

and the standard deviation is

$$\sigma = \sqrt{(235)(.8)(.2)} = 6.13$$

At least one person holding a reservation will be deprived of a seat if $X \geq 201$ because the plane holds only 200 people. Once again, we use the normal approximation (Table A.4) to obtain the following probability:

$$\begin{array}{cc} \textbf{Binomial} & \textbf{Normal} \\ (n = 235, \ p = .8) & (\mu = 188, \ \sigma = 6.13) \end{array}$$

$$P(X \geq 201) \cong P(X \geq 200.5)$$

$$= P\left[Z \geq \frac{200.5 - 188}{6.13} \right]$$

$$= P(Z \geq 2.04)$$

$$= .5 - .4793$$

$$= .0207$$

So on approximately 2 flights out of 100, at least one person will be unable to secure a seat.*

---

* Using Excel (see Figure 5.6, bottom panel) or MINITAB, the exact value of $P(X \leq 200)$ is .9821, and so the exact answer here is $P(X \geq 201) = 1 - P(X \leq 200) = .0179$. This value is quite close to the normal approximation (.0207), and so we again conclude that approximately 2% of the flights will end up with at least one passenger without a seat.

EXERCISES 6.26–6.33

UNDERSTANDING THE MECHANICS

6.26 Let the random variable X have a binomial distribution. For which of the following cases would it be reasonable to approximate the binomial distribution with the normal distribution?

    a. $n = 50, \ p = .12$
    b. $n = 100, \ p = .1$
    c. $n = 11, \ p = .6$
    d. $n = 100, \ p = .99$

6.27 Suppose that X is a binomial random variable with $n = 50$ and $p = .2$.

    a. Are these values of n and p sufficient to have a reasonably good approximation to the binomial distribution using a normal distribution?

    b. Use the normal approximation to find the probability that X is larger than 8.

    c. Use the normal approximation to find the probability that X is at least 7 but less than 11.

6.28 Let X be a binomial random variable with $n = 20$ and $p = .5$. Find the following probabilities by using the normal approximation and also by using the binomial distribution.

    a. $P(X \leq 12)$
    b. $P(X > 5)$
    c. $P(6 \leq X < 15)$

APPLYING THE NEW CONCEPTS

6.29 A travel agency promotes vacation packages by phoning households at random in the evening hours. Historically, only 65% of heads of households are at home when the agency phones. If 30 households are phoned on a given evening, what is the probability that the agency will find between 15 and 25 households, inclusive, with the head of the household at home?

6.30 Many of Citicorp's customers need to make financial transactions to European and South American countries. Because Citicorp has branches overseas in these areas, its cus-tomers enjoy Citicorp's efficiency in transferring money for international operations conducted by small and large firms. In Florida, an estimated 25% of consumer banking is with non-U.S. citizens.

(Adapted from *The American Banker,* "Citi Exec Helps Pilot Consumer Bank Overhaul," June 20, 1997, p. 1.)

    a. Suppose that 100 customers are selected at random. What is the probability that between 20 and 30, inclusively, are non-U.S. citizens?

    b. If 100 customers were selected at random and less than 14 were non-U.S. citizens, would this be considered unusual? Why?

6.31 In 1998, South Korea's benchmark three-year corporate bond yield went to 17.8%. Many bankers believed that this rate will result in major corporate bankruptcies. One measure of the severity of the banking problem is to consider the number of nonperforming loans—those that haven't been serviced in more than three months. This estimate was 15.6%.

(Adapted from *The Wall Street Journal,* "South Korea Risks Repeating Last Year's Economic Decline," May 15, 1998, p. A12.)

    a. Suppose that 40 loans were randomly selected in South Korea in 1998. What is the probability that no more than seven loans are nonperforming loans? What do you need to assume about the 40 loans?

    b. In part (a), would no more than two nonperforming loans be considered unusual? Why?

USING THE COMPUTER

6.32 Generate 20 random observations from a binomial distribution with $n = 12$ and $p = .6$. Find the mean in Excel, by clicking on **Tools ➤ Data Analysis ➤ Random Number Generation.** Put "1" into the box **Number of Random Variables.** Type "20" in the **Number of Random Numbers** box. Select **Binomial** for the **Distribution** box. Fill in the values for the parameters and type in a cell for the **Output Range** box. Find the sample mean and standard deviation for this data set. Repeat this process with samples of size 50 and 100 and compare the estimates of the mean and standard deviation for sample sizes of 20, 50, and 100.

6.33 Show the accuracy of the normal approximation to probabilities of the individual outcomes in a binomial experiment with $n = 15$ and $p = .3$. In Excel, put the values of "0" through "15" in the first 16 cells of column A. In B1, put "=A1 − .5". In C1, put "=A1 + .5". In D1 put "=NORMSDIST((C1 − 4.5)/1.7748) − NORMSDIST((B1 − 4.5)/1.7748)". In E1 put "=BINOMDIST(A1, 15, .3, 0)". Drag the cells B1 through E1 through the 16th row. Note that column D has the normal approximation, while column E has the exact binomial probabilities. How accurate is the normal approximation?

6.9 OTHER CONTINUOUS DISTRIBUTIONS (OPTIONAL)

The normal distribution is one example of a continuous distribution. A normal random variable X is a continuous random variable; that is, over some specific range, *any* value of X is possible. We used X to represent the lifetime of an Everglo bulb to illustrate a continuous random variable because any value between 280 hours and 520 hours (see Figure 6.2) is possible. In fact, any value less than 280 or more than 520 is also possible, although not likely to occur.

In the Everglo example, a normal distribution seemed appropriate because the histogram of 200 sample bulbs in Figure 6.2 revealed a concentration of burnout times in the "middle" and not nearly as many burnout times around 300 or 500. These features give the normal curve its "mound" in the center and "tails" on each end.

There are many continuous distributions that do not resemble a normal curve in appearance. For example, consider the following two situations, in which a random variable, X, ranges from 1 to 10.

SITUATION 1.   The chance that X is between 1.0 and 1.5

$$= \text{the chance that } X \text{ is between 1.5 and 2.0}$$

$$= \text{the chance that } X \text{ is between 2.0 and 2.5}$$

$$\vdots$$

$$= \text{the chance that } X \text{ is between 9.0 and 9.5}$$

$$= \text{the chance that } X \text{ is between 9.5 and 10.0}$$

SITUATION 2.   The larger X is, the less likely it is to occur. Thus, the chance that X is between 1.0 and 1.5

$$> \text{the chance that } X \text{ is between 1.5 and 2.0}$$

$$> \text{the chance that } X \text{ is between 2.0 and 2.5}$$

$$\vdots$$

$$> \text{the chance that } X \text{ is between 9.0 and 9.5}$$

$$> \text{the chance that } X \text{ is between 9.5 and 10.0}$$

These two cases can be represented by two other frequently occurring continuous distributions. Situation 1 can be represented by a uniform random variable; situation 2 could be described using an exponential random variable.

Although there are other random variables that apply to these two situations, the uniform and exponential distributions fit many of the applications encountered in business.

THE UNIFORM DISTRIBUTION

Consider spinning the minute hand on a clock face. Define a random variable X to be the stopping point of the minute hand. It seems reasonable to assume, for example, that the probability that X is between 2 and 4 is *twice* the probability of observing a value of X between 8 and 9. In other words, the probability that X is in any particular interval is *proportional* to the width of that interval.

FIGURE 6.33

Relative frequency histogram of a sample of 150 cups of soda.

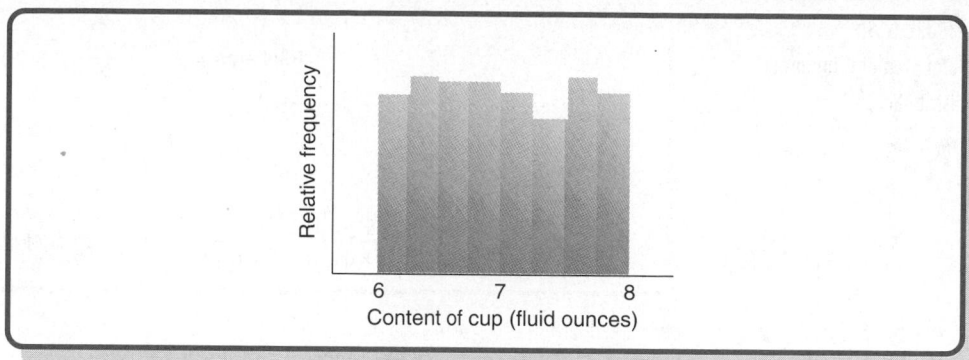

FIGURE 6.34

Uniform distribution for X = soda content (compare with Figure 6.33).

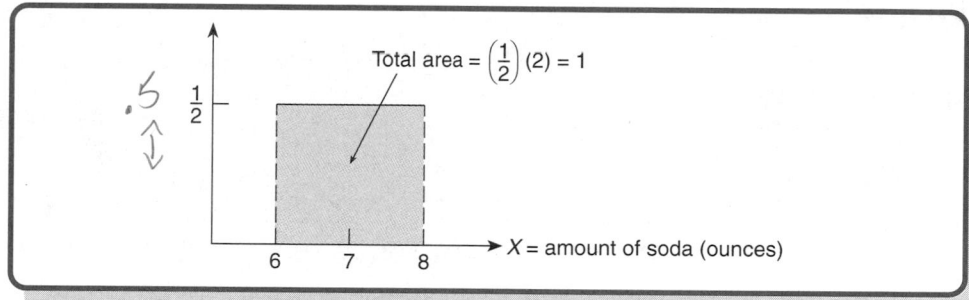

A random variable of this nature is a **uniform random variable.** The values of such a variable are evenly distributed over some interval because the random variable occurs *randomly* over this interval. Unlike the normal random variable, values of the uniform random variable do not tend to be concentrated about the mean.

Assume that the manager of Dixie Beverage Service is concerned about the amount of soda that is released by the dispensing machine that the company is now using. He is considering the purchase of a new machine that electronically controls the cutoff time and is supposed to be very accurate. The present machine cuts off mechanically, and he suspects that the device shuts off the fluid flow *randomly* anywhere between 6 and 8 ounces. To test the present system, a sample of 150 cups is taken from the machine, and the amount of soda released into each cup is recorded. The relative frequency histogram made from these 150 observations is shown in Figure 6.33.

Would you be tempted to describe the population of *all* cup contents using a normal curve? We hope not, because there is no evidence of a declining number of observations in the tails. A word of warning here: though we often have a tendency to think of all continuous random variables as being normally distributed, as this application demonstrates this is certainly not the case. Instead, this distribution is a flat or uniform distribution. The random variable X = cup contents is a uniform random variable. The corresponding smooth curve describing the population is shown in Figure 6.34. Notice that the total area here is given by a rectangle, and, as is true of all continuous random variables, this total area must be 1. The area of a rectangle is given by (width) · (height). By making the height of this curve (a straight line, actually) equal to .5, the total area is

$$(8 - 6)(.5) = 1.0$$

In general, the curve defining the probability distribution for a uniform random variable is as shown in Figure 6.35. The total area is

$$(b - a)\left[\frac{1}{b - a}\right] = 1.0$$

FIGURE 6.35
Total area of a uniform distribution.

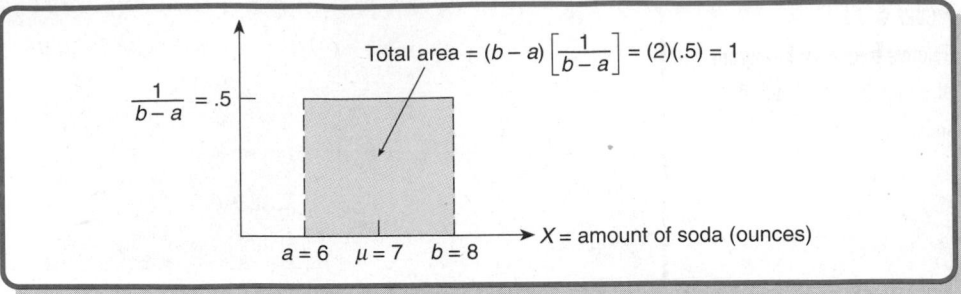

FIGURE 6.36
The probability that X exceeds 7.5. The shaded area represents the percentage of cups containing more than 7.5 ounces.

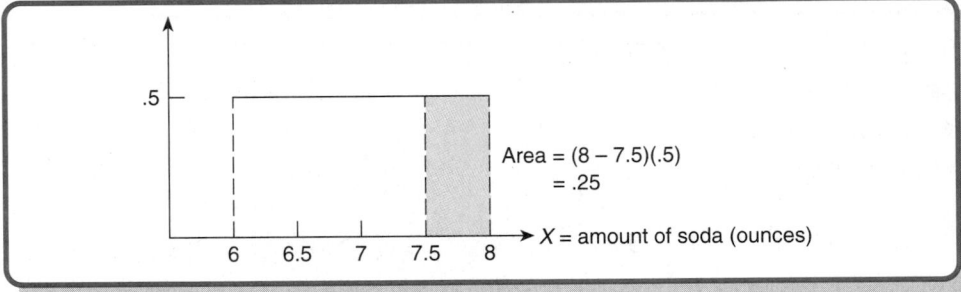

MEAN AND STANDARD DEVIATION

Refer to Figure 6.35. The mean (μ) of X is the value midway between a and b, namely,

$$\mu = \frac{a+b}{2}$$

The standard deviation (σ) of X is, as before, a measure of how much variation there would be in X if you were to observe it indefinitely. Unlike the standard deviation of a normal distribution, σ for a uniform distribution is hard to represent graphically as a particular distance on the probability curve. Its value, however, is given by

$$\sigma = \frac{b-a}{\sqrt{12}}$$

DETERMINING PROBABILITIES

As it is for all continuous random variables, a probability based on a uniform random variable is determined by finding an area under a curve. Suppose, for example, the manager of Dixie Beverage Service would like to know what percentage of the cups will contain more than 7.5 ounces, using the present machines. In Figure 6.36, the shaded area is a rectangle, so its area is easy to find:

$$\text{area} = (\text{width}) \cdot (\text{height}) = (8 - 7.5) \cdot .5 = .25$$

So 25% of the cups will contain more than 7.5 ounces.

EXAMPLE 6.9

What is the probability that a cup will contain between 6.5 and 7.5 ounces? What is the average content?

FIGURE 6.37
The probability that X is
between 6.5 and 7.5.

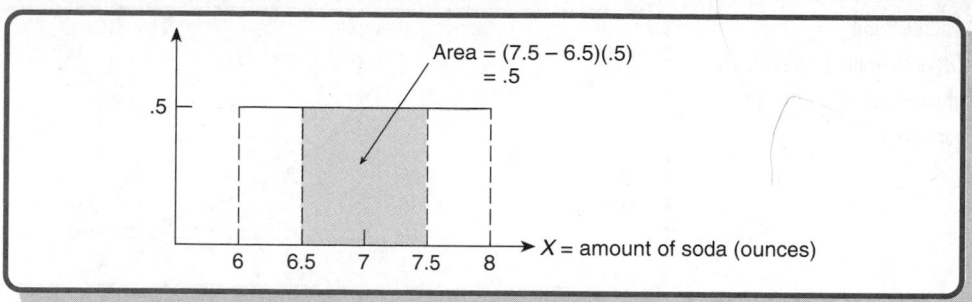

The first result is the same as the percentage of cups containing between 6.5 and 7.5 ounces. Based on Figure 6.37, we conclude that

$$P(6.5 < X < 7.5) = .5$$

The average cup content (mean of X) is

$$\mu = \frac{6+8}{2} = 7 \text{ ounces}$$

The standard deviation of X is

$$\sigma = \frac{8-6}{\sqrt{12}} = 0.58 \text{ ounce}$$

Notice that, as with the normal random variable, the probability that X is equal to any particular value is zero. So,

$$P(X = 6.5) = P(X = 7.5) = 0$$

As a result,

$$P(6.5 \leq X \leq 7.5) = P(6.5 < X < 7.5) = .5$$

Simulation is an area of statistics that relies heavily on the uniform distribution. In fact, the uniform distribution is the underlying mechanism for this often-complex procedure. So, although not as many "real-world" populations have uniform distributions as have normal ones, the uniform distribution is extremely important in the application of statistics.

THE EXPONENTIAL DISTRIBUTION

The final continuous distribution we will discuss is the **exponential distribution.** Similar to the uniform random variable, the exponential random variable is used in a variety of applications in statistics. One application is observing the time between arrivals at, for example, a drive-up bank window. Another situation that often fits the exponential distribution is observing the lifetime of certain components in a machine.

Chapter 5 discussed the Poisson random variable, which often is used to describe the *number* of arrivals over a specified time period. If the random variable Y, representing the number of arrivals over period T, follows a Poisson distribution, then X, representing the *time between* successive arrivals, will be an **exponential random variable.** The exponential random variable has many applications when describing any situation in which people or objects have to wait in line. Such a line is called a **queue.** People, machines, or telephone calls may wait in a queue.

FIGURE 6.38
Curve showing the distribution of an exponential random variable.

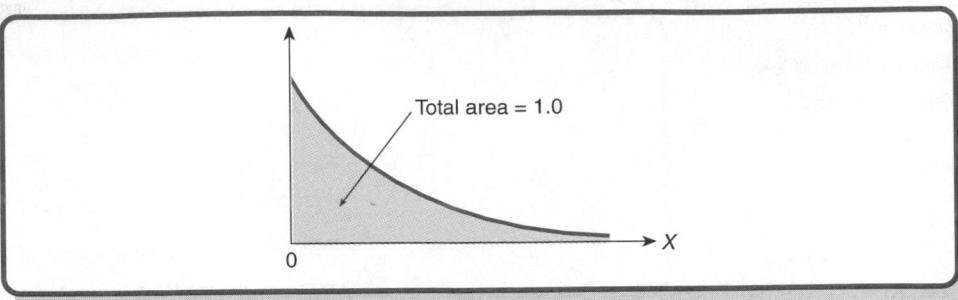

FIGURE 6.39
Curve used for determining a probability for an exponential random variable.

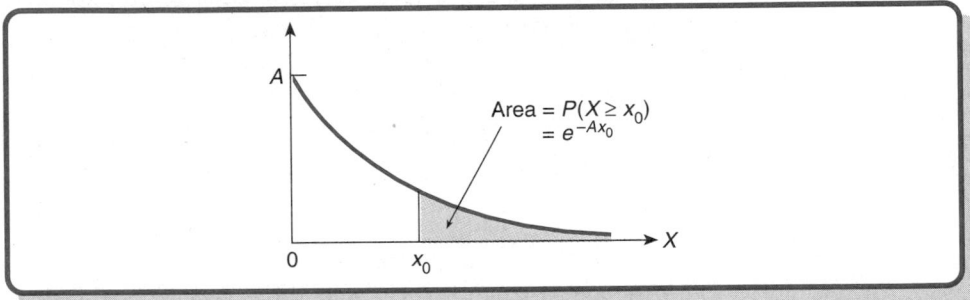

Continuous distribution

THE EXPONENTIAL RANDOM VARIABLE. The shape of the exponential distribution is represented by a curve that steadily decreases as the value of the random variable, X, increases. Thus, the larger X is, the probability of observing a value of X at least this large decreases exponentially. This type of curve is illustrated in Figure 6.38.

DETERMINING PROBABILITIES. Determining areas for exponential random variables is not as simple as for uniform ones, but it is easier than for normal random variables because exponential probabilities can be derived on a calculator. Table A.2 also can be used to determine the probability for an exponential random variable.

As Figure 6.39 illustrates, for an exponential random variable, X, the probability that X exceeds or is equal to a specific value, x_0, is

$A = \frac{1}{mean}$

$$P(X \geq x_0) = e^{-Ax_0}$$

The parameter A is related to the Poisson random variable we used when discussing arrivals. In fact, the Poisson distribution for arrivals per unit time and the exponential distribution for time *between* arrivals provide two alternative ways of describing the same thing. For example, if the number of arrivals per unit time follows a Poisson distribution with an average of $A = 6$ per hour, then an alternate way of describing this situation is to say that the time between arrivals is exponentially distributed with mean time between arrivals equal to $1/A = 1/6$ hour (10 minutes).

In general, $1/A$ is the average (mean) value of the exponential random variable, X. It is also equal to the standard deviation of X. So,

$$\mu = 1/A$$

$$\sigma = 1/A$$

 In applications using this distribution, the value of A either will be given or can be estimated in some way.

FIGURE 6.40

Curve showing the probability that X exceeds .5 [$P(X > .5)$].

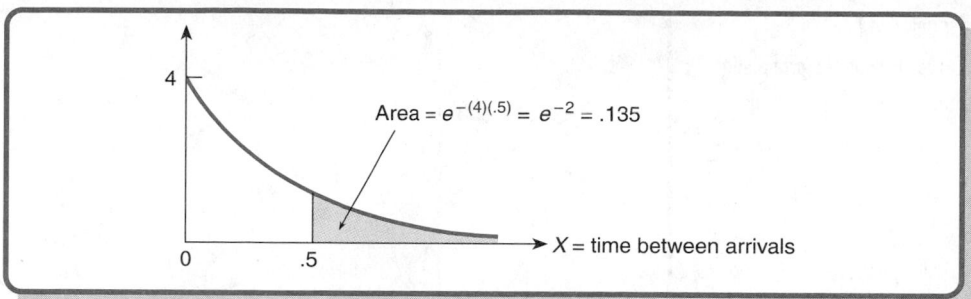

Area $= e^{-(4)(.5)} = e^{-2} = .135$

X = time between arrivals

EXAMPLE 6.10

The owner of the Downtown Haircut Emporium believes the best way to run his barber-shop is to rely on walk-in customers and not to schedule appointments. From past experience, the arrival of customers follows a Poisson distribution with an average arrival rate of $A = 4$ customers per hour.

1. If the owner just witnessed the arrival of a customer, what is the probability that there will be a new arrival within 30 minutes?
2. If X represents the time between successive arrivals, what are the mean and standard deviation of X?

SOLUTION 1

To determine this probability, we must first convert 30 minutes to .5 hour, since the arrival rate is 4 *per hour.* The desired probability then is $P(X \le .5)$. Referring to Figure 6.40, the probability that X *exceeds* .5 is

$$P(X > .5) = P(X \ge .5)$$

$$= e^{-(4)(.5)}$$

$$= e^{-2}$$

$$= .135$$

Consequently, $P(X \le .5) = 1 - .135 = .865$, and so 86.5% of the time, the time between successive arrivals will not exceed 30 minutes.

SOLUTION 2

Both the mean and standard deviation of X (the time between successive arrivals) are $1/A = 1/4$ hour (15 minutes).

EXAMPLE 6.11

The exponential distribution is widely used in the area of **reliability engineering** to describe the time to failure of a component or system. The parameter μ is called the *mean time to failure* and $A = 1/\mu$ is the *failure rate of the system.* Suppose that an automobile battery has a useful life described by the exponential distribution with a mean of 1000 days.

1. What is the probability that a battery will fail before its expected lifetime of 1000 days?
2. If the battery has a 12-month (365-day) warranty, what fraction of the batteries fail during the warranty period?

SOLUTION 1

The battery lifetime (X) follows an exponential distribution with $\mu = 1000$ and $A = 1/1000 = .001$. Referring to Figure 6.41, we wish to find the probability that X is less than 1000:

$$P(X < 1000) = 1 - e^{-(.001)(1000)} = 1 - e^{-1} = .632$$

FIGURE 6.41

Curve showing the probability that X is less than 1000 days.

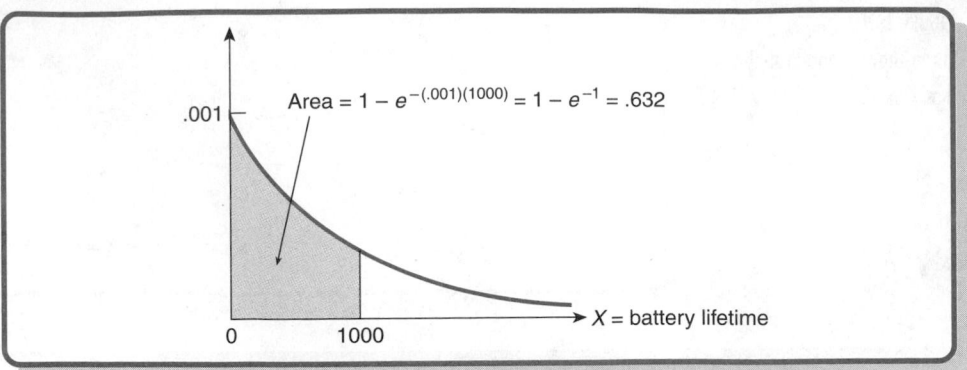

FIGURE 6.42

Curve showing the probability that X is less than 365 days.

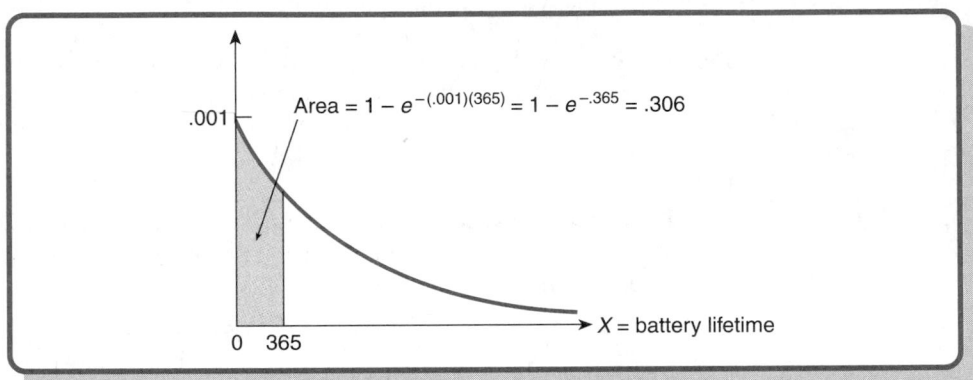

Consequently, there is a 63% chance that the battery will fail prior to its mean lifetime of 1000 days. This value is larger than 50% since this distribution is not symmetric and is positively skewed.

SOLUTION 2

According to Figure 6.42, the probability that the battery fails before the warranty expires is

$$P(X \le 365) = 1 - e^{-(.001)(365)} = 1 - e^{-.365} = .306$$

The manufacturer will be forced to replace 30.6% of the batteries during the one-year warranty period. This large percentage is encountered despite the fact that the average lifetime of the battery is nearly three years because of the positive skewness and the heavy concentration of probability on the "low end" of the distribution.

EXERCISES 6.34–6.45

UNDERSTANDING THE MECHANICS

6.34 Find the probability that the random variable X is between 2 and 4 for each of the following distributions.
   a. X is uniform from 0 to 4.
   b. X is uniform from 1 to 6.
   c. X is uniform from 2 to 4.

6.35 Let X be a random variable with a uniform distribution between 55 and 70.

   a. What is the probability that X is between $\mu - \sigma$ and $\mu + \sigma$?
   b. Find the value of x such that the $P(X \le x) = .80$.

6.36 Suppose that the distribution of a random variable X is approximately exponential with a mean of 10.
   a. What is $P(X \ge 8)$?
   b. What is $P(X \le 11)$?
   c. What is $P(6 \le X \le 10)$?
   d. What is the standard deviation of X?

APPLYING THE NEW CONCEPTS

6.37 The rate at which a swimming pool is filled is uniformly distributed between 20 and 26.3 gallons per minute.

a. What is the probability that the filling rate at any one time is between 21.3 and 24.6 gallons per minute?

b. What is the mean rate at which the swimming pool is filled?

c. What is the standard deviation of the rate at which the swimming pool is filled?

6.38 Suppose that customers arrive at a bank to either deposit money or withdraw money. Assume that the interarrival time (time between arrivals) is exponentially distributed with a mean of 4 minutes.

a. What is the probability that the interarrival time is greater than 5 minutes?

b. What is the probability that the interarrival time is between 1 minute and 4 minutes?

c. What is the standard deviation of the interarrival time?

6.39 The time intervals (in operating hours) between successive failures of air conditioning equipment in certain aircraft is believed to follow an exponential distribution. Assume that the mean time between failures is 300 hours. What is the probability that air conditioning equipment in a particular aircraft will fail after 200 operating hours?

6.40 From surveys, Holiday Inn knew that guests found the bathrooms at its hotels to be dirty. If the company shifted from tubs to shower stalls, it would mean much less dingy grout and an end to dark showers and discolored shower curtains. Moreover, consultants estimate that the cleaning time required for each guest room would fall to 13 minutes on average from the current 23 minutes required for guest rooms with tubs. That translates into a savings of $150 per room per year in maintenance costs.

(Adapted from *The Wall Street Journal,* "Shower or Bath? It's A Hotel's Tough Call," May 14, 1998, p. B1.)

a. Assume that the time to clean a guest room is uniformly distributed between 15 and 31 minutes for guest rooms with bathtubs. What is the standard deviation of the time that it takes to clean a guest room which has a tub?

b. What is the probability that a guest room with a tub is cleaned in less than 25 minutes?

6.41 Yellow Rose taxi company estimates that it makes an average of $415 in profits per day. Assuming that the daily profit follows an exponential distribution, what is the probability that on a given day at least $500 in profits will be made?

6.42 The president of Bright-Light Candles estimates that the average burning time of their "medium-K" candles is 40 hours. Assuming that burning time follows an exponential distribution, calculate the probability that a given medium-K candle will burn for at least 50 hours?

6.43 AT&T has an exclusive agreement with Nokia, a Finnish telecommunications equipment company, giving AT&T exclusive distribution rights to the Nokia 6162 digital multinetwork phone for one year. These phones sell for between $199 and $229, weigh less than 6 oz each, and have standard extended-life batteries with a mean life of 200 hours of standby time. Assuming that the extended-life batteries have a life that is exponentially distributed with a mean of 200 hours, what is the probability that an extended-life battery will last longer than 200 hours?

(Adapted from *The Baltimore Sun,* "AT&T Offers Flat-Rate Wireless Service," May 8, 1998, p. 2C.)

USING THE COMPUTER

6.44 An engineer would like to know the reliability of an insulating fluid. The life of the insulating fluid is exponentially distributed. Let X be an exponential random variable with a mean life of three hours. Then the reliability of the fluid at four hours would be 1 minus the cumulative exponential distribution function at four hours. In Excel, type into a cell "=1 – EXPONDIST(4, 1/3,1)". Find the reliability of the fluid at five hours and at six hours.

6.45 [DATA SET EX6-45] *Variable description:*

BotErr : Error in manufacturing bottom half of rod
TopErr : Error in manufacturing top half of rod

A quality-control engineer is monitoring the production of a metal rod that is made in two parts. The bottom (steel) part is manufactured to a length of 1 meter. The top (aluminum) part is also manufactured to a length of 1 meter. The errors in manufacturing these rods are recorded for 400 observations in variables **BotErr** and **TopErr.**

a. Plot a histogram of **BotErr** and a histogram of **TopErr.** Which of the following distributions most closely fits this data: Normal, Exponential, or Uniform?

b. Define the variable **TotalErr** to be equal to **BotErr + TopErr.** Plot a histogram of the data for this variable. What is the approximate shape of the distribution?

SUMMARY

A random variable that can assume any value over a specific range is a **continuous random variable.** Many business applications have continuous probability distributions that can be approximated using a normal, uniform, or exponential random variable. Each of these distributions has a unique curve that can be used to determine probabilities by finding the corresponding area under this curve. The **normal** distribution is characterized by a bell-shaped curve with values concentrated about the mean. The **uniform** distribution (curve) is flat; values of this random variable are evenly distributed over a specified range. The **exponential** distribution has a shape that steadily decreases as the value of the random variable increases. Table A.2 (or a good calculator) can be used to derive probabilities for the exponential distribution.

We discussed examples illustrating the shape of each distribution. The exact curve for a particular random variable is specified using one or two *parameters* that describe the corresponding population. As in the case of a discrete random variable, the population consists of what you would obtain if the random variable was observed indefinitely. The resulting average value and standard deviation represent the **mean** and **standard deviation** of the random variable and corresponding population.

There are infinitely many normal random variables, one for each mean (μ) and positive standard deviation (σ). If $\mu = 0$ and $\sigma = 1$, this normal random variable is the **standard normal** random variable, Z. Consequently, there is only *one* normal random variable of this type. Table A.4 gives the probabilities (areas) under the standard normal curve. You can also use this table to determine a probability for any normal random variable if you first **standardize** the variable by defining $Z = (X - \mu)/\sigma$. For this situation, Z represents the number of standard deviations that X is to the right (Z is positive) or left (Z is negative) of the mean.

SUMMARY OF FORMULAS

1. Standardizing a normal random variable (X)

$$Z = \frac{X - \mu}{\sigma}$$

2. Approximating a binomial random variable (X) using a standard normal random variable (Z)

$$P(X \le b) = P\left(Z \le \frac{b + .5 - \mu}{\sigma}\right)$$

$$P(X \ge a) = P\left(Z \ge \frac{a - .5 - \mu}{\sigma}\right)$$

$$P(a \le X \le b) = P\left(\frac{a - .5 - \mu}{\sigma} \le Z \le \frac{b + .5 - \mu}{\sigma}\right)$$

where $\mu = np$ and $\sigma = \sqrt{np(1-p)}$.

3. Uniform distribution

$$\mu = \frac{a + b}{2} \quad \text{and} \quad \sigma = \frac{b - a}{\sqrt{12}}$$

$$P(X \le x_0) = \frac{x_0 - a}{b - a} \quad \text{for } a \le x_0 \le b$$

4. Exponential distribution

$$P(X \le x_0) = 1 - e^{-A x_0} \quad \text{for } x_0 \ge 0$$

where $A = 1/\mu$, $\mu = \dfrac{1}{A}$, and $\sigma = \dfrac{1}{A}$.

REVIEW EXERCISES 6.46–6.75

6.46 A plant manager knows that the number of boxes of supplies received weekly is normally distributed with a mean of 200 and a standard deviation of 20. What percentage of the time will the number of boxes received weekly be:

    a. Greater than 200?

    b. Less than 160?

    c. Between 180 and 210?

6.47 Refer to Exercise 6.46. Determine the number of boxes, say x, such that:

    a. 50% of the time the number of boxes received weekly are less than x.

    b. 20% of the time the number of boxes received are greater than x.

    c. 80% of the time the number of boxes are less than x.

6.48 Which distribution, the normal or exponential distribution, would be most suitable for approximating the distributions of the following quantities.

    a. The time between arrivals at a bank drive-up window.

    b. The heights of seniors in a high school class.

c. The time between placement and execution of a market order on the New York Stock Exchange.

6.49 A quality-control engineer of a high-tech company noted that 4% of all parts provided by the company's main supplier were of inferior quality (nonconforming items). Out of a sample of 300 parts provided by the company's main supplier, what is the probability that more than 10 parts are of inferior quality?

6.50 The Supreme Court overturned the Communications Decency Act, a law that would have limited communications on the World Wide Web. To shield children from inappropriate Internet sites, several software companies are selling software to block slices of the Internet that parents deem objectionable. Assume that the software costs are normally distributed with an average of $30 with a standard deviation of $5. What percentage of this software is selling between $25 and $40?

(Adapted from *The Dallas Morning News*, "Deregulating Cyberspace," June 27, 1997, p. 1D.)

6.51 Automotive analysts contend that a weak Japanese yen enables Japanese automakers to keep a lid on the price of vehicles sold in the U.S. because it is cheaper for them to develop and build autos at home. GM, Ford, and Chrysler have stepped up plans for aggressive cost cutting when the yen reaches a very high level. Suppose that an analyst believes that for 1998, the value of the yen to the dollar will follow approximately a normal distribution with a mean of 140 yen to the dollar and a standard deviation of 5 yen to the dollar. Find the values, symmetrical about the mean of 140, between which the price of yen to the dollar should lie 60% of the time.

(Adapted from *USA Today*, "Another Strike Against GM," June 16, 1998, p. 4B.)

6.52 The National Restaurant Association (NRA), an industry trade group, thinks that business meals, which were once 100% tax deductible, should be at least 80% deductible. Furthermore the NRA wants the proposed deduction to apply to companies with annual sales of $5 million or less. For these companies the average business meal per person is $22.52. Assume that the standard deviation of the price of a business meal per person for these companies is $4.00. Also assume that the price of a business meal per person for companies with annual sales of $5 million or less is approximately normally distributed.

(Adapted from *Phoenix New Times*, "Second Helpings," June 11, 1998, Food section, p. 1.)

a. What percent of the business meals are between $20 and $30 for these companies?

b. What is the cost of a business meal for these companies such that 40% of the business meals cost at least that amount?

6.53 The examination committee of the Institute of Chartered Accountants passes only 20% of those who take the examination. If the scores follow a normal distribution with an average of 72 and a standard deviation of 18, what is the passing score?

6.54 The shelf life of cookies made by a small bakery is considered to be exponentially distributed with a mean equal to 3 days. What percentage of the boxes of cookies placed on the shelf today would still be considered marketable after 2.75 days?

6.55 The time that a certain drug has an effect on a normal human being is considered to be exponentially distributed when a standard dose is taken. If the average length of time that the drug has an effect is 30 hours, what is the probability that any given normal person will be affected by the drug for at least 32 hours? What is the standard deviation for the length of time that the drug affects a person?

6.56 Becoming an entrepreneur can be a radical career change. Last year American credit card companies wrote off at least $2 billion attributable to failed businesses, estimates Frederick, Md.–based RAM Research Group. Fully half of all new businesses fail in their first six years. Close to 5% go belly-up, owing money to creditors each year.

(Adapted from *Forbes*, "Go Ahead: Buy the Dream," June 15, 1998, p. 146.)

a. If 100 entrepreneurial enterprises were randomly selected, what is the probability that more than 45 of these enterprises failed in their first six years?

b. If 100 entrepreneurial enterprises were randomly selected, what is the probability that at least six enterprises will go belly-up, owing money to creditors? Is it advisable to approximate this probability using the normal approximation to the binomial distribution?

6.57 Clearvision Company manufactures picture tubes for color television sets and claims that the life spans of their tubes are exponentially distributed with a mean of 1800 hours. What percentage of the picture tubes will last no more than 1600 hours?

6.58 The amount of time each day that the copying machine is used at a certain business is approximately exponentially distributed with a mean of 3.5 hours. What is the probability that the copying machine will be used at least 2 hours a day?

6.59 The diameter of a special aluminum pipe made by Everything Aluminum Inc. is normally distributed with a mean of 3.00 centimeters and a standard deviation of .1 centimeter. Calculate the proportion of pipes whose diameters are more than 3.15 centimeters.

6.60 Professor Marcus Felson of the University of Southern California is an expert on crime-rate trends. He notes that, yearly fluctuations aside, the overall crime rate in the United States remains three to four times higher than it was in the early 1960s. Firearms were the weapon of choice in approximately two-thirds of all homicides in 1992, continuing a steady rise from three-fifths in 1988.

(Source: Adapted from *Dallas Morning News*, "Crime Statistics Down for '92, Despite Increase in Rape, Assault," Oct. 3, 1993, p. 6A.)

   a. If 40 homicides from 1992 were randomly selected, what is the probability that exactly 26 homicides involved the use of firearms?
   b. If 40 homicides from 1992 were randomly selected, what is the probability that between 20 and 30 homicides involved the use of firearms?

6.61 A manufacturer of heating elements for water heaters ships boxes that contain 100 elements. A quality-control inspector randomly selects a box in each shipment and accepts the shipment if there are 5 or fewer defective heating elements in the box. Assuming that the manufacturer has had a rate of 6% defective items, what is the probability that a shipment of heating elements will pass the inspection?

6.62 In a NBC News Poll, respondents were asked to name the most important issues that they would like the federal government to do something about. Approximately 49% of the respondents would like to see the government overhaul social programs, and 17% would like to see the government overhaul the health care system.

(Adapted from *The Wall Street Journal*, "Global Engagement?" May 15, 1988, p. A16.)

   a. If 50 respondents were randomly selected, what is the probability that no more than 25 respondents would like to see the government overhaul social programs?
   b. If 50 respondents were randomly selected, what is the probability that no more than nine respondents would like to see the government overhaul the health care system?
   c. Why do you think that the probabilities in parts (a) and (b) are close?

6.63 A paint sprayer coats a metal surface with a layer of paint between 0.5 and 1.5 millimeters thick. The thickness of the coat of paint is approximately uniformly distributed.
   a. What are the mean and standard deviation of the thickness of the coat of paint on the metal surface?
   b. What is the probability that paint from this sprayer on any given metal surface will be between 1.0 and 1.3 millimeters thick?

6.64 The rate at which a sack of soybeans is filled varies uniformly from 50 to 65 pounds per hour. What percentage of the time is the rate greater than 55 pounds per hour?

6.65 If X is a uniform random variable that represents the percentage of time each day that a machine does not work, what is the probability that X is greater than the mean percentage of time that the machine does not work?

6.66 If the random variable X has a uniform distribution between -10 and 10, find the value of x such that $P[X \geq x] = .25$.

6.67 In 1990, the average person was expected to live to age 75, six years longer than in 1960. The population of the United States is getting older as Baby Boomers age and people live longer.

(Source: Adapted from *Dallas Morning News*, "A '90s Generation Gap," by Kimberly Good, Oct. 31, 1993, p. 1A.)

   a. If the lifespan of Americans is exponentially distributed with a mean of 75 years, what is the probability that a person lives beyond 80 years?
   b. If it can be assumed that the lifespan of Americans is approximately normally distributed with a mean of 75 years and a standard deviation of 15 years, what is the probability that a person lives beyond 80 years? How does this probability compare to that in part (a)?

6.68 The random variable X is normally distributed with mean μ and variance σ^2. Find k if $P(\mu - k\sigma \le X \le \mu + k\sigma) = .67$.

6.69 If the random variable X is normally distributed with mean 25, find the variance if $P(X \ge 29) = .27$.

6.70 The random variable X is normally distributed such that $P(X \le 10) = .12$ and $P(X \ge 15) = .4$. Find the mean and variance of the random variable X.

6.71 After a \$2 billion investment, Sprint is offering businesses the Integrated On-Demand Network (ION). This digital service allows customers to simultaneously hold a phone conversation, send faxes, watch video, and log onto the Internet over a single line. Sprint is pricing the ION access so that 90% of the sales are priced between \$110 and \$150. If the sales of the ION access can be considered to be approximately normally distributed with a mean of \$130, what is the standard deviation of the sales prices?

(Adapted from *USA Today,* "Sprint Starts Up Single-Line Service," June 3, 1998, p. 1B.)

6.72 The mechanics at Quick Brown Fox can tune up a car in an average of 30 minutes with a standard deviation of 5 minutes. If a car arrives for a tune-up 25 minutes before closing, what is the probability that the car will be serviced by closing, assuming that the time it takes for a tune-up is normally distributed.

6.73 A study by the University of Toronto found that drivers in the Toronto metropolitan area who use a cell phone are four times more likely to get in an accident than drivers without cell phones and that their accident rate is equal to that of a driver who is legally intoxicated. The study doesn't suggest that cell phones cause accidents but that cell phone users need to be very careful when driving and using a cell phone.

(Adapted from *Chicago Tribune,* "Driven to Distraction," June 14, 1998, p. 20L.)

    a. Suppose that a Canadian driver in Toronto has a accident rate of .25 per year, assuming that the driver does not use a car cell phone. Assume that those drivers who use a car cell phone have an accident rate four times this rate. If the length of time between car accidents is exponentially distributed, what is the probability that an accident will occur within two years for a driver in Toronto who does not use a car cell phone?

    b. In part (a), what is the probability that a driver in Toronto who uses a car cell phone will be involved in an accident within the next two years?

6.74 Sometimes discrete distributions can have a shape that approximates the shape of the normal distribution. Consider the Poisson distribution. For a mean of 1, 3, and 6, the probability of a Poisson random variable being equal to the integer values 0 through 15 is illustrated in the following graph. Would you say that the shape of the distribution is looking more like the shape of a normal distribution as the mean increases? Plot the probabilities of a Poisson for a mean of 9. In Excel, put "0" through "15" in the first 16 rows of column A. In B1, type in "=Poisson(A1, 9, 0)". Drag this cell to B16. Highlight B1 through B16. Click on **Chart Wizard ➤ Line.** Select the chart subtype that says **Line with markers displayed at each data value.** Describe the shape of the distribution.

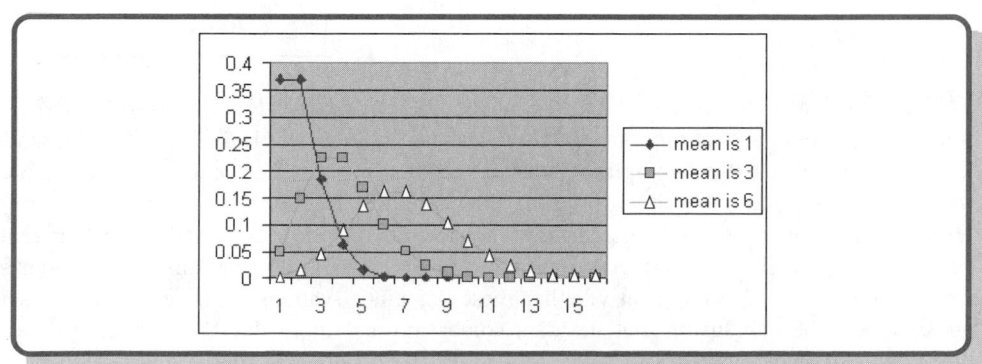

6.75 Data were collected from two computer service divisions of a large semiconductor company. In division A, the salaries were approximately normally distributed with a mean of $5000 per month and a standard deviation of $1000 per month. In division B, the salaries were approximately normally distributed with a mean of $7000 and a standard deviation of $1500 per month. In Excel, type in the two rows displayed below, with the upperleft most cell starting in cell A1.

	A	B	C	D	E	F	G
1	0	=NORMDIST(A1,$D$2,$E$2,0)	=NORMDIST(A1,$F$2,$G$2,0)	mean1	std1	mean2	std2
2	0.25	=NORMDIST(A2,$D$2,$E$2,0)	=NORMDIST(A2,$F$2,$G$2,0)	5	1	7	1.5

Now highlight the first two rows of columns A, B, and C. Drag these rows down through the 41st row. Highlight columns A and B from row 1 to row 41. Click on **Chart Wizard ➤ Scatter Plot with Data Values Connected by Smooth Lines ➤ Next ➤ Series.** Add series two by first clicking on the **Add** button and then entering the range of values in column A into **X Values** and the range of values in column C into **Y Values.** The resulting graph presented below will be displayed.

a. The units in the plot are in thousands of dollars. What range of salaries appears to be at least somewhat likely to occur in both groups?

b. If an employee is selected at random from division A, what is the probability that the employee's salary falls within the range in part (a)?

c. Do a "what if" analysis by changing the mean values in cells D2 and F2. What mean salaries for divisions A and B would allow almost no overlap in salaries?

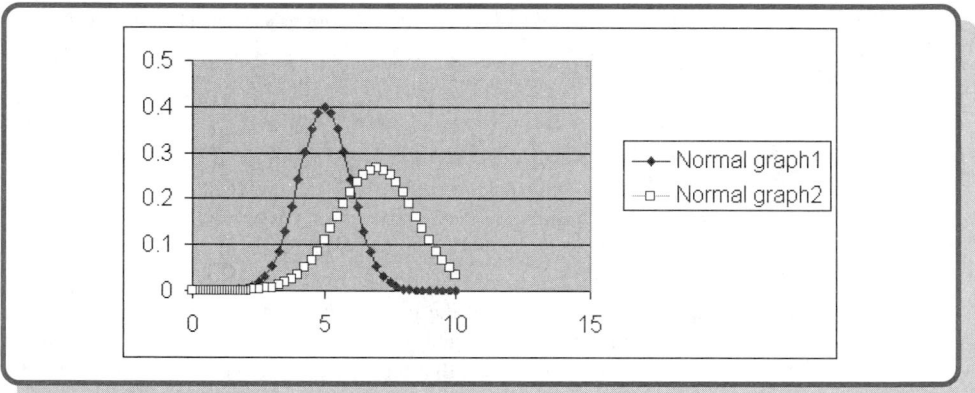

COMPUTER EXERCISES USING THE DATABASES

EXERCISE 1—APPENDIX E

Select 100 observations at random from the database and use a convenient statistical computer package to estimate the mean and standard deviation of the variable HPAYRENT (house payments or apartment/house rents). Find the percentage of the observations between $\bar{x} \pm s$, $\bar{x} \pm 2s$, and $\bar{x} \pm 3s$. Comment on whether these percentages support the conclusion that the data come from a normally distributed population.

EXERCISE 2—APPENDIX E

Select 150 observations at random from the database and, with reference to the variable OWNORENT, calculate the proportion of those observations that indicate the house is owned rather than rented. If a random sample of 20 observations were chosen from this set of 150 observations with replacement, what is the probability that more than half of the homes in the sample of 20 are owned by their occupants? Is the normal approximation appropriate for this situation?

EXERCISE 3—APPENDIX F

Select 100 observations at random from the database on the variable EMPLOYEES (number of employees). Use a convenient statistical computer package to construct a histogram. What type of distribution does the histogram approximate? normal? uniform? exponential? none of these?

EXERCISE 4—APPENDIX F

Repeat Exercise 3 using the variable SALES.

INSIGHTS FROM STATISTICS IN ACTION: CHANGES IN THE SOCIAL SECURITY SYSTEM AND ITS EFFECT ON THE DISTRIBUTION OF RETIREMENT FUNDS FOR WORKING AMERICANS

In the Statistics in Action discussion at the beginning of this chapter, we examined the question of whether the Social Security Administration should invest a portion of their funds in private accounts. Suppose that a particular poll asked three different age groups what proportion of their contributed Social Security would they want put in a private account, assuming that the Social Security system will not go bankrupt. The data are listed below. Ana-

lysts use data such as this to construct histograms and then identify a statistical distribution that may describe the observed distribution of the data. The normal distribution has been shown to approximately fit many such situations. These distributions can assist actuaries in figuring what it will take to make Social Security a viable option for workers.

Under 30 Years of Age	At Least 30 Years Old but Less Than 50 Years Old	50 Years of Age or Over
.95	.95	.03
.90	.57	.91
.62	.78	.12
.58	.54	.83
.92	.42	.93
.77	.58	.71
.85	.67	.63
.75	.20	.32
.63	.37	.51
.92	.64	.42
.69	.65	.05
.98	.01	.94
.85	.42	.15
.81	.88	.85
.52	.67	.26
.67	.34	.73
.57	.26	.34
.64	.34	.66
.73	.39	.46

Under 30 Years of Age	At Least 30 Years Old but Less Than 50 Years Old	50 Years of Age or Over
.77	.48	.53
.99	.40	.08
.81	.46	.99
.78	.51	.18
.92	.53	.88
.89	.83	.18
.71	.50	.76
.68	.19	.29
.61	.73	.68
.59	.29	.38
.50	.15	.59
.90	.66	.46
.70	.93	.10
.51	.77	.30
.80	.17	.60
.60	.54	.80

1. Plot a histogram of the data for each of the age groups. In practice, the distribution of data never conforms exactly to a particular distribution. However, approximate distributions are often used to conveniently describe the distribution and to find probabilities. What continuous distribution approximates the distribution of each of these data sets?

2. Find the sample mean and sample standard deviation for each of the distributions. If a distribution is approximately uniform, use the formulas for the mean and standard deviation to compute these values and compare to the sample mean and sample standard deviation.

3. For the age group of at least 30 but less than 50 years of age, calculate the z score for a value of .05. Interpret this value.

4. Using the approximate distributions from Question 1, what is the probability that a working American chooses to put at least 60% of their Social Security contribution into a private account assuming that the individual is less than 30 years old?

5. Answer Question 4 assuming that a working American is at least 30 but less than 50 years old. Also answer Question 4 assuming that the age is 50 or more. Compare the results.

6. Between what two values is 68% of the data for each distribution assuming that the mean is in the middle? How do these compare across age groups?

Source: *USA Today,* "System Is Face-to-Face With Change," July 27, 1998, p. 7A.

CHAPTER 6 APPENDIX: DATA ANALYSIS WITH MINITAB

NORMAL PROBABILITIES

Probabilities, cumulative probabilities, and inverse cumulative probabilities can be calculated for a number of continuous distributions in MINITAB. The examples below will demonstrate how to find the cumulative probabilities for a specified value of a normal random variable. The probability density function option for the continuous random variables gives the value of the bell-shaped curve corresponding to a value of the random variable and is not to be used as a probability. In fact the probability of a point for any continuous distribution is defined to be zero, since it only makes sense to talk about the probability of a continuous set of values for a continuous random variable.

To obtain a cumulative probability for the normal distribution, click **Calc ➤ Probability Distributions ➤ Normal,** and type in the value for the mean and standard deviation. In this example, the standard normal is used so a mean of 0 and a standard deviation of 1 are typed into the user form. Select **Cumulative probability** and then specify a value of the random variable in the **Input constant** option. In this example, the probability that a standard normal random variable is less than 2 will be found. The input column option can be used to find the cumulative probability for many values of the normal random variable. The user form should look like the one below. The output is displayed in the session window and follows the user form.

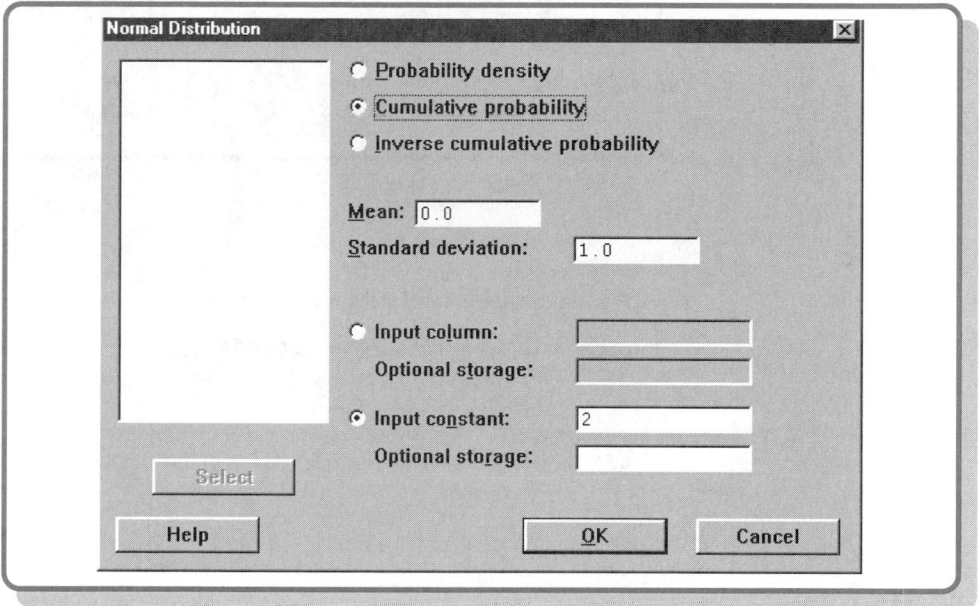

CUMULATIVE DISTRIBUTION FUNCTION

```
Normal with mean = 0 and standard deviation = 1.00000
         x       P( X <= x)
    2.0000        0.9772
```

EXPONENTIAL PROBABILITIES

To obtain a cumulative probability for the exponential distribution, click **Calc ➤ Probability Distributions ➤ Exponential,** and type in the value of the mean. In this example, a mean of 1 is used. Select **Cumulative probability** and then specify a value of the random variable in the **Input constant** option. In this example, the probability that an exponentially distributed random variable is less than 2 will be found. The input column option can be used to find the cumulative probability for many values of an exponentially distributed random variable. The user form should look like the one below. The output is displayed in the session window and follows the user form.

CUMULATIVE DISTRIBUTION FUNCTION

Exponential with mean = 1.00000

x	P(X <= x)
2.0000	0.8647

STATISTICAL INFERENCE AND SAMPLING

STATISTICS IN ACTION: WHAT IS THE AVERAGE GATE-TO-TAKEOFF TIME AT AIRPORTS?

Bringing a book to read, a laptop computer to play games, or stationary to write letters may be a good suggestion to cope with flight-departure delays at many of the nation's airports. While one bad experience with a delayed flight may bias a flier to believe that the time to take-off must be frustratingly long at most airports, a comparative look at the gate-to-takeoff times at airports across the United States can provide a clearer picture as to how serious this problem is. A census could be taken of all the airports in the United States to provide the average gate-to-takeoff time. Statistical sampling can provide this same information to within a certain margin of error at a specified level of confidence. The advantage to this procedure is that the average gate-to-take off time can be obtained far more economically and effectively when compared to a census.

Taxi-out time is the term used by many airlines for the time that a plane takes to leave its gate and take off. However, the actual time that it takes the plane to leave the ground after taxiing out from the gate varies widely because of congestion, weather, and occasional mechanical concerns. Some sprawling airports, such as Dallas/Fort Worth, have long distances separating runways and gates. At Dallas Love Field, the distance is much shorter. The Federal Aviation Administration projects that arrivals and departures at large airports will rise 34% to 18.3 million by 2010. Congress is considering a bill that would add dozens of flights to two of the most congested U.S. airports: Chicago O'Hare and Ronald Reagan Washington National. Expansion projects at airports typically move slowly because of environmental and financial concerns.

Finding the average time for the gate-to-takeoff time can be used by airport authorities to determine if the delays are unacceptably long, thus infuriating passengers as well as increasing costs to airlines. Taxiway delays cost carriers $2.4 billion a year in wasted fuel and labor,

according to the Air Transport Association. By sampling the gate-to-takeoff time, analysts can convince airport authorities to redesign domestic airports or provide additional resources when the average gate-to-takeoff time becomes unacceptably high. For example, at Newark airport, radar equipment will be added to enable controllers in the tower to locate planes on the runways and taxiways when bad weather conditions obscure visibility.

When the time from gate-to-takeoff is consistently above a certain level, airport authorities examine several factors. The first is scheduling. Airlines schedule many flights at the same hours because that is when demand is greatest. Obviously, no one wants to lose customers. "De-peaking" flights is one strategy that is used. Another factor that is considered is the shortage of air traffic controllers. The National Air Traffic Controllers Association says that the number of air traffic controllers will continue to increase, especially at airports that are seeing an increase in the total number of flights arriving and departing.

Then there is the weather factor. While most airline schedules are made out as if the sun shines every day, there are certain weather patterns that can be taken into consideration during planning. For example, at San Francisco International Airport, the morning fog routinely rolls into the bay area. Weather is the most difficult factor to control, but routinely high gate-to-take off times can force airport authorities to deal with the weather patterns by creating contingency plans.

When you have completed this chapter, you will be able to examine a sample of gate-to-takeoff times from various U.S. airports and be able to:

- View the average of these times as an **estimate** of the average gate-to-takeoff time for all major U.S. airports;
- Discuss the reliability of this estimate and what you can do to come up with a "better" estimate; and
- Discuss how many airports should be included in the sample so that the estimated average time from gate to takeoff at all major U.S. airports is within, say, three minutes of the actual average time.

A Look Back/Introduction

The previous three chapters laid the foundation for using statistical methods in decision making. Any such decision will have uncertainty associated with it, but we can attempt to measure this uncertain outcome using a probability. Random variables (both discrete and continuous) allow you to represent certain outcomes of an experiment and their corresponding probabilities conveniently. If the experiment involves a particular discrete situation (such as a binomial random variable), you can easily determine the probability of certain events or determine the mean (average) value of the related distribution.

If the random variable of interest is continuous, you can make probability statements after assuming the probability distribution involved (such as normal, exponential, uniform, or others we have not discussed). Both discrete and continuous random variables come into play in all areas of decision making. They allow us to make decisions concerning a large population using the information contained in a much smaller sample.

Such decision making lies in the area of **statistical inference,** which this chapter introduces by demonstrating how to estimate something about a population (such as its average value, μ) by using the corresponding value from a sample (such as the sample average $\overline{X}$). Recall that μ (belonging to the population) is a *parameter* and $\overline{X}$ (belonging to the sample) is a *statistic*. When dealing with a normal population, for example, what does one do if the population mean, μ, is unknown? So far in the text, this value has been specified for you. In this chapter, we discuss methods of estimating population parameters using sample statistics, along with several methods of gathering sample data.

7.1 Random Sampling and the Distribution of the Sample Mean

In Chapter 3, you learned how to calculate the mean of a sample, $\overline{X}$. This sample is drawn from a population having a particular distribution, such as normal, exponential, or uniform. If you were to obtain another sample (you probably will not, as most decisions are made from just one sample), would you get the same value of $\overline{X}$? Assuming that the new sample was made up of different individuals than was the first sample, then almost certainly the two $\overline{X}$'s would not be the same. So, $\overline{X}$ itself is a random variable. We will demonstrate that if a sample is large enough, $\overline{X}$ is very nearly *normally* distributed regardless of the shape of the sampled population. That is, if you were to obtain many large samples, calculate the resulting $\overline{X}$'s, and then make a histogram of these $\overline{X}$'s, *this histogram would always approximately resemble a bell-shaped (normal) curve.*

SIMPLE RANDOM SAMPLES

In Chapters 1 and 4, the concept of a simple random sample was introduced. The mechanics of obtaining a random sample range from drawing names out of a hat to using a computer to generate lists of random numbers. For extremely large populations, one is often forced to select individuals (elements) from the population in a *nearly* random manner.

The underlying assumption behind a random sample of size *n* is that any sample of size *n* has the same chance (probability) of being selected. To be completely assured of obtaining a random sample from a *finite* population, you should number the members of the population from 1 to *N* (the population size) and, using a set of *n* random numbers, select the corresponding sample of *n* population elements for your sample.

This procedure was described in Chapter 4 and is often used in practice, particularly when you have a sampling situation that needs to be legally defensible, as is the case in many statistical audits. However, for situations in which the population is extremely large, this strategy may be impractical, and instead you can use a sampling plan that is nearly random. Several other sampling procedures are discussed in the last section of this chapter.

The main point of all this lengthy discussion is that practically all the procedures presented in subsequent chapters relating to decision making and estimation assume that you are using a random sample. In the chapters that follow, the word *sample* will mean *simple random sample*.

ESTIMATION

The idea behind statistical inference has two components:

1. The *population* consists of everyone of interest. By "everyone" we mean measurements taken from all people, machine parts, daily sales, or whatever else you are interested in measuring or observing. The mean value (for example, average height, average income) of everyone in this population is μ and generally is not known.
2. The *sample* is randomly drawn from this population. Elements of the sample thus are part of the population—but certainly not all of it. The exception to this is a *census*, a sample that consists of the entire population.

The sample values should be selected randomly, one at a time, from the entire population. Figure 7.1 emphasizes our central point—namely, an unknown population **parameter** (such as μ = the mean value for the entire population) can be **estimated** using the corresponding sample **statistic** (such as $\bar{X}$ = the mean of your sample).

FIGURE 7.1

The sample mean, $\bar{X}$, is used to estimate the population mean, μ. In general, sample statistics are used to estimate population parameters.

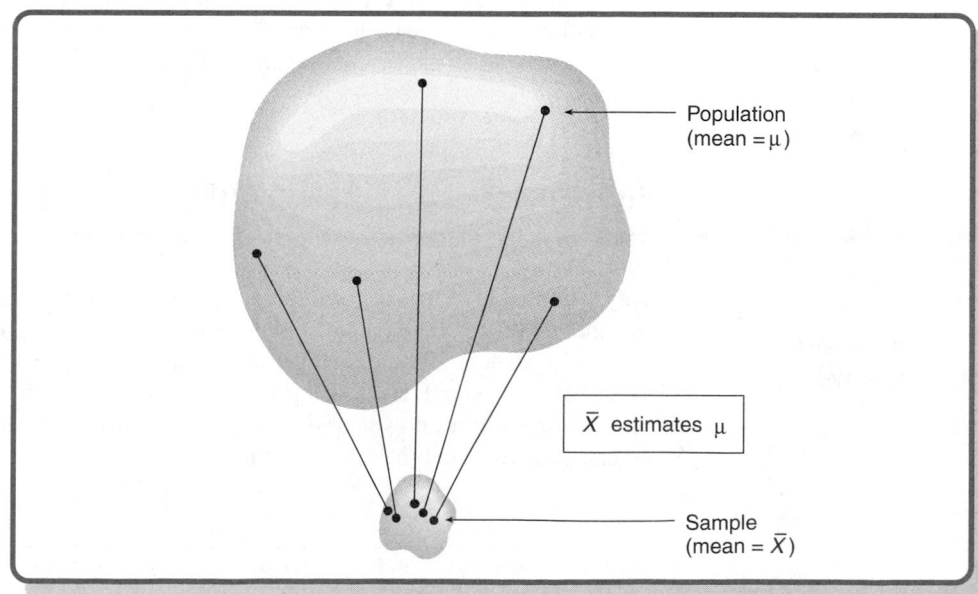

It makes sense, doesn't it? It would be most desirable to know the average value for everyone in the population, but in practice this is nearly always impossible. It may take too much time or money, we may not be able to obtain values for them all even if we want to, or the process of measuring the individual items may destroy them (such as measuring the lifetime of a light bulb). In many instances, estimating the population value using a sample estimate is the best we can do.

EXAMPLE 7.1

In Example 6.3, the funds dispensed by an automatic teller machine (ATM) were believed to follow a normal distribution with a mean of $\mu = \$3700$ and a standard deviation of $\sigma = \$625$. There is no way of *knowing* that μ is $3700 unless the population of all daily dispersements is examined. Assume that

$$X = \text{daily funds released by this ATM}$$

is a normal random variable, but do not assume anything about the mean and standard deviation. Ignoring the standard deviation, estimating the mean, μ, involves obtaining a random sample of daily dispersements. Suppose you obtain a random sample of size $n = 10$, with the following results (in dollars):

3880   3460   3530   4240   3470   3770   3990   4550   3310   2300

What is the estimate of μ, based on these values?

SOLUTION

The sample mean is $\bar{x} = \$3650.00$. Thus, based on these 10 sample values, our best estimate of μ is $\bar{x} = \$3650.00$.*

DISTRIBUTION OF $\overline{X}$

Referring to Example 7.1, the value of $\overline{X}$ would almost certainly change if you were to obtain another sample. The question of interest here is, if we *were* to obtain many values of $\overline{X}$, how would they behave? If we observed values of $\overline{X}$ indefinitely, where would they center; that is, what is the **mean** of the distribution for the random variable, $\overline{X}$? Is the variation of the $\overline{X}$ values more, less, or the same as the variation of individual observations? This variation is measured by the **standard deviation** of the distribution for $\overline{X}$.

In Example 6.2, it was assumed that the average lifetime of an Everglo light bulb was $\mu = 400$ hours, with a population standard deviation of $\sigma = 50$ hours. This result does not imply that if you obtain a random sample of these bulbs, the resulting sample mean, $\overline{X}$, always will be 400. Rather, a little head scratching should convince you that $\overline{X}$ will not be exactly 400, but $\overline{X}$ should be *approximately* 400.

| **MICROSOFT® EXCEL APPLICATION** | **USE DATA7-2** |

EXAMPLE 7.2

Determining the Distribution of the Sample Mean

Twenty samples of 10 Everglo bulbs each and the calculated $\overline{X}$'s for each sample are shown in Table 7.1. The data are contained in columns 1 to 20 in dataset DATA7-2. For now we will assume that the population parameters are $\mu = 400$ hours and $\sigma = 50$ hours (Figure 7.2). (1) Using Excel, determine the mean and standard deviation of the means of these 20 samples. What do you observe here? (2) Construct a histogram of these 20 means. What can you say about the "shape" of the $\overline{X}$ values?

---

* The notation $\hat{\mu}$ is commonly used in place of $\bar{x}$ to denote an *estimate* of μ. For this example, the estimate of μ is $\hat{\mu} = \$3650.00$.

TABLE 7.1

Twenty samples of 10 Everglo bulbs.

Sample 1	Sample 2	Sample 3	Sample 4	Sample 5
308	431	416	373	354
419	448	361	451	385
389	380	389	329	449
432	371	497	460	419
362	387	400	481	483
302	410	489	350	396
440	400	406	431	317
430	426	333	356	457
375	381	307	410	404
383	361	375	353	480
$\bar{x} = 384.0$	399.5	397.3	399.4	414.4
$s = 49.30$	28.54	60.51	53.99	54.25

Sample 6	Sample 7	Sample 8	Sample 9	Sample 10
404	372	449	403	354
390	404	389	350	446
390	493	397	565	343
454	344	428	354	458
386	396	374	358	404
385	441	502	412	468
384	373	365	441	416
351	438	402	340	340
392	360	416	359	409
396	367	316	446	408
$\bar{x} = 393.2$	398.8	403.8	402.8	404.6
$s = 25.45$	46.10	50.32	68.93	46.28

Sample 11	Sample 12	Sample 13	Sample 14	Sample 15
329	429	461	448	457
473	286	399	386	432
336	382	416	375	425
356	380	378	488	391
385	423	359	447	429
365	388	408	429	448
419	329	393	377	416
448	438	374	380	429
459	423	440	372	414
449	378	454	408	315
$\bar{x} = 401.9$	385.6	408.2	411.0	415.6
$s = 54.12$	47.91	34.60	40.12	39.73

Sample 16	Sample 17	Sample 18	Sample 19	Sample 20
491	439	331	418	428
353	336	427	422	368
375	425	445	341	445
536	419	420	485	429
447	346	401	442	475
415	408	389	470	437
322	392	363	404	475
350	409	439	370	458
453	313	352	539	308
343	334	346	435	408
$\bar{x} = 408.5$	382.1	391.3	432.6	423.1
$s = 71.46$	45.28	41.35	56.78	51.48

FIGURE 7.2
Assumed distribution of
Everglo bulb lifetimes.

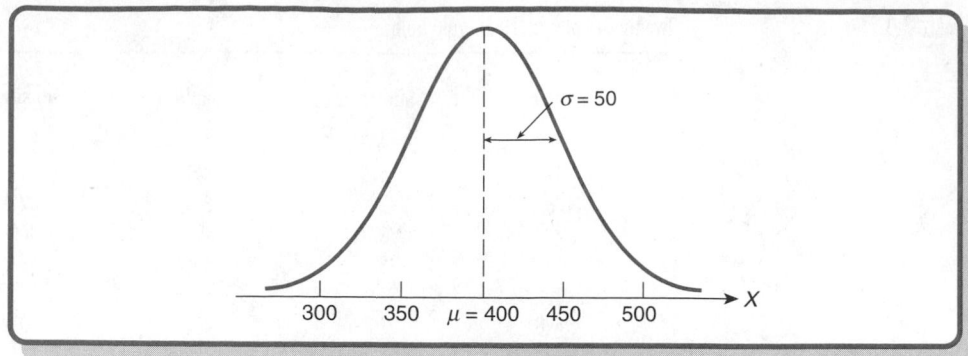

FIGURE 7.3
Sample means created using
KGP Data Analysis ➤ Means and CIs for Multiple Samples.

	Q	R	S	T	U	V	W	X	Y	Z
1	439	331	418	428	**Multiple Samples**		**Frequency Distribution Table**			
2	336	427	422	368	SAMPLE	MEANS	CLASS	CLASS LIMITS	FREQUENCY	
3	425	445	341	445	1	384.00	1	377 and under 384	1	
4	419	420	485	429	2	399.50	2	384 and under 391	2	
5	346	401	442	475	3	397.30	3	391 and under 398	3	
6	408	389	470	437	4	399.40	4	398 and under 405	7	
7	392	363	404	475	5	414.40	5	405 and under 412	3	
8	409	439	370	458	6	393.20	6	412 and under 419	2	
9	313	352	539	308	7	398.80	7	419 and under 426	1	
10	334	346	435	408	8	403.80	8	426 and under 433	1	
11					9	402.80		TOTAL	20	
12					10	404.60				
13					11	401.90				
14					12	385.60				
15					13	408.20				
16					14	411.00				
17					15	415.60				
18					16	408.50				
19					17	382.10				
20					18	391.30				
21					19	432.60				
22					20	423.10		*Pop*		
23					SUMMARY FOR X-BARs					
24					Mean	402.89		*400*		
25					St. Dev.	12.78		*50*		

File Edit View Insert Format Tools Data KGP Data Analysis Window Help

Frequency Histogram \ DATA7-2

SOLUTION TO 1

Rather than using Excel to determine the 20 means one at a time, use the Excel KGP Data Analysis. First you must open file DATA7-2. Then click on **KGP Data Analysis ➤ Means and CIs for Multiple Samples.** Enter "A1:T10" as the **Input Range,** "50" as the **Population Std. Dev.,** and "U1" as the **Output Range.** Make sure the button alongside **Means** at the bottom of the form is selected. The output from this macro is shown in Figure 7.3 and does not include the frequency distribution in cells W1:Y11. Examining cell V24, we conclude that the average of the 20 sample means is 402.89 hours, and so the $\bar{X}$ values appear to be centered approximately at $\mu = 400$ hours. Look at the 20 standard deviations in Table 7.1. These values are in the neighborhood of $\sigma = 50$, as they should be. However, the standard deviation of the 20 $\bar{X}$ values (contained in cell V25) is 12.78, so we conclude that the $\bar{X}$ values have much less variation than the individual observations in each of the samples.

SOLUTION TO 2

To obtain the frequency distribution of the twenty sample means in Figure 7.3 and corresponding histogram, click on **KGP Data Analysis ➤ Quantitative Data Charts/Tables ➤ Histogram/Freq. Charts.** You will then see the input form for this macro (see Figure 2.3 on page 37). For the **Input Range,** enter "V3:V22," and for the **Output Range,** enter "W1." Also, click on the circle to the left of **Number of Classes** and enter "7" in the text

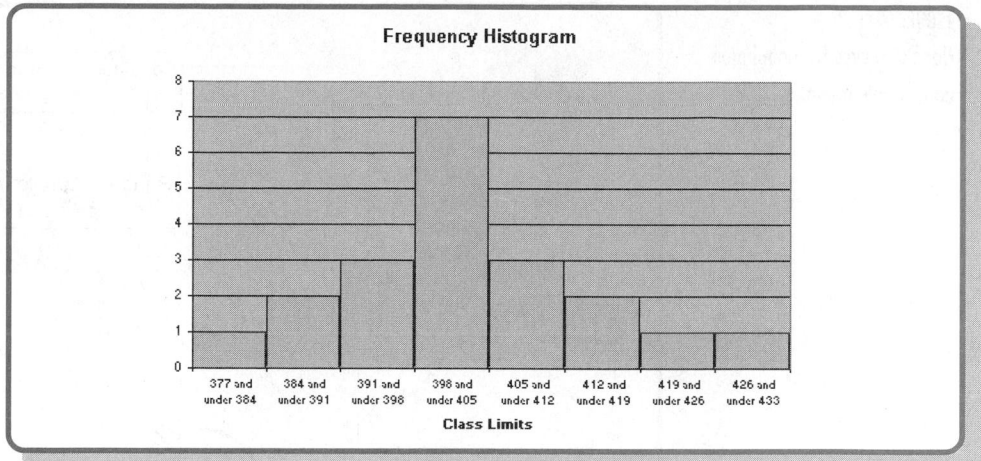

FIGURE 7.4

Excel histogram of 20 sample means.

box. Finally, click on the check box for **Frequencies** in the **Table** list and the check box for **Frequency Histogram** in the **Chart Output Options** list. This will result in the frequency distribution table shown in Figure 7.3 and the histogram in Figure 7.4 (obtained by clicking on the **Frequency Histogram** tab at the bottom of your spreadsheet). Notice that the procedure produced eight classes, rather than the requested seven. As mentioned in earlier chapters, this Excel macro creates a frequency distribution containing an easy-to-interpret class width and classes, and very often will modify the intended number of classes to achieve this.

Based on the histogram in Figure 7.4 and the solution to (1), it seems reasonable to assume that the values of $\overline{X}$ follow a normal distribution centered at $\mu = 400$ hours but one that is much narrower than the population of individual lifetimes described in Figure 7.2.

In the previous example, we observed that the values of $\overline{X}$ were centered about the mean of the population, μ. In addition, the standard deviation of the $\overline{X}$ values was considerably less than the standard deviation of the population, σ. In general, what can you say about the mean and standard deviation of the random variable $\overline{X}$? This is summarized as follows:

Mean of the random variable $\overline{X}$ is

$$\mu_{\overline{X}} = \mu \tag{7.1}$$

Standard deviation of the random variable $\overline{X}$ is

$$\sigma_{\overline{X}} = \frac{\sigma}{\sqrt{n}} \tag{7.2}$$

For the previous example, $\mu = 400$, $\sigma = 50$, and $n = 10$. As a result, the mean and standard deviation of the $\overline{X}$ values, if samples of size 10 were obtained *indefinitely,* are

$$\mu_{\overline{X}} = 400 \qquad \text{and} \qquad \sigma_{\overline{X}} = \frac{50}{\sqrt{10}} = 15.8$$

Recall that the mean and standard deviation of the 20 observed $\overline{X}$ values was 402.89 and 12.78, respectively. These values will tend toward 400 and 15.81 if we were to take additional samples of size 10. These results are summarized in Figure 7.5, where $\mu_{\overline{X}} = 400$ and $\sigma_{\overline{X}} = 15.81$.

FIGURE 7.5

Normal curves for population and sample mean.

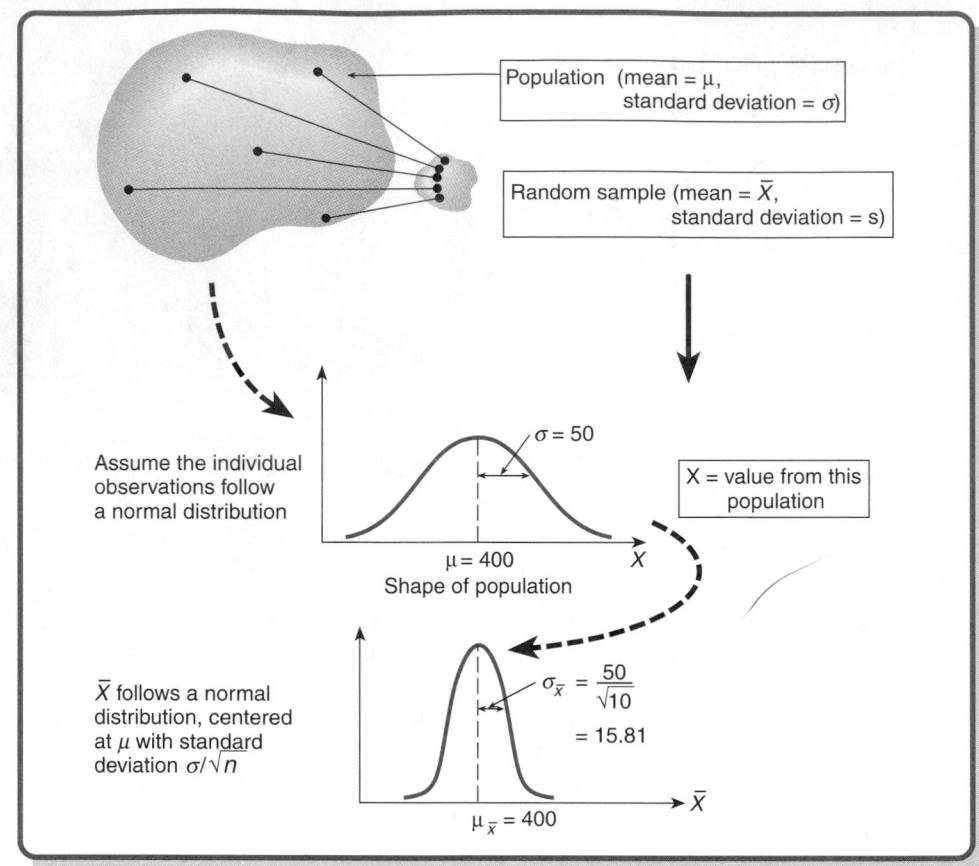

7.2 THE CENTRAL LIMIT THEOREM

In the previous example, we observed that the shape of the $\bar{X}$ curve was approximately normal. This is not a surprising result, considering that the population from which the samples were obtained followed an assumed normal curve; that is, the random variable X = lifetime of Everglo bulb is a normal random variable. What may surprise you is that the random variable $\bar{X}$ follows an approximate normal curve *regardless of the shape of the population curve*, *provided large samples are obtained*. This is summarized in the **Central Limit Theorem.**

CENTRAL LIMIT THEOREM   CLT

When obtaining large samples (generally $n > 30$) from any population, the sample mean $\bar{X}$ will follow an approximate normal distribution.

Based on the Central Limit Theorem and equations 7.1 and 7.2, whenever large samples are obtained from *any* population, the sample mean, $\bar{X}$, will follow an approximate normal distribution with mean μ and standard deviation $\sigma / \sqrt{n}$. In practice, you are likely to obtain your one and only sample of size n. However, these results allow you to make probability statements regarding $\bar{X}$, as illustrated in the examples to follow.

COMMENTS

1. Not having to know the shape of the sampled population for large samples makes the Central Limit Theorem a very strong tool in statistics. For example, if you repeatedly took large samples from a population with an exponential distribution (look ahead to Figure 7.11), the resulting $\bar{X}$'s would follow a *normal* (not an exponential) curve.

2. Based on equations 7.1 and 7.2, the mean of $\bar{X}$ is μ and the standard deviation of $\bar{X}$ is $\sigma / \sqrt{n}$ for *any* sample size *n*. However, for $\bar{X}$ to be approximately normally distributed, a large value of *n* is necessary if the population is not assumed to be normally distributed.

3. If the population from which you are sampling is a normal population, the Central Limit Theorem isn't necessary. For this situation, the random variable $\bar{X}$ is *exactly* normally distributed, with mean μ and standard deviation $\sigma / \sqrt{n}$. For Example 7.2, we can say that the random variable $\bar{X}$ follows an exact normal distribution with mean = 400 and standard deviation $50 / \sqrt{10} = 15.81$.

Basically, equations 7.1 and 7.2 along with the Central Limit Theorem state that the normal curve (distribution) for $\bar{X}$ is centered at the same value as the population distribution but has a much smaller standard deviation. Notice that as the sample size, *n*, increases, $\sigma / \sqrt{n}$ decreases, and so the spread relative to the mean of the $\bar{X}$ curve (that is, the variation in the $\bar{X}$ values) decreases. In the Everglo bulb example, if we repeatedly obtained samples of size 100 (rather than 10), the corresponding $\bar{X}$ values would lie even closer to $\mu_{\bar{X}} = 400$ because now $\sigma_{\bar{X}}$ would equal $50 / \sqrt{100} = 5$ (see Figure 7.6).

For the 20 values of $\bar{X}$ in Table 7.1, it was assumed that the population mean was *known* to be $\mu = 400$, so each of the $\bar{X}$ values estimates μ with a certain amount of error. The more variation in the $\bar{X}$ values, the more error we encounter using $\bar{X}$ as an estimate of

FIGURE 7.6

Normal curves for the sample mean ($n = 10, 20, 50, 100$).

The highes + sharper the peak the lower the std Dev. — getter closer to actual mean.

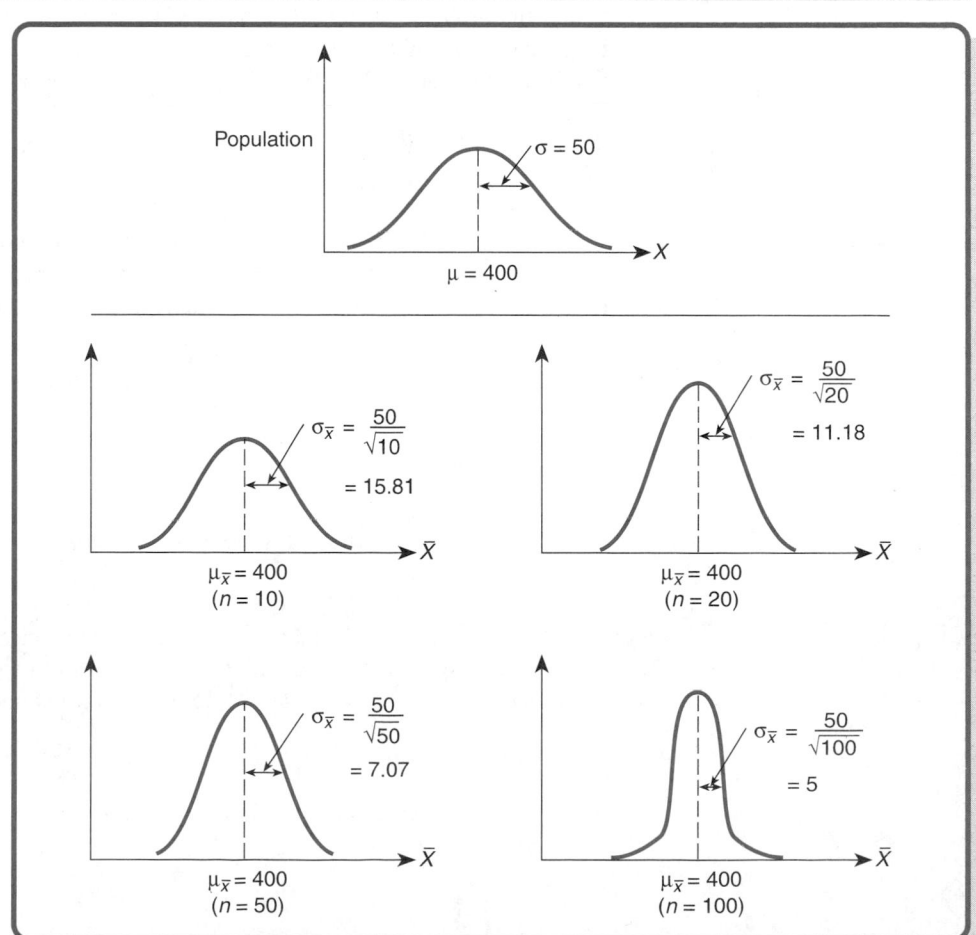

μ. Consequently, the standard deviation of $\overline{X}$ also serves as a measure of the error that will be encountered using a sample mean to estimate a population mean. The standard deviation of the $\overline{X}$ distribution is often referred to as the **standard error** of $\overline{X}$.

> Standard error of $\overline{X}$ = standard deviation of the probability distribution for $\overline{X}$
>
> $$= \frac{\sigma}{\sqrt{n}}$$

The previous discussion has described the probability distribution of the sample mean, $\overline{X}$. This distribution is referred to as the *sampling distribution* of $\overline{X}$.

DEFINITION

The probability distribution of a sample statistic is its **sampling distribution.**

To summarize this section: For large samples, the sampling distribution of $\overline{X}$ is approximately normal, centered at μ, with a standard deviation (standard error) of $\sigma/\sqrt{n}$, regardless of the shape of the sampled population.

EXAMPLE 7.3

Electricalc has determined that the assembly time for a particular electrical component is normally distributed with a mean of 20 minutes and a standard deviation of 3 minutes.

1. What is the probability that an employee in the assembly division takes longer than 22 minutes to assemble one of these components?
2. What is the probability that the average assembly time for 15 such employees exceeds 22 minutes?
3. What is the probability that the average assembly time for 15 employees is between 19 and 21 minutes?

SOLUTION 1

The random variable X here is the assembly time for a component. It is assumed to be a normal random variable, with μ = 20 minutes and σ = 3 minutes (Figure 7.7). We wish to determine $P(X > 22)$. Standardizing this variable and using Table A.4, we obtain

$$P(X > 22) = P\left[\frac{X - 20}{3} > \frac{22 - 20}{3}\right]$$

$$= P(Z > .67)$$

$$= .5 - .2486 = .2514$$

Therefore, a randomly chosen employee will require longer than 22 minutes to assemble the component with probability .25.

SOLUTION 2

Figure 7.7 does *not* apply to this question, because we are concerned with the *average* time for 15 employees, not an individual employee. Using comment 3 on page 261, we know that the curve describing $\overline{X}$ (an average of 15 employees) is normal with

$$\text{mean} = \mu_{\overline{X}} = \mu = 20 \text{ minutes}$$

$$\text{standard deviation (standard error)} = \sigma_{\overline{X}} = \frac{\sigma}{\sqrt{n}}$$

$$= \frac{3}{\sqrt{15}} = .77 \text{ minutes}$$

(See Figure 7.8.)

FIGURE 7.7

Assembly time for the population of electrical components. (See Example 7.3.)

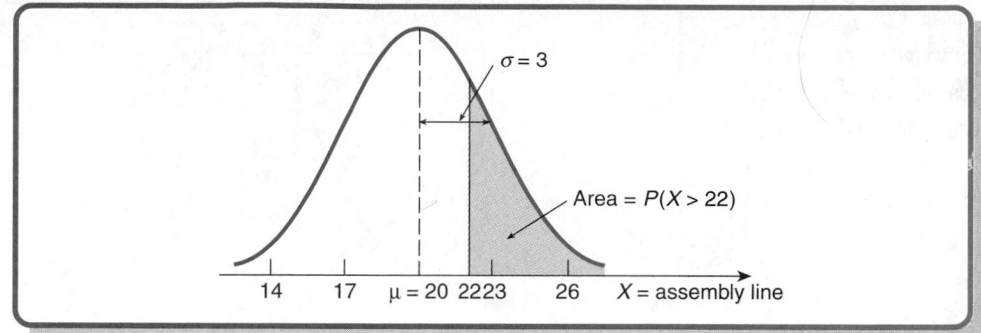

FIGURE 7.8

Curve for $\overline{X}$ = average of 15 employees' assembly times. Shaded area shows $P(\overline{X} > 22)$.

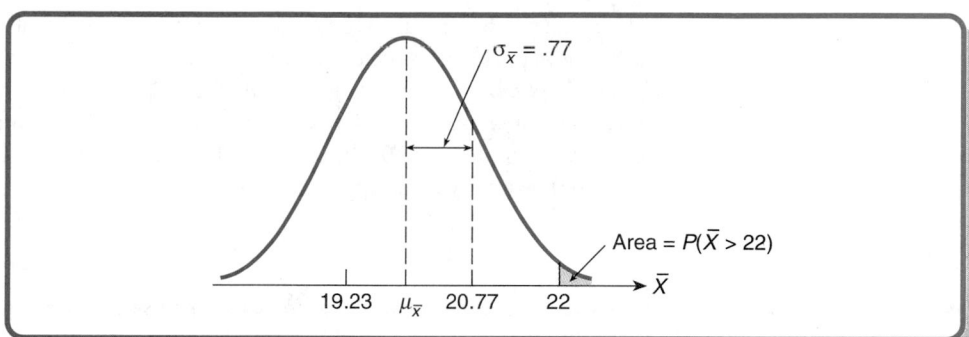

This procedure is the same as in solution 1, except now the standard deviation of this curve is .77 rather than 3:

$$P(\overline{X} > 22) = P\left[\frac{\overline{X} - 20}{.77} > \frac{22 - 20}{.77}\right]$$

$$= P(Z > 2.60)$$

$$= .5 - .4953 = .0047$$

So an average assembly time for a sample of 15 employees will be more than 22 minutes with less than 1% probability; that is, it is very unlikely that an average of 15 assembly times will exceed 22 minutes.

SOLUTION 3

The curve for this solution is shown in Figure 7.9. We wish to find $P(19 > \overline{X} > 21)$.

$$P(19 < \overline{X} < 21) = P\left[\frac{19 - 20}{.77} < \frac{\overline{X} - 20}{.77} < \frac{21 - 20}{.77}\right]$$

$$= P(-1.30 < Z < 1.30)$$

$$= .4032 + .4032 + .8064$$

Thus, a sample of 15 employees will produce an average assembly time between 19 and 21 minutes with probability about .81.

FIGURE 7.9
Curve for average assembly
time of 15 employees. Shaded
area shows $P(19 < \bar{X} < 21)$.

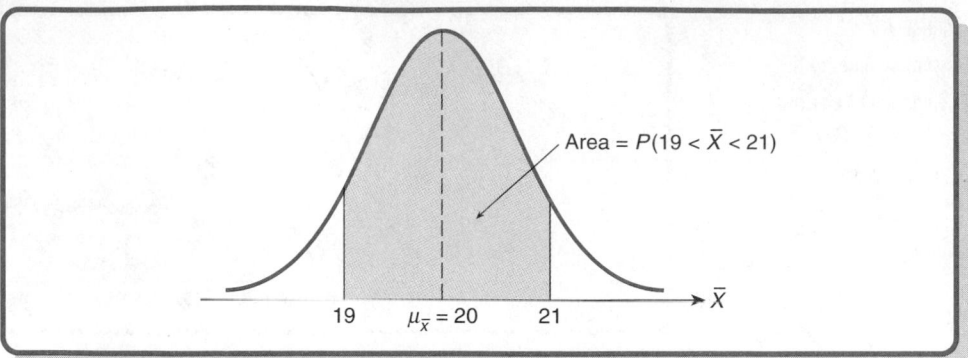

In Example 7.3, it was assumed that the individual assembly times followed a normal distribution. *However, remember that the strength of the Central Limit Theorem is that this assumption is not necessary for large samples.* We can answer questions 2 and 3 for *any* population whose mean is 20 minutes and standard deviation is 3 minutes, provided we take a *large* sample ($n > 30$). In this case, the normal distribution of $\bar{X}$ may not be exact, but it provides a very good approximation.

EXAMPLE 7.4

The price-earnings (P/E) ratio of a stock is usually considered by analysts who put together financial portfolios. Suppose a population of all P/E ratios has a mean of 10.5 and a standard deviation of 4.5.

1. What is the probability that a sample of 40 stocks will have an average P/E ratio less than 9?
2. What assumptions about the population of all P/E ratios are necessary in your answer to question 1?

SOLUTION 1

By the Central Limit Theorem and equations 7.1 and 7.2, $\bar{X}$ is approximately a normal random variable with mean $= \mu = 10.5$ and standard deviation $= \sigma / \sqrt{n} = 4.5 / \sqrt{40} = .71$. So

$$Z = \frac{\bar{X} - 10.5}{.71}$$

is approximately a standard normal random variable, and consequently

$$P(\bar{X} < 9) = P\left[\frac{\bar{X} - 10.5}{.71} < \frac{9 - 10.5}{.71}\right]$$

$$= P(Z < -2.11) = .0174$$

SOLUTION 2

No assumptions regarding the shape of the P/E ratio population are necessary. This population may be normal or it may not be—it simply does not matter because we are using a fairly large sample ($n = 40$). The distribution of $\bar{X}$ is approximately normal, regardless of the shape of the population of all P/E ratios. Our only assumptions in solution 1 were that $\mu = 10.5$ and $\sigma = 4.5$.

EXERCISES 7.1–7.8

UNDERSTANDING THE MECHANICS

7.1 A sample of $n = 100$ observations from a normal population is drawn. The population mean is 500 and the population standard deviation is 200. Find the following.

  a. $P(\bar{X} > 480)$
  b. $P(460 < \bar{X} < 480)$
  c. $P(\bar{X} < 530)$

7.2 A population has a mean of 200 and a standard deviation of 50. Let $\bar{X}$ be used to estimate the mean of the population from a random sample of size 100. Find the following probabilities.

  a. $P(\bar{X} \leq 205)$
  b. $P(\bar{X} \geq 190)$
  c. $P(195 \leq \bar{X} \leq 210)$
  d. $P(188 \leq \bar{X} \leq 198)$

APPLYING THE NEW CONCEPTS

7.3 Surveys indicate that an adult between the ages of 20 and 30 years of age spends a mean of four hours per day either watching TV or listening to the radio. The standard deviation of the amount of time spent doing these activities is one hour.

  a. If a sample of 50 adults between the ages of 20 and 30 years of age was drawn, what does the Central Limit Theorem tell us about the distribution of the sample mean of the time spent by the adults either watching TV or listening to the radio?

  b. If the sample size were to increase to 100, how would this change the distribution of the sample mean of the time spent by the adults either watching TV or listening to the radio?

7.4 Five machines produce electronic components. The number of components produced per hour is normally distributed with a mean of 25 and a standard deviation of 4.

  a. What percentage of the time does a machine produce more than 27 components per hour?

  b. What percentage of the time is the average rate of output of the five machines more than 27 components per hour?

7.5 A quality engineer knows from past data that in a shipment lot, the number of wire cables that have tensile strengths below

the lower specification limit follows a Poisson distribution with a mean of 50. For a sample of 45 shipment lots, what is the probability that the sample mean for the number of wire cables with tensile strengths below the lower specification limit exceeds 53?

7.6 The average length of actual running time (excluding advertisements) for television feature films is 1 hour and 40 minutes, with a standard deviation of 15 minutes. If a sample of 49 TV feature films is taken at random, what is the probability that the average running time for this group is 1 hour and 45 minutes or more?

7.7 As the European Union becomes a reality, regional airports must face the difficulties encountered from the loss of profits generated by duty-free shopping. Duty-free revenue has allowed many of Europe's regional airports to expand. A survey of authorities that run regional airports showed that business travelers would be required to pay an average of $35 more per round trip flight once duty-free shopping is abolished. Suppose that the standard deviation of the amount that a business traveler would have to pay is $10. What is the probability that from a random sample of 30 regional airports selected in an independent study that the sample mean would be at least $27?

(Adapted from *London Financial Times,* "Business Travel Duty-Free Abolition," June 1, 1998, p. 13.)

7.8 Several communities surrounding the Dallas/Fort Worth metroplex are trying to cope with a small tax base. One such community is Keller, a community north of Fort Worth. Keller's land use committee is charged with developing the city's first comprehensive land use plan in 10 years. More than 54% of Keller is residential, and less than 6% of the land is commerical. The average household pays $600 in taxes annually.

(Adapted from *Dallas Morning News,* "In the News," March 30, 1998, p. 5A.)

  a. Suppose that a random sample of 40 households in Keller was randomly obtained. What is the probability that the average of the taxes paid by the 40 households is more than $630? Assume that the standard deviation is $100.

  b. Do a "what if" analysis by changing the standard deviation to $200 or $250 and answering part (a). Do you think that the probability will increase or decrease? Why?

A LOOK AT THE SAMPLING DISTRIBUTION OF $\bar{X}$ FOR NORMAL POPULATIONS

The Central Limit Theorem tells us that $\bar{X}$ tends toward a normal distribution as the sample size increases. If you are dealing with a population that has an assumed normal distribution (as in Example 7.3), then $\bar{X}$ is normal regardless of the sample size. However, as the sample size increases, the variability of $\bar{X}$ decreases, as is illustrated in Figure 7.6. This means that for large sample sizes, if you were to get many samples and corresponding values of $\bar{X}$, these values of $\bar{X}$ would be more concentrated around the middle, with very few extremely large or extremely small values.

Look at Figure 7.6, which illustrates the assumed normal distribution of all Everglo bulbs. We know (using Table A.4) that 95% of a normal curve is contained within 1.96 standard deviations of the mean. For a sample size of $n = 10$ from a normal population with $\mu = 400$ and $\sigma = 50$, $\sigma_{\bar{X}} = 15.81$. Now,

$$\mu_{\bar{X}} - 1.96\sigma_{\bar{X}} = 400 - 1.96(15.81) = 369.0$$

and

$$\mu_{\bar{X}} + 1.96\sigma_{\bar{X}} = 400 + 1.96(15.81) = 431.0$$

TABLE 7.2

Sample from a normal population with $\mu = 400$ and $\sigma = 50$; 95% of the time, the value of $\overline{X}$ will be between $\mu_{\overline{x}} - 1.96\sigma_{\overline{x}}$ and $\mu_{\overline{x}} + 1.96\sigma_{\overline{x}}$. Refer to Figure 7.6 for the values of $\sigma_{\overline{x}}$.

Sample Size	$\sigma_{\overline{x}}$	$\mu_{\overline{x}} - 1.96\sigma_{\overline{x}}$	$\mu_{\overline{x}} + 1.96\sigma_{\overline{x}}$	Conclusion
$n = 10$	15.81	369.0	431.0	95% of the time, the value of $\overline{X}$ will be between 369.0 and 431.0
$n = 20$	11.18	378.1	421.9	95% of the time, the value of $\overline{X}$ will be between 378.1 and 421.9
$n = 50$	7.07	386.1	413.9	95% of the time, the value of $\overline{X}$ will be between 386.1 and 413.9
$n = 100$	5	390.2	409.8	95% of the time, the value of $\overline{X}$ will be between 390.2 and 409.8

Thus, if we repeatedly obtain samples of size 10, 95% of the resulting $\overline{X}$ values will lie between 369.0 and 431.0.

This result and the corresponding results using $n = 20$, 50, and 100 are contained in Table 7.2, which reemphasizes that for larger samples, you are much more likely to get a value of $\overline{X}$ that is close to $\mu = 400$. In practice, you typically do not know the value of μ. However, by using a larger sample size, you are more apt to obtain an $\overline{X}$ that is a good estimate of the unknown μ.

APPLYING THE CENTRAL LIMIT THEOREM TO NONNORMAL POPULATIONS

The real strength of the Central Limit Theorem is that $\overline{X}$ will tend toward a normal random variable regardless of the shape of your population. You need a large sample ($n > 30$) to obtain a nearly normal distribution for $\overline{X}$. The Central Limit Theorem also holds when sampling from a discrete population.

Figures 7.10, 7.11, and 7.12 illustrate the distribution of $\overline{X}$ for three nonnormal populations. Notice that the uniform population (Figure 7.10) is at least symmetric about the mean, so the distribution of the sample mean, $\overline{X}$, tends toward a normal distribution for

FIGURE 7.10

Distribution of $\overline{X}$ for a uniform population.

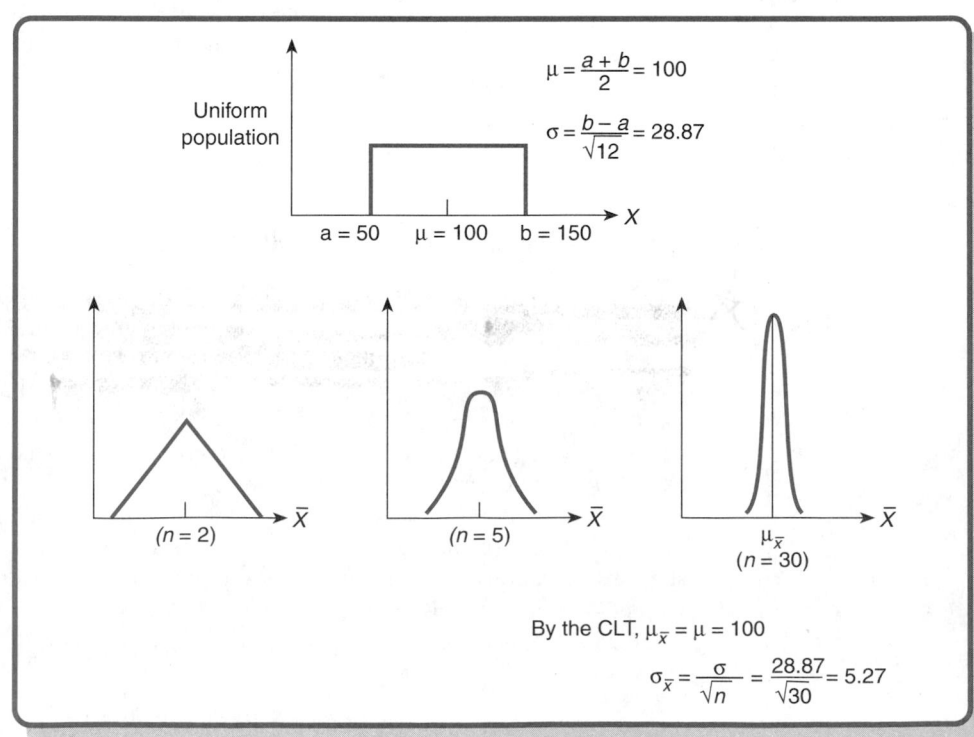

FIGURE 7.11

Distribution of $\overline{X}$ for an exponential population.

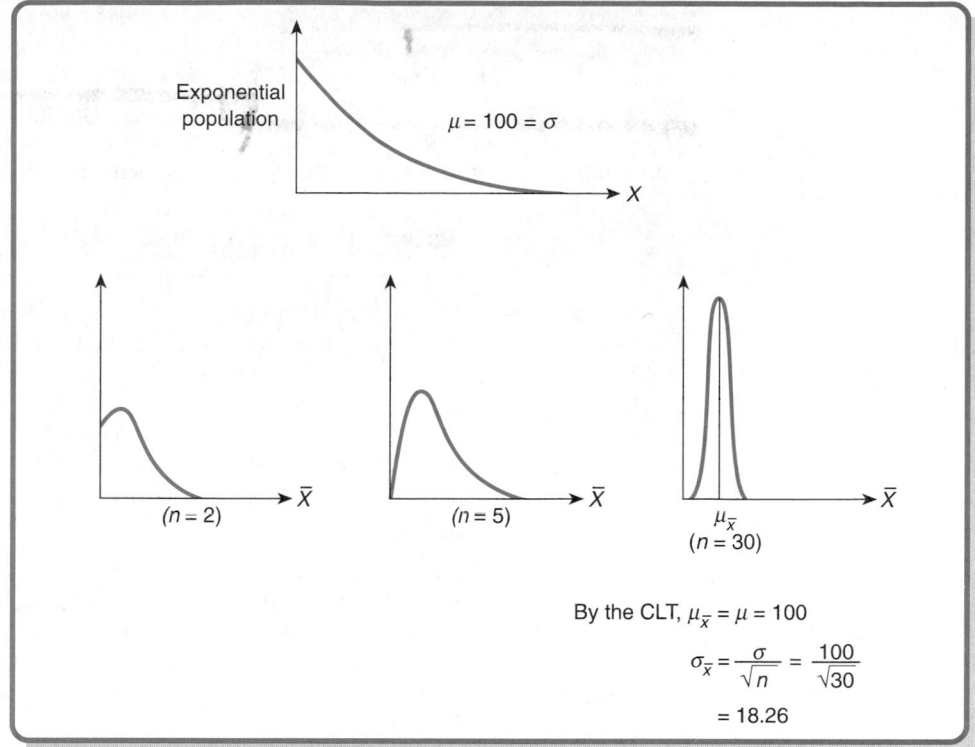

FIGURE 7.12

Distribution of $\overline{X}$ for a U-shaped population.

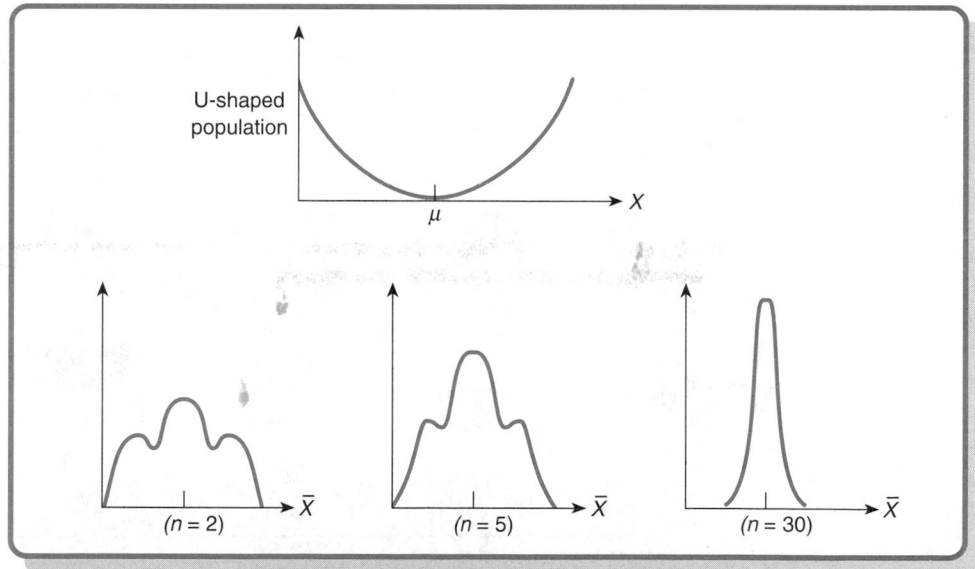

much smaller sample sizes. The U-shaped distribution (Figure 7.12) is another continuous distribution. It is characterized by many small and large values, with few values in the middle. This distribution is symmetric about the mean, but its shape is opposite to that of a normal distribution. Here, $\overline{X}$ requires a large sample ($n > 30$) to attain an approximate normal distribution.

SAMPLING FROM A FINITE POPULATION

In the previous discussion, we assumed that the population was large enough that the sample was extremely small by comparison. We will now consider whether our results, including the Central Limit Theorem, apply when the exact size of the population is known and the sample is a large portion of the population.

SAMPLING WITH REPLACEMENT.   When you return each element of the sample to the population before taking the next sample element, you are sampling *with replacement*. This sampling procedure is not common; people generally obtain their sample all at once, making it impossible to sample with replacement. When sampling with replacement, it is possible to obtain the same element more than once. For example, the same person could be chosen all three times in a sample of size $n = 3$. When sampling with replacement, the previous results apply exactly as before, without any adjustments necessary.

SAMPLING WITH REPLACEMENT FROM A FINITE POPULATION

When sampling with replacement from a finite population with mean μ and standard deviation σ, the sample mean $\bar{X}$ tends toward a normal distribution with

$$\text{mean} = \mu_{\bar{X}} = \mu \qquad (7.3)$$

$$\text{standard deviation (standard error)} = \sigma_{\bar{X}} = \frac{\sigma}{\sqrt{n}} \qquad (7.4)$$

where n = sample size.

SAMPLING WITHOUT REPLACEMENT.   We first encountered the problem of sampling without replacement from a finite population in Chapter 5, where the hypergeometric distribution considered the population size (N) and the binomial distribution did not. It is easy to show that, for this situation,

$$\begin{bmatrix} \text{variance of hypergeometric} \\ \text{random variable} \end{bmatrix} = \begin{bmatrix} \text{variance of corresponding} \\ \text{binomial random variable} \end{bmatrix} \cdot \begin{bmatrix} \frac{N-n}{N-1} \end{bmatrix}$$

because

$$\frac{k(N-k)n(N-n)}{N^2(N-1)} = n\frac{k}{N}\left[1 - \frac{k}{N}\right] \cdot \left[\frac{N-n}{N-1}\right]$$

$$= np(1-p) \cdot \left[\frac{N-n}{N-1}\right]$$

where $p = k/N$. Here, $(N-n)/(N-1)$ is called the **finite population correction (fpc) factor.** When the sample size, n, is very small compared with the population size, N, the fpc factor is nearly 1 and can be ignored. In fact, as discussed in Chapter 5, the binomial distribution serves as a good approximation to the hypergeometric whenever $n/N < .05$. The same result applies to sampling situations as well. We can express this as a rule: The fpc can be ignored whenever $n/N < .05$.

For this situation, the standard error of $\bar{X}$ includes the finite population correction.

SAMPLING WITHOUT REPLACEMENT FROM A LARGE, FINITE POPULATION

When sampling without replacement from a large finite population (of size N), with mean μ and standard deviation σ, the sample mean $\bar{X}$ tends toward a normal distribution with

$$\text{mean} = \mu_{\bar{X}} = \mu \qquad (7.5)$$

$$\text{standard deviation (standard error)} = \sigma_{\bar{X}} = \frac{\sigma}{\sqrt{n}} \cdot \sqrt{\frac{N-n}{N-1}} \qquad (7.6)$$

where n = sample size.*

---

* The standard error in equations 7.2, 7.4, and 7.6 assumes that the population standard deviation σ is known. If this parameter is estimated from the sample and the sample standard deviation (s) is substituted for σ, the resulting standard error is referred to as the "estimated standard error." For this situation, the fpc in equation 7.6 becomes $(N-n)/N$ rather than $(N-n)/(N-1)$. Section 7.6 contains additional discussion on this topic.

FIGURE 7.13

Distribution of sample mean of annual salaries (assuming $\mu = \$48,000$, $\sigma = \$8500$). The shaded area represents the solution to Example 7.5, $P(\bar{X} \leq 43,900)$.

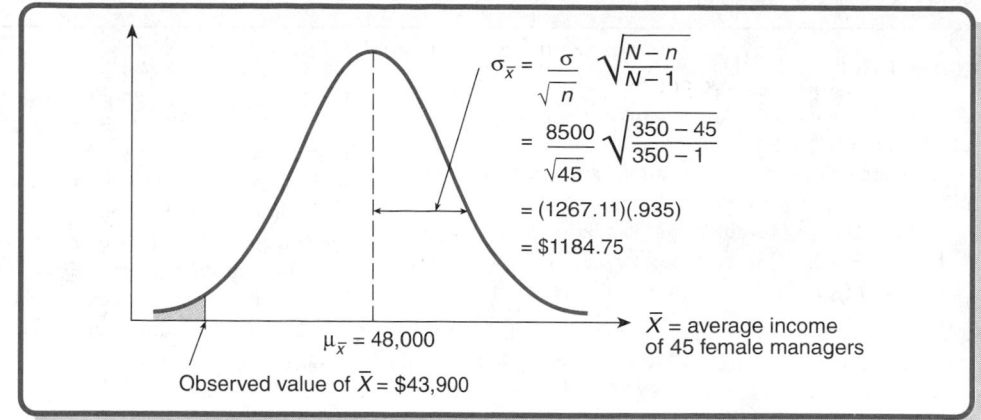

$$\sigma_{\bar{x}} = \frac{\sigma}{\sqrt{n}} \sqrt{\frac{N-n}{N-1}}$$

$$= \frac{8500}{\sqrt{45}} \sqrt{\frac{350-45}{350-1}}$$

$$= (1267.11)(.935)$$

$$= \$1184.75$$

$\mu_{\bar{x}} = 48,000$ $\bar{X}$ = average income of 45 female managers

Observed value of $\bar{X} = \$43,900$

The fpc recognizes that our estimate is better for a finite population than for an infinite population and shrinks the size of the standard error. In fact, when the sample size (*n*) and the population size (*N*) are the same, the fpc is 0, making the standard error equal to 0. This value is correct, since repeated samples of size $n = N$ would produce the same sample, namely the entire population, and consequently, the same value of $\bar{X}$. Since there is no variation in the $\bar{X}$ values, the standard deviation of $\bar{X}$ (standard error) *should* be zero. *As a final note, remember that although the effect of the fpc is negligible when n/N <.05, it can (and some will argue "should") always be used to derive a more accurate standard error.*

EXAMPLE 7.5

A group of women managers at Compumart is considering filing a sex-discrimination suit. A recent report stated that the average annual income of all employees in middle management positions at Compumart is $48,000 and the standard deviation is $8500. A random sample of 45 women taken from a population of 350 female middle managers at Compumart had an average income of $\bar{x} = \$43,900$. If the population of all female incomes at this level is assumed to have the same mean ($48,000) and standard deviation ($8500) as the distribution of incomes for all employees, what is the probability of observing a value of $\bar{X}$ this low?

SOLUTION

Because we have a large sample, we can assume (using the Central Limit Theorem) that the curve describing $\bar{X}$ is normal, as shown in Figure 7.13. Here, $n = 45$ and $N = 350$. We need to find $P(\bar{X} \leq 43,900)$. Standardizing and using Table A.4, we find that

$$P(\bar{X} \leq 43,900) = P\left[Z \leq \frac{43,900 - 48,000}{1184.75}\right]$$

$$= P(Z \leq -3.46) = .0003$$

So, if the female population has an average salary of $48,000 (and standard deviation of $8500), then the chance of obtaining an $\bar{X}$ as low as $43,900 is extremely small. If we assume that the standard deviation is correct, then, based strictly on this set of data, our conclusion would be that the average salary for women at this level is not $48,000 but is less than $48,000.

With the type of question asked in Example 7.5, there is always the chance that we will reach an incorrect decision using the sample data; there is always the chance of error due to sampling. This possible error will be a concern whenever you test a hypothesis. For now, remember that when dealing with sample data, statistics never *prove* anything. They do, however, *support or fail to support* a claim (such as $\mu < \$48,000$).

EXERCISES 7.9–7.18

UNDERSTANDING THE MECHANICS

7.9 tells you it's Z.

tells you to use FCP

7.9 A finite population is approximately normally distributed with a mean of 20 and a standard deviation of 6. Let $\bar{X}$ be used to estimate the mean of this population from sampling 40 observations without replacement.

    a. Find $P(\bar{X} \leq 21)$ if the finite population is of size 100.

    b. Find $P(\bar{X} \leq 21)$ if the finite population is of size 300.

    c. Find $P(\bar{X} \leq 21)$ if the finite population is of size 1000.

7.10 Consider a finite population whose distribution can be approximated by a normal distribution. Assume that the population is of size 400 with a mean of 100 and a standard deviation of 25. Let $\bar{X}$ be used to estimate the mean of the population from a sample of size 30.

    a. Find $P(95 \leq \bar{X} \leq 105)$ if sampling is performed without replacement.

    b. Find $P(95 \leq \bar{X} \leq 105)$ if sampling is performed with replacement.

APPLYING THE NEW CONCEPTS

7.11 The electric bill for 250 households in a small midwestern town was found to have a mean of $120 with a standard deviation of $25 for the month of November. If 10 households are selected at random from the 250 households, what is the probability that the sample mean will be between $110 and $130? What are you assuming about the population?

7.12 General Appliances has 70 microwave ovens that need repair. The mean cost of repair for the 70 microwaves is $80. The standard deviation of the cost is $35. The cost can be considered to be approximately normally distributed.

    a. If a sample of 10 of the 70 microwaves is selected without replacement, what is the probability that the mean cost for the sample is greater than $100?

    b. If a sample of 10 of the 70 microwaves is selected with replacement, what is the probability that the mean cost of the sample is greater than $100?

7.13 The mean daily time spent on the telephone by the 60 personnel managers of Retail Products is 1.25 hours; the standard deviation is .62 hours. Assuming that the time spent on the telephone is approximately normally distributed, what is the probability that the mean daily time spent on the telephone by 10 different personnel managers selected at random is greater than 1.5 hours?

7.14 Explain how the finite population correction factor is affected as the finite population size gets large for a fixed sample size.

7.15 A shipment of 200 treated lumber boards arrives at a construction site. The lengths of the lumber boards are approximately normally distributed with a mean of 10 feet and a standard deviation of .14 feet. Would it be considered unusual for a quality inspector to find a sample of 20 lumber boards with a mean of 9.92 feet or less?

7.16 The unification of Germany in 1990 spurred optimistic anticipation that East Germany's factory workers would be just as productive as those of West Germany. However, even in 1997, the average productivity of East Germany's factory work-

ers was 54% less than the productivity levels of West Germany's factory workers. Suppose that there are 75 automotive plants throughout East Germany and that the average productivity of these 75 plants was 54% less than productivity levels in West Germany, with a standard deviation of 4%. Assume that 25 of these automotive plants were randomly sampled and that the percent of productivity that each plant was below the standard levels in West Germany was recorded. What is the probability that the sample mean will be between 52% and 56%? What are you assuming here about the distribution of the data?

(Adapted from *The Wall Street Journal*, "Why Eastern Germany Still Lags," June 11, 1998, p. A22.)

USING THE COMPUTER

7.17 Generate a random sample of 10 observations from a normal population with a mean of 100 and a standard deviation of 20. Repeat this 30 times. Find the sample means for each of the 30 samples. Plot a histogram and describe the distribution of the sample means. In Excel, click on **Tools ➤ Data Analysis ➤ Random Number Generation.** For the number of variables type in "30", and for the number of random numbers type in "10". Select the normal distribution and type into the parameter boxes the mean of 100 and the standard deviation of 20. Type in "A1" for the output range. Click "OK", and then in cell A11 type in "=Average(A1:A10)". Drag cell A11 to cell AD11. Highlight A11 through AD11 and click "copy". Click on A13 and then on **Edit ➤ Paste Special** and click on the options values and transpose. The 30 averages will appear in column A starting in cell A13. To plot a histogram, click on **KGP Data Analysis ➤ Quantitative Data Charts/Tables ➤ Histogram/Freq. Charts.** Specify the input as being cells A13:A42. After clicking on the OK button, view the shape of the histogram. From cells A13:A42, find the sample mean and standard deviation of these values by using the menu provided from clicking on **Paste Function ➤ Statistical.**

7.18 Plot the normal distribution bell-shaped curve for values between 40 and 60 for a normal population with a mean of 50 and a standard deviation of 5. In addition, plot a similar normal curve except with a standard deviation of 5/sqrt(25). This standard deviation is selected to illustrate the effect of obtaining samples of size 25. Comment on the shape of the two distributions. To obtain this plot in Excel, first put integer values from 40 to 60 in column A, starting in cell A1. In cell B1, type in "=NORMDIST(A1, 50, 5, 0)". Drag this cell to B21. Likewise, type into cell C1 "=NORMDIST(A1, 50, 5/sqrt(25), 0)". Drag this cell to C21. Now use the Chart Wizard to obtain a line plot of the normal curve values in columns B and C. The result should be the chart presented below after proper labeling.

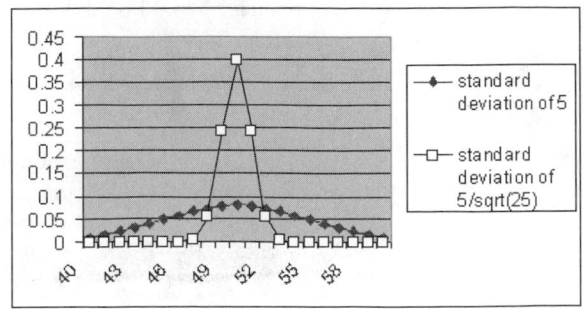

7.3 CONFIDENCE INTERVALS FOR THE MEAN OF A NORMAL POPULATION (σ KNOWN)

Return to the situation where we have obtained a sample from a normal population with unknown mean, μ. We first consider a case in which we know σ, the standard deviation of the normal random variable (Figure 7.14). (The situation where both μ and σ are unknown is dealt with in the next section.)

We know that to estimate μ, the average of the entire population, we obtain a sample from this population and calculate $\overline{X}$, the average of the sample. The sample mean, $\overline{X}$, is the estimate of μ and is also called a **point estimate**, because it consists of a single number.

In Example 7.3, it was assumed that the assembly time for a particular electrical component followed a normal distribution, with $\mu = 20$ minutes and $\sigma = 3$ minutes. What if μ is not known for *all* workers? A random sample of 25 workers' assembly times was obtained with the following results (in minutes):

> 22.8, 29.3, 27.2, 30.2, 24.0, 23.2, 22.9, 30.3, 27.1, 31.2, 27.0, 32.0, 28.6, 24.1, 28.9, 26.8, 26.6, 23.4, 25.1, 26.6, 25.7, 28.1, 31.5, 24.8, 25.2

Based on these data,

$$\text{estimate of } \mu = \text{sample mean, } \overline{X}$$

$$= \frac{22.8 + 29.3 + \cdots + 25.2}{25} = 26.9 \text{ minutes}$$

Is this large value of $\overline{X}$ (= 26.9) due to random chance? We know that 50% of the samples drawn will have $\overline{X}$ larger than 20, even if $\mu = 20$ (Figure 7.15). Or is this value large because μ is a value larger than 20? In other words, does this value of $\overline{X}$ provide just cause for concluding that μ is larger than 20? We tackle this type of question in Chapter 8.

FIGURE 7.14

An example where the standard deviation σ is known but the mean μ is unknown.

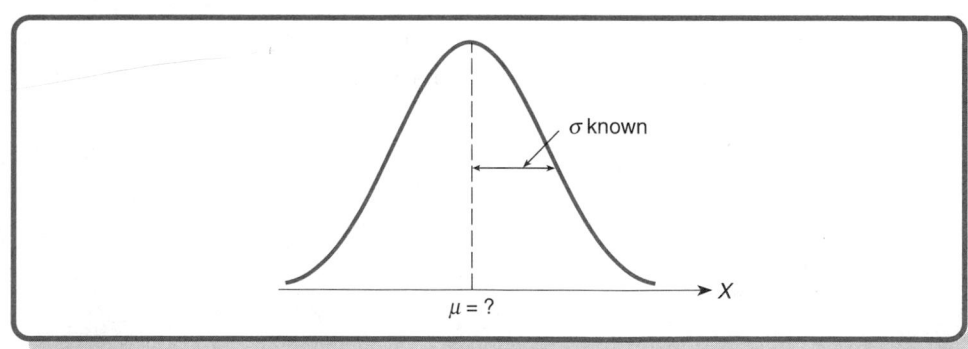

FIGURE 7.15

Distribution of $\overline{X}$ if $\mu = 20$ minutes.

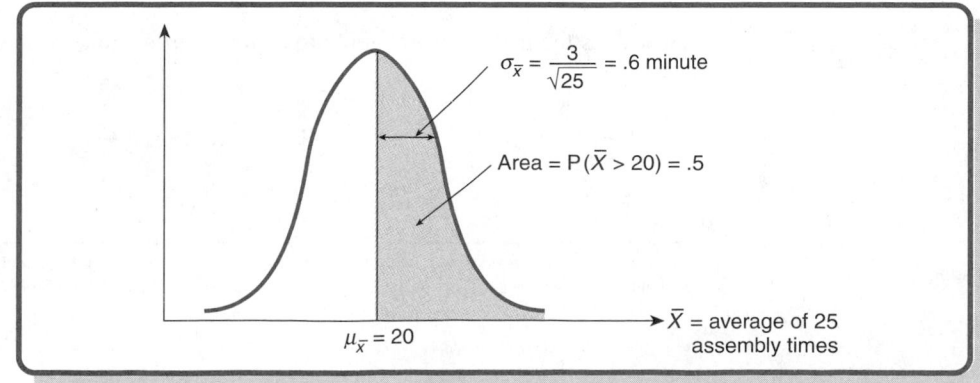

FIGURE 7.16
$P(-1.96 \leq Z \leq 1.96) = .95.$

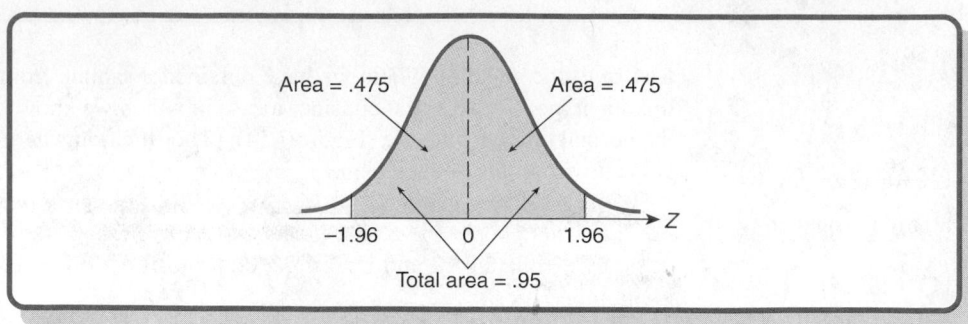

How accurate is a derived estimate of the population mean, μ? The accuracy depends, for one thing, on the sample size. We can measure the precision of this estimate by constructing a **confidence interval.** By providing the confidence interval, one can make such statements as "I am 95% confident that the average assembly time, μ, is between 25.7 minutes and 28.1 minutes." For this illustration, (25.7, 28.1) is called a 95% confidence interval for μ. The following discussion demonstrates how to construct such a confidence interval.

Using comment 3 on page 261, we know that $\overline{X}$ is a normal random variable with

$$\mu_{\overline{X}} = \mu$$

$$\sigma_{\overline{X}} = \frac{\sigma}{\sqrt{n}}$$

where μ and σ represent the mean and standard deviation of the population.* To standardize $\overline{X}$, you subtract the mean (μ) of $\overline{X}$ and divide by the standard deviation ($\sigma / \sqrt{n}$) of $\overline{X}$. Consequently,

$$Z = \frac{\overline{X} - \mu}{\sigma / \sqrt{n}}$$

is a standard normal random variable. Consider the following statement and refer to Figure 7.16:

$$P(-1.96 \leq Z \leq 1.96) = .95$$

so

$$P\left(-1.96 \leq \frac{\overline{X} - \mu}{\sigma / \sqrt{n}} \leq 1.96\right) = .95$$

After some algebra and rearrangement of terms, we get

$$P\left(\overline{X} - 1.96 \frac{\sigma}{\sqrt{n}} \leq \mu \leq \overline{X} + 1.96 \frac{\sigma}{\sqrt{n}}\right) = .95$$

How does the last statement apply to a *particular* sample mean, $\overline{x}$? Consider the interval

$$\left(\overline{x} - 1.96 \frac{\sigma}{\sqrt{n}}, \; \overline{x} + 1.96 \frac{\sigma}{\sqrt{n}}\right) \tag{7.7}$$

Confidence Interval

---

* This discussion ignores the finite population correction (fpc) factor defined in the previous section. For the case of sampling without replacement, where the population size (N) is known, see the discussion of simple random sampling in Section 7.6.

FIGURE 7.17
$1.28 = Z_{.1}$, $1.645 = Z_{.05}$, and
$1.96 = Z_{.025}$.

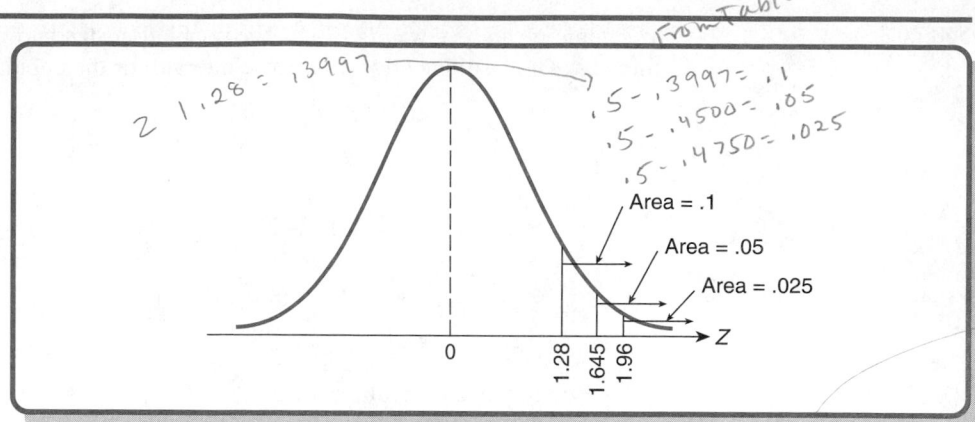

[handwritten notes in margins]

Ex .10 is
10% risk of rejecting H₀ when it is correct

For Hypoth Testing

Significance Level alpha ∝

90% confident that it is betw x̄ + +

10% = .10
5% = .05
1% = .01

Convertin CI Levels to Z
∝/2 :
Z or ⊕ = 1.645
90% = Z .05
95% = Z .025   Z or ⊕ = 1.96
99% = Z .005   Z or ⊕ = 2.58
10% = Z .45   Z or ⊕ = .0199

Using the values from our assembly-time example, we have $\bar{x} = 26.9$, $\sigma = 3$, and $n = 25$. The resulting 95% confidence interval is

$$\left(26.9 - 1.96 \cdot \frac{3}{\sqrt{25}}, \ 26.9 + 1.96 \cdot \frac{3}{\sqrt{25}} \right)$$

or

$$(25.72, 28.08)$$

Since μ is unknown, we do not know whether μ lies between 25.72 and 28.08 minutes. However, if you were to obtain random samples repeatedly, calculate $\bar{x}$, and determine the intervals defined by formula 7.7, then 95% of these intervals would contain μ and 5% would not. For this reason, formula 7.7 is called a **95% confidence interval** for μ. Using our assembly-time illustration, we are 95% confident that the average assembly time, μ, lies between 25.72 and 28.08 minutes.

NOTATION.   Let Z_a denote the value of Z such that the area *to the right* of this value is equal to a. How can we determine $Z_{.025}$, $Z_{.05}$, and $Z_{.1}$ (Figure 7.17)? Using Table A.4, $Z_{.025} = 1.96$, $Z_{.05} = 1.645$, and $Z_{.1} = 1.28$.

When defining a confidence interval for μ, we can define a 99% confidence interval, a 95% confidence interval, a 90% confidence interval, or whatever. The specific percentage represents the **confidence level**. The *higher* the confidence level, the *wider* the confidence interval. The confidence level is written as $(1 - \alpha) \cdot 100\%$, where $\alpha = .01$ for a 99% confidence interval, $\alpha = .05$ for a 95% confidence interval, and so on. Thus, a $(1 - \alpha) \cdot 100\%$ confidence interval for the mean of a normal population, μ, is

$$\left[\bar{x} - Z_{\alpha/2}\left(\frac{\sigma}{\sqrt{n}} \right), \ \bar{x} + Z_{\alpha/2}\left(\frac{\sigma}{\sqrt{n}} \right) \right] \tag{7.8}$$

According to the Central Limit Theorem, formula 7.8 provides an approximate confidence interval for the mean of any population, provided the sample size, n, is large (n > 30).

EXAMPLE 7.6   Determine a 90% and a 99% confidence interval for the average assembly time of all workers using the 25 observations given on page 271.

SOLUTION

The sample mean here was $\bar{x} = 26.9$. The population standard deviation is assumed to be 3 minutes. The resulting 90% confidence interval for the population mean μ is

$$26.9 - Z_{.05}\left(\frac{3}{\sqrt{25}}\right) \quad \text{to} \quad 26.9 + Z_{.05}\left(\frac{3}{\sqrt{25}}\right)$$

$$= 26.9 - 1.645\left(\frac{3}{\sqrt{25}}\right) \quad \text{to} \quad 26.9 + 1.645\left(\frac{3}{\sqrt{25}}\right)$$

$$= 26.9 - .99 \quad \text{to} \quad 26.9 + .99$$

$$= 25.91 \text{ minutes} \quad \text{to} \quad 27.89 \text{ minutes}$$

The 99% confidence interval for μ is

$$26.9 - Z_{.005}\left(\frac{3}{\sqrt{25}}\right) \quad \text{to} \quad 26.9 + Z_{.005}\left(\frac{3}{\sqrt{25}}\right)$$

$$= 26.9 - 2.575\left(\frac{3}{\sqrt{25}}\right) \quad \text{to} \quad 26.9 + 2.575\left(\frac{3}{\sqrt{25}}\right)$$

$$= 26.9 - 1.54 \quad \text{to} \quad 26.9 + 1.54$$

$$= 25.36 \text{ minutes} \quad \text{to} \quad 28.44 \text{ minutes}$$

Consequently, we are 90% confident that the mean assembly time for all workers is between 25.91 and 27.89 minutes. We are also 99% confident that this parameter is between 25.36 and 28.44 minutes, based on the results of this sample. Notice that the width of the interval increases as the confidence level increases when using the same sample data.

DISCUSSING A CONFIDENCE INTERVAL

The narrower your confidence interval, the better, for the same level of confidence. Suppose Electricalc spent $50,000 investigating the average time necessary to assemble their electrical components. Part of this study included obtaining a confidence interval for the average assembly time, μ. Which statement would they prefer to see?

1. I am 95% confident that the average assembly time is between 2 minutes and 50 minutes.
2. I am 95% confident that the average assembly time is between 25 minutes and 27 minutes.

The information contained in the first statement is practically worthless, and that's $50,000 down the drain. The second statement contains useful information; μ is narrowed down to a much smaller range.

  Given the second statement, can you tell what the corresponding value of $\bar{X}$ was that produced this confidence interval? For any confidence interval for μ, $\bar{X}$ (the estimate of μ) is always *in the center*. So $\bar{X}$ must have been 26 minutes.

  For the 90% confidence interval in Example 7.6, the following conclusions are valid:

1. I am 90% confident that the average assembly time for the population (μ) lies between 25.91 and 27.89 minutes.
2. If I repeatedly obtained samples of size 25, then 90% of the resulting confidence intervals would contain μ and 10% would not. (Question from the audience: Does this confidence interval [25.91, 27.89] contain μ? Your response: I don't know. All I can say is that this procedure leads to an interval containing μ 90% of the time.)

3. I am 90% confident that my estimate of μ (namely, $\bar{x} = 26.9$) is within .99 minute of the actual value of μ.

Here .99 is equal to $1.645 \cdot (\sigma / \sqrt{n})$. This quantity is referred to as the **maximum error, E.**

$$E = \text{maximum error} = Z_{\alpha/2}\left(\frac{\sigma}{\sqrt{n}}\right) \qquad (7.9)$$

Be careful! The following statement is *not* correct: The probability that μ lies between 25.91 and 27.89 is .90. What is the probability that the number 27 lies in this confidence interval? How about 24? The answer to the first question is 1, and to the second, 0, because 27 lies in the confidence interval and 24 does not. So what is the probability that μ lies in the confidence interval? Remember that μ is a fixed number; we just do not know what its value is. It is *not* a random variable, unlike its estimator, $\bar{X}$. As a result, this probability is either 0 or 1, not .90. Therefore, remember that once you have inserted your sample results into formula 7.8 to obtain your confidence interval, the word *probability* can no longer be used to describe the resulting confidence interval.

EXAMPLE 7.7

Refer to the 20 samples of Everglo bulbs in Table 7.1. Using sample 1, what is the resulting 95% confidence interval for the population mean, μ? Assume that σ is 50 hours.

SOLUTION

Here, $n = 10$ and $\bar{x} = 384.0$. The confidence level is 95%, so $Z_{\alpha/2} = Z_{.025} = 1.96$ (from Table A.4). Therefore, the resulting 95% confidence interval for μ is

$$384.0 - 1.96\left(\frac{50}{\sqrt{10}}\right) \quad \text{to} \quad 384.0 + 1.96\left(\frac{50}{\sqrt{10}}\right)$$

$$= 384.0 - 31.0 \quad \text{to} \quad 384.0 + 31.0$$

$$= 353.0 \quad \text{to} \quad 415.0$$

So we are 95% confident that μ lies between 353 and 415 hours. Also, we are 95% confident that our estimate of μ ($\bar{x} = 384.0$) is within 31.0 hours of the actual value.

USING EXCEL TO DETERMINE A CONFIDENCE INTERVAL FOR A POPULATION MEAN (σ KNOWN)

You can determine this type of confidence interval very easily using Excel. The two commands that are necessary are AVERAGE and CONFIDENCE, as illustrated in Figure 7.18. To see how this works, enter the 10 values from Example 7.7 into column A. In cell B1, click on the **Paste Function** icon (f_x) and **Statistical** under **Function Category** and **AVERAGE** under **Function Name.** Enter "A1:A10" in the Number1 box, as shown in the top panel of Figure 7.18, and then click on "OK." To obtain the maximum error, E, click on cell B2. Then click on the **Paste Function** icon and **Statistical** under **Function Category** and **CONFIDENCE** under **Function Name.** Fill in the values as shown in the bottom panel of Figure 7.18, and click on "OK." The number in cell B2 is the value of E.

To determine the confidence interval, you must add and subtract the values in cells B1 and B2. So, (1) in cell B3, enter "=B1-B2"; (2) in cell B4, enter "=B1+B2"; (3) in cell C3, enter "LL" (for Lower Limit); and (4) in cell C4, enter "UL" (Upper Limit). The results of all this are shown in Figure 7.19, which agree with the solution found in Example 7.7.

FIGURE 7.18
Excel screens for commands
AVERAGE and CONFIDENCE.

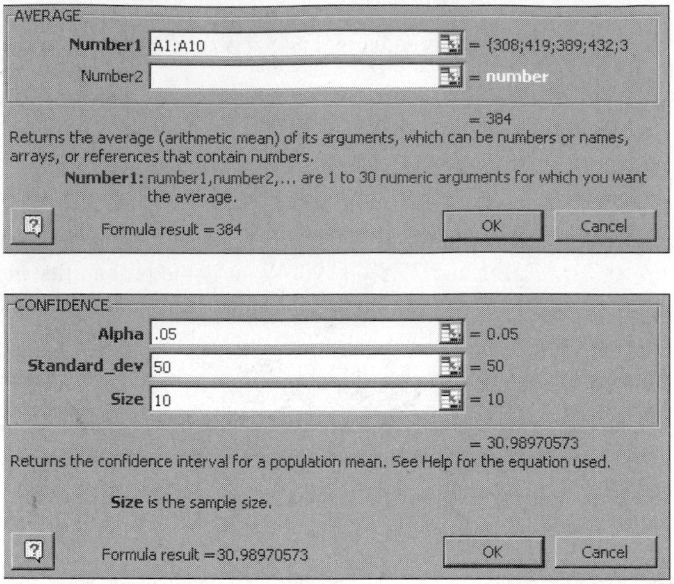

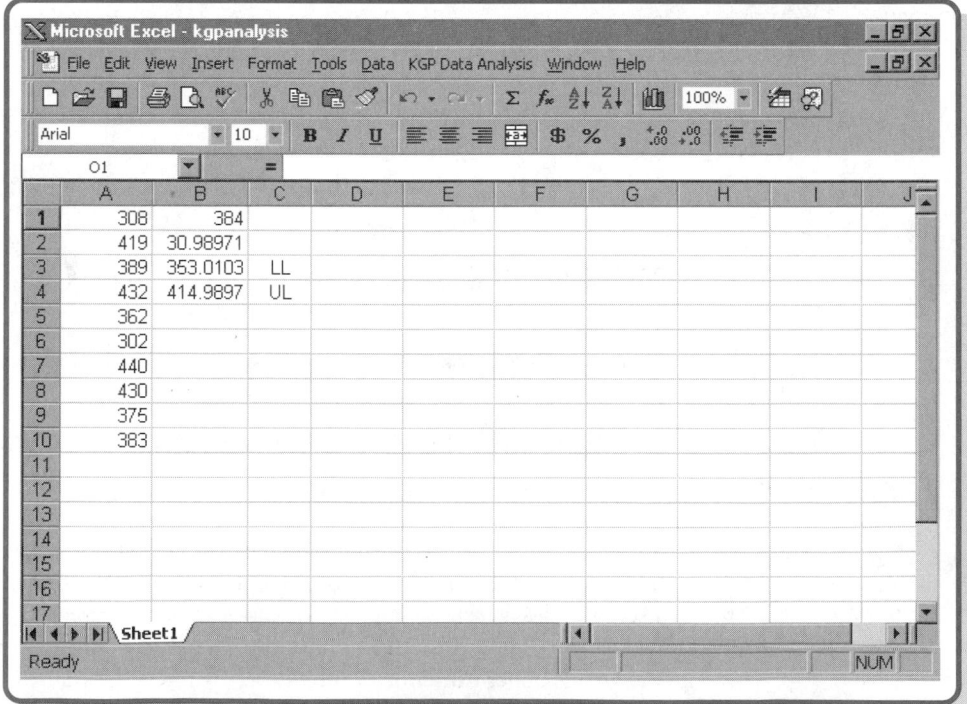

FIGURE 7.19
Excel spreadsheet containing a
95% confidence interval in
cells B3 and B4.

MICROSOFT® EXCEL APPLICATION   **USE DATA7-2**

EXAMPLE 7.8
How Many Confidence
Intervals Contain the
Population Mean?

Referring to Example 7.7, if the procedure of obtaining samples of size 10 were repeated indefinitely, we would expect 95% of the resulting confidence intervals to contain the population mean (known to be $\mu = 400$ here), and 5% would not. To illustrate this, repeat Example 7.7 using all 20 samples contained in DATA7-2.

FIGURE 7.20

Confidence intervals created using **KGP Data Analysis ➤ Means and CIs for Multiple Samples.**

File Edit View Insert Format Tools Data KGP Data Analysis Window Help								
	P	Q	R	S	T	U	V	W	X	Y
1	491	439	331	418	428	**Multiple Samples**				
2	353	336	427	422	368	SAMPLE	MEANS	E	Lower 95%	Upper 95%
3	375	425	445	341	445	1	384.00	30.99	353.01	414.99
4	536	419	420	485	429	2	399.50	30.99	368.51	430.49
5	447	346	401	442	475	3	397.30	30.99	366.31	428.29
6	415	408	389	470	437	4	399.40	30.99	368.41	430.39
7	322	392	363	404	475	5	414.40	30.99	383.41	445.39
8	350	409	439	370	458	6	393.20	30.99	362.21	424.19
9	453	313	352	539	308	7	398.80	30.99	367.81	429.79
10	343	334	346	435	408	8	403.80	30.99	372.81	434.79
11						9	402.80	30.99	371.81	433.79
12						10	404.60	30.99	373.61	435.59
13						11	401.90	30.99	370.91	432.89
14						12	385.60	30.99	354.61	416.59
15						13	408.20	30.99	377.21	439.19
16						14	411.00	30.99	380.01	441.99
17						15	415.60	30.99	384.61	446.59
18						16	408.50	30.99	377.51	439.49
19						17	382.10	30.99	351.11	413.09
20						18	391.30	30.99	360.31	422.29
21						19	432.60	30.99	401.61	463.59
22						20	423.10	30.99	392.11	454.09
23						SUMMARY FOR X-BARs				
24						Mean	402.89			
25						St. Dev.	12.78			
26										

DATA7-2

SOLUTION

To make your life a bit easier, we have written an Excel macro inside KGP Data Analysis that will construct these 20 intervals. First, open file DATA7-2. Then click on **KGP Data Analysis ➤ Means and CIs for Multiple Samples.** Click on **Means and CIs** at the bottom of the input form and enter "A1:T10" as the **Input Range,** "50" as the **Population Std. Dev.,** "95" as the **Confidence Level,** and "U1" as the **Output Range.** The output from this macro is shown in Figure 7.20. Notice that all the samples contain the known mean (μ = 400) except sample 19 (highlighted). In practice, however, the population mean is *unknown,* so all we can say is that this procedure will produce a confidence interval containing the population mean 95% of the time.

EXERCISES 7.19–7.30

UNDERSTANDING THE MECHANICS

7.19 A random sample of 100 observations is obtained from a normally distributed population with a standard deviation of 10. What is a 95% confidence interval for the mean of the population if the sample mean is 40?

7.20 Construct a 90% confidence interval for the mean of a normally distributed population with a variance of 144 using the following data from a simple random sample.

    43 30 50 33 63 65 53 72 45 69
    66 63 58 73 62 57 58 78 55 70

7.21 Fifty observations are randomly selected from a normally distributed population with a population standard deviation of 25. The sample mean is 175.
- **a.** Find a 90% confidence interval for the mean.
- **b.** Find a 95% confidence interval for the mean.
- **c.** Find a 99% confidence interval for the mean.

APPLYING THE NEW CONCEPTS

7.22 The monthly advertising expenditure of Discount Hardware Store is normally distributed with a standard deviation of $100. If a sample of 10 randomly selected months yields a mean advertising expenditure of $380 monthly, what is a 90% confidence interval for the mean of the store's monthly advertising expenditure?

7.23 In analyzing the operating cost for a huge fleet of delivery trucks, a manager takes a sample of 25 cars and calculates the sample mean and sample standard deviation. Then he finds a 95% confidence interval for the mean cost to be $253 to $320. He reasons that this interval contains the mean operating cost for the fleet of delivery trucks since the sample mean is contained in the interval. Do you agree? How would you interpret this confidence interval?

7.24 The perfectionist owner of Kwik Kar Kare has reduced an oil-change job to a science and wants to keep it that way. The owner constantly monitors the performance of the staff. This week, 15 oil-change jobs were sampled with a sample mean of 9.8 minutes per job. Experience has shown that the times follow a normal distribution, and the standard deviation of the population is known to be 1.2 minutes. Based on this week's sample, construct a 90% confidence interval for the population mean (average time for an oil-change job).

7.25 Ozone alerts can affect the events of many cities across the United States. Ozone is a nearly invisible gas formed when fuel byproducts—oxides of nitrogen and hydrocarbons—are heated by the summer sun. This makes ozone an irritant to the respiratory tract. The federal Environmental Protection Agency is particularly concerned when the ozone limits are above 80 ppb (parts per billion). Suppose that a random sample of counties in the Midwest revealed an average of 75 ppb. Assume that the population standard deviation of the ppb of ozone in the midwest is 6 ppb. Construct a 95% confidence interval for the population mean using

(Adapted from *The Wall Street Journal,* "Pollution from Ozone Is a Lot More Harmful to Us Than It Looks," June 22, 1998, p. B1.)

    a. a sample of size 20
    b. a sample of size 50
    c. a sample of size 200

7.26 A quality-control engineer is concerned about the breaking strength of a metal wire manufactured to stringent specifications. A sample of size 25 is randomly obtained, and the breaking strengths are recorded. The breaking strength of the wire is considered to be normally distributed with a standard deviation of 3. Find a 95% confidence interval for the mean breaking strength of the wire.

    26, 27, 18, 23, 24, 20, 21, 24, 19, 27, 25, 20, 24, 21, 26, 19, 21, 20, 25, 20, 23, 25, 21, 20, 21

7.27 Federal law requires GTE to allow competing long-distance carriers to use its infrastructure, and it regulates how much GTE can charge for the service. To compensate for the lost revenue from new federal regulations related to long-distance access charges, GTE has asked the Idaho Public Utilities Commission for permission to approve hikes in basic monthly rates. Commission members will schedule public meetings and seek written comments from customers before making a decision. Suppose that the standard deviation of charges to business customers by GTE in Idaho is $10. A concerned business association surveyed 20 business members to collect data on the monthly charges paid to GTE to reveal how high current charges were. Construct a 90% confidence interval on the average business cus-

tomer's monthly bill to GTE using the data below. What assumption is necessary for this to be a reliable confidence interval?

| 35 | 45 | 57 | 21 | 46 | 78 | 52 | 32 | 24 | 81 |
| 34 | 29 | 45 | 51 | 33 | 26 | 46 | 37 | 40 | 34 |

(Adapted from *Spokane Spokesman-Review,* "GTE Requests Rate Increase In North Idaho," May 30, 1998, p. B2.)

7.28 As the sample size increases, would a confidence interval given by equation 7.8 get smaller or larger? For a given random sample, would the confidence interval given by equation 7.8 for a 90% confidence interval be wider or narrower than that obtained using an 80% confidence level?

USING THE COMPUTER

7.29 **[DATA SET EX7-29]** *Variable description:*

Billing: Amount billed by a marital counselor

An auditor reviewed the billings by a marital counselor. The auditor knows that past billings have been approximately normally distributed with a standard deviation of $50. A random sample of 60 billings is recorded for variable Billing.

    a. Find a 95% confidence interval for the mean number of billings. In Excel, click on **KGP Data Analysis ➤ One Population Inference.** Use the **Population Mean (*z* statistic)** option. Fill in the input range and type in "5" for the alpha level, since the confidence level is 95%. Click on **Confidence Interval** and type in a standard deviation of "50." Select an output range and click on OK.

    b. In part (b), change the standard deviation to 25. How much has the length of the confidence interval changed?

7.30 **[DATA SET EX7-30]** *Variable description:*

Savings: Amount in a personal savings account

The marketing department of Gibraltar State Bank is interested in the average monthly balance in personal savings accounts in which individuals have a direct deposit for their checks from work. The bank has found that the monthly balances on personal savings accounts to be normally distributed with a standard deviation of 200. A random sample of 100 monthly balances of personal savings accounts is drawn, and the data are labeled as Savings.

    a. Find a 90% confidence interval on the mean amount of the monthly balances in personal savings accounts. Interpret this interval. In Excel, click on **KGP Data Analysis ➤ One Population Inference,** and use the confidence interval option. Use the **Population Mean (*z* statistic)** option in the first box.

    b. Repeat part (a) using a 90% confidence interval. Compare the length of the confidence intervals.

7.4 CONFIDENCE INTERVALS FOR THE MEAN OF A NORMAL POPULATION (σ UNKNOWN)

If σ is unknown, it is impossible to determine a confidence interval for μ using formula 7.8 because we are unable to evaluate the standard error $\sigma/\sqrt{n}$. Let us take another look at how we estimate the parameters of a normal population.

When a population mean is unknown, we can estimate it using the sample mean. The logical thing to do if σ is unknown is to replace it by its estimate, the standard deviation of the sample, *s*. But consider what happens when

$$\frac{\bar{X} - \mu}{\sigma/\sqrt{n}}$$

is replaced by

$$\frac{\overline{X} - \mu}{s / \sqrt{n}}$$

This is no longer a standard normal random variable, Z. However, it does follow another identifiable distribution, the **t distribution.** Its complete name is *Student's t distribution,* named after W. S. Gosset, a statistician in a Guinness brewery who used the pen name Student. The distribution of

$$\frac{\overline{X} - \mu}{s / \sqrt{n}}$$

will follow a t distribution, *provided* the population from which you are obtaining the sample is normally distributed.

The t distribution is similar in appearance to the standard normal (Z) distribution in that it is symmetric about zero. Unlike the Z distribution, however, its shape depends on the sample size, n. Consequently, when you use the t distribution, you must take into account the sample size. This is accomplished by using **degrees of freedom.** For this application using the t distribution,

$$\text{degrees of freedom} = \text{df} = n - 1$$

The value of df $= n - 1$ can be explained by observing that for a given value of $\overline{X}$, only $n - 1$ of the sample values are free to vary. For example, in a sample of size $n = 3$, if $\overline{x} = 5.0, x_1 = 2$, and $x_2 = 7$, then x_3 must be 6 because this is the only value providing a sample mean equal to 5.0.

Two t distributions are illustrated in Figure 7.21. Notice that the t distributions are symmetrically distributed about zero but have wider tails than does the standard normal, Z. Observe that as n increases, the t distribution tends toward the standard normal, Z. In fact, for $n > 30$, there is little difference between these two distributions. Values having a specified tail area under a t curve are provided in Table A.5 for various df. So, for large samples ($n > 30$), it does not matter whether σ is known (Z distribution, Table A.4) or σ is unknown (t distribution, Table A.5) because the t and Z curves are practically the same. For this reason, the t distribution often is referred to as the **small-sample distribution** for $\overline{X}$. The Z table can be used as an approximation even if σ is unknown, provided n is larger than 30. *Remember, however, that a more accurate confidence interval is always obtained using the t table when the sample standard deviation (s) is used in the construction of this interval.*

Using the t distribution, then, a $(1 - \alpha) \cdot 100\%$ confidence interval for μ is

$$\overline{x} - t_{\alpha/2, n-1}\left(\frac{s}{\sqrt{n}}\right) \qquad \text{to} \qquad \overline{x} + t_{\alpha/2, n-1}\left(\frac{s}{\sqrt{n}}\right) \qquad\qquad \textbf{(7.10)}$$

where $t_{\alpha/2, n-1}$ denotes the t value from Table A.5 using a t curve with $n - 1$ df and a right-tail area of $\alpha/2$.

FIGURE 7.21

The *t* distribution.

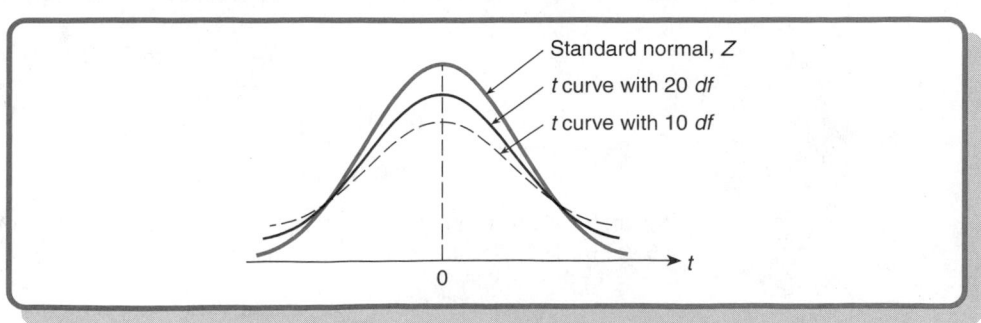

Standard normal, Z

t curve with 20 *df*

t curve with 10 *df*

0

Do you remember our sample of 25 assembly times that produced a point estimate for μ having a value of $\bar{x} = 26.9$ minutes? This estimate was used in Example 7.6, where it was assumed that the population standard deviation was $\sigma = 3$, in constructing a confidence interval for μ. Furthermore, the assembly times were assumed to follow a *normal* distribution.

Suppose that we do not know σ, either. Then the point estimate of the population standard deviation is

$$s = \sqrt{\frac{(22.8^2 + 29.3^2 + \cdots + 25.2^2) - (22.8 + 29.3 + \cdots + 25.2)^2/25}{24}}$$

$$= \sqrt{\frac{18,285.14 - (672.6)^2/25}{24}}$$

$$= \sqrt{7.896} = 2.81 \text{ minutes}$$

Using Table A.5 to find a 90% confidence interval for μ, you first determine that

$$t_{\alpha/2, n-1} = t_{.05, 24} = 1.711$$

The resulting 90% confidence interval is

$$26.9 - 1.711\left(\frac{2.81}{\sqrt{25}}\right) \quad \text{to} \quad 26.9 + 1.711\left(\frac{2.81}{\sqrt{25}}\right)$$

$$= 26.9 - .96 \quad \text{to} \quad 26.9 + .96$$

$$= 25.94 \quad \text{to} \quad 27.86$$

Using these data, we are 90% confident that the estimate for the mean of this normal population ($\bar{x} = 26.9$) is within .96 minute of the actual value. Comparing this result with Example 7.6, we notice little difference in the two 90% confidence intervals. Their agreement is due mostly to the fact that the estimate of σ ($s = 2.81$) is very close to the assumed value of $\sigma = 3$.

EXAMPLE 7.9

The output voltage of power supplies manufactured by Clark Products is believed to follow a normal distribution. Of primary concern to the company is the average output voltage of a particular power supply unit, believed to be 10 volts. Eighteen observations taken at random from this unit are:

10.85, 11.40, 10.81, 10.24, 10.23, 9.49, 9.89, 10.11, 10.57, 11.21, 10.10, 11.22, 10.31, 11.24, 9.51, 10.52, 9.92, 8.33

What is the 95% confidence interval for the average output voltage for this power supply unit?

SOLUTION

Your point estimate of σ is $s = .767$ volt. Also, your point estimate of μ is $\bar{x} = 10.331$ volts. A 95% confidence interval for the average output voltage (μ) is

$$10.331 - t_{.025, 17}\left(\frac{.767}{\sqrt{18}}\right) \quad \text{to} \quad 10.331 + t_{.025, 17}\left(\frac{.767}{\sqrt{18}}\right)$$

$$= 10.331 - 2.11\left(\frac{.767}{\sqrt{18}}\right) \quad \text{to} \quad 10.331 + 2.11\left(\frac{.767}{\sqrt{18}}\right)$$

$$= 10.331 - .381 \quad \text{to} \quad 10.331 + .381$$

$$= 9.950 \quad \text{to} \quad 10.712$$

We are 95% confident that the average output voltage of this power supply unit is between 9.950 and 10.712 volts. Notice here that the maximum error is

$$E = 2.11\left(\frac{.767}{\sqrt{18}}\right) = .381 \text{ volt}$$

which implies that we are 95% confident that $\bar{X}$ is within .381 volt of the actual average voltage.

USING EXCEL TO DETERMINE A CONFIDENCE INTERVAL FOR A POPULATION MEAN (σ UNKNOWN)

Excel provides this type of confidence interval as an option in its DESCRIPTIVE STATISTICS command. To illustrate this procedure using Example 7.9, enter the 18 voltage values in column A. Then click on **Tools ➤ Data Analysis ➤ Descriptive Statistics** and fill in the boxes as illustrated in Figure 7.22. Be sure to click on the small boxes alongside **Summary Statistics** and **Confidence Level for Mean.** This produces columns B and C in Figure 7.23.

FIGURE 7.22

Input screen for using Excel's DESCRIPTIVE STATISTICS to determine a confidence interval for a population mean (σ unknown).

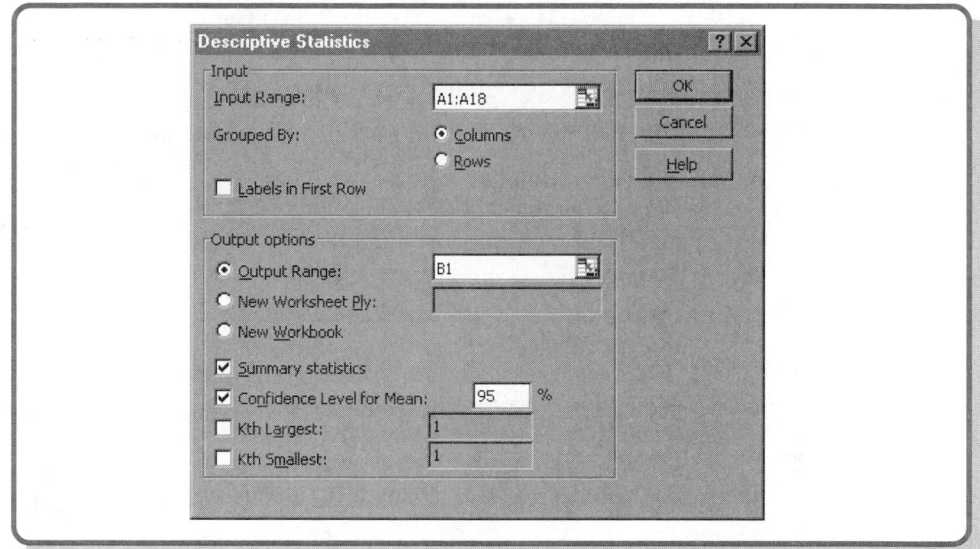

FIGURE 7.23

The Excel spreadsheet containing the 95% confidence interval in cells D1 and D2.

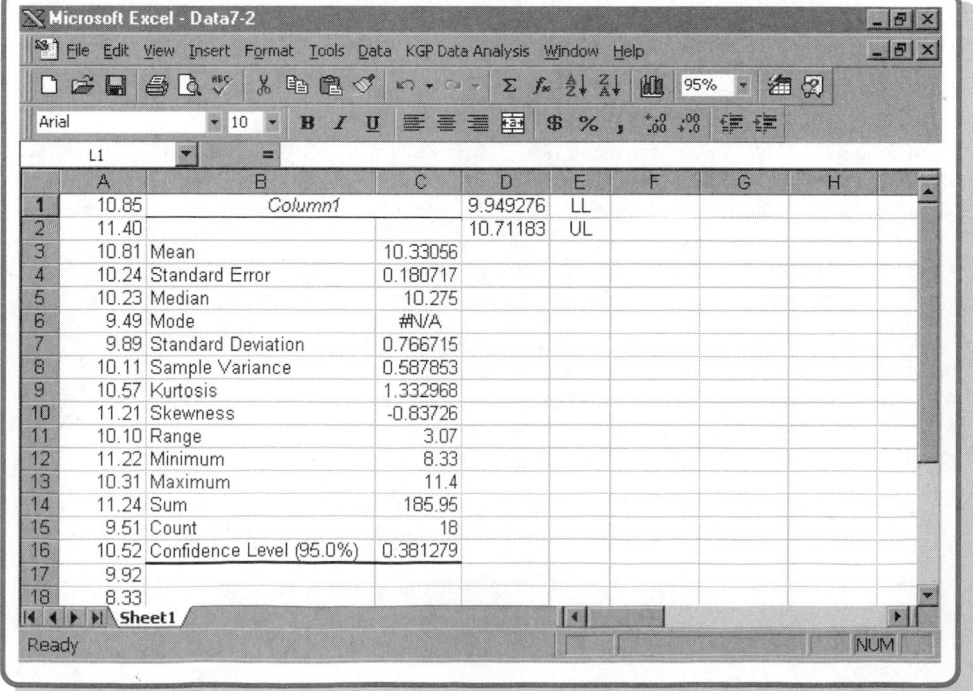

Referring to Figure 7.23, to obtain the confidence interval, we need to subtract and add cells C3 (the sample mean) and C16 (the maximum error, E). To do this, (1) click on cell D1 and enter "=c3-c16", (2) click on cell D2 and enter "=c3+c16", (3) enter "LL" in cell E1, and (4) enter "UL" in cell E2. The resulting confidence interval is shown in Figure 7.23, and this interval agrees with the solution to Example 7.9.

EXERCISES 7.31–7.42

UNDERSTANDING THE MECHANICS

7.31 For a t distribution with 20 degrees of freedom, what is the t value such that the following are true?
  a. 90% of the area under the t distribution is to the right of the t value.
  b. 10% of the area under the t distribution is to the right of the t value.
  c. 5% of the area under the t distribution is to the left of the t value.

7.32 A t distribution has 30 degrees of freedom.
  a. Find the area to the right of 2.750.
  b. Find the area to the left of 1.697.
  c. Find the area to the left of –1.310.
  d. Find the area between –2.042 and 2.042.

7.33 A random sample of size 20 is selected from a normally distributed population. The sample mean is 50 and the sample standard deviation is 10.
  a. Find a 90% confidence interval for the population mean.
  b. Find a 95% confidence interval for the population mean.
  c. Find a 99% confidence interval for the population mean.

APPLYING THE NEW CONCEPTS

7.34 The manager of a gift shop would like to estimate the average retail price of a particular greeting card by its competitors. A random sample of 20 retail stores in a 100-mile radius of the store were selected. The sample mean and standard deviation were $2.05 and $0.40, respectively. Find a 99% confidence interval for the mean price of the greeting card.

7.35 The mean monthly expenditure on gasoline per household in Middletown is determined by selecting a random sample of 36 households. The sample mean is $68, with a sample standard deviation of $17.
  a. What is a 95% confidence interval for the mean monthly expenditure on gasoline per household in Middletown?
  b. What is a 90% confidence interval for the mean monthly expenditure on gasoline per household in Middletown?

7.36 Second Federal Savings and Loan would like to estimate the mean number of years in which 30-year mortgages are paid off. Eighteen paid-off 30-year mortgages are randomly selected, and the numbers of years in which the loans were paid in full are

  19.6, 20.8, 29.6, 6.3, 3.1, 10.6, 30.0, 21.7, 10.5, 26.3, 10.7, 6.1, 7.3, 12.6, 9.8, 27.4, 20.1, 10.8

Assuming that the number of years in which 30-year mortgages are paid off is normally distributed, construct an 80% confidence interval for the mean number of years in which the mortgages are paid off.

7.37 An apartment-finder service would like to estimate the average cost of a one-bedroom apartment in Kansas City. A random sample of 41 apartment complexes yielded a mean of $310 with a standard deviation of $29. Construct a 90% confidence interval for the mean cost of one-bedroom apartments in Kansas City.

7.38 In his book *Privacy for Sale*, Jeffrey Rothfeder explains the story of Safeway Stores' installation of dashboard computers on 782 trucks. The computer gave a report showing any abnormal condition. For instance, if a truck's engine idled for 25 minutes on a trip for which the average idling time was only 10 minutes, then the driver would be questioned and possibly suspended.

Assume that a Canadian plant manager wished to determine an estimate of the mean idle time for the trucks. Idle times from a random sample of size 51 were recorded. The sample mean was 11.5 minutes, and the sample standard deviation was 5.3 minutes. Find a 90% confidence interval on the mean idle time for the trucks.

(Source: Adapted from "Experts Urge More Controls on Workplace Spying Gadgets," by Claire Bernstein, *Toronto Star*, Dec. 31, 1993, p. B1.)

7.39 An investment advisor believes that the return on interest-sensitive stocks is approximately normally distributed. A sample of 24 interest-sensitive stocks was selected, and their yearly return (including dividends and capital appreciation) was as follows (in percentages):

$\bar{x} = 10.99$

11.1, 12.5, 13.6, 9.1, 8.7, 10.6, 12.5, 15.6, 13.8, 8.0, 10.9, 7.6, 5.2, 1.2, 12.8, 16.7, 13.9, 10.1, 9.6, 10.8, 11.6, 12.3, 12.9, 11.6

Find a 90% confidence interval for the mean yearly return on interest-sensitive stocks.

7.40 Monthly fees by Internet service providers are competitive. The following 15 Internet service providers and their monthly fees in dollars were randomly sampled from an extensive list of Internet providers in *Computer Currents*. Find a 90% confidence interval on the mean monthly fee by Internet providers.

(Source: *Computer Currents*, "Internet Service Providers," Oct 1998, p. 90.)

Provider	Monthly Fee
Fast Lane	20
FlashNet	14
Industrial Strength Internet	12
IDT	30
Internet Global	25
Internet Texas	21
Mesh Net	17
Mind Spring	27
Netcom	20

Provider	Monthly Fee
Netgazer Solutions	15
NorthStar Technologies	16
SouthNet Telecom	18
Vnet Internet Access	25
WebUSA	20
WhyWeb	16

USING THE COMPUTER

7.41 [DATA SET EX7-41] *Variable description:*

Satisfact: Satisfaction rating on tile installation.

Home Interiors is interested in the satisfaction rating that it receives from its customers one year after it has installed tile flooring. The manager has collected a sample of 40 ratings by customers. The sample results are listed in variable Satisfact. The rating scale is between 1 and 10, with 10 representing the highest possible satisfaction and 1 representing total dissatisfaction with the job. Find a 95% confidence interval for the mean of Satisfact. In Excel, click on **KGP Data Analysis ➤ One Population Inference.** Use the **Population Mean with Est. Std. Dev. (*t* statistic)** option. Interpret the confidence interval.

7.42 [DATA SET EX7-42] *Variable description:*

ServiceTime: Time that it takes for a photocopy repair person to respond to a call about a malfunctioning photocopier.

A supplier of photocopying machines is interested in the time that it takes for a repair person to respond to a request for service when a photocopier is malfunctioning. A random sample of 35 calls is selected, and times in minutes are recorded for the repair person to respond. The variable ServiceTime is the label for the number of minutes to respond.

 a. Find a 90% confidence interval for the mean of Ser- viceTime. In Excel, click on **KGP Data Analysis ➤ One Population Inference.** Use the **Population Mean with Est. Std. Dev. (*t* statistic)** option. Interpret the confidence interval.

 b. Find a 99% confidence interval and compare the lengths of the confidence intervals.

7.5 SELECTING THE NECESSARY SAMPLE SIZE

SAMPLE SIZE FOR KNOWN σ

How large a sample do you need? This is often difficult to determine, although a carefully chosen *large* sample generally provides a better representation of the population than does a smaller sample. Acquiring large samples can be costly and time-consuming. Why obtain a sample of size $n = 1000$ if a sample size of $n = 500$ will provide sufficient accuracy for estimating a population mean? This section will show you how to determine what sample size is necessary when the maximum error, E, is specified in advance.

  In Example 7.7, we assumed that the lifetime of Everglo bulbs is normally distributed with standard deviation $\sigma = 50$ hours but unknown mean μ. Based on the results of sample 1 from Table 7.1, we concluded that we were 95% confident that the estimate of μ ($\bar{x} = 384.0$) was within 31.0 hours of the actual value of μ for $n = 10$. How large a sample is necessary if we want our point estimator ($\bar{x}$) to be within 15 hours of the actual value of μ, with 95% confidence? The value 15 here is the maximum error, E, defined in equation 7.9. We would like the estimate of μ (that is, $\bar{x}$) to be within 15 of the actual value, so

$$E = 15 = Z_{\alpha/2}\left(\frac{50}{\sqrt{n}}\right)$$

Because the confidence level is 95%, $Z_{\alpha/2} = Z_{.025} = 1.96$. Consequently,

$$15 = (1.96)\frac{50}{\sqrt{n}}$$

$$\sqrt{n} = \frac{(1.96)(50)}{15} = 6.53$$

Squaring both sides of this statement produces

$$n = (6.53)^2 = 42.68$$

To be a bit conservative, this number should always be rounded *up*. So a sample size of $n = 43$ will produce a confidence interval with $E \leq 15$ hours. Your point estimate of μ $\bar{x}$, will then be within 15 hours of the actual value, with 95% confidence.

This sequence of steps can be summarized by the following expression:

$$n = \left[\frac{Z_{\alpha/2} \cdot \sigma}{E} \right]^2 \tag{7.11}$$

SAMPLE SIZE FOR UNKNOWN σ *(Sigma)*

Equation 7.11 works if σ is known, but it does not apply to situations where both μ and σ *mean std dv* are unknown. There are two approaches to the latter situation.

A PRELIMINARY SAMPLING

If you have already obtained a small sample, you have an estimate of σ, namely, the sample standard deviation, *s*. Replacing σ by *s* in equation 7.11 gives you the desired sample size, *n*. Assuming that the resulting value of *n* is greater than 30, the $Z_{\alpha/2}$ notation in equation 7.11 is still valid because the actual *t* distribution here will be closely approximated by the standard normal distribution.

When you do obtain the confidence interval using the larger sample, the resulting maximum error, *E*, may not be exactly what you originally specified, because the new sample standard deviation will not be the same as that belonging to the smaller original sample.

EXAMPLE 7.10

In Example 7.9, Clark Products obtained 18 observations of the output voltages for a particular power supply unit. For these data,

$$\bar{x} = 10.331 \text{ volts}$$

$$s = .767 \text{ volt}$$

How large a sample would they need for $\bar{X}$ to be within .2 volts of the actual average output voltage with 95% confidence?

SOLUTION

Based on the results of the original sample, *s* = .767, so

$$n = \left[\frac{Z_{\alpha/2} \cdot s}{E} \right]^2 = \left[\frac{(1.96)(.767)}{.2} \right]^2 = 56.5$$

We round this number up to 57. Consequently, they would need 57 observations to make a statement with this much precision, that is, within .2 volt. Of course, they already have 18 observations that can be included in the larger sample.

OBTAINING A ROUGH APPROXIMATION OF σ

We know from the empirical rule and Table A.4 that 95.4% of the population will lie between μ – 2σ and μ + 2σ. Because (μ + 2σ) – (μ – 2σ) = 4σ, this is a span of 4 standard deviations. One method of obtaining an estimate of σ is to ask a person who is familiar with the data to be collected these questions:

1. What do you think will be the highest value in the sample (*H*)?
2. What will be the lowest value (*L*)?

The approximation of σ is then obtained by assuming that μ + 2σ = *H* and μ – 2σ = *L*, so

$$H - L = (\mu + 2\sigma) - (\mu - 2\sigma) = 4\sigma$$

Consequently,

$$\sigma \cong \frac{H - L}{4} \qquad (7.12)$$

In other words, a rough approximation of σ is the *anticipated range* $(H - L)$ divided by 4. This (somewhat conservative) estimate of σ can be used in equation 7.11 to determine the necessary sample size, n.

EXAMPLE 7.11

The manager of quality assurance for a division that produces hair dryers is interested in the average number of switches that can be tested by the division's employees. Assuming that the number of switches that are tested each hour by an employee follows a normal distribution (centered at μ), the manager wants to estimate μ with 90% confidence. Also, this estimate must be within one unit (switch) of μ. The manager estimates that H is 45 switches and L is 25 switches. How large a sample will be necessary?

SOLUTION

Based on $H = 45$ switches and $L = 25$ switches,

$$\sigma \cong \frac{45 - 25}{4} = 5 \text{ switches}$$

The sample size necessary to obtain a maximum error of $E = 1$ is

$$n = \left[\frac{(1.645)(5)}{1} \right]^2 = 67.7$$

Thus, a sample size of 68 should produce a value of E close to one switch. The value will not be exactly one because the sample standard deviation, s, probably will not be exactly 5. Estimating σ in this manner, however, produces a value that is in the neighborhood of σ.

EXERCISES 7.43–7.53

UNDERSTANDING THE MECHANICS

7.43 Assume that a 90% confidence interval on the mean is to be constructed with a maximum error of E. The population standard deviation is equal to 50. How large a sample is required if:
  a. $\bar{X}$ is to be within 10 units of the population mean.
  b. $\bar{X}$ is to be within 15 units of the population mean.
  c. $\bar{X}$ is to be within 5 units of the population mean.

7.44 A pilot study yielded the following random sample of 15 observations from a normally distributed population.

69 50 74 40 24 50 49 60 52 44 49 52 39 47 48

  a. Using the sample standard deviation as an estimate for the population standard deviation, what is the necessary sample size for the sample mean to be within 3 units of the population mean with 95% confidence?
  b. Repeat part (a) using the highest and lowest values of the observations to estimate the population standard deviation.

APPLYING THE NEW CONCEPTS

7.45 The Chamber of Commerce of Tampa, Florida, would like to estimate the mean amount of money spent by a tourist to within $100 with 95% confidence. If the amount of money spent by tourists is considered to be normally distributed with a standard deviation of $200, what sample size would be necessary for the Chamber of Commerce to meet their objective in estimating this mean amount?

7.46 Security Savings and Loan Association's manager would like to estimate the mean deposit by a customer into a savings account to within $500. If the deposits into savings accounts are considered to be normally distributed with a standard deviation of $1250, what sample size would be necessary to be 90% confident?

7.47 If a sample size of 70 was necessary to estimate the mean of a normal population to within 1.2 with 90% confidence, what is the approximate value of the standard deviation of the population?

7.48 The marketing agency for computer software of Personal Micro Systems would like to estimate with 95% confidence the mean time that it takes for a beginner to learn to use a standard software package. Past data indicate that the learning time can be approximated by a normal distribution with a standard deviation of 20 minutes. How large a sample size should the marketing agency choose if the mean time to learn to use the software package is to be estimated within 8 minutes with 90% confidence?

7.49 In an effort to lure vacationers to exotic locations, several vacation packages to world-class golf destinations, such as Scotland, New Zealand, and Maui, are offered by the major airlines and vacation agencies. The prices range from $1200 to $4000. Suppose that a travel agency wished to obtain a 90% confidence interval on the mean price of an exotic golf vacation offered by numerous vacation agencies throughout the United States. What sample size would be necessary to estimate the mean price to within $250?

(Adapted from *USA Today*, "Charting a Course For World-Class Tee Times," April 17, 1998, p. D1.)

7.50 A chemist at International Chemical would like to measure the adhesiveness of a new wood glue. From past experiments, a measure used to indicate adhesiveness has ranged from 7.3 to 11.1 units. To be 98% confident, how large a sample would be necessary to estimate the mean adhesiveness to within .5 units?

7.51 For the Canadian government and casino operators, gambling has provided the basis for a very profitable marriage. There are now 55 casinos in Canada, earning $2.5 billion a year, of which the government pockets $1.2 billion. The lion's share of that action is in Central Canada, which has five glitzy casinos—Niagara Falls, Windsor, and Casino Rama near Orillia in Ontario and Hull and Montreal in Quebec. A survey at one of these casinos revealed that the Canadian households that gamble spend between $100 and $3200 annually in gambling. What sample size would be necessary to estimate the average amount spent by Canadian households that visit the casinos so that the estimate of the average is within $150 with 95% confidence.

(Adapted from *Maclean Hunter Limited*, "The Curse of Casinos," May 11, 1998, p. 44.)

USING THE COMPUTER

7.52 To understand the quality of the approximation of the population standard deviation by using the highest and lowest values in a random sample, this exercise considers a simulation of observations from a population to calculate the approximation of the standard deviation.

a. Generate a random sample of 20 observations from a normal population with a mean of 100 and a standard deviation of 10. Repeat this 30 times. In Excel, click on **Tools ➤ Data Analysis ➤ Random Number Generation.** For the number of variables, type in "30," and for the number of random numbers, type in "10." Select the normal distribution and type into the parameter boxes the mean of "100" and the standard deviation of "10." Type in "A1" for the output range, and then click "OK."

b. Calculate the approximation of the population standard deviation for each of the 30 samples in part (a) using the formula: $(H - L)/4$. In Excel, type in cell A11: "=(MAX(A1:A10) – MIN(A1:A10))/4". Drag cell A11 through AD11.

c. Obtain a histogram of the approximations of the population standard deviation. Find the average of the 30 estimates. Considering that the actual population standard deviation is 10, comment on the accuracy of the estimates. In Excel, highlight A11 through AD11 and click **Copy.** Click on A13, then on **Edit ➤ Paste Special,** and then on the options **Values** and **Transpose.** The 30 averages will appear in column A starting in cell A13. To plot a histogram, click on **KGP Data Analysis ➤ Quantitative Data Charts/Tables ➤ Histogram/Freq. Charts.** Specify the input as cells A13:A42. After clicking on the "OK" button, view the shape of the histogram. From cells A13:A42, find the sample average by typing in a cell "=Average(A13:A42)".

7.53 To understand how the sample size increases as the confidence level increases to maintain a specified maximum error, calculate the required sample for $\sigma = 10$, $E = 1$, and for confidence levels of 90%, 92%, 94%, 96%, 98%, and 99%. In Excel, type into cells A1 through A6 the numbers ".95", ".96", ".97", ".98", ".99", and ".995". In cell B1, type in "=(NORMSINV(A1) *10/1)^2" for the formula for n. Drag cell B1 through cell B6. Comment on the changes in the required sample size as the confidence level increases. Note that the alpha level is divided by two in the formula for n. Thus, for example, it is necessary to use .95 in the NORMSINV formula when a confidence level of 90% is required. Likewise, it is necessary to use .96 in the NORMSINV formula for a confidence level of 92%, and so on.

7.6 BOOTSTRAP CONFIDENCE INTERVALS (OPTIONAL)

Around 1980, a new method of deriving confidence intervals, known as bootstrapping, entered the statistical scene. This procedure falls in the category of "computer-intensive" procedures and is especially useful for deriving confidence intervals from small samples. Deriving a confidence interval using the bootstrap sampling procedure has one distinct advantage: it derives a confidence interval *without making any assumptions about the distribution of the underlying population.* At first glance, use of this technique appears a bit magical but numerous published studies have demonstrated its rather remarkable reliability.

How Bootstrapping Works

The bootstrap method derives a sampling distribution by repeatedly resampling with replacement from an initial sample. Applying this procedure to estimating a population mean, you begin by obtaining a simple random sample (of size n) in the usual manner, exactly as discussed so far in this chapter. Keep in mind that a "simple random sample" implies that the sample was selected *without replacement* from the population. You next obtain a sample of size n from *the initial sample* by randomly selecting n elements *with replacement*. This implies that a particular sample element may be selected more than once. Determine the mean ($\overline{X}$) of this sample. Now repeat the procedure of sampling from the sample (with replacement) and finding $\overline{X}$, say, 200 times. The value 200 is arbitrary (generally, between 100 and 1000) and will be referred to as B. You now have $B = 200$ sample means, all derived by taking samples of size n, with replacement, from the original sample of size n.

Once the B sample means are derived, arrange them in order from smallest to largest. For a 90% confidence interval, you would simply count in $200(1 - .90)/2 = 10$ from each end of the ordered array. In general, you count in $B(\alpha/2)$ from each end, where $(1 - \alpha) \cdot 100\%$ is the confidence level. You now will have found the sample mean in the 10th spot (10 values in from the left end) and in the 191st spot (10 values in from the right end) in the array of ordered sample means. These two values represent the lower limit (the smaller sample mean) and the upper limit (the larger sample mean) of the 90% confidence interval for the population mean, μ.

An Example.   We'll illustrate the bootstrapping technique using the 18 sample values in Example 7.9 (output voltages) and the Excel macro contained in KGP Data Analysis. Referring to Figure 7.24, enter the sample values in column A and then click on **KGP Data Analysis ➤ Bootstrapped Confidence Interval for Mean.** In the resulting input screen, enter (1) "A1:A18" for the **Sample Input Range,** (2) "18" for the **Sample Size,** (3) "200" for the **Number of Samples,** (4) "95" for the **Confidence Level,** and (5) "B1" for the **Output Range.** What you will not see when running this macro are the 200

FIGURE 7.24

Excel spreadsheet using **KGP Data Analysis ➤ Bootstrapped Confidence Interval for Mean.**

	A	B	C	D	E	F	G	H	I
1	10.85		Bootstrap Sampling						
2	11.40	95% CI for Population Mean							
3	10.81	9.958	to	10.662					
4	10.24								
5	10.23								
6	9.49								
7	9.89								
8	10.11								
9	10.57								
10	11.21								
11	10.10								
12	11.22								
13	10.31								
14	11.24								
15	9.51								
16	10.52								
17	9.92								
18	8.33								

sample means generated by Excel, since the Excel procedure will simply output the mean in the $200(.05/2) = 5$th location and in the 196th location of the ordered array. According to Figure 7.24, the 5th largest of the 200 sample means is 9.958, and the 196th largest sample mean is 10.662. Consequently, the 95% confidence interval for the mean output voltage using the bootstrap procedure is from 9.958 to 10.662. Notice that this interval is quite close to that obtained in Example 7.9—namely, 9.950 to 10.712. Keep in mind one important point: the bootstrap interval *did not* assume that the population of voltage values follows a normal distribution, whereas use of the *t*-table in Example 7.9 did require this assumption.

Use of bootstrap estimation is gaining popularity because of the ever-increasing speed of desktop PCs, which allow you to construct a bootstrap confidence interval in a matter of seconds. As mentioned at the start of this section, bootstrap procedures are especially useful for dealing with small samples since (1) no population assumptions are necessary and (2) the Central Limit Theorem is not available to derive a confidence interval (as in Section 7.3) because of the small sample size. Bootstrap results may appear magical at first since we obtain all this information from a single sample, but in fact, bootstrap estimation is well grounded in statistical theory.* A final word here: it is important to keep in mind that any bootstrap procedure is sensitive to how representative the initial sample is of the underlying population. Deriving a bootstrap confidence interval from a haphazard or non-random sample would produce highly unreliable results.

---

* For more information on the application and theory of bootstrap procedures, refer to the extra bootstrap readings at the end of this chapter. The 1981 article by Efron is often quoted as the pioneer article in this area. A comprehensive discussion of bootstrap techniques is contained in the 1993 book by Efron and Tibshirani; pages 184–188 discuss a more complicated, but more reliable, bootstrap method referred to as the BC_a (bias-corrected and accelerated) method. An excellent discussion of bootstrap inference applied to auditing is the 1990 article by Biddle, Bruton, and Siegel.

EXERCISES 7.54–7.63

7.54 Construct a 95% confidence interval for the population mean using the random sample presented below by bootstrapping 100 times. In Excel, click on **KGP Data Analysis ➤ Bootstrapped Confidence Interval for Mean.**

| 112 | 150 | 130 | 140 | 129 | 121 | 153 | 172 |
| 132 | 126 | 114 | 156 | 166 | | | |

7.55 Because of the expensive nature of testing the strength of a specialized metal covering, a quality engineer is only able to collect 10 observations. The data are coded and presented below. Since it cannot be verified that the data are from a normally distributed population, and the sample size is small, the engineer does not want to use the confidence interval procedure using the *t* distribution. Obtain a bootstrapped 95% confidence interval by selecting 150 bootstrap samples.

| 23 | 26 | 18 | 32 | 24 | 27 | 23 | 28 | 25 | 19 |

7.56 The Texas Department of Transportation is interested in obtaining a preliminary sample of the time that workers in Arlington, Texas, travel to work. A random sample of 40 commuters was selected, and their travel times to work were recorded. The data are presented below in minutes.

35	45	22	21	18	20	14	45	33	46
12	22	34	41	17	13	18	63	31	78
41	14	54	42	33	16	70	15	55	38
23	49	67	38	96	52	41	18	73	17

a. Plot a histogram of the data. Would you describe these data as being approximately bell shaped?

b. Obtain a bootstrapped confidence interval for the mean time to work by selecting 100 bootstrap samples. How would you interpret this interval?

7.57 The American Marketing Association sponsored a project to determine the average amount that women between the ages of 20 and 25 spend on clothes annually. A pilot study at the university town of College Station yielded the following data for 30 women. The data are presented in units of thousands of dollars.

2500	1300	4500	900	750	3400
1300	2300	5200	1100	2100	1600
6400	980	2400	2100	580	1890
840	1030	4300	2300	1230	840
630	790	4500	3040	840	2500

a. Find a 90% bootstrapped confidence interval for the mean annual amount spent by women on clothes. Select 100 bootstrapped samples.

b. Find a 90% confidence interval for the mean annual amount spent by women on clothes using a *t* distribution.

c. Compare the confidence intervals in parts (a) and (b).

7.58 Refer to Exercise 7.27. Construct a 90% bootstrapped confidence interval for the average business customer's monthly bill to GTE. Select 100 bootstrapped samples. Compare this confidence interval to that obtained in Exercise 7.27.

7.59 Refer to Exercise 7.39. Construct a 90% bootstrapped confidence interval for the mean yearly return on interest-sensitive stocks by using 150 bootstrapped samples. Compare this confidence interval to that obtained in Exercise 7.39.

7.60 Refer to Exercise 7.40. Find a 90% bootstrapped confidence interval for the mean monthly fee by Internet providers. Select 200 bootstrapped samples. Compare this confidence interval to that obtained in Exercise 7.40.

7.61 Refer to Exercise 7.41. Find a 95% bootstrapped confidence interval for the mean of the variable Satisfact by selecting 100 bootstrapped samples. Compare this confidence interval to that obtained in Exercise 7.41.

7.62 Repeat Exercise 7.41 except use 400 bootstrapped samples. Do you notice much of a difference in the length of the confidence interval?

7.63 Refer to Exercise 7.42. Find a 90% bootstrapped confidence interval for the mean of the variable ServiceTime by selecting 100 bootstrapped samples. Compare this confidence interval to that obtained in Exercise 7.42.

7.7 OTHER SAMPLING PROCEDURES (OPTIONAL)

To discuss methods of sampling other than simple random sampling, we need to define several terms. These definitions also apply to simple random sampling.

1. **Population.** As before, population refers to the collection of people or objects about which we are trying to learn something. It may be as large as the set of all voting adults in the United States or as small or smaller than the set of all top-level managers in a particular company. In this section, we will assume that we are sampling from a *finite* population.
2. **Sampling unit.** A sampling unit is a collection of elements or an individual element selected from the population. Elements within one sampling unit must not overlap with the elements in other sampling units.
3. **Cluster.** A cluster is a sampling unit that is a group of elements from the population, such as all adults in a particular city block.
4. **Sampling frame.** A sampling frame is a list of population elements from which the sample is to be selected. Ideally, the sampling frame should be identical to the population. In many situations, however, this is impossible, in which case the frame must be *representative* of the population.
5. **Strata.** Strata are nonoverlapping subpopulations. For example, the population of all cigarette smokers can be split into two strata—men and women. You can then use **stratified sampling,** in which your total sample consists of a sample selected from each individual stratum.
6. **Sampling design.** A sampling design specifies the manner in which the sampling units are to be selected for your sample. Examples include simple random sampling, systematic sampling, stratified sampling, and cluster sampling.

SIMPLE RANDOM SAMPLING

The results obtained when using a simple random sample were presented earlier and are summarized here for the usual case of sampling without replacement, where every sample of n elements (from a population of size N) has an equal chance of being selected.

According to the Central Limit Theorem, for large samples the distribution of the sample mean, $\bar{X}$, is approximately normal, without making any assumptions concerning the shape of the population being sampled. The resulting confidence interval for the population mean, μ, is an *approximate* confidence interval for this parameter. If you have reason to believe that the population has a normal distribution with mean μ, the confidence interval is exact.

COMMENTS

1. In this section, we provide the *estimated* standard error of the estimator, rather than the *actual* standard error discussed earlier using equation 7.6. The standard error calculated from equation 7.6 is employed in the (somewhat unusual) situation where the population standard deviation (σ) is known. Typically, this parameter is unknown and is replaced by the sample standard deviation (s). The approximate confidence interval is written using the estimated standard error $s_{\bar{X}}$) and the standard normal Z value, assuming a large sample. When sampling from an assumed normal population, the Z value should be replaced by the corresponding t value with $n-1$ df.

2. Notice that the finite population correction (fpc) in equation 7.6 (the actual standard error) is $(N - n)/(N - 1)$, and that for the estimated standard error the fpc is $(N - n)/N$. For this situation, it would be desirable for the square of $s_{\overline{X}}$ (the estimated variance of $\overline{X}$) to be the square of $\sigma_{\overline{X}}$ (the actual variance of $\overline{X}$), on the average, if we were to obtain samples of size n indefinitely. This property is achieved if we set the fpc equal to $(N - n)/N$ in equation 7.14.

SIMPLE RANDOM SAMPLING

Population mean: μ
Estimator:

$$\overline{X} = \frac{\sum x}{n} \tag{7.13}$$

Estimated standard error of $\overline{X}$:

$$s_{\overline{X}} = \sqrt{\frac{s^2}{n} \cdot \frac{N - n}{N}} \tag{7.14}$$

Approximate confidence interval: $\overline{X} \pm Z_{\alpha/2} s_{\overline{X}}$

EXAMPLE 7.12

The fill weight of the can for a particular brand of coffee is supposed to be 13 ounces. A random sample of 40 cans from a batch containing 500 cans produced a mean of 13.12 ounces and a standard deviation of .014 ounces. Determine the (approximate) 95% confidence interval for the mean fill weight based on these sample results.

SOLUTION

Using equation 7.14, the estimated standard error is

$$s_{\overline{X}} = \sqrt{\frac{(.014)^2}{40} \cdot \frac{500 - 40}{500}} = .002123$$

The resulting 95% confidence interval is

$$13.12 \pm 1.96(.002123)$$

that is, 13.1158 to 13.1242 ounces. This confidence interval indicates a slight overfill in the can-filling process.

SYSTEMATIC SAMPLING

For large populations, obtaining a random sample can be quite cumbersome. Perhaps you have just informed a group of bank tellers that you need a random sample of their customers over the next few days. For them to select people randomly would be nearly impossible. A much easier scheme would be to have them select, say, every tenth customer to be included in the sample. This is systematic sampling.

Other situations where systematic sampling is advantageous include the following.

1. The sampling frame consists of N records on a magnetic tape or disk. The sample of n is obtained by sampling every kth record, where k is an integer approximately equal to N/n. For example, if there are $N = 9435$ records and you need a sample of size $n = 100$, selecting every $9435/100 \cong 94$th record would result in a systematic sample. Typically, a random starting point (record) is determined (between 1 and 94 here), and then every kth record is selected for your sample.

2. The sampling frame consists of a collection of files stored consecutively by date of birth. A quick (although not necessarily reliable) method of obtaining a "nearly ran-

dom" sample is to select every kth file for your sample. (What could cause the sample selected from such a list *not* to be random?)

3. A bank (or any service establishment) wants a sample of customers to determine their reaction to a proposed new service. The bank president knows that on the average they see 520 customers a day. If a sample of $n = 50$ is desired, they could elect to interview every $520/50 \approx 10$th customer. This is a situation where a simple random sample is not advisable, since it would be very difficult to randomly select customers during the working day.

There are many situations in which it is dangerous to use symmetric sampling. If there are obvious patterns contained in the sample frame listing, your sample may be far from random. If elements are stored according to days, for example, your sample could consist of data that all belong to Tuesday. If the data are cyclic, your sample might consist of all the peaks or all the valleys of the population. *Basically, systematic sampling works best when the order of your sampling frame is fairly random with respect to the measurement of interest.*

Despite its dangers, systematic sampling can provide an easy method of obtaining a representative sample. If the order of your population is in fact random (no cycles, no obvious patterns of any kind), a systematic sample can be analyzed as though it were a simple random sample.

STRATIFIED SAMPLING

Suppose that you have been asked by a local auto dealer to determine the average dollar amount of "extras" (such as air conditioning, automatic transmission, exterior trim) for new-car buyers during the past year. One possibility would be to take a simple random sample of say, 40 purchases. Suppose that you've been told that the car salesforce has noticed a tremendous difference in these amounts depending on whether the buyer is a single male, a single female, or a married couple. This suggests the use of a stratified sample containing these three strata. They also inform you that there are roughly the same number of single male and single female buyers, but the number of married buyers is approximately the size of these two groups combined. You could elect to get random samples of 10 single male buyers, 10 single female buyers, and 20 married couples for a total sample size of 40. This is *proportional stratified sampling.*

Stratified sampling is used whenever the population can be partitioned into two or more nonoverlapping groups (strata), where the variation within the strata is less than the variation within the entire population. The cost of obtaining the stratified sample may be less than that of collecting a random sample of the same size, especially if the strata are determined geographically (generally not a good idea).

The advantages of stratified sampling are:

1. By stratifying, we can obtain more information from the sample because data are more homogeneous within each stratum; consequently, confidence intervals are narrower than those obtained through random sampling.
2. We do obtain a cross section of the entire population.
3. We do obtain an estimate of the mean within each stratum as well as an estimate of μ for the entire population.

We use the following notation:

$$n_i = \text{sample size in stratum } i$$

$$N_i = \text{number of elements in stratum } i$$

$$N = \text{total population size} = \sum N_i$$

$$n = \text{total sample size} = \sum n_i$$

$$\bar{X}_i = \text{sample mean in stratum } i$$

$$s_i = \text{sample standard deviation in stratum } i$$

STRATIFIED SAMPLING

Population mean: μ
Estimator:

$$\overline{X}_{st} = \frac{\sum N_i \overline{X}_i}{N} \qquad (7.15)$$

Estimated standard error of $\overline{X}_{st}$:

$$s_{\overline{X}_{st}} = \sqrt{\sum \left(\frac{N_i}{N}\right)^2 \left(\frac{N_i - n_i}{N_i}\right) \frac{s_i^2}{n_i}} \qquad (7.16)$$

Approximate confidence interval: $\overline{X}_{st} \pm Z_{\alpha/2} s_{\overline{X}_{st}}$

(mean + or - the error.)

To increase the precision of this sampling procedure, the estimated standard error of $\overline{X}_{st}$ should be "small." Consequently, you should attempt to create strata such that the individual variances, s_i^2, are as small as possible. In this way, the point estimates provided by $\overline{X}_{st}$ would not drastically vary if you were to obtain repeated stratified samples of size n.

One method often used to select the strata sample sizes is *proportional stratified sampling*, where each sample size is proportional to the stratum size.* The sample size for the ith stratum is defined by

$$n_i = n\left(\frac{N_i}{N}\right)$$

Assume that you would like to obtain a sample of size 40 from the auto dealer and you elect to use a stratified sample with proportional sample sizes. A search of the records for the past year indicates that there have been $N = 2840$ new-car purchases, with $N_1 = 685$ being single male purchasers (stratum 1), $N_2 = 720$ being single female purchasers (stratum 2), and the remaining $N_3 = 1435$ purchasers belonging to the married couple stratum (stratum 3).

Your sample sizes are:

$$n_1 = 40\left(\frac{685}{2840}\right) \approx 10 \qquad n_2 = 40\left(\frac{720}{2840}\right) \approx 10 \qquad n_3 = 40\left(\frac{1435}{2840}\right) \approx 20$$

Simple random samples of size $n_1 = 10$, $n_2 = 10$, and $n_3 = 20$ are obtained from the three strata, and the dollar amounts of the purchased extras for these 40 new-car sales are recorded. The sample results are given in Table 7.3.

The estimate of the average dollar amount spent on extras, μ, is

$$\overline{X}_{st} = \frac{(685)(5889.2) + (720)(4072.4) + (1435)(7296.3)}{2840}$$

$$= \frac{17,436,420.5}{2840} = \$6,139.58$$

Also,

$$s_{\overline{X}_{st}}^2 = \left(\frac{685}{2840}\right)^2 \left(\frac{685-10}{685}\right)\frac{(779.99)^2}{10} + \left(\frac{720}{2840}\right)^2 \left(\frac{720-10}{720}\right)\frac{(832.59)^2}{10}$$

$$+ \left(\frac{1435}{2840}\right)^2 \left(\frac{1435-20}{1435}\right)\frac{(934.71)^2}{20}$$

$$= 18,878.77$$

---

* More precision often can be obtained by considering the variation within each stratum and obtaining larger samples from strata with more variation. In particular, set $n_i = n[N_i s_i/(\sum N_i s_i)]$, where s_i is the sample standard deviation in the ith stratum. This method of determining the sample sizes is called *Neyman allocation* and reduces to proportional sampling if the strata standard deviations are equal or ignored.

TABLE 7.3

Illustration of stratified sampling. Each stratum represents the gender/marital status of the new automobile purchaser. The samples consist of the dollar amounts of the purchased extra items.

Single Male Purchasers (Stratum 1)	Single Female Purchasers (Stratum 2)	Married Purchasers (Stratum 3)
6353	3960	8449
6755	3952	6632
5681	4107	6661
4202	4970	7169
5773	4213	7339
5993	4496	8661
5369	4874	6413
6317	4543	8752
5547	2054	6021
6902	3355	6317
		7758
		6149
		7613
		8164
		7514
		6719
		8941
		6170
		7641
		6843

N_i	685	720	1435
n_i	10	10	20
$\bar{X}_i$	5889.2	4072.4	7296.3
s_i	779.99	832.59	934.71

Consequently, the estimated standard error is

$$s_{\bar{X}_{st}} = \sqrt{18,878.77} = \$137.40$$

The corresponding approximate 95% confidence interval for the average amount spent on extras is

$$\$6139.58 - (1.96)(137.40) \qquad \text{to} \qquad \$6139.58 + (1.96)(137.40)$$

that is, $5870.28 to $6408.88. As a result, we are 95% confident that the average amount is between $5870.28 and $6408.88.

CLUSTER SAMPLING

We can sample clusters (groups) within the population rather than collecting individual elements one at a time. For example, to determine the opinions of the members of a particular labor union, you might interview everyone attending several of the local meetings. Of course, the danger here is that possibly (1) the people attending the local meetings that were sampled (clusters) do not represent the population of all voting members, and (2) the people attending the local meetings do not provide an adequate representation of the local members. As a general rule, it is advisable to select many small clusters rather than a few large clusters to obtain a more accurate representation of your population.

Cluster sampling is preferred to (and less costly than) random and stratified sampling when:

1. The only sampling frame that can be constructed consists of clusters (for example, all people in a particular household, city block, or zip code).
2. The population is extremely spread out, or it is impossible to obtain data on all the individual members.

When using cluster sampling, you should *randomly* select a set of clusters (once they have been clearly defined) for sampling. You can then include all individuals within each cluster selected for the sample (**single-stage cluster sampling**) or randomly select individuals from the sampled clusters to be included in the sample (**two-stage cluster sampling**).

We use the following notation:

M = total number of clusters in the population

m = number of clusters randomly selected for the sample

n_i = number of elements in sample cluster i

$\bar{n}$ = average cluster size of the sampled clusters ($\bar{n} = \sum n_i/m$)

N = total population size (N = total of all M cluster sizes that make up the population)

$\bar{N}$ = average cluster size for the population ($\bar{N} = N/M$)

T_i = total of all observations within cluster i (required for the sampled clusters only)

CLUSTER SAMPLING (SINGLE STAGE)

Population mean: μ
Estimator:

$$\bar{X}_c = \frac{\sum T_i}{\sum n_i} \tag{7.17}$$

Estimated standard error of $\bar{X}_c$:

$$s_{\bar{X}_c} = \sqrt{\left(\frac{M-m}{mM\bar{N}^2}\right)\frac{\sum(T_i - \bar{X}_c n_i)^2}{m-1}} \tag{7.18}$$

If $\bar{N}$ is unknown, this can be replaced by its estimate, $\bar{n}$.

Approximate confidence interval: $\bar{X}_c \pm Z_{\alpha/2} s_{\bar{X}_c}$

As marketing director for a cable-television company in a large city, you are trying to decide whether to begin a major advertising campaign to reach tenants in local high-rise apartment buildings. Your staff disagree about whether this is a good idea. One group of your employees feels that people living in high-rise apartments are always on the go and are not likely to spend much time watching television—cable or network. The others tend to believe that such tenants have no grass to mow or leaves to rake and so have a great deal of time to spend watching television.

Rather than drawing a sample from all high-rise tenants, you construct a sampling frame consisting of all 18 ($= M$) high-rise apartment complexes. From these, you randomly select a sample of $m = 4$ complexes (clusters). Each tenant in these four complexes is then asked how many hours per week he or she watches television. You obtain the following results:

	Complex 1	Complex 2	Complex 3	Complex 4
Number of units (n_i)	260	220	310	274
Total number of hours per cluster (complex)	2475	2750	3160	4110

N = the total number of units in the 18 high-rise complex (population) = 4590

$$\overline{N} = \frac{4590}{18} = 255$$

You begin by noting

$$\sum (T_i - \overline{X}_c n_i)^2 = \sum T_i^2 - 2\overline{X}_c \sum T_i n_i + \overline{X}_c^2 \sum n_i^2 \qquad (7.19)$$

Using the sample data,

$$\sum T_i = 2475 + \cdots + 4110 = 12{,}495$$

$$\sum n_i = 260 + \cdots + 274 = 1064$$

$$\sum T_i^2 = (2475)^2 + \cdots + (4110)^2 = 40{,}565{,}825$$

$$\sum T_i n_i = (2475)(260) + \cdots + (4110)(274) = 3{,}354{,}240$$

$$\sum n_i^2 = (260)^2 + \cdots + (274)^2 = 287{,}176$$

As a result,

$$\overline{X}_c = \frac{\sum T_i}{\sum n_i} = \frac{12{,}495}{1064} = 11.743$$

Also, using equation 7.19,

$$\frac{\sum (T_i - \overline{X}_c n_i)^2}{m-1} = [40{,}565{,}825 - (2)(11.743)(3{,}354{,}240)$$

$$+ (11.743)^2 (287{,}176)] \div 3$$

$$= 463{,}051.49$$

Consequently,

$$s_{\overline{X}_c}^2 = \frac{18-4}{(4)(18)(255)^2} \cdot 463{,}051.49 = 1.385$$

and so

$$s_{\overline{X}_c} = \sqrt{1.385} = 1.177$$

The resulting approximate 95% confidence interval for the average number of television hours (for all 18 complexes) is

$$11.743 - 1.96(1.177) \qquad \text{to} \qquad 11.743 + 1.96(1.177)$$

$$= 9.44 \text{ hours} \qquad \text{to} \qquad 14.05 \text{ hours}$$

Therefore, we are 95% confident that μ lies between 9.44 and 14.05 hours and that we have estimated μ to within 2.3 hours. This example has illustrated single-stage cluster sampling, where everyone in the selected clusters (apartment complexes) was used in the sample. Another look at this example indicates that it might be more practical to use a two-stage sampling procedure, where each of the four sample clusters is also sampled to obtain the final sample.

EXERCISES 7.64–7.69

UNDERSTANDING THE MECHANICS

7.64 Construct a 95% confidence interval for the mean of the population using the following statistics.

Stratum 1	Stratum 2	Stratum 3
$n_1 = 20$	$n_2 = 10$	$n_3 = 15$
$\bar{X}_1 = 34$	$\bar{X}_2 = 22$	$\bar{X}_3 = 25$
$s_1^2 = 40$	$s_2^2 = 144$	$s_3^2 = 81$
$N_1 = 160$	$N_2 = 50$	$N_3 = 100$

7.65 The following data are collected on three strata, with $N_1 = 80$, $N_2 = 112$, $N_3 = 40$. Construct a 90% confidence interval on the mean of the population.

Stratum 1	Stratum 2	Stratum 3
6 8 6 12 10	10 14 18 22 12	42 32 36 24 14
8 6 8 2 6	28 34 8 16 14	52 18 16
4 8 10 4 14	18 14 18 26 22	
	24 8 6 16 12	
	18 22	

APPLYING THE NEW CONCEPTS

7.66 Basic Microcomputers would like to market its version of the professional computer. To price the professional computer and its peripheral equipment properly, a survey is taken among the lower-middle-, upper-middle-, and high-income groups to find out what a businessperson would be willing to pay. The survey was restricted to a certain city in an industrial area. A stratified sample among these three groups yielded the following statistics. Construct a 90% confidence interval for the mean price that a professional businessperson would be willing to pay, in units of thousands of dollars.

Income Level	N_i	n_i	$\bar{X}_i$	s_i^2
Lower-middle	8,641	56	2.3	1.6
Upper-middle	14,683	95	4.6	1.9
High	7,457	49	4.8	1.4
	30,781	200		

7.67 A market-research firm would like to estimate the average number of hours that a householder spends shopping each week. Four neighborhoods were selected from a total of 24 neighborhoods for sampling purposes. Find a 90% confidence interval for the mean number of hours that a householder spends shopping each week from the following data (units are in hours per week):

1	2	3	4
2.3	5.4	1.6	5.6
1.1	4.2	0.9	4.1
4.3	3.6	4.6	2.3
0.5	7.2	5.4	7.3
3.7	8.4	5.6	6.1
4.6	11.8	4.6	4.7
10.1	2.1	7.1	5.8
6.3	1.5	3.2	4.8
7.8	8.1	4.5	5.3
8.4	4.1	3.1	1.9
7.9	3.4	2.6	8.4
10.6			

7.68 In what situation is the use of systematic sampling appropriate? Explain how a systematic sample would be taken from a file of students listed by social security number.

7.69 The administration of Digital Systems would like to obtain an estimate of the amount of time workers spend on physical exercise. Five departments out of 20 in Digital Systems were selected for sampling purposes. Find a 95% confidence interval for the mean time that an employee spends on physical fitness per week given the following data (units are in hours per week):

1	2	3	4	5
1.1	2.3	3.5	7.9	0.1
0.2	0.4	4.6	1.3	0.0
2.3	0.3	1.5	2.5	7.6
4.6	1.0	0.7	5.7	5.1
0.1	4.6	3.6	7.8	4.0
0.0	8.3	9.5	10.3	3.0
2.6	7.1	0.8	0.6	6.5
6.8	0.2			
1.1	2.7			

SUMMARY

This chapter introduced you to **statistical inference,** an extremely important area of statistics. Inference procedures were used to estimate a certain unknown *parameter* (such as the mean, μ, or the standard deviation, σ) of a population by using the corresponding sample *statistic* (such as the sample mean, $\bar{X}$, or the sample standard deviation, *s*).

The **Central Limit Theorem** states that for large samples, the sample mean $\bar{X}$ always follows an approximate normal distribution. If, in addition, you assume that the population is normally distributed, then $\bar{X}$ will follow an exact normal distribution. The strength of the Central Limit Theorem is that no assumptions need be made concerning the shape of the population, provided the sample is large ($n > 30$). The Central Limit Theorem allows you to make probability statements concerning $\bar{X}$, such as $P(\bar{X} < 150)$. When sampling without replacement from a finite population, the standard deviation of the normal distribution for $\bar{X}$ (the **standard error**) is obtained by including a **finite population correction factor (fpc)**, which adjusts the standard error by including the effect of the known population size, N.

The probability distribution of a sample statistic is its **sampling distribution.** Consequently, according to the Central Limit Theorem, the sampling distribution of $\bar{X}$ is approximately normal, regardless of the shape of the sampled population.

The sample mean, $\bar{X}$, provides a **point estimate** of μ because it estimates this parameter using a single number. A **confidence interval** for μ measures the precision of the point estimate. If the population standard deviation σ is known, the standard normal table (Table A.4) is used to derive the confidence interval. If σ is unknown, it can be replaced by its estimate—the sample standard deviation, s. This provided an introduction to the t **distribution.** The corresponding confidence interval for μ is constructed using the t table (Table A.5) and assumes that the sampled population is normally distributed (that is, μ is the mean of a normal population). For sample sizes (n) greater than 30, the standard normal table can be used to construct an approximate confidence interval for the population mean when σ is unknown. A summary of this procedure is contained in Figure 7.25.

For many applications, the precision of the point estimate, $\bar{X}$, is specified using the **maximum error, E.** When constructing a confidence interval, E is the amount that is added to and subtracted from the point estimate to obtain the endpoints of the desired interval. The sample size n necessary to achieve a desired accuracy can be obtained using a specified value of E. The population standard deviation can be estimated from a preliminary sample, or a rough approximation procedure can be used.

Use of **bootstrapping** techniques to derive confidence intervals was introduced about 20 years ago. It is a computer-intensive procedure that does require a great deal of computer calculations but, because of the much-improved speed of desktop PCs, can provide a very reliable confidence interval in a matter of seconds. The main advantage of using a bootstrap procedure is that the resulting confidence interval is derived without making *any* assumptions about the shape of the population from which the sample was obtained.

Simple random sampling is employed when every sample of n elements has an equal chance of being selected. Other sampling procedures can often be used to obtain a more precise estimate of the population mean, μ, providing much narrower confidence intervals for this parameter or less costly estimates of the population mean. These sampling techniques include systematic, stratified, and cluster sampling. **Systematic** sampling selects a random starting point and then selects every kth value for some counting number $k > 0$. This procedure assumes that the population is stored sequentially in some manner, such as in a computer file. **Stratified** sampling is used whenever the population can be partitioned into two or more nonoverlapping groups (strata) where the variation within the strata is less than the variation within the entire population. **Cluster** sampling involves sampling groups of people (clusters) within the population, rather than selecting individual elements one at a time.

FIGURE 7.25

The correct table to use for constructing a confidence interval for a population mean. *Note:* In all cases, if the population size (N) is known, the fpc can be used to derive a more precise standard error. This adjustment is negligible if $n/N < .05$.

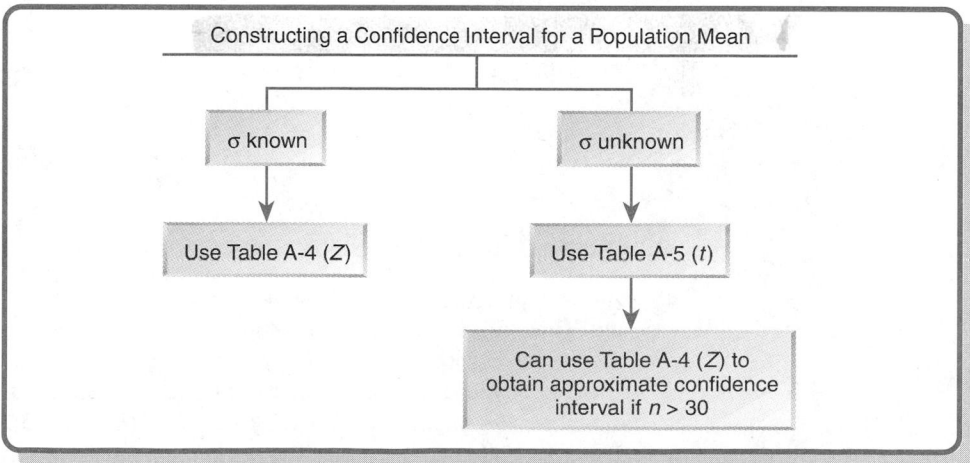

SUMMARY OF FORMULAS

1. Standard error of $\bar{X}$ (simple random sample):

$$\frac{\sigma}{\sqrt{n}} \quad (N \text{ unknown or infinite})$$

$$\frac{\sigma}{\sqrt{n}}\sqrt{\frac{N-n}{N-1}} \quad (N \text{ known})$$

where $(N-n)/(N-1)$ is the finite population correction (fpc).

2. Estimated standard error of $\bar{X}$ (simple random sample):

$$\frac{s}{\sqrt{n}} \quad (N \text{ unknown or infinite})$$

$$\frac{s}{\sqrt{n}}\sqrt{\frac{N-n}{N}} \quad (N \text{ known})$$

where $(N-n)/N$ is the finite population correction (fpc).

3. Confidence interval for a population mean (large simple random sample, σ known):

$$\bar{X} \pm Z_{\alpha/2}\frac{\sigma}{\sqrt{n}}$$

Note: Include the fpc in Formula 1 if N is known.

4. Confidence interval for the mean of a normal population (simple random sample, σ unknown):

$$\bar{X} \pm t_{\alpha/2,n-1}\frac{s}{\sqrt{n}}$$

Note: Include the fpc in Formula 2 if N is known.

5. Necessary sample size (simple random sample):

$$n = \left[\frac{Z_{\alpha/2}\cdot\sigma}{E}\right]^2$$

where E is the specified maximum error.

STRATIFIED SAMPLING

1. Estimator of population mean:

$$\bar{X}_{st} = \frac{\sum N_i \bar{X}_i}{N}$$

where $\bar{X}_i$ is the ith stratum mean and N_i is the size of the ith stratum in the population.

2. Estimated standard error of $\bar{X}_{st}$:

$$s_{\bar{X}_{st}} = \sqrt{\sum \left(\frac{N_i}{N}\right)^2 \left(\frac{N_i - n_i}{N_i}\right)\frac{s_i^2}{n_i}}$$

3. Approximate confidence interval:

$$\bar{X}_{st} \pm Z_{\alpha/2}s_{\bar{X}_{st}}$$

CLUSTER SAMPLING

1. Estimator of population mean:

$$\bar{X}_c = \frac{\sum T_i}{\sum n_i}$$

where T_i is the total of the observations in the ith cluster.

2. Estimated standard error of $\bar{X}_c$:

$$s_{\bar{X}_c} = \sqrt{\left(\frac{M-m}{mM\bar{N}^2}\right)\frac{\sum(T_i - \bar{X}_c n_i)^2}{m-1}}$$

If $\bar{N}$ is unknown, $\bar{N}$ can be replaced by its estimate, $\bar{n}$.

3. Approximate confidence interval:

$$\bar{X}_c \pm Z_{\alpha/2}s_{\bar{X}_c}$$

ADDITIONAL BOOTSTRAP READINGS

1. Biddle, G. C., C. M. Bruton, and A. F. Siegel. "Computer-Intensive Methods in Auditing: Bootstrap Difference and Ratio Estimation" *Auditing: A Journal of Practice & Theory,* vol. 3, no. 3, Fall 1990, pp. 92–114.
2. Efron, B. "Nonparametric Estimates of Standard Error: The Jackknife, the Bootstrap, and Other Resampling Methods" *Biometrika,* 1981, pp. 589–99.
3. Efron, B., and R. J. Tibshirani. *An Introduction to the Bootstrap.* New York: Chapman & Hall, 1993.

REVIEW EXERCISES 7.70–7.87

7.70 After taking a random sample of 40 customers and asking them the amount of time they spend shopping at a particular store, a 95% confidence interval is computed to be 10 to 32 for the average time spent shopping. An analyst can correctly make which of the following statements:

a. I am 95% confident that the average time that a customer spends shopping is between 10 and 32 minutes.

b. The probability is .95 that the midpoint of the interval is equal to the population mean.

c. The mean of the population is between 10 and 32.

d. If I repeatedly obtained samples of size 40, then 95% of the resulting confidence intervals would contain the mean time that customers spend shopping.

7.71 An accounting firm has a large pool of secretaries. It is assumed that the time it takes a secretary to type a certain legal document is normally distributed with a mean time of 30 minutes and a standard deviation of 4 minutes.

a. What is the probability that a secretary will spend less than 27 minutes typing the legal document?

b. In a randomly selected sample of six secretaries, what is the probability that the average time that it takes them to type the legal document is less than 27 minutes?

7.72 Airline officials say the number of children flying alone has risen significantly over the past few years. Northwest Airlines and Delta Airlines have doubled the extra fee charged for unaccompanied children traveling on connecting flights, and Delta has added a charge for children flying alone on direct flights. To obtain a 90% confidence interval on the average number of unaccompanied children per flight on its Chicago to Baltimore flight, suppose that Delta airlines recorded the following number of unaccompanied children on a random sample of 60 flights. Use a computer package to find the confidence interval. What interpretation would you give to this confidence interval?

3	4	3	10	6	8	1	5	7	2
4	6	1	3	11	5	8	3	2	6
4	7	1	0	8	12	6	3	6	9
11	2	9	6	2	4	10	12	2	5
3	5	6	2	9	7	1	2	11	4
6	5	1	4	9	2	5	12	3	7

(Adapted from *The New York Times*, "Northwest and Delta Raise Baby-Sitting Fees," June 21, 1998, section 5, p. 3.)

7.73 A quality-assurance inspector believes that the weight of a machine bearing produced by a certain manufacturing process approximately follows a uniform distribution. A sample of 50 machine bearings yielded a sample mean of .211 pounds with a standard deviation of .05. Find a 90% confidence interval for the mean weight of the machine bearings produced by this manufacturing process.

7.74 Mail strikes in Toronto had many businesspersons thinking about alternatives to the mail system. Courier service is popular but somewhat expensive. The minimal charges range from $10 to $40 depending on how far the letter is going. What sample size would be necessary to estimate the mean charge by a courier service in the Toronto metropolitan area to within $2 with 90% confidence?

(Adapted from *Toronto Star*, "Communications Alternatives to the Mail Ample but Expensive Couriers, Faxes, Telegrams Provide Costly Choices," Nov 21, 1997, p. B1.)

7.75 A random variable is found to range from a high of 50 to a low of 25 from past data. The distribution of the random variable can be approximated by a normal distribution. To estimate the mean of the random variable to within 2.1, what sample size would be necessary in selecting a random sample to achieve a 99% confidence level?

7.76 Direct marketing efforts—including catalogs, direct mail and e-mail—refer more potential customers to Web sites and result in higher average order sizes, according to market research company Binary Compass Enterprises, Los Angeles. This marketing research company revealed that 5153 online buyers have placed orders over the Internet, with the average order size being $213 with a standard deviation of $50. Find the probability that 500 randomly selected online buyers selected from the 5153 buyers who have placed orders over the Internet have an average order size between $210 and $215?

(Adapted from *Direct Marketing News*, "DM Drives More Traffic, Higher Average Orders," Web marketing news section, p. 21.)

7.77 The research and development department of a large oil company employs 253 engineers who have an average of 6.2 years of practical experience with a standard deviation of 2.1 years.

a. If a sample of 35 engineers is selected randomly without replacement, what is the probability that the average number of years of experience of the sample will be greater than 6.8 years?

b. If a sample of 35 engineers is selected randomly with replacement, what is the probability that the average number of years of experience will be greater than 6.8 years?

7.78 A confidence interval for the mean of a normally distributed population is found to range from 70.1 to 80.2. What is the level of confidence for the confidence interval if the sample size is 36 and the population standard deviation is 13.2?

7.79 The tensile strength of a high-powered copper coil used in giant power transformers is believed to follow a normal distribution. A sample of 14 high-powered copper coils yields the following tensile strength (in units of thousands of pounds per square inch). Construct a 90% confidence interval for the mean tensile strength of copper coils.

$$6.1, 2.6, 3.5, 4.3, 3.1, 5.2, 3.6, 3.5, 5.4, 4.2, 3.2, 2.8, 4.0, 3.7$$

7.80 Motorola, one of the largest makers of modems that link personal computer users to the Internet and other users, is considering selling the consumer-oriented modem business because falling prices have eroded profits. The company does not want to sell its more profitable modem business in which modems connect to corporate networks and tap the internet via cable TV lines. Assume that the director of global product marketing is interested in obtaining an estimate of the price of a 56K modem on the market—those modems that transmit data at 56 kilobytes per second. The following data (units are in dollars) resulted from a random sample of 25 vendors selling the 56K modem.

85 92 125 88 99 106 135 129 79 84 110 95 108 81 85 95 112 79 137 119 113 84 78 99 103

(Adapted from *USA Today,* "Motorola Says It's Ready to Hang Up Low-End Modems," October 8, 1997, p. 2B.)

a. Use a computer package to find a 90% confidence interval on the mean price of a 56K modem.

b. Find the confidence interval in part (a) with a 99% confidence level and compare the results to the 90% confidence interval.

7.81 Cereal companies like Kellogg view Europe and Asia as an opportunity for growth at a time when the United States market is in a decline. In Italy, for example, American cereals like Corn Flakes have been available in that country since the 1950s. But until this decade, they were considered a niche product. Suppose that Kellogg wishes to estimate the annual consumption by adults in Italy. How large would the sample size need to be to estimate the mean annual consumption of cereal (in pounds) to within .2 pounds with 95% confidence if the standard deviation of the amount of cereal consumed is estimated to be 1.2 pound?

(Adapted from *The Wall Street Journal,* "Europe Is Deaf to Snap! Crackle! Pop!" June 22, 1998, p. B1.)

7.82 A personnel administrator for Teltronix would like to estimate the amount of term life insurance that an employee carries. Three strata are used for finding a stratified random sample of all employees. From the data, construct a 95% confidence interval for the mean amount of term life insurance that an employee carries (given in units of thousands of dollars).

Stratum	N_i (Total Number in Company)	n_i	$\bar{X}_i$	s_i
Employees paid by the hour	350	67	28.5	5.7
Engineers and technicians	112	22	80.6	10.3
Management	57	11	125.2	13.6
	519	100		

7.83 A machine at a manufacturing plant fills sacks with 10 pounds of oats. Each case contains 10 sacks of oats. The quality-control engineer would like to find a 99% confidence interval for the mean weight per sack of oats. Using cases as clusters, construct the confidence interval if eight cases are chosen at random. Assume that there is a total of 50 cases from which to choose.

Cases	Sacks Per Case	Weight of Case	Cases	Sacks Per Case	Weight of Case
1	10	96.7	5	10	110.8
2	10	99.8	6	10	104.6
3	10	103.5	7	10	93.5
4	10	92.7	8	10	112.3

7.84 After having lagged the returns by domestic U.S. mutual funds, mutual funds investing in Europe had a spectacular 1997 year. There's new economic life in the Old World low inflation, government restraint and the drive toward economic unification has boosted mutual funds investing in Europe, with some funds returning more than 35%. Consider the 20 observations below to be 1997 returns (in percentage) from a random sample of closed-end mutual funds investing primarily in Europe.

$$24.3 \quad 25.8 \quad 18.5 \quad 39.5 \quad 25.9 \quad 33.2 \quad 41.2 \quad 13.6 \quad 37.5 \quad 28.3$$
$$36.5 \quad 19.3 \quad 23.7 \quad 32.8 \quad 40.3 \quad 22.5 \quad 27.5 \quad 21.8 \quad 30.5 \quad 33.6$$

(Adapted from *Toronto Star*, "Smart Money," April 29, 1998, Business section, p. E3.)

    a. Use a computer package to find a 90% confidence interval on the mean performance.
    b. Find a 95% confidence interval.
    c. Find a 99% confidence interval.
    d. Comment on how the length of the confidence intervals changes with the confidence levels.

7.85 A binomial random variable can be thought of as a sum of 1s and 0s, where 1 respresents a success on a trial and 0 represents a failure on a trial. Dividing the binomial random variable by n gives an estimate of the proportion of successes. This estimate of the proportion is equivalent to a sample mean of 1s and 0s. What is the approximate distribution of the estimate of the proportion of successes for a large number of trials? (Hint: What does the Central Limit Theorem say?)

7.86 To understand how the required sample size changes with a change in the maximum error for a confidence interval, plot n against the values of $E = 8, 9, 10, \ldots 20$, when the population standard deviation is equal to 100, and the confidence level is 95%. The plot should look like the one displayed below. Comment on the relationship between n and E. In Excel, type in "8", "9", "10", $\ldots$, "20" in cells A1 through A13. In cell B1 type in "=(1.96*100/A1)^2". Drag B1 through B13. Then click on the **Chart Wizard** to form a line graph.

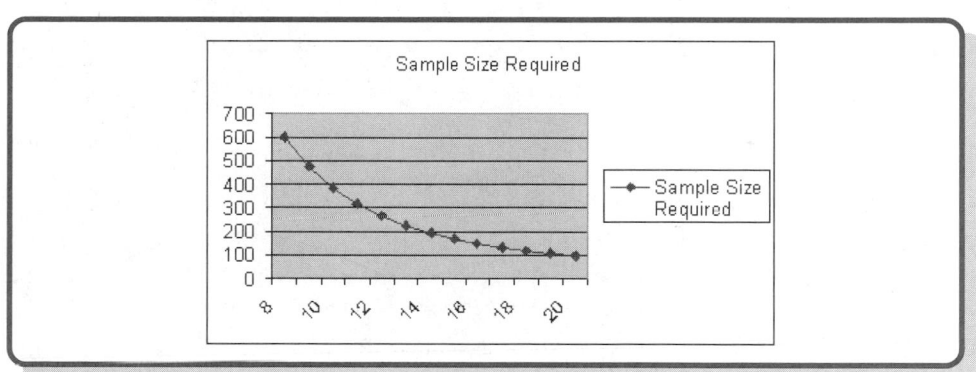

7.87 According to the Central Limit Theorem, the distribution of the sample mean should be approximately normal for large sample sizes. To illustrate this, first simulate 30 samples of size 10 from an exponentially distributed random variable. An exponentially distributed random variable can be generated by calculating $-ln$(random number), where ln is the natural log function. Second, simulate 30 samples of size 20 from the same population. Compare the histograms. Continue this for a much larger sample size. The two histograms presented on the next page are examples of simulations with samples of size 20 and 30. In Excel to simulate 30 samples of size 10 from an exponentially distributed random variable, first type "=-ln(RND())" in cell A1. The function RND() generates a random number. Now drag cell A1 to A10, and then drag across to cell AD10. The columns represent 30 samples. Type "=AVERAGE(A1:A10)" in cell A11. Drag cell A11 to AD11. Highlight row A11. Click on **Edit ➤ Copy.** Then click on AD13 and then on **Edit ➤ Paste Special.** Select **Values** and **Transpose.** Click "OK". The sample means will appear in cells A13 to A32. Now form a histogram of these values. Repeat this using 30 samples of size 20. What do you observe?

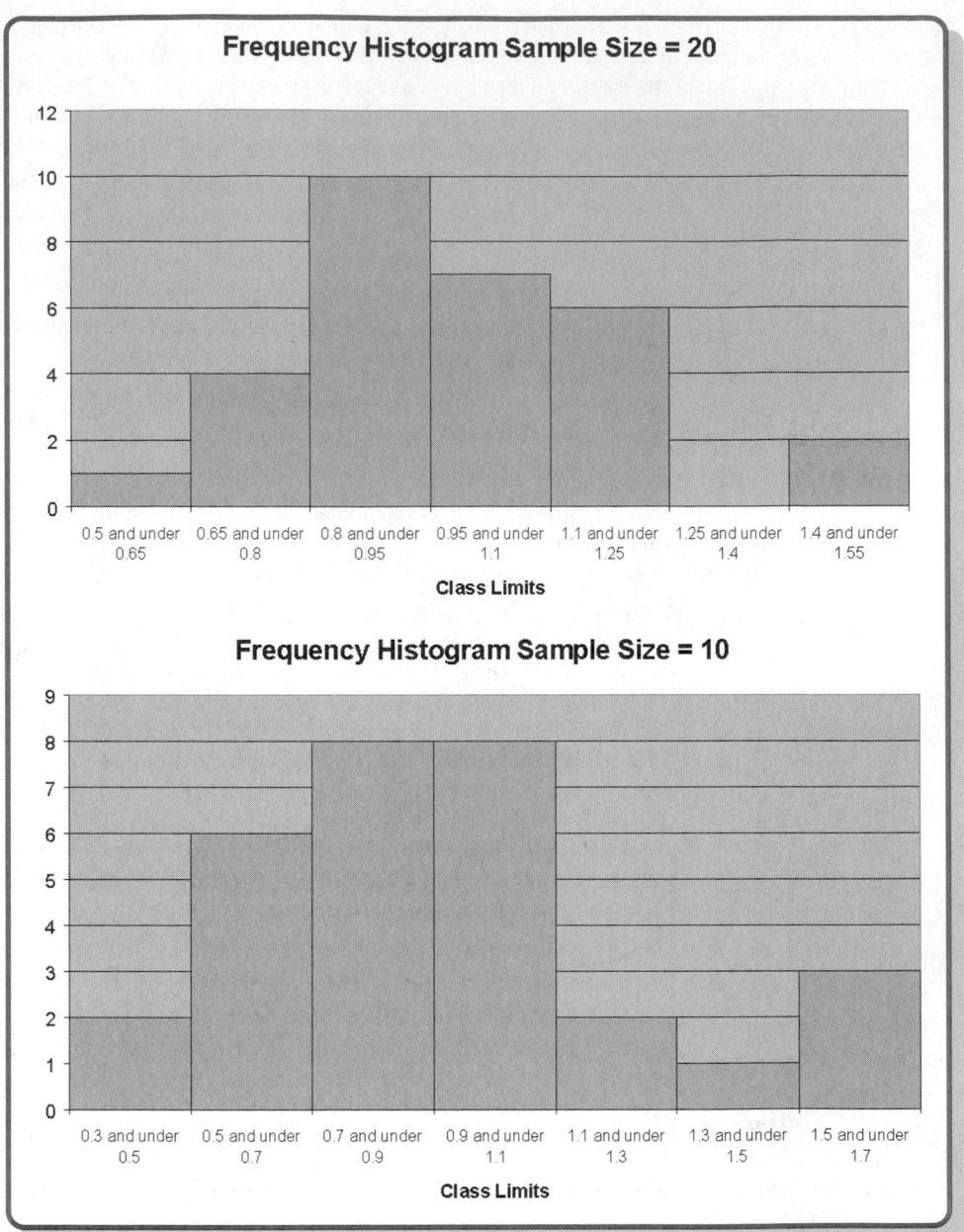

COMPUTER EXERCISES USING THE DATABASES

EXERCISE 1—APPENDIX E

Select the first 500 observations of the database as the population of interest. Estimate the mean of HPAYRENT (house payment or house/apartment rent) for this population by taking a simple random sample of size 40. Also estimate the mean by taking a stratified sample proportional to the size of the two strata. Let stratum 1 be the group of observations in which a secondary wage earner (variable INCOME2) has a positive income, and let stratum 2 be the group of observations in which there is no

secondary wage earner. Compare the confidence intervals on mean house payment/rent (HPAYRENT) for both the simple random sample and the stratified random sample.

Note: The MINITAB procedure to select the first 500 rows is

```
MTB > COPY C1-C9 INTO C11-C19;
SUBC > USE ROWS 1:500.
```

To obtain the simple random sample of size 40, use

```
MTB > RANDOM 40 FROM C17, PUT INTO C20
```

EXERCISE 2—APPENDIX E
EXERCISE 2—APPENDIX E

Select a simple random sample of 32 observations from the database. Calculate a 95% confidence interval on the mean income of the principal wage earner (variable INCOME1). Select another simple random sample of size 60 from this database. Calculate a 95% confidence interval on the mean income of the principal wage earner. Comment on the widths of these two confidence intervals.

EXERCISE 3—APPENDIX F

Generate 20 random samples of size 10 using the data for the variable ASSETS (current assets). For each sample determine the sample mean. Construct a histogram of these 20 sample means. Also find the mean and the variance of these 20 values. Repeat this procedure for samples of size 25 and 40. Does the Central Limit Theorem appear to be operating correctly here? Discuss.

INSIGHTS FROM STATISTICS IN ACTION: WHAT IS THE AVERAGE GATE-TO-TAKEOFF TIME AT AIRPORTS?

The Statistics in Action introductory case study discussed the problem of excessive gate-to-takeoff times at many major U.S. airports. To understand what the average gate-to-takeoff time is for airports across the United States, consider the random sample below. Thirty airports were randomly selected from the major airports across the United States. Assume the population size of all major airports across the United States to be large relative to the sample below.

Airport	Time from Gate-to-Takeoff (in Minutes)
Newark International	25.3
Honolulu International	19.2
JFK International	24.8
El Paso International	8.6
Dallas Love Field	7.4
Denver International	14.7
Los Angeles International	14.8
Hartsfield Atlanta International	17.2
Omaha Eppley Airfield	10.1
Miami International	19.2
Chicago Midway	9.3
Bangor International	9.9
Milwaukee International	11.4
Memphis International	14.6
San Diego International	11.7
Lubbock International	7.0
Detroit Metropolitan	17.7
Philadelphia International	16.1
Washington Dulles International	14.7
Boise Air Terminal	8.7
Indianapolis International	10.8
Syracuse Hancock International	10.7

Airport	Time from Gate-to-Takeoff (in Minutes)
Raleigh-Durham International	10.4
Albuquerque International	10.0
Norfolk International	9.1
Los Angeles International	14.8
Cleveland Hopkins International	14.2
Kansas City International	10.6
George Bush Intercontinental	15.2
Salt Lake City International	15.9

1. Should a census be taken instead of a random sample to obtain the average gate-to-takeoff time? For what reasons would a researcher want to use a random sample instead of a census?

2. Find a 90% confidence interval for the mean gate-to-takeoff time using the above data. Use the t distribution.

3. What is the interpretation of the confidence interval in Part 2 in the context of this problem? If you repeatedly obtained samples of 30 and repeated Part 2, what general statement can you make about the true mean gate-to-takeoff time for airports across the United States?

4. What sample size would be necessary for the sample mean gate-to-takeoff time to be within one minute of the actual average gate-to-takeoff time with 95% confidence?

5. Construct a histogram of the data. Comment on the shape of the data. Using the Central Limit Theorem, can we say that the distribution of the sample mean (not the sample data) is approximately normally distributed?

Source: *USA Today*, "Just Plane Stuck," July 27,1998, p. 1B. Copyright 1998, *USA TODAY*. Reprinted with permission.

Handwritten notes (left margin):
If told or you know it's a normal Dist. of population—OK
If you know it's not normal— Take larger sample or do non-parametric technique
Du: Normal Plot or Histogram or Stem + leaf to See data
See Shape to see if data is normally distributed
☆ test question

Chapter 7 Appendix: Data Analysis with MINITAB

CONFIDENCE INTERVALS ON THE MEAN USING THE NORMAL DISTRIBUTION

To obtain a one population confidence interval on the mean using the normal distribution click on **Stat ➤ Basic Statistics ➤ 1-Sample Z.** For this example, the 20 samples of 10 Everglo bulbs in Table 7.1 are used to obtain 20 confidence intervals for the mean. Type in the variables c1–c20 in the Variables box. Also type in "95.0" in the Level box for a 95% confidence interval as well as the population standard deviation; in this case, 50 is used.

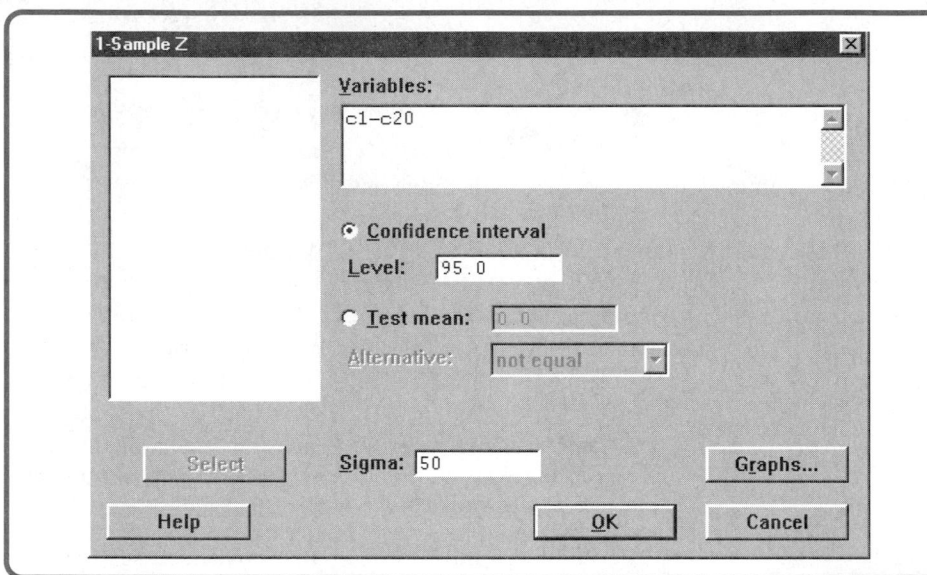

The output will appear in the session window and will look as follows.

Handwritten note: Since Sample size is 10, N=10, 20 sets of Data. you need to know σ or else use "t dist." table to get one.

Z CONFIDENCE INTERVALS *of σ (population)*

The assumed sigma = 50.0

Variable	N	Mean	StDev	SE Mean	95.0 % CI
C1	10	384.0	49.3	15.8	(353.0, 415.0)
C2	10	399.5	28.5	15.8	(368.5, 430.5)
C3	10	397.3	60.5	15.8	(366.3, 428.3)
C4	10	399.4	54.0	15.8	(368.4, 430.4)
C5	10	414.4	54.3	15.8	(383.4, 445.4)
C6	10	393.2	25.4	15.8	(362.2, 424.2)
C7	10	398.8	46.1	15.8	(367.8, 429.8)
C8	10	403.8	50.3	15.8	(372.8, 434.8)
C9	10	402.8	68.9	15.8	(371.8, 433.8)
C10	10	404.6	46.3	15.8	(373.6, 435.6)
C11	10	401.9	54.1	15.8	(370.9, 432.9)
C12	10	385.6	47.9	15.8	(354.6, 416.6)
C13	10	408.2	34.6	15.8	(377.2, 439.2)
C14	10	411.0	40.1	15.8	(380.0, 442.0)
C15	10	415.6	39.7	15.8	(384.6, 446.6)
C16	10	408.5	71.5	15.8	(377.5, 439.5)

Handwritten note (bottom): SE means are all same because $\sigma_{\bar{x}} = \dfrac{\sigma}{\sqrt{n}}$

19 of these
(CI) intervals will
contain the mean
of pop.

$$\frac{95(20)}{100} = 19$$

(Std. Error of mean)

Variable	N	Mean	StDev	SE Mean	95.0 % CI
C17	10	382.1	45.3	15.8	(351.1, 413.1)
C18	10	391.3	41.4	15.8	(360.3, 422.3)
C19	10	432.6	56.8	15.8	(401.6, 463.6)
C20	10	423.1	51.5	15.8	(392.1, 454.1)

$\bar{x}_{20}$

To obtain histograms of several of these columns of data, click on the Graphs button of the **1-Sample Z** user form. The following user form will appear. MINITAB cannot open too many histograms at once. So if 20 histograms are requested, it will display several of these and then ask that some of the previously opened histograms be closed before continuing to display the rest of the histograms. Note that dot plots or box plots of the data may be selected as well.

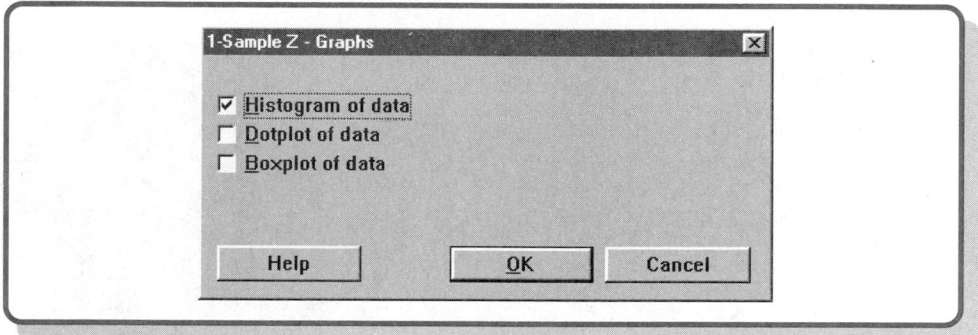

CONFIDENCE INTERVALS ON THE MEAN USING THE *t* DISTRIBUTION

To obtain a one population confidence interval on the mean using the *t* distribution, click on **Stat ➤ Basic Statistics ➤ 1-Sample *t*.** For 20 samples of 10 Everglo bulbs, type in the variables c1–c20 in the **Variables** box. Also type in 95.0 in the **Level** box for a 95% confidence interval. This user form is very similar to the 1-Sample Z user form, except that the population standard deviation box does not appear. The user form for obtaining a confidence interval on the mean using a *t* distribution is displayed below.

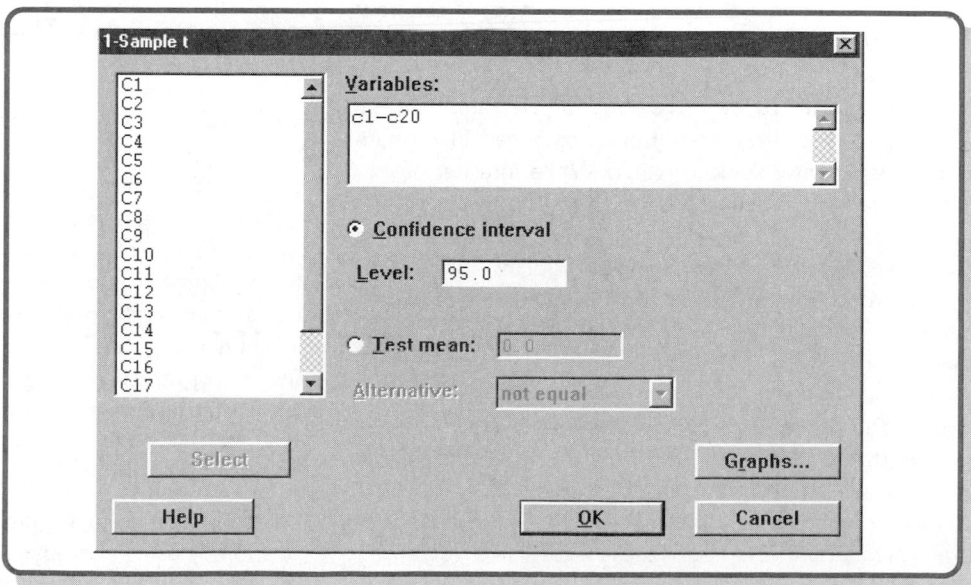

HYPOTHESIS TESTING FOR THE MEAN AND VARIANCE OF A POPULATION

STATISTICS IN ACTION: DRAMATIC CHANGES IN THE RADIO INDUSTRY

Government data on radio station ownership show that radio is undergoing an unprecedented wave of consolidation, taking it from a kitchen-table culture of mom-and-pop businesses to one at home in the boardrooms of the nation's largest companies. Historically, one of the most regulated industries, radio has seen many changes after passage of the Telecom Act's radio provision, which allows firms to own a greater number of radio stations.

The sales of 4,407 radio stations in 1996 and 1997 are valued at $32.4 billion. Consolidation in the industry has resulted in a loss of 700 individual owners since March 1996. Changes in the industry have resulted in many opportunities for large firms. However, one factor that needs to be battled is the declining listenership. Multimedia experts believe that the number of hours that the typical adult listens to the radio is 22 hours per week.

The decline in listenership has not stopped the flow of advertising revenue to radio. For many years, radio has drawn about 7% of all advertising revenues, and this percentage appears to be increasing. To give radio further challenges, Web sites offer music, packaged in formats borrowed from traditional radio. While Internet advertising totals more than $1 billion annually, analysts believe less than 1% of that goes to radio Internet. Unless songs are played on PCs with high-speed modems, sound quality for Internet stations isn't up to FM radio standards. Perhaps just as important as Internet radio, people one day may have the option of listening to satellite stations. A recent survey indicated that 20% of radio listeners would be willing to pay for satellite radio.

With the industry makeup shifting, multimedia experts are interested in the average number of radio stations owned by large companies as well as their average revenue. Surveys allow these experts to get timely information, without waiting for the results from reports from all owners of radio stations across the United

States. Using hypothesis testing, researchers can assess whether their beliefs in the average number of radio stations owned or average revenue has changed significantly.

If the average revenue per station in a sample of stations is different one year from the preceding year, is it safe to assume that the average revenue has decreased for *all* stations in the population? The answer is *no* unless you can demonstrate that the sample average differs *significantly* from the preceding year's value. When you have completed this chapter, you will be able to

- Determine what is meant by a "significant difference";
- Understand the various types of error that can result when trying to infer something about a population by using a sample; and
- Determine the effects on these errors when the sample size is increased.

A Look Back/Introduction

We have seen that statistical inference is used to estimate a population parameter using a sample statistic. For the rest of this book, the mean (μ) and standard deviation (σ) of the parent population will be unknown and will have to be estimated from the sample. Do not forget that even though you have estimated μ or σ, these values still are unknown and will forever remain unknown.

As a measure of how reliable your point estimate of the population mean μ really is, you can determine a confidence interval for this parameter. For a given confidence level, the narrower your resulting confidence interval is, the more faith you can have in the ability of your sample mean, $\overline{X}$, to provide an accurate estimate of the population mean. Also, when the Central Limit Theorem is applicable, you need not worry about the shape of the parent population (normal, exponential, and so on) when making probability statements regarding $\overline{X}$, provided you have a large sample (generally, $n > 30$). When you do have a large sample, the distribution of $\overline{X}$ closely approximates the normal. You can thus construct confidence intervals for population means without worrying about the nature of the parent population, simply because it doesn't matter.

Next, we turn to the situation in which someone makes a claim regarding the value of the population mean, μ. For example, when dealing with the lifetime of Everglo light bulbs in Chapter 6, we assumed that the population average of *all* bulbs was $\mu = 400$ hours. Where did this value come from? Suppose that Everglo advertisements claim that the average lifetime of the bulbs is 400 hours. By testing a sample of bulbs, can we prove this statement? The answer is an emphatic no; the only way to know the value of μ exactly is to obtain data for *all* Everglo bulbs; that is, obtain the entire population.

The sample, however, may allow us to reject the claim that μ is 400 hours, but since the sample is only a portion of the population, this conclusion may be incorrect. Such is the nature of hypothesis testing.

8.1 Hypothesis Testing on the Mean of a Population: Large Sample

A newspaper article claims that the average height of adult males in the United States is not the same as it was 50 years ago; it claims the average height is now 5.9 feet (approximately 5'11"). Your firm manufactures clothing, so the value of this population mean is of vital interest to you. To investigate the article's claim, you randomly select 75 males and measure their heights.* Your results for $n = 75$ are $\overline{x} = 5.76$ feet and $s = .48$ feet.

Let μ represent the population average (mean) of all U.S. male heights. We do have a point estimate of μ; $\overline{x} = 5.76$ feet is an estimate of μ. Keep in mind that the actual value of μ is unknown (although it *does exist*) and will remain that way. What we can do is estimate μ using the sample data. This situation can be summarized by considering the following pair of hypotheses:

Null Hypothesis	Alternative Hypothesis
H_0: $\mu = 5.9$	H_a: $\mu \neq 5.9$

H_0 asserts that the value of μ that has been claimed to be correct is in fact correct. H_a asserts that μ is some value other than 5.9 feet. The alternative hypothesis typically contains the conclusion that the researcher is attempting to demonstrate using the sample data. In our height example, if you do not believe that the average height is 5.9 feet and you expect the data to demonstrate that μ has some other value, H_a is $\mu \neq 5.9$.

---

* The size of this sample is unrealistically small (yet large, statistically).

DEFINITION

1. **Null hypothesis** (H_0). A statement (equality or inequality) concerning a population parameter; the researcher wishes to discredit this statement.
2. **Alternative hypothesis** (H_a). A statement in contradiction to the null hypothesis; the researcher wishes to support this statement.

The task of all hypothesis testing is to either **reject** H_0 or **fail to reject** H_0. Notice that we do not say "reject H_0 or accept H_0." This is an important distinction.

In our study of male heights, the (point) estimate of μ is $\bar{x} = 5.76$ feet. Should we reject H_0, given that it claims that μ is 5.9? First, we need not worry about the shape of the underlying population of male heights because, by the Central Limit Theorem, $\bar{X}$ is approximately normally distributed for large samples, regardless of the shape of this population. So, $\bar{X}$ is approximately a normal (and thus continuous) random variable. What is the probability that *any* continuous random variable is equal to a certain value? In particular, what is the probability that $\bar{X}$ is exactly equal to 5.9 feet? The answer to both questions is zero. Thus we see that we cannot reject H_0 simply because $\bar{X}$ is not equal to 5.9 feet. What we do is allow H_0 to stand, provided $\bar{X}$ is "close to" 5.9 feet, and reject H_0 otherwise. To define what "close" means, we need to take an in-depth look at what happens when you test hypotheses.

TYPE I AND TYPE II ERRORS

Because the sample does not consist of the entire population, there always is the possibility of drawing an incorrect conclusion when inferring the value of a population parameter using a sample statistic. When testing hypotheses, there are two types of possible errors:

TYPE I ERROR.   A Type I error occurs if you rejected H_0 when in fact it is true. For example, a Type I error would occur if you were to reject the claim (hypothesis) that the population mean is 5.9 feet when in fact it really is true.

TYPE II ERROR.   A Type II error occurs if you fail to reject H_0 when in fact H_0 is not true. For example, a Type II error occurs if you fail to reject the hypothesis that the population mean is 5.9 feet when in fact the mean is *not* 5.9 feet.

	Actual Situation	
Conclusion	H_0 **True**	H_0 **False**
Fail to reject H_0	Correct decision	Type II error
Reject H_0	Type I error	Correct decision

For any test of hypothesis, define

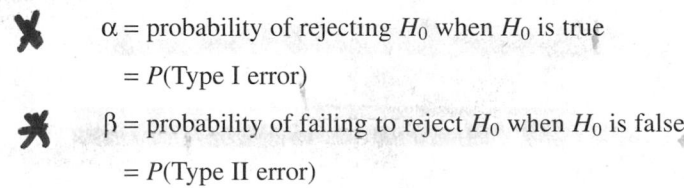

$$\alpha = \text{probability of rejecting } H_0 \text{ when } H_0 \text{ is true}$$

$$= P(\text{Type I error})$$

$$\beta = \text{probability of failing to reject } H_0 \text{ when } H_0 \text{ is false}$$

$$= P(\text{Type II error})$$

For any test of hypothesis, you would like to have control over n (the sample size), α (the probability of a Type I error), and β (the probability of a Type II error). However, in reality, you can control only two of these: n and α, n and β, or α and β. *In other words, for a fixed sample size, you cannot predetermine both α and β.*

Suppose you decide to set $\alpha = .02$. Then the procedure you use to test H_0 versus H_a will reject H_0 when it is true with a probability of .02. You may wonder why we do not set $\alpha = 0$, so that we would never have a Type I error. The thought of never rejecting a correct

H_0 sounds appealing, but the bad news is that β (the probability of a Type II error) is then equal to 1; that is, you will *always* fail to reject H_0 when it is false. If we set $\alpha = 0$, then the resulting test of H_0 versus H_a will automatically fail to reject H_0: $\mu = 5.9$ whenever μ is, in fact, any value other than 5.9 feet. If, for example, μ is 7.5 feet (hardly the case, but interesting), we would still fail to reject H_0—not a good situation at all. We therefore need a value of α that offers a better compromise between the two types of error probabilities.

The value of α you select depends on the relative importance of the two types of error. For example, consider the following hypotheses and decide if the Type I error or the Type II error is the more serious: You have just been examined by a physician using a sophisticated medical device, where the hypotheses under consideration are:

H_0: you do not have a particular serious disease

H_a: you do have the disease

$\quad\alpha = P(\text{rejecting } H_0 \text{ when it is true})$

$\quad\quad = P(\text{device indicates that you have the disease when you do not have it})$

$\quad\beta = P(\text{fail to reject } H_0 \text{ when in fact it is false})$

$\quad\quad = P(\text{device indicates that you do not have the disease when you do have it})$

For this situation, the Type I error (measured by α) is not nearly as serious as the Type II error (measured by β). Provided the treatment for the disease does you no serious harm if you are well, the Type I error is not serious. But the Type II error means you fail to receive the treatment even though you are ill.

We never set β in advance, only α. This will allow us to carry out a test of H_0 versus H_a. *The smaller α is, the larger β is. Consequently, if you want β to be small, you choose a large value of α.* For most situations, the range of acceptable α values is .01 to .1.

Acceptable
values of α

.01   .1

For the medical-device problem, you could choose a value of α near .1 or possibly larger, due to the seriousness of a Type II error. On the other hand, if you are more worried about Type I errors for a particular test (such as rejecting an expensive manufactured part that really is good), a small value of α is in order. What if there is no basic difference in the effect of these two errors? If there is no significant difference between the effects of a Type I error versus a Type II error, researchers often choose $\alpha = .05$.

PERFORMING A STATISTICAL TEST

The claim that the average adult male height is 5.9 feet resulted in the following pair of hypotheses:

$$H_0: \mu = 5.9$$

$$H_a: \mu \neq 5.9$$

We decide to use a test that carries a 5% risk of rejecting H_0 when it is correct; that is, $\alpha = .05$. In hypothesis testing, α is referred to as the **significance level** of your test. Using $n = 75$, $\bar{x} = 5.76$ ft, and $s = .48$ ft, we wish to carry out the resulting statistical test of H_0 versus H_a. We decided to let H_0 stand (not reject it) if $\bar{X}$ was "close to" 5.9 feet. In other words, we will reject H_0 if $\bar{X}$ is "too far away" from 5.9 feet. We write this as follows:

$$\text{reject } H_0 \text{ if } |\bar{X} - 5.9| \text{ is "too large"}$$

or, by standardizing $\bar{X}$, we can

$$\text{reject } H_0 \text{ if } \left|\frac{\bar{X} - 5.9}{\sigma/\sqrt{n}}\right| \text{ is "too large"}$$

FIGURE 8.1

The shaded area represents the significance level, α.

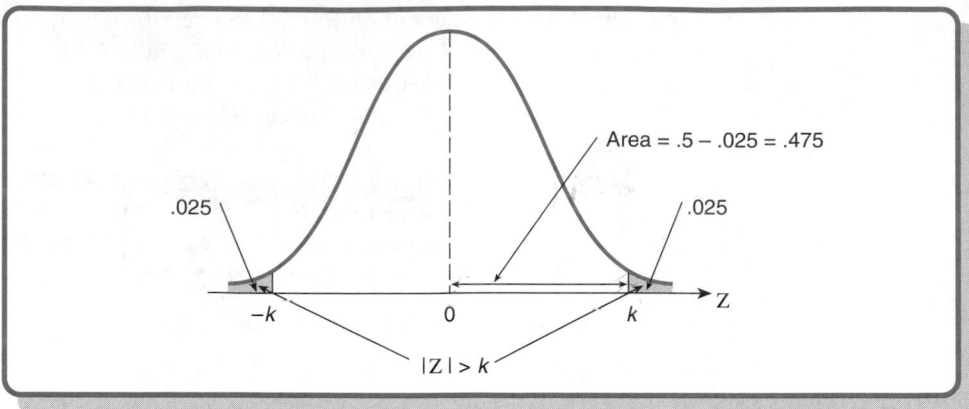

We rewrite the last statement as

$$\text{reject } H_0 \text{ if } \left| \frac{\overline{X} - 5.9}{\sigma / \sqrt{n}} \right| > k, \text{ for some } k$$

What is the value of k? Here is where the value of α has an effect. If H_0 is true and the sample size is large, then using the results of section 7.2, $\overline{X}$ is approximately a normal random variable with

$$\text{mean} = \mu = 5.9 \quad \text{and} \quad \text{standard deviation} = \frac{\sigma}{\sqrt{n}}$$

So, if H_0 is true, $(\overline{X} - 5.9)/(\sigma / \sqrt{n})$ is approximately a standard normal random variable, Z, for large samples. In this case, we reject H_0 if $|Z| > k$, for some k. Suppose $\alpha = .05$. Then,

$$.05 = \alpha = P(\text{rejecting } H_0 \text{ when it is true})$$

$$= P\left(\left| \frac{\overline{X} - 5.9}{\sigma / \sqrt{n}} \right| > k, \text{ when } \mu = 5.9 \right)$$

$$= P(|Z| > k)$$

To find the value of k that satisfies this statement, consider Figure 8.1. When $|Z| > k$, either $Z > k$ or $Z < -k$, as illustrated. Since $P(|Z| > k) = .05$, the total shaded area is .05, with .025 in each tail due to the symmetry of this curve. Consequently, the area between 0 and k is .475, and, using Table A.4, $k = 1.96$. So our test of H_0 versus H_a is

$$\text{reject } H_0 \text{ if } \left| \frac{\overline{X} - 5.9}{\sigma / \sqrt{n}} \right| > 1.96$$

and fail to reject H_0 otherwise. So,

$$\text{reject } H_0 \text{ if } \frac{\overline{X} - 5.9}{\sigma / \sqrt{n}} > 1.96$$

or

$$\text{reject } H_0 \text{ if } \frac{\overline{X} - 5.9}{\sigma / \sqrt{n}} < -1.96$$

This test will reject H_0 when it is true 5% of the time. This means that there is a 5% risk of making a Type I error.

FIGURE 8.2

Distribution of $\overline{X}$ if H_0 is true (H_0: $\mu = 5.9'$).

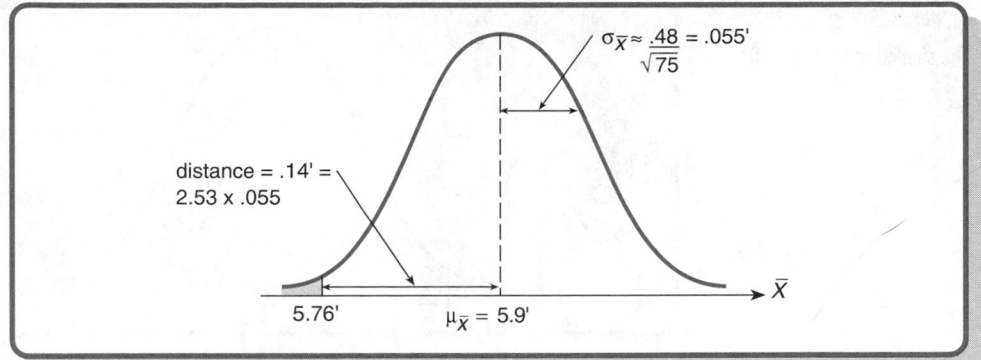

$\sigma_{\overline{X}} \approx \dfrac{.48}{\sqrt{75}} = .055'$

distance = .14' = 2.53 x .055

5.76'

$\mu_{\overline{X}} = 5.9'$

$\overline{X}$

Using the sample data, we obtained $n = 75$, with $\overline{x} = 5.76$ feet and $s = .48$ feet. Is $\overline{x} \doteq 5.76$ feet far enough away from 5.9 feet for us to reject H_0? This was not at all obvious at first glance; it may have seemed that this value of $\overline{X}$ is "close enough to" 5.9 for us not to reject H_0. Such is not the case, however, because

$$Z = \frac{\overline{X} - 5.9}{\sigma / \sqrt{n}} \approx \frac{\overline{X} - 5.9}{s / \sqrt{n}} = \frac{5.76 - 5.9}{.48 / \sqrt{75}} = -2.53 = Z^*$$

where Z^* is the **computed value** of Z. Notice that for the large-sample case, you can substitute for $\sigma / \sqrt{n}$ (typically unknown) its sample estimate $s / \sqrt{n}$.

CONCLUSION. Because $-2.53 < -1.96$, we reject H_0. Based on the sample results and a value of $\alpha = .05$, the average population male height (μ) is not equal to 5.9 feet.

Another way of phrasing this result is to say that if H_0 is true (that is, if $\mu = 5.9$ feet), the value of $\overline{X}$ obtained from the sample (5.76 feet) is 2.53 standard deviations to the left of the mean using the normal curve for $\overline{X}$ (Figure 8.2). Because a value of $\overline{X}$ this far away from the mean is very unlikely (that is, with probability less than $\alpha = .05$), our conclusion is that H_0 is not true, and so we reject it.

COMMENTS

1. In the preceding procedure, the sample standard deviation (s) was used in place of the population standard deviation (σ). In Chapter 7, we mentioned that $(\overline{X} - 5.9)/(s / \sqrt{n})$ actually follows a t distribution when sampling from a *normal* population, but that for large sample sizes, it can be approximated well using the standard normal (Z) distribution. This section deals with large samples from *any* population, and so $(\overline{X} - 5.9)/(s / \sqrt{n})$ will follow approximately a standard normal distribution for this situation.

2. When testing $\mu = $ (some value) versus $\mu \neq$ (some value), the null hypothesis, H_0, always contains the $=$, and the alternative hypothesis, H_a, always contains the $\neq$. In our example, this resulted in splitting the significance level, α, in half and including one-half in each tail of the test statistic, Z. Consequently, a test of H_0: $\mu = $ (some value) versus H_a: $\mu \neq$ (some value) is referred to as a **two-tailed test.**

EXAMPLE 8.1

Using the data from our example of male heights, what would be the conclusion using a significance level α of .01?

SOLUTION

1st way to do Statistic test

The only thing that we need to change from our previous solution is the value of k. Now,

$$P(|Z| > k) = \alpha = .01$$

as shown in Figure 8.3. Using Table A.4, $k = 2.575$, and the test is (see Figure 8.4):

$$\text{reject } H_0 \text{ if } Z > 2.575 \quad \text{or} \quad Z < -2.575$$

FIGURE 8.3

The shaded area is $\alpha = .01$.

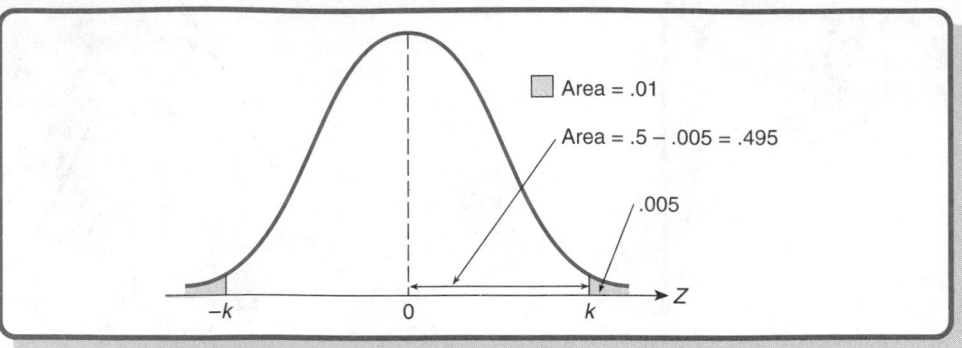

FIGURE 8.4

We reject H_0 if Z^* falls within either tail—the rejection region for $\alpha = .01$.

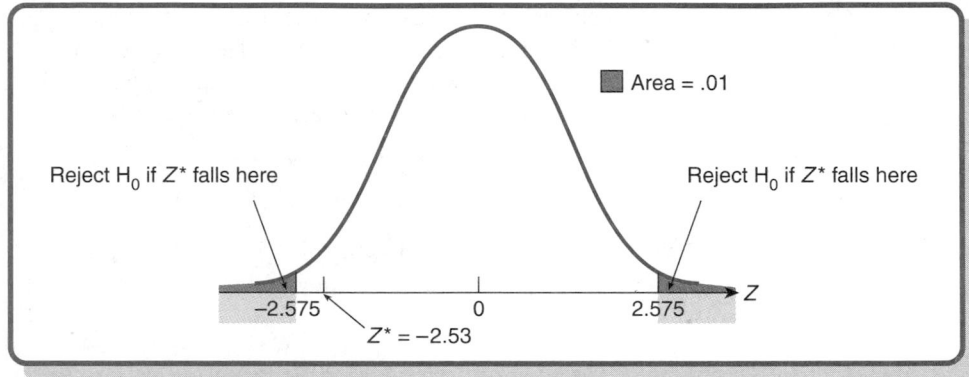

What is the computed value of Z? Our data values have not changed, so the value of this expression is the same: $Z^* = -2.53$.

The region defined by values of Z to the right of 2.575 and to the left of -2.575 in Figure 8.4 is the **rejection region.** The value of k (2.575) defining this region is the **critical value.** Z^* fails to fall in this region, so we fail to reject H_0. In other words, for $\alpha = .01$, the value of $\overline{X}$ is "close enough" to 5.9 to let H_0 stand; there is insufficient evidence to conclude that μ is different from 5.9 feet.

Clearly then, the choice of the significance level, α, is a delicate matter. It is important to remember that a value of α must be selected prior to obtaining the sample and should reflect the impact of a Type I versus a Type II error.

ACCEPTING H_0 OR FAILING TO REJECT H_0

It may appear that there is no difference between "accepting" and "failing to reject" a null hypothesis, but there *is* a difference between these two statements. When you test a hypothesis, H_0 is *presumed innocent* until it is demonstrated to be guilty. In Example 8.1, using $\alpha = .01$ we failed to reject H_0. Now, how certain are we that μ is *exactly* 5.9 feet? After all, our estimate of μ is 5.76 feet. Clearly, we do not believe that μ is precisely 5.9 feet. There simply was not enough evidence to *reject* the claim that $\mu = 5.9$ feet.

For any hypothesis-testing application, the only hypothesis that can be *accepted* is the alternative hypothesis, H_a. Either there is sufficient evidence to *support* H_a (we reject H_0) or there is not (we fail to reject H_0). The focus of our attention is whether there is sufficient evidence within the sample data to conclude that H_a is correct. By failing to reject H_0, we are simply saying that the data do not allow us to support the claim made in H_a (such as $\mu \neq 5.9$ feet) and not that we accept the statement made in H_0 (such as $\mu = 5.9$ feet).

THE FIVE-STEP PROCEDURE FOR HYPOTHESIS TESTING

The discussion up to this point has concentrated on hypothesis testing on the unknown mean of a particular population. We want to emphasize that the shape of the parent population is not important, provided you have a large sample. In other words, the population may be a normal (bell-shaped) one or it may not—it simply does not matter for large samples. Once the level of significance (α) has been determined, the steps carried out when attempting to reject or failing to reject a claim regarding the population mean μ are:

Step 1. *Set up the null hypothesis, H_0, and the alternative hypothesis, H_a.* If the purpose of the hypothesis test is to test whether the population mean is equal to a particular value (say, μ_0), the "equal hypothesis" always is stated in H_0 and the "unequal hypothesis" always is stated in H_a.

Step 2. *Define the test statistic.* The test statistic will be evaluated, using the sample data, to determine if the data are compatible with the null hypothesis. For tests regarding the mean of a population using a *large sample* (generally, $n > 30$), the test statistic is approximately a standard normal random variable given by the equation

$$Z = \frac{\overline{X} - \mu_0}{\sigma / \sqrt{n}} \approx \frac{\overline{X} - \mu_0}{s / \sqrt{n}} \qquad\qquad (8.1)$$

use this formula

where μ_0 is the value of μ specified in H_0.

Step 3. *Define a rejection region,* having determined a value for α, the significance level. In this region the value of the test statistic will result in rejecting H_0.

Step 4. *Calculate the value of the test statistic, and carry out the test.* State your decision: to reject H_0 or to fail to reject H_0.

Step 5. *Give a conclusion* in the terms of the original problem or question. This statement should be free of statistical jargon and should merely summarize the results of the analysis.

Steps 1 through 5 apply to all tests of hypothesis in this and subsequent chapters. The form of the test statistic and rejection region change for different applications, but the sequence of steps always is the same.

EXAMPLE 8.2

Remember that Everglo light bulbs are advertised as lasting 400 hours on the average. As manager of the quality assurance department, you need to examine this claim closely. If the average lifetime is, in fact, less than 400 hours, you can expect at least a half-dozen government watchdog agencies knocking on your door. If the light bulbs last longer than the 400 hours (on the average) claimed, you want to revise your advertising accordingly. To check this claim, you have tested the lifetimes of 100 bulbs, each under the same circumstances (power load, room temperature, and so on). The results of this sample are $n = 100$, $\overline{x} = 411$ hours, and $s = 42.5$ hours. What conclusion would you reach using a significance level of .1?

$.1 \div 2 =$ $\alpha = .1$ $\alpha/2 = .05$ $.5 - .05 = .45$
$Z = 1.645$

SOLUTION

Step 1. *Define the hypotheses.* We will test H_0: $\mu = 400$ versus H_a: $\mu \neq 400$.

Step 2. *Define the test statistic.* The proper test statistic for this problem is

$$Z = \frac{\overline{X} - 400}{\sigma / \sqrt{n}} \approx \frac{\overline{X} - 400}{s / \sqrt{n}}$$

Step 3. *Define the rejection region.* The steps for finding the rejection region are shown in Figure 8.5. We conclude:

reject H_0 if $Z > 1.645$ or $Z < -1.645$

FIGURE 8.5

See Example 8.2; the rejection region is $|Z| > 1.645$.

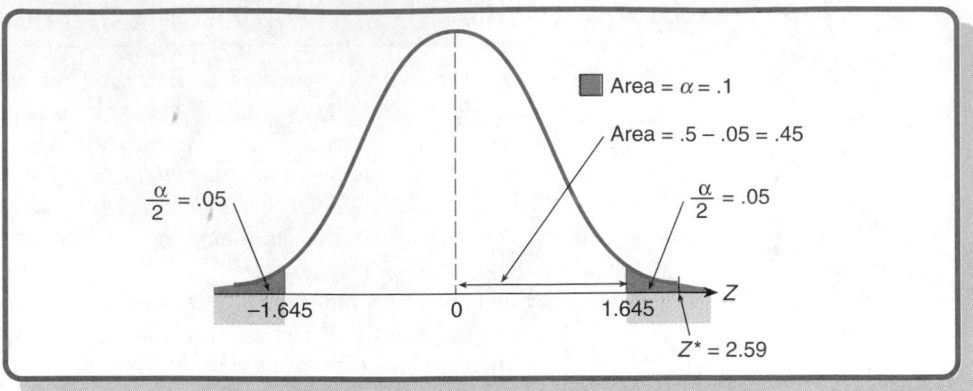

Step 4. *Calculate the value of the test statistic and carry out the test.* The computed value of Z is

$$Z^* \approx \frac{411 - 400}{42.5 / \sqrt{100}} = \frac{11}{4.25} = 2.59$$

Since $2.59 > 1.645$, our decision is to reject H_0. In Figure 8.5, Z^* falls in the rejection region.

Step 5. *State a conclusion.* Based on the sample data, there is sufficient evidence to conclude that the average lifetime of Everglo bulbs is not 400 hours.

COMMENTS

In Example 8.2, $\bar{X}$ was "far enough away from" 400 for us to reject the claim that the average lifetime is 400 hours (H_0). However, remember that you cannot decide what is "far enough away from" without also considering the value of the standard deviation ($s = 42.5$ hours in Example 8.2). This is why the value of s (or σ, if it is known) is a vital part of the test statistic. Essentially, when the sample contains much variation (s is large), the sample mean

($\bar{X}$) is a less reliable estimator of the population mean and it is more difficult for $\bar{X}$ to be significantly different than the hypothesized value (400, in the previous value).

Examine the test statistic in Example 8.2. Observe that for *small s*, it is "easier" to reject H_0. As s becomes smaller, the absolute value of the test statistic, Z, becomes larger, and the test statistic is more likely to be in the rejection region for a given value of α.

CONFIDENCE INTERVALS AND HYPOTHESIS TESTING

What is the relationship, if any, between a 95% confidence interval and performing a *two-tailed* test using $\alpha = .05$? There is a very simple relationship here: When testing H_0: $\mu = \mu_0$ versus H_a: $\mu \neq \mu_0$ using the five-step procedure and a significance level, α, H_0 will be rejected if and only if μ_0 lies outside the $(1 - \alpha) \cdot 100\%$ confidence interval for μ.

The five-step procedure and the confidence interval procedure always lead to the same result. In fact, you can think of a confidence interval as that set of values of μ_0 that would not be rejected by a *two-tailed* test of hypothesis.

In our example involving heights of U.S. males, a sample of 75 heights produced $\bar{x} = 5.76$ feet and $s = .48$ feet. The resulting 95% confidence interval for μ is

$$\bar{X} - k\left[\frac{\sigma}{\sqrt{n}}\right] \quad \text{to} \quad \bar{X} + k\left[\frac{\sigma}{\sqrt{n}}\right]$$

What is the value of k? For large sample sizes, the standard normal table (Table A.4) gives us the probability points we need. The value of k that provides a 95% confidence interval here is the *same* value of k that provides a two-tailed area under the Z curve equal to $1 - .95 = .05$. In other words, we use the same k value that we used in a two-tailed test of H_0 versus H_a—namely, $k = 1.96$. Since we are dealing with large samples, $\sigma / \sqrt{n}$ can be approximated by $s / \sqrt{n}$, and the resulting 95% confidence interval for μ is

$$\overline{X} - 1.96\left(\frac{\sigma}{\sqrt{n}}\right) \quad \text{to} \quad \overline{X} + 1.96\left(\frac{\sigma}{\sqrt{n}}\right)$$

$$\approx \overline{X} - 1.96\frac{s}{\sqrt{n}} \quad \text{to} \quad \overline{X} + 1.96\frac{s}{\sqrt{n}}$$

$$= 5.76 - 1.96\left(\frac{.48}{\sqrt{75}}\right) \quad \text{to} \quad 5.76 + 1.96\left(\frac{.48}{\sqrt{75}}\right)$$

$$= 5.76 - .11 \quad \text{to} \quad 5.76 + .11$$

$$= 5.65 \quad \text{to} \quad 5.87$$

The value of μ we are investigating here is $\mu = 5.9$ feet, and the corresponding hypotheses are H_0: $\mu = 5.9$ and H_a: $\mu \neq 5.9$. For $\alpha = .05$, our result using the two-tailed test was to reject H_0. Using the confidence interval procedure, we obtain the same result because 5.9 does not lie in the 95% confidence interval.

Thus, if you already have computed a confidence interval for μ, you can tell at a glance whether to reject H_0 for a two-tailed test, provided the significance level, α, for the hypothesis test and the confidence level, $(1 - \alpha) \cdot 100\%$, match up.

EXAMPLE 8.3

Repeat the example involving the heights of U.S. males, but using a 99% confidence interval. Is the result the same as in Example 8.1, where we failed to reject H_0: $\mu = 5.9$ using $\alpha = .01$?

SOLUTION

Using $\alpha = .01$, we failed to reject H_0 because the absolute value of the test statistic did not exceed the critical value of $k = 2.575$. The corresponding 99% confidence interval for μ is

$$\overline{X} - 2.575\left(\frac{\sigma}{\sqrt{n}}\right) \quad \text{to} \quad \overline{X} + 2.575\left(\frac{\sigma}{\sqrt{n}}\right)$$

$$\approx 5.76 - 2.575\left(\frac{.48}{\sqrt{75}}\right) \quad \text{to} \quad 5.76 + 2.575\left(\frac{.48}{\sqrt{75}}\right)$$

$$= 5.76 - .143 \quad \text{to} \quad 5.76 + .143$$

$$= 5.617 \quad \text{to} \quad 5.903$$

Because 5.9 does (barely) lie in this confidence interval, our decision is to fail to reject H_0—the same conclusion reached in Example 8.1.

THE POWER OF A STATISTICAL TEST

Up to this point, the probability of a Type II error, β, has remained a phantom—we know it is there, but we don't know what it is. One thing we can say is that a *wide* confidence interval for μ means that the corresponding two-tailed test of H_0 versus H_a has a *large* chance of failing to reject a false H_0; that is, β is large. Now,

$$\beta = P(\text{fail to reject } H_0 \text{ when } H_0 \text{ is false})$$

which means that

$$1 - \beta = P(\text{rejecting } H_0 \text{ when } H_0 \text{ is false})$$

The value of $1 - \beta$ is referred to as the **power** of the test. Since we like β to be small, we prefer the power of the test to be large. Notice that $1 - \beta$ represents the probability of making a *correct* decision in the event that H_0 is false, because in this case we *should* reject it. The more powerful your test is, the better.

Determining the power of your test (hence, β) is not difficult. We will illustrate this procedure for the previous two-tailed test of H_0: $\mu = \mu_0$ versus H_a: $\mu \neq \mu_0$, for some μ_0. We will first consider the case where σ is known and then discuss the situation where σ is unknown.

POWER OF THE TEST: σ KNOWN. In Example 8.2 we looked at the data on Everglo light bulbs, where the hypotheses were H_0: $\mu = 400$ hours and H_a: $\mu \neq 400$ hours. Assume that the actual population standard deviation is known to be $\sigma = 50$ hours. For this situation, our test statistic is (using a sample size of $n = 100$):

$$Z = \frac{\overline{X} - 400}{\sigma / \sqrt{n}} = \frac{\overline{X} - 400}{50 / \sqrt{100}}$$

$$= \frac{\overline{X} - 400}{5}$$

Proceeding as in Example 8.2, using $\alpha = .10$, we reject H_0 if $Z > 1.645$ or $Z < -1.645$, that is, if $|Z| > 1.645$. So reject H_0 if $(\overline{X} - 400)/5 > 1.645$ [same as $\overline{X} > 400 + (1.645)(5) = 408.225$] or if $(\overline{X} - 400)/5 < -1.645$ [same as $\overline{X} < 400 - (1.645)(5) = 391.775$]. This way of representing the rejection region is illustrated in Figure 8.6, using the shaded area under curve A. The power of this test is

$$1 - \beta = P(\text{rejecting } H_0 \text{ if } H_0 \text{ is false})$$

$$= P(\text{rejecting } H_0 \text{ if } \mu \neq 400)$$

What is the power of this test if μ is not 400 but is 403? What you have here is a value of $1 - \beta$ for *each* value of $\mu \neq 400$.

Recall that we reject H_0 if $\overline{X} > 408.225$ or $\overline{X} < 391.775$. The probability of this occurring if $\mu = 403$ is illustrated as the lined area under curve B in Figure 8.6. Now, if $\mu = 403$ and $\sigma = 50$ (assumed), then

$$Z = \frac{\overline{X} - 403}{50 / \sqrt{n}} = \frac{\overline{X} - 403}{5}$$

is a standard normal random variable. So, in Figure 8.6, the striped area to the right of 408.225 is

$$P(\overline{X} > 408.225) = P\left[\frac{\overline{X} - 403}{5} > \frac{408.225 - 403}{5}\right]$$

$$= P\left[Z > \frac{5.225}{5}\right]$$

$$= P(Z > 1.04)$$

$$= .5 - .3508$$

$$= .1492$$

Also, the striped area to the left of 391.775 is

$$P(\overline{X} < 391.775) = P\left[\frac{\overline{X} - 403}{5} < \frac{391.775 - 403}{5}\right]$$

$$= P(Z < -2.24)$$

$$= .5 - .4875$$

$$= .0125$$

FIGURE 8.6

The shaded area is the probability of rejecting H_0 if $\mu = 400$ (that is, $\alpha = .10$), and the striped area is the probability of rejecting H_0 if $\mu = 403$ (that is, the power of the test $1 - \beta$ when $\mu = 403$).

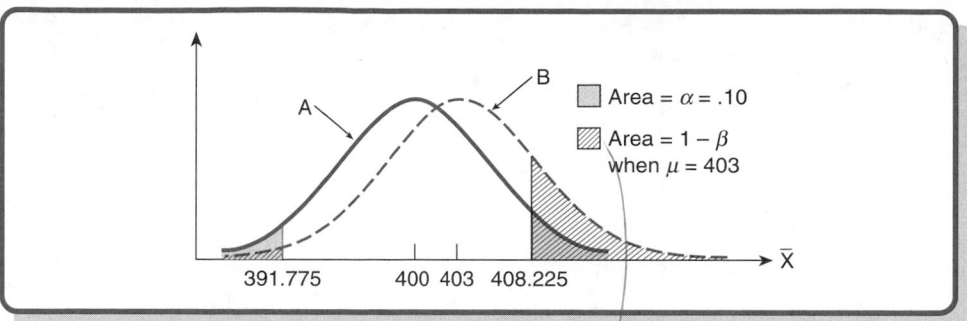

Adding these two areas, we find that, if $\mu = 403$, the power of the test of H_0: $\mu = 400$ versus H_a: $\mu \neq 400$ is

$$1 - \beta = .1492 + .0125 = .1617$$

This means that if $\mu = 403$, the probability of making a Type II error (not rejecting H_0) is $\beta = 1 - .1617 = .8383$ (rather high).

This procedure is summarized in the following box. Notice that in the previous discussion, $Z_{\alpha/2} = Z_{.05} = 1.645$, $z_1 = 1.645 - (403 - 400) / (50 / \sqrt{100}) = 1.04$, and $z_2 = -1.645 - (403 - 400) / (50 / \sqrt{100}) = -2.24$.

POWER OF TEST FOR H_0: $\mu = \mu_0$ VERSUS H_a: $\mu \neq \mu_0$

1. Determine

$$z_1 = Z_{\alpha/2} - \frac{\mu - \mu_0}{\sigma / \sqrt{n}}$$

and

$$z_2 = -Z_{\alpha/2} - \frac{\mu - \mu_0}{\sigma / \sqrt{n}}$$

where $Z_{\alpha/2}$ is the value of Z from Table A.4 having a right-tailed area of $\alpha/2$ and μ is the specific value of the population mean (403 in Figure 8.6).

2. Power of test = $P(Z > z_1) + P(Z < z_2)$.

The power of your test increases (β decreases) as μ moves away from 400, as illustrated in Figure 8.7. Using the five-step procedure, which uses the test statistic $Z = (\overline{X} - 400)/(\sigma / \sqrt{n})$, the resulting power curve is the solid-line curve in Figure 8.7. It is symmetric, and its lowest point is located at $\mu = 400$. For this value of μ, H_0 is actually true, so that a Type II error was not committed. Nevertheless, the value on the power curve corresponding to $\mu = 400$ is always

$$P(\text{rejecting } H_0 \text{ if } \mu = 400) = \alpha = .10 \text{ (for this example)}$$

The *steeper* your power curve is, the better. You are more apt to reject H_0 as μ moves away from 400—certainly a nice property. If we assume that the sampled population is normally distributed, Figure 8.7 illustrates that the power curve using the five-step procedure lies above (is steeper than) the power curve for any other testing procedure. To illustrate briefly another testing procedure, rather than basing the test statistic on the sample mean $\overline{X}$, we could derive a test statistic using the sample *median*. The resulting power curve for this

FIGURE 8.7
Power curve for H_0: $\mu = 400$
versus H_a: $\mu \neq 400$.

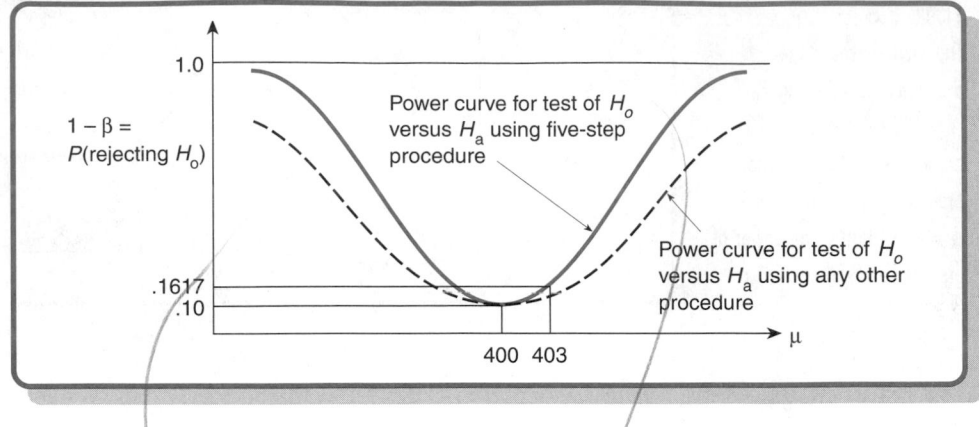

procedure would lie *below* the one using $\bar{X}$, indicating that the test using the sample median is less powerful and thus inferior. So, in this sense, the five-step procedure defines the best (most powerful) test of H_0: $\mu = \mu_0$ versus H_a: $\mu \neq \mu_0$.

POWER OF THE TEST: σ UNKNOWN. When σ is unknown, we are forced to *approximate* the power of the test by replacing σ with the sample estimate, s. We are dealing with large samples, so we can use Table A.4 (the Z table).

In our discussion of the power of our test for Everglo bulb lifetimes, we treated the population standard deviation, σ, as known. If we make no assumptions about this parameter, we need to approximate the power of the test for $\mu = 403$. We assume $s = 42.5$ hours (as before) and use $\alpha = .10$.

We now reject H_0 if

$$\bar{X} > 400 + 1.645\left[\frac{s}{\sqrt{n}}\right] \quad \text{or} \quad \bar{X} < 400 - 1.645\left[\frac{s}{\sqrt{n}}\right]$$

So, H_0 is rejected, provided

$$\bar{X} > 400 + 1.645\left[\frac{42.5}{\sqrt{100}}\right] = 406.99$$

or

$$\bar{X} < 400 - 1.645\left[\frac{42.5}{\sqrt{100}}\right] = 393.01$$

The resulting power of the test for $\mu = 403$ is approximately equal to

$$P(\bar{X} > 406.99 \text{ if } \mu = 403) + P(\bar{X} < 393.01 \text{ if } \mu = 403)$$

$$= P\left[Z > \frac{406.99 - 403}{42.5/\sqrt{100}}\right] + P\left[Z < \frac{393.01 - 403}{42.5/\sqrt{100}}\right]$$

$$= P(Z > .94) + P(Z < -2.35)$$

$$= (.5 - .3264) + (.5 - .4906) = .1736 + .0094$$

$$= .183$$

So there is an 18% chance of rejecting the null hypothesis if the population mean is, in fact, equal to 403.

EXERCISES 8.1–8.16

UNDERSTANDING THE MECHANICS

8.1 A random sample is drawn to test the claim that the population mean is not equal to 100.
  a. What is the null hypothesis?
  b. What is the alternative hypothesis?
  c. What are the different combinations of decisions and true states of nature?
  d. Will the hypothesis test procedure prove that the claim is right or wrong?

8.2 State what type of error can be made in the following situations:
  a. The conclusion is to reject the null hypothesis.
  b. The conclusion is to fail to reject the null hypothesis.
  c. The calculated value of the test statistic does not fall in the rejection region.

8.3 State whether each of the following statements is true or false, and explain why.
  a. The probability of the Type I error and the probability of the Type II error always add to 1.
  b. Increasing the value of α increases the value of β.
  c. A large value for the power at a specified value of the alternative hypothesis indicates a small value for the probability of a Type II error, given the specified value stated in the alternative hypothesis.
  d. The smaller the specified value of α is, the larger the rejection region.

APPLYING THE NEW CONCEPTS

8.4 State the null and alternative hypotheses for the following situations.
  a. Federal inspectors claim that a supplier of metal sheets for aircraft is producing sheets below specifications.
  b. *NewsMonth* magazine claims that its subscribers have an annual income over $60,000.
  c. The median number of children by a married couple in Massachusetts is two in 1990. A social worker would like to show that in 1999 the median number of children by a married couple in this state has changed.
  d. A study on chief executive officers (CEOs) would like to state that the average age of CEOs is greater than 55.

8.5 The mean of a normally distributed population is believed to be equal to 50.1. A sample of 36 observations is taken, and the sample mean is found to be 53.2. The alternative hypothesis is that the population mean is not equal to 50.1. Complete the hypothesis test, assuming that the population standard deviation is equal to 4. Use a .05 significance level.

8.6 More people are choosing to get married in the Caribbean as the cost of a traditional wedding increases. In fact, weddings in the Caribbean, with the cost of travel, can cost the bride's father between $5,000 and $10,000. As an additional benefit, the wedding can roll right into the honeymoon. While the disadvantage of such far-away weddings is difficult for many relatives and close friends, the savings over a $25,000 to $30,000 traditional wedding can make the decision easy. Suppose that a Caribbean resort wished to promote their location as a low-cost alternative to the traditional wedding and advertised that the average wedding with travel expenses is $7,500. To confirm this figure, 50 previously held weddings on the Caribbean island are randomly sampled. The data are presented below in dollars. Using a .05 significance level, is there sufficient evidence to indicate that the average cost of a wedding in the Caribbean differs from $7,500?

6,300	8,400	9,000	7,400	7,000	8,100	6,500	8,400
7,700	7,300	5,800	9,700	6,800	6,400	8,300	7,700
5,100	5,800	8,700	9,500	7,800	8,000	7,200	7,500
6,500	9,700	7,400	7,800	6,700	8,900	7,500	8,700
7,700	6,900	7,100	8,200	6,400	7,600	8,700	7,800
9,600	9,200	7,700	5,700	7,900	8,800	9,000	7,300
8,300	8,100						

(Adapted from *USA Today*, "Here Come the Isles: Exotic Ways to Wed," June 19, 1998, p. 4D.)

8.7 The weights of a fish in a certain pond that is regularly stocked are considered to be normally distributed with a mean of 3.1 pounds and a standard deviation of 1.1 pounds. A random sample of size 30 is selected from the pond, and the sample mean is found to be 2.4 pounds. Is there sufficient evidence to indicate that the mean weight of the fish differs from 3.1 pounds? Use a 10% significance level.

8.8 A crime reporter was told that, on the average, 3000 burglaries per month occurred in his city. The reporter examined past data, which were used to compute a 95% confidence interval for the number of burglaries per month. The confidence interval was from 2176 to 2784. At a 5% level of significance, do these data tend to support the alternative hypothesis, H_a: $\mu \neq 3000$?

8.9 A 95% confidence interval for the mean time that it takes a city bus to complete its route is 2.2 hours to 2.6 hours. The time that it takes the bus to complete its route is normally distributed. Is there sufficient evidence to indicate that the mean time to complete the route is different from 2.0 hours? Use a 5% significance level.

8.10 The life span of an electronic chip used in a high-powered microcomputer is estimated to be 625.35 hours from a random sample of 40 chips. The life of an electronic chip is considered to be normally distributed with a population variance of 400 hours.
  a. Find a 90% confidence interval for the mean life of the electronic chips.
  b. Is the true mean life of the electronic chips different from 633 hours? Use a 10% significance level.

8.11 The $450 million Stade de France, built specifically for the 1998 World Cup soccer championship, has 80,000 seats with no pillars or obstructed views. Soccer is so popular that the global television audience will outdraw that of the Olympics. Tickets sold through travel agencies were priced up to $600 for early matches before the World Cup championship. Suppose that a travel agency wished to know the mean selling price of the early matches and a random sample revealed a mean of $430 with a standard deviation of $130.

(Adapted from *USA Today*, "Frank Talk About State-of-the-Art Stadium," May 12, 1988, p. 8C.)

a. Find an interval with a 90% confidence level for estimating the true mean selling price for the early matches. Assume a sample size of 100.

b. Is there sufficient evidence to indicate that the true mean selling price for the early matches differs from $500? Use a 10% significance level.

8.12 The hypotheses for a situation are:

$$H_0: \mu = 20$$

$$H_a: \mu \neq 20$$

If the population of interest is normally distributed, what is the power of the test for the mean if μ is actually equal to 22? Assume that a sample of size 49 is used and the sample standard deviation is 4.2. Use a significance level of .05.

8.13 Windows 98, which was released in June 1998, offers support for technologies that have not caught on to the mass market. One such technology is WebTV for Windows. This technology allows suitably equipped computers to be used as TV receivers so that a user can watch TV while cruising the Web or crunching numbers. A TV tuner card is needed and costs vary with an ATI card being the more expensive option. Assume that the mean price for a card to connect the PC to a TV is $215 for the population of sales prices for this card. Furthermore, assume the price of these cards can be approximated by a normal distribution with a population standard deviation of $40. Suppose that a marketing analyst randomly samples 25 stores and wishes to test a hypothesis about the mean of this population using a .10 significance level. What would be the power of the statistical test if the hypotheses are as presented below? Compare and comment on the power for the two hypotheses.

(Adapted from *USA Today*, "Windows 98 is an Upgrade That Bears Scrutiny," June 25, 1998, p. 5D.)

a. $H_0: \mu = 200$, $H_0: \mu \neq 200$
b. $H_0: \mu = 160$, $H_0: \mu \neq 160$

8.14 An electro-optical firm currently uses a laser component in producing sophisticated graphic designs. The time it takes to produce a certain design with the current laser component is 70 seconds, with a standard deviation of 8 seconds. A new laser component is bought by the firm because it is believed that the time it takes this laser to produce the same design is not equal to 70 seconds; the new component also has a standard deviation of 8 seconds. The research-and-development department is interested in constructing the power curve for testing the claim that the time it takes to produce the same design by the new laser component is not equal to 70 seconds. Graph the power function for a sample of size 25 and a significance level of .05.

Using the Computer

8.15 Generate 100 random samples each of size 30 from a normal population with a mean of 50 and a standard deviation of 10. Perform the Z test for each of the 100 random samples using a σ of 10. For a 5% significance level, the critical values are −1.96 and 1.96. Count the number of Z test values that fall in the critical region. How many Z tests would you expect to result in a conclusion of reject the null hypothesis? In Excel, click on **Tools ➤ Data Analysis ➤ Random Number Generation,** and then select **Normal** for the distribution. Type in "100" for the number of variables and "30" for the number of random numbers. For the mean and standard deviation, type in "50" and "10," respectively. Type in cell "A" for the ouput range. Click "OK" and the columns A through CV should have 30 observations each. Now type "=average(A1:A30)" in cell A31. In cell A32, type "=(A31 − 50)/(10/sqrt(30))". In cell A33, type "=if(ABS(A32) > 1.96,1,0)". Now highlight cells A31, A32, and A33. Click on **Copy.** Holding the shift key, move the cursor to CV31 and move the cursor down to CV33. This will highlight all the three rows below the data. Now release the shift key and click on **Paste.** In cell A34, type "=sum(A33:CV33)". Cell A34 gives the count of the number of test statistic values that resulted in rejecting the null hypothesis.

8.16 **[DATA SET EX8-16]** *Variable description:*

KiloUsage: Weekly kilowatt usage of electrical components in a factory.

The plant manager of a paper factory has retooled the plant. Some of the new tools are energy efficient and some require more energy to operate. The manager knows that historical monthly kilowatt usage was 3,200 hours per week with a standard deviation of 500 hours per week. The manager selects 40 weeks at random over the 18 months since the seminar. These values are in the variable KiloUsage and represent the number of hours of kilowatt usage per week.

a. Plot a histogram of the data. Describe the shape of the distribution.

b. Is there sufficient evidence for the plant manager to claim that the retooling has changed the average weekly kilowatt usage of the paper plant? Use a 5% significance level and use the historical standard deviation of 500 kilowatts in the statistical test. In Excel, click on **KGP Data Analysis ➤ One Population Inference.** Fill in the user form, selecting the *z* statistic.

8.2 One-Tailed Test for the Mean of a Population: Large Sample

There are many situations in which you are interested in demonstrating that the mean of a population is *larger* or *smaller* than some specified value. For example, as a member of a consumer-advocate group, you may be attempting to demonstrate that the average weight of a bag of sugar for a particular brand is not 10 pounds (as specified on the bag) but is in fact less than 10 pounds. Because the situation that you (the researcher) are attempting to demonstrate goes into the alternative hypothesis, the resulting hypotheses would be H_0: $\mu \geq 10$ and H_a: $\mu < 10$. *Remember that we said it is standard practice always to put the equals sign in the null hypothesis.* In the testing procedure only the **boundary value** is important, and so the hypotheses may be written as

$$H_0: \mu = 10$$

$$H_a: \mu < 10$$

In this way, we can identify the distribution of $\bar{X}$ when H_0 is true—namely, $\bar{X}$ is approximately a normal random variable centered at 10 with standard deviation $\sigma/\sqrt{n}$ (or $s/\sqrt{n}$ if σ is unknown). Because the focus of our attention is on H_a (can we support it or not?), which of the two ways you use to write H_0 is not an important issue. The procedure for testing H_0 versus H_a is the same regardless of how you state H_0.

The resulting test is referred to as a **one-tailed test,** and it uses the same five-step procedure as the two-tailed test. The only change we make is to modify the rejection region: All the error is in a single tail.

EXAMPLE 8.4

A foreign car manufacturer advertises that its newest model, the Bullet, rarely stops at gas stations. In fact, they claim its EPA rating for highway driving is at least 32.5 mpg. However, the results of a recent independent study determined the mpg for 50 identical models of the Bullet, with these results: $n = 50$, $\bar{x} = 30.4$ mpg, and $s = 5.3$ mpg. This report failed to offer any conclusion, and you have been asked to interpret these results by someone who has always felt that the 32.5 figure is too high. What would be your conclusion using a significance level of $\alpha = .05$?

SOLUTION

Step 1. *An important point to be made here is that H_0 and H_a (as well as α) must be defined* before *you observe any data.* In other words, *do not let the data dictate your hypotheses;* this approach would introduce a serious bias into your final outcome. For this application, we want to demonstrate that the population mean, μ, is less than 32.5 mpg, and so this goes into H_a. The appropriate hypotheses then are $H_0: \mu \geq 32.5$ and $H_a: \mu < 32.5$.

Step 2. The test statistic for a large-sample one-tailed test is the same as that for a large-sample two-tailed test, namely,

$$Z = \frac{\bar{X} - \mu_0}{\sigma/\sqrt{n}} \approx \frac{\bar{X} - \mu_0}{s/\sqrt{n}}$$

Here,

$$Z \approx \frac{\bar{X} - 32.5}{s/\sqrt{n}}$$

Step 3. What happens to Z when H_a is true? Here we would expect $\bar{X}$ to be less than 32.5 (because μ is), so the value of Z should be negative. Consequently, our procedure will be to reject H_0 if Z lies "too far to the left" of 0; that is,

$$\text{reject } H_0 \text{ if } Z \approx \frac{\bar{X} - 32.5}{s/\sqrt{n}} < k \quad \text{for some } k < 0$$

Since $\alpha = .05$, we will choose a value of k (the critical value) such that the resulting test will reject H_0 (shoot down the mpg claim) when it is true, with a 5% risk of an incorrect decision. This amounts to defining a rejection region in the *left tail* of the Z curve, the shaded area in Figure 8.8. Using Table A.4, we see that the critical value is $k = -1.645$, and the resulting test of H_0 versus H_a is

$$\text{reject } H_0 \text{ is } Z \approx \frac{\bar{X} - 32.5}{s/\sqrt{n}} < -1.645$$

FIGURE 8.8

The one-tailed rejection region is $Z < -1.645$. We reject H_0 if $Z = (\overline{X} - 32.5)/(\sigma/\sqrt{n}) < -1.645$.

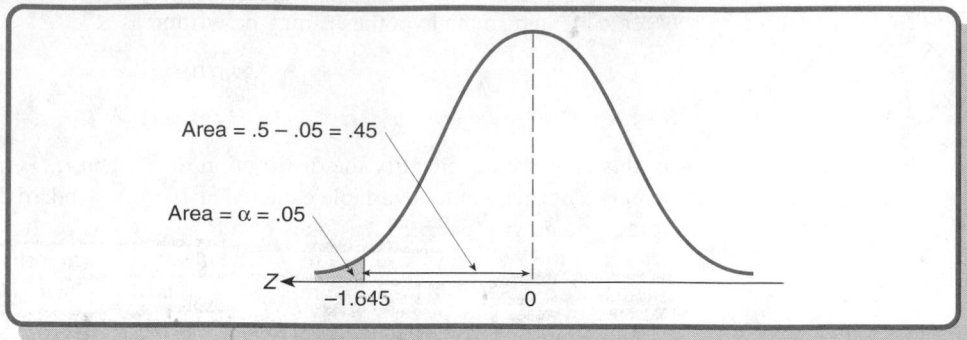

Step 4. Using the sample results, the value of the test statistic is

$$Z^* \approx \frac{30.4 - 32.5}{5.3/\sqrt{50}} = -2.80$$

Because $-2.80 < -1.645$, the decision is to reject H_0.

Step 5. The results of this study support the claim that the average mileage for the Bullet is *less than* 32.5 mpg. This result would provide just cause for claiming false advertising by the auto manufacturer.

ONE-TAILED TEST OR TWO-TAILED TEST?

The decision to use a one-tailed test or a two-tailed test depends on what you are attempting to demonstrate. For example, when the quality-control department of a manufacturing facility receives a shipment from one of its vendors and wants to determine if the product meets minimal specifications, a one-tailed test is appropriate. If the product does not meet specifications, it will be rejected. This type of problem was first encountered in Chapter 5, where we examined lot acceptance sampling. Here, the product is *not* checked to see whether it *exceeds* specifications, because any product that exceeds specifications is acceptable.

On the other hand, the vendors who supply the products would generally run two-tailed tests to determine two things. First, they must know if the product meets the minimal specifications of their customers before they ship it. Second, they must determine whether the product greatly exceeds specifications because this can be very costly in production (making a product that uses too much raw material costs them extra money).

The testing of electric fuses is a classic example of a two-tailed test. A fuse must break when it reaches the prescribed temperature or a fire will result. However, the fuse must not break before it reaches the prescribed temperature or it will shut off the electricity when there is no need to do so. Therefore, the quality-control procedures for testing fuses must be two-tailed.

MICROSOFT® EXCEL APPLICATION   USE DATA8-5

EXAMPLE 8.5

Using Excel to Calculate the Large-Sample Test Statistic for Testing a Population Mean

The mean consumption of electricity for the month of June at the Southern States Power Company (SSPC) historically has been 918 kilowatt-hours per residential customer. As part of its request for a rate increase, SSPC is arguing that the power consumption for June of the current year is substantially higher. To demonstrate this, they hired an independent consulting firm to examine a random sample of 60 customer accounts. The sample results, contained in data set DATA8-5, consist of the 60 kilowatt-hours for June of the current year. Can you conclude that the average consumption for all users during June of this year (denoted by μ) is larger than 918? Use $\alpha = .01$.

SOLUTION

Step 1. The hypotheses here are H_0: $\mu \leq 918$ and H_a: $\mu > 918$.

Step 2. The correct test statistic is

$$Z = \frac{\overline{X} - 918}{\sigma / \sqrt{n}} \approx \frac{\overline{X} - 918}{s / \sqrt{n}}$$

Approximating $\sigma / \sqrt{n}$ using $s / \sqrt{n}$ is valid since we are dealing with a large sample here.

Step 3. For this situation, what happens to Z if H_a is true? The value of $\overline{X}$ should then be *larger* than 918 (on the average), resulting in a positive value of Z. So we

$$\text{reject } H_0 \text{ if } Z \approx \frac{\overline{X} - 918}{s / \sqrt{n}} > k \quad \text{for some } k > 0$$

Examine the standard normal curve in Figure 8.9, where the area corresponding to α is the shaded part of the *right tail;* using Table A.4, the critical value is $k = 2.33$. The test of H_0 versus H_a will be

$$\text{reject } H_0 \text{ if } Z > 2.33$$

Step 4. To carry out the test of hypothesis using Excel, begin by opening file DATA8-5. The first step is to determine the standard deviation of the 60 sample values. Referring to Figure 8.11, type "Stand. Dev." in cell B1 and "=STDEV(A2:A61)" in cell B2. The value of 173.92 should appear in cell B2. Although 173.92 is the sample standard deviation, the *Z test procedure will treat this value as the standard deviation of the population.* Next, click on **KGP Data Analysis ➤ One Population Inference** and fill in the various boxes as illustrated in Figure 8.10. The input range is A1:A61, since there are 60 data values and cell A1 contains the label "KW-Hours" (be sure to click on the box alongside **Labels**). By specifying the output range as C1 (upper-left corner), you obtain the output shown in Figure 8.11. The computed value of the test statistic is

$$Z^* = \frac{952.58 - 918}{173.92 / \sqrt{60}} = 1.540$$

Because $1.540 < 2.33$ (the rounded value in cell D9), the decision is to fail to reject H_0. A valuable piece of information is contained in cell D8. It is called the *p-value* for the test of hypothesis and will be discussed in Section 8.3.

Step 5. At the .01 significance level, there is insufficient evidence to support the power company's claim that the power consumption for June has increased.

FIGURE 8.9

One-tailed rejection region; reject H_0 if $Z > 2.33$.

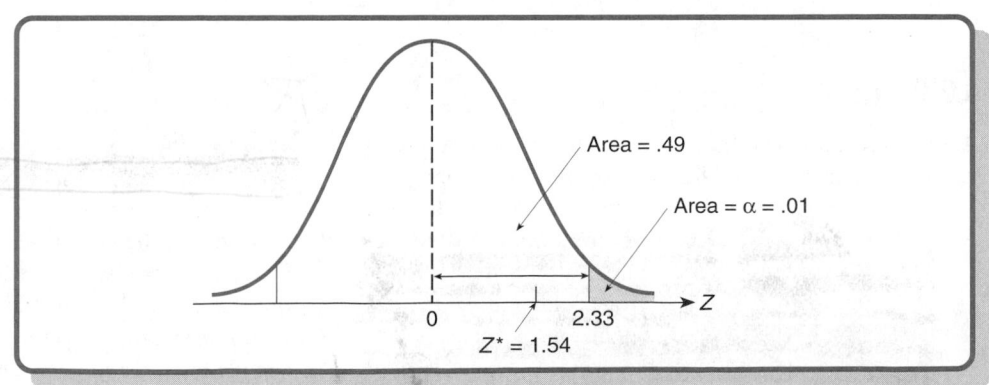

Area = .49

Area = α = .01

0

2.33

$Z^* = 1.54$

FIGURE 8.10

Excel input screen for testing a population mean using **KGP Data Analysis ➤ One Population Inference.**

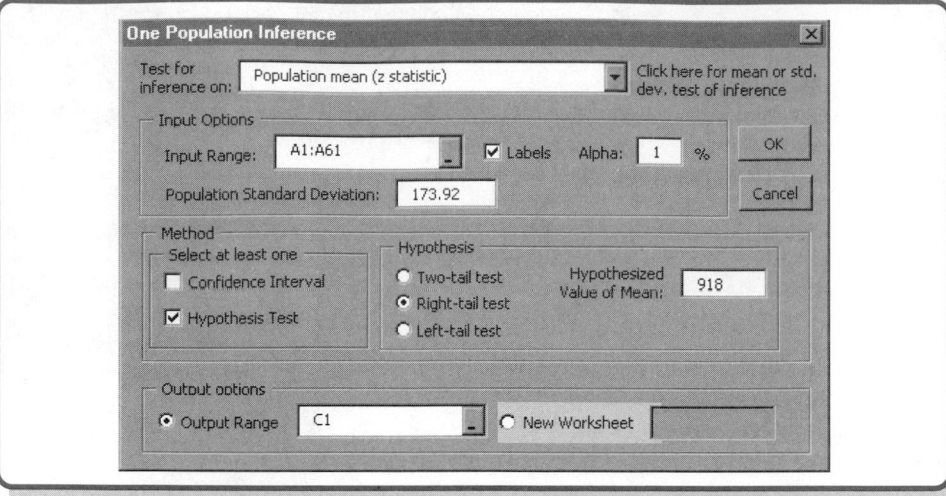

FIGURE 8.11

Excel spreadsheet and output using **KGP Data Analysis ➤ One Population Inference** (refer to Figure 8.10 for input screen; Sample standard deviation is in cell B2).

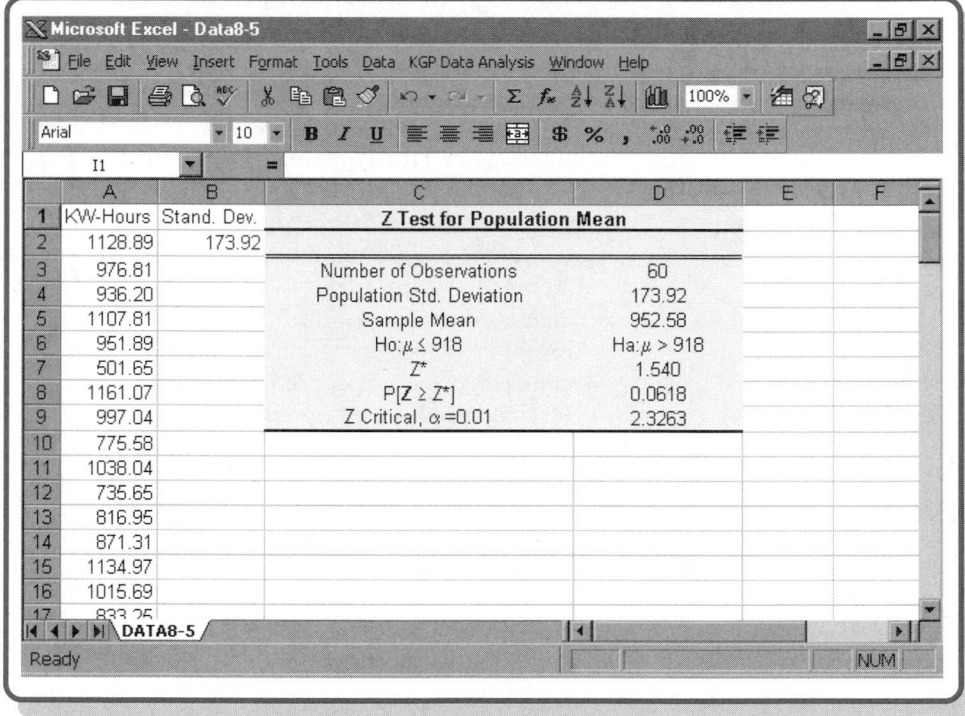

COMMENTS

1. This result is very much tied to the value of α. Using α = .10 in Example 8.5, we would obtain the *opposite* conclusion—which you may find somewhat disturbing. You often hear the expression that "statistics lie." This is not true—statistics are merely mistreated, either intentionally or accidentally. One can often obtain the desired conclusion by choosing the value of α that produces the desired conclusion. We therefore reemphasize that you must choose α by

weighing the seriousness of a Type I versus a Type II error *before* seeing the data. A partial remedy for this dilemma is discussed in Section 8.3.

2. To calculate the power of a one-sided test, refer to the box on page 317. We modify this procedure for a one-sided test as outlined in the following boxes.

3. A summary of the procedure for carrying out a large-sample test on a population mean is contained in the third box.

POWER OF TEST FOR H_0: $\mu \leq \mu_0$ VERSUS H_a: $\mu > \mu_0$

1. Determine

$$z_1 = Z_\alpha - \frac{\mu - \mu_0}{\sigma / \sqrt{n}}$$

where Z_α is the value of Z from Table A.4 having a right-tailed area of α and μ is the specific value of the population mean.

2. Power of the test is $P(Z > z_1)$

POWER OF TEST FOR H_0: $\mu \geq \mu_0$ VERSUS H_a: $\mu < \mu_0$

1. Determine

$$z_2 = -Z_\alpha - \frac{\mu - \mu_0}{\sigma / \sqrt{n}}$$

where Z_α is the value of Z from Table A.4 having a right-tailed area of α and μ is the specific value of the population mean.

2. Power of the test is $P(Z < z_2)$

LARGE-SAMPLE TESTS ON A POPULATION MEAN

Two-Tailed Test

$$H_0: \mu = \mu_0$$

$$H_a: \mu \neq \mu_0$$

reject H_0 if $|Z^*| > Z_{\alpha/2}$

where Z^* is the computed value of $Z \approx \dfrac{\bar{X} - \mu_0}{s / \sqrt{n}}$ ($Z_{\alpha/2} = 1.96$ for $\alpha = .05$).

One-Tailed Test

$H_0: \mu \leq \mu_0$	$H_0: \mu \geq \mu_0$
$H_a: \mu > \mu_0$	$H_a: \mu < \mu_0$
reject H_0 if $Z^* > Z_\alpha$	reject H_0 if $Z^* < -Z_\alpha$
($Z_\alpha = 1.645$ for $\alpha = .05$)	($-Z_\alpha = -1.645$ for $\alpha = .05$)

Will not cover

EXERCISES 8.17–8.26

UNDERSTANDING THE MECHANICS

8.17 Set up the null hypothesis and the alternative hypothesis for each of the following situations.

a. An automotive analyst believes that the miles per gallon on a new model is less than what the company is advertising. A random sample of data is taken to support the analyst's belief.

b. A phone company claims that the average customer pays less than $30 a month. A random sample of data is taken to verify this claim.

c. A marketing research firm believes that the average number of hours per week that Americans watch television differs from 15 hours a week. A sample of data is taken to support this belief.

8.18 A random sample of 64 observations was selected. Test that the mean of the population is less than 106 using a significance level of .05. The following statistics were calculated from the random sample:

$$\Sigma(x_i - \bar{x})^2 = 2016 \qquad \Sigma x = 6592$$

8.19 A random sample of 49 observations from a normal population yields a sample mean of 85 with a standard deviation of 14.

a. Test the claim that the population mean differs from 81. Use a .05 significance level.

b. Test the claim that the population mean is greater than 85. Use a .05 significance level.

APPLYING THE NEW CONCEPTS

8.20 Bobby Marks is seriously considering investing in the grocery business in the southeastern United States. He believes that the industry's average return on sales (ROS) is less than 5%. A random sample of 46 such businesses in various sectors of the southeastern United States revealed that

$$\bar{x} = 4.6\% \qquad s = 1.2\%$$

Test Marks' belief concerning the ROS of the grocery business in the southeastern United States, using a 5% significance level.

8.21 The idea of a smart mower has been on drawing boards for years. In 1988, the Lawn Ranger, a lawn mower guided by remote control was introduced to the public, but few of them sold. In 1994 the Turtle was patented and sold for about $2000. Its computer guides it to cut grass. However, tall grass and a cloudy day can stall out the lawn mower. Michael Gaffney of the Professional Lawn Care Association of America believes that walk-behind lawn mowers will be popular for some time, with the average lawn mower costing $275. Suppose that a venture capitalist, who is interested in putting a new remote control lawn mower on the market, is advised that this novel lawn mower will be a profitable investment in the Richmond, Virginia, area if the average cost of a push lawn mower sold in that area exceeds $350. A random sample of 100 lawn mower owners was obtained. The sample mean was $375 with a standard deviation of $150. Should the venture capitalist invest in marketing the new lawn mower? Use a significance level of .05.

(Adapted from *USA Today*, "It's Like George Jetson's Lawn Mower," May 12, 1998, p. 2D.)

8.22 Nouriel Roubini started a Web site on the subject of the Asian economic crisis to keep his students informed. However, now World Bank big shots scour the Roubini site, especially for ammunition for use in their battles with the IMF over Asia policy. Mr. Roubini believes that the average number of times per day that his papers are downloaded is less than 300. He wishes to test this hypothesis with a random sample of 60 days.

(Adapted from *The Wall Street Journal*, "Internet Hot Spot Emerges From Asian Economic Crisis," June 23, 1998, p. B1.)

    a. With a sample mean of 283 and a sample standard deviation of 58, what can Mr. Roubini conclude using a significance level of .05?

    b. If the significance level were .10 instead of .05, would the conclusion be different?

8.23 In an attempt to get AIDS drugs to thousands of HIV-infected people in Africa, Asia, and South America, several major pharmaceutical companies are slashing their prices, in some cases by 50% to 75%. The manager of a medical center working under the United Nations' AIDS program is interested in the average cost of widely used anti-HIV drugs in the South African region. The manager believes that the cost is less than $280 per month. Assume that the costs of these anti-HIV drugs are approximately normally distributed with a standard deviation of $100. What is the power of the statistical test to test the manager's belief if the sample size is 35 and the true mean cost is $240 for the anti-HIV drugs in South Africa? Use a significance level of .05.

(Adapted from *The Wall Street Journal*, "AIDS Medicine Will Cost Less in Poor Nations," June 23, 1998, p. B1.)

8.24 As part of a massive marketing blitz, Proctor and Gamble (P&G) distributed thousands of samples of its olestra-made chips, Fat-Free Pringles, to lunchtime crowds in 20 major cities. P&G is hoping that many people who do not eat snacks to avoid fat will enjoy the Wow! brand of chips made with P&G's olestra. Suppose that a marketing analyst believes that on a scale from 1 to 10 (with 10 equal to incredibly delicious to 1 equal to awful) that the average rating by consumers is greater than 6 and wishes to perform a statistical test with a .05 significance level. Assume that the analyst has historical data on similar types of potato chips and knows that the population standard deviation is 2.5. What is the power of the hypothesis test to test the analyst's belief if the analyst randomly samples 35 consumers from a population in which the true mean rating is 7?

(Adapted from *The Wall Street Journal*, "P&G Puts Lots of Chips on Plan To Give Away Fat-Free Pringles," June 23, 1998, p. B6.)

USING THE COMPUTER

8.25 **[DATA SET EX8-25]** *Variable description:*

CartridgLife: Number of pages that a cartridge can be used to print.

An office supply company would like to advertise that its new and improved ink jet cartridges last longer than the previous ones. From past tests, the old cartridges had a life of 2,375 pages with a standard deviation of 250 pages. The company believes that the new the life of the new ink jet cartridges will be longer than the old cartridges and that the standard deviation of the life of the new cartridges is the same. A random sample of 100 new cartridges were used in a study and their life is recorded in variable CartridgLife in units of pages.

    a. Using a significance level of .10, is there sufficient evidence that the new cartridges last longer?

    b. Explain how practical and statistical significance are important in determining whether the company should advertise the new cartridges as lasting longer?

    c. Should the standard deviation also have decreased to really have an improved cartridge? Explain.

8.26 **[DATA SET EX8-26]** *Variable description:*

TraceElem: The number of parts per million of trace chemicals used in a plant with a smelter.

The plant manager wishes to claim its plant was within the standards set by the Occupational Safety and Health Act (OSHA). Inspectors previously have been concerned that the smelter at the plant did not meet these standards. The plant manager randomly tests 200 pockets of air around the plant. This data are listed in variable TraceElem and are specified in units of per milligram per cubic meter of air. The standard set by OSHA on these trace elements is .0016 per milligram per cubic meter of air.

    a. What are the null and alternative hypotheses to test the claim that the plants have fewer parts per million of the trace elements than allowed by OSHA's standards?

    b. Which error is worse—Type I or Type II in this study?

    c. Using a .01 significance level, is there sufficient evidence to conclude that the plant meets the standards set by OSHA on the trace elements. Find the standard deviation of the data and then use the Z test with this value.

8.3 REPORTING TESTING RESULTS USING A *p*-VALUE

In Example 8.1, we noted that for one value of α we rejected H_0, and for another (seemingly reasonable) value of α we failed to reject H_0. Is there a way of summarizing the results of a test of hypothesis that allows you to determine whether these results are barely significant (or insignificant) or overwhelmingly significant (or insignificant)? Did we barely reject H_0, or did H_0 go down in flames?

A convenient way to summarize your results is to use a *p*-value, often called the *observed* α or *observed significance* level.

> The ***p*-value** is the value of α at which the hypothesis test procedure changes conclusions based on a given set of data. It is the largest value of α for which you will fail to reject H_0.

Consequently, the *p*-value is the point at which the five-step procedure leads us to switch from rejecting H_0 to failing to reject H_0 for a given set of data.

DETERMINING THE *p*-VALUE

The *p*-value for *any* test is determined by replacing the area corresponding to α by the area corresponding to the *computed* value of the test statistic. In our discussion and Example 8.1, using α = .05 you reject H_0 and using α = .01 you fail to reject H_0. We know that the *p*-value here is between .01 and .05. For this example, the computed value of the test statistic was $Z^* = -2.53$, where the hypotheses are H_0: μ = 5.9 feet and H_a: μ ≠ 5.9 feet. The Z curve for this situation is shown in Figure 8.12.

For which value of α does the testing procedure change the conclusions here? In Figure 8.12, if you were using a predetermined significance level α, you would split α in half and put α/2 into each tail. So the total tail area represents α. Using Figure 8.13, we reverse

FIGURE 8.12
Rejection regions for α = .01, .05.

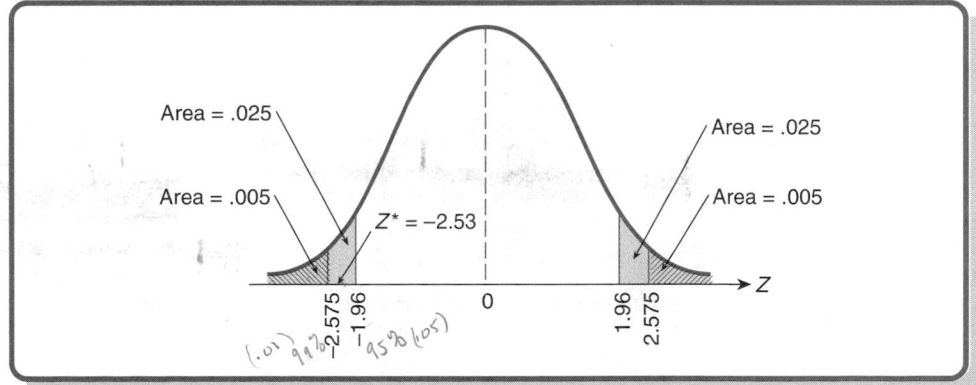

FIGURE 8.13
p-value is determined by replacing the area corresponding to α (see Figure 8.12) by the area corresponding to Z^*. Here $Z^* = -2.53$, and the *p*-value = $2 \cdot .0057 = .0114$ (total shaded area).

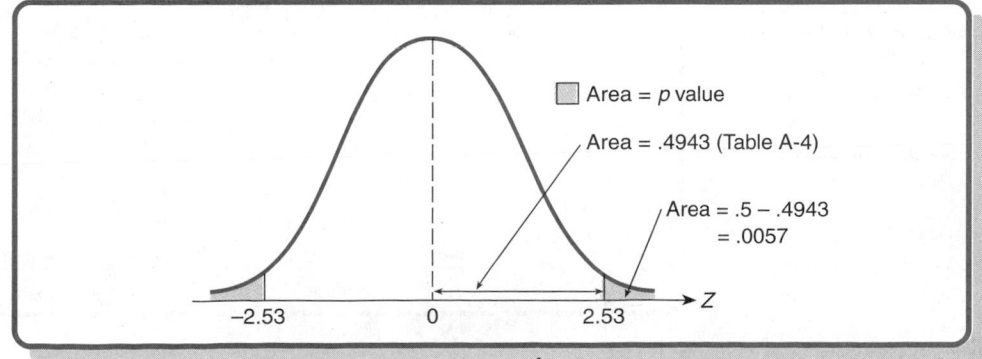

Remark

Ha must prove something, not disprove.

this procedure by finding the *total* tail area corresponding to a two-tailed test with $Z^* = -2.53$; we add the area to the left of -2.53 (.0057) to that to the right of 2.53 (also .0057). This total area is .0114, which is the *p*-value for this application. Thus, if you choose a value of $\alpha > .0114$ (such as .05), you will reject H_0. If you choose a value of $\alpha < .0114$ (such as .01), you will fail to reject H_0.

PROCEDURE FOR FINDING THE *p*-VALUE

1. For H_a: $\mu \neq \mu_0$

$$p = 2 \cdot (\text{area outside of } Z^*)$$

Reason: When using a significance level α, the value of α represents a *two-tailed* area.

2. For H_a: $\mu > \mu_0$

$$p = \text{area to the right of } Z^*$$

Reason: When using a significance level α, the value of α represents a *right-tailed* area.

3. For H_a: $\mu < \mu_0$

$$p = \text{area to the left of } Z^*$$

Reason: When using a significance level α, the value of α represents a *left-tailed* area.

EXAMPLE 8.6

What is the *p*-value for Example 8.5?

SOLUTION

The results of the sample were $n = 60$, $\bar{x} = 952.58$ kilowatt-hours, and $s = 173.92$ kilowatt-hours. The corresponding value of the test statistic was

$$Z^* \approx \frac{952.58 - 918}{173.92 / \sqrt{60}} = 1.54$$

The alternative hypothesis is H_a: $\mu > 918$, so the *p*-value will be the area to the *right* of the computed value, 1.54, as illustrated in Figure 8.14. Notice that the inequality in H_a determines the *direction* of the tail area to be found. The *p*-value here is .0618, which is consistent with the results of Example 8.5, where we concluded that for $\alpha = .01$, you fail to reject H_0 and for $\alpha = .10$, you reject H_0. That is, the *p*-value is between .01 and .10.

FIGURE 8.14

p-value for $Z^* = 1.54$.

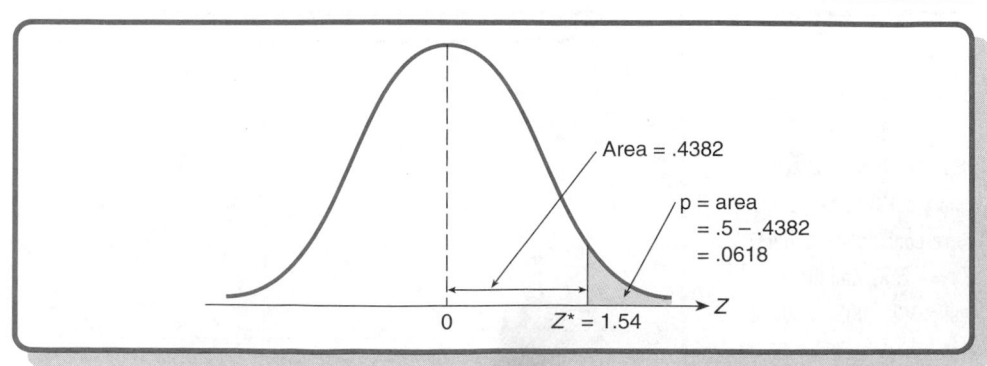

INTERPRETING THE *p*-VALUE

We will consider two ways of using the *p*-value to arrive at a conclusion. The first is the **classical approach** that we have used up to this point: We choose a value for α and base our decision on this value. When using a *p*-value in this manner, the procedure is:

reject H_0 if *p*-value $< \alpha$

fail to reject H_0 if *p*-value $\geq \alpha$

The second approach is a **general rule of thumb** that applies to most business applications of hypothesis testing on μ. We previously stated that typical values of α range from .01 to .10, implying that for most applications we will not see values of α smaller than .01 or larger than .1. With this in mind, the following rule can be defined:

reject H_0 if the *p*-value is small ($p < .01$)

fail to reject H_0 if the *p*-value is large ($p > .1$)

Consequently, if $.01 \leq$ *p*-value $\leq .1$, the data are *inconclusive.*

The advantage of this approach is that you avoid having to choose a value of α; the disadvantage is that you may arrive at an inconclusive result.

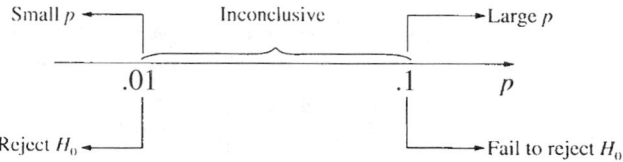

Now for a brief disclaimer: This rule does not apply to all situations. If a Type I error would be extremely serious and you prefer a very small value of α using the classical approach, then you can lower the .01 limit. Similarly, you might raise the .1 limit if the Type II error is extremely critical and you prefer a large value for α. However, this rule gives a working procedure for most applications in business.

What can you conclude if the *p*-value is $p = .0001$? This value is extremely small compared with *any* reasonable value of α. So we would strongly reject H_0. Consequently, if you are making an investment decision based on these results, for example, you can breathe a little easier. This data set supports H_a overwhelmingly. On the other hand, if $p = .65$, this value is large compared with any reasonable value of α. Without question, we would fail to reject H_0.

There is yet one other interpretation of the *p*-value, summarized in the following box.

ANOTHER INTERPRETATION OF THE *p*-VALUE

1. For a two-tailed test where H_a: $\mu \neq \mu_0$, the *p*-value is the probability that the value of the test statistic, Z^*, will be at least as large (in absolute value) as the observed Z^*, if μ is in fact equal to μ_0.
2. For a one-tailed test where H_a: $\mu > \mu_0$, the *p*-value is the probability that the value of the test statistic, Z^*, will be at least as large as the observed Z^*, if μ is in fact equal to μ_0.
3. For a one-tailed test where H_a: $\mu < \mu_0$, the *p*-value is the probability that the value of the test statistic, Z^*, will be at least as small as the observed Z^*, if μ is in fact equal to μ_0.

In Example 8.6, we determined the *p*-value to be .0618; the computed value of the test statistic was $Z^* = 1.54$; the hypotheses were H_0: $\mu \leq 918$ and H_a: $\mu > 918$. So the probability of observing a value of Z^* as large as 1.54 (that is, $Z^* \geq 1.54$) if μ is 918 is $p = .0618$.

Based on this description of the *p*-value, if *p* is small, conclude that H_0 is not true and reject it. We obtain precisely the same result using the classical and rule-of-thumb options of the *p*-value. *Small values of p favor H_a, and large values favor H_0.*

MICROSOFT® EXCEL APPLICATION   USE DATA8-7

EXAMPLE 8.7

Using Excel to Calculate the Z Statistic and Corresponding *p*-Value.

In Examples 2.1, 3.4, and 6.8 we examined the inside diameter of a certain machined part produced by Allied Manufacturing having specification (spec) limits of 10.1 millimeters (the lower limit) and 10.3 millimeters (the upper limit). Your advice to Allied was that, based on the sample of 100 diameters, the process was producing parts that were, on the average, too large, with a large percentage of the parts exceeding the upper spec limit. The quality-improvement team at Allied took your advice and attempted to modify the manufacturing process to produce parts that were closer to the target diameter of 10.2 millimeters. After this modification, another sample of 100 parts was obtained (stored in data set DATA8-7). They would like to know whether there is sufficient evidence to indicate that the average diameter (μ) differs from 10.2 millimeters. In particular:

1. What is your conclusion based on the corresponding *p*-value, using $\alpha = .05$?
2. Without specifying a value of α, what would be your conclusion based on the calculated *p*-value?
3. Interpret the *p*-value for this application.
4. What can you advise Allied about the present manufacturing process?

SOLUTION 1

Begin by opening dataset DATA8-7. The first 16 values are visible in column A of Figure 8.15, a rather busy Excel spreadsheet. The first step is to determine the standard deviation of the 100 sample values. Referring to Figure 8.15, type "Stand. Dev." in cell B1 and "=STDEV(A2:A101)" in cell B2. The value of .0334 should appear in cell B2. To carry out the test of hypothesis, click on **KGP Data Analysis ➤ One Population Inference.** Referring to Figure 8.10, enter (1) "A1:A101" for the **Input Range,** (2) "5" in the **Alpha** box, (3) ".0334" in the **Population Standard Deviation** box, (4) "two-tail test" in the **Hypothesis** section, (5) "10.2" for the **Hypothesized Value of Mean,** and (6) "B4" for the Output Range. Be sure to click on the box alongside **Labels.** The resulting output is contained in Figure 8.15 (cells B4:C12).

FIGURE 8.15

Excel spreadsheet for Example 8.7.

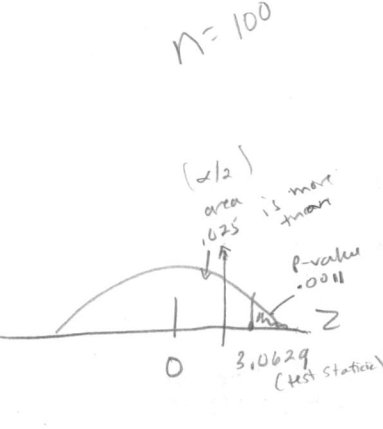

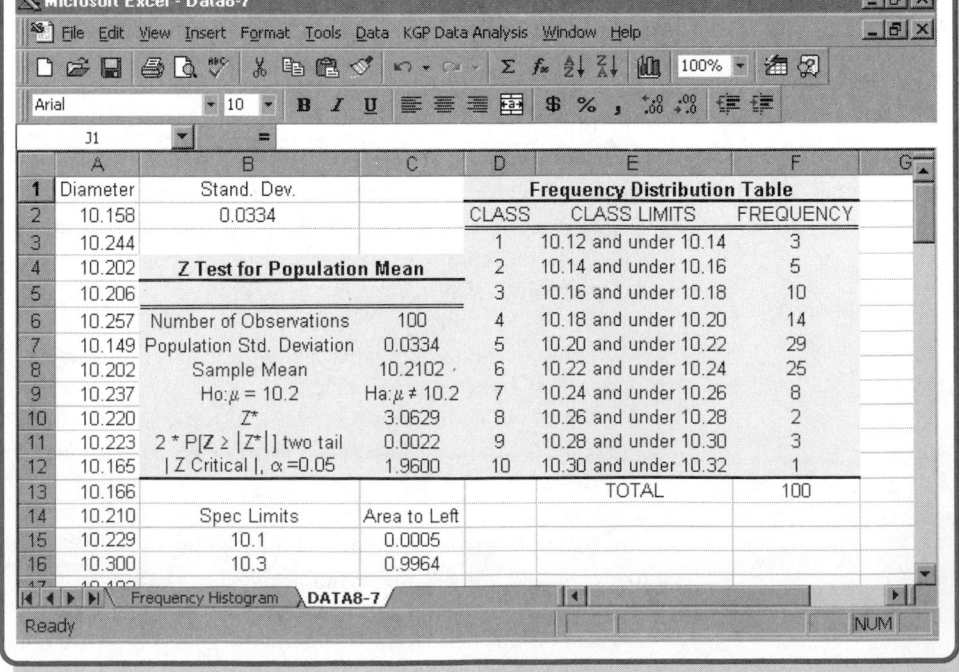

The calculated value of the test statistic is $Z^* = 3.06$, with a corresponding *p*-value of $p = .0022$, illustrated in Figure 8.16. Because *p* is less than $\alpha = .05$, we reject H_0 and conclude that the mean diameter is not 10.2 millimeters. Put another way, the sample mean $\bar{x} = 10.2102$ is *significantly different* from 10.2—certainly not obvious at first glance.

SOLUTION 2

We use the general rule of thumb for interpreting the *p*-value. Since $p = .0022$, this value is small ($<.01$) and so we reject H_0. Although this is the same conclusion reached in Solution 1, this is not always the case.

SOLUTION 3

We can make the following statements:

1. The significance level at which the conclusion indicated by the testing procedure changes is $\alpha = .0022$.
2. The largest significance level for which we fail to reject the null hypothesis is $\alpha = .0022$.
3. The probability of observing a value of the test statistic as large (in absolute value) as the one obtained (that is, ≥ 3.06), is .0022 if, in fact, the population mean is 10.2 millimeters.

SOLUTION 4

Take a look at the sorted sample data and the sample histogram. Next, determine what percentage of the produced parts in the population can be expected to lie outside the spec limits, using Excel's NORMDIST function.

To obtain the histogram in Figure 8.17, click on **KGP Data Analysis ➤ Quantitative Data Charts/Tables ➤ Histogram/Freq. Charts.** Fill in the input range (A1:A101) and the output range (D1). Be sure to click on the box alongside **Labels.** Also, click on the

---

FIGURE 8.16

Illustration of the *p*-value for Example 8.7.

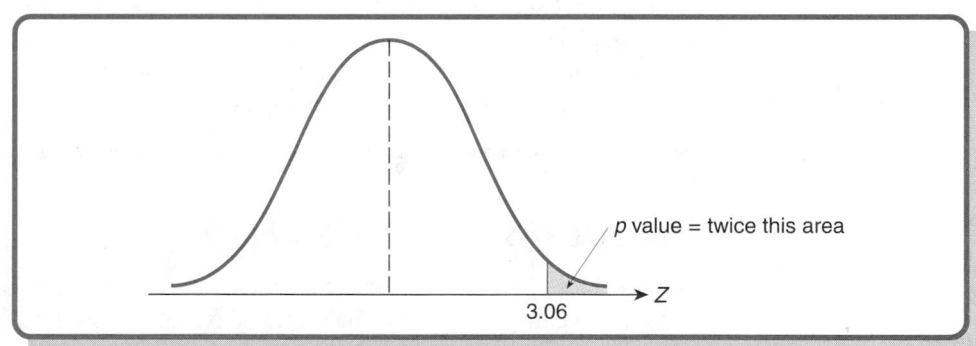

FIGURE 8.17

Excel-generated histogram of 100 inside diameters (Example 8.7).

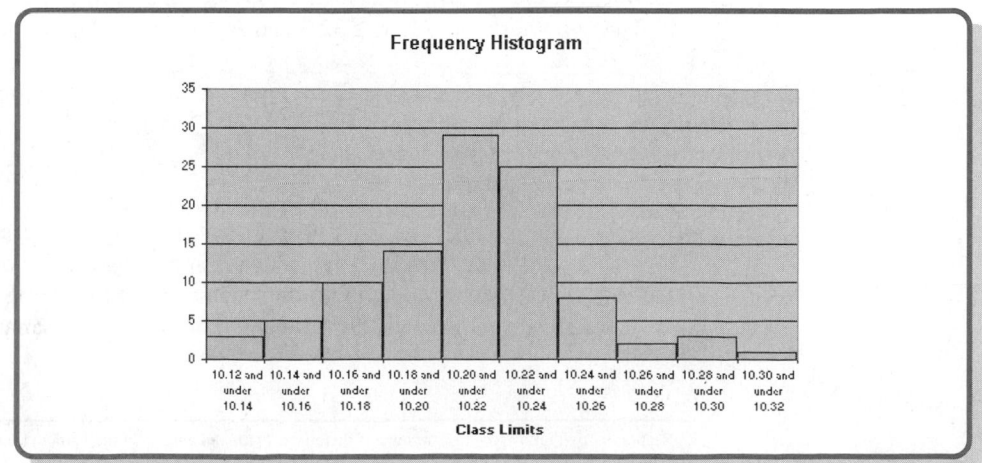

white square alongside **Frequencies** in the **Table** section and **Frequency Histogram** in the **Chart Output Options** section. You will then obtain the output in cells D1:F13 (Figure 8.15) and the Figure 8.17 histogram. Based on this histogram, it appears safe to assume that the sample was selected from a normal population.

To determine the percentage of produced parts in the population that can be expected outside the spec limits, examine cells B14:C16 in Figure 8.15. Type in the contents of cells B14, B15, B16, and C14. The areas under the normal curve in cells C15 and C16 are obtained by clicking on the **Paste Function** icon (**ƒ∗**) and clicking on **Statistical** under **Function Category** and **NORMDIST** under **Function Name.** The resulting input screen was first introduced in Figure 6.29. To obtain the Value of .0005 in cell C15, enter 10.1 for the **Value of X,** 10.2102 for the **Mean,** .0334 for the **Standard Deviation,** and "true" in the **Cumulative** box. The value of .9964 in cell C16 is obtained by replacing 10.1 with 10.3 in the previous sentence. The value in cell C15 implies that we can expect .05% of the parts to be less than the lower spec limit of 10.1. The value of .9964 in cell C16 is the area to the *left* of 10.3 under the normal curve, since the NORMDIST function always returns the value to the left of the specified X value. Consequently, we can expect .36% (that is, $100 - 99.64$) of the parts to exceed the upper spec limit of 10.3 and so $.05 + .36 = .41\%$ of the population will be outside the spec limits.

RECOMMENDATION. Prior to the quality-improvement effort, the mean diameter was 10.275 millimeters and 17% of the sample exceeded the upper spec limit. In one sense, the quality of the process has been improved, since the estimated mean of the new process (10.2102) is much closer to 10.2 than before, and none of the sample values lie outside the spec limits of 10.1 millimeters and 10.3 millimeters. Despite this good news, we can still expect .41% of the population to lie outside the spec limits, which translates to 4100 nonconforming parts per million.

We also observe additional variation in this sample, since the sample standard deviation has increased from .0267 (before the quality-improvement effort) to .0334 (refer to Solution 1).* Overall, the team should be commended for improving the process. But based on Solution 1, efforts should be made to move the process even closer to 10.2 millimeters and to reduce the process variation.

PRACTICAL VERSUS STATISTICAL SIGNIFICANCE

Researchers often calculate what appears to be a conclusive result without considering the practical significance of their findings. For example, consider a situation similar to the one described in Example 8.4; this time, a sample of 1000 Bullets, tested under normal highway conditions, results in a sample average of $\bar{x} = 32.32$ mpg, with a standard deviation of $s = 2.15$ mpg. Advertising for this car claims that the mpg under test conditions is at least 32.5 mpg. Is there sufficient evidence to reject this claim?

The hypotheses are H_0: $\mu \geq 32.5$ and H_a: $\mu < 32.5$. The value of the test statistic is

$$Z^* \approx \frac{\bar{X} - 32.5}{s / \sqrt{n}} = \frac{32.32 - 32.5}{2.15 / \sqrt{1000}} = -2.65$$

The p-value here is the area to the left of -2.65 under the Z curve, as illustrated in Figure 8.18. This value (from Table A.4) is .004. Based on this small p-value, we reject H_0 and conclude (as we did in Example 8.4) that the mpg for these cars under normal highway conditions is less than 32.5. Statistically speaking, this is correct, and the data to provide sufficient evidence to support the statement that their mpg claim is overstated. As a consumer, however, how concerned would you be that the sample average ($\bar{x} = 32.32$) is

---

* Section 9.4 will allow you to determine if there is a *significant* change in the variation for the "before" and "after" processes (populations).

FIGURE 8.18
p-value for $Z^* = -2.65$.

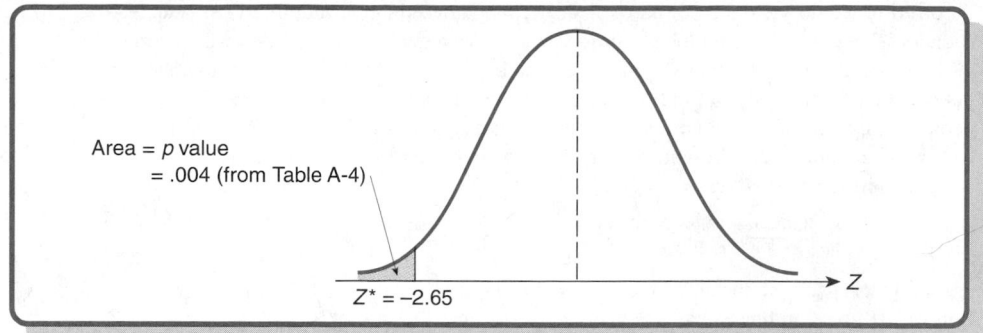

Area = *p* value
= .004 (from Table A-4)

$Z^* = -2.65$

(only) .18 mpg under the advertised level? In other words, in a practical sense, how misleading is the Bullet advertising?

What we have seen is that $\bar{X}$ is far enough away from 32.5 (in a statistical sense) to conclude that μ is less than 32.5 mpg. However, perhaps in the eyes of a consumer about to invest $25,000 in a new car, this value of $\bar{X}$ is really "close enough" to 32.5.

Moral: It is possible for a statistically significant result to be of no particular practical significance, depending on the context of the analysis.

EXERCISES 8.27–8.36

UNDERSTANDING THE MECHANICS

8.27 Consider a hypothesis test with the null hypothesis $\mu = 100$ versus the alternative hypothesis $\mu \neq 100$. State the conclusion to the hypothesis test if the *p*-value is .03 and the significance level is

  a. .10
  b. .05
  c. .01

8.28 Using the rule-of-thumb option (not selecting a value of α) in the interpretation of the *p*-value, state whether the test statistic would be statistically significant in the following situations.

  a. $p = .57$
  b. $p = .008$
  c. $p = .12$
  d. $p = .04$

8.29 Find the *p*-values for the following situations, with calculated test statistics given by Z^*.

  a. $H_0: \mu = 50$, $H_a: \mu \neq 50$, $Z^* = 2.53$
  b. $H_0: \mu \leq 50$, $H_a: \mu > 50$, $Z^* = 2.53$
  c. $H_0: \mu = 10$, $H_a: \mu \neq 10$, $Z^* = 1.87$
  d. $H_0: \mu \leq 10$, $H_a: \mu > 10$, $Z^* = 1.87$

APPLYING THE NEW CONCEPTS

8.30 A pharmaceutical firm found from a random sample of 100 volunteers that the average time it takes a new drug to take effect is 3.5 minutes. It is well known that the mean time for the old drug was 3.7 minutes. The mean time for the new drug was found to be significantly less than the mean time for the old drug, via a statistical analysis of the data. Explain the difference between "significance" in a statistical sense and "significance" in a practical sense for this situation.

8.31 Growth in Tommy Hilfiger Corp.'s casual-menswear business is slowing, so the company is introducing pricey women's apparel under its "Red" and "White" labels, with suits that range from $450 to $1500. A women's retail specialist would like to test that the mean price for Tommy Hilfiger's women's suits differs from $(450 + 1500)/2 = 975$. Suppose that a random sample of 60 stores revealed a sample mean of $925 with a standard deviation of $200. Test the retail specialist's belief.

(Adapted from *The Wall Street Journal*, "Hilfiger's Fashion Empire Starts to Show Some Wear," June 12, 1998, p. B4.)

  a. Find the observed significance level and interpret it.
  b. What conclusion would follow if the significance level was specified as 5%?

8.32 The producer of Take-a-Bite, a snack food, claims that each package weighs 175 grams. A representative of a consumer advocate group selected a random sample of 70 packages. From this sample, the mean and standard deviation were found to be 172 grams and 8 grams, respectively.

  a. Find the *p*-value for testing the claim that the mean weight of Take-a-Bite is less than 175 grams.
  b. Interpret the *p*-value in part (a).

8.33 A marketing-research analyst is interested in examining the statement made by the makers that brand A cigarettes contain less than 3 milligrams of tar. The marketing-research analyst randomly selected 60 cigarettes and found the mean amount of tar to be 2.75 milligrams with a standard deviation of 1.5 milligrams. Do the data support the claim? Find the *p*-value.

8.34 Alice Chang and her husband Jau Huang are the co-founders of a multimedia software start-up company named CyberLink, based in Taiwan. These founders are interested in the average number of hours that engineers would be willing to work for the company if they were given a small salary but a large quantity of stock with the anticipation that an initial public offering would yield a nice return. A consultant advised the founders that engineers would be willing to work an average of 70 hours per week under those terms. The idea that they could get rich in a short period of time is very enticing to many engineers in Taiwan. Suppose that a sample of 50 start-up companies was randomly selected and the number of hours that the typical engineer worked was recorded.

(Adapted from *The Wall Street Journal*, "Taiwan Doesn't Shield Firms: Only Strong Survive," June 23, 1998, p. 2B.)

a. Does a sample mean of 62 hours and a standard deviation of 20 hours indicate that the average work time that an engineer would be willing to work for a start-up company differs from 70 hours a week? Interpret the *p*-value.

b. From the *p*-value in part (a), would you expect a 99% confidence interval for the mean number of weekly hours that an engineer would be willing to work for a start-up company to include 70? Find a 99% confidence interval for this mean.

Using the Computer

8.35 [DATA SET EX8-35] *Variable description:*

CostGoods: Cost of goods by shoplifters

A manager of a New York retail store believes that the average cost of goods shoplifted by those customers that have shoplifted

is greater than $75. A random sample of 60 customers that have shoplifted is selected, and the selling price of the goods shoplifted was recorded.

a. Test that the average cost of goods shoplifted among the population of shoplifters at the retail store is greater than $75. Use the general rule of thumb concerning the *p*-value to arrive at a conclusion.

b. How would you interpret the results of the hypothesis test in part (a) for the manager?

8.36 [DATA SET EX8-36] *Variable description:*

StressIndex: Stress index for managers

An industrial psychologist has a stress test that is used to determine the amount of stress that managers are under. A value of 80 or higher indicates "high stress." The industrial psychologist believes that the managers at a large, profitable pharmaceutical firm are not under "high stress" and that the average stress index is less than 80 for managers of the company. A random sample of 50 managers is selected, and their stress index was recorded.

a. Test that the data support the industrial psychologist's belief.

b. What conclusion would you reach if the significance level was .10? .05? .01?

8.4 Hypothesis Testing on the Mean of a Normal Population: Small Sample

Our approach to hypothesis testing with small samples when the standard deviation, σ is unknown uses the same technique we used for dealing with confidence intervals on the mean of a population: we switch from the standard normal distribution, Z, to the t distribution. However, we need to examine the distribution of the population when the sample is small—the population distribution determines the procedure that we use. In this section, we have reason to believe that the population has a *normal distribution*. When it does not, we use a nonparametric procedure, which is discussed in Chapter 19.

Certain variations from a normal population *are* permissible with the small-sample test. If a test of hypothesis is still reliable when slight departures from the assumptions are encountered, the test is said to be **robust.** If you believe the parent population to be reasonably symmetric, the level of your confidence interval and Type I error (α) will be quite accurate, even if the population has heavy tails (unlike the normal distribution), as shown in Figure 8.19(a). However, when using small samples, the small-sample test is *not* robust for populations that are heavily skewed [see Figure 8.19(b)]. A nonparametric procedure offers a much better solution for this situation. For larger sample sizes, a histogram of your data often can detect whether a population is heavily skewed in one direction.

To reemphasize, the discussion in this section assumes a normal population. In other words, if X is an observation from this population, then X is a normal random variable with unknown mean μ. Also, we assume that σ is unknown. (If σ is known, the resulting test statistic is $Z = (\bar{X} - \mu_0)/(\sigma/\sqrt{n})$, and the five-step procedure of Section 8.1 allows you to do hypothesis testing on μ.)

The only distinction between using a small and a large sample is the identification of the test statistic. Using the discussion from Chapter 7, if we define the test statistic as

$$t = \frac{\bar{X} - \mu_0}{s/\sqrt{n}} \qquad (8.2)$$

FIGURE 8.19
(a) Small-sample test is valid.
(b) Small-sample test is not valid.

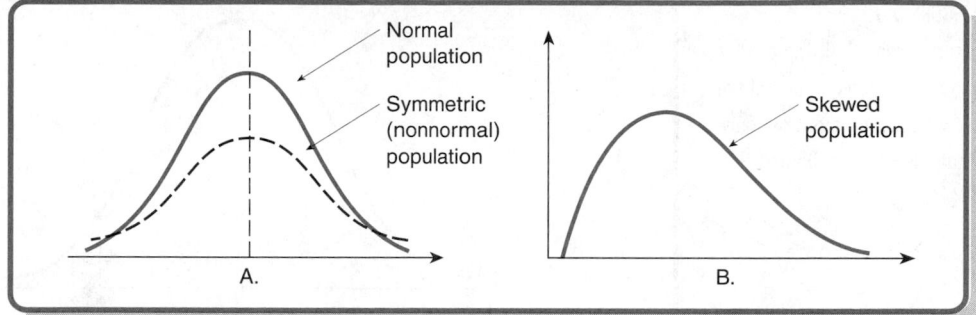

we now have a t distribution with $n-1$ degrees of freedom (df). The procedure to use for testing H_0: $\mu = \mu_0$ and H_a: $\mu \neq \mu_0$ is the same five-step procedure, except that the rejection region is defined using the t table (Table A.5) rather than the Z table (Table A.4). This procedure also applies to a one-tailed test.

EXAMPLE 8.8

You may recall from Example 7.9 that Clark Products manufactures a power supply with an output voltage that is believed to be normally distributed with a mean of 10 volts. During the design stage, the quality-engineering staff recorded 18 observations of the output voltage of a particular power supply unit. They decide to use a significance level of .05, since the implications of making a Type I error (rejecting a correct H_0) and a Type II error (failing to reject an incorrect H_0) appear to be the same. Is there evidence to indicate that the average output voltage is not 10 volts?

SOLUTION

Step 1. When a question is phrased "Is there evidence to indicate that . . . ," what follows is the *alternative hypothesis*. For this application then, the alternative hypothesis is that the mean is unequal to 10 volts, and the resulting hypotheses are H_0: $\mu = 10$ and H_a: $\mu \neq 10$.

Step 2. The test statistic here is

$$t = \frac{\bar{X} - 10}{s / \sqrt{n}}$$

Step 3. Using a significance level of .05 and Figure 8.20, the corresponding two-tailed procedure is to

reject H_0 if $|t| > t_{.025,17} = 2.11$

because df $= n - 1 = 17$.

FIGURE 8.20

t distribution; the rejection region is the lightly shaded area to the right of 2.11 and to the left of −2.11, for Example 8.8.

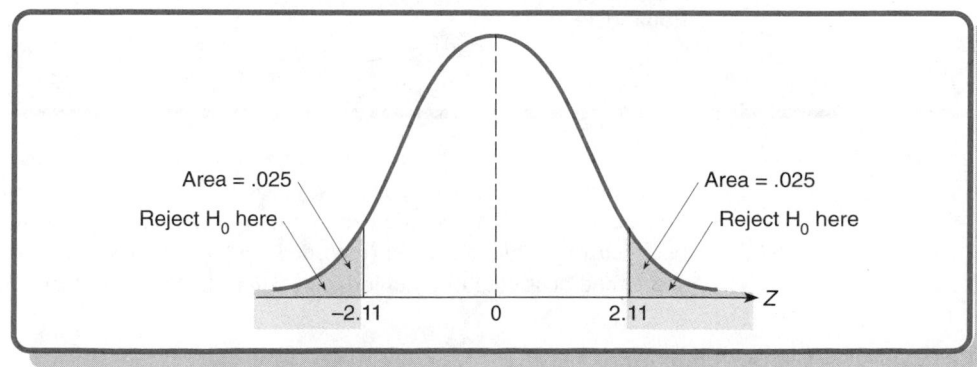

FIGURE 8.21

t curve with 17 df. The *p*-value is twice the area to the right of *t** = 1.83, so we can say only that it is between .05 and .10.

You can only approximate p-value for t-dist.

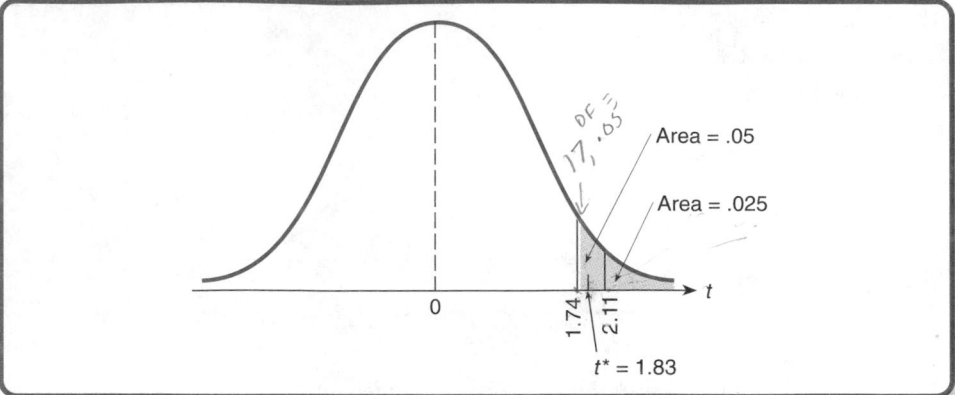

Step 4. For these data, $n = 18$, $\bar{x} = 10.331$ volts and $s = .767$ volts. The value of the test statistic is

$$t^* = \frac{10.331 - 10}{.767 / \sqrt{18}} = 1.83$$

Because $1.83 < 2.11$, we fail to reject H_0.

Step 5. There is insufficient evidence to indicate that the average output voltage is different from 10 volts.

DF = 1.740

What is the *p*-value in Example 8.8, and what can we conclude based on this value? We run into a slight snag when dealing with the *t* distribution, because we are not able to determine precisely the *p*-value. You can see this in Figure 8.21, using Table A.5 (17 df). The *p*-value is twice the area to the right of $t^* = 1.83$. The best we can do here is to say that *p* is *between* (2)(.025) and (2)(.05), that is, between .05 and .10. (*Note:* A reliable computer package or sophisticated calculator will provide the exact *p*-value. Using Excel or MINITAB, this value is $p = .0847$.)

Using the classical approach and $\alpha = .05$ we *can* say that *p* is greater than .05, despite not knowing *p* exactly. Consequently, we fail to reject H_0. *This procedure* always *produces the same result as the five-step procedure.*

Suppose we choose not to select a significant level (α) but prefer to base our conclusion strictly on the calculated *p*-value. We use the rule of thumb and decide whether *p* is small (<.01), large (>.1), or in between. Despite not having an exact value of *p*, we can say that this *p*-value falls in the inconclusive range. These data values do not provide us with any strong conclusion. One approach available to Clark Products is to obtain some additional data.

EXAMPLE 8.9

An auditing firm was hired to determine if a particular defense plant was overstating the value of their inventory items. It was decided that 15 items would be randomly selected. For each item, the recorded amount, the audited (exact) amount, and the difference between these two amounts (recorded – audited) were determined. Of particular interest was whether it could be demonstrated that the average difference exceeds $25, in which case the defense plant would be subject to a loss of contract and financial penalties. The following 15 differences were obtained (in dollars):

$$17, 35, 31, 22, 50, 42, 56, 23, 27, 38, 20, 25, 43, 45, 21$$

So $n = 15$, $\bar{x} = \$33.00$, and $s = \$12.15$. Set up the appropriate hypotheses and test them using a significance level of $\alpha = .05$. The population of differences is believed to be normally distributed.

SOLUTION

Step 1. The hypotheses are H_0: $\mu \leq 25$ and H_a: $\mu > 25$, where μ is the average difference between the recorded and audited amounts for *all* the inventory items.

Steps 2, 3.

$$\text{reject } H_0 \text{ if } t = \frac{\bar{X} - 25}{s/\sqrt{n}} > t_{.05,14} = 1.761,$$

where the df $= n - 1 = 14$.

Step 4. The calculated t is

$$t^* = \frac{33 - 25}{12.15/\sqrt{15}} = 2.55$$

Because 2.55 exceeds the tabulated value of 1.761, we reject H_0. Also, the p-value (using Table A.5 and 14 df) is the area to the right of 2.55. It is between .01 and .025, so it is less than $\alpha = .05$, and so (as before) we reject H_0.

Step 5. These data indicate that the defense plant is overstating the value of their inventory items by more than \$25.

To obtain the Excel solution shown in Figure 8.22, enter the 15 values in cells A1:A15. Next, click on **KGP Data Analysis ➤ One Population Inference.** Referring to Figure 8.10, use the down arrow in the top box to select **Population Mean with Est. Std. Dev. (*t* statistic).** The resulting input screen is very similar to that in Figure 8.10. Enter "A1:A15" for the **Input Range,** but don't click on the **Labels** box (unless you inserted a label in cell A1). Enter 5 in the **Alpha** box (this is the default value), click on **Hypothesis Test** and **Right-Tail Test,** and enter "25" for the **Hypothesized Value of Mean** and "B1" for the **Output Range.** The p-value here is .012 and is in agreement with the solution to Example 8.9—namely that the p-value is between .01 and .025.

FIGURE 8.22

Portion of Excel spreadsheet containing the sample values and output for Example 8.9.

17	t Test for Population Mean	
35		
31	Number of Observations	15
22	Sample Standard Deviation	12.148
50	Sample Mean	33.000
42	Ho:$\mu \leq 25$	Ha:$\mu > 25$
56	T*	2.551
23	P[T $\geq$ T*]	0.012
27	T Critical, α=0.05	1.761
38		
20		
25		
43		
45		
21		

SMALL-SAMPLE TESTS ON A NORMAL POPULATION MEAN

Two-Tailed Test

$$H_0: \mu = \mu_0$$

$$H_a: \mu \neq \mu_0$$

$$\text{reject } H_0 \text{ if } |t^*| > t_{\alpha/2, n-1}$$

where n = sample size and t^* is the computed value of

$$t = \frac{\overline{X} - \mu_0}{s / \sqrt{n}}$$

One-Tailed Test

$H_0: \mu \leq \mu_0$	$H_0: \mu \geq \mu_0$
$H_a: \mu > \mu_0$	$H_a: \mu < \mu_0$
reject H_0 if $t^* > t_{\alpha, n-1}$	reject H_0 if $t^* < -t_{\alpha, n-1}$

EXERCISES 8.37–8.46

UNDERSTANDING THE MECHANICS

8.37 Find the t statistic and carry out the statistical test for the following situations in sampling data from a normally distributed population. Use a significance level of .05.

   a. $H_0: \mu = 50$, $H_a: \mu \neq 50$, $\overline{x} = 56$, $s = 24$, $n = 15$
   b. $H_0: \mu \leq 50$, $H_a > 50$, $\overline{x} = 56$, $s = 24$, $n = 15$
   c. $H_0: \mu \geq 113.7$, $H_a < 113.7$, $\overline{x} = 111.6$, $s = 2.5$, $n = 30$
   d. $H_0: \mu = 85$, $H_a \neq 85$, $\overline{x} = 78$, $s = 25$, $n = 25$

8.38 Find the p-value for the following situations, with calculated test statistics given by t^*.

   a. $H_0: \mu = 72.5$, $H_a: \mu \neq 72.5$, $t^* = 2.72$, $n = 12$
   b. $H_0: \mu \leq 72.5$, $H_a: \mu > 72.5$, $t^* = 2.72$, $n = 12$
   c. $H_0: \mu = 180.7$, $H_a: \mu \neq 180.7$, $t^* = 1.3$, $n = 41$
   d. $H_0: \mu \leq 180.7$, $H_a: \mu > 180.7$, $t^* = 1.3$, $n = 41$

8.39 The following data were collected using a random sample from a normally distributed population. Test that the mean of the population differs from 20. Use a significance level of .05.

$$18, 12, 24, 20, 19, 16, 21, 14, 22, 18$$

APPLYING THE NEW CONCEPTS

8.40 Easy-Fly Airline took a random sample of 25 flights to determine if the mean time it takes for luggage to reach the travelers departing from a flight is less than 15 minutes. The sample mean was found to be 13.8 minutes with a standard deviation of 4 minutes.

   a. Using a significance level of .05, what conclusion can be reached based on the random sample?

   b. What assumption about the data is necessary for the hypothesis test to be valid in this situation?

8.41 The Hungarian-born executive Zsolt Rummy, chairman of Zoltek Company, claims that his company is the world's largest producer of carbon fiber, the strong yet lightweight material used in everything from aircraft to golf clubs. To maintain profitability, the cost of producing carbon fiber is very important. Zoltek has production lines in both Texas and Hungary. A financial analyst interested in estimating the earnings of the company wants to test that the cost of producing a pound of carbon differs from its average cost of $6 per pound last year. Twenty days are randomly selected from the first 6 months of 1998, and the cost per pound of carbon is recorded. The data are presented below. Using a .05 significance level, what conclusion can the financial analyst make? Assume that the distribution of the cost per pound of carbon can be approximated by a normal distribution. $u = 6$ $\overline{x} = 6.36$ $n = 20$ $s = .662$

6.3	6.8	7.5	6.0	5.3	6.2	5.4	7.3	6.1	6.4
6.1	6.5	5.7	6.3	7.2	6.9	6.2	7.0	5.9	6.1

(Adapted from *The Wall Street Journal*, "Zoltek Touts Potential for Carbon Fiber; Its Shares Reflect Immediate Concerns," June 12, 1998, p. B11.)

8.42 The senior executive of a publishing firm would like to train employees to read faster than 1000 words per minute. A random sample of 21 employees underwent a special speed-reading course. This sample yielded a mean of 1018 words per minute with a standard deviation of 30 words per minute. Do the data support the belief that the speed-reading course will enable the employees to read more than 1000 words per minute at a significance level of .05? Assume that the reading speeds of persons who have taken the course are normally distributed.

8.43 It is believed that the mean aptitude test score for engineers graduating from Safire University is greater than 180. Assume that the scores are normally distributed. A random sample of 26 engineers yielded a mean score of 186 with a standard deviation of 10.2. Do these data support the belief? Use the p-value.

8.44 In an effort to control cost, a quality-control inspector is interested in whether the mean number of ounces of sauce dispensed by bottle-filling machines differs from 16 ounces. From the bottling process, the inspector collects the following measurements.

16.3, 16.2, 15.8, 15.4, 16.0, 15.6, 15.5, 16.1, 15.9, 16.1

Test at a .05 significance level that the bottle-filling machines need adjusting.

USING THE COMPUTER

8.45 [DATA SET EX8-45] *Variable description:*

Expend: Expenditure per night by guests sharing the same room

The manager at the Ocean Breeze Hotel believes the average expenditure per night for guests sharing the same room is greater than $200. A random sample of 25 rooms was selected, and the expenditure by the guests per night was recorded.

a. Test the manager's belief that the average expenditure for guests sharing the same room is greater than $200. At what significance level can the null hypothesis be rejected?

b. What assumption are you making about the sampled population?

8.46 [DATA SET EX8-46] *Variable description:*

Time: Time, in minutes, to correct a defective aluminum sheet

A quality inspector is interested in the average time it takes to correct defective sheets of aluminum manufactured at the plant. A random sample of 25 sheets of defective aluminum sheets was selected, and the time to correct the defect was recorded.

a. Suppose that the quality inspector believes the average time to correct a defective sheet of aluminum is different from 20 minutes, a time given in a recent report on the operations of the company. Test the quality inspector's belief. Use the general rule of thumb for interpreting the *p*-value.

b. Construct a histogram and determine if the data can be assumed to come from an approximately normal population.

8.5 INFERENCE FOR THE VARIANCE AND STANDARD DEVIATION OF A NORMAL POPULATION (OPTIONAL)

Our discussion in Chapters 7 and 8 has been concerned with the mean of a particular random variable or population. In other words, we are trying to decide or estimate what is occuring *on the average.* Suppose someone involved with a production process that manufactures 2-inch bolts has just been informed that, without a doubt, these bolts are 2 inches long, on the average. Is there anything else this person might like to know about the production process? Suppose that half of the bolts produced are 1 inch long and the other half are 3 inches. The report was accurate—on the average, they *are* 2 inches long.* However, such a production process certainly will not satisfy the customers, and this company soon will be out of the bolt business.

What was missing in the report was the amount of *variation* in this production process. If the variation were zero, every bolt would be exactly 2 inches long—an ideal situation. In practice, there always will be a certain amount of variation in any mechanical or production process. So we are concerned about not only the mean length μ of the population of bolts but also the variance σ^2 or standard deviation σ of the lengths of these bolts. If the variance is *too large,* the process is not operating correctly and needs adjustment. *Consequently, a key element of statistical quality improvement (Chapter 12) is the act of monitoring and attempting to reduce process variation. A process that is "in control" is one that is consistent and contains only random variation.*

The variance of a population also is of vital interest to someone making investment decisions. Here the *risk* of a venture (or portfolio) often is measured by the variance of the return paid by the venture in the past. Often, financial analysts prefer a financial package with a relatively small average return (based on past history) that appears to be low risk on the basis of only small fluctuations in its past performance.

In the inference procedures for a population variance (and standard deviation) to follow, we will assume that the population of interest is normally distributed. Unlike the *t* test, the hypothesis-testing procedures and confidence intervals for the variance are very sensitive to departures from the normal population—notably, heavy tails in the distribution or heavy skewness will have a large effect. In other words, the following tests of hypothesis are less robust than are those we discussed earlier.

_____

* A statistician often is described as someone who thinks that if half of you is in an oven and the other half is in a deep freeze, on the average you are very comfortable.

FIGURE 8.23
Shape of a chi-square distribution.

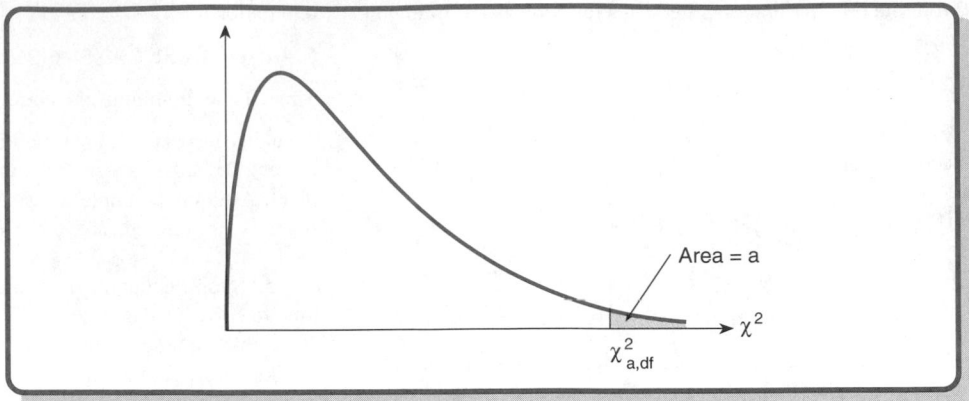

CONFIDENCE INTERVAL FOR THE VARIANCE AND STANDARD DEVIATION

The point estimate of a population variance is the obvious one—namely, the sample variance, which was discussed in Chapter 7, where we used the variance, s^2, of a sample to estimate the variance, σ^2, of the much larger population.*

When constructing a confidence interval for μ using a small sample, we used the t distribution. Such a distribution is referred to as a **derived distribution** because it was derived to describe the behavior of a particular test statistic. This type of distribution is not used to describe a population, as is the normal distribution in many applications. For example, you will *not* hear a statement such as, "Assume that these data follow a t distribution"—normal, exponential, uniform, maybe, but not a t distribution. The t random variable merely offers us a method of testing and constructing confidence intervals for the mean of a *normal* population when the standard deviation is unknown and is replaced by its estimate.

Another such continuous derived distribution, the **chi-square** (pronounced "ky square") distribution, written as χ^2, allows us to determine confidence intervals and perform tests of hypothesis on the variance and standard deviation of a normal population. The shape of this distribution is illustrated in Figure 8.23. Notice that unlike the Z and t curves, the χ^2 distribution is not symmetric and is definitely skewed right.

For chi-square, as for all continuous distributions, a probability corresponds to an area under a curve. Also, the shape of the chi-square curve, like that of its cousin the t distribution, depends on the sample size n. As before, this will be specified by the corresponding degrees of freedom (df).

When using the χ^2 distribution to construct a confidence interval or perform a test of hypothesis on a population variance or standard deviation, the degrees of freedom are given by

$$df = n - 1$$

Let $\chi^2_{a,df}$ be the χ^2 value whose area to the right is a, using the proper df.

EXAMPLE 8.10

Using a chi-square curve with 12 df, determine $P(\chi^2 > 18.5494)$ and $P(\chi^2 < 6.30380)$.

SOLUTION

Tabulated values for the χ^2 distribution are contained in Table A.6. This table contains *right-tailed* areas (probabilities). Based on this table (see Figure 8.24),

$$P(\chi^2 > 18.5494) = .1$$

---

* The notation $\hat{\sigma}^2$ is often used to represent an estimate of σ^2. Consequently, $s^2 = \hat{\sigma}^2$.

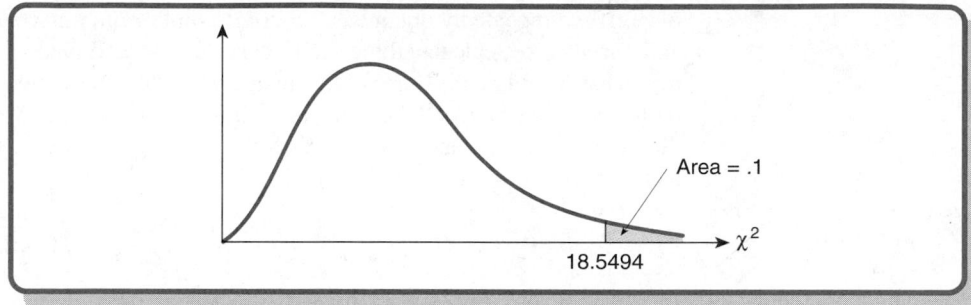

FIGURE **8.24**

χ^2 curve with 12 df. The shaded area represents $P(\chi^2 > 18.5494)$.

This can be written as

$$\chi^2_{.1,12} = 18.5494$$

For $\chi^2 = 6.30380$, Table A.6 informs us that the area to the right of 6.30380 is .900. Because the total area is 1, the area to the left of 6.30380 is $1 - .900 = .1$, and so $P(\chi^2 < 6.30380) = .1$. As a result, we can say that

$$P(6.30380 \le \chi^2 \le 18.5494) = 1 - .1 - .1 = .8$$

That is, 80% of the time a χ^2 value (with 12 df) will be between 6.30380 and 18.5494.

EXAMPLE **8.11**

Using Example 8.10, determine a and b that satisfy

$$P(a < \chi^2 < b) = .95, \qquad \text{with df} = 12$$

Choose a and b so that an equal area occurs in each tail.

SOLUTION

Figure 8.25 shows the areas for a and b. Using Table A.6,

$$a = \chi^2 \text{ value whose left-tailed area is } .025$$
$$= \chi^2 \text{ value whose area to the right is } .975$$
$$= 4.40$$

and

$$b = \chi^2 \text{ value whose right-tailed area is } .025$$
$$= 23.3$$

FIGURE **8.25**

χ^2 curve with 12 df.

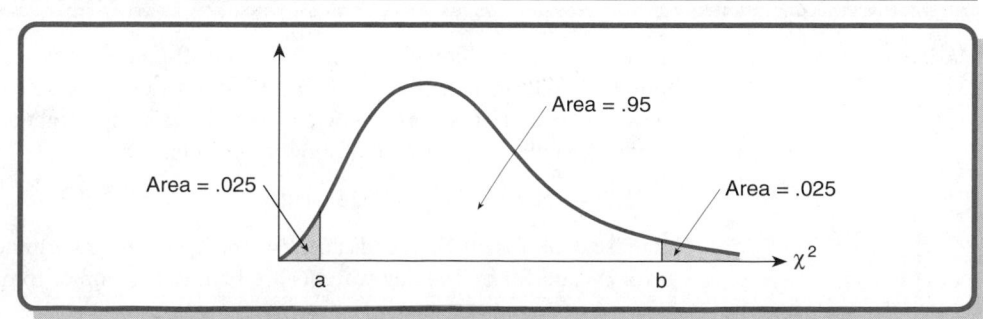

To derive a confidence interval for σ^2, we need to examine the sampling distribution of s^2. If we repeatedly obtained a random sample from a normal population with mean μ and variance σ^2, calculated the sample variance s^2, and made a histogram of these s^2 values, what would be the shape of this histogram? It can be shown that the shape will depend on the sample size n and the value of σ^2 but *not* on the value of the population mean μ. In fact, the values of n and σ^2, along with the random variable s^2, can be combined to define a chi-square random variable, given by

$$\chi^2 = \frac{(n-1)s^2}{\sigma^2} \tag{8.3}$$

having a chi-square distribution with $n-1$ df. Therefore, the sampling distribution for s^2 can be defined using the chi-square distribution in equation 8.3.

For example, a sample size of $n = 13$ results in 12 df. From Example 8.11, it follows that

$$P(4.40 < \chi^2 < 23.3) = .95$$

So,

$$P\left[4.40 < \frac{12s^2}{\sigma^2} < 23.3\right] = .95 \qquad \text{using equation 8.3}$$

or

$$P\left[\frac{12s^2}{23.3} < \sigma^2 < \frac{12s^2}{4.40}\right] = .95$$

As in all confidence interval constructions, the parameter (σ^2) is bounded between two limits defined by a random variable (s^2). This means that a 95% confidence interval for σ^2 is

$$\frac{12s^2}{23.3} \qquad \text{to} \qquad \frac{12s^2}{4.40}$$

In general, the following procedure can be used to construct a confidence interval for σ^2 or σ. A $(1-\alpha)\cdot 100\%$ confidence interval for σ^2 is

$$\frac{(n-1)s^2}{\chi^2_{\alpha/2,n-1}} \qquad \text{to} \qquad \frac{(n-1)s^2}{\chi^2_{1-\alpha/2,n-1}} \tag{8.4}$$

The corresponding confidence interval for σ is

$$\sqrt{\frac{(n-1)s^2}{\chi^2_{\alpha/2,n-1}}} \qquad \text{to} \qquad \sqrt{\frac{(n-1)s^2}{\chi^2_{1-\alpha/2,n-1}}} \tag{8.5}$$

EXAMPLE 8.12

Vitamix Dog Chow comes in 10-, 25-, and 50-pound bags. The owners are concerned about the variation in the weight of the 50-pound bags because they have recently acquired a new mechanical packaging device. A random sample of the weights of 15 bags (in pounds) was obtained, with the following results:

51.2, 47.5, 50.8, 51.5, 49.5, 51.1, 51.3, 50.7, 46.7, 49.2, 52.1, 48.3, 51.6, 49.2, 51.5

For these data, $\bar{x} = 50.15$ pounds and $s = 1.651$ pounds. Determine a 90% confidence interval for σ^2 and for σ. The bag weights are believed to come from a normal population.

SOLUTION

The corresponding 90% confidence interval for σ^2 is

$$\frac{(15-1)(1.651)^2}{\chi^2_{.05,14}} \quad \text{to} \quad \frac{(15-1)(1.651)^2}{\chi^2_{.95,14}} = \frac{(14)(1.651)^2}{23.7} \quad \text{to} \quad \frac{(14)(1.651)^2}{6.57}$$

$$= 1.61 \quad \text{to} \quad 5.81$$

The 90% confidence interval for σ would be

$$\sqrt{1.61} \quad \text{to} \quad \sqrt{5.81}$$

that is, 1.27 pounds to 2.41 pounds.

HYPOTHESIS TESTING FOR THE VARIANCE AND STANDARD DEVIATION

For many applications, we are concerned that the standard deviation or variance of our population may be exceeding some specified value. If this claim is supported, then, for example, we may wish to shut down a production process and make adjustments that will reduce this excessive variation. As you could with the tests of hypothesis examined so far, you can (although this is not the usual case) perform a two-tailed test where either too much variation or too little variation is the topic of concern.

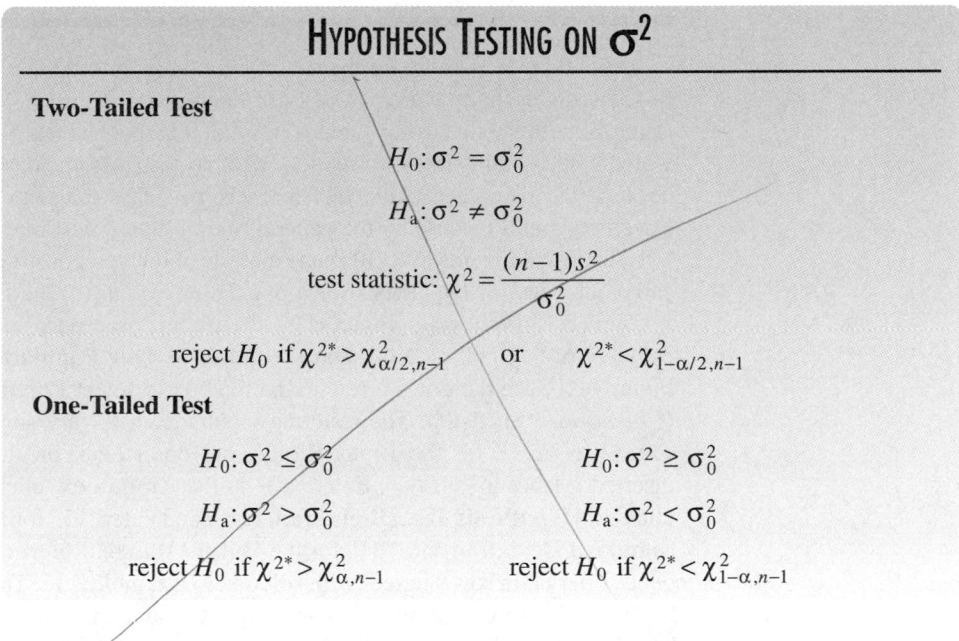

HYPOTHESIS TESTING ON σ^2

Two-Tailed Test

$$H_0: \sigma^2 = \sigma_0^2$$

$$H_a: \sigma^2 \neq \sigma_0^2$$

test statistic: $\chi^2 = \dfrac{(n-1)s^2}{\sigma_0^2}$

reject H_0 if $\chi^{2*} > \chi^2_{\alpha/2,n-1}$ or $\chi^{2*} < \chi^2_{1-\alpha/2,n-1}$

One-Tailed Test

$$H_0: \sigma^2 \leq \sigma_0^2 \qquad\qquad H_0: \sigma^2 \geq \sigma_0^2$$

$$H_a: \sigma^2 > \sigma_0^2 \qquad\qquad H_a: \sigma^2 < \sigma_0^2$$

reject H_0 if $\chi^{2*} > \chi^2_{\alpha,n-1}$ reject H_0 if $\chi^{2*} < \chi^2_{1-\alpha,n-1}$

EXAMPLE 8.13

Example 8.12 was concerned with the variation of the actual weight of a (supposedly) 50-pound bag of Vitamix Dog Chow. Based on earlier production tests, management is convinced that the average weight of all bags being produced is, in fact, 50 pounds. However, the production supervisor has been informed that at least 95% of the bags produced *must* be within 1 pound of the specified weight (50 pounds). Using a significance level of $\alpha = .1$, what can we conclude? Assume a normal distribution for the bag weights.

What is the supervisor being told about σ? Remember that for a normal population, 95% of the observations will lie within two standard deviations of the mean (empirical rule, Chapter 3). So, if two standard deviations are equivalent to 1 pound, then the supervisor is being told that σ must be no more than .5 pound. Is there any evidence to conclude that this is not the case—that is, that σ is larger than .5 pound? Let's investigate.

SOLUTION

Step 1. The appropriate hypotheses are H_0: $\sigma \le .5$ and H_a: $\sigma > .5$ (production is not meeting required standards).

(Note that these hypotheses are precisely the same as H_0: $\sigma^2 \le .25$ and H_a: $\sigma^2 > .25$. Whether you write H_0 and H_a in terms of σ or σ^2 does not matter; the testing procedure is the same in either case.)

Step 2. The test statistic is

$$\chi^2 = \frac{(15-1)s^2}{(.5)^2} = \frac{14s^2}{.25}$$

which has a chi-square distribution with 14 df.

Step 3. Using $\alpha = .1$ and Table A.6, the rejection region for this test is

$$\text{reject } H_0 \text{ if } \chi^2 > 21.1$$

Step 4. The computed value using the sample data is

$$\chi^2 = \frac{(15-1)(1.651)^2}{(.5)^2} = 152.6$$

Since $152.6 > 21.1$, we reject H_0. This is hardly a surprising result; the point estimate of σ is $s = 1.651$, quite a bit larger than .5.

Step 5. We conclude rather convincingly that σ is larger than .5 pound. The bagging procedure has far too much variation in the weight of the bags produced.

Note that the *p*-value for the test of hypothesis in Example 8.13 is the area to the right of 152.6 under the χ^2 curve with 14 df (illustrated in Figure 8.26). All we are able to determine about this value using Table A.6 is that it is much smaller than .005 (the smallest tabulated value). Using this information, we arrive at the same decision—namely, reject H_0—because (1) using the classical approach, p is less than $\alpha = .10$, or (2) the *p*-value is extremely small ($< .01$) by the general rule of thumb described in Section 8.3.

The Excel macros in KGP Data Analysis allow you construct a confidence interval and carry out a test of hypothesis for a population variance. The Excel solution to Examples 8.12 and 8.13 is shown in Figure 8.27. To use this procedure, enter the 15 sample values in cells A1:A15. Click on **KGP Data Analysis ➤ One Population Inference.** Referring to Figure 8.10, use the down arrow in the top box to select **Population Standard Deviation (Chi-Square Statistic).** The resulting input screen is very similar to that in Figure 8.10. Enter "A1:A15" for the **Input Range,** but don't click on the **Labels** box (unless you inserted a label in cell A1). Enter "10" in the **Alpha** box, click on **Confidence Interval,** click on **Hypothesis Test (Right-Tail Test),** and enter ".5" for the **Hypothesized Value of Standard Deviation** and "B1" for the **Output Range.** Referring to Figure 8.27, the confidence interval in row 9 agrees with solution to Example 8.12. The calculated chi-square statistic is 152.71 (slightly more accurate than the solution to Example 8.13), and the *p*-value in cell C7 is zero to four decimal places. This solution supports the earlier conclusion that the bagging procedure contains excessive variation in the bag weights.

FIGURE 8.26

Illustration of the *p*-value for Example 8.13.

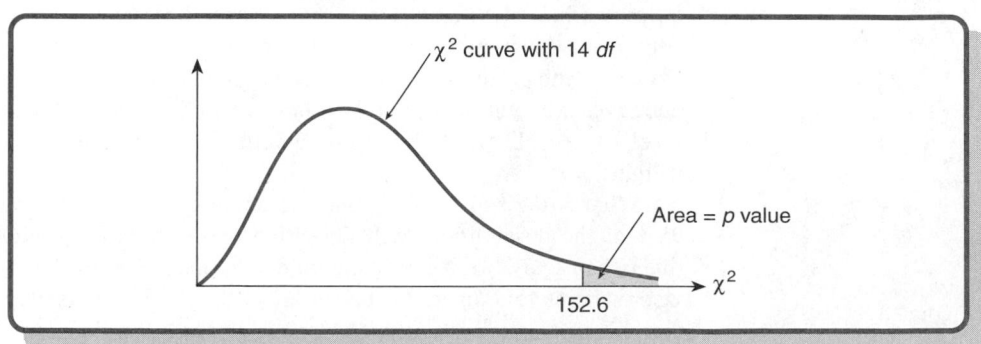

FIGURE 8.27

Excel spreadsheet for solution to Examples 8.12 and 8.13.

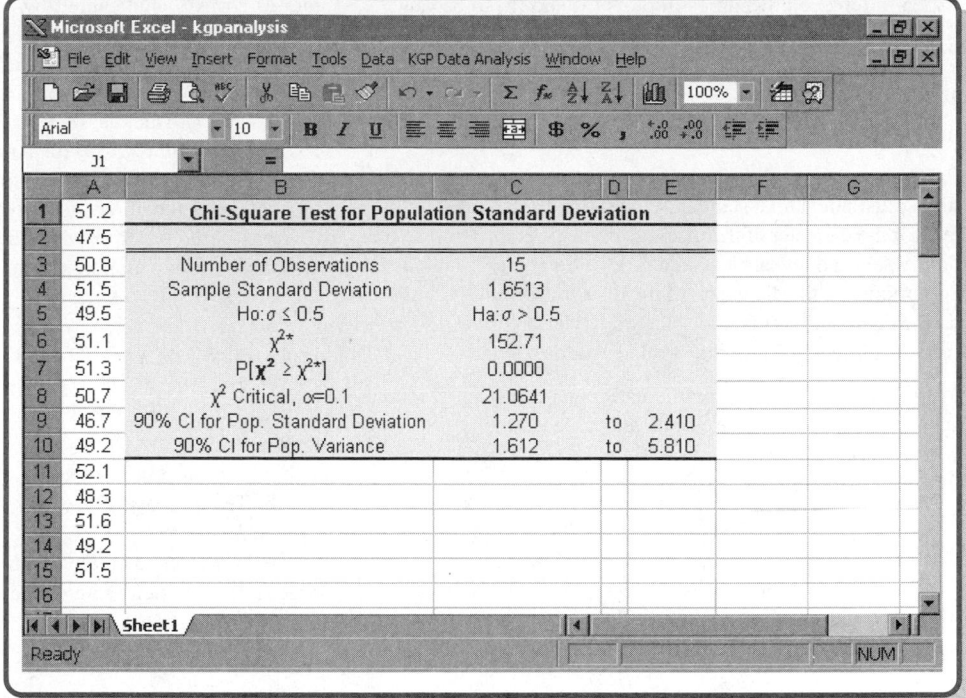

EXERCISES 8.47–8.56

UNDERSTANDING THE MECHANICS

8.47 Find the rejection region for testing H_0: $\sigma^2 = 100$ and H_a: $\sigma^2 \neq 100$ using the chi-square statistic for the following values of n and α.

    a. $n = 11$, $\alpha = .10$
    b. $n = 31$, $\alpha = .05$
    c. $n = 8$, $\alpha = .01$
    d. $n = 81$, $\alpha = .05$

8.48 A sample of size 25 from a normally distributed population yields a sample standard deviation of 12.8. At the 10% significance level, determine if there is sufficient evidence to indicate that the population standard deviation is greater than 11.3.

8.49 A random sample of 12 observations from an approximately normally distributed population is as follows.

$$5, 8, 13, 7, 14, 10, 6, 12, 9, 11, 8, 4$$

    a. Construct a 90% confidence interval for the population variance.

    b. Construct a 90% confidence interval for the population standard deviation.

    c. Test that the population standard deviation is less than 5. Use a .10 significance level.

APPLYING THE NEW CONCEPTS

8.50 According to Sanford C. Bernstein, a New York money management firm, the standard deviation of the daily closing prices of stocks on the New York Stock Exchange has been 13% in the 1990s. Suppose that the chairperson of a family of mutual funds wishes to determine if the standard deviation of equity mutual funds during the 1990s differs from 13%. The chairperson believes that the return by equity mutual funds can be approximated by a normal distribution. Assume that a sample of 25 equity mutual funds revealed a standard deviation of 9.8%.

(Source: Adapted from "The New Perilous Stock Market," by Susan E. Kuyn, *Fortune,* Dec. 27, 1993, p. 48.)

    a. Construct a 95% confidence interval for the population variance of equity mutual funds.

    b. Construct a 95% confidence interval for the population standard deviation of equity mutual funds.

    c. Is there sufficient evidence to indicate that the standard deviation of equity mutual funds differs from 13%? Use a .05 significance level.

8.51 As the stock market surges upward amid low inflation, consumers need to sock away a smaller portion of their income to achieve their saving goals, leaving them with more to spend. The University of Michigan's consumer-sentiment index is an indicator of consumers' contentment with the economy. In 1998, it remained quite high, and consumers' spending continued to increase. Suppose that financial advisors are concerned with the variability of the index. To be able to predict future changes in consumer sentiment, a low variance for the consumer-sentiment index is desirable. Assume that a financial advisor randomly selected 15 values of the consumer-sentiment index over the past two years and found a standard deviation of 1.7.

(Adapted from *The Wall Street Journal,* "Consumer Spending Rose Faster in April Than Income, and the Savings Rate Fell," June 1, 1998, p. A4.)

    a. Find a 90% confidence interval for the standard deviation of the consumer-sentiment index.

    b. What conclusion would result from the financial advisor testing that the population standard deviation of the consumer-sentiment index was less than three using a significance level of .05?

c. What assumptions must hold about the data for the statistical inference procedures in parts (a) and (b) to be valid?

8.52 For a random variable χ^2, which has chi-square distribution with 18 df, determine the values of a and b such that $P(a \leq \chi^2 \leq b) = .90$ and such that the areas in each tail are equal, that is, $P(0 \leq \chi^2 < a) = P(b < \chi^2)$.

8.53 A production manager in charge of manufacturing plastic discs must maintain a standard deviation of less than 2 millimeters for the diameter of the disc. A sample of 26 plastic discs randomly selected reveals a standard deviation of 1.85 millimeters. Assuming that the diameters of the disc are normally distributed, do the data indicate that the standard deviation of the disc is less than 2 millimeters? Use the p-value criteria.

8.54 The salaries for mathematics teachers in secondary schools in Connecticut are believed to be normally distributed with a variance greater than $3000. Test this belief using the following sample statistics:

$$\sum(x - \bar{x})^2 = 45,130$$

$$n = 14$$

where X represents a math teacher's salary. Use a 1% significance level.

Using the Computer

8.55 [DATA SET EX8-55] *Variable description:*

ThicknessProcess1: Thickness of metal strips in first manufacturing process
ThicknessProcess2: Thickness of metal strips in second manufacturing process
ThicknessProcess3: Thickness of metal strips in third manufacturing process

A quality engineer is experimenting with three machinery processes to determine which is the most acceptable. The processes produce metal strips that are targeted to be 5 centimeters thick and have a standard deviation no more than .25 centimeter thick. The consistency of the thickness of these strips is very important to the companies purchasing the strips. If the thicknesses vary too much, the strips will not fit properly into the structure of a military aircraft. Since the quality engineer has been empowered by the new management of the company to make decisions at the process level, the engineer decides to sample 20 strips manufactured by each process. The thickness is recorded in centimeters in the three variables ThicknessProcess1, ThicknessProcess2, and ThicknessProcess3.

a. Obtain three histograms of the variables: ThicknessProcess1, ThicknessProcess2, and ThicknessProcess3. In Excel, click on **KGP Data Analysis ➤ Quantitative Data Charts/Tables ➤ Stacked Histograms.**

b. From the three histograms in part (a), rank the histograms in the order of which has the most variation, the second most variation, and the third most variation.

c. Test H_0: $\mu = 5$ versus H_a: $\mu \neq 5$ using ThicknessProcess1.

d. Test H_0: $\sigma \geq .25$ versus H_a: $\sigma < .25$ using ThicknessProcess1.

e. Test H_0: $\mu = 5$ versus H_a: $\mu \neq 5$ using ThicknessProcess2.

f. Test H_0: $\sigma \geq .25$ versus H_a: $\sigma < .25$ using ThicknessProcess2.

g. Test H_0: $\mu = 5$ versus H_a: $\mu \neq 5$ using ThicknessProcess3.

h. Test H_0: $\sigma \geq .25$ versus H_a: $\sigma < .25$ using ThicknessProcess3.

i. Is your perception of the amount of variation in the processes consistent with the results obtained in parts (d), (f), and (h)?

8.56 [DATA SET EX8-56] *Variable description:*

CostTuneUp: The cost of tuning up a 1999 Buick LeSabre

To understand how prices vary, a news reporter took a 1999 Buick LeSabre with 25,000 miles on it for a tune-up at 30 different automotive locations in the Chicago area. The reporter did not explain to the automotive managers that he was checking out the automotive prices of a tune-up at various automotive garages. The reporter simply asked the automotive manager to look at the car and give an estimate on the price of a tune-up. No work was done. The reporter has learned that the standard deviation of the price of a tune-up in the Cleveland metroplex is equal to $5. The reporter believes that the standard deviation of a tune-up is greater in the Chicago metroplex area.

a. Test the hypothesis that the standard deviation of the variable CostTuneUp is greater than $5. Use a 5% significance level.

b. Suppose that the reporter notices that the third value in the random sample (the value of $104.50) is unusually large and decides to delete this value from the sample. What would be your conclusion in part (a) with this value removed?

Summary

In Chapter 7 you were introduced to the topic of **statistical inference** through discussion of the concept of estimating a population parameter (such as μ or σ) from the corresponding sample estimate. The reliability of using the sample mean to estimate μ was measured via a confidence interval. This chapter presented the other side of statistical inference—**hypothesis testing** regarding these two population parameters, along with a method of deriving a confidence interval for the population standard deviation or variance.

For testing against a hypothetical value of the population mean (μ), we introduced a procedure that used the standard normal (Z) distribution for large samples ($n > 30$) and the t distribution for small samples. For small samples, the hypotheses are concerned with the mean of a normal population. However, the Central Limit Theorem allows us to discuss the mean of any continuous population when we have a large sample.

The two hypotheses under investigation are the **null hypothesis,** H_0, and the **alternative hypothesis,** H_a. Typically, a claim that one is attempting to demonstrate goes into the alternative hypothesis.

Since any test of hypothesis uses a sample to infer something about a population, errors can result. Two specific errors are of great concern when you use the hypothesis-testing procedure. A **Type I error** occurs in the event you reject a null hypothesis when in fact it is true; a **Type II error** occurs when you fail to reject a null hypothesis when in fact it is not true.

The probability of a Type I error is the **significance level** of the test and is written as α. The probability of a Type II error is β; large values of β are associated with small values of α, and vice versa. To define a test of hypothesis, you **select a value of α** that considers the cost of rejecting a correct H_0 and failing to reject an incorrect H_0. Typical values of α range from .01 to .1.

The **power** of a statistical test is defined as $1 - \beta$ and is equal to the probability of rejecting H_0 when it is in fact false. The value of β (and so $1 - \beta$) depends on the actual value of the parameter under investigation, and so the power of the test can be obtained for each possible value of this parameter. The resulting set of power values defines a **power curve** for this test of hypothesis.

A five-step procedure was defined for any test of hypothesis:

Step 1. Set up H_0 and H_a.
Step 2. Define the **test statistic**, which is evaluated using the sample data.
Step 3. Define a **rejection region**, using the value of α, by selecting a **critical value** from the appropriate table.
Step 4. Calculate the value of the test statistic from the sample data and carry out the test. This will result in rejecting H_0 or failing to reject H_0.

Step 5. Give a conclusion in the language of the problem.

A test such as H_0: $\mu = 50$ versus $H_a \neq 50$ is called a **two-tailed test,** because we reject H_0 whenever the sample estimate of μ ($\overline{X}$) is either too large (test statistic is in the right tail) or too small (test statistic is in the left tail). Similarly, a test on the population variance (or standard deviation) such as H_0: $\sigma^2 = .2$ versus H_a: $\sigma^2 \neq .2$ also is a two-tailed test.

H_0: $\mu \leq 50$ vs H_a: $\mu > 50$ or H_0: $\mu \geq 50$ vs H_a: $\mu < 50$

and

H_0: $\sigma^2 \leq .2$ vs H_a: $\sigma^2 > .2$ or H_0: $\sigma^2 \geq .2$ vs H_a: $\sigma^2 < .2$

are all examples of **one-tailed tests** of hypothesis, since the rejection region lies in either the left tail *or* the right tail.

The tests on a population variance introduce the **chi-square distribution, χ^2**. This distribution was used to construct confidence intervals for σ^2 and σ as well as to define a distribution for the test statistic when performing a test of hypothesis on the variance or standard deviation.

Finally, we discussed why you should always include a **p-value** in the results of any hypothesis test. This value measures the strength of your point estimate (such as $\overline{X}$ or s^2). When using a predetermined significance level, α, you reject H_0 whenever the p-value is less than α and fail to reject H_0 otherwise. Another option is not to select the somewhat arbitrary value of α but simply to reject H_0 whenever the p-value is "small" (say, <.01), to fail to reject H_0 if it is "large" (say, >.1), or to decide that the data are inconclusive if the p-value lies between these two values. You can also use the p-value to measure the enthusiasm (p-value very small) with which you reject H_0 or the authority (p-value quite large) with which you fail to reject H_0.

SUMMARY OF FORMULAS

1. Test statistic for hypothesis testing on a population mean:

$$\frac{\overline{X} - \mu_0}{s / \sqrt{n}}$$

This statistic has approximately a standard normal distribution (Z) for *large samples* from any population, and a *t* distribution with $n - 1$ df for *small samples* from a normal population.

2. Power of a test for H_0: $\mu = \mu_0$ versus H_a: $\mu \neq \mu_0$ (large sample):

$$\text{Power} = P(Z > z_1) + P(Z < z_2)$$

where Z is the standard normal random variable,

$$z_1 = Z_{\alpha/2} - \frac{\mu - \mu_0}{\sigma / \sqrt{n}}$$

$$z_2 = -Z_{\alpha/2} - \frac{\mu - \mu_0}{\sigma / \sqrt{n}}$$

and μ is the specified value of the population mean.

3. Power of a test for H_0: $\mu \leq \mu_0$ versus H_a: $\mu > \mu_0$ (large sample):

$$\text{Power} = P(Z > z_1)$$

where Z is the standard normal random variable and

$$z_1 = Z_\alpha - \frac{\mu - \mu_0}{\sigma / \sqrt{n}}$$

4. Power of a test for H_0: $\mu \geq \mu_0$ versus H_a: $\mu < \mu_0$ (large sample):

$$\text{Power} = P(Z < z_2)$$

where Z is the standard normal random variable and

$$z_2 = -Z_\alpha - \frac{\mu - \mu_0}{\sigma / \sqrt{n}}$$

5. Confidence interval for a normal population variance (σ^2):

$$\frac{(n-1)s^2}{\chi^2_{\alpha/2,n-1}} \quad \text{to} \quad \frac{(n-1)s^2}{\chi^2_{1-\alpha/2,n-1}}$$

6. Confidence interval for a normal population standard deviation (σ):

$$\sqrt{\frac{(n-1)s^2}{\chi^2_{\alpha/2,n-1}}} \quad \text{to} \quad \sqrt{\frac{(n-1)s^2}{\chi^2_{1-\alpha/2,n-1}}}$$

7. Test statistic for hypothesis testing on a normal population variance or standard deviation:

$$\chi^2 = \frac{(n-1)s^2}{\sigma_0^2}$$

where σ_0^2 is the hypothesized variance.

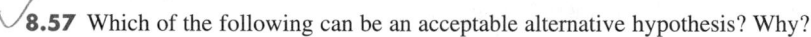

REVIEW EXERCISES 8.57–8.82

8.57 Which of the following can be an acceptable alternative hypothesis? Why?
  a. H_a: $\mu = 10$
  b. H_a: $\mu \neq 10$
  c. H_a: $\mu \leq 10$
  d. H_a: $\mu > 10$

8.58 The manager of Jack-Be-Nimble Candle Company would like to claim that a certain type of their candles burns more than 14 hours. To test this claim, the manager randomly selects 50 candles and finds that the sample mean is equal to 14.75 hours with a standard deviation of 1.8 hours.
  a. What are the null and alternative hypotheses?
  b. Which error would you consider to be more serious, Type I or Type II?
  c. At a significance level of .05, what is your conclusion?

8.59 Which of the following statements are true about a hypothesis test? Why?
  a. The probability of a Type I error and the significance level are the same.
  b. For a fixed sample size, the probability of a Type II error increases as the probability of a Type I error decreases.
  c. The null hypothesis is rejected if the p-value is greater than the significance level.
  d. A Type I error and a Type II error are the only ways that a wrong conclusion can occur.

8.60 The manager of the Train Depot Restaurant believes that the average time customers wait before being served is 10 minutes. To test the belief, the manager selects 50 customers at random and determines that the average waiting time is 11.9 minutes with a standard deviation of 1.4 minutes.
  a. Find a 95% confidence interval for the mean waiting time of a customer.
  b. Do the data indicate that the mean waiting time differs from 10 minutes, at a 5% significance level?

8.61 Calculate the power of the test for the mean of a normally distributed population with known population variance for the following situations, assuming that the true population mean is 10 and the known population standard deviation is 3.1. Use a significance level of .05.
  a. H_0: $\mu = 11$, H_a: $\mu \neq 11$, $n = 14$.
  b. H_0: $\mu = 9.5$, H_a: $\mu \neq 9.5$, $n = 25$.
  c. H_0: $\mu = 8$, H_a: $\mu \neq 8$, $n = 40$.

8.62 A supervisor is interested in whether a new machine will produce a batch of cylinders more quickly than the current machines do. A trial test of 23 batches of cylinders on the new machine yielded a sample mean of 8.5 minutes with a sample standard deviation of 1.2 minutes. The old machine is known to have a mean time of 9 minutes. Assume that the time required to produce a batch of cylinders follows a normal distribution.

a. Assuming a significance level of .10, what managerial conclusion can be given in testing that the mean time for the new machine is less than 9 minutes?

b. Explain how statistical significance and practical significance play a role in determining decisions made by the supervisor with regard to the new machine.

8.63 A manufacturer of drugs and medical products claims that a new antiinflammatory drug will be effective for 4 hours after the drug is administered in the prescribed dosage. A random sample of 50 volunteers demonstrated that the average effective time is 3.70 hours with a sample standard deviation of .606 hours. Use the p-value criteria to determine if there is sufficient evidence to support the hypothesis that the mean effective time of the drug differs from 4 hours.

8.64 Indicate what the p-values are for the following situations, in which the mean of a normally distributed population is being tested.

a. H_0: $\mu = 31.6$, H_a: $\mu \neq 31.6$ (population variance is known), $Z^* = 2.16$

b. H_0: $\mu = 4.07$, H_a: $\mu \neq 4.07$ (population variance is known), $Z^* = -1.35$

c. H_0: $\mu = 87.6$, H_a: $\mu \neq 87.6$ (population variance is unknown), $t^* = 2.51$, $n = 15$

d. H_0: $\mu = 195.3$, H_a: $\mu \neq 195.3$ (population variance is unknown), $t^* = -1.71$, $n = 25$

8.65 The economic crisis that Japan has faced in 1998 has forced many Japanese banks to examine their policies in making loans. Under the tutelage of the International Monetary Fund, many of the banks are being forced to abandon the "crony capitalism" that led to Japan's economic woes and adopt financial systems more akin to that in the USA, where bank loans are granted not on who you know but on how much money the borrower is making. Many of the loans made in prior years were primarily based on tight links between banks, businesses, and bureaucrats. Assume that 61 vice presidents of lending institutions in Japan were randomly selected and asked to respond on a 5-point Likert scale, with 5 being strongly agree and 1 being strongly disagree to the statement: The primary basis in qualifying a customer for a loan is his or her potential to repay the loan. The sample mean was found to be 4.2 with a standard deviation of .8. Suppose that financial consultants to the IMF are interested in whether the mean score to this question differs from 4.

(Adapted from *USA Today*, "All Eyes on Japan as Crisis Turns a Year Old," July 2, 1998, p. 3B.)

a. Use the Z test to test whether the data indicate that the mean score differs from 4. Use a significance level of .05.

b. Use the t test instead of the Z test in part (a). How much does the rejection region change?

8.66 The vice president of academic affairs at a small private college believes that the average full-time student who lives off campus spends about $300 per month for housing. A random sample of 200 full-time students living off campus spent an average of $305 per month with a standard deviation of $70 a month.

a. Find the p-value to determine whether there is sufficient evidence to indicate that a full-time student spends more than $300 per month on housing.

b. Would you reject the null hypothesis for the test in part (a) if $\alpha = .01$? if $\alpha = .05$? if $\alpha = .10$?

8.67 A marketing analyst is looking at the feasibility of opening a new movie theater in a small town. The town currently has only two movie theaters. The movie theater would be a practical investment if the average family in the town spends at least 14 hours at the movies each year. A random sample of 80 households yielded a sample mean of 14.5 hours per year with a standard deviation of 1.4.

a. Find the 95% confidence interval for the mean time that a family spends per year at the movies.

b. Is there sufficient evidence to indicate that the mean time that a family spends at the movies is greater than 14 hours per year? Use a .05 significance level.

8.68 International students having little financial support from home can apply for a loan through Citibank's Student Loan Corp. unit. If the student attends Harvard, no upfront fees and no co-signer are required. What's in it for Citibank? It hopes that a relationship can be established that will carry forward with the student's career. The president of the Student Loan Corp. is interested in the mean loan value. The president figures that a $50,000 loan would cover a student's primary expenses.

(Adapted from *The Wall Street Journal*, "Harvard and Citibank Team Up on Low-Rate Loans for MBA Students," July 2, 1998, p. 1.)

a. To test at the .10 significance level if the mean loan that a student would need over a two-year period differs from this amount, a random sample of students who have graduated and made loans was sampled. The resulting mean was $46,700 with a standard deviation of $14,500. The sample size was 50. What conclusion can the President make?

b. Discuss potential problems in sampling from students who have already graduated when making conclusions about expenses for future students.

8.69 In 1998, 30% of all travelers used e-tickets for airline travel. Electronic ticketing allows passengers to not have to worry about a paper ticket, and it costs the airline companies less to handle an e-ticket than a paper ticket. However, the American Society of Travel Agents (ASTA) has received reports of passengers having problems with their e-tickets, particularly with connecting flights. Suppose that the ASTA randomly sampled 20 airports and collected the number of complaints that the airport had with e-tickets for the month of July. The data are presented below. Test the hypothesis that the mean number of e-ticketing complaints per airport for the month of July is less than 15. Use a 10% significance level. What managerial decision should the ASTA make based on the results of this test?

| 18 | 12 | 17 | 13 | 11 | 10 | 17 | 16 | 9 | 17 |
| 14 | 13 | 15 | 18 | 14 | 8 | 19 | 18 | 10 | 15 |

(Adapted from *USA Today*, "E-tickets not Error-free," June 23, 1998, p. 5B.)

8.70 The owners of a shopping center are contemplating increasing the parking space in front of the shopping center. The owners would like to demonstrate that the average driver parks for more than .75 hours. The length of time parked is considered to be normally distributed. A random sample of 45 parked cars is observed; the average time parked was .80 hours with a standard deviation of .12. Do the data support the idea that the average driver parks for more than .75 hours? Use a 10% significance level.

8.71 Dow Jones & Co. said that it plans to cut 4.9% of its Ottaway Newspapers, Inc., staff. The publisher said that it will take a third quarter charge in 1998 of $5 million to pay severance and related costs. Suppose that the company decided to poll 20 of its employees to ask the likelihood of accepting a buyout. The employees responded on a scale from 1 to 10, with 10 indicating that the employee would accept any reasonable buyout and 1 indicating that the employee would be totally unwilling to accept any type of buyout. The poll revealed a mean likelihood value of 6.5.

(Adapted from *The Wall Street Journal*, "Dow Jones Proposes to Trim 125 Jobs at Its Ottaway Unit," June 30, 1998, p. B8.)

a. To reach its goal of eliminating 4.9% of Ottaway Newspapers staff, a consultant believes that the likelihood value should be greater than 6. Is there sufficient evidence that the company's goal will be reached with respect to eliminating jobs? Assume that the sample standard deviation is 1.3 and that the significance level is .05.

b. If you were a consultant being paid to advise Ottaway Newspapers on how to reach their goal of eliminating 4.9% of their staff, would you want to use a small significance level or a large significance level in part (a)? Explain.

8.72 From a normally distributed population, a random sample of size 22 yields the following statistic:

$$\Sigma(x - \bar{x})^2 = 1.67$$

a. Find a 95% confidence interval for the population variance.
b. Find a 95% confidence interval for the population standard deviation.
c. Test the null hypothesis that the population variance is equal to .07. Use a two-tailed test and a .05 significance level.

8.73 Using a significance level of .05, perform the hypothesis test for the standard deviation of a normally distributed population, given the following information:

$$H_0: \sigma \geq 20.6 \qquad \Sigma(x - \bar{x})^2 = 6100$$
$$H_a: \sigma < 20.6 \qquad n = 18$$

8.74 Eastern State Bank currently operates five drive-in teller windows. Management is concerned about the variability of the time spent waiting by a customer using the windows. A sample of 24 customers was taken, and the sample standard deviation was found to be 4.7 minutes. Management would like to keep the standard deviation below 4 minutes and may consider adding another drive-in teller window.

a. Test the null hypothesis that the standard deviation of a customer's waiting time is less than or equal to 4 minutes. Use a 10% significance level.

b. What assumption should be made about the distribution of the waiting time of customers who use the drive-in teller windows?

8.75 An investment counselor would like to know how much variability there is in the yield of money market funds. The yields of these funds can be considered to be approximately normally distributed for the time frame of interest. A sample of 21 money market funds yields a sample standard deviation of .7%. At the .05 significance level, is there sufficient evidence to indicate that the standard deviation of the yields of money market funds is greater than .6%?

8.76 A large university had recently converted to a computerized registration system for enrollment. After the first semester, administrators found that the average time spent registering per student was quite satisfactory, yet there still continued to be substantial complaints and dissatisfaction among students. Further study indicated that although the *average* time might seem satisfactory, there might be too much *variation* in the registration times. It was decided to study the situation during the next semester's registration period. If the standard deviation was greater than 20 minutes, six additional computer terminals would be installed; otherwise, two new computer terminals would be installed. From a random sample, the following data were obtained:

$$\Sigma(x - \overline{x})^2 = 6900 \qquad n = 18$$

Assume the population is normally distributed.

    a. Is there sufficient evidence to indicate that the population standard deviation exceeds 20 minutes? Use a 5% significance level.

    b. What is the decision indicated by the test: install six new terminals or two new terminals?

    c. State the *p*-value for the test.

8.77 The U.S. Treasury Department is starting to use a new system for paying the government's bills and for accepting payment. It is called the e-check program. With this system, a check is sent by e-mail. The company or the government makes out a digital check using special software, signs it with a secure digital "signature," and e-mails it to the creditor. Suppose that a banking analyst believes that for this program to become viable, the banking community needs to be very supportive. Assume that a poll of 75 bankers rated the acceptance of this new payment system on a scale from 1 to 10, with 10 indicating complete acceptance and 1 indicating that the new payment system would never be acceptable. Use a computer package to analyze the data below. Construct a 90%, 95%, and 99% confidence interval on the mean acceptance of this new payment system by the banking community.

8	5	8	4	9	3	7	5	10	2	7	6	3	5	8
7	8	9	5	7	8	5	9	4	10	3	7	4	8	9
3	8	5	8	9	8	7	10	1	3	8	9	7	8	9
5	8	3	7	5	9	3	9	3	7	4	8	9	10	2
4	8	5	8	4	3	8	4	9	4	9	5	9	5	9

(Adapted from *The Wall Street Journal*, "Treasury Department to Inaugurate Internet-Payment Plan Called 'Echeck'," June 30, 1998, p. B12.)

8.78 Many business failures have been attributed to the lack of successful integration of engineering and marketing. Examples include Texas Instrument's disastrous early entry into the desktop personal computer business, Medical Electronics, Inc.'s, ineffective introduction of a key portable heart monitoring product, and Hewlett-Packard's early foray into the laptop business with a technology-laden, 23-pound portable. To understand if communications between marketing and engineering managers have improved, a survey was conducted of 60 randomly selected managers of Fortune 500 companies. Thirteen items were answered pertaining to communication frequency. The numerical responses were summed to form one score on communication frequency. Suppose that a communication score of less than 40 indicated that there were serious communication problems. Assume that the results of the survey yielded the results:

$$\overline{x} = 38, \ s^2 = 4$$

(Adapted from *Journal of Marketing*, "Enhancing Communication Between Marketing and Engineering: The Moderating Role of Relative Functional Identification," 1997, vol. 61, no. 3, p. 54.)

    a. What is the *p*-value for testing that a serious communications problem exists between marketing and engineering managers? What conclusion would be researched at a .01 significance level? At a .05 level?

    b. Find a 95% confidence interval for the population standard deviation. Use this confidence interval to test the hypothesis that the standard deviation of the population differs from 2.5 assuming a .05 significance level.

8.79 [DATA EX8-79] *Variable description:*

RecycledAlum: Amount of recycled aluminum scraps from manufactured castings

An operations manager has purchased new energy-efficient machinery to manufacture aluminum castings. Historically, the amount of aluminum that is left as scrap after a casting is manufactured averages 2.1 ounces. With the new machinery, 35 castings were manufactured and the amounts of scrap in ounces from this test run were used as the values of the variable RecycledAlum. The manager ran a hypothesis test at the 5% significance level and also obtained a 95% confidence interval. The results of this analysis follow. The manager is interested in whether the average recycled aluminum scraps differ from the historical amount of 2.6 ounces.

a. What are the results of the hypothesis test at the 5% significance level? Is the corresponding confidence interval consistent with the results of the test?

t Test for Population Mean			
Number of Observations	35		
Sample Standard Deviation	1.024629		
Sample Mean	2.188571		
Ho:μ = 2.6	Ha:$\mu \neq$ 2.6		
T*	-2.375536		
2 * P[T $\geq$ |T*|] two tail	0.023303		
| T Critical |, α =0.05	2.032243		
95% CI for Pop. Mean	1.836599	to	2.540544

b. The manager believes that the data may not be from a normal distribution. Therefore, she decides to obtain a confidence interval using the bootstrap approach (see section 7.6). Obtain a 95% confidence interval using 150 bootstrapped samples of size 35. Does the manager have enough evidence from this confidence interval to conclude at the 5% significance level that the amount of aluminum scraps differs from the historical amount of 2.6 ounces? Does this support the conclusion in part (a)?

8.80 [DATA SET EX8-80] *Variable description:*

JITscore: Manager's rating of supplier-manufacturer relationship

A consulting firm's study of 100 manufacturers who have recently implemented just-in-time (JIT) purchasing of parts needed to manufacture goods revealed how managers rate this process with respect to lowering ordering costs. Each manager rated the process on a 100-point scale, with 100 representing a maximum possible reduction in ordering costs and 0 representing the highest increase in ordering costs relative to historical costs. A value of 50 would indicate that JIT purchasing has neither increased nor decreased ordering costs. These data are the values for the variable JITscore. The consulting firm decided to test the hypothesis that the ratings are significantly higher than 70 with a 5% significance level. If there is evidence that the average rating is greater than 70, then the firm will recommend the procedure to its clients.

a. Below are the results of a two-tailed hypothesis test conducted at the 10% significance level. Explain how an analyst can use this output to conduct the hypothesis test in which the firm is interested with a significance level of 5%.

t Test for Population Mean	
Number of Observations	100
Sample Standard Deviation	18.564316
Sample Mean =0.1	73.250000
Ho:μ = 70	Ha:$\mu \neq$ 70
T*	1.750670
2 * P[T $\geq$ |T*|] two tail	0.083100
| T Critical |, α	1.660392

b. Run the corresponding one-tail hypothesis test in which the consulting firm is interested using a 5% significance level. Compare this result to that obtained from the computer printout in part (a).

8.81 Simulate 200 sample variances by calculating the variance of 200 random samples of size 15 from a normal population with mean 100 and standard deviation 5. Calculate the test statistics for testing that the population variance is equal to 25. Plot the histogram of the values of the test statistic. Also plot a histogram of 200 observations from the chi-square distribution with 14 degrees of freedom. Compare the shapes of the two plots. If the mean of the population were to change from 100 to 500, how do you think the plot would change? Try it. If the standard deviation of the normal population were to change from 5 to 30, how would the plot change? Try it. In Excel, to obtain 200 sample standard deviations assuming a sample size of 15 from a normal population with a mean of 100 and a standard deviation of 5, click on **Tools ➤ Data Analysis ➤ Random Number Generation.** Type in "200" for the **Number of Variables,** "15" for the **Number of Random Numbers,** select **Normal** for the distribution with parameters 100 and 5. Select cell A1 for the output. Then click on the OK button. In cell A16, type in "var(A1:A15)" and drag to cell GR16. Row 16 displays the sample variances. To calculate the value of the test statistic, type "=A16*(15-1)/25" in cell A17. Highlight row 17, click on **copy,** and do a **paste special** (click on the options of values and transpose) into column A starting in cell A18. This will produce a column of test statistic values. Plot a histogram of the test statistic values. Now to generate 200 observations of the chi-square distribution, first generate 200 observations from the uniform distribution starting in cell C19 (use **Tools ➤ Data Analysis ➤ Random Number Generation**). In cell D19, type Chiinv(C19, 14) and drag to D218). These values are random observations from a population having a chi-square distribution. Plot a histogram of these values. The plots below represent the histogram of the test statistic for testing the population variance and the histogram of the observations from a population with a chi-square distribution.

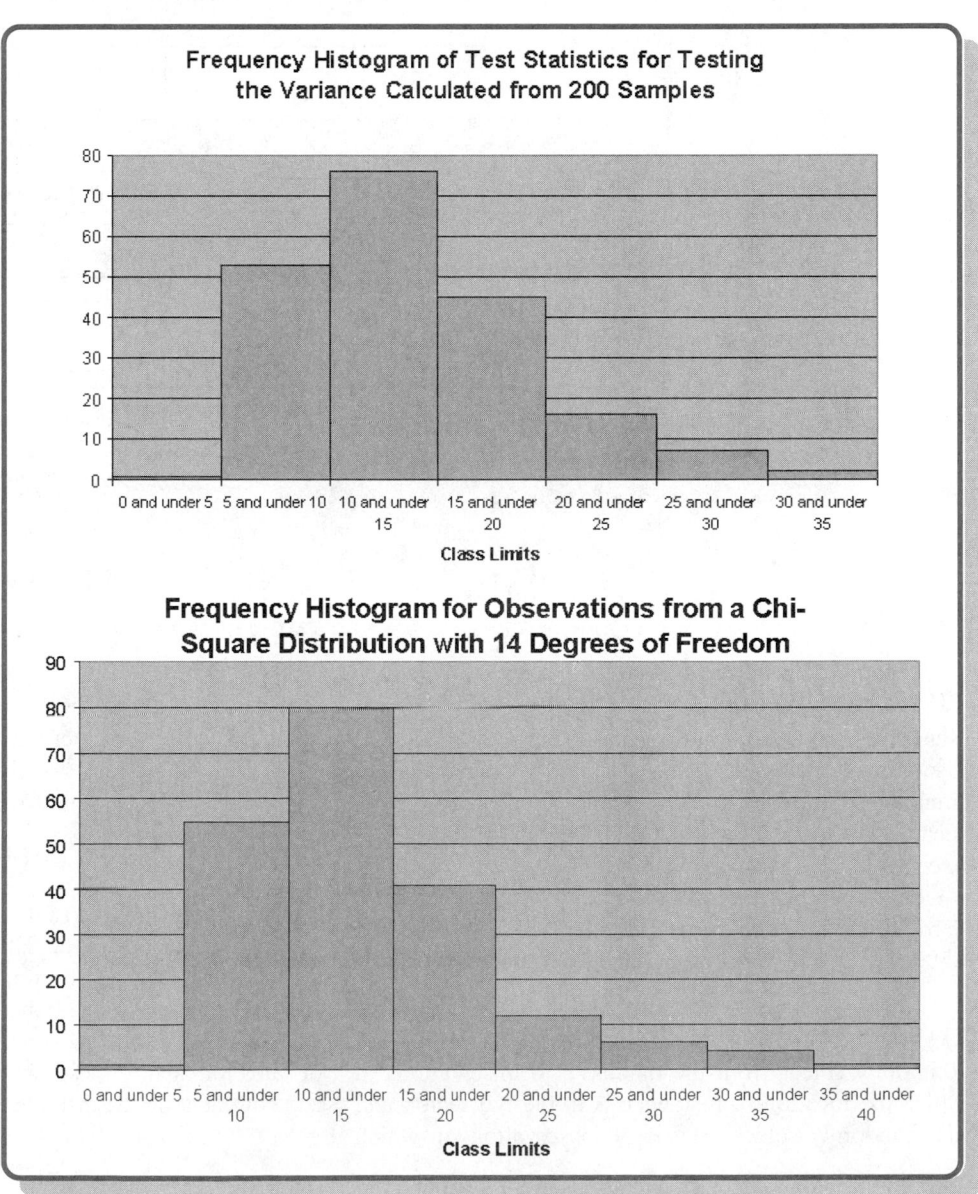

8.82 Graph the power function for testing the null hypothesis of $\mu = 100$ against the alternative hypothesis of $\mu \neq 100$ when the true value of the mean ranges from 80 to 120. Do this for $n = 40$ and $n = 70$ when the population standard deviation is known to be 25. For which values of the mean does the power function change very little? To obtain a graph of the power function in Excel, put the values 80, 81, . . . , 120 in cells A2 to A42. Then in cells A1 through G1, put the titles presented below. In cells B2 through G2, put in the formulas presented below.

A	B	C	D	E	F	G
True Mean	Term needed in z1 and z2	z1	z2	P(Z > z1)	P(Z < z2)	Power
80	=(A2-100)*SQRT(40)/25	=1.96 - B2	=-1.96-B2	=1-NORMSDIST(C2)	=NORMSDIST(D2)	=E2 + F2

Now highlight the region: cells B1 through G1 and B2 through G2. Click on **Copy.** Now highlight rows 3 through 42 for columns B through G. Click on **Paste.** Use the line chart subtype option of the **Chart Wizard** to plot the power function. A graph of the power function for $n = 40$ is presented below.

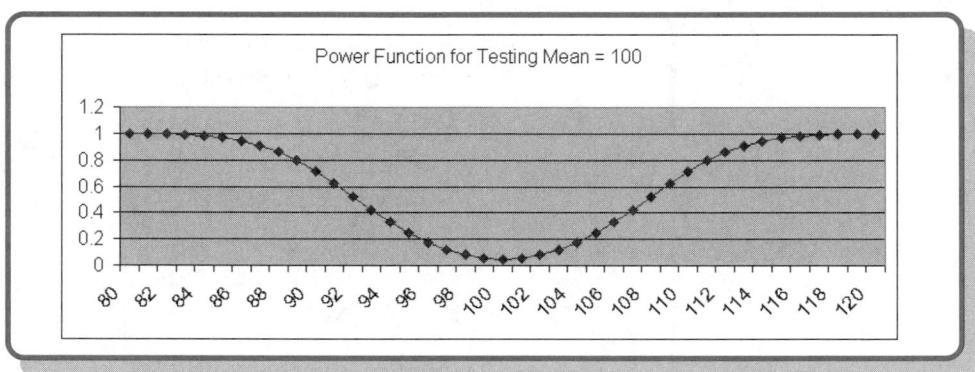

COMPUTER EXERCISES USING THE DATABASES

EXERCISE 1—APPENDIX E
Randomly select 100 observations from the database. Use a convenient statistical computer package to determine whether the sample evidence indicates that the mean of the variable TOTLDEBT (total indebtedness) exceeds $14,000 at the .05 significance level. Also determine whether the sample evidence indicates that the standard deviation of the variable TOTLDEBT exceeds $4000 at the .05 significance level.

EXERCISE 2—APPENDIX E
Randomly select from the database 30 observations in which the location of residence is in the NE sector, and also randomly select another 30 observations in which the location of residence is in the NW sector. Find separate 90% confidence intervals on the mean of the variable INCOME1 (income of principal wage earner) from each of these two sets of data. Comment on the difference in the confidence intervals.

EXERCISE 3—APPENDIX F
Randomly select from the database 30 observations from companies with a bond rating of A and 30 observations from companies with a bond rating of C. Find separate 95% confidence intervals on the mean of sales minus cost of sales for each of these two random samples. Compare and comment on the differences.

INSIGHTS FROM STATISTICS IN ACTION: DRAMATIC CHANGES IN THE RADIO INDUSTRY

The Statistics in Action section at the beginning of this chapter described the changes taking place in the radio industry with an ever-increasing level of consolidation. Financial analysts will want to closely monitor and form conclusions about the average number of radio stations owned and the average revenue per station. Some multi-media experts are also interested in the amount of variability (or variance) in the number of radio stations owned. If the variance is increasing, this may indicate that a few companies own many radio stations, while at the same time several companies own very few radio stations. Consider the following list to be a sample of large public companies that have bought radio stations and their revenue from operating radio stations during 1998.

Owner	Number of Radio Stations Owned	Revenue for 1998 (in thousands)
Susquehanna Radio	21	141.4
CBS	160	1529.4
Heftel Broadcasting	39	155.5
Chancellor Media	108	996.0
Emmis Broadcasting	13	156.7
Jacor Communications	204	602.2
Cox Radio	59	246.9
Capstar Broadcasting Partners	299	537.7
Clear Channel Comm.	196	452.3
ABC Radio	29	310.4

1. Compute 95% and 99% confidence intervals for the mean revenue for 1998 for large companies that have acquired radio stations.
2. Compute 95% and 99% confidence intervals for the mean number of radio stations owned by companies that have acquired radio stations.
3. Compute 95% and 99% confidence intervals for the standard deviation of the revenue for 1998.
4. Determine if the mean revenue for 1998 for the large companies is different from a mean of 225. Use a significance level of .05. What is the conclusion using a .10 significance level?
5. Test whether the mean number of radio stations owned by the companies is different from 50. Use a significance level of .05. What is the conclusion using a .10 significance level?
6. Determine if the standard deviation of the revenue for 1998 for the large companies is significantly different from 300. Use a significance level of .05. What is the conclusion using a .10 significance level?
7. The CEO for one of the radio station conglomerates has reviewed the confidence intervals constructed in the prior questions. She is concerned about the widths of these confidence intervals—that is, she would like to see the maximum error reduced. What can you advise her as to how to reduce this maximum error? What effect do you think this will have on the Type I and Type II errors in Question 5?

Sources: *The Wall Street Journal,* "Amid Consolidation, Fear of Less Diversity, Choice," July 7, 1998, p. 1; and *The Wall Street Journal,* "Radio Stations Make Waves on the Web," July 23, 1998, p. B1. Republished by permission of Dow Jones, Inc. via Copyright Clearance Center, Inc. © 1998, Dow Jones and Company, Inc. All Rights Reserved Worldwide.

CHAPTER 8 APPENDIX: DATA ANALYSIS WITH MINITAB

HYPOTHESIS TEST FOR A ONE-POPULATION MEAN USING THE NORMAL DISTRIBUTION

To obtain a Z test statistic for testing a hypothesis on the mean of a single population, click on **Stat ➤ Basic Statistics ➤ 1-Sample Z.** The user form is the same as that used in obtaining a confidence interval on the mean using the normal distribution. For this example the kilowatt data in DATA8-5 is used. In this example an alternative hypothesis of "greater than" is selected for a hypothesized mean of 918. Note that an alpha value is not assigned, since a *p*-value is reported for the test. If **Graphs** is clicked, a histogram will also be displayed. The histogram will include a 95% confidence interval on the mean. The hypothesized value of the mean will also be displayed below the histogram. The value of the population standard deviation is assumed to be 173.92, the estimate from the sample. The Z test can be used in place of the *t* test for large sample sizes. The output follows the user form. In addition, the histogram and confidence interval are also displayed. The hypothesized mean (918) and the sample mean (952.8) are also displayed in this graph.

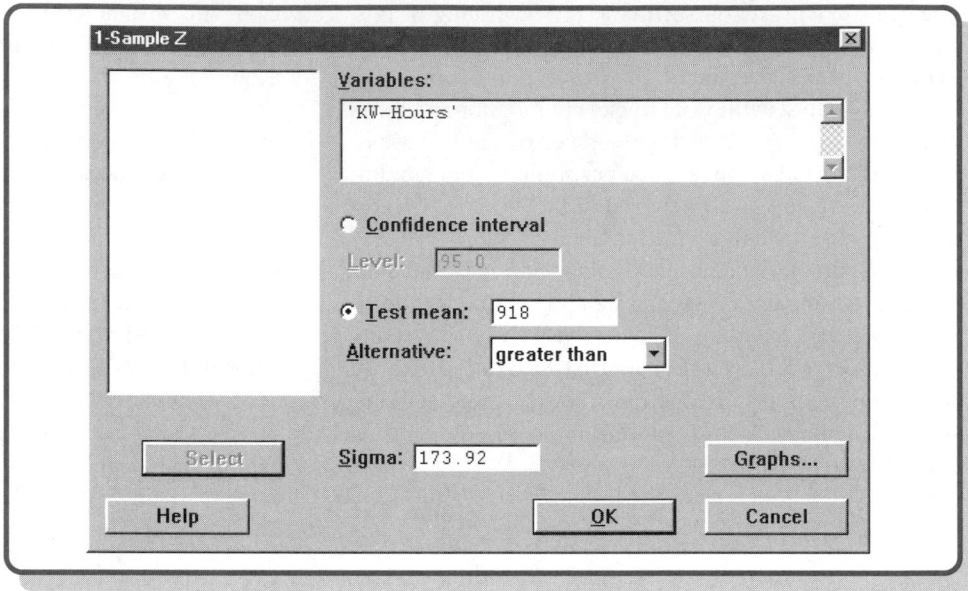

Z-Test

```
Test of mu = 918.0 vs mu > 918.0
The assumed sigma = 174
```

Variable	N	Mean	StDev	SE Mean	Z	P
KW-Hours	60	952.6	173.9	22.5	1.54	0.062

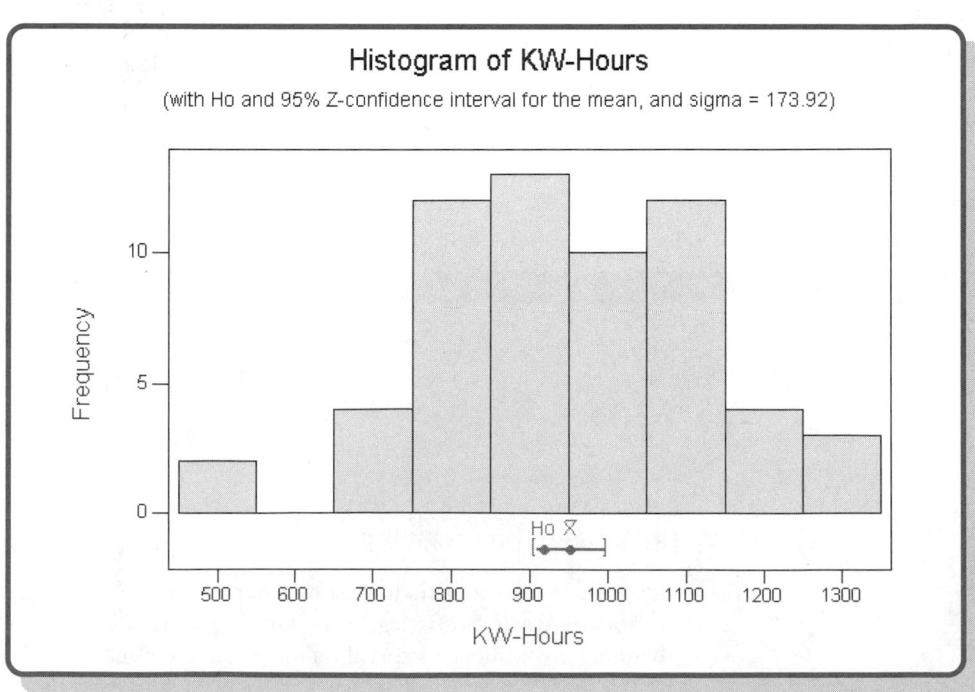

HYPOTHESIS TEST FOR A ONE-POPULATION MEAN USING THE *t* DISTRIBUTION

To obtain a *t* test statistic for testing a hypothesis on the mean of a single population, click on **Stat ➤ Basic Statistics ➤ 1-Sample t.** The user form is the same as that used in obtaining a *t* test on the mean using the normal distribution, except there is not a box for specifying the value of the standard deviation, σ.

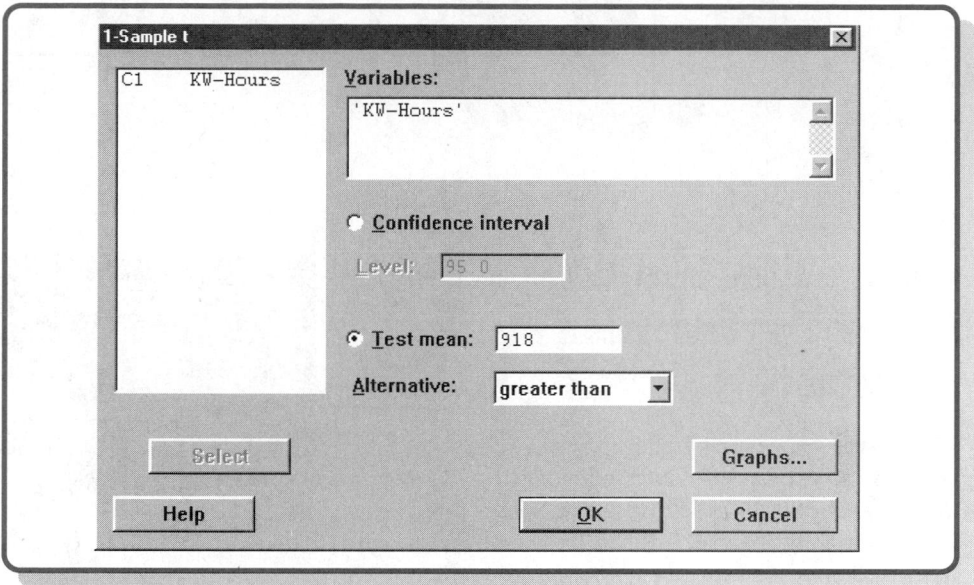

T-Test of the Mean

```
Test of mu = 918.0 vs mu > 918.0
```

Variable	N	Mean	StDev	SE Mean	T	P
KW-Hours	60	952.6	173.9	22.5	1.54	0.064

INFERENCE PROCEDURES FOR TWO POPULATIONS

STATISTICS IN ACTION: COLLISIONS INVOLVING LIGHT TRUCKS AND SPORT UTILITY VEHICLES WITH CARS: ASSESSING THE IMPACT

The increasing popularity of light trucks and sport utility vehicles (SUVs) can be witnessed along any highway or in any parking lot. Since 1985, the presence of light trucks has increased more than 50%. In the United States, light trucks account for more than 40% of new vehicle sales and sport utility vehicles have gained similar popularity. Once considered farm, work, or off-road vehicles, small trucks and sport utility vehicles are now used for primary transportation and as the family car.

It seems only natural that as the number of light trucks increases, the number of accidents involving light trucks will similarly increase. But over the years that light trucks gained popularity, the typical passenger car became smaller and lighter. While this has certainly been driven by the need for more fuel-efficient automobiles, according to the National Traffic Highway Safety Administration (NTHSA), in collisions involving a car and a light truck, 80% of the fatalities are occupants of the cars.

Light trucks not only have a more rigid structure that is carried higher off the ground, light trucks outweigh cars by an average of 900 pounds. In a collision with a car, the truck's higher ground clearance causes the truck to override the car's occupant protection features. The truck's stiffer structure better withstands collision forces, leaving the car to endure greater deformation. Being heavier, trucks deliver more momentum to the collision. Studies indicate a 100-pound reduction in the truck's weight could prevent 40 fatalities and 601 moderate-to-critical injuries each year. Unless additional safety improvements are added, similar *reduction* in the weight of cars could add 302 fatalities and 1,823 moderate-to-critical injuries each year.

Adding weight to the cars will reduce fatalities and serious injuries yet can lead to noncompliance with federally mandated fuel efficiency. Both safety advocates

and environmentalists suggest raising light trucks' Corporate Average Fuel Economy (CAFE) above the current 20.7 miles per gallon. Such legislation would require smaller, lighter, and more fuel-efficient trucks, thus hopefully saving lives and reducing injuries.

The automotive insurance industry has begun examining the disproportionate damage that cars sustain in collisions with trucks and SUVs. The insurance industry would like automakers to design vehicles that are more equally paired in crashes. Liability rate increases as much as 20% are possible for drivers of the light trucks and sport utility vehicles. Car owners may see premium reductions as much as 10%.

But how do you determine if the average amount of damage is different for cars hit by another car versus those hit by an SUV? Can you compare the means from two samples and see if one is larger than the other? The answer is *no* because this may happen simply by chance, and you need to determine if the sample means are *significantly* different.

When you have completed this chapter, you will be able to:

- Discuss what is meant by a "significant difference" between two sample means;
- Set up hypotheses that will demonstrate that, in fact, repair costs for car/SUV collisions are larger than costs for car/car collisions; and
- Carry out a hypothesis test and be able to discuss the findings.

A LOOK BACK/INTRODUCTION

We have learned to describe and summarize data from a single population using a statistic (such as the sample mean, $\overline{X}$) or a graph (such as a histogram). Chapters 7 and 8 introduced you to statistical inference, where we (1) attempted to estimate a parameter (such as the mean, μ) from this population by using the corresponding sample statistic and (2) arrived at a conclusion about this parameter (such as $\mu > 5.9$ ft) by performing a test of hypothesis. The concept behind hypothesis testing was described, and we paid special attention to the errors (Type I and Type II) that can occur when we use a sample to infer something about a population.

Next we learn how to compare two populations. Questions of interest here include:

1. Are the values in population 1 larger, on the average, than those in population 2? (For example, are men taller, on the average, than women?)
2. Do the values in population 1 exhibit more variation than those in population 2? (For example, do male heights vary more than female heights?)

The two populations under observation may or may not be normally distributed. When we compare two population means using large samples, once again using the Central Limit Theorem, the type of distribution simply does not matter. For small samples, we need to examine the distributions of the populations so that we can use the proper procedure to construct confidence intervals and perform tests of hypothesis.

This chapter discusses two different sampling situations. In the first, random samples from two populations are obtained *independently* of each other; in the second, corresponding data values from the two samples are matched up, or paired. Paired samples are *dependent*.

9.1 INDEPENDENT VERSUS DEPENDENT SAMPLES

When making comparisons between the means of two populations, we need to pay particular attention to how we intend to collect sample data. For example, how would you determine if tire brand A lasts longer than brand B? You might decide to put one of each brand on the rear wheels of ten cars and measure the tires' wear. Or you might randomly select ten brand A and ten brand B tires, attach them to a machine that wears them down for a certain time, and then measure the resulting tire wear. If you use the first procedure (putting both brands of tire on the same car), you obtain *dependent* samples; in the latter situation, you obtain *independent* samples.

Consider another situation. Suppose you are interested in male heights as compared with female heights. You obtain a sample of $n_1 = 50$ male heights and $n_2 = 50$ female heights. You obtain these data:

Observation	Male Heights	Observation	Female Heights
1	5.92 ft	1	5.36 ft
2	6.13 ft	2	5.64 ft
3	5.78 ft	3	5.44 ft
⋮	⋮	⋮	⋮
50	5.81 ft	50	5.52 ft

Is there any need to match up 5.92 with 5.36, 6.13 with 5.64, 5.78 with 5.44, and so on? The male heights were randomly selected and the female heights were obtained independently, so there is no reason to match up the first male height with the first female height, the second male height with the second female height, and so on. Nothing relates male 1 with female 1 other than the accident of their being selected first—these are **independent samples.**

What if you wish to know whether husbands are taller than their wives? To collect data, you select 50 married couples. Suppose you obtain the 100 observations from the previous male and female height example. Now, is there a reason to compare the first male height with the first female height, the second with the second, and so on? The answer is a definite yes, since each pair of heights belongs to a married couple. The resulting two samples are **dependent,** or **paired, samples.**

In summary,

1. If there is a definite reason for pairing (matching) corresponding data values, the two samples are **dependent** samples.
2. If the two samples were obtained independently and there is no reason for pairing the data values, the resulting samples are **independent** samples.

Why does this distinction matter? *If you are trying to decide whether male heights are, on the average, greater than female heights, the procedure that you use for testing this depends on whether the samples are obtained independently.*

Applications of dependent samples in a business setting include data from the following situations.

1. Comparisons of *before versus after.* Sample 1: person's weight before a diet plan is begun. Sample 2: person's weight 6 months after starting the diet. Why do we pair the data? We pair them because each pair of observations belongs to the same person.
2. Comparisons of people with *matching characteristics.* Sample 1: salary for a male employee at Company ABC. Sample 2: salary for a female employee at Company ABC, where the woman's education and job experience are equal to the man's. Why do we pair the data? We pair them because the two paired employees are identical in their job qualifications.
3. Comparisons of observations *matched by location.* Sample 1: sales of brand A tires for a group of *n* stores. Sample 2: sales of brand B tires for the same group of stores. Why do we pair the data? We pair them because both observations were obtained from the same store. Your data consist of sales (weekly, monthly, and so on) from a sample of stores selling these two brands.
4. Comparisons of observations *matched by time.* Sample 1: sales of restaurant A during a particular week. Sample 2: sales of restaurant B during this week. Why do we pair the data? We pair them because each pair of observations corresponds to the same week of the year.

EXERCISES 9.1–9.8

APPLYING THE NEW CONCEPTS

9.1 For each of the following situations, state whether paired samples or independent samples are involved.

a. A marketing strategist selects a random sample of teenagers and a random sample of consumers 20 years old or older to rate a new mouthwash.

b. Ten different supermarkets were randomly selected. The price of whole milk and the price of skim milk were recorded from each store.

c. Mortgage rates by institutional lenders on the east coast and west coast were studied. Random samples of 50 lending institutions on each coast were selected, and their 30-year fixed mortgage rates were recorded.

9.2 Two private colleges decided to compare the mean SAT scores of their incoming freshmen. One college gathered 98 scores and the other took a sample of 52 scores. Do the two sets of data represent dependent or independent samples?

9.3 A medical institution is examining the effectiveness of a newly developed drug. The drug was administered to 18 patients whose health condition before and after taking the drug was recorded. Is this a case of dependent or independent samples?

9.4 The advertising division of a chemical company would like to see how two different dishwashing detergents are rated by homemakers. Homemakers are chosen at random. They assign a value from 0 to 10 to each product. They assign a value of 0 to the product if they think the detergent is worthless and 10 to the detergent if they believe it is the best on the market. How can dependent samples be chosen? How can independent samples be chosen?

9.5 The career placement center at Safire University conducts a survey of beginning salaries for MBAs with no on-the-job experience. Ten pairs of men and women are chosen randomly such that each pair of one man and one woman has nearly identical qualifications. Can the sample of observations from men be independent of the sample of observations from women?

9.6 A retail store would like to compare sales from two different arrangements of displaying its merchandise. Sales are recorded for a 30-day period with one arrangement and then sales are recorded for another 30-day period for the alternative arrangement. Would the data for each of the two 30-day periods be independent or dependent?

9.7 Fifty people were randomly selected to rate particular brands of soft drink on a scale from 1 to 10, with 10 being the highest rating. If 25 people rated brand A and the other 25 people rated brand B, would the samples from these two groups be independent or dependent?

9.8 In Exercise 9.7 suppose the 50 people were each asked to rate both brand A and brand B. Would the sample of 50 observations of brand A be independent of the sample of 50 observations of brand B?

9.2 COMPARING TWO MEANS USING TWO LARGE, INDEPENDENT SAMPLES

When comparing the means of two independent samples from different populations, we can use Figure 9.1 to help visualize the situation. The two populations are shown to be normally distributed, but, because we will be using large samples (generally, $n_1 > 30$ and $n_2 > 30$) from these populations, this is *not* a necessary assumption. For these populations,

$$\mu_1 = \text{mean of population 1}$$

$$\mu_2 = \text{mean of population 2}$$

$$\sigma_1 = \text{standard deviation of population 1}$$

$$\sigma_2 = \text{standard deviation of population 2}$$

For example, if we wished to compare U.S. adult male and female heights:

$$\mu_1 = \text{average of all female heights}$$

$$\mu_2 = \text{average of all male heights}$$

$$\sigma_1 = \text{standard deviation of all female heights}$$

$$\sigma_2 = \text{standard deviation of all male heights}$$

The point estimates discussed in earlier chapters apply here as well—we simply have two of everything because we are dealing with two populations.

The procedure we follow is to obtain a random sample of size n_1 from population 1 and then obtain another sample of size n_2, completely independent of the first sample, from population 2. So, $\overline{X}_1$ is our best (point) estimate of μ_1. Likewise, $\overline{X}_2$ estimates μ_2. The sample standard deviations (s_1 and s_2) provide the best estimates of the population standard deviations (σ_1 and σ_2).

CONSTRUCTING A CONFIDENCE INTERVAL FOR $\mu_1 - \mu_2$

Ace Delivery Service operates a fleet of delivery vans in the Houston area. They prefer to have all their drivers charge their gasoline using the same brand of credit card. Presently, they all use a Texgas credit card. Ace management has decided that perhaps Quik-Chek, a chain of convenience stores that also sells gasoline but does not accept credit cards, is worth investigating. A random sample of gas prices at 35 Texgas stations and 40 Quik-Chek stores

FIGURE 9.1

Example of two populations.
Does $\mu_1 = \mu_2$?

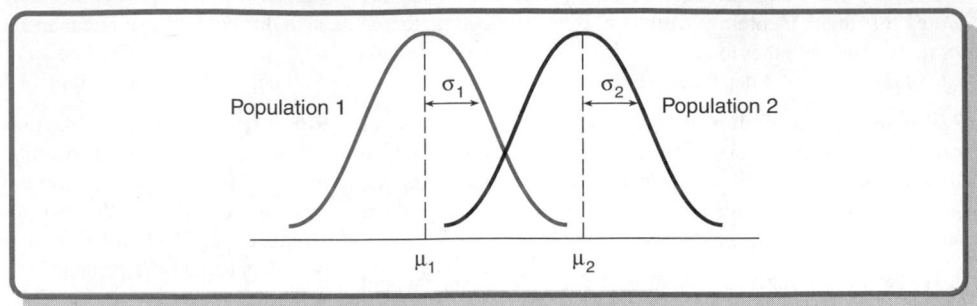

in the Houston area is obtained. The cost of 1 gallon of regular gasoline is recorded; the data are summarized:

Sample 1 (Texgas)	Sample 2 (Quik-Chek)
$n_1 = 35$	$n_2 = 40$
$\bar{x}_1 = \$1.48$	$\bar{x}_2 = \$1.39$
$s_1 = \$.12$	$s_2 = \$.10$

Let μ_1 be the average price of regular gasoline at *all* Texgas stations in the Houston area, and let μ_2 be the average price of regular gasoline at all Quik-Chek stores in the Houston area.

When dealing with these two populations, the parameter of interest is $\mu_1 - \mu_2$, rather than the individual values of μ_1 and μ_2. Here, $\mu_1 - \mu_2$ represents the difference between the average gasoline prices at the Texgas stations and Quik-Chek stores. If we conclude that $\mu_1 - \mu_2 > 0$, then $\mu_1 > \mu_2$. In this case, the gasoline *is* more expensive at the Texgas stations.

The point estimator of $\mu_1 - \mu_2$ is the obvious one: $\bar{X}_1 - \bar{X}_2$. For our data, the (point) estimate of $\mu_1 - \mu_2$ is $\bar{x}_1 - \bar{x}_2 = 1.48 - 1.39 = .09$. How much more expensive is the gasoline from all of the Texgas stations, on the average? We do not know because this is $\mu_1 - \mu_2$, but we *do* have an estimate of this value—namely, 9¢.

What kind of random variable is $\bar{X}_1 - \bar{X}_2$? First, because the samples are moderately large, we know by using the Central Limit Theorem that $\bar{X}_1$ is approximately a normal random variable with mean μ_1 and variance σ_1^2/n_1 and that $\bar{X}_2$ is approximately a normal random variable with mean μ_2 and variance σ_2^2/n_2. Because these are two independent samples, it follows that $\bar{X}_1 - \bar{X}_2$ is also approximately a normal random variable with mean $\mu_1 - \mu_2$ and variance $(\sigma_1^2/n_1) + (\sigma_2^2/n_2)$. Note that the variance of $\bar{X}_1 - \bar{X}_2$ is obtained by *adding* the variances for $\bar{X}_1$ and $\bar{X}_2$.

By standardizing this normal distribution, we obtain an approximate standard normal random variable defined by

$$Z = \frac{(\bar{X}_1 - \bar{X}_2) - (\mu_1 - \mu_2)}{\sqrt{\dfrac{\sigma_1^2}{n_1} + \dfrac{\sigma_2^2}{n_2}}} \tag{9.1}$$

We do not need normal populations. The results of equation 9.1 are approximately valid *regardless* of the shape of the two populations, provided both samples are large (from the Central Limit Theorem). We pointed out that the two populations illustrated in Figure 9.1 need not follow a normal distribution. In fact, they can have any shape, such as exponential, uniform, or possibly a discrete distribution of some sort.

We can now derive a confidence interval for $\mu_1 - \mu_2$. From Table A.4, we know that for the standard normal random variable Z,

$$P(-1.96 < Z < 1.96) = .95$$

Using equation 9.1 (and rearranging the inequalities), we can make the following statement about a random interval prior to obtaining the sample data:

$$P\left[(\overline{X}_1 - \overline{X}_2) - 1.96\sqrt{\frac{\sigma_1^2}{n_1} + \frac{\sigma_2^2}{n_2}} < \mu_1 - \mu_2 < (\overline{X}_1 - \overline{X}_2) + 1.96\sqrt{\frac{\sigma_1^2}{n_1} + \frac{\sigma_2^2}{n_2}}\right] = .95$$

This produces the following $(1 - \alpha) \cdot 100\%$ confidence interval for $\mu_1 - \mu_2$ (large samples, where σ_1 and σ_2 are known):

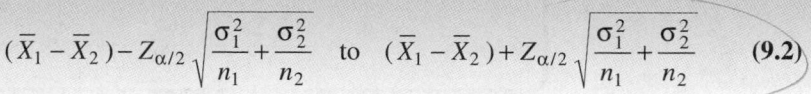

$$(\overline{X}_1 - \overline{X}_2) - Z_{\alpha/2}\sqrt{\frac{\sigma_1^2}{n_1} + \frac{\sigma_2^2}{n_2}} \quad \text{to} \quad (\overline{X}_1 - \overline{X}_2) + Z_{\alpha/2}\sqrt{\frac{\sigma_1^2}{n_1} + \frac{\sigma_2^2}{n_2}} \qquad \textbf{(9.2)}$$

If σ_1 and σ_2 are *unknown*, we have:

$$(\overline{X}_1 - \overline{X}_2) - Z_{\alpha/2}\sqrt{\frac{s_1^2}{n_1} + \frac{s_2^2}{n_2}} \quad \text{to} \quad (\overline{X}_1 - \overline{X}_2) + Z_{\alpha/2}\sqrt{\frac{s_1^2}{n_1} + \frac{s_2^2}{n_2}} \qquad \textbf{(9.3)}$$

Notice that this interval is very similar to the confidence interval for a single population mean using a large sample, namely,

$$(\text{point estimate}) \pm Z_{\alpha/2} \cdot (\text{standard deviation of the point estimator})$$

To construct the confidence interval if σ_1 and σ_2 are unknown (the usual case), you simply substitute the sample estimates in their place *provided* you have large samples ($n_1 > 30$ and $n_2 > 30$). Consequently, the confidence interval in equation 9.2 is exact (σ_1, σ_2 known) and the confidence interval in equation 9.3 is approximate (σ_1, σ_2 unknown).

EXAMPLE 9.1

Using the data from the two gas-price samples, construct a 90% confidence interval for $\mu_1 - \mu_2$.

SOLUTION

To begin with, the estimate of μ_1 is $\overline{x}_1 = \$1.48$, and the estimate of μ_2 is $\overline{x}_2 = \$1.39$. We are constructing a 90% confidence interval, so (using Table A.4) we find that $Z_{.05} = 1.645$ (Figure 9.2). The resulting 90% confidence interval for $\mu_1 - \mu_2$ is

$$(\overline{X}_1 - \overline{X}_2) - 1.645\sqrt{\frac{s_1^2}{n_1} + \frac{s_2^2}{n_2}} \quad \text{to} \quad (\overline{X}_1 - \overline{X}_2) + 1.645\sqrt{\frac{s_1^2}{n_1} + \frac{s_2^2}{n_2}}$$

$$= (1.48 - 1.39) - 1.645\sqrt{\frac{(.12)^2}{35} + \frac{(.10)^2}{40}} \text{ to } (1.48 - 1.39) + 1.645\sqrt{\frac{(.12)^2}{35} + \frac{(.10)^2}{40}}$$

$$= .09 - (1.645)(.0257) \quad \text{to} \quad .09 + (1.645)(.0257)$$

$$= .09 - .042 \quad \text{to} \quad .09 + .042$$

$$= .048 \quad \text{to} \quad .132$$

We can summarize this result in several ways:

1. We are 90% confident that $\mu_1 - \mu_2$ lies between .048 and .132.
2. We are 90% confident that the average price of Texgas regular gasoline is between 4.8¢ and 13.2¢ higher than the regular gasoline at Quik-Chek.
3. We are 90% confident that our estimate of $\mu_1 - \mu_2$ ($\overline{X}_1 - \overline{X}_2 = .09$) is within 4.2¢ of the actual value.

FIGURE 9.2

Finding the pair of Z values containing 90% of the area under the curve. The values are −1.645 and 1.645.

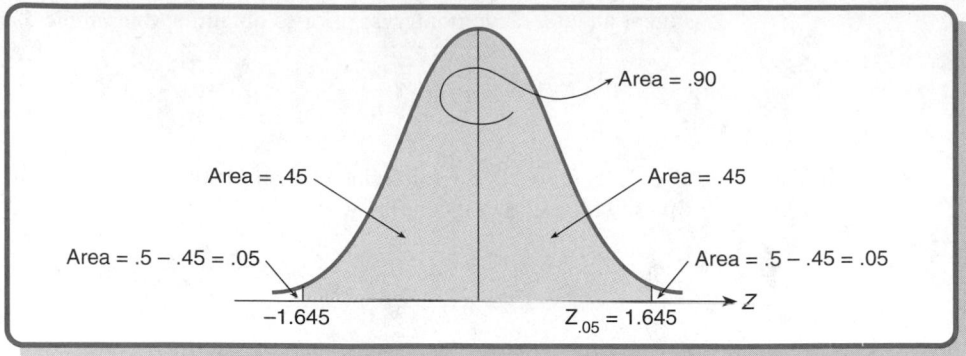

[handwritten: When we don't know σ We use s.]

The confidence intervals defined in equations 9.2 and 9.3 will contain $\mu_1 - \mu_2$ 90% of the time. In other words, if you repeatedly obtained independent samples and repeated the procedure in Example 9.1, 90% of the corresponding confidence intervals would contain the unknown value of $\mu_1 - \mu_2$, and 10% of them would not.

SAMPLE SIZES

The amount that you add to and subtract from your point estimate to obtain the confidence interval is the **maximum error, E.** For Example 9.1, this value is $E = .042$ (4.2¢). If you think that E is too large and you would like it to be smaller, one recourse is to *obtain larger samples* from your two populations. To determine how large a sample you need, one procedure is to select equal sample sizes. Consider the illustration in Example 9.1, and suppose that you want large enough sample means so that the difference in sample means is within 2¢ (rather than the 4.2¢ in Example 9.1) of the difference in population means, with 90% confidence. So $E = .02$. By insisting on equal sample sizes, where $n_1 = n_2 = n$ (say), then

$$.02 = 1.645 \sqrt{\frac{(.12)^2}{n} + \frac{(.10)^2}{n}}$$

[handwritten: use algebra solve for n₁, n₂]

After some algebraic manipulation, we have

$$n = \frac{(1.645)^2 \, [(.12)^2 + (.10)^2\,]}{(.02)^2} \approx 166 \qquad \text{(by rounding up)}$$

In general, this value is

$$n = \frac{Z_{\alpha/2}^2 \, (s_1^2 + s_2^2)}{E^2} \tag{9.4}$$

In this illustration, the total sample size is $n_1 + n_2 = 166 + 166 = 332$. A better way to proceed here is to find the values of n_1 and n_2 that **minimize the total sample size.** The values of n_1 and n_2 that accomplish this are

$$n_1 = \frac{Z_{\alpha/2}^2 s_1 \, (s_1 + s_2)}{E^2} \tag{9.5}$$

$$n_2 = \frac{Z_{\alpha/2}^2 s_2 \, (s_1 + s_2)}{E^2} \tag{9.6}$$

FIGURE 9.3

Hypothesis testing for two populations. Sample 1: size, n_1, mean, $\overline{X}_1$, and standard deviation, s_1. Sample 2: size, n_2, mean, $\overline{X}_2$, and standard deviation, s_2. Is $\mu_1 < \mu_2$?

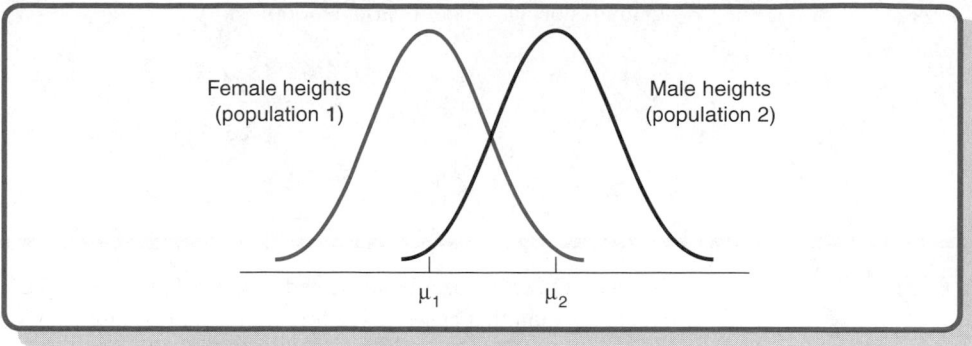

For this illustration, $Z_{\alpha/2} = Z_{.05} = 1.645$, $s_1 = .12$, $s_2 = .10$, and $E = .02$. Consequently,

$$n_1 = \frac{(1.645)^2\,(.12)(.22)}{(.02)^2} \approx 179$$

$$n_2 = \frac{(1.645)^2\,(.10)(.22)}{(.02)^2} \approx 149$$

and the total sample size is $179 + 149 = 328$.

A derivation of this result is contained in Appendix B. Keep in mind that when you use these values of n_1 and n_2, the resulting value of E may not be exactly what you previously specified—because the values of s_1 and s_2 in the new samples will change. If no prior estimates of σ_1 and σ_2 are available, each can be roughly estimated using the high/low procedure discussed in Section 7.5.

Using equations 9.5 and 9.6, observe that if $s_1 = s_2$, your total sample size ($n_1 + n_2$) will be the smallest when $n_1 = n_2$. If $s_1 > s_2$, you will select $n_1 > n_2$, and if $s_1 < s_2$, you will select $n_1 < n_2$. Finally, note that the ratio of the sample sizes (n_1/n_2) is the same as the ratio of the estimated standard deviations (s_1/s_2).

HYPOTHESIS TESTING FOR μ_1 AND μ_2 (LARGE SAMPLES)

Are men on the average taller than women? How do you answer such a question? We know that we can start by getting a sample of male heights and independently obtaining a sample of female heights. Figure 9.3 illustrates the two corresponding populations.

We proceed as before and put the claim that we are trying to demonstrate into the *alternative* hypothesis. The resulting hypotheses are

$H_0: \mu_1 \geq \mu_2$ (men are not taller, on the average)

$H_a: \mu_1 < \mu_2$ (men are taller, on the average)

We have estimators of μ_1 and μ_2, namely, $\overline{X}_1$ and $\overline{X}_2$. A sensible thing to do would be to reject H_0 if $\overline{X}_1$ is "significantly smaller" than $\overline{X}_2$. In this case, the obvious conclusion is that μ_1 (the average of all female heights in your population) is smaller than μ_2 (for male heights).

To define "significantly larger," we need to know what chance we are willing to take of rejecting H_0 when in fact it is true. This chance is α (the significance level) and, as before, it is determined prior to seeing any data. Typical values range from .01 to .1, with $\alpha = .05$ generally providing a good trade-off between Type I and Type II errors. The test statistic here is the same as the one used to derive a confidence interval for $\mu_1 - \mu_2$. We are dealing with large samples ($n_1 > 30$ and $n_2 > 30$), so the test statistic is approximately a standard normal random variable, defined by

$$Z = \frac{\overline{X}_1 - \overline{X}_2}{\sqrt{\dfrac{\sigma_1^2}{n_1} + \dfrac{\sigma_2^2}{n_2}}} \qquad\qquad (9.7)$$

EXAMPLE 9.2

The Ace Delivery people suspected that the gasoline at the Quik-Chek stores was less expensive than that at Texgas before they obtained any data. (*Note:* This is important! Do not let the data dictate your hypotheses for you. If you do, you introduce a serious bias into your testing procedure, and the "true" significance level may no longer be the predetermined α.) Here, μ_1 represents the average price at all of the Texgas stations and μ_2 is the average price at the Quik-Chek stores in the area. Is $\mu_2 < \mu_1$? Or, put another way, is $\mu_1 > \mu_2$? Use a significance level of .05.

SOLUTION

Step 1. *Define the hypotheses.* The question is whether the data support the claim that $\mu_1 > \mu_2$, so we put this statement in the alternative hypothesis.

$$H_0: \mu_1 \le \mu_2 \qquad \text{(Texgas is less expensive or the same.)}$$

$$H_a: \mu_1 > \mu_2 \qquad \text{(Quik-Chek is less expensive.)}$$

As in Chapter 8, the equals sign goes into H_0 for a one-tailed test. In other words, the case where $\mu_1 = \mu_2$ is contained in the null hypothesis.

Step 2. *Define the test statistic.* This is the statistic that you evaluate using the sample data. Its value will either support the alternative hypothesis or it will not. The test statistic for this situation is given by equation 9.7:

$$Z = \frac{\overline{X}_1 - \overline{X}_2}{\sqrt{\dfrac{\sigma_1^2}{n_1} + \dfrac{\sigma_2^2}{n_2}}}$$

Step 3. *Define the rejection region.* In Figure 9.4, where should the null hypothesis H_0 be rejected? We simply ask, what happens to Z when H_a is true? In this case ($\mu_1 > \mu_2$), we *should* see $\overline{X}_1 > \overline{X}_2$. In other words, Z will be positive. So we reject H_0 if Z is "too large," that is,

$$\text{reject } H_0 \text{ if } Z > k \quad \text{for some } k > 0$$

Using $\alpha = .05$, we use Table A.4 to find the corresponding value of Z (that is, k). In Figure 9.4, $k = 1.645$. This is the same value and rejection region we obtained in Chapter 8 when using Z for a one-tailed test in the right tail. The test is

$$\text{reject } H_0 \text{ if } Z > 1.645$$

FIGURE 9.4

Z curve showing rejection region for Example 9.2.

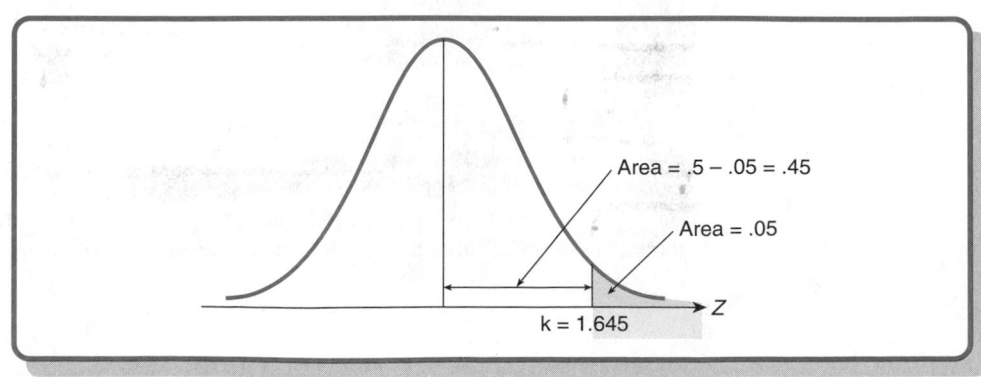

Area = .5 − .05 = .45

Area = .05

$k = 1.645$

Step 4. *Evaluate the test statistic and carry out the test.* The data collected showed $n_1 = 35$, $\bar{x}_1 = 1.48$, $s_1 = .12$ (from the Texgas sample) and $n_2 = 40$, $\bar{x}_2 = 1.39$, $s_2 = .10$ (from the Quik-Chek sample). Based on these sample results, can we conclude that $\bar{x}_1 = 1.48$ is *significantly larger* than $\bar{x}_2 = 1.39$? If we can, the decision will be to reject H_0. The following value of the test statistic will answer our question.

$$Z = \frac{\overline{X}_1 - \overline{X}_2}{\sqrt{\dfrac{\sigma_1^2}{n_1} + \dfrac{\sigma_2^2}{n_2}}} \approx \frac{\overline{X}_1 - \overline{X}_2}{\sqrt{\dfrac{s_1^2}{n_1} + \dfrac{s_2^2}{n_2}}} = \frac{1.48 - 1.39}{\sqrt{\dfrac{(.12)^2}{35} + \dfrac{(.10)^2}{40}}}$$

$$= \frac{.09}{.0257} = 3.50 = Z*$$

Because $3.50 > 1.645$, we reject H_0; $\bar{x}_1$ *is* significantly larger than $\bar{x}_2$. Therefore, we claim that $\mu_1 > \mu_2$.

Step 5. *State a conclusion.* We conclude that the Quik-Chek stores *do* charge less for gasoline (on the average) than do the Texgas stations. If the locations of these stores are equally convenient to Ace Delivery Service, buying gas from Quik-Chek appcars to be a money-saving alternative.

COMMENT

In Step 4, we replaced the unknown population variances (σ_1^2 and σ_2^2) with their sample estimates (s_1^2 and s_2^2). This is appropriate whenever the sample sizes are large, generally, $n_1 > 30$ and $n_2 > 30$.

Using the corresponding *p*-value for the data in Example 9.2, what would you conclude using the classical approach (with $\alpha = .05$)? For this example, the *p*-value will be the area under the Z curve (Z is our test statistic) to the right (we reject H_0 in the right tail for this example) of the calculated test statistic, $Z* = 3.50$. In general,

$$p = p\text{-value} = \begin{cases} \text{area to the right of } Z* \text{ for } H_a\text{: } \mu_1 > \mu_2 \\ \text{area to the left of } Z* \text{ for } H_a\text{: } \mu_1 < \mu_2 \\ 2 \cdot (\text{tail area of } Z*) \text{ for } H_a\text{: } \mu_1 \neq \mu_2 \end{cases} \qquad \textbf{(9.8)}$$

These three alternative hypotheses are your choices for this situation. Once again, H_0: $\mu_1 = \mu_2$ versus H_a: $\mu_1 \neq \mu_2$ is a two-tailed test, and the first two alternative hypotheses represent one-tailed tests.

Returning to our example, we can see from Figure 9.5 that the resulting *p*-value is $p = .0002$ (very small). Using the classical approach, because p is smaller than the significance level of .05, we reject H_0—the same conclusion as before. In fact, this procedure *always* leads to the same conclusion as the five step-solution, as we saw in Chapter 8.

FIGURE 9.5

Z curve showing *p*-value for $Z* = 3.50$.

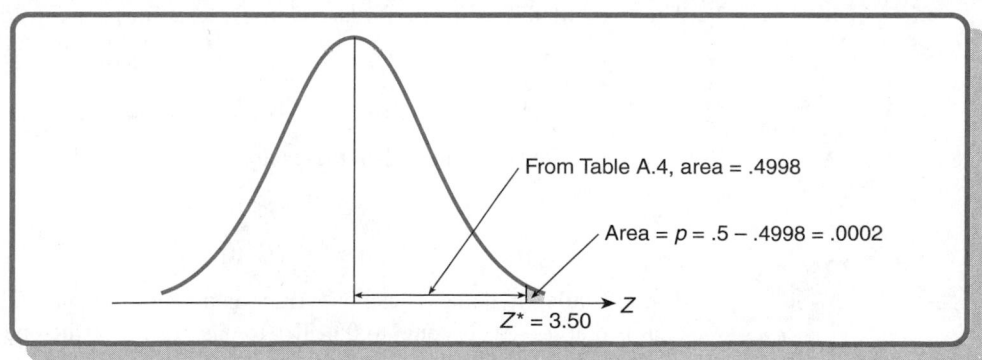

From Table A.4, area = .4998

Area = $p = .5 - .4998 = .0002$

$Z* = 3.50$

If we elect not to select a significance level α and instead use only the *p*-value to make a decision, we proceed as before:

Reject H_0 if *p* is small ($p < .01$).

Fail to reject H_0 if *p* is large ($p > .1$).

Data are inconclusive if *p* is neither small nor large ($.01 \le p \le .1$).

For this example, $p = .0002$ is clearly small, and so we again reject H_0. The Quik-Chek gasoline definitely appears to be less expensive than the Texgas gasoline. As was pointed out in the previous chapter, you often encounter a result that is *statistically* significant but not significant in a *practical sense*. To illustrate, suppose that the *p*-value of .0002 was the result of two very large samples and that the difference in gasoline price for the two samples was $\bar{x}_1 - \bar{x}_2 = .008$. You might not view this difference (less than 1¢) as being worth the inconvenience of having to pay cash for all gasoline purchases.

COMMENTS

There may well be situations where the severity of the Type I error requires a significance level smaller than .01 on the low end, or the impact of a Type II error dictates a significance level larger than .1 on the upper end. This rule is thus only a general yardstick that applies to most, but certainly not all, business applications.

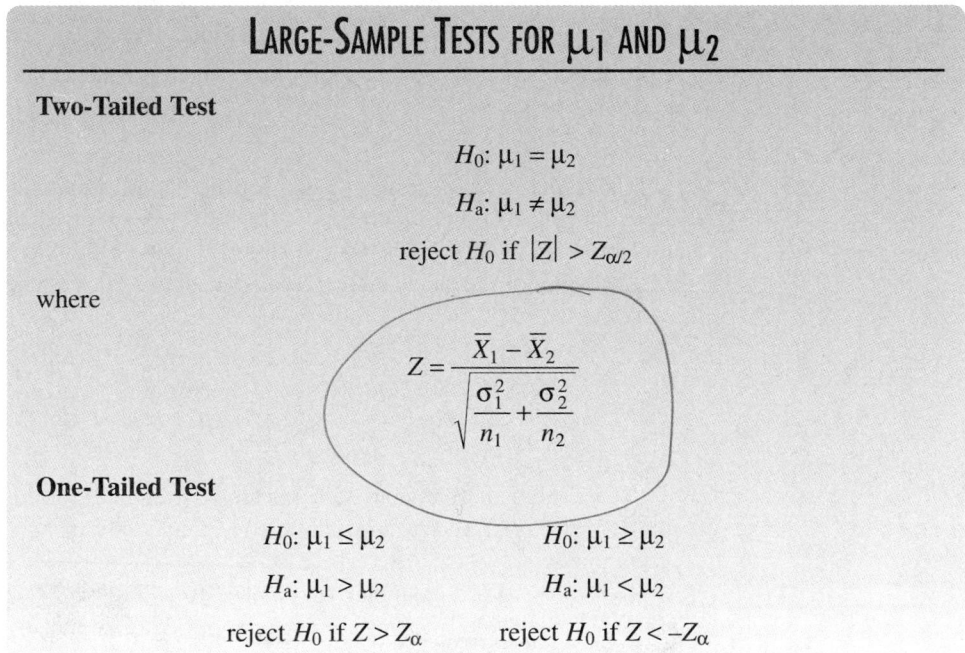

LARGE-SAMPLE TESTS FOR μ_1 AND μ_2

Two-Tailed Test

$$H_0: \mu_1 = \mu_2$$

$$H_a: \mu_1 \ne \mu_2$$

reject H_0 if $|Z| > Z_{\alpha/2}$

where

$$Z = \frac{\bar{X}_1 - \bar{X}_2}{\sqrt{\dfrac{\sigma_1^2}{n_1} + \dfrac{\sigma_2^2}{n_2}}}$$

One-Tailed Test

$H_0: \mu_1 \le \mu_2$	$H_0: \mu_1 \ge \mu_2$
$H_a: \mu_1 > \mu_2$	$H_a: \mu_1 < \mu_2$
reject H_0 if $Z > Z_{\alpha}$	reject H_0 if $Z < -Z_{\alpha}$

TWO-SAMPLE PROCEDURE FOR ANY SPECIFIED VALUE OF $\mu_1 - \mu_2$

The two-tailed hypotheses for large sample tests for μ_1 and μ_2 can be written as

$$H_0: \mu_1 - \mu_2 = 0$$

$$H_a: \mu_1 - \mu_2 \ne 0$$

The right-sided one-tailed hypotheses are

$$H_0: \mu_1 - \mu_2 \le 0$$

$$H_a: \mu_1 - \mu_2 > 0$$

The left-tailed hypotheses can be written in a similar manner. The point is that H_0 (so far) claims that $\mu_1 - \mu_2$ is equal to 0 or lies to one side of 0 (the one-tailed tests).

Suppose the claim is that $\mu_1 - \mu_2$ is more than ten. To demonstrate that this is true, we must make our alternative hypothesis H_a: $\mu_1 - \mu_2 > 10$; the corresponding null hypothesis is H_0: $\mu_1 - \mu_2 \leq 10$.

In general, to test that $\mu_1 - \mu_2 =$ (some specified value, say D_0), the five-step procedure still applies, but the test statistic is now

$$Z = \frac{(\overline{X}_1 - \overline{X}_2) - D_0}{\sqrt{\dfrac{\sigma_1^2}{n_1} + \dfrac{\sigma_2^2}{n_2}}} \qquad (9.9)$$

Equation 9.9 applies to both one-tailed and two-tailed tests. It can be used to compare two means directly (for example, H_0: $\mu_1 = \mu_2$ versus H_a: $\mu_1 \neq \mu_2$) by setting $D_0 = 0$, as in Example 9.2.

EXAMPLE 9.3

In Example 9.2, we decided that Ace Delivery Service would save money if they purchased their gasoline from Quik-Chek because that store's average gasoline price appeared to be less than that of the Texgas stations. Because Quik-Chek does not accept credit cards, the owner of Ace is willing to purchase their gasoline only if their average price is more than 6¢ per gallon less than Texgas's. Do the data indicate that it is? (α is still .05.)

SOLUTION

The question now is whether the data support the claim that the difference between the two means (Texgas and Quik-Chek) is larger than 6¢. So the hypotheses are H_0: $\mu_1 - \mu_2 \leq .06$ and H_a: $\mu_1 - \mu_2 > .06$, where μ_1 is Texgas's mean and μ_2 is Quik-Check's mean. The test statistic is

$$Z = \frac{(\overline{X}_1 - \overline{X}_2) - .06}{\sqrt{\dfrac{\sigma_1^2}{n_1} + \dfrac{\sigma_2^2}{n_2}}} \approx \frac{(\overline{X}_1 - \overline{X}_2) - .06}{\sqrt{\dfrac{s_1^2}{n_1} + \dfrac{s_2^2}{n_2}}}$$

The computed value of Z is

$$Z^* \approx \frac{(1.48 - 1.39) - .06}{\sqrt{\dfrac{(.12)^2}{35} + \dfrac{(.10)^2}{40}}} = \frac{.03}{.0257} = 1.17$$

The testing procedure is exactly as it was previously—reject H_0 if $Z^* > 1.645$. Because $1.17 < 1.645$, we fail to reject H_0. The difference between the two sample means (9¢) was *not* significantly larger than the hypothesized value of 6¢.

These data provide insufficient evidence to conclude that Quik-Chek is more than 6¢ less expensive (on the average) than Texgas. If Ace's owner thinks that not using credit cards would be too much trouble for a savings of less than 6¢ per gallon, Ace should use the Texgas gasoline.

USING EXCEL TO CARRY OUT A TWO-SAMPLE Z TEST

Excel has a built-in function to carry out the two-sample Z test. This procedure will ask for the two population variances and assumes they are known. If in fact these two variances are estimated from the two samples, then a better way to go is to use an Excel two-sample t test procedure discussed in the next section. This comment applies to any situation where the sample variances are used in the test statistic but, as we have emphasized in this section, the Z statistics in equations 9.7 and 9.9 are quite reliable, provided both sample sizes are large.

To use Excel on Example 9.3, click on **Tools ➤ Data Analysis ➤ z:Test Two-Sample for Means,** and you should see the input form in Figure 9.6. The first 17 values for the two

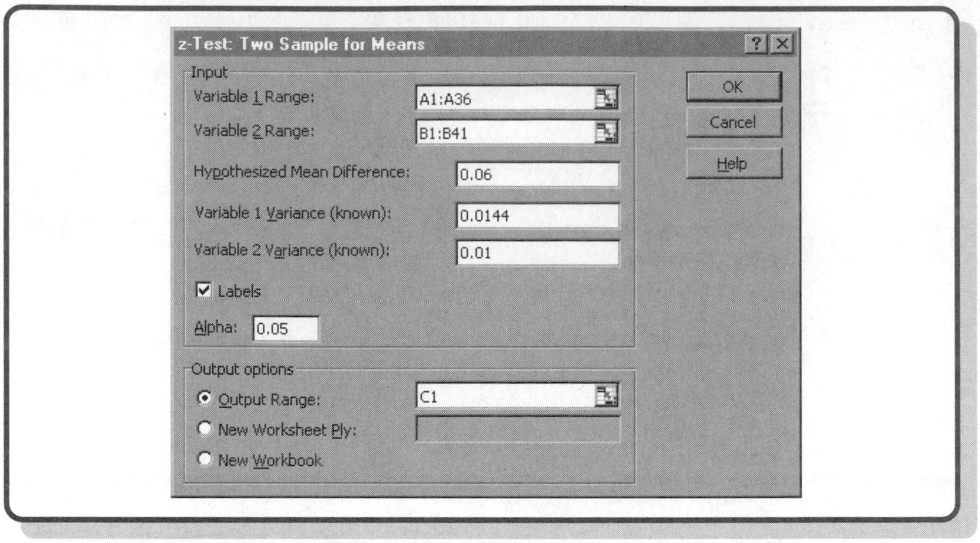

FIGURE 9.6

Input Screen for Excel's **Tools ➤ Data Analysis ➤ z Test: Two-Sample for Means.**

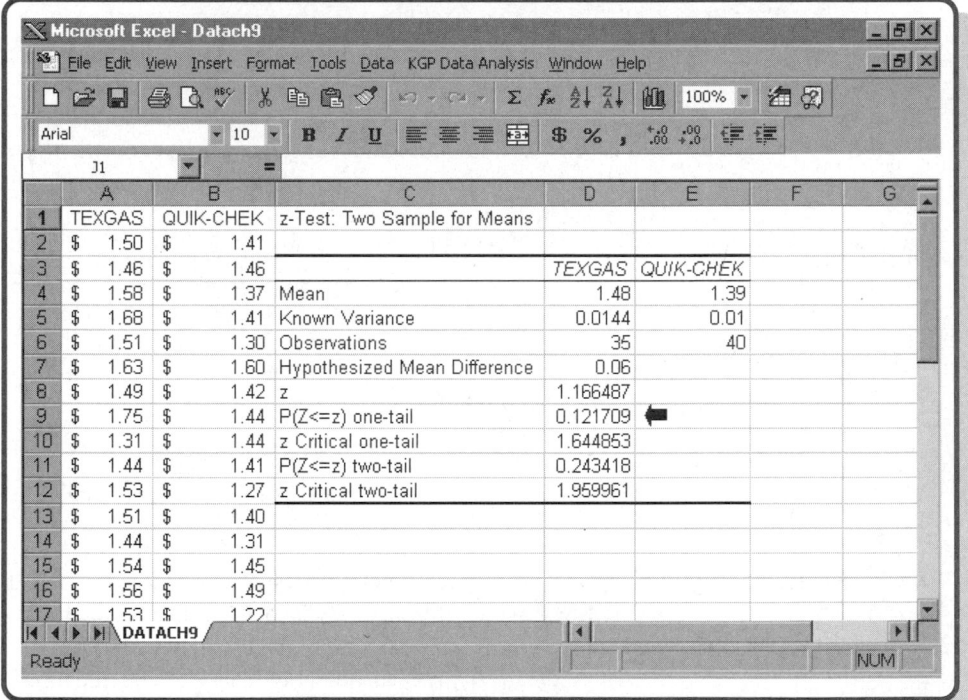

FIGURE 9.7

Excel spreadsheet using **Tools ➤ Data Analysis ➤ z Test: Two-Sample for Means.**

samples are visible in Figure 9.7, and these two columns contain the labels **TEXGAS** and **QUIK-CHEK.** Fill in the various boxes as shown in Figure 9.6 and be sure to click on the box marked **Labels.** Notice that you specify the two variances that, for now, are assumed to be known and equal to $(.12)^2 = .0144$ and $(.10)^2 = .01$. The **Hypothesized Mean Difference** value is .06. If you were using Excel on Example 9.2, this value would be zero. After clicking on "OK," you should obtain the output in cells C1:E12 in Figure 9.7.

In Figure 9.7, the calculated value of Z is 1.166487 and agrees with Example 9.3, where we obtained $Z^* = 1.17$. The arrow inserted into Figure 9.7 highlights the p-value, which is now .1217.* Since this is larger that .05, we fail to reject H_0 and arrive at the same conclusion reached in the solution to Example 9.3.

---

* In this chapter, Excel's one-tailed p-values are correct *provided* a true statement is obtained when the population means in the **alternative** hypothesis are replaced by the sample means. For this example, you would examine $\bar{x}_1 - \bar{x}_2 > .06$. Using $\bar{x}_1 = 1.48$ and $\bar{x}_2 = 1.39$, you obtain a true statement since $.09 > .06$. Consequently, the Excel p-value of .1217 is correct. If you had obtained a false statement, the correct p-value is 1 minus Excel's p-value (.8783 here).

EXERCISES 9.9–9.24

UNDERSTANDING THE MECHANICS

9.9 Random samples of sizes $n_1 = 48$ and $n_2 = 60$ from two normally distributed populations were selected, with the following results.

Population 1	Population 2
$\bar{x}_1 = 50$	$\bar{x}_2 = 56$
$s_1 = 12.6$	$s_2 = 14.2$

a. Find a 90% confidence interval for the difference in the means of the two populations $(\mu_2 - \mu_1)$.

b. Test that the mean of population 1 is less than the mean of population 2 using a 10% significance level.

9.10 Two independent random samples, each of size 80, were selected. Sample means were $\bar{X}_1 = 110$ and $\bar{X}_2 = 105$. Sample variances were $s_1^2 = 49$ and $s_2^2 = 25$.

a. Find a 99% confidence interval for the difference of the population means.

b. Test that the difference in the population means is not equal to 3. Use a .05 significance level. Find the p-value.

9.11 Find the values of n_1 and n_2 that minimize the total sample size if the maximum error of estimating the mean difference of two populations is equal to 1.2 with a 95% confidence level. The sample standard deviations from a preliminary study are $s_1 = 3$ and $s_2 = 6$.

APPLYING THE NEW CONCEPTS

9.12 First National Bank and City National Bank are competing for customers who would like to open IRAs (individual retirement accounts). Thirty-two weeks are randomly selected for First National Bank and another 32 weeks are randomly selected for City National. The total amount deposited into IRAs is noted for each week. A summary of data (deposits in thousands of dollars) from the survey is as follows. First National: $\bar{x} = 4.1$, $s = 1.2$. City National: $\bar{x} = 3.5$, $s = 0.9$. Use a 98% confidence interval to estimate the difference in the mean weekly deposits into IRAs for each bank.

9.13 Two discount stores in a popular shopping mall have their merchandise laid out differently. Both stores claim that the arrangement of goods in their store makes the customer buy more on impulse. A survey of 100 customers from each store is taken. Each customer is asked how much money he or she spent on merchandise he or she did not originally intend to buy before walking into the store. The results are as follows. Discount store 1, $\bar{x} = \$15.50$, $s = \$3.20$. Discount store 2: $\bar{x} = \$19.40$, $s = \$4.80$. Find a 90% confidence interval for the difference in the mean amount of cash spent per customer on impulse buying for the two different stores. Is layout affecting impulse buying? How do you know?

9.14 Military managers have had to learn to make the military operations more economical by using the just-in-time system. Consider the following data measuring the time (in days) to deliver tank parts to NATO bases in Europe from the factory in 1992 and in 1999. Assume that the population variances for the two time frames are known to be 28 and 14 for time periods 1992 and 1999, respectively.

1992	1999
20	13
16	15
12	14
19	18
25	12
14	13
21	16
17	17
16	19
22	13

a. Is the mean time for 1999 less than that for 1992? Use a 10% significance level.

b. What assumptions do you need for the validity of the test in part (a)?

9.15 The manager of an information systems support group would like to test the hypothesis that easy listening music increases the productivity of programmers. Samples of two separate groups of 50 programmers were randomly selected from programmers across the company. The same computer programming task was given to each group and a rating on a scale from 1 to 100 was recorded for each individual programmer. The first group was given the task with easy listening music playing, whereas the second group did the task without music. The results revealed that the easy listening music group had a mean rating of 71 with a sample variance of 30.2. The second group had a mean rating of 67 with a sample variance of 28.1. Use a significance level of 10% to test for the manager's belief.

9.16 Refer to Exercise 9.15.

a. Find a 90% confidence interval for the difference in the mean ratings of the two groups.

b. Can the information in part (a) be used to test the hypothesis in Exercise 9.15? Why or why not?

c. If the same programmers were used in each group in Exercise 9.15, would the assumptions for the validity of the test change?

9.17 Travel agencies plan vacation packages for tourists mostly in the summer. Car rental rates can make a big difference in the cost of a vacation package, with New York City averaging more than $75 a day in the summer and Orlando averaging $45. Suppose that a travel agency believes that the rates drop somewhat during the last week of August but that the difference in the rates for New York City and Orlando still stay about the same. A preliminary survey showed that the standard deviation of the daily car rental rates from either city was approximately $15. What sample size would be required for samples from both cities if a desired maximum error of estimating the mean difference in daily rental costs is to be within $5 with 90% confidence?

(Adapted from *The Wall Street Journal*, "The Dow Jones Travel Index," July 17, 1998, p. W6.)

9.18 A production manager wishes to determine if there is a difference in the number of production units produced by the night shift and the day shift. A random sample of night and day shifts is selected, and the number of production units for each shift is recorded. The following statistics resulted.

	$\bar{x}$	s	n
Day shift	27.4	6.4	60
Night shift	18.3	5.9	60

a. Find a 90% confidence interval on the difference in the mean number of production units for the two shifts.

b. Calculate a 99% confidence interval for part (a).

c. Compare the two confidence intervals in parts (a) and (b), and comment on the length of the intervals.

9.19 Eurostat, a statistical office of the European Union, reports that on average a person in Ireland bought one more movie ticket per year than a person in Britain. To confirm this report, a marketing entertainment researcher sampled 100 Irish and 150 British citizens. The researcher wished to test the belief that the difference in the average number of movie tickets purchased per year by British and Irish citizens was not equal to one. The results of the sample survey were as follows:

	$\bar{x}$	s_i	n_i
Ireland	3.4	1.5	100
Britain	2.1	1.7	150

At the .10 significance level, do the data support the researchers belief that the difference in the average number of movie tickets purchased per year by British and Irish citizens was not equal to one. Report the *p*-value and interpret it.

(Adapted from *USA Today*, "Irish Eyes Watching Movies," May 26, 1998, p. 1D.)

9.20 Mad property tax disease is starting to grip business and homeowners in many provinces in Canada as properties get evaluated using market value assessment (MVA). Tenants in commercial buildings expect to see an approximate 10% to 30% jump in rents by the end of 1998. Suppose that an economist wished to show that the average percent increase in Toronto exceeds that in Quebec by more than 3 percent. A random sample of 100 properties in Quebec and 100 properties in Toronto affected by MVA revealed the average percent increase in rent.

City	$\bar{x}$	s
Quebec	17	5
Toronto	24	10

Report the *p*-value for testing the economist's belief. Should the economist be concerned with the actual distribution of the data?

(Adapted from *Toronto Sun*, "Tax Revolt Sweeps Province Business Owners across Ontario," June 28, 1998, p. 69.)

9.21 The financial analyst of Hogan Securities believes there is no difference in the annual average returns for steel industry stocks and mineral industry stocks. Using the following information, test the hypothesis that there is no significant difference in the average returns for these two types of stocks. Steel industry stocks: $\bar{x} = 9\%$, $n = 33$, $s = 2.4\%$. Mineral industry stocks: $\bar{x} = 11\%$, $n = 41$, $s = 4\%$. Use a 10% significance level.

9.22 From an initial study of a sample of the length of time that it takes for a package to be delivered by two different express mail companies, it was found that the standard deviation of times to send a package is 1.5 days for company A and 2.3 days for company B. Let E be the maximum error of estimating the mean difference in the times with a 90% confidence interval. If E is taken to be .6, find the values of n_1 and n_2 that minimize the total sample size.

USING THE COMPUTER

9.23 **[DATA SET EX9-23]** *Variable description:*

Loss1994: Loss from reselling leased car in 1994
Loss1997: Loss from reselling leased car in 1997

Automotive leasing companies usually resell returned leased cars at a loss from their national resale value when the lease terms expired. Automobile analysts believe that the loss from reselling these returned vehicles was at least $200 more in 1997 than in 1994. Suppose that a sample of 40 lease cars resold in 1994 and a sample of 40 lease cars resold in 1997 were randomly selected and their loss was recorded in dollars.

(Adapted from *USA Today*, "Lease Losses," May 6, 1998, p. B1.)

a. Find the mean and standard deviation of both samples. Use the stacked histogram option on the KGP menu to view the two sets of data. What differences do you observe?

b. Use the Z test for testing the hypothesis that the mean loss for 1997 is at least $200 more than in 1994. Use a significance level of .10.

c. Explain how practical significance of the results may differ from the statistical significance of the results for this problem.

9.24 **[DATA SET EX9-24]** *Variable description:*

SalesCareer: Monthly sales by salespersons who say that they want to make a career out of sales
SalesNonCareer: Monthly sales by salespersons who say that they will eventually change to a profession that does not involve sales.

A sales manager believes that salespersons who wish to remain in sales as a career will sell at least $400 more than those who have decided that they will eventually change to a profession that does not involve sales. Across the company, 50 of each type of salesperson is selected, and each person's average monthly sales for the past six months is recorded in either the variables SalesCareer or SalesNonCareer. The units are in thousands of dollars. Test the sales manager's belief using a 5% significance level. What managerial conclusion can you give for this situation?

9.3 Comparing Two Normal Population Means Using Two Small, Independent Samples

When dealing with *small* samples from two populations, we need to consider the assumed distribution of the populations because the Central Limit Theorem no longer applies. This section is concerned with comparing two population means when two small, independent random samples are used. It differs from the previous section in two respects:

1. We are dealing with *small samples.**
2. We have reason to believe that the two populations of interest are *normal* populations. In Figures 9.1 and 9.3, where we had large sample sizes, this assumption was not necessary. When you use small samples from two populations, one or both of which appear to be *not* normally distributed, a nonparametric procedure is the proper method for analyzing such data. (This procedure is discussed in Chapter 19.)

In Chapter 8, we showed that when going from large samples to small samples from normal populations, the confidence interval and hypothesis-testing procedures both remained exactly the same, except that we used the *t* distribution rather than the *Z* distribution to describe the test statistic. We will use the same approach for small samples from two populations.

Confidence Interval for $\mu_1 - \mu_2$ (Small, Independent Samples)

When using large samples from two populations to compare μ_1 and μ_2, we used the approximate *Z*-statistic defined by

$$Z \approx \frac{\overline{X}_1 - \overline{X}_2}{\sqrt{\dfrac{s_1^2}{n_1} + \dfrac{s_2^2}{n_2}}}$$

When using small samples ($n_1 < 30$ or $n_2 < 30$), this statistic no longer approximates the standard normal. To make matters more complicated, it is not a *t* random variable either. However, this expression is *approximately* a *t* random variable if a somewhat complicated expression is used to derive the degrees of freedom (df). So we define

$$t' = \frac{\overline{X}_1 - \overline{X}_2}{\sqrt{\dfrac{s_1^2}{n_1} + \dfrac{s_2^2}{n_2}}} \qquad (9.10)$$

This statistic approximately follows a *t* distribution with df given by

$$\text{df for } t' = \frac{\left[\dfrac{s_1^2}{n_1} + \dfrac{s_2^2}{n_2} \right]^2}{\dfrac{\left(\dfrac{s_1^2}{n_1} \right)^2}{n_1 - 1} + \dfrac{\left(\dfrac{s_2^2}{n_2} \right)^2}{n_2 - 1}} \qquad (9.11)$$

Admittedly, equation 9.11 is a bit messy, but a good calculator or computer package makes this calculation relatively painless. To be on the conservative side, if df as calculated is not an integer (1, 2, 3, . . .), it should be rounded to the nearest integer. As a check

---

* Strictly speaking, this section applies to any situation where the population standard deviations (σ_1 and σ_2) are unknown and the sample standard deviations (s_1 and s_2) are used in the test statistic. This statement is applicable for *any* sample sizes, n_1 and n_2, but it is especially critical when dealing with small samples, where the *Z* test from Section 9.2 is no longer reliable.

of your calculations, the df should be between A and B, where A is the smaller of $(n_1 - 1)$ and $(n_2 - 1)$ and B is $(n_1 - 1) + (n_2 - 1)$.

When finding the df, you can scale *both* s_1 and s_2 any way you wish, provided you scale them both the same way. By scaling, we mean that you can use s_1 and s_2 as is, or you can move the decimal point to the right or left. The resulting df will be the same *regardless* of the scaling used. However, when you evaluate the test statistic, t', or later perform a test of hypothesis, you must return to the *original* values of s_1 and s_2.

To derive an approximate confidence interval for $\mu_1 - \mu_2$, we use the same logic as in the previous (large samples) procedure. Thus, a $(1 - \alpha) \cdot 100\%$ confidence interval for $\mu_1 - \mu_2$ (small samples) is:

$$(\overline{X}_1 - \overline{X}_2) - t_{\alpha/2,\,df} \sqrt{\frac{s_1^2}{n_1} + \frac{s_2^2}{n_2}} \quad \text{to} \quad (\overline{X}_1 - \overline{X}_2) + t_{\alpha/2,\,df} \sqrt{\frac{s_1^2}{n_1} + \frac{s_2^2}{n_2}} \quad \textbf{(9.12)}$$

where df is specified in equation 9.11. If df is not an integer, round this value to the nearest integer.

EXAMPLE 9.4

Checkers Cab Company is trying to decide which brand of tires to use for the coming year. Based on current price and prior experience, they have narrowed their choice to two brands, Beltex and Roadmaster. A recent study examined the durability of these tires by using a machine with a metallic device that wore down the tires. The time it took (in hours) for the tire to blow out was recorded.

Because the test for each tire took a great deal of time and the tire itself was ruined by the test, small samples (15 of each brand) were used. Notice that these are *independent* samples; there is no reason to match up the first Beltex tire with the first Roadmaster tire in the sample, the second Beltex with the second Roadmaster, and so on. (As discussed in Section 9.1, they would be dependent samples if the tires were tested by putting one of each brand on the rear wheels of 15 different cars.) To compensate for any machine fatigue, the order of selection for the 30 tires was determined randomly.

The blowout times (hours) were as follows:

Beltex	Roadmaster	Beltex	Roadmaster
3.82	4.16	2.84	3.65
3.11	3.92	3.26	3.82
4.21	3.94	3.74	4.55
2.64	4.22	3.04	3.82
4.16	4.15	2.56	3.85
3.91	3.62	2.58	3.62
2.44	4.11	3.15	4.88
4.52	3.45		

Construct a 90% confidence interval for $\mu_1 - \mu_2$, letting μ_1 be the average blowout time for *all* Beltex tires and μ_2 be the average blowout time for *all* Roadmaster tires.

SOLUTION

Here is a summary of the data from these two samples.

Sample 1 (Beltex)	Sample 2 (Roadmaster)
$n_1 = 15$	$n_2 = 15$
$\overline{x}_1 = 3.33$ hr	$\overline{x}_2 = 3.98$ hr
$s_1 = .68$ hr	$s_2 = .38$ hr

Your next step is to get a t-value from Table A.5. To do this, you first must calculate the correct df using equation 9.11:

$$df = \frac{\left[\dfrac{(.68)^2}{15} + \dfrac{(.38)^2}{15}\right]^2}{\dfrac{\left[\dfrac{(.68)^2}{15}\right]^2}{14} + \dfrac{\left[\dfrac{(.38)^2}{15}\right]^2}{14}}$$

$$= \frac{(.0404)^2}{.0000679 + .00000662} = 21.9$$

Rounding to the nearest integer, we use df = 22. Using Table A.5:

$$t_{.10/2,22} = t_{.05,22} = 1.717$$

The resulting 90% confidence interval for $\mu_1 - \mu_2$ is

$$(\overline{X}_1 - \overline{X}_2) - t_{.05,22}\sqrt{\frac{s_1^2}{n_1} + \frac{s_2^2}{n_2}} \text{ to } (\overline{X}_1 - \overline{X}_2) + t_{.05,22}\sqrt{\frac{s_1^2}{n_1} + \frac{s_2^2}{n_2}}$$

$$= (3.33 - 3.98) - 1.717\sqrt{\frac{(.68)^2}{15} + \frac{(.38)^2}{15}} \text{ to } (3.33 - 3.98) + 1.717\sqrt{\frac{(.68)^2}{15} + \frac{(.38)^2}{15}}$$

$$= -.65 - .35 \text{ to } -.65 + .35$$

$$= -1.00 \text{ hr to } -.30 \text{ hr}$$

So we are 90% confident that the average blowout time for the Beltex tires is between 18 minutes (.3 hours) and 1 hour *less* than the average for the Roadmaster tires. Based on these results, Roadmaster appears to be the better (longer-wearing) tire.

HYPOTHESIS TESTING FOR μ_1 AND μ_2 (SMALL, INDEPENDENT SAMPLES)

The five-step procedure for testing hypotheses concerning μ_1 and μ_2 with large samples also applies to the small-sample situation. The only difference is that Table A.5 is used (rather than Table A.4) to define the rejection region.

EXAMPLE 9.5

In Example 9.4 a confidence interval was constructed for the difference in average blowout times for Beltex and Roadmaster tires. Can we conclude that these average blowout times are in fact not the same? Use a significance level of .10.

SOLUTION

Step 1. We are testing for a difference between the two means (not that Roadmaster is longer-wearing than Beltex or vice versa). The corresponding appropriate hypotheses are $H_0: \mu_1 = \mu_2$ and $H_a: \mu_1 \neq \mu_2$.

Step 2. The test statistic is

$$t' = \frac{\overline{X}_1 - \overline{X}_2}{\sqrt{\dfrac{s_1^2}{n_1} + \dfrac{s_2^2}{n_2}}}$$

which approximately follows a t distribution with df given by equation 9.11.

Step 3. You next need the df in order to determine your rejection region. In Example 9.4 we found that df = 22. Because $H_a: \mu_1 \neq \mu_2$, we will reject H_0 if t' is too large ($\overline{X}_1$ is significantly *larger* than $\overline{X}_2$) or if t' is too small ($\overline{X}_1$ is significantly *smaller* than $\overline{X}_2$). As in previous two-tailed tests using the Z or t statistic, H_0 is rejected if the absolute value of t exceeds the value from the table corresponding to $\alpha/2$. Using Table A.5, the rejection region for this situation will be

$$\text{reject } H_0 \text{ if } |t'| > t_{\alpha/2,df} = t_{.05,22} = 1.717$$

Step 4. The value of the test statistic is

$$t'* = \frac{3.33 - 3.98}{\sqrt{\dfrac{(.68)^2}{15} + \dfrac{(.38)^2}{15}}} = \frac{-.65}{.20} = -3.25$$

Because $|t'*| = 3.25 > 1.717$, we reject H_0. Consequently, the difference between the sample means $(-.65)$ *is* significantly large (in absolute value), which leads to a rejection of the null hypothesis.

Step 5. There *is* a significant difference in the average blowout times for the two brands.

COMMENTS

The hypotheses in Example 9.5 could be written as H_0: $\mu_1 - \mu_2 = 0$ and H_a: $\mu_1 - \mu_2 \neq 0$. Having already determined a 90% confidence interval for $\mu_1 - \mu_2$, a much simpler way to perform this two-tailed test (using $\alpha = .10$) would be to reject H_0 if 0 does not lie in the confidence interval for $\mu_1 - \mu_2$ and fail to reject H_0 otherwise. The confidence interval according to Example 9.4 is $(-1.00, -.30)$, which does not contain zero, and so we reject H_0 (as before).

This alternative method of testing H_0 versus H_a holds only for a two-tailed test in which the significance level of the test, α, and the confidence level $[(1 - \alpha) \cdot 100\%]$ of the confidence interval "match up." For example, a significance level of $\alpha = .05$ would correspond to a 95% confidence interval, a value of $\alpha = .10$ would correspond to a 90% confidence interval, and so on.

Notice that the procedure in this section for testing μ_1 versus μ_2 and constructing confidence intervals for $\mu_1 - \mu_2$ made no mention as to whether the population variances (or standard deviations) were equal or not. In fact, we can say that this procedure did not assume that $\sigma_1 = \sigma_2$; it also did *not* assume that $\sigma_1 \neq \sigma_2$. Next, we will examine a special case where we have reason to believe that the standard deviations *are* equal. For this situation, we will define another t test to detect any difference between the population means.

USING EXCEL TO CARRY OUT A TWO-SAMPLE t TEST

The Excel procedure to use here is the **Two-Sample t Test Assuming Unequal Variances.** The name of this procedure will make more sense after you read the Special Case of Equal Variances discussion to follow. Actually, a better title for the Excel procedure would have been Two-Sample t Test Not Assuming Equal Variances, since using this procedure simply makes no assumptions about whether or not the population variances are the same.

Applying the Excel function to Example 9.5, click on **Tools ➤ Data Analysis ➤ Two-Sample t Test Assuming Unequal Variances** and fill in the input screen as indicated in Figure 9.8. Since we are only comparing the two population means, the value in the **Hypothesized Mean Difference** box is zero. Enter a value of .10 in the **Alpha** box, and be sure to enter a check next to **Labels** since the data contain labels in the first row. The resulting output is shown in Figure 9.9, where the value of the test statistic is again -3.25 (cell D9) and the calculated p-value is .00367 (cell D12). Based on this extremely small p-value, we once again reject H_0.

SPECIAL CASE OF EQUAL VARIANCES

There are some situations in which we are willing to assume that the population variances (σ_1^2 and σ_2^2) are equal. This situation is common in many long-running production processes for which, based on past experience, you are convinced that the variation within population 1 is the same as the variation within population 2.

Another situation in which we may assume σ_1 and σ_2 are equal arises when we obtain two *additional* samples from the two populations, which we use strictly to determine if the population standard deviations are equal. If there is not sufficient evidence to indicate that $\sigma_1 \neq \sigma_2$, then there is no harm in assuming that $\sigma_1 = \sigma_2$. (A procedure for comparing the population standard deviations is discussed in upcoming Section 9.4.)

FIGURE 9.8

Excel input screen for **Tools ➤ Data Analysis ➤ t Test: Two-Sample Assuming Unequal Variances.**

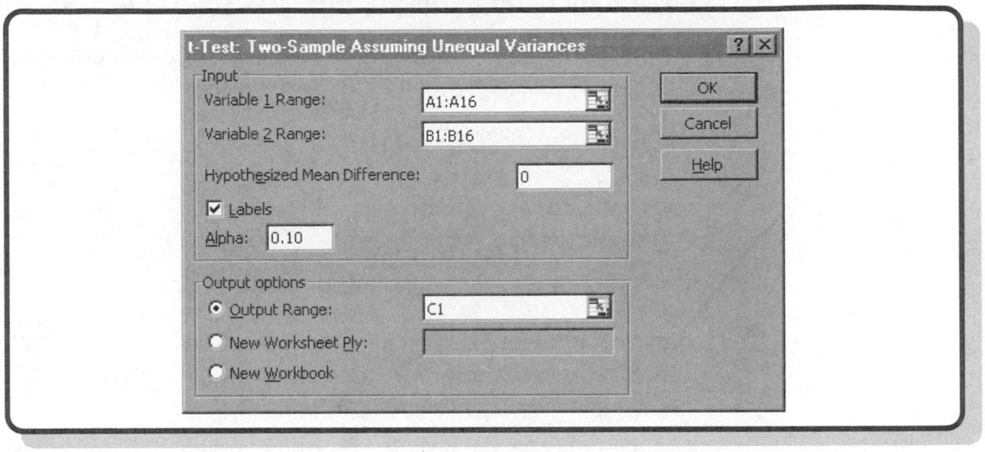

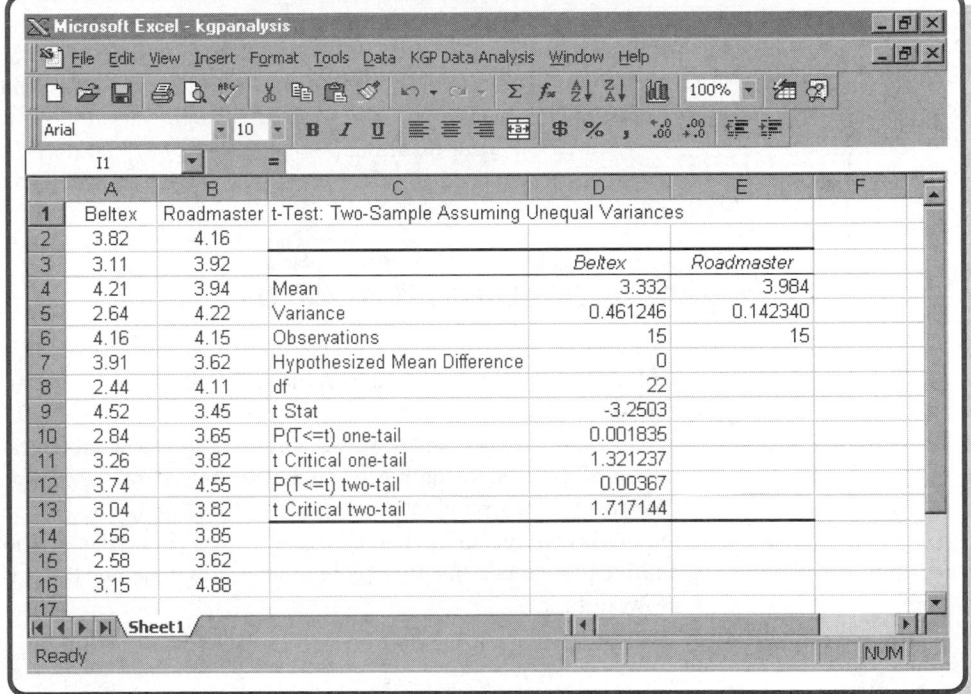

FIGURE 9.9

Excel spreadsheet using **Tools ➤ Data Analysis ➤ t Test: Two-Sample Assuming Unequal Variances.**

Why make the assumption that $\sigma_1 = \sigma_2$? Remember, we are still interested in the means, μ_1 and μ_2. As before, we would like to obtain a confidence interval for $\mu_1 - \mu_2$ and to perform a test of hypothesis. If, in fact, σ_1 is equal to σ_2, we can construct a slightly stronger test of μ_1 versus μ_2. By stronger, we mean that we are *more likely* to reject H_0 when it is actually false. This test is said to be more **powerful.**

For this case, because we believe that $\sigma_1^2 = \sigma_2^2 = \sigma^2$ (say), it makes sense to combine—or **pool**—our estimate of σ_1^2 (s_1^2) with the estimate of σ_2^2 (s_2^2) into one estimate of this common variance (σ^2). The resulting estimate of σ^2 is called the **pooled sample variance** and is written s_p^2. This estimate is merely a *weighted average* of s_1^2 and s_2^2, defined by

$$s_p^2 = \frac{(n_1 - 1)s_1^2 + (n_2 - 1)s_2^2}{n_1 + n_2 - 2} \qquad (9.13)$$

Notice that s_p^2 gives more weight to the sample variance from the larger sample. Also, if the sample sizes are the same, then s_p^2 is simply the average of s_1^2 and s_2^2.

Constructing Confidence Intervals for $\mu_1 - \mu_2$

To construct the confidence interval, we make two changes in the previous procedure. First, t' is replaced by

$$t = \frac{\overline{X}_1 - \overline{X}_2}{\sqrt{\dfrac{s_p^2}{n_1} + \dfrac{s_p^2}{n_2}}} \qquad (9.14)$$

$$= \frac{\overline{X}_1 - \overline{X}_2}{s_p \sqrt{\dfrac{1}{n_1} + \dfrac{1}{n_2}}} \qquad (9.15)$$

Here (unlike the previous test statistic), t exactly follows a t distribution (assuming the two populations follow normal distributions).

Second, the df for t are much easier to derive:

$$df = n_1 + n_2 - 2$$

So you avoid the difficult df calculation in equation 9.11, but you need to derive the pooled variance, s_p^2, using the individual sample variances, s_1^2 and s_2^2.

As a check, your resulting pooled value for s_p^2 should be between s_1^2 and s_2^2, since it is a weighted average of these two values. It may be easier to check that s_p is between s_1 and s_2.

Hypothesis Testing for μ_1 and μ_2

In hypothesis testing for $\mu_1 - \mu_2$, the previous procedure applies, except that t' is replaced by t and the df used in Table A.5 is $df = n_1 + n_2 - 2$ rather than the df value from equation 9.11.

In Examples 9.4 and 9.5, we examined the blowout times for two brands of tires as measured by a machine performing a stress test of the sampled tires. Assume we have determined from previous tests that the *variation* of the blowout times is not affected by the tire brand. Assuming that σ_1^2 (Beltex) $= \sigma_2^2$ (Roadmaster), how can we construct a 90% confidence interval for $\mu_1 - \mu_2$ and determine whether there is a difference in the mean blowout times?

Sample 1 (Beltex)	**Sample 2 (Roadmaster)**
$n_1 = 15$	$n_2 = 15$
$\overline{x}_1 = 3.33$ hr	$\overline{x}_2 = 3.98$ hr
$s_1 = .68$ hr	$s_2 = .38$ hr

Our first step is to pool the sample variances:

$$s_p^2 = \frac{(15-1)(.68)^2 + (15-1)(.38)^2}{15+15-2} = \frac{(14)(.4624) + (14)(.1444)}{28}$$

$$= \frac{8.495}{28} = .303$$

$$s_p = \sqrt{.303} = .55 \text{ hr}$$

As a check, is .55 between .38 and .68? Yes. Consequently, $s_p^2 = .303$ is our estimate of the common variance (σ^2) of the two tire populations. To find the 90% confidence interval for $\mu_1 - \mu_2$, we use

CI=

$$(\overline{X}_1 - \overline{X}_2) - t_{\alpha/2,\mathrm{df}}\sqrt{\frac{s_p^2}{n_1} + \frac{s_p^2}{n_2}} \quad \text{to} \quad (\overline{X}_1 - \overline{X}_2) + t_{\alpha/2,\mathrm{df}}\sqrt{\frac{s_p^2}{n_1} + \frac{s_p^2}{n_2}} \quad \textbf{(9.16)}$$

where df $= n_1 + n_2 - 2$ and $\alpha = .10$.

Because $n_1 + n_2 - 2 = 28$, we find (from Table A.5) that $t_{.05,28} = 1.701$. Next,

$$\sqrt{\frac{s_p^2}{n_1} + \frac{s_p^2}{n_2}} = s_p\sqrt{\frac{1}{n_1} + \frac{1}{n_2}} = .55\sqrt{\frac{1}{15} + \frac{1}{15}} = .20$$

The resulting confidence interval is

$$(3.33 - 3.98) - (1.701)(.20) \quad \text{to} \quad (3.33 - 3.98) + (1.701)(.20)$$

$$= -.65 - .34 \quad \text{to} \quad -.65 + .34$$

$$= -.99 \quad \text{to} \quad -.31$$

Comparing this result to the confidence interval in Example 9.4, you see little difference in the two confidence intervals, although the interval using the pooled variance is a bit narrower. Oftentimes these intervals can differ considerably, depending on the relative sizes of n_1 and n_2 as well as the relative values of s_1^2 and s_2^2.

Now we wish to test H_0: $\mu_1 = \mu_2$ versus H_a: $\mu_1 \neq \mu_2$. For this particular example, we can, as noted earlier, reject H_0 (using $\alpha = .10$) because zero does not lie in the previously derived confidence interval for $\mu_1 - \mu_2$. In the five-step procedure, there are only two changes we need to make when using the pooled sample variances. First, when defining our rejection region, we use $n_1 + n_2 - 2 = 28$ df. From Table A.5, the test procedure is to

$$\text{reject } H_0 \text{ if } |t| > t_{\alpha/2,\mathrm{df}}$$

where $t_{.05,28} = 1.701$.

Second, the form of the test statistic is now

$$t = \frac{\overline{X}_1 - \overline{X}_2}{s_p\sqrt{\dfrac{1}{n_1} + \dfrac{1}{n_2}}} \quad \textbf{(9.17)}$$

Here,

$$t = \frac{3.33 - 3.98}{.55\sqrt{\dfrac{1}{15} + \dfrac{1}{15}}} = \frac{-.65}{.20} = -3.25$$

Because $|-3.25| = 3.25 > 1.701$, we reject H_0; once again the two sample means are significantly different. We conclude that there is a difference in the population mean blowout times for the two brands of tires.

USING EXCEL TO CARRY OUT A TWO-SAMPLE t TEST ASSUMING EQUAL VARIANCES

An Excel solution for the preceding example can be carried out by clicking on **Tools ➤ Data Analysis ➤ t Test: Two-Sample Assuming Equal Variances.** The input screen for this procedure is identical to that shown in Figure 9.8 (except for the title) and so fill in the same values as in this figure. The output is shown in Figure 9.10 where (1) the calculated t value is -3.25, (2) the corresponding two-tailed p-value is $.002997$, and (3) the pooled standard deviation is the square root of the pooled variance—that is, $\sqrt{.301793} = .55$. As in Example 9.5 (Figure 9.9), we obtain a very small p-value when pooling the sample variances. For this particular example, we observe little difference in the two solutions.

FIGURE 9.10

Excel output using **Tools ➤ Data Analysis ➤ t Test: Two Sample Assuming Equal Variances.**

t-Test: Two-Sample Assuming Equal Variances		
	Beltex	*Roadmaster*
Mean	3.332	3.984
Variance	0.461246	0.142340
Observations	15	15
Pooled Variance	0.301793	
Hypothesized Mean Difference	0	
df	28	
t Stat	-3.2503	
P(T<=t) one-tail	0.001499	
t Critical one-tail	1.312526	
P(T<=t) two-tail	0.002997	
t Critical two-tail	1.70113	

FIGURE 9.11

Frequency polygons of the two samples obtained before and after the process adjustment.

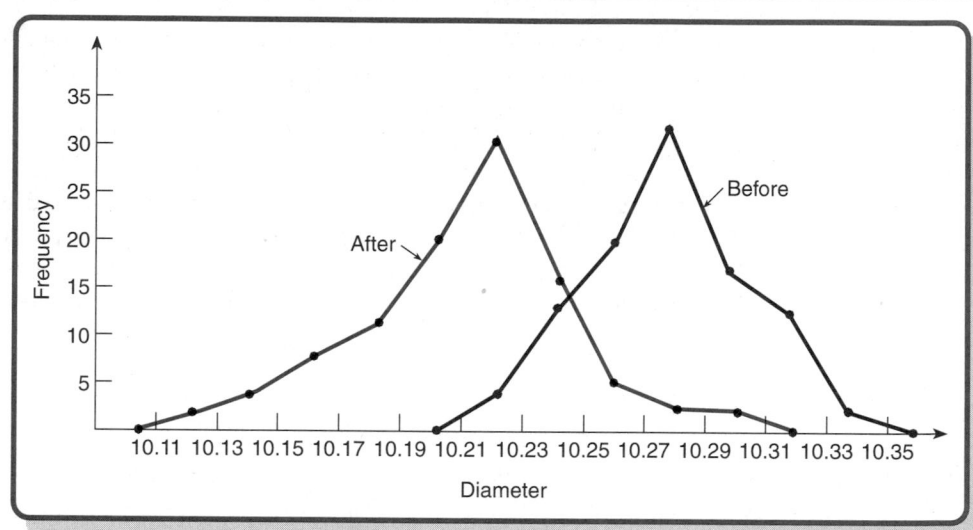

MICROSOFT® EXCEL APPLICATION   USE DATA9-6

EXAMPLE 9.6

Using Excel to Compare Two Population Means

In Examples 3.4 and 8.7, we examined the inside diameters of a certain machined part produced by Allied Manufacturing. Data set DATA9-6 contains the samples from Example 3.4 (100 measurements obtained *before* a quality-improvement effort) and Example 8.7 (100 measurements *after* this effort).

Column A contains the 100 measurements from Example 8.7.

Column B contains the 100 measurements from Example 3.4.

Prior to obtaining the second set of data, Allied wanted to know if there was sufficient evidence using a significance level of .05 to say that the mean of the process after the adjustment (data in column A) is less than the mean before the adjustment (data in column B).

What would you tell Allied? Did their adjustment to improve the quality of these parts produce a process having a smaller mean? They are not willing to assume the two population variances are equal. If you *were* to pool the sample variances (and assume equal population variances), would this change your conclusion?

SOLUTION

A nice way to compare the two samples is to use the sample results to construct a pair of frequency polygons, plotted in the same graph (Figure 9.11). From this graph, it is readily apparent that there was a shift in the means after the adjustment. Also, the polygon for the "after" sample is wider than the "before" polygon, indicating more variation in the process after the adjustment. To determine if the "after" sample mean is *sig-*

FIGURE 9.12
Excel spreadsheet for solutions to Example 9.6.

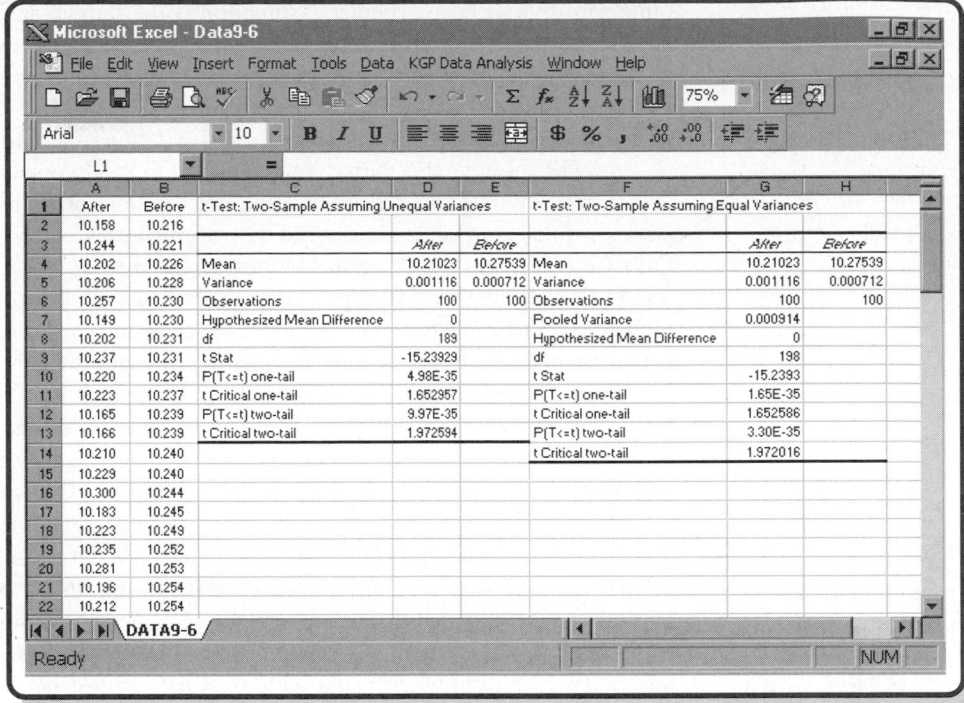

nificantly less than the "before" sample mean, the next step is to carry out the test of hypothesis.

Letting population 1 represent the process measurements *after* the adjustment and population 2 represent the measurements *before* the adjustment, the hypotheses under investigation are

$$H_0: \mu_1 \geq \mu_2$$

$$H_a: \mu_1 < \mu_2$$

An Excel solution not assuming equal variances is shown in Figure 9.12 (cells C1:E13). The calculated t statistic in cell D9 is -15.2393 and the p-value (in cell D10) is nearly zero.* The output using the equal variances procedure is contained in cells F1:G14 and is very similar to the previous solution—namely the calculated test statistic is -15.2393, and the p-value (in cell G11) is nearly zero.

CONCLUSION.   Due to the extremely large sample sizes, both test statistics could be very closely approximated by the standard normal (Z) statistic used in Section 9.2. As a result, whether or not you pool is not a critical issue for very large sample sizes. The p-value is nearly zero (and less than $\alpha = .05$), and so we reject H_0. There is strong evidence to indicate that the process mean after the quality-improvement adjustment is less than the mean before the adjustment.

TO POOL OR NOT TO POOL?   You might think, based on the previous examples, that it really does not matter whether you assume $\sigma_1 = \sigma_2$ or not. The two confidence intervals were nearly the same and the tests of hypothesis results were very close, differing only in their df for the test statistic. However, this is not always the case. *Unless you have strong evidence that the variances are the same,* we suggest you not pool the sample variances *and use the test statistic defined in equation 9.10.* If you assume that $\sigma_1 = \sigma_2$ and use the t test

---

* The value 4.98E-35 is written using **exponential notation,** which is very useful for representing very small or very large numbers. This particular value is actually 4.98, with the decimal place moved 35 places to the left—that is, a decimal point, followed by 34 zeros, followed by 498. This is a *very* small number (nearly zero). Also, be sure to refer to the footnote at the beginning of this section when interpreting Excel's one-tailed p-values.

statistic in equation 9.17 but in fact $\sigma_1 \neq \sigma_2$, your results can be unreliable. This test is quite sensitive to this particular assumption if the sample sizes (n_1 and n_2) are unequal. Also, if σ_1 and σ_2 *are* the same, we would expect s_1 and s_2 to be nearly the same. If, in addition, $n_1 = n_2$ (or nearly so), then the computed values of t' and t will be practically identical (including the df). What this means is that you have little to gain by pooling the variances (and using t) but a great deal to lose if your assumption is incorrect.

We will show you in the next section how to use two samples to test the hypothesis that $\sigma_1 = \sigma_2$. With those results in hand, one possible procedure to use when testing the *means* would be: (1) if you reject H_0: $\sigma_1 = \sigma_2$, then use t' to test H_0: $\mu_1 = \mu_2$, and (2) if you fail to reject H_0: $\sigma_1 = \sigma_2$, then use t to test H_0: $\mu_1 = \mu_2$.

At first glance this may appear to be statistically sound, but it has some problems. The main one is that these two tests use the same data, and so the tests are not performed independently of one another. Also, your actual significance level may not be the α that you had previously chosen before you saw any data. This *can* be a valid procedure if you obtain separate samples—one to test the σ values and the other to test the μ values. Again, however, caution is in order, since the test of H_0: $\sigma_1 = \sigma_2$ is very sensitive to the assumption of normal populations, and so using small samples to carry out this test can be unreliable. Consequently, if there is reason to believe that the standard deviations might not be equal, a safe procedure is to proceed as if they weren't; that is, use the t' statistic to test the means.

The next section provides a procedure for testing the standard deviations from two normal populations using independent samples. By comparing the standard deviations using separate data from the two populations, one can decide whether the pooling procedure should be used when using additional data to test μ_1 versus μ_2. If you reject H_0: $\sigma_1 = \sigma_2$, then the t'-statistic in equation 9.10 is the proper test statistic to use on a test for the means because it does *not* assume that the population standard deviations are equal. On the other hand, if you fail to reject H_0, then the t statistic in equation 9.17, which *does* assume that $\sigma_1 = \sigma_2$, is the recommended test statistic for testing μ_1 versus μ_2.

SMALL-SAMPLE TESTS FOR μ_1 AND μ_2

Two-Tailed Test

$$H_0: \mu_1 - \mu_2 = D_0$$

$$H_a: \mu_1 - \mu_2 \neq D_0$$

$$(D_0 = 0 \text{ for } H_0: \mu_1 = \mu_2)$$

$$\text{reject } H_0 \text{ if } |T| > t_{\alpha/2, df}$$

where, not assuming $\sigma_1 = \sigma_2$:

$$T = t' = \frac{(\overline{X}_1 - \overline{X}_2) - D_0}{\sqrt{\dfrac{s_1^2}{n_1} + \dfrac{s_2^2}{n_2}}}$$

$$df = \frac{\left[\dfrac{s_1^2}{n_1} + \dfrac{s_2^2}{n_2}\right]^2}{\dfrac{\left(\dfrac{s_1^2}{n_1}\right)^2}{n_1 - 1} + \dfrac{\left(\dfrac{s_2^2}{n_2}\right)^2}{n_2 - 1}}$$

Or, assuming $\sigma_1 = \sigma_2$:

$$T = t = \frac{(\overline{X}_1 - \overline{X}_2) - D_0}{s_p \sqrt{\dfrac{1}{n_1} + \dfrac{1}{n_2}}}$$

$$df = n_1 + n_2 - 2$$

where

$$s_p = \sqrt{\frac{(n_1 - 1)s_1^2 + (n_2 - 1)s_2^2}{n_1 + n_2 - 2}}$$

One-Tailed Test

$H_0: \mu_1 - \mu_2 \leq D_0$

$H_a: \mu_1 - \mu_2 > D_0$

$(D_0 = 0 \text{ for } H_0: \mu_1 \leq \mu_2)$

reject H_0 if $T > t_{\alpha, \text{df}}$

$H_0: \mu_1 - \mu_2 \geq D_0$

$H_a: \mu_1 - \mu_2 < D_0$

$(D_0 = 0 \text{ for } H_0: \mu_1 \geq \mu_2)$

reject H_0 if $T < -t_{\alpha, \text{df}}$

EXERCISES 9.25–9.36

UNDERSTANDING THE MECHANICS

9.25 Independent random samples were selected from two normal populations. The following statistics were calculated.

	Sample 1	Sample 2
	$n_1 = 12$	$n_2 = 15$
	$\bar{x}_1 = 10.0$	$\bar{x}_2 = 12.00$
	$s_1 = 2.04$	$s_2 = 1.4$

a. Calculate the pooled estimate of the variance for the populations.

b. Find a 90% confidence interval for $\mu_1 - \mu_2$ using the pooled estimate of the variance for the populations.

c. Find a 90% confidence interval for $\mu_1 - \mu_2$ not assuming that the population variances are equal.

9.26 The observations below resulted from independent random samples selected from approximate normal populations.

Sample 1	Sample 2
4.5	6.5
7.0	5.4
3.1	7.8
6.2	8.1
5.8	7.9
6.1	

a. Conduct a test of hypothesis to determine if the mean of the second population is greater than the mean of the first population. Assume that the population variances are equal. Use a .05 significance level.

b. Perform the statistical test in part (a), but don't assume that the population variances are equal.

APPLYING THE NEW CONCEPTS

9.27 The president of a personnel agency is interested in examining the annual mean salary differences between vice presidents of banks and vice presidents of savings and loan institutions. A random sample of eight of each kind of vice president was selected. Their annual salaries (in dollars) were as follows:

n	Banks	Savings and Loan Institutions	n	Banks	Savings and Loan Institutions
1	84,320	73,420	5	48,940	88,670
2	67,440	49,580	6	56,790	59,640
3	98,590	58,750	7	77,610	65,590
4	111,780	101,400	8	62,000	74,810

Conduct a test of hypothesis to determine if there is a significant difference in the average salary for the two vice president groups. The salaries for both groups are considered to be approximately normally distributed. Use a significance level of .05. Do not assume that the population variances are equal.

9.28 Construct a 90% confidence interval for the difference in the means of the salaries for vice presidents in the banking industry and for vice presidents of savings and loan institutions for Exercise 9.27. Do not assume that the population variances are equal.

9.29 Using the data in Exercise 9.27, test the same hypothesis, but assume that the population variances *are* equal.

9.30 The production supervisor of Dow Plast is conducting a test of the tensile strengths of two types of copper coils. The relevant data are as follows. Coil A: $\bar{x} = 118$, $s = 17$, $n = 9$. Coil B: $\bar{x} = 143$, $s = 24$, $n = 16$. The tensile strengths for the two types of copper coils are approximately normally distributed. Based on the p-value, do the data support the conclusion that the mean tensile strengths of the two coils are different at a significance level of 7%? Do not assume that the population variances are equal.

9.31 Construct a 99% confidence interval for $\mu_A - \mu_B$ in Exercise 9.30. Do not assume that the population variances are equal.

9.32 Using a pooled estimate of the variance, perform the test of hypothesis in Exercise 9.30. Compare the two answers.

9.33 Master-McNeil, Inc., a corporate product and naming firm in Berkeley, California, believes that technology companies that have words such as **cyber, link,** and **Web** in their name have had greater growth over the past year than technology companies that do not. To test this belief, a random sample of technology companies with and without these words in their company title are sampled and their percentage growth rates in 1998 are recorded. Is there sufficient evidence to support Master-McNeil's belief using a significance level of .10? Assume equal population variances.

Growth Rate of Technology Companies with Cyber Term in the Company Name	Growth Rate of Technology Companies without Cyber Term in the Company Name
30	15
21	20
8	12
7	40
12	27
29	13
41	6
15	17
22	7
25	24

(Adapted from *The Wall Street Journal*, "Tired of 'Wired'," July 2, 1998, p. 1.)

9.34 The gap of 23% between average pay for private workers and lower pay for the 1.8 million federal employees was, by law, to be almost wiped out by the year 2003, beginning in 1994. However, President Clinton is extending that deadline to the year 2005. Suppose that the American Federation of Government Employees believes that the mean difference in salaries for newly hired accountants in industry and in the government working in the Washington, D.C., area is greater than $5000. Use the following data from a random sample of accountants and test the belief of the American Federation of Government Employees. Do not assume that the population variances for the salaries of accountants working for the government and for industry are equal.

Salaries of Accountants Working for the Government	Salaries of Accountants Working for Industry
35,000	38,000
43,000	39,000
36,500	48,000
38,000	46,250
41,000	39,300
42,500	44,100
34,350	37,250
40,120	47,300
34,000	39,500
37,400	44,000

(Adapted from *The Wall Street Journal*, "Federal-Worker Unions Battle for Pay Matching the Private Sector," June 30, 1998, p. 1.)

USING THE COMPUTER

9.35 When assuming that population variances may not be equal, the degrees of freedom for the t' statistic decrease as one

of the population variances becomes much larger than the other. To understand this relationship, put a value of 10 in the first 15 rows of column A and the values 10 through 150 in increments of 10 in the first 15 rows of column B. Type the formulas presented below into the cells C1 through F1 and drag these down to row 15. Then plot the degrees of freedom that appear in column F with the variances that appear in column B. The graph should look like that given below. Comment on how quickly the degrees of freedom change as the variance of one group increases while the other group's variance remains constant.

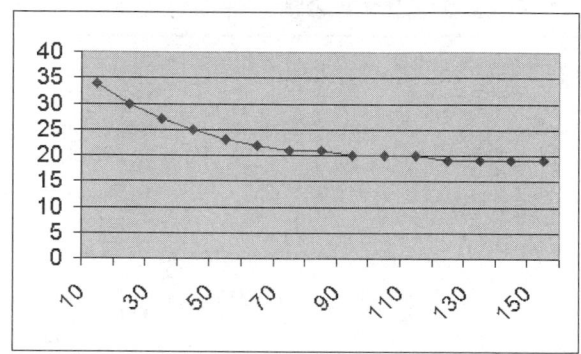

9.36 [DATA SET EX9-36] *Variable description:*

AgesMetro: Ages of patients admitted to Metro Clinic
AgesLake: Ages of patients admitted to Lakeview Clinic

MedicAid is an emergency medical clinic with two branches. The Metro Clinic Branch is in the center of town and services many lower-income individuals. The Lakeview Clinic branch operates in a higher-income suburb. The owner of MedicAid wants to examine the ages of individuals admitted to the two branches. The ages (at last birthday) are assumed to be normally distributed. Ages from 30 randomly selected patients at each site are contained in variable AgesMetro and AgesLake.

a. Using Excel, click on **KGP ➤ Quantitative Data Charts/Tables ➤ Stacked Histograms** and comment on whether the data are approximately normally distributed.

b. Assuming equal population variances, find a 90% confidence interval for the difference in the ages of patients at the two clinics (Metro–Lakeview). Interpret this confidence interval for the owner of MedicAid.

9.4 COMPARING THE VARIANCES OF TWO NORMAL POPULATIONS USING INDEPENDENT SAMPLES

Once again we concentrate on independent samples from two normal populations, only this time we focus our attention on the *variation* of these populations rather than on their averages (see Figure 9.13). When estimating and testing σ_1 versus σ_2, we will not be concerned about μ_1 and μ_2. They may be equal, or they may not—it simply does not matter for this test procedure.

In business applications, you may want to compare the variation of two different production processes or compare the risk involved with two proposed investment portfolios. As mentioned previously, when testing for population *means* using small, independent samples, you must pay attention to the population standard deviations (variances). Based on your belief that σ_1 does or does not equal σ_2, you select your corresponding test statistic for testing the means, μ_1 and μ_2. As a reminder, it is *not* a safe procedure to use the *same*

FIGURE 9.13

Compare two standard deviations. Does $\sigma_1 = \sigma_2$?

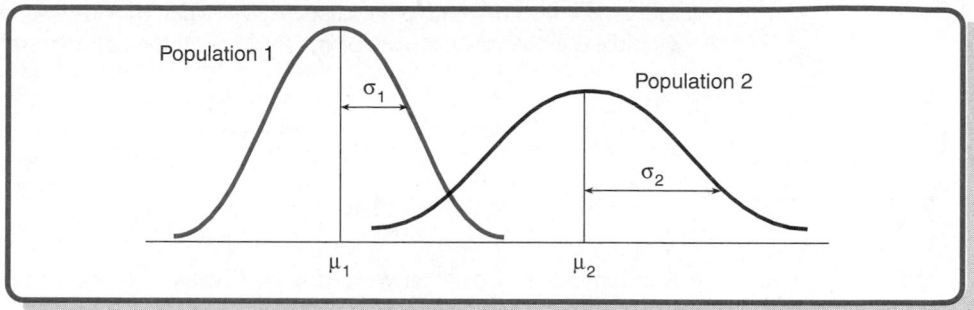

FIGURE 9.14

Shape of the F distribution.

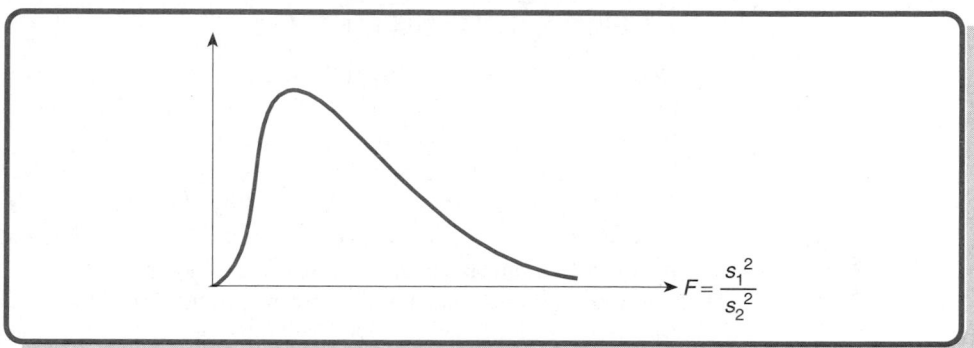

data set to test both $\sigma_1 = \sigma_2$ and $\mu_1 = \mu_2$. A proper procedure would be to test σ_1 and σ_2 using one set of samples (as outlined in this section) and to obtain another set of samples *independently* of the first to test the means.

In the previous section, when trying to decide if $\mu_1 = \mu_2$, we examined the *difference* between the point estimators, $\overline{X}_1 - \overline{X}_2$. If $\overline{X}_1 - \overline{X}_2$ was large enough (in absolute value), we rejected H_0: $\mu_1 = \mu_2$. When looking at the variances, we use the **ratio of the sample variances,** s_1^2 and s_2^2, to derive a test of hypothesis and construct confidence intervals. We do this because the distribution of $s_1^2 - s_2^2$ is difficult to describe mathematically, but s_1^2/s_2^2 does have a recognizable distribution when in fact σ_1^2 and σ_2^2 are equal. So we define

$$F = \frac{s_1^2}{s_2^2} \tag{9.18}$$

If you were to obtain sets of two samples repeatedly, calculate s_1^2/s_2^2 for each set, and make a histogram of these ratios, the shape of this histogram would resemble the curve in Figure 9.14, the **F distribution.** Its shape resembles the chi-square curve—it is nonsymmetric, skewed right (right-tailed), and the corresponding random variable is never negative. There are many F curves, depending on the sample sizes, n_1 and n_2. The shape of the F curve becomes more symmetric as the sample sizes, n_1 and n_2, increase. As later chapters will demonstrate, the F distribution has a large variety of applications in statistics. Right-tail areas for this random variable have been tabulated in Table A.7. As a final note here, *the F-statistic in equation 9.18 is highly sensitive to the assumption of normal populations. For larger data sets, it is recommended that you examine the shape of the sample data when using this particular F-statistic.*

When using the t and χ^2 statistics, we needed a way to specify the sample size(s) because the shapes of these curves change as the sample size changes. The same applies to the F distribution. There are two samples here, one from each population, and we need to specify *both* sample sizes. As before, we use the degrees of freedom (df) to accomplish this:

$$v_1 = \text{df for numerator} = n_1 - 1$$

$$v_2 = \text{df for denominator} = n_2 - 1$$

So, the F-statistic shown in Figure 9.14 follows an F distribution with v_1 and v_2 df provided $\sigma_1^2 = \sigma_2^2$ ($\sigma_1 = \sigma_2$). What happens to F when $\sigma_1 \neq \sigma_2$? Suppose that $\sigma_1 > \sigma_2$? Then we would expect s_1 (the estimate of σ_1) to be larger than s_2 (the estimate of σ_2); we should see

$$s_1^2 > s_2^2$$

or

$$F = \frac{s_1^2}{s_2^2} > 1$$

Similarly, if $\sigma_1 < \sigma_2$, then we expect an F-value < 1. We will use this reasoning to define a test of hypothesis for σ_1 versus σ_2.

HYPOTHESIS TESTING FOR $\sigma_1 = \sigma_2$

Does $\sigma_1 = \sigma_2$? We use the usual five-step procedure for testing a hypothesis concerning the two variances. Your choice of hypotheses is (as usual) a two-tailed test or a one-tailed test. For the two-tailed test the hypotheses are H_0: $\sigma_1 = \sigma_2$ ($\sigma_1^2 = \sigma_2^2$) and H_a: $\sigma_1 \neq \sigma_2$ ($\sigma_1^2 \neq \sigma_2^2$). For the one-tailed test the hypotheses are H_0: $\sigma_1 \leq \sigma_2$ and H_a: $\sigma_1 > \sigma_2$ [Figure 9.15(a)] or H_0: $\sigma_1 \geq \sigma_2$ and H_a: $\sigma_1 < \sigma_2$ [Figure 9.15(b)].

Notice that the hypotheses can be written in terms of the standard deviations (σ_1 and σ_2) or the variances (σ_1^2 and σ_2^2); if $\sigma_1 > \sigma_2$, then $\sigma_1^2 > \sigma_2^2$.

Right-tail areas under an F curve are provided in Table A.7. Notice that we have a table for areas of .1 [Table A.7(a)], .05 [Table A.7(b)], .025 [Table A.7(c)], and .01 [Table A.7(d)]. These are the most commonly used values. For each table, the df for the numerator (v_1) run across the top, and the df for the denominator (v_2) run down the left margin. A portion of Table A.7(a) is shown in Table 9.1.

Suppose we want to know which F-value has a right-tail area of .10 using 6 and 8 df. Let the F-value whose right-tail area is a, where the df are v_1 and v_2, be

$$F_{a,v_1,v_2}$$

For example, using Table 9.1, $F_{.10,6,8} = 2.67$ (Figure 9.16).

FINDING LEFT-TAIL F-VALUES. Notice that Table A.7 contains *right-tail* values only. However, we can use the following rule to determine left-tail values:

$$F \text{ value } (\mathrm{df} = v_1, v_2) \text{ having a left-tail area of } a$$

$$= \frac{1}{F \text{ value } (\mathrm{df} = v_2, v_1) \text{ having a right-tail area of } a}$$

Take a look at Figure 9.17. From Figure 9.16, we know that the F-value having a right-tail area of .10 is 2.67, where the df are 6 and 8. For this curve, what F-value has a left-tail area equal to .10? First, you switch the df to 8 and 6. Using Table 9.1 [or Table A.7(a)], find the F-value having a right-tail area = .10, where now the df are $v_1 = 8$ and $v_2 = 6$. This

FIGURE 9.15

Unequal population variances.

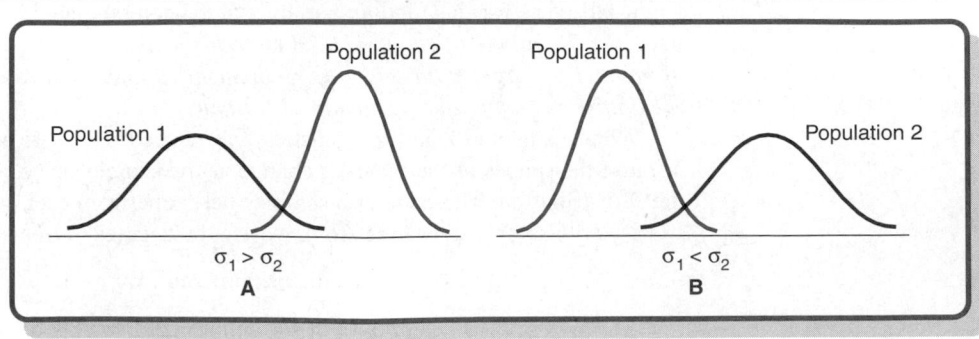

$\sigma_1 > \sigma_2$

A

$\sigma_1 < \sigma_2$

B

value is 2.98. Consequently, for the F curve with 6 and 8 df, the value having a *left*-tail area of .10 is $1/2.98 = .336$.

Since the area to the left of .336 is .10, the area to the right of this value is .90, and using the previously introduced notation we can say that

$$.336 = F_{1-.10,6,8} = F_{.9,6,8}$$

In general, we have

$$F_{1-a,v_1,v_2} = \frac{1}{F_{a,v_2,v_1}} \tag{9.19}$$

TABLE 9.1   Portion of F distribution table containing values with tail areas of .10 [Table A-7(a)].

V_2 \ V_1	1	2	3	4	5	6	7	8	9
1	39.86	49.50	53.59	55.83	57.24	58.20	58.91	59.44	59.86
2	8.53	9.00	9.16	9.24	9.29	9.33	9.35	9.37	9.38
3	5.54	5.46	5.39	5.34	5.31	5.28	5.27	5.25	5.24
4	4.54	4.32	4.19	4.11	4.05	4.01	3.98	3.95	3.94
5	4.06	3.78	3.62	3.52	3.45	3.40	3.37	3.34	3.32
6	3.78	3.46	3.29	3.18	3.11	3.05	3.01	2.98	2.96
7	3.59	3.26	3.07	2.96	2.88	2.83	2.78	2.75	2.72
→ 8	3.46	3.11	2.92	2.81	2.73	2.67	2.62	2.59	2.56
9	3.36	3.01	2.81	2.69	2.61	2.55	2.51	2.47	2.44
10	3.29	2.92	2.73	2.61	2.52	2.46	2.41	2.38	2.35

FIGURE 9.16

F curve with 6 and 8 df. Shaded area is the probability that F exceeds 2.67 [2.67 is from Table A.7(a)].

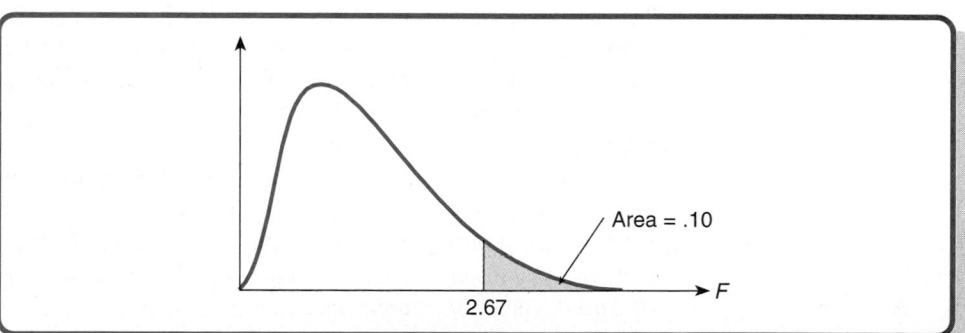

FIGURE 9.17

F curve with 6 and 8 df for probability that F is less than .336.

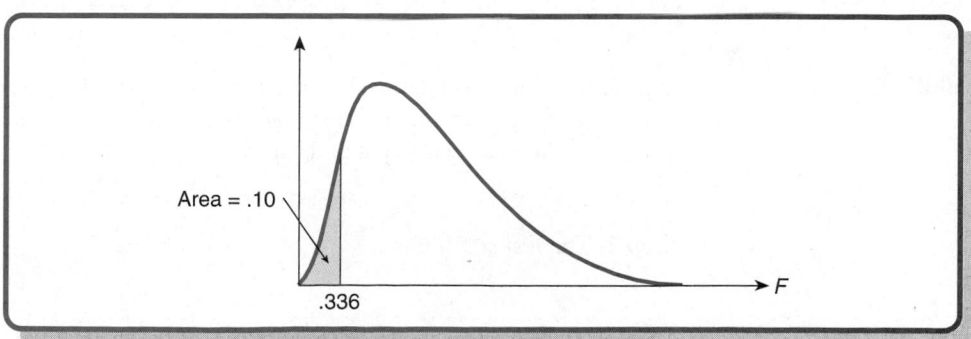

To test H_0 versus H_a, we use equation 9.18 as the test statistic. This procedure is summarized in the accompanying box.

HYPOTHESIS TESTS FOR σ_1 AND σ_2

Two-Tailed Test

$$H_0: \sigma_1 = \sigma_2$$

$$H_a: \sigma_1 \neq \sigma_2$$

$$F = \frac{s_1^2}{s_2^2}$$

Reject H_0 if $F > F_{\alpha/2, v_1, v_2}$ (right tail)

or if $F < F_{1-\alpha/2, v_1, v_2}$ (left tail)

where $v_1 = n_1 - 1$ and $v_2 = n_2 - 1$.

One-Tailed Test

$H_0: \sigma_1 \leq \sigma_2$	$H_0: \sigma_1 \geq \sigma_2$
$H_a: \sigma_1 > \sigma_2$	$H_a: \sigma_1 < \sigma_2$
$F = \dfrac{s_1^2}{s_2^2}$	$F = \dfrac{s_1^2}{s_2^2}$
Reject H_0 if $F > F_{\alpha, v_1, v_2}$	Reject H_0 if $F < F_{1-\alpha, v_1, v_2}$
where $v_1 = n_1 - 1$	where $v_1 = n_1 - 1$
and $v_2 = n_2 - 1$.	and $v_2 = n_2 - 1$.

EXAMPLE 9.7

The management of Case Automotive Products is considering the purchase of some new equipment that will fill 1-quart containers with a recently introduced radiator additive. They have narrowed their choice of brand of filling machine to brand 1 and brand 2. Although brand 1 is considerably less expensive than brand 2, they suspect that the contents delivered by the brand 1 machine will have more variation than would be obtained using brand 2. In other words, brand 1 is more apt to slightly (or severely) overfill or underfill containers. The Case people realize that they must use a container slightly larger than 1 quart in any event, to allow for heat expansion and overfill of their product.

The Case production department was able to obtain data on the performance of both brands for a sample of 25 containers using brand 1 and 20 containers using brand 2. Using their summary information, can you confirm Case's suspicions? Use $\alpha = .05$. All mean and standard deviation measurements are in fluid ounces.

Brand 1	Brand 2
$n_1 = 25$	$n_2 = 20$
$\bar{x}_1 = 31.8$	$\bar{x}_2 = 32.1$
$s_1 = 1.21$	$s_2 = .72$

SOLUTION

Step 1. The purpose of the test is to determine if one standard deviation (or variance) is *larger* than the other; this calls for a one-tailed test. The suspicion is that σ_1 is larger than σ_2, so this statement is put in the alternative hypothesis. The resulting hypotheses are

$$H_0: \sigma_1 \leq \sigma_2 \qquad H_a: \sigma_1 > \sigma_2$$

Step 2. The test statistic is

$$F = \frac{s_1^2}{s_2^2}$$

Step 3. Because the df are $v_1 = 25 - 1 = 24$ and $v_2 = 20 - 1 = 19$, we find $F_{.05,24,19} = 2.11$. The test of H_0 versus H_a will be to

$$\text{reject } H_0 \text{ if } F > 2.11$$

Step 4. The computed F-value is

$$F^* = \frac{(1.21)^2}{(.72)^2} = 2.82$$

Because $2.82 > 2.11$, we reject H_0.

Step 5. On the basis of these data and this significance level, Case is correct in its belief that the variation in the containers filled by brand 1 exceeds that of the containers filled by brand 2.

MICROSOFT® EXCEL APPLICATION   USE DATA9-6

EXAMPLE 9.8
Using Excel to Compare Two Population Variances

In Example 9.6, we compared the means of two processes—before and after a quality improvement adjustment to reduce the process mean. Allied Manufacturing would like to use these samples strictly to compare the two population variances to determine if they differ (assuming a significance level of .10). Column A in dataset DATA9-6 contains 100 sample values obtained *after* the adjustment, and column B contains 100 sample values obtained *before* the adjustment. To obtain an Excel solution, click on **Tools ➤ Data Analysis ➤ F Test: Two-Sample for Variances.** The input screen is very similar to that shown in Figure 9.8.

SOLUTION

The resulting output is contained in Figure 9.18. The one-tailed *p*-value is .013094 and is in cell D9. Since this is a two-tailed test (H_a states that the two standard deviations differ), you will need to double this value. To do this, type "*p*-value (2-tailed)" in cell C11 and "=2*D9" in cell D11. This produces the two-tailed *p*-value of .026188 in Figure 9.18.

FIGURE 9.18
Excel spreadsheet for **Tools ➤ Data Analysis ➤ F Test: Two-Sample for Variances** (*p*-value (2 tailed) added).

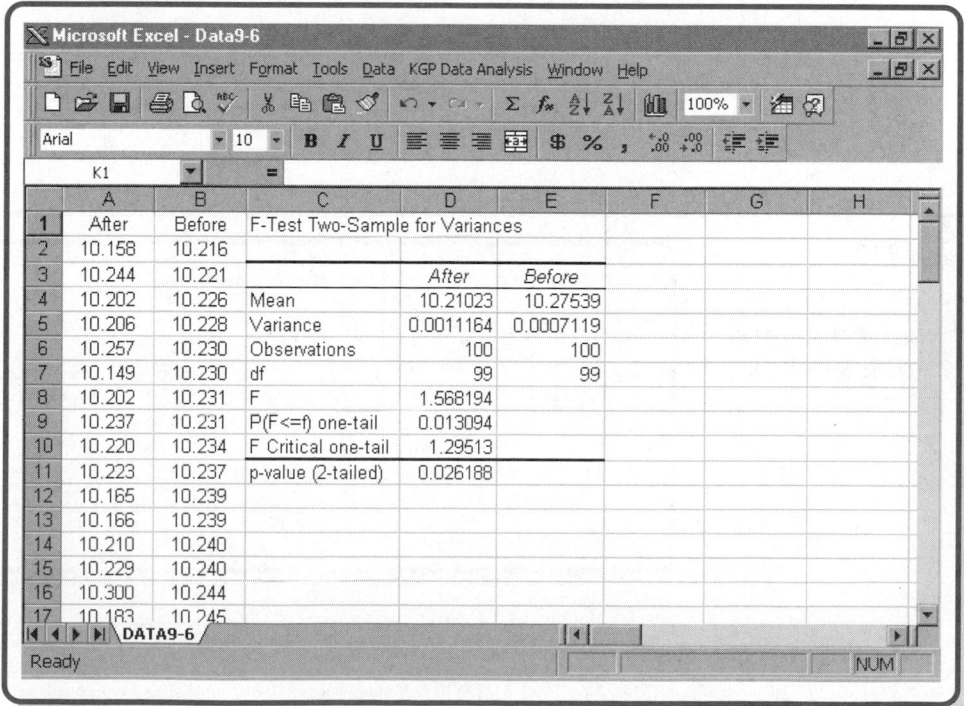

Since the p-value of .026188 is less than .10, we reject H_0 and conclude that the two population (process) variances *are* different. In fact, we see a noticeable increase in the process variation after the adjustment—a concern for the quality-improvement team at Allied.

COMMENT

If this had been the first step in our investigation of these two processes, and additional *small* samples were to be obtained to compare the two process means, the correct procedure would be to use the t' statistic described earlier, which does not assume that σ_1 and σ_2 are equal, provided both populations are believed to be normally distributed.*

CONFIDENCE INTERVAL FOR $\dfrac{\sigma_1^2}{\sigma_2^2}$

Consider an F curve with v_1 and v_2 df. To construct a 95% confidence interval for σ_1^2/σ_2^2, you proceed as you did when performing a two-tailed test of σ_1 versus σ_2, by finding both left-tailed and right-tailed F-values. Let F_L and F_R denote the left- and right-tailed F-values, respectively. Using equation 9.19 and Figure 9.19,

$$F_R = F_{.025,v_1,v_2} \quad \text{and} \quad F_L = \frac{1}{F_{.025,v_2,v_1}}$$

where $F_{.025,v_1,v_2}$ and $F_{.025,v_2,v_1}$ are obtained from Table A.7(c). *Remember:* Be sure to switch the df when finding the left-tailed value, F_L. The confidence interval for σ_1^2/σ_2^2 is then

$$\frac{s_1^2/s_2^2}{F_R} \quad \text{to} \quad \frac{s_1^2/s_2^2}{F_L}$$

In general, we have a $(1 - \alpha) \cdot 100\%$ confidence interval for σ_1^2/σ_2^2 (independent samples):

$$\frac{s_1^2/s_2^2}{F_R} \quad \text{to} \quad \frac{s_1^2/s_2^2}{F_L} \qquad \textbf{(9.20)}$$

where

$$F_R = F_{\alpha/2,v_1,v_2}$$

$$F_L = \frac{1}{F_{\alpha/2,v_2,v_1}}$$

$$v_1 = n_1 - 1$$

$$v_2 = n_2 - 1$$

FIGURE 9.19

F curve with v_1 and v_2 df showing *F* values used for a 95% confidence interval.

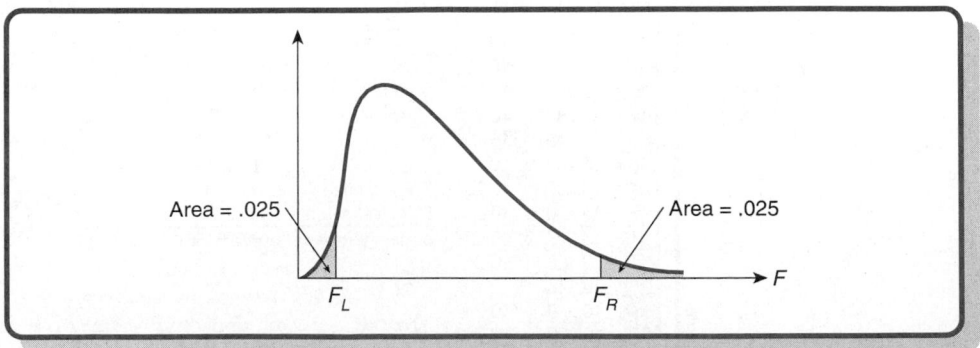

* Recently, attention has been given to whether this *F*-test is an effective "screening procedure" for determining which *t* test is appropriate for subsequent tests of the population means. (See the article by Markowski and Markowski in *The American Statistician*, Nov. 1990, p. 322.) In particular, when the two sample sizes are unequal, the *F*-test tends incorrectly to fail to reject H_0: $\sigma_1 = \sigma_2$ for situations where use of the *t* statistic in equation 9.14 (which assumes $\sigma_1 = \sigma_2$) is *not* appropriate.

EXAMPLE 9.9

Using the Case Automotive Products data in Example 9.7, determine a 95% confidence interval for σ_1^2/σ_2^2.

SOLUTION

Here, $n_1 = 25$, $s_1 = 1.21$, and $n_2 = 20$, $s_2 = .72$. So we need

$$F_R = F_{.025,24,19} = 2.45$$

$$F_L = \frac{1}{F_{.025,19,24}}$$

$$\approx \frac{1}{2.33} \quad (\text{using } F_{.025,20,24})$$

$$= .43$$

The 95% confidence interval for σ_1^2/σ_2^2 is

$$\frac{(1.21)^2 / (.72)^2}{2.45} \quad \text{to} \quad \frac{(1.21)^2 / (.72)^2}{.43} = 1.15 \quad \text{to} \quad 6.57$$

As a result, we are 95% confident that σ_1^2/σ_2^2 is between 1.15 and 6.57. This means that we are 95% confident that σ_1^2 is between 1.15 and 6.57 *times as large* as σ_2^2.

EXAMPLE 9.10

For the Case Automotive Products data in Example 9.7, determine a 95% confidence interval for σ_1/σ_2. Use the results of Example 9.9.

SOLUTION

This is obtained simply by finding the *square root* of each endpoint of the confidence interval for σ_1^2/σ_2^2. Your 95% confidence interval for σ_1/σ_2 will be

$$\sqrt{1.15} \quad \text{to} \quad \sqrt{6.57} = 1.07 \quad \text{to} \quad 2.56 \text{ (fluid ounces)}$$

EXERCISES 9.37–9.46

UNDERSTANDING THE MECHANICS

9.37 Find the rejection region for each of the following situations.
   a. H_0: $\sigma_1^2 = \sigma_2^2$ versus H_a: $\sigma_1^2 \neq \sigma_2^2$, $n_1 = 20$, $n_2 = 15$, $\alpha = 05$
   b. H_0: $\sigma_1^2 \geq \sigma_2^2$ versus H_a: $\sigma_1^2 < \sigma_2^2$, $n_1 = 5$, $n_2 = 15$, $\alpha = .10$
   c. H_0: $\sigma_1 \leq \sigma_2$ versus H_a: $\sigma_1 > \sigma_2$, $n_1 = 19$, $n_2 = 11$, $\alpha = .01$

9.38 Independent samples from a normally distributed population were selected. The following statistics were calculated.

Sample 1	Sample 2
$n_1 = 13$	$n_2 = 25$
$\bar{x}_1 = 45$	$\bar{x}_2 = 48$
$s_1^2 = 4.1$	$s_2^2 = 9.2$

   a. Do the data support the claim that the population variances are not equal? Use a .05 significance level. Find the *p*-value.
   b. Calculate a 95% confidence interval for σ_1/σ_2.

9.39 The following data were collected from normally distributed populations.

Sample 1	Sample 2
7.1	7.3
9.2	6.4
8.4	9.4
1.8	5.6
2.5	7.3
3.7	6.8
4.5	7.1
	8.0

   a. Do the data provide sufficient evidence that the standard deviation of the second population is less than the standard deviation of the first population? Use a .05 significance level.
   b. Find the *p*-value in part (a).

APPLYING THE NEW CONCEPTS

9.40 The Water Pollution Prevention Council (WPPC) had recommended that the discharge of industrial waste and effluents into rivers in the district should be done at a slow and steady rate of 100 pound/hour (i.e., 2400 pound/day). Industrial plants tended to concentrate their effluent discharge activity in the night shift. The WPPC found that although companies might technically achieve an average discharge rate of 2400 pound/day, the rivers could not cope with the erratic rate of discharge. The effluents needed to be released throughout the day, rather than all at night. It was recommended that the true variance of the discharge rate should not exceed 600. The following results were obtained from samples of 21 observations each.

Factory A: variance 585
Factory B: variance 618

At a 5% significance level, is there sufficient evidence to conclude that the variance for factory A is less than that for factory B?

9.41 A lot of investors have been reading about something called the "new-fund effect." That's the tendency of new funds to outperform their older peers because of any one of a number of factors: better access to initial public offerings, more motivated managers, or better spreads on trades. However, despite the potential growth benefits of new funds, their volatility may make it difficult for some investors. Consider a sample of 10 newly created mid-cap mutual funds and a sample of 10 newly created small-cap mutual funds randomly selected from all mutual funds that are less than 18 months old. Is there sufficient evidence to conclude that there is a significant difference in the variance of newly created mid-cap and small-cap mutual funds? Use a .10 significance level.

Annualized Performance of New Mid-Cap Funds	Annualized Performance of New Small-Cap Funds
13.7	15.3
7.9	9.8
13.6	13.5
11.4	8.6
14.6	15.2
9.5	14.9
10.8	11.5
11.3	25.2
12.0	6.3
12.7	12.4

(Adapted from *Chicago Tribune,* "Early Birds Sometimes Can Fly Higher," July 3, 1998, p. 3.)

9.42 The quality-improvement department of a company that manufactures wall clocks is studying the variability of two recently developed types of wall clocks. Using the following information, test the hypothesis that $H_0: \sigma_1 = \sigma_2$, using a significance level of .05. Assume that the samples are taken from populations that are approximately normally distributed. Clock 1: $n = 25$, $s = 1.8$. Clock 2: $n = 21$, $s = 1.39$.

9.43 Construct a 95% confidence interval for σ_1^2/σ_2^2 using the data in Exercise 9.42.

9.44 The following is a summary of the mean annual return ($\bar{X}$) and variance (s^2) of the annual return for common stocks in three different industries. Computer industry: $n = 16$, $\bar{x} = 14.3\%$, $s^2 = 5.6$. Steel industry: $n = 9$, $\bar{x} = 8.5\%$, $s^2 = 11.2$. Oil-and-gas industry: $n = 13$, $\bar{x} = 11.8\%$, $s^2 = 16.4$. Using these data, can we conclude that computer stocks are less risky than oil and gas stocks? Use a significance level of .05. Assume that the mean annual returns for these industries are approximately normally distributed.

USING THE COMPUTER

9.45 **[DATA SET EX9-45]** *Variable description:*

TraditStu: Grades in capstone MBA course for traditional students
NonTraditStu: Grades in capstone MBA course for nontraditional students

An associate dean at the University of North Texas was interested in whether the variation in scores for nontraditional students in the capstone MBA course is greater than that of the traditional student. A nontraditional student is one that has been out of school for more than 10 years. Fifty final grade scores were recorded for each of the types of students.

    a. Using a 5% significance level, can the associate dean conclude that the variation in scores is greater for nontraditional students. When using Excel's **F Test: Two-Sample for Variances** procedure, make sure that the group with the larger variance is designated as the first group.

    b. Subtract five points from each grade of the nontraditional student. Do you think that these new grades would affect the F test in part (a)? Try it.

9.46 **[DATA SET EX9-46]** *Variable description:*

FluidMach1: Amount of fluid dispensed by vending machine 1
FluidMach2: Amount of fluid dispensed by vending machine 2

The manager of a vending-machine company decided to purchase one of two types of dispensers to put in her vending machines. Both dispensers are supposed to dispense, on the average, 6 ounces of fluid into a plastic cup. The amount dispensed is approximately normally distributed. However, to test this claim, the manager would first like to know whether the variability in the amount of fluid dispensed is the same for both dispensers. Random samples of 16 cups with fluid dispensed by machine 1 and 16 cups with fluid dispensed by machine 2 are selected. The number of ounces of fluid in each cup is recorded in variables FluidMach1 and FluidMach2.

    a. Find a 95% confidence interval for the ratio of the variances of the amount of fluid coming from machines 1 and 2.

    b. Test for a difference in the variances of the amount of fluid from machines 1 and 2 at the .05 significance level.

    c. Can part (a) be used to test for a difference in the variances of the two machines? If so, how?

9.5 COMPARING THE MEANS OF TWO NORMAL POPULATIONS USING PAIRED SAMPLES

The final section of this chapter examines the situation in which the two samples are *not* obtained independently. All discussion up to this point has assumed that the two samples *are* independent. By not independent, we mean that the corresponding elements from the two samples are *paired*. Perhaps each pair of observations corresponds to the same city, the same week, the same married couple, or even the same person. Our discussion focuses on comparing the two population means for the situation in which two *dependent* samples are obtained from the two populations.

When attempting to estimate or test for the difference between two population means, your first question always should be, is there any natural reason to pair the first observation from sample 1 with the first observation from sample 2, the second with the second, and so on? If there is no reason to pair these data and the samples were obtained independently, the previous methods for finding confidence intervals and testing μ_1 versus μ_2 apply. If the data were gathered such that pairing the values is necessary, then it is *extremely* important that you recognize this and treat the data in a different manner. We can still determine confidence intervals and perform a test of hypothesis, but the procedure is different.

As an illustration, Metalloy manufactures metal hinges. The hardness of these hinges is tested by pressing a rod with a pointed tip into the hinge with a specified force and measuring the depth of the depression caused by the tip. Two tips are available for the hardness tester, and it is suspected that tip #1 produces higher hardness readings, on the average. To control for variation in the hardness of the hinges, it was decided to use paired samples in which *both* tips were used to test the hardness of the *same* metal hinge. The following coded data were obtained using 12 randomly selected hinges. The letter d represents the *difference* of each pair of hardness values (Tip #1 – Tip #2).

Hinge	1	2	3	4	5	6	7	8	9	10	11	12
Tip #1	39	32	42	49	45	47	45	48	38	48	41	47
Tip #2	35	34	38	48	47	43	41	47	35	46	37	44
d	4	–2	4	1	–2	4	4	1	3	2	4	3
d^2	16	4	16	1	4	16	16	1	9	4	16	9

$$\sum d = 4 - 2 + 4 + \cdots + 3 = 26$$
$$\sum d^2 = 16 + 4 + 16 + \cdots + 9 = 112$$

Each pair of values was obtained from the same metal hinge, so these data values clearly need to be paired—they are dependent samples. It seems reasonable to examine the difference of the two values for each hinge, so these differences (d), along with the d^2 values, are also shown. We have thus reduced the problem from two sets of values to a single set. The parameter of interest here is the **difference** of the population means, μ_d. Put another way, μ_d is the **mean of the population differences.**

Since we have a single set of sample values (the 12 differences) and a single parameter (μ_d), the results of Sections 7.4 and 8.4 can be used to construct a confidence interval and perform a test of hypothesis, *provided we have reason to believe that the population differences are normally distributed.* As a result, we need not worry about large versus small samples, because we will use the t distribution for our confidence intervals and tests of hypothesis, regardless of the sample sizes. Of course, if the number of differences is large (generally, >30), this distribution is closely approximated by the standard normal distribution.

If you have reason to suspect that the population of differences is *not* normally distributed, then one alternative is to use a nonparametric procedure, in particular, the Wilcoxon signed rank test (discussed in Chapter 19).

CONFIDENCE INTERVAL FOR μ_d USING PAIRED SAMPLES

The statistic used to derive a confidence interval for μ_d and perform a test of hypothesis using *dependent* samples is

$$t_D = \frac{\overline{X}_1 - \overline{X}_2}{s_d / \sqrt{n}} = \frac{\overline{d}}{s_d / \sqrt{n}} \qquad (9.21)$$

where

$$n = \text{the number of pairs of observations}$$

$$s_d = \text{the standard deviation of the } n \text{ differences}$$

$$s_d = \sqrt{\frac{\sum d^2 - (\sum d)^2 / n}{n-1}}$$

$$\text{df for } t_D = n - 1$$

This is a *t random variable with* $n - 1$ df. Notice that the numerator of t_D is the same as before, namely, $\overline{X}_1 - \overline{X}_2$, which is also represented by $\overline{d} = \sum d/n$, the mean of the differences. The mean of the differences $\overline{d}$ always is equal to $\overline{X}_1 - \overline{X}_2$ (this can help you in checking your arithmetic when computing the d's).

Based on the discussion in Section 7.4, we obtain a $(1 - \alpha) \cdot 100\%$ confidence interval for μ_d:

$$\overline{d} - t_{\alpha/2, n-1} \frac{s_d}{\sqrt{n}} \quad \text{to} \quad \overline{d} + t_{\alpha/2, n-1} \frac{s_d}{\sqrt{n}} \qquad (9.22)$$

EXAMPLE 9.11

Using the hardness data, derive a 95% confidence interval for μ_d, where

$$\mu_d = \text{average difference in hardness}$$

SOLUTION

We have

$$\overline{d} = \frac{\sum d}{n} = \frac{26}{12} = 2.167$$

Notice that

$$\overline{x}_1 = \frac{39 + 32 + \cdots + 47}{12} = 43.417$$

and

$$\overline{x}_2 = \frac{35 + 34 + \cdots + 44}{12} = 41.25$$

so $\overline{d} = \overline{x}_1 - \overline{x}_2 = 2.167$. It checks! Also,

$$s_d = \sqrt{\frac{\sum d^2 - (\sum d)^2 / n}{n-1}} = \sqrt{\frac{112 - (26)^2 / 12}{11}}$$

$$= \sqrt{\frac{55.667}{11}} = \sqrt{5.061} = 2.250$$

The resulting 95% confidence interval for μ_d is

$$\overline{d} - t_{.025, 11} \frac{s_d}{\sqrt{n}} \quad \text{to} \quad \overline{d} + t_{.025, 11} \frac{s_d}{\sqrt{n}}$$

$$= 2.167 - 2.201 \frac{2.250}{\sqrt{12}} \quad \text{to} \quad 2.167 + 2.201 \frac{2.250}{\sqrt{12}}$$

$$= 2.167 - 1.430 \quad \text{to} \quad 2.167 + 1.430$$

$$= .737 \quad \text{to} \quad 3.597$$

Based on these data, we are 95% confident that the hardness reading using tip #1 is between .737 and 3.597 *more* than the tip #2 reading. Notice that this is quite a wide confidence interval, due to the small sample sizes.

HYPOTHESIS TESTING USING PAIRED SAMPLES

The test statistic for testing the means is the same as that in Section 8.4, except that we use the sample differences.

$$t_D = \frac{\bar{d} - D_0}{s_d / \sqrt{n}} \tag{9.23}$$

where D_0 is the hypothesized value of μ_d. When testing H_0: $\mu_d = D_0$ versus H_a: $\mu_d \neq D_0$, reject H_0 if $|t_D| > t_{\alpha/2, n-1}$. Here, $t_{\alpha/2, n-1}$ is obtained from Table A.5 using $n-1$ df. One-tailed tests are performed in a similar manner by placing α in either the right tail (H_a: $\mu_d > D_0$) or in the left tail (H_a: $\mu_d < D_0$). A summary is provided in the box on paired sample tests for μ_d and D_0 on page 398.

EXAMPLE 9.12

Consider the previous hardness data collected by Metalloy. Can you confirm the suspicion that the average difference in hardness readings (tip #1 – tip #2) is positive? Use a significance level of $\alpha = .05$.

SOLUTION

Step 1. We are attempting to demonstrate that the average difference in hardness readings is positive; this claim goes into the alternative hypothesis. The resulting hypotheses are

$$H_0: \mu_d \leq 0$$

$$H_a: \mu_d > 0$$

Step 2. We are dealing with paired data, so the correct test statistic is

$$t_D = \frac{\bar{d}}{s_d / \sqrt{n}}$$

Step 3. What happens to t_D when H_a is true? If $\mu_d > 0$, then we would expect $\bar{d}$ to be *positive*. So, the test procedure is to

reject H_0 if $t_D > k$, for some $k > 0$

What is k? As before, this depends on α, and in the usual manner, we have

reject H_0 if $t_D > t_{\alpha, n-1}$

where $t_{\alpha, n-1}$ is obtained from Table A.5. For this situation, $t_{.05,11} = 1.796$, and so we

reject H_0 if $t_D > 1.796$

Step 4. Using the sample data,

$$t_D^* = \frac{2.167}{2.250/\sqrt{12}} = 3.34$$

Because 3.34 > 1.796, we reject H_0.

Step 5. The average hardness reading using tip #1 is higher than that using tip #2.

Using Excel to Compare Means Using Paired Samples

An Excel solution to Example 9.12 is provided in Figure 9.20 (cells C1:E14). First, you must enter the 12 values for tip #1 in cells A2:A13 and the 12 values for tip #2 in cells B2:B13. Type "Tip #1" in cell A1 and "Tip #2" in cell B1. To obtain the output in Figure 9.20, click on **Tools ➤ Data Analysis ➤ t Test: Paired Two-Sample for Means.** The input screen is very similar to that in Figure 9.8. Enter "A1:A13" for the variable 1 range and "B1:B13" for the variable 2 range. Be sure to click on the box to the left of **Labels** (since these two columns contain a label in the first row) and the (default) value of alpha should be .05. The resulting *p*-value (highlighted with an arrow) in cell D11 is .003318, which, using $\alpha = .05$, again results in rejecting H_0 since the *p*-value is less than α.

What happens if you fail to pair these observations and perform a regular two-sample *t* test, as we did in Section 9.3 for small, *independent* samples? The results are summarized in cells F1:H13 in Figure 9.20, where we observe an interesting result. The *t* value (using the test statistic from equation 9.10) now is 1.02, with a corresponding *p*-value of $p = .159$ (highlighted with an arrow). This means that, using this test, we now *fail to reject* H_0. We are unable to demonstrate a difference between the average hardness readings, which, according to the paired sample test, is *not* a correct conclusion. The incorrect solution in cells F1:H13 shows convincingly that failing to pair the observations when you should can cause you to obtain an incorrect result. More importantly, there is nothing to warn you that this has occurred.

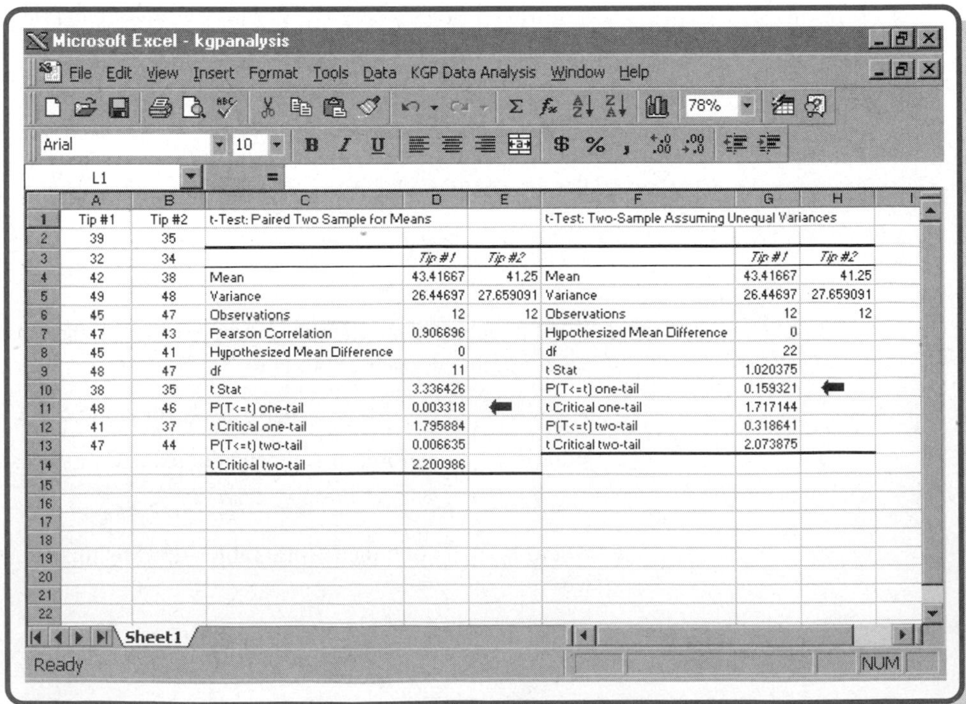

	A	B	C	D	E	F	G	H
1	Tip #1	Tip #2	t-Test: Paired Two Sample for Means			t-Test: Two-Sample Assuming Unequal Variances		
2	39	35						
3	32	34		Tip #1	Tip #2		Tip #1	Tip #2
4	42	38	Mean	43.41667	41.25	Mean	43.41667	41.25
5	49	48	Variance	26.44697	27.659091	Variance	26.44697	27.659091
6	45	47	Observations	12	12	Observations	12	12
7	47	43	Pearson Correlation	0.906696		Hypothesized Mean Difference	0	
8	45	41	Hypothesized Mean Difference	0		df	22	
9	48	47	df	11		t Stat	1.020375	
10	38	35	t Stat	3.336426		P(T<=t) one-tail	0.159321	
11	48	46	P(T<=t) one-tail	0.003318		t Critical one-tail	1.717144	
12	41	37	t Critical one-tail	1.795884		P(T<=t) two-tail	0.318641	
13	47	44	P(T<=t) two-tail	0.006635		t Critical two-tail	2.073875	
14			t Critical two-tail	2.200986				

Figure 9.20 Excel spreadsheet for **Tools ➤ Data Analysis ➤ t Test: Paired Two-Sample for Means** and **Tools ➤ Data Analysis ➤ t Test: Two-Sample Assuming Unequal Variances.**

EXAMPLE 9.13

The market research staff at Allied Foods is considering two different packaging designs for an instant breakfast cereal that Allied is about to introduce. The first type of container under consideration is a rectangular box, whereas the second container type has a cylindrical shape.

The staff decides to conduct a pilot study by placing the product in both containers and locating the two types at opposite ends of the breakfast cereal section in ten different supermarkets. All the containers are placed at eye level to remove any effect due to the height of the display. The main question under consideration is whether there is any difference in the sales of the two types of container. From the following data, can you conclude that there is a difference in sales for the rectangular and cylindrical containers? Use $\alpha = .05$ to define your test.

Supermarket	1	2	3	4	5	6	7	8	9	10
Rectangular	194	152	160	172	118	110	137	126	176	145
Cylindrical	184	161	153	184	105	123	155	111	156	129

SOLUTION

The data were gathered by collecting a pair of observations from each supermarket, so this is a clear-cut case of dependent sampling. Your next step should be to determine the paired differences. Define d to be the rectangular box sales minus the cylindrical box sales.

Supermarket	1	2	3	4	5	6	7	8	9	10	Total
d	10	−9	7	−12	13	−13	−18	15	20	16	29
d^2	100	81	49	144	169	169	324	225	400	256	1917

Step 1. We are attempting to detect a difference in the two means: a two-tailed test is in order. Let

μ_d = average difference in sales for the two container types.

The correct hypotheses are

$$H_0: \mu_d = 0$$

$$H_a: \mu_d \neq 0$$

Steps 2, 3. Using the t_D test statistic, the test will be to

$$\text{reject } H_0 \text{ if } |t_D| > t_{\alpha/2, n-1}$$

where $t_{\alpha/2, n-1} = t_{.025,9} = 2.262$.

Step 4. Using the sample data,

$$\bar{d} = \frac{\sum d}{n} = \frac{29}{10} = 2.9$$

$$s_d = \sqrt{\frac{\sum d^2 - (\sum d)^2 / n}{n-1}}$$

$$= \sqrt{\frac{1917 - (29)^2 / 10}{9}}$$

$$= \sqrt{\frac{1832.9}{9}} = 14.271$$

From these values we obtain

$$t_D^* = \frac{\bar{d}}{s_d / \sqrt{n}} = \frac{2.9}{14.271 / \sqrt{10}} = .643$$

Because $.643 < 2.262$, we fail to reject H_0.

Step 5. Based on these data, there is *insufficient evidence* to conclude that the container type has an effect on sales.

PAIRED SAMPLE TESTS FOR μ_d

Two-Tailed Test

$$H_0: \mu_d = D_0$$

$$H_a: \mu_d \neq D_0$$

$$\text{reject } H_0 \text{ if } |t_D^*| > t_{\alpha/2,\,n-1}$$

where

1. Each difference, d, is (sample 1 value – sample 2 value)

2. $t_D = \dfrac{\bar{d} - D_0}{s_d / \sqrt{n}}$

3. $\bar{d} = \bar{X}_1 - \bar{X}_2 = \dfrac{\sum d}{n}$

4. $s_d = \sqrt{\dfrac{\sum d^2 - (\sum d)^2 / n}{n-1}}$

5. df for $t_D = n - 1$

One-Tailed Test

$$H_0: \mu_d \leq D_0 \qquad\qquad H_0: \mu_d \geq D_0$$

$$H_a: \mu_d > D_0 \qquad\qquad H_a: \mu_d < D_0$$

$$\text{reject } H_0 \text{ if } t_D^* > t_{\alpha,\,n-1} \qquad \text{reject } H_0 \text{ if } t_D^* < -t_{\alpha,\,n-1}$$

EXERCISES 9.47–9.56

UNDERSTANDING THE MECHANICS

9.47 From each of two normally distributed populations, random samples were selected. The observations in the first sample are paired with the observations in the second sample. The following statistics were calculated: $\bar{x}_1 = 5.17$, $\bar{x}_2 = 3.16$, $s_d = 2.4$, $n = 13$.

a. Do the data provide sufficient evidence that the mean of population 1 is greater than the mean of population 2? Use a .05 significance level.

b. Find the p-value for the test statistic in part (a).

9.48 The following data were gathered by collecting pairs of observations from two normally distributed populations.

Pair	Sample 1	Sample 2
1	73	63
2	62	69
3	70	63
4	70	80
5	18	5
6	11	20
7	39	57
8	30	15
9	87	67
10	46	30

a. Is there sufficient evidence to conclude that the mean of the second population is less than the mean of the first population? Use a .05 significance level.

b. Find the p-value for the test statistic in part (a).

9.49 Consider the following pairs of observations. Assume that the population differences are normally distributed.

Pair	1	2	3	4	5	6	7	8	9	10	11	12
Sample 1	93	84	53	87	83	76	95	84	68	80	74	50
Sample 2	89	86	48	85	85	72	91	83	65	78	69	47

a. Do the data support the conclusion that the means of the two populations are significantly different? Use a .10 significance level.

b. Find a 90% confidence interval for the mean difference of the two populations.

APPLYING THE NEW CONCEPTS

9.50 The controller of a fast-food chain is interested in determining whether there is any difference in the weekly sales of restaurant 1 and restaurant 2. The weekly sales are approximately normally distributed. The sales, in dollars, for seven randomly selected weeks are:

Week	Restaurant 1	Restaurant 2
1	4100	3800
2	1800	4600
3	2200	5100
4	3400	3050
5	3100	2800
6	1100	1950
7	2200	3400

a. Should this problem be analyzed using an independent or dependent sample t statistic?

b. Using a significance level of .01, is there evidence to support the conclusion that there is a significant difference in the weekly sales of the two restaurants?

9.51 China's one-child policy, which limits most families to one baby to restrict population growth, seems to be making parents and grandparents in China willing to spend a larger portion of their disposable income on their children. Walt Disney Co. has been selling the Disney Babies line of T-shirts since 1993 in China. Suppose that a market analyst believes that these T-shirts sell for $7.00 (dollar equivalent to the Chinese yuan) more than a local children's T-shirt. Suppose that 25 retail stores were randomly sampled in Shanghai and at each store, the price of a Disney T-Shirt and the price of a local children's T shirt were recorded. If the mean difference was $9.50 with a standard deviation of the differences, s_d, equal to $2.80, is there sufficient evidence to support the marketing analyst's belief? Use a significance level of .01.

(Adapted from *The Wall Street Journal,* "Chinese Babies Are Coveted Consumers," May 15, 1998, p. B1.)

9.52 The challenge of inspecting and maintaining an expanded fleet of aging planes is causing government regulators to closely observe data collected from various airline companies. One measure of alarm is the number of unscheduled landings by an airline company. Suppose that airline regulators are interested in a 90% confidence interval for the mean monthly difference in unscheduled landings by US Airways and Midwest Express Airlines. Using the following data, determine this confidence interval (US Airways – Midwest Express). What assumptions about the data are necessary to ensure the validity of this confidence interval?

Month of 1998	Number of Unscheduled Landings by US Airways	Number of Unscheduled Landings by Midwest Express
Jan.	5	2
Feb.	2	3
Mar.	8	5
Apr.	10	8
May	4	1
June	12	9
July	6	10
Aug.	7	7

(Adapted from *The Wall Street Journal,* "Northwest's Aging Jets Lead to Some Service Disruptions," June 12, 1998, p. A7.)

9.53 Some stock market analysts have speculated that parts of U.S. West Communications might be worth more than the whole. For example, the company's communication systems serving dense business centers (such as Minneapolis and Seattle) could be sold to companies such as SBC Communications. However, regulatory hurdles make these transactions difficult to assess financially. Suppose that a stock market analyst randomly sampled 10 acquisition experts and asked each to predict the return (in percent) on an investment in U.S West held to the year 2000 if 1) it does business as usual and keeps all its assets, and 2) if it breaks up its communication systems and sells all its parts.

(Adapted from *The Wall Street Journal,* "U.S. West Communications May Be Vulnerable to Rivals," May 13, 1998, p. B4.)

Acquisition Expert	Return on Investment If Company Does Not Break Up	Return on Investment If Company Breaks Up
1	12.5	18.6
2	15.7	13.0
3	16.8	17.5
4	20.1	23.0
5	16.0	18.5
6	20.0	17.0
7	17.0	18.0
8	21.0	21.0
9	22.0	23.0
10	18.0	20.0

	Company Does Not Break Up	Company Breaks Up
Mean	17.91	18.96
Variance	8.37	8.96
Observations	10	10.00
Pearson correlation	0.59	
Hypothesized mean difference	0.00	
df	9	
t Stat	−1.25	
P(T<=t) one-tail	0.12	
t Critical one-tail	1.83	
P(T<=t) two-tail	0.24	
t Critical two-tail	2.26	

a. Is there sufficient evidence to conclude that acquisition analysts believe that the return on investment in U.S. West is greater if the company breaks up? Use a .10 significance level.

b. What assumptions are necessary to justify the use of the test procedure in part (a)?

c. How would the data have to be sampled to test the hypothesis in part (a) using a t test with independent samples?

9.54 Using the data in Exercise 9.53, do a "what if" analysis by changing the tenth acquisition analyst's return for U.S. West breaking up. How large would this value have to be to make the test in Exercise 9.53 part (a) significant?

USING THE COMPUTER

9.55 [DATA SET EX9-55] *Variable description:*

PercentReworkPrior: Percent of materials that need rework prior to using quality control charts
PercentReworkPost: Percent of materials that need rework after use of quality control charts is implemented.

The vice president of a manufacturing firm wishes to determine if the implementation of quality control charts at assembly lines will decrease the amount of rework required at each of the assembly lines. There are 35 assembly lines that the vice president selects randomly from plants at various locations. The percent of rework during the month prior to requiring workers to use control charts and the percent of rework afterward is recorded as a percent for variables PercentReworkPrior and PercentReworkPost, respectively.

a. Put PercentReworkPost – PercentReworkPrior in a separate column. Using a one population t statistic, test that the mean difference is less than zero. Use a 1% significance level.

b. Use the *t* statistic for paired samples to test that Percent-ReworkPost is less than PercentReworkPrior. Use a 1% significance level.

c. What similarities do you notice in the analyses in parts (a) and (b)?

d. What assumptions are necessary for the analysis in part (b) to be valid?

e. Do a "what if" analysis by eliminating any pair that has a percentage of rework above 10%. How do the conclusions to part (b) change?

9.56 [DATA SET EX9-56] *Variable description:*

ThisyearSales: Annual sales of retail stores with advertising on cable channels
LastyearSales: Annual sales of retail stores without advertising on cable channels

Cable television has allowed local retail stores to advertise on certain cable channels. A random sample of 40 retail stores that advertised this year but did not advertise last year was selected. The annual sales were recorded in units of thousands of dollars under the variable names ThisyearSales and LastyearSales.

a. Is there enough evidence to infer at the 5% significance level that the mean sales from this year is greater than the mean sales for last year for retail stores that started advertising on cable this year?

b. Can you say that advertising on cable channels increased the sales of the local retail stores? Could anything else possibly cause this increase? What assumptions need to hold to say that the effect of advertising on cable had a significant positive effect on sales?

c. Do a "what if" analysis by subtracting $15 thousand from the sales of each of the sales in ThisyearSales. Repeat part (a). What conclusion do you get?

SUMMARY

This chapter has presented an introduction to **statistical inference for two populations.** We examined tests of hypothesis and confidence intervals for the means and variances (for example, whether they are equal) of two populations, using both independent and dependent samples.

When we used large **independent samples** to test the population means, we defined a test statistic having approximately a standard normal distribution, and we also used this test statistic to define a confidence interval for $\mu_1 - \mu_2$. For small independent samples ($n_1 < 30$ or $n_2 < 30$), hypothesis testing on μ_1 versus μ_2 is concerned with means from two normal populations. For this situation, although we are concerned with the means, we must pay special attention to whether we also have reason to believe that the population standard deviations (σ_1 and σ_2) are equal.

If we do not assume that the σ values are equal, we use a test statistic for μ_1 versus μ_2 having an *approximate* *t* distribution. This statistic also results in an approximate confidence interval for $\mu_1 - \mu_2$. If we assume that the σ values are equal, we use a procedure that pools the sample variances and results in a test statistic having an *exact*

t distribution. We also derived a confidence interval for $\mu_1 - \mu_2$ for this situation.

To determine whether two population variances (or standard deviations) are the same, we introduced the **F distribution.** This distribution is nonsymmetric (right skew) and assumes that two independent samples were obtained from normal populations. Probabilities (areas under the curve) for the *F* random variable are contained in Table A.7. Using this distribution, we can perform two-tailed tests (such as H_a: $\sigma_1 \neq \sigma_2$) or one-tailed tests (such as H_a: $\sigma_1 > \sigma_2$) on the two standard deviations. We also use it to construct a confidence interval for σ_1^2/σ_2^2 or σ_1/σ_2.

When two samples are obtained such that corresponding observations are paired (matched), the resulting samples are **dependent** or **paired.** When using two such samples, we defined a *t*-statistic to test the mean of the population differences, μ_d, and to construct a confidence interval for μ_d. We need not be concerned about whether the population standard deviations are equal for this situation because the test statistic uses the differences between the paired observations, a new variable.

SUMMARY OF FORMULAS

LARGE INDEPENDENT SAMPLES

1. Confidence interval for $\mu_1 - \mu_2$ (σ_1, σ_2 known):

$$(\overline{X}_1 - \overline{X}_2) \pm Z_{\alpha/2} \sqrt{\frac{\sigma_1^2}{n_1} + \frac{\sigma_2^2}{n_2}}$$

2. Confidence interval for $\mu_1 - \mu_2$ (σ_1, σ_2 unknown):

$$(\overline{X}_1 - \overline{X}_2) \pm Z_{\alpha/2} \sqrt{\frac{s_1^2}{n_1} + \frac{s_2^2}{n_2}}$$

3. Hypothesis testing for μ_1 and μ_2: Test statistic is

$$Z = \frac{(\overline{X}_1 - \overline{X}_2) - D_0}{\sqrt{\dfrac{\sigma_1^2}{n_1} + \dfrac{\sigma_2^2}{n_2}}} \approx \frac{(\overline{X}_1 - \overline{X}_2) - D_0}{\sqrt{\dfrac{s_1^2}{n_1} + \dfrac{s_2^2}{n_2}}}$$

where D_0 is the hypothesized value of $\mu_1 - \mu_2$.

SAMPLE SIZES (MINIMIZING $n = n_1 + n_2$)

$$n_1 = \frac{Z_{\alpha/2}^2 s_1 (s_1 + s_2)}{E^2}$$

$$n_2 = \frac{Z_{\alpha/2}^2 s_2 (s_1 + s_2)}{E^2}$$

SMALL, INDEPENDENT SAMPLES

1. Confidence interval for $\mu_1 - \mu_2$ (not assuming $\sigma_1 = \sigma_2$):

$$(\overline{X}_1 - \overline{X}_2) \pm t_{\alpha/2,\mathrm{df}} \sqrt{\frac{s_1^2}{n_1} + \frac{s_2^2}{n_2}}$$

where

$$\mathrm{df} = \frac{\left[\dfrac{s_1^2}{n_1} + \dfrac{s_2^2}{n_2}\right]^2}{\dfrac{\left(\dfrac{s_1^2}{n_1}\right)^2}{n_1 - 1} + \dfrac{\left(\dfrac{s_2^2}{n_2}\right)^2}{n_2 - 1}}$$

2. Confidence interval for $\mu_1 - \mu_2$ (assuming $\sigma_1 = \sigma_2$):

$$(\overline{X}_1 - \overline{X}_2) \pm t_{\alpha/2,\mathrm{df}} \sqrt{\frac{s_p^2}{n_1} + \frac{s_p^2}{n_2}}$$

where

$$\mathrm{df} = n_1 + n_2 - 2$$

and

$$s_p^2 = \frac{(n_1 - 1)s_1^2 + (n_2 - 1)s_2^2}{n_1 + n_2 - 2}$$

3. Hypothesis testing for μ_1 and μ_2 (not assuming $\sigma_1 = \sigma_2$): Test statistic is

$$t' = \frac{(\overline{X}_1 - \overline{X}_2) - D_0}{\sqrt{\dfrac{s_1^2}{n_1} + \dfrac{s_2^2}{n_2}}}$$

where D_0 is the hypothesized value of $\mu_1 - \mu_2$.

where

$$\mathrm{df} = \frac{\left[\dfrac{s_1^2}{n_1} + \dfrac{s_2^2}{n_2}\right]^2}{\dfrac{\left(\dfrac{s_1^2}{n_1}\right)^2}{n_1 - 1} + \dfrac{\left(\dfrac{s_2^2}{n_2}\right)^2}{n_2 - 1}}$$

4. Hypothesis testing for μ_1 and μ_2 (assuming $\sigma_1 = \sigma_2$): Test statistic is

$$t = \frac{(\overline{X}_1 - \overline{X}_2) - D_0}{s_p \sqrt{\dfrac{1}{n_1} + \dfrac{1}{n_2}}}$$

where

$$\mathrm{df} = n_1 + n_2 - 2$$

and

$$s_p = \sqrt{\frac{(n_1 - 1)s_1^2 + (n_2 - 1)s_2^2}{n_1 + n_2 - 2}}$$

COMPARING VARIANCES (OR STANDARD DEVIATIONS)

1. Confidence interval for σ_1^2/σ_2^2:

$$\frac{s_1^2 / s_2^2}{F_R} \quad \text{to} \quad \frac{s_1^2 / s_2^2}{F_L}$$

where $F_R = F_{\alpha/2,\nu_1,\nu_2}$, $F_L = 1/F_{\alpha/2,\nu_2,\nu_1}$, $\nu_1 = n_1 - 1$, and $\nu_2 = n_2 - 1$.

2. Hypothesis testing for σ_1^2/σ_2^2: Test statistic is

$$F = \frac{s_1^2}{s_2^2}$$

DEPENDENT (PAIRED) SAMPLES

1. Confidence interval for μ_d:

$$\overline{d} \pm t_{\alpha/2,n-1} \frac{s_d}{\sqrt{n}}$$

where

$n =$ number of paired observations

$\overline{d} =$ average of n differences

$s_d =$ standard deviation of n differences

2. Hypothesis testing for μ_d: Test statistic is

$$t_D = \frac{\overline{d} - D_0}{s_d / \sqrt{n}} \quad (\mathrm{df} = n - 1)$$

where D_0 is the hypothesized value of μ_d.

REVIEW EXERCISES 9.57–9.72

9.57 Independent random samples are selected from two normally distributed populations. Determine the value of the test statistic and the p-value from the hypothesis test in each of the following cases.

    a. H_0: $\mu_1 - \mu_2 = 0$, H_a: $\mu_1 - \mu_2 \neq 0$, $n_1 = 64$, $n_2 = 38$, $\bar{x}_1 = 5.6$, $\bar{x}_2 = 6.9$, $s_1 = 48$, $s_2 = 17$

    b. H_0: $\mu_1 - \mu_2 \leq 90$, H_a: $\mu_1 - \mu_2 > 90$, $n_1 = 24$, $n_2 = 26$, $\bar{x}_1 = 180$, $\bar{x}_2 = 80$, $s_1 = 24$, $s_2 = 20$

    c. H_0: $\mu_1 - \mu_2 \geq 203$, H_a: $\mu_1 - \mu_2 < 203$, $n_1 = 100$, $n_2 = 100$, $\bar{x}_1 = 525$, $\bar{x}_2 = 325$, $s_1 = 450$, $s_2 = 165$

9.58 A sandwich shop wishes to test the effectiveness of its coupons. The manager believes that the business brought in by the responses to the coupon in the *Highland Village Daily* is equal to the business brought in by the responses to the coupon placed in the *Green Sheet*. The amount spent by each customer using a coupon is recorded (in dollars) and can be considered to be normally distributed. Test the manager's belief with a significance level of .01. *Highland Village Daily*: $n = 32$, $\bar{x} = 9.50$, $s = 26.3$. *Green Sheet*: $n = 39$, $\bar{x} = 11.80$ $s = 29.4$.

9.59 Dairy Castle wanted to boost the sales of their "Country Baskets." They thought that it might be helpful to hang posters that picture the item. They recorded the number of Country Baskets sold during lunchtime for one week at their various stores. They repeated the sampling for another week when the poster advertising was used. Assume that weekly sales are normally distributed. Is there sufficient evidence to say that hanging the posters improved sales of the Country Baskets? Use a .05 significance level.

Store	Before	After	Store	Before	After
1218	215	240	1270	201	220
1224	180	220	1282	207	215
1236	150	190	1292	195	219
1252	180	175	1304	180	195

9.60 For the 12 months ending July 1, 1998, many mutual funds that invested overseas performed very well. Suppose that a financial analyst would like to determine if the performance by global funds (funds investing anywhere in the world) and international funds (funds investing outside of the United States) differed during this period of time. Consider 10 mutual funds randomly selected from the global funds and eight mutual funds randomly selected from the international funds. The financial analyst would like to test that global funds have outperformed international funds during this period.

Global Funds	Performance	International Funds	Performance
Janus Worldwide	26.36	GAM Intl.	26.51
GAM:Global	32.18	First Amer: Intl	26.95
Gabelli Couch Potato	47.79	Driehaus: Intl Gro.	31.56
Warb Pincus GI	26.38	Waddel&Reed:Intl	37.03
Montgomery:GI Opp	27.15	United Intl Growth	34.50
Phoenix Worldwide	31.45	Amer Cent: TC Intl	25.75
Forum:Austin GLBL	28.75	BJB:Intl Equity	25.99
Dreyfus Prem WW	27.31	BEA Intl Equity	26.12
IDDA GL Val.	41.2		
Righttime Gr.	69.7		

t TEST: TWO-SAMPLE ASSUMING EQUAL VARIANCES

	Global	International
Mean	35.827	29.30125
Variance	192.0672011	19.83972679
Observations	10	8
Pooled variance	116.7176811	
Hypothesized mean difference	0	

t Test: Two-Sample Assuming Equal Variances (continued)

	Global	International
df	16	
t Stat	1.273417599	
P(T<=t) one-tail	0.110530042	
t Critical one-tail	1.745884219	
P(T<=t) two-tail	0.221060084	
t Critical two-tail	2.119904821	

(Adapted from *The Wall Street Journal*, "Top-Performing Funds in Selected Sectors," July 6, 1998, p. R18.)

a. What conclusion can the financial analyst state from the statistical analysis using a two-sample *t* test assuming equal variances if the significance level is .10?

b. Do you think that the conclusion would change if you used the two-sample *t* test not assuming equal population variances? Try it.

9.61 A last-minute New York–Los Angeles ticket is almost $2000 round trip. While many airline fares have increased in price during 1998, the walk-up airfares have mostly softened, particularly in areas where low-cost carriers have a well-traveled route. Airlines and analysts say that lower fuel prices have kept costs down. Suppose that an airline analyst believes that the walk-up price for the Dallas to Chicago (Midway) round-trip airfare exceeds the price of a Dallas to St. Louis round trip by more than $100. A random sample revealed that the average walk-up price for a ticket from Dallas to Chicago is $440, whereas the random sample of walk-up airfares for the Dallas to St. Louis route revealed an average price of $310. If the sample size is 10 for each of the round-trip routes and the significance level is .01, what conclusion can the airline analyst make? Use a sample standard deviation of 20 for the Dallas to Chicago airfare and a sample standard deviation of 15 for the Dallas to St. Louis airfare. Assume that population variances are equal and that the data come from approximately normally distributed populations.

(Adapted from *The Wall Street Journal*, "Coming Down," July 17, 1998, p. W6.)

9.62 In 1998, companies in South Korea struggled to survive the contracting economy. Many of these companies fell further behind in meeting their payrolls, adding to labor unrest. South Korea's Ministry of Labor said that total unpaid wages more than tripled in the first 6 months of 1998. Policy makers worried that rising labor unrest could derail economic overhaul in Korea. A labor dispute in Korea is defined as labor unrest that interrupts work for a day or more at a time. Suppose that a labor commission would like to test the hypothesis that the average number of labor disputes per company exceeds the number of labor disputes from a year ago by at least four. A random sample of 19 companies and their number of labor disputes in 1997 and in 1998 are recorded below. At the .05 significance level, what conclusion can the labor commission state from the analysis presented below.

(Adapted from *The Wall Street Journal*, "South Korean Paychecks, Patience Vanish," July 6, 1998, p. A12.)

t Test: Paired Two Sample for Means

	Number of Disputes in 1998	Number of Disputes in 1997
Mean	9.842	3.632
Variance	12.918	4.579
Observations	19	19
Pearson correlation	−0.073	
Hypothesized mean difference	4.000	
df	18	
t Stat	2.233	
P(T<=t) one-tail	0.019	
t Critical one-tail	1.734	
P(T<=t) two-tail	0.038	
t Critical two-tail	2.101	

9.63 Analysis of real estate volatility, both in the U.S. and the U.K., suggests that it is indeed less volatile than stocks or bonds. But in both markets, it underperforms. Robin Goodchild, research director of a European pension fund, randomly sampled 21 funds from each of three types of portfolios: one for real estate ventures, one for strictly bonds, and one with large-cap stocks. The standard deviation was recorded for each: .2 percent for real estate, .6 percent for bonds, and .8 percent for large-cap stocks.

(Adapted from *The London Financial Times,* "An Asset Apart," May 29, 1998, p. 13.)

a. What is a 95% confidence interval for the ratio of the standard deviation of the large-cap stock portfolio to the standard deviation of the real estate portfolio?

b. What is a 95% confidence interval for the ratio of the standard deviation of the bond portfolio to that of the real estate portfolio?

c. Compare and interpret the confidence intervals in parts (a) and (b).

9.64 A study by two professors at Wright State University compared the standard deviation of the annual performance of lump-sum investing in the stock market and of investing by dollar-cost averaging. From 1926 to 1971, the standard deviations of the annual performance for the lump-sum investor and for the dollar-cost-averaging investor were 22.81 and 13.21%, respectively. Suppose an investor wishes to find a confidence interval for the difference in the average performance of n_1 growth mutual funds selected at random for lump-sum investing and n_2 growth mutual funds selected at random for dollar-cost averaging over the past 15 years. Assume that the standard deviations found by the professors at Wright State University approximate the standard deviations of the annual performance of lump-sum investing and dollar-cost averaging over the past 15 years. Find n_1 and n_2 if the maximum error of estimating the mean difference in performance of the two investments is taken to be 4% with 90% confidence.

(Source: Adapted from "Reducing Risk Reduces Return; New Study Examines Popular Dollar-Cost Averaging Technique," by Linda Stern, *Washington Post,* Jan. 9, 1994, p. H14.)

9.65 A new packaging method that is proposed has an average output yield of finished units approximately the same as the existing packaging method. This new packaging method will be adopted if the variability in the number of finished units is less, thus providing greater process control. At a .05 significance level, is there sufficient evidence to conclude that the variance of the number of finished units is less for the new packaging method.

	Existing Packaging Method	**New Packaging Method**
Days sampled	9	9
s^2	1190	465

9.66 Determine which of the following sets of hypotheses are equivalent.

a. H_0: $\sigma_1^2/\sigma_2^2 \leq 1$ and H_a: $\sigma_1^2/\sigma_2^2 > 1$

b. H_0: $\sigma_2^2/\sigma_1^2 \geq 1$ and H_a: $\sigma_2^2/\sigma_1^2 < 1$

c. H_0: $\sigma_2^2 \geq \sigma_1^2$ and H_a: $\sigma_2^2 < \sigma_1^2$

d. H_0: $\sigma_1 \leq \sigma_2$ and H_a: $\sigma_1 > \sigma_2$

9.67 A study is designed to determine the effect of an office-training course on typing productivity. Ten typists are randomly selected and are asked to type 15 pages of equally difficult text before and after completing the training course. Their productivity is measured by the total number of errors made.

Typist	Before	After	Typist	Before	After
1	30	27	6	33	31
2	19	14	7	28	22
3	36	31	8	30	25
4	42	37	9	27	30
5	35	29	10	34	33

Assume that the total number of errors can be approximated by a normal distribution. Test the claim that taking the office-training course leads to a reduction in the average number of errors made by a typist. Use a significance level of .05.

9.68 Suppose that a sample of size 16 is chosen from population 1 and a sample of size 26 is drawn from population 2. Assume that both populations are normally distributed. If a 90% confidence interval for the ratio of the variance of population 1 to the variance of population 2 is .367 to 1.753, what is the point estimate of the ratio of the two population variances?

9.69 Government auditors say that up to 15% of Medicare's $22.7 billion in annual payments to the nursing home industry is wasted or fraudulent. About 1.5 million Americans live in nursing homes. Spending on long-term elderly care approaches $100 billion a year. In addition to Medicare, many patients receive state Medicaid benefits, which can finance as much as a third of the expense. To trim the cost of Medicare, effective July 1998, Medicare payments to the nursing home industry have a cap. Suppose that a social worker is interested in the percentage of nursing home expense paid by the individuals in nursing homes and the percentage paid by Medicare. A random sample of 20 patients living in nursing homes was obtained and the percentages paid by the patient and by Medicare are recorded. The results are presented below. Data are presented in units of percent.

Patient	Percentage Paid by Patient	Percentage Paid by Medicare
1	40	45
2	33	35
3	32	43
4	45	42
5	43	34
6	38	45
7	43	32
8	41	46
9	40	33
10	46	32
11	34	40
12	35	38
13	45	32
14	43	31
15	43	40
16	41	36
17	31	41
18	42	32
19	48	30
20	40	39

t TEST: PAIRED TWO SAMPLE FOR MEANS

	Paid by Patient	Paid by Medicare
Mean	40.15	37.3
Variance	23.71315789	27.48421053
Observations	20	20
Pearson correlation	−0.476029648	
Hypothesized mean difference	0	
df	19	
t Stat	1.466826723	
P(T<=t) one-tail	0.079390254	
t Critical one-tail	1.729131327	
P(T<=t) two-tail	0.158780509	
t Critical two-tail	2.093024705	

(Adapted from *USA Today*, "Medicare Cap Set for Nursing Homes," July 1, 1998, p. B1.)

a. Is there sufficient evidence to support that the amount paid by the patient on a nursing home is more than that paid by Medicare? Use a .10 significance level.

b. If patient 10 is removed from the data, how will the analysis change? Rerun the paired t test with this observation omitted.

9.70 The controversy over sulfur reductions in gasoline is part of a debate being played out by automobile makers, automobile supply companies, and oil companies. The automobile makers and suppliers want the sulfur levels to be very low so that very little damage would occur to auto-emission control devices. The oil companies believe that small refineries will have to bear too much cost if the sulfur levels are too low. An analyst with the Environmental Protection Agency (EPA) believes that the automobile makers and suppliers want a sulfur level that is more than 100 parts per million lower than that suggested by oil companies. Assume that the analyst with the EPA randomly collects data from nine oil company advisors and 14 automobile advisors, and she records their suggested levels of future sulfur levels. An analysis of the data is presented below.

Advisors to Oil Companies	Advisors to Automobile Companies
150	40
145	35
160	43
136	46
150	42
180	39
140	41
135	40
125	42
	40
	43
	42
	41
	40

t Test: Two-Sample Assuming Equal Variances

	Advisors to Oil Companies	Advisors to Automobile Companies
Mean	146.78	41.00
Variance	259.69	6.15
Observations	9	14
Pooled variance	102.74	
Hypothesized mean difference	100.00	
df	21	
t Stat	1.33	
P(T<=t) one-tail	0.098	
t Critical one-tail	1.72	
P(T<=t) two-tail	0.20	
t Critical two-tail	2.08	

t Test: Two-Sample Assuming Unequal Variances

	Advisors to Oil Companies	Advisors to Automobile Companies
Mean	146.78	41.00
Variance	259.69	6.15
Observations	9	14
Hypothesized mean difference	100.00	
df	8	
t Stat	1.07	
P(T<=t) one-tail	0.16	
t Critical one-tail	1.86	
P(T<=t) two-tail	0.32	
t Critical two-tail	2.31	

(Adapted from *The Wall Street Journal*, "Auto and Oil Companies Disagree on How to Curb Sulfur Pollution," May 13, 1998, p. B4.)

a. To test the EPA analyst's belief that the automobile makers and suppliers want a sulfur level that is more than 100 parts per million lower than that suggested by oil companies, what are the null and alternative hypotheses?

b. Examining the Excel printout, why do you believe that the two t test procedures give different conclusions for testing the hypothesis in part (a), assuming a significance level of .10?

c. Which t test would you recommend? Why?

9.71 **[DATA SET EX9-71]** *Variable description:*

WithAdditive: Miles per gallon of trucks with gasoline additive
WithoutAdditive: Miles per gallon of trucks without gasoline additive

An engineer is experimenting with a gasoline additive that may help some trucks with heavy loads. However, the engineer is uncertain that the additive will be beneficial for all types of trucks. The engineer believes that the additive may increase the variability of the gas mileage among the trucks but believes that the mean miles per gallon for all trucks may not change very much. A random sample of 50 trucks used by the company is selected. Twenty-five of these use the additive, and the other 25 trucks do not. Each truck carries the same load and makes the same trip. The miles per gallon values are recorded as variables WithAdditive and WithoutAdditive. To assist in interpreting the data, a histogram is displayed for each group, the first histogram is for the WithAdditive values and the second histogram is for the WithoutAdditive values. Use the Excel printouts to make conclusions about the population means and variances. Write a managerial report explaining the effect of the additive on the gas mileage of the trucks. Assume that the significance level is 10%.

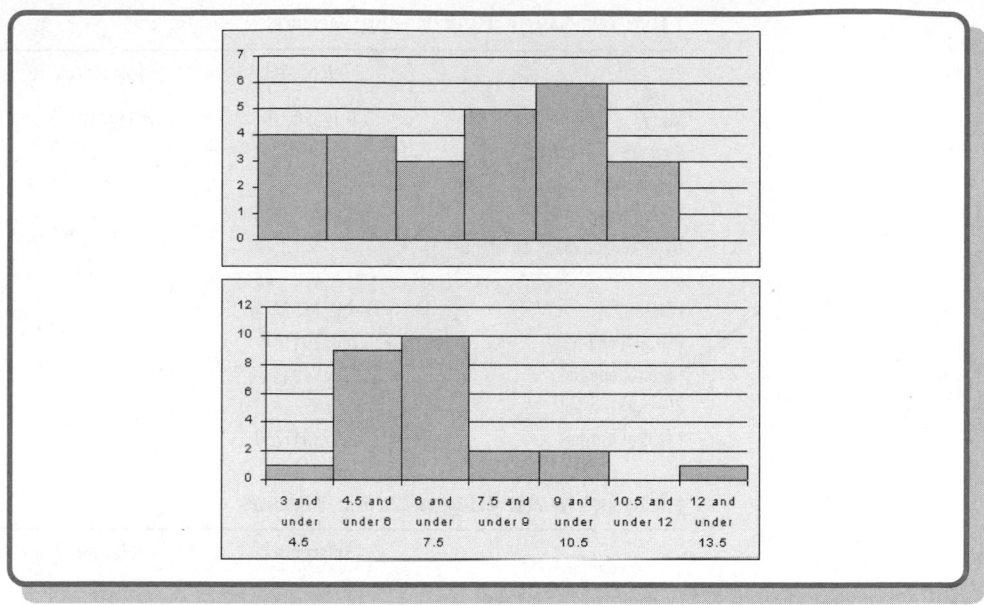

F Test: Two-Sample for Variances

	WithAdditive	WithoutAdditive
Mean	7.446325771	6.759547982
Variance	6.470830688	3.682136708
Observations	25	25
df	24	24
F	1.757357535	
P(F<=f) one-tail	0.087240708	
F Critical one-tail	1.983757159	

t Test: Two-Sample Assuming Unequal Variances

	WithAdditive	WithoutAdditive
Mean	7.446325771	6.759547982
Variance	6.470830688	3.682136708
Observations	25	25
Hypothesized Mean Difference	0	
df	45	
t Stat	1.077679817	
P(T<=t) one-tail	0.143459994	
t Critical one-tail	1.679427442	
P(T<=t) two-tail	0.286919989	
t Critical two-tail	2.014103302	

9.72 [DATA SET EX9-72] *Variable description:*

Tolerance1: Tolerances for machine 1
Tolerance2: Tolerances for machine 2

A quality engineer wishes to compare the diameters of ball bearings produced by two machines. The ball bearings are supplied to a manufacturer that specifies that the diameters are 580 microns, with a certain tolerance—that is, the diameter of each ball bearing minus 580 microns. A random sample of 50 ball bearings is selected from machine 1, and another 15 are selected from machine 2. The tolerances for machine 1 and machine 2 are contained in variables Tolerance1 and Tolerance2, respectively. Use the printouts below to decide whether the machines differ in their mean tolerances assuming that the significance level is 5%. Which procedure did you select? Why?

t Test: Two-Sample Assuming Equal Variances

	Tolerance1	Tolerance2
Mean	−0.125900351	0.320702112
Variance	0.816490143	0.10031569
Observations	50	15
Pooled variance	0.657340265	
Hypothesized mean difference	0	
df	63	
t Stat	−1.871112714	
P(T<=t) one-tail	0.032987412	
t Critical one-tail	1.669402536	
P(T<=t) two-tail	0.065974825	
t Critical two-tail	1.998341759	

t Test: Two-Sample Assuming Unequal Variances

	Tolerance1	Tolerance2
Mean	−0.125900351	0.320702112
Variance	0.816490143	0.10031569
Observations	50	15
Hypothesized mean difference	0	
df	61	
t Stat	−2.943688773	
P(T<=t) one-tail	0.002291397	
t Critical one-tail	1.670218808	
P(T<=t) two-tail	0.004582795	
t Critical two-tail	1.999624146	

Computer Exercises Using the Databases

EXERCISE 1—APPENDIX E

Choose at random 10 observations from the database in which the family owns their home and 10 observations in which the family rents their home. (Refer to the variable OWNORENT.) Do the data support the conclusion that the home payment for homeowners is larger than the home payment for renters? Use a .05 significance level. What assumptions are necessary to ensure that the test procedure is valid? Do not assume equal population variances.

EXERCISE 2—APPENDIX E

Choose at random 10 observations from the database from a family of size 2 and 10 observations from a family of size 4. Do the data support the conclusion that the monthly utility expenditure (variable UTILITY) is larger for a family of size 4? Use a .05 significance level. Do not assume equal population variances.

EXERCISE 3—APPENDIX F

From the database, choose a random sample of 12 companies with an A bond rating and another random sample of 12 companies with a C bond rating. Do the data support the conclusion that the net income of companies with a C bond rating is less than the net income of companies with an A rating? Use a .05 significance level. Do not assume equal population variances.

EXERCISE 4—APPENDIX F

From the database, choose a random sample of 15 companies with a B bond rating and another random sample of 15 companies with a C bond rating. Do the data support the conclusion that the variances of the current assets of the companies with B bond ratings and C bond ratings differ significantly at the .05 level?

INSIGHTS FROM STATISTICS IN ACTION: COLLISIONS INVOLVING LIGHT TRUCKS AND SPORT UTILITY VEHICLES WITH CARS: ASSESSING THE IMPACT

At the beginning of this chapter, the Statistics in Action case study discussed the ever-increasing problem of light trucks and sport utility vehicles (SUVs) causing excessive damage when striking a much lighter automobile. The concept of testing for a difference between two population means presented in this chapter can be used to determine the extent of this problem. Are the average repair costs for car/SUV collisions actually larger than for car/car collisions? To guide you through the process of answering such a question, first consider the following list of questions.

1. a. If an automotive analyst wished to show that damage to cars involved in collisions with trucks and sport utility vehicles, cars sustained more than $2000 worth of damage than cars involved in collisions with other cars, how would you set up the hypotheses?

   b. If a random sample of 25 cars involved in accidents with other cars showed an average amount of damage of $5810 and a random sample of 25 cars involved in accidents with trucks or sport utility vehicles showed an average amount of damage $8000, would this data support the alternative hypothesis in part (a). Assume that the population standard deviation for the amount of damage for cars in either group is $1500. Use a significance level of .05.

2. What assumptions are necessary for the test in Question 1 to be valid?

3. If you use a t test in Question 1 and assume that the standard deviation of $1500 was a pooled standard deviation, would the results of the test change?

4. Suppose a consultant for an insurance company wished to compare the results of the amount of damage sustained by the Ford Explorer in the National Highway Traffic Safety Administration's (NHTSA) annual crash test and the amount of damaged sustained in similar accidents using real-world data. Automakers have rejected calls to make trucks such as the Explorer lighter, arguing that these trucks often have quite a lot of damage in accidents as noted from real-world accidents. When these trucks hit cars at a right angle they often have little damage, while the cars suffer badly. However, in head-on collisions the consultant believes that these trucks sustain more damage than that indicated by NHTSA's crash tests. A preliminary study showed that the standard deviation of the damage resulting either from the crash tests or from real-world data was approximately $1500. What sample size would be required for both groups if a desired maximum error for the mean difference in damage is to be within $500 with a 90% confidence?

Sources: *Motor Trend*, "Cars and Trucks Mismatched in Highway Crashes." Oct. 1997, vol. 49, no. 10, p. 28. *The Dallas Morning News*, Oct. 17, 1997, vol. 149, no. 17, p. 1A, 15A. Adapted from *The Wall Street Journal*, "Tests Question Whether Light Trucks Are Much Deadlier Than Cars in Crashes," June 1, 1998, p. A4.

CHAPTER 9 APPENDIX: DATA ANALYSIS WITH MINITAB

INFERENCE PROCEDURE FOR INDEPENDENT SAMPLES FROM TWO POPULATIONS

To test a hypothesis about the means of two populations with independent samples, click on **Stat ➤ Basic Statistics ➤ 2-Sample t.** For this example, the data in Example 9.4 are used. The names of the two types of tires—Beltex and Roadmaster—are typed into the boxes under the selection of **Samples in Different Columns.** If the data were to appear together in one column, another column would be needed to indicate (usually with a 1 or a 2) from which population each sample value was obtained. Since the alternative in Example 9.4 is that the means of the two populations are not equal, the **not equal** option is selected in the **Alternative:** box. No significance level is set for the hypothesis test, but any level of confidence can be typed into the **Confidence Level:** box. For this example, the population variances will not be assumed to be equal, so the **Assume equal variances** box is not checked. The user form and output appear below. MINITAB always rounds the df value *down* to the nearest integer (21, here). To obtain a dot plot or box plot, click on **Graphs.** For this example, dot plots will be presented after the output below.

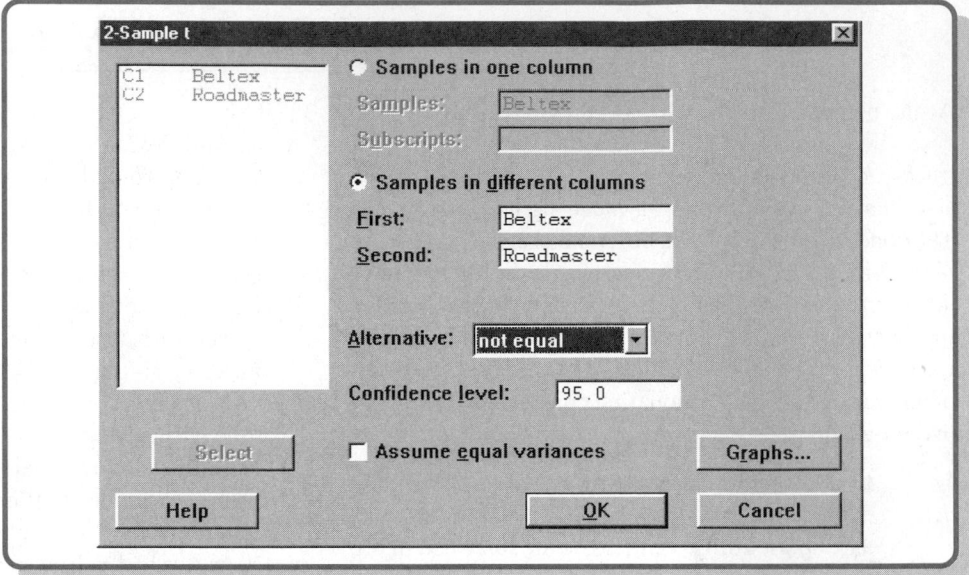

Two Sample T-Test and Confidence Interval

Two sample T for Beltex vs Roadmaster

	N	Mean	StDev	SE Mean
Beltex	15	3.332	0.679	0.18
Roadmast	15	3.984	0.377	0.097

95% CI for mu Beltex − mu Roadmast: (−1.07, −0.235)
T-Test mu Beltex = mu Roadmast (vs ≠): T = −3.25   P = 0.0038
DF = 21

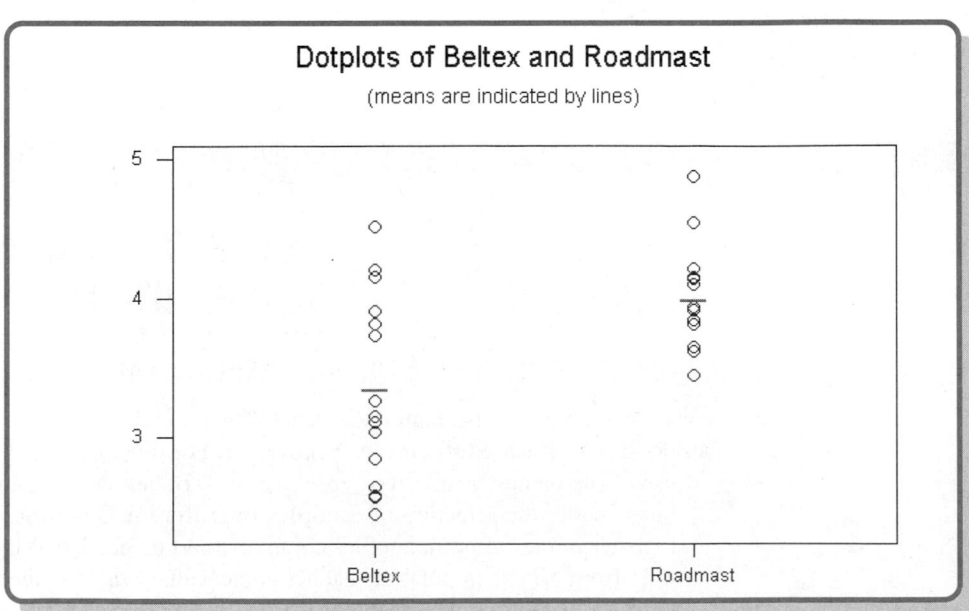

Dotplots of Beltex and Roadmast
(means are indicated by lines)

INFERENCE PROCEDURE FOR DEPENDENT SAMPLES FROM TWO POPULATIONS

To test a hypothesis about a difference in the means of two populations with dependent samples, click on **Stat ➤ Basic Statistics ➤ Paired t.** For this example, the metal hinge data in Example 9.11 are used. The differences are calculated by subtracting the first sample from the second sample. The names of the two types of hinges—Tip 1 and Tip 2—are typed into the boxes **First sample** and **Second sample** under the selection of **Samples in Different Columns.** Click on **Options** to input the hypothesized mean, the confidence level for the confidence interval on the difference for the means, and the type of alternative hypothesis. For this example the alternative hypothesis is selected to be **not equal,** and a 95% confidence level is selected for the confidence interval on the difference of the two population means. The **Graphs** button can be clicked to obtain histograms, dot plots, or box plots of the differences in the observations. The user forms are presented below with the output following.

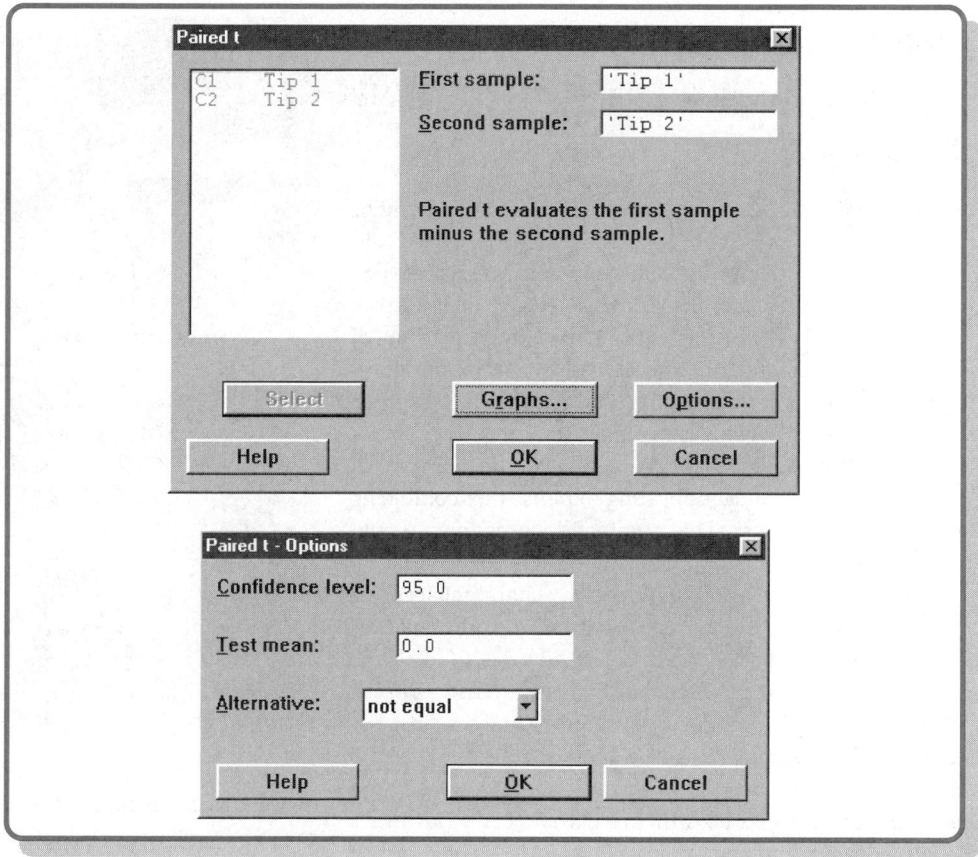

Paired T-Test and Confidence Interval

```
Paired T for Tip 1 - Tip 2

                N       Mean      StDev    SE Mean
Tip 1          12      43.42       5.14       1.48
Tip 2          12      41.25       5.26       1.52
Difference     12      2.167       2.250      0.649

95% CI for mean difference: (0.737, 3.596)
T-Test of mean difference = 0 (vs not = 0): T-Value = 3.34
P-Value = 0.007
```

ESTIMATION AND TESTING
FOR POPULATION PROPORTIONS

STATISTICS IN ACTION: LARGE WASTE MANAGMENT FIRMS ARE SHIFTING TO A MANAGEMENT STRATEGY OF "WASTE INTERNALIZATION"

It's a simple business, but America's waste management companies are constantly considering the gritty and unglamourous details of pursuing marketshare. For example, in several major U.S. markets, such as Houston, New York City, and Pittsburgh, the combination of Waste Management, Inc., and USA Waste raise anticompetitive concerns. USA Waste had proposed a merger with the much-larger Waste Management. The companies would be able to cut at least $800 million out of their combined annual operating expenses by combining overlapping business. The combined companies would have about $12 billion in sales, $9 billion of that in North American waste business. That equates to approximately 22.5% of the North American market estimated at about $40 billion.

The U.S. Justice Department's antitrust division believe that such a merger would violate antitrust statutes. For example, in some areas of the country, the antitrust division believes that the companies own anywhere from 60% to 80% of the dump sites. With more dump capacity and haulers accustomed to shipping trash longer distances to get better dumping fees, big waste companies have figured out that overhead costs can be reduced significantly by buying more dump sites. Thus, big haulers, such as USA Waste and Waste Management, Inc., have shifted to a strategy known as "waste internalization," or hauling trash to their own dump sites. In the Houston area, USA Waste is trying to purchase enough dump sites to haul almost all of its trash to its own disposal facilities.

When you have completed this chapter, you will be able to determine if the percentage of dump sites owned

by USA Waste is more/less/different than the percentage owned by Waste Management, Inc., based on sample results. In particular, this chapter will show you how to:

- Construct a confidence interval for a single population *proportion* (e.g., the proportion of dump sites owned by USA Waste);
- Construct a confidence interval for the difference in two population proportions;
- Determine if USA Waste owns more than half of the dump sites in the population, based on sample results;
- Determine if USA Waste owns a higher proportion of dump sites than its main competitor.

A LOOK BACK/INTRODUCTION

By now you should be comfortable with the concepts of estimation and hypothesis testing. If, for example, you have reason to believe that the population is normally distributed, you can then estimate the necessary population parameters (such as the mean and standard deviation) using the corresponding sample statistics. You should be well aware that there always is the risk of arriving at an incorrect conclusion when using sample information to infer something about an entire population. We can use the Central Limit Theorem to relax the assumptions regarding normality when making inferences about population means if large samples are used.

Chapters 7, 8, and 9 concentrated primarily on normal populations. We provided you with confidence intervals for the mean and the variance of a single normal population. We examined how to check a statement regarding one of these parameters (such as $\mu < 100$ or $\sigma > .5$) using a test of hypothesis. Then this concept was extended to comparing the means or variances of two normal populations.

Now we return to the *binomial* situation, in which we are interested in the *proportion* of your population that has a certain attribute. Attributes can include personal attributes, such as willingness to buy a product or being in favor of a proposed labor contract. We can also examine proportions as they relate to a particular physical attribute, such as the proportion of defective components in a batch.

We are interested in a single parameter, referred to as **p,** which is the **proportion** of the population having this attribute. For example, suppose that a recent report claims that only 10% of all registered voters in a certain area are in favor of forced busing for school children ($p = .10$). Or suppose it has been reported that a lower proportion of families with children favor busing than do those without children. How can we estimate the actual proportions here and test these claims?

Examining a population proportion plays a *vital* role in describing and monitoring the quality of a production process. Here, the parameter of interest is the proportion (p) of nonconforming units being produced by the process. Based on the results of a statistical sample, we can decide if the parameter p is too large (process is out of control) or acceptable (process is in control). This topic will be discussed further in Chapter 12.

10.1 ESTIMATION AND CONFIDENCE INTERVALS FOR A POPULATION PROPORTION

A test for a population *proportion* is a binomial situation. Using the definitions from Chapter 5, each member of your population is either a *success* or a *failure*. These words can be misleading; it is necessary only that each person (or object) in your population either have a certain attribute (a success) or not have it (a failure). So we define p to be the proportion of successes in the population—that is, the proportion that have a certain attribute.

Do not confuse the notation $p = $ a population proportion with the previously used notation for a *p*-value. They do not mean the same thing. We hope that the context will make it clear which of the two *p*'s is being described.

In Chapter 5 we assumed that p is known. For any binomial situation, perhaps p is known, or more likely it was estimated in some way. This chapter examines how you can estimate p by using a sample from the population. Also, you can support (or fail to support) claims concerning the value of p. The final section in this chapter compares two samples from two separate populations.

POINT ESTIMATE FOR A POPULATION PROPORTION

Auditors often deal with sample results concerned with a population proportion. This type of sampling is called **attribute sampling,** since the parameter of interest is the proportion of the population having a certain attribute. Suppose that Cassidy Electronics is under an audit investigation (perhaps, routine) to determine the proportion of payroll checks in the current fiscal year containing calculation errors. The proportion of interest is the proportion of payroll checks containing such an error. A random sample of 250 payroll checks turned up 14 containing calculation errors. What can you say about the proportion (p) of all payroll checks in this fiscal year that contain errors in calculation?

We view this as a binomial situation and define a "success" as a payroll check containing an error and a "failure" as a check containing no error. Consequently, p is the proportion of successes in the population (proportion of all payroll checks containing an error). Remember that p, like μ and σ previously, will remain *unknown* forever unless a complete 100% audit is conducted. To *estimate p,* we obtain a random sample and observe the proportion of successes in the sample. We use $\hat{p}$ (read as "p hat") to denote the estimate of p. Consequently, $\hat{p}$ (the proportion of successes in the sample) estimates p (the proportion of successes in the population). Here, $\hat{p}$ = proportion of payroll checks containing calculation errors = 14/250 = .056.

In general,

$$\hat{p} = \text{estimate of } p$$

$$= \text{proportion of sample having a specified attribute}$$

$$= \frac{x}{n} \tag{10.1}$$

where n = sample size and x = the number of sample observations having this attribute.

The symbol $\hat{}$ is used to denote an *estimate.* Distinguish between $\hat{p}$ obtained from sample information and p, the population proportion being estimated by $\hat{p}$. This is the same type of difference that we previously recognized between a sample mean, $\overline{X}$ (often referred to as $\hat{\mu}$), and a population mean, μ.

The mean of the random variable $\hat{p}$ is the (unknown) value of p. In other words, the average value of $\hat{p}$ is the parameter it is estimating. Such an estimator is said to be **unbiased.** If we obtained random samples indefinitely, the resulting $\hat{p}$'s—on the average—will equal p. This is a desirable property for a sample estimator to have. We have actually discussed two other unbiased estimators previously; $\overline{X}$ is an unbiased estimator of a population mean (μ) and s^2 is an unbiased estimator of a population variance (σ^2).

CONFIDENCE INTERVALS FOR A POPULATION PROPORTION (USING A SMALL SAMPLE)

The calculations involved in determining a confidence interval for p using a small sample are fairly complex. To make them easier, we have listed 90% and 95% confidence intervals for sample sizes of $n = 5, 6, \ldots , 20$ in Table A.8. For sample sizes other than these, you can (1) use the large-sample confidence interval (described next) or (2) extend Table A.8 by consulting your local statistician.

Using Table A.8 is much like using Table A.1, the table of binomial probabilities. Let n = sample size and x = the observed number of successes in your sample. Based on these values, the confidence interval (p_L, p_U) can be obtained directly from the table.

EXAMPLE 10.1

A private company is considering the purchase of 200 Beagle microcomputers to monitor seismic activity. These computers will be placed in outdoor stations where they must be able to operate in extremely cold weather. If the computers will operate in temperatures as low as −10°F, the company will purchase them. Beagle, anxious to demonstrate the relia-

See A.8 table on page A-22

n = 15   *12 work*

12/15 = .8

bility of their system, has agreed to subject 15 computers to a "cold test." Let p = proportion of *all* Beagle computers that will function at $-10°F$.

Of the 15 example computers, three of them stopped operating at or above $-10°F$. What can you say about p? Construct a 95% confidence interval for p.

SOLUTION

Let a success be that a computer *survives* the cold test (still functions at $-10°F$). We observe 12 successes out of 15 in the sample. So,

$$\hat{p} = \frac{12}{15} = .8$$

point estimate for population — Find CI at 95%

Using Table A.8 for $n = 15$, $x = 12$, and $\alpha = .05$, we find $p_L = .519$ and $p_U = .957$. The corresponding 95% confidence interval for p is

$$p_L \quad \text{to} \quad p_U = .519 \quad \text{to} \quad .957$$

So we are 95% confident that the actual (population) percentage of Beagle computers that can function at $-10°F$ is between 51.9% and 95.7%.

COMMENTS

One of the purposes of this section (omitted in many textbooks) is to demonstrate that confidence intervals for a population proportion (p) are typically very wide when using a small sample. In Example 10.1, the company considering the purchase of the Beagle microcomputers still is pretty much in the dark regarding the proportion of computers that will survive the cold test. They are 95% confident that this proportion is between 52% and 96%— a very wide range. The moral of this section is: *To obtain a useful (narrow) confidence interval for p, obtain a large sample.*

CONFIDENCE INTERVALS FOR A POPULATION PROPORTION (USING A LARGE SAMPLE)

When dealing with large samples, the Central Limit Theorem once again provides us with a reliable method of determining approximate confidence intervals for a population proportion. For each element in your sample, assign a value of 1 if this observation is a success (has the attribute) or 0 if this observation is a failure (does not have the attribute). Using the audit results at Cassidy Electronics to illustrate, for *each* payroll check in the sample we assign 1 if this check contains an error and 0 otherwise. So what is $\hat{p}$? We can write it as

$$\hat{p} = \frac{\overbrace{1 + 1 + \cdots + 1}^{14 \text{ times}} + \overbrace{0 + 0 + \cdots + 0}^{236 \text{ times}}}{250} = \frac{14}{250} = .056$$

In this sense, then, $\hat{p}$ is a **sample average**: it is an average of 0s and 1s. *As a result, we can apply the Central Limit Theorem to $\hat{p}$ and conclude that $\hat{p}$ is (approximately) a normal random variable for large samples.* This works reasonably well provided np and $n(1-p)$ are both greater than 5. So the distribution of $\hat{p}$ [large sample; $np > 5$ and $n(1-p) > 5$] can be summarized: $\hat{p}$ is (approximately) a normal random variable with

$$\text{mean} = p$$

$$\text{standard deviation (standard error)} = \sqrt{\frac{p(1-p)}{n}}$$

By standardizing this result, we have

$$Z = \frac{\hat{p} - p}{\sqrt{\dfrac{p(1-p)}{n}}} \tag{10.2}$$

which is approximately a standard normal random variable. This variable allows us to use Table A.4 to construct a confidence interval for p. This confidence interval is obtained in the identical manner used to construct previous confidence intervals with the standard normal distribution, namely,

$$\text{(point estimate)} \pm Z_{\alpha/2} \cdot \text{(standard deviation of point estimator)} \quad \textbf{(10.3)}$$

The standard deviation of $\hat{p}$ (that is, the **standard error of** $\hat{p}$) in the denominator of equation 10.2 contains the unknown parameter, p. To estimate this standard error, it would seem logical to replace $p(1-p)/n$ with $\hat{p}(1-\hat{p})/n$. However, it can be shown that if we were to sample indefinitely, $\hat{p}(1-\hat{p})/n$ on the average *underestimates* $p(1-p)/n$. In fact, an unbiased estimator of $p(1-p)/n$ is obtained by using

$$\frac{\hat{p}(1-\hat{p})}{n-1}$$

and so the *estimated standard error* of $\hat{p}$ is

$$s_{\hat{p}} = \sqrt{\frac{\hat{p}(1-\hat{p})}{n-1}} \quad \textbf{(10.4)}$$

Using the estimated standard error, a $(1-\alpha) \cdot 100\%$ confidence interval for p (large sample; $n\hat{p}$ and $n(1-\hat{p})$ both > 5) is

$$C.I. = \qquad \hat{p} - Z_{\alpha/2}\sqrt{\frac{\hat{p}(1-\hat{p})}{n-1}} \quad \text{to} \quad \hat{p} + Z_{\alpha/2}\sqrt{\frac{\hat{p}(1-\hat{p})}{n-1}} \quad \textbf{(10.5)}$$

EXAMPLE 10.2

Using the audit results (14 errors in 250 payroll checks), what is a 90% confidence interval for the proportion of all payroll checks in this fiscal year that contain calculation errors?

SOLUTION

Using Table A.4, $Z_{\alpha/2} = Z_{.05} = 1.645$. Also, $\hat{p} = 14/250 = .056$. So the 90% confidence interval for p is

$$.056 - 1.645\sqrt{\frac{(.056)(.944)}{249}} \quad \text{to} \quad .056 + 1.645\sqrt{\frac{(.056)(.944)}{249}}$$

$$= .056 - .015 \quad \text{to} \quad .056 + .015$$

$$= .041 \quad \text{to} \quad .071$$

Based on the sample results, we are 90% confident that the percentage of payroll checks containing calculation errors is between 4.1% and 7.1%.

EXAMPLE 10.3

Remember that in lot acceptance sampling, we either accept or reject a batch (lot) of components, parts, or assembled products based on tests using a random sample drawn from the lot.

Suppose we draw a sample of size 150 from a lot of calculators. We test each of the sampled calculators and find 13 defectives. Determine a 95% confidence interval for the proportion of defectives in the entire batch.

SOLUTION

Let p = proportion of defective calculators in the batch. Based on the sample of 150 calculators, we have

$$\hat{p} = \frac{13}{150} = .0867$$

Because $Z_{.025} = 1.96$, the 95% confidence interval for p is

$$.0867 - 1.96\sqrt{\frac{(.0867)(.9133)}{149}} \quad \text{to} \quad .0867 + 1.96\sqrt{\frac{(.0867)(.9133)}{149}}$$

$$= .0867 - .045 \quad \text{to} \quad .0867 + .045$$

$$= .042 \quad \text{to} \quad .132$$

Consequently, we are 95% confident that our estimate $\hat{p} = .0867$ is within .045 of the actual value of p. In other words, this sample estimates the actual percentage of defective calculators to within 4.5%, with 95% confidence.

CHOOSING THE SAMPLE SIZE (ONE POPULATION)

Suppose that you want your point estimate, $\hat{p}$, to be within a certain amount of the actual proportion, p. In Example 10.3 the *maximum error, E,* was $E = .045$, that is, 4.5%. In general, larger samples will yield lower maximum errors. What if the buyer's specifications necessitate that we estimate the parameter p to within 2% with 95% confidence? Now,

$$E = 1.96\sqrt{\frac{\hat{p}(1-\hat{p})}{n-1}} \tag{10.6}$$

We have an earlier estimate of p ($\hat{p} = .0867$) using the sample of size 150; this value can be used in equation 10.6. The purpose is to extend this sample in order to obtain this specific maximum error, E. The specified value of E is .02, so

$$E = .02 = 1.96\sqrt{\frac{(.0867)(.9133)}{n-1}}$$

Therefore,

$$\sqrt{\frac{(.0867)(.9133)}{n-1}} = \frac{.02}{1.96}$$

Squaring both sides and rearranging leads to

$$n = \frac{(1.96)^2(.0867)(.9133)}{(.02)^2} + 1 = 761.5$$

Rounding up (*always*), we come to the conclusion that a sample of size $n = 762$ calculators will be necessary to estimate p to within 2%.

By solving equation 10.6 for n, we arrive at the following equation, which provides the necessary sample size to estimate p with a specified maximum error, E, and confidence level $(1 - \alpha) \cdot 100\%$:

$$n = \frac{Z_{\alpha/2}^2 \hat{p}(1-\hat{p})}{E^2} + 1 \tag{10.7}$$

In this illustration, we used an estimate of p from a prior sample to determine the necessary sample size using equation 10.7. If the sample of size n based on this equation is our first and only sample, then we *have no estimate of p.* There is a conservative

FIGURE 10.1

Curve of values of $\hat{p}(1 - \hat{p})$.

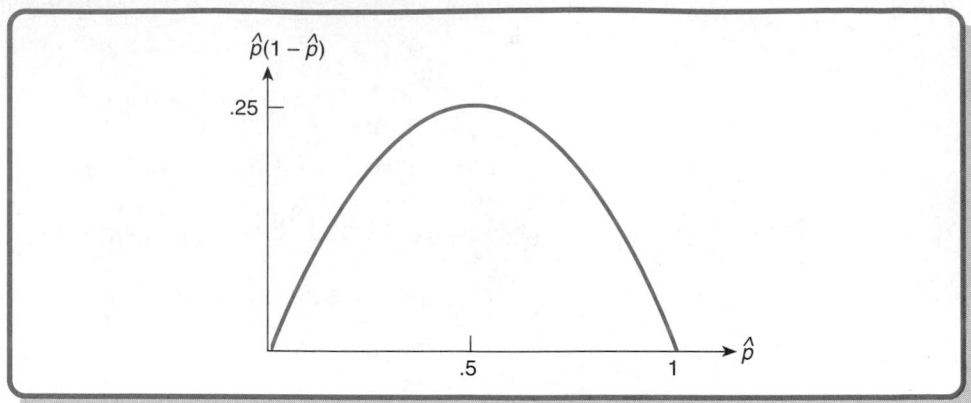

procedure we can follow here that will guarantee the accuracy (E) that we require. Look at the curve of different values of $\hat{p}(1 - \hat{p})$ in Figure 10.1. Consider these values:

$\hat{p}$	$\hat{p}(1 - \hat{p})$
.2	.16
.4	.24
.5	.25
.7	.21
.9	.09

Note that the largest value of $\hat{p}(1 - \hat{p})$ is .25.

   If we make $\hat{p}(1 - \hat{p})$ in equation 10.7 *as large as possible,* we will obtain a value of n that will result in a maximum error that is sure to be less than the specified value. So we can formulate this rule: If no prior estimate of p is available, a conservative procedure to determine the necessary sample size from equation 10.7 is to use $\hat{p} = .5$.

EXAMPLE 10.4

The insurance company underwriting the dental plan for Cassidy Electronics wishes to obtain a single sample that will estimate, to within 2% with 90% confidence, the proportion (p) of employees who would purchase the dental insurance. They have *no* prior knowledge of this proportion. Their intent is to obtain a large enough sample the first time so that they can estimate the population proportion with this much accuracy. How large a sample is required?

SOLUTION

We have no prior knowledge of p, so we use $\hat{p} = .5$ in equation 10.7 to obtain a sample size of

$$n = \frac{(1.645)^2\,(.5)(.5)}{(.02)^2} + 1 = 1692.3$$

   To obtain an estimate of p with a maximum error of $E = .02$, we will need a sample size of $n = 1693$ employees. With a sample of this size, we can safely say that the point estimate, $\hat{p}$, will be within 2% of the actual value of p, with 90% confidence (however, this is a very large sample).

EXERCISES 10.1–10.15

UNDERSTANDING THE MECHANICS

.05

10.1 Construct 95% confidence intervals on the proportion for the following values of n and x, where n is the number of observations and x is the number of people having a specified attribute.

a. $n = 15$ and $x = 7$
b. $n = 20$ and $x = 11$
c. $n = 30$ and $x = 15$
d. $n = 50$ and $x = 25$

10.2 In each situation, determine whether the sample size is large enough to conclude that the Z statistic is appropriate to use in a confidence interval.

    a. $n = 12$, $\hat{p} = .6$
    b. $n = 20$, $\hat{p} = .45$
    c. $n = 100$, $\hat{p} = .98$
    d. $n = 200$, $\hat{p} = .98$
    e. $n = 500$, $\hat{p} = .98$
    f. $n = 15$, $\hat{p} = .50$

10.3 A pollster wants to determine the necessary sample size to estimate p with a specified maximum error, E, and a confidence level of 95%. Find this sample size assuming that a prior estimate of the proportion, $\hat{p}$, is known.

    a. $\hat{p} = .4$ and $E = .05$
    b. $\hat{p} = .2$ and $E = .1$
    c. $\hat{p} = .72$ and $E = .08$

APPLYING THE NEW CONCEPTS

10.4 According to a poll by Crowne Plaza Hotels and Resorts, 11.1% of the men that travel on business and 33.3% of the women that travel on business usually bring a friend or spouse.

(Source: Adapted from *USA Today*, "Men vs. Women: Business Travel Difference," October 27, 1998, p. 1B.)

    a. Construct a 90% confidence interval for the percent of men that bring a friend or spouse assuming that the sample size was 9. Use Table A.8. (Hint: Obtain the value of x in Table A.8 by multiplying the percentage by the sample size and rounding to the nearest integer.)
    b. Construct a 90% confidence interval for the percent of women that bring a friend or spouse, assuming that the sample size was 9. Use Table A.8.
    c. Find the confidence interval in part (a), assuming a sample size of 90. Compare the length of the confidence interval to that obtained in part (a).
    d. Find the confidence interval in part (b), assuming a sample size of 90. Compare the length of the confidence interval to that obtained in part (b).

10.5 An investment firm surveyed 18 randomly selected economists. The survey found that 13 of them felt that the economy of the United States would not slip into a recession for at least a year. Use Table A.8 to construct 90% and 95% confidence intervals for the percentage of economists who believe that a recession will not occur in the United States for at least a year.

10.6 A math workshop will be offered only if the student demand is sufficiently high. What is the required sample size necessary to estimate with 90% confidence the proportion of students who would register for the workshop if we specify a value of .03 for the maximum error, E?

10.7 In Exercise 10.6, if a previous study indicated that the proportion of students who would register for the workshop was .968, estimate the necessary sample size for a maximum error, E, of 3%.

10.8 Winthrop Boat Lines is exploring the possibility of offering a ferry service between the cities of Patna and Madura, provided there is sufficient demand to make it feasible. The firm randomly interviewed 210 commuters from the two cities, and 146 of them indicated they would patronize the ferry service instead of the present bus service. Estimate the population proportion p of commuters from the two cities who would prefer the ferry service. Construct a 95% confidence interval for p.

10.9 In Exercise 10.8, if the maximum error is $E = .01$, estimate the necessary sample size at the 95% confidence level. Use the value obtained in Exercise 10.8 for the estimate of p.

10.10 About 2.8 million people are paid from the public purse at all levels of government across Canada. That was the average for the first quarter of 1998, according to data from Statistics Canada's Public Institutions Division show. The total includes all federal, provincial, and municipal workers, from mandarins to office cleaners, the military, crown corporation, and government business enterprise staffers, nurses, local police and fire personnel, teachers, public transit workers and on to drivers who chauffeur politicians around. It comes to about 18 percent of the labor force. Suppose that an economist wished to estimate the proportion of public employees in the Toronto area.

(Adapted from *The Toronto Star*, "2.8 Million Jobs Paid Out of Taxes," July 3, 1998, News section, p. 1.)

    a. What is an estimate of the sample size required to estimate the proportion of public employees in the Toronto area to within .01 with 99% confidence?
    b. How would the required sample size change if the estimate of the proportion in part (a) is to be within .005?

10.11 A manufacturer of microcomputers purchases electronic chips from a supplier that claims its chips are defective only 5% of the time. Determine the sample size that would be required to estimate the true proportion of defective chips if we wanted our estimate, $\hat{p}$, to be within 1.25% of the true proportion, with 99% confidence.

10.12 Congressional elections, midterm between presidential elections are considered to be important by both parties to maintain control of the House and Senate. The party in the White House during the midterm elections usually loses House seats. A 1998 October Gallup poll revealed that among likely voters, 49% would vote Republican. The margin of error was reported to be 4%. Assuming that the confidence level is 95%, approximate the number of voters that were sampled in the Gallup poll.

(Source: *USA Today*, "Poll Finds Parties Are in Dead Heat," Oct 27, 1998, p. 1A.)

10.13 Pacific of Lynnwood, Washington, distributes baseball cards featuring major league baseball players in uniform to retail stores. However, Major League Baseball Properties, Inc., (MLBP) has sued Pacific because their team logos and uniforms were being printed on the baseball cards without their permission. To convince the judge in the lawsuit, MLBP conducted a survey of 228 people in 12 shopping malls and found that 34% of those interviewed believed that Pacific had the blessings of MLBP from the way that Pacific was marketing the cards.

(Source: *The Wall Street Journal*, "Judge Flips Baseball-Card Case Straight out of His Courtroom," May 15, 1998, p. B1.)

    a. What is a 90% confidence interval on the proportion of buyers who believe that Pacific had the blessings of MLBP to print the team logos and uniforms?
    b. For a 90% confidence interval on the proportion of buyers who believe that Pacific had the blessings of MLBP, find the required sample size for a maximum error, E, of 4%?
    c. What do you think the confidence interval would need to look like to convince the judge that most of the baseball card buyers thought that Pacific had the blessings of MLBP (when Pacific really did not) and to convince the judge that Pacific was using marketing practices that misled the consumer?

USING THE COMPUTER

10.14 As the maximum error in estimating the proportion increases, the required sample size for estimating p with a fixed confidence level decreases. Put the values of .02, .025, .03, .035, .04, .045, .05, .055, .06, .065, and .07 in column A of a spreadsheet. Put the value of "1.96" in cell C1. In cell B1, type in "=(\$C\$1^2)*(0.5)*(1-0.5)/A1^2" and drag down to cell B11. This is the formula for the sample size when the confidence level is 95%, and no prior estimate of the proportion is available. The plot of the values in columns A and B should look like the graph presented below. Do a "what if" analysis and see how the graph changes when 90% and 99% confidence levels are used.

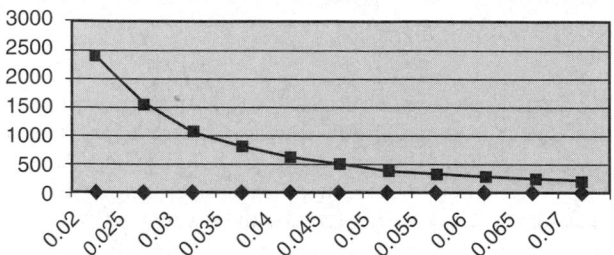

10.15 **[DATA SET EX10-15]** *Variable description:*

Error: Coded values of 0s and 1s for no error and error found, respectively

An internal auditor at a manufacturing plant needs to estimate the proportion of invoices that are in error. A random sample of 100 invoices is selected with an error being recorded as a 1, and a 0 indicating no error.

a. Order the 0s and 1s in the variable Error. What is the estimate of the proportion? What is the estimated standard error of $\hat{p}$?

b. In Excel, click on **Tools ➤ Data Analysis ➤ Descriptive Statistics.** Do your estimates agree with the output for the mean and standard error?

c. Compute a 95% confidence interval on the proportion of invoices in error using the calculations in part (a).

d. From the KGP Data Analysis menu, find a 95% confidence interval for the proportion. Compare this confidence interval to that obtained in part (c).

10.2 HYPOTHESIS TESTING FOR A POPULATION PROPORTION

How can you statistically reject a statement such as, at least 60% of all heavy smokers will contract a serious lung or heart ailment before age 65? Perhaps someone merely took a wild guess at the value of 60%, and it is your job to gather evidence that will either shoot down this claim or let it stand if there is insufficient evidence to conclude that this percentage actually is less than 60%. We set up hypotheses and test them much as we did before, only now we are concerned about a population proportion, p, rather than the mean or standard deviation of a particular population.

HYPOTHESIS TESTING USING A SMALL SAMPLE

Because confidence intervals can be used to perform a test of hypothesis, we will use Table A.8 to conduct such a test. Table A.8 contains sample sizes of $n = 5$ to 20 and $\alpha = .05$ and .10. If the sample size exceeds 20 and np and $n(1 - p)$ are both greater than 5, the large-sample approximation will provide an accurate test. For sample sizes contained in Table A.8, use the procedure outlined in the accompanying box.

HYPOTHESIS TESTING (SMALL SAMPLE; n BETWEEN 5 AND 20)

Two-Tailed Test

$$H_0: p = p_0$$

$$H_a: p \neq p_0$$

1. Obtain the $(1 - \alpha) \cdot 100\%$ confidence interval from Table A.8; that is, (p_L, p_U), using $x =$ the observed number of successes.
2. Reject H_0 if p_0 does not lie between p_L and p_U.
3. Fail to reject H_0 if $p_L \leq p_0 \leq p_U$.

> **One-Tailed Test**
>
> | H_0: $p \le p_0$ | H_0: $p \ge p_0$ |
> |---|---|
> | H_a: $p > p_0$ | H_a: $p < p_0$ |
>
> 1. Obtain the $(1 - 2\alpha) \cdot 100\%$ confidence interval from Table A.8; that is, (p_L, p_U), using $x =$ the observed number of successes.
> 2. Reject H_0 if $p_0 < p_L$.
> 3. Fail to reject H_0 if $p_0 \ge p_L$.
>
> 1. Obtain the $(1 - 2\alpha) \cdot 100\%$ confidence interval from Table A.8; that is, (p_L, p_U), using $x =$ the observed number of successes.
> 2. Reject H_0 if $p_0 > p_U$.
> 3. Fail to reject H_0 if $p_0 \le p_U$.

Notice that for a one-tailed test, we *double* α when finding the confidence interval for p from Table A.8. For example, if $\alpha = .05$, then $2\alpha = .10$, and so we retrieve a 90% confidence interval from the table. As a result, this particular binomial table can be used only when $\alpha = .025$ or $.05$ for a one-tailed test.

EXAMPLE 10.5

In Example 10.1, suppose that the company interested in the Beagle microcomputers will purchase them if Beagle's claim that the proportion, p, of all Beagle computers that can survive these cold temperatures is greater than .75 (75%) can be shown to be true. Do the data support this claim using $\alpha = .05$? $p+\ est\hat{i}mate = 12/15 = .8$

SOLUTION

The claim under investigation goes into the alternative hypothesis. The appropriate hypotheses are

$$H_0: p \le .75 \qquad \text{and} \qquad H_a: p > .75 \qquad one-tailed$$

We observed, in the sample of 15 computers, $x = 12$ successes (computers that survived). Because $\alpha = .05$, we double this $(2\alpha = .10)$ and refer to Table A.8 for a 90% confidence interval for p when $n = 15$, $x = 12$. This confidence interval is:

$$(p_L, p_U) = (.560, .943)$$

We will reject H_0 provided $p_0 = .75$ lies to the left of p_L. Because .75 is greater than $p_L = .560$, we fail to reject H_0.

Based on the evidence gathered from this sample, we cannot demonstrate that p is greater than the required 75%. Notice that we are not *accepting* H_0—we simply *fail to reject* it. This means that the point estimate $\hat{p} = 12/15 = .8$ is not enough larger than .75 to justify the claim made in H_a. The fact that $\hat{p}$ exceeds .75 may be due to the sampling error that is possible when using a sample statistic ($\hat{p}$) to infer something about a population parameter (p).

COMMENTS

In the same sense that confidence intervals for a proportion, p, are typically very wide, it is usually very difficult to obtain a significant result (reject H_0) when using a small sample. The moral mentioned in the confidence interval section applies here as well: *To obtain a reasonably powerful test on a population proportion, use a large sample.*

HYPOTHESIS TESTING USING A LARGE SAMPLE

The standard five-step procedure is used for testing H_0 versus H_a when attempting to support a claim regarding a binomial parameter, p, using a large sample. The approximate standard normal random variable given by equation 10.2 is used as a test statistic for this situation.

The rejection region for this test is defined by determining the distribution of the test statistic, given that H_0 is true. This means that the unknown value of p in equation 10.2 is replaced by the value of p specified in H_0 (say, p_0). For a one-tailed test, the boundary value of p in H_0 is used. This procedure is summarized in the following box.

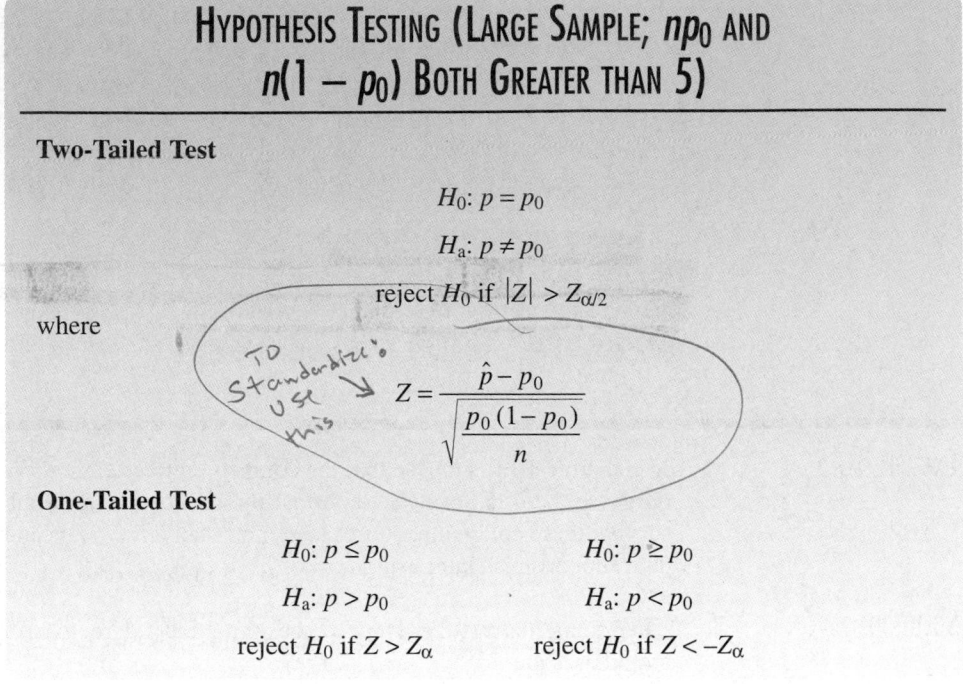

HYPOTHESIS TESTING (LARGE SAMPLE; np_0 AND $n(1 - p_0)$ BOTH GREATER THAN 5)

Two-Tailed Test

$$H_0: p = p_0$$

$$H_a: p \neq p_0$$

reject H_0 if $|Z| > Z_{\alpha/2}$

where

TO Standardize, use this →

$$Z = \frac{\hat{p} - p_0}{\sqrt{\dfrac{p_0 (1 - p_0)}{n}}}$$

One-Tailed Test

$$H_0: p \leq p_0 \qquad\qquad H_0: p \geq p_0$$

$$H_a: p > p_0 \qquad\qquad H_a: p < p_0$$

reject H_0 if $Z > Z_\alpha$ \qquad reject H_0 if $Z < -Z_\alpha$

Notice that the form of the test statistic is that used in many of the previous large sample test statistics, namely,

$$Z = \frac{\text{(point estimate)} - \text{(hypothesized value)}}{\text{(standard deviation of point estimator)}} \qquad\qquad \textbf{(10.8)}$$

EXAMPLE 10.6

In Example 10.2, we estimated the proportion of payroll checks containing a calculation error. The audit plan also specifies that a more detailed inspection of the Cassidy Electronics payroll checks be conducted if there is evidence to indicate that this proportion* exceeds .03. Using a significance level of 10%, can you conclude that the percentage of checks in error exceeds 3%?

SOLUTION

Step 1. Your hypotheses should be

$$H_0: p \leq .03$$

$$H_a: p > .03$$

Step 2. Since $np_0 = (250)(.056) = 14$ and $n(1 - p_0) = (250)(.944) = 236$ are both greater than 5, the large-sample test statistic can be used, namely,

$$Z = \frac{\hat{p} - p_0}{\sqrt{\dfrac{p_0 (1 - p_0)}{n}}} = \frac{\hat{p} - .03}{\sqrt{\dfrac{(.03)(.97)}{250}}}$$

---

* Auditing textbooks often refer to this value as the *maximum tolerable error rate* (MTER).

FIGURE 10.2

Z curve showing *p*-value for Example 10.6.

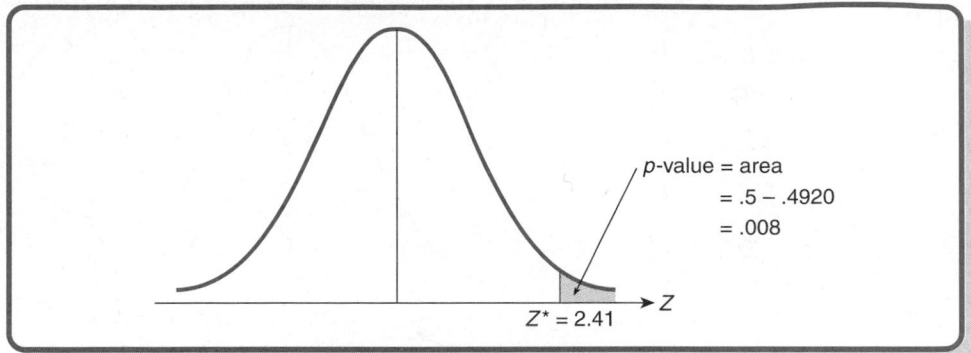

p-value = area
= .5 − .4920
= .008

$Z^* = 2.41$

Step 3. The testing procedure, using $\alpha = .10$, will be to

$$\text{reject } H_0 \text{ if } Z > Z_{.10} = 1.28$$

Step 4. Using the sample data, $\hat{p} = 14/250 = .056$, so

$$Z^* = \frac{.056 - .03}{\sqrt{\dfrac{(.03)(.97)}{250}}} = \frac{.026}{.0108} = 2.41$$

Because 2.41 > 1.28, we reject H_0 in favor of H_a.

Step 5. This sample indicates that the percentage of payroll checks in error *does* exceed 3%. In other words, at a significance level of $\alpha = .10$, the sample percentage containing an error (5.6%) *is* significantly greater than 3%, and, as a result, the alternative hypothesis is supported.

In Example 10.6, the computed test statistic was $Z^* = 2.41$. Figure 10.2 shows the Z curve and the calculated *p*-value, which is .008. Using the classical approach, because .008 is less than $\alpha = .10$, we reject H_0. If we choose to base our conclusion strictly on the *p*-value (without choosing a significance level, α), this value would be classified as "small"—it is less than .01. This means that using the classical approach, we would reject H_0 for both $\alpha = .10$ and $\alpha = .01$.

EXAMPLE 10.7

In Example 10.3, we estimated the proportion of calculators that were defective in a batch (lot). The company has determined that a good target for this defective percentage is 4%. The sample of 150 had 13 defectives. Can we conclude that the actual proportion of defective calculators is different from 4%? Use $\alpha = .05$.

SOLUTION

Step 1. We wish to see if p is *different* from 4%, so we should use a two-tailed test with hypotheses

$$H_0: p = .04$$

$$H_a: p \neq .04$$

Step 2. Here $np_0 = (150)(.04) = 6$ and $n(1 - p_0) = (150)(.96) = 144$. Both are greater than 5, so the appropriate test statistic is

$$Z = \frac{\hat{p} - p_0}{\sqrt{\dfrac{p_0(1 - p_0)}{n}}} = \frac{\hat{p} - .04}{\sqrt{\dfrac{(.04)(.96)}{150}}}$$

Step 3. With $\alpha = .05$, the test procedure of H_0 versus H_a will be to

$$\text{reject } H_0 \text{ if } |Z| > 1.96$$

FIGURE 10.3

Z curve showing *p*-value (twice the shaded area) for Example 10.7.

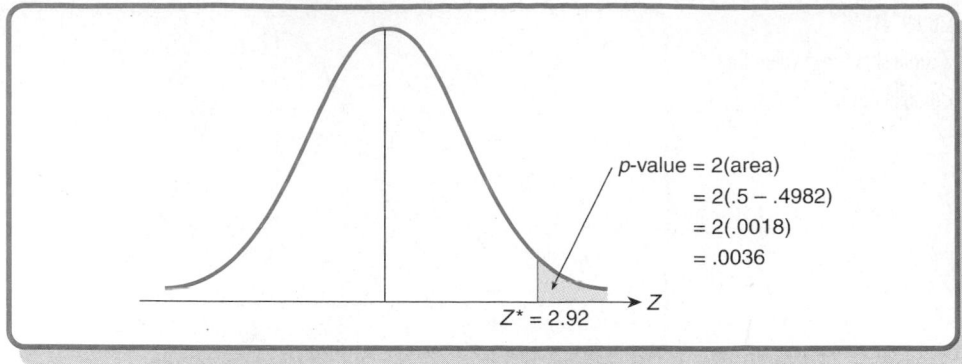

p-value = 2(area)
= 2(.5 − .4982)
= 2(.0018)
= .0036

$Z^* = 2.92$

FIGURE 10.4

Excel solution to Example 10.7 using **KGP Data Analysis ➤ Inference on Proportions ➤ One Population Proportion.**

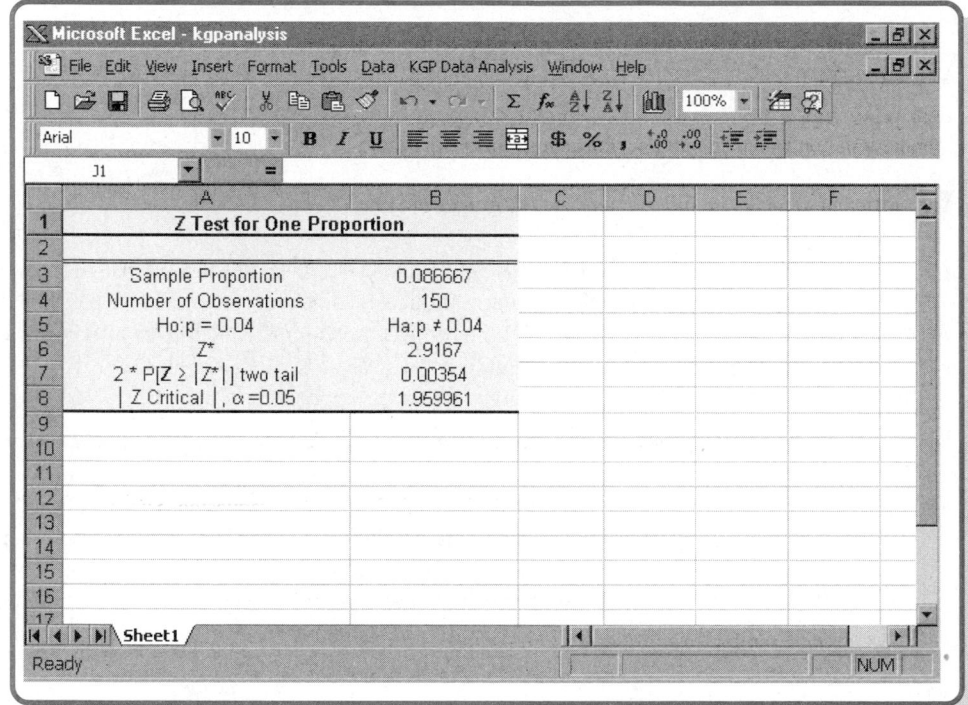

	A	B
1	**Z Test for One Proportion**	
2		
3	Sample Proportion	0.086667
4	Number of Observations	150
5	Ho:p = 0.04	Ha:p ≠ 0.04
6	Z^*	2.9167
7	2 * P[Z ≥ |Z*|] two tail	0.00354
8	| Z Critical |, α=0.05	1.959961

Step 4. Using $\hat{p} = 13/150 = .0867$,

$$Z^* = \frac{.0867 - .04}{\sqrt{\dfrac{(.04)(.96)}{150}}} = \frac{.0467}{.016} = 2.92$$

Because 2.92 > 1.96, we reject H_0.

Step 5. The company is *not* meeting their target percentage of defectives. As a reminder, because $\alpha = .05$, 5% of the time this particular test will reject H_0 when in fact it is true.

In Example 10.7, $Z^* = 2.92$. What is the *p*-value? This is a two-tailed test, so we need to *double* the right-tail area, as illustrated in Figure 10.3. So $p = 2 \cdot .0018 = .0036$. Thus, using either the classical procedure (comparing the *p*-value to $\alpha = .05$) or basing our decision strictly on the *p*-value, we reject H_0 because of this extremely small *p*-value.

An Excel solution to Example 10.7 using the macro from KGP Data Analysis is shown in Figure 10.4. To obtain this solution, click on **KGP Data Analysis ➤ Inference on Pro-**

portions ➤ **One Population Proportion.** Next, (1) enter 13 in the **Number of Successes** box; (2) enter 150 in the **Sample Size box;** (3) enter 5 in the **Alpha** box; (4) click on the box alongside **Hypothesis Test,** then on **Two-Tail Test,** and enter .04 in the **Hypothesized Value of Proportion** box; and (5) enter "A1" in the **Output Range** box. The resulting output in Figure 10.4 agrees with the previous solution. The Excel p-value in cell B7 (namely, .00354) is slightly more accurate than the one illustrated in Figure 10.3. Based on this small p-value, we conclude that the percentage of defective calculators is *not* 4%.

Exercises 10.16–10.30

Understanding the Mechanics

10.16 In each case, test the hypothesis H_0: $p = p_0$ against H_a: $p \neq p_0$ for a random sample of size n.
  a. $n = 12$, $\hat{p} = .33$, $p_0 = .25$, $\alpha = .05$
  b. $n = 20$, $\hat{p} = .40$, $p_0 = .20$, $\alpha = .10$
  c. $n = 40$, $\hat{p} = .925$, $p_0 = .75$, $\alpha = .01$
  d. $n = 100$, $\hat{p} = .08$, $p_0 = .13$, $\alpha = .05$
  e. $n = 280$, $\hat{p} = .85$, $p_0 = .87$, $\alpha = .10$

10.17 A random sample of 25 observations yielded a value of $\hat{p} = .60$. Test each of the following hypotheses and find the p-values.
  a. H_0: $p = .71$ versus H_a: $p \neq .71$
  b. H_0: $p \geq .71$ versus H_a: $p < .71$
  c. H_0: $p \leq .51$ versus H_a: $p > .51$

Applying the New Concepts

10.18 An official for a computer firm was told by an independent source that 20% of the employees of the computer firm perceived that there was sex discrimination in the salary structure of the company. A quick random survey by the official of 18 employees found that 3 of the employees thought there was sex discrimination in the salary structure of the company. Is there sufficient evidence in the official's survey to indicate that the figure of 20% given by the independent source is in error? Conduct a hypothesis test using a significance level of .10 and using Table A.8.

10.19 Using the data in Exercise 10.5, test the hypothesis that the proportion of economists who believe that a recession will not occur in the United States for at least a year is more than 50%, using a .05 level of significance. Use Table A.8.

10.20 There are about 87 million households in the United States. In 1970, about 71% of the households were occupied by married couples. In the last 15 years, the trend toward living alone has accelerated. One market researcher believes that at present the proportion of households occupied by married couples is 58%. A random sample of 20 households reveals that 12 are occupied by married couples. At a significance level of 10%, are you in a position to contradict the market researcher and say that this person is probably wrong?

10.21 In order for $np > 5$ and $n(1 - p) > 5$, how large must n be if $p = .03$?

10.22 A random sample of 40 coffee drinkers was asked to taste-test a new coffee brand. The responses follow, with 1 representing "like the brand," 2 representing "indifferent to the brand," and 3 representing "do not like the brand." Do the data support the conclusion that more than half of the coffee drinkers like the new coffee brand? Use a .10 significance level.

1	3	1	3	3	1	2	1	1	1
1	1	1	2	1	1	3	1	2	1
1	2	1	1	1	2	1	1	3	2
1	1	2	1	3	1	3	1	2	1

10.23 In January of 1998, American Airlines created the AAdvantage Executive Platinum program for its frequent flier passengers. Membership requires that a customer fly 100,000 miles a year. American's move is an example of airlines focusing on their best and highest paying customers. This elite level will allow members to reserve an upgrade to first class 100 hours before their flights versus 72 hours previously allowed for AAdvantage members. Frequent Flyer magazine previously found that 71% of its surveyed readers had difficulty getting upgrades when requested. Suppose that Frequent Flyer takes another survey after the Executive Platinum program has been in effect for a year and from a sample of 200 readers, 125 readers said that they had difficulty getting upgrades when requested.

(Adapted from *The Wall Street Journal*, "American Adds Perks to Frequent Flying," January 21, 1998, p. 2B.)

  a. Do the data from the new survey support the belief that the percentage of readers who have had difficulty in upgrading to first class is less than 71%? Use a .10 significance level.
  b. List any assumptions that you made about the data in testing the hypothesis in part (a).

10.24 A manager at National Insurance believes that out of the total number of automobile-accident claims settled in a particular month, there are more claims related to speeding by the driver than there are claims that are not related to speeding. From a random sample of 75 claims, 40 were found to be associated with speeding. Test the manager's belief. Use a significance level of .05.

10.25 A consumer group would like to determine the proportion of dealers who charge more than $450 monthly for a 36-month lease on a BMW 323i. The consumer group found a 90% confidence interval for the proportion of dealers in the midwest United States to be 24% to 38%. Suppose that the consumer group wished to find a 90% confidence interval to estimate the proportion to within 4% with 90% confidence. What sample size is necessary?

(Adapted from *The Wall Street Journal*, "Drive Buys," Oct 25, 1998, p. W7.)

10.26 An instructor believes that of the students who take a certain course, there are more students who have not taken the prerequisites for the course than students who have taken the prerequisites. The instructor randomly selected 70 students and found that only 30 students had taken the prerequisites for the course. Do these data support the instructor's belief? Use a significance level of .10.

10.27 Based on the *p*-value for Exercise 10.26, would you reject the null hypothesis at the .01 level?

10.28 Wal-Mart developed a strategy to attract Christmas shoppers. It broadcasted a live concert by country superstar Garth Brooks in its 2,390 stores during December 1998. Nationwide, Wal-Mart's directors believe that 40% of its shoppers are mothers with children. Suppose that managers for stores in the Houston area believe that this figure is different for the Houston area. A random sample of 300 shoppers in the Houston area revealed 135 shoppers were mothers with children.

(Adapted from *The Wall Street Journal*, "Wal-Mart's Garth-Quake May Spur Sales," Nov 2, 1998, p. B1.)

   a. Find a 95% confidence interval for estimating the proportion of shoppers that are mothers with children.

   b. Test at the .05 significance level that the percentage of shoppers that are mothers with children differs from the national proportion. How can the confidence interval in part (a) be used to test this?

Using the Computer

10.29 [DATA SET EX10-29] *Variable description:*

WatchHomShp: A *Yes* indicates that a family watches a televised home shopping program, and a *No* indicates that they do not

A marketing agency wishes to determine if more than 50% of the families in the Chicago metropolitan area have ever watched a televised home shopping program. A random sample of 100 adults was selected through telephone interviews. A *Yes* reply indicated that the family has watched the program, and a *No* reply indicated that the family has never watched the program. These are the values for the variable WatchHomShp. Test to determine whether there is sufficient evidence to conclude that the true proportion is greater than 50%. Use the *p*-value to support your conclusion.

10.30 [DATA SET EX10-30] *Variable description:*

ReadReport: A 1 indicates that a shareholder reads the annual report, and a 0 indicates that the shareholder does not

The vice president of a public utilities company believes that less than 60% of the shareholders of the company read the annual report. From a random sample of 200 shareholders, a 1 or a 0 is listed for the variable ReadReport. Test the vice president's belief. Use a .01 significance level.

10.3 Comparing Two Population Proportions (Large, Independent Samples)

Consider the following questions:

> *Is the divorce rate higher in California than it is in New York?*
>
> *Is there a higher rate of lung cancer among cigarette smokers than there is among nonsmokers?*
>
> *Is there any difference in the proportion of engines rebuilt by Engine Masters that fail during the one-year warranty period and the proportion of engines rebuilt by Freed Motors that fail during the warranty period?*

These questions are concerned with proportions from *two* populations. Our method of estimating these proportions will be exactly as it was for one population. We simply have two of everything—two populations, two samples, two estimates, and so on. In this section, it is assumed that the two samples are obtained *independently*.

For example, consider the question concerning the proportion of engines that fail during the warranty period. Population 1 is all engines rebuilt by Engine Masters, with p_1 = proportion of all engines rebuilt by Engine Masters that fail during the warranty period, n_1 = sample size for the Engine Masters engines, and x_1 = number of engines in the Engine Masters sample that fail. Population 2 is all engines rebuilt by Freed Motors, where p_2, n_2, and x_2 are the corresponding values for this population.

Define a "success" to be that an engine fails during the warranty period. (Keep in mind that "success" is merely a label for the trait you are interested in. It need not be a desirable trait.) Our unbiased point estimator of p_1 will be as before:

$$\hat{p}_1 = \frac{\text{observed number of successes in the sample}}{\text{sample size}}$$

$$= \frac{\text{number of engines in the Engine Masters sample}}{\text{that fail during the warranty period}}{n_1}$$

That is, the unbiased point estimator of p_1 is

$$\hat{p}_1 = \frac{x_1}{n_1} \qquad (10.9)$$

Similarly, the unbiased point estimator of p_2, obtained from the second sample, is

$$\hat{p}_2 = \frac{x_2}{n_2} \qquad (10.10)$$

For the two-population case, the parameter of interest will be the *difference* between the two population proportions, $p_1 - p_2$. The next section discusses a method of estimating $p_1 - p_2$ by using a point estimate along with a corresponding confidence interval.

CONFIDENCE INTERVAL FOR $p_1 - p_2$ (LARGE, INDEPENDENT SAMPLES)

The logical estimator of $p_1 - p_2$ is $\hat{p} - \hat{p}_2$, the difference between the sample estimators. What kind of random variable is $\hat{p}_1 - \hat{p}_2$? We are dealing with large, independent samples (where $n_1 \hat{p}_1$, $n_1(1 - \hat{p}_1)$, $n_2 \hat{p}_2$, and $n_2(1 - \hat{p}_2)$ are each larger than 5), so it follows that $\hat{p}_1 - \hat{p}_2$ is (approximately) a normal random variable with

$$\text{mean} = p_1 - p_2$$

and

$$\text{standard deviation} = \sqrt{\frac{p_1(1-p_1)}{n_1} + \frac{p_2(1-p_2)}{n_2}}$$

In Section 10.1, we observed that $\hat{p}_1$ is a sample mean, where the sample consists of observations that are either a 1 (a particular event occurred) or a 0 (this event did not occur). Because the two samples are obtained independently, the results extend to this situation, leading to the approximate normal distribution for $\hat{p}_1 - \hat{p}_2$. Since $\hat{p}_1$ and $\hat{p}_2$ are unbiased estimators of p_1 and p_2, respectively, the mean of the estimator $\hat{p}_1 - \hat{p}_2$ is $p_1 - p_2$; that is, $\hat{p}_1 - \hat{p}_2$ is an unbiased estimator of $p_1 - p_2$. Notice that the variance of $\hat{p}_1 - \hat{p}_2$ is obtained by *adding* the variance of $\hat{p}_1$, or $p_1(1 - p_1)/n_1$, to the variance of $\hat{p}_2$, or $p_2(1 - p_2)/n_2$.

To derive a confidence interval for $p_1 - p_2$, we must estimate the unknown population parameters, p_1 and p_2, using the corresponding sample estimates, $\hat{p}_1$ and $\hat{p}_2$. The same argument used to derive the one-population estimated standard error in equation 10.4 can be used here to derive the estimated standard deviation of $\hat{p}_1 - \hat{p}_2$ (that is, the **standard error of $\hat{p}_1 - \hat{p}_2$**). This estimated standard error is

$$s_{\hat{p}_1 - \hat{p}_2} = \sqrt{\frac{\hat{p}_1(1-\hat{p}_1)}{n_1 - 1} + \frac{\hat{p}_2(1-\hat{p}_2)}{n_2 - 1}} \qquad (10.11)$$

The resulting confidence interval for $p_1 - p_2$ using large samples [$n_1 \hat{p}_1$, $n_1(1 - \hat{p}_1)$, $n_2 \hat{p}_2$, and $n_2(1 - \hat{p}_2)$ each greater than 5] is

$$(\hat{p}_1 - \hat{p}_2) - Z_{\alpha/2} \sqrt{\frac{\hat{p}_1(1-\hat{p}_1)}{n_1 - 1} + \frac{\hat{p}_2(1-\hat{p}_2)}{n_2 - 1}}$$

$$\text{to} \quad (\hat{p}_1 - \hat{p}_2) + Z_{\alpha/2} \sqrt{\frac{\hat{p}_1(1-\hat{p}_1)}{n_1 - 1} + \frac{\hat{p}_2(1-\hat{p}_2)}{n_2 - 1}} \qquad (10.12)$$

where $\hat{p}_1 = x_1/n_1$ and $\hat{p}_2 = x_2/n_2$ are the sample proportions. Observe that the construction of this confidence interval was the "usual" procedure employing Table A.4 and described in equation 10.3.

EXAMPLE 10.8

Of a random sample of 100 rebuilt engines from Engine Masters (population 1), 28 failed within the 12-month warranty period. A second sample, obtained independent of the first, consisted of 150 engines rebuilt by Freed Motors (population 2), 48 of which failed during the 12-month warranty period. Both sets of engines were subjected to the same weather conditions, engine stress, and maintenance program. Construct a 90% confidence interval for $p_1 - p_2$.

SOLUTION

We have $\hat{p}_1 = 28/100 = .28$ and $\hat{p}_2 = 48/150 = .32$. Also, $Z_{\alpha/2} = Z_{.05} = 1.645$, using Table A.4. The resulting confidence interval for $p_1 - p_2$ is

$$(.28 - .32) - 1.645\sqrt{\frac{(.28)(.72)}{99} + \frac{(.32)(.68)}{149}}$$

$$\text{to}\quad (.28 - .32) + 1.645\sqrt{\frac{(.28)(.72)}{99} + \frac{(.32)(.68)}{149}}$$

$$= -.04 - .097 \quad \text{to} \quad -.04 + .097$$

$$= -.137 \quad \text{to} \quad .057$$

This confidence interval leaves us unable to conclude that either manufacturer produces a better engine. We are 90% confident that the percentage of Engine Masters engines failing during the warranty period is between 13.7% *lower* and 5.7% *higher* than for the Freed Motors engines.

EXAMPLE 10.9

The Redican Corporation manufactures 1-quart metal cans to hold canned vegetable juice. A can is *nonconforming* if it is out of round or has a leak in the side weld. The cans are produced during two shifts, shift 1 (the day shift) and shift 2 (the night shift). The quality supervisor suspects that the proportion of nonconforming cans produced during the day shift (p_1) is *lower* than that for the night shift (p_2), since the day shift has better qualified workers. To investigate this, random samples of 500 cans were obtained from each shift. The results were as follows. Of the $n_1 = 500$ cans from the day shift, $x_1 = 70$ were nonconforming, and of the $n_2 = 500$ cans from the night shift, $x_2 = 110$ were nonconforming. Determine a 95% confidence interval for $p_1 - p_2$.

SOLUTION

The proportion estimates are

$$\hat{p}_1 = \frac{70}{500} = .14 \qquad \hat{p}_2 = \frac{110}{500} = .22$$

The 95% confidence interval for $p_1 - p_2$ is

$$(.14 - .22) - 1.96\sqrt{\frac{(.14)(.86)}{499} + \frac{(.22)(.78)}{499}}$$

$$\text{to}\quad (.14 - .22) + 1.96\sqrt{\frac{(.14)(.86)}{499} + \frac{(.22)(.78)}{499}}$$

$$= -.08 - .047 \quad \text{to} \quad -.08 + .047$$

$$= -.127 \quad \text{to} \quad -.033$$

So we are 95% confident that (1) our estimate of the difference in proportions (shift 1 minus shift 2), namely, $\hat{p}_1 - \hat{p}_2 = -.08$, is within 4.7% of the actual value, and (2) the proportion of nonconforming cans during shift 1 is between 3.3% and 12.7% *lower* than for shift 2.

Choosing the Samples Sizes (Two Populations)

In Chapter 9, we discussed how to select samples from two populations when the desired accuracy of the point estimate of the difference between two population means is specified—this is the maximum error, E. If E is 10 pounds, for instance, then what sample sizes (n_1 and n_2) are necessary for the point estimate of $\mu_1 - \mu_2$ (namely, $\bar{X}_1 - \bar{X}_2$) to be within 10 pounds of the actual value, with 95% (of whatever) confidence? Using the results contained in Appendix B at the end of the text, values of n_1 and n_2 were provided in Chapter 9 to minimize the total sample size, $n_1 + n_2$, for this specific value of E.

We encounter a similar situation when dealing with two population proportions, p_1 and p_2. If a maximum error of $E = .10$, for instance, is specified, then the question of interest is, what sample sizes (n_1 and n_2) are necessary for the point estimate of $p_1 - p_2$ (namely, $\hat{p}_1 - \hat{p}_2$) to be within .10 of the actual value, with 95% (or whatever) confidence?

The maximum error, E, always is the amount that you *add to* and *subtract from* the point estimate when determining a confidence interval. When dealing with two proportions, E is

$$E = Z_{\alpha/2} \sqrt{\frac{\hat{p}_1 (1 - \hat{p}_1)}{n_1 - 1} + \frac{\hat{p}_2 (1 - \hat{p}_2)}{n_2 - 1}} \qquad \text{(10.13)}$$

To evaluate this expression, you will need estimates of p_1 and p_2. You have two options. If you have previously obtained small samples from these two populations, you can use the resulting sample estimates $\hat{p}_1$ and $\hat{p}_2$. The purpose then will be to extend these samples to obtain better accuracy in the point estimate, $\hat{p}_1 - \hat{p}_2$. If no information regarding p_1 and p_2 is available, then you can use the conservative approach discussed in Section 10.1 by letting $\hat{p}_1 = \hat{p}_2 = .5$.

By applying the results of Appendix B to this situation, the sample sizes n_1 and n_2 that minimize the total sample size $n_1 + n_2$ are given by

$$n_1 = \frac{Z_{\alpha/2}^2 (A + B)}{E^2} + 1 \qquad \text{(10.14)}$$

$$n_2 = \frac{Z_{\alpha/2}^2 (C + B)}{E^2} + 1 \qquad \text{(10.15)}$$

where

$$A = \hat{p}_1 (1 - \hat{p}_1)$$

$$B = \sqrt{\hat{p}_1 \hat{p}_2 (1 - \hat{p}_1)(1 - \hat{p}_2)}$$

$$C = \hat{p}_2 (1 - \hat{p}_2)$$

To determine A, B, and C, the estimates $\hat{p}_1$ and $\hat{p}_2$ can be obtained by using one of the two options described in the previous paragraph.

Example 10.10

Using the situation described in Example 10.9, determine what sample sizes are necessary for the estimate of the difference between the two proportions to be within .03 of the actual difference, with 99% confidence, if (1) the results from Example 10.9 are available, and (2) no sample information is available.

Solution 1

The specified maximum error is $E = .03$. Sample data have been collected regarding these proportions, so we use the corresponding estimates to determine the sample sizes necessary to obtain this degree of accuracy. Using Table A.4, $Z_{\alpha/2} = Z_{.005} = 2.575$. Here, $\hat{p}_1 = .14$ and $\hat{p}_2 = .22$. Consequently,

$$A = \hat{p}_1 (1 - \hat{p}_1)$$

$$= .1204$$

$$B = \sqrt{\hat{p}_1 \hat{p}_2 (1 - \hat{p}_1)(1 - \hat{p}_2)}$$

$$= .1437$$

$$C = \hat{p}_2 (1 - \hat{p}_2)$$

$$= .1716$$

To obtain the *smallest possible* total sample size for the required accuracy, the two sample sizes should be

$$n_1 = \frac{(2.575)^2 (.1204 + .1437)}{(.03)^2} + 1 \approx 1947$$

(remember—always round up) and

$$n_2 = \frac{(2.575)^2 (.1716 + .1437)}{(.03)^2} + 1 \approx 2324$$

providing a total sample size of $n_1 + n_2 = 4271$ cans.

SOLUTION 2

If no prior estimates of p_1 and p_2 are available, using $\hat{p}_1 = \hat{p}_2 = .5$ will result in sample sizes, n_1 and n_2 that will provide a maximum error *no larger than* the specified value of $E = .03$. Here, $A = (.5)(.5) = .25$. Similarly, $B = C = .25$, so

$$\dot{n}_1 = n_2 = \frac{(2.575)^2 (.25 + .25)}{(.03)^2} + 1 \approx 3685$$

Consequently, a total sample size of $n_1 + n_2 = 7370$ cans will be necessary for $\hat{p}_1 - \hat{p}_2$ to be within .03 of the actual value of $p_1 - p_2$, with 99% confidence.

HYPOTHESIS TESTING FOR p_1 AND p_2 (LARGE, INDEPENDENT SAMPLES)

Suppose that a recent report stated that, based on a sample of 500 people, 35% of all cigarette smokers had at some time in their lives developed a particular fatal disease. On the other hand, 25% of the nonsmokers in the sample acquired the disease. Can we conclude from this sample that, because $\hat{p}_1 = .35 > \hat{p}_2 = .25$, the proportion ($p_1$) of all smokers who will acquire the disease exceeds the proportion (p_2) for nonsmokers? In other words, is $\hat{p}_1$ *significantly* larger than $\hat{p}_2$? After all, even if $p_1 = p_2$, there is a 50–50 chance that $\hat{p}_1$ will be larger than $\hat{p}_2$, because for large samples, the distribution of $\hat{p}_1 - \hat{p}_2$ is approximately a bell-shaped (normal) curve centered at $p_1 - p_2$, which, if $p_1 = p_2$, would be zero.

Are the results of the sample significant, or are they due simply to the sampling error that is always present when estimating from a sample? Your alternative hypothesis can be that two proportions are *different* (a two-tailed test) or that one *exceeds* the other (a one-tailed test). As before, we will assume that the two random samples are obtained *independently*. The possible hypotheses are these:

FOR A TWO-TAILED TEST

$H_0: p_1 = p_2$

$H_a: p_1 \neq p_2$

FOR A ONE-TAILED TEST

$$H_0: p_1 \leq p_2 \qquad H_0: p_1 \geq p_2$$
$$\text{or}$$
$$H_a: p_1 > p_2 \qquad H_a: p_1 < p_2$$

One possible test statistic to use here would be the standard normal (Z) statistic that was used to derive a confidence interval for $p_1 - p_2$, namely,

[handwritten: TO Standardize Use this One]

$$Z = \frac{\hat{p}_1 - \hat{p}_2}{\sqrt{\dfrac{\hat{p}_1(1-\hat{p}_1)}{n_1 - 1} + \dfrac{\hat{p}_2(1-\hat{p}_2)}{n_2 - 1}}} \qquad (10.16)$$

In previous tests of hypothesis, we always examined the distribution of the test statistic when H_0 was *true*. For a one-tailed test, we assumed the boundary condition of H_0, which in this case is $p_1 = p_2$. Because of this, whenever we obtained a value of the test statistic in one of the tails, our decision was to reject H_0 because this value would be very unusual if H_0 were true. This reasoning was used for test statistics that followed a Z, t, χ^2, or F distribution.

We use the same approach here. If $p_1 = p_2 = p$ (for example), we can improve the test statistic in equation 10.16. For this situation, p is the proportion of successes in the combined population. Our best estimate of p is the proportion of successes in the *combined sample*. So define

[handwritten: Even though Bottom of page say to use this) one]

$$\bar{p} = \frac{x_1 + x_2}{n_1 + n_2}$$

Thus, assuming $p_1 = p_2$, $\hat{p}_1 - \hat{p}_2$ is approximately a normal random variable with

$$\text{mean} = p_1 - p_2 = 0$$

and

$$\text{standard deviation} = \sqrt{\frac{p_1(1-p_1)}{n_1} + \frac{p_2(1-p_2)}{n_2}}$$

$$\approx \sqrt{\frac{\bar{p}(1-\bar{p})}{n_1} + \frac{\bar{p}(1-\bar{p})}{n_2}}$$

The resulting test statistic for p_1 versus p_2 (large, independent samples; $n_1\hat{p}_1$, $n_1(1-\hat{p}_1)$, $n_2\hat{p}_2$, and $n_2(1-\hat{p}_2)$ are each greater than 5) is

[handwritten: TO Standardize, use this]

$$Z = \frac{\hat{p}_1 - \hat{p}_2}{\sqrt{\dfrac{\bar{p}(1-\bar{p})}{n_1} + \dfrac{\bar{p}(1-\bar{p})}{n_2}}} \qquad (10.17)$$

where

$$\hat{p}_1 = \frac{x_1}{n_1} \qquad \hat{p}_2 = \frac{x_2}{n_2} \qquad \bar{p} = \frac{x_1 + x_2}{n_1 + n_2}$$

Observe that the form of this test statistic is the same as for the single-population case described in equation 10.8. The test procedure is the standard routine when using the Z distribution.*

---

* As a final word here, always use the Z statistic in equation 10.17 to test two proportions. Equation 10.16 is included for discussion purposes only in this section and should never be used as the test statistic.

FOR A TWO-TAILED TEST

$$H_0: p_1 = p_2$$

$$H_a: p_1 \neq p_2$$

$$\text{reject } H_0 \text{ if } |Z| > Z_{\alpha/2}$$

where Z is defined in equation 10.17.

FOR A ONE-TAILED TEST

$$H_0: p_1 \leq p_2 \qquad\qquad H_0: p_1 \geq p_2$$

$$H_a: p_1 > p_2 \qquad \text{or} \qquad H_a: p_1 < p_2$$

$$\text{reject } H_0 \text{ if } Z > Z_\alpha \qquad\qquad \text{reject } H_0 \text{ if } Z < -Z_\alpha$$

EXAMPLE 10.11

Using the engine failure data from Example 10.8, determine whether there is any difference between the proportion of Engine Masters engines (population 1) and the proportion of Freed Motors engines (population 2) that failed in the one-year warranty period. Let $\alpha = .10$.

SOLUTION

The five-step procedure is the correct one. The confidence interval derived in Example 10.8 would produce the same result as the five-step procedure *if* the test statistic were the one defined in equation 10.16. *The correct procedure here is to use the Z-statistic in equation 10.17 as your test statistic.*

Step 1. Since we are looking for a difference between p_1 and p_2, define

$$H_0: p_1 = p_2$$

$$H_a: p_1 \neq p_2$$

Step 2. The test statistic is

$$Z = \frac{\hat{p}_1 - \hat{p}_2}{\sqrt{\dfrac{\bar{p}(1-\bar{p})}{n_1} + \dfrac{\bar{p}(1-\bar{p})}{n_2}}}$$

Step 3. Using $\alpha = .10$, then $Z_{\alpha/2} = Z_{.05} = 1.645$. The test procedure will be to

$$\text{reject } H_0 \text{ if } |Z| > 1.645$$

Step 4. Since $n_1 = 100$, $x_1 = 28$, and $n_2 = 150$, $x_2 = 48$, then

$$\bar{p} = \frac{x_1 + x_2}{n_1 + n_2} = \frac{76}{250} = .304$$

Therefore, our estimate of the proportion of engines failing within the warranty period for the combined population (if $p_1 = p_2$) is $\bar{p} = .304$ (30.4%). Also, $\hat{p}_1 = 28/100 = .28$ and $\hat{p}_2 = 48/150 = .32$. The value of the test statistic is

$$Z^* = \frac{.28 - .32}{\sqrt{\dfrac{(.304)(.696)}{100} + \dfrac{(.304)(.696)}{150}}} = \frac{-.04}{.059} = -.68$$

Because $|Z^*| = .68 < 1.645$, we fail to reject H_0.

FIGURE 10.5

Z curve showing p-value
(twice the shaded area) for
Example 10.11.

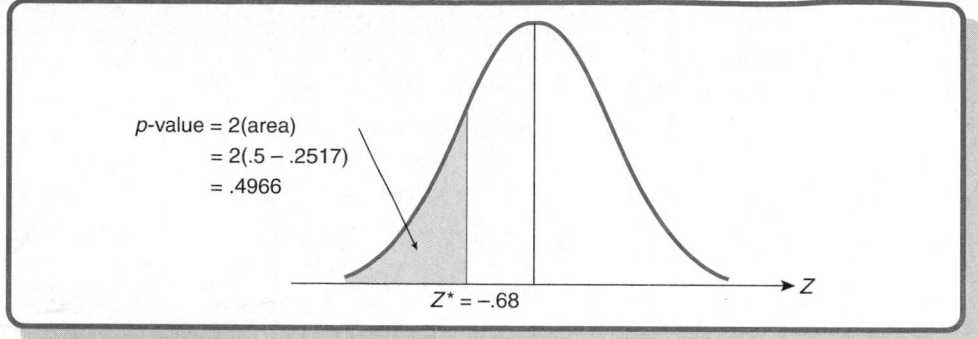

p-value = 2(area)
= 2(.5 − .2517)
= .4966

$Z^* = -.68$

Step 5. There is *insufficient evidence* to conclude that a difference exists between the two brands of engines as far as engine durability during the warranty period is concerned.

The Z curve and calculated p-value for Example 10.11 are shown in Figure 10.5. The p-value is twice the shaded area (this was a two-tailed test) and is .4966, which is extremely large. Using the classical approach, because $.4966 > \alpha = .10$, we fail to reject H_0—there is insufficient evidence to indicate a difference in engine durability. As a reminder, this reasoning *always* leads to the same conclusion as the five-step procedure. Because .4966 exceeds *any* reasonable value of α, we fail to reject H_0 quite strongly for this application.

EXAMPLE 10.12

In Example 10.9, we examined the proportions of nonconforming metal cans produced by Redican during the day shift (p_1) and the night shift (p_2). Based on these data, can you conclude that the proportion of nonconforming cans during the day shift is lower than during the night shift? Use the p-value and a significance level of .05.

SOLUTION

Step 1. We wish to know whether the data warrant the conclusion that p_1 is *smaller* than p_2. Placing this in the alternative hypothesis leads to

$$H_0: p_1 \geq p_2$$

$$H_a: p_1 < p_2$$

Steps 2 and 3. Using the test statistic in equation 10.17, the resulting one-tailed test procedure would be to

$$\text{reject } H_0 \text{ if } Z < -Z_{.05} = -1.645$$

This is the same as rejecting H_0 if the resulting p-value $< .05$.
Step 4. We have

$$\hat{p}_1 = \frac{70}{500} = .14 \quad \text{and} \quad \hat{p}_2 = \frac{110}{500} = .22$$

Also,

$$\bar{p} = \frac{(70+110)}{(500+500)} = \frac{180}{1000} = .18$$

Consequently,

$$Z^* = \frac{.14 - .22}{\sqrt{\dfrac{(.18)(.82)}{500} + \dfrac{(.18)(.82)}{500}}} = \frac{-.08}{.0243} = -3.29$$

FIGURE 10.6

Z curve showing the calculated
p-value for Example 10.12.

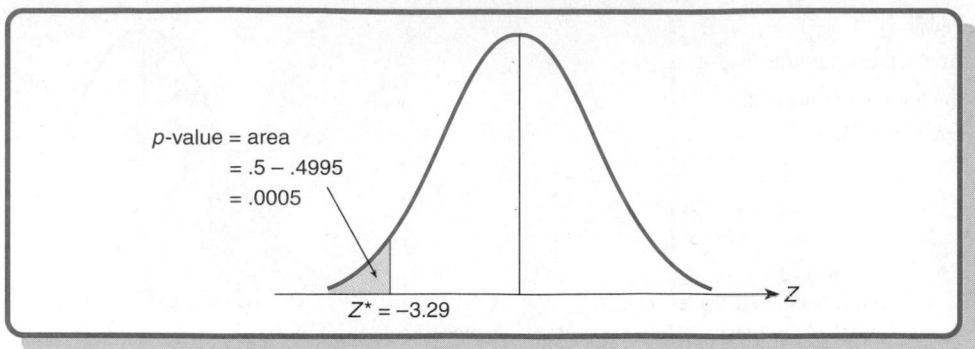

FIGURE 10.7

Excel solution to Example
10.12 using **KGP Data
Analysis ➤ Inference on
Proportions ➤ Two
Population Proportions.**

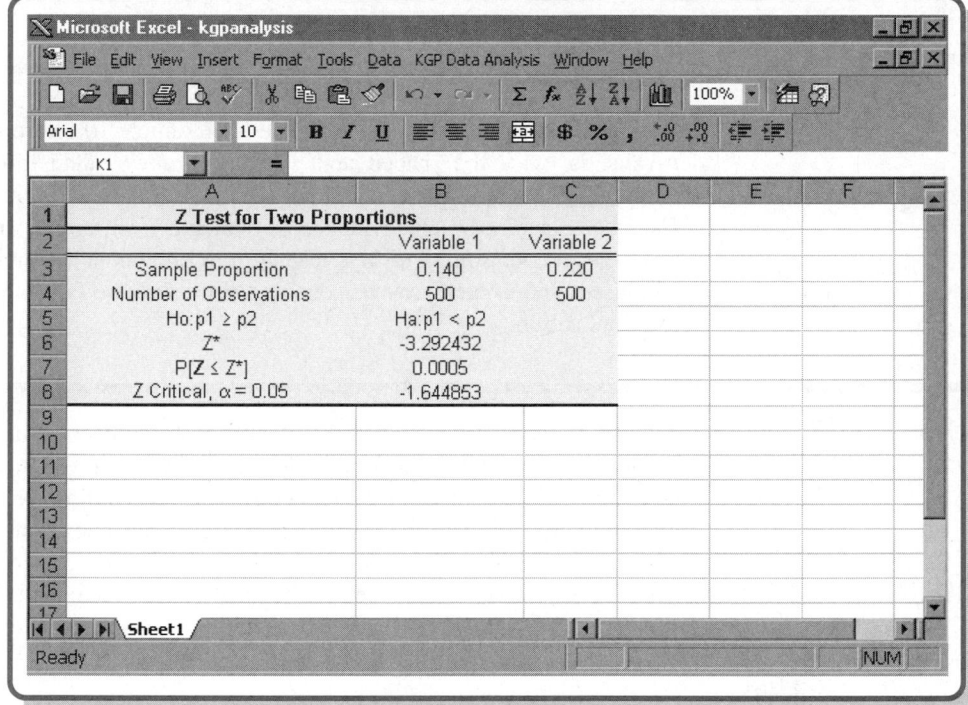

The *Z* curve and calculated *p*-value of .0005 are shown in figure 10.6. H_0 is
rejected since (1) –3.29 is less than –1.645 and, as a result, (2) the *p*-value of .0005
is less than $\alpha = .05$. Condition (2) is actually a restatement of condition (1), since
.0005 is the area to the left of –3.29 and .05 is the area to the left of –1.645.

Step 5. There *is* evidence that the proportion of nonconforming cans is smaller during the
day shift.

An Excel solution to Example 10.12 using the macro from KGP Data Analysis is
shown in Figure 10.7. To obtain this solution, click on **KGP Data Analysis ➤ Inference
on Proportions ➤ Two Population Proportions.** Under Sample 1, enter "70" in the
Number of Successes box and "500" in the **Sample Size** box. In the Sample 2 boxes, enter
"110" and "500." Next, enter 5 in the **Alpha** box and click on the box alongside **Hypothesis Test.** Finally, click on **Left-Tail Test"** and enter "A1" in the **Output Range** box. The
resulting output agrees with the previous solution. In particular, the small *p*-value of .0005
(in cell B7, Figure 10.7) supports the alternative hypothesis that the proportion of defective cans *is* smaller during the day shift.

Exercises 10.31–10.39

Understanding the Mechanics

10.31 Using random samples from population 1 and population 2, the following sample sizes and number of successes were observed:

$$n_1 = 50, \qquad x_1 = 40, \qquad n_2 = 80, \qquad x_2 = 70$$

a. Construct a 90% confidence interval for the difference in the proportions of successes for the two populations.

b. Test the hypothesis that the proportions of successes for the two populations differ. Use a .05 significance level.

c. Find the *p*-value for the test in part (b).

10.32 Determine what sample sizes are necessary for the estimate of the difference between two proportions to be within .03 of the actual difference with 95% confidence if:

a. Previous estimates of p_1 and p_2 are known to be .18 and .26.

b. No prior estimates of p_1 and p_2 are available.

Applying the New Concepts

10.33 How does the value of the test statistic given in equation 10.17 change if $\hat{p}_1$, the proportion of successes for sample 1, is replaced by the proportion of failures for sample 1 and if $\hat{p}_2$, the proportion of successes for sample 2, is replaced by the proportion of failures for sample 2?

10.34 Many employees are learning the economics of health care as they watch their deductibles rise. In the past, most health maintenance organizations (HMOs) let patients see doctors with no copayment. In 1997, almost 75% of the HMOs required an initial copayment. A health care analyst is interested in whether there is a difference in the proportion of employees in 1997 and in 1999 that used an HMO requiring an initial copayment. A random sample of 500 employees in 1997 and another sample of 500 employees in 1999 revealed that 390 and 430 employees, respectively, from 1997 and 1999 were required to pay an initial copayment when visiting the doctor. Based on these data, can the analyst conclude that the proportion of employees in 1997 and 1999 differ? Use a 10% significance level.

(Adapted from *USA Today,* "Workers' Health Care Costs Rise As Costs to Employees Drop," Oct 23, 1998, p. 10A.)

10.35 The owner of two hotels in Atlanta is interested in the proportion of "no-shows" on Friday night. The manager believes that the proportion of no-shows does not differ significantly between the two hotels. Assume that preliminary estimates of the proportion of no-shows are 15% at hotel A and 19% at hotel B. How many random Friday nights would the owner need to select from each hotel to estimate the difference in the proportions of no-shows to within .20 with 95% confidence, minimizing the total sample size?

10.36 Very few metropolitan areas in the United States have more than 25% of the adult population possessing a passport. New York City and San Francisco have the highest percentages of adults possessing a current U.S. passport. Suppose that a survey by a travel agency was conducted to determine if there is a significant difference in the proportion of adults in these two cities that possess a current passport. If a random sample of 300 adults from each city revealed that 105 and 90 adults from San Francisco and New York City, respectively, hold a current passport, what conclusion can the travel agency make? Use a 5% significance level.

(Adapted from *USA Today,* "Passports at the Ready," Sept. 25–27, 1998, p. 1A.)

10.37 A quality engineer wishes to determine if there is a difference in the number of nonconforming bottle-top seals produced by two different assembly-line processes. A bottle-top seal is nonconforming if the seal is not airtight. To investigate this, the engineer samples 300 bottle-top seals from each assembly-line process. The samples reveal that one process produced 8 nonconforming items and the other produced 12 nonconforming items. Based on these data, can the engineer conclude that there is a significant difference in the number of nonconforming bottle-top seals produced by the two assembly-line processes? Use the *p*-value to support your conclusion.

Using the Computer

10.38 **[DATA SET EX10-38]** *Variable description:*

MalesInterested: A *Yes* indicates that a male is interested in a sales manager position, and a *No* indicates no interest
FemalesInterested: A *Yes* indicates that a female is interested in a sales manager position, and a *No* indicates no interest

The vice president at Global Life Insurance Company is interested in the proportion of male college business students and female college business students that would be willing to interview for a sales manager position at the company. Random samples of 170 males and 115 females from college business students were selected. Responses were recorded as *Yes* or *No* and are listed in variables MalesInterested and FemalesInterested. Test that the proportion of male students exceeds the proportion of female students interested in this position. Use the *p*-value of test statistic as the basis for your conclusion.

10.39 **[DATA SET EX10-39]** *Variable description:*

ManufactA: A 1 indicates a defective motor and a 0 indicates that the motor is not defective from manufacturer A
ManufactB: A 1 indicates a defective motor and a 0 indicates that the motor is not defective from manufacturer B

Two manufacturers supply rebuilt motors to an air conditioning repair company. The manager at the air conditioning repair company believes that the proportion of defective motors from the two manufacturers differs. A random sample of 150 rebuilt motors from manufacturer A and 150 rebuilt motors from manufacturer B were selected. Variables ManufactA and ManufactB contain a 1 or a 0 to indicate a defective or nondefective motor.

a. Use the two-sample proportions test to test that there is sufficient evidence to indicate a difference. Use a 5% significance level.

b. What is the estimate of the pooled proportion, $\bar{p}$?

c. Use the Z statistic to test for a difference in the means of the two variables. Assign σ the value of $\sqrt{2\bar{p}(1-\bar{p})}$. What resemblance is there to the test in part (a)?

You will often encounter a situation in which you are concerned with a population **proportion** rather than the mean or variance. For example, the parameter of interest might be the proportion (p) of executives earning more than \$100,000 annually, rather than the average salary (μ) or the standard deviation (σ) of the salaries. The usual procedure of estimating a population parameter using the sample estimator, $\hat{p}$, allows us to derive a point estimate and construct a confidence interval for p. When the sample is small, Table A.8 provides an exact confidence interval for p. For large samples, the Central Limit Theorem can be applied to determine an approximate confidence interval, provided that *both* $n\hat{p}$ and $n(1 - \hat{p})$ are greater than 5.

When the desired accuracy of the point estimator, $\hat{p}$, is specified in advance, you can determine the sample size necessary to obtain this degree of accuracy for a certain confidence level. To derive this sample size, an estimate of p is necessary. You can calculate this value using a previous sample estimate or, if no information is available, using a conservative procedure and making $\hat{p} = .5$.

When you investigate a statement concerning a population proportion, you can use a statistical test of

SUMMARY

hypothesis. For small samples, the confidence interval from Table A.8 provides an exact procedure for either a one- or two-tailed test. For tests of a hypothesis when a large sample is used, a test statistic having an approximate standard normal distribution can be used.

To compare **two population proportions** (p_1 and p_2), two *independent* random samples are obtained, one from each population. Procedures for large, independent samples generally provide an accurate confidence interval or test of hypothesis whenever $n_1\hat{p}_1$, $n_1(1 - \hat{p}_1)$, $n_2\hat{p}_2$, and $n_2(1 - \hat{p}_2)$ each exceed 5. Using a standard normal approximation, we can construct a confidence interval for $p_1 - p_2$. If the accuracy of this estimate is specified, the sample sizes necessary to obtain this level of accuracy as well as to minimize the total sample size $n_1 + n_2$ can be obtained.

Two population proportions can be compared by using two large, independent samples to evaluate a test statistic having an approximate standard normal distribution. We examined procedures for a one-tailed test (for example, H_a: $p_1 > p_2$) or a two-tailed test (H_a: $p_1 \neq p_2$). The rejection regions for these tests are defined using the areas from Table A.4.

SUMMARY OF FORMULAS

SINGLE POPULATION
1. Point estimate of population proportion (p):

$$\hat{p} = \frac{x}{n}$$

   where

   x = number of sample items having the selected attribute
   n = sample size

2. Confidence interval for p (large sample):

$$\hat{p} \pm Z_{\alpha/2} \sqrt{\frac{\hat{p}(1-\hat{p})}{n-1}}$$

3. Sample size necessary to obtain maximum error (E) with $(1 - \alpha) \cdot 100\%$ confidence:

$$n = \frac{Z_{\alpha/2}^2 \, \hat{p}(1-\hat{p})}{E^2} + 1$$

4. Test statistic for hypothesis testing on p (large sample):

$$Z = \frac{\hat{p} - p_0}{\sqrt{\dfrac{p_0(1-p_0)}{n}}}$$

   where p_0 is the hypothesized value of p.

TWO POPULATIONS (LARGE, INDEPENDENT SAMPLES)
1. Confidence interval for $p_1 - p_2$:

$$(\hat{p}_1 - \hat{p}_2) \pm Z_{\alpha/2} \sqrt{\frac{\hat{p}_1(1-\hat{p}_1)}{n_1 - 1} + \frac{\hat{p}_2(1-\hat{p}_2)}{n_2 - 1}}$$

2. Samples sizes necessary to obtain maximum error
    (E) with $(1 - \alpha) \cdot 100\%$ confidence (total sample
    size minimized):

$$n_1 = \frac{Z_{\alpha/2}^2 \, (A + B)}{E^2} + 1$$

$$n_2 = \frac{Z_{\alpha/2}^2 \, (C + B)}{E^2} + 1$$

where

$$A = \hat{p}_1 (1 - \hat{p}_1)$$

$$B = \sqrt{\hat{p}_1 \hat{p}_2 \, (1 - \hat{p}_1)(1 - \hat{p}_2)}$$

$$C = \hat{p}_2 (1 - \hat{p}_2)$$

3. Test statistic for hypothesis testing on p_1 and p_2:

$$Z = \frac{\hat{p}_1 - \hat{p}_2}{\sqrt{\dfrac{\bar{p}(1 - \bar{p})}{n_1} + \dfrac{\bar{p}(1 - \bar{p})}{n_2}}}$$

where

$$\bar{p} = \frac{x_1 + x_2}{n_1 + n_2}$$

REVIEW EXERCISES 10.40–10.63

10.40 Conduct the test indicated in each of the following cases for a random sample of size n with an estimate of the population proportion given by $\hat{p}$.

    a. H_0: $p = p_0$ versus H_a: $p \neq p_0$, $n = 10$, $\hat{p} = .60$, $p_0 = .30$, $\alpha = .10$

    b. H_0: $p = p_0$ versus H_a: $p \neq p_0$, $n = 20$, $\hat{p} = .40$, $p_0 = .15$, $\alpha = .05$

    c. H_0: $p = p_0$ versus H_a: $p \neq p_0$, $n = 100$, $\hat{p} = .10$, $p_0 = .16$, $\alpha = .01$

    d. H_0: $p \leq p_0$ versus H_a: $p > p_0$, $n = 150$, $\hat{p} = .88$, $p_0 = .83$, $\alpha = .05$

10.41 An advertising agent for Computerized Telephone Systems claims that the proportion of installed telephone systems that have maintenance problems during the first three years is less than 10%. A random sample of 19 computerized telephone systems that were installed within the last three years was taken, and one of the telephone systems was found to have needed repairs.

    a. Test the advertising agent's claim at the .05 significance level. Use Table A.8.

    b. Find a 90% confidence interval for the true proportion of installed telephone systems that have maintenance problems.

10.42 Fifteen male customers were asked which of two electric shavers, brand 1 or brand 2, they preferred. Nine of them preferred brand 1.

    a. At the .05 level of significance, can it be concluded that brand 1 was preferred to brand 2 by male shoppers? Use Table A.8.

    b. Find a 95% confidence interval for the proportion of male shoppers who preferred brand 1 over brand 2. Use Table A.8.

    c. Assume you have no prior knowledge of p (the proportion of males who preferred brand 1 over brand 2). Estimate the sample size that is required to estimate p, with 90% confidence, assuming a maximum error of .08.

10.43 A small sample ($n = 15$) is drawn from a lot of dry-cell batteries. Each of the batteries was tested; seven were defective. Determine a 95% confidence interval for the proportion of defectives in the entire batch. Use Table A.8.

10.44 William's Packaging is interested in estimating the proportion of its employees who would attend an alcohol-awareness program. In a random sample of 70 employees, 39 said that they would attend the program. Calculate the estimate of the proportion of all employees who would attend the program. Find a 90% confidence interval for this proportion.

10.45 A week before the congressional elections at the midterm of President Clinton's second term, voters were asked if their vote for Congress was meant to send a signal of support for or against President Clinton or no signal at all. An NBC news poll found that only 23% of the voters said that their vote was cast as a signal of opposition. Suppose that a pollster wished to find out the percentage of voters casting their vote in opposition during the elections. If the maximum error of the estimate of the proportion is 3%, what sample size is large enough to estimate the population proportion with this much accuracy at the 95% confidence level?

(Adapted from *The Wall Street Journal*, "Impeachment Politics," Nov. 2, 1998, p. A36.)

10.46 According to a Gallup study conducted for Pitney Bowes, a major supplier of fax machines, the use of fax machines is skyrocketing among Canadian companies. Canada's largest corporations faxed 38% more documents in 1993 than they did in 1992. Also, 66% of fax users in the survey had no idea how much it costs to send a fax. Suppose that another survey was conducted by an independent pollster of 100 Canadian companies and estimated that Canada's largest corporations faxed 33% more documents in 1993 than in 1992. The pollster also found that 61% of 282 fax users had no idea how much it costs to send a fax.

(Source: "Fax Users Ignore High Cost of Sending," by Dana Flavelle, *Toronto Star*, Oct. 1, 1993, p. B1.)

    a. Is there sufficient evidence to conclude that the actual proportion of fax users in Canadian companies who have no idea how much it costs to send a fax differs from 66%? Use the *p*-value to interpret the results of the hypothesis test.

    b. What is an appropriate test statistic to test whether there is sufficient evidence to conclude that the increase in documents faxed at Canada's largest corporations in 1993 differs from 38%? Why?

10.47 *People's Choice,* a monthly magazine, claimed that more than 40% of its subscribers had an annual income of $50,000 or more. In a random sample of 62 subscribers, 30 had incomes of $50,000 or more. Does this information substantiate the magazine's claim? Use a significance level of .10.

10.48 Marketing researchers like to contrast cities to gain insight into how consumers will react to different marketing strategies. One example is the difference between New York City and San Diego. The median age in San Diego is 43.8 versus 48 in New York City. Also New York City has about 15% of its population making over $100,000 annually versus 10% for San Diego. Suppose that a marketing researcher is interested in the percentage of adults that watch TV sports. A random sample of 250 for each city yielded 98 and 108 for New York City and San Diego, respectively. Can the marketing researcher conclude that the proportion of adults in San Diego that watch TV sports is greater than that in New York City? Use a 5% significance level.

(Adapted from *USA Today*, "Tale of Two Cities," Oct. 20, 1998, p. 1A.)

10.49 A statistician reported to a car insurance company a confidence interval for the proportion of convertible cars that had been involved in major accidents during the past year. The 95% confidence interval for *p* was reported to be the interval from .10 to .36.

    a. What is the statistician's estimate of *p?*

    b. What is the maximum error of estimate (*E*) of the proportion for this confidence interval?

    c. Approximately what sample size did the statistician use?

10.50 The rise in the number of TV viewers watching cable TV is directly proportionate to investments in TV programming. TV viewers will watch the channel where the hot program is. Cable TV has been successful at offering many hot programs, thus giving the network programs a smaller viewership. In 1997, 36% of prime-time viewing was done on cable. Suppose that Nielsen Media Research found a confidence interval on the current proportion of viewers who watch cable during prime time to be 30.35% to 49.65% from a random sample of 100 TV viewers.

(Adapted from *USA Today*, "Cable Keeps Coming on Strong," July 17, 1998, p. 2E.)

    a. What is the estimate of the proportion of TV viewers who watch cable during prime time?

    b. What is the confidence level?

10.51 Must a confidence interval for a proportion contain the true proportion of the population? Explain what the "level of confidence" means for a confidence interval.

10.52 A market-research firm believed that the proportion of households with more than four family members in county 1 was greater than the probability of households with more than four family members in county 2. The firm gathered random samples of size 180 and 155 from counties 1 and 2, respectively. The number of households with more than four members were 74 from county 1 and 61 from county 2. From these data, can we conclude that the proportion of households with more than four members is higher in county 1 than in county 2? Use a significance level of .01.

10.53 Calculate the *p*-value for Exercise 10.52. Using the *p*-value, would you reject the null hypothesis at the .05 level?

10.54 Construct a 95% confidence interval for the difference of the two proportions in Exercise 10.52.

10.55 A market-research firm is interested in testing the hypothesis that the proportion of students who own a car is the same for the local state university campus and a local private college. They interviewed 240 students from the state university and 270 from the private college. The number of students who did not own a car was 78 at the state university and 82 at the private college. Using a .02 significance level, test the hypothesis.

10.56 For Exercise 10.55, construct a 95% confidence interval for the difference of the true proportions of students who own cars at the two campuses.

10.57 Two machines are used in a production process to cut metal circles from thin sheets of steel. If the circumference of the steel circles are larger than 9.01 inches or smaller than 9.00 inches, the steel circles are considered to be *nonconforming*. The quality supervisor suspected that the number of nonconforming steel circles produced by the older machine was larger than that for the newer machine. The supervisor randomly selected 400 steel circles from each machine. The data revealed that of the 400 steel circles from the older machine, 86 were nonconforming, and of the 400 steel circles from the newer machine, 56 were nonconforming.

a. Determine a 95% confidence interval for the difference in the proportion of nonconforming steel circles produced by the machines.

b. How much larger would the sample size need to be for the difference between the two proportions in part (a) to be within .05 of the actual difference with 95% confidence?

10.58 The Travel Industry Association approximates the number of U.S. travelers heading outside the U.S. This agency believes that the number of U.S. travelers heading abroad in 1999 is a record 57.4 million. However, overseas travels account for just 5% of the total travel by Americans. Suppose that the association wishes to obtain a 95% confidence interval on the differnce in the proportions of Americans living in Los Angeles and living in New York City that travel overseas.

(Adapted from *USA Today*, "Travel Forecast: Mostly Sunny, Chance Clouds," Oct 27, 1998.)

a. What sample sizes are necessary to obtain a maximum error of 3%? Assume that the initial estimates of the proportions for the two cities is 5%.

b. Suppose the preliminary estimates of 5% for each city were not available, what sample size would be necessary?

10.59 The top reason that adult online shoppers give for shopping via the computer is convenience. In fact, a preliminary estimate of the percentage of adults giving this reason is 71% according to a USA poll. Suppose that a market analyst wishes to obtain a 95% confidence interval on the difference in proportions of men and women that shop via the computer primarily because of convenience.

(Adapted from *USA Today*, "Where Net Shoppers Shop," Apr. 29, 1998, p. B1.)

a. What sample sizes are necessary to obtain a maximum error of 3%? Assume that the initial estimates of the proportions for the men and women is 71%.

b. Suppose the preliminary estimates of 71% were not available, what sample size would be necessary?

10.60 The aging of industrial societies is of concern to many economists. Many economists believe that the proportion of the population in France and the United Kingdom to be approximately the same. This would imply that both of these countries will have similar difficulties in adjusting social benefits to support the increasing size of its senior citizens. To check that the current population in the major metropolitan areas of London and Paris have similar proportions of its populations over age 65, a random sample is taken by a concerned economist. Suppose that 1000 citizens from the London metropolitan area and 1000 citizens from the Paris metropolitan area revealed that 15.5% and 16.4% of the population of these respective areas had citizens over age 65.

(Adapted from *USA Today*, "Aging Industrial Societies," Aug. 12, 1998, p. 1A.)

a. Construct a 90% confidence interval on the difference in the proportion of citizens from Paris and the proportion of citizens from London that are over 65 years of age.

b. If a 90% confidence interval for the difference of proportions in part (a) are required to have a maximum error of .02, what sample sizes are required for sampling from each city?

c. How do you think the economist should interpret the confidence interval in part (a)?

10.61 The percentages of consumer loans 30 days or more past due in the first quarter of 1993 for the states of Connecticut and Rhode Island were 4.68 and 3.63, respectively. Suppose that an economist from the American Bankers Association wished to determine a confidence interval for the difference in the percentages of consumer loans 30 days or more past due during the first quarter of 1994 for these two states.

(Source: Adapted from *Dallas Morning News*, "Delinquent Consumer Loans Fall to Lowest Level in 4 Years," June 15, 1993, p. 4D.)

a. Determine what sample sizes are necessary for the estimate of the difference between these two proportions to be within .04 of the actual difference with 95% confidence.

b. Find the sample sizes in part (a) using a 99% confidence level. Compare the sample sizes for both confidence levels.

c. Are the requirements of $n_1\hat{p}_1 > 5$, $n_1(1 - \hat{p}_1) > 5$, $n_2\hat{p}_2 > 5$, and $n_2(1 - \hat{p}_2) > 5$ satisfied for the validity of a confidence interval on $p_1 - p_2$?

10.62 The rate at which borrowers have defaulted on student loans has been steadily declining. Thanks to Congress' willingness to give borrowers more flexibility in repaying loans, President Clinton proclaimed the declining default rate as "a shining example of government providing opportunity with accountability." Suppose that the Education Department believes that the default rate is lower for students graduating from private schools than from public schools. A random sample of 500 students from each sector yielded default rates of 8.0% and 8.8% from students having attended private and public schools, respectively.

(Adapted from *USA Today*, "Loans, Grants, Jobs Pay the Way," Oct. 27, 1998, p. 1D.)

a. Test the Education Department's belief. What is the *p*-value?

b. Suppose that the same proportions were found with sample size 1000 from each sector. How does the *p*-value change?

10.63 Using the random number generator in Excel, **Tools ➤ Data Analysis,** generate 40 binomial observations in column A assuming that the parameters are $n = 20$ and $p = .5$. In column B, divide the values from column A by 20. These will be sample proportions. Then in columns C and D calculate the lower and upper bound for a 90% confidence interval on the proportion. Obtain a graph of the upper and lower bounds. The results should be similar to that shown below. Should each interval contain the proportion $p = .5$? How many intervals do contain $p = .5$? How many would you expect to contain $p = .5$? Why?

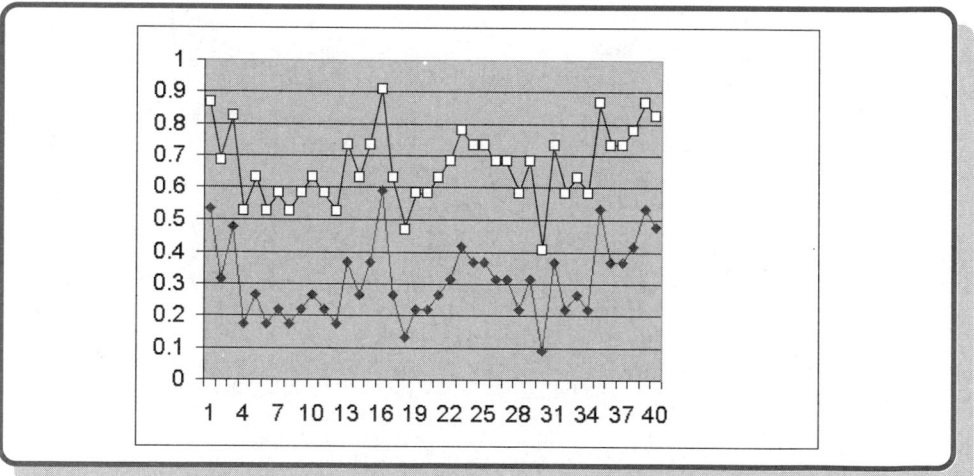

COMPUTER EXERCISES USING THE DATABASES

EXERCISE 1—APPENDIX E

Randomly select 100 observations from the database. Find a 95% confidence interval on the proportion of households that own their homes. (Refer to the variable OWNORENT.)

EXERCISE 2—APPENDIX E

Randomly select 100 observations from the database. Estimate the proportion of observations from the NE sector in which the households own their homes. (Refer to the variables LOCATION and OWNORENT.) Also estimate the proportion of observations from the NW sector in which the households own their homes. Find a 95% confidence interval on the difference of the proportions of house owners for the two sectors.

EXERCISE 3—APPENDIX F
Randomly select 100 observations from the database. Find a 95% confidence interval on the proportion of companies with a positive net income. (Refer to the variable NETINC.)

EXERCISE 4—APPENDIX F
Randomly select 100 observations from the database. Estimate the proportion of observations from companies with an A bond rating that have a positive net income. (Refer to the variables BONDRATE and NETINC.) Also estimate the proportion of observations from companies with a B bond rating that have a positive net income. Find a 95% confidence interval on the difference of the proportions of companies with positive net income between those with A bond ratings and those with B bond ratings.

INSIGHTS FROM STATISTICS IN ACTION: LARGE WASTE MANAGMENT FIRMS ARE SHIFTING TO A MANAGEMENT STRATEGY OF "WASTE INTERNALIZATION"

The Statistics in Action introductory case study at the beginning of this chapter examined the less-than-glamourous world of waste management companies. Two large companies, USA Waste and Waste Management, Inc., had considered a merger but were denied by the antitrust division of the U.S. Justice Department.

In this section, we take a closer look at these two companies and examine their marketshares within two particular regions in Michigan. Consider a random sample of 20 and 30 dump sites selected from two large metropolitan regions in Michigan for the years 1997 and 1998. One region is in central Michigan, and the other area is in eastern Michigan. The number of dump sites owned by USA Waste and Waste Management is recorded from this sample in the table below.

Number of Dump Sites Owned by USA Waste and Waste Management

Metropolitan Area	No. of Dump Sites	Owned by USA Waste 1997	Owned by USA Waste 1998	Owned by Waste Management 1997	Owned by Waste Management 1998
Central	20	5	8	6	8
East	30	2	9	4	15
Total	50	7	17	10	23

1. For each of the metropolitan areas, present a bar chart showing the number of dump sites owned by USA Waste and by Waste Management during the years 1997 and 1998. Comment on the shape of the chart.
2. For the Central metropolitan area, find a 90% confidence interval for the proportion of sites owned by USA Waste during 1997. For the Central metropolitan area, find a 95% confidence interval for the proportion of dump sites owned by USA Waste during 1998. Interpret these confidence intervals.
3. Using the combined number of dump sites from both metropolitan areas, test that the total proportion of dump sites owned by the two companies in 1998 is greater than 65%. Use a .10 significance level.
4. Test that in 1997, Waste Management owned a larger proportion of the dumps in central Michigan than in eastern Michigan. Test that in 1998, Waste Management owned a larger proportion of dumps in eastern Michigan than in central Michigan. Use a .10 significance level.
5. How do you think the U.S. Justice's antitrust department will view the results of this analysis?

Source: Adapted from *The Wall Street Journal*, "USA Waste Is on a Mission to Expand in Trash Business," May 15, 1998, p. B4.

CHAPTER 10 APPENDIX: DATA ANALYSIS WITH MINITAB

HYPOTHESIS TESTING FOR A POPULATION PROPORTION

To test a hypothesis about the proportion of a single population, click on **Stat ➤ Basic Statistics ➤ 1 Proportion.** The user form below will appear. If data were entered into a column with two distinct values, then the radial button **Samples in columns** should be clicked and the column names typed in below. However, if the number of successes and failures are known then click on the radial button labeled **Summarized data** and type in the number of trials and successes. For this example, the data in Example 10.3 and Example 10.7 are used. Click on the **Options** button. The second user form presented below will appear. Type in the confidence level for a confidence interval, input the hypothesized value of the proportion (.04 for this example), indicate the alternative as being "not equal", and check if the normal approximation is to be used. The output appears below the user forms. In this example the normal approximation was selected, so the first output with the title **Test and Confidence Interval for One Proportion** uses the Z test. For comparison purposes, the second output with the title **Test and Confidence Interval for One Proportion** does not use the Z test and gives an exact confidence interval and *p*-value.

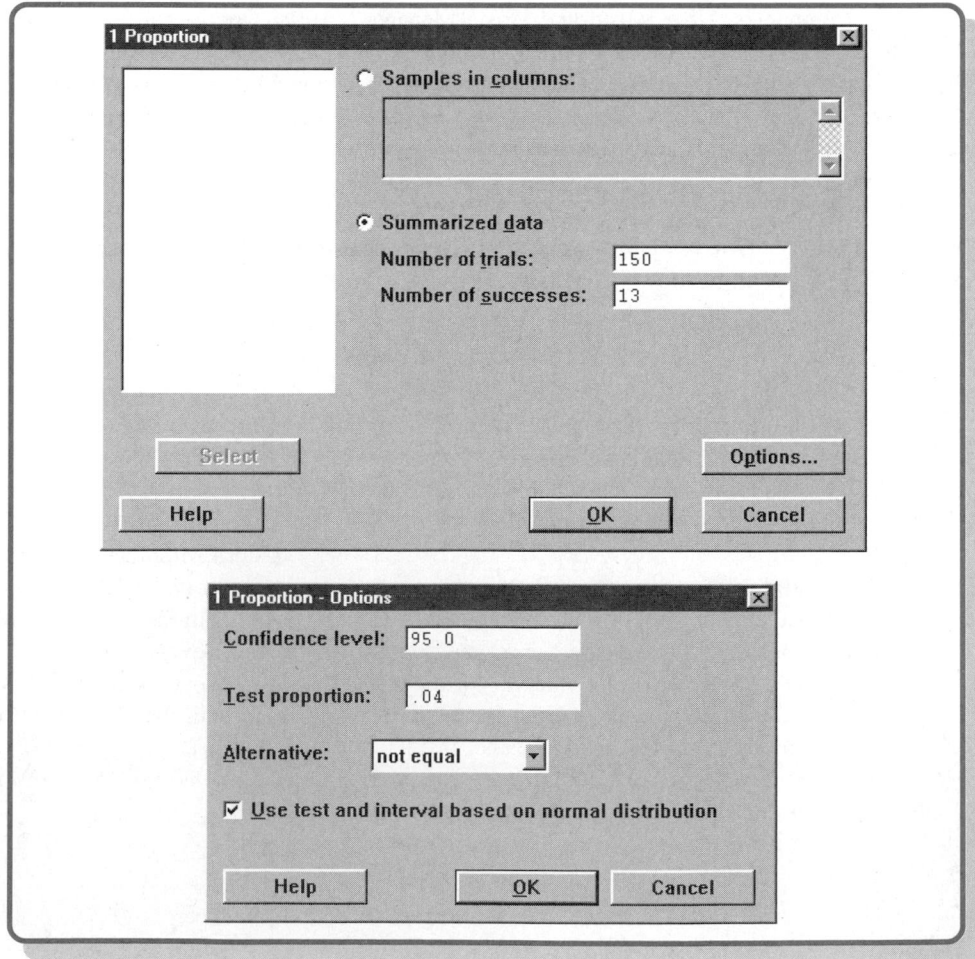

```
MTB > POne 150 13;
SUBC>   Confidence 95.0;
SUBC>   Test .04;
SUBC>   Alternative 0;
SUBC>   UseZ.
```

Test and Confidence Interval for One Proportion

```
Test of p = 0.04 vs p not = 0.04

Sample    X    N   Sample p        95.0 % CI          Z-Value   P-Value
1        13  150   0.086667  (0.041643, 0.131691)      2.92     0.004
```

Test and Confidence Interval for One Proportion

```
Test of p = 0.04 vs p not = 0.04

                                                       Exact
Sample    X    N   Sample p        95.0 % CI          P-Value
1        13  150   0.086667  (0.046955, 0.143643)      0.023
```

To test a hypothesis about the proportions of two populations, click on **Stat ➤ Basic Statistics ➤ 2 Proportions.** The user form below will appear. If the raw data were entered into a single column with a separate column indicating the population to which the data values belong, then click on the radial button **Samples in one column.** If the raw data are entered into two separate columns—one for each group—then click on **Samples in different columns.** If the number of successes and failures are known, then click on the radial button labeled **Summarized data** and type in the number of trials and successes. For this example, the data in Example 10.9 and Example 10.12 are used. Click on the **Options** button. The second user form presented below will appear. Type in the confidence level for the confidence interval, input the hypothesized value of the proportion (0.0 for this example), indicate the alternative as being "less than", and check if the pooled estimate of the proportion is to be used. Note that the pooled estimate only should be used if the test difference is equal to 0.0. The output appears below the user forms.

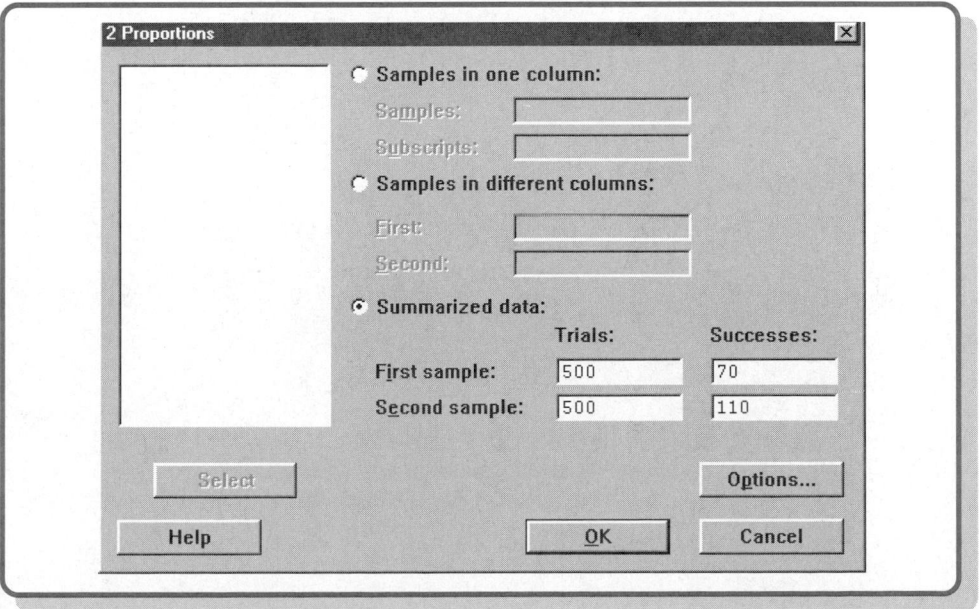

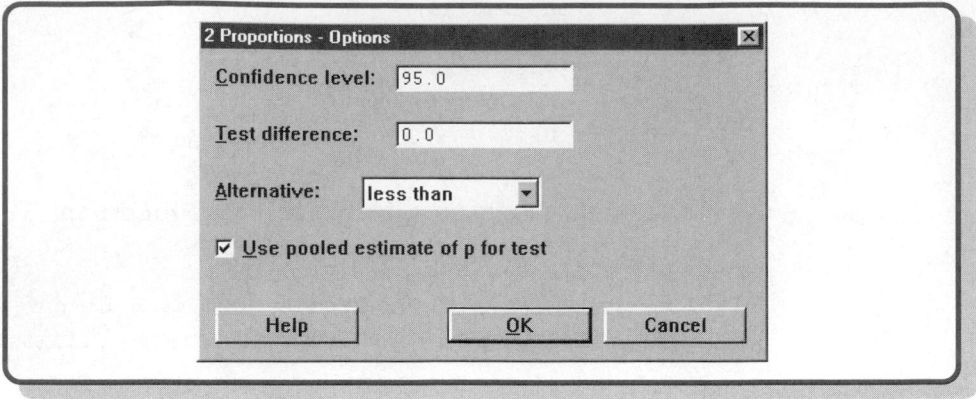

```
MTB > PTwo 500 70 500 110;
SUBC>    Confidence 95.0;
SUBC>    Test 0.0;
SUBC>    Alternative -1;
SUBC>    Pooled.
```

Test and Confidence Interval for Two Proportions

Sample	X	N	Sample p
1	70	500	0.140000
2	110	500	0.220000

Estimate for p(1) – p(2): -0.08
95% CI for p(1) – p(2): (-0.127365, -0.0326353)
Test for p(1) – p(2) = 0 (vs < 0): Z = -3.29 P-Value = 0.000

ANALYSIS OF VARIANCE

STATISTICS IN ACTION: AUTOMOTIVE INSURANCE RATES AND CATEGORY OF DRIVER

Auto insurance rates are headed down, according to Sean Mooney, economist for the Insurance Information Institute. The drop in rates is credited to safer cars, low inflation, and the fact that some antifraud precautions the industry put in place a few years ago are working as intended. But Mooney says that not every insurer is ready to pass its savings along to the consumer. Supposedly, the automotive insurance companies are afraid that they will never get their rates up again. Consumers should shop around for car insurance companies that are willing to share the wealth.

Even members in Congress are pushing for lower automotive insurance rates. Dick Armey, a Texas Republican, has his name on a bill that he contends will drop auto insurance premiums by as much as 25%. Americans pay an average annual premium of $774.12 for a vehicle with liability, comprehensive, and collision coverage. By comparison, Texans spend an average of $820.38 annually. Mr. Armey claims that for his beloved Ford pickup truck and his wife's Mercury Cougar, he spends nearly $1,100 to insure two 10-year-old vehicles with minimum coverage. He believes that the cost of litigation, as well as fraud and abuse, keep these rates high.

Mr. Armey proposes to give the consumers a choice when dealing with their insurance companies. He believes that the consumer should have the option of giving up his/her right to claim pain and suffering damages. In exchange, insurance companies would promptly respond to other damages, such as lost wages and economic losses. Automotive insurance rates should substantially drop for consumers choosing this option.

Most states require liability insurance for motor vehicles registered within the state. Although every driver is required to have basic automobile liability insurance, insurance companies and brokers offer a variety of policy options. Auto insurance companies base their insurance rates on factors such as age, sex, years of dri-

ving experience, driving record, value and type of vehicle, and place of residence. Currently, most states limit the criteria that insurance companies can use to base their rates. For example, car insurance companies are not allowed to base their rates primarily on zip codes.

Liability insurance pays for damages caused by the insured driver and may be the only insurance required by law. Liability insurance typically makes up about half of a policy's total cost. Other types of coverage provide for catastrophes such as theft, vandalism, or storm damage.

This chapter explains how you can examine differences across different groups. For example, you might consider four different groups of drivers (say, younger males, younger females, older males, and older females) and investigate differences in annual premiums for these four groups. If you are in one of the first two categories and you've ever attempted to purchase auto insurance, you might suspect that there is indeed a difference in premium rates across these four groups.

When you've completed this chapter, you will be able to determine:

*   If the four (or however many) sample means are significantly different and what this implies;

*   A confidence interval for, say, the average premium for a young female driver;

*   A confidence interval for, say, the *difference* between annual premiums for older male drivers and younger male drivers; and

*   The difference between independent and dependent (blocked) samples.

A LOOK BACK/INTRODUCTION

In Chapter 9, we considered a question of the type, do men have the same heights as women? By this we mean, is the *average* height of males equal to the average height of females? We were interested in the means of two populations and performed a test of hypothesis, using, for example, $H_0: \mu_M = \mu_F$ and $H_a: \mu_M \neq \mu_F$. Such tests work well when dealing with two populations, but how can we compare the means of more than two populations? For example, we might wish to examine the average sales of salespeople trained using five different training programs to see whether they are the same. Our hypotheses become

$$H_0: \mu_1 = \mu_2 = \mu_3 = \mu_4 = \mu_5$$

$$H_a: \text{not all } \mu\text{'s are equal}$$

We test such a hypothesis by first collecting five samples, one from each of the training programs (populations). We will see that to compare these five means one pair at a time is *not* the correct approach: this procedure results in ten different pairwise tests, and what was intended to be a testing procedure with, say, a .05 significance level results in a much higher significance level. In other words, the overall significance level, α, is *larger* than the predetermined value. The correct procedure for this situation is to examine the *variation* of the sales values, both (1) within each of the samples (examining the variability of each sample alone) and (2) among the five samples (for example, are the values in sample 1 larger or smaller, on the average, than the values in the other samples?).

In Chapter 9, we saw that when trying to decide if $\bar{X}_1$ is "significantly different" from $\bar{X}_2$, a key part of the answer rested on the values of s_1 and s_2, the variation *within* the two samples. Both s_1 and s_2 affect the width of the confidence interval for $\mu_1 - \mu_2$. Consequently, we infer something about the *means* of several populations by utilizing the *variation* of the resulting samples. Hence the term *analysis of variance*—our next topic.

11.1 COMPARING TWO MEANS: ANOTHER LOOK

We begin with an example. The manufacturer of a small battery-powered tape recorder decides to include four alkaline batteries with their product. Two battery suppliers are being considered; each has its own brand (brand 1 and brand 2). The supervising inspector of incoming quality wants to know if the average lifetimes of the two brands are the same. Based on past experience, she believes that the battery lifetimes follow a *normal* distribution. A simple experiment is conducted: each of 10 batteries (5 of each brand) is connected to a test device that places a small drain on the battery power and records the battery lifetime. The following results (in hours) are obtained:

Brand 1	Brand 2
43	30
48	26
38	37
41	31
51	34

Let μ_1 be the average lifetime (if observed indefinitely) for brand 1 and μ_2 be the average for brand 2. We wish to determine whether the data allow us to conclude that $\mu_1 \neq \mu_2$, using $\alpha = .10$.

We examined the same type of question in Chapter 9; we are dealing with two small independent samples. In Chapter 9 we advised against assuming that σ_1 was equal to σ_2. As a result, we generally used a t test that did *not* pool the sample variances. However, when examining more than two normal populations (the main concern of this chapter), the following testing procedure for detecting a difference in the population means requires that the populations have the *same* distribution if, in fact, the population means are equal. Consequently, it can be used only when we are willing to assume that the *population variances are equal* (or approximately equal). The analysis of variance procedure is *not* extremely sensitive to departures from this assumption, especially if equal-sized samples are obtained from each population. A procedure for verifying this assumption (similar to the F-test used to compare two variances in Chapter 9) is discussed in this chapter.

As a result, we will assume that we have reason to believe that the variation of the brand 1 lifetimes is the same as for brand 2, that is, $\sigma_1 = \sigma_2$. Using the approach discussed in Chapter 9, we first find

$$s_p^2 = \text{pooled variance} = \frac{(n_1 - 1)s_1^2 + (n_2 - 1)s_2^2}{n_1 + n_2 - 2}$$

where n_1, n_2 = sample sizes for brand 1, brand 2 and s_1^2, s_2^2 = sample variances for brand 1, brand 2. Using the sample data,

Brand 1	Brand 2
$n_1 = 5$	$n_2 = 5$
$\overline{x}_1 = 44.2$ hr	$\overline{x}_2 = 31.6$ hr
$s_1 = 5.263$ hr	$s_2 = 4.159$ hr

Consequently,

$$s_p^2 = \frac{(4)(5.263)^2 + (4)(4.159)^2}{8} = \frac{180.0}{8} = 22.5$$

and so

$$s_p = \sqrt{22.5} = 4.74 \text{ hr}$$

The appropriate hypotheses are H_0: $\mu_1 = \mu_2$ and H_a: $\mu_1 \neq \mu_2$. The resulting test statistic is

$$t = \frac{\overline{X}_1 - \overline{X}_2}{s_p \sqrt{\dfrac{1}{n_1} + \dfrac{1}{n_2}}}$$

$$= \frac{44.2 - 31.6}{4.74 \sqrt{\dfrac{1}{5} + \dfrac{1}{5}}} = \frac{12.6}{2.998} = 4.20$$

That is, $t^* = 4.20$.

We are dealing with a two-tailed test using a t statistic with $(n_1 - 1) + (n_2 - 1) = 4 + 4 = 8$ df, so the test procedure is to

$$\text{reject } H_0 \text{ if } |t^*| > t_{\alpha/2,\text{df}} = t_{.05,8} = 1.86$$

Comparing $t^* = 4.20$ to 1.86, we reject H_0 and conclude that the mean lifetimes for the two brands are not the same. Looking at the sample data, we can say that $\bar{x}_1 = 44.2$ is significantly different from $\bar{x}_2 = 31.6$.

THE ANALYSIS OF VARIANCE APPROACH

We need to introduce two new terms. The previous example examined the effect of one **factor** (brand), consisting of two **levels** (brand 1 and brand 2). If you want to extend this to four brands (say, brands 1, 2, 3, and 4), then you still have *one* factor but you now have *four* levels.

The purpose of **analysis of variance (ANOVA)** is to determine whether this factor has a *significant effect* on the variable being measured (battery lifetime, in our example). If, for instance, the brand factor *is* significant, the mean lifetimes for the different brands will not be equal. Consequently, testing for equal means among the various brands is the same as attempting to answer the question, is there a significant effect on battery lifetime due to this factor?

This section examines the effect of a single factor on the variable being measured, **one-factor ANOVA.** Extensions of this technique include ANOVA procedures that determine the effect of two or more factors operating simultaneously. These factors may be *qualitative* (such as brand in the previous illustration) or *quantitative* (such as several levels of advertising expenditure).

All 10 values in the battery lifetimes example are different, and we observe a variation in these values. We will look at two *sources of variation:* (1) variation *within* the samples (levels) and (2) variation *between* the samples.

WITHIN-SAMPLE VARIATION

When you obtain a sample, you usually obtain different values for each observation. The five sample values for brand 1 vary about the mean $\bar{x}_1 = 44.2$ hours, as measured by $s_1 = 5.26$ hours. Likewise, the five values in the second sample also exhibit some variation ($s_2 = 4.16$) about $\bar{x}_2 = 31.6$ hours. These are the **within-sample variations.** They are used when estimating the common population variance, say σ^2. This procedure tends to provide an accurate estimate of σ^2, whether or not the sample means are equal.

BETWEEN-SAMPLE VARIATION

When you compare the two samples, you observe that the values for brand 1 are *larger*, on the average, than those for brand 2. This is summarized in the sample means, where $\bar{x}_1 = 44.2$ appears to be considerably larger than $\bar{x}_2 = 31.6$. So there is a variation in the ten values due to the *brand*; that is, due to the factor. This is **between-sample variation.** In general, if this variation is large, we expect considerable variation among the sample means. The between-sample variation is also used in another estimate of the common variance, σ^2, *provided the population means are equal. In other words, if the means are equal, the between-sample and within-sample estimates of σ^2 should be nearly the same.* As we will see later in this section, we can derive a test of hypothesis procedure for determining whether the means are equal by comparing these two estimates.

MEASURING VARIATION

When using the ANOVA approach, we measure these two sources of variation by calculating various **sums of squares, SS.** We determine

SS(factor), which measures between-sample variation [also called SS(between)]

SS(error), which measures within-sample variation [also called SS(within)]

SS(total) = SS(between) + SS(within) = SS(factor) + SS(error)

Each of the first two sums of squares will have corresponding degrees of freedom, df, which are determined from the number of terms that make up this particular SS. The df for our example are given by

$$\text{df for factor} = (\text{number of levels}) - 1$$

$$= (\text{number of brands}) - 1$$

$$= 2 - 1 = 1$$

$$\text{df for error} = (n_1 - 1) + (n_2 - 1)$$

$$= n_1 + n_2 - 2 = 5 + 5 - 2 = 8$$

We will show how to determine these sums of squares and how we combine them and their df into another test statistic for testing H_0: $\mu_1 = \mu_2$ against H_a: $\mu_1 \neq \mu_2$. The beauty of this approach is that it extends nicely to the situation in which you wish to compare more than two means using a *single* test.

DETERMINING SS(FACTOR).   SS(factor) is the sum of squares that determines whether the values in one sample are larger or smaller on the average than the values in the second sample:

$$SS(\text{factor}) = n_1(\bar{x}_1 - \bar{x})^2 + n_2(\bar{x}_2 - \bar{x})^2 \qquad \textbf{(11.1)}$$

where, $\bar{x}_1$, $\bar{x}_2$ are the two sample means and

$$\bar{x} = \frac{\sum(\text{all data values})}{n} = \frac{n_1\bar{x}_1 + n_2\bar{x}_2}{n_1 + n_2}$$

and $n = n_1 + n_2 = $ total sample size.
   There is another method of determining this sum of squares that is much easier using a calculator.

$$SS(\text{factor}) = \left[\frac{T_1^2}{n_1} + \frac{T_2^2}{n_2}\right] - \frac{T^2}{n} \qquad \textbf{(11.2)}$$

where $T_1 = $ total of the sample 1 observations, $T_2 = $ total of the sample 2 observations, and $T = $ grand total $= T_1 + T_2$.

DETERMINING SS(TOTAL).   SS(total) is a measure of the variation in all $n = n_1 + n_2$ data values. You obtain its value as though you were finding the *variance* of these n values, except that you do not divide by $n - 1$:

$$SS(\text{total}) = \sum(x - \bar{x})^2 \qquad \textbf{(11.3)}$$

or (after some algebra similar to that used in Chapter 3),

$$SS(\text{total}) = \sum x^2 - \frac{(\sum x)^2}{n} = \sum x^2 - \frac{T^2}{n} \qquad \textbf{(11.4)}$$

DETERMINING SS(ERROR).   SS(error) is the measure of the variation *within* each of the samples. Its value simply is the *numerator of the pooled variance, s_p^2,* obtained using the previous *t* test. Thus,

$$SS(\text{error}) = \underbrace{\sum(x - \bar{x}_1)^2}_{\text{first sample}} + \underbrace{\sum(x - \bar{x}_2)^2}_{\text{second sample}} \qquad \textbf{(11.5)}$$

and therefore,

$$SS(error) = \sum x^2 - \left[\frac{T_1^2}{n_1} + \frac{T_2^2}{n_2} \right] \qquad \textbf{(11.6)}$$

Given that

$$SS(total) = SS(factor) + SS(error)$$

a much easier way to find this value is

$$SS(error) = SS(total) - SS(factor) \qquad \textbf{(11.7)}$$

Let us return to the battery lifetimes example. To find the SS(factor) here, we first determine

$$T_1 = 43 + 48 + 38 + 41 + 51 = 221$$

$$T_2 = 30 + 26 + 37 + 31 + 34 = 158$$

$$T = T_1 + T_2 = 221 + 158 = 379$$

So, using equation 11.2,

$$SS(factor) = \frac{221^2}{5} + \frac{158^2}{5} - \frac{379^2}{10}$$

$$= 14,761 - 14,361.4 = 396.9$$

To find SS(total), the only new term we need to evaluate is

$$\sum x^2 = \text{sum of each data value squared}$$

$$= 43^2 + 48^2 + \cdots + 31^2 + 34^2 = 14,941$$

So, using equation 11.4 [the value 14,364.1 was obtained in SS(factor)],

$$SS(total) = \sum x^2 - \frac{T^2}{n}$$

$$= 14,941 - 14,364.1 = 576.9$$

Finally, we find SS(error) by subtraction:

$$SS(error) = SS(total) - SS(factor)$$

$$= 576.9 - 396.9 = 180.0$$

ANOVA Test for $H_0: \mu_1 = \mu_2$ Versus $H_a: \mu_1 \neq \mu_2$

To begin with, the procedure we are about to define is valid for a *two-tailed test only*. In other words, the alternative hypothesis must be that the two means differ, not that one is larger than the other (a one-tailed test). (When examining more than two means, the alternative hypothesis will be that *at least* two of the means are unequal and H_0 will be that all the means are equal.) The next step when using the ANOVA procedure is to determine something resembling an "average" sum of squares, referred to as a **mean square**. We compute a mean square for only SS(factor) and SS(error), not for SS(total).

$$MS(factor) = \frac{SS(factor)}{\text{df for factor}} = \frac{SS(factor)}{1} \qquad \textbf{(11.8)}$$

Note that the df for this term always is (number of levels) – 1. In this section, we are dealing with two levels (populations), and so here df is 1.

$$MS(\text{error}) = \frac{SS(\text{error})}{\text{df for error}} = \frac{SS(\text{error})}{n_1 + n_2 - 2} \qquad (11.9)$$

We denote the common variance of the two normal populations as σ^2. So $\sigma^2 = \sigma_1^2 = \sigma_2^2$. If the null hypothesis (H_0: the means are equal) is true, then, because the populations have identical means and variances, this implies that under H_0 we are dealing with a *single population*. The ANOVA procedure is based on a comparison between two separate estimates of the variance, σ^2. The first estimate is derived using the variation among the sample means (only two in the previous example). The other estimate is determined using the variation *within* each of the samples.

The ANOVA procedure is based on a comparison of these two estimates of σ^2 because they should be approximately equal *provided H_0 is true*. We have derived these two estimates:

$MS(\text{factor})$ = estimate of σ^2 based on the variation among the sample means

$MS(\text{error})$ = estimate of σ^2 based on the variation within each of the samples

Our new test statistic for testing H_0: $\mu_1 = \mu_2$ versus H_a: $\mu_1 \neq \mu_2$ is the *ratio* of these two estimates:

$$F = \frac{\left(\begin{array}{c}\text{estimated population variance based on} \\ \text{the variation among the sample means}\end{array}\right)}{\left(\begin{array}{c}\text{estimated population variance based on} \\ \text{the variation within each of the samples}\end{array}\right)} = \frac{MS(\text{factor})}{MS(\text{error})} \qquad (11.10)$$

This test statistic follows an F distribution, which was first introduced in Chapter 9 as a ratio of two variance estimates. The degrees of freedom (df) for the F statistic in equation 11.10 are the df for factor and the df for error; that is, in our present example, the df for F are 1 and $(n_1 + n_2 - 2)$. *Because the F statistic is based on a comparison of two variance estimates, this technique is called analysis of variance.*

This is our second encounter with the F distribution. In Chapter 9, we used this distribution to compare two population variances (σ_1^2 and σ_2^2). The shape of this distribution is illustrated in Figure 11.1 and is tabulated in Table A.7. Remember that the shape of the F curve is affected by both the df for the numerator (1 here) and the df for the denominator (here, $n_1 + n_2 - 2$).

DEFINING THE REJECTION REGION

What happens to the F statistic when H_a is true, that is, when $\mu_1 \neq \mu_2$? In this case, we would expect $\bar{X}_1$ and $\bar{X}_2$ to be "far apart." As a result, the estimate of the variance σ^2 using the *between-sample* variation (measured by $MS(\text{factor})$) will be *larger* than the estimate of σ^2 based on the *within-sample* variation (measured by $MS(\text{error})$). This implies that we should

FIGURE 11.1

Shape of the *F* distribution shown by *F* curve with 1 and $n_1 + n_2 - 2$ df.

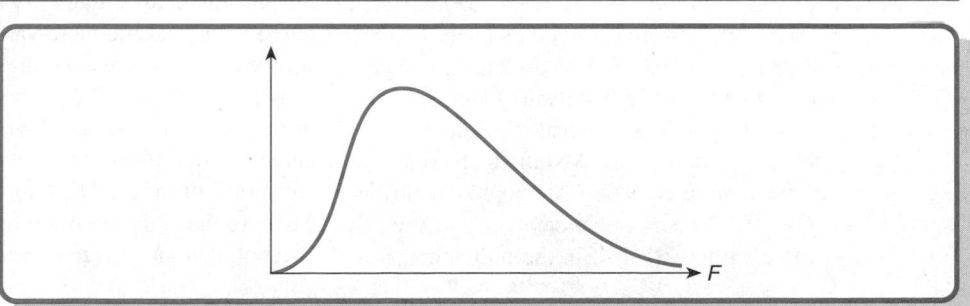

reject H_0 in favor of H_a whenever the ratio of these two estimates is large—in which case the computed F-value is in the right tail. Consequently, the test procedure will be to

$$\text{reject } H_0 \text{ if } F^* > F_{\alpha, v_1, v_2}$$

where v_1 = df for numerator = (number of levels) − 1 = 1, v_2 = df for denominator = $n_1 + n_2 - 2$, and F_{α, v_1, v_2} is obtained from Table A.7 with a right-tail area = α.

EXAMPLE 11.1

Using the data from the battery lifetimes example and the previously calculated sums of squares, test H_0: $\mu_1 = \mu_2$ versus H_a: $\mu_1 \neq \mu_2$, where μ_1 = average lifetime for brand 1, if observed indefinitely, and μ_2 = average for brand 2. Use a significance level of $\alpha = .10$.

SOLUTION

Step 1. The hypotheses are as defined—H_0: $\mu_1 = \mu_2$ and H_a: $\mu_1 \neq \mu_2$.
Step 2. The test statistic is

$$F = \frac{\text{MS(factor)}}{\text{MS(error)}}$$

Step 3. The rejection region [using Table A.7(a)] is

$$\text{reject } H_0 \text{ if } F > F_{.10, 1, 8} = 3.46$$

Step 4. From the previous calculations, SS(factor) = 396.9 and SS(error) = 180. So,

$$\text{MS(factor)} = \frac{\text{SS(factor)}}{1} = \frac{396.9}{1} = 396.0$$

and

$$\text{MS(error)} = \frac{\text{SS(error)}}{n_1 + n_2 - 2} = \frac{180.0}{8} = 22.5$$

The resulting value of the test statistic is

$$F^* = \frac{396.9}{22.5} = 17.64$$

Because $17.64 > 3.46$, we reject H_0.
Step 5. These data indicate that the mean lifetimes for brand 1 and brand 2 are *not* the same.

COMMENTS

Compare our first treatment of the battery lifetimes problem with Example 11.1. Both solutions led to the same conclusion, namely, that the two average lifetimes are not the same. In fact, the two solutions *always* lead to the same conclusion when comparing *two* means. Furthermore, the p-values for the two solutions *are the same,* as illustrated in Figure 11.2. The values were obtained using a computer program (available in many statistical packages) that provides an exact p-value for a t or F-statistic, given the computed value and corresponding degrees of freedom.

The computed value of the F-statistic is equal to the square of the computed value of the t statistic because $17.64 = (4.20)^2$. This is true whenever you have an F-statistic or table value with 1 df in the numerator, So

$$F^* = (t^*)^2$$

Furthermore, the table values satisfy the same relationship, for example,

$$F_{.10, 1, 8} = 3.46 = (1.86)^2 = [t_{.05, 8}]^2$$

We see that the two tests are *identical;* they produce the same conclusion and p-value. Furthermore, the computed value and the table value for the F-statistic are the squares of the corresponding values using the t statistic. This comparison applies *only* when the F-statistic has 1 df in the numerator—that is, when there are two factor levels (as in this illustration). As mentioned previously, the advantage of the ANOVA approach is that it extends very easily to the situation of comparing means for more than two populations (covered in the next section).

FIGURE 11.2

p-values for the solution to the battery lifetimes example. (a) Solution using pooled variance t test. (b) Solution using ANOVA (see Example 11.1).

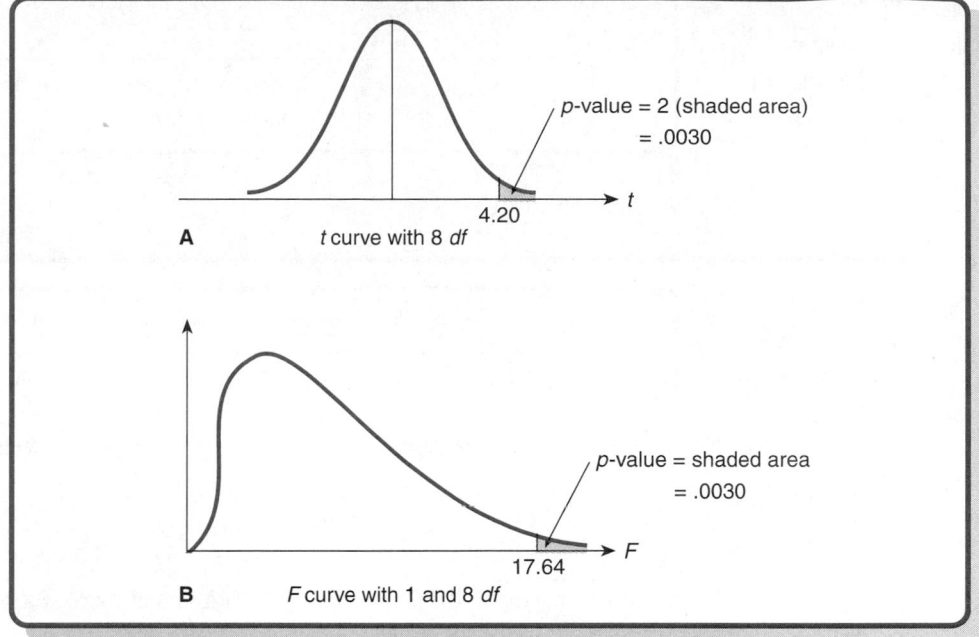

THE ANOVA TABLE

Rather than carrying out the five-step procedure using the F-statistic, an easier method is to use an **ANOVA table** of the various sums of squares. The format of this table is as follows:*

Source	df	SS	MS	F
Factor	1	SS(factor)	$\text{MS(factor)} = \dfrac{\text{SS(factor)}}{1}$	$\dfrac{\text{MS(factor)}}{\text{MS(error)}}$
Error	$n-2$	SS(error)	$\text{MS(error)} = \dfrac{\text{SS(error)}}{n-2}$	
Total	$n-1$	SS(total)		

To fill in this table, you compute the necessary sums of squares along with the mean squares and insert them. Notice that $n = n_1 + n_2 =$ total sample size and that column 3 (MS) = column 2 (SS) divided by column 1 (df).

The ANOVA table for Example 11.1 follows.

Source	df	SS	MS	F
Factor	1	396.9	396.9	17.64
Error	8	180.0	22.5	
Total	9	576.9		

SUMMARY OF THE ANOVA APPROACH FOR ONE-FACTOR TESTS

In Example 11.1 we concluded that a difference existed between the two *means* because the variation *between* the two samples (measured by MS(factor)) was much greater than the variation *within* the samples (measured by MS(error)). Thus, the ratio of these values was very large and F^* fell in the rejection region. Consequently, we rejected $H_0: \mu_1 = \mu_2$.

---

* The headings under the "Source" column will vary, depending on the computer package. SS(factor) often is labeled "between groups" (Excel), "treatment," or "among groups"; SS(error) often is labeled "within groups" (Excel), "residual" or "error" (MINITAB).

FIGURE 11.3
Dot-array diagram of replicates in Example 11.1.

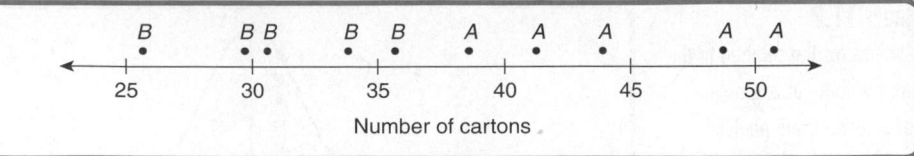

FIGURE 11.4
Dot-array diagram where between-sample and within-sample variations are nearly the same. The *F* statistic would not lie in the rejection region.

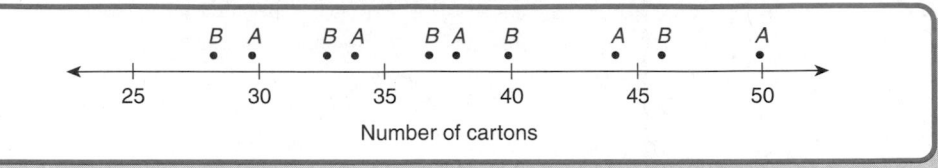

What this means in the language of ANOVA is that there *is* a significant effect on battery lifetime due to the brand factor.

To carry out the *F*-test, we first randomly obtain observations, called **replicates,** from each population. Example 11.1 used five replicates from each of the two battery brand populations. It is *not necessary* to obtain the same number of replicates from each population.

Figure 11.3 is a dot-array diagram of the data in Example 11.1, where the symbol A represents a value from brand 1, and B represents brand 2. You do not need to be an expert statistician to observe that a clear difference exists between the lifetimes of the two brands of batteries. The variation within the A's alone and the B's alone is the within-sample variation. Because the distances from the A values to the B values are much larger than the distances among the A values alone, the between-sample variation is quite large, as we have already observed.

Suppose instead that your dot-array diagram looks like Figure 11.4. Now the two sources of variation appear to be nearly the same, and there is no obvious difference between the two brands. The resulting *F*-statistic here would not lie within the rejection region, and we would not be able to demonstrate, using the ANOVA approach, a difference between the two mean lifetimes.

11.2 ONE-FACTOR ANOVA COMPARING MORE THAN TWO MEANS

In the previous section, we examined a single *factor* with two *levels*. Our concern was whether there was any difference between the two levels of this factor. We performed a test of hypothesis on the means of two populations. Because we were dealing with the effect of a single factor, this was a one-factor (or one-way) ANOVA.

In general, one-factor ANOVA techniques can be used to study the effect of any single factor on performance, sales, and the like. This factor can consist of any number of levels— say, k levels. To determine if the levels of this factor affect our measured observations, we examine the hypotheses

$$H_0: \mu_1 = \mu_2 = \cdots = \mu_k$$

$$H_a: \text{not all } \mu\text{'s are equal}$$

Suppose we are interested in the average lifetimes of not two but five brands of batteries. Is there any difference in these five mean lifetimes? To answer this question, we test

$$H_0: \mu_1 = \mu_2 = \mu_3 = \mu_4 = \mu_5$$

$$H_a: \text{not all } \mu\text{'s are equal}$$

Note that the complement of H_0 is *not* H_a: $\mu_1 \neq \mu_2 \neq \mu_3 \neq \mu_4 \neq \mu_5$. This alternative hypothesis is "too strong," and the correct form of H_a is that at least two of the means differ or, as stated here, not all of the means are equal.

We have a single factor (brand) consisting of five levels (brand 1, brand 2, . . . , brand 5). One possibility is to examine these samples one pair at a time using the t statistic discussed in the previous section. This appears to be a safe way to proceed here, although there are $_5C_2 = 10$ such pairs of tests to perform this way. The main problem with performing many tests of this nature is determining the probability of making an incorrect decision. In particular, what value does α have, where α is the probability of rejecting H_0: all μ's are equal, when in fact it is true? You set α in advance but, after performing ten of these pairwise tests ($\mu_1 = \mu_2$, $\mu_1 = \mu_3$, . . .), for instance, what is your *overall* probability of concluding that at least one pair of means are not equal when they actually are? This is a difficult question. The overall probability is not the significance level, α, with which you selected for just one pair. *So we need an approach that will test for the equality of these five means using a single test. This is what the ANOVA approach does.*

ASSUMPTIONS BEHIND THE ANOVA ANALYSIS

When using the ANOVA procedure, there are three key assumptions that must be satisfied. They are basically the same requirements that were necessary when testing two means using small, independent samples and the pooled variance approach. These requirements are:

1. The replicates (observations) are obtained *independently* and *randomly* from each of the populations. The value of one observation has no effect on any other replicates within the same sample or within the other samples.
2. The replicates from each population follow (approximately) a *normal* distribution.
3. The normal populations all have a *common variance,* σ^2. We expect the values in each sample to vary about the same amount. The ANOVA procedure will be much less sensitive to violations of this requirement when we obtain samples of equal size from each population.

DERIVING THE SUM OF SQUARES

When examining k populations, for example, the data will be configured somewhat like this:

	Level 1	Level 2	$\cdots$	Level k
	$\vdots$	$\vdots$		$\vdots$
	n_1 replicates	n_2 replicates	$\cdots$	n_k replicates
	$\vdots$	$\vdots$		$\vdots$
Totals	T_1	T_2	$\cdots$	T_k

These resemble the data from Example 11.1, where $k = 2$ and $n_1 = n_2 = 5$ replicates. To derive the sum of squares for this situation, we extend the results in equations 11.2, 11.4, and 11.6 to

$$\text{SS(factor)} = \left[\frac{T_1^2}{n_1} + \frac{T_2^2}{n_2} + \cdots + \frac{T_k^2}{n_k} \right] - \frac{T^2}{n} \qquad (11.11)$$

$$\text{SS(total)} = \sum x^2 - \frac{T^2}{n} \qquad (11.12)$$

$$\text{SS(error)} = \sum x^2 - \left[\frac{T_1^2}{n_1} + \frac{T_2^2}{n_2} + \cdots + \frac{T_k^2}{n_k} \right] \qquad (11.13)$$

$$= \text{SS(total)} - \text{SS(factor)} \qquad (11.14)$$

Here, n = the total number of observations = $n_1 + n_2 + \cdots + n_k$, and $T = \sum x$ = the sum of all n observations = $T_1 + T_2 + \cdots + T_k$. Also, to find $\sum x^2$, we square each of the n observations and sum the results.

THE ANOVA TABLE

The good news is that the format of the ANOVA table is the same regardless of the number of populations (levels), k. The only change from the two-population case is that

$$\text{df for factor} = k - 1$$

$$\text{df for error} = n - k$$

As before, the total df are $n - 1$. The resulting ANOVA table follows.

Source	df	SS	MS	F
Factor	$k - 1$	SS(factor)	$\text{MS(factor)} = \dfrac{\text{SS(factor)}}{k - 1}$	$\dfrac{\text{MS(factor)}}{\text{MS(error)}}$
Error	$n - k$	SS(error)	$\text{MS(error)} = \dfrac{\text{SS(error)}}{n - k}$	
Total	$n - 1$	SS(total)		

Note that

$$
\begin{aligned}
\text{MS(factor)} &= \frac{\text{SS(factor)}}{\text{df for factor}} \\
&= \frac{\text{SS(factor)}}{k - 1} \qquad \text{(11.15)} \\
\text{MS(error)} &= \frac{\text{SS(error)}}{\text{df for error}} \\
&= \frac{\text{SS(error)}}{n - k} \qquad \text{(11.16)}
\end{aligned}
$$

The test statistic for testing H_0: $\mu_1 = \mu_2 = \cdots = \mu_k$ versus H_a: not all μ's are equal is

$$F = \frac{\text{MS(factor)}}{\text{MS(error)}}$$

which has an F distribution with $k - 1$ and $n - k$ df.

As in the two-sample case, the procedure is to reject H_0 when the variation among the sample means (measured by MS(factor)) is *large* compared to the variation within the samples (measured by MS(error)). Consequently, the test will be to reject H_0 whenever F lies in the *right-tailed* rejection region defined by the significance level, α.

EXAMPLE 11.2

The manufacturer of the small battery-powered tape recorder (discussed at the start of this chapter) also manufactures battery powered AM/FM radio sets that include the required batteries. This unit uses a smaller battery, and four suppliers (brands) of this battery are being considered. Past experience has indicated that the battery lifetimes are normally distributed. The supervising inspector of incoming quality again wants to know whether there is any difference among the average lifetimes of the four battery brands. Twenty-four batteries (six of each brand) are placed on a test device that slowly drains the battery power and records the battery lifetime. The following data (in hours) were obtained:

	Brand 1	**Brand 2**	**Brand 3**	**Brand 4**
	41	32	35	33
	35	37	30	27
	48	46	24	36
	40	53	26	35
	45	41	28	27
	52	43	31	25
Total (T)	261	252	174	183
Average ($\overline{X}$)	43.5	42.0	29.0	30.5
Variance (s^2)	37.1	52.8	15.2	22.3

The four sample averages are $\overline{x}_1 = 43.5$, $\overline{x}_2 = 42.0$, $\overline{x}_3 = 29.0$, and $\overline{x}_4 = 30.5$. Brands 1 and 2 appear to be outlasting brands 3 and 4. In other words, it appears that there is a significant *between-group variation*. But do these sample means provide sufficient evidence to reject H_0: $\mu_1 = \mu_2 = \mu_3 = \mu_4$, where each μ_i represents the average of *all* lifetimes for brand *i*? Use the ANOVA procedure to answer this question with $\alpha = .05$.

SOLUTION

The requirements for this analysis are (1) the samples were obtained randomly and independently from each of the four populations, and (2) the battery lifetimes for each brand follow a *normal* distribution with a *common variance,* say, σ^2.

$$SS(factor) = \left[\frac{T_1^2}{n_1} + \frac{T_2^2}{n_2} + \frac{T_3^2}{n_3} + \frac{T_4^2}{n_4} \right] - \frac{T^2}{n}$$

So $n = n_1 + n_2 + n_3 + n_4 = 24$, and

$$T = \sum x = T_1 + T_2 + T_3 + T_4$$

$$= 261 + 252 + 174 + 183 = 870$$

Therefore,

$$SS(factor) = \frac{261^2}{6} + \frac{252^2}{6} + \frac{174^2}{6} + \frac{183^2}{6} - \frac{870^2}{24}$$

$$= 32{,}565 - 31{,}537.5 = 1027.5$$

$$SS(total) = \sum x^2 - \frac{T^2}{n}$$

$$= [41^2 + 35^2 + \cdots + 27^2 + 25^2] - \frac{870^2}{24}$$

$$= 33{,}202 - 31{,}537.5 = 1664.5$$

$$SS(error) = SS(total) - SS(factor)$$

$$= 1664.5 - 1027.5 = 637$$

The ANOVA table for this analysis follows.

Source	df	SS	MS	F
Factor	$k - 1 = 3$	1027.5	$1027.5/3 = 342.5$	$342.5/31.85 = 10.75$
Error	$n - k = 20$	637	$637/20 = 31.85$	
Total	23	1664.5		

The computed F-value from the ANOVA table is $F^* = 10.75$. Since $\alpha = .05$, we use Table A.7 to find that $F_{.05,3,20} = 3.10$. Comparing these two values, $F^* = 10.75 > 3.10$, so we reject H_0.

We conclude that the average lifetimes for the four brands are not the same. This confirms our earlier suspicion based on the variation among the four sample means. Our results indicate that the brand factor *does* have a significant effect on battery lifetime.

The Assumptions behind ANOVA and a Test for Equal Variances

Using *independent random samples* is of extreme importance with the ANOVA procedure. The F-test used for comparing the population means in the ANOVA table is very sensitive to departures from this assumption, so the safest way to guard against incorrect conclusions is to use random sampling techniques. In many situations, however, such as when using the same set of people for before-and-after experiments, this may be difficult or impossible. One solution to this problem is to modify your study design, for example, by using a randomized block design, discussed later in this chapter.

Lack of **normality** within the populations is not a critical matter provided the departure is not too extreme. The F-test used to test the means is not severely affected by populations that are somewhat nonnormal in nature. One way of making the ANOVA procedure even less sensitive to this requirement is to use *large samples*.

If the *variances* of the population *are not equal,* the F-test used in the ANOVA procedure for testing the means is only slightly affected, provided the *sample sizes are equal* (or nearly so). However, for this case, there is a very simple test of hypothesis for verifying this requirement.

In Chapter 9 an F-test was defined for determining whether two normal population variances (or standard deviations) are equal. A similar test is used when you are comparing more than two normal population variances, provided the sample sizes are equal.* Here the hypotheses are

$$H_0: \sigma_1^2 = \sigma_2^2 = \cdots = \sigma_k^2$$

H_a: at least two variances are unequal (the k variances are not the same)

We warned you in Chapter 9 about the dangers of using the same data to test both the variances *and* the means. This warning also applies to tests of more than two populations. A better procedure is to use a different data set for testing H_0: the variances are equal. This requires a much larger data set than is necessary if you use the same data for both tests. The test for equal variances is the Hartley test; the test statistic is defined to be

$$H = \frac{\text{maximum } s^2}{\text{minimum } s^2} \qquad (11.17)$$

which is simply the ratio of the largest sample variance divided by the smallest of these k variances.

If H_0 is false, the test statistic will be "large," so the testing procedure is to reject H_0 if the computed value of H lies in the right tail. The rejection region for a 5% level of significance can be obtained from Table A.14. This region depends on the number (k) of populations or levels and the number of observations in *each* sample.

Suppose we use the battery lifetime data from Example 11.2, only for testing the hypotheses

$$H_0: \sigma_1^2 = \sigma_2^2 = \sigma_3^2 = \sigma_4^2$$

H_a: at least two variances are unequal

Using $\alpha = .05$ and Table A.14, because $k = 4$ and there are six observations in each sample, the test is to

reject H_0 if $H > 13.7$

Using the data summary in Example 11.2, the minimum s^2 is 15.2 and the maximum s^2 is 52.8. Consequently,

$$H = \frac{52.8}{15.2} = 3.47$$

---

* When the sample sizes are unequal, a computationally more difficult test for equal variances can be performed, derived by M. S. Bartlett. For details, see M. Kutner, C. Nachtschiem, W. Wasserman, and J. Neter, *Applied Linear Statistical Models*, 4th ed. (Homewood, Ill.: Richard D. Irwin, 1996).

which is less than 13.7, and so the conclusion is that we have no reason to suspect unequal variances for this situation.

If other data are available for testing the means, the requirement of equal variances behind the ANOVA procedure appears to be met.

CONFIDENCE INTERVALS IN ONE-FACTOR ANOVA

When we deal with normal populations, as we do here, we can supply:

1. A point estimate of each mean, μ_i; for example, an estimate of μ_2 is $\overline{X}_2$.
2. A point estimate of each mean difference, $\mu_i - \mu_j$; for example, an estimate of $\mu_1 - \mu_3$ is $\overline{X}_1 - \overline{X}_3$.

When using the ANOVA procedure, the populations are believed to have a common variance, say σ^2. To estimate this variance, we use an estimate of σ^2 that does not depend on whether the population means are equal—the *within*-sample variation, measured by MS(error). The point estimate of σ^2 is

$$s_p^2 = \text{pooled variance}$$

$$= \text{MS(error)}$$

where MS(error) is defined in equation 11.16.

In previous chapters, we always supplied a confidence interval along with a point estimate to provide a measure of how reliable this estimate really is. The narrower the confidence interval, the more faith you have in your point estimate. A $(1 - \alpha) \cdot 100\%$ confidence interval for μ_i is

$$\overline{X}_i - t_{\alpha/2, n-k} s_p \sqrt{\frac{1}{n_i}} \quad \text{to} \quad \overline{X}_i + t_{\alpha/2, n-k} s_p \sqrt{\frac{1}{n_i}} \qquad \textbf{(11.18)}$$

where

$$k = \text{number of populations (levels)}$$

$$n_i = \text{number of replicates in the } i\text{th sample}$$

$$n = \text{total number of observations}$$

$$s_p = \sqrt{\text{MS(error)}}$$

$t_{\alpha/2, \text{df}}$ is the value from Table A.5 with df = df for error = $n - k$, and right-tail area = $\alpha/2$.

A $(1 - \alpha) \cdot 100\%$ confidence interval for $\mu_i - \mu_j$ is

$$(\overline{X}_i - \overline{X}_j) - t_{\alpha/2, n-k} s_p \sqrt{\frac{1}{n_i} + \frac{1}{n_j}} \quad \text{to} \quad (\overline{X}_i - \overline{X}_j) + t_{\alpha/2, n-k} s_p \sqrt{\frac{1}{n_i} + \frac{1}{n_j}} \qquad \textbf{(11.19)}$$

EXAMPLE 11.3

Using the battery lifetime data from Example 11.2, construct a 95% confidence interval for the average lifetime of brand 1. Also determine a 95% confidence interval for the difference between the average lifetimes of brands 1 and 3.

SOLUTION

First, your point estimate of μ_1 is $\overline{x}_1 = 43.5$. Using the ANOVA table from Example 11.2,

$$s_p^2 = \text{MS(error)} = 31.85$$

and so

$$s_p = \sqrt{31.85} = 5.64$$

Because $n = 24$ and $k = 4$, the resulting 95% confidence interval for μ_1 is

$$43.5 - t_{.025,20}\,(5.64)\sqrt{\frac{1}{6}} \quad \text{to} \quad 43.5 + t_{.025,20}\,(5.64)\sqrt{\frac{1}{6}}$$

$$= 43.5 - (2.086)(5.64)(.408) \quad \text{to} \quad 43.5 + (2.086)(5.64)(.408)$$

$$= 43.5 - 4.80 \quad \text{to} \quad 43.5 + 4.80$$

$$= 38.7 \quad \text{to} \quad 48.3$$

As a result, we are 95% confident that the average lifetime of the brand 1 battery is between 38.7 and 48.3 hours.

The 95% confidence interval for $\mu_1 - \mu_3$ is

$$(\overline{X}_1 - \overline{X}_3) - t_{.025,20}\,s_p\sqrt{\frac{1}{n_1} + \frac{1}{n_3}} \quad \text{to} \quad (\overline{X}_1 - \overline{X}_3) + t_{.025,20}\,s_p\sqrt{\frac{1}{n_1} + \frac{1}{n_3}}$$

$$= (43.5 - 29.0) - (2.086)(5.64)\sqrt{\frac{1}{6} + \frac{1}{6}} \quad \text{to} \quad (43.5 - 29.0) + (2.086)(5.64)\sqrt{\frac{1}{6} + \frac{1}{6}}$$

$$= 14.5 - (2.086)(5.64)(.577) \quad \text{to} \quad 14.5 + (2.086)(5.64)(.577)$$

$$= 14.5 - 6.79 \quad \text{to} \quad 14.5 + 6.79$$

$$= 7.71 \quad \text{to} \quad 21.29$$

Based on this confidence interval, we are 95% confident that the average lifetime for brand 1 is between 7.71 and 21.29 hours *higher* than the average lifetime for brand 3.

A Word of Warning

The procedure we used in Example 11.3 for determining confidence intervals is reliable, providing you decide which intervals you want computed *before* you observe your data. For example, constructing a confidence interval for the difference of two population means having the corresponding largest and smallest sample means is not an accurate procedure. If you do this, you let the data dictate which confidence interval you determine.

When using the procedure in Example 11.3 to construct confidence intervals for the difference of two population means, it is important to keep the number of such intervals as small as possible, because the probability of any one interval containing the true population difference is $1 - \alpha$, but the probability that *all* the intervals contain their respective population differences is not $1 - \alpha$. In other words, if $\alpha = .05$, the overall confidence level of this procedure is not 95%; it is something much less than 95%. *To compare all possible pairs of means effectively, you need to use a technique that will allow you to make all possible comparisons between population means while maintaining the Type I error rate at α.* This is called a **multiple comparisons** procedure; one such procedure is discussed following Example 11.5.

EXAMPLE 11.4

The manager of Autoplex, a local car dealership, is interested in examining the average dollar amount of "extras" (such as air conditioning, automatic transmission, exterior trim) for new-car buyers during the past year. In particular, she wants to compare average purchases for three groups: single male purchasers, single female purchasers, and married purchasers. Data from a sample of 20 purchasers contained 5 in each of the first two groups and 10 in the married group.* The sample results (in dollars) are:

---

* A similar data set was presented in Chapter 7 in the discussion on stratified sampling. Knowledge of this sampling procedure is not necessary for the discussion here. However, it is worth mentioning that stratified sampling is more effective if there *is* large variation between the groups (strata)—that is, H_0: $\mu_1 = \mu_2 = \mu_3$ is rejected.

	Single Male Purchasers	Single Female Purchasers	Married Purchasers
	5,375	4,802	8,314
	6,913	4,123	5,906
	6,283	3,567	6,025
	5,809	4,355	7,577
	5,346	4,982	6,071
			8,000
			6,489
			7,720
			6,968
			7,538
Total (T)	29,726	21,829	70,608
$\bar{X}_i$	5,945.20	4,365.80	7,060.80

What would be the conclusion using a significance level of .10?

SOLUTION

Examining the sample means, it appears at first glance that there is considerable variation in the sample means; that is, the three population means are not all equal. But is there a significant difference among these three sample means? An ANOVA analysis will clarify this. The necessary requirements here are:

1. The dollar amounts were obtained randomly and independently from each of the three populations (groups).
2. The dollar amounts for each of the three populations follow a normal distribution, with means μ_1, μ_2, μ_3. The amounts in each of the three populations are required to have the same variation.

Because the sample sizes are not the same, the Hartley test for equal variances cannot be used here. As discussed earlier, we prefer not to use the same data for testing both the means and the variances, and so a better procedure would be to obtain additional data (with equal sample sizes) for testing the equality of these three variances. Despite the lack of a Hartley test, we'll proceed by first calculating the necessary sum of squares:

$$SS(\text{factor}) = \left[\frac{T_1^2}{n_1} + \frac{T_2^2}{n_2} + \frac{T_3^2}{n_3} \right] - \frac{T^2}{n}$$

where

$$T = \Sigma x = T_1 + T_2 + T_3$$

$$= 29,726 + 21,829 + 70,608 = 122,163$$

$$n = n_1 + n_2 + n_3$$

$$= 5 + 5 + 10 = 20$$

So

$$SS(\text{factor}) = \frac{29,726^2}{5} + \frac{21,829^2}{5} + \frac{70,608^2}{10} - \frac{122,163^2}{20}$$

$$= 770,577,029.8 - 746,189,928.4 = 24,387,101.4$$

$$SS(\text{total}) = \Sigma x^2 - \frac{T^2}{n}$$

$$= (5375^2 + 6913^2 + \cdots + 6968^2 + 7538^2) - \frac{122,163^2}{20}$$

$$= 780,700,667 - 746,189,928.4 = 34,510,738.6$$

$$SS(\text{error}) = SS(\text{total}) - SS(\text{factor})$$

$$= 34,510,738.6 - 24,387,101.4 = 10,123,637.2$$

Finally, because $k = 3$ and $n = 20$,

$$\text{df for factor} = k - 1 = 2$$

$$\text{df for error} = n - k = 17$$

$$\text{df for total} = n - 1 = 19$$

The resulting ANOVA table is

Source	df	SS	MS	F
Factor	2	24,387,101.4	12,193,550.7	20.48
Error	17	10,123,637.2	595,508.1	
Total	19	34,510,738.6		

The hypotheses are

$$H_0: \mu_1 = \mu_2 = \mu_3$$

$$H_a: \text{not all } \mu\text{'s are equal}$$

where each μ_i represents the average dollar amount of extras for each of the three purchase groups.

We will reject H_0 if

$$F^* > F_{.10,2,17} = 2.64$$

Because $20.48 > 2.64$, H_0 is rejected. There is strong evidence to indicate a difference in the buying behavior for these three groups.

The factor in Example 11.4 was the type of purchaser, and it had three levels. The results indicate that this factor had a significant effect on the amount of extras purchased.

EXAMPLE 11.5

In Example 11.4, before the data were obtained, the manager at Autoplex decided to construct a 95% confidence interval for the average dollar amount of the married purchasers and the difference between the average dollar amounts for the married purchasers and the single male purchasers. What are the confidence intervals?

SOLUTION

The point estimates are

for μ_3: $\bar{x}_3 = \$7,060.80$

for $\mu_3 - \mu_1$: $\bar{x}_3 - \bar{x}_1 = \$7,060.80 - \$5,945.20 = \$1,115.60$

To construct the confidence intervals, you first need an estimate of the common variance of these three populations. Based on the results of Example 11.4, this is

$$s_p^2 = \text{MS(error)} = 595,508.1$$

So

$$s_p = \sqrt{595,508.1} = 771.69$$

Because $n = 20$, $k = 3$, and $n_3 = 10$, the 95% confidence interval for μ_3 (the mean for the married purchasers) is

$$\bar{x}_3 - t_{.025,17} s_p \sqrt{\frac{1}{n_3}} \quad \text{to} \quad \bar{x}_3 + t_{.025,17} s_p \sqrt{\frac{1}{n_3}}$$

$$= 7060.80 - (2.110)(771.69)(.316) \quad \text{to} \quad 7060.80 + (2.110)(771.69)(.316)$$

$$= 7060.80 - 514.53 \quad \text{to} \quad 7060.80 + 514.53$$

$$= \$6,546.27 \quad \text{to} \quad \$7,575.33$$

The 95% confidence interval for $\mu_3 - \mu_1$ is

$$(\bar{x}_3 - \bar{x}_1) - t_{.025,17} s_p \sqrt{\frac{1}{n_3} + \frac{1}{n_1}} \quad \text{to} \quad (\bar{x}_3 - \bar{x}_1) + t_{.025,17} s_p \sqrt{\frac{1}{n_3} + \frac{1}{n_1}}$$

$$= (7060.80 - 5945.20) - (2.110)(771.69)(.548) \quad \text{to}$$

$$(7060.80 - 5945.20) + (2.110)(771.69)(.548)$$

$$= 1115.60 - 892.29 \quad \text{to} \quad 1115.60 + 892.29$$

$$= \$223.31 \quad \text{to} \quad \$2007.89$$

Consequently, we are 95% confident that the average dollar amount of the purchased extras for the married group is between \$223.31 and \$2,007.89 *higher* than for the single male group.

Multiple Comparisons: A Follow-Up to the One-Factor ANOVA Procedure

If the one-factor ANOVA procedure leads to a rejection of H_0: all populations means are equal, a logical question would be, which means do differ? In other words, rejecting the ANOVA null hypothesis informs us that the means are not all the same but provides no clue as to which of the population means are different. As we discussed prior to Example 11.4, performing a series of t tests to compare all possible pairs of means is not a good idea, since the chances of making at least one Type I error (concluding that a difference exists between two population means when in fact they are the same) using such a procedure is much larger than the predetermined α used for each of the t tests.

What is needed is a technique that compares all possible pairs of means in such a way that the probability of making **one or more** Type I errors is α. This is a *multiple comparisons procedure*. There are several methods available for making multiple comparisons; the one presented here is **Tukey's** test for multiple comparisons (Tukey is pronounced too′-key).

Tukey's procedure is based on a statistical test that uses the largest and smallest sample means. The form of this statistic is

$$Q = \frac{\text{maximum } (\bar{X}_i) - \text{minimum } (\bar{X}_i)}{\sqrt{\text{MS(error)} / n_r}} \qquad \textbf{(11.20)}$$

where

1. Maximum $(\bar{X}_i)$ and minimum $(\bar{X}_i)$ are the largest and smallest sample means, respectively.
2. MS(error) is the pooled sample variance.
3. n_r is the number of replicates in each sample.

Notice that Tukey's procedure assumes that each sample contains the same number (n_r) of replicates. Critical values of the Q statistic are contained in Table A.16. Define

$Q_{\alpha,k,v}$ = critical value of the Q statistic from Table A.16, using a significance level of α; k is the number of sample means (groups), and v is the df associated with MS(error)

MULTIPLE COMPARISONS PROCEDURE: ONE-FACTOR ANOVA

1. Find $Q_{\alpha,k,v}$ using Table A.16.
2. Determine

$$D = Q_{\alpha,k,v} \cdot \sqrt{\frac{MS(error)}{n_r}}$$

where MS(error) is the pooled sample variance and n_r is the number of replicates in each sample. For one-factor ANOVA, MS(error) is the same as s_p^2.
3. Place the sample means in order, from smallest to largest.
4. If two sample means differ by more than D, the conclusion is that the corresponding population means are unequal. In other words, if $\left| \bar{X}_i - \bar{X}_j \right| > D$, this implies that $\mu_i \neq \mu_j$.

To illustrate this procedure, reconsider Example 11.2. There we concluded that the average lifetime on a test device was not the same for the four brands of batteries. The four sample means were

$$\text{Brand 1: } \bar{x}_1 = 43.5$$

$$\text{Brand 2: } \bar{x}_2 = 42.0$$

$$\text{Brand 3: } \bar{x}_3 = 29.0$$

$$\text{Brand 4: } \bar{x}_4 = 30.5$$

For this study, there were $n_r = 6$ replicates in each sample, with a resulting pooled variance of $s_p^2 = MS(error) = 31.85$. The study contained $k = 4$ groups and the df for the error sum of squares was $v = n - k = 24 - 4 = 20$. Using a significance level of .05, we begin by finding $Q_{.05,4,20}$ in Table A.16. This value is 3.96. Next we determine

$$D = Q_{.05,4,20} \cdot \sqrt{\frac{MS(error)}{n_r}}$$

$$= 3.96 \sqrt{\frac{31.85}{6}} = 9.12$$

The sample means, in order, are

$$\overline{29.0, \ 30.5,} \quad \overline{42.0, \ 43.5}$$

Any two sample means are significantly different using the Tukey procedure if they differ by an amount greater than $D = 9.12$. Here there are four significant differences, namely,

$$\bar{x}_1 - \bar{x}_3 = 43.5 - 29.0 = 14.5 > 9.12$$

$$\bar{x}_2 - \bar{x}_3 = 42.0 - 29.0 = 13.0 > 9.12$$

$$\bar{x}_1 - \bar{x}_4 = 43.5 - 30.5 = 13.0 > 9.12$$

$$\bar{x}_2 - \bar{x}_4 = 42.0 - 30.5 = 11.5 > 9.12$$

The conclusion from the multiple comparisons analysis is that $\mu_1 \neq \mu_3$, $\mu_1 \neq \mu_4$, $\mu_2 \neq \mu_3$, and $\mu_2 \neq \mu_4$. There is no evidence of a difference between the brand 1 and the brand 2 populations or between the brand 3 and the brand 4 populations. This is indicated by the two overbars connecting these two pairs of sample means. In general, there is no evidence to indicate a difference in the population means for any group of sample means under such a bar.

MICROSOFT® EXCEL APPLICATION   USE DATA11-6

EXAMPLE 11.6
Using Excel for One-Factor
ANOVA

LensPro manufactures corrective eyeglasses. Many of their "rimless" frames use a light nylon line (similar to fishing line) to secure the lenses to the frame. LensPro is evaluating the line produced by five different vendors (suppliers). Using a testing device, they determined the breaking strength of 25 different lines obtained independently from each supplier. These breaking strengths are contained in column A for vendor 1, B for vendor 2, . . . , and E for vendor 5.

Using a significance level of .05, do you believe there is sufficient evidence to indicate a difference in average breaking strength for these five suppliers? If so, which of the suppliers would you recommend to LensPro?

In addition, (1) carry out the Hartley test for equal variances using a significance level of .05, (2) determine a 95% confidence interval for the mean breaking strength for vendor 4, and (3) determine a 95% confidence interval for the difference of the mean breaking strengths for vendors 2 and 4 (vendor 4 minus vendor 2).

SOLUTION

The five vertical dotplots in Figure 11.5 (generated using MINITAB) provide an excellent visual examination of the data.* A glance at this graph suggests that the breaking strengths for vendors 1 and 4 are larger than for the other three vendors. Can we in fact demonstrate this? Let's continue.

Begin by opening the dataset DATA11-6. You should see five columns of 25 values each, with labels in the first row. Click on **KGP Data Analysis ➤ ANOVA.** When using this procedure, you *must* include labels in the first row identifying each of the groups. The resulting input screen is shown in Figure 11.6 and should be filled in as shown. The next section will discuss use of the term *experimental design* and mentions that a *completely randomized design* means the same as *one-factor ANOVA.* The resulting Excel-generated ANOVA table is shown in Figure 11.7. Notice that Excel uses "Between Groups" rather than "Factor" in cell F14 and "Within Groups" rather than "Error" in cell F15.

Since the extremely small *p*-value (zero to four decimal places) is less than the 5% significance level, we conclude that the five average breaking strengths are not all the same. To carry out a multiple comparisons procedure (obtained by checking the **Tukey Test for Difference Between Means** box in Figure 11.6), refer to cells F20:J28 in Figure 11.8. The

FIGURE 11.5

Dotplots of nylon line breaking strengths for five vendors.

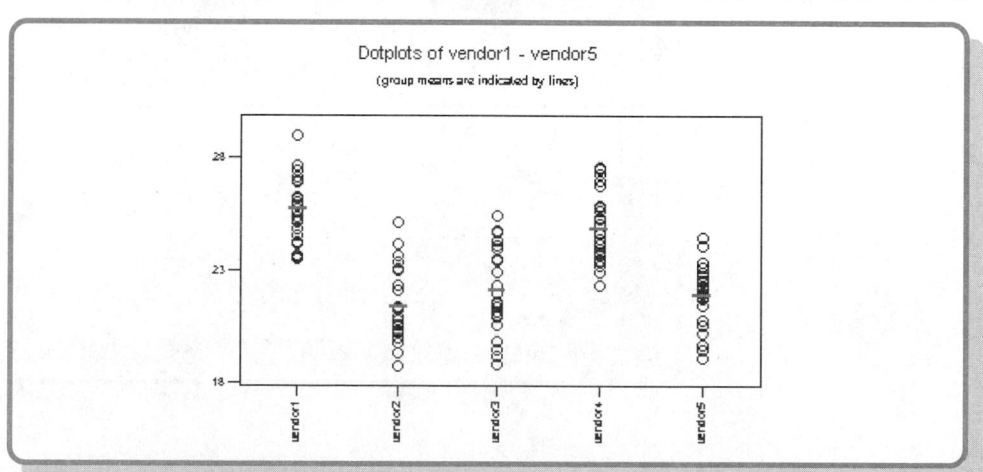

---

* To obtain the graph in Figure 11.5, read the data into columns C1–C5. Name the columns "vendor 1", . . . , "vendor 5". Click on **Stat ➤ ANOVA ➤ Oneway (Unstacked).** In the Response box, enter "C1–C5", click on **Graphs** and the box alongside **Dotplots of data.** Another interesting representation here is obtained by also clicking on the box alongside **Boxplots of data.** In this way, you get five box plots arranged side-by-side.

FIGURE 11.6

Excel input screen using **KGP Data Analysis ➤ ANOVA.**

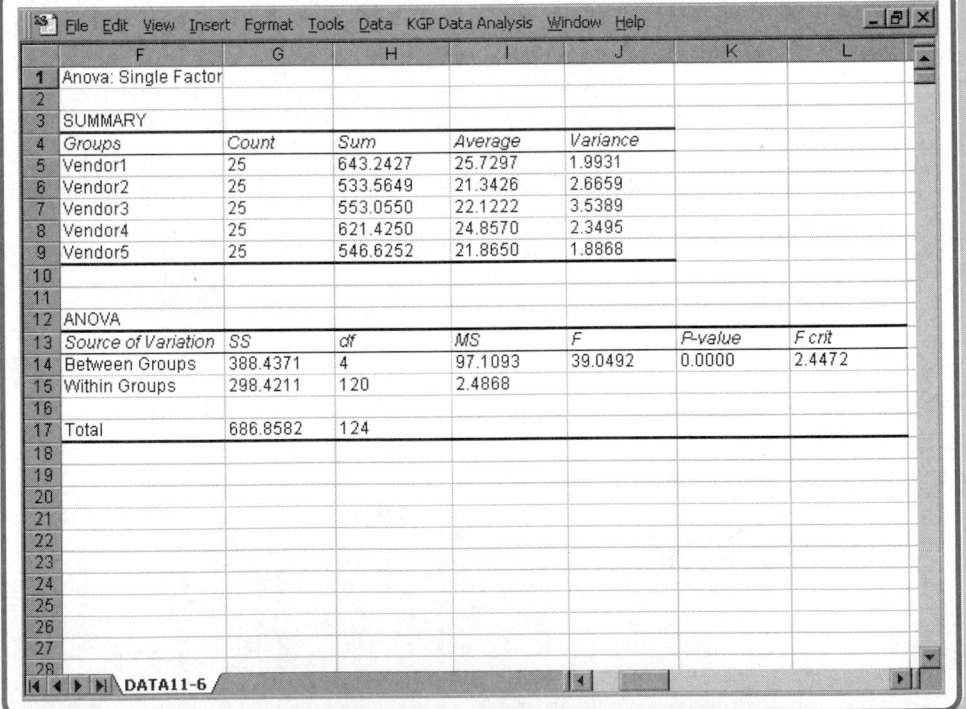

FIGURE 11.7

Portion of Excel spreadsheet containing the one-factor ANOVA output.

	F	G	H	I	J	K	L
1	Anova: Single Factor						
2							
3	SUMMARY						
4	Groups	Count	Sum	Average	Variance		
5	Vendor1	25	643.2427	25.7297	1.9931		
6	Vendor2	25	533.5649	21.3426	2.6659		
7	Vendor3	25	553.0550	22.1222	3.5389		
8	Vendor4	25	621.4250	24.8570	2.3495		
9	Vendor5	25	546.6252	21.8650	1.8868		
10							
11							
12	ANOVA						
13	Source of Variation	SS	df	MS	F	P-value	F crit
14	Between Groups	388.4371	4	97.1093	39.0492	0.0000	2.4472
15	Within Groups	298.4211	120	2.4868			
16							
17	Total	686.8582	124				
18							

DATA11-6

value of D is in the cell labeled **Distance** and is equal to D = 1.236. What pairs of sample means differ by more than 1.236? These are means 1 and 2, 1 and 3, 1 and 5, as well as 4 and 2, 4 and 3, 4 and 5. This is illustrated in cells F26:J28 in Figure 11.8, where the two overbars connect the sample means in row 28 for vendors 2, 3, and 5 and also for vendors 1 and 4. Your recommendation to LensPro would be to use either vendor 1 or vendor 4, based on the breaking strength alone. Other considerations here might consist of cost, sup-

FIGURE 11.8

Remainder of Excel solution to Example 11.6.

	F	G	H	I	J	K	L
19							
20	TUKEY MULTIPLE COMPARISON TEST						
21	Critical Q	Distance	Alpha				
22	3.92	1.2363	0.05				
23							
24	Means joined by a double line are not significantly different.						
25							
26							
27	Vendor2	Vendor5	Vendor3	Vendor4	Vendor1		
28	21.3426	21.8650	22.1222	24.8570	25.7297		
29							
30	HARTLEY TEST FOR HOMOGENEITY OF VARIANCE						
31	Hartley Test	Critical Value	Alpha				
32	1.8756	3.54	0.05				
33							
34							
35							
36	95% CI FOR MEAN OF Vendor4						
37	Mean of Vendor4	Critical t	Standard error	Lower Limit	Upper Limit		
38	24.8570	1.98	0.3154	24.2325	25.4815		
39							
40							
41							
42	95% CI FOR Vendor4 - Vendor2						
43	Difference	Critical t	Standard error	Lower Limit	Upper Limit		
44	3.5144	1.9799	0.4460	2.6313	4.3975		
45							

plier dependability, or other "quality" factors (such as durability and breaking strength variability).

The bottom portion of Figure 11.8 indicates that the test statistic value for the Hartley test is H = 1.8756. This is less than the critical value of 3.54, and so the assumption of equal variances appears to be satisfied. The 95% confidence interval for the mean breaking strength for vendor 4 is from 24.2325 to 25.4815, and the 95% confidence interval for $\mu_4 - \mu_2$ is from 2.6313 to 4.3975. This implies that we are 95% confident that the average breaking strength for vendor 4 is between 2.6 and 4.4 *higher* than for vendor 2.

ONE-FACTOR ANOVA PROCEDURE

Requirements

1. The replicates are obtained *independently* and *randomly* from each of the populations. The value of one observation has no effect on any other replicates within the same sample or within the other samples.
2. The observations (replicates) from each population follow (approximately) a *normal* distribution.
3. The normal populations all have a *common variance*, σ^2. We expect the values in each sample to vary about the same amount. The ANOVA procedure will be much less sensitive to this requirement when we obtain samples of equal size from each population.

Hypotheses

$$H_0: \mu_1 = \mu_2 = \cdots = \mu_k$$

$$H_a: \text{not all } \mu\text{'s are equal}$$

Note that H_a is not the same as H_a': all μ's are unequal; H_a states that *at least two* of the μ's are different.

Sum of Squares

$$SS(\text{factor}) = \left[\frac{T_1^2}{n_1} + \frac{T_2^2}{n_2} + \cdots + \frac{T_k^2}{n_k}\right] - \frac{T^2}{n}$$

where $n = n_1 + n_2 + \cdots + n_k$ and $T = \sum x = T_1 + T_2 + \cdots + T_k$.

$$SS(\text{total}) = \sum x^2 - \frac{T^2}{n}$$

$$SS(\text{error}) = SS(\text{total}) - SS(\text{factor})$$

$$= \sum x^2 - \left[\frac{T_1^2}{n_1} + \frac{T_2^2}{n_2} + \cdots + \frac{T_k^2}{n_k}\right]$$

Degrees of Freedom

$$\text{df for factor} = k - 1$$

$$\text{df for error} = n - k$$

$$\text{df for total} = n - 1$$

Note that $(k - 1) + (n - k) = n - 1$.

ANOVA Table

Source	df	SS	MS	F
Factor	$k - 1$	SS(factor)	$MS(\text{factor}) = \dfrac{SS(\text{factor})}{k - 1}$	$\dfrac{MS(\text{factor})}{MS(\text{error})}$
Error	$n - k$	SS(error)	$MS(\text{error}) = \dfrac{SS(\text{error})}{n - k}$	
Total	$n - 1$	SS(total)		

where MS = mean square = SS/df.

Testing Procedure

$$\text{reject } H_0 \text{ if } F^* > F_{\alpha, k-1, n-k}$$

where $F_{\alpha, k-1, n-k}$ is obtained from Table A.7.

EXERCISES 11.1–11.18

UNDERSTANDING THE MECHANICS

11.1 Consider the following data collected for a completely randomized design.

> Group 1: 5, 7, 2, 8, 5
> Group 2: 8, 10, 6, 9, 14

a. Find the pooled standard deviation that is used in the two-sample t statistic assuming equal population variances.

b. Find the MSE that is used in the completely randomized design.

c. Is the square of the pooled standard deviation equal to the MSE?

d. Find the t statistic assuming equal population variances and the F-statistic for the completely randomized design.

e. Is the square of the t statistic equal to the F-statistic in part (d)?

f. Construct the ANOVA table.

g. Find a 95% confidence interval for the difference in the two means.

11.2 Use the following ANOVA table to answer the succeeding questions.

Source	df	SS	MS	F
Factor		180		
Error	36			
Total	39	241		

a. Complete the ANOVA table, and determine the value of the F-statistic for testing the null hypothesis that the means of the populations are equal.

b. Do the data provide sufficient evidence to indicate that a difference exists in the means of the populations? Use a .01 significance level.

c. If the number of observations from the random samples of each population are equal, what is the number of observations selected from each population?

d. If $T_1 = 95$, $T_2 = 67$, $T_3 = 70$, and $T_4 = 64$, what pairs of population means are significantly different according to Tukey's multiple comparisons procedure? Use a .01 significance level.

11.3 Four independent samples are collected from four normally distributed populations. The data are as follows:

Group 1	Group 2	Group 3	Group 4
12	14	17	10
11	12	18	9
14	16	20	13
10	15	22	12
12		23	
10			

a. Construct an ANOVA table. The SST is equal to 309.158. The sums for groups 1, 2, 3, and 4 are 69, 57, 100, and 44, respectively.

b. Conduct a test of the null hypothesis that the group means are equal. Use a 5% significance level.

c. Find a 95% confidence level for the mean of Group 1. Find a 95% confidence level for the mean of Group 3.

d. Find a 95% confidence interval for the difference between Group 1 and Group 3.

e. Using a 5% significance level, determine if there is a difference in the variance of the four groups. Assume equal sample sizes of $n_r = 5$.

f. Would you recommend that the same data be used to test both the variances and the means for a completely randomized design?

APPLYING THE NEW CONCEPTS

11.4 A 1993 survey indicated that for a majority of Canadians, price is more important than brand loyalty when it comes to buying groceries. Research on the buying patterns of the consumer is important to large manufacturing companies. "Consumers have adopted a much more aggressive approach to shopping," says Gord James, vice president of strategic planning for the Quaker Oats Company of Canada, Ltd. A survey by the Grocery Products Manufacturers of Canada found that on the average, in Canada, men spend $44 a week on groceries, compared to $36 a week for women.

(Source: "Men Spend More on Food, Survey Finds," by Lynne Ainsworth, *Toronto Star*, Sept. 16, 1993, p. A4.)

a. Suppose that the survey included 200 men and 200 women in the random sample and that the Σx^2, where x is weekly expenditure on groceries, is 600,000 for men and 450,000 for women. Construct the ANOVA table for this completely randomized design.

b. Do the data support the conclusion that the weekly expenditures of men and women in Canada differ? Use a .05 significance level.

c. Use the two-sample t test to test for any differences in the mean weekly grocery expenditure for Canadian men and Canadian women. Use a .05 significance level. Assume equal population variances.

d. What is the relationship between the t test in part (c) and the F-test in part (a)?

11.5 The science of ergonomics studies the influence of "human factors" in technology, i.e., how human beings relate to and work with machines. With the widespread use of computers for data processing, computer scientists and psychologists are getting together to study human factors. One typical study investigated the productivity of secretaries with different word processing programs. An identical task was given to 18 secre-

taries, randomly allocated to three groups. Group 1 used a primarily menu-driven program. Group 2 used a command-driven program, and Group 3 used a mixture of both approaches. The secretaries all had about the same level of experience, typing speed, and computer skills. The time (in minutes) taken to complete the task was observed. The results were as follows:

Group 1 (Menu-Driven)	Group 2 (Command-Driven)	Group 3 (Mixed)
12	14	10
15	11	8
11	13	9
12	12	10
10	11	7
13	14	8

a. Do the necessary calculations to construct an ANOVA table, and test the hypothesis that there is no difference between the three types of word processing programs (i.e., on the average, the time taken to complete the task is about the same). Use $\alpha = .05$.

b. State the p-value for the test.

c. Does the type of word processing software used affect the performance of the secretaries?

d. If the secretaries had different levels of experience, typing speed, and computer skills, how would it affect the data? (Would it be an extraneous source of variation, or "noise"? Would it tend to increase the "within-sample" variation, the "between-sample" variation, both, or neither?)

e. Using a significance level of .05, perform a multiple comparisons procedure (if appropriate).

11.6 A small engine-repair shop can special-order parts from any one of the three different warehouses and receive a substantial discount on the price. The manager of the shop is concerned with the length of time that it takes to special-order a part from one of the warehouses. The number of days it takes to special-order a part is recorded for 15 randomly selected orders from each of the three warehouses, as shown in the following table. Do the data indicate that there is a difference in the mean times that it takes to special-order a part from a warehouse? Use a .05 significance level. State the p-value.

Warehouse

A	13 17 14 10 9 15 18 11 13 18 16 13 15 12 16
B	7 12 8 15 6 10 12 10 8 14 10 6 9 13 11
C	10 12 18 19 9 15 20 11 15 13 17 13 10 14 16

11.7 A sales manager wanted to know whether there was a significant difference in the monthly sales of three sales representatives. John is strictly on commission. Randy is on commission and a small salary, and Ted is on a small commission and a salary. Eight months were chosen at random. The data represent monthly sales.

John	969	905	801	850	910	1030	780	810
Randy	738	773	738	805	850	800	690	720
Ted	751	764	701	810	840	790	720	735

a. Using a significance level of .05, test the hypothesis that there is no difference in the mean monthly sales. (Coding the data may make the computations easier.)

b. What is the p-value?

c. Using a significance level of .05, perform a multiple comparisons procedure, if appropriate.

11.8 An instructor wanted to test whether there was a difference in the effectiveness of four different teaching techniques. Four groups of students were taught using one of the four teaching techniques. If the instructor examined the groups of mean differences one pair at a time, how many t tests would have to be performed? What is the advantage of using an ANOVA procedure instead?

11.9 Astral Airlines recently introduced a nonstop flight between Houston and Chicago. The vice president of marketing for Astral decided to run a test to see whether Astral's passenger load was similar to that of its two major competitors. Ten daytime flights were picked at random from each of the three airlines and the percent of unfilled seats on each flight was as follows:

Astral	10	14	12	10	8	13	11	8	12	9
Competitor 1	12	9	8	9	9	10	12	7	11	10
Competitor 2	15	10	15	8	14	9	8	11	10	12

Use a significance level of .05 and perform an ANOVA procedure. Find the p-value.

11.10 The revved-up economy of 1998 produced record profits for many of the partner law firms, with the average profit per partner being approximately $600,000. However, the inflation-adjusted profits per partner—the key measure of law-firm wealth—is only now matching the booming levels of the early 1980s. Suppose that a corporate partner is interested in whether there is a significant difference in the average partner's annual profit for three different geographical regions in the eastern United States. The results of the survey by this partner are presented below.

Geographical Region	Sample Size	Average Annual Profit (in thousands of dollars)
Northeastern states	12	802
Mid-Atlantic states	12	690
Southeastern states	10	557

(Adapted from *The Wall Street Journal,* "Big Law Firms' Profits Evoke 1980s Boom Times," June 30, 1998, p. B1.)

a. Assume that the SSE for the data is 1,811,685. Do the data suggest that a significant difference exists in the average annual profit for partner firms across the three geographical regions of the United States? Use a .10 significance level.

b. Find a 90% confidence interval for the difference in the average annual profit for the Northeastern states and the Southeastern states. Would you expect 0 to be between the upper and lower endpoints of this interval? Why?

c. What assumption must be made to assure the validity of the F test in part (a)?

11.11 T. Sharkey, J. Lim, and K. Kim of the University of Toledo explain that before U.S. companies can export, they must overcome a "threshold fear" based on a lack of knowledge and skills associated with export barriers. These researchers conducted a survey of nonexporting companies, marginal exporters, and active exporters to determine these companies' perceptions to strategic limitations due to export barriers. From this study, the following mean perceptions were computed. A scale from 1 to 5 was used to measure the degree of perceived strategic limitations.

	Sample Mean
Nonexporters	3.2740
Marginal exporters	3.1751
Active exporters	2.8634

(Source: Adapted from "Export Development and Perceived Export Barriers: An Empirical Analysis of Small Firms." *Management International Review,* vol. 29 (1989), pp. 33–40.)

a. Use a multiple comparison procedure to determine which population means differ at a .05 significance level. Assume that the value of the MSE is .9617, that the error degrees of freedom is 414, and that there are 139 observations from each group.

b. In part (a), which population means would be different at the .01 level?

11.12 The workers at a calculator assembly plant wish to bargain for more breaks during the work day. The manager believes that increasing the number of 15-minute breaks will affect productivity. The workers currently receive three breaks during the 8-hour work day. The manager decides to run a test by choosing four groups of five workers each and giving one group three breaks, the next group four breaks, and so on. The number of calculators assembled per day is recorded for five days. Test the manager's claim using an ANOVA procedure with a .10 significance level. Find the p-value. Using a significance level of .05, perform a multiple comparisons procedure, if appropriate.

3 breaks	200	205	197	210	205
4 breaks	210	203	201	197	199
5 breaks	198	190	185	188	180
6 breaks	197	180	190	192	175

11.13 Some four thousand teams participate in the CNBC/ MCI tournament of buying and selling stocks in a make-believe portfolio initially worth $10,000 in cash over 61 trading days. Team players look for news on the stocks and statistics on the Internet using on-line services such as Infospace and Datek Online for news and real-time stock quotes. A finance professor was interested in whether there is a significant difference among aggressive trading (high turnover), moderate trading, and a buy-and-hold approach (low turnover). Assume that from a random sample of 25 teams from each of the three categories that the factor sum of squares was equal to 12 and that the total sum of squares was equal to 616.

(Adapted from *The Wall Street Journal,* "He Was a Teenage Day-Trader," Apr. 22, 1998, p. C1.)

a. What conclusion can the finance professor make in testing whether there is a difference based on trading strategy? Use the p-value to base your conclusions.

b. Should a multiple comparisons procedure be used for further analysis? Why?

c. What requirements on the data must be met to ensure that the analysis is valid?

11.14 A shoe manufacturer wanted to test whether there is a difference in the amount of wear on four different designs of rubber soles for a particular jogging shoe. Before collecting a lot of data on the effect of the designs on the wear, a small pilot study was performed to determine whether the population variances for the different groups were the same. The manufacturer used six joggers for each design in the pilot study. After running 200 miles, the joggers turned in their shoes. The manufacturer used an index to indicate the amount of rubber left on the sole. The pilot study yielded the following standard deviations: $s_1 = 3.12$, $s_2 = 11.61$, $s_3 = 12.48$, $s_4 = 7.31$.

a. Do the data provide sufficient evidence that a difference exists in the population standard deviations for the four designs? Use a .05 significance level.

b. If an ANOVA procedure is used for a larger set of data to determine whether there is a difference in the average amount of wear on the four different designs of rubber soles, are you safe in assuming that the population variances are equal?

c. What requirements on the data are necessary for the validity of the statistical test procedure in part (a)?

11.15 Three machines package 50-pound sacks of pinto beans. A preliminary test is performed using data from a pilot study to determine whether a difference exists among the variances of the amount of beans packaged for each machine. Use a 5% significance level in conducting a test for equality of variances for each of the machines from the following sample data (in pounds):

Machine 1	Machine 2	Machine 3
52	50	48
51	49	46
48	51	51
50	50	50
46	52	52
55	53	50
53	55	51
49	50	52
56	49	50
51	51	51
56	50	49
45	49	50
50	48	50

11.16 A sales manager would like to determine whether there is a difference in the variance of the sales of three salespersons. Three independent samples of daily sales (in hundreds of dollars) are collected. Using a 5% significance level, determine whether the data indicate a difference in the variance of the sales of the three salespersons.

Salesperson 1	Salesperson 2	Salesperson 3
1.2	2.5	1.4
1.1	2.1	1.8
1.4	2.3	1.5
1.6	2.0	1.6
1.4	2.3	1.4
1.0	2.2	1.7
1.3	2.3	1.3
1.8	2.4	1.2
1.4	2.3	1.5
1.5	2.5	1.6

USING THE COMPUTER

11.17 [DATA SET EX11-17] *Variable description:*

Closing1: Willingness to develop a long-term buying relationship from salesperson using closing technique 1.

Closing2: Willingness to develop a long-term buying relationship from salesperson using closing technique 2.

Closing3: Willingness to develop a long-term buying relationship from salesperson using closing technique 3.

The effectiveness of closing techniques has been debated among sales strategists. Closing technique 1 is the most aggressive technique with closing technique 2 being moderately aggressive and closing technique 3 being a no-pressure technique. To determine the impact that each of the techniques has on developing a long term buying relationship, 60 purchasing executives, 20 per technique, were subjected to each of the closing techniques and then asked to rate their willingness to develop a long-term buying relationship with the salesperson. The rating scales ranges from 1 (not willing at all) to 9 (extremely willing).

a. Examine the three means in the printout. Which pairs of sample means appear to be significantly different?

b. Do the data provide sufficient evidence to conclude that the mean rating differs across the three closing techniques? Use a 5% significance level.

c. Examine the printout showing Tukey's multiple comparisons procedure using a 5% significance level. Does this agree with your response to part (a)?

d. Do a "what if" analysis by adding 10 to all the ratings. What parts of the analysis does this change?

e. Do a "what if" analysis by multiplying all the ratings by 10. What parts of the ANOVA table and multiple comparisons procedure change?

Anova: Single Factor

Summary

Groups	Count	Sum	Average	Variance
Closing1	20	115.000	5.750	2.724
Closing2	20	97.000	4.850	2.134
Closing3	20	137.000	6.850	4.450

ANOVA

Source of Variation	SS	df	MS	F	P-value	F crit
Between Groups	40.133	2	20.067	6.468	0.0029	3.159
Within Groups	176.850	57	3.103			
Total	216.983	59				

Tukey Multiple Comparisons Test

Critical Q	Distance	Alpha
3.4	1.339	0.05

Means joined by a double line are not significantly different.

Closing2	Closing1	Closing3
4.850	5.750	6.850

Hartley Test for Homogeneity of Variance

Hartley Test	Critical Value	Alpha
2.085	2.95	0.05

11.18 [DATA SET EX11-18] *Variable description:*

LifeA: Life of battery A
LifeB: Life of battery B
LifeC: Life of battery C
LifeD: Life of battery D

A manager must decide which of four batteries is best for his delivery service company to purchase. The manager assigns a quality engineer to perform an accelerated life testing experiment on the batteries to determine their expected life. After the experiment, the quality engineer records the expected life of each battery using the variables LifeA, LifeB, LifeC, and LifeD in units of months. Fifty batteries of each type are used in the experiment.

a. Use the **Stacked Histogram** option in the KGP Data Analysis menu to examine histograms of the life expectancies of the batteries. How would you describe the differences?

b. Construct an ANOVA table. At a 5% significance level, do the data indicate a difference in the expected life of the four brands of batteries?

c. Use a multiple comparisons procedure to examine the differences. Use a 5% significance level.

d. What recommendation should the quality engineer make to the manager?

11.3 DESIGNING AN EXPERIMENT

The previous section introduced you to one-factor (or one-way) ANOVA. In this type of analysis, you randomly obtain samples from each of the k populations (levels) describing a single factor. The variable that is being measured (such as battery lifetime) is referred to as the **dependent** variable. Since replicates (repeat observations) are obtained in a completely random manner from each population, this type of sampling plan is called a **completely randomized design.** This section discusses other experimental designs, including the randomized block design and the two-way factorial design.

Suppose that the human resource director at Blackburn Industries is interested in examining the cost of dental claims filed by Blackburn employees. Let us consider using the amounts of these claims to examine various group differences; we will need to determine what type of design would be appropriate for each situation.

SITUATION 1: THE COMPLETELY RANDOMIZED DESIGN

One question of interest to the human resource director is whether the average annual amount claimed on the dental insurance plan differs among the four employee classifications. These classifications range from category 1 (consisting of production-line workers) to category 4 (consisting of upper-level management). Replicates are obtained randomly within each population (category), and the four samples are not related in any way. This illustration consists of one factor (employee classification) consisting of four levels. The question of interest here is, is there a difference in the average annual dental claims among the four types of employees? The corresponding null hypothesis is

$$H_0: \mu_1 = \mu_2 = \mu_3 = \mu_4$$

Essentially, this type of analysis (called one-way ANOVA) will fail to reject H_0 if the sample means are "close together" and reject this hypothesis otherwise.

SITUATION 2: THE RANDOMIZED BLOCK DESIGN

Suppose instead that the human resource director at Blackburn Industries wished to investigate family dental claims. In particular, she wished to know if there was a difference in the amounts claimed (1) by the husband, (2) by the wife, and (3) per child in the family. For the study she randomly selected 15 (or however many) families having at least one child and recorded these three amounts for each family. This is an example of a **randomized block design.** The configuration of the sample results would resemble the following scheme, where each x represents a dollar amount.

Family	Husband	Wife	Per Child	
1	x	x	x	(1st block)
2	x	x	x	(2nd block)
$\vdots$				
15	x	x	x	(15th block)

This design consists of one *factor* (say, family member) with three levels (husband/wife/per child). Unlike the completely randomized design, the three samples *are not independent,* since the data are grouped (blocked) by family. For example, the first husband value is not independent of the first wife value, since they both belong to the same family. We encountered this very same design in Chapter 9, where we compared two population means using paired (that is, blocked) samples. When using the randomized block design, you can compare the means of more than two populations using a blocking strategy to gather your data.

The question of interest here is, is there a difference in the husband, wife, and per-child claims? In a situation similar to that of the completely randomized design, the question of interest is whether the factor of interest (family member type, here) has a significant effect on the value of the dependent variable (amount of the annual claim, here). *The difference between the randomized block design and the completely randomized situation is that here we use a blocking strategy rather than independent samples to obtain a more precise test for examining differences in the factor level means.* The null hypothesis for this illustration is that the group (factor level) means are identical, that is,

$$H_0: \mu_H = \mu_W = \mu_C$$

where μ_H is the average annual amount claimed by the husband, μ_W is the average amount for the wife, and μ_C is the average amount claimed per child.

The analysis for the randomized block design is discussed in the next section, but essentially this procedure removes the effects of the blocks (families, here) before testing for a difference between the factor level means. Consequently, this design removes the block effect from the error sum of squares in the completely randomized design. Several examples in the next section illustrate this technique.

SITUATION 3: THE TWO-WAY FACTORIAL DESIGN

The **two-way factorial design** is very similar to situation 1, the one-way analysis of variance, except now *two* factors are of interest to the individual conducting the study. Suppose that the human resource director at Blackburn Industries decides to examine the dental claims for all the unmarried employees. She wants to investigate the effect of gender (factor A) and employee classification (factor B) on the amount of the annual claims. As before, employee classification ranges from category 1 (production-line workers) to category 4 (upper-level management). The previous one-way ANOVA illustration examined only the effect of employee classification on the amount of dental claims. The inclusion of the gender factor accomplishes two things: first, you can determine if the gender of the employee has an effect on the amount of the annual claim, and second, you can investigate whether the relationship between employee classification and the amount of the annual claim is different for male and female employees. In other words, whether factor B relates to the dependent variable (amount of annual dental claim) depends on the level of factor A. This type of effect is called **interaction** between factors *A* and *B*. *This differs from the randomized block design, where it is assumed that no interaction is present between the factor of interest and the blocks.*

Consequently, there are three sets of hypotheses that can be tested using the two-way factorial design. The corresponding null hypotheses are:

$H_{0,A}$: factor *A* (gender) is not significant

$H_{0,B}$: factor *B* (employee classification) is not significant

$H_{0,AB}$: there is no interaction between factor *A* and factor *B*

The first two hypotheses are similar to those tested in one-way ANOVA, but the third hypothesis is unique to the two-way (or higher) factorial design.

To collect data for this design, the human resource director would obtain an amount for *every* combination of a factor A level and a factor B level. This particular illustration consists of two levels for factor A (male/female) and four levels for factor B (category 1/. . ./ category 4) and is called a **2 × 4 factorial design.** Consequently, data are collected for eight possible factor level combinations, referred to as **treatments.** Data values within the same treatment are termed **replicates.** Furthermore, it is necessary when using this

FIGURE 11.9

Illustration of a 2 × 4 factorial design using three replicates.

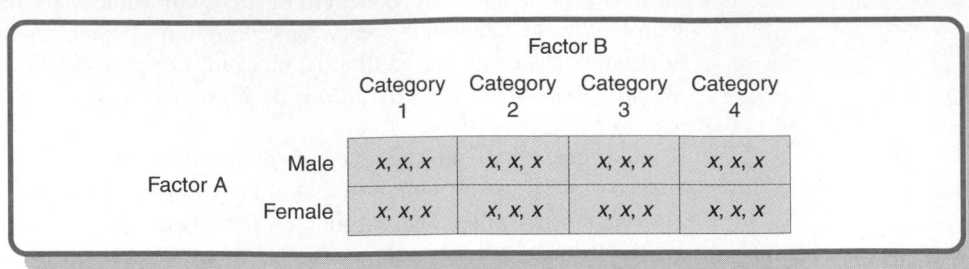

FIGURE 11.9

Illustration of a 2 × 4 factorial design using three replicates.

type of design *to obtain more than one replicate for each treatment.* An illustration using three replicates (two would be sufficient) is shown in Figure 11.9. Each x represents the amount of the annual dental claim. The actual two-way analysis of variance for this illustration is demonstrated in Section 11.5.

EXERCISES 11.19–11.22

UNDERSTANDING THE MECHANICS

11.19

a. Name the three types of experimental design discussed in the preceding section.

b. Which design or designs do not involve the necessity of having replicates?

c. What is "interaction" between factors? Which design permits testing for interaction?

d. In each of the three designs, how many dependent variables are there?

e. If a one-way (one-factor) ANOVA design has four levels of the factor and six replicates at each level, how many treatments are being considered and how many total observations are there?

f. If a 4×6 two-way factorial design is chosen for an ANOVA-based experiment, what are the number of treatments being considered and the *minimum* number of total observations necessary?

g. What is the advantage of blocking and when is it necessary?

h. What are some potential problems that can arise with the randomized block design?

APPLYING THE NEW CONCEPTS

11.20 Quality managers believe that involving suppliers in fundamental design, production, and logistical decisions of a manufacturing firm can have an impact on productivity. In fact, researchers are investigating the effects of supply chain management on manufacturing performance. Suppose that a researcher wishes to determine if there is a significant difference in manufacturing performance as measured by time-to-complete an order in manufacturing organizations with high, medium, and low levels of importance placed on supplier selection criteria. The manufacturing performance is recorded using a self-reporting rating from 1 to 10.

(Source: Adapted from *Decision Sciences Institute 1998 Proceedings*, "Building Supply Chains: A Key to Enhanced Manufacturing Performance," p. 1184–86.)

a. What design is appropriate to test whether there is a difference in the levels of importance placed on supplier selection criteria?

b. Suppose that another factor is also considered: firm size (small, medium, and large). What design is appropriate to test whether there is a difference based on the two factors? Should the interaction effect be tested?

c. Is it necessary for the researcher to obtain more than one replicate for each of the combinations of factor levels in part (b)? What is the minimum number of observations for this design?

11.21 Suppose a supervisor is interested in the productivity of three different machines used to assemble electronics components.

a. What design would be appropriate to test whether there is a difference in the productivity of the machines?

b. Suppose that 20 operators use the machines over three shifts to assemble the components. How can a randomized block design be used?

c. How can one be assured that observations within each block are randomized?

11.22 Toymakers have recognized that children love to imitate adults. A toy analyst wished to determine the differences in perception by 9- and 10-year-old girls over the Milton Bradley games: Mall Madness, Game of Life, and Payday. Each game teaches youngsters that buying store items comes at a cost. The analyst would like to select 9- and 10-year-old girls to play a game and then have a monitor rate the excitement the girls displayed on a scale from 1 to 10.

(Source: *USA Today*, "Toying With Money Messages," Nov. 27, 1998, p. 3B.)

a. Explain how a completely randomized design can be used to test whether there is a difference in excitement among the three games.

b. Explain how a randomized block design can be used to test whether there is a difference in excitement among the three games.

11.4 RANDOMIZED BLOCK DESIGN

The previous section described the difference between the randomized block and completely randomized designs. Rather than obtaining independent samples from the k populations, the data for a randomized block design are organized into homogeneous units referred to as **blocks.** *Within* each block, any predictable difference in the observations is due to the effect of the factor of interest, such as gender or employee classification.

Consider the situation discussed in Section 9.5. Metalloy manufactures metal hinges, and as part of the quality inspection these hinges are subjected to a hardness test in which a rod with a pointed tip is pressed into a hinge and the depth of the depression caused by the tip is measured. Two tips are available for the hardness tester. Twelve hinges were randomly selected, and both tips were used to test the hardness of each metal hinge. The coded data from this hardness test are as follows.

Hinge	Tip #1	Tip #2	Hinge	Tip #1	Tip #2
1	39	35	7	45	41
2	32	34	8	48	47
3	42	38	9	38	35
4	49	48	10	48	46
5	45	47	11	41	37
6	47	43	12	47	44

Once again, there is a single factor of interest, namely, the tip used for the test. But are the 24 sample observations in fact replicates? Replicates (by definition) are obtained under (nearly) identical circumstances, so that any variation in the values within any one sample is due strictly to chance. In this situation, the hinge used in the test heavily influences each sample value. Also, each pair of values is obtained from the same hinge, and so these samples are *not independent,* violating a key assumption of the completely randomized design.

This situation fits the *paired sample* design discussed in Section 9.5, provided we assume that the population of differences (tip #1 minus tip #2) is normally distributed. We will now extend our discussion of Section 9.5 to consider more than two populations.

To determine whether there is a factor (tip) effect in these 24 observations, we must first account for the block (hinge) effect. If we ignore this effect, we could easily come to an incorrect conclusion regarding a difference in the effect of the two tips. This same point was made in Section 9.5, where a crucial question was whether to pair (block) the data. Figure 9.20 illustrated how one can arrive at an incorrect conclusion by failing to block the data.

Metalloy also makes a larger, softer hinge that requires a hardness test as part of the quality inspection. For this test, there are three tips available for inserting into the rod that is then pressed into the hinge with a specified force. The question of interest, as before, is whether there is a difference in the average reading for the three tips. Using 10 hinges, an experiment was conducted in which all three tips were applied to each of the metal hinges. The results were:

Hinge	Tip #1	Tip #2	Tip #3	Hinge	Tip #1	Tip #2	Tip #3
1	68	72	65	6	80	91	86
2	40	43	42	7	47	58	50
3	82	89	84	8	55	68	52
4	56	60	50	9	78	77	75
5	70	75	68	10	53	65	60

The data from this situation constitute a randomized block design with a single factor (tip used in the rod) containing three levels (tip #1, tip #2, tip #3) as well as 10 blocks (hinge 1, . . . , hinge 10). The general appearance of such a design is shown in Table 11.1.

When using the randomized block design, the various levels should be applied in a *random* manner within each block. In the hardness testing, the test should *not* always use

TABLE 11.1   The randomized block design.

Block	FACTOR LEVEL (POPULATION) 1	2	3	$\cdots$	k	Total
1	x	x	x	$\cdots$	x	S_1
2	x	x	x	$\cdots$	x	S_2
3	x	x	x	$\cdots$	x	S_3
$\vdots$						$\vdots$
b	x	x	x	$\cdots$	x	S_b
Total	T_1	T_2	T_3	$\cdots$	T_k	T
Sample Mean	$\overline{X}_1$	$\overline{X}_2$	$\overline{X}_3$	$\cdots$	$\overline{X}_k$	

tip #1 first, tip #2 second, and tip #3 last. Instead, the three tips should be applied in a randomized order for each hinge—hence the name *randomized block design*.

The requirements for the randomized block design are:

1. The populations within each factor level/block combination (hinge-and-tip combination in our example) are normally distributed, and the sample observation within each factor level/block combination is randomly selected.
2. These normal populations have a common variance, σ^2.

Furthermore, we assume that the factor effects are the same within each block; that is, there is no interaction effect between the factor and the blocks.

The analysis using the randomized block design is similar to that for the one-factor ANOVA, except that the total sum of squares (SS(total)) has an additional component. Now,

$$SS(total) = SS(factor) + SS(blocks) + SS(error)$$

where SS(blocks) measures the variation due to the blocks. Consequently, this design extracts the block effect, as measured by SS(blocks), from the error of sum of squares in the completely randomized design.

If you use the randomized block design when blocking is not necessary, SS(blocks) will be very small in comparison to the other sums of squares. Referring to Table 11.1, this will occur when S_1, S_2, . . . , S_b are nearly the same. If all the S_i's are equal, then SS(blocks) = 0. The effect of the blocks will be significant whenever you observe a lot of variation in these block totals.

The sum of squares for the randomized block design is thus

$$SS(factor) = \frac{1}{b}[T_1^2 + T_2^2 + \cdots + T_k^2] - \frac{T^2}{bk} \qquad (11.21)$$

where

k = number of factor levels in the design

b = number of blocks in the design

n = number of observations = bk

$T_1, T_2, \ldots, T_k$ represent the totals for the k factor levels

$S_1, S_2, \ldots, S_b$ are the totals for the b blocks

$T = T_1 + T_2 + \cdots + T_k$

$\quad = S_1 + S_2 + \cdots + S_b$ = total of all observations

$$SS(blocks) = \frac{1}{k}[S_1^2 + S_2^2 + \cdots + S_b^2] - \frac{T^2}{bk} \qquad \text{(11.22)}$$

$$SS(total) = \sum x^2 - \frac{T^2}{bk} \qquad \text{(11.23)}$$

where $\sum x^2 =$ sum of the squares for each of the $n \ (= bk)$ observations.

$$SS(error) = SS(total) - SS(factor) - SS(blocks) \qquad \text{(11.24)}$$

The degrees of freedom are

$$\text{df for factor} = k - 1$$

$$\text{df for blocks} = b - 1$$

$$\text{df for error} = (k - 1)(b - 1)$$

$$\text{df for total} = bk - 1$$

The ANOVA table for a blocked design is very similar to the one-factor ANOVA table. There is one additional row because you now include the effect of the various blocks in your design:

Source	df	SS	MS	F
Factor	$k-1$	SS(factor)	$MS(factor) = \dfrac{SS(factor)}{k-1}$	$F_1 = \dfrac{MS(factor)}{MS(error)}$
Blocks	$b-1$	SS(blocks)	$MS(blocks) = \dfrac{SS(blocks)}{b-1}$	$F_2 = \dfrac{MS(blocks)}{MS(error)}$
Error	$(k-1)(b-1)$	SS(error)	$MS(error) = \dfrac{SS(error)}{(k-1)(b-1)}$	
Total	$bk-1$	SS(total)		

where

$$MS(factor) = \frac{SS(factor)}{k-1}$$

$$MS(blocks) = \frac{SS(blocks)}{b-1}$$

$$MS(error) = \frac{SS(error)}{(k-1)(b-1)}$$

HYPOTHESIS TESTING

Is there a difference in the average reading for the three tips in the previous illustration? In other words, does the tip used have a significant effect on the hardness reading? The hypotheses for this situation are H_0: $\mu_1 = \mu_2 = \mu_3$ and H_a: not all the means are equal. We determine the test statistic exactly as we did for the one-factor ANOVA:

$$F_1 = \frac{MS(factor)}{MS(error)} \qquad \text{(11.25)}$$

where the mean square values are obtained from the ANOVA table. Notice that the MS(factor) value is the *same* regardless of whether you block. However, when you use the block effect in the design, the SS(error) is smaller than the SS(error) value obtained using the completely randomized design. The df in the error term are different for the two designs, so it does not necessarily follow that the MS(error) is smaller in the randomized block design. If there is considerable variation among the block totals, then quite likely MS(error) *will* be smaller in the randomized block design. You are thus more likely to detect a difference in these k means when a difference does exist. Had you not included the block effect, the block variation would have been included in SS(error), resulting in a smaller F-value. This value often becomes small enough not to fall in the rejection region, leading you to conclude that no difference exists. *But perhaps there is a difference among these means (the factor does have a significant effect) that will go undetected if an incorrect experimental design is used.*

For the randomized block design, the test will be to

$$\text{reject } H_0 \text{ if } F_1 > F_{\alpha, v_1, v_2}$$

where $v_1 = k - 1$ and $v_2 = (k - 1)(b - 1)$. So, once again, we reject H_0 if the F-statistic falls in the right-tail rejection region, this time using Table A.7 with $v_1 = k - 1$, the df for factor, and $v_2 = (k - 1)(b - 1)$, the df for error.

Now suppose we wish to determine whether the effect of the hinge used for the hardness test is significant. We are attempting to determine whether there is a block effect, so the hypotheses are

H_0': there is no effect due to the hinges (blocks) (the block means are equal)

H_a': there is an effect due to the hinges (the block means are not all equal)

The corresponding test uses the "other" F-statistic from the randomized block ANOVA table, namely,

$$F_2 = \frac{\text{MS(blocks)}}{\text{MS(error)}} \qquad (11.26)$$

and the test procedure is to

$$\text{reject } H_0' \text{ if } F_2 > F_{\alpha, v_1', v_2'}$$

where $v_1' = b - 1$ and $v_2' = (k - 1)(b - 1)$.

Let us reexamine our data. We will use $\alpha = .05$. Here, $k = 3$ levels (tips), $b = 10$ blocks (hinges), and $n = bk = 30$ observations.

Hinge	Tip #1	Tip #2	Tip #3	Totals
1	68	72	65	205
2	40	43	42	125
3	82	89	84	255
4	56	60	50	166
5	70	75	68	213
6	80	91	86	257
7	47	58	50	155
8	55	68	52	175
9	78	77	75	230
10	53	65	60	178
Total	629	698	632	1959
$\overline{X}$	62.9	69.8	63.2	

$$\text{SS(factor)} = \frac{1}{10}[629^2 + 698^2 + 632^2] - \frac{1959^2}{30}$$

$$= 128{,}226.9 - 127{,}922.7 = 304.2$$

$$\text{SS(blocks)} = \frac{1}{3}[205^2 + 125^2 + \cdots + 178^2] - \frac{1959^2}{30}$$

$$= 133{,}627.7 - 127{,}922.7 = 5705.0$$

$$SS(\text{total}) = [68^2 + 40^2 + \cdots + 75^2 + 60^2] - \frac{1959^2}{30}$$

$$= 134{,}107 - 127{,}922.7 = 6184.3$$

$$SS(\text{error}) = SS(\text{total}) - SS(\text{factor}) - SS(\text{blocks})$$

$$= 6184.3 - 304.2 - 5705.0 = 175.1$$

So

$$MS(\text{factor}) = \frac{SS(\text{factor})}{k-1}$$

$$= \frac{304.2}{2} = 152.1$$

$$MS(\text{blocks}) = \frac{SS(\text{blocks})}{b-1}$$

$$= \frac{5705.0}{9} = 633.9$$

$$MS(\text{error}) = \frac{SS(\text{error})}{(k-1)(b-1)}$$

$$= \frac{175.1}{18} = 9.73$$

The resulting ANOVA table is

Source	df	SS	MS	F
Factor	2	304.2	152.1	$152.1/9.73 = 15.63$ (F_1)
Blocks	9	5705.0	633.9	$633.9/9.73 = 65.15$ (F_2)
Error	18	175.1	9.73	
Total	29	6184.3		

We first consider the hypotheses

$$H_0: \mu_1 = \mu_2 = \mu_3$$

$$H_a: \text{not all } \mu\text{'s are equal}$$

where

$$\mu_1 = \text{average reading using tip \#1 (estimate is } \bar{x}_1 = 62.9)$$

$$\mu_2 = \text{average reading using tip \#2 (estimate is } \bar{x}_2 = 69.8)$$

$$\mu_3 = \text{average reading using tip \#3 (estimate is } \bar{x}_3 = 63.2)$$

Because $F_1 = 15.63 > F_{.05,2,18} = 3.55$, we reject H_0 and conclude that there *is* a difference in the hardness readings for the three tips. This is not a surprising result, because it appears that the tip #2 readings were much higher than for tips #1 and #3. This means that the factor (tip used) *does* have a significant effect on the hardness reading.

We also wish to test

$$H_0': \text{there is no block effect}$$

$$H_a': \text{there is a block effect}$$

$S_1, S_2, \ldots, S_{10}$ appear to contain considerable variation, so our initial guess is that there is a block effect. Carrying out the statistical test, we see that

$$F_2 = 65.15 > F_{.05,9,18} = 2.46$$

Consequently, we strongly reject H_0' in favor of H_a'. The effect of the hinge used for the hardness test *is* significant.

FIGURE 11.10

Excel spreadsheet containing the hardness data with labels for the rows and columns.

	A	B	C	D
1	Hinge	Tip #1	Tip #2	Tip #3
2	1	68	72	65
3	2	40	43	42
4	3	82	89	84
5	4	56	60	50
6	5	70	75	68
7	6	80	91	86
8	7	47	58	50
9	8	55	68	52
10	9	78	77	75
11	10	53	65	60

FIGURE 11.11

Portion of Excel spreadsheet containing the solution for the hardness testing data.

File Edit View Insert Format Tools Data KGP Data Analysis Window Help

	E	F	G	H	I	J	K
1	Anova: Two-Factor Without Replication						
2							
3	SUMMARY	Count	Sum	Average	Variance		
4	1	3	205.0000	68.3333	12.3333		
5	2	3	125.0000	41.6667	2.3333		
6	3	3	255.0000	85.0000	13.0000		
7	4	3	166.0000	55.3333	25.3333		
8	5	3	213.0000	71.0000	13.0000		
9	6	3	257.0000	85.6667	30.3333		
10	7	3	155.0000	51.6667	32.3333		
11	8	3	175.0000	58.3333	72.3333		
12	9	3	230.0000	76.6667	2.3333		
13	10	3	178.0000	59.3333	36.3333		
14							
15	Tip #1	10	629.0000	62.9000	216.3222		
16	Tip #2	10	698.0000	69.8000	209.0667		
17	Tip #3	10	632.0000	63.2000	227.9556		
18							
19							
20	ANOVA						
21	Source of Variation	SS	df	MS	F	P-value	F crit
22	Factor	304.2000	2	152.1000	15.6327	0.0001	3.5546
23	Blocks	5704.9667	9	633.8852	65.1500	0.0000	2.4563
24	Error	175.1333	18	9.7296			
25							
26	Total	6184.3000	29				
27							
28							

Sheet1

An Excel solution for this problem is shown in Figure 11.11. To obtain this solution, first enter the thirty data values in cells B2:D11 and the corresponding labels as shown in Figure 11.10. Then click on **KGP Data Analysis ➤ ANOVA.** In the resulting input screen (see Figure 11.6), enter "A1:D11" in the **Input Range** box, and enter "E1" in the **Output Range** box. In the **Experimental Design** frame, click on **Randomized Block.** The alpha value should be 5%. Your resulting output will be that shown in Figure 11.11, except rows 22 and 23 will be interchanged and will have different labels (**Rows** and **Columns**). Excel's ANOVA table will have the block row (labeled **Rows**) first, followed by the factor row (labeled **Columns**).

To swap these two rows (as in Figure 11.11), highlight the cells in E22:K22. Move the cursor up from the bottom toward this row and stop when it becomes a white arrow. Drag this row down one row *while holding down the shift key.* Release the mouse button, then the shift key. You have now swapped these two rows in the ANOVA table. Finally, type "Factor" in cell E22 and "Blocks" in cell E23. Notice that the output contains the (very small) p-values in cells J22 and J23, along with the critical F values for $\alpha = .05$ in cells K22 and K23. Since both p-values are less than .05, this supports the earlier conclusion that there is a difference in the three tips, and there is a significant block effect.

COMMENTS

Notice that the block (hinge) effect is highly significant here, indicating much variation in the totals for each row (hinge). This indicates that there is very little uniformity in the hardness of the hinges being produced, regardless of what tip is used for measurement. Consequently, Met-alloy has a serious problem in the quality of the hinges being produced. As Chapter 12 ("Quality Improvement") will point out, one indicator of poor quality is too much variation in the quality characteristic being measured (hardness, here).

What would the result have been had we treated these 30 observations as replicates, ten from each of the three tips? In other words, what would happen if we failed to recognize that blocking was necessary and we incorrectly used the one-factor ANOVA? Because both SS(factor) and SS(total) do not change, the only difference is a new SS(error). Therefore,

$$SS(error) = SS(total) - SS(factor)$$

$$= 6184.3 - 304.2$$

$$= 5880.1$$

Also, in the one-factor ANOVA design,

$$df \text{ for total} = (df \text{ for factor}) + (df \text{ for error})$$

So,

$$df \text{ for error} = (df \text{ for total}) - (df \text{ for factor})$$

$$= 29 - 2 = 27$$

The resulting F-value will be

$$F = \frac{MS(factor)}{MS(error)} = \frac{304.2 / 2}{5880.1 / 27} = .70$$

Because $F^* = .70$ is *much less* than $F_{.05,2,27} = 3.35$, *we fail to detect a difference in the three means,* μ_1, μ_2, and μ_3. This is the effect of assuming independence among the samples when it does not exist. This example emphasizes that failing to recognize the need for a randomized block design can have serious consequences!

EXAMPLE 11.7

The human resource director at Blackburn Industries is investigating dental claims submitted by married employees having at least one child. Of interest is whether the average annual dollar amounts of dental work claimed by the husband, by the wife, and per child are the same. Data were collected by randomly selecting 16 families and recording these three dollar amounts (total claims for the year by the husband, by the wife, and per child). The results of the sample are shown below. Can the human resource director conclude that there is a difference in the three population means using a significance level of .05?

Family	Husband	Wife	Per Child	Total
1	78	84	112	274
2	105	80	274	459
3	95	184	305	584
4	85	158	280	523
5	148	180	263	591
6	284	208	145	637
7	124	145	340	609
8	118	75	130	323
9	153	112	239	504
10	143	204	262	609

Family	Husband	Wife	Per Child	Total
11	84	110	182	376
12	106	172	248	526
13	218	185	320	723
14	145	90	226	461
15	175	304	152	631
16	128	161	217	506
Total	2189	2452	3695	8336
$\bar{X}$	\$ 136.81	\$ 153.25	\$ 230.94	

SOLUTION

The hypotheses for this situation are

$$H_0: \mu_H = \mu_W = \mu_C$$

$$H_a: \text{not all three means are equal}$$

where μ_H is the average annual amount claimed by the husband, μ_W is the average for the wife, and μ_C is the average amount per child.

The various block and factor totals shown are obtained by summing across and down the array of data.

$$SS(\text{factor}) = \frac{1}{16}[2189^2 + 2452^2 + 3695^2] - \frac{8336^2}{48}$$

$$= 1,528,565.625 - 1,447,685.33 = 80,880.29$$

$$SS(\text{blocks}) = \frac{1}{3}[274^2 + 459^2 + \cdots + 506^2] - \frac{8336^2}{48}$$

$$= 1,520,999.33 - 1,447,685.33 = 73,314$$

$$SS(\text{total}) = (78^2 + 105^2 + \cdots + 152^2 + 217^2) - \frac{8336^2}{48}$$

$$= 1,699,824 - 1,447,685.33 = 252,138.67$$

$$SS(\text{error}) = SS(\text{total}) - SS(\text{factor}) - SS(\text{blocks})$$

$$= 97,944.38$$

The corresponding ANOVA table follows. Note that the df for the factor are $3 - 1 = 2$, for blocks are $16 - 1 = 15$, and for total are $48 - 1 = 47$, leaving $47 - 2 - 15 = 30$ df for error.

Source	df	SS	MS	F
Factor	2	80,880.29	40,440.14	40440.14/3264.81 = 12.39
Blocks	15	73,314	4,887.60	4887.60/3264.81 = 1.50
Error	30	97,944.38	3,264.81	
Total	47	252,138.67		

To test $H_0: \mu_H = \mu_W = \mu_C$, we use $F_1 = 12.39$. Since $12.39 > F_{.05,2,30} = 3.32$, we reject H_0 and conclude that the three average claim amounts are not equal. By observing the sample means, we notice that the claims per child are considerably higher than those for the husband and wife.

As a final note, the block (family) effect is *not* significant here, since $F_2 = 1.50 < F_{.05,15,30} = 2.01$. This does not mean that including the block effect in the analysis was a mistake, since the samples were clearly *not* obtained independently. Furthermore, there is no guarantee that the block effect will once again turn out to be insignificant for the next set of data in this situation.

Constructing a Confidence Interval for the Difference between Two Population Means

Due to a possible block effect with this type of design, you cannot determine a confidence interval for an individual factor-level mean, μ_i. You can, however, construct a confidence interval for the difference between any *pair* of means, $\mu_i - \mu_j$. Remember: (1) We must determine which confidence intervals we will construct *before* observing the data (don't let the data dictate which confidence intervals to construct), and (2) this procedure is satisfactory provided you compare only a very small number of pairs (say, one or two pairs).

The second comment is very important! If you wish to compare a large number of population means, such as all possible pairs, a multiple comparisons procedure should be used (discussed following Example 11.8). In this way you can be sure that the probability of making one or more Type I errors (concluding that two means differ when, in fact, they are equal), is the predetermined significance level, α.

When using the randomized block design, our estimate of the common variance, σ^2, is now

$$s^2 = \text{estimate of } \sigma^2$$

$$= \text{MS(error)} = \frac{\text{SS(error)}}{(k-1)(b-1)} \tag{11.27}$$

Thus, a $(1 - \alpha) \cdot 100\%$ confidence interval for $\mu_i - \mu_j$ is

$$(\overline{X}_i - \overline{X}_j) - t_{\alpha/2,\text{df}} \cdot s \cdot \sqrt{\frac{1}{b} + \frac{1}{b}} \text{ to } (\overline{X}_i - \overline{X}_j) + t_{\alpha/2,\text{df}} \cdot s \cdot \sqrt{\frac{1}{b} + \frac{1}{b}} \tag{11.28}$$

where df = degrees of freedom for the t statistic (Table A.5) = $(k - 1)(b - 1)$; b = number of blocks; k = number of factor levels; and s is determined from equation 11.27.

EXAMPLE 11.8

Assume you have not yet observed the dental claim data in Example 11.7, and you decided to construct a 95% confidence interval for the difference between the average annual claim for the wife and the average annual claim per child. What does this confidence interval tell you?

SOLUTION

Using the ANOVA table for these data,

$$s^2 = \text{MS(error)} = 3264.81$$

and so $s = 57.1385$. Also, $t_{.025,30} = 2.042$ using Table A.5. The resulting 95% confidence interval for $\mu_C - \mu_W$ is

$$(\overline{X}_C - \overline{X}_W) - t_{.025,30} \, s \sqrt{\frac{1}{16} + \frac{1}{16}} \text{ to } (\overline{X}_C - \overline{X}_W) + t_{.025,30} \, s \sqrt{\frac{1}{16} + \frac{1}{16}}$$

$$= (230.94 - 153.25) - (2.042)(57.1385)(.3536) \quad \text{to}$$

$$(230.94 - 153.25) + (2.042)(57.1385)(.3536)$$

$$= 77.69 - 41.26 \quad \text{to} \quad 77.69 + 41.26$$

$$= 36.43 \quad \text{to} \quad 118.95$$

We are thus 95% confident that the average annual claim per child is between \$36.43 and \$118.95 *higher* than the average annual claim for the wife.

The Excel generated 95% confidence interval for $\mu_C - \mu_W$ is shown in Figure 11.12. To obtain this solution, enter the data in cells A1:D17, including the labels as shown in

FIGURE 11.12
Excel spreadsheet with ANOVA table and confidence interval for Examples 11.7 and 11.8.

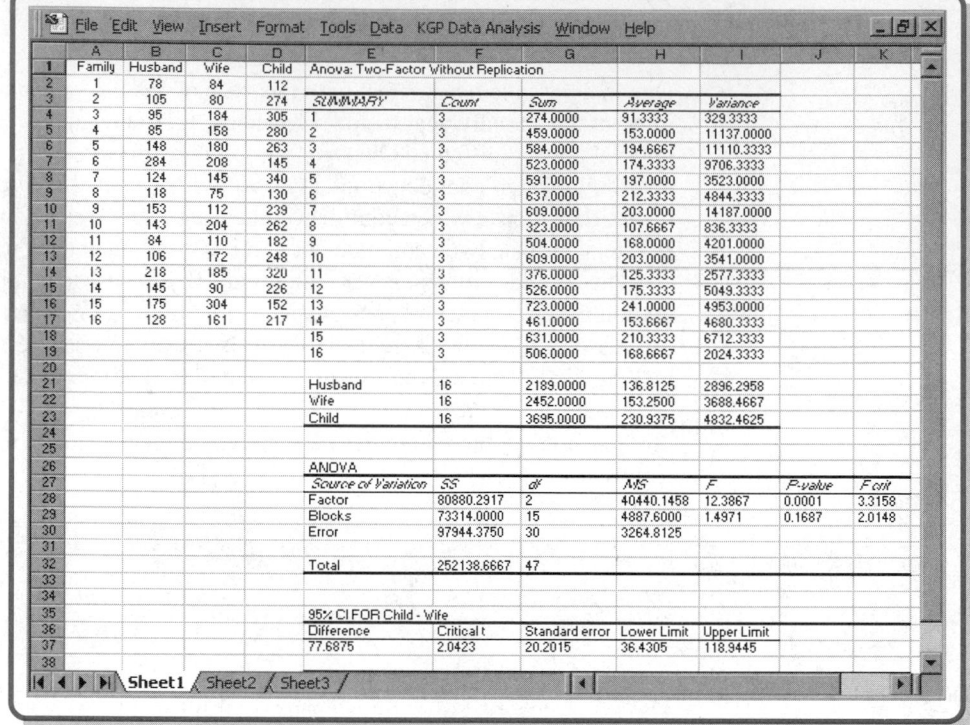

Figure 11.12, and then click on **KGP Data Analysis ➤ ANOVA.** In the resulting input screen (see Figure 11.6), enter "A1:D17" in the **Input Range** box and enter "E1" in the **Output Range** box. In the **Experimental Design** frame, click on **Randomized Block.** Be sure to click on the check box alongside **Confidence Interval for Difference Between Two Means** and enter 3 in the top box (First Group) and 2 in the bottom box (Second Group). The alpha value should be 5%. The resulting confidence interval in cells H37 and I37 agrees with the previous result.

MULTIPLE COMPARISONS PROCEDURE: RANDOMIZED BLOCK DESIGN

If the null hypothesis that the factor-level means are equal, is rejected, then Tukey's multiple comparisons procedure (introduced in section 11.2) can be applied to the randomized block design. In this way, you can determine which pairs of factor-level means are different while preserving your experimentwise significance level, α.

The number of means being compared is k, where $k =$ the number of factor levels. For example, in Example 11.7, there are $k = 3$ different levels (husband, wife, child), and it was observed in the solution to this example that the per-child average cost in the sample appeared to be considerably different than the other two sample averages. The follow-up questions here are: Is $\mu_H \neq \mu_W$? Is $\mu_H \neq \mu_C$? Is $\mu_W \neq \mu_C$?

For the randomized block design, we use Table A.16 to find $Q_{\alpha,k,v}$, where $\alpha =$ the experimentwise significance level, $k =$ number of factor-level means, and $v =$ df associated with MS(error) $= (k-1)(b-1)$, where b is the number of blocks in the design. We conclude that any two population means (μ_i and μ_j) are unequal, provided

$$|\bar{X}_i - \bar{X}_j| > D$$

where

$$D = Q_{\alpha,k,(k-1)(b-1)} \sqrt{\frac{MS(error)}{b}}$$

In Example 11.7, $\alpha = .05$, $k = 3$, $b = 16$, and MS(error) = 3264.81. Referring to Table A.16, we first locate $Q_{.05,3,(3-1)(16-1)} = Q_{.05,3,30} = 3.49$. Next, we find

$$D = 3.49\sqrt{\frac{3264.81}{16}} = 49.85$$

Examining the three sample means, we see that

$$\bar{X}_C - \bar{X}_H = 230.94 - 136.81 = 94.13 > 49.85$$

$$\bar{X}_C - \bar{X}_W = 230.94 - 153.25 = 77.69 > 49.85$$

$$\bar{X}_W - \bar{X}_H = 153.25 - 136.81 = 16.44 < 49.85$$

and so we conclude that the average per-child claim differs from the average claim for the husbands and the average claim for the wives, but we cannot distinguish between the average claims for the husband and wife populations. This is illustrated by an overbar connecting the husband and wife sample means.

$$\overline{\begin{array}{ccc} 136.81 & 153.25 \end{array}} \quad 230.94$$
$$\begin{array}{ccc} \text{(H)} & \text{(W)} & \text{(C)} \end{array}$$

MICROSOFT® EXCEL APPLICATION   USE DATA11-9

EXAMPLE 11.9
Using Excel to Carry Out a Randomized Block Analysis

Allied Container Corporation manufactures corrugated boxes that are sold to other businesses for use as shipping containers. They currently have three different brands of machine under consideration that are used to manufacture the boxes from corrugated sheets. They are about to purchase new machines, and it is suspected that the average number of boxes produced per hour by an individual worker is not the same for each machine. To verify this, they conducted an experiment in which each of 20 randomly selected workers ran each machine (in random order) for one hour. At the end of each hour, the number of boxes produced on that particular machine was recorded. The results are in data set DATA11-9, where columns A, B, C contain the number of boxes produced on machines A, B, and C, respectively. The 20 rows consist of the blocks (workers), so that row 1 contains the boxes produced by worker 1 on the three machines, row 2 corresponds to worker 2, and so on.

Using a significance level of .05, what can you tell Allied about the average output of these three machines?

SOLUTION

Begin by opening dataset DATA11-9. You should observe three columns of 20 values with corresponding labels, as shown in Figure 11.13. Click on **KGP Data Analysis ➤ ANOVA.** In the resulting input screen (see Figure 11.6), enter "A1:D21" in the **Input Range** box and enter "E1" in the **Output Range** box. Be sure to click on the checkbox alongside **Tukey Test for Difference Between Means** and leave the alpha value set at 5%. You will see the ANOVA table in cells E30:K36 in Figure 11.3, except rows 32 and 33 will be reversed. To swap these two rows, refer to the discussion of Figure 11.11, which mentioned that Excel's ANOVA table contains the block effect values in the first row and the factor effect values in the second row. After swapping these two rows, type "Factor (Machines)" in cell E32 and "Blocks (Workers)" in cell E33.

To carry out a multiple comparisons procedure, refer to cell F41, where Tukey's D value is 240.6. Which pairs of sample means differ by more than 240.6? These would be machines A and B, since $6388.05 - 6010.05 = 378$, and machines A and C, since $6270.35 - 6010.05 = 260.3$. Consequently, you are able to demonstrate that machines B and C are superior to machine A but are unable to show that machine B is superior to machine C. This is illustrated at the bottom of Figure 11.13 by the overbar connecting the sample means for machines B and C (no significant difference between these two machines), but there is no bar connecting machines A and B and machines A and C.

FIGURE 11.13
Excel solution for Example
11.9 using **KGP Data
Analysis ➤ ANOVA.**

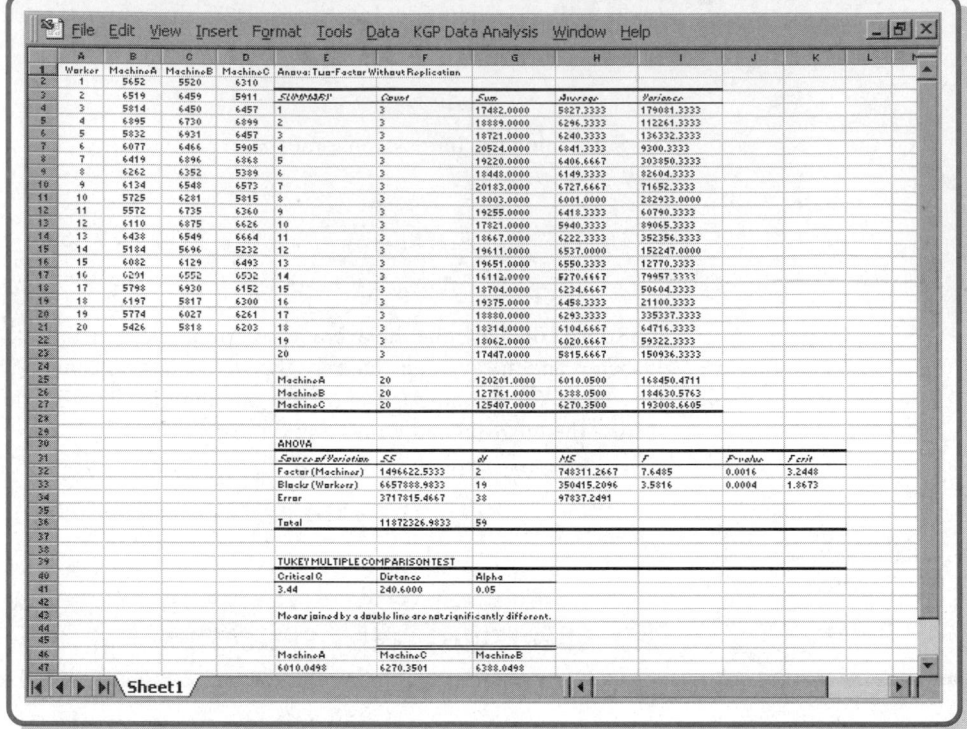

RECOMMENDATION. When purchasing new machines, remove machine A from consideration. machines B and C are both outperforming machine A, but neither is clearly superior; so either brand machine should be considered for new purchases.

EXERCISES 11.23–11.37

UNDERSTANDING THE MECHANICS

11.23 A randomized block design resulted in the values given in the following ANOVA table.

Source	df	SS	MS	F
Factor		70.0	10	
Blocks		52.8		
Error	21			
Total	31	168.2		

a. Complete the ANOVA table.

b. Conduct a hypothesis test to determine whether there is a significant difference in the levels of the factor. Base your conclusions on the *p*-value.

11.24 The following data were collected on two factor levels with 10 blocks.

	Factor Level	
Block	**1**	**2**
1	13	15
2	4	7
3	9	8
4	3	6

	Factor Level	
Block	**1**	**2**
5	2	4
6	18	17
7	13	19
8	7	8
9	9	10
10	5	6

a. Specify the null and alternative hypotheses for testing whether a difference in the factor levels exists.

b. Specify the null and alternative hypotheses for testing whether there is a block effect.

c. Construct an ANOVA table for this randomized block design.

d. What conclusions do the data support? Use a .05 significance level.

e. Construct a 95% confidence interval for the difference between the mean values for the two factor levels.

f. Use a paired *t* test to test for a difference in the factor levels. Use a .05 significance level.

g. What is the relationship between the *t* test in part (f) and the *F*-test in part (d) for testing whether a difference in factor levels exists?

11.25 A randomized block design yielded the following totals for four blocks and four levels of the factor.

Blocks: $S_1 = 85$, $S_2 = 92$, $S_3 = 91$, $S_4 = 120$
Factor Levels: $T_1 = 60$, $T_2 = 120$, $T_3 = 105$, $T_4 = 103$

a. Construct the ANOVA table, and assume that the total sum of squares is 709.

b. Do the data provide sufficient evidence to indicate that the factor levels differ? Use a .05 significance level.

c. Is there sufficient evidence to conclude that blocking was effective in reducing the experimental error? Use a .05 significance level.

d. Use a multiple comparisons procedure to determine which pairs of factor-level means differ. Use a .05 significance level.

APPLYING THE NEW CONCEPTS

11.26 A travel agency is interested in the response time for receiving information from the tourism bureaus within various states in the Southeastern United States. According to Harper's Hideaway Report newsletter, Hawaii has the shortest response time, but several states can take as long as three months. To determine if there is a difference in the time that it takes South Carolina, Georgia, and Florida to respond to tourists requests, six letters requesting information on various local state activities were sent to each of the states. The response times (in days) are recorded below.

Letter	South Carolina	Georgia	Florida
1	10	18	8
2	16	12	11
3	25	20	18
4	13	27	17
5	11	14	19
6	21	19	10

(Adapted from *The Wall Street Journal*, "How Efficient Is Your State's Tourism Bureau?" July 17, 1998, p. W6.)

a. Why is this design considered a randomized block design? Determine whether the mean response time for a request from a potential tourist differs across the three states. Use a .05 significance level.

b. Should a multiple comparisons procedure be used to determine which pairs of states differ in their mean response time? If so, determine which states differ and use a significance level of .05.

c. What requirements on the data are necessary for the validity of the statistical test in part (a)?

11.27 The study in Exercise 11.5 was modified such that only six secretaries were used. Each secretary had a different typing speed. Each secretary tested all three word processing software packages. The same task could not be used for testing all three packages, since the "learning effect" would come into play, so each secretary performed three separate tasks. However, the tasks were of essentially the same length and difficulty level. Furthermore, which task was assigned to which word processor was randomly determined, and the order in which the three word processors were tested was also randomly decided. The secretaries relaxed between tasks to avoid "fatigue effects." Thus, a randomized block design was achieved, with secretaries constituting blocks and the three observations (levels of the fac-

tor) within each block being randomized. The following data were obtained (the secretary's typing speed in words per minute is given in parentheses for reference purposes, and the body of the table contains the time taken to complete the tasks):

Secretary	Group 1 (Menu-Driven)	Group 2 (Command-Driven)	Group 3 (Mixed)
1 (75 wpm)	9	10	7
2 (65 wpm)	12	11	9
3 (55 wpm)	12	14	11
4 (50 wpm)	13	13	11
5 (45 wpm)	16	15	13
6 (30 wpm)	18	16	15

a. Compute the ANOVA table for the preceding data.

b. Conduct a hypothesis test to address the question of whether there is a difference between the three word processors (as measured by the performance of the secretaries). Use $\alpha = .10$.

c. Determine the p-value. Does the conclusion change at $\alpha = .05$ and at $\alpha = .01$.?

d. Is the block (secretary's) effect significant at $\alpha = .01$?

11.28 An analyst with a marketing firm wished to know if there was a difference in the number of responses from advertising a certain product at three different times on television. Ten days were randomly selected to run a commercial with a call-in phone number at each of the three times. The number of responses was recorded for 16 products:

Product	Noon	5:00 P.M.	10:30 P.M.
1	12	18	14
2	12	30	22
3	5	4	3
4	21	20	24
5	13	19	14
6	17	16	15
7	35	37	33
8	20	29	20
9	7	5	8
10	35	39	37
11	17	15	16
12	31	45	40
13	15	25	21
14	18	29	18
15	7	10	6
16	20	17	18

a. At the .05 significance level, is there sufficient evidence to conclude that the mean number of responses at noon, 5:00 P.M., and 10:30 P.M. are different?

b. Find a 90% confidence interval for the difference in the mean number of responses for noon and 5:00 P.M.

11.29 In Exercise 11.28, subtract 3.0 from each of the observations in the table. Perform the ANOVA procedure at the .05 significance level and test the hypothesis that the three different times of day have no effect. Is the sum of squares the same for the coded data as for the original data? If any set of data is coded by adding (or subtracting) the same number to (or from) the value of each observation, how will the sum of squares be affected?

11.30 A quality-control engineer wishes to investigate the spray pattern delivered by three different windshield washer spray nozzles. The engineer uses eight different windshield designs with the three different spray nozzles. A score is given to each spray pattern to indicate the effectiveness of the spray pattern in cleaning the windshield. The experimental data are given below. Do the data provide sufficient evidence to indicate that there is a difference in the effectiveness of the three different windshield washer spray nozzles at the .05 significance level? Is there a significant difference due to blocks?

	Spray Nozzles		
Windshield	1	2	3
1	67.2	75.3	70.1
2	63.5	72.1	68.7
3	50.8	65.1	62.5
4	71.3	78.8	71.8
5	78.1	79.9	79.0
6	69.5	74.8	64.3
7	74.6	79.6	70.8
8	70.1	76.8	69.8

11.31 In a randomized block design, if the df for the error sum of squares is given as 12 and the df for the factor sum of squares is 3, can you find the number of blocks used in the experiment? If yes, how many were used? If the total sum of squares is given as 520, the error sum of squares as 110, and the sum of squares due to blocks as 280, can you find the F-test for this experiment? If yes, what is it?

11.32 A machine-shop supervisor is interested in knowing whether there is a significant difference among the production times of three machines running six different jobs.

	1	2	3	4	5	6
Machine 1	4.2	2.1	1.3	7.1	6.0	3.4
Machine 2	6.1	2.9	2.0	7.8	6.8	4.3
Machine 3	5.3	2.1	1.4	7.3	5.8	3.1

a. At the .01 level, test the hypothesis that there is no mean difference in the production time for each of the three machines.

b. Is the test for blocks significant at the .05 level?

c. Find a 90% confidence interval for the difference in mean production time for machine 1 and machine 2.

11.33 When the Dow Jones Industrial Average drops several hundred points in a single day, journalists can choose either of two ways to present the news: a misleading but scary story or a valid but boring news story. For example, reporting the 300-point decline in the Dow Jones on August 4, 1998, could be reported in absolute numbers or in terms of percentage. The percentage is 3.4%, and there have been more than 215 one-day drops of more than 3.4% since the index has been recorded. But the absolute point decline is the third largest decline in the history of the Dow Jones Industrial Average. Suppose that a journalist wishes to determine if there was a difference in the way that three leading newspapers presented this event. The newspapers selected were the *Baltimore Sun,* the *Los Angeles Times,* and the *St. Louis Post-Dispatch.* A random sample of 10 business executives was selected to rate the presentation of this story on a scale from 1 to 10, with 1 representing "strongly agree that the story is misleading" and 10 representing "strongly disagree that the story is misleading." The results follow.

Business Executive	Baltimore Sun	Los Angeles Times	St. Louis Post-Dispatch
1	3	4	5
2	4	4	8
3	2	5	3
4	7	8	6
5	1	4	2
6	4	3	7
7	2	8	8
8	4	4	3
9	2	5	7
10	3	3	5

(Adapted from *USA Today,* "When the Market Falls, Media Stoke Investors' Fear," Aug. 12, 1998, p. 13A.)

a. What makes this design a randomized block design? What are the blocks?

b. Assume that the necessary assumptions required for the randomized block design to be valid are satisfied. Do the data provide sufficient evidence at the .10 level of significance to conclude that the mean ratings by the business executives differ across newspapers?

c. Use the Tukey multiple-comparisons procedure to determine which pairs of treatment means differ in part (a). Use a .05 significance level.

11.34 Linoleum Unlimited is experimenting with three types of adhesives for laying linoleum. Each glue is tested on five different surfaces. The adhesiveness of the glue is measured, and the coded results are as follows. Construct the ANOVA table and test the hypothesis that there is no difference in the three types of adhesives at the .10 level of significance.

Surface	Adhesive 1	Adhesive 2	Adhesive 3
1	1.5	2.1	2.4
2	1.6	1.8	1.9
3	2.4	2.5	2.4
4	3.1	3.4	3.1
5	4.5	4.2	4.0

11.35 An analyst of the Canadian mineral industry is conducting a study of the production of gold for the years 1991, 1992, and 1993. As part of the analyst's study, eight randomly selected Canadian mining firms are selected, and each firm's production for these years is recorded. The production figures, in units of 1000's of ounces, are as follows.

Company	1991	1992	1993
1	179	165	155
2	300	300	320
3	785	1200	1400
4	370	400	380
5	312	370	600
6	76	80	110
7	733	700	710
8	46	45	48

a. Is there sufficient evidence to indicate a difference in the mean production for the years 1991, 1992, and 1993? Construct the ANOVA table, and test at the 10% significance level.

b. Is the effect due to the blocks significant at the .10 level?

c. Construct a 90% confidence interval for the difference in mean production for the years 1991 and 1993.

(Adapted from "Resources and Penny Mines," *Investor Digest*, vol. 25, no. 9 (May 1993).)

USING THE COMPUTER

11.36 [DATA SET EX11-36] *Variable description:*

WaitRestauA: Wait time at restaurant A
WaitRestauB: Wait time at restaurant B
WaitRestauC: Wait time at restaurant C

The manager of three steak restaurants would like to know if there is a difference in the length of time that a customer has to wait on Saturday evening to be seated. Data are recorded over a 24-week period and the average wait time per customer on a Saturday evening is recorded. Times are recorded in minutes.

a. Determine if there is sufficient evidence to conclude that a difference in waiting time exists among the three restaurants using a significance level of 5%.

b. Determine if there is a difference based on week using a significance level of 5%.

c. Which pairs of restaurants have different waiting times at a 5% significance level?

d. Do a "what if" analysis by eliminating week 13. Do any of the conclusions change?

11.37 [DATA SET EX11-37] *Variable description:*

Morale97: Morale of employee in 1997
Morale98: Morale of employee in 1998
Morale99: Morale of employee in 1999

The manager of a large factory is interested in determining if there has been a change in the morale of employees over the past three years. Thirty employees are randomly selected to provide a score between 1 and 10 indicating the morale level for each of the employees for each of the years 1997, 1998, and 1999. A score of 10 indicates the highest possible level of morale.

a. Test the hypothesis that the mean morale score has not changed over the three years. Use a 5% significance level.

b. Is there an effect due to blocks? Use a 5% significance level.

c. Should a multiple comparisons procedure be performed to determine which years differ with respect to morale?

11.5 THE TWO-WAY FACTORIAL DESIGN

The two-way factorial design was introduced in Section 11.3. For this type of experiment, the researcher is considering two factors of interest, say, factor A and factor B. Of concern will be whether the individual factors have a significant effect on the observed variable (called the dependent variable) as well as the combined effect of the two factors.

Consider a simple example in which the dependent variable is the score on a test designed to measure assertiveness and managerial potential. The factors are gender and marital status (single or married). Each of these two factors consists of two levels. Suppose we observed a significant difference between the male and female scores. Thus we would conclude that factor A (gender) is significant. The analysis procedure to investigate this hypothesis is described in this section. If a significant difference between the scores of the single and married subjects is observed, then we would conclude that factor B (marital status) is also significant.

Suppose that a closer look at the scores revealed that the married males and single females scored high, but the single males and married females scored low on the test, as illustrated in Figure 11.14.

Consequently, the relationship between gender and the dependent variable (exam score) *depends upon the marital status,* since this relationship is different for the single and married groups. Similarly, the relationship between marital status and the dependent variable depends upon the particular level of factor A (gender). This example illustrates **interaction** between factors A and B. A method of detecting interaction using a simple graph, along with a statistical test of hypothesis, will be explained in this section.

FIGURE 11.14
Scores on assertiveness/managerial potential exam.

	Single	Married
Male	Low	High
Female	High	Low

FIGURE 11.15

Layout for two-way factorial design.

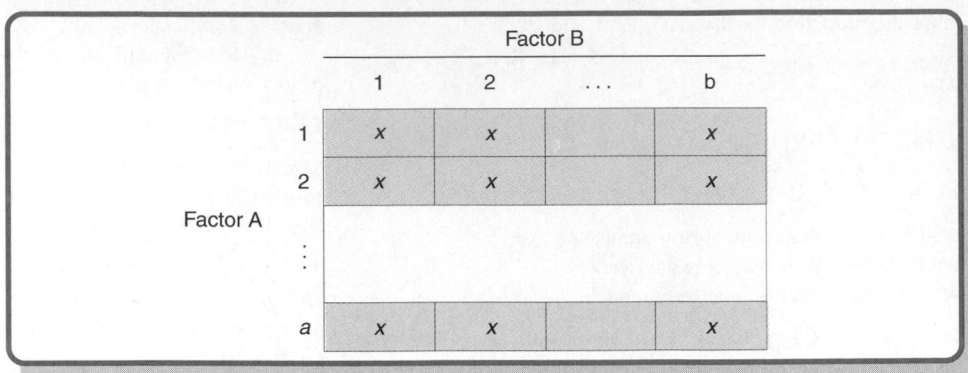

DEGREES OF FREEDOM

In a two-way factorial design, each level of factor A is combined with each level of factor B when obtaining the sample data. Suppose that factor A has a levels and factor B has b levels, as shown in Figure 11.15. Each x represents a test score.

If we record one observation for each factor A and factor B combination (referred to as a **treatment**), then we have $n = ab$ total observations. The df for each factor is one less than the number of levels and the df for the interaction term is the product of the factor A df and the factor B df. Consequently,

$$\text{df for factor } A = a - 1$$

$$\text{df for factor } B = b - 1$$

$$\text{df for interaction} = (a - 1)(b - 1)$$

$$\text{df for total} = n - 1 = ab - 1$$

We have a bit of a problem here. This design, like all experimental designs, must contain a source of variation due to error, that is, the unexplained variation. Suppose $a = 4$ and $b = 3$. Then the remaining df for error is (df for total) – (df for factor A) – (df for factor B) – (df for interaction), which in this case is $11 - 3 - 2 - 6 = 0$. It can be shown that the error df is zero *regardless* of the values of a and b. Since it will be necessary to measure this unexplained variation, this design requires that you obtain repeat observations (**replicates**) for each treatment. An illustration (using two replicates) including the various totals needed to carry out the analysis is shown in Figure 11.16. *In general, you will need two or more replicates at each treatment.* The number of replicates at each treatment need not be the same, but we consider here only the case where there are r replicates at each treatment.

In the replicated design, the degrees of freedom are

$$\text{df for factor } A = a - 1$$

$$\text{df for factor } B = b - 1$$

$$\text{df for interaction} = (a - 1)(b - 1)$$

$$\text{df for total} = \text{number of observations} - 1$$

$$= abr - 1$$

$$\text{df for error} = (abr - 1) - (a - 1) - (b - 1) - (a - 1)(b - 1)$$

$$= ab(r - 1)$$

SUM OF SQUARES AND MEAN SQUARES

The necessary sums of squares can be computed in a manner similar to that used in the previous designs. Using Figure 11.16, the following expressions give the corresponding sums of squares.

FIGURE 11.16

Illustration of two replicates in a two-way factorial design ($r = 2$).

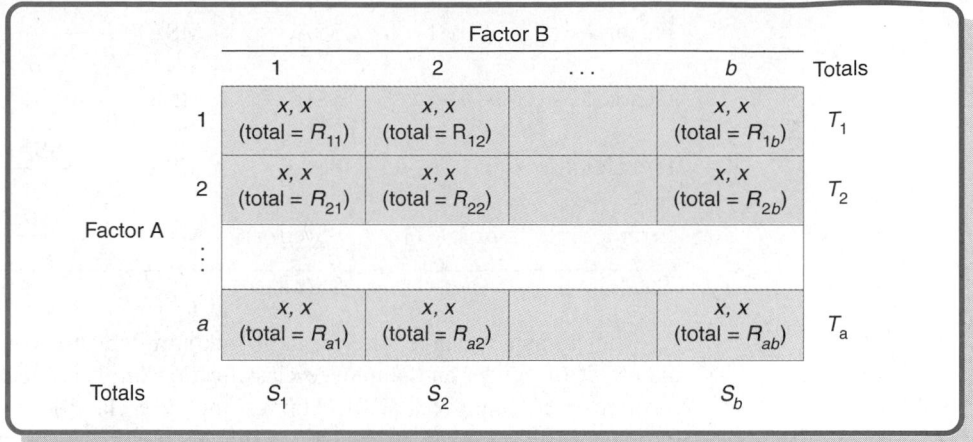

factor A: $SSA = \dfrac{1}{br}[T_1^2 + T_2^2 + \cdots + T_a^2] - \dfrac{T^2}{abr}$ **(11.29)**

where T = total of all $n = abr$ observations (that is, $T = T_1 + T_2 + \cdots + T_a$).

factor B: $SSB = \dfrac{1}{ar}[S_1^2 + S_2^2 + \cdots + S_b^2] - \dfrac{T^2}{abr}$ **(11.30)**

interaction: $SSAB = \dfrac{1}{r}[\sum R^2] - SSA - SSB - \dfrac{T^2}{abr}$ **(11.31)**

where the sum in the brackets is the sum of all the squares of the replicate totals, illustrated in Figure 11.16.

total: $SS(\text{total}) = \sum x^2 - \dfrac{T^2}{abr}$ **(11.32)**

where $\sum x^2$ is the sum of the squares for each of the $n = abr$ observations. By subtraction,

$SS(\text{error}) = SS(\text{total}) - SSA - SSB - SSAB$ **(11.33)**

The corresponding mean squares can be obtained by dividing each sum of squares by the corresponding degrees of freedom. Thus we have

$$MSA = \dfrac{SSA}{a-1}$$ **(11.34)**

$$MSB = \dfrac{SSB}{b-1}$$ **(11.35)**

$$MSAB = \dfrac{SSAB}{(a-1)(b-1)}$$ **(11.36)**

$$MS(\text{error}) = \dfrac{SS(\text{error})}{ab(r-1)}$$ **(11.37)**

This analysis can be summarized in the following ANOVA table:

Source	df	SS	MS	F
Factor A	$a-1$	SSA	$MSA = \dfrac{SSA}{a-1}$	$F_1 = \dfrac{MSA}{MS(error)}$
Factor B	$b-1$	SSB	$MSB = \dfrac{SSB}{b-1}$	$F_2 = \dfrac{MSB}{MS(error)}$
Interaction	$(a-1)(b-1)$	SSAB	$MSAB = \dfrac{SSAB}{(a-1)(b-1)}$	$F_3 = \dfrac{MSAB}{MS(error)}$
Error	$ab(r-1)$	SS(error)	$MS(error) = \dfrac{SS(error)}{ab(r-1)}$	
Total	$abr-1$	SS(total)		

The human resource director at Blackburn Industries is interested in examining the effect of gender and employee classification on the annual amount of dental claims for unmarried employees at Blackburn. Employee classifications range from category 1 (production-line workers) to category 4 (upper-level management). By utilizing a two-way factorial design, she can study the effect of gender (factor A) and employee classification (factor B), as well as the interaction effect between gender and employee classification, on the amount of the annual dental claims. These factors result in a 2×4 factorial design, since factor A consists of two levels and factor B has four levels. She decided to use three replicates for each of the eight treatment combinations, requiring annual claims from 24 different employees. The sample results are as follows, where the values in parentheses are the replicate totals for each of the treatments.

Employee Classification (Factor B)

		Category 1	Category 2	Category 3	Category 4	Total	Average
Gender (Factor A)	Male	190, 225, 200 (615)	135, 180, 100 (415)	260, 330, 350 (940)	305, 275, 240 (820)	2790	232.50
	Female	235, 190, 270 (695)	275, 305, 285 (865)	160, 205, 140 (505)	155, 110, 75 (340)	2405	200.42
	Total	1310	1280	1445	1160	5195	
	Average	218.33	213.33	240.83	193.33		

Using the previous discussion, the necessary sums of squares can be derived.

$$SSA = \frac{1}{(4)(3)}(2790^2 + 2405^2) - \frac{5195^2}{24} = 6176.04$$

$$SSB = \frac{1}{(2)(3)}(1310^2 + 1280^2 + 1445^2 + 1160^2) - \frac{5195^2}{24} = 6853.12$$

$$SSAB = \frac{1}{3}(615^2 + 415^2 + 940^2 + 820^2 + 695^2 + 865^2 + 505^2 + 340^2)$$

$$-6176.04 - 6853.12 - \frac{5195^2}{24} = 98578.13$$

$$SS(total) = (190^2 + 225^2 + 200^2 + \cdots + 155^2 + 110^2 + 75^2) - \frac{5195^2}{24}$$

$$= 131173.96$$

Consequently,

$$SS(error) = 131173.96 - 6176.04 - 6853.12 - 98578.13 = 19566.67$$

The degrees of freedom here will be:

$$\text{Gender factor:} \quad a - 1 = 2 - 1 = 1$$

$$\text{Employee classification factor:} \quad b - 1 = 4 - 1 = 3$$

$$\text{Interaction:} \quad (a - 1)(b - 1) = (1)(3) = 3$$

$$\text{Error:}\quad ab(r-1) = (2)(4)(3-1) = 16$$

$$\text{Total:}\quad abr - 1 = (2)(4)(3) - 1 = 24 - 1 = 23$$

These calculations and the resulting mean squares can be summarized in the following ANOVA table.

Source	df	SS	MS	F
Gender	1	6,176.04	6,176.04	$F_1 = 6{,}176.04/1{,}222.92 = 5.05$
Employee classification	3	6,853.12	2,284.37	$F_2 = 2{,}284.37/1{,}222.92 = 1.87$
Interaction	3	98,578.13	32,859.38	$F_3 = 32{,}859.38/1{,}222.92 = 26.87$
Error	16	19,566.67	1,222.92	
Total	23	131,173.96		

HYPOTHESIS TESTING.   When using a two-way factorial design, you can test for the significance of factor A, factor B, and the interaction of the two factors. For factor A, the null hypothesis is that the means are equal across the factor A levels. Written another way, we can define the following hypotheses:

$$H_{0,A}: \text{factor A is not significant } (\mu_M = \mu_F)$$

$$H_{a,A}: \text{factor A is significant } (\mu_M \neq \mu_F)$$

The corresponding test statistic is

$$F_1 = \frac{\text{MSA}}{\text{MS(error)}} \tag{11.38}$$

and the testing procedure is to reject $H_{0,A}$ if

$$F_1 > F_{\alpha, v_1, v_2}$$

where F_{α, v_1, v_2} is from Table A.7, $v_1 = $ df for factor A $= a - 1$, and $v_2 = $ df for error $= ab(r-1)$.

Similarly, to test for equal means of the factor B levels, we can define the hypotheses:

$$H_{0,B}: \text{factor B is not significant } (\mu_1 = \mu_2 = \mu_3 = \mu_4)$$

$$H_{a,B}: \text{factor B is significant (not all } \mu_i\text{'s are equal)}$$

The test statistic for determining the factor B effect is

$$F_2 = \frac{\text{MSB}}{\text{MS(error)}} \tag{11.39}$$

and factor B is significant ($H_{0,B}$ is rejected) if

$$F_2 > F_{\alpha, v_1, v_2}$$

where $v_1 = $ df for factor B $= b - 1$, and $v_2 = $ df for error $= ab(r-1)$.

The final set of hypotheses is concerned with the interaction effect between the two factors. The hypotheses for this procedure can be stated

$$H_{0,AB}: \text{there is no significant interaction between factor A and factor B}$$

$$H_{a,AB}: \text{there is significant interaction between factor A and factor B}$$

The test statistic is the remaining F statistic in the ANOVA table, namely,

$$F_3 = \frac{\text{MSAB}}{\text{MS(error)}} \tag{11.40}$$

and the test procedure is to reject $H_{0,AB}$ if

$$F_3 > F_{\alpha, v_1, v_2}$$

where $v_1 = $ df for interaction $= (a - 1)(b - 1)$ and $v_2 = $ df for error $= ab(r - 1)$.

MULTIPLE COMPARISONS PROCEDURE: TWO-WAY FACTORIAL DESIGNS

The method of multiple comparisons discussed in section 11.2 for the one-factor ANOVA procedure (Tukey's method) can be used to examine pairwise differences between the various treatment means in two-way factorial designs. Since factor A has a levels and factor B has b levels, there are ab such means that can be compared, one pair at a time.

For the two-way factorial design, we use Table A.16 to find $Q_{\alpha,k,v}$, where α is the desired experimentwise significance level, $k = ab$ is the number of treatment means, and v is the degrees of freedom associated with MS(error). Any two (sample) treatment means differing by more than

$$D = Q_{\alpha,k,v} \cdot \sqrt{\frac{MS(error)}{r}}$$

will imply that the corresponding population means are unequal. This procedure is illustrated in the next example.

EXAMPLE 11.10

Using the previous ANOVA table constructed using the dental claims and the two factors, gender (factor A) and employee classification (factor B), determine whether (1) factor A is significant, (2) factor B is significant, (3) there is significant interaction between gender and employee classification, and (4) which pairs of the eight (population) treatment means are unequal. Use a significance level of .05.

SOLUTION 1

The df for the F-statistic are $v_1 = 1$ and $v_2 = 16$. Using Table A.7, $F_{.05,1,16} = 4.49$, and the test is to reject $H_{0,A}$ if $F_1 > 4.49$. Since $F_1 = 5.05 > 4.49$, we conclude that the gender factor *is* significant. Examining the raw data, we observe that the sample mean for the males is $2790/12 = 232.50$, and the female average is $2405/12 = 200.42$. Thus we conclude that the difference between these sample means *is* significant, with higher dental claims occurring in the male population.

SOLUTION 2

For the employee classification factor, the df for the F-statistic are $v_1 = 3$ and $v_2 = 16$, with a corresponding table value of $F_{.05,3,16} = 3.24$. Since $F_2 = 1.87 < 3.24$, the employee classification factor is *not* significant. Taking a closer look, we observe that the high (low) female values were balanced by the low (high) male values within each employee classification category. Consequently, there is insignificant variation in the means for the four employee classification groups, leading to the "fail to reject $H_{0,B}$" conclusion.

SOLUTION 3

The discussion in the solution to part 2 indicates the presence of interaction between the two factors. The four male means are $615/3 = 205$ (category 1), $415/3 = 138.33$ (category 2), $940/3 = 313.33$ (category 3), and $820/3 = 273.33$ (category 4). The corresponding means for the female sample are 231.67, 288.33, 168.33, and 113.33. These means are shown in Figure 11.17(a), where interaction effect is very apparent, since the male and female lines *are not parallel*. When no interaction exists between the two factors, such a graph should contain lines that are *nearly parallel,* as illustrated in Figure 11.17(b).

The statistical test here supports this conclusion, since there is significant interaction provided F_3 is larger than $F_{.05,3,16} = 3.24$. Here, $F_3 = 26.87$, and so we once again conclude that there is significant interaction between gender and employee classification for this population.

Since the two lines in Figure 11.17(a) are not parallel, the relationship between employee classification and the amount of dental claims is not the same for males and females. In particular, the amount of dental claims is low for category 4 females and high for category 4 males. Also, the amount is high for category 2 females and low for cate-

FIGURE 11.17

Illustration of interaction effect. (a) Interaction effect in Example 11.10. (b) Hypothetical situation containing no significant interaction between gender and employee classification.

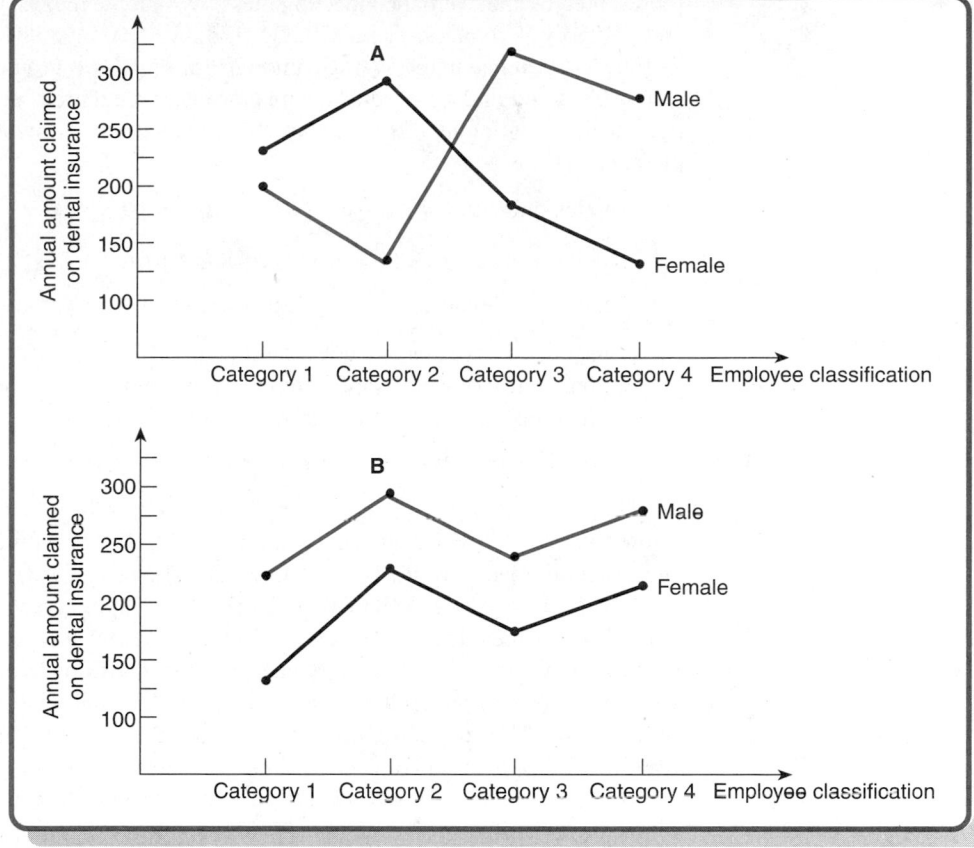

gory 2 males. *This type of discussion should always be included in the analysis whenever the interaction effect is significant.*

SOLUTION 4

A multiple comparisons analysis will determine whether the average annual amount for category 1 males is the same as for category 4 males, the average for category 2 males is the same for category 3 females, and so forth. There are $2 \cdot 4 = 8$ means here, providing $_8C_2 = 28$ possible pairwise comparisons. In general, for a two-way factorial design there are $_{ab}C_2$ possible pairs of means that can be compared using the multiple comparisons procedure.

The critical value corresponding to $\alpha = .05$, $k = 8$, and $v = 16$ (the df associated with the error sum of squares) from Table A.16 is $Q_{.05,8,16} = 4.90$. Since MS(error) = 1222.92 and there are $r = 3$ replicates at each treatment level, we next determine

$$D = Q_{\alpha,k,v} \cdot \sqrt{\frac{\text{MS(error)}}{r}}$$

$$= 4.90 \sqrt{\frac{1222.92}{3}} = 98.93$$

Consequently, any pair of sample treatment means differing by more than 98.93 will imply that the corresponding population means are unequal.

The eight sample means are obtained by dividing the corresponding replicate totals (R) by $r = 3$. Placing them in order, we obtain

113.33	138.33	168.33	205.00	231.67	273.33	288.33	313.33
(F, 4)	(M, 2)	(F, 3)	(M, 1)	(F, 1)	(M, 4)	(F, 2)	(M, 3)

Here, M and F represent the gender (factor A) and 1, 2, 3, and 4 represent the employee classification (factor B).

Since $250.00 - 138.33 = 66.67 < 98.93$, we *cannot* conclude that $\mu_{M,1} \neq \mu_{M,2}$. This is represented by the overbar connecting these two sample means. Consider category 4 males and category 4 females. Here $273.33 - 133.33 = 160 > 98.93$, and so we conclude that there *is* a difference in the average amounts for these two groups; that is, $\mu_{M,4} \neq \mu_{F,4}$. This can be observed in the preceding sample means, since there is no overbar connecting these two means. Continuing this procedure, we arrive at the following summary for the multiple comparisons analysis:

males only: $\mu_{M,2} \neq \mu_{M,4}$, $\mu_{M,2} \neq \mu_{M,3}$, $\mu_{M,1} \neq \mu_{M,3}$

females only: $\mu_{F,4} \neq \mu_{F,1}$, $\mu_{F,4} \neq \mu_{F,2}$, $\mu_{F,3} \neq \mu_{F,2}$

males and females: $\mu_{F,4} \neq \mu_{M,4}$, $\mu_{F,4} \neq \mu_{M,3}$, $\mu_{F,2} \neq \mu_{M,2}$, $\mu_{F,3} \neq \mu_{M,4}$, $\mu_{F,3} \neq \mu_{M,3}$

Consequently, we observe three significant differences in each of the male and female populations and five significant differences in the amount of annual dental claims when comparing employee classifications across both genders.

The Excel solution for this example is shown in Figure 11.18. The data should be entered in cells A1:E7 using the format in Figure 11.18, with the factor A labels in column A and the factor B labels in the first row. The procedure to follow here is to click on **KGP Data Analysis ➤ ANOVA.** In the resulting input screen, click on "Two-Way Factorial" and "Tukey Test for Difference Between Means." Next, enter (1) "A1:E7" in the **Input Range** box, (2) "3" in the **Number of Replications** box, and (3) "F1" in the **Output Range** box. The resulting output contains summary information and the ANOVA table in rows 23 through 30. In the ANOVA table, the word *Sample* was changed to *Gender,* *Columns* was changed to *Emp. Classification,* and *Within* was changed to *Error.*

The *p*-value for gender (factor A) is .039 and supports the earlier conclusion that the gender factor is significant, since $.039 < .05$. The employee classification factor (factor B) is not significant, as in the earlier solution, since its *p*-value (.176) exceeds .05. The Excel solution supports the finding that the interaction between these two factors is significant, since the *p*-value for the interaction effect is nearly zero. Also, Figure 11.18 contains the critical *F* values at the .05 significance level (in cells L25:L27), used in the earlier solution to Example 11.10.

FIGURE 11.18

Excel spreadsheet solution for Example 11.10 using **KGP Data Analysis ➤ ANOVA.**

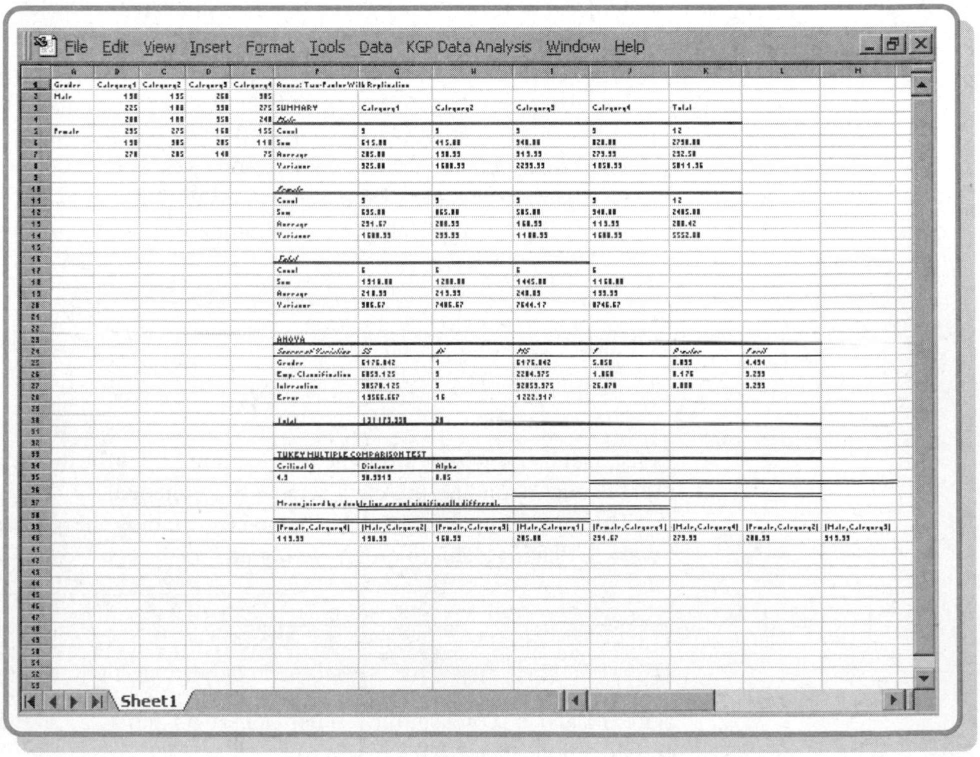

Exercises 11.38–11.43

Understanding the Mechanics

11.38 The data for a 2×3 factorial experiment are presented here. For each factor-level combination there are two replicates.

		Level of Factor A		
		1	**2**	**3**
Level of	**1**	20.6, 22.6	21.3, 23.1	21.1, 20.1
Factor B	**2**	22.6, 23.4	24.3, 22.9	22.2, 23.4

a. Calculate the treatment means. Plot the treatment means using the y-axis for the value of the mean and the x-axis for the levels of factor A. Plot two curves, one for each level of factor B. Do you think the factors interact?

b. Construct an ANOVA table for the factorial experiment.

c. Is there sufficient evidence to conclude that there is interaction between the factors using a .05 significance level? Do the results of this test support what you observed visually in part (a)?

d. Is there sufficient evidence to conclude that the levels of factor A differ? Use a .05 significance level.

e. Is there sufficient evidence to conclude that the levels of factor B differ? Use a .05 significance level.

f. If appropriate, determine which treatment means differ by using a multiple comparisons procedure at the .05 significance level.

Applying the New Concepts

11.39 The comparative study of word processing software in Exercise 11.27 was modified to take into account different types of keyboards: enhanced keyboard, modified keyboard, and standard keyboard. Keyboard layout and type of software could not be assumed to be independent, because it was possible that a certain type of software might actually be enhanced by a certain type of keyboard (e.g., one with special function keys). In other words, interaction between factors was possible. Therefore, a 3×3 factorial design was implemented. The following table gives the completion time in minutes, with three replicates for each treatment "cell."

	Software Type		
Keyboard Type	**Group 1 (Menu-Driven)**	**Group 2 (Command-Driven)**	**Group 3 (Mixed)**
Enhanced	9, 8, 10	8, 7, 7	8, 10, 10
Modified	14, 14, 13	10, 14, 12	12, 10, 14
Standard	15, 18, 17	18, 16, 15	15, 15, 14

a. Calculate the ANOVA table for the preceding experiment.

b. Assume that the assumptions of an ANOVA have been satisfied. Is there a difference in the three word processors, as measured by the productivity of the secretaries? Use $\alpha = .05$.

c. Do the different keyboards seem to affect productivity, as measured by completion times? Use $\alpha = .05$.

d. Is there a significant interaction between software type and keyboard type, at $\alpha = .05$?

e. For parts (b), (c), and (d), find the corresponding p-value for each test.

11.40 A manufacturer is interested in the number of defective components produced by its employees. A consultant recommends that each employee follow one of three proposed systematic procedures. To determine whether there was a difference in the three procedures, an experiment was conducted with one factor having three levels: less than a year of experience, 1 to 4 years experience, and over 4 years experience. The second factor was the systematic procedure, one level for each of the three proposed procedures. Data from the experiment, with three replicates per treatment, are as follows and show the average number of nondefective components produced per day over a one-week period for each employee:

	Procedure		
Experience	**1**	**2**	**3**
Less than a year	12.6, 15.7, 10.5	8.6, 9.9, 11.2	13.6, 12.8, 10.2
Between 1 and 4 years	13.7, 14.2, 15.8	9.2, 12.6, 13.1	12.1, 11.8, 14.1
Over 4 years	17.5, 19.8, 20.4	16.4, 17.1, 14.2	16.5, 18.7, 17.0

At the 10% significance level, is there a difference in the results of the three systematic procedures?

11.41 To investigate the effects of changes in inventory control policies for serial production systems, Dr. Henry Person collected data with the observed response being the number of units of system output in a 2×2 experiment. The factor CV (coefficient of variation of processing times at each work station) had two levels: CV = 5% and CV = 50%. The factor DT (down time rate at each work station also had two levels: DT = 10% and DT = 30%. One hundred observations were collected in each combination of factor levels. The sum of squares for CV, DT, CV $\times$ DT, and Error were 11,718.06, 19,010.02, 632.52, and 671,215.97 respectively. Construct an ANOVA table and explain what conclusions can be drawn using a 5% significance level.

(Source: *Decision Sciences Institute 1998 Proceedings*, "Impacts of Inventory Controls on Just-In-Time and Push Systems," p. 1181–83.)

11.42 A real estate broker wished to determine whether the Southern states and Midwestern states differ with respect to the median price of a new home for large and small metropolitan areas. Use the following data to test the location factor (Southern and Midwestern) and the city size factor (large and small metropolitan area) as well as the interaction of these two factors. Use a multiple comparisons test to examine pairwise differences. Use a significance level of 5%.

Midwestern and Small Metropolitan Area	Median Price of a New Home
Cedar Rapids, Iowa	105900
Champaign, Illinois	91400
Moline, Illinois	79500
Topeka, Kansas	78900
South Bend, Indiana	84700
Peoria, Illinois	86900

Midwestern and Large Metropolitan Area	Median Price of a New Home
Chicago, Illinois	169200
St. Louis, Missouri	104400
Cincinnati, Ohio	117900
Columbus, Ohio	123200
Des Moines, Iowa	109700
Lincoln, Nebraska	99100

Southern and Small Metropolitan Area	Median Price of a New Home
Corpus Christi, Texas	87100
Amarillo, Texas	77900
Little Rock, Arkansas	93600
Baton Rouge, Louisiana	98700
Ocala, Florida	70,300
Chattanooga, Tennessee	99500

Southern and Large Metropolitan Area	Median Price of a New Home
Atlanta, Georgia	116800
New Orleans, Louisiana	104700
Dallas, Texas	122600
Oklahoma City, Oklahoma	83800
Houston, Texas	100700
Birmingham, Alabama	120500

(Source: Adapted from *USA Today*, "Home Prices Climb," Nov. 23, 1998, p. 10B.)

USING THE COMPUTER

11.43 [DATA SET EX11-43] *Variable description:*

ExpLevel: Low (1) or High (2) experience level of operator
SpeedA: Number of nonconforming items for speed level A
SpeedB: Number of nonconforming items for speed level B
SpeedC: Number of nonconforming items for speed level C
SpeedD: Number of nonconforming items for speed level D

A quality engineer believes that there are two factors affecting the number of nonconforming items produced by a machine. The first factor is the experience level of the operator denoted by 1 and 2 for low and high experience, respectively. The variables SpeedA, SpeedB, SpeedC, and SpeedD are used to record the number of nonconforming items for four different machine speed levels. There are eight replicates for each of the factor level combinations.

   a. Interpret the results of the two-way factorial experiment using a 5% significance level. How do you interpret the interaction term?

   b. Which pairs of treatment means are significantly different? Use a significance level of 5%.

   c. Do a "what if" analysis by deleting the last two replicates in each cell and performing the steps in parts (a) and (b).

SUMMARY

The **analysis of variance (ANOVA)** procedure is a method of detecting differences between the means of two or more normal populations. The various populations represent the *levels* of a *factor* under observation. The factor might consist of, for example, different locations (does the crime rate differ among five cities?), brand (does one brand outsell the others?), or time periods (is average attendance the same each day of the week?).

Samples for this analysis must be obtained independently of each other. The ANOVA technique measures sources of variation among the sample data by computing various **sums of squares.** The variation from one level (population) to the next is measured by the factor sum of squares (SS(factor)), which is large when there is great variation among the sample means. The variation *within* the samples is measured by the error sum of squares (SS(error)). Each of these SS has a corresponding df, which is divided into the SS to produce a **mean square,** MS.

The ratio of MS(factor) to MS(error) produces an *F*-statistic that is used to test for equal means within the various populations. If the *F*-value is large (significant), we conclude that the means are not all the same, which implies that the factor of interest *does* have a significant effect on the variable under observation, called the **dependent** variable.

When we analyze the effect of a single factor, we perform a one-factor ANOVA and use a **completely randomized design.** The results of this analysis, including the various sums of squares, mean squares, and df, are summarized in an **ANOVA table.** If the ANOVA procedure concludes that the population means are not the same, a follow-up analysis can be conducted to determine which of the population means are unequal. This analysis is a **multiple comparisons procedure** and should be performed only in the event that the ANOVA null hypothesis of equal means is rejected.

When samples are not obtained in an independent manner, a **randomized block design** often can be used to test for differences in the population means. Again, there is a single factor of interest, but to determine the effect of this factor, the sample data are organized into *blocks.* For this situation, the samples are not independently obtained, but data within the same block may be gathered from the same city or person or at the same point in time. By including a block effect in the ANOVA procedure, we can analyze the factor of interest (the population means) using an *F*-test. In addition, another *F*-statistic can be used for determining whether there is a significant block effect within the sample data. If the null hypothesis of equal factor-level means is rejected, a multiple comparisons procedure for the randomized block design should be carried out to determine which pairs of factor-level means are unequal.

The other experimental design that was discussed was the **two-way factorial** design, where the effect of two factors can be investigated. Observations are obtained for each combination of factor levels, called **treatments.** For such a design, it is necessary to obtain two or more independent replicates for each treatment.

The two-way factorial design allows the researcher to investigate the effect of each factor individually, as well as the combined effect of the two factors, which is referred to as the **interaction** effect. A multiple comparisons analysis for the two-way factorial design will determine which pairs of treatment means are unequal.

SUMMARY OF FORMULAS

COMPLETELY RANDOMIZED DESIGN (ONE-FACTOR ANOVA)

$$SS(\text{factor}) = \left[\frac{T_1^2}{n_1} + \frac{T_2^2}{n_2} + \cdots + \frac{T_k^2}{n_k} \right] - \frac{T^2}{n}$$

$$SS(\text{total}) = \sum x^2 - \frac{T^2}{n}$$

$$SS(\text{error}) = SS(\text{total}) - SS(\text{factor})$$

$$MS(\text{factor}) = \frac{SS(\text{factor})}{k-1}$$

$$MS(\text{error}) = \frac{SS(\text{error})}{n-k} = s_p^2$$

where

n = total number of observations

k = number of groups (populations) to be compared

T_i = total of sample values for the ith group

T = grand total = $T_1 + T_2 + \cdots + T_k$

1. Test statistic:

$$F = \frac{MS(\text{factor})}{MS(\text{error})}$$

2. Confidence interval for μ_i:

$$\overline{X}_i \pm t_{\alpha/2, n-k} s_p \sqrt{\frac{1}{n_i}}$$

3. Confidence interval for $\mu_i - \mu_j$:

$$(\overline{X}_i - \overline{X}_j) \pm t_{\alpha/2, n-k} s_p \sqrt{\frac{1}{n_i} + \frac{1}{n_j}}$$

4. Multiple comparisons:

$$\mu_i \neq \mu_j \quad \text{provided } |\overline{X}_i - \overline{X}_j| > D$$

where

$$D = Q_{\alpha, k, v} \sqrt{\frac{MS(\text{error})}{n_r}}$$

v = df for error

n_r = number of replicates in each sample.

RANDOMIZED BLOCK DESIGN

$$SS(\text{factor}) = \frac{1}{b}[T_1^2 + T_2^2 + \cdots + T_k^2] - \frac{T^2}{bk}$$

$$SS(\text{blocks}) = \frac{1}{k}[S_1^2 + S_2^2 + \cdots + S_b^2] - \frac{T^2}{bk}$$

$$SS(\text{total}) = \sum x^2 - \frac{T^2}{bk}$$

$$SS(\text{error}) = SS(\text{total}) - SS(\text{factor}) - SS(\text{blocks})$$

$$MS(\text{factor}) = \frac{SS(\text{factor})}{k-1}$$

$$MS(\text{blocks}) = \frac{SS(\text{blocks})}{b-1}$$

$$MS(\text{error}) = \frac{SS(\text{error})}{(k-1)(b-1)}$$

where

b = number of blocks

k = number of factor levels

T = total of all bk observations

1. Test statistic for factor effect:

$$F_1 = \frac{MS(\text{factor})}{MS(\text{error})}$$

2. Test statistic for block effect:

$$F_2 = \frac{MS(\text{blocks})}{MS(\text{error})}$$

3. Confidence interval for $\mu_i - \mu_j$:

$$(\overline{X}_i - \overline{X}_j) \pm t_{\alpha/2, \text{df}} \cdot s \cdot \sqrt{\frac{1}{b} + \frac{1}{b}}$$

where

$$\text{df} = (k-1)(b-1)$$

$$s = \sqrt{MS(\text{error})}$$

4.   Multiple comparisons:

$$D = Q_{\alpha, k, (k-1)(b-1)} \sqrt{\frac{MS(error)}{b}}$$

TWO-WAY FACTORIAL DESIGN

$$SSA = \frac{1}{br}[T_1^2 + T_2^2 + \cdots + T_a^2] - \frac{T^2}{abr}$$

$$SSB = \frac{1}{ar}[S_1^2 + S_2^2 + \cdots + S_b^2] - \frac{T^2}{abr}$$

$$SSAB = \frac{1}{r}[\sum R^2] - SSA - SSB - \frac{T^2}{abr}$$

$$SS(total) = \sum x^2 - \frac{T^2}{abr}$$

$$SS(error) = SS(total) - SSA - SSB - SSAB$$

$$MSA = \frac{SSA}{a-1}$$

$$MSB = \frac{SSB}{b-1}$$

$$MSAB = \frac{SSAB}{(a-1)(b-1)}$$

$$MS(error) = \frac{SS(error)}{ab(r-1)}$$

where

a = number of levels for factor A

b = number of levels for factor B

r = number of replicates for each factor A, factor B combination (treatment)

R = sum of replicates for each treatment

T = grand total of all observations

1.   Test statistic for factor A effect:

$$F_1 = \frac{MSA}{MS(error)}$$

2.   Test statistic for factor B effect:

$$F_2 = \frac{MSB}{MS(error)}$$

3.   Test statistic for interaction effect:

$$F_3 = \frac{MSAB}{MS(error)}$$

4.   Multiple comparisons:

$$D = Q_{\alpha, ab, ab(r-1)} \sqrt{\frac{MS(error)}{r}}$$

REVIEW EXERCISES 11.44–11.65

11.44 A researcher wished to determine if there was a difference in the time required to complete three types of tasks. The data for the experiment are as follows. The time is given in units of minutes.

Task 1	Task 2	Task 3
66	80	49
90	58	60
75	79	56
63	61	68
71	68	53
72	73	58
80	77	59
55	82	70

   a. How many factors are there in this experiment? How many factor levels are there? How many replicates for each level are there?

   b. What is the name of this experimental design? Are the samples and observations within each factor level required to be independent for this design?

   c. Construct the ANOVA table. What conclusion is supported by the data at the .05 significance level?

   d. Compare all pairs of means by using a multiple comparisons procedure at the .05 significance level.

11.45 Political parties in Germany are very interested in the projected economic expansion of that country because of the fall elections in 1998. German unemployment in April 1998 exceeded 12%, and this was the highest unemployment for that month since the 1930s. Assume that a political analyst working for the German government randomly sampled economists from each of the six economic institutes in Germany and asked for their estimate of the country's economic growth (in percentage) for 1999. A summary of the survey results are presented below.

Summary Group	Count	Sum	Average	Variance
Institute 1	4	9	2.25	0.07
Institute 2	4	10	2.5	0.026667
Institute 3	4	8	2	0.086667
Institute 4	4	9.6	2.4	0.053333
Institute 5	4	8.4	2.1	0.06
Institute 6	4	8.8	2.2	0.06

(Adapted from *The Wall Street Journal*, "German Growth Seen Accelerating in 1999," May 13, 1998, p. A15.)

a. Assume that the SS(total) is equal to 1.758333. What conclusion can the political analyst draw from the data? Use a significance level of .05.

b. Test for the equality of group variances. Use a .05 significance level. What assumption concerning the population variances is required for an ANOVA procedure to be valid?

11.46 The results of a one-factor ANOVA for four groups with six replicates per group yielded the following statistics:

$$\bar{x}_1 = 85, \bar{x}_2 = 90, \bar{x}_3, = 58, \bar{x}_4 = 53, MSE = 198.73$$

Perform a multiple comparisons procedure at the .05 significance level.

11.47 The following table gives scores on an index that measures leadership ability, for respondents at three levels of management. It is assumed that the populations are normal and independent and the observations are randomly obtained. High scores represent greater leadership ability.

Supervisor	Middle-Level Manager	Upper-Level Manager
18	36	55
21	60	42
16	21	68
45	31	33
20	40	48

a. Compute the ANOVA table.

b. Is there a difference, on the average, between the leadership scores of the three groups? Use $\alpha = .05$. Find the p-value.

c. What is the 95% confidence interval for the mean leadership score of middle-level managers?

d. What is the 99% confidence interval for the difference between mean scores for the upper-level managers and the middle-level managers?

e. Using a significance level of .05, perform a multiple comparisons procedure, if appropriate.

11.48 The study in Exercise 11.47 has been modified to cover the leadership scores of individual managers who advanced from the post of supervisor to upper-level manager. Fifteen persons were initially studied, but only 10 actually went all the way to upper-level managerial positions. Since the same managers were used, a "randomized block" design was obtained, with three scores for each manager. Assume that the populations are normally distributed. The following table lists the leadership scores for the 10 managers who completed the study.

Respondent	Supervisor	Middle-Level Manager	Upper-Level Manager
1	25	30	30
2	16	35	48
3	17	18	20
4	30	25	20
5	35	30	32
6	28	29	28
7	29	30	35
8	30	40	48
9	27	29	35
10	40	30	32

a. Compute the ANOVA table.

b. Test the hypothesis that the means for the three classes are equal, at $\alpha = .05$. Can you conclude that, on the average, leadership scores remain stable, or do they tend to change as the persons move up the managerial scale?

c. Is there a significant difference among the managers' mean leadership scores? Use $\alpha = .05$.

11.49 Exercise 11.47 was further modified to take into account the influence of gender. Thus, a 3×2 two-way factorial design was implemented. It was decided to have three replicates for each cell. The leadership ability scores are given in the following table.

Gender	Supervisor	Middle-Level Manager	Upper-Level Manager
Male	16, 17, 25	18, 25, 30	20, 30, 42
Female	18, 20, 28	20, 28, 30	30, 41, 55

a. Compute the ANOVA table.

b. At $\alpha = .10$, test for a significant difference in leadership scores among the three groups of managers.

c. At $\alpha = .10$, is there a difference between the leadership scores of males and females?

d. Test for interaction between managerial level and gender at $\alpha = .10$.

e. Find the p-value for the three preceding hypothesis tests. Do the conclusions change at $\alpha = .05$ or $\alpha = .01$?

11.50 A court decision in Chicago supported university students who did not want their mandatory fees to finance liberal campus groups. This decision currently affects Wisconsin, Illinois, and Indiana. But this action could eventually spark challenges from students in other universities across the nation. Suppose that two universities in Ohio—University of Ohio and Ohio State University—were used to conduct an experiment to determine if senior students feel differently about this issue than freshmen students. Students were asked to respond on a scale from 1 to 7, with 1 representing "strongly opposed to any fees going to finance campus groups" and 7 representing "strongly support fees going to finance campus groups." The following table displays the results of the survey.

University	Seniors	Freshmen
University of Ohio	3,3,1,3,2,3,3,4,1,2,3,5	4,3,6,4,7,2,5,3,6,6,4,7
Ohio State University	4,1,2,5,2,3,2,3,1,2,5,4	4,7,2,3,5,2,3,6,7,5,4,6

(Adapted from *USA Today,* "Court Rules Students Can Limit Who Gets Campus Funding," Aug. 12, 1998, p. 1A.)

a. Construct the ANOVA table for this experiment.

b. Is there an interaction effect between universities and the classification of a student (senior versus freshman)? Use a significance level of .05.

c. Assume that the ANOVA assumptions are satisfied. Is there a difference between the students at the University of Ohio and Ohio State University using a significance level of .05?

d. Is there an effect based on classification of student at the .05 significance level?

e. Graphically display the relationship between seniors' and freshmen's responses and the university they are attending.

11.51 Assume four samples of size 10 are taken from four normally distributed populations with a common variance. The total sum of squares is 221.6, and the error sum of squares is 3.7. Test the null hypothesis that there is no difference in the means of the populations at the .05 level. Find the p-value.

11.52 An engineer wishes to design the flashlight batteries that provide the brightest light but do not burn out the light bulb prematurely. An experiment is conducted to determine the life of flashlight light bulbs at voltage levels of 3.5, 4.0, and 4.5. Ten light bulbs were used at each of these levels, and the data collected on the life of the light bulbs are as follows, in coded form.

Voltage Level 3.5	Voltage Level 4.0	Voltage Level 4.5
19	12	15
15	25	17
29	18	13
21	13	28
18	21	10
36	19	16
14	26	19
31	15	13
23	20	10
19	17	9

a. Compute the ANOVA table.

b. Is there a difference among the lifetimes of the light bulbs for the three groups? Use a .05 significance level.

c. What is a 95% confidence interval for the mean lifetime of the light bulbs in the group with the voltage level of 3.5?

d. What is the 99% confidence interval for the difference in mean lifetimes between the group with a voltage level of 3.5 and the group with a voltage level of 4.0?

e. Using a significance level of .05, perform a multiple comparisons procedure, if appropriate.

11.53 A quality engineer wishes to investigate the severity of cracks that develop on a casting design that is manufactured by three different processes. The engineer conducts an experiment in which three castings, one from each process, are subjected to extreme heat. A score is given to the severity of the crack. Various temperature levels are used, and the data are as follows. Using a .05 significance level, what conclusions can be made from this experiment?

Temperature Level	Process 1	Process 2	Process 3
1	7.6	8.0	7.9
2	6.0	7.3	7.4
3	9.9	9.9	10.0
4	7.8	8.0	8.6
5	6.8	7.3	7.7
6	9.6	9.7	9.9
7	7.1	7.8	7.9
8	7.4	8.0	8.2

11.54 Suppose it is known in a randomized block design that the mean square for blocks is 75, the error mean square is 291, the total sum of squares is 5083, and five blocks and four factor levels are used in the experiment. What would be the value of the F-test for testing the hypothesis that there is no difference in the mean levels of the factor?

11.55 Complete the following ANOVA table for a two-way factorial design.

Source	df	SS	MS	F
Factor A	1		3,088	
Factor B		3,400		
Interaction	3	49,000		
Error				
Total	23	63,000		

11.56 Fifteen university campuses of similar size were selected to determine which of three methods of advertising a blood-donation drive was most effective. Five randomly selected campuses advertised in the university newspaper (method 1). Another five advertised only by posters and signs around campus (method 2). The remaining five had each professor credit five points to the student's last test if the student contributed (method 3). The following table gives the percentage of the student body that contributed:

Method 1	.10	.15	.19	.21	.25
Method 2	.20	.18	.20	.23	.19
Method 3	.29	.20	.25	.30	.25

Do these data provide sufficient evidence at the .01 level of significance to reject the null hypothesis that there is no difference in the effectiveness of the three methods of advertising?

11.57 Sample data from three normally distributed populations were generated by a computer program for a simulation study. Do the data provide evidence to indicate that at least two of the population variances are not equal? Use a .05 significance level.

Sample 1	Sample 2	Sample 3	Sample 1	Sample 2	Sample 3
38	45	28	33	47	30
37	47	27	32	45	31
35	43	31	39	43	32
40	44	30	37	42	31
39	42	31	36	44	29
35	44	32	35	45	30
34	45	29			

11.58 Three different investment advisers were asked to give a performance rating from 0 to 100 on the risk-adjusted performances of 12 randomly selected aggressive growth mutual funds. From the following data, is there sufficient evidence to conclude that the three investment advisers differ in their mean performance ratings? Use a .05 significance level.

Mutual Funds	Investment Advisers			Mutual Funds	Investment Advisers		
	A	B	C		A	B	C
1	81	76	70	7	88	75	83
2	83	72	75	8	51	55	53
3	51	51	43	9	41	37	45
4	96	92	90	10	88	90	87
5	67	70	68	11	59	61	60
6	71	64	71	12	78	73	74

11.59 In a 3×3 factorial experiment with two replicates per treatment, how many error df are there? If a one-way ANOVA was used with three levels and six observations per level, how many error df are there? If the error df are very small for a two-way factorial experiment, how can one increase the error df?

11.60 Password protection of computer resources has been a concern for security analysts for some time. Many bank accounts are guarded only by a four- or five-digit personal identification number (PIN). Two researchers performed a laboratory experiment to assess the effect of two factors on the creation of passwords/PINs. In this experiment, the lengths of passwords/PINs were recorded. One factor, called "Password/PINs," consisted of two levels, with some subjects being told to create a password and some subjects being told to create a PIN. The other factor, called "keyboard presence," consisted of two levels, with some subjects using a standard touchtone keypad and some subjects using no keypad. The sum of squares for "Password/PINs," the sum of squares for "keypad presence," and the total sum of squares were, respectively, 1.78, 13.05, and 332.28.

(Source: "An Investigation of Keyboard Interface Security," *Information and Management,* vol. 24 (1993), pp.53–59.)

   a. Assume that in each cell of the factorial experiment there were 28 students and that the sum of squares for interaction was 2.04. Construct the ANOVA table for this experiment.
   b. What conclusions do the data support with regard to the lengths of Passwords/PINs created? Use a .05 significance level.
   c. What requirements must hold on the data in order for the factorial experiment to be valid?

11.61 A manager of Bookstop would like to determine if rankings of hardcover books are different across type (fiction and nonfiction) and cost (high [over $10] and low [$10 or less]). Consider the following data to be a random sample of hardcover books and their sales rankings.
   a. Use an appropriate experimental design to analyze the two factors, type and cost, using a 5% significance level.
   b. Should you perform a multiple comparisons procedure? If so, use a 5% significance level.
   c. Do a "what if" analysis by dividing each ranking by 50 and analyzing the data. What changes occur in the ANOVA results?

Book Title	Fiction and over $10
All Through the Night	22
Rainbow Six	33
The Path of Daggers	2
Cold Mountain	31
The Present	34
	Fiction and $10 or less
Animorphs: The Pretender	19
Cat & Mouse	8
Special Delivery	48
Deception on His Mind	35
The MacGregor Grooms	7

	Nonfiction and over $10
Chicken Soup for The Teenage Soul II	3
In the Meantime	12
The 9 Steps to Financial Freedom	29
Sugar Busters	20
The Seat of the Soul	11
	Nonfiction and $10 or less
The Perfect Storm	46
Dr. Atkins' New Diet Revolution	4
The Virtues of Aging	26
Protein Powder	21
Don't Sweat the Small Stuff	25

(Source: Adapted from *USA Today*, "Best-Selling Books," Nov. 5, 1998, p. 8D.)

11.62 The weak performance of Latin American mutual funds relative to domestic U.S. funds has sapped the assets of these funds in the late 1990s. The percentage of funds actually invested in Latin America has dropped off partly because of the very strong performance of the United States stock market and the poor performance of Asian financial markets. However, with private-equity funds, a longer-term view is held. Most private-equity funds hold investments for five years or so, then exit through an initial public offering or a strategic sale. Suppose that each of the ten private-equity funds investing in Latin America are presented below with the percentage of their assets in the IPO (initial public offering) market for the years 1996, 1997, and 1998. The IPO market is a very risky part of the stock market, particularly in countries outside of the U.S. Using a .05 significance level, explain what conclusions financial analysts can make using the following data to support these statements.

Private-Equity Fund	**1996**	**1997**	**1998**
Aig/Ge Capital Latin American Infrastructure	10.7	15.7	7.5
Hicks, Muse, Tate & Furst Latin American Fund	11.3	20.2	8.9
Exxel Capital Partners	16.9	24.7	16.8
G.P. Capital Partners II	14.5	12.5	18.5
CVC/Opportunity Equity Partners	17.4	14.5	19.5
G.P. Capital Partners	16.5	15.5	14.4
Latin American Capital Partners II	10.4	21.5	12.2
Newbridge Latin America	8.9	13.3	9.7
TCW/Latin America Equity Partners	13.9	14.5	12.5
Latin American Private Equity Fund	7.4	13.5	8.5

(Adapted from *The Wall Street Journal*, "U.S. Deal Makers Snap Up Stakes in Latin Companies Bucking Area Stock Slump," July 23, 1998, p. A13.)

11.63 [DATA SET EX11-63] *Variable description:*

Schedule1: productivity of each employee on work schedule 1.
Schedule2: productivity of each employee on work schedule 2.
Schedule3: productivity of each employee on work schedule 3.

The manager of an electronics factory wishes to determine the effect of three different work schedules on the productivity of assemblers of electrical components. Work schedule 1 is a five-day work week, 8 hours a day. Work schedule 2 is a week consisting of four days at 9 hours a day and 4 hours on the fifth day. Work schedule 3 is a four-day week, 10 hours a day. A random sample of eight employees was selected for each work schedule. The productivity of each employee was recorded for a week, and productivity was measured in terms of total dollar worth of units produced. The productivity figures are recorded using variables Schedule1, Schedule2, and Schedule3.

    a. Consider the three histograms stacked in order from Schedule1 (first one) to Schedule3 (last one). From these histograms, what conclusions would you make?

    b. Consider the Excel printout. What conclusions can you make assuming a 5% significance level? Is the Tukey procedure consistent with the results of the ANOVA table?

    c. Suppose that observations 33 and 49 for Schedule 2 were mistyped as 25341 and 25473, and should have been 20500 and 20200. Do a "what if" analysis by changing these values and analyzing the data again. What changes take place in the variances of the three groups?

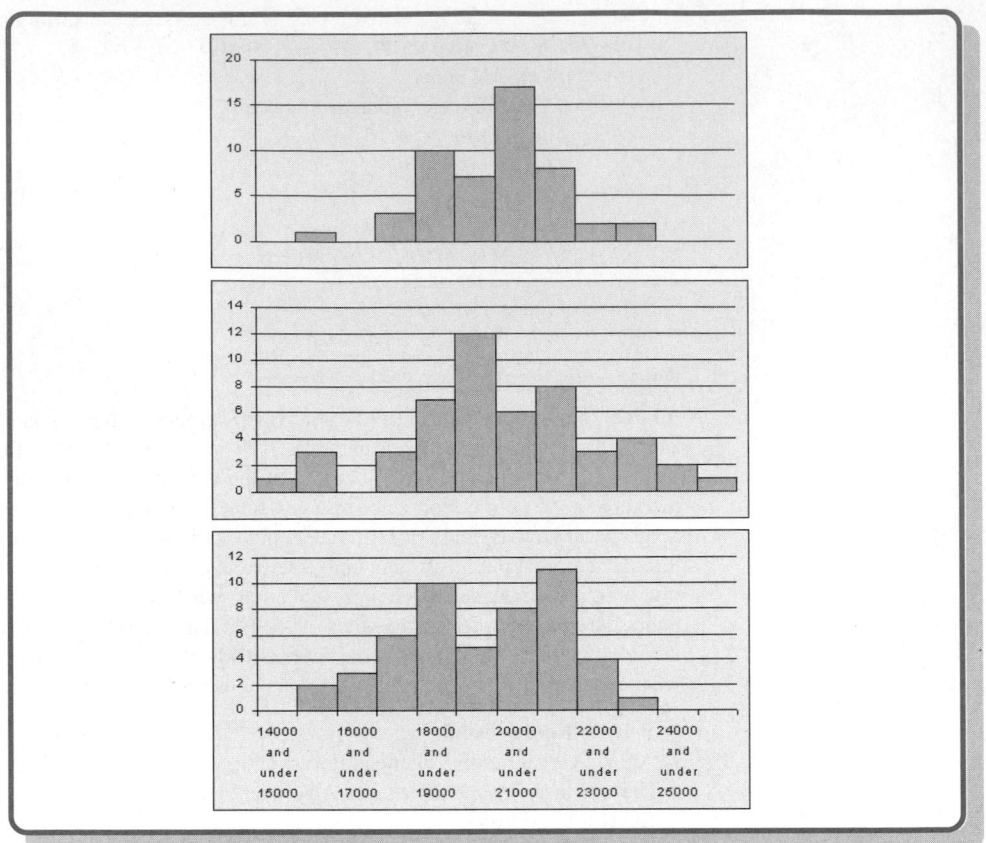

ANOVA

Source of Variation	SS	df	MS	F	P-value	F crit
Between Groups	10148561.45	2	50743280.7	1.21	0.30	3.06
Within Groups	615589918.92	147	4187686.5			
Total	625738480.37	149				

Tukey Multiple Comparisons Test

Critical Q	Distance	Alpha
3.36	972.39	0.05

Means joined by a double line are not significantly different.

Schedule3	Schedule1	Schedule2
19628.00	20056.70	20250.54

Hartley Test for Homogeneity of Variance

Hartley Test	Critical Value	Alpha
2.31	1.85	0.05

11.64 [DATA EX11-64] *Variable description:*

Tastetester: taste tester from 1 to 20
Plant1: rating for potato chips from plant 1
Plant2: rating for potato chips from plant 2
Plant3: rating for potato chips from plant 3

A manufacturer of potato chips wants to ensure that its three different plants are producing potato chips with the same high standards. Twenty potato chip bags from each of the three plants were randomly selected. Twenty taste-testers rated the quality of the manufactured potato chips on a scale from 1 (lowest quality) to 10 (highest quality). Stem-and-leaf plots of the ratings for each plant follows.

a. What interpretation can you give to the stem-and-leaf plots?

b. What conclusions can you draw from the ANOVA table and Tukey's multiple comparisons procedure? Use a 5% significance level.

c. Do a "what if" analysis by considering only the first ten observations rather than the entire set of twenty observations. What conclusions change?

Plant1		Plant2		Plant3	
Stem and Leaf		**Stem and Leaf**		**Stem and Leaf**	
STEM	LEAF UNIT = 0.1	STEM	LEAF UNIT = 0.1	STEM	LEAF UNIT = 0.1
5	4 7	5	6	3	5
6	0 1 7 8	6	3 3 5 5 7 8 9 9	4	5
7	0 1 2 2 3 4 6 8 8	7	0 1 2 4 5 6 7 8	5	0 6 8 8
8	9	8	0 1 9	6	0 0 1 1 5 6 7
9	1 5 5 5			7	0 1 5 7 9
				8	7
				9	1

ANOVA

Source of Variation	SS	df	MS	F	P-value	F crit
Rows	22.06	19	1.16	0.82	0.67	1.87
Columns	10.79	2	5.39	3.82	0.03	3.24
Error	53.73	38	1.41			
Total	86.58	59				

Tukey Multiple Comparisons Test

Critical Q	Distance	Alpha
3.44	0.91466647	0.05

Means joined by a double line are not significantly different.

Plant3	Plant2	Plant1
6.46	7.14	7.48

11.65 [DATA EX11-65] *Variable description:*

Experience: A value from 1 through 4 describing the experience of the programmer
HelpSysA: Time required to write a program using Help System A
HelpSysB: Time required to write a program using Help System B
HelpSysC: Time required to write a program using Help System C

An information systems researcher wishes to determine whether the type of help system available to programmers has an effect on the time required to write a program. The researcher also knows that the experience of a programmer can influence the time (in minutes) required to write a program. An experiment is set up with three different help systems and four levels of programming experience (1 for almost no experience, 2 for no more than two years' experience but some previous experience, 3 for less than five years' but more than two years' experience, and 4 for more than five years' experience).

a. The mean times for each help system and experience level are presented below. In addition a graph displays the means versus the experience level. Interpret this graph. Do you believe that there is an interaction effect?

b. Analyze the data using a significance level of 5%. Write a summary of your findings.

Exper	HelpSys A	HelpSys B	HelpSys C
1	31	34	39.5
2	33	30.5	30.5
3	26	25.5	23.5
4	24.5	23.5	18

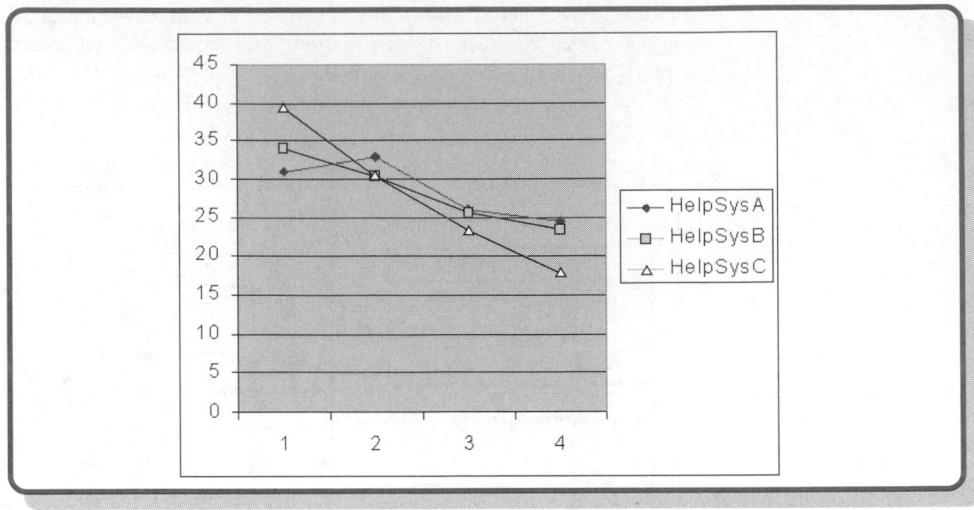

COMPUTER EXERCISES USING THE DATABASES

EXERCISE 1—APPENDIX E
From the database, randomly select 10 observations each from the NE sector, the NW sector, and SE sector (variable LOCATION). Using a .05 significance level, is there sufficient evidence to conclude that the mean house payment or apartment/house rent (variable HPAYRENT) is significantly different for the three locations? Include a multiple comparisons procedure, if appropriate.

EXERCISE 2—APPENDIX E
Select at random 12 observations for each level of two factors from the database. Factor A has two levels: a nonzero income from the secondary wage earner, and no secondary income (variable INCOME2). Factor B has two levels: own one's residence and rent one's residence (variable OWNORENT). Determine the effect of these two factors on house payment or house/apartment rent (variable HPAYRENT). Set up an ANOVA table that includes interaction. What conclusions can be drawn at the .05 significance level?

EXERCISE 3—APPENDIX F
From the database, select at random six observations from each bond rating and region combination. (Refer to variables BONDRATE and REGION.) Determine the effect of bond rating and region on the assets (variable ASSETS). Use a .05 significance level. Discuss the effect of interaction.

EXERCISE 4—APPENDIX F
Repeat Exercise 3, but determine the effect of bond rating (BONDRATE) and region (REGION) on the net income (NETINC) instead of assets.

INSIGHTS FROM STATISTICS IN ACTION: AUTOMOTIVE INSURANCE RATES AND CATEGORY OF DRIVER

At the beginning of this chapter, the Statistics in Action case study explained the effort by some politicians to curtail the ever-increasing cost of auto insurance. Efforts are underway to provide the auto owner with more options when selecting an auto insurance policy and to pass on a portion of the recent auto insurance company savings back to the consumer. As a first step, let's assume you were charged with demonstrating that there is a difference in annual premiums for different age and gender categories. The table below provides rates for minimum liability insurance required by the state of Texas. The insurance companies listed represent companies that sell more than 80% of the automotive liability insurance in the Dallas area.

Rates given in the table provide 1996–1997 rates for 21 companies and four categories of drivers. Driver A is an adult male between age 25 and 64 or female between age 21 and 64 who drives to and from work and has no at-fault accidents or major traffic convictions. Driver B is a single male under age 21 who has no at-fault accidents or major traffic convictions. Driver C is a single female under age 21 who has no at-fault accidents or major traffic convictions. Driver D is an adult male or female over age 64 who drives only for pleasure and errands and has no at-fault accidents or major traffic convictions.

You can use the analysis of variance procedure to test for mean price differences between both the different insurance companies and categories of drivers. Which types of testing would be beneficial in your selecting an insurance policy? Do you already have some suspicion as to what the testing of driver categories may demonstrate?

1996–1997 Automotive Liability Insurance Rates—23 Insurance Companies Selling More Than 80% of Policies in Dallas, Texas

Insurance Company	Driver Category			
	A	B	C	D
Allstate Indemnity	506	1608	1238	420
Allstate Insurance	552	1758	1352	462
Allstate Property & Casualty	522	1662	1280	436
Beacon National	447	1420	1092	372
Farmers Texas County Mutual	788	2244	1626	690
First Preferred	383	1217	936	319
Government Employees (GEICO)	420	1290	1018	282
Liberty Mutual	440	1481	1110	330
Mid-Century	446	1666	1280	344
Nationwide Mutual	411	1306	1005	297
Petrolia	553	1758	1352	460
Potomac	509	1232	1249	425
Progressive County Mutual	526	1291	992	625
Prudential Property & Casualty	474	1509	1162	338
Southern Farm Bureau Casualty	372	1183	910	309
State Farm County Mutual	624	1986	1529	452
State Farm Mutual	480	1528	1176	348
Teachers	422	1610	1240	352
Texas Farm Bureau Mutual	534	1699	1307	445
Texas Farmers	552	1758	1352	462
United Services Automobile Association (USAA)	291	1118	830	253

1. What statistical procedure would you use to test for price differences among the four categories of drivers? State the appropriate null and alternative hypotheses.

2. Using insurance companies as blocks, perform a randomized block procedure to test for differences in the mean price for the four categories of drivers. Use a significance level of .05.

3. If appropriate, perform a multiple comparisons test to isolate any differences in mean liability costs for the four categories of drivers. Use a .05 significance level. Do the results agree with your experience or expectation?

4. From the results of the multiple comparisons test, do you believe that a 95% confidence interval for the mean price difference between driver categories A and D will include 0? Why?

5. Construct a 95% confidence interval for the mean price difference between driver categories A and D. Does this agree with your response in Question 4?

6. What other ANOVA procedure might you have used for comparing mean prices of the different drivers? Discuss why this procedure would not be appropriate.

Sources: "Auto Insurance Rates Vary Widely," Terrence Stutz/Austin Bureau, *The Dallas Morning News*, July 30, 1997, p. 1A. Reprinted with permission of *The Dallas Morning News*.

"Armey Pushes Bill to Cut Auto Insurance Premiums," Catalina Camia, *The Dallas Morning News*, May 31, 1998, p. 10A. Reprinted with permission of *The Dallas Morning News*.

"Take Advantage of New Cut-rate Car Insurance," *USA Today*, June 14, 1998, p. 20.

Chapter 11 Appendix: Data Analysis with MINITAB

ANALYSIS OF VARIANCE

To perform a one-factor ANOVA procedure, click on **Stat ➤ ANOVA ➤ One-Way** (unstacked) if the data are entered with each group in a separate column. If the data are entered with the dependent variable in one column and the factor levels in a separate column, then click on **Stat ➤ ANOVA ➤ One-Way.** To perform a multiple comparisons test, you must use **Stat ➤ ANOVA ➤ One-Way** for stacked data.

To demonstrate the ANOVA procedure in MINITAB, data set DATA11-6 is used. After clicking on **Stat ➤ ANOVA ➤ One-Way** (unstacked), the following user form appears. In the **Responses** box, type "C1-C5." Click on **Graphs** to obtain the second user form. The dot plots that appear in Figure 11.5 can be obtained by clicking on the dot plot radial button. The one-way ANOVA printout appears after the user forms. Following the output is the user form necessary if values of the dependent variable were entered in one column and the factor levels were listed in another.

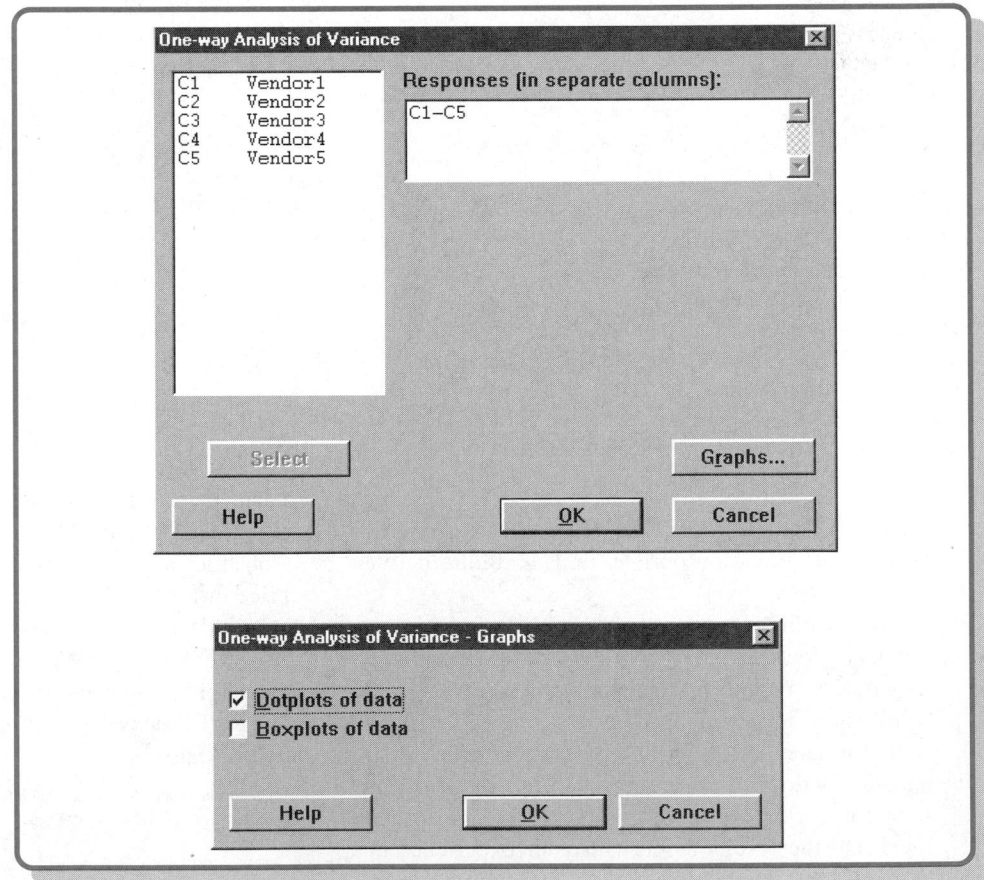

One-way Analysis of Variance

```
Analysis of Variance
Source      DF       SS      MS        F       P
Factor       4   388.44   97.11    39.05   0.000
Error      120   298.42    2.49
Total      124   686.86
                                  Individual 95% CIs For Mean
                                  Based on Pooled StDev
Level        N     Mean    StDev   -+---------+---------+---------+-----
vendor1     25   25.730    1.412                                (---*---)
vendor2     25   21.343    1.633   (---*---)
vendor3     25   22.122    1.881       (---*---)
vendor4     25   24.857    1.533                        (---*---)
vendor5     25   21.865    1.374        (---*---)
                                  -+---------+---------+---------+-----
Pooled StDev =  1.577            20.8      22.4      24.0      25.6
```

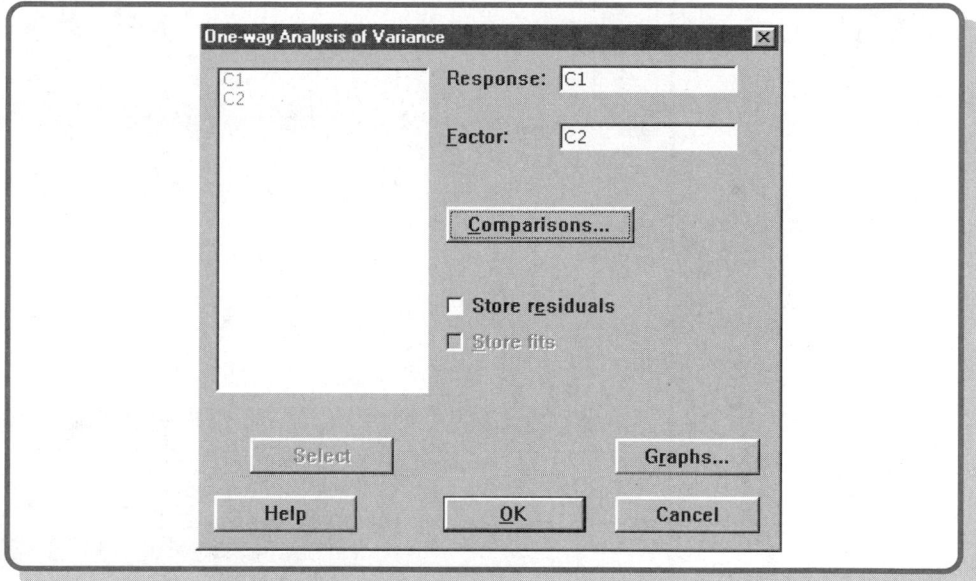

To perform a randomized block procedure or a two-way ANOVA procedure in MINITAB, click on **Stat ➤ ANOVA ➤ Two-Way.** To use this procedure, the data must have two factors (one of which could be a block) and the same number of observations appearing in each cell. A printout is presented of the data in section 11.4 with type of tip being one factor and the hinge being the other factor (block for this example). Note that the values in column C2 are 1, 2, or 3, indicating the type of tip, and the values in column C3 are from 1 to 10 and identify the hinge. Following the data spreadsheet is the user form for the two-way ANOVA. In the **Response** box, type the name or column number of the response variable. In the **Row Factor** box type one of the columns identifying the levels of the factor. Do the same with the **Column Factor** box. Check the **Display Means** box to display the mean for each factor level and to display a 95% confidence interval for each level. Check **Store Residuals** or **Store Fits** to store these values in the spreadsheet. If the model does not have an interaction term, then check the **Fit Additive Model** option. For a randomized block design with only one observation per cell, there is no interaction term in the model. Therefore, for this design the **Fit Additive Model** option will have no affect on the ANOVA output. The MINITAB output appears after the user form for this example. A histogram of the residuals, a normal plot of the residuals, a plot of the residuals versus the fits, and a plot of the residuals versus the order can be obtained by clicking on the **Graph** option and choosing the desired plot options.

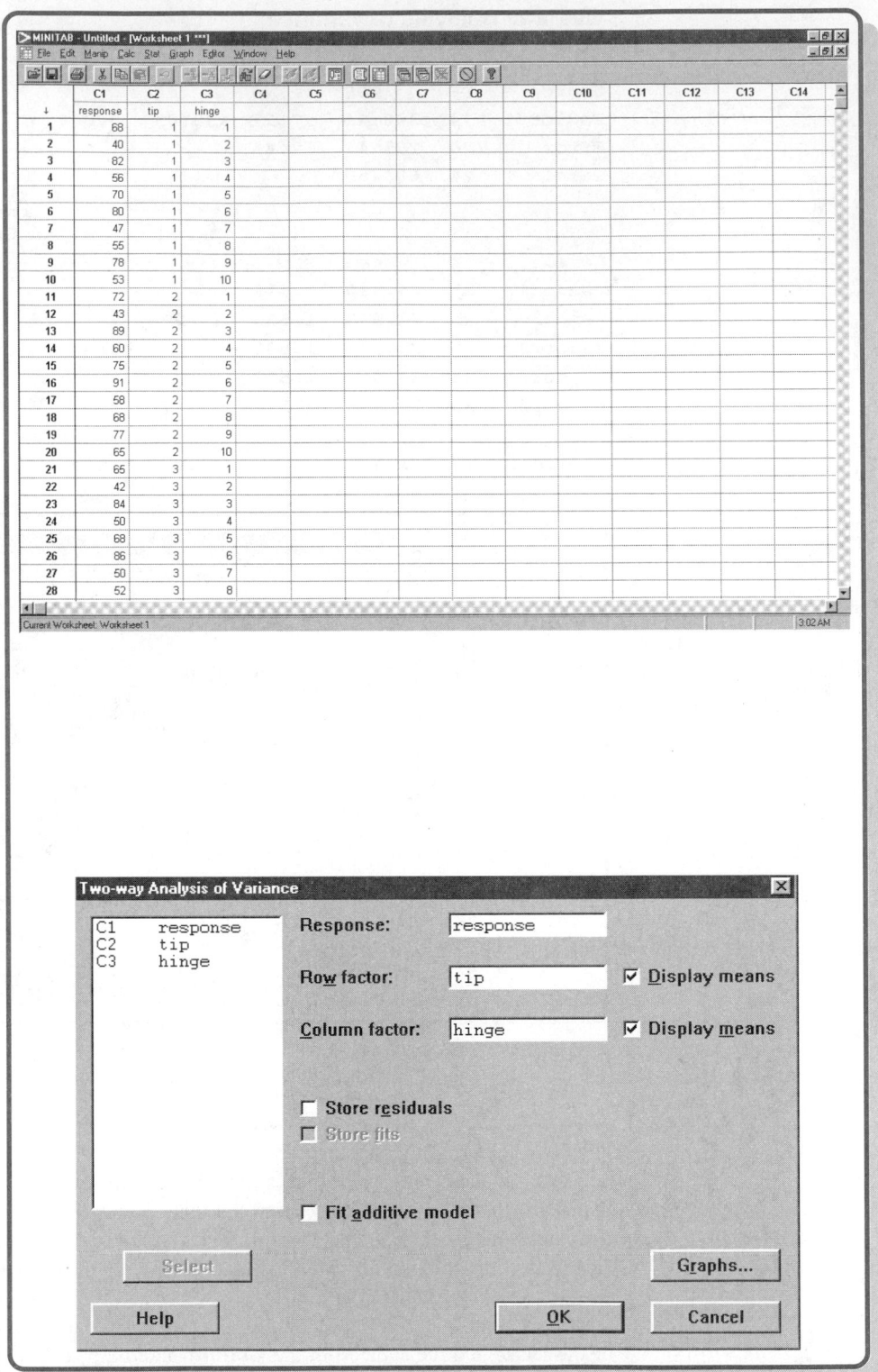

```
MTB > Twoway C1 C2 C3;
SUBC> Means C2 C3.
```

Two-way Analysis of Variance

```
Analysis of Variance for response
Source    DF        SS        MS        F        P
tip        2     304.20    152.10    15.63    0.000
hinge      9    5704.97    633.89    65.15    0.000
Error     18     175.13      9.73
Total     29    6184.30
                              Individual 95% CI
Tip      Mean      --------+---------+---------+---------+---
1        62.90        (------*------)
2        69.80                              (------*------)
3        63.20        (------*------)
                      --------+---------+---------+---------+---
                          63.00     66.00     69.00     72.00

                              Individual 95% CI
Hinge    Mean      -----+---------+---------+---------+------
1        68.3                         (--*-)
2        41.7        (--*-)
3        85.0                                     (--*-)
4        55.3               (--*-)
5        71.0                          (-*--)
6        85.7                                     (-*--)
7        51.7              (-*--)
8        58.3                 (--*-)
9        76.7                            (-*--)
10       59.3                 (--*-)
                   -----+---------+---------+---------+------
                      45.0      60.0      75.0      90.0
```

QUALITY IMPROVEMENT

STATISTICS IN ACTION: SIX SIGMA MEANS BEING 99.9997% PERFECT

According to corporate managers, Six Sigma is either a revolution slashing trillions of dollars from corporate inefficiency or the most maddening management fad yet devised to keep front-line workers too busy collecting data to do their jobs. General Electric, the company most smitten with Six Sigma, became the first company worth more than $300 billion based on its current stock price. Motorola, the company that founded Six Sigma, is still struggling with shrinking profits and downsizing.

In 1985, Six Sigma was founded by Bill Smith, a studious mid-level engineer at Motorola. At that time, Motorola was facing extinction, having lost its radio and TV businesses to Japan. By 1988, Motorola had won the first-ever Malcolm Baldrige award for quality.

Implementing Six Sigma is expensive, but at least 30 large companies have embraced it. Six Sigma is capturing widespread attention because of two heavyweight disciples: CEOs Jack Welch of GE and Larry Bossidy of Allied Signals. Larry Bossidy is quoted as saying, "The fact is, there is more reality with this than anything that has come down in a long time in business. The more you get involved with it, the more you are convinced." Not all large companies have had success with Six Sigma. For example, John Akers promised to turn IBM around with Six Sigma. But the attempt was abandoned after Akers was ousted in 1993.

The Six Sigma movement is trying to insert the science of hard-nosed statistics into the foggy philosophy of quality. A good company can operate at four sigma, which means they are 99% perfect. Six Sigma means being 99.9997% correct. At first glance, four sigma might not seem that much worse than Six Sigma. However, think of it this way. The savings for an automaker that has to repair 6,210 cars for every one million made at Four Sigma would be considerable if only 3.4 cars would need to be repaired at Six Sigma. Raytheon figures it spends 25% of each sales dollar fixing problems when operating at four sigma. This figure drops to 1% if quality and efficiency are raised to Six Sigma.

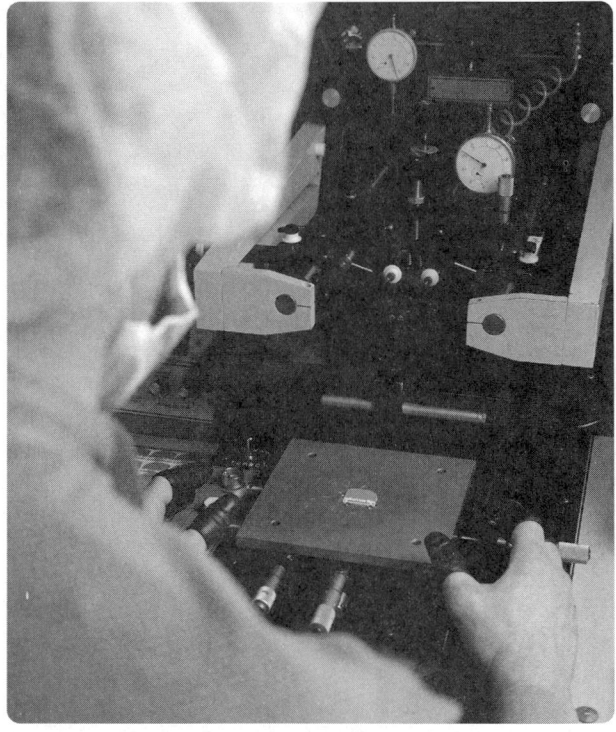

A key question for any manufacturing process is whether the process is *capable* of producing a satisfactory number of usable (conforming) items. If a machine part is either too small or too large, it simply will not fit and is considered to be unusable (nonconforming). The *quality* of the process is poor whenever the number of items not meeting the process specifications is considered to be excessively high. The Six Sigma concept attempts to reduce this number and raise process quality.

When you have completed this chapter, you will have a firm grasp of what is meant by the increasingly popular word *quality*. In particular, you will be able to:

- Discuss the essential concepts behind Total Quality Management and the Malcolm Baldrige National Quality Award;
- Construct control charts that monitor the stability of a process; and
- Determine if a particular process is capable of meeting the corresponding process specifications.

A Look Back/Introduction

Previous chapters have introduced you to various statistical measures, such as the sample mean (a measure of *location*) and the sample range (a measure of *dispersion* or *variation*). When examining a population, knowledge of these measures can tell you a great deal about the population. For example, if your company advertises 10-pound bags of dog food but a large random sample of bags produces an average ($\bar{x}$) of 8.7 pounds, the company will undoubtedly encounter many angry consumers and may well be out of the dog food business if the sample is representative of all bags being produced.

Similarly, too much variation in the bag weights would indicate that the *production process* is too erratic. The company would then lose money due to dissatisfied customers (whose bags weigh under 10 pounds) or excess product being packaged (in bags that weigh over 10 pounds). Ideally, this production process could be fine-tuned to always produce 10-pound bags with no variation, but realistically, such a goal is nearly impossible. Our example, however, points out the need to be *on target* and *consistent*.

In part, **quality improvement is the study of variability.** Recently, it has received a great deal of national attention, as more and more companies are facing competitors who focus on quality and offer less expensive, more reliable products. This chapter will examine the human side of quality management along with many of the popular tools for implementing quality standards in manufacturing and service industries. Many of the statistical measures and procedures from the earlier chapters will be used to develop simple, yet powerful, methods of monitoring and controlling process location and variation.

12.1 Quality Improvement: Concepts and Strategies

Rarely a day goes by in which we're not bombarded by such statements as, "Quality is our most important job at Company A," or "Company B is a leader in quality." It is safe to say that a focus on quality is taking over American business; however, using the word "quality" in one's advertising is not what this movement is all about. Rather, the current focus on quality represents a change in the entire corporate culture, from the top on down, ranging from a dramatic change in how we manage and treat company employees all the way to using statistical methods to monitor and improve a production or service process.

New ideas within U.S. business organizations generally encounter a great deal of resistance. The "Doing business as usual" and "If it ain't broke, don't fix it" philosophies have prevailed, we would argue, for too long. New ideas require change. Change means more work, and we all seem to have enough work. American manufacturing organizations were first to notice that, in fact, many parts of their businesses were broken. As they began to lose an ever-increasing share to overseas competition, they began to take a closer look at their manufacturing processes and management styles. It has become clear to an increasing number of both manufacturing and service organizations that what worked in the past may not be the ideal path into the twenty-first century.

In the 1980s, General Motors recognized that their many layers of management bureaucracy and lack of customer focus needed a fresh approach. When they created the Saturn division, their first new division in over 50 years, a new philosophy was carved out—one that contained fewer (and more accessible) management divisions and that empowered their employees to satisfy customer needs. Many other American business organizations have revolutionized the way they do business—not always by choice, since for many it was the only available path to survival.

A recent convert to the "Not doing business as usual" approach is the U.S. government. A 1993 report, *Creating a Government That Works Better and Costs Less, Report of* *the National Performance Review,* prepared by Vice President Al Gore, gives a very candid* assessment of why the federal government must change its organizational philosophy. An interesting aspect of this report is that it does not stop at criticizing the past and offering very broad-based solutions, but rather provides very specific suggestions and action items for bringing about very dramatic changes. Here are two quotes from the NPR report.

> *The federal government is not simply broke; it is broken. Ineffective regulation of the financial industry brought us the savings and loan debacle. Ineffective education and training programs jeopardize our competitive edge. Ineffective welfare and housing programs undermine our families and cities. (p. 1)*

> *Some may say that the task is too large; that we should not attempt it because we are bound to make mistakes; that it cannot be done. But we have no choice. Our government is in trouble. It has lost its ethic of public service; and, most importantly, it has lost the faith of the American people. . . .*
> *In times such as these, the most dangerous course is to do nothing. We must have the courage to risk change. (p. 9)*

The report proposes to invent a governmental system that puts people first. It recommends:

- cutting unnecessary spending and red tape;
- serving its customers;
- empowering its employees;
- helping communities solve their own problems;
- fostering excellence.

This will be accomplished by:

- creating a clear sense of mission;
- steering more, rowing less;
- delegating authority and responsibility;
- replacing regulations with incentives;
- developing budgets based on outcomes;
- exposing federal operations to competition;
- searching for markets, not administrative solutions;
- measuring government success by customer satisfaction.

Certainly the skeptics will question whether this is simply another government mandate that will fall on deaf ears when confronted by special-interest legislators and administrators who oppose changing a system that has stood firm these many years. Nevertheless, the report contains a long list of corrective actions (such as "All agencies will begin developing and using measurable objectives and reporting results") that describe a new management philosophy for the federal government.

The NPR report is available at the National Performance Review Web site (www.npr.gov). The 1998 Web site contains a list of their major accomplishments during the past year, including dollars saved through fraud detection and electronic fund transfers, improvements in worker safety and environmental protection, improvements in the IRS's and the Social Security Administration's customer service, and more cost-effective postal service.

Actually, this new philosophy (as the report is quick to point out) has its roots in the **Total Quality Management** (TQM) movement that has produced an abundance of positive results in U.S. manufacturing and service organizations. The TQM approach represents a basic change in how we view employees, competition, education, and business strategies. What U.S. businesses have discovered is that we live at a time when changes are occurring constantly and institutions that are based on assumptions that do not allow reaction to such changes have difficulty surviving. As mentioned in the NPR report, the

---

* This report will be referred to as the NPR report in subsequent discussion. The National Performance Review is now known as the National Partnership for Reinventing Government.

federal government has begun to realize that existing policies, rules, regulations, and procedures that served us well at one time need a serious overhaul in order to meet the demands of tomorrow. The use of TQM can offer solutions to such organizations.

What is TQM? There are many definitions of TQM in the literature. Essentially, TQM embraces a management philosophy that will allow a firm to meet or surpass customer expectations. TQM focuses on continuous quality improvement, teamwork, and paying close attention to the voice of the customer. TQM is an integrated management system that involves everyone in the organization (as well as outside suppliers) and uses quantitative methods to monitor and continuously improve the quality of a process.

THE QUALITY GURUS

Surprising to many people is that the quality message has been preached in the United States for many years. People simply ignored the message because there was little foreign competition. The corporate mind set was "we are invincible" and the corporate strategy became "new challenge, old response." The early quality messengers, most notably W. Edwards Deming and Joseph M. Juran, warned that past success does not guarantee survival tomorrow. In 1979, another quality expert, Philip B. Crosby, began offering organizations a quality-management/improvement program. Although these three individuals appear to have different messages, there are many similarities in their guidelines for building quality-focused organizations. We will briefly examine the key points of the Deming, Juran, and Crosby quality-improvement programs.

W. EDWARDS DEMING. The year 1993 marked the end of an era in the world of quality improvement as Dr. W. Edwards "Ed" Deming passed away at the age of 93. He was lecturing and delivering his typically unflattering message to corporate executives up until shortly before his death. A classic quote from Dr. Deming is: "The basic cause of sickness in American industry and resulting unemployment is failure of top management to manage." Deming insisted on working with top management of companies seeking his services, and, as the previous quote makes clear, he was quick to point out that they were a significant part of any corporate difficulties. He denounced production quotas, performance ratings, and individual bonuses as being detrimental to quality improvement.

Dr. Deming mellowed slightly during his final years but was best known for his confrontive style and often sarcastic response to what he considered a less-than-intelligent question. This is perhaps due to the fact that he was largely ignored in this country for decades. In 1950, he took his message to Japan and was very instrumental in turning Japanese industry into a world economic power. When he was "discovered" much later in the United States, his presence filled lecture halls with people anxious to hear what these "new" ideas were all about. In fact, they were the same ideas he had advocated many years before.

Deming's philosophy centers around a 14-point program on managing productivity and quality. This program is discussed at length in his book *Out of the Crisis,* in which he paints a rather gloomy picture about the survival of American business if it continues to do business as usual. Deming's 14 points are:

1. Create constancy of purpose for improvement of product and service.
2. Adopt the new philosophy.
3. Cease dependence on inspection to achieve quality.
4. End the practice of awarding business on the basis of price tag alone. Instead, minimize total cost by working with a single supplier.
5. Improve, constantly and forever, every process for planning, production, and service.
6. Institute training on the job.
7. Adopt and institute leadership.
8. Drive out fear.
9. Break down barriers between staff areas.
10. Eliminate slogans, exhortations, and targets for the workforce.

11. Eliminate numerical quotas for the workforce and numerical goals for management.
12. Remove barriers that rob people of pride of workmanship. Eliminate the annual rating or merit system.
13. Institute a vigorous program of education and self-improvement for everyone.
14. Put everybody in the company to work to accomplish the transformation.

Deming advocates the use of statistical methods and statistical charts (discussed in sections 12.4, 12.5, and 12.6) to monitor and correct production processes. While continuous improvement is also preached by Juran and Crosby, Deming stresses that continuous improvement is the only way to retain customers. Ford Motor Company has used the Deming approach since 1981 and has been praised for the improved quality of its automobiles. But, as stressed by Deming's fifth point, this is a never-ending process whereby Ford Motor Company constantly strives continually to improve their products.

JOSEPH M. JURAN.   Juran's quality philosophy urges managers to adopt a more internal focus on quality improvement. The "customer" may be the next person down the production line, and it is important to realize that each step in a process affects the next. Juran calls this "identifying the customer." It is important from Juran's point of view to examine the entire production process for problems and to train employees to do the same. He is an advocate of using quality teams for problem solving and for helping the company internalize the "quality first" mind-set. Both Juran and Crosby believe that by concentrating on reducing waste and minimizing the number of defective products, the quality focus can lead to savings that far exceed the cost of implementing and sustaining such a program.

The core of Juran's philosophy is contained in the *Juran Trilogy*—quality planning, quality control, and quality improvement. Quality planning concentrates on (1) identifying who the customers are and their needs; (2) developing product features that respond to those needs, and processes that can produce those product features; and (3) transferring this plan throughout the entire organization. Quality control measures the performance of the production or service process against the quality goals and then acts on those differences. The quality-improvement phase emphasizes the importance of achieving continuous quality improvement for the entire life of the product or service.

PHILIP B. CROSBY.   Crosby's methods are filled with catchy slogans, such as "zero defects" and "quality is free." The latter slogan is the title of his first and most popular book. This particular aspect of Crosby's approach goes against the grain of Deming's tenth point (Eliminate slogans, exhortations, and targets for the workforce), but has made Crosby's message a very popular one. Unlike Deming and Juran, Crosby is an excellent motivational speaker, and his enthusiastic approach has produced a great many quality "converts."

Crosby's approach is largely nontechnical. Similar to Deming, he also has a 14-point program, which addresses such issues as management commitment, quality-improvement teams, quality measurement, corrective action, quality awareness, goal setting, and the importance of employee recognition. His particular style and message have been very instrumental in helping organizations adjust their attitude toward quality. He emphasizes early training for *all* managers, and his program provides them, many would argue, with an excellent guide for becoming better employee leaders rather than merely employee managers.

SIMILARITIES AND DIFFERENCES.   Deming, Juran, and Crosby all agree on one thing: For a quality program to succeed, the quality commitment must cut across the entire organization. They also agree on the following points.

*   Attack the system, not the employee.
*   Identify the customer—internal or external.
*   Satisfy or exceed customer requirements.
*   Teamwork and training are essential.
*   Create an atmosphere of continuous improvement.
*   Management, not the front-line worker, is responsible for poor quality.

Some areas where these three individuals differ include the following.

- Juran and Deming rely heavily on statistical methods; Crosby doesn't.
- Crosby's nontechnical approach focuses on getting an organization started on quality improvement and committed to this purpose. Deming and Juran have a more nuts-and-bolts approach to achieving this end.
- Deming believes in starting with top management commitment, whereas Juran believes this effort can begin with middle management and filter up and down the organization.
- Deming places a great deal of emphasis on studying variation (see section 12.4).
- Deming describes fear in negative terms when he discusses eliminating fear in the workplace. Juran believes that fear can bring out the best in people when they are confronted with the possibility of their company's going under.

As a final word, we would argue that it is more beneficial to concentrate on the similarities of these (or any espoused) quality philosophies. It is more important to do *something* in the area of quality improvement than to spend countless hours arguing which program is superior. In fact, most quality programs that are implemented end up as a hybrid of these ideas and the company's own contributions when the final quality-improvement strategy is agreed upon.

SOME KEY DEFINITIONS

As we have seen, the term *quality* means slightly different things to different people. We will define a **quality product or service** to be one that meets or surpasses the needs and expectations of the customer; that is, quality means general excellence in the eyes of the customer. Here are other key terms that will be used in the sections to follow.

PROCESS.   Any combination of people, machinery, material, and methods that is intended to produce a product or service.

QUALITY CHARACTERISTICS.   Features of a product that describe its fitness for use, such as length, weight, taste, appearance, reliability. For a service organization these could include promptness of service (e.g., check-in time at a hotel, response time to a police call), number of customer complaints, or level of employee attitude.

STATISTICAL PROCESS CONTROL (SPC).   The application of statistical quality-control methods to measuring and analyzing the variation found in processes.

CONTROL CHART.   A statistical chart used to monitor various aspects of a process (such as the process average) and to determine if the process is in control (stable) or out of control (unstable).

12.2 THE MALCOLM BALDRIGE NATIONAL QUALITY AWARD AND ISO 9000 REGISTRATION

MALCOLM BALDRIGE AWARD

The Malcolm Baldrige National Quality Award (MBNQA) was established by Congress in 1987. The award was named after the former Secretary of Commerce who was killed in a rodeo accident earlier the same year. The MBNQA was modeled, in part, after the Deming Award, named after W. Edwards Deming, presented annually *in Japan* for over 45 years to the organization that best demonstrates dramatic quality improvement.

Recent winners of the MBNQA, through 1998, are listed in Table 12.1. There can be at most two winners each year within each of three categories—manufacturing companies, small businesses, and service companies. Federal Express Corporation was the first service company winner in 1990; in 1992, AT&T became the only company to win two Baldrige awards in the same year. Also, 1992 marked the first time two service companies

TABLE 12.1

Recent Winners of the Malcolm Baldrige National Quality Award.

	Manufacturing Companies	Small Business	Service Companies
1990	Cadillac Motor Car Div. IBM Rochester	Wallace Co. Inc.	Federal Express Corp.
1991	Solectron Corp. Zytec Corp.	Marlow Industries	
1992	AT&T Network Systems Group— Transmission Systems Business Unit Texas Instruments Inc.—Defense Systems & Electronics Group	Granite Rock Co.	AT&T Universal Card Services The Ritz-Carlton Hotel Co.
1993	Eastman Chemical Company (a division of Eastman Kodak Company)	Ames Rubber Corporation	
1994		Wainwright Industries, Inc.	AT&T Consumer Communications Services GTE Directories Corporation
1995	Armstrong World Industries Building Products Operations Corning Telecommunications Products Division		
1996	ADAC Laboratories	Custom Research, Inc. Trident Precision Manufacturing, Inc.	Dana Commercial Credit Corp.
1997	3M Dental Products Division Solectron Corp.		Merrill Lynch Credit Corp. Xerox Business Services
1998	Boeing Aircraft and Tanker (A & T) Solar Turbines, Inc.	Texas Nameplate Co. Inc.	

won the award. In 1997, Xerox joined the group of two-time winners, and in 1994, AT&T became the only three-time winner. The examination process includes on-site visits for those companies passing an initial screening. As you can see from Table 12.1, there need not be an MBNQA winner within all three categories if the Baldrige examiners find no company in a particular category (such as small businesses, 1997 and service companies, 1998) that meet the rather strict, yet very objective, criteria.

The MBNQA was established to raise awareness about quality management in the United States, and to recognize U.S. companies that have a world-class system for managing their operations and people and for satisfying their customers. A company applying for this award must provide evidence, in minute detail, describing its achievements and improvements in the following areas:

- leadership
- strategic planning
- customer and market focus
- information and analysis
- human resource focus
- process management
- business results

Each of these seven categories receives a score, ranging from 80 (strategic planning, customer and market focus, and information and analysis) to 450 (business results). The total score is 1000 points. Figure 12.1 also contains a breakdown of the points within each category. For example, the 80 points within category 3 (Customer and Market Focus) is broken down into two subcategories: customer and market knowledge (40 points) and customer satisfaction and relationship enhancement (40 points).

FIGURE 12.1

Categories and maximum points awarded for the Malcolm Baldrige National Quality Award.

Examination Categories		Points
1.0 Leadership		110
1.1 Leadership system	80	
1.2 Company responsibility and citizenship	30	
2.0 Strategic planning		80
2.1 Strategy development process	40	
2.2 Company strategy	40	
3.0 Customer and market focus		80
3.1 Customer and market knowledge	40	
3.2 Customer satisfaction and relationship enhancement	40	
4.0 Information and analysis		80
4.1 Selection and use of information and data	25	
4.2 Selection and use of comparative information and data	15	
4.3 Analysis and review of company performance	40	
5.0 Human resource focus		100
5.1 Work systems	40	
5.2 Employee education, training, and development	30	
5.3 Employee well-being and satisfaction	30	
6.0 Process management		100
6.1 Management of product and service processes	60	
6.2 Management of support processes	20	
6.3 Management of supplier and partnering processes	20	
7.0 Business results		450
7.1 Customer satisfaction results	125	
7.2 Financial and market results	125	
7.3 Human resource results	50	
7.4 Supplier and partner results	25	
7.5 Company-specific results	125	
TOTAL POINTS		1000

CATEGORY 1: LEADERSHIP.   This category examines:

- The company's leadership system; and
- How the company's values are integrated into its management system and are reflected in the manner in which the company addresses its public concern.

CATEGORY 2: STRATEGIC PLANNING.   This category looks at:

- How the company sets strategic directions and how it develops the critical strategies and action plans to support the directions; and
- How plans are deployed and how performance is tracked.

CATEGORY 3: CUSTOMER AND MARKET FOCUS.   This category focuses on:

- How the company determines requirements, expectations, and preferences of customers and markets; and
- How the company builds relationships with customers and determines their satisfaction.

CATEGORY 4: INFORMATION AND ANALYSIS.   This category examines:

- The selection, management, and effectiveness of use of information and data to support key company processes and action plans; and
- The company's performance management system.

CATEGORY 5: HUMAN RESOURCE FOCUS.   This category assesses:

- How the company enables employees to develop and utilize their full potential; and
- The company's efforts to build and maintain a work environment and work climate conducive to performance excellence.

CATEGORY 6: PROCESS MANAGEMENT.   This category looks at:

- The key aspects of process management, including customer-focused design and product and service delivery/support; and
- How key processes are designed, implemented, managed, and improved to achieve better performance.

CATEGORY 7: BUSINESS RESULTS.   This category examines:

- The company's performance and improvement in key business areas: customer satisfaction, financial and marketplace performance, human resource results, supplier and partner performance, and operational performance; and
- Performance levels relative to competitors.

Few awards or programs have affected American business as the Baldrige Award has. It's been called "U.S. industry's rough equivalent to the Nobel Prize" (*Computerworld,* Oct. 10, 1990). Initiated in obscurity not long ago, it has rapidly become a glittering prize for executives, who see it as an official recognition of their behind-the-scenes efforts to improve quality. Companies considering applying for this award must examine their motives carefully. If this is merely an attempt for the company to look good, and management is not fully aligned with the values of quality, the application process and resulting disappointment can have a serious negative (and often costly) effect on the organization.

An important point to be made here is that the principal benefit of the application process is the internal changes required, not the award itself, as Baldrige winners are quick to point out. Companies are using these criteria as a self-assessment tool. Whether or not they win the award, such quality-driven companies undoubtedly will be better able to survive and thrive in an increasingly competitive and quality-conscious marketplace.

ISO 9000 REGISTRATION

As the emerging global economy invites new and expanded international trade and business, corporations are finding that continued success requires doing business beyond the borders of their host country. As new worldwide markets bring together once foreign customers and companies, standardized business practice will facilitate successful business relations. Industry standards and practices unique to individual countries and continents become a problem when expanding markets, much like a language barrier.

Acknowledging, controlling, and reducing process variation lies at the heart of most quality control endeavors. Conflicting business practices among various international industries represent one possible source of variation. In response to this problem, the International Organization for Standards for Quality Management issued the ISO 9000 standards as a series of guidelines. Revised in 1994, the ISO 9000 standards now represent the worldwide benchmark standards for process quality systems. ISO 9000 does not specify how business and industry processes must be performed but instead ISO 9000 defines required actions that must be carried out within those processes to ensure quality products. Businesses and corporations that subscribe to ISO practices operate their systems in like fashion. In this sense, ISO 9000 significantly reduces process variation among companies in the worldwide business community.

ISO 9000 requires companies to establish and maintain procedural control by concentrating on procedure documentation. Employee training and awareness in quality procedures is required and documented. ISO 9000 mandates that ISO registered businesses have written procedures that are understood and followed by all company employees. ISO requires a documented and established system as well as universal conformance to that system.

Registration to ISO 9000 standards is increasingly becoming a prerequisite for doing business. Nonregistered companies are often blocked from entering the competition. The European business community led the adoption of ISO standards and is now nearly an exclusively ISO community. Major U.S. corporations are following suit. Required ISO registration of suppliers is commonplace, and in many instances an invitation to bid on a contract is predicated upon ISO registration. ISO 9000 registration requires application to a register, quality system documentation reviews, pre-assessment to identify noncompliant procedures, final assessment and registration or corrective action, and periodic surveillance audits for verifying continued compliance.

It is worth noting that ISO 9000 registration does not necessarily imply that the registered companies have good product quality. The ISO standards do not require a company to supply references to quality results or customer satisfaction. A registered company is not required to document attempted improvements in the product quality. As a result, ISO 9000 registration does not mean that all registered companies have similar levels of product quality.

COMPARING THE BALDRIGE AWARD AND ISO 9000 REGISTRATION

Quite often, the Baldrige Award criteria and the ISO 9000 standards are considered to be equivalent in their purpose and content. Such is not the case, however, since there are many notable differences. In particular, the Baldrige Award depends heavily on results and customer satisfaction, whereas ISO 9000 registration does not assess outcome-oriented results nor require demonstration of high/improving quality. The Baldrige Award is just that, an "award" or "form of recognition." On the other hand, ISO 9000 registration provides customers with some assurance that a registered supplier has a documented quality system in place and is following it. Although many companies are using the Baldrige Award and ISO 9000 standards compatibly, there is no guarantee that an ISO registration will translate into a high Baldrige Award assessment score.

EXERCISES 12.1–12.8

12.1 What are the basic elements of TQM?

12.2 Briefly detail the areas of common agreement between Deming, Juran, and Crosby.

12.3 Cite the appropriate term associated with each of the following definitions.

a. A feature/characteristic of a product or service that imparts its fitness for use.

b. A chart used to monitor and control some aspect of a process.

c. A combination of people, machinery, material, and methods used to produce a product or service.

12.4 For each of the following statements, indicate to which of the seven MBNQA categories the statement corresponds.

a. Companies should have well-defined programs for developing their employees and involving them in quality-improvement activities.

b. Firms must have well-established and well-documented systems for collecting and analyzing data concerning product/service quality.

c. Top management must signal a commitment to quality values by being responsible members of society through fulfilling their societal or public obligations.

d. Firms should be able to establish that their levels of quality meet or exceed those of direct product/service competitors.

12.5 If a firm is unsuccessful in winning the Baldrige Award, its efforts will have been wasted. Do you agree or disagree with this statement, and why?

12.6 Based on the discussion of the NPR report, label each of the following statements as true or false. Why?

a. Government employees should be encouraged to think of their agency more along the lines of a for-profit business with corresponding incentives for better performance, reduced levels of management, focus on employee empowerment, customer satisfaction, and so forth.

b. Some government agencies, such as the Internal Revenue Service (IRS), need not be customer focused, since they have little to gain by having satisfied customers.

c. Government watchdog agencies, such as the Office of Inspector General, should increase efforts to police violations of government regulations and to recover monetary settlements from those who violate those regulations.

d. Government agencies should attempt to be less autocratic and allow state and local agencies to improve the quality of their performance.

12.7 Roughly half of the MBNQA point total comes from which two categories? Consider a company or business you have worked for (in any capacity) prior to or during your college years. How do these two categories apply to this company, and what advice would you offer this company to improve in these two areas?

12.8 Do you see the seven examination categories for the MBNQA as distinct and nonoverlapping? Would you expect efforts within certain categories to have an impact on improvement efforts in other categories? If so, which categories?

12.3 QUALITY-IMPROVEMENT TOOLS

This textbook has emphasized the use of statistical graphs for examining sample data. This is especially important in the quality area, where such graphs allow you to understand the reasons for quality problems and to find solutions for eliminating them. They provide a means of conveying information that is more easily understood by a group of people, such as those attending a staff meeting or a team assigned to examine a particular quality problem. They allow you to see an entire process or to focus on a particular problem area within the process.

Recall that we defined a *process* as any combination of people, machinery, material, and methods that is intended to produce a product or service. The use of statistical graphs can provide you with various recordings of this process, ranging from an instant snapshot, such as a **histogram,** to charts recorded over time. This latter category of graphs includes **control charts,** the subject of the remaining sections of this chapter. Histograms, introduced in Chapter 2, provide a summary of a set of sample data, constructed by condensing the data into classes (groups) and constructing bars of height equal to the frequency (or relative frequency) of each class.

Another popular quality-improvement tool, the **Pareto chart,** was introduced in the Chapter 2 exercises (see Exercises 2.33, 2.34, and 2.57). This is an enhanced bar chart useful for identifying quality problems with the largest impact, and for displaying the relative importance of different categories of information. Another statistical graph in the category of quality-improvement tools is the **scatter diagram.** The scatter diagram is useful whenever your sample observations contain information on two variables, say $X = $ percent of steel used in a rubber tire mixture and $Y = $ corresponding tire durability. (The scatter diagram will be explained in Chapter 14, which also analyzes the relationship between these two variables.)

Two other methods of graphing a process include the **flowchart** and the **cause-and-effect diagram** (also known as the *fishbone* or *Ishikawa diagram*). The best way to understand a process is to draw a picture of it—that's basically what a flowchart is. The purpose of a cause-and-effect diagram is to examine a phase of the process in more detail and to relate causes and effects within the process.

FLOWCHARTS

When a product moves down an assembly line, the process flow is readily apparent, so a flowchart likely isn't necessary. However, if the flow of material during a production process is unpredictable (as in a job-shop manufacturing facility), or is not flowing smoothly, such a chart can be very useful in studying the process. While not statistical in nature, a flowchart can often identify key areas where a data collection and/or analysis would be beneficial. A popular use of flowcharts is to analyze the delivery of a service for which the flow of paper and sequence of actions may not be readily apparent.

Flowcharts should be used as a first-step examination of a process. In this way, all people who work in the process can understand it. Better understanding leads to more suggestions for improvement and more enthusiasm, since employees can see better how they fit into the overall picture. The flowchart provides a basic diagram of the *entire* process and so leads to better communication among everyone involved. Let's examine an example.

Metro Delivery Service provides package delivery services in a large metropolitan area. They have a money-back guarantee that any package brought to any of their dropoff stations will be delivered to anywhere within its area in 90 minutes or less. Metro achieved initial success with their innovative use of bicycles and motorbikes for delivering small packages. The bulk of their business, however, consists of delivering larger packages requiring an automobile or van. Lately, the owner of Metro had noticed a lack of consistency in meeting the 90-minute deadline. Metro management immediately began to blame the problem on what they perceived to be a careless attitude among the company drivers.

FIGURE 12.2

Flowchart of package delivery process for Metro Delivery Service.

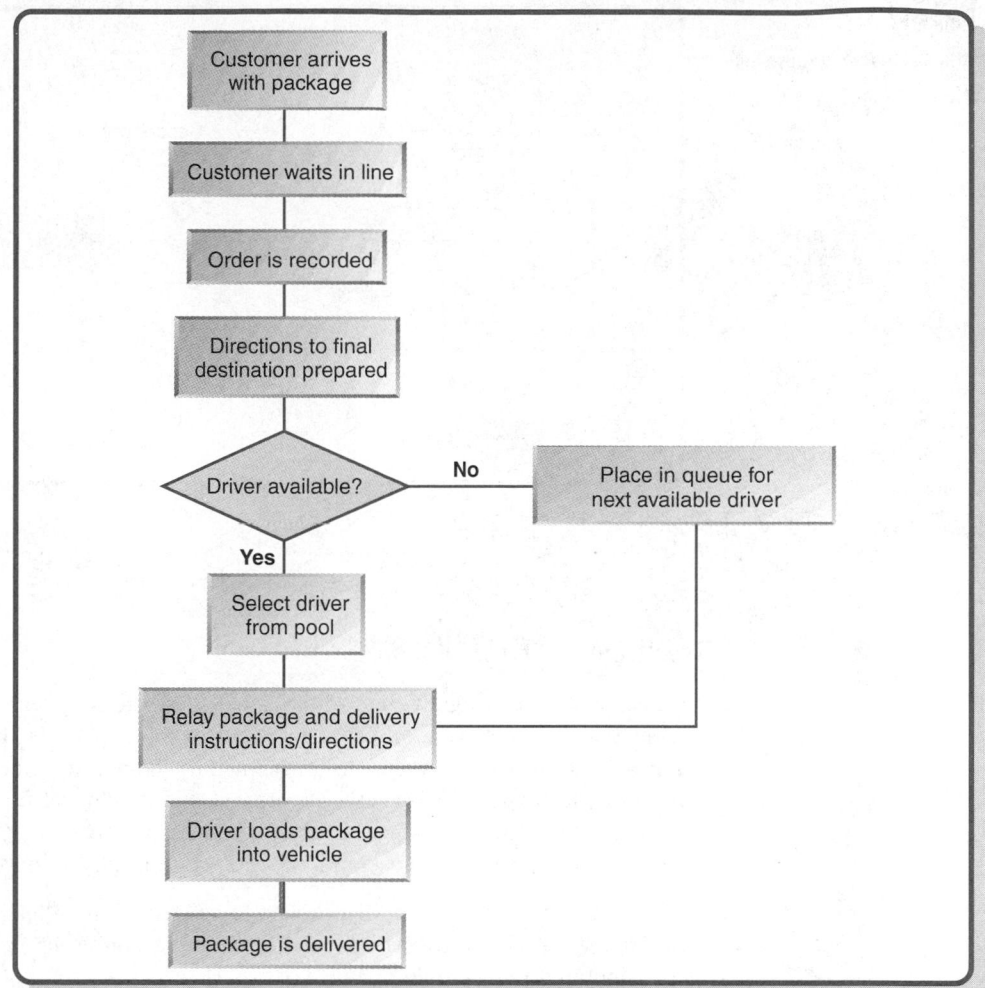

However, the owner of Metro had attended several quality-improvement seminars and suspected that company performance could best be improved by making changes to the process itself.

A team of employees from all phases of the delivery process was formed and charged with taking a *systematic* look at the entire delivery process, beginning with a customer's arrival at a dropoff station and ending with the package's delivery. The flowchart in Figure 12.2 was the result.

The chart in Figure 12.2 is a very basic one and doesn't provide a great deal of detail. Nevertheless, it is a good starting point for the team to begin discussing the various operations and potential bottlenecks (the points at which the flow is constricted) within the delivery process. Final versions of a flowchart most often are *very* detailed, so that each employee can see precisely where his or her job fits into the flow of the entire process.

The symbols used in Figure 12.2 consist of rectangular boxes (□) and diamond boxes (◊). The rectangles represent each step of the process; the diamonds are points where a decision must be made; typically requiring a yes or no response. A decision point does occur in this flowchart, since the dispatch supervisor must determine whether a driver is available at the time a package is due to leave the station.

The quality-improvement team at Metro was able to use this flowchart to discuss the delivery operation and to study potential problem areas. Their next concern was to explore why a package arrived late at its destination—a topic best examined using a cause-and-effect diagram.

FIGURE 12.3

Basic structure of a cause-and-effect diagram.

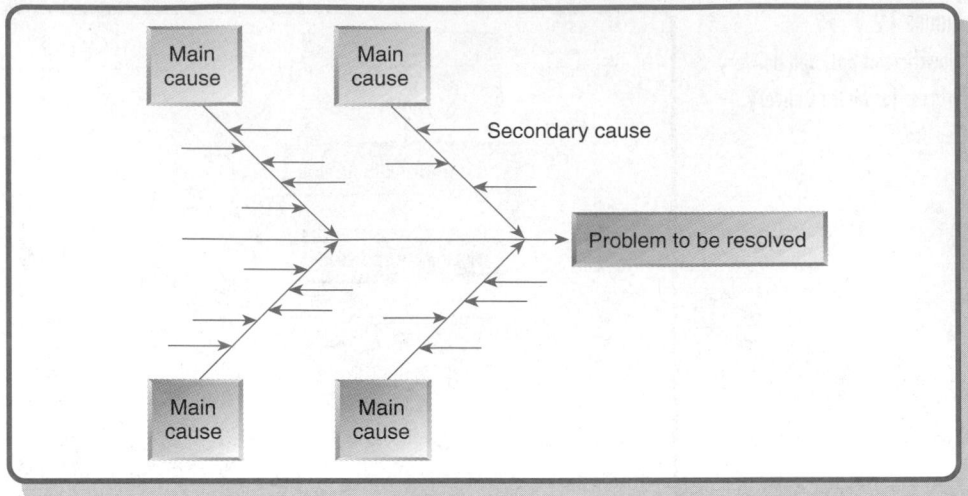

CAUSE-AND-EFFECT DIAGRAMS

Cause and effect diagrams are often called **fishbone diagrams** or **Ishikawa diagrams,** named after their originator, Dr. Kaoru Ishikawa. In the 1940s, Ishikawa found that many Japanese plant personnel were overwhelmed by the many factors that could influence the outcome of a particular process. He created this very powerful diagram to represent the relationships between potential problems and their sources.

The basic form of a cause-and-effect diagram is shown in Figure 12.3. It contains:

1. a horizontal arrow with the problem to be studied in a box at its far right;
2. major branches off the horizontal arrow representing the primary (main) causes contributing to this problem; and
3. additional arrows within each major branch making up the secondary causes that contribute to the main problem within that major branch.

If you examine the shape of Figure 12.3, you'll see that it does indeed resemble the skeleton of a fish, which is why *fishbone diagram* is the more popular name for this chart. Although Figure 12.3 shows only two levels of arrows off the horizontal arrow (primary and secondary causes), this procedure of subdividing the possible causes can be continued for additional levels in Step 3 until all variables have been accounted for.

The team at Metro Delivery Service began by identifying four primary causes for the late delivery of a package: taking the order; assigning the driver to the order; traffic conditions; and the delivery vehicle. Secondary causes within each of these primary branches were brainstormed; the result of this effort was the cause-and-effect diagram in Figure 12.4. While developing this chart, the individuals on the team discovered: (1) there was a feeling that everyone was working together (a true "team spirit"); (2) the chart enabled them to discuss the delivery process better; and (3) they were able to view the entire delivery process as a system rather than as a collection of disjointed activities.

A final word regarding this example: The logical next step for Metro would be to observe the process (obtain sample data) and construct a **Pareto chart*** for each of the four major branches; summarizing the frequency of secondary causes within each branch. In this way, they could attack the problem by putting their resources into those areas that would bring about the greatest improvement in performance.

---

* Pareto charts were discussed in the exercises at the end of Section 2.6 in Chapter 2.

FIGURE 12.4   Cause-and-effect diagram for Metro Delivery Service.

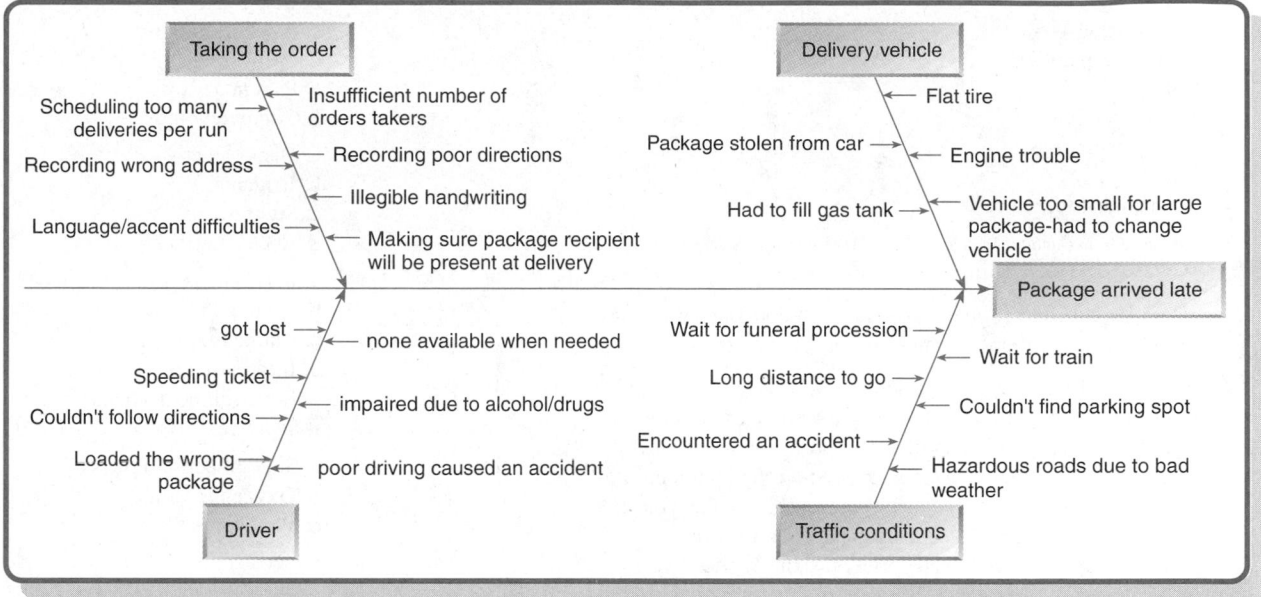

EXERCISES 12.9–12.19

12.9 Describe reasons for using each of the following graphical quality improvement tools. What information does each graph best present?

    a. Pareto chart

    b. Fishbone diagram

    c. Flowchart

    d. Control chart

    e. Scatter diagram

12.10 For each of the following scenarios, select the graphical tools noted in Exercise 12.9 as the most appropriate for analyzing the given scenario. Explain the reasons for each of your selections.

    a. A university is interested in the relationship between a student's grade point average and the student's starting salary after graduating from college. The university's assessment office has interviewed students prior to and after earning a degree. How can this office show this relationship?

    b. An appliance manufacturer maintains records for all warranty services performed. Data analysis for warranty service related to their stoves and ovens has revealed cooking temperature problems generate over 60 percent of the warranty calls. The service manager wishes to investigate possible causes for the temperature problems. What analysis should the manager next perform?

    c. A production supervisor has listed all operations required in a manufacturing facility for each product. The supervisor wishes to examine methods for streamlining production. How should the supervisor compile and present the operations?

    d. A restaurant manager notices that the catering service provided by the restaurant has received numerous complaints.

Problems occur during recording of orders as well as with delivery of the food. What type of chart should the manager use to understand the many factors that could influence the quality of the catering service?

    e. Every hour an inspector randomly selects five bearings and measures their inside and outside diameters. The inspector wishes to investigate the ability of the manufacturing process to produce dimensionally acceptable bearings. What graphical technique should be used?

12.11 Create a flowchart showing the steps that a traveler would take when entering an airport servicing a large metropolitan area. Be sure to include points such as using remote or infield parking, outdoor porter service for checking baggage or indoor ticket counter service, and whether the traveler stops at any of the specialty shops in the airport. Once you have completed the flowchart, use your experiences with airport facilities to identify potential delays that a traveler could have in the process.

12.12 Small and specialized production companies often do not produce in sufficient quantity to provide a statistically significant number of observations. Some special order products may be produced in lots of less than ten. Single unit production is not rare. Although process control charts may be of little use in these instances, statistical quality control procedures can help identify problem areas. Identifying each step in the manufacturing process and then recording instances of error or difficulty in those areas permit the use of Pareto analysis for identifying improvement opportunities. Ten operations were identified, and the number of defects or problems with the operations was recorded over a 10-week period.

Operation	Number of Defects
Milling	11
Lathe operations	21
Drilling	4
Heat treating	9
Surface preparation	27
Testing	10
Surface coating	32
Layout operations	18
Metallurgy	16
Dimensional tolerance	19

(Source: Adapted from *Quality,* "Tracking Attribute Data Improves Supplier Rating," Oct. 1997, p. 46–48.)

Construct a Pareto chart for the above data and note operations where further investigation and analysis may be needed.

12.13 Review the mistakes (i.e., defects) you have made on the quizzes and examinations that you have completed thus far in this course. Create categories of the reasons for those mistakes (e.g., made a simple math error, pressed wrong button on the calculator, transposed digits), attribute each mistake you made to one of the categories you have created, and construct a Pareto chart. Which of your categories has the highest frequency of mistakes? How can you use this information to improve your future scores?

12.14 The process of purchasing a new car can be very frustrating for the careful buyer. Construct a fishbone diagram to demonstrate the potential problems and their sources in this process. Consider the initial stage of viewing many automobiles and the closing stage of negotiating a contract on the purchase of a new automobile.

12.15 Construct a fishbone diagram for your progress through your statistics course. Consider the various stages in the course such as lectures, exams, and projects. What conditions can cause a student to have difficulties at each stage?

12.16 Manufacturing companies probably provided the first American applications of the statistical quality control principles advanced by Deming and others. Successes achieved in the manufacturing sector have prompted the adoption of quality practices in other segments of U.S. enterprise. Many service industries now use quality control tools for understanding their processes, their customers, and for providing consistent and quality service. A hospital utilized fishbone diagrams as part of their analysis in efforts to reduce pain in cases of outpatient surgery. The sources and causes they identified are given below.

Main Causes of Outpatient Discomfort	Elements of Each Main Cause
Environment	a. Temperature
	b. Cleanliness
	c. Humidity
	d. Ventilation
	e. Lighting
Equipment	a. Operating table
	b. Headlight
	c. Rolling sitting stool
	d. Instrument sets
	e. Power drill
	f. Suction pump
	g. Standing stool

Main Causes of Outpatient Discomfort	Elements of Each Main Cause
People	a. Same-day surgery nurses
	b. Surgeon
	c. Anesthesiologist
	d. Scrub nurse
	e. Patient
	f. Circulating nurse
Supplies	a. Disposables
	b. Irrigants
	c. Sutures
	d. Local anesthetics
Methods	a. Intravenous
	b. By mouth
	c. Antinausea
	d. Intramuscular
	e. Reversal medications
	f. Sedative
Measurements	a. State of consciousness
	b. Oxygen saturation
	c. Vital signs
	d. Pain

(Source: *Quality Progress,* "Charting New Territory," Vol. 30, No. 2, Feb. 1997, p. 63–66.)

a. Use the above causes and elements to construct a cause-and-effect diagram that can be used to better understand causes of patient discomfort.

b. What steps should hospital staff take next for improved patient comfort?

12.17 It so happens that pizza is the preferred food of most college students; thus, chances are good that you are a pizza expert. Create a flowchart of the process that the local pizzeria must go through to make and deliver your pizza. Begin your flowchart with the taking of your order by phone, and enumerate all decisions and activities that must take place, culminating in the delivery of the pizza to your door. What potential bottlenecks exist in the pizza making/delivery process?

12.18 A major crisis facing education today is the dropout rate for high school students. As a concerned citizen, you have volunteered to help examine this problem and to try to identify root causes of student dropout.

a. Construct a fishbone diagram where the primary causes are Students, Faculty/Staff, Curriculum, and Family.

b. For the Student branch, what are some possible secondary causes (e.g., low self-esteem and peer pressure)?

c. For the Faculty/Staff branch, possible secondary causes are disinterest of teachers and class size. What are some others?

d. Secondary causes for the Curriculum branch might include lack of basic skills and language barriers. Can you think of other causes?

e. Possible secondary causes for the Family branch are lack of parental interest in education and truancy not being monitored. What are some others?

12.19 A quality-improvement team at PQ Systems, Inc., a software and training organization in Dayton, Ohio, was formed to improve the process of technical support. While the answers of most callers to the technical support line were answered immediately, some calls required follow-up and a return call. Regretably, the resolution of some calls was taking far too long. The team brainstormed to identify the root causes of delay in the resolution of calls. The following table categorizes these causes.

Main Causes of Delay in Call Resolution	Elements of Each Main Cause
Customer	a. Customer not at home
	b. Customer had to get more information/data
	c. Customer not sure what questions to ask
	d. Customer unfamiliar with use of computer
	e. Customer unfamiliar with use of software
	f. Customer frustrated

Main Causes of Delay in Call Resolution	Elements of Each Main Cause
Analyst	a. Analyst not available
	b. Analyst not sure where to find information
	c. Analyst frustrated
	d. Analyst insufficiently trained
	e. Answer given by analyst too abstract
Software	a. Error that has not been encountered before
	b. Existing error with unknown status
	c. Software too complex
	d. Third-party software involved
Hardware	a. Hardware malfunction
	b. Third-party hardware involved

(Source: Barbara A. Cleary, "Company Cares About Customers' Calls," *Quality Progress* 26, no. 11 (Nov. 1993): 69–73.)

Using the information in the table, construct a cause-and-effect diagram that can be used to improve the quality of technical support at PQ Systems.

12.4 PROCESS VARIATION AND CONTROL CHARTS

Variation exists in every process and in nearly every sample of measurements. Even the best automatic machine tools cannot make every unit exactly the same. Along with machine inconsistencies, there is variation introduced due to:*

- people
- materials
- production methods
- the environment

Consequently, the measured quality of a manufacturer's product is always subject to a certain amount of variation as a result of chance. We refer to this situation as a *stable* system of *chance causes* of variation. Variation within this stable pattern is random and inevitable. Variations *outside* this stable pattern is another matter. Once discovered, causes for such variation (called *assignable causes*) should be searched out and corrected. Detection of such variation is a key objective of quality control, and is the subject of the remaining sections in this chapter.

For a production process, one of the goals of a quality-improvement program is to reduce the variability in the process, with an eye toward eliminating this process variation—an impossible task, but a goal nonetheless. By keeping a close watch on process variation and not overreacting to chance variation, a company can bring about dramatic improvements in product quality and a reduction of spoilage and rework. This can be illustrated in a very striking and entertaining way using a favorite device of Dr. Deming—the funnel experiment.

THE DEMING FUNNEL EXPERIMENT

The funnel experiment was often used by Dr. W. Edwards Deming in his lectures to illustrate that reacting to chance (random) variation has an adverse effect on overall process variation. Despite the good intentions of a machine operator to "fix" the system and move

* These sources of variation also are the key components of any cause-and-effect (fishbone) diagram, which was discussed in the previous section.

FIGURE 12.5   Deming funnel experiment [panel (a)] and MINITAB simulation output using control strategies 1, 2, and 3 [panels (b), (c), and (d)].

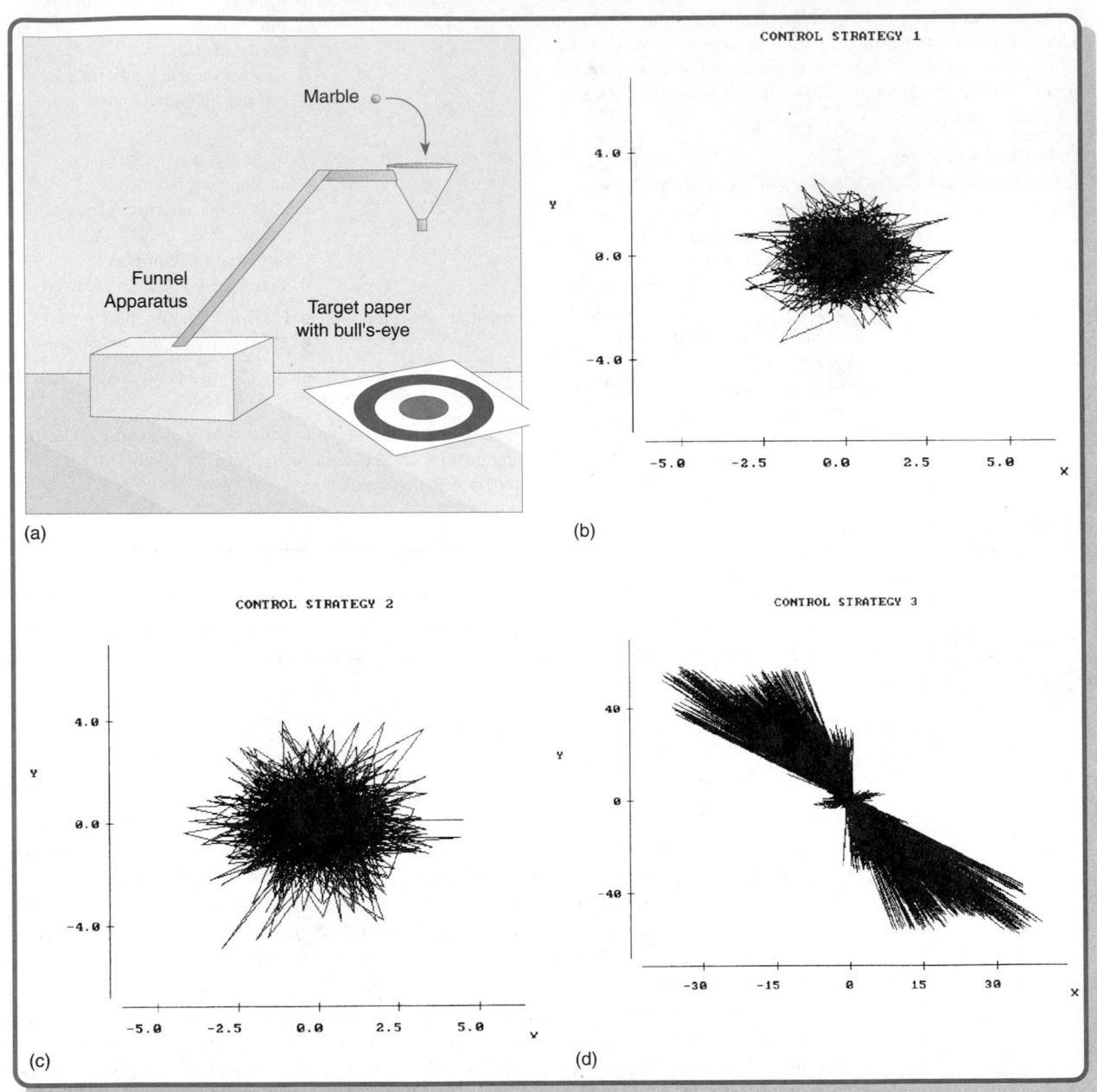

it closer to the process target, such manipulations only make matters worse. In fact, the more diligent the operator, the worse the result.

The device used by Deming was a funnel, mounted on a stand, that is placed directly over a target having a bull's-eye directly in the center, illustrated in Figure 12.5(a). A marble is dropped through the funnel, hits the target, and rolls a short distance away. The target bull's-eye represents the process target (such as a stated length or weight), and the final resting place of the marble represents the value of the final product. The direction and distance from the bull's-eye represent random variation within the manufacturing process. Despite the operator's best efforts, the marble will not come to rest directly on the bull's-eye each time.

STRATEGY 1.   The recommended strategy would be not to react to this random variation and not to move the funnel. The diligent operator, on the other hand, could measure the distance and direction that the marble strayed from the bull's-eye and move the funnel that distance in the opposite direction. Two possible alternative strategies here would be the following.

STRATEGY 2.   Measure the distance from the marble's resting place to the bull's-eye. Move the funnel an equal distance, but in the opposite direction. This will be called the "error relative to the previous position" strategy.

STRATEGY 3.   Measure the distance from the marble's resting place to the bull's-eye. Move the funnel this distance, in the opposite direction, starting at the bull's-eye. This procedure could be called the "error relative to the bull's-eye" strategy.

A sequence of MINITAB commands was used to simulate this funnel experiment 1000 times; the results are given in Figure 12.5.* The bull's-eye is in the center of each graph, at the point $X = 0$, $Y = 0$. Control strategy 1 is where we do not react to chance variation and the funnel is not moved (no machine adjustments are made in an attempt to fix the process). Figure 12.5(b), is an illustration of this strategy, with, as expected, a certain amount of random variation. Parts (c) and (d) represent the outcome of strategies 2 and 3, respectively. The result of strategy 2 is stable, but contains more variation than the "leave it alone" strategy (strategy 1)—in fact, it can be shown that the variation within this process is *twice* that in part (b). The error relative to the bull's-eye strategy (strategy 3) used in part (d) is unstable, contains a great deal of variation, and resembles a bow tie. The error associated with this strategy will eventually wander off to infinity.

The point of the funnel experiment is to make clear that a machine operator can only be held accountable for what is under his or her control. If the goal is to reduce process variation, then we can *improve the process* by building a better funnel or by moving the funnel closer to the target. It is management's responsibility to examine the process carefully and to provide resources and training for making process improvements. As Deming, and others, have said, "Attack the system, not the employee."

CONTROL CHARTS

In a sense, control charts form the foundation of the inspection side of statistical quality control. These charts were first introduced by W. A. Shewhart at Bell Telephone Laboratories in 1924. Essentially, control charts allow you to monitor a process (usually, but not necessarily, a manufacturing process) to determine if the process is "in control" or "out of control."

DEFINITION

A process is **in control** if the observed variation is due to inherent or natural variability. This variability is the cumulative effect of many small, essentially uncontrollable, causes.

It is important to note that a process may be in control yet entirely unsatisfactory. For example, your process of producing 10-pound bags of dog food may be perfectly in control, with little variation, yet a closer look may reveal that the process appears to be centered at 8.7 pounds, which would certainly be unacceptable to dog owners who check the weight of the bags.

---

* This sequence of MINITAB commands (a MINITAB macro) is on the disk that comes with the textbook. If the disk is in drive A, then type EXECUTE 'A:FUNNEL' while in MINITAB. The result will be modified versions of Figure 12.5(b), (c), and (d). This macro is a revised version of the one in the *MINITAB Users' Group Newsletter,* 14, (Oct. 1991).

FIGURE 12.6

General form of a control chart.

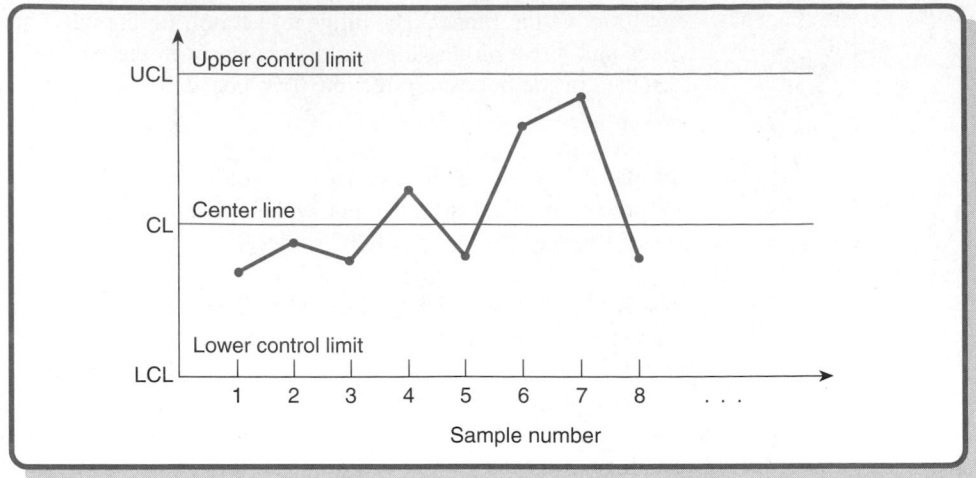

DEFINITION

A process is *out of control* if a relatively large variation is introduced that can be traced to an *assignable cause*. Such causes are generally the result of an improperly adjusted machine, an operator error, or defective raw material.

During the in-control state, we say that the variation is due to **chance cause.** Such variation can be reduced by careful analysis of the process, but it can never be completely eliminated. On the other hand, variation during an out-of-control state is due to one or more assignable causes. Such causes are avoidable and cannot be overlooked.

The purpose of the control chart is to detect the presence of an out-of-control state, during which a large portion of the process output will not be conforming to requirements. If an assignable cause can be determined, corrective action is taken and an attempt is made to return the process to an in-control state. As Figure 12.5 illustrates, while a process is believed to be in control it should not be adjusted or tampered with, since such well-meaning adjustments generally result in an *increase* in process variation.

The general form of a control chart is shown in Figure 12.6. The chart contains a **center line (CL),** which represents the average value of the quality characteristic corresponding to the in-control state. The other two horizontal lines are the **control limits;** the *upper control limit* (UCL) and the *lower control limit* (LCL) are the same distance from the center line. *These limits are chosen so that if the process is in control, nearly all the plotted points will be between the two control limits.* For example, a plotted point might represent the average weight of a sample of five filled coffee cans. As long as the plotted averages fall within the control limits, the process is determined to be in control, with only chance variation present.

The process of using a control chart to monitor and improve process quality is shown in Figure 12.7.

When measuring a quality characteristic such as the weight of a filled coffee can, the resulting data are referred to as **variables data.** Conversely, when counting the number of solder defects in the coffee can, such data are referred to as **attribute data.** Chapter 1 referred to variables data as *continuous* data and to attribute data as *discrete* data. The type of control chart that is needed for a particular situation depends on what quality characteristic is being measured and what type of data is being collected. For the filled weight of the coffee cans, we would undoubtedly be interested in the average weight of each sample of five cans and would construct a control chart referred to as an $\bar{X}$ chart ($\bar{X}$ is read as "X bar"). We would also want to maintain a control chart for the *variation* within each sam-

FIGURE 12.7

The application of control charts.

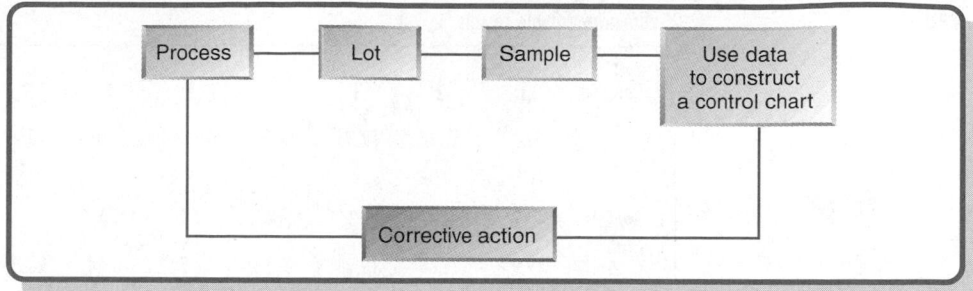

ple. The control chart to use for this situation would be an R chart, where R represents the sample range.

Since control charts are typically used to monitor *small* samples, the sample range is generally used to measure sample variation. The range is easier to calculate than is the sample standard deviation (s), and provides nearly as much information about the sample variation for sample sizes under 10. For sample sizes of 10 or more, the sample standard deviation should be used to measure sample variation, producing $\bar{X}$ and s charts. For a more thorough discussion of these charts, refer to the book by D. C. Montgomery in the list of Further Reading later in the chapter.

One cautionary note regarding the use of control charts: Most processes cannot be expected to remain stable over an extended period of time. A change in raw materials, tooling, or work shifts or any other major change in process operating conditions can change the process distribution. New control limits should be determined if the control chart is to retain its effectiveness.

12.5 CONTROL CHARTS FOR VARIABLES DATA: THE $\bar{X}$ AND R CHARTS

Variables data are obtained by observing a continuous variable, which has *no gaps* in the values it can have, over the range of possible values. A corresponding control chart could be constructed for controlling and analyzing a process whose quality characteristic is a continuous variable, such as weight, length, or concentration.

The first step is to obtain data for construction of the control chart. A number of preliminary samples (say, m of these) is obtained, each of size n, when the process is thought to be in control. Typically, m ranges from 20 to 25, and the sample size, n, is 4, 5, or 6. Define $\bar{X}_1, \bar{X}_2, \ldots, \bar{X}_m$ to be the m sample averages. Also define $R_1, R_2, \ldots, R_m$ to be the m sample ranges.

For example, suppose the quality characteristic is the weight of a filled coffee can produced by International Food Products. The first three samples are (data in ounces):

Sample	Data	$\bar{X}$	R
1	19.8, 20.1, 20.2, 19.9, 20.0	20.00	20.2 – 19.8 = .4
2	20.3, 19.9, 19.8, 19.8, 20.1	19.98	20.3 – 19.8 = .5
3	20.0, 19.7, 20.2, 19.8, 19.7	19.88	20.2 – 19.7 = .5

For these samples, $\bar{X}_1 = 20.00$, $\bar{X}_2 = 19.98$, $\bar{X}_3 = 19.88$, $R_1 = .4$, $R_2 = .5$, and $R_3 = .5$. These results and those for the next 17 samples are shown in Table 12.2.

In the quality-control context, the population consists of the *process* values. Thus we speak of the process mean, the process standard deviation, and so on. The best estimator of μ, the process mean, is

$$\bar{\bar{X}} = \frac{\bar{X}_1 + \bar{X}_2 + \cdots + \bar{X}_m}{m} \qquad (12.1)$$

Preliminary sample results.

Sample	1	2	3	4	5	6	7	8	9	10
$\overline{X}$	20.00	19.98	19.88	19.94	20.04	20.06	20.02	19.82	20.02	20.06
R	.4	.5	.5	.4	.6	.3	.4	.4	.5	.7
Sample	11	12	13	14	15	16	17	18	19	20
$\overline{X}$	19.94	19.86	19.90	20.12	19.92	20.04	20.06	19.98	19.88	20.08
R	.4	.3	.2	.5	.5	.4	.3	.5	.6	.4

Factors for constructing an R chart.

n	d_2	d_3	D_3	D_4
2	1.128	.853	0	3.267
3	1.693	.888	0	2.574
4	2.059	.880	0	2.282
5	2.326	.864	0	2.114
6	2.534	.848	0	2.004
7	2.704	.833	.076	1.924
8	2.847	.820	.136	1.864
9	2.970	.808	.184	1.816
10	3.078	.797	.223	1.777

For our coffee-can filling example, the process consists of taking empty coffee cans and filling them with a prescribed amount of coffee. The quality characteristic is the filled weight of the can. The estimate of the process average is

$$\overline{\overline{X}} = \frac{20.00 + 19.98 + \cdots + 20.08}{20}$$

$$= \frac{399.60}{20} = 19.98 \ ounces$$

We also need an estimate of the process standard deviation (σ). As mentioned earlier, there is more than one way to estimate this parameter, but since the sample sizes are small (under 10), the best way to proceed is to use the sample ranges (R) and carry out the following steps:

1. Determine the average of the m values of R. Call this $\overline{R}$.
2. Select the value of d_2 from Table 12.3 using the corresponding sample size, n.
3. Estimate σ using

$$\hat{\sigma} = \frac{\overline{R}}{d_2} \tag{12.2}$$

For the coffee-can illustration,

$$\overline{R} = \frac{.4 + .5 + \cdots + .4}{20}$$

$$= \frac{8.8}{20} = .44$$

FIGURE 12.8

Tail area outside ±3 for the
standard normal curve.

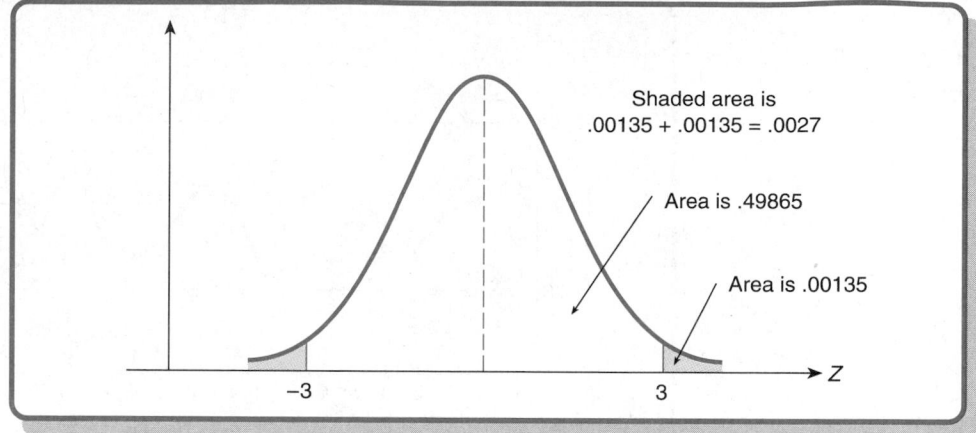

Using Table 12.3, the estimate of the process standard deviation is

$$\hat{\sigma} = \frac{\bar{R}}{d_2} = \frac{.44}{2.326} = .189 \; ounce$$

In Chapter 7, a procedure was outlined for constructing a confidence interval for the population mean using the results of a *single* sample. When constructing a control chart for the process average, a similar procedure is followed using the results of *multiple* samples (*m* of them). The center line and control limits are defined below:

$$\text{UCL} = \bar{\bar{X}} + 3\frac{\hat{\sigma}}{\sqrt{n}} = \bar{\bar{X}} + 3\frac{(\bar{R}/d_2)}{\sqrt{n}}$$

$$\text{Center Line} = \bar{\bar{X}} \qquad\qquad (12.3)$$

$$\text{LCL} = \bar{\bar{X}} - 3\frac{\hat{\sigma}}{\sqrt{n}} = \bar{\bar{X}} - 3\frac{(\bar{R}/d_2)}{\sqrt{n}}$$

Notice that the control limits take on the appearance of a confidence interval where the value 3 replaces the value previously obtained from the standard normal (Z) table or the t table. The resulting control limits are referred to as the **3-sigma control limits.** It should be mentioned that the value 3 can be changed to fit the quality requirements of the process. Essentially, using this value produces control limits that will be exceeded approximately 27 times in ten thousand (.0027) if the process average and variation remain stable. Assuming a normal (or nearly normal) process, the value .0027 is obtained by finding the combined tail area under a standard normal curve outside ±3 (see Figure 12.8). In Chapter 7, a confidence interval for a population mean was constructed using a single sample. Control limits in a control chart are derived using many small samples instead of a single larger sample. Tying these two topics together, it may be helpful for you to view an $\bar{X}$ chart as a **99.7% confidence interval** for the population mean derived using many small samples. Here, 99.7% is $(1 - .0027) \times 100\%$, where .0027 is the probability of a sample mean lying outside the control limits if the process is on target (centered correctly) and remains stable.

For the coffee can illustration, $\bar{\bar{X}} = 19.98$ and $\hat{\sigma} = .189$, so the control limits would be

$$\text{UCL} = 19.98 + 3\frac{.189}{\sqrt{5}} = 19.98 + .25 = 20.23$$

$$\text{Center Line} = 19.98$$

$$\text{LCL} = 19.98 - 3\frac{.189}{\sqrt{5}} = 19.98 - .25 = 19.73$$

FIGURE 12.9
$\overline{X}$ chart for coffee-can
example.

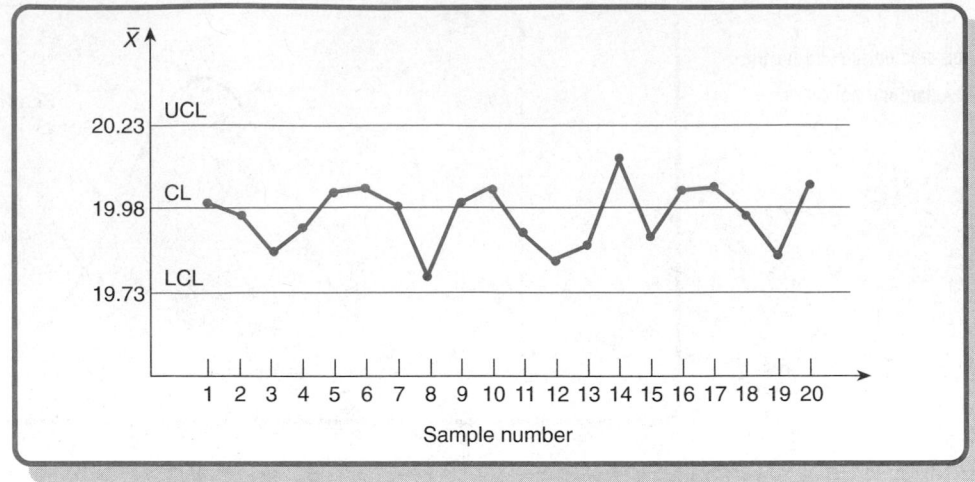

The control chart is shown in Figure 12.9. Notice that all 20 of the sample means are within the control limits, indicating that the control chart is ready for use. If one or more of the sample means falls outside the control limits a search should be made to determine whether there is an assignable cause behind these extreme sample values. If such a cause is found, this sample should be removed and the control limits (including the center line) should be rederived.

THE *R* CHART

To monitor the process variability, we use an *R* chart to plot values of the sample range, *R*. As we do with the $\overline{X}$ chart, we conclude that the sample *variability* is out of control when a sample range falls outside the control limits of the *R* chart. If the sample range falls within the control limits, the process variation is in control, that is, stable. Note that it is possible for a sample range to be out of control while the corresponding sample mean ($\overline{X}$) is well in control; that is, a sample can contain extreme variation but be centered properly.

The center line for the *R* chart is the average ($\overline{R}$) of the *m* ranges. For the summary data in Table 12.2, we have already determined that $\overline{R} = .44$. The 3-sigma control limits are derived by again adding and subtracting three times the estimated standard deviation of $\overline{R}$, say, $s_{\overline{R}}$. The value of $s_{\overline{R}}$ can be derived using

$$s_{\overline{R}} = \overline{R}\left(\frac{d_3}{d_2}\right)$$ (12.4)

where the values of d_2 and d_3 are provided in Table 12.3.

The control limits for the *R* chart are

$$\text{UCL} = \overline{R} + 3s_{\overline{R}} = \overline{R} + 3\overline{R}\left(\frac{d_3}{d_2}\right) = \left(1 + 3\frac{d_3}{d_2}\right)\overline{R}$$

$$\text{LCL} = \overline{R} - 3s_{\overline{R}} = \overline{R} - 3\overline{R}\left(\frac{d_3}{d_2}\right) = \left(1 - 3\frac{d_3}{d_2}\right)\overline{R}$$

By defining

$$D_3 = 1 - 3\frac{d_3}{d_2} \quad \text{and} \quad D_4 = 1 + 3\frac{d_3}{d_2}$$ (12.5)

FIGURE 12.10
R chart for the coffee-can
example.

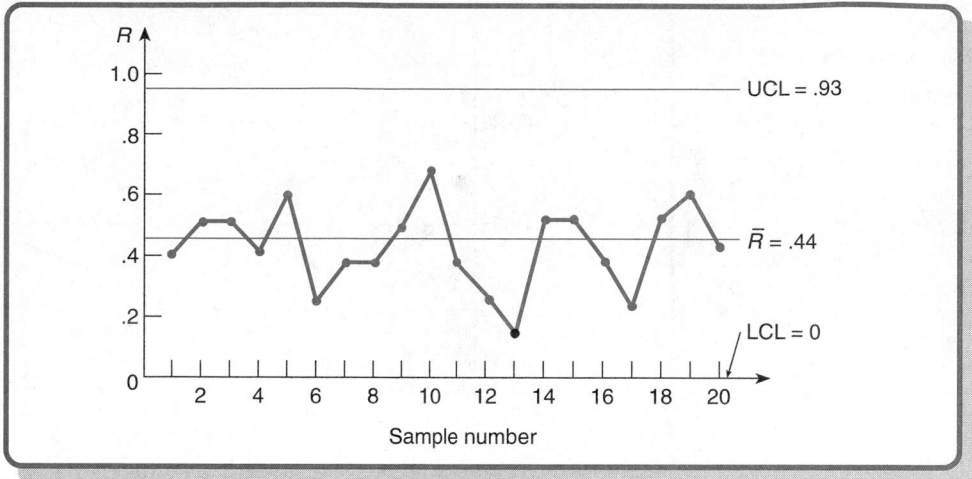

the R chart can be defined using

$$UCL = D_4\bar{R}$$

$$\text{Center Line} = \bar{R} \tag{12.6}$$

$$LCL = D_3\bar{R}$$

COMMENTS

1. Values of D_3 and D_4 are provided in Table 12.3.
2. Since a sample range is never negative, D_3 is defined to be zero whenever the expression in equation (12.5) is negative, that is, for $n = 2, 3, 4, 5,$ and 6.

For our previous example, in which the quality characteristic is the filled weight of a coffee can, the limits for the R chart are easily found:

$$UCL = (2.114)(.44) = .93$$

$$\text{Center line} = .44$$

$$LCL = 0$$

This R chart is shown in Figure 12.10. Note that all the sample ranges appear to be in control, so the R chart is ready for use. If future range values fall within these limits, we conclude that the process variation is in control. Our procedure is the same as for the $\bar{X}$ chart: If any of the values in Figure 12.10 had fallen outside the control limits, a search would have been made for an assignable cause (or causes) for these sample points. Samples for which such a cause is found should be removed and the R chart derived again.

EXAMPLE 12.1

Following the construction of the control charts using the data in Table 12.2 (shown in Figures 12.9 and 12.10), samples of five filled coffee cans were obtained every half hour over a three-hour period. The data for these samples are as follows (in ounces).

Sample	Data
1	19.9, 19.7, 19.9, 20.2, 20.3
2	20.1, 20.3, 19.6, 19.8, 19.5
3	19.9, 20.1, 20.3, 19.9, 19.9
4	20.1, 19.9, 20.0, 20.1, 20.3
5	20.0, 19.5, 19.5, 20.1, 20.2
6	19.7, 19.8, 20.3, 19.7, 20.1

FIGURE 12.11
Control charts for
Example 12.1.

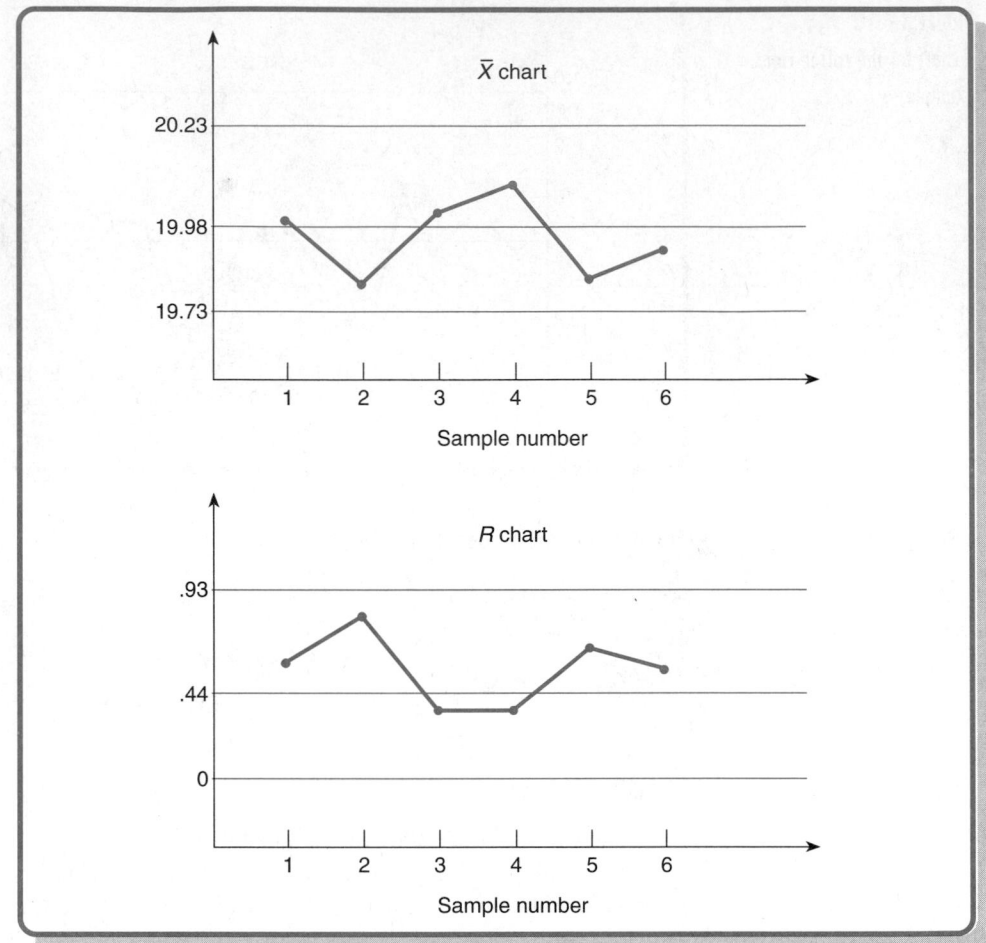

Using the proper control charts, determine whether the process location and variability are in control during this three-hour period.

SOLUTION

The first step is to find the sample averages and ranges.

Sample	1	2	3	4	5	6
$\bar{X}$	20.00	19.86	20.02	20.08	19.86	19.92
R	.6	.8	.4	.4	.7	.6

Each sample mean is plotted in the $\bar{X}$ chart and each sample range in the R chart. Both charts are shown in Figure 12.11. Since all points in the two charts are within the control limits, we conclude that the process is in control (stable) and that no adjustments to the process are necessary.

STEPS FOR MAKING $\bar{X}$ AND R CHARTS

1. Collect m samples of data, each of size n (in our first example, $m = 20$ samples of $n = 5$ observations each).
2. Compute the average of each subgroup ($\bar{X}_1, \bar{X}_2, \bar{X}_3, \ldots, \bar{X}_m$).
3. Compute the range for each subgroup ($R_1, R_2, R_3, \ldots, R_m$).
4. Find the overall mean, $\bar{\bar{X}}$, where $\bar{\bar{X}}$ is the average of the m values of $\bar{X}$.
5. Find the average range, $\bar{R}$, where $\bar{R}$ is the average of the m values of R.
6. To estimate σ (say, $\hat{\sigma}$), compute $\bar{R}/d_2$, where d_2 can be found using Table 12.3.

7. Compute the 3-sigma control limits for the $\bar{X}$ control chart:

$$\text{UCL} = \bar{\bar{X}} + 3\frac{\hat{\sigma}}{\sqrt{n}}$$

$$\text{CL} = \bar{\bar{X}}$$

$$\text{LCL} = \bar{\bar{X}} - 3\frac{\hat{\sigma}}{\sqrt{n}}$$

8. Compute the 3-sigma control limits for the R control chart.

$$\text{UCL} = D_4\bar{R} \qquad \text{(using Table 12.3)}$$

$$\text{CL} = \bar{R}$$

$$\text{LCL} = D_3\bar{R} \qquad \text{(using Table 12.3)}$$

9. Construct the control charts by plotting the $\bar{X}$ and R points for each subgroup on the same vertical line.

PATTERN ANALYSIS FOR $\bar{X}$ CHARTS

So far, our discussion of control charts has focused on determining out-of-control conditions by identifying a point beyond the 3-sigma control limits on the $\bar{X}$ or R charts. For $\bar{X}$ charts, a closer look at the pattern of the control chart points (all of which may be within the control limits) may also reveal a process that is out of control and requiring attention. For example, six points in a row, all increasing or decreasing, indicates an out-of-control process, possibly due to a gradual wearing down of a machine part or due to operator fatigue. While the process may be not outside the control limits, it can be improved by identifying and eliminating this source of variation (an assignable cause).

Pattern analysis is concerned with recognizing systematic or nonrandom patterns in an $\bar{X}$ control chart and identifying the source of such process variation. To help us detect nonrandom patterns in $\bar{X}$ charts, we divide each chart into **zones:**

Zone A contains the area between the 2- and the 3-sigma limits, both above and below the center line.

Zone B contains the area between the 1- and the 2-sigma limits, both above and below the center line.

Zone C contains the area between the center line and the 1-sigma limit, both above and below the center line.

Specific patterns indicating nonrandom variation can be summarized as follows:*

Pattern	Description
1	One point beyond zone A
2	Nine points in a row in zone C or beyond, all on one side of the center line
3	Six points in a row, all increasing or all decreasing
4	Fourteen points in a row, alternating up and down
5	Two out of three points in a row in zone A or beyond
6	Four out of five points in a row in zone B or beyond (on one side of center line)
7	Fifteen points in a row in zones C (above or below center line)
8	Eight points in a row beyond zones C (above or below center line)

These patterns are illustrated in Figure 12.12, where A, B, and C refer to zones A, B, and C. Note that pattern 1 illustrates what we have, up to this point, identified as an out-of-control state.

---

* There is no general agreement about the set of nonrandom patterns. This set is used by MINITAB.

FIGURE 12.12
Eight patterns requiring a search for assignable causes due to nonrandom variation. The dotted lines indicate the nonrandom pattern.

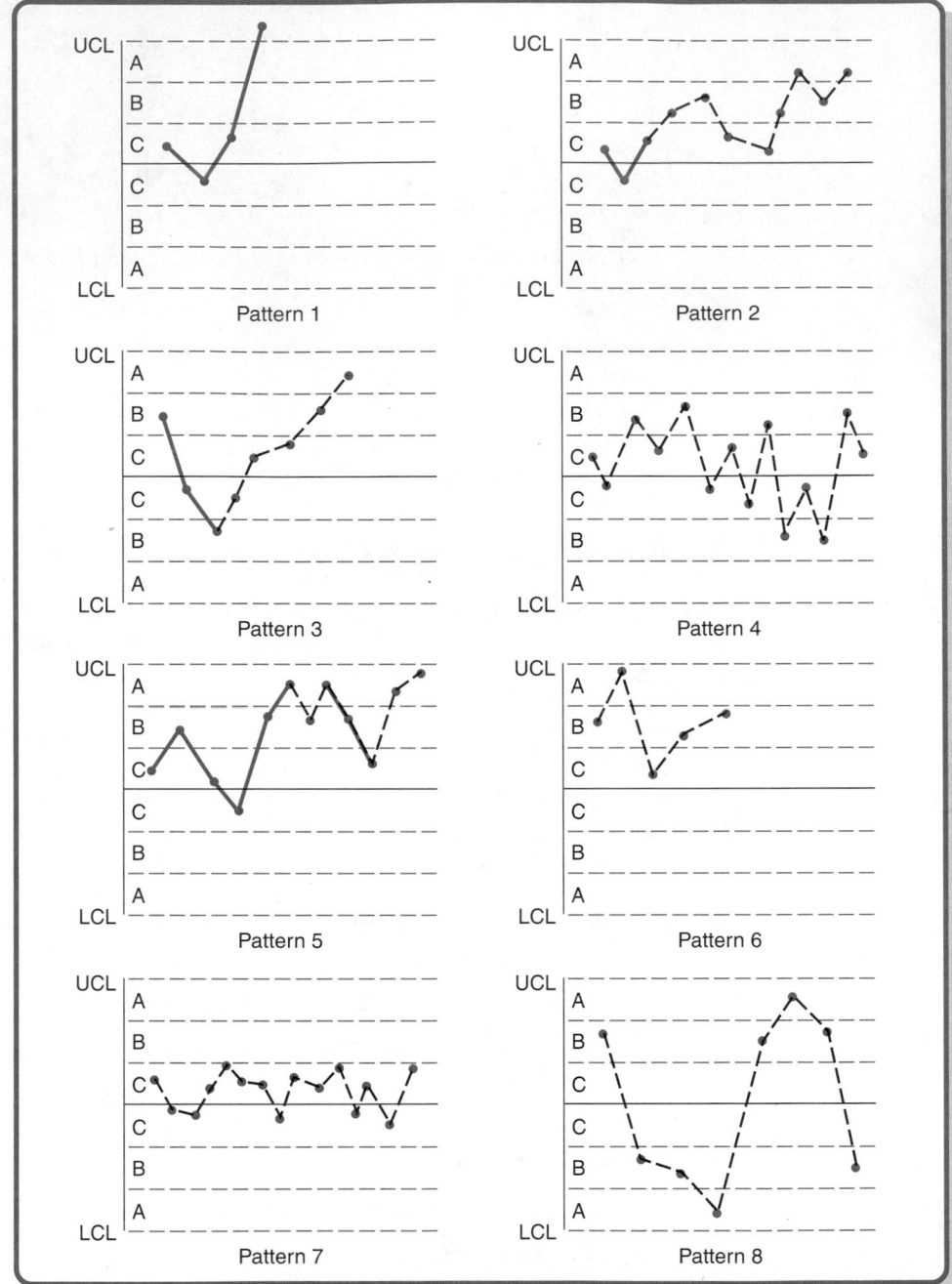

We will not attempt in this discussion to interpret the causes behind these nonrandom patterns; rather, these patterns should point out to you that *there is more to control chart inspection than looking for points outside the control limits*. The ability to interpret a particular pattern in terms of assignable causes requires a great deal of experience and knowledge of the process. For more information on pattern interpretation, see the textbook by Montgomery listed in the Other Textbooks and Articles section at the end of this chapter.

MINITAB will construct these zones in the $\bar{X}$ chart and will search for the eight patterns. The instructions for carrying out this analysis are contained in the end-of-chapter MINITAB appendix. If MINITAB does detect a pattern, the sample at which the pattern is completed is flagged by placement of a value (1 for pattern 1, 2 for pattern 2, and so forth) directly above or below the plotted point.

FIGURE 12.13
MINITAB $\bar{X}$ chart with zones A, B, and C, containing three nonrandom patterns.

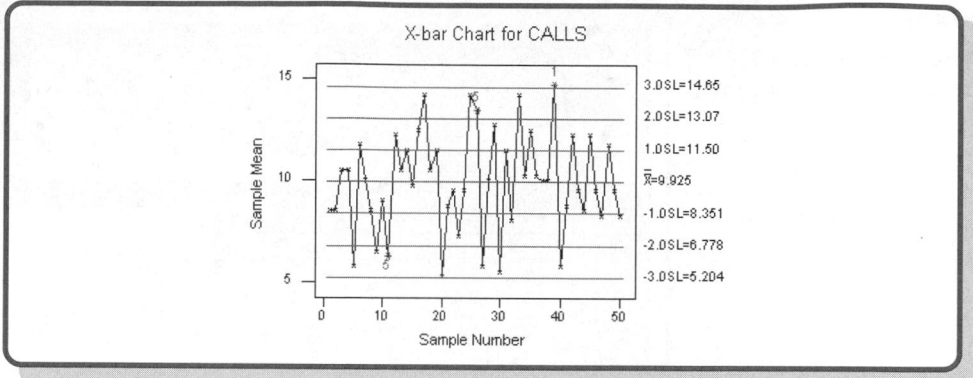

Suppose that Home Security Protection is a company that installs and maintains home security systems. They are interested in monitoring the number of calls that come into their office as a result of a home system triggering an alarm because of an intruder or false alarm. The company obtains a sample of 50 consecutive days and records the number of calls between midnight and 6 A.M., 6 A.M. and noon, noon and 6 P.M., and 6 P.M. and midnight—a total of four observations for each of the 50 days. The resulting $\bar{X}$ chart is shown in Figure 12.13, where several nonrandom patterns are detected. The glaring pattern occurs in sample 39, where the plotted mean lies above the upper control limit (pattern 1). Two instances of pattern 5 (two out of three points in a row in zone A or beyond) are observed in samples 9, 10, 11 and in samples 24, 25, 26. Home Security Protection clearly has a process that is not in control, and they should take a closer look at what assignable causes are contributing to this excessive variation.

MICROSOFT® EXCEL APPLICATION   USE DATA12-2

EXAMPLE 12.2
Excel-Generated $\bar{X}$ and R Charts

The control charts in Figures 12.9 and 12.10 were derived for the 20-ounce cans of ground coffee produced by International Food Products. Management decided to repeat this procedure on their 50-ounce coffee cans, sold mostly to restaurants and hospitals. Twenty samples of five cans each were obtained every 30 minutes, and the resulting 100 observations are contained in a single column. Analyze these data by first constructing an R chart using Excel and, if in control, then constructing the $\bar{X}$ chart. Are these control charts ready for use?

SOLUTION

Excel does not have the capability of constructing control charts using its built-in graphical tools, but they are constructed easily using the KGP Data Analysis macros that accompany this textbook. Begin by opening file DATA12-2. The first 16 observations are shown in Figure 12.14. To obtain the R chart, click on **KGP Data Analysis ➤ Quantitative Data Charts/Tables ➤ Control Charts.** Select **R Chart** and enter "A1:A100" in the **Input Range** box and "B1" in the **Output Range** box. Also, enter "5" in the **Sample Size** box and "R Chart for Coffee Cans" as the chart title.

DISCUSSION. The resulting summary information is in columns B and C in Figure 12.14 and the corresponding R chart is in Figure 12.15. All 20 of the sample ranges lie between the upper control limit of 1.918 and the (inactive) lower control limit of zero. From a variability standpoint, this process is in control. In general, *if the* R *chart signals an out-of-control process, there is no point in continuing and attempting to interpret the corresponding* $\bar{X}$ *chart.*

FIGURE 12.14
Excel spreadsheet using KGP
Data Analysis (Example 12.2).

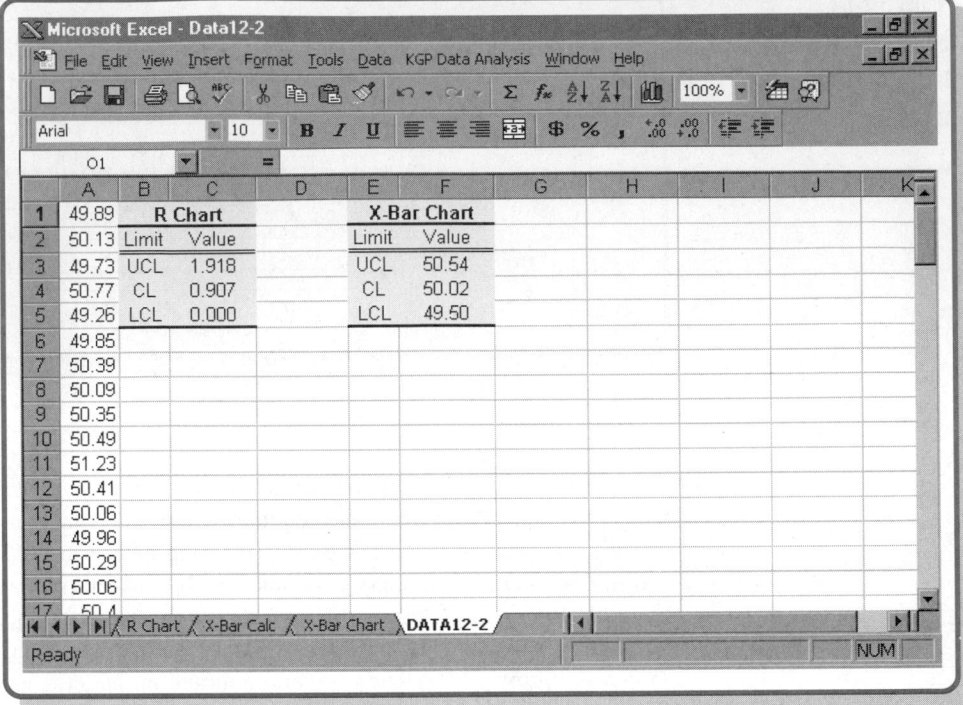

FIGURE 12.15
Excel *R* chart using KGP Data
Analysis (Example 12.2).

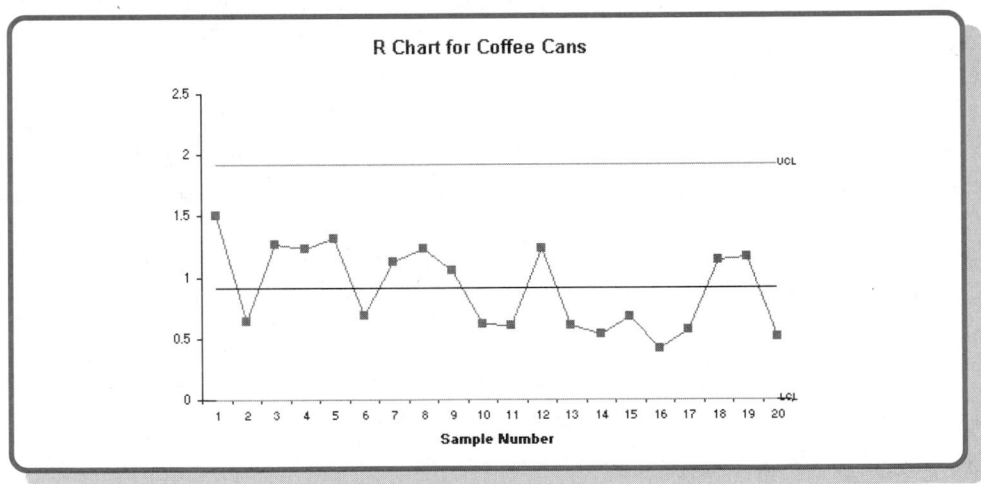

To construct the $\bar{X}$ chart using Excel, repeat the preceding procedure, except select **X Bar Chart** in the input screen and enter "X-Bar Chart for Coffee Cans" as the chart title. Enter "E1" in the **Output Range** box. The resulting summary information is in columns E and F in Figure 12.14 and the $\bar{X}$ chart is shown in Figure 12.16. None of the samples indicate an out-of-control condition since all the plotted means lie between 49.50 and 50.54. A closer look at the $\bar{X}$ chart fails to uncover any nonrandom patterns.* The *R* chart and $\bar{X}$ chart for this process are ready for use.

---

* This conclusion is supported when the authors used MINITAB to search for nonrandom patterns in the $\bar{X}$ chart using this set of data.

FIGURE 12.16

Excel $\bar{X}$ chart using KGP Data Analysis (Example 12.2).

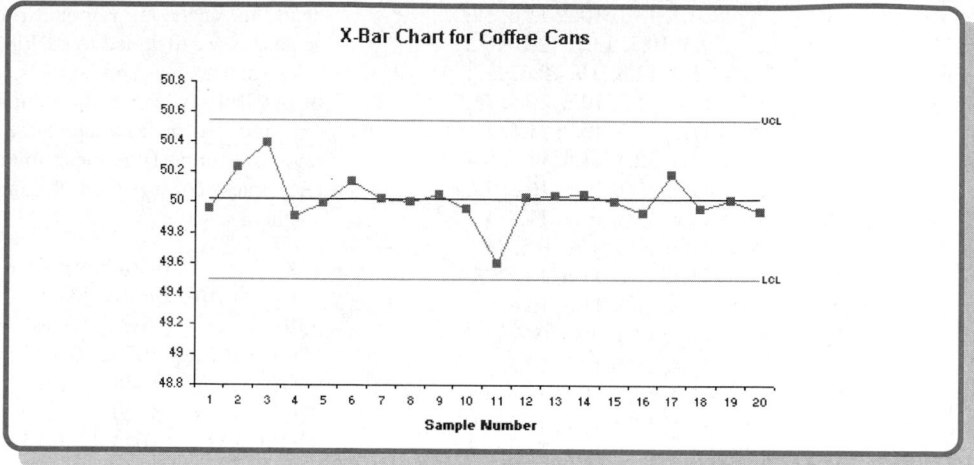

EXERCISES 12.20–12.32

UNDERSTANDING THE MECHANICS

12.20 Thirty samples of size 5 are drawn from a process. The mean of the sample means for the batches of size 5 is equal to 130, and the mean of the range of the observations of the batches is equal to 10.

    a. Find the centerline and control limits for the $\bar{X}$ chart.

    b. Find the boundaries for the A, B, and C zones of the $\bar{X}$ chart.

    c. Find the centerline and control limits for the R chart.

12.21 Construct an $\bar{X}$ and R chart for the following data, assuming a sample size of 5.

Sample Number	Sample Mean	Sample Range
1	380	27
2	420	28
3	435	31
4	425	42
5	422	33
6	433	36
7	430	18
8	445	42
9	430	38
10	409	38
11	403	33
12	418	28
13	400	22
14	401	25
15	409	35
16	450	70
17	429	31
18	490	85
19	412	21
20	500	95

12.22 Samples of five cups of beer are taken at five-hour intervals from various depths in the brew kettle, and the alcohol content, as a percentage of volume, is measured. The following table relates the sample means and ranges for the last 10 samples.

Sample	Mean	Range	Sample	Mean	Range
1	2.8	0.9	6	3.3	0.2
2	4.2	0.2	7	2.9	0.9
3	3.7	0.6	8	2.7	0.3
4	3.9	1.1	9	3.4	0.5
5	2.6	0.5	10	2.8	1.0

    a. Construct an R chart that can be used to control the alcohol content of the beer.

    b. Construct an $\bar{X}$ chart that can be used to control the alcohol content of the beer.

    c. Perform a pattern analysis of the $\bar{X}$ chart from part (b) by checking for nonrandom patterns.

12.23 A drill press operator selects samples of eight metal bushings and measures and records the internal diameter of the bushings at 15-minute intervals for the first two hours of her shift. The following are the sample ranges of the internal diameter measurements:

Sample	Range (mm)	Sample	Range (mm)
1	1.26	5	1.42
2	1.20	6	1.44
3	1.39	7	0.99
4	1.62	8	1.21

    a. Construct an R chart using these data.

    b. What are your observations concerning the pattern of these data?

APPLYING THE NEW CONCEPTS

12.24 Concerned with reducing costs, a delivery manager uses control charts for monitoring gas mileage of delivery fleet vehicles. Each week the manager randomly selects mileage and fuel records for five vehicles. The fleet of delivery vehicles consists of identical make and model trucks. Data for 25 weeks are presented on the following page:

Week	Miles per Gallon
1	12.3, 13.1, 10.2, 11.6, 12.2
2	9.3, 10.5, 13.1, 12.2, 10.3
3	11.3, 12.6, 9.9, 10.6, 11.4
4	12.0, 11.3, 10.2, 10.6, 11.6
5	11.2, 12.3, 10.9, 11.5, 11.8
6	13.1, 12.2, 11.8, 11.2, 9.4
7	11.2, 11.7, 10.8, 10.1, 12.4
8	12.6, 11.3, 10.4, 11.7, 13.2
9	11.5, 12.6, 9.7, 10.5, 10.7
10	13.1, 12.7, 11.6, 12.3, 12.8
11	12.3, 11.2, 11.6, 13.4, 9.4
12	11.3, 12.6, 9.8, 10.7, 11.1
13	10.4, 11.3, 12.3, 12.6, 11.9
14	12.4, 13.5, 10.8, 11.6, 10.7
15	13.1, 12.0, 10.9, 11.8, 11.1
16	11.5, 11.3, 12.2, 10.9, 11.8
17	11.3, 12.6, 12.1, 10.9, 11.8
18	12.4, 10.7, 9.6, 13.6, 11.1
19	11.5, 12.3, 12.2, 11.8, 11.6
20	11.3, 10.8, 11.4, 12.0, 11.9
21	12.6, 10.2, 13.5, 12.1, 12.8
22	10.9, 11.4, 10.5, 13.2, 12.7
23	13.2, 12.8, 11.9, 12.7, 13.1
24	9.4, 11.6, 12.8, 13.0, 12.3
25	12.2, 11.5, 12.9, 10.6, 10.1

a. Construct an R chart for gasoline mileage.
b. Construct an $\overline{X}$ chart for gasoline mileage.
c. Comment on any nonrandom patterns in the $\overline{X}$ chart.

12.25 A drill press operator selects samples of eight bronze bushings and measures and records the internal diameter of the bushings at 15-minute intervals for the first two hours of her shift. The following are the sample ranges of the internal diameter measurements:

Sample	Range (in.)	Sample	Range (in.)
1	.016	5	.007
2	.014	6	.010
3	.012	7	.012
4	.010	8	.013

a. Construct an R chart using these data.
b. What are your observations concerning the pattern of these data?

12.26 The drill press operator in Exercise 12.25 continues to sample eight bushings for the next two hours of her shift and gathers the following internal diameter sample ranges:

Sample	Range (in.)	Sample	Range (in.)
1	.013	5	.019
2	.015	6	.021
3	.015	7	.022
4	.018	8	.023

a. What pattern has emerged during the last two hours of operation?
b. What are the likely consequences if nothing is done to correct the process?
c. What are some possible causes for the new pattern of variation?

12.27 Selit Corporation's vice president of sales uses control charts for analyzing regional sales activity. Five sales representatives are assigned to each region, and the mean quarterly sales volumes for each region's sales representatives are given below. If the Mid-Atlantic region is considered to be a southern region, then there are three northern and three southern regions. Compute the mean total northern and southern quarterly sales, construct an $\overline{X}$ chart for northern sales and for southern sales.

Mean Sales By Region ($1000)

Yr/Qtr	North-east	South-west	North-west	North Central	Mid-Atlantic	South Central
92Q1	$924	$1056	$1412	$431	$539	$397
92Q2	928	1048	1280	470	558	391
92Q3	956	1129	1129	439	591	414
92Q4	1222	1073	1181	431	556	407
93Q1	748	1157	1149	471	540	415
93Q2	962	1146	1248	496	590	442
93Q3	983	1064	1103	506	606	384
93Q4	1024	1213	1021	573	643	448
94Q1	991	1088	1085	403	657	441
94Q2	978	1322	1125	440	602	366
94Q3	1040	1256	910	371	596	470
94Q4	1295	1132	999	405	640	426
95Q1	765	1352	883	466	691	445
95Q2	1008	1353	851	536	723	455
95Q3	1038	1466	997	551	701	363
95Q4	952	1196	878	670	802	462
96Q1	1041	1330	939	588	749	420
96Q2	1020	1003	834	699	762	454
96Q3	976	1197	688	743	807	447
96Q4	1148	1337	806	702	781	359

(Source: Adapted from *Quality Progress,* "How to Teach Others to Apply Statistical Thinking," June 1997, p. 67–79.)

12.28 Refer to the data for the six regions in Exercise 12.27.
    a. Construct an $\overline{X}$ chart for the six regions combined.
    b. Compare the chart from part (a) with the charts constructed in Exercise 12.27.

USING THE COMPUTER

12.29 **[DATA SET EX12-29]** *Variable description:*

DelivTimes: Time in minutes that it takes to deliver a pizza

The owner of Pizza New York has built a solid business by promising timely and consistent home delivery service. She maintains a control chart procedure for monitoring these delivery times and searches for an assignable cause whenever an out-of-control condition appears. The data recorded in the variable DelivTimes are the delivery times for 200 trips over 50 randomly selected days, with 4 trips observed on each day. Use appropriate control charts to determine if this process is out of control.

12.30 **[DATA SET EX12-30]** *Variable description:*

BoltLen: Length of a bolt produced for a military aircraft

A quality engineer is interested in the precision of the production of bolts for a tactical military aircraft. A special computerized instrument is used to measure the exact length of the bolts. Forty samples of size 10 each are randomly selected, and the length is recorded in centimeters. The ideal length is 9 centimeters.

a. Construct an $\bar{X}$ chart and an R chart.

b. What is the first indication (if any) of the process being out of control?

12.31 **[DATA SET EX12-31]** *Variable description:*

BatteryLife: Life of a 12-volt battery in hours from accelerated life testing.

The production plant manager has used control charts to monitor the quality of 12-volt batteries manufactured at the plant. A sample of three 12-volt batteries is selected every hour. These batter-ies are subjected to an accelerated life testing procedure. The life of each of the 120 samples of batteries of size 3 is recorded in BatteryLife. Construct the necessary charts to determine if you have any reservations about this process based on these charts.

12.32 Assume that a manufacturing process produces axle shafts having a mean diameter of 3.5 inches and a standard devi-ation of 0.010 inches. If the axle diameter from this process is a normally distributed random variable and 20 samples of 10 axles are periodically checked, estimate the upper and lower process control limits. Now use Excel's random number generator to produce 20 samples of 10 axles from a normal distribution hav-ing a mean of 3.5 and a standard deviation equal to 0.010. Con-struct an $\bar{X}$ chart for these observations and compare the control limits to the ones you estimated above.

12.6 CONTROL CHARTS FOR ATTRIBUTE DATA: THE *p* AND *c* CHARTS

Many quality characteristics cannot be measured. In these situations, an item is typically classified as either *conforming* or *nonconforming,* where the word *conforming* implies that the item conforms to specifications imposed upon the process (such as no surface scratches). Such quality characteristics are called **attributes.** The data gathered on these characteristics consist of counts or values based on counts, such as proportions. Examples of such data would be the number of blemishes in a square yard of sheet metal (monitored using a *c* chart) or the proportion of nonconforming computer chips in a container of 200 chips (monitored using a *p* chart).

CONTROL CHART FOR THE PROPORTION NONCONFORMING: THE *p* CHART

The proportion nonconforming is defined as the number of nonconforming items in a pop-ulation divided by the population size. It is denoted by *p,* and it corresponds to the bino-mial parameter *p* discussed in Chapters 5 and 10, where (as in Chapter 10) the value of *p* is unknown. Consequently, the process involved must satisfy the assumptions behind a binomial situation, described in Chapter 5, section 4 (page 180). When using a *p* chart, we concentrate on the parameter *p* and observe when this proportion appears to be out of con-trol. If an item is judged on more than one quality characteristic, it is said to be noncon-forming if the item does not conform to standard on one or more of these characteristics.

The reasons for using a *p* chart include the following:

1. Quality measurements are not possible.
2. Quality measurements are possible, but not practical (such as determining the atmo-spheric pressure at which an electrical component is destroyed).
3. Many characteristics on each part are being judged during inspection.
4. The main question of interest is, "will the process be able to produce conforming prod-ucts over time?"

The construction of a *p* chart is done in basically the same way as for an $\bar{X}$ or an R chart. A collection of samples (usually, 20 to 25) is obtained while the process is believed to be in control. Let T_i be the number of nonconforming items in the ith sample, and let n be the sample size. The resulting proportion nonconforming is $p_i = T_i/n$. For example, if sample 4 contains 150 items, 3 of which are nonconforming, then $n = 150$, $T_4 = 3$, and $p_4 = 3/150 = .02$.

The five-step procedure for constructing a *p* chart follows, and is illustrated in the next example.

STEPS FOR MAKING *p* CHARTS (CONSTANT SAMPLE SIZE).

1. Collect m samples of data (typically, 20 to 25), each of size, n.

2. Determine the proportion nonconforming for each sample. Call this value p_i.

$$p_i = \frac{T_i}{n}$$

where T_i is the number of nonconforming items in sample i and n is the sample size.

3. Find $\bar{p}$, the overall proportion nonconforming.

$$\bar{p} = \frac{\text{total number of nonconforming units}}{\text{total sample size}}$$

That is,

$$\bar{p} = \frac{\sum T_i}{mn}$$

Note: $\bar{p}$ is merely the average of the m values of p_i.

4. Compute the 3-sigma control limits:

$$\text{UCL} = \bar{p} + 3\sqrt{\frac{\bar{p}(1-\bar{p})}{n}}$$

$$\text{CL} = \bar{p} \qquad\qquad\text{(12.7)}$$

$$\text{LCL} = \bar{p} - 3\sqrt{\frac{\bar{p}(1-\bar{p})}{n}}$$

5. Draw in the control lines and plot the values of p_i.

EXAMPLE 12.3

Repeated samples of 150 coffee cans are inspected to determine whether a can is out of round (the cylindrical shape of the can has been distorted) or whether it contains leaks due to improper construction. Such a can is said to be nonconforming, and p represents the proportion of nonconforming cans in the population. Twenty preliminary samples (150 cans each) are obtained.

Sample Number	Number of Nonconforming Cans	p_i
1	7	.047
2	4	.027
3	1	.007
4	3	.020
5	4	.027
6	8	.053
7	10	.067
8	5	.033
9	2	.013
10	7	.047
11	6	.040
12	8	.053
13	0	.000
14	9	.060
15	3	.020
16	1	.007
17	4	.027
18	5	.033
19	7	.047
20	2	.013
	96	

Construct the p chart for these data.

FIGURE 12.17

p chart for Example 12.3.

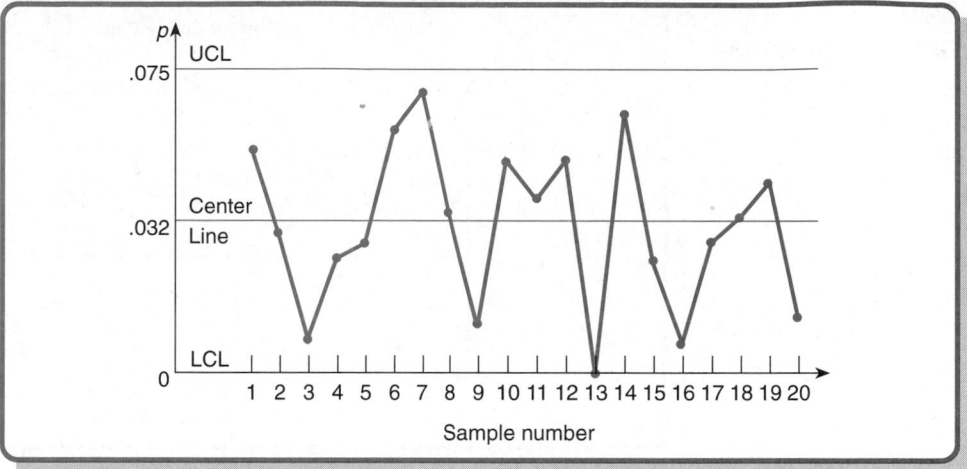

SOLUTION

Steps 1 and 2 have been completed. The next step is to determine the overall proportion nonconforming, $\bar{p}$, which is found by dividing the total number of nonconforming items (96) by the total sample size (20 · 150 = 3000). Consequently,

$$\bar{p} = \frac{96}{3000} = .032$$

The control limits are then easily derived:

$$UCL = .032 + 3\sqrt{\frac{(.032)(.968)}{150}} = .075$$

$$\text{Center Line} = .032$$

$$LCL = .032 - 3\sqrt{\frac{(.032)(.968)}{150}} = -.011 \quad (\text{set } LCL = 0)$$

Since a negative proportion is impossible, the LCL is set equal to zero and is inactive. The resulting *p* chart is shown in Figure 12.17. Since none of the 20 sample proportions are outside the control limits, the *p* chart has been established and is ready for use.

The KGP Data Analysis macros provide an easy-to-use procedure for constructing a *p* chart. Begin by entering the number of nonconforming cans (7, 4, 1, . . .) in column A. Click on **KGP Data Analysis ➤ Quantitative Data Charts/Tables ➤ Control Charts.** Select **p Chart** and enter "A1:A20" in the **Input Range** box and "B1" in the **Output Range** box. Also, enter "150" in the **Sample Size** box and "P Chart for Coffee Cans" as the chart title. Select "count" in the **Nonconforming Input** section since the data consist of the *number* of nonconforming cans in each sample of 150 rather than the *proportion* of nonconforming cans in each sample. The resulting chart in Figure 12.18 agrees with the one in Figure 12.17, so once again we conclude that the process is in control, and the *p* chart is ready for use.

EXAMPLE 12.4

Continuing with Example 12.3, the next five coffee can samples (each of size 150) produced 5, 2, 11, 6, and 8 nonconforming cans, respectively. Do the sample proportions indicate that the process is in control for each of these samples?

FIGURE 12.18
Excel *p* chart using KGP Data
Analysis (Example 12.3).

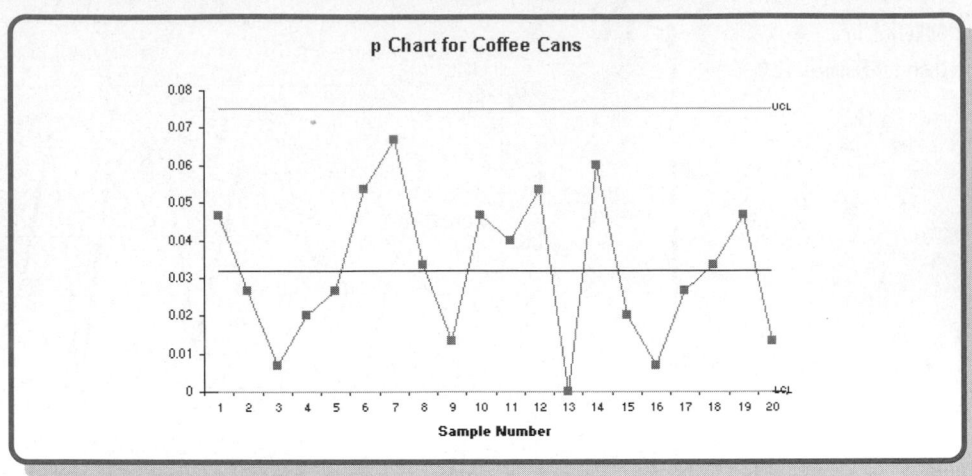

FIGURE 12.18
Excel *p* chart using KGP Data
Analysis (Example 12.3).

SOLUTION

The five sample proportions are

$$5/150 = .033$$

$$2/150 = .013$$

$$11/150 = .073$$

$$6/150 = .040$$

$$8/150 = .053$$

Each of these proportions falls within the control limits in Figure 12.17, so the conclusion would be that the process is in control during this period.

Notice that the third sample came close to exceeding the upper control limit of .075, and it may be tempting to react and start tampering with the process to "fix it." But this action would defeat the purpose of a control chart, since we conclude that the occurrence of 11 nonconforming cans is due simply to chance variation and no process adjustment is called for. As was pointed out earlier, such well-meaning overadjustments result in *increased* process variation rather than improved product quality.

CONTROL CHART FOR NUMBER OF NONCONFORMITIES: THE *c* CHART

The *p* chart dealt with monitoring the proportion (or in a sense, the number) of *nonconforming units* in a sample of *n* units. Since it is quite possible for a unit to have more than one nonconformity, we must also consider the *number of nonconformities per unit*. The *c* chart can be used for controlling a single type of nonconformity or for controlling all types of nonconformities without distinguishing between types. Situations in which a *c* chart could be used would include monitoring the number of scratches on a CRT casing, the number of minor blemishes on a rubber tire, the number of loose bolts on a manufactured assembly, and so forth.

The assumption behind the process is that the number of nonconformities occurring in a unit satisfies the assumptions behind the Poisson process, described in Chapter 5, section 6, page 194. An important characteristic of the Poisson random variable is that the mean and variance are identical, and so the standard deviation is the square root of the mean. Therefore, the control chart for the number of nonconformities per unit (say, *c*) is very easy to construct. The method for constructing a *c* chart is described in the following five-step procedure.

STEPS FOR MAKING A *c* CHART.

1. Collect *m* samples of data (typically, 20 to 25 units), where each sample is obtained by observing a single unit.
2. Determine the number of nonconformities for the *i*th unit. Call this value c_i.
3. Find the *average* number of nonconformities per unit, $\bar{c}$, where

$$\bar{c} = \frac{\sum c_i}{m}$$

4. Compute the 3-sigma control limits:*

$$UCL = \bar{c} + 3\sqrt{\bar{c}}$$

$$\text{Center Line} = \bar{c} \qquad\qquad (12.8)$$

$$LCL = \bar{c} - 3\sqrt{\bar{c}}$$

5. Construct the control chart by drawing in the control lines and plotting the values of c_i.

EXAMPLE 12.5

An automobile assembly worker is interested in monitoring and controlling the number of minor paint blemishes appearing on the outside door panel on the driver's side of a certain make of automobile. The following data were obtained, using a sample of 25 door panels.

Panel	1	2	3	4	5	6	7	8	9	10	11	12	13	14
Number of Paint Blemishes	1	0	3	3	1	2	5	0	2	1	2	0	8	0

Panel	15	16	17	18	19	20	21	22	23	24	25
Number of Paint Blemishes	2	1	4	0	2	4	1	1	0	2	3

Construct the control chart for this situation and determine whether all the plotted points are in control.

SOLUTION

The average number of nonconformities (minor paint blemishes) for the sample of 25 door panels is $\bar{c}$, where

$$\bar{c} = \frac{1 + 0 + 3 + \cdots + 2 + 3}{25}$$

$$= \frac{48}{25} = 1.92$$

The limits and center line for the resulting *c* chart are

$$UCL = 1.92 + 3\sqrt{1.92} = 6.08$$

$$\text{Center Line} = 1.92$$

$$LCL = 1.92 - 3\sqrt{1.92} = -2.24 \quad (\text{set } LCL = 0)$$

Since the Poisson variable is never negative, the LCL is set equal to zero here and is inactive.

You can easily construct a *c* chart using KGP Data Analysis. Begin by entering the number of paint blemishes (1, 0, 3, 3, . . .) in column A. Click on **KGP Data Analysis ➤ Quantitative Data Charts/Tables ➤ Control Charts**. Select **c Chart** and enter "A1:A25" in the **Input Range** box and "B1" in the **Output Range** box. Also, enter

---

* If the mean of the process is known, its value may be substituted for $\bar{c}$ in the control limits and center line.

FIGURE 12.19

Excel *c* chart using KGP Data
Analysis (Example 12.5).

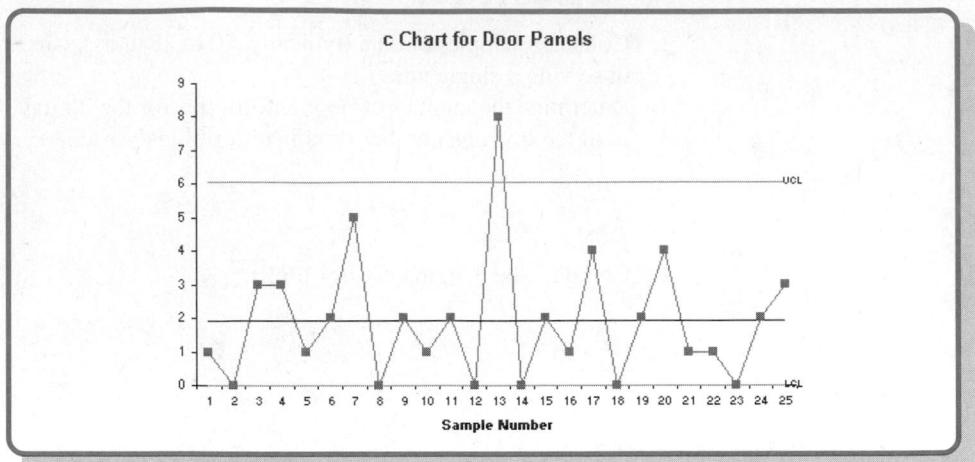

"c Chart for Door Panels" as the chart title. The resulting *c* chart is shown in Figure 12.19. Notice that the thirteenth sample contains an out-of-control observation. If control limits for current or future production are to be meaningful, they must be based on data from a process that is *in control.*

The next step here would be to examine the 13th observation to determine if an assignable cause can be located. If it can, the observation should be removed, the control limits recomputed (using 24 samples), and the procedure continued until all observations are in control. If no assignable cause is found, you have one of two choices (1) retain this observation and keep the present control limits, or (2) drop this observation, assuming that an assignable cause exists but was not identified.

EXAMPLE 12.6

It was discovered that defective paint was used during sample number 13 in Example 12.5. Since this is a legitimate assignable cause, the observation was removed from the sample. Construct the modified control limits for the *c* chart, and determine if the control chart is ready for use.

SOLUTION

Removing the 13th observation produces a new total of $48 - 8 = 40$ and an average of

$$\bar{c} = \frac{40}{24} = 1.67$$

The resulting control limits are

$$UCL = 1.67 + 3\sqrt{1.67} = 5.55$$

$$\text{Center Line} = 1.67$$

$$LCL = 1.67 - 3\sqrt{1.67} = -2.21 \quad (\text{set } LCL = 0)$$

Reviewing the 24 samples, all of the number of nonconformities fall within the revised control limits, so the *c* chart has been established.

COMMENTS

1. At first glance, it may seem strange that lower control limits are used for *p* charts and *c* charts. After all, why should we be concerned when, say, a sample proportion (p_i) falls below the lower control limit? Keep in mind that a plotted point outside a control limit does not necessarily indicate that something *bad* happened, merely that something *unusual* has occurred. Whether this point lies above the UCL or below the LCL, a

search should be made for an assignable cause. Perhaps this small proportion is due to extremely good raw material or to a change in operator skill/attitude. In either case, management should investigate the reasons behind this unusual event.

2. Any control chart should be modified when it appears that a substantial decrease in variability has produced a process that is more consistent. As product quality improves, the definition of what is "in control" should also change to reflect the new standards resulting from the improved process. One always hopes that *this year's control limits will not be acceptable on next year's control chart.*

EXERCISES 12.33–12.44

UNDERSTANDING THE MECHANICS

12.33 Discuss the difference between a *p* chart and a *c* chart. What type of data are required for their use? What do you control using each of these charts? How is a *p* chart similar to an $\bar{X}$ chart?

12.34 Indicate whether a *p* or a *c* chart would be appropriate for controlling:
  a. The number of defective micro-switches in a sample of 25
  b. The number of surface flaws in the reflecting mirror of a telescope
  c. The number of underfilled containers in one hour of production
  d. The number of broken light bulbs in a carton of 50 packages
  e. The number of knots in a sheet of paneling

12.35 For an in-control process, the percentage of defectives is 5%. Find the 3-sigma upper and lower control limits in which each sample consist of 100 observations.

12.36 Samples of 200 floppy diskettes are taken from each production run, and the diskettes are checked for bad sectors. The following are the number of diskettes found with bad sectors for the past eight production runs:

Run	Bad Diskettes	Run	Bad Diskettes
1	13	5	23
2	15	6	26
3	14	7	29
4	19	8	37

  a. What control chart is appropriate in this instance?
  b. Construct the appropriate control chart.
  c. Is this process in control?

APPLYING THE NEW CONCEPTS

12.37 Consider a hospital that uses control charts for monitoring patient sedation. After administering sedation, nurses record their impressions of the patients at 10- to 15-minute intervals. Patients who were asleep or awake and pain free were considered acceptable and fulfilled the objective of conscious sedation. Other patient conditions were deemed unacceptable. Twenty-five entries each day over a 15-day period are given below:

								Day						
1	2	3	4	5	6	7	8	9	10	11	12	13	14	15
								Unacceptable						
17	7	5	9	5	14	5	0	6	7	13	14	8	5	0
								p						
.680	.280	.200	.360	.200	.560	.200	0.00	.240	.280	.520	.560	.320	.200	0.00

  a. Construct a *p* chart using these data.
  b. Is this process in control?
  c. What assignable cause might be the cause of any out-of-control observations? What should the hospital do?

12.38 Six operators produce boots at a leather goods manufacturing facility. Each day 50 pairs of boots are inspected from each worker and the number of defects are recorded. Data collected during the past two weeks follow.

Operator	Mon.	Tue.	Wed.	Thu.	Fri.	Total
Steve	2	1	2	2	2	
	0	2	1	2	3	17
Mary	1	3	0	2	1	
	4	2	0	0	2	15
Carlos	2	0	1	0	1	
	2	0	2	1	1	10
John	4	4	5	5	6	
	4	3	4	5	6	46
Andrew	2	1	1	0	2	
	2	1	1	0	2	12
Betty	2	0	0	1	3	
	2	1	0	0	2	11

  a. Construct an appropriate type of control chart for the number of defects using the ten data points for the two-week period. Note that 300 pairs of boots are inspected each day.
  b. Can the process be considered as in control?
  c. Construct Pareto charts for the number of defects by worker.
  d. What corrective measures do you suggest?

12.39 Eight-foot × 4-foot sheets of oak paneling are inspected, and the number of surface nonconformities noted. The following are the number of nonconformities found in the last 14 samples.

Sample	Nonconformities	Sample	Nonconformities
1	5	7	4
2	7	8	4
3	3	9	3
4	8	10	6
5	5	11	15
6	7	12	8
7	6	14	2

  a. What type of control chart is appropriate to use in this instance?
  b. Construct the appropriate control chart.
  c. Is this process in control?

12.40 Bill 3 was passed in November 1989 in the province of Manitoba, Canada. Bill 3 was among the most stringent drinking-and-driving legislation ever enacted in North America. Its proponents pointed to the decrease in alcohol-related traffic fatalities in the year following the passage of Bill 3. Its critics, however, maintained that the decrease in alcohol-related fatalities was due simply to random chance. The following data represent the proportion of total traffic fatalities that were alcohol-related for the 1973 to 1990 time period. For the sake of simplicity, assume that there was a constant 250 traffic fatalities per year for the period in question.

Year	Alcohol-Related Fatalities	Year	Alcohol-Related Fatalities
1973	0.4940	1982	0.4500
1974	0.4455	1983	0.4000
1975	0.5354	1984	0.3916
1976	0.5398	1985	0.4440
1977	0.4865	1986	0.5380
1978	0.4038	1987	0.4301
1979	0.6425	1988	0.4744
1980	0.4457	1989	0.4277
1981	0.5357	1990	0.4211

(Source: Fred A. Spiring, "A Bill's Effect on Alcohol-Related Traffic Fatalities," *Quality Progress* 27, no. 2 (Feb. 1994): 35–38.)

  a. Construct a *p* chart for these data.
  b. Does the *p* chart in part (a) indicate an in-control state?
  c. Would you agree with the proponents of Bill 3 that the legislation was successful in significantly reducing alcohol-related traffic fatalities?

USING THE COMPUTER

12.41 [DATA SET EX12-41] *Variable description:*

NumAirBubbles: Number of air bubbles in the production of picture windows

A quality engineer is interested in the quality of picture windows produced at his plant. Every 50th window produced is selected, and a sample of 40 windows is obtained where the number of air bubbles is recorded. Construct a control chart to determine those samples where the chart indicates that the process is out of control.

12.42 [DATA SET EX12-42] *Variable description:*

NumAbsences: Number of absences per day from a plant with 200 employees

The production manager of a plant is concerned about the affect that too many absences may have on the productivity of a plant. The manager does not mind some absences per day, as employees may use sick time, personal leave, or comp time. If too few absences are occurring, this may indicate that in the future too many employees will be absent on the same day. Also many absences are sometimes followed by very few absences. The manager would like to gain insight into the process from a control chart of the number of absences per day from a total of 200 employees over 30 working days. What conclusions can you reach?

12.43 [DATA SET EX12-43] *Variable description:*

NumErrAcct: Number of errors found in purchase orders

A manager of an accounting office is concerned that purchase orders may contain too many errors and hence result in excessive returned merchandise. To gain insight into the process in which purchase orders are filled out, 35 purchase orders are randomly selected and the number of errors are recorded in the variable NumErrAcct. What control chart is appropriate for this situation? Construct this chart and discuss the results.

12.44 [DATA SET EX12-44] *Variable description:*

SuppA: Number of defective cases in sampled batch of 150 cases from supplier A
SuppB: Number of defective cases in sampled batch of 120 cases from supplier B

A recording studio and production company use two suppliers for their clear plastic cassette tape cases. A case is considered defective if it is scratched, cloudy, cracked, or otherwise unusable. Data from 50 samples collected from each of the two suppliers are recorded in the variables SuppA and SuppB.
  a. Construct the appropriate control chart for each of the two suppliers.
  b. Do either of these two processes indicate an out-of-control condition?
  c. Comment on the performance of the two suppliers. Which would you prefer to use?

12.7 PROCESS CAPABILITY

We have dealt with control charts that monitor a process to determine whether it is operating in control. But the term "in control" merely indicates that the process is performing within natural variation *as measured by past performance*. It is entirely possible that the process might be in control but not be *capable* of meeting the process requirements, referred to as **specification limits.**

For example, suppose the process that produces piston rings is operating in control, with the inside diameter of the rings centered at 12.1 cm with a standard deviation of .03 cm. However, the product specifications state that in order to be of acceptable quality, the piston rings must have an inside diameter between 11.95 and 12.05 cm. The value 11.95 is called the **lower spec limit** (LSL) and 12.05 is the **upper spec limit** (USL). From this information, we would have to conclude that the piston rings process is incapable of meeting the required specifications (specs) (see Figure 12.20).

FIGURE 12.20

Spec limits versus process performance.

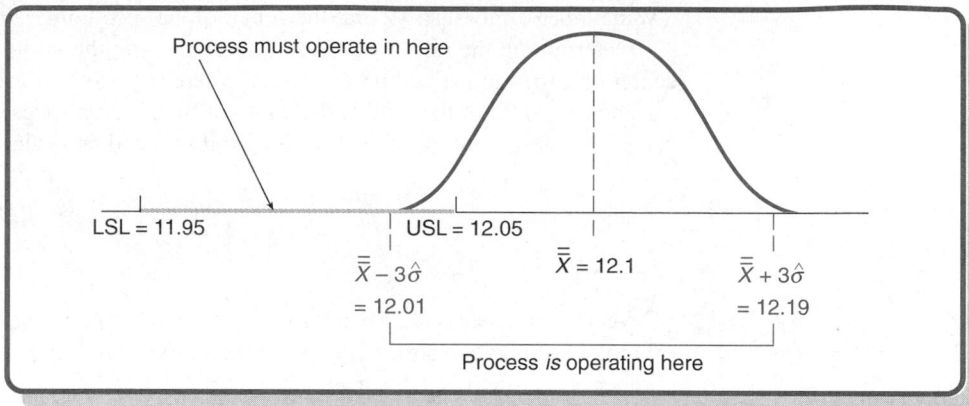

FIGURE 12.21

Visual inspection of process capability.

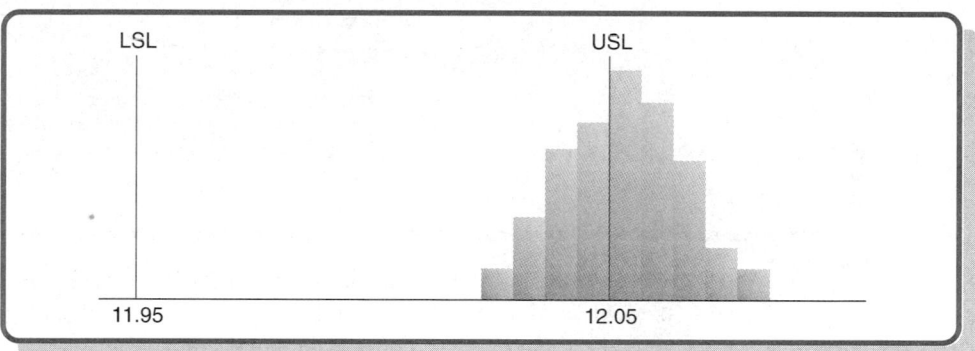

In Figure 12.20, the difference between 12.19 and 12.01 is 6 standard deviations (estimated) and is referred to as the **process spread:**

$$\text{process spread} = 6\hat{\sigma} \tag{12.9}$$

For this illustration, $6\hat{\sigma} = 12.19 - 12.01 = .18$ cm.

A visual method of checking process capability is to obtain a fairly large sample and plot a histogram against the required spec limits. In the preceding example, the quality characteristic of interest is the inside diameter of a piston ring; suppose that the histogram of inside diameters looks like the one in Figure 12.21. Visually, it is clear that the process is centered at a value much too large and that the process is not capable of meeting the required specifications.

This section will introduce three descriptors of process capability that *measure* how well the process is conforming to the required specifications. We will move away from a subjective visual assessment of process capability toward an objective measure that is based on facts (sample information) rather than opinion.

PROCESS CAPABILITY RATIOS, C_p AND C_{pk}

When computing the first measure (C_p), the assumptions are:

1. The process output is centered within specification.
2. The process is normally distributed.
3. The process is stable (in control).

The measure C_p is simply a comparison of the process capability with the specifications, and it is a valid indicator *only* if the above assumptions are true. It is clear from Figure 12.21

that assumption 1 is violated for the piston ring illustration, since the process is centered at a value much larger than 12 cm (the center of the spec limits).

Determining the ratio C_p is similar to comparing the width of a car driving down the center of a road to the width of the road, where the width of the car is the process spread, $6\hat{\sigma}$, and the width of the road is the width of the process specs (USL – LSL). The process capability ratio C_p for a two-sided spec limit is found by dividing these two "widths":

$$C_p = \frac{\text{USL} - \text{LSL}}{6\hat{\sigma}} \qquad \textbf{(12.10)}$$

Very often process specifications are one-sided, specifying only a lower spec limit (for example, the bursting strength of a glass bottle) or an upper spec limit (for example, the number of missing rivets in an aircraft assembly). For these situations, we compare the distance between the sample mean and the spec limit with three standard deviations:

$$C_p = \frac{\text{USL} - \overline{X}}{3\hat{\sigma}} \qquad \text{(upper spec limit only)} \qquad \textbf{(12.11)}$$

$$C_p = \frac{\overline{X} - \text{LSL}}{3\hat{\sigma}} \qquad \text{(lower spec limit only)} \qquad \textbf{(12.12)}$$

EXAMPLE 12.7

The specification limits for the filled weight of a coffee can are 20 ± 1 (ounces); that is, the USL is 21 oz and the LSL is 19 oz. A sample of 100 cans provides a mean of 19.98 oz and an estimated standard deviation of .189 oz. Determine the capability ratio, C_p.

SOLUTION

The process spread is $(6)(.189) = 1.134$ oz. The value of C_p can be found from equation 12.10:

$$C_p = \frac{21 - 19}{1.134} = 1.76$$

EXAMPLE 12.8

The bursting strength of a particular soft drink container has a lower spec limit of 200 psi (pounds per square inch). A sample of 100 containers produced a sample mean of 226 psi and a standard deviation of 11.3 psi. What is the capability ratio, C_p?

SOLUTION

Using equation 12.12,

$$C_p = \frac{226 - 200}{3(11.3)} = \frac{26}{33.9} = .77$$

INTERPRETING C_p

A general rule for interpreting C_p is as follows:*

$$C_p \geq 1.33 \qquad \text{good}$$
$$1 \leq C_p < 1.33 \qquad \text{adequate}$$
$$C_p < 1 \qquad \text{inadequate}$$

---

* A more precise interpretation of C_p should consider whether the process is new or existing and whether the quality characteristic is of critical importance (such as one related to consumer safety). See the reference by Montgomery in the Further Reading section for more detail.

FIGURE 12.22

The C_{pk} ratio considers the distance from the process center to the nearest spec limit.

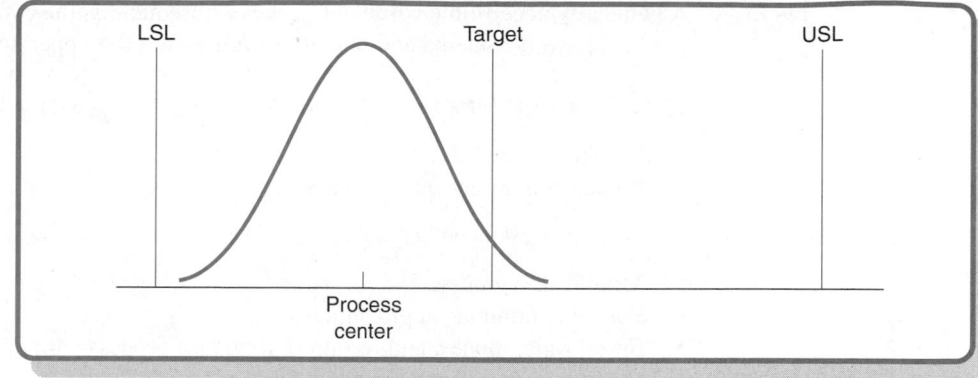

For Example 12.7, the value of $C_p = 1.76$ would be in the "good" category, and we would conclude that the *potential* capability of the coffee-can process to meet the product specs is very good, with little chance of producing a nonconforming (out-of-spec) product. The term *potential* is needed here, since *no attention has been paid to where the process is centered when determining this capability ratio.* The C_{pk} capability ratio (discussed next) considers this very important aspect of the process performance.

A value of $C_p = .77$ was determined for Example 12.8, indicating that this process has a tendency to operate dangerously close to the lower spec limit. We can expect that an unsatisfactory number of containers will have a bursting strength below the lower spec limit of 200 psi.

CONSIDERATION OF PROCESS LOCATION: USE OF C_{pk}

When determining the C_p ratio, we used the analogy of comparing the width of a car (the process spread) to the width of the road (the difference between the spec limits), while *assuming* that the car is traveling down the center of the road. The C_p ratio is a measure of potential capability.

The C_{pk} process capability ratio not only compares the width of the car to the width of the road but also questions whether the car is on or off the center stripe. This ratio examines the distance from the process center to the *nearest* spec limit (assuming both an upper and a lower spec limit), as illustrated in Figure 12.22.

The assumptions behind the use of the C_{pk} ratio are:

1. The process may or may not be centered in spec.
2. The process is normally distributed.
3. The process is stable.
4. Control charts will be used to monitor the process over time.

PROCEDURE FOR FINDING C_{pk}.

1. Determine $R_L = \dfrac{\overline{X} - \text{LSL}}{3\hat{\sigma}}$

2. Determine $R_U = \dfrac{\text{USL} - \overline{X}}{3\hat{\sigma}}$

3. $C_{pk} = $ Minimum of R_L and R_U

Referring to Example 12.7, we have $\bar{x} = 19.98$ oz, $\hat{\sigma} = .189$ oz, LSL $= 19$ oz, and USL $= 21$ oz. Consequently,

$$R_L = \frac{19.98 - 19}{3(.189)} = 1.73$$

$$R_U = \frac{21 - 19.98}{3(.189)} = 1.80$$

and so C_{pk} is the minimum of 1.73 and 1.80, that is, $C_{pk} = 1.73$.

The value of C_{pk} will always be less than or equal to the corresponding value of C_p. **A generally acceptable value of C_{pk} is 1.** Consequently, the coffee-can process in Example 12.7 is well centered and operating well within the upper and lower spec limits.

TAKING C_{pk} ONE STEP FURTHER.   If the process is capable ($C_{pk} > 1$):

- Monitor the process.
- Pursue continuous improvement.

   If the process is not capable ($C_{pk} \leq 1$):

- Monitor the process.
- Pursue continuous improvement.
- Invest time, money, and resources to reduce process variation.
- Consider removing this product from production.

Although the fourth statement under $C_{pk} \leq 1$ may appear to be a bit drastic, it is worthy of serious consideration, given the present world of increasing product quality requirements and consumer quality demands.

CONSIDERATION OF THE PROCESS TARGET: USE OF C_{pm}

When using the C_p ratio or the C_{pk} ratio, we divide by either $3s$ or $6s$, where s is the sample standard deviation. The value of s is a measure of the variation about the process mean (center). An alternative here is to replace s with an estimate of the variation about the process *target* (T), assumed here to be midway between the upper spec limit and the lower spec limit; that is, $T = (\text{USL} + \text{LSL})/2$. Denoting this estimate by s', then,

$$
\begin{aligned}
s' &= \sqrt{\frac{\sum(x-T)^2}{n-1}} \\
&= \sqrt{\frac{\sum(x-\bar{x})^2}{n-1} + \frac{n(\bar{x}-T)^2}{n-1}} \\
&= \sqrt{s^2 + \frac{n(\bar{x}-T)^2}{n-1}}
\end{aligned}
\tag{12.13}
$$

Consider the ratio defined by

$$
C_{pm} = \frac{\text{USL} - \text{LSL}}{6s'}
\tag{12.14}
$$

This index will decrease as s' increases, due to a shift from the process target. When the process variance (s^2) changes and the process mean drifts from T concurrently, the C_{pm} index has the ability to detect these changes. *We suggest you interpret the C_{pm} index using the same guidelines for interpreting the C_p ratio discussed previously.* In particular, this implies that a C_{pm} ratio less than 1 is an indicator of a process that cannot adequately meet the process specifications.

EXAMPLE 12.9

SOLUTION

Determine the C_{pm} ratio for the coffee-can illustration in Example 12.7.

The sample size is $n = 100$, the target value is $T = 20$ oz, the sample mean is $\bar{x} = 19.98$ oz, and the sample standard deviation is $s = .189$ oz. Consequently,

$$
s' = \sqrt{.189^2 + \frac{100(19.98-20)^2}{99}} = .1901
$$

and

$$C_{pm} = \frac{21-19}{6(.1901)} = \frac{2}{1.141} = 1.75$$

Since $1.75 > 1.33$, we once again conclude that this process is capable of meeting the process specifications.

DETERMINING THE PERCENT NONCONFORMING

Another method of measuring process capability is to estimate the number of nonconforming units, that is, those outside the spec limits. The basic assumption behind this procedure is that we have reason to believe that the process is *normally distributed.* If there is reason to doubt this assumption (such as, when a process has been shown to be out of control), then the results of this section are unreliable. There is nothing new about the procedure we will use here, since we learned in Chapter 6 that the percent nonconforming can be determined by finding the corresponding area under a normal curve. The mean and standard deviation are estimated using the sample statistics, again assuming that the process is in control during the collection of this sample. This procedure is illustrated in the following example.

EXAMPLE 12.10

A machine is used to fill plastic containers of motor oil, each of which is supposed to contain 32 fluid ounces. The process specs are $32 \pm .5$ fluid ounces. A sample of 75 containers produces a mean of $\bar{x} = 31.92$ fluid ounces and a standard deviation of $s = .16$. Describe the process capability.

SOLUTION

The sample standard deviation is the estimated process standard deviation, that is, $\hat{\sigma}$. First we determine the process capability ratio C_{pk}.

$$R_L = \frac{31.92-31.5}{3(.16)} = \frac{.42}{.48} = .88$$

$$R_U = \frac{32.5-31.92}{3(.16)} = \frac{.58}{.48} = 1.21$$

Consequently,

$$C_{pk} = \text{minimum of .88 and } 1.21$$

$$= .88$$

which is an unacceptable value.

To find the value of C_{pm}, we use equation 12.13 to calculate the variation about the process target, $T = 32$. This is

$$s' = \sqrt{(.16)^2 + \frac{75(31.92-32)^2}{74}} = .179$$

The resulting ratio is

$$C_{pm} = \frac{32.5-31.5}{6(.179)} = .93 < 1$$

So, both the C_{pk} and C_{pm} ratios indicate a process incapable of meeting process specifications. The small value of C_{pm} is due to the variation about the process center, as measured by $s = .16$, and the slight drift from the process target equal to $\bar{x} - T = 31.92 - 32 = -.08$.

To estimate the percent nonconforming, we examine the tails of a normal curve outside the lower and upper spec limits of 31.5 and 32.5. These tail areas are shaded in Figure 12.23, where the curve is centered at $\bar{x} = 31.92$ with a standard deviation of $\hat{\sigma} = .16$.

FIGURE 12.23

Tail areas represent the proportion of nonconforming units.

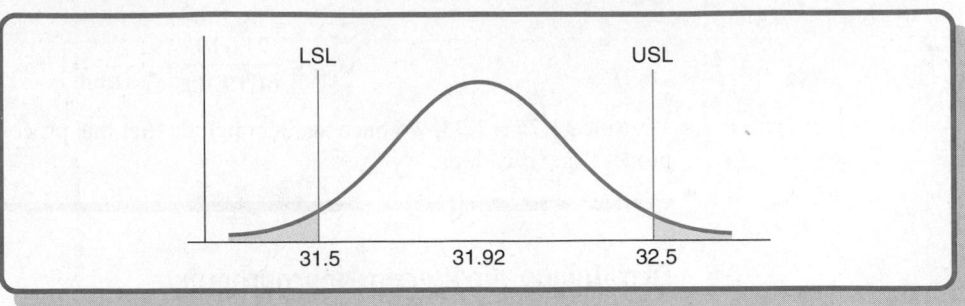

TABLE 12.4

Determining the number of nonconforming units per million produced using C_{pk}.

C_{pk}	Number of Nonconforming Units per Million Produced
.5	133,614
.75	24,448
1.00	2,700
1.30	96
1.50	6.8
2.00	.002

The standardized values for the spec limits are

$$\text{standardized LSL} = \frac{31.5 - 31.92}{.16} = -2.62$$

$$\text{standardized USL} = \frac{32.5 - 31.92}{.16} = 3.62$$

The proportion nonconforming will be

(the proportion to the left of −2.62 under a Z curve)

+ (the proportion to the right of 3.62 under a Z curve)

= .0044 + .0002 (approximately) = .0046

So, an estimated .46% of the oil containers will be nonconforming. At first glance, this appears to be a reasonably "small" number. However, when discussing the proportion of units nonconforming, it is common to talk in terms of number of units nonconforming *per million* units produced. For this example, the estimated number of nonconforming oil containers per million produced is (.0046)(1,000,000) or 4,600, a number that should be large enough to get management's attention.

The expected number of nonconforming units per million produced, *provided the process is centered in the specs,* can be estimated roughly from the value of C_{pk} using Table 12.4. This table is constructed using the procedure discussed in the previous example.

Since Table 12.4 assumes the process is centered exactly on target (midway between the spec limits), it provides a measure of the *potential* number of nonconforming units per million produced, given the variation of the process. Since the process in the previous example was very nearly centered on target (32 fluid ounces) with a C_{pk} of .88, we would expect Table 12.4 to provide a crude estimate of the number nonconforming, namely, between 2,700 and 24,448. The actual number of nonconforming units per million produced was estimated to be 4,600.

EXERCISES 12.45–12.55

UNDERSTANDING THE MECHANICS

12.45 What phenomena does process capability measure?

12.46 How does the measure of process capability C_{pm} differ from both C_p and C_{pk}?

12.47 For each of the following well-centered processes (i.e., A–D), a sample of size 325 is collected and the standard deviation of the process estimated. Calculate C_p, and indicate whether you believe the process capability to be "good," "adequate," or "inadequate."

Process	Specifications	Sample Standard Deviation
A	0.65 ± 0.07	0.03
B	29.3 ± 2.5	0.74
C	99.5 ± 7.2	1.11
D	0.25 ± 0.02	0.006

12.48 For each of the following processes (i.e., A–D), a sample of size 400 is collected in order to estimate the process mean and variability.

Process	Specifications	Mean	Sample Standard Deviation
A	124.0 ± 8.5	117.6	2.56
B	0.66 ± 0.08	0.67	0.022
C	89.2 ± 2.0	90.0	0.72
D	0.13 ± 0.03	0.132	0.009

a. Indicate which measure of process capability (C_p vs. C_{pk}) appears the more appropriate to use for each process, and state why.

b. Compute the appropriate measure of process capability for each process.

c. Using Table 12.4, estimate the number of nonconforming units per million for processes B and D.

12.49 Verify in equation 12.13 that

$$\frac{\Sigma(x-T)^2}{n-1} = s^2 + \frac{n(\bar{x}-T)^2}{n-1}$$

APPLYING THE NEW CONCEPTS

12.50 A process used to fill small cartridges with CO_2 has an upper specification limit of 250 psi (i.e., pounds per square inch). A sample of 150 CO_2 cartridges produces a sample mean of 228.8 psi and a standard deviation of 6.2 psi.

a. What is the capability ratio C_p for this process?

b. What proportion of the CO_2 cartridges will exceed the upper specification limit?

12.51 Answer the following questions using the data from Exercise 12.50.

a. Assuming that the process target is 225 psi, compute C_{pm}, considering only the upper specification limit.

b. Assuming that the process target is 229 psi, compute C_{pm}, considering only the upper specification limit.

c. What happens to C_{pm} as the process mean and target converge (i.e., get closer to one another), given a constant process variability?

12.52 In a process evaluation study, the lower glue joint gaps of corrugated boxes are measured in units of 1/128 inch. The process target is 31 units, and the specification limits are set at 31 ± 16 units. A sample of 160 total boxes is taken by selecting 16 samples of 10 boxes each. The following are the means and ranges for the 16 samples. You may assume that this process is in control. (Hint: $\hat{\sigma} = \bar{R}/d_2$)

Sample	Mean	Range	Sample	Mean	Range
1	27	9	9	29	10
2	28	12	10	32	15
3	30	14	11	30	18
4	36	20	12	31	19
5	35	22	13	29	9
6	33	18	14	34	21
7	34	16	15	35	19
8	30	12	16	36	20

(Source: Boris Iglewicz and David Hoaglin, "Use of Boxplots for Process Evaluation," *Journal of Quality Technology* 19, no. 4 (Oct. 1987): 180.)

a. Compute C_{pm} for this process.

b. Compute C_p for this process.

c. What is your assessment of the capability of this process?

d. Using Table 12.4, estimate the number of nonconforming units per million for this process.

e. Compute the number of nonconforming units.

12.53 A decision must be made between two experimental processes for producing silicon chips. The specification limits on the thickness of the chips is 0.125 ± 0.003 mm. Samples of 500 chips are drawn from experimental runs for each process, and means and standard deviations are recorded:

Process	Sample Mean	Sample Standard Deviation
A	0.1254	0.0008
B	0.1231	0.0003

a. Which of the two processes is better centered?

b. Calculate C_{pk} for both processes.

c. Which process do you recommend, and why?

12.54 Three processes in your manufacturing facility have been producing unacceptably high numbers of nonconforming parts. You have drawn normally distributed samples of 375 from each process. The sample means and standard deviations are as follows:

Process	Specifications	Sample Mean	Sample Standard Deviation
A	51.0 ± 1.2	51.2	1.1
B	102.5 ± 8.9	108.1	2.3
C	3.4 ± 0.5	3.7	0.4

a. Calculate the z-scores for the specification limits and the spread between specification limits (in standard deviations) for each process.

b. The plant manager wants to know your thoughts regarding this predicament. Considering the calculated z-scores and spreads, do you believe that the problem is attributable to improper centering of the process, excessive process variability, or both? Discuss your answer for each process individually.

12.55 [DATA SET EX12-55] *Variable description:*

Sample: Sample number
MeanFill: Mean amount filled in 2-liter container (in ml)
Range: Range of values for the amount filled in the 2-liter container

Rapid development and introduction of new brands and flavors of soft drinks require new and modified plant operations for handling the new product. New product lines require new processes, materials, packaging, and often new machinery. Statistical process control is used to measure and regulate performance of these new systems. A soft drink producer has introduced a new 2-liter container and purchased new filling machinery. The target fill for each container is 2 liters (2000 ml) plus or minus 5 ml. Five bottles are randomly sampled each hour, and the content volumes are measured. The data presented below for 30 hours of inspection would be typical of that found in a beverage manufacturing plant. Assuming the process is in control, determine the capability index or indices for the new machinery. What are your recommendations?

Sample	Mean Fill (ml)	Range
1	2002.1	3.7
2	2002.2	2.2
3	2002.6	2.6
4	2002.3	2.2
5	2002.6	2.1
6	2002.1	7.1

Sample	Mean Fill (ml)	Range
7	2002.1	4.4
8	2003.2	3.8
9	2002.1	1.4
10	2002.4	2.6
11	2002.5	4.1
12	2001.1	4.7
13	2003.2	3.1
14	2002.1	3.4
15	2001.6	3.7
16	2001.9	3.0
17	2002.7	2.3
18	2001.7	2.4
19	2003.9	1.8
20	2002.6	2.0
21	2001.6	3.3
22	2003.7	4.0
23	2003.3	7.1
24	2003.1	5.0
25	2001.5	4.5
26	2003.9	4.5
27	2002.9	2.8
28	2002.8	3.8
29	2003.0	4.0
30	2001.7	3.3

(Source: Adapted from "New Horizons in Beverage Manufacturing," *Beverage World,* July 15, 1997, p. 84–85.)

SUMMARY

American manufacturing and service industries are continuing to undergo an evolution that emphasizes quality. The need for tools to monitor quality has sparked a renewed interest in the everyday application of statistical thinking. Decisions are routinely based on *facts* gathered from sample data.

This chapter has examined both the management and the statistical sides of quality improvement. **Total Quality Management** (TQM) is a customer-focused management strategy that emphasizes a respect for employees and a constant effort at improving product or service quality. The basic philosophies of the early quality pioneers, **Deming, Juran,** and **Crosby,** were explained, noting both similarities and differences in their approaches to quality improvement.

Companies in the United States demonstrating a high degree of quality emphasis both internally and externally are recognized each year through the **Malcolm Baldrige National Quality Award** (MBNQA). Recipients of this award have exhibited and documented that they have a world-class system for managing their operations/ employees and satisfying their customers. The **ISO 9000**

guidelines require businesses to provide evidence of the establishment of a quality system that is understood and followed by all company employees. Registration to ISO 9000 standards increasingly is becoming a prerequisite for doing business. The Baldrige Award criteria are more customer focused, whereas ISO 9000 registration provides a common basis for assuring buyers that specific (documented) quality practices are being followed by their suppliers.

A **process** can be any combination of resources, such as people, machines, and/or material that lead to a product or service. **Statistical process control** (SPC) is the application of statistical procedures intended to measure, analyze, and control this process.

To monitor a process, you must first define what it is you wish to measure or count. For measurement data, what you are measuring is the **quality characteristic** and such measurements result in **variables data.** Examples of variables data include the weight or length of a manufactured unit. When counting, you obtain **attribute data,** such as the number of nonconformities per unit.

Two of the quality-improvement tools were explained in Chapter 2, namely, the **histogram** and **Pareto chart.** Two additional tools for describing a process were introduced in this chapter, the flowchart and the cause-and-effect diagram. A **flowchart** is a diagram of an entire process that can be used to view the process as a system and allow you to search for potential problem areas or opportunities for improvement. The **cause-and-effect diagram** can be used to represent the relationships between potential problems within a process and their possible causes.

Another quality-improvement tool, a **control chart,** can be set up to monitor a process to determine whether it is in control (stable) or out of control (unstable). Provided the plotted points for a control chart stay within the **upper control limit** (UCL) and the **lower control limit** (LCL), the process is exhibiting natural variation and is said to be in control. If a plotted point exceeds either of the limits, a search is made for an **assignable cause,** that is, an explanation (such as defective raw material) for this extreme value in the control chart. Control charts for variables data consist of the $\bar{X}$ **chart** for monitoring the process center and the R **chart** for monitoring the process variation. For attribute data, the most commonly used control charts are the p **chart** for observing and controlling the proportion of nonconforming units and the c **chart** for the number of nonconformities per unit.

Control charts enable the front-line worker to distinguish between random variation (**chance cause**) and that due to an assignable cause. One of Deming's main points is that a process should not be "tampered with" when it is exhibiting chance variation. This was illustrated using the **Deming funnel experiment,** which demonstrated how such manipulations will actually have an adverse effect on process variation.

For most production situations, a process must conform to certain requirements referred to as **specification (spec) limits.** These may be imposed by an outside purchaser or internally by the company's engineering staff. The ability of the process to conform to these specifications is the **process capability.** If a "large" percentage of the units produced can be expected to lie outside the spec limits, we would conclude that the process is not capable of performing to specification. Measures of process capability consist of the C_p ratio, which does not consider where the process is centered, the C_{pk} ratio, which does, and the C_{pm} ratio, which includes the effect of a drift away from the process target. The C_p ratio measures how well the process *should* perform (the difference of the spec limits) compared with how well the process *is* performing (the **process spread,** defined as 6 standard deviations).

SUMMARY OF FORMULAS

CONTROL CHARTS

1. $\bar{X}$ Chart:

$$UCL = \bar{\bar{X}} + 3\frac{\hat{\sigma}}{\sqrt{n}}$$

$$CL = \bar{\bar{X}}$$

$$LCL = \bar{\bar{X}} - 3\frac{\hat{\sigma}}{\sqrt{n}}$$

where $\bar{\bar{X}} = \sum \bar{X}_i/m$ and $\hat{\sigma} = \bar{R}/d_2$ (values of d_2 provided in Table 12.3).

2. R chart:

$$UCL = D_4\bar{R}$$

$$CL = \bar{R}$$

$$LCL = D_3\bar{R}$$

(values of D_3 and D_4 provided in Table 12.3).

3. p chart:

$$UCL = \bar{p} + 3\sqrt{\frac{\bar{p}(1-\bar{p})}{n}}$$

$$CL = \bar{p}$$

$$LCL = \bar{p} - 3\sqrt{\frac{\bar{p}(1-\bar{p})}{n}}$$

4. c chart:

$$UCL = \bar{c} + 3\sqrt{\bar{c}}$$

$$CL = \bar{c}$$

$$LCL = \bar{c} - 3\sqrt{\bar{c}}$$

where $\bar{c}$ = average number of nonconformities per unit.

PROCESS CAPABILITY

1. Process spread: $6\hat{\sigma}$ where $\hat{\sigma} = s$ (sample standard deviation).

2. $C_p = \dfrac{\text{USL} - \text{LSL}}{6\hat{\sigma}}$ (two-sided spec limit)

   $C_p = \dfrac{\text{USL} - \overline{X}}{3\hat{\sigma}}$ (upper spec limit only)

   $C_p = \dfrac{\overline{X} - \text{LSL}}{3\hat{\sigma}}$ (lower spec limit only)

3. C_{pk} = minimum of R_L and R_U where

   $R_L = \dfrac{\overline{X} - \text{LSL}}{3\hat{\sigma}}$ $R_U = \dfrac{\text{USL} - \overline{X}}{3\hat{\sigma}}$

4. $C_{pm} = \dfrac{\text{USL} - \text{LSL}}{6s'}$ where

   $s' = \sqrt{s^2 + \dfrac{n(\overline{x} - T)^2}{n-1}}$

   and T = process target = (USL + LSL)/2.

FURTHER READING

Crosby, Philip. *Quality is Still Free: Making Quality Certain in Uncertain Times,* New York: McGraw Hill, 1996.

Deming, W. Edwards. *Out of the Crisis,* Cambridge, MA: Mass. Institute of Technology, Center for Advanced Engineering Study, 1986.

Dobyns, Lloyd, and Clare Crawford-Mason. *Quality or Else: The Revolution in World Business,* Boston, MA: Houghton-Mifflin, 1993.

Juran, J. M. *Managerial Breakthrough,* New York: McGraw-Hill, 1995.

———. *Juran on Leadership for Quality,* New York: Free Press, 1989.

———. *Juran on Quality by Design,* New York: Free Press, 1992.

———. *Quality Control Handbook,* 4th ed. New York: McGraw-Hill, 1988.

Juran, J. M., and Frank M. Gryna. *Quality Planning and Analysis,* New York: McGraw-Hill, 1993.

Paradis, W. P., and Fen Small. *Demystifying ISO 9000,* Reading, MA: Addison-Wesley, 1996.

Rosander, A. C. *Deming's 14 Points Applied to Services,* Houston: Marcel-Dekker, 1991.

Stamatis, D. H. *Documenting and Auditing for ISO 9000 and QS 9000,* Burr Ridge, IL: Irwin Professional Publications, 1996.

Walton, Mary. *The Deming Management Method,* New York: Perigee Books, 1988.

OTHER TEXTBOOKS AND ARTICLES

Kane, V. E. "Process Capability Indices," *Journal of Quality Technology* 18, no. 1 (1986): 41.

Montgomery, D. C. *Introduction to Statistical Quality Control,* 3rd ed. New York: Wiley, 1996.

Shewhart, W. A. "Quality Control Charts," *Bell System Technical Journal* (1926).

Information on the Malcolm Baldrige National Quality Award: Malcolm Baldrige National Quality Award Office, NIST, Administration Bldg., Rm. A537, Gaithersburg, MD 20899-0001, (301) 975-2036.

REVIEW EXERCISES 12.56–12.73

12.56 What are the different types of variation? Are there differences in our ability to diagnose and control the different types of variation? Explain.

12.57 Identify the quality guru(s) associated with each of the following notions or terms.
   a. Management, particularly top management, is most responsible for poor quality.
   b. Fear can be channeled constructively into quality-improvement efforts.

c. Zero defects

d. The problem is the system, not the people.

e. Quality is free.

f. The use of statistical methods is imperative to quality improvement.

g. The overriding objective of quality improvement is to exceed customer requirements and expectations.

12.58 Under what conditions would C_p, C_{pk}, and C_{pm} all be equal?

12.59 Briefly explain, in one sentence each, the seven categories of the Malcolm Baldrige National Quality Award (MBNQA).

12.60 Chapter 3 presented the empirical rule, indicating that for a "bell-shaped" distribution, approximately 99.7 percent of all observations will lie within ± 3 standard deviations of the mean. Chapter 7 contained discussion showing the distribution of sample means taken from a normal distribution is also normal, with a mean equal to that of the parent distribution and a standard deviation of $\sigma / \sqrt{n}$ Briefly, discuss process control limits in terms of the Chapter 7 results.

12.61 Differentiate between specification limits and control limits. Is there a measure that conveys the relationship between the two? Explain.

12.62 Classify the following as attribute or variables data:

a. the refractive index of a lens

b. the number of typographical errors in a legal document

c. the number of defective tires in a production batch

d. the voltage output of a transformer

e. the torque of an electric motor

12.63 Explain the primary difference between the measures of process capability C_p and C_{pk}. When is each appropriate to use?

12.64 The specification limits for the tear strength of a cardboard container are 150 ± 2 ft-lb. A normally distributed sample of 100 containers yields a mean tear strength of 150.3 ft-lb with a standard deviation of 0.7 ft-lb.

a. Calculate C_{pk}.

b. Estimate the number of containers nonconforming per million by using Table 12.4.

c. Calculate the number of containers nonconforming per million.

12.65 The quality-improvement team at PQ Systems, Inc. (see Exercise 12.19), decided that it would concentrate on controlling the amount of time it took for a technical support analyst to resolve an outstanding call. Samples of six calls requiring follow-up were randomly selected for each of 20 days, and the response time noted. The following data represent the sample mean response times, in minutes, for the 20-day period. The mean range (i.e., $\overline{R}$) for the 20 samples is 78.52.

Day	Mean	Day	Mean
1	85	11	240
2	32	12	52
3	174	13	54
4	54	14	22
5	50	15	24
6	53	16	25
7	23	17	29
8	31	18	49
9	33	19	68
10	40	20	73

(Source: Barbara A. Cleary, "Company Cares About Customers' Calls," *Quality Progress* 26, no. 11 (Nov. 1993): 69–73.)

a. Construct an $\overline{X}$ chart that can be used to control call response times.

b. Perform a pattern analysis of the $\overline{X}$ chart from part (a) by checking for nonrandom patterns.

12.66 Indicate whether an $\overline{X}$, R, p, or c chart would be best for controlling:

a. the number of defective resistors in a container of 500 resistors

b. the mean cranking amperage of a sample of car batteries

c. the discrepancy in time it takes to perform an identical oil change

d. the number of scratches and other imperfections in an 8-foot $\times$ 4-foot sheet of paneling

e. the mean length of a sample of bolts

f. the number of nonconforming sprocket sets in a container of 250

12.67 A number of graphical tools for quality improvement were mentioned in this chapter. The following statements correspond to one of these tools. Identify the graphical tool associated with each statement.

    a. This tool shows the relationship, if any, between two variables.

    b. This tool graphically illustrates a process by showing the activities engaged in and decisions made.

    c. This tool can be used to monitor and control a process over time.

    d. This tool is used to identify the quality problem(s) with the largest impact.

    e. This tool shows the main/subcauses responsible for a quality problem.

12.68 Samples of five 100-pound bags of pinto beans are taken hourly and weighed. The mean weights of the last 16 samples are as follows. The mean range for the last 16 samples is 12.7 pounds ($\bar{R} = 12.7$).

Sample	Weight (Pounds)	Sample	Weight (Pounds)
1	102.3	9	100.8
2	99.8	10	100.2
3	101.8	11	103.2
4	99.2	12	100.5
5	103.1	13	98.2
6	102.5	14	96.4
7	98.7	15	92.3
8	103.1	16	89.9

    a. Construct an $\bar{X}$ chart using these data.

    b. Do you have any recommendations concerning this control chart?

12.69 Part of the processing of lumber involves kiln drying. Once the lumber is cut into boards, it is then stacked onto carts that are wheeled into the kiln for drying. In order that warm air can circulate between the boards, spacers are inserted between the boards, and the carts have pilings that elevate the stack of wood. It is critical that the spacers be placed precisely in line with each other so that the weight of the wood can be transferred to the pilings of the cart. If a spacer is out of line, weight will be transferred to the board itself, causing it to warp. The loss due to warpage in the average mill runs in the millions of dollars per year.

    Workers inspect the alignment of spacers by holding a straight stick (i.e., like a yardstick, but longer) against the side of the stack of wood. Any spacer not partially covered by the stick is considered misaligned. Each stack uses 360 spacers. The following data represent the number of misaligned spacers out of 360 for the last 14 carts inspected.

Cart	Misaligned Spacers	Cart	Misaligned Spacers
1	8	8	5
2	10	9	4
3	9	10	7
4	5	11	11
5	6	12	5
6	9	13	8
7	7	14	10

(Source: Robert G. Maki and Michael R. Milota, "Statistical Quality Control Applied to Lumber Drying," *Quality Process* 26, no. 12 (Dec. 1993): 75–79.)

    a. What type of chart is appropriate to use in this instance?

    b. Construct the appropriate control chart.

    c. Is this process in control or out of control?

12.70 The lower specification limit for an inflatable air bladder to be used in an automobile seat is 230 psi. A sample of 100 bladders failed at a mean of 236.1 psi with a standard deviation of 1.8 psi.

    a. Calculate the process capability ratio C_p.

    b. What proportion of the air bladders will fail at less than 230 psi?

12.71 The Palmer House, a landmark Chicago hotel, periodically receives complaints from guests regarding low water pressure. To remedy the problem, the engineering department can adjust the flow of water, therefore water pressure, to the various floors of the hotel. Management wishes to establish a control chart to control the number of complaints about low water pressure. It is decided that the number of complaints received per day will be recorded by floor of the hotel. The following are the number of complaints received per floor (10 in all) for the last two days.

Sample	Complaints	Sample	Complaints	Sample	Complaints
1	3	8	2	15	4
2	1	9	1	16	4
3	0	10	0	17	0
4	2	11	4	18	2
5	5	12	3	19	2
6	0	13	2	20	1
7	2	14	1		

a. What type of chart is appropriate to use in this instance?

b. Construct the appropriate control chart.

c. Plot the data and control limits. Is this process in control or out of control?

12.72 Rural ambulance and rescue squads are largely staffed by volunteer emergency medical technicians (EMTs). As the number of rural jobs decline and EMTs begin commuting to work in more populated areas, ambulance and rescue services find it increasingly difficult responding to all calls. The chief of one such rural squad used control charts to gain a better understanding of her community's need for service and to improve the squad's ability to respond to all calls. The control chart below shows the number of daily calls for which the squad was unable to respond ("dropped calls") over a seven-week period. Comment on any patterns that you observe. What recommendations would you make? (Hint: Look for a cyclical pattern.) Note that this example illustrates that control charts are useful to service organizations as well as to manufacturing-oriented organizations.

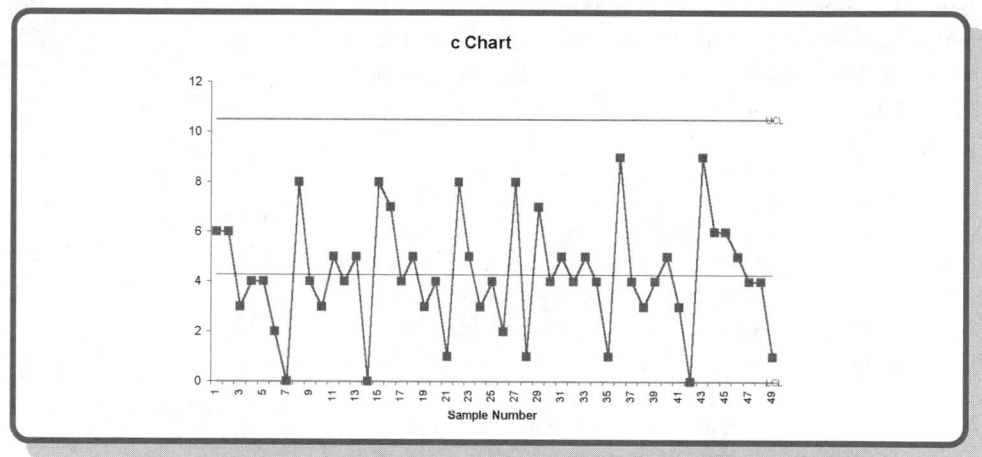

12.73 [DATA SET EX12-73] *Variable description:*

WidthCircuit: The width of a circuit path in a computer chip (in microns)

A computer chip manufacturer monitors the quality of its computer chips by selecting a batch of 10 computer chips and measuring the width of the circuit path. If this path is too wide or too narrow, the computer CPU may malfunction. Is there a pattern that may indicate that the following $\bar{X}$ chart, in which 30 batches were sampled, is out of control? Construct an R chart and explain if there is a similar indication that the process is out of control.

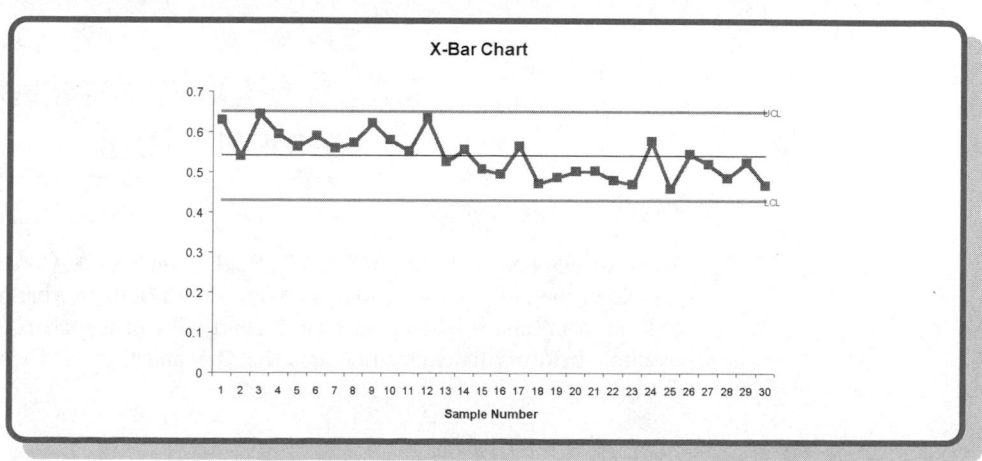

The Statistics in Action case study at the start of this chapter discussed the efforts of several companies to implement the Six Sigma concept into their production processes. In essence, this policy states that a single-sided spec limit is at least six standard deviations (sigmas) away from the mean, allowing for a 1.5 sigma shift for the process average. This rather convoluted concept has come under fire by authorities in the field (see "The Confusion over Six-Sigma Quality" in *Quality Progress,* Vol. 27, No. 11, Nov. 1994, p. 83–85.) The defect rates of 3.4 parts per million (Six-Sigma) and 6,210 parts per million (four-sigma) mentioned in the opening Statistics in Action discussion, are the results of this definition of K-sigma quality (for any $K = 1, 2, 3, \ldots$), first introduced by Motorola Corporation.

Using this definition, one would subtract 1.5 from the value of K and examine the standard normal (Z) curve to the right of $K - 1.5$. For example, for a Six-Sigma policy, examine the area to the right of $6 - 1.5 = 4.5$ under the Z curve. This is .0000034, which translates to 3.4 nonconforming parts per million or "being 99.9997% perfect." Similarly, for a four-sigma plan, the number of nonconforming items per million is $P(Z > 2.5) \times 10^6 = 6,210$.

Assessing the capability of a system is part of the Six Sigma movement. Consider a process evaluation study in which the lower glue gaps of corrugated boxes are measured in units of 1/128 inch. The process target is 31 units and the specification limits are set at 31 ± 16 units. A sample of 160 total boxes is taken by selecting 16 samples of 10 boxes each. The following are the means and ranges for the 16 samples. You may assume that this process is in control. (Hint: $\hat{\sigma} = \bar{R}/d_2$.)

INSIGHTS FROM STATISTICS IN ACTION: SIX SIGMA MEANS BEING 99.9997% PERFECT

Sample	Mean	Range
1	27	9
2	28	12
3	30	14
4	36	20
5	35	22
6	33	18
7	34	16
8	30	12
9	29	10
10	32	15
11	30	18
12	31	19
13	29	9
14	34	21
15	35	19
16	36	20

1. Compute C_{pm} for this process.
2. Compute C_p for this process.
3. What is your assessment of the capability of this process?
4. Using Table 12.4, estimate the number of nonconforming boxes per million produced for this process. Is this process meeting the six sigma requirements?
5. Compute the number of nonconforming boxes per million produced.
6. What recommendations and comments would you provide to management?

Sources: *USA Today,* "Firms Aim for Six Sigma Efficiency," July 21, 1998, p. 1B. *Journal of Quality Technology,* "Use of Boxplots for Process Evaluations," Vol. 19, No. 4, Oct. 1987, p. 180, Reprinted with permission.

CHAPTER 12 APPENDIX: DATA ANALYSIS WITH MINITAB

QUALITY IMPROVEMENT

To construct a control chart in MINITAB, click on **Stat ➤ Control Charts,** and then click on one of the options listed, such as **Xbar-R** (for both an *X*bar and an *R* chart), **Xbar** (for only an *X*bar chart), **R** (for only an *R* chart), **P** (for a *p* chart), or **C** (for a *c* chart). The example below will demonstrate only the *X*bar and *R* chart. The user form for the *X*bar and

R chart is displayed below using the coffee data in Example 12.2. The two control charts are illustrated immediately following. The data can be inputted in one column, and the size of each sample can be typed in the option box labeled **Subgroup size.**

The Xbar and R charts are typically used to track the process level and process variation for samples of less than or equal to 10. Otherwise, the Xbar and S charts should be used. MINITAB's Xbar and R charts use the estimate of the process variation, σ, based on the subgroup ranges. However, an option is to use a pooled standard deviation or an historical value for σ.

Similar charts can be obtained for p charts and c charts. To test for patterns in the Xbar chart, click on **Tests,** click on **Perform all Eight Tests,** and **OK.** Then click on **Estimate,** and under **Methods of Estimating Sigma,** click on **Rbar** and then **OK.** Finally, click on **Options,** and in the **Sigma Limit Positions** box, enter "1 2 3." The resulting MINITAB output was previously introduced in Figure 12.13. To examine the process capability of a process, click on **Stat ► Quality Tools,** and select **Capability Analysis (Normal).** Enter the lower and upper spec limits as "49" and "51," respectively. To enter the target value of "50," click on **Options** and enter this value in the target box. The output for the example with 20 samples of coffee data is displayed below the capability analysis user form.

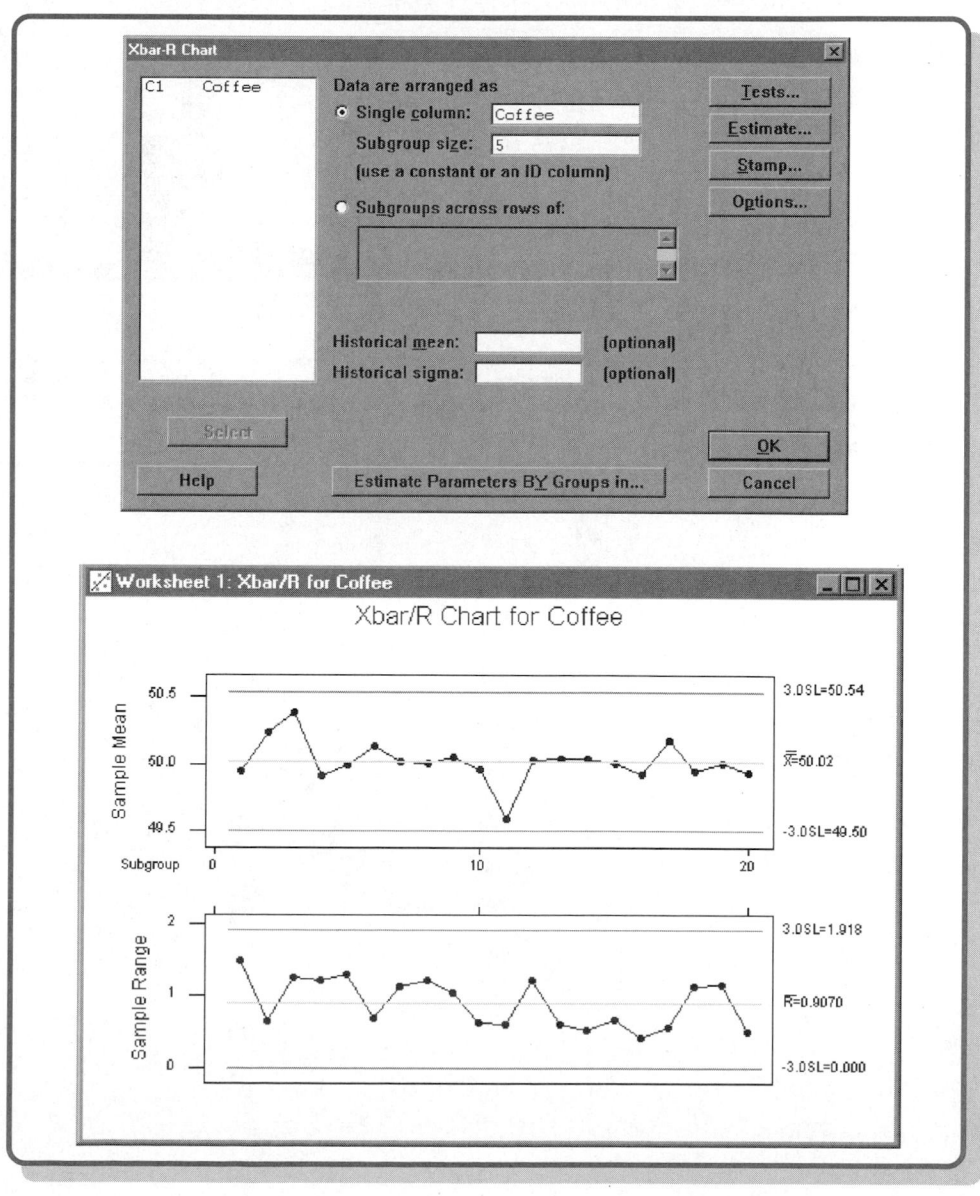

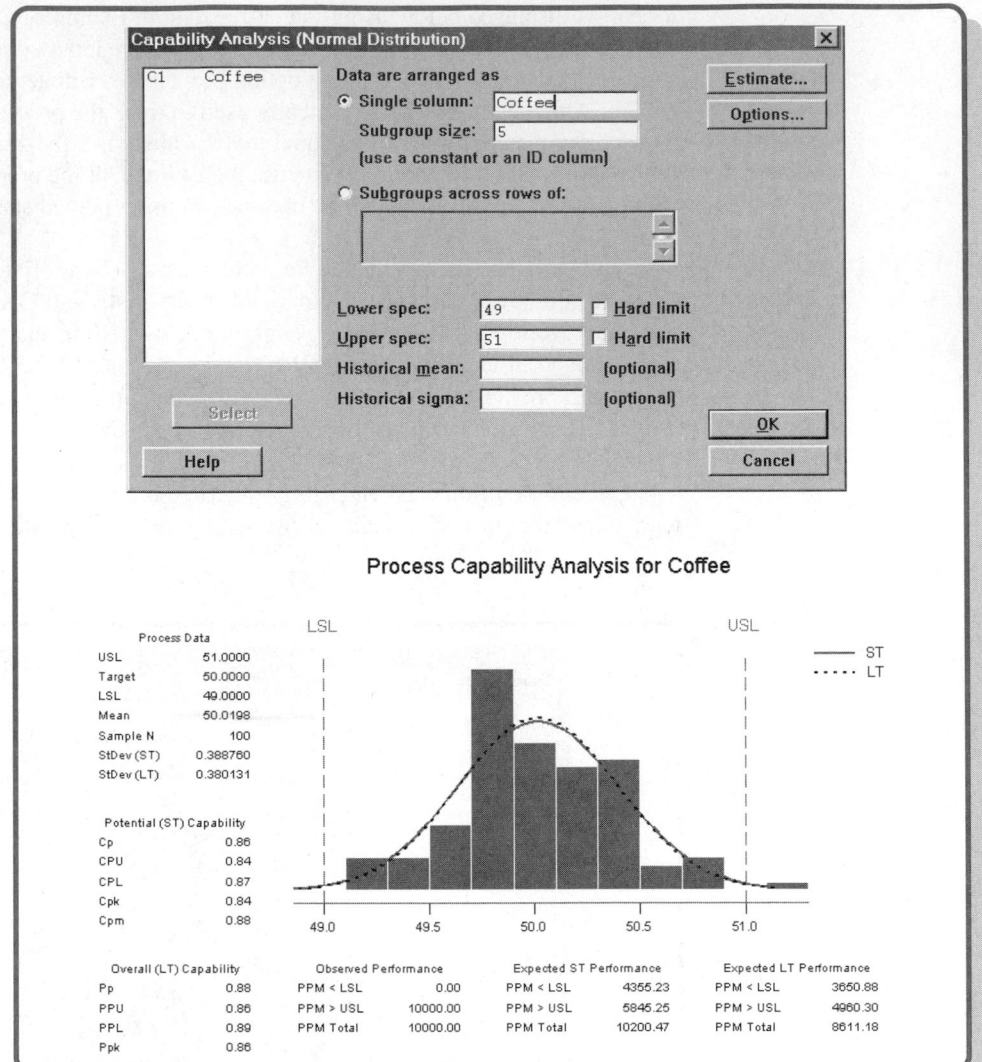

Process Capability Analysis for Coffee

APPLICATIONS OF THE CHI-SQUARE STATISTIC

STATISTICS IN ACTION: BUYING AND SELLING VACATIONS IN THE CORPORATE WORKPLACE

Approximately 24% of large companies are buying and selling vacations. Human resource experts are examining the relationships between characteristics of an employee's job (such as salary and length of time on the job) and their participation in buying and selling vacation programs within the corporation. When offered, approximately 25% of the employees usually participate. Although buying and selling unused vacation days can bring a financial windfall, only 6% of the workers are estimated to have sold vacations, while 24% buy more vacation days. Some companies, such as 7-Eleven, allow workers to buy and sell vacations via an automated telephone menu system. Some 5,000 transactions take place annually.

Buying and selling vacation days like a commodity is very popular at Freddie Mac, where every full-time employee gets two week's paid vacation. Some 82% of the employees participate in buying or selling back unused days. For some workers, the vacation days are like a savings plan. When big bills arrive, they sell their vacation days. While employees generally enjoy the flexibility of buying and selling vacation days, there are potential problems with excessive buying and selling. Allowing too many employees to buy an excessive number of vacation days can leave staffs too thin to have time off for vacations already bought.

Selling vacation days is most popular among highly compensated executives who usually have less opportunity to take a vacation. Texas Instruments pays only 75% for unused vacation days because the company encourages its employees to take time off. Buying extra days of vacation can be painful to employees whose salary is just barely sufficient to meet expenses.

How would you determine if the number of employees that participate in such a program is related to the

number of years that they have been with the company? Or if the number of bought vacation days is related to salary? This chapter introduces *tests of independence* and will enable you to:

- Determine if two classifications are independent (not related);
- Measure the strength of the relationship between two classifications using a test of hypothesis and corresponding *p*-value; and
- Determine if the proportions of employees purchasing vacation days across different salary levels is the same this year as last year, based on a sample of current employees.

A LOOK BACK/INTRODUCTION

We have now examined several topics in *descriptive* and *inferential* statistics. The descriptive area introduced you to both the numeric methods (for example, mean, median, and variance) and the graphic methods (for example, histogram and scatter diagram) of describing data. In inferential statistics, we discussed point estimation, confidence intervals, and tests of hypothesis. In the remaining chapters, we turn our attention to other applications of the material from these earlier chapters.

In Chapter 8, we introduced the chi-square (χ^2) distribution. We used this distribution to test that the variance of a normal distribution was equal to a specified value. The shape of the chi-square distribution is skewed right (with a right tail) and is nonnegative. The shape of a chi-square curve and areas (probabilities) under such a curve are contained in Table A.6. The test statistic in Chapter 8 had a chi-square distribution. This chapter introduces you to additional applications of statistics by using the chi-square distribution to answer such questions as:

> Do reported percentages of market share accurately describe the product mix for the new cars sold this past year in Minneapolis, Minnesota?

> Does a person's age have an influence on buying behavior?

13.1 CHI-SQUARE GOODNESS-OF-FIT TESTS

THE BINOMIAL SITUATION

In the binomial situation (introduced in Chapter 5) the following four conditions must be satisfied:

1. The experiment consists of n repetitions, called *trials*.
2. The trials are *independent*.
3. Each trial has two (and only two) possible outcomes, referred to as *success* and *failure*.
4. The probability of a success for each trial is p, where p remains the same for each trial. For a large finite population, p is the *proportion* of successes in this population.

Consequently, the binomial distribution applies to applications where there are only two possible outcomes, such as:

The person selected is a male or a female.

The product tested is either defective or not defective.

A new-car buyer buys either an American-made car or a foreign-made car.

INFERENCES FOR THE BINOMIAL SITUATION

Estimating the binomial parameter, p, was covered in Chapter 10. We obtained a random sample of size n and observed the number of successes, x. The estimator of p, the proportion of successes in the *population*, was $\hat{p} = x/n =$ the proportion of successes in the *sample*. We also discussed hypothesis testing for p. For example, we discussed a binomial situation in which a calculator was either defective (with probability p) or not defective. The hypothetical value of p was .04, and we determined whether the results of the sample (13 defectives out of 150) indicated a departure from this percentage. Here $\hat{p} = 13/150 = .0867$. So, 8.67% of the sampled calculators were defective. Is this percentage large enough for us to conclude that p is different from .04, or is this large value of $\hat{p}$ just due to the fact that we tested a sample and not the entire population—that is, is this sampling error?

The resulting value of the test statistic was

$$Z^* = \frac{\hat{p} - .04}{\sqrt{\dfrac{(.04)(.96)}{150}}} = \frac{.0867 - .04}{.016} = 2.92$$

By comparing $Z^* = 2.92$ with the value 1.96 in Table A.4, we rejected H_0 using $\alpha = .05$; that is, the proportion of defective calculators was not 4%. The corresponding p-value was .0036.

ANOTHER TEST FOR $H_0: p = p_0$ VERSUS $H_a: p \neq p_0$

There is another test for a *two-tailed* test on p. This new test extends easily to a situation in which there are *more than two possible outcomes* for each trial: the **multinomial situation.**

To demonstrate this new testing procedure, the **chi-square goodness-of-fit** test, let's look at the lot sampling example. Note that the population consists of two **categories**—defective (category 1) and nondefective (category 2). Let $p_1 =$ the proportion of defectives in the population and $p_2 =$ the proportion of nondefectives in the population. In the previous solution, $p_1 = p$ and $p_2 = 1 - p$.

We *observed* 13 sample values in category 1 (defective) and 137 in category 2. So define

$$O_1 = 13$$

$$O_2 = 137$$

How many units do we *expect* to see in each category if H_0 is *true?* The hypotheses here can be written

$$H_0: p_1 = .04, p_2 = .96$$

$$H_a: p_1 \neq .04, p_2 \neq .96$$

This means that if H_0 is true, then, on the average, 4% of the sample values should be defective (category 1) and 96% should be nondefective (category 2). Define

$E_1 =$ expected number of sample values in category 1 if H_0 is true

$\quad = (150)(.04) = 6.0$

$E_2 =$ expected number of sample values in category 2 if H_0 is true

$\quad = (150)(.96) = 144.0$

We next define a test statistic that has an approximate chi-square distribution:

$$\chi^2 = \sum \frac{(O - E)^2}{E} \tag{13.1}$$

where the summation is over all categories (two here). In previous uses of this distribution, its shape depended on the sample size, specified by the degrees of freedom (df). Now the shape depends on the number of categories, and

$$df = \text{number of categories} - 1$$

For the binomial situation,

$$df = 2 - 1 = 1$$

Therefore, for any *binomial* application, the test statistic in equation 13.1 has a *chi-square distribution with 1 df.*

EXAMPLE 13.1

Analyze the lot sampling data using the chi-square test statistic and a significance level of $\alpha = .05$.

SOLUTION

Step 1. The hypotheses are

$$H_0: p_1 = .04, p_2 = .96$$

$$H_a: p_1 \neq .04, p_2 \neq .96$$

Step 2. The test statistic is

$$\chi^2 = \sum \frac{(O-E)^2}{E}$$

$$= \frac{(O_1 - E_1)^2}{E_1} + \frac{(O_2 - E_2)^2}{E_2}$$

Step 3. If H_0 is not true (H_a is true), we expect the observed values to be different from the expected values, resulting in a *large* value for χ^2. So the procedure is to reject H_0 if the chi-square test statistic lies in the *right* tail. Consequently, we

reject H_0 if $\chi^2 > \chi^2_{.05,1}$

where $\chi^2_{.05,1}$ is the χ^2 value having a right-tail area of .05 with 1 df. Using Table A.6, this value is 3.84. Therefore, we

reject H_0 if $\chi^2 > 3.84$

Step 4. We have

$$O_1 = 13 \qquad E_1 = 6$$

$$O_2 = 137 \qquad E_2 = 144$$

(Note that $O_1 + O_2 = E_1 + E_2 = n = 150$.) The calculated value of the test statistic is

$$\chi^{2}* = \frac{(13-6)^2}{6} + \frac{(137-144)^2}{144}$$

$$= 8.17 + .34 = 8.51$$

This value is larger than 3.84, so we rejected H_0.

Step 5. We conclude, as before, that the proportion of defectives (p_1) is not .04.

The *p*-value for Example 13.1 using the chi-square analysis is shown in Figure 13.1; it is the shaded area to the right of 8.51. Using Table A.6, all we can say is that this value is less than .005. The actual value is .0036 (calculated using a statistical software package). This is the *same* p-value we obtained when $Z*$ was used to perform this test of hypothesis.

In the lot sampling example, we observe some quite fascinating (would you believe mildly interesting?) parallels with Chapter 11. In Chapter 11, we noted that when using the F-test from the ANOVA procedure to test $H_0: \mu_1 = \mu_2$, we obtained an F-value that was the *square* of the t value obtained using the corresponding t test. Also, the value from the F table used to define the rejection region was the square of the corresponding t value. This relationship held only when testing the equality of two means. Finally, the *p*-values from the two tests were identical; it made no difference which test we used for a two-tailed test on two means because the results were the same for both procedures. However, the ANOVA technique also could be used for comparing the means of more than two populations.

FIGURE 13.1

p-value for Example 13.1 using the chi-square analysis.

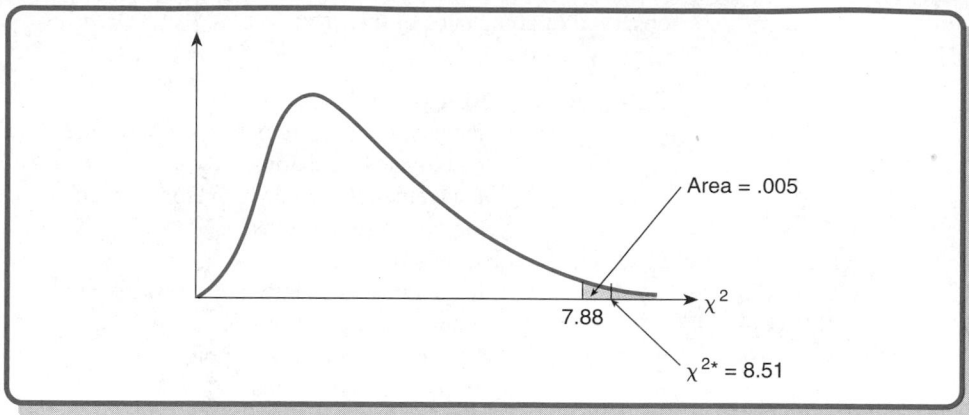

Using the results from the lot-sampling example in this chapter, we again find that:

1. $\chi^{2*} = 8.51 = (2.92)^2 = (Z^*)^2$.
2. The table values for the rejection region are 1.96 for the Z test and $3.84 = (1.96)^2$ for the χ^2 test.
3. The *p*-value for each test was the same.

So again we have two testing procedures that produce identical conclusions. *The chi-square test, however, extends easily to the multinomial situation.* The chi-square goodness-of-fit test is an *extension* of the Z test used to test a binomial parameter. Furthermore, there is a definite relationship between the standard normal distribution (Z) and the chi-square distribution: the *square* of Z always is a chi-square random variable with 1 df.

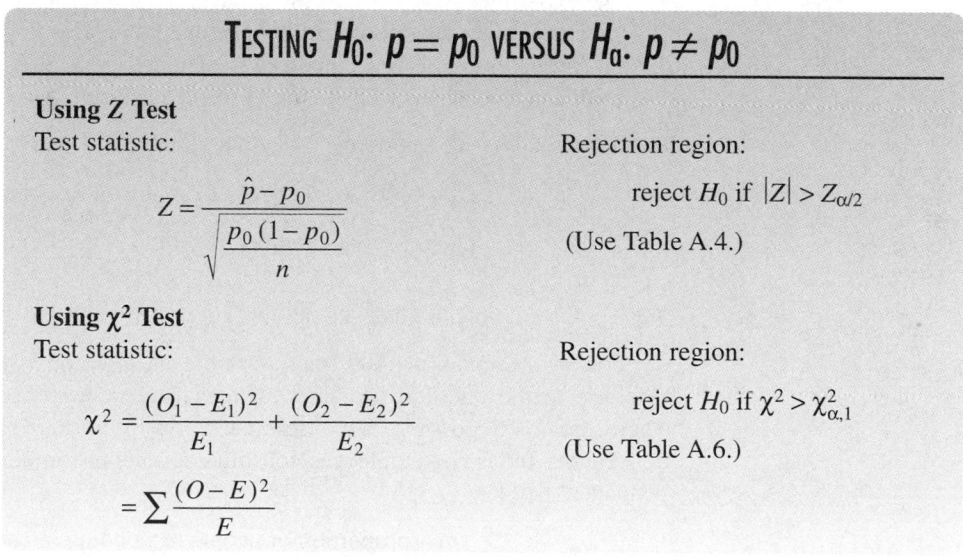

TESTING $H_0: p = p_0$ VERSUS $H_a: p \neq p_0$

Using Z Test

Test statistic:

$$Z = \frac{\hat{p} - p_0}{\sqrt{\dfrac{p_0(1 - p_0)}{n}}}$$

Rejection region:

reject H_0 if $|Z| > Z_{\alpha/2}$

(Use Table A.4.)

Using χ^2 Test

Test statistic:

$$\chi^2 = \frac{(O_1 - E_1)^2}{E_1} + \frac{(O_2 - E_2)^2}{E_2}$$

$$= \sum \frac{(O - E)^2}{E}$$

Rejection region:

reject H_0 if $\chi^2 > \chi^2_{\alpha,1}$

(Use Table A.6.)

THE MULTINOMIAL SITUATION

The multinomial situation is identical to the binomial situation, except that there are k possible outcomes on each trial rather than two. Here, k is any integer that is at least 2.

Suppose that the management of Tucker Industries is concerned with how company employees feel about management; in particular, do the employees feel that management is responsive to employee suggestions? A quality consultant has informed the Tucker team charged with examining this situation that traditionally the following percentages are observed in companies of this size:

Category	Description	Percentage of Employees in this Category
1	Management is extremely responsive to employee suggestions	.05
2	Management is somewhat responsive to employee suggestions	.30
3	No opinion	.20
4	Management is usually not responsive to employee suggestions	.40
5	Management is rarely responsive to employee suggestions	.05

The Tucker team would like to verify these percentages among their own employees and obtains responses to the question "Is management responsive to employee suggestions?" from a random sample of 500 employees. Possible responses to this question are the five categories just listed, and the following frequencies are observed in each category for this sample:

Category	Frequency
1	32
2	142
3	87
4	221
5	18
	500

The assumptions necessary for a multinomial experiment are:

1. The experiment consists of n independent repetitions (trials).
2. Each trial outcome falls in exactly one of k categories.
3. The probabilities of the k outcomes are denoted by $p_1, p_2, \ldots, p_k$, where these probabilities (proportions) remain the same on each trial. Also, $p_1 + p_2 + \cdots + p_k = 1$.

For this situation, we can define k random variables as the k observed values, where

$$O_1 = \text{observed number of sample values in category 1}$$

$$O_2 = \text{observed number of sample values in category 2}$$

$$\vdots$$

$$O_k = \text{observed number of sample values in category } k$$

For our example, $n = 500$ trials, where each trial consists of obtaining an employee response to the question dealing with management response to employee suggestions. There are $k = 5$ possible responses (categories) for this experiment. Assuming these 500 Tucker Industries employees constitute a random sample, then these trials are independent. Also, let:

$$p_1 = \text{proportion of people responding in category 1}$$

$$p_2 = \text{proportion of people responding in category 2}$$

$$\vdots$$

$$p_5 = \text{proportion of people responding in category 5}$$

The five random variables in our example are:

$$O_1 = \text{observed number of Tucker employees in the sample responding in category 1}$$

$$\vdots$$

$$O_5 = \text{observed number of Tucker employees in the sample responding in category 5}$$

Thus this example fits the assumptions for the multinomial situation.

HYPOTHESIS TESTING FOR A MULTINOMIAL SITUATION

The hypotheses for the Tucker Industries example are

$$H_0: p_1 = .05, p_2 = .30, p_3 = .20, p_4 = .40, p_5 = .05$$

$$H_a: \text{at least one of the } p_i\text{'s is incorrect}$$

Notice that H_a is *not* $p_1 \neq .05$, $p_2 \neq .30$, . . . , $p_5 \neq .05$. This hypothesis is too strong and is not the opposite of H_0.

Let $p_{1,0}$ be any specified value of p_1, $p_{2,0}$ any specified value of p_2, and so on. The hypotheses to test the multinomial parameters are

$$H_0: p_1 = p_{1,0}, p_2 = p_{2,0}, \quad . . . \quad , p_k = p_{k,0}$$

$$H_a: \text{at least one of the } p_i\text{'s is incorrect}$$

Using the observed values $(O_1, O_2, . . .)$, the point estimates here are

$$\hat{p}_1 = \text{estimate of } p_1 = O_1/n$$

$$\hat{p}_2 = \text{estimate of } p_2 = O_2/n$$

$$\vdots$$

To test H_0 versus H_a, we use the previously stated chi-square statistic. To define the rejection region, notice that when H_a is true, we would expect the O's and E's to be "far apart," because the E's are determined by assuming that H_0 is true. In other words, if H_a is true, the chi-square test statistic should be large. Consequently, we always reject H_0 when χ^{2*} lies in the *right tail* when using this particular statistic.

To test H_0 versus H_a, compute

$$\chi^2 = \sum \frac{(O - E)^2}{E} \qquad\qquad (13.2)$$

where

1. The summation is across all categories (outcomes).
2. The O's are the *observed* frequencies in each category using the sample.
3. The E's are the *expected* frequencies in each category if H_0 is true, so

$$E_1 = np_{1,0}$$

$$E_2 = np_{2,0}$$

$$E_3 = np_{3,0}$$

$$\vdots$$

4. The df for the chi-square statistic are $k - 1$, where k is the number of categories.

To carry out the test,

$$\text{reject } H_0 \text{ if } \chi^2 > \chi^2_{\alpha,df}$$

Notice that the hypothetical proportions (probabilities) for each of the categories are specified in H_0. Consequently, we will complete the analysis by concluding that at least one of the proportions is incorrect (we reject H_0) or that there is not enough evidence to conclude that these proportions are incorrect (we fail to reject H_0). We do not *accept H_0*: we never conclude that these specified proportions *are* correct. We act like the juror who acquits a defendant not because he or she is convinced that this person is innocent but rather because there was not sufficient evidence for conviction.

When we introduced the ANOVA technique, we mentioned that this procedure allowed us to determine whether many population means were equal using a *single* test. This technique was preferable to using many *t* tests to test the equality of two means, one pair at a time, because these tests would not be independent, and the overall significance level would be difficult to determine. We encounter the same situation here. *It is much better to use a chi-square goodness-to-fit test to test* all *of the proportions at once rather than using many Z tests to test the individual proportions.*

EXAMPLE 13.2

What do the observed number of Tucker Industries employees in each category for the sample of 500 employees tell us about the mix of responses to this question for all Tucker employees? Do they conform to the percentages cited by the quality consultant? Use a significance level of .05.

SOLUTION

Step 1. Let p_1 = proportion of all Tucker employees that would respond in category 1 to this question; that is, they feel that management is extremely responsive to employee suggestions. Similarly, define p_2, p_3, p_4, and p_5 to be the corresponding percentages for categories 2, 3, 4, and 5. The hypotheses under investigation are:

$$H_0: p_1 = .05, p_2 = .30, p_3 = .20, p_4 = .40, p_5 = .05$$

$$H_a: \text{at least one of these } p_i\text{'s is incorrect}$$

Step 2. The test statistic is

$$\chi^2 = \sum \frac{(O-E)^2}{E}$$

where the summation is over the five categories.

Step 3. Your test procedure here is to

$$\text{reject } H_0 \text{ if } \chi^2 > \chi^2_{\alpha,df}$$

The df is (number of categories) − 1, so df = 5 − 1 = 4. The chi-square value from Table A.6 is $\chi^2_{.05,4} = 9.49$, and we

$$\text{reject } H_0 \text{ if } \chi^2 > 9.49$$

Step 4. The observed values are

$$O_1 = 32, O_2 = 142, O_3 = 87, O_4 = 221, O_5 = 18$$

The expected values when H_0 is true are obtained by multiplying $n = 500$ by each of the proportions in H_0. So

$$E_1 = (500)(.05) = 25$$

$$E_2 = (500)(.30) = 150$$

$$E_3 = (500)(.20) = 100$$

$$E_4 = (500)(.40) = 200$$

$$E_5 = (500)(.05) = 25$$

In general, do not round the expected values, because they are averages.
   The computed value of the chi-square test statistic is

$$\chi^2* = \frac{(32-25)^2}{25} + \frac{(142-150)^2}{150} + \frac{(87-100)^2}{100} + \frac{(221-200)^2}{200} + \frac{(18-25)^2}{25}$$

$$= 8.242$$

Because 8.242 does not exceed 9.49, we fail to reject H_0.

Step 5. There is insufficient evidence to indicate that the proportion of Tucker employees in each response category differs from the proportions stated by the quality consultant. In other words, the observed values were "close enough" to the expected values under H_0 to let this hypothesis stand. Examining categories 4 and 5, this indicates that 45% of the Tucker employees feel that management is not responsive on some level to employee suggestions. Obviously, there is a great deal of room for improvement in this area of management relations.

In Example 13.2, the proportions under investigation were specified directly. We can also use the chi-square statistic when the proportions are implied.

EXAMPLE 13.3

Allied Health Corporation owns and operates hospitals in the southeast. Three of their hospitals were recently audited by federal auditors to determine if the three hospitals were in compliance with Medicare billing regulations. According to the auditors, a billing selected for audit had an equal probability of being from each of the three hospitals. A random sample of the audited billings revealed the following number of billings selected from each hospital: hospital 1: 485, hospital 2: 405, hospital 3: 310; total = 1200. Using a significance level of .01, what can you conclude about the auditors' selection of billings?

SOLUTION

Step 1. Let p_1 = proportion of audited billings from hospital 1, p_2 = proportion from hospital 2, and p_3 = proportion from hospital 3. If an audited billing has an equal probability of belonging to each hospital, then each of these proportions will be 1/3, providing the values for H_0:

$$H_0: p_1 = 1/3, p_2 = 1/3, p_3 = 1/3$$

$$H_a: \text{at least one of these proportions is incorrect}$$

Steps 2, 3. The test procedure will be to

$$\text{reject } H_0 \text{ if } \chi^2 > \chi^2_{.01,2} = 9.21$$

because df $= k - 1 = 3 - 1 = 2$. The value of χ^2 is determined from equation 13.2.

Step 4. The observed and expected values are

O	E (if H_0 is true)	$\hat{p}$
$O_1 =$ 485	$E_1 = (1200)(1/3) =$ 400	485/1200 = .404
$O_2 =$ 405	$E_2 = (1200)(1/3) =$ 400	405/1200 = .338
$O_3 =$ 310	$E_3 = (1200)(1/3) =$ 400	310/1200 = .258
1200	1200	1.0

$$\chi^{2*} = \frac{(485-400)^2}{400} + \frac{(405-400)^2}{400} + \frac{(310-400)^2}{400}$$

$$= 18.06 + .06 + 20.25 = 38.4$$

So we reject H_0 because $38.4 > 9.21$.

Step 5. There *is* an unequal distribution of hospital selection here. Your next step should be to examine the three values making up this large χ^2 value. This large value is due to the 18.06 (the number of billings from hospital 1 was larger than expected under H_0) and the 20.25 (the number of billings from hospital 3 was smaller than expected under H_0). This discrepancy can also be seen in the values of $\hat{p}$ from step 4.

The p-value for the results in Example 13.3 is shown in Figure 13.2. Using Table A.6 and 2 df, the largest value here is 10.6, with a corresponding right-tail area of .005. All you can say using this table is that the p-value is less than .005. At any rate, it is small and would lead you to reject H_0 for the most common values of α.

FIGURE 13.2
Shaded area is *p*-value for
Example 13.3.

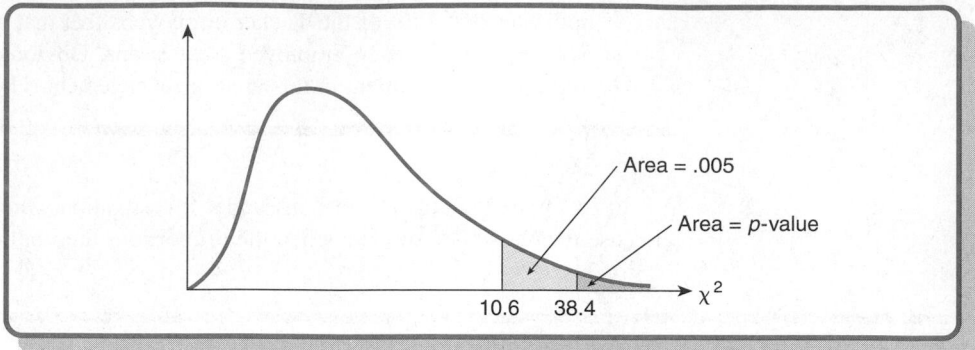

POOLING CATEGORIES

When using the chi-square procedure of comparing observed and expected values, we determine the difference between these two values for each category, square it, and *divide by the expected value, E.* If one value of E is very small (say, less than 5), then this computation produces an extremely *large* contribution to the final χ^2 value from this category. In other words, this small expected value produces an inflated chi-square value, with the result that we reject H_0 when perhaps we should not have. To prevent this from occurring, we use the following rule: When using equation 13.2, each expected value, E, should be at least 5.*

If you encounter an application where one or more of the expected values is less than 5, you can handle this situation by *pooling* your categories such that each of the new categories has an expected value that is at least 5.

EXAMPLE 13.4

The analysis in Example 13.2 was repeated for Metro Elevators, a small subsidiary of Tucker Industries. Metro installs and repairs escalators and elevators for use in commercial buildings. Independent of the Tucker sample in Example 13.2, Metro obtained a random sample of 75 of their employees, since they suspected that their responses to the question dealing with how well management responds to employee suggestions would be considerably different from the stated proportions in Example 13.2. The following data were obtained:

Category	Frequency
1	9
2	31
3	12
4	18
5	5
	75

Do the data from Metro appear to contradict the stated proportions in Example 13.2? Use $\alpha = .05$.

SOLUTION

Category	Observed (O)	Expected (E), if H_0 is True
1	$O_1 = 9$	$E_1 = (75)(.05) = 3.75$
2	$O_2 = 31$	$E_2 = (75)(.30) = 22.50$
3	$O_3 = 12$	$E_3 = (75)(.20) = 15.00$
4	$O_4 = 18$	$E_4 = (75)(.40) = 30.00$
5	$O_5 = 5$	$E_5 = (75)(.05) = 3.75$

---

* This rule is somewhat arbitrary and a bit conservative, but is commonly used. Another procedure for pooling requires that all the expected values be 3 or more, while yet another procedure requires that no more than 20% of all the expected values be less than 5, with none less than 1.

Notice that the first and last expected values are less than 5. As a result, it will be necessary to pool (combine) categories 1 and 2 and categories 4 and 5. The new summary is obtained by summing O_1 and O_2 (= 40), E_1 and E_2 (= 26.25), O_4 and O_5 (= 23), and E_4 and E_5 (= 33.75).

New Category	Name	Observed (O)	Expected (E), if H_0 is True
1	Management is responsive	40	26.25
2	No opinion	12	15.00
3	Management is not responsive	23	33.75
		75	75

Now each of the expected values is at least 5, and we can continue the analysis. The hypotheses using the new categories are

$$H_0: p_1 = .35, p_2 = .20, p_3 = .45$$

H_a: at least one of these proportions is incorrect

The value of $p_1 = .35$ is obtained by summing the previous first two proportions (.05 + .30), and the value of $p_3 = .45$ is the sum of the previous last two proportions (.40 + .05).

The computed chi-square value is now

$$\chi^{2*} = \frac{(40-26.25)^2}{26.25} + \frac{(12-15)^2}{15} + \frac{(23-33.75)^2}{33.75}$$

$$= 7.202 + .600 + 3.424 = 11.226$$

This value exceeds the Table A.6 value of $\chi^2_{.05,2} = 5.99$, so we reject H_0 and conclude that the mix of responses to this question at Metro Elevator is not the same as the proportions stated in Example 13.2. The main contributors to this large chi-square value came from the first and third categories, since we observed more people stating that management is responsive than we expected under H_0 (40 versus 26.25) and fewer people stating that management is not responsive than expected (23 versus 33.75).

USING EXCEL TO PERFORM A MULTINOMIAL GOODNESS-OF-FIT TEST

The KGP Data Analysis package provides an easy method of carrying out a multinomial goodness-of-fit test. We will illustrate this procedure using Example 13.2, which tested five proportions. First, enter the five observed values (32, 142, 87, 221, 18) in column A and the five proportions (.05, .30, .20, .40, .05) in column B. Click on **KGP Data Analysis ➤ Chi Square Tests.** Enter "A1:A5" for the **Input Range of Observed Frequencies** and "B1:B5" for the **Input Range of Hypothesized Proportions.** You can enter "C1" for the **Output Range.** The default alpha value is 5%, and so there is no need to change this value.

The resulting output is shown in Figure 13.3, where column J (a blank column) is hidden. The computed chi-square value (8.242) is the same as that obtained in the solution to Example 13.2, and based on the p-value of .0831 (in cell L9), we again fail to reject H_0 since the p-value exceeds $\alpha = .05$. As a reminder, you should follow up this conclusion with a discussion of why the large chi-square value occurred, as was done in step 5 of the Example 13.2 solution.

TESTING A HYPOTHESIS ABOUT A DISTRIBUTIONAL FORM

In this discussion of the goodness-of-fit test, we examine such questions as:

Is it true that these data came from a binomial distribution with probability of success, p, equal to .2?

Does this particular set of data violate the assumption that the number of defects in this product follow a Poisson distribution?

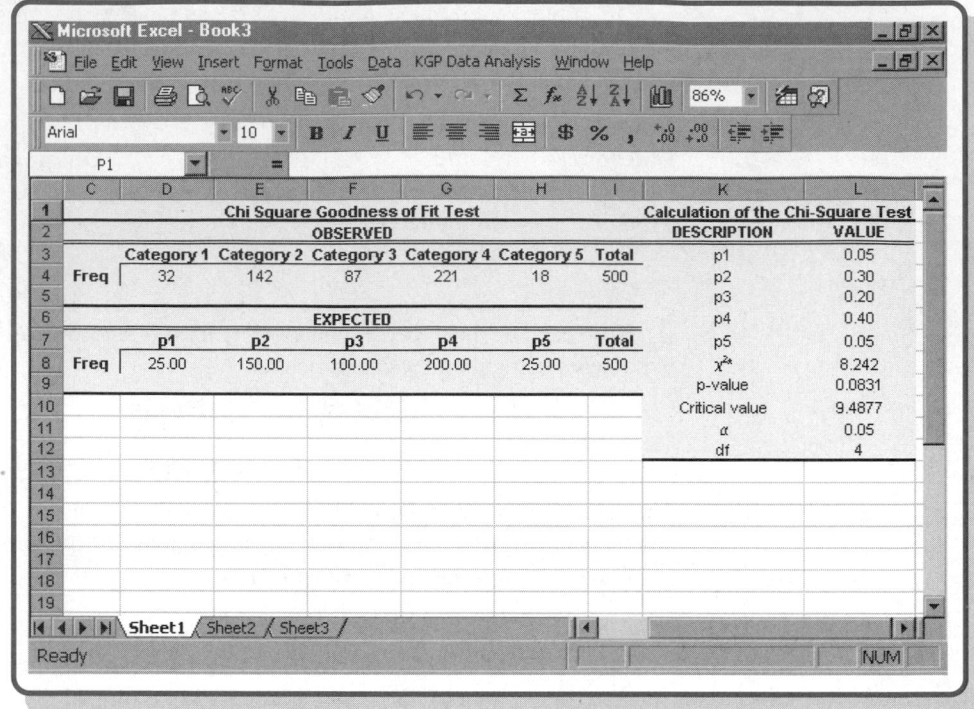

Is there any reason to doubt the assumption that the weights of all Rice Krinkle cereal boxes follow a normal distribution using a recently obtained sample of boxes?

The first two questions concern *discrete* distributions (binomial and Poisson). The final question is concerned with whether the data came from a particular *continuous* (in this case, normal) distribution. We illustrate the chi-square technique using a goodness-of-fit test for a discrete situation. (The goodness-of-fit test for the normal distribution is illustrated in Exercise 13.13.)

Suppose that Blitz laundry detergent is well known for its obnoxious commercials, which advertise that 20% of all Blitz boxes contain a valuable discount coupon. The commercials also claim that the boxes containing coupons are randomly distributed across all stores carrying the product. A recent study obtained a random sample of ten Blitz boxes from each of 100 different stores. The results were

Of 10 Boxes, Number Containing Coupons	**Number of Stores**
0	9
1	31
2	29
3	18
>3	13
	100

We wish to know whether these data appear to come from a binomial distribution with $p = .2$, using $\alpha = .05$.

Your immediate reaction may well be that this problem does not fit a multinomial situation. However, there are 100 independent trials, each trial consisting of randomly selecting ten boxes of Blitz detergent. Also, we can set up five categories here, namely:

Category 1: Observe 0 coupons in the ten boxes (probability p_1)

Category 2: Observe 1 coupon in the ten boxes (probability p_2)

Category 3: Observe 2 coupons in the ten boxes (probability p_3)

Category 4: Observe 3 coupons in the ten boxes (probability p_4)

Category 5: Observe > 3 coupons in the ten boxes (probability p_5)

So we *do* have a multinomial situation here. The hypotheses can be stated as

H_0: the data follow a binomial distribution with $p = .2$

H_a: the data do not follow a binomial distribution with $p = .2$

If H_0 is true, how often should we observe zero coupons in ten boxes? Each multinomial trial fits a binomial situation, where a success consists of a box containing a coupon. We repeat the trial ten times and count the number of successes (coupons). According to Table A.1, with $n = 10$ and probability of success $p = .2$, you should observe zero coupons out of ten boxes 10.7% of the time. So, if H_0 is true, $p_1 = .107$. Similarly, if H_0 is true, we should see one success out of ten trials 26.8% of the time. In other words, $p_2 = .268$. Therefore another way to state your hypotheses is

H_0: $p_1 = .107$, $p_2 = .268$, $p_3 = .302$, $p_4 = .201$, $p_5 = .122$

H_a: at least one of these p_i's is incorrect

We obtain p_5 by finding the probability of more than three successes in ten trials:

$$1 - (\text{probability of 3 or less}) = 1 - (p_1 + p_2 + p_3 + p_4)$$

$$= 1 - .878 = .122$$

So this is a multinomial test of hypothesis in disguise. Next, we compute the expected values, E.

Category	Observed (O)	Expected (E), if H_0 is True
0 boxes	9	$(100)(.107) = 10.7$
1 box	31	$(100)(.268) = 26.8$
2 boxes	29	$(100)(.302) = 30.2$
3 boxes	18	$(100)(.201) = 20.1$
>3 boxes	13	$(100)(.122) = 12.2$
	100	100

Make sure that all the E's (do not worry about the O's) are at least 5. In this case, all E's are greater than 5, so no pooling of categories is necessary.

To define the rejection region, we notice that there are $k =$ five categories. So the df in the chi-square statistic is df $= k - 1 = 4$. Also, $\chi^2_{.05,4} = 9.49$, and so the test procedure will be to

reject H_0 if $\chi^2 > 9.49$

The value of our test statistic is

$$\chi^{2*} = \frac{(9-10.7)^2}{10.7} + \frac{(31-26.8)^2}{26.8} + \cdots + \frac{(13-12.2)^2}{12.2}$$

$$= 1.25$$

Because 1.25 is less than 9.49, we fail to reject H_0 and conclude that there is no evidence to suggest that these data have violated the binomial assumption. These 100 observations suggest that we have no reason to accuse Blitz of false advertising for their claim that 20% of their boxes contain coupons.

In summary, you can refer to the following guidelines if you are trying to perform a test of hypothesis on a binomial parameter, p (for example, H_0: $p = .2$).

1. If you have a *single* sample of size n, then the results of Chapter 10 apply; you have a binomial experiment.
2. If you have *many* samples of size n, then the results of this section apply; this problem can be expressed as a multinomial experiment. The chi-square goodness-of-fit procedure allows you to perform a test on the population proportion, p, as well as determine if the population follows a binomial distribution. The previous example illustrates this type of situation.

DISTRIBUTIONAL FORM WITH UNKNOWN PARAMETERS

In the Blitz cereal example, H_0 not only stated that the data followed a binomial distribution, it also specified a value of the binomial parameter p (namely, $p = .2$). Often your only concern is whether the data follow a particular distribution (such as binomial, Poisson, or normal), and the values of the corresponding parameters are not present.

For example, suppose that the manager of Case Electronics has always assumed that the weekly sales of his top-of-the-line telephone answering machine followed a Poisson distribution. Data from a 50-week period were gathered, with the following results:

Units Sold	Number of Weeks	Units Sold	Number of Weeks
0	1	5	7
1	3	6	5
2	6	7	3
3	11	8	4
4	10	>8	0
			50

How can we test the hypothesis that the number of units sold follows a Poisson distribution, using $\alpha = .1$?

The correct hypotheses here are

H_0: weekly sales follow a Poisson distribution

H_a: weekly sales do not follow a Poisson distribution

The probability function for the Poisson distribution has one parameter, μ, because this function (from equation 5.15) is given by

$$P(X = x) = \frac{\mu^x e^{-\mu}}{x!}$$

for $x = 0, 1, 2, \ldots$, where $x =$ the number of units sold during a particular week.

However, the value of μ was not specified in H_0. In this case, we estimate any unknown parameter (μ, here) from the sample information and replace each parameter by its estimate in the probability function. In this way, we can estimate all the expected frequencies ($E_1, E_2, E_3, \ldots$).

Whenever you estimate unknown parameters for use with the chi-square test, you need to *adjust the corresponding degrees of freedom*, df. In general, the df for the chi-square goodness-of-fit statistic is given by

df = (number of classes) – 1 – (number of estimated parameters)

For the Poisson situation, you are estimating only one parameter, μ, and so the df = (number of classes) – 1 – 1 = (number of classes) – 2. The same argument holds true for a test of hypothesis on a binomial distribution where the single parameter, p, is unspecified in H_0 and is instead estimated from the sample information.

ESTIMATING μ

Because μ is the mean of the telephone answering machine sales population, we estimate it using the average (mean) of the sample. In the sample, we observe 1 value of zero, 3 values of one, 6 values of two, and so on for all 50 values. The sample average, our estimate of μ, will be

$$\hat{\mu} = \frac{(0)(1) + (1)(3) + (2)(6) + \cdots + (8)(4)}{50}$$

$$= \frac{206}{50} = 4.12$$

Rounding this to $\hat{\mu} = 4.1$, the estimated probability function is

$$P(X = x) = \frac{(4.1)^x e^{-4.1}}{x!}$$

for $x = 0, 1, 2, \ldots$.

We can now use Table A.3 (the Poisson table) to estimate the expected number of weeks with zero sales, with one sale, and so on. We are *estimating* each expected value, so we denote each of them as $\hat{E}$.

X	$P(X = x)$	$\hat{E}$	O
0	.0166	$(.0166)(50) = \quad .83$	1
1	.0679	$(.0679)(50) = 3.39$	3
2	.1393	$(.1393)(50) = 6.97$	6
3	.1904	$(.1904)(50) = 9.52$	11
4	.1951	$(.1951)(50) = 9.76$	10
5	.1600	$(.1600)(50) = 8.00$	7
6	.1093	$(.1093)(50) = 5.46$	5
7	.0640	$(.0640)(50) = 3.20$	3
8	.0328	$(.0328)(50) = 1.64$	4
>8	.0246	$(.0246)(50) = \underline{\ 1.23}$	$\underline{\ 0}$
	1	50	50

Notice that, for the category $X > 8$, the corresponding probability is $1 - (.0166 + .0679 + \cdots + .0640 + .0328) = .0246$.

The next step always is to check your expected frequencies ($\hat{E}$) to see if pooling is necessary. Each $\hat{E}$ value must be at least 5, so it is necessary to pool the first three classes $(.83 + 3.39 + 6.97 = 11.19)$ and the last three classes $(3.20 + 1.64 + 1.23 = 6.07)$. Now you can evaluate the chi-square statistic.

X	$\hat{E}$	O	$(O - \hat{E})$	$(O - \hat{E})^2/\hat{E}$
≤2	11.19	10	−1.19	.127
3	9.52	11	1.48	.230
4	9.76	10	.24	.006
5	8.00	7	−1.00	.125
6	5.46	5	−.46	.039
≥7	$\underline{6.07}$	$\underline{7}$	$\underline{.93}$	$\underline{.142}$
	50	50	0	.669

(check)

$$\chi^2 = \sum \frac{(O - \hat{E})^2}{\hat{E}} = .669$$

The degrees of freedom for the corresponding test are

$$df = (\text{number of classes}) - 1 - (\text{number of estimated parameters})$$

$$= 6 - 1 - 1 = 4$$

The resulting test, using Table A.6 and $\alpha = .1$, is

$$\text{reject } H_0 \text{ if } \chi^2 > 7.779$$

Because $.669 < 7.779$, we fail to reject H_0 and conclude that there is not enough evidence to indicate that the Poisson distribution assumption is incorrect.

EXERCISES 13.1–13.15

UNDERSTANDING THE MECHANICS

13.1 Test H_0: $p_1 = .2$, $p_2 = .5$, $p_3 = .3$ for a multinomial experiment with the following data. Use a .05 significance level.

Category	1	2	3
Observed frequency	18	53	29

13.2 Consider a multinomial experiment with five categories and a sample of size 50. Test H_0: $p_1 = .30$, $p_2 = .30$, $p_3 = .20$, $p_4 = .15$, $p_5 = .05$. Use a .10 significance level. Are all expected frequencies greater than 5?

Category	1	2	3	4	5
Observed frequency	11	20	7	10	2

13.3 Do the following data appear to come from a binomial distribution with $p = .5$? Test using a .05 significance level.

Value of Binomial Random Variable	Observed Frequency
0	2
1	11
2	34
3	31
4	18
5	5

APPLYING THE NEW CONCEPTS

13.4 The credit card industry is very competitive, with about 3 billion solicitations each year. In 1998, Visa had about 47% of the market, compared with nearly 26% for Mastercard, 20% for American Express, and 7% for other credit cards. To check if these percentages still held in 1999, a financial analyst randomly sampled 200 households and asked which credit card they primarily used. The results were as follows.

Visa	Mastercard	American Express	Other
110	40	39	11

(Adapted from *USA Today*, "Credit Card Firms Face Justice Suit," July 17, 1998, p. 1B.)

a. What are the expected values for each category? Should the expected values be above a certain value for the chi-square test to be valid?

b. Does this survey indicate that the population percentages using these credit cards differ from the previous year? Use a .10 significance level.

13.5 A stockbroker believes that when too many of the stock market newsletters are bullish on the market (that is, they predict that stock prices will go higher), the stock market will most likely fall. Thirty-two randomly selected stock market newsletters were each placed in one of three categories:

Bearish on Stock Market	Neutral on Stock Market	Bullish on Stock Market
9	10	13

Test the null hypothesis that the newsletters are equally divided among the three categories. Use a .05 significance level.

13.6 Economists believe that the average holiday spending for Americans is $800. The amount of time to pay off this holiday expense is two months or less for about 35% of the population and more than two months for the rest of the population. To check this claim, suppose that a random sample of 500 American adults was selected, and the following results were recorded.

Two Months or Less to Pay Off Holiday Bills	More than Two Months to Pay Off Holiday Bills
165	335

(Source: Adapted from *USA Today*, "Holiday Hangover," Dec. 15, 1998, p. 1B.)

a. Is there sufficient evidence indicating that the percentage of the population paying off their holiday bills in two months or less differs from 35%?

b. Use the Z test to test the belief in part (a). Use a 10% significance level.

c. What relationship exists between the test statistic in parts (a) and (b)?

13.7 Market analysts believe that nationwide, approximately 50% of the population purchase a movie video at a video store on the spur of the moment. These analysts also believe that approximately 40% who purchase a movie video do so after thinking about the movie earlier in the same day. Approximately 5% of the population think of the movie they purchased one or two days ahead, and 5% think of the movie more than two days ahead of the purchase. Suppose that this survey was repeated in St. Louis with the 200 video buyers. Determine whether the responses for this group are similar to what would be expected in the nationwide survey. Use a 5% significance level.

Spur of the Moment	Earlier the Same Day	One to Two Days Ahead	More than Two Days Ahead
91	75	18	16

(Adapted from *The Dallas Morning News*, "TECHBITS," July 14, 1997, p. D2.)

13.8 Electrical fuses are packaged in lots of 20. The quality-control department claims that on the average only about 10% of the fuses in each package of 20 fuses are defective. A random sample of 40 packages was selected and the results were:

Defective Fuses	Packages
0	7
1	12
2	10
3	7
4	1
5	1
>5	2

Do these data appear to have come from a binomial distribution with $p = .10$? Use a significance level of .05.

13.9 A temporary manpower service has 20 competent computer programmers that can be assigned to a company on a weekly basis. The manager of the manpower service agency believes that the number of programmers assigned to a job during a week follows a binomial distribution with $p = .05$. A random sample of 100 weeks is selected. Seven classes are used to summarize the frequency of different numbers of programmers assigned to a job during a week. Test that the following data follow a binomial distribution with $p = .05$. Use a .10 significance level.

Class	Number of Programmers Assigned to a Job During a Week	Observed Frequencies
1	0	29
2	1	40
3	2	18
4	3	9
5	4	3
6	5	1
7	6 or more	0

13.10 An auditor believes that the number of errors per 25 invoices in the records of a discount furniture store chain follow a Poisson distribution with a mean of 2.2. To test the auditor's belief, 25 stores were randomly selected and the number of errors were tabulated.

Errors per 25 Invoices	Stores	Errors per 25 Invoices	Stores
0	3	4	2
1	5	5	2
2	7	6	1
3	4	>6	1

Do these data appear to have come from a Poisson distribution with a mean of 2.2? Use a .10 significance level.

13.11 On each flight of Astral Airways, 12 randomly selected passengers are asked if they would be willing to pay a 5% airfare increase to fly on an airline that had an open bar in the airplane. Results of the survey from 50 different flights were as follows:

Yes Answers	Flights	Flights	Yes Answers
0	3	4	7
1	10	5	3
2	13	6	2
3	12	>6	0

Use a chi-square goodness-of-fit test to determine whether these data came from a binomial distribution. Let the significance level be .05. [Hint: p must be estimated using (total number of people who said yes)/(total number asked).]

13.12 An assembly-line operation coats moving sheets of steel with a plastic film. If the thickness of the plastic coating at any point is less than 5mm, then a nonconformity is present. A quality inspector samples 150 lots of 1-meter by 10-meter sheets that have been coated. The number of nonconformities is believed to follow a Poisson distribution. Eight classes are used to classify the frequencies of each number of nonconformities per lot. Test the hypothesis that the data follow a Poisson distribution. Use a .05 significance level.

Class	Number of Nonconformities per Lot	Observed Frequency
1	0	21
2	1	43
3	2	37
4	3	25
5	4	12
6	5	7
7	6	5
8	7 or more	0

13.13 To perform certain statistical tests on a set of data, the assumption of normality is required. It is thought that the percentage gain over the past three years in mutual funds that have balanced portfolios of both long-term growth stocks and income-oriented stocks is normally distributed, with a mean of 35% and a standard deviation of 10%. A sample of 75 mutual funds of this type is selected to test this assumption of normality using a chi-square goodness-of-fit test. For the intervals listed, probabilities can be found from the normal table (Table A.4). To find the expected frequencies in the third column, the sample size is multiplied by each probability. If the differences between the observed and expected frequencies are large, then the chi-square statistic based on the observed and expected frequencies would be large and would cause the null hypothesis (that the data were sampled from a normally distributed population with mean = 35 and standard deviation = 10) to be rejected.

Percentage Gain Interval	Probability	Expected Frequency	Observed Frequency
less than 20	.0668	5.01	7
20 and less than 30	.2417	18.1275	15
30 and less than 40	.3830	28.725	26
40 and less than 50	.2417	18.1275	21
50 or more	.0668	5.01	6

At the 5% significance level, complete the chi-square goodness-of-fit test by calculating the chi-square statistic presented in this chapter and by using a tabulated chi-square value for the critical value of the rejection region. The degrees of freedom is taken to be equal to the number of intervals minus one.

USING THE COMPUTER

13.14 [DATA SET EX13-14] Variable description:

Knowledge/skills: a score from 1 through 5, with 5 indicating the highest knowledge level of technology skill

Corporations spending millions of dollars on information technology are interested in assessing the impact of this technology in the workplace. To assess a user's knowledge in their technology application, a typical question might be "For your requirements, how would you rate your knowledge/skills in using this application compared to someone who is knowledgeable/skillful enough to make full use of this application in your job." The response is measured on a 5-point scale: 1 = less than 20% of full use, 2 = 20%–39% of full use, 3 = 40%–59% of full use, 4 = 60%–79% of full use, and 5 = 80% or more of full use. Suppose that 100 employees using technology applications in the workplace respond to the survey. Test that the employees are equally divided among the five knowledge/skills levels using a 5% significance level. (Hint: First use the histogram command to obtain a frequency distribution.)

(Source: Adapted from *Proceedings of the 1998 Decision Sciences Institute,* "A Confirmatory Factor Analysis of the Impact of Information Technology Instrument," p. 955–57.)

13.15 [DATA SET EX13-15] *Variable description:*

LateFlights: Number of late flights per day

A manager for Easy Fly Airlines believes that the number of late flights per day between Boston and New York follows a binomial distribution, with $p = .35$. Easy Fly airlines schedules 10 shuttle flights per day between these cities. A random sample of 100 days was selected, and the number of late flights was recorded for each day.

a. Obtain a discrete histogram for the variable LateFlights.

b. Obtain the binomial probabilities for $n = 10$ and $p = .35$. Using Excel, type "0" through "10" in column C. In D1 type "=Binomdist(C1,10,.35,False)" and drag down through cell D11.

c. Using the probabilities in part (b), obtain a column of expected values. Pool cells if necessary.

d. Test that the variable LateFlights follows a binomial distribution, with $p = .35$. Use a 5% significance level.

e. Do a "what if" analysis by using a value of $p = .20$ and repeating the analysis. What conclusion do you reach?

13.2 CHI-SQUARE TESTS OF INDEPENDENCE

In the previous section, we classified each member of a population into one of many categories. This classification was one-dimensional, because each member was classified using only *one* criterion (brand, color, and so on). In this section, we extend classification to a two-dimensional situation, in which each element in the population is classified according to two criteria, such as gender and income level (high, medium, or low). The question of interest is, are these two variables (classifications) *independent?* For example, if gender and income level are not independent, perhaps gender discrimination is present in the salary structure of a company. If a person's salary is not related to gender, these two classifications *would* be independent.

In Chapter 4, we examined a survey concerned with the age and gender of the purchasers of a recently released microcomputer. The results were summarized in a *contingency* (or *cross-tab*) table. This table consisted of **cells,** where each cell contains the **frequency** of people in the sample who satisfy each of the various cross-classifications:

Gender	Age <30	Age 30–45	Age >45	Total
Male	60	20	40	120
Female	40	30	10	80
Total	100	50	50	200

This 2×3 contingency table shows that there were 60 people who were both male *and* under 30. In Chapter 4, we determined various probabilities for a person selected at random from this group of 200, such as the probability that this person is both a male and over 45 years. Now we will view these data as the results of a particular experiment (survey) and attempt to determine whether the variables—age and gender—are independent for this application. Put another way, is the age structure of the male buyers the same as that of the female purchasers? The hypotheses are

H_0: the classifications (age and gender) are independent

H_a: the classifications are dependent

This problem can also be viewed as a multinomial experiment containing 200 trials and $(2)(3) = 6$ possible categories for each trial outcome.

DERIVING A TEST OF HYPOTHESIS FOR INDEPENDENT CLASSIFICATIONS

CALCULATING THE EXPECTED VALUES. We want to decide whether the data about the purchasers exhibit random variation or a pattern of some type due to a dependency between age and gender. If these classifications *are* independent (H_0 is true), how many people would you expect in each cell? Consider the upper right cell, which shows males over 45 years. The expected number of sample observations in this cell is $200 \cdot P$(sampled purchaser is a male and over 45). Assuming independence, this is $200 \cdot P$(sampled purchaser is a male) $\cdot P$(sampled purchaser is over 45), using the multiplicative rule for independent events discussed in Chapter 4.

What is P(sampled purchaser is a male)? We do not know, because we do not have enough information to determine what percentage of *all* purchasers are male. However, we can *estimate* this probability using the percentage of males in the sample: 120/200 = .6.

Similarly, P(sampled purchaser is over 45) can be estimated by the fraction of people over 45 in the sample—namely, 50/200. So, our estimate of the expected number of observations for this cell is

$$\hat{E} = 200 \cdot \frac{120}{200} \cdot \frac{50}{200} = \frac{(120)(50)}{200} = 30$$

So, for this cell, the observed frequency is $O = 40$, and our estimate of the expected frequency (if H_0 is true) is $\hat{E} = 30$. In general,

$$\hat{E} = \frac{(\text{row total for this cell}) \cdot (\text{column total for this cell})}{n}$$

where n = total sample size. A summary of the calculations can be tabulated as follows.

Gender	Age	Observed (O)	Expected ($\hat{E}$), If H_0 Is True
Male	<30	60	(120)(100)/200 = 60
	30–45	20	(120)(50)/200 = 30
	>45	40	(120)(50)/200 = 30
Female	<30	40	(80)(100)/200 = 40
	30–45	30	(80)(50)/200 = 20
	>45	10	(80)(50)/200 = 20
		200	200

The easiest way to represent these 12 values is to place the expected value in parentheses alongside the observed value in each cell:

Gender	Age <30	Age 30–45	Age >45	Total
Male	60 (60)	20 (30)	40 (30)	120
Female	40 (40)	30 (20)	10 (20)	80
Total	100	50	50	200

POOLING

At this point, you need to check your expected values. If any one of them is less than 5, you need to combine the column (or row) in which this small value occurs with another column (or row) to comply with our earlier requirement that all expected values in the chi-square statistic are at least 5. The observed and expected values for this new column (row) are obtained by summing the values for the two columns (rows).

THE TEST STATISTIC

The test statistic for testing H_0: the classifications are independent versus H_a: the classifications are dependent is the usual chi-square statistic, which in this case compares each *observed* frequency with the corresponding *expected* frequency estimate.

$$\chi^2 = \sum \frac{(O - \hat{E})^2}{\hat{E}} \tag{13.3}$$

where the summation is over all cells of the contingency table.

DEGREES OF FREEDOM

In the multinomial situation, the degrees of freedom for the chi-square statistic were $k - 1$, where k = the number of categories (outcomes). In this situation, there were k values of $(O - \hat{E})$. However, because the sum of the observed frequencies is the same as the sum of

FIGURE 13.4

Expected value estimates for an $r \times c$ contingency table.

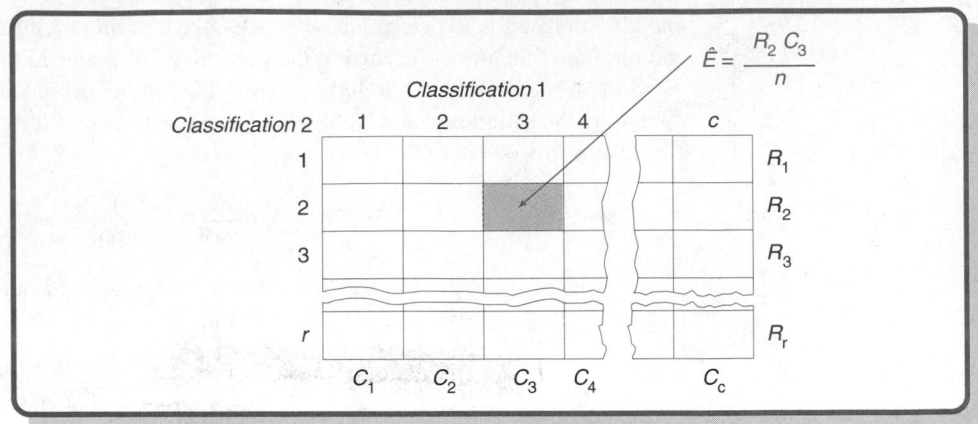

the expected frequencies, the sum of the k values of $(O - \hat{E})$ is *always zero*. This means that, of these k values, only $k - 1$ are free to vary, resulting in $k - 1$ df for the chi-square statistic.

Take a close look at the observed and expected frequencies in the contingency table for age and gender of purchasers. Notice that (1) for each row, sum of O's = sum of $\hat{E}$'s and (2) for each column, sum of O's = sum of $\hat{E}$'s. In general, if classification 1 has c categories and classification 2 has r categories, you construct an **$r \times c$ contingency table** (Figure 13.4). Of the c values of $(O - \hat{E})$ in each row, only $c - 1$ are free to vary. Similarly, only $r - 1$ of the values in each column are free to assume any value. So, for this contingency table, only $(r - 1)(c - 1)$ values are free to vary. Therefore, for the chi-square test of independence,

$$\text{df} = (r - 1)(c - 1) \qquad\qquad (13.4)$$

TESTING PROCEDURE

When H_0 is not true, the expected frequencies and observed frequencies will be very different, producing a large χ^2 value. We again reject H_0 if the value of the test statistic falls in the *right-tail* rejection region, so we

$$\text{reject } H_0 \text{ if } \chi^2 > \chi^2_{\alpha, df}$$

where df $= (r - 1)(c - 1)$.

In summary, the chi-square test for independence hypotheses are

H_0: the row and column classifications are independent (not related)

H_a : the classifications are dependent (related or associated in some way)

The test statistic is

$$\chi^2 = \sum \frac{(O - \hat{E})^2}{\hat{E}}$$

where

1. The summation is over all cells of the contingency table consisting of r rows and c columns.
2. O is the observed frequency in this cell.
3. $\hat{E}$ is the estimated expected frequency for this cell.

$$\hat{E} = \frac{\left(\begin{array}{c}\text{total of row in}\\\text{which the cell lies}\end{array}\right)\left(\begin{array}{c}\text{total of column in}\\\text{which the cell lies}\end{array}\right)}{(\text{total of all cells})}$$

4. The degrees of freedom for the chi-square statistic are df $= (r - 1)(c - 1)$.

The test procedure is (using Table A.6):

$$\text{reject } H_0 \text{ if } \chi^2 > \chi^2_{\alpha, df}$$

We can now return to our question of whether the age and gender of microcomputer purchasers are independent. Step 1 (statement of hypotheses) and step 2 (definition of test statistic) of our five-step procedure have been discussed already. Assume that a significance level of $\alpha = .1$ was specified. For step 3, the df are $(2-1)(3-1) = 2$. Using Table A.6, $\chi^2_{.1,2} = 4.61$. So we will reject H_0 if $\chi^2 > 4.61$. For step 4, referring to the contingency table,

$$\chi^{2*} = \frac{(60-60)^2}{60} + \frac{(20-30)^2}{30} + \frac{(40-30)^2}{30} + \frac{(40-40)^2}{40}$$
$$+ \frac{(30-20)^2}{20} + \frac{(10-20)^2}{20}$$
$$= 0 + 3.33 + 3.33 + 0 + 5 + 5$$
$$= 16.66$$

This exceeds the table value of 4.61, so we reject H_0. We thus conclude that the age and gender classifications are *not* independent (step 5).

If the results of the chi-square test lead to a conclusion that the classifications are not independent, a closer look at the individual terms in the chi-square statistic can often reveal what the relationship is between these two variables. Examining the six terms, we observe four large values, namely, 3.33 (male/age 30–45), 3.33 (male/age over 45), 5 (female/age 30–45), and 5 (female/age over 45). We obtained more men (and fewer women) over 45 years than we would expect if there was no dependency. Similarly, there were fewer men (and more women) between 30 and 45 years.

We can find the *p*-value for this situation also, given $\chi^{2*} = 16.66$. Using a χ^2 curve with 2 df, the area to the right of 16.66, using Table A.6, is <.005. The *p*-value indicates the **strength** of the dependency between two classifications. *The smaller the p-value is, the more you tend to support the alternative hypothesis, which indicates a stronger dependency between the two variables.* For the age and gender illustration, $p < .005$, so we conclude that the age and gender of these purchasers are strongly related.

It is worth mentioning at this point that it is possible that examining one category (such as gender) can fail to show any differences among subcategories (male versus female), but when the category is examined along with another category (such as age classification), patterns can emerge. Such a technique is often useful in detecting job discrimination within companies. For example, no gender discrimination may be evident in a sample, but when it is examined along with race or age categories, certain discriminatory practices can be identified.

EXAMPLE 13.5

The personnel director at PCSoft, a computer software development firm, is interested in determining whether an employee's educational level has an effect on his or her job knowledge. An exam was given to a sample of 120 employees, and the director would like to know whether there is a difference in exam performance among three groups: (1) those with a high school diploma only, (2) those with a bachelor's degree only, and (3) those with a master's degree.

Rather than using the actual exam scores and performing a one-factor analysis of variance (ANOVA, discussed in Chapter 11), she rated each person's exam performance as high, average, or low. The results of the study are:

	High	Average	Low	Total
Master's degree	4	20	11	35
Bachelor's degree	12	18	15	45
High school diploma	9	22	9	40
Total	25	60	35	120

Does job knowledge as measured by the exam appear to be related to the level of an employee's education, at this particular firm? Use $\alpha = .05$.

SOLUTION

Step 1. This problem calls for a chi-square test of independence, with hypotheses

H_0: exam performance is independent of educational level

H_a: these classifications are dependent

Steps 2, 3. Your test statistic is the chi-square statistic in equation 13.3. The table of frequencies here is a 3×3 contingency table, which means that the degrees of freedom are df $= (3-1)(3-1) = 4$. From Table A.6, we determine that $\chi^2_{.05,4} = 9.49$, so the testing procedure is to

reject H_0 if $\chi^2 > 9.49$

Step 4. Computing the expected frequency estimates in the usual way, we arrive at the following table:

(handwritten annotation: Row total · col total / 120 = 35·25/120)

	High	Average	Low	Total
Master's degree	4 (7.29)	20 (17.5)	11 (10.21)	35
Bachelor's degree	12 (9.38)	18 (22.5)	15 (13.12)	45
High school diploma	9 (8.33)	22 (20.0)	9 (11.67)	40
Total	25	60	35	120

To illustrate the calculations, the 11.67 in the lower right cell is $(40 \cdot 35)/120$. The computed chi-square value is

$$\chi^{2}* = \frac{(4-7.29)^2}{7.29} + \frac{(20-17.5)^2}{17.5} + \cdots + \frac{(9-11.67)^2}{11.67} = 4.67$$

This value is less than 9.49, and so we fail to reject H_0.

Step 5. We see no evidence of a relationship between job knowledge as measured by the exam and level of education.

We do not conclude that these data demonstrate that the two classifications are clearly *independent,* because this would amount to accepting H_0. We are simply unable to demonstrate that a relationship exists.

You can carry out a test of independence using Excel, but you will need to first construct a table of the expected frequencies—a somewhat tedious procedure. The analysis is much simpler using the macro contained in KGP Data Analysis. We will illustrate this procedure using Example 13.5. Begin by entering the nine observed frequencies in cells A1:C3 by placing "4," "12," and "9" (the HIGH values) in column A, the three AVERAGE frequencies ("20," "18," "22") in column B and the LOW frequencies ("11," "15," "9") in column C. Click on **KGP Data Analysis ➤ Chi Square Tests** and select **Independence of Rows and Columns.** Enter "A1:C3" in the **Input Range of Observed Frequencies** box and "D1" for the **Output Range.** The default alpha value is 5%, and so there is no need to change this value.

The resulting output in Figure 13.5 agrees with the previous solution—namely, there is no evidence of a relationship between exam score (job knowledge) and level of education. Excel also provides a *p*-value of .323 in Figure 13.5 (cell K4), and so once again we fail to reject H_0, since this value is larger than $\alpha = .05$.

COMMENTS

In Example 13.5, the personnel director recorded the exam performance as high, average, or low rather than listing the actual exam score. Why would anyone take *interval/ratio* data (the exam scores) and convert them to seemingly weaker *ordinal* data (the exam performance classifications)? Do you lose useful information by doing this? When using the ANOVA procedure in Chapter 11, we were forced to assume that these data came from *normal*

FIGURE 13.5

Excel spreadsheet for chi-square test of independence using KGP Data Analysis (Example 13.5).

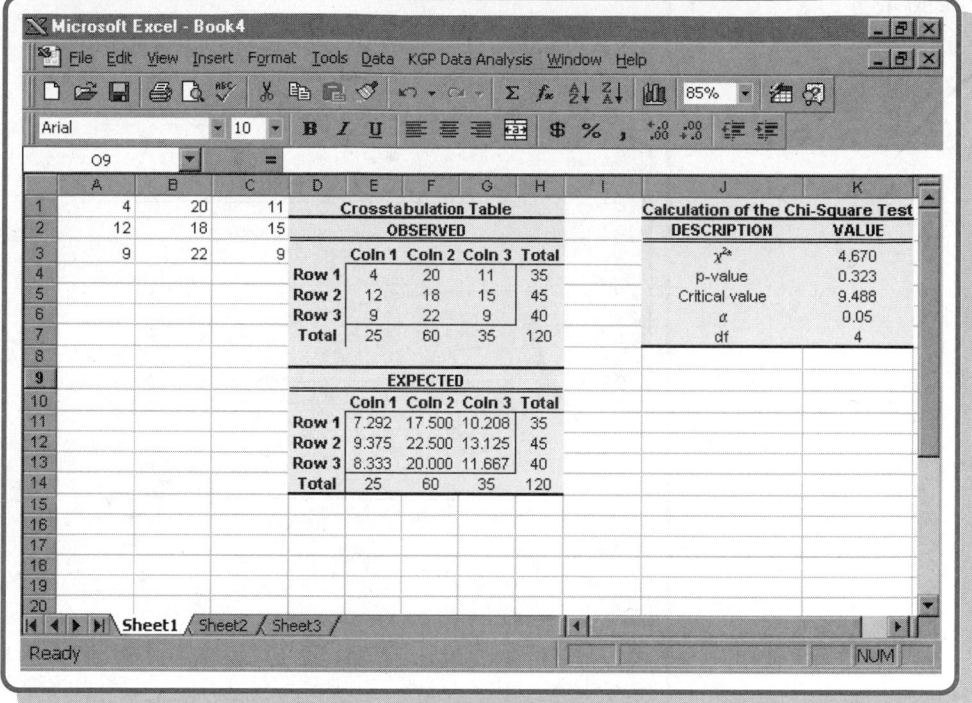

populations with equal variances. In this chapter, *no* assumptions regarding the populations (aside from the randomness of the sample) were necessary. So, by converting the exam scores to a form suitable for a contingency table and using the chi-square test of independence, we can avoid the assumptions of normality and equal variances.

This question introduces **nonparametric statistics**, often called *distribution-free* statistics. The beauty of these procedures is that they require only very weak assumptions regarding the populations. However, if the data *do* satisfy the requirements of the ANOVA procedure (or nearly so), the nonparametric test is less sensitive to differences among the populations (such as educational level) and so is less *powerful* than the ANOVA *F* test. Additional nonparametric tests of hypothesis are discussed in Chapter 19.

MICROSOFT® EXCEL APPLICATION   USE DATA13-6

EXAMPLE 13.6

An Excel Test of Independence and Corresponding *p*-Value

In Example 4.3, a quality engineer at Microtek obtained a random sample 200 electrical components produced over a one-week period. Each component was inspected and classified as (1) OK, (2) OK after rework (repair), or (3) scrap (unusable). Which of the three Microtek plants produced the part (Memphis, Miami, Pittsburgh) was also recorded. The same sample results are stored in columns A and B of data set DATA13-6, where

Column A = city producing the component: 1 = Memphis
2 = Miami
3 = Pittsburgh

Column B = component quality: 1 = OK
2 = OK after rework
3 = scrapped

Using Excel, construct a contingency table. This will be the same contingency table derived in Example 4.3. Using a significance level of .10, determine whether these two categories (city and product quality) are independent. What is the resulting *p*-value?

FIGURE 13.6

Excel contingency table for Example 13.6.

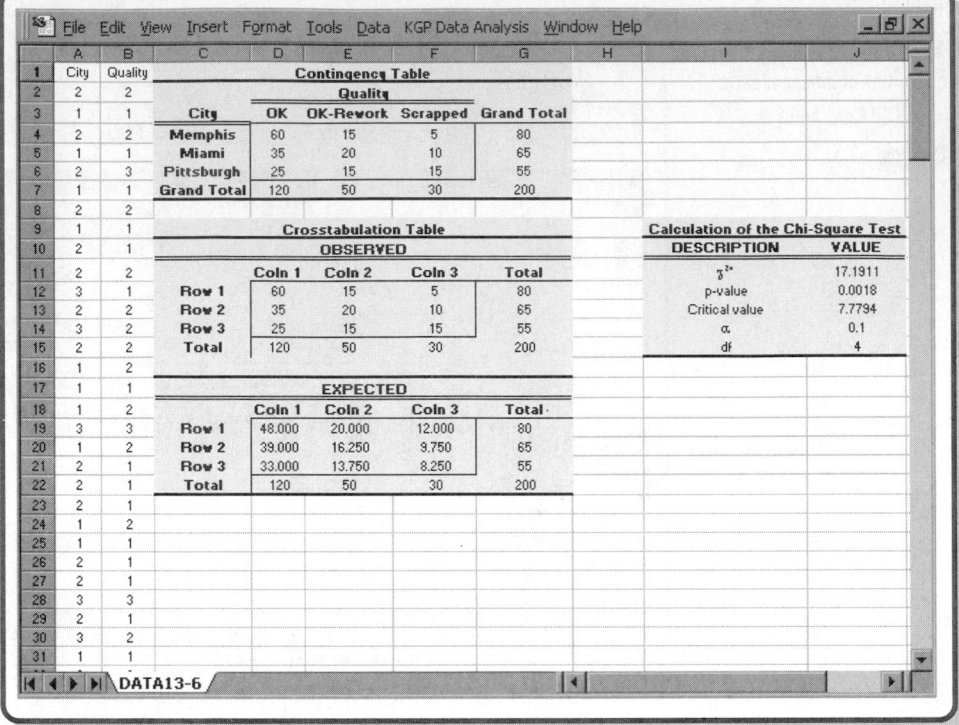

SOLUTION

To construct the contingency table using Excel, first open the Excel file DATA13-6. You should then see the first two columns labeled **City** and **Quality** in Figure 13.6. The Excel Tool Pack does not contain a procedure for constructing a contingency table from these two columns; however, the KGP Data Analysis add-ins do allow you to do this. Click on **KGP Data Analysis ➤ Qualitative Data Charts ➤ Contingency Table.** It is important when using this procedure to make sure that the two columns of data contain labels in the top row (**City** and **Quality** here). Enter "A1:A201" in the top box. This is the input range for the row variable (**City**) and includes the label. Repeat this for the column variable (**Quality**) by typing "B1:B201" in the second box. Enter "A202" as the **Output Range** and click on "OK." You will then obtain the output shown in Figure 13.6 by cutting the output in cells A202:E208 and pasting it into cells C1:G7. To make this table easier to interpret, enter the city names in cells C4, C5, and C6 and the quality labels in cells D3, E3, and F3 (as in Figure 13.6).

To carry out the test of independence, click on **KGP Data Analysis ➤ Chi Square Tests,** and select **Independence of Rows and Columns** in the top list. Enter "D4:F6" in the **Input Range of Observed Frequencies** box. These are the nine observed values in Figure 13.6, created by the preceding procedure. Enter "C9" for the **Output Range.** Also, the value of alpha needs to be changed from the default value of 5% to 10%. The resulting output is shown below the previously created contingency table in Figure 13.6. The computed chi-square value is seen to be 17.1911, with a corresponding p-value of .0018.

Since the p-value is less than .10, we conclude that these two categories (city and product quality) are dependent; that is, they are related in some way. Also, due to the small size of this p-value, we can say that the categories are *strongly* related. To determine this relationship, we compare the observed and expected values. Notice that (1) a superior product is coming from Memphis, since we observed more "OK" and fewer "scrap" components than expected under H_0, and (2) an inferior product is being produced in Pittsburgh, since we observed fewer "OK" and more "scrap" components than expected under H_0. Our advice to Microtek would be to examine these two production processes (Memphis and Pittsburgh) to determine why there is this pattern of product quality.

TEST OF INDEPENDENCE WITH FIXED MARGINAL TOTALS (TEST OF HOMOGENEITY)

We use a slightly different interpretation of the previous chi-square procedure when we determine *in advance* the number of observations to be sampled within each column (or row). In the previous discussion, the row and column totals were random variables because we had no way of knowing what they would be before the sample was obtained. In this discussion, the contingency table is the same, except that the column (or row) totals are predetermined.

Assume Delmar International, a textile manufacturer, has facilities located in Dallas, Boston, Seattle, and Toronto. Over the years, Delmar has gone to great lengths to discourage the formation of labor unions at these plants, including constructing employee recreational centers and offering better-than-average employee benefits. Management suspects, however, that there is growing interest among the employees in forming a union. Of particular interest is whether employee interest in a union differs among the four plants.

The Dallas and Toronto plants are considerably larger than the other two, so Delmar obtains a random sample of 200 employees from each of these two plants and 100 from each of the two smaller facilities. The results of the survey are:

	Dallas	Boston	Seattle	Toronto	Total
Interested	120	41	45	112	318
Not interested	35	38	40	36	149
Indifferent	45	21	15	52	133
Total	200	100	100	200	600

In the previous tests of independence, we had a *single* population, where each member was classified according to two criteria, such as age and gender. Now we have four distinct populations, namely, the Delmar employees in each of the four cities. Consequently, we obtained a random sample from each one. The column totals (sample sizes) were determined in advance. This example differs from our previous ones, where we had no idea what the row or column totals would be before the sample was obtained.

The question of interest here becomes, is interest in a labor union the same in each of the four cities? In other words, we are trying to determine whether these four populations can be viewed as belonging to the *same* population (in terms of this criterion). Identical populations are said to be **homogeneous.** Consequently, the test of hypothesis here is a **test of homogeneity** as well as a test for independence. The null hypothesis can be written as

H_0: the four populations are homogeneous in their interest in a union

The procedure for analyzing a contingency table is the *same* whether or not the column (or row) totals are fixed in advance.

An Excel solution using $\alpha = .05$ is provided in Figure 13.7.* The expected cell frequencies are computed by finding

$$\hat{E} = \frac{(\text{row total})(\text{column total})}{600}$$

The computed chi-square value is

$$\chi^{2*} = \frac{(120 - 106.0)^2}{106} + \frac{(41 - 53.0)^2}{53} + \cdots + \frac{(52 - 44.333)^2}{44.333} = 34.163$$

The degrees of freedom here are $(3 - 1)(4 - 1) = 6$, so we reject H_0 if $\chi^2 > 12.59$, where 12.59 is $\chi^2_{.05,6}$. The computed value (34.163) exceeds the tabled value, so we reject H_0. We conclude that these four populations are *not* homogeneous. The employee interest in a labor union is not identical at each of the four locations.

---

* To obtain this solution, follow the procedure used in the Excel solution to Example 13.5. Enter "A1:D3" in the **Input Range** box.

FIGURE 13.7

Excel spreadsheet for chi-square test of homogeneity using KGP Data Analysis.

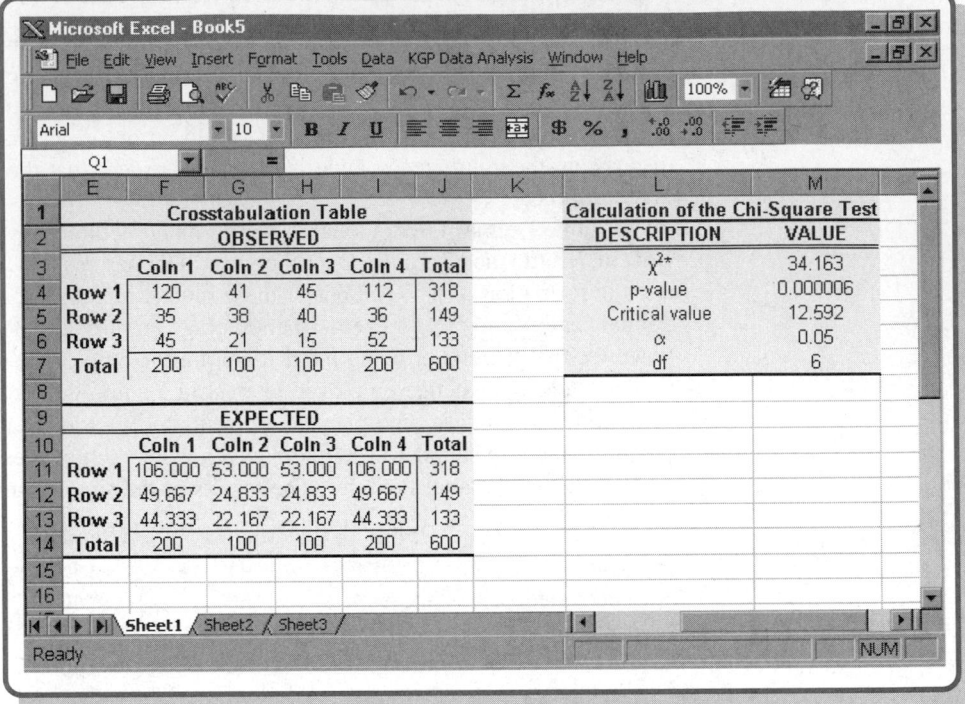

Examining the individual terms of the chi-square value in Figure 13.7, we note that the larger plants (Dallas and Toronto) had a higher proportion of employees interested in forming a union. In Dallas, for example, if these classifications were independent, we would expect 106 employees to be interested; instead, we observed 120. The same argument applies to the Toronto plant.

The p-value for this analysis is .000006, contained in cell M4, Figure 13.7. Because of this extremely small value, we reject H_0 and conclude that employees at these four plants have considerably different views in regard to the formation of a labor union.

EXAMPLE 13.7

Masuturi, a manufacturer of printed circuit boards, has determined that boards classified as nonconforming nearly always have one of three defects: a component on the board is either missing, damaged, or raised (installed improperly). The boards are produced on three machines (A, B, and C). Machine A is 90% computer-controlled and produces twice as many boards per day as machines B and C, which are 50% computer-controlled. To determine whether there is a relationship between the type of nonconformity and the machine, a sample of 500 nonconforming boards was obtained, 250 from machine A and 125 each from machines B and C, since machine A produces twice as many boards as machines B and C. The following data were obtained:

Type of Nonconformity

Machine	Missing	Damaged	Raised	Total
A	50	80	120	250
B	60	55	10	125
C	65	45	15	125
Total	175	180	145	500

Is the type of nonconformity related to the machine used for production? Use a significance level of .10.

SOLUTION

Step 1. The hypotheses for this test of homogeneity are

H_0: the three machine populations are homogeneous in the types of nonconformity produced

H_a: the three machine populations are not homogeneous in the types of nonconformity produced

Steps 2, 3. Your test statistic is the chi-square statistic in equation 13.3 with degrees of freedom $(3-1)(3-1)=4$. Using Table A.6, the testing procedure is to

$$\text{reject } H_0 \text{ if } \chi^2 > 7.78$$

Step 4. Computing the expected frequencies in the usual way produces the following table:

	Type of Nonconformity			
Machine	**Missing**	**Damaged**	**Raised**	**Total**
A	50 (87.5)	80 (90.0)	120 (72.5)	250
B	60 (43.75)	55 (45.0)	10 (36.25)	125
C	65 (43.75)	45 (45.0)	15 (36.25)	125
Total	175	180	145	500

The computed chi-square value is

$$\chi^{2*} = \frac{(50-87.5)^2}{87.5} + \frac{(80-90)^2}{90} + \cdots + \frac{(15-36.25)^2}{36.25}$$

$$= 16.071 + 1.111 + 31.121 + 6.036 + 2.222 + 19.009 + 10.321 + 0.000 + 12.457$$

$$= 98.35$$

This value is greater than 7.78, so we reject H_0.

Step 5. There is evidence to indicate that the three machine populations are not homogeneous; that is, the type of nonconformity *is* related to the machine used for production of the circuit boards. Comparing the observed and expected values, we observed more raised component nonconformities than expected on machine A and fewer than expected on machines B and C. Also, we observed fewer missing-component nonconformities than expected on machine A and more than expected on machines B and C.

EXERCISES 13.16–13.25

UNDERSTANDING THE MECHANICS

13.16 Consider the following contingency table.

	Column	
Row	**1**	**2**
1	12	20
2	8	13
3	10	7

a. Formulate the hypotheses for a chi-square test of independence.

b. Calculate the expected cell frequencies.

c. Calculate the chi-square statistic.

d. At the .05 significance level, what conclusion do the data support?

e. If the column totals had been determined in advance, that is, before the observations were sampled, what would be the hypotheses of interest?

13.17 Test the null hypothesis of independence of the two classifications A and B in the accompanying table. Combine any row or column to comply with the requirement that all expected cell frequencies are at least 5. Base your conclusions on the *p*-value.

	B			
A	B_1	B_2	B_3	B_4
A_1	10	6	3	2
A_2	13	7	8	4
A_3	3	15	2	1

13.18 A survey included 100 males and 100 females. Forty percent of the males were for issue X and the remaining were against. Forty-eight percent of the females were for the same issue, with the remaining being against.

    a. Construct a contingency table.

    b. State an appropriate null and alternative hypothesis that would be of interest.

    c. Would you reject the null hypothesis at a 10% significance level?

13.19 A manager asks 100 customers in stores A, B, and C if they prefer brand X, brand Y, or brand Z . The results are as follows:

	Store A	Store B	Store C
Brand X	42	36	39
Brand Y	28	28	31
Brand Z	30	36	30
Total	100	100	100

    a. State the null and alternative hypothesis.

    b. Should any cells be pooled?

    c. Calculate the chi-square test statistic.

    d. Is there sufficient evidence to reject the null hypothesis at the 1% significance level?

Applying the New Concepts

13.20 An insurance company claims that full-size cars are more prone to automobile accidents and hence should be subject to a higher insurance premium. To test the validity of the claim, an auto firm gathered a random sample:

Car Size	At Least One Accident	No Accidents
Full size	24	13
Compact	36	117
Small	108	214

Formulate the necessary hypotheses and test at the 10% significance level. Also calculate the p-value. Based on this value, would you reject the null hypothesis that car size and occurrence of accidents are independent at the 1% level?

13.21 The Meyers-Briggs Type Indicator (MBTI) is a personality scale that can be used to classify qualities like Extrovert (E), Introvert (I), Intuitive (N), Feeling (F), Sensing (S), Thinking (T), Judging (J), Perceptive (P). Thus, EN means extrovert-intuitive, SP means sensing-perceptive. Consider the following hypothetical frequencies for a cross-tabulation of four types of personality using the MBTI against profession.

Profession	Personality (MBTI)				
	EN	IF	SP	JT	Total
Computer programmer	4	6	5	6	21
Accountant	3	7	5	5	20
Marketer	9	3	7	4	23
Educator	5	5	5	5	20
Total	21	21	22	20	84

    a. From the table, can you conclude at a 1% significance level, whether personality type and profession are related?

    b. State the p-value for your test.

13.22 A quality manager was interested in whether three shifts were homogeneous with respect to the number of resulting defects when producing products A, B, and C. Four hundred defects from the past three months were sampled from each of the three shifts.

    a. What conclusion can you give the quality manager using the following data? Use a 10% significance level.

    b. Do a "what if" analysis by using only shifts 1 and 2. What conclusion do you reach using a 10% significance level?

	Product A	Product B	Product C	Total
Shift 1	120	138	142	400
Shift 2	115	142	143	400
Shift 3	155	120	125	400

13.23 In 1999, one in every eight households in the United States and Canada has at least one adult working full-time from home, for himself/herself or an employer. That number will rise to one in every five households by the year 2002. The Census Bureau is very concerned about keeping track of household growth patterns. Suppose that an analyst with the Census Bureau is interested in whether there is a relationship between the type of company a person is employed by (service company or a manufacturing company) and the reason a person is working at home. These reasons are (1) a tight labor market (not enough space at the company), (2) growth in computer networks (all work can be conveniently completed on the computer by e-mailing co-workers), and (3) changing worker values (worker prefers or needs to stay at home). The analyst selects 100 at-home workers from workers employed by service companies and 100 at-home workers from those employed by manufacturing companies. The results of the survey are presented below. Are the two types of companies homogeneous with respect to the reason workers are primarily staying at home? Use a .01 significance level.

Type of Company	Reason for Working at Home		
	Tight Labor Market	Growth in Computer Networks	Changing Worker Values
Service	35	45	20
Manufacturing	21	37	42

(Adapted from *The Wall Street Journal,* "Families, Communities Can Benefit From Rise in Home-Based Work," May 13, 1998, p. B1.)

Using the Computer

13.24 [DATA SET EX13-24] *Variable description:*

Age: Labeled as "18–34 years old" or "More than 34 years old"
Donate: Labeled as "Does donate to charity" or "Does not donate to charity"

The percentage of American adults nationwide that donate to charitable organizations is surprisingly high and typically increases with age. For age categories 18 to 34 years of age, approximately 70% of the population donates to charities. For the age category over 34, approximately 80% donate to charities. Suppose that a new survey is conducted for the Atlanta, GA, metroplex to determine whether there is a relationship between age and charity donation status.

    a. Test that a relationship exists. From the p-value, what conclusion would you draw at a 5% significance level? At a 1% significance level?

b. Do a "what if" analysis by selecting only the first 100 observations (through row 101) in part (a). How does the *p*-value change?

(Source: Adapted from *USA Today*, "Giving Season," Dec. 15, 1998, p. 1A.)

13.25 [DATA SET EX13-25] *Variable description:*

Salary: Row categories listed under Salary are "Less than $40,000," "Between $40,000 and less than $70,000" and "More than $70,000"

GM: Frequency of individuals preferring GM cars for each row
Ford: Frequency of individuals preferring Ford cars for each row

Imports: Frequency of individuals preferring import cars for each row

Market analysts are interested in the relationship between buyers' income and the type of car they prefer to drive. A study in which 500 recent automobile buyers were randomly selected revealed a possible relationship between a buyer's preference and his/her income bracket.

a. Is there sufficient evidence to indicate that a relationship exists between automobile preference and salary level using a 5% significance level?

b. Do a "what if" analysis by considering only GM and Ford. Does this change your response to part (a)?

SUMMARY

When performing a two-tailed test of hypothesis on a binomial parameter (for example, $p = .75$) we can use a chi-square test statistic. The advantage of this approach is that it extends easily to the **multinomial situation,** where each trial can result in any specified number of outcomes. For example, the roll of a single die has six possible outcomes on each roll.

In the multinomial situation, the probability of observing each possible outcome may be specified (such as 1/6 for each outcome in the single die illustration). To test the hypothesis, a random sample of observations is obtained, and a chi-square test statistic is evaluated either to reject or to fail to reject this set of probabilities (percentages). Such a test is referred to as a **chi-square goodness-of-fit test.** The form of this chi-square test statistic is

$$\chi^2 = \sum \frac{(O - E)^2}{E}$$

where

1. *O* represents the *observed* frequency of observations in a particular category (such as the observed number of 3s in 60 rolls of a single die).
2. *E* is the *expected* frequency for this category. For example, we would expect to see $60 \cdot 1/6 = 10$ values of 3 in the die illustration.
3. The chi-square value is obtained by summing over all categories of the multinomial random variable.
4. Categories must be combined (pooled) together whenever an expected value (*E*) for a particular category is less than 5.

The chi-square goodness-of-fit procedure can be used to determine whether a certain set of sample data came from a specified probability distribution. For example, you might attempt to determine whether the number of nonconformities in a particular product follows a Poisson distribution. By collecting a random sample and counting the number of nonconformities in each product, you can compare the observed values (how many 0's, how many 1's, and so on) with what you would expect if the null hypothesis (H_0: the data are from a Poisson distribution) is true. If the calculated chi-square value is significantly large (in the right tail), this hypothesis will be rejected. Whenever any of the parameters for this distribution are unknown (such as μ for the Poisson illustration), they can be estimated using the sample data. The degrees of freedom of the chi-square test statistic are reduced by one for *each* estimated parameter.

Finally, this chi-square statistic can be used to test whether two classifications (such as age and performance) used to define a contingency table are independent. This is the **chi-square test of independence.** The expected value within each cell of the contingency table is determined under the assumption that H_0 is true, for H_0: the row and column classifications are independent. This also leads to a right-tailed rejection region using the chi-square statistic.

This procedure can be used as a **test for homogeneity** when fixed sample sizes are used for each row or column of the table. If the column totals are fixed in advance, this test will determine whether the populations defined by the column categories are homogeneous (identical) with respect to the variable defining the rows. A similar argument applies when the row totals are predetermined. The test statistic used for a test of homogeneity is the same chi-square statistic used in the test of independence.

SUMMARY OF FORMULAS

CHI-SQUARE TEST STATISTIC:

$$\chi^2 = \sum \frac{(O-E)^2}{E}$$

summed over all categories for a goodness-of-fit test and over all cells for a test of independence or homogeneity. In the latter case, each expected value (E) is replaced by its estimate, $\hat{E}$.

ESTIMATED EXPECTED VALUE FOR A TEST OF INDEPENDENCE/HOMOGENEITY:

$$\hat{E} = \frac{(\text{row total for cell})(\text{column total for cell})}{n}$$

where n is the total of all cells in the contingency table.

REVIEW EXERCISES 13.26–13.52

13.26 Sears charges a 21% annual rate with the proprietary Sears credit card. Sears has issued 24 million new credit cards over the past four years. Historically, 5% of all accounts end up not being closed out without being paid in full. Suppose that a financial analyst wished to determine if the current percentage of accounts that have not been paid in full is different from 5%.

(Adapted from *The Wall Street Journal*, "Come See the Softer Side of Sears—Its Earnings," July 23, 1998, p. B1.)

    a. What conclusion can the analyst make using a 5% significance level if a random sample of 100 accounts revealed that eight accounts were closed out and had not been paid in full? Use the Z test.

    b. Use the chi-square goodness-of-fit test instead of the Z test in part (a).

    c. What is the relationship between the test statistics in parts (a) and (b)?

13.27 Russia's last czar, Nicholas II, and his family were buried in St. Petersburg's Peter and Paul Fortress in July 1998 on the anniversary of their murder. In a survey of Russian citizens across several major cities in Russia, respondents were asked how they primarily view the czar. The results are as follows:

25% Innocent victim of Bolsheviks
22% Not good ruler but redeemed by martyr's death
16% Brought poverty, catastrophe to Russia
15% Responsible for what happened after 1917
22% No opinion on the czar

Suppose that a political analyst wished to determine if these same percentages held for the residents of St. Petersburg. Two hundred residents of St. Petersburg were selected for the survey. Using the following data, test that the distribution of the responses appears to be the same as the distribution in the national survey. Use a 1% significance level.

(Adapted from *USA Today*, "Russia's Last Royal Burial," July 17, 1998, p. A1.)

Category	Number of Respondents Selecting this Category
Innocent victim of Bolsheviks	45
Not good ruler but redeemed by martyr's death	50
Brought poverty, catastrophe to Russia	40
Responsible for what happened after 1917	34
No opinion on the czar	31

13.28 A large department store in New York City has five entrances and exits. It is believed that the proportion of shoppers entering or leaving the store is approximately the same for each of the five doorways on any single day. The number of customers entering or leaving the store is tallied at each doorway for three randomly selected days:

Doorways	Customers
1	150
2	123
3	126
4	163
5	152

Do the data justify the statement that all five entrances and exits are used equally often? Use a 5% significance level.

13.29 Many Canadians believe that certain medical procedures (such as cosmetic procedures) should not be covered by OHIP (Ontario Health Insurance Plan). However, there is strong support for including annual health exams as an item paid for by OHIP. A 1994 poll showed that out of 1002 Ontario adults surveyed, 752 supported OHIP paying for annual health exams, 208 were against it, and 42 were undecided.

(Source: "OHIP Should Cover Annual Health Exams, Star Poll Told," by Lisa Priest, *Toronto Star,* Jan. 23, 1994, p. A1.)

a. Suppose that a previous survey indicated that 72% of Ontario adults supported OHIP paying for annual health exams, 24% were against it, and 4% were undecided. Do the new data suggest that these percentages have changed? Use a 5% significance level.

b. What requirements on the data are necessary for the test procedure in part (a) to be valid?

13.30 A car-rental company has 15 cars to rent. The owner believes that the number of cars rented daily is binomially distributed. He also believes that each car has a 30% chance of being rented each day. Forty-five randomly selected days are chosen and the number of cars rented are recorded. From the data, test the hypothesis that the daily rental of cars is binomially distributed with $p = .30$. Use a 5% significance level.

Cars Rented	Days Occurred	Cars Rented	Days Occurred
0	0	5	12
1	3	6	6
2	3	7	3
3	6	≥8	3
4	9		

13.31 An advertising firm believes that the number of daily responses to an advertisement in the *Wall Street Journal* follows a Poisson distribution. Forty days were randomly selected, and the following data were collected:

Responses	Days	Responses	Days
0	0	4	6
1	8	5	6
2	8	6	2
3	10		

Can you conclude that the data did come from a Poisson distribution? Use a 1% level of significance.

13.32 The assistant dean of the College of Business at Oceanside University believes that the number of students dropping a class is Poisson distributed. Fifty classes, all containing the same number of students, were randomly selected. The number of withdrawals from the classes was recorded. Based on the following data, what conclusion can be drawn about whether these data come from a Poisson distribution? Use a significance level of 5% to justify your conclusion.

Drops	Classes	Drops	Classes
0	0	5	4
1	2	6	6
2	6	7	4
3	10	>7	0
4	18		

13.33 Favin Copiers Inc. has repairpersons who are used to traveling to sites where a Favin copier needs repair. For a certain metropolitan area, the company has 10 repairpersons who stand by for calls to repair a copier. A manager believes that the number of repairpersons used each day is binomially distributed with $p = .3$, where p is the probability that a repairperson is sent out on any given day. One hundred days of operation yielded the following results:

Number of Repairpersons Sent Out	Days with the Number of Repairpersons Sent Out
0	4
1	10
2	21
3	27
4	18
5	12
6	5
7	3
8 or more	0

Test the goodness-of-fit of the data to a binomial distribution with $p = .3$. Use a significance level of .05.

13.34 A computer generates 100 observations from a normally distributed population with mean 35 and standard deviation 2. The results of the 100 observations generated are:

Interval	Observed Frequency	Interval	Observed Frequency
less than 32	6	35 but less than 36	19
32 but less than 33	9	36 but less than 37	15
33 but less than 34	12	37 but less than 38	11
34 but less than 35	23	38 or more	5

Use the chi-square goodness-of-fit procedure in Exercise 13.13 to test whether there is enough evidence to support the conclusion that the generated numbers did not come from a normally distributed population with mean = 35 and standard deviation = 2. Use a 1% significance level.

13.35 The vice president of a national firm wants to know the response of workers at a certain plant to a proposal to relocate the plant. Forty workers were randomly selected from each of the five divisions at the plant and asked if they favored a relocation of the plant.

Division	Favored	Do Not Favor	Total
A	15	25	40
B	18	22	40
C	24	16	40
D	17	23	40
E	20	20	40

Do the data indicate that the divisions are not homogeneous with respect to the proportion of workers who favor a relocation of the plant? Use a .05 significance level.

13.36 In the first quarter of 1998, the economy expanded at a sizzling 5.4%. In the second quarter of 1998, the economy expansion dropped to 1.0%. Economic experts were surveyed to determine if they believed the economy would slip into a recession. While few economists predicted a recession, many were concerned about factors that could affect economic growth. Suppose that a survey of 100 economists was conducted to determine whether the Asian monetary crisis, the General Motors strike, the big backlog of unsold goods, or some other factor would primarily affect the growth of the economy in 1999. Test the belief that the responses of the economists are evenly divided among the four categories. Use a .05 significance level.

(Adapted from *USA Today*, "Slip Doesn't Mean Recession—Experts," July 17, 1998, p. 1A.)

Category	Frequency
Asian monetary crisis	22
General Motors strike	17
Backlog of unsold goods	40
Other	21

13.37 An immigration attorney was investigating which industries to target for obtaining new clients who might have problems with changes in the immigration laws. Five industries were selected. Twenty workers were chosen in each industry, and their visa status was verified. The data are summarized as follows:

Visa Status	Industry					Total
	A	B	C	D	E	
Illegal alien	8	10	5	10	1	34
Legal resident	4	2	6	4	9	25
U.S. citizen	8	8	9	6	10	41
Total	20	20	20	20	20	100

a. Are the five industries homogeneous with respect to the visa status of their workers? Use $\alpha = .05$.

b. State the p-value.

13.38 Polls in February 1994 showed that a majority of Canadians would vote for a significant reduction in immigration if a referendum was held. In 1994, about 45% of the individuals immigrating to Canada got in solely because of their family ties, 44% were selected for skills and business credentials, and 11% came as refugees fleeing persecution. Suppose that a 1998 survey was taken to determine if these same percentages still held. Assume that 150 immigrants were randomly selected, and the following data were recorded.

Reason for Immigrating to Canada	Number
Family ties	60
Skills and business credentials	71
Fleeing persecution	19

Does the distribution of immigrants in the three categories appear to be the same as in 1994? Test at the .10 significance level.

(Source: Adapted from "Nose to Nose on Immigration," *Toronto Star*, Feb. 5, 1994, p. B1.)

13.39 An experiment is set up to test whether a person, upon having lost either a $10 bill or a $10 ticket, will be willing to purchase a $10 admission to see a play. (In the case of the lost ticket, the $10 admission is for a replacement ticket.) Sixty subjects were randomly assigned to have either "lost" the $10 bill or "lost" a $10 ticket. The results are shown in the following table:

Type of Loss	Purchase	No Purchase	Total
$10 Bill	25	5	30
$10 Ticket	15	15	30

(Source: "Social Interaction Effects in the Framing of Buying Decisions," by Arch Woodside and Alan Singer, *Psychology and Marketing,* vol. 11(1) (Jan./Feb. 1994), pp. 27–34.)

a. At a significance level of .05, determine if the subjects having either type of loss are homogeneous in their ticket-purchasing behavior.

b. Find the p-value for the test in part (a) and interpret it.

13.40 A Gallup survey of how parents of 10th graders plan to pay for their college found current income to be the top choice, with savings not far behind. To understand if a relationship existed between how parents plan to pay and the highest level of education of either parent, 600 parents of 10th graders were sampled yielding the following data. Formulate the necessary hypotheses and test using a 5% significance level.

(Source: Adapted from *USA Today*, "College: Pay As They Go," Oct. 25, 1998, p. D1.)

How Parents Plan to Pay for College	No College Degree	Undergraduate Degree	Graduate Degree
Current Income	58	63	60
Savings	32	80	48
Borrowed Funds	50	67	38
Other (second job, relatives, etc.)	30	40	34
Total	170	250	180

13.41 A record company wanted to survey its customers regarding music preferences. A random sample of 258 frequent customers of the record company was selected, and information was gathered on their music preference and job classification. From the following data, can the null hypothesis of independence between type of music preferred and working status be rejected at the 10% significance level?

Job Classification	Country and Western	Rock	Classical	Jazz	Total
Clerical	25	40	17	5	87
Managerial	21	25	29	15	90
Blue collar	27	33	14	7	81
Total	73	98	60	27	258

13.42 The personnel department of a particular firm wants to know if an employee's age is associated with productivity (given in items per hour). The manager of the personnel department draws a random sample of 60 employees from each of the age classifications listed. Do the data support the hypothesis that the five age categories are not homogeneous with respect to productivity? Use a 10% significance level.

Age	4–5 Items	6–7 Items	≥8 Items	Total
20 and under 30	15	25	20	60
30 and under 40	13	29	18	60
40 and under 50	16	26	18	60
50 and under 60	19	26	15	60
60 and under 70	22	24	14	60

13.43 A vice president at Edwards Brokerage firm is interested in what mutual fund investors with Internet access do when they visit the company's Web site. Investors are categorized as either short- or long-term investors and also by the information they request. Requested information is either: (1) check mutual fund price, (2) buy/sell mutual funds, (3) download prospectus, and (4) other. A random sample of 800 investors each from long- and short-term investors is drawn. Do the data indicate a lack of homogeneity among the two types of investors? Use a 10% significance level.

(Source: Adapted from *USA Today*, "Visiting Their Money," Oct. 27, 1998, p. 1B.)

Type of Information Requested	Short-Term Investors	Long-Term Investors
Check fund price	210	206
Buy/sell fund	407	298
Download prospectus	93	192
Other	90	104

13.44 Axiom Market Research published the following data concerning education level and attendance at "regular" theater performances. A sample size of 950 was selected. Do the data indicate, at the .05 significance level, a relationship between level of education and regular theater attendance?

Education	Attend More than Once per Year	Attend No More than Once per Year	Total
College graduate	82	120	202
Some college	75	131	206
High school graduate	106	215	321
Not a high school graduate	51	170	221

13.45 A sample of households classified as having incomes below the poverty level revealed the following distribution of persons by age:

Age	Frequency
0 to <5	27
5 to <18	53
18 to <22	16
22 to <45	60
45 to <65	26
65 to <72	18
Total	200

a. Compute the mean and standard deviation for this distribution.

b. Using a 10% significance level, determine with a chi-square test whether the data fit a normal population.

c. Find the p-value for the test.

d. Does your conclusion change if $\alpha = .05$ or $\alpha = .01$?

13.46 In an effort to monitor the service of its employees, a parcel-delivery firm keeps a tally of the number of packages misrouted each week at each of its 25 distribution centers, with the following results:

Misrouted Packages	Distribution Centers
0	5
1	6
2	8
3	6
>3	0

Do these data appear to come from a Poisson distribution? Use a .05 significance level.

13.47 In the field of organizational psychology, extensive study has been made of different leadership styles. One researcher refers to two extremes as authoritarian versus democratic; another refers to task-oriented versus people-oriented; yet others have their own labels for these qualities. Whatever the label, do these different styles affect the morale of the subordinates? To address this issue, a researcher established a ranking scale for worker morale, based on interviews, and grouped the workers into low, acceptable, and high morale categories. These were cross-classified against the leadership style of the supervisor. The following contingency table summarizes the results.

Worker Morale	Leadership Style Authoritarian	Leadership Style Democratic	Total
Low	10	5	15
Acceptable	8	12	20
High	6	9	15
Total	24	26	50

a. Apply the chi-square test of independence to these data, at a 5% significance level.
b. State the p-value for your test.
c. Is worker morale related to the supervisor's leadership style, or are these qualities independent?

13.48 Kingston Pencils is considering a new bonus plan. Under the current bonus plan, the amount of bonus is not linked to production but only linked to profits. According to the proposed bonus plan, the amount of bonus will be linked to the quantity produced but will be subject to the amount of profits. The controller of Kingston is interested in examining whether employee opinion of the bonus plan is independent of job classification.

Employee	Favorable	Unfavorable
White collar	67	28
Blue color	43	19

Calculate the p-value and interpret it.

13.49 Nonresponse bias is a problem for many sample surveys. One way to minimize the "refusal to respond" is to include an incentive as a reward for participating in the survey. An experiment was carried out in which a survey instrument was sent to a control group, which did not receive any reward for participating in the survey, and also to a group in which each participating member received a digital clock pen. The results of the experiment are as follows. Do the data provide sufficient evidence to indicate that the incentive and failure to respond are related? Base your conclusion on the p-value.

	Control	Pen
Completed questionnaire	213	227
Refused to complete questionnaire	66	77

(Source: Adapted from S. Pharr, R. Stuefen, and M. Wilber, "The Effects of Nonmonetary Incentives Upon Survey Refusal Tendencies of the Affluent Consumer Population," *Journal of Applied Business Research* 6, no. 3 (1990): 88.)

13.50 The percentage of time that each of the following carriers has been on time has been reported to be from 70% to 80%: United, Northwest, Alaska, America West, and TWA. Suppose that an airline consultant wished to determine if these carriers are homogeneous with respect to the number of times that they are on time. A random sample of 50 flights from each of these airlines was selected, and the number of times that the airline was on time was recorded. The contingency table below shows the observed frequencies. At a .10 significance level, is there evidence to support the statement that these airlines are not homogeneous with respect to being on time?

(Adapted from *USA Today*, "Worst On-Time Arrivals in May," July 17, 1998, p. B1.)

	On Time	Not On Time
United	35	15
Northwest	31	19
Alaska	45	5
America West	38	12
TWA	33	17

13.51 [DATA SET EX13-51] *Variable description:*

DouglasorNoble: Indicates whether an on-line buyer purchases a Douglas fir or a Noble fir
OnlineSite: Indicates which of the four on-line sites that the buyer used in purchasing a Christmas tree

While Internet sales of Christmas trees still only represent about 5% of the Christmas tree market, experts say that this market segment could potentially grow rapidly. Some on-line buyers like the home-delivery aspect of the service, particularly if they are too busy to shop for a tree. To better understand the relationship between the type of tree and the on-line site where buyers purchase their trees, a random sample of 300 on-line buyers was selected, and the data in DouglasorNoble and OnlineSite were collected.

    a. Form a contingency table of the data.

    b. Can you conclude that the type of tree ordered and the on-line site are independent at the 5% significance level?

    c. Do a "what if" analysis by removing the site www.mtnstarfarms.com from the contingency table. Does this change your conclusion in part (b)?

13.52 [DATA SET EX13-52] *Variable description:*

Return: Percentage return on equity

An analyst for the computer industry believes that the distribution of the percentage return on equity for all computer software firms is approximately normally distributed. A random sample of 250 firms with at least some software business was selected to verify this belief.

    a. Find the mean and standard deviation of the data.

    b. Standardize the data by subtracting the mean and dividing by the standard deviation.

    c. Construct a histogram of the data using a class width of 1.

    d. Under the assumption of a standard normal distribution, find the expected probabilities for the intervals of data, keeping in mind that the first and last intervals are open intervals.

    e. Compute the chi-square goodness-of-fit test statistic.

    f. What conclusion can you draw using a 5% significance level?

COMPUTER EXERCISES USING THE DATABASES

EXERCISE 1—APPENDIX E
Randomly select 100 observations from the database. Determine whether the variable family size (FAMLSIZE) has a distribution that is significantly different from the binomial distribution. Use a .05 significance level.

EXERCISE 2—APPENDIX E
Randomly select 200 observations from the database. Are the categories own or rent one's residence (variable OWNORENT) and family size (variable FAMLSIZE) independent? Use a .05 significance level.

EXERCISE 3—APPENDIX F
Randomly select 100 observations from the database. Determine whether the total asset value (variable TOTAL) has a distribution that is significantly different from the normal distribution. Use a .05 significance level. (*Hint:* See Exercise 13.13.)

EXERCISE 4—APPENDIX F
Randomly select 100 observations from the database. Are the categories bond rating (BONDRATE) and positive or negative net income (NETINC) independent? Use a .05 significance level.

INSIGHTS FROM STATISTICS IN ACTION: BUYING AND SELLING VACATIONS IN THE CORPORATE WORKPLACE

The purchase of vacation days from other employees within a company was discussed in the introductory Statistics in Action section. While this may be appealing to employees needing extra income or wanting longer vacations, the resulting largely unpredictable shifts in the day-to-day labor force often pose significant headaches within human resource (HR) departments.

Suppose that an HR executive takes a survey of 680 employees at a company where buying and selling vacation days is very popular to determine if there is a relationship between the employees that have participated in the buying and selling of vacation days and the number of years that an individual has been with the company. Among the 350 employees that have participated in the program, a contingency table is constructed to determine if the number of days bought is dependent on the salary level of the employee.

Number of Years with the Company	Number of Employees That Participated	Number of Employees That Did Not Participate
Less than 2 years	50	100
2 years but less than 5 years	70	70
5 years but less than 10 years	95	105
10 years but less than 15 years	75	50
More than 15 years	60	5

Salary Level (in Thousands of Dollars)	Bought Less than 5 Days	Bought at Least 5 Days but Less than 10 Days	Bought 10 Days or More
Less than 30	16	4	0
At least 30 but less than 50	32	44	10
At least 50 but less than 75	40	30	14
At least 75 but less than 100	33	34	10
More than 100	37	30	16

1. Do the data support that there is a relationship between the number of years that an employee is with a company and the number of employees that participate in corporate buy-and-sell vacation programs? Use a .05 significance level.

2. Find the expected frequency for each combination of salary level category and number of days bought category. Are any of the expected frequencies less than five? If so, combine rows or columns so that the degrees of freedom is as large as possible.

3. If you do not combine the rows and columns in question 2, what is the result of the statistical analysis for testing independence of salary level and the number of days bought? Use a .05 significance level.

4. To eliminate the cell or cells with an expected frequency below five, researchers combine either the rows or columns so that the degrees of freedom are the largest. What is the best way to merge rows or columns to eliminate cell(s) with an expected frequency below five for this problem?

5. Now combining either rows or columns to eliminate expected frequencies below five, what conclusion would result from testing the hypothesis in part 3? Use a .05 significance level.

Source: *USA Today,* "Vacation As a Commodity: Sell It or Buy More," July 17, 1998, p. B1.

CHAPTER 13 APPENDIX: DATA ANALYSIS WITH **MINITAB**

APPLICATIONS OF THE CHI-SQUARE STATISTIC

To perform chi-square tests of independence with a two-dimensional set of data, select up to seven columns to list the frequencies for each cell and then use the **Chi-Square Test** option from the menu. This test can be obtained by clicking **Stat ➤ Tables ➤ Chi-Square Test.** The user form shown below will appear. The data used in Example 13.5 are used. These data are typed in columns C1, C2, and C3. The output follows the user form. If the data are not in the form of a contingency table, such as the data used in Example 13.6, then put these data in two columns (one for each dimension) and click on **Stat ➤ Tables ➤ Cross Tabulation.** Check **Chi-Square Analysis** as one of the options.

MINITAB does not perform a chi-square goodness-of-fit test. However, if the observed frequencies are put in column C1 and the expected frequencies are put in column C2, then the commands below can be used to obtain the chi-square statistic and its p-value. In the last line, replace DF with the actual degrees of freedom (DF = 4, here).

```
MTB > LET C3 = (C1 - C2)**2 / C2
MTB > SUM C3, put into C4
MTB > CDF (C4);
SUBC> CHISQUARE (DF).
```

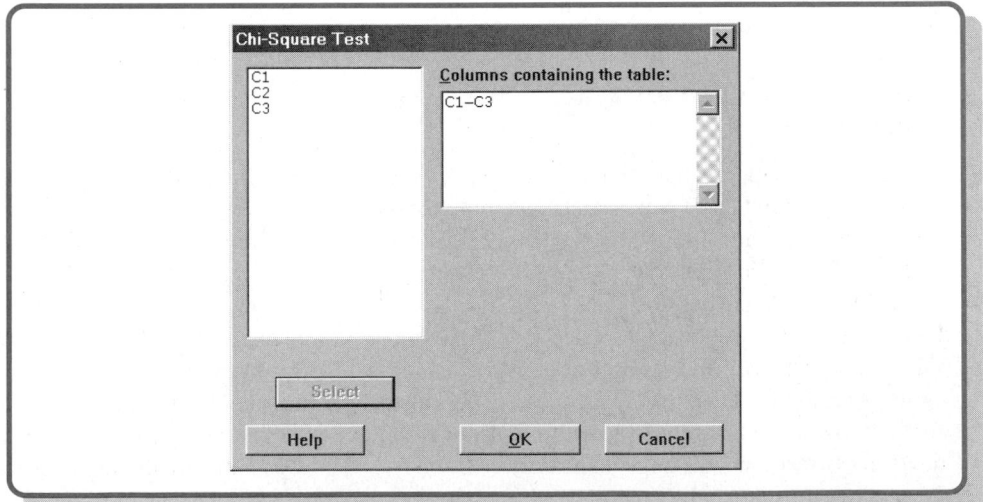

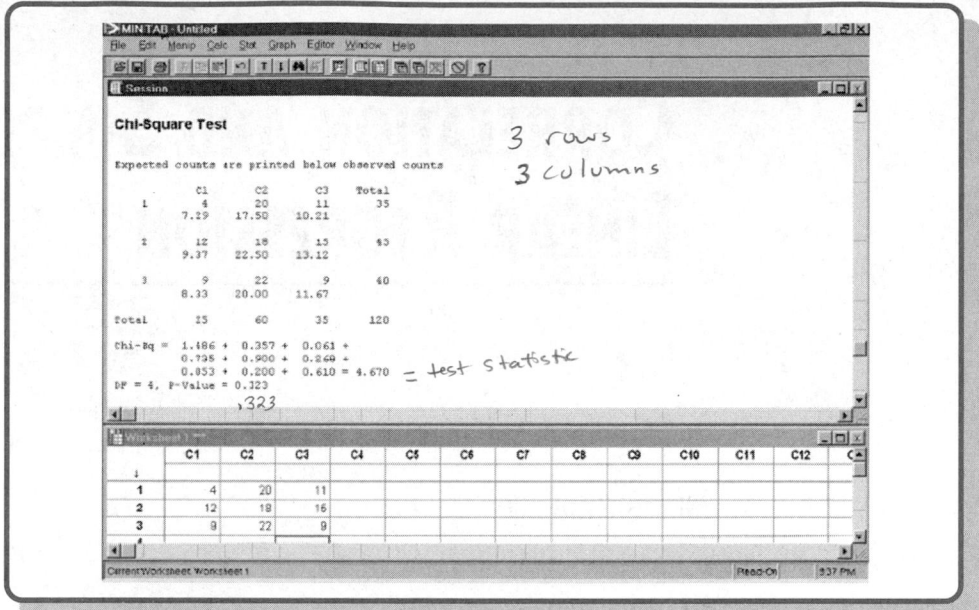

$\alpha = .05$

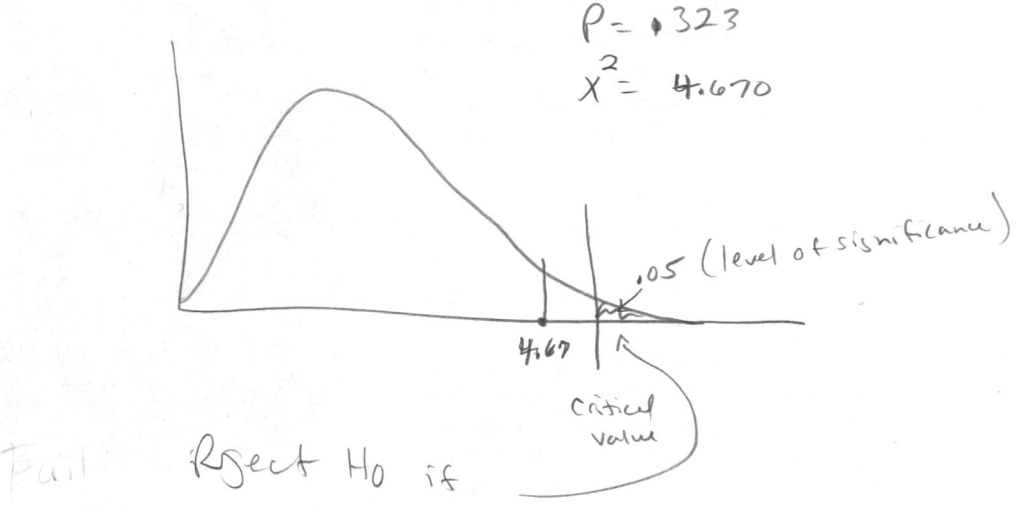

$P = .323$

$X^2 = 4.670$

.05 (level of significance)

4.67

critical value

Fail   Reject H_0 if

Fail to reject if $P \geq \alpha .05$
          it is, so

Fail to reject H_0
Rows + columns are independent

CHAPTER 14

CORRELATION AND SIMPLE LINEAR REGRESSION

STATISTICS IN ACTION: UNEMPLOYMENT AND ITS RELATIONSHIP TO PUBLIC SOCIAL EXPENDITURE AS A PERCENTAGE OF GDP: AN INTERNATIONAL CONCERN

Prime Minister Tony Blair of Great Britain has been promoting Britain's New Deal as a way to stem the tide of unemployment benefits. The rest of Europe is watching. One area where Europe needs to change the most, but has changed the least, is welfare reform. Under Britain's New Deal, hundreds of unemployed youths are being coaxed, prodded and, eventually, pushed off the dole under the new leadership.

To workers in Continental Europe, threatening to throw people off the dole if they don't find work may seem draconian. However, critics believe that generous benefits have made it comfortable for some Europeans to stay unemployed. Prime Minister Blair's solution is that young people should be prodded to take a job, any job, as opposed to holding out for the ideal job. With a jobless rate of 6.5%, the United Kingdom has one of the lowest unemployment rates in Europe. But unemployment in the United Kingdom among young people is much higher, at 10%. In Britain, long-term unemployment is defined as not having worked in six months.

Many political analysts believe that public social expenditure, as a large percentage of GNP, contributes to unemployment. Currently, the United States has one of smallest unemployment rates and spends far less than most European countries on social expenditure as a percentage of GDP (gross domestic product). For all the talk about welfare reform, Western Europe still spends 30% of government budgets on welfare and social programs overall. Sweden has the highest at 35%, compared with 15.8% in the U.S. and 13.8% in Japan, according to the Organization for Economic Cooperation and Development.

Statistical analysis on the relationship of social expenditure to the unemployment rate may convince many politicians that the risks of curtailing social programs are worth it. The extensive welfare state defined

postwar Europe and bolstered its self-image, making it different and—in Europe's mind—better than other parts of the world. In a sign of how entrenched the entitlement culture remains in Europe, long-term unemployed workers in France have not only staged demonstrations but have occupied government offices in a bid to get more benefits. Britain's bold move toward overhauling its 50-year-old welfare system is making many workers and unemployed working groups feel uneasy, particularly on the continent.

While Europe has taken many steps in the 1990s to become more competitive and regain its economic vitality, further progress is difficult. That is why still-generous welfare handouts need to be seriously curtailed. That may be too difficult to accept.

This chapter will examine a sample of two variables (say, X = social expenditure as a percentage of GDP, and

Y = unemployment rate for 12 countries) and will determine if there is a basic linear relationship between them. By this we mean that if these 12 sample observations are plotted in a simple X-Y graph (called a scatter plot), there is a straight line that does a good job of "slicing through" the 12 observations.

When you have completed this chapter, you will be able to:

* Measure the strength of the linear relationship between two variables (say, X and Y);

* Construct the best line through a sample of such data;
* Predict the value of one variable (say, Y = unemployment rate) using the other variable (say, X = social expenditure as a percentage of GDP) as a predictor, if a significant linear relationship exists; and
* Determine which observations would be considered as outliers and which observations, if removed, would have a dramatic effect on the best line through the observations.

A LOOK BACK/INTRODUCTION

The early chapters discussed methods of reducing a set of values for one variable to a graph (such as a histogram) or a numerical measure (such as a mean). A **variable** here is a characteristic of the population being measured or observed. For example, the variable of interest might be an individual's height or income. The sample then consists of random observations of the variable describing a given population.

In this chapter we discuss the situation in which the population and sample consist of measurements not of *one* variable but of *two*. As a result, we not only can describe each variable individually—we can also describe how the two variables are related. The relationship between the two variables can be described using a simple graph or a numerical measure (statistic). We can then use the sample results to form a conclusion about the population from which the sample was obtained. If we believe that a linear relationship between the two variables exists, the next step is to construct the "best-fitting" line through the points defined by the sample bivariate data.

Finally, we turn our attention to the question of what we are estimating when sampling from a population of bivariate data. How can we determine whether a significant linear relationship exists? To answer this question, we introduce the concept of a **statistical model** and the assumptions behind it. Various tests of hypothesis examine the adequacy of this model (is it a good one?), and an assortment of confidence intervals measure the reliability of the corresponding estimates using this model.

14.1 BIVARIATE DATA AND CORRELATION

With bivariate data, each observation consists of data on two variables. For example, you obtain a sample of people and record their ages (X) and liquid assets (Y). Or, for each month, you record the average interest rate (X) and the number of new housing starts (Y). These data are *paired*.

Suppose that a real-estate developer is interested in determining the relationship between family income (X, in thousands of dollars) of the local residents and the square footage of their homes (Y, in hundreds of square feet). A random sample of ten families is obtained with the following results:

Income (X)	32	36	55	47	38	60	66	44	70	50
Square footage (Y)	16	17	26	24	22	21	32	18	30	20

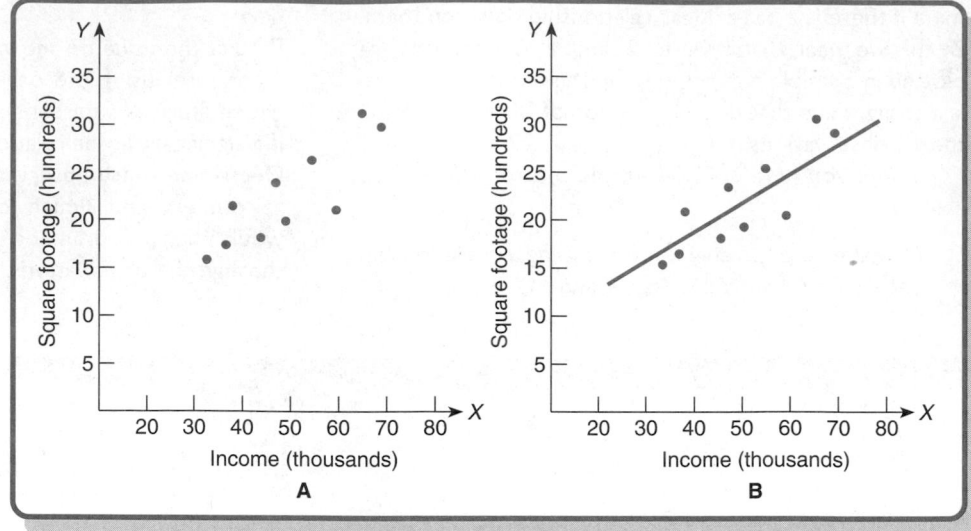

Bivariate data can be represented graphically using a **scatter diagram.** In this graph, each observation is represented by a point, where the X axis is always horizontal and the Y axis is vertical. A scatter diagram of the real-estate data is shown in Figure 14.1a. The underlying pattern here appears to be that larger incomes (X) are associated with larger home sizes (Y). In this example X and Y have a **positive (direct) relationship**. A **negative (inverse) relationship** occurs when Y decreases as X increases—for example, when Y is the demand for a particular consumer product and X is the selling price.

We next try to determine whether we can estimate this relationship by means of a straight line. One possible line is sketched in Figure 14.1b; it passes among these points and has a positive slope. To measure the strength of the linear relationship between these two variables, we determine the coefficient of correlation.

COEFFICIENT OF CORRELATION

It is often difficult to determine whether a *significant* linear relationship exists between X and Y by inspecting a scatter diagram of the data. A second procedure is to include a *measure* of this linearity—the sample coefficient of correlation. It is computed from the sample data by combining these pairs of values into a single number, written as r. The sample **coefficient of correlation, r,** measures the strength of the linear relationship that exists within a sample of n bivariate data. Its value is given by

$$r = \frac{\sum(x-\bar{x})(y-\bar{y})}{\sqrt{\sum(x-\bar{x})^2}\sqrt{\sum(y-\bar{y})^2}} \qquad (14.1)$$

$$= \frac{\sum xy - (\sum x)(\sum y)/n}{\sqrt{\sum x^2 - (\sum x)^2/n}\sqrt{\sum y^2 - (\sum y)^2/n}} \qquad (14.2)$$

where $\sum x$ = sum of X values, $\sum x^2$ = sum of X^2 values, $\sum y$ = sum of Y values, $\sum y^2$ = sum of Y^2 values, $\sum xy$ = sum of XY values, $\bar{x} = \sum x/n$, and $\bar{y} = \sum y/n$. When using a calculator to determine a coefficient of correlation, equation 14.2 provides a computationally easier procedure. Notice that the summations in the denominator of equation 14.1 are the numerators for the sample variances of X and Y.

SUM OF SQUARES

We will introduce a shorthand notation at this point, related to the notation in Chapter 11 for ANOVA. Let

$$SS_X = \text{sum of squares for } X$$

$$= \sum (x - \bar{x})^2$$

$$= \sum x^2 - \frac{(\sum x)^2}{n} \tag{14.3}$$

$$SS_Y = \text{sum of squares for } Y$$

$$= \sum (y - \bar{y})^2$$

$$= \sum y^2 - \frac{(\sum y)^2}{n} \tag{14.4}$$

$$SCP_{XY} = \text{sum of cross products for } XY$$

$$= \sum (x - \bar{x})(y - \bar{y})$$

$$= \sum xy - \frac{(\sum x)(\sum y)}{n} \tag{14.5}$$

Using this notation, we can write r as   *Condensed formula*

$$r = \frac{SCP_{XY}}{\sqrt{SS_X}\sqrt{SS_Y}} \tag{14.6}$$

The following are some important properties of the sample correlation coefficient r.

1. r ranges from -1.0 to 1.0.
2. The larger $|r|$ (absolute value of r) is, the stronger is the linear relationship.
3. r near zero indicates that there is no linear relationship between X and Y, and the scatter diagram *typically* (although not necessarily) appears to have a shotgun effect (Figure 14.2a). Here, X and Y are uncorrelated.
4. $r = 1$ or $r = -1$ implies that a perfect linear pattern exists between the two variables in the sample, that is, a single line will go *through* each point. Here we say that X and Y are **perfectly correlated** (Figure 14.2b and c).
5. Values of $r = 0$, 1, or -1 are rare in practice. Several other values of the correlation coefficient are illustrated in Figure 14.2d, e, and f.
6. The sign of r tells you whether the relationship between X and Y is a positive (direct) or a negative (inverse) one.
7. The value of r tells you very little about the slope of the line through these points (except for the sign of r). If r is positive, the line through these points has positive slope, and similarly, this line will have negative slope if r is negative. However, a set of data with $r = .9$ will not necessarily have a steeper line passing through it than will a set of data with $r = .4$. All you will observe in the first data set is a set of points that is very close to some straight line with positive slope, but you know nothing (except for the sign) about the slope of this line. See Figure 14.3, where both sets of data have an r value of .9.

FIGURE 14.2
Scatter diagrams for various values of the sample correlation coefficient.

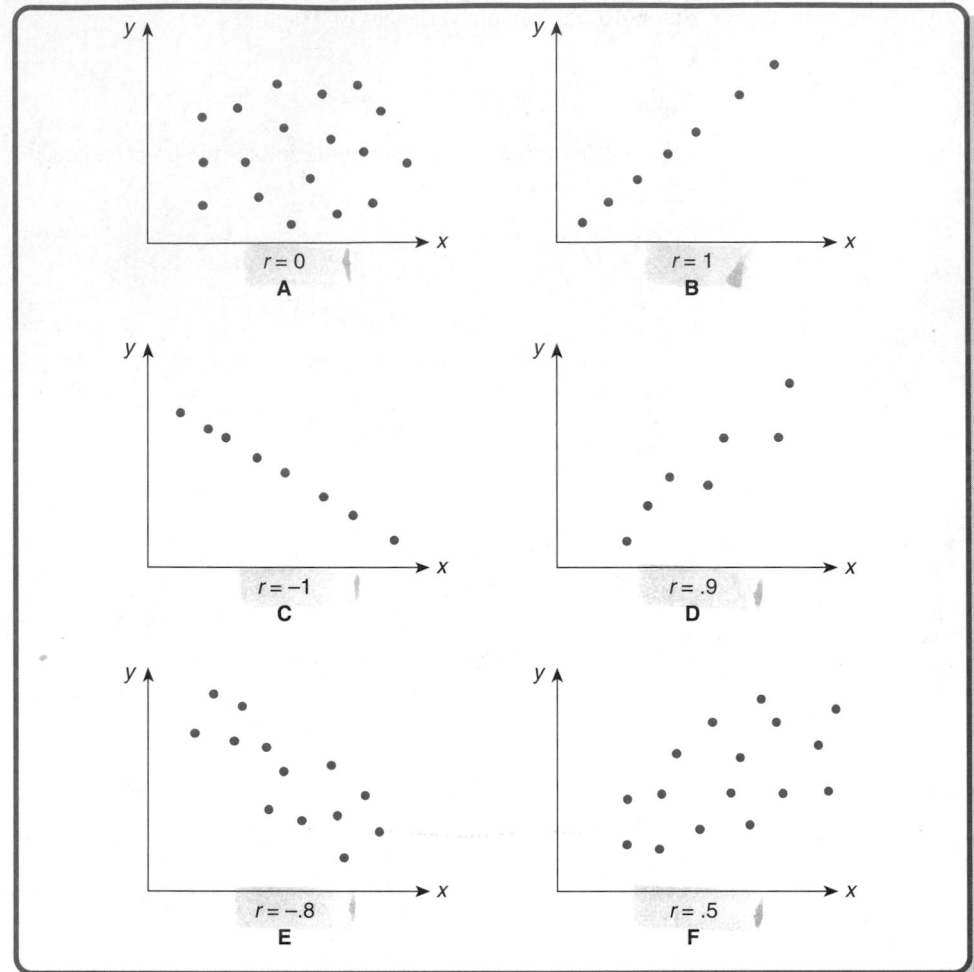

FIGURE 14.3
Although (a) has a large slope and (b) has a small slope, both are scatter diagrams for $r = .9$.

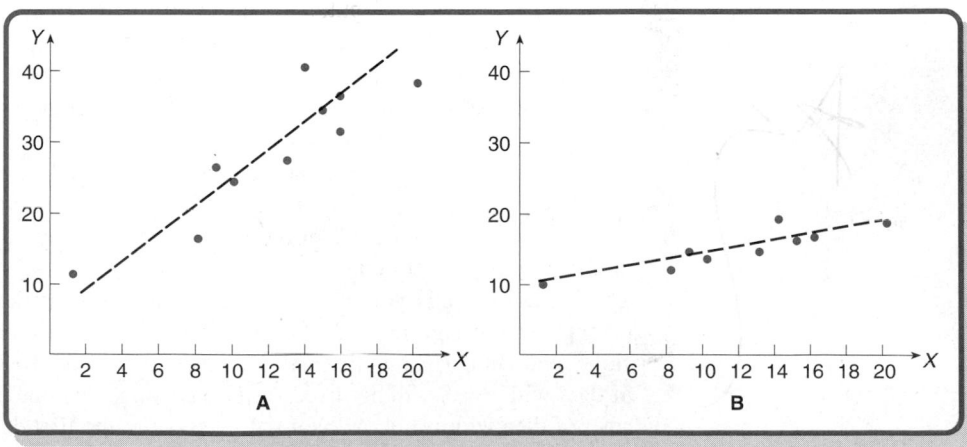

EXAMPLE 14.1

Determine the sample correlation coefficient for the real-estate data in Figure 14.1.

SOLUTION

Your calculations can be organized as follows:

Family	X (Income)	Y (Square Footage)	XY	X^2	Y^2
1	32	16	512	1,024	256
2	36	17	612	1,296	289
3	55	26	1,430	3,025	676
4	47	24	1,128	2,209	576
5	38	22	836	1,444	484
6	60	21	1,260	3,600	441
7	66	32	2,112	4,356	1,024
8	44	18	792	1,936	324
9	70	30	2,100	4,900	900
10	50	20	1,000	2,500	400
	498	226	11,782	26,290	5,370

Using the totals from this table,

$$SS_X = 26,290 - \frac{(498)^2}{10} = 1489.6$$

$$SS_Y = 5370 - \frac{(226)^2}{10} = 262.4$$

$$SCP_{XY} = 11,782 - \frac{(498)(226)}{10} = 527.2$$

This value of the sample correlation coefficient is

$$r = \frac{SCP_{XY}}{\sqrt{SS_X}\sqrt{SS_Y}}$$

$$= \frac{527.2}{\sqrt{1489.6}\sqrt{262.4}} = \frac{527.2}{625.2} = .843$$

USING EXCEL. For large data sets, the easiest way to obtain a scatter diagram and calculate the value of r is to use a computer. At the end of the chapter, we will show you how to do this using MINITAB. The Excel result is shown in Figure 14.4. To obtain this output, follow this sequence:

1. Click on the **Chart Wizard** icon (   ) ➤ **XY (Scatter)** ➤ **Next.** Enter "A1:B10" in the **Data Range** box (click on **Next**). Click on the **Titles** tab and enter "Real Estate Data" for the chart title, "Income" in the **Value (X) Axis** box, and "Footage" in the **Value (Y) Axis** box. Click on **Finish.**
2. Drag the plot so that the upper left corner is in cell C1 as shown in Figure 14.4. The resulting plot will begin the X and Y axes at zero. To obtain the more focused plot in Figure 14.4, *right* click on any of the values along the X axis, click on **Format Axis,** and then click on the **Scale** tab. Set the minimum value to 30 and the maximum value to 75. Repeat this for the Y axis by right clicking on any of the Y axis values, clicking on the **Scale** tab, and setting the minimum value to 15 and the maximum value to 35.
3. Enter "Correlation Coefficient" in cell A11. Click on (activate) cell A12 and click on the **Paste** function icon (   ) ➤ **Statistical** ➤ **CORREL.** Enter "A1:A10" for **Array 1** and "B1:B10" for **Array 2.** The resulting correlation coefficient ($r = .843$) should appear in cell A12.

FIGURE 14.4

Excel-generated scatter diagram and correlation coefficient for real estate data.

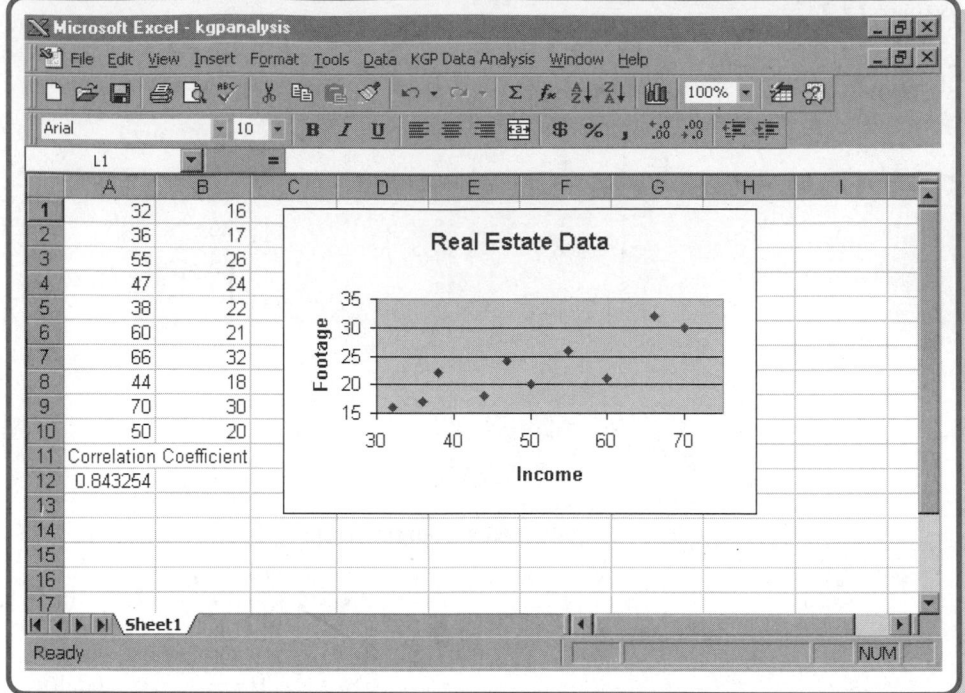

COVARIANCE

Another commonly used measure of the association between two variables, X and Y, is the sample covariance, written cov(X, Y). It is similar to the sample correlation between these two variables. For one thing, the covariance and correlation always have the *same sign*. Consequently, if large values of X are associated with large values of Y, then both the covariance and correlation are positive. Similarly, both values are negative whenever large values of X are associated with small values of Y. For any two variables, X and Y, the sample **covariance** between these variables is defined in the following box.

DEFINITION

The sample covariance between two variables, cov(X, Y) is a measure of the joint variation of the two variables, X and Y, and is defined to be

$$\text{cov}(X, Y) = \frac{1}{n-1}\sum(x - \bar{x})(y - \bar{y}) \qquad (14.7)$$

$$= \frac{1}{n-1}\text{SCP}_{XY} \qquad (14.8)$$

In Example 14.1, the sample covariance between income (X) and home size (Y) is

$$\text{cov}(X, Y) = \frac{1}{n-1}\text{SCP}_{XY} = \frac{1}{9}(527.2) = 58.58$$

To see how the sample covariance and sample correlation (r) are related, let

$$s_X = \text{standard deviation of the } X \text{ values } = \sqrt{\frac{\text{SS}_X}{n-1}}$$

and

$$s_Y = \text{standard deviation of the } Y \text{ values} = \sqrt{\frac{SS_Y}{n-1}}$$

Then

$$r = \text{sample correlation between } X \text{ and } Y$$

$$= \frac{\text{cov}(X, Y)}{s_X s_Y} \tag{14.9}$$

In Example 14.1,

$$s_X = \sqrt{\frac{1489.6}{9}} = 12.865 \qquad \text{and} \qquad s_Y = \sqrt{\frac{262.4}{9}} = 5.400$$

so

$$r = \frac{58.58}{(12.865)(5.400)} = .843 \qquad \text{(as before)}$$

The correlation between two variables is used more often than the covariance because r always ranges from -1 to 1. The covariance, on the other hand, has no limits and can assume any value. Furthermore, the units of measurement for a covariance are difficult to interpret. For example, the previously calculated covariance is 58.58 (thousands of dollars) · (hundreds of square feet)—a somewhat meaningless unit of measurement. So, in a sense, the correlation is a scaled version of the covariance and has no units of measurement (a nice feature). To illustrate, the sample correlation between body weight and height will be the same whether you use the metric or the English systems to obtain the sample data. The covariance, however, will *not* be the same for these two situations. The covariance does have its applications, however, particularly in financial analyses, such as determining the risk associated with a number of interrelated investment opportunities.

As a final look at these two measures, you can consider the correlation between two variables to be the covariance between the **standardized** variables. By defining

$$X' = \frac{X - \bar{X}}{s_X} \qquad \text{and} \qquad Y' = \frac{Y - \bar{Y}}{s_Y}$$

then

$$\text{cov}(X', Y') = \text{correlation between } X \text{ and } Y = r$$

LEAST SQUARES LINE

If we believe that two variables do exhibit an underlying linear pattern, how can we determine a straight line that best passes through these points? So far, we have demonstrated only the calculations necessary to compute a correlation coefficient. We next illustrate how to construct a line through a set of points exhibiting a linear pattern; we look at the assumptions behind this procedure in the next section.

Look at the scatter diagram in Figure 14.1b, which shows one possible line through these points. The scatter diagram and line are repeated in Figure 14.5, which also shows the vertical distances from each point to the line ($d_1, d_2, \ldots$).

Is line L the best line through these points? Because we would like the distances d_1, $d_2, \ldots, d_{10}$ to be small, we define the best line to be the one that minimizes

$$\sum d^2 = d_1^2 + d_2^2 + d_3^2 + \cdots + d_{10}^2 \tag{14.10}$$

FIGURE 14.5
Vertical distances from line L
to real-estate data (Example
14.1), represented by
$d_1, d_2, \ldots, d_{10}$.

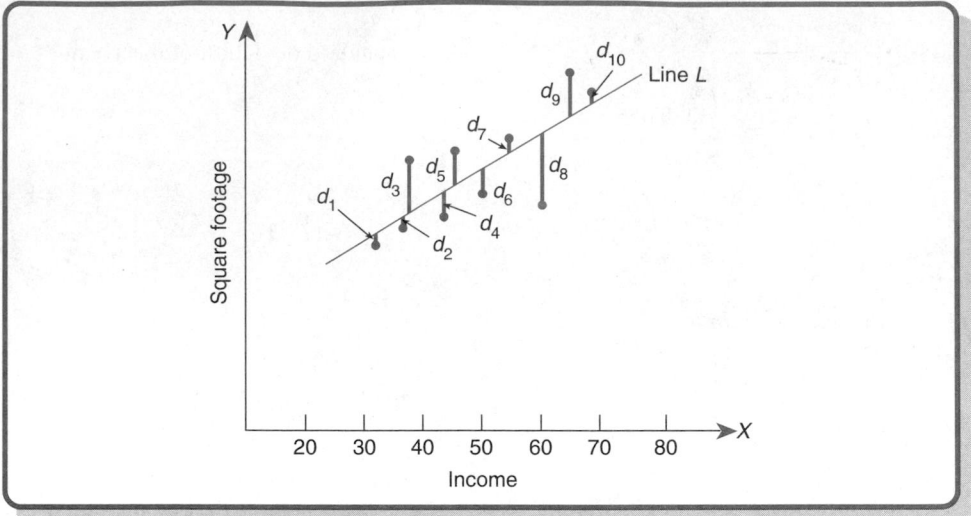

We square each distance because some of these distances are positive (the point lies *above* line L) and some are negative (the point lies *below* line L.) If we did not square each distance, d, the positive d's might cancel out the negative ones. This means that using $(d_1 + d_2 + \cdots + d_{10})$ as a *measure of fit* is *not* a good idea. A better method is to determine which line makes equation 14.10 as small as possible; this line is called the **least squares line.** Deriving this line in general requires the use of calculus (derivatives, in particular).*

Because we intend to use this line to predict Y for a particular value of X, we use the notation $\hat{Y}$ (Y-hat) to describe the equation of the line. We can now define, for the least squares line, the b_0 and b_1 that minimize $(d_1^2 + d_2^2 + \cdots + d_n^2)$, given by

$$b_1 = \frac{SCP_{XY}}{SS_X} \qquad (14.11)$$

$$b_0 = \bar{y} - b_1 \bar{x} \qquad (14.12)$$

where SS_X and SCP_{XY} are as defined in equations 14.3 and 14.5. Also, $\bar{x} = \sum x/n$ and $\bar{y} = \sum y/n$. The resulting least squares line is

$$\hat{Y} = b_0 + b_1 X$$

In Figure 14.6, notice that each distance, d, is actually $Y - \hat{Y}$ and consists of the **residual,** encountered by using the straight line to estimate the value of Y at this point. So

$$\sum d^2 = \sum (y - \hat{y})^2$$

This term is the **sum of squares of error** (or *residual sum of squares*) and is written **SSE.** Consequently, the least squares line is the one that makes SSE as small as possible.

---

* For the mathematically curious, we provide a condensed derivation of these coefficients. To minimize $\sum d^2$, first write this expression as

$$f(b_0, b_1) = \sum d^2 = \sum (y - \hat{y})^2$$
$$= \sum (y - b_0 - b_1 x)^2$$

because $\hat{y} = b_0 + b_1 x$.

To minimize this function, determine the partial derivatives with respect to b_0 (written as f_{b_0} and with respect to b_1 (written as f_{b_1}). These are

$$f_{b_0} = 2\sum (y - b_0 - b_1 x)(-1) = -2[\sum y - nb_0 - b_1 \sum x]$$

$$f_{b_1} = 2\sum (y - b_0 - b_1 x)(-x) = -2[\sum xy - b_0 \sum x - b_1 \sum x^2]$$

Setting $f_{b_0} = f_{b_1} = 0$ and solving for b_0 and b_1 results in equations 14.11 and 14.12.

FIGURE 14.6

The least squares line for Example 14.1. Each $d = Y - \hat{Y}$, the error encountered by using the straight line to estimate the value of Y at the corresponding point.

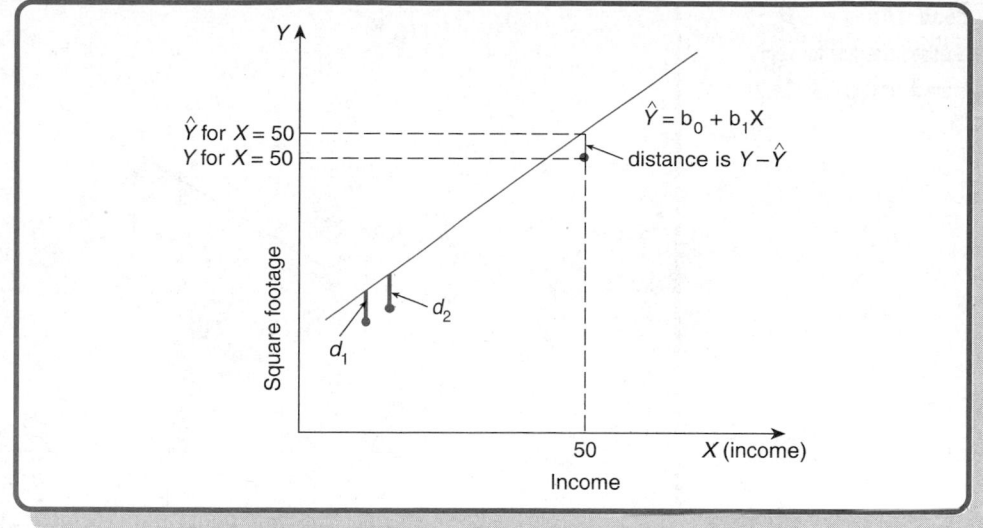

$$SSE = \Sigma d^2 = \Sigma(y - \hat{y})^2 \qquad\qquad (14.13)$$

There is another method of determining SSE when using the least squares line, which avoids having to determine the value of $\hat{Y}$ at each point:

$$SSE = SS_Y - \frac{(SCP_{XY})^2}{SS_X} \qquad\qquad (14.14)$$

EXAMPLE 14.2

Determine the least squares line for the real-estate data we used in Example 14.1. What is the SSE?

SOLUTION

Using the calculations from Example 14.1, $SCP_{XY} = 527.2$, $SS_X = 1489.6$, and $SS_Y = 262.4$, leading to

$$b_1 = \frac{SCP_{XY}}{SS_X}$$

$$= \frac{527.2}{1489.6} = .3539$$

$$SSE = 262.4 - \frac{(527.2)^2}{1489.6}$$

and

$$b_0 = \bar{y} - b_1\bar{x}$$

SCP+y   *mean of y*

$$= 22.6 - \left(\frac{527.2}{1489.6}\right)(49.8) = 4.975$$

SSx

because

$$\bar{y} = \frac{\Sigma y}{n} = \frac{226}{10} = 22.6 \qquad \text{and} \qquad \bar{x} = \frac{\Sigma x}{n} = \frac{498}{10} = 49.8$$

So the equation of the best (least squares) line through these points is

$$\hat{Y} = 4.975 + .3539X$$

B_0 + B_1 is (slope)

FIGURE 14.7

Least squares line for real-
estate data (Example 14.2).

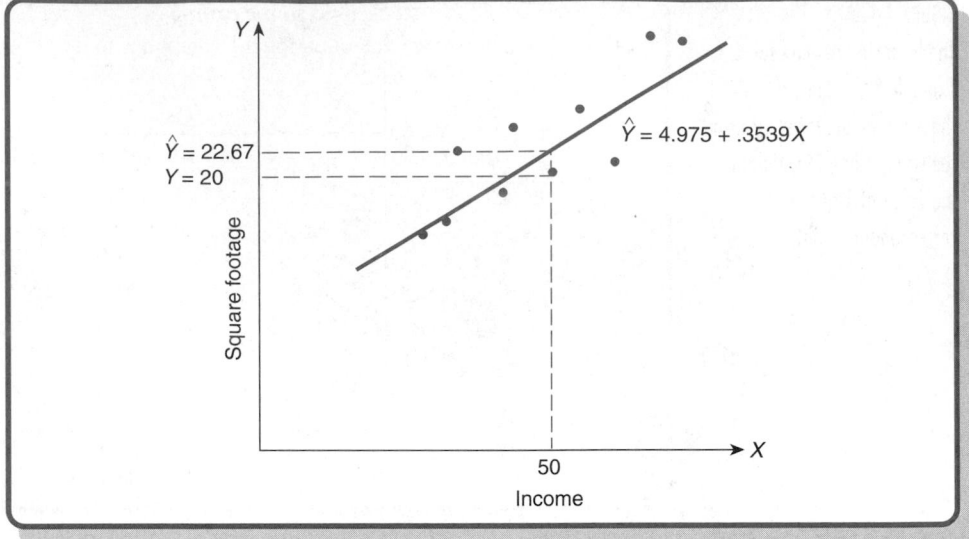

This equation tells us that in the sample data an increase of $1000 in income ($X$ increases by 1) is accompanied by an increase of 35.39 square feet in home size (Y increases by .3539), on the average. For this illustration (and many others in practice), the *intercept, b_0*, has no real meaning because it corresponds to an income of zero dollars. Furthermore, an income of zero is considerably outside the range of the incomes in the sample. It is unsafe to assume that the linear relationship between X and Y present over the range of sample incomes ($32,000 to $70,000) exists outside this range—in particular, all the way to an income of zero. The *slope, b_1*, generally is the more informative value.

In Figure 14.7, the actual value of Y (in the sample data) for $X = 50$ is $Y = 20$ (the last pair of X, Y values). The predicted value of Y using the least squares line is

$$\hat{Y} = 4.975 + (.3539)(50) = 22.670$$

The residual at this point is

$$\text{residual} = Y - \hat{Y} = 20 - 22.670 = -2.670$$

Repeating this for the other nine points leads to the following results. Notice that the sum of the residuals when using the least squares line is zero. This is always true.

X	Y	$\hat{Y}$	$Y - \hat{Y}$	$(Y - \hat{Y})^2$
32	16	16.300	−0.300	0.090
36	17	17.715	−0.715	0.511
55	26	24.440	1.560	2.434
47	24	21.608	2.392	5.722
38	22	18.423	3.577	12.795
60	21	26.209	−5.209	27.134
66	32	28.332	3.668	13.454
44	18	20.547	−2.547	6.487
70	30	29.748	0.252	0.064
50	20	22.670	−2.670	7.129
			0	75.82

⌐ Rounded

As you can see, calculating the SSE (=75.82) using the table and equation 14.13 is tedious. Using equation 14.14 instead leads to

$$\text{SSE} = 262.4 - \frac{(527.2)^2}{1489.6}$$

$$= 262.4 - 186.59$$

$$= 75.81$$

This calculated SSE value is slightly more accurate than the value obtained by summing the squared residuals and will be used in the examples to follow.

Remember, however, that equation 14.13 applies to *any* line that you choose to construct through these points, whereas equation 14.14 applies only to the SSE for the least squares line.

In Example 14.2, we attempted to predict the size of a home (Y) using the corresponding income (X). The variable Y is the **dependent variable,** and X is the **independent variable.** By passing a straight line through the sample points with Y as the dependent variable, we are **regressing** Y on X. *In linear regression, you regress the dependent variable, Y, which you are trying to predict, on the independent (or predictor or explanatory) variable, X.*

EXERCISES 14.1–14.12

UNDERSTANDING THE MECHANICS

14.1 Consider the following table.

X	Y	XY	X²	Y²
3	8			
10	22			
2	6			
5	9			
4	8			

Totals $\Sigma x = \underline{24}$ $\Sigma y = \underline{53}$ $\Sigma xy = \underline{\quad}$ $\Sigma x^2 = \underline{\quad}$ $\Sigma y^2 = \underline{\quad}$

a. Find the totals for each column in the table.

b. Use the totals in the table to calculate the slope and the intercept for the least squares line.

c. Calculate the sample correlation of X and Y.

14.2 The following pairs of measurements were observed.

X	10	12	11	8	6	5
Y	9	7	6	11	15	19

a. Draw a scatter diagram of X and Y.

b. What relationship does the scatter diagram suggest about X and Y?

c. Find the least squares line.

d. Verify that the sum of the deviations from the least squares line is zero.

APPLYING THE NEW CONCEPTS

14.3 Tony's used-car lot has been paying car salespeople the highest commission in town. Tony decides to compile data to substantiate his belief that monthly net earnings increase when the car salespeople are highly paid. Fifteen months are chosen:

Net Earnings (Y)	Total Commissions Paid (X)	Net Earnings (Y)	Total Commissions Paid (X)
10,780	3,680	11,915	3,161
15,120	5,160	25,160	7,540
18,195	5,180	26,151	8,216
21,690	7,150	18,630	6,051
14,691	5,030	15,551	4,980
16,151	5,210	16,980	5,801
11,015	2,991	24,130	7,160
10,151	3,151		

a. Graph the data and draw a line through them, using the "eyeball" method.

b. Calculate the least squares line. How does it compare to the line in part (a)?

14.4 The supervisor of a group of assembly-line workers wanted to compare last year's productivity (X) to this year's productivity (Y) for each of the 20 employees that she supervises. In the past, an approximate linear relationship has existed between these two variables. Last year the average productivity per worker was 9.5 items per hour. This year, the average productivity per worker is 12.1 items per hour. The supervisor found the following sums for her 20 employees:

$$SCP_{XY} = 0.4$$

$$SS_X = 0.3$$

$$SS_Y = 0.8$$

a. Calculate the correlation coefficient.

b. Calculate the least squares line.

c. Calculate the sum of squares for error.

14.5 Because $b_0 = \bar{y} - b_1\bar{x}$, we can replace b_0 in $\hat{Y} = b_0 + b_1X$ by $\bar{y} - b_1\bar{x}$. Hence, we have $\hat{Y} = \bar{y} + b_1(X - \bar{x})$. From this equation, show that the point $(\bar{x}, \bar{y})$ always falls on the least squares line.

14.6 Compare the formulas for the sample correlation, r, and the slope of the least squares line, b_1, and verify that $b_1 = r\sqrt{SS_Y/SS_X}$. What can we say about the sign of r and b_1?

14.7 Generale Bank agreed to a takeover from the Dutch-Belgian bank and insurance concern, named Fortis Group. This acquisition would propel Fortis to the top league of Europe's largest financial institutions and speed up other cross-border mergers in the European financial-services sector, an industry roiled by mounting competition and the launch of a single European currency. Generale Bank management advisor is interested in the relationship between the market capitalization of Europe's main bank insurance concerns and their total assets. The following data are listed as a random sample of these European companies with their market capitalization and total assets in billions of dollars.

European Bank Insurance Firm	Market Capitalization	Total Assets
Deutsche Bank	46.3	585.0
Credit Suisse	59.1	370.0
ING Group	49.4	309.4
Benelux Bank	23.8	168.0
Generale Bank	9.8	160.8
CGER-ASLK	33.6	328.8

(Adapted from *The Wall Street Journal,* "Belgium's Largest Bank Agrees to Be Acquired by Fortis Group," May 13, 1998, p. C14.)

a. Graph the data. Estimate the intercept and slope of the regression equation from viewing the graph. Also, estimate the correlation coefficient.

b. Calculate the least squares line. Interpret the coefficients of the regression equation. How closely do the calculated values of the least squares line agree with your estimates from part (a)?

c. Calculate the correlation coefficient and compare to your estimate from part (a).

14.8 The owner of Grandmother's Cake Shop would like to predict the quantity of cakes sold when they are marked at low prices. There are no restrictions on the quantity, because the shop can easily bake several cakes in an hour if the demand is stronger than predicted. Past data show the following results.

Number of Cakes Sold (Y)	Price of Cake (X)	Number of Cakes Sold (Y)	Price of Cake (X)
14	2.30	16	1.99
16	2.10	17	1.90
17	1.80	15	2.25
17	1.89	14	2.39
13	2.50	13	2.70
12	2.80		

a. Find the least squares line for X and Y.

b. Graph the data and the least squares line.

c. Suppose that the manager believes that there is a strong linear relationship between Y and X^2. Find the prediction equation for Y using X^2 only.

d. Compare the SSE for the least squares line found in part (a) with the least squares line found in part (c).

14.9 According to U.S. House Budget Committee Chairman Martin Sabo, Democrat from Minnesota, one of the most disturbing trends in the American economy is the ongoing polarization of income. The chairman is concerned about the high poverty rate in several states. Consider the following random sample of 10 states, giving the median 1992 income, in dollars, and poverty rate, in percentage.

State	Median Income	Poverty Rate
Arizona	29,593	15.1
Colorado	32,716	10.6
Connecticut	41,059	9.4
Florida	27,456	15.3
Louisiana	25,479	24.2
Michigan	32,347	13.5
New Jersey	39,227	10.0
New Mexico	26,158	21.0
Rhode Island	30,636	12.0
Virginia	38,223	9.4

(Source: Adapted from *Dallas Morning News,* "Number of Poor Americans Up in '92, Census Bureau Says," Oct. 5, 1993, p. 7A.)

a. Use simple linear regression to model the relationship between the poverty rate (Y) and the median income (X).

b. Calculate the error sum of squares for the regression line.

14.10 Many of Japan's technology giants found themselves saddled with aging product line ups, a general falloff in consumer demand in Japan, and a strong yen that made their products more expensive overseas. Given that the electronics industry has been one of the main drivers for the Japanese economy, predicting the earnings for the Japanese electronics companies can be important in determining the direction of Japan's economy. Consider the following table listing the 1997 pretax profits (in billions of dollars) and the forecasted 1998 profits.

Electronics Company	Profits in 1997	Projected Profits in 1998
Hitachi	.69	.69
Toshiba	.98	.08
Sony	2.43	3.12
Fujitsu	1.11	1.32
Mitsubishi Electric	.07	−.08
Matsushita	2.59	2.90
Nec	.94	1.09

(Source: *The Wall Street Journal,* "Japan's Electronics Makers Expect Slump," Jan. 21, 1998, p. A17.)

a. Calculate the least squares line. Interpret the coefficients of the least squares line in the context of this problem.

b. Calculate the error sum of squares.

c. Graph the data, and draw the least squares line through them.

USING THE COMPUTER

14.11 [DATA SET EX14-11] *Variable description:*

NumberYears: Number of years invested in a retirement plan
ValuePlan: The value of a retirement plan

A financial planner wishes to determine the relationship between the number of years that employees have invested in a company's retirement program and the value of their retirement package at that time. The data in NumberYears are in years, and the data in ValuePlan are in units of thousands of dollars.

a. Find the correlation between NumberYears and ValuePlan.

b. From the value of the correlation in part (a), do you think that the plot of $Y =$ ValuePlan and $X =$ NumberYears will be approximately linear? Plot the values.

c. Multiply ValuePlan by 1.5 and add 5 (thousand). Do you think that the value of the correlation in part (b) will be affected? Try it.

14.12 [DATA SET EX14-12] *Variable description:*

AskPrice: Asking price of a car
SellPrice: Selling price of a car

A car dealer is interested in the relationship between the original asking price of a new car and the final selling price of the car. The car dealer selected a random sample of 50 car deals. The asking and selling prices were recorded as variables AskPrice and SellPrice, respectively. The units of the data are in thousands of dollars.

a. Graph the data. Estimate the intercept and slope of the regression equation from viewing the graph. Estimate the value of the correlation from viewing the graph.

b. Calculate the correlation coefficient and find the coefficients of the least squares line. Compare your answers to that in part (a).

14.2 THE SIMPLE LINEAR REGRESSION MODEL

When we construct a straight line through a set of data points, we are attempting to predict the behavior of a dependent variable, Y, using a straight line equation with one predictor (independent) variable, X. Examples 14.1 and 14.2 examined the relationship in a particular community between the square footage (Y) of a particular home and the income of the owner (X).

Another applicant is attempting to predict the sales (Y) of a certain brand of shampoo using the amount of advertising expenditure (X) as the independent variable. We expect that as more advertising dollars are spent, the sales will increase. In other words, we expect a *positive* relationship for this situation.

Regression analysis is a method of studying the relationship between two (or more) variables, one purpose being to arrive at a method for predicting a value of the dependent variable. In **simple linear regression,** we use only *one* predictor variable, X, to describe the behavior of the dependent variable, Y. Also, the relationship between X and Y is assumed to be basically linear.

We have learned the mechanics of constructing a line through a set of bivariate sample values. We are now ready to introduce the concept of a statistical model.

DEFINING THE MODEL

Return to Example 14.2 and Figure 14.4. This set of sample data contained a value of $X = 50$ and $Y = 20$. Consider the population of *all* houses in this community where the owner's income is 50 (that is, $50,000). Will they all have the same square footage? Unless this is a very boring-looking neighborhood, certainly not. Does this mean that the straight line predictor is of no use? The answer again is no; we do not expect things in this world to be that perfectly predictable. When you use the equation of a straight line to predict the square footage, you should be aware that there will be a certain amount of *error* present in this estimate. This is similar to the situation in which we estimate the mean, μ, of a population and the sample mean, $\bar{X}$, always estimates this parameter with a certain amount of inherent error.

When we elect to use a straight-line predictor, we employ a **statistical model** of the form

$$Y = \beta_0 + \beta_1 X + e \qquad\qquad (14.15)$$

where (1) $\beta_0 + \beta_1 X$ is the *assumed* line about which *all* values of X and Y will fall, called the **deterministic** portion of the model, and (2) e is the error component, referred to as the **random** part of the model.

In other words, there exists some (unknown) line about which all X, Y values can be expected to fall. Notice that we said "about which," not "on which"—hence the necessity of the error term, e, which is the unexplained error that is part of the simple linear model. Because this model considers only one independent variable, the effect of other predictor variables (perhaps unknown to the analyst) is contained in this error term.

We emphasize that the deterministic portion, $\beta_0 + \beta_1 X$, refers to the straight line for the *population* and will remain unknown. However, by obtaining a random sample of bivariate data from this population, we are able to estimate the unknown parameters, β_0 and β_1.

Thus b_0 is the **intercept** of the sample regression line and is the estimate of the population intercept, β_0. The value of b_0 can be calculated using equation 14.12. Similarly, b_1 is the **slope** of the sample regression line and is the estimate of the population slope, β_1. The value of b_1 can be calculated using equation 14.11.

ASSUMPTIONS FOR THE SIMPLE LINEAR REGRESSION MODEL

We can construct a least squares line through *any* set of sample points, whether or not the pattern is linear. We could construct a least squares line through a set of sample data exhibiting no linear pattern at all. However, to have an effective predictor and a model that will enable us to make statistical decisions, certain assumptions are necessary.

We treat the values of X as fixed (nonrandom) quantities when using the simple linear regression model. For any given value of X, the only source of variation comes from the error component, e, which is a random variable. In fact, there are many random variables here, one for each possible value of X. The assumptions used with this model are concerned with the nature of these random variables.

The first three assumptions are concerned with the behavior of the error component for a fixed value of X. The fourth assumption deals with the manner in which the error components (random variables) affect each other.

ASSUMPTION 1. *The mean of each error component is zero.* This is the key assumption behind simple linear regression. Look at Figure 14.8, where we once again examine a value of $X = 50$. Considering all homes (in this community) whose owners have an income of $50,000 ($X = 50$), we have already decided that these homes do not all have the same square footage, Y. In fact, the square-footage values will be scattered about the (unknown) line $Y = \beta_0 + \beta_1 X$, with some values lying above the line (e is positive) and some falling below it (e is negative). Consider the average of *all* Y values with $X = 50$. This is written as

$$\mu_{Y|50}$$

which is the mean of Y *given* $X = 50$. Our assumption here is that the point $(50, \mu_{Y|50})$ *lies on this line;* that is, for *any* value of X, the point $(x, \mu_{Y|x})$ *lies on the line* $Y = \beta_0 + \beta_1 X$ (such as $\mu_{Y|35}$ in Figure 14.8). Put another way, the error is zero, *on the average*.

FIGURE 14.8

Illustration of assumption 1; see text.

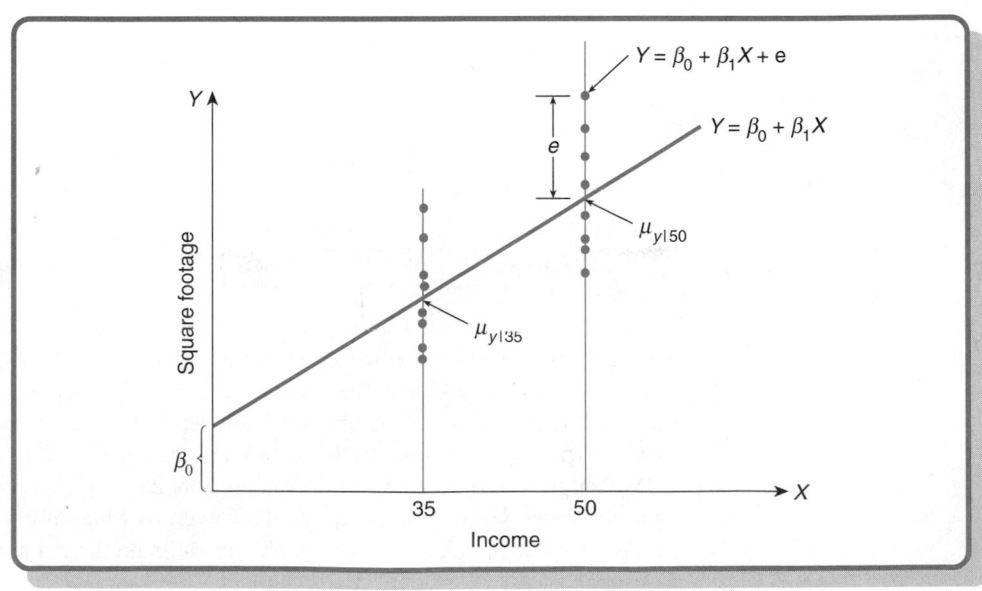

● **ASSUMPTION 2.** *Each error component (random variable) follows an approximate normal distribution.* In our sample of ten homes and incomes, we had one family with $X = 50$ and $Y = 20$. Figure 14.8 illustrates what we might expect if we were to examine other homes whose owners had an income of $50,000. We assume here that if we were to obtain 100 homes, for example, whose owners had this income, a histogram of the resulting errors (e) would be bell-shaped in appearance. So we would expect a concentration of errors near zero (from assumption 1), with half of them positive and half of them negative.

● **ASSUMPTION 3.** *The variance of the error component, σ_e^2, is the same for each value of X.* For each value of X, the errors illustrated in Figure 14.8 have so far been assumed to follow a normal distribution with a mean of zero. So each error, e, is from such a normal population. The variance of this population is σ_e^2. The assumption here is that σ_e^2 *does not change* as the value of X changes. This is the assumption of **homoscedasticity.** A situation where this assumption is violated is illustrated in Figure 14.9, where we once again consider what might occur if we *were* to obtain (we will not, actually) many values of Y for $X = 35$ and also for $X = 60$. If Figure 14.9 were the result, assumption 3 would be violated, because the errors would be much larger (in absolute value) for the $60,000-income homes than they would for the $35,000-income homes. Figure 14.9 illustrates **heteroscedasticity,** which does pose a problem when we try to infer results from a linear regression equation.

You might argue that, proportionally, the errors for $X = 60$ seem about the same as those for $X = 35$, which means that you would expect larger errors for larger values of X here. If this is the case, the confidence intervals and tests of hypothesis that we are about to develop for the simple linear regression model are *not appropriate*. There are methods of "repairing" this situation, by applying a *transformation* to the dependent variable, Y, such as $\sqrt{Y}$ or $\log(Y)$. By using this "new" dependent variable rather than the original Y, the resulting errors often will exhibit a nearly constant variance. Such transformations, however, are beyond the scope of this text.

A summary of the first three assumptions is shown in Figure 14.10. Note that the distribution of errors is *identical* for each illustrated value of X; namely, it is a normal distribution with mean = 0 and variance σ_e^2.

● **ASSUMPTION 4.** *The errors are independent of each other.* This implies that the error encountered for one value of Y is unaffected by the error for any other value of Y. To illustrate, consider the real-estate data and suppose that the sample is *not* random but that instead the sample houses are all located on a certain street. The first house has a positive error when predicting the square footage. If the probability is greater than .5 that the next

FIGURE 14.9

A violation of assumption 3; see text.

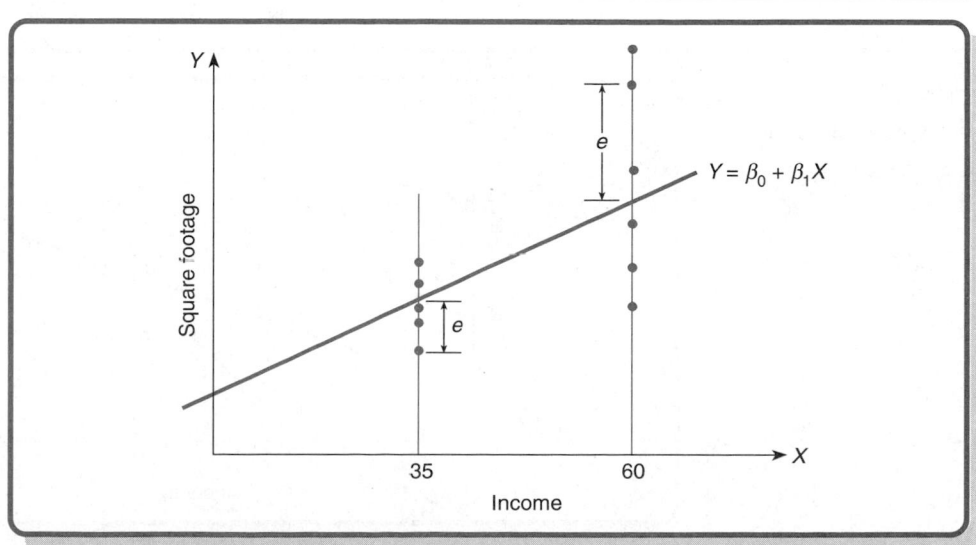

house in the sample also has a positive error (that is, if its location makes it probable that it will be a certain size), then the assumption of independence is violated. In other words, the sample was poorly chosen because the houses on one street are likely to be more or less the same size and their owners are likely to have similar incomes. The nonrandom sample led to a violation of assumption 4.

We can draw two conclusions from these assumptions. First, each value of the dependent variable, Y, is a normal random variable with mean $= \beta_0 + \beta_1 X$ and variance σ_e^2. Second, the error components come from the same normal population, *regardless of the value of X*. In other words, it makes sense to examine the residuals resulting from each value of X in the sample, to construct a histogram of these residuals, and to determine whether its appearance is bell-shaped (normal), centered at zero. A key assumption when using simple linear regression is that the errors follow a normal distribution with a mean of zero. Constructing a histogram of the sample residuals provides a convenient method of determining whether this assumption is reasonable for a particular application.

This discussion is continued in section 14.6 (Examining the Residuals). This section will demonstrate graphical methods for checking these assumptions (including a histogram of the residuals), along with various numerical measures that identify "unusual" and "influential observations" in the sample data.

Estimating the Error Variance, σ_e^2

The variance of the error components, σ_e^2, measures the variation of the error terms resulting from the simple linear regression model. The value of σ_e^2 severely affects our ability to use this model as an effective predictor for a given situation. Suppose, for example, that σ_e^2 is very large in Figure 14.10. This means that if we were to obtain many observations (square footage values, Y) for a *fixed* value of X (say, income = $50,000), these Y values would vary a great deal, decreasing the accuracy of our model; we would prefer that these values were grouped closely about the mean, $\mu_{Y|50}$.

In practice, σ_e^2 typically is unknown and must be estimated from the sample. To estimate this variance, we first determine the sum of squares of error, SSE, using SSE $= \Sigma(y - \hat{y})^2$ or equation 14.14. Estimating β_0 and β_1 for the simple regression model results in a loss of 2 df, leaving $n - 2$ df for estimating the error variance. Consequently,

$$s^2 = \hat{\sigma}_e^2 = \text{estimate of } \sigma_e^2 = \frac{\text{SSE}}{n-2} \qquad (14.16)$$

FIGURE 14.10

Illustration of assumptions 1, 2, 3; see text.

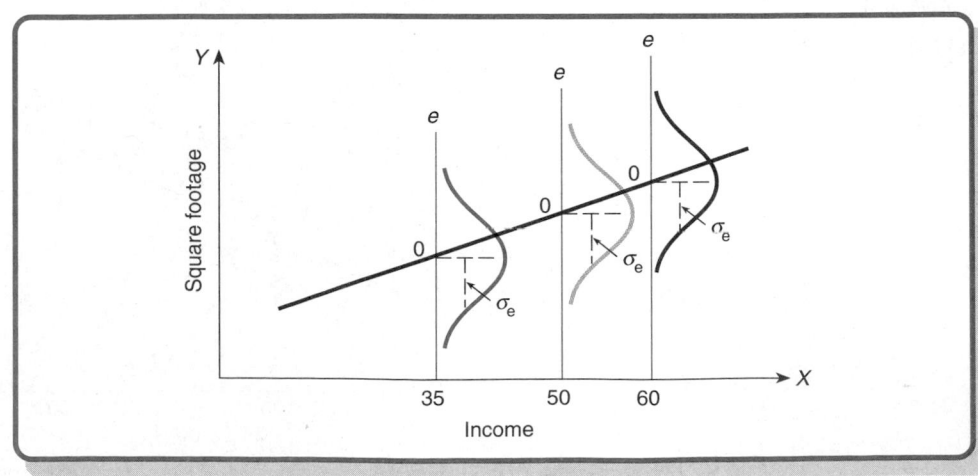

Same as Chalk board example he gave

where

$$SSE = \sum(y - \hat{y})^2 = SS_Y - \frac{(SCP_{XY})^2}{SS_X}$$

Note that SSE is the expression that was minimized in Figure 14.5 when determining the "best" line through the sample points. In Figure 14.5, each distance d corresponds to $y - \hat{y}$.

We can determine the estimate of σ_e^2 and σ_e for the real-estate data in Example 14.2, where we calculated the value of SSE to be 75.81. Our estimate of σ_e^2 is

$$s^2 = \frac{SSE}{n-2} = \frac{75.81}{8} = 9.476$$

and so $s = \sqrt{9.476} = 3.078$ provides an estimate of σ_e. The values of s^2 and s are a measure of the variation of the Y values about the least squares line.

COMMENTS

We know from the empirical rule that approximately 95% of the data from a normal population should lie within two standard deviations of the mean. For this example, this rule implies that approximately 95% of the residuals should lie within $2(3.078) = 6.16$ of the mean. In the table in Example 14.2, the sample residuals are in the fourth column. Their sum is *always* zero, when using the least squares line; therefore, their mean is *zero*. So, approximately 95% of the residuals should be no larger (in absolute value) than 6.16. In fact, all of them are less than 6.16—not a surprising result, given that we had only 10 values in the sample.

EXERCISES 14.13–14.22

UNDERSTANDING THE MECHANICS

14.13 The residuals of a least squares line are as follows.

$Y - \hat{Y}$: .4 .2 3 −.1 .2 .1 −.3 −.4 −.2 −3 .1 .3 .4

  −3 .3 −.1 3 −.2 −.3 −.4

a. Find the estimate of the error variance, s^2.

b. Are approximately 95% of the residuals within $2s$ of the mean of the residuals? What does your answer indicate about the appropriateness of the data for a regression analysis procedure?

14.14 Consider the following set of residuals, resulting from a regression analysis.

$Y - \hat{Y}$	X	$Y - \hat{Y}$	X
.4	1.0	2.0	4.0
−.4	1.5	−3.0	5.0
−1.0	1.6	4.2	6.0
1.2	2.0	−3.4	7.0
−1.6	2.5	−5.0	8.0
−1.0	3.0	7.6	9.0

a. Construct a graph of the residuals versus the X values.

b. Does it appear that the equal variance assumption of regression analysis is violated?

APPLYING THE NEW CONCEPTS

14.15 The following data show the number of total annual bankruptcy petitions filed in the northern district of a southern state (in thousands) and the size of the permanent staff at the U.S. Bankruptcy Court for that district.

Bankruptcies in Thousands (X)	Permanent Staff at U.S. Bankruptcy Court (Y)
2.1	15
3.8	18
4.1	18
10.0	59
3.2	14
3.9	18
6.1	24

a. Compute the least squares line.

b. Identify the values of the slope and the intercept for the simple linear regression model.

c. Estimate the variance of the error for the model.

d. Find the residuals $(Y - \hat{Y})$ for all the Y values.

14.16 What assumptions need to be made about the error component of a linear model in order that statistical inference can be used?

14.17 The following is a list of sample errors $(Y - \hat{Y})$ from a linear regression application:

2.1, −.3, 1.4, −2.8, −3.9, 4.2, 3.6, 4.3, 1.8, −2.7, −.8, 1.2, .9, −1.1, −4.5, −5.2, −1.3, .5, .9, −.6, 1.5, 2.1, −2.2, .9

Do the data appear to conform to the empirical rule that approximately 95% of the errors should lie within two standard deviations of the mean? Construct a histogram for the residuals.

14.18 Let X be the distance an employee lives from his or her job. Let Y be the average time that it takes the employee to drive to work. Data from 30 employees gave the following sample statistics.

$$SCP_{XY} = 8.4 \qquad SS_X = 9.4 \qquad SS_Y = 12.2$$

a. Find the estimate of the error variance.

b. Find the interval in which approximately 68% of the error values should fall.

14.19 Title insurance premiums (Y) charged by title companies can be thought of as a function of the number of title policies issued (X). The table below lists several title companies in Fort Worth, Texas, the local title insurance premiums (in thousands of dollars) and the number of policies issued (in thousands) for a one-year period ending March 31, 1997. Find the residual for each premium.

Title Company	Local Title Insurance Premiums	Number of Policies Issued
Alamo Title Co.	9,498	14.1
First American Title Insurance Co.	7,487	10.6
Rattikin Title Co.	6,413	15.9
Safeco Land Title of Tarrant	5,526	15.8
Commonwealth Land Title Co.	5,168	18.6
Old Republic Title Co.	1,747	2.3
Commerce Land Title Inc.	818	.6

(Source: *The Business Press*, "The List," June 20, 1997, p. 12.)

14.20 Why is $\Sigma(y - \hat{y})^2$ used in estimating the variance of the error term instead of $\Sigma(y - \hat{y})$?

USING THE COMPUTER

14.21 [DATA SET EX14-21] *Variable description:*

InterpersonalScore: Employer's rating of an employee's interpersonal skills

JobPerformScore: Employer's rating of an employee's performance on the job

C-Cubed is a collaboration between the Fort Worth, Texas, Chamber of Commerce and the local school district. This partnership is designed to provide local businesses with successful employees according to "Learn to Work," an article in *The Fort Worth Star-Telegram*, June 29, 1997, p. 1E. One skill that often is not taught in school, but that appears to be essential to long-term job success is interpersonal skills. Suppose that in a survey of Fort Worth businesses, 70 employees who obtained jobs through the C-Cubed effort were selected. The employers were asked to rate the employees on interpersonal skills and on job performance on a scale from 1 to 10, with 10 representing perfect satisfaction.

a. Find the least squares line for predicting JobPerformScore from InterpersonalScore. Interpret the slope of this line.

b. Construct a histogram of the residuals. Do the residuals appear to follow a normal distribution.

14.22 [DATA SET EX14-22] *Variable description:*

SpecialNumber: Number of special parts ordered
SpecialCost: Dollar cost of special parts ordered

A sales manager for a car dealership mails an order for special parts each week. The manager is interested in the relationship between the number of special parts ordered and the total cost of the special order. One hundred special parts orders were randomly selected. The number of special parts and the total cost of these parts are recorded as variables SpecialNumber and SpecialCost, respectively.

a. Find the least squares line and interpret the coefficients.

b. What is the shape of the histogram of the residuals?

c. Sometimes researchers make a transformation on the data to make the residuals conform better to a normal distribution. Suppose that the square of SpecialCost is used instead of the original values. Describe the shape of the histogram in which this value is used as the dependent variable. Would you say that the error component of this regression model follows an approximately normal distribution?

14.3 INFERENCE ON THE SLOPE, β_1

PERFORMING A TEST OF HYPOTHESIS ON THE SLOPE OF THE REGRESSION LINE

Under the assumptions of the simple linear regression model outlined in the previous section, we are now in a position to determine whether a linear relationship exists between the variables X and Y. Examining the estimate of the slope, b_1, will provide information as to the nature of this relationship.

Consider the *population* slope, β_1. Three possible situations are demonstrated in Figure 14.11. What can you say about using X as a predictor of Y in Figure 14.11a? When $\beta_1 = 0$, the population line is perfectly horizontal. As a result, the value of Y is the *same* for each value of X, and so X is not a good predictor of Y; the value of X provides no information regarding the value of Y. In the event $\beta_1 = 0$, the best predictor of Y is given by $\hat{Y} = \bar{y}$, and so $\beta_1 \neq 0$ is equivalent to saying that $\hat{Y}$ (using X as a predictor) is superior to using the sample mean ($\hat{Y} = \bar{y}$) as a predictor.

To determine whether X provides information in predicting Y, the hypotheses are

$$H_0: \beta_1 = 0 \quad \text{(X provides no information)}$$

$$H_a: \beta_1 \neq 0 \quad \text{(X does provide information)}$$

OTHER ALTERNATIVE HYPOTHESES.   If we are attempting to demonstrate that a significant *positive* linear relationship exists between X and Y, the appropriate alternative hypothesis would be $H_a: \beta_1 > 0$. For example, do the data in Example 14.1 support the hypothesis that owners with large incomes have larger homes?

FIGURE 14.11

Three possible population slopes (β_1).

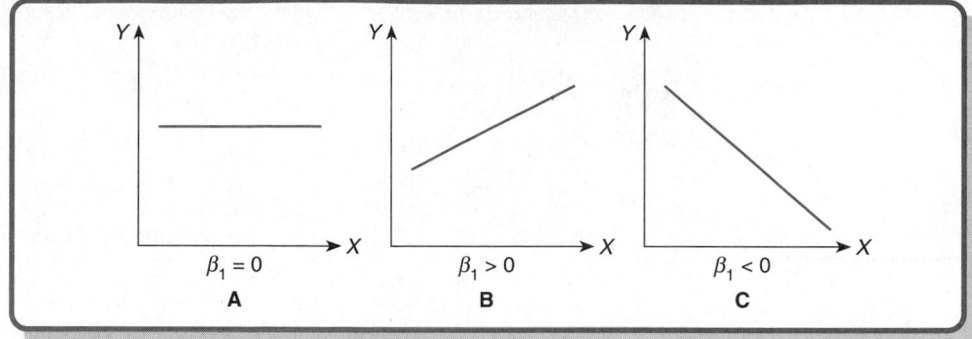

When the purpose of the analysis is to determine whether a *negative* linear relationship exists between X and Y, the alternative hypothesis should be H_a: $\beta_1 < 0$. For example, you would expect such a relationship between the number of new housing starts (Y) and the interest rate (X) (as the interest rate increases, you would expect the number of new houses under construction to decrease).

THE TEST STATISTIC.   We use the point estimate of β_1 (that is, b_1) in the test statistic to determine the nature of β_1. What is b_1? a constant? a variable? Suppose that we obtained a different set of data and recalculated b_1. The new value would not be exactly the same as the previous value, implying that b_1 is actually a variable. To be more precise, under the assumptions of the previous section, b_1 is a *normal* random variable with mean $= \beta_1$ and variance $= \sigma_{b_1}^2 = \sigma_e^2/SS_X$. Notice that b_1 is, on the average, equal to β_1; that is, b_1 is an *unbiased* estimator of β_1. The variance $\sigma_{b_1}^2$ is a parameter describing the variation in the b_1 values if we were to obtain random samples of n observations indefinitely.

If we replace the unknown σ_e^2 by its estimate, s^2, then the *estimated* variance of b_1 is $s_{b_1}^2 = s^2/SS_X$. As a result

$$t = \frac{b_1 - \beta_1}{s/\sqrt{SS_X}} = \frac{b_1 - \beta_1}{s_{b_1}} \qquad (14.17)$$

has a t distribution with $n - 2$ df. If the null hypothesis is H_0: $\beta_1 = 0$, the test statistic becomes

$$t = \frac{b_1}{s/\sqrt{SS_X}} \qquad (14.18)$$

A summary of the testing procedure is shown in the accompanying box.

TEST OF HYPOTHESIS ON THE SLOPE OF THE REGRESSION LINE

Two-Tailed Test

$$H_0: \beta_1 = 0$$
$$H_a: \beta_1 \neq 0$$

Test statistic:

$$t = \frac{b_1}{s_{b_1}}$$

where $s_{b_1} = s/\sqrt{SS_X}$ and df $= n - 2$.

Test:

$$\text{reject } H_0 \text{ if } |t| > t_{\alpha/2, n-2}$$

One-Tailed Test

$$H_0: \beta_1 \leq 0 \qquad\qquad\qquad H_0: \beta_1 \geq 0$$
$$H_a: \beta_1 > 0 \qquad\qquad\qquad H_a: \beta_1 < 0$$

Test statistic: Test statistic:

$$t = \frac{b_1}{s_{b_1}} \qquad\qquad\qquad t = \frac{b_1}{s_{b_1}}$$

where $s_{b_1} = s / \sqrt{SS_X}$ and   where $s_{b_1} = s / \sqrt{SS_X}$ and
df $= n - 2$.   df $= n - 2$.

Test: Test:

$$\text{reject } H_0 \text{ if } t > t_{\alpha, n-2} \qquad\qquad \text{reject } H_0 \text{ if } t < -t_{\alpha, n-2}$$

EXAMPLE 14.3

Is there sufficient evidence, using the real-estate data in Example 14.1, to conclude that a positive linear relationship exists between income (X) and home size (Y)? Use $\alpha = .05$.

SOLUTION

Step 1. The hypotheses indicated here are

$$H_0: \beta_1 \leq 0$$
$$H_a: \beta_1 > 0$$

Step 2. The test statistic is

$$t = \frac{b_1}{s_{b_1}}$$

which has a t distribution with $n - 2 = 8$ df.

Step 3. The testing procedure is to

$$\text{reject } H_0 \text{ if } t > t_{.05,8} = 1.860$$

The t curve is shown in Figure 14.12.

FIGURE 14.12

t curve with 8 df showing rejection region (shaded) for Example 14.3.

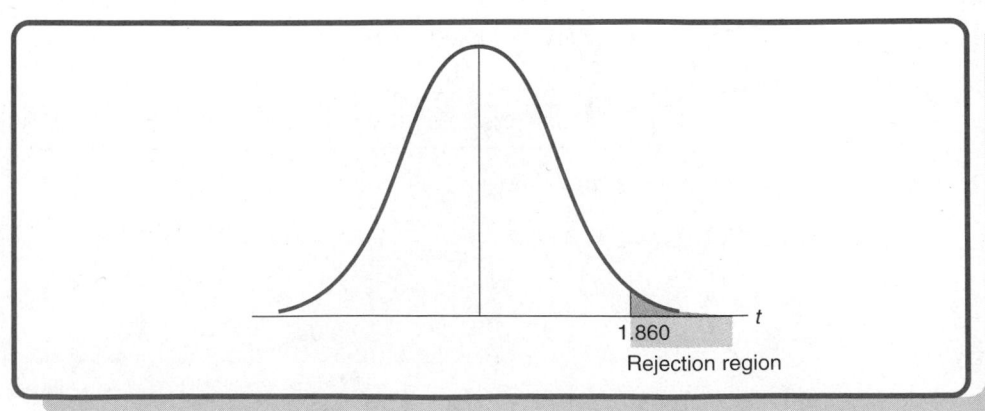

Step 4. We previously determined that $SS_X = 1489.6$, $b_1 = .3539$, and $s = 3.078$. The calculated test statistic is then

$$t^* = \frac{.3539}{3.078 / \sqrt{1489.6}} = \frac{.3539}{.0797} = 4.44$$

where $s_{b_1} = .0797$. Because $4.44 > 1.86$, we reject H_0.

Step 5. Based on these ten observations, we conclude that a positive linear relationship does exist between income and home size.

USING EXCEL.   An Excel solution to Example 14.3 is shown in Figures 14.14 and 14.15. After clicking on **Tools ➤ Data Analysis ➤ Regression,** enter the input and output ranges as shown in Figure 14.13. Be sure to click on the **Residuals** box. Some of the more interesting portions of the output are highlighted (shaded) in Figure 14.14 and are discussed below.

Cell(s)	Contents
B27, B28	The least squares equation is $\hat{Y} = 4.975 + .3539X$.
C28	The standard deviation of b_1 is $s_{b_1} = .07976$.
D28	The value of the test statistic is $t^* = b_1/s_{b_1} = 4.44$.
E28	The p-value for the t-test is .0022. Since this value is less than .05 (α), we can conclude that a positive linear relationship exists between income and home size.
B17	The estimated standard deviation of the error components is $s = 3.078$.
C23	The value of SSE is 75.81. The construction of this ANOVA table is discussed in Chapter 15.

The ten predicted Y values ($\hat{Y}$ values) and corresponding residuals ($Y - \hat{Y}$ values) are shown in Figure 14.15. These values were previously calculated without the use of a computer in the solution to Example 14.2. The Excel calculated residuals contain more accuracy but do agree with the values in the Example 14.2 solution to two decimal places.

FIGURE 14.13

Excel input screen using **Tools ➤ Data Analysis ➤ Regression.**

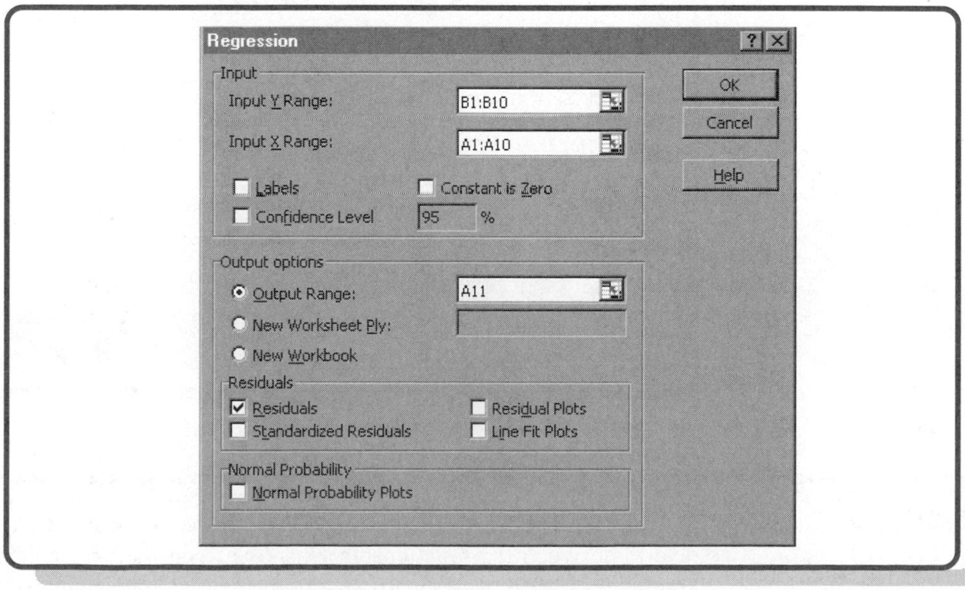

FIGURE 14.14

Excel solution to Example 14.3.

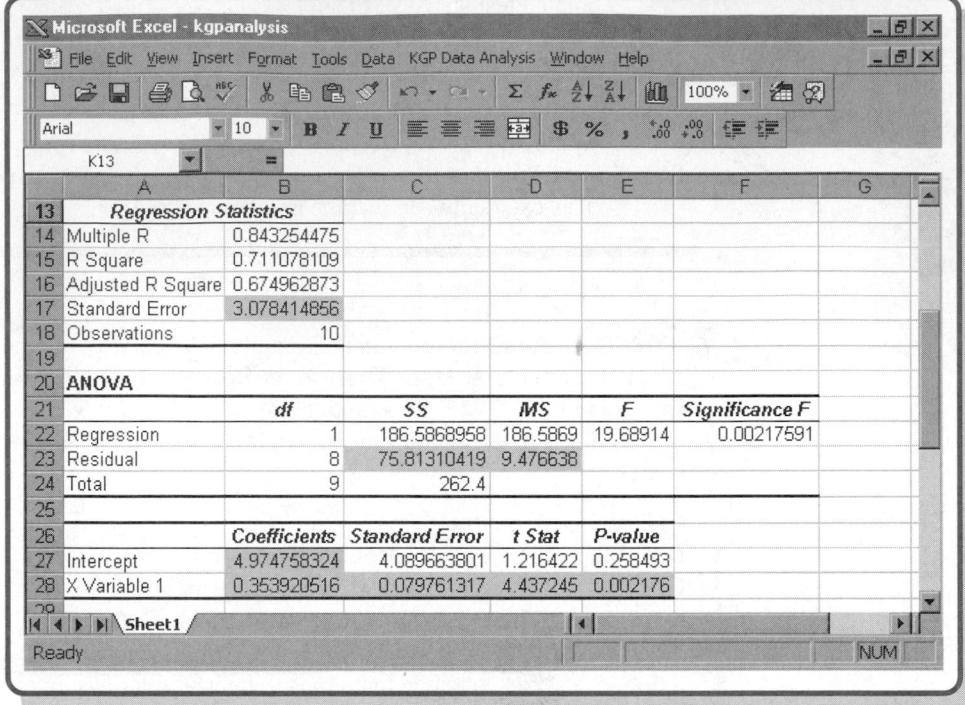

FIGURE 14.15

Excel-generated predicted *Y* values and residuals (Example 14.3).

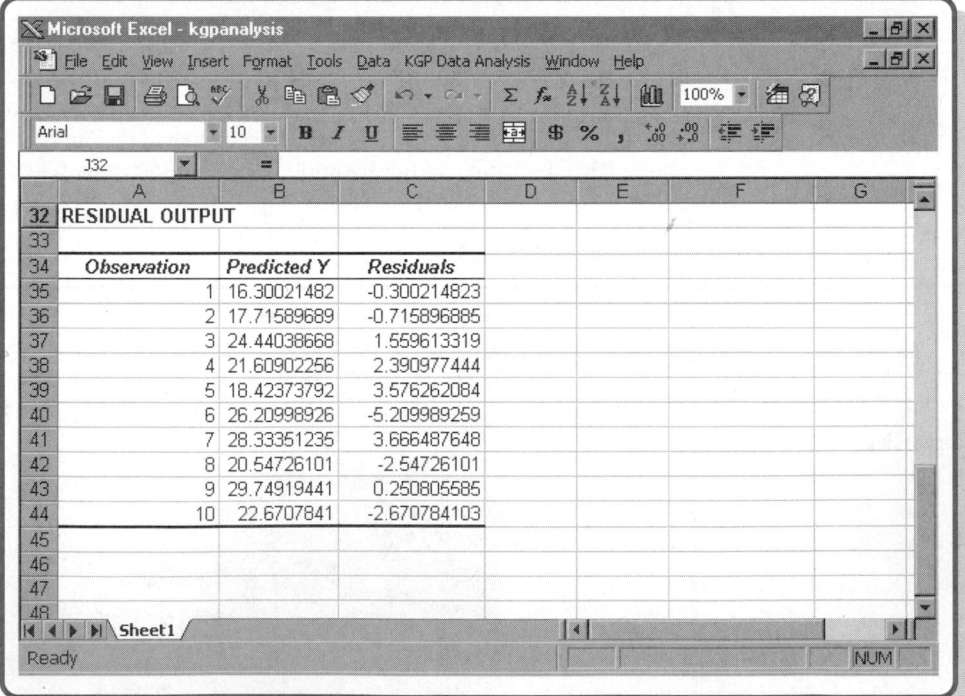

EXAMPLE 14.4

The firm of Smithson Financial Consultants has been hired by Blackburn Industries to determine whether a relationship exists between the age of unmarried male Blackburn employees (that is, never married, divorced, or widowed male employees) and the amount of individual liquid assets. The main question of interest is whether a linear relationship exists between these two variables, where *X* is defined as the age of the employee and *Y* is the *percentage* of annual income allocated to liquid assets (such as cash, savings accounts,

FIGURE 14.16

Scatter diagram and least squares line for age (X) and percentage of annual income invested in liquid assets (Y).

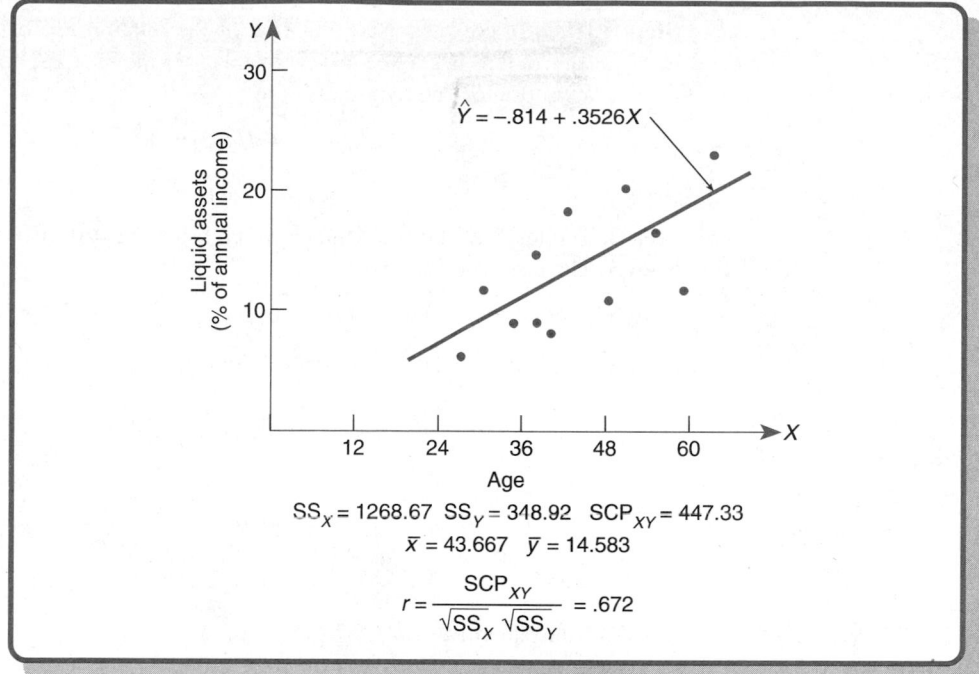

$$SS_X = 1268.67 \quad SS_Y = 348.92 \quad SCP_{XY} = 447.33$$
$$\bar{X} = 43.667 \quad \bar{Y} = 14.583$$

$$r = \frac{SCP_{XY}}{\sqrt{SS_X}\sqrt{SS_Y}} = .672$$

and tradable stocks and bonds). A random sample of 12 unmarried male employees is selected, and the following data are obtained:

Age (X)	Liquid Assets (Y, Percentage of Annual Income)	Age (X)	Liquid Assets (Y, Percentage of Annual Income)
38	16	58	13
48	12	31	13
38	10	42	20
28	7	35	10
40	9	54	18
50	22	62	25

A scatter diagram of these 12 observations is provided in Figure 14.16, with a summary of the calculations. Using $\alpha = .10$, do you think that an employee's age provides useful information for predicting the percentage of total income allocated to liquid assets?

SOLUTION

To derive the least squares regression line, we determine

$$b_1 = \frac{SCP_{XY}}{SS_X} = \frac{447.33}{1268.67} = .3526$$

and

$$b_0 = \bar{y} - b_1\bar{x}$$

$$= 14.583 - (.3526)(43.667) = -.814$$

Consequently, the least squares line is

$$\hat{Y} = -.814 + .3526X$$

Notice that the slope of this line is positive. As the following test of hypothesis will conclude, this slope is significant. Consequently, a higher percentage invested in liquid assets is associated with the *older* employees. According to these data, each additional year of age is accompanied by an increase of .35 percent of income allocated to liquid assets, on the average, for the unmarried male population at Blackburn.

To carry out a test of hypothesis, we follow the usual five-step procedure.

Step 1. Because the suspected direction of the relationship between these two variables (positive or negative) is unknown before the data are obtained, a two-tailed test is appropriate. The hypotheses are

$$H_0: \beta_1 = 0$$

$$H_a: \beta_1 \neq 0$$

Step 2. The test statistic is $t = b_1/s_{b_1}$, which has $n - 2 = 10$ df.

Step 3. The test procedure is to

$$\text{reject } H_0 \text{ if } |t| > t_{.10/2,10} = t_{.05,10} = 1.812$$

Step 4. Based on the data summary in Figure 14.16 and using equation 14.14,

$$\text{SSE} = \text{SS}_Y - \frac{(\text{SCP}_{XY})^2}{\text{SS}_X}$$

$$= 348.92 - \frac{(447.33)^2}{1268.67}$$

$$= 348.92 - 157.73 = 191.19$$

Consequently,

$$s^2 = \frac{\text{SSE}}{n-2} = \frac{191.19}{10} = 19.12$$

and so

$$s_{b_1} = \frac{s}{\sqrt{\text{SS}_X}} = \frac{\sqrt{19.12}}{\sqrt{1268.67}} = .1228$$

The computed value of the test statistic is therefore:

$$t^* = \frac{b_1}{s_{b_1}}$$

$$= \frac{.3526}{.1228} = 2.87$$

Because $t^* = 2.87$ exceeds the table value of 1.812, we reject H_0 in support of H_a.

Step 5. Our conclusion is that age is a useful (although imperfect) predictor of percentage of income invested in liquid assets for this particular population.

One thing to keep in mind is that *statistical* significance does not always imply *practical* significance. In other words, rejection of H_0: $\beta_1 = 0$ (statistical significance) does not mean that precise prediction (practical significance) follows. It *does* demonstrate to the researcher that, within the sample data at least, this particular independent variable has an association with the dependent variable.

CONFIDENCE INTERVAL FOR β_1

Following our usual procedure of providing a confidence interval with a point estimate, we use the t distribution of the previous test statistic and equation 14.17 to define a confidence interval for β_1. The narrower this confidence interval is, the more faith we have in our estimate of β_1 and in our model as an accurate, reliable predictor of the dependent variable. A $(1 - \alpha) \cdot 100\%$ confidence interval for β_1 is

$$b_1 - t_{\alpha/2, n-2} s_{b_1} \qquad \text{to} \qquad b_1 + t_{\alpha/2, n-2} s_{b_1}$$

EXAMPLE 14.5

Construct a 90% confidence interval for the population slope, β_1, using the real-estate data in Examples 14.1 and 14.3.   C.I. $= b_1 +- t\alpha/2, n - 2 s_{b_1}$

SOLUTION

All the necessary calculations have been completed; $b_1 = .3539$ and $s_{b_1} = .0797$ (from Example 14.3). Using $t_{.05,8} = 1.860$, the resulting confidence interval is

$$.3539 - (1.860)(.0797) \qquad \text{to} \qquad .3539 + (1.860)(.0797)$$

$$= .3539 - .148 \qquad \text{to} \qquad .3539 + .148$$

$$= .206 \qquad \text{to} \qquad .502$$

So we are 90% confident that the value of the estimated slope ($b_1 = .3539$) is within .148 of the actual slope, β_1. The large width of this interval is due in part to the lack of information (small sample size) used to derive the estimates; a larger sample would decrease the width of this confidence interval.

COMMENTS

A failure to reject H_0 when performing a hypothesis test on β_1 does not always indicate that no relationship exists between the two variables. Some form of nonlinear relationship may exist between these variables. For example, in Figure 14.17, there is clearly a strong curved (**curvi-** linear) relationship between X and Y. However, the least squares line through these points is horizontal, leading to a t value equal to zero and a failure to reject H_0. Furthermore, the sample correlation coefficient, r, for these data is zero.

Of course, you may fail to reject H_0 as the result of a type II error. In other words, you failed to reject H_0 when in fact a significant linear relationship does exist. This situation is more apt to occur when using a small sample to test the null hypothesis.

More often, a failure to reject H_0 occurs when there is no visible relationship between the two variables within the sample data. To determine whether there is no relationship or that there is a nonlinear one, you should inspect either a scatter diagram of the data, a scatter diagram of the residuals, or, better yet, both. The latter diagram is a picture of the residuals $(Y - \hat{Y})$ plotted against the independent variable, X. Residual plots are discussed further in Section 14.6 and in Chapter 15.

In many situations, a business analyst has the opportunity to select the values of the independent variable, X, *before* the sample is obtained. At first glance, it might appear that the precision of b_1 (as an estimator of β_1) is unaffected by the X values. This is partially but not completely true. Because a narrow confidence interval for β_1 lends credibility to our model, we may choose to decrease the width of this confidence interval by decreasing s_{b_1}. Now $s_{b_1} = s / \sqrt{SS_X}$, so if we make SS_X large, the resulting s_{b_1} will be small. Therefore,

FIGURE 14.17

Curvilinear relationship. The horizontal line is the least squares line.

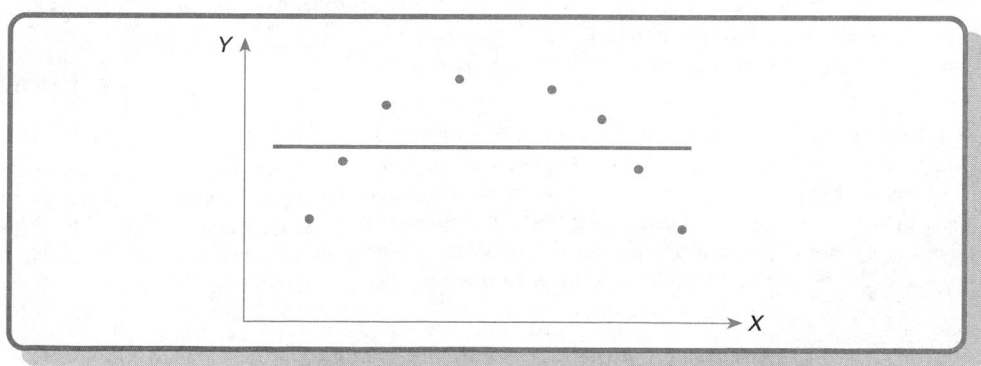

given the opportunity, select a set of X values having a *large variance*. You can accomplish this by choosing a great many X values on the lower end of your range of interest, a large number of values at the upper end, and some values in between to detect any curvature that exists (as in Figure 14.17).

EXERCISES 14.23–14.32

UNDERSTANDING THE MECHANICS

14.23 The following statistics were calculated in a regression analysis procedure.

$$b_0 = -10.8$$

$$b_1 = 3.0$$

$$s_{b_1} = 1.624$$

$$n = 21$$

a. Test the null hypothesis that the slope of the regression line is zero at the .01 significance level.

b. Calculate a 99% confidence interval for the slope of the regression line.

14.24 Consider the following pairs of measurements.

X	5	6	7	9	3	10	12
Y	4	8	12	18	1	20	26

a. Is there sufficient evidence using the observed data to conclude that a positive linear relationship exists between X and Y? Use a 5% significance level.

b. Find the p-value for the test statistic in part (a).

APPLYING THE NEW CONCEPTS

14.25 It is believed that the size of the U.S. population (X) is a variable that influences personal consumption expenditure for housing (Y). However, the relationship historically does not appear to be linear. Therefore, a log transformation of housing expenditure is used. Fifteen observations are taken over previous years. The units of Y are millions and the units of X are billions.

X	Log Y	X	Log Y	X	Log Y
183.69	3.935	196.56	4.241	207.66	4.631
186.54	4.001	198.71	4.305	209.90	4.722
189.24	4.060	200.71	4.379	211.91	4.818
191.89	4.117	202.68	4.465	213.85	4.923
194.30	4.182	205.05	4.542	215.97	5.009

From the data, does there appear to be a significant positive linear relationship between X and log Y? Use a significance level of .05.

14.26 The life of a lawn-mower engine can be extended by frequent oil changes. An experiment was conducted in which 20 lawn mowers were used over many years with different time intervals between oil changes. Let X be the number of hours of operation between oil changes. Let Y be the number of years that the engine was able to perform adequately.

X	Y	X	Y	X	Y
11.25	12.1	22.0	9.5	25.5	6.1
15.5	11.8	22.5	9.2	26.0	5.4
17.5	11.5	23.0	8.4	26.5	4.8
20.5	10.1	23.5	8.8	27.0	4.6
19.5	9.9	24.0	7.1	28.0	4.8
18.5	9.7	24.5	7.2	30.0	4.1
21.5	10.1	25.0	5.8		

a. Graph the data and the least squares line.

b. Is there sufficient evidence to conclude, at the 10% significance level, that a negative linear relationship exists between Y and X? What is the critical region?

14.27 Typically baseball fans pay for parking and a hot dog and soda when watching a baseball game. A random sample of seven minor league stadiums was selected and the ticket price (X) as well as the additional expenses of a hot dog and a soda (Y) were recorded. Obtain the least squares line for Y and $\sqrt{X}$. Comment on whether the slope of the regression line is positive using a 1% significance level.

City	Ticket Price (X)	Additional Expense (Y)
New Haven (Ravens)	16	3.60
Reading, PA (Phillies)	8	3.25
Indianapolis (Indians)	12	4.00
Peoria (Chiefs)	7	2.25
San Antonio (Missions)	10	2.75
Adelanto, CA (High Desert Mavericks)	6	2.00
San Jose (Giants)	16	4.60

14.28 A medical researcher was interested in the amount of weight loss caused by a particular diuretic. In a controlled experiment with 18 rats, the amount of weight loss was recorded after 1 month of daily dose of the diuretic. Let X be the amount, in milligrams, of diuretic given. Let Y be the weight loss in pounds.

X	Y	X	Y	X	Y
.10	.05	.25	.35	.40	.44
.10	.08	.25	.31	.40	.47
.15	.11	.30	.41	.45	.51
.15	.13	.30	.42	.45	.52
.20	.19	.35	.43	.50	.54
.20	.21	.35	.42	.50	.53

Is there sufficient evidence to conclude that a significant positive relationship exists between the amount of diuretic given and the amount of weight loss? Use a significance level of 10%. Find a 90% confidence interval for the slope of the regression equation used to predict Y.

14.29 Analysts who study trends in travel expenses believe there is a relationship between the average room rate at hotels and the average daily car-rental rate. Listed below are the daily room rates and daily car rental rates for 15 cities across the United States.

City	Daily Room Rate	Daily Car-Rental Rate
Atlanta	151	52
Boston	220	57
Chicago	188	54
Cleveland	157	50
Dallas	144	50
Denver	136	45
Houston	138	52
Miami	148	36
Minneapolis	155	54
New Orleans	156	46
New York	209	69
Pittsburgh	125	45
San Francisco	195	62
Seattle	156	49
Washington, D.C.	176	54

(Source: Adapted from *The Wall Street Journal*, "Dow Jones Travel Index: Trends in Travel Costs," July 11, 1997, p. B2.)

a. Find a 90% confidence interval for the slope of the regression line with Y = daily car-rental rate and X = daily room rates.

b. Use the confidence interval in part (a) to determine if a linear relationship exists between Y and X at the 10% significance level.

14.30 An investment counselor wanted to know the relationship between the price/earnings ratio (Y) and the yield (X) for high-yield stocks. If a stock yielded over 5.5%, it was considered to be a high-yield stock. Twenty-five high-yield stocks were randomly selected. The following sample statistics were found:

$$SCP_{XY} = -10.4$$

$$SS_X = 11.4$$

$$SS_Y = 21.4$$

a. Test that the slope of the regression equation used to predict the price/earnings ratio from the yield of a stock is negative. Use a 10% significance level.

b. Find a 95% confidence interval for the slope in part (a).

USING THE COMPUTER

14.31 **[DATA SET EX14-31]** *Variable description:*

FurniturePrice: Price of furniture sold
TimeToSell: Time that it took for a furniture item to sell
Experience: Length of time the salesperson has been in sales

The furniture store business can be tricky. "Furniture customers are fickle, with tastes varying widely across the country. They enter a store to get ideas and browse, not necessarily to buy," says Troy Peery Jr., president of Heilig-Meyers Company (*Forbes*, "Sofa With Your Stereo, Sir," July 7, 1997, p. 46). Suppose that a furniture manager wished to determine if there is a linear relationship between the selling price of furniture and either the amount of time that it took for the furniture to sell or the number of years of experience of the salesperson who sold the furniture. The units for TimeToSell are months and the units for Experience are years.

a. Look at a plot of FurniturePrice and TimeToSell and a plot of FurniturePrice and Experience. Comment on the linear relationship in each plot. Which would you use to construct a prediction equation?

b. For the variables selected in part (a) to construct a prediction equation, is there sufficient evidence to conclude that a positive relationship exists at a 1% significance level?

c. Do a "what if" analysis by multiplying TimeToSell by 2 and find the test statistic for testing whether a positive relationship exists. Compare this to your result in part (b).

14.32 **[DATA SET EX14-32]** *Variable description:*

ExpenditureR&D: Percentage of total revenue spent on research and development (R&D)
PEratio: Price/earnings ratio for a company

A financial analyst is interested in the relationship between a company's P/E (price/earnings) ratio and the percentage of total revenue spent by the company on R&D. A random sample of 100 companies was selected and the data were recorded in variables ExpenditureR&D and PEratio, respectively.

a. Plot the variables X = ExpenditureR&D and Y = PEratio. Estimate the intercept and slope and interpret these values.

b. Find 90%, 95%, and 99% confidence intervals for the slope of the regression line. How much does the width of the confidence interval change as the confidence level is increased?

14.4 MEASURING THE STRENGTH OF THE MODEL

We have already used the sample coefficient of correlation, r, as a measure of the amount of linear association within a sample of bivariate data. The value of r is given by

$$r = \frac{SCP_{XY}}{\sqrt{SS_X}\sqrt{SS_Y}} \qquad (14.19)$$

The possible range for r is -1 to 1.
    Comparing the equations for r and b_1 we see that

$$r = b_1 \sqrt{\frac{SS_X}{SS_Y}}$$

Because SS_X and SS_Y are *always greater than zero*, r and b_1 have the same sign. Thus, if a positive relationship exists between X and Y, then both r and b_1 will be greater than zero. Similarly, they are both less than zero if the relationship is negative.

When you determine r, you use a sample of observations; r is a *statistic*. What does r estimate? It is actually an estimate of ρ (rho, pronounced "roe"), the **population correlation coefficient.** To grasp what ρ is, imagine obtaining *all* possible X, Y values and using equation 14.19 to determine a correlation. The resulting value is ρ.

The population slope, β_1, and ρ are closely related. In particular, $\beta_1 = 0$ if and only if $\rho = 0$. This leads to another method of determining whether the simple linear regression model (using X to predict Y) is satisfactory. The hypotheses are

$$H_0:\ \rho = 0 \qquad \text{(no linear relationship exists between } X \text{ and } Y\text{)}$$

$$H_a:\ \rho \neq 0 \qquad \text{(a linear relationship does exist)}$$

In a similar manner, alternative hypotheses can be set up to demonstrate a positive relationship ($H_a:\ \rho > 0$) or a negative relationship ($H_a:\ \rho < 0$). The test statistic uses the point estimate of ρ (that is, r) and is defined by

$$t = \frac{r}{\sqrt{\dfrac{1 - r^2}{n - 2}}} \qquad\qquad (14.20)$$

where $n =$ the number of observations in the sample. It is also a t statistic with $n - 2$ df. Although equations 14.18 and 14.20 appear to be unrelated, the two are algebraically equivalent and *their values for t are always the same.*

Thus, the t tests for $H_0:\ \beta_1 = 0$ and $H_0:\ \rho = 0$ produce identical results, provided both tests use the same level of significance. Performing both tests is therefore unnecessary; they both produce the same conclusion. Remember, if you have already computed the sample correlation coefficient, r, equation 14.20 offers a much easier method of determining whether the simple linear model is statistically significant. Notice also in equation 14.20 that the significance of the t value depends on the sample size, n. As a result, *if the sample size is large enough, then virtually any value of r can produce a "significantly large" value of t.*

EXAMPLE 14.6

Use equation 14.20 to determine whether a positive linear relationship exists between $X =$ income and $Y =$ home square footage, based on the real-estate data from Example 14.1. Use $\alpha = .05$.

SOLUTION

The hypotheses to be used here are $H_0:\ \rho \leq 0$ versus $H_a:\ \rho > 0$. In Example 14.1, we found that $r = .843$. This leads to a computed test statistic value of

$$t^* = \frac{r}{\sqrt{\dfrac{1 - r^2}{n - 2}}} = \frac{.843}{\sqrt{\dfrac{1 - (.843)^2}{8}}}$$

$$= \frac{.843}{.190} = 4.44$$

Because this value is the same as the one obtained in Example 14.3 (testing $H_0:\ \beta_1 \leq 0$ versus $H_a:\ \beta_1 > 0$), we draw the same conclusion. A positive linear relationship *does* exist between these two variables. In other words, r is large enough to justify this conclusion.

Remember, there is no harm in using equation 14.20 as a substitute for equation 14.18 with $H_0:\ \beta_1 = 0$ (or ≤ 0, or ≥ 0), particularly if you have already determined the value of r.

DANGER OF ASSUMING CAUSALITY

A word of warning is in order here—namely, that high statistical correlation does not imply *causality*. Even if the correlation between X and Y is extremely high (say, $r = .95$), a unit increase in X does not necessarily *cause* an increase in Y. All we know is that in the sample data, as X increased, so did Y. As a simple example, consider X = percentage of gray hairs and Y = blood pressure. One might expect to observe a high correlation between these two variables, but it is probably absurd to say that an additional gray hair will *cause* a person's blood pressure to increase. What is actually happening is that there is another variable, in this case age, that is causing both percentage of gray hair and blood pressure to increase.

In many business and economics applications, we observe highly correlated variables when each pair of observations corresponds to a particular time period. For example, we would expect a high correlation between average annual wages (X) and the U.S. gross national product (GNP; Y) when measured over time. Even though wages may be a good predictor of GNP, this correlation does not imply that an increase in wages *causes* an increase in GNP. It is much more likely that a third factor—inflation—caused both wages and GNP to increase.

COEFFICIENT OF DETERMINATION

In our earlier discussion of ANOVA techniques, we used the expression SS(total) = $\Sigma(y - \overline{y})^2$ to measure the tendency of a set of observations to group about the mean. If this value was large, then the observations (data) contained much variation and were *not* all clustered about the mean, $\overline{y}$.

In the simple linear regression model, $SS_Y = \Sigma(y - \overline{y})^2$ is computed in the same way and (as before) measures the total variation in the values of the dependent variable.

$$SS_Y = \text{total variation of the dependent variable observations}$$

When comparing the sum of squares of error, SSE, to the total variation, SS_Y, we use the ratio SSE/SS_Y. If all $\hat{Y}$ values are equal to their respective Y values, there is a perfect fit, with SSE = 0 and $r = 1$ or -1. Our model explains 100% of this total variation, and the unexplained variation is zero.

In general, SSE/SS_Y (expressed as a percentage) is the **percentage of unexplained variation.** Recall from equations 14.14 and 14.19 that

$$SSE = SS_Y - \frac{(SCP_{XY})^2}{SS_X} \quad \text{and} \quad r^2 = \frac{(SCP_{XY})^2}{SS_X SS_Y}$$

Thus

$$r^2 = 1 - \frac{SSE}{SS_Y}$$

As a result, r^2 may be interpreted as a measure of the *explained variation* in the dependent variable using the simple linear model; r^2 is the **coefficient of determination.**

$$r^2 = \text{coefficient of determination}$$

$$= 1 - \frac{SSE}{SS_Y} \tag{14.21}$$

$$= \text{percentage of explained variation in the dependent}$$
$$\text{variable using the simple linear regression model}$$

For this model, we can determine r^2 simply by squaring the coefficient of correlation. In Chapter 15, we will predict the dependent variable, Y, using *more than one* predictor (independent) variable. To derive the coefficient of determination in this case, we must first calculate SSE and then use equation 14.21. So, although this definition may appear to be unnecessary, it will enable us to compute this value when we use a multiple linear regression model.

EXAMPLE 14.7

What percentage of the total variation of the home sizes is explained by means of the single predictor, income, using the real-estate data from Example 14.1?

SOLUTION

We previously calculated r to be .843, so the coefficient of determination is

$$r^2 = (.843)^2 = .71$$

Therefore, we have accounted for 71% of the total variation in the home sizes by using income as a predictor of home size.

Notice that we could have determined this value by using the calculations from Examples 14.1 and 14.2, where

$$r^2 = 1 - \frac{SSE}{SS_Y}$$

$$= 1 - \frac{75.81}{262.4} = .71$$

TOTAL VARIATION, SS_Y

In Chapter 11, when discussing the ANOVA procedure, we partitioned the total variation in the observations, measured by SS(total), into two sums of squares, namely, SS(factor) and SS(error). The resulting equation was

$$SS(\text{total}) = SS(\text{factor}) + SS(\text{error})$$

In a similar fashion, we can partition the total variation of the Y values in linear regression, measured by SS_Y, into two other sums of squares. In Figure 14.18, notice that the value of $y - \overline{y}$ can be written as the sum of two deviations, namely,

$$y - \overline{y} = (\hat{y} - \overline{y}) + (y - \hat{y})$$

By squaring and summing over *all* the data points in the sample, we can show that*

$$\Sigma(y - \overline{y})^2 = \Sigma(\hat{y} - \overline{y})^2 + \Sigma(y - \hat{y})^2$$

The summation on the left of the equals sign is SS_Y. The second summation on the right is the sum of squares of error, SSE. The first summation on the right is defined to be the **sum of squares of regression, SSR.**

$$\Sigma(\hat{y} - \overline{y})^2 = SSR$$

As a result, we have

$$SS_Y = SSR + SSE \qquad (14.22)$$

---

* This result follows since it can be shown that $\Sigma(\hat{y} - \overline{y})(y - \hat{y}) = 0$ when using the least squares line.

FIGURE 14.18

Splitting $(y - \overline{y})$ into two deviations, $(\hat{y} - \overline{y}) + (y - \hat{y})$.

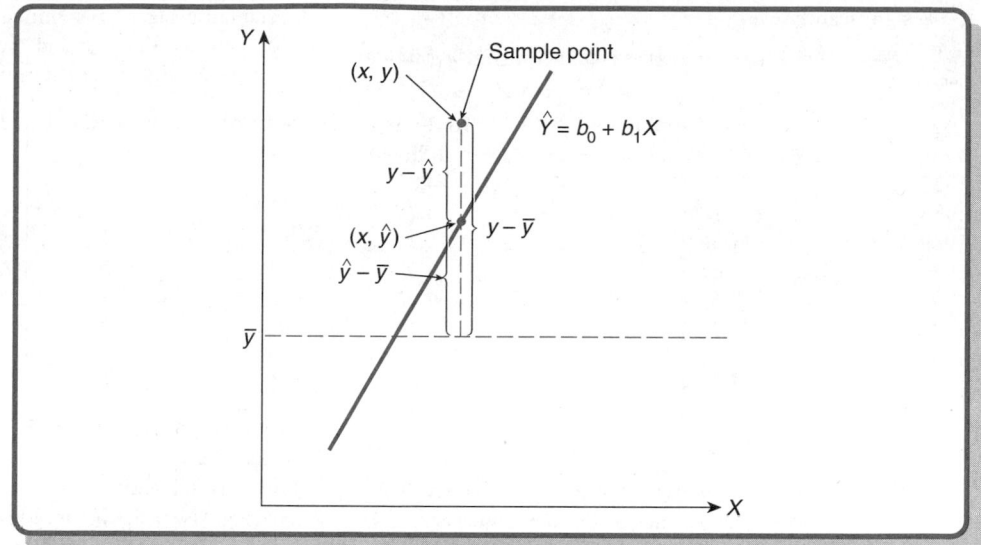

By comparing equations 14.14 and 14.22, we see that a simple way to calculate the sum of squares of regression is

$$SSR = \frac{(SCP_{XY})^2}{SS_X} \qquad (14.23)$$

The regression sum of squares, SSR, measures the variation in the Y values that would exist if differences in X were the *only* cause of differences among the Y's. If this were the case, then all the (X, Y) points would lie exactly on the regression line. In practice, this does not happen when using a simple linear regression model. Otherwise, we would have a deterministic phenomenon, not an object of statistical investigation. Consequently, the sample points can be assumed to lie about the regression line rather than on this line. This variation *about* the regression line is measured by the error sum of squares, SSE.

EXERCISES 14.33–14.42

UNDERSTANDING THE MECHANICS

14.33 Consider the following pairs of measurements.

X	10	5	8	9	11	4	6	7
Y	9	20	14	11	8	20	18	15

a. Specify the null and alternative hypotheses you would use to test whether the population correlation between the variables X and Y is nonzero.

b. Calculate the estimate of the population correlation coefficient between X and Y.

c. Calculate the coefficient of determination.

d. Using a .05 significance level, test the hypothesis in part (a).

APPLYING THE NEW CONCEPTS

14.34 The manager of a company that relies on traveling salespersons to sell the company's products wants to examine the relationship between sales and the amount of time a salesperson spends with each established customer who regularly orders the company's products. The manager collects data on 12 salespersons. Let Y represent sales per month and X represent hours spent with customers per month.

X	Y	X	Y	X	Y
3.2	412	6.1	715	5.1	570
4.6	500	4.2	500	7.1	800
3.9	450	5.6	610	6.5	725
5.3	610	5.3	600	7.8	850

Can one conclude that the population correlation coefficient between X and Y is positive? Use a 10% significance level. Can one conclude that spending more time with customers increases sales?

14.35 From 1987 to 1996, the revenue and the number of employees at Electronic Data Systems Corp. (EDS) have generally been in an uptrend. To understand the relationship between revenue and number of employees, construct a prediction equation of revenue from number of employees. What percentage of the total variation in revenue is explained using the number of employees? Does this indicate there is a linear relationship between revenue and number of employees? Use a 5% significance level.

(Source: *Dallas Morning News*, "Reinventing EDS," July 1, 1997, Business Section, p. 1.)

Year	Number of Employees (in Thousands)	Revenue (in Billions)
1987	43.4	4.33
1988	50.4	4.74
1989	56.9	5.37
1990	61.5	6.02
1991	65.2	7.03
1992	71.0	8.16
1993	69.7	8.51
1994	81.5	9.96
1995	96.0	12.4
1996	100.5	14.4

14.36 The demand and supply of new apartments are typically not in balance in most large cities across the United States. In Dallas, the demand for apartments has been difficult to predict. The demand for new apartments has generally been greater than the supply of new units. However, since 1996, the supply of new units has exceeded demand, which has kept rental prices stable. Consider the data below to be a random sample of yearly data listing the demand for new apartments and the supply of new units. The data are in units of thousands.

Demand for New Apartment Units	Supply of New Apartment Units
4.1	9.5
9.2	3.1
10.5	1.8
3.2	.7
−3.0	3.8
5.5	2.5
8.1	2.8
5.3	3.8
7.1	6.0
11.0	12.1
10.3	11.5
10.0	14.5

(Source: Adapted from *The Dallas Morning News*, "Apartment Pipeline," Aug. 8, 1997, p. D1.)

a. Calculate the correlation coefficient between the demand and supply of apartment units.

b. What is the coefficient of determination for predicting the demand of apartment units from the supply of new units? Interpret this value.

c. Do the data support the belief that a nonzero correlation exits? Use a .10 significance level.

14.37 Ten cards numbered 1 through 10 are shuffled, and a person is asked to pick one. The card is replaced and the deck reshuffled. Then the person is asked to draw a second card. If the second card is higher than the first, the dealer gives $.85 to the player. If the second card is not higher than the first, the player pays $1.15 to the dealer. A sample of 15 pairs of draws is taken to see whether there is any correlation between the first and the second cards.

a. Would you expect to observe significant correlation here? Why or why not?

b. Find the coefficient of determination for the following data, and test using a 5% significance level that there is no correlation between the first and the second cards. Interpret the value of the coefficient of determination.

First Card (X)	Second Card (Y)	First Card (X)	Second Card (Y)
7	3	10	5
3	10	3	6
8	2	4	3
5	8	6	1
2	7	7	8
7	9	8	4
9	4	2	6
1	1		

14.38 Refer to Exercise 14.25. Use equation 14.20 to test that there is no linear relationship between the size of the U.S. population and the logarithm of personal consumption expenditure on housing. Use a significance level of 5%.

14.39 For the data in Exercise 14.26, test that there is no linear relationship between the number of hours of operation between oil changes and the number of years that the engine was able to perform adequately. Use equation 14.20 and test with a 10% significance level. Is the result the same as in Exercise 14.26?

14.40 A sample of 35 pairs of observations is taken, and a sample correlation coefficient is computed to be $r = .48$. Do the data provide sufficient evidence to reject the null hypothesis of no correlation? Use a 1% significance level.

USING THE COMPUTER

14.41 **[DATA SET EX14-41]** *Variable description:*

SatDishAdv: Amount spent on local advertising (excludes national advertising)
SatDishSales: Annual sales of satellite dishes

Tandy Corp.'s Radio Shack units have used their marketing muscle to promote many of their products. Through Radio Shack's ubiquitous neighborhood stores, Tandy has become the leading retailer for home satellite equipment (*Dallas Morning News*, "Radio Shack No. 1 for Dishes," July 14, 1997, p. D2). Suppose that a company analyst wished to determine if there is a linear relationship between the amount spent on local advertising (SatDishAdv) and the annual sales of satellite dishes (SatDishSales). Fifty stores are randomly selected and the data are recorded in units of thousands of dollars.

a. Find the correlation between $X = $ SatDishAdv and $Y = $ SatDishSales. Based on this value, do you think that the data will support the alternative hypothesis that the population correlation is positive? Use a 5% significance level.

b. Find the value of the *t* statistic for testing that the slope of the regression equation is greater than zero. What conclusion can you make using a 5% significance level? Compare the value of this *t* statistic with that calculated in part (a).

c. Find the predicted values of SatDishSales. What is the correlation between these values and the original values of SatDishSales? Compare this to the correlation obtained in part (a).

14.42 [DATA SET EX14-42] *Variable description:*

AnnualInc: Yearly income
VacationExp: Expenditure on vacation

A marketing analyst is interested in the relationship between the yearly income of recently married couples and their vacation expenditure for the year. A random sample of 100 married couples is selected, and the data are recorded in variables Annual-Inc and VacationExp in units of thousands of dollars. If a relationship exists, the marketing analyst will use an estimate of a

married couple's income to determine which type of promotional vacation information to mail to them.

a. Test whether a linear relationship exists between the variables Y = VacationExp and X = AnnualInc. Use a 1% significance level.

b. Sometimes a transformation of one of the variables will result in a better linear relationship with the other variable. Take the natural log of AnnualInc. Find the correlation between these values and VacationExp. Is there sufficient evidence to conclude that a nonzero correlation exists at the 1% significance level?

14.5 ESTIMATION AND PREDICTION USING THE SIMPLE LINEAR MODEL

We have concentrated on predicting a value of the dependent variable (Y) for a given value of X. In the previous examples, we used a person's income, X, to predict the size of that person's home (Y). Notice in Figure 14.8 that we can also use the least squares line to estimate the *average (mean)* value of Y for a specified value of X. So we can use this line in two different situations.

SITUATION 1.   The regression equation $\hat{Y} = b_0 + b_1 X$ estimates the **mean** value of Y for a specified value of the independent variable, X. For $X = x_0$, this value would be written $\mu_{Y|x_0}$ (the mean of Y given $X = x_0$).

For example, the least squares line passing through the real-estate data in Example 14.1 is $\hat{Y} = 4.975 + .3539X$. The average square footage for *all* homes in the population with an income of \$50,000 ($X = 50$) is $\mu_{Y|50}$. Its estimate is provided by the corresponding value on the least squares line, namely,

$$\hat{Y} = 4.975 + (.3539)(50) = 22.67$$

So the estimate of the average square footage of all such homes is 2267 square feet (Figure 14.7).

SITUATION 2.   An **individual** predicted value of Y also uses the regression equation $\hat{Y} = b_0 + b_1 X$ for a specified value of X. This value of Y is denoted by Y_{x_0} for $X = x_0$. This application is the more common one in business, because a regression equation is generally used for individual forecasts.

For example, assume the Jenkins family resides in our sample community and has an income of \$50,000. A prediction of their home size (Y_{50}) is also

$$\hat{Y} = 4.975 + (.3539)(50) = 22.67$$

which is 2267 square feet (Figure 14.7).

We see that the least squares line can be used to estimate average values (situation 1) or predict individual values (situation 2). Since $\mu_{Y|50}$ *is a parameter, we use* $\hat{Y}$ *to* estimate *this value. On the other hand,* Y_{50} *represents a particular value of a dependent (random) variable, and so* $\hat{Y}$ *is used to* predict *this value. In the first situation, we can determine a confidence interval for* $\mu_{Y|50}$; *in the second situation, we determine a prediction interval for* Y_{50}.

CONFIDENCE INTERVAL FOR $\mu_{Y|x_0}$ (SITUATION 1)

We have already established that the point estimate of $\mu_{Y|x_0}$ is the corresponding value of $\hat{Y}$. The reliability of this estimate depends on (1) the number of observations in the sample, (2) the amount of variation in the sample, and (3) the value of $X = x_0$. A confidence interval for $\mu_{Y|x_0}$ takes all three factors into consideration.

A $(1 - \alpha) \cdot 100\%$ confidence interval for $\mu_{Y|x_0}$ is

$$\hat{Y} - t_{\alpha/2, n-2} s \sqrt{\frac{1}{n} + \frac{(x_0 - \bar{x})^2}{SS_X}} \quad \text{to} \quad \hat{Y} + t_{\alpha/2, n-2} s \sqrt{\frac{1}{n} + \frac{(x_0 - \bar{x})^2}{SS_X}} \quad \textbf{(14.24)}$$

EXAMPLE 14.8

Determine a 95% confidence interval for the average home size of families with an income of $45,000, using the real-estate data from Example 14.1.

SOLUTION

We previously determined that $n = 10$, $\bar{x} = 49.8$, $SS_X = 1489.6$, and $s = 3.078$. The point estimate for the average square footage, $\mu_{Y|45}$, is

$$\hat{Y} = 4.975 + .3539(45)$$

$$= 20.90 \ (2090 \text{ square feet})$$

Obtaining $t_{.025,8} = 2.306$ from Table A.5, the 95% confidence interval for $\mu_{Y|45}$ is

$$20.90 - (2.306)(3.078)\sqrt{\frac{1}{10} + \frac{(45 - 49.8)^2}{1489.6}} \quad \text{to} \quad 20.90 + (2.306)(3.078)\sqrt{\frac{1}{10} + \frac{(45 - 49.8)^2}{1489.6}}$$

$$= 20.90 - (2.306)(3.078)(.340) \quad \text{to} \quad 20.90 + (2.306)(3.078)(.340)$$

$$= 20.90 - 2.41 \quad \text{to} \quad 20.90 + 2.41$$

$$= 18.49 \quad \text{to} \quad 23.31$$

We are thus 95% confident that the average home size for families earning $45,000 is between 1849 and 2331 square feet.

USING EXCEL TO CONSTRUCT CONFIDENCE INTERVALS. Excel does not provide confidence and prediction intervals in its statistical tool package, but the KGP Data Analysis add-ins will allow you to compute these intervals. To carry out this analysis, enter "Income" in cell A1 and "Footage" in cell B1. Next, enter the income values in cells A2:A11 and the square footage values in cells B2:B11 and then click on **KGP Data Analysis ➤ Regression.** Enter "B1:B11" in the **Y Range** box and "A1:A11" in the **Contiguous X Range** box.* At the bottom of the form, click on **Confidence and Prediction Intervals** and enter "A2:A11" in the accompanying box. The default confidence level is 95%, and you can select any level by typing a value in the **Confidence Level** box. The resulting output is shown in Figure 14.19.

The column labeled **Std. Error Prediction** contains the standard deviation of the predicted Y values. Writing this as $s_{\hat{Y}}$,

$$s_{\hat{Y}} = s\sqrt{\frac{1}{n} + \frac{(x_0 - \bar{x})^2}{SS_X}} \qquad \textbf{(14.25)}$$

For each value of X *in the sample* (say, x_0), the corresponding confidence interval for $\mu_{Y|x_0}$ is

$$\hat{Y} - t \cdot s_{\hat{Y}} \qquad \text{to} \qquad \hat{Y} + t \cdot s_{\hat{Y}}$$

where $t = t_{\alpha/2, n-2}$, as before, and $\hat{Y}$ is contained in the column labeled **Predicted Value.**

Using the Excel output in Figure 14.19, we can find the confidence intervals corresponding to X values of 32 and 50. The remaining eight confidence intervals are constructed in a similar manner.

For X = 32 in the first row, the confidence interval is

$$16.300 - (2.306)(1.721) \qquad \text{to} \qquad 16.300 + (2.306)(1.721)$$

$$= 12.33 \qquad \text{to} \qquad 20.27$$

---

* Chapter 15 will explore the use of more than one independent (explanatory) variable. These columns may or may not be adjacent (contiguous) in your spreadsheet. The KGP Data Analysis regression procedure, unlike the standard Excel procedure, allows for either option. In this chapter, always use the **Contiguous X Range** box.

FIGURE 14.19

Excel confidence and prediction intervals for real estate data using KGP Data Analysis (see Figure 14.4).

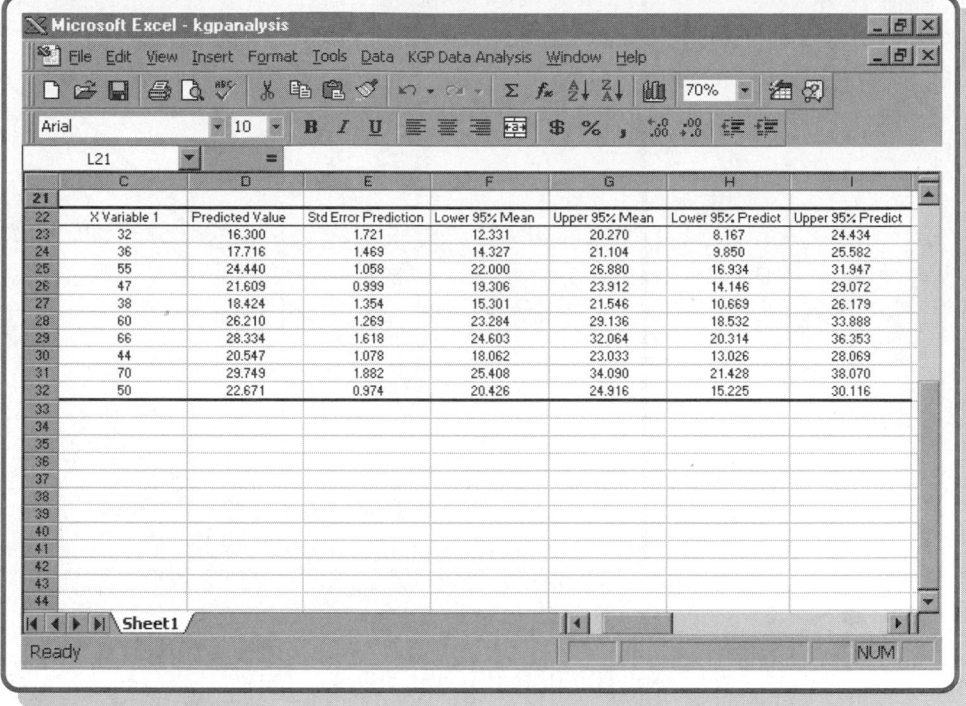

For $X = 50$ in the last row, the confidence interval is

$$22.671 - (2.306)(.974) \qquad \text{to} \qquad 22.671 + (2.306)(.974)$$

$$= 20.43 \qquad \text{to} \qquad 24.92$$

Notice that the confidence interval is much wider for $X = 32$ than for $X = 50$.

All 10 confidence intervals are shown in columns F and G in Figure 17.19 under the headings **Lower 95% Mean** and **Upper 95% Mean.** The intervals in the first and last rows (for $X = 32$ and $X = 50$) agree with the previously calculated confidence intervals for the average square footage using these two incomes. For values of X not in the sample, simply construct a new column containing these values and enter this range in the **Contiguous X Range** box.

By connecting the upper end of the confidence intervals for all ten data points and connecting the lower limits, we obtain Figure 14.20. Equation 14.23 indicates that the confidence interval is narrowest when $(x_0 - \bar{x})^2 = 0$, that is, at $X = x_0 = \bar{x}$. For values of X to the left or right of $\bar{x}$, the confidence interval is wider. *In other words, the farther x_0 is from $\bar{x}$, the less reliable is the estimate.*

THE DANGER OF EXTRAPOLATION.   Extrapolation is the process of calculating an estimate corresponding to a value of X outside the range of the data used to derive the prediction equation (the least squares line). For example, in Figure 14.20 the least squares line could be used to estimate the average home size for families with an income of $100,000. Although we *can* estimate $\mu_{Y|100}$, the corresponding confidence interval for this parameter will be extremely wide, so the point estimate, $\hat{Y}$, will have little practical value.

To use the simple regression model effectively for estimation, you need to stay within the range of the sampled values for the independent variable, X. This process is called **interpolation.** If you use values outside this range, you need to be aware that given *another* set of data, you would quite likely obtain a considerably different estimate. Furthermore, you have no assurance that the linear relationship still holds outside the range of your sample data.

FIGURE 14.20
95% confidence intervals for the real-estate data derived from Excel output shown in Figure 14.19.

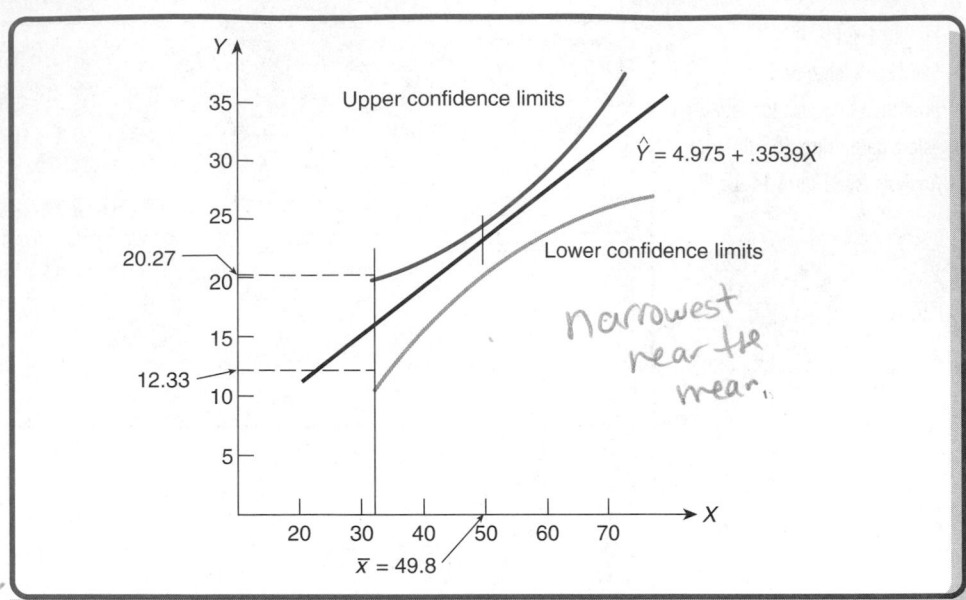

PREDICTION INTERVAL FOR Y_{x_0} (SITUATION 2)

The procedure of predicting individual values is used more often in business applications. The regression equation is generally used to **forecast** (predict) a future value of the dependent variable for a particular value of the independent variable. When attempting to predict a single value of the dependent variable, Y, using the simple linear regression model, we begin, as before, with $\hat{Y}$. Substituting $X = x_0$ into the regression equation provides the best prediction of Y_{x_0}. For example, if the Johnson family has an income of \$45,000, our best guess as to their home size (using this particular model) is $\hat{Y}$ for $X = 45$. From the results of Example 14.8, this is 20.90, or 2090 square feet.

We do not use the term *confidence interval* for this procedure because what we are estimating (Y_{x_0}) is not a parameter. It is a value of a random variable, so we use the term **prediction interval.**

The variability of the error in predicting a single value of Y is more than that for estimating the average value of Y (situation 1). It can be shown that an estimate of the variance of the error ($Y - \hat{Y}$), when using $\hat{Y}$ to predict an individual Y for $X = x_0$, is*

$$s_Y^2 = s^2\left(1 + \frac{1}{n} + \frac{(x_0 - \bar{x})^2}{SS_X}\right) \qquad \textbf{(14.26)}$$

This result can be used to construct a $(1 - \alpha) \cdot 100\%$ prediction interval for Y_{x_0}, as follows:

$$\hat{Y} - t_{\alpha/2, n-2}\, s\sqrt{1 + \frac{1}{n} + \frac{(x_0 - \bar{x})^2}{SS_X}} \quad \text{to}$$

$$\hat{Y} + t_{\alpha/2, n-2}\, s\sqrt{1 + \frac{1}{n} + \frac{(x_0 - \bar{x})^2}{SS_X}} \qquad \textbf{(14.27)}$$

---

* This follows since $Y = \hat{Y} + e$ and, as a result, $s_Y^2 = s_{\hat{Y}}^2 + s_e^2$. Substituting equation 14.25 for $s_{\hat{Y}}^2$ and s^2 for s_e^2 produces the desired result.

Notice that the only difference between this prediction interval and the confidence interval in equation 14.24 is the inclusion of "1+" under the square root sign. The other two terms under the square root are usually quite small, so this "1+" has a large effect on the width of the resulting interval. Be aware that our warning about extrapolating outside the range of the data applies here as well. In equations 14.26 and 14.27, the distance from the mean $(x_0 - \bar{x})$ is squared, which increases the risk of predicting beyond the range of the sampled data.

EXAMPLE 14.9

We previously determined that if the Johnson family has an income of $45,000, the best prediction of their home size is $\hat{Y} = 20.90$. Determine a 95% prediction interval for this situation.

SOLUTION

We can use the calculations from Example 14.8 to derive the prediction interval for Y_{45}. The result is

$$20.90 - (2.306)(3.078)\sqrt{1 + \frac{1}{10} + \frac{(45 - 49.8)^2}{1489.6}} \quad \text{to}$$

$$20.90 + (2.306)(3.078)\sqrt{1 + \frac{1}{10} + \frac{(45 - 49.8)^2}{1489.6}}$$

$$= 20.90 - (2.306)(3.078)(1.056) \quad \text{to} \quad 20.90 + (2.306)(3.078)(1.056)$$

$$= 20.90 - 7.49 \quad \text{to} \quad 20.90 + 7.49$$

$$= 13.41 \quad \text{to} \quad 28.39$$

Comparing this interval to the confidence interval for $\mu_{Y|45}$ in Example 14.8, we see that individual predictions are considerably less accurate than estimations for the mean home size. Of course, we could reduce the width of this interval by obtaining additional data. Expecting accurate results from a sample of ten observations is being a bit optimistic.

USING EXCEL FOR CONSTRUCTING PREDICTION INTERVALS. Prediction intervals can be determined without any calculations by using the **KGP Data Analysis ➤ Regression** procedure discussed immediately following the solution to Example 14.8. From Figure 14.19, we observe the following prediction intervals:

$X = 32$: prediction interval for Y_{32} is from 8.167 to 24.434

$X = 50$: prediction interval for Y_{50} is from 15.225 to 30.116

Notice that these intervals are considerably wider than the corresponding confidence intervals.

Figure 14.21 shows the prediction intervals for all 10 data points; the upper and lower limits have been connected. The increased width of a prediction interval versus a confidence interval is quite apparent from this graph. Also, like the width of a confidence interval, the width of a prediction interval increases as the value of X strays from $\bar{x}$.

14.6 EXAMINING THE RESIDUALS

CHECKING THE MODEL ASSUMPTIONS

When using a linear regression model, you should keep two things in mind. First, no distributional assumptions are necessary to derive the least squares estimates of β_0 and β_1. The regression coefficients b_0 and b_1 from the sample regression line are the "best" estimates in the least squares sense.

Second, several key assumptions *are* required for the validity of any constructed confidence intervals and tests of hypothesis. If these assumptions are violated, you may still

FIGURE 14.21

The 95% prediction and confidence intervals for the real-estate data. Calculated values on the Y axis are for X = 32.

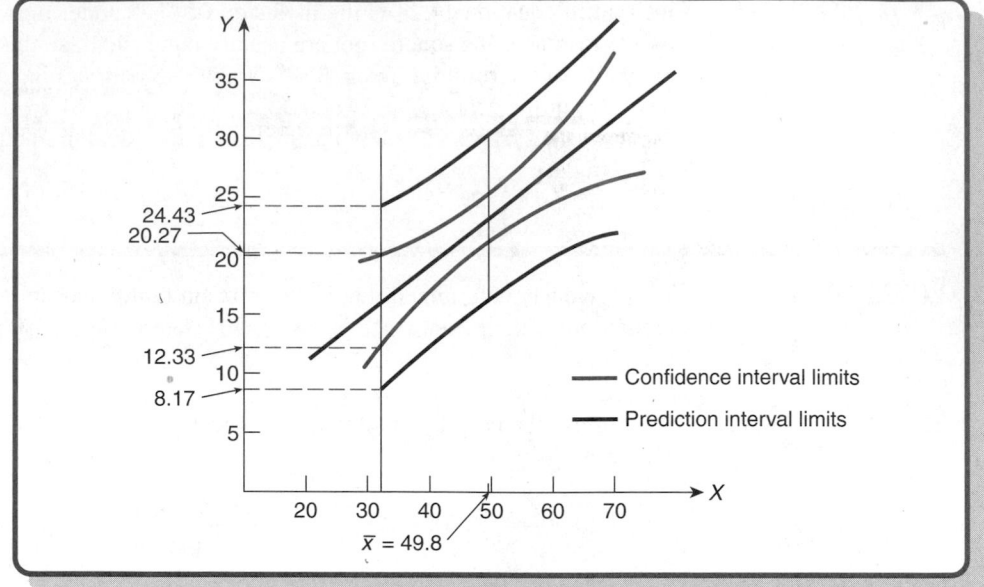

have an accurate prediction, $\hat{Y}$, but the validity of the inference procedures will be highly questionable.

Your final step in any regression analysis should be to verify your assumptions.

ASSUMPTION 1. *The errors are normally distributed with a mean of zero.* An easy method to determine whether the errors follow a normal distribution centered at zero is to let the computer construct a histogram of the sample residuals $(Y - \hat{Y})$. Since the residuals *always* sum to zero when using the least squares line, the residual histogram is typically centered at zero. The plot should reveal whether the distribution of residuals is severely skewed. Remember that an exact normal distribution is not necessary here; problems arise only when the distribution is severely skewed and does not resemble a normal distribution. (The Excel procedure to obtain this histogram is illustrated in upcoming Example 14.10.)

More sophisticated methods of checking this assumption involve the use of a *probability plot* or a *chi-square goodness-of-fit test*. We do not discuss the probability plot technique here, except to say that you plot the residuals in a specialized type of graph. If the resulting graph is linear in appearance, the normality assumption has been verified.

The goodness-of-fit test was discussed in Chapter 13, where we used a chi-square statistic to test the hypothesis that a particular set of data (in this case, the regression residuals) came from a specific (normal, here) distribution. Exercise 13.13 at the end of Section 13.1 discusses how to use the chi-square test for a suspected *normal* population.

If you have reason to believe that this assumption of your model has been violated, then you need to search for another model. This new model may include additional predictor variables (the subject of Chapter 15) that have been overlooked. Another possibility is to transform the dependent variable (for example, use $\sqrt{Y}$ rather than Y) or to transform the independent variable. As your model tends to "improve," you should observe the residuals tending toward a normal distribution.

ASSUMPTION 2. *The variance of the errors remains constant. For example, you should not observe larger errors associated with larger values of X.* When the residuals $(Y - \hat{Y})$ are plotted against the independent variable, X, we hope to observe *no pattern* (a "shotgun blast" appearance) in this graph, as in Figure 14.22(a). Remember—the assumption is essentially that the errors consist of what engineers call *noise*, with no observable pattern.

A common violation of this assumption of equal variances occurs when the value of the residual increases as X increases, as illustrated in Figure 14.22(b). In this graph, the variance of the residual increases with X, producing a funnel appearance. This has a seri-

FIGURE 14.22

Examination of the residuals. (*a*) The shotgun effect (no violation of assumptions 1 and 2). (*b*) A violation of the equal variance assumption (assumption 2).

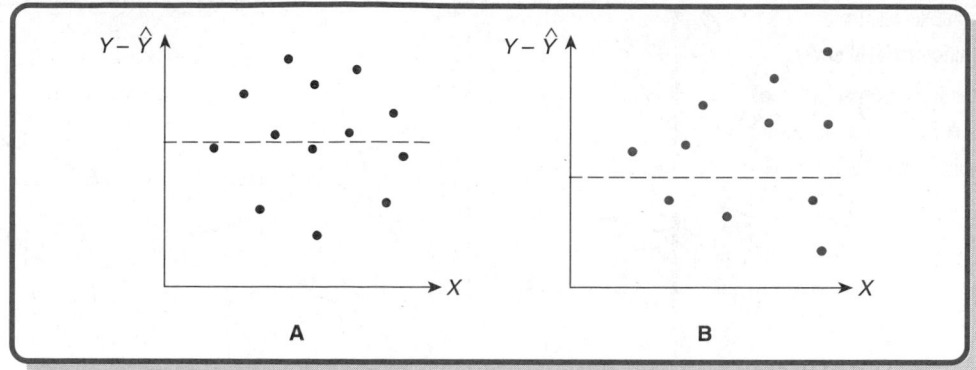

ous effect on the validity of the *t* tests discussed in this chapter, which determine the strength of the regression model.

When you encounter a violation of this type, you need to resort to more advanced modeling techniques, such as *weighted least squares* or *transformations* of your dependent variable.*

ASSUMPTION 3.   *The errors are independent.* To examine this assumption after the regression equation has been determined involves using the residual from each of the sample observations. For given values of *X,* the actual error is

$$e = Y - (\beta_0 + \beta_1 X)$$

The β's are unknown, so we estimate the error by using the residual for this particular observation,

$$Y - \hat{Y} = Y - (b_0 + b_1 X)$$

When your regression data consist of *time-series* data, your errors often are not independent. This type of data has the following appearance:

Time	Y	X
1989	*	*
1990	*	*
1991	*	*
⋮	⋮	⋮

(* denotes a numeric value)

Also remember that your error component includes the effect of variables missing from your model. Chapter 15 deals with regression models containing more than one predictor variable. In many business applications, there is a positive relationship between time-related predictor variables, such as prices and wages, because they increase over time.

This relationship can produce a set of residuals in your regression analysis that are not independent of one another but instead display a pattern similar to the one in Figure 14.23. This plot contains the sample residuals on the vertical axis and time on the horizontal axis. If this assumption were *not* violated here, we would observe the shotgun appearance as in Figure 14.22(a). Instead we notice that adjacent residuals have roughly the same value and so are correlated with each other. This is **autocorrelation.**

To be more specific, the pattern in Figure 14.23 is one of *positive* autocorrelation. Negative autocorrelation exists when most of the neighboring residuals are very unequal in size (such as a positive residual, followed by a negative residual, followed by a positive

---

* See J. Neter, M. Kutner, and C. Nachtscheim, *Applied Linear Regression Models,* 3rd ed. (Homewood, Ill.: Richard D. Irwin, 1996).

FIGURE 14.23
Autocorrelated errors.

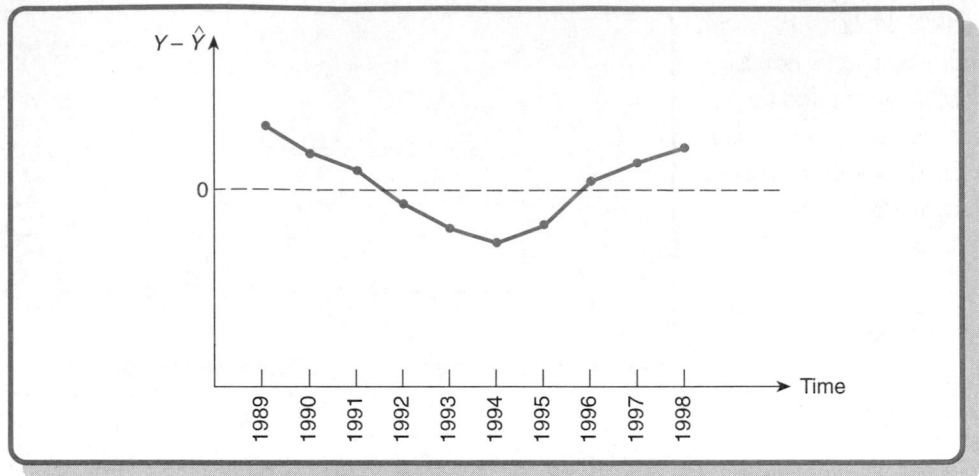

residual, and so on). The amount of autocorrelation that exists in residuals is measured by the **Durbin-Watson statistic.** Chapter 17 discusses the calculation of this statistic and its use in detecting autocorrelated residuals.

The problem of autocorrelated errors is the most difficult of the three assumptions to correct. The error term is not noise, as we originally assumed, but instead has a definite pattern (as in Figure 14.23). Several ways of treating this problem are discussed in Chapter 17.

COMMENT

Practically all computer packages can provide the value of the Durbin-Watson statistic when performing a linear regression analysis. When your data are *not* collected over time (but rather from different families, cities, companies, or the like), this statistic is meaningless and should be ignored. For this situation, assumption 3 is not of vital concern and is often taken for granted.

CHECKING FOR OUTLIERS AND INFLUENTIAL OBSERVATIONS

A closer look at the regression data and computer solution can reveal some rather interesting and important details concerning the least squares line. Of particular interest is whether there are one or more **outliers** in the sample observations. These points are generally fairly obvious in a scatter diagram, since such points do not seem to "fit" with the remaining observations. An outlier can have a dramatic effect on the least squares line, because the regression line will be pulled in the direction of the outlier, reducing the effectiveness of the regression line as a predictor. Such observations need to be detected and studied to determine if an error was made in the recording of this data point and whether this observation should be corrected or removed from the sample data.

Also of interest is the determination of whether the sample outliers are very influential in determining the fitted regression line (the least squares line). A point is said to have a *strong influence* on the regression line if removal of this observation produces a dramatic shift in the regression line if the line is recalculated from the remaining points. These observations may be extreme in their X value, Y value, or both.

Figure 14.24 contains three outliers (points A, B, and C). Point A has an X value close to the average of the X values in the sample, but has an extremely large Y value. As we will demonstrate, this observation will not have a large influence on the regression line, due to the number of sample observations having similar X values. Point B has a large X value, but the Y value is consistent with the line determined from the remaining observations; it will not have a very strong influence on the regression line. Point C is another matter—it has an extremely large X value and a Y value that is not consistent with the regression line

FIGURE 14.24

Excel illustration of outliers and influential observations.

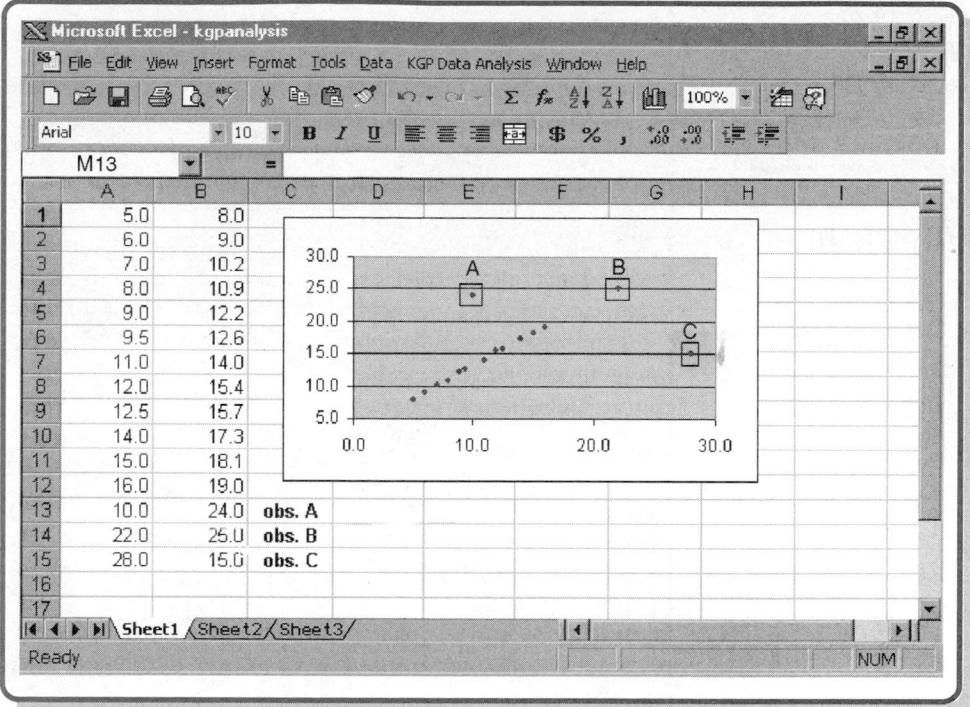

through the remaining observations. Removal of this observation would produce a drastically different least squares line; this point is an **influential observation.**

IDENTIFYING OUTLYING VALUES OF THE INDEPENDENT VARIABLE. Observations having extremely large or small values of the independent variable (*X*) can be detected by computing **sample leverages.** An observation whose value of the independent variable is distant from the sample mean of the *X* values ($\bar{x}$) is said to have high leverage. In Figure 14.24, point C would be a high leverage observation and point B has a potentially high leverage. The leverage of the *i*th observation is measured by h_i, where

$$h_i = \frac{1}{n} + \frac{(x_i - \bar{x})^2}{\text{SS}_X}$$ (14.28)

and $\text{SS}_X = \sum x^2 - (\sum x)^2/n$.

Consider the real-estate data in Examples 14.1, 14.2, and 14.3. Suppose one additional observation is added to this data set. In Figure 14.25(a), this observation is $X = 115$ and $Y = 48$ (a family with a large income and a large house). In Figure 14.25(b), the additional observation is $X = 115$ and $Y = 29$ (a family with a large income and a small house for this income). The leverage value for the additional observation *will be the same* in both cases, since it depends on the *X* value only. In either case, the average of the 11 *X* values in the sample is now

$$\bar{x} = 55.727$$

Also,

$$\text{SS}_X = 39,515 - \frac{(613)^2}{11} = 5354.18$$

Consequently, the leverage of the new observation is

$$h_{11} = \frac{1}{11} + \frac{(115 - 55.727)^2}{5354.18} = .747$$

FIGURE 14.25

(a) Original real-estate data, with a new observation ($X = 115$, $Y = 48$).

(b) Original real-estate data, with a new observation ($X = 115$, $Y = 29$).

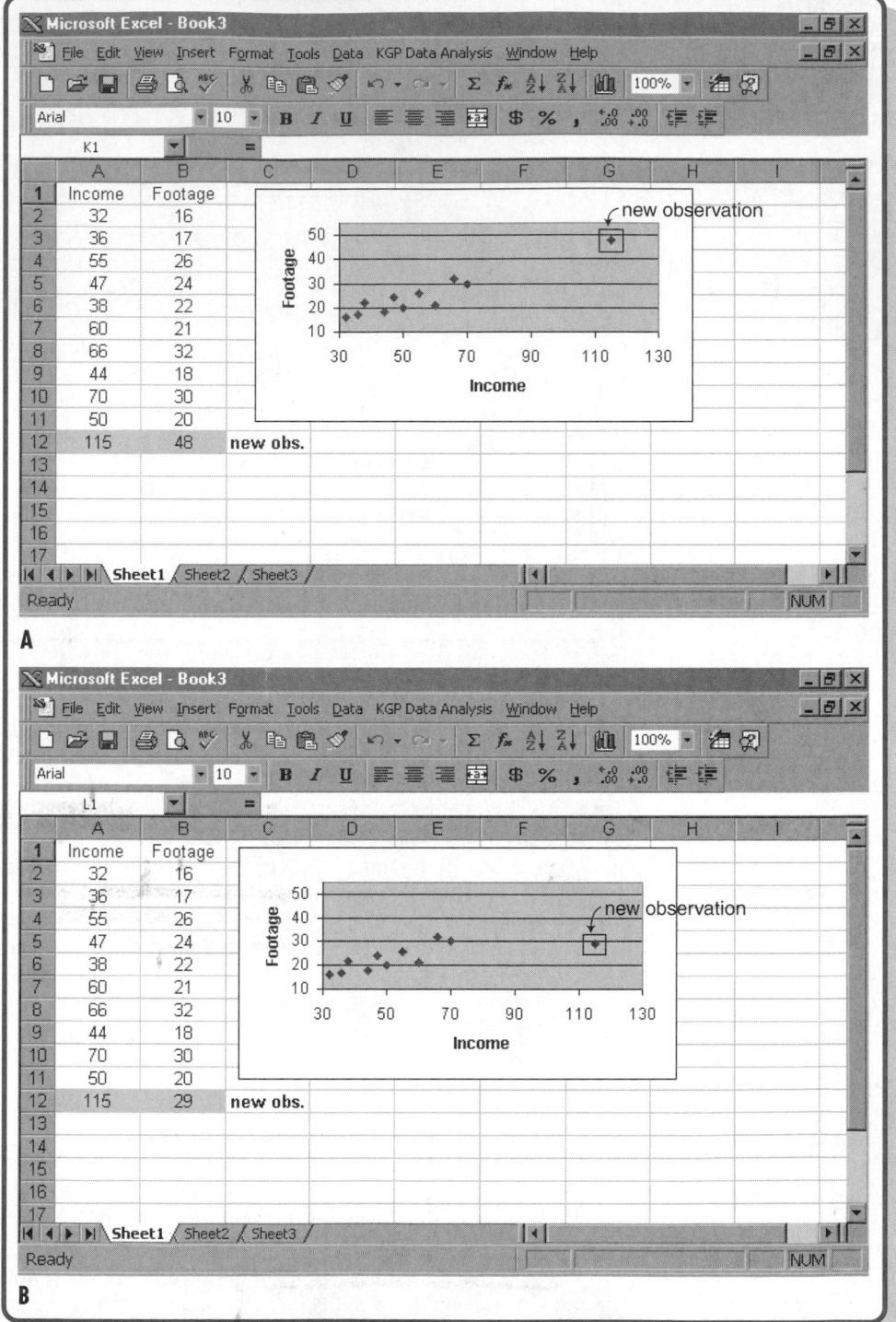

Commonly accepted procedures for simple linear regression are to conclude that a **sample observation has an outlying X value if its leverage value is larger than $4/n$ or larger than $6/n$, where n is the number of sample observations.** MINITAB uses the "larger than $6/n$" rule, and we will accept that decision rule in our discussion. Here, $6/n = 6/11 = .545$; and since $.747 > .545$, we conclude that the 11th observation does have an unusually large income (X). Since the leverage value depends strictly on the X value, it is impossible to say whether the new observation exerts a large influence on the regression equation. We will demonstrate shortly that the new observation in Figure 14.25(a) is *not* an influential observation, whereas in Figure 14.25(b) it is.

Compare the leverage value in equation 14.28 and the confidence interval for the mean value of Y at $X = x_0$ given in equation 14.24. If a confidence interval is calculated at the ith observation (x_i, y_i), then the leverage for this observation, h_i, is the quantity under the square root sign in equations 14.24 and 14.25. As a result, the standard deviation of the predicted Y value in equation 14.25 can be written

$$s_{\hat{Y}} = s\sqrt{h_i} \tag{14.29}$$

The corresponding confidence interval for $\mu_{Y|x_i}$ is

$$\hat{Y} - t_{\alpha/2,n-2}\,s\sqrt{h_i} \quad \text{to} \quad \hat{Y} + t_{\alpha/2,n-2}\,s\sqrt{h_i} \tag{14.30}$$

and the prediction interval for Y_{x_i} in equation 14.27 is

$$\hat{Y} - t_{\alpha/2,n-2}\,s\sqrt{1+h_i} \quad \text{to} \quad \hat{Y} + t_{\alpha/2,n-2}\,s\sqrt{1+h_i} \tag{14.31}$$

Consequently, as the leverage of the ith observation increases (x_i moves farther from $\bar{x}$), the confidence interval for $\mu_{Y|x_i}$ and the prediction interval for Y_{x_i} become wider. The smallest possible leverage value is $h_i = 1/n$, and this occurs only if $x_i = \bar{x}$.

IDENTIFYING OUTLYING VALUES OF THE DEPENDENT VARIABLE. Sample observations having unusually large or small values of the dependent variable (Y) can generally be detected using the sample **standardized residuals.** Recall that the residual at the ith observation is $Y - \hat{Y}$, and that this residual estimates the error in the model at this observation. Since one of the model assumptions is that each error has a mean of zero, then to standardize the ith residual we simply divide by its estimated standard deviation. The estimated standard deviation of the ith residual can be written as

$$s\sqrt{1-h_i} \tag{14.32}$$

where h_i is the leverage for this observation, defined in equation 14.28, and s (rather, s^2) is defined in equation 14.16. Consequently,

$$\text{standardized residual} = \frac{Y_i - \hat{Y}_i}{s\sqrt{1-h_i}} \tag{14.33}$$

A recommended procedure is to identify an observation as having an outlying value of Y if its standardized residual is larger than 2 or less than –2. MINITAB will automatically inform you which (if any) of your observations have standardized residuals larger than 2 in absolute value.

Using Excel (or MINITAB) and Figure 14.25(a), the following results can be obtained:

Least squares line: $\hat{Y} = 3.752 + .3796X$

$$SSE = 77.18 \quad \text{and} \quad s = \sqrt{\frac{77.18}{9}} = 2.93$$

For $X = 115$, $\hat{Y} = 47.41$, and

$$\text{Standardized residual of observation 11} = \frac{48 - 47.41}{2.93\sqrt{1-.747}} = .40$$

Consequently, observation 11 does not contain an extreme value of the dependent variable. We would still classify this observation as an outlier due to the large value of the independent variable ($X = 115$) and the correspondingly large leverage value ($h_{11} = .747$).

For Figure 14.25(b), the results are:

$$\text{Least squares line: } \hat{Y} = 13.746 + .1693X$$

$$\text{SSE} = 146.14 \quad \text{and} \quad s = \sqrt{\frac{146.14}{9}} = 4.03$$

For $X = 115$, $\hat{Y} = 33.22$, and

$$\text{Standardized residual of observation } 11 = \frac{29 - 33.22}{4.03\sqrt{1 - .747}} = -2.08$$

Since $-2.08 < -2$, observation 11 is extreme in both the Y value *and* the X value.

IDENTIFYING INFLUENTIAL OBSERVATIONS.   On occasion, you may have one or two observations that have a very large impact on the sample regression line. If such an observation were deleted from the sample, the new values of the intercept (b_0) and/or the slope (b_1) would be much different. If such an observation exists, a little investigation may be in order to determine if this sample value should be modified or removed. If an error was made while recording this observation, then, if possible, the regression analysis should be rerun using the corrected value.

Very often, it is impossible to recapture this observation. For example, it may have been recorded during an expensive experiment, which would necessitate rerunning the experiment. Perhaps, this observation occurred during a point in time that has since passed. For such situations, you could remove this observation and rerun the regression analysis.

On the other hand, if this observation was recorded correctly, simply removing this observation from the data set is ill-advised. This observation may be trying to tell you something; in particular, your model (using a straight line to predict Y) may be inappropriate, or the situation you're attempting to model is simply not as predictable as you expected. Perhaps additional independent variables should be considered (discussed in Chapter 15).

Determining influential observations uses the strategy for identifying outliers that was just discussed, since such observations are characterized by large leverage values (unusual values of X) and/or large standardized residuals (unusual values of Y).

A commonly used measure of influence is **Cook's distance measure,** which combines the leverage value and standardized residual into one overall value. Cook's distance measure for the ith observation is given by

$$D_i = \frac{1}{2}\frac{h_i}{1 - h_i}(\text{standardized residual})^2$$

$$= \frac{(Y_i - \hat{Y}_i)^2}{2s^2}\left(\frac{h_i}{(1 - h_i)^2}\right) \tag{14.34}$$

For example, in Figure 14.25(a), at observation 11,

$$Y = 48, \quad \hat{Y} = 47.41, \quad s = 2.93, \quad h_{11} = .747$$

and so

$$D_{11} = \frac{(48 - 47.41)^2}{2(2.93)^2}\left(\frac{.747}{(1 - .747)^2}\right) = .24$$

For Figure 14.25(b), at observation 11,

$$Y = 29, \quad \hat{Y} = 33.22, \quad s = 4.03, \quad h_{11} = .747$$

FIGURE 14.26

Another look at Figure 14.24, with calculated leverages, standardized residuals, and Cook distance measures.

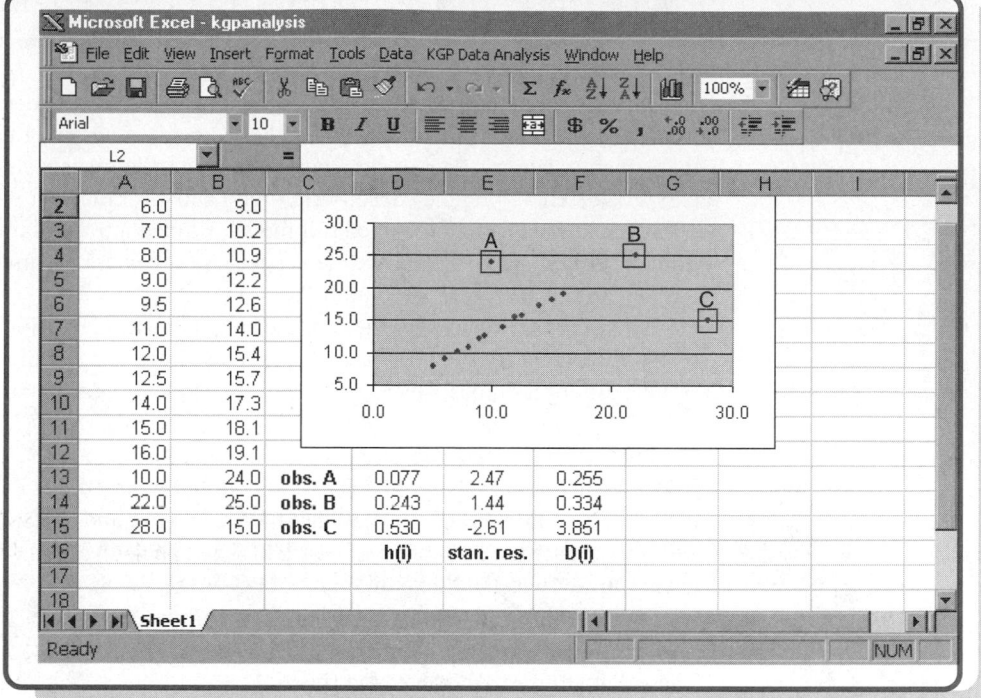

TABLE 14.1

Summary of Figures 14.24 and 14.26.

Point	Outlying in X Value $(h_i > .4)$	Outlying in Y Value $(\|\text{stand. res.}\| > 2)$	Influential Observation $(D_i > .8)$
A	No	Yes	No
B	No	No	No
C	Yes	Yes	Yes

Cooks Distance measure (handwritten annotation)

and

$$D_{11} = \frac{(29-33.22)^2}{2(4.03)^2}\left(\frac{.747}{(1-.747)^2}\right) = 6.40$$

For simple linear regression, we recommend you conclude that the *i*th observation is influential if the corresponding D_i measure is larger than .8.* For Figure 14.25(a), the new observation is *not* considered influential: .24 < .8, and so, despite the large leverage value, this observation would not seriously affect the regression results if it were removed from the sample. In Figure 14.25(b), the new observation *would* be labeled as influential, because 6.40 > .8.

A final look at Figure 14.24 is contained in Figure 14.26, where the leverage value, standardized residual, and Cook's distance measure are shown for each of the three outliers. These results are summarized in Table 14.1, where the cutoff for the leverage values is $h_i = 6/n = 6/15 = .4$.

---

* The cutoff value for Cook's distance measure in simple linear regression can also be defined using the F distribution: tail area = .5, df = 2 and $n - 2$. For nearly all sample sizes, the value .8 provides a reliable, and slightly conservative, approximation to this F-value.

EXAMPLE 14.10
A Full Excel Simple Linear Regression Analysis

The editor of a monthly automotive magazine is interested in determining how well automotive manufacturers are meeting federal mandates concerning the average fuel economy that a manufacturer's fleet of cars must reach. The editor suspects that a linear relationship exists between X = engine capacity (in liters) and Y = miles per gallon (mpg). A sample of 60 different models was obtained (all models having a manual transmission) and is found in data set DATA14-10. The engine capacities (X values) are in column A, and the miles per gallon (Y values) are in column B.

Determine the appropriateness of the simple linear regression model, and examine the residuals (1) to detect any outliers, (2) to determine if any outliers would be classified as influential observations, and (3) to verify the model assumptions.

SOLUTION

Begin by opening data file DATA14-10 into columns A and B. The labels **Capacity** and **MPG** should be in cells A1 and B1, as shown in Figure 14.27. To obtain a scatter diagram of the observations, click on the **Chart Wizard** icon and select **XY(Scatter) ➤ Next.** If necessary, enter the data range as "A1:B61," and click on **Next.** Click on the **Titles** tab and enter **Capacity** as the X axis title and **MPG** as the Y axis title. You may enter a chart title if you wish. After clicking on **Finish,** you will see the scatter diagram in Figure 14.27, where a negative relationship is observed between X = capacity and Y = miles per gallon. There is one unusual observation (boxed).

To obtain the regression equation, use the KGP Data Analysis option since it identifies outliers and influential observations. Click on **KGP Data Analysis ➤ Regression** and enter "B1:B61" in the **Y Range** box and "A1:A61" in the **X Range** box. Enter "C18" as the output range, directly below the previously created scatter diagram. Select **Residuals, Standardized Residuals, Leverages,** and **Cook's Ds** in the **Data** frame, and **Residual Plots** in the **Plots** frame. The resulting regression equation from Figure 14.28 is $\hat{Y} = 55.494 - 5.981X$. Since the X coefficient is negative, there is indeed a negative relationship, and each additional liter of engine capacity in the data is accompanied by a decrease of approximately six miles per gallon (on the average).

FIGURE 14.27
Excel plot of X = engine capacity versus Y = miles per gallon (Example 14.10).

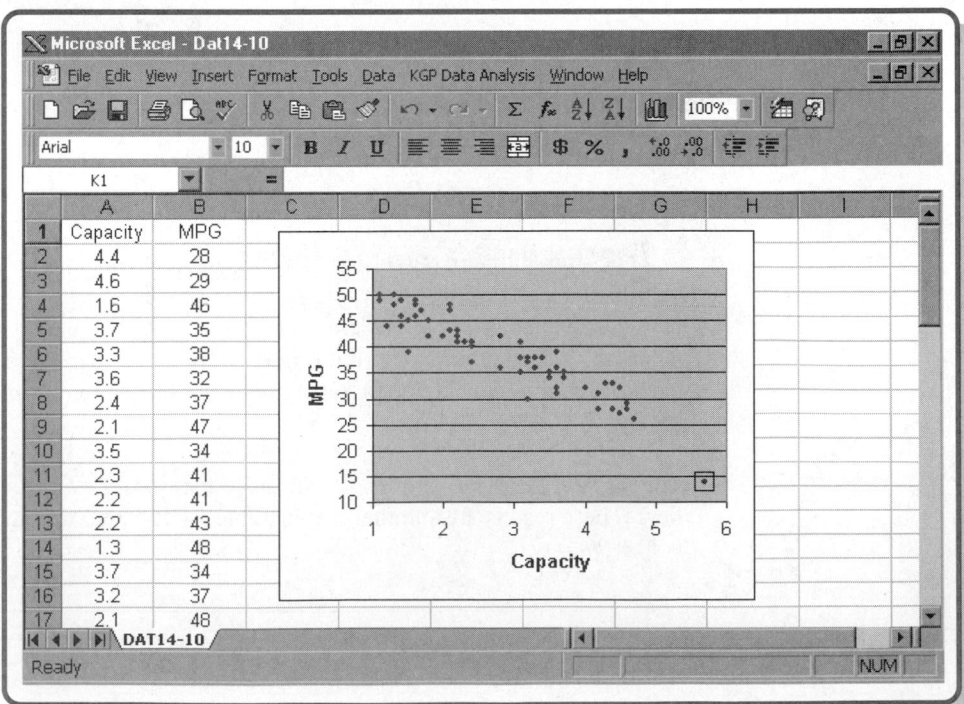

A scan of the standardized residuals and Cook's distance measures reveals three "suspicious" or "interesting" observations—namely, observations 28, 51, and 60. These three observations are highlighted in Figure 14.29, which contains an abbreviated listing of the residuals, standardized residuals, leverages, and Cook's measures. The leverage cutoff here is 6/60 = .1 and a complete scan of the leverage column indicates that observation 28 is the only observation with a leverage value exceeding .1. It also has a standardized residual larger than 2 in absolute value, and so this observation contains outlying values of both the independent and dependent variables. This is, in fact, the "unusual" observation identified in the lower-right corner of the scatter diagram (Figure 14.27). Observations 51 and 60 also contain outlying values of Y, since their standardized residuals exceed 2 in absolute value.

All of the Cook's D values are under .8. Upon closer examination, it was discovered that observation 28 was from a Lamborghini and was, in fact, correctly recorded. No recording error was discovered for observations 51 and 60.

Figure 14.30 is a plot of the residuals, where the $Y - \hat{Y}$ values are plotted against the corresponding X values. The three boxed values correspond to observations 28 (labeled C), 51 (labeled B), and 60 (labeled A). In this plot, the three large residuals are very obvious. No pattern is detected in the residual plot, and assumption 2 appears to be satisfied.

A histogram of the residuals is shown in Figure 14.31. First, locate the residuals in your spreadsheet. Similar to Figure 14.29, the *full* set of residuals would occupy cells E42:E101. To obtain the residual histogram in Figure 14.31, click on **KGP Data Analysis ➤ Quantitative Data Charts/Tables ➤ Histogram/Freq. Charts.** Enter "E42:E101" in the **Input Range** box, "J1" in the **Output Range** box, and "8" in the **Number of Classes** box. Finally, click on the check boxes for **Frequencies** and **Frequency Histogram,** and then **OK.** The resulting histogram in Figure 14.31 appears to be approximately normally distributed with a mean of zero (assumption 1). The three residuals in the left-most two boxes correspond to observations 28, 51, and 60. There is no need to check assumption 3, since the regression data were not time-ordered.

CONCLUSION.   The model appears to be an excellent one, providing a highly significant t statistic ($t = -19.46$, p-value ≈ 0) and $r^2 = 86.7\%$; that is, engine capacity explains 86.7% of

---

FIGURE 14.28

Excel regression equation for Example 14.10.

SUMMARY OUTPUT					
Regression Statistics					
Multiple R	0.9312				
R Square	0.8672				
Adjusted R Square	0.8649				
Standard Error	2.7539				
Observations	60				
ANOVA					
	df	SS	MS	F	Significance F
Regression	1	2872.302	2872.302	378.723	4.18426E-27
Residual	58	439.882	7.584		
Total	59	3312.183			
	Coefficients	Standard Error	t Stat	P-value	
Intercept	55.494	0.937	59.206	1.43654E-53	
Capacity	-5.981	0.307	-19.461	4.18426E-27	

DAT14-10

FIGURE 14.29
Excel output containing standardized residuals, leverages, and Cook's distance measures using KGP Data Analysis.

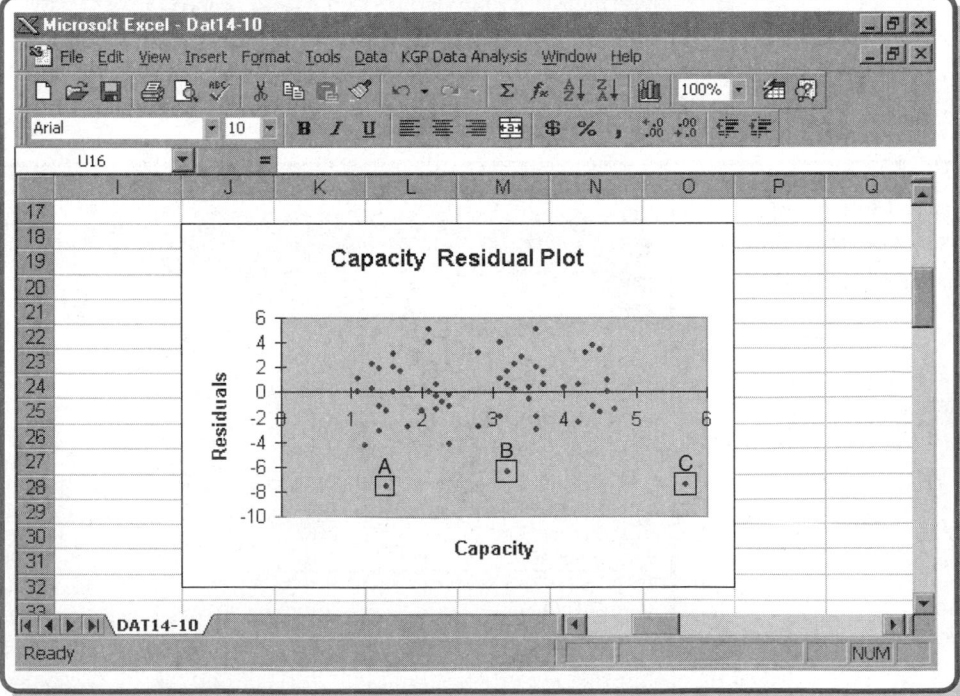

	File Edit View Insert Format Tools Data KGP Data Analysis Window Help					
	C	D	E	F	G	H
39	RESIDUAL OUTPUT					
41	Observation	Predicted MPG	Residuals	Standardized Residuals	Leverages	Cook's D
42	1	29.1759	-1.1759	-0.4376	0.0477	0.0048
43	2	27.9797	1.0203	0.3813	0.0561	0.0043
44	3	45.9240	0.0760	0.0281	0.0353	0.0000
45	4	33.3630	1.6370	0.6024	0.0263	0.0049
46	5	35.7555	2.2445	0.8231	0.0195	0.0067
68	25	41.1388	-0.1388	-0.0509	0.0189	0.0000
69	26	33.9611	-2.9611	-1.0885	0.0242	0.0147
70	27	44.7277	0.2723	0.1004	0.0297	0.0002
71	28	21.4001	-7.4001	-2.8642	0.1199	0.5586
72	29	35.1574	2.8426	1.0431	0.0208	0.0116
73	30	48.9147	1.0853	0.4051	0.0536	0.0046
95	50	28.5778	-1.5778	-0.5884	0.0518	0.0094
96	51	36.3537	-6.3537	-2.3287	0.0184	0.0510
97	52	30.3722	0.6278	0.2327	0.0403	0.0011
98	53	45.3259	1.6741	0.6180	0.0323	0.0064
99	54	27.9797	0.0203	0.0076	0.0561	0.0000
100	55	31.5685	0.4315	0.1594	0.0340	0.0004
101	56	41.1388	-1.1388	-0.4175	0.0189	0.0017
102	57	47.7184	2.2816	0.8480	0.0455	0.0171
103	58	42.9333	0.0667	0.0245	0.0232	0.0000
104	59	29.7741	3.2259	1.1980	0.0439	0.0329
105	60	46.5221	-7.5221	-2.7855	0.0384	0.1550

DAT14-10

FIGURE 14.30
Excel residual plot using KGP Data Analysis (Example 14.10).

the variation in the mpg values. All of the model assumptions appear to be satisfied. All three of the apparent outliers could be retained in the model, since none of these observations produced a significant Cook's distance measure, and no error was made in the recording of these values. Consideration could be given to removing the Lamborghini from the population and from the sample, and restricting the discussion to less exotic automobiles.

FIGURE 14.31
Histogram of residuals
using KGP Data Analysis
(Example 14.10).

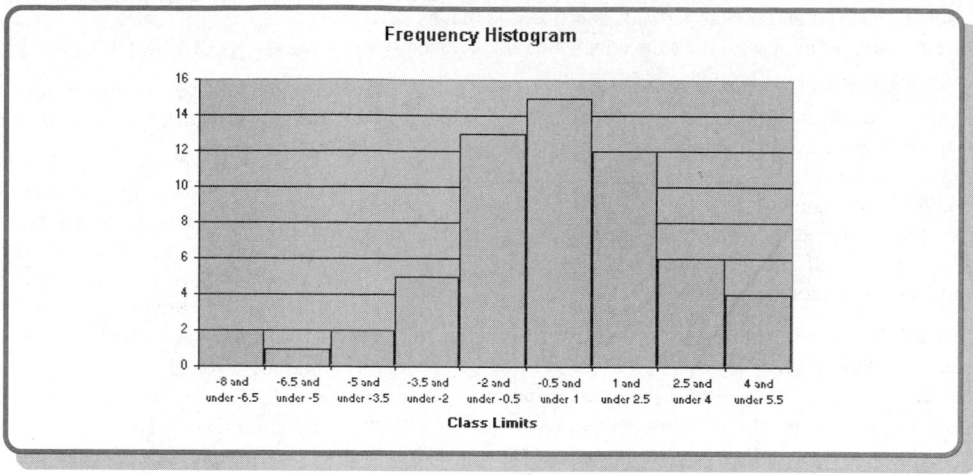

EXERCISES 14.43–14.57

UNDERSTANDING THE MECHANICS

14.43 Consider the following pairs of observations.

X	1	4	3	5	7	2	6	20
Y	3	12	10	12	19	7	17	60

   a. Calculate the least squares line.
   b. Determine a 95% confidence interval for the mean value of Y using X = 6.
   c. Determine a 95% prediction interval for the Y value using X = 6.
   d. Calculate the standardized residuals, the leverage values, and the values of Cook's D for each observation.
   e. Can any observation be considered influential?

14.44 Determine if any observation is an outlier and if any observation is an influential observation from the accompanying data set.

X	5	8	30	12	18	10	11	6	15	14
Y	7	12	45	17	25	15	14	8	14	21

APPLYING THE NEW CONCEPTS

14.45 For the data in Exercise 14.3, find a 95% confidence interval on the mean monthly net earnings for an X value equal to $5000 in commissions. Interpret this interval. Find the 95% prediction interval on the monthly net earnings for an X value equal to $5000 in commissions. Interpret this interval.

14.46 For the data in Exercise 14.8, find a 90% confidence interval for the mean number of cakes sold when the independent variable $X^2 = (2.00)^2 = 4.00$. Determine if any observation can be considered influential for the simple regression model in which Y is regressed on X^2.

14.47 For the data in Exercise 14.15, find a 95% confidence interval for the mean size of the permanent staff for 6000 annual bankruptcies. Calculate the standardized residual, the leverage value, and the value of Cook's D for each observation. Comment on these values.

14.48 For the data in Exercise 14.19, calculate the standardized residual, the leverage value, and the value of Cook's D for each observation. Comment on these values. Can any observation be considered influential?

14.49 For the data in Exercise 14.25, find the 90% prediction interval for the log of personal consumption expenditure for an X value of 200 billion people. Transform the interval, by replacing each endpoint by 10^z, where z is the value of the endpoint. What does this transformed prediction interval represent?

14.50 Consumer Reports rates eyeglasses sold through various outlets. Ratings are based on at least 200 responses from each chain store and more than 1000 responses for larger chains. Eyeglass price is the median amount that respondents paid for a complete pair of glasses. Ratings range from 0 to 100 with 100 representing a perfect score.

Eyeglass Company	Rating	Eyeglass Price
LensCrafters	74	190
Opti-World	73	181
Visionworks	72	183
Pearle Vision Express	71	203
Sam's Club Vision Center	70	135
EyeMasters	70	203
Empire Vision Center	69	138
Texas State Optical	69	173
Eye World	69	181
Sterling Optical	69	170
Sears Optical	64	159
J.C. Penney	63	166
America's Best Contacts & Eyeglasses	57	109

(Source: *Consumer Reports*, "Ratings: Eyeglass Stores," July 1997, p. 14.)

   a. Let Y = Rating and X = Eyeglass Price. Find the least squares line. Do the data support the conclusion that there is a linear relationship between X and Y? Use a 1% significance level.
   b. Find the standardized residual, leverage value, and Cook's D for each observation.

c. Delete the observation that you would consider to be the most influential and repeat part (a). Is it possible that by deleting an influential observation, the conclusion that a linear relationship exists may no longer be supported?

14.51 For the data in Exercise 14.26, find the 99% confidence interval for the average number of years that a lawn mower will be able to function properly if the number of hours of operation between oil changes is 23 hours. What is the standard deviation for the predicted value of the number of years that a single lawnmower will be able to perform adequately if the number of hours of operation between oil changes is 23?

14.52 For a fixed value of X, which interval is larger, the confidence interval for the mean value of Y at X (equation 14.24) or the prediction interval for a predicted value of Y at X (equation 14.27)? What value can you assign to X to achieve the narrowest confidence interval for the mean value of Y at X or for the predicted value of Y at X?

14.53 A sample of 200 executives who work in Chicago was taken to find out how much of their own money the executives invest each year in stock of the company that they work for. The following regression equation was developed, where X is the income (in thousands) of an executive and Y is the amount of money (in thousands) he or she invests each year in the company. The prediction equation is

$$\hat{Y} = 9.5 + 0.05X$$

Based on the regression equation, can the following statement be made? A Chicago-area executive who earns $15,000 a year would invest about $10,250 in company stock. Comment.

14.54 When cyclical consumer stocks perform well in the United States, their counterparts in Europe also tend to move in tandem. Twelve cyclical consumer industry groups were randomly selected, and their performance for the first four months of 1998 was recorded. Data are presented in percentages.

Industry Group	United States	Europe
Airlines	15.85	16.52
Clothing/Fabrics	14.77	18.11
Auto Manufacturers	30.68	43.23
Auto Parts & Equipment	15.09	29.39
Casinos	7.23	32.40
Home Construction	24.79	23.42
Home Furnishings	21.04	28.34
Lodging	4.90	42.09
Media	15.49	6.72
Recreation Products	20.32	13.57
Restaurants	23.73	13.99
Specialty Retailers	21.97	1.90

(Source: Adapted from *The Wall Street Journal,* "Dow Jones Global Industry Groups," Apr. 23, 1998, p. C21.)

a. Calculate the least squares line for predicting $Y =$ performance of cyclical consumer industry group in the U.S. from $X =$ performance of European counterpart.

b. Determine a 95% prediction interval for the performance of a cyclical consumer industry group in the U.S. if the performance of that group in Europe is 14%.

c. Find the standardized residual, leverage value, and value of Cook's D for each observation.

d. Determine if any of the observations are influential.

USING THE COMPUTER

14.55 [DATA SET EX14-55] *Variable description:*

NumberTourist: Number of tourists visiting water park daily
AmountSpent: Amount spent by the tourists daily

The manager of a water park would like to investigate the relationship between the number of tourists who visit her water park daily and the amount of revenue generated. A random sample of 40 days is selected, and data on daily attendance (X) and amount spent by tourists (Y) are recorded. The amount spent is in units of thousands.

a. Find the predicted values and the residual values. Verify that the residuals sum to zero.

b. Do any of the observations have an unusually large value for Cook's D?

c. Construct a residual plot of AmountSpent and the residuals. Do you notice any pattern? Does this violate any assumptions of the regression analysis model?

14.56 [DATA SET EX14-56] *Variable description:*

WebSalary: Salary paid to the Web general manager
ComputerExp: Years experience working in a computer environment

The average size of the Internet staff at companies surveyed by Buck Consultants in Stamford, Conn., is approximately 14. The salary of the Web general manager averages $73,000, but this varies by experience (*The Dallas Morning News,* "Companies Forming Web Site Departments to Handle Online Work," July 9, 1997, p. 10D). Suppose that a consultant wished to determine if there is a linear relationship between WebSalary and ComputerExp. Data were collected on 60 Web general managers with salary recorded in thousands of dollars and computer experience recorded in years.

a. Plot $Y =$ WebSalary and $X =$ ComputerExp. Comment on the fit. Do you notice any outliers or influential observations?

b. Calculate the leverage values, standardized residuals, and Cook's D values to identify unusual observations. Compare these to those found in part (a). Which observation appears to be the most influential?

14.57 [DATA SET EX14-57] *Variable description:*

CEO_Compens: Total compensation of the chief executive officer (CEO)
CompanyProfit: Annual company after-tax profit

A financial researcher is interested in the relationship between the total compensation of the CEO of a corporation and the after-tax profit of the company. A random sample of 50 CEOs was selected. Total compensation includes salary, bonus, and stock options in thousands of dollars, and company profit is measured in units of millions of dollars.

a. Plot $Y =$ CEO_Compens and $X =$ CompanyProfit. Comment on the fit of the data.

b. Calculate the leverage values, standardized residuals, and Cook's D to identify unusual observations.

c. Eliminate the most influential observation and perform part (b) again. What changes, if any, do you note.

SUMMARY

When dealing with a pair of variables (say, X and Y), we generally are interested in determining whether the variables are related in some manner. If a relationship does exist, perhaps the **independent** variable (X) can be used to predict values of the **dependent** variable (Y). If a significant linear relationship exists within the sample data, both the direction (positive or negative) and the strength of this linear relationship can be measured using the sample **coefficient of correlation,** r. The sample correlation coefficient is an estimate of the population coefficient of correlation, ρ. Another commonly used measure of association between two variables is the sample **covariance.**

Whenever a sample of bivariate data contains a significant linear pattern, we determine the **least squares line** through the data points and generate an equation that can be used to predict values of the dependent variable. To describe accurately the assumptions behind this procedure, we introduced the concept of a **statistical model** consisting of a **deterministic** portion (the straight line) and a **random error** component. This model can be written as $Y = \beta_0 + \beta_1 X + e$, where $\beta_0 + \beta_1 X$ is the deterministic component and e represents the error component. When we perform any test of hypothesis regarding the underlying bivariate population, we must be careful to satisfy the necessary assumptions behind this procedure. These assumptions will be examined again in Chapter 15.

By regressing Y on X we are able to determine the least squares line, $\hat{Y} = b_0 + b_1 X$. The value of b_0 is the **intercept** of the least squares line and estimates the population intercept β_0. The **slope** of the least squares line, b_1, estimates the population slope β_1. One question of interest is, if we regress X on Y (that is, switch the independent and dependent variables), can we rearrange the previous equation and say that $\hat{X} = (-b_0/b_1) + (1/b_1)Y$? The answer is no, although the coefficient of correlation, r, is the same in either case.

Various methods for determining the utility of the model as a predictor of the dependent variable include: (1) a t test for detecting a significant slope, b_1 (a value of $\beta_1 = 0$ indicates that X has no predictive ability); (2) a t test for determining whether the sample correlation, r, is significantly large (a value of $\rho = 0$ indicates that there is no linear relationship between the two variables); and (3) a confidence interval for the slope, β_1. The two t tests appear to be quite different, but their computed values (and df) are *identical;* there is no point in performing both tests.

Another measure of how well the model provides estimates that fit the sample data is given by the **coefficient of determination,** r^2. For simple linear regression (one independent variable), this is the square of the correlation coefficient. Another definition of the coefficient of determination can also be used to examine more than one independent variable (called multiple linear regression), namely, $r^2 = 1 - (SSE/SS_Y)$. Here, SSE is the sum of squared errors and SS_Y represents the total variation in the sample Y values. For example, if $r^2 = .85$, then 85% of the variation in the sample Y values has been explained using this model.

The value of $\hat{Y}$ from the least squares regression line at a specific value of X (say, $X = x_0$), can be used to estimate an *average* value of Y, given this value of X (written $\mu_{Y|x_0}$). The value of $\hat{Y}$ centers a *confidence interval* for $\mu_{Y|x_0}$. Similarly, we can use the $\hat{Y}$ value to center a *prediction interval* for an individual value of the dependent variable, given this specific value of X (written Y_{x_0}). The value of $\hat{Y}$ can be used to *estimate* the value of $\mu_{Y|x_0}$ or *predict* the value of Y_{x_0}.

Examination of the residuals [values of $(Y - \hat{Y})$] is an important step during a regression analysis. These values can be used to verify the model assumptions as well as to indicate sample observations that appear to be *outliers* or observations that are very influential in determining the least squares line. The calculated **sample leverages** will identify observations that have unusual values of the independent variable, X; that is, such observations have values of X that are distant from the sample mean of the X values ($\bar{x}$). Observations that have unusually large or small values of the dependent variable, Y, can generally be detected during an inspection of the **standardized residuals.** Observations that have a large impact in the calculation of the least squares line are referred to as **influential observations.** These sample points can be determined using the calculated **Cook's distance measures.**

SUMMARY OF FORMULAS

CORRELATION BETWEEN TWO VARIABLES

$$r = \frac{SCP_{XY}}{\sqrt{SS_X}\,\sqrt{SS_Y}}$$

where

$$SCP_{XY} = \sum xy - \frac{(\sum x)(\sum y)}{n}$$

$$SS_X = \sum x^2 - \frac{(\sum x)^2}{n}$$

$$SS_Y = \sum y^2 - \frac{(\sum y)^2}{n}$$

LEAST SQUARES LINE

$$\hat{Y} = b_0 + b_1 X$$

where

$$b_1 = \frac{SCP_{XY}}{SS_X} \quad \text{and} \quad b_0 = \bar{y} - b_1 \bar{x}$$

ESTIMATE OF THE RESIDUAL VARIANCE

$$\hat{\sigma}_e^2 = s^2 = \frac{SSE}{n-2}$$

where

$$SSE = \sum (y - \hat{y})^2$$

$$= SS_Y - \frac{(SCP_{XY})^2}{SS_X}$$

t STATISTIC FOR DETECTING A SIGNIFICANT SLOPE

$$t = \frac{b_1}{s_{b_1}}$$

$(df = n - 2)$, where

$$s_{b_1} = \frac{s}{\sqrt{SS_X}}$$

CONFIDENCE INTERVAL FOR THE SLOPE, β_1

$$b_1 - t_{\alpha/2, n-2} s_{b_1} \quad \text{to} \quad b_1 + t_{\alpha/2, n-2} s_{b_1}$$

t STATISTIC FOR DETECTING A SIGNIFICANT CORRELATION

$$t = \frac{r}{\sqrt{\dfrac{1 - r^2}{n - 2}}}$$

$(df = n - 2)$

COEFFICIENT OF DETERMINATION

$$r^2 = \text{square of correlation coefficient}$$

$$= 1 - \frac{SSE}{SS_Y}$$

CONFIDENCE INTERVAL FOR THE AVERAGE VALUE OF Y AT A SPECIFIC VALUE OF X (SAY x_0)

$$\hat{Y} \pm t_{\alpha/2, n-2}\, s \sqrt{\frac{1}{n} + \frac{(x_0 - \bar{x})^2}{SS_X}}$$

PREDICTION INTERVAL FOR A PARTICULAR VALUE OF Y AT A SPECIFIC VALUE OF X (SAY, x_0)

$$\hat{Y} \pm t_{\alpha/2, n-2}\, s \sqrt{1 + \frac{1}{n} + \frac{(x_0 - \bar{x})^2}{SS_X}}$$

LEVERAGE OF THE iTH OBSERVATION

$$h_i = \frac{1}{n} + \frac{(x_i - \bar{x})^2}{SS_X}$$

STANDARDIZED RESIDUAL OF THE iTH OBSERVATION

$$\frac{Y_i - \hat{Y}_i}{s\sqrt{1 - h_i}}$$

COOK'S DISTANCE MEASURE FOR THE iTH OBSERVATION

$$D_i = \frac{(Y_i - \hat{Y}_i)^2}{2s^2} \left(\frac{h_i}{(1 - h_i)^2} \right)$$

REVIEW EXERCISES 14.58–14.73

14.58 The following statistics were calculated from pairs of observations where X represents the independent variable and Y represents the dependent variable.

$$\Sigma x = 511 \qquad \Sigma y = 314 \qquad \Sigma xy = 19{,}064$$

$$\Sigma x^2 = 34{,}234.5 \qquad \Sigma y^2 = 13{,}036 \qquad n = 8$$

a. Determine the least squares line.
b. Determine the sample correlation coefficient between X and Y.
c. Determine if there is a linear relationship between X and Y at the .10 significance level.
d. Find a 90% confidence interval for the slope of the regression line.
e. Find a 90% confidence interval for the mean of Y if $X = 60$.
f. Find a 90% prediction interval for Y if $X = 60$.
g. What are the necessary assumptions for the validity of the procedure in parts (c), (d), (e), and (f)?

14.59 The performance of many mutual funds are correlated with the performance of the S&P 500. Large funds often become so large that they begin to mimic the overall stock market. To understand the relationship between the S&P 500, and the total return of the Windsor II Fund, fourteen years of performance are listed below.

Year	Yearly Performance of Windsor II Ending October 31 (in Percentage)	Yearly Performance of S&P 500 Ending October 31 (in Percentage)
1985	.2	1.8
1986	35.6	33.2
1987	.9	6.4
1988	20.5	14.8
1989	24.7	26.4
1990	−17.5	−7.5
1991	36.6	33.5
1992	12.5	10.0
1993	19.5	14.9
1994	2.2	3.9
1995	23.1	26.4
1996	27.2	24.1
1997	31.3	32.1
1998	16.5	22.0

(Source: *Vanguard Windsor II Annual Report,* October 31, 1998, p. 0.)

a. Find the least squares line for the data using X = performance (in percentage) of the S&P 500 and Y = performance (in percentage) of the Windsor II fund.
b. Find the coefficient of determination and interpret it.
c. Find the 95% confidence interval for the slope of the regression line. Interpret the confidence interval in the context of this problem.
d. What assumptions are necessary for the interpretation of the confidence interval to be valid?
e. Find the 95% confidence interval for the mean value of Y when $X = 15\%$.

14.60 Dolls-R-Us believes that television advertising is the most effective way to market their new line of dolls. The sales manager recorded the amount of money spent on advertising and the amount of sales for 20 randomly selected months. The average cost for television advertising for the 20 months was $110,000. The average sales volume for the 20 months was $675,000. The following sample statistics were found from the data for the 20 months.

$$\text{SCP}_{XY} = 198.4 \qquad \text{SS}_X = 205.3 \qquad \text{SS}_Y = 341.6$$

where Y represents the sales volume (in thousands) and X represents the television advertising costs (in thousands of dollars).

a. Calculate the least squares line.
b. Calculate the coefficient of determination.

c. Calculate the sum of squares of error.

d. What is the estimate of the variance of the error component for the model?

e. Is there sufficient evidence from the data to conclude at the .01 significance level that a positive relationship exists between X and Y?

f. Find a 95% prediction interval for the monthly sales volume if the television advertising expenditure during one particular month is $120,000.

14.61 A car rental agency has a fleet of 200 cars available for rent at Kennedy airport in New York City. The owner of the agency uses a regression equation for estimating the company's daily revenue based on the number of incoming flights that day. The regression equation is $\hat{Y} = 2500 + 21.4X$, where X is the number of daily incoming flights and Y is the daily revenue in dollars. The data used to find the least squares line are based on a sample of 100 randomly selected days in 1998. Can the following statement be made based on regression analysis? If Kennedy airport increases its daily incoming flights by 50 flights next year, then the car agency can expect to make an additional daily revenue of $1,070. Comment.

14.62 Each week, a realtor advertises the houses she manages that are available for rent. The number of telephone calls from people inquiring about the advertisement were recorded for several weeks, during which various sizes of the advertisement were used. Is there sufficient evidence from the following data to conclude at the .10 significance level, that a nonzero correlation exists?

X (Height of Ad, Inches)	Y (Number of Inquiries)	X (Height of Ad, Inches)	Y (Number of Inquiries)
0.5	3	2.5	10
1.0	4	3.0	14
1.5	6	3.5	12
2.0	5	4.0	18

14.63 The manager of a firm that specializes in assisting individuals in filling out federal income tax forms obtained data from the Internal Revenue Service pertaining to deductions for charitable contributions. The following table provides a distribution of charitable contributions of eight groups with different adjusted gross incomes.

Median Adjusted Gross Income (In Thousands of Dollars) (X)	Percentage in Group Making Charitable Contributions (Claiming Itemized Deductions) (Y)
5.0	17.0
7.5	36.0
12.5	40.5
17.5	38.5
25.0	29.2
40.0	14.0
75.0	4.2
100.0	1.5

a. Obtain the least squares line for these data.

b. Identify the values of the intercept, the slope, and the variance of the error for the simple linear regression model.

c. Find the residuals for all the Y values.

d. If the correlation between X and Y above was very strong, would it then be correct to conclude that an increase in income causes people to become less charitable?

14.64 As the average occupancy rate increases in city hotels, the average price also tends to increase. Consider the ten cities selected below to be a random sample in which occupancy rate (in percentage) and average price (in dollars) of a room overnight are recorded. Find a 95% prediction interval for the price of a room if the occupancy rate is 72%. Interpret this interval.

(Source: Adapted from *The Dallas Morning News,* "Hotel Construction Leads to Lower Occupancy in DFW," July 25, 1997, p. 2D.)

City	Occupancy Rate	Average Price
Atlanta	68.0	98.78
Chicago	62.8	101.32
Dallas-Fort Worth	68.4	87.16

City	Occupancy Rate	Average Price
Denver	70.9	109.96
Miami	84.2	141.59
New Orleans	75.4	122.94
New York	76.8	173.61
Phoenix	83.6	144.60
San Antonio	62.7	72.80
San Francisco	73.3	125.73
Seattle	66.8	102.60

14.65 One management policy is based on the hypothesis that the more productive a worker is, the more satisfied the worker will be. A scale from 1 to 10 is used to measure productivity, with ten being assigned to an extremely productive worker. A second scale from 1 to 10 is used to measure satisfaction. The worker assigns him- or herself a 10 if he or she is satisfied in every aspect of the job. Twenty employees were selected randomly from the production-and-research department of Tellon Oil. The results of the data collection are as follows:

Satisfaction (Y)	Productivity (X)	Satisfaction (Y)	Productivity (X)
5	4	9	7
2	3	7	5
9	8	4	4
9	9	8	7
5	6	9	8
3	5	10	9
5	4	5	6
7	7	1	2
9	8	7	8
2	3	9	9

   a. Draw a scatter diagram of the data.

   b. Test the hypothesis, at a 5% significance level, that there is a positive linear relationship between productivity and satisfaction.

   c. Find a 99% confidence interval for the slope of the regression equation.

   d. Calculate the coefficient of determination.

   e. Find a 99% prediction interval for the satisfaction of a particular worker whose measure of productivity is 7.

14.66 A certain risk-averse investor calculates the beta for a stock before investing in the stock. By regressing the weekly percent return of, say, stock XYZ on the weekly percent return of the Standard and Poor's 500 Index (S&P 500), the investor can determine the stock's beta, which is equal to the slope of the regression line. The following data represent the weekly return over 20 weeks for both the S&P 500 and stock XYZ.

Week	S&P 500 (in Percent) (X)	Stock XYZ (in Percent) (Y)	Week	S&P 500 (in Percent) (X)	Stock XYZ (in Percent) (Y)
1	.51	.95	11	−1.12	−1.13
2	.22	.66	12	−.80	−.74
3	−.43	−.21	13	1.55	2.32
4	−2.51	−3.00	14	2.34	3.34
5	3.05	4.11	15	−.50	−.40
6	.40	.75	16	2.81	4.00
7	−.21	.01	17	3.33	4.63
8	1.80	2.64	18	−1.64	−1.83
9	2.55	4.51	19	1.75	2.58
10	3.80	6.12	20	2.20	3.11

   a. Calculate the least squares line.

   b. A slope greater than one indicates that the stock is more volatile than the S&P market index. Interpret the coefficients of the regression equation.

   c. Graph the data and the least squares line. Comment on the fit.

14.67 Diane's Beauty Salon is currently hiring beauticians at its new location in a popular mall. Diane wants to know what percentage of commission to pay the beauticians based on experience. A survey of 12 licensed beauticians was taken with the following results.

Percentage of Commission (Y)	Years of Experience (X)	Percentage of Commission (Y)	Years of Experience (X)
24	2	25	4
18	1	44	12
30	5	33	8
41	10	24	3
35	8	20	1
35	7	40	10

a. Find the least squares line.

b. Calculate the sum of squares due to error.

c. Test the null hypothesis that there is no linear relationship between years of experience and percentage of commissions paid. Use a significance level of .05.

d. Find a 90% confidence interval for the slope of the regression line.

14.68 A regression line is fitted to a set of data and the values of $(Y - \hat{Y})$ are calculated. Does the following set of sample errors appear to conform to the empirical rule that 95% of the data should lie within two standard deviations of the mean? Construct a histogram for the residuals. Comment on the shape of the histogram.

$$1.1, -0.8, 2.6, 1.5, 0.2, -0.4, 0.8, -1.8, -2.3, 0.9, -2.7, 3.1, -1.0, 0.9, 4.5,$$
$$-3.4, -0.1, -0.2, 2.4, -1.7, -0.7$$

14.69 Economists generally believe that liberal welfare programs tend to increase a country's unemployment rate. Critics of social programs say that generous benefits have made it comfortable for some Europeans to stay unemployed. The figures presented below represent the unemployment rate of various European countries, the U.S., and Japan. The units are in percentage.

Country	Unemployment Rate	Public Social Expenditure as a Percentage of GDP
Japan	3.7	13.1
United States	4.4	16.2
Norway	3.3	26.1
Netherlands	4.6	27.0
Denmark	5.2	32.5
United Kingdom	6.2	24.2
Sweden	8.6	35.1
Germany	10.1	27.4
Italy	12.3	24.3
France	11.4	30.2
Finland	13.8	34.1
Spain	18.5	22.3

(Source: Adapted from *The Wall Street Journal*, "All of Europe Watches As Britain's Tony Blair Hacks Away at Welfare," June 25, 1998, p. A18.)

a. Plot the values of Y = Unemployment Rate and X = Public Social Expenditure As a Percentage of GDP. Does the least squares line appear to provide a good fit when eyeballing the scatterplot?

b. Calculate the correlation between X and Y.

c. Test that there is a linear relationship between X and Y. Use a 5% significance level.

d. What are the residuals for the Y values?

e. Find the standardized residuals, the leverage values, and the values of Cook's D.

f. What observations (if any) would you identify as influential?

14.70 **[DATA SET EX14-70]** *Variable description:*

ApprecRank: Rank of stock in 30 DJI with regard to performance
DividendRank: Rank of stock in 30 DJI with regard to dividend growth

Some security analysts believe that share prices are a function of future dividend flows. Fads and fashions may come and go, but this relationship appears to have withstood the test of time. To confirm the wisdom of this belief, consider the 30 Dow Jones Industrial (DJI) stocks ranked by appreciation ApprecRank and by dividend growth as given in variable DividendRank.

a. Plot the values of Y = ApprecRank and X = DividendRank. Does the least squares line appear to be a good fit when eyeballing the scatterplot?

b. Test that there is a linear relationship between X and Y. Use a 5% significance level.

c. Construct a histogram of the residuals. Do they appear to be approximately normally distributed?

14.71 [DATA SET EX14-71] *Variable description:*

Total: Total amount of soup purchased over the past six months
Campbell: Amount of Campbell soup purchased over the past six months
Pet: Amount of Pet soup purchased over the past six months
Private: Amount of soup with a private label purchased over the past six months

"Never underestimate the power of marketing" is Campbell Soup Company's motto. According to an article in the *Wall Street Journal* ("Campbell's New Ads Heat Up Soup Sales," Mar. 17, 1994, p. B5), Campbell increased its ad budget for its soups by 30% to 40% in 1994. The company has used Olympic medal winners to promote its soup. Suppose that an analyst for the food industry is interested in the relationship of the total purchase of soup by a family and the purchase of three types of soup. The analyst randomly selected 50 soup-eating families in the Philadelphia area, and over a six-month period, each family's total purchase of soups, the amount purchased of Campbell Soup, the amount purchased of Pet Soup, and the amount purchased of soups with a private store label were recorded. The correlations of these variables are displayed below in a matrix format using the "correl" function in Excel.

    a. Interpret the values of the correlations in this matrix. Which correlations are different from zero at the 5% significance level?

    b. Would you say that the variable Campbell is a good predictor of Private? Why?

    c. Which variable would you say is the best predictor of the total amount of soup purchased over the past six months?

    d. Interpret the slope of the regression equation for the predictor selected in part (c). What is a 95% confidence interval for the slope of the regression line?

	A	B	C	D	E	F	G	H
1	Total	Campbell	Pet	Private				
2	336.61	133.93	91.51	43.32				
3	347.2	137.2	116.26	41.85		Total	Campbell	Pet
4	376.53	161.16	129.21	73.97	Campbell	0.826098		
5	368.04	159.01	111.81	70.39	Pet	0.587812	0.310694	
6	379.81	178.23	101.29	78.39	Private	0.297726	-0.0508	0.111523
7	373.76	161.55	143.02	42.46				
8	335.35	135.44	80.6	49.33				
9	283.75	50.8	109.59	39.35				
10	338.78	151.66	70.13	32.3				

14.72 [DATA SET EX14-72] *Variable description:*

City: Name of city in the NE United States
StateIncomeTax: Average state income tax paid in various NE cities
PropertyTax: Average property tax paid in various NE cities
SalesTax: Average property tax paid in various NE cities
TotalTax: Average total tax paid in various NE cities

Cities in the northeastern United States have attempted to lower the total amount of taxes that local residents pay. However, the typical resident living in the northeastern U.S. will pay at least $6000 in state and local taxes. Suppose that an economist would like to determine if a linear relationship exists between the total tax paid by a resident and each of the variables: state income tax, property tax, and sales tax. The units for the tax data are in thousands of dollars.

(Source: Adapted from *Kiplinger's Personal Finance Magazine*, "Tax Tidings From Back East," June 1997, p. 57.)

    a. Based on the computer printouts below, which variable (StateIncomeTax, PropertyTax, or SalesTax) would you use in a prediction equation for TotalTax? Why?

    b. Use the equation that you selected and find the most influential observation.

    c. Did deleting the most influential observation found in part (b) produce a large change in the value of the coefficient of determination?

SUMMARY OUTPUT USING STATEINCOMETAX (CONTINUED ON NEXT PAGE)

Regression Statistics

Multiple R	0.215656869
R Square	0.046507885
Adjusted R Square	-0.017058256
Standard Error	1.708594077
Observations	17

ANOVA (CONTINUED)

	df	SS	MS	F	Significance F
Regression	1	2.135888301	2.135888301	0.731646	0.405806262
Residual	15	43.78940582	2.919293721		
Total	16	45.92529412			

	Coefficients	Standard Error	t Stat	P-value	Lower 95%	Upper 95%
Intercept	6.271478335	1.283551792	4.886034497	0.000198	3.535651	9.007306
StateIncomeTax	0.419892282	0.49089377	0.855362826	0.405806	−0.626424	1.466208

SUMMARY OUTPUT USING PROPERTYTAX

Regression Statistics

Multiple R	0.63288412
R Square	0.400542309
Adjusted R Square	0.360578463
Standard Error	1.35475141
Observations	17

ANOVA

	df	SS	MS	F	Significance F
Regression	1	18.39502337	18.39502337	10.022617	0.006396
Residual	15	27.53027075	1.835351383		
Total	16	45.92529412			

	Coefficients	Standard Error	t Stat	P-value	Lower 95%	Upper 95%
Intercept	4.605982643	0.915314337	5.032132084	0.000149	2.655035	6.556930
PropertyTax	0.708557483	0.223812598	3.16585165	0.006396	0.231512	1.185603

SUMMARY OUTPUT USING SALESTAX

Regression Statistics

Multiple R	0.667151878
R Square	0.445091628
Adjusted R Square	0.408097737
Standard Error	1.303439812
Observations	17

ANOVA

	df	SS	MS	F	Significance F
Regression	1	20.44096395	20.44096395	12.031490	0.003438
Residual	15	25.48433017	1.698955345		
Total	16	45.92529412			

	Coefficients	Standard Error	t Stat	P-value	Lower 95%	Upper 95%
Intercept	1.282140069	1.766501535	0.725807504	0.479129	−2.483071	5.047351
SalesTax	11.31165771	3.261118279	3.468643802	0.003438	4.360744	18.262571

14.73 **[DATA SET EX14-73]** *Variable description:*

QuarterlyPerf: Quarterly performance of a high-yield mutual fund
AssetChange: Change in the high-yield mutual fund's asset size

Mutual fund managers sometimes impose a redemption fee on mutual funds to discourage short-term trading. This prevents the fund's asset size from decreasing when performance falls. One fund that doesn't have a redemption fee is Fidelity's New Markets Income Fund, which is a high-yield fund. According to an article in the *Wall Street Journal* ("Fidelity Investments See Big Outflow from Its

Developing-Countries Fund," Mar. 17, 1994, p. A2), money gushed out of this fund over a two-month period because of poor performance, thus contributing to a shrinkage of more than 40% in the fund's size. Suppose that the fund manager wished to determine the relationship between the quarterly performance of mutual funds that impose a redemption fee and the percentage change in their asset size over the quarter. Thirty high-yield mutual funds were randomly selected and a plot of the data is displayed below.

a. Let $Y =$ QuarterlyPerf and $X =$ AssetChange. From the plot of the data, which observations, if any, appear to be either outliers or influential observations?

b. Find the value of Cook's D for each observation. Remove the observation with the largest value of Cook's D.

c. Compare the coefficient of determination using the original data set and the data set with the removed observation.

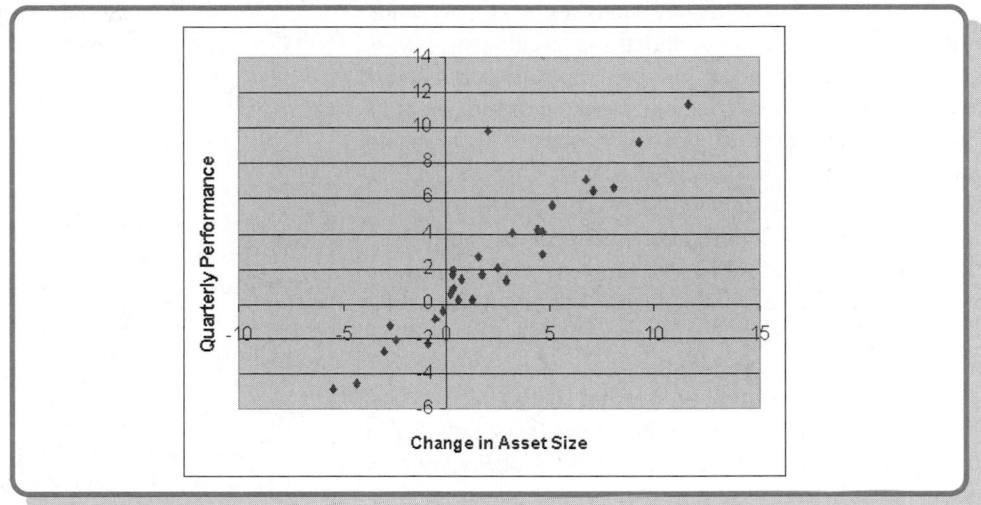

COMPUTER EXERCISES USING THE DATABASES

EXERCISE 1—APPENDIX E

From the database, randomly select 50 observations. Compute the sample correlation between the variable HPAYRENT (house payment or rent) and the variable UTILITY (monthly utility expenditure). Is there evidence to conclude that a positive correlation exists? Use a .05 significance level.

EXERCISE 2—APPENDIX E

Randomly select 50 observations from the database. Plot the values of total indebtedness (TOTLDEBT) and total income (INCOME1 + INCOME2). Also plot the values of TOTLDEBT and HPAYRENT (house payment or rent). Choose the graph that appears to have a stronger linear relationship between the graphed variables. Test to determine if the predictor variable significantly contributes to the prediction of total indebtedness. Use a significance level of .10.

EXERCISE 3—APPENDIX F

Randomly select 50 observations from the database. Compute the sample correlation between the variable NETINC (net income) and each of the variables SALES (gross sales) and COSTSALE (cost of sales). Select the variable from the latter two that has the highest correlation with net income. Regress net income on this variable and determine if this variable significantly contributes to the prediction of net income. Use a .05 significance level.

EXERCISE 4—APPENDIX F

Randomly select 50 observations from the database. Compute the regression line for predicting total assets (TOTAL) from current assets (ASSETS). Also compute the regression line for predicting total assets using current liabilities (LIABIL). Test for the adequacy of the fit of these two regression lines to the data. Use a .10 significance level. Which of these two regression lines has a higher value for the coefficient of determination and what does the higher value indicate?

INSIGHTS FROM STATISTICS IN ACTION: UNEMPLOYMENT AND ITS RELATIONSHIP TO PUBLIC SOCIAL EXPENDITURE AS A PERCENTAGE OF GDP: AN INTERNATIONAL CONCERN

At the start of this chapter, the Statistics in Action section introduced the idea that perhaps a relationship exists between a country's unemployment rate and public social expenditures, expressed as a percentage of the country's gross domestic product (GDP). Analysts are trying to understand the benefits to curtailing welfare programs. Political and economic analysts would like to be able to model the relationship between public social expenditure as a percentage of GDP and unemployment rate. Do countries that have smaller welfare programs generally have smaller unemployment rates? Regression analysis can assist in modeling this relationship.

Consider the following set of data collected on twelve countries. Both the public social expenditure as a percentage of GDP (X) and the countries unemployment rate (Y) are listed.

Country	Social Expenditure as a Percentage of GDP (X)	Unemployment Rate in Percentage (Y)
Japan	13.8	3.6
Sweden	35.2	8.7
Finland	32.4	12.5
United Kingdom	22.9	6.5
United States	15.8	4.6
France	30.1	12.1
Spain	22.0	19.2
Italy	24.2	12.1
Germany	27.1	10.3

Country	Social Expenditure as a Percentage of GDP (X)	Unemployment Rate in Percentage (Y)
Netherlands	26.5	4.5
Norway	23.2	4.0
Denmark	31.5	5.1

1. Graph the data in this table. Do you believe that a linear trend exists?
2. Find the regression equation. Is the value of r^2 very high? What is the interpretation of the r^2 value in the context of this problem? Do you consider the regression equation computed to be an acceptable predictor?
3. What observation has the largest standardized residual? Delete this observation from the data set and find the resulting regression equation?
4. Compare the r^2 found in part (2) with that found in part (3). Would you consider the deleted observation influential? Look at the observation that was deleted. Why do you believe that it is an influential observation?
5. What is the largest standardized residual for the regression equation found in part (3)? Do you think that any of the remaining observations are influential? Does there appear to be a relationship between unemployment rate and public social expenditure, using a .10 significance level?

Source: *The Wall Street Journal,* "All of Europe Watches As Britain's Tony Blair Hacks Away at Welfare," June 25, 1998, p. A18.

CHAPTER 14 APPENDIX: DATA ANALYSIS WITH MINITAB

CORRELATION AND SIMPLE LINEAR REGRESSION

To do a correlation analysis of two or more variables in MINITAB, click on **Stat ➤ Basic Statistics ➤ Correlation.** The user form displayed on the next page will appear. Select as many variables as desired to obtain a correlation matrix. If only two variables are used, then no matrix will appear. For Example 14.1 using the real estate data, the output will appear as shown below the user form. If p-values are desired for testing whether the correlation differs from zero, check the **Display p-values** box.

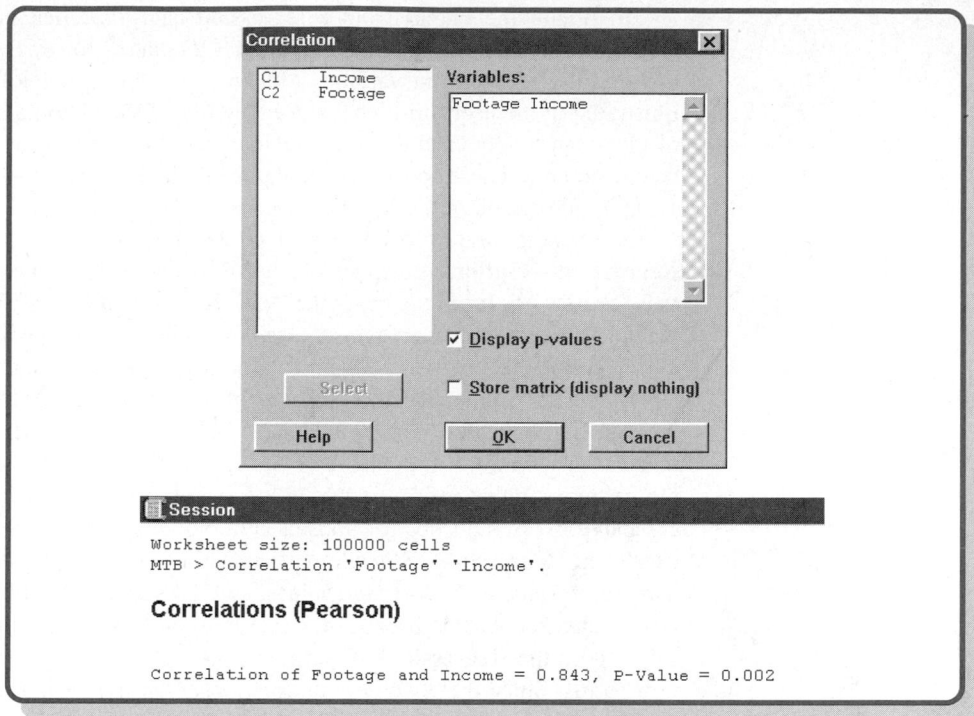

To obtain a plot of the independent variable and the dependent variable, click on **Graph ➤ Plot.** The user form and output for Example 14.1 appear below.

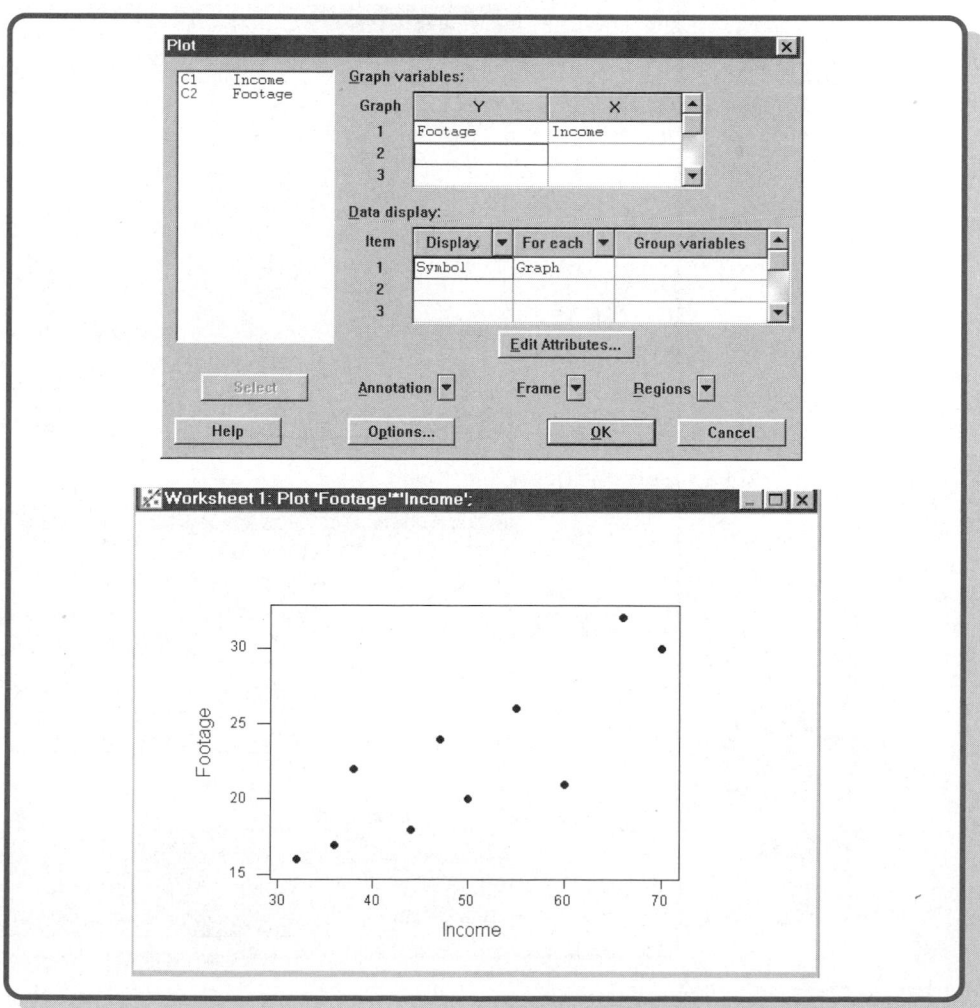

To obtain the output from a regression analysis, click on **Stat ➤ Regression ➤ Regression.** Enter the dependent variable ("Footage" for this example) in the **Response** box and the independent variable ("Income" for this example) in the **Predictors** box as illustrated in the user form labeled **Regression.** If the **Graphs** button is clicked, a variety of plots can be obtained using the residuals (either the regular residuals or the standardized residuals). These options are contained in the **Regression—Graphs** user form. In this example, the graph of the residuals versus income is displayed.

By clicking on the **Options** button on the **Regression** user form, the user form labeled **Regression—Options** is displayed. For this example, 50 is entered in the **Prediction intervals for new observations** box. Since 95 is entered in the **Confidence level** box, this means that a 95% prediction interval on footage for an income of 50 will be displayed. In addition, a 95% confidence interval on the mean footage for an income of 50 will be displayed.

By clicking on the **Results** button on the **Regression** user form, the display of the output can be controlled. The default is "In addition, sequential sums of squares and the unusual observations in the table of fits and residuals" is checked. This option is used in this example so that any outliers or influential observations are displayed. To obtain a more extensive list of statistics for unusual observations, click on the **Storage** button, and the user form **Regression—Storage** will appear. Note that this user form can store the standardized residuals, the leverage values, and the values of Cook's D. For this example, no box is checked in this user form since unusual observations will appear from the box selected on the **Regression—Results** user form. The output for this example follows the user forms. Since there were no unusual observations for this set of data, no observation is indicated as having a large residual or as being influential.

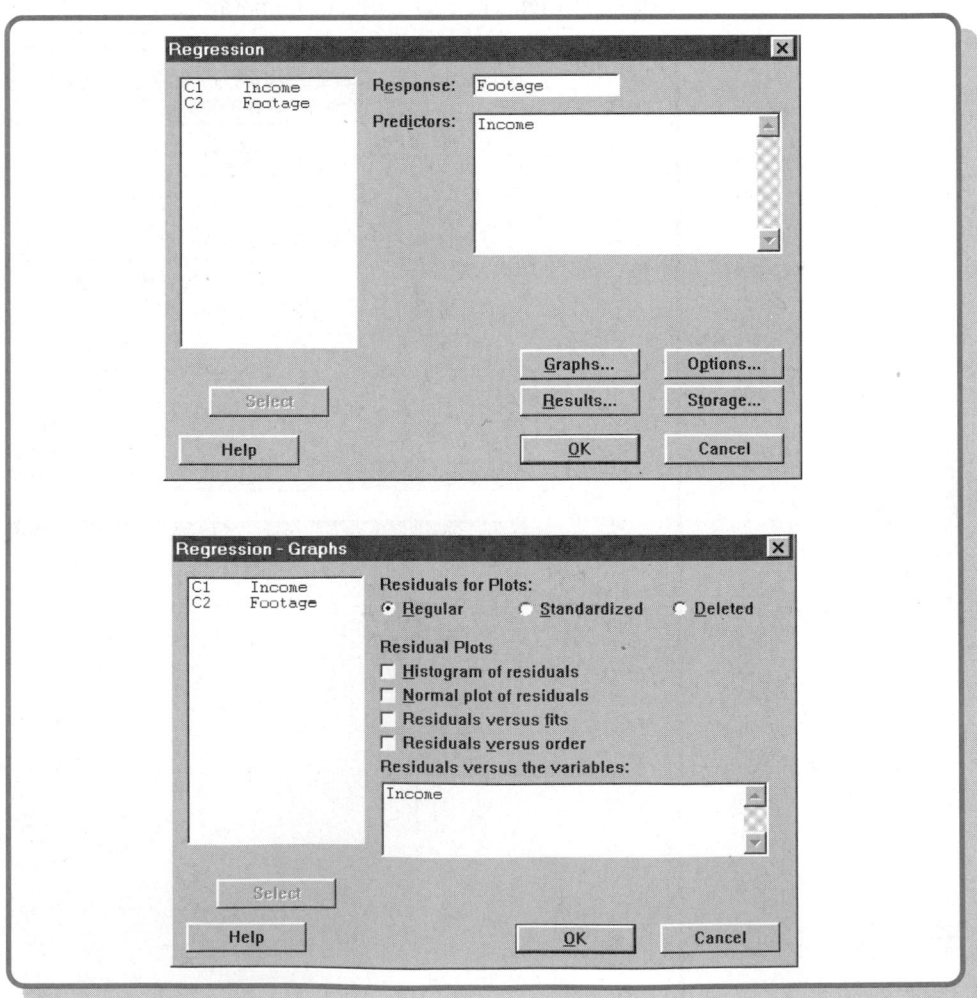

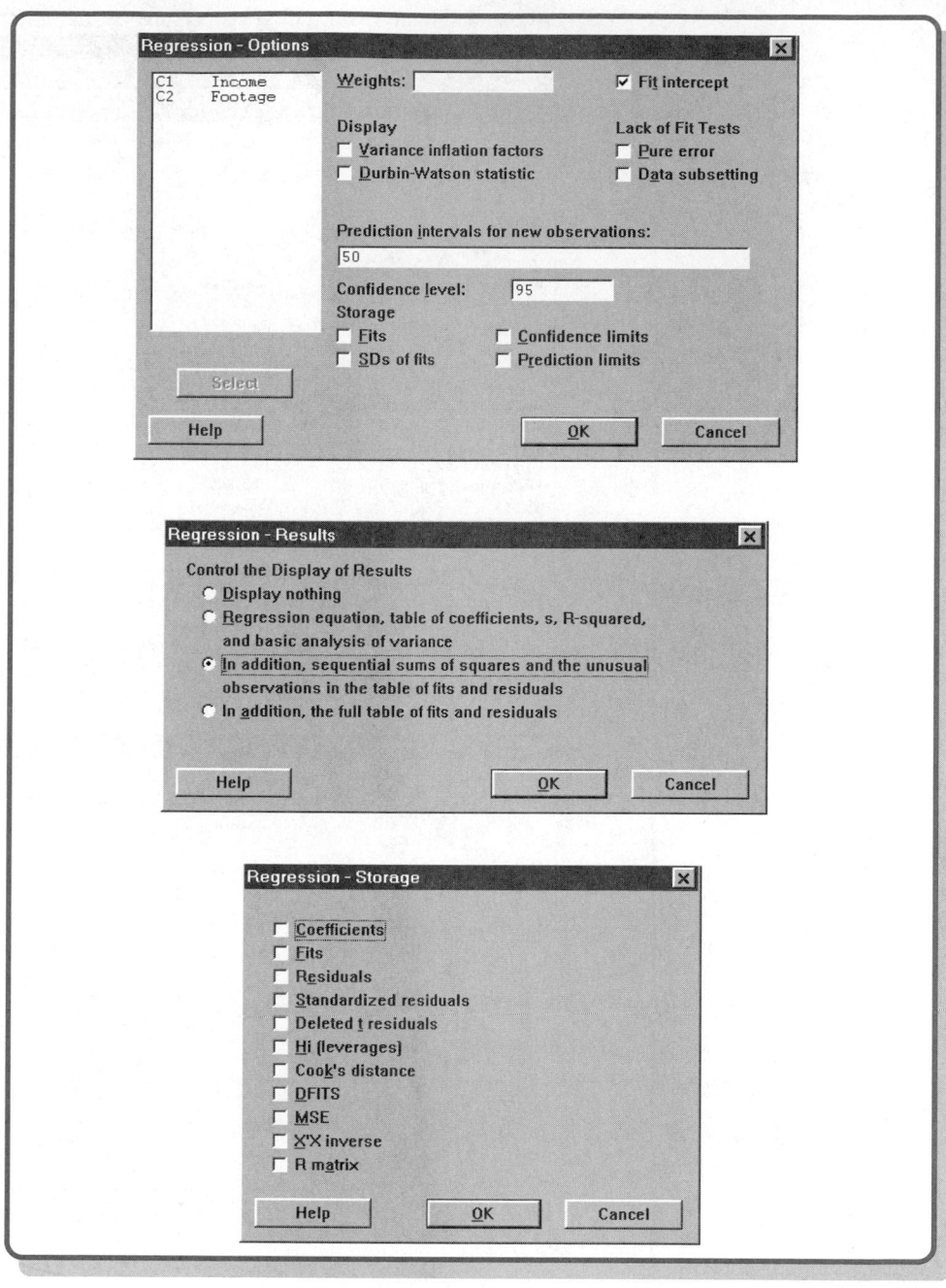

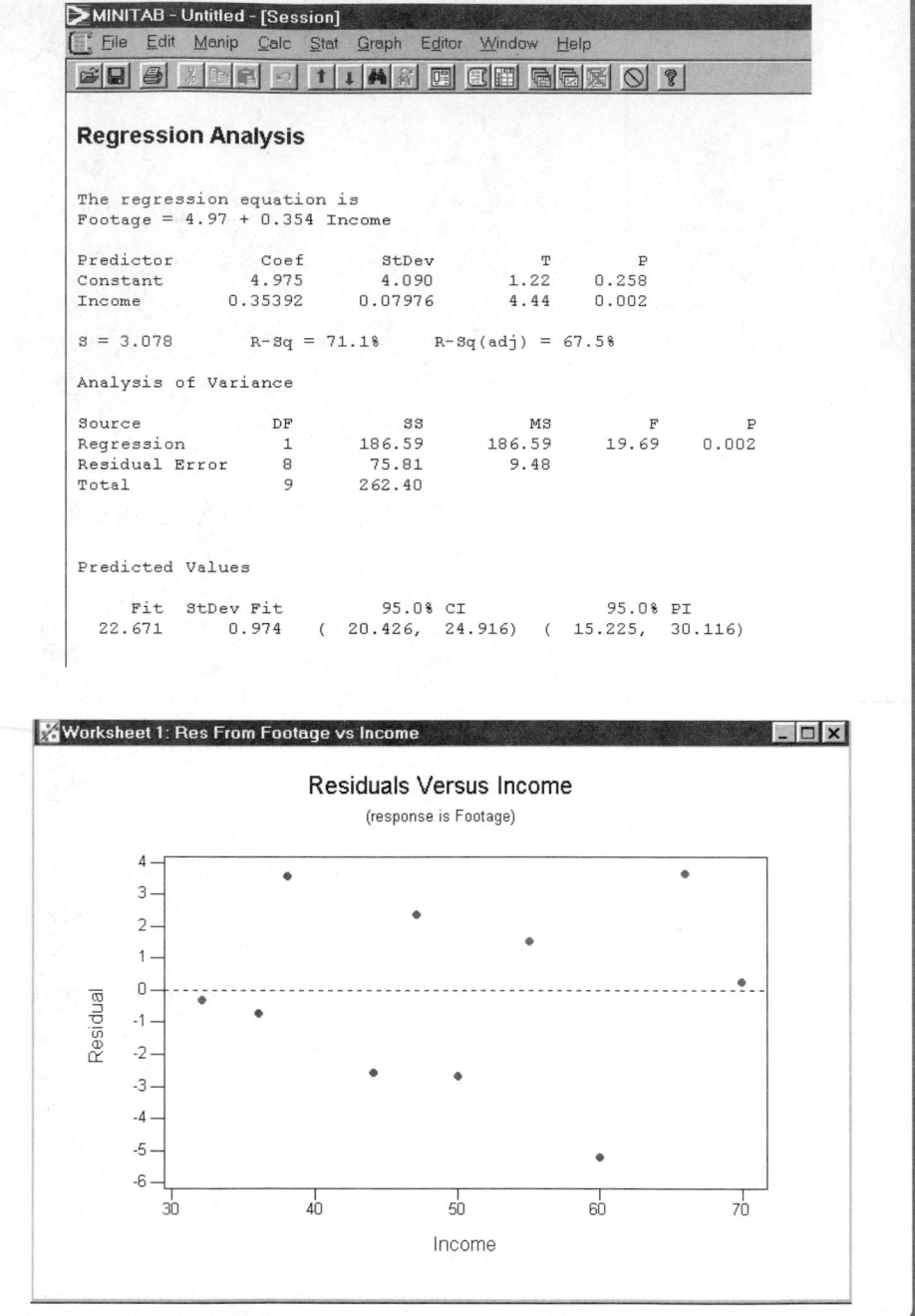

MULTIPLE LINEAR REGRESSION

STATISTICS IN ACTION: PERSONAL COMPUTER PRICES DROP AS TECHNOLOGY IMPROVES

Computer industry analysts believe that today's personal computers (PCs) will be the Model Ts of the Digital Age. The flood of new buyers of the PCs increased the penetration of PCs to 43% of U.S. homes. Not too long ago, a gigabyte of hard disc space seemed unthinkable. The *Wall Street Journal* reports that the average PC user should have at least a 233 MHz processor, with no less than 32 megabytes of RAM memory, and preferably 64 for good performance. A 6-gigabyte machine with a 56K modem may sound fancy, but today's most advanced personal computers may be near the low end of the market in less than a year. How accurately can the price of a PC be predicted? What components of a PC are important predictors of its price? Multiple regression analysis can assist computer industry analysts in modeling the price of a home computer.

From January 1997 to January 1998, the average selling price of a home PC dropped 30%, to $1,169. By Christmas 1998, top PC makers offered $600 machines— setting the stage for PCs to find their way into 60% of U.S. homes by 2002, according to projections by Forrester Research, Inc. If these figures are accurate, then the home-PC business will have steady growth for several years, and the American society will be in for another profound change because of technology. Why? Because the PC will no longer be a staple of just white-collar households. It will be nearly as ubiquitous as the telephone some time in the not-too-distant future.

The new cheap PCs are bringing blue-collar households into the Digital Age. Currently the median income of people intending to buy these cheap PCs have a median income between $27,000 and $50,000, according to Forrester Research, Inc. Millions more citizens will discover how to shop, chat, and explore cyberspace as these PCs become truly affordable. Investors have noticed this revolutionary change in the American society. Shares of companies such as Yahoo!, Inc., and Excite have prices in the stratosphere. The assumption that investors are mak-

ing is that the millions of consumers snapping up cheap PCs will bring more traffic to the Web sites, thus driving up advertising rates and generating many more transactions. Electronic commerce means big business to many online merchants, such as Amazon.com.

According to International Data Corp., computer makers around the world will ship approximately 13.4% more PCs each year. But because of price cuts, their revenues will be up only 4.4%. Intel posted its first year-to-year profit decline since 1989. "As the price drops, computer manufacturers are forced to get volumes up," says Arno A. Penzias, a Nobel prize-winning physicist, who is now chief scientist of the Bell Laboratories unit of Lucent Technologies, Inc. "The only way to do that is to make things less intimidating. The real winners are people who can make these things look friendly."

Can you accurately predict the price of a PC given its characteristics, such as processor speed and size of the hard drive? This chapter builds on the previous simple linear regression chapter by attempting to improve the accuracy of the prediction of a dependent variable (Y) by considering more than one predictor variable ($X_1, X_2, \ldots$).

When you have completed this chapter, you will be able to:

- Construct a prediction equation containing more than one predictor variable;

- Measure how well these predictor variables do, in fact, predict the dependent variable and which ones could be removed without a significant reduction in the prediction accuracy;

- Construct a model that includes *interactions* between the predictor variables and *quadratic effects* of the predictor variables; and

- Discuss why a regression equation containing 50 predictor variables is not a good idea.

A LOOK BACK/INTRODUCTION

We used the technique of simple linear regression in Chapter 14 to explain the behavior of a dependent variable using a single predictor (independent) variable. For example, we can attempt to explain the amount of new housing construction using the interest rate as a predictor variable.

To define this procedure in statistical terms, we introduced the concept of a statistical model. This model consists of two parts. The first part, the deterministic component, is assumed to be $Y = \beta_0 + \beta_1 X$ (a straight line), implying that the underlying pattern for the X and Y variables is linear. If a simple linear regression model is appropriate for the construction illustration, a scatter diagram of the new housing starts (Y) and the corresponding interest rates (X) should reveal a basic linear pattern. We never expect all the sample data to lie *exactly* on a straight line; we realize that with any statistical model there is error involved. This error makes up the random component. The actual model used for simple linear regression is $Y = \beta_0 + \beta_1 X + e$, where e represents the distance from the actual Y value to the line passing through all X, Y values. The value of e is the error and represents the error component of the model. The assumptions behind the use of this model deal with the behavior of these error terms—are they normally distributed, centered at zero, with the same variance? Are they independent?

In the construction example, it seems reasonable to assume that the volume of housing construction is affected not only by the interest rate but also by many other factors (variables) as well, including cost of materials, geographic location, and unemployment rate in the area. We next look at statistical models that predict the dependent variable (such as $Y =$ the number of new housing starts) as a function of *more than one* independent variable. The concept and assumptions are the same as before—now we are merely concerned with more than one predictor variable. When we include these additional variables, the predictive ability of the model should be significantly improved. This procedure is called multiple linear regression, and it is a very useful statistical technique.

15.1 THE MULTIPLE LINEAR REGRESSION MODEL

PREDICTION USING MORE THAN ONE VARIABLE

To explain or predict the behavior of a certain dependent variable using more than one predictor variable, we use a **multiple linear regression** model. The form of this model is

$$Y = \beta_0 + \beta_1 X_1 + \beta_2 X_2 + \cdots + \beta_k X_k + e \qquad \text{(15.1)}$$

where $X_1, X_2, \ldots, X_k$ are the k independent (predictor) variables and e is the error associated with this model.

Notice that equation 15.1 is similar to the equation for the simple linear regression model, except that the *deterministic component* is now

$$\beta_0 + \beta_1 X_1 + \cdots + \beta_k X_k \tag{15.2}$$

rather than $\beta_0 + \beta_1 X$. Once again the error term, e, is included to provide for deviations about the deterministic component.

What is the appearance of the deterministic portion in equation 15.2? In Chapter 14, where we discussed simple linear regression, the deterministic portion was a straight line. In the case of multiple linear regression, the deterministic portion is more difficult (usually impossible) to represent graphically. If your model contains two predictor variables, X_1 and X_2, the deterministic component becomes a plane, as shown in Figure 15.1. Consequently, the key assumption behind the use of this particular model is that the Y values will lie in this plane, *on the average,* for any particular values of X_1 and X_2.

In Chapter 14, we examined the relationship between the square footage of a home (Y) and the corresponding household income (X). The results were:

- least squares line: $\hat{Y} = 4.975 + .3539X$
- correlation between X and Y: $r = .843$
- coefficient of determination: $r^2 = .711$
- a significant linear relationship exists

We now want to include two additional variables in this model. The real-estate developer performing the study suspects that (1) larger families have larger homes and (2) the size of the home is affected by the amount of formal education (years of college) of the wage earner(s) in the home. We now have three independent variables:

X_1 = annual income (thousands of dollars)

X_2 = family size

X_3 = combined years of formal education (beyond high school) for all household wage earners

FIGURE 15.1

The multiple linear regression model (two independent variables).

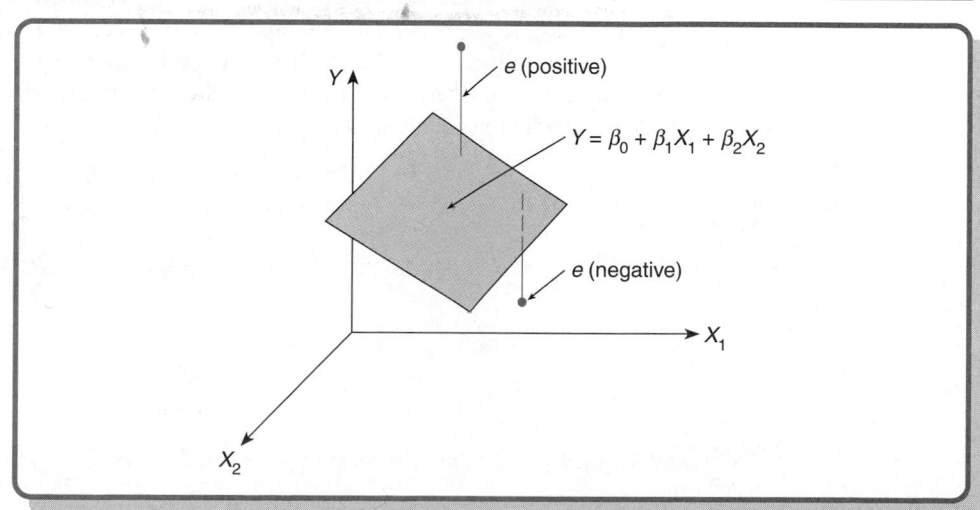

The same 10 families were used in the study, but data were collected on the two additional variables, X_2 and X_3.*

Family	Y (Home Square Footage)	X_1 (Income)	X_2 (Family Size)	X_3 (Years of Formal Education)
1	16	32	2	4
2	17	36	2	8
3	26	55	3	7
4	24	47	4	0
5	22	38	4	2
6	21	60	3	10
7	32	66	6	8
8	18	44	3	8
9	30	70	5	2
10	20	50	3	6

The data configuration now has four columns (including Y) and 10 rows (called *observations*). Our task is to use the data on all *three* variables (X_1, X_2, and X_3) to provide a better estimate of home size (Y).

THE LEAST SQUARES ESTIMATE.   Using Figure 15.1, we proceed as we did for simple regression and determine an estimate of the β's that will make the sum of squares of the residuals as small as possible. A **residual** is defined as the difference between the actual Y value and its estimate; that is, $Y - \hat{Y}$. In other words, we attempt to find the $b_0, b_1, \ldots, b_k$ that minimize the sum of squares of error,

$$\text{SSE} = \sum(Y - \hat{Y})^2 \tag{15.3}$$

where now $\hat{Y} = b_0 + b_1X_1 + b_2X_2 + \cdots + b_kX_k$ and $b_0, b_1, \ldots, b_k$ are called the **least squares estimates** of $\beta_0, \beta_1, \ldots, \beta_k$.

By determining the estimated *regression coefficients* ($b_0, b_1, \ldots, b_k$) that minimize SSE rather than $\sum(Y - \hat{Y})$, we once again avoid the problem of positive errors canceling out negative ones. Another advantage of this procedure is that, by means of a little calculus, we can show that a fairly simple expression exists for these sample regression coefficients. Because this expression involves the use of *matrix notation,* we omit this result.†

There is only one way to solve a multiple regression problem in practice, and that is with the help of a computer. All computer packages determine the values of $b_0, b_1, \ldots, b_k$ in the same way—namely, by minimizing SSE. As a result, these values will be identical (except for numerical rounding errors), regardless of which computer program you use.

In the example where we attempt to predict home size using the three predictor variables, the prediction equation is

$$\hat{Y} = b_0 + b_1X_1 + b_2X_2 + b_3X_3$$

where

$$\hat{Y} = \text{predicted home size}$$

$$X_1 = \text{income}$$

$$X_2 = \text{family size}$$

$$X_3 = \text{years of education}$$

and b_0, b_1, b_2, and b_3 are the least squares estimates of β_0, β_1, β_2, and β_3.

---

* A sample of size 10 is unrealistically small in practice.

† Information on this expression is presented in T. Sincich and W. Mendenhall, *A Second Course in Business Statistics: Regression Analysis,* 5th ed. (Upper Saddle River, NJ: Prentice-Hall, 1996); J. Neter, M. Kutner, and C. Nachtscheim, *Applied Linear Regression Models,* 3rd ed. (Homewood, Ill.: Richard D. Irwin, 1996).

FIGURE 15.2

Excel multiple regression solution to predicting house size using three predictor variables.

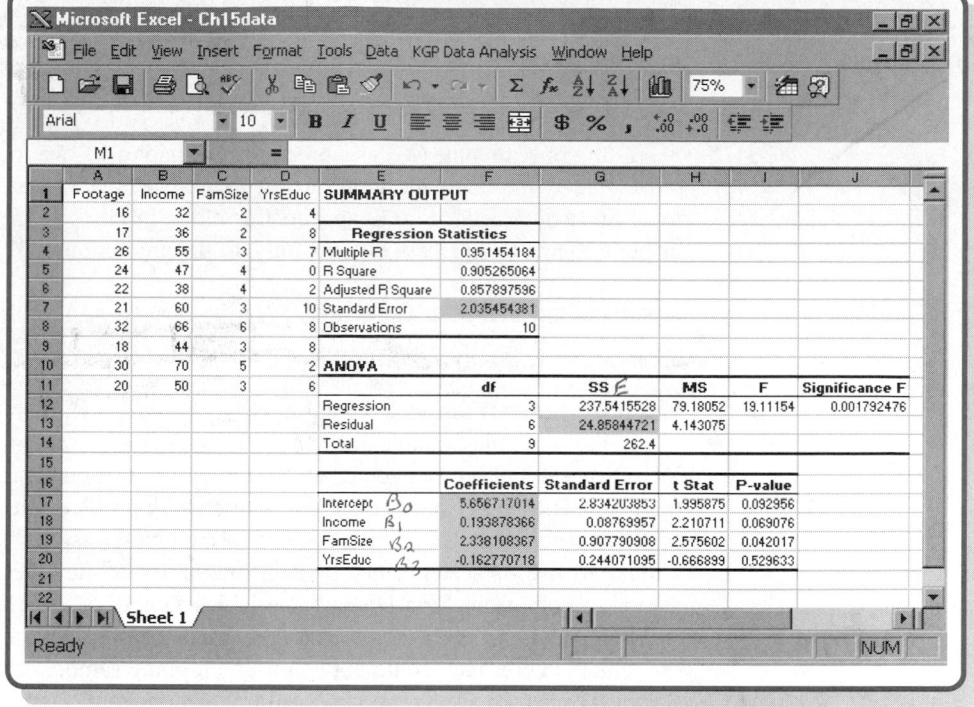

Figure 15.2 contains the Excel solution using the data we presented. To obtain this solution, type "Footage", "Income", "FamSize", and "YrsEduc" in cells A1:D1 and enter the 10 rows of data in cells A2:D11. Click on **Tools ➤ Data Analysis ➤ Regression,** and enter "A1:A11" as the **Input Y Range,** "B1:D11" as the **Input X Range,** and "E1" as the **Output Range.** Be sure to click on the box alongside **Labels,** since there are labels in the first row. According to this output, the best prediction equation (in the least squares sense) for home size is

$$\hat{Y} = 5.657 + .194X_1 + 2.338X_2 - .163X_3$$

So this solution minimizes SSE. But what is the SSE here? We need to determine how well this equation "fits" the ten observations in the data set. Consider the first family, where $X_1 = 32$ (income = \$32,000), $X_2 = 2$ (family size = 2, such as an adult couple with no children), and $X_3 = 4$ (combined years of college = 4). The predicted home size here is

$$\hat{Y} = 5.657 + .194(32) + 2.338(2) - .163(4) = 15.886$$

Consequently, the predicted home size is 1589 square feet. The actual square footage for this observation is 1600 ($Y = 16$), so the sample residual here is $Y - \hat{Y} = 16 - 15.886 = .114$.

Using this procedure on the remaining nine observations, we get the following results:

Y	$\hat{Y}$	$Y - \hat{Y}$	$(Y - \hat{Y})^2$
16	15.886	0.114	0.01300
17	16.010	0.990	0.98010
26	22.195	3.805	14.47803
24	24.121	−0.121	0.01464
22	22.051	−0.051	0.00260
21	22.676	−1.676	2.80898
32	31.179	0.821	0.67404
18	19.900	−1.900	3.61000
30	30.593	−0.593	0.35165
20	21.388	−1.388	1.92654
		0	24.86 = SSE

↑—approximately

The computed value for the error sum of square is SSE = 24.86. This value also is highlighted in cell G13 in Figure 15.2. This result implies that for *any* other values of b_0, b_1, b_2, and b_3, if we were to find the corresponding $\hat{Y}$'s and the resulting SSE = $\Sigma(Y - \hat{Y})^2$ using these values, this new SSE would be *larger* than 24.86. Thus, $b_0 = 5.657$, $b_1 = .194$, $b_2 = 2.338$, and $b_3 = -.163$ minimize the error sum of squares, SSE. Put still another way, these values of b_0, b_1, b_2, and b_3 provide the **best fit** to our data.

Using only income (X_1) as a predictor in Chapter 14, we found the SSE to be 75.81 in our table. By including the additional two variables, the SSE has been reduced from 75.81 to 24.86 (a 67% reduction). It appears that either family size (X_2), years of education (X_3), or both contribute, perhaps significantly, to the prediction of Y.

INTERPRETING THE REGRESSION COEFFICIENTS.   When using a multiple linear regression equation, such as $Y = \beta_0 + \beta_1 X_1 + \beta_2 X_2 + \beta_3 X_3 + e$, what does β_2 represent? Very simply, it reflects the change in Y that can be expected to accompany a change of one unit in X_2, *provided all other variables* (namely, X_1 and X_3) *are held constant.*

In the previous example, the sample estimate of β_2 was $b_2 = 2.338$. Can we expect an increase of 2.338 on the average as X_2 (the family size) increases by one if X_1 and X_3 are held constant? This type of argument is filled with problems, as we demonstrate later. The primary problem is that a change in one of the predictor variables (such as X_2) always (or almost always) is accompanied by a change in one of the other predictors (say, X_1) in the sample observations. Consequently, variables X_1 and X_2 are related in some manner, such as $X_1 \cong 1 + 5X_2$. In other words, a situation in which X_2, for instance, changed and the others remained constant would not be observed in the sample data.

In the case (typically not observed in business applications) where the predictor variables *are* totally unrelated, a unit change in X_2, for example, can be expected to be accompanied by a change of β_2 in the dependent variable.

In general, it is not safe to assume that the predictor variables are unrelated. As a result, the b's usually do not reflect the true "partial effects" of the predictor variables, and you should avoid such conclusions. Section 15.4 discusses methods of dealing with this type of situation.

THE ASSUMPTIONS BEHIND THE MULTIPLE LINEAR REGRESSION MODEL

The form of the multiple linear regression model is given by equation 15.1, which contains a linear combination of the k predictor (independent) variables as well as the error component, e. The assumptions for the case of $k > 1$ predictors are exactly the same as for $k = 1$ independent variable (simple linear regression). These assumptions, discussed in Chapter 14, are:

1. The errors follow a normal distribution, centered at zero, with common variance, σ_e^2.
2. The errors are (statistically) independent.

The case for $k = 2$ predictor variables can be represented graphically, as shown in Figures 15.1 and 15.3. Using Figure 15.3, consider the situation in which $X_1 = 30$ and $X_2 = 8$. If you *were* to obtain repeated values of Y for these values for X_1 and X_2, you would obtain some Y's above the plane and some below. The assumptions are that the *average* value of Y with $X_1 = 30$ and $X_2 = 8$ lies *on* the plane and that, moreover, these errors are normally distributed.

The final part of assumption 1 is that the variation about this plane does not depend on the values of X_1 and X_2. You should see roughly the same amount of variation if you obtain repeated values of Y corresponding to $X_1 = 50$ and $X_2 = 2$ as you observed for $X_1 = 30$ and $X_2 = 8$. The variance of these errors, if you could observe Y indefinitely, is σ_e^2.

Finally, assumption 2 means that the error encountered at $X_1 = 50$ and $X_2 = 2$, for instance, is not affected by a known error at any other point, such as $X_1 = 30$ and $X_2 = 8$. The error associated with one pair of X_1, X_2 values has no effect on any other error.

FIGURE 15.3
FIGURE 15.3
The errors in multiple linear
regression ($k = 2$).

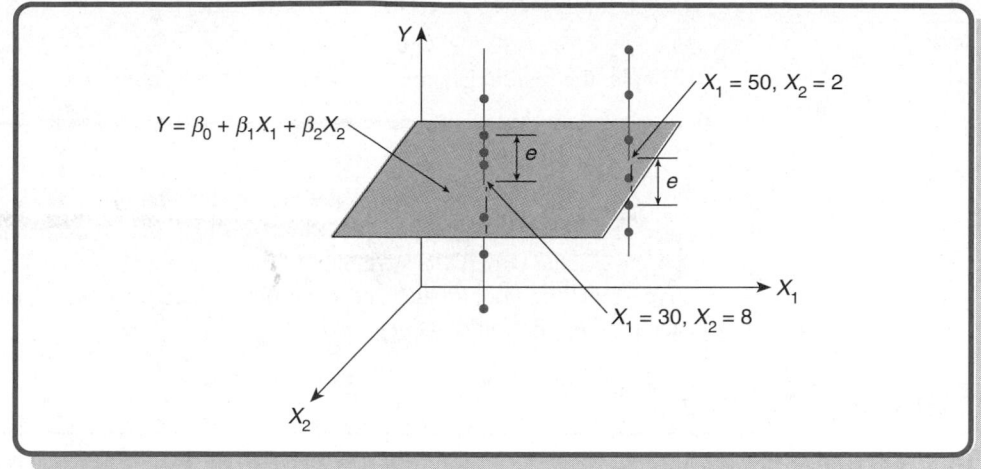

AN ESTIMATE OF σ_e^2.   When using a straight line to model a relationship between Y and a single predictor, the estimate of σ_e^2 was given by equation 14.16, where

$$s^2 = \hat{\sigma}_e^2 = \frac{\text{SSE}}{n-2}$$

In general, for k predictors and n observations, the estimate of this variance is

$$s^2 = \hat{\sigma}_e^2 = \frac{\text{SSE}}{n-(k+1)} = \frac{\text{SSE}}{n-k-1} \qquad \textbf{(15.4)}$$

The value of s^2 is critical in determining the reliability and usefulness of the model as a predictor. If $s^2 = 0$, then SSE $= 0$, implying that $Y = \hat{Y}$ for each of the observations in the sample data. This rarely happens in practice, but it does point out that a small s^2 is desirable. As s^2 increases, you can expect more error when predicting a value of Y for specified values of $X_1, X_2, \ldots, X_k$. In the next section, we use s^2 as a key to determining whether the model is satisfactory and which of the independent variables are useful in the prediction of the dependent variable.

The square root of this estimated variance is the **residual standard deviation.**

$$s = \sqrt{\frac{\text{SSE}}{n-k-1}} \qquad \textbf{(15.5)}$$

In the Excel solution in Figure 15.2, the value of s is highlighted in cell F7. The residual standard deviation is often called the **standard error.**

EXAMPLE 15.1

Determine the estimate of σ_e^2 and the residual standard deviation (standard error) for the real-estate data on page 676.

SOLUTION

This example contained $n = 10$ observations and $k = 3$ predictor variables. The resulting error sum of squares was SSE $= 24.86$ (from Figure 15.2). Therefore,

$$s^2 = \hat{\sigma}_e^2$$

$$= \frac{24.86}{10-3-1} = \frac{24.86}{6} = 4.14$$

and

$$s = \sqrt{4.14} = 2.035$$

That is, the residual standard deviation is 203.5 square feet.

If a particular regression model meets all the required assumptions, then the next question of interest is whether this set of independent variables provides an accurate method of predicting the dependent variable, Y. The next section shows how to calculate the predictive ability of your model and determine which variables contribute significantly to an accurate prediction of Y.

EXERCISES 15.1–15.8

UNDERSTANDING THE MECHANICS

15.1 The prediction equation $\hat{Y} = 3.0 - 2.1X_1 + 7X_2 + 1.4X_3$ was calculated from a data set with 20 observations.
  a. What is the error degrees of freedom?
  b. If X_1 is increased by 2 and X_2 is increased by 1 with X_3 remaining constant, what is the net change in $\hat{Y}$?

15.2 The following data were collected.

Y	X_1	X_2
5.4	11	3.1
7.7	14	5.1
9.1	17	5.4
8.8	17	4.4
6.2	11	3.5
7.0	12	3.8
8.4	14	4.9
7.1	13	4.0

The regression equation for this data is $\hat{Y} = .214 + .341X_1 + .608X_2$. Calculate the estimate of the variance of the error component of the model.

APPLYING THE NEW CONCEPTS

15.3 An oil-service company decided to fit a least squares equation to a set of data to predict the total cost of building a well. The independent variables are $X_1 =$ drilling days, $X_2 =$ total depth, and $X_3 =$ intermediate casing depth. After calculating the least squares equation, the residuals were calculated to find out whether the assumptions of regression analysis are satisfied. The following are the residuals from 20 observations:

–0.8, 1.5, –3.7, 4.1, –3.1, –5.2, 4.3, –2.1, –1.6, 4.1, 0.9, –0.3, 4.5, –4.2, 3.2, –2.7, 1.7, –2.2, 3.4, –1.8

Do the residuals $Y - \hat{Y}$ appear to conform to the empirical rule that approximately 95% of the data should lie within two standard deviations of the mean?

15.4 What assumptions need to be made about the error component of a multiple linear regression model in order that the results of statistical inference can be used?

15.5 Tony owns a used-car lot. He would like to predict monthly sales volume. Tony believes that sales volume (given in thousands) is directly related to the number of salespeople

employed and the number of cars on the lot for sale. The following data were collected over a period of 10 months:

Monthly Sales Volume (Y)	Salespeople (X_1)	Cars (X_2)
5.8	4	20
7.5	5	15
11.4	7	25
7.0	3	17
5.1	2	18
8.1	4	25
13.3	8	30
15.0	9	35
8.3	5	20
6.8	4	23

  a. Using a computerized statistical package, determine the least squares prediction equation for these data.
  b. Find the value of SSE.

15.6 Using the multiple regression model $\hat{Y} = b_0 + b_1X_1 + b_2X_2 + b_3X_3$, where do you expect the average value of Y to fall for $X_1 = 3$, $X_2 = 4.1$, and $X_3 = 5.6$?

USING THE COMPUTER

15.7 [DATA SET EX15-7] *Variable description:*

Close: Closing price for used microcomputer and related equipment
SellerAsk: Asking price for used microcomputer and related equipment
BuyerBid: Price that a buyer is willing to pay for used microcomputer and related equipment

According to *The Dallas Morning News*, "PC Market," Aug. 4, 1997, p. 2D, the used personal computer market is active with buyers and sellers of used microcomputers and assorted parts, particularly notebook computers. The spread (difference between initial bid and initial asking price) may be anywhere from a couple of hundred dollars to over a thousand dollars. Suppose that a random sample of 60 negotiated sales of microcomputer and related equipment is selected, and the variables Close, SellerAsk, and BuyerBid are recorded in units of thousands of dollars.

  a. Find the prediction equation for the dependent variable Close and independent variable SellerAsk. What is the value of the residual standard deviation?

b. Find the prediction equation of the dependent variable Close and the independent variables SellerAsk and BuyerBid. Compare the standard deviation of this model to that in part (a).

c. Construct a histogram of the residuals for the model in part (b).

15.8 [DATA SET EX15-8] *Variable description:*

InvestKnow: Investment knowledge
Age: Age of viewer
AnnualInc: Annual income of viewer

According to the *Toronto Star* ("Mutual Fund Investing on Video," Dec. 12, 1993, p. D2), the Investment Funds Institute of Canada (IFIC) has produced a sophisticated half-hour video that covers the basic principles of investing in mutual funds.

Many Canadian mutual fund companies have ordered large quantities to distribute to their clients as promotional tools. Suppose that an investment counselor was hired by the IFIC to assess the knowledge level of an investor after the investor views the film. The counselor randomly selected 50 Canadian investors and collected data on an investment test and on each person's age (in years) and income (in thousands of dollars).

a. Find the regression equation to predict InvestKnow using the variables Age and AnnualInc. If Age is held constant, but the AnnualInc of the viewer changes by $20,000, by how much does the predicted value of InvestKnow change?

b. Verify that the sum of the residuals is zero. What is the mean of the residuals? Do approximately 95% of the residuals lie within two standard deviations of the mean?

15.2 HYPOTHESIS TESTING AND CONFIDENCE INTERVALS FOR THE β PARAMETERS

Multiple linear regression is a popular tool in the application of statistical techniques to business decisions. However, this modeling procedure does not always result in an accurate and reliable predictor. When the independent variables that you have selected account for very little of the variation in the values of the dependent variable, the model (as is) serves no useful purpose.

The first thing we demonstrate is how to determine whether your overall model is satisfactory. We begin by summarizing a regression analysis in an analysis of variance (ANOVA) table, much as we did in Chapter 11.

THE ANOVA TABLE

The summary ANOVA table contains the usual headings.

Source	df	SS	MS	F
Regression	k	SSR	MSR	MSR/MSE
Residual	$n - k - 1$	SSE	MSE	
Total	$n - 1$	SST		

where $n =$ number of observations and $k =$ number of independent variables.

$$\text{SST} = \text{total sum of squares}$$

$$= \text{SS}_Y$$

$$= \Sigma(Y - \bar{Y})^2 = \Sigma Y^2 - \frac{(\Sigma Y)^2}{n} \tag{15.6}$$

$$\text{SSE} = \text{sum of squares for error}$$

$$= \Sigma(Y - \hat{Y})^2 \tag{15.7}$$

$$\text{SSR} = \text{sum of squares for regression}$$

$$= \Sigma(\hat{Y} - \bar{Y})^2$$

$$= \text{SST} - \text{SSE} \tag{15.8}$$

$$\text{MSR} = \text{mean square for regression}$$

$$= \frac{\text{SSR}}{k} \tag{15.9}$$

$$\text{MSE} = \text{mean square for error}$$

$$= \frac{\text{SSE}}{n - k - 1} \tag{15.10}$$

Practically all computer packages provide you with this ANOVA summary as part of the standard output. The ANOVA section of the Excel solution for the real-estate model is in Figure 15.4(a). Notice that

$$SST = SS_Y$$

$$= (16^2 + 17^2 + \cdots + 20^2) - \frac{(16 + 17 + \cdots + 20)^2}{10} = 262.4$$

This is the same value of SS_Y we obtained for the same example in Chapter 14, when we used only income (X_1) as the predictor variable. This is hardly surprising because *this value is strictly a function of the Y values* and is unaffected by the model that we are using to predict Y. The total sum of squares (SST) measures the total variation in the values of the dependent variable. Its value is the same, regardless of which predictor variables are included in the model.

The df for the regression source of variation is k = the number of predictor variables in the analysis. The df for the error sum of squares is $n - k - 1$, where n = the number of observations in the sample data.

As in the case of simple linear regression, the sum of squares of regression (SSR) measures the variation *explained* by the model—the variation in the Y values that would exist if differences in the values of the predictor variables were the only cause of differences among the Y's. On the other hand, the sum of squares of error (SSE) represents the variation *unexplained* by the model. The easiest way to determine the sum of squares of regression is to subtract:

$$SSR = SST - SSE$$

The error mean square is $MSE = SSE/(n - k - 1) = 24.858/(10 - 4) = 4.14$. This is the same as the *estimate* of σ_e^2 determined in Example 15.1. So,

$$s^2 = \hat{\sigma}_e^2 = MSE$$

FIGURE 15.4

Excel output (see Figure 15.2). (a) Prediction equation and ANOVA table using X_1, X_2, and X_3. (b) Prediction equation and ANOVA table using X_1 and X_2.

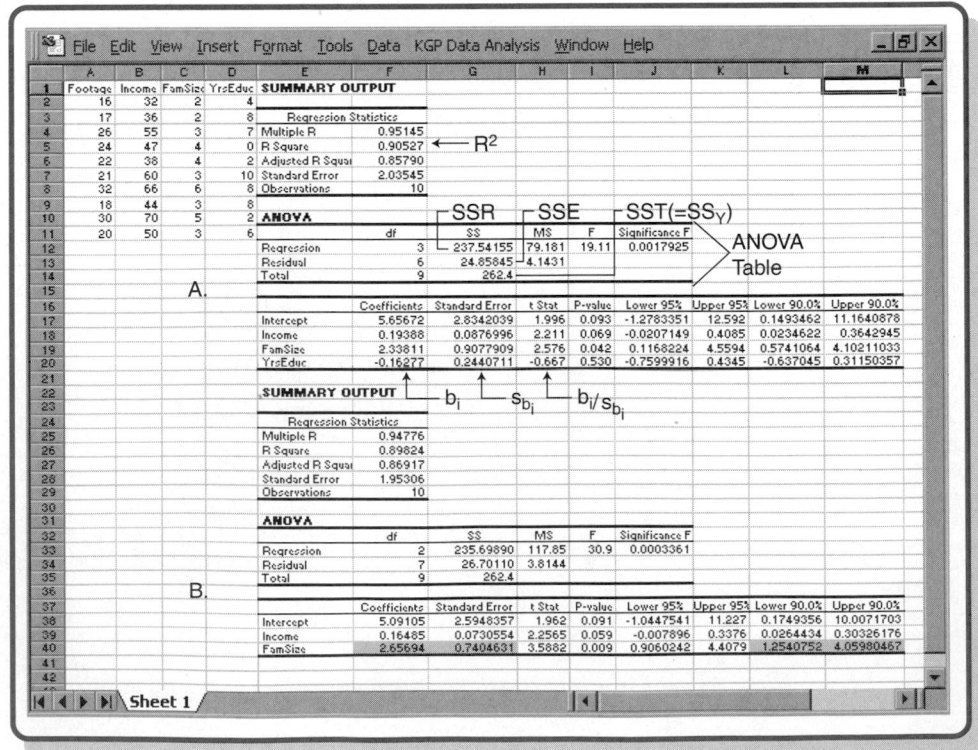

A Test for H_0: All β's $= 0$

We have yet to make use of the F-value calculated in the ANOVA table, where

$$F = \frac{\text{MSR}}{\text{MSE}} \qquad (15.11)$$

When using the simple regression model, we previously argued that one way to determine whether X is a significant predictor of Y is to test H_0: $\beta_1 = 0$, where β_1 is the coefficient of X in the model $Y = \beta_0 + \beta_1 X + e$. If you reject H_0, the conclusion is that the independent variable X *does* contribute significantly to the prediction of Y. For example, in Example 14.3, by rejecting H_0: $\beta_1 = 0$, we concluded that income (X_1) was a useful predictor of home size (Y) using the simple linear model.

We use a similar test as the first step in the multiple regression analysis, where we examine the hypotheses

$$H_0: \beta_1 = \beta_2 = \cdots = \beta_k = 0$$

$$H_a: \text{at least one of the β's} \neq 0$$

If we *reject* H_0, we can conclude that at least one (but maybe not all) of the independent variables contributes significantly to the prediction of Y. If we *fail to reject* H_0, we are unable to demonstrate that any of the independent variables (or combination of them) helps explain the behavior of the dependent variable, Y. For example, in our housing example, if we were to fail to reject H_0, this would imply that we are unable to demonstrate that the variation in the home sizes (Y) can be explained by the effect of income, family size, and years of education.

Test Statistic for H_0 Versus H_a. The test statistic used to determine whether our multiple regression model contains at least one explanatory variable is the F statistic from the preceding ANOVA table.

When testing H_0: all β's $= 0$ (this set of predictor variables is no good at all) versus H_a: at least one $\beta \neq 0$ (at least one of these variables is a good predictor), the test statistic is

$$F = \frac{\text{MSR}}{\text{MSE}}$$

which has an F distribution with k and $n - k - 1$ df. The expression $n - k - 1$ can be written as $n - (k + 1)$, where $k + 1$ is the number of coefficients (β's) estimated including the constant term.

Notice that the df for the F-statistic comes directly from the ANOVA table. The testing procedure is to

$$\text{reject } H_0 \text{ if } F > F_{\alpha, v_1, v_2}$$

where (1) $v_1 = k$, $v_2 = n - k - 1$ and (2) F_{α, v_1, v_2} is the corresponding F-value in Table A.7 having a *right-tail area* $= \alpha$ (Figure 15.5).

EXAMPLE 15.2

Using the real-estate data and the model we developed, what can you say about the predictive ability of the independent variables, income (X_1), family size (X_2), and years of education (X_3)? Use $\alpha = .10$.

SOLUTION

Step 1. The hypotheses are

$$H_0: \beta_1 = \beta_2 = \beta_3 = 0$$

$$H_a: \text{at least one } \beta \neq 0$$

FIGURE 15.5

F curve with k and $n-k-1$ df. The lightly shaded area is the rejection region.

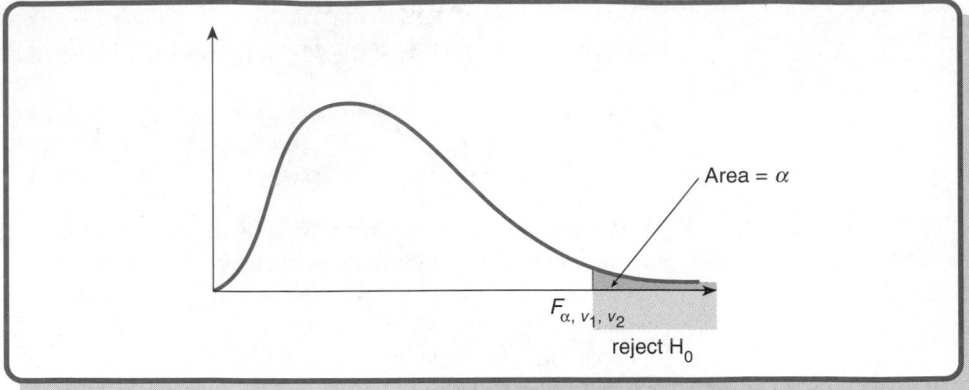

Remember that your hope here is to reject H_0. If you are unable to demonstrate that any of your independent variables have any predictive ability, then you will fail to reject H_0.

Step 2. The test statistic is

$$F = \frac{\text{MSR}}{\text{MSE}}$$

The mean squares are obtained from the ANOVA summary of the regression analysis (see Figure 15.4).

Step 3. The df for the F statistic are $k = 3$ and $n - k - 1 = 10 - 3 - 1 = 6$. So we will

reject H_0 if $F > F_{.10,3,6} = 3.29$

Step 4. According to Figure 15.4(a), the computed F-value is

$$F^* = \frac{79.18}{4.14} = 19.1$$

Because $F^* > 3.29$, we reject H_0.

Step 5. The three independent variables *as a group* constitute a good predictor of home size. This does *not* imply that all three variables have significant predictive ability; however, at least one of them does. The next section shows how you can tell *which* of these predictor variables significantly contributes to the prediction of home size.

A Test for H_0: $\beta_i = 0$

Assuming that you rejected the null hypothesis that all of the β's are zero, the next logical question would be, which of the independent variables contributes to the prediction of Y?

In Example 15.2, we rejected the null hypothesis, so at least one of these three independent variables affects the variation of the ten home sizes in the sample. To determine the contribution of each variable, we perform three separate t tests:

$$H_0: \beta_1 - 0 \ (X_1 \text{ docs not contribute})$$

$$H_a: \beta_1 \neq 0 \ (X_1 \text{ does contribute})$$

$$H_0: \beta_2 = 0 \ (X_2 \text{ does not contribute})$$

$$H_a: \beta_2 \neq 0 \ (X_2 \text{ does contribute})$$

$$H_0: \beta_3 = 0 \ (X_3 \text{ does not contribute})$$

$$H_a: \beta_3 \neq 0 \ (X_3 \text{ does contribute})$$

One-tailed tests also can be used here, but we will demonstrate this procedure using two-tailed tests. This means that we are testing to see whether this particular X contributes to the prediction of Y, but we are not concerned about the direction (positive or negative) of this relationship.

When income (X_1) was the only predictor of home size (Y), we used a t test to determine whether the simple linear regression model was adequate. In Example 14.3, the value of the test statistic was derived, where

$$t = \frac{b_1}{s_{b_1}} \tag{15.12}$$

Also, b_1 is the estimate of β_1 in the simple regression model, and s_{b_1} is the (estimated) standard deviation of b_1. Excel refers to s_{b_1} as the **standard error** of b_1.

All computer packages provide both the estimated coefficient (b_1) and its standard error (s_{b_1}). In Example 14.3, the computed value of this t statistic was $t^* = 4.44$. This result led us to conclude that income was a good predictor of home size because a significant positive relationship existed between these two variables.

We use the same t statistic procedure to test the effect of the individual variables in a multiple regression model. When examining the effect of an individual independent variable, X_i, on the prediction of a dependent variable, the hypotheses are

$$H_0: \beta_i = 0$$

$$H_a: \beta_i \neq 0$$

The test statistic is

$$t = \frac{b_i}{s_{b_i}}$$

where (1) b_i is the estimate of β_i, (2) s_{b_i} is the (estimated) standard error of b_i, and (3) the df for the t statistic is $n - k - 1$.

The test of H_0 versus H_a is to

$$\text{reject } H_0 \text{ if } |t| > t_{\alpha/2, n-k-1}$$

where $t_{\alpha/2, n-k-1}$ is obtained from Table A.5.

We can now reexamine the real-estate data in Example 15.2.

$X_1 = $ INCOME. Consider the hypotheses

$$H_0: \beta_1 = 0$$

$$H_a: \beta_1 \neq 0$$

As in Example 15.2, we use $\alpha = .10$.

According to Figure 15.4(a), $b_1 = .194$ and $s_{b_1} = .0877$. Also contained in the output is the computed value of

$$t^* = \frac{b_1}{s_{b_1}} = \frac{.194}{.0877} = 2.21$$

Why is this value of t^* *not* the same as the value of t calculated for this variable in Chapter 14, when income was the only predictor of Y? When there are three predictors in the model, t^* for income is 2.21. When income is the only predictor in the model, $t^* = 4.44$. The difference in the two values is simply that $t^* = 2.21$ provides a measure of the contribution of $X_1 = $ income, *given that X_2 and X_3 already have been included in the model.* A large value of t^* indicates that X_1 contributes significantly to the prediction of Y, even if X_2 and X_3 have been included previously as predictors.

The hypotheses can better be stated as

H_0: income *does not* contribute to the prediction of home size, *given* that family size and years of education already have been included in the model

H_a: income *does* contribute to this prediction, given that family size and years of education already have been included in the model

or as

$$H_0: \beta_1 = 0 \quad \text{(if } X_2 \text{ and } X_3 \text{ are included)}$$

$$H_a: \beta_1 \neq 0$$

Because $t^* = 2.21$ exceeds the table value of $t_{\alpha/2, n-k-1} = t_{.05, 10-3-1} = t_{.05,6} = 1.943$, we conclude that income contributes significantly to the prediction of home size and should be kept in the model. An easier procedure to use here is to compare the corresponding p-value to the significance level (α). The p-value is in cell I18 in Figure 15.4(a) and is equal to .069. Since this is less than $\alpha = .10$, we reject H_0 and again conclude that income is a significant predictor.

X_2 = FAMILY SIZE.   Using a similar argument, the following test of hypothesis will determine the contribution of family size, X_2, as a predictor of the home square footage, given that X_1 and X_3 already have been included. The hypotheses here are

$$H_0: \beta_2 = 0 \quad \text{(if } X_1 \text{ and } X_3 \text{ are included)}$$

$$H_a: \beta_2 \neq 0$$

According to Figure 15.4(a), the computed t statistic here is

$$t^* = \frac{b_2}{s_{b_2}} = \frac{2.3381}{.9078} = 2.576$$

This value also exceeds $t_{.05,6} = 1.943$ (p-value of .042 is less than .10), and so family size provides useful information in predicting the square footage of a home. We conclude that we should keep X_2 in the model.

X_3 = YEARS OF EDUCATION.   To test

$$H_0: \beta_3 = 0 \quad \text{(if } X_1 \text{ and } X_2 \text{ are included)}$$

$$H_a: \beta_3 \neq 0$$

we once again use the t statistic.

$$t = \frac{b_3}{s_{b_3}}$$

Using Figure 15.4, the computed value of this statistic is

$$t^* = \frac{-.1628}{.2441} = -.67$$

Because $|t^*| = .67$, which does *not* exceed $t_{.05,6} = 1.943$, we fail to reject H_0. Here, the p-value of .530 exceeds the significance level of .10. We conclude that, given the values of X_1 = income and X_2 = family size, the level of a family's education appears not to contribute to the prediction of the size of their home. This means that X_3 can be ignored in the final prediction equation, leaving only X_1 and X_2.

COMMENTS

As a word of warning, you should *not* simply remove this term from the equation containing all three variables. Since the predictor variables are typically related in some manner, the sample regression coefficients (b_0, b_1, . . .) change as variables are added to or deleted from the model. Referring to Figure 15.4(a), the final prediction equation is not $\hat{Y} = 5.657 + .194X_1 + 2.338X_2$. Instead, the coefficients of X_1 and X_2 should be derived by repeating the analysis using only these two variables. According to Figure 15.4(b), this prediction equation is $\hat{Y} = 5.091 + .165X_1 + 2.657X_2$.

A CONFIDENCE INTERVAL FOR β_i

Using what you believe to be the "best" model, you can easily construct a $(1 - \alpha) \cdot 100\%$ confidence interval for β_i based on the previous t statistic:

$$b_i - t_{\alpha/2, n-k-1} s_{b_i} \quad \text{to} \quad b_i + t_{\alpha/2, n-k-1} s_{b_i} \qquad (15.13)$$

Once again, k represents the number of predictor variables used to estimate β_i.

EXAMPLE 15.3

Suppose you decide to retain only X_1 = income and X_2 = family size in the prediction equation. Referring to Figure 15.4(b), construct a 90% confidence interval for β_2, the coefficient for X_2.

SOLUTION

Since this model contains $k = 2$ predictor variables, we first find $t_{\alpha/2, n-k-1} = t_{.05,7} = 1.895$. Using cells F40 and G40 (highlighted) in Figure 15.4(b), the confidence interval for β_2 is

$$2.6569 - (1.895)(.7405) \quad \text{to} \quad 2.6569 + (1.895)(.7405)$$

$$= 2.6569 - 1.4032 \quad \text{to} \quad 2.6569 + 1.4032$$

$$= 1.25 \quad \text{to} \quad 4.06$$

Therefore, we are 90% confident that the estimate of β_2 (that is, $b_2 = 2.6569$) is within 1.4032 of the actual value of β_2. Notice that this is an extremely wide confidence interval. As usual, increasing the sample size would help to reduce the width of this confidence interval. When creating Figure 15.4(b), if you enter 90% as the confidence level, Excel will determine this confidence interval for you (cells L40 and M40 in Figure 15.4(b)).

MICROSOFT® EXCEL APPLICATION   USE DATA15-4

EXAMPLE 15.4

An Excel Multiple Regression Analysis

The management of BB Investments decided to develop a model to predict the amount of money invested by various clients in their portfolio of high-risk securities. It was generally agreed that the income of the investor should be a major factor in predicting his or her annual investment and would explain a major portion of the variability in the amount invested. In addition, the investor's willingness to assume risk also was influenced by the investor's view of present and future economic conditions. On the assumption that the investors would use economic forecasts and economists' indices of future expectations, the financial group at BB Investments constructed an economic index that ranged from 0 to 100. When applied to any particular point in time, this index was tied to the expected increase in interest rates and borrowing levels, the expected increase in manufacturing

FIGURE 15.6

Excel regression solution for Example 15.4.

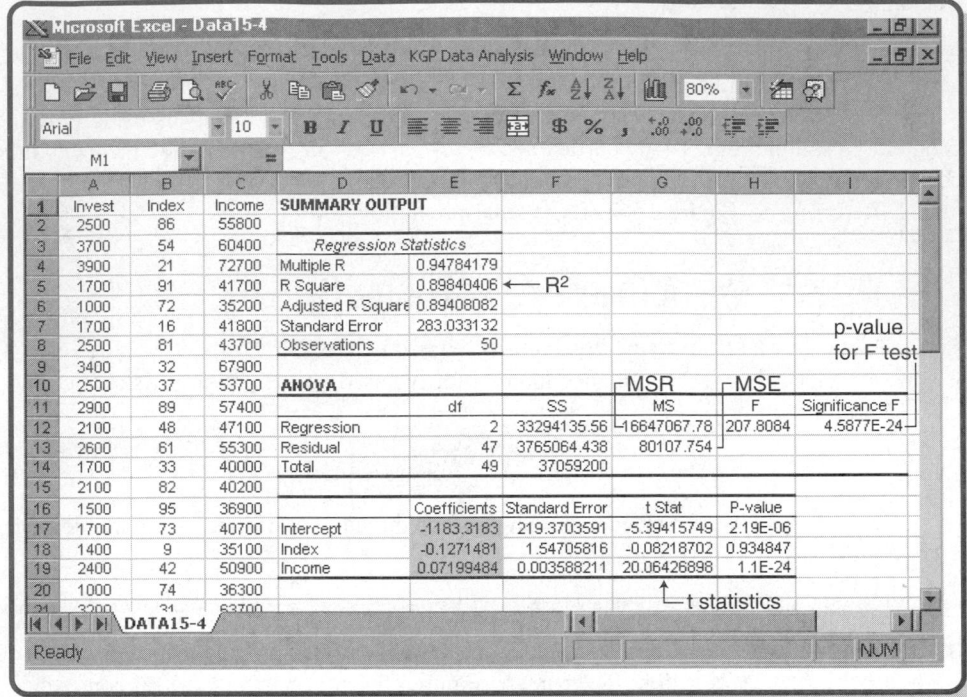

costs because of the rate of inflation, and the expected level of price inflation at the retail level. This meant that the *lower* the index, the *better* the future economic conditions were expected to be.

Data were obtained by randomly selecting 50 high-risk portfolio customers and recording their incomes and the amounts of their investments. The income figures represent annual incomes and the economic index values are the index values at the time the investment was made. Determine the adequacy of this model and the predicted investment for an investor with an income of $48,500 at a time when the economic index has a value of 72.

SOLUTION

The Excel regression solution is shown in Figure 15.6. To obtain this solution, first open data set DATA15-4. The first 20 rows are shown in columns A, B, and C in Figure 15.6. Next, click on **Tools ➤ Data Analysis ➤ Regression,** and enter "A1:A51" as the **Input Y Range,** "B1:C51" as the **Input X Range,** and "D1" as the **Output Range.** Finally, click on the box alongside **Labels** (since there are labels in the first row) and on "OK."

The least squares equation (highlighted) is

$$\hat{Y} = -1183.3 - .127X_1 + .072X_2$$

The predicted investment is

$$\hat{Y} = -1183.3 - .127(72) + .072(48,500)$$

$$= -1183.3 - 9.1 + 3492.0 = 2299.6$$

that is, approximately $2300. Note that, following the same argument used in Chapter 14, $2300 also serves as an estimate of the average investment whenever $X_1 = 72$ and $X_2 = $48,500$. This topic is explored further in Section 15.5, where we discuss the construction of a confidence interval for an *average* investment or a prediction interval for an *individual* investment.

The first test of hypothesis determines whether these two variables *as a group* provide a useful model for predicting the amount of an investment:

$$H_0: \beta_1 = \beta_2 = 0$$

$$H_a: \beta_1 \neq 0, \beta_2 \neq 0, \text{ or both} \neq 0$$

Using the ANOVA table, the value of the F-statistic is

$$F^* = \frac{MSR}{MSE} = \frac{16,647,067.78}{80,107.754} = 207.81$$

The df here are $v_1 = k = 2$ and $v_2 = n - k - 1 = 50 - 2 - 1 = 47$. Because $F_{.10,2,47}$ is not in Table A.7(a), we use the nearest value, $F_{.10,2,40} = 2.44$. The computed F^* exceeds this value, so we reject H_0 and conclude that at least one of these two independent variables is a significant predictor of investment amounts. We could have avoided any table look-up here by simply comparing the p-value for the F-test (nearly zero) to the significance level of $\alpha = .10$. Since the p-value is less than α, H_0 is rejected rather soundly and we arrive at the same conclusion.

THE t TESTS. Because we rejected H_0: $\beta_1 = \beta_2 = 0$, the next step is to examine the t tests to determine which of the two independent variables are useful predictors. The t value from Table A.5 is $t_{\alpha/2, n-k-1} = t_{.05,47} \approx 1.684$. We can either compare the t values to 1.684 or compare the corresponding p-values to $\alpha = .10$. The p-value for X_1 = economic index is $.935 > .10$, and the p-value for X_2 = income is approximately zero and is $< .10$. The large p-value (and small t statistic) for X_1, implies that, given the presence of X_2 in the model, X_1 does not contribute useful information to the prediction of the amount of an investment. Conversely, for X_2, the small p-value (and large t statistic of 20.06) indicates that the investor's income *is* an excellent predictor of the amount of an investment. It was the contribution of this variable and not of X_1 that produced the extremely large F-value obtained previously.

As we have seen, a quick glance at the computer output allows you to determine whether your model is useful as a whole and, furthermore, which variables are useful predictors. But beware—the analysis is not over! *Before you form your conclusions from this analysis and make critical decisions based on several tests of hypotheses, you need to be sure that none of the assumptions of the multiple linear regression model (discussed earlier) have been violated.* We will discuss this problem in the final section of this chapter, where we conclude the analysis by examining the sample *residuals*, $Y - \hat{Y}$.

The use of t tests allows you to determine the predictive contribution of each independent variable, provided you want to examine the contribution of *one* such variable while assuming that the remaining variables are included in the equation. The next section shows you how to extend this procedure to a situation in which you wish to determine the contribution of any *set* of predictor variables by using a single test.

EXERCISES 15.9–15.20

UNDERSTANDING THE MECHANICS

15.9 The following regression equation was calculated from a data set of 20 observations: $\hat{Y} = -1.0 + 2.5X_1 + 4.0X_2$. The value of MSR and MSE are .465 and .004, respectively. The standard deviations of the regression coefficients of X_1 and X_2 are .26 and .21, respectively.

a. Test the hypothesis that at least one of the regression coefficients is not equal to zero. Use a .05 significance level.

b. Test H_0: $\beta_1 = 0$ versus H_a: $\beta_1 \neq 0$. Use a .05 significance level.

c. Test H_0: $\beta_2 = 0$ versus H_a: $\beta_2 \neq 0$. Use a .05 significance level.

15.10 A researcher wished to test that a model with five independent variables contributed to the prediction of a certain dependent variable. From 51 observations, the researcher calculated SST to be equal to 215 and SSE to be equal to 180. Construct an ANOVA table.

APPLYING THE NEW CONCEPTS

15.11 Many chief executives (CEOs) have been under serious criticism from organized labor for the fat paychecks CEOs take home. Many of the CEOs have advocated sacrifice and leaner paychecks for large groups of employees of their companies. An experiment was set up in which 15 observations were taken on the variables:

Y = CEOs pay (in thousands of dollars)

X_1 = company's net profit (in millions of dollars)

X_2 = number of employees (in thousands)

A computer package gave the following sample statistics:

$$b_1 = .1336 \qquad b_2 = -.86$$

$$s_{b_1} = .0424 \qquad s_{b_2} = .39$$

a. Given that X_2 is in the model, does X_1 contribute to predicting the dependent variable at the .05 significance level?

b. Given that X_1 is in the model, does X_2 contribute to predicting the dependent variable at the .05 significance level?

15.12 Brown and Gilbert's law firm would like to predict the salary for a legal secretary based on years of college education (X_1), typing speed in words per minute (X_2), and years of experience (X_3). The following data were collected:

Y	X_1	X_2	X_3	Y	X_1	X_2	X_3
15,120	2	65	2	12,500	0	45	.5
12,500	1	45	2	15,800	2.5	60	2
26,000	3.5	85	9	19,600	1	70	3
19,000	0	55	11	21,800	3	75	6
16,000	4	85	1	12,400	0	60	.5
15,000	0	65	1	22,500	2	75	7

a. Using a computerized statistical package, determine the least squares prediction equation.

b. What is the value of the residual standard deviation?

c. Do the variables X_1, X_2, and X_3 contribute to predicting salaries at the .10 significance level?

d. Find a 90% confidence interval for β_1.

e. Test the null hypothesis that $\beta_1 = 0$ at the 10% significance level.

f. Interpret the results of the hypothesis test in part (e).

15.13 The total value of a baseball franchise is affected by several factors, including gate receipts and player costs. Typically high gate receipts make a franchise valuable, provided that its operating expenses are not excessive. High player costs affect a franchise's operating costs. However, to attract some of the best players, player costs may have to be high. The table below displays 10 baseball franchises along with gate receipts, player costs, and franchise value. All units are in millions of dollars.

Franchise	Gate Receipts	Player Costs	Franchise Value
New York Yankees	42.6	63.0	241
Baltimore Orioles	51.0	55.8	207
Atlanta Braves	40.1	55.4	199
Colorado Rockies	46.0	41.6	184
Los Angeles Dodgers	31.9	39.1	178
Cleveland Indians	48.0	51.4	175
Texas Rangers	35.5	42.8	174
Boston Red Sox	39.0	42.2	172
Chicago Cubs	28.3	32.2	165
Toronto Blue Jays	36.3	30.7	155

(Source: *Financial World,* "Franchise," June 17, 1997.)

a. Interpret the following computer printout. Interpret the confidence interval for the regression coefficient of player costs.

b. What is the predicted franchise value for the Los Angeles Dodgers?

SUMMARY OUTPUT FOR EXERCISE 15.13

Regression Statistics

Multiple R	0.906330628
R Square	0.821435207
Adjusted R Square	0.770416695
Standard Error	11.90501689
Observations	10

ANOVA

	df	SS	MS	F	Significance F
Regression	2	4563.894011	2281.947005	16.10072836	0.00240594
Residual	7	992.1059893	141.729427		
Total	9	5556			

	Coefficients	Standard Error	t Stat	P-value	Lower 95%	Upper 95%
Intercept	104.920706	22.52617818	4.657723346	0.002320706	51.6547969	158.1866
Gate Receipts	−0.76089757	0.744637315	−1.021836477	0.340868178	−2.5216838	0.999889
Player Costs	2.431005727	0.50393784	4.82401902	0.001912586	1.23938294	3.622629

15.14 The model $\hat{Y} = 3.2 + 6.1X_1 + 5.2X_2$ was calculated to fit 20 data points pertaining to the growth rate of a hog. The variable X_1 represents the daily food consumption of the hog and X_2 represents the age of the hog. If the standard deviation of the estimate of β_1 is 2.5, what is a 95% confidence interval for the parameter β_1?

15.15 The tensile strength (Y) of a paper product is related both to the amount of hardwood in the pulp (X_1) and to the amount of time the paper spent soaking in a preparatory solution prior to cutting (X_2). A quality engineer collected ten samples of the variables Y, X_1, and X_2. Complete the following ANOVA table to test the null hypothesis that the independent variables X_1 and X_2 are not useful predictors of the tensile strength of the paper product.

Source	df	SS	MS	F
Regression			582.83	
Error				
Total		1300.90		

15.16 Datamatics Equipment, a Seattle-based electronics firm, is interested in identifying variables in the manufacturing environment that have a linear relationship with the number of line shortages on the manufacturing floor. The sample data used in a regression analysis are as follows:

Week	Y	X_1	X_2	X_3	Week	Y	X_1	X_2	X_3
1	293	205	5.936	343	9	420	365	4.780	453
2	348	215	5.815	259	10	407	329	4.905	460
3	416	227	4.983	250	11	397	345	5.009	426
4	445	301	4.841	236	12	430	249	4.869	408
5	453	362	4.755	243	13	497	356	4.791	324
6	392	358	4.775	303	14	534	424	4.754	330
7	382	302	4.813	411	15	547	430	4.598	283
8	365	246	4.909	420					

where

Y = number of line shortages with back-order status for a given week

X_1 = number of delinquent purchase orders for a given week

X_2 = inventory level (in millions of dollars) for prior weeks

X_3 = number of purchased items for prior weeks

The least squares regression equation was found to be:

$$\hat{Y} = 710.9 + 0.4767X_1 - 70.90X_2 - 0.2525X_3$$

a. Does the complete model significantly contribute to predicting the dependent variable? Use a 10% significance level.

b. If s_{b_2} is 36.886, find a 95% confidence interval for β_2.

c. Interpret the results of the hypothesis test in part (a), and interpret the confidence interval in part (b).

15.17 The least squares equation $\hat{Y} = 3.4 + 1.2X_1 + 4.3X_2$ was obtained. The sample residuals of the 20 observations used in fitting the regression equation are:

4.1, –3.2, 1.5, 6.7, 6.4, 3.8, –4.2, –2.4, 1.6, –8.7, –3.1, 1.2, –5.1, 2.1, 0.6, 5.4, 3.4, –7.1, –6.2, 3.2

Given that the value of SST is 510, test the null hypothesis that the variables X_1 and X_2 do not contribute to predicting the variation in the dependent variable. Use a 5% significance level.

15.18 Money magazine picks selected stocks and lists their five-year projected earnings growth, their price/earnings (PE) ratio, and their target return. All units are in percentage. A rationale is also provided as to why each stock will outperform the market. For example, Cisco systems is cited as driving technological change as opposed to being driven by it. Cisco systems has a Research and Development (R&D) budget of more than 500 million.

Stock	Five-Year Earnings Growth	Price/ Earnings	Target Return
AirTouch Comm	38	41	57
Amgen	16	20	19
Cisco Systems	35	20	45
Coca-Cola	18	37	11
Colgate-Palmolive	13	22	15
CUC International	25	22	48
Enron	15	14	30
Hewlett-Packard	16	15	25
Dome Depot	25	23	12
Intel	20	16	14
Johnson & Johnson	15	24	13
Merck	14	23	24
Monsanto	17	23	14
Nike	18	17	43
Sun Microsystems	20	13	39

(Source: *Money*, "Our Picks for the 21st Century," June 1997, p. 60.)

a. Find the regression equation for predicting a stock's target return from its five-year earnings growth and PE ratio.

b. Given that PE is in the model, does a stock's five-year earnings growth contribute to the prediction of the target return? Use a 5% significance level.

c. Given that a stock's five-year earnings growth is in the model, does PE contribute to the prediction of the target return? Use a 5% significance level.

d. Find a 95% confidence interval for the regression coefficient of five-year earnings growth variable.

USING THE COMPUTER

15.19 [DATA SET EX15-19] *Variable description:*

CellularBill: Bill for monthly use of cellular phone
MinutesTalked: Total number of minutes that the cellular phone was used
MonthlyCharge: Fixed monthly charge for making phone calls.

The wireless phone market is taking a bigger and bigger share of the total phone market. Many phone companies are offering free off-peak calls. Many companies are launching PCS—short for personal communications services (*Business Week,* "Talk Keeps Getting Cheaper," June 16, 1997, p. 37). Suppose that a communications consultant wished to determine the relationship between the variables CellularBill and the independent variables MinutesTalked and MonthlyCharge.

a. Perform a regression analysis on these data and explain what conclusions the data support at a 5% significance level.

b. Construct a histogram of the residuals and comment on the shape of the distribution.

15.20 [DATA SET EX15-20] *Variable description:*

SalesDec98: Store sales for the month of Dec 1998
SalesDec97: Store sales for the month of Dec 1997
SalesNov98: Store sales for the month of Nov 1998

A management consulting agency is interested in the relationship between the sales of a chain of video stores for the current month of December 1999 with the sales from stores in December 1998 and November 1999. The agency randomly samples 35 stores and records the stores sales for these months in units of thousands of dollars. The agency believes that sales from the previous December may be a better predictor of sales than sales from the previous month.

a. Find the regression equation to predict SalesDec98 using SalesDec97 and SalesNov98. Find a 95% confidence interval for the regression coefficients. What explanation would you give to management?

b. Find the regression equation to predict SalesDec98 from SalesDec97. Find a 95% confidence interval for the regression coefficient of SalesDec97. Does this confidence interval change much from that found in part (a)?

15.3 DETERMINING THE PREDICTIVE ABILITY OF CERTAIN INDEPENDENT VARIABLES

We can extend the procedure we used to examine the contribution of each independent variable, one at a time, using a *t* test.

Assume that the personnel director of an accounting firm has developed a regression model to predict an individual's performance on the CPA exam. The multiple linear regression model contains eight independent variables, three of which (say, X_6, X_7, X_8) describe the physical attributes of each individual (say, height, weight, and age). Can all three of these variables be removed from the analysis without seriously affecting the predictive ability of the model?

To answer this question, we return to a statistic described in Chapter 14 that measures how well a model captures the variation in the values of the dependent variable.

COEFFICIENT OF DETERMINATION

The total variation of the sampled dependent variable is determined by

$$SST = \text{total sum of squares}$$

$$= SS_Y$$

$$= \Sigma(Y - \bar{Y})^2$$

$$= \Sigma Y^2 - \frac{(\Sigma Y)^2}{n}$$

where n = number of observations. To determine what percentage of this variation has been explained by the predictor variables in the regression equation, we determine the **coefficient of determination, R^2**.

$$R^2 = 1 - \frac{SSE}{SST} \qquad (15.14)$$

The range for R^2 is 0 to 1. If $R^2 = 1$, then 100% of the total variation has been explained, because in this case $SSE = \Sigma(Y - \hat{Y})^2 = 0$, and so $Y = \hat{Y}$ for each observation in the sample; that is, the model provides a *perfect predictor*. This does not occur in practice, but the main point is that a large value of R^2 is generally desirable for a regression application. It should be mentioned that $R^2 = 1$ whenever the number of observations (n) is equal to the number of estimated coefficients ($k + 1$). This does not mean that you have a "wonderful" model; rather, you have inadequate data. As a result, you need to guard against using too small a sample in your regression analysis. *A general rule of thumb is to use a sample containing at least three times as many (unique) observations as the number of predictor variables (k) in the model.*

H_0: **ALL β's = 0.**   A test statistic for testing H_0: all β's = 0 was introduced in equation 15.11, which used the ratio of two mean squares from the ANOVA table. Another way to calculate this F-value is to use

$$F = \frac{R^2/k}{(1-R^2)/(n-k-1)} \tag{15.15}$$

This version of the F statistic is used to answer the question, Is the value of R^2 significantly large? If H_0 is rejected, then the answer is yes, and so this group of predictor variables has at least some predictive ability for predicting Y.

The F-value computed in this way will be exactly the *same* as the one computed using $F = MSR/MSE$, except for possible rounding error (see Example 15.5).

Once again, remember that *statistical* significance does not always imply *practical* significance. A large value of R^2 (rejecting H_0) does not imply that precise prediction (practical significance) will follow. However, it does inform the researcher that these predictor variables, as a group, are associated with the dependent variable.

EXAMPLE 15.5

In Chapter 14, we determined that $X =$ income explained 71% of the total variation of the home sizes (Y) in the sample, since the computed value of r^2 was .711. What percentage is explained using all three predictors (income, family size, and years of education)?

SOLUTION

The coefficient of determination using X_1 only is .711. Using the Excel solution in Figure 15.4(a), the coefficient of determination using X_1, X_2, and X_3 is

$$R^2 = 1 - \frac{SSE}{SST}$$

$$= 1 - \frac{24.858}{262.4} = .905$$

Consequently, 90.5% of this variation has been explained using the three independent variables.

The F-value determined in Example 15.2 for testing H_0: $\beta_1 = \beta_2 = \beta_3 = 0$ can be duplicated using equation 15.15 because

$$F = \frac{.905/3}{(1-.905)/(10-3-1)} = \frac{.905/3}{.095/6} = 19.1 \text{ (as before)}$$

COMMENTS

1. In Example 15.5, notice that the value of R^2 *increased* when we went from using one independent variable to using three. As you add variables to your regression model, R^2 *never decreases*. However, the increase may not be a significant one. If adding 10 more predictor variables to your model causes R^2 to increase from .91 to .92, this is not a *significant* increase. Therefore, do not include these 10 variables; they clutter up your model and are likely to add spurious predictive ability to it.

2. Nearly every computer package (including Excel and MINITAB) will provide a value in the output, referred to as the **adjusted R^2**. This particular statistic does *not* necessarily increase as additional predictor variables are added to the model, and many researchers use this value to determine the predictive contribution of a variable added to the model. The adjusted R^2 is found by dividing SSE and SST by their respective degrees of freedom.

$$R^2 \text{ (adj)} = 1 - \frac{SSE/(n-k-1)}{SST/(n-1)} \tag{15.16}$$

Referring to Example 15.5 and Figure 15.4(a), the adjusted R^2 value is

$$R^2 \text{ (adj)} = 1 - \frac{24.858/6}{262.4/9} = 1 - \frac{4.143}{29.156} = .858$$

which is also given in cell F6 in Figure 15.4(a).

How can we tell if adding (or removing) a certain set of X variables causes a *significant* increase (or decrease) in R^2?

THE PARTIAL F-TEST

Consider the situation in which the personnel director is trying to determine whether to retain three variables (X_6 = height, X_7 = weight, X_8 = age) as predictors of a person's performance on a CPA exam. We know one thing—R^2 *will* be higher with these three variables included in the model. If we do not observe a *significant* increase, however, our advice would be to remove these variables from the analysis. To determine the extent of this increase, we use another F-test.

We define two models—one contains X_6, X_7, and X_8, and one does not:

Complete model: uses all predictor variables, including X_6, X_7, and X_8

Reduced model: uses the same predictor variables as the complete model except X_6, X_7, and X_8

Also, let

$$R_c^2 = \text{the value of } R^2 \text{ for the complete model}$$

$$R_r^2 = \text{the value of } R^2 \text{ for the reduced model}$$

Do X_6, X_7, and X_8 contribute to the prediction of Y? We will test

H_0: $\beta_6 = \beta_7 = \beta_8 = 0$ (they do not contribute)

H_a: at least one of the β's $\neq 0$ (at least one of them does contribute)

The test statistic here is

$$F = \frac{(R_c^2 - R_r^2)/v_1}{(1 - R_c^2)/v_2} \tag{15.17}$$

where v_1 = number of β's in H_0 and $v_2 = n - 1 - $ (number of X's in the complete model).

For this illustration, $v_1 = 3$ because there are three β's in H_0. Assuming that there are eight predictor variables in the complete model, then $v_2 = n - 1 - 8 = n - 9$. Here, n is the total number of observations (rows) in the data. This F-statistic measures the *partial* effect of these three variables; it is a **partial F-statistic.**

Equation 15.17 resembles the F-statistic given in equation 15.15, which we used to test H_0: all β's = 0. If all the β's are zero, then the reduced model consists of only a constant term, and the resulting R^2 will be zero; that is, $R_r^2 = 0$. Setting $R_r^2 = 0$ in equation 15.17 produces equation 15.15, where $v_1 = k$ and $v_2 = n - k - 1$.

These variables (as a group) contribute significantly if the computed partial F-value in equation 15.17 exceeds F_{α,v_1,v_2} from Table A.7.

EXAMPLE 15.6

The personnel director gathered data from 30 individuals using all eight independent variables. These data were entered into a computer, and a multiple linear regression analysis was performed. The resulting R^2 was .857.

Next, variables X_6, X_7, and X_8 were omitted, and a second regression analysis was performed. The resulting R^2 was .824. Do the variables X_6, X_7, and X_8 (height, weight, and age) appear to have any predictive ability? Use $\alpha = .10$.

SOLUTION

Here, $n = 30$ and

$$R_c^2 = .857 \text{ (complete model)}$$

$$R_r^2 = .824 \text{ (reduced model)}$$

Based on the previous discussion, the value of the partial F-statistic is

$$F^* = \frac{(.857 - .824)/3}{(1 - .857)/(30 - 1 - 8)} = \frac{.033/3}{.143/21} = 1.61$$

The procedure is to reject H_0: $\beta_6 = \beta_7 = \beta_8 = 0$ if $F^* > F_{.10,3,21} = 2.36$. The computed F-value does not exceed the table value, so we fail to reject H_0. We conclude that these variables should be removed from the analysis because including them in the model fails to produce a significantly larger R^2.

The partial F-test also can be used to determine the effect of adding a *single* variable to the model.

EXAMPLE 15.7

Using the real-estate data analyzed in Example 15.2, determine whether X_2 = family size contributes to the prediction of home size, given that X_1 = income and X_3 = years of education are included in the model. Use a significance level of $\alpha = .10$.

SOLUTION

We test the hypotheses

$$H_0: \beta_2 = 0 \qquad \text{(if } X_1 \text{ and } X_3 \text{ are included)}$$

$$H_a: \beta_2 \neq 0$$

The complete model uses X_1, X_2, and X_3. Using Example 15.5,

$$R_c^2 = .905$$

The reduced model uses only X_1 and X_3. Figure 15.8 contains the Excel solution using this model and the KGP Data Analysis regression procedure. When using the standard Excel regression analysis, the X variables must be in adjacent (contiguous) columns, whereas the KGP Data Analysis procedure does not have this restriction. To obtain the output in Figure 15.8, click on **KGP Data Analysis ➤ Regression.** You will then see the input form shown in Figure 15.7. When using this form, you *must* have labels in the first

FIGURE 15.7

Input screen using **KGP Data Analysis ➤ Regression.**

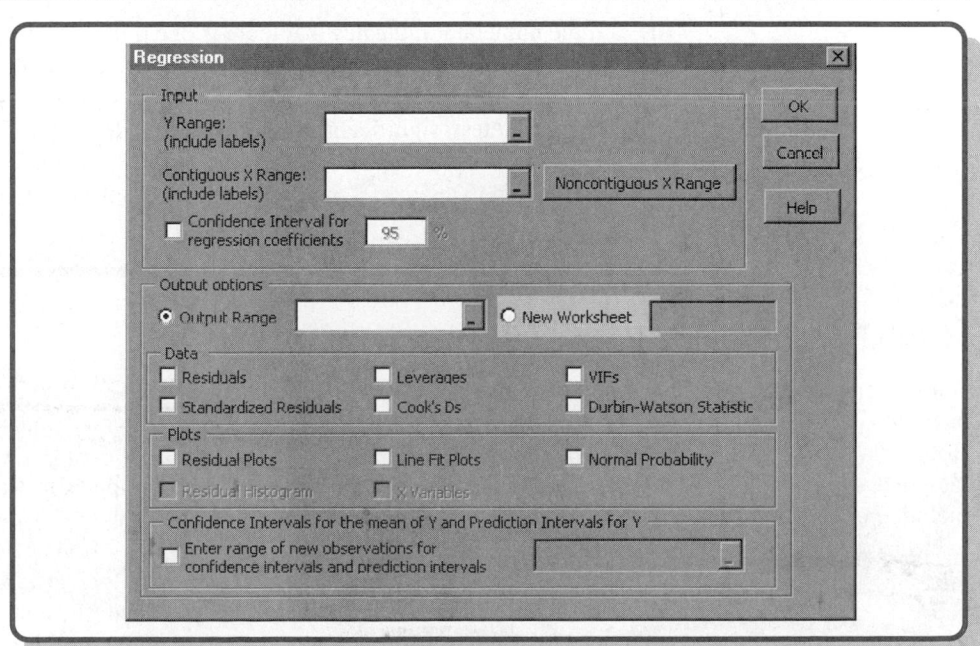

FIGURE 15.8

Excel output using $X_1 =$ income and $X_3 =$ years of education as predictors.

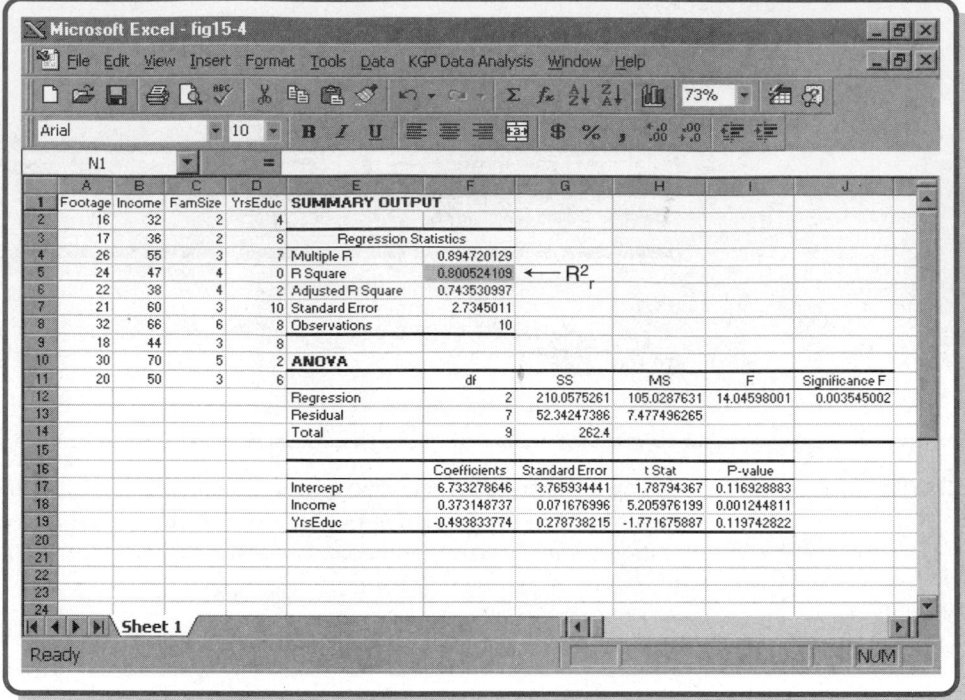

row for all of your variables. Enter "A1:A11" as the **Y Range,** which includes the label in cell A1. Next, click on **Noncontiguous X Range** and enter "2" as the number of X variables, "B1:B11" for **X Column 1,** and "D1:D11" for **X Column 2.** Finally, enter "E1" as the **Output Range.** Using the Figure 15.8 output, the coefficient of determination using the reduced model is

$$R_r^2 = .801$$

The value of the partial F-statistic is

$$F^* = \frac{(.905 - .801)/1}{(1 - .905)/(10 - 1 - 3)} = \frac{.104/1}{.095/6} = 6.6$$

The 1 in the numerator indicates that there is one β in H_0; subtracting the 3 in the denominator indicates that there are three X's in the complete model.

This value does exceed $F_{.10,1,6} = 3.78$, and so $X_2 =$ family size does (as suspected from the earlier t test) significantly improve the model's predictive ability when included with X_1 and X_3. In other words, there is a significant increase in R^2 (from .801 to .905) when X_2 is added to the model, and as a result, our conclusion is to retain this variable in the model.

COMMENTS

Both Example 15.7 and the t test for X_2 discussed on page 686 dealt with testing H_0: $\beta_2 = 0$ versus H_a: $\beta_2 \neq 0$. Both tests attempted to determine whether X_2 should be included as a predictor given that X_1 and X_3 were already included as predictor variables. Note: (1) the partial F-value = 6.6 = $(2.576)^2 = (t \text{ value})^2$, and (2) the p-value using the t test (.042) = the p-value using the F-test (not shown).

We can see that these tests are *identical:* they result in exactly the same p-value and the same conclusion. This result demonstrates that to determine the predictive ability of an individual independent variable, we can compute the partial F-statistic or the somewhat simpler t statistic. Some computer packages use the F-statistics to summarize the individual predictors, whereas others (such as Excel and MINITAB) use the t values to measure the influence of each predictor. You should use whatever is provided (the F statistic or t statistic) to measure the partial effect of each variable; both sets of statistics accomplish the same thing.

FIGURE 15.9

Excel scatter diagram of data and least squares trend line for inspection expense example.

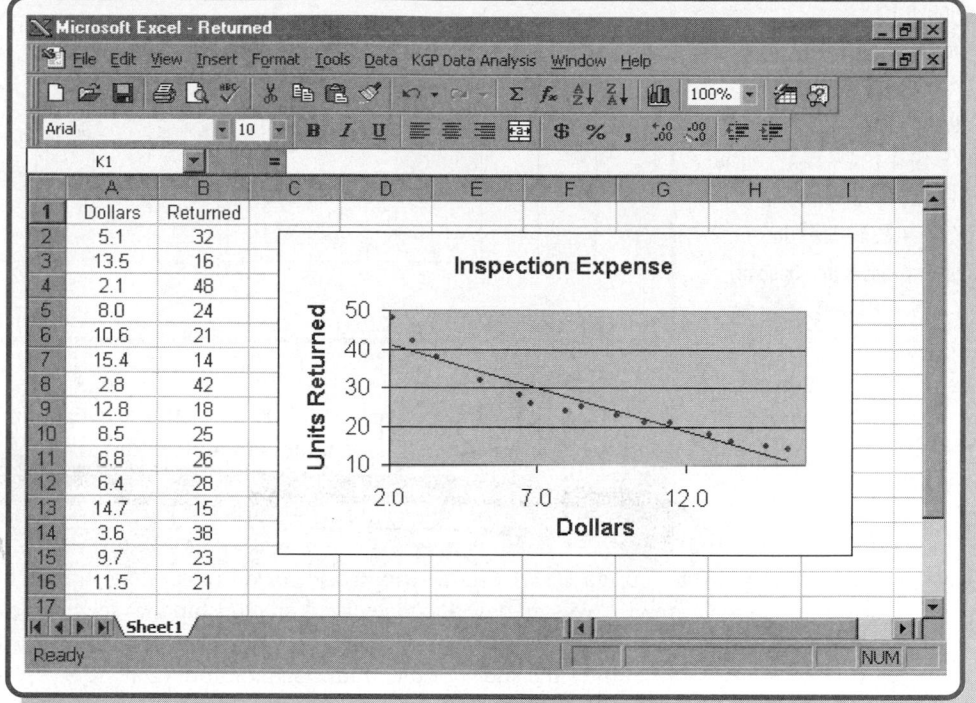

USING CURVILINEAR MODELS: POLYNOMIAL REGRESSION

Motormax produces electric motors for use in home furnaces. The company has formed a team of employees to examine the relationship between the dollars spent per week in inspecting finished products (X) and the number of motors produced during that week that were returned to the factory by the customer (Y). Motormax suspects that the number of returned motors will decrease as the amount spent on inspection increases but that after a certain point the decrease will slow down, that is, the number of returned motors will continue to decrease but at a slower rate. In other words, after spending a certain amount on inspecting finished product, they will reach a point where there will be little decrease in the number of returned motors, even though they spend a much larger amount on inspection.

The following data were gathered from company records covering 15 (nonconsecutive) weeks (the inspection expenditure (X) is in thousands of dollars).

Week	Units Returned (Y)	Inspection Expenditures (X)	Week	Units Returned (Y)	Inspection Expenditures (X)
1	32	5.1	9	25	8.5
2	16	13.5	10	26	6.8
3	48	2.1	11	28	6.4
4	24	8.0	12	15	14.7
5	21	10.6	13	38	3.6
6	14	15.4	14	23	9.7
7	42	2.8	15	21	11.5
8	18	12.8			

The sample values and scatter diagram are shown in Figure 15.9. This chart can be obtained using Excel's Chart Wizard and selecting the **XY (Scatter)** option. The data range is A1:B16. Once you have the plot, you can right click on any of the 15 plotted points and click on **Add Trendline ➤ Linear** to obtain the trend line in Figure 15.9. The last five values are above the trend line, and so it appears that Motormax seems to have a point—the number of returned motors does appear to level off after a certain amount of inspection expense.

FIGURE 15.10

Quadratic curves. (a) Graph of $Y = 34 - 12X + 2X^2$. In general, this is the shape of $Y = \beta_0 + \beta_1X + \beta_2X^2$, where $\beta_2 > 0$. (b) Graph of $Y = 6 + 12X - 2X^2$. In general, this is the shape of $Y = \beta_0 + \beta_1X + \beta_2X^2$, where $\beta_2 < 0$.

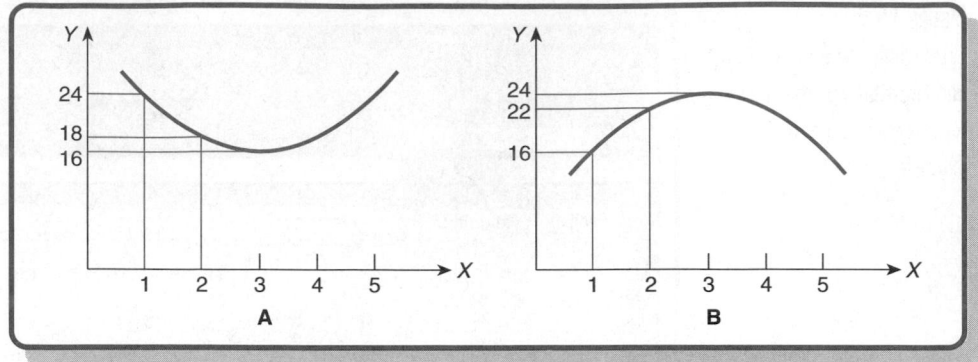

Does the simple linear model $Y = \beta_0 + \beta_1X + e$ capture the relationship between inspection expenditure (X) and number of units returned (Y)? Although Y does decrease as X increases here, the linear model does not capture the "slowing down" of Y for larger values of X. The least squares line (contained in Figure 15.9) overpredicts Y for the middle range of X but underpredicts Y for small or large values of X.

Figure 15.10 shows **quadratic curves** rather than straight lines. If we include X^2 in the model, we can describe the curved relationship that seems to exist between the number of returned motors and inspection expense. More specifically, the left half of Figure 15.10(a) resembles the shape of the scatter diagram in Figure 15.9.

Consider the model

$$Y = \beta_0 + \beta_1X + \beta_2X^2 + e \qquad (15.18)$$

Is this a linear regression model? At first glance, it would appear not to be. However, by the word *linear* we really mean that the model is **linear in the unknown β's,** not in X. In equation 15.18, there is no term such as β_1/β_2 or $\beta_1\beta_2$. So the model is linear in the β's, and this is a (multiple) linear regression application.

The model in equation 15.18 is a **curvilinear model** and is an example of **polynomial regression.** Such models are very useful when a particular independent variable and dependent variable exhibit a definite increasing and/or decreasing relationship that is nonlinear.

SOLVING FOR β_0, β_1, AND β_2.   Equation 15.18 represents a multiple regression model containing two predictors, namely, $X_1 = X$ and $X_2 = X^2$. The data for the model then are

Y	X_1	X_2
32	5.1	26.01 ($= 5.1^2$)
16	13.5	182.25 ($= 13.5^2$)
48	2.1	4.41
⋮	⋮	⋮
23	9.7	94.09
21	11.5	132.25

These data for Y, X_1, and X_2 are your input to the multiple linear regression computer program. You can simplify this task by letting the computer build the $X_2 = X^2$ column of data by squaring the entries in the $X_1 = X$ column.

EXAMPLE 15.8

Determine the Excel solution using the model $Y = \beta_0 + \beta_1X + \beta_2X^2 + e$ for the Motormax data shown in Figure 15.11. Also,

1. Predict the number of returned motors for a week in which Motormax spends $20,000 on inspecting final product.
2. What do the F- and t tests tell you about this model? Use $\alpha = .10$.

FIGURE 15.11
Excel solution to Example 15.8 using $Y = \beta_0 = \beta_1 X + \beta_2 X^2$.

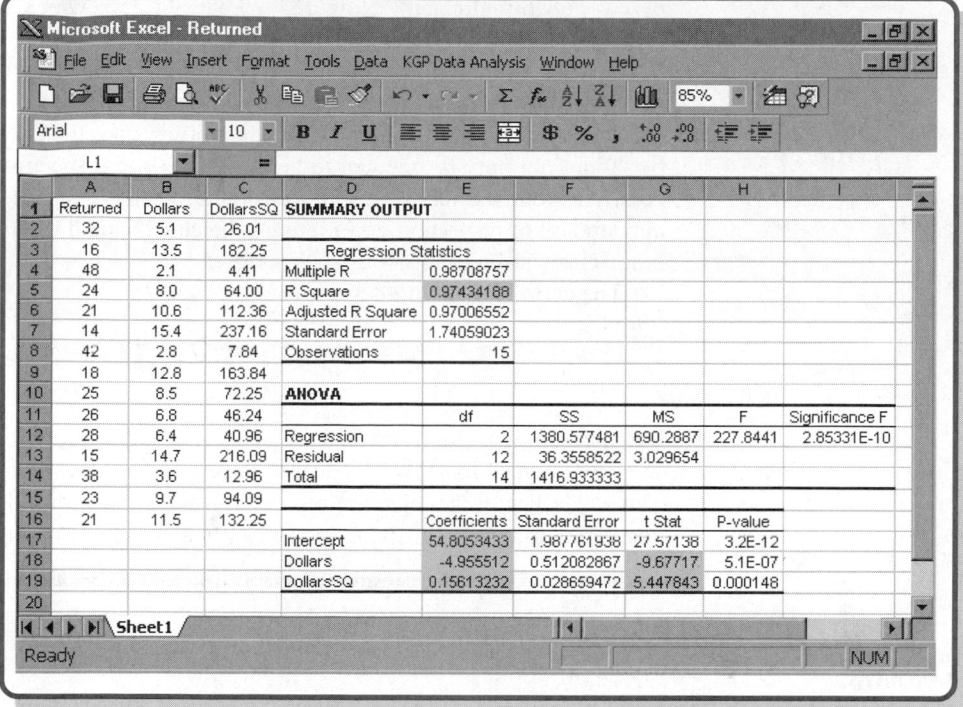

SOLUTION 1

To obtain the Excel solution in Figure 15.11, enter the data and labels in cells A1:B16 as shown. In cell C1, type "DollarsSQ" and in cell C2, type "=B2*B2". Drag cell C2 down through cell C16. This will produce the X^2 values in column C. Next, click on **Tools ➤ Data Analysis ➤ Regression,** and enter "A1:A16" as the **Input Y Range,** "B1:C16" as the **Input X Range,** and "D1" as the **Output Range.** Finally, click on the box alongside **Labels** (since there are labels in the first row) and on "OK."

The regression coefficients are in cells E17:E19 (highlighted). The predicted number returned for $X_1 = 20$ (thousand) is

$$\hat{Y} = 54.8 - 4.96(20) + .156(20)^2 = 18.0$$

That is, 18 units.

SOLUTION 2

We first examine the F-test. Our first test of hypothesis determines whether the overall model has predictive ability.

$$H_0: \beta_1 = \beta_2 = 0$$

$$H_a: \text{at least one of the } \beta\text{'s} \neq 0$$

Using the R^2 value from Figure 15.11 (in cell E5) and equation 15.15,

$$F^* = \frac{.97434 / 2}{.02566 / (15 - 2 - 1)} = \frac{.97434 / 2}{.02566 / 12} = 227.8$$

As we might have suspected, this model does have significant predictive ability; $F^* = 227.8$ exceeds $F_{\alpha, k, n-k-1} = F_{.10,2,12} = 2.81$ from Table A.7.

Now we want to look at the t tests (same as partial F tests). Here, we examine each variable in the model, namely, X and X^2. The t value from Table A.5 is $t_{.10,12} = 1.356$ for a one-tailed test. We want to determine first whether $X_1 = $ inspection expenditure should be included in the model. Increased expenditure should be associated with decreased returns, so β_1 should be less than zero. We will therefore use a one-tailed procedure to test $H_0: \beta_1 \geq 0$ versus $H_a: \beta_1 < 0$.

According to Figure 15.11, the computed t statistic is $t^* = b_1/$(standard deviation of b_1) $= -9.68$ (highlighted). Now, $t^* = -9.68 < -1.356$, which means that the expenditure variable should be retained as a predictor of returns.

Next, we want to determine whether $X_2 =$ (inspection expenditures)^2 contributes significantly to the prediction of number returned. We are asking whether including the *quadratic term* was necessary. If this model is the correct one, then according to Figure 15.10(a), β_2 should not only be unequal to zero but also, more specifically, should be greater than zero. This follows since if the number of returned motors does, in fact, level off after a certain amount of inspection expenditures, the curve should resemble the left half of the quadratic curve in Figure 15.10(a).

The appropriate hypotheses are

$$H_0: \beta_2 \leq 0$$

$$H_a: \beta_2 > 0$$

We reject H_0 if $t > t_{.10,12} = 1.356$.

From Figure 15.11, we see that $t^* = b_2/$(standard deviation of b_2) $= 5.45$ (highlighted). This value lies in the rejection region, so we conclude that $\beta_2 > 0$, which means that the quadratic term, X^2, contributes significantly and in the correct direction.

COMMENTS

There are three points you should note about the curvilinear model.

1. Curvilinear models often are used for situations in which the rate of increase or decrease in the dependent variable is not constant when plotted against a particular independent variable. The use of X^2 (and in some cases, X^3) in your model allows you to capture this nonlinear relationship between your variables.
2. There are other methods available for modeling a nonlinear relationship, including

$$Y = \beta_0 + \beta_1 \left(\frac{1}{X} \right) + \text{error}$$

and

$$Y = \beta_0 + \beta_1 e^{-x} + \text{error}$$

These models also are (simple, here) linear regressions; they are linear in the unknown parameters.

Unlike the quadratic model discussed previously, these models involve a **transformation** of the independent variable, X. When replacing X by the transformed X (such as $1/X$ or e^{-x}) in the model, one obtains many other curvilinear models that may better fit a set of sample data displaying a nonlinear pattern.

3. Avoid using the model $Y = \beta_0 + \beta_1 X + \beta_2 X^2 + e$ for values of X outside the range of data used in the analysis. Extrapolation is extremely dangerous when using this modeling technique. Consider Figure 15.10(a), and suppose that values of X between 1 and 3 were used to derive the estimate of β_0, β_1, and β_2. Figure 15.12 shows the results. For values of X larger than 3, the predicting equation will turn up, whereas the actual relationship will probably continue to level off. So this model works for interpolation (for values of X between 1 and 3, here) but is extremely unreliable for extrapolation.

FIGURE 15.12

Error resulting from extrapolation. See text and Figure 15.10(a).

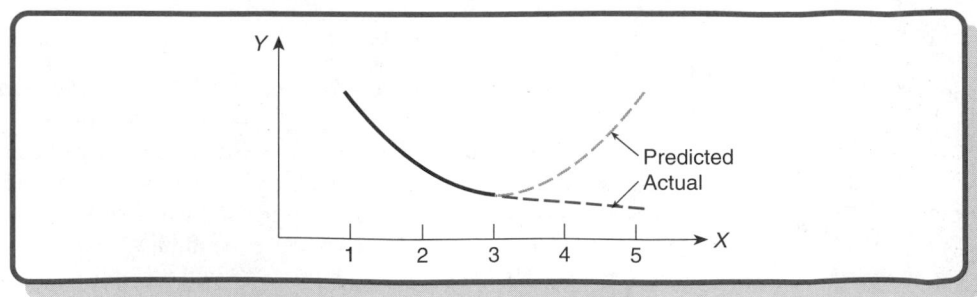

EXERCISES 15.21–15.30

UNDERSTANDING THE MECHANICS

15.21 The SSE and SST for a regression equation with three independent variables were found to be 26 and 250, respectively. The number of observations was 10.
  a. Calculate the R^2 value.
  b. Calculate the adjusted R^2 value.

15.22 A researcher collected data from 28 individuals. Seven independent variables were used to predict a dependent variable. The value of R^2 for this model was .87. When the variables X_1 and X_3 were omitted from the model, R^2 was .84. Do the variables X_1 and X_3 contribute to the prediction of the dependent variable? Use a .10 significance level.

APPLYING THE NEW CONCEPTS

15.23 The manager of the personnel department of a computer firm is interested in knowing the relationship between the pay raise (Y) given to an employee of the firm and the following variables: yearly performance evaluation (X_1), years with the company (X_2), and number of credit hours of computer courses that the employee has taken in college (X_3). After observing 50 employees under different values of X_1, X_2, and X_3, the manager wishes to test that X_2 and X_3 contribute to predicting the variation in pay raises. The coefficient of determination for the model involving just Y and X_1 is .71. The coefficient of determination for the model with X_1, X_2, and X_3 is .82. Do the additional independent variables contribute significantly to the model? Use a 5% significance level.

15.24 According to Professor David Douglas of the University of Arkansas in "The Changing Language Mix in Information Systems Curricula" in the *1998 Proceedings of Decison Sciences Institute,* the computer programming courses of COBOL, C, C++, Java, and Visual Basic will be among the dominant programming languages expected of future information systems graduates. Suppose that a career placement director wished to determine the relationship between a student's starting salary and two independent variables: a proficiency score in programming languages and a score measuring interpersonal skills. Data collected from 83 graduates of an information systems program yielded a coefficient of determination of .64.
  a. Using a significance level of 1%, what conclusion can you make about the contribution that these two prediction scores make to the prediction of starting salaries?
  b. What is the value of the adjusted R^2? How does this compare with the value of R^2?

15.25 The dean of the college of business at Fargo University would like to see whether several variables affect a student's grade point average. Thirty first-year students were randomly selected and data were collected on the following variables:

Y = grade point average for the first year

X_1 = average time spent per month at fraternity or sorority functions

X_2 = average time spent per month working part time

X_3 = total number of hours of coursework attempted

The SSE for the least squares line involving only Y and X_1 was found to be 5.21. The SSE for the complete model was found to be 4.31. The SST is 24.1. At the 5% significance level, test the null hypothesis that the independent variables X_2 and X_3 do not contribute to predicting the variation in Y given that X_1 is already in the model.

15.26 The market capitalization of major oil companies is partly driven by the company's oil/gas reserves. Royal Dutch Shell Group has by far the largest amount of oil/gas reserves, exceeding 19 billion barrel equivalents of oil and gas. This company also has the largest market capitalization. Suppose that an energy consultant wished to determine the relationship between an oil company's oil/gas reserves (in units of billions of barrel equivalents of oil and gas) and market capitalization (in units of billions of dollars).

Oil Company	Market Capitalization (Y)	Oil/Gas Reserves (X)	Square of Oil/ Gas Reserves (X^2)
Enron	13.1	1.2	1.44
Repsol	12.3	1.4	1.96
Phillips	12.0	2.5	6.25
Arco	13.8	4.2	17.64
Texaco	25.3	4.8	23.04
Amoco	31.1	6.8	46.24
Chevron	51.3	7.1	50.41
Mobil	53.2	7.4	54.76
Exxon	174.9	14.2	201.64
RD Shell Group	181.7	19.4	376.36

(Source: Adapted from *The Wall Street Journal,* "BP-Amoco Would Set New Standards," Aug. 13, 1998, p. A3.)

  a. The R^2 for the regression equation $\hat{Y} = -18.035 + 10.856X$ is 91.78%. Test that the variable oil/gas reserves contributes to the prediction of market capitalization. Use a 1% significance level.
  b. The R^2 for the regression equation $\hat{Y} = -9.045 + 7.857X + .150X^2$ is 92.29%. Test that the variable oil/gas reserves and the square of this variable contribute to the prediction of market capitalization. Use a 1% significance level.
  c. What is the adjusted value of R^2 for the model in parts (a) and (b)? Since the value of the adjusted R^2 does not increase in value for the model in part (b), what conclusion can you make about the appropriateness of adding the square term to the model?

15.27 Professor Xenophon Koufteros of The University of Texas at El Paso and Professors Mark Vonderembse and William Doll of The University of Toledo have performed a large-scale study to understand the impact that manufacturing practices have on throughput time reduction. A random sample of 244 firms was used to collect data on throughput time (TT) as well as on pull production (PP) and quality improvement effort (QI). For the regression equation predicting TT using PP and QI, the MSE was .85851 and the total sum of squares was 242.67012. Use the table below to determine which independent variables should be included in the model assuming a 5% significance level. What is the value of R^2? How does this compare to the value of the adjusted R^2?

(Source: *1998 Proceedings of the Decision Sciences Institute,* "How to Cut Manufacturing Throughput Time," p. 1433–35.)

Variable	Coefficient	Standard Deviation
Pull Production (PP)	−.1268	.0586
Quality Improvement Effort (QI)	−.291539	.2061

15.28 An economist would like to examine the relationship between personal savings and the following independent variables:

$$X_1 = \text{total personal income}$$

$$X_2 = \text{yield on U.S. Government securities}$$

$$X_3 = \text{consumer price index}$$

The following data were collected for 14 randomly selected months:

Y	X_1	X_2	X_3	Y	X_1	X_2	X_3
80.2	2077.2	12.036	233.2	107.4	2179.4	9.259	249.4
91.6	2086.4	12.814	236.4	116.8	2205.7	10.321	252.7
87.4	2101.0	15.526	239.8	102.1	2234.3	11.580	253.9
104.9	2102.1	14.003	242.5	97.9	2257.6	13.888	256.2
116.2	2114.1	9.150	244.9	93.3	2276.6	15.661	258.4
109.1	2127.1	6.995	247.6	83.6	2300.7	14.724	260.5
110.1	2161.2	8.126	247.8	91.0	2318.2	14.905	263.2

a. Using a computerized statistical package, determine the least squares equation for these data.

b. Use only the variables X_1 and X_2. What is the new prediction equation?

c. Does the variable X_3 contribute to predicting the variation in personal savings, given that X_1 and X_2 are in the model? Use a 10% significance level.

Using the Computer

15.29 **[DATA SET EX15-29]** *Variable description:*

CompPerf: Computer performance
CompEffic: Self-perception of computer self-efficacy
Loyalty: Self-perception of company loyalty
CompanyYrs: Number of years with the company

Professor Bassam Hasan of Macon State College and Professor Brian Reithel of University of Mississippi have investigated computer performance with measures of self-efficacy. They employ social cognitive theory (SCT) to develop a model to predict computer performance. Self-efficacy refers to "people's judgements of their capabilities to organize and execute courses of action required to attain designated types of performance," according to their study in "Performance In Computer Training: Identifying Critical Factors," in the *1998 Proceedings of Decison Sciences Institute.* Suppose that a random sample of 25 employees working in the Information Technology Department of a corporation are sampled. The dependent variable is computer performance, and the independent variables are measures of computer self-efficacy, company loyalty, and number of years with the company. The variables computer self-efficacy and loyalty are measured on a scale from 1 to 7, and computer performance is a score from 1 to 100.

a. Find the regression equation predicting CompPerf using CompEffic. Comment on the fit of the regression line to the data.

b. Find the regression equation predicting CompPerf using CompEffic, Loyalty, and CompanyYrs. Using a 5% significance level, do the variables Loyalty and CompanyYrs contribute to the prediction of CompPerf, given that CompEffic is in the model?

15.30 **[DATA SET EX15-30]** *Variable description:*

NintendoExpend: Amount of money spent by a family on Nintendo games
GamesExpend: Amount of money spent by a family on computer games other than Nintendo
TimeOwnGames: Length of time that a family has owned computer games

Nintendo of Canada Ltd. reported an 11% drop in hardware sales after six strong years of double-digit increases, according to the *Toronto Star* ("Nintendo Sales Miss Intended Mark," Jan. 5, 1994, p. D2). The company claims that more than one in three Canadian families own a Nintendo system. Suppose that an analyst wished to determine the relationship between the amount of money spent on Nintendo games (NintendoExpend) and the independent variables GamesExpend and TimeOwnGames. A random sample of 35 Canadian families who have purchased Nintendo games was obtained.

a. Do the variables GamesExpend and TimeOwnGames contribute to the prediction of NintendoExpend? Use a 5% significance level.

b. Take the natural logarithm of NintendoExpend and use this variable as the dependent variable in part (a). Do you believe that this model explains the relationship between the dependent and independent variables better than in part (a)?

15.4 The Problem of Multicollinearity

Another possible title for this section is: What do the individual b_i's tell you? We discuss one of the common problems in the use (or misuse) of multiple linear regression—namely, trying to extract more information from the results than they actually contain.

We examine the validity of such statements as: Because $b_1 = 10$, increasing X_1 by 1 while *holding X_2 constant* will result in an increase of 10 in Y.

Assume that a sample of 10 employees at Bellaire Industries was examined in an effort to determine the ability of age (X_1) and years of experience (X_2) to predict an employee's salary (Y). The following data were obtained:

Employee	Y (Salary)	X_1 (Age)	X_2 (Years of Experience)
1	62	52	33
2	45	47	21
3	55	38	14
4	38	25	3
5	52	44	18
6	70	55	30
7	41	36	8
8	48	40	15
9	43	32	7
10	58	50	27

First, we can ask how well X_1 (age) predicts Y (salary).

An Excel solution using the model $Y = \beta_0 + \beta_1 \cdot (age) + e$ is shown in Figure 15.13. Notice the computed t value. Now, $k = 1$ because this model considers only one independent variable, so the tabulated value for comparison (using $\alpha = .10$) is $t_{\alpha/2, n-k-1} = t_{.05, 10-1-1} = t_{.05,8} = 1.860$. The value of $t^* = 4.60$ is considerably larger than 1.86, so X_1 (age) is an excellent predictor of Y (salary).

What is the correlation between X_1 and Y? It seems reasonable that it would be quite large, because age has been shown to be a good predictor. This correlation is highlighted in cell G3 in Figure 15.13, and its value is .852. To obtain the array of correlations in cells G3, G4 and H4, click on **Tools ➤ Data Analysis ➤ Correlation** and enter "A1:C11" as the **Input Range** and "F1" as the **Output Range.** Be sure to click on the box alongside **Labels** (there are labels in the first row). Since the correlation between these two variables is .852, we conclude that there is a *positive* relationship between age and salary, as we would expect.

Next, we determine how well X_2 (years of experience) predicts Y (salary). The solution using $Y = \beta_0 + \beta_1 \cdot (years\ of\ experience) + e$ is shown in Figure 15.14. Once again, the computed t value $= t^* = 5.21$ is much larger than $t_{.05,8} = 1.860$, and the correlation between these two variables (highlighted in cell G4) is .879. This result is not surprising; we might expect people with more years of experience to have higher salaries. Consequently, a significant positive relationship appears to exist between these two variables.

FIGURE 15.13
Excel solution to
$\hat{Y} = b_0 + b_1 \cdot (age)$.
Correlation between salary
and age is in cell G3.

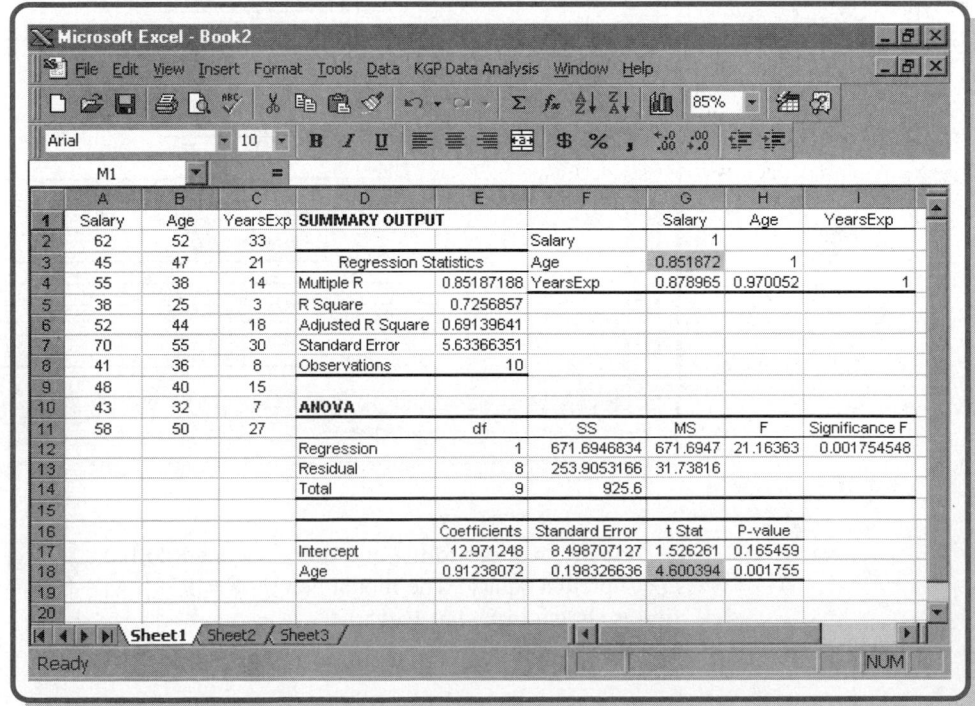

FIGURE 15.14

Excel solution to $\hat{Y} = b_0 + b_1 \cdot$ (years of experience). Correlation between salary and years of experience is in cell G4.

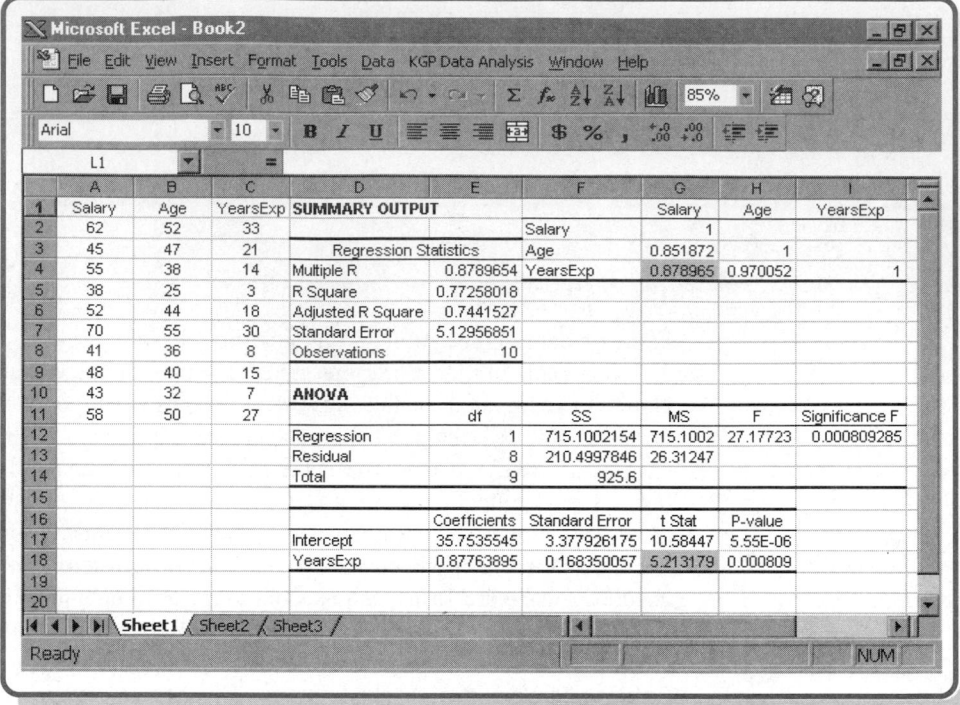

FIGURE 15.15

Excel solution to $\hat{Y} = b_0 + b_1 \cdot (\text{age}) + b_2 \cdot$ (years of experience). Correlation between age (X_1) and years of experience (X_2) is in cell H4.

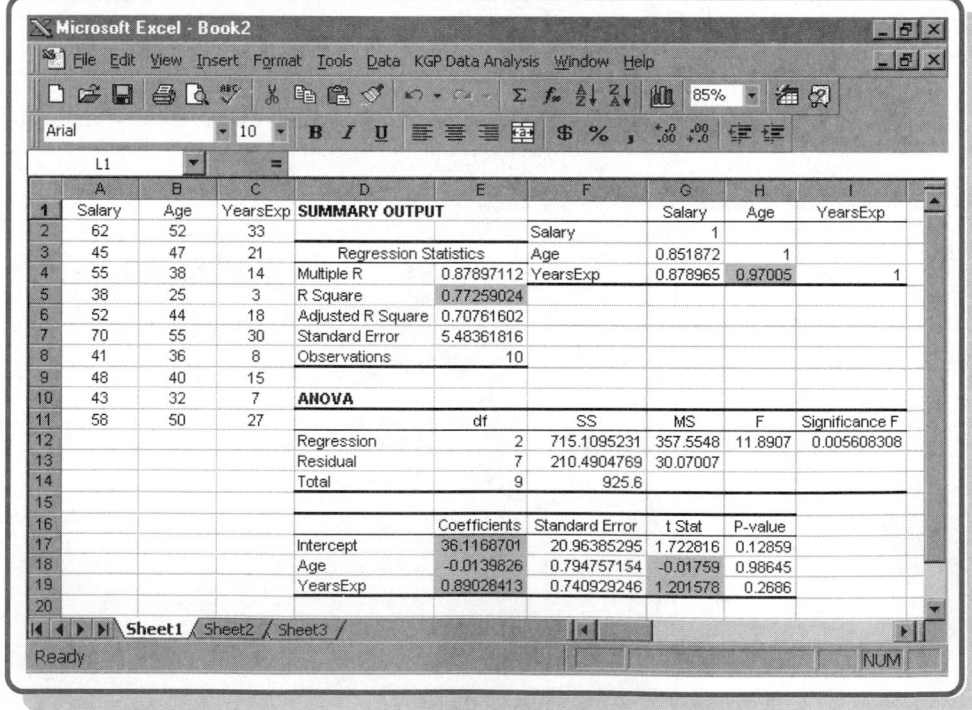

Finally, we turn to the question, how well do both X_1 (age) and X_2 (years of experience) predict salary? The model here is $Y = \beta_0 + \beta_1 X_1 + \beta_2 X_2 + e$. The least squares solution is shown in Figure 15.15.

$$\hat{Y} = 36.1 - .014 X_1 + .890 X_2$$

A few seemingly bizarre things show up here.

The coefficient of X_1 is $b_1 = -.014$. This result would appear to indicate that larger values of X_1 (older people) produce smaller salaries. But we know from our first analysis that the *opposite* is true. We would have expected a *positive* value of b_1 here, and so the coefficient of X_1 appears to have the wrong sign.

The small t values also are puzzling. The value of the F-statistic (using Figure 15.15) is

$$F^* = \frac{R^2/2}{(1-R^2)/(10-1-2)} = \frac{.7726/2}{.2274/7} = 11.89$$

This value is also contained in the ANOVA table, where

$$F^* = \frac{MSR}{MSE} = \frac{357.55}{30.07} = 11.89$$

Using $\alpha = .10$, this value is much larger than $F_{.10,2,7} = 3.26$, and so the model does provide a very good predictor of Y. The coefficient of determination is $R^2 = .77$; these two predictor variables explain 77% of the total variation in the ten salary values.

The t values are very small; both are smaller in absolute value than $t_{\alpha/2,n-k-1} = t_{.05,10-2-1} = t_{.05,7} = 1.895$. Does this imply that both predictors are weak and should be removed from the model? Certainly not, as our previous analysis made clear.

This example demonstrates the problem of **multicollinearity.** In multiple regression models, it is desirable for each independent variable, X, to be highly correlated with Y, but it is *not* desirable for the X's to be highly correlated *with each other.* In business applications of multiple linear regression, the independent variables typically have a certain amount of pairwise correlation (usually positive). Extremely high correlation between any pair of variables can cause a variety of problems, as we will show.

The (sample) correlation between X_1 and X_2 is

$$r = \frac{\sum X_1 X_2 - (\sum X_1)(\sum X_2)/n}{\sqrt{\sum X_1^2 - (\sum X_1)^2/n}\ \sqrt{\sum X_2^2 - (\sum X_2)^2/n}}$$

This value, using the highlighted correlation in Figure 15.15, is $r = .970$. Notice in the data set that nearly every time X_1 increases, so does X_2; X_1 and X_2 are highly correlated. As a result, these data contain a great deal of multicollinearity.

Implications

First of all, the correlation of X_1 and X_2 explains the small t values. Remember that each t value describes the contribution of that particular independent variable *after* all other independent variables have been included in the model. X_1 is very nearly a linear function of X_2 (as evidenced by $r = .970$), so it contributes very little to the prediction of Y, given that X_2 is in the model. The same argument applies to X_2. This means that neither X_1 nor X_2 is a strong predictor given that the other variable is included—not that each one is a weak predictor by itself.

The second implication of the multicollinearity is that the situation in which X_1 increases by 1 while X_2 remains constant never occurred in the sample data—as X_1 increased by 1, X_2 always changed also, because X_1 and X_2 are highly correlated.

Finally, the sample coefficients (b_1 and b_2) of our independent variables have very large variances. If we took another sample from this population, the values of b_1 and b_2 probably would change dramatically—this is not a good situation. In fact, as this example has demonstrated, these coefficients can even have the "wrong" sign, a sign different from that obtained when regressing X_1 or X_2 alone on Y.

Detecting Multicollinearity: Variance Inflation Factors

Whenever you perform a multiple regression analysis, it is always a good idea to examine the pairwise correlations between all of your variables, including the dependent variable. In this way, you can often detect two variables that are contributing to the multicollinearity problem.

These correlations can be obtained using a single command with most computer packages. The Excel procedure to generate a table (often called a **correlation matrix**) of pairwise correlations was discussed in the creation of Figure 15.13. This output indicates that the correlation between Y and X_1 is .852, that between Y and X_2 is .879, and that between X_1 and X_2 is .970. The high correlation between X_1 and X_2 is the reason multicollinearity exists for this illustration.

Since the correlation of any variable with itself is 1, this particular correlation matrix can be written as

$$
\begin{array}{c c}
 & \begin{array}{ccc} Y & X_1 & X_2 \end{array} \\
\begin{array}{c} Y \\ X_1 \\ X_2 \end{array} &
\left[\begin{array}{ccc}
1.0 & .852 & .879 \\
.852 & 1.0 & .970 \\
.879 & .970 & 1.0
\end{array} \right]
\end{array}
$$

An examination of pairwise correlations is not a foolproof method of detecting multicollinearity problems, since a particular independent variable may be nearly a linear combination of several other independent variables, but still not be highly correlated pairwise with any of them. Consequently, an examination of the correlation matrix would fail to detect this relationship.

Suppose a regression analysis contains 10 predictor variables and that variable X_6 is nearly a linear combination of X_3, X_5, and X_9. Consequently,

$$X_6 \approx a_0 + a_1 X_3 + a_2 X_5 + a_3 X_9$$

for some set of constants a_0, a_1, a_2, and a_3. How can we detect if such a relationship exists? This is accomplished very simply, by treating X_6 as a dependent variable and using variables X_3, X_5, and X_9 as independent variables in a regression analysis. If this relationship is present in the data, the resulting R^2 will be very high. This large value of R^2 is your warning that this independent variable is contributing to the multicollinearity problem.

Fortunately, it is not necessary to examine each independent variable in this way. Most computer packages will compute a statistic referred to as a **variance inflation factor** for each independent variable. The variance inflation factor for variable X_j is defined as

$$\text{VIF}_j = \frac{1}{1 - R_j^2} \tag{15.19}$$

where R_j^2 is the coefficient of determination obtained by regressing X_j on the remaining $k - 1$ independent variables. If R_j^2 is large (close to 1.0), then VIF_j will be large. *A commonly used procedure here is to conclude that severe multicollinearity exists in the sample data if the maximum VIF_j is larger than 10.*

The Excel regression procedure does not provide the variance inflation factors, but these values are available when using **KGP Data Analysis ➤ Regression.** Using this on the previous illustration with age and years of experience as predictors of salary (see Figure 15.15), enter "A1:A11" in the **Y Range** box and "B1:C11" as the **Contiguous X Range.** These ranges *must* include labels in the first row. Next, enter "D1" as the **Output Range** and be sure to click on the box alongside **VIFs.** The resulting output is shown in Figure 15.16, where the VIFs (both equal to 16.9) are highlighted in cells K18 and K19. Note that the VIFs for both X_1 and X_2 are equal (such is always the case when using only two predictor variables), and both exceed 10. In Figure 15.15, we saw that the correlation between X_1 and X_2 is .970. When regressing X_1 on X_2 (or vice versa), the resulting R^2 is the square of this correlation; that is, $R_1^2 = R_2^2 = (.970)^2 = .941$. The resulting values for VIF_1 and VIF_2 are

$$\text{VIF}_1 = \text{VIF}_2 = \frac{1}{1 - .941} = 16.9$$

which agree with the Excel results. The easiest way out of this dilemma is to remove one of these predictor variables from the model. The best procedure here would be to retain $X_2 =$ years of experience, because it has the highest correlation with Y.

FIGURE 15.16

Excel solution to $\hat{Y} = b_0 + b_1 \cdot (\text{age}) + b_2 \cdot (\text{years of experience})$ using KGP Data Analysis regression procedure, including calculation of variance inflation factors.

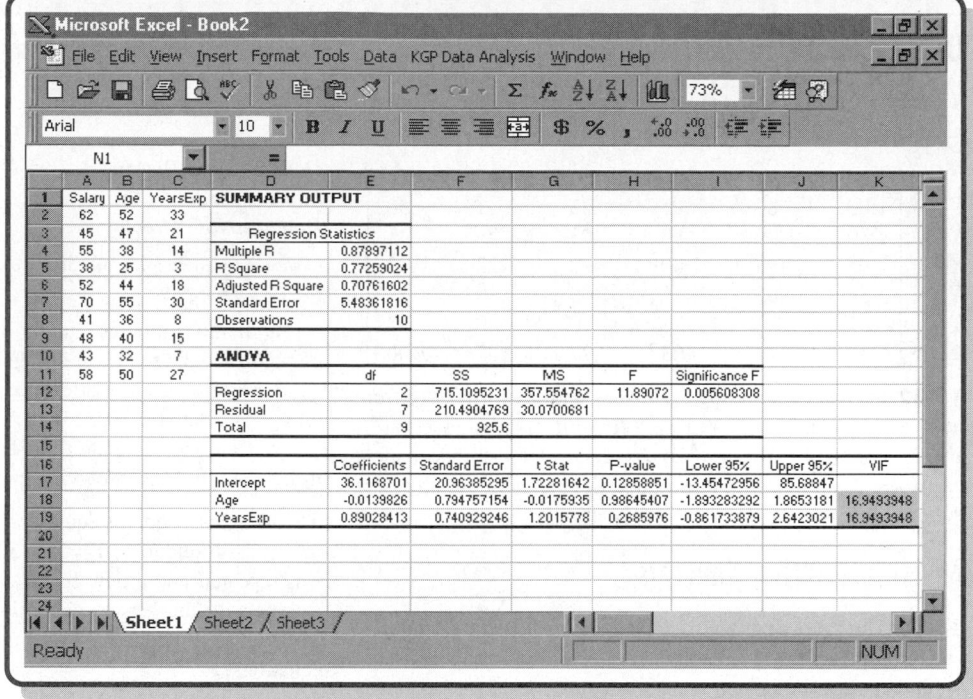

A FINAL LOOK AT MULTICOLLINEARITY

Another method of eliminating correlated predictor variables is to use a **stepwise** selection procedure. This technique of selecting the variables to be used in a multiple linear regression equation is discussed in the next section. Essentially, it selects variables one at a time and generally (although not always) does not insert into the regression equation a variable that is highly correlated with a variable already in the equation. In the previous example, a stepwise procedure would have selected variable X_2 (the single best predictor of Y) and then informed the user that X_1 did not significantly improve the prediction of Y, given that X_2 was already included in the prediction equation.

Other, more advanced methods of detecting and treating the multicollinearity problem are beyond the scope of this text. One of the more popular procedures is *ridge regression.**

We have seen that the problem of multicollinearity enters into our regression analysis when an independent variable is highly correlated with one or more other independent variables. Multicollinearity produces inflated regression coefficients that can even have the wrong sign. Also, the resulting t statistics can be small, making it difficult to determine the predictive ability of an individual variable. Therefore, $b_1, b_2, \ldots$ tell us nothing about the partial effect of each variable, unless we can demonstrate that there is no correlation among our predictor variables. In business applications, correlation (in particular, *positive* correlation) among the independent variables is far from unusual.

As a final note, care should be taken in the selection of a model not to include variables that will be likely to produce multicollinearity. The detection and correction of the multicollinearity problem is often difficult to accomplish, and the methods discussed in this section are open to debate. The treatments of multicollinearity discussed so far are highly data dependent; that is, a new set of data could very well produce different results. Also, examining pairwise correlations may well miss the presence of multicollinearity, since multicollinearity will exist when one predictor variable is nearly a linear combination of two or more predictor variables and is not highly correlated with either of them. *In short, there is no easy way out of the multicollinearity problem.*

---

* For an excellent discussion of this topic, see J. Neter, M. Kutner, and C. Nachtsheim, *Applied Linear Regression Models,* 3rd ed. (Homewood, Ill.: Richard D. Irwin, 1996).

EXERCISES 15.31–15.38

UNDERSTANDING THE MECHANICS

15.31 Which independent variables appear to contribute to high multicollinearity? Use the following correlation matrix.

	Y	X_1	X_2	X_3	X_4	X_5
Y	1.00	.80	.95	.32	.41	.50
X_1	.80	1.00	.98	.03	.25	.41
X_2	.95	.98	1.00	.12	.22	.03
X_3	.32	.03	.12	1.00	.10	.27
X_4	.41	.25	.22	.10	1.00	.97
X_5	.50	.41	.03	.27	.97	1.00

15.32 R^2 from regressing X_1 on X_2 and X_3 is .93. R^2 from regressing X_2 on X_1 and X_3 is .89. R^2 from regressing X_3 on X_1 and X_2 is .80. What is the VIF for each of these independent variables, assuming that these three independent variables are the only variables in a regression equation?

APPLYING THE NEW CONCEPTS

15.33 The following table displays the top 10 prime-time television programs in April 1998 along with their rating and share of the market (both in units of percentage). Market share is defined as the percentage of all switched-on sets turned to the show in question.

Program Name	Rating	Share of Market
E.R.	30.6	33
Seinfeld	18.9	23
CBS Sunday movie,		
The Echo of Thunder	16.4	26
Veronica's Closet	15.9	24
Friends	15.3	26
Just Shoot Me	14.4	24
60 Minutes	12.5	23
Dateline NBC Tuesday	12.0	21
Law and Order	11.9	20
Dateline NBC Monday	11.5	20

(Source: Adapted from *The Wall Street Journal*, "Top 10 Prime-Time Programs," Apr. 23, 1998, p. A16.)

a. In the computer printout, with share of market regressed on rating and the square of rating, is multicollinearity a concern?

b. From the correlation between rating and the square of rating, calculate the VIF for each of the independent variables.

c. Can one calculate the VIFs from the correlation values if there are more than two independent variables?

15.34 A least squares equation fit to a set of data for an experiment was found to be $\hat{Y} = 30 - 501X_1 + 300X_2$. The experiment was repeated and a new set of data from the same population was fit with the least squares line $\hat{Y} = -20 + 309X_1 - 151X_2$. Is there any explanation for these two different prediction equations?

15.35 The following set of data was collected:

Y	X_1	X_2	Y	X_1	X_2
2.02	1.01	.97	4.20	1.61	2.62
7.95	2.34	5.50	2.62	1.19	1.42
2.61	1.21	1.49	.07	.07	.01
.31	.23	.05	1.53	.80	.67
1.63	.85	.72	6.19	2.03	4.17

SUMMARY OUTPUT FOR EXERCISE 15.33

Regression Statistics	
Multiple R	0.91045
R Square	0.82891
Adjusted R Square	0.78003
Standard Error	1.79618
Observations	10

ANOVA

	df	SS	MS	F	Significance F
Regression	2	109.41628	54.70814	16.95721	0.00207
Residual	7	22.58372	3.22625		
Total	9	132			

	Coefficients	Standard Error	t Stat	P-value	Lower 95%	Upper 95%
Intercept	11.64160	7.30247	1.59420	0.15492	-5.62598	28.90919
Rating	0.89455	0.77799	1.14982	0.28798	-0.94511	2.73421
Rating Squared	-0.00671	0.01838	-0.36531	0.72567	-0.05018	0.03675

Correlation between Rating and Rating Squared	0.99077

a. Construct the correlation matrix for the variables. Does multicollinearity appear to be a problem?

b. Find the coefficient of determination for the model using only X_1. Then find it using only X_2.

c. The coefficient of determination for the complete model is .9996. Does it appear that both variables, X_1 and X_2, should stay in the model?

15.36 Consider the following set of data for 12 emerging growth-oriented companies. Y represents the growth rate of a company for the current year, X_1 represents the growth rate of the company for the previous year, and X_2 represents the percent of the market that does not use the company's product or a similar product. All values are percentages.

Y	X_1	X_2	Y	X_1	X_2
20	10	30	30	15	60
24	12	35	36	42	38
18	15	25	47	45	40
33	30	40	35	32	32
27	19	32	28	24	31
20	24	20	32	20	50

a. Construct the correlation matrix for the variables. Does multicollinearity appear to be a problem?

b. Find the coefficient of determination for the model with only X_1 included in the model.

c. Find the coefficient of determination for the model with only X_2 in the model.

d. The coefficient of determination for the complete model is .896. Does it appear from observing the values of the coefficient of determination in parts (a) and (b) that both variables X_1 and X_2 should stay in the model?

USING THE COMPUTER

15.37 [DATA SET EX15-37] *Variable description:*

StockPercent: Percentage of portfolio in stocks
BondPercent: Percentage of portfolio in bonds
Performance: Percentage return of the portfolio six months later

During the 11 years that the *Wall Street Journal* has tracked asset-allocation advice offered by major investment firms, strategists have recommended holding an average of 12% cash. In 1998, the average was only 6% ("The Wisdom of Wall Street Is Decidedly Short on Cash," Apr. 30, 1998, p. C1). Suppose that 50 financial strategists were asked what percentage of their portfolio should be in stocks and bonds. The performance of the corresponding portfolio was recorded six months later.

a. Regress Performance on StockPercent and BondPercent. Does the model contribute to the prediction of Performance using a 5% significance level?

b. Does each of the independent variables contribute to the prediction of Performance assuming the other independent variable is included in the model? Use a 5% significance level.

c. Find the VIF of StockPercent and BondPercent. Do you believe that there is a multicollinearity problem within the data?

15.38 [DATA SET 15-38] *Variable description:*

SalesMonth: Sales of discount department store during the previous month
AgeStore: Age of the store
ExperManager: Years of experience of store manager

Many of the newly opened discount department stores sell more merchandise than similar older stores. However, over time these stores' sales tend to level off. To understand the relationship between the sales of a discount department store and the age of a store, a manager randomly selected 35 stores with approximately the same square footage. The sales of the previous month and the age of the store are recorded as variables SalesMonth (in thousands of dollars) and AgeStore (in years). A regional executive is interested in the relationship between SalesMonth and the independent variables AgeStore and ExperManager (years of experience of store manager).

a. Construct the model in which the regional executive is interested. Comment on the contribution of the independent variables used to predict SalesMonth assuming a significance level of 5%.

b. Add the squares of the variables AgeStore and ExperManager to the model in part (a) and comment on the appropriateness of adding these terms.

c. Find the correlations between the independent variables in part (b). What conclusion can you make about possible problems with multicollinearity?

d. Find the VIFs for the independent variables in part (b). What conclusion can you make about the level of multicollinearity?

15.5 DUMMY VARIABLES AND ADDITIONAL TOPICS IN MULTIPLE LINEAR REGRESSION

The use of **dummy,** or **indicator,** variables in a regression analysis allows you to include *qualitative* variables in the model. For example, if you wanted to include an employee's gender as a predictor variable in a regression model, define

$$X_1 = \begin{cases} 1 & \text{if female} \\ 0 & \text{if male} \end{cases}$$

Note that the choice of which gender is assigned the value of 1, male or female, is arbitrary. The estimated value of Y will be the same, regardless of which coding procedure is used.

Returning to the data we used in Example 15.2, the real-estate developer noticed that all the houses in the population were from three neighborhoods, A, B, and C. Taking note of which neighborhood each of the sampled houses was from led to the following data (in the discussion following Example 15.2, X_3 = years of education was shown to be a weak predictor and so is removed from the model here):

Family	Home Square Footage (Y)	Income (X_1)	Family Size (X_2)	Neighborhood
1	16	32	2	B
2	17	36	2	C
3	26	55	3	A
4	24	47	4	C
5	22	38	4	B
6	21	60	3	C
7	32	66	6	B
8	18	44	3	B
9	30	70	5	A
10	20	50	3	A

Using these data, we can construct the necessary dummy variables and determine whether they contribute significantly to the prediction of home size (Y).

One way to code neighborhoods would be to define

$$X_3 = \begin{cases} 0 & \text{if neighborhood A} \\ 1 & \text{if neighborhood B} \\ 2 & \text{if neighborhood C} \end{cases}$$

However, this type of coding has many problems. First, because $0 < 1 < 2$, the codes imply that neighborhood A is smaller than neighborhood B, which is smaller than neighborhood C. Furthermore, any difference between neighborhoods A and C receives twice the weight (because $2 - 0 = 2$) of any difference between neighborhoods A and B or B and C. So this coding transforms data that are actually *nominal* to data that are *interval,* a much stronger type.

A better procedure is to use the necessary number of dummy variables (coded 0 or 1) to represent the neighborhoods. We needed one dummy variable with two categories (male and female) to specify a person's gender. To represent the three neighborhoods, we use two dummy variables by letting

$$X_3 = \begin{cases} 1 & \text{if house is in A} \\ 0 & \text{otherwise} \end{cases} \quad \text{and} \quad X_4 = \begin{cases} 1 & \text{if house is in B} \\ 0 & \text{otherwise} \end{cases}$$

Note that as for the male/female dummy variable, this coding is arbitrary as far as the prediction, $\hat{Y}$, is concerned. We could have assigned $X_3 = 0$ and $X_4 = 0$ to neighborhood A, with $X_3 = 1$ for B and $X_4 = 1$ for C.

What happened to neighborhood C? It is not necessary to develop a third dummy variable here because we have the following scheme:

House is in Neighborhood	X_3	X_4
A	1	0
B	0	1
C	0	0

In fact, it can be shown that a third dummy variable is not only unnecessary, it is very important that you not include it. If you attempted to use three such dummy variables in your model, you would receive a message in your computer output informing you that "no solution exists" for this model. Suppose we had introduced a third dummy variable (say, X_5) that was equal to 1 if the house was in neighborhood C. For each observation in the sample, we would have

$$X_5 = 1 - X_3 - X_4$$

Whenever any one predictor variable is a linear function (including a constant term) of one or more other predictors, then mathmematically *no solution* exists for the least squares coefficients, since you have multicollinearity at its worst. To arrive at a usable equation, any such predictor variable must not be included.

FIGURE 15.17

Excel solution (partial output) to real-estate dummy variable problem. (a) Solution using X_1, X_2, X_3, and X_4. (b) Solution using variables X_1 and X_2.

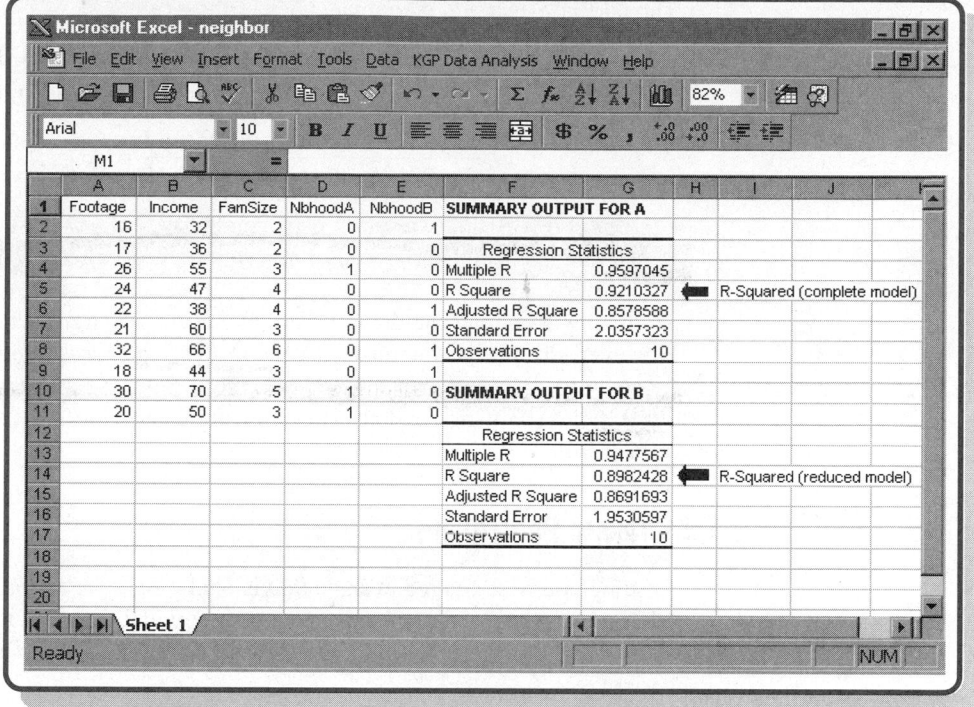

The resulting model here is*

$$Y = \beta_0 + \beta_1 X_1 + \beta_2 X_2 + \beta_3 X_3 + \beta_4 X_4 + e$$

The final array of data (ready for input into a computer program) is

Row	Y	X_1	X_2	X_3	X_4	Row	Y	X_1	X_2	X_3	X_4
1	16	32	2	0	1	6	21	60	3	0	0
2	17	36	2	0	0	7	32	66	6	0	1
3	26	55	3	1	0	8	18	44	3	0	1
4	24	47	4	0	0	9	30	70	5	1	0
5	22	38	4	0	1	10	20	50	3	1	0

where Y = square footage of home, X_1 = income, X_2 = family size, $X_3 = 1$ if neighborhood A, and $X_4 = 1$ if neighborhood B.

An abbreviated Excel solution using all four predictors is shown in Figure 15.17(a). To determine whether the particular neighborhood has any effect on the prediction of home size, we test

$$H_0: \beta_3 = \beta_4 = 0 \qquad \text{(if } X_1 \text{ and } X_2 \text{ are included)}$$

$$H_a: \beta_3 \text{ or } \beta_4 \text{ (or both)} \neq 0$$

In the complete model, the variables are X_1, X_2, X_3, and X_4, and from Figure 15.17(a),

$$R_c^2 = .921$$

In the reduced model, the variables are X_1 and X_2 only, and from Figure 15.17(b),

$$R_r^2 = .898$$

---

* Models that include dummy variables typically contain terms that reflect any interaction between the dummy variables and the other quantitative variables. For this model, this would amount to adding four additional terms to the model, namely, $X_1 X_3$, $X_1 X_4$, $X_2 X_3$, and $X_2 X_4$. Such a model would require a larger sample size (n) than that used in this illustration, since the model would then contain $k = 8$ predictor variables. This topic is explored further in Section 15.6.

At first glance, it does not appear that X_3 and X_4 produced a significant increase in R^2. The partial F-test will determine whether this is true.

$$F = \frac{(R_c^2 - R_r^2)/(\text{number of } \beta\text{'s in } H_0)}{(1 - R_c^2)/[n - 1 - (\text{number of } X'\text{s in the complete model})]}$$

$$= \frac{(.921 - .898)/2}{(1 - .921)/(10 - 1 - 4)} = \frac{.023/2}{.079/5} = .73$$

Using $\alpha = .10$, this result is considerably less than $F_{.10,2,5} = 3.78$, so there is no evidence that the neighborhood dummy variables significantly improve the prediction of home size.

In this example, the dummy variables were not significant predictors in the model. However, do not let this mislead you. In many business applications, dummy variables representing location, weather conditions, yes/no situations, time, and many other variables can have a tremendous effect on improving the results of a multiple regression model.

STEPWISE PROCEDURES

Assume you wish to predict annual divisional profits for a large corporation using, among other techniques, a multiple linear regression model. Your strategy is to consider any variable that you think *could* have an effect on these profits. You have identified twelve such variables.

One possibility is to include all these variables in your model and to use the t tests to decide which variables are significant predictors. However, this procedure invites multicollinearity, because your model is more apt to include correlated predictors, severely hindering the interpretation of your model. In particular, two independent variables that are very highly correlated may both have small t values (as we saw in Section 15.4), causing you possibly to discard both of them from the model—this is *not* the right thing to do because you possibly should have retained one of them.

A better way to proceed here is to use one of the several stepwise selection procedures. These techniques either choose or eliminate variables, one at a time, in an effort not to include those variables that either have no predictive ability or are highly correlated with other predictor variables. A word of caution—these procedures do not provide a guarantee against multicollinearity; however, they greatly reduce the chances of including a large set of correlated independent variables.

These procedures consist of three different selection techniques: (1) forward regression, (2) backward regression, and (3) stepwise regression.

FORWARD REGRESSION.   The forward regression method of model selection puts variables into the equation, one at a time, beginning with that variable having the highest correlation (or R^2) with Y. For sake of argument, call this variable X_1.

Next, it examines the remaining variables for the variable that, when included with X_1, has the highest R^2. That predictor (with X_1) is inserted into the model. This procedure continues until adding the "best" remaining variable at that stage results in an insignificant increase in R^2 according to the partial F-test.

BACKWARD REGRESSION.   Backward regression is the opposite of forward regression: it begins with *all* variables in the model and, one by one, removes them. It begins by finding the "worst" variable—the one that causes the smallest decrease in R^2 when removed from the complete model. If the decrease is insignificant, this variable is removed, and the process continues.

The variable among those remaining in the model that causes the smallest decrease in the new R^2 is considered next. You continue this procedure of removing variables until a significant drop in R^2 is obtained, at which point you replace this significant predictor and terminate the selection.

FIGURE 15.18

Possible solution using stepwise regression on divisional profits data.

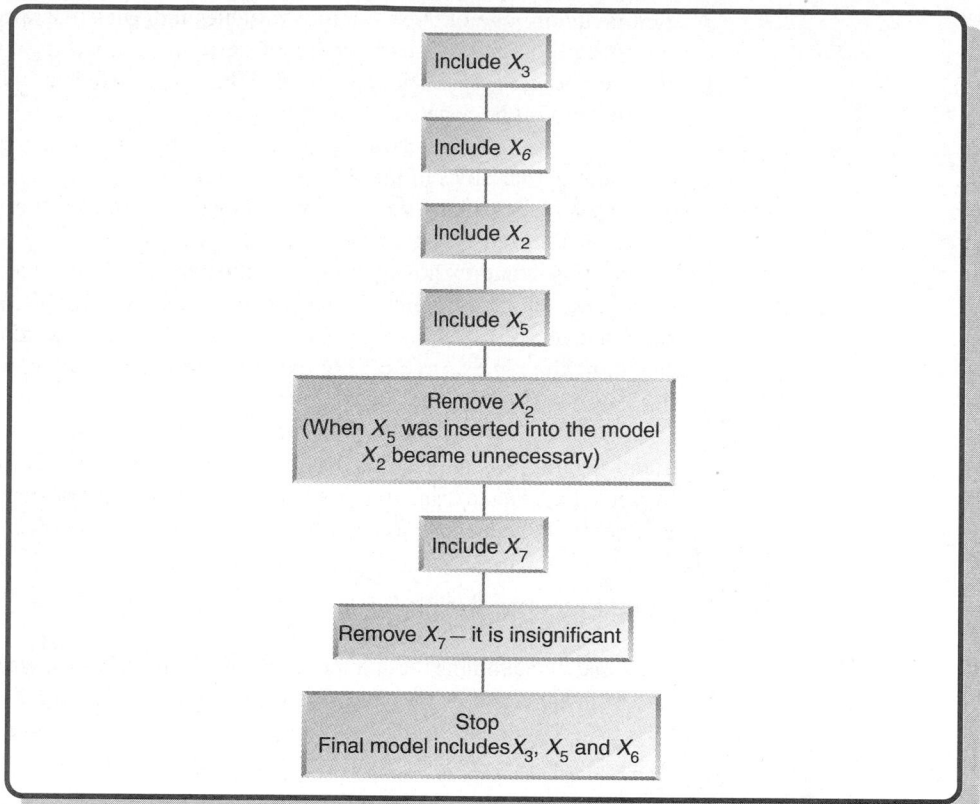

Will the model resulting from a backward regression be the same as that obtained using forward regression? Not necessarily; usually, however, the resulting models are very similar. Of course, if two variables are highly correlated, the forward procedure could choose one of the correlated predictors, whereas the backward procedure could choose the other.

STEPWISE REGRESSION.   Stepwise regression is a modification of forward regression. *It is the most popular and flexible of the three selection techniques.* It proceeds exactly as does forward regression, except that at each stage it can *remove* any variable whose partial F-value indicates that this variable does not contribute, given the present set of independent variables in the model. Like forward regression, it stops when the "best" variable among those remaining produces an insignificant increase in R^2.

Figure 15.18 illustrates this procedure for the example on predicting divisional profits (the data are not shown). Data from all 12 independent variables, as well as from Y, are used as input to a stepwise regression program. One possible outcome from this analysis is shown in Figure 15.18.

The stepwise solution for the data we used to predict home size is contained in the end-of-chapter MINITAB appendix. As we previously determined, X_3 = educational level does not contribute significantly, and so the resulting prediction equation includes only X_1 = income and X_2 = family size. This equation is

$$\hat{Y} = 5.091 + .165X_1 + 2.66X_2$$

USING DUMMY VARIABLES IN FORWARD OR STEPWISE REGRESSION.   We emphasized that $C - 1$ dummy variables should be used to represent C categories if *all* the dummy variables were to be inserted into the regression equation. When using a forward or stepwise regression procedure, this may not be the best way to proceed, as the following illustration shows.

Suppose you are using nine dummy (indicator) variables to represent 10 cities. The dependent variable is monthly sales, and the purpose is to determine which city (or cities) exhibits very large or very small sales. If a forward or stepwise selection procedure is used, then including one of these dummy variables indicates that specifying this particular city significantly improves the prediction of sales. In other words, it indicates that sales for this city are not just average but are much higher (its coefficient will be positive) or lower (its coefficient will be negative) than average.

When you use the forward or stepwise techniques, you probably will not include all nine dummy variables in the model. Your ability to predict sales (Y) is unaffected by not defining a tenth dummy variable and, in fact, as pointed out earlier, the regression analysis will not accept all ten dummy variables.

For this situation, however, there is the danger of not detecting extremely high or low sales in the tenth city, which did not receive a dummy variable. When including these variables one at a time in the regression equation using a forward or stepwise procedure, we can allow the regression model to examine the effect of all ten cities. We do this by defining ten such dummy variables, one for each city.*

Because a forward regression procedure generally will not attempt to include all ten dummy variables, you are able to investigate the existence of high or low sales in each of the ten cities. When using dummy variables in a forward or stepwise regression procedure, it is perfectly acceptable to use C such variables to represent C categories.

Examining the Residuals

The topic of examining the sample residuals (values of $Y - \hat{Y}$) was introduced in Section 14.6 for the linear regression model containing one predictor variable. These values can be used to verify the model assumptions discussed on page 678 as well as to identify outliers and observations that are very influential in determining the least squares prediction equation.

Checking the Model Assumptions

An important step in a regression analysis is to verify the model assumptions. If one or more of these assumptions are violated, the results of the F-test and the t tests discussed in this chapter are, at best, questionable. The procedure for verifying these assumptions is nearly identical to that used in simple linear regression, described in detail in Section 14.6.

Checking Assumption 1. *The errors are normally distributed, with a mean of zero.* Construct a histogram of the sample residuals. This plot should resemble a normal curve centered at zero. Remember that an exact normal curve is not necessary here, but the inference results from this chapter are suspect if this distribution is severely skewed.

Checking Assumption 2. *The variance of the errors remains constant.* In Chapter 14, the sample residuals were plotted against the independent variable, X. For the multiple regression analysis, there is more than one independent variable and so one alternative is to plot the residuals versus the predicted ($\hat{Y}$) values. This plot should contain no pattern. This is the "shotgun blast" appearance illustrated in Figure 14.22(a), where now the horizontal axis is $\hat{Y}$ rather than X. Beware of situations where the larger residuals are associated with the larger $\hat{Y}$ values, as illustrated in Figure 14.22(b), where again the horizontal axis is $\hat{Y}$.

Checking Assumption 3. *The errors are independent.* This is an important assumption whenever the sample data are obtained in a sequential manner—in particular, across time. Such data are referred to as *time series data,* where, for example, each row (value of Y and the predictor variables) corresponds to a particular year. This assumption can be tested using the **Durbin-Watson statistic,** defined in Chapter 17, which discusses the use of multiple linear regression models on time series data.

---

* This problem is discussed in D. Dorsett and J. T. Webster, "Guidelines for Variable Selection Problems When Dummy Variables Are Used," *The American Statistician* 37, no. 4 (1983): 337.

DETECTING SAMPLE OUTLIERS

As in Chapter 14, we will:

- Detect sample observations with outlying values of the predictor variables using **sample leverages.**
- Detect observations with outlying values of the dependent variable, Y, using the **standardized residuals.**
- Classify an observation as "influential" using the corresponding **Cook's distance measure.**

For the multiple linear regression model, no simple formula exists for the leverage value (h_i) of the ith observation. Nearly all computerized statistical packages will provide you with these leverage values via a simple command. The instructions when using MINITAB are contained in the end-of-chapter appendix for Chapter 14. The output using Excel will be shown in upcoming Example 15.9. *A suggested procedure here is to conclude that an observation has outlying values of the predictor variables if its leverage value is larger than $2(k + 1)/n$ or larger than $3(k + 1)/n$, where k is the number of predictor variables and n is the number of observations (rows of data).* Since MINITAB and the KGP Data Analysis regression procedure within Excel use the "larger than $3(k + 1)/n$" rule, we will use this decision rule in the discussion to follow.

The standardized residual, as in Chapter 14, is defined as

$$\text{Standardized residual} = \frac{Y_i - \hat{Y}_i}{s\sqrt{1 - h_i}} \tag{15.20}$$

where $s = \sqrt{MSE}$ and MSE is as defined in equation 15.10. *A recommended procedure is to identify an observation as having an outlying value of Y if its standardized residual is larger than 2 or less than –2.* MINITAB will flag automatically any observation having such a standardized residual.

Influential observations are those that, if removed, result in a considerably different regression equation. Such observations may have been improperly recorded (an error was made) or, if recorded correctly, may be a signal that your model is inadequate. A search for additional predictor variables could be made that, when inserted into the existing model, results in a better "model fit." Influential observations will be identified by using Cook's distance measure, where this measure for the ith observation is defined as

$$D_i = \left(\frac{1}{k+1}\right)\left(\frac{h_i}{1-h_i}\right) (\text{standardized residual})^2$$

$$= \frac{(Y_i - \hat{Y}_i)^2}{(k+1)s^2}\left[\frac{h_i}{(1-h_i)^2}\right] \tag{15.21}$$

A suggested procedure here is to conclude that the ith observation is influential if the corresponding D_i measure is larger than DMAX, where DMAX depends on the number of predictor variables and is as specified in Table 15.1. For a more accurate procedure, you can set $DMAX = F_{.5,k+1,n-k-1}$. The values in Table 15.1 closely approximate these median F-values.

TABLE 15.1

Critical values for Cook's distance measure, D_i using k predictor variables. An observation is classified as influential if $D_i >$ DMAX.

k	1 or 2	3 or 4	≥ 5
DMAX	.8	.9	1.0

EXAMPLE 15.9
An Excel Residual Analysis

An Excel analysis of the residuals using the investment data in Example 15.4 follows. Since this sample consists of a random sample of 50 investment clients, and is not time ordered, assumption 3 was not investigated.

SOLUTION

To obtain the Excel output in Figure 15.19, click on **KGP Data Analysis ➤ Regression.** Referring to the input screen in Figure 15.7, enter "A1:A51" in the **Y Range** box, "B1:C51" in the **Contiguous X Range** box, and "D1" in the **Output Range** box. Be sure to click on the boxes for **Residuals, Standardized Residuals, Leverages,** and **Cook's Ds.** The maximum standardized residual, leverage value, and Cook's D are provided in cells I2:I4. To obtain these values, first type in the labels in cells H1:H4 of Figure 15.19. In cell I2, type "=max(G26:G75)" to obtain the maximum standardized residual, since these values occupy cells G26:G75 in Figure 15.19. Repeat this using "=max(H26:H75)" in cell I3 for the maximum leverage and "=max(I26:I75)" in cell I4 for the maximum Cook's D.

A histogram of the residuals is shown in Figure 15.20. To obtain the histogram, click on **KGP Data Analysis ➤ Quantitative Data Charts/Tables ➤ Histogram/Freq. Charts.** Enter "F26:F75" in the **Input Range** box, "K1" in the **Output Range** box, and "7" in the **Number of Classes** box. Finally, click on the check boxes for **Frequencies** and **Frequency Histogram,** and then "OK." Except for a very slight positive skew, the residuals appear to be approximately normally distributed, centered at zero, and so we conclude that assumption 1 is satisfied.

The residuals are plotted against the predicted Y values ($\hat{Y}$ values) in Figure 15.21. This plot can be obtained by clicking on **Excel Chart Wizard ➤ XY (Scatter) ➤ Next.** The data range is E26:F75, since the predicted Y values are in cells E26:E75, and the residuals are in F26:F75. Using Figure 15.21 as a guide, you can input the various titles by clicking on the **Titles** tab. Once you have clicked on **Finish,** and you have the plot on your spreadsheet, the minimum and maximum values on the vertical axis can be set at –600 and 600

FIGURE 15.19
Excel regression output using KGP Data Analysis (Example 15.9).

	File Edit View Insert Format Tools Data KGP Data Analysis Window Help								
	A	B	C	D	E	F	G	H	I
1	Invest	Index	Income	SUMMARY OUTPUT				Maximum	
2	2500	86	55800					Stand. Resid.	1.99005
3	3700	54	60400	Regression Statistics				Leverage	0.13557
4	3900	21	72700	Multiple R	0.947841788			Cook's D	0.11589
5	1700	91	41700	R Square	0.898404055				
6	1000	72	35200	Adjusted R Square	0.894080823				
7	1700	16	41800	Standard Error	283.0331323				
8	2500	81	43700	Observations	50				
9	3400	32	67900						
10	2500	37	53700	ANOVA					
11	2900	89	57400		df	SS	MS	F	Significance F
12	2100	48	47100	Regression	2	33294135.56	16647067.78	207.8084449	4.5877E-24
13	2600	61	55300	Residual	47	3765064.438	80107.754		
14	1700	33	40000	Total	49	37059200			
15	2100	82	40200						
16	1500	95	36900		Coefficients	Standard Error	t Stat	P-value	Lower 95%
17	1700	73	40700	Intercept	-1183.318266	219.3703591	-5.394157491	2.19372E-06	-1624.634089
18	1400	9	35100	Index	-0.127148104	1.54705816	-0.082187023	0.934847013	-3.239424746
19	2400	42	50900	Income	0.071994836	0.003588211	20.06426898	1.09643E-24	0.064776292
20	1000	74	36300						
21	3200	31	63700						
22	2500	12	46800						
23	4500	25	75200	RESIDUAL OUTPUT					
24	2400	24	42400						
25	2000	88	42000	Observation	Predicted Invest	Residuals	Standardized Residuals	Leverages	Cook's D
26	2900	53	54600	1	2823.0588	-323.0588	-1.1797	0.0639	0.0317
27	3600	40	61600	2	3158.3038	541.6962	1.9445	0.0312	0.0406
28	2800	81	60000	3	4048.0362	-148.0362	-0.5500	0.0958	0.0107
29	2200	44	50600	4	1807.2959	-107.2959	-0.3951	0.0793	0.0045
30	3800	36	66300	5	1341.7453	-341.7453	-1.2549	0.0742	0.0420
31	4300	50	70900	6	1824.0315	-124.0315	-0.4572	0.0812	0.0062
32	3300	95	66600	7	1952.5570	547.4430	1.9901	0.0553	0.0773

| ◄ ◄ ► ►| \ DATA15-4 / |

FIGURE 15.20

Excel histogram of residuals
using KGP Data Analysis
(Example 15.9).

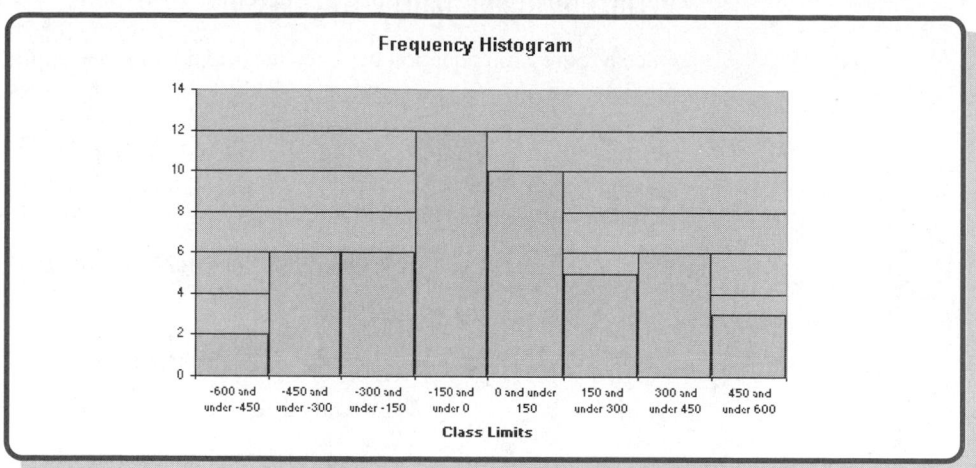

FIGURE 15.20

Excel histogram of residuals
using KGP Data Analysis
(Example 15.9).

FIGURE 15.21

Excel residual plot for
Example 15.9.

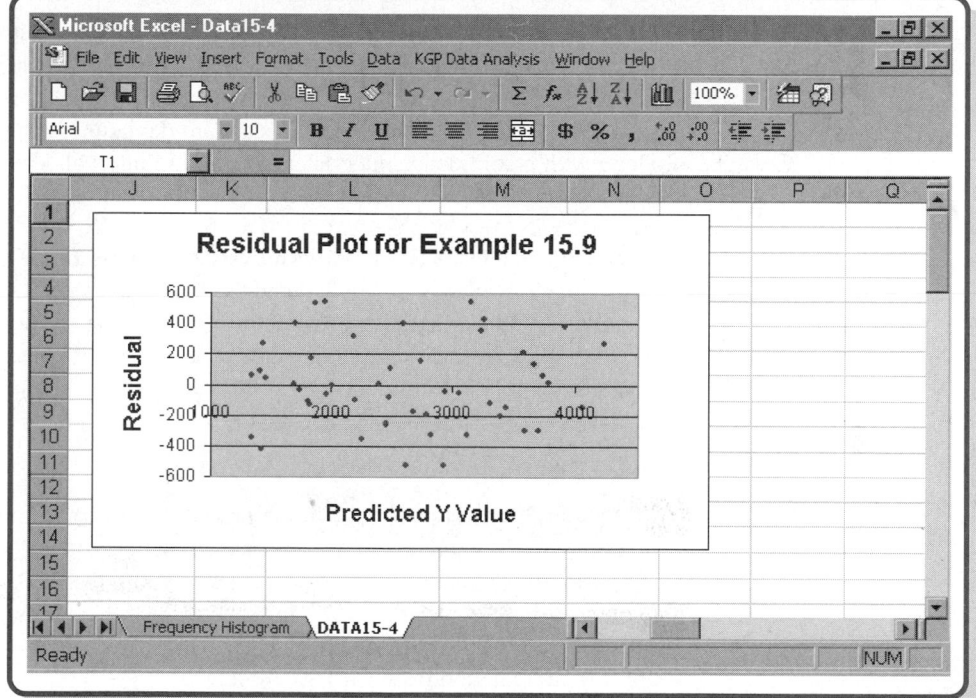

respectively, by right clicking on this axis and then clicking on **Format Axis** and the **Scale** tab. Also, the decimal places can be set at zero for both axes by repeating this procedure on both axes using the **Number** tab. No pattern is observed in this plot, and assumption 2 appears to be satisfied.

Using the maximum values in I2:I4 in Figure 15.19, we see that none of the standardized residuals are greater than 2 in absolute value, and so there are no observations with an outlying Y value. None of the leverage (h_i) values exceed $3(2 + 1)/50 = 9/50 = .18$, and so there are no observations with unusually large or small values of the predictor variables. Finally, there are no influential observations, since all of the Cook distance measures are less than .8 (from Table 15.1).

PREDICTION USING MULTIPLE REGRESSION

Once a regression equation has been derived, its primary application generally is to derive predicted values of the dependent variable. Computer packages provide an easy method of deriving such an estimate. To illustrate, consider the regression equation we developed for the real-estate data. For this illustration we include $X_3 =$ years of formal education, although, as we demonstrated in Section 15.2, this variable could be dropped without any significant loss in the prediction of home size. The resulting prediction equation was

$$\hat{Y} = 5.657 + .194X_1 + 2.338X_2 - .163X_3$$

Consider a situation in which

$$X_1 = \text{income} = 46 \text{ (thousands of dollars)}$$

$$X_2 = \text{family size} = 4$$

$$X_3 = \text{years of formal education} = 8 \text{ (years)}$$

The predicted home size (Y) here is

$$\hat{Y} = 5.657 + .194(46) + 2.338(4) - .163(8) = 22.63 \text{ (2263 square feet)}$$

PREDICTION USING EXCEL.   The standard statistical tool package with Excel does not allow for new value prediction. However, the KGP Data Analysis add-ins will allow you to predict values of the dependent variable using one or more new observations. For each observation, it will also provide the estimated standard deviation (standard error) of the predicted Y, along with a confidence interval and prediction interval. The easiest way to accomplish this is to simply attach the new observations at the end of your sample values. Referring to Figure 15.2, the new observation ($X_1 = 46$, $X_2 = 4$, $X_3 = 8$) can be typed into cells B12, C12, and D12. Click on **KGP Data Analysis ➤ Regression.** Using the input screen in Figure 15.7, the **Y Range** is "A1:A11," and the (contiguous) **X Range** is "B1:D11." Click on the box inside **Confidence and Prediction Intervals** at the bottom of the input form and enter "B12:D12" as the range of new observations. The regression output using this input information is shown in Figure 15.22. The predicted Y value in cell H25 is $\hat{Y} = 22.625$ and agrees with the previous result.

CONFIDENCE AND PREDICTION INTERVALS.   In the preceding illustration, what does $\hat{Y} = 22.625$ estimate? For ease of notation, let X_0 represent the set of X values used for this estimate; that is, $X_0 = (46, 4, 8)$, where $X_1 = 46$, $X_2 = 4$, and $X_3 = 8$. This value of $\hat{Y}$ estimates (1) the *average* home size of all families with this specific set of X values, written $\mu_{Y|X_0}$ and (2) the home size for an *individual* family having this specific set of X values, written Y_{X_0}.

Using the notation from Chapter 14, let

$$s_{\hat{Y}} = \text{the standard deviation (standard error) of the predicted } Y \text{ mean}$$

To determine the reliability of this particular point estimate, $\hat{Y}$, you can (1) derive a *confidence interval* for $\mu_{Y|X_0}$ if your intent is to estimate the *average* value of Y given X_0 (not the usual situation) or (2) derive a *prediction interval* for Y_{X_0} if the purpose is to forecast an *individual* value of Y given this specific set of values for the predictor variables. In business applications, deriving a specific forecast is, by far, the more popular use of linear regression.

These intervals are summarized as follows. A $(1 - \alpha) \cdot 100\%$ confidence interval for $\mu_{Y|X_0}$ is

$$\hat{Y} - t_{\alpha/2, n-k-1} s_{\hat{Y}} \qquad \text{to} \qquad \hat{Y} + t_{\alpha/2, n-k-1} s_{\hat{Y}} \qquad\qquad \textbf{(15.22)}$$

FIGURE 15.22

Prediction for new data using Excel and KGP Data Analysis. For the input data, see Figure 15.2.

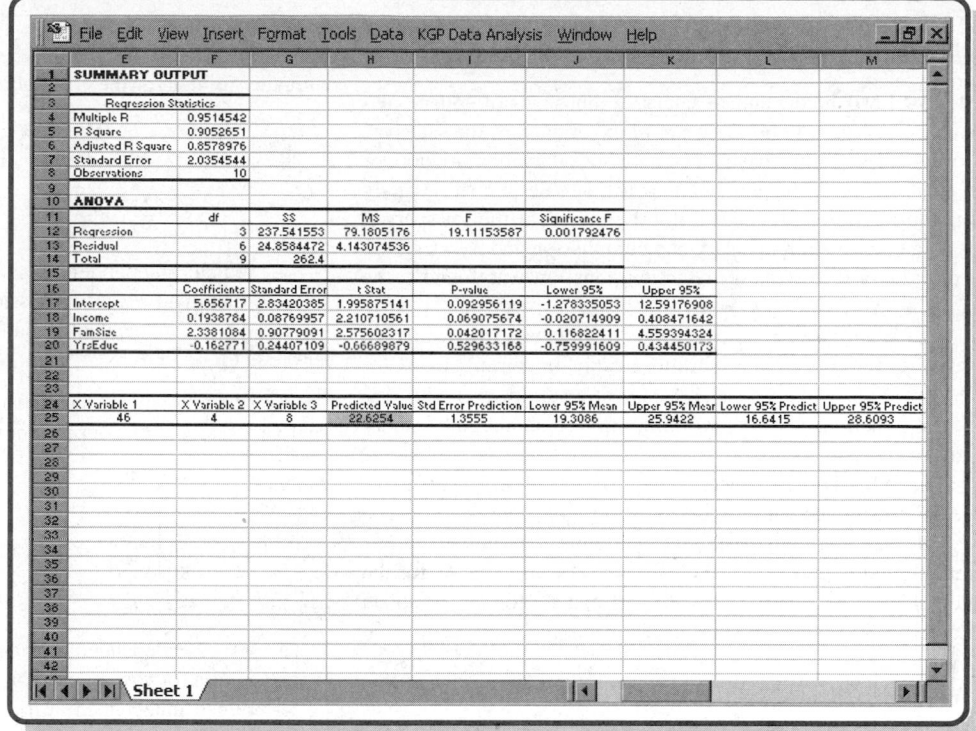

A $(1 - \alpha) \cdot 100\%$ prediction interval for Y_{X_0} is

$$\hat{Y} - t_{\alpha/2, n-k-1} \sqrt{s^2 + s_{\hat{Y}}^2} \qquad \text{to} \qquad \hat{Y} + t_{\alpha/2, n-k-1} \sqrt{s^2 + s_{\hat{Y}}^2} \qquad \textbf{(15.23)}$$

where s^2 is the MSE value in the regression ANOVA table and is defined in equation 15.4.

USING EXCEL TO DETERMINE THE INTERVALS.   In Figure 15.22 (cell I25), the standard deviation of the predicted Y mean is labeled **StdErrorPrediction** and is equal to $s_{\hat{Y}} = 1.3555$. The 95% confidence interval for $\mu_{Y|X_0}$ is derived by first using Table A.5 to obtain $t_{\alpha/2, n-k-1} = t_{.025, 10-3-1} = t_{.025, 6} = 2.447$. The resulting confidence interval is

$$22.625 - (2.447)(1.3555) \qquad \text{to} \qquad 22.625 + (2.447)(1.3555)$$

$$= 22.625 - 3.317 \qquad \text{to} \qquad 22.625 + 3.317$$

$$= 19.308 \qquad \text{to} \qquad 25.942$$

Consequently, we have estimated the average home size for families with $X_1 = 46$, $X_2 = 4$, $X_3 = 8$ to within 331.7 square feet of the actual mean with 95% confidence. The KGP Data Analysis regression procedure within Excel computes this interval for you and is contained in cells J25 and K25 in Figure 15.22.

The prediction interval from equation 15.23 is derived by using MSE $= 4.1431$ from Figure 15.22 to obtain

$$22.625 - 2.447\sqrt{4.1431 + (1.3555)^2} \qquad \text{to} \qquad 22.625 + 2.447\sqrt{4.1431 + (1.3555)^2}$$

$$= 22.625 - 5.984 \qquad \text{to} \qquad 22.625 + 5.984$$

$$= 16.641 \qquad \text{to} \qquad 28.609$$

This means that we have predicted the home size of an individual family with $X_1 = 46$, $X_2 = 4$, and $X_3 = 8$ to within 598.4 square feet of the actual value with 95% confidence. This same prediction interval will be provided by the KGP Data Analysis regression procedure and is contained in cells L25 and M25 in Figure 15.22.

EXERCISES 15.39–15.54

UNDERSTANDING THE MECHANICS

15.39 Let Y be the annual salary, in thousands of dollars, of a salesperson. Let X_1 be the years of experience of the salesperson. A salesperson's pay can come from salary, commission, or a combination of the two. Let $X_2 = 1$ if the salesperson is strictly on commission and $X_2 = 0$ if not. Let $X_3 = 1$ if the salesperson is on a combination of salary and commission and $X_3 = 0$ if not. From 20 observations a prediction equation was found to be $\hat{Y} = 7 + 5X_1 + 4X_2 + 7X_3$.

a. What is the predicted salary of a salesperson with five years' experience who is working strictly on commissions?

b. What is the predicted salary of a salesperson with five years' experience who is working on a combination of salary and commissions?

c. What is the predicted salary of a salesperson with five years' experience who is working strictly on salary?

d. Test the hypothesis that the dummy variables improve the prediction of a salesperson's salary. Assume that R^2 for the model including only X_1, is .70 and that R^2 for the complete model is .80. Use a .05 significance level.

APPLYING THE NEW CONCEPTS

15.40 If an economist is interested in examining the relationship between household income and household recreational expenses over time, then the economist would use *time series* data. However, if an economist is interested in estimating household recreational expenses as a function of household income, then he or she would use *cross-sectional* data. A set of cross-sectional data were collected from a sample of 30 households in a large metropolitan area. The independent variables are yearly household income (in thousands), X_1, and house payment (either rent or mortgage), X_2. The dependent variable was annual household recreational expenses. The least squares line is $\hat{Y} = 51.3 + 12.3X_1 + .11X_2$. Given that the standard deviations of the estimates of the coefficients of X_1 and X_2 are 5.59 and .048, test the hypothesis that the variable X_1 contributes to the prediction of Y, given that X_2 is in the model. Also, test that X_2 contributes to the prediction of Y, given that X_1 is in the model. Use a .05 significance level.

15.41 Nebraska Associated Insurance handles workers' compensation insurance for three large manufacturing firms. The insurance company believes that the following independent variables are important in determining the total amount of compensation paid for each claim from the three manufacturers:

　　age

　　gender

　　marital status

　　length of employment

　　type of injury (to a limb, to the head, or to other parts of the body)

　　manufacturer employing the worker

Set up an appropriate regression model to predict total amount of compensation paid based on the independent variables. Define your variables.

15.42 Data are collected for the variables, Y, X_1, and X_2. A computer printout of the correlation matrix is:

$$\begin{array}{c c} & \begin{array}{ccc} Y & X_1 & X_2 \end{array} \\ \begin{array}{c} Y \\ X_1 \\ X_2 \end{array} & \left[\begin{array}{ccc} 1 & .49 & .30 \\ .49 & 1 & .12 \\ .30 & .12 & 1 \end{array}\right] \end{array}$$

a. Which independent variable, X_1 or X_2, would be selected first in a forward regression procedure?

b. Which independent variable, X_1 or X_2, would be a better predictor of Y? Why?

15.43 The following is a correlation matrix for three independent variables and one dependent variable:

$$\begin{array}{c c} & \begin{array}{cccc} Y & X_1 & X_2 & X_3 \end{array} \\ \begin{array}{c} Y \\ X_1 \\ X_2 \\ X_3 \end{array} & \left[\begin{array}{cccc} 1 & .25 & .36 & .59 \\ .25 & 1 & .54 & .22 \\ .36 & .54 & 1 & .31 \\ .59 & .22 & .31 & 1 \end{array}\right] \end{array}$$

a. Which independent variable would be chosen for the first stage of a forward regression procedure?

b. Which independent variable would be chosen for the first step of a stepwise regression procedure?

15.44 The least squares regression equation

$$\hat{Y} = 1.5 + 3.5X_1 + 7.5X_2 - 150X_3$$

has the following t values for the independent variables:

Null Hypothesis	t Statistic
$\beta_1 = 0$	4.5
$\beta_2 = 0$	1.89
$\beta_3 = 0$	1.52

Twenty observations were used in calculating the least squares equation. In the first stage of a backward selection procedure, which independent variable would be eliminated first? Use a 5% level of significance.

15.45 Describe the main difference between the forward selection procedure and the stepwise selection procedure in regression analysis.

15.46 Industrial managers involved in quality improvement in international trade keep tabs of consultants specializing in ISO 9000. The number of clients that the consultants have registered is correlated with the year that the consultants established themselves and whether they also specialize in ISO 14000. A quality manager wished to determine the relationship between the number of clients registered with the independent variables year established (X_1) and a dummy variable (X_2) that is equal to 1 if the consultant specializes in ISO 14000 as well and 0 if he/she does not. Refer to the computer printout on the next page.

(Source: Adapted from *Quality Digest*, "ISO 9000 Register and Consultants Guide," May 1997, p. 23–30.)

a. Do the variables X_1 and X_2 contribute to the prediction of the number of clients registered? Use a 5% significance level.

b. Calculate the residual for each consultant. How many residuals lie within 2 standard deviations of zero?

c. What is the 95% prediction interval for the number of clients registered in the year 1991 for a consultant who does not specialize in ISO 14000? How does this compare to the 95% confidence interval for the mean number of clients registered in the year 1991 for consultants who do not specialize in ISO 14000?

Consultants	Number of Clients	Year Established	1 if Specialize in ISO 14000, and 0 if not
Unique Development Corp	36	1987	0
Huntington Quality Associates	24	1991	1
ISO 9000 Quality Systems Management	17	1994	0
Jerry L. Anderson	7	1991	0
Marshall-Qualtec Inc.	30	1989	1
Pleiades International Inc.	36	1991	1
Quality Solutions	18	1990	0
Quality Systems Enhancement Inc.	37	1992	1
Tetris	14	1992	0
Canadian QA Quality Management	45	1988	1
WorldSource One Inc.	7	1994	0

15.47 Which of the standard assumptions of regression appear to have been violated in the data from the following table, which lists the dependent variable and the residual values?

$\hat{Y}$	$Y - \hat{Y}$	$\hat{Y}$	$Y - \hat{Y}$
1.5	.12	5.0	−1.45
2.1	−.70	5.5	1.61
3.5	−.91	6.0	1.79
4.0	1.02	7.0	−2.40
4.5	−1.18	7.5	2.10

15.48 How should a graph of the residuals $(Y - \hat{Y})$ plotted against the predicted values $\hat{Y}$ look if the standard assumptions of regression are satisfied?

15.49 A set of 20 observations is used to obtain the least squares line

$$\hat{Y} = 1.5 + 3.6X_1 + 4.9X_2$$

a. Given that the estimated standard deviation of Y at $X_1 = 1.0$ and $X_2 = 2.0$ is 3.4, find a 90% confidence interval for the mean value of Y at $X_1 = 1.0$ and $X_2 = 2.0$.

b. Given that the MSE from this analysis is 21.5, then, using the information in part (a), find a 90% prediction interval for an individual value of Y at $X_1 = 1.0$ and $X_2 = 2.0$.

15.50 The first quarter of 1998 saw the Standard & Poor's 500 Index surge nearly 14%. Nine of the 14 major brokerage firms did even better than the index in recommending companies to investors. Investors are often interested in whether a brokerage firm's previous performance can be used to predict current performance. Let Y represent the current quarter's performance. Let X_1 and X_2 represent the performance for one year and five years, respectively. Consider the performance data below for 14 major brokerage houses. Performance is measured in percentage.

SUMMARY OUTPUT FOR EXERCISE 15.46

Regression Statistics	
Multiple R	0.85483
R Square	0.73073
Adjusted R Square	0.66342
Standard Error	7.54772
Observations	11

ANOVA

	df	SS	MS	F	Significance F
Regression	2	1236.8012	618.4006	10.8552	0.0053
Residual	8	455.7442	56.9680		
Total	10	1692.5455			

	Coefficients	Standard Error	t Stat	P-value	Lower 95%	Upper 95%
Intercept	5602.0173	2212.8530	2.5316	0.0352	499.1660	10704.8687
X1	-2.8049	1.1112	-2.5241	0.0356	-5.3674	-0.2424
X2	14.7211	4.7407	3.1052	0.0145	3.7890	25.6532

X Variable 1	X Variable 2	Predicted Value	Std Error Prediction	Lower 95% Mean	Upper 95% Mean	Lower 95% Predict	Upper 95% Predict
1991	1	32.1561	3.4905	24.1068	40.2053	12.9799	51.3323
1991	0	17.4350	3.1035	10.2782	24.5917	-1.3841	36.2540

Firm	Quarter Ending 3/31/98 (Y)	One Year Performance (X_1)	Five-Year Performance (X_2)
Lehman Brothers	16.6	62.4	162.4
Everen	12.5	59.4	177.0
A. G. Edwards	18.0	58.1	239.7
Wheat First	22.6	57.8	175.0
Edwards Jones	15.8	56.8	152.4
Raymond James	16.5	56.4	247.4
Prudential	14.7	56.0	127.6
Paine Weber	21.0	53.1	292.2
Goldman Sachs	12.6	50.1	169.4
Merril Lynch	14.5	46.2	200.1
Credit Suisse F.B.	11.6	46.2	178.3
Bear Stearns	14.4	45.7	177.9
Salomon S. B.	11.5	44.3	172.0
Morgan Stanley	13.6	39.0	125.4

(Source: Adapted from *Wall Street Week*, "Brokerage Houses' Stock Picks Sparkle," May 7, 1998, p. C1.)

a. The prediction equation for these data is $\hat{Y} = -.342 + .1982X_1 + .0291X_2$. Predict Y for each of the brokerage houses.

b. Calculate the residuals $Y - \hat{Y}$ for each firm.

c. Calculate the residual standard deviation.

d. How many residuals lie within two standard deviations of the mean of the error terms? How many observations would you expect to lie outside of two standard deviations, assuming that the residuals are approximately normally distributed?

15.51 Explain the difference between a confidence interval for the mean value of Y at particular values of the independent variables and a prediction interval for a future value of Y at particular values of the independent variables. Will the prediction interval for Y always be larger than the corresponding confidence interval for particular values of the independent variables?

15.52 A real-estate firm would like to determine the monthly income (Y) of homeowners in a certain section of town by using the monthly mortgage payment (X_1), the market value of the homeowner's car(s) (X_2), and the age of the homeowner (X_3). The following data were collected from 15 randomly selected households, (Y, X_1, and X_2 are in dollars; X_3 in years):

Y	X_1	X_2	X_3	Y	X_1	X_2	X_3
2963	820	7,800	32	2950	975	6,580	34
2100	710	5,100	33	3460	1120	7,900	33
2820	520	10,500	26	3180	635	9,450	36
3350	630	9,500	30	3350	758	12,600	31
2640	925	6,260	35	3267	810	10,630	29
2225	725	4,380	30	2120	710	5,340	28
1630	538	3,760	27	2280	504	4,690	32
3070	679	7,350	37				

Use a computerized statistical package to answer the following questions:

a. What is the mean income for a homeowner with $X_1 = 800$, $X_2 = 7000$, and $X_3 = 30$?

b. Find a 95% confidence interval for the mean monthly income of a homeowner with $X_1 = 800$, $X_2 = 7000$, and $X_3 = 30$.

c. Find a 95% prediction interval for the income of a homeowner with $X_1 = 800$, $X_2 = 7000$, and $X_3 = 30$.

d. Examine the residuals to determine if any outliers or influential observations are present in the data.

USING THE COMPUTER

15.53 [DATA SET EX15-53] *Variable description:*

Magazine: Name of widely circulated magazine
TotalRev: Total revenue for the magazine from all sources
AdRev: Revenue from advertisements in the magazine
SubscriberRev: Revenue for the magazine from subscribers

Magazines obtain revenue from advertisements, subscribers, newsstands, and general circulation. The amount of revenue from advertisements and subscribers tends to be rather stable for most widely circulated magazines. To understand the relationship between AdRev and SubscriberRev in predicting TotalRev, 16 widely circulated magazines were randomly selected. Data for each of the variables were recorded in units of thousands of dollars.

(Source: *Advertising Age*, "Top 300 Magazines by Gross Revenue," June 16, 1997, p. S6.)

a. Using a significance level of 1%, comment on the contribution of AdRev and SubscriberRev in predicting TotalRev.

b. Interpret the 95% prediction interval for a magazine's total revenue given that the revenue from advertisements is $200,000 and the revenue from subscribers is $100,000.

c. Are there any influential observations? If so, eliminate the most influential observation and comment on the increase or decrease in the coefficient of determination.

15.54 [DATA SET EX15-54] *Variable description:*

Funding: Level of funding approved for research proposal
Theory: Score on theoretical soundness
Usefulness: Score on usefulness of applications
Reviewer: 1 if reviewer is from the business research institute and 0 if the reviewer is external to the institute

A business research institute receives research proposals for possible funding. These research proposals come from universities engaged in long-term business projects. Each proposal is evaluated in two areas: theoretical soundness and usefulness of applications. The proposal is reviewed by either someone at the business research institute or someone externally. A committee within the institute considers the scores and qualifications of the reviewer and then may approve some level of funding. A researcher wished to determine the relationship of the level of funding with the scores given by the reviewer and with whether the reviewer is from the business research institute or external to it. The researcher randomly sampled 35 proposals that have received some level of funding. The level of funding is recorded in units of thousands of dollars.

a. Find a 95% confidence interval for the mean level of funding for a proposal with scores of 7 for theoretical soundness and 7 for applications by a reviewer in the business research institute. Interpret the interval in the context of the problem.

b. In part (a), if the confidence interval for the mean level of funding was changed to a prediction interval for the same values of the scores by a reviewer in the business research institute, what is the resulting interval and how would you interpret it?

c. From the histogram of the residuals, does it appear that the errors are approximately normal?

d. Do any of the observations have values of Cook's D greater than .9?

15.6 MODEL BUILDING

Linear regression models can provide you with a variety of predictive equations that attempt to explain the behavior of a particular dependent variable. These go beyond the straight line obtained in Chapter 14 and the flat plane of this chapter, using two independent (predictor) variables, illustrated in Figure 15.1. This section will introduce you to the more flexible linear models, which include the effect of **interaction** terms and **quadratic** terms.

INTERACTION EFFECTS

An interaction effect between two predictor variables, say, X_1 and X_2, implies that how these two variables occur *together* has an impact on the prediction of the dependent variable. This is the same type of effect observed in two-way factorial designs, discussed in Chapter 11, where the effect of one factor on the dependent variable depends on the level of the second factor. A linear regression model containing two predictor variables and an interaction term can be written

$$Y = \beta_0 + \beta_1 X_1 + \beta_2 X_2 + \beta_3 X_1 X_2 + e \qquad (15.24)$$

where the *interaction term* is the product of X_1 and X_2, and e is the error associated with the model. Since the error term is assumed to have a mean of zero, an alternate form of this model is

$$\mu_Y = \beta_0 + \beta_1 X_1 + \beta_2 X_2 + \beta_3 X_1 X_2 \qquad (15.25)$$

where μ_Y is the mean of the random variable Y.

To illustrate an interaction effect, consider the model

$$\mu_Y = 10 + 15X_1 + 4X_2 - 5X_1 X_2$$

Suppose we set $X_2 = 2$. Then we have

$$\mu_Y = 10 + 15X_1 + 4(2) - 5X_1(2)$$
$$= 10 + 15X_1 + 8 - 10X_1$$
$$= 18 + 5X_1$$

For $X_2 = 5$, the model becomes

$$\mu_Y = 10 + 15X_1 + 4(5) - 5X_1(5)$$
$$= 10 + 15X_1 + 20 - 25X_1$$
$$= 30 - 10X_1$$

These two lines are shown in Figure 15.23(a). Due to presence of the interaction term, the relationship between Y and X_1 is highly dependent on the value of X_2. This is not the case if the interaction effect is missing from the model, illustrated in Figure 15.23(b). Without the interaction term, the model becomes

$$\mu_Y = 10 + 15X_1 + 4X_2$$

where for $X_2 = 2$, we have $\mu_Y = 10 + 15X_1 + 4(2) = 18 + 15X_1$ and for $X_2 = 5$, the model becomes $\mu_Y = 10 + 15X_1 + 4(5) = 30 + 15X_1$. Notice in Figure 15.23(b) that the two lines are parallel, indicating the absence of an interaction effect between these two variables.

FIGURE 15.23

Illustration of interaction effect. (a) Interaction is present in the model $\mu_Y = 10 + 15X_1 + 4X_2 - 5X_1X_2$. (b) Interaction is absent in the model $\mu_Y = 10 + 15X_1 + 4X_2$.

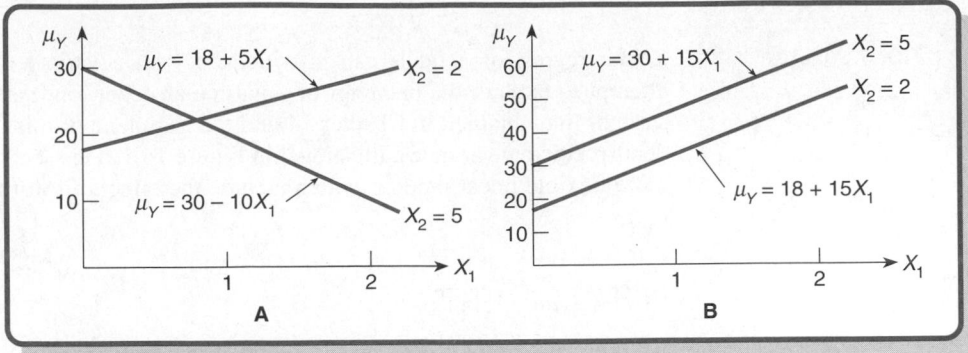

QUADRATIC EFFECTS

Quadratic effects were discussed in Section 15.3, which introduced curvilinear models. An example of a curvilinear model using a single predictor variable (say, X_1) is

$$Y = \beta_0 + \beta_1 X_1 + \beta_2 X_1^2 + e \qquad (15.26)$$

Such a model is useful whenever the effect of X_1 is nonlinear; in particular, the change in Y for a given change in X_1 tends to increase or decrease as X_1 gets larger. Such a relationship can be seen in Figure 15.9, where the change in Y tends to "slow down" for larger values of the predictor variable. Including quadratic terms in the multiple regression model allows you to capture such relationships between the dependent variable and the various predictor variables.

SECOND-ORDER MODELS

The multiple linear regression model introduced in equation 15.1 is

$$Y = \beta_0 + \beta_1 X_1 + \beta_2 X_2 + \cdots + \beta_k X_k + e$$

This model is referred to as a **first-order model,** since no interaction terms or quadratic terms are included.

A **complete second-order model** is one that includes all possible interaction and quadratic terms. For the cases of two and three predictor variables, this model becomes

$$Y = \beta_0 + \beta_1 X_1 + \beta_2 X_2 + \beta_3 X_1 X_2 + \beta_4 X_1^2 + \beta_5 X_2^2 + e \qquad (15.27)$$

$$Y = \beta_0 + \beta_1 X_1 + \beta_2 X_2 + \beta_3 X_3 + \beta_4 X_1 X_2 + \beta_5 X_1 X_3 + \beta_6 X_2 X_3$$
$$+ \beta_7 X_1^2 + \beta_8 X_2^2 + \beta_9 X_3^2 + e \qquad (15.28)$$

Such a model is linear in the unknown β parameters, and so is considered to be a multiple linear regression model. It will provide you with a much more powerful modeling tool than will a first-order model. Construction of a second-order model is illustrated in Example 15.10.

MICROSOFT® EXCEL APPLICATION   USE DAT15-10

EXAMPLE 15.10

Construction of a Second-Order Model

A financial analyst at a major lending institution is interested in predicting the annual sales for defense-related companies. As a possible set of predictor variables, she decides to use the number of employees, current assets, current liabilities, and total assets. Data from a

FIGURE 15.24
Excel regression solution using
KGP Data Analysis and all four
predictor variables.

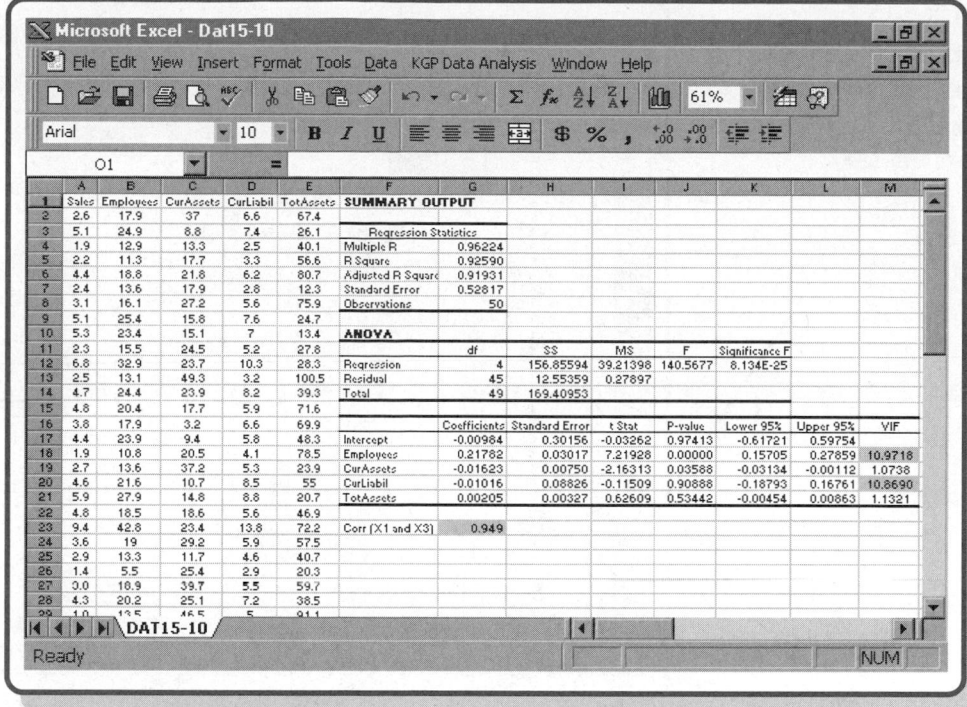

FIGURE 15.24
Excel regression solution using KGP Data Analysis and all four predictor variables.

random sample of 50 such industries is contained in dataset DAT15-10, where each column of data is described as follows:

Column	Contains
A	Y = annual sales (units of \$10,000,000)
B	X_1 = number of employees (units of 100)
C	X_2 = current assets (units of \$100,000)
D	X_3 = current liabilities (units of \$100,000)
E	X_4 = total assets (units of \$100,000)

Construct an appropriate second-order model based on this set of sample data. Use a significance level of .10.

SOLUTION

The first look at the data will be a first-order model containing all four predictor variables. The Excel solution using these variables is shown in Figure 15.24. This output, which includes the four variance inflation factors, can be obtained by clicking on **KGP Data Analysis ➤ Regression.** The **Y Range** is "A1:A51," and the (contiguous) **X Range** is "B1:E51." Both ranges must include labels in the first row. It will be necessary to click on the box alongside VIFs. The variance inflation factors for X_1 and X_3 (highlighted) are both larger than 10, indicating a high correlation between these two variables. This correlation (highlighted in cell G23) is .949. This correlation can be obtained by typing "=correl (B2:B51,D2:D51)" in cell G23. As a result, it was decided to drop X_3 (current liabilities) from the model, since the analyst, rather arbitrarily, elected to keep the number of employees (X_1) in the prediction equation.

The regression analysis was repeated using predictor variables, X_1, X_2, and X_4 in Figure 15.25. Since the range of the predictor variables is noncontiguous, it was necessary to use the KGP Data Analysis regression procedure. By (1) clicking on **KGP Data Analysis ➤ Regression;** (2) entering "A1:A51" as the **Y Range;** (3) clicking **Noncontiguous X Range;** (4) entering "3" as the number of X variables (followed by "OK") with ranges B1:B51, C1:C51, and E1:E51; and (5) entering "F1" as the **Output Range,** the Excel output in Figure 15.25 was obtained. All of the variance inflation factors are now well under 10. Due to the large p-value for X_4 = total assets (highlighted in cell J20), this variable was dropped from the model. *Note:* It is possible that an interaction effect exists between X_1 and X_4 or between X_2 and X_4, which will not be detected once X_4 is dropped from the model.

FIGURE 15.25

Excel regression solution using
KGP Data Analysis and X_1, X_2,
and X_4.

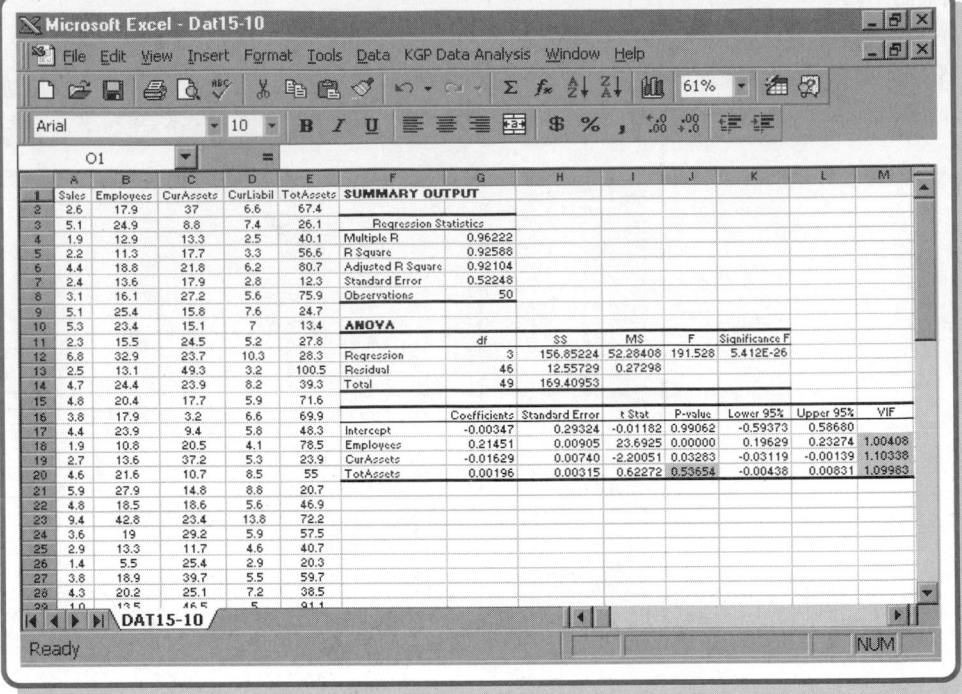

FIGURE 15.26

Excel regression solution using
X_1, X_2, X_1X_2, and quadratic
terms.

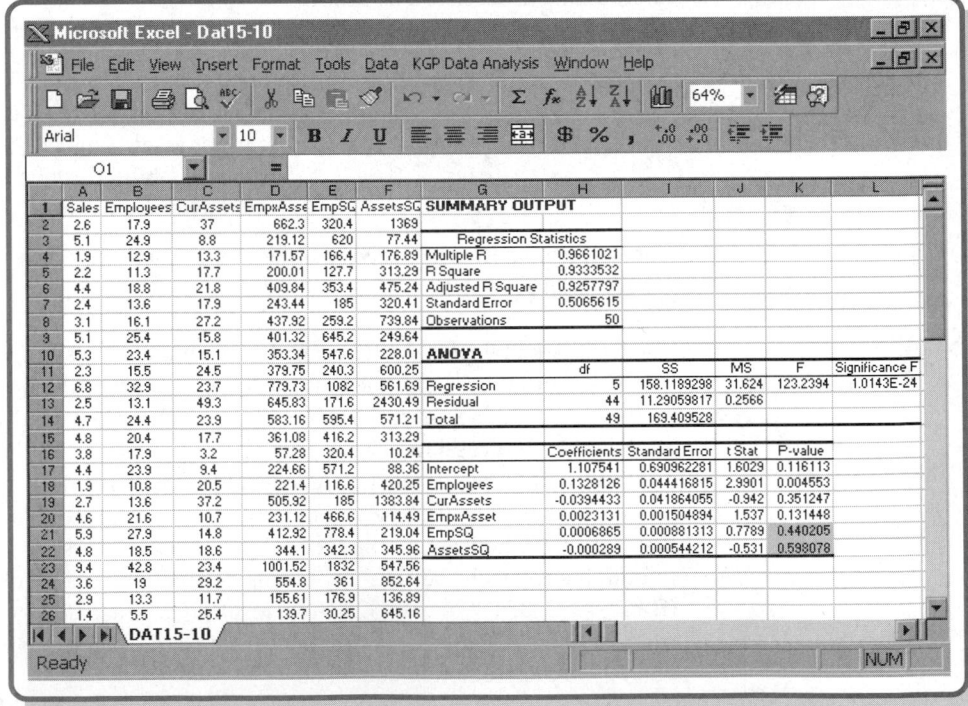

In Figure 15.26, the interaction effect between X_1 and X_2 (that is, X_1X_2) along with the quadratic terms (X_1^2 and X_2^2) were included. The interaction column can be obtained by typing "=B2*C2" in cell D2 and dragging this cell down through cell D51. The quadratic column for X_1 can be built by typing "=B2*B2" in cell E2 and dragging down through cell E51. This should be repeated for the second quadratic term by typing "=C2*C2" in cell F2 and dragging down through cell F51. The titles "EmpxAsset", "EmpSQ", and "AssetsSQ" should be typed in the top row (cells D1, E1, and F1). Referring to the high-

FIGURE 15.27

Excel regression solution using X_1, X_2, and X_1X_2.

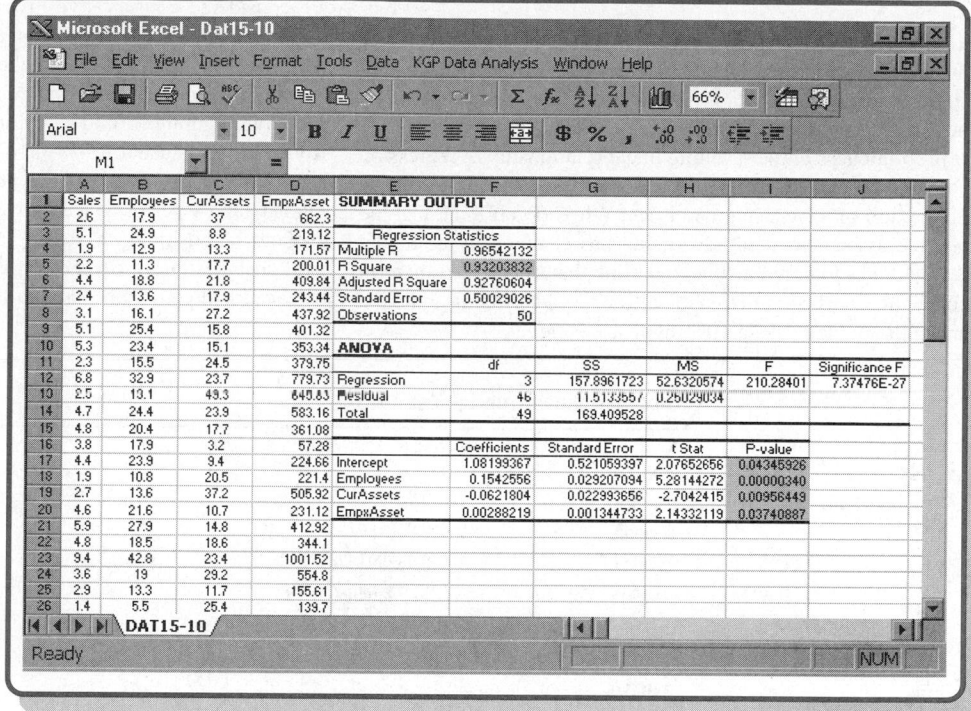

lighted *p*-values in Figure 15.26, the *p*-values for the quadratic terms appear quite large, and so the analyst decided to re-run the regression analysis without these terms in the model. This output is shown in Figure 15.27.

The R^2 value using the five predictors in Figure 15.26 is .933. The R^2 value with the quadratic terms removed is .932 (highlighted in Figure 15.27). Consequently, the two quadratic terms do not contribute significantly to the prediction of sales. This is confirmed using the partial *F*-value, where

$$F = \frac{(.933 - .932)/2}{(1 - .933)/(50 - 1 - 5)} = .33$$

which is less than $F_{.10,2,44} \approx 2.44$. The *p*-values for the remaining three predictors are less than .10, and so the resulting prediction equation is

$$\hat{Y} = 1.0820 + 0.1543X_1 - 0.0622X_2 + 0.0029X_1X_2$$

The final step in the analysis would be to examine the residuals as outlined in Example 15.9.

EXERCISES 15.55–15.60

UNDERSTANDING THE MECHANICS

15.55 Consider a regression model with a continuous independent variable X_1 and with an independent variable X_2 that is equal to 1 for training method A and 0 for training method B. Twenty observations were used to yield the following prediction equation.

$$\hat{Y} = 10.1 + 5X_1 + 8X_2 - 10X_1X_2$$

a. For training method A, what is the prediction equation?
b. For training method B, what is the prediction equation?
c. Are the prediction lines parallel in parts (a) and (b)?

15.56 Consider the following two regression models that were fit using 25 observations:

Model 1: $\hat{Y} = 13 + 2X_1 + 3X_2 + 6X_1^2 + 7X_2^2 - 20X_1X_2$

Model 2: $\hat{Y} = 10 + 14X_1 + 2X_2$

a. What terms in Model 1 indicate a quadratic effect?
b. If the coefficients of determination for Model 1 and Model 2 are .61 and .52, respectively, do the second-order terms contribute to the prediction of Y in Model 1? Use a .05 significance level.

Applying the New Concepts

15.57 A marketing researcher is interested in whether the interaction of advertising and price affect sales. The following computer printout displays a regression analysis of the contribution of advertising and price on sales. Comment on the appropriateness of the resulting linear relationship. A regression analysis is also provided for the same model but includes the interaction of advertising and price. Why do you think that the p-value associated with advertising has changed in the model that includes interaction? Do you think that the interaction term contributes to the prediction of sales when advertising and price are in the model? Use a 10% significance level.

15.58 Balanced mutual funds and convertible mutual funds are considered conservative investments. The standard deviation of a mutual fund's performance is a measure of the level of risk. If two mutual funds have the same performance, then the one with the smaller standard deviation is considered more conservative. A mutual fund's performance is also affected by a front-end load, usually 4% or higher for load funds and no charge for no-load funds. The asset size can sometimes affect a mutual fund's performance, since smaller funds can move in and out of positions in stocks rather quickly. The following table displays the five-year performance (in percentage) of 15 balanced and convertible mutual funds along with each fund's

Summary Output for Exercise 15.57

Regression Statistics

Multiple R	0.984261019
R Square	0.968769754
Adjusted R Square	0.963091528
Standard Error	111.4304063
Observations	14

ANOVA

	df	SS	MS	F	Significance F
Regression	2	4236871.4	2118435.7	170.6113	5.25007E-09
Residual	11	136584.09	12416.7354		
Total	13	4373455.49			

	Coefficients	Standard Error	t Stat	P-value	Lower 95%	Upper 95%	VIF
Intercept	−3487.886	402.32131	−8.6694041	3.02E-06	−4373.389681	−2602.3823	
price	26.61620811	4.90601983	5.42521414	0.000209	15.81812582	37.4142904	1.00259
ad	6.844391846	0.39427939	17.3592434	2.43E-09	5.976588329	7.71219536	1.00259

Summary Output

Regression Statistics

Multiple R	0.99179144
R Square	0.98365026
Adjusted R Square	0.97874534
Standard Error	84.5605478
Observations	14

ANOVA

	df	SS	MS	F	Significance F
Regression	3	4301950.63	1433983.54	200.5435008	3.141E-09
Residual	10	71504.8624	7150.48624		
Total	13	4373455.49			

	Coefficients	Standard Error	t Stat	P-value	Lower 95%	Upper 95%	VIF
Intercept	2200.1765	1909.99153	1.15192998	0.276145139	−2055.550566	6455.90356	
price	−51.93048	26.3008498	−1.9744792	0.076572324	−110.5324354	6.67147522	50.035
ad	−3.6836857	3.50256396	−1.0517112	0.317682354	−11.48788591	4.12051447	137.39
price*ad	0.14531379	0.04816743	3.01684784	0.012965072	0.037990063	0.25263752	194.73

asset size (in millions of dollars), risk (as measured by standard deviation), and a dummy variable, with 1 representing a fund with a front-end load and 0 representing a no-load fund.

Balanced or Convertible Fund	Five-Year Performance (Y)	Asset Size (X_1)	Risk (X_2)	Load (1) or No-Load (0) (X_3)
CGM Mutual	15.1	1,183	10.9	0
Davis Convertible Securities	17.5	51	9.8	1
Franklin Convertible Securities	16.2	170	7.9	1
Value Line Convertible	14.5	79	7.1	0
Dodge & Cox Balanced	15.7	4,169	7.7	0
Chubb Total Return	15.3	33	8.4	1
Mainstay Total Return	13.7	1,118	9.8	1
IDS Mutual	13.2	3,098	7.2	1
Hotchkis & Wiley Balanced Income	12.1	88	5.8	0
Wellesley Income	12.0	6,918	7.2	0
USAA Growth & Tax Strategy	11.2	185	5.9	0
Smith Barney Convertible	10.8	41	6.3	1
Van Kampen American Cap Harbor	11.6	377	7.7	1
Phoenix Convertible	10.5	194	5.9	1
Lindner Dividend	11.4	2,075	6.1	0

(Source: "Retirement Guide," Fortune, August 18, 1997, page 100)

a. Is there sufficient evidence that the model with only X_2 and X_2^2 contributes to the prediction of Y? Use a 10% significance level.

b. Do you think that X_1, X_3, and $X_2 * X_3$ contribute to the model when X_2 and X_2^2 are in the model? Use a 10% significance level. Comment on the effect of multicollinearity.

15.59 [DATA EX15-59] *Variable description:*

ReturnEquity: The return on equity of a stock in France's stock market
PE: Price/Earnings ratio of a stock in France's stock market
PBook: Price/Book value ratio for a stock in France's stock market

To understand the relationship between the return on equity (in percentage) with the price/earnings ratio and price/book value of a large-cap stock in France's stock market, an international investor selected 18 large-cap stocks from this market. Usually the higher the values of PE and PBook, the higher the value of ReturnEquity. Construct a complete second-order model to predict ReturnEquity from PE and PBook. Compare this model to the first-order model and determine whether the quadratic terms and interaction term contribute to the prediction of ReturnEquity. Use a 5% significance level.

(Source: Adapted from *Business Week,* "The Business Week Global 1000," July 7, 1997, p. 60.)

15.60 [DATA SET EX15-60] *Variable description:*

Tasktime: Time required to complete a task
Aptitude: Score on aptitude test
Exper: On-the-job experience

A manager in charge of a production process is interested in the amount of time, Y, in minutes (Tasktime) that it takes a production worker to perform a certain task relative to his or her score on an aptitude test (Aptitude) and relative to the person's on-the-job experience (Exper) in years. The manager uses a first-order regression model with Aptitude and Exper to predict Tasktime. In addition, the manager uses a second-order regression model with Aptitude, the square of Aptitude, Exper, the square of Exper, and the interaction of Aptitude and Exper. Test that the second-order terms contribute to the model using a 5% significance level.

SUMMARY OUTPUT FOR EXERCISE 15.58

Regression Statistics

Multiple R	0.7847528
R Square	0.615837
Adjusted R Square	0.5518098
Standard Error	1.4827703
Observations	15

ANOVA

	df	SS	MS	F	Significance F
Regression	2	42.29404077	21.14702038	9.618369049	0.003214352
Residual	12	26.38329256	2.198607714		
Total	14	68.67733333			

	Coefficients	Standard Error	t Stat	P-value	Lower 95%	Upper 95%
Intercept	−12.65165	10.64646862	−1.188342371	0.25768539	−35.84831179	10.54501226
x2	5.7192249	2.693129349	2.123635412	0.055176766	−0.148599821	11.58704953
x2*x2	−0.289622	0.164891544	−1.756439157	0.104476745	−0.64888977	0.069645841

(CONTINUED ON NEXT PAGE)

SUMMARY OUTPUT FOR EXERCISE 15.58 (CONTINUED)

Regression Statistics

Multiple R	0.8460454
R Square	0.7157928
Adjusted R Square	0.5578999
Standard Error	1.4726618
Observations	15

ANOVA

	df	SS	MS	F	Significance F
Regression	5	49.1587396	9.83174793	4.5334071	0.02422662
Residual	9	19.5185937	2.16873263		
Total	14	68.6773333			

	Coefficients	Standard Error	t Stat	P-value	Lower 95%	Upper 95%	VIF
Intercept	−22.862205	14.1803979	−1.6122401	0.1413686	−54.940518	9.216108	
x1	−0.0003456	0.00025095	−1.3771092	0.2017594	−0.0009133	0.000222	1.625351
x2	8.6250871	3.60381363	2.39332217	0.0403371	0.47268803	16.77749	208.6636
x3	−2.7002352	4.0937225	−0.6596039	0.526025	−11.960886	6.560415	28.84879
x2x3	0.1594412	0.55199712	0.2888443	0.7792431	−1.089264	1.408146	34.57355
x2*x2	−0.4667688	0.21318029	−2.1895496	0.0562916	−0.9490165	0.015479	194.7752

SUMMARY

Multiple linear regression offers a method of predicting (or modeling) the behavior of a particular **dependent** variable (Y) using two or more **independent (predictor)** variables. As in the case of simple linear regression, which uses one predictor variable, the regression coefficients are those that minimize

$$\text{SSE} = \text{sum of squares of error} = \sum(Y - \hat{Y})^2$$

To use this technique properly, you must pay special attention to the assumptions behind it: (1) the regression errors follow a normal distribution, centered at zero, with a common variance and (2) the errors are statistically independent. An estimate of this common variance is

$$\hat{\sigma}_e^2 = s^2 = \text{MSE} = \frac{\text{SSE}}{n - k - 1}$$

To determine the adequacy of the regression model, you can test the entire set of predictor variables using an F-test with k and $n - k - 1$ degrees of freedom:

$$F = \frac{\text{MSR}}{\text{MSE}} = \frac{R^2 / k}{(1 - R^2) / (n - k - 1)}$$

The contribution of an individual predictor variable (say, X_i) can be tested using a t statistic with $n - k - 1$ df:

$$t = \frac{b_i}{s_{b_i}}$$

where s_{b_i} represents the estimated standard deviation of b_i. Here b_i is the least squares estimate of the population parameter, β_i, and centers the confidence interval for this parameter.

The **coefficient of determination, R^2,** describes the percentage of the total variation in the sample Y values explained by this set of predictor variables. To determine the contribution of a particular subset of the predictor variables—such as X_2 and X_4—R^2 is computed with X_2 and X_4 included and then with X_2 and X_4 excluded from the regression equation. A **partial F-test** is then used to determine whether the resulting decrease in R^2 is significant. The **adjusted value of R^2,** $R^2(\text{adj})$, is a statistic that, unlike R^2, does not necessarily increase as variables are added to the model. $R^2(\text{adj})$ helps distinguish variables that significantly improve the model from those that do not.

When a **curvilinear** pattern exists between two variables, X and Y, this nonlinear relationship often can be modeled by including an X^2 term in the regression equation. The resulting equation is

$$\hat{Y} = b_0 + b_1 X + b_2 X^2$$

This type of model often works well in situations where Y (for example, sales) appears to increase more slowly as the independent variable, X (for example, the amount of shelf space devoted to this product) continues to increase.

The problem of **multicollinearity** arises in the application of multiple linear regression whenever one or more of the predictor variables are a nearly linear combination of the remaining predictor variables. The most common form of multicollinearity occurs when two predictor variables are highly correlated. The resulting regression equation contains coefficients that are highly inflated (have a large variance), with t statistics that are extremely small, despite the fact that one or more of these seemingly insignificant variables are very useful predictors. The presence of multicollinearity within a specific data set can be detected by computing a **variance inflation factor** for each predictor variable. This value is large (>10) whenever the corresponding predictor variable produces a large R^2 value when regressed on the remaining predictor variables.

Stepwise techniques allow you to insert variables one at a time into the equation (**forward regression**), remove them one at a time after initially including all variables in the equation (**backward regression**), or perform a combination of the two by inserting variables one at a time but removing a variable that has become redundant at any stage (**stepwise regression**). Once the variables for the model have been selected, **residual plots** should be obtained (1) to examine the underlying assumptions that are necessary in a regression analysis, and (2) to search for outlying and influential observations. Sample observations that have unusually large or small values for the predictor variables can be detected using **sample leverages (h_i).** By computing the **standardized residuals,** you can identify observations having an outlying value of the dependent variable, Y. **Cook's distance measures (D_i)** can be used to determine if any of the sample observations have a large effect on determining the regression equation.

Dummy variables can be used in a regression application to represent the categories of a qualitative variable (such as city). If all dummy variables are to be inserted into the equation, then $C-1$ such variables should be defined to represent C categories. If a forward or stepwise selection procedure is used to define the final regression equation, then a better procedure is to define C dummy variables to represent this situation.

Use of a computer package is essential in the derivation of a multiple regression equation. In this chapter, we used Excel and MINITAB. They provide the sampling coefficients (b_0, b_1, b_2, . . .), the statistics necessary to perform any test of hypothesis, and those needed for the prediction and confidence intervals for any specific set of predictor variable values. A **confidence interval** is derived whenever the predicted Y value is used to estimate the average value of the dependent variable for a specific set of X values. When the predicted Y value is used to predict an individual value of Y for a specific set of X values, a **prediction interval** can be used to place bounds on the actual Y value.

A linear regression model containing a strictly linear combination of the predictor variables (such as $Y = \beta_0 + \beta_1 X_1 + \beta_2 X_2 + e$) is a **first-order model.** A **complete second-order model** (such as $Y = \beta_0 + \beta_1 X_1 + \beta_2 X_2 + \beta_3 X_1 X_2 + \beta_4 X_1^2 + \beta_5 X_2^2 + e$) includes **interaction** terms (such as $\beta_3 X_1 X_2$) and **quadratic** terms (such as $\beta_4 X_1^2$). The second-order model provides an extremely powerful modeling device, since any curvilinear effects of the predictor variables (using the quadratic terms) and any interactive effects between the predictor variables can be captured.

SUMMARY OF FORMULAS

$$H_0: \text{all } \beta\text{'s} = 0$$

$$H_a: \text{at least one } \beta \neq 0$$

$$F = \frac{\text{MSR}}{\text{MSE}} = \frac{R^2/k}{(1-R^2)/(n-k-1)}$$

$$(\text{df} = k \text{ and } n-k-1)$$

$$H_0: \beta_i = 0$$

$$H_a: \beta_i \neq 0$$

$$(\text{or } H_a: \beta_i > 0)$$

$$(\text{or } H_a: \beta_i < 0)$$

$$t = \frac{b_i}{s_{b_i}}$$

$$(\text{df} = n - k - 1)$$

CONFIDENCE INTERVAL FOR β_i

$$b_i - t_{\alpha/2, n-k-1} s_{b_i} \quad \text{to} \quad b_i + t_{\alpha/2, n-k-1} s_{b_i}$$

COEFFICIENT OF DETERMINATION

$$R^2 = 1 - \frac{\text{SSE}}{\text{SST}}$$

where

$$SST = \sum(Y - \bar{Y})^2 = \sum Y^2 - \frac{(\sum Y)^2}{n}$$

and

$$SSE = \sum(Y - \hat{Y})^2$$

COEFFICIENT OF DETERMINATION (ADJUSTED)

$$R^2 (\text{adj}) = 1 - \frac{SSE/(n-k-1)}{SST/(n-1)}$$

PARTIAL F-TEST

H_0: $X_i, X_{i+1}, \ldots, X_j$ do not contribute

H_a: at least one of them contributes

$$F = \frac{(R_c^2 - R_r^2)/v_1}{(1 - R_c^2)/v_2}$$

where (1) R_c^2 is the R^2 including the variables in H_0 (the complete model), (2) R_r^2 is the R^2 excluding the variables in H_0 (the reduced model), (3) $v_1 = $ the number of β's in H_0, (4) $v_2 = n - 1 - $ (number of X's in the complete model), and (5) the degrees of freedom for the F statistic are v_1 and v_2.

VARIANCE INFLATION FACTOR FOR THE jTH PREDICTOR VARIABLE

$$VIF_j = \frac{1}{1 - R_j^2}$$

where R_j^2 is the coefficient of determination obtained by regressing the jth predictor variable on the remaining $k - 1$ predictor variables.

STANDARDIZED RESIDUAL

$$\text{Standardized residual} = \frac{Y_i - \hat{Y}_i}{s\sqrt{1 - h_i}}$$

where h_i is the corresponding leverage value, $s = \sqrt{MSE}$, and $MSE = SSE/(n - k - 1)$.

COOK'S DISTANCE MEASURE

$$D_i = \frac{(Y_i - \hat{Y}_i)^2}{(k+1)s^2}\left[\frac{h_i}{(1 - h_i)^2}\right]$$

REVIEW EXERCISES 15.61–15.76

15.61 The following information is selected from a computer printout of a multiple regression analysis:

Predictor	Coefficient	S.D.
Constant	-1.0	.396
X₁	4.8	.512
X₂	5.9	.42

Analysis of Variance

Source	df	SS	MS	F
Model	2		147.65	
Residual				
Total	19	314.80		

a. Write the multiple regression equation.
b. What percentage of the total variation in Y is explained by the model?
c. Does the model with X_1 and X_2 contribute to the prediction of Y? Use a .05 significance level.
d. Does X_1 contribute to this model given that X_2 is in the model? Use a .05 significance level.
e. Does X_2 contribute to this model given that X_1 is in the model? Use a .05 significance level.

15.62 A company has opened several outdoor ice-skating rinks and would like to know what factors affect the attendance at the rinks. The manager believes that the following variables affect attendance:

$X_1 = $ temperature (forecasted high)

$X_2 = $ wind speed (forecasted high)

$$X_3 = 1 \text{ if weekend and 0 otherwise}$$

$$X_4 = X_1 X_2$$

The following least squares model was found from 30 days of data:

$$\hat{Y} = 250 + 4.8X_1 - 30X_2 + 1.3X_3 + 35X_4$$

a. What is the predicted attendance on a weekend if the forecasted high temperature is 28°F and the forecasted high wind speed is 12 miles per hour?

b. If the coefficient of determination for the model is .67, test that the overall model contributes to predicting the attendance at the ice-skating rinks. Use a .05 significance level. What is the value of the adjusted R^2?

c. If the standard deviation of the estimate of the coefficient of X_2 is 2.01, does the variable wind speed contribute to predicting the variation in attendance, assuming that the variables X_1, X_3, and X_4 are in the model? Use a .05 significance level.

15.63 To understand the linear relationship between business performance among wood manufacturers within the state of Minnesota, a random sample of 107 manufacturers was selected. The independent variables were the number of employees, production competence, and manufacturing strategy implementation. These independent variables were entered in the model sequentially as indicated in the table. Determine if the variable entered into the model at each step contributes to the prediction of business performance. Use a 10% significance level.

Independent Variables Included in the Model to Predict Business Performance	R-Square for the Model in Units of Percentage
Employee size	8.17%
Employee size Production competence	19.28%
Employee size Production competence Manufacturing strategy	21.05%

(Source: *1998 Proceedings of the Institute of Decision Sciences,* "An Analysis of the Relationship between Production Competence, Manufacturing Strategy Implementation, and Business Performance," p. 1298–1300.)

15.64 A real-estate agent wanted to explore the feasibility of using multiple regression analysis in appraising the value of single-family homes within a certain community. The following variables were used:

$$Y = \text{selling price of a house (in dollars)}$$

$$X_1 = \text{total living area (in square feet)}$$

$$X_2 = \begin{cases} 1 & \text{if in neighborhood 1} \\ 0 & \text{if not} \end{cases}$$

$$X_3 = \begin{cases} 1 & \text{if in neighborhood 2} \\ 0 & \text{if not} \end{cases}$$

$$X_4 = \begin{cases} 1 & \text{if lot size is larger than the typical house lot} \\ 0 & \text{if not} \end{cases}$$

The data are as follows:

Y	X_1	X_2	X_3	X_4	Y	X_1	X_2	X_3	X_4
63,000	2020	1	0	1	31,350	640	0	1	0
36,000	980	1	0	0	49,400	1910	0	0	1
44,000	1230	0	0	1	31,000	900	1	0	0
37,000	980	0	1	0	56,000	1890	1	0	0
28,000	640	0	1	0	63,500	1900	0	0	1
28,000	720	0	1	0	49,000	2080	1	0	1
56,000	2400	1	0	1	63,000	1900	0	0	1
28,600	670	0	1	0					

Using a computerized statistical package, find the following:

    a. The least squares equation

    b. The 95% confidence interval for the coefficient of total living area

    c. The 95% prediction interval for selling price given that $X_1 = 1800$, $X_2 = 1$, $X_3 = 0$, and $X_4 = 0$

    d. The overall F-test for the model and the resulting conclusion using a 5% significance level

15.65 To predict the asking price of a used Chevrolet Camaro, the following data were collected on the car's age, condition, and mileage and on whether the seller is an individual or a dealer.

Asking Price (Y)	Age (in Years) (X_1)	Mileage (in Thousands) (X_2)	Condition (Excellent, Average, Poor) (X_3)	(X_4)	Dealer or Individual (X_5)
3,000	9	70	1	0	0
2,700	9	99	0	1	0
2,995	8	120	0	1	0
5,500	7	56	1	0	1
3,988	7	50	0	1	0
3,900	7	83	0	1	0
2,800	7	106	0	1	0
6,800	6	70	0	0	1
6,295	6	66	1	0	1
3,700	6	60	0	1	0
7,450	5	55	1	0	1
6,800	5	67	0	1	0
6,795	5	62	1	0	0
6,476	5	60	0	1	0
6,450	5	55	0	1	0
4,800	5	75	0	1	0
9,695	4	44	1	0	1
9,675	4	37	0	0	1
9,595	4	44	1	0	0
8,500	4	55	1	0	0
7,995	4	46	0	1	0
6,995	4	56	0	1	0
6,450	4	65	0	1	0
14,350	3	29	0	0	1
11,965	3	23	0	1	1
11,850	3	27	0	0	1
11,000	3	31	1	0	1
7,600	3	45	0	1	0
19,888	2	18	0	0	1
16,000	2	19	0	0	1
17,650	1	9	0	0	1

The dummy variable X_3 is equal to 1 if the car is in average condition, 0 if not. The variable X_4 is equal to 1 if the car is in poor condition, 0 if not. The dummy variable X_5 is equal to 1 if the seller is a dealer and is equal to zero if the seller is an individual. Use a computerized statistical package to answer the following questions.

    a. Find the least squares equation.

    b. Does the overall model contribute significantly to predicting the asking price of a used Chevrolet Camaro? Use a .01 significance level.

    c. Find a 95% prediction interval for the asking price of a 5-year-old Camaro in average condition with 70,000 miles, sold by an individual.

    d. Calculate the correlation matrix of all the variables. Would you suspect any multicollinearity problems by observing the correlations in this matrix?

    e. Do a forward regression analysis using a significance level of .10.

    f. Examine the residuals. Do you detect the presence of any outliers or influential observations?

15.66 The owner of a photographic laboratory would like to explore the relationship between her weekly profits (Y) and

X_1 = number of rolls of film sold

X_2 = number of enlargements given out free for advertising purposes

X_3 = number of prints

X_4 = number of reprints

Several weeks were selected randomly, and the following data were collected.

Y	X_1	X_2	X_3	X_4	Y	X_1	X_2	X_3	X_4
350	50	15	130	50	358	62	17	125	35
414	61	18	150	39	392	55	19	150	36
385	71	12	125	45	415	59	24	157	44
429	86	21	141	36	380	63	28	140	38
415	90	22	133	40					

Use a computerized statistical package.

a. Find the least squares prediction equation.

b. Test the null hypothesis that X_4 does not contribute to predicting the variation in Y given that X_1, X_2, and X_3 are already in the model. Use a .05 significance level.

c. Find the 90% confidence interval for the mean value of Y given $X_1 = 85$, $X_2 = 20$, $X_3 = 135$, and $X_4 = 37$.

d. Find the coefficient of determination for the complete model and interpret its value.

e. Examine the residuals. Do you detect any outliers or influential observations?

15.67 Use a computerized statistical package to analyze the following data:

Y	X_1	X_2	X_3	Y	X_1	X_2	X_3
154	30	1	1	220	34	5	25
223	41	3	9	210	38	4	16
201	33	5	25	230	44	3	9
177	31	4	16	265	51	2	4
143	25	3	9	306	55	5	25
155	29	2	4	170	31	4	16

a. Find the least squares prediction equation.

b. Find the coefficient of determination for the model.

c. Test at the .10 significance level that X_2 and X_3 contribute to the prediction of Y, given that X_1 is in the model.

d. Test at the .10 significance level that X_1 contributes to the prediction of Y, given that X_2 and X_3 are in the model.

e. Plot the residuals of the complete model versus the predicted values. Do the residuals appear to be random? Are there any outliers or influential observations?

15.68 Complete the following ANOVA table for testing whether a model with five independent variables contributes significantly to the prediction of the dependent variable:

Source	df	SS	MS	F
Regression		95.6		
Error	20	159.0		
Total				

15.69 [DATA SET EX15-69] *Variable description:*

IQ5yr: IQ level of a 5 year old
IncHouse: Average annual income of household over past five years
BothWork: 0 if only one parent works, and 1 if both parents work

Family income appears to be correlated with a child's IQ at the age of five. According to an article in the *Toronto Star* ("Poverty Lowers Kids' IQs," Mar. 30, 1993, p. C8), persistent poverty during the first five years of life leaves children 9.1 IQ points lower at age five than children who suffer no poverty during that period. Suppose that a researcher studying the relationship between income and child IQ-level selected a random sample of 50 Canadian families. The researcher collected data on IQs of children five years of age, the average annual income of the family over the past five years, and whether both parents work. An effort was made to include families with very low income levels in this study.

a. Test at the 5% significance level that the square of IncHouse and the interaction of IncHouse and BothWork contribute to predicting IQ5yr given that the first order terms are included in the model.

b. Why is it inappropriate to include the square of BothWork in the regression model?

15.70 By using independent variables in a model, a stepwise procedure can sometimes produce a spurious "significant" model. Using Excel, use the **Random Number Generation** option under **Data Analysis** to generate values of 50 standard normal (mean = 0, standard deviation = 1) random variables of size 30 (place in columns A through AX). Then in cell B40, type "=correl($A$1:$A$30, B1:B30)" and drag over to cell AX40. Note that row 40 will contain the correlations of 49 random variables with the first random variable. Pick the column with the highest correlation and run a regression analysis. What is the p-value for this regression equation? Note that all of the random variables are independent, and none of the variables should be good predictors of the first random variable. However, by chance, a supposed good predictor may appear. What do the results of this procedure imply about the interpretation of the stepwise selection procedure in adding a predictor variable to a regression model?

15.71 As interest rates increased on bonds in the first quarter of 1994, in general the yield on utility stocks increased and the corresponding price decreased. Consider the following 10 utility stocks to be a random sample of utility stocks.

Company	Yield (X_1)	52-Week Return (Y)
SCEcorp.	8.35%	−24.64%
Houston Industries	7.92	−12.80
Detroit Edison	7.36	−13.81
American Electric Power	7.36	−2.03
Public Service Enterprises	7.29	−4.05
Consolidated Edison	6.45	−6.51
Pacific Gas & Electric	6.37	−4.32
Peoples Energy	6.21	−1.09
PECO Energy	5.43	−0.97
Panhandle Eastern	3.84	1.96

(Source: *Wall Street Journal,* "Comparing the Yields," Mar. 18, 1994, p. C1.)

a. Construct the ANOVA table for testing the regression equation $\hat{Y} = b_0 + b_1X_1 + b_2X_2$, where $X_2 = X_1^2$ and X_1 is the yield of the utility stock. Use a statistical computer package. Test the model at the .10 significance level.

b. What are the values of R^2 and $R^2(\text{adj})$? Should these values be equal? Explain.

c. Find a 95% significance interval on the mean value for the 52-week return for a utility stock yielding 6.5%.

15.72 A random sample of 12 countries was selected. The exports of the United States to these countries and the imports from these countries to the United States were as follows for 1991, in millions of dollars.

Country	Imports	Exports	Country	Imports	Exports
Japan	487,129	421,730	Venezuela	8,178	4,656
China	91,510	48,125	Italy	11,764	8,569
Taiwan	18,969	6,278	Republic of Korea	17,018	15,594
Canada	23,023	13,182	Sweden	4,524	3,286
Germany	91,064	85,149	Columbia	2,736	1,952
Saudi Arabia	26,136	21,302	Brazil	6,716	6,147

(Source: *The World Almanac and Book of Facts,* "U.S. Foreign Trade with Leading Countries," 1993, p. 662.)

a. Let Y be amount of imports and X_1 be amount of exports. Also let X_2 be a dummy variable that takes on the value of 1 if the country is in eastern Asia and 0 if the country is not in eastern Asia. Let X_3 be the interaction of X_1 and X_2. Use a statistical computer package to find the least squares equation.

b. Find the least squares equation that would be determined using a backward regression procedure. Use a .10 significance level.

15.73 **[DATA SET EX15-73]** *Variable description:*

Age: Age of teacher
Cost500: Quarterly cost for a teacher who has elected a $500,000 policy
Cost1000: Quarterly cost for a teacher who has elected a $1,000,000 policy

Teachers Insurance and Annuity Association (TIAA) offers teachers preferred rates on annual renewable term life insurance. The cost for this insurance is determined by the person's age and the amount of insurance desired. An analysis of the cost was conducted using multiple regression with the dependent variable being the quarterly cost of a policy. The independent variables are age and a dummy variable labeled indicator500_or_1000 (a 1 indicating a $500,000 policy and a 0 indicating a $1,000,000 policy).

(Source: Adapted from TIAA CREF pamphlet, "Life Insurance Made Simple," 1998.)

    a. Using the printout below, comment on the fit of this model. Which observation, if eliminated, do you think would result in a better fit. Eliminate this observation and rerun the analysis. Note that you will need to create a column for the dependent variable consisting of Cost500 and Cost1000 stacked into a single column. Also an indicator (dummy) variable will need to be created with zeros and ones to denote either the $500,000 policy or the $1,000,000 policy.

    b. Form an interaction variable between the indicator variable and the age variable. Run the multiple regression model in part (a) with this variable added. Comment on the fit.

SUMMARY OUTPUT

Regression Statistics	
Multiple R	0.950198302
R Square	0.902876812
Adjusted R Square	0.89762691
Standard Error	90.48703582
Observations	40

ANOVA

	df	SS	MS	F	Significance F
Regression	2	2816307.165	1408153.582	171.979745	1.84278E-19
Residual	37	302952.4351	8187.903652		
Total	39	3119259.6			

	Coefficients	Standard Error	t Stat	P-value
Intercept	−415.1261391	52.59855713	−7.892348416	1.90023E-09
Age	15.40563549	0.990839557	15.54806263	8.31039E-18
Indicator500_or_1000	289.3	28.61451319	10.11025412	3.39981E-12

RESIDUAL OUTPUT

Observation	Predicted Y	Residuals	Standardized Residuals	Leverages	Cook's D
1	−29.985251799	171.985251799	2.025036475	0.119064748	0.184749668
2	16.231654676	136.768345324	1.595781420	0.102877698	0.097340854
3	47.042925659	116.957074341	1.357390555	0.093285372	0.063187523
4	93.259832134	81.740167866	0.942148709	0.080695444	0.025972112
5	124.071103118	64.928896882	0.745468388	0.073501199	0.014695582
6	170.288009592	33.711990408	0.385192733	0.064508393	0.003410447
7	201.099280576	21.900719424	0.249598302	0.059712230	0.001318756
8	247.316187050	−6.316187050	−0.071778723	0.054316547	0.000098641
9	278.127458034	−14.127458034	−0.160344778	0.051918465	0.000469315
10	324.344364508	−35.344364508	−0.400773892	0.050119904	0.002825004
11	355.155635492	−41.155635492	−0.466668575	0.050119904	0.003830340
12	401.372541966	−52.372541966	−0.594421415	0.051918465	0.006449764
13	432.183812950	−45.183812950	−0.513480104	0.054316547	0.005047919
14	478.400719424	−48.400719424	−0.551613722	0.059712230	0.006440972
15	509.211990408	−26.211990408	−0.299497837	0.064508393	0.002061781
16	555.428896882	−108.428896882	−1.244905102	0.073501199	0.040982723
17	586.240167866	−97.240167866	−1.120803896	0.080695444	0.036755948
18	632.457074341	−88.457074341	−1.026622784	0.093285372	0.036144605

Observation	Predicted Y	Residuals	Standardized Residuals	Leverages	Cook's D
19	663.268345324	−49.268345324	−0.574851658	0.102877698	0.012631645
20	709.485251799	−15.485251799	−0.182330749	0.119064748	0.001497745
21	259.314748201	0.685251799	0.008068482	0.119064748	0.000002933
22	305.531654676	−22.531654676	−0.262894135	0.102877698	0.002641862
23	336.342925659	−33.342925659	−0.386974218	0.093285372	0.005135536
24	382.559832134	−59.559832134	−0.686495029	0.080695444	0.013789330
25	413.371103118	−65.371103118	−0.750545492	0.073501199	0.014896436
26	459.588009592	81.588009592	−0.932223462	0.064508393	0.019975384
27	490.399280576	−77.399280576	−0.882104766	0.059712230	0.016471062
28	536.616187050	−91.616187050	−1.041149167	0.054316547	0.020753485
29	567.427458034	−79.427458034	−0.901491130	0.051918465	0.014834668
30	613.644364508	−77.644364508	−0.880418550	0.050119904	0.013633224
31	644.455635492	−63.455635492	−0.719530888	0.050119904	0.009105821
32	690.672541966	−44.672541966	−0.507027435	0.051918465	0.004692646
33	721.483812950	−5.483812950	−0.062319416	0.054316547	0.000074355
34	767.700719424	30.299280576	0.345315093	0.059712230	0.002524134
35	798.511990408	96.488009592	1.102470654	0.064508393	0.027937604
36	844.728896882	−16.728896882	−0.192069547	0.073501199	0.000975541
37	875.540167866	30.459832134	0.351084323	0.080695444	0.003606544
38	921.757074341	86.242925659	1.000925625	0.093285372	0.034357796
39	952.568345324	185.431654676	2.163573659	0.102877698	0.178933523
40	998.785251799	289.214748201	3.405352541	0.119064748	0.522446862

15.74 [DATA SET EX15-74] *Variable description:*

RatingPeers: Performance rating by peers on a team
TimeJobRelated: Hours per week spent doing job-related tasks
Education: Education level equal to 1 for college graduate and 0 if not a college graduate
YearsJob: Years on the job

A large semiconductor plant uses "empowered" teams to perform certain projects. The performance of each team member is evaluated by the team on a scale from 1 to 10. A manager wishes to study the relationship between the performance ratings and the variables TimeJobRelated, Education, and YearsJob. The regression analysis with only TimeJobRelated as a predictor shows an R^2 of 22.3%. Would you include Education and YearsJob in the prediction equation to increase the R^2 to 38.2%? Use a 5% significance level.

SUMMARY OUTPUT

Regression Statistics	
Multiple R	0.48570004
R Square	0.23590453
Adjusted R Square	0.20268299
Standard Error	1.52779107
Observations	25

ANOVA

	df	SS	MS	F	Significance F
Regression	1	16.57465253	16.5747	7.10095	0.013840222
Residual	23	53.68534747	2.33415		
Total	24	70.26			

	Coefficients	Standard Error	t Stat	P-value	Lower 95%	Upper 95%
Intercept	−0.7157087	2.762304748	−0.2591	0.79786	−6.42996366	4.9985463
TimeJobRelated	0.17319386	0.064994146	2.66476	0.01384	0.038743409	0.3076443

SUMMARY OUTPUT

Regression Statistics

Multiple R	0.6182944
R Square	0.3822879
Adjusted R Square	0.2940434
Standard Error	1.437598
Observations	25

ANOVA

	df	SS	MS	F	Significance F
Regression	3	26.859551	8.95318366	4.3321408	0.01586491
Residual	21	43.400449	2.06668805		
Total	24	70.26			

	Coefficients	Standard Error	t Stat	P-value	Lower 95%	Upper 95%
Intercept	−0.9786549	2.64089744	−0.37057664	0.7146646	−6.47070274	4.51339292
TimeJobRelated	0.1548929	0.06173445	2.50901927	0.0203771	0.02650908	0.28327675
Education	1.1946801	0.59264515	2.01584392	0.0567901	−0.03779315	2.42715339
YearsJob	0.1171507	0.11234573	1.04276966	0.3089114	−0.11648506	0.35078651

15.75 [DATA SET EX15-75] *Variable description:*

MonthlyPay: Monthly payment for a leased truck
StickerPrice: Sticker price of truck
OwnPickUp3: 1 if the customer leased a pickup within the past three years, and 0 if not
OwnPickUpGT3: 1 if the customer leased a pickup more than three years ago, and 0 if not

Owning a pick-up truck through a lease arrangement has become popular with many pick-up drivers. Recently, Dodge upscaled its pick-ups to the Quad Cab model. Spruced up with CD players, keyless entry, and automatic transmissions, pick-ups have taken a larger part of the market share of automotive sales (*The Wall Street Journal,* "Drive Buys," May 8, 1998, p. W4). Suppose that a lease manager wished to determine if there is a relationship between the monthly payment for a leased pick-up and the variables StickerPrice, OwnPickUp3, and OwnPickUpGT3. The manager believes that the monthly price that a customer is willing to negotiate may be influenced by whether they have previously leased a pick-up. A random sample of 14 pick-up lease agreement customers was selected. The data on StickerPrice is in units of thousands of dollars.

a. Interpret the coefficients in the regression model. Do the independent variables contribute to the prediction of monthly payment at the 5% significance level?

b. Are there any outliers or influential observations?

c. Eliminate the most influential observation and run the regression analysis again. Interpret the coefficients of this model. Do the independent variables contribute to the prediction of monthly payment at the 5% significance level?

SUMMARY OUTPUT

Regression Statistics

Multiple R	0.941890346
R Square	0.887157423
Adjusted R Square	0.85330465
Standard Error	49.38638683
Observations	14

ANOVA

	df	SS	MS	F	Significance F
Regression	3	191753.0163	63917.6721	26.206344	4.71408E-05
Residual	10	24390.15204	2439.0152		
Total	13	216143.1683			

	Coefficients	Standard Error	t Stat	P-value	Lower 95%	Upper 95%
Intercept	−163.2625997	73.02360287	−2.23575109	0.0493587	−325.9693545	−0.5558449
StickerPrice	19.62576855	2.248387679	8.72881876	5.444E-06	14.61604774	24.635489
OwnPickUp3	195.1025757	39.94847761	4.88385509	0.0006383	106.0918053	284.11335
OwnPickUpGT3	58.46083195	35.48437318	1.64750922	0.1304729	−20.60329225	137.52496

RESIDUAL OUTPUT

Observation	Predicted MonthlyPay	Residuals	Standardized Residuals	Leverages	Cook's D
1	619.389091809	−28.621291809	−0.727684509	0.365724850	0.07633136
2	420.430193362	−31.767233362	−0.724867602	0.212542904	0.03545496
3	454.532635973	13.202044027	0.293552447	0.170729079	0.00443529
4	419.206252579	24.842107421	0.551135309	0.166998292	0.01522378
5	573.511188067	−46.139028067	−1.085381224	0.259103119	0.10299579
6	154.258377128	−67.738377128	−2.084713368	0.567125139	1.42347303
7	354.857690068	51.391509932	1.299455556	0.358723408	0.23614415
8	378.408612331	−51.761172331	−1.294325468	0.344297700	0.21991477
9	325.002563530	55.742556470	1.280231389	0.222711370	0.11740241
10	426.317923928	81.320116072	1.852194357	0.209670198	0.22753146
11	589.950438981	2.572961019	0.062694445	0.309452155	0.00044035
12	537.377337601	0.369662399	0.009687948	0.403057587	0.00001584
13	491.082960149	−1.634280149	−0.037060104	0.202693628	0.00008729
14	432.205654493	−1.779574493	−0.040468680	0.207170572	0.00010698

15.76 [DATA SET EX15-76] *Variable description:*

AppraisedVal: Appraised value of home
LotSize: Size of the lot on which the home is built
HouseSize: Square footage of the house
HouseAge: Age of the house

A real-estate broker is interested in predicting the appraised value of homes in a certain subdivision. The broker selected a random sample of 20 homes. The variable AppraisedVal is recorded in units of thousands of dollars, LotSize and HouseSize are recorded in square feet, and HouseAge is recorded in years. The correlations of LotSize, HouseSize, and HouseAge with AppraisedVal are presented below.

  a. Which variable would you place in a model using the forward selection procedure?

  b. Construct a regression equation with the variable selected in part (a). Does this independent variable contribute to the prediction of AppraisedVal at a 5% significance level?

  c. Add another independent variable to the model in part (b). Which variable would a forward selection procedure pick? Does this added variable contribute to the prediction of AppraisedVal at a 5% significance level?

  d. Should the third variable be added to the model using a 5% significance level?

  e. Find the VIFs for the independent variables that you believe should be included in the model and comment on whether a multicollinearity problem exists.

Correlation of AppraisedVal and LotSize	0.01499
Correlation of AppraisedVal and HouseSize	0.91204
Correlation of AppraisedVal and HouseAge	0.57869

COMPUTER EXERCISES USING THE DATABASES

EXERCISE 1—APPENDIX E

From the database, randomly select 50 observations. Regress the variable HPAYRENT (house payment or apartment/house rent) on the prediction variables INCOME1 (primary income), INCOME2 (secondary income), and FAMLSIZE (size of family). Find the coefficient of determination for the complete model. Find a 90% confidence interval on the mean value of HPAYRENT for families having a principal income of $45,000, a secondary income of $22,000 and a family size equal to three.

EXERCISE 2—APPENDIX E

Using the data from the previous problem along with dummy variables representing the LOCATION of the residences, do both a forward regression analysis and a backward regression analysis with a significance level of .10. Compare the two resulting models.

EXERCISE 3—APPENDIX F

From the database, randomly select 50 observations. Consider a multiple regression model, where the dependent variable is SALES and predictor variables are COSTSALE (sales cost), EMPLOYEE (number of employees), NETINC (net income), ASSETS, and TOTAL. Using these predictor variables, what percentage of the variation in the SALES values has been explained? Construct a histogram of the residuals. Do the regression assumptions appear to be satisfied?

EXERCISE 4—APPENDIX F

Using the data from the previous exercise perform both a forward regression analysis and a backward regression analysis, with a significance level of .10. Compare the resulting models.

INSIGHTS FROM STATISTICS IN ACTION: PERSONAL COMPUTER PRICES DROP AS TECHNOLOGY IMPROVES

The case study presented in the Statistics in Action section at the beginning of this chapter introduced the concept of a linear model containing more than one predictor variable. It posed the question: Can the price of a personal computer package be predicted based on its components, such as processor speed, size of the hard drive, and whether the package includes a monitor and/or a printer?

Below are the advertised price (after rebates, if applicable) and specifications for 20 computers that appeared in newspaper advertisements during April and May 1998. The first column represents the dependent variable, price in dollars. The five columns to the right of price are the predictor variables: processor speed, megabytes of RAM, size of hard drive in gigabytes, and two indicator variables—Monitor (1 for yes and 0 for no) and Printer (1 for yes and 0 for no). From data such as these, computer industry analysts can determine the most significant relationships of PC components to the price of a PC.

Price ($)	Mhz Speed	MB RAM	GB HardDrive	Monitor	Printer
799.92	233	32	2.1	0	0
1499.06	266	48	4.0	1	1
2599.92	400	64	12.0	0	0
1649.00	266	48	6.0	1	1
1699.99	300	64	5.7	1	0
1549.99	266	48	6.0	1	1
1799.99	300	64	4.0	1	1
1399.99	266	32	5.7	1	1

Price ($)	Mhz Speed	MB RAM	GB HardDrive	Monitor	Printer
1099.99	233	32	2.1	1	1
1649.93	266	48	6.0	1	1
1099.97	233	32	3.2	1	1
1799.99	300	48	6.4	1	1
2199.99	333	64	7.0	1	1
1499.93	266	48	4.0	1	1
1199.95	266	32	4.3	1	0
1399.99	266	32	4.3	1	1
1999.99	333	64	8.0	0	0
2599.99	400	64	12.0	0	0
1299.99	266	32	4.3	1	1
1349.70	233	48	4.0	1	1

Before using computer software to perform a regression analysis, answer the following questions.

1. From your own experience, which predictor variable do you believe would be the best predictor of a PC price? Which of the predictor variables do you believe would be the least influential?
2. Graph price with each of the variables: Speed, RAM, and HardDrive Size. Comment on how linear the fit is. From these graphs, which variable seems to have the steepest slope?
3. What other variables do you believe could have been added to this study to provide accurate predictor variables of the price of a PC?

Using computer software, conduct a multiple regression analysis using all five predictor variables and answer the following questions.

4. How significant is the overall regression model? Which of the predictor variables are significant? Use a .10 significance level.
5. Interpret the value of R^2 for the overall regression model. How does the adjusted R^2 compare to this value? Why are they different?
6. Delete any predictors that are not significant at the .10 level. Find the regression model without these predictors. How has R^2 changed? Would you expect it to change much?
7. Using the regression model from part 6, generate a 95% confidence interval for the price of a 333 MHz computer having a 8 GB hard drive, 64 MB RAM, and a printer. Interpret this confidence interval in the context of the problem.

Source: *Business Week,* "Cheap PCs," March 23, 1998, p. 28.

CHAPTER 15 APPENDIX: DATA ANALYSIS WITH MINITAB

MULTIPLE LINEAR REGRESSION

The instructions presented in the appendix for chapter 14 on simple regression also apply to multiple regression. Many of the options mentioned in chapter 15, such as VIFs, appear on the user forms presented in the appendix for chapter 14. These procedures will therefore not be repeated here. In this appendix, only a brief example using the real estate data from section 1 of chapter 15 will be used to illustrate prediction and confidence intervals and bands including quadratic terms and also to illustrate MINITAB's stepwise procedure.

To display confidence bands or prediction intervals for a single independent variable with either linear, quadratic, or cubic terms, click on **Stat ➤ Regression ➤ Fitted Line Plot.** The following user form will be displayed. Enter the dependent variable ("Footage" for this example) in the **Response** box and one of the independent variables in the "Predictor" box. Click on either **Linear, Quadratic,** or **Cubic** terms. For this example income is used as the predictor, and **Quadratic** is selected. The output follows the user form. Next, a plot of the regression line with the data points and bands for prediction and confidence intervals is displayed.

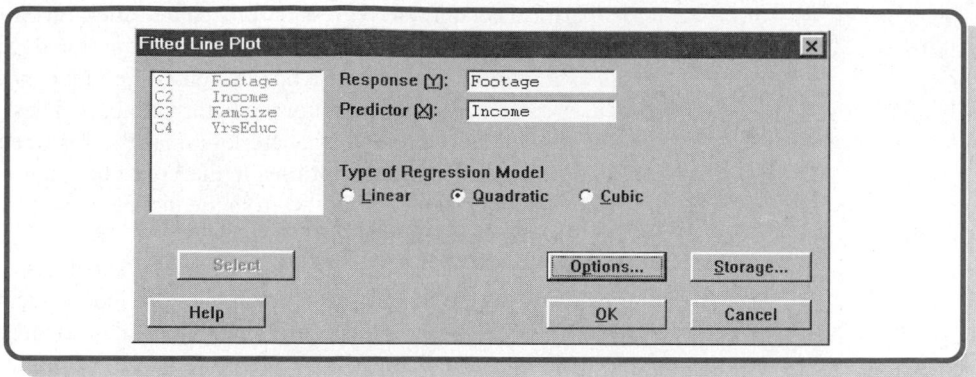

```
Session
|
Macro is running ... please wait

Polynomial Regression


Y = 15.7528 - 9.47E-02X + 4.40E-03X**2
R-Sq = 72.4 %

Analysis of Variance

SOURCE            DF         SS        MS         F          P
Regression         2    189.948   94.9740   9.17599   1.11E-02
Error              7     72.452   10.3503
Total              9    262.400


SOURCE      DF    Seq SS        F         P
Linear       1   186.587  19.6891   2.18E-03
Quadratic    1     3.361  0.324741  0.586587

MTB >
```

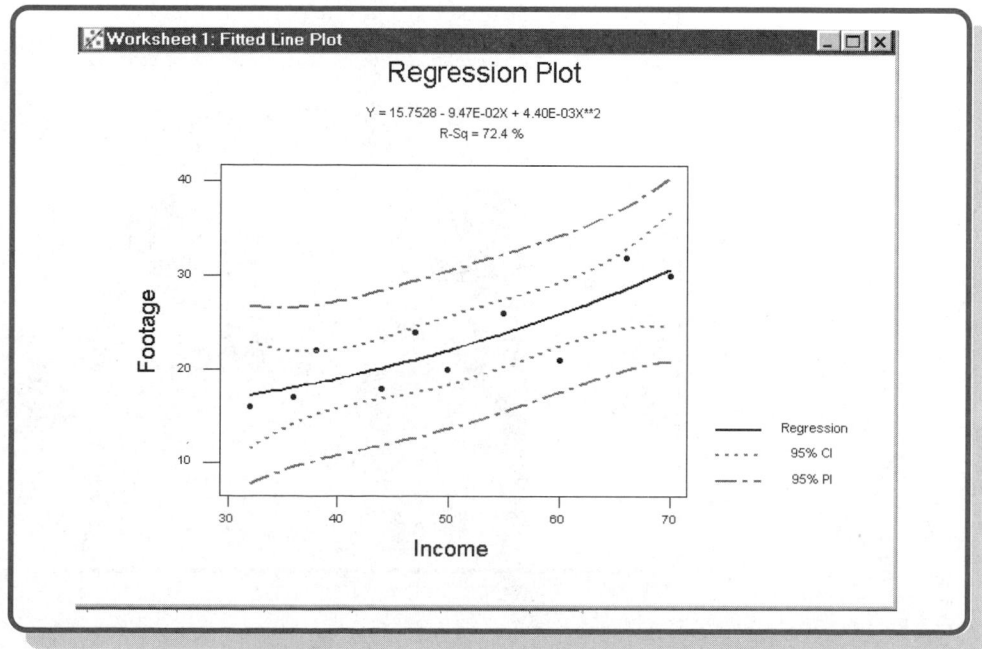

To perform a stepwise regression procedure, click on **Stat ➤ Regression ➤ Stepwise.** The following user form will be displayed. Enter the dependent variable ("Footage" for this example) in the **Response** box and enter the independent variables. In the **Enter** box, a user can enter a starting set of predictor variables. These variables may be dropped from the model if their F-statistics are less than the **F to remove** value, which can be seen/modified by clicking on **Options.** In the **Force** box, a user can enter a set of predictor variables that cannot be removed from the model, even when their F-statistics are less than the **F to remove** value under **Options.**

If **Options** is clicked, the next user form will appear. An F value can be entered in these boxes (4 is the default) to control when an independent variable will enter or be removed from a regression procedure. A number can be entered to show the best (number selected) alternate predictors. If the user prefers to be prompted for intervention, then the **Take _____ steps between pauses** option can be used. In step 1 of the stepwise procedure, an F-statistic for each predictor already in the model is calculated. If the F-statistic for any predictor is less than the value specified in the **F to remove** text box under **Options,** MINITAB removes the predictor with the lowest F-statistic and prints output from the resulting model. In step 2, MINITAB calculates an F-statistic for each predictor not in the current model. If any value is greater than the value specified in the **F to enter** text box in the **Options** for any predictor, MINITAB enters the predictor with the highest F-statistic and prints the output from the resulting model. These steps are repeated until no variables meet the criteria for addition or removal.

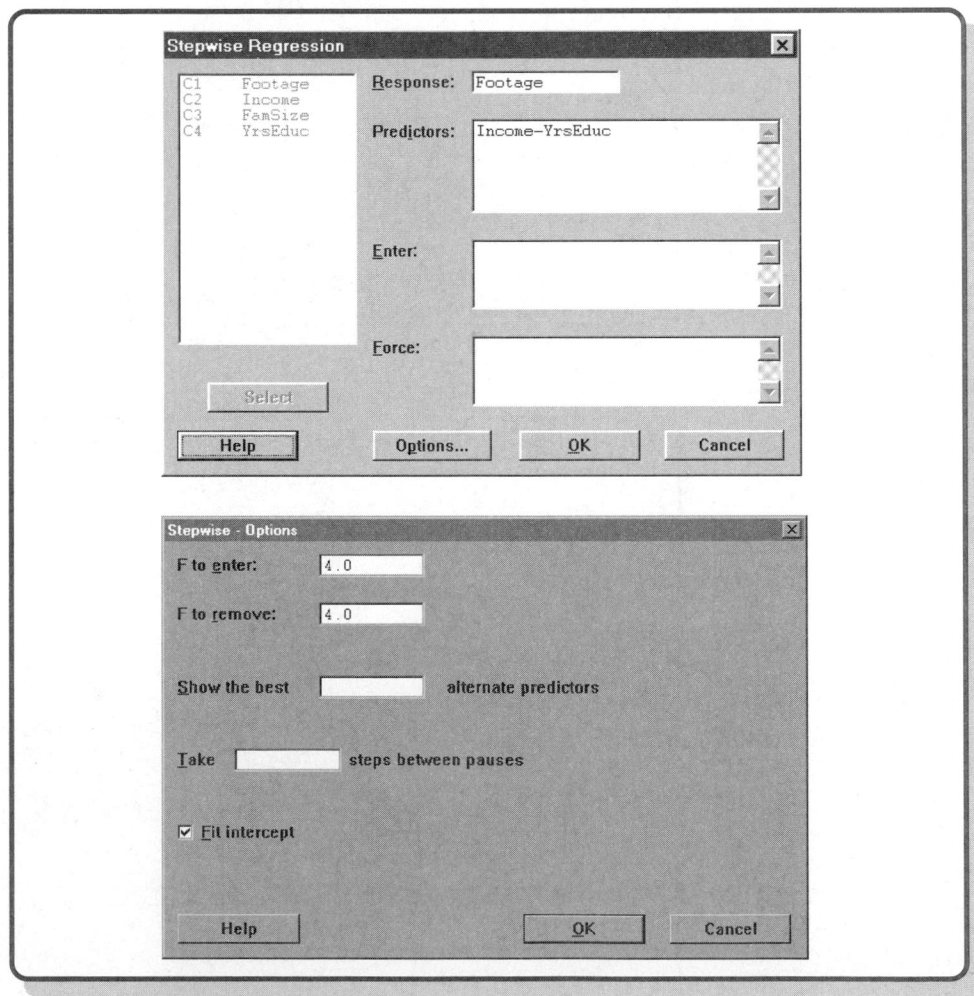

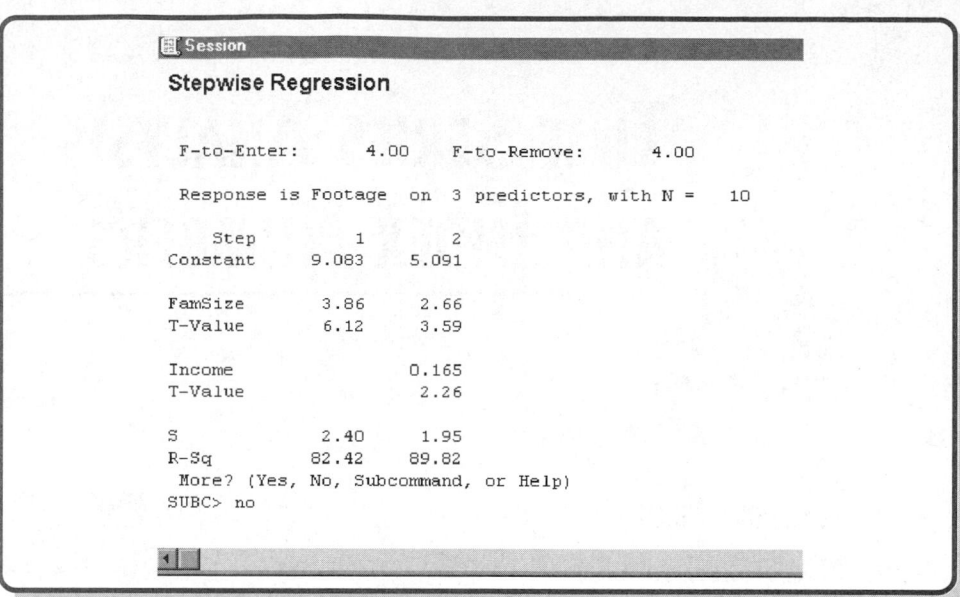

Session

Stepwise Regression

```
   F-to-Enter:      4.00    F-to-Remove:      4.00

   Response is Footage  on  3 predictors, with N =    10

        Step        1        2
   Constant     9.083    5.091

   FamSize       3.86     2.66
   T-Value       6.12     3.59

   Income                0.165
   T-Value                2.26

   S             2.40     1.95
   R-Sq         82.42    89.82
    More? (Yes, No, Subcommand, or Help)
   SUBC> no
```

TIME SERIES ANALYSIS AND INDEX NUMBERS

STATISTICS IN ACTION: WHICH WAY IS THE EMPLOYMENT COST INDEX HEADED?

Employers are watching the employment cost index to determine their overall cost and to perhaps pass costs onto the consumer by raising prices. The employment cost index is the government's broadest measure of compensation to workers. Strong gains in this index are good news to many Americans who are working or seeking work. However, strong gains are a headache for employers who are trying to remain competitive and control costs.

In June 1998, Federal Reserve Chairman Alan Greenspan told Congress that despite the Asian financial crisis's damping effect on the U.S. economy, he was worried more about inflation than recession. Part of his concern lay in the employment cost index. Since this index had been increasing during 1997 and 1998, the concern was that employers would raise prices to cover the costs. The United States was experiencing the tightest labor market in a generation in 1997 and 1998. High labor costs have historically been associated with inflation.

Surprisingly, the employment cost index did not increase as much as expected from 1993 through 1995, despite a robust economy. During that period of time, health care costs were declining and cost-saving gains from the advent of managed health care were being realized. As health maintenance organizations increased premiums and the cost of employees' paid vacation time increased, the employment cost index started heading up.

While regression analysis can be used to predict the employment cost index, using a forecasting procedure that takes into account seasonality may help the prediction of the forecast. The more accurate the prediction, the more likely a manager is to make the correct decision about cost and the company's budgetary projections. Many economic time series display seasonal fluctuations inherent in the business cycle. Analyses that adequately describe the seasonal components of the

data are essential for predicting business-related variables accurately. For example in 1998, some of the biggest increases in second-quarter compensation costs were in the construction and real-estate sectors, which not surprisingly were very robust sectors of the economy. Seasonal fluctuations in the economy can influence this sector.

This chapter examines data in the form of a time series—that is, a variable (such as the employment cost index) recorded across time. Of particular interest is whether the time series contains effects because of *seasonality* (within-year recurrent fluctuations), *trend* (a long-term growth or decline), or *cyclical activity* (unpredictable fluctuations about the trend, generally caused by economic conditions).

When you have completed this chapter, you will be able to:

- Describe and measure the various *components* (such as seasonality, trend, and cyclical activity) that make up a time series;

- Make simple forecasts by considering the trend and seasonal components; and

- Discuss a popular time series, the Consumer Price Index (CPI).

A Look Back/Introduction

The previous two chapters introduced you to a method of predicting the value of a dependent variable using the technique of linear regression. You determined a set of one or more predictor (independent) variables ($X_1, X_2, \ldots$) that could be used to model the behavior of the dependent variable, Y.

When the dependent variable is measured over *time*, there is another method of describing the behavior of this variable—**time series analysis.** For example, consider the following data, where Y is the amount of electrical power consumed in Pine Bluff over a ten-year period:

Year	Power Consumption (Million kwh)
1989	95
1990	145
1991	174
1992	200
1993	224
1994	245
1995	263
1996	275
1997	283
1998	288

This is an example of a (very short) time series. Typically, a time series covers many more periods, especially when measured for each month, week, or even day. To describe the behavior of the variable Y, we examine the past data and, rather than searching for a number of predictor variables, we try to capture the patterns that exist in the Y observations over a period of time. In other words, we assume that *time-related patterns can serve as predictors*. In this illustration, one pattern is clear—the power consumption values increase from one year to the next.

The process of using the patterns contained in the past data to predict future values is referred to as **forecasting.** Forecasting using time series data has both advantages and disadvantages. The primary advantage of using time series analysis is that often you can describe your variable of interest, Y, by using only a sample of past observations. Inherent to this type of forecasting procedure is the assumption that past patterns will continue into the future. The disadvantage of time series forecasting is that the past observations often contain patterns that are difficult to extract and, as a result, the models can become very complex.

In this chapter, we will concentrate on methods of *describing* a time series by isolating its various *components* (for example, sales in December are always much higher than the yearly average). In the next chapter, methods of forecasting are discussed. We should note at this point that in general, there is no single best forecasting technique. Instead, the forecaster should attempt to match the forecasting technique to patterns observed in the time series data. Consequently, this chapter and the next chapter are highly intertwined, since by describing the nature of the time series (Chapter 16), you will have a better idea as to which forecasting technique to employ (Chapter 17).

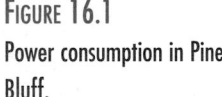

16.1 COMPONENTS OF A TIME SERIES

A **time series** represents a variable observed across time. The time increment can be years, quarters, months, or even days. The values of the time series can be presented in a table or illustrated using a scatter diagram. Usually, the points in the graph are connected by straight lines, making it easier to detect any existing patterns; such a graph is called a **line graph.**

The time series for the power-consumption data is shown in Figure 16.1. As we noted, the power-consumption values increase steadily from one year to the next. This long-term movement in the time series is called a *trend*. These values exhibit a definite increasing trend (or growth). Trend is only one of several components that describe the behavior of any time series. The **components** of a time series are:

> trend (TR)
> seasonal variation (S)
> cyclical variation (C)
> irregular activity (I)

The purpose of time series analysis is to describe a particular data set by estimating the various components that make up this time series. We examine each of these components individually, although time series data usually contain a mixture of all four. This section will *not* attempt to measure these components, but rather will introduce you to the nature of each component. The remainder of this chapter demonstrates methods of capturing and measuring these individual components.

TREND (TR)

The **trend** is a steady increase or decrease in the time series. If a particular time series is neither increasing nor decreasing over its range of time, it contains *no trend*. The trend reflects any long-term growth or decline in the observations. For example, a trend may be due to inflation, increases in the population, increases in personal income, market growth or decline, or changes in technology. Each of these factors could have a long-term effect on the variable of interest and would be reflected in the trend in the corresponding time series.

This long-term growth or decay pattern can take a variety of shapes. If the rate of change in Y from one time period to the next is relatively constant, the trend is a **linear trend:**

$$TR = b_0 + b_1 t$$

(for some b_0 and b_1), where the predictor variable is time t.

FIGURE 16.1
Power consumption in Pine Bluff.

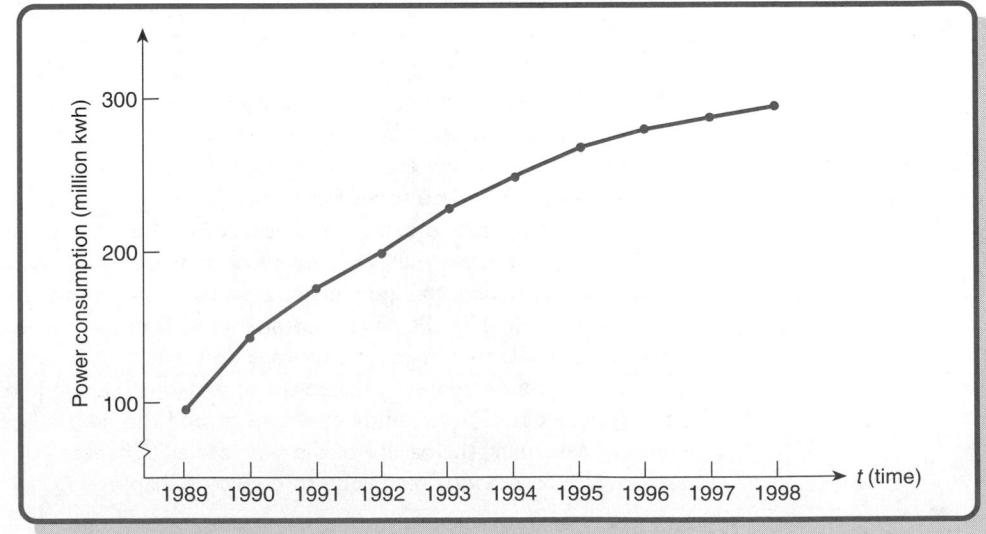

When the time series appears to be slowing down or accelerating as time increases, then a nonlinear trend may be present. It may be a **quadratic trend**

$$TR = b_0 + b_1 t + b_2 t^2$$

or a **decaying trend**

$$TR = b_0 + b_1 \left(\frac{1}{t} \right) \qquad \text{or} \qquad TR = b_0 + b_1 e^{-t}$$

These trend equations can be derived from the linear regression equations developed in Chapter 14 (for linear or decaying trend) and Chapter 15 (for quadratic trend). The linear trend equation is an application of *simple* linear regression, whereas the quadratic trend uses a *multiple* regression equation using two predictors, t and t^2. Simple linear regression techniques also can be used to derive b_0 and b_1 for the decaying trend equations, where values of t are replaced by the values of $1/t$ or e^{-t} in the data input.

The number of employees from 1991 to 1998 at Video-Comp, an expanding microcomputer-software firm, are recorded in the following table and illustrated in Figure 16.2.

Year	Number of Employees (Thousands)
1991	1.1
1992	2.4
1993	4.6
1994	5.4
1995	5.9
1996	8.0
1997	9.7
1998	11.2

The underlying long-term growth trend in this time series appears to be nearly *linear*, as represented by the trend line in Figure 16.2. To determine the equation of this line, we use the technique of simple linear regression, where X = the predictor variable = time and Y = the number of employees. We can estimate the existing trend using

$$\hat{y}_t = b_0 + b_1 t$$

where t represents the time variable and y_t is the value of Y at time period t. Here b_0 and b_1 are the least squares regression coefficients for a straight line predictor. The procedure of deriving these least squares estimates is developed later in the chapter. Figure 16.3 shows an *increasing* linear trend (y_t increases over time) and a decreasing linear trend (y_t decreases over time).

FIGURE 16.2

Number of employees at Video-Comp (an example of linear trend).

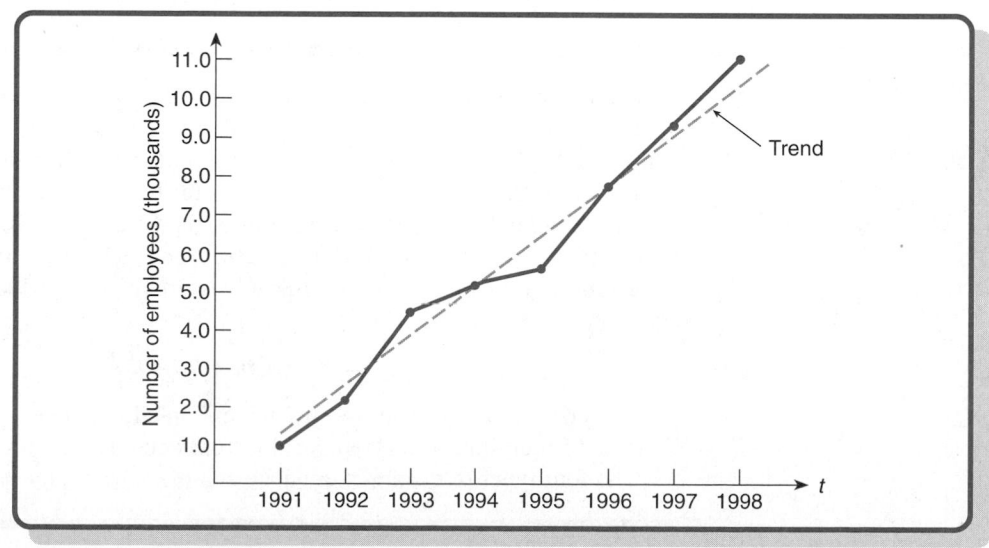

FIGURE 16.3

(a) Increasing linear trend: $TR = b_0 + b_1t$ ($b_1 > 0$).

(b) Decreasing linear trend: $TR = b_0 + b_1t$ ($b_1 < 0$).

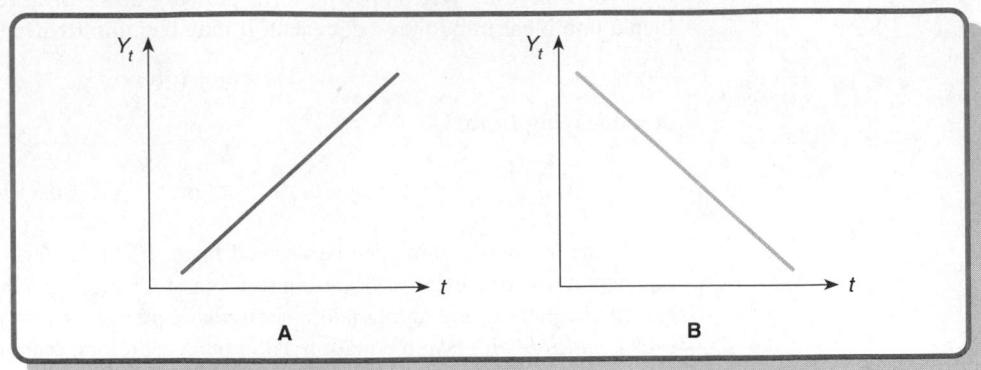

FIGURE 16.4

Quadratic trend. (a) Y increases at a decreasing rate. (b) Y decreases at an increasing rate. (c) Y decreases at a decreasing rate. (d) Y increases at an increasing rate.

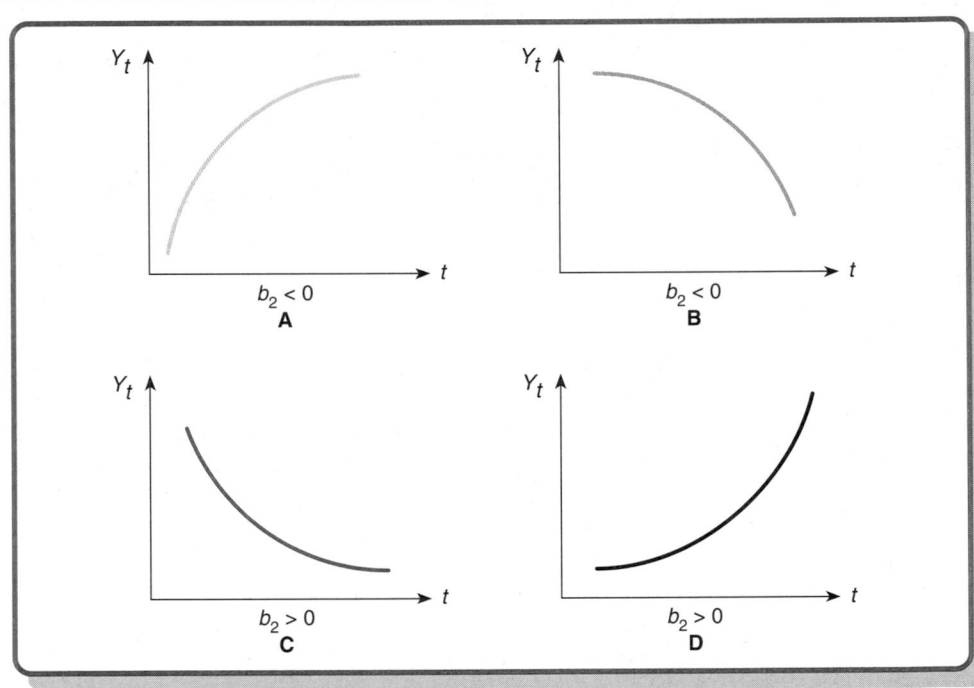

EXAMPLE 16.1

What type of trend exists in the power-consumption data (Figure 16.1)?

SOLUTION

Although this time series increases steadily, *it increases at a decreasing rate;* it starts off with large increases from one time period to the next, but these increments gradually become smaller. When the growth is linear, the values increase at a nearly constant rate. Figure 16.1 is an illustration of **quadratic trend,** where the time series randomly fluctuates about a quadratic (or curvilinear) level over time. This trend is captured by the equation

$$\hat{y}_t = b_0 + b_1t + b_2t^2$$

To derive these estimates, we use the multiple linear regression approach discussed in Chapter 15 (curvilinear models). Section 16.2 demonstrates this technique.

The four types of quadratic trend are summarized in Figure 16.4.

FIGURE 16.5

Illustration of seasonal variation. These are monthly observations; compare with annual data in Figure 16.1.

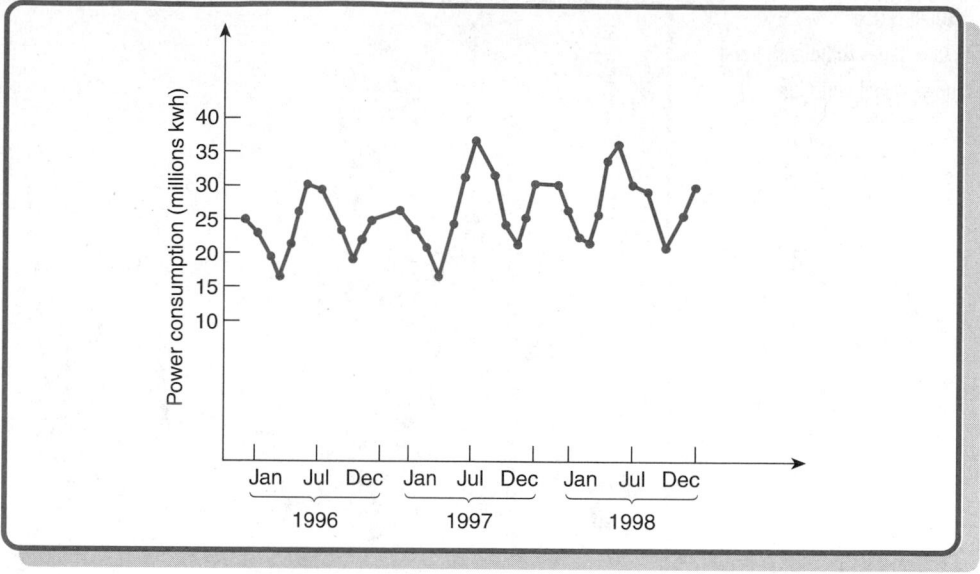

SEASONALITY (S)

Seasonal variation, or **seasonality,** refers to periodic increases or decreases that occur *within a calendar year* in a time series. They are very predictable because they occur every year. When a time series consists of annual data (as in Figure 16.1), you cannot see what is going on within each year. Data reported in annual increments therefore cannot be used to examine seasonality. Seasonality may or may not exist; annual increment data are not in a form that will show whether it does.

When time series data are quarterly or monthly, seasonal variation may be evident. For example, if the power-consumption data were available for each month over these 10 years, then the resulting time series would contain $12 \cdot 10 = 120$ observations. A plot of monthly data for the last 3 years (36 observations) is shown in Figure 16.5. The seasonal effects here consist of

> *Extremely high power consumption during the hot summer months (July and August)*
>
> *Very high consumption during the coldest part of the winter (December and January)*
>
> *Gradually declining consumption during the spring, reaching a low level in April and then increasing until July*
>
> *Gradually declining power consumption during the fall, but beginning to increase in November*

The key is that these movements in the time series follow the same pattern each year and so probably are due to seasonality. An analysis of seasonal variation is often a crucial step in planning sales and production. Just because your sales drop from one month to the next does not necessarily mean that it is time to panic. If a review of past observations indicates that sales *always* drop between these two months, then quite likely there is no cause for concern. On the production side, if sales always are extremely high in December, then you will need to increase production in the months prior to December so that you will have the necessary inventory level for this peak month. Measurement of this seasonal component is discussed later.

As mentioned earlier, a time series often contains the effect of trend and seasonality (as well as cyclical and irregular activity). The sales of Wildcat sailboats, illustrated in Figure 16.6, contain a strong linear trend as well as definite seasonal variation. In particular, the highest sales occur in the summer months of each year.

FIGURE 16.6

A time series containing trend
and seasonal variation.

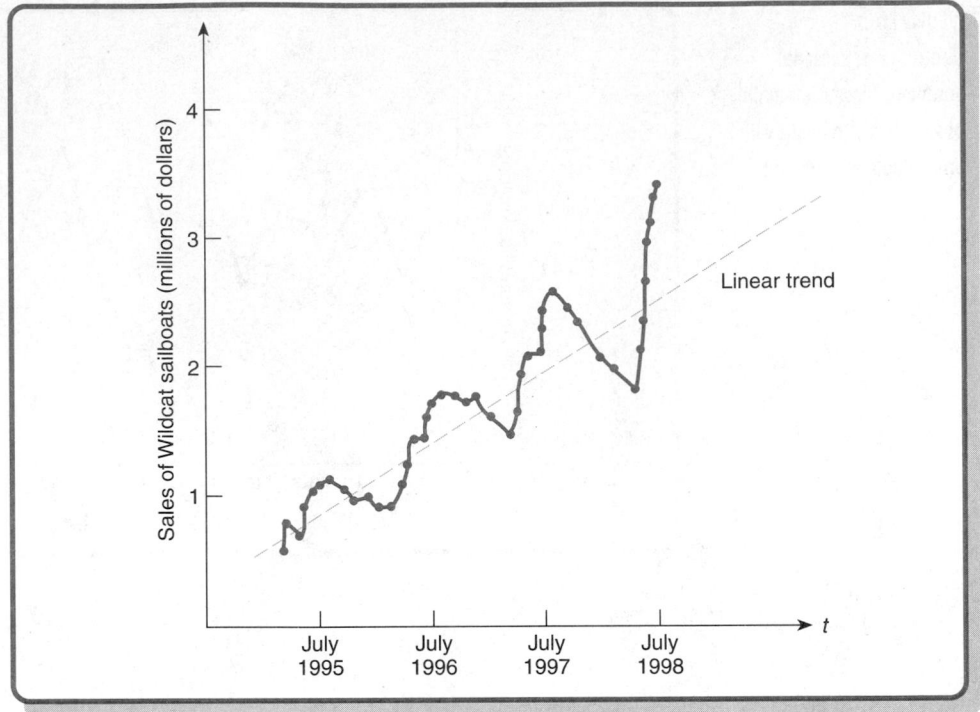

As manager of Wildcat Enterprises, would you be concerned that the sales of these boats in December 1998 were lower than those in July 1998? There may or may not be a problem; this seasonal pattern exists in Figure 16.6 despite an overall growth. More data would be required to determine whether the December sales were lower than expected for that month. What would you think if sales in July 1999 were lower than those in July 1998? This event should definitely concern you. This is a year-to-year comparison, and seasonal variation or not, we would expect the sales for July 1999 to be larger than for July 1998 if the long-term growth trend in Figure 16.6 is still present. Lower sales in July 1999 would indicate a possible leveling off or a drop in boat sales in 1999.

Cyclical Variation (C)

Cyclical variation describes a gradual cyclical movement about the trend; it is generally attributable to business and economic conditions. The length of a cycle is the **period** of that cycle. The period of a cycle can be measured from one **peak** to the next, one **trough** (valley) to the next, or from the time value at which the cycle crosses the horizontal line (where no cyclic activity exists) to the value where it completes the cycle and returns to this point. Figure 16.7 shows that the cycle length can be measured from P_1 to P_2, from V_1 to V_2, or from Z_1 to Z_2. In the illustrations to follow, we use the Z_1 to Z_2 approach.

In business applications, cycles typically are long-term movements, with periods ranging from two to ten years. The primary difference between the cyclical and seasonal factors is the period length. Seasonal effects take place *within* one year, whereas the period for cyclical activity is usually *more than* one year.

Cyclical activity need not follow a definite, recurrent pattern. The cycles generally represent conditions within the economy, where a peak occurs at the height of an expansion (prosperity) period and is generally followed by a period of contraction in economic activity. The low point (trough) of each cycle usually takes place at the low point of an economic recession or depression. This low point is then followed by a gradual increase during the recovery period.

FIGURE 16.7
The cycle can be measured from P_1 to P_2, from V_1 to V_2, or from Z_1 to Z_2.

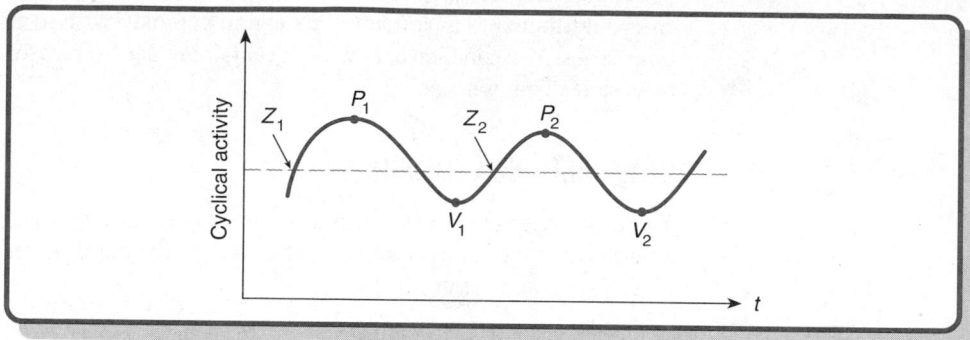

FIGURE 16.8
Annual taxes paid by Lindale Textiles (illustration of cyclical activity; Example 16.2).

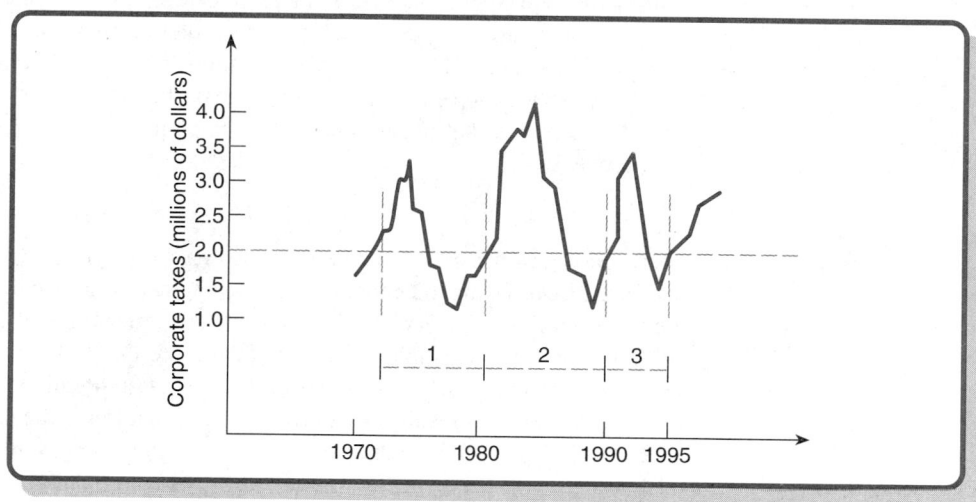

EXAMPLE 16.2

The annual corporate taxes paid by Lindale Textiles (a clothing manufacturer) over a 25-year period are shown in Figure 16.8. How many cycles do you observe?

SOLUTION

The year 1972 began a cycle lasting approximately eight years. There are three cycles contained within the time series, which ends in the midst of an "up cycle." Notice that the cycle lengths are not the same.

IRREGULAR ACTIVITY (I)

Irregular activity consists of what is "left over" after accounting for the effect of any trend, seasonality, or cyclical activity. These values should consist of noise, much like the error term in the linear regression models discussed in the previous chapters. *The irregular activity should contain no observable or predictable pattern.* An extremely large irregular component can be caused by a measurement error in the variable. Such an outlier should always be checked to ensure its accuracy.

The irregular component (1) measures the random movement in your time series and (2) represents the effect introduced by unpredictable rare events, such as earthquakes, oil embargoes, or strikes.

If a noticeable jump in the resulting irregular components (when plotted across time) can be attributed to a particular rare event, you may wish to eliminate such data from the time series. You can then examine the remaining data to measure more accurately the other time series components.

COMBINING THE COMPONENTS

The time series components can be combined in various ways to describe the behavior of a particular time series. One method is to describe the time series variable, y_t, as a *sum* of these four components

$$y_t = TR_t + S_t + C_t + I_t$$

This is called the **additive structure.** The implication here is that any seasonal effects are additive from one year to the next. For example, if the seasonal effect of December for a time series representing sales is an increase of 250 units over the average yearly sales, then this same increase will occur each year regardless of the sales volume. Whether the average yearly sales are 1000 units or 10,000 units, December should show a sales volume of approximately 1250 (the first case) or 10,250 (the latter case).

Better success has been achieved by describing a time series using the **multiplicative structure,** where

$$y_t = TR_t \cdot S_t \cdot C_t \cdot I_t$$

Here, the seasonal effect increases or decreases according to the underlying trend and cyclical effect. Using the previous illustration, the difference between the December sales and the yearly average will be *higher* for the latter case (where the yearly average is 10,000 units). For example, for the first case, the December sales might be 1250 (a 25% increase over the yearly average) and, for the latter situation, it might be 12,500 (also a 25% increase). This result follows from the implication in the multiplicative structure that as the sales increase from one year to the next, the changes in volume due to seasonality also increase. For our illustration, this shift was 250 units for the first case and 2500 units for the second case.

EXERCISES 16.1–16.6

APPLYING THE NEW CONCEPTS

16.1 Suppose that the sales of a retail store can best be described by a multiplicative structure with respect to trend, seasonality, cyclical variation, and irregular activity. Describe the seasonal effect on sales over time if the trend is increasing.

16.2 The following data set shows the percentage of disposable income (DPI) set aside as personal savings by people in the United States for the years 1983–1992.

Year	Percentage of DPI Set Aside as Savings
1983	5.4
1984	6.1
1985	4.4
1986	4.1
1987	3.2
1988	4.2
1989	4.6
1990	5.1
1991	4.7
1992	4.8

(Source: *The World Almanac and Book of Facts,* 1994, p. 116.)

a. Plot the data against time.
b. Describe the trend.

16.3 Construction in the housing industry usually appears to peak in the middle of the summer and to bottom out around January. If the number of new housing starts are the same for the month of March and the month of July in a particular year, of what concern would these figures be to housing construction companies? Would they be pleased, worried, or indifferent? Why?

16.4 The end-of-year inventory levels, in dollars, of West Coast Distributing are given in the following table. Estimate the period of the cyclical component by graphing the data.

Year	Inventory	Year	Inventory
1987	80	1994	80
1988	75	1995	83
1989	71	1996	80
1990	73	1997	77
1991	82	1998	79
1992	76	1999	84
1993	78		

16.5 To which of the four components of a time series would each of the following influences on housing starts contribute?
  a. Presidential election year
  b. Start of the school year in September
  c. Long-term growth of the housing industry
  d. Shortage of lumber because of a strike

Month	1998	1999	Month	1998	1999
Jan	1.2	2.2	July	2.9	3.8
Feb	1.4	2.4	Aug	3.2	4.0
Mar	1.3	2.3	Sept	2.5	3.5
Apr	1.5	2.4	Oct	2.4	3.0
May	1.5	2.5	Nov	2.3	2.8
June	2.3	3.5	Dec	2.1	2.5

16.6 Describe in words both the trend and the seasonal components for the following sales figures (in thousands of dollars). (*Hint:* Draw a graph for each.)

16.2 MEASURING TREND: NO SEASONALITY

Suppose that you have a time series containing trend and cyclical activity but no seasonality. For example, the employment data in Figure 16.2 are annual and so contain no seasonality. The same is true for the annual power-consumption data in Figure 16.1. When data are collected on a yearly basis, we are not concerned with any seasonality in the data; we need data from quarterly or shorter intervals to identify any seasonality. Yearly data may have trend (TR), cyclical activity (C), or irregular activity (I). If we observe a strong linear trend (as in Figure 16.2) or a quadratic trend (Figure 16.4), we can estimate it using the least squares technique developed in Chapters 14 and 15. We use simple linear regression for linear trends and multiple linear regression for quadratic trends.

LINEAR TREND

We begin by **coding** the variable to make the calculations (or computer input) easier.

We can find an equation for the trend line in Figure 16.2 passing through the eight observations in the time series. The least squares trend line through these eight values is sketched in Figure 16.9. The equation of the trend line is

$$\hat{y}_t = TR_t = b_0 + b_1 t$$

where t represents the time variable. For this equation, TR_t represents the trend component of the sample observation at time period t and is simply a new name for the trend effect that this equation allows us to estimate.

We could use $t = 1991, 1992, \ldots$ to represent time, but a much simpler method is to *code* the data, as illustrated in Figure 16.9. By using $t = 1, 2, \ldots$, the estimate, $\hat{y}_t$, is not affected and the calculations are easier. You are able to code the predictor variable, t, because the sample values are equally spaced—they are all one year apart. As we saw in Chapter 14, this equal spacing does not occur in all simple regression applications. Continuing the scheme in Figure 16.9, $t = 9$ represents the year 1999, and the estimated number of employees for 1999 (using trend only) is

$$\hat{y}_9 = b_0 + b_1(9)$$

FIGURE 16.9

Least squares trend line using coded time data (compare with Figure 16.2): $\hat{y}_t = b_0 + b_1 t$.

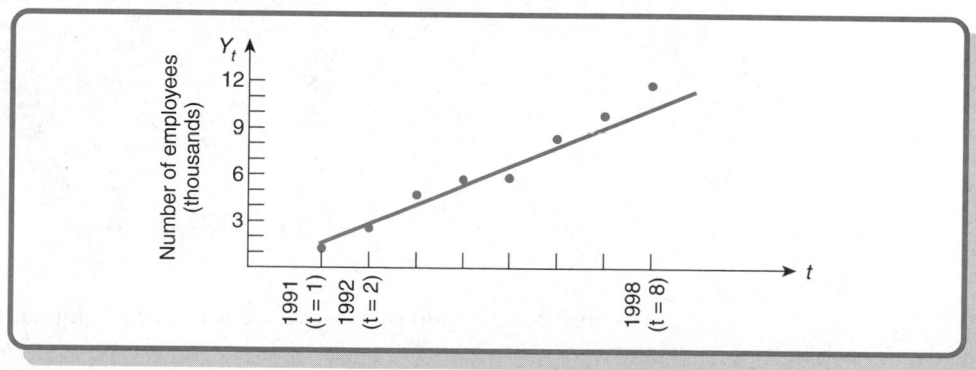

To derive the "best" line through the time series data, we use the least squares estimates discussed in Chapter 14; the independent variable here is time, t. The data are

t	y_t	
1	1.1	$(= y_1)$
2	2.4	$(= y_2)$
3	4.6	$\vdots$
4	5.4	
5	5.9	
6	8.0	
7	9.7	
8	11.2	

The calculations are

$$\Sigma t = 1 + 2 + \cdots + 8 = 36$$

$$\Sigma t^2 = 1 + 4 + \cdots + 64 = 204$$

$$\Sigma y_t = 1.1 + 2.4 + \cdots + 11.2 = 48.3$$

$$\Sigma y_t^2 = (1.1)^2 + (2.4)^2 + \cdots + (11.2)^2 = 375.63$$

$$\Sigma t y_t = (1)(1.1) + (2)(2.4) + \cdots + (8)(11.2) = 276.3$$

In Chapter 14, when we regressed the variable Y on a single variable X, the estimate for the slope of the least squares line (from equation 14.11) was given by

$$b_1 = \frac{SCP_{XY}}{SS_X} = \frac{\Sigma xy - (\Sigma x)(\Sigma y)/n}{\Sigma x^2 - (\Sigma x)^2/n}$$

where n was the number of sample observations. To determine a linear trend line for a time series, this equation becomes

$$b_1 = \frac{\Sigma t y_t - (\Sigma t)(\Sigma y_t)/T}{\Sigma t^2 - (\Sigma t)^2/T} \qquad (16.1)$$

where T = the number of observations in the time series.

The sample estimate of the intercept is

$$b_0 = \bar{y} - b_1 \bar{x} = \bar{y}_t - b_1 \bar{t} \qquad (16.2)$$

where $\bar{y}_t = (y_1 + y_2 + \cdots + y_T)/T$.

Because the time variable, t, *always* is 1, 2, . . . , T, there is an easier way to calculate Σt, Σt^2, and $\bar{t}$.

$$\Sigma t = 1 + 2 + \cdots + T$$

$$= \frac{T(T+1)}{2} \qquad (16.3)$$

$$\Sigma t^2 = 1 + 4 + \cdots + T^2$$

$$= \frac{T(T+1)(2T+1)}{6} \qquad (16.4)$$

$$\bar{t} = \frac{\Sigma t}{T} = \frac{T+1}{2} \qquad (16.5)$$

We use these equations to derive the least squares line in Figure 16.9. Using equations 16.3 and 16.4,

$$\Sigma t = \frac{T(T+1)}{2} = \frac{(8)(9)}{2} = 36$$

and

$$\Sigma t^2 = \frac{T(T+1)(2T+1)}{6} = \frac{(8)(9)(17)}{6} = 204$$

Also,

$$\bar{t} = \frac{\Sigma t}{T} = \frac{36}{8} = 4.5$$

This value can also be found using equation 16.5:

$$\bar{t} = \frac{T+1}{2} = \frac{9}{2} = 4.5$$

So we can now calculate

$$b_1 = \frac{\Sigma t y_t - (\Sigma t)(\Sigma y_t)/T}{\Sigma t^2 - (\Sigma t)^2 / T}$$

$$= \frac{276.3 - (36)(48.3)/8}{204 - (36)^2/8} = \frac{58.95}{42} = 1.4036$$

and

$$b_0 = \bar{y}_t - b_1 \bar{t}$$

$$= \frac{48.3}{8} - (1.4036)(4.5) = 6.0375 - 6.3162 = -.279$$

The trend line for this time series is

$$\hat{y}_t = -.279 + 1.404t$$

We conclude that the number of employees appears to increase at the rate of 1404 per year, on the average.

The trend line is derived using the same least squares procedure discussed in Chapter 14—you can use the computer instructions contained in the simple linear regression illustrations. A computer solution using Excel is shown in Figure 16.10. Enter the values 1 though 8 in column A and the time series values in column B.* To obtain the linear trend equation, click on **Tools ➤ Data Analysis ➤ Regression.** Enter "B1:B8" as the **Input Y Range,** "A1:A8" as the **Input X Range,** and "C1" as the **Output Range.** The regression coefficients in cells D17 and D18 agree with the previously derived trend equation.

Figure 16.10 contains the t statistic; you may be tempted to use it to determine whether time is a significant predictor of Y = number of employees. However, to use this statistic, you must assume that the errors about the trend line are completely *independent* of one another and contain *no observable pattern.* Do not forget that there may well be considerable cyclical activity about the trend line, and this cyclical activity will be contained in the residuals of the regression analysis. Thus there probably will be a cyclical pattern to these residuals, so the assumption of complete independence is not met. The errors are therefore *autocorrelated* and any test of hypothesis is invalid.

This situation poses no serious problems at this point, however, because *our intent is simply to describe the time series by measuring the various components, and not to perform a statistical test of hypothesis.* If, however, the residuals about the trend line appear to be extremely large, it suggests that a linear trend component is not appropriate.

---

* You can generate 1, 2, . . . , 8 in column A by typing "1" in cell A1 and "2" in cell A2, highlighting these two cells, and dragging them though cell A8. This technique will be especially useful for very long time series.

FIGURE 16.10

Excel solution of least squares trend line.

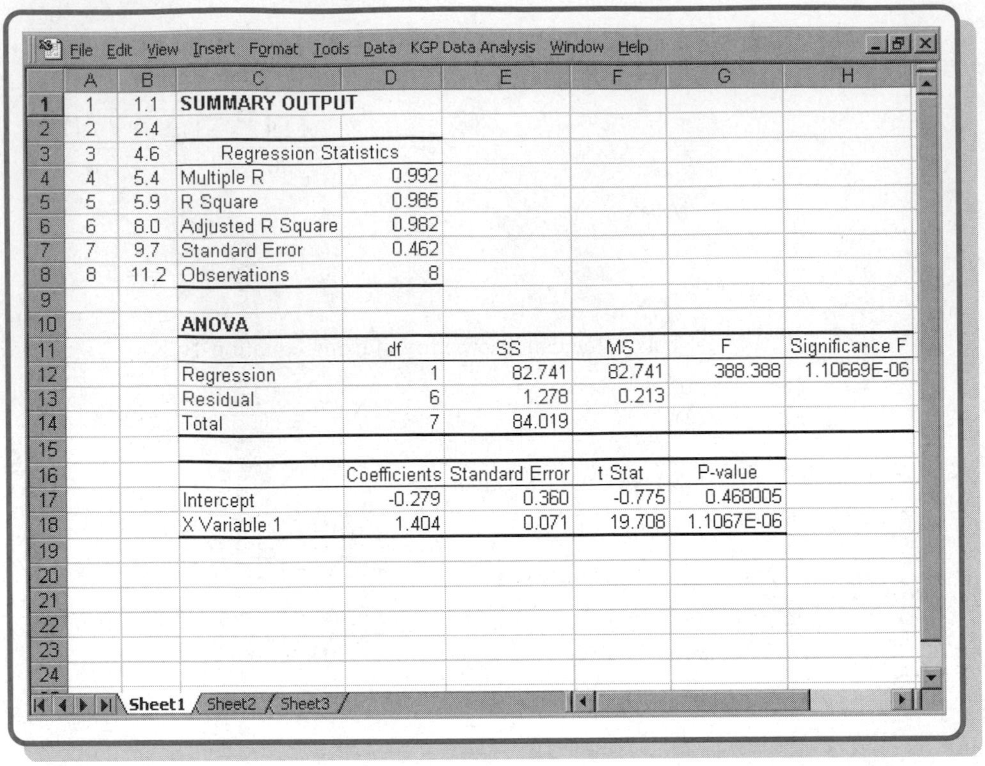

	A	B	C	D	E	F	G	H
	File Edit View Insert Format Tools Data KGP Data Analysis Window Help							
1	1	1.1	SUMMARY OUTPUT					
2	2	2.4						
3	3	4.6	Regression Statistics					
4	4	5.4	Multiple R	0.992				
5	5	5.9	R Square	0.985				
6	6	8.0	Adjusted R Square	0.982				
7	7	9.7	Standard Error	0.462				
8	8	11.2	Observations	8				
9								
10			ANOVA					
11				df	SS	MS	F	Significance F
12			Regression	1	82.741	82.741	388.388	1.10669E-06
13			Residual	6	1.278	0.213		
14			Total	7	84.019			
15								
16				Coefficients	Standard Error	t Stat	P-value	
17			Intercept	-0.279	0.360	-0.775	0.468005	
18			X Variable 1	1.404	0.071	19.708	1.1067E-06	
19								
20								
21								
22								
23								
24								

Sheet1 / Sheet2 / Sheet3 /

QUADRATIC TREND

The nature of a quadratic trend is illustrated in Figure 16.4. This type of trend is common for a time series that increases or decreases rapidly and then gradually levels off over the observed values. We discussed a similar situation in Chapter 15, where a quadratic model of the form

$$\hat{Y} = b_0 + b_1 X + b_2 X^2$$

was used to capture a curvilinear relationship between two variables. We use exactly the same technique to describe a quadratic trend; now X is replaced by time, t.

The power-consumption time series in Figure 16.1 indicates that as time increases, the amount of power consumption (y_t) also increases, but at a decreasing rate. More specifically, the increase for 1994 to 1995 is 18; for 1995 to 1996 is 12 (12 < 18); for 1996 to 1997 is 8 (8 < 12); and for 1997 to 1998 is 5 (5 < 8).

When you observe a series where the *changes* from one year to the next are not (approximately) constant but seem to be either increasing or decreasing with time, these changes indicate a quadratic trend. The equation of this curvilinear (quadratic) trend is

$$\hat{y}_t = b_0 + b_1 t + b_2 t^2$$

To derive the least squares estimates b_0, b_1, and b_2, we use the multiple linear regression procedure of Chapter 15.

What would be the input to a computer program (such as Excel or MINITAB) for the power-consumption data? For the regression program, you have two predictor variables, $X_1 = t$ and $X_2 = t^2$. The resulting data configuration is

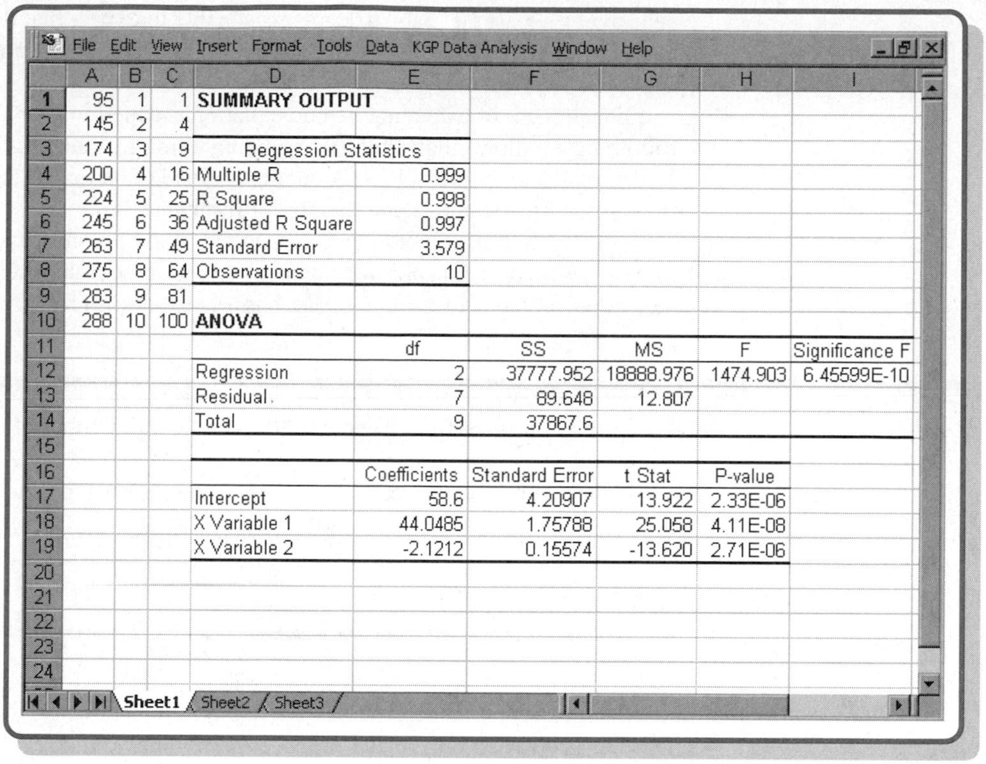

FIGURE 16.11

Excel solution for quadratic trend (power consumption data).

			yₜ	t	t²	
			y_t	t	t^2	
			95	1	1	(for 1989)
			145	2	4	(for 1990)
			174	3	9	(for 1991)
			200	4	16	⋮
			224	5	25	
			245	6	36	
			263	7	49	
			275	8	64	
			283	9	81	(for 1997)
			288	10	100	(for 1998)

Figure 16.11 contains the Excel solution for the quadratic trend equation. To obtain this equation, click on **Tools ➤ Data Analysis ➤ Regression.** You should enter the time series values in column A (as in Figure 16.11) and the values 1 though 10 in column B. To obtain column C, enter "=B1*B1" in cell C1 and drag this cell through cell C10. Enter "A1:A10" as the **Input Y Range,** "B1:C10" as the **Input X Range,** and "D1" as the **Output Range.** The regression coefficients in cells E17: E19 provide the quadratic trend equation

$$y_t = 58.6 + 44.0485t - 2.1212t^2$$

To illustrate the use of this equation, the actual value for the second time period is $y_2 = 145$ and the predicted value is

$$\hat{y}_2 = 58.6 + 44.0485(2) - 2.1212(2)^2 = 138.21$$

A First Look at Forecasting: Extending the Trend

Whenever a time series contains very little seasonality (such as *annual* data, which have *no* seasonality) and a strong trend, an easy method of providing future forecasts is to project the observed growth pattern, as measured by the trend equation, into the future. For example, if a city's tax revenues have increased steadily by approximately $15,000 per year over the past 10 years, it seems reasonable to expect that this pattern will continue, at least for a short time. (Of course, assuming that such a growth will continue indefinitely is a hazardous gamble at best!)

The process of extending a trend equation is called **forecasting,** or **extrapolation.** The following examples illustrate that extending a straight-line trend equation can provide useful estimates of future values. A quadratic trend equation is, however, useful only *within* the range of the sample data, that is, for **interpolation.**

This method of forecasting is but one of many possible ways of predicting the future time series values by capturing patterns present in the past observations. Chapter 17 examines other methods of using the past observations to forecast future values.

EXAMPLE 16.3

Using the trend line from Figure 16.9, estimate the number of employees in 1999.

SOLUTION

$t = 9$ corresponds to the year 1999, so the *forecast* for this year is

$$\hat{y}_9 = -.279 + 1.404(9) = 12.357$$

that is, 12,357 employees.

As mentioned earlier, the basic assumption when using the trend line to determine a forecast is that this same pattern *will continue* into the future. This may or may not be true. Very often a time series will increase at a more or less constant rate and then begin to level off. One example is the sales of an innovative product. Such a time series will grow from one year to the next as people think that they just have to have this product, but eventually a saturation point is reached and the sales grow at a much smaller rate. If the historical data used to determine the trend line are collected during the growth stage, then you will stop short of and miss the "slowing down" of the time series, severely overestimating the sales. This problem is not a flaw in the technique; any time series model makes predictions by capturing the pattern(s) in the past observations and extending this pattern beyond the last year of the data. It does, however, place a great deal of responsibility on the person who uses the data to predict beyond the data range. If you do not know what underlying factors are driving the trend, serious errors can result.

Very often, a nonlinear growth rate can be described accurately by including a quadratic term in the trend equation. However, using such an equation to forecast *future* values is not a reliable procedure, as the following example demonstrates.

EXAMPLE 16.4

Using the trend equation from Figure 16.11

$$\hat{y}_t = \text{TR}_t = 58.6 + 44.0485t - 2.1212t^2$$

what is your forecast for the power consumption during 1999? during 2000? Use only the trend equation.

SOLUTION

The year 1999 corresponds to $t = 11$ (the last year of your data is $t = 10$ for 1998). Your forecast for 1999 is

$$\hat{y}_{11} = 58.6 + 44.0485(11) - 2.1212(11)^2 = 286.46$$

that is, 2,864,600 kilowatt-hours. For the year 2000, your forecast is

$$\hat{y}_{12} = 58.6 + 44.0485(12) - 2.1212(12)^2 = 281.72$$

FIGURE 16.12

Illustration of how quadratic trend equations will reverse direction. The quadratic trend equation is $y_t = b_0 + b_1 t + b_2 t^2$, where $b_2 < 0$ in part (a) and $b_2 > 0$ in part (b).

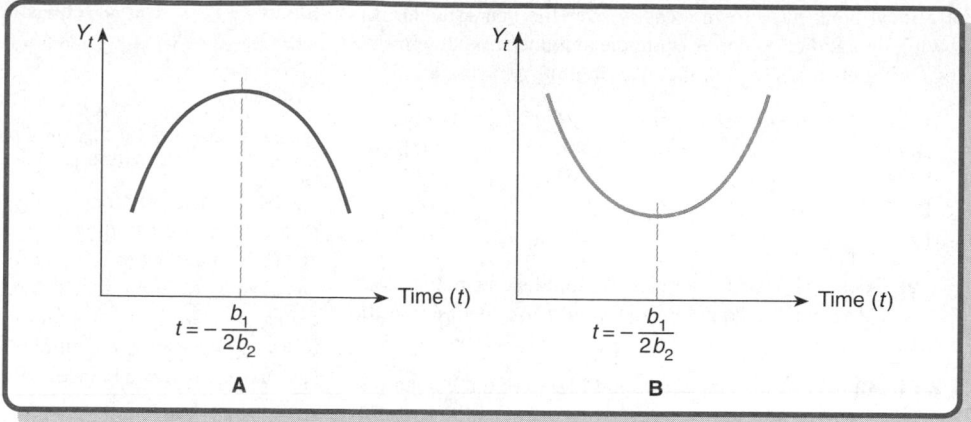

The sermon we delivered about projecting a trend line beyond the range of the data applies to a quadratic trend as well: by forecasting with such an equation, you assume that this quadratic (curved) pattern observed in the time series observations will continue.

In addition, there is another danger when forecasting with a quadratic trend equation. Every such equation looks like Figure 16.12(a) or (b). In other words, the curve reaches a peak or trough at $t = -b_1/(2b_2)$ and then reverses direction. This change in direction is generally not seen in the sample data and produces trend estimates that are contrary to the pattern seen in the sample data. For example, rather than producing trend estimates that "slow down" with increasing time, the estimates after a certain point [namely, after $t = -b_1/(2b_2)$] will reverse direction.

The forecasts for power consumption (Example 16.4) for 1999 and 2000 provide a good illustration of this problem. Notice that the predicted value for 1999 is less than the actual value for 1998, despite a steadily increasing pattern in the time series data. Even worse, the year 2000 estimate is less than that for 1999. These values imply that the trend equation is decreasing during the years after 1998. We see that the trend equation forecasts appear to be poor estimates—we have no reason to suspect a downturn in the amount of power consumption in these future years. The trend is appropriately described by the quadratic curve, but only within the range of the data. This curve will peak at $t = -44.0485/2(-2.1212) = 10.38$ (between 1998 and 1999) and then begin to decline. Because we have no reason to believe that the demand for electrical power will decrease, the quadratic equation is no longer appropriate outside the range of the sample data.

To describe the trend *within* the years of your time series data, the quadratic trend equation may work well. However, remember that, *as a forecasting procedure, it is very dangerous; do not use it for this purpose.*

This section has demonstrated how you can derive linear or quadratic trend equations by using linear regression techniques. Extending such a trend equation into the future is a method of statistical forecasting, a subject that is discussed at length in Chapter 17.

EXERCISES 16.7–16.16

UNDERSTANDING THE MECHANICS

16.7 The following table displays annual observations from 1994 to 1999.

Year	Time (t)	y_t	ty_t
1994	1	30	
1995	2	120	
1996	3	180	
1997	4	220	
1998	5	280	
1999	6	320	
	$\Sigma t =$	$\Sigma y_t =$	$\Sigma ty_t =$

a. Complete the table.
b. Determine the least squares line.
c. What is the predicted value for the year 2000?

16.8 Using the following statistics, fit a linear trend line for time periods $t = 1, 2, \ldots, 10$.

$$\Sigma y_t = 1300, \ \Sigma ty_t = 7484$$

APPLYING THE NEW CONCEPTS

16.9 Explain why a prediction equation with a quadratic trend may be dangerous to use in forecasting even though a quadratic trend fits the historic data very well.

16.10 The amount of money deposited into savings accounts at a local bank has grown steadily over the years, as the following data indicate (deposits are the amount of money in savings accounts at the end of the year, in units of $100,000):

Year	Deposits	Year	Deposits
1992	2.1	1996	10.3
1993	4.2	1997	13.3
1994	6.4	1998	14.9
1995	8.5	1999	16.7

a. Does it appear that a quadratic trend exists in the data?

b. Calculate the equation you would use to describe the trend.

16.11 An insurance company would like to find the trend line for the amount of insurance sold annually (in millions of dollars) across time. The variable time is represented by t and is equal to 1, 2, . . . , 8 for the past eight years. The following statistics were collected:

$$\sum ty_t = 394.5 \qquad \sum y_t = 29.4$$

Find the trend line for these time series data.

16.12 Due to rising competition from overseas, an electronics firm has been losing its share of the market. The following data show the percent of the market that the firm has captured for the past seven years.

Year	Share of Market
1993	4.7
1994	4.3
1995	3.9
1996	3.8
1997	3.6
1998	3.0
1999	2.9

a. Does the trend appear to be linear?

b. Find the equation to estimate the trend for the time series data.

c. What would be your estimate of the electronics firm's share of the market in 2000?

16.13 Broadcast TV still commands the lion's share of advertising dollars. However, by the year 2005, market researchers predict advertisers will spend $14.5 billion on cable. Average time spent weekly watching cable television per household has been steadily increasing since 1988. Find the least squares prediction equation that best describes this trend. What is your estimate for the average weekly time spent watching cable television per household in the year 2005?

Year	Average Weekly Time Spent Watching Cable Television per Household, in Hours
1988	9.4
1989	14.3
1990	16.1
1991	17.4
1992	17.5
1993	19.4
1994	19.0

Year	Average Weekly Time Spent Watching Cable Television per Household, in Hours
1995	22.1
1996	22.9
1997	24.0

(Source: Adapted from *The Wall Street Journal*, "In Battle for TV Ads, Cable Is Now the Enemy," May 6, 1998, p. B1.)

16.14 From 1990 to 1997, the New York Stock Exchange has restricted program trading when the Dow Jones Industrial Average (DJIA) climbs or falls more than 50 points from its previous closing level. As the DJIA reached new records, it has been easier to activate the 50-point collar on program trading. The following data show the number of times that the 50-point collar has been activated since 1990.

Year	Percentage of Trading Days That the 50-Point Collar Was Activated
1990	23
1991	17
1992	15
1993	10
1994	17
1995	20
1996	30
1997	77

(Source: *The Wall Street Journal*, "Big Board May Loosen Its 'Collar'," Mar. 23, 1998, p. C1.)

a. Estimate a linear trend and a quadratic trend for these data. Which do you think is a better fit?

b. What is your estimate of the percentage of trading days that the 50-point collar was activated in 1998?

Using the Computer

16.15 [DATA SET EX16-15] *Variable description:*

Year: Year from 1977 to 1996
Ratio: Ratio of capital spending to cash flow for the Standard & Poor's Industrials

The money that many companies are spending on capital investment has gone heavily into cost-cutting technology, aided by tumbling computer prices, rather than new buildings and factories that add capacity. Therefore, the ratio of capital spending to cash flow has recently been near historic lows. The following table contains data on the ratio of capital spending to cash flow for the Standard & Poor's Industrials from 1977 to 1997 (displayed in units of percent).

Year	Ratio of Capital Spending to Cash Flow
1977	80.1
1978	89.3
1979	98.4
1980	103.9
1981	110.5
1982	116.3
1983	95.3
1984	94.3
1985	93.5
1986	91.8

Year	Ratio of Capital Spending to Cash Flow
1987	85.4
1988	83.1
1989	82.1
1990	81.8
1991	82.3
1992	78.4
1993	76.2
1994	70.1
1995	68.5
1996	66.4
1997	62.2

(Source: Adapted from *The Wall Street Journal*, "With Dow 9000 Nearby, Stocks Get Boost As Corporate America Tightens Its Belt," Mar. 23, 1998, p. C1.)

a. Without performing any calculations, determine whether the ratio of capital spending to cash flow is trending upward, downward, or contains no trend.

b. Plot the data against time. Do you think there is a linear or quadratic trend present? Estimate the appropriate trend line.

16.16 [DATA SET EX16-16] *Variable description:*

Year: Year from 1975 to 2000
Bonus: Annual bonus in thousands of dollars

A new vice president of a local bank is interested in examining the annual bonuses paid to her predecessors. She also realizes that stockholders of the bank are concerned about exorbitant bonuses. Do you believe that a linear or quadratic trend is present? What are the estimates of the expected annual bonuses for 2001 and 2002?

16.3 MEASURING CYCLICAL ACTIVITY: NO SEASONALITY

Practically every time series in a business setting contains a certain amount of cyclical activity. Cyclical activity is a gradual movement about the trend. It is generally due to economic or other long-term conditions. The overall U.S. economy tends to fluctuate through "good times" and "bad times," producing (rather unpredictable) upward and downward variation about the long-term growth or decline in a time series.

One way of describing the cyclical activity component is to represent it as a fraction of the trend. This procedure provides accurate measures of the cyclical activity provided the time series contains *little irregular activity*. Assuming that each time series observation is the *product* of its components, then

$$y_t = TR_t \cdot C_t \cdot I_t$$

because we are dealing with data containing no seasonality.

If we represent a small irregular activity component as i_t (rather than I_t), then a time series containing little irregular variation (noise) can be written as

$$y_t = TR_t \cdot C_t \cdot i_t$$

The cyclical components are then obtained by dividing each observation, y_t, by its corresponding estimate using trend only, $\hat{y}_t$.

$$\text{ratio of data to trend} = \frac{y_t}{\hat{y}_t} = \frac{\cancel{TR}_t \cdot C_t \cdot i_t}{\cancel{TR}_t} = C_t \cdot i_t$$

where y_t = actual time series observation at time period t and $\hat{y}_t = TR_t$ = the estimate of y_t using trend only. Notice that the resulting ratios still contain some irregular activity. (A method of reducing the irregular activity within these values is illustrated in Section 16.6.)

An estimate of the cyclical components can be obtained by ignoring the irregular activity components in these ratios and defining

$$C_t \cong \frac{y_t}{\hat{y}_t} \tag{16.6}$$

Assuming that we are dealing with data containing no seasonality (such as annual data), equation 16.6 provides a convenient method of determining the cycles present in the data. If $C_t > 1$, the actual y_t is larger than that predicted by trend alone. Consequently, this value is somewhere in a cycle *above* the trend line. A similar argument indicates a cycle below the trend line whenever $C_t < 1$ (Figure 16.13).

FIGURE 16.13

A complete cycle within a time series.

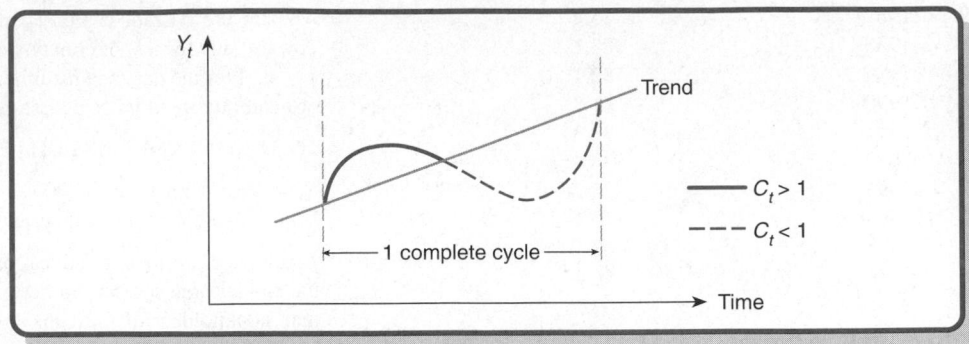

TABLE 16.1

Trend and cyclical activity (Example 16.5).

t	y_t	$\hat{y}_t$	$C_t \cong \dfrac{y_t}{\hat{y}_t}$
1	1.1	1.125	.978
2	2.4	2.529	.949
3	4.6	3.933	1.169
4	5.4	5.337	1.012
5	5.9	6.741	.875
6	8.0	8.145	.982
7	9.7	9.549	1.016
8	11.2	10.953	1.022

The third column is the trend component, and the fourth column is the cyclical component as a fraction of the trend.

EXAMPLE 16.5

For the data in Figure 16.9, we determined a least squares trend line for the number of employees (y_t) over an eight-year period at Video-Comp. We observed a linear trend with the corresponding equation

$$\hat{y}_t = -.279 + 1.404t$$

where $t = 1$ represents 1991, $t = 2$ is for 1992, and so on. Determine and graph the cyclical activity over this period.

SOLUTION

We can obtain Table 16.1 by using the preceding trend line. Here $\hat{y}_1 = -.279 + 1.404(1) = 1.125$, $\hat{y}_2 = -.279 + 1.404(2) = 2.529$, and so on.

To examine the cyclical activity, we can describe each component as a percentage of the trend. For example, in Table 16.1, during the first time period, the actual number of employees is 97.8% of the trend value: C_1 is .978. An illustration of the trend and cyclical activity is shown in Figure 16.14. The cycles fluctuate about the trend line. Between the years $t = 2$ (1992) and $t = 3$ (1993), $y_t = \hat{y}_t$ and a cycle begins. This cycle is completed somewhere between $t = 6$ (1996) and $t = 7$ (1997), where, once again, $y_t = \hat{y}_t$. As discussed earlier, you can also measure cycles from peak to peak or from trough to trough.

The summary of the cyclical variation (components) over the eight years is contained in Table 16.1 and Figure 16.15. The four-year cycle we described is more evident in this

FIGURE 16.14

Cyclical activity about a trend line (Example 16.5).

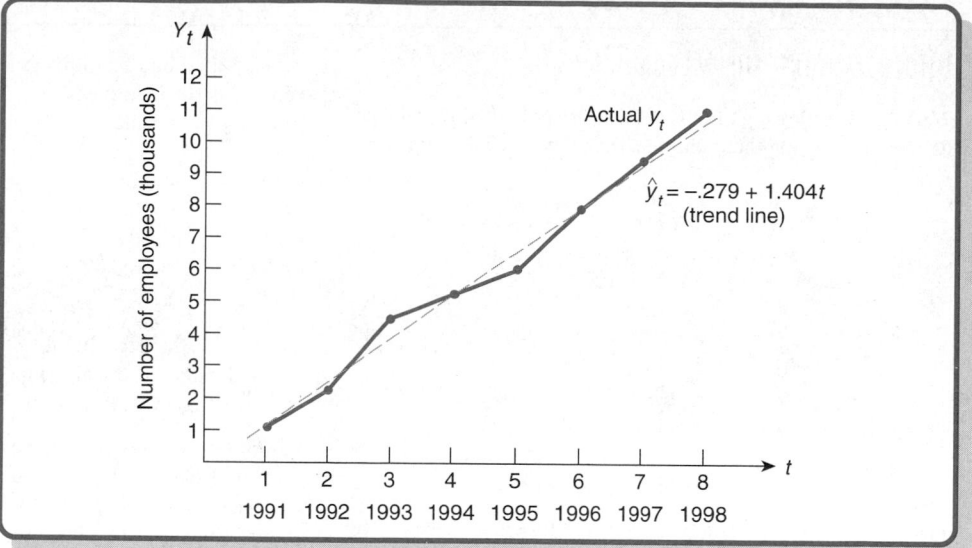

FIGURE 16.15

Cyclical components (Example 16.5).

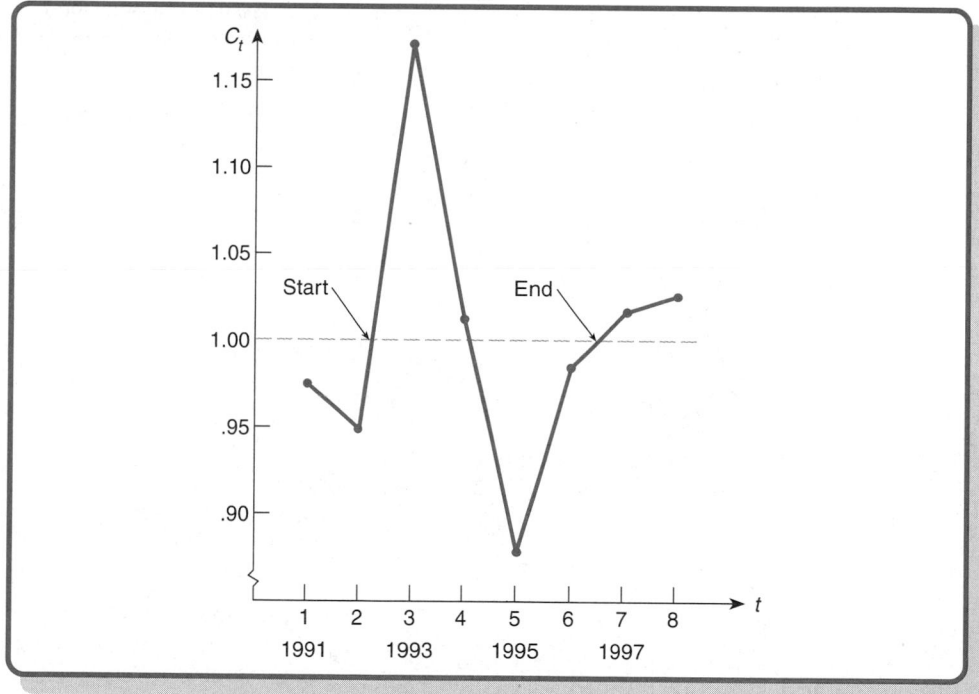

graph. The graph clearly indicates the beginning of the cycle, where $C_t = 1$. The cycle's peak occurs at $t = 3$ (1993), the trough is at $t = 5$ (1995), and the cycle is finally complete when C_t is again equal to 1, toward the end of 1996.

In summary, cyclical variation represents an upward or downward movement about the overall growth or decline (that is, the trend) in the time series data. Such cycles typically last more than one year. For annual data, these components can be estimated by dividing each observation (y_t) by its corresponding estimate using the trend equation ($\hat{y}_t$).

EXERCISES 16.17–16.26

UNDERSTANDING THE MECHANICS

16.17 The following time series data are presented with the predicted values using the trend line. Find the cyclical components.

t	y_t	$\hat{y}_t$
1	1.0	1.493
2	2.0	2.752
3	5.0	4.012
4	5.5	5.271
5	6.0	6.530
6	8.0	7.790
7	10.0	9.049
8	11.0	10.309
9	11.3	11.568
10	11.8	12.827

16.18 Estimate the length of the cycle for each of the following three time series

a. t	C_t	**b.** t	C_t	**c.** t	C_t
1	1.0	1	.3	1	3.1
2	.9	2	.7	2	2.2
3	1.7	3	1.3	3	1.2
4	.8	4	2.0	4	.9
5	1.5	5	1.5	5	.6
6	.9	6	.8	6	.3
7	1.4	7	.4	7	.7
8	.8	8	.9	8	.9
9	1.6	9	1.2	9	1.3
10	.7	10	2.4	10	1.8
		11	1.6	11	4.0
		12	.8	12	2.5
		13	.5	13	1.0
				14	.6

APPLYING THE NEW CONCEPTS

16.19 A food-store chain has the following record for yearly sales volume (in hundreds of thousands of dollars) for the past 9 years:

Year	Sales Volume	Year	Sales Volume
1991	7	1996	17
1992	15	1997	12
1993	10	1998	8
1994	5	1999	17
1995	11		

   a. Find the trend line.
   b. Find the cyclical components.
   c. Estimate the period of the cycle.

16.20 Residential Construction of America has been growing over the long term. Because the construction company is sensitive to cyclical variations in the economy, the level of employment for the company changes from year to year, as can be seen by the following data:

Year	Full-Time Employees (in Hundreds)	Year	Full-Time Employees (in Hundreds)
1987	2.4	1994	11.7
1988	9.2	1995	17.3
1989	11.1	1996	23.1
1990	8.5	1997	28.7
1991	10.5	1998	29.3
1992	6.8	1999	25.2
1993	5.4		

   a. Find the trend line.
   b. Find the cyclical components.
   c. Estimate the period of the cycle.

16.21 Few objects convey wealth and power like a private airplane and many companies are presently using them. Casket salesmen for Hillenbrand Industries, Inc., use them to escort funeral directors when visiting showrooms. Lumber buyers for Home Depot, Inc., based in Atlanta, fly on private airplanes to purchase inventory at out-of-the-way mills. Corning, Inc.'s technicians use them to shuttle between the company's headquarters in upstate New York and its optical-fiber plant in Wilmington, N.C. The following data illustrate the number of U.S. companies from 1988 to 1998 who operate turbine-powered aircraft in units of thousands.

Year	Number of U.S. Companies Operating Turbine-Powered Aircraft
1988	7.1
1989	6.7
1990	6.6
1991	6.5
1992	6.6
1993	6.7
1994	6.8
1995	7.8
1996	7.4
1997	7.5
1998	8.0

(Source: Adapted from *The Wall Street Journal,* "Not Just for Highfliers, Corporate Planes Take Off," Jan. 8, 1999, p. B1.)

   a. Find the trend line.
   b. Determine the cyclical activity.
   c. Does the period of the cycle appear to be longer or shorter than five years?

16.22 For the data in Exercise 16.12, estimate the cyclical components.

16.23 A production manager is interested in the competitiveness of his company in manufacturing air conditioning compressors for automobiles. Data are collected over a ten year period, and the compressor cost per unit compressor is recorded. Determine the cyclical components for each year. Do you believe that the length of the cycle is longer than three years?

Year	Dollar Cost per Unit Compressor
1990	100.4
1991	103.6
1992	105.2
1993	102.3
1994	99.8
1995	104.3
1996	107.8
1997	101.6
1998	98.4
1999	103.1

16.24 Recently sales among Japan's top shipbuilders reached a record six trillion yen ($48 billion dollars). Conventional wisdom in the 1980s had it that countries such as South Korea and Taiwan would overtake Japan in the shipbuilding industry, just as Japan had done to U.S. shipyards. For a while, that happened. Japan fell behind South Korea in 1993 in tonnage. Now Japan's shipbuilders rank among the world's most profitable shipbuilders. Consider the total sales of the top 10 Japanese shipbuilders, presented below in terms of billions of dollars.

Year	Total Sales in Billions of Dollars
1986	32.1
1987	30.2
1988	30.9
1989	33.5
1990	39.3
1991	42.0
1992	42.3
1993	43.0
1994	43.1
1995	45.3
1996	48.1

(Adapted from *The Wall Street Journal,* "Defying the Odds, Japan Shipbuilders Beat Back Their Hungry Competitors," Feb. 12, 1998, p. A19.)

a. Estimate the trend equation. How would you interpret the coefficients of the equation?

b. Estimate the cyclical components.

c. Construct a bar chart of the total sales using time as the horizontal axis and describe the pattern.

USING THE COMPUTER

16.25 [DATA SET EX16-25] *Variable description:*

Year: Year, 1983 through 1999
Applicants: Number of applicants for the supervisory positions

The manager of a paper plant needs to hire new supervisors every year because of growth in the company, turnover in the company, and promotions within the company. The manager decided to collect data from 1983 through 1999 to determine the cyclical activity. Determine the length of the cycles for this data set.

16.26 [DATA SET EX16-26] *Variable description:*

Year: Year, 1992 through 1998
Quarter: One through four for the four quarters of the year
UnemployRate: Unemployment rate in percentage for each quarter

The quarterly unemployment rate for the United States was recorded from 1992 through 1998. The unemployment rate was seasonally adjusted for students looking for work. This period of time was highly influenced by the spread of new technology and an increasingly strong economy. Therefore, the unemployment rate was in a sustained downward trend. Estimate the approximate period of the cycle for the unemployment rate between 1992 and 1998.

(Source: Adapted from *The Wall Street Journal,* "Wages for Low-Paid Workers Rose in 1997," Mar. 23, 1998, p. A2.)

16.4 TYPES OF SEASONAL VARIATION

Seasonality causes another type of variation about the trend in a time series. Seasonality generally is present when the data are quarterly or monthly. It can also occur for weekly or even daily data. For example, recurrent daily effects can be expected to occur in the check-processing volume in a bank. **Seasonality** is any recurrent, constant source of variation caused by events at the particular time of year rather than by any long-term influence (as in cyclical activity). For example, one would expect to sell more snowmobiles in January than in July. In a sense, the seasonal variation appears as a cycle within a year; we do not refer to this as cyclical variation, however, due to its recurrent nature.

We will discuss two types of seasonal variation: additive and multiplicative.

ADDITIVE SEASONAL VARIATION

One encounters **additive seasonal variation** when the amount of the variation due to seasonality *does not depend on the level* y_t. This type of seasonal variation is illustrated in Figure 16.16, which shows the sales of snowmobiles over a three-year period at the Outdoor Shop. Notice that the amount of variation for each of the winter quarters remains the same (100 units), even as the unit sales increase over the three years. For an actual application, we assume an additive effect of seasonality if these increments are of nearly the same magnitude over the observed time series.

FIGURE 16.16

Snowmobile sales at the Outdoor Shop (additive seasonal variation).

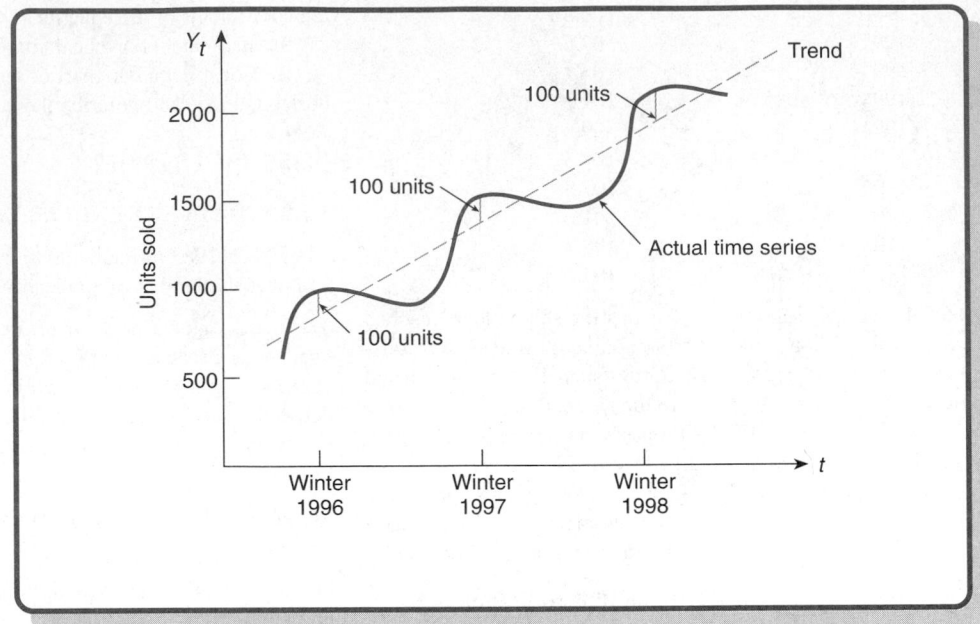

Assume that the sales data for Jetski snowmobiles from sales area 1 were recorded quarterly over the five-year period from 1994 through 1998. The following trend line was derived:

$$TR_t = \hat{y}_t = 100 + 20t$$

The seasonal indexes for a seasonal time series represent the incremental effect of the seasons alone, apart from any trend or cyclical activity. For the Jetski data in sales area 1, these indexes were found to be

$S_1 = +60$ (winter quarter) $S_3 = -40$ (summer quarter)

$S_2 = +30$ (spring quarter) $S_4 = -20$ (fall quarter)

In a time series decomposition (where we actually derive these seasonal indexes), additive seasonal variation assumes that the seasonal index for, say, the winter quarter is the *same* for each year. Using the additive model, this implies that the store will sell 60 more Jetski units in the winter quarter than would be predicted by trend alone during any year. This implies that $S_1 = S_5 = S_9 = \cdots = +60$.

To estimate y_t using only the trend and seasonality, we *add* the two corresponding components.

t (Time)	$TR_t + S_t$ (Sales Estimate)
1 (winter 1994)	$[100 + 20(1)] + 60 = 180$
2 (spring 1994)	$[100 + 20(2)] + 30 = 170$
3 (summer 1994)	$[100 + 20(3)] - 40 = 120$
4 (autumn 1994)	$[100 + 20(4)] - 20 = 160$
5 (winter 1995)	$[100 + 20(5)] + 60 = 260$
6 (spring 1995)	$[100 + 20(6)] + 30 = 250$
7 (summer 1995)	$[100 + 20(7)] - 40 = 200$
8 (autumn 1995)	$[100 + 20(8)] - 20 = 240$
$\vdots$	$\vdots$

A graph of the estimated sales is shown in Figure 16.17. Notice that as the overall level of sales increases, the deviation from the trend line (due to seasonality) remains the same. If the past observations in the time series indicate that higher levels of sales produce wider seasonal fluctuations, this is an indication of multiplicative seasonal variation.

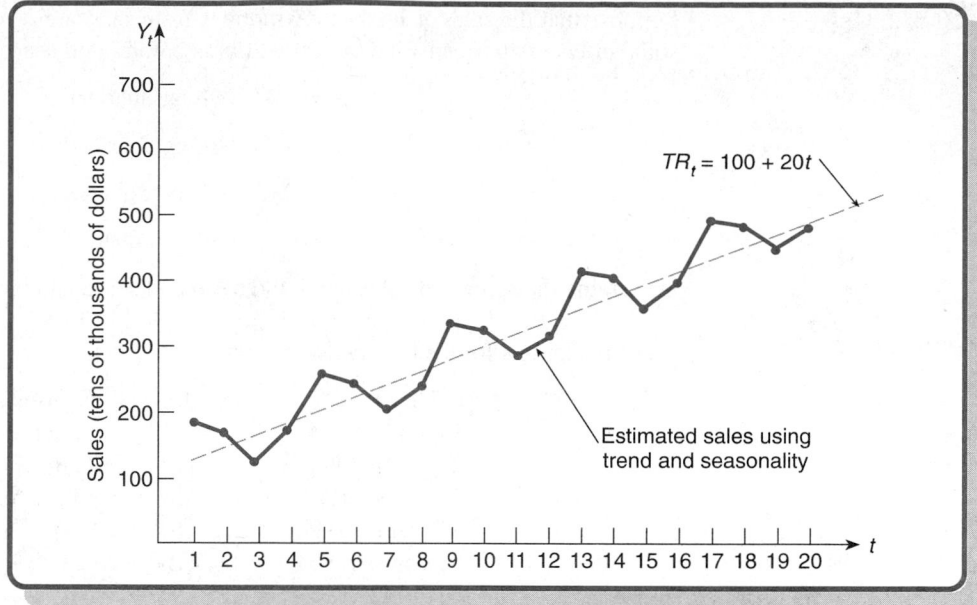

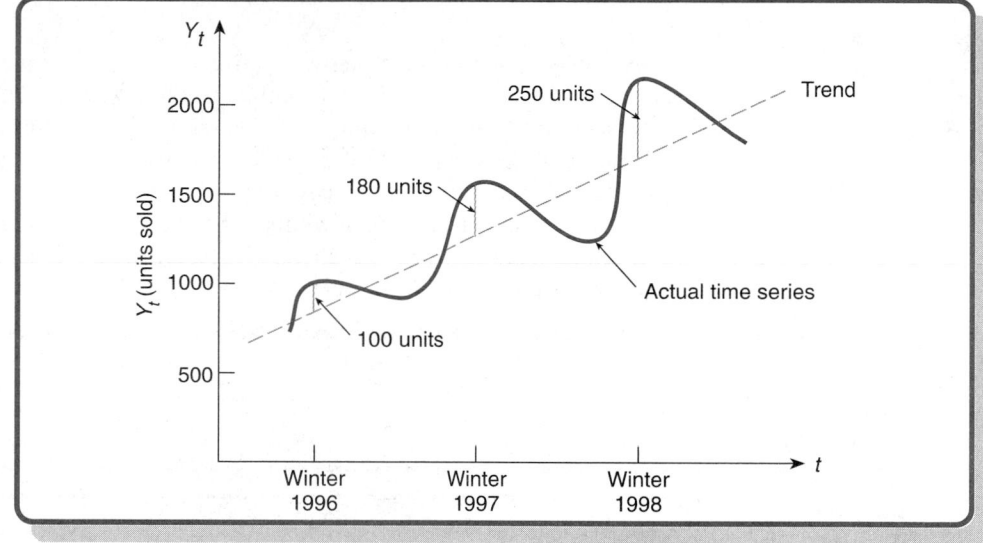

MULTIPLICATIVE SEASONAL VARIATION

Figure 16.6 shows **multiplicative seasonal variation** in the time series for the sale of Wildcat sailboats. Notice that in each successive year, the difference between the actual value and the trend value for July is larger. In multiplicative seasonal variation, the seasonal fluctuation is *proportional* to the trend level for each observation. Figure 16.18 is a general illustration of multiplicative seasonability; it shows the sales of heat pumps over a three-year period at Handy Home Center.

Considering only the effects of trend and seasonality, an estimate for a time series observation is given by

$$\text{estimate of } y_t = \text{TR}_t \cdot S_t$$

As in additive seasonal variation, the seasonal indexes, S_t, remain constant from one year to the next. When dealing with quarterly data, this means that $S_1 = S_5 = S_9 = \cdots$, $S_2 = S_6 = S_{10} = \cdots$, and so on. The next section discusses a method for determining these indexes for the case of multiplicative seasonality.

EXAMPLE 16.6

Suppose that the sales of Jetski snowmobiles from sales area 2 contain multiplicative seasonal effects with trend = $TR_t = 100 + 20t$ (as before) and seasonal indexes

$$S_1 = 1.4 \quad \text{(winter quarter)}$$

$$S_2 = 1.2 \quad \text{(spring quarter)}$$

$$S_3 = 0.6 \quad \text{(summer quarter)}$$

$$S_4 = 0.8 \quad \text{(autumn quarter)}$$

Determine the estimated sales using the trend and seasonal components.

SOLUTION

The calculations for the first two years are

t (Time)	$TR_t \cdot S_t$ (Estimate)
1 (winter 1994)	$[100 + 20(1)](1.4) = 168$
2 (spring 1994)	$[100 + 20(2)](1.2) = 168$
3 (summer 1994)	$[100 + 20(3)](.6) = 96$
4 (autumn 1994)	$[100 + 20(4)](.8) = 144$
5 (winter 1995)	$[100 + 20(5)](1.4) = 280$
6 (spring 1995)	$[100 + 20(6)](1.2) = 264$
7 (summer 1995)	$[100 + 20(7)](.6) = 144$
8 (autumn 1995)	$[100 + 20(8)](.8) = 208$
⋮	⋮

A graph of the estimated sales over a five-year period is shown in Figure 16.19. Notice that seasonal patterns do exist, but (unlike additive variation) these fluctuations increase as the sales level rises. For a time series representing sales, this type of variation seems to make sense. If the volume of sales doubles, it is reasonable to expect a larger effect due to seasonality than occurred previously.

Remember that in practice, few time series exhibit exact additive or multiplicative seasonal effects. However, you can classify a great many time series as essentially belonging to one or the other of these two classes.

FIGURE 16.19

Jetski sales from sales area 2 (multiplicative seasonal variation).

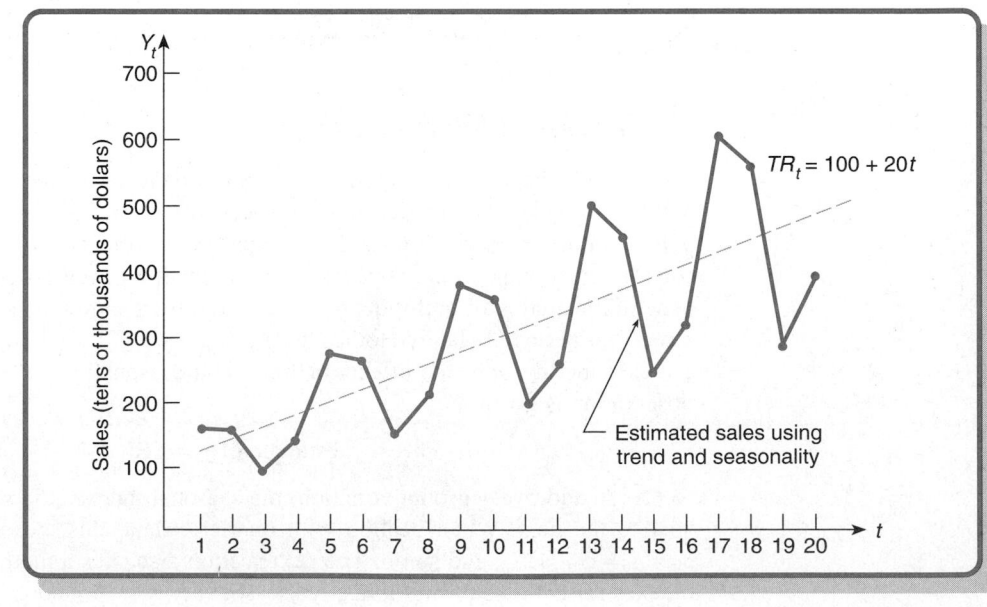

In the discussion to follow, we assume that any seasonality in the time series is *multiplicative*. Most analysts (including those in the U.S. Census Bureau) have had better success describing time series in this manner. The decomposition method to be discussed assumes that each observation is the *product* of its various components. So, the *component structure* is assumed to be

$$y_t = \mathrm{TR}_t \cdot S_t \cdot C_t \cdot I_t \tag{16.7}$$

where the components representing seasonality, trend, cyclical variation, and noise are multiplied by one another.*

Four-Step Procedure (Multiplicative Components)

Based on the multiplicative component structure in equation 16.7, the following four-step procedure can be used to decompose a time series containing the effects of all four components.

Step 1. *Determine a seasonal index, S_t, for each time period.* For quarterly data, this involves determining four such indexes, S_1, S_2, S_3, and S_4. When the time series contains monthly observations, 12 seasonal indexes (S_1 through S_{12}) must be calculated, one for each month.

Step 2. *Deseasonalize the data.* This step is often referred to as *adjusting for seasonality;* the seasonal component is eliminated. Because we are using a multiplicative structure, we divide each observation by its corresponding seasonal index. So

$$\text{deseasonalized observation} = d_t = \frac{y_t}{S_t}$$

where

$$S_t = \begin{cases} S_1,\, S_2,\, S_3,\, \text{or } S_4 & \text{(quarterly data)} \\ S_1,\, S_2,\, \ldots,\, \text{or } S_{12} & \text{(monthly data)} \end{cases}$$

Because $y_t = \mathrm{TR}_t \cdot S_t \cdot C_t \cdot I_t$,

$$d_t = \frac{y_t}{S_t} = \frac{\mathrm{TR}_t \cdot \cancel{S_t} \cdot C_t \cdot I_t}{\cancel{S_t}} = \mathrm{TR}_t \cdot C_t \cdot I_t$$

Step 3. *Determine the trend component, TR_t.* The trend is estimated by passing a least squares line through the *deseasonalized* data. The technique is identical to that discussed in Section 16.2 (which assumed no seasonality), except that we use the d_t values rather than the original time series. This process is illustrated in the next section.

Step 4. *Determine the cyclical component, C_t.* You obtain C_t by first dividing each deseasonalized observation, d_t, by the corresponding trend value from step 3. So the cyclical estimates are derived by first calculating (for each time period)

$$\frac{d_t}{\hat{d}_t} = \frac{d_t}{\mathrm{TR}_t} = \frac{\cancel{\mathrm{TR}_t} \cdot C_t \cdot I_t}{\cancel{\mathrm{TR}_t}} = C_t \cdot I_t$$

Notice that the resulting series contains cycles and irregular activity (but no trend or seasonality). A method for reducing the irregular component in these ratios is discussed in Section 16.6. The resulting values are the cyclical components, C_t.

We do not use the cyclical components to attempt to forecast future values of the time series because their behavior (and period) generally cannot be predicted.

---

* Similar methods for determining the components of a time series containing additive seasonality also exist. Chapter 17 contains a brief discussion of this topic. For a fuller discussion of such techniques, see B. L. Bowerman and R. T. O'Connell, *Forecasting and Time Series: An Applied Approach,* 3d ed., (North Scituate, Mass.: Duxbury Press, 1993).

The cyclical components can be used in forecasting if one is willing to assume a particular phase in the business cycle. If one assumes, for example, that the cycle is in the midst of an upturn, a value of C_t (such as $C_t = 1.2$) can be assigned to this particular time period. In the discussion to follow, the cyclical components are obtained strictly as a means of *describing* the cyclical activity within a recorded time series.

EXERCISES 16.27–16.34

UNDERSTANDING THE MECHANICS

16.27 Assuming additive seasonal variation, find the estimate of y_t for $t = 1, 2, 3, 4$. These time periods represent four quarters.

$$TR_t = 21 + 4.5t$$

$$S_1 = 12 \qquad S_3 = -8$$

$$S_2 = 6 \qquad S_4 = -4$$

16.28 Assuming multiplicative seasonal variation, find the estimates of y_t for $t = 1, 2, 3, 4$. These time periods represent four quarters.

$$TR_t = 100 - 3t$$

$$S_1 = .82 \qquad S_3 = 1.30$$

$$S_2 = .64 \qquad S_4 = 1.24$$

APPLYING THE NEW CONCEPTS

16.29 For a six-year period (1994 to 1999) quarterly sales data (in thousands) were used to arrive at the following trend line and seasonal indexes.

$$TR_t = 35 + 2.3t \qquad \text{for } t = 1, 2, \ldots, 24$$

$$S_1 = -8.7 \qquad S_3 = 8.4$$

$$S_2 = 2.5 \qquad S_4 = 3.1$$

Estimate the sales figures for the four quarters in 1998 using an additive equation containing only the trend and seasonality components.

16.30 Advanced Digital Components has experienced rapid growth during the past several years. The quarterly data for the past four years give the following trend line and seasonal indexes. Sales units are in tens of thousands.

$$TR_t = 0.85 + 0.8t \qquad \text{for } t = 1, 2, \ldots, 16$$

$$S_1 = 0.82 \qquad S_3 = 1.20$$

$$S_2 = 1.36 \qquad S_4 = 0.62$$

Estimate the sales figures for the four quarters in the most recent year using a multiplicative equation containing only the trend and seasonality components.

16.31 Monthly data from the years 1995 through 1999 were used to find the following trend line and seasonal indexes:

$$TR_t = 1.3 + 0.5t \qquad \text{for } t = 1, 2, \ldots, 60$$

$S_1 = 0.5$	$S_4 = 1.3$	$S_7 = 2.4$	$S_{10} = 0.2$
$S_2 = 0.8$	$S_5 = 1.1$	$S_8 = 3.1$	$S_{11} = 0.2$
$S_3 = 0.6$	$S_6 = 1.4$	$S_9 = 0.3$	$S_{12} = 0.1$

Assuming a multiplicative model containing only the trend and seasonality components, estimate the data for the 12 months of 1998.

16.32 The manager of a local utility company is interested in estimating the deseasonalized quarterly usage of electric power consumption by the average household. Using deseasonalized data, the manager wants to see if a clear pattern exists. Average electrical usage is collected quarterly from 1997 through 1999 in units of millions of kilowatt hours. Assume that the data are subject to additive seasonal variation and that the seasonal indexes are $S_1 = 12.4$, $S_2 = -5.8$, $S_3 = 7.2$, and $S_4 = -6.8$. Deseasonalize the data and determine if any patterns are revealed in these seasonally adjusted values.

Year	Quarter	Electrical Usage
1997	1	62
	2	46
	3	61
	4	49
1998	1	66
	2	52
	3	67
	4	55
1999	1	76
	2	60
	3	75
	4	63

USING THE COMPUTER

16.33 [DATA SET EX16-33] *Variable description:*

Year: Year from 1995 to 1998
Quarter: One through four for the four quarters of the year
AluminumProd: Number of metric tons of aluminum produced per quarter

The Aluminum Association records the number of metric tons in units of millions for each quarter. A strong economy typically increases the demand for aluminum. However, aluminum tends to be a cyclical commodity. Assume that the seasonal indexes are $S_1 = 1.041$, $S_2 = .953$, $S_3 = .994$, and $S_4 = 1.012$. If the production of aluminum is subject to multiplicative seasonal variation, what are the deseasonalized production figures per quarter from 1995 to 1998?

(Source: Adapted from *The Wall Street Journal,* "Aluminum Production," July 14, 1998, p. A1.)

16.34   [DATA SET EX16-34] *Variable description:*

Year: Year from 1992 to 1997
Quarter: One through four for the four quarters of the year
ChinaGDP: Growth rate of China's Gross Domestic Product on
a quarterly basis

In 1993, China had a very enviable growth rate of over 12%.
Now, the Chinese government is trying to maintain a growth
rate of 8%. From 1993 to 1997, China's rate of growth has
slowed, although the government is still implementing policies
to stimulate domestic consumption. Assuming additive seasonality, calculate the deseasonalized data recorded in units of percentage given the following seasonal indexes:

$$S_1 = 1.0, \ S_2 = 2.1, \ S_3 = -2.2, \text{ and } S_4 = -.5$$

(Source: Adapted from *The Wall Street Journal,* "China's Growth Target Defended," July 15, 1998, p. A9.)

16.5 MEASURING SEASONALITY

Seasonality often is present in time series data collected over months or quarters. This effect is observed when, for example, some months are always higher than the average for the year. For example, if the recorded values of the time series indicate that July sales are 25% higher than the average for the year, the July index should be 1.25 using the multiplicative structure.

We derive a seasonal index for each period during the year (4 for quarterly data, 12 for monthly data). We begin by developing a new series that contains *no seasonality.* This new series is obtained from the original time series and consists of the **centered moving averages.** This method provides an excellent way of isolating the seasonal components from the original time series. In addition to containing no seasonality, the centered moving averages are *smoother* (contain less irregular activity) than the original time series. Consequently, the moving averages give you a clearer picture of any existing trend within a time series containing significant seasonality and irregular activity. Other methods of smoothing a time series will be discussed in Chapter 17.

CENTERED MOVING AVERAGES

To illustrate the calculation of a moving average, consider a time series containing quarterly observations, as shown in Table 16.2.* Here,

$$(1) = \text{sum of } y_1 \text{ through } y_4$$

$$= 85 + 41 + 92 + 45 = 263$$

$$(2) = \text{sum of } y_2 \text{ through } y_5$$

$$= 41 + 92 + 45 + 90 = 268$$

$$(3) = \text{sum of } y_3 \text{ through } y_6$$

$$= 92 + 45 + 90 + 43 = 270$$

and so on.

Because each total contains four observations (one from each quarter), any quarterly seasonal effects have been removed. Consequently, there is no seasonality in the moving totals 263, 268, 270, and so on, in Table 16.2.

The first moving total in Table 16.2 is equal to $y_1 + y_2 + y_3 + y_4$. If we were to position this total in the center of these values, it would lie between $t = 2$ and $t = 3$, at $t = 2.5$. The second moving total is equal to $y_2 + y_3 + y_4 + y_5$; again, we position this total in the center between $t = 3$ and $t = 4$, at $t = 3.5$.

We then add the first two moving totals. Notice that four values went into each of these totals, so that a total of *eight* values makes up this sum. The sum of the first two moving totals is $263 + 268 = 531$. The average for the 8 months in the first two moving totals is $531/8 = 66.38$. This is a **centered moving average.** The position of this centered moving average is midway between $t = 2.5$ and $t = 3.5$, at $t = 3$. We therefore conclude that 66.38 is the centered moving average corresponding to $t = 3$.

---

* An example using monthly data is given in Section 16.6.

TABLE 16.2

Time series with quarterly observations.

Time	Quarter	t	y_t	Moving Totals
1990	1	1	85	(1) 263
	2	2	41	(2) 268
	3	3	92	(3) 270
	4	4	45	and so on
1991	1	5	90	
	2	6	43	
	3	7	95	
	4	8	47	
1992	1	9	92	
	⋮		⋮	

EXAMPLE 16.7

Continue the procedure using Table 16.2 and determine the centered moving average for (1) $t = 4$ and (2) $t = 5$.

SOLUTION 1

Here we obtain

$$268 = y_2 + y_3 + y_4 + y_5$$

(positioned at $t = 3.5$) and

$$270 = y_3 + y_4 + y_5 + y_6$$

(positioned at $t = 4.5$). So the average of the eight numbers making up $268 + 270 = 538$ would be positioned midway between 3.5 and 4.5, at $t = 4$. Consequently, the centered moving average for $t = 4$ is

$$\frac{268 + 270}{8} = 67.25$$

SOLUTION 2

Proceeding as before,

$$270 = y_3 + y_4 + y_5 + y_6$$

(positioned at $t = 4.5$) and

$$273 = y_4 + y_5 + y_6 + y_7$$

(positioned at $t = 5.5$). Therefore, the centered moving average for $t = 5$ is

$$\frac{270 + 273}{8} = 67.88$$

Assume quarterly sales data at Video-Comp were recorded over a four-year period. We now want to determine the centered moving averages for these data, shown in Table 16.3. There appears to be a definite seasonal effect within this time series; the highest sales occur in the fourth quarter of each year. Table 16.4 shows the centered moving averages for these data. The *first moving total* is

$$139 = y_1 + y_2 + y_3 + y_4$$

$$= 20 + 12 + 47 + 60$$

TABLE 16.3

Sales data for Video-Comp (millions of dollars).

Year	Quarter 1	Quarter 2	Quarter 3	Quarter 4
1995	20	12	47	60
1996	40	32	65	76
1997	56	50	85	100
1998	75	70	101	123

TABLE 16.4

Moving averages for Video-Comp sales data.

Year	Quarter	t	y_t	Moving Total	Centered Moving Average	Ratio to Moving Average
1995	1	1	20	—	—	—
	2	2	12		—	—
				139		
	3	3	47		37.25	1.26
				159		
	4	4	60		42.25	1.42
				179		
1996	1	5	40		47.00	.85
				197		
	2	6	32		51.25	.62
				213		
	3	7	65		55.25	1.18
				229		
	4	8	76		59.50	1.28
				247		
1997	1	9	56		64.25	.87
				267		
	2	10	50		69.75	.72
				291		
	3	11	85		75.13	1.13
				310		
	4	12	100		80.00	1.25
				330		
1998	1	13	75		84.50	.89
				346		
	2	14	70		89.38	.78
				369		
	3	15	101		—	—
	4	16	123	—	—	—

Its actual location is $t = 2.5$; it is positioned between $t = 2$ and $t = 3$. Similarly, the next moving total is centered at $t = 3.5$ and so appears between $t = 3$ and $t = 4$ in the table. This total is

$$159 = y_2 + y_3 + y_4 + y_5$$

$$= 12 + 47 + 60 + 40$$

Each moving total is centered midway between the values making up this total. For example, the last moving total, 369, is centered between $t = 14$ and $t = 15$, at $t = 14.5$. Here,

$$369 = y_{13} + y_{14} + y_{15} + y_{16}$$

$$= 75 + 70 + 101 + 123$$

The *centered moving average* at time t is the average of the moving total immediately preceding this time value and the total immediately following it. This means that, for $t = 3$,

$$37.25 = \frac{139 + 159}{8}$$

For $t = 4$,

$$42.25 = \frac{159 + 179}{8}$$

and so on. Consequently, for $t = 3$, $y_3 = 47$ and the centered moving average is 37.25.

This procedure produces 12 centered moving averages; we are unable to compute this value for $t = 1, 2, 15,$ or 16. Notice that the first two of these values of t are for quarters 1 and 2, whereas the remaining two correspond to quarters 3 and 4. In general, if our time series contains T observations, we can derive $T - 4$ centered moving averages using quarterly data or $T - 12$ averages for monthly data.

The moving totals and centered moving averages are formed by summing over the four quarters (seasons), so there is no seasonality present in these values. Furthermore, the irregular component has been reduced because averages always contain less random variation (noise) than do the individual values making up these averages. Representing this reduced irregular activity component as i_t (rather than I_t), we can represent a centered moving average at time t as

centered moving average at time $t = \text{TR}_t \cdot C_t \cdot i_t$

Because of this averaging procedure, the moving averages contain much less irregular activity and so are much "smoother" than the original time series. This procedure thus is referred to as **smoothing** the time series to get a clearer picture of any existing trend as well as of its shape (straight line or curve).

The centered moving averages in Table 16.4 show a steadily increasing trend. Because the differences between any two adjacent moving averages are nearly the same, this trend is very *linear*. The trend is more apparent in Figure 16.20, which contains the original data with the moving averages.

To determine the four quarterly seasonal indexes, the first step is to divide each observation, y_t, by its corresponding centered moving average; the result is shown in the last column in the table.

for $t = 3$:   ratio = 47/37.25 = 1.26   (belongs to quarter 3, 1995)

for $t = 4$:   ratio = 60/42.25 = 1.42   (belongs to quarter 4, 1995)

$\vdots$

for $t = 14$:   ratio = 70/89.38 = .78   (belongs to quarter 2, 1998)

FIGURE 16.20

Smoothing a time series using moving averages (Video-Comp sales data).

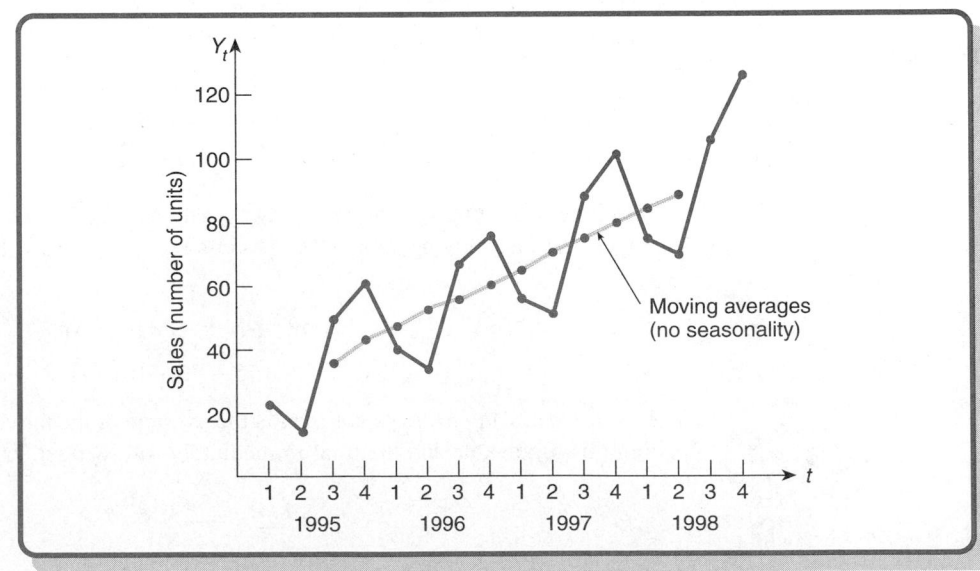

When we divide y_t by its corresponding centered moving average, we obtain

$$\text{ratio} = \frac{y_t}{\text{centered moving average}} = \frac{\cancel{PR}_t \cdot S_t \cdot \cancel{C}_t \cdot I_t}{\cancel{PR}_t \cdot \cancel{C}_t \cdot i_t}$$

$$= S_t \cdot I_t$$

Consequently, these ratios contain the seasonal effects as well as the irregular activity (noise) components. The following discussion illustrates how you can reduce the effect of the irregular activity factor by combining these ratios into a set of four seasonal indexes, one for each quarter.

COMPUTING A SEASONAL INDEX

The purpose of a seasonal index is to indicate how the time series value for each quarter (or month) compares with the average for the year. The following discussion will assume that we are dealing with a time series containing quarterly data. In the next section, we illustrate this procedure using monthly data.

We begin by collecting the ratios to moving average, placing each of them in its respective quarter. In Table 16.4, we see that 1.26 belongs to quarter 3, 1.42 to quarter 4, .85 to quarter 1, and so on. Table 16.5 is the result. Notice that there are three ratios for each quarter. In general, you always will obtain (total number of years − 1) ratios under each quarter (or month). The time series in this example contains four years; therefore, it has three ratios. To obtain a "typical" ratio for each quarter, you have several options, including

1. Determining an average of these ratios
2. Finding the median of these values
3. Eliminating the largest and smallest ratio within each quarter and computing a mean of the remaining ratios; this is called a **trimmed mean.**

We will follow the first procedure and calculate a mean ratio for each quarter, as illustrated in Table 16.5. When the time series contains five or more years of data, a trimmed mean offers you protection against an outlier ratio dominating the index for this quarter. Using the median ratios also helps guard against this type of situation.

A FINAL ADJUSTMENT

The last step in computing the seasonal indexes is to make sure that the four computed ratio averages **sum to 4** (or 12, for monthly indexes). This is accomplished by (1) adding the four averages computed in the table (call this SUM) and (2) multiplying each average by 4/SUM. The modified average obtained in this process is the seasonal index for that quarter.

TABLE 16.5

Ratios for each quarter.

	Quarter 1	Quarter 2	Quarter 3	Quarter 4
	—	—	1.26	1.42
	.85	.62	1.18	1.28
	.87	.72	1.13	1.25
	.89	.78	—	—
Total	2.61	2.12	3.57	3.95
Average	0.870	0.707	1.190	1.317

EXAMPLE 16.8

SOLUTION

Using Table 16.5, determine the four seasonal indexes.

First,

$$\text{SUM} = .870 + .707 + 1.190 + 1.317 = 4.084$$

This means that we need to multiply each of the four averages in Table 16.5 by $4/4.084 = .9794$.

Quarter	Seasonal Index
1	$(0.870)(.9794) = 0.852$
2	$(0.707)(.9794) = 0.692$
3	$(1.190)(.9794) = 1.166$
4	$(1.317)(.9794) = \underline{1.290}$
	4.0

The indexes for quarters 1 and 2 are below 1.0, so the sales during these quarters typically are below the yearly average. On the other hand, quarters 3 and 4 have seasonal indexes of 1.166 and 1.290, so the sales for these quarters are higher than the average for the year.

This procedure for determining seasonal effects works well, provided the ratios in Table 16.5 are reasonably *stable*. In Example 16.8, all the ratios for quarter 2 are small (near .7) and all the ratios for quarter 4 are large (near 1.3). If strong seasonality is present, such will be the case.

Seasonal indexes can be updated as you obtain an additional year's observations on the variable of interest. You have the option of deleting the most distant year's observations prior to recalculating these values. This procedure leads to seasonal indexes that change slowly over the years.

In summary, to calculate the seasonal indexes:

1. Derive the *moving* totals by summing the observations for 4 (quarterly data) or 12 (monthly data) consecutive time periods.
2. Average and center the totals by finding the *centered moving averages.*
3. Divide each observation by its corresponding centered moving average.
4. Place the ratios from step 3 in a table headed by the 4 quarters or 12 months.
5. For each column in this table, determine the mean of these ratios; these are the unadjusted seasonal indexes.
6. Make a final adjustment to guarantee that the final seasonal indexes sum to 4 (quarterly data) or 12 (monthly data); these adjusted means are the seasonal indexes.

DESEASONALIZING THE DATA

To remove the seasonality from the data, we deseasonalize the time series. The resulting series contains no seasonal effects and consists of the trend, cyclical activity, and, of course, irregular activity. We write deseasonalized data as d_t.

$$d_t = \frac{y_t}{\text{corresponding seasonal index}}$$

$$= \frac{\text{TR}_t \cdot S_t \cdot C_t \cdot I_t}{S_t} = \text{TR}_t \cdot C_t \cdot I_t$$

The deseasonalized sales values from Table 16.3 are contained in Table 16.6. These values contain trend, cyclical effects, and irregular activity. Notice how the trend is much more apparent in the deseasonalized values than in the original time series.

Table 16.6   Deseasonalized sales.

Year	t	y_t	Seasonal Index (S_t)	Deseasonalized Values $d_t = \dfrac{y_t}{S_t}$
1995	1	20	.852	23.47
	2	12	.692	17.34
	3	47	1.166	40.31
	4	60	1.290	46.51
1996	5	40	.852	46.95
	6	32	.692	46.24
	7	65	1.166	55.75
	8	76	1.290	58.91
1997	9	56	.852	65.73
	10	50	.692	72.25
	11	85	1.166	72.90
	12	100	1.290	77.52
1998	13	75	.852	88.03
	14	70	.692	101.16
	15	101	1.166	86.62
	16	123	1.290	95.35

In Table 16.6, we obtained deseasonalized values for all 16 of the original observations, including the two quarters on each end. We can use the "new" deseasonalized series to determine the trend and cyclical components of the original time series. This will be illustrated in the next section, where we apply the four-step procedure: (1) computing seasonal indexes, (2) deseasonalizing the data, (3) computing the trend components from the deseasonalized time series (d_t), and finally (4) calculating the cyclical activity.

COMMENTS

Monthly values in the *Wall Street Journal* and other business publications are often stated as "seasonally adjusted." This simply means these values have been deseasonalized to reflect "real" changes in the variable. For example, the number of unemployed workers always increases in May because college students are looking for summer or long-term employment. To determine if there has actually been an increase in the unemployment rate, a deseasonalized (seasonally adjusted) value is generally quoted in the article or news release.

EXERCISES 16.35–16.44

UNDERSTANDING THE MECHANICS

16.35 Complete the following table.

Year	Quarter	t	y_t	Moving Total	Centered Moving Average	Ratio to Moving Average
1998	1	1	10			
	2	2	6	—		
	3	3	23	69		
	4	4	30	79		
1999	1	5	20	88		
	2	6	15	95		
	3	7	30	101		
	4	8	36	—		

16.36 Find the deseasonalized values for the following monthly time series data.

Year	t	y_t	Seasonal Index (S_t)
1999	1	20	1.12
	2	19	.98
	3	17	.96
	4	16	.93
	5	15	.92
	6	11	.90
	7	18	1.05
	8	19	1.06
	9	20	1.07
	10	22	1.05
	11	19	.96
	12	18	1.00

APPLYING THE NEW CONCEPTS

16.37 Explain why a moving average is a smoothing technique.

16.38 The following table presents the ratio to moving average figures for sales at Zano Systems, a supplier of photocopy machines. Find the seasonal indexes.

Year	Quarter 1	Quarter 2	Quarter 3	Quarter 4
1994			.88	.87
1995	1.14	1.25	.83	.86
1996	1.19	1.22	.94	.88
1997	1.23	1.35	.90	.72
1998	1.16	1.32	.94	.81
1999	1.10	1.21		

16.39 The following table presents the ratio to moving average figures for the cost of a bushel of grapefruit in a certain county in Florida. Find the seasonal indexes.

Year	Jan	Feb	Mar	Apr	May	June
1995						
1996	.90	.87	.95	.93	1.00	1.04
1997	.87	.84	.81	.88	1.01	1.02
1998	.81	.75	.82	.89	1.05	1.04
1999	.87	.81	.77	.98	1.01	1.06

Year	July	Aug	Sept	Oct	Nov	Dec
1995	1.06	1.10	1.12	1.02	1.03	.99
1996	1.08	1.14	1.15	1.06	1.04	.97
1997	1.01	1.15	1.07	1.03	1.00	.90
1998	1.10	1.21	1.18	1.10	1.07	.97
1999						

16.40 The sale of grass sod is a seasonal business. Green Garden Supplies does most of its business in May, June, July, and August. The following table presents their monthly sales (in thousands of dollars). Find the seasonal indexes. For what month is the seasonal index the largest?

Year	Jan	Feb	Mar	Apr	May	June
1995	.1	.1	1.2	2.2	4.1	4.5
1996	.1	.2	1.4	2.0	4.0	4.2
1997	.1	.2	1.3	2.2	4.3	4.4
1998	.1	.3	1.4	2.3	4.4	4.6
1999	.1	.3	1.5	2.3	4.6	4.8

Year	July	Aug	Sept	Oct	Nov	Dec
1995	5.5	5.3	3.5	1.1	.2	.1
1996	5.3	5.0	3.2	1.0	.1	.1
1997	5.6	5.3	3.5	1.1	.2	.1
1998	5.8	5.5	3.7	1.3	.3	.1
1999	6.0	5.6	3.7	1.4	.4	.1

16.41 The following table represents the ratio to moving average figures for the number of people below the poverty level in a certain county. Find the seasonal indexes.

Year	Quarter 1	Quarter 2	Quarter 3	Quarter 4
1995			.84	.83
1996	1.12	1.29	.91	.89
1997	1.17	1.24	.92	.90
1998	1.15	1.30	.92	.88
1999	1.13	1.26		

16.42 The amount of beverage sold at Chesapeake Restaurant varies according to the time of the year. The manager would like to know which quarter is most affected by seasonal variation. Business at Chesapeake Restaurant has steadily increased over the past four years. What advice can you give the manager? The following data are in units of thousands of dollars.

Year	Quarter	Beverage Sales
1996	1	22
	2	21
	3	26
	4	27
1997	1	25
	2	24
	3	29
	4	30
1998	1	29
	2	28
	3	35
	4	37
1999	1	34
	2	33
	3	40
	4	42

USING THE COMPUTER

16.43 [DATA SET EX16-43] *Variable description:*

Year: Year from 1995 to 1998
Month: One through twelve for the months of the year
JoblessFemale: Percentage of unemployed females who are married and in the civilian labor force

Unemployment among married females is typically higher than unemployment among married males. From 1995 to 1998, the strong economy has produced a much tighter job market and therefore, the difference in the unemployment rates of married males and females has narrowed. Find the seasonal indexes for the percentage of unemployed females who are married and in the civilian labor force.

16.44 [DATA SET EX16-44] *Variable description:*

Year: Year from 1994 to 1999
Quarter: One through four for the four quarters of the year
CellularLines: Number of cellular telephone lines in Brazil

The state-owned telephone company of Brazil, Telecommunicacoes Brasileiros (Telebras), is fighting vast inefficiencies because they need to compete with foreign telecommunication companies offering digital technology. Suppose that a manager of the Telebras system is interested in the seasonal indexes for the number of cellular telephone lines in Brazil. Compute the seasonal indexes for these data (in units of millions). For which quarter is this index the smallest? The largest?

(Source: Adapted from *The Wall Street Journal*, "Telebras Wards Off Competition," July 15, 1998, p. A9.)

Table 16.7

Total U.S. retail trade (excluding automotive group) (billions of dollars).

1994	1995	1996	1997
119.402	127.550	130.900	140.539
117.954	123.440	133.434	136.278
136.853	141.594	146.628	155.319
135.441	140.627	147.447	151.703
141.180	149.643	158.666	164.132
141.864	148.708	152.745	157.726
141.164	145.846	152.803	160.679
146.759	151.856	159.851	165.064
140.513	144.856	147.371	155.001
144.393	146.450	156.473	163.314
151.838	157.284	164.872	168.301
191.472	194.854	201.187	209.406

Source: U.S. Department of Commerce, Bureau of the Census, *Current Business Report.* These reports are only available electronically using Internet address **http://www.census.gov.**

16.6 A Time Series Containing Seasonality, Trend, and Cycles

During the summer of 1998, the owner of an import/export company decided to investigate the past behavior of U.S. retail trade figures for the years 1994 through 1997. He collected the data in Table 16.7 using monthly figures released by the U.S. Department of Commerce. He suspected that these data would indicate high retail trade during December (due to holiday sales) with much lower activity during January and possibly February. For the remaining months, he had no idea whether seasonal effects would be present. He also suspected there would be a steadily increasing trend due to inflation and population growth.

The four-step procedure for decomposing (a gruesome term, we'll admit) a time series into the seasonal, trend, and cyclical components was introduced in Section 16.4. We demonstrate this method of describing a time series by using the monthly retail trade data in the example to follow (Example 16.9).

MICROSOFT® EXCEL APPLICATION   USE DATA16-9

Example 16.9
A Time Series Decomposition Using Excel

The U.S. monthly retail data for 1994–1997 are contained in data set DATA16-9. Perform a time series decomposition of these data, and discuss the results.

Solution

Begin by entering the 48 observations into column A. Click on **KGP Data Analysis ➤ Time Series Analysis ➤ Decomposition.** Select 12 as the number of time periods per year, and enter "A1:A48" in the **Input Range** box, "B1" in the **Output Range** box, and "1994" in the **First Year** box. Also, click on "A Single Column" since the data are stored in a single column (column A). The resulting output will be contained in five sheets, labeled **Components, Cyclical, Trend, Seasonal,** and **Plots.**

Step 1. *Determine the seasonal indexes.* The first step is to determine the moving totals and centered moving averages for the 48 observations in Table 16.7. This portion of the output is in the sheet labeled **Seasonal** and will be identical to the results contained in Table 16.8. Notice that when using monthly data, there is no monthly

TABLE 16.8

Moving averages and ratios to moving average for U.S. monthly retail trade data. This output is contained in the Excel sheet labeled **Seasonal.**

Year	Month	t (1)	y_t (2)	Moving total (3)	Centered Moving Average (4)	Ratio to Moving Average (5)
1994	Jan	1	119.402			
	Feb	2	117.954			
	Mar	3	136.853			
	Apr	4	135.441			
	May	5	141.180			
	June	6	141.864			
	July	7	141.164	1708.833	142.742	0.989
	Aug	8	146.759	1716.981	143.310	1.024
	Sept	9	140.513	1722.467	143.736	0.978
	Oct	10	144.393	1727.208	144.150	1.002
	Nov	11	151.838	1732.394	144.719	1.049
	Dec	12	191.472	1740.857	145.357	1.317
1995	Jan	13	127.550	1747.701	145.837	0.875
	Feb	14	123.440	1752.383	146.244	0.844
	Mar	15	141.594	1757.480	146.638	0.966
	Apr	16	140.627	1761.823	146.904	0.957
	May	17	149.643	1763.880	147.217	1.016
	June	18	148.708	1769.326	147.585	1.008
	July	19	145.846	1772.708	147.865	0.986
	Aug	20	151.856	1776.058	148.421	1.023
	Sept	21	144.856	1786.052	149.047	0.972
	Oct	22	146.450	1791.086	149.541	0.979
	Nov	23	157.284	1797.906	150.201	1.047
	Dec	24	194.854	1806.929	150.746	1.293
1996	Jan	25	130.900	1810.966	151.204	0.866
	Feb	26	133.434	1817.923	151.827	0.879
	Mar	27	146.628	1825.918	152.265	0.963
	Apr	28	147.447	1828.433	152.787	0.965
	May	29	158.666	1838.456	153.521	1.034
	June	30	152.745	1846.044	154.101	0.991
	July	31	152.803	1852.377	154.766	0.987
	Aug	32	159.851	1862.0169	155.286	1.02
	Sept	33	147.371	1864.860	155.767	0.946
	Oct	34	156.473	1873.551	156.307	1.001
	Nov	35	164.872	1877.807	156.712	1.052
	Dec	36	201.187	1883.273	157.147	1.280
1997	Jan	37	140.539	1888.254	157.683	0.891
	Feb	38	136.278	1896.130	158.228	0.861
	Mar	39	155.319	1901.343	158.763	0.978
	Apr	40	151.703	1908.973	159.366	0.952
	May	41	164.132	1915.814	159.794	1.027
	June	42	157.726	1919.243	160.279	0.984
	July	43	160.679	1927.462		
	Aug	44	165.064			
	Sept	45	155.001			
	Oct	46	163.314			
	Nov	47	168.301			
	Dec	48	209.406			

average for $t = 1$ through $t = 6$ (January through June 1994) and for $t = 43$ through 48 (July through December 1997). The first moving total is

$$1708.833 = y_1 + y_2 + \cdots + y_{12}$$

$$= 119.402 + 117.954 + \cdots + 191.472$$

This value is positioned midway between $t = 1$ and $t = 12$, that is, at $t = 6.5$ (between $t = 6$ and $t = 7$). The next moving total is

$$1716.981 = y_2 + y_3 + \cdots + y_{13}$$

$$= 117.954 + 136.853 + \cdots + 127.550$$

which is centered at $t = 7.5$ (between $t = 7$ and $t = 8$). So the first *centered moving average* is positioned midway between $t = 6.5$ and $t = 7.5$, at $t = 7$. This is

$$142.742 = \frac{1708.833 + 1716.981}{24}$$

Notice that we divide by 24, because 24 observations went into the sum of these two moving totals.

The final centered moving average is

$$160.279 = \frac{1919.243 + 1927.462}{24}$$

and corresponds to $t = 42$.

The Excel output and Table 16.8 also contain each ratio to moving average (column 2 divided by column 4). To illustrate:

$$0.989 = \frac{141.164}{142.742} \qquad 1.024 = \frac{146.759}{143.310}$$

and so on. These ratios are summarized in the top portion of the **Seasonal** Excel spreadsheet (under **Summary of Ratios**) and in Table 16.9, both of which also contain the average of the three values for each time period.

The final step is to adjust each of these averages in Table 16.9 so they sum to 12 (because there are 12 time periods per year). Here,

$$SUM = .877 + .861 + \cdots + 1.297 = 12.004$$

and so

$$S_1 = \text{seasonal index for January}$$

$$= .877\left(\frac{12}{12.004}\right) = .877$$

$$S_2 = \text{seasonal index for February}$$

$$= .861\left(\frac{12}{12.004}\right) = .861$$

$$\vdots$$

$$S_{12} = \text{seasonal index for December}$$

$$= 1.297\left(\frac{12}{12.004}\right) = 1.296$$

The final collection of seasonal indexes is

Month	Seasonal Index	Month	Seasonal Index
Jan.	.877	July	.987
Feb.	.861	Aug.	1.025
Mar.	.969	Sept.	.965
Apr.	.958	Oct.	.994
May	1.025	Nov.	1.049
June	.994	Dec.	1.296

TABLE 16.9   Summary of ratios. This output is in the Excel sheet labeled **Seasonal.**

					MONTH (PERIOD)							
	Jan	Feb	Mar	Apr	May	Jun	Jul	Aug	Sep	Oct	Nov	Dec
1994							0.989	1.024	0.978	1.002	1.049	1.317
1995	0.875	0.844	0.966	0.957	1.016	1.008	0.986	1.023	0.972	0.979	1.047	1.293
1996	0.866	0.879	0.963	0.965	1.034	0.991	0.987	1.029	0.946	1.001	1.052	1.280
1997	0.891	0.861	0.978	0.952	1.027	0.984						
Average	0.877	0.861	0.969	0.958	1.026	0.994	0.988	1.026	0.965	0.994	1.049	1.297

The sum of these seasonal indexes $(S_1 + S_2 + \cdots + S_{12})$ is 12.000. Due to rounding, this sum may not be exactly 12 on occasion, and this is perfectly acceptable.

We observe (1) a large seasonal index for December $(S_{12} = 1.296)$, indicating large retail trade for this month, (2) low indexes for January and February, and (3) very little seasonality for any of the remaining months.

Step 2. *Deseasonalize the data.* We obtain the deseasonalized values (which contain no seasonality) by dividing each observation by its corresponding seasonal index. These values are contained in the Excel spreadsheet labeled **Trend** (under the column labeled D(t)) and are shown in Table 16.10. The trend is more apparent now because the deseasonalized values tend to increase over time.

Step 3. *Determine the trend components.* A common method for estimating trend (and the one we use) is to construct a least squares trend line (or curve) through the deseasonalized data. From the moving averages in the Excel output (under the column **Centered Average** in the sheet labeled **Seasonal**), also shown in Table 16.8, it appears that a straight line trend equation will be appropriate; these values tend to increase at a fairly steady rate.

The calculations for the trend line are identical to those discussed in Section 16.2, using the d_i values in place of the original observations, y_i. A summary of these calculations is given in Table 16.11. The least squares line through the deseasonalized data is contained at the top of the Excel sheet labeled **Trend** and is given by

$$TR_t = \hat{y}_t = b_0 + b_1 t$$

where

$$b_1 = \frac{\sum t d_t - (\sum t)(\sum d_t)/T}{\sum t^2 - (\sum t)^2/T}$$

$$= \frac{182,507.088 - (1176)(7254.796)/48}{38,024 - (1176)^2/48} = \frac{4764.586}{9212} = .51722$$

and

$$b_0 = \bar{d}_t - b_1 \bar{t}$$

$$= \frac{7254.796}{48} - (.51722)\frac{1176}{48} = 151.142 - 12.672 = 138.470$$

Consequently, the equation of the trend equation is given by

$$TR_t = \hat{d}_t = 138.470 + .517t$$

This equation agrees with the Excel result and implies that, apart from seasonal fluctuations, the U.S. retail trade is increasing at an average rate of $517 million each month. A graph of the deseasonalized data and corresponding trend line is shown in Figure 16.21.

TABLE 16.10   Deseasonalized monthly retail trade values. This output is in the Excel sheet labeled **Trend**.

Year	Month	t	y_t	S_t	$d_t = \dfrac{y_t}{S_t}$
1994	Jan	1	119.402	0.877	136.163
	Feb	2	117.954	0.861	136.980
	Mar	3	136.853	0.969	141.285
	Apr	4	135.441	0.958	141.416
	May	5	141.180	1.025	137.688
	June	6	141.864	0.994	142.727
	July	7	141.164	0.987	142.995
	Aug	8	146.759	1.025	143.154
	Sept	9	140.513	0.965	145.631
	Oct	10	144.393	0.994	145.310
	Nov	11	151.838	1.049	144.730
	Dec	12	191.472	1.296	147.711
1995	Jan	13	127.550	0.877	145.455
	Feb	14	123.440	0.861	143.351
	Mar	15	141.594	0.969	146.179
	Apr	16	140.627	0.958	146.831
	May	17	149.643	1.025	145.941
	June	18	148.708	0.994	149.613
	July	19	145.846	0.987	147.738
	Aug	20	151.856	1.025	148.126
	Sept	21	144.856	0.965	150.133
	Oct	22	146.450	0.994	147.381
	Nov	23	157.284	1.049	149.921
	Dec	24	194.845	1.296	150.320
1996	Jan	25	130.900	0.877	149.276
	Feb	26	133.434	0.861	154.957
	Mar	27	146.628	0.969	151.376
	Apr	28	147.447	0.958	153.951
	May	29	158.666	1.025	154.741
	June	30	152.745	0.994	153.674
	July	31	152.803	0.987	154.785
	Aug	32	159.851	1.025	155.924
	Sept	33	147.371	0.965	152.739
	Oct	34	156.473	0.994	157.467
	Nov	35	164.872	1.049	157.154
	Dec	36	201.187	1.296	155.206
1997	Jan	37	140.539	0.877	160.268
	Feb	38	136.278	0.861	158.259
	Mar	39	155.319	0.969	160.349
	Apr	40	151.703	0.958	158.395
	May	41	164.132	1.025	160.072
	June	42	157.726	0.994	158.685
	July	43	160.679	0.987	162.763
	Aug	44	165.064	1.025	161.009
	Sept	45	155.001	0.965	160.647
	Oct	46	163.314	0.994	164.352
	Nov	47	168.301	1.049	160.422
	Dec	48	209.406	1.296	161.546

TABLE 16.11

Calculations for trend line (U.S. monthly retail trade data).

t	d_t	$t \cdot d_t$	t^2
1	136.163	136.163	1
2	136.980	273.960	4
3	141.285	423.855	9
4	141.416	565.664	16
⋮	⋮	⋮	⋮
45	160.647	7229.115	2025
46	164.352	7560.129	2116
47	160.422	7539.834	2209
48	161.546	7754.208	2304
1,176	7,254.796	182,507.088	38,024

FIGURE 16.21

Deseasonalized data and trend line (monthly U.S. retail trade).

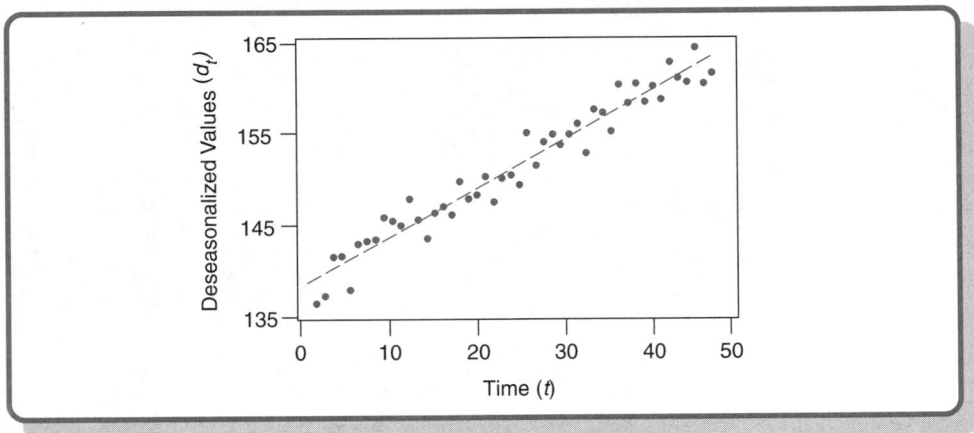

Step 4. *Determine the cyclical activity.* We begin by following the procedure outlined in Section 16.3. We divide each deseasonalized observation by the corresponding trend value:

$$\frac{d_t}{\text{TR}_t} = \frac{d_t}{\hat{d}_t} = \frac{\text{TR}_t \cdot C_t \cdot I_t}{\text{TR}_t} = C_t \cdot I_t$$

The resulting values contain cyclical effects as well as an irregular activity component. One method of reducing the irregular effect is to compute a series of *three-period* moving averages on the $C_t \cdot I_t$ values. This procedure greatly reduces the irregular activity effect, and the moving averages provide a much better estimate of the cyclical components. The choice of a three-period moving average is somewhat arbitrary; however, when we use an odd number of terms, the moving averages need not be centered.

A partial solution, using the first six rows of the Excel output under the column **Ratio** in the sheet labeled **Seasonal,** is shown in Table 16.12. We see that the cyclical component for $t = 2$ is C_2, where

$$C_2 = \frac{.9797 + .9819 + 1.0090}{3} = .990$$

and the cyclical component for $t = 3$ is

$$C_3 = \frac{.9819 + 1.0090 + 1.0062}{3} = .999$$

TABLE 16.12

Calculating the cyclical components for the U.S. monthly retail trade data.

t	d_t	$\hat{d}_t$	$\dfrac{d_t}{\hat{d}_t}(= C_t \cdot I_t)$	Three-Month Moving Average (C_t)
1	136.163	$138.470 + .517(1) = 138.987$	0.9797	—
2	136.980	$138.470 + .517(2) = 139.504$	0.9819	0.990
3	141.285	$138.470 + .517(3) = 140.021$	1.0090	0.999
4	141.416	$138.470 + .517(4) = 140.539$	1.0062	0.997
5	137.688	$138.470 + .517(5) = 141.056$	0.9761	0.997
6	142.727	$138.470 + .517(6) = 141.573$	1.0082	0.997
⋮	⋮	⋮	⋮	⋮

FIGURE 16.22

Plot of cyclical activity (monthly U.S. retail trade data).

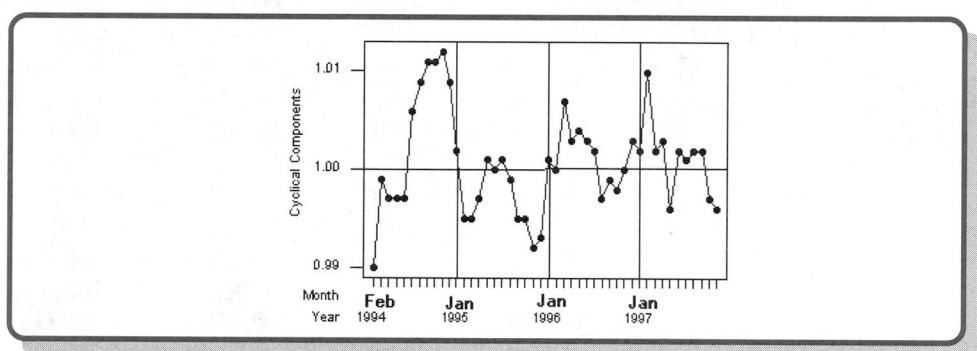

Similarly,

$$C_4 = \frac{1.0090 + 1.0062 + .9761}{3} = .997$$

and

$$C_5 = \frac{1.0062 + .9761 + 1.0082}{3} = .997$$

The complete set of smoothed cyclical values is contained in the Excel sheet labeled **Cyclical** (under the column titled **C(t)**). These components are reproduced in Table 16.13 (far right column) and plotted in Figure 16.22. Observe the start of a cycle beginning mid-1994 and ending in May 1995. There are three very weak cycles between May 1995 and June 1997. The data end in the midst of downward cycle with cyclical components less than 1. Since the cyclical components range from .99 to 1.01, we can say that there was very mild cyclical activity during these four years. In previous editions of this textbook, the cyclical components for the U.S. retail trade data ranged from .97 to 1.03 (1980–1983), .97 to 1.01 (1984–1987), .98 to 1.02 (1987–1990) and .97 to 1.04 (1989–1992).

Once the steps in the previous sections have been completed, the various components can be combined for any specified value of t.

TABLE 16.13   Cyclical components (monthly U.S. retail trade data). This output is in the Excel sheet labeled **Cyclical.**

Year	Month	d_t	$\hat{d}_t$ (TR$_t$)	$\dfrac{d_t}{\hat{d}_t}(= C_t \cdot I_t)$	Three-Month Moving Average (C_t)
1994	Jan	136.163	138.987	0.9797	—
	Feb	136.980	139.504	0.9819	0.990
	Mar	141.285	140.021	1.0090	0.999
	Apr	141.416	140.539	1.0062	0.997
	May	137.688	141.056	0.9761	0.997
	June	142.727	141.573	1.0082	0.997
	July	142.995	142.090	1.0064	1.006
	Aug	143.154	142.607	1.0038	1.009
	Sept	145.631	143.125	1.0175	1.011
	Oct	145.310	143.642	1.0116	1.011
	Nov	144.730	144.159	1.0040	1.012
	Dec	147.711	144.676	1.0210	1.009
1995	Jan	145.455	145.194	1.0018	1.002
	Feb	143.351	145.711	0.9838	0.995
	Mar	146.179	146.228	0.9997	0.995
	Apr	146.831	146.745	1.0006	0.997
	May	145.941	147.262	0.9910	1.001
	June	149.613	147.780	1.0124	1.000
	July	147.738	148.297	0.9962	1.001
	Aug	148.126	148.814	0.9954	0.999
	Sept	150.133	149.331	1.0054	0.995
	Oct	147.381	149.849	0.9835	0.995
	Nov	149.921	150.366	0.9970	0.992
	Dec	150.320	150.883	0.9963	0.993
1996	Jan	149.276	151.400	0.9860	1.001
	Feb	154.957	151.917	1.0200	1.000
	Mar	151.376	152.435	0.9931	1.007
	Apr	153.951	152.952	1.0065	1.003
	May	154.741	153.469	1.0083	1.004
	June	153.674	153.986	0.9980	1.003
	July	154.785	154.503	1.0018	1.002
	Aug	155.924	155.021	1.0058	0.997
	Sept	152.739	155.538	0.9820	0.999
	Oct	157.467	156.055	1.0090	0.998
	Nov	157.154	156.572	1.0037	1.000
	Dec	155.206	157.090	0.9880	1.003
1997	Jan	160.268	157.607	1.0169	1.002
	Feb	158.259	158.124	1.0009	1.010
	Mar	160.349	158.641	1.0108	1.002
	Apr	158.395	159.158	0.9952	1.003
	May	160.072	159.676	1.0025	0.996
	June	158.685	160.193	0.9906	1.002
	July	162.763	160.710	1.0128	1.001
	Aug	161.009	161.227	0.9986	1.002
	Sept	160.647	161.745	0.9932	1.002
	Oct	164.352	162.262	1.0129	0.997
	Nov	160.422	162.779	0.9855	0.996
	Dec	161.546	163.296	0.9893	—

EXAMPLE 16.10   Determine the four components for (1) August 1994 and (2) March 1997.

SOLUTION 1   The value of t for August 1994 is $t = 8$. The seasonal index for August is $S_8 = 1.025$. The trend component (from Table 16.13) is $TR_8 = 142.607$. The cyclical component (far right column of Table 16.13) is 1.009. Therefore,

$$S_8 \cdot TR_8 \cdot C_8 = (1.025)(142.607)(1.009) = 147.488$$

The actual observation for August 1994 is $y_8 = 146.759$. Since $y_8 = S_8 \cdot TR_8 \cdot C_8 \cdot I_8$,

$$I_8 = \frac{y_8}{S_8 \cdot TR_8 \cdot C_8} = \frac{146.759}{147.488} = .995$$

and the final decomposition is

$$y_8 = 146.759 = S_8 \cdot TR_8 \cdot C_8 \cdot I_8 = (1.025)(142.607)(1.009)(.995)$$

SOLUTION 2   For $t = 39$ (March 1997), we have $S_{39} =$ seasonal index for March $= S_3 = .969$. Also, $TR_{39} = 158.641$ and $C_{39} = 1.002$, from Table 16.13. Consequently,

$$I_{39} = \frac{y_{39}}{S_{39} \cdot TR_{39} \cdot C_{39}} = \frac{155.319}{154.031} = 1.008$$

The combined decomposition for this observation is

$$y_{39} = 155.319 = S_{39} \cdot TR_{39} \cdot C_{39} \cdot I_{39} = (.969)(158.641)(1.002)(1.008)$$

The components for all but the first and last observations are contained in the Excel spreadsheet labeled **Components** under the heading **Time Series Components.** The same components are shown in Table 16.14.

SUMMARY OF TIME SERIES DECOMPOSITION

The time series decomposition procedure allows you to examine the presence of

> *Trend (a long-term growth or decline)*
>
> *Seasonality (a within-year recurrent pattern)*
>
> *Cyclical activity (upward or downward variation about the trend)*

The remaining component (what is left after removing the effect of these three factors) is irregular activity. Having determined these four components, you are able to describe a particular time series by carefully examining and plotting the calculated components.

A summary of the components for the U.S. retail trade time series is contained in Table 16.14. The irregular activity components (I_t) are determined by continuing the procedure in Example 16.10. Graphs of these components are shown in Figure 16.23. These four graphs will be on the Excel sheet labeled **Plots** when using **KGP Data Analysis ➤ Time Series Analysis ➤ Decomposition.** Notice that the graph of the irregular activity components contains no obvious pattern, as we would expect. By combining the various graphs of the time series components into a single set of graphs (Figure 16.23), we can tell at a glance what is the nature of the series. The conclusions we can reach from this figure include the following.

1. There is a strong linear trend that increases over the four-year period.
2. There is a strong retail trade peak each December, followed by weak trading in January and February.
3. There is very weak cyclic activity observed over this four-year period. There is a clear cycle between May 1994 and May 1995. Retail trade for 1997 ends in the midst of a downward cycle.

Other methods of time series analysis are discussed in Chapter 17, where we examine time series forecasting.

TABLE 16.14   Time series components for U.S. retail trade data. This output is in the Excel sheet labeled **Components.**

Year	Month	y_t	TR_t	S_t	C_t	I_t
1994	Jan	119.402	138.987	0.877	—	—
	Feb	117.954	139.504	0.861	0.990	0.992
	Mar	136.853	140.021	0.969	0.999	1.010
	Apr	135.441	140.539	0.958	0.997	1.009
	May	141.180	141.056	1.025	0.997	0.979
	June	141.864	141.573	0.994	0.997	1.011
	July	141.164	142.090	0.987	1.006	1.000
	Aug	146.759	142.607	1.025	1.009	0.995
	Sept	140.513	143.125	0.965	1.011	1.006
	Oct	144.393	143.642	0.994	1.011	1.001
	Nov	151.838	144.159	1.049	1.012	0.992
	Dec	191.472	144.676	1.296	1.009	1.012
1995	Jan	127.550	145.194	0.877	1.002	1.000
	Feb	123.440	145.711	0.861	0.995	0.989
	Mar	141.594	146.228	0.969	0.995	1.005
	Apr	140.627	146.745	0.958	0.997	1.003
	May	149.643	147.262	1.025	1.001	0.990
	June	148.708	147.780	0.994	1.000	1.013
	July	145.846	148.297	0.987	1.001	0.995
	Aug	151.856	148.814	1.025	0.999	0.996
	Sept	144.856	149.331	0.965	0.995	1.011
	Oct	146.450	149.849	0.994	0.995	0.988
	Nov	157.284	150.366	1.049	0.992	1.005
	Dec	194.854	150.883	1.296	0.993	1.003
1996	Jan	130.900	151.400	0.877	1.001	0.985
	Feb	133.434	151.917	0.861	1.000	1.020
	Mar	146.628	152.435	0.969	1.007	0.987
	Apr	147.447	152.952	0.958	1.003	1.004
	May	158.666	153.469	1.025	1.004	1.004
	June	152.745	153.986	0.994	1.003	0.995
	July	152.803	154.503	0.987	1.002	1.000
	Aug	159.851	155.021	1.025	0.997	1.009
	Sept	147.371	155.538	0.965	0.999	0.983
	Oct	156.473	156.055	0.994	0.998	1.011
	Nov	164.872	156.572	1.049	1.000	1.003
	Dec	201.187	157.090	1.296	1.003	0.985
1997	Jan	140.539	157.607	0.877	1.002	1.015
	Feb	136.278	158.124	0.861	1.010	0.991
	Mar	155.319	158.641	0.969	1.002	1.008
	Apr	151.703	159.158	0.958	1.003	0.992
	May	164.132	159.676	1.025	0.996	1.006
	June	157.726	160.193	0.994	1.002	0.989
	July	160.679	160.710	0.987	1.001	1.012
	Aug	165.064	161.227	1.025	1.002	0.997
	Sept	155.001	161.745	0.965	1.002	0.992
	Oct	163.314	162.262	0.994	0.997	1.016
	Nov	168.301	162.779	1.049	0.996	0.990
	Dec	209.406	163.296	1.296	—	—

FIGURE 16.23

Excel plots of monthly U.S. retail trade data using **KGP Data Analysis ➤ Time Series Analysis ➤ Decomposition.**

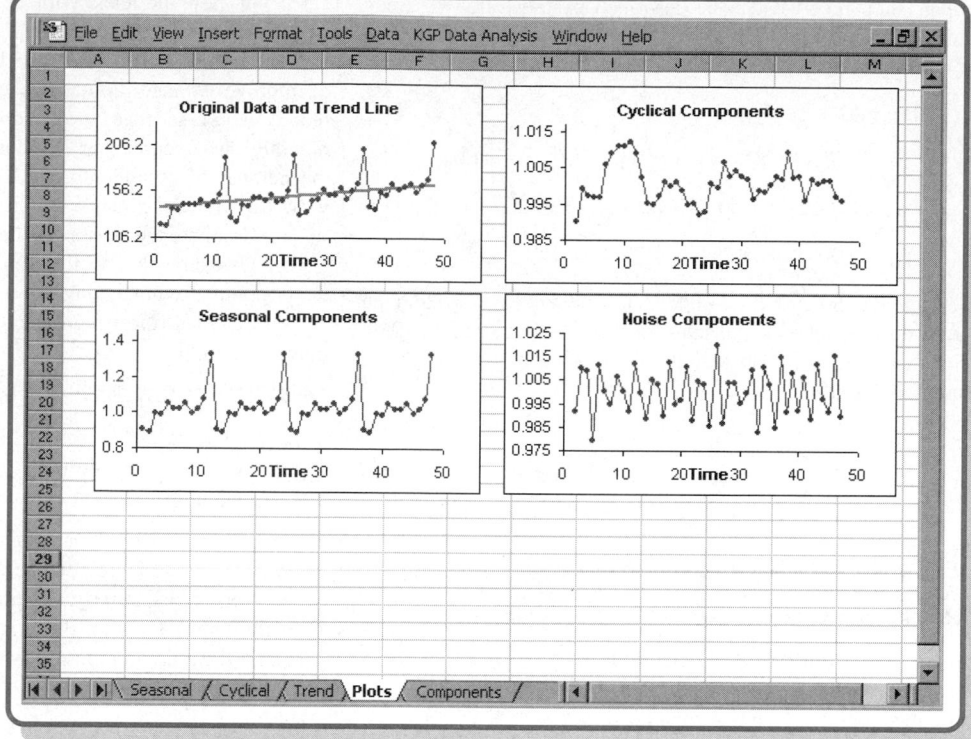

EXERCISES 16.45–16.52

UNDERSTANDING THE MECHANICS

16.45 For the month of January 1999, a researcher finds that the seasonal index is 1.2, the trend value is 100, and the cyclical component is .90. What is the irregular component if the actual observation for January 1999 is 110?

16.46 Given the following ratio to moving averages, determine the seasonal indexes.

Year	Month	Ratio to Moving Average	Year	Month	Ratio to Moving Average
1996	July	1.046	1998	Jan	.856
	Aug	1.057		Feb	.826
	Sept	.993		Mar	.969
	Oct	1.015		Apr	.952
	Nov	.996		May	1.021
	Dec	1.217		June	1.011
1997	Jan	.851		July	1.019
	Feb	.858		Aug	1.071
	Mar	.978		Sept	1.005
	Apr	.968		Oct	1.088
	May	1.010		Nov	1.026
	June	1.011		Dec	1.218
	July	1.020	1999	Jan	.881
	Aug	1.051		Feb	.843
	Sept	1.195		Mar	.982
	Oct	1.012		Apr	.956
	Nov	1.038		May	1.012
	Dec	1.252		June	1.003

APPLYING THE NEW CONCEPTS

16.47 Shipments abroad represent a larger share of Texas's total production than in any other state. Thus, exports buoy Texas's economy when foreign economies are robust, but it becomes a hazard if exports shrink. In 1998, the ill effects of Asia's economy dampened the continual rise in Texas's exports in the past couple of years according to "Texas, It Appears, Isn't Immune to Asia After All" in the *Wall Street Journal,* July 15, 1998, p. T1. Suppose that the following data are representative of the deseasonalized exports in units of billions of dollars. Determine the cyclical components for all four quarters of 1998.

Year	Quarter	Deseasonalized Exports
1996	1	15.0
	2	15.0
	3	15.1
	4	15.9
1997	1	17.0
	2	18.0
	3	18.8
	4	17.9
1998	1	19.2
	2	18.8
	3	19.0
	4	20.1
1999	1	20.8
	2	21.7
	3	22.9
	4	23.1

16.48 The amount of monthly business that an automotive repair shop receives can be described by the following trend line and seasonal indexes for the time periods January 1996 ($t = 1$) to the present. Sales are in units of thousands of dollars.

$$TR_t = 12 + .5t$$

$$S_1 = .90, S_2 = .84, S_3 = 1.00, S_4 = 1.00, S_5 = 1.02,$$

$$S_6 = 1.04, S_7 = 1.00, S_8 = 1.00, S_9 = 1.00, S_{10} = .99,$$

$$S_{11} = 1.00, S_{12} = 1.21$$

Assume that no cyclical component is present ($C_t = 1.0$). Given the following set of actual sales for the first six months of 1999, calculate the irregular activity component for the first six months of 1999.

	1999					
	Jan	**Feb**	**Mar**	**Apr**	**May**	**Jun**
Sales	10.6	10.5	12.0	12.5	12.9	12.8

USING THE COMPUTER

16.49 [DATA SET EX16-49] *Variable description:*

Year: Years from 1996 through 1999
Months: Months are numbered from 1 through 12
Membership: The monthly membership

The membership of a local spa fluctuates seasonally. The manager of the spa is interested in knowing what the trend line is for the spa's membership. The membership data are recorded monthly. Estimate the trend line and use it to predict the deseasonalized membership for January 2000.

16.50 [DATA SET EX16-50] *Variable description:*

Year: Years from 1996 through 1999
Months: Months are numbered from 1 through 12
BagComplaints: Number of baggage complaints per 1000 fliers

Airline companies are examining their baggage complaints and enforcing new policies with respect to carry-on luggage. According to "Frequent Fliers Like Limits" (in *USA Today,* Dec. 17, 1998, p. 3B), United Airlines is spending $10 million to improve its handling of checked bags, an area in which its record is worse than most competitors. Suppose that the monthly data recorded in BagComplaints is representative of the number of complaints per 1000 fliers over the past four years for United Airlines.

  a. Compute the seasonal indexes for BagComplaints.
  b. Calculate the cyclical components for 1998 using a three-month moving average.
  c. Calculate the irregular components for the first three months of 1999.

16.51 [DATA SET EX16-51] *Variable description:*

Year: Years from 1994 through 1999
Quarter: Quarters are numbered from 1 through 4
LoanApp: Number of loan applications

The manager of a branch bank is having difficulty in staffing. A good measure of banking business is the number of loan applications received quarterly. Quarterly data are collected from 1994 through 1999. Plot the original data and the trend line. Also plot the noise components over time and determine if any pattern is apparent in this plot.

16.52 [DATA SET EX16-52] *Variable description:*

Year: Years from 1995 through 1999
Quarter: Quarters are numbered from 1 through 4
Enroll: Enrollment in a retirement education seminar

A stock brokerage firm offers a free retirement seminar on a quarterly basis. Since many of the participants in the seminar will invest in financial products offered by the firm, the manager of the brokerage firm wishes to determine the trend and seasonal components of the enrollment. Plot the trend line using the deseasonalized data. Also construct a plot of the seasonal components.

16.7 INDEX NUMBERS

How many times have you heard a remark such as "Fifteen years ago we could have bought that house for $70,000. Now it's worth $180,000." Or "My weekly grocery bill used to be $25. Today, it's almost $100." Many people like to talk about the prices back in the "good old days," but were goods and services actually less expensive in those days?

Perhaps a particular item consumed a greater proportion of the typical consumer's consumable income (purchasing power) in years past. To compare effectively the change in the price or value of a certain item (or group of items) between any two time periods, we use an index number. An **index number** (or index) measures the change in a particular item (typically a product or service) or a collection of items between two time periods.

The average hourly wages for production employees at Kessler Toy Company in 1980, 1985, 1990, and 1998 are shown in Table 16.15. Suppose we wish to compare the average

TABLE 16.15   Average hourly wage of production employees at Kessler Toy Company.

	1980	**1985**	**1990**	**1998**
Wage	$ 7.05	$ 8.50	$ 10.90	$ 12.50
Index (base = 1980)	100	120.6	154.6	177.3

wages for 1985, 1990, and 1998 with those for 1980. By computing a ratio for each pair of wages (expressed as a *percentage* of the 1980 wage), we obtain the following set of index numbers:

$$\text{index number for 1985:} \qquad \left(\frac{8.50}{7.05}\right) \cdot 100 = 120.6$$

$$\text{index number for 1990:} \qquad \left(\frac{10.90}{7.05}\right) \cdot 100 = 154.6$$

$$\text{index number for 1998:} \qquad \left(\frac{12.50}{7.05}\right) \cdot 100 = 177.3$$

When calculating an index number, we follow standard practice—round to the nearest tenth (as in Table 16.15) and omit the percent sign. For this application, all wages were compared to those in 1980, the **base year.** The index number for the base year is always 100.

When each index number uses the same base year, the resulting set of values is an **index time series.** An index time series is a set of index numbers determined from the same base year. The purpose of such a time series is to measure the yearly values in *constant* units (dollars, people, and so on). Because these values define a time series, they can be analyzed and decomposed by using the methods described previously. Our purpose in this section is simply to describe how to *construct* a time series of this type.

PRICE INDEXES

Index numbers are derived for a variety of products (goods or services) as well as locations. For example, you may wish to compare the relative costs of consumer items in Los Angeles and Minneapolis if you are considering a move. Such information is readily available or can be determined from a number of business publications or government reports. The Department of Labor and the Bureau of Labor Statistics release reports (many of them monthly) on the price and quantity of many consumer items and agricultural commodities. Often these are recorded for specific U.S. cities, providing geographical comparisons.

We focus our attention on comparison of *prices* from one year to the next; such comparisons are **price indexes.** The most popular of these indexes is the Consumer Price Index (CPI), which combines a large number (thousands) of prices for consumer goods (such as food and housing) and family services (such as health care and recreation) into a single index. It is often called the cost-of-living index.

An index that includes more than one item is an **aggregate index.** We examine two methods of calculating an aggregate price index.

Say we wish to measure the change in the prices of several items from 1990 to 1998, using a single price index. Table 16.16 shows four items; 1990 is the base year. Let P_0 denote the price for a particular item in the base year (1990) and P_1 represent this price during the reference year (1998). So

$$\Sigma P_0 = \text{sum of sampled prices for 1990}$$

$$= .75 + .95 + .89 + 31 = \$33.59$$

and

$$\Sigma P_1 = \text{sum of sampled prices for 1998}$$

$$= 1.35 + 1.79 + 1.85 + 55 = \$59.99$$

The ratio of these sums represents the **simple aggregate price index** for this application.

$$\text{simple aggregate price index} = \left(\frac{\Sigma P_1}{\Sigma P_0}\right) \cdot 100 \qquad \textbf{(16.8)}$$

TABLE 16.16   Prices of four items in 1990 and 1998.

Item	1990	1998
Eggs	.75 (doz)	1.35 (doz)
Chicken	.95 (lb)	1.79 (lb)
Cheese	.89 (lb)	1.85 (lb)
Auto battery	$31.00 (each)	$55.00 (each)

For our example,

$$\text{index} = \left(\frac{59.99}{33.59} \right) \cdot 100 = 178.6$$

It might be tempting to conclude that, based on the prices of these four items, all prices increased by 78.6% between 1990 and 1998. Two problems arise here. The first is whether these sampled items are *representative* of the population of all price changes over this eight-year period. This is not a new problem—the same concern arose when we first introduced statistical sampling.

The second problem is that this index does not take into account the amounts of these items that are typically purchased by consumers. A significant change in the price for any single item will have a dramatic effect on the simple aggregate index, regardless of the demand for this product. The increase of $24 in the price of an automobile battery dominated the computed value of the aggregate price index; however, a typical consumer will spend much more annually on chicken than on car batteries. *The simple aggregate price index assumes that equal amounts of each item are purchased.*

For this reason, the next step is to include a measure of the quantity (Q) of each item in the price index. (We discuss methods of selecting the item quantities later.) The resulting index is known as a **weighted aggregate price index.**

$$\text{weighted aggregate price index} = \left(\frac{\sum P_1 Q}{\sum P_0 Q} \right) \cdot 100 \qquad \textbf{(16.9)}$$

EXAMPLE 16.11   Assume that a representative family each year purchases 1 automobile battery and each month consumes 6 dozen eggs, 15 pounds of chicken, and 8 pounds of cheese. Using 1990 as the base year and equation 16.9, determine the weighted aggregate price index for 1998. Use the data in Table 16.16.

SOLUTION   The choice of time units on the quantities, Q, is arbitrary, but it is essential that we be consistent across all items. Converting the family purchases to annual units, we have $6 \cdot 12 = 72$ dozen eggs, $15 \cdot 12 = 180$ pounds of chicken, $8 \cdot 12 = 96$ pounds of cheese, and 1 car battery (Table 16.17).

The weighted aggregate price index for 1998 (using 1990 as the base year) is

$$\text{index} = \left(\frac{\sum P_1 Q}{\sum P_0 Q} \right) \cdot 100 = \left(\frac{652}{341.44} \right) \cdot 100 = 191.0$$

In this index, the increase of 91% between 1990 and 1998 is not as severely affected by the price change for the car battery as was the simple aggregate price index, which ignored annual demand for each item. All widely used business price indexes are based on some variation of the weighted aggregate price index in equation 16.9.

TABLE 16.17

Calculated aggregate price index.

Item	1990			1998		
	P_0	Q	$P_0 Q$	P_1	Q	$P_1 Q$
Eggs	.75	72	$ 54.00	1.35	72	$ 97.20
Chicken	.95	180	171.00	1.79	180	322.20
Cheese	.89	96	85.44	1.85	96	177.60
Auto battery	31.00	1	31.00	55.00	1	55.00
			$\sum P_0 Q = 341.44$			$\sum P_1 Q = 652.00$

SELECTION OF THE QUANTITY, Q. Because the weights in a weighted aggregate price index usually reflect the quantities consumed, a problem arises when these quantities cannot be assumed to remain constant over the time span of the index. In Example 16.11, the same quantities, Q, were applied to both time periods, so we are assuming an equal demand for the two years.

We have two options here: (1) Use the quantities for the base year (1990, here) and (2) use the quantities for the reference year (1998, here). The first method is the *Laspeyres index;* the second is the *Paasche index.*

$$\text{Laspeyres index} = \left(\frac{\sum P_1 Q_0}{\sum P_0 Q_0} \right) \cdot 100 \qquad \textbf{(16.10)}$$

where Q_0 represents a base-year quantity.

$$\text{Paasche index} = \left(\frac{\sum P_1 Q_1}{\sum P_0 Q_1} \right) \cdot 100 \qquad \textbf{(16.11)}$$

where Q_1 represents a reference-year quantity.

Each of these indexes has strengths and weaknesses. The main advantage of the Laspeyres index is that the same base-year quantities apply to all future reference years. This greatly simplifies updating of this index, particularly given that most aggregate business indexes contain a large number of items. Its main disadvantage is that it tends to give more weight to those items that show a dramatic price increase. When a particular commodity's price increases sharply, it is typically accompanied by a decrease in the demand (measured by Q) for this item, or perhaps another item may be substituted by the consumer. The Laspeyres index fails to adjust for this situation. The advantages of this index outweigh its disadvantages, however, and it is more popular than the Paasche index.

The complexity of updating the reference-year quantities for the Paasche index make it difficult (and often impossible) to apply. Furthermore, because it reflects *both* price and quantity changes, we cannot use it to reflect price changes between two time periods. Its obvious advantage is that it uses current-year quantities, which provide a more realistic and up-to-date estimate of total expense.

We have seen that there is no completely reliable and accurate method of describing aggregate price changes. All such indexes include inaccuracies introduced by using a sample of items in the index as well as by the quantities to be used for weighting. Nevertheless, we treat such an index like any other sample estimate: We use the index as an estimate of relative price changes and realize that it is subject to a certain amount of error.

COMMENTS

1. The most widely used Laspeyres index is the Consumer Price Index (CPI), which is based on thousands of items, ranging from the price of housing to medical expenditures. The CPI is used as a measure of inflation and the cost of living in the United States. It is published monthly and is utilized by the federal government (and some private companies), which bases payment (or salary) adjustments on increases or decreases in the CPI. For example, social security payments and retirement benefits for federal civil service employees are tied to this index.

2. The CPI can be used to *deflate* a time series, providing a better comparison of dollar amounts across time. A value is deflated by *dividing* the actual dollar amount for this time period by the corresponding value of the CPI and then multiplying by 100. For example, if your current hourly wage is $18 and the CPI for this year is 150, then the deflated amount is $(18/150)(100) = \$12$. Consequently, the $12 amount can be compared to the hourly wage for the base year (or any other deflated wage value) to determine if there has been a change in "real" wages. This technique can also be applied to the Gross National Product (GNP) to detect real changes in the total value of goods and services.

EXERCISES 16.53–16.62

UNDERSTANDING THE MECHANICS

16.53 The following data are the selling prices of a particular chemical.

Year	1990	1992	1994	1996	1999
Price	24	28	34	44	50

    a. Construct an index time series for the years 1990, 1992, 1994, 1996, and 1999 using 1990 as the base year.

    b. Repeat part (a) using 1992 as the base year.

16.54 Consider the following prices and quantities of four items.

	1994		1999	
	P_0	Q_0	P_1	Q_1
Item 1	1.50	60	3.00	50
Item 2	2.00	100	2.25	90
Item 3	1.70	80	2.00	100
Item 4	4.00	20	3.50	50

    a. Construct the Laspeyres index.

    b. Construct the Paasche index.

APPLYING THE NEW CONCEPTS

16.55 A typical family in Jackson, Miss., had the following weekly buying patterns in 1994 and 1999 (prices are in dollars). Use 1994 as the base year.

Item	1994 Unit Price	1994 Quantity	1999 Unit Price	1999 Quantity
Meat	1.03	2	1.25	2
Milk	.97	3	1.19	2
Fish	.98	2	1.05	3
Oranges	.65	3	.75	4
Bread	.40	1	.62	2

    a. Find the simple aggregate price index.

    b. Construct the Laspeyres index.

    c. Construct the Paasche index.

16.56 Explain the meaning, including the advantages and disadvantages, of the Paasche and Laspeyres weighted indexes. Comment on whether the indexes can be used as a representation of buying pattern.

16.57 The following table reflects the typical family's buying habits per 6 months on repairs for the family car. Use 1993 as the base year.

Item	1993 Price	1993 Quantity	1999 Price	1999 Quantity
Lube job	3.50	2	5.00	1
Oil change	9.50	3	13.00	2
Tune-up	29.95	1	39.95	1
New tires	35.95	2	49.00	2

    a. Find the simple aggregate price index.

    b. Construct the Laspeyres index.

    c. Construct the Paasche index.

16.58 A conglomerate is considering buying one or more of three companies. The closing prices of the stocks of these three companies for the years 1991 to 1999 are:

Year	Better Foods	Friendly Insurance	Chock Full of Computer Chips
1991	13.500	20.125	39.25
1992	13.750	20.250	35.50
1993	14.250	20.500	31.75
1994	15.125	21.750	34.25
1995	15.500	21.500	37.75
1996	16.000	21.750	39.75
1997	16.125	22.500	40.00
1998	16.250	23.750	39.50
1999	16.750	23.500	42.25

Find an appropriate index to measure the change in the price of these three stocks for the years 1994, 1995, 1997, and 1999 using 1991 as the base year.

16.59 Suppose that, for a certain basket of goods, the Paasche index for 1999 is 115 and the Laspeyres index is 97. Assuming that the base year is 1993, interpret the meaning of the value of the two indexes.

16.60 The number of housing starts for four counties for the years 1997, 1998, and 1999 is:

County	1997	1998	1999
Brooks	1304	1505	1580
Litton	1264	1759	1987
Riverbed	1135	1443	1565
Tannon	1401	1605	1615

a. Compare the housing starts for Litton county for the years 1998 and 1999 using 1997 as the base year.

b. Compare the aggregate of housing starts for the years 1998 and 1999 for the four counties using 1997 as the base year.

16.61 Resource-based industries are an important component of the Canadian economy. Consider the following short list on Canadian mineral production (in millions of kilograms) and price per kilogram (in Canadian dollars) for 1988 through 1990.

Mineral	Quantity			Price		
	1988	1989	1990	1988	1989	1990
Zinc	1370	1272	1285	1.65	2.15	1.92
Copper	758	704	779	3.16	3.39	3.20
Nickel	198	195	196	14.04	15.59	10.29

(Source: *Canada Year Book*, pp. 408–409.)

a. Calculate the Laspeyres index for 1989 and 1990 using 1988 as the base year.

b. Calculate the Paasche index for 1989 and 1990 using 1988 as the base year.

c. Compare the two indexes.

16.62 Indexes are often confusing to investors. For example, the Dow Jones Industrial Average (DJIA) is a price-weighted index incorporating a multiplier that changes over time. In Dec. 1997, the multiplier could be interpreted to mean that a gain in the DJIA of 3.93 would result from a gain of one dollar in any one of the 30 companies that make up the DJIA. But the price-weighted DJIA also means that higher-priced stocks have a bigger impact than lower-priced stocks. Say that hypothetically an investor had bought equal dollar amounts of each Dow stock at the close of the market one day. The next day, if the Dow's 15 highest-priced stocks had each declined 5% and the 15 lowest-priced stocks each gained 5%, the DJIA would have declined 197 points or 1.5% for the day. How would the investor have fared? Does this explain how the DJIA can be confusing for investors who may not understand how a price-weighted index works?

(Source: "The Numbers Game," *Stages: The Fidelity Investments Magazine of Personal Finance*, Winter 1998, p. 21.)

SUMMARY

A variable recorded over time is a **time series.** You obtain a sample of values for this variable by recording its past observations. Because such a sample is not a random one, it is extremely difficult (if not impossible) to obtain any tests of hypothesis or confidence intervals. Consequently, we resort to describing the past observations by deriving the components of the time series. This process is called **time series decomposition.** The components of a time series are (1) **trend** (a long-term growth or decline in the observations), (2) **seasonality** (within-year recurrent fluctuations), (3) **cyclical activity** (upward and downward movements of various lengths about the trend), and (4) **irregular activity** (what remains after the other three components have been removed).

We described methods of estimating these components for a time series. We first specify how we believe the components interact with one another, thus describing the time series variable, y_t. The **additive** structure assumes that each observation is the *sum* of its components. In particular, this structure implies that seasonal fluctuations during a particular year are not affected by the base volume for that year. In the **multiplicative** structure, each value of y_t is the *product* of the four components. In this framework, the seasonal fluctuation for a specific month (or quarter) is more apt to be a constant *percentage* of the base volume for that year; for example, sales in December might be 35% higher than the average (base) sales for that particular year. The multiplicative structure was assumed for practically all of the illustrations in this chapter and is used more commonly in practice. The Bureau of the Census uses a variation of this procedure for their time series decomposition analyses.

We described a four-step procedure for deriving these components for a particular time series, based on the multiplicative structure. The steps were: (1) determine a **seasonal index** for each month (monthly data) or quarter (quarterly data); (2) **deseasonalize** the data by dividing each observation by its corresponding seasonal index; (3) determine the **trend components** by deriving a least squares line or quadratic curve through the deseasonalized values; and (4) determine the **cyclical components** by, for each time period, dividing each deseasonalized value by its estimate using the trend equation and smoothing these values by computing three-period moving averages.

An **index time series,** often used by business analysts, is a time-related sequence of index numbers in which each value is a measure of the change in a particular item (or group of items) from one year to the next. **Price indexes** are used to compare prices over time.

An **aggregate price index** is used to compare the relative price of a set of items for any year to the price during the base year. The index for the base year always is 100. The prices for the items can be averaged (**simple** aggregate price index) or weighted by the corresponding quantity of each item (**weighted** aggregate price index).

Methods of selecting these quantities include using base-year quantities (the **Laspeyres index**) or using the reference-year quantities (the **Paasche index**). The most popular Laspeyres index in practice is the Consumer Price Index (CPI).

FURTHER READING

Bowerman, B. L., and R. T. O'Connell. *Forecasting and Time Series: An Applied Approach,* 3rd ed. North Scituate, Mass: Duxbury Press, 1993.

Brockwell, P. J., and R. A. Davis. *Introduction to Time Series and Forecasting,* New York: Springer-Verlag, 1996.

Hamilton, J. D. *Time Series Analysis,* Princeton, NJ: Princeton University Press, 1994.

Makridakis, S., S. C. Wheelwright, and R. J. Hyndman. *Forecasting: Methods and Applications,* 3rd ed. New York: Wiley, 1997.

SUMMARY OF FORMULAS

LINEAR TREND LINE

$$\hat{y}_t = b_0 + b_1 t$$

where

$$t = 1, 2, \ldots, T$$

$$b_1 = \frac{\sum t y_t - (\sum t)(\sum y_t)/T}{\sum t^2 - (\sum t)^2/T}$$

$$b_0 = \bar{y}_t - b_1 \bar{t}$$

Shortcut:

$$\sum t = 1 + 2 + \cdots + T$$

$$= \frac{T(T+1)}{2}$$

$$\sum t^2 = 1 + 4 + \cdots + T^2$$

$$= \frac{T(T+1)(2T+1)}{6}$$

$$\bar{t} = \frac{\sum t}{T} = \frac{T+1}{2}$$

DESEASONALIZED VALUE OF y_t

$$d_t = \frac{y_t}{\text{corresponding seasonal index}}$$

SIMPLE AGGREGATE PRICE INDEX

$$\left(\frac{\sum P_1}{\sum P_0}\right) \cdot 100$$

WEIGHTED AGGREGATE PRICE INDEX

$$\left(\frac{\sum P_1 Q}{\sum P_0 Q}\right) \cdot 100$$

LASPEYRES INDEX

$$\left(\frac{\sum P_1 Q_0}{\sum P_0 Q_0}\right) \cdot 100$$

where Q_0 represents a base-year quantity.

PAASCHE INDEX

$$\left(\frac{\sum P_1 Q_1}{\sum P_0 Q_1}\right) \cdot 100$$

where Q_1 represents a reference-year quantity.

REVIEW EXERCISES 16.63–16.79

16.63 Each of the following influences on the variation in profits of a national chain of department stores would contribute to which of the four components of a time series?
 a. The long-term growth of the economy
 b. The resignation of top managers in the company
 c. Annual demand in spring and summer for garden equipment
 d. The closing of several other department stores

16.64 A manufacturer of tractors has built a record number of tractors for every year for the past seven years. Given in thousands, the figures show the number of tractors built from 1993 to 1999.

Year	Tractors Built
1993	10.75
1994	11.78
1995	12.59
1996	13.4
1997	14.3
1998	15.7
1999	16.8

Find the least squares prediction equation that you would use to forecast the trend. What would you estimate the number of tractors built in 1999 to be?

16.65 Luz Chemicals, which manufactures a special-purpose baking soda, is interested in estimating the equation of the trend line for their monthly sales data (in tons) for the year 1999.

Month	Baking Soda Sales	Month	Baking Soda Sales
Jan.	28	July	34
Feb.	33	Aug.	34
Mar.	39	Sept.	35
Apr.	33	Oct.	36
May	38	Nov.	31
June	31	Dec.	37

 a. Without considering the seasonality present in the monthly sales, estimate the trend line equation.
 b. Using the equation obtained in part (a), estimate the sales (in tons) for the month of February 2000.

16.66 Telemex, a supplier of telephone systems, has experienced moderate to rapid growth over a 12-year period. The data show the annual sales figures (in tens of thousands of dollars).

Year	Sales	Year	Sales
1988	3.1	1994	18.8
1989	6.3	1995	18.4
1990	10.5	1996	20.0
1991	10.2	1997	21.3
1992	11.5	1998	29.0
1993	14.7	1999	28.3

 a. Find the trend line.
 b. Find the cyclical components.
 c. Graph the data and estimate the period of the cycle.

16.67 The percentage of people 18 and over who smoke regularly has trended downward for the United States population. Other countries, while experiencing a decline in the percentage of smokers, have not seen the dramatic results seen in the U.S. For example, Norway has banned tobacco advertising since 1975. In 1974, 41% of the adult population smoked. In 1994, 34% of the adult Norwegians smoke. The following data display the percentage of adult smokers in Norway from 1974 to 1994.

Year	Percentage of Adult Smokers in Norway	Year	Percentage of Adult Smokers in Norway
1974	41.1	1985	38.0
1975	40.3	1986	37.4
1976	40.4	1987	37.9
1977	39.8	1988	38.6
1978	39.9	1989	36.1
1979	38.5	1990	35.8
1980	39.1	1991	35.7
1981	37.8	1992	34.5
1982	38.6	1993	35.1
1983	39.0	1994	34.2
1984	38.6		

(Source: Adapted from *The Wall Street Journal*, "Ad Bans Abroad Haven't Snuffed Out Smoking," June 12, 1997, p. B1.)

a. Find the least squares trend line for predicting the percentage of Norwegian smokers over time.

b. Determine the cyclical components.

16.68 Suppose that for the month of January 1999, the marketing department of a firm finds that the seasonal index is 1.20, the trend line value is $17,000 in sales, and the cyclical component is .79. What is the irregular component if the actual sales figure for January 1999 is $16,500?

16.69 As the economy has strengthened in the mid-1990s, the average cost for office rent has trended upward. The following data display the average per-square-foot annual office rent for the Dallas area. Plot these data. Would you suggest using a linear or quadratic trend line to fit the data? Determine the cyclical components.

Year	Per-Square-Foot Cost for Dallas Office Space	Year	Per-Square-Foot Cost for Dallas Office Space
1986	19.15	1992	13.31
1987	18.81	1993	12.75
1988	15.34	1994	13.6
1989	15.25	1995	15.5
1990	15.10	1996	17.4
1991	14.85	1997	19.26

(Source: Adapted from *The Dallas Morning News*, "A Rude Awakening," Aug. 4, 1997, p. 1D.)

16.70 The following table lists the number of building permits per month for nonresidential construction during the four-year period 1996 through 1999 in Parkins, Neb.

Year	Jan	Feb	Mar	Apr	May	June	July	Aug	Sept	Oct	Nov	Dec
1991	21	22	23	24	25	28	29	30	27	26	20	20
1992	21	24	23	25	26	25	29	32	32	27	20	18
1993	17	18	21	24	22	28	29	30	27	26	22	20
1994	17	21	23	23	24	29	31	22	28	22	21	29

a. Determine the seasonal indexes.

b. Determine the cyclical components for 1998 using a three-month moving average.

c. Determine the irregular component for July of 1998.

16.71 The average monthly utility bill for residents of the small community of Ridgecrest for the years 1996 through 1999 is:

Year	Jan	Feb	Mar	Apr	May	June	July	Aug	Sept	Oct	Nov	Dec
1996	190	180	179	130	135	145	148	153	145	153	170	185
1997	197	193	185	150	151	159	163	165	160	159	180	185
1998	215	205	193	175	171	179	185	184	180	180	173	190
1999	235	225	205	180	182	190	195	198	188	185	195	201

a. Determine the seasonal indexes.
b. Determine the trend.
c. Determine the cyclical components for 1997 using a three-period moving average.
d. Determine the irregular components for June and July 1997.

16.72 The weekly buying pattern of a typical family in a suburb of Atlanta, Ga., for 1993 and 1999 follows.

Item	1993 Unit Price	1993 Quantity	1999 Unit Price	1999 Quantity
Chicken	2.40	1	2.75	2
Milk	1.02	3	1.19	2
Bread	.39	2	.45	2
Ground beef	1.59	3	1.89	2
Tomatoes	.39	2	.78	2

Using 1993 as the base year,
a. Find the simple aggregate price index.
b. Calculate the Laspeyres index.
c. Calculate the Paasche index.
d. Compare the indexes in parts (b) and (c).

16.73 The president of R&B Home Builders uses a housing index to obtain information about the direction of the housing market. The index for the four quarters of 1996, 1997, 1998, and 1999 yields these data:

Year	Quarter 1	Quarter 2	Quarter 3	Quarter 4
1996	157	155	154	147
1997	142	145	140	142
1998	143	153	152	150
1999	163	165	162	160

a. Determine the seasonal indexes for each quarter.
b. Determine the trend line.
c. Determine the cyclical components for 1997 using a three-period moving average.
d. Determine the irregular components for the first and second quarter of 1997.

16.74 Scanners convert photos, drawings, or print into the ones and zeros of computer code. These devices have become popular to businesses since images can be posted on Web sites or e-mailed on the Internet. According to "Scanner Prices Plunge as Supplies Soar," (*Wall Street Journal,* Dec. 17, 1998, p. B1), a confluence of factors has caused a steady decline in scanner prices. These factors include production capacity that has sharply outpaced demand and Asian manufacturers that need to sell their products to raise cash. "It is the bloodiest peripheral category I have seen," says Guerrino De Luca, a former Apple Computer, Inc., executive. Consider the following prices of a typical flatbed color scanner.

Year	Quarter	Price	Year	Quarter	Price
1996	1	720	1998	1	320
	2	660		2	261
	3	580		3	182
	4	540		4	165
1997	1	522	1999	1	170
	2	463		2	136
	3	378		3	80
	4	344		4	69

a. Compute the seasonal indexes.
b. Determine the trend line.
c. Calculate the cyclical components for 1998.
d. Calculate the irregular components for 1998.

16.75 The number of defaults per month on business loans at First State Bank are given over a five-year period. Find the seasonal indexes.

Year	Jan	Feb	Mar	Apr	May	June	July	Aug	Sept	Oct	Nov	Dec
1995	54	53	52	50	48	46	48	50	52	56	58	60
1996	58	54	53	50	50	45	46	49	51	55	57	62
1997	53	52	48	47	47	44	45	48	49	52	55	60
1998	58	51	50	49	45	43	44	49	50	51	58	63
1999	59	58	56	52	54	49	50	51	54	58	60	64

16.76 The following data are the total amount of mortgage assets held by U.S. life insurance companies for 1979, 1982, 1985, and 1988 (in millions of dollars).

Year	Total Mortgages	Year	Total Mortgages
1979	111,421	1985	171,797
1982	141,989	1988	232,863

(Source: *Moody's Bank and Finance Manual* (1990): a12.)

The total amount of mortgages is an aggregate. Find the simple aggregate index for the years 1979, 1982, 1985, and 1988, using 1979 as the base year.

16.77 [DATA SET EX16-77] *Variable description:*

Year: Year from 1995 to 1998
Month: Month of year indicated by 1 through 12
CapUtil: Capacity utilization in percentage

Capacity utilization measures the extent to which the nation's capital is being used in the production of goods. The utilization rate rises and falls with business cycles. Economists closely watch capacity utilization for signs of inflation pressures. There is a common belief that when utilization rises above a value between 82% and 85%, price pressures increase, resulting in inflation.

(Source: Adapted from *The Wall Street Journal*, "Capacity Utilization," Dec. 17, 1998, p. A1.)

   a. Describe the plot of these data. Determine the seasonal indexes.
   b. What are the cyclical and irregular components for 1998?

16.78 [DATA SET EX16-78] *Variable description:*

Time: Monthly data over 25 months, numbered 1 through 25
Y1: Data collected from sales of Business A
Y2: Data collected from sales of Business B

The data on sales from Business A and Business B were collected to determine if sales exhibited additive variation or multiplicative variation. Plots of these data are presented below. What type of variation do these plots exhibit? Draw a trend line for each time series. Estimate the length of the cycle.

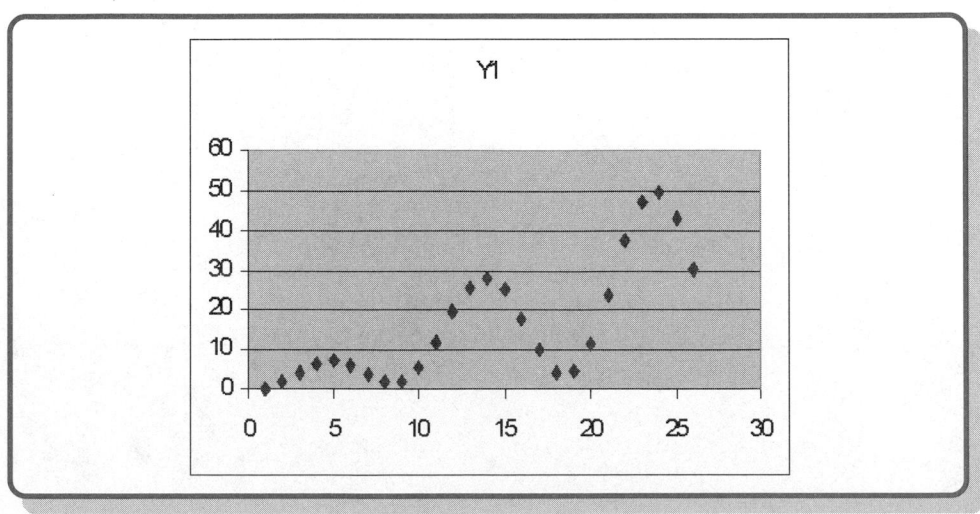

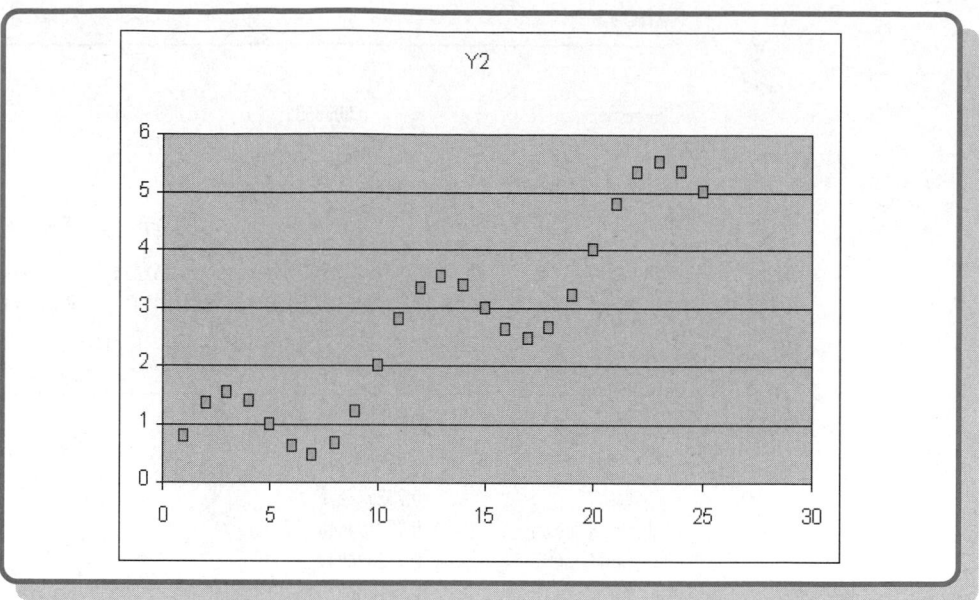

16.79 **[DATA SET EX16-79]** *Variable description:*

Time: Time periods numbered 1 through 20
Observ: Observation at specified time period

Examining a plot of the residuals versus the time variable may be helpful in developing an improved model to predict the observed values. If the least squares model of Observ regressed on Time is the appropriate model, the following plot of the residuals versus Time ideally should exhibit no pattern.

    a. An estimate of eight periods was obtained for the length of the cycle that appears in the plot. Does this estimate appear reasonable to you? Would you say that the pattern approximately resembles the graph made by a sin function?

    b. Examine the ANOVA table presented for the model with Observ regressed on Time. What conclusion can you draw from this ANOVA table?

    c. To obtain an improved model for predicting Observ, the variable Time is replaced by the variable sin((2*3.14/8)*Time), where the 8 represents the cycle length. This new variable is labeled TimeTransformed. Examine the ANOVA table presented for the model with Observ regressed on the transformed values of Time. What conclusion can you draw?

    d. If you think that a different cycle length should be used, rerun the analysis using the transformed time variable with your proposed cycle length.

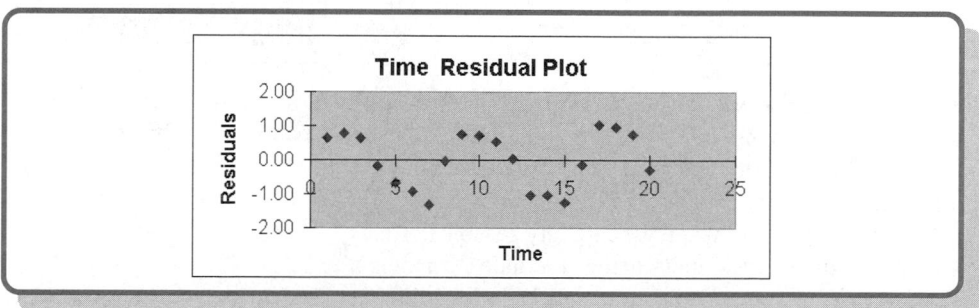

SUMMARY OUTPUT

Regression Statistics	
Multiple *R*	0.028134805
R Square	0.000791567
Adjusted *R* Square	−0.05472001
Standard Error	0.823218329
Observations	20

ANOVA

	df	SS	MS	F	Significance F
Regression	1	0.0096635	0.009663496	0.014259	0.9062707
Residual	18	12.1983915	0.677688417		
Total	19	12.208055			

	Coefficients	Standard Error	t Stat	P-value	Lower 95%	Upper 95%
Intercept	10.11152632	0.38241081	26.44152853	7.42E-16	9.3081104	10.91494
Time	−0.00381203	0.03192304	−0.11941314	0.906271	−0.0708799	0.063256

SUMMARY OUTPUT USING TRANSFORMED TIME VARIABLE

Regression Statistics

Multiple R	0.965682296
R Square	0.932542296
Adjusted R Square	0.928794646
Standard Error	0.213896049
Observations	20

ANOVA

	df	SS	MS	F	Significance F
Regression	1	11.38452765	11.38452765	248.833869	5.5356E-12
Residual	18	0.823527355	0.04575152		
Total	19	12.208055			

	Coefficients	Standard Error	t Stat	P-value	Lower 95%	Upper 95%
Intercept	9.940516317	0.048544047	204.7731274	9.1458E-32	9.83852898	10.042504
TimeTransformed	1.082725903	0.068637867	15.77446888	5.5356E-12	0.93852298	1.2269288

INSIGHTS FROM STATISTICS IN ACTION: WHICH WAY IS THE EMPLOYMENT COST INDEX HEADED?

The introductory case study in the Statistics in Action section discussed how many employers are keeping a sharp eye on the employment cost index, one of the government's measures of employee compensation. Of particular interest to many analysts are any seasonal effects within this time series and whether the index contains a steady growth (trend). For example, if the index is higher in the fourth quarter of 1998 than in the previous quarter, is this due to an unexpected gain, or does the index always increase when going from the third quarter to the fourth quarter?

The data following represent the employment cost index from 1992 to 1998. The overall trend within the data is upward. However, the data may have interesting seasonality.

Year	Quarter	Count	Employ Cost Index
1992	1	1	130.284
	2	2	135.716
	3	3	140.624
	4	4	143.587
1993	1	5	134.583
	2	6	140.330
	3	7	145.686
	4	8	148.613
1994	1	9	138.890
	2	10	144.681
	3	11	150.348
	4	12	152.922

Year	Quarter	Count	Employ Cost Index
1995	1	13	142.918
	2	14	148.732
	3	15	154.257
	4	16	156.745
1996	1	17	147.062
	2	18	153.342
	3	19	158.577
	4	20	161.604
1997	1	21	151.621
	2	22	157.636
	3	23	163.493
	4	24	166.937
1998	1	25	156.625
	2	26	163.153
	3	27	169.378
	4	28	173.281

1. Examine the data carefully, using no statistical procedures and make a judgmental assessment about the trend as well as about the existence and type of seasonality. After finishing the remainder of the questions, compare the results of your "eyeball method" with the statistical decomposition results.

2. Assuming that seasonality is multiplicative in nature, determine the seasonal indexes, deseasonalize the data, determine the trend components, determine the cyclical activity, and compute the noise (irregular) components.

3. Prepare forecasts of the employment cost index for the four quarters of 1999 using only the trend equation. Use the seasonal indexes to adjust the deseasonalized forecasts.

4. How far into the future do you think that a researcher could predict with this model and still obtain accurate predictions? Graph the data and examine the trend line going through the data. What type of economic events do you think could make the forecast invalid for predicting the employment cost index?

Source: Adapted from *The Wall Street Journal*, "Compensation Costs Climb for Employers," July 31, 1998, p. A2. Republished by permission of Dow Jones, Inc. via Copyright Clearance Center, Inc. (© 1998) Dow Jones and Company, Inc. All Rights Reserved Worldwide.

CHAPTER 16 APPENDIX: DATA ANALYSIS WITH MINITAB

TIME SERIES ANALYSIS

For multiplicative or additive decomposition of a time series in MINITAB, click on **Stat ➤ Time Series ➤ Decomposition.** MINITAB uses a different procedure than the Excel macros to determine the trend and seasonal components. Also it does not determine a cyclical component in the decomposition of a time series. The sales data for Video-Comp in Table 16.3 will be used to illustrate MINITAB's decomposition procedure.

In the user form displayed below for the decomposition procedure, the variable **Sales** (in column C1) is entered into the **Variable** box. The seasonal length is entered as 4, since the data are quarterly. Under **Model Type,** select **Multiplicative** and under **Model Components,** select **Trend plus seasonal.** Since the first observation starts in period 1, "1" is entered into the **First obs. is in seasonal period** box. To obtain a forecast, check the box **Generate forecasts.** In this example "1" is entered into the box **Number of forecasts** and "16" is entered into the box **Starting from origin.** This means that a forecast will be generated for time period 17. To replace the default title with your own custom title, type the desired text in this box. This title will be used for all three sets of plots that will appear in the output. The **Title** box is optional, and the name of the data is entered into this box. If the **Results** button is clicked, the **Decomposition-Results** user form appears. This user form allows for control of the output. In this example, the **Display plot** and the **Summary table and results table** options have been selected. The output from this selection follows the user forms.

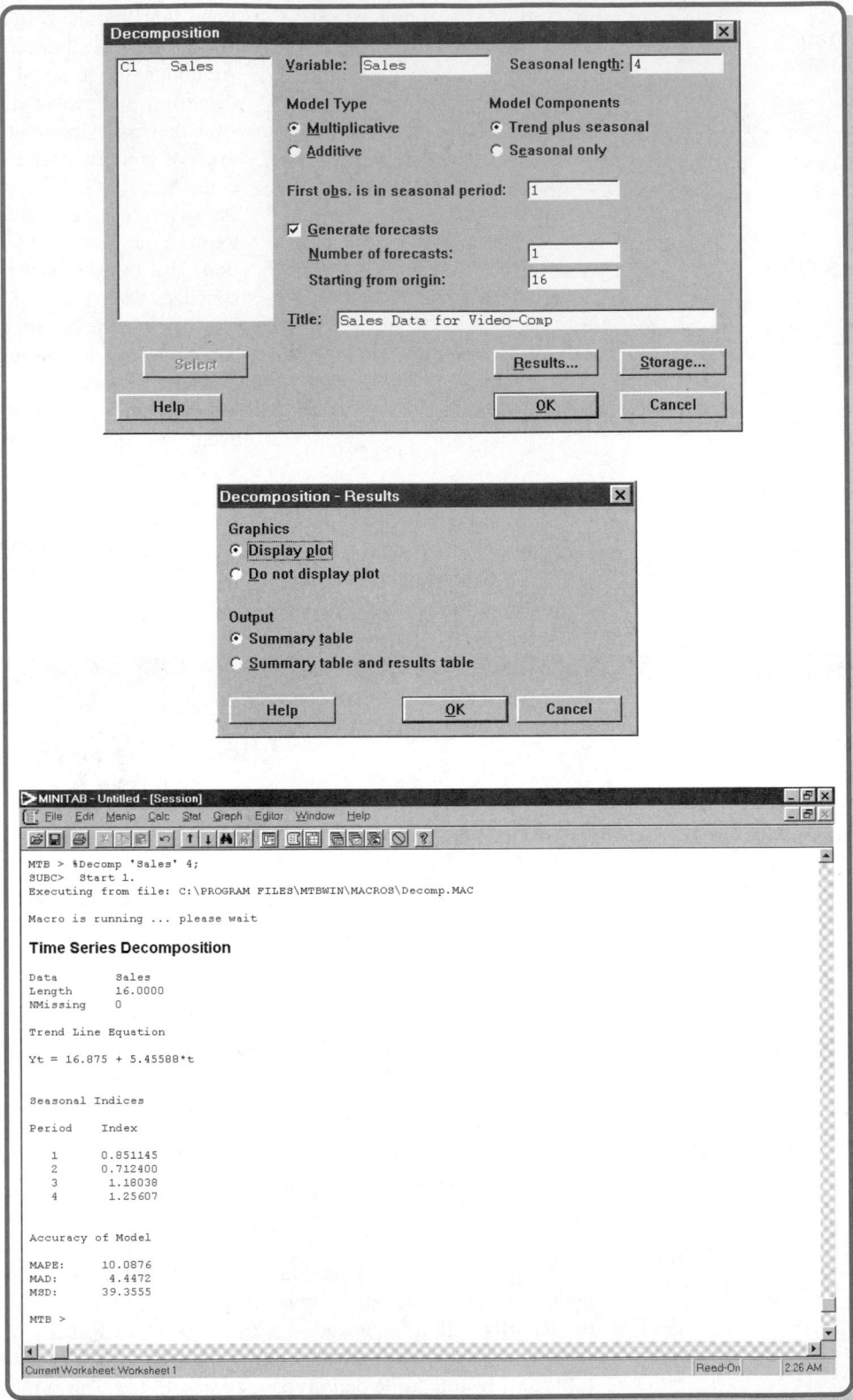

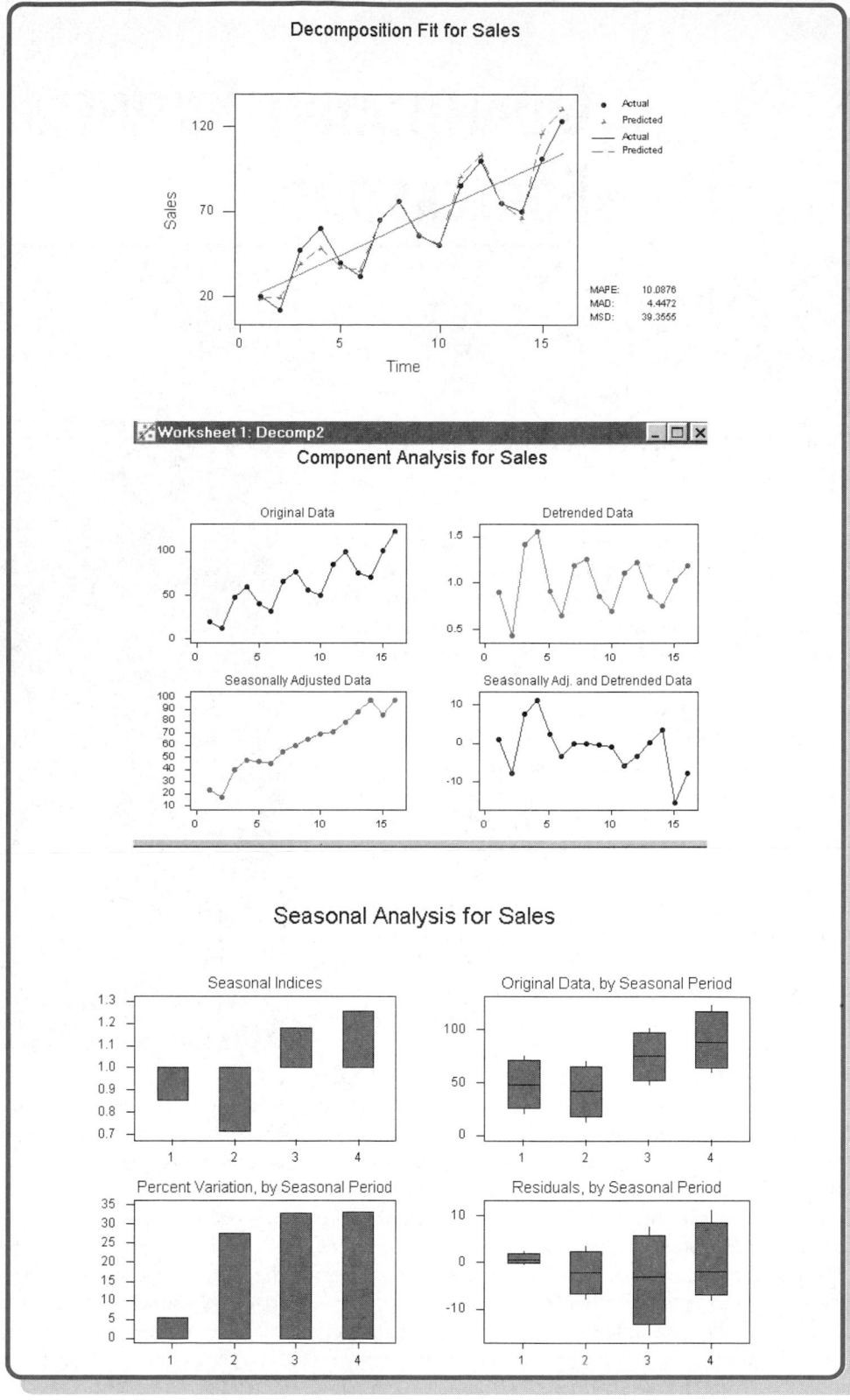

QUANTITATIVE BUSINESS FORECASTING

STATISTICS IN ACTION: THE CONSUMER PRICE INDEX— DUE FOR A CHANGE?

In late 1997, the U.S. Department of Labor issued a report that stated during 1997, consumers enjoyed the lowest inflation rate in 11 years as the Consumer Price Index (CPI) rose a scant 1.7 percent. Analysts also predicted continued stability for 1998. "I do not think it gets much better than this," said Sung Won Sohn, chief economist at Norwest Corp. in Minneapolis, Minnesota.

In late 1996 and early 1997, news articles began reporting that the procedure used to calculate the CPI was about to change since a study conducted at Stanford University concluded that the CPI had overstated past inflation by an average of 1.3 percentage points per year. The three main reasons for this are that the CPI (1) does not allow for substitution of goods or markets, (2) does not adequately account for quality improvements, and (3) introduces new products into its calculations much too slowly, causing the index to understate declining prices for rapidly evolving products, such as personal computers.

So why should we be concerned about this? The CPI now affects the cost-of-living increases on Social Security payments, veterans benefits, and pensions for government workers. Many collective bargaining agreements and rental-rate increases are tied to changes in the CPI. The CPI also affects a host of welfare programs and is used to help determine the direction of interest rates. The bottom line: an inaccurate CPI enriches some Americans at the expense of others.

But in 1997, the index was not revised substantially and it appears that this matter is still under review. As mentioned, the index increased less than 2% from 1996, due in part to a sharp drop in energy prices and a very small increase in food prices. Analysts predicted that inflation would remain in control during 1998, and some predicted the Fed would lower interest rates (they did!) to offset the effects of the Asian economic crisis. The Asian countries were expected to try to boost their

troubled economies in 1998 by exporting goods made cheaper by their devalued currencies. But economists argued that services represent the bulk of the U.S. economy, and the country is largely immune from foreign price competition.

To better get a handle on time series data, such as the CPI, you could begin by examining its components (trend, seasonal, cyclical) as outlined in the previous chapter. Perhaps you are interested in forecasting this time series into the future by capturing past patterns and extending them into the future or possibly coming up with a set of predictor variables to use in a multiple regression model.

This chapter will enable you examine time series data with the intent of forecasting future values. With such an analytical crystal ball, the future becomes less mysterious and less ominous. By combining the procedures described in the previous chapter with various forecasting methods introduced in this chapter, you will be able to:

- Discuss several forecasting procedures and evaluate their performance;

- Carry out a multiple regression analysis using time series data; and
- Discuss the pros and cons of using a time series forecasting model versus a multiple linear regression model.

A LOOK BACK/INTRODUCTION

We have introduced you to several methods of capturing the behavior of a dependent variable, Y. The first procedure was linear regression, which used a set of predictor (independent) variables to explain the observed values of the dependent variable. In simple linear regression, a single predictor is used. When we had two or more predictor variables, we used a multiple linear regression model to attempt to account for the variation in the observed values of the dependent variable. These calculations were considerably more complex, and a computer solution was used to estimate the linear relationship between the dependent variable (Y) and the predictor variables ($X_1, X_2, \ldots$).

The success or failure of this technique lies in your ability to arrive at a set of predictor variables that can accurately predict past (and future) values of the dependent variable. Suppose your model fails to fit adequately the observed values of Y, with a resulting large sum of squares for error (SSE) and a low value of R^2 (coefficient of determination). Do these results imply that multiple linear regression is not a reliable method of prediction for this situation? This could be the case, but it is just as likely that you omitted one or more key variables that would have significantly improved your prediction accuracy.

The time series decomposition technique, presented in the previous chapter, uses a different approach. This procedure attempts to explain each observed value by means of its various components. These components include trend (long-term growth or decline in the time series), seasonality (predictable variation within each year), and cyclical activity (generally due to unpredictable swings in the national or international economy).

The key distinction between these two procedures is that the time series approach does not search for explanatory (predictor) variables. Rather, it seeks to capture the past behavior of the time series by analyzing its various components. More complex time series techniques (which were not discussed) use past observations to predict the value for the future. You can use a time series approach to forecast future values by "extending" the pattern into the future. For example, if your company sales have been increasing approximately 150,000 units each year over the past six years, a reasonable forecast for next year would be a sales volume of 150,000 more than the present year's value.

Statistical forecasting is, in one sense, an extension of the prediction of a dependent variable. However, we now enter a more uncertain world—that of extrapolation. In previous chapters, we warned you of the dangers of this procedure, because outside the range of your data, the predicted values become less reliable. We can only hope that tomorrow's world will be similar to today's and that patterns observed over the past will continue. This uncertainty makes forecasting fascinating. We live in an uncertain world, and a reasonably accurate forecast can be extremely valuable for a marketing or production strategy.

This chapter introduces many (certainly not all) methods of using quantitative techniques for predicting future values of the variable of interest. We demonstrate how to forecast future values by using the past observations (the time series approach) as well as by using the multiple linear regression method. By applying the proper forecast method, you often can make the future considerably less uncertain.

17.1 METHODS OF FORECASTING

Forecasting procedures come in a variety of shapes and colors. You can arrive at a sales forecast by simply assembling a panel of experts and arriving at a collective "guess" or by constructing a highly complex statistical model that attempts to predict the future using past data. In the broadest sense, forecasting methods can be classified as **qualitative** (the panel of experts procedure) or **quantitative** (the statistical forecasting procedure). Quantitative forecasting can be carried out using two different approaches, namely, **regression** models (with several predictor variables) or **time series** models, which utilize past observations of the dependent variable to arrive at forecasted values.

QUALITATIVE FORECASTING

There are many instances when a qualitative approach to forecasting is appropriate. When no past data are available, it is impossible to construct a quantitative model to predict future values. This situation can occur when you intend to introduce a new product and no past sales data exist. Furthermore, when you introduce this product, it becomes a guessing game as to what the response will be from competitors in the field. Will they respond to your entry into the market? When will they respond? Will they lower their price to increase the demand for their product? Will they attempt to "copy" your product, and how soon can this be accomplished? Such questions do require expert opinion.

One popular method of qualitative forecasting is the **Delphi method.** With this procedure, you assemble individuals from the sales force and the market research staff and ask them to supply their predictions based on their knowledge of the area. This can be accomplished through a questionnaire or any other written set of specific questions. After this step, members of the team are informed as to the responses of the entire group and asked to reevaluate their opinions based on this new information. In this way, members of the team may be able to arrive at a "best educated" prediction of competitor response to their market entry. Of course, it is also entirely possible that no collective agreement will be reached after several rounds of this process.

We do not pursue qualitative forecasting methods in this chapter. The interested reader is referred to the text by Bowerman and O'Connell (see the Further Reading section at the end of the chapter) for additional qualitative procedures. The remainder of the chapter focuses on the use of quantitative forecasting techniques.

QUANTITATIVE FORECASTING

With a quantitative forecasting procedure, you predict future behavior of a dependent variable using information from previous time periods. This can be accomplished in one of two ways: using a *regression* model or using a *time series* model.

REGRESSION MODELS. The multiple regression approach consists of using regression models where variation of the dependent variable is explained using several independent (predictor) variables. One main advantage of this approach is that you can measure the effect of changes in one or more of the predictor variables. Furthermore, this type of model is generally easily understood by those individuals responsible for making the final forecast decision, since it is clear which variables are assumed to have an effect on the value of the dependent variable. A drawback of this type of model as a forecasting instrument is that to predict future values of the dependent variable, it is necessary to predict future values of the predictor variables, which, in many instances, may be as uncertain as future values of the dependent variable. This forecasting procedure is discussed in Section 17.9.

TIME SERIES MODELS. A time series forecast is made by capturing the patterns that exist in the past observations and extending them into the future. Consider the annual data reflecting

FIGURE 17.1

Sales for Clayton Corporation.

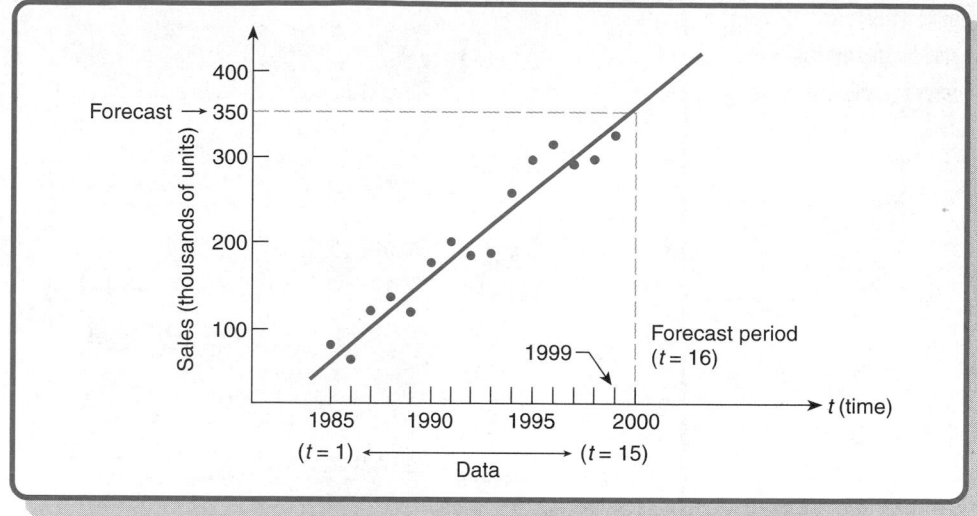

the sales of the Clayton Corporation between 1985 and 1999, shown in Figure 17.1. The data reflect a strong linear trend, as shown by the line passing through the points. To estimate the sales for the year 2000, one simple method would be to extend this line to 2000, as illustrated in Figure 17.1. By graphically extending this line and observing the estimated value, we obtain

$$\hat{y}_{16} = \text{forecast for the year } 2000 \cong 350$$

that is, 350,000 units. This procedure, along with methods of dealing with trend and seasonality, is discussed later in the chapter.

At first glance, it might appear that time series forecasting is easier to apply than are multiple regression models. After all, there is no need to search for a reliable set of predictor variables. It is true that time series predictors can be simple and straightforward, as is the so-called naive forecast discussed in the next section. *Frequently, however, extracting the complex and interrelated structure of an observed time series requires sophisticated and complex prediction equations.*

As in Chapter 16, we do not put any statistical bounds (such as a 95% confidence interval) on the predicted values. Rather, we suggest alternative methods of forecasting and demonstrate a way of determining the "best" forecasting procedure for a particular set of data. Of course, all forecasts are subject to error and are based on the assumption that the past historical patterns (such as the straight line in Figure 17.1) continue into the future.

In Sections 17.2 through 17.8, we examine several time series models and methods of evaluating the predictive ability of each procedure when applied to a particular set of time series data.

The procedure for selecting a forecasting model is summarized in Figure 17.2. Steps 1 through 5 are the model selection and forecasting stage. Steps 6 and 7 are the model review phase, during which you reevaluate your forecasting procedure. This step allows you to update your model using the latest observations or to consider changing your forecasting model by returning to step 2. Any forecasting technique should be reviewed; you must reexamine the forecast errors (that is, the difference between the forecasted values and the previous observations).

Remember that any quantitative forecasting technique can never replace the forecast of an individual (or team of people) who uses his or her expertise and knowledge of unpredictable future events (such as strikes, wars, or market shifts) to make forecasts. Rather, the quantitative forecast is one tool the forecaster uses. A forecast is an excellent baseline that can be modified by informed judgment.

FIGURE 17.2

A step-by-step procedure for forecasting with time series data.

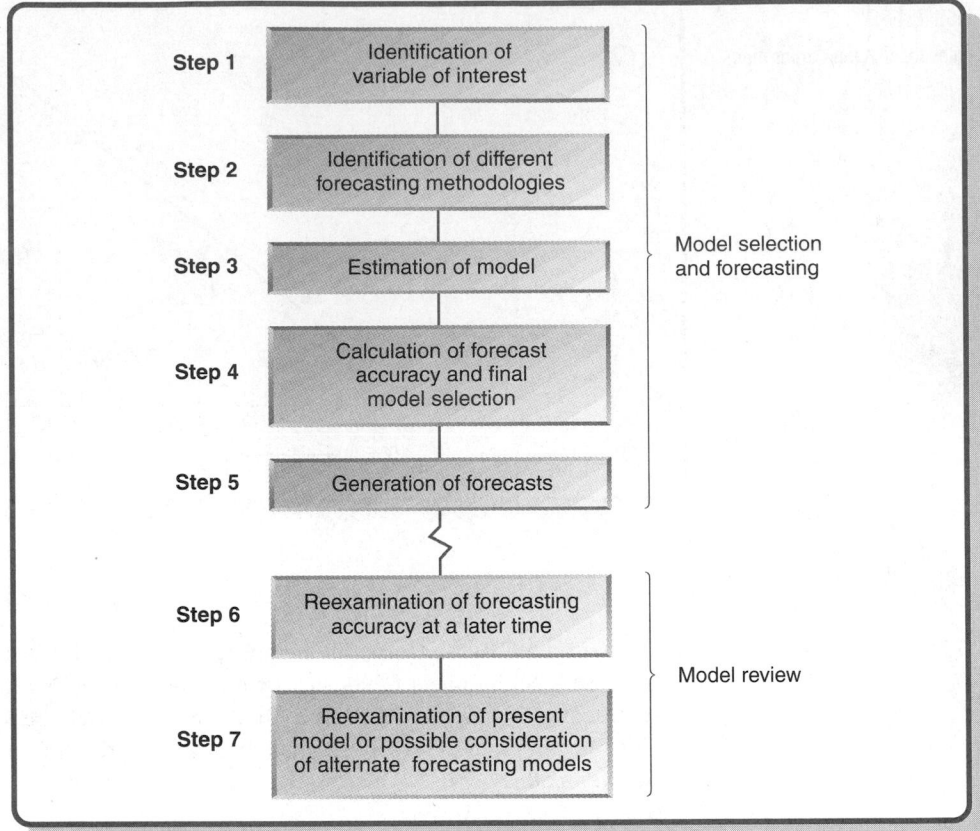

17.2 THE NAIVE FORECAST

Simply put, the naive forecast procedure states that the estimate of Y for tomorrow is the actual value from today. In general,

$$\hat{y}_{t+1} = y_t \qquad t = 1, 2, 3, \ldots \qquad \textbf{(17.1)}$$

or any time period, t.

Once again, the "hat" notation is used to denote an estimate. Equation 17.1 reads: "y hat for time period $t + 1$ is y for time t." Here, $\hat{y}_{t+1}$ presents the *forecast* for time period $t + 1$.

This method of forecasting often works well for data that are recorded for smaller time intervals (such as daily or weekly) and contain no apparent upward or downward trend among the observed values. Data of this type are not apt to shift direction suddenly from one day to the next, and the naive forecast can provide a simple, yet fairly reliable, estimate of the next day's value. On more than one occasion, this predictor has outperformed much more complex forecasting equations—particularly when applied to a difficult-to-predict time series, such as an individual stock market price. It provides an inexpensive, easy method of forecasting.

EXAMPLE 17.1

The weekly closing price for a share of Keller Toy Company stock was recorded over a 12-week period. Using the following data, determine a forecast for week 13.

Week	Price	Week	Price	Week	Price
1	60	5	64½	9	63¼
2	62¼	6	62	10	62½
3	61¾	7	63½	11	61
4	63	8	64	12	61½

FIGURE 17.3

Excel input screen using **KGP Data Analysis ➤ Time Series Analysis ➤ Forecasting** using the naive forecast procedure (Examples 17.1 and 17.2).

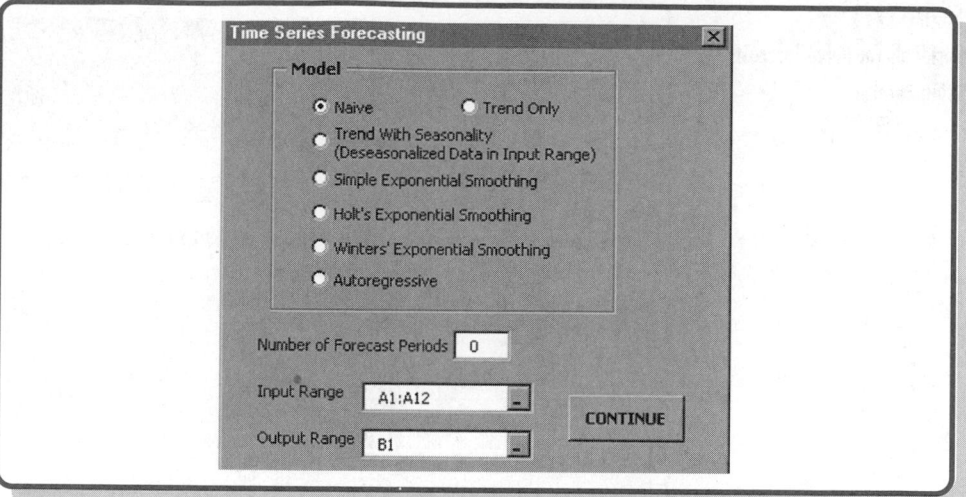

SOLUTION

The observed value for the last time period is $y_{12} = 61\frac{1}{2}$, so your forecast for the next time period is

$$\hat{y}_{13} = y_{12} = 61\frac{1}{2}$$

Notice that we are careful to distinguish between a *forecast,* such as $\hat{y}_{13}$, and an *observed* value, such as y_{12}.

One method of checking to see whether a particular forecasting technique is appropriate for your time series involves applying this procedure to each period of the observed data. For example, in Example 17.1, what would we have predicted for the fifth week using the naive forecasting equation 17.1? In other words, suppose we are at the end of the fourth week and need a forecast for $t = 5$. Using the naive predictor,

$$\hat{y}_5 = y_4 = 63$$

The actual value turned out to be $y_5 = 64\frac{1}{2}$, providing a **residual** of

$$\text{residual} = y_5 - \hat{y}_5 = 64\frac{1}{2} - 63 = 1\frac{1}{2}$$

The time series forecasting tools provided in the KGP Data Analysis Excel add-ins will allow you to carry out all of the forecasting procedures discussed in this chapter. By clicking on **KGP Data Analysis ➤ Time Series Analysis ➤ Forecasting,** you will see the screen in Figure 17.3. Using this input form will be illustrated in the following example.

EXAMPLE 17.2

Apply the naive forecasting procedure to the 12 time periods in Example 17.1 and determine the residual for each week.

SOLUTION

The procedure cannot be applied during the first time period ($t = 1$) because $\hat{y}_1 = y_0$, where y_0 is the closing price for the week preceding the observations in the table. If this value is available, then the forecast value for $t = 1$ can be determined; it is equal to this value. Otherwise, the forecast for this time period is left blank.

To obtain a solution using Excel, begin by entering the 12 stock prices in column A as seen in Figure 17.4. Next, click on **KGP Data Analysis ➤ Time Series Analysis ➤ Forecasting** and enter "A1:A12" as the **Input Range** and "B1" as the **Output Range.** For this example, enter "0" in the **Number of Forecast Periods** box. By clicking on **Continue,** you will obtain the output in Figure 17.4, which contains the 11 values of $\hat{y}_t$ (in the **YHAT** column) and the 11 residuals.

FIGURE 17.4

Residuals for naive forecasts using Excel.

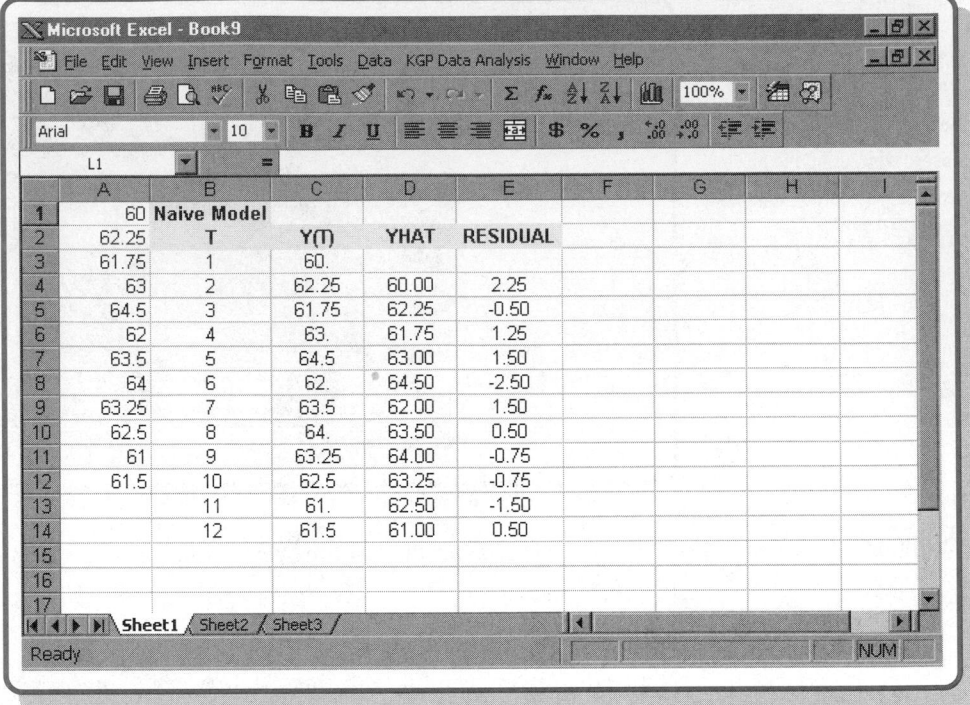

When we first introduced the concept of a residual (or error) in the chapters dealing with linear regression, we stressed that small residuals were desirable. When the residuals were near zero for regression applications, this meant that the model did a good job of "fitting" the sample observations.

The same idea applies to evaluating the effectiveness of a forecasting procedure. Small residuals indicate that this particular forecast technique would have done a good job of predicting the past values of this time series. A method of combining these residuals into a single measure (much like the SSE in linear regression) will be introduced in a later section.

EXERCISES 17.1–17.5

APPLYING THE NEW CONCEPTS

17.1 Explain the distinction between the technique of time series analysis and that of multiple regression analysis.

17.2 Why is validation important in regression analysis and in time series analysis? That is, why is it important to reexamine the forecasting accuracy of a model at a later time?

17.3 The table below lists the number of new apartment buildings (in thousands) built in Houston for the time period 1989 to 1998. Use the naive model to obtain forecast for the time periods between 1990 and 1998. Which time periods would you say the naive model predicted poorly?

Year	Number of New Apartments
1989	1.5
1990	2.4
1991	2.5

Year	Number of New Apartments
1992	4.0
1993	1.1
1994	6.1
1995	5.5
1996	5.4
1997	5.3
1998	14.2

(Source: Adapted from *The Wall Street Journal,* "Houston Is Facing an Oversupply of Apartments," July 15, 1999, p. T4.)

17.4 While the United States has been enjoying a strong economy, global economic growth declined in 1998. The IMF tried to reverse downward economic trends in Third World countries by recommending increases in interest rates to keep each country's currency from depreciating and to prevent foreign capital from fleeing. Suppose that a naive model was used to forecast global economic growth on a monthly basis during 1998. Using the following data measuring global economic growth in annualized percentage, find the residual for each period. What is the largest residual using the naive model?

Month	Global Economic Growth
January	3.7
February	3.5
March	3.2
April	3.0
May	3.4
June	3.3

Month	Global Economic Growth
July	3.1
August	2.8
September	2.7
October	2.3
November	2.4
December	2.1

(Source: Adapted from *The Wall Street Journal*, "IMF Again Lowers Forecast for Global Growth," Dec. 22, 1998, p. A2.)

17.5 What advantages and disadvantages can you think of in using the naive model to forecast?

17.3 PROJECTING THE LEAST SQUARES TREND EQUATION

For data containing a strong linear or curvilinear trend, one method of predicting future values of the time series is to extend the trend line (or curve) into the forecast periods. This method was illustrated in Figure 17.1, where the data from 1985 to 1999 demonstrated a very strong linear growth over those 15 years.

Suppose that a simple linear regression analysis is performed on these data, using the 15 sales values as the dependent variable and $t = 1, 2, \ldots, 15$ as the predictor variable (as discussed in Chapter 16). The resulting least squares line, shown in Figure 17.1, turns out to be

$$\hat{y}_t = 32 + 20t$$

The estimated forecast for the year 2000 in the earlier discussion was $\hat{y}_{16} = 350$. This value was determined simply by extending the least squares line into this time period and "eyeballing" the estimate for 2000. The actual forecast is

$$\hat{y}_{16} = 32 + 20(16) = 352$$

So, our estimate of sales for the year 2000 is 352,000 units, based on the linear trend equation.

Referring to Figure 17.3, you could also have obtained this trend equation by clicking on the **Trend Only** button after entering the 15 sales values in column A.

A TIME SERIES CONTAINING TREND AND SEASONALITY

The previous procedure can be adapted to situations in which the time series contains significant trend *and* seasonality. Such a situation can occur when the data are monthly or quarterly, with seasonal fluctuations about a linear or curvilinear trend.

The quarterly sales for Video-Comp over a four-year period (1995–1998) are contained in Table 16.3 on page 775 and are illustrated in Figure 17.5. The deseasonalized sales figures (often called *seasonally adjusted* sales) are summarized in Table 16.6 on page 779 and also are graphed in Figure 17.5. Notice that the extreme seasonal fluctuations of the original time series were removed when these values were divided by the appropriate seasonal index. The indexes for this application were derived in Example 16.8, and they indicated low sales for the first two quarters, above-average sales for the third quarter, and extremely high sales during the fourth (holiday) quarter. The corresponding indexes were

$$S_1 = .852 \qquad S_3 = 1.166$$

$$S_2 = .692 \qquad S_4 = 1.290$$

To forecast future values when using seasonal data, you once again determine the least squares line (or curve), except that now you use the *deseasonalized data* (say, d_t) as your dependent variable. Once you have calculated the trend forecast, you obtain your final

FIGURE 17.5

Quarterly sales at Video-Comp.

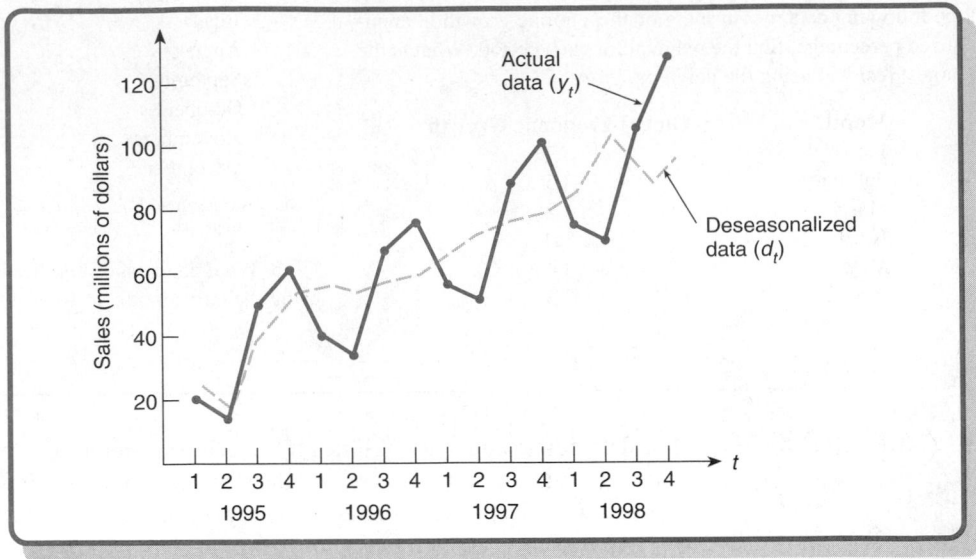

forecast by multiplying this deseasonalized estimate by the corresponding seasonal index. So the procedure for extending trend and seasonal components is:

1. Calculate the deseasonalized (seasonally adjusted) data from the original time series $(y_1, y_2, \ldots, y_T)$. Call these values $d_1, d_2, \ldots, d_T$.
2. Construct a least squares line through the deseasonalized data, where $(t = 1, 2, \ldots, T)$.

$$\hat{d}_t = b_0 + b_1 t$$

3. Calculate the forecast for time period $T + 1$ using

$$\hat{y}_{T+1} = (\hat{d}_{T+1}) \cdot (\text{seasonal index for } t = T + 1)$$

$$= [b_0 + b_1(T + 1)] \cdot (\text{seasonal index for } t = T + 1)$$

EXAMPLE 17.3

Using the Video-Comp data, what would be your forecast for the first-quarter sales for 1999? second-quarter sales?

SOLUTION

The trend line through the deseasonalized data is contained in Figure 17.7 and illustrated in Figure 17.6. To obtain this solution, enter the 16 deseasonalized values in column A and click on **KGP Data Analysis ➤ Time Series Analysis ➤ Forecasting.** Select the **Trend with Seasonality** option and enter "2" as the **Number of Forecast Periods,** select "4" as the **Number of Periods per Year,** enter "A1:A16" as the **Input Range,** and "B1" as the **output range.** After clicking on **Continue,** select **Linear** in the **Trend** frame and enter the four seasonal indexes (.852, .692, 1.166, 1.290) by repeatedly entering a value and then clicking on the **Next Period** button. The resulting output is shown in Figure 17.7. The least squares trend line is

$$\hat{d}_t = 19.372 + 5.0375t$$

This equation tells us that, apart from seasonal variation, the sales at Video-Comp are increasing by approximately $5 million each quarter. Using this equation and Figure 17.6, your deseasonalized forecast for the first quarter of 1999 (time period 17) is

$$\hat{d}_{17} = 19.372 + 5.0375(17)$$

$$= 105.01$$

FIGURE 17.6

Trend line through
deseasonalized data (quarterly
sales, Video-Comp).

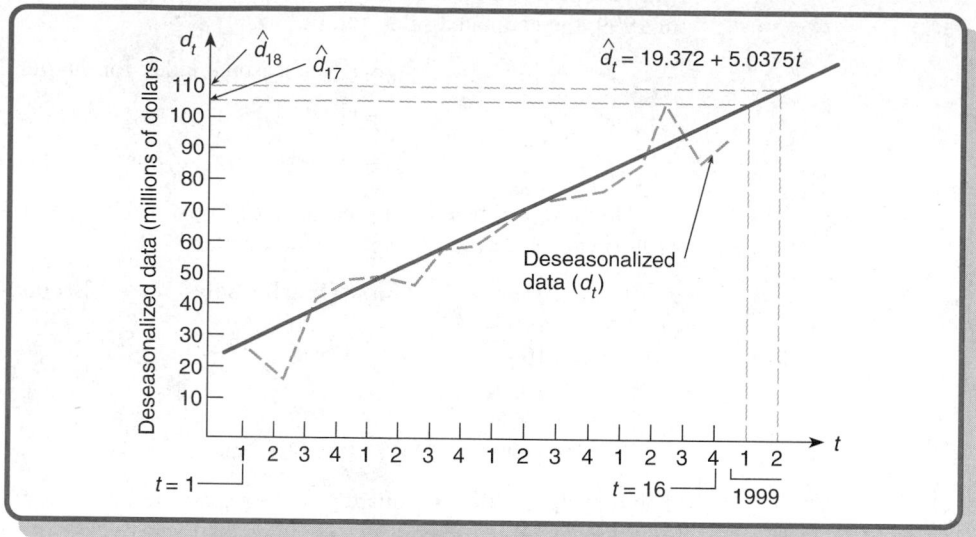

FIGURE 17.7

Excel solution for
deseasonalized trend line and
forecasting two periods ahead.

	A	B	C	D	E	F	G	H
1	23.47	**Linear Trend with Seasonality Model is Y(T) = 19.372 + 5.0375T**						
2	17.34	T	Y(T)	YHAT	RESIDUAL		**Seasonal Factors**	
3	40.31	1	23.47	24.409	-0.939		0.852	
4	46.51	2	17.34	29.446	-12.106		0.692	
5	46.95	3	40.31	34.484	5.826		1.166	
6	46.24	4	46.51	39.521	6.989		1.290	
7	55.75	5	46.95	44.559	2.391			
8	58.91	6	46.24	49.596	-3.356			
9	65.73	7	55.75	54.634	1.116			
10	72.25	8	58.91	59.671	-0.761			
11	72.90	9	65.73	64.709	1.021			
12	77.52	10	72.25	69.746	2.504			
13	88.03	11	72.9	74.784	-1.884			
14	101.16	12	77.52	79.821	-2.301			
15	86.62	13	88.03	84.859	3.171			
16	95.35	14	101.16	89.896	11.264			
17		15	86.62	94.934	-8.314			
18		16	95.35	99.971	-4.621			
19								
20		Forecasts						
21		17	89.5					
22		18	76.2					
23								
24								
25								

Now, the sales for the first quarter of each year are lower than the yearly average, as
reflected in the seasonal index of $S_1 = .852$ (from Example 16.8). Consequently, your
actual forecast for this time period is contained in cell C21 (Figure 17.7) and is equal to

$$\hat{y}_{17} = \hat{d}_{17} \cdot \text{(seasonal index for quarter 1)}$$

$$= 105.01 \cdot .852$$

$$= 89.5 \text{ (million dollars)}$$

This procedure can be used to forecast any future time period. For the second quarter of 1999, the estimated sales will be

$$\hat{y}_{18} = \hat{d}_{18} \cdot \text{(seasonal index for quarter 2)}$$

$$= [19.372 + 5.0375(18)] \cdot .692$$

$$= (110.05)(.692) = 76.2 \quad \text{(million dollars)}$$

Do these estimates seem reasonable? Look at the observed (1995–1998) and forecast (1999) values for the first and second quarters:

Year	First-Quarter Sales	Second-Quarter Sales
1995	20	12
1996	40	32
1997	56	50
1998	75	70
1999	89.5	76.2

The forecast for the first quarter of 1999 seems to be about what we would expect, based on the past first-quarter sales. The predicted sales value for the second quarter of 1999 seems to be on the low side, with an increase of only 6.2 from the second quarter of 1998. Remember, however, that this forecasting technique contains the effect of *all* the quarters observed over the four years. By examining the past sales during the second quarter only, we are ignoring the remaining quarters, and perhaps an explanation for this seemingly low forecast lies in these values.

It is possible that this forecasting procedure is not a good one for the application in Example 17.3—there may be a better way to obtain a forecast for this situation. We show you several ways to forecast a time series and then determine which of these does the best job for a particular set of observed values. *No one procedure always performs well for all applications.*

EXERCISES 17.6–17.10

UNDERSTANDING THE MECHANICS

17.6 Several sets of quarterly data have been gathered over a 3-year period from 1997 to 1999. Find the forecasts for the four quarters of 2000 for each of the following models. Assume $t = 1, 2, \ldots$

    a. $\hat{d}_t = 5.2 + .8t$, $S_1 = .81$, $S_2 = .93$, $S_3 = 1.19$, $S_4 = 1.07$
    b. $\hat{d}_t = 10.5 + 5t$, $S_1 = .66$, $S_2 = 1.08$, $S_3 = 1.19$, $S_4 = 1.07$
    c. $\hat{d}_t = 50 - 2t$, $S_1 = 1.10$, $S_2 = 1.16$, $S_3 = .90$, $S_4 = .84$

APPLYING THE NEW CONCEPTS

17.7 What is an advantage of using the least squares trend line over the naive forecast procedure?

17.8 The Learning Company sells educational material to households online. The company usually receives many online requests during the third and fourth quarters, which have seasonal indexes of 1.6 and 1.7, respectively. The quarterly number of online requests (deseasonalized) resulting in sales are presented below. Find the least squares trend line for the deseasonalized data and find the forecast for the number of online requests resulting in sales during the third and fourth quarters of 1999.

Year	Quarter 1	Quarter 2	Quarter 3	Quarter 4
1994	69	56	60	57
1995	68	65	68	71
1996	75	72	69	74
1997	72	79	80	81
1998	78	85	88	90

USING THE COMPUTER

17.9 **[DATA SET 17-9]** *Variable description:*

Year: Year starting in 1995 through 1998
Month: Numbered from 1 through 12 for the twelve months of the year
HousePermits: Number of new housing permits issued to build houses (deseasonalized)

A real estate developer is interested in forecasting the number of new housing permits issued for the first three months of 1999. She knows that the seasonal indexes for those three months are .7, .6, and 1.1. Monthly deseasonalized data have been collected from 1995 through 1998. Find the least squares trend line for the deseasonalized data and find the forecasts that the developer needs.

17.10 [DATA SET 17-10] *Variable description:*

Year: Year starting in 1996 and ending in 1999
Quarter: Numbered from 1 to 4 for each of the four quarters of the year
PretaxProf: Deseasonalized pretax profit per quarter

The German software company, SAP, has benefitted from the year-2000 computer problem. In addition, the company is the biggest maker of enterprise-resource-planning software, known as ERP. The company's programs automate manufacturing, human resources, and other nuts-and-bolts functions to give companies insight into the profitability of their internal operations according to "European Software Highflier SAP Comes Back to Earth" (*The Wall Street Journal,* Jan. 6, 1999, p. B8). Like most high-tech companies, the profits depend on cycles in the economy. Assume that deseasonalized pretax profit (converted into U.S. dollars from German marks) is collected from 1996 through 1999. If the quarterly indexes are .7, 1.0, .8, and 1.5, respectively, for quarters 1 through 4, what is the forecast of pretax profit for the four quarters of the year 2000?

17.4 SIMPLE EXPONENTIAL SMOOTHING

In Chapter 16, we introduced the concept of smoothing a time series by computing a set of centered *moving averages.* The moving averages were used to derive the various seasonal indexes, but they also provided a "new" time series with considerably less random variation (irregular activity) and no seasonality. Because the moving average series was much smoother, it provided a clearer picture of any existing trend or cyclical activity.

Another method of smoothing a time series, which also serves as a forecasting procedure is **exponential smoothing.** Unlike moving averages, this technique uses all the preceding observations to determine a smoothed value for a particular time period. The method described in this section is called **simple** (or single) **exponential smoothing** and works well for a time series containing *no trend* (Figure 17.8). A time series (such as the one in this figure) is said to be **stationary** if the data exhibit no trend and the variance about the mean ($\bar{y}_t$) remains constant over time. *Simple exponential smoothing generally will track the original time series well, provided this series is stationary.* We extend the simple exponential smoothing procedure to a series containing trend and seasonality in later sections.

The simplest way to determine a smoothed value for time period t using exponential smoothing is to find a weighted sum of the actual observation for this time period, y_t, and the previous smoothed value, S_{t-1}.

$$S_t = \text{smoothed value for time period, } t$$
$$= Ay_t + (1 - A)S_{t-1} \qquad t = 2, 3, 4, \ldots \qquad \textbf{(17.2)}$$

where A is any number between 0 and 1.

The value of A is the **smoothing constant.** Small values of A produce smoothed values giving less weight to the corresponding observation, y_t. You should use such values (say, $A < .1$) for a volatile time series containing considerable irregular activity (noise). In this way, you give more weight to the previous smoothed value, S_{t-1}, rather than to the original observation, y_t. You can use larger values of A for a more stable time series.

FIGURE 17.8

Illustration of a stationary time series.

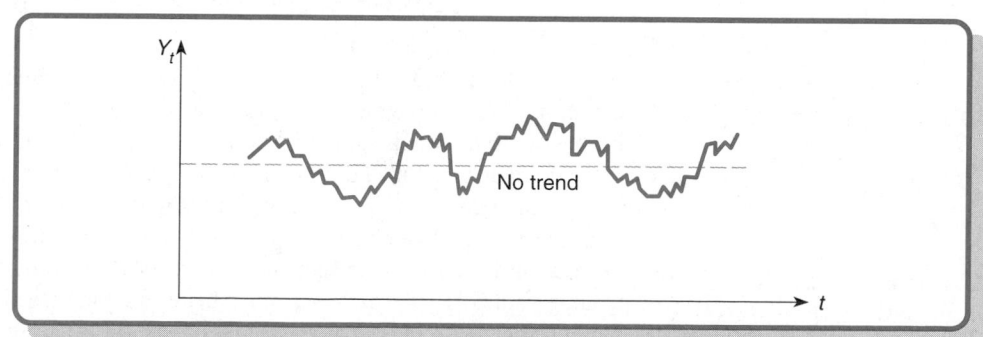

TABLE 17.1   Actual and smoothed values for attendance at Jefferson Civic Center.

Year	t	y_t	$S_t (A = .1)$	$S_t (A = .5)$	$S_t (A = .9)$
1986	1	5.0	5.0	5.0	5.0
1987	2	8.0	5.3	6.5	7.7
1988	3	2.1	4.98	4.3	2.66
1989	4	7.1	5.19	5.7	6.66
1990	5	4.8	5.15	5.25	4.99
1991	6	2.0	4.84	3.62	2.30
1992	7	7.8	5.13	5.71	7.25
1993	8	5.0	5.12	5.36	5.23
1994	9	14.1	6.02	9.73	13.21
1995	10	13.0	6.72	11.36	13.02
1996	11	13.5	7.39	12.43	13.45
1997	12	14.2	8.07	13.32	14.12
1998	13	14.0	8.67	13.66	14.01

The smoothing procedure used here begins by setting the first smoothed value, S_1, equal to the first observation, y_1. So,

$$S_1 = y_1$$

Then,

$$S_2 = Ay_2 + (1 - A)S_1$$
$$= Ay_2 + (1 - A)y_1$$
$$S_3 = Ay_3 + (1 - A)S_2$$
$$S_4 = Ay_4 + (1 - A)S_3$$

and so on.

The average attendance (y_t, in thousands) for major events held at the Jefferson County Civic Center for the past 13 years is contained in Table 17.1. We determine the exponentially smoothed values using three smoothing constants, $A = .1$, $A = .5$, and $A = .9$.

The actual time series and the three smoothed series are shown in Table 17.1 and Figure 17.9. For $A = .1$,

$$S_1 = y_1 = 5.0$$
$$S_2 = (.1)y_2 + (.9)S_1$$
$$= (.1)(8.0) + (.9)(5.0) = 5.3$$
$$S_3 = (.1)y_3 + (.9)S_2$$
$$= (.1)(2.1) + (.9)(5.3) = 4.98$$

and so on.

Notice that the average attendance, y_t, had a significant jump in 1994, when (it turns out) the facility was completely refurnished, providing better seating and more accessible snack booths. With the small value of $A = .1$, the smoothed values did not "track" the original series very well after this point. In general, when you use exponential smoothing with a small smoothing constant, the resulting series will be slow to detect any turning points or shifts in the observed values. However, such values of A provide considerable smoothing, as is evident from the values between the years 1986 and 1993.

The large value of $A = .9$ provides much better tracking (see Figure 17.9) but not much smoothing. Larger smoothing constants are more useful for a time series that does not con-

FIGURE 17.9

Smoothed values for attendance data (Table 17.2).

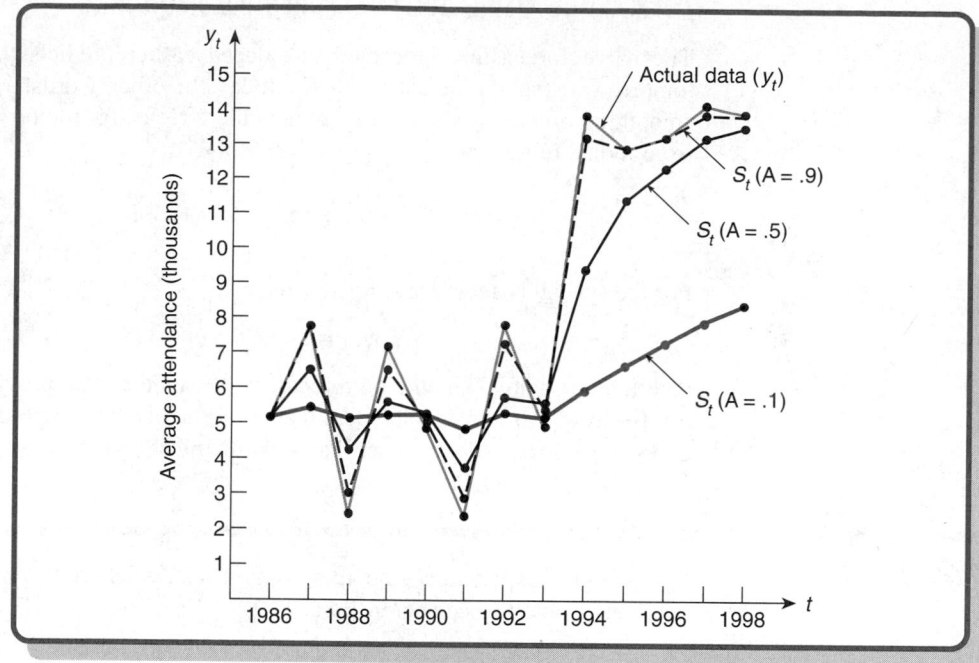

tain a great deal of random fluctuation. Using $A = .5$ offers a compromise between these two extreme smoothing constants. Later we discuss methods of comparing the tracking ability of different values of A, in an effort to determine the best smoothing constant for a particular series.

To see why this procedure is called *exponential smoothing,* we look at how each smoothed value is obtained. First, $S_1 = y_1$. Then,

$$S_2 = Ay_2 + (1 - A)S_1$$

$$= Ay_2 + (1 - A)y_1$$

$$S_3 = Ay_3 + (1 - A)S_2$$

$$= Ay_3 + (1 - A)[Ay_2 + (1 - A)y_1]$$

$$= Ay_3 + A(1 - A)y_2 + (1 - A)^2 y_1$$

$$S_4 = Ay_4 + (1 - A)S_3$$

$$= Ay_4 + (1 - A)[Ay_3 + A(1 - A)y_2 + (1 - A)^2 y_1]$$

$$= Ay_4 + A(1 - A)y_3 + A(1 - A)^2 y_2 + (1 - A)^3 y_1$$

In general,

$$S_t = Ay_t + A(1 - A)y_{t-1} + A(1 - A)^2 y_{t-2} + \cdots + A(1 - A)^{t-2} y_2 + (1 - A)^{t-1} y_1$$

For example, if $A = .5$, then

$$S_t = .5y_t + .25y_{t-1} + .125y_{t-2} + .062y_{t-3} + \cdots$$

Therefore, each smoothed value is actually a weighted sum of *all the previous observations.* Because the more recent observations have the largest weight, they have a larger effect on the smoothed value. Notice that the weights on the observations are decreasing exponentially. Except for observation y_1, the weight given to a particular observation is some constant (namely, $1 - A$) *times* the weight given to the preceding observation. That is why this procedure is called exponential smoothing.

FORECASTING USING SIMPLE EXPONENTIAL SMOOTHING

The naive forecasting procedure introduced earlier predicts the time series value for tomorrow using the actual value for today. In other words, $\hat{y}_{t+1} = y_t$. The exponential smoothing process is similar, except now the forecast for tomorrow is the smoothed value from today. In general,

$$\hat{y}_{t+1} = S_t \qquad t = 1, 2, 3, \ldots \qquad \textbf{(17.3)}$$

For the special case where $A = 1$, we have

$$\hat{y}_{t+1} = S_t = 1y_t + (1 - 1)S_{t-1} = y_t$$

and the exponential smoothing forecast is the same as that provided by the naive predictor. Because A is considerably less than 1 in practice, the smoothed forecast makes use of all the past observations, rather than only the most recent measurement.

EXAMPLE 17.4

Using simple exponential smoothing with $A = .1$, what are the predicted values and residuals for the attendance data in Table 17.1?

SOLUTION

Suppose the year is 1986 ($t = 1$) and you want a forecast for 1987 ($t = 2$). You need the smoothed value for 1986: $\hat{y}_2 = S_1 = 5.0$. Next, the year is 1987, and you need a forecast for 1988. Here, $\hat{y}_3 = S_2 = 5.3$ (from Table 17.1).

To obtain an Excel solution, enter the 13 time series values in column A. Click on **KGP Data Analysis ➤ Time Series Analysis ➤ Forecasting** and select **Simple Exponential Smoothing.** Enter "0" as the **Number of Forecast Periods,** "A1:A13" as the **Input Range,** and "B1" as the **Output Range.** After clicking on **Continue,** select **Smoothing Constant(s) Will be Provided** and enter ".1" as the smoothing constant (A). You will obtain the output in Figure 17.10 after clicking on **Continue.**

How well does this forecasting procedure perform here? We cannot use Figure 17.9 to compare the $\hat{y}$'s and the y's because, for each time period t, we have plotted y_t and S_t. The predicted value at t, however, is $\hat{y}_t = S_{t-1}$, not S_t. So we need to shift the smoothed values in Figure 17.9 one period to the right. This is shown in Figure 17.11, which contains a plot of the values in Figure 17.10 for $A = .1$.

As we might expect from Figure 17.11, the residuals using this method are quite large from 1994 on because this value of A produces smoothed values that fail to adapt to the shift that occurred in 1994. This series was not a good one for simple exponential smoothing because of this sudden shift. However, between the years 1986 and 1993 (a relatively stationary set of observations), the smoothed time series contains much less noise using $A = .1$ and gives a clear indication of the lack of any trend.

Simple exponential smoothing is a popular method of forecasting, particularly when there are hundreds or perhaps thousands of forecasts to be updated for each time period. Such is the case for many inventory-control systems, which are used to predict future demand levels for each item in inventory by means of a computerized forecasting procedure. Simple exponential smoothing often is used for such situations because each forecast, $\hat{y}_{t+1}$, requires only two values: the current observation, y_t, and the previous smoothed value, S_{t-1}. There is no need to store all the previous observations. *Computationally, this procedure is very simple and requires less computer time than do more sophisticated forecasting techniques.*

FIGURE 17.10

Forecasts and residuals using Excel and KGP Data Analysis to do simple exponential smoothing on attendance data ($A = .1$).

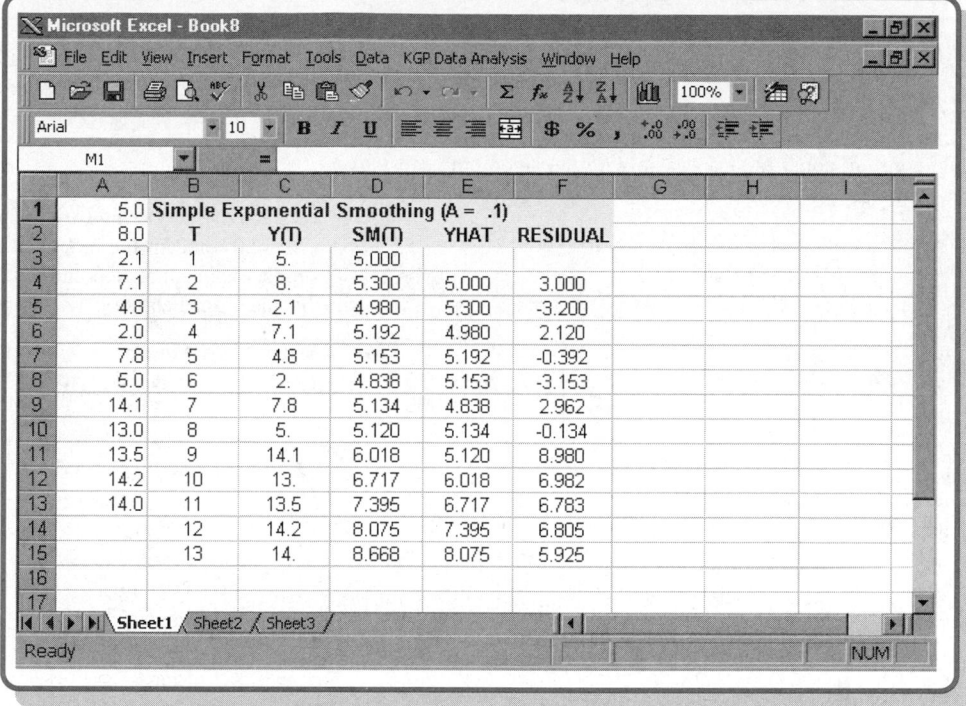

FIGURE 17.11

Predicted versus actual values for attendance data (Table 17.3).

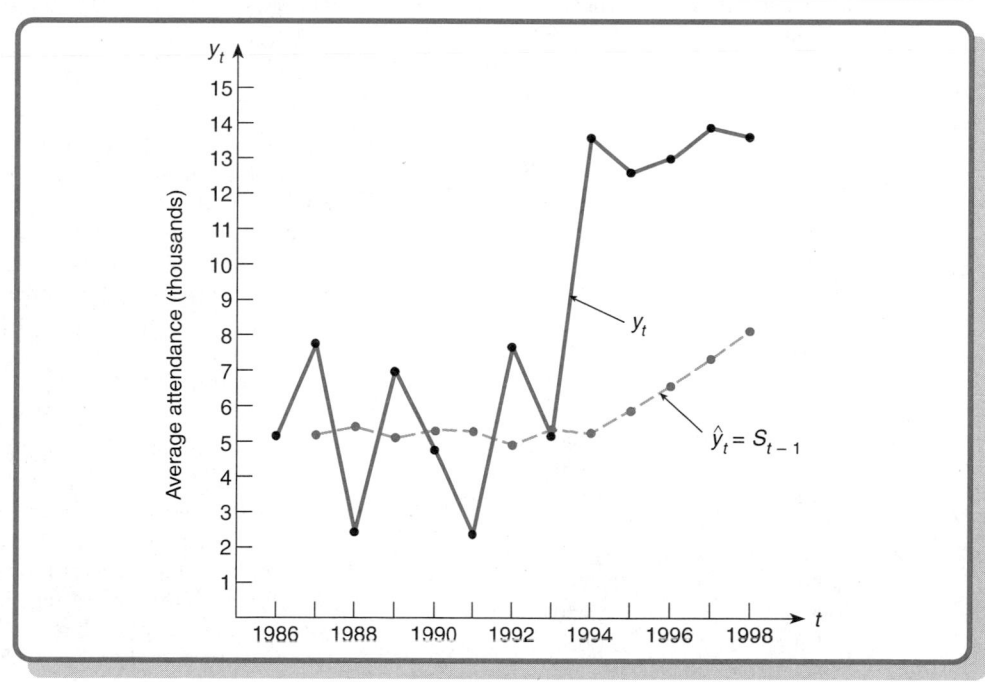

EXERCISES 17.11–17.15

UNDERSTANDING THE MECHANICS

17.11 Calculate the smoothed values for the following time series data. Use simple exponential smoothing with the smoothing constant equal to .1 and also with the smoothing constant equal to .3.

Year	t	y_t	S_t ($A = .1$)	S_t ($A = .3$)
1985	1	2	2	2
1986	2	3		
1987	3	2		
1988	4	5		
1989	5	8		
1990	6	7		
1991	7	5		
1992	8	8		
1993	9	10		
1994	10	9		
1995	11	8		
1996	12	10		
1997	13	7		
1998	14	9		
1999	15	7		

APPLYING THE NEW CONCEPTS

17.12 The trend in the price of Texas homes is up since 1992. However, the price of the average home in Texas is nowhere near as costly as during the 1980 boom. On an inflation-adjusted basis, the average price of a Texas home hit a 20-year low at $106,793 in 1991. During the 1998 and 1999 period, economists believe a four-and-a-half month supply of homes was on the Texas market, compared to a normal inventory of nine to 10 months.

Year	Average Home Sale Prices in Texas
1979	119,105
1980	120,500
1981	129,200
1982	130,350
1983	137,650
1984	141,100
1985	134,200
1986	131,700
1987	118,750
1988	112,425
1989	110,900
1990	108,300
1991	106,793
1992	108,450
1993	111,650
1994	113,210
1995	115,350
1996	118,900
1997	121,300
1998	122,100

(Source: Adapted from *The Wall Street Journal*, "Housing," Dec. 30, 1998, p. T3.)

a. Using simple exponential smoothing with $A = .25$, find the residuals for 1997 and 1998.

b. Repeat part (a) with $A = .5$ and compare the residuals for 1997 and 1998.

17.13 The Purchasing Managers' Index tracks overall business activity at 300 industrial companies, in percent. A reading above 50% means the industrial economy is expanding. Using simple exponential smoothing with $A = .2$, predict the value of this index for February, March, and April 1997.

Year	Month	Purchasing Managers' Index
1996	May	49.5
	June	54.5
	July	50.2
	August	52.5
	September	50.3
	October	49.7
	November	54.5
	December	55.0
1997	January	52.3
	February	53.5
	March	54.7
	April	53.9

(Source: Adapted from *The Dallas Morning News*, "Incomes, Spending Creep Up Mere 0.1%," June 3, 1997, p. 7D.)

USING THE COMPUTER

17.14 [DATA SET 17-14] *Variable description:*

Year: 1983 to 1999

ProductivityIndex: An index to measure the overall productivity of a paper plant

The plant manager has developed a productivity index measuring plant productivity for plants that manufacture paper products. This measure has been recorded yearly and fluctuates with the demand for paper products and the number of employees hired. Use simple exponential smoothing with $A = .15$, to forecast the productivity index for the year 2000.

17.15 [DATA SET EX17-15] *Variable description:*

Year: Year from 1984 to 1999
RefinanceNum: Number of home loans refinanced

The trend in interest rates over the past decade has been generally downward. So as mortgage interest rates dip, homeowners consider refinancing home loans. Suppose that the manager of First State Bank in Denton, Texas, is interested in forecasting the number of homeowners refinancing their home mortgage for a better interest rate. Using simple exponential smoothing with $A = .2$, predict the number of homeowners refinancing at First State Bank in the years 1998 and 1999 and comment on the accuracy.

17.5 EXPONENTIAL SMOOTHING FOR A TIME SERIES CONTAINING TREND

The simple exponential smoothing technique discussed in the previous section always will lag behind a time series that contains a steadily increasing or decreasing trend. A procedure known as *Holt's two-parameter linear exponential smoothing* allows you to estimate separately the smoothed value of the time series as well as the average trend gain at each point in time. The resulting smoothed values track the past time series observations more accurately. We refer to this procedure as **linear exponential smoothing.** There are two equations for this method. The first, for smoothing the observations, is

$$S_t = Ay_t + (1 - A)(S_{t-1} + b_{t-1}) \qquad t = 2, 3, 4, \ldots \qquad \textbf{(17.4)}$$

The second, for smoothing the trend, is

$$b_t = B(S_t - S_{t-1}) + (1 - B)b_{t-1} \qquad t = 2, 3, 4, \ldots \qquad \textbf{(17.5)}$$

where (1) S_t is the smoothed value for time period t, (2) b_t is the smoothed *trend* estimate for this time period, and (3) A and B are smoothing constants between 0 and 1.

SMOOTHING THE OBSERVATIONS (EQUATION 17.4)

Equation 17.4 is similar to the equation used for simple exponential smoothing, except that S_{t-1} is replaced by $(S_{t-1} + b_{t-1})$ to include the effect of the trend. The smoothing constant for this equation is $0 < A < 1$; typically, $A \leq .3$.

SMOOTHING THE TREND (EQUATION 17.5)

Equation 17.5 is a new addition to the smoothing process and represents the smoothed trend. It uses a separate smoothing constant, B, to smooth the trend values. This constant also is generally less than or equal to .3. This smoothed trend estimate is updated by using a weighted sum of (1) the difference between the last two smoothed values (an estimate of the current "trend") and (2) the previous smoothed trend estimate. Such a procedure significantly reduces any randomness (irregular activity) in the trend values across time.

FORECASTING USING LINEAR EXPONENTIAL SMOOTHING

Linear exponential forecasting uses both the smoothed observations and the smoothed trend estimates. The forecast for time period $t + 1$ is the current smoothed value plus the current smoothed trend value.

$$\hat{y}_{t+1} = S_t + b_t \qquad t = 1, 2, 3, \ldots \qquad \textbf{(17.6)}$$

We also can use this procedure to forecast any number of time periods into the future, say, m periods. Here,

$$\hat{y}_{t+m} = S_t + mb_t \qquad t = 1, 2, 3, \ldots \qquad \textbf{(17.7)}$$

The forecast using equation 17.6 is the **one-step ahead forecast,** and the value from equation 17.7 is the ***m*-step ahead forecast.**

TABLE 17.2

Summary for linear exponential smoothing.

Year	t	Actual Observation (y_t)	Smoothed Observation (S_t)	Smoothed Trend (b_t)	Forecast ($\hat{y}_t$)	Residual ($y_t - \hat{y}_t$)
1980	1	y_1	$S_1 = y_1$	b_1	—	—
1981	2	y_2	S_2	b_2	$\hat{y}_2$	$y_2 - \hat{y}_2$
1982	3	y_3	S_3	b_3	$\hat{y}_3$	$y_3 - \hat{y}_3$
1983	4	y_4	S_4	b_4	$\hat{y}_4$	$y_4 - \hat{y}_4$
⋮						

SUMMARIZING THE RESULTS

To summarize the necessary calculations for linear exponential smoothing, you can use the format in Table 17.2. The initial year for this time series is 1980. As we did for simple exponential smoothing, we continue to set the first smoothed value, S_1, equal to the first observation, y_1. A new problem arises here: the initial estimate of the trend, b_1. We examine two procedures for estimating this value.

PROCEDURE 1.   Let $b_1 = 0$. Provided you have a large number of years in your observed time series, this procedure provides an adequate initial estimate for the trend. The smoothed trend value soon "catches up" with the actual trend of the series.

PROCEDURE 2.   You can obtain a more accurate estimate of b_1 by using the first five (or so) time periods to estimate the initial trend. A least squares line is constructed through these five observations (exactly as discussed in Chapter 16), with the resulting equation $\hat{y}_t = a + bt$. The value of b provides an initial trend estimate.

We demonstrate this technique in Example 17.5, which uses both procedures to obtain the initial trend estimate, b_1.

EXAMPLE 17.5

The time series in the following table contains the city taxes (in thousands of dollars) collected in Jackson City over the past 20 quarters. Using procedures 1 and 2 to calculate an initial trend estimate, obtain the smoothed values, S_t, for each time period. Also, determine the predicted values, $\hat{y}_t$, using smoothing constants $A = .1$ and $B = .3$.

Year	Quarter	Taxes Collected	Year	Quarter	Taxes Collected
1994	1	76	1997	1	403
	2	93		2	282
	3	108		3	288
	4	128		4	387
1995	1	196	1998	1	484
	2	175		2	384
	3	141		3	330
	4	236		4	497
1996	1	256			
	2	190			
	3	227			
	4	299			

TABLE 17.3

Solution to Example 17.5 using linear exponential smoothing ($A = .1$, $B = .3$).

t	y_t	S_t	b_t	$\hat{y}_t$	$y_t - \hat{y}_t$
1	76.0	76.000	0.000		
2	93.0	77.700	0.510	76.000	17.000
3	108.0	81.189	1.404	78.210	29.790
4	128.0	87.133	2.766	82.593	45.407
5	196.0	100.509	5.949	89.899	106.101
6	175.0	113.313	8.005	106.458	68.542
7	141.0	123.286	8.596	121.318	19.682
8	236.0	142.293	11.719	131.882	104.118
9	256.0	164.211	14.779	154.013	101.987
10	190.0	180.091	15.109	178.990	11.010
11	227.0	198.380	16.063	195.200	31.800
12	299.0	222.899	18.600	214.443	84.557
13	403.0	257.649	23.445	241.499	161.501
14	282.0	281.184	23.472	281.094	0.906
15	288.0	302.991	22.972	304.656	−16.656
16	387.0	332.067	24.803	325.963	61.037
17	484.0	369.583	28.617	356.870	127.130
18	384.0	396.781	28.191	398.201	−14.201
19	330.0	415.475	25.342	424.972	−94.972
20	497.0	446.435	27.028	440.817	56.183

SOLUTION

A summary of the results using procedure 1 (setting $b_1 = 0$) is shown in Table 17.3. To illustrate the necessary calculations here, consider $t = 10$.

1. $y_{10} = 190$
2. $S_{10} = .1y_{10} + .9(S_9 + b_9) = .1(190) + .9(164.211 + 14.779) = 180.091$
3. $b_{10} = .3(S_{10} - S_9) + .7(b_9) = .3(180.091 - 164.211) + .7(14.779) = 15.109$
4. $\hat{y}_{10} = S_9 + b_9$ (from equation 17.6) $= 164.211 + 14.779 = 178.990$
5. Residual for $t = 10$ is $y_{10} - \hat{y}_{10} = 190 - 178.990 = 11.010$

The KGP Data Analysis tool pack allows you to perform linear exponential smoothing within Excel using either procedure 1 or procedure 2. To obtain a procedure 2 solution, begin by entering the 20 city tax values in column A and clicking on **KGP Data Analysis ➤ Time Series Analysis ➤ Forecasting.** Select **Holt's Exponential Smoothing** and enter "0" as the **Number of Forecast Periods,** "A1:A20" as the **Input Range,** and "B1" as the **Output Range.** After clicking on **Continue,** select **Procedure 2** in the next screen and click on **OK.** In the next screen, select **Smoothing Constant(s) Will Be Provided** and enter ".1" as smoothing constant A and ".3" as smoothing constant B. After clicking on **Continue,** you will obtain the output in Figure 17.12. The columns in the Excel output correspond to those in Table 17.3 where the column labeled **YHAT** corresponds to the $\hat{y}_t$ column and the **RESIDUAL** column contains the $y_t - \hat{y}_t$ values.

The values of y_t and $\hat{y}_t$ (the predicted value for that time period) are shown in Figure 17.13. For this particular example, procedure 2, which used the first 5 quarters to obtain the initial trend estimate, estimated (and smoothed) the past values more accurately. The value of b_1 (in cell E3) is 27.5.

FIGURE 17.12

Excel solution to Example 17.5 using KGP Data Analysis (linear exponential smoothing with procedure 2, $A = .1$, $B = .3$).

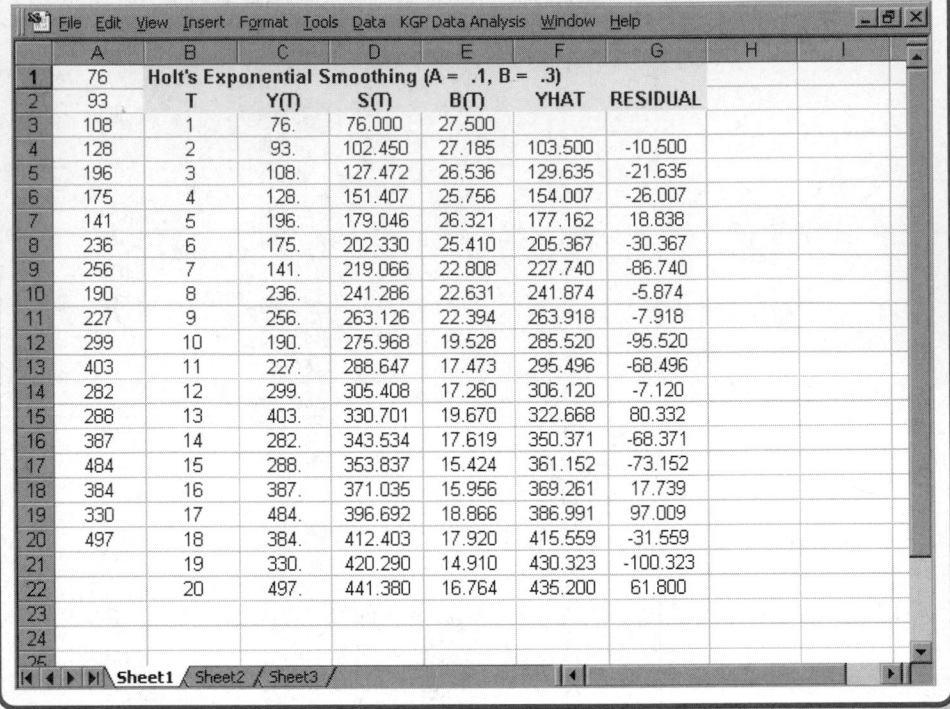

	A	B	C	D	E	F	G	H	I
1	76	Holt's Exponential Smoothing (A = .1, B = .3)							
2	93	T	Y(T)	S(T)	B(T)	YHAT	RESIDUAL		
3	108	1	76.	76.000	27.500				
4	128	2	93.	102.450	27.185	103.500	-10.500		
5	196	3	108.	127.472	26.536	129.635	-21.635		
6	175	4	128.	151.407	25.756	154.007	-26.007		
7	141	5	196.	179.046	26.321	177.162	18.838		
8	236	6	175.	202.330	25.410	205.367	-30.367		
9	256	7	141.	219.066	22.808	227.740	-86.740		
10	190	8	236.	241.286	22.631	241.874	-5.874		
11	227	9	256.	263.126	22.394	263.918	-7.918		
12	299	10	190.	275.968	19.528	285.520	-95.520		
13	403	11	227.	288.647	17.473	295.496	-68.496		
14	282	12	299.	305.408	17.260	306.120	-7.120		
15	288	13	403.	330.701	19.670	322.668	80.332		
16	387	14	282.	343.534	17.619	350.371	-68.371		
17	484	15	288.	353.837	15.424	361.152	-73.152		
18	384	16	387.	371.035	15.956	369.261	17.739		
19	330	17	484.	396.692	18.866	386.991	97.009		
20	497	18	384.	412.403	17.920	415.559	-31.559		
21		19	330.	420.290	14.910	430.323	-100.323		
22		20	497.	441.380	16.764	435.200	61.800		
23									
24									

FIGURE 17.13

Predicted values using linear exponential smoothing ($A = .1$, $B = .3$).

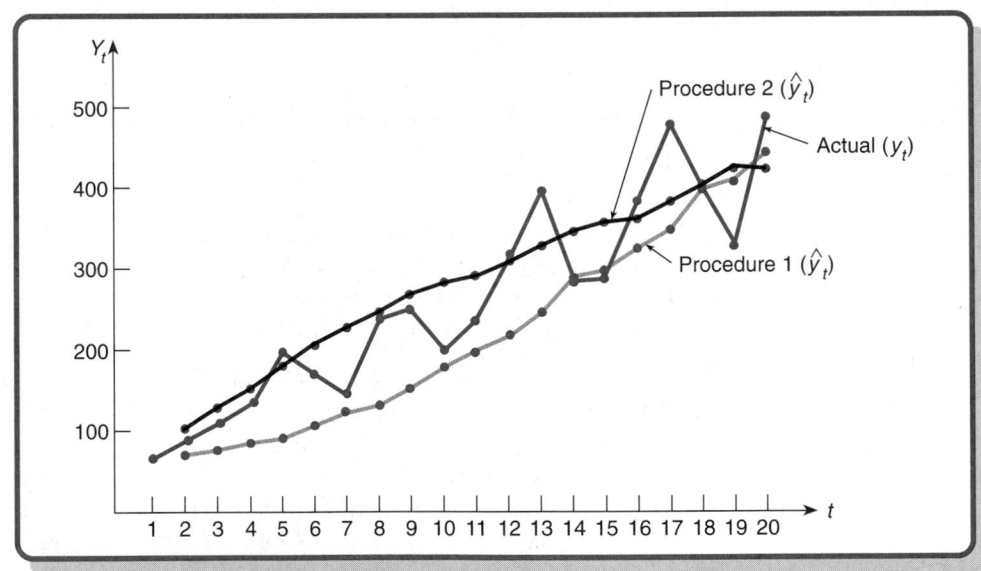

EXERCISES 17.16–17.20

UNDERSTANDING THE MECHANICS

17.16 The following values were found from a time series data set. Use Holt's two-parameter linear exponential smoothing technique to answer parts (a) and (b).

$$Y_{10} = 12.0 \qquad S_8 = 11.0$$
$$S_9 = 11.5 \qquad b_8 = .5$$

a. Find the smoothed value at time $t = 10$ with $A = .1$ and $B = .2$.

b. Find the smoothed value at time $t = 10$ with $A = .25$ and $B = .10$.

APPLYING THE NEW CONCEPTS

17.17 The growth of the chip industry is vital to the tax base of many counties across the United States. For example, in

Washington County, Oregon, Intel is the county's biggest property tax payer. In 1998, Intel paid about $10 million, about three times as much as the next-biggest property tax payer. Annual revenue for the computer chip industry is presented below in units of billions of dollars. Forecast the 1999 annual revenue using Holt's two-parameter linear exponential smoothing technique with an initial estimate of zero for the slope and with $A = .3$ and $B = .2$.

Year	Annual Revenue for Chip Industry	Year	Annual Revenue for Chip Industry
1988	46.3	1994	100.7
1989	48.6	1995	143.3
1990	50.5	1996	130.1
1991	62.3	1997	131.4
1992	69.5	1998	128.7
1993	75.8		

(Source: Adapted from *USA Today*, "States Bet Smarter on Chip Plants," Dec. 17, 1998, p. 2B.)

17.18 More than 20% of the American population live in households wired for e-mail. Though no one keeps track of the recipients of all the messages, communications analysts say inter-family e-mail accounts for a large percentage of the traffic. The estimated number of messages per day per person since 1989 are presented below.

Year	Estimated Messages per Day per Person	Year	Estimated Messages per Day per Person
1989	1.7	1994	2.2
1990	1.8	1995	2.4
1991	2.0	1996	2.5
1992	2.1	1997	2.7
1993	2.1	1998	3.1

(Source: Adapted from *The Wall Street Journal*, "Getting the Message," June 7, 1997, p. R22.)

a. Using zero as an initial estimate of the slope, find the predicted value for the estimated number of messages received per day per person at households that are wired for e-mail. Let $A = .25$ and $B = .1$.

b. Using the least squares estimate from the first five years for the slope, redo part (a). Compare the predicted value from part (a) to the predicted value using this procedure.

Using the Computer

17.19 [DATA SET EX17-19] *Variable description:*

Year: Year from 1980 to 1999
LaborForce: Number of employees in the nonagricultural sector of St. Charles county
Value of Smoothing constant A: .5
Value of Smoothing constant B: .3

St. Charles County has a large agricultural population. However, as farming becomes more modernized, fewer employees have been needed in this sector of the population. Manufacturing and service facilities have gradually increased the number of employees in the nonagricultural industry. Using linear exponential smoothing with zero as the initial value estimate of the slope, forecast the number of employees in this sector of the economy for St. Charles County for the year 2000. Do a "what if" analysis by using the data from 1989 to 1999. How sensitive is the value of the forecast to this change?

17.20 [DATA SET EX17-20] *Variable description:*

Year: Year from 1985 to 1998
TouristExp: Amount of money spent by tourists visiting Pensacola Beach during the summer months
Value of smoothing constant A: .4
Value of smoothing constant B: .25

Pensacola Beach in the panhandle of Florida has some of the finest beaches on the Gulf of Mexico. The flow of tourists to the area is sometimes interrupted by unpredictable weather and by hurricanes. Suppose that from 1985 to 1998, data were collected on the amount of money in dollars spent by tourists over the summer months. Using the first five years of data to estimate the slope, what is the predicted amount of money spent by tourists during the summer months for the year 1999?

17.6 Exponential Smoothing Method for Trend and Seasonality

As discussed earlier, seasonality is present in a time series whenever certain months or quarters are consistently higher or lower than the yearly average. In such cases, an extension of Holt's method, **Winters' linear and seasonal exponential smoothing,** offers additional flexibility. This three-parameter technique (that is, there are three smoothing constants) not only smooths the past observation and trend estimates (as does linear exponential smoothing) but also provides smoothed seasonality factors for each time period.

The smoothing equations for Winters' method are, for smoothing the observations,

$$S_t = A\left(\frac{y_t}{F_{t-L}}\right) + (1 - A)(S_{t-1} + b_{t-1})$$

$$t = L+1, \ L+2, \ L+3, \ \ldots \tag{17.8}$$

for smoothing the seasonality factors,

$$F_t = B\left(\frac{y_t}{S_t}\right) + (1-B)F_{t-L}$$

$$t = L+1,\ L+2,\ L+3,\ \dots \tag{17.9}$$

and for smoothing the trend estimates,

$$b_t = C(S_t - S_{t-1}) + (1-C)b_{t-1}$$

$$t = L+1,\ L+2,\ L+3,\ \dots \tag{17.10}$$

Here, (1) S_t is the smoothed observation for time period t; (2) F_t is the smoothed seasonality factor for this time period; (3) b_t is the smoothed estimate of trend; (4) L is the number of periods per year ($L = 4$ for quarterly data and $L = 12$ for monthly data); and (5) A, B, and C are the three smoothing constants.

Equations 17.8 and 17.10 are similar to the corresponding equations from the linear exponential smoothing procedure, except that S_t now consists of deseasonalized smoothed values. These values are obtained by dividing each observation, y_t, by the smoothed seasonal factor from one year before that observation, F_{t-L}.

FORECASTING USING LINEAR AND SEASONAL EXPONENTIAL SMOOTHING

The procedure for forecasting using Winters' exponential smoothing method is similar to that used for Holt's. Here, the forecast for a particular quarter (month) includes the effect of all three smoothing equations. The forecast for m periods ahead is

$$\hat{y}_{t+m} = (S_t + mb_t) \cdot F_{t+m-L} \tag{17.11}$$

The term $(S_t + mb_t)$ represents the smoothed *deseasonalized* estimate and includes the smoothed trend effect. The seasonality is included in the final estimate by multiplying by the smoothed seasonality factor for the quarter (or month) one year previous to the forecast time period, namely, F_{t+m-L}. This procedure is much like that used in Section 17.3, where the deseasonalized estimate was multiplied by the corresponding seasonal index to arrive at the final forecast.

When using this procedure on the past observations, you would, for example, determine $\hat{y}_{10}$ by assuming observations, $y_1, y_2, \dots, y_9$ are available. You would do a one-step ahead forecast ($m = 1$) using the smoothed seasonal value from the previous year; that is, $F_{10-4} = F_6$, assuming quarterly data. As a result,

$$\hat{y}_{10} = [S_9 + (1)b_9] \cdot F_6$$

Similarly,

$$\hat{y}_{11} = [S_{10} + (1)b_{10}] \cdot F_7$$

$$\hat{y}_{12} = [S_{11} + (1)b_{11}] \cdot F_8$$

and so on.

Forecasting *beyond* the range of your observations (extrapolating) is illustrated in Example 17.7.

When dealing with quarterly data, your first set of predicted values will be

$$\hat{y}_5 = [S_4 + (1)b_4] \cdot F_1$$

$$\hat{y}_6 = [S_5 + (1)b_5] \cdot F_2$$

$$\hat{y}_7 = [S_6 + (1)b_6] \cdot F_3$$

TABLE 17.4

Summary of linear and seasonal exponential smoothing (using procedure 1).

Year	Qtr.	t	Actual Observations (y_t)	Smoothed Observations (S_t)	Smoothed Seasonal Factors (F_t)	Smoothed Trend (b_t)	Forecast $(\hat{y}_t)$	Residual $(y_t - \hat{y}_t)$
1993	1				(1) 1.0			
(year 0)	2				1.0			
	3			(3)	1.0	(2)		
	4			$S_0 = y_4$	1.0	$b_0 = 0$		
1994	1	1	y_1	S_1	F_1	b_1	$\hat{y}_1 = S_0$	$y_1 - \hat{y}_1$
(year 1)	2	2	y_2	S_2	F_2	b_2	$\hat{y}_2 = S_0$	$y_2 - \hat{y}_2$
	3	3	y_3	S_3	F_3	b_3	$\hat{y}_3 = S_0$	$y_3 - \hat{y}_3$
	4	4	y_4	S_4	F_4	b_4	$\hat{y}_4 = S_0$	$y_4 - \hat{y}_4$
1995	1	5	y_5	S_5	F_5	b_5	$\hat{y}_5$	$y_5 - \hat{y}_5$
(year 2)	2	6	y_6	S_6	F_6	b_6	$\hat{y}_6$	$y_6 - \hat{y}_6$
	$\vdots$							

and so on. If the time series consists of monthly observations ($L = 12$), then you begin your predicted values with

$$\hat{y}_{13} = [S_{12} + (1)b_{12}] \cdot F_1$$

$$\hat{y}_{14} = [S_{13} + (1)b_{13}] \cdot F_2$$

$$\hat{y}_{15} = [S_{14} + (1)b_{14}] \cdot F_3$$

and so on.

SUMMARIZING THE RESULTS

A method of summarizing the necessary calculations is shown in Table 17.4. Suppose that the original year of the observed time series is 1994, with quarterly observations. Initial estimates must be supplied for (1) the seasonal factors for each quarter of 1993, (2) the trend estimate for quarter 4, 1993, and (3) the smoothed value corresponding to quarter 4, 1993.

Once again, we will examine two procedures for this situation—one is quick and easy, and the other is more accurate but requires additional calculations. Procedure 1 is used in Table 17.4. Both procedures are demonstrated in Example 17.6. These are not the only procedures—can you think of one or two others?

PROCEDURE 1.

1. Set the initial seasonal factors equal to 1.
2. Set the initial trend estimate (b_0) equal to 0.
3. Set the initial smoothed value for quarter 4, 1993 (S_0), equal to the actual value for quarter 4, 1994 (y_4). This value is also the *forecast value* ($\hat{y}_t$) for each of the four quarters in 1994.

PROCEDURE 2.

1. Use the first two years of data to determine the seasonal indexes. These are the four values for F_t in 1993. Actually, any number of years of data can be used here.
2. Deseasonalize the data for the first two years (or any number of years), and calculate the least squares line through these deseasonalized values, d_t. Call this line $\hat{d}_t = a + bt$. The initial trend estimate (b_0) is b.
3. The initial smoothed value for quarter 4, 1993, is $S_0 = [a + b(0)] \cdot$ (seasonal index for quarter 4 in step 1) $= a \cdot$ (seasonal index), where a is the intercept of the least squares line in step 2. Also, S_0 is the *forecast value* ($\hat{y}_t$) for each of the 4 quarters in 1994.

EXAMPLE 17.6

The quarterly taxes from Jackson City in Example 17.5 indicated significant seasonality. In particular, the first-quarter taxes appeared to be considerably larger than those for the yearly average. Using the linear and seasonal exponential smoothing procedures, determine the smoothed value, S_t, and predicted value, $\hat{y}_t$, for each time period. Use smoothing constants $A = .1$, $B = .3$, and $C = .2$.

SOLUTION

The computed results using procedure 1 are summarized in Table 17.5, where $b_0 = 0$, $S_0 = y_4$, and the initial seasonal factors are each 1.

The KGP Data Analysis tool pack allows you to perform linear and seasonal exponential smoothing within Excel using either procedure 1 or procedure 2. To obtain a procedure 2 solution, begin by entering the 20 city tax values in column A and clicking on **KGP Data Analysis ➤ Time Series Analysis ➤ Forecasting.** Select **Winters' Exponential Smoothing** and enter "0" as the **Number of Forecast Periods.** Select 4 as the number of periods per year, and enter "A1:A20" as the **Input Range** and "B1" as the **Output Range.** After clicking on **Continue,** select **Procedure 2** in the next screen and click on **OK.** In the next screen, select **Smoothing Constant(s) Will Be Provided** and enter ".1" as smoothing constant A, ".3" as smoothing constant B, and ".2" as smoothing constant C. After clicking on **Continue,** you will obtain the output in Figure 17.14. The columns in the Excel output correspond to those in Table 17.5 where the column labeled **YHAT** contains the $\hat{y}_t$ values and the **RESIDUAL** column corresponds to the $y_t - \hat{y}_t$ column. Finally, for column D to contain the years (1994, . . . , 1998), select column D in your output (it should be black), click on **Insert ➤ Columns,** and enter the years in cells D3, D7, D11, D15, and D19.

TABLE 17.5

Solution using linear and seasonal exponential smoothing, procedure 1 ($A = .1$, $B = .3$, $C = .2$).

	t	y_t	S_t	F_t	b_t	$\hat{y}_t$	$y_t - \hat{y}_t$
				1.0			
				1.0			
				1.0			
			128	1.0	0.0		
1994	1	76.0	122.800	0.886	−1.040	128.000	−52.000
	2	93.0	118.884	0.935	−1.615	128.000	−35.000
	3	108.0	116.342	0.978	−1.801	128.000	−20.000
	4	128.0	115.887	1.031	−1.531	128.000	0.000
1995	5	196.0	125.050	1.090	0.608	101.281	94.719
	6	175.0	131.815	1.053	1.839	117.450	57.550
	7	141.0	134.699	0.999	2.048	130.779	10.221
	8	236.0	145.954	1.207	3.889	141.034	94.966
1996	9	256.0	158.342	1.248	5.589	163.356	92.644
	10	190.0	165.589	1.081	5.921	172.547	17.453
	11	227.0	177.082	1.084	7.035	171.334	55.666
	12	299.0	190.477	1.316	8.307	222.235	76.765
1997	13	403.0	211.193	1.446	10.789	248.112	154.888
	14	282.0	225.870	1.131	11.567	239.967	42.033
	15	288.0	240.265	1.118	12.132	257.347	30.653
	16	387.0	256.568	1.374	12.966	332.116	54.884
1998	17	484.0	276.049	1.538	14.269	389.793	94.207
	18	384.0	295.231	1.182	15.252	328.427	55.573
	19	330.0	308.943	1.103	14.944	347.212	−17.212
	20	497.0	327.681	1.417	15.703	444.893	52.107

With procedure 2, the first two years were used to obtain the initial seasonal factors by finding the four seasonal indexes as described in Chapter 16. These values (contained in cells C4:C7) are

$$\text{quarter } 1 = 1.23 \qquad \text{quarter } 3 = .91$$

$$\text{quarter } 2 = 0.98 \qquad \text{quarter } 4 = .88$$

Next, the data from the first two years were deseasonalized by dividing by the corresponding seasonal index to obtain the deseasonalized values, d_t. A least squares line through these eight values using the simple linear regression procedure from Chapter 16 produced:

$$\hat{d}_t = 43.8 + 23.1t$$

The value of 23.1 became the initial slope estimate, b_0. Finally, the initial smoothed value for quarter 4, 1993, is

$$S_0 = (43.8)(\text{initial seasonal index for quarter 4})$$

$$= (43.8)(.88) = 38.5$$

Also, $S_0 = 38.5$ becomes the forecast value ($\hat{y}_t$) for each of the quarters in 1994.

The calculations required here can be illustrated using Table 17.5 and $t = 10$ for procedure 1.

1. $y_{10} = 190$

2. $S_{10} = .1\left(\dfrac{y_{10}}{F_{10-4}}\right) + .9(S_9 + b_9)$

$$= .1\left(\frac{y_{10}}{F_6}\right) + .9(S_9 + b_9)$$

$$= .1\left(\frac{190}{1.053}\right) + .9(158.342 + 5.589) = 165.589$$

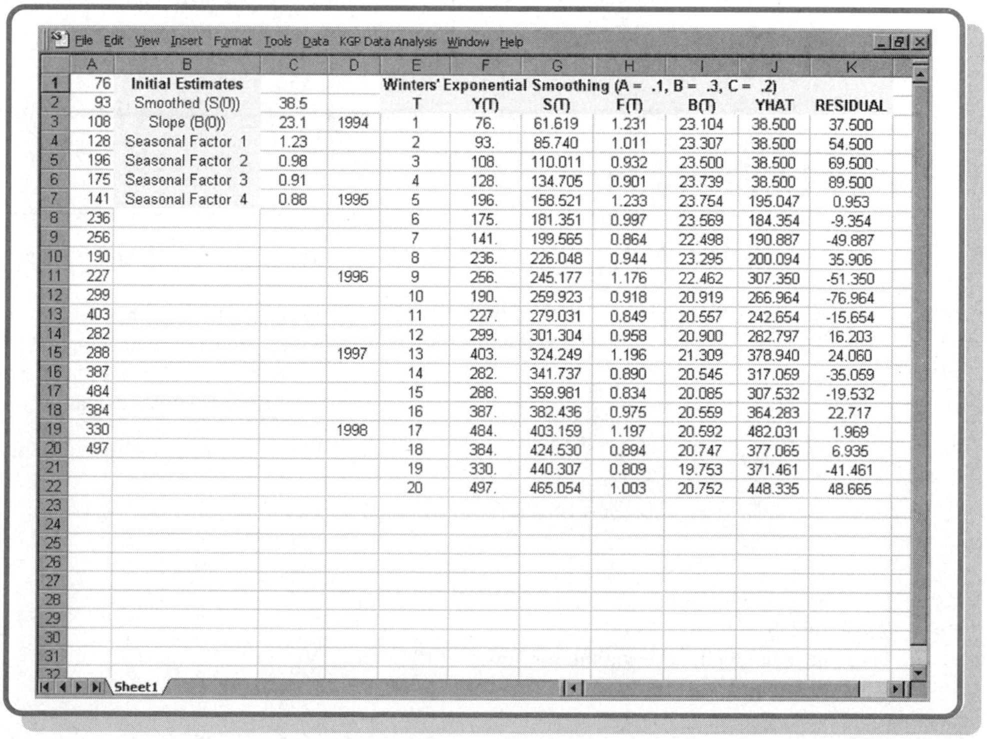

FIGURE 17.14

Excel solution to Example 17.6 using KGP Data Analysis (linear and seasonal exponential smoothing with procedure 2, $A = .1$, $B = .3$, $C = .2$).

	A	B	C	D	E	F	G	H	I	J	K
1	76	Initial Estimates				Winters' Exponential Smoothing (A = .1, B = .3, C = .2)					
2	93	Smoothed (S(0))	38.5		T	Y(T)	S(T)	F(T)	B(T)	YHAT	RESIDUAL
3	108	Slope (B(0))	23.1	1994	1	76.	61.619	1.231	23.104	38.500	37.500
4	128	Seasonal Factor 1	1.23		2	93.	85.740	1.011	23.307	38.500	54.500
5	196	Seasonal Factor 2	0.98		3	108.	110.011	0.932	23.500	38.500	69.500
6	175	Seasonal Factor 3	0.91		4	128.	134.705	0.901	23.739	38.500	89.500
7	141	Seasonal Factor 4	0.88	1995	5	196.	158.521	1.233	23.754	195.047	0.953
8	236				6	175.	181.351	0.997	23.569	184.354	-9.354
9	256				7	141.	199.565	0.864	22.498	190.887	-49.887
10	190				8	236.	226.048	0.944	23.295	200.094	35.906
11	227			1996	9	256.	245.177	1.176	22.462	307.350	-51.350
12	299				10	190.	259.923	0.918	20.919	266.964	-76.964
13	403				11	227.	279.031	0.849	20.557	242.654	-15.654
14	282				12	299.	301.304	0.958	20.900	282.797	16.203
15	288			1997	13	403.	324.249	1.196	21.309	378.940	24.060
16	387				14	282.	341.737	0.890	20.545	317.059	-35.059
17	484				15	288.	359.981	0.834	20.085	307.532	-19.532
18	384				16	387.	382.436	0.975	20.559	364.283	22.717
19	330			1998	17	484.	403.159	1.197	20.592	482.031	1.969
20	497				18	384.	424.530	0.894	20.747	377.065	6.935
21					19	330.	440.307	0.809	19.753	371.461	-41.461
22					20	497.	465.054	1.003	20.752	448.335	48.665

FIGURE 17.15

Forecasted values using linear and seasonal exponential smoothing ($A = .1$, $B = .3$, $C = .2$).

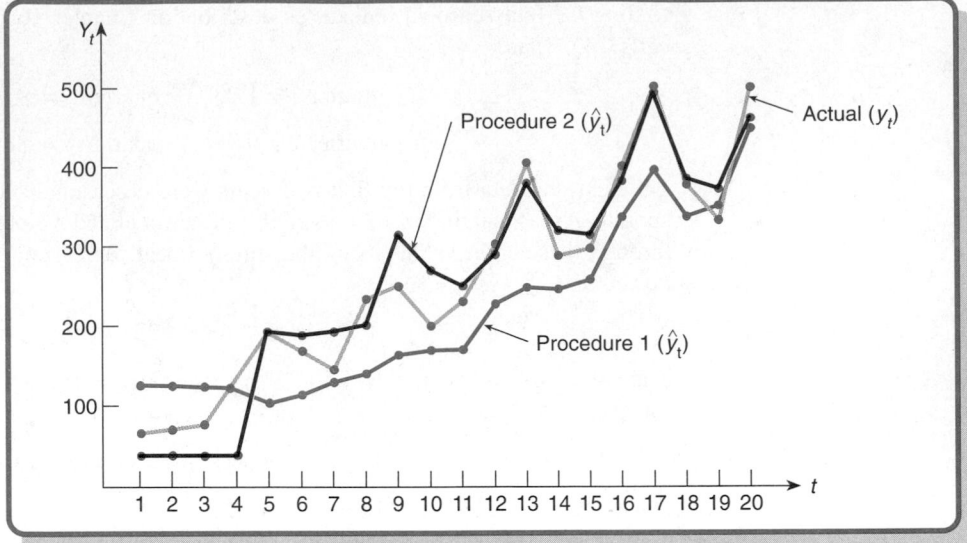

3. $F_{10} = .3\left(\dfrac{y_{10}}{S_{10}}\right) + .7 F_6$

    $= .3\left(\dfrac{190}{165.589}\right) + .7(1.053) = 1.081$

4. $b_{10} = .2(S_{10} - S_9) + .8 b_9$
    $= .2(165.589 - 158.342) + .8(5.589) = 5.921$

5. $\hat{y}_{10} = [S_9 + (1)(b_9)]F_6$ (from equation 17.11)
    $= (158.342 + 5.589)1.053$ (computer-stored value is 1.05256)
    $= 172.547$

6. Residual for $t = 10$ is: $y_{10} - \hat{y}_{10} = 190 - 172.547 = 17.453$

A graphical illustration of the actual observations, y_t, and the predicted value for each time period, $\hat{y}_t$, is shown in Figure 17.15. Once again, the more complex procedure 2 performed better than did procedure 1; for the last ten quarters, procedure 2 tracked the actual time series extremely well.

EXERCISES 17.21–17.26

UNDERSTANDING THE MECHANICS

17.21 The following values were used in the analysis of a time series data set with Winters' linear and seasonal smoothing technique.

$$b_8 = .8 \qquad F_{10} = .9$$

$$S_9 = 16 \qquad F_6 = .8$$

$$S_8 = 14 \qquad Y_{10} = 16$$

$$S_7 = 13 \qquad L = 4$$

a. Find the smoothed observation for time $t = 10$ with $A = .2$, $B = .1$, and $C = .1$.

b. Find the smoothed observation for time $t = 10$ with $A = .1$, $B = .3$, and $C = .3$.

APPLYING THE NEW CONCEPTS

17.22 Ektronics manufactures electronic testing and measuring instruments. The company has managed to capture a large share of the market over the past four years. Sales of its equipment (in ten thousands) are recorded monthly for 1996–1999.

Year	Jan	Feb	Mar	Apr	May	June
1996	1.0	1.1	1.2	1.7	1.9	2.3
1997	1.7	1.4	1.5	1.7	2.4	2.7
1998	1.9	2.0	2.1	2.3	3.1	3.5
1999	2.9	2.8	2.7	3.4	3.7	4.1

Year	Jul	Aug	Sep	Oct	Nov	Dec
1996	2.7	3.1	2.5	2.3	2.0	1.9
1997	3.3	3.9	3.4	3.0	2.6	2.0
1998	4.1	4.7	4.3	3.4	2.9	2.8
1999	4.6	5.0	4.7	4.0	3.7	3.6

Use Winters' linear and seasonal smoothing technique to find the smoothed values for the first four months of 1994. Let $A = .2$, $B = .1$, and $C = .1$. Using procedure 1, set the initial estimates of the seasonal factors to 1.0 and let $b_0 = 0$.

17.23 The earnings per share of Mecta Mining, a large producer of silver, are:

Year	Quarter 1	Quarter 2	Quarter 3	Quarter 4
1996	.25	.20	.27	.30
1997	.26	.24	.34	.37
1998	.30	.27	.38	.45
1999	.36	.32	.47	.50

Using the linear and seasonal exponential smoothing procedure, determine the predicted value for each quarter of 2000. Use procedure 2 and the first two years of data to obtain b_0, S_0, and the four initial seasonal factors (F). Let $A = .3$, $B = .2$, and $C = .1$.

17.24 To attract workers in a tight job market, employers have been spending more in terms of total compensation to employees. The government's broadest measure of compensation is the employment cost index. This index has been rising since 1995. One reason for the rise is health care. For example, health maintenance organizations have raised the premiums that employers pay. The following data represent the year-to-year percentage change in total employment compensation. Determine the predicted values for the first two quarters of 1999 by using Winters' linear and seasonal smoothing technique with procedure 2 and the first two years of data to obtain b_0, S_0, and the four initial seasonal factors. Let $A = .2$, $B = .3$, and $C = .3$.

Year	Quarter 1	Quarter 2	Quarter 3	Quarter 4
1995	3.2	3.0	2.9	3.0
1996	3.3	3.1	3.0	3.1
1997	3.4	3.2	3.1	3.2
1998	3.6	3.5	3.4	3.6

(Source: Adapted from *The Wall Street Journal*, "Compensation Costs Climb for Employers," July 31, 1998, p. A2.)

USING THE COMPUTER

17.25 [DATA SET EX17-25] *Variable description:*

Year: Year from 1994 through 1999
Quarter: Quarter represented by 1 through 4
Membership: Membership at the Fitness and Health Center
Value of smoothing constant A: .1
Value of smoothing constant B: .2
Value of smoothing constant C: .2

The membership at the Fitness and Health Center has increased over the past 6 years (1994–1999). The manager of the center is interested in knowing the forecasted membership for the first quarter of the year 2000. The information is important in deciding whether to open a new center. Find this forecast using Winters' linear and seasonal smoothing technique with procedure 1, setting the initial estimates of the seasonal factors to 1.0 and let $b_0 = 0$.

17.26 [DATA SET EX17-26] *Variable description:*

Year: Year from 1992 through 1999
Quarter: Quarter represented by 1 through 4
PriceSqFt: Average price per square foot to build a new home in Calgary, Canada
Value of smoothing constant A: .1
Value of smoothing constant B: .15
Value of smoothing constant C: .15

The average price per square foot to build a new home in Calgary, Canada, has fluctuated over the years. Quarterly data from 1992 to 1999 were collected. Find the forecasted values for the four quarters of the year 2000. This information is important to builders who are deciding on the number of new homes to build in the area. Use procedure 2 and the first two years of data to obtain b_0, S_0, and the four initial seasonal factors.

17.7 CHOOSING THE APPROPRIATE FORECASTING PROCEDURE

Our purpose in showing you several different forecasting techniques is to point out that, unfortunately, no one procedure works well all the time. One method may work well on a particular steadily increasing time series that has little random fluctuation but perform poorly on a series that has considerable seasonality or random fluctuation.

As you gain more experience in time series applications, you will be better able to choose an appropriate forecasting technique. One factor to consider is the length of your forecast. We classify the forecast period as

Short-term forecast: one to three months

Medium-range forecast: greater than three months but less than two years

Long-range forecast: two years or more

The exponential smoothing procedures are excellent for *short-term* forecasts, whereas the component decomposition method (in Section 17.3) is useful in medium- and long-range forecasting. The latter also is a popular procedure for many short-term applications, including inventory control and production planning.

One method of deciding whether a certain forecast technique is appropriate in a particular situation is to determine how well the procedure "fits" the observed time series. You accomplish this by pretending that, in each time period, the next observation is unknown and letting the forecasting procedure "predict" the next value (the $\hat{y}_t$ values in the previous examples). Next, you compare the predicted ($\hat{y}_t$) values with the observed values (y_t).

The three most popular methods of comparing the predicted and observed values use measures involving the residuals. These measures are the mean absolute deviation, the predictive mean squared error, and the mean absolute percentage error.

The **mean absolute deviation (MAD)** is the average of the absolute values of each residual. Let

$$e_t = \text{residual at time } t$$
$$= y_t - \hat{y}_t$$

The mean absolute deviation is defined as

$$\text{MAD} = \frac{\Sigma |e_t|}{n} \tag{17.12}$$

where n is the number of *predicted* values obtained from the past data. For example, when using linear exponential smoothing on 20 data values, you obtain 19 predicted values because $\hat{y}_1$ is unavailable, so n is 19 and not 20.

The **predictive mean squared error (MSE)** is similar to the MAD, except we find the average of the *squared* residuals.

$$\text{(predictive) MSE} = \frac{\Sigma e_t^2}{n} \tag{17.13}$$

where, again, n is the number of predicted values.*

The **mean absolute percentage error (MAPE)** considers the *relative* error of each forecast. The relative error at time period t is defined as e_t/y_t. The mean absolute percentage error is defined to be

$$\text{MAPE} = \frac{\Sigma \left| \dfrac{e_t}{y_t} \right|}{n} \tag{17.14}$$

where n is the number of predicted values.

If, during a particular time period, the actual value is $y_t = 50$ and the forecast value is $\hat{y}_t = 60$, the absolute percentage error is

$$\left| \frac{50 - 60}{50} \right| = .2$$

So, the error at this time period is 20% of the actual value. Consequently, for a particular time series, the MAPE is the sum of the absolute percentage error for each predicted value divided by the number of predicted values.

The MSE severely penalizes large residuals because it *squares* each value. Consequently, you use the MSE for situations in which you prefer several small residuals to one large value and wish to be warned if there is one larger residual. The primary advantage of using the MAPE is that it can be used to compare the predictive ability of a certain forecasting technique on two different time series. By using relative error, rather than actual error, the effect of the magnitude of the time series observations has been removed from the predictive measure.

---

* The MSE that we compute as a measure of how well a forecasting procedure fits the observed data is not the same as the MSE computed in a normal ANOVA table. The ANOVA MSE is equal to SSE/(degrees of freedom for residual). In contrast, the predictive MSE is not used in any test of hypothesis and is merely the average of the squared deviations.

TABLE 17.6

Comparison of the mean absolute deviation (MAD), the mean squared error (MSE), and the mean absolute percentage error (MAPE).

FORECAST	y_t	$\hat{y}_t$	$e_t = y_t - \hat{y}_t$	$\lvert e_t \rvert$	e_t^2	$\left\lvert \dfrac{e_t}{y_t} \right\rvert$
Method 1	36	32	4	4	16	.111
	42	46	−4	4	16	.095
	45	49	−4	4	16	.089
				12	48	.295

MAD = 12/3 = 4.0
MSE = 48/3 = 16.0
MAPE = .295/3 = .098

FORECAST	y_t	$\hat{y}_t$	$e_t = y_t - \hat{y}_t$	$\lvert e_t \rvert$	e_t^2	$\left\lvert \dfrac{e_t}{y_t} \right\rvert$
Method 2	36	34	2	2	4	.056
	42	40	2	2	4	.048
	45	52	−7	7	49	.156
				11	57	.260

MAD = 11/3 = 3.67
MSE = 57/3 = 19.0
MAPE = .260/3 = .087

To illustrate these measures, consider Table 17.6. For forecasting method 1, there are no large residuals, whereas method 2 results in one large residual. So the MSE is smaller for method 1, but the MAD is smaller for method 2. When using any of these measures, the *smaller* the value, the *more accurate* your forecast procedure.

There is no concensus among statisticians as to which measure is preferable. Instead, it depends on the results of having large forecast residuals. If a large error is disastrous (such as in predicting the inventory level of an expensive product), then using the MSE is preferable. On the other hand, if you can afford to overlook a single severe miss provided the general tracking is close, then the MAD serves better. When comparing the predictive accuracy of two different time series, the MAPE is the appropriate measure.

When using the KGP Data Analysis tools within Excel, the resulting spreadsheet will contain the corresponding MSE, MAD, and MAPE. To avoid any possible confusion, these values were not shown in the previous Excel solutions (Figures 17.4, 17.7, 17.10, 17.12, and 17.14). If you use Excel on the previous examples, you will see these three measures at the bottom of your spreadsheet.

EXAMPLE 17.7

We used two types of exponential smoothing to smooth (and predict) the city taxes collected in Jackson City over the past five years. Data from the past 20 quarters are contained in the table in Example 17.5, in which we used linear exponential smoothing (with smoothing constants $A = .1$ and $B = .3$) to reduce randomness within the observations and trend values. The results are summarized in Table 17.3 and Figure 17.12, using the two procedures for providing initial estimates.

Example 17.6 examined the same data using linear and seasonal exponential smoothing, with smoothing constants $A = .1$, $B = .3$, and $C = .2$. A much better fit was obtained using the more sophisticated method of providing initial smoothed estimates (procedure 2). These results are summarized in Tables 17.5 and Figure 17.14 and are presented graphically in Figure 17.15.

Determine the predictive MSE for each of these four methods. Using the appropriate procedure, determine the forecasted tax revenue for each quarter of 1999.

SOLUTION

1. *Linear exponential smoothing (procedure 1).* The residuals from this forecasting procedure are contained in Table 17.3. The computed predictive mean squared error is

$$\text{MSE} = \frac{(17.000)^2 + (29.790)^2 + \cdots + (56.183)^2}{19} = 5670.08$$

2. *Linear exponential smoothing (procedure 2).* Based on Figures 17.12 and 17.13, we would expect a much smaller predictive MSE here. There are no surprises, because

$$\text{MSE} = \frac{(-10.500)^2 + (-21.635)^2 + \cdots + (61.800)^2}{19} = 3426.50$$

3. *Linear and seasonal exponential smoothing (procedure 1).* These residuals are listed in Table 17.5, with a corresponding predictive mean squared error of

$$\text{MSE} = \frac{(-52.000)^2 + (-35.000)^2 + \cdots + (52.107)^2}{20} = 4414.91$$

(Note that we divide by 20 here because 20 predicted values are available using this procedure.)

A warning: It is not valid to conclude, based on the large MSE value, that this forecasting method is less appropriate than linear exponential smoothing. Remember that we are at the mercy of the particular values of the smoothing constants, A, B, and C. Perhaps a different set of constants would have resulted in a significantly smaller MSE. Finding the best set of constants for any one application involves finding the set of values for A, B, and C that *minimize* the resulting predictive MSE. This (not insignificant) computational burden is one of the drawbacks of using Holt's and Winters' exponential smoothing techniques.

4. *Linear and seasonal exponential smoothing (procedure 2).* In Figures 17.14 and 17.15, we observed excellent agreement between the actual time series, y_t, and the predicted series, $\hat{y}_t$, using the smoothed estimates. A very small predictive MSE value would be expected here, and such is the case:

$$\text{MSE} = \frac{(37.500)^2 + (54.500)^2 + \cdots + (48.665)^2}{20} = 1849.80$$

We conclude that the best choice of these four alternatives is the linear and seasonal exponential smoothing method using procedure 2 to derive the original estimates.

5. *Forecasted tax revenue.* Using equation 17.11 and the results in Figure 17.14, the forecasts for 1999 would be as follows. For the first quarter (one step ahead): $t = 20$, $L = 4$, $m = 1$, and

$$\hat{y}_{21} = [S_{20} + (1)b_{20}] \cdot F_{17}$$
$$= [464.654 + (1)(20.752)](1.197) = 581$$

For the second quarter (two steps ahead): $t = 20$, $L = 4$, $m = 2$, and

$$\hat{y}_{22} = [S_{20} + (2)b_{20}] \cdot F_{18}$$
$$= [464.654 + (2)(20.752)] \cdot (.894) = 453$$

For the third quarter (three steps ahead): $t = 20$, $L = 4$, $m = 3$, and

$$\hat{y}_{23} = [S_{20} + (3)b_{20}] \cdot F_{19}$$
$$= [464.654 + (3)(20.752)](.809) = 426$$

For the fourth quarter (four steps ahead): $t = 20$, $L = 4$, $m = 4$, and

$$\hat{y}_{24} = [S_{20} + (4)b_{20}] \cdot F_{20}$$
$$= [464.654 + (4)(20.752)] \cdot (1.003) = 549$$

SELECTING THE SMOOTHING CONSTANTS

As mentioned earlier, the computed MSE (or MAD or MAPE) value for any exponential smoothing procedure is determined not only by the procedure itself but also by the value of the necessary smoothing constants. In Example 17.6, the smoothing constants were $A = .1$, $B = .3$, and $C = .2$, with a corresponding MSE value of 1849.80, using procedure 2. By changing these constants, you might improve the fit (lower the MSE), or you might obtain a less desirable solution (a larger MSE).

To illustrate this point, using Example 17.6 and procedure 2, for

$$A = .1, B = .4, C = .3: \qquad \text{MSE} = 1767.94 \text{ (an improvement)}$$

$$A = .2, B = .2, C = .2: \qquad \text{MSE} = 2145.64$$

To arrive at the smallest possible predictive MSE, you must examine a variety of values, compute the MSE for each combination, and select the set of values that provides the smallest MSE. For example, if you consider all nonzero values of A, B, and C between 0 and 1, in increments of .05, you will need $(1/.05)^3 = 20^3 = 8,000$ different passes through the procedure to determine the corresponding 8,000 MSE values. The set of A, B, and C values that provides the smallest MSE is the one you should use in forecasting future values of the time series.

When using the KGP Data Analysis tools within Excel, you will have the option of specifying the smoothing constants or letting Excel determine the optimal smoothing constants. If you elect to use the latter procedure, you will be asked whether you want the smoothing constants that provide the minimum MAD, minimum MSE, or minimum MAPE. This Excel routine falls under the category of **automated forecasting procedures.** By selecting this option, Excel will determine the optimal smoothing constants by searching in increments of .05. For Example 17.6 using linear and seasonal exponential smoothing (Winters' method) and procedure 2, the optimal smoothing constants are $A = .1$, $B = .6$, and $C = 0$. The smoothing constant for the trend values (B) is rather large for this illustration; however, this set of smoothing constants does provide a minimum MSE of 1682.06. As a final word here: by utilizing optimal smoothing constants, you can drastically simplify the calculations necessary to fit a model to your time series. On the negative side, however, such a "black box" procedure implies that you sacrifice some control and knowledge of the fitting process.

Determining and using optimal smoothing constants does take away one main advantage of exponential smoothing—namely, the computational simplicity of this procedure in calculating and updating smoothed estimates. If you are using this method to perform a small number of forecasts, then this poses no problem. On the other hand, if the technique is being used to forecast future demand levels continuously for thousands of inventory items, then this added complexity is a cause for concern. You will have to consider complexity versus cost on an individual application basis.

You can increase the computational burden (but also improve the accuracy) even more by using different values of the smoothing constant(s) at different times in the analysis of a time series. Such techniques are computer controlled. The constant(s) are changed automatically to adapt the process to shifts in the structure of the time series, using **adaptive control procedures.**

We showed you several forecasting procedures and methods for comparing the predictive accuracy of these techniques. Our purpose is to give you an arsenal of methodologies that will allow you to apply each procedure to a particular time series and then summarize and compare the resulting residuals. In this way, you can determine the most accurate procedure for a particular time series and use this method to arrive at a forecast.

Next we turn to another forecasting model, the autoregressive model. With this procedure, we again use the past observations to predict future values but in a slightly different way: we use the past values as variables in a regression equation.

EXERCISES 17.27–17.34

UNDERSTANDING THE MECHANICS

17.27 Consider the following data and their forecasts.

Year	Actual	Forecast
1990	10	—
1991	11	10
1992	14	12
1993	18	15
1994	22	17
1995	20	19
1996	19	21
1997	24	23
1998	26	24
1999	40	28

a. Compute the MAD, MAPE, and MSE for these forecasts.

b. Eliminate the data for year 1999. Then recompute the MAD, MAPE, and MSE.

c. Compare the MAD, MAPE, and MSE values in parts (a) and (b).

17.28 The following monthly data were collected. Using the naive model, find the MAD, MAPE, and predictive MSE.

Year	Jan	Feb	Mar	Apr	May	Jun
1996	1	2	2	3	3	4
1997	3	4	4	5	4	6
1998	5	6	7	7	7	6
1999	7	8	8	10	9	11

Year	Jul	Aug	Sep	Oct	Nov	Dec
1996	5	5	6	5	5	4
1997	7	8	10	9	9	8
1998	7	8	9	12	11	10
1999	12	14	14	12	13	11

17.29 Two forecasting procedures produce the following sets of forecast errors:

Year	Month	Procedure 1	Procedure 2
1998	Jan	+5	+1
	Feb	+7	−2
	Mar	+6	+3
	Apr	+2	−1
	May	−1	+2
	June	−2	0
	July	−3	+1
	Aug	+2	+1
	Sept	+4	0
	Oct	+7	−1
	Nov	+6	+2
	Dec	+1	+1
1999	Jan	−3	−3
	Feb	−5	+1
	Mar	−4	0
	Apr	+3	−2
	May	+2	−19
	June	−1	−20

Compute the MAD and predictive MSE for each forecasting procedure. Comment on the adequacy of the forecasting procedure.

APPLYING THE NEW CONCEPTS

17.30 The following data represent the number of single-family housing starts in a certain sector of the state of California. The units are in 10,000s.

Year	Quarter 1	Quarter 2	Quarter 3	Quarter 4
1996	.6	.8	1.4	.8
1997	.9	1.1	1.7	1.3
1998	1.2	1.4	2.1	1.6
1999	1.4	1.7	2.6	1.9

a. Using the simple exponential procedure with $A = .3$, find the predicted number of housing starts for each time period, omitting the first time period. Find the predictive MSE and MAD.

b. Use Holt's two-parameter linear exponential smoothing technique to obtain a forecast for each time period, omitting the first time period. Let $A = .3$ and $B = .2$. Use the least squares estimate of the slope from the first five periods for the initial value of the slope. Find the predictive MSE and MAD.

c. Compare the forecasts obtained in parts (a) and (b).

17.31 An investor who invested $10,000 into the T. Krow long-term-growth mutual fund would have realized a gain of 93% after five years. The following table shows the value of the $10,000 investment over this period of time.

Year	Quarter 1	Quarter 2	Quarter 3	Quarter 4
1995	10,031	9,638	12,591	12,480
1996	12,691	11,745	13,721	13,980
1997	13,043	12,680	15,376	15,860
1998	14,932	14,280	17,035	17,210
1999	16,830	15,923	18,671	19,300

a. Use Winters' linear and seasonal smoothing technique to find the forecasted value of the original $10,000 invested for each of the quarters of 1997, 1998, and 1999. Let $A = .2$, $B = .1$, and $C = .1$. Using procedure 1 and Winters' technique, set the initial estimates of the seasonal factors to 1.0 and $b_0 = 0$. Find the predictive MSE.

b. Redo question (a) with $A = .1$, $B = .2$, and $C = .2$. Find the predictive MSE.

c. Compare the forecasts from parts (a) and (b) using the predictive MSEs.

17.32 Explain how the MAD, MAPE, and the predictive MSE differ in what they measure. Why should the sum of the forecast errors divided by the number of forecasts not be used to compare two forecasting procedures?

USING THE COMPUTER

17.33 [DATA SET EX17-33] *Variable description:*

Year: Year from 1993 through 1999
Quarter: Quarter represented by 1 through 4
AirTripCost: Cost in dollars for a round trip ticket between Seattle and Albuquerque
Value of smoothing constant A: .22
Value of smoothing constant B: .12
Value of smoothing constant C: .10

The cost of a round-trip airline ticket on Sunset Airlines is recorded for each quarter over the years 1993 through 1999. Use Winters' technique to find smoothed values for each of the quarters of 1998 and 1999. This information is important to companies planning their travel budget for the upcoming year. Use procedure 2 and the first two years of data to obtain b_0, S_0, and the four initial seasonal factors. Find the MAPE using this procedure and determine the quarterly forecast of the airfares for the year 2000.

17.34 [DATA SET EX17-34] *Variable description:*

Year: Year from 1992 through 1999
Quarter: Quarter represented by 1 through 4
SubNewsletter: Number of subscriptions to stock market newsletter

Value of smoothing constant *A*: .25
Value of smoothing constant *B*: .22
Value of smoothing constant *C*: .25

The number of subscribers to a stock market investment newsletter has fluctuated over the years. Data on the number of subscriptions for each quarter of the years 1992 through 1999 are collected. The editor of the newsletter will use this information to decide on the future price of the newsletter. For the given smoothing constants, find the predictive MSE using Winters' linear and seasonal exponential smoothing technique. Use Winters' technique with procedure 1, setting the initial estimates of the seasonal factors to 1.0 and let $b_0 = 0$ to find smoothed values for each of the quarters of 1998 and 1999. Change the values of *A*, *B*, and *C* to .10, .05, and .05, respectively. Compare the predictive MSEs for the two sets of smoothing constants.

17.8
AUTOREGRESSIVE FORECASTING TECHNIQUES

So far, the forecasting procedures have used either a member of the exponential smoothing family or the method of time series decomposition. The exponential smoothing technique greatly reduces the randomness (irregular activity) within the observed time series, as well as smoothing any existing trend or seasonal effects.

For the case of simple exponential smoothing, the forecast for the next time period ($\hat{y}_{t+1}$) is the smoothed value for the current period (S_t). When you use the other exponential smoothing procedures, your forecast includes the effect of the smoothed seasonality or trend.

The time series decomposition method determines the various components in each observation, including seasonality, trend, cycles, and random activity. Forecasts are derived by extending the trend and seasonal components into the future. Unlike exponential smoothing, this method can provide reliable long-range forecasts. Naturally, the longer this forecast period is, the less reliable your forecasted value becomes.

This section examines yet another method of forecasting, a method that can be used when the time series variable is related to past values of itself. By regressing y_t on some combination of its past values, we are able to derive a forecasting equation. So we return to multiple linear regression, except now the dependent variable is y_t, and the predictor variables are the past values, $y_{t-1}, y_{t-2}, \ldots$. This forecasting technique is **autoregression;** we are essentially regressing the time series variable on itself.

We can expect the autoregressive forecast technique to perform reasonably well for a time series that (1) is not extremely volatile and does not contain extreme amounts of random movement and (2) requires a short-term or medium-range forecast (that is, less than two years). The fact that the autoregressive procedure does not perform well on a time series containing a great deal of irregular activity is not a serious disadvantage; practically all forecasting techniques perform poorly in this situation.

Suppose we attempt to predict the values of y_t using the previous two observations. The prediction equation is

$$\hat{y}_t = b_0 + b_1 y_{t-1} + b_2 y_{t-2} \qquad t = 3, 4, 5, \ldots \qquad (17.15)$$

The values of b_0, b_1, and b_2 are the least squares regression estimates, obtained from any multiple linear regression computer package. There are two predictor variables here: the **lagged variables,** y_{t-1} and y_{t-2}. Equation 17.15 is a **second-order** autoregressive equation because it uses the first two lagged terms. In general, a *p*th-order autoregressive equation is written

$$\hat{y}_t = b_0 + b_1 y_{t-1} + b_2 y_{t-2} + \cdots + b_p y_{t-p}$$

$$t = p + 1, p + 2, \ldots \qquad (17.16)$$

TABLE 17.7   Input for the second-order autoregresive predictor.

y_t	y_{t-1}	y_{t-2}
60	—	—
62.25	60	—
61.75	62.25	60
63	61.75	62.25
64.5	63	61.75
62	64.5	63
63.5	62	64.5
64	63.5	62
63.25	64	63.5
62.5	63.25	64
61	62.5	63.25
61.5	61	62.5

We illustrate the computer-input procedure for the second-order equation with an example. Earlier, we used the naive forecasting procedure (forecast for tomorrow is the observed value for today) to predict the closing price of Keller Toy company stock. The closing prices for a 12-week period are shown on page 812, and the predicted values are summarized in Figure 17.4.

Suppose we use the second-order autoregressive equation (17.15) to predict these values. The input data required by the linear regression routine consist of the actual time series data and the two columns of lagged data, as illustrated in Table 17.7. The 10 input rows are below the horizontal line. Notice that we lose the first two observations due to the missing values for the lagged variables. If these data are available from the two weeks prior to week 1, they can be used to fill in the missing values, providing 12 rows of data.

A computer solution to this problem using Excel is in Figure 17.16. To obtain this solution, enter the 12 prices in column A. Copy and paste the first 11 values in column B (cells B2:B12), as shown in Figure 17.16. Copy and paste the first 10 values into column C (cells C3:C12). Click on **Tools ➤ Data Analysis ➤ Regression** and enter "A3:A12" as the **Input Y Range** and "B3:C12" as the **Input X Range.** The resulting prediction equation using the highlighted cells is

$$\hat{y}_t = 45.5 + .278y_{t-1} - .004y_{t-2}$$

Also, $R^2 = .068$, indicating that the two lagged variables account for only 7% of the total variation in the 10 time series values used as input (y_3 through y_{12}).

To determine whether this is the best way to forecast a particular time series, we can use the procedure discussed in the previous section. This involves calculating an MSE (or MAPE or MAD), using the autoregressive technique on the past observations and comparing this MSE with the MSE using other forecasting methods. For example, we obtain an improvement over the naive forecasting procedure here because, using Figure 17.16, the SSE value in cell F13 is 10.926 and the

$$\text{(predictive) MSE} = \frac{10.926}{10} = 1.09 \text{ (for autoregressive forecaster)}$$

From Figure 17.4,

$$\text{(predictive) MSE} = \frac{(2.25)^2 + (-.5)^2 + \cdots + (.5)^2}{11} = \frac{21.5}{11}$$

$$= 1.95 \text{ (for naive forecaster)}$$

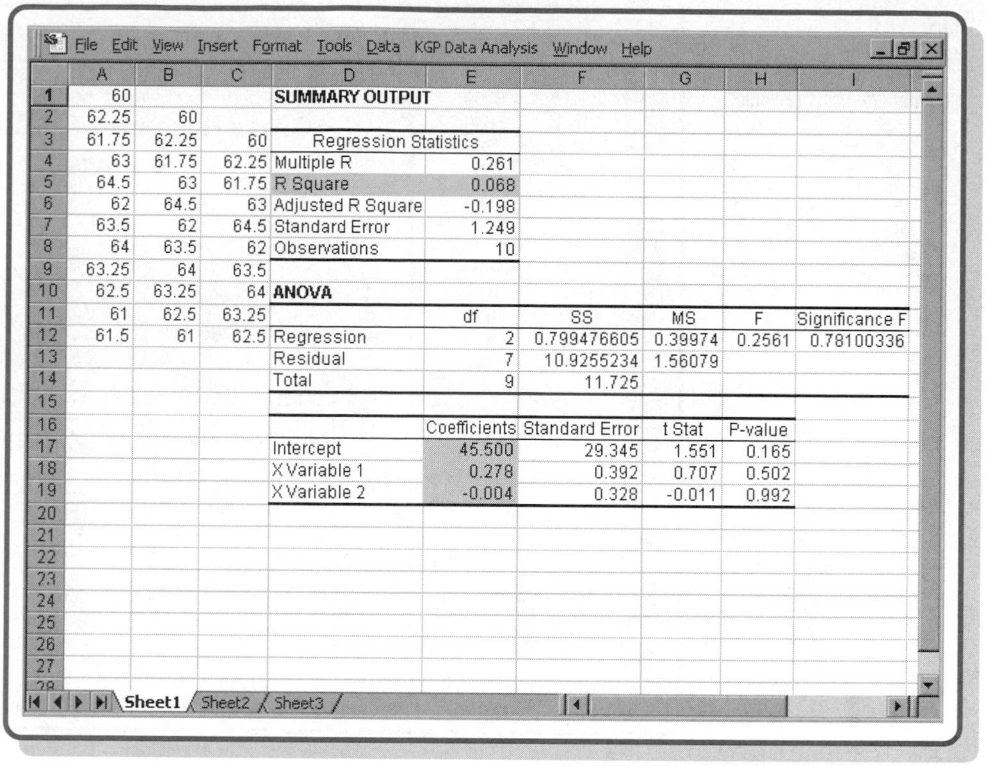

	A	B	C	D	E	F	G	H	I
1	60			**SUMMARY OUTPUT**					
2	62.25	60							
3	61.75	62.25	60	Regression Statistics					
4	63	61.75	62.25	Multiple R	0.261				
5	64.5	63	61.75	R Square	0.068				
6	62	64.5	63	Adjusted R Square	-0.198				
7	63.5	62	64.5	Standard Error	1.249				
8	64	63.5	62	Observations	10				
9	63.25	64	63.5						
10	62.5	63.25	64	**ANOVA**					
11	61	62.5	63.25		df	SS	MS	F	Significance F
12	61.5	61	62.5	Regression	2	0.799476605	0.39974	0.2561	0.78100336
13				Residual	7	10.9255234	1.56079		
14				Total	9	11.725			
15									
16					Coefficients	Standard Error	t Stat	P-value	
17				Intercept	45.500	29.345	1.551	0.165	
18				X Variable 1	0.278	0.392	0.707	0.502	
19				X Variable 2	-0.004	0.328	-0.011	0.992	

FIGURE 17.16
Excel solution for second-order autoregression.

So, despite the low value of R^2, we obtain a better fit to the observed data using the second-order autoregressive technique. This value of R^2, however, does indicate that the search for a more accurate forecasting procedure should continue.

MICROSOFT® EXCEL APPLICATION — USE DATA17-8

EXAMPLE 17.8
A Forecasting Analysis Using Excel

An analyst with Fulton Financial Services is interested in forecasting the annual gross revenues for the Coca Cola Company for 1997 using annual data from the past 15 years (1982–1996). These data (in millions of dollars) are contained in dataset DATA17-8 and are graphed in Figure 17.17.

To obtain the time series graph in Figure 17.17, click on the **Chart Wizard** icon and select **XY** (**Scatter**). Select the graph whose description is **Scatter with Data Points Connected by Lines** and click on **Next.** Click on the **Titles** tab and fill in the appropriate boxes using the titles in Figure 17.17. Once you have the graph on your spreadsheet, you can resize it by dragging any of the square boxes (handles) around the graph border. Also, you can begin the vertical axis at 5000 by right clicking on this axis, selecting **Format Axis,** clicking on the **Minimum** box, and entering "5000."

The analyst has decided to examine six different forecasting equations:

Equation A: The naive method ($\hat{y}_t = y_{t-1}$)

Equation B: Linear trend ($\hat{y}_t = b_0 + b_1 t$)

Equation C: Linear and quadratic trend ($\hat{y}_t = b_0 + b_1 t + b_2 t^2$)

Equation D: First order autoregressive ($\hat{y}_t = b_0 + b_1 y_{t-1}$)

Equation E: Simple exponential smoothing (optimal smoothing constant)

Equation F: Linear exponential smoothing (optimal smoothing constants)

FIGURE 17.17

Excel time series plot of Coca-Cola Company gross revenues.

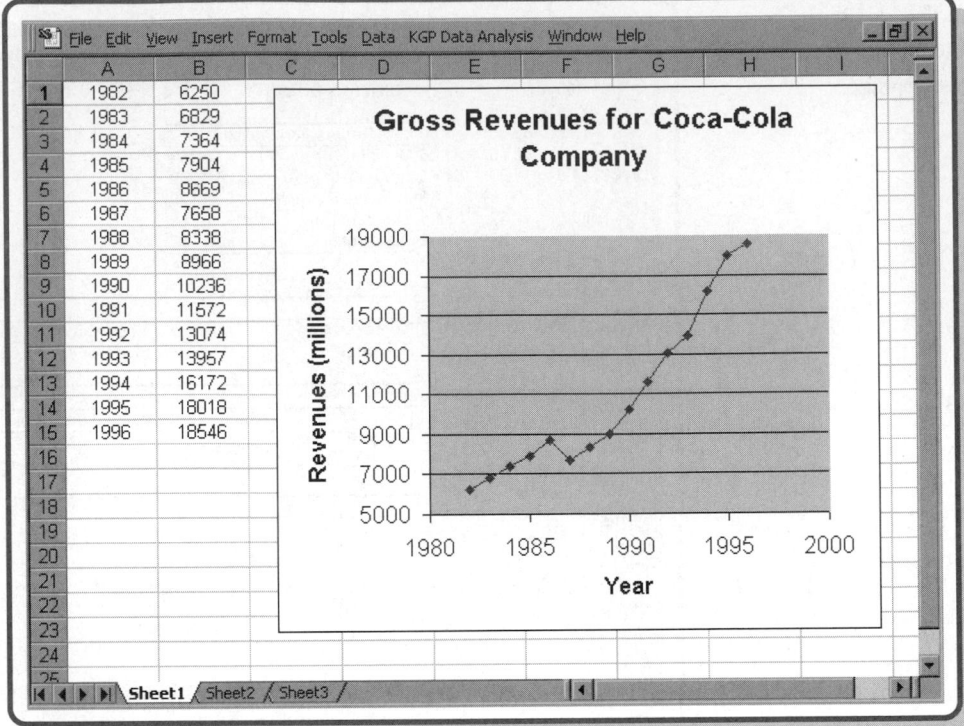

TABLE 17.8

Excel steps and results for six forecasting procedures using KGP Data Analysis (Example 17.8).

Equation	Click On	Select/Enter	MAD
A	Naive		1022.7
B	Trend Only	Linear	1151.2
C	Trend Only	Linear and Quadratic	464.0
D	Autogressive	1 = Number of Lagged Variables	454.3
		1 = Lag Period	
E	Simple Exponential Smoothing	Optimal Smoothing Constant	1022.7
		Minimize MAD	
F	Holt's Exponential Smoothing	Procedure 2	542.1
		Optimal Smoothing Constants	
		Minimize MAD	

The analyst decided to use the mean absolute deviation (MAD) as a measure of the predictive accuracy, since he did not want one or two large residuals to have a dramatic effect on this measure. Using each of these forecasting equations, determine which method provides the minimum MAD value and use this equation to forecast the gross revenues for 1997.

SOLUTION

When you click on **KGP Data Analysis ➤ Time Series Analysis ➤ Forecasting,** you will see the screen in Figure 17.3. For each option, you can enter "1" as the number of forecast periods, "B1:B15" as the **Input Range,** and "C1" as the **Output Range.** For each forecast procedure, use the instructions in Table 17.8.

CONCLUSION

Because of the underlying trend in the data, it is not surprising that the naive and simple exponential smoothing methods performed poorly. The minimum MAD is obtained using the first-order autoregressive procedure (equation D). From the Excel output using this method, the prediction equation is $\hat{y}_t = -63.205 + 1.0909 y_{t-1}$, and so the 1997 forecast is

$$\hat{y}_{16} = -63.205 + 1.0909(18{,}546)$$

$$= 20{,}168.6 \text{ (million dollars)}$$

The MAD using the linear and trend equation (equation C) was a very close second for this particular time series. From the Excel solution using this procedure, the forecast for 1997 is 21,027.7, about 4% higher than the autoregressive forecast. Both methods predict roughly a 10% increase in revenues from 1996 to 1997.

ESTIMATING AUTOCORRELATIONS

There are several methods of calculating the correlation between a time series, y_t, and its past values. For example, in Table 17.7,

y_t	y_{t-1}	y_{t-2}
61.75	62.25	60
63	61.75	62.25
⋮	⋮	⋮
61.5	61	62.5

To find the correlation between y_t and y_{t-1}, we could use the equation for the sample correlation coefficient, r, defined in Chapter 14. We could also find the correlation between y_t and y_{t-2} using the same procedure. However, the generally accepted method of computing such correlations is to use equation 17.17.

$$r_k = \frac{\sum_{t=1}^{T-k}(y_t - \bar{y})(y_{t+k} - \bar{y})}{\sum_{t=1}^{T}(y_t - \bar{y})^2} \tag{17.17}$$

where (1) k is the lag under consideration, (2) r_k is the **sample autocorrelation** for lag k, (3) $\bar{y}$ is the average of the observed time series—that is,

$$\bar{y} = \frac{1}{T}\sum_{t=1}^{T} y_t$$

and (4) T is the number of observations in the time series.

There are three points to remember about the formula in equation 17.17:

1. The value of r_k using this formula will not agree with the value obtained using the correlation formula for r from Chapter 14, particularly for small sample sizes.
2. This formula is computationally more efficient.
3. This formula helps identify a time series that is not stationary.

EXAMPLE 17.9

Determine r_1 and r_2 using the following time series:

t	y_t
1	5
2	12
3	20
4	15
5	13

SOLUTION

Here $T = 5$ and

$$\bar{y} = \frac{1}{5}(5 + 12 + 20 + 15 + 13) = 13$$

Consequently, r_1 (correlation between y_t and y_{t-1})

$$= \frac{(y_1 - \bar{y})(y_2 - \bar{y}) + (y_2 - \bar{y})(y_3 - \bar{y}) + (y_3 - \bar{y})(y_4 - \bar{y}) + (y_4 - \bar{y})(y_5 - \bar{y})}{(y_1 - \bar{y})^2 + (y_2 - \bar{y})^2 + \cdots + (y_5 - \bar{y})^2}$$

$$= \frac{(-8)(-1) + (-1)(7) + (7)(2) + (2)(0)}{(-8)^2 + (-1)^2 + (7)^2 + (2)^2 + (0)^2} = \frac{15}{118} = .13$$

Also,

$$r_2 = \frac{(y_1 - \bar{y})(y_3 - \bar{y}) + (y_2 - \bar{y})(y_4 - \bar{y}) + (y_3 - \bar{y})(y_5 - \bar{y})}{118}$$

$$= \frac{(-8)(7) + (-1)(2) + (7)(0)}{118} = \frac{-58}{118} = -.49$$

A graphical representation of these autocorrelations is a **correlogram.** The correlogram for Example 17.9 contains the values of r_1 and r_2, as illustrated in Figure 17.18. By inspecting a correlogram, you can determine which lagged variables appear to contribute to the prediction of your time series variable. *The autoregressive equation includes those lagged variables for which the corresponding autocorrelation is large in absolute value.* Statistical procedures for identifying significantly large autocorrelations are discussed in Bowerman and O'Connell (1993), and also in Makridakis, Wheelwright, and Hyndman (1997) (see Further Reading at the end of the chapter).

DETECTING SEASONALITY

The autoregressive forecasting approach does allow you to detect seasonality in your time series data. If seasonality is present in quarterly data, we expect a significant positive correlation between y_t and t_{t-4}, that is, r_4 will be large, implying that the y value of one year ago is a good predictor of the y value today. Similarly, for monthly data, we can expect r_{12} to be large if there is significant seasonality.

FIGURE 17.18
Correlogram for
Example 17.9.

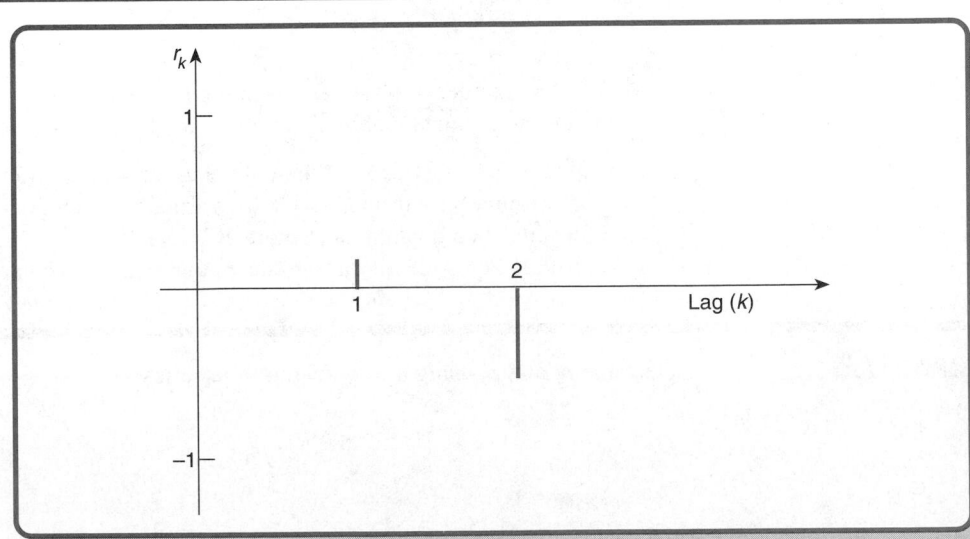

EXAMPLE 17.10

Table 17.9 contains data for the quarterly profits from Ken's Auto Paint Shop. Which lagged variables appear to be correlated with y_t = profit during time period t?

SOLUTION

The Excel output for the autocorrelation equation (17.17) is shown in Figure 17.19. Here the *autocorrelation function* computes the first $10 + \sqrt{T}$ autocorrelations, where T (20 here) is the number of observations in the time series. If $10 + \sqrt{T}$ is not an integer, it is rounded *down* to the nearest integer, which is 14 in this case. To obtain the results in Figure 17.19, click on **KGP Data Analysis ➤ Time Series Analysis ➤ Autocorrelations** and enter "A1:A20" as the **Input Range** and "B1" as the **Output Range.**

The seasonality pattern of four-quarter duration can be seen from the resulting auto-correlations in Figure 17.19. The large r_k values are $r_4 = .678$, $r_8 = .512$, and $r_{12} = .388$. Notice that $r_4 > r_8 > r_{12}$, which is typical of strong four-period seasonality. The large value of r_4 is your clue that such seasonality exists, and the large values of r_8 and r_{12} confirm this suspicion.

Using y_{t-4} as the predictor variable, the resulting autoregression equation is contained in Figure 17.20. To obtain this Excel solution, click on **KGP Data Analysis ➤ Time Series Analysis ➤ Forecasting** and select the **Autoregressive** option. Enter "0" as the

TABLE 17.9

Quarterly profits of Ken's Auto Paint Shop (in thousands of dollars).

Quarter	1994	1995	1996	1997	1998
Spring	5.56	5.11	4.12	6.31	4.81
Summer	16.36	15.21	14.33	15.02	16.82
Fall	2.12	5.72	5.25	2.83	4.75
Winter	3.15	2.65	6.75	4.56	8.54

FIGURE 17.19

Excel autocorrelations for Example 17.10 using KGP Data Analysis.

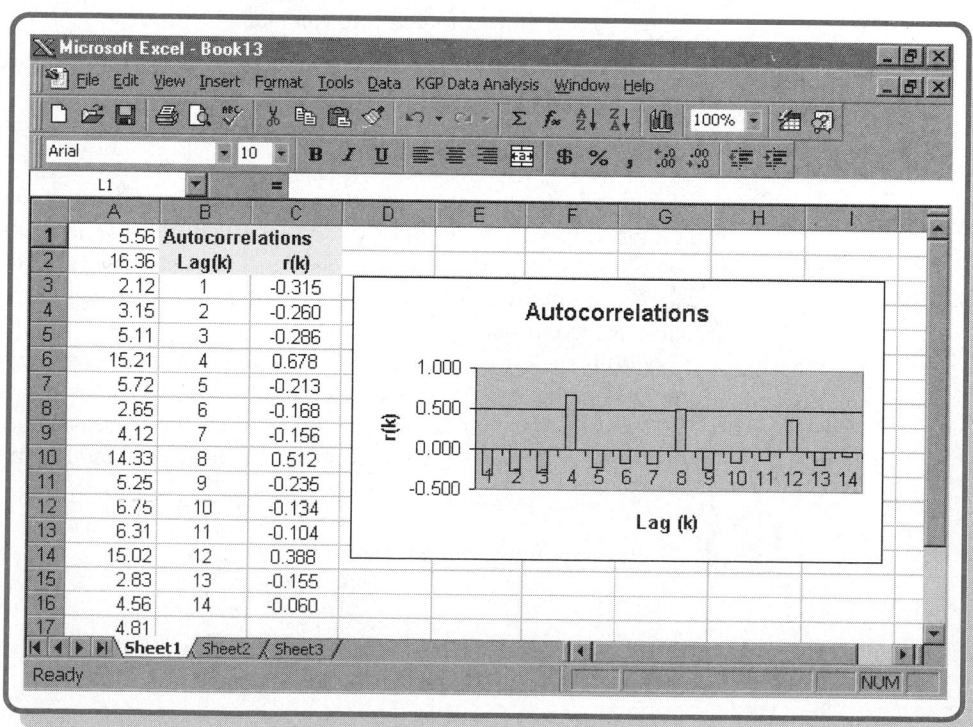

FIGURE 17.20
Excel solution for
Example 17.10 using
KGP Data Analysis.

	A	B	C	D	E	F	G	H	I	J	K
							File Edit View Insert Format Tools Data KGP Data Analysis Window Help				
1	5.56	**Autoregressive Model**									
2	16.36	T	Y(T)	YHAT	RESIDUAL		Lag	Coef.			
3	2.12	1	5.56				Constant	1.420			
4	3.15	2	16.36				4	0.870			
5	5.11	3	2.12								
6	15.21	4	3.15								
7	5.72	5	5.11	6.256	-1.146						
8	2.65	6	15.21	15.649	-0.439						
9	4.12	7	5.72	3.264	2.456						
10	14.33	8	2.65	4.159	-1.509						
11	5.25	9	4.12	5.864	-1.744						
12	6.75	10	14.33	14.648	-0.318						
13	6.31	11	5.25	6.395	-1.145						
14	15.02	12	6.75	3.725	3.025						
15	2.83	13	6.31	5.003	1.307						
16	4.56	14	15.02	13.883	1.137						
17	4.81	15	2.83	5.986	-3.156						
18	16.82	16	4.56	7.291	-2.731						
19	4.75	17	4.81	6.908	-2.098						
20	8.54	18	16.82	14.483	2.337						
21		19	4.75	3.881	0.869						
22		20	8.54	5.386	3.154						
23											
24		Forecasts									
25											
26		MSE	4.025								
27		MAD	1.786								
28		MAPE	34.300								
29											
30											

Sheet1 / Sheet2 / Sheet3 /

Number of Forecast Periods, "A1:A20" as the **Input Range,** and "B1" as the **Output Range.** In the next screen, enter "1" as the **Number of Lagged Predictor Variables** and "4" as the **Lag Period.** The resulting equation from Figure 17.20 is

$$\hat{y}_t = 1.420 + .870 y_{t-4}$$

The corresponding predictive MSE in cell C26 is 4.025. To decide whether this procedure performs well for this time series, we need to compare this MSE with the MSE obtained using other forecasting techniques.

REMOVING NONSTATIONARITY

The autoregressive procedures discussed so far are effective if the time series is *stationary*— that is, if it contains no trend and has constant variance about the mean, $\bar{y}$. One method of detecting nonstationarity in a time series is to examine the correlogram. *If you notice that the autocorrelations in the correlogram do not die down rapidly* (*say after the second or third lag*), *then your time series is* not stationary.

With such a time series, an autoregressive procedure is *not appropriate,* unless you modify the time series to make it more stationary. That is, the data should be transformed to a stationary series before attempting to determine seasonality. This can be achieved by using the **differencing** method, which replaces y_t by the first difference, defined by

$$y_t' = y_t - y_{t-1}$$

To illustrate this technique, consider the series

$$2, 5, 8, 11, 14, \ldots$$

This series clearly contains a linear trend; each value is three more than the preceding value. The first differences are

$$y'_2 = 5 - 2 = 3$$

$$y'_3 = 8 - 5 = 3$$

$$y'_4 = 11 - 8 = 3$$

$$y'_5 = 14 - 11 = 3$$

and so on. These values contain no trend, and so the resulting series of first differences is stationary.

If this procedure has been successful in producing a stationary time series, the resulting correlogram (using the y'_t values) should die out quickly. If such is not the case, using the *second* differences of the original time series values ($y_1, y_2, \ldots, y_T$) often will produce a stationary series. Here, the second differences can be found by deriving the first differences of the y'_t values, namely,

$$y''_t = y'_t - y'_{t-1} = y_t - 2y_{t-1} + y_{t-2}$$

You generally can achieve stationarity in your original time series by continuing to take differences until the autocorrelations of the "new" series drop to near zero after two or three time lags (except for possible large values, or spikes, due to seasonal effects). It usually is necessary to determine only first- or second-order differences when dealing with a nonstationary time series.

EXAMPLE 17.11

In Chapter 16, we examined the quarterly sales data of Video-Comp, shown in Table 16.3 on page 775. These data contained a strong linear trend and a definite seasonal pattern, with low sales in the first two quarters and high sales in the final two quarters. A graph of the data is contained in Figure 17.5. Is the seasonal effect more apparent using the original data or the first differences?

SOLUTION

The Excel autocorrelations using the original data are summarized and plotted in Figure 17.21. To obtain this spreadsheet, enter the 16 values in column A and click on **KGP Data Analysis ➤ Time Series Analysis ➤ Autocorrelations.** Enter "A1:A16" as the **Input Range** and "B1" as the **Output Range.** You can see the nonstationarity of this series—the autocorrelations fail to die out after two or three periods. Because of the strong trend component, the seasonal effect is not apparent.

The first differences are formed by subtracting adjacent y_t values:

	First Differences
y_t	$y'_t = y_t - y_{t-1}$
20	*
12	−8
47	35
60	13
40	−20
⋮	⋮

The Excel autocorrelations using the first differences are shown in Figure 17.22. To insert the labels in cells A1:C1, place the cursor on cell A1 and click on **Insert ➤ Rows.** Type in the labels in these three cells. To form column B, copy cells A2:A16 into cells B3:B17. To create column C, type "=A3-B3" in cell C3 and drag this cell through cell C17. Click on **KGP Data Analysis ➤ Time Series Analysis ➤ Autocorrelations.** Enter "C3:C17" as the **Input Range** and "D1" as the **Output Range.** The output in Figure 17.22 will be the result.

Now the seasonality pattern is much clearer, with large negative values for r_2, r_6, and r_{10} as well as large positive values for r_4, r_8, and r_{12}. The negative values are a result of a high (low) sales value in time period t followed by a low (high) sales figure two quarters

FIGURE 17.21

Excel autocorrelations using KGP Data Analysis on sales data in Example 17.11.

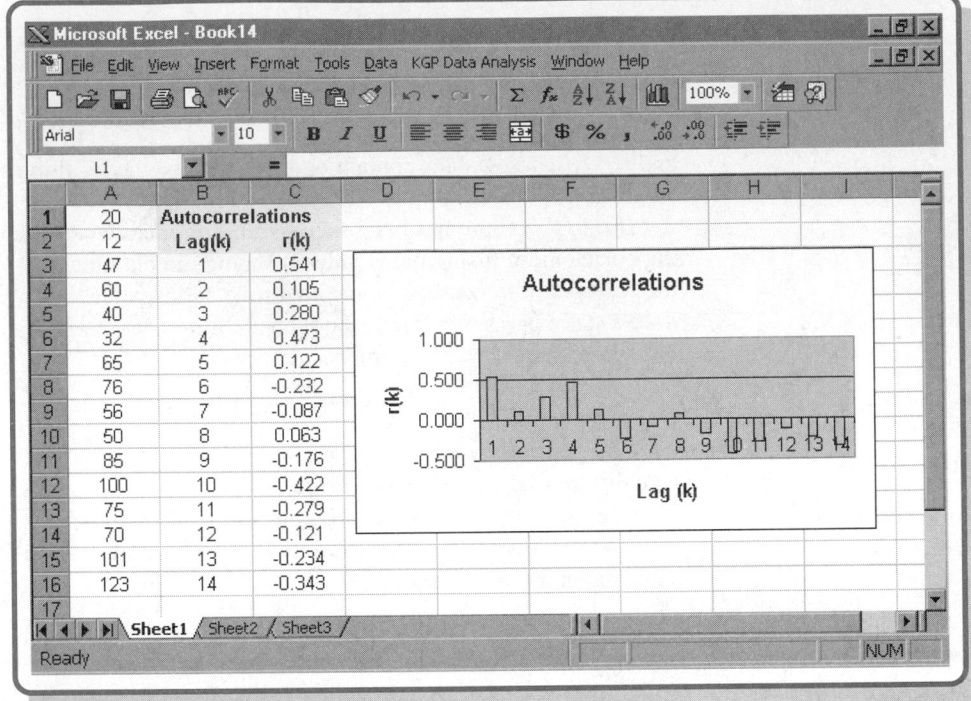

FIGURE 17.22

Excel autocorrelations using first differences (Example 17.11).

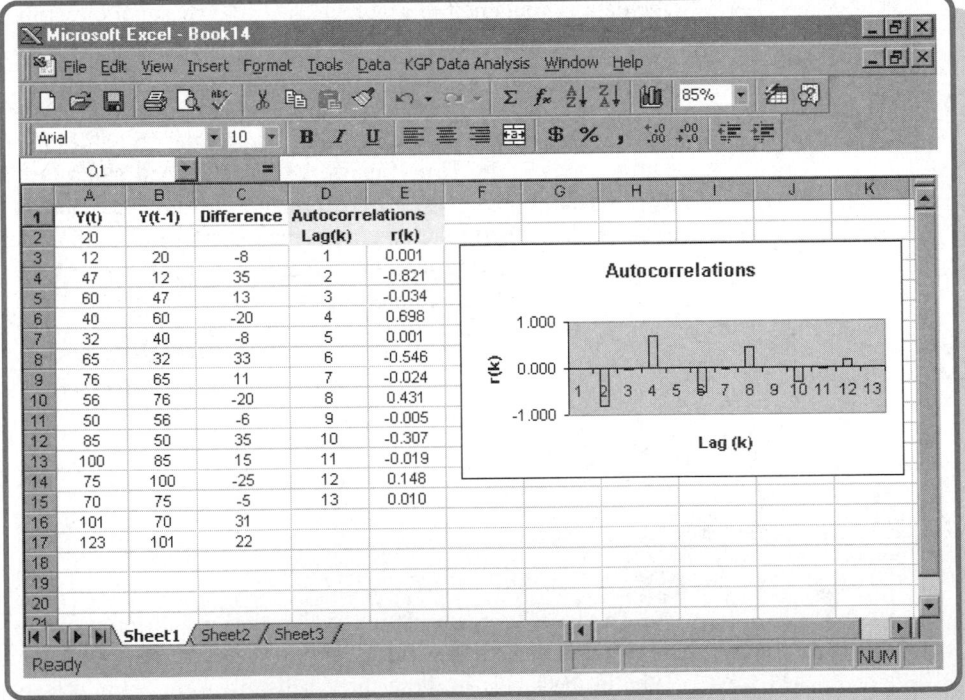

later. Similarly, the large value of r_4 indicates a strong four-quarter seasonal effect; the (somewhat) large values of r_8 and r_{12} support this conclusion.

If you wished to use an autoregressive model for this application, you would use y_t' (not y_t) as your dependent variable because the y_t' values *are* stationary. An excellent set of predictor variables (using Figure 17.22) would be y_{t-2}' and y_{t-4}'.

EXERCISES 17.35–17.43

UNDERSTANDING THE MECHANICS

17.35 The following quarterly data were collected. Find the predictive MSE using the autoregressive model

$$\hat{y}_t = 8.468 + .7093y_{t-1} - .0169y_{t-2}$$

Year	Quarter 1	Quarter 2	Quarter 3	Quarter 4
1997	12	15	20	18
1998	18	23	27	30
1999	30	31	25	27

APPLYING THE NEW CONCEPTS

17.36 The debt-to-equity capitalization ratio for Dooper Industries, a maker of machinery parts, has never been above 20% for the past six years, as a result of excellent management. These ratios (given as a percentage) for the past six years are as follows:

Year	Quarter 1	Quarter 2	Quarter 3	Quarter 4
1994	12	15	18	13
1995	11	14	16	12
1996	10	16	19	12
1997	11	17	20	14
1998	12	15	18	12
1999	11	14	17	13

a. Find the autocorrelations for lags of $k = 1, 2, 3,$ and 4.

b. Using a computer package, find the coefficients for the autoregressive process

$$\hat{y}_t = b_0 + b_1y_{t-1} + b_2y_{t-2} + b_3y_{t-3} + b_4y_{t-4}$$

17.37 The percentage of Medical International's total revenue derived from freestanding centers for cardiac rehabilitation is given for the past 16 years:

Year	Percentage of Revenue	Year	Percentage of Revenue
1984	45	1992	42
1985	47	1993	43
1986	46	1994	40
1987	43	1995	37
1988	40	1996	35
1989	36	1997	37
1990	35	1998	40
1991	39	1999	43

a. Find the autocorrelation for lags $k = 1, 2, 3,$ and 4.

b. Fit a first-order autoregressive equation to the data.

17.38 How should the graph of a correlogram look if the time series is stationary?

17.39 Refer to Exercise 17.23. Find the autocorrelations for the earnings per share of Mecta Mining. Would you say that the data appear to be stationary?

17.40 The number of manufacturing workers has increased and decreased partially because of economic cycles. Plants have been built and shut down to correspond to changing economic conditions. The following data show the number of manufacturing workers (in units of millions) in the United States from 1980 to 1998.

Year	Number of Manufacturing Workers	Year	Number of Manufacturing Workers
1980	22.1	1990	17.1
1981	21.2	1991	17.2
1982	20.3	1992	16.6
1983	20.8	1993	17.3
1984	19.4	1994	17.4
1985	18.4	1995	17.8
1986	18.9	1996	18.1
1987	19.5	1997	18.3
1988	18.5	1998	18.5
1989	18.3		

(Source: Adapted from *The Wall Street Journal*, "Jobless Rate Skidded to 4.4% in November," Dec. 7, 1998, p. A2.)

a. Calculate the first differences for the time series.

b. Calculate the autocorrelations for the original data and the first differences.

c. Do the autocorrelations describe a stationary time series?

17.41 Determine whether the following data are stationary. If the data are not stationary, take differences until it becomes clear that the resulting time series is stationary. The data represent quarterly interest (in thousands of dollars) paid by a local savings and loan association to depositors who have regular saving accounts.

Year	Quarter 1	Quarter 2	Quarter 3	Quarter 4
1995	25	38	15	21
1996	46	57	36	32
1997	65	80	54	49
1998	84	97	77	70
1999	104	109	96	90

USING THE COMPUTER

17.42 **[DATA SET EX17-42]** *Variable description:*

Year: Year from 1988 through 1999
Attendance: Number of moviegoers per year

The number of people going to the movies had been in a decline during the 1980s but has steadily increased during the 1990s. This number is collected as variable Attendance and is measured in billions. Comment on the correlogram for attendance over these years. Take the first differences of the attendance data. Compare the correlogram of the first differences to that of the original data.

(Source: Adapted from *USA Today*, "The Box Office by Year," Dec. 28, 1998, p. D1.)

17.43 **[DATA SET EX17-43]** *Variable description:*

Time: Monthly time periods numbered 1 through 48
PartTimeCost: Cost of part-time help per month

A construction firm hires part-time help as its business increases. The monthly cost measured in thousands of dollars for part-time help is recorded for four years. Find the predictive MSE for the first-order autoregressive equation. Also find the predictive MSE for the second-order autoregressive equation. Compare the two predictive MSEs.

17.9 THE OTHER SIDE OF FORECASTING: LINEAR REGRESSION USING TIME SERIES DATA

We have already used linear regression procedures in many of the time series forecasting techniques we have discussed. For instance, simple linear regression was used to describe the *trend* present in time series data. Multiple linear regression was used in the previous section to predict a future time series value using the past one or more observations. This was the autoregressive forecasting method, where, for example,

$$\hat{y}_t = b_0 + b_1 y_{t-1} + b_2 y_{t-2}$$

Here the predictor variables are the *lagged* time series variables, y_{t-1} and y_{t-2}.

Often, you will wish to combine one or more autoregressive terms and several time-related predictor variables into the regression equation, such as

$$\hat{y}_t = b_0 + b_1 y_{t-1} + b_2 y_{t-2} + b_3 X_{1,t} + b_4 X_{2,t} + b_5 X_{3,t}$$

Or you can omit the autoregressive terms and use an equation such as

$$\hat{y}_t = b_0 + b_1 X_{1,t} + b_2 X_{2,t} + b_3 X_{3,t}$$

Data that are to be used in a multiple regression model and that are obtained at a single point in time are referred to as **cross-sectional data.** The resulting regression predictor variables are usually labeled as $X_1, X_2, \ldots, X_k$. Chapter 15 focused on regression applications dealing with cross-sectional data, such as data gathered from ten different households at one point in time. This chapter examines regression applications where the data are gathered across time, that is, **time series data.** The corresponding regression variables are written as $X_{1,t}, X_{2,t}, \ldots, X_{k,t}$ to denote the values of these variables during time period t. For example, $X_{2,5}$ represents the observed value of variable X_2 during the fifth time period. Whether using cross-sectional or time series data, the regression model (with corresponding formulas and assumptions) developed in Chapter 15 is applicable.

Linear regression techniques on time series data offer a variety of opportunities for better forecasting precision, including (1) the use of dummy variables to capture *additive* seasonality and (2) the use of lagged independent variables to allow for time-delay effects between the dependent and predictor variables. *On the other hand, when this technique is used on time series data, it becomes increasingly difficult to satisfy the linear regression assumptions discussed in Chapter 15.* In particular, the error term from one time period often is related to the previous errors, violating the assumption of independent errors. This means that we can expect to find that the *residuals* are *autocorrelated.* The degree of autocorrelation in the residuals can be measured and tested for significance by calculating the **Durbin-Watson statistic,** which is obtained from the residuals.

These matters are discussed in the remaining sections of this chapter. We look at how regression techniques expand the area of time series analysis but also present a new set of problems.

USE OF DUMMY VARIABLES FOR SEASONALITY

We introduced the concept of additive seasonality previously. Essentially, this type of seasonal effect is present whenever the amount of the seasonal variation is unaffected by the underlying trend in the time series, as illustrated in Figure 16.16 on page 768. Notice that even as the sales grow over time, the seasonal effect remains the same.

Ignoring any cyclical activity, each observation, y_t, can be described by

$$y_t = \mathrm{TR}_t + S_t + I_t$$

where (1) TR_t is the trend component described by a straight line ($\mathrm{TR}_t = \beta_0 + \beta_1 t$) or a quadratic curve ($\mathrm{TR}_t = \beta_0 + \beta_1 t + \beta_2 t^2$), (2) S_t is the seasonal effect, and (3), I_t is the irregular activity component.

Both the trend and seasonal components can be obtained by using multiple linear regression. The seasonal effects are captured by including a set of *dummy variables* in the regression equation. This type of variable was first introduced in Chapter 15, where we used a set of dummy variables to represent the categories of a *qualitative* variable—such as seasons of the year, in this application.

We use the same procedure for defining dummy variables here—we define one less dummy variable than the number of seasons (categories), L. Because $L = 4$ for quarterly data, we need $L - 1 = 3$ dummy variables. One possible scheme is to define

$$Q_1 = \begin{cases} 1 & \text{if quarter 1} \\ 0 & \text{otherwise} \end{cases} \quad Q_2 = \begin{cases} 1 & \text{if quarter 2} \\ 0 & \text{otherwise} \end{cases} \quad Q_3 = \begin{cases} 1 & \text{if quarter 3} \\ 0 & \text{otherwise} \end{cases} \quad (17.18)$$

With this procedure, no dummy variable is defined for the fourth quarter. The resulting coefficient of Q_1, Q_2, or Q_3 in the prediction equation will compare the effect of that quarter *against the fourth quarter.* For example, if the coefficient of Q_2 from your computer solution is –5, then, apart from any changes due to trend, quarter 2 produces a value of the dependent variable *five* less than during quarter 4. Quarter 4 is called the **base** quarter. Remember that the base period you select has absolutely no *effect* on the predicted values, $\hat{y}_t$.

For monthly data, you define $L - 1 = 12 - 1 = 11$ dummy variables. As before, you can omit the dummy variables for any one month, which then becomes the base month for all the computed dummy variable coefficients. If you omitted a variable for December, then December would be the base month, and your corresponding set of dummy variables would be

$$M_1 = \begin{cases} 1 & \text{if January} \\ 0 & \text{otherwise} \end{cases} \quad M_2 = \begin{cases} 1 & \text{if February} \\ 0 & \text{otherwise} \end{cases} \cdots M_{11} = \begin{cases} 1 & \text{if November} \\ 0 & \text{otherwise} \end{cases} \quad (17.19)$$

The quarterly sales at Video-Comp were examined in Examples 16.8 and 17.3, assuming *multiplicative* seasonality. The vice president of retail marketing, in reviewing this solution, thinks that the seasonal fluctuations do not appear to be increasing along with the trend and so believes that additive seasonality actually is present. We use the dummy variable approach to model the seasonality and calculate the forecasts for the first four quarters of 1999. We want to know whether this approach appears to provide a good fit to the four years of observed sales.

The prediction equation is

$$\hat{y}_t = \hat{\text{TR}}_t + \hat{S}_t$$

where (1) $\hat{\text{TR}}_t = b_0 + b_1 t$ (the trend appears to be nearly linear) and (2) $\hat{S}_t = b_2 Q_1 + b_3 Q_2 + b_4 Q_3$. Here, Q_1, Q_2, and Q_3 are the dummy variables defined in equation 17.18.

The input configuration used by the computer program consists of 16 rows and five columns:

y_t	t	Q_1	Q_2	Q_3	y_t	t	Q_1	Q_2	Q_3
20	1	1	0	0	56	9	1	0	0
12	2	0	1	0	50	10	0	1	0
47	3	0	0	1	85	11	0	0	1
60	4	0	0	0	100	12	0	0	0
40	5	1	0	0	75	13	1	0	0
32	6	0	1	0	70	14	0	1	0
65	7	0	0	1	101	15	0	0	1
76	8	0	0	0	123	16	0	0	0

The Excel solution for b_0, b_1, . . . , b_4 is shown in Figure 17.23. Begin by entering the data into cells "A1:E16," and then click on **Tools ➤ Data Analysis ➤ Regression.** Enter "A1:A16" as the **Input Y Range** and "B1:E16" as the **Input X Range.** The output

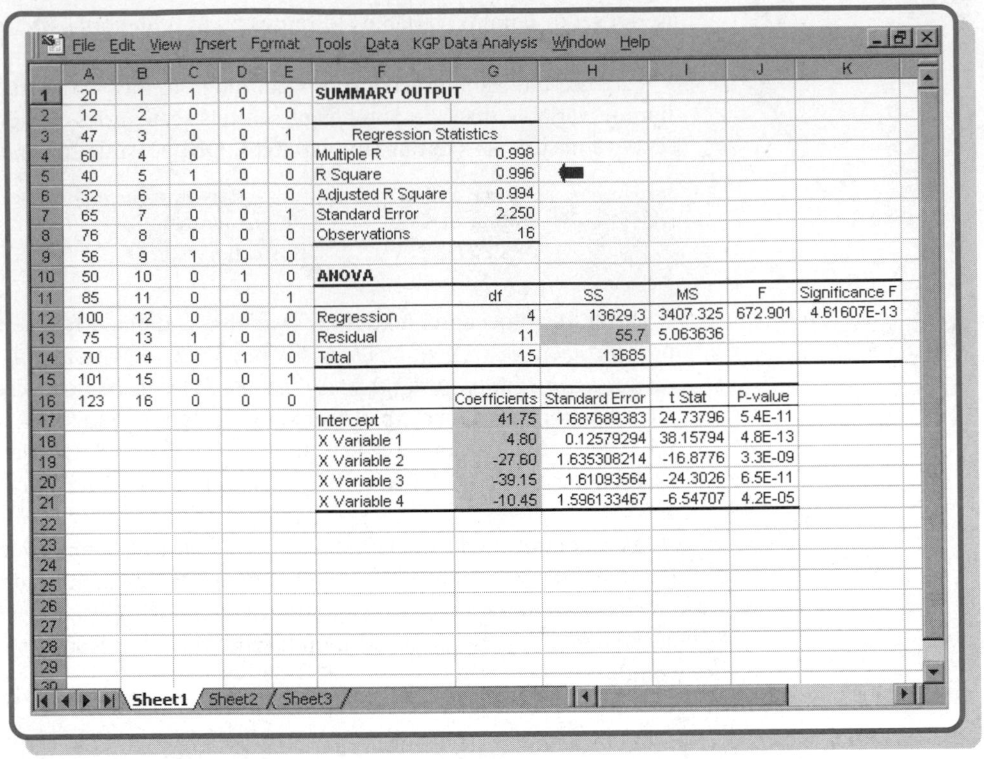

FIGURE 17.23
Excel solution using dummy variables to represent quarterly sales at Video-Comp.

	A	B	C	D	E	F	G	H	I	J	K
						File Edit View Insert Format Tools Data KGP Data Analysis Window Help					
1	20	1	1	0	0	SUMMARY OUTPUT					
2	12	2	0	1	0						
3	47	3	0	0	1	Regression Statistics					
4	60	4	0	0	0	Multiple R	0.998				
5	40	5	1	0	0	R Square	0.996				
6	32	6	0	1	0	Adjusted R Square	0.994				
7	65	7	0	0	1	Standard Error	2.250				
8	76	8	0	0	0	Observations	16				
9	56	9	1	0	0						
10	50	10	0	1	0	ANOVA					
11	85	11	0	0	1		df	SS	MS	F	Significance F
12	100	12	0	0	0	Regression	4	13629.3	3407.325	672.901	4.61607E-13
13	75	13	1	0	0	Residual	11	55.7	5.063636		
14	70	14	0	1	0	Total	15	13685			
15	101	15	0	0	1						
16	123	16	0	0	0		Coefficients	Standard Error	t Stat	P-value	
17						Intercept	41.75	1.687689383	24.73796	5.4E-11	
18						X Variable 1	4.80	0.12579294	38.15794	4.8E-13	
19						X Variable 2	-27.60	1.635308214	-16.8776	3.3E-09	
20						X Variable 3	-39.15	1.61093564	-24.3026	6.5E-11	
21						X Variable 4	-10.45	1.596133467	-6.54707	4.2E-05	

Sheet1 / Sheet2 / Sheet3 /

range in Figure 17.23 was selected as F1. The resulting equation using the highlighted cells is

$$\hat{y}_t = 41.75 + 4.8t - 27.6Q_1 - 39.15Q_2 - 10.45Q_3 \qquad (17.20)$$

Notice that $R^2 = .996$, which indicates a very strong fit to the 16 observations. How does this method of forecasting compare to the one used in Example 17.3, where we assumed *multiplicative* seasonality in the quarterly sales data? Comparing the two MSE's in Table 17.10, it appears that the seasonality effect is in fact additive, and the marketing vice president was correct.

From equation 17.20, we find that

1. The sales are increasing at an average rate of 4.8 (million dollars) per quarter.
2. Apart from trend effects, sales for the first quarter are 27.6 (million dollars) less than the sales for the fourth quarter.
3. Apart from trend effects, sales for the second quarter are 39.15 (million dollars) less than for the fourth quarter.
4. Sales for the third quarter are 10.45 (million dollars) lower than those during the fourth quarter, ignoring trend effects.

After you have decided to use the additive seasonality equation, to determine the 1999 forecasts you use the appropriate value for t, with the 0 or 1 values for the dummy variables.

Forecast for first quarter of 1999: here, $Q_1 = 1$, $Q_2 = 0$, $Q_3 = 0$, and

$$\hat{y}_{17} = 41.75 + 4.8(17) - 27.6(1) - 39.15(0) - 10.45(0)$$

$$= 95.75 \text{ (million dollars)}$$

Forecast for second quarter of 1999: here, $Q_2 = 1$ (all other Q's $= 0$) and

$$\hat{y}_{18} = 41.75 + 4.8(18) - 27.6(0) - 39.15(1) - 10.45(0)$$

$$= 89$$

TABLE 17.10

Summary of multiplicative versus additive seasonal forecasting (quarterly sales of Video-Comp).

	MULTIPLICATIVE SEASONALITY				ADDITIVE SEASONALITY		
t	y_t	$\hat{y}_t$	$y_t - \hat{y}_t$	t	y_t	$\hat{y}_t$	$y_t - \hat{y}_t$
1	20	20.80	−.80	1	20	18.95	1.05
2	12	20.38	−8.38	2	12	12.20	−.20
3	47	40.21	6.79	3	47	45.70	1.30
4	60	50.98	9.02	4	60	60.95	−.95
5	40	37.96	2.04	5	40	38.15	1.85
6	32	34.32	−2.32	6	32	31.40	.60
7	65	63.70	1.30	7	65	64.90	.10
8	76	76.98	−.98	8	76	80.15	−4.15
9	56	55.13	.87	9	56	57.35	−1.35
10	50	48.26	1.74	10	50	50.60	−.60
11	85	87.20	−2.20	11	85	84.10	.90
12	100	102.97	−2.97	12	100	99.35	.65
13	75	72.30	2.70	13	75	76.55	−1.55
14	70	62.21	7.79	14	70	69.80	.20
15	101	110.69	−9.69	15	101	103.30	−2.30
16	123	128.96	−5.96	16	123	118.55	4.45

Forecasting equation:

$$\hat{y}_t = (19.372 + 5.0375t) \cdot S_t$$

$$S_1 = S_5 = S_9 = \cdots = .852$$
$$S_2 = S_6 = S_{10} = \cdots = .692$$
$$S_3 = S_7 = S_{11} = \cdots = 1.166$$
$$S_4 = S_8 = S_{12} = \cdots = 1.290$$

$$\text{predictive MSE} = \frac{\sum(y_t - \hat{y}_t)^2}{16}$$

$$= \frac{425.36}{16} = 26.58$$

Forecasting equation:

$$\hat{y}_t = 41.75 + 4.8t - 27.6Q_1$$
$$- 39.15Q_2 - 10.45Q_3$$

$$\text{predictive MSE} = \frac{\sum(y_t - \hat{y}_t)^2}{16}$$

$$= \frac{55.7}{16} = 3.48$$

Forecast for third quarter of 1999: now, $Q_3 = 1$ (all other Q's $= 0$) and

$$\hat{y}_{19} = 41.75 + 4.8(19) - 27.6(0) - 39.15(0) - 10.45(1)$$

$$= 122.5$$

Forecast for the fourth quarter of 1999: since $Q_1 = Q_2 = Q_3 = 0$,

$$\hat{y}_{20} = 41.75 + 4.8(20) - 27.6(0) - 39.15(0) - 10.45(0)$$

$$= 137.75$$

EXERCISES 17.44–17.49

UNDERSTANDING THE MECHANICS

17.44 The following multiple regression equation was fit to quarterly data.

$$\hat{y}_t = 100 + 2t + 3t^2 + Q_1 + 5Q_2 - 2Q_3$$

where

$$Q_1 = \begin{cases} 1 & \text{if quarter 1} \\ 0 & \text{otherwise} \end{cases} \quad Q_2 = \begin{cases} 1 & \text{if quarter 2} \\ 0 & \text{otherwise} \end{cases}$$

$$Q_3 = \begin{cases} 1 & \text{if quarter 3} \\ 0 & \text{otherwise} \end{cases}$$

a. Describe the underlying trend for this model.

b. Assuming that time period 1 represents the first quarter of 1991, what is the predicted value for the fourth quarter of 1992?

c. Apart from the trend, are the predicted values higher in the second quarter or in the first quarter?

APPLYING THE NEW CONCEPTS

17.45 While many investors consider only the absolute yield on long-term treasury bonds, financial analysts recommend that investors consider the real yield. The real yield is the current yield minus the inflation rate as measured by the Gross Domestic Product deflator. Real yields have varied between 3.7% and 5.5% since 1991. So even if the absolute yield on a long-term treasury bond is lower than it used to be, the real yield may still make it a good buy. Determine the multiple regression equation that takes into account trend and additive seasonality.

Year	Quarter 1	Quarter 2	Quarter 3	Quarter 4
1991	4.1	3.7	4.3	4.5
1992	4.6	4.5	4.7	4.9
1993	4.9	4.1	4.0	4.3
1994	4.3	4.2	4.7	5.2
1995	5.3	3.9	4.0	4.2
1996	4.3	4.2	5.0	5.3
1997	5.5	5.0	5.1	5.3

(Source: Adapted from *Fortune*, "Buy Treasurys Now," June 16, 1997, p. 224–27.)

17.46 Quality Homes, Inc., builds single-family houses in several large cities. The number of carpenters that it hires fluctuates with the demand for housing. For the six years shown, find a multiple regression equation to predict the number of carpenters on the payroll at Quality Homes. The multiple regression equation should take into account the trend and the monthly seasonality. What percentage of the total variation has been explained using these variables?

Year	Jan	Feb	Mar	Apr	May	Jun
1994	145	148	150	169	197	250
1995	155	150	166	178	220	290
1996	180	195	210	213	255	308
1997	230	245	258	290	330	342
1998	285	298	310	345	396	408
1999	350	361	372	395	420	439

Year	Jul	Aug	Sep	Oct	Nov	Dec
1994	267	290	280	230	180	160
1995	320	325	300	270	200	190
1996	350	368	345	320	280	250
1997	394	405	380	350	310	290
1998	451	465	441	430	390	370
1999	480	495	483	450	420	410

17.47 Refer to Exercise 17.23. Determine the multiple regression equation that takes into account trend and additive seasonality when predicting the earnings per share of Mecta Mining. What percentage of the variation is explained by this equation?

17.48 Explain the difference between multiplicative seasonality and additive seasonality. Which forecasting techniques are best suited for each of these situations?

USING THE COMPUTER

17.49 **[DATA SET EX17-49]** *Variable description:*

Time: Time periods numbered from 1 through 24 for 24 quarters
AdvDolls-R-Us: Quarterly television advertising expenses for Dolls-R-Us
X_1: Dummy variable equal to 1 to indicate the first quarter
X_2: Dummy variable equal to 1 to indicate the second quarter
X_3: Dummy variable equal to 1 to indicate the third quarter

The sales manager at Dolls-R-Us recorded the quarterly television expenses from 1994 through 1999 in thousands of dollars. Regress AdvDolls-R-Us on the variable Time. Also regress AdvDolls-R-Us on the variables Time, X_1, X_2, and X_3. Compare the predictive MSEs for these two models.

USE OF LAGGED INDEPENDENT VARIABLES

When using multiple linear regression on time series data, we can represent the model as

$$y_t = \beta_0 + \beta_1 X_{1,t} + \beta_2 X_{2,t} + \cdots + \beta_k X_{k,t} + e_t$$

where each $X_{i,t}$ represents the value of predictor variable X_i in time period t, and e_t is the error component for this period.

Look at the data in Table 17.11, which consist of semiannual figures for 1990 through 1997. Our object is to predict the number of home loans financed by Liberty Savings and Loan. The predictor variables were chosen to be average interest rate (X_1), advertising expenditure (X_2), an election-year dummy variable ($X_3 = 1$ for a presidential election year and 0 otherwise), and a seasonal dummy variable, where $X_4 = 1$ for the first six months of each year and $X_4 = 0$ for the final six months.

A financial analyst at Liberty Savings saw two problems with the data in Table 17.11. First, she thought that the number of home loans during a particular six-month period should be more affected by the *previous* six-month interest rate, due to the time delay between loan application and actual funding. The value of y_t increases by 1 each time a loan is funded, not when the application is turned in. This time delay generally runs between three and six months. For the same reason, she believed that the effect of any

TABLE 17.11   Housing data for Liberty Savings and Loan.

Year	t	Number of Home Loans Y_t	Average Interest Rate ($X_{1,t}$)	Advertising Expenditure (Thousands of Dollars) ($X_{2,t}$)	Election Year Variable ($X_{3,t}$)	Seasonal Variable ($X_{4,t}$)
1990	1	122	7.6	10.4	0	1
	2	118	8.0	6.7	0	0
1991	3	88	7.0	7.5	0	1
	4	122	9.5	7.8	0	0
1992	5	114	7.0	5.1	1	1
	6	133	7.3	6.8	1	0
1993	7	110	8.4	6.8	0	1
	8	90	8.7	9.1	0	0
1994	9	92	8.3	7.5	0	1
	10	97	7.8	5.1	0	0
1995	11	117	6.4	8.8	0	1
	12	102	6.9	4.3	0	0
1996	13	140	6.4	7.1	1	1
	14	140	6.2	8.6	1	0
1997	15	121	6.0	8.8	0	1
	16	126	6.5	5.4	0	0

increased (or decreased) advertising would be reflected in the loan amounts of the next period.

The procedure to follow in this situation is to lag the predictor variable by the corresponding time lag. For this example, we can lag X_1 and X_2 by one time period, resulting in the following regression model:

$$y_t = \beta_0 + \beta_1 X_{1,t-1} + \beta_2 X_{2,t-1} + \beta_3 X_{3,t} + \beta_4 X_{4,t} + e_t$$

The other problem the financial analyst foresaw with using the regression variables in Table 17.11 is a common difficulty in applying regression techniques to a forecasting situation. If we had not lagged X_1 and X_2, then any forecast for 1998 would involve *specifying values for X_1 and X_2 for this future time period*. Because these values may be just as difficult to predict as the dependent variable, our model has little potential as a forecaster. By lagging these variables, we have removed this problem for a one-period-ahead forecast, because now the lagged values for tomorrow are the actual values for today.

A portion of the input data using the lagged predictors is:

y_t	$X_{1,t-1}$	$X_{2,t-1}$	$X_{3,t}$	$X_{4,t}$
118	7.6	10.4	0	0
88	8.0	6.7	0	1
122	7.0	7.5	0	0
114	9.5	7.8	1	1
133	7.0	5.1	1	0
110	7.3	6.8	0	1
90	8.4	6.8	0	0
⋮				

The resulting prediction equation using the highlighted cells in Figure 17.24 is

$$\hat{y}_t = 182.079 - 10.353 X_{1,t-1} + 0.210 X_{2,t-1}$$

$$+ 24.737 X_{3,t} + 1.569 X_{4,t} \qquad (17.21)$$

FIGURE 17.24
Excel solution using lagged interest and advertising variables (data from Table 17.11).

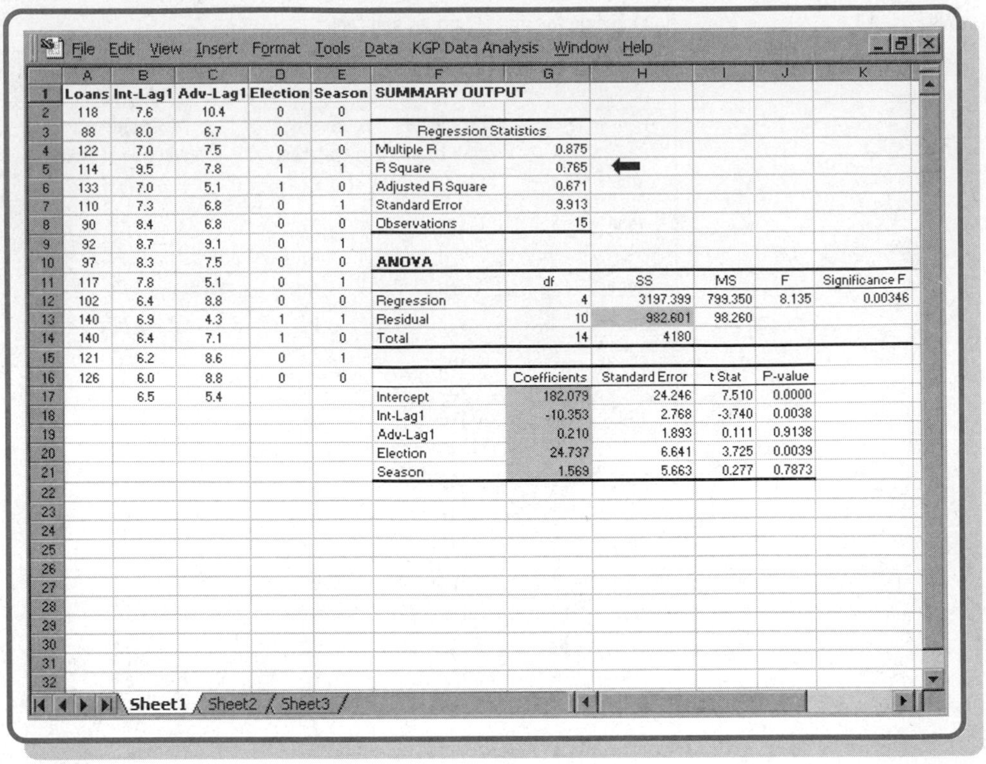

Loans	Int-Lag1	Adv-Lag1	Election	Season
118	7.6	10.4	0	0
88	8.0	6.7	0	1
122	7.0	7.5	0	0
114	9.5	7.8	1	1
133	7.0	5.1	1	0
110	7.3	6.8	0	1
90	8.4	6.8	0	0
92	8.7	9.1	0	1
97	8.3	7.5	0	0
117	7.8	5.1	0	1
102	6.4	8.8	0	0
140	6.9	4.3	1	1
140	6.4	7.1	1	0
121	6.2	8.6	0	1
126	6.0	8.8	0	0
	6.5	5.4		

SUMMARY OUTPUT

Regression Statistics	
Multiple R	0.875
R Square	0.765
Adjusted R Square	0.671
Standard Error	9.913
Observations	15

ANOVA

	df	SS	MS	F	Significance F
Regression	4	3197.399	799.350	8.135	0.00346
Residual	10	982.601	98.260		
Total	14	4180			

	Coefficients	Standard Error	t Stat	P-value
Intercept	182.079	24.246	7.510	0.0000
Int-Lag1	-10.353	2.768	-3.740	0.0038
Adv-Lag1	0.210	1.893	0.111	0.9138
Election	24.737	6.641	3.725	0.0039
Season	1.569	5.663	0.277	0.7873

To obtain the Excel solution in Figure 17.24, enter the values for the five variables in Table 17.11 into columns A through E *exactly as they appear in this table.* To lag the interest and advertising variables, place the cursor in cell B1 and click on **Insert ➤ Cells.** Select **Shift Cells Down.** Repeat this for the advertising variable by first placing the cursor in cell C1. You can now replace any remaining values in the first row with the labels **Loans, Int-Lag1, Adv-Lag1, Election,** and **Season,** as shown in Figure 17.24. If you want, you can delete cells B17 and C17. To obtain the regression analysis in Figure 17.24, click on **Tools ➤ Data Analysis ➤ Regression.** Enter "A1:A16" as the **Input Y Range** and "B1:E16" as the **Input X Range.** Be sure to click on the box alongside **Labels.**

We can draw several conclusions from Figure 17.24:

1. Based on the t values and a significance level of .10, the lagged interest rate variable ($X_{1,t-1}$) and the election year variable ($X_{3,t}$) are the only significant predictors of the number of home loans financed by Liberty.
2. Because $R^2 = .765$, we can say that 76.5% of the total variation of the y_t values has been explained using these four variables.
3. The predictive mean squared error (for comparison purposes) is

$$\text{(predictive) MSE} = \frac{\text{SSE}}{15} = \frac{982.601}{15} = 65.5$$

To illustrate the effect of lagging the independent variables, Figure 17.25 contains the solution to this example lagging neither X_1 nor X_2. Two things are striking. First, the R^2 drops from .765 to .520. Second, the interest variable, X_1, is *no longer significant,* based on its small t value.

In each application, try lagging the independent variables that could possibly have a delayed action on the dependent variable. You could also vary the lag period to account for predictor effects that show up several periods later.

What would be the forecast for the first half of 1998 using predictive equation 17.21? Here $X_{1,t-1} = X_{1,16}$ = interest rate for the last half of 1997 = 6.5 and $X_{2,t-1} = X_{2,16} = 5.4$. Also, $X_{3,17} = 0$ (1998 is not an election year) and $X_{4,17} = 1$ (for the first half of 1998). So,

$$\hat{y}_t = 182.079 - 10.353(6.5) + 0.210(5.4) + 24.737(0) + 1.569(1) = 117.5$$

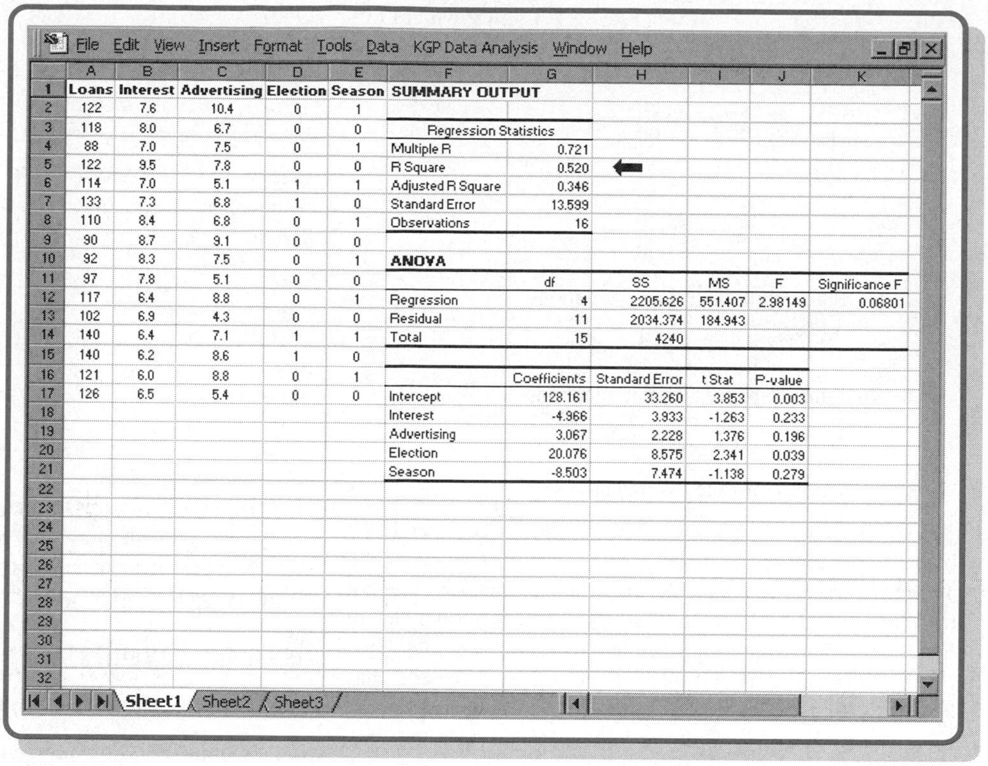

Loans	Interest	Advertising	Election	Season
122	7.6	10.4	0	1
118	8.0	6.7	0	0
88	7.0	7.5	0	1
122	9.5	7.8	0	0
114	7.0	5.1	1	1
133	7.3	6.8	1	0
110	8.4	6.8	0	1
90	8.7	9.1	0	0
92	8.3	7.5	0	1
97	7.8	5.1	0	0
117	6.4	8.8	0	1
102	6.9	4.3	0	0
140	6.4	7.1	1	1
140	6.2	8.6	1	0
121	6.0	8.8	0	1
126	6.5	5.4	0	0

SUMMARY OUTPUT

Regression Statistics	
Multiple R	0.721
R Square	0.520
Adjusted R Square	0.346
Standard Error	13.599
Observations	16

ANOVA

	df	SS	MS	F	Significance F
Regression	4	2205.626	551.407	2.98149	0.06801
Residual	11	2034.374	184.943		
Total	15	4240			

	Coefficients	Standard Error	t Stat	P-value
Intercept	128.161	33.260	3.853	0.003
Interest	-4.966	3.933	-1.263	0.233
Advertising	3.067	2.228	1.376	0.196
Election	20.076	8.575	2.341	0.039
Season	-8.503	7.474	-1.138	0.279

FIGURE 17.25 Excel solution without lagging the interest and advertising variables (data from Table 17.11).

This result is very close to the actual value for the first half of 1997 (121), not a surprising result, since the interest rate changed very little during 1996 and 1997 and neither 1997 nor 1998 was an election year.

EXERCISES 17.50–17.55

APPLYING THE NEW CONCEPTS

17.50 What is the importance of using lagged independent variables in a regression equation?

17.51 The following table lists the food price index (FPI) and the per-capita income (PCI) index for a certain third-world nation. The indexes are listed in six-month increments.

Year	Month	Y: FPI	X: PCI	Year	Month	Y: FPI	X: PCI
1991	June	109	104	1996	June	114	115
	Dec	101	116		Dec	104	127
1992	June	104	124	1997	June	107	112
	Dec	107	120		Dec	102	141
1993	June	105	167	1998	June	110	124
	Dec	114	133		Dec	105	162
1994	June	108	188	1999	June	113	184
	Dec	126	148		Dec	120	140
1995	June	112	101				
	Dec	100	158				

a. Find the simple regression equation

$$\hat{y}_t = b_0 + b_1 X_t$$

b. Find the simple regression equation

$$\hat{y}_t = b_0 + b_1 X_{t-1}$$

c. Compare R^2 for the two equations found in parts (a) and (b).

17.52 Credit Corp finances small home-improvement projects for one year or less. Usually the company does not screen clients rigorously, because a mechanics lien is placed on the home. Credit Corp has found that a significant correlation exists between the interest rate on loans and the number of defaults. The following data give the average interest rate charged during that quarter and the number of times a loan holder was more than 30 days behind on a payment.

Year	Quarter	Average Interest Rate (Y)	Times Behind on a Loan Payment (X)
1996	1	8.5	53
	2	8.0	45
	3	9.0	44
	4	9.5	47
1997	1	9.0	49
	2	10.0	46
	3	10.5	49
	4	10.0	52

Year	Quarter	Average Interest Rate (Y)	Times Behind on a Loan Payment (X)
1998	1	10.5	50
	2	11.25	51
	3	11.50	55
	4	11.00	57
1999	1	12.25	52
	2	12.50	60
	3	12.00	63
	4	11.50	58

a. Find the simple regression equation

$$\hat{y}_t = b_0 + b_1 X_t$$

b. Find the simple regression equation

$$\hat{y}_t = b_0 + b_1 X_{t-1}$$

c. Compare R^2 for the two equations.

17.53 The United States' current account is considered the broadest measure of U.S. transactions with the rest of the world. The current account measures not only merchandise trade but trade in services and investment earnings between the United States and other countries. Since the global economy has been trending downward in 1998, the U.S. current account deficit has been widening. Some economists worry that if the common European currency turns out to be a big success, investors may find alternative places to invest, thus making it more costly for the U.S. to finance its deficit. The following data show the U.S. current account deficit measured in millions of dollars for the period from 1996 through 1998. Determine the multiple regression equation to predict the current account deficit. Use the independent variable representing time and dummy variables to represent additive seasonality. Find the predictive MSE.

Year	Quarter 1	Quarter 2	Quarter 3	Quarter 4
1996	26.1	28.4	33.5	30.2
1997	32.6	34.3	39.7	40.1
1998	45.4	51.3	62.5	63.2

(Source: Adapted from *The Wall Street Journal*, "U.S. Current-Account Deficit Widens to Record," Dec. 10, 1998, p. A2.)

17.54 Refer to Exercise 17.36. The following is the level of inventory of Dooper Industries in units of 10,000 for the years 1994 to 1999.

Year	Quarter 1	Quarter 2	Quarter 3	Quarter 4
1994	4.8	6.1	4.2	3.8
1995	4.2	5.2	4.1	3.3
1996	5.0	6.4	4.2	3.2
1997	5.5	6.8	4.2	3.1
1998	5.1	6.1	4.0	3.8
1999	4.2	5.9	4.1	3.7

Find the multiple regression equation to predict the debt-to-equity capitalization ratio for Dooper Industries using one variable to represent seasonality and a second variable, level of inventory lagged by one quarter. Find R^2.

Using the Computer

17.55 [DATA SET EX17-55] *Variable description:*

SalesMonthly: Sales per month at Friendly Ford
AdvExpend: Monthly advertising expenditure at Friendly Ford

The dealer at Friendly Ford recorded the monthly advertising expenditure and monthly sales as variables SalesMonthly and AdvExpend, respectively, in thousands of dollars for 1997, 1998, and 1999. Create another variable, say AdvExpendLag, which is equal to the value of AdvExpend for the prior month. That is, AdvExpendLag is AdvExpend lagged by one period. Regress SalesMonthly on AdvExpend. Also, regress SalesMonthly on AdvExpendLag. Compare the values of R^2 for these two models.

17.10 The Problem of Autocorrelation: The Durbin-Watson Statistic

A problem you will encounter frequently when using multiple linear regression on time series data is that the residual terms (e_t) are not independent. We discussed autoregressive forecasting, in which an observation (y_t) is related to its past values. For this situation, we said that significant autocorrelation was present in the *observations*.

When we have an autocorrelated time series, we simply regress y_t on the past values. However, when a particular model dealing with least squares estimates of the unknown parameters (such as multiple linear regression) results in **autocorrelated residuals,** problems do arise. In particular, all tests of hypothesis, including the *t*-tests for individual predictors, become extremely suspect.

Detecting Autocorrelated Residuals

The Durbin-Watson statistic frequently is used to test for significant autocorrelation in the residuals. If its value is very small, significant *positive* autocorrelation exists. This means that each value of e_t is very close to its neighbors, e_{t-1} and e_{t+1}. A large value indicates high *negative* autocorrelation, where each e_t value is very different from the adjacent residuals.

The value of the Durbin-Watson statistic (DW) is determined using each residual value, e_t, and its previous value, e_{t-1}.

$$DW = \frac{\sum_{t=2}^{T}(e_t - e_{t-1})^2}{\sum_{t=1}^{T}e_t^2} \qquad (17.22)$$

where T is the number of observations in the time series.

The range of possible values for the Durbin-Watson statistic is from 0 to 4. The **ideal value of DW** is 2. When $DW = 2$, the errors are completely uncorrelated, and there is no violation of the independent errors assumption. As DW decreases from 2, positive auto-correlation of the errors increases. Values between 2 and 4 indicate various degrees of negative autocorrelation.*

The common problem of autocorrelated errors results from *positive* correlation between neighboring errors. When this situation occurs, the errors are not independent of one another; instead, each error is largely determined by its previous value. This implies that a similar behavior will exist for the estimated residuals in the regression model—that is, we can expect the estimated residuals to be positively correlated. The test for autocor-relation using the DW statistic is unique in that there is a certain range of DW values for which we can neither reject H_0: no autocorrelation exists, nor fail to reject it. The testing procedure uses Table A.9; the value of k in Table A.9 represents the number of predictor variables in the regression equation. The hypotheses are

$$H_0: \text{no autocorrelation exists}$$

$$H_a: \text{positive autocorrelation exists}$$

The testing procedure, using the values of d_L and d_U from Table A.9, is

Reject H_0 if $DW < d_L$.

Fail to reject H_0 if $DW > d_U$.

The test is inconclusive if $d_L \leq DW \leq d_U$.

The assumption behind the Durbin-Watson test is that the errors follow a normal distribu-tion. An alternative to the Durbin-Watson procedure for detecting significant autocorrela-tions is the **runs test,** discussed in Chapter 19 (in Example 19.2). The runs test does *not* assume that the errors are normally distributed.

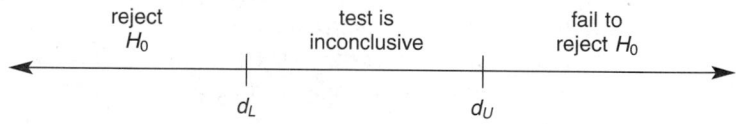

EXAMPLE 17.12

Determine the value of the Durbin-Watson statistic if equation 17.21 is used on the home-loan data in Table 17.11. Use $\alpha = .05$.

SOLUTION

Using Figure 17.24 to obtain the estimated values from equation 17.21, Table 17.12 shows the necessary calculations to compute the Durbin-Watson statistic.

Using Table 17.12, the Durbin-Watson statistic for this situation is

$$DW = \frac{2878.5}{982.6} = 2.93$$

---

* The Durbin-Watson statistic can be approximated using the autocorrelation of lag 1 (called r_1) discussed in Section 17.8. This approximation is $2(1 - r_1)$. Since r_1 ranges from -1 to 1, the value of DW ranges from 0 to 4, with positive autocorrelation occur-ring for values of r_1, close to 1, that is, for values of DW close to 0.

TABLE 17.12

Calculating the Durbin-Watson statistic for Example 17.12.

t	y_t	$\hat{y}_t$	$e_t = y_t - \hat{y}_t$	$e_t - e_{t-1}$	$(e_t - e_{t-1})^2$	e_t^2
1	122	—	—	—	—	—
2	118	105.585	12.415	—	—	154.138
3	88	102.235	−14.235	−26.650	710.247	202.642
4	122	111.187	10.813	25.049	627.428	116.927
5	114	111.674	2.326	−8.488	72.040	5.409
6	133	135.419	−2.419	−4.745	22.512	5.852
7	110	109.503	0.497	2.916	8.503	0.247
8	90	96.546	−6.546	−7.043	49.600	42.848
9	92	95.493	−3.493	3.053	9.320	12.200
10	97	97.728	−0.728	2.765	7.643	0.530
11	117	103.969	13.031	13.759	189.306	169.796
12	102	117.672	−15.672	−28.702	823.816	245.599
13	140	137.855	2.145	17.816	317.414	4.599
14	140	142.051	−2.051	−4.196	17.603	4.207
15	121	121.269	−0.269	1.782	3.174	0.073
16	126	121.813	4.187	4.457	19.863	17.534
					2878.5*	982.6**

*Numerator for *DW*.
**Denominator for *DW* (= SSE in Figure 17.24).

Using $\alpha = .05$, $n = 15$, $k = 4$, and Table A.9, $d_L = .69$ and $d_U = 1.97$. Notice that the value of n is 15, because only 15 values of y_t were estimated. Also, equation 17.21 uses four variables to predict y_t, and so $k = 4$. The test of hypothesis will be to

Reject H_0 if $DW < .69$.

Fail to reject H_0 if $DW > 1.97$.

The test is inconclusive if $.69 \leq DW \leq 1.97$.

Because $2.93 > 1.97$, we conclude that there is no evidence of positive autocorrelation. In fact, since $2.93 > 2$, this suggests the possible presence of negative autocorrelation. To test for significant negative autocorrelation, the alternative hypothesis becomes H_a: negative autocorrelation exists. The test statistic is now $4 - DW$ (rather than DW), and the test procedure remains the same; that is,

Reject H_0 if $(4 - DW) < d_L (= .69)$

Fail to reject H_0 if $(4 - DW) > d_U (= 1.97)$

The test is inconclusive if $d_L \leq (4 - DW) \leq d_U$

Here, $4 - DW = 4 - 2.93 = 1.07$, which falls in the grey area between .69 and 1.97. Consequently, negative autocorrelation *could* exist, but this test is inconclusive. We should note that this result is approximate, since we have redefined the hypotheses "in midstream" rather than (as required) prior to obtaining the sample results.

Although Excel does not currently provide the value of the Durbin-Watson statistic, this value is available when using the KGP Data Analysis package. When you click on **KGP Data Analysis ➤ Regression,** you will see the input screen in Figure 15.7. Enter the Y and X ranges as before when generating Figure 17.24 and be sure to click on the box alongside **Durbin-Watson Statistic.** Note that the X columns (variables) are contiguous (adjacent) for this application. The calculated Durbin-Watson value of 2.93 is shown at the bottom of the regression output in Figure 17.26 and agrees with the results of Example 17.12.

FIGURE 17.26

Value of Durbin-Watson statistic using **KGP Data Analysis ➤ Regression.**

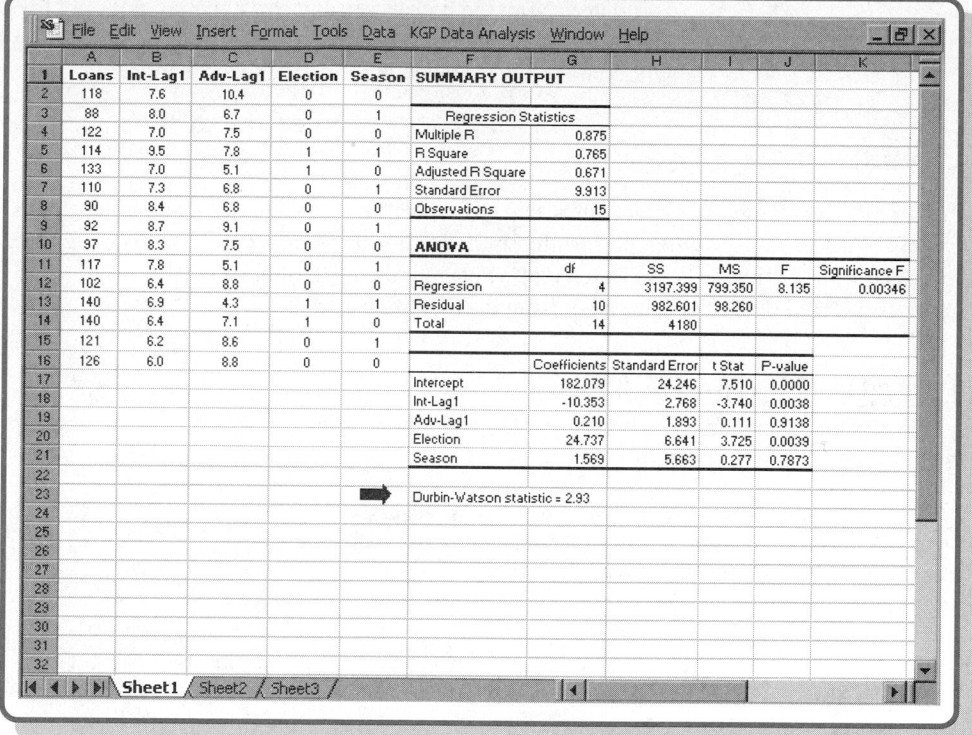

PROCEDURES FOR CORRECTING AUTOCORRELATED ERRORS

All is not lost if the Durbin-Watson test concludes that significant autocorrelation is present in the residuals. We do not attempt to describe fully all the remedies for this situation. (For discussions of these methods, consult Bowerman and O'Connell (1993) and Makridakis, Wheelwright, and Hyndman (1997) in the Further Reading at the end of this chapter.) However, the following procedures are often used to modify the model such that the "new" residuals are uncorrelated.

1. Replace y_t by the *first difference,* as discussed in Section 17.8. The new dependent variable is

$$y'_t = y_t - y_{t-1}$$

2. Replace y_t by the *percentage change* during year t,

$$z_t = \left(\frac{y_t - y_{t-1}}{y_{t-1}} \right) 100$$

3. Include the lagged dependent variables, $y_{t-1}, y_{t-2}, \ldots$, as predictors of y_t in the regression equation. This is a modification of the autoregressive technique in Section 17.8; now the lagged dependent variables are used with $X_{1,t}, X_{2,t}, \ldots$ (which might also be lagged) to predict the time series variable, y_t.

4. Improve the existing model by attempting to discover other significant predictor variables. Because the residuals include the effect of these missing variables, residual autocorrelation often can be improved by including these additional variables. This procedure offers the best solution to the autocorrelation problem but, unfortunately, is easier said than done.

5. Because the errors are autocorrelated, you can *model the error term* in much the same way we handled the situation of autocorrelated observations. This modeling involves describing each residual, e_t, by its previous values, such as

$$e_t = \phi_1 e_{t-1} + \phi_2 e_{t-2} + \cdots + \phi_j e_{t-j} + u_t$$

The value of j is arbitrary and represents the maximum period over which errors are correlated. Now the problem becomes estimating not only the coefficients of the predictor variables (β_0, β_1, β_2, . . .) but also ϕ_1, ϕ_2, ... The hope is that the new error term, u_t, will contain mostly noise with little autocorrelation.

COMMENTS

Practically all computer packages can provide the Durbin-Watson statistic when performing multiple linear regression. In Section 14.6, we stated that when your data are *not* collected over time (but rather from different families, cities, companies, and so on), *this statistic is meaningless* and should be ignored. We mention this again as a reminder.

EXERCISES 17.56–17.62

UNDERSTANDING THE MECHANICS

17.56 Test that there is a positive autocorrelation in a data set of 16 observations with four independent variables for each of the following values of the Durbin-Watson test statistics. Use a .05 significance level.
  a. 2.50
  b. .40
  c. 1.01

APPLYING THE NEW CONCEPTS

17.57 What type of autocorrelation is indicated by a value of the Durbin-Watson statistic equal to 0? 2? 4?

17.58 Find the value of the Durbin-Watson statistic for the following yearly data.

Year	Data	Year	Data
1984	32	1992	42
1985	40	1993	48
1986	48	1994	54
1987	52	1995	64
1988	41	1996	42
1989	31	1997	35
1990	28	1998	32
1991	27	1999	27

  a. Use the model $\hat{y}_t = b_0 + b_1 y_{t-1}$.
  b. Test for positive autocorrelation. Use a significance level of .05.

17.59 Test for positive autocorrelation in the residuals of the fourth-order process in Exercise 17.36. Use a significance level of .05.

17.60 The "Misery Index" has been often referred to by politicians when it is to their advantage. This index is a combination of the national unemployment rate and inflation rate. The values for this index in percentage are presented below for the years 1978 through 1998.

Year	Misery Index
1978	15.1
1979	19.4

Year	Misery Index
1980	19.9
1981	18.3
1982	15.4
1983	12.3
1984	11.5
1985	10.4
1986	8.1
1987	10.6
1988	9.7
1989	10.3
1990	12.5
1991	10.4
1992	9.9
1993	9.6
1994	8.5
1995	8.3
1996	8.9
1997	6.6
1998	6.5

(Source: Adapted from *The Wall Street Journal*, "Happy Days: Are They Here Again?" Dec 10, 1998, p. A9.)

  a. Use the model $\hat{y}_t = b_0 + b_1 y_{t-1}$ to fit the data. Calculate the residuals.
  b. Find the value of the Durbin-Watson statistic and test for positive autocorrelation at the 5% significance level.

17.61 Test for positive autocorrelation in the residuals of the multiple regression equation in Exercise 17.46. Use a significance level of .05.

USING THE COMPUTER

17.62 **[DATA SET EX17-62]** *Variable description:*

Time: Monthly time periods numbered 1 through 60.
GrossRev: Monthly gross revenue at Cinemark Theatres

The owner of Cinemark Theatres recorded the monthly gross revenue in thousands of dollars from 1995 through 1999. Regress GrossRev on the independent variable Time. What is the Durbin-Watson statistic for this regression model? Does positive autocorrelation exist at the 5% significance level?

In this chapter, we have looked briefly at several popular **forecasting** techniques. To cover all aspects of time series forecasting would fill an entire textbook. It is a fascinating side of statistics because anyone having a reliable "crystal ball" technique for predicting the future definitely is one step ahead of the game. We hope that this chapter has whetted your appetite to pursue further reading in this area.

Forecasting methods can be divided into two broad categories: qualitative procedures and quantitative techniques. When arriving at a **qualitative** forecast, expert opinion is used to arrive at a "best educated" estimate of future behavior. One such method is the **Delphi method,** which requires input from a team of experts. Each team member is then informed as to the responses from all other members and asked to reevaluate his or her opinion in light of this information. This process is continued for several rounds until each member of the team feels confident in his or her final decision.

Quantitative forecasting, the main emphasis of this chapter, dealt with two (sometimes overlapping) sets of procedures: time series techniques and multiple linear regression on time series data. **Time series procedures** attempt to capture the past behavior of the time series and use this information to predict future values. No external predictors are considered; only the past observations are used to describe and predict the future value of the time series variable. Time series methods include (1) the **decomposition** procedure, which extracts and extends the trend and seasonal components, (2) **exponential smoothing,** which reduces randomness and forecasts future values by using the smoothed values, and (3) **autoregressive** forecasting, which predicts future values by using a linear combination of past values.

There are various exponential smoothing procedures; the proper one to use depends on the nature of the time series. **Simple exponential smoothing** works best when the time series contains neither trend nor seasonality. **Linear exponential smoothing** is better for a time series that does contain trend but has no seasonality, and **linear and seasonal exponential smoothing** should be used for a time series that has both components.

EXPONENTIAL SMOOTHING

	STRUCTURE OF TIME SERIES	
TYPE	Contains Trend	Contains Seasonality
Simple Exponential Smoothing	NO	NO
Linear Exponential Smoothing	YES	NO
Linear and Seasonal Exponential Smoothing	YES	YES

SUMMARY

There are many factors that determine the strengths of any forecasting procedure, including the (1) time horizon of the forecast, (2) stationary of the data, and (3) presence of trend, seasonality, or cyclical activity. To measure the forecast accuracy of a particular method, you can calculate the predictive mean squared error (MSE), the mean absolute deviation (MAD), or the mean absolute percentage error (MAPE). The **MSE** is found by squaring each of the residuals obtained by applying this technique to the past observations and then deriving the average of these squared residuals. This measure is very sensitive to one or two very large residuals. The **MAD** is calculated by averaging the absolute values of the residuals and is less sensitive to a single large residual. The **MAPE** uses the *relative* error of each forecast value to arrive at a measure of prediction accuracy. It is very useful for comparing the accuracy of a particular forecasting technique on two different time series, since the effect of the magnitude of the observations has been removed.

The advantage of the time series methods is that there is no need to search for external predictors to explain the behavior of the dependent variable. One disadvantage is that the patterns within the observed values can be extremely complex and difficult to determine. Such methods often are hard to "sell" to managers, who may not be able to understand the technique.

Multiple linear regression forecasting requires additional input data; for each time period, data are recorded for each predictor (independent) variable as well as for the dependent variable, y_t. Such data are **time series data,** since the variables are observed across time. This situation differs from many of the earlier applications of linear regression, which used data gathered at one point in time, that is, **cross-sectional data.** In a time series regression model, the predictor variables can include **lagged** dependent or lagged predictor variables as well as **dummy** variables to represent seasonality or the occurrence (or nonoccurrence) of a particular event (such as an election year).

When you use multiple linear regression techniques on time series data, you often will violate the assumption of independent errors. The **Durbin-Watson statistic** can be used to test for significant autocorrelation in the regression residuals. If significant autocorrelation is present, the tests of hypothesis and confidence intervals contained in the regression output are unreliable.

The advantages of multiple linear regression on time series data include: (1) it is a very flexible approach, in that a wide variety of explanatory variables can be included in the model; (2) it allows for lagging the predictor variables, including lagged values of the dependent variable; and (3) it is generally easier to explain to managers, who can see easily which variables are predicting the behavior of the dependent variable. On the other hand, residual autocorrelation often is a problem. It may be caused by missing variables in the prediction equation, which typically are extremely difficult to determine. Also, a very complex pattern within the observed time series may be difficult to capture using a linear combination of predictor variables. Finally, forecasting with this technique becomes extremely difficult unless lagged variables are used. Dummy variables can be included, provided that they can be predicted with certainty. A dummy variable representing an election year would be acceptable, whereas one representing the occurrence (or nonoccurrence) of an earthquake would not be.

FURTHER READING

Bowerman, B. L., and R. T. O'Connell. *Time Series and Forecasting: An Applied Approach,* 3rd ed. North Scituate, Mass: Duxbury Press, 1993.

Brockwell, P. J., and R. A. Davis. *Introduction to Time Series and Forecasting,* New York: Springer-Verlag, 1996.

Hamilton, J. D. *Time Series Analysis.* Princeton, NJ: Princeton University Press, 1994.

Hanke, J., and A. Reitsch. *Business Forecasting,* 6th ed. Upper Saddle River, NJ: Prentice Hall, 1996.

Makridakis, S., S. C. Wheelwright, and R. J. Hyndman. *Forecasting: Methods and Applications,* 3rd ed. New York: Wiley, 1997.

Sincich, T., and W. Mendenhall. *A Second Course in Statistics: Regression Analysis,* 5th ed. Upper Saddle River, NJ: Prentice-Hall, 1996.

SUMMARY OF FORMULAS

FORECASTING MODELS

1. Naive:

$$\hat{y}_{t+1} = y_t$$

2. Using seasonality and trend:

$$\hat{y}_{t+1} = [b_0 + b_1(t+1)]$$
$$\cdot \text{(seasonal index for period } t+1)$$

3. Simple exponential smoothing:

$$\hat{y}_{t+1} = S_t$$

where

$$S_t = Ay_t + (1-A)S_{t-1}$$
$$0 < A < 1.$$

4. Using Holt's method (exponential smoothing for a time series containing trend):

$$\hat{y}_{t+1} = S_t + b_t$$

where

$$S_t = Ay_t + (1-A)(S_{t-1} + b_{t-1})$$
$$b_t = B(S_t - S_{t-1}) + (1-B)b_{t-1}$$
$$0 < A < 1, \quad 0 < B < 1$$

5. Using Winters' method (exponential smoothing for a time series containing trend and seasonality):

$$\hat{y}_{t+m} = (S_t + mb_t) \cdot F_{t+m-L}$$

where

m = number of periods ahead to be forecast

$L = 4$ for quarterly data, 12 for monthly data

$$S_t = A\left(\frac{y_t}{F_{t-L}}\right) + (1-A)(S_{t-1} + b_{t-1})$$

$$F_t = B\left(\frac{y_t}{S_t}\right) + (1-B)F_{t-L}$$

$$b_t = C(S_t - S_{t-1}) + (1-C)b_{t-1}$$

$$0 < A < 1, \quad 0 < B < 1, \quad 0 < C < 1$$

6. Using a pth-order autoregressive model:

$$\hat{y}_{t+1} = b_0 + b_1 y_t + b_2 y_{t-1} + \cdots + b_p y_{t-p+1}$$

ADDITIONAL FORMULAS

1. Sample autocorrelation of lag k:

$$r_k = \frac{\sum\limits_{t=1}^{T-k}(y_t - \bar{y})(y_{t+k} - \bar{y})}{\sum\limits_{t=1}^{T}(y_t - \bar{y})^2}$$

2. Durbin-Watson statistic:

$$DW = \frac{\sum\limits_{t=2}^{T}(e_t - e_{t-1})^2}{\sum\limits_{t=1}^{T} e_t^2}$$

MEASUREMENTS OF FORECAST ERROR

$$MAD = \frac{\sum |e_t|}{n}$$

$$(\text{predictive}) \ MSE = \frac{\sum e_t^2}{n}$$

$$MAPE = \frac{\sum \left| \dfrac{e_t}{y_t} \right|}{n}$$

REVIEW EXERCISES 17.63–17.76

17.63 A set of monthly data has been gathered over three years from January 1997 to December 1999. From these data, the seasonal indexes for the 12 months are found to be

$S_1 = 0.75$	$S_2 = 0.85$	$S_3 = 0.95$	$S_4 = 0.99$	$S_5 = 0.90$	$S_6 = 1.01$
$S_7 = 1.20$	$S_8 = 1.10$	$S_9 = 1.15$	$S_{10} = 1.05$	$S_{11} = 1.11$	$S_{12} = 0.94$

The least squares line through the deseasonalized data is found to be

$$\hat{d}_t = 2.73 + 0.62t$$

for the 36 monthly periods. Find the forecast for monthly periods 37, 38, 39, 40, and 41.

17.64 The estimated monthly retail sales (in millions of dollars) for variety stores are shown in the table. Using simple exponential smoothing with $A = .1$, find the forecasted yield for October using the data from the previous months.

Month	Retail Sales	Month	Retail Sales
Jan	525	June	537
Feb	534	July	543
Mar	529	Aug	543
Apr	531	Sept	543
May	540		

(Source: *Current Business Reports*, 1993, Bureau of the Census, p. 5.)

17.65 The number of employees at Computeron has fluctuated over the past nine years. The following table lists the number of employees on the payroll at Computeron at the end of each year for the years 1991 to 1999. The company would like you to forecast employment in 2000 by using the linear exponential smoothing technique.

Year	Employees	Year	Employees
1991	1030	1996	1075
1992	1020	1997	1130
1993	1941	1998	1135
1994	1050	1999	1175
1995	1062		

    a. Using the initial estimate of the slope to be zero with $A = .2$ and $B = .2$, determine the predicted value for the employment at the end of 2000.

    b. Using the least squares estimate for the slope from the first three years of data, redo part (a).

    c. Compare the predicted values in parts (a) and (b).

17.66 Two forecasting procedures were used to forecast the 12 quarters from 1997 to 1999. The forecast errors for each quarter are given. Compute the predictive MSE and MAD for each forecasting procedure. Interpret the results.

Year	Quarter	Procedure 1 Forecast Error	Procedure 2 Forecast Error
1997	1	−1.0	.7
	2	.5	−.5
	3	−2.1	−.2
	4	2.5	.9
1998	1	.9	.1
	2	2.1	.2
	3	−1.3	−.3
	4	1.6	.9
1999	1	2.7	11.2
	2	−1.9	−.1
	3	2.4	.2
	4	−1.2	−.2

17.67 The amount of money spent on research and development by Energy Today in finding economical uses of alternative fuels is given over a four-year period. Units are in $10,000.

Year	Quarter 1	Quarter 2	Quarter 3	Quarter 4
1996	4.2	4.5	4.8	4.0
1997	4.3	4.7	5.6	4.4
1998	4.6	4.9	5.7	4.5
1999	4.7	5.0	5.8	4.7

Use Holt's two-parameter linear exponential smoothing technique to obtain a forecast for each of the quarters except for the first time period. Let $A = .3$ and $B = .2$. Use the least squares estimate of the trend from the first five periods for the initial value of the slope. Calculate the predictive MSE.

17.68 The increase in government income (in billions of dollars) from 1989 to 1993 is illustrated by the data in the table.

Year	Quarter 1	Quarter 2	Quarter 3	Quarter 4
1989	599.4	607.5	616.5	626.7
1990	643.7	655.8	663.9	675.8
1991	693.3	698.2	701.2	705.0
1992	717.8	726.2	730.7	738.7
1993	757.4	761.3		

(Source: *Survey of Current Business,* 1993, U.S. Department of Commerce, Bureau of Economic Analysis, p. 82.)

a. Determine whether the data are stationary. If the data are not stationary, take differences until it becomes clear that the resulting time series is stationary.

b. Fit a first-order autoregressive equation to the difference data. Does this appear to be a satisfactory fit?

17.69 National Finance Company provides short-term loans to consumers to finance household goods. The amount of interest received quarterly is given below in units of $10,000.

Year	Quarter 1	Quarter 2	Quarter 3	Quarter 4
1995	20	31	39	42
1996	28	35	43	45
1997	31	38	45	49
1998	35	40	43	52
1999	38	44	48	56

Determine the multiple regression equation that takes into account trend and seasonality.

17.70 An independent gas station allows its customers to buy gasoline on credit. The amount of credit on the books for the 20 quarters of the years 1995 through 1999 follows. Find the multiple regression equation that takes into account trend and seasonality. The figures in the table are in units of $10,000.

Year	Quarter 1	Quarter 2	Quarter 3	Quarter 4
1995	2.3	2.7	3.4	3.0
1996	2.4	3.0	3.6	3.2
1997	2.6	3.1	3.8	3.4
1998	3.0	3.3	4.0	3.2
1999	3.2	3.4	4.4	3.5

17.71 Using Holt's two-parameter linear exponential technique, find the smoothed value at time $t = 12$, where the observed value at $t = 12$ is 13.6 and the observed value at $t = 11$ is 12.1. Also let $S_{11} = 7.4$, $S_{10} = 10.4$, $b_{11} = 0.6$, $A = .1$, and $B = .2$.

17.72 In Holt's two-parameter linear exponential smoothing technique, why do you think the values of A and B are typically less than or equal to .3?

17.73 Explain what you should look for in determining the appropriate forecasting procedure.

17.74 The Gross Domestic Product (GDP) is considered an important measure of U.S. output. The quarterly GDP values (in billions of dollars) are provided in the table.

Year	Quarter 1	Quarter 2	Quarter 3	Quarter 4
1989	5113.1	5201.7	5281.0	5337.0
1990	5375.4	5443.3	5514.6	5597.9
1991	5631.7	5697.7	5758.6	5803.7
1992	5908.7	5991.4	6059.5	6194.4
1993	6261.6	6327.6	6395.9	6450.0

(Source: Adapted from *Economic Indicators,* Dec. 1993, Department of Commerce, Bureau of Economic Analysis, p. 1.)

Use Winters' linear and seasonal smoothing technique to find the smoothed values for Quarter 4 of 1993. Let $A = .2$, $B = .1$, and $C = .1$. Using procedure 1, set the initial estimates of the seasonal factors to 1.0 and let $b_0 = 0$.

17.75 [DATA SET EX17-75] *Variable description:*

Year: Years from 1995 to 1998
Month: Month of the year
FactoryPay: Average weekly earnings of factory workers reported monthly

Average weekly earnings of factory workers have fluctuated with cycles in the economy but generally have trended upward. These data represent earnings before taxes and other deductions and include overtime pay. Find the predictive MSE using the following autoregressive equation.

$$\hat{y}_t = b_0 + b_1 y_{t-1} + b_2 y_{t-2} + b_3 y_{t-3}$$

(Source: Adapted from *The Wall Street Journal,* "Weekly Earnings," July 23, 1998, p. A1.)

17.76 [DATA SET EX17-76] *Variable description:*

Time: Quarterly time periods numbered 1 through 20
NetProf: Quarterly net profit for school supply store
X_1: Dummy variable equal to 1 to indicate the first quarter
X_2: Dummy variable equal to 1 to indicate the second quarter
X_3: Dummy variable equal to 1 to indicate the third quarter

The manager of a school supply store kept track of the store's quarterly net profit, measured in thousands of dollars, for the five years since the store's opening. As the store's business grew, the manager noticed that profits were magnified according to seasonal effect. Therefore, by multiplying the Time variable by the dummy variables, the manager created new variables: TimeX1, TimeX2, and TimeX3. These variables are used to include the effects of interaction between the time variable and the dummy variables representing the quarter.

    a. From the computer printout, would you say that the interaction terms are useful in explaining quarterly net profit?

    b. What is the predictive MSE for the model using all of the independent variables, including the interaction terms? Use the computer to run a regression analysis for the model using all the independent variables but excluding the interaction terms, and find the predictive MSE. Compare these two predictive MSEs.

SUMMARY OUTPUT

Regression Statistics

Multiple R	0.9970122
R Square	0.9940333
Adjusted R Square	0.9905528
Standard Error	1.1999653
Observations	20

ANOVA

	df	SS	MS	F	Significance F
Regression	7	2878.6505	411.235786	285.5969	2.22086E-12
Residual	12	17.279	1.43991667		
Total	19	2895.9295			

	Coefficients	Standard Error	t Stat	P-value	Lower 95%	Upper 95%
Intercept	−0.1	1.2585342	−0.0794575	0.937978	−2.842110415	2.6421104
Time	0.545	0.09486558	5.74497065	9.24E-05	0.33830565	0.7516943
X1	0.1275	1.61271494	0.07905923	0.938289	−3.386303943	3.6413039
X2	−0.71	1.66488425	−0.4264561	0.677326	−4.337471113	2.9174711
X3	0.3	1.72070585	0.17434706	0.8645	−3.449095933	4.0490959
TimeX1	−0.2925	0.13416019	−2.1802294	0.049873	−0.584809952	−0.00019
TimeX2	0.58	0.13416019	4.32318985	0.000991	0.287690048	0.87231
TimeX3	1.855	0.13416019	13.8267537	9.83E-90	1.562690048	2.14731

17.77 The manager of the school supply store in Exercise 17.76 decided to investigate another regression model, involving four independent variables. The independent variables contain quarterly net profit lagged by one through four periods and are labeled as NetProfLag1, NetProfLag2, NetProfLag3, and NetProfLag4.

a. From the computer printout, which lagged variables are useful in explaining quarterly net profit?

b. Compare the predictive MSE for this model with that found in Exercise 17.76 part (b).

SUMMARY OUTPUT

Regression Statistics

Multiple R	0.97892864
R Square	0.95830129
Adjusted R Square	0.94313812
Standard Error	3.07675185
Observations	16

ANOVA

	df	SS	MS	F	Significance F
Regression	4	2393.07895	598.269738	63.1992749	1.6143E-07
Residual	11	104.130421	9.46640194		
Total	15	2497.20938			

	Coefficients	Standard Error	t Stat	P-value	Lower 95%	Upper 95%
Intercept	5.11893227	1.74265482	2.93743329	0.01350962	1.28337294	8.9544916
NetProfLag1	−0.0614597	0.07275105	−0.8447948	0.41622153	−0.2215838	0.0986644
NetProfLag2	−0.1286208	0.08929934	−1.4403333	0.1776229	−0.3251674	0.0679258
NetProfLag3	-0.0339803	0.09040588	−0.3758637	0.71416607	−0.2329624	0.1650018
NetProfLag4	1.17197573	0.08949793	13.0950045	4.718E-08	0.97499203	1.3689594

INSIGHTS FROM STATISTICS IN ACTION: THE CONSUMER PRICE INDEX: DUE FOR A CHANGE?

The introductory Statistics in Action section at the beginning of this chapter discussed the problem of trying to measure the rate of inflation based on the Consumer Price Index (CPI). This index contains the prices of about 90,000 items and services, 75% of which are related to housing (41%), transportation (17%), and food (17%). Many financial analysts believe the CPI overstates the rate of inflation, and a 1996 Stanford University study supports this argument.

Suppose that a labor union representative is in the process of preparing a budget for 1998 and would like to forecast the CPI index for these months. Use the following monthly CPI data to answer the questions immediately following.

Year	Jan	Feb	Mar	Apr	May	June	July	Aug	Sep	Oct	Nov	Dec
1980	77.8	78.9	80.1	77.8	81.8	82.7	82.7	83.3	84.0	84.8	85.5	86.3
1981	87.0	87.9	88.5	89.1	89.8	90.6	91.6	92.3	93.2	93.4	93.7	94.0
1982	94.3	94.6	94.5	94.9	95.8	97.0	97.5	97.7	97.9	98.2	98.0	97.6
1983	97.8	97.9	97.9	98.6	99.2	99.5	99.9	100.2	100.7	101.0	101.2	101.3
1984	101.9	102.4	102.6	103.1	103.4	103.7	104.1	104.5	105.0	105.3	105.3	105.3
1985	105.5	106.0	106.4	106.9	107.3	107.6	107.8	108.0	108.3	108.7	109.0	109.3
1986	109.6	109.3	108.8	108.6	108.9	109.5	109.5	109.7	110.2	110.3	110.4	110.5
1987	111.2	111.6	112.1	112.7	113.1	113.5	113.8	114.4	115.0	115.3	115.4	115.4
1988	115.7	116.0	116.5	117.1	117.5	118.0	118.5	119.0	119.8	120.2	120.3	120.5
1989	121.1	121.6	122.3	123.1	123.8	124.1	124.4	124.6	125.0	125.6	125.9	126.1
1990	127.4	128.0	128.7	128.9	129.2	129.9	130.4	131.6	132.7	133.5	133.8	133.8
1991	134.6	134.8	135.0	135.2	135.6	136.0	136.2	136.6	137.2	137.4	137.8	137.9
1992	138.1	138.6	139.3	139.5	139.7	140.2	140.5	140.9	141.3	141.8	142.0	141.9
1993	142.6	143.1	143.6	144.0	144.2	144.4	144.4	144.8	145.1	145.7	145.8	145.8
1994	146.2	146.7	147.2	147.4	147.5	148.0	148.4	149.0	149.4	149.5	149.7	149.7
1995	150.3	150.9	151.4	151.9	152.2	152.5	152.5	152.9	153.2	153.7	153.6	153.5
1996	154.4	154.9	155.7	156.3	156.6	156.7	157.0	157.3	157.8	158.3	158.6	158.6
1997	159.1	159.6	160.0	160.2	160.1	160.3	160.5	160.8	161.2	161.6	161.5	161.3

1. Use the Excel decomposition program to examine the trend and seasonality within the CPI data. In particular, do you observe much seasonality within the data?
2. Based on your analysis in question 1, which of the three exponential smoothing techniques do you think would be most appropriate?
3. Determine the predictive MSE for each of the three methods of exponential smoothing. Use procedure 2 and the optimal smoothing constants.
4. Which of the three smoothing models provides the minimum predictive MSE? Based on your answer, determine the forecasts for the first six months of 1998.
5. Find the autocorrelations using the raw data and the first differences. Which of the two provides a stationary series?
6. Use a second-order autoregressive model with the stationary series found in question 5 to predict the CPI index for the first two months of 1998. What is the predictive MSE using this model?

Sources: *The Dallas Morning News*, "CPI Change to Affect Everyone, Like It or Not," Dec. 15, 1996, p. 6H.

The Dallas Morning News, "1997 a Good Year for Consumers, Offering Lowest Inflation since '86," Jan. 14, 1998, p. 17A.

CHAPTER 17 APPENDIX: DATA ANALYSIS WITH **MINITAB**

QUANTITATIVE BUSINESS FORECASTING

For trend analysis, exponential smoothing, and autoregressive models, MINITAB has various procedures which can be viewed by clicking on **Stat ➤ Time Series.** Because MINITAB uses a different algorithm from Excel in deriving the initial estimates, the results from MINITAB and Excel will generally differ. By clicking on the **Trend Analysis** option, a general trend model can be fit to the time series data and provide forecasts. The following user form, entitled Trend Analysis, will appear. Choose from among the linear, quadratic, exponential growth/decay, or S-curve models. The deseasonalized Video-Comp sales data are used in this example using the linear model selection. The graph of the linear trend equation appears as the output to this procedure. Use this procedure to fit the trend when there is no seasonal component to your time series. In the MINITAB output, MSD is the mean squared deviation and is the same as the mean squared error (MSE) defined in equation 17.13. Also, MINITAB's MAPE is the MAPE defined in equation 17.14, multiplied by 100.

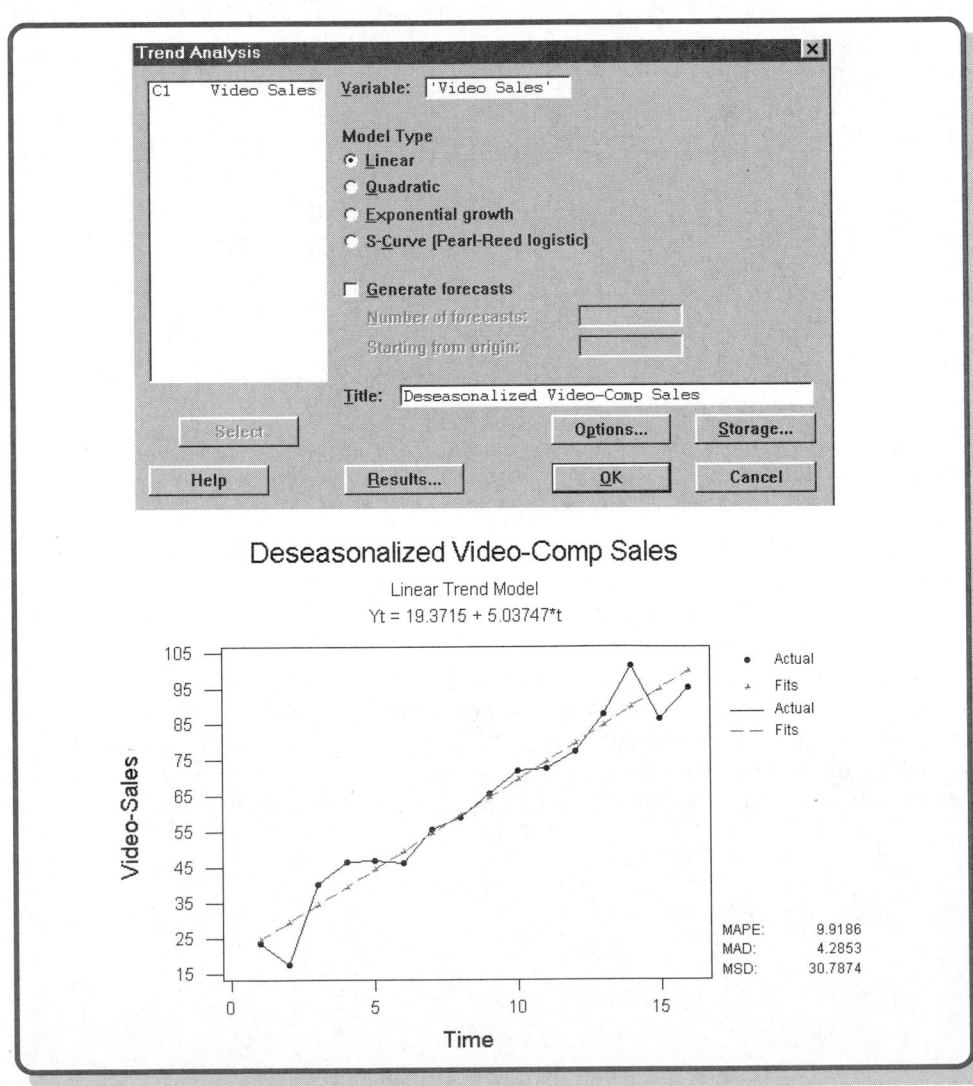

To select the single exponential smoothing model with either optimal or specified weights, click on the **Single Exp Smoothing** option. Short-term forecasts can be selected as an option. These forecasts appear in red on the time series plot along with 95% prediction interval bands. If the **Start From Origin** box is left blank, MINITAB generates forecasts from the end of the data. The user form for the attendance data in Table 17.1 is used to illustrate this procedure. The graph that follows displays the output using this procedure.

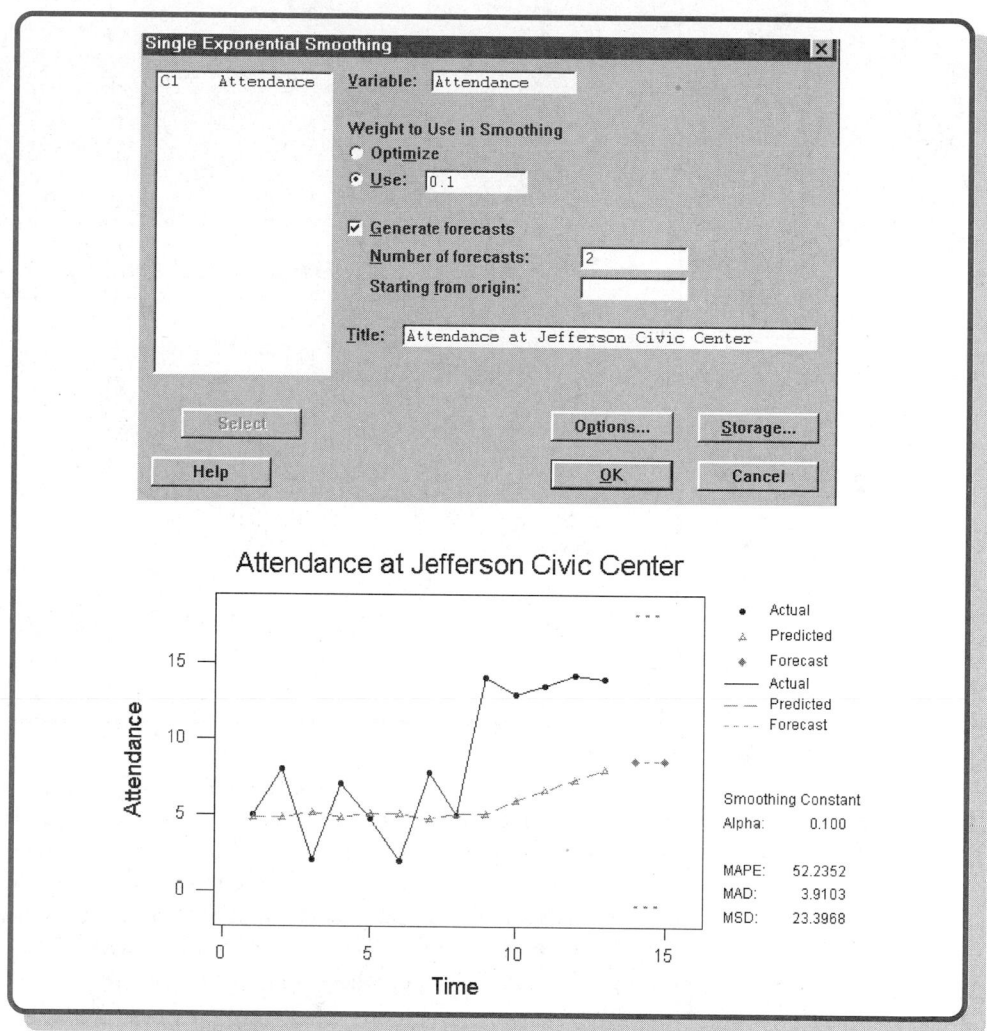

To select Holt's two-parameter linear exponential smoothing model with either optimal or specified weights, click on the **Double Exp Smoothing** option. The user form for this procedure is similar to that for the Single Exp Smoothing option except that a smoothing weight for trend is used. The user form for the Jackson City's tax data in Example 17.5 is used to illustrate this procedure. The graph that follow displays the output when using this procedure.

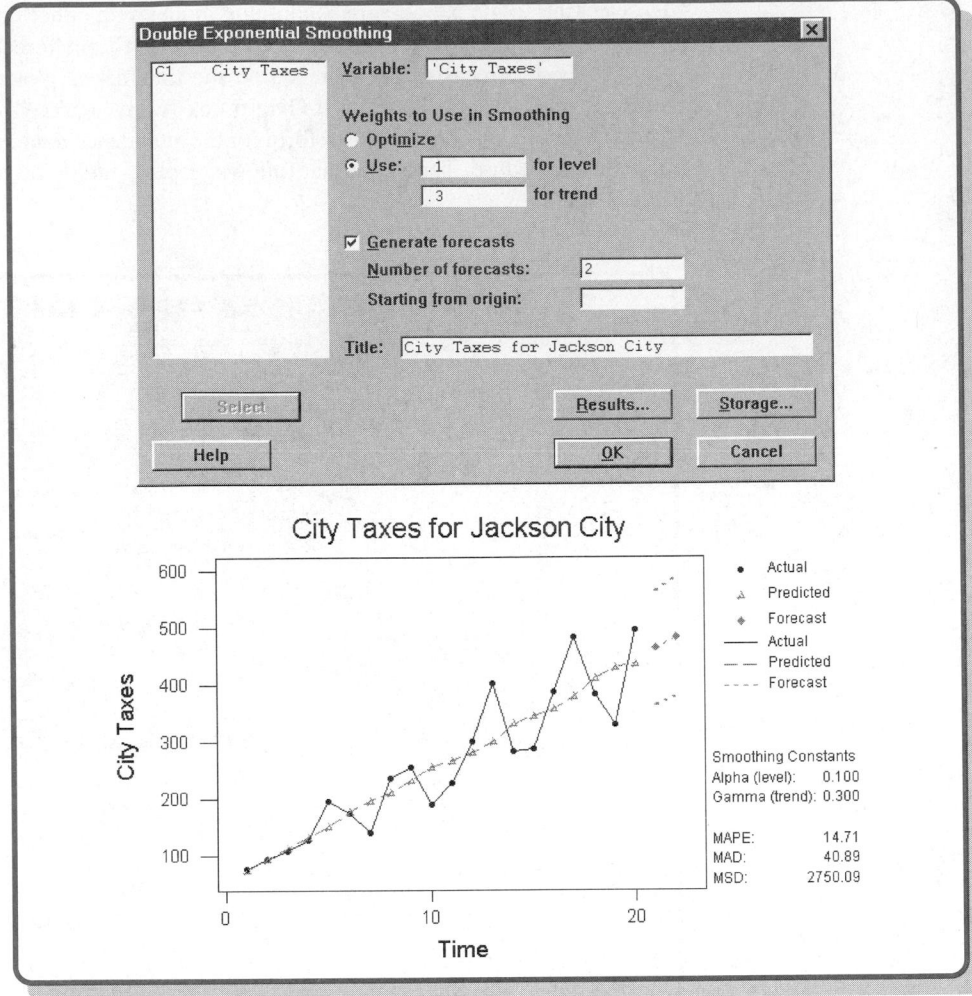

By clicking on the **Winters' Method** option, Winters' linear and seasonal exponential smoothing (either additive or multiplicative seasonality) can be used with either optimal or specified weights. Chapter 17 uses Winters' method to model only multiplicative seasonality. The user form for this procedure is similar to that for the **Double Exp Smoothing** option except that a smoothing weight for seasonality is used. The user form for Jackson City's tax data in Example 17.5 is used to illustrate this procedure. The graph that follows displays the output when using this procedure.

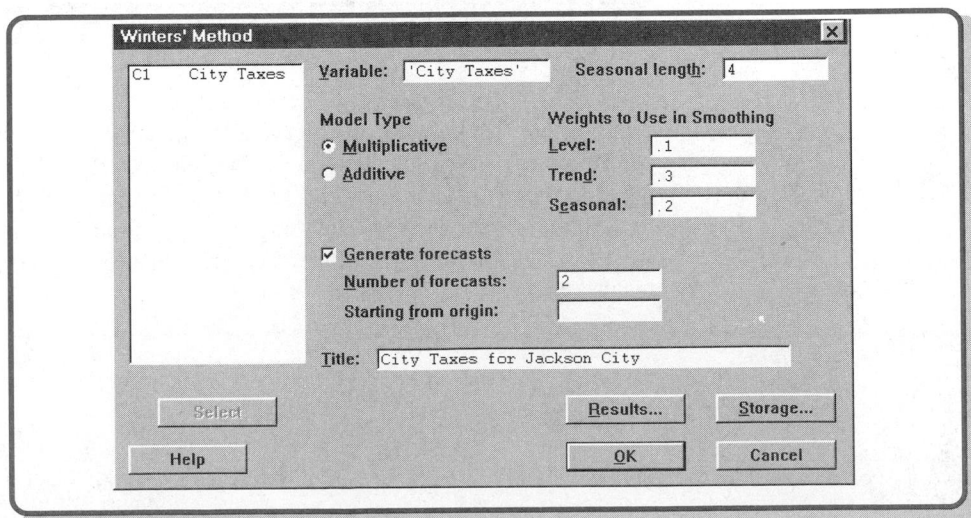

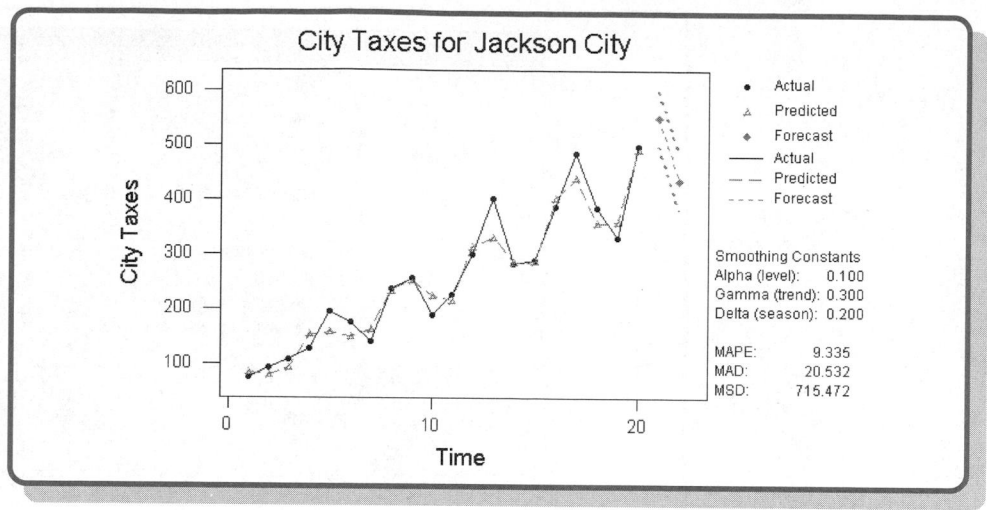

Clicking on **Stat ➤ Time Series ➤ Lag** will produce the user form labeled **Lag** as displayed below. **Lag** computes the lagged values for a column and stores them in a new column. To lag a time series, MINITAB moves the data down the column and inserts a missing value symbol at the top of the column. The number of missing value symbols inserted depends upon the length of the lag. Quarterly profits of Ken's Auto Paint Shop are listed in column C1, labeled **Profits.** The first lag of these data will appear in column C2 after the **OK** button is clicked.

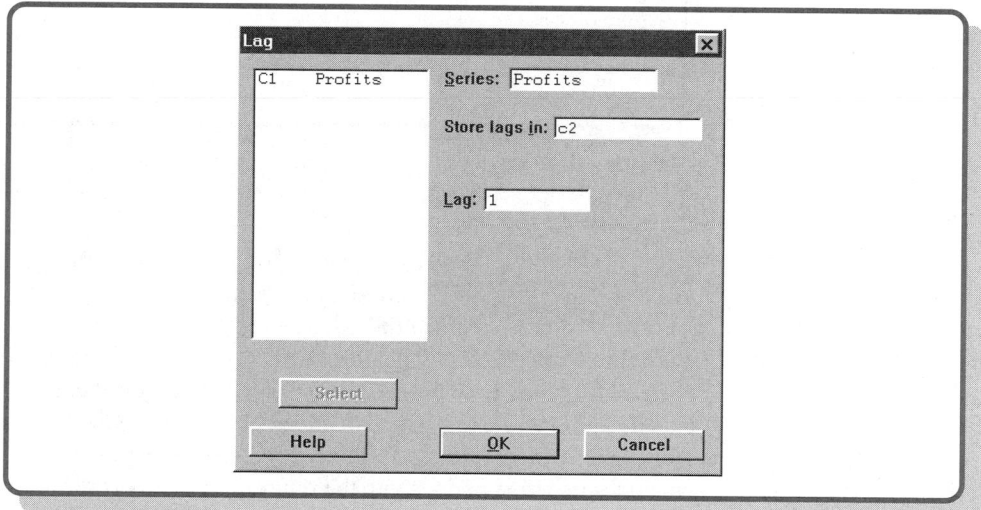

Clicking on **Stat ➤ Time Series ➤ Autocorrelation** will produce the user form labeled **Autocorrelation Function** as displayed below. The options on this user form produce a plot of the autocorrelations of a time series. From this plot, decisions can be made as to the choice of terms to include in an autoregressive model. Quarterly profits of Ken's Auto Paint Shop are listed in column C1, labeled **Profits.** The resulting graph includes confidence limits for the correlations and is displayed after the user form. The column labeled T and LBQ are the associated t-statistics and Ljung-Box Q statistics that are used to determine an appropriate model. In this example, the default number of lags was used. The default number is $n/4$ for a series with less than or equal to 240 observations, and $\sqrt{n} + 45$ for a series with more than 240 observations, where n is the number of observations in the series.

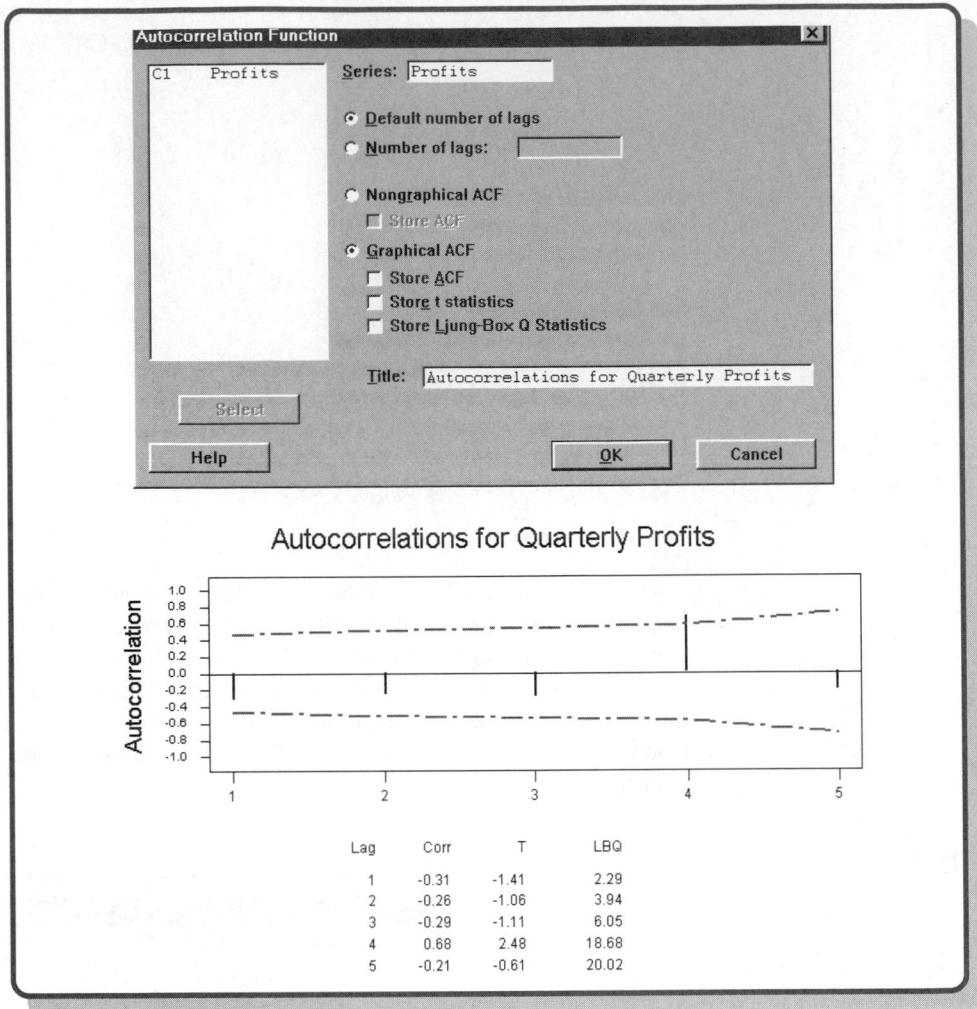

The ARIMA option may be used to produce an autoregressive model. The user form labeled ARIMA can be used to model patterns in a time series. In this example, quarterly profits of Ken's Auto Paint Shop, listed in Table 17.9, are used. In the user form a 4 typed into the **Autoregressive (Nonseasonal)** box indicates that the first four lagged terms will be used in an autoregressive model. By clicking on the **Forecast** button, the user form labeled **ARIMA-Forecasts** will appear. In this example, the origin is stated as five, since four lagged time periods are used. Seventeen forecasts will be shown in the output. This includes two time periods into the future. The forecasts for this model and their confidence intervals are presented following this user form.

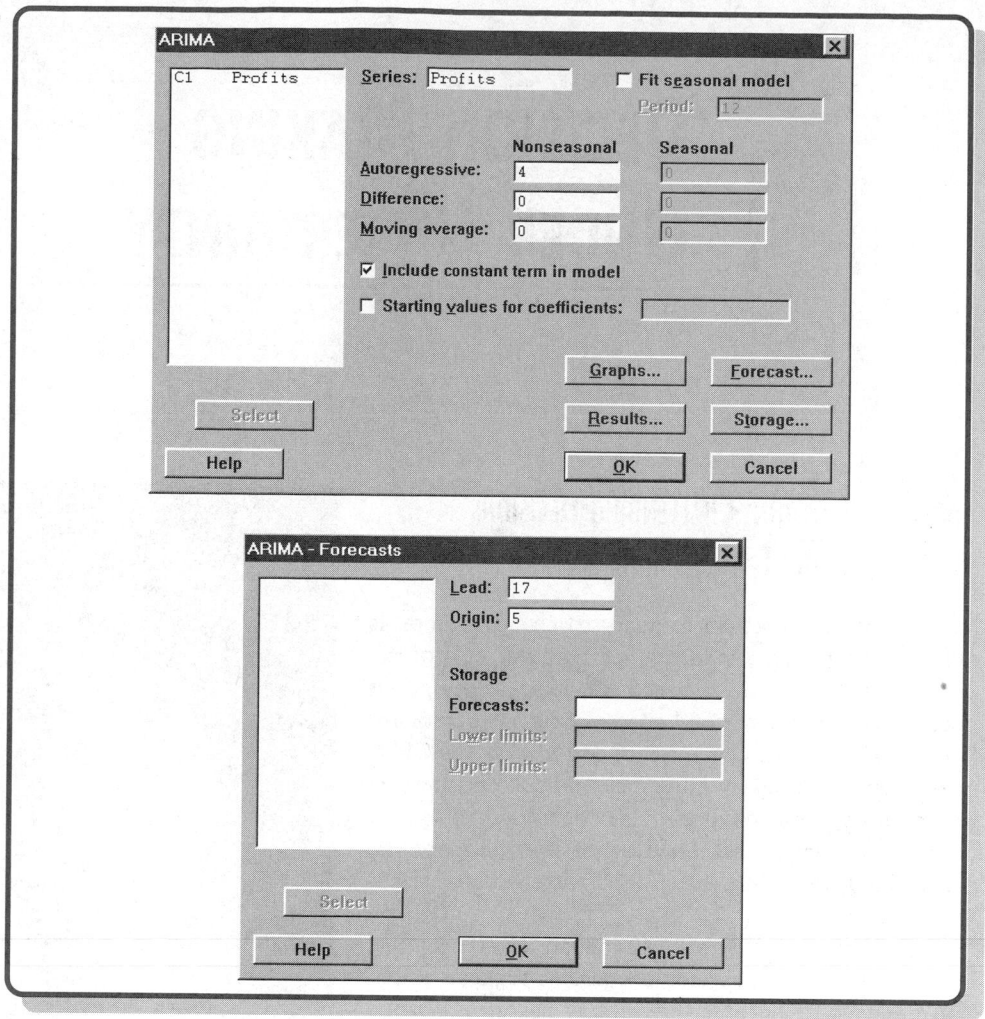

```
            Forecasts from period 5

                                 95 Percent Limits
       Period      Forecast        Lower        Upper         Actual
           6        17.1934      13.1681      21.2188        15.2100
           7         4.0170      -0.1101       8.1440         5.7200
           8         3.3784      -0.8601       7.6169         2.6500
           9         3.8137      -0.5731       8.2006         4.1200
          10        17.2130      11.5532      22.8728        14.3300
          11         5.5584      -0.1441      11.2610         5.2500
          12         3.6957      -2.1066       9.4980         6.7500
          13         2.4243      -3.6334       8.4820         6.3100
          14        16.8297       9.9022      23.7572        15.0200
          15         6.9463       0.0128      13.8797         2.8300
          16         4.2614      -2.7337      11.2565         4.5600
          17         1.1232      -6.2130       8.4594         4.8100
          18        16.1480       8.1769      24.1191        16.8200
          19         8.1743       0.2023      16.1463         4.7500
          20         5.0796      -2.9199      13.0792         8.5400
          21        -0.0103      -8.4229       8.4024
          22        15.2209       6.3529      24.0889
```

DECISION MAKING UNDER UNCERTAINTY

STATISTICS IN ACTION: CHALLENGING DECISIONS FOR CEOS OF THE TOBACCO INDUSTRY

Few companies have had to adapt to changing times as much as the tobacco industry. In May 1960, 66% of the population said that the tobacco industry was doing all it could to reduce the harmful effects of cigarette smoking. In June 1998, that percentage dropped to 17%. The CEOs of the tobacco industry must make critical decisions on how to sway public opinion. In fact, decision making may be the most important function of the CEOs of the tobacco industry since these decisions can have nationwide implications.

The tobacco industry's $40 million advertising blitz in spring of 1998 against comprehensive tobacco legislation, designed to increase the price of cigarettes, warned that there were "some" who sought to resurrect "the big tax bill." The industry was able to tailor its ads to aid specific members of Congress in the elections in the fall of 1998. Spending by private industry is not limited and in some cases may not even be publicly disclosed under federal law. The tobacco industry has to make big decisions with its money. Should it run hard-hitting ads, or should it provide individual campaign donations to obtain legislation that is favorable to the tobacco industry?

In a television ad campaign, the tobacco industry could decide to support those who voted to kill legislation that would raise the tax on cigarettes. In fact, a $40 million ad campaign in the spring of 1998 helped to convince congressional members that public opinion could be swayed on the issue of raising taxes on cigarettes. The National Center for Tobacco-Free Kids ran some TV ads featuring former Surgeon General C. Everett Koop warning viewers to consider the source of the tobacco ads. However, very few of these type of ads ran compared to the number from the tobacco industry.

CEOs at many of today's corporations face tough decisions. They rely on the dynamics of the political and

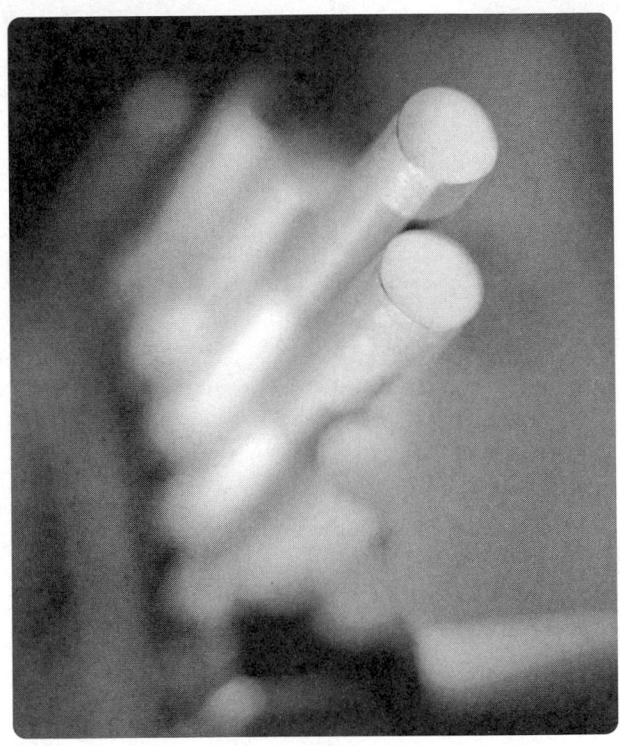

economic events of the time. The CEOs of the tobacco industry have many critical decisions to make in implementing a strategy for the industry to continue to be profitable. According to the Center for Responsive Politics, tobacco companies and political action committees had donated $5.3 million for the 1998 election cycle. That is more than double the amount they had given in the last non-presidential election cycle.

Decision making in the face of uncertainty can be a tricky, yet at the same time fascinating, venture. When dealing with a structured decision problem, you will need to examine such questions as: Am I a risk taker or am I risk averse? Should I attempt to purchase outside data and/or a consultant to better predict the best course of action?

This chapter will explore several decision strategies and will enable you to:

- Explain the difference between a conservative and a risky decision strategy;
- Discuss the pros and cons of maximizing your *expected* payoff in a decision problem;
- Perform a sensitivity analysis that examines how sensitive your decision solution is to unknown future conditions;
- Calculate the *risk* associated with a particular course of action; and
- Construct a decision tree to help visualize the decision problem and to allow for revising the probabilities of future events in light of new information about the future.

A LOOK BACK/INTRODUCTION

You have been exposed to decision making in which you use a statistical test of hypothesis. The final step for any test of hypothesis is to reject or fail to reject the null hypothesis, H_0. The previous chapters examined a number of such tests, ranging from a decision regarding two means (for example, is $\mu_1 > \mu_2$?) to selecting predictor variables for a multiple regression equation.

The previous tests of hypothesis concentrated on the *probabilistic* aspects of decision making. For example, if the probability of observing a t value as large as the computed sample value was less than a predetermined significance level α, we rejected H_0 and decided to keep a particular predictor variable in the regression equation. Such procedures are intended to help you make statistical decisions regarding certain population **parameters,** such as the mean (μ) or standard deviation (σ) of a normal population, the population coefficient (β) for a certain independent variable in a regression equation, or the proportion of successes (p) for a binomial situation.

We now examine a different side of decision making, a side that is particularly useful when money is involved. This area of statistics allows the decision maker to consider the various benefits and losses associated with each possible alternative in an effort to find the best decision. For example, if your aging car one day rolls over and goes to that great garage in the sky, you may be faced with the decision of buying a new car or leasing one. If you are lucky enough to have the option of buying a new car that runs well and will incur few repair bills, perhaps your best bet would be to purchase it. Other factors to consider would be the length of time that you intend to keep the car and the tax advantages for each alternative. The main problem, however, is that the future reliability of the new car is uncertain.

The problem of decision making in such a situation would be greatly simplified if you had a crystal ball. A perfect predictor would tell you whether the new car you are thinking of buying is a lemon. Unfortunately, no such device exists, so you need to develop various decision strategies to deal with future uncertainties. Certain strategies are conservative; you stand neither to gain nor to lose a large amount. Other procedures attempt to measure the likelihood of future events by using probabilities. If you are a gambler at heart, strategies exist that allow you to defy odds in hopes of a big payoff.

If your life savings are at stake, you may elect to use a more conservative strategy in your investment decisions; gambling with these funds could be too dangerous. On the other hand, you may have certain reserve funds that you would be willing to invest in more speculative ventures, hoping for a large return at the risk of losing your investment. The purchase of a lottery ticket is a small-scale example of such an investment.

This chapter examines the various strategies available to the decision maker and illustrates these techniques for different business situations.

18.1 DEFINING THE DECISION PROBLEM

When confronted with making a decision in the face of uncertainty, you essentially need to be concerned with two basic questions:

1. What are my possible **actions** (alternatives) for this problem?
2. What is it about the future that affects the desirability of each action?

For the buy versus lease example, you are faced with two possible actions,

Action	Description
A_1	Purchase the car
A_2	Lease the car

When you are trying to decide between these two options, what would you like to know? One possibility is to describe the future (as it applies to this decision) by means of three events, or **states of nature.**

S_1: the new car will have less-than-average repair costs.
S_2: the new car will have average repair costs.
S_3: the new car will have above-average repair costs.

These future states of nature are **outcomes.** *The key distinction between an action and a state of nature is that the action taken is* under your control, *whereas the state of nature that occurs is strictly a matter of chance.* We will assume that *one and only one* of the states of nature will occur in the future; that is, they are *mutually exclusive.*

Other questions that require the decision maker to specify corresponding states of nature are ones such as:

What will be the future demand for a new computer software package?
How long will it be until the newly purchased electrical pump breaks down and needs to be replaced?
Will the stock market turn up or down in the next three months?
Will this year's winter be milder or colder than the average for the past 20 years?

Associated with each action (A) and state of nature (S) is a corresponding **payoff** or **profit.** We will assume that the payoff associated with each particular state of nature and action is known with certainty. These payoffs can be summarized in a **payoff table,** as shown in Table 18.1. The entry corresponding to action A_2 (row 2) and state of nature S_3 (column 3), for example, is denoted by π_{23} and is the payoff associated with action A_2 should state of nature S_3 occur.

Mr. Larson is owner of Sailtown, a store in southern Minnesota specializing in the sale of small sailboats. Each spring he is forced to place an order for his entire stock of Bluefin sailboats to be sold during the summer months because the Bluefin manufacturer is unable to supply any additional boats once the summer has begun.

TABLE 18.1   Payoff table.

	STATES OF NATURE				
Action	S_1	S_2	S_3	$\cdots$	S_n
A_1	π_{11}	π_{12}	π_{13}		π_{1n}
A_2	π_{21}	π_{22}	π_{23}		π_{2n}
A_3	π_{31}	π_{32}	π_{33}		π_{3n}
$\vdots$					
A_k	π_{k1}	π_{k2}	π_{k3}		π_{kn}

Mr. Larson's main concern when ordering his summer inventory is the demand for his product during the next five months. He has discovered that this demand seems to be largely dependent on economic conditions, in particular on the prevailing interest rate. He has four possible actions (order quantities).

A_1: purchase 50 boats
A_2: purchase 75 boats
A_3: purchase 100 boats
A_4: purchase 150 boats

The states of nature for this problem are

S_1: the interest rate increases significantly (more than 1.5%) from the current rate.
S_2: the interest rate holds steady.
S_3: the interest rate drops significantly (more than 1.5%).

Based on his expected sales under each condition, the payoff table in Table 18.2 was constructed. To demonstrate how the payoffs were determined, consider $\pi_{42} = 5$, which is the resulting profit if he orders 150 sailboats (action A_4) and if the interest rate remains basically unchanged (state of nature S_2). Mr. Larson believes that, for S_2, the resulting demand will be 100 sailboats. His profit per sale is $300, and his cost for holding and returning an unsold boat at the end of the fall season is $500. Consequently, if the demand is for 100 boats and he decides to stock 150, he ends up selling 100 boats and returning 50 of them to the manufacturer. The resulting dollar amounts are

$$\text{profit for selling 100 boats} = 100 \cdot \$300 = \$30{,}000$$

$$\text{loss for returning 50 boats} = 50 \cdot \$500 = \underline{\$25{,}000}$$

$$\text{net payoff} = \pi_{42} = \$5{,}000$$

So Mr. Larson calculates that the interest rate holding steady is equivalent to a demand for 100 sailboats. Similarly, he determines that an increase in the interest rate will result in a demand for 50 boats, whereas a decrease in the interest rate will produce a demand for 150 boats (Table 18.3).

TABLE 18.2

Profit table for Sailtown (thousands of dollars).

	Average Interest Rate		
Amount Ordered	Increases (S_1)	Steady (S_2)	Decreases (S_3)
50 (A_1)	15	15	15
75 (A_2)	2.5	22.5	22.5
100 (A_3)	−10	30	30
150 (A_4)	−35	5	45

TABLE 18.3

Demand for sailboats for each state of nature.

State of Nature	Interest Rate	Corresponding Demand
S_1	Increases	50
S_2	Holds steady	100
S_3	Decreases	150

TABLE 18.4   Payoff for Sailtown under S_1 (Example 18.1).

Action	Revenue for Boats Sold	Loss Due to Returned Boats	Net Payoff
A_1	$50 \cdot 300 = \$15,000$	$0 \cdot 500 = \$0$	$\$15,000$
A_2	$50 \cdot 300 = \$15,000$	$25 \cdot 500 = \$12,500$	$\$2,500$
A_3	$50 \cdot 300 = \$15,000$	$50 \cdot 500 = \$25,000$	$-\$10,000$
A_4	$50 \cdot 300 = \$15,000$	$100 \cdot 500 = \$50,000$	$-\$35,000$

EXAMPLE 18.1

Using Table 18.3, determine the payoff for each of the four alternatives if the interest rate increases over the summer months. What would be the best action to take if you knew that this particular state of nature would occur?

SOLUTION

We are given that state of nature S_1 will occur. Mr. Larson thinks that under this state of nature, 50 people will walk in his front door wanting to purchase a Bluefin sailboat. Under this assumption, the payoffs in Table 18.4 can be derived.

If we know that the interest rate will increase during the summer months, Table 18.4 tells us that the ideal action is to purchase 50 boats (action A_1).

Is action A_1 the ideal action for each state of nature? Given state of nature S_2 and using Table 18.2, the payoffs are $\$15,000$ (for A_1), $\$22,500$ (for A_2), $\$30,000$ (for A_3), and $\$5000$ (for A_4). In this case, you would achieve maximum profit by purchasing 100 boats (action A_3). The S_3 column of Table 18.2 shows that action A_4 (purchasing 150 boats) provides the maximum profit in the event that the interest rate declines.

This example illustrates **decision making under certainty.** Although the decision maker will never have this luxury, the technique at least enables him or her to determine the maximum profit under each state of nature. Also, if the *same action* provides the maximum payoff regardless of the state of nature, then this particular action is the obvious choice for this situation. Such was not the case in Table 18.2. There is no obviously superior action here, so we need to consider more elaborate decision strategies.

EXERCISES 18.1–18.5

UNDERSTANDING THE MECHANICS

18.1 Assume there are three actions that a decision maker can take and four states of nature (S_1, S_2, S_3, and S_4). Under A_1, the payoff is $\$500$ regardless of the state of nature. Under A_2, the payoffs are $\$400$, $\$500$, $\$10,000$, and $\$20,000$ for S_1, S_2, S_3, and S_4, respectively. Under A_3 the payoffs are $-\$500$, $\$0$, $\$10,000$, and $\$30,000$, respectively. Construct the payoff table. What is the best action to take under each state of nature?

APPLYING THE NEW CONCEPTS

18.2 Would the following decisions be made under certainty or uncertainty?

a. A software corporation needs to decide whether to price a new income tax program above the market, at the market, or below the market.

b. A manager needs to decide whether to purchase steel rods from one of two suppliers. Each supplier offers rods at the same price and the same quality.

c. A car buyer must decide whether to borrow $\$10,000$ at 7% for three years or at 9% for five years.

d. A banker must decide if a customer is creditworthy.

18.3 A seminar on sales motivation is being given at a local hotel. The cost of handouts and materials per attendee is $\$10$. The total cost of the hotel arrangements is $\$75$. Each attendee pays $\$25$ for the seminar. The coordinator of the seminar must plan the number of handouts and materials. The coordinator must plan for 7, 8, 9, 10, 11, 12, or 13 attendees. Construct the payoff table if the demand is 5, 6, 7, 8, 9, 10, 11, 12, or 13 attendees.

18.4 The Jones family has moved out of their house and now has it up for sale. They need to decide whether to price their house at the top of market ($88,000), at the market ($85,000), or below the market ($82,000). Each month that it takes to sell the house, the Jones family loses $700 from making the monthly payment. Construct a payoff table that shows the selling price of the home minus $700 for each month the house remains unsold. Use S_1 = sold in 1 month, S_2 = sold in 2 months, . . . , S_6 = sold in 6 months.

18.5 Mini-Super, a convenience food store, orders milk each week. The store pays $1.10 per gallon and sells the milk for $2.00 per gallon. Unsold milk at the end of the week is given to an orphanage. The manager must decide on ordering 100 gallons, 125 gallons, or 150 gallons per week. Construct the payoff table for this problem if demand is 100 gallons, 125 gallons, or 150 gallons a week.

18.2 DECISION STRATEGIES

When the action providing a maximum payoff depends on an uncertain state of nature, the decision maker is forced to consider all the values in the payoff table to choose the most attractive action. The various strategies discussed here allow you to choose a procedure that best fits your style of making decisions. We begin with a conservative strategy: the minimax procedure.

THE CONSERVATIVE (MINIMAX) STRATEGY

A conservative strategy is basically one that, when choosing between a savings account and an extremely risky venture, selects the savings account. It does this because, under the *worst* conditions, the loss is smaller with a savings account than with the high-risk venture.

We examined the ideal action for Mr. Larson to take in the event that he knew that the interest rate was going to increase (S_1 in Table 18.2). This action was to order 50 boats for a payoff of $\pi_{11} = 15$ (thousand). If he had taken action A_2 instead, his profit would be only $2500. For this situation, we say that the opportunity loss is $15,000 – $2500 = $12,500.

The **opportunity loss,** L_{ij}, is the difference between the payoff for action i and the payoff for the action that would have the largest payoff under state of nature j.*

The opportunity loss is not a loss in the accounting sense; rather, it describes how much more profit you *would have made* had you chosen the best action for this state of nature. In our example, the opportunity loss for action A_3 (assuming state of nature S_1) is

$$\text{opportunity loss} = L_{31} = 15 - (-10)$$

$$= 25 \text{ (thousand dollars)}$$

and this value for action A_4 (under S_1) is

$$\text{opportunity loss} = L_{41} = 15 - (-35)$$

$$= 50 \text{ (thousand dollars)}$$

EXAMPLE 18.2

Construct the remaining opportunity losses for Mr. Larson, and summarize them in an opportunity loss table.

SOLUTION

Keep in mind that opportunity losses are determined one *column* at a time in Table 18.2 by assuming that each individual state of nature occurs and then looking for the best action under this condition. This procedure is exactly the same as the one we used when discussing the unrealistic situation of decision making under certainty.

If the interest rate holds steady (S_2 occurs), the best action is to stock 100 boats (action A_3) with a payoff of $\pi_{32} = 30$. Table 18.5 shows the opportunity loss for this situation.

Similarly, action A_4 (stock 150 boats) is the ideal action in the event the interest rate decreases (S_3) and sales increase, as shown in Table 18.6.

---

* Some textbooks refer to opportunity loss as *regret* and to the minimax strategy as the *minimax regret strategy.*

TABLE 18.5

Opportunity loss for assumption: S_2 occurs; best action: A_3; maximum payoff: 30.

Action	Payoff	Opportunity Loss
A_1	15	$L_{12} = 30 - 15 = 15$
A_2	22.5	$L_{22} = 30 - 22.5 = 7.5$
A_3	30	$L_{32} = 30 - 30 = 0$
A_4	5	$L_{42} = 30 - 5 = 25$

TABLE 18.6

Opportunity loss for assumption: S_3 occurs; best action: A_4; maximum payoff: 45.

Action	Payoff	Opportunity Loss
A_1	15	$L_{13} = 45 - 15 = 30$
A_2	22.5	$L_{23} = 45 - 22.5 = 22.5$
A_3	30	$L_{33} = 45 - 30 = 15$
A_4	45	$L_{43} = 45 - 45 = 0$

TABLE 18.7

Opportunity loss table for Sailtown decision problem (thousands of dollars).

Action	STATE OF NATURE S_1	S_2	S_3
A_1	0	15	30
A_2	12.5	7.5	22.5
A_3	25	0	15
A_4	50	25	0

We format these results in an **opportunity loss table,** as shown in Table 18.7. Notice that each column of an opportunity loss table contains a zero and that all values in this table are nonnegative (≥ 0).

THE MINIMAX STRATEGY.   The minimax strategy is to:

1. Construct an opportunity loss table by using the maximum payoff for each state of nature.
2. Determine the maximum opportunity loss for each action.
3. Find the minimum value of the opportunity losses found in step 2; the corresponding action is the one selected by the minimax strategy.

The minimax strategy is a very conservative approach that does not search for large payoffs; rather, it selects the action that has the smallest "worst case" opportunity loss.

The minimax procedure begins by examining the worst possible situation for each action. So you examine Table 18.7 one *row* at a time and determine the largest opportunity loss for each action. Thus, we have

Action	Maximum Opportunity Loss
A_1	30
A_2	22.5
A_3	25
A_4	50

This is the *max* part of the minimax strategy. The *mini* side is finding the *minimum* of these four values. In this way, you attempt to offset the worst possible situation scenario. For this example, with values of 30, 22.5, 25, and 50, the minimum is 22.5, which belongs to action A_2, so the **minimax decision** is to order 75 sailboats.

In actual practice, a decision analysis rarely begins in the form of a payoff table. Instead, this table perhaps can be constructed using the information available and then the appropriate decision strategy can be applied to arrive at the corresponding action. This method is illustrated in the next example.

EXAMPLE 18.3

Recently, GTE Southwest offered their residential and business customers a plan to help reduce long-distance costs. The plan was called *1 + Saver* and provided four options for each customer.

Option 1: a 10% discount at a cost of $1 per month (action A_1)
Option 2: a 15% discount at a cost of $6 per month (action A_2)
Option 3: a 20% discount at a cost of $15 per month (action A_3)
Option 4: a 30% discount at a cost of $50 per month (action A_4)

These discounts applied to any direct-dialed long-distance call placed with GTE Southwest that did not involve operator-handled or credit card calls. As an employee of Worldwide Import Distributors, you have been asked to select one of these options for your company's future long-distance calls. Company records show that previous long-distance charges can be summarized using four states of nature:

S_1: long-distance charges = $100
S_2: long-distance charges = $200
S_3: long-distance charges = $300
S_4: long-distance charges = $400

Construct a payoff table for this situation and select one of these four options using the minimax strategy.

SOLUTION

The payoff table is constructed by determining the discount amount and subtracting the corresponding monthly charge for this option. For example, if the monthly long-distance charges are approximately $300 ($S_3$) then using option 2 (action A_2), the payoff (savings) is ($300)(.15) − $6 = $39. The resulting payoff table is shown in Table 18.8.

If state of nature S_2 should occur, the best action is A_3, with a savings (payoff) of $25 and an opportunity loss of zero. Consequently, A_1 has an opportunity loss of $25 − $19 = $6. Continuing in this way, you can construct Table 18.9.

Next, we find the maximum opportunity loss for each action.

Action	Maximum Opportunity Loss
A_1	31
A_2	16
A_3	5
A_4	29

TABLE 18.8

Payoff table for Worldwide Import Distributors (dollars).

	STATE OF NATURE			
Action	**$100 ($S_1$)**	**$200 ($S_2$)**	**$300 ($S_3$)**	**$400 ($S_4$)**
Option 1 (A_1)	9	19	29	39
Option 2 (A_2)	9	24	39	54
Option 3 (A_3)	5	25	45	65
Option 4 (A_4)	−20	10	40	70

TABLE 18.9

Opportunity loss table for Worldwide Import Distributors (dollars).

Action	STATE OF NATURE				
	$100 ($S_1$)	$200 ($S_2$)	$300 ($S_3$)	$400 ($S_4$)	Maximum
Option 1 (A_1)	0	6	16	31	31
Option 2 (A_2)	0	1	6	16	16
Option 3 (A_3)	4	0	0	5	5
Option 4 (A_4)	29	15	5	0	29

Finally we select the minimum of these values: $5, corresponding to action A_3. The minimax decision is to use option 3 with a 20% discount and a fixed charge of $15 per month. This action is fairly conservative here and is the one that minimizes the maximum difference between the savings received and the savings that could have been received if the state of nature (actual long-distance charges) had been known in advance.

THE GAMBLER (MAXIMAX) STRATEGY

The maximax strategy is the opposite of the minimax procedure and appeals to those who are gamblers at heart. The **maximax strategy** is to choose that action having the largest possible payoff. It is not a recommended procedure for most business decisions because, by choosing that action with the largest payoff, it fails to consider the possibility of large accounting losses or opportunity losses.

EXAMPLE 18.4

Using the information in Table 18.2, which action should Sailtown select using the maximax strategy?

SOLUTION

Of the 12 payoffs in Table 18.2, the largest is 45, which corresponds to action A_4. If Sailtown is desperate for a large payoff, the appropriate action using this strategy would be to order 150 sailboats for the summer months. Of course, the company also stands to lose the most using this action; the loss will be $35,000 if the interest rate increases.

EXAMPLE 18.5

Based on the payoff table in Table 18.8 and the maximax strategy, which of the four long-distance discount options would you select?

SOLUTION

The maximum savings is $70 per month, corresponding to option 4. So, if you want to gamble for a large savings, the corresponding action would be option 4, which has a 50% discount and a monthly charge of $50. Interestingly, the minimax procedure (typically, very conservative) selected option 3 with a maximum payoff of $65, only $5 less than obtained using the maximax procedure.

EXERCISES 18.6–18.10

UNDERSTANDING THE MECHANICS

18.6 Given the following payoff table, construct the opportunity loss table and find the minimax decision.

Action	S_1	S_2	S_3	S_4
A_1	–5	–1	0	3
A_2	–6	–2	1	7
A_3	–6	–3	2	8
A_4	–8	–4	1	9

18.7 Can each of the following tables be considered opportunity loss tables? Why?

   a.

Action	S_1	S_2	S_3
A_1	0	9	100
A_2	100	1	2
A_3	20	4	0

   b.

Action	S_1	S_2	S_3
A_1	0	20	4
A_2	8	0	2
A_3	–1	5	0

APPLYING THE NEW CONCEPTS

18.8 The owner of a small commercial building can either pay $1000 per year to insure the $200,000 building or not insure and save $1000 per year. If the states of nature are complete loss of the commercial building or no loss at all, what would the payoff table and opportunity loss table be for this situation? What is the minimax decision?

18.9 A retail store manager must decide on the store's inventory of jeans for the next month. The table gives the store's payoff for three levels of demand and three levels of inventory. What is the minimax decision? What is the maximax decision?

Action (Inventory Level)	Demand		
	Low	**Medium**	**High**
Low	4,000	4,000	4,000
Medium	1,000	7,000	7,000
High	–4,000	3,000	11,000

18.10 Refer to Exercise 18.5. Construct the opportunity loss table for the actions of the manager of Mini-Super. What is the minimax decision? What is the maximax decision?

THE STRATEGIST (MAXIMIZING EXPECTED PAYOFF)

In many respects, a more sensible approach to many decision problems is to consider the likelihood that each state of nature will occur. In this way, you can use any information you have to help evaluate the possibilities of each of the states of nature. If you believe strongly that the chance of the interest rate declining is small, a decision strategy that uses this information would be useful. The strategy discussed here differs from previous procedures, in that we begin by determining the *probability* associated with each state of nature.

SELECTING THE PROBABILITIES. The probability for each state of nature measures to what degree you believe this state of nature will occur in the future. One way to obtain these probabilities is from past experience—referred to as **empirical evidence.** For example, if, under similar conditions in the past, the stock market declined 15% of the time, we would set

$$P(\text{stock market declines}) = .15$$

In this way, you can determine the probability for each state of nature. Because we are assuming that one (and only one) of these states *must* occur, these probabilities must sum to 1.

Another method of selecting these probabilities is the **subjective approach.** With this procedure, an individual or group of individuals will select each probability such that (1) each value represents their confidence that each state of nature will occur and (2) the probabilities sum to 1.

To someone unfamiliar with the concept of a probability, you can pose the question, given this set of circumstances 100 different times, how often do you think the stock market will decline? If the answer is about 15 times, then once again you have

$$P(\text{stock market declines}) = .15$$

If the resulting probabilities do not sum to 1 on the first pass, you can state that these probabilities are *all* a little too small (or large) and try again. By continuing in this manner, you eventually will arrive at a set of probabilities for this situation.

TABLE 18.10

Probabilities for S_1, S_2, and S_3 from Table 18.2.

State of Nature	Probability
S_1: Interest rate increases	$P(S_1) = .3$
S_2: Interest rate remains unchanged	$P(S_2) = .2$
S_3: Interest rate decreases	$P(S_3) = .5$

The strengths and weaknesses of using these probabilities in the decision process lie in the accuracy of their values. If they are inaccurate, you may well choose an action that incurs a small (or negative) payoff. As a result, this strategy can lead to poor decisions, particularly if the action chosen was based on unreliable subjective probabilities. Nevertheless, it continues to be a popular decision strategy because it allows the decision maker to place probabilities on the unknown future and consider the alternatives.

THE DECISION STRATEGY.   When using probabilities for each of the states of nature, you determine the *average* payoff for each action in the long run—the average payoff if you repeatedly took this action. This is the **expected payoff** for each action. The strategy in this case is to choose that action having the *largest* expected payoff.

Consider Table 18.2. Suppose that the owner of Sailtown believes there is a 30% chance that the interest rate will increase over the summer months. This can be written as

$$P(S_1) = .3$$

The chance of the interest rate holding steady is believed to be 20%, whereas the probability of a drop in the rate is 50% (Table 18.10).

One of the alternatives for this problem was to stock 150 sailboats (action A_4). Using Table 18.2, the respective payoffs are a loss of \$35,000 should the interest rate increase (S_1), a profit of \$5000 if it holds steady (S_2), and a profit of \$45,000 if it decreases (S_3). So, if you repeatedly took this action (under the same conditions facing the owner of Sailtown), then you would

lose \$35,000, 30% of the time (S_1 occurs)
make \$5000, 20% of the time (S_2 occurs)
make \$45,000, 50% of the time (S_3 occurs)

We discussed this situation in Chapter 5, where we examined *discrete random variables*. The random variable for this situation is

$$X = \text{payoff under action } A_4$$

Based on the preceding discussion, we have

$$X = \begin{cases} -35 & \text{with probability } .3 \\ 5 & \text{with probability } .2 \\ 45 & \text{with probability } .5 \\ & \overline{1.0} \end{cases} \qquad (18.1)$$

The expected payoff for this action is simply the *mean of the random variable, X*. In Chapter 5, this was defined to be

$$\text{expected payoff for } A_4 = \text{mean of } X$$

$$= \Sigma(\text{each value of } X)(\text{its probability})$$

$$= (-35)(.3) + (5)(.2) + (45)(.5) = 13$$

This implies that, if the owner of Sailtown repeatedly ordered 150 sailboats (under similar conditions), he would make a profit of \$13,000 on the average.

COMMENT

The decision strategy when using expected payoffs is to select that action having the largest expected payoff. At first glance this may appear to be an inappropriate strategy for a one-time decision analysis. The underlying philosophy behind this approach is that whatever is best in the long run is best for the short-term decision problem (such as a one-time decision problem). For each action under consideration, you can think of the corresponding expected payoff as a *weighted average* of the possible payoffs for this action, where the weight for a particular state of nature is its probability of occurring. In this way, states of nature with a higher chance of occurring receive a larger weight. For instance, if a state of nature has a 90% chance of occurring, then it receives a weight of .9 (out of a maximum possible 1.0) in the weighted average (expected payoff) for each action being considered. The remaining state-of-nature weights total only .1, so we reflect the small chance of these states' occurring when determining each expected payoff.

EXAMPLE 18.6

Determine the expected payoff for each of the actions in Table 18.2. Using this procedure, how many sailboats should Mr. Larson order?

SOLUTION

Based on the four expected payoffs, the appropriate action is to order 100 sailboats (A_3) with an expected (average) payoff of $18,000 (Table 18.11). If Mr. Larson chooses this alternative, his payoff for a one-time decision will be not a profit of $18,000 but, rather, a loss of $10,000 [with probability $P(S_1) = .3$] or a gain of $30,000 [with probability $P(S_2) + P(S_3) = .7$]. Mr. Larson will select this action if he believes that his long-term gain under this alternative has been maximized. In a sense, he has measured the uncertainty of the future in order to select the best action.

EXAMPLE 18.7

In Example 18.3, the minimax strategy was used to select one of the four long-distance discounts offered by GTE Southwest. Suppose that you took a closer look at recent long-distance charges and arrived at the following set of probabilities for the four states of nature:

$$P(S_1) = .1 \quad P(S_2) = .3 \quad P(S_3) = .4 \quad P(S_4) = .2$$

If you elect to use the expected payoff strategy, which of the long-distance options offers the largest expected savings?

SOLUTION

The expected payoffs for the four options (actions) are:

A_1: $(.1)(9) + (.3)(19) + (.4)(29) + (.2)(39) = \$26.00$

A_2: $(.1)(9) + (.3)(24) + (.4)(39) + (.2)(54) = \$34.50$

A_3: $(.1)(5) + (.3)(25) + (.4)(45) + (.2)(65) = \$39.00$

A_4: $(.1)(-20) + (.3)(10) + (.4)(40) + (.2)(70) = \$31.00$

TABLE 18.11

Expected payoffs for Sailtown (thousands of dollars).

Action	Expected Payoff
A_1: Order 50 sailboats	$(15)(.3) + (15)(.2) + (15)(.5) = 15$
A_2: Order 75 sailboats	$(2.5)(.3) + (22.5)(.2) + (22.5)(.5) = 16.5$
A_3: Order 100 sailboats	$(-10)(.3) + (30)(.2) + (30)(.5) = 18$
A_4: Order 150 sailboats	$(-35)(.3) + (5)(.2) + (45)(.5) = 13$

TABLE 18.12

Profit table for Omega computer-price problem (millions of dollars).

Selling Price	<6 Months (S₁)	6–12 Months (S₂)	12–18 Months (S₃)	>18 Months (S₄)
A_1: $1500	250	320	350	400
A_2: $1750	150	260	300	370
A_3: $2000	120	290	380	450
A_4: $2500	80	280	410	550

Consequently, A_3 has the largest expected payoff. Both the minimax and expected payoff strategies indicate that the best action is option 3, with the 20% discount and a fixed charge of $15 per month.

EXAMPLE 18.8

Omega is about to introduce a new line of microcomputers. Their main concern is what selling price they should charge for their computers. The managers can estimate accurately the demand at each price; they are primarily concerned about the time it will take their competitors to catch up and introduce a similar product. They intend to determine a selling price and then not change it for the next two years. They decide to structure the decision problem using four possible alternatives (actions):

A_1: set selling price at $1500
A_2: set selling price at $1750
A_3: set selling price at $2000
A_4: set selling price at $2500

The states of nature specify the amount of time until a similar product is introduced by one of their competitors:

$$S_1 = \text{less than 6 months}$$

$$S_2 = 6 \text{ to } 12 \text{ months}$$

$$S_3 = 12 \text{ to } 18 \text{ months}$$

$$S_4 = \text{longer than 18 months}$$

The next step for this decision problem is to construct a payoff table. This is *not* an easy step because the managers must consider price-demand, cost-volume, and consumer-preference information in order to specify a payoff for each action under each state of nature. After many meetings between the production and marketing staffs, Table 18.12 was derived, showing projected profits over the next two years.

What is the appropriate action (selling price) if:

1. The minimax strategy is used?
2. Omega decides to maximize the expected payoff?

Use

$$P(S_1) = .1 \qquad P(S_2) = .5 \qquad P(S_3) = .3 \qquad P(S_4) = .1$$

SOLUTION 1

Using the minimax strategy, we first construct an opportunity loss table for this situation (Table 18.13). We do this by considering each state of nature and finding the action with the largest payoff under each state. The opportunity loss for each action is the maximum payoff under this state of nature minus the payoff for this particular action.

TABLE 18.13

Construction of opportunity loss table for Omega (Example 18.8).

State of Nature	Action with Largest Payoff	Opportunity Loss
S_1	A_1	for A_1: $250 - 250 = 0$ for A_2: $250 - 150 = 100$ for A_3: $250 - 120 = 130$ for A_4: $250 - 80 = 170$
S_2	A_1	for A_1: $320 - 320 = 0$ for A_2: $320 - 260 = 60$ for A_3: $320 - 290 = 30$ for A_4: $320 - 280 = 40$
S_3	A_4	for A_1: $410 - 350 = 60$ for A_2: $410 - 300 = 110$ for A_3: $410 - 380 = 30$ for A_4: $410 - 410 = 0$
S_4	A_4	for A_1: $550 - 400 = 150$ for A_2: $550 - 370 = 180$ for A_3: $550 - 450 = 100$ for A_4: $550 - 550 = 0$

TABLE 18.14

Opportunity loss table for Omega computer-price problem (millions of dollars).

Selling Price	<6 Months (S_1)	6–12 Months (S_2)	12–18 Months (S_3)	>18 Months (S_4)
A_1: $1500	0	0	60	150
A_2: $1750	100	60	110	180
A_3: $2000	130	30	30	100
A_4: $2500	170	40	0	0

Next, we find the maximum opportunity loss *for each action* (row in Table 18.14).

Action	Maximum Opportunity Loss
A_1	150
A_2	180
A_3	130
A_4	170

The minimum of these values is 130 for A_3. The minimax strategy would be to select a selling price of $2000 for the next two years.*

SOLUTION 2

The expected profit for each action is summarized in Table 18.15.

The maximum expected profit is 330, for action A_1. So the strategy here is to set the selling price at $1500, with an expected payoff of $330 million. Notice, however, that the

---

* The minimax procedure is often confused with the *maximin* strategy, which examines the minimum payoff for each action and selects that action having the maximum of these minimum payoffs. For this application, the minimum payoffs for each action are A_1: 250, A_2: 150, A_3: 120, and A_4: 80. The maximum value here is 250 (belonging to A_1), and the maximin strategy is to select action A_1. The conclusions resulting from minimax and maximin are not the same here because the minimax strategy (which selects that action minimizing the maximum opportunity loss) is to use action A_3. Both strategies typically are very conservative.

TABLE 18.15   Expected profits for Omega (Example 18.8).

Action	Expected Payoff
A_1	$(.1)(250) + (.5)(320) + (.3)(350) + (.1)(400) = 330$
A_2	$(.1)(150) + (.5)(260) + (.3)(300) + (.1)(370) = 272$
A_3	$(.1)(120) + (.5)(290) + (.3)(380) + (.1)(450) = 316$
A_4	$(.1)(80) + (.5)(280) + (.3)(410) + (.1)(550) = 326$

three largest expected values are quite close to each other, implying that one of the other alternatives might surpass A_1 if the state of nature probabilities are adjusted slightly. The preference for A_1 may be very sensitive to these probabilities. This situation should concern a decision maker, especially if the probabilities are determined subjectively.

Example 18.8 suggests another important element of the decision process—a sensitivity analysis.

SENSITIVITY ANALYSIS

Typically, there is no way to determine a state of nature probability with certainty. You can consider past observations and derive an empirical estimate or merely make up a value that measures your belief that this event will occur (the subjective approach). The next step when using the maximum expected payoff strategy is to examine what happens to this solution under other sets of realistic probabilities. This examination is called a **sensitivity analysis.**

In Example 18.6, the expected payoff procedure selected action A_3. By ordering 100 sailboats, Sailtown achieved a maximum expected payoff of $18,000. The state of nature probabilities used here were

$$P(S_1) = .3 \text{ (interest rate increases)}$$

$$P(S_2) = .2 \text{ (interest rate remains unchanged)}$$

$$P(S_3) = .5 \text{ (interest rate decreases)}$$

Although Mr. Larson and his financial advisor are uncertain as to the precise values of these probabilities, they believe that:

1. There is no more than a 50% chance that the interest rate will increase ($P(S_1) \le .5$).
2. There is no more than a 30% chance that the rate will remain unchanged ($P(S_2) \le .3$).
3. The probability that the rate will decrease is between .3 and .5.

They decide to examine the expected payoffs under the probability conditions listed in Table 18.16. The expected payoffs under each set of probabilities are determined as in Example 18.6. As an illustration, using $P(S_1) = .4$ and $P(S_2) = P(S_3) = .3$, the expected payoff for action A_4 is $(.4)(-35) + (.3)(5) + (.3)(45) = 1$ (that is, $1000).

The sensitivity summary in Table 18.16 indicates that action A_1 (ordering 50 sailboats) may be much more attractive than we thought. In fact, if there is more than a 30% chance that the interest rate will increase ($P(S_1) > .3$), this action produces the largest expected payoff. Under this decision, Mr. Larson can expect to sell all his inventory, resulting in a profit of $15,000 *regardless of the state of nature.* Consequently, Sailtown would be seeking an expected gain of $3000 ($18,000 for A_3 minus $15,000 for A_1) by speculating on the uncertain future.

TABLE 18.16

Summary of sensitivity analysis (boxed values represent the action with the largest expected payoff).

			EXPECTED PAYOFF			
$P(S_1)$	$P(S_2)$	$P(S_3)$	A_1	A_2	A_3	A_4
.4	.2	.4	15	14.5	14	5
.4	.3	.3	15	14.5	14	1
.4	.1	.5	15	14.5	14	9
.5	.2	.3	15	12.5	10	–3
.5	.1	.4	15	12.5	10	1
.3	.3	.4	15	16.5	18	9
.3	.2	.5	15	16.5	18	13

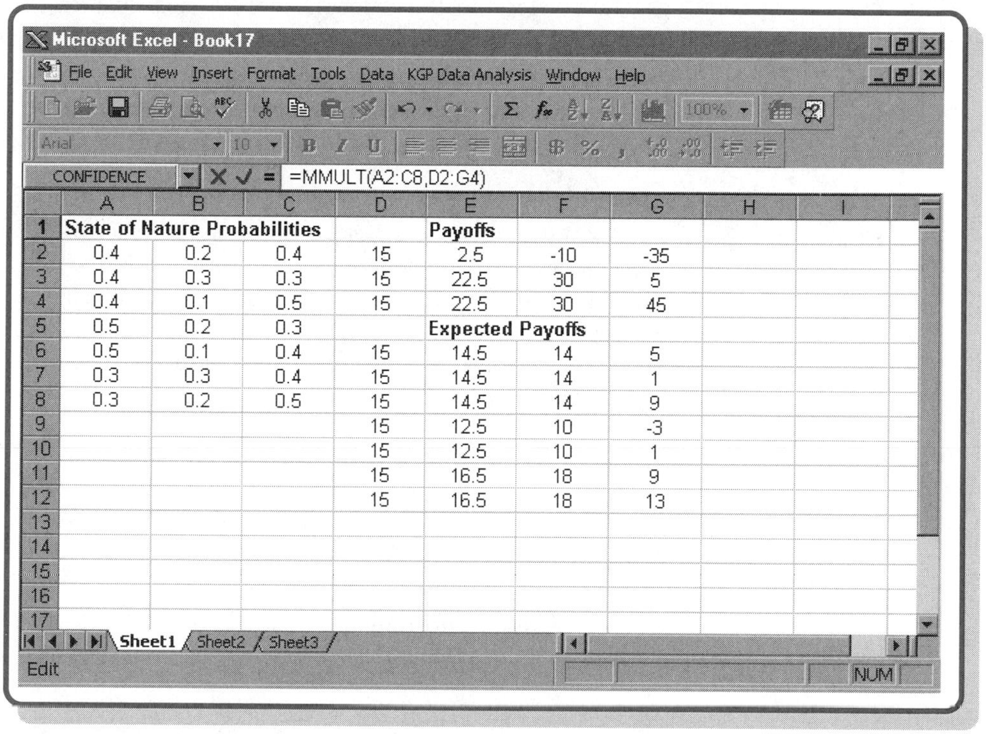

FIGURE 18.1

Sensitivity analysis using Excel. The expected payoffs are those in Table 18.16.

Without such a sensitivity analysis, Mr. Larson would not have noticed these results. In five of the six cases using probabilities other than those used in Example 18.6, action A_1 produced the maximum expected payoff. If Mr. Larson is uncertain in his original determination of these probabilities, this action is a better solution to his decision problem.

An easy method of performing the rather lengthy sensitivity analysis calculations is to use a spreadsheet package (such as Excel) or a statistical package (such as MINITAB). Any such computer package will refer to an array of numbers as a *matrix*. For this application, the state of nature probabilities represent one matrix (say, A), and the array of payoffs (B) constitute another matrix. In general, two matrices can be multiplied (written $A \cdot B$ or simply AB), provided the number of *columns* in A and the number of *rows* in B are the same. This is always the case here since, for the Sailtown analysis, there are three columns in the State of Nature Probabilities matrix and three rows in the Payoffs matrix. This can be seen in Figure 18.1, where Excel is used to multiply the two matrices, the result of which is the matrix (array) of *expected* payoff amounts.

To obtain the expected payoff matrix in Figure 18.1, first enter the two matrices and corresponding titles in columns A1:C8 and D1:G4. Enter "Expected Payoffs" in cell E5. Under the Payoffs array, highlight (select) a block of cells containing seven rows (number of rows in matrix *A*) and four columns (number of columns in matrix *B*). These are cells D6:G12 in Figure 18.1. The Excel command for multiplying two matrices is "=MMULT(array1,array2)". In the formula bar, enter "=MMULT(A2:C8,D2:G4)" followed by Control + Shift + Enter (hold down these three keys at the same time). Excel then will fill in cells D6:G12 with the expected payoff amounts.

EVALUATING RISK

Using the preceding sensitivity analysis and the payoffs in Table 18.2, we noticed that the payoff for action A_1 was 15 (thousand dollars), regardless of the state of nature. Action A_4, on the other hand, has possible payoffs of –35, 5, and 45, implying that you will encounter a higher risk using A_4 rather than A_1. In fact, action A_1 has *no* risk because its payoff is known with certainty.

Take a closer look at action A_4. In discussing equation 18.1, we remarked that the payoff for this action, *X*, is a random variable, where

$$X = \begin{cases} -35 & \text{with probability .3} \\ 5 & \text{with probability .2} \\ 45 & \text{with probability .5} \end{cases}$$

The expected payoff for this action is the *mean* of *X*.

A risky alternative (action) is one that has larger probabilities attached to extremely large or small payoffs. A good measure of this risk is simply the *variance* of *X;* the variance of the possible payoffs for each action is a measure of the risk associated with this alternative. The larger the variance is, the more risk will be incurred using this action. The variance of this *discrete* random variable is found in the same way as in Chapter 5 and is summarized here.

Let X_i be the payoff associated with action A_i. Then

$$X_i = \begin{cases} x_1 & \text{with probability } p_1 \\ x_2 & \text{with probability } p_2 \\ \vdots \\ x_n & \text{with probability } p_n \end{cases}$$

where *n* represents the number of states of nature.

The **expected payoff** for this action is the mean of X_i, where

$$\text{expected payoff} = \mu_i = \sum xp \qquad \textbf{(18.2)}$$

The **risk** associated with action A_i is the variance of X_i. So,

$$\text{risk} = \sum p(x - \mu_i)^2$$
$$= \sum x^2 p - \mu_i^2 \qquad \textbf{(18.3)}$$

EXAMPLE 18.9

Compute the risk for each of the actions in Table 18.2, using the state of nature probabilities from Example 18.6. Based on these results and the sensitivity analysis in Table 18.16, which action appears to be the best one for this situation?

SOLUTION

Using equation 18.3, we can find the risk associated with each of the four alternatives, as shown in Table 18.17. The purpose of examining the risk for each action is that often the decision maker will prefer a less risky alternative over a riskier action with a larger

TABLE 18.17

Risk calculations for Sailtown decision problem.

Action	Expected Payoff (μ_i)	Risk (Using Equation 18.3)
A_1	15	$[(15)^2(.3) + (15)^2(.2) + (15)^2(.5)] - 15^2 = 0$
A_2	16.5	$[(2.5)^2(.3) + (22.5)^2(.2) + (22.5)^2(.5)] - 16.5^2 = 84$
A_3	18	$[(-10)^2(.3) + (30)^2(.2) + (30)^2(.5)] - 18^2 = 336$
A_4	13	$[(-35)^2(.3) + (5)^2(.2) + (45)^2(.5)] - 13^2 = 1216$

TABLE 18.18

Risk calculations for Worldwide Import Distributors problem.

Action	Expected Payoff (μ_i)	Risk (Using Equation 18.3)
A_1	26.00	$[(9)^2(.1) + (19)^2(.3) + (29)^2(.4) + (39)^2(.2)] - 26^2 = 81$
A_2	34.50	$[(9)^2(.1) + (24)^2(.3) + (39)^2(.4) + (54)^2(.2)] - 34.5^2 = 182.25$
A_3	39.00	$[(5)^2(.1) + (25)^2(.3) + (45)^2(.4) + (65)^2(.2)] - 39^2 = 324$
A_4	31.00	$[(-20)^2(.1) + (10)^2(.3) + (40)^2(.4) + (70)^2(.2)] - 31^2 = 729$

expected payoff. In this example, action A_1 has no risk and also has a maximum expected payoff for most of the situations examined in the sensitivity analysis. On the other hand, action A_3 (the other suggested approach) carries the second-largest risk, as measured in Table 18.17. For these reasons, the soundest alternative appears to be action A_1, with a known payoff of $15,000.

EXAMPLE 18.10

Which of the long-distance options facing Worldwide Import Distributors (Example 18.7) has the least amount of risk?

SOLUTION

The risk for each of the four options is computed in Table 18.18. The four options show an increasing amount of risk as the discount rate increases, with option 1 (a 10% discount and a monthly charge of $1) having the lowest risk but also the lowest expected monthly savings.

EXAMPLE 18.11

Which of the alternatives in Example 18.8 has the least amount of risk?

SOLUTION

As before, the risk associated with each action is the variance of the corresponding random variable, shown in Table 18.19. The most desirable action for Omega is A_1 (selling price = $1500) because it wins on two counts: it not only has the largest expected profit, it also has the smallest risk. For a great many decision problems, this will not be the case, and so the decision maker will have to decide how much risk he or she is willing to assume in an effort to gain a higher expected profit. *If a heavy loss would be devastating to a company, it may be forced into adopting strategies that select alternatives with reasonably attractive profits but considerably less risk.*

TABLE 18.19   Risk calculations for Omega decision problem.

Action	Expected Payoff (μ_i)	Risk (Using Equation 18.3)
A_1	330	$[(250)^2(.1) + (320)^2(.5) + (350)^2(.3) + (400)^2(.1)] - 330^2 = 1,300$
A_2	272	$[(150)^2(.1) + (260)^2(.5) + (300)^2(.3) + (370)^2(.1)] - 272^2 = 2,756$
A_3	316	$[(120)^2(.1) + (290)^2(.5) + (380)^2(.3) + (450)^2(.1)] - 316^2 = 7,204$
A_4	326	$[(80)^2(.1) + (280)^2(.5) + (410)^2(.3) + (550)^2(.1)] - 326^2 = 14,244$

EXERCISES 18.11–18.16

UNDERSTANDING THE MECHANICS

18.11 Consider the accompanying payoff table. What is the expected payoff of each action? What is the expected risk of each action? The probabilities of S_1, S_2, and S_3 are .2, .4, and .4, respectively.

Action	S_1	S_2	S_3
A_1	40	8	0
A_2	10	60	20
A_3	0	20	80

APPLYING THE NEW CONCEPTS

18.12 The manager of a hardware store orders several cords of split logs to be sold to customers for firewood. More wood typically is sold when a winter is colder than usual. The manager figures that the chance of an extremely cold winter (S_1) is 0.25, the chance of a normal winter (S_2) is 0.50, and the chance of a relatively mild winter (S_3) is 0.25. The manager must decide on ordering either 50, 40, 30 or 20 cords of wood. The payoff table follows.

Action	S_1	S_2	S_3
A_1 (50)	5500	2670	1300
A_2 (40)	4000	3200	1150
A_3 (30)	3000	2800	1400
A_4 (20)	2800	2500	1180

a. What is the minimax decision?
b. What is the decision based on the maximum expected payoff?
c. What is the risk of each action?
d. What is the decision based on minimum risk?

18.13 Programs need to be printed for a theatrical performance. The programs are sold at the entrance of the theater before the performance starts. The director of the theater believes that there is a 35% chance that there will be a heavy turnout (S_1), a 50% chance for a normal turnout (S_2), and a 15% chance for a low turnout (S_3). The director must decide to have 200 copies (A_1), 300 copies (A_2), 400 copies (A_3), or 500 copies

(A_4) of the program printed. The payoff table follows. Unsold programs would result in a loss.

Action	S_1	S_2	S_3
A_1	100	100	100
A_2	150	140	110
A_3	200	160	75
A_4	250	120	–50

a. Find the minimax decision.
b. Find the decision based on the maximum expected payoff.
c. Find the risk associated with each decision.

18.14 A manager must decide on how to price a contract. The contract can either be accepted for 1 year, 2 years, or 3 years. Find the decision, based on the maximum expected payoff. The probabilities that the contract is accepted for 1, 2, and 3 years are .4, .4, and .2, respectively.

Contract Price	1 Year	2 Years	3 Years
Low	10,000	15,000	20,000
High	3,000	10,000	30,000

18.15 The marketing department of a soft drink company wishes to determine the maximum expected payoff from introducing a new crystal-clear drink. What decision should the marketing department make using the payoff table below? Assume that the probability that the market share is less than 1% is .20, that the probability that market share is at least 1% and less than 4% is .50, and that the probability that the market share is at least 4% is .30.

Investment Level	Market Share		
	<1%	1%–4%	≥4%
Low	300,000	400,000	500,000
Medium	–100,000	900,000	1,000,000
High	–400,000	300,000	3,000,000

18.16 In Exercise 18.8, what is the maximum expected payoff if the probability of a complete loss of the commercial building is .05? Assume that the probability of no loss is 0.95. Find the risk associated with each action.

DOMINATED ACTIONS AND THE VALUE OF A CRYSTAL BALL

In a decision problem, we often can eliminate an action from consideration if another action in the problem has a larger payoff, regardless of the state of nature. Consider actions A_1 and A_2 from Table 18.12. Notice that the payoff for A_1 exceeds that for A_2 for all four states of nature. In this case, we say that A_1 **dominates** A_2. Action A_i dominates A_j if the payoff for A_i is greater than or equal to that for A_j under each state of nature. For at least one state of nature, the payoff for A_i must exceed that for A_j. In our example, there is no reason to consider A_2 for any decision strategy because A_1 produces a larger profit, regardless of what happens in the future. We say that action A_2 is inadmissible; it will not be included in the group of actions to be considered in the problem solution. Action A_i is **inadmissible** if it is dominated by any other action. Consequently, A_i is **admissible** if no other action under consideration dominates it.

EXAMPLE 18.12

Which of the actions in Table 18.2 are admissible?

SOLUTION

The procedure here is to determine whether any of these actions are dominated by any other action. For example, for actions A_2 and A_3, A_2 has a larger payoff, given state of nature S_1, but A_3 produces a bigger profit, given S_3. Therefore, neither of these two actions dominates the other. Comparing the remaining pairs of actions produces a similar argument; no one action produces a larger payoff for all states of nature. This implies that *all four* actions are admissible, and so they will all be considered in the search for the best action under the selected decision strategy.

Note that there is no serious harm in considering a dominated action; such an action never is selected by any of the decision strategies. By eliminating a dominated action from consideration, however, we simplify the decision process, since we have fewer actions to consider.

EXPECTED VALUE OF PERFECT INFORMATION

When using the strategy of maximizing expected profit, one value of interest is how much you would be willing to pay for a predictor that could tell you the future state of nature correctly 100% of the time. For example, you might have the (very unrealistic) situation of a consulting firm that predicts the future correctly all the time or, just as farfetched, a crystal ball. Because the future is in fact never perfectly predictable, any information about the future will be imperfect. Consequently, you use the value of a perfect predictor to evaluate any cost that you might incur for such imperfect information.

In Example 18.6, what would Mr. Larson, the owner of Sailtown, expect to make if a perfect predictor existed? Referring to Table 18.2, because $P(S_1) = .3$, the crystal ball will predict state of nature S_1 30% of the time. In this case, Mr. Larson inspects this column of Table 18.2, realizes that action A_1 has the largest payoff, and so orders 50 sailboats. His profit for this decision will be 15 (thousand dollars).

Now suppose the crystal ball predicts that the interest rate will remain unchanged (S_2 occurs). In this event, Mr. Larson will order 100 sailboats (A_3), because this is the largest payoff in the column under S_2 in Table 18.2. His profit will be 30. Finally, if he is informed that S_3 will occur, he selects action A_4, with a payoff of 45, because this produces the largest profit given that the interest rate will decrease.

In the long run, with a perfect predictor, Mr. Larson would make

$15,000 30% of the time   (when S_1 occurs)
$30,000 20% of the time   (when S_2 occurs)
$45,000 50% of the time   (when S_3 occurs)

These results mean that his *expected payoff with a perfect predictor* is

$$(15,000)(.3) + (30,000)(.2) + (45,000)(.5) = \$33,000$$

Finally, recall that the action that maximized the expected payoff (from Example 18.6) was A_3, with a value of \$18,000. So, Mr. Larson would make \$33,000 on the average *with* a crystal ball, and he would earn \$18,000 on the average *without* it by taking action A_3 each time. This means that the maximum price he should be willing to pay for a perfect predictor is

$$\$33,000 - 18,000 = \$15,000$$

This is the expected value of perfect information.

When you use expected payoffs in your decision strategy, you select that action (say, A') having the largest expected payoff. The **expected value of perfect information (EVPI)** is

> EVPI = (average payoff using a perfect predictor) – (average payoff for A')   **(18.4)**

EXAMPLE 18.13

In Example 18.8, the managers of Omega attempted to choose a selling price for their new computer. The states of nature for this problem were concerned with the amount of time until a major competitor introduced a similar product. The payoffs for this situation are summarized in Table 18.12. Assuming that $P(S_1) = .1$, $P(S_2) = .5$, $P(S_3) = .3$, and $P(S_4) = .1$, determine the expected value of perfect information.

SOLUTION

The action having the largest expected profit (according to Example 18.8) is A_1, with an expected value of 330. Consequently, the payoff with a selling price of \$1500 would be \$330 million on the average.

Given a perfect predictor, the following payoffs are possible:

State of Nature (S_i)	Maximum Payoff	Probability $P(S_i)$
S_1	250 (for A_1)	.1
S_2	320 (for A_1)	.5
S_3	410 (for A_4)	.3
S_4	550 (for A_4)	.1

Consequently, the expected payoff using a perfect predictor is

$$(.1)(250) + (.5)(320) + (.3)(410) + (.1)(550) = 363 \text{ (million dollars)}$$

From these results, the expected value of perfect information (from equation 18.4) is

$$\text{EVPI} = 363 - 330 = 33 \text{ (million dollars)}$$

So what is the maximum amount that Omega Corporation should be willing to pay an outside consulting firm for information regarding the time until a competitor introduces a similar model into the market? This is what the EVPI represents—an upper limit for the price of *any* information regarding the future. If Omega elects to pay an outside firm for information, they realize that the predicted state of nature could be wrong (that is, this information will be imperfect). For this reason, this information is worth *considerably less* than the EVPI of \$33 million. Its value will depend in part on the reliability of the consulting firm, as measured by the latter's past performance in similar situations. This topic is pursued further in Section 18.4.

EXERCISES 18.17–18.23

UNDERSTANDING THE MECHANICS

18.17 The maximum payoff for four states of nature are presented here with the probabilities of each state of nature.

State of Nature	Maximum Payoff	Probability $P(S_i)$
S_1	500 (for A_3)	.2
S_2	400 (for A_1)	.4
S_3	150 (for A_4)	.3
S_4	200 (for A_1)	.1

Determine the EVPI if the largest expected value is given by A_3, with an expected value of 180.

18.18 Consider the accompanying payoff table, with $P(S_1) = .3$, $P(S_2) = .4$, and $P(S_3) = .3$. Find the EVPI. Are all actions admissible?

Action	S_1	S_2	S_3
A_1	30	2	2
A_2	5	10	1
A_3	1	1	5

APPLYING THE NEW CONCEPTS

18.19 Greetings Card Shop must decide on whether to order 1500, 2000, or 2500 holiday cards before the holiday season. The card shop makes a profit of 50¢ on each card it sells and loses 30¢ on each card that remains unsold. If the demand for holiday cards is strong (S_1), 2500 cards should sell. If the demand is average (S_2), 2000 cards should sell. If the demand is weak (S_3), 1,500 cards should sell. The manager of Greetings believes that the following probabilities are representative of past sales: $P(S_1) = .40$, $P(S_2) = .40$, and $P(S_3) = .20$. What is the maximum amount that the manager of Greetings would be willing to pay for perfect information regarding the demand for holiday cards?

18.20 If the EVPI for a certain company is $40,000 and the average payoff based on the decision from the maximum expected payoff is $25,000, what is the maximum payoff using a perfect market predictor?

18.21 A manager uses a computerized planning system to maintain an inventory of raw materials for a certain manufacturing operation. The manager knows from experience that the probabilities of low demand (S_1), medium demand (S_2), and high demand (S_3) for the inventory of raw materials are .30, .40, and .30, respectively. The following payoff table gives the amounts of money the manager can save the company by ordering the monthly supply of raw materials given by A_1 (low supply), A_2 (medium supply), and A_3 (high supply). What is the maximum amount the manager would be willing to pay a consultant for advice regarding the company's demand for raw materials?

Action	S_1	S_2	S_3
A_1	10,500	8,000	5,000
A_2	−1,000	15,000	10,000
A_3	−4,000	3,000	30,000

18.22 Refer to Exercise 18.12. What is the maximum that the manager of the hardware store would be willing to pay to obtain perfect information regarding the type of winter for the current year?

18.23 Refer to Exercise 18.13. What is the EVPI for the manager of the theater, regarding attendance turnout? Are any of the actions inadmissible?

18.3 THE CONCEPT OF UTILITY

We have concentrated on choosing the best action under various decision strategies by using the values contained in the payoff table. For example, one strategy determines the action having the largest expected payoff. Another (the minimax procedure) examines opportunity losses derived from the payoff table. Still another strategy examines expected payoffs. In other words, each action is evaluated by the corresponding *dollar amount* resulting from a particular strategy.

There are many instances in which it is more advantageous *not* to use expected payoffs, particularly when large amounts of money are at stake. Anyone who purchases an insurance policy or buys a lottery ticket generally is trying neither to minimize expected losses nor maximize expected gains. Rather, such a person *gambles* his or her money, trying to guard against a heavy loss (insurance) or hoping to strike it rich (lottery).

There is something else besides money involved in the decision to purchase an insurance policy or a lottery ticket. In the case of insurance, suppose you have a $150,000 home insured for the full amount. For most people, a gift of $150,000 would be nice (in fact, *very* nice) but a $150,000 loss would be totally devastating—this is the underlying concept behind the insurance philosophy. A gain of $150,000 does not have the same effect on the positive side as does a $150,000 loss on the negative side.

When you fail to purchase insurance, you are betting that your house will not go up in smoke. Your *risk* here is that the house may burn. When we look at expected payoffs only, we ignore risk. On the other hand, we also discussed a method of examining the risk of each action by finding the variance of the respective payoffs. What we need is a method that combines the decision maker's attitude toward the payoff with the corresponding risk of each alternative. An action with a possible higher payoff (or loss, in the case of insurance) often contains more risk. We measure the attractiveness of each outcome using utility values, which we will now develop.

> The **utility value** of a particular outcome is used to measure both the attractiveness and the risk associated with this dollar amount.

CONSTRUCTING A UTILITY VALUE

Suppose you have $10,000 saved up for college expenses one year before you begin your freshman year. A friend of yours has offered you part interest in an oil-drilling venture for your $10,000. If the venture fails, you lose your entire investment, but if it succeeds, your payoff will be $40,000. According to the latest geological survey, the probability of hitting oil is .3. Also, if oil exists, the expected life of the venture is one year, with the payoff of $40,000.

Your other option is to invest the money for one year in a money market account at an expected interest rate of 12%. If you choose to maximize your expected payoff (dollars on hand at the end of the year), which action should you select?

The decision problem involves two actions,

A_1: put the $10,000 into the money market (interest = 12%)
A_2: invest $10,000 in the oil venture

with two states of nature

S_1: oil does not exist on the site
S_2: oil does exist on the site

Your corresponding payoffs, should you select the oil investment, are

$0   if S_1 occurs (and you lose your investment)

$40,000   if S_2 occurs

The payoff table is shown next, with the corresponding state-of-nature probabilities in parentheses. The expected payoffs here are

	S_1(.7)	S_2(.3)
A_1	11,200	11,200
A_2	0	40,000

for action A_1: 11,200(.7) + 11,200(.3) = 11,200
for action A_2:   (0)(.7)   + (40,000)(.3) = 12,000

The oil venture (A_2) has a larger expected payoff, so, using this decision strategy, you would elect to gamble your money in hopes of a large payoff. But is this a realistic strategy? Assume that the loss of your $10,000 would result in your not going to college. All things considered, this would be disastrous. Although the large payoff would be terrific, the high probability of a heavy loss might make you wonder if the gamble is a good idea.

The problem in this illustration is that a large payoff often is very attractive, but it is offset by a risk associated with it. We say that the **utility** associated with a gain of, say, $100,000 without risk is *higher* than the utility of this amount with a high risk. For each decision problem, we ask the decision maker to determine the utility value associated with the various payoffs in the problem. In this way, the person can build in his or her attitudes with regard to avoiding risk or preferring a gamble with a big payoff (a *risk taker*).

To illustrate the construction of a utility value, consider the payoff table we just constructed. There are many ways to proceed here, although all the various ways of assigning utility values produce the *same* decision when using these values to arrive at the best alternative. We use a two-step procedure:

Step 1. Assign a utility value of 0 to the smallest payoff amount (π_{min}) and a value of 100 to the largest (π_{max}). For this example, the utility values would be written as $U(0) = 0$ and $U(40,000) = 100$, because $\pi_{min} = 0$ and $\pi_{max} = 40,000$. *All utility values range from 0 to 100.* Whether you assign utility values from 0 to 1, 0 to 100, 1 to 5, or any range does not matter. It is not the actual value of the utility that is important but rather its value *relative* to the range of all values.

There is one other payoff in the table to consider, namely, $11,200. What is the utility of this dollar amount to the decision maker (you, in this case)? We consider both the attractiveness and the risk involved with this payoff in the following situation.

Consider the largest payoff of $40,000 and the smallest of $0. You need to decide what the probability, *P*, would have to be before you would consider

$$\$11,200 \text{ with certainty}$$

to be as attractive as

$$\$40,000 \text{ with probability } P \text{ and } \$0 \text{ with probability } 1 - P$$

Suppose you decide that you would need at least a 50% chance of striking oil. So, $P = .5$. We next define the utility of the $11,200 payoff by using

$$\text{utility value} = P \cdot 100$$

$$= .5 \cdot 100 = 50$$

That is,

$$U(11,200) = 50$$

A graphical illustration of these utilities is shown in Figure 18.2. An easy way to measure your attitude toward risk is to connect the lower left (utility = 0) and upper right (utility = 100) corners. If the utility values you have assigned fall *above* this line, you tend to avoid risk. If they fall *below* the line, you are a risk taker. For this example, $U(11,200) = 50$ lies above the diagonal line, indicating that, for this situation, you are a risk avoider. A summary of this procedure is step 2 of the utility value assignment.

Step 2. The utility value for any payoff (say, π_{ij}) under consideration is found by using

$$U(\pi_{ij}) = P \cdot 100$$

where *P* is the probability such that

$$\pi_{ij} \text{ with certainty}$$

is equally as attractive as

$$\pi_{max} \text{ with probability } P \quad \text{and} \quad \pi_{min} \text{ with probability } 1 - P$$

and π_{max} and π_{min} are determined in step 1.

FIGURE 18.2

Illustration of utility values for oil venture.

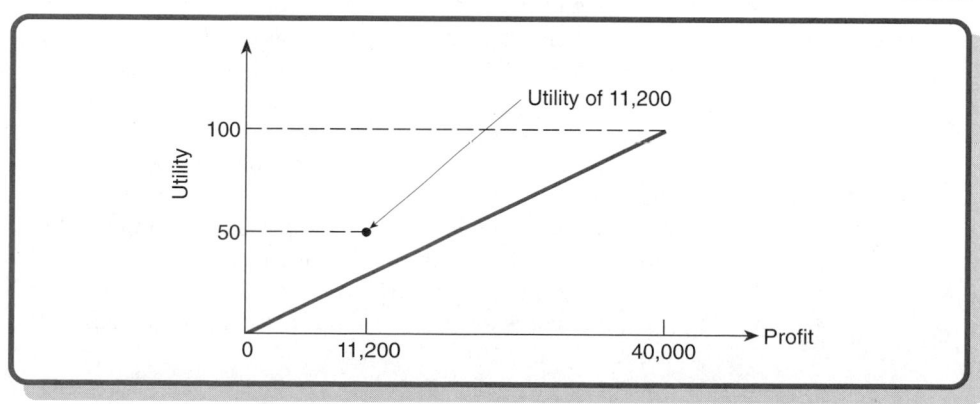

The resulting table of utility values for this example is

Action	S_1: Oil Venture Is Unsuccessful (.7)	S_2: Oil Venture Is Successful (.3)
A_1: money-market account	50	50
A_2: oil venture	0	100

Notice that we return to the *original* probabilities for the states of nature (.7 and .3) when constructing this table. The values of .5 and .5 were used only to measure your willingness to take a risk. They do not change the fact that S_1 will occur 70% of the time (even though you may wish it would occur only 50% of the time).

To use the utility values in choosing one of the alternative actions, we proceed exactly as before, except that we select that action having the largest expected utility *rather than the largest expected payoff.*

> expected utility for each action = $\sum$(each utility value) · (its probability)   **(18.5)**

EXAMPLE 18.14

Using the preceding table, which action, based on expected utility, is the more attractive of the two?

SOLUTION

A_1: expected utility = $(50)(.7) + (50)(.3) = 50$

A_2: expected utility = $(0)(.7) + (100)(.3) = 30$

Because action A_1 (the money market account) has a larger expected utility, we choose this action over the riskier oil venture, A_2. This choice was also suggested by Figure 18.2, which indicated that, for this application, you are a risk avoider.

DETERMINING UTILITY VALUES FOR LARGE DECISION PROBLEMS

Whenever your payoff table contains a large number of values, there is an alternative to the two-step procedure just described. The main problem here is the second step, which requires that the decision maker determine the utility of *each* payoff contained in the pay-off table. This can be quite difficult, because there is a requirement for step 2: If

$$\text{payoff } \pi_{ij} < \text{payoff } \pi_{st}$$

then it is necessary that

$$U(\pi_{ij}) < U(\pi_{st})$$

This means that if one payoff is larger than another, the corresponding utility values must be in the *same order.*

When forced to determine the utility of many payoffs, some of which are nearly the same, the decision maker may rate one payoff lower than another, but the utility values may be in the opposite order. One way to avoid this situation is *not* to use step 2 on every payoff involved in the problem; rather, you use this step on *between five and ten payoff values over the range of payoffs* for this problem. Consequently, you would examine $\pi_{\min}$ and $\pi_{\max}$ from step 1 and select, say, six payoffs between these values. These *need not* be actual payoff values from the payoff table. You then use the step 2 procedure to determine the utility value (U) for each of these six payoffs.

Your next step is to plot these values in a graph and connect them to form a **utility curve.** The utility of each value in the payoff table can be obtained by approximating it from the resulting graph. Because of the requirement for step 2, you need to make sure that the utility curve always *increases as the payoff increases.* We will demonstrate this technique in Example 18.15.

TABLE 18.20   Utilities for Example 18.15.

	PAYOFF					
	100	150	200	300	400	500
Probability (*P*)	.20	.40	.55	.75	.90	.97
Utility [*P*(100)]	20	40	55	75	90	97

EXAMPLE 18.15

Table 18.12 contains the various payoffs for the selling-price decision facing the Omega Corporation. The minimum payoff is $\pi_{min} = 80$ (million dollars), and the maximum is $\pi_{max} = 550$. So, for step 1, we have

$$U(80) = 0 \quad \text{and} \quad U(550) = 100$$

Describe a procedure for determining the utility of the remaining 14 values.

SOLUTION

One method, of course, is to have the decision maker choose 14 corresponding utility values using step 2 on each payoff. An easier procedure is to request this information for payoffs of, say, 100, 150, 200, 300, 400, and 500. Notice that these payoffs are not necessarily contained in Table 18.12, but they do cover the range from 80 to 550. For a payoff of 200, we ask for that value of *P* such that a payoff of 200 (million dollars) with certainty is equally as attractive as a payoff of 550 with probability *P* and a payoff of 80 with probability $1 - P$. Suppose the decision maker's response is $P = .55$. Then the utility value of this payoff is

$$U(200) = .55 \cdot 100 = 55$$

Consider the set of probabilities (*P*) and corresponding utilities in Table 18.20. It will be much easier for the decision maker to supply these six values than to choose the 14 values remaining in Table 18.12. *A key ingredient to making any quantitative procedure usable is to keep it reasonably simple!*

The utilities for this problem are plotted in Figure 18.3; the curve through these points represents the decision maker's utility curve. Notice that the utility values *do* increase as the payoffs increase, so the requirement for step 2 is satisfied. As in Figure 18.2, the utility values lie *above* the line connecting the corners, indicating that this individual is a risk avoider.

EXAMPLE 18.16

Using the utility curve in Figure 18.3, determine the utility for each payoff in Table 18.12. Which action (selling price) has the largest expected utility?

SOLUTION

From step 1, we have $U(80) = 0$ and $U(550) = 100$. The remaining utilities can be estimated from the utility curve constructed in Example 18.15. This process is illustrated for payoffs of 260 (action A_2, state of nature S_2) and 350 (action A_1, state of nature S_3) in Figure 18.3. Consequently,

$$U(260) = 68 \qquad U(350) = 84$$

Continuing this procedure results in Table 18.21. The expected utilities are, for example,

$$\text{expected utility for } A_2 = (.1)(40) + (.5)(68) + (.3)(75) + (.1)(87) = 69.2$$

FIGURE 18.3
Utility curve for Omega
computer-price decision
(Example 18.15).

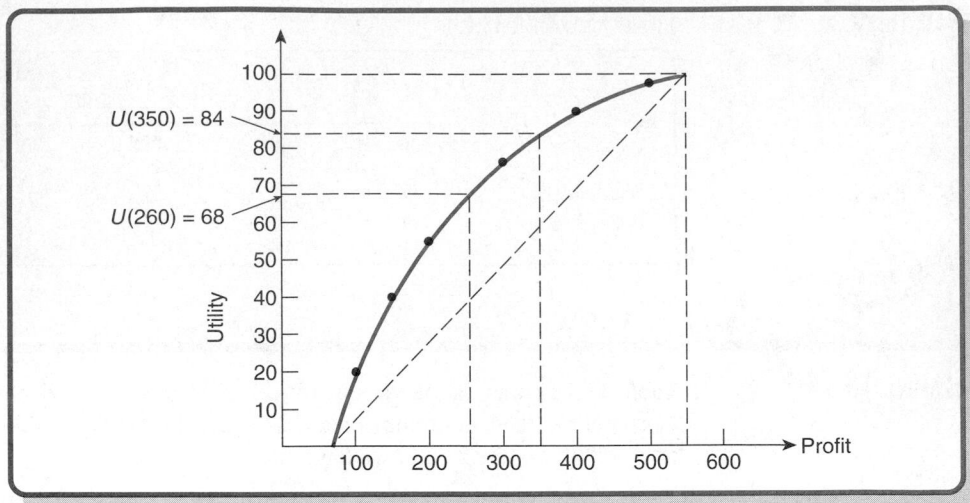

TABLE 18.21

Utility table for Omega computer-price decision problem (Example 18.16).

Action	S_1 (.1)	S_2 (.5)	S_3 (.3)	S_4 (.1)	Expected Utility
A_1: price = $1500	67	79	84	90	80.4
A_2: price = $1750	40	68	75	87	69.2
A_3: price = $2000	30	74	88	94	75.8
A_4: price = $2500	0	72	91	100	73.3

If we choose that action with the largest expected utility, our decision is to select action A_1 (selling price $1500). For this application, A_1 maximizes both expected payoff (see Example 18.8) and expected utility.

SHAPE OF UTILITY CURVES

The shape of a decision maker's utility curve indicates his or her preference for or aversion to risk. There are essentially three categories of people in regard to risk: (1) the risk avoider, (2) the risk neutral, and (3) the risk taker.

The basic shapes of the utility curves for each of these classifications are shown in Figure 18.4. Notice that in all three situations, the utility curves increase as the payoff increases. Variations of these curves also can occur; for example, a person may prefer a risk for small payoffs but then avoid a risk for large payoffs. A utility curve for such a person is S-shaped.

An individual who is **risk neutral** will have resulting utility values that lie close to the line connecting the corners. It makes no difference whether you maximize expected payoff or expected utility—the resulting best action for this person is the *same* in either case. Very wealthy people often demonstrate this behavior because, for them, the utility of each dollar remains nearly constant.

Most people are **risk avoiders,** particularly when large payoffs or losses are involved. For two actions with equal expected payoffs, the risk avoider prefers the one with the smaller risk. This person also prefers a smaller expected payoff with a small risk over a larger expected payoff with a large risk. The **risk taker,** on the other hand, is the gambler; he or she prefers an action with a possible large payoff, even if the risk is more severe.

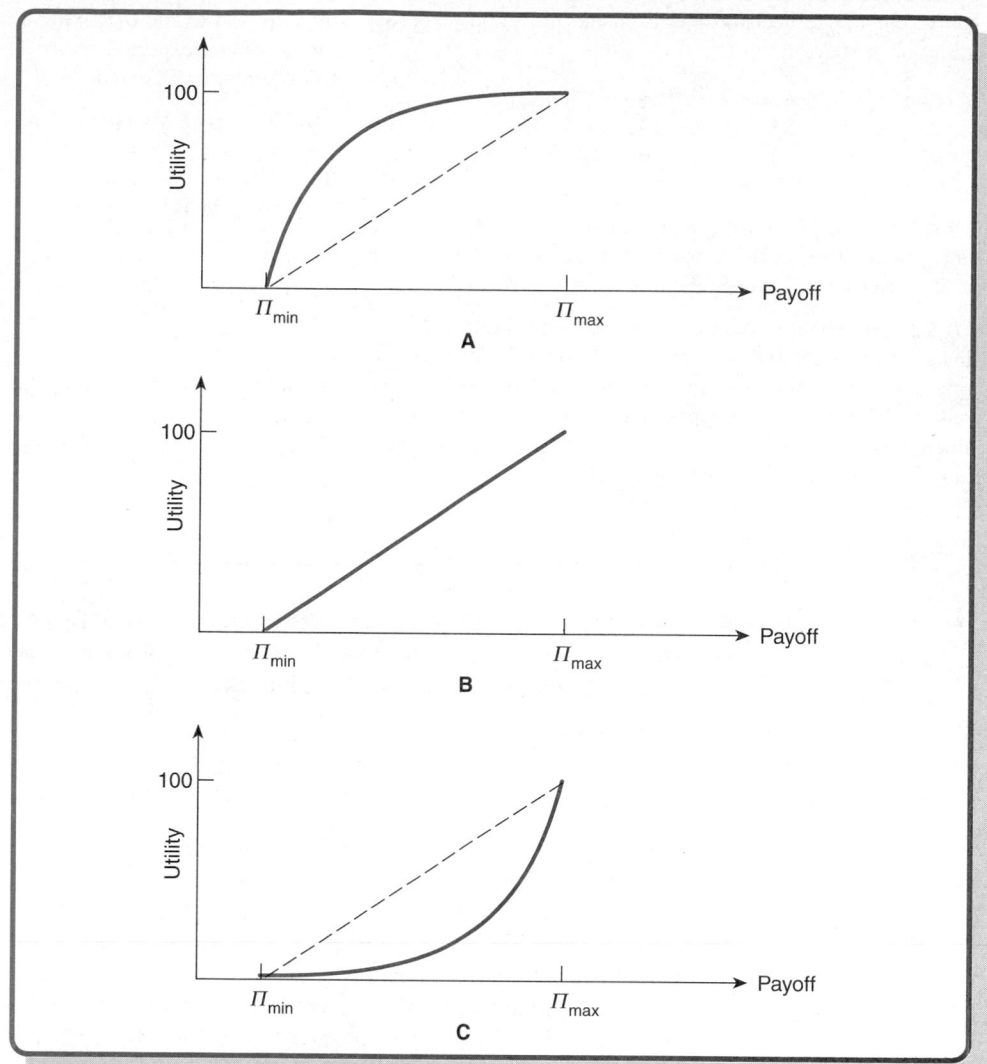

FIGURE 18.4

Three classes of utility curves: (a) the risk avoider, (b) the risk neutral, (c) the risk taker.

In summary, utility values allow the decision maker to combine both payoff and risk into a single measure. However, the assignment of these values is subjective and special care must be taken in their determination.

EXERCISES 18.24–18.30

UNDERSTANDING THE MECHANICS

18.24 Examine each of the following functions over the specified range of values. Can the function be considered to be a utility function? If yes, is the decision maker a risk avoider, risk neutral, or a risk taker?

  a. $U(x) = 100x^3$ for x between 0 and 1

  b. $U(x) = .01x - 100$ for x between 10,000 and 20,000

  c. $U(x) = 4 - x^2$ for x between 2 and 10

18.25 Consider the accompanying payoff table and the following utility function for money. All four states of nature are equally likely.

$$U(x) = 10\sqrt{x} \qquad \text{for } 0 \le x \le 100$$

Action	S_1	S_2	S_3	S_4
A_1	4	100	49	9
A_2	81	25	36	25
A_3	100	16	25	9

  a. Find the decision based on the maximum expected payoff.

  b. Find the decision based on the maximum expected utility of the payoff.

APPLYING THE NEW CONCEPTS

18.26 Suppose a person is risk neutral and has the utility function $U(x) = 3x/2$. In the following payoff table, $P(S_1) = .20$, $P(S_2) = .40$, $P(S_3) = .30$, and $P(S_4) = .10$. Show that the decision based on the maximum expected payoff is equivalent to the decision based on the maximum expected utility of the payoff.

Action	S_1	S_2	S_3	S_4
A_1	50	10	30	10
A_2	20	20	30	60
A_3	10	50	10	20

18.27 Repeat Exercise 18.26 using the utility function $U(x) = 1.2x$. Does the decision based on the maximum expected utility differ from that obtained in Exercise 18.26?

18.28 A decision maker assigns a probability value of P such that a payoff of $50,000 with certainty is equally as attractive as a payoff of $500,000 with probability P and as a payoff of 0 with probability $1 - P$. Suppose the decision maker's utility function is defined such that $U(0) = 0$, $U($500,000$) = 100$, and $U($50,000$) = 75$. What is the value of P?

18.29 If the utility curve of the manager of the hardware store in Exercise 18.12 is $U(x) = \log_{10}(x)$, find the decision based on the maximum expected utility. Is the manager risk neutral, a risk taker, or a risk avoider?

18.30 Suppose a money manager is a risk avoider with the utility function $U(x) = (x\sqrt{x})/33.75$, where x can range from 0 to 225. In the following payoff table, $P(S_1) = .25$, $P(S_2) = .30$, $P(S_3) = .40$, and $P(S_4) = .05$.

Action	S_1	S_2	S_3	S_4
A_1	151	33	95	40
A_2	75	75	97	180
A_3	29	162	30	50

  a. Find the decision based on the maximum expected payoff.

  b. Find the decision based on the maximum expected utility of the payoff.

18.4 DECISION TREES AND BAYES' RULE

This section describes the decision tree, a device useful for structuring and illustrating the uncertain outcomes associated with any decision problem. A decision tree graphically represents the entire decision problem, including a representation of:

1. The possible actions facing the decision maker.
2. The outcomes (states of nature) that can occur.
3. The relationships between these actions and outcomes.

The decision tree makes it easier for you to compute the expected values and to understand the process of making a decision. We will demonstrate how to construct a decision tree and discuss a procedure for using the tree to examine the alternatives and arrive at a decision.

The basic idea behind a decision tree was introduced in Chapter 4, which discussed **tree diagrams.** These diagrams can be very useful for determining probabilities in applications that lend themselves to a treelike structure. For example, if a defective part is discovered during final inspection, what is the probability that it was produced during the third shift? Because the Chapter 4 discussion was not concerned with making decisions, no mention was made then of "possible actions" or "states of nature."

CONSTRUCTING DECISION TREES

A convenient way of representing a set of alternatives and states of nature is to use a decision tree. A **decision tree** is a picture of the actions under consideration and the states of nature that affect the probability of each action. It is a convenient way of illustrating the entire decision problem, because you can tell at a glance exactly which alternatives are being considered and what the payoff is under each state of nature.

In Example 18.8, Omega needed to make a decision about the selling price of their new computer. A decision tree for this situation is shown in Figure 18.5.

A decision tree represents a sequence of *decisions,* represented by boxes, and *outcomes* left strictly to chance, represented by circles. The boxes are decision nodes, and the circles are chance nodes.

When you reach a **decision node,** you need to make a decision at this point in the decision tree. The path you select reflects your choice of the best action to take at this point. This decision is under your control. The paths away from a **chance node** represent states of nature (S_1, S_2, . . .). There is no choice for you to make here; rather, each of these paths will occur with a certain probability, written as $P(S_1)$, $P(S_2)$, ...

FIGURE 18.5

Decision tree for the Omega computer-price problem.

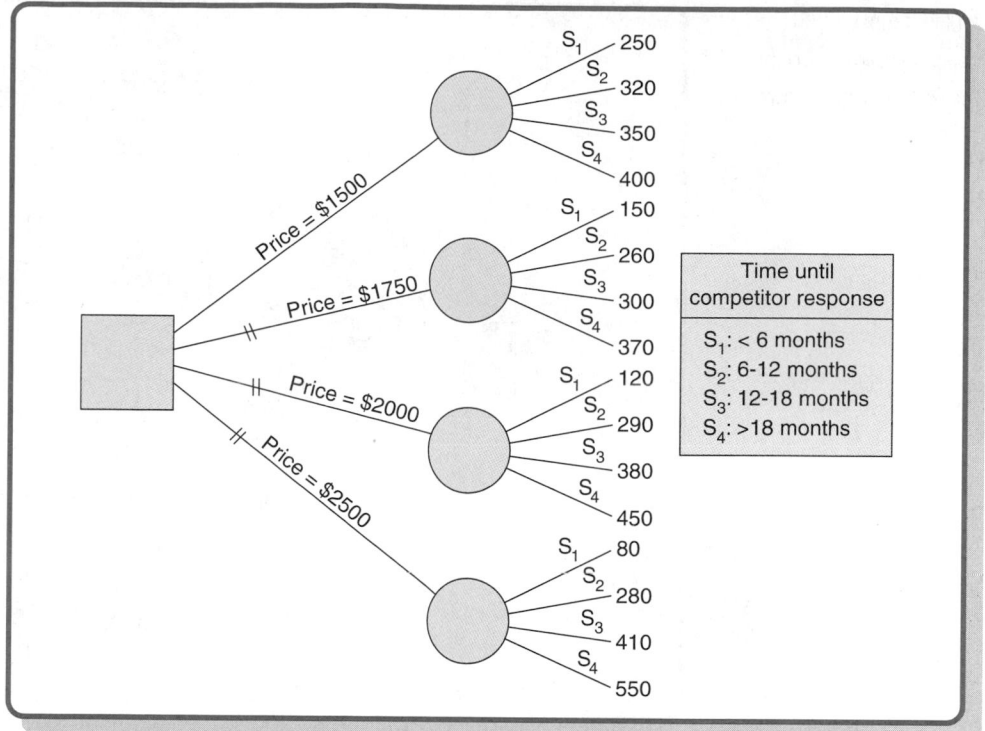

The final step in completing a decision tree is to determine a dollar amount (or utility amount, if you are using utility values) within each chance node and decision node. The amount placed inside a chance node is the *expected payoff* at this point, using the probability for each state of nature. Consider the top chance node in Figure 18.5. Using the state-of-nature probabilities from Example 18.8, the completed tree (Figure 18.6) contains the expected payoff for each selling price. To illustrate, the expected payoff for a selling price of $1500 is

$$(.1)(250) + (.5)(320) + (.3)(350) + (.1)(400) = 330$$

In Figure 18.6, the amount in each *decision* node is not an expected value, because there are no probabilities associated with the paths leading away from this point. Instead, the dollar (or utility) amount, or the expected dollar (or utility) amount, associated with the *best* action at this point is contained within the box. Of the four paths leading away from the decision node in Figure 18.6, action A_1 (price = $1500) has the largest expected payoff, so this amount goes into the box. On the remaining three paths at this node, a double vertical bar across the path indicates that we have struck out these alternatives because they are not the ones to use at this point in the decision path.

Our conclusion from reading this tree would be to select a selling price of $1500 for an expected payoff of 330 (million dollars).

EXAMPLE 18.17

SOLUTION

Structure the decision problem with the Sailtown data from Table 18.2 as a decision tree.

The decision path begins with a decision node (how many sailboats to purchase), followed by a sequence of chance nodes reflecting the change in the interest rate. Figure 18.7 contains the completed tree for this problem. As in the previous analysis, when you are maximizing expected payoffs, your best alternative is to order 100 sailboats (action A_3) with an expected payoff of 18 (thousand dollars).

FIGURE 18.6

Completed decision tree for the Omega computer-price problem.

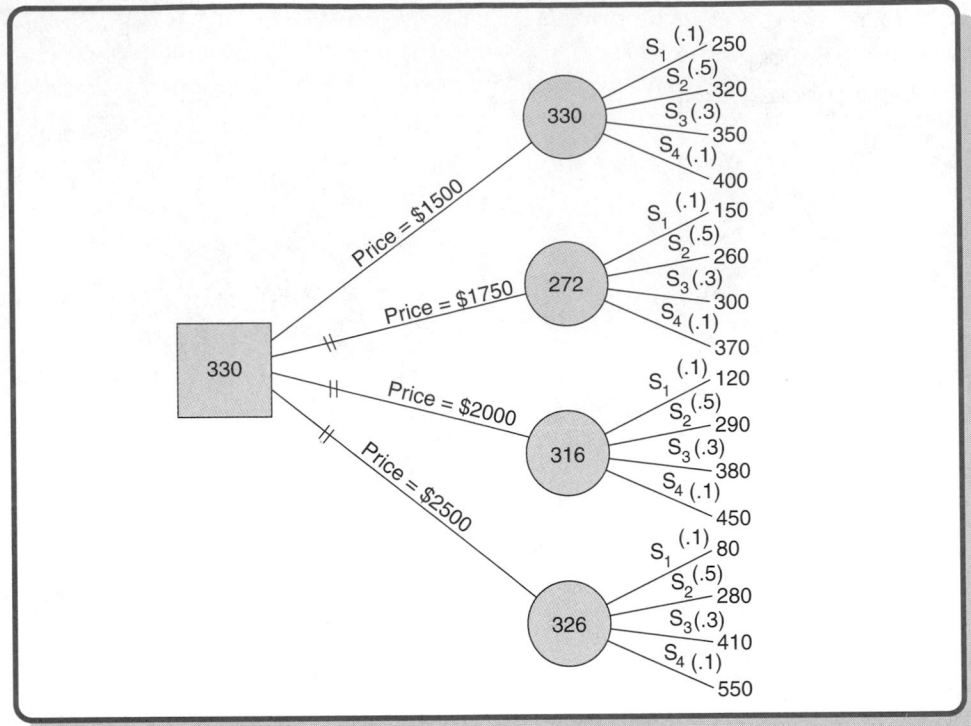

FIGURE 18.7

Decision tree for Sailtown decision problem (Example 18.17).

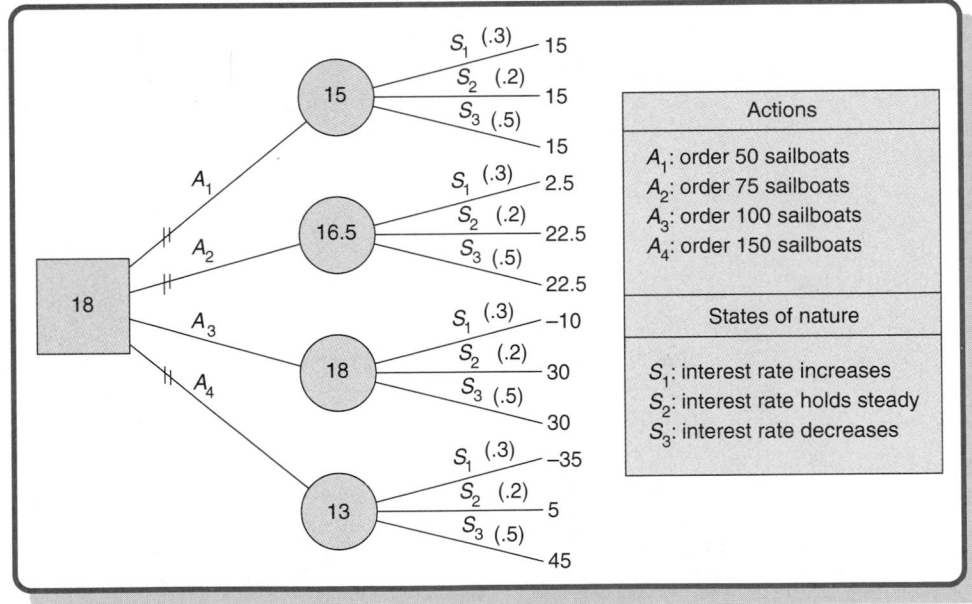

Once again you should perform a follow-up *sensitivity analysis* to determine how sensitive this solution is to the state-of-nature probabilities. When you summarize the results of a sensitivity analysis, you can construct a decision tree for each set of probabilities under consideration, and it will indicate the optimum path under this condition.

AN APPLICATION OF DECISION TREES: USING BAYES' RULE TO MAXIMIZE PROFITS

Bayes' Rule (attributed to the English clergyman, Thomas Bayes) was introduced in Chapter 4. This rule allows you to revise a probability in light of certain information that is provided. For example, suppose we know that 30% of the manufactured parts at your plant are produced during the third (late-night) shift. This probability is referred to as a **prior probability,** since it is a probability obtained *prior* to any known information, such as "I know this part is defective." The probability that the part was produced during the third shift *given that it is defective* is a **posterior probability.** It is the revised probability that a part was produced during the third shift, in light of the information that the part is defective.

To apply Bayes' Rule, a decision problem is structured into a decision tree (or tree diagram in Chapter 4) beginning with a set of paths, such as shift 1, shift 2, and shift 3. Determining a posterior probability is equivalent to finding the probability that the new information (part is defective) was arrived at along a certain path, such as path 3 belonging to shift 3. This type of situation was illustrated in Example 4.7, where, using Bayes' Rule,

$$P(\text{shift 3} \mid \text{part is defective}) = \frac{\text{third path}}{\text{sum of paths}}$$

$$= \frac{(.3)(.15)}{.091} = .495$$

That is, given that a defective part is discovered, there is nearly a 50–50 chance that it was produced during the third shift.

In general, Bayes' Rule states that given the final event (new information) B, the probability that the event was reached along the ith path corresponding to event E_i is

$$P(E_i \mid B) = \frac{P(E_i \text{ and } B)}{P(B)} = \frac{i\text{th path}}{\text{sum of paths}} \qquad (18.6)$$

In Table 18.2, the probability that the interest rate will increase (S_1) was $P(S_1) = .3$. What if a reliable consulting firm using various economic indicators predicted that the interest rate would increase? The value of $P(S_1) = .3$ was a subjective estimate, measuring Mr. Larson's belief that the rate would increase; it is a prior probability. In light of the *new information* obtained from the consulting firm, we would expect the probability of S_1 to increase if, in fact, the firm is reliable. This probability, $P(S_1 \mid$ firm predicts a rate increase), is a posterior probability.

An excellent opportunity to use Bayes' Rule arises whenever you want to determine posterior probabilities based on recent information regarding the states of nature in your decision problem. This information can come from such sources as an outside consulting firm or a questionnaire developed by your company's marketing staff. Based on the new information, you can maximize your expected payoff (or utility) by replacing the prior probabilities with their corresponding posterior probabilities.

EXAMPLE 18.18

Now take another look at the Sailtown example. Mr. Larson, the owner, has decided to purchase the services of an outside consultant in an effort to determine more accurately the movement of the interest rate over the summer months. The information supplied by the consultant will be one of the following:

I_1:   consultant predicts an increase in the interest rate
I_2:   consultant predicts no change in this rate
I_3:   consultant predicts a drop in this rate

The information in Table 18.22 also was provided; it describes the past performance of this consultant when predicting interest rates. The values in the table contain conditional probabilities for the consultant's prediction under each state of nature. For example, $.7 = P(I_1 \mid S_1)$, $.4 = P(I_1 \mid S_2)$, and so forth. These probabilities mean that she predicted interest rate increases 70% of the times they actually occurred, and when there was no change in the interest rate, she predicted an increase 40% of the time. If the consultant is

TABLE 18.22   Conditional probabilities for consultant [= $P(I \mid S)$] (Example 18.18).

| | ACTUALLY OCCURRED | | |
Consultant Predicted	An Increase (S_1)	No Change (S_2)	A Decrease (S_3)
I_1 an increase	.7	.4	.2
I_2 no change	.2	.5	.2
I_3 a decrease	.1	.1	.6
	1.0	1.0	1.0

FIGURE 18.8   Decision tree, given information I_1.

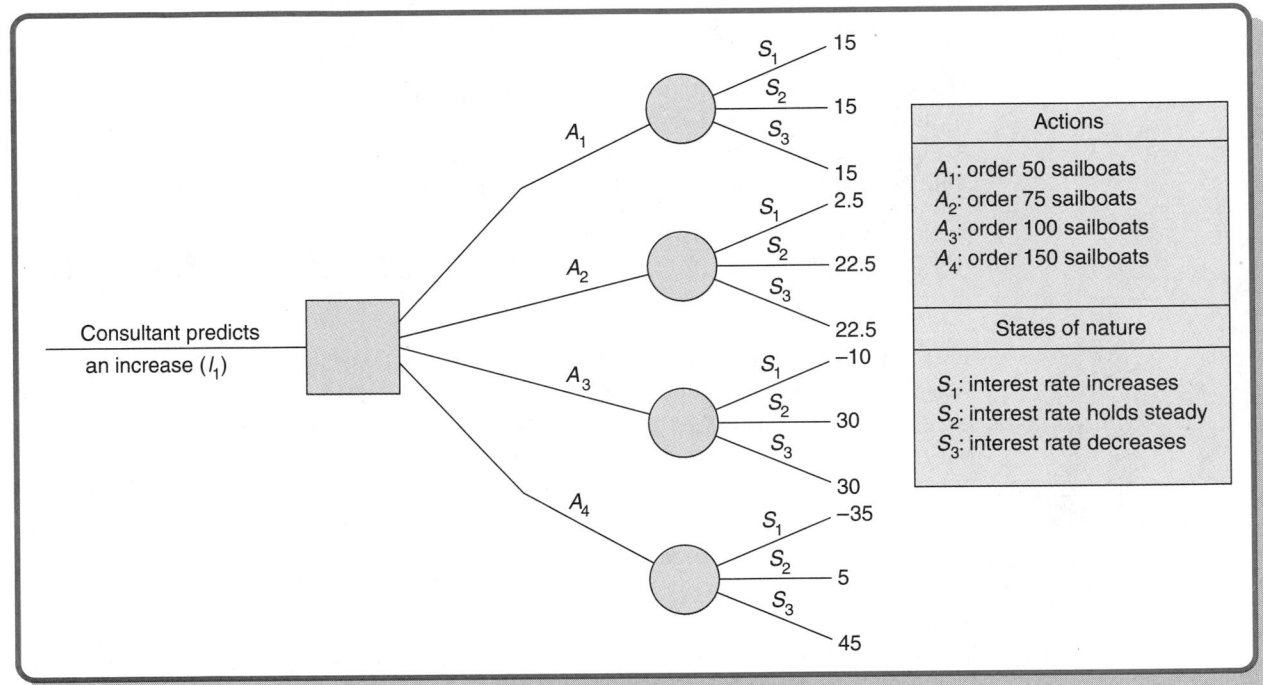

extremely reliable, the numbers from the upper left to the lower right (.7, .5, and .6) should be near 1, and the remaining values should be small.

The consultant predicts an increase (I_1) in the interest rate. What is the best action for Mr. Larson to take in light of this information? What is his expected profit?

SOLUTION   Figure 18.8 shows the new decision tree. Notice that Figures 18.7 and 18.8 are very similar, including the payoff amounts. The big difference is that the prior probabilities of $P(S_1) = .3$, $P(S_2) = .2$, and $P(S_3) = .5$ will be revised in light of the new information: $P(S_1)$ will be replaced by $P(S_1 \mid I_1)$, $P(S_2)$ by $P(S_2 \mid I_1)$, and $P(S_3)$ by $P(S_3 \mid I_1)$.

DERIVING THE POSTERIOR PROBABILITIES

To derive the posterior probabilities, we begin by constructing a tree diagram with the new information as the event on the *far right,* as shown in Figure 18.9. We can then obtain the probabilities along the various branches from the prior probabilities and the information in Table 18.22.

FIGURE 18.9

Partial tree diagram for deriving posterior probabilities; new information is the event on the far right.

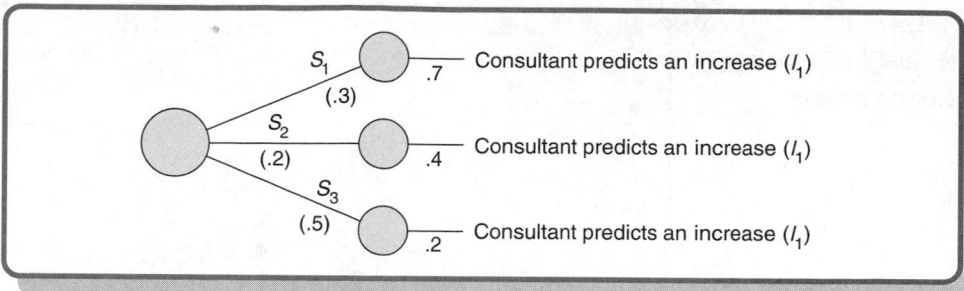

Using Bayes' rule,

$$P(I_1) = \text{sum of the paths}$$

$$= (.3)(.7) + (.2)(.4) + (.5)(.2) = .39$$

The posterior probabilities are given by

$$P(S_1 \mid I_1) = \frac{\text{first path}}{\text{sum of the paths}}$$

$$= \frac{.21}{.39} = .538$$

$$P(S_2 \mid I_1) = \frac{\text{second path}}{\text{sum of the paths}}$$

$$= \frac{.08}{.39} = .205$$

$$P(S_3 \mid I_1) = \frac{\text{third path}}{\text{sum of the paths}}$$

$$= \frac{.10}{.39} = .256$$

Placing these values in the decision tree results in Figure 18.10. The expected payoffs using the posterior probabilities are found in the usual manner. For action A_2,

$$\text{expected payoff} = (.538)(2.5) + (.205)(22.5) + (.256)(22.5) = 11.72$$

Our conclusion is that, given information that the consultant has predicted a rise in the interest rate, Mr. Larson's best alternative is to order 50 sailboats (action A_1) with an expected payoff of 15 (thousand dollars). Remember that, given no information at all, we use the *prior* probabilities to select that action having the largest expected payoff. These expected values were summarized in Table 18.11, where action A_3 (ordering 100 sailboats) provided the largest expected value. Notice also in Table 18.11 that the expected payoff for action A_2, given no information from the consultant, is 16.5. In other words, our revised expected payoff for this action, given the consultant's forecast, drops from 16.5 to 11.72.

EVALUATING SAMPLE INFORMATION: DETERMINING EXPECTED PAYOFF

By combining a decision tree with Bayes' Rule for calculating posterior probabilities, the decision maker is able to determine whether purchasing new information is a good idea. We will refer to this new information as **sample information.** Such information may be collected from one of many sources, including a sample of questionnaires, a recently released

FIGURE 18.10

Completed decision tree using posterior probabilities.

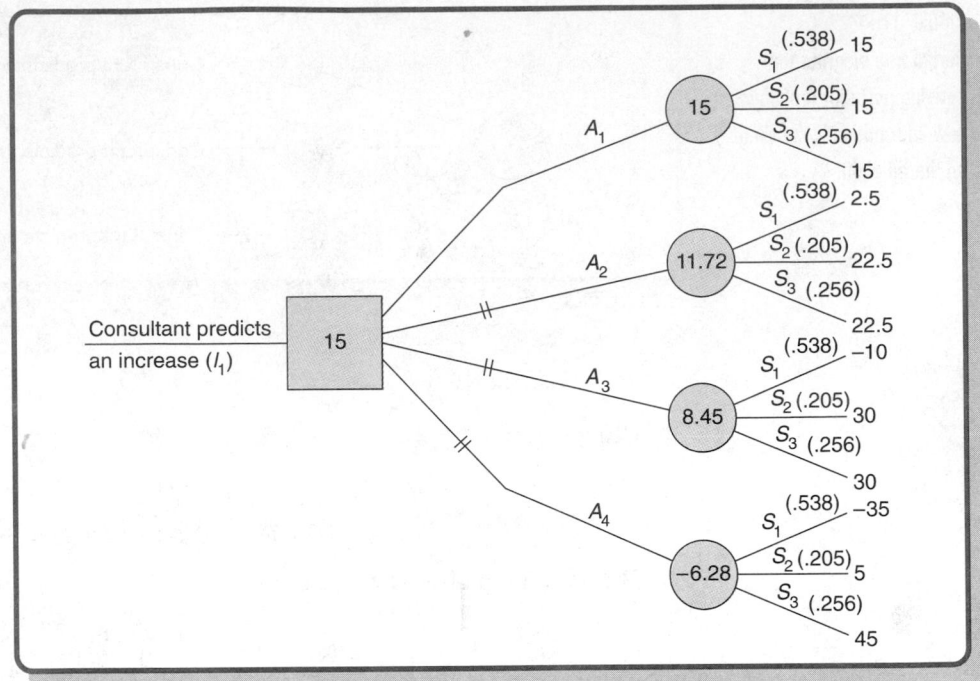

government report, or, as in the previous example, an outside consultant. Typically, such information costs money; by using a decision-tree analysis, you will be able to decide between:

1. Not purchasing any additional information and using the prior probabilities to determine that action with the maximum expected payoff (or utility).
2. Purchasing this information because the expected payoff (or utility) for this decision is larger than that obtained using prior probabilities only.

In Example 18.18, the owner of Sailtown used information provided by a consultant to revise his prior probabilities regarding a possible change in the interest rate. Based on the information provided (the interest rate will increase), Mr. Larson derived the posterior probabilities and decided to purchase 50 sailboats (action A_1).

Was it a good idea for Mr. Larson to purchase the consultant's services in the first place? The cost of this information was $2500. We previously found the expected value of perfect information (EVPI) for this situation to be $15,000. The consultant's fee is considerably less than this amount, so Mr. Larson was willing to evaluate the alternative of purchasing this information.

To construct a decision tree for the full problem, we begin exactly as we did in Figure 18.7. Our next step is to include an additional branch for purchasing information from the consultant. To complete this branch, we can use a two-step procedure (refer to Figure 18.11).

Step 1. The next node will be a *chance* node, representing the possible information to be provided. In Figure 18.11 this is

I_1:   consultant predicts an increase in the interest rate
I_2:   consultant predicts no change in the interest rate
I_3:   consultant predicts a decrease in the interest rate

FIGURE 18.11   Completed decision tree for Sailtown decision problem.

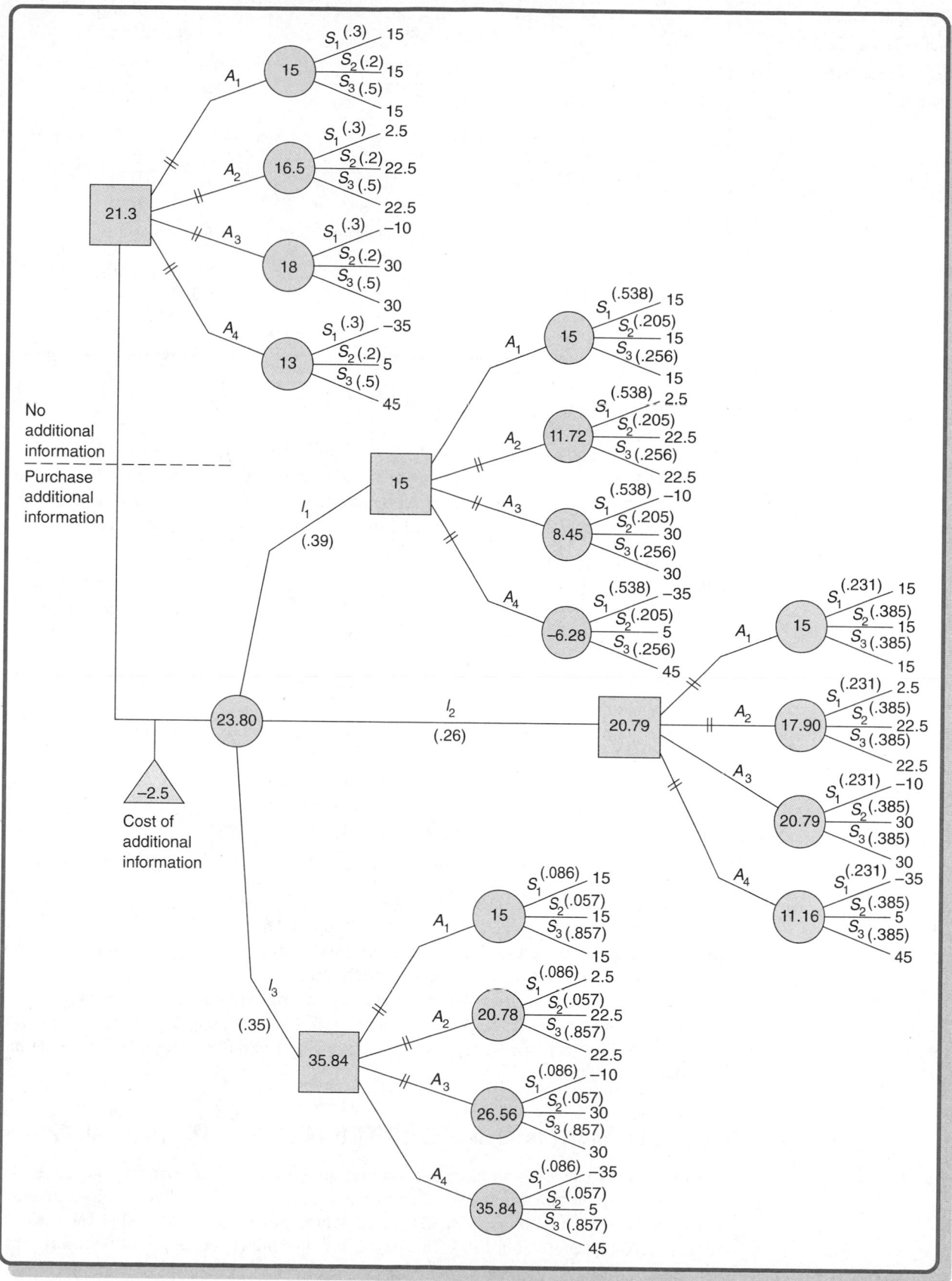

FIGURE 18.12
Deriving the posterior probabilities for the Sailtown decision problem (see Table 18.22).

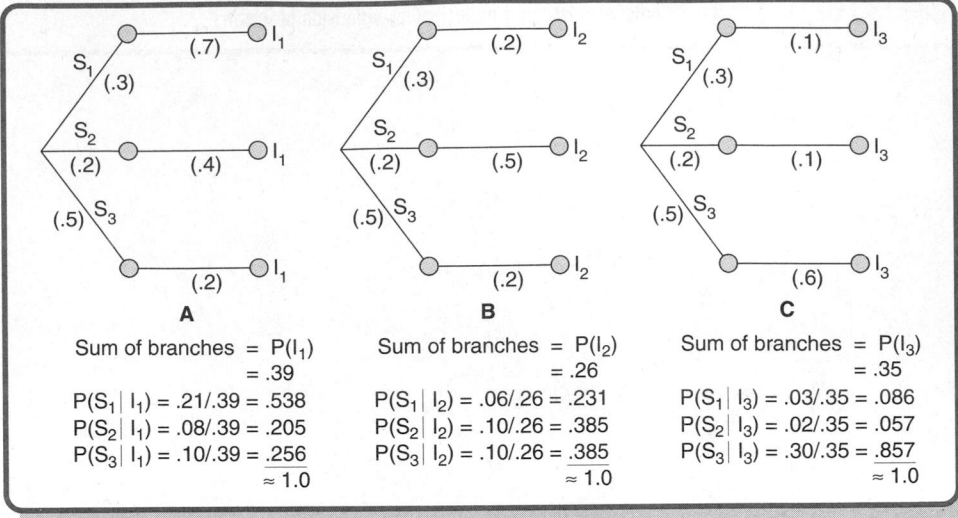

Sum of branches $= P(I_1)$ = .39
$P(S_1 \mid I_1) = .21/.39 = .538$
$P(S_2 \mid I_1) = .08/.39 = .205$
$P(S_3 \mid I_1) = .10/.39 = \underline{.256}$
≈ 1.0

Sum of branches $= P(I_2)$ = .26
$P(S_1 \mid I_2) = .06/.26 = .231$
$P(S_2 \mid I_2) = .10/.26 = .385$
$P(S_3 \mid I_2) = .10/.26 = \underline{.385}$
≈ 1.0

Sum of branches $= P(I_3)$ = .35
$P(S_1 \mid I_3) = .03/.35 = .086$
$P(S_2 \mid I_3) = .02/.35 = .057$
$P(S_3 \mid I_3) = .30/.35 = \underline{.857}$
≈ 1.0

Step 2. For each branch representing $I_1, I_2, \ldots$ in step 1, we reconstruct the decision tree in Figure 18.7 because the possible actions and states of nature from this point on are the *same as before*. However, the probabilities for $S_1, S_2, \ldots$ will be the *posterior* probabilities rather than the prior probabilities in Figure 18.7.

Having constructed the decision tree, you next need to calculate the posterior probabilities. This calculation was illustrated in Example 18.18, where I_1 occurred (the consultant predicted an increase in the interest rate). Notice that the tree for this situation in Figure 18.10 becomes a portion of the large tree in Figure 18.11. A summary of the posterior probabilities is contained in Figure 18.12.

Also contained in Figure 18.12 are the probabilities for each of the possible predictions by the consultant. Here, $P(I_1) = .39$, $P(I_2) = .26$, and $P(I_3) = .35$. Because this prediction is *not* under your control, step 1 constructs a chance node including these three probabilities at this point.

We find the expected payoff given each of the consultant's predictions (15, 20.79, and 35.84) by using the posterior probabilities, as in Example 18.18 and Figure 18.12. We then calculate the expected payoff when using the consultant, where

expected payoff with consultant $= (.39)(15) + (.26)(20.79) + (.35)(35.84) = 23.80$

From this amount you need to subtract the cost of this information (2.5 thousand dollars), providing a net expected payoff of 21.3 (thousand dollars). Because this exceeds the four expected payoffs where no additional information is purchased, this action maximizes the expected payoff and provides the best alternative.

We thus conclude that the owner of Sailtown was right to purchase the services of the external consultant. The best action for him to take for each prediction is summarized in Table 18.23. The net profit is obtained for each case by subtracting the cost of information, 2.5 (thousand dollars).

EVALUATING SAMPLE INFORMATION: EXPECTED VALUE OF SAMPLE INFORMATION

For the Sailtown decision problem, the top portion of the decision tree corresponded to the situation where no sample information was obtained (labeled "No additional information" in Figure 18.11). The maximum expected payoff here was $18,000, derived in Table 18.11, for action A_3 (order 100 sailboats). This payoff is called the **expected payoff without sample information.**

TABLE 18.23   Best actions for Mr. Larson, given the consultant's advice.

Consultant Predicts	Best Action
A rise in the interest rate (I_1)	Order 60 sailboats (A_1) Expected payoff: 15 Net profit: 12.5
No change in the interest rate (I_2)	Order 100 sailboats (A_3) Expected payoff: 20.79 Net profit: 18.29
A drop in the interest rate (I_3)	Order 150 sailboats (A_4) Expected payoff: 35.84 Net profit: 33.34

The bottom portion of the decision tree in Figure 18.11 represents the decision and chance nodes when sample information is purchased from the outside consultant. The values derived at each node are affected in large part by the consultant's ability to predict accurately, as measured in Table 18.22. The net expected payoff of using this strategy (hiring the consultant) was calculated to be $21,300. Thus, we see a net *expected gain* of $21,300 – $18,000 = $3300 when hiring the consultant. This value is the **expected value of sample information** (**EVSI**). In general,

$$\text{EVSI} = (\text{expected payoff when obtaining sample information})$$
$$- (\text{expected payoff without obtaining sample information}) \qquad \textbf{(18.7)}$$

In Section 18.2 for the Sailtown illustration, we previously determined the value of having a perfect predictor to be

$$\text{EVPI} = \left(\begin{array}{c} \text{expected payoff using} \\ \text{a perfect predictor} \end{array} \right) - \left(\begin{array}{c} \text{largest expected payoff} \\ \text{of available actions} \end{array} \right)$$

The subtracted amount in the EVPI (largest expected payoff of available actions) is the same as the subtracted amount in the EVSI (expected payoff without obtaining sample information), and so

$$\text{EVPI} = \$33,000 - \$18,000 = \$15,000$$

It seems reasonable (and is always true) that the EVSI will be smaller than the EVPI. For this example it is considerably smaller. This indicates that the consultant's accuracy and information are far from perfect. An easy method of evaluating the sample information is to divide the EVSI value by the EVPI value and to express the result as a percentage. This value is the **efficiency of the sample information.** So

$$\text{efficiency of the sample information} = \frac{\text{EVSI}}{\text{EVPI}} \cdot 100 \qquad \textbf{(18.8)}$$

For the Sailtown example, this efficiency is $3,300/15,000 \cdot 100 = 22.0\%$. The efficiency of a perfect predictor would be 100%. The rather poor efficiency rating for the consultant's sample information again demonstrates that perhaps Mr. Larson at Sailtown would be better off investigating other sources of predicting interest rate movement.

EXERCISES 18.31–18.46

UNDERSTANDING THE MECHANICS

18.31 Complete the following decision tree, and determine the decision based on the maximum expected payoff. Let $P(S_1) = .4$, $P(S_2) = .2$, $P(S_3) = .1$, and $P(S_4) = .3$.

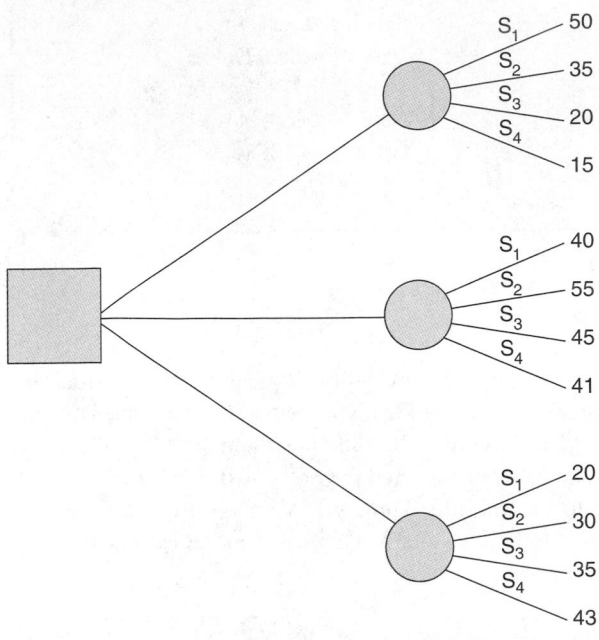

18.32 Let A_1, A_2, A_3, A_4, and A_5 comprise a set of outcomes. Find the probabilities of A_1, A_2, A_3, A_4, and A_5 given that event B occurs. Use the following probabilities.

$$P(A_1) = .2 \qquad P(A_2) = .1 \qquad P(A_3) = .1$$

$$P(A_4) = .3 \qquad P(A_5) = .3$$

$$P(B\,|\,A_1) = .5 \qquad P(B\,|\,A_2) = .3 \qquad P(B\,|\,A_3) = .5$$

$$P(B\,|\,A_4) = .2 \qquad P(B\,|\,A_5) = .1$$

18.33 Consider the following payoff table, which lists the utilities of the payoff to an investor who needs to decide on one of three different investment strategies: A_1, A_2, and A_3. The investor believes that there are four different states of nature that can affect the return on the investment. States S_1, S_2, S_3, and S_4 are believed to occur with probabilities .1, .3, .4, and .2, respectively.

Action	S_1	S_2	S_3	S_4
A_1	30	25	32	45
A_2	35	15	40	42
A_3	44	27	20	18

Construct a decision tree to find the decision based on the maximum expected utility of the payoff.

18.34 Sullivan and Orr, in an article in *Industrial Engineering* on using simulation analysis to determine optional decisions, describe a company that was contemplating making an investment of $150,000 in a new product line. Because of the uncer-

tainty of the market, the following probabilities were assigned to the event that the product will be discontinued in either 8, 10, 12, or 14 years: .1, .2, .5, and .2, respectively. Suppose that a manager of the company could invest in one of three products: A_1, A_2, and A_3. Consider the following payoff table, which lists the utilities of the payoff to a manager who must decide on one of the three actions. States S_1, S_2, S_3, and S_4 refer to a market life of 8, 10, 12, or 14 years, respectively.

Action	S_1	S_2	S_3	S_4
A_1	480	750	2950	4900
A_2	−360	1240	3800	6210
A_3	−1180	1500	5300	7360

(Source: W. Sullivan and R. G. Orr, "Monte Carlo Simulation Analyzes Alternatives in Uncertain Economy," *Industrial Engineering* (Nov. 1982): 43–49.)

Construct a decision tree to find the decision based on the maximum expected utility of the payoff.

18.35 An accountant who operates an income tax service for small businesses needs to decide on one of the following strategies: Lay off two staff employees (A_1); maintain staff at current levels (A_2); increase the staff size by one employee (A_3); increase the staff size by two employees (A_4). A weekly payoff table is presented here, with the probability of each state of nature in parentheses. The states of nature are: Business will decrease (S_1); business will stay the same (S_2); business will increase moderately (S_3); and business will increase rapidly (S_4).

Action	S_1 (.15)	S_2 (.25)	S_3 (.25)	S_4 (.35)
A_1	1451	1840	2050	2300
A_2	−1091	1685	2430	2900
A_3	−2015	1100	3060	3561
A_4	−3460	−1350	3340	4300

a. Construct a decision tree.
b. Calculate the maximum expected payoff.

18.36 Refer to Exercise 18.35. Let I_1 represent the event that the consultant predicts that business will decline, I_2 that the consultant predicts business will remain the same, I_3 that the consultant predicts business will increase moderately, and I_4 that the consultant predicts business will increase rapidly. The consultant's service costs the accountant $400. The following table lists the conditional probabilities for predictions made by the consultant.

	State of Nature			
Prediction	S_1	S_2	S_3	S_4
I_1	.80	.10	.20	.10
I_2	.10	.70	.20	.20
I_3	.05	.10	.50	.30
I_4	.05	.10	.10	.40

a. What is the EVSI?
b. What is the efficiency of the additional information from the consultant?
c. Was the consultant's fee of $400 too high?

18.37 Let A_1, A_2, A_3, A_4, and A_5 be a set of outcomes with $P(A_1) = .1$, $P(A_2) = .3$, $P(A_3) = .3$, $P(A_4) = .1$, and $P(A_5) = .2$. If it is given that $P(B|A_1) = .3$, $P(B|A_2) = .1$, $P(B|A_3) = .2$, $P(B|A_4) = .5$, and $P(B|A_5) = .5$, what are the probabilities $P(A_1|B)$, $P(A_2|B)$, $P(A_3|B)$, $P(A_4|B)$, and $P(A_5|B)$?

18.38 A survey shows that 30% of the fashions that were found to be unprofitable were marketed by the major fashion clothes stores; 60% of the fashions found to be profitable were marketed by the major fashion clothes stores. If 70% of all fashions are profitable to market, find the probability that a fashion will be profitable if the major fashion clothes stores market it. What is the probability that the major fashion clothes stores market a particular fashion?

18.39 David, Harold, and Daniel are three salespeople at Southeast Insurance. David sells 40% of all insurance policies, Harold sells 33%, and Daniel sells 27%. The percent of policies sold by David that are whole-life insurance policies is 5%; for Harold this percentage is 8% and for Daniel, 10%. If a whole-life insurance policy at Southeast Insurance is selected at random, what is the probability that the insurance policy was sold by Harold?

18.40 Refer to Exercise 18.33. What is the efficiency of additional sample information obtained by the investor if the EVSI is 1.5?

18.41 The investor in Exercise 18.33 subscribes to the stock market newsletter *Prudent Investor*. The newsletter forecasts state of nature S_1. Let I be the event that the newsletter forecasts S_1. The stock market newsletter has the following record: $P(I|S_1) = .6$, $P(I|S_2) = .2$, $P(I|S_3) = .3$, and $P(I|S_4) = .1$. Using revised probabilities based on the additional information, find the decision based on the maximum expected utility of the payoff.

18.42 Five legal secretaries type legal documents at a certain law firm. Secretary A types 10% of the work load, secretary B types 20%, secretary C types 20%, secretary D types 40%, and secretary E types 10%. The error rates for each of the secretaries are:

Secretary	Performance
A	.04
B	.06
C	.08
D	.03
E	.09

If a typographical error is found on a legal document, which secretary is most likely responsible?

18.43 A decision maker must determine whether to conduct an experiment that will give one of three predictions, I_1, I_2, or I_3. If the experiment indicates I_1 and the decision maker uses this information, the expected profit is $15,000. If I_2 is indicated, the expected profit is $5000. But if I_3 is indicated, the expected profit is only $1000. If the experiment is not performed, the maximum expected profit would be $4000. Assuming that each of the predictions I_1, I_2, and I_3 is equally likely, is it worthwhile to conduct an experiment that costs $2000?

18.44 Nutritious Cereals would like to market a new multigrain cereal. The manager is trying to decide whether to produce the cereal in large quantities (A_1), moderate quantities (A_2), or small quantities (A_3). The manager believes that the probability of strong demand (S_1) is .4, of moderate demand (S_2) is .4, and of weak demand (S_3) is .2. A survey that can be conducted would predict strong demand (I_1), moderate demand (I_2), or weak demand (I_3). Historical data show the following conditional probabilities with regard to the predictions of the survey [$P(I|S)$]:

Prediction	S_1	S_2	S_3
I_1	0.8	0.3	0.3
I_2	0.1	0.5	0.1
I_3	0.1	0.2	0.6

The profit resulting from the different actions of Nutritious Cereal with regard to marketing the product is given in the following payoff table, in thousands of dollars.

Action	S_1	S_2	S_3
A_1	88	53	20
A_2	75	66	32
A_3	57	50	39

If the survey costs $20,000 to conduct, should the management of Nutritious Cereals undertake it?

18.45 Refer to Figure 18.11 for the Sailtown decision problem. Assume that the payoff table has been changed to the following.

Action	S_1	S_2	S_3
A_1	25	25	25
A_2	12.5	32.5	32.5
A_3	0	40	40
A_4	−25	15	55

a. What is the expected gain from hiring the consultant?
b. What is the efficiency of the information obtained by the consultant?

18.46 A financial planner presents an investor with three states of nature and four actions. The payoff table is presented here. The probabilities of the states are given in parentheses. The conditional probabilities that the financial planner makes predictions I_1, I_2, and I_3 represent the forecasted states of nature S_1, S_2, and S_3, respectively. Would it be worth paying $2000 for the financial planner's advice?

Action	S_1 (.4)	S_2 (.3)	S_3 (.3)
A_1	10,000	13,000	16,000
A_2	8,000	23,000	25,000
A_3	8,000	20,000	40,000

Prediction	S_1	S_2	S_3
I_1	.8	.4	.2
I_2	.1	.4	.2
I_3	.1	.2	.6

This chapter presented a different approach to using probabilities—arriving at a **decision** when the future is uncertain. For example, should you lease a building or incur the extra expense of building one? Should your recently acquired inheritance be put in the bank or should you take advantage of a reliable (in the past, at least) stockmarket report and invest in a newly formed corporation?

When facing such a problem, the decision maker must define the possible **actions** or **alternatives** (such as lease versus purchase or bank versus stocks) and **states of nature** that describe the uncertain future (such as company sales will be below expected, equal to expected, or greater than expected). For each action and state of nature, the decision maker must determine the corresponding **payoff** amount. These values can be summarized in a **payoff table.** This is certainly the most difficult and crucial step in the decision process, because each payoff value must reflect such factors as future costs to the company and responses of competitors. Any action whose payoff is less than that belonging to another action *regardless of the state of nature* is said to be **dominated** and can be removed from consideration.

Different strategies exist for any decision problem. If you elect to describe the uncertain future by assigning a probability to each state of nature, then a popular strategy is to select the action that **maximizes the expected payoff.** Typically, these probabilities are subjective, so any decision based on this method always should be followed up by a **sensitivity analysis** that repeats the decision procedure under various sets of probabilities. In other words, we use a "what-if" process that says, If the future is described by the following set of probabilities, then the best action using this strategy is. . . .

The minimax and maximax procedures do not require state-of-nature probabilities. The **minimax** strategy is very conservative. It begins by constructing an opportunity loss table that summarizes, for each state of nature, the loss the decision maker incurs by failing to take the most profitable action, given that this state of nature occurs. The action to take using this strategy is the one that minimizes the maximum opportunity loss for each of the actions under consideration. The **maximax** strategy is suited to the gambler; it selects that action having the largest possible payoff. Because it fails to take into consideration any heavy losses, it is not appropriate for most business decisions.

SUMMARY

When using the expected payoff strategy, you should examine not only the payoffs that you can expect in the long run from each action but also the **risk** associated with each action. Here you measure the variation in the possible payoffs corresponding to each alternative. You often will select a less risky alternative and sacrifice a small amount of expected payoff. When you use the expected payoff strategy, a useful piece of information is the **expected value of perfect information** (**EVPI**), which is how much a decision maker should be willing to pay for a perfect prediction of tomorrow's state of nature, that is, for a crystal ball. Because any information about the future probably will be imperfect (for example, a consultant might be wrong), such information should cost considerably less than the EVPI.

It is not necessary to set up a decision problem by defining a payoff table in financial units. An alternative is to use **utility values,** which measure both the attractiveness and the risk associated with each dollar amount. For example, a $100,000 gain might be attractive, but a $100,000 loss may be disastrous to a struggling company. The utility value for each dollar amount can be summarized in a **utility curve.** You can use the shape of this curve to identify a decision maker as a **risk avoider,** a **risk neutral,** or a **risk taker.**

A complex decision problem can be summarized best using a **decision tree.** The tree identifies clearly the actions under consideration, the states of nature for the problem, and the expected payoffs for various segments of the decision analysis. **Bayes' Rule** puts such a tree to good use by allowing the decision maker to revise the subjective probability for each state of nature (the **prior probabilities**) in light of new information about the future. This new information could be a recent stock market analysis or predictions made by a consulting firm. The revised probabilities are **posterior probabilities.** Bayes' rule allows you to analyze a decision problem by determining the expected payoff of (1) not purchasing this information and using the prior probabilities or (2) purchasing this information and basing your decision on the results of this prediction. Using the posterior probabilities and the **expected value of sample information** (**EVSI**), you can determine the reliability of the source of this purchased information. A measure of how well the EVSI compares to the EVPI is the **efficiency of the sample information** obtained by dividing EVSI by EVPI, expressed as a percentage.

SUMMARY OF FORMULAS

EXPECTED PAYOFF

$$\mu_i = \Sigma xp$$

RISK

$$\Sigma x^2 p - \mu_i^2$$

EXPECTED VALUE OF PERFECT INFORMATION

EVPI = (expected payoff using a perfect predictor) – (largest expected payoff of available actions)

EXPECTED UTILITY

$$\Sigma [(\text{utility}) \cdot (\text{corresponding probability})]$$

BAYES' RULE

$$P(E_i \mid B) = \frac{P(E_i \text{ and } B)}{P(B)} = \frac{i\text{th path}}{\text{sum of paths}}$$

EXPECTED VALUE OF SAMPLE INFORMATION

EVSI = (expected payoff when obtaining sample information) – (expected payoff without obtaining sample information)

EFFICIENCY OF THE SAMPLE INFORMATION

$$\frac{\text{EVSI}}{\text{EVPI}} \cdot 100$$

REVIEW EXERCISES 18.47–18.59

18.47 Consider the accompanying payoff table.

Action	S_1	S_2	S_3	S_4
A_1	10	18	20	40
A_2	6	16	30	50
A_3	6	14	30	60
A_4	4	12	16	55

a. Construct the opportunity loss table.
b. What is the minimax decision?
c. What is the maximax decision?

18.48 A computer company is considering marketing software that will take daily financial data, compute various statistics, and give a complete financial analysis as well as an up-to-date forecast of financial conditions. The introduction of the software will cost approximately $200,000 in fixed cost. A profit of $20 is expected from the sale of each financial software package. The vice president of the company believes that sales will amount to 5,000, 10,000, 15,000, 20,000 or 25,000 packages of the software. Construct the opportunity loss table. What is the minimax decision?

18.49 Refer to Example 18.8. The managers at Omega have decided that a sensitivity analysis should be made before making a decision. Rework Example 18.8 using the following sets of probabilities. How sensitive is the decision based on the maximum expected payoff?

$P(S_1)$	$P(S_2)$	$P(S_3)$	$P(S_4)$
.1	.5	.2	.2
.1	.5	.1	.3
.1	.5	.3	.1
.1	.5	.2	.2
.2	.5	.2	.1

18.50 S & W Bookstore competes with the bookstore on a university campus for selling textbooks to students. *Introductory Statistics* is one of the textbooks that sells in large quantities. The manager of S & W Bookstore believes that there is a 30% chance that there will be a heavy enrollment (S_1)

in this course. The probabilities for a normal enrollment (S_2) and a low enrollment (S_3) are .55 and .15, respectively. The manager must decide whether to order either 300, 400, or 500 copies of the textbooks. The payoff table follows.

Action	S_1	S_2	S_3
A_1 (300)	830	750	710
A_2 (400)	1230	1125	620
A_3 (500)	1850	910	330

    a. Are all the actions admissible?
    b. What is the minimax decision?
    c. What is the decision based on the maximum expected payoff?
    d. What is the risk of each action?
    e. What is the decision based on minimum risk?
    f. What is the EVPI?

18.51 Suppose you have $500 you would like to invest in either a no-load mutual fund that invests completely in stocks (A_1) or a fixed money market account that yields 12% for one year (A_2). Assume there are two states of nature: The stock market goes up (S_1), and the stock market goes down (S_2). An investment advisor gives you the following payoff table. Determine what value your personal utility function would have for the payoffs.

Action	S_1	S_2
A_1	1100	−600
A_2	750	750

18.52 Refer to Example 18.10. Assume that the probabilities of S_1, S_2, S_3, and S_4 are .2, .2, .4, and .2, respectively. Compute the risk for each action. Which action has the least risk?

18.53 Given the following expected payoffs, compute the efficiency of the sample information.

Expected payoff from sample information: 21
Largest expected payoff of available actions: 18
Expected payoff using a perfect predictor: 30

18.54 Refer to Exercise 18.50. Assume that the manager at S & W Bookstore has obtained additional information from a consultant that the enrollment in the introductory statistics course will be heavy (I_1). Evidence from the consultant's previous performance indicates the following probabilities: $P(I_1 | S_1) = .6$, $P(I_1 | S_2) = .2$, and $P(I_1 | S_3) = .2$. Determine the decision based on the maximum expected payoff, using the revised probabilities.

18.55 Refer to Exercise 18.54. Suppose that the consultant's predictions I_2 and I_3, which represent a normal enrollment and a low enrollment, respectively, have the following conditional probabilities: $P(I_2 | S_1) = .1$, $P(I_2 | S_2) = .5$, $P(I_2 | S_3) = .3$, $P(I_3 | S_1) = .3$, $P(I_3 | S_2) = .3$, $P(I_3 | S_3) = .5$. Would the consultant's fee of $350 make it worthwhile for S & W Bookstore to hire this consultant?

18.56 A manufacturing firm receives electronic components from three suppliers. Supplier A provides 48% of the components, supplier B provides 22%, and supplier C provides 30%. The proportion of defective products from suppliers A, B, and C are .0009, .005, and .002, respectively. If an electronic component is found to be defective, which of the three suppliers is most likely responsible?

18.57 Examine each of the following utility functions over the specified range of values. Describe the decision maker's attitude toward risk.
    a. $U(x) = 4(x - 4)^2$ for x between 4 and 9
    b. $U(x) = 2(x - 5)$ for x between 5 and 55
    c. $U(x) = (10\sqrt{x - 10})$ for x between 10 and 110

18.58 A brokerage firm is conducting a seminar to explain the use of technical indicators in adjusting one's portfolio. The seminar director can decide to have either one (A_1), two (A_2), or three (A_3) guest speakers present at the seminar. Usually the more guest speakers, the more inclined the attendees will be to invest their money with the brokerage firm. The director believes that there is a 40% chance for a heavy turnout (S_1), a 35% chance for a normal turnout (S_2), and a 25% chance for a low turnout (S_3). The cost incurred to have the three guest speakers with a normal or low turnout would cause a loss. The payoff table is as follows.

Action	S_1	S_2	S_3
A_1	450	400	350
A_2	700	500	200
A_3	800	−100	−300

a. Find the minimax decision.
b. Find the decision based on the maximum expected payoff.
c. Find the risk associated with each action.

18.59 Employees at a certain company use three methods of transportation to work. Fifty-five percent of the employees drive their own car, while 25% carpool and 20% use the city bus. Of the employees who drive their own car to work, 70% are male. Of the employees who carpool, 30% are male. Of the employees who use the city bus, 20% are male. What is the probability that a male employee drives his car to work?

Insights from Statistics in Action: Challenging Decisions for CEOs of the Tobacco Industry

The introductory Statistics in Action section in this chapter discussed the many problems facing the CEOs of the tobacco industry. One of their main concerns is trying to achieve a better public image while at the same time aggressively dealing with the latest flood of tobacco-related lawsuits.

Suppose that the CEO of a particular tobacco company is wrestling with the problem of what percentage of the company's image improvement funds should go toward running hard-hitting TV and radio ads and what percentage should be spent on congressional election contributions. Consider the following three decisions that this CEO might have to make:

Strategy A. Devote 80% of the funds to run the ads and 20% of the funds to contribute to the election of congressional members.
Strategy B. Devote 50% of the funds to run the ads and 50% of the funds to contribute to the election of congressional members.
Strategy C. Devote 20% of the funds to run the ads and 80% of the funds to contribute to the election of congressional members.

Suppose that the following table of probabilities was provided for each strategy. In addition, a payoff table for a local retail store is illustrated below, with the payoff representing the additional number of packs of cigarettes expected to be sold under each state of nature.

Table of Probabilities of Each State Under a Specific Strategy

Strategy	State 1: Price of a Pack of Cigarettes Is Raised by $1.10	State 2: Price of a Pack of Cigarettes Is Raised by 50 Cents	State 3: Price of a Pack of Cigarettes Is Not Raised
A	.2	.5	.3
B	.3	.3	.4
C	.4	.1	.5

Payoff Table for Each State Under a Specific Strategy—Number of Packs of Cigarettes Sold Weekly

Strategy	State 1: Price of a Pack of Cigarettes Is Raised by $1.10	State 2: Price of a Pack of Cigarettes Is Raised by 50 Cents	State 3: Price of a Pack of Cigarettes Is Not Raised
A	−50	100	200
B	−50	100	200
C	−50	100	200

1. Set up a decision tree for the decisions and states of nature (amount that a pack of cigarettes will increase).
2. Determine the decision based on the maximum expected payoff for this particular retail store.
3. How sensitive is the decision in question (2) to the given probabilities? Vary the probabilities slightly and determine the decision based on the maximum expected payoff for a pack of cigarettes.

Source: Adapted from *The Wall Street Journal*, "Despite Polls, GOP Doesn't Fear Voter Heat on Tobacco," June 25, 1998, p. A24.

NONPARAMETRIC STATISTICS

STATISTICS IN ACTION: MARKETING ATHLEISURE SHOES: DEALING WITH FICKLE CONSUMERS

Today dozens of shoe marketers cater to the skate/surf/snow board market versus only a handful in 1993. The shoe industry has been marked by cyclical shifts and fast-changing tastes. As teens tune into the Internet, MTV, and other fast-paced media, image is more fleeting than ever. Statistical surveys are typically taken of target consumers to discover how they rank a particular style of shoe. For example, a relatively new brand on the market in 1997, Airwalk had an average rank of 12 in a survey of teenagers—that is, Airwalk was the twelfth "coolest" brand among the popular styles shown to teenagers.

Airwalk, a shoe company named after a skateboard maneuver, used advertising to market an image that is part urban hip and part California beach culture. It shifted consumer taste from pricey, high-tech white sneakers to low-tech suede skateboard shoes, sandals, and other "athleisure" shoes. These types of shoes combine performance with a casual, fashionable look. Chief Executive George Yohn believes that Airwalk can retain its performance image by staying close to its extreme sports roots—that is, by sponsoring sports events. Yearly sales of traditional athletic shoes have stalled at about 344 million pairs since 1995.

The big challenge for Airwalk is to remain fresh enough to retain and attract teen consumers. Quirky, cutting-edge ads, a hallmark of Airwalk's early success, continue to be shown on cable TV, with $3.5 million ad blitzes during the back-to-school season. Airwalk knows that its market is 12 to 18 year olds. However, the company would like to target a larger group, the 8 to 24 year olds.

Nike, Reebok, Fila, Adidas, Converse, and Skechers are also toeing the line with the promotion of athleisure shoes. Their sales exceed Airwalk's. In fact, Nike has a marketing war chest that is nearly as big as Airwalk's sales. Airwalk has to maintain its counterculture image

and keep its customers interested in its products if it is to compete with the larger companies. In 1999 and 2000, Airwalk is hoping that its new casual-tech line will appeal to a broader target audience.

Surveys of customers and their rankings of Airwalk's products and its competitors are important to the decision-making process at many of the local stores that sell Airwalk's shoes. In these surveys, ordinal data are often collected—that is, the respondent usually *ranks* the products by preference. The Analysis of Variance chapter (Chapter 11) discussed how to compare two or more groups when the data of interest are interval or ratio. For example, if we were comparing the prices or measures of durability, an ANOVA test would likely be appropriate. However, when comparing customer rankings for several groups (brands), we need to use a nonparametric test to determine if there is a difference across the various brands. Even if the sample is relatively small, nonparametric statistics can help local shoe managers determine whether there is a difference in the preference of consumers among several brands.

When you have completed this chapter, you will be able to:

- Discuss when the use of a nonparametric test is appropriate;

- Compare the various nonparametric tests to the corresponding ANOVA tests;
- Determine if a sequence (say, H, H, T, T, T, H, T, . . .) was generated in a random manner, where, here, H = flipping a heads with a coin and T = flipping a tail; and
- Discuss an alternative to the simple linear regression equation derived in Chapter 14 that is much less sensitive to outliers in your data.

A LOOK BACK/INTRODUCTION

Although last, this chapter is far from the least in importance. **Nonparametric** statistical techniques are used extensively for a variety of business-related applications.

In the previous chapters, we introduced a large assortment of tests of hypothesis. These tests generally were concerned with such quantities as the mean and the variance of a population. A mean, variance, or proportion is referred to as a *parameter* in statistics, and so these tests are called *parametric* tests of hypothesis. The common underlying assumption in testing a parameter from a continuous population is that this population has a *normal* distribution. Any time you use a *t*-statistic, you assume a normal population distribution. When you test more than two means using the ANOVA procedure, you also assume that the shape of the populations is normal.

What can you do if you have reason to believe that the populations under study are not normally distributed? For example, suppose that data collected previously from these populations have been extremely skewed (not symmetric). One option when dealing with means or proportions is to collect large samples. In such a situation, the Central Limit Theorem assures us that the distribution of the sample estimators is approximately normal *regardless* of the population distribution. The other alternative, particularly for small or moderate sample sizes, is to use a nonparametric statistical procedure that deals with cases in which the assumptions of normality are not true.

Many of the nonparametric statistical tests try to answer the same sorts of questions as do those tests discussed previously. With these tests, however, the assumptions can be relaxed considerably. In earlier chapters, means and medians were referred to as *measures of central tendency*. A nonparametric test concerning such a measure does not assume an underlying normal population—unlike its parametric counterpart. Consequently, nonparametric methods are used for situations that violate the assumptions of the parametric procedures.

A common method for practically all nonparametric techniques is the use of **ranks.** Given a set of data, we obtain a set of ranks by replacing each data value by its relative *position*. To illustrate this idea, consider the following eight observations.

$$10.8, 6.4, 11.7, 5.3, 9.5, 2.5, 15.1, 10.4$$

Arranged in order, these are

Position	1	2	3	4	5	6	7	8
Value	2.5	5.3	6.4	9.5	10.4	10.8	11.7	15.1

We say that the rank of the value 2.5 is 1, the rank of the value 5.3 is 2, and so forth. Replacing each value by its rank and maintaining the original order produces

$$6, 3, 7, 2, 4, 1, 8, 5$$

Most nonparametric procedures use these eight *ranks* rather than the original data values. *By using ranks, we are able to relax the assumptions regarding the underlying populations and develop tests that apply to a wider variety of situations.*

You often will encounter an application in which a numeric measurement is extremely difficult to obtain, but a rank value is not. One example is a consumer taste test; each participant finds it much easier to rank several different brands of soft drinks than to assign a numeric value to each one. The data for analysis consist of the rank assigned to each brand.

Such data are said to be *ordinal* because only the relative position of each value has any meaning (see Chapter 1). This form of data is "weaker" than the *interval* form, for which not only the positions but also the *differences* between data values are meaningful. In this text, we have dealt mostly with interval or ratio data. Data consisting of temperatures, for example, are interval data; the difference between 60°F and 70°F is the same as the difference between 65°F and 75°F (10°F). When dealing with ranks, this is not the case; there is no reason to assume that the difference between ranks 1 and 3 is the same as that between ranks 3 and 5.

In Chapter 13 we introduced one nonparametric procedure that used the chi-square statistic to test for goodness-of-fit or independence between two classifications. In this chapter, we examine other popular nonparametric methods used in a business setting. These tests of hypothesis by no means constitute all the nonparametric techniques used in practice, but they should provide you with a basis for knowing how and when to apply such a method to a particular set of sample data.

19.1 A Test for Randomness: The Runs Test

The concept of *randomness* is a crucial assumption behind a great many statistical procedures. In the earlier chapters, all samples were assumed to be random. The reliability of any statistical test—even if run on a high-powered computer—is suspect if the sample was not obtained in a random manner. Similarly, the t and F-tests in linear regression contain the assumption that the resulting sample residuals are *independent,* with no observable pattern. This assumption implies that the *signs* of these errors should be random.

When you examine a sequence of observations or residuals, one method of detecting a lack of randomness is to observe the number of runs contained in the sequence. For a sequence containing two possible values (A and B, $+$ and $-$, and so on), a **run** consists of a string of identical values.

Suppose we flip a coin 10 times, where each flip results in a head (H) or a tail (T). Consider the following three outcomes, each containing five heads and five tails.

Sequence 1	H	H	H	H	H	T	T	T	T	T
Sequence 2	H	T	H	T	H	T	H	T	H	T
Sequence 3	T	H	H	H	T	H	T	H	T	T

Only sequence 3 exhibits a random pattern. To see why, we will examine each sequence.

SEQUENCE 1.   These 10 observations contain only two runs:

$$\underset{\text{Run 1}}{\underline{H\ H\ H\ H\ H}} \quad \underset{\text{Run 2}}{\underline{T\ T\ T\ T\ T}}$$

The small number of runs is unlikely if this sequence was generated in a random manner.

SEQUENCE 2.   At first glance, this pattern may appear to be random, but there are an excessive number of runs (10):

$$\underline{H}\ \underline{T}\ \underline{H}\ \underline{T}\ \underline{H}\ \underline{T}\ \underline{H}\ \underline{T}\ \underline{H}\ \underline{T}$$
$$\overset{\nwarrow}{\text{Run 1}} \qquad\qquad \overset{\nearrow}{\text{Run 10}}$$

TABLE 19.1   Partial list of the 252 arrangements for $n_1 = 5$ and $n_2 = 5$.

Arrangement Number	Arrangement	Number of Runs	
1	HHHHHTTTTT	2	← sequence 1
2	HHHHTHTTTT	4	
3	HHHHTTHTTT	4	
4	HHHHTTTHTT	4	
5	HHHHTTTTHT	4	
⋮			
130	THHHHTTTHT	5	
131	THHHHTTTTH	4	
132	THHHTHHTTT	5	
133	THHHTHTHTT	7	← sequence 3
134	THHHTHTTHT	7	
⋮			
248	TTTTHHHHTH	4	
249	TTTTHHHTHH	4	
250	TTTTHHTHHH	4	
251	TTTTHTHHHH	4	
252	TTTTTHHHHH	2	

Once again, the process that generated this sequence is unlikely to be random because of the large number of runs.

SEQUENCE 3. This sequence seems to be a compromise between the first two, exhibiting neither too few runs nor too many.

$$\underline{T}\ \underline{HHH}\ \underline{T}\ \underline{H}\ \underline{T}\ \underline{H}\ \underline{TT}$$

↰— Run 1   ↰— Run 7

It appears that the sequence was generated in a random manner.

In this section, we use the runs test statistical procedure to test for randomness using the number of observed runs.

THE RUNS TEST (SMALL SAMPLES)

Consider a sequence of n observations, containing n_1 symbols of the first type (H, in our example) and n_2 symbols of the second type (T). So, $n = n_1 + n_2$. Let

R = number of runs within these n observations

The situation we consider here is for small samples, where $n_1 \leq 20$ and $n_2 \leq 20$. We will demonstrate that this particular nonparametric technique is indeed distribution free; that is, it makes no assumptions about the population of H's and T's.

For the coin-tossing illustration, there are $n_1 = 5$ H's and $n_2 = 5$ T's. How many such arrangements (permutations) of these 10 symbols are there?* There are 252, partially listed in Table 19.1. This value in general can be found using

$$\text{number of arrangements} = A = \frac{n!}{n_1!\, n_2!} \tag{19.1}$$

---

* The formula for the number of permutations given in Chapter 4 does not apply here because the 10 objects (symbols) are not all different (distinct).

TABLE 19.2

Distribution of runs for $n_1 = 5$ and $n_2 = 5$.

Number of Runs (R)	Number of Times R Occurred	Relative Frequency	Cumulative Relative Frequency
2	2	.008	.008
3	8	.032	.040
4	32	.127	.167
5	48	.190	.357
6	72	.286	.643
7	48	.190	.833
8	32	.127	.960
9	8	.032	.992
10	2	.008	1.000
	252	1.000	

where $n = n_1 + n_2$. For this illustration,

$$A = \frac{10!}{5!5!} = \frac{(10)(9)(8)(7)(6)}{(5)(4)(3)(2)} = 252$$

Each of these 252 arrangements is equally likely to occur, *providing* the process generating this sequence is *random,* so each has probability $1/252 = .004$.

A tally of all 252 arrangements would reveal the distribution of runs described in Table 19.2. Using the far-right column of Table 19.2, we can say, for example, that $P(R \leq 4) = .167$, since 16.7% of the arrangements had 4 or fewer runs. This probability is obtained *without* assuming any probability distribution for the underlying population (process) that generated a sequence of $n_1 = 5$ values of H and $n_2 = 5$ values of T. This is the beauty of nonparametric methods.

The hypotheses under investigation here are

H_0: the sequence was generated in a random manner

H_a: the sequence was not generated in a random manner

As mentioned earlier, we reject H_0 whenever the number of runs is too small (say, whenever $R \leq k_1$) or too large (say, whenever $R \geq k_2$).

For a significance level of $\alpha = .05$, what we need is the *largest* value of k_1 such that

$$P(R \leq k_1) \leq \frac{\alpha}{2} = .025$$

and the *smallest* value of k_2 such that

$$P(R \geq k_2) \leq \frac{\alpha}{2} = .025$$

For the case of $n_1 = 5$ and $n_2 = 5$, what are k_1 and k_2? Referring to Table 19.2, we see that for $k_1 = 2$ and $k_1 = 3$ we have $P(R \leq 2) = .008$ and $P(R \leq 3) = .040$.

Consequently, $k_1 = 2$. Also from Table 19.2,

$$P(R \geq 9) = 1 - P(R \leq 8)$$

$$= 1 - .960 = .040$$

and

$$P(R \geq 10) = 1 - P(R \leq 9)$$

$$= 1 - .992 = .008$$

and so $k_2 = 10$. Thus we reject H_0 if $R \leq 2$ or $R \geq 10$.

TABLE 19.3

A portion of Table A.15 for the runs test. For each pair of numbers, the top value is k_1 and the bottom value is k_2. This table assumes $\alpha = .05$.

THE SMALLER OF n_1 AND n_2	THE LARGER OF n_1 AND n_2					
	5	**6**	**7**	**8**	**9**	**10**
2						
3		2 8	2 8	2 8	2 8	2 8
4	2 9	2 9	2 10	3 10	3 10	3 10
5	2 10	3 10	3 11	3 11	3 12	3 12
6		3 11	3 12	3 12	4 13	4 13
7			3 13	4 13	4 14	5 14
8				4 14	5 14	5 15
9					5 15	5 16
10						6 16

Table A.15 contains values of k_1 and k_2 for values of n_1 and $n_2 \le 20$. A portion of this table is shown in Table 19.3. For each pair of numbers, the top number is k_1 and the bottom number is k_2. For the case of $n_1 = 5$ and $n_2 = 5$ (boxed in Table 19.3), we see that $k_1 = 2$ and $k_2 = 10$, as before.

We can summarize this testing procedure as follows:

HYPOTHESES.

H_0: the sequence was generated in a random manner

H_a: the sequence was not generated in a random manner

TEST STATISTIC (FOR SMALL SAMPLES). R, where R denotes the number of runs in the sequence.

PROCEDURE.

Reject H_0 if $R \le k_1$ or $R \ge k_2$

where k_1 and k_2 are the top and bottom values, respectively, in Table A.15. This table assumes $\alpha = .05$.

EXAMPLE 19.1

Using a significance level of .05, determine which of the three sequences of H's and T's in the earlier discussion were generated in a random manner.

SOLUTION

Using Table 19.3 (or Table A.15), we previously determined that $k_1 = 2$ and $k_2 = 10$, and so we reject H_0 if $R \le 2$ or $R \ge 10$. The results are:

For sequence 1: $R = 2$, so reject H_0

For sequence 2: $R = 10$, so reject H_0

For sequence 3: $R = 7$, so fail to reject H_0

For the first two sequences we conclude that these arrangements were not the result of a random process. For the third sequence, we have no reason to suspect the presence of a nonrandom process.

THE RUNS TEST (LARGE SAMPLES)

For large samples ($n_1 > 20$ or $n_2 > 20$), the approximate distribution for R if the generating process is random will be *normal* with mean

$$\mu_R = 1 + \frac{2n_1n_2}{n_1 + n_2} \tag{19.2}$$

and standard deviation

$$\sigma_R = \sqrt{\frac{2n_1n_2(2n_1n_2 - n_1 - n_2)}{(n_1 + n_2)^2(n_1 + n_2 - 1)}} \tag{19.3}$$

By standardizing R in the usual way, we obtain the following summary.

HYPOTHESES.

H_0: pattern was generated in a random manner

H_a: pattern was not generated in a random manner

TEST STATISTIC (FOR LARGE SAMPLES).

$$Z = \frac{R - \mu_R}{\sigma_R} \tag{19.4}$$

where (1) R denotes the number of runs in the data sequence, and (2) μ_R and σ_R are the mean and standard deviation of this random variable, defined in equations 19.2 and 19.3.

The testing procedure using the standard normal random variable is the same as in previous tests using Z. For the randomness test, a nonrandom pattern is indicated by a Z value in the right tail (too many runs) or in the left tail (too few runs).

EXAMPLE 19.2

The president of Northside National Bank requested the savings-account balances for 45 randomly selected accounts of nonmarried customers. When she examined the data, she began to question the randomness of the procedure used to select the accounts. Letting M denote the account of a male and F the account of a female, the following sequence was obtained, listed in the order in which they were selected for the supposedly random sample.

M M F F F F M F F M M M M M M F F F F M M F

M M F F M F F F F F M M M M M F F F F M M M

Based upon this sequence, would you conclude that this sample consists of 45 randomly selected males and females? Use $\alpha = .05$.

SOLUTION   This sequence contains $R = 15$ runs. Also,

$$n_1 = \text{number of males} = 22$$

$$n_2 = \text{number of females} = 23$$

For these values of n_1 and n_2, the mean number of runs if H_0 is true is

$$\mu_R = 1 + \frac{(2)(22)(23)}{45} = 23.49$$

This implies that, on the average, whenever $n_1 = 22$ and $n_2 = 23$, you will obtain 23.49 runs.

The sample contains only 15 runs, so it could be that this sequence exhibits a nonrandom pattern, due to insufficient runs. However, this depends heavily on the standard deviation of R; therefore, to complete the analysis, we next find

$$\sigma_R = \sqrt{\frac{(2)(22)(23)[(2)(22)(23) - 45]}{(45)^2 (44)}} = \sqrt{10.9832} = 3.314$$

To determine whether $R = 15$ is sufficiently small to reject the random sequence hypothesis, we calculate the test statistic.

$$Z* = \frac{15 - 23.49}{3.314} = -2.56$$

The test procedure here (using $\alpha = .05$) is to

$$\text{reject } H_0 \text{ if } |Z| > 1.96$$

The computed Z value does have an absolute value larger than 1.96, and so we reject H_0. There is evidence that the male-female sequence is nonrandom, indicating a lack of randomness in the sampling procedure used in selecting the individual accounts from the bank records.

The standard statistical tool package within Excel does not perform any of the nonparametric tests within this chapter. However, the Excel macros within the KGP Data Analysis add-ins do provide all of these tests, including the runs test. To obtain the solution for Example 19.2, click on **KGP Data Analysis ➤ Nonparametric Procedures.** Select **Runs Test** and in the **Runs Test Using** box, click on **Series Values.*** Enter "A1:A45" in the **Input Range** box and "B1" in the **Output Range** box. The resulting output in Figure 19.1 is identical to the previous solution. Since the p-value of .0104 is less than the significance level of .05, once again the decision is to reject H_0 and conclude that the male-female sequence was generated in a nonrandom manner.

We encounter another application of the runs test when we examine the residuals from a linear regression analysis. A key assumption when using linear regression is that the errors are *independent.* Consequently, we should observe a random pattern in the sample residuals. If the observations in our data set are recorded across time (say, 24 consecutive months), this often results in residuals that are *not* independent. In this case, we would say that the errors are correlated—more precisely, that they are *autocorrelated,* since they are correlated with each other. In Chapter 17, we computed the Durbin-Watson (*DW*) statistic to measure the degree of autocorrelation.

The DW statistic assumes that the errors follow a normal distribution, as do all the tests of hypothesis when using a linear regression model. The nonparametric runs test also can be used to examine the residuals, by recording the *sign* (+ or −) of each residual and counting the number of runs. This test is valid regardless of the distribution of the errors and can be used for any model that assumes the errors are uncorrelated.

---

* The **Series Signs** option for the runs test will be illustrated in the next example.

FIGURE 19.1
Excel runs test using **KGP
Data Analysis** ➤
Nonparametric Procedures
(Example 19.2).

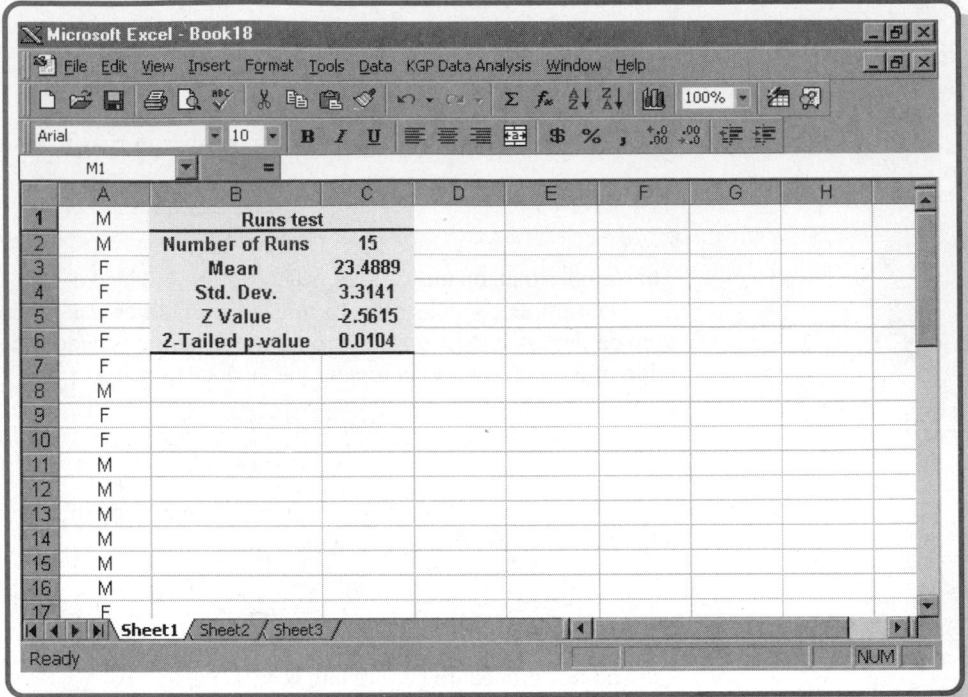

MICROSOFT® EXCEL APPLICATION   USE DATA19-3

EXAMPLE 19.3
An Excel Runs Test

A financial analyst with Case Automated Equipment is examining the company's quarterly sales for the past 10 years. She suspects there is a strong trend and cyclical component in the seasonally adjusted (deseasonalized) sales figures due to steadily increasing sales and cyclical movement in the general U.S. economy.* The seasonally adjusted quarterly sales figures are contained in column B in data set DATA19-3. Using the runs test, and a significance level of $\alpha = .05$, determine if there is cylical activity present when regressing the seasonally adjusted sales values against time. The time variable ($t = 1, 2, \ldots, 40$) is contained in column A.

SOLUTION

Begin by opening DATA19-3. There should be labels in the first row (**Time** and **Sales**), providing a total of 41 rows. To carry out the regression analysis, click on **KGP Data Analysis** ➤ **Regression.** Enter "B1:B41" as the **Y Range,** "A1:A41" as the (contiguous) **X Range,** and "C1" as the **Output Range.** Be sure to click on the box alongside **Residuals** inside the **Data** frame and on the **Residual Plots** box inside the **Plots** frame. The resulting output is shown in Figures 19.2 and 19.3. The residuals (partially shown) are contained in cells E25:E64.

If cyclical activity is present in the residuals, we would expect to see too *few* runs, since a positive (negative) residual is likely to be preceded and followed by a positive (negative) residual. Since neighboring residuals are likely to have the same sign if the residuals contain cyclical activity, this implies that the residuals will be *positively* autocorrelated. The resulting hypotheses under investigation are

$$H_0\text{: no autocorrelation exists}$$

$$H_a\text{: positive autocorrelation exists}$$

---

* A procedure for deseasonalizing time series data was discussed in Section 16.5.

FIGURE 19.2
Excel regression solution and runs test for Example 19.3 using KGP Data Analysis.

File Edit View Insert Format Tools Data KGP Data Analysis Window Help

	A	B	C	D	E	F	G	H
1	Time	Sales	SUMMARY OUTPUT			Runs test		
2	1	66.726				Number of Runs	7	
3	2	83.330	Regression Statistics			Mean	20.95000	
4	3	131.933	Multiple R	0.966387383		Std. Dev.	3.11346	
5	4	129.594	R Square	0.933904574		Z Value	-4.48054	
6	5	147.617	Adjusted R Square	0.932165221		2-Tailed p-value	7.4521E-06	
7	6	181.917	Standard Error	34.76022879				
8	7	175.724	Observations	40				
9	8	170.846						
10	9	179.688	ANOVA					
11	10	193.306		df	SS	MS	F	Significance F
12	11	212.337	Regression	1	648753.8503	648753.8503	536.9263229	5.08782E-24
13	12	199.606	Residual	38	45914.3932	1208.273505		
14	13	171.588	Total	39	694668.2435			
15	14	201.454						
16	15	204.120		Coefficients	Standard Error	t Stat	P-value	
17	16	219.663	Intercept	69.51555769	11.20154259	6.205891479	2.97177E-07	
18	17	184.244	Time	11.03256182	0.476122847	23.1716707	5.08782E-24	
19	18	229.150						
20	19	201.720						
21	20	226.171						
22	21	278.248	RESIDUAL OUTPUT					
23	22	285.802						
24	23	320.338	Observation	Predicted Sales	Residuals			
25	24	338.583	1	80.548119512	-13.822119512			
26	25	375.325	2	91.580681332	-8.250681332			
27	26	391.877	3	102.613243152	29.319756848			
28	27	434.485	4	113.645804972	15.948195028			
29	28	443.277	5	124.678366792	22.938633208			
30	29	436.220	6	135.710928612	46.206071388			
31	30	456.062	7	146.743490432	28.980509568			

DATA19-3

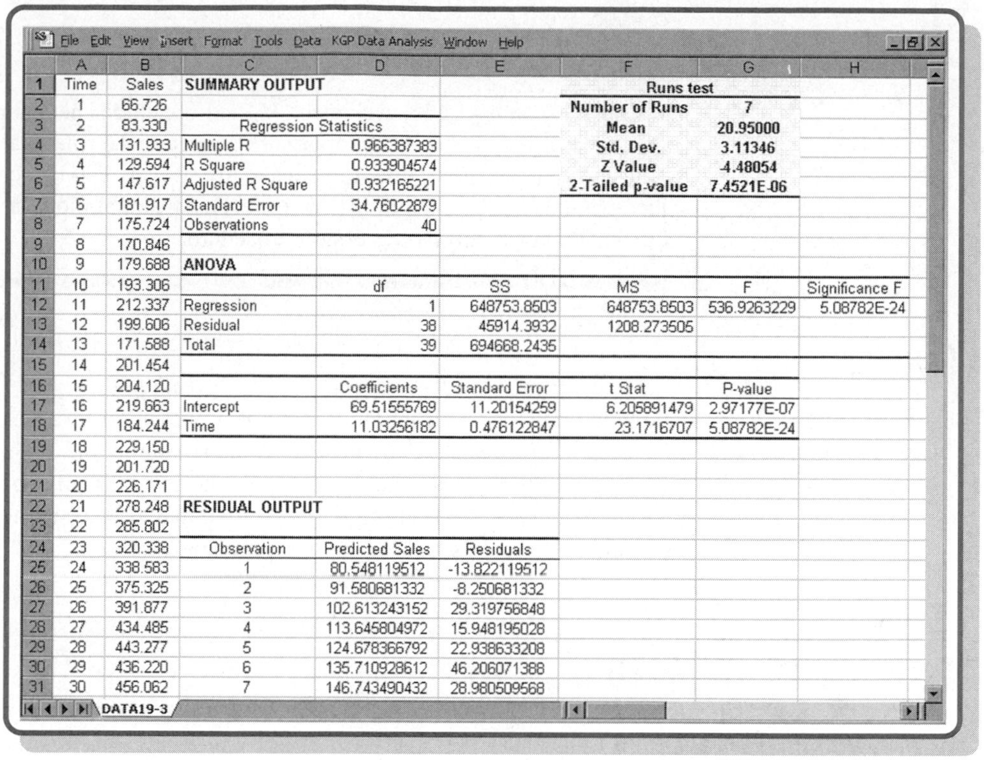

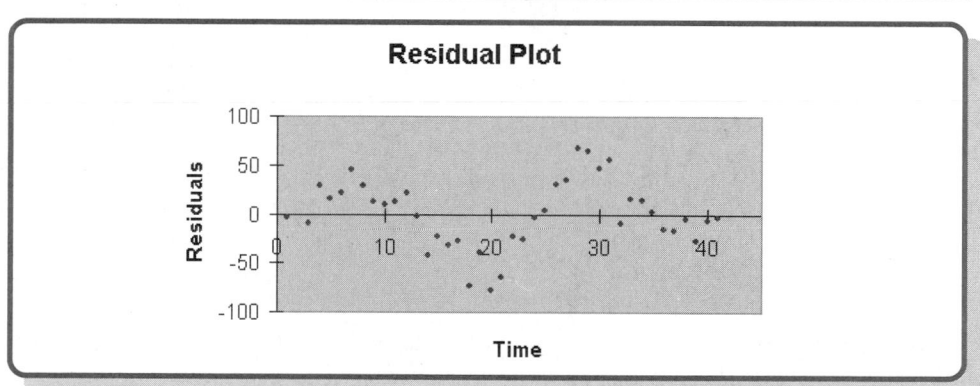

FIGURE 19.3
Excel residual plot using KGP Data Analysis (Example 19.3).

To carry out the runs test using Excel, click on **KGP Data Analysis ➤ Nonparametric Procedures.** Select **Runs Test** and click on **Series Signs** in the **Runs Test Using** box and enter "E25:E64" in the **Input Range** box and "F1" in the **Output Range** box. The resulting output is contained in cells F1:G6 in Figure 19.2. An examination of the residuals reveals $n_1 = 21$ negative residuals and $n_2 = 19$ positive residuals. The first residual value in this example is negative, and as a result, n_1 is a count of the negative residuals, and n_2 represents the number of positive residuals.

According to the output, $\mu_R = 1 + [(2)(21)(19)/40] = 20.95$. The output also contains

$$\sigma_R = \sqrt{\frac{(2)(21)(19)[(2)(21)(19) - 21 - 19]}{(40)^2(39)}} = 3.113$$

and the value of the test statistic (Z^*), where

$$Z^* = \frac{7 - 20.95}{3.113} = -4.48$$

Under H_a, we expect a small number of runs; that is, this is a *left-tailed* test. Since $\alpha = .05$, we

$$\text{reject } H_0 \text{ if } Z < -1.645$$

Because $-4.48 < -1.645$, we reject H_0 and conclude that there are too few runs in this sequence of residuals. This supports the hunch of the financial analyst that the seasonally adjusted sales figures contain cyclical activity. This can be seen in the scatter diagram of the residuals versus time in Figure 19.3. This residual plot was generated using the previous KGP Data Analysis regression procedure.

COMMENTS

1. When you perform a one-tailed runs test, you should divide the two-tailed Excel *p*-value by 2 and then compare it to the level of significance (α) to make a decision. In the previous example, the resulting *p*-value is $.00001/2 \approx .000005$ (extremely small).

2. For a one-tailed test, be sure that the sign of the Z value is compatible with your one-tailed alternative hypothesis; that is, it should be positive when testing H_a: too many runs, and negative when testing H_a: too few runs.

EXERCISES 19.1–19.10

UNDERSTANDING THE MECHANICS

19.1 Using a significance level of .05, determine if each of the two sequences of 0's and 1's is generated in a random manner.
   a. 1 0 1 0 0 1 0 1 0 1
   b. 1 0 0 1 0 1 1 0 1 1

19.2 A sequence contains high and low numbers. Let n_1 and n_2 equal the number of high and low numbers, respectively, in a sequence. Let R equal the number of runs. Would you conclude that the following sequences were generated in a random manner? Use a .05 significance level.
   a. $n_1 = 23$, $n_2 = 24$, $R = 15$
   b. $n_1 = 35$, $n_2 = 30$, $R = 21$
   c. $n_1 = 50$, $n_2 = 50$, $R = 35$

19.3 At the .10 significance level, can you conclude that the even and odd numbers presented here are randomly generated?

2 4 5 1 3 7 9 2 1 9 2 4 6 8 2 4 1 3 5 1 4 2 7 4 8 7 9 2 1 9
7 3 5 2 4 4 8 6 9 1 9 7 4 8 2

APPLYING THE NEW CONCEPTS

19.4 Ozark County Bank is taking applications for the position of loan officer. The following sequence lists the order in which either a male (M) or a female (F) applied for the position. Is there evidence to indicate that the sequence is not randomly generated? Use a .05 significance level.

M M M F M M F M M F M F F M M F M M M F F F F
M M F F F

19.5 After a television debate between two political candidates, a telephone line is open to viewers wishing to express their opinions on whether the Democratic (D) or the Republican (R) candidate won the debate. The following sequence represents 19 opinions of viewers in the order in which they telephoned. Using a runs test and a significance level of 5%, does the sequence indicate a nonrandom order?

R R D D R D D R R R R D D R D R D D D

19.6 Conduct a runs test on the following sequence of 3's and 4's to see if there is evidence that the sequence is not randomly generated. Use a 5% significance level.

3 3 3 4 4 3 4 3 4 3 3 3 3 4 4 3 4 4 3 3 3 3 4 3

19.7 A certain computer program generates a sequence of random digits. Test whether there is any evidence that the following sequence of numbers is nonrandom, by considering the sequence of odd and even numbers. Use a 5% significance level.

9 8 5 3 1 1 2 2 7 4 4 3 7 3 8 1 6 5 8 4 7 9 1

19.8 For years, magazines have been the preferred way for pharmaceutical companies to advertise drugs. According to "TV Gets Most Drug-Ad Spending, but Magazines Have Equal Impact," (*The Wall Street Journal,* Jan. 14, 1999, p. B8), conventional wisdom on Madison Avenue is that magazines often are a better way to target specific audiences with complicated messages. With magazines, companies can reach audiences they want without paying for the audience that is not being targeted. The following table lists annual advertising expenditure (in millions of dollars) by the top 10 prescription drug advertisers for the years from 1987 to 1998.
   a. Fit a regression equation through the data using year as the independent variable.
   b. Find the 12 residuals using the regression equation in part (a).
   c. Use a runs test to determine if the sequence of positive and negative residuals in part (b) appear to be randomly generated over time. Use a 5% significance level.

Year	Advertising Expenditure		Year	Advertising Expenditure
1987	160.8		1993	160.8
1988	145.3		1994	170.4
1989	152.8		1995	193.5
1990	160.3		1996	285.1
1991	166.5		1997	403.6
1992	174.5		1998	360.7

USING THE COMPUTER

19.9 [DATA SET EX19-9] *Variable description:*

Response: A participant's response to a survey question

A survey is used to assess workers' satisfaction and productivity. Each response is coded as 1, 2, 3, or 4. As a way of determining if a participant's responses were randomly generated, a runs test is used by determining the runs above and below 2.5. For the data in Response, is there evidence to indicate that the sequence of 40 questions is not randomly generated? Use a 5% significance level.

19.10 [DATA SET EX19-10] *Variable description:*

Time: Time period numbered 1 through 40
RetailIndex: Retail sales index for county in southern California

A marketing analyst is examining the retail sales index for a county in southern California over a 10-year period. The retail sales index values (RetailIndex) are deseasonalized figures recorded each quarter, hence making 40 time periods available for analysis. Using the runs test, determine if there is cyclical activity present in the residuals when regressing the seasonally adjusted retail sales index against time. Use a 5% significance level.

19.2 NONPARAMETRIC TESTS OF CENTRAL TENDENCY: TWO POPULATIONS

Chapter 3 introduced you to measures of central tendency. The more commonly used measures are the mean and median, which attempt to identify the middle of a set of sample data. In Chapter 9, we introduced two populations, where the question of interest was whether the two means were the same (a two-tailed test) or whether one mean exceeded the other (a one-tailed test). A two-population test is illustrated in Figure 19.4, where the variable of interest is height.

The main assumption in Figure 19.4 is that the two populations are normally distributed. When you sample from these populations, if both sample sizes (n_1 and n_2) are *large,* you can remove this assumption. However, there is a need for a nonparametric technique for this two-population situation when (1) you have small samples and you suspect that one or both populations do not follow a normal distribution or (2) your data are such that only the relative ranks are available within each sample, such as in a consumer taste test (in other words, you are dealing with *ordinal data*). *The t tests from Chapter 9 assumed that the measurement scale of the data was at least interval, so these tests are inappropriate for data consisting of ranks.*

When dealing with samples from two populations in Chapter 9, we also looked at two situations:

1. The two samples are *independent.* In Figure 19.4, this would mean that a sample of n_1 female heights is obtained independently of the n_2 male heights. There is no reason to match up the first male height with the first female height, the second male height with the second female height, and so on in the two samples.
2. The two samples are *dependent,* or *paired.* This might occur in Figure 19.5 if the question were, are husbands taller than wives? The data then consist of n_1 wives and $n_2 = n_1$ husbands.

FIGURE 19.4

Two-population test of hypothesis for means.

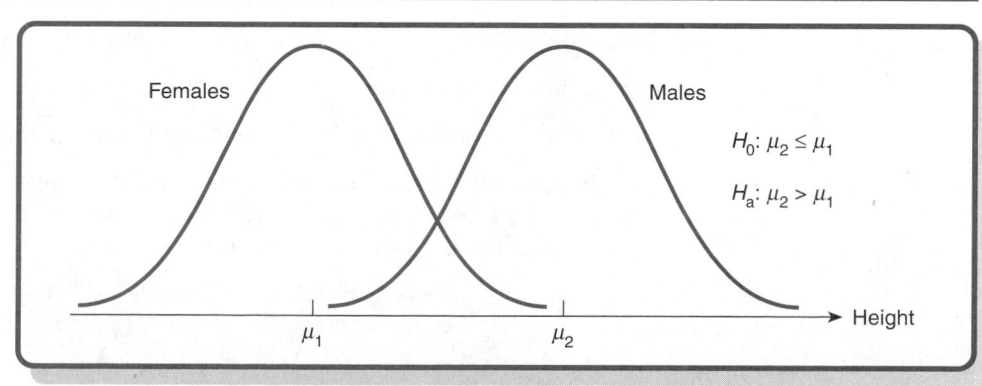

FIGURE 19.5

Illustration of dependent (paired) samples.

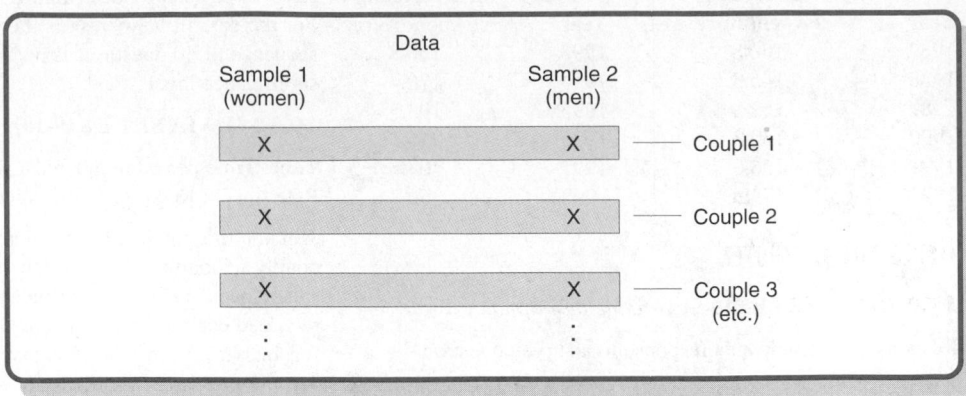

This portion of the chapter discusses the nonparametric counterparts to these two parametric tests of hypothesis. The assumptions behind the application of these methods are considerably weaker than those for the *t* tests in Chapter 9. These nonparametric techniques, named after the people responsible for their development, are the Mann-Whitney *U* test— a nonparametric procedure for situation 1 (two independent samples)—and the Wilcoxon signed rank test—a nonparametric procedure for situation 2 (two paired samples).

The parametric tests in Chapter 9 were concerned with population means. If two populations have different means, we say that these populations differ in **location.** This implies that population 1 is shifted to the left or right of population 2. When defining the corresponding nonparametric test, the hypotheses will be stated in terms of differing location rather than differing means.

THE MANN-WHITNEY *U* TEST FOR INDEPENDENT SAMPLES

The **Mann-Whitney *U* test** is named after H. B. Mann and R. Whitney, who developed this test in the 1940s. The purpose of this procedure is to provide a test for differing location that does not require the assumption of normal populations. The test is an alternative to the *t* tests from Chapter 9, which are based on this assumption.

The two-tailed hypotheses for the Mann-Whitney test can be written

H_0: the two populations have identical probability distributions

H_a: the two populations differ in location

To use the Mann-Whitney nonparametric technique, we begin by combining (pooling) the two samples into one large sample and then determining the rank of each observation in the pooled sample. Next, let

T_1 = sum of the ranks of the observations from the first sample in this pooled sample

T_2 = sum of the ranks of the observations from the second sample

The procedure is (if $n_1 = n_2$)

reject H_0 if T_1 is "significantly different" from T_2

To illustrate this technique, consider the following pooled sample, where the pooled observations have been arranged in order from smallest to largest. Here *A* represents a value from population *A* and *B* is a value from population B.

Value	A	A	A	A	A	B	B	B	B	B
Rank	1	2	3	4	5	6	7	8	9	10

For this pooled sample, we have

$$n_1 = 5$$

T_1 = sum of ranks of the five A observations in the pooled sample

$$= 1 + 2 + 3 + 4 + 5 = 15$$

$$n_2 = 5$$

T_2 = sum of the ranks of the B observations

$$= 6 + 7 + 8 + 9 + 10 = 40$$

Now consider another pooled sample:

Value	A	B	B	A	B	A	A	A	B	B
Rank	1	2	3	4	5	6	7	8	9	10

For this situation, the values are $T_1 = 1 + 4 + 6 + 7 + 8 = 26$ and $T_2 = 2 + 3 + 5 + 9 + 10 = 29$.

In the first pooled sample, there is clear evidence that the second population is shifted to the right of the first population, as indicated by the large difference between $T_1 = 15$ and $T_2 = 40$. This difference is also evident when you examine this pooled sample because the values from population A are all less than those from population B. From a parametric view, this implies that $\mu_B > \mu_A$. The Mann-Whitney procedure will result in rejecting H_0: the two populations have identical probability distributions in favor of H_a: the two populations differ in location (or H_a: population A is shifted to the left of population B, had we used a one-tailed test). For the second set of ten pooled observations, there is no indication of a difference in population location; the A and B values are fairly well mixed in the combined sample, as evidenced by the values of $T_1 = 26$ and $T_2 = 29$, which are nearly equal. The Mann-Whitney test will lead to a failure to reject the null hypothesis.

MANN-WHITNEY TEST FOR SMALL SAMPLES. For this test of hypothesis, small samples are defined as both $n_1 \leq 10$ and $n_2 \leq 10$. *Regardless* of the sample sizes, the procedure begins by finding T_1 and T_2 as described previously and then letting

$$U_1 = n_1 n_2 + \frac{n_1(n_1 + 1)}{2} - T_1 \qquad (19.5)$$

and

$$U_2 = n_1 n_2 + \frac{n_2(n_2 + 1)}{2} - T_2 \qquad (19.6)$$

The Mann-Whitney test is summarized in the accompanying box.

THE MANN-WHITNEY TEST FOR SMALL SAMPLES

Null hypothesis:

H_0: the two populations have identical probability distributions

Assumptions:

1. Random samples are obtained from each population.
2. The two samples are independent of one another—respective observations are not paired.
3. The sample data are at least ordinal.
4. If the two populations differ, they differ only in location—that is, the two populations have the same variation and shape.

Procedure:

1. Assume that $n_1 \leq n_2$ (if this is not the case, reverse your populations, so that n_1 is the smaller sample size).
2. Determine U_1 and U_2 from equations 19.5 and 19.6.
3. Use the value from Table A.10 to test H_0 versus H_a, where, once again, small p-values lead to rejecting H_0.

Two-Sided Test	One-Sided Test	
H_a: the two populations differ in location	H_a: population 1 is shifted to the right of population 2	H_a: population 1 is shifted to the left of population 2
Reject H_0 if Table A.10 value for U is less than $\alpha/2$, where U = minimum of U_1 and U_2.	Reject H_0 if Table A.10 value for U is less than α, where $U = U_1$.	Reject H_0 if Table A.10 value for U is less than α, where $U = U_2$.

EXAMPLE 19.4

Turner Electronics manufactures the outside computer casing for a new line of fax machines. They are considering two suppliers, Vendor A and Vendor B. Of concern to Turner is the durability of these casings, and they have designed a test that measures their breaking strength. A weight is dropped from a 2-inch height onto the casing, and the test determines at what maximum weight the casing cracks or becomes otherwise unusable. A random sample of eight casings from Vendor A and nine from Vendor B were subjected to the test, with the following results.

Maximum Weight in Pounds

Vendor A	92.9	78.4	70.0	75.6	110.0	83.1	75.4	98.5	
Vendor B	82.8	102.8	97.0	88.7	107.0	97.2	68.9	76.3	87.3

The quality engineers at Turner have no reason to believe the weight amounts are normally distributed, so they elect to use the Mann-Whitney procedure to determine if there is a difference between the casing strengths from the two vendors. Using $\alpha = .05$, is there a difference between the two suppliers?

SOLUTION

The hypotheses are

H_0: the two populations have identical probability distributions

H_a: the two populations differ in location

The pooled sample (ordered) here is:

68.9, 70.0, 75.4, 75.6, 76.3, 78.4, 82.8, 83.1, 87.3, 88.7, 92.9, 97.0, 97.2, 98.5, 102.8, 107.0, 110.0

Next we indicate from which sample each value in the pooled sample came.

Rank	Vendor A Sample	Vendor B Sample	Ranks for Vendor A Sample	Ranks for Vendor B Sample
1		68.9		1
2	70.0		2	
3	75.4		3	
4	75.6		4	
5		76.3		5
6	78.4		6	
7		82.8		7
8	83.1		8	
9		87.3		9

Rank	Vendor A Sample	Vendor B Sample	Ranks for Vendor A Sample	Ranks for Vendor B Sample
10		88.7		10
11	92.9		11	
12		97.0		12
13		97.2		13
14	98.5		14	
15		102.8		15
16		107.0		16
17	110.0		17	
			$T_1 = 65$	$T_2 = 88$

Using equations 19.5 and 19.6,

$$U_1 = (8)(9) + \frac{(8)(9)}{2} - 65 = 43$$

$$U_2 = (8)(9) + \frac{(9)(10)}{2} - 88 = 29$$

Because this is a two-sided alternative, we let $U =$ the minimum of 29 and 43, so $U = 29$.

For $n_1 = 8$, $n_2 = 9$, and $U = 29$, the value in Table A.10 is .2707. Because this value is greater than $\alpha/2 = .025$, we fail to reject H_0. Based on these data, there is insufficient evidence to indicate a difference in the casing strength for the two vendors.

The p-value for this test is $(2)(.2707) = .5414$, which is extremely large. For a one-sided test, the p-value would be obtained by finding the value from Table A.10, *not* by doubling it.

TIES.   When the pooled sample contains two or more identical observations, each is assigned a rank equal to the *average* of the ranks of the tied observations. For example, if there are two observations tied for sixth and seventh place, each is assigned a rank of 6.5. The rank of the next largest sample value is 8. We illustrate this procedure in the next section. Because of ties, the Mann-Whitney U statistic may not be a counting number (integer). If for example, $U = 42.5$,* then you should always round this value *up* to the next integer (43, here) when consulting Table A.10.

MANN-WHITNEY TEST FOR LARGE SAMPLES.   Whenever n_1 or n_2 is greater than 10, a large-sample approximation can be used for the distribution of the Mann-Whitney U statistic. For this case, we can use either U_1 or U_2 in the test statistic for both one-sided *and* two-sided tests. The following discussion uses U_2.

In the event that the two populations have identical probability distributions (that is, H_0 is true), the U_2 statistic is approximately *normally* distributed with mean

$$\mu_{U_2} = \frac{n_1 n_2}{2} \tag{19.7}$$

and standard deviation

$$\sigma_{U_2} = \sqrt{\frac{n_1 n_2 (n_1 + n_2 + 1)}{12}} \tag{19.8}$$

The rejection region for the various alternative hypotheses are defined in the accompanying box.

---

* The value to the right of the decimal point will always be .5 if U is not an integer.

The corresponding test statistic here is

$$Z = \frac{U_2 - \mu_{U_2}}{\sigma_{U_2}}$$ (19.9)

THE MANN-WHITNEY TEST FOR LARGE SAMPLES

Null hypothesis:

H_0 : the two populations have identical probability distributions

Assumptions: Same as for small samples.

Procedure: Determine

$$U_2 = n_1 n_2 + \frac{n_2(n_2 + 1)}{2} - T_2$$

where T_2 = sum of the ranks for the second sample in the pooled sample.

Two-Sided Test	One-Sided Test	
H_a: the two populations differ in location	H_a: population 1 is shifted to the right of population 2	H_a: population 1 is shifted to the left of population 2
Reject H_0 if $|Z| > Z_{\alpha/2}$ where (1) Z is defined in equation 19.9 and (2) $Z_{\alpha/2}$ is the value from Table A.4 having a right-tail area of $\alpha/2$.	Reject H_0 if $Z > Z_\alpha$.	Reject H_0 if $Z < -Z_\alpha$.

EXAMPLE 19.5

Food World operates two supermarkets in a large metropolitan area. One of their services to customers is to cash personal checks at no charge. The owner of Food World is concerned that one of the stores (store A), situated in a low-income neighborhood, may have a greater number of checks returned due to insufficient funds in the customers' checking accounts than does store B, which is located in a higher-income area. Data were collected for 12 randomly selected six-month periods from store A; the data consisted of the number of returned checks over this period. Similar data were collected for 15 randomly selected six-month periods for store B.

Store A	42	65	38	55	71	60	47	59	68	57	76	42			
Store B	22	17	35	19	8	24	42	14	28	17	10	15	20	45	50

The pooled sample and corresponding ranks are summarized in Table 19.4. Notice that there are two values of 17, which are tied for fifth and sixth place. Consequently, each is given a rank of $(5 + 6)/2 = 5.5$. Similarly, there is a three-way tie for fourteenth, fifteenth, and sixteenth place, so a rank of $(14 + 15 + 16)/3 = 15$ is given to each.

Using $\alpha = .05$, is there sufficient evidence to indicate that store A has a larger number of returned checks than does store B?

SOLUTION

The hypotheses for this situation are

H_0: the two populations have identical probability distributions

H_a: population A is shifted to the right of population B

The test procedure is to

reject H_0 if $Z > 1.645$

where $1.645 = Z_{.05}$ is obtained from Table A.4. From Table 19.4, we find that

TABLE 19.4   Pooled sample for Example 19.5.

Rank	Store A Sample	Store B Sample	Ranks for Store A	Ranks for Store B
1		8		1
2		10		2
3		14		3
4		15		4
5		17		5.5
6		17		5.5
7		19		7
8		20		8
9		22		9
10		24		10
11		28		11
12		35		12
13	38		13	
14	42		15	
15		42		15
16	42		15	
17		45		17
18	47		18	
19		50		19
20	55		20	
21	57		21	
22	59		22	
23	60		23	
24	65		24	
25	68		25	
26	71		26	
27	76		27	
			$T_1 = 249$	$T_2 = 129$

T_2 = sum of ranks for store B

$$= 1 + 2 + 3 + 4 + 5.5 + 5.5 + \cdots + 15 + 17 + 19 = 129$$

and so

$$U_2 = (12)(15) + \frac{(15)(16)}{2} - 129 = 171$$

Also, the mean and standard deviation of the U_2 statistic are

$$\mu_{U_2} = \frac{(12)(15)}{2} = 90$$

and

$$\sigma_{U_2} = \sqrt{\frac{(12)(15)(28)}{12}} = 20.49$$

The value of the resulting test statistic is

$$Z = \frac{U_2 - \mu_{U_2}}{\sigma_{U_2}} = \frac{171 - 90}{20.49} = 3.95$$

This exceeds 1.645, and so we reject H_0 and conclude that store A does in fact have a larger volume of returned checks than store B.

FIGURE 19.6
Excel solution to Example 19.5
using the Mann-Whitney test
within **KGP Data Analysis
➤ Nonparametric
Procedures.**

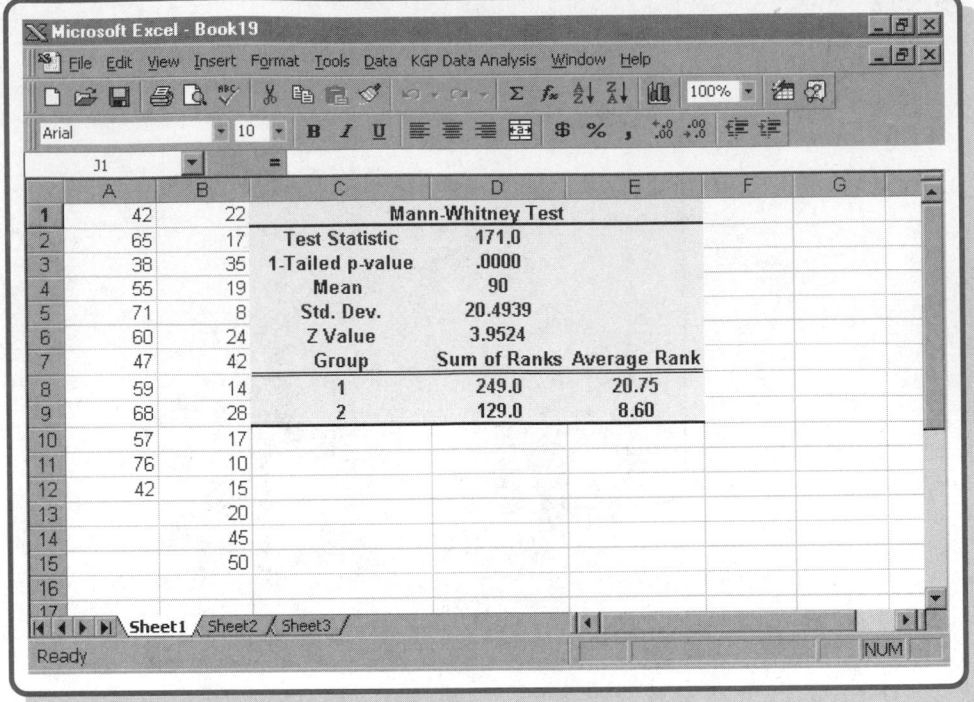

An Excel solution for Example 19.5 is contained in Figure 19.6. To obtain this solution, click on **KGP Data Analysis ➤ Nonparametric Procedures.** Select **Comparing Two Groups** and click on **Mann-Whitney Test** and then on **OK.** In the next form, enter "A1:A12" as the **Input Range** for sample 1 and "B1:B15" for sample 2. Enter "C1" as the **Output Range** and select **Population 1 Is Shifted to the Right of Population 2** as the alternative hypothesis.

The Excel analysis uses the values in Table A.10 to determine p-values if both n_1 and n_2 are less than or equal to 10. If either sample size is more than 10, the p-value is determined using the value of the large-sample Z statistic. For this example, both n_1 and n_2 exceed 10, so the p-value is computed as the area to the right of $Z^* = 3.95$. In Figure 19.6, this very small p-value (zero to four decimal places) again supports the alternative hypothesis and leads to the conclusion that store A has a larger volume of returned checks than store B.

WILCOXON SIGNED RANK TEST FOR PAIRED SAMPLES

When your sample data consist of *paired* observations from two populations, the Mann-Whitney procedure from the previous section does not apply because it assumes *independent* samples. By *paired observations,* we mean that respective observations from each sample are matched with one another. Examples of paired observations include husband-wife, brother-sister, and before-after combinations.

A method of testing population means under this type of sampling procedure was introduced in Chapter 9, where we used a t test on the sample differences. However, as in all t tests, a key assumption using this method of testing two means is that the differences are *normally distributed. When small samples from suspected nonnormal populations are used, a nonparametric technique is required.* The **Wilcoxon signed rank test** is used for such situations.

The Wilcoxon test begins like its parametric counterpart, the paired-sample t test, by subtracting the data pairs and using the differences to perform the test. As in the paired-sample t test, the hypotheses are written in terms of the location of the probability distribution for the population differences.

TABLE 19.5

Sales (thousands of dollars) for 10 cities.

City	Sales Before	Sales After
Denver	61	63
Boston	50	57
Salt Lake City	18	34
Seattle	56	48
Miami	29	44
Dallas	25	38
Atlanta	34	28
Baltimore	48	68
Topeka	37	57
Minneapolis	14	26

TABLE 19.6

Illustration of Wilcoxon signed rank procedure (Example 19.6).

Sales After	Sales Before	Difference (After − Before)	|Difference|	Rank
63	61	2	2	1
57	50	7	7	3
34	18	16	16	8
48	56	−8	8	4 (−)
44	29	15	15	7
38	25	13	13	6
28	34	−6	6	2 (−)
68	48	20	20	9.5
57	37	20	20	9.5
26	14	12	12	5

The steps involved in applying the Wilcoxon test are:

1. Determine the difference for each sample pair.
2. Arrange the *absolute value* of these differences in order, assigning a rank to each.
3. Let T_+ = sum of the ranks having a positive value and T_- = sum of the ranks for the negative values.
4. T_+, T_-, or T = the minimum of T_+ and T_- is used to define a test of H_0 versus H_a.

To demonstrate the test, suppose we are interested in determining the effects of a vigorous six-month advertising campaign. Sales figures are collected before and after the campaign from ten different cities. The results are shown in Table 19.5. We determine the paired differences and rank the corresponding absolute values in order. Ties are handled as before by assigning a rank equal to the average of the tied positions. Also, if a pair of observations has a difference equal to zero, then this pair is *deleted* from the sample, and n is reduced by 1. Other methods exist for handling zero differences, but this procedure is the simplest, and it works well provided there are not many zero differences.

According to Table 19.6, the negative differences are −6 and −8. Their corresponding ranks are 2 and 4. Therefore,

$$T_- = 2 + 4 = 6$$

A rule that can simplify the calculations here and serve as a check for arithmetic is that

$$T_+ + T_- = \frac{n(n+1)}{2}$$

where n = the number of sample pairs. In our example, $n = 10$, so

$$T_+ + T_- = \frac{(10)(11)}{2} = 55$$

which means that $T_+ = 55 - T_- = 55 - 6 = 49$.

THE WILCOXON SIGNED RANK TEST FOR SMALL SAMPLES (PAIRED). Once T_+ and T_- have been obtained, you can use the Wilcoxon signed rank test for testing hypotheses about the location of the population differences.

THE WILCOXON SIGNED RANK TEST FOR SMALL SAMPLES (PAIRED)

Null hypothesis:

$$H_0 : \text{the population differences are centered at } 0$$

Assumptions:

1. Each data pair is randomly selected.
2. The absolute values of the differences can be ranked.

Procedure:

1. Determine the n differences using each sample pair, where each difference is defined to be sample 1 – sample 2.
2. Assign a rank to the absolute value of each difference; define T_+ = sum of the ranks of the positive values and T_- = sum of the ranks of the negative values.

Table A.11 is used to define the rejection region for the following tests.

Two-Sided Test	**One-Sided Test**	
H_a: the population differences are not centered at 0	H_a: the population differences are centered at a value > 0	H_a: the population differences are centered at a value < 0
Using the two-sided value from Table A.11, reject H_0 if $T \leq$ table value, where $T =$ minimum of T_+ and T_-.	Using the one-sided value from Table A.11, reject H_0 if $T_- \leq$ table value.	Using the one-sided value from Table A.11, reject H_0 if $T_+ \leq$ table value.

EXAMPLE 19.6

Table 19.5 contains the sales results from 10 cities before and after the six-month advertising campaign. Using $\alpha = .05$, are we able to conclude that there was a significant increase in sales after the advertising campaign?

SOLUTION

The hypotheses here can be stated as (A = after, B = before)

H_0: the population differences are centered at 0.

H_a: the population differences are centered at a value > 0.

We refer to the "after" population as population 1 and the "before" population as population 2 to correspond to the difference column in Table 19.6 [our procedure assumes that each difference is sample 1 (A) – sample 2 (B)].

The values of T_+ and T_- also are derived from Table 19.6, where

$$T_- = 6 \quad \text{and} \quad T_+ = 49$$

The one-sided value in Table A.11 corresponding to $n = 10$ and $\alpha = .05$ is 11. Consequently, the test is to

$$\text{reject } H_0 \text{ if } T_- \leq 11$$

Because the value of T_- is smaller than 11, we reject H_0 and conclude that there is sufficient evidence of a sales increase after the advertising campaign.

THE WILCOXON SIGNED RANK TEST FOR LARGE SAMPLES (PAIRED).   For samples consisting of $n > 15$ pairs, a large-sample approximation to the Wilcoxon test statistic can be used. An advantage to using this procedure is that p-values are much easier to determine. (A p-value is once again a measure of the strength of your conclusion.)

When using the large-sample procedure, we can define a test using either T_+ or T_-. The following hypothesis tests use T_+, the sum of the ranks for the positive differences. If the population differences are centered at zero (that is, H_0 is true), then T_+ is approximately a normal random variable with mean

$$\mu_{T_+} = \frac{n(n+1)}{4} \tag{19.10}$$

and standard deviation

$$\sigma_{T_+} = \sqrt{\frac{n(n+1)(2n+1)}{24}} \tag{19.11}$$

The corresponding test statistic is

$$Z = \frac{T_+ - \mu_{T_+}}{\sigma_{T_+}} \tag{19.12}$$

The one- and two-sided large-sample procedures are summarized in the accompanying box.

THE WILCOXON SIGNED RANK TEST FOR LARGE SAMPLES (PAIRED)

Null hypothesis:

H_0: the population differences are centered at 0.

Assumptions: Same as for small samples.

Procedure: (1) and (2) are the same as for small samples. Each paired difference is defined to be sample 1 − sample 2.

Two-Sided Test

H_a: the population differences are not centered at 0

Reject H_0 if $|Z| > Z_{\alpha/2}$, where Z is defined in equation 19.12 and $Z_{\alpha/2}$ is the value from Table A.4 having a right-tail area of $\alpha/2$.

One-Sided Test

H_a: the population differences are centered at a value > 0

Reject H_0 if $Z > Z_{\alpha}$.

H_a: the population differences are centered at a value < 0

Reject H_0 if $Z < -Z_{\alpha}$.

EXAMPLE 19.7

The paper produced by Glendale Container Corporation has historically contained 2% hardwood in the paper pulp. A quality engineer at Glendale believed that a 10% hardwood concentration would improve the tensile strength of the paper. Management has decided to adopt the 10% concentration, despite the slightly higher cost, if in fact the tensile strength can be demonstrated to be larger at the 10% level. An experiment is performed in which the plant runs two batches of paper a day, one at 2% concentration and one at 10% concentration. A section of paper from each of the two batches is cut, dried, and tested. The following tensile strength data were obtained:

Day	2%	10%	Day	2%	10%
1	125	119	11	113	148
2	133	120	12	131	116
3	132	139	13	128	107
4	116	148	14	119	142
5	130	148	15	112	106
6	135	109	16	111	142
7	119	137	17	128	112
8	112	116	18	135	145
9	122	122	19	106	131
10	137	131	20	118	146

Use the Wilcoxon signed rank test to determine whether the quality engineer's belief—that the tensile strength is larger for the 10% hardwood concentration—is correct. Let $\alpha = .05$.

SOLUTION

If we let the 2% population be population 1, then the correct hypotheses are

H_0: the population differences are centered at 0

H_a: the population differences are centered at a value < 0

The alternative hypothesis agrees with Table 19.7, in which each difference is calculated using the 2% value (sample 1) minus the 10% value (sample 2). Because the values for day 9 are the same, the difference is zero, so this sample is removed from the analysis, leaving $n = 19$ pairs in the sample.

Based on a significance level of $\alpha = .05$, the proper test is to

reject H_0 if $Z < -1.645$

For a value of $n = 19$, the mean of T_+ (assuming H_0 is true) is

$$\mu_{T_+} = \frac{(19)(20)}{4} = 95$$

with a standard deviation of

$$\sigma_{T_+} = \sqrt{\frac{(19)(20)(39)}{24}} = 24.85$$

Table 19.7 informs us that $T_+ = 60$, and so the value of the test statistic here is

$$Z^* = \frac{60 - 95}{24.85} = -1.41$$

This value is not less than -1.645, so there is insufficient evidence to conclude that the 10% concentration produces a larger tensile strength. Glendale Container should continue to use the less expensive 2% hardwood concentration.

TABLE 19.7

Paired samples for Example 19.7.

HARDWOOD CONCENTRATION 2%	HARDWOOD CONCENTRATION 10%	Difference (2%–10%)	Rank of Absolute Value		+ Ranks	− Ranks
125	119	6	3		3*	
133	120	13	7		7	
132	139	−7	5	(−)		5
116	148	−32	18	(−)		18
130	148	−18	10.5	(−)		10.5†
135	109	26	15		15	
119	137	−18	10.5	(−)		10.5†
112	116	−4	1	(−)		1
122	122	0	—	removed, so use $n = 19$ pairs		
137	131	6	3		3*	
113	148	−35	19	(−)		19
131	116	15	8		8	
128	107	21	12		12	
119	142	−23	13	(−)		13
112	106	6	3		3*	
111	142	−31	17	(−)		17
128	112	16	9		9	
135	145	−10	6	(−)		6
106	131	−25	14	(−)		14
118	146	−28	16	(−)		16
					$T_+ = 60$	$T_- = 130$

*Three-way tie; assigned rank = (2 + 3 + 4)/3 = 3.
†Two-way tie; assigned rank = (10 + 11)/2 = 10.5.

FIGURE 19.7

p-value for Example 19.7.

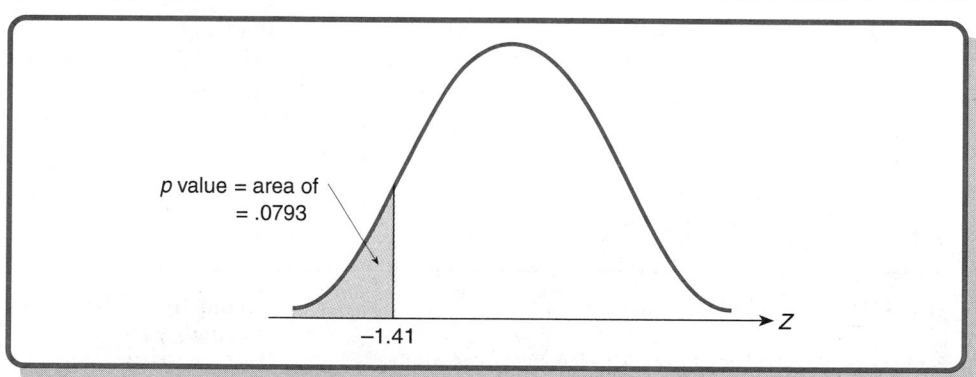

p value = area of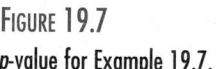
= .0793

−1.41

Z

The p-value for this test is obtained in the usual manner by finding, in this case, the area under a standard normal curve to the left of the calculated test statistic of $Z^* = -1.41$. According to Figure 19.7 and Table A.4, the p-value is .0793. Using our rule-of-thumb procedure from before, this p-value is neither large (>.1) nor small (<.01), but it *is* greater than $\alpha = .05$, which leads us to fail to reject H_0.

FIGURE 19.8

Excel solution to Example 19.7 using the Wilcoxon test within **KGP Data Analysis ➤ Nonparametric Procedures.**

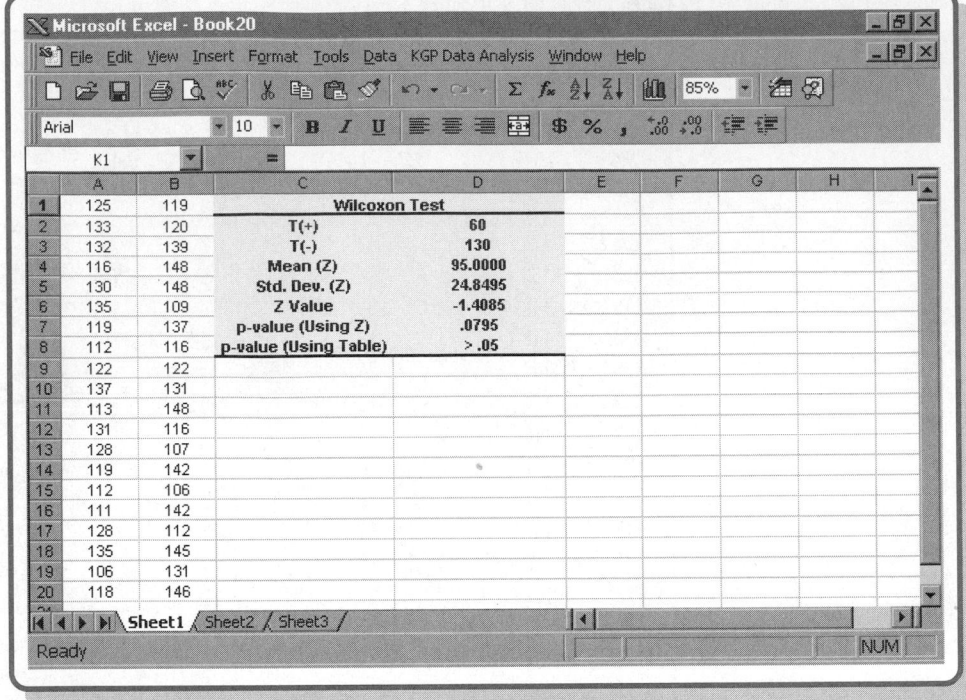

An Excel solution for Example 19.7 is contained in Figure 19.8. To obtain this solution, click on **KGP Data Analysis ➤ Nonparametric Procedures.** Select **Comparing Two Groups** and click on **Wilcoxon Test** and then on **OK.** In the next form, enter "A1:B20" as the **Input Range,** enter "C1" as the **Output Range,** and select **Differences (Pop. 1 – Pop. 2) Center is < 0** as the alternative hypothesis. In Figure 19.8, the p-value using the large-sample Z statistic is .0795. This is slightly more accurate than the p-value illustrated in Figure 19.7, since a more accurate value of the Z statistic was used.

Using Table A.11, $\alpha = .05$, and $n = 19$ (remember: there was one tie), the null hypothesis will be rejected if $T_+ \le 54$. Since $60 > 54$, we fail to reject H_0 as before, and we also can say that the corresponding p-value is $> .05$. For $n \le 50$, the KGP Data Analysis Wilcoxon test will provide a p-value using Table A.11. For this example, Excel will output **p-value (Using Table)** and **> .05.** This p-value and the large-sample p-value (.0795) both exceed .05, leading to the conclusion that there is insufficient evidence to indicate that the 10% concentration produces a larger tensile strength than the 2% concentration.

EXERCISES 19.11–19.35

UNDERSTANDING THE MECHANICS

19.11 Data were collected from 10 randomly selected observations of population A and from 15 randomly selected observations of population B. The Mann-Whitney statistic can be used to test whether population A is shifted to the right of population B. The sum of the ranks for the observations from population A is 196. The sum of the ranks for the observations from population B is 129. Using a significance level of .05, is there sufficient evidence to indicate that population A is shifted to the right of population B?

19.12 Random samples of sizes 13 and 15 were drawn from populations 1 and 2, respectively. Using a significance level of .10, determine if the two populations differ in location.

Sample from Population 1			Sample from Population 2		
24	18	8	17	6	30
14	12	12	31	13	26
9	28	33	27	20	20
12	25		21	27	33
36	15		34	16	18

19.13 Ten pairs of observations from two populations were randomly selected. The sum of ranks of the positive differences (T_+) and the sum of ranks of the negative differences (T_-) were found to be 50 and 5, respectively. Can you conclude that the population differences are centered at a value greater than 0? Use a .05 significance level.

19.14 Consider the following pairs of observations. Use the Wilcoxon signed rank test to determine whether the population differences are centered at a value different from 0. Use a .10 significance level.

Pair	Sample A	Sample B
1	121	112
2	132	124
3	131	141
4	122	140
5	114	152
6	101	112
7	131	152
8	124	125
9	140	110
10	141	135
11	113	138
12	139	118
13	125	110
14	120	135
15	115	110
16	128	118
17	136	141
18	106	130
19	112	132
20	118	124

APPLYING THE NEW CONCEPTS

19.15 An engineer is proposing a new manufacturing process to increase the tensile strength of a certain wire. Eleven samples of wire manufactured under the proposed process are collected, and 14 samples are collected from wire manufactured under the existing process. Using the following data and a 10% significance level, test the hypothesis that there is greater tensile strength in the proposed technique.

Proposed Technique (PSI)	Existing Technique (PSI)	Proposed Technique (PSI)	Existing Technique (PSI)
1.4	1.2	2.2	1.8
2.1	1.6	2.0	1.7
1.8	1.7	1.9	2.0
1.7	1.7	2.0	1.8
1.6	2.0		1.9
1.9	1.3		1.6
1.4	1.4		2.1

19.16 The head lawyer of the Brown and Smith firm would like to know whether there is a difference in the number of errors made by the two secretaries employed in the firm. Five randomly selected documents are given to secretary A to type, and five are given to secretary B. The number of errors per document is shown in the following table. Using a 5% level of significance, test the hypothesis that there is no difference in the number of errors made by each secretary.

Secretary A	Secretary B
3	2
5	0
4	4
2	3
0	1

19.17 The profits of many banks worldwide fell in 1992 from the previous year. A random sample of 10 banks with assets of more than $70 billion was selected. Another random sample of 10 banks with assets of $70 billion or less was also selected. The percentage change in profit from 1991 is presented here for each bank. Using a .05 significance level, can you conclude that there is a difference in percentage change in profits from 1991 for banks with assets over $70 billion and for banks with assets of $70 billion or less? (*Hint:* When ranking the data, rank the most negative value 1, the next most negative value 2, and so on.)

Banks with Assets over $70 Billion in 1992	Percentage Change in Assets from 1991
Royal Bank of Canada (Canada)	−89.5
Bank of Yokohama (Japan)	−48.3
Canadian Imperial Bank (Canada)	−98.6
J. P. Morgan (U.S.)	20.6
Banco DiRoma (Italy)	−28.3
Generale Bank (Belgium)	18.6
Hok Kaido Takushoku (Japan)	39.6
Bank of Montreal (Canada)	4.2
Banco Bilbao Vizcaya (Spain)	−28.2
National Australia	−8.7

Banks with Assets of $70 Billion or Less in 1992	Percentage Change in Assets from 1991
HoKuriku (Japan)	−37.3
Banque Indosuez (France)	−86.7
Commonwealth Bank (Australia)	−54.6
Joyo Bank (Japan)	−16.5
BancoEspanol DeCredito (Spain)	−83.9
Banc One Corp. (U.S.)	47.6
Hiroshima Bank (Japan)	−20.2
Toronto-Dominion (Canada)	−20.6
Credit Commercial deFrance (France)	13.6
Banco DeSantader (Spain)	−15.6

(Source: "The 100 Largest Commercial Banking Companies," *Fortune*, Aug. 23, 1993, p. 168.)

19.18 Two samples of light bulbs are taken from the brands Everglo and Britelite. The following table gives the life of bulbs for the collected samples. At the 1% level, is there sufficient evidence to indicate that Britelite bulbs last longer than do Everglo bulbs?

Everglo (Hours)	Britelite (Hours)	Everglo (Hours)	Britelite (Hours)
1134	1405	1107	1290
1255	1251	1095	1210
1313	1106	1401	1198
1012	1384	1109	1203
1265	1193	1150	1295
1375	1208		1102
1102	1110		1185

19.19 An economist wishes to compare the percentage increase in personal income for two suburbs of Chicago. Using the data in the following table, test at the 5% significance level the hypothesis that there is no difference in the percentage increase in personal income.

Suburb A (%)	Suburb B (%)	Suburb A (%)	Suburb B (%)	Process 1	Process 2	Process 1	Process 2
5.2	2.6	1.3	11.3	10	13	16	19
3.1	9.7	8.4	8.1	15	19	15	5
10.6	1.2	9.1	4.2	13	14	12	19
11.4	1.4	11.3	1.6	25	18	11	20
1.2	5.0	12.1	2.7	18	20	17	15
0.0	9.8	9.8	7.9				

19.20 A supermarket manager was curious as to which of the two vending machines located at opposite ends of the store was used more during peak hours. During the peak hours on 12 randomly selected days, the number of users was counted for machine A. During the peak hours on another randomly selected 12 days, the number of users was counted for machine B. From the data on the following page, test at the 5% level of significance the hypothesis that there is no difference in the use of the two vending machines.

Vending Machine A	Vending Machine B	Vending Machine A	Vending Machine B
10	9	13	9
12	11	19	8
13	14	11	12
11	10	10	13
10	13	15	14
15	14	12	11

19.21 Airline fares to international locations can vary according to the geographical location in the United States. A travel agency wished to determine if there is a difference in the airfare from major cities located in the northern and eastern sector of the U.S. (denoted by N/E Region) versus those cities located in the southern and eastern sector of the U.S. (denoted by S/E Region). Use the following data to test if there is evidence that a difference exists in the one-way airfare to Tokyo from these two regions. Use a 10% significance level.

S/E Region	Air Fare from City in the S/E Region
Atlanta	438
Miami	495
Orlando	495
Birmingham	485
New Orleans	480
Memphis	478
Houston	385

N/E Region	Air Fare from City in the N/E Region
Boston	470
Washington, D.C.	495
New York City	480
Philadelphia	470
Cleveland	478
Newark	480
Baltimore	495

(Adapted from *USA Today,* "Get Great Low Fares to Japan with Northwest Airlines," May 7, 1998, p. 11A.)

19.22 The number of defective electronic components in lots of two different processes are:

a. Use a *t* test, assuming equal population variances, to test that the two processes differ in location with respect to the number of defective terms. Use a .05 significance level.

b. Use the Mann-Whitney test to perform part (a).

c. Which test is preferable for this type of data?

19.23 What assumption needs to be made about the sample data used in the Wilcoxon signed rank test? What assumption needs to be made about the distribution of the populations?

19.24 From 12 paired observations, it is found that by ranking the magnitude of the differences of the observations in each pair, T_+ (the sum of the ranks of the positive differences) is 27. Using a .05 significance level, can it be concluded that there is a difference in the location of the two populations?

19.25 A psychologist conducts a seminar to increase a person's self-esteem. A before-and-after test that measures each person's self-esteem is given to nine individuals. Using the following scores and a 5% significance level, is there evidence to conclude that the scores after the seminar are greater than the scores before the seminar?

Before	After	Before	After
70	74	55	58
72	88	43	41
75	71	51	63
61	62	84	80
82	89		

19.26 An insurance company believes that employees who have a college degree when hired progress faster in the company than those who do not. Pairs of employees are randomly selected; each pair consists of two people hired at the same time, one person with a college degree and the other without a college degree. The percentage increase in pay for these employees after three years is shown here. At the 10% level of significance, can you conclude that employees who have a college degree when hired progress faster than those who do not?

Without College Degree (%)	With College Degree (%)	Without College Degree (%)	With College Degree (%)
10	13	12	13
9	10	9	8
8	6	18	16
13	13	9	12
14	18	15	17
7	10	10	9
12	11	11	13
11	15	10	9
16	20		

19.27 Seven randomly selected faculty members were asked to evaluate two research project proposals on a scale from 0 to 10, with a higher score indicating a more acceptable proposal.

The scores follow. Using a 5% significance level, can you conclude that the proposal for research project 2 is more acceptable than the proposal for research project 1?

Research Project 1	Research Project 2
5	7
3	5
6	9
7	6
8	9
4	6
7	10

19.28 The increase or decrease in help-wanted advertisements is an indicator of economic expansion or contraction, respectively. A sample of newspapers across the New Mexico, Texas, and Oklahoma region was selected to obtain a reading on the direction of the economy in that region. The number of help-wanted ads in November 1997 and November 1998 was recorded as an index, with 1989 being the base year. Test that the number of help-wanted ads in November 1998 have declined for the region. Use a 5% significance level.

Location of Newspaper	Help-wanted Index Nov. 1997	Help-wanted Index Nov. 1998
Albuquerque	150	145
Amarillo	132	121
Austin	210	205
Dallas	141	132
El Paso	185	180
Ft. Worth	155	164
Houston	111	95
Oklahoma	152	163
San Antonio	205	205
Tulsa	203	190

(Source: Adapted from *The Wall Street Journal,* "Tracking Texas: The Help-Wanted Index," Jan. 6, 1999, p. T1.)

19.29 The manager of a calculator-assembly plant wanted to know whether machine operators with little experience produced more defective calculators than did the experienced machine operators. The number of defective calculators produced by 20 randomly selected experienced machine operators in one week was recorded. Then, these 20 experienced operators were replaced by inexperienced machine operators and the number of defective calculators produced at these positions was recorded for one week. If the operators at each position can be considered to be a pair, use the Wilcoxon test to test that the experienced operators produced fewer defective calculators. Use a 5% significance level.

Experienced Employees	Inexperienced Employees	Experienced Employees	Inexperienced Employees
10	14	13	19
13	14	18	21
15	12	19	18
18	25	10	13
14	13	19	26
10	15	25	26
30	21	15	17
14	18	21	20
22	23	20	28
15	13	12	19

19.30 The manager of an insurance company sent 10 randomly selected salespeople to a sales-motivation lecture given by several top-selling insurance salespeople. The manager recorded the dollar amount (in hundreds of thousands) of insurance sold by the 10 salespeople during the four months prior to attending the lecture and the four months after the lecture. At the 5% significance level, is there evidence to suggest that the sales-motivation lecture improved sales?

Before Lecture	After Lecture	Before Lecture	After Lecture
1.2	1.9	6.2	6.3
1.8	3.4	1.5	1.4
3.8	3.1	3.3	4.9
1.9	4.5	2.4	3.5
5.8	5.0	3.1	3.0

19.31 A paired-difference experiment yielded a value of 280 for the sum of the ranks of the positive differences from 30 observations. Using a 5% significance level, is there evidence to suggest that the population differences are not centered at zero?

Using the Computer

19.32 [DATA SET EX19-32] *Variable description:*

GasMileageReg: Gas mileage of a Jeep Cherokee with regular unleaded gasoline
GasMileageSup: Gas mileage of a Jeep Cherokee with supreme unleaded gasoline

A researcher working for Consumer Issues must determine if there is a difference in gas mileage of a Jeep Cherokee when regular unleaded gasoline is used and when supreme unleaded gasoline is used. A random sample of one hundred 1999 Jeep Cherokees was used in the study. Fifty of the jeeps were tested with regular unleaded gasoline and the other half with supreme unleaded gasoline. Each Jeep was driven by a randomly selected owner of a Jeep Cherokee. Using the variables GasMileageReg and GasMileageSup, interpret the results of a nonparametric test to determine if a difference exists at the 5% significance level. Explain how the practical significance of the results may differ from the statistical significance of the results for this problem.

19.33 [DATA SET EX19-33] *Variable description:*

StressA: Stress measurement for Tube A
StressB: Stress measurement for Tube B

A quality engineer is interested in determining if the stress level for Tube A is less than the stress level for Tube B. Forty-five measurements of each tube were randomly selected, and a stress test revealed each tube's stress measurement. Do the data indicate that the stress level for Tube A is less than the stress level for Tube B? Use a 1% significance level.

19.34 [DATA SET EX19-34] *Variable description:*

Design1: Sales using conservative style
Design2: Sales using flashy style

The management at Lion Foods is interested in placing its breakfast cereal in two different packaging designs. The first design (Design1) has a conservative style. The second design

(Design2) has a flashy style. Management decides to place the products with both designs at opposite ends of the breakfast section in 25 different supermarkets. Can you conclude there is a difference in sales (number of boxes sold) for the two designs? Use a 5% significance level.

19.35 [DATA SET EX19-35] *Variable description:*

Employee: Number indicating the employee, numbered from 1 to 35

SatisfactionBef: Job satisfaction score before promotion

SatisfactionAft: Job satisfaction score after promotion

An industrial psychologist believes that an employee's level of satisfaction with his/her job changes as the employee gets promoted. Thirty-five employees were randomly selected. A year before each employee received a promotion, a job satisfaction score was recorded. Then a year after the employee was promoted, a job satisfaction score was recorded.

a. Do the data indicate a difference in job satisfaction scores before and after promotion? Use a 5% significance level.

b. Using the paired *t* test, how would you answer part (a)?

c. Why do you believe that the results in parts (a) and (b) differ?

19.3 COMPARING MORE THAN TWO POPULATIONS: THE KRUSKAL-WALLIS TEST AND THE FRIEDMAN TEST

THE KRUSKAL-WALLIS TEST

When comparing the means of more than two populations, a popular technique is the ANOVA procedure discussed in Chapter 11. One of the assumptions behind this technique is that you are dealing with normally distributed populations; the *F* test used in the ANOVA table is invalid unless all of the populations are nearly normally distributed with equal variances.

The nonparametric counterpart to the one-way ANOVA method is the **Kruskal-Wallis test.** It is named after W. H. Kruskal and W. A. Wallis, who published their results in 1952. This test, like many other nonparametric procedures, is relatively new, unlike most of the parametric hypothesis tests, which were developed much earlier. *The assumption of normal populations is* not necessary *for the Kruskal-Wallis test, making it an ideal technique for samples exhibiting a nonsymmetric (skewed) pattern.* It is also less sensitive than the ANOVA procedure to the assumption of equal variances. This test also is useful when the data consist of rankings (ordinal data) within each sample.

The assumption of normal populations becomes quite critical when dealing with small samples. As we've seen in many of the earlier tests of hypothesis, this assumption can be relaxed when larger samples are used, due to the Central Limit Theorem. However, many experiments of a business nature dealing with product comparisons result in the destruction of the product being tested. Consequently, small samples are often a necessity for such experiments, and nonparametric techniques are widely used to analyze the resulting data.

The Kruskal-Wallis test is actually an extension of the Mann-Whitney *U* test discussed earlier for *two* independent samples. Both procedures require that the sample values have a measurement scale that is at least ordinal (that is, each sample can be ranked from smallest to largest).

The hypotheses for this situation are similar to the Mann-Whitney hypotheses in that they are stated in terms of differing population locations. The Kruskal-Wallis hypotheses are

H_0: the k populations have identical probability distributions

H_a: at least two of the populations differ in location

PROCEDURE.   You first obtain random samples of size $n_1, n_2, \ldots, n_k$ from each of the k populations. The total sample size is $n = n_1 + n_2 + \cdots + n_k$. As with the Mann-Whitney procedure, you next pool the samples and arrange them in order, assigning a rank to each. For ties, you assign the average rank to the tied positions.

Let T_i = the total of the ranks from the ith sample. The Kruskal-Wallis test statistic (KW) is

$$KW = \frac{12}{n(n+1)} \sum_{i=1}^{k} \frac{T_i^2}{n_i} - 3(n+1) \qquad \text{(19.13)}$$

The distribution of the KW statistic approximately follows a chi-square distribution with $k - 1$ df. This approximation is good even if the sample sizes are small. To test H_0 versus H_a, the procedure is to

$$\text{reject } H_0 \text{ if } KW \text{ is "large"}$$

that is, if KW is in the right tail of the chi-square curve. This right-tail critical value is obtained from Table A.6, using a significance level $= \alpha$ and df $= k - 1$.

THE KRUSKAL-WALLIS TEST

Hypotheses:

$$H_0: \text{the } k \text{ populations have identical probability distributions}$$
$$H_a: \text{at least two of the populations differ in location}$$

Assumptions:

1. Random samples are obtained from each of the k populations.
2. The individual samples are obtained independently.
3. Values within each sample can be ranked.
4. If any two populations differ, they differ only in location—that is, all k populations have the same variation and shape.

Procedure: The individual samples are pooled and then ranked from smallest to largest. Letting $T_i =$ the sum of the ranks of the ith sample, the KW statistic is determined using equation 19.13. The null hypothesis, H_0, is rejected if

$$KW > \chi^2_{\alpha, df}$$

where $\chi^2_{\alpha, df}$ is the value from Table A.6 corresponding to df $= k - 1$, with a right-tail area $= \alpha$.

EXAMPLE 19.8

Drexton Industries has a number of different brands of copying machines at their main facility. A critical factor in the attractiveness of each brand is the amount of time in which a machine is not working and is waiting for repair (downtime). Management requested a study to be made on four different brands of machines to determine whether there is a difference in the amount of downtime for these brands. Data were collected by finding the total downtime per month for 20 randomly selected months. In this way, the downtimes for five randomly selected months were obtained for each of the four brands of machine. These results are shown in Table 19.8.

Do these data indicate a difference in the amount of downtime for the four brands? Use $\alpha = .05$.

TABLE 19.8

Amount of downtime for copying machines (Example 19.8).

Brand 1	Rank	Brand 2	Rank	Brand 3	Rank	Brand 4	Rank
28	12	5	1	10	3	45	18
41	17	16	6	8	2	30	13
34	15	20	8	18	7	49	19
52	20	24	9	14	4	32	14
25	10	15	5	26	11	36	16
	$T_1 = 74$		$T_2 = 29$		$T_3 = 27$		$T_4 = 80$

FIGURE 19.9

p-value for *KW* statistic;
χ^2 curve with 3 df
(Example 19.8).

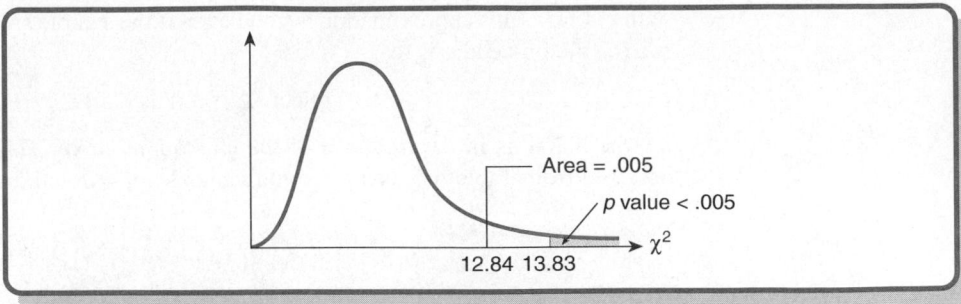

SOLUTION

There are $k = 4$ populations here, so we need the $\chi^2_{.05,3}$ value from Table A.6. Based on this value, the testing procedure is to

$$\text{reject } H_0 \text{ if } KW > \chi^2_{.05,3} = 7.81$$

From Table 19.8, we are able to compute the value of the *KW* statistic using the ranks of the observations in the pooled sample:

$$KW = \frac{12}{(20)(21)}\left[\frac{74^2}{5} + \frac{29^2}{5} + \frac{27^2}{5} + \frac{80^2}{5}\right] - 3(21) = 13.83$$

As a check of your calculations at this point, make sure the ranks sum to $n(n + 1)/2$. For this example, $n = $ total number of observations $= 20$, and so the total of the ranks should be $(20)(21)/2 = 210$; here, $74 + 29 + 27 + 80 = 210$.

The calculated *KW* value exceeds 7.81, and so our conclusion is that there is a difference in downtime among the four brands. From the small values of T_2 and T_3, it appears that these two brands have much less downtime and are superior in this respect to brands 1 and 4.

Finally, the *p*-value here is <.005, indicating a very strong conclusion. In other words, these data indicate a clear difference in location for the four brands. This *p*-value is illustrated in Figure 19.9.

To obtain the Excel solution for Example 19.8, click on **KGP Data Analysis ➤ Nonparametric Procedures.** Select **Comparing More Than Two Groups** and click on **Kruskal-Wallis Test** and then on **OK.** In Figure 19.10, the four samples were placed in the first four columns. *Note:* In general, these columns must be contiguous (adjacent). To carry out the test, enter "A1" as the **Upper Left Corner of the Sample Data,** "E1" as the **Output Range,** and "4" as the **Number of Groups.** After clicking on **OK,** enter "5" as the **Number of Values** in each of the four samples, and then click on **OK** again. From Figure 19.10, the actual *p*-value is .0031 < .05, and so this output supports the conclusion that there is a difference in downtime for the four brands.

THE FRIEDMAN TEST

The topic of comparing more than two population means using dependent samples was introduced in Chapter 11, where we examined the randomized block design. Such a design consists of a single factor of interest with k levels, with the sample data organized into blocks. For this situation, the samples are not independently obtained, but data within the same block may be gathered from the same city or person or at the same point in time.

The key assumption behind the use of the randomized block design is that the variable being measured (the *dependent* variable) is normally distributed within each factor level/block combination. There are two situations for a blocked design where the use of the parametric randomized block technique is inappropriate, requiring the use of a nonparametric procedure:

1. You have no evidence to support the assumption of normality.

FIGURE 19.10

Excel solution to Example 19.8 using the Kruskal-Wallis test within **KGP Data Analysis** ➤ **Nonparametric Procedures.**

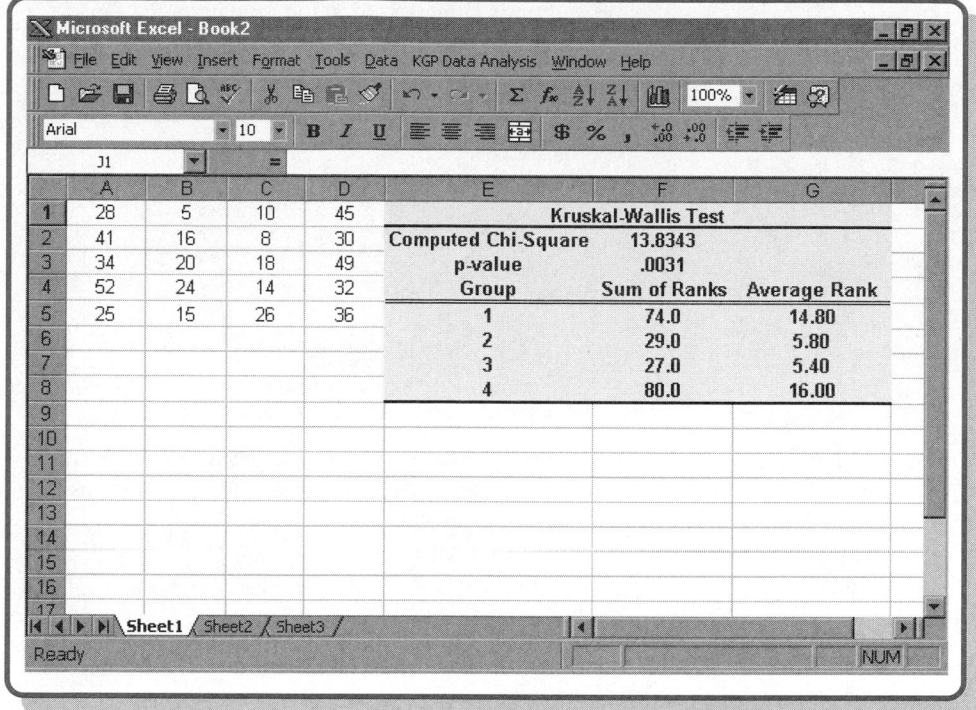

or

2.   The sample data are ordinal (that is, consist of rankings).

When confronted with either of these two situations, the nonparametric **Friedman** test provides a correct method of testing for differences in location for the k factor-level populations. The corresponding hypotheses are

H_0: the k populations have identical probability distributions

H_a: at least two of the populations differ in location

PROCEDURE.   The k observations *within each block* are rank ordered, using the usual procedure of assigning the average of the tied positions in the event of ties within a block. Of course, this step is omitted if ordinal data are obtained initially, such as asking 50 people to rank order four particular products (or brands) according to a specified set of criteria. For this illustration, you would have $b = 50$ blocks and $k = 4$ populations defined by the four products. In addition, to remove potential bias introduced by fatigue, familiarity, and so on, the order in which the four brands are evaluated should be *randomly* determined for each person.

Define $T_i =$ the total of the ranks for the ith population. The test statistic for the Friedman test is defined as

$$FR = \frac{12}{bk(k+1)} \sum_{i=1}^{k} T_i^2 - 3b(k+1) \qquad (19.14)$$

where $b =$ number of blocks and $k =$ number of factor levels (populations).

The distribution of the FR statistic approximately follows a chi-square distribution with $k - 1$ df. This approximation works well provided the number of blocks (b) or the number of factor levels (k) exceeds five. Like the Kruskal-Wallis test procedure, the Friedman test procedure is to reject H_0 if FR lies in the right-tail of the chi-square curve; that is,

reject H_0 if $FR > \chi^2_{\alpha,df}$

where $\chi^2_{\alpha,df}$ is the value from Table A.6 corresponding to df $= k - 1$ and right-tail area $= \alpha$. This procedure is summarized in the accompanying box.

THE FRIEDMAN TEST

Hypotheses:

H_0: the k populations have identical probability distributions

H_a: at least two of the populations differ in location

Assumptions:

1. The factor levels are applied in a random manner within each block.
2. The number of blocks (b) or the number of factor levels (k) exceeds five.
3. Values within each block can be ranked.

Procedure: Values are ranked within each block. Letting $T_i =$ sum of the ranks within the ith factor level, the FR statistic is calculated using equation 19.14. The null hypothesis is rejected if

$$FR > \chi^2_{\alpha,df}$$

where $\chi^2_{\alpha,df}$ is the chi-square value (Table A.6) with df $= k - 1$ and right-tail area $= \alpha$.

EXAMPLE 19.9

In a study of the perceived attractiveness of new car warranties, a newspaper writer sent the warranties of three competing brands of automobiles (Starfire, RX1000, and Bullet) to 10 different editors of automotive magazines. At first, it was decided to have each editor assign a score from 0 (worst) to 100 (best) for each of the three warranties and use a randomized block analysis. Here the ten editors would represent the $b = 10$ blocks, and the factor of interest would be brand of automobile, consisting of $k = 3$ levels. However, after much discussion, it became clear that each editor had his or her own set of criteria for judging a warranty, not to mention different weights for each of these various criteria.

Consequently, it was decided simply to ask each editor to rank the three warranties, rather than determine a score for each one. The warranties were assigned in a random manner for each editor. The results are summarized in Table 19.9. Use the Friedman test and a

---

TABLE 19.9

Results of new-car warranty ranking (Example 19.9).

Starfire	RX1000	Bullet
3	2	1
2	1	3
3	1	2
2	1	3
3	2	1
2	1	3
1	2	3
2	1	3
3	1	2
1	2	3
$T_1 = 22$	$T_2 = 14$	$T_3 = 24$

significance level of .10 to determine if there is a difference in the perceived quality of the three warranties.

SOLUTION

The computed value of the Friedman statistic is

$$FR = \frac{12}{(10)(3)(4)}[22^2 + 14^2 + 24^2] - 3(10)(4) = 125.6 - 120 = 5.6$$

Referring to the chi-square table (A.6), using $k - 1 = 2$ df and right-tail area $= .10$, the test procedure is to

$$\text{reject } H_0 \text{ if } FR > 4.60517$$

Since $5.6 > 4.60517$, we reject H_0 and conclude that there *is* a difference in the perceived quality of the three warranties. The apparent reason for this result is the fact that the RX1000 warranty was ranked first or second by all 10 editors and far outranked the warranties for the Starfire and the Bullet.

An Excel solution for Example 19.9 is shown in Figure 19.11. Select **Comparing More than Two Groups** and click on **Friedman Test** and then on **OK.** To carry out the test, enter "A1" as the **Upper Left Corner of the Sample Data,** "D1" as the **Output Range,** "3" as the **Number of Factor Levels,** and "10" as the **Number of Blocks.** Be sure to select **Each Row is a Block** (this is the default selection) since the rows constitute the blocks. From Figure 19.11, the computed chi-square value is once again equal to 5.6, and the corresponding *p*-value is .0608. This *p*-value indicates a fairly weak result, but one that is statistically significant at a level of $\alpha = .10$. As in the previous solution, the conclusion here is that there is a difference in the perceived quality of the three warranties.

FIGURE 19.11

Excel solution to Example 19.9 using the Friedman test within **KGP Data Analysis ➤ Nonparametric Procedures.**

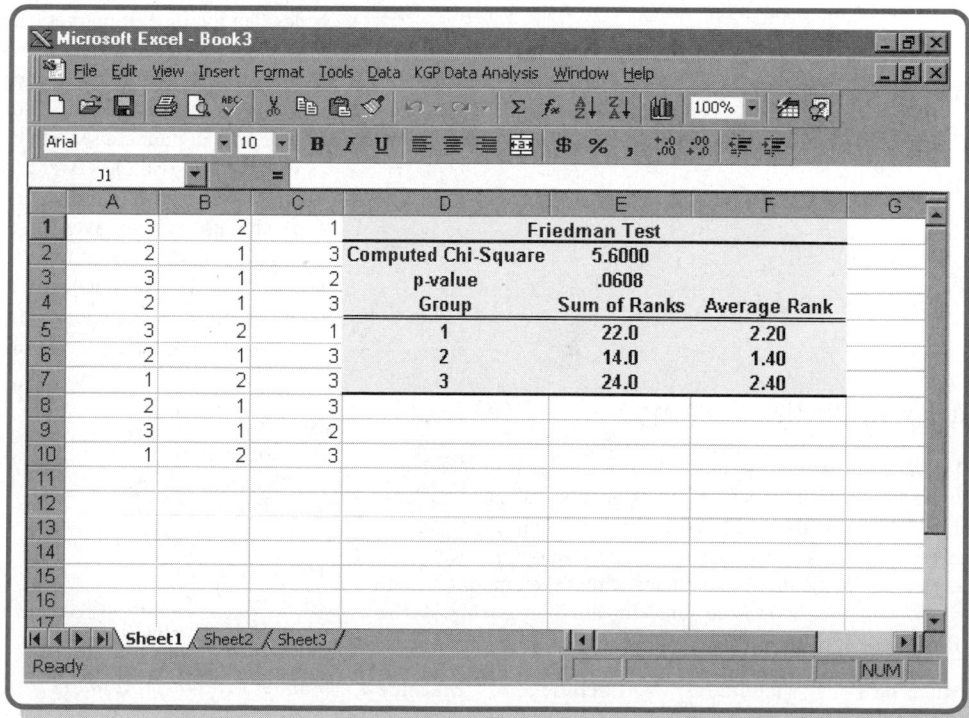

EXERCISES 19.36–19.54

UNDERSTANDING THE MECHANICS

19.36 Samples of size 5 are randomly selected from four populations. A Kruskal-Wallis test is used to test if at least two of the populations differ in location. The sums of the ranks for samples 1, 2, 3, and 4 are 69, 34, 32, and 75, respectively. Do these data indicate a difference in the locations of at least two populations? Use a significance level of .05.

19.37 Use the Kruskal-Wallis statistic on the following data to determine if at least two populations differ in location. Use a .10 significance level.

Sample from Population 1	Sample from Population 2	Sample from Population 3
3.9	1.7	4.6
2.6	2.1	2.3
2.5	2.3	2.1
3.8	3.4	3.8
2.2	1.8	1.5
4.4	3.1	3.1
2.0	2.9	2.3
1.9	2.8	2.6

19.38 A randomized block design is used to analyze data from a single factor with three levels and with the sample data organized into 10 blocks. The totals of the ranks of the sample from populations 1, 2, and 3 are $T_1 = 20$, $T_2 = 14$, and $T_3 = 26$, respectively. Determine if there is a difference in location for at least two of the populations. Use the Friedman test with a .05 significance level.

19.39 The data presented here are collected using a randomized block design. Conduct a Friedman test to determine if at least two of the populations differ in location. Use a .10 significance level.

Block	A	B	C
1	15	28	31
2	10	11	15
3	5	9	3
4	10	3	8
5	39	41	50
6	16	13	18
7	27	23	25
8	2	2	9
9	1	6	12

APPLYING THE NEW CONCEPTS

19.40 Four machines are used to package 16-ounce bags of puffed wheat. Each machine is designed to package the bags so that the average bag has 16 ounces of cereal in it. From the data, in which samples of eight bags were randomly selected from each machine, is there an indication that the amount of puffed wheat packaged is not the same for all four machines? Use a .05 significance level.

Machine 1	Machine 2	Machine 3	Machine 4
15.9	16.1	15.8	16.4
15.8	16.3	15.9	16.5

Machine 1	Machine 2	Machine 3	Machine 4
16.0	16.0	16.0	16.0
15.7	15.9	16.1	16.1
16.1	16.4	16.0	16.4
16.2	15.8	16.4	16.3
15.6	16.2	16.1	16.1
15.8	16.1	15.7	16.4

19.41 Thirty new employees were selected to test two training programs. Ten of them (group A) were randomly selected for a self-paced training program. Another 10 (group B) were randomly selected for a classroom training program. The remaining 10 employees (group C) were not given any training. After the completion of the experiment, the manager evaluated the 30 employees on their productivity over a two-week span. The following ranks were given by the manager, with the highest rankings being given to those who were not productive.

Program A	Program B	Program C
6	5	1
22	21	10
25	15	11
26	4	13
20	8	2
30	12	3
16	18	7
23	24	14
28	27	17
9	29	19

From the data, is there a difference in the productivity of the three groups? Use a .05 significance level.

19.42 Mark Hulbert, editor of *Hulbert Financial Digest,* concedes that the type of market letter you want to follow during a bull market is one that recommends taking certain risks. But he is quick to point out that those gains can quickly evaporate during a down market if an investor continues to take such risks. That is why certain conservative investment styles can perform as well as high-risk ones over a long cycle. The following table shows a sample of newsletters that can be categorized as endorsing either high, average, or low risks. Each newsletter's performance is measured over an 11-year period ending January 1, 1999. Do the data provide sufficient evidence that the returns from these categories of stock market newsletters differ? Use a 5% significance level.

Newsletter	Performance in Percentage	Category of Risk
Addison-Report	8.4	Low
BI Research	11.6	High
Big Picture	7.1	High
Bob Brinker's Market Timer	8.8	Average
Cabot Market Letter	6.2	High
Chartist	15.0	High
Dow Theory Forecasts	9.5	Average
Equities Special Situations	4.2	High
Fabian Investment Resource	10.6	Low
Fidelity Monitor	15.1	Average

Newsletter	Performance in Percentage	Category of Risk
Fund Advice.com	10.1	Low
Fundline	14.8	Average
Granville Market Letter	−16.6	High
Growth Stock Outlook	6.8	Low
Insiders	13.2	High
Investment Quality Trends	13.6	Low
Investment Reporter	11.3	High
LaLoggie's Special Situation Investor	5.2	Average
Margo's Small Stocks	5.4	High
Market Logic	6.9	Average
Medical Technology Stock Letter	1.3	High
Mutual Fund Forecaster	10.1	Average
Mutual Fund Investing	7.6	Low
Mutual Fund Strategists	7.7	Average
No-Load Fund X	11.5	Average
Professional Tape Reader	1.1	Low
Systems and Forecasts	12.2	Low

(Source: Adapted from *Forbes*, "The Forbes/Hulbert Investment Letter Survey," Jan. 25, 1999, p. 112–13.)

19.43 The management of a company that markets Soft and Fresh Detergent would like to increase sales of detergent by including a free drinking glass in the box, including a coupon worth 50 cents toward the next purchase, or using a colorful see-through plastic container for the detergent. Thirty stores in different cities were randomly selected to market the detergent in one of the three ways (10 stores for each way). The number of boxes sold in these stores over a one-month period follows. Do the data indicate a difference in the number of boxes sold for each of the marketing strategies? Use a 5% significance level.

Free Glass	Coupon	See-Through Plastic Container
350	320	374
310	315	371
250	300	332
380	315	361
290	390	356
270	311	349
340	318	331
310	330	322
290	340	368
375	314	351

19.44 The number of hours it takes three workers to complete a task is given in the following table. The task is assigned to each worker four times. Do the data indicate a significant difference in the time it takes each worker to complete the task? Use a significance level of .05.

Worker 1	Worker 2	Worker 3
3.1	3.4	3.5
3.4	3.3	3.2
3.0	3.4	3.3
3.1	3.2	3.1

19.45 The number of cars passing each of three different intersections in Crossroads City between 5:00 P.M. and 5:30 P.M. is given in the following table for randomly selected days. Fifteen days were randomly selected, and then the amount of traffic was recorded for 5 of the 15 days at each intersection. Test the null hypothesis that there is no difference in the amount of traffic at each intersection between 5:00 P.M. and 5:30 P.M. Use a 10% significance level.

Intersection 1	Intersection 2	Intersection 3
440	480	433
420	392	406
530	386	427
401	456	338
454	427	397

19.46 A manager believes that the higher-salaried employees in a certain company are more satisfied with their jobs than are the lower-salaried employees. A sample of 10 employees from each of the salary levels indicated by the following table was taken. Is there a significant difference in the satisfaction level, measured on a scale of 1 to 10 (10 being a perfectly satisfied employee), for the three groups? Use a significance level of 5%.

$25,000 to $40,000	$40,000 to $60,000	Over $60,000
4	7	8
3	8	7
7	6	6
6	7	7
5	9	5
9	3	9
1	4	10
8	9	3
7	6	8
6	7	7

19.47 The yields on short-term, tax-exempt mutual funds have tended to fluctuate less than intermediate and long-term bond funds. A money manager is interested in whether the annualized compounded percentage given in short-term tax-exempt mutual funds differs over the one-year period, the three-year period, and the five-year period ending on January 1, 1999. Do the following data (measured in percentage annualized returns) indicate a difference in the performance of short-term, tax-exempt mutual funds over these three periods of time? Use a 5% significance level.

Short-Term, Tax-Exempt Mutual Fund	1-Year Performance	3-Year Performance	5-Year Performance
CMA Tax-Exempt	2.98	3.22	3.18
Smith Barney Muni MM	2.94	3.12	3.15
Vanguard Muni: Tax-Exempt	3.34	3.54	3.59
Fidelity Muni MM	3.13	3.36	3.52
Schwab: Muni MM	2.92	3.07	3.09
Paine Weber RMA Tax-Free	2.93	3.08	3.10
Fidelity Spartan Muni MM	3.26	3.12	3.52
Strong Muni MM	3.54	3.69	3.80
Active Assets Tax-Free	2.95	3.13	3.14
Centennial Tax-Free	2.95	3.13	3.14

(Source: Adapted from *The Wall Street Journal*, "Fund Performance Derby," Jan. 22, 1999, p. C21.)

19.48 In Exercise 11.7, can you conclude that there is a significant difference in the monthly sales of the three salespeople, using the Kruskal-Wallis test statistic? Use a 5% significance level. When would you prefer the Kruskal-Wallis test to the usual ANOVA procedure?

19.49 The vice president of quality assurance at an airline company is interested in whether its three quality engineers are usually in agreement on the ratings they give to different airplane seating designs. Seven different designs are chosen at random and the quality engineers are asked to rate the comfort to the passengers on a scale from 1 to 10, with 10 representing the highest level of comfort possible. Do the given data indicate a difference in the ratings of the three quality engineers? Use a .10 significance level.

Design	Quality Engineer 1	Quality Engineer 2	Quality Engineer 3
1	5	7	8
2	4	3	5
3	6	5	4
4	9	7	8
5	5	7	4
6	8	7	6
7	9	6	8

19.50 The manager at a manufacturing plant is interested in whether there is a significant difference in the number of times four machines need to be readjusted after going out of control. Eight months are randomly selected, and the number of times the machines are readjusted per month is recorded. Do the data support the conclusion that some machines need more adjusting than others? Use a .05 significance level.

Month	Machine 1	Machine 2	Machine 3	Machine 4
1	5	6	3	6
2	4	3	7	5
3	4	5	6	3
4	5	3	4	7
5	4	4	5	6
6	10	11	9	11
7	15	18	13	16
8	3	4	5	4

Using the Computer

19.51 [DATA SET EX19-51] *Variable description:*

Supplier1Rating: Rating by supervisor on the quality of parts supplied by supplier 1
Supplier2Rating: Rating by supervisor on the quality of parts supplied by supplier 2
Supplier3Rating: Rating by supervisor on the quality of parts supplied by supplier 3

The vice president of an industrial firm wished to determine if the supervisors in the firm's manufacturing plant perceived a difference in the quality of parts provided by three suppliers.

Sixty supervisors were randomly selected to participate in the study, and twenty of the supervisors were assigned to rate a particular supplier. The supervisors responded with a number between 1 and 7, where 1 represented the "highest quality" and 7 represented the "lowest quality." What conclusion can you draw from the standard, one-way ANOVA and from the Kruskal-Wallis test? Use a 5% significance level.

19.52 [DATA SET EX19-52] *Variable description:*

NonExporter: Knowledge level of international trade regulations and barriers by companies that do not export
MarginalExporter: Knowledge level of international trade regulations and barriers by companies that do some exporting
ActiveExporter: Knowledge level of international trade regulations and barriers by companies that export most of their products

International marketing researchers conducted a study to determine if there is a difference in the knowledge level of companies that were classified as doing no exporting, some exporting, or high levels of exporting. A scale from 1 to 10 was used to measure the degree of perceived knowledge of international trade. Thirty companies were selected for NonExporter and MarginalExporter, while 25 companies were selected for ActiveExporter. Using an appropriate nonparametric test, what conclusion can you draw? Use a 1% significance level.

19.53 [DATA SET EX19-53] *Variable description:*

StoreNum: A number from 1 through 20 to indicate the convenience store
Quarter1Sales: Sales during quarter 1
Quarter2Sales: Sales during quarter 2
Quarter3Sales: Sales during quarter 3
Quarter4Sales: Sales during quarter 4

The president of a chain of convenience stores is interested in determining if a difference exists in the sales of its stores over the four quarters of last year. A random sample of 20 convenience stores was selected. Can the president conclude from this sample that a difference exists in the quarterly sales of the convenience stores? Use a 5% significance level.

19.54 [DATA SET EX19-54] *Variable description:*

EngineerNum: A number from 1 through 30 indicating a particular engineer
Task1Time: Completion time for task 1
Task2Time: Completion time for task 2
Task3Time: Completion time for task 3
Task4Time: Completion time for task 4

A manager is interested in the time required for mechanical engineers to complete four types of tasks. Thirty mechanical engineers are randomly selected. Each engineer completes the four tasks and the times are recorded. Compare the results using a randomized block design and using the Friedman test. What conclusions can you make? Base your decisions on the *p*-value.

19.4 A MEASURE OF ASSOCIATION: SPEARMAN'S RANK CORRELATION

Whenever you encounter data describing two variables (say, X and Y), one measure of interest is the degree of **association** between X and Y. Are large values of X associated with large values of Y (a *positive* relationship)? Or do you observe smaller values of Y with larger values of X (a *negative* relationship)? Another possibility is that no relationship is observed between these two variables.

Consider the following data, in which a sample of ten families is used to determine the relationship (if any) that exists between X = market value of the family's home and Y = their total indebtedness (excluding the home mortgage; in thousands of dollars). Included in Y are any charge accounts, automobile loans, and other current liabilities.

Family	X (Market Value of Home)	Y (Total Indebtedness)
1	85	12
2	147	27
3	340	45
4	94	10
5	120	17
6	105	4
7	135	20
8	162	25
9	480	35
10	88	14

The president of Metro Savings and Loan believes that larger home values are associated with larger indebtedness, that is, a positive relationship exists between these two variables. His belief is confirmed by the scatter plot contained in Figure 19.12.

FIGURE 19.12

Excel scatter plot of home value versus debt.

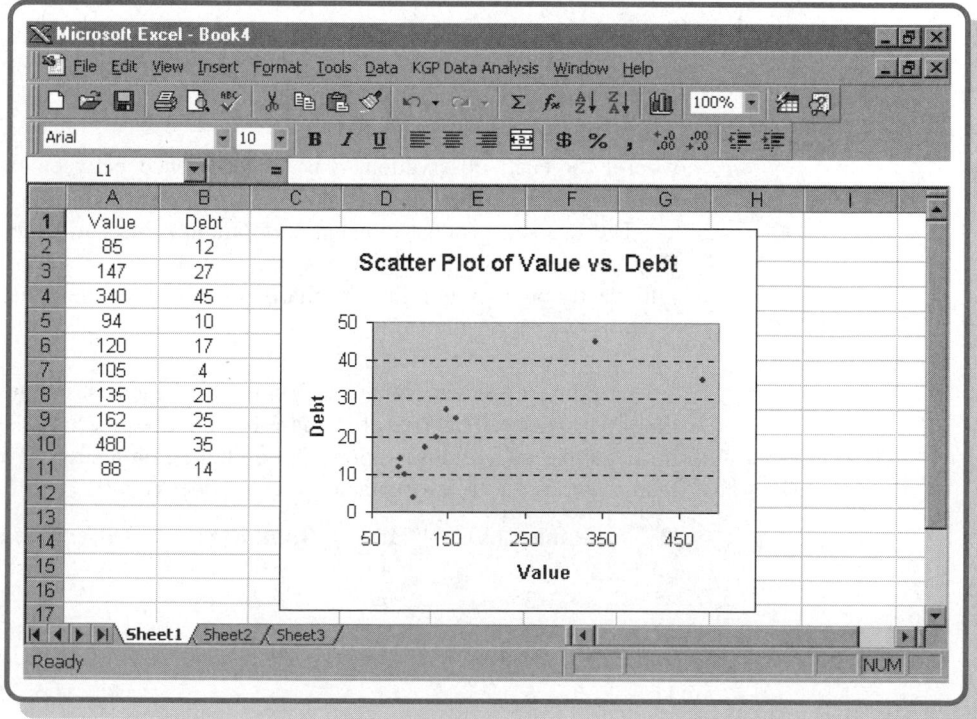

One method of measuring the association between two variables is the correlation coefficient, r, introduced in Chapter 14; r is also referred to as the Pearson product moment correlation. The equation used to determine this measure is

$$r = \frac{\sum xy - (\sum x)(\sum y)/n}{\sqrt{\sum x^2 - (\sum x)^2/n} \sqrt{\sum y^2 - (\sum y)^2/n}}$$ (19.15)

where n represents the number of observations (pairs).

The value of r, often called the *sample correlation coefficient,* measures the amount of linearity that exists between the sample values of X and Y. It is used to estimate ρ (rho), the *population* correlation coefficient. The value of ρ can be thought of as the correlation between *all* possible X, Y pairs, not just those contained in the sample.

In the previous discussions, a significant relationship between X and Y existed if we were able to reject H_0: $\rho = 0$. The test statistic here was a t statistic, so this test assumes a normal distribution for the X, Y variables.

An alternative to this procedure is a measure of association derived from the *ranks* of the X and Y variables. *This nonparametric measure does not assume a normal distribution; it assumes only that the values within the X and Y samples can be ranked.* For data such as the home price versus debt values, each of the X and Y values can also be replaced by their ranks. If we use these ranks in place of the actual data in equation 19.15, we obtain another measure of association, called the **Spearman rank correlation coefficient, r_s:**

$$r_s = \frac{\sum R(x)R(y) - [\sum R(x)][\sum R(y)]/n}{\sqrt{\sum R^2(x) - [\sum R(x)]^2/n} \sqrt{\sum R^2(y) - [\sum R(y)]^2/n}}$$ (19.16)

where $R(x)$ = rank of the X observation and $R(y)$ = rank of the Y observation.

If there are no ties, a second formula provides a much easier method of finding r_s. If there are a few ties, this formula still serves as a very good approximation to r_s. The short-cut method of finding r_s is

$$r_s = 1 - \frac{6\sum d^2}{n(n^2 - 1)}$$ (19.17)

where, for each observation, d is the difference between the X and Y ranks; that is, $d = R(x) - R(y)$.

The Pearson product moment correlation, r, measures the amount of *linear* relationship between X and Y and ranges from -1 to 1. Also, $r = 1$ or -1 only if all of the points fall exactly on a straight line. Similarly, the range for the Spearman rank correlation is

$$-1 \leq r_s \leq 1$$

One difference here is that r_s will equal 1 if Y increases in the sample observations every time X increases. This rate of increase need not be linear, as is illustrated in Figure 19.13 for a sample of five observations that do not lie on a straight line. Consequently, r is less than 1 but, as the following table shows, r_s does equal 1.

X	Rank $R(X)$	Y	Rank $R(Y)$	Difference of Ranks (d)	d^2
3	1	4	1	$1 - 1 = 0$	0
5	2	7	2	$2 - 2 = 0$	0
7	3	8	3	$3 - 3 = 0$	0
9	4	10	4	$4 - 4 = 0$	0
11	5	16	5	$5 - 5 = 0$	0
					$\sum d^2 = \overline{0}$

FIGURE 19.13

Measure of association. Pearson product moment correlation, r, and Spearman rank correlation, r_s.

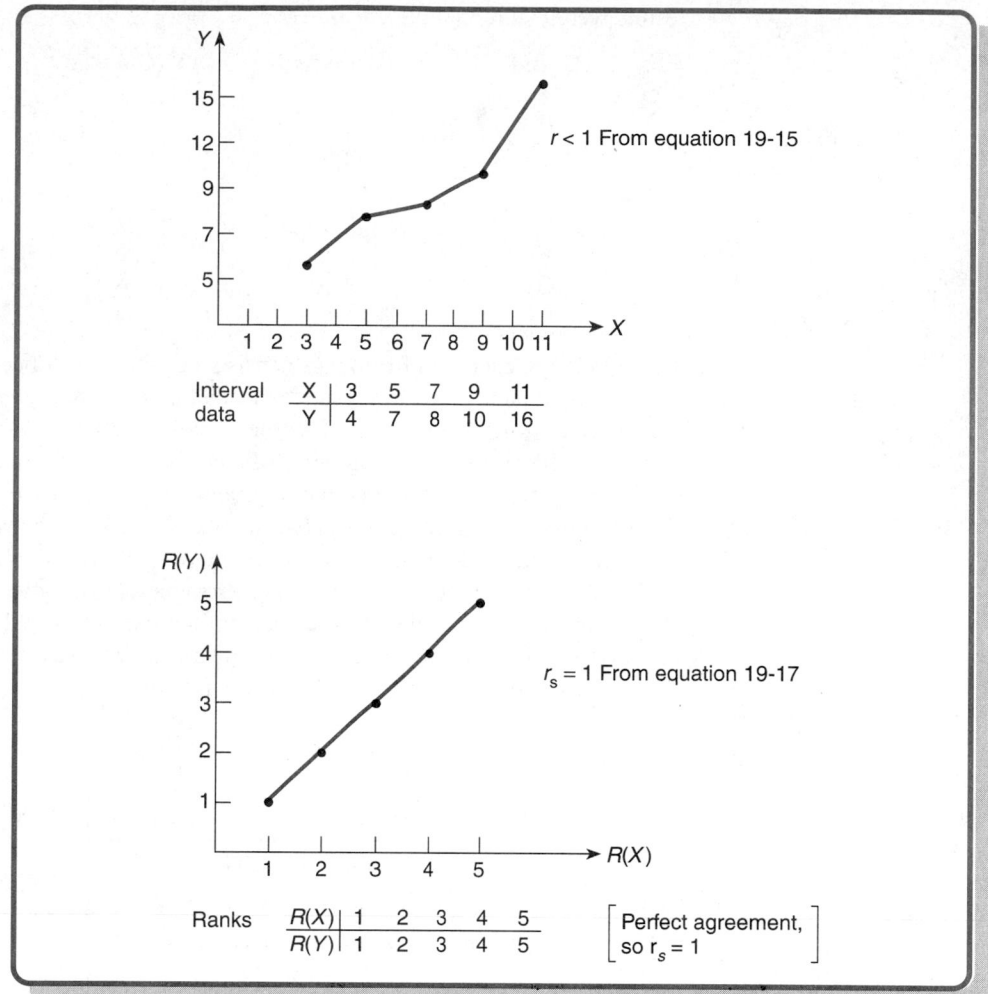

Interval data

X	3	5	7	9	11
Y	4	7	8	10	16

Ranks

R(X)	1	2	3	4	5
R(Y)	1	2	3	4	5

$$\begin{bmatrix} \text{Perfect agreement,} \\ \text{so } r_s = 1 \end{bmatrix}$$

You can also see in Figure 19.13 that the pairwise ranks *are* perfectly linear; this is why $r_s = 1$.

$$r_s = 1 - \frac{6 \sum d^2}{n(n^2 - 1)}$$

$$= 1 - \frac{(6)(0)}{(5)(24)} = 1$$

When it is possible to calculate both, the values of r and r_s are generally not the same, although they are usually quite close and they will have the same sign. A positive value indicates a *positive* relationship between the two variables. Similarly, if r_s and r are negative, then a *negative* relationship exists (Y decreases as X increases). If the values of r and r_s are nearly the same, there is usually high linearity between the two variables.

As we discussed earlier, *nonparametric methods are well suited for situations in which (1) the data are* ordinal *or (2) the distribution of the population(s) from which the data are obtained is suspected to be nonnormal.* When using data of the ordinal type, it is no longer appropriate to use the Pearson coefficient of correlation (r) to perform a t test to determine whether a significant linear relationship exists. This procedure requires interval or ratio data. Similarly, when dealing with nonnormal populations, the t test is no longer valid because the normality assumption is a vital part of this procedure.

Suppose that Mr. Roberts and Mr. Clauson each evaluated eight brands of television sets by inspecting eight different sets. After inspecting the sets, rather than assigning each of them a score of some kind, they merely ranked them from 1 (best) to 8 (worst). The results were

Brand	X (Roberts)	Y (Clauson)	Difference
A	1	2	−1
B	4	3	1
C	2	1	1
D	6	6	0
E	8	7	1
F	3	5	−2
G	7	8	−1
H	5	4	1

Notice that each set of rankings consists of ordinal data because the only meaningful information contained within these values is the *order*, not the difference between them. For example, Mr. Roberts' three favorite brands were brands A (first), C (second), and F (third). We have no way of knowing whether brand A was much better than brand C or only slightly better; the same is true for brand C versus brand F. Consequently, there is no way of knowing if the distances between ranks 1 and 2 and between ranks 2 and 3 are the same, and so these differences are meaningless.

The Spearman rank correlation, r_s, is also a measure of how well the two people agree. The larger this value is, the more agreement there is between the two sets of rankings. A value of $r_s = 1$ would indicate perfect agreement, whereas perfect disagreement would result in a value of $r_s = -1$. Here the rank correlation is

$$r_s = 1 - \frac{6 \sum d^2}{n(n^2 - 1)}$$

$$= 1 - \frac{6[(-1)^2 + (1)^2 + \cdots + (-1)^2 + (1)^2]}{8(64 - 1)} = 1 - \frac{(6)(10)}{(8)(63)} = .881$$

This value appears to be quite large, although we will need a formal testing procedure to determine whether there is *significant* agreement between the two testers (discussed next).

EXAMPLE 19.10

Refer to the table for the home values and debt data. The president of Metro Savings and Loan would like a measure of association between these two variables. Based on past experience, he is reluctant to assume that the home values are normally distributed; they usually are skewed right. There generally are enough homes with an extremely large market value (two, here) to produce a skewed distribution (see Figure 19.12). He asks you to use the Spearman measure of correlation and determine the value of r_s.

SOLUTION

The ranks are calculated as follows:

Family	X	Rank $R(X)$	Y	Rank $R(Y)$	Difference (d)	d^2
1	85	(1)	12	(3)	−2	4
2	147	(7)	27	(8)	−1	1
3	340	(9)	45	(10)	−1	1
4	94	(3)	10	(2)	1	1
5	120	(5)	17	(5)	0	0
6	105	(4)	4	(1)	3	9
7	135	(6)	20	(6)	0	0
8	162	(8)	25	(7)	1	1
9	480	(10)	35	(9)	1	1
10	88	(2)	14	(4)	−2	4

$$\sum d^2 = 22$$

Then,

$$r_2 = 1 - \frac{(6)(22)}{(10)(99)} = .867$$

Based on this value, it appears that a significant positive relationship exists between the market value of a family's home and their total debts.

To determine whether a derived value of r_s is "large enough" to support a conclusion, as in Example 19.10, we develop a test of hypothesis that uses the rank correlation, r_s, as the test statistic.

To obtain the Excel solution for Spearman's rank correlation in Figure 19.14, click on **KGP Data Analysis ➤ Nonparametric Procedures.** Select **Regression/Correlation Analysis** and click on **Spearman Rank Correlation.** Enter "A2:B11" as the **Input Range** and "C1" as the **Output Range.** The value of r_s from Figure 19.14 agrees exactly with the previous result, since there were no ties within the X and Y values. The Excel calculated value uses equation 19.16 rather than the easier-to-calculate-by-hand equation 19.17.

A TEST FOR HYPOTHESIS USING THE RANK CORRELATION

In Chapter 14, we used the Pearson correlation coefficient, r, to determine whether a linear relationship existed between two variables, X and Y. This relationship could be either positive (Y increases as X increases) or negative (Y decreases as X increases). When using Spearman's rank correlation, r_s, we drop the word "linear" in the hypotheses and test

H_0: no association exists between the X and Y variables

H_a: association does exist between the X and Y variables

You can also perform one-sided tests, as summarized in the accompanying box. In this way, you can test for a significant positive or negative relationship between the two variables.

FIGURE 19.14

Spearman rank correlation using Excel and **KGP Data Analysis ➤ Nonparametric Procedures.**

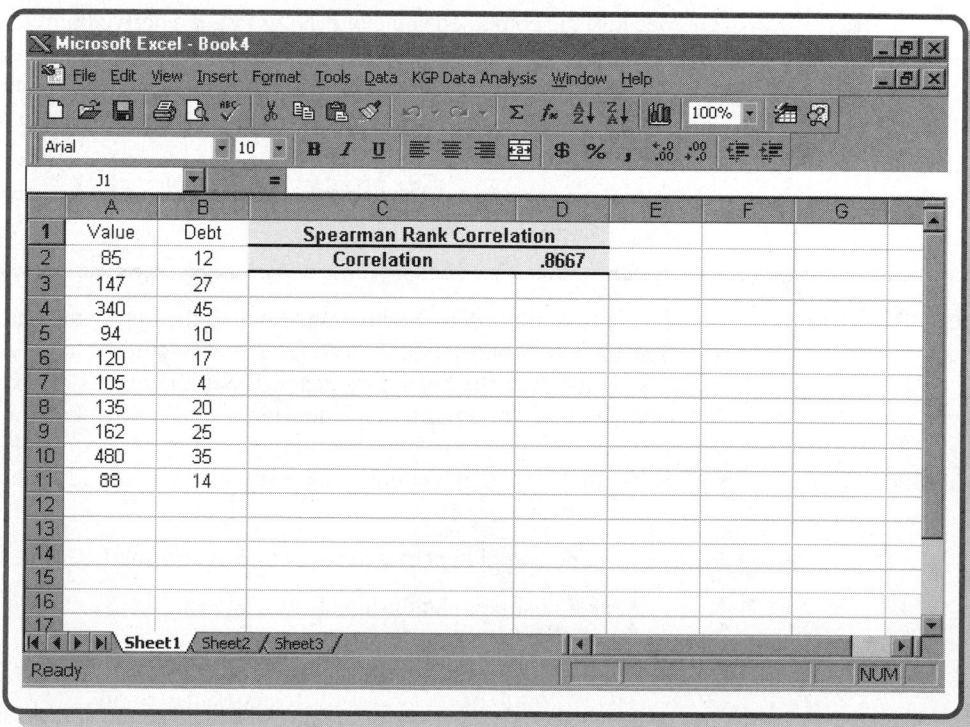

THE SPEARMAN TEST FOR RANK CORRELATION

Two-Sided Test

H_0: no association exists between X and Y

H_a: association does exist between X and Y

Assumption: Sample values for each variable can be ranked.

Procedure: Determine the value from Table A.12 using the sample size, n, and the column corresponding to $\alpha/2$.

Reject H_0 if $|r_s| >$ (table value).

One-Sided Test

H_0: no association exists between X and Y

H_a: a positive relationship exists between X and Y

Use the column in Table A.12 corresponding to α.

Reject H_0 if $r_s >$ (table value).

H_0: no association exists between X and Y

H_a: a negative relationship exists between X and Y

Use the column in Table A.12 corresponding to α.

Reject H_0 if $r_s < -$(table value).

EXAMPLE 19.11

In the television-ranking example, is there sufficient evidence to indicate that there was general agreement between the rankings made by Mr. Roberts and those made by Mr. Clauson? Use $\alpha = .05$.

SOLUTION

The appropriate hypotheses here are

H_0: no association exists between the two ranks

H_a: a positive association exists between the two ranks

According to Table A.12, using $\alpha = .05$ and $n = 8$, the testing procedure is to

reject H_0 if $r_s > .643$

Because the computed value of r_s is .881 (as we derived previously), we reject H_0 and conclude that there *was* significant agreement between the two sets of rankings.

The p-value for this result can be obtained by looking across the row in Table A.12 corresponding to $n = 8$. Here we find that .881 corresponds to $\alpha = .005$. Consequently, the p-value here is .005.

EXAMPLE 19.12

The president of Metro Savings and Loan is attempting to demonstrate that a positive relationship exists between $X =$ market value of a family's home and $Y =$ their total indebtedness (excluding the home mortgage). Using the results of Example 19.10, is there sufficient evidence of a positive relationship between these two variables? Use $\alpha = .05$.

SOLUTION

In Example 19.10, the sample rank correlation was found to be $r_s = .867$. Using Table A.12 for $\alpha = .05$ and $n = 10$, we test

H_0: no association exists between the home market value and total indebtedness

H_a: a positive relationship exists

using

reject H_0 if $r_s > .564$

The computed value of .867 exceeds the table value, so we reject H_0 and conclude that there is a tendency for larger values of $X =$ home value and $Y =$ family indebtedness to be paired together. This large value of r_s also is off the right side of Table A.12, indicating that for this test the p-value is <.005. This extremely small value is strong evidence of a positive relationship between these two variables.

EXERCISES 19.55–19.65

UNDERSTANDING THE MECHANICS

19.55 The rank correlation between 15 pairs of observations is .42. Using a .05 significance level, determine if a positive relationship exists between the two variables sampled.

19.56 Consider the following 13 pairs of observations. Calculate the Spearman rank correlation. Determine if an association exists between the X and Y variables. Use a .10 significance level.

X	Y
78	4
370	25
150	15
125	10
90	4
110	7
84	2
290	35
135	17
75	3
130	11
380	26
140	18

19.57 Using the following data, is there sufficient evidence to conclude that a positive association exists between the ranks of the X variable and the ranks of the Y variable at the .05 significance level?

X	Y
78	36
80	42
82	41
83	45
74	30
75	28
76	30
81	38
80	39

APPLYING THE NEW CONCEPTS

19.58 A factory wants to know what the relationship is between the age of its machines and the number of breakdowns per year. Ten machines were selected at random, and the following table was constructed. Using the Spearman test for rank correlation, is there a relationship between the age of the machine and the number of breakdowns per year? Use a 10% significance level.

Age (Years)	Breakdowns per Year	Age (Years)	Breakdowns per Year
2	6	7	20
4	10	5	16
5	12	6	15
8	24	3	10
6	17	4	12

19.59 A physician would like to know the relationship between a person's diastolic blood pressure and the average number of hours spent exercising each week. Twenty people of age 30 years were selected randomly. Is there an indication from the data that there may be a negative relationship between exercise and blood pressure? Test with the Spearman test for rank correlation, and use a 1% significance level.

Diastolic Blood Pressure	Hours Exercised	Diastolic Blood Pressure	Hours Exercised
74	9	80	8
70	10	64	18
62	16	56	20
58	15	68	10
82	6	72	11
84	3	78	8
90	0	84	7
84	4	88	4
72	12	70	12
70	9	66	15

19.60 Between 1991 and 1993, Rolls-Royce Motor Company increased productivity 30%. During that period, cars spent only 32 days in the factory instead of the more traditional 76 days. The number of man-hours required to assemble a Jaguar was reduced to 251, down from 418 only two years before that. Today most Rolls-Royce cars and Jaguars are sold in the United States. A breakdown of the markets for these cars is presented here.

	Number of Cars Sold	
Market in 1992	**Jaguar**	**Rolls**
U.S.	8681	392
Britain	5607	382
Europe (continental)	5025	294
Japan	1501	91
Asia and Africa	740	134
Middle East	250	67

(Source: Adapted from "Shaking Up Jaguar," *Fortune*, Sept. 6, 1993, pp. 65–68.)

a. Calculate the Pearson product moment correlation of the number of Jaguars and Rolls Royces sold in different parts of the world.

b. Calculate the Spearman rank correlation coefficient for the number of Jaguars and Rolls Royces sold in different parts of the world.

c. Suppose the number of Rolls Royces sold in the United States was 1500 instead of 392. What would be the values of the correlations in parts (a) and (b)? Which correlation is affected the most by this change in the number of Rolls Royces sold in the United States?

19.61 The rankings for 10 of the best-selling books in 1997 are presented below.

Ranking for the Week of Dec. 21, 1997	Ranking for the Week of Dec. 14, 1997	Book Title/Author
1	1	*Don't Sweat the Small Stuff* By Carlson
2	2	*Cold Mountain* By Frazier
3	4	*Midnight in the Garden of Good and Evil* By Berendt
4	5	*Chicken Soup for the Mother's Soul* By Canfield, Hansen, Hawthorne, Shimoff
5	3	*Chicken Soup for the Teenage Soul* By Canfield, Hansen, Hawthorne, Shimoff
6	8	*Angela's Ashes* By Frank McCourt
7	9	*Dark Tower IV: Wizard and Glass* By Stephen King
8	6	*Joy of Cooking* By Rombauer, M. Becker, and E. Becker
9	7	*Chicken Soup for the Woman's Soul* By Canfield, Hansen, Hawthorne, and Shimoff
10	10	*Power Plays: Politika* By Clancy and Greenberg

Test the null hypothesis that there is a positive relationship between the rankings of the top-selling books for the week of Dec. 14 and the week of Dec. 21, 1997. Use a .05 significance level.

(Source: Adapted from *USA Today,* "Best-Selling Books," Dec. 31, 1997, p. 5D.)

19.62 A supervisor at a computer firm wanted to determine whether a relationship existed between the level of an employee's job satisfaction (measured from 1 to 10) and the number of years the employee has been employed with the firm. Test the null hypothesis that there is no relationship and use a 10% significance level.

Level of Satisfaction	Number of Years Employed at the Firm
6	1
3	5
7	10
5	12
8	6
4	5
3	2
9	10
7	7
8	12
7	16

Using the Computer

19.63 [DATA SET EX19-63] *Variable description:*

Economist: Name of ecomonist
Bondrate: Interest rate for the 30-year bond
Unemploy: Unemployment rate

Predicting the U.S. economy has typically been a tricky game for economists and financial analysts. A survey was conducted by *The Wall Street Journal* to predict the mid-year (1999) 30-year bond's interest rate and the unemployment rate. The prediction was made by participants in December 1998. Assume that a financial strategist believes that unemployment and the 30-year bond's interest rate will move in opposite directions. Test for a negative relationship between Bondrate and Unemploy using a 5% significance level.

(Source: Adapted from *The Wall Street Journal,* "A Sampling of Interest-Rate, Economic and Currency Forecasts," Jan. 4, 1999, p. A2.)

19.64 [DATA SET EX19-64] *Variable description:*

NumNewCars: Number of new cars sold monthly
MonthlyRate: Monthly interest rate, in percent, for financing new cars

A car dealer believes there is a negative relationship between the number of cars sold monthly and the average monthly interest rate for financing new cars. Thirty months were randomly selected to obtain the data. At a 5% significance level, test the car dealer's belief using the variables NumNewCars and MonthlyRate. Why do you think the Pearson correlation is smaller than the Spearman rank correlation coefficient?

19.65 [DATA SET EX19-65] *Variable description:*

DayNum: Number from 1 through 30 identifying a particular day
MedSales: Daily sales of allergy-related, over-the-counter medicines
PollenIndex: Daily pollen index

An especially bad allergy season may drive up daily sales of over-the-counter allergy remedies. According to an article in *The Wall Street Journal* ("Gesundheit! As Allergy Season Blooms, Sniffers Take Whatever Promises Relief," Apr. 21, 1994, p. B1), about 35 million Americans suffer from rhinitis, the sneezing and runny-nose condition that results from pollen. Approximately 53% of these allergy sufferers rely on over-the-counter products for relief. Suppose a marketer wishes to determine whether a positive relationship exists between the daily pollen count and the daily allergy remedy sales at a popular pharmacy. Thirty days are randomly selected and the variables MedSales and PollenIndex are recorded. What conclusions can you make using a 5% significance level?

19.5 AN ALTERNATIVE TO THE LEAST SQUARES REGRESSION LINE: A NONPARAMETRIC APPROACH

The previous section examined the relationship between two variables using the Spearman rank correlation. This same situation was explored in Chapter 14, which discussed the calculation of the coefficient of correlation (r) for two variables, X and Y, as well as the least squares line that "best" passed through the set of sample observations. The least squares line has an interesting property—it passes through the point $(\bar{x}, \bar{y})$, where $\bar{x}$ is the mean of the X values and $\bar{y}$ is the mean of the Y values. However, when the sample data contain one or two outliers (points at a considerable distance from the remaining points), this can have a drastic effect on the least squares line. Such an outlier, in an effort to minimize the squared distances, will pull the line toward this point.

An alternative to this procedure is a line of "best fit" that passes through the **median** of the X and Y values rather than through the means. Consequently, we will force the point (median of X values, median of Y values) to lie on the new line called the **regression line through the medians.** This regression line will be much less affected by the presence of an outlier or two and will do a better job of "passing through" the remaining points. We will write the regression line through the medians as

$$\hat{Y} = B_0 + B_1 X$$

DETERMINATION OF B_0 AND B_1

The sample data consist of n points—say, point 1, point 2, . . . , point n—where the coordinates of point i are (X_i, Y_i). For points i and j, define the slope of the line connecting them to be

$$S_{ij} = \frac{Y_j - Y_i}{X_j - X_i} \tag{19.18}$$

To determine the slope of the sample regression line, B_1, we begin by determining all possible slopes, S_{ij}, for which (1) $i < j$ and (2) the denominator is non-zero—that is, $X_i \neq X_j$. If no two X values are the same, there will be $n(n-1)/2$ such S_{ij} values. Next, we arrange the S_{ij}'s in order, from smallest to largest. The *median* of these slopes is B_1—that is,

$$B_1 = \text{median of slopes, } S_{ij} \tag{19.19}$$

The intercept of this line is B_0, where

$$B_0 = (\text{median of } Y \text{ values}) - B_1 \cdot (\text{median of } X \text{ values}) \tag{19.20}$$

To illustrate, consider five points, one of which (namely, $X = 25$, $Y = 55$) appears to be an outlier.

X	5	8	12	20	25
Y	10	15	18	23	55

Using the formulas from Chapter 14, the least squares line using these five values is (see Figure 19.15)

$$\hat{Y} = -2.34 + 1.896X$$

To determine the regression line through the medians, we determine the $(5)(4)/2 = 10$ slopes, S_{ij}. These are

$$\frac{15-10}{8-5}, \frac{18-10}{12-5}, \frac{23-10}{20-5}, \frac{55-10}{25-5}, \frac{18-15}{12-8}, \frac{23-15}{20-8}, \frac{55-15}{25-8}, \frac{23-18}{20-12}, \frac{55-18}{25-12}, \frac{55-23}{25-20}$$

That is,

$$1.67, 1.14, .87, 2.25, .75, .67, 2.35, .625, 2.85, 6.4$$

FIGURE 19.15   Least squares regression line through the means and regression line through the medians.

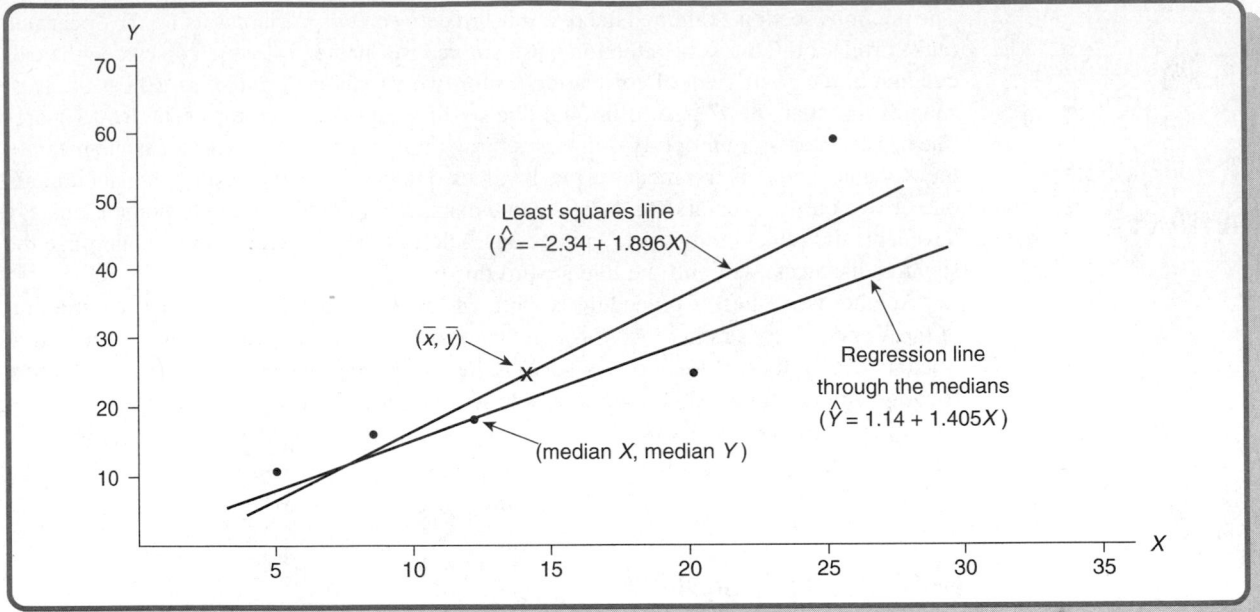

Next, we arrange these values in order:

$$.625, .67, .75, .87, \mathbf{1.14}, \mathbf{1.67}, 2.25, 2.35, 2.85, 6.4$$

The median of these ten values is

$$B_1 = \frac{1.14 + 1.67}{2} = 1.405$$

Finally, the median of the X values is 12, and the median of the Y values is 18. Consequently,

$$B_0 = 18 - (1.405)(12) = 1.14$$

The regression line through the medians is

$$\hat{Y} = 1.14 + 1.405X$$

The least squares regression line and the regression line through the medians are illustrated in Figure 19.15. Notice how the median regression line is less affected by the presence of the outlier in the upper right corner.

EXAMPLE 19.13

In Examples 19.10 and 19.12, the president of Metro Savings and Loan determined the rank correlation to be $r_s = .867$ between $X =$ market value of a family's home and $Y =$ total indebtedness (excluding the home mortgage) and concluded that a positive relationship exists between these two variables. A glance at the scatter plot in Figure 19.12 revealed two observations with large values of X (namely, $X = 340$ and $X = 480$). To lessen the impact of these two observations, it was decided to use the regression line through the medians, rather than the least squares line, for prediction purposes. Determine this line and the predicted debt for a family with a home having a market value of $250,000.

SOLUTION

The first step is to determine the $(10)(9)/2 = 45$ slopes, S_{ij}. The ordered slopes are contained in Table 19.10. The median value (the 23rd value in the center boxed location) is $B_1 = .1294$. Also, the median X value is 127.5, and the median Y value is 18.5, and so $B_0 = 18.5 - (.1294)(127.5) = 2.00$. The resulting regression line through the medians is

$$\hat{Y} = 2.00 + .1294X$$

TABLE 19.10

The 45 slopes, S_{ij}, for the home value versus debt data (Example 19.13).

−.6667	−.5882	−.5455	−.4000	−.2222
−.1333	−.0714	.0240	.0314	.0435
.0500	.0536	$\boxed{.0582}$	.0648	.0827
.0933	.0938	.1124	.1220	.1230
.1273	.1277	$\boxed{.1294}$	.1423	.1429
.1486	.1600	.1688	.1745	.1852
.1905	.2000	$\boxed{.2203}$	.2206	.2419
.2439	.2692	.3208	.3684	.3704
.5333	.5476	.5833	.6667	.8677

The predicted debt value for a family with a home value of \$250,000 ($X = 250$) is

$$\hat{Y} = 2.00 + .1294(250) = 34.35$$

That is, \$34,350.

CONFIDENCE INTERVAL FOR THE SLOPE, β_1

In deriving a confidence interval for the slope of the (population) regression line, β_1, in Chapter 14, a critical assumption was that the residuals were normally distributed. An alternative to this procedure is to remove this assumption by deriving a *nonparametric* confidence interval for β_1. This confidence interval can be used as a follow up to either the least squares regression line procedure or the regression line through the medians procedure.

To derive this interval, we begin by examining the ordered slopes, S_{ij}. If the regression line through the medians is being used, these values have already been determined in the calculation of B_1. Suppose that n_1 slopes have been derived. If no two X values are equal, then we previously stated that $n_1 = n(n-1)/2$, where n is the number of sample observations.

To construct, say, a 90% confidence interval for β_1, we consult Table A-17, using the column labeled $V_{1-(.10/2)} = V_{.95}$. In general, for a $(1 - \alpha) \times 100\%$ confidence interval, use the column labeled $V_{1-\alpha/2}$ in Table A.17. This confidence interval procedure is based on a nonparametric technique developed by M. G. Kendall around 1940—hence, the title of Table A.17. Next, using the value of n (the number of sample observations) in the far left column of the table, find the corresponding value (say, n_2) from the table. Define

$$k = \frac{1}{2}(n_1 - n_2)$$

and round this value *downward* if it is not a counting number.

To derive the confidence interval, let L = lower and U = upper

S_L = the kth ordered slope, S_{ij}, starting from the *smallest* value

S_U = the kth ordered slope, S_{ij}, starting from the *largest* value

  = the $(n_1 - k + 1)$th ordered slope, S_{ij}, starting from the smallest value

The $(1 - \alpha) \times 100\%$ confidence interval for β_1 is then (S_L, S_U).

EXAMPLE 19.14

Using the home value versus debt data and the calculations in Example 19.13, construct a 90% confidence interval for the slope of the regression line.

SOLUTION

The $n_1 = 45$ ordered slopes, S_{ij}, are contained in Table 19.10. Using Table A.17 with $n = 10$ under the $V_{.95}$ column, we find that $n_2 = 19$. Thus,

$$k = \frac{1}{2}(45 - 19) = 13$$

FIGURE 19.16

Excel regression line through the medians and confidence interval for the slope using **KGP Data Analysis ➤ Nonparametric Procedures.**

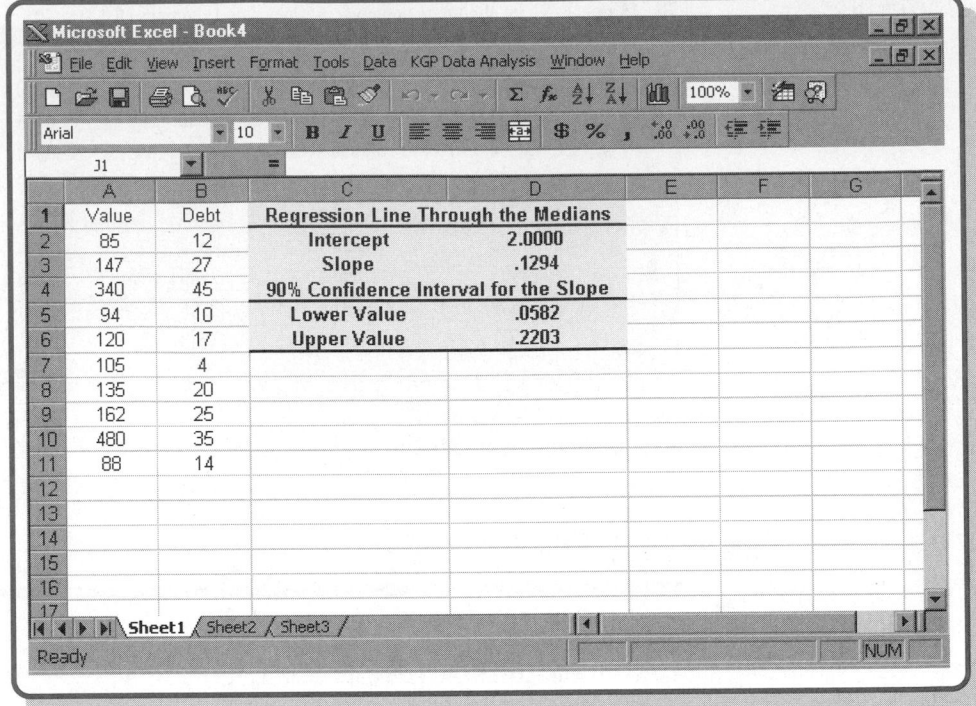

Consequently, S_L is the 13th value in Table 19.10, beginning with the smallest value. This value is the top boxed value in Table 19.10—that is, $S_L = .0582$. The upper confidence limit, S_U, is the 13th value beginning with the largest value (the bottom boxed value)—that is, $S_U = .2203$. The 90% confidence interval for β_1 is then .0582 to .2203. This implies that we are 90% confident that the slope of the regression line through the population (β_1) is between .0582 and .2203. The beauty of this procedure is that no assumption of normally distributed residuals was necessary here.

To obtain the Excel-generated regression line through the medians and confidence interval for β_1 shown in Figure 19.16, click on **KGP Data Analysis ➤ Nonparametric Procedures.** Select **Regression/Correlation Analysis** and click on **Regression Line Through the Medians** inside the **Bivariate Data** frame and on **OK.** Enter "A2:A11" as the **Range for X** and "B2:B11" as the **Range for Y.** Also, enter "C1" as the **Output Range** and click on the **90% Confidence Level.** Both the regression line and the 90% confidence interval agree with the earlier solutions to Examples 19.13 and 19.14. Based on the value of $B_1 = .1294$, we conclude that an increase of one thousand dollars in home value is accompanied by an average increase in $129 in total indebtedness, since the units for X and Y are in thousands of dollars.

MICROSOFT® EXCEL APPLICATION   USE DATA14-10

EXAMPLE 19.15

An Excel Regression Line Through the Medians

In Example 14.10, the editor of a monthly automotive magazine carried out a regression analysis using X = engine capacity in liters as a predictor of Y = miles per gallon. The regression equation was derived from a sample of 60 different automobile models and the resulting least squares prediction equation was $\hat{Y} = 55.494 - 5.981X$. The correlation

FIGURE 19.17

Excel generated regression line through the medians (Example 19.15).

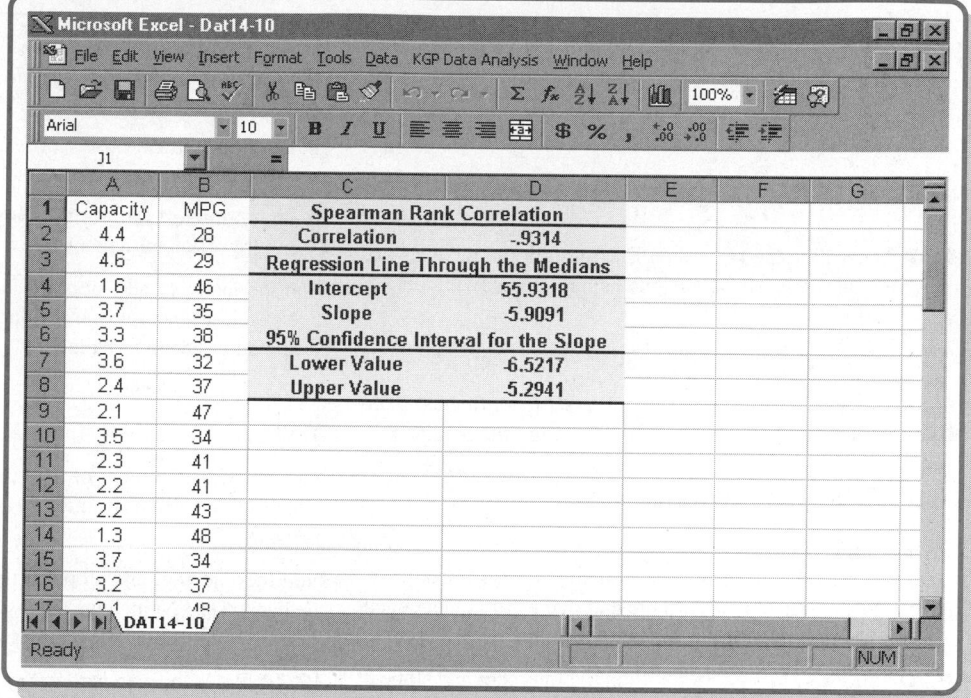

between these two variables was –.931, indicating a strong negative relationship between these two variables—that is, a larger engine implies less miles per gallon, as one would expect. One observation, the boxed observation in Figure 14.27, was determined to have an outlying value of both X and Y. This observation was for a Lamborghini, a somewhat unusual and expensive automobile. This observation was also determined to be influential—that is, removal of this observation would produce a noticeable shift in the regression line.

In reviewing these results, the editor elected to keep the Lamborghini observation in the sample and to use the regression line through the medians for prediction purposes. Determine this line. Does it appear to be considerably different from the least squares line?

SOLUTION

The Excel solution in Figure 19.17 can be obtained by clicking on **KGP Data Analysis ➤ Nonparametric Procedures,** selecting **Regression/Correlation Analysis,** and clicking on both boxes inside the **Bivariate Data** frame. Next, enter "A2:A61" as the **Range for X** (don't include the label in the first row) and "B2:B61" as the **Range for Y.** Also, enter "C1" as the **Output Range** and click on any of the confidence levels (say, 95%). According to Figure 19.17, the regression line through the medians is

$$\hat{Y} = 55.9318 - 5.9091X$$

Comparing this to the least squares line, we observe very little difference here, since: (1) using the least squares line, each additional liter of engine capacity is accompanied by an average decrease of 5.98 miles per gallon, and (2) this decrease is 5.91 miles per gallon using the median regression line.

An interesting observation here is that both the correlation (r) and rank correlation (r_s) are equal to –.931, indicating a strong negative relationship. Unless you are dealing with ordinal data, it is unusual to see such close agreement between these two measures of association.

EXERCISES 19.66–19.74

UNDERSTANDING THE MECHANICS

19.66 Determine the slope of the regression line through the medians for the following values of X and Y.

X	0	3	7
Y	5	10	13

19.67 Determine the regression line through the medians and compare with the least squares line using the following data.

X	50	10	16	24	40
Y	110	20	30	36	46

19.68 Refer to Exercise 19.67. Find a 90% confidence interval for the slope of the regression line through the medians.

APPLYING THE NEW CONCEPTS

19.69 Refer to Exercise 19.58. Find the intercept and slope of the regression line through the medians. Use breakdowns per year as the dependent variable and age as the independent variable.

19.70 Refer to Exercise 19.59. Find the intercept and slope of the regression line through the medians. Use diastolic blood pressure as the dependent variable and hours exercised as the independent variable.

19.71 Refer to Exercise 19.62. Find a 90% confidence interval on the slope of the regression line through the medians. Use level of satisfaction as the dependent variable and number of years employed by the firm as the independent variable.

USING THE COMPUTER

19.72 Refer to Exercise 19.63.

[DATA SET EX19-63] *Variable description:*

Economist: Name of ecomonist
Bondrate: Interest rate for the 30-year bond
Unemploy: Unemployment rate

Find the intercept and slope of the regression line through the medians. Use Unemploy as the dependent variable and Bondrate as the independent variable.

19.73 Refer to Exercise 19.64.

[DATA SET EX19-64] *Variable description:*

NumNewCars: Number of new cars sold monthly
MonthlyRate: Monthly interest rate, in percent, for financing new cars

Find the intercept and slope of the regression line through the medians. Use NumNewCars as the dependent variable and MonthlyRate as the independent variable.

19.74 Refer to Exercise 19.65.

[DATA SET EX19-65] *Variable description:*

DayNum: Number from 1 through 30 to identify the day
MedSales: Daily sales of allergy-related, over-the-counter medicines
PollenIndex: Daily pollen index

Find a 90% confidence interval for the slope of the regression line through the medians. Use MedSales as the dependent variable and PollenIndex as the independent variable.

SUMMARY

A key step in applying any statistical technique correctly is to make sure that it is appropriate for the type of data that is involved. For example, performing a t test using a small sample containing *ordinal* data (such as a set of consumer rankings) is never correct. For situations in which your data are ordinal or from populations that you suspect are nonnormally distributed, a **nonparametric technique** is often preferable. This chapter has introduced some (certainly not all) of the more popular nonparametric procedures.

The **runs test** examines a sequence containing an arrangement of two symbols (M or F, yes or no, + or –, and so on) to determine whether the sequence was generated in a random manner. We defined tests for both small samples (using Table A.15) and large samples (using a test statistic having an approximate normal distribution and Table A.4).

The **Mann-Whitney U test** is a nonparametric procedure for determining whether two populations differ in location using two independent samples. Unlike its counterpart, the t test, this test does not require that the populations be normally distributed. By combining (pooling) the samples and finding the ranks of the combined sample, you can calculate a value of the test statistic. This method can be applied both to small samples (using Table A.10) and to large samples (using an approximate normal distribution and Table A.4).

The **Wilcoxon signed rank test** is a nonparametric procedure used for determining whether the population of differences is centered at zero when dealing with two dependent (paired) samples. The Wilcoxon technique determines the differences of the paired observations and then calculates a value of the test statistic using the ranks of these differences. Both small samples (using Table A.11)

FIGURE 19.18

Summary of nonparametric tests of central tendency.

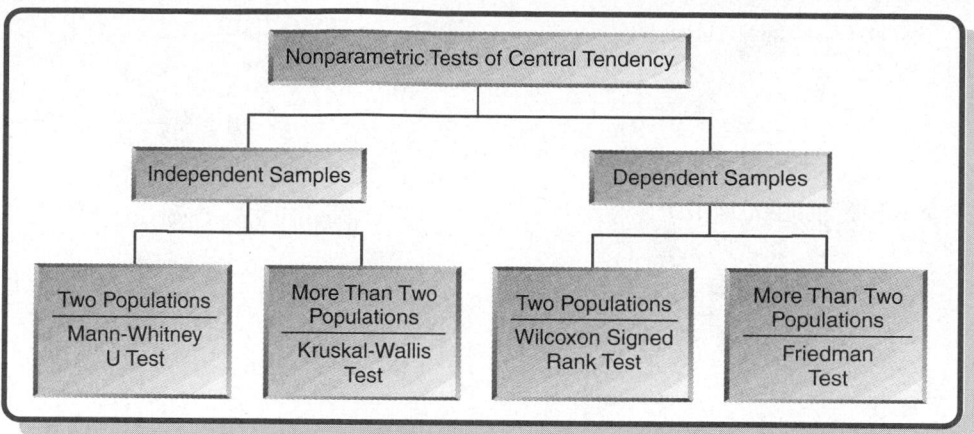

and large samples (using an approximate normal distribution and Table A.4) can be tested.

The **Kruskal-Wallis test** is an extension of the Mann-Whitney test. It is used to test whether two or more populations differ in location when using independent samples. As in the Mann-Whitney procedure, the samples are pooled and then ranked from smallest to largest. The resulting ranks are then used to define a test statistic. This statistic has an approximate chi-square distribution (tabulated in Table A.6), even for fairly small sample sizes.

A nonparametric alternative to the randomized block technique (discussed in Chapter 11) is the **Friedman test.** The Friedman test does not require normal populations with equal variances, unlike the randomized block procedure. Values are ranked within each block and then summed for the various populations under consideration. The Friedman test statistic is calculated using these sums and has an approximate chi-square distribution.

These tests are summarized in Figure 19.18.

Another nonparametric technique, the **Spearman rank correlation,** allows you to measure the *association* between sample values on two variables that consist of ordinal data. If the data are of the interval or ratio type, they can be converted to ordinal data by using the ranks of these values. The Spearman rank correlation coefficient, denoted as r_s, is a nonparametric measure of association between the observations of these two variables. This statistic is computed using the ranks of the observations and can be used to test for a significant relationship between the two variables.

An alternative to the least squares regression line from Chapter 14 is the **regression line through the medians.** This regression line has the nice property of being relatively unaffected by the presence of one or two outlying observations in the sample data. This procedure also allows you to compute a confidence interval for the slope of the population regression line without assuming the residual population is normally distributed.

SUMMARY OF FORMULAS

RUNS TEST (LARGE SAMPLE, R = NUMBER OF RUNS)

$$\mu_R = 1 + \frac{2n_1 n_2}{n_1 + n_2}$$

$$\sigma_R = \sqrt{\frac{2n_1 n_2 (2n_1 n_2 - n_1 - n_2)}{(n_1 + n_2)^2 (n_1 + n_2 - 1)}}$$

Test statistic (large samples):

$$Z = \frac{R - \mu_R}{\sigma_R}$$

MANN-WHITNEY U TEST

$$U_1 = n_1 n_2 + \frac{n_1 (n_1 + 1)}{2} - T_1$$

$$U_2 = n_1 n_2 + \frac{n_2 (n_2 + 1)}{2} - T_2$$

$$\mu_{U_2} = \frac{n_1 n_2}{2}$$

$$\sigma_{U_2} = \sqrt{\frac{n_1 n_2 (n_1 + n_2 + 1)}{12}}$$

Test statistic (large samples):

$$Z = \frac{U_2 - \mu_{U_2}}{\sigma_{U_2}}$$

WILCOXON SIGNED RANK TEST

$$\mu_{T_+} = \frac{n(n+1)}{4}$$

$$\sigma_{T_+} = \sqrt{\frac{n(n+1)(2n+1)}{24}}$$

Test statistic (large samples):

$$Z = \frac{T_+ - \mu_{T_+}}{\sigma_{T_+}}$$

KRUSKAL-WALLIS TEST

Test statistic:

$$KW = \frac{12}{n(n+1)} \sum_{i=1}^{k} \frac{T_i^2}{n_i} - 3(n+1)$$

FRIEDMAN TEST

Test statistic:

$$FR = \frac{12}{bk(k+1)} \sum_{i=1}^{k} T_i^2 - 3b(k+1)$$

SPEARMAN RANK CORRELATION

$$r_s = \frac{\sum R(x)R(y) - [\sum R(x)][\sum R(y)]/n}{\sqrt{\sum R^2(x) - [\sum R(x)]^2/n} \sqrt{\sum R^2(y) - [\sum R(y)]^2/n}}$$

$$= 1 - \frac{6\sum d^2}{n(n^2-1)} \quad \text{(if no ties)}$$

REGRESSION LINE THROUGH THE MEDIANS

Equation of line: $\hat{Y} = B_0 + B_1 X$

Slope of the line connecting observations i and j:

$$S_{ij} = \frac{Y_j - Y_i}{X_j - X_i}$$

B_1 = median of S_{ij} values

B_0 = (Median Y value) $- B_1 \cdot$ (Median X value)

REVIEW EXERCISES 19.75–19.96

19.75 Consider the following sequence of regression residuals, where the dependent variable is regressed on time. Using the runs test on positive and negative residuals, is there evidence to indicate that the residuals are not in random order? Use a 5% significance level.

Residual	Time	Residual	Time
−1.2	1	3.7	16
−2.6	2	−2.1	17
4.0	3	−1.7	18
−3.1	4	3.8	19
1.5	5	.7	20
.6	6	−2.1	21
−3.4	7	−1.5	22
−1.0	8	1.3	23
1.5	9	−.7	24
1.6	10	.8	25
1.8	11	−.2	26
−.5	12	−.3	27
−1.0	13	−.5	28
2.0	14	−.8	29
−1.6	15	1.0	30

19.76 A radio station requests that people telephone the station to express their opinion on the new property tax the city is levying. An F represents a person telephoning in who is for the tax, and an A represents one against it. Test whether the following sequence of people telephoning the radio station is nonrandomly generated. Use a 5% significance level.

FAFAAAFAAFAAAFFAFAFAAAFAA

19.77 The manager of a small-town savings and loan association is interested in finding out whether there is a relationship between the average monthly balance of a savings account and the age of the savings account. Fifteen accounts were selected at random. Do the data indicate a relationship at the .05 significance level?

Average Monthly Balance	Age of Account (Years)	Average Monthly Balance	Age of Account (Years)
2510	1.5	6148	3.8
3612	2.6	5134	4.7
5634	3.5	2614	1.1
3698	1.8	2581	1.9
3978	2.1	2501	0.5
6751	4.3	3986	4.2
5869	10.1	6645	4.1
		3582	2.3

19.78 Explain the difference in the assumptions necessary to perform parametric tests and nonparametric tests on two population means.

19.79 A statistician wants to determine whether two populations differ in location. After collecting a sample of size eight from each population, the statistician finds that the sum of the ranks of the observations in population 1 is 60. Is there evidence to indicate that there is a difference in location for the two populations? Use a 5% significance level.

19.80 An economist believes that the cost of a typical basket of goods bought by a family of four costs more in Atlanta, Georgia, than it does in Houston, Texas. Seven grocery stores were randomly selected in each of the two cities to collect the following data (cost of basket of goods, in dollars). Test that there is no difference in the cost of the basket of goods for the two cities. Use a 10% significance level.

Atlanta	Houston
30	37
33	36
41	39
43	40
37	32
39	36
41	32

19.81 Politicians often refer to various polls to assess the confidence adults have that their children will enjoy a higher standard of living than themselves. Use the following data to regress the percentage who expect their children to have a higher standard of living (Y) on the independent variable time (t). Calculate the residuals. Use a runs test to determine if the sequence of positive and negative residuals appears to be randomly generated with respect to time. Use a 5% significance level.

Year	Quarter	Time Period (t)	Percentage Expecting Children to Have a Higher Standard of Living (Y)
1995	1	1	51.1
	2	2	44.2
	3	3	41.6
	4	4	40.3
1996	1	5	41.5
	2	6	42.7
	3	7	46.5
	4	8	48.7
1997	1	9	51.6
	2	10	53.8
	3	11	58.6
	4	12	60.3
1998	1	13	63.1
	2	14	62.4
	3	15	61.3
	4	16	61.7

(Source: Adapted from *The Wall Street Journal*, "And Are Confident That Our Children Will Enjoy a Higher Standard of Living," Dec. 10, 1998, p. A14.)

19.82 Vulcan Construction believes that a minicourse in safety to increase the employees' awareness of potential accidents would reduce the incidence of on-the-job accidents. The following data represent the number of accidents reported at 15 construction sites for the month before and the month after the workers attended the minicourse. Do the data indicate that the minicourse reduced accidents? Use a 5% significance level.

Before	After	Before	After
4	3	11	6
5	6	7	7
7	6	8	5
8	5	5	3
7	8	10	11
10	3	9	4
12	2	11	9
9	8		

19.83 A cooking contest was conducted: Two top chefs baked chicken and then asked 12 tasters to judge the quality of the cooking on a scale from 1 to 10, 10 being the highest score. Test the null hypothesis that there was no difference between the taster's judgment of the two chefs' quality of cooking at a significance level of .05.

Taster	Chef A	Chef B	Taster	Chef A	Chef B
1	8	7	7	9	9
2	6	10	8	10	7
3	5	9	9	9	10
4	10	4	10	8	6
5	5	8	11	4	9
6	3	7	12	7	3

19.84 Paint A, paint B, and paint C were painted on metallic surfaces and then subjected to high temperatures. Nine replications of the experiment were made. A measure of the cohesiveness of the paint was then taken. The following coded data represent the cohesiveness of the individual paints. Test the hypothesis that there was no difference in the cohesiveness for the three paints. Use a 10% significance level.

Paint A	Paint B	Paint C	Paint A	Paint B	Paint C
1.3	2.1	3.4	1.6	1.9	2.5
1.6	2.7	2.8	2.6	2.3	2.4
3.1	1.6	1.9	2.7	1.8	1.9
2.6	1.9	2.0	1.9	1.6	1.7
4.3	1.6	2.8			

19.85 A chemist was interested in knowing whether three different drugs used for insomnia were equally effective. Three groups of mice, with 10 mice to a group, were used. Each group of mice was given the adult-equivalent dosage of one of the three drugs. The time, in minutes, it took for the mice to fall asleep was recorded. Using the following data, test the null hypothesis that each drug is equally effective in reducing sleep latency. Use a significance level of .05.

Drug 1	Drug 2	Drug 3	Drug 1	Drug 2	Drug 3
32	38	31	41	35	30
35	37	33	28	39	28
40	42	29	34	40	33
30	44	34	39	41	37
33	37	31	28	42	35

19.86 An automobile worker would like to know whether there is any difference in the comfort of three different cars. Three groups of five drivers were selected to judge the riding comfort of the three cars; one of the three cars was assigned to each group. The drivers rated the comfort of each car on a scale from 1 to 5, 5 being the most comfortable. Test that there is no difference in the comfort of the three cars from these data. Use a .05 significance level.

Car 1	Car 2	Car 3
2	5	4
4	3	1
4	4	2
3	3	5
5	2	4

19.87 The Food and Drug Administration approved the use of acesulfame potassium, a noncaloric sweetner, for use in diet beverages. "This could be a boon for the (soft drink) business—there's a massive palate fatigue out there, and consumers are waiting for something new to stimulate them," says the president of Bevmark, a New York consulting firm. As the following data illustrate, the marketshare for diet drinks measured as a percentage has been declining.

Year	Marketshare of Diet Drinks
1990	30.1
1991	29.8
1992	29.7
1993	26.8
1994	26.5
1995	23.8
1996	24.2
1997	21.0
1998	23.7

(Source: Adapted from *The Wall Street Journal*, "New Sweetner Could Energize Diet-Soda Sales," July 1, 1998, p. B1.)

a. At the 5% significance level, is there sufficient evidence to indicate a negative relationship between the percent of marketshare for diet drinks and time.

b. What is the slope of the regression line using time to predict marketshare of diet drinks?

c. What is the slope of the regression line through the medians to predict marketshare of diet drinks?

d. Compare the results from part (a) with part (b). Comment on why you think the slopes are similar.

19.88 A company uses four advertising methods to increase sales: newspaper, mailers, television, and radio. Four 6-month periods were randomly selected, and sales (in thousands of dollars) were recorded monthly for one of the 6-month periods for each advertising method. Do the following data indicate a difference in sales promotion for the four advertising methods? Use a .05 significance level.

Newspaper	Mailers	Television	Radio
2.1	4.1	5.1	4.2
5.6	2.6	4.2	4.3
6.2	2.1	3.7	4.0
3.4	3.3	2.0	3.1
3.1	3.0	3.6	3.8
4.1	3.1	3.1	3.7

19.89 The following data represent the years of job-related experience and last year's salary (in thousands of dollars) for 10 randomly selected realtors. Do the data indicate a positive relationship? Use a 5% significance level.

Years of Experience	Annual Salary	Years of Experience	Annual Salary
13.2	42.5	7.8	38.4
10.1	36.8	5.4	29.6
4.6	15.9	3.8	21.6
5.7	27.6	9.6	33.7
6.7	34.3	8.4	35.3

19.90 The *Wall Street Journal* presents investment performance results using a panel of professionals (PROS), a portfolio of stocks selected at random (DARTS), and the Dow Jones Industrial Average (DJIA). The following data measured in percent illustrate the results of the three investment categories.

Time Period	PROS	DARTS	DJIA
January–June 1997	20.2	18.0	16.2
February–July 1997	29.3	−13.9	20.8
March–August 1997	20.7	.1	8.3
April–September 1997	50.3	35.6	20.2
May–October 1997	38.4	20.7	3.0
June–November 1997	−3.5	6.5	3.8
July–December 1997	−14.1	6.5	−.7
August 1997–January 1998	14.3	−9.0	−.3
September 1997–February 1998	10.9	−3.3	10.7
October 1997–March 1998	5.5	−13.3	7.6

Time Period	PROS	DARTS	DJIA
November 1997–April 1998	17.4	–10.5	22.5
December 1997–May 1998	0.0	28.5	10.6
January–June 1998	24.4	3.2	15.0
February–July 1998	39.3	–10.1	7.1
March–August 1998	–18.8	–20.4	–13.1
April–September 1998	–20.1	–34.2	–11.8

(Source: Adapted from *The Wall Street Journal*, "The Scoreboard since the Beginning," Oct. 7, 1998, p. C18.)

a. At the 5% significance level, is there an association between PROS and DARTS?

b. At the 5% significance level, is there an association between PROS and DJIA?

c. Compare the slope of the regression equation through the medians in predicting PROS's performance from DARTS to the slope of the regression equation through the medians in predicting PROS's performance from DJIA.

19.91 A cable television company is interested in whether there is a difference in viewers' preference for three movie channels. Listed are rankings from 1 to 3 given to the three movie channels—channel 22, channel 29, and channel 32—by each household. A ranking of 1 indicates the most desirable channel. Do the data provide sufficient evidence to indicate that there is a difference in the preference for these channels? Use a .10 significance level.

Household	Channel 22	Channel 29	Channel 32	Household	Channel 22	Channel 29	Channel 32
1	1	3	2	6	1	3	2
2	3	2	1	7	3	1	2
3	1	2	3	8	2	3	1
4	2	3	1	9	1	3	2
5	3	2	1	10	3	2	1

19.92 Lifetime Exterior sells three types of siding: vinyl, aluminum, and steel. The manager is interested in whether one type of siding is sold more than another. Twelve salespersons are randomly selected and the number of sales of each type of siding is recorded over a 6-month period. From the data, can the manager conclude that not all types of siding sell equally well? Use a .05 significance level.

Salesperson	Vinyl	Aluminum	Steel	Salesperson	Vinyl	Aluminum	Steel
1	9	5	8	7	8	14	10
2	6	10	11	8	9	8	3
3	13	9	7	9	6	9	5
4	11	10	6	10	11	15	17
5	15	12	11	11	25	21	15
6	21	22	14	12	10	19	20

19.93 The Forbes Index is a measure of U.S. economic activity composed of eight equally weighted elements: (1) the cost of services relative to all consumer prices, (2) the level of new orders for durable goods compared with manufacturer's inventory, (3) total industrial production, (4) new housing starts, (5) personal income, (6) new claims for unemployment compensation, (7) total retail sales, and (8) total consumer installment.

Year	Forbes Index	Year	Forbes Index
1983	185	1992	215
1984	180	1993	235
1985	195	1994	263
1986	210	1995	270
1987	230	1996	280
1988	235	1997	285
1989	327	1998	290
1990	315	1999	304
1991	210		

(Source: Adapted from *Forbes*, "The Forbes/Bridge Economic Forecast Report," Jan 25, 1999, p. 48.)

a. Find the regression line predicting the Forbes Index from time ($t = 1, 2, \ldots$).

b. Find the regression line through the medians to predict the Forbes Index from time ($t = 1, 2, \ldots$).

c. Compare the slopes of the lines in parts (a) and (b).

19.94 According to a *Wall Street Journal* article ("Acid-Based Wrinkle Creams: Fountain of Youth or Snake Oil?" Apr. 13, 1994, p. B1), alpha-hydroxy acid (AHA), which is a chemical used in leather tanners and tile cleaners, has emerged as a lucrative discovery for the cosmetic industry. Avon Products says its Anew line, which uses AHA, sold more than $175 million worldwide in 1993. Suppose a researcher wished to determine whether there was a significant difference between the performance of a leading facial cosmetic without AHA and one with AHA. Assume that 20 randomly selected women used the two products on opposite sides of their face for a two-month period. At the end of this period, each woman assigned two scores from 1 to 25 measuring the performance of each facial cosmetic. From the following computer printout, do the data indicate a difference in the performance of the two products, one with AHA and one without AHA? Use the *p*-value to base your conclusion.

Person	No AHA	With AHA	Person	No AHA	With AHA
1	14	16	11	9	13
2	22	23	12	7	7
3	18	13	13	8	12
4	16	20	14	10	14
5	11	12	15	13	14
6	12	17	16	23	16
7	20	14	17	12	16
8	15	17	18	10	11
9	20	20	19	10	14
10	18	24	20	9	12

Wilcoxon Test

$T(+)$	49
$T(-)$	122
Mean (Z)	85.5000
Std. Dev. (Z)	22.9619
Z Value	−1.5896
p-value (Using Z)	.1119
p-value (Using Table)	>.10

19.95 A home builder records the number of new construction permits issued by a county in Georgia. From a plot of the number of new construction permits over a 24-month period, the builder estimates a cyclical trend of eight months. The builder examines two regression equations to predict the new permits: one with time (Time) as the independent variable and the other with time and the new permits lagged by eight months (PermitsLag8) as the independent variables. Examine the computer printouts displaying the regression analysis for each equation. Explain the importance of using the runs test in examining the residuals.

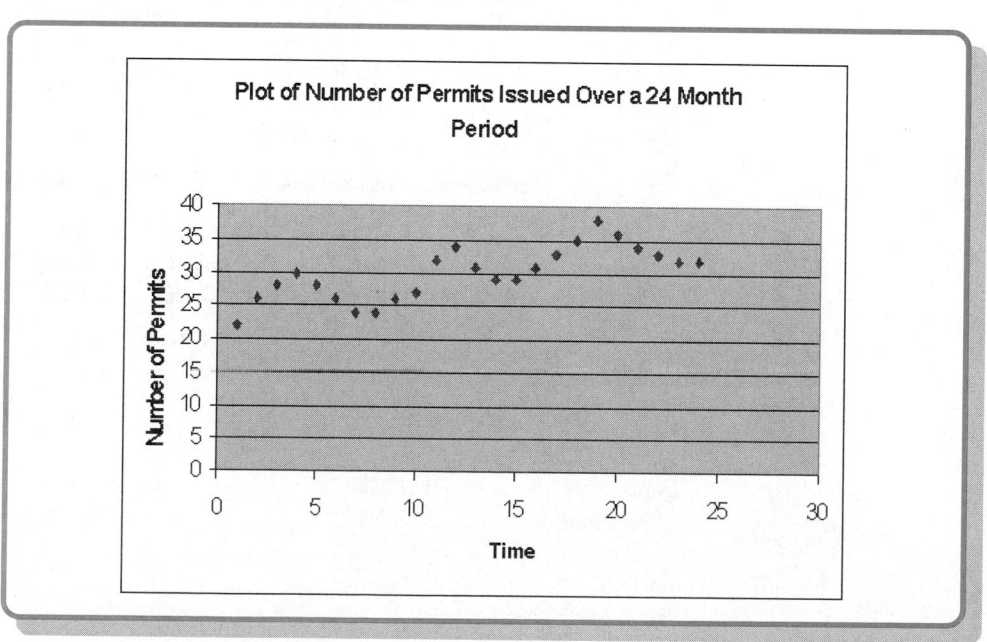

Summary Output Using Time

Regression Statistics

Multiple R	0.76703517
R Square	0.58834295
Adjusted R Square	0.56963126
Standard Error	2.70831686
Observations	24

ANOVA

	df	SS	MS	F	Significance F
Regression	1	230.6304348	230.6304	31.4425	1.22733E-05
Residual	22	161.3695652	7.33498		
Total	23	392			

	Coefficients	Standard Error	t Stat	P-value	Lower 95%	Upper 95%
Intercept	24.4021739	1.141150626	21.38383	3.3E-16	22.03556982	26.768778
Time	0.44782609	0.079863907	5.607365	1.2E-05	0.282198303	0.6134539

Runs Test for Regression Equation with Time

Number of Runs	7
Mean	13
Std. Dev.	2.395648229
Z Value	−2.50454133
2-Tailed p-value	0.012261059

Summary Output Using Time and PermitsLag8

Regression Statistics

Multiple R	0.802082959
R Square	0.643337072
Adjusted R Square	0.588465853
Standard Error	2.042109863
Observations	16

ANOVA

	df	SS	MS	F	Significance F
Regression	2	97.78723502	48.893617	11.72449	0.001229354
Residual	13	54.21276498	4.1702126		
Total	15	152			

	Coefficients	Standard Error	t Stat	P-value	Lower 95%	Upper 95%
Intercept	11.23065191	1.141150626	21.38383	3.3E-16	22.03556982	26.768778
Time	0.116328106	0.079863907	5.607365	1.2E-05	0.282198303	0.6134539
PermitsLag8	0.674718008	0.203682993	3.312588	0.005610	0.234687738	1.1147482

Runs Test for Regression Equation with Time and PermitsLag8

Number of Runs	6
Mean	8.875
Std. Dev.	1.899835519
Z Value	−1.513288898
2-Tailed p-value	0.130206339

19.96 Many medical and business studies employ a small sample size. With these studies, a few outliers in the study may produce unreliable results. For example, a study by S. S. Hecht and J. P. Richie ("Smoking Study Sparks Debate on Race Issues," reported by Marilyn Chase in *The Wall Street Journal,* Apr. 5, 1994, p. B1) proposed that black smokers may be less able than white smokers to detoxify the potent cancer-causing chemical NNK, which is found exclusively in tobacco and tobacco smoke. However, Harold Freeman, past president of the American Cancer Society, said that the Hecht-Richie study is small, preliminary, and "far from having statistical power." To understand how outliers can effect the results of a study with a small sample size, consider three groups, each with 10 persons. Analyze the the following data and explain why you think the standard, one-way ANOVA procedure and the Kruskal-Wallis test give different results. Using a 10% significance level, what conclusion would you say the data support?

Group1	Group2	Group3
49.1593	46.4225	50.6839
53.5741	53.3554	54.8528
44.9120	49.3443	53.8545
46.9572	48.0674	51.2132
44.8286	47.2626	51.3544
48.5120	48.4098	52.3400
50.3776	48.9766	50.4343
48.9633	53.7594	50.4988
49.4788	48.5630	55.5222
52.4239	56.6518	45.0034

ANOVA: SINGLE FACTOR

SUMMARY

Groups	Count	Sum	Average	Variance
Group1	10	489.18692	48.91869	8.13957
Group2	10	500.81291	50.08129	11.07443
Group3	10	515.75761	51.57576	8.74712

ANOVA

Source of Variation	SS	df	MS	F	P-value
Between Groups	35.483635752	2	17.74182	1.90355	0.16851
Within Groups	251.650148681	27	9.32038		
Total	287.133784434	29			

KRUSKAL-WALLIS TEST

Computed Chi-Square	4.9316	
p-value	.0849	
Group	Sum of Ranks	Average Rank
1	120.0	12.00
2	141.0	14.10
3	204.0	20.40

INSIGHTS FROM STATISTICS IN ACTION: MARKETING ATHLEISURE SHOES— DEALING WITH FICKLE CONSUMERS

The introductory Statistics in Action section in this chapter discussed the intense rivalry between athletic and leisure shoe companies, including Nike, Reebok, Adidas, and Airwalk. This discussion introduced the idea of comparing brands of shoes by having the respondents *rank* the brands rather than provide a numerical score of some kind. When dealing with such ordinal data, the analysis of variance (ANOVA) methods of Chapter 11 are no longer appropriate, since they require interval/ratio data.

A local store is interested in comparing customer preference for four brands of "athleisure" shoes. The store owner asked 25 customers to rank the top of the line athleisure shoe by Nike, Reebok, Adidas, and Airwalk. Since these data are ordinal, a nonparametric test of hypothesis is in order. The following sample results were obtained.

Consumer Surveyed	Nike	Reebok	Adidas	Airwalk
1	1	3	4	2
2	4	2	1	3
3	2	4	3	1
4	1	3	4	2
5	2	4	1	2
6	3	2	1	4
7	4	2	3	1
8	3	4	2	1
9	3	1	2	4
10	2	4	1	3
11	1	3	4	2
12	4	2	3	1
13	3	2	4	1
14	3	2	1	4
15	3	4	1	2
16	3	2	4	3
17	1	4	2	3
18	2	3	4	1
19	3	2	1	4
20	4	3	2	1
21	4	3	1	2
22	1	3	2	4
23	2	1	4	3
24	2	3	4	1
25	4	2	3	1

1. What statistical test procedure would you use for the data collected to test the belief that there is a difference in the preference of consumers for the four brands of athleisure shoes? What statistical test would you use if instead of ranks, the consumers provided a rating response on a continuous scale from 1 to 100, and these data were approximately normally distributed?

2. Analyze the belief in question (1) using a .05 significance level. Should we be concerned with which pairs of brands are different with respect to preference considering the outcome of this analysis?

3. What conclusions would you provide to management on the results of your analysis? Do you think the results would likely be different if you had a larger sample size?

4. Would it be easier for the respondents to provide ranks of the shoes that it preferred than to provide a rating response on a scale from 1 to 100? Which type of response provides more information?

5. Could the Kruskal-Wallis test be used to analyze these data? When would this test be appropriate?

Source: Adapted from *USA Today*, "Battle's Afoot: Airwalk Tries Not to Trip," July 31, 1998, p. 1B.

COMPUTER EXERCISES USING THE DATABASES

EXERCISE 1—APPENDIX E

Choose ten observations at random from the database of households that own their home and another ten observations at random from households that rent their home (refer to variable OWNORENT). Using the Mann-Whitney test, is there sufficient evidence to conclude that the income of the principal wage earner is significantly different for the households that own their home and for the households that rent their home? Use a .05 significance level.

EXERCISE 2—APPENDIX E

Choose 12 observations at random from the database of households that have a secondary income (INCOME2) above $25,000. Choose another 12 observations from households that have a secondary income (INCOME2) that is positive and less than $25,000. Also, choose a random sample of 12 observations from households with no secondary income. Can one conclude that there is a difference in the house payment or apartment/house rent (HPAYRENT) for the three groups? Use the Kruskal-Wallis test with a .05 significance level.

EXERCISE 3—APPENDIX F

Randomly select 12 observations from the database of companies with an A bond rating, 12 of companies with a B bond rating, and 12 of companies with a C bond rating. Can one conclude that there is a difference in the TOTAL (long-term assets) for the three groups? Use the Kruskal-Wallis test with a .05 significance level.

EXERCISE 4—APPENDIX F

Choose 25 observations at random from the database. Is there evidence that a positive relationship exists between EMPLOYEE (the number of employees) and SALES (the amount of sales)? Use Spearman's rank correlation coefficient, and test at the .01 significance level. Determine the regression line through the medians using this set of data. Interpret the slope of this line.

CHAPTER 19 APPENDIX: DATA ANALYSIS WITH MINITAB

NONPARAMETRIC STATISTICS

For nonparametric statistical analysis, MINITAB has various procedures that can be viewed by clicking **Stat ➤ Nonparametrics.** To perform the runs tests, click **Stat ➤ Nonparametrics ➤ Runs Test.** The user form labeled **Runs Test** will appear. The data in Example 19.2 are used to illustrate this procedure. Since numerical values must be used for this test, a male is coded as a 0, and a female is coded as a 1. Note that the **Above and Below the Mean** option has been selected in this example, since the mean will be some number between 0 and 1. The other option (**Above and Below**) could have been used with any number between 0 and 1. The output follows the user form.

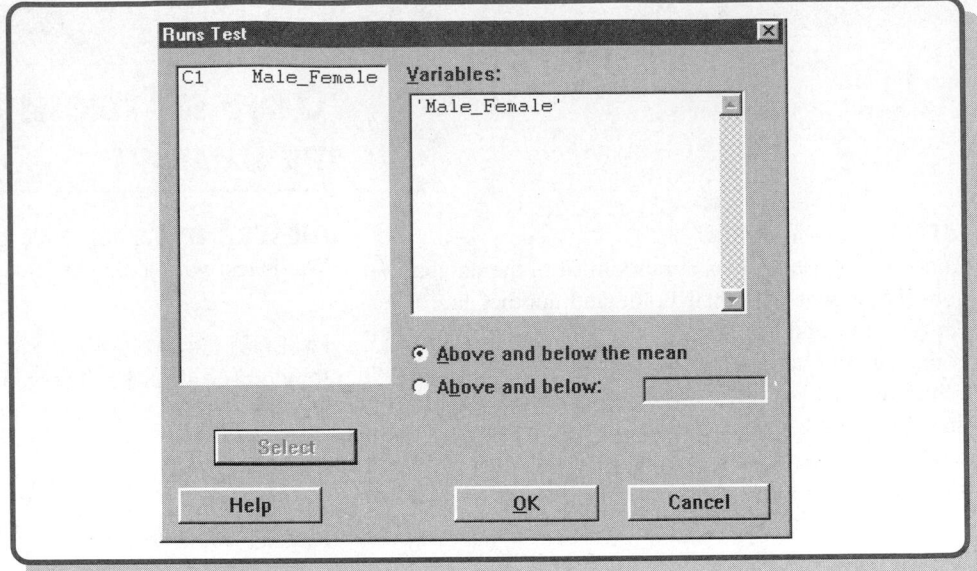

Runs Test

```
Male_Fem

K =      0.5111


The observed number of runs = 15
The expected number of runs = 23.4889
23 Observations above K    22 below
           The test is significant at   0.0104
```

To perform the Mann-Whitney test, click **Stat ➤ Nonparametrics ➤ Mann-Whitney.** The user form labeled **Mann-Whitney** will appear. The data in Example 19.5 are used to illustrate this procedure. In the Alternative box, select **Greater Than,** since the alternative hypothesis is that population *A* is shifted to the right of population *B.* A 95% confidence interval will also be printed, since 95 (default value) was entered in the **Confidence Level** box. The output follows the user form. The Mann-Whitney statistic is represented by *W.*

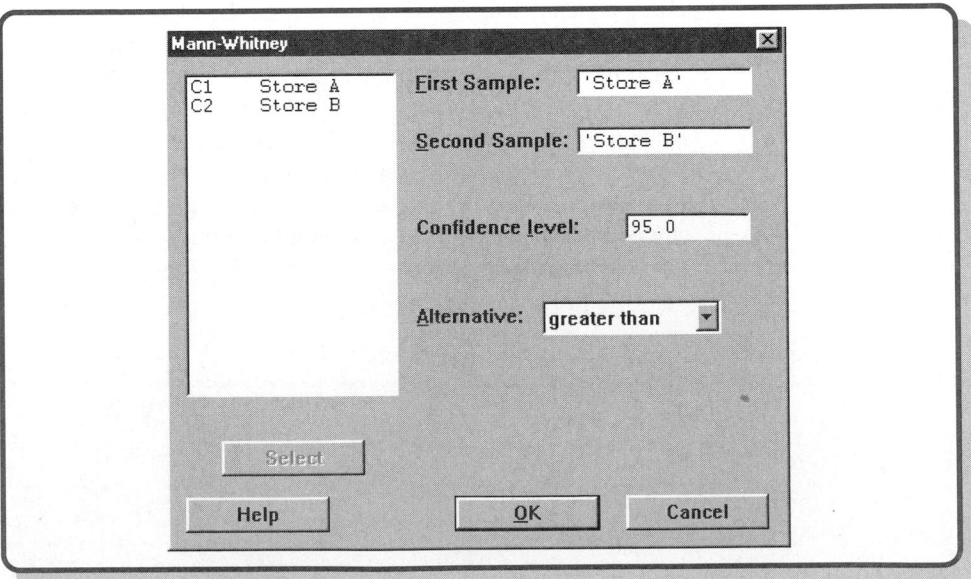

Mann-Whitney Confidence Interval and Test

```
Store A     N = 12      Median =    58.00
Store B     N = 15      Median =    20.00
Point estimate for ETA1-ETA2 is    33.00
95.2 Percent CI for ETA1-ETA2 is (21.99,44.00)
W = 249.0
Test of ETA1 = ETA2 vs ETA1 > ETA2 is significant at 0.0000
The test is significant at 0.0000 (adjusted for ties)
```

To perform the Kruskal-Wallis test, click **Stat ➤ Nonparametrics ➤ Kruskal-Wallis.** The user form labeled **Kruskal-Wallis** will appear. The data in Example 19.8 are used to illustrate this procedure. In one column (C1, labeled **Brand**), observed values are entered. In another column (C2, labeled **Factor Levels**), the levels of the factor are entered. These two columns (C1 and C2) are then selected for input into the **Response** and **Factor** boxes. Click on **OK,** and the output immediately following appears. Note that the Kruskal-Wallis statistic is denoted by the letter H.

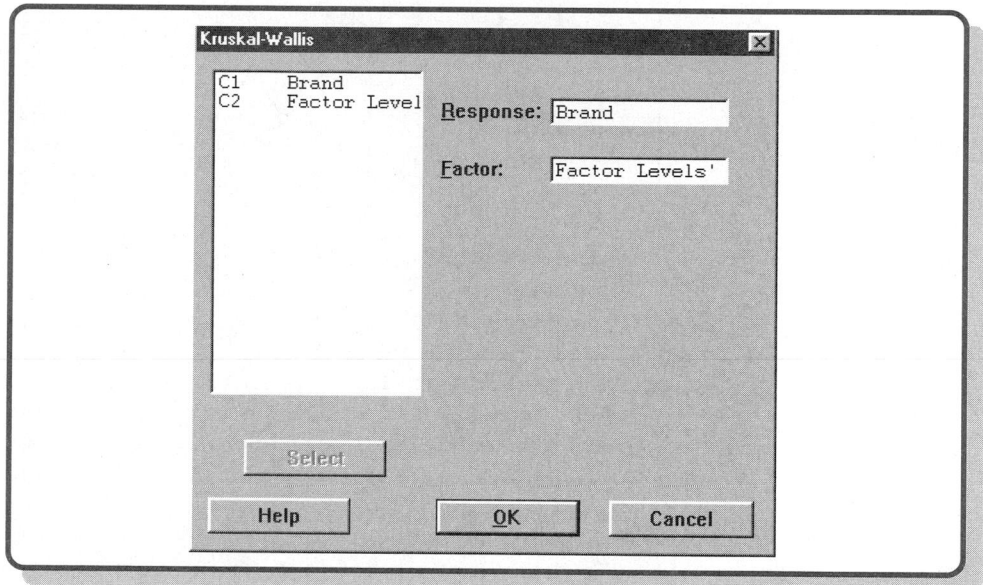

Kruskal-Wallis Test

```
Kruskal-Wallis Test on Brand

Factor L    N     Median    Ave Rank       Z
1           5     34.00       14.8       1.88
2           5     16.00        5.8      -2.05
3           5     14.00        5.4      -2.23
4           5     36.00       16.0       2.40
Overall    20                 10.5

H = 13.83   DF = 3   P = 0.003
```

To perform the Freidman test, click **Stat ➤ Nonparametrics ➤ Friedman.** The user form labeled Friedman will appear. The data in Example 19.9 are used to illustrate this procedure. The observed data must be entered in one column (C1, labeled **EditorRanks**). In another column (C2, labeled **Brand**), the treatment levels are entered. Finally, in still another column (C3, labeled **Editor**), the block number is entered. The following MINITAB worksheet displays the necessary columns for this test. In the user form, labeled **Friedman,** enter the three columns (C1, C2, and C3, respectively) into the boxes **Response, Treatment,** and **Blocks.** The output follows the user form. Note that the Friedman statistic is represented by the letter S. The Wilcoxon Signed Rank test is not available in MINITAB. However, the Friedman test can be used to perform a two-tailed Wilcoxon Signed Rank test by using each pair as a block and the two groups as the treatment levels.

MINITAB - Untitled - [Worksheet 1 *]**

File Edit Manip Calc Stat Graph Editor Window Help

↓	C1	C2	C3	C4	C5	C6	C7	C8
	EditorRanks	Brand	Editor					
1	3	1	1					
2	2	2	1					
3	1	3	1					
4	2	1	2					
5	1	2	2					
6	3	3	2					
7	3	1	3					
8	1	2	3					
9	2	3	3					
10	2	1	4					
11	1	2	4					
12	3	3	4					
13	3	1	5					
14	2	2	5					
15	1	3	5					
16	2	1	6					
17	1	2	6					
18	3	3	6					
19	1	1	7					
20	2	2	7					
21	3	3	7					
22	2	1	8					
23	1	2	8					
24	3	3	8					
25	3	1	9					
26	1	2	9					
27	2	3	9					
28	1	1	10					

Current Worksheet: Worksheet 1

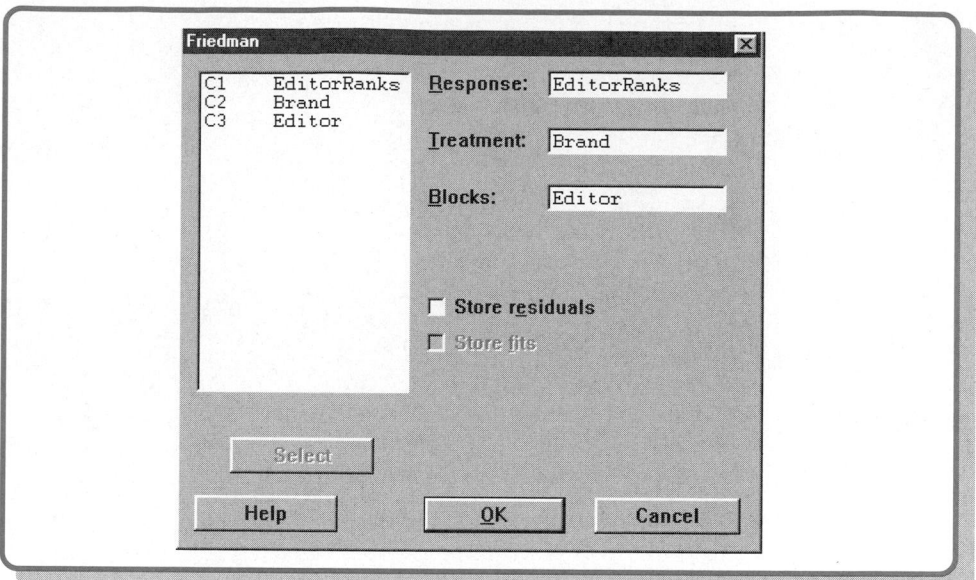

Friedman Test

```
Friedman test for EditorRa by Brand blocked by Editor

S = 5.60   DF = 2   P = 0.061

                        Est      Sum of
Brand           N      Median    Ranks
1               10     2.0000    22.0
2               10     1.3333    14.0
3               10     2.6667    24.0

Grand median  =       2.0000
```

APPENDIXES

APPENDIX A   TABLES

TABLE A.1   Binomial probabilities $[{}_nC_x p^x(1-p)^{n-x}]$.

n	x	0.01	0.05	0.10	0.20	0.30	0.40	P 0.50	0.60	0.70	0.80	0.90	0.95	0.99	x
2	0	980	902	810	640	490	360	250	160	090	040	010	002	0+	0
	1	020	095	180	320	420	480	500	480	420	320	180	095	020	1
	2	0+	002	010	040	090	160	250	360	490	640	810	902	980	2
3	0	970	857	729	512	343	216	125	064	027	008	001	0+	0+	0
	1	029	135	243	384	441	432	375	288	189	096	027	007	0+	1
	2	0+	007	027	096	189	288	375	432	441	384	243	135	029	2
	3	0+	0+	001	008	027	064	125	216	343	512	729	857	970	3
4	0	961	815	656	410	240	130	062	026	008	002	0+	0+	0+	0
	1	039	171	292	410	412	346	250	154	076	026	004	0+	0+	1
	2	001	014	049	154	265	346	375	346	265	154	049	014	001	2
	3	0+	0+	004	026	076	154	250	346	412	410	292	171	039	3
	4	0+	0+	0+	002	008	026	062	130	240	410	656	815	961	4
5	0	951	774	590	328	168	078	031	010	002	0+	0+	0+	0+	0
	1	048	204	328	410	360	259	156	077	028	006	0+	0+	0+	1
	2	001	021	073	205	309	346	312	230	132	051	008	001	0+	2
	3	0+	001	008	051	132	230	312	346	309	205	073	021	001	3
	4	0+	0+	0+	006	028	077	156	259	360	410	328	204	048	4
	5	0+	0+	0+	0+	002	010	031	078	168	328	590	774	951	5
6	0	941	735	531	262	118	047	016	004	001	0+	0+	0+	0+	0
	1	057	232	354	393	303	187	094	037	010	002	0+	0+	0+	1
	2	001	031	098	246	324	311	234	138	060	015	001	0+	0+	2
	3	0+	002	015	082	185	276	312	276	185	082	015	002	0+	3
	4	0+	0+	001	015	060	138	234	311	324	246	098	031	001	4
	5	0+	0+	0+	002	010	037	094	187	303	393	354	232	057	5
	6	0+	0+	0+	0+	001	004	016	047	118	262	531	735	941	6
7	0	932	698	478	210	082	028	008	002	0+	0+	0+	0+	0+	0
	1	066	257	372	367	247	131	055	017	004	0+	0+	0+	0+	1
	2	002	041	124	275	318	261	164	077	025	004	0+	0+	0+	2
	3	0+	004	023	115	227	290	273	194	097	029	003	0+	0+	3
	4	0+	0+	003	029	097	194	273	290	227	115	023	004	0+	4
	5	0+	0+	0+	004	025	077	164	261	318	275	124	041	002	5
	6	0+	0+	0+	0+	004	017	055	131	247	367	372	257	066	6
	7	0+	0+	0+	0+	0+	002	008	028	082	210	478	698	932	7
8	0	923	663	430	168	058	017	004	001	0+	0+	0+	0+	0+	0
	1	075	279	383	336	198	090	031	008	001	0+	0+	0+	0+	1
	2	003	051	149	294	296	209	109	041	010	001	0+	0+	0+	2
	3	0+	005	033	147	254	279	219	124	047	009	0+	0+	0+	3
	4	0+	0+	005	046	136	232	273	232	136	046	005	0+	0+	4
	5	0+	0+	0+	009	047	124	219	279	254	147	033	005	0+	5
	6	0+	0+	0+	001	010	041	109	209	296	294	149	051	003	6
	7	0+	0+	0+	0+	001	008	031	090	198	336	383	279	075	7
	8	0+	0+	0+	0+	0+	001	004	017	058	168	430	663	923	8
9	0	914	630	387	134	040	010	002	0+	0+	0+	0+	0+	0+	0
	1	083	299	387	302	156	060	018	004	0+	0+	0+	0+	0+	1
	2	003	063	172	302	267	161	070	021	004	0+	0+	0+	0+	2
	3	0+	008	045	176	267	251	164	074	021	003	0+	0+	0+	3
	4	0+	001	007	066	172	251	246	167	074	017	001	0+	0+	4
9	5	0+	0+	001	017	074	167	246	251	172	066	007	001	0+	5
	6	0+	0+	0+	003	021	074	164	251	267	176	045	008	0+	6
	7	0+	0+	0+	0+	004	021	070	161	267	302	172	063	003	7
	8	0+	0+	0+	0+	0+	004	018	060	156	302	387	299	083	8
	9	0+	0+	0+	0+	0+	0+	002	010	040	134	387	630	914	9
10	0	904	599	349	107	028	006	001	0+	0+	0+	0+	0+	0+	0
	1	091	315	387	268	121	040	010	002	0+	0+	0+	0+	0+	1
	2	004	075	194	302	233	121	044	011	001	0+	0+	0+	0+	2
	3	0+	010	057	201	267	215	117	042	009	001	0+	0+	0+	3
	4	0+	001	011	088	200	251	205	111	037	006	0+	0+	0+	4
	5	0+	0+	001	026	103	201	246	201	103	026	001	0+	0+	5
	6	0+	0+	0+	006	037	111	205	251	200	088	011	001	0+	6
	7	0+	0+	0+	001	009	042	117	215	267	201	057	010	0+	7
	8	0+	0+	0+	0+	001	011	044	121	233	302	194	075	004	8
	9	0+	0+	0+	0+	0+	002	010	040	121	268	387	315	091	9
	10	0+	0+	0+	0+	0+	0+	001	006	028	107	349	599	904	10

TABLE A.1 — Binomial probabilities $[_nC_x p^x(1-p)^{n-x}]$ (continued).

n	x	0.01	0.05	0.10	0.20	0.30	0.40	0.50	0.60	0.70	0.80	0.90	0.95	0.99	x
11	0	895	569	314	086	020	004	0+	0+	0+	0+	0+	0+	0+	0
	1	099	329	384	236	093	027	005	001	0+	0+	0+	0+	0+	1
	2	005	087	213	295	200	089	027	005	001	0+	0+	0+	0+	2
	3	0+	014	071	221	257	177	081	023	004	0+	0+	0+	0+	3
	4	0+	001	016	111	220	236	161	070	017	002	0+	0+	0+	4
	5	0+	0+	002	039	132	221	226	147	057	010	0+	0+	0+	5
	6	0+	0+	0+	010	057	147	226	221	132	039	002	0+	0+	6
	7	0+	0+	0+	002	017	070	161	236	220	111	016	001	0+	7
	8	0+	0+	0+	0+	004	023	081	177	257	221	071	014	0+	8
	9	0+	0+	0+	0+	001	005	027	089	200	295	213	087	005	9
	10	0+	0+	0+	0+	0+	001	005	027	093	236	384	329	099	10
	11	0+	0+	0+	0+	0+	0+	0+	004	020	086	314	569	895	11
12	0	886	540	282	069	014	002	0+	0+	0+	0+	0+	0+	0+	0
	1	107	341	377	206	071	017	003	0+	0+	0+	0+	0+	0+	1
	2	006	099	230	283	168	064	016	002	0+	0+	0+	0+	0+	2
	3	0+	017	085	236	240	142	054	012	001	0+	0+	0+	0+	3
	4	0+	002	021	133	231	213	121	042	008	001	0+	0+	0+	4
	5	0+	0+	004	053	158	227	193	101	029	003	0+	0+	0+	5
	6	0+	0+	0+	016	079	177	226	177	079	016	0+	0+	0+	6
	7	0+	0+	0+	003	029	101	193	227	158	053	004	0+	0+	7
	8	0+	0+	0+	001	008	042	121	213	231	133	021	002	0+	8
	9	0+	0+	0+	0+	001	012	054	142	240	236	085	017	0+	9
	10	0+	0+	0+	0+	0+	002	016	064	168	283	230	099	006	10
	11	0+	0+	0+	0+	0+	0+	003	017	071	206	377	341	107	11
	12	0+	0+	0+	0+	0+	0+	0+	002	014	069	282	540	886	12
13	0	878	513	254	055	010	001	0+	0+	0+	0+	0+	0+	0+	0
	1	115	351	367	179	054	011	002	0+	0+	0+	0+	0+	0+	1
	2	007	111	245	268	139	045	010	001	0+	0+	0+	0+	0+	2
	3	0+	021	100	246	218	111	035	006	001	0+	0+	0+	0+	3
	4	0+	003	028	154	234	184	087	024	003	0+	0+	0+	0+	4
	5	0+	0+	006	069	180	221	157	066	014	001	0+	0+	0+	5
	6	0+	0+	001	023	103	197	209	131	044	006	0+	0+	0+	6
	7	0+	0+	0+	006	044	131	209	197	103	023	001	0+	0+	7
	8	0+	0+	0+	001	014	066	157	221	180	069	006	0+	0+	8
	9	0+	0+	0+	0+	003	024	087	184	234	154	028	003	0+	9
	10	0+	0+	0+	0+	001	006	035	111	218	246	100	021	0+	10
	11	0+	0+	0+	0+	0+	001	010	045	139	268	245	111	007	11
	12	0+	0+	0+	0+	0+	0+	002	011	054	179	367	351	115	12
	13	0+	0+	0+	0+	0+	0+	0+	001	010	055	254	513	878	13
14	0	869	488	229	044	007	001	0+	0+	0+	0+	0+	0+	0+	0
	1	123	359	356	154	041	007	001	0+	0+	0+	0+	0+	0+	1
	2	008	123	257	250	113	032	006	001	0+	0+	0+	0+	0+	2
	3	0+	026	114	250	194	085	022	003	0+	0+	0+	0+	0+	3
	4	0+	004	035	172	229	155	061	014	001	0+	0+	0+	0+	4
	5	0+	0+	008	086	196	207	122	041	007	0+	0+	0+	0+	5
	6	0+	0+	001	032	126	207	183	092	023	002	0+	0+	0+	6
	7	0+	0+	0+	009	062	157	209	157	062	009	0+	0+	0+	7
	8	0+	0+	0+	002	023	092	183	207	126	032	001	0+	0+	8
	9	0+	0+	0+	0+	007	041	122	207	196	086	008	0+	0+	9
	10	0+	0+	0+	0+	001	014	061	155	229	172	035	004	0+	10
	11	0+	0+	0+	0+	0+	003	022	085	194	250	114	026	0+	11
	12	0+	0+	0+	0+	0+	001	006	032	113	250	257	123	008	12
	13	0+	0+	0+	0+	0+	0+	001	007	041	154	356	359	123	13
	14	0+	0+	0+	0+	0+	0+	0+	001	007	044	229	488	869	14
15	0	860	463	206	035	005	0+	0+	0+	0+	0+	0+	0+	0+	0
	1	130	366	343	132	031	005	0+	0+	0+	0+	0+	0+	0+	1
	2	009	135	267	231	092	022	003	0+	0+	0+	0+	0+	0+	2
	3	0+	031	129	250	170	063	014	002	0+	0+	0+	0+	0+	3
	4	0+	005	043	188	219	127	042	007	001	0+	0+	0+	0+	4
	5	0+	001	010	103	206	186	092	024	003	0+	0+	0+	0+	5
	6	0+	0+	002	043	147	207	153	061	012	001	0+	0+	0+	6
	7	0+	0+	0+	014	081	177	196	118	035	003	0+	0+	0+	7
	8	0+	0+	0+	003	035	118	196	177	081	014	0+	0+	0+	8
	9	0+	0+	0+	001	012	061	153	207	147	043	002	0+	0+	9
	10	0+	0+	0+	0+	003	024	092	186	206	103	010	001	0+	10
	11	0+	0+	0+	0+	001	007	042	127	219	188	043	005	0+	11
	12	0+	0+	0+	0+	0+	002	014	063	170	250	129	031	0+	12
	13	0+	0+	0+	0+	0+	0+	003	022	092	231	267	135	009	13

TABLE A.1 — Binomial probabilities $[_nC_x p^x(1-p)^{n-x}]$ (continued).

n	x	0.01	0.05	0.10	0.20	0.30	0.40	P 0.50	0.60	0.70	0.80	0.90	0.95	0.99	x
	14	0+	0+	0+	0+	0+	0+	001	005	031	132	343	366	130	14
	15	0+	0+	0+	0+	0+	0+	0+	0+	005	035	206	463	860	15
16	0	852	440	185	028	003	0+	0+	0+	0+	0+	0+	0+	0+	0
	1	138	371	329	113	023	003	0+	0+	0+	0+	0+	0+	0+	1
	2	010	146	274	211	073	015	002	0+	0+	0+	0+	0+	0+	2
	3	0+	036	142	246	146	047	008	001	0+	0+	0+	0+	0+	3
	4	0+	006	051	200	204	101	028	004	0+	0+	0+	0+	0+	4
	5	0+	001	014	120	210	162	067	014	001	0+	0+	0+	0+	5
	6	0+	0+	003	055	165	198	122	039	006	0+	0+	0+	0+	6
	7	0+	0+	0+	020	101	189	175	084	018	001	0+	0+	0+	7
	8	0+	0+	0+	006	049	142	196	142	049	006	0+	0+	0+	8
	9	0+	0+	0+	001	018	084	175	189	101	020	0+	0+	0+	9
	10	0+	0+	0+	0+	006	039	122	198	165	055	003	0+	0+	10
	11	0+	0+	0+	0+	001	014	067	162	210	120	014	001	0+	11
	12	0+	0+	0+	0+	0+	004	028	101	204	200	051	006	0+	12
	13	0+	0+	0+	0+	0+	001	008	047	146	246	142	036	0+	13
	14	0+	0+	0+	0+	0+	0+	002	015	073	211	274	146	010	14
	15	0+	0+	0+	0+	0+	0+	0+	003	023	113	329	371	138	15
	16	0+	0+	0+	0+	0+	0+	0+	0+	003	028	185	440	852	16
17	0	843	418	167	022	002	0+	0+	0+	0+	0+	0+	0+	0+	0
	1	145	374	315	096	017	002	0+	0+	0+	0+	0+	0+	0+	1
	2	012	158	280	191	058	010	001	0+	0+	0+	0+	04	0+	2
	3	001	042	156	239	124	034	005	0+	0+	0+	0+	0+	0+	3
	4	0+	008	060	209	187	080	018	002	0+	0+	0+	0+	0+	4
	5	0+	001	018	136	208	138	047	008	001	0+	0+	0+	0+	5
	6	0+	0+	004	068	178	184	094	024	003	0+	0+	0+	0+	6
	7	0+	0+	001	027	120	193	148	057	010	0+	0+	0+	0+	7
	8	0+	0+	0+	008	064	161	186	107	028	002	0+	0+	0+	8
	9	0+	0+	0+	002	028	107	186	161	064	008	0+	0+	0+	9
	10	0+	0+	0+	0+	010	057	148	193	120	027	001	0+	0+	10
	11	0+	0+	0+	0+	003	024	094	184	178	068	004	0+	0+	11
	12	0+	0+	0+	0+	001	008	047	138	208	136	018	001	0+	12
	13	0+	0+	0+	0+	0+	002	018	080	187	209	060	008	0+	13
	14	0+	0+	0+	0+	0+	0+	005	034	124	239	156	042	001	14
	15	0+	0+	0+	0+	0+	0+	001	010	058	191	280	158	012	15
	16	0+	0+	0+	0+	0+	0+	0+	002	017	096	315	374	145	16
	17	0+	0+	0+	0+	0+	0+	0+	0+	002	022	167	418	843	17
18	0	834	397	150	018	002	0+	0+	0+	0+	0+	0+	0+	0+	0
	1	152	376	300	081	013	001	0+	0+	0+	0+	0+	0+	0+	1
	2	013	168	284	172	046	007	001	0+	0+	0+	0+	0+	0+	2
	3	001	047	168	230	105	025	003	0+	0+	0+	0+	0+	0+	3
	4	0+	009	070	215	168	061	012	001	0+	0+	0+	0+	0+	4
	5	0+	001	022	151	202	115	033	004	0+	0+	0+	0+	0+	5
	6	0+	0+	005	082	187	166	071	014	001	0+	0+	0+	0+	6
	7	0+	0+	001	035	138	189	121	037	005	0+	0+	0+	0+	7
	8	0+	0+	0+	012	081	173	167	077	015	001	0+	0+	0+	8
	9	0+	0+	0+	003	039	128	186	128	039	003	0+	0+	0+	9
	10	0+	0+	0+	001	015	077	167	173	081	012	0+	0+	0+	10
	11	0+	0+	0+	0+	005	037	121	189	138	035	001	0+	0+	11
	12	0+	0+	0+	0+	001	014	071	166	187	082	005	0+	0+	1
	13	0+	0+	0+	0+	0+	004	033	115	202	151	022	001	0+	13
	14	0+	0+	0+	0+	0+	001	012	061	168	215	070	009	0+	14
	15	0+	0+	0+	0+	0+	0+	003	025	105	230	168	047	001	15
	16	0+	0+	0+	0+	0+	0+	001	007	046	172	284	168	013	16
	17	0+	0+	0+	0+	0+	0+	0+	001	013	081	300	376	152	17
	18	0+	0+	0+	0+	0+	0+	0+	0+	002	018	150	397	834	18
19	0	826	377	135	014	001	0+	0+	0+	0+	0+	0+	0+	0+	0
	1	159	377	285	068	009	001	0+	0+	0+	0+	0+	0+	0+	1
	2	014	179	285	154	036	005	0+	0+	0+	0+	0+	0+	0+	2
	3	001	053	180	218	087	018	002	0+	0+	0+	0+	0+	0+	3
	4	0+	011	080	218	149	047	007	0+	0+	0+	0+	0+	0+	4
	5	0+	002	027	164	192	093	022	002	0+	0+	0+	0+	0+	5
	6	0+	0+	007	096	192	145	052	008	0+	0+	0+	0+	0+	6
	7	0+	0+	001	044	152	180	096	024	002	0+	0+	0+	0+	7
	8	0+	0+	0+	017	098	180	144	053	008	0+	0+	0+	0+	8
	9	0+	0+	0+	005	051	146	176	098	022	001	0+	0+	0+	9
	10	0+	0+	0+	001	022	098	176	146	051	005	0+	0+	0+	10
	11	0+	0+	0+	0+	008	053	144	180	098	017	0+	0+	0+	11

TABLE A.1   Binomial probabilities $[_nC_x p^x (1-p)^{n-x}]$ *(continued)*.

n	x	0.01	0.05	0.10	0.20	0.30	0.40	P 0.50	0.60	0.70	0.80	0.90	0.95	0.99	x
	12	0+	0+	0+	0+	002	024	096	180	152	044	001	0+	0+	12
	13	0+	0+	0+	0+	0+	008	052	145	192	096	007	0+	0+	13
	14	0+	0+	0+	0+	0+	002	022	093	192	164	027	002	0+	14
	15	0+	0+	0+	0+	0+	0+	007	047	149	218	080	011	0+	15
	16	0+	0+	0+	0+	0+	0+	002	018	087	218	180	053	001	16
	17	0+	0+	0+	0+	0+	0+	0+	005	036	154	285	179	014	17
	18	0+	0+	0+	0+	0+	0+	0+	001	009	068	285	377	159	18
	19	0+	0+	0+	0+	0+	0+	0+	0+	001	014	135	377	826	19
20	0	818	358	122	012	001	0+	0+	0+	0+	0+	0+	0+	0+	0
	1	165	377	270	058	007	0+	0+	0+	0+	0+	0+	0+	0+	1
	2	016	189	285	137	028	003	0+	0+	0+	0+	0+	0+	0+	2
	3	001	060	190	205	072	012	001	0+	0+	0+	0+	0+	0+	3
	4	0+	013	090	218	130	035	005	0+	0+	0+	0+	0+	0+	4
	5	0+	002	032	175	179	075	015	001	0+	0+	0+	0+	0+	5
	6	0+	0+	009	109	192	124	037	005	0+	0+	0+	0+	0+	6
	7	0+	0+	002	054	164	166	074	015	001	0+	0+	0+	0+	7
	8	0+	0+	0+	022	114	180	120	036	004	0+	0+	0+	0+	8
	9	0+	0+	0+	007	065	160	160	071	012	0+	0+	0+	0+	9
	10	0+	0+	0+	002	031	117	176	117	031	002	0+	0+	0+	10
	11	0+	0+	0+	0+	012	071	160	160	065	007	0+	0+	0+	11
	12	0+	0+	0+	0+	004	036	120	180	114	022	0+	0+	0+	12
	13	0+	0+	0+	0+	001	015	074	166	164	054	002	0+	0+	13
	14	0+	0+	0+	0+	0+	005	037	124	192	109	009	0+	0+	14
	15	0+	0+	0+	0+	0+	001	015	075	179	175	032	002	0+	15
	16	0+	0+	0+	0+	0+	0+	005	035	130	218	090	013	0+	16
	17	0+	0+	0+	0+	0+	0+	001	012	072	205	190	060	001	17
	18	0+	0+	0+	0+	0+	0+	0+	003	028	137	285	189	016	18
	19	0+	0+	0+	0+	0+	0+	0+	0+	007	058	270	377	165	19
	20	0+	0+	0+	0+	0+	0+	0+	0+	001	012	122	358	818	20

TABLE A.2   Values of e^{-a}.

a	e^{-a}	a	e^{-a}	a	e^{-a}	a	e^{-a}
0.00	1.000000	2.60	.074274	5.10	.006097	7.60	.000501
0.10	.904837	2.70	.067206	5.20	.005517	7.70	.000453
0.20	.818731	2.80	.060810	5.30	.004992	7.80	.000410
0.30	.740818	2.90	.055023	5.40	.004517	7.90	.000371
0.40	.670320	3.00	.049787	5.50	.004087	8.00	.000336
0.50	.606531	3.10	.045049	5.60	.003698	8.10	.000304
0.60	.548812	3.20	.040762	5.70	.003346	8.20	.000275
0.70	.496585	3.30	.036883	5.80	.003028	8.30	.000249
0.80	.449329	3.40	0.33373	5.90	.002739	8.40	.000225
0.90	.406570	3.50	.030197	6.00	.002479	8.50	.000204
1.00	.367879	3.60	.027324	6.10	.002243	8.60	.000184
1.10	.332871	3.70	.024724	6.20	.002029	8.70	.000167
1.20	.301194	3.80	.022371	6.30	.001836	8.80	.000151
1.30	.272532	3.90	.020242	6.40	.001661	8.90	.000136
1.40	.246597	4.00	.018316	6.50	.001503	9.00	.000123
1.50	.223130	4.10	.016573	6.60	.001360	9.10	.000112
1.60	.201897	4.20	.014996	6.70	.001231	9.20	.000101
1.70	.182684	4.30	.013569	6.80	.001114	9.30	.000091
1.80	.165299	4.40	.012277	6.90	.001008	9.40	.000083
1.90	.149569	4.50	.011109	7.00	.000912	9.50	.000075
2.00	.135335	4.60	.010052	7.10	.000825	9.60	.000068
2.10	.122456	4.70	.009095	7.20	.000747	9.70	.000061
2.20	.110803	4.80	.008230	7.30	.000676	9.80	.000056
2.30	.100259	4.90	.007447	7.40	.000611	9.90	.000050
2.40	.090718	5.00	.006738	7.50	.000553	10.00	.000045
2.50	.082085						

TABLE A.3

Poisson probabilities $\left[\dfrac{e^{-\mu}\mu^{x}}{x!}\right]$.

x	μ = 0.005	0.01	0.02	0.03	0.04	0.05	0.06	0.07	0.08	0.09
0	0.9950	0.9900	0.9802	0.9704	0.9608	0.9512	0.9418	0.9324	0.9231	0.9139
1	0.0050	0.0099	0.0192	0.0291	0.0384	0.0476	0.0565	0.0653	0.0738	0.0823
2	0.0000	0.0000	0.0002	0.0004	0.0008	0.0012	0.0017	0.0023	0.0030	0.0037
3	0.0000	0.0000	0.0000	0.0000	0.0000	0.0000	0.0000	0.0001	0.0001	0.0001

x	0.1	0.2	0.3	0.4	0.5	0.6	0.7	0.8	0.9	1.0
0	0.9048	0.8187	0.7408	0.6703	0.6065	0.5488	0.4966	0.4493	0.4066	0.3679
1	0.0905	0.1637	0.2222	0.2681	0.3033	0.3293	0.3476	0.3595	0.3659	0.3679
2	0.0045	0.0164	0.0333	0.0536	0.0758	0.0988	0.1217	0.1438	0.1647	0.1839
3	0.0002	0.0011	0.0033	0.0072	0.0126	0.0198	0.0284	0.0383	0.0494	0.0613
4	0.0000	0.0001	0.0002	0.0007	0.0016	0.0030	0.0050	0.0077	0.0111	0.0153
5	0.0000	0.0000	0.0000	0.0001	0.0002	0.0004	0.0007	0.0012	0.0020	0.0031
6	0.0000	0.0000	0.0000	0.0000	0.0000	0.0000	0.0001	0.0002	0.0003	0.0005
7	0.0000	0.0000	0.0000	0.0000	0.0000	0.0000	0.0000	0.0000	0.0000	0.0001

x	1.1	1.2	1.3	1.4	1.5	1.6	1.7	1.8	1.9	2.0
0	0.3329	0.3012	0.2725	0.2466	0.2231	0.2019	0.1827	0.1653	0.1496	0.1353
1	0.3662	0.3614	0.3543	0.3452	0.3347	0.3230	0.3106	0.2975	0.2842	0.2707
2	0.2014	0.2169	0.2303	0.2417	0.2510	0.2584	0.2640	0.2678	0.2700	0.2707
3	0.0738	0.0867	0.0998	0.1128	0.1255	0.1378	0.1496	0.1607	0.1710	0.1804
4	0.0203	0.0260	0.0324	0.0395	0.0471	0.0551	0.0636	0.0723	0.0812	0.0902
5	0.0045	0.0062	0.0084	0.0111	0.0141	0.0176	0.0216	0.0260	0.0309	0.0361
6	0.0008	0.0012	0.0018	0.0026	0.0035	0.0047	0.0061	0.0078	0.0098	0.0120
7	0.0001	0.0002	0.0003	0.0005	0.0008	0.0011	0.0015	0.0020	0.0027	0.0034
8	0.0000	0.0000	0.0001	0.0001	0.0001	0.0002	0.0003	0.0005	0.0006	0.0009
9	0.0000	0.0000	0.0000	0.0000	0.0000	0.0000	0.0001	0.0001	0.0001	0.0002

x	2.1	2.2	2.3	2.4	2.5	2.6	2.7	2.8	2.9	3.0
0	0.1225	0.1108	0.1003	0.0907	0.0821	0.0743	0.0672	0.0608	0.0550	0.0498
1	0.2572	0.2438	0.2306	0.2177	0.2052	0.1931	0.1815	0.1703	0.1596	0.1494
2	0.2700	0.2681	0.2652	0.2613	0.2565	0.2510	0.2450	0.2384	0.2314	0.2240
3	0.1890	0.1966	0.2033	0.2090	0.2138	0.2176	0.2205	0.2225	0.2237	0.2240
4	0.0992	0.1082	0.1169	0.1254	0.1336	0.1414	0.1488	0.1557	0.1622	0.1680
5	0.0417	0.0476	0.0538	0.0602	0.0668	0.0735	0.0804	0.0872	0.0940	0.1008
6	0.0146	0.0174	0.0206	0.0241	0.0278	0.0319	0.0362	0.0407	0.0455	0.0504
7	0.0044	0.0055	0.0068	0.0083	0.0099	0.0118	0.0139	0.0163	0.0188	0.0216
8	0.0011	0.0015	0.0019	0.0025	0.0031	0.0038	0.0047	0.0057	0.0068	0.0081
9	0.0003	0.0004	0.0005	0.0007	0.0009	0.0011	0.0014	0.0018	0.0022	0.0027
10	0.0001	0.0001	0.0001	0.0002	0.0002	0.0003	0.0004	0.0005	0.0006	0.0008
11	0.0000	0.0000	0.0000	0.0000	0.0000	0.0001	0.0001	0.0001	0.0002	0.0002
12	0.0000	0.0000	0.0000	0.0000	0.0000	0.0000	0.0000	0.0000	0.0000	0.0001

x	3.1	3.2	3.3	3.4	3.5	3.6	3.7	3.8	3.9	4.0
0	0.0450	0.0408	0.0369	0.0334	0.0302	0.0273	0.0247	0.0224	0.0202	0.0183
1	0.1397	0.1304	0.1217	0.1135	0.1057	0.0984	0.0915	0.0850	0.0789	0.0733
2	0.2165	0.2087	0.2008	0.1929	0.1850	0.1771	0.1692	0.1615	0.1539	0.1465
3	0.2237	0.2226	0.2209	0.2186	0.2158	0.2125	0.2087	0.2046	0.2001	0.1954
4	0.1734	0.1781	0.1823	0.1858	0.1888	0.1912	0.1931	0.1944	0.1951	0.1954
5	0.1075	0.1140	0.1203	0.1264	0.1322	0.1377	0.1429	0.1477	0.1522	0.1563
6	0.0555	0.0608	0.0662	0.0716	0.0771	0.0826	0.0881	0.0936	0.0989	0.1042
7	0.0246	0.0278	0.0312	0.0348	0.0385	0.0425	0.0466	0.0508	0.0551	0.0595
8	0.0095	0.0111	0.0129	0.0148	0.0169	0.0191	0.0215	0.0241	0.0269	0.0298
9	0.0033	0.0040	0.0047	0.0056	0.0066	0.0076	0.0089	0.0102	0.0116	0.0132
10	0.0010	0.0013	0.0016	0.0019	0.0023	0.0028	0.0033	0.0039	0.0045	0.0053
11	0.0003	0.0004	0.0005	0.0006	0.0007	0.0009	0.0011	0.0013	0.0016	0.0019
12	0.0001	0.0001	0.0001	0.0002	0.0002	0.0003	0.0003	0.0004	0.0005	0.0006
13	0.0000	0.0000	0.0000	0.0000	0.0001	0.0001	0.0001	0.0001	0.0002	0.0002
14	0.0000	0.0000	0.0000	0.0000	0.0000	0.0000	0.0000	0.0000	0.0000	0.0001

x	4.1	4.2	4.3	4.4	4.5	4.6	4.7	4.8	4.9	5.0
0	0.0166	0.0150	0.0136	0.0123	0.0111	0.0101	0.0091	0.0082	0.0074	0.0067
1	0.0679	0.0630	0.0583	0.0540	0.0500	0.0462	0.0427	0.0395	0.0365	0.0337
2	0.1393	0.1323	0.1254	0.1188	0.1125	0.1063	0.1005	0.0948	0.0894	0.0842
3	0.1904	0.1852	0.1798	0.1743	0.1687	0.1631	0.1574	0.1517	0.1460	0.1404
4	0.1951	0.1944	0.1933	0.1917	0.1898	0.1875	0.1849	0.1820	0.1789	0.1755

TABLE A.3   Poisson probabilities $\left[\dfrac{e^{-\mu}\mu^x}{x!}\right]$ *(continued).*

μ										
x	4.1	4.2	4.3	4.4	4.5	4.6	4.7	4.8	4.9	5.0
5	0.1600	0.1633	0.1662	0.1687	0.1708	0.1725	0.1738	0.1747	0.1753	0.1755
6	0.1093	0.1143	0.1191	0.1237	0.1281	0.1323	0.1362	0.1398	0.1432	0.1462
7	0.0640	0.0686	0.0732	0.0778	0.0824	0.0869	0.0914	0.0959	0.1002	0.1044
8	0.0328	0.0360	0.0393	0.0428	0.0463	0.0500	0.0537	0.0575	0.0614	0.0653
9	0.0150	0.0168	0.0188	0.0209	0.0232	0.0255	0.0280	0.0307	0.0334	0.0363
10	0.0061	0.0071	0.0081	0.0092	0.0104	0.0118	0.0132	0.0147	0.0164	0.0181
11	0.0023	0.0027	0.0032	0.0037	0.0043	0.0049	0.0056	0.0064	0.0073	0.0082
12	0.0008	0.0009	0.0011	0.0014	0.0016	0.0019	0.0022	0.0026	0.0030	0.0034
13	0.0002	0.0003	0.0004	0.0005	0.0006	0.0007	0.0008	0.0009	0.0011	0.0013
14	0.0001	0.0001	0.0001	0.0001	0.0002	0.0002	0.0003	0.0003	0.0004	0.0005
15	0.0000	0.0000	0.0000	0.0000	0.0001	0.0001	0.0001	0.0001	0.0001	0.0002
x	5.1	5.2	5.3	5.4	5.5	5.6	5.7	5.8	5.9	6.0
0	0.0061	0.0055	0.0050	0.0045	0.0041	0.0037	0.0033	0.0030	0.0027	0.0025
1	0.0311	0.0287	0.0265	0.0244	0.0225	0.0207	0.0191	0.0176	0.0162	0.0149
2	0.0793	0.0746	0.0701	0.0659	0.0618	0.0580	0.0544	0.0509	0.0477	0.0446
3	0.1348	0.1293	0.1239	0.1185	0.1133	0.1082	0.1033	0.0985	0.0938	0.0892
4	0.1719	0.1681	0.1641	0.1600	0.1558	0.1515	0.1472	0.1428	0.1383	0.1339
5	0.1753	0.1748	0.1740	0.1728	0.1714	0.1697	0.1678	0.1656	0.1632	0.1606
6	0.1490	0.1515	0.1537	0.1555	0.1571	0.1584	0.1594	0.1601	0.1605	0.1606
7	0.1086	0.1125	0.1163	0.1200	0.1234	0.1267	0.1298	0.1326	0.1353	0.1377
8	0.0692	0.0731	0.0771	0.0810	0.0849	0.0887	0.0925	0.0962	0.0998	0.1033
9	0.0392	0.0423	0.0454	0.0486	0.0519	0.0552	0.0586	0.0620	0.0654	0.0688
10	0.0200	0.0220	0.0241	0.0262	0.0285	0.0309	0.0334	0.0359	0.0386	0.0413
11	0.0093	0.0104	0.0116	0.0129	0.0143	0.0157	0.0173	0.0190	0.0207	0.0225
12	0.0039	0.0045	0.0051	0.0058	0.0065	0.0073	0.0082	0.0092	0.0102	0.0113
13	0.0015	0.0018	0.0021	0.0024	0.0028	0.0032	0.0036	0.0041	0.0046	0.0052
14	0.0006	0.0007	0.0008	0.0009	0.0011	0.0013	0.0015	0.0017	0.0019	0.0022
15	0.0002	0.0002	0.0003	0.0003	0.0004	0.0005	0.0006	0.0007	0.0008	0.0009
16	0.0001	0.0001	0.0001	0.0001	0.0001	0.0002	0.0002	0.0002	0.0003	0.0003
17	0.0000	0.0000	0.0000	0.0000	0.0000	0.0001	0.0001	0.0001	0.0001	0.0001
x	6.1	6.2	6.3	6.4	6.5	6.6	6.7	6.8	6.9	7.0
0	0.0022	0.0020	0.0018	0.0017	0.0015	0.0014	0.0012	0.0011	0.0010	0.0009
1	0.0137	0.0126	0.0116	0.0106	0.0098	0.0090	0.0082	0.0076	0.0070	0.0064
2	0.0417	0.0390	0.0364	0.0340	0.0318	0.0296	0.0276	0.0258	0.0240	0.0223
3	0.0848	0.0806	0.0765	0.0726	0.0688	0.0652	0.0617	0.0584	0.0552	0.0521
4	0.1294	0.1269	0.1205	0.1162	0.1118	0.1076	0.1034	0.0992	0.0952	0.0912
5	0.1579	0.1549	0.1519	0.1487	0.1454	0.1420	0.1385	0.1349	0.1314	0.1277
6	0.1605	0.1601	0.1595	0.1586	0.1575	0.1562	0.1546	0.1529	0.1511	0.1490
7	0.1399	0.1418	0.1435	0.1450	0.1462	0.1472	0.1480	0.1486	0.1489	0.1490
8	0.1066	0.1099	0.1130	0.1160	0.1188	0.1215	0.1240	0.1263	0.1284	0.1304
9	0.0723	0.0757	0.0791	0.0825	0.0858	0.0891	0.0923	0.0954	0.0985	0.1014
10	0.0441	0.0469	0.0498	0.0528	0.0558	0.0588	0.0618	0.0649	0.0679	0.0710
11	0.0245	0.0265	0.0285	0.0307	0.0330	0.0353	0.0377	0.0401	0.0426	0.0452
12	0.0124	0.0137	0.0150	0.0164	0.0179	0.0194	0.0210	0.0227	0.0245	0.0264
13	0.0058	0.0065	0.0073	0.0081	0.0089	0.0098	0.0108	0.0119	0.0130	0.0142
14	0.0025	0.0029	0.0033	0.0037	0.0041	0.0046	0.0052	0.0058	0.0064	0.0071
15	0.0010	0.0012	0.0014	0.0016	0.0018	0.0020	0.0023	0.0026	0.0029	0.0033
16	0.0004	0.0005	0.0005	0.0006	0.0007	0.0008	0.0010	0.0011	0.0013	0.0014
17	0.0001	0.0002	0.0002	0.0002	0.0003	0.0003	0.0004	0.0004	0.0005	0.0006
18	0.0000	0.0001	0.0001	0.0001	0.0001	0.0001	0.0001	0.0002	0.0002	0.0002
19	0.0000	0.0000	0.0000	0.0000	0.0000	0.0000	0.0000	0.0001	0.0001	0.0001
x	7.1	7.2	7.3	7.4	7.5	7.6	7.7	7.8	7.9	8.0
0	0.0008	0.0007	0.0007	0.0006	0.0006	0.0005	0.0005	0.0004	0.0004	0.0003
1	0.0059	0.0054	0.0049	0.0045	0.0041	0.0038	0.0035	0.0032	0.0029	0.0027
2	0.0208	0.0194	0.0180	0.0167	0.0156	0.0145	0.0134	0.0125	0.0116	0.0107
3	0.0492	0.0464	0.0438	0.0413	0.0389	0.0366	0.0345	0.0324	0.0305	0.0286
4	0.0874	0.0836	0.0799	0.0764	0.0729	0.0696	0.0663	0.0632	0.0602	0.0573
5	0.1241	0.1204	0.1167	0.1130	0.1094	0.1057	0.1021	0.0986	0.0951	0.0916
6	0.1468	0.1445	0.1420	0.1394	0.1367	0.1339	0.1311	0.1282	0.1252	0.1221
7	0.1489	0.1486	0.1481	0.1474	0.1465	0.1454	0.1442	0.1428	0.1413	0.1396
8	0.1321	0.1337	0.1351	0.1363	0.1373	0.1382	0.1388	0.1392	0.1395	0.1396
9	0.1042	0.1070	0.1096	0.1121	0.1144	0.1167	0.1187	0.1207	0.1224	0.1241
10	0.0740	0.0770	0.0800	0.0829	0.0858	0.0887	0.0914	0.0941	0.0967	0.0993
11	0.0478	0.0504	0.0531	0.0558	0.0585	0.0613	0.0640	0.0667	0.0695	0.0722

TABLE A.3   Poisson probabilities $\left[\dfrac{e^{-\mu}\mu^{x}}{x!}\right]$ (continued).

	μ									
x	7.1	7.2	7.3	7.4	7.5	7.6	7.7	7.8	7.9	8.0
12	0.0283	0.0303	0.0323	0.0344	0.0366	0.0388	0.0411	0.0434	0.0457	0.0481
13	0.0154	0.0168	0.0181	0.0196	0.0211	0.0227	0.0243	0.0260	0.0278	0.0296
14	0.0078	0.0086	0.0095	0.0104	0.0113	0.0123	0.0134	0.0145	0.0157	0.0169
15	0.0037	0.0041	0.0046	0.0051	0.0057	0.0062	0.0069	0.0075	0.0083	0.0090
16	0.0016	0.0019	0.0021	0.0024	0.0026	0.0030	0.0033	0.0037	0.0041	0.0045
17	0.0007	0.0008	0.0009	0.0010	0.0012	0.0013	0.0015	0.0017	0.0019	0.0021
18	0.0003	0.0003	0.0004	0.0004	0.0005	0.0006	0.0006	0.0007	0.0008	0.0009
19	0.0001	0.0001	0.0001	0.0002	0.0002	0.0002	0.0003	0.0003	0.0003	0.0004
20	0.0000	0.0000	0.0001	0.0001	0.0001	0.0001	0.0001	0.0001	0.0001	0.0002
21	0.0000	0.0000	0.0000	0.0000	0.0000	0.0000	0.0000	0.0000	0.0001	0.0001

x	8.1	8.2	8.3	8.4	8.5	8.6	8.7	8.8	8.9	9.0
0	0.0003	0.0003	0.0002	0.0002	0.0002	0.0002	0.0002	0.0002	0.0001	0.0001
1	0.0025	0.0023	0.0021	0.0019	0.0017	0.0016	0.0014	0.0013	0.0012	0.0011
2	0.0100	0.0092	0.0086	0.0079	0.0074	0.0068	0.0063	0.0058	0.0054	0.0050
3	0.0269	0.0252	0.0237	0.0222	0.0208	0.0195	0.0183	0.0171	0.0160	0.0150
4	0.0544	0.0517	0.0491	0.0466	0.0443	0.0420	0.0398	0.0377	0.0357	0.0337
5	0.0882	0.0849	0.0816	0.0784	0.0752	0.0722	0.0692	0.0663	0.0635	0.0607
6	0.1191	0.1160	0.1128	0.1097	0.1066	0.1034	0.1003	0.0972	0.0941	0.0911
7	0.1378	0.1358	0.1338	0.1317	0.1294	0.1271	0.1247	0.1222	0.1197	0.1171
8	0.1395	0.1392	0.1388	0.1382	0.1375	0.1366	0.1356	0.1344	0.1332	0.1318
9	0.1256	0.1269	0.1280	0.1290	0.1299	0.1306	0.1311	0.1315	0.1317	0.1318
10	0.1017	0.1040	0.1063	0.1084	0.1104	0.1123	0.1140	0.1157	0.1172	0.1186
11	0.0749	0.0776	0.0802	0.0828	0.0853	0.0878	0.0902	0.0925	0.0948	0.0970
12	0.0505	0.0530	0.0555	0.0579	0.0604	0.0629	0.0654	0.0679	0.0703	0.0728
13	0.0315	0.0334	0.0354	0.0374	0.0395	0.0416	0.0438	0.0459	0.0481	0.0504
14	0.0182	0.0196	0.0210	0.0225	0.0240	0.0256	0.0272	0.0289	0.0306	0.0324
15	0.0098	0.0107	0.0116	0.0126	0.0136	0.0147	0.0158	0.0169	0.0182	0.0194
16	0.0050	0.0055	0.0060	0.0066	0.0072	0.0079	0.0086	0.0093	0.0101	0.0109
17	0.0024	0.0026	0.0029	0.0033	0.0036	0.0040	0.0044	0.0048	0.0053	0.0058
18	0.0011	0.0012	0.0014	0.0015	0.0017	0.0019	0.0021	0.0024	0.0026	0.0029
19	0.0005	0.0005	0.0006	0.0007	0.0008	0.0009	0.0010	0.0011	0.0012	0.0014
20	0.0002	0.0002	0.0002	0.0003	0.0003	0.0004	0.0004	0.0005	0.0005	0.0006
21	0.0001	0.0001	0.0001	0.0001	0.0001	0.0002	0.0002	0.0002	0.0002	0.0003
22	0.0000	0.0000	0.0000	0.0000	0.0001	0.0001	0.0001	0.0001	0.0001	0.0001

x	9.1	9.2	9.3	9.4	9.5	9.6	9.7	9.8	9.9	10.0
0	0.0001	0.0001	0.0001	0.0001	0.0001	0.0001	0.0001	0.0001	0.0001	0.0000
1	0.0010	0.0009	0.0009	0.0008	0.0007	0.0007	0.0006	0.0005	0.0005	0.0005
2	0.0046	0.0043	0.0040	0.0037	0.0034	0.0031	0.0029	0.0027	0.0025	0.0023
3	0.0140	0.0131	0.0123	0.0115	0.0107	0.0100	0.0093	0.0087	0.0081	0.0076
4	0.0319	0.0302	0.0285	0.0269	0.0254	0.0240	0.0226	0.0213	0.0201	0.0189
5	0.0581	0.0555	0.0530	0.0506	0.0483	0.0460	0.0439	0.0418	0.0398	0.0378
6	0.0881	0.0851	0.0822	0.0793	0.0764	0.0736	0.0709	0.0682	0.0656	0.0631
7	0.1145	0.1118	0.1091	0.1064	0.1037	0.1010	0.0982	0.0955	0.0928	0.0901
8	0.1302	0.1286	0.1269	0.1251	0.1232	0.1212	0.1191	0.1170	0.1148	0.1126
9	0.1317	0.1315	0.1311	0.1306	0.1300	0.1293	0.1284	0.1274	0.1263	0.1251
10	0.1198	0.1210	0.1219	0.1228	0.1235	0.1241	0.1245	0.1249	0.1250	0.1251
11	0.0991	0.1012	0.1031	0.1049	0.1067	0.1083	0.1098	0.1112	0.1125	0.1137
12	0.0752	0.0776	0.0799	0.0822	0.0844	0.0866	0.0888	0.0908	0.0928	0.0948
13	0.0526	0.0549	0.0572	0.0594	0.0617	0.0640	0.0662	0.0685	0.0707	0.0729
14	0.0342	0.0361	0.0380	0.0399	0.0419	0.0439	0.0459	0.0479	0.0500	0.0521
15	0.0208	0.0221	0.0235	0.0250	0.0265	0.0281	0.0297	0.0313	0.0330	0.0347
16	0.0118	0.0127	0.0137	0.0147	0.0157	0.0168	0.0180	0.0192	0.0204	0.0217
17	0.0063	0.0069	0.0075	0.0081	0.0088	0.0095	0.0103	0.0111	0.0119	0.0128
18	0.0032	0.0035	0.0039	0.0042	0.0046	0.0051	0.0055	0.0060	0.0065	0.0071
19	0.0015	0.0017	0.0019	0.0021	0.0023	0.0026	0.0028	0.0031	0.0034	0.0037
20	0.0007	0.0008	0.0009	0.0010	0.0011	0.0012	0.0014	0.0015	0.0017	0.0019
21	0.0003	0.0003	0.0004	0.0004	0.0005	0.0006	0.0006	0.0007	0.0008	0.0009
22	0.0001	0.0001	0.0002	0.0002	0.0002	0.0002	0.0003	0.0003	0.0004	0.0004
23	0.0000	0.0001	0.0001	0.0001	0.0001	0.0001	0.0001	0.0001	0.0002	0.0002
24	0.0000	0.0000	0.0000	0.0000	0.0000	0.0000	0.0000	0.0001	0.0001	0.0001

TABLE A.4

Areas of the standard normal distribution. The entries in this table are the probabilities that a standard normal random variable is between 0 and z (the shaded area).

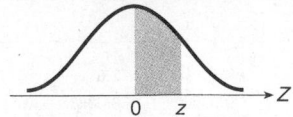

z	SECOND DECIMAL PLACE IN z									
	0.00	0.01	0.02	0.03	0.04	0.05	0.06	0.07	0.08	0.09
0.0	0.0000	0.0040	0.0080	0.0120	0.0160	0.0199	0.0239	0.0279	0.0319	0.0359
0.1	0.0398	0.0438	0.0478	0.0517	0.0557	0.0596	0.0636	0.0675	0.0714	0.0753
0.2	0.0793	0.0832	0.0871	0.0910	0.0948	0.0987	0.1026	0.1064	0.1103	0.1141
0.3	0.1179	0.1217	0.1255	0.1293	0.1331	0.1368	0.1406	0.1443	0.1480	0.1517
0.4	0.1554	0.1591	0.1628	0.1664	0.1700	0.1736	0.1772	0.1808	0.1844	0.1879
0.5	0.1915	0.1950	0.1985	0.2019	0.2054	0.2088	0.2123	0.2157	0.2190	0.2224
0.6	0.2257	0.2291	0.2324	0.2357	0.2389	0.2422	0.2454	0.2486	0.2517	0.2549
0.7	0.2580	0.2611	0.2642	0.2673	0.2704	0.2734	0.2764	0.2794	0.2823	0.2852
0.8	0.2881	0.2910	0.2939	0.2967	0.2995	0.3023	0.3051	0.3078	0.3106	0.3133
0.9	0.3159	0.3186	0.3212	0.3238	0.3264	0.3289	0.3315	0.3340	0.3365	0.3389
1.0	0.3413	0.3438	0.3461	0.3485	0.3508	0.3531	0.3554	0.3577	0.3599	0.3621
1.1	0.3643	0.3665	0.3686	0.3708	0.3729	0.3749	0.3770	0.3790	0.3810	0.3830
1.2	0.3849	0.3869	0.3888	0.3907	0.3925	0.3944	0.3962	0.3980	0.3997	0.4015
1.3	0.4032	0.4049	0.4066	0.4082	0.4099	0.4115	0.4131	0.4147	0.4162	0.4177
1.4	0.4192	0.4207	0.4222	0.4236	0.4251	0.4265	0.4279	0.4292	0.4306	0.4319
1.5	0.4332	0.4345	0.4357	0.4370	0.4382	0.4394	0.4406	0.4418	0.4429	0.4441
1.6	0.4452	0.4463	0.4474	0.4484	0.4495	0.4505	0.4515	0.4525	0.4535	0.4545
1.7	0.4554	0.4564	0.4573	0.4582	0.4591	0.4599	0.4608	0.4616	0.4625	0.4633
1.8	0.4641	0.4649	0.4656	0.4664	0.4671	0.4678	0.4686	0.4693	0.4699	0.4706
1.9	0.4713	0.4719	0.4726	0.4732	0.4738	0.4744	0.4750	0.4756	0.4761	0.4767
2.0	0.4772	0.4778	0.4783	0.4788	0.4793	0.4798	0.4803	0.4808	0.4812	0.4817
2.1	0.4821	0.4826	0.4830	0.4834	0.4838	0.4842	0.4846	0.4850	0.4854	0.4857
2.2	0.4861	0.4864	0.4868	0.4871	0.4875	0.4878	0.4881	0.4884	0.4887	0.4890
2.3	0.4893	0.4896	0.4898	0.4901	0.4904	0.4906	0.4909	0.4911	0.4913	0.4916
2.4	0.4918	0.4920	0.4922	0.4925	0.4927	0.4929	0.4931	0.4932	0.4934	0.4936
2.5	0.4938	0.4940	0.4941	0.4943	0.4945	0.4946	0.4948	0.4949	0.4951	0.4952
2.6	0.4953	0.4955	0.4956	0.4957	0.4959	0.4960	0.4961	0.4962	0.4963	0.4964
2.7	0.4965	0.4966	0.4967	0.4968	0.4969	0.4970	0.4971	0.4972	0.4973	0.4974
2.8	0.4974	0.4975	0.4976	0.4977	0.4977	0.4978	0.4979	0.4979	0.4980	0.4981
2.9	0.4981	0.4982	0.4982	0.4983	0.4984	0.4984	0.4985	0.4985	0.4986	0.4986
3.0	0.4987	0.4987	0.4987	0.4988	0.4988	0.4989	0.4989	0.4989	0.4990	0.4990
3.1	0.4990	0.4991	0.4991	0.4991	0.4992	0.4992	0.4992	0.4992	0.4993	0.4993
3.2	0.4993	0.4993	0.4994	0.4994	0.4994	0.4994	0.4994	0.4995	0.4995	0.4995
3.3	0.4995	0.4995	0.4995	0.4996	0.4996	0.4996	0.4996	0.4996	0.4996	0.4997
3.4	0.4997	0.4997	0.4997	0.4997	0.4997	0.4997	0.4997	0.4997	0.4997	0.4998
3.5	0.4998									
4.0	0.49997									
4.5	0.499997									
5.0	0.4999997									

Reprinted with permission from *Standard Mathematical Tables*, 15th ed., © CRC Press. Inc., Boca Raton, FL.

TABLE A.5

Critical values of *t*.

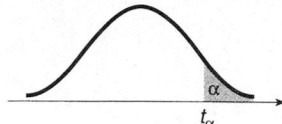

DEGREES OF FREEDOM	$t_{.100}$	$t_{.050}$	$t_{.025}$	$t_{.010}$	$t_{.005}$
1	3.078	6.314	12.706	31.821	63.657
2	1.886	2.920	4.303	6.965	9.925
3	1.638	2.353	3.182	4.541	5.841
4	1.533	2.132	2.776	3.747	4.604
5	1.476	2.015	2.571	3.365	4.032
6	1.440	1.943	2.447	3.143	3.707
7	1.415	1.895	2.365	2.998	3.499
8	1.397	1.860	2.306	2.896	3.355
9	1.383	1.833	2.262	2.821	3.250
10	1.372	1.812	2.228	2.764	3.169
11	1.363	1.796	2.201	2.718	3.106
12	1.356	1.782	2.179	2.681	3.055
13	1.350	1.771	2.160	2.650	3.012
14	1.345	1.761	2.145	2.624	2.977
15	1.341	1.753	2.131	2.602	2.947
16	1.337	1.746	2.120	2.583	2.921
17	1.333	1.740	2.110	2.567	2.898
18	1.330	1.734	2.101	2.552	2.878
19	1.328	1.729	2.093	2.539	2.861
20	1.325	1.725	2.086	2.528	2.845
21	1.323	1.721	2.080	2.518	2.831
22	1.321	1.717	2.074	2.508	2.819
23	1.319	1.714	2.069	2.500	2.808
24	1.318	1.711	2.064	2.492	2.797
25	1.316	1.708	2.060	2.485	2.787
26	1.315	1.706	2.056	2.479	2.779
27	1.314	1.703	2.052	2.473	2.771
28	1.313	1.701	2.048	2.467	2.763
29	1.311	1.699	2.045	2.462	2.756
30	1.310	1.697	2.042	2.457	2.750
35	1.306	1.690	2.030	2.438	2.724
40	1.303	1.684	2.021	2.423	2.704
50	1.299	1.676	2.009	2.403	2.678
60	1.296	1.671	2.000	2.390	2.660
120	1.289	1.658	1.980	2.358	2.617
∞	1.282	1.645	1.960	2.326	2.576

TABLE A.6   Critical values of χ^2.

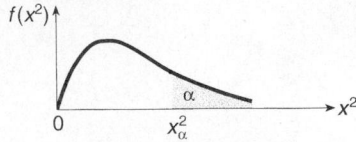

DEGREES OF FREEDOM	$\chi^2_{.995}$	$\chi^2_{.990}$	$\chi^2_{.975}$	$\chi^2_{.950}$	$\chi^2_{.900}$
1	0.0000393	0.0001571	0.0009821	0.0039321	0.0157908
2	0.0100251	0.0201007	0.0506356	0.102587	0.210720
3	0.0717212	0.114832	0.215795	0.351846	0.584375
4	0.206990	0.297110	0.484419	0.710721	1.063623
5	0.411740	0.554300	0.831211	1.145476	1.61031
6	0.675727	0.872085	1.237347	1.63539	2.20413
7	0.989265	1.239043	1.68987	2.16735	2.83311
8	1.344419	1.646482	2.17973	2.73264	3.48954
9	1.734926	2.087912	2.70039	3.32511	4.16816
10	2.15585	2.55821	3.24697	3.94030	4.86518
11	2.60321	3.05347	3.81575	4.57481	5.57779
12	3.07382	3.57056	4.40379	5.22603	6.30380
13	3.56503	4.10691	5.00874	5.89186	7.04150
14	4.07468	4.66043	5.62872	6.57063	7.78953
15	4.60094	5.22935	6.26214	7.26094	8.54675
16	5.14224	5.81221	6.90766	7.96164	9.31223
17	5.69724	6.40776	7.56418	8.67176	10.0852
18	6.26481	7.01491	8.23075	9.39046	10.8649
19	6.84398	7.63273	8.90655	10.1170	11.6509
20	7.43386	8.26040	9.59083	10.8508	12.4426
21	8.03366	8.89720	10.28293	11.5913	13.2396
22	8.64272	9.54249	10.9823	12.3380	14.0415
23	9.26042	10.19567	11.6885	13.0905	14.8479
24	9.88623	10.8564	12.4011	13.8484	15.6587
25	10.5197	11.5240	13.1197	14.6114	16.4734
26	11.1603	12.1981	13.8439	15.3791	17.2919
27	11.8076	12.8786	14.5733	16.1513	18.1138
28	12.4613	13.5648	15.3079	16.9279	18.9392
29	13.1211	14.2565	16.0471	17.7083	19.7677
30	13.7867	14.9535	16.7908	18.4926	20.5992
40	20.7065	22.1643	24.4331	26.5093	29.0505
50	27.9907	29.7067	32.3574	34.7642	37.6886
60	35.5346	37.4848	40.4817	43.1879	46.4589
70	43.2752	45.4418	48.7576	51.7393	55.3290
80	51.1720	53.5400	57.1532	60.3915	64.2778
90	59.1963	61.7541	65.6466	69.1260	73.2912
100	67.3276	70.0648	74.2219	77.9295	82.3581

TABLE A.6   Critical values of χ^2 (continued).

DEGREES OF FREEDOM	$\chi^2_{.100}$	$\chi^2_{.050}$	$\chi^2_{.025}$	$\chi^2_{.010}$	$\chi^2_{.005}$
1	2.70554	3.84146	5.02389	6.63490	7.87944
2	4.60517	5.99147	7.37776	9.21034	10.5966
3	6.25139	7.81473	9.34840	11.3449	12.8381
4	7.77944	9.48773	11.1433	13.2767	14.8602
5	9.23635	11.0705	12.8325	15.0863	16.7496
6	10.6446	12.5916	14.4494	16.8119	18.5476
7	12.0170	14.0671	16.0128	18.4753	20.2777
8	13.3616	15.5073	17.5346	20.0902	21.9550
9	14.6837	16.9190	19.0228	21.6660	23.5893
10	15.9871	18.3070	20.4831	23.2093	25.1882
11	17.2750	19.6751	21.9200	24.7250	26.7569
12	18.5494	21.0261	23.3367	26.2170	28.2995
13	19.8119	22.3621	24.7356	27.6883	29.8194
14	21.0642	23.6848	26.1190	29.1413	31.3193
15	22.3072	24.9958	27.4884	30.5779	32.8013
16	23.5418	26.2962	28.8454	31.9999	34.2672
17	24.7690	27.5871	30.1910	33.4087	35.7185
18	25.9894	28.8693	31.5264	34.8053	37.1564
19	27.2036	30.1435	32.8523	36.1908	38.5822
20	28.4120	31.4104	34.1696	37.5662	39.9968
21	29.6151	32.6705	35.4789	38.9321	41.4010
22	30.8133	33.9244	36.7807	40.2894	42.7956
23	32.0069	35.1725	38.0757	41.6384	44.1813
24	33.1963	36.4151	39.3641	42.9798	45.5585
25	34.3816	37.6525	40.6465	44.3141	46.9278
26	35.5631	38.8852	41.9232	45.6417	48.2899
27	36.7412	40.1133	43.1944	46.9630	49.6449
28	37.9159	41.3372	44.4607	48.2782	50.9933
29	39.0875	42.5569	45.7222	49.5879	52.3356
30	40.2560	43.7729	46.9792	50.8922	53.6720
40	51.8050	55.7585	59.3417	63.6907	66.7659
50	63.1671	67.5048	71.4202	76.1539	79.4900
60	74.3970	79.0819	83.2976	88.3794	91.9517
70	85.5271	90.5312	95.0231	100.425	104.215
80	96.5782	101.879	106.629	112.329	116.321
90	107.565	113.145	118.136	124.116	128.229
100	118.498	124.342	129.561	135.807	140.169

TABLE A.7

Percentage points of the F distribution. (a) $\alpha = .10$

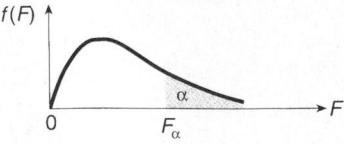

	ν_1	NUMERATOR DEGREES OF FREEDOM								
ν_2		1	2	3	4	5	6	7	8	9
	1	39.86	49.50	53.59	55.83	57.24	58.20	58.91	59.44	59.86
	2	8.53	9.00	9.16	9.24	9.29	9.33	9.35	9.37	9.38
	3	5.54	5.46	5.39	5.34	5.31	5.28	5.27	5.25	5.24
	4	4.54	4.32	4.19	4.11	4.05	4.01	3.98	3.95	3.94
	5	4.06	3.78	3.62	3.52	3.45	3.40	3.37	3.34	3.32
	6	3.78	3.46	3.29	3.18	3.11	3.05	3.01	2.98	2.96
	7	3.59	3.26	3.07	2.96	2.88	2.83	2.78	2.75	2.72
	8	3.46	3.11	2.92	2.81	2.73	2.67	2.62	2.59	2.56
	9	3.36	3.01	2.81	2.69	2.61	2.55	2.51	2.47	2.44
	10	3.29	2.92	2.73	2.61	2.52	2.46	2.41	2.38	2.35
	11	3.23	2.86	2.66	2.54	2.45	2.39	2.34	2.30	2.27
	12	3.18	2.81	2.61	2.48	2.39	2.33	2.28	2.24	2.21
	13	3.14	2.76	2.56	2.43	2.35	2.28	2.23	2.20	2.16
	14	3.10	2.73	2.52	2.39	2.31	2.24	2.19	2.15	2.12
	15	3.07	2.70	2.49	2.36	2.27	2.21	2.16	2.12	2.09
	16	3.05	2.67	2.46	2.33	2.24	2.18	2.13	2.09	2.06
	17	3.03	2.64	2.44	2.31	2.22	2.15	2.10	2.06	2.03
	18	3.01	2.62	2.42	2.29	2.20	2.13	2.08	2.04	2.00
	19	2.99	2.61	2.40	2.27	2.18	2.11	2.06	2.02	1.98
	20	2.97	2.59	2.38	2.25	2.16	2.09	2.04	2.00	1.96
	21	2.96	2.57	2.36	2.23	2.14	2.08	2.02	1.98	1.95
	22	2.95	2.56	2.35	2.22	2.13	2.06	2.01	1.97	1.93
	23	2.94	2.55	2.34	2.21	2.11	2.05	1.99	1.95	1.92
	24	2.93	2.54	2.33	2.19	2.10	2.04	1.98	1.94	1.91
	25	2.92	2.53	2.32	2.18	2.09	2.02	1.97	1.93	1.89
	26	2.91	2.52	2.31	2.17	2.08	2.01	1.96	1.92	1.88
	27	2.90	2.51	2.30	2.17	2.07	2.00	1.95	1.91	1.87
	28	2.89	2.50	2.29	2.16	2.06	2.00	1.94	1.90	1.87
	29	2.89	2.50	2.28	2.15	2.06	1.99	1.93	1.89	1.86
	30	2.88	2.49	2.28	2.14	2.05	1.98	1.93	1.88	1.85
	40	2.84	2.44	2.23	2.09	2.00	1.93	1.87	1.83	1.79
	60	2.79	2.39	2.18	2.04	1.95	1.87	1.82	1.77	1.74
	120	2.75	2.35	2.13	1.99	1.90	1.82	1.77	1.72	1.68
	∞	2.71	2.30	2.08	1.94	1.85	1.77	1.72	1.67	1.63

(left vertical axis label) DENOMINATOR DEGREES OF FREEDOM

TABLE A.7   (a) $\alpha = .10$ *(continued)*

ν_2	\multicolumn{10}{c}{NUMERATOR DEGREES OF FREEDOM}
	10	12	15	20	24	30	40	60	120	∞
1	60.19	60.71	61.22	61.74	62.00	62.26	62.53	62.79	63.06	63.33
2	9.39	9.41	9.42	9.44	9.45	9.46	9.47	9.47	9.48	9.49
3	5.23	5.22	5.20	5.18	5.18	5.17	5.16	5.15	5.14	5.13
4	3.92	3.90	3.87	3.84	3.83	3.82	3.80	3.79	3.78	3.76
5	3.30	3.27	3.24	3.21	3.19	3.17	3.16	3.14	3.12	3.10
6	2.94	2.90	2.87	2.84	2.82	2.80	2.78	2.76	2.74	2.72
7	2.70	2.67	2.63	2.59	2.58	2.56	2.54	2.51	2.49	2.47
8	2.54	2.50	2.46	2.42	2.40	2.38	2.36	2.34	2.32	2.29
9	2.42	2.38	2.34	2.30	2.28	2.25	2.23	2.21	2.18	2.16
10	2.32	2.28	2.24	2.20	2.18	2.16	2.13	2.11	2.08	2.06
11	2.25	2.21	2.17	2.12	2.10	2.08	2.05	2.03	2.00	1.97
12	2.19	2.15	2.10	2.06	2.04	2.01	1.99	1.96	1.93	1.90
13	2.14	2.10	2.05	2.01	1.98	1.96	1.93	1.90	1.88	1.85
14	2.10	2.05	2.01	1.96	1.94	1.91	1.89	1.86	1.83	1.80
15	2.06	2.02	1.97	1.92	1.90	1.87	1.85	1.82	1.79	1.76
16	2.03	1.99	1.94	1.89	1.87	1.84	1.81	1.78	1.75	1.72
17	2.00	1.96	1.91	1.86	1.84	1.81	1.78	1.75	1.72	1.69
18	1.98	1.93	1.89	1.84	1.81	1.78	1.75	1.72	1.69	1.66
19	1.96	1.91	1.86	1.81	1.79	1.76	1.73	1.70	1.67	1.63
20	1.94	1.89	1.84	1.79	1.77	1.74	1.71	1.68	1.64	1.61
21	1.92	1.87	1.83	1.78	1.75	1.72	1.69	1.66	1.62	1.59
22	1.90	1.86	1.81	1.76	1.73	1.70	1.67	1.64	1.60	1.57
23	1.89	1.84	1.80	1.74	1.72	1.69	1.66	1.62	1.59	1.55
24	1.88	1.83	1.78	1.73	1.70	1.67	1.64	1.61	1.57	1.53
25	1.87	1.82	1.77	1.72	1.69	1.66	1.63	1.59	1.56	1.52
26	1.86	1.81	1.76	1.71	1.68	1.65	1.61	1.58	1.54	1.50
27	1.85	1.80	1.75	1.70	1.67	1.64	1.60	1.57	1.53	1.49
28	1.84	1.79	1.74	1.69	1.66	1.63	1.59	1.56	1.52	1.48
29	1.83	1.78	1.73	1.68	1.65	1.62	1.58	1.55	1.51	1.47
30	1.82	1.77	1.72	1.67	1.64	1.61	1.57	1.54	1.50	1.46
40	1.76	1.71	1.66	1.61	1.57	1.54	1.51	1.47	1.42	1.38
60	1.71	1.66	1.60	1.54	1.51	1.48	1.44	1.40	1.35	1.29
120	1.65	1.60	1.55	1.48	1.45	1.41	1.37	1.32	1.26	1.19
∞	1.60	1.55	1.49	1.42	1.38	1.34	1.30	1.24	1.17	1.00

TABLE A.7

Percentage points of the F distribution. (b) $\alpha = .05$

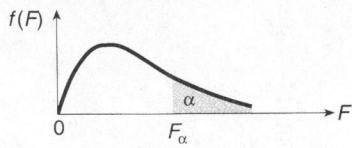

ν_2	NUMERATOR DEGREES OF FREEDOM ν_1								
	1	2	3	4	5	6	7	8	9
1	161.4	199.5	215.7	224.6	230.2	234.0	236.8	238.9	240.5
2	18.51	19.00	19.16	19.25	19.30	19.33	19.35	19.37	19.38
3	10.13	9.55	9.28	9.12	9.01	8.94	8.89	8.85	8.81
4	7.71	6.94	6.59	6.39	6.26	6.16	6.09	6.04	6.00
5	6.61	5.79	5.41	5.19	5.05	4.95	4.88	4.82	4.77
6	5.99	5.14	4.76	4.53	4.39	4.28	4.21	4.15	4.10
7	5.59	4.74	4.35	4.12	3.97	3.87	3.79	3.73	3.68
8	5.32	4.46	4.07	3.84	3.69	3.58	3.50	3.44	3.39
9	5.12	4.26	3.86	3.63	3.48	3.37	3.29	3.23	3.18
10	4.96	4.10	3.71	3.48	3.33	3.22	3.14	3.07	3.02
11	4.84	3.98	3.59	3.36	3.20	3.09	3.01	2.95	2.90
12	4.75	3.89	3.49	3.26	3.11	3.00	2.91	2.85	2.80
13	4.67	3.81	3.41	3.18	3.03	2.92	2.83	2.77	2.71
14	4.60	3.74	3.34	3.11	2.96	2.85	2.76	2.70	2.65
15	4.54	3.68	3.29	3.06	2.90	2.79	2.71	2.64	2.59
16	4.49	3.63	3.24	3.01	2.85	2.74	2.66	2.59	2.54
17	4.45	3.59	3.20	2.96	2.81	2.70	2.61	2.55	2.49
18	4.41	3.55	3.16	2.93	2.77	2.66	2.58	2.51	2.46
19	4.38	3.52	3.13	2.90	2.74	2.63	2.54	2.48	2.42
20	4.35	3.49	3.10	2.87	2.71	2.60	2.51	2.45	2.39
21	4.32	3.47	3.07	2.84	2.68	2.57	2.49	2.42	2.37
22	4.30	3.44	3.05	2.82	2.66	2.55	2.46	2.40	2.34
23	4.28	3.42	3.03	2.80	2.64	2.53	2.44	2.37	2.32
24	4.26	3.40	3.01	2.78	2.62	2.51	2.42	2.36	2.30
25	4.24	3.39	2.99	2.76	2.60	2.49	2.40	2.34	2.28
26	4.23	3.37	2.98	2.74	2.59	2.47	2.39	2.32	2.27
27	4.21	3.35	2.96	2.73	2.57	2.46	2.37	2.31	2.25
28	4.20	3.34	2.95	2.71	2.56	2.45	2.36	2.29	2.24
29	4.18	3.33	2.93	2.70	2.55	2.43	2.35	2.28	2.22
30	4.17	3.32	2.92	2.69	2.53	2.42	2.33	2.27	2.21
40	4.08	3.23	2.84	2.61	2.45	2.34	2.25	2.18	2.12
60	4.00	3.15	2.76	2.53	2.37	2.25	2.17	2.10	2.04
120	3.92	3.07	2.68	2.45	2.29	2.17	2.09	2.02	1.96
∞	3.84	3.00	2.60	2.37	2.21	2.10	2.01	1.94	1.88

TABLE A.7   (b) $\alpha = .05$ *(continued)*

ν_2	NUMERATOR DEGREES OF FREEDOM ν_1									
	10	12	15	20	24	30	40	60	120	∞
1	241.9	243.9	245.9	248.0	249.1	250.1	251.1	252.2	253.3	254.3
2	19.40	19.41	19.43	19.45	19.45	19.46	19.47	19.48	19.49	19.50
3	8.79	8.74	8.70	8.66	8.64	8.62	8.59	8.57	8.55	8.53
4	5.96	5.91	5.86	5.80	5.77	5.75	5.72	5.69	5.66	5.63
5	4.74	4.68	4.62	4.56	4.53	4.50	4.46	4.43	4.40	4.36
6	4.06	4.00	3.94	3.87	3.84	3.81	3.77	3.74	3.70	3.67
7	3.64	3.57	3.51	3.44	3.41	3.38	3.34	3.30	3.27	3.23
8	3.35	3.28	3.22	3.15	3.12	3.08	3.04	3.01	2.97	2.93
9	3.14	3.07	3.01	2.94	2.90	2.86	2.83	2.79	2.75	2.71
10	2.98	2.91	2.85	2.77	2.74	2.70	2.66	2.62	2.58	2.54
11	2.85	2.79	2.72	2.65	2.61	2.57	2.53	2.49	2.45	2.40
12	2.75	2.69	2.62	2.54	2.51	2.47	2.43	2.38	2.34	2.30
13	2.67	2.60	2.53	2.46	2.42	2.38	2.34	2.30	2.25	2.21
14	2.60	2.53	2.46	2.39	2.35	2.31	2.27	2.22	2.18	2.13
15	2.54	2.48	2.40	2.33	2.29	2.25	2.20	2.16	2.11	2.07
16	2.49	2.42	2.35	2.28	2.24	2.19	2.15	2.11	2.06	2.01
17	2.45	2.38	2.31	2.23	2.19	2.15	2.10	2.06	2.01	1.96
18	2.41	2.34	2.27	2.19	2.15	2.11	2.06	2.02	1.97	1.92
19	2.38	2.31	2.23	2.16	2.11	2.07	2.03	1.98	1.93	1.88
20	2.35	2.28	2.20	2.12	2.08	2.04	1.99	1.95	1.90	1.84
21	2.32	2.25	2.18	2.10	2.05	2.01	1.96	1.92	1.87	1.81
22	2.30	2.23	2.15	2.07	2.03	1.98	1.94	1.89	1.84	1.78
23	2.27	2.20	2.13	2.05	2.01	1.96	1.91	1.86	1.81	1.76
24	2.25	2.18	2.11	2.03	1.98	1.94	1.89	1.84	1.79	1.73
25	2.24	2.16	2.09	2.01	1.96	1.92	1.87	1.82	1.77	1.71
26	2.22	2.15	2.07	1.99	1.95	1.90	1.85	1.80	1.75	1.69
27	2.20	2.13	2.06	1.97	1.93	1.88	1.84	1.79	1.73	1.67
28	2.19	2.12	2.04	1.96	1.91	1.87	1.82	1.77	1.71	1.65
29	2.18	2.10	2.03	1.94	1.90	1.85	1.81	1.75	1.70	1.64
30	2.16	2.09	2.01	1.93	1.89	1.84	1.79	1.74	1.68	1.62
40	2.08	2.00	1.92	1.84	1.79	1.74	1.69	1.64	1.58	1.51
60	1.99	1.92	1.84	1.75	1.70	1.65	1.59	1.53	1.47	1.39
120	1.91	1.83	1.75	1.66	1.61	1.55	1.50	1.43	1.35	1.25
∞	1.83	1.75	1.67	1.57	1.52	1.46	1.39	1.32	1.22	1.00

DENOMINATOR DEGREES OF FREEDOM

TABLE A.7   Percentage points of the F distribution. (c) $\alpha = .025$

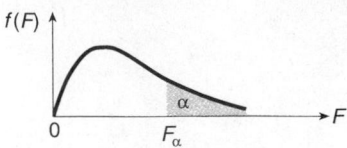

v_2 \ v_1	NUMERATOR DEGREES OF FREEDOM								
	1	2	3	4	5	6	7	8	9
1	647.8	799.5	864.2	899.6	921.8	937.1	948.2	956.7	963.3
2	38.51	39.00	39.17	39.25	39.30	39.33	39.36	39.37	39.39
3	17.44	16.04	15.44	15.10	14.88	14.73	14.62	14.54	14.47
4	12.22	10.65	9.98	9.60	9.36	9.20	9.07	8.98	8.90
5	10.01	8.43	7.76	7.39	7.15	6.98	6.85	6.76	6.68
6	8.81	7.26	6.60	6.23	5.99	5.82	5.70	5.60	5.52
7	8.07	6.54	5.89	5.52	5.29	5.12	4.99	4.90	4.82
8	7.57	6.06	5.42	5.05	4.82	4.65	4.53	4.43	4.36
9	7.21	5.71	5.08	4.72	4.48	4.32	4.20	4.10	4.03
10	6.94	5.46	4.83	4.47	4.24	4.07	3.95	3.85	3.78
11	6.72	5.26	4.63	4.28	4.04	3.88	3.76	3.66	3.59
12	6.55	5.10	4.47	4.12	3.89	3.73	3.61	3.51	3.44
13	6.41	4.97	4.35	4.00	3.77	3.60	3.48	3.39	3.31
14	6.30	4.86	4.24	3.89	3.66	3.50	3.38	3.29	3.21
15	6.20	4.77	4.15	3.80	3.58	3.41	3.29	3.20	3.12
16	6.12	4.69	4.08	3.73	3.50	3.34	3.22	3.12	3.05
17	6.04	4.62	4.01	3.66	3.44	3.28	3.16	3.06	2.98
18	5.98	4.56	3.95	3.61	3.38	3.22	3.10	3.01	2.93
19	5.92	4.51	3.90	3.56	3.33	3.17	3.05	2.96	2.88
20	5.87	4.46	3.86	3.51	3.29	3.13	3.01	2.91	2.84
21	5.83	4.42	3.82	3.48	3.25	3.09	2.97	2.87	2.80
22	5.79	4.38	3.78	3.44	3.22	3.05	2.93	2.84	2.76
23	5.75	4.35	3.75	3.41	3.18	3.02	2.90	2.81	2.73
24	5.72	4.32	3.72	3.38	3.15	2.99	2.87	2.78	2.70
25	5.69	4.29	3.69	3.35	3.13	2.97	2.85	2.75	2.68
26	5.66	4.27	3.67	3.33	3.10	2.94	2.82	2.73	2.65
27	5.63	4.24	3.65	3.31	3.08	2.92	2.80	2.71	2.63
28	5.61	4.22	3.63	3.29	3.06	2.90	2.78	2.69	2.61
29	5.59	4.20	3.61	3.27	3.04	2.88	2.76	2.67	2.59
30	5.57	4.18	3.59	3.25	3.03	2.87	2.75	2.65	2.57
40	5.42	4.05	3.46	3.13	2.90	2.74	2.62	2.53	2.45
60	5.29	3.93	3.34	3.01	2.79	2.63	2.51	2.41	2.33
120	5.15	3.80	3.23	2.89	2.67	2.52	2.39	2.30	2.22
∞	5.02	3.69	3.12	2.79	2.57	2.41	2.29	2.19	2.11

DENOMINATOR DEGREES OF FREEDOM

TABLE A.7   (c) $\alpha = .025$ *(continued)*

v_2	NUMERATOR DEGREES OF FREEDOM									
	10	12	15	20	24	30	40	60	120	∞
1	968.6	976.7	984.9	993.1	997.2	1001	1006	1010	1014	1018
2	39.40	39.41	39.43	39.45	39.46	39.46	39.47	39.48	39.49	39.50
3	14.42	14.34	14.25	14.17	14.12	14.08	14.04	13.99	13.95	13.90
4	8.84	8.75	8.66	8.56	8.51	8.46	8.41	8.36	8.31	8.26
5	6.62	6.52	6.43	6.33	6.28	6.23	6.18	6.12	6.07	6.02
6	5.46	5.37	5.27	5.17	5.12	5.07	5.01	4.96	4.90	4.85
7	4.76	4.67	4.57	4.47	4.42	4.36	4.31	4.25	4.20	4.14
8	4.30	4.20	4.10	4.00	3.95	3.89	3.84	3.78	3.73	3.67
9	3.96	3.87	3.77	3.67	3.61	3.56	3.51	3.45	3.39	3.33
10	3.72	3.62	3.52	3.42	3.37	3.31	3.26	3.20	3.14	3.08
11	3.53	3.43	3.33	3.23	3.17	3.12	3.06	3.00	2.94	2.88
12	3.37	3.28	3.18	3.07	3.02	2.96	2.91	2.85	2.79	2.72
13	3.25	3.15	3.05	2.95	2.89	2.84	2.78	2.72	2.66	2.60
14	3.15	3.05	2.95	2.84	2.79	2.73	2.67	2.61	2.55	2.49
15	3.06	2.96	2.86	2.76	2.70	2.64	2.59	2.52	2.46	2.40
16	2.99	2.89	2.79	2.68	2.63	2.57	2.51	2.45	2.38	2.32
17	2.92	2.82	2.72	2.62	2.56	2.50	2.44	2.38	2.32	2.25
18	2.87	2.77	2.67	2.56	2.50	2.44	2.38	2.32	2.26	2.19
19	2.82	2.72	2.62	2.51	2.45	2.39	2.33	2.27	2.20	2.13
20	2.77	2.68	2.57	2.46	2.41	2.35	2.29	2.22	2.16	2.09
21	2.73	2.64	2.53	2.42	2.37	2.31	2.25	2.18	2.11	2.04
22	2.70	2.60	2.50	2.39	2.33	2.27	2.21	2.14	2.08	2.00
23	2.67	2.57	2.47	2.36	2.30	2.24	2.18	2.11	2.04	1.97
24	2.64	2.54	2.44	2.33	2.27	2.21	2.15	2.08	2.01	1.94
25	2.61	2.51	2.41	2.30	2.24	2.18	2.12	2.05	1.98	1.91
26	2.59	2.49	2.39	2.28	2.22	2.16	2.09	2.03	1.95	1.88
27	2.57	2.47	2.36	2.25	2.19	2.13	2.07	2.00	1.93	1.85
28	2.55	2.45	2.34	2.23	2.17	2.11	2.05	1.98	1.91	1.83
29	2.53	2.43	2.32	2.21	2.15	2.09	2.03	1.96	1.89	1.81
30	2.51	2.41	2.31	2.20	2.14	2.07	2.01	1.94	1.87	1.79
40	2.39	2.29	2.18	2.07	2.01	1.94	1.88	1.80	1.72	1.64
60	2.27	2.17	2.06	1.94	1.88	1.82	1.74	1.67	1.58	1.48
120	2.16	2.05	1.94	1.82	1.76	1.69	1.61	1.53	1.43	1.31
∞	2.05	1.94	1.83	1.71	1.64	1.57	1.48	1.39	1.27	1.00

DENOMINATOR DEGREES OF FREEDOM

TABLE A.7   Percentage points of the *F* distribution. (d) $\alpha = .01$

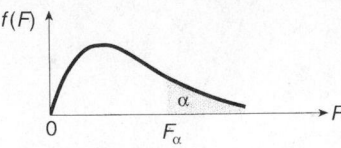

ν_1		NUMERATOR DEGREES OF FREEDOM							
ν_2	1	2	3	4	5	6	7	8	9
1	4,052	4,999.5	5,403	5,625	5,764	5,859	5,928	5,982	6,022
2	98.50	99.00	99.17	99.25	99.30	99.33	99.36	99.37	99.39
3	34.12	30.82	29.46	28.71	28.24	27.91	27.67	27.49	27.35
4	21.20	18.00	16.69	15.98	15.52	15.21	14.98	14.80	14.66
5	16.26	13.27	12.06	11.39	10.97	10.67	10.46	10.29	10.16
6	13.75	10.92	9.78	9.15	8.75	8.47	8.26	8.10	7.98
7	12.25	9.55	8.45	7.85	7.46	7.19	6.99	6.84	6.72
8	11.26	8.65	7.59	7.01	6.63	6.37	6.18	6.03	5.91
9	10.56	8.02	6.99	6.42	6.06	5.80	5.61	5.47	5.35
10	10.04	7.56	6.55	5.99	5.64	5.39	5.20	5.06	4.94
11	9.65	7.21	6.22	5.67	5.32	5.07	4.89	4.74	4.63
12	9.33	6.93	5.95	5.41	5.06	4.82	4.64	4.50	4.39
13	9.07	6.70	5.74	5.21	4.86	4.62	4.44	4.30	4.19
14	8.86	6.51	5.56	5.04	4.69	4.46	4.28	4.14	4.03
15	8.68	6.36	5.42	4.89	4.56	4.32	4.14	4.00	3.89
16	8.53	6.23	5.29	4.77	4.44	4.20	4.03	3.89	3.78
17	8.40	6.11	5.18	4.67	4.34	4.10	3.93	3.79	3.68
18	8.29	6.01	5.09	4.58	4.25	4.01	3.84	3.71	3.60
19	8.18	5.93	5.01	4.50	4.17	3.94	3.77	3.63	3.52
20	8.10	5.85	4.94	4.43	4.10	3.87	3.70	3.56	3.46
21	8.02	5.78	4.87	4.37	4.04	3.81	3.64	3.51	3.40
22	7.95	5.72	4.82	4.31	3.99	3.76	3.59	3.45	3.35
23	7.88	5.66	4.76	4.26	3.94	3.71	3.54	3.41	3.30
24	7.82	5.61	4.72	4.22	3.90	3.67	3.50	3.36	3.26
25	7.77	5.57	4.68	4.18	3.85	3.63	3.46	3.32	3.22
26	7.72	5.53	4.64	4.14	3.82	3.59	3.42	3.29	3.18
27	7.68	5.49	4.60	4.11	3.78	3.56	3.39	3.26	3.15
28	7.64	5.45	4.57	4.07	3.75	3.53	3.36	3.23	3.12
29	7.60	5.42	4.54	4.04	3.73	3.50	3.33	3.20	3.09
30	7.56	5.39	4.51	4.02	3.70	3.47	3.30	3.17	3.07
40	7.31	5.18	4.31	3.83	3.51	3.29	3.12	2.99	2.89
60	7.08	4.98	4.13	3.65	3.34	3.12	2.95	2.82	2.72
120	6.85	4.79	3.95	3.48	3.17	2.96	2.79	2.66	2.56
∞	6.63	4.61	3.78	3.32	3.02	2.80	2.64	2.51	2.41

DENOMINATOR DEGREES OF FREEDOM

TABLE A.7   (d) $\alpha = .01$ *(continued)*

v_2	NUMERATOR DEGREES OF FREEDOM									
	10	12	15	20	24	30	40	60	120	∞
1	6,056	6,106	6,157	6,209	6,235	6,261	6,287	6,313	6,339	6,366
2	99.40	99.42	99.43	99.45	99.46	99.47	99.47	99.48	99.49	99.50
3	27.23	27.05	26.87	26.69	26.60	26.50	26.41	26.32	26.22	26.13
4	14.55	14.37	14.20	14.02	13.93	13.84	13.75	13.65	13.56	13.46
5	10.05	9.89	9.72	9.55	9.47	9.38	9.29	9.20	9.11	9.02
6	7.87	7.72	7.56	7.40	7.31	7.23	7.14	7.06	6.97	6.88
7	6.62	6.47	6.31	6.16	6.07	5.99	5.91	5.82	5.74	5.65
8	5.81	5.67	5.52	5.36	5.28	5.20	5.12	5.03	4.95	4.86
9	5.26	5.11	4.96	4.81	4.73	4.65	4.57	4.48	4.40	4.31
10	4.85	4.71	4.56	4.41	4.33	4.25	4.17	4.08	4.00	3.91
11	4.54	4.40	4.25	4.10	4.02	3.94	3.86	3.78	3.69	3.60
12	4.30	4.16	4.01	3.86	3.78	3.70	3.62	3.54	3.45	3.36
13	4.10	3.96	3.82	3.66	3.59	3.51	3.43	3.34	3.25	3.17
14	3.94	3.80	3.66	3.51	3.43	3.35	3.27	3.18	3.09	3.00
15	3.80	3.67	3.52	3.37	3.29	3.21	3.13	3.05	2.96	2.87
16	3.69	3.55	3.41	3.26	3.18	3.10	3.02	2.93	2.84	2.75
17	3.59	3.46	3.31	3.16	3.08	3.00	2.92	2.83	2.75	2.65
18	3.51	3.37	3.23	3.08	3.00	2.92	2.84	2.75	2.66	2.57
19	3.43	3.30	3.15	3.00	2.92	2.84	2.76	2.67	2.58	2.49
20	3.37	3.23	3.09	2.94	2.86	2.78	2.69	2.61	2.52	2.42
21	3.31	3.17	3.03	2.88	2.80	2.72	2.64	2.55	2.46	2.36
22	3.26	3.12	2.98	2.83	2.75	2.67	2.58	2.50	2.40	2.31
23	3.21	3.07	2.93	2.78	2.70	2.62	2.54	2.45	2.35	2.26
24	3.17	3.03	2.89	2.74	2.66	2.58	2.49	2.40	2.31	2.21
25	3.13	2.99	2.85	2.70	2.62	2.54	2.45	2.36	2.27	2.17
26	3.09	2.96	2.81	2.66	2.58	2.50	2.42	2.33	2.23	2.13
27	3.06	2.93	2.78	2.63	2.55	2.47	2.38	2.29	2.20	2.10
28	3.03	2.90	2.75	2.60	2.52	2.44	2.35	2.26	2.17	2.06
29	3.00	2.87	2.73	2.57	2.49	2.41	2.33	2.23	2.14	2.03
30	2.98	2.84	2.70	2.55	2.47	2.39	2.30	2.21	2.11	2.01
40	2.80	2.66	2.52	2.37	2.29	2.20	2.11	2.02	1.92	1.80
60	2.63	2.50	2.35	2.20	2.12	2.03	1.94	1.84	1.73	1.60
120	2.47	2.34	2.19	2.03	1.95	1.86	1.76	1.66	1.53	1.38
∞	2.32	2.18	2.04	1.88	1.79	1.70	1.59	1.47	1.32	1.00

DENOMINATOR DEGREES OF FREEDOM

TABLE A.8   Confidence interval for a population proportion, small sample.

n = 5   α = .05   α = .10

x	P_L	P_U	P_L	P_U
x = 1	0.005	0.716	0.010	0.657
2	0.053	0.853	0.076	0.811
3	0.147	0.947	0.189	0.924
4	0.284	0.995	0.343	0.990

n = 6   α = .05   α = .10

x	P_L	P_U	P_L	P_U
x = 1	0.004	0.641	0.009	0.582
2	0.043	0.777	0.063	0.729
3	0.118	0.882	0.153	0.847
4	0.223	0.957	0.271	0.937
5	0.359	0.996	0.418	0.991

n = 7   α = .05   α = .10

x	P_L	P_U	P_L	P_U
x = 1	0.004	0.579	0.007	0.521
2	0.037	0.710	0.053	0.659
3	0.099	0.816	0.129	0.775
4	0.184	0.901	0.225	0.871
5	0.290	0.963	0.341	0.947
6	0.421	0.996	0.479	0.993

n = 8   α = .05   α = .10

x	P_L	P_U	P_L	P_U
x = 1	0.003	0.527	0.006	0.471
2	0.032	0.651	0.046	0.600
3	0.085	0.755	0.111	0.711
4	0.157	0.843	0.193	0.807
5	0.245	0.915	0.289	0.889
6	0.349	0.968	0.400	0.954
7	0.473	0.997	0.529	0.994

n = 9   α = .05   α = .10

x	P_L	P_U	P_L	P_U
x = 1	0.003	0.482	0.006	0.429
2	0.028	0.600	0.041	0.550
3	0.075	0.701	0.098	0.655
4	0.137	0.788	0.169	0.749
5	0.212	0.863	0.251	0.831
6	0.299	0.925	0.345	0.902
7	0.400	0.972	0.450	0.959
8	0.518	0.997	0.571	0.994

n = 10   α = .05   α = .10

x	P_L	P_U	P_L	P_U
x = 1	0.003	0.445	0.005	0.394
2	0.025	0.556	0.037	0.507
3	0.067	0.652	0.087	0.607
4	0.122	0.738	0.150	0.696
5	0.187	0.813	0.222	0.778
6	0.262	0.878	0.304	0.850
7	0.348	0.933	0.393	0.913
8	0.444	0.975	0.493	0.963
9	0.555	0.997	0.606	0.995

n = 11   α = .05   α = .10

x	P_L	P_U	P_L	P_U
x = 1	0.002	0.413	0.005	0.364
2	0.023	0.518	0.033	0.470
3	0.060	0.610	0.079	0.564
4	0.109	0.692	0.135	0.650
5	0.167	0.766	0.200	0.729
6	0.234	0.833	0.271	0.800
7	0.308	0.891	0.350	0.865

n = 11   α = .05   α = .10

x	P_L	P_U	P_L	P_U
8	0.390	0.940	0.436	0.921
9	0.482	0.977	0.530	0.967
10	0.587	0.998	0.636	0.995

n = 12   α = .05   α = .10

x	P_L	P_U	P_L	P_U
x = 1	0.002	0.385	0.004	0.339
2	0.021	0.484	0.030	0.438
3	0.055	0.572	0.072	0.527
4	0.099	0.651	0.123	0.609
5	0.152	0.723	0.181	0.685
6	0.211	0.789	0.245	0.755
7	0.277	0.848	0.315	0.819
8	0.349	0.901	0.391	0.877
9	0.428	0.945	0.473	0.928
10	0.516	0.979	0.562	0.970
11	0.615	0.998	0.661	0.996

n = 13   α = .05   α = .10

x	P_L	P_U	P_L	P_U
x = 1	0.002	0.360	0.004	0.316
2	0.019	0.454	0.028	0.410
3	0.050	0.538	0.066	0.495
4	0.091	0.614	0.113	0.573
5	0.139	0.684	0.166	0.645
6	0.192	0.749	0.224	0.713
7	0.251	0.808	0.287	0.776
8	0.316	0.861	0.355	0.834
9	0.386	0.909	0.427	0.887
10	0.462	0.950	0.505	0.934
11	0.546	0.981	0.590	0.972
12	0.640	0.998	0.684	0.996

n = 14   α = .05   α = .10

x	P_L	P_U	P_L	P_U
x = 1	0.002	0.339	0.004	0.297
2	0.018	0.428	0.026	0.385
3	0.047	0.508	0.061	0.466
4	0.084	0.581	0.104	0.540
5	0.128	0.649	0.153	0.610
6	0.177	0.711	0.206	0.675
7	0.230	0.770	0.264	0.736
8	0.289	0.823	0.325	0.794
9	0.351	0.872	0.390	0.847
10	0.419	0.916	0.460	0.896
11	0.492	0.953	0.534	0.939
12	0.572	0.982	0.615	0.974
13	0.661	0.998	0.703	0.996

n = 15   α = .05   α = .10

x	P_L	P_U	P_L	P_U
x = 1	0.002	0.319	0.003	0.279
2	0.017	0.405	0.024	0.363
3	0.043	0.481	0.057	0.440
4	0.078	0.551	0.097	0.511
5	0.118	0.616	0.142	0.577
6	0.163	0.677	0.191	0.640
7	0.213	0.734	0.244	0.700
8	0.266	0.787	0.300	0.756
9	0.323	0.837	0.360	0.809
10	0.384	0.882	0.423	0.858
11	0.449	0.922	0.489	0.903
12	0.519	0.957	0.560	0.943
13	0.595	0.983	0.637	0.976
14	0.681	0.998	0.721	0.997

TABLE A.8

Confidence interval for a population proportion, small sample *(continued)*.

n = 16		α = .05		α = .10	
		P_L	P_U	P_L	P_U
x =	1	0.002	0.302	0.003	0.264
	2	0.016	0.383	0.023	0.344
	3	0.040	0.456	0.053	0.417
	4	0.073	0.524	0.090	0.484
	5	0.110	0.587	0.132	0.548
	6	0.152	0.646	0.178	0.609
	7	0.198	0.701	0.227	0.667
	8	0.247	0.753	0.279	0.721
	9	0.299	0.802	0.333	0.773
	10	0.354	0.848	0.391	0.822
	11	0.413	0.890	0.452	0.868
	12	0.476	0.927	0.516	0.910
	13	0.544	0.960	0.583	0.947
	14	0.617	0.984	0.656	0.977
	15	0.698	0.998	0.736	0.997

n = 17		α = .05		α = .10	
		P_L	P_U	P_L	P_U
x =	1	0.001	0.287	0.003	0.250
	2	0.015	0.364	0.021	0.326
	3	0.038	0.434	0.050	0.396
	4	0.068	0.499	0.085	0.461
	5	0.103	0.560	0.124	0.522
	6	0.142	0.617	0.166	0.580
	7	0.184	0.671	0.212	0.636
	8	0.230	0.722	0.260	0.689
	9	0.278	0.770	0.311	0.740
	10	0.329	0.816	0.364	0.788
	11	0.383	0.858	0.420	0.834
	12	0.440	0.897	0.478	0.876
	13	0.501	0.932	0.539	0.915
	14	0.566	0.962	0.604	0.950
	15	0.636	0.985	0.674	0.979
	16	0.713	0.999	0.750	0.997

n = 18		α = .05		α = .10	
		P_L	P_U	P_L	P_U
x =	1	0.001	0.273	0.003	0.238
	2	0.014	0.347	0.020	0.310
	3	0.036	0.414	0.047	0.377
	4	0.064	0.476	0.080	0.439
	5	0.097	0.535	0.116	0.498
	6	0.133	0.590	0.156	0.554
	7	0.173	0.643	0.199	0.608
	8	0.215	0.692	0.244	0.659
	9	0.260	0.740	0.291	0.709
	10	0.308	0.785	0.341	0.756
	11	0.357	0.827	0.392	0.801
	12	0.410	0.867	0.446	0.844

n = 18		α = .05		α = .10	
		P_L	P_U	P_L	P_U
	13	0.465	0.903	0.502	0.884
	14	0.524	0.936	0.561	0.920
	15	0.586	0.964	0.623	0.953
	16	0.653	0.986	0.690	0.980
	17	0.727	0.999	0.762	0.997

n = 19		α = .05		α = .10	
		P_L	P_U	P_L	P_U
x =	1	0.001	0.260	0.003	0.226
	2	0.013	0.331	0.019	0.296
	3	0.034	0.396	0.044	0.359
	4	0.061	0.456	0.075	0.419
	5	0.091	0.512	0.110	0.476
	6	0.126	0.565	0.147	0.530
	7	0.163	0.616	0.188	0.582
	8	0.203	0.665	0.230	0.632
	9	0.244	0.711	0.274	0.680
	10	0.289	0.756	0.320	0.726
	11	0.335	0.797	0.368	0.770
	12	0.384	0.837	0.418	0.812
	13	0.435	0.874	0.470	0.853
	14	0.488	0.909	0.524	0.890
	15	0.544	0.939	0.581	0.925
	16	0.604	0.966	0.641	0.956
	17	0.669	0.987	0.704	0.981
	18	0.740	0.999	0.774	0.997

n = 20		α = .05		α = .10	
		P_L	P_U	P_L	P_U
x =	1	0.001	0.249	0.003	0.216
	2	0.012	0.317	0.018	0.283
	3	0.032	0.379	0.042	0.344
	4	0.057	0.437	0.071	0.401
	5	0.087	0.491	0.104	0.456
	6	0.119	0.543	0.140	0.508
	7	0.154	0.592	0.177	0.558
	8	0.191	0.639	0.217	0.606
	9	0.231	0.685	0.259	0.653
	10	0.272	0.728	0.302	0.698
	11	0.315	0.769	0.347	0.741
	12	0.361	0.809	0.394	0.783
	13	0.408	0.846	0.442	0.823
	14	0.457	0.881	0.492	0.860
	15	0.509	0.913	0.544	0.896
	16	0.563	0.943	0.599	0.929
	17	0.621	0.968	0.656	0.958
	18	0.683	0.988	0.717	0.982
	19	0.751	0.999	0.784	0.997

TABLE A.9   Critical values for the Durbin-Watson DW statistic. (a) $\alpha = .05$

n	k = 1 d_L	k = 1 d_U	k = 2 d_L	k = 2 d_U	k = 3 d_L	k = 3 d_U	k = 4 d_L	k = 4 d_U	k = 5 d_L	k = 5 d_U
15	1.08	1.36	0.95	1.54	0.82	1.75	0.69	1.97	0.56	2.21
16	1.10	1.37	0.98	1.54	0.86	1.73	0.74	1.93	0.62	2.15
17	1.13	1.38	1.02	1.54	0.90	1.71	0.78	1.90	0.67	2.10
18	1.16	1.39	1.05	1.53	0.93	1.69	0.82	1.87	0.71	2.06
19	1.18	1.40	1.08	1.53	0.97	1.68	0.86	1.85	0.75	2.02
20	1.20	1.41	1.10	1.54	1.00	1.68	0.90	1.83	0.79	1.99
21	1.22	1.42	1.13	1.54	1.03	1.67	0.93	1.81	0.83	1.96
22	1.24	1.43	1.15	1.54	1.05	1.66	0.96	1.80	0.86	1.94
23	1.26	1.44	1.17	1.54	1.08	1.66	0.99	1.79	0.90	1.92
24	1.27	1.45	1.19	1.55	1.10	1.66	1.01	1.78	0.93	1.90
25	1.29	1.45	1.21	1.55	1.12	1.66	1.04	1.77	0.95	1.89
26	1.30	1.46	1.22	1.55	1.14	1.65	1.06	1.76	0.98	1.88
27	1.32	1.47	1.24	1.56	1.16	1.65	1.08	1.76	1.01	1.86
28	1.33	1.48	1.26	1.56	1.18	1.65	1.10	1.75	1.03	1.85
29	1.34	1.48	1.27	1.56	1.20	1.65	1.12	1.74	1.05	1.84
30	1.35	1.49	1.28	1.57	1.21	1.65	1.14	1.74	1.07	1.83
31	1.36	1.50	1.30	1.57	1.23	1.65	1.16	1.74	1.09	1.83
32	1.37	1.50	1.31	1.57	1.24	1.65	1.18	1.73	1.11	1.82
33	1.38	1.51	1.32	1.58	1.26	1.65	1.19	1.73	1.13	1.81
34	1.39	1.51	1.33	1.58	1.27	1.65	1.21	1.73	1.15	1.81
35	1.40	1.52	1.34	1.58	1.28	1.65	1.22	1.73	1.16	1.80
36	1.41	1.52	1.35	1.59	1.29	1.65	1.24	1.73	1.18	1.80
37	1.42	1.53	1.36	1.59	1.31	1.66	1.25	1.72	1.19	1.80
38	1.43	1.54	1.37	1.59	1.32	1.66	1.26	1.72	1.21	1.79
39	1.43	1.54	1.38	1.60	1.33	1.66	1.27	1.72	1.22	1.79
40	1.44	1.54	1.39	1.60	1.34	1.66	1.29	1.72	1.23	1.79
45	1.48	1.57	1.43	1.62	1.38	1.67	1.34	1.72	1.29	1.78
50	1.50	1.59	1.46	1.63	1.42	1.67	1.38	1.72	1.34	1.77
55	1.53	1.60	1.49	1.64	1.45	1.68	1.41	1.72	1.38	1.77
60	1.55	1.62	1.51	1.65	1.48	1.69	1.44	1.73	1.41	1.77
65	1.57	1.63	1.54	1.66	1.50	1.70	1.47	1.73	1.44	1.77
70	1.58	1.64	1.55	1.67	1.52	1.70	1.49	1.74	1.46	1.77
75	1.60	1.65	1.57	1.68	1.54	1.71	1.51	1.74	1.49	1.77
80	1.61	1.66	1.59	1.69	1.56	1.72	1.53	1.74	1.51	1.77
85	1.62	1.67	1.60	1.70	1.57	1.72	1.55	1.75	1.52	1.77
90	1.63	1.68	1.61	1.70	1.59	1.73	1.57	1.75	1.54	1.78
95	1.64	1.69	1.62	1.71	1.60	1.73	1.58	1.75	1.56	1.78
100	1.65	1.69	1.63	1.72	1.61	1.74	1.59	1.76	1.57	1.78

TABLE A.9   Critical values for the Durbin-Watson DW statistic. (b) $\alpha = .01$

n	k = 1 d_L	k = 1 d_U	k = 2 d_L	k = 2 d_U	k = 3 d_L	k = 3 d_U	k = 4 d_L	k = 4 d_U	k = 5 d_L	k = 5 d_U
15	0.81	1.07	0.70	1.25	0.59	1.46	0.49	1.70	0.39	1.96
16	0.84	1.09	0.74	1.25	0.63	1.44	0.53	1.66	0.44	1.90
17	0.87	1.10	0.77	1.25	0.67	1.43	0.57	1.63	0.48	1.85
18	0.90	1.12	0.80	1.26	0.71	1.42	0.61	1.60	0.52	1.80
19	0.93	1.13	0.83	1.26	0.74	1.41	0.65	1.58	0.56	1.77
20	0.95	1.15	0.86	1.27	0.77	1.41	0.68	1.57	0.60	1.74
21	0.97	1.16	0.89	1.27	0.80	1.41	0.72	1.55	0.63	1.71
22	1.00	1.17	0.91	1.28	0.83	1.40	0.75	1.54	0.66	1.69
23	1.02	1.19	0.94	1.29	0.86	1.40	0.77	1.53	0.70	1.67
24	1.04	1.20	0.96	1.30	0.88	1.41	0.80	1.53	0.72	1.66
25	1.05	1.21	0.98	1.30	0.90	1.41	0.83	1.52	0.75	1.65
26	1.07	1.22	1.00	1.31	0.93	1.41	0.85	1.52	0.78	1.64
27	1.09	1.23	1.02	1.32	0.95	1.41	0.88	1.51	0.81	1.63
28	1.10	1.24	1.04	1.32	0.97	1.41	0.90	1.51	0.83	1.62
29	1.12	1.25	1.05	1.33	0.99	1.42	0.92	1.51	0.85	1.61
30	1.13	1.26	1.07	1.34	1.01	1.42	0.94	1.51	0.88	1.61
31	1.15	1.27	1.08	1.34	1.02	1.42	0.96	1.51	0.90	1.60
32	1.16	1.28	1.10	1.35	1.04	1.43	0.98	1.51	0.92	1.60
33	1.17	1.29	1.11	1.36	1.05	1.43	1.00	1.51	0.94	1.59
34	1.18	1.30	1.13	1.36	1.07	1.43	1.01	1.51	0.95	1.59
35	1.19	1.31	1.14	1.37	1.08	1.44	1.03	1.51	0.97	1.59
36	1.21	1.32	1.15	1.38	1.10	1.44	1.04	1.51	0.99	1.59
37	1.22	1.32	1.16	1.38	1.11	1.45	1.06	1.51	1.00	1.59
38	1.23	1.33	1.18	1.39	1.12	1.45	1.07	1.52	1.02	1.58
39	1.24	1.34	1.19	1.39	1.14	1.45	1.09	1.52	1.03	1.58
40	1.25	1.34	1.20	1.40	1.15	1.46	1.10	1.52	1.05	1.58
45	1.29	1.38	1.24	1.42	1.20	1.48	1.16	1.53	1.11	1.58
50	1.32	1.40	1.28	1.45	1.24	1.49	1.20	1.54	1.16	1.59
55	1.36	1.43	1.32	1.47	1.28	1.51	1.25	1.55	1.21	1.59
60	1.38	1.45	1.35	1.48	1.32	1.52	1.28	1.56	1.25	1.60
65	1.41	1.47	1.38	1.50	1.35	1.53	1.31	1.57	1.28	1.61
70	1.43	1.49	1.40	1.52	1.37	1.55	1.34	1.58	1.31	1.61
75	1.45	1.50	1.42	1.53	1.39	1.56	1.37	1.59	1.34	1.62
80	1.47	1.52	1.44	1.54	1.42	1.57	1.39	1.60	1.36	1.62
85	1.48	1.53	1.46	1.55	1.43	1.58	1.41	1.60	1.39	1.63
90	1.50	1.54	1.47	1.56	1.45	1.59	1.43	1.61	1.41	1.64
95	1.51	1.55	1.49	1.57	1.47	1.60	1.45	1.62	1.42	1.64
100	1.52	1.56	1.50	1.58	1.48	1.60	1.46	1.63	1.44	1.65

TABLE A.10   Distribution function for the Mann-Whitney U statistic.* This table contains the value of $P(U \le U_0)$, where $n_1 \le n_2$.

$n_2 = 3$ U_0	n_1 1	2	3
0	.25	.10	.05
1	.50	.20	.10
2		.40	.20
3		.60	.35
4			.50

$n_2 = 4$ U_0	n_1 1	2	3	4
0	.2000	.0667	.0286	.0143
1	.4000	.1333	.0571	.0286
2	.6000	.2667	.1143	.0571
3		.4000	.2000	.1000
4		.6000	.3143	.1714
5			.4286	.2429
6			.5714	.3429
7				.4429
8				.5571

$n_2 = 5$ U_0	1	2	n_1 3	4	5
0	.1667	.0476	.0179	.0079	.0040
1	.3333	.0952	.0357	.0159	.0079
2	.5000	.1905	.0714	.0317	.0159
3		.2857	.1250	.0556	.0278
4		.4286	.1964	.0952	.0476
5		.5714	.2857	.1429	.0754
6			.3929	.2063	.1111
7			.5000	.2778	.1548
8				.3651	.2103
9				.4524	.2738
10				.5476	.3452
11					.4206
12					.5000

*Computed by M. Pagano, Dept. of Statistics, University of Florida. Reprinted by permission from *Statistics for Management and Economics*, 5th ed., by William Mendenhall and James E. Reinmuth. Copyright © 1986 by PWS-KENT Publishers, Boston.

TABLE A.10 Distribution function for the Mann-Whitney U statistic *(continued)*.

$n_2 = 6$ U_0	1	2	3	4	5	6
0	.1429	.0357	.0119	.0048	.0022	.0011
1	.2857	.0714	.0238	.0095	.0043	.0022
2	.4286	.1429	.0476	.0190	.0087	.0043
3	.5714	.2143	.0833	.0333	.0152	.0076
4		.3214	.1310	.0571	.0260	.0130
5		.4286	.1905	.0857	.0411	.0206
6		.5714	.2738	.1286	.0628	.0325
7			.3571	.1762	.0887	.0465
8			.4524	.2381	.1234	.0660
9			.5476	.3048	.1645	.0898
10				.3810	.2143	.1201
11				.4571	.2684	.1548
12				.5429	.3312	.1970
13					.3961	.2424
14					.4654	.2944
15					.5346	.3496
16						.4091
17						.4686
18						.5314

$n_2 = 7$ U_0	1	2	3	4	5	6	7
0	.1250	.0278	.0083	.0030	.0013	.0006	.0003
1	.2500	.0556	.0167	.0061	.0025	.0012	.0006
2	.3750	.1111	.0333	.0121	.0051	.0023	.0012
3	.5000	.1667	.0583	.0212	.0088	.0041	.0020
4		.2500	.0917	.0364	.0152	.0070	.0035
5		.3333	.1333	.0545	.0240	.0111	.0055
6		.4444	.1917	.0818	.0366	.0175	.0087
7		.5556	.2583	.1152	.0530	.0256	.0131
8			.3333	.1576	.0745	.0367	.0189
9			.4167	.2061	.1010	.0507	.0265
10			.5000	.2636	.1338	.0688	.0364
11				.3242	.1717	.0903	.0487
12				.3939	.2159	.1171	.0641
13				.4636	.2652	.1474	.0825
14				.5364	.3194	.1830	.1043
15					.3775	.2226	.1297
16					.4381	.2669	.1588
17					.5000	.3141	.1914
18						.3654	.2279
19						.4178	.2675
20						.4726	.3100
21						.5274	.3552
22							.4024
23							.4508
24							.5000

TABLE A.10　　　　　Distribution function for the Mann-Whitney U statistic *(continued)*.

$n_2 = 8$ U_0	1	2	3	4	5	6	7	8
0	.1111	.0222	.0061	.0020	.0008	.0003	.0002	.0001
1	.2222	.0444	.0121	.0040	.0016	.0007	.0003	.0002
2	.3333	.0889	.0242	.0081	.0031	.0013	.0006	.0003
3	.4444	.1333	.0424	.0141	.0054	.0023	.0011	.0005
4	.5556	.2000	.0667	.0242	.0093	.0040	.0019	.0009
5		.2667	.0970	.0364	.0148	.0063	.0030	.0015
6		.3556	.1394	.0545	.0225	.0100	.0047	.0023
7		.4444	.1879	.0768	.0326	.0147	.0070	.0035
8		.5556	.2485	.1071	.0466	.0213	.0103	.0052
9			.3152	.1414	.0637	.0296	.0145	.0074
10			.3879	.1838	.0855	.0406	.0200	.0103
11			.4606	.2303	.1111	.0539	.0270	.0141
12			.5394	.2848	.1422	.0709	.0361	.0190
13				.3414	.1772	.0906	.0469	.0249
14				.4040	.2176	.1142	.0603	.0325
15				.4667	.2618	.1412	.0760	.0415
16				.5333	.3108	.1725	.0946	.0524
17					.3621	.2068	.1159	.0652
18					.4165	.2454	.1405	.0803
19					.4716	.2864	.1678	.0974
20					.5284	.3310	.1984	.1172
21						.3773	.2317	.1393
22						.4259	.2679	.1641
23						.4749	.3063	.1911
24						.5251	.3472	.2209
25							.3894	.2527
26							.4333	.2869
27							.4775	.3227
28							.5225	.3605
29								.3992
30								.4392
31								.4796
32								.5204

TABLE A.10   Distribution function for the Mann-Whitney U statistic *(continued)*.

$n_2 = 9$	U_0	1	2	3	4	n_1 5	6	7	8	9
	0	.1000	.0182	.0045	.0014	.0005	.0002	.0001	.0000	.0000
	1	.2000	.0364	.0091	.0028	.0010	.0004	.0002	.0001	.0000
	2	.3000	.0727	.0182	.0056	.0020	.0008	.0003	.0002	.0001
	3	.4000	.1091	.0318	.0098	.0035	.0014	.0006	.0003	.0001
	4	.5000	.1636	.0500	.0168	.0060	.0024	.0010	.0005	.0002
	5		.2182	.0727	.0252	.0095	.0038	.0017	.0008	.0004
	6		.2909	.1045	.0378	.0145	.0060	.0026	.0012	.0006
	7		.3636	.1409	.0531	.0210	.0088	.0039	.0019	.0009
	8		.4545	.1864	.0741	.0300	.0128	.0058	.0028	.0014
	9		.5455	.2409	.0993	.0415	.0180	.0082	.0039	.0020
	10			.3000	.1301	.0559	.0248	.0115	.0056	.0028
	11			.3636	.1650	.0734	.0332	.0156	.0076	.0039
	12			.4318	.2070	.0949	.0440	.0209	.0103	.0053
	13			.5000	.2517	.1199	.0567	.0274	.0137	.0071
	14				.3021	.1489	.0723	.0356	.0180	.0094
	15				.3552	.1818	.0905	.0454	.0232	.0122
	16				.4126	.2188	.1119	.0571	.0296	.0157
	17				.4699	.2592	.1361	.0708	.0372	.0200
	18				.5301	.3032	.1638	.0869	.0464	.0252
	19					.3497	.1942	.1052	.0570	.0313
	20					.3986	.2280	.1261	.0694	.0385
	21					.4491	.2643	.1496	.0836	.0470
	22					.5000	.3035	.1755	.0998	.0567
	23						.3445	.2039	.1179	.0680
	24						.3878	.2349	.1383	.0807
	25						.4320	.2680	.1606	.0951
	26						.4773	.3032	.1852	.1112
	27						.5227	.3403	.2117	.1290
	28							.3788	.2404	.1487
	29							.4185	.2707	.1701
	30							.4591	.3029	.1933
	31							.5000	.3365	.2181
	32								.3715	.2447
	33								.4074	.2729
	34								.4442	.3024
	35								.4813	.3332
	36								.5187	.3652
	37									.3981
	38									.4317
	39									.4657
	40									.5000

TABLE A.10   Distribution function for the Mann-Whitney U statistic (continued).

$n_2 = 10$ U_0	1	2	3	4	5	6	7	8	9	10
0	.0909	.0152	.0035	.0010	.0003	.0001	.0001	.0000	.0000	.0000
1	.1818	.0303	.0070	.0020	.0007	.0002	.0001	.0000	.0000	.0000
2	.2727	.0606	.0140	.0040	.0013	.0005	.0002	.0001	.0000	.0000
3	.3636	.0909	.0245	.0070	.0023	.0009	.0004	.0002	.0001	.0000
4	.4545	.1364	.0385	.0120	.0040	.0015	.0006	.0003	.0001	.0001
5	.5455	.1818	.0559	.0180	.0063	.0024	.0010	.0004	.0002	.0001
6		.2424	.0804	.0270	.0097	.0037	.0015	.0007	.0003	.0002
7		.3030	.1084	.0380	.0140	.0055	.0023	.0010	.0005	.0002
8		.3788	.1434	.0529	.0200	.0080	.0034	.0015	.0007	.0004
9		.4545	.1853	.0709	.0276	.0112	.0048	.0022	.0011	.0005
10		.5455	.2343	.0939	.0376	.0156	.0068	.0031	.0015	.0008
11			.2867	.1199	.0496	.0210	.0093	.0043	.0021	.0010
12			.3462	.1518	.0646	.0280	.0125	.0058	.0028	.0014
13			.4056	.1868	.0823	.0363	.0165	.0078	.0038	.0019
14			.4685	.2268	.1032	.0467	.0215	.0103	.0051	.0026
15			.5315	.2697	.1272	.0589	.0277	.0133	.0066	.0034
16				.3177	.1548	.0736	.0351	.0171	.0086	.0045
17				.3666	.1855	.0903	.0439	.0217	.0110	.0057
18				.4196	.2198	.1099	.0544	.0273	.0140	.0073
19				.4725	.2567	.1317	.0665	.0338	.0175	.0093
20				.5275	.2970	.1566	.0806	.0416	.0217	.0116
21					.3393	.1838	.0966	.0506	.0267	.0144
22					.3839	.2139	.1148	.0610	.0326	.0177
23					.4296	.2461	.1349	.0729	.0394	.0216
24					.4765	.2811	.1574	.0864	.0474	.0262
25					.5235	.3177	.1819	.1015	.0564	.0315
26						.3564	.2087	.1185	.0667	.0376
27						.3962	.2374	.1371	.0782	.0446
28						.4374	.2681	.1577	.0912	.0526
29						.4789	.3004	.1800	.1055	.0615
30						.5211	.3345	.2041	.1214	.0716
31							.3698	.2299	.1388	.0827
32							.4063	.2574	.1577	.0952
33							.4434	.2863	.1781	.1088
34							.4811	.3167	.2001	.1237
35							.5189	.3482	.2235	.1399
36								.3809	.2483	.1575
37								.4143	.2745	.1763
38								.4484	.3019	.1965
39								.4827	.3304	.2179
40								.5173	.3598	.2406
41									.3901	.2644
42									.4211	.2894
43									.4524	.3153
44									.4841	.3421
45									.5159	.3697
46										.3980
47										.4267
48										.4559
49										.4853
50										.5147

TABLE A.11

Critical values of the Wilcoxon signed rank test ($n = 5, \ldots, 50$).

1-sided	2-sided	$n = 5$	$n = 6$	$n = 7$	$n = 8$	$n = 9$	$n = 10$
$\alpha = .05$	$\alpha = .10$	1	2	4	6	8	11
$\alpha = .025$	$\alpha = .05$		1	2	4	6	8
$\alpha = .01$	$\alpha = .02$			0	2	3	5
$\alpha = .005$	$\alpha = .01$				0	2	3

1-sided	2-sided	$n = 11$	$n = 12$	$n = 13$	$n = 14$	$n = 15$	$n = 16$
$\alpha = .05$	$\alpha = .10$	14	17	21	26	30	36
$\alpha = .025$	$\alpha = .05$	11	14	17	21	25	30
$\alpha = .01$	$\alpha = .02$	7	10	13	16	20	24
$\alpha = .005$	$\alpha = .01$	5	7	10	13	16	19

1-sided	2-sided	$n = 17$	$n = 18$	$n = 19$	$n = 20$	$n = 21$	$n = 22$
$\alpha = .05$	$\alpha = .10$	41	47	54	60	68	75
$\alpha = .025$	$\alpha = .05$	35	40	46	52	59	66
$\alpha = .01$	$\alpha = .02$	28	33	38	43	49	56
$\alpha = .005$	$\alpha = .01$	23	28	32	37	43	49

1-sided	2-sided	$n = 23$	$n = 24$	$n = 25$	$n = 26$	$n = 27$	$n = 28$
$\alpha = .05$	$\alpha = .10$	83	92	101	110	120	130
$\alpha = .025$	$\alpha = .05$	73	81	90	98	107	117
$\alpha = .01$	$\alpha = .02$	62	69	77	85	93	102
$\alpha = .005$	$\alpha = .01$	55	61	68	76	84	92

1-sided	2-sided	$n = 29$	$n = 30$	$n = 31$	$n = 32$	$n = 33$	$n = 34$
$\alpha = .05$	$\alpha = .10$	141	152	163	175	188	201
$\alpha = .025$	$\alpha = .05$	127	137	148	159	171	183
$\alpha = .01$	$\alpha = .02$	111	120	130	141	151	162
$\alpha = .005$	$\alpha = .01$	100	109	118	128	138	149

1-sided	2-sided	$n = 35$	$n = 36$	$n = 37$	$n = 38$	$n = 39$
$\alpha = .05$	$\alpha = .10$	214	228	242	256	271
$\alpha = .025$	$\alpha = .05$	195	208	222	235	250
$\alpha = .01$	$\alpha = .02$	174	186	198	211	224
$\alpha = .005$	$\alpha = .01$	160	171	183	195	208

1-sided	2-sided	$n = 40$	$n = 41$	$n = 42$	$n = 43$	$n = 44$	$n = 45$
$\alpha = .05$	$\alpha = .10$	287	303	319	336	353	371
$\alpha = .025$	$\alpha = .05$	264	279	295	311	327	344
$\alpha = .01$	$\alpha = .02$	238	252	267	281	297	313
$\alpha = .005$	$\alpha = .01$	221	234	248	262	277	292

1-sided	2-sided	$n = 46$	$n = 47$	$n = 48$	$n = 49$	$n = 50$
$\alpha = .05$	$\alpha = .10$	389	408	427	446	466
$\alpha = .025$	$\alpha = .05$	361	379	397	415	434
$\alpha = .01$	$\alpha = .02$	329	345	362	380	398
$\alpha = .005$	$\alpha = .01$	307	323	339	356	373

From F. Wilcoxon and R. A. Wilcox, "Some Rapid Approximate Statistical Procedures," 1964.
Reprinted by permission of Lederle Labs, a division of the American Cyanamid Co.

TABLE A.12

Critical values of Spearman's rank correlation coefficient.

n	$\alpha = .05$	$\alpha = .025$	$\alpha = .01$	$\alpha = .005$
5	0.900	—	—	—
6	0.829	0.886	0.943	—
7	0.714	0.786	0.893	—
8	0.643	0.738	0.833	0.881
9	0.600	0.683	0.783	0.833
10	0.564	0.648	0.745	0.794
11	0.523	0.623	0.736	0.818
12	0.497	0.591	0.703	0.780
13	0.475	0.566	0.673	0.745
14	0.457	0.545	0.646	0.716
15	0.441	0.525	0.623	0.689
16	0.425	0.507	0.601	0.666
17	0.412	0.490	0.582	0.645
18	0.399	0.476	0.564	0.625
19	0.388	0.462	0.549	0.608
20	0.377	0.450	0.534	0.591
21	0.368	0.438	0.521	0.576
22	0.359	0.428	0.508	0.562
23	0.351	0.418	0.496	0.549
24	0.343	0.409	0.485	0.537
25	0.336	0.400	0.475	0.526
26	0.329	0.392	0.465	0.515
27	0.323	0.385	0.456	0.505
28	0.317	0.377	0.448	0.496
29	0.311	0.370	0.440	0.487
30	0.305	0.364	0.432	0.478

*From E. G. Olds, "Distribution of Sums of Squares of Rank Differences for Small Samples," *Annals of Mathematical Statistics*, Vol. 9 (1938). Reprinted with permission of the Institute of Mathematical Statistics.

TABLE A.13   Random numbers.

12651	61646	11769	75109	86996	97669	25757	32535	07122	76763
81769	74436	02630	72310	45049	18029	07469	42341	98173	79260
36737	98863	77240	76251	00654	64688	09343	70278	67331	98729
82861	54371	76610	94934	72748	44124	05610	53750	95938	01485
21325	15732	24127	37431	09723	63529	73977	95218	96074	42138
74146	47887	62463	23045	41490	07954	22597	60012	98866	90959
90759	64410	54179	66075	61051	75385	51378	08360	95946	95547
55683	98078	02238	91540	21219	17720	87817	41705	95785	12563
79686	17969	76061	83748	55920	83612	41540	86492	06447	60568
70333	00201	86201	69716	78185	62154	77930	67663	29529	75116
14042	53536	07779	04157	41172	36473	42123	43929	50533	33437
59911	08256	06596	48416	69770	68797	56080	14223	59199	30162
62368	62623	62742	14891	39247	52242	98832	69533	91174	57979
57529	97751	54976	48957	74599	08759	78494	52785	68526	64618
15469	90574	78033	66885	13936	42117	71831	22961	94225	31816
18625	23674	53850	32827	81647	80820	00420	63555	74489	80141
74626	68394	88562	70745	23701	45630	65891	58220	35442	60414
11119	16519	27384	90199	79210	76965	99546	30323	31664	22845
41101	17336	48951	53674	17880	45260	08575	49321	36191	17095
32123	91576	84221	78902	82010	30847	62329	63898	23268	74283
26091	68409	69704	82267	14751	13151	93115	01437	56945	89661
67680	79790	48462	59278	44185	29616	76531	19589	83139	28454
15184	19260	14073	07026	25264	08388	27182	22557	61501	67481
58010	45039	57181	10238	36874	28546	37444	80824	63981	39942
56425	53996	86245	32623	78858	08143	60377	42925	42815	11159
82630	84066	13592	60642	17904	99718	63432	88642	37858	25431
14927	40909	23900	48761	44860	92467	31742	87142	03607	32059
23740	22505	07489	85986	74420	21744	97711	36648	35620	97949
32990	97446	03711	63824	07953	85965	87089	11687	92414	67257
05310	24058	91946	78437	34365	82469	12430	84754	19354	72745
21839	39937	27534	88913	49055	19218	47712	67677	51889	70926
08833	42549	93981	94051	28382	83725	72643	64233	97252	17133
58336	11139	47479	00931	91560	95372	97642	33856	54825	55680
62032	91144	75478	47431	52726	30289	42411	91886	51818	78292
45171	30557	53116	04118	58301	24375	65609	85810	18620	49198
91611	62656	60128	35609	63698	78356	50682	22505	01692	36291
55472	63819	86314	49174	93582	73604	78614	78849	23096	72825
18573	09729	74091	53994	10970	86557	65661	41854	26037	53296
60866	02955	90288	82136	83644	94455	06560	78029	98768	71296
45043	55608	82767	60890	74646	79485	13619	98868	40857	19415
17831	09737	79473	75945	28394	79334	70577	38048	03607	06932
40137	03981	07585	18128	11178	32601	27994	05641	22600	86064
77776	31343	14576	97706	16039	47517	43300	59080	80392	63189
69605	44104	40103	95635	05635	81673	68657	09559	23510	95875
19916	52934	26499	09821	97331	80993	61299	36979	73599	35055
02606	58552	07678	56619	65325	30705	99582	53390	46357	13244
65183	73160	87131	35530	47946	09854	18080	02321	05809	04893
10740	98914	44916	11322	89717	88189	30143	52687	19420	60061
98642	89822	71691	51573	83666	61642	46683	33761	47542	23551
60139	25601	93663	25547	02654	94829	48672	28736	84994	13071

TABLE A.14   Critical values of Hartley's *H*-statistic, $\alpha = .05$. n = number of observations in each sample; k = number of samples.

n	k										
	2	3	4	5	6	7	8	9	10	11	12
3	39.0	87.5	142	202	266	333	403	475	550	626	704
4	15.4	27.8	39.2	50.7	62.0	72.9	83.5	93.9	104	114	124
5	9.60	15.5	20.6	25.2	29.5	33.6	37.5	41.1	44.6	48.0	51.4
6	7.15	10.8	13.7	16.3	18.7	20.8	22.9	24.7	26.5	28.2	29.9
7	5.82	8.38	10.4	12.1	13.7	15.0	16.3	17.5	18.6	19.7	20.7
8	4.99	6.94	8.44	9.70	10.8	11.8	12.7	13.5	14.3	15.1	15.8
9	4.43	6.00	7.18	8.12	9.03	9.78	10.5	11.1	11.7	12.2	12.7
10	4.03	5.34	6.31	7.11	7.80	8.41	8.95	9.45	9.91	10.3	10.7
11	3.72	4.85	5.67	6.34	6.92	7.42	7.87	8.28	8.66	9.01	9.34
13	3.28	4.16	4.79	5.30	5.72	6.09	6.42	6.72	7.00	7.25	7.48
16	2.86	3.54	4.01	4.37	4.68	4.95	5.19	5.40	5.59	5.77	5.93
21	2.46	2.95	3.29	3.54	3.76	3.94	4.10	4.24	4.37	4.49	4.59
31	2.07	2.40	2.61	2.78	2.91	3.02	3.12	3.21	3.29	3.36	3.39
61	1.67	1.85	1.96	2.04	2.11	2.17	2.22	2.26	2.30	2.33	2.36
∞	1.00	1.00	1.00	1.00	1.00	1.00	1.00	1.00	1.00	1.00	1.00

TABLE A.15

Critical values for the number of runs R, in samples of size (n_1, n_2). The null hypothesis is rejected if $R \leq k_1$ or $R \geq k_2$, where for each n_1 and n_2 the top value is k_1 and the bottom value is k_2.

THE SMALLER OF n_1 AND n_2 (rows) vs **THE LARGER OF n_1 AND n_2** (columns). Each cell shows k_1 (top) / k_2 (bottom).

	5	6	7	8	9	10	11	12	13	14	15	16	17	18	19	20
2								2/6	2/6	2/6	2/6	2/6	2/6	2/6	2/6	2/6
3		2/8	2/8	2/8	2/8	2/8	2/8	2/8	2/8	3/8	3/8	3/8	3/8	3/8	3/8	3/8
4	2/9	2/9	2/10	3/10	3/10	3/10	3/10	3/10	3/10	3/10	3/10	4/10	4/10	4/10	4/10	4/10
5	2/10	3/10	3/11	3/11	3/12	3/12	4/12	4/12	4/12	4/12	4/12	4/12	4/12	5/12	5/12	5/12
6		3/11	3/12	3/12	4/13	4/13	4/13	4/13	5/14	5/14	5/14	5/14	5/14	5/14	6/14	6/14
7			3/13	4/13	4/14	5/14	5/14	5/14	5/15	5/15	6/15	6/16	6/16	6/16	6/16	6/16
8				4/14	5/14	5/15	5/15	6/16	6/16	6/16	6/16	6/17	7/17	7/17	7/17	7/17
9					5/15	5/16	6/16	6/16	6/17	7/17	7/18	7/18	7/18	8/18	8/18	8/18
10						6/16	6/17	7/17	7/18	7/18	7/18	8/19	8/19	8/19	8/20	9/20
11							7/17	7/18	7/19	8/19	8/19	8/20	9/20	9/20	9/21	9/21
12								7/19	8/19	8/20	8/20	9/21	9/21	9/21	10/22	10/22
13									8/20	9/20	9/21	9/21	10/22	10/22	10/23	10/23
14										9/21	9/22	10/22	10/23	10/23	11/23	11/24
15											10/22	10/23	11/23	11/24	11/24	12/25
16												11/23	11/24	11/25	12/25	12/25
17													11/25	12/25	12/26	13/26
18														12/26	13/26	13/27
19															13/27	13/27
20																14/28

TABLE A.16

Critical values of the studentized range (Q) distribution. The values listed in the table are the critical values of Q for $\alpha = .05$ and $\alpha = .01$, as a function of degrees of freedom for MS(error) and k (the number of means).

df for MS(ERROR) (v)	α	2	3	4	5	6	7	8	9	10	11
5	.05	3.64	4.60	5.22	5.67	6.03	6.33	6.58	6.80	6.99	7.17
	.01	5.70	6.98	7.80	8.42	8.91	9.32	9.67	9.97	10.24	10.48
6	.05	3.46	4.34	4.90	5.30	5.63	5.90	6.12	6.32	6.49	6.65
	.01	5.24	6.33	7.03	7.56	7.97	8.32	8.61	8.87	9.10	9.30
7	.05	3.34	4.16	4.68	5.06	5.36	5.61	5.82	6.00	6.16	6.30
	.01	4.95	5.92	6.54	7.01	7.37	7.68	7.94	8.17	8.37	8.55
8	.05	3.26	4.04	4.53	4.89	5.17	5.40	5.60	5.77	5.92	6.05
	.01	4.75	5.64	6.20	6.62	6.96	7.24	7.47	7.68	7.86	8.03
9	.05	3.20	3.95	4.41	4.76	5.02	5.24	5.43	5.59	5.74	5.87
	.01	4.60	5.43	5.96	6.35	6.66	6.91	7.13	7.33	7.49	7.65
10	.05	3.15	3.88	4.33	4.65	4.91	5.12	5.30	5.46	5.60	5.72
	.01	4.48	5.27	5.77	6.14	6.43	6.67	6.87	7.05	7.21	7.36
11	.05	3.11	3.82	4.26	4.57	4.82	5.03	5.20	5.35	5.49	5.61
	.01	4.39	5.15	5.62	5.97	6.25	6.48	6.67	6.84	6.99	7.13
12	.05	3.08	3.77	4.20	4.51	4.75	4.95	5.12	5.27	5.39	5.51
	.01	4.32	5.05	5.50	5.84	6.10	6.32	6.51	6.67	6.81	6.94
13	.05	3.06	3.73	4.15	4.45	4.69	4.88	5.05	5.19	5.32	5.43
	.01	4.26	4.96	5.40	5.73	5.98	6.19	6.37	6.53	6.67	6.79
14	.05	3.03	3.70	4.11	4.41	4.64	4.83	4.99	5.13	5.25	5.36
	.01	4.21	4.89	5.32	5.63	5.88	6.08	6.26	6.41	6.54	6.66
15	.05	3.01	3.67	4.08	4.37	4.59	4.78	4.94	5.08	5.20	5.31
	.01	4.17	4.84	5.25	5.56	5.80	5.99	6.16	6.31	6.44	6.55
16	.05	3.00	3.65	4.05	4.33	4.56	4.74	4.90	5.03	5.15	5.26
	.01	4.13	4.79	5.19	5.49	5.72	5.92	6.08	6.22	6.35	6.46
17	.05	2.98	3.63	4.02	4.30	4.52	4.70	4.86	4.99	5.11	5.21
	.01	4.10	4.74	5.14	5.43	5.66	5.85	6.01	6.15	6.27	6.38
18	.05	2.97	3.61	4.00	4.28	4.49	4.67	4.82	4.96	5.07	5.17
	.01	4.07	4.70	5.09	5.38	5.60	5.79	5.94	6.08	6.20	6.31
19	.05	2.96	3.59	3.98	4.25	4.47	4.65	4.79	4.92	5.04	5.14
	.01	4.05	4.67	5.05	5.33	5.55	5.73	5.89	6.02	6.14	6.25
20	.05	2.95	3.58	3.96	4.23	4.45	4.62	4.77	4.90	5.01	5.11
	.01	4.02	4.64	5.02	5.29	5.51	5.69	5.84	5.97	6.09	6.19
24	.05	2.92	3.53	3.90	4.17	4.37	4.54	4.68	4.81	4.92	5.01
	.01	3.96	4.55	4.91	5.17	5.37	5.54	5.69	5.81	5.92	6.02
30	.05	2.89	3.49	3.85	4.10	4.30	4.46	4.60	4.72	4.82	4.92
	.01	3.89	4.45	4.80	5.05	5.24	5.40	5.54	5.65	5.76	5.85
40	.05	2.86	3.44	3.79	4.04	4.23	4.39	4.52	4.63	4.73	4.82
	.01	3.82	4.37	4.70	4.93	5.11	5.26	5.39	5.50	5.60	5.69
60	.05	2.83	3.40	3.74	3.98	4.16	4.31	4.44	4.55	4.65	4.73
	.01	3.76	4.28	4.59	4.82	4.99	5.13	5.25	5.36	5.45	5.53
120	.05	2.80	3.36	3.68	3.92	4.10	4.24	4.36	4.47	4.56	4.64
	.01	3.70	4.20	4.50	4.71	4.87	5.01	5.12	5.21	5.30	5.37
∞	.05	2.77	3.31	3.63	3.86	4.03	4.17	4.29	4.39	4.47	4.55
	.01	3.64	4.12	4.40	4.60	4.76	4.88	4.99	5.08	5.16	5.23

From E. S. Pearson and H. O. Hartley (eds.), *Biometrika Tables for Statisticians*, 3rd ed., 1966. Reproduced by permission of *Cambridge University Press*.

TABLE A.17

Quantiles of the Kendall Test Statistic

n	$V_{.90}$	$V_{.95}$	$V_{.975}$	$V_{.990}$	$V_{.995}$
4	4	4	6	6	6
5	6	6	8	8	10
6	7	9	11	11	13
7	9	11	13	15	17
8	10	14	16	18	20
9	12	16	18	22	24
10	15	19	21	25	27
11	17	21	25	29	31
12	18	24	28	34	36
13	22	26	32	38	42
14	23	31	35	41	45
15	27	33	39	47	51
16	28	36	44	50	56
17	32	40	48	56	62
18	35	43	51	61	67
19	37	47	55	65	73
20	40	50	60	70	78
21	42	54	64	76	84
22	45	59	69	81	89
23	49	63	73	87	97
24	52	66	78	92	102
25	56	70	84	98	108
26	59	75	89	105	115
27	61	79	93	111	123
28	66	84	98	116	128
29	68	88	104	124	136
30	73	93	109	129	143
31	75	97	115	135	149
32	80	102	120	142	158
33	84	106	126	150	164
34	87	111	131	155	173
35	91	115	137	163	179
36	94	120	144	170	188
37	98	126	150	176	196
38	103	131	155	183	203
39	107	137	161	191	211
40	110	142	168	198	220
41	114	146	174	206	228
42	119	151	181	213	235
43	123	157	187	221	245
44	128	162	194	228	252
45	132	168	200	236	262
46	135	173	207	245	271
47	141	179	213	253	279
48	144	186	220	260	288
49	150	190	228	268	296
50	153	197	233	277	305
51	159	203	241	285	315
52	162	208	248	294	324
53	168	214	256	302	334
54	173	221	263	311	343
55	177	227	269	319	353
56	182	232	276	328	362
57	186	240	284	336	372
58	191	245	291	345	381
59	197	251	299	355	391
60	202	258	306	364	402

From W. J. Conover, *Practical Nonparametric Statistics,* 2/e, Table A-12, 1980, John Wiley & Sons, New York. Reprinted with permission.

APPENDIX B DERIVATION OF MINIMUM TOTAL SAMPLE SIZE

CLAIM. When obtaining two independent samples, the maximum error for the difference of the two population means, $\mu_1 - \mu_2$, is

$$E = Z_{\alpha/2}\sqrt{\frac{\sigma_1^2}{n_1} + \frac{\sigma_2^2}{n_2}} \qquad (\sigma_1, \sigma_2 \text{ known})$$

or is estimated using

$$E = Z_{\alpha/2}\sqrt{\frac{s_1^2}{n_1} + \frac{s_2^2}{n_2}} \qquad (\sigma_1, \sigma_2 \text{ unknown})$$

For a specific value of E, the sample sizes, n_1 and n_2, that minimize the total sample size, $n = n_1 + n_2$, are given by

$$n_1 = \frac{Z_{\alpha/2}^2 s_1 (s_1 + s_2)}{E^2} \qquad \text{and} \qquad n_2 = \frac{Z_{\alpha/2}^2 s_2 (s_1 + s_2)}{E^2}$$

PROOF. For ease of notation, define

$$Z = Z_{\alpha/2} \qquad x = n_1$$

$$a = s_1 \qquad y = n_2$$

$$b = s_2$$

(For the case where the σ's are known, then $a = \sigma_1$ and $b = \sigma_2$.) Now,

$$E = Z\sqrt{\frac{a^2}{x} + \frac{b^2}{y}}$$

is fixed. Solving for y yields

$$y = \frac{Z^2 b^2 x}{E^2 x - Z^2 a^2}$$

The total sample size is $n = x + y$, and so

$$n = f(x) = x + \frac{Z^2 b^2 x}{E^2 x - Z^2 a^2}$$

To determine the value of x that minimizes $n = f(x)$, the procedure will be to find $f'(x)$, set it equal to zero, and solve for x.

$$f'(x) = 1 + \frac{(E^2 x - Z^2 a^2)(Z^2 b^2) - Z^2 b^2 x (E^2)}{(E^2 x - Z^2 a^2)^2} = 1 - \frac{Z^4 a^2 b^2}{(E^2 x - Z^2 a^2)^2}$$

Now,

$$f'(x) = 0$$

iff $x^2 (E^4) + x(-2Z^2 E^2 a^2) + (Z^4 a^4 - Z^4 a^2 b^2) = 0$

iff $x = \dfrac{2Z^2 E^2 a^2 \mp \sqrt{4Z^4 E^4 a^4 - 4Z^4 E^4 a^2 (a^2 - b^2)}}{2E^4} = \dfrac{Z^2 a^2 \mp Z^2 ab}{E^2}$

Now,

$$f''(x) = \frac{2Z^4 E^2 a^2 b^2 (E^2 x - Z^2 a^2)}{(E^2 x - Z^2 a^2)^4}$$

Consequently,

$$f''(x) > 0 \qquad \text{iff } (E^2x - Z^2a^2) > 0$$

Letting

$$x = \frac{Z^2a^2 + Z^2ab}{E^2}$$

then

$$E^2x - Z^2a^2 = Z^2ab > 0$$

because a and b are > 0. Letting

$$x = \frac{Z^2a^2 - Z^2ab}{E^2}$$

then

$$E^2x - Z^2a^2 = -Z^2ab < 0$$

CONCLUSION.

1. $f(x)$ has a local minimum at

$$x = \frac{Z^2a(a+b)}{E^2}$$

2. $f(x)$ has a local maximum at

$$x = \frac{Z^2a(a-b)}{E^2}$$

Because we are restricted to values of x (that is, n_1) such that $f(x) =$ total sample size is positive, and because $f(x)$ approaches ∞ as x approaches ∞, for the admissible values of x, $f(x)$ has a global minimum at

$$x = n_1 = \frac{Z^2a(a+b)}{E^2} = \frac{Z^2s_1(s_1+s_2)}{E^2}$$

Solving for n_2, we previously stated that

$$y = \frac{Z^2b^2x}{E^2x - Z^2a^2}$$

Substituting

$$x = \frac{Z^2s_1(s_1+s_2)}{E^2}$$

into this expression produces

$$y = n_2 = \frac{Z^2s_2(s_1+s_2)}{E^2}$$

APPENDIX C   INTRODUCTION TO EXCEL

Spreadsheet applications originated with business professionals, such as accountants, who needed an electronic version of a paper spreadsheet. These spreadsheets or worksheets consisted of row and column grids in which entries were placed. The computational abilities and flexibility of spreadsheet applications using Microsoft Excel have come a long way from the introduction of VisiCalc (short for visible calculator), the first marketed spreadsheet application.

When you first open Excel, a window opens with an empty worksheet appearing. Excel offers 13 different toolbars to accomplish a number of tasks, some of which are illustrated in the following worksheet. Click on the white paper-shaped icon in the upper left corner (□ on the standard toolbar) to obtain a new worksheet quickly. Another way to open a new worksheet is to click on **File** on the menu bar and then click on **New.** The following window will be displayed when opening a new Worksheet.

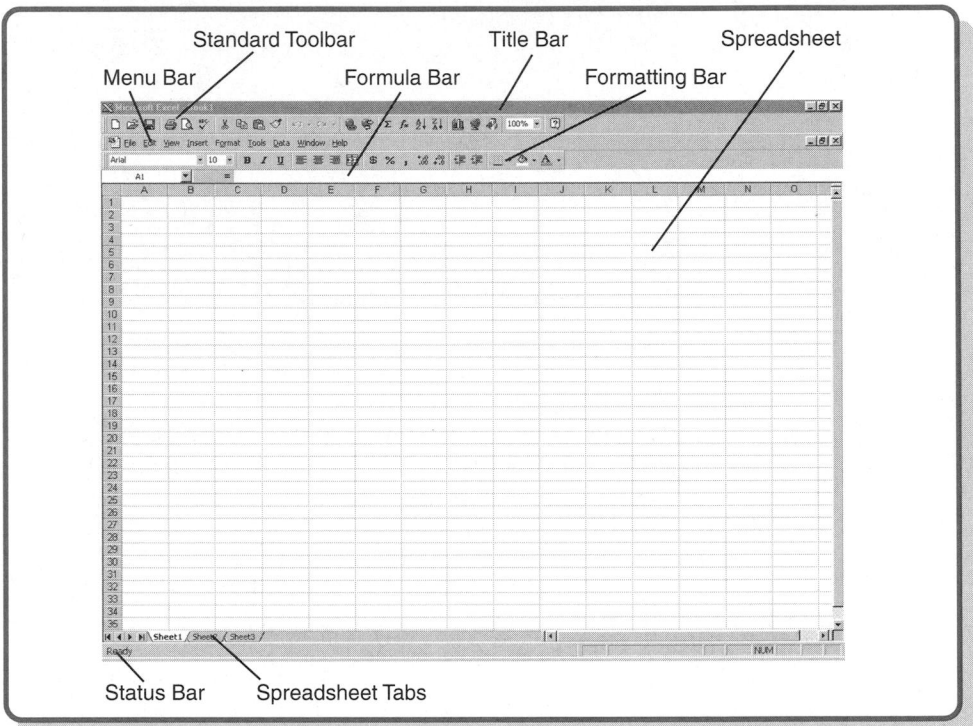

STARTING AND EXITING EXCEL

* To start in Windows 98 or Windows NT 4.0
  From the Taskbar, choose **Start ➤ Programs ➤ Microsoft Office ➤ Microsoft Excel**
* To exit Excel
  Choose **File ➤ Exit** or click on the **Close** button (X) in the upper right corner.

ENTERING DATA IN A SPREADSHEET

Click on a cell in the spreadsheet to *activate* the cell. Then type in the information you want. If your mouse pointer is in the spreadsheet, it will initially have the shape of a white plus sign. Then as you click on a cell or click on the formula bar, the mouse pointer changes into a "I-beam" shape. If the mouse pointer is moved to the menu or toolbar, it will have the shape of an arrow. These shapes are to help you understand what Excel is expecting you to do. You can enter data into any one of the spreadsheets indicated at the bottom of the window. Click on the arrows in the bottom left corner of the window to move to another spreadsheet as illustrated below.

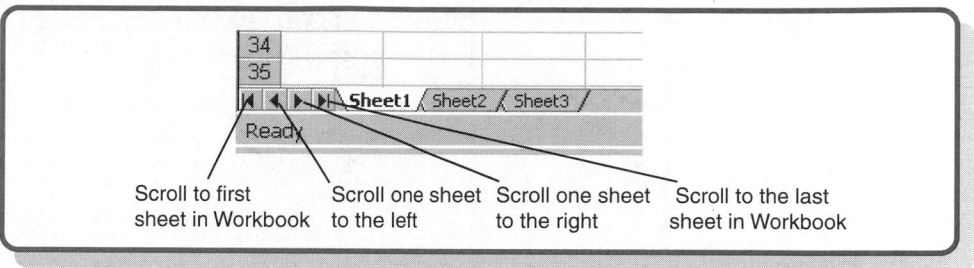

USING EXCEL'S HELP: THE OFFICE ASSISTANT

Hitting F1 is the universal help command and this also works in Excel. One of the noticeable features about Excel is that it has an animated cartoonlike character to assist in answering questions. There are actually nine different Office Assistants, each as capable as the next. The one used below is the Office Assistant that appears if you do not select one. This Office Assistant is known as Clippit. We will illustrate how to obtain information on moving and copying cells by using Clippit. Simply type **move or copy cells** into the white text box and click on **Search.** By clicking on the radial button next to **Move or copy cell data,** the help screen that follows will appear. Notice that there are several topics from which to select. If the **Move or copy characters within a cell** is selected, the next help screen will appear. This help screen provides a step-by-step procedure for moving or copying characters within a cell.

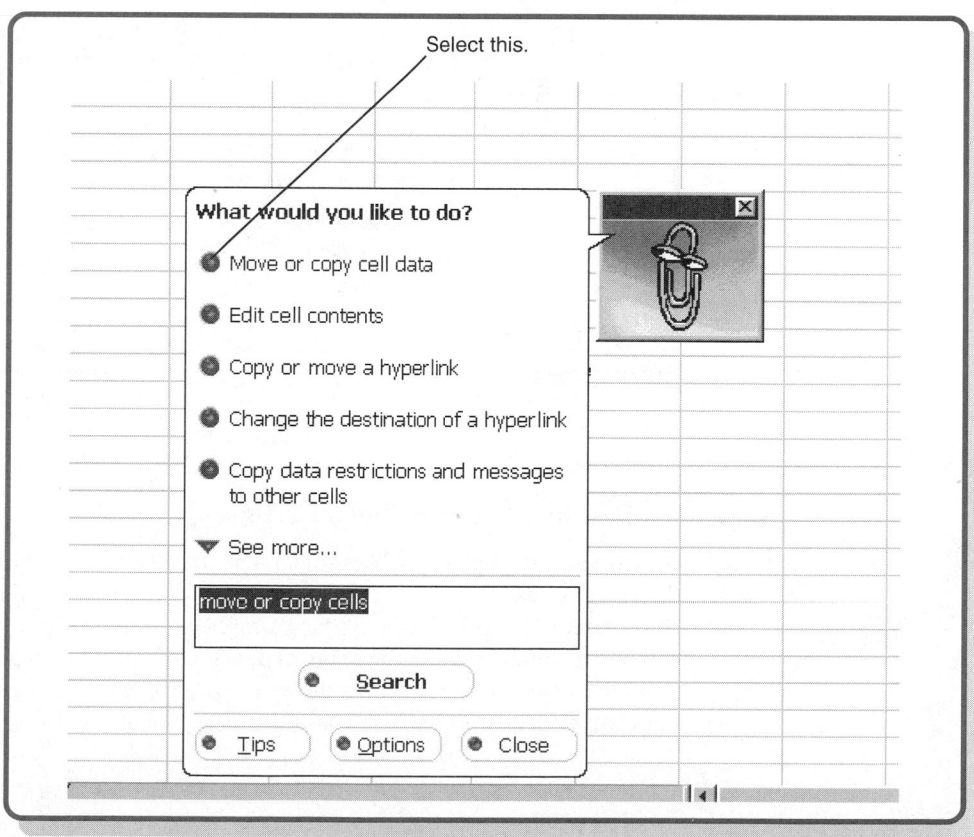

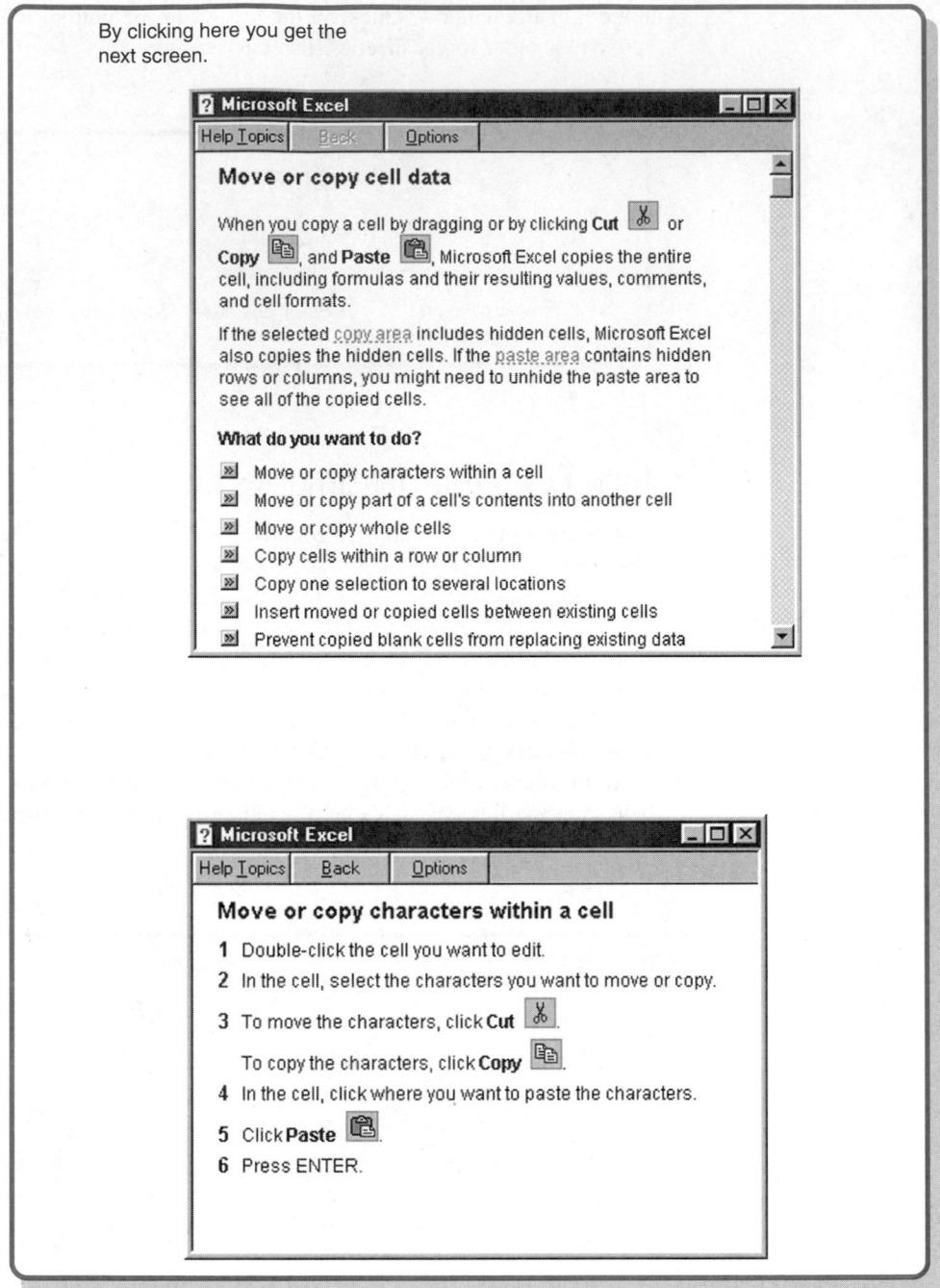

By clicking here you get the next screen.

MOVING OR COPYING A RANGE OF DATA

An easy way to copy or cut (delete) a range of cells is to first highlight those cells and then do a right click. Be sure to keep the mouse pointer in the central area of the highlighted cells. After the pop-up menu appears, simply click either **Copy** or **Cut.** Then highlight one cell where you would like the range of data to appear. If you select more than one cell, then you must select a region that is the exact same size of the region copied or cut. Next hit the **Control** key with the V key and the range of entries will appear.

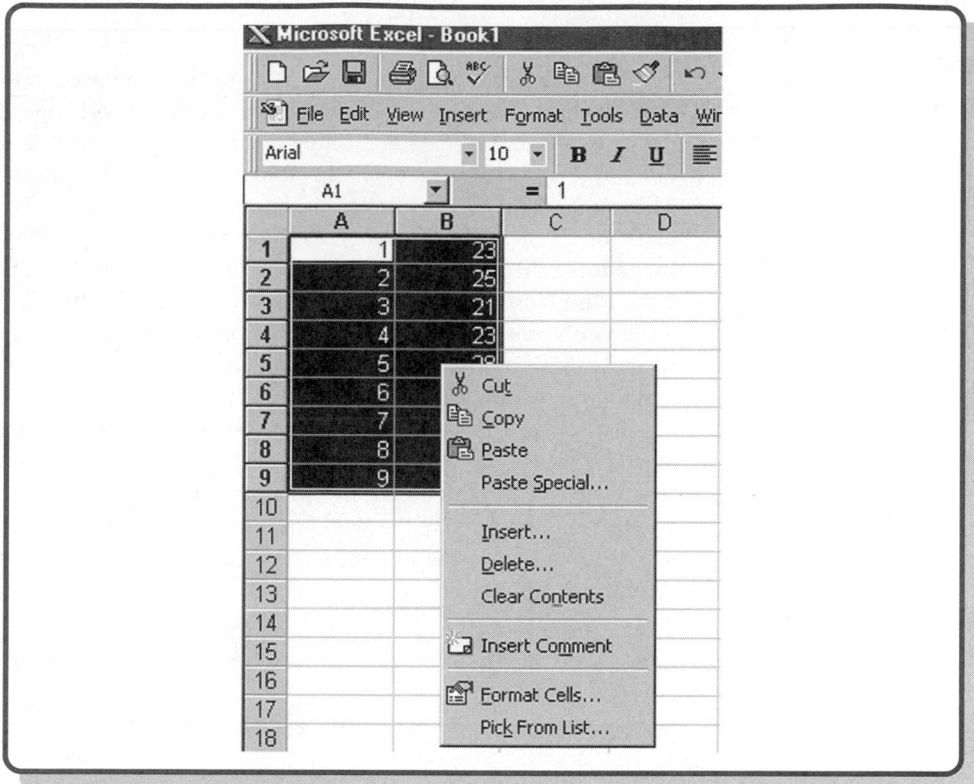

To move cells, simply highlight the cells and then put the mouse pointer on the border of the selection. Notice that the pointer takes the shape of an arrow as illustrated below. Now drag the cells; that is, left click and hold while moving the cells to the desired area. To copy the cells, hold down the **Control** key while dragging.

ENTERING FORMULAS AND FUNCTIONS INTO CELLS

Calculations, formulas and functions are often entered into cells. A formula is an equation that analyzes data on a worksheet and must begin with the equals sign. Formulas perform operations such as addition, multiplication, exponentiation, and comparison on worksheet values. By using functions, formulas can combine values from several cells or do mathematical operations on the values from several cells. You can use the **Paste** function (*fx* on the standard toolbar) to enter functions. Formulas can refer to cells on the same worksheet, cells on sheets in the same workbook, or cells on sheets in other workbooks. The following example adds the value of cell C6 and 50 and then divides the result by the sum of cells A1 through A10.

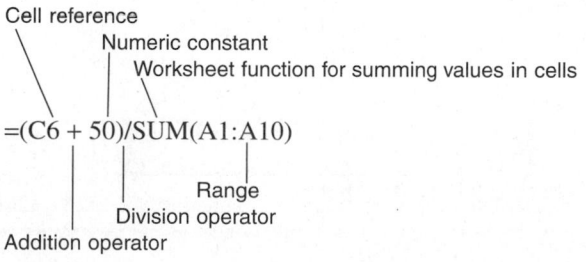

OPENING AND SAVING FILES

Perhaps the quickest way to open a file is to click on the open folder icon (on the standard toolbar). The **Open** userform displayed below will appear. In the **Look in** box, click the drive, folder, or Internet location that contains the workbook. In the folder list, double-click folders until you open the folder that contains the workbook you want. Only Microsoft Excel files are listed in the dialog box initially. To open another type of file, click the file format you want in the **Files of type** box, and then double-click the file name in the folder list. You can also type the file name extension in the **File name** box, and then click **Find Now.** For example, type "*.wk4" to find Lotus 1-2-3 Release 4.0 files. To open a file you've used recently, click the file name at the bottom of the **File** menu. If the list of recently used files isn't displayed, click **Options** on the **Tools** menu, click the **General** tab, and then select the **Recently used file list** check box.

To save a workbook with all of its spreadsheets, click on the diskette icon (on the standard toolbar) or click on **File** and select **Save** or **Save as.** The **Save as** userform displayed after the **Open** userform will appear. In the **Save in** box, select the drive and folder where you want to save the workbook. To save the workbook in a new folder, click **Create New Folder.** In the **File name** box, type a name for the workbook. You can use long, descriptive file names.

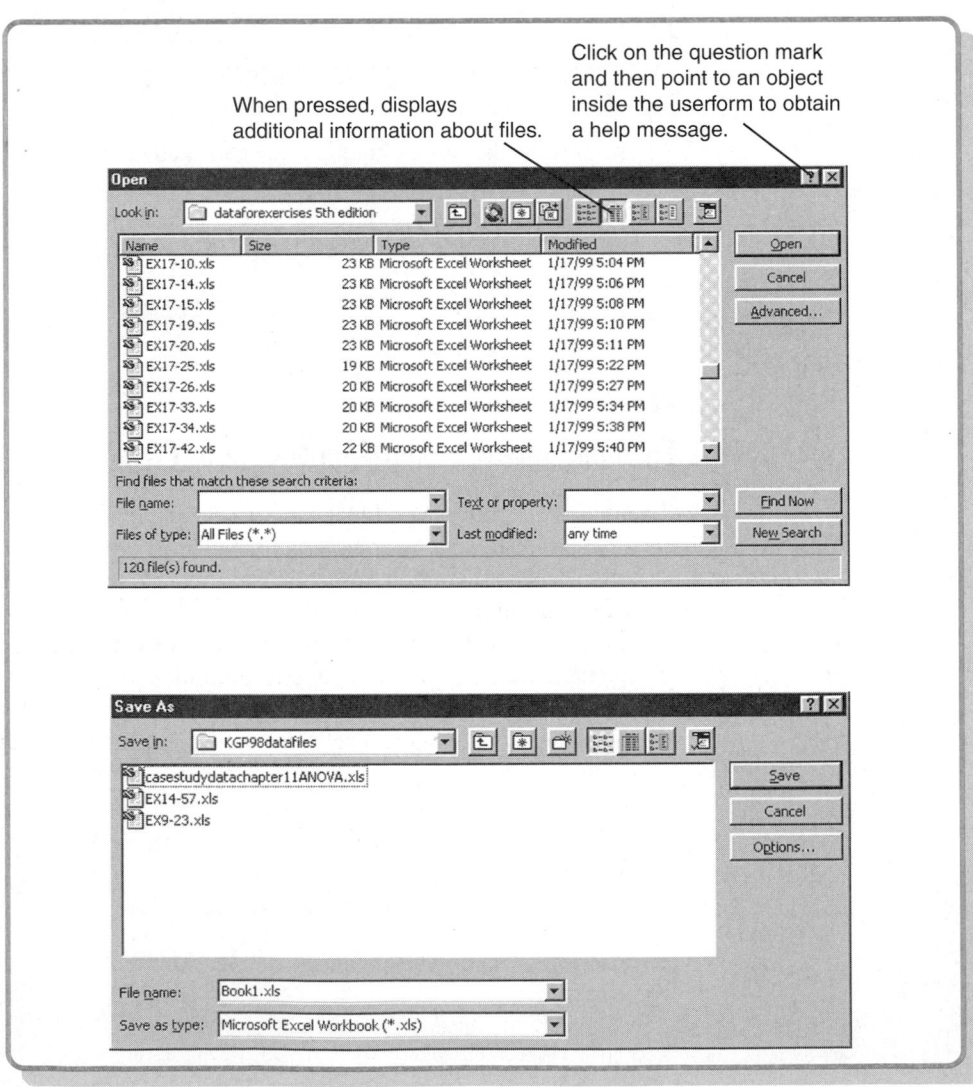

USING ADD-INS

Add-ins are preprogramed procedures that add optional commands and features to Microsoft Excel. Before you can use an add-in, you must install it on your computer and then load it in Microsoft Excel. Add-ins (*.xla files) are installed by default in the Library folder in the Microsoft Excel folder. Loading an add-in makes the feature available in Microsoft Excel and adds any associated commands to the appropriate menus. To conserve memory, unload add-ins you do not often use. Unloading an add-in removes its features and commands from Microsoft Excel, but the add-in program remains on your computer so you can easily load it again. To add Excel Add-ins, click on **Tools** and select **Add-Ins** as illustrated below.

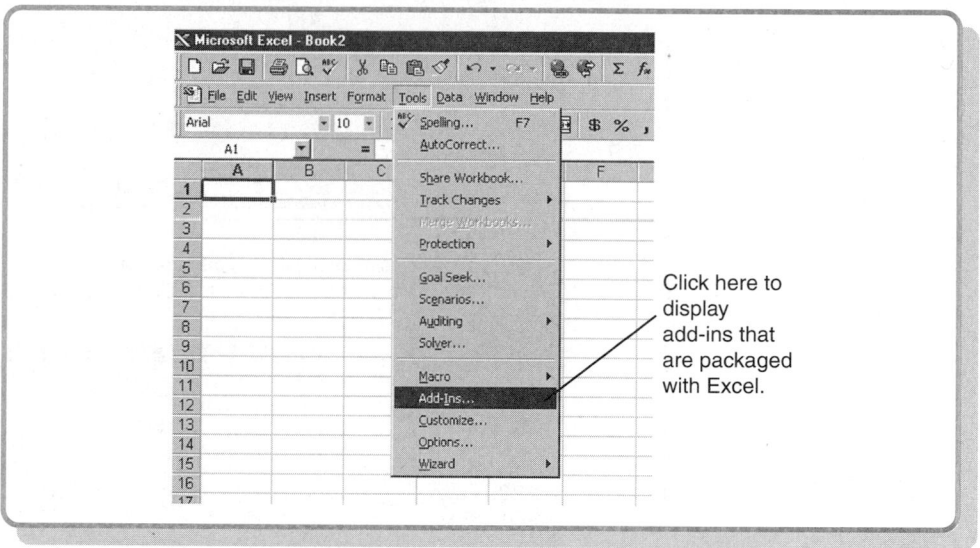

If the **Typical** option of the Microsoft Excel/Office setup program was selected, the (Data) Analysis ToolPak add-ins used in this text will not appear. After selecting **Add-Ins** from the **Tools** menu, the following userform will appear. For this textbook, it is necessary to have the Analysis ToolPak and Analysis ToolPak-VBA add-ins checked.

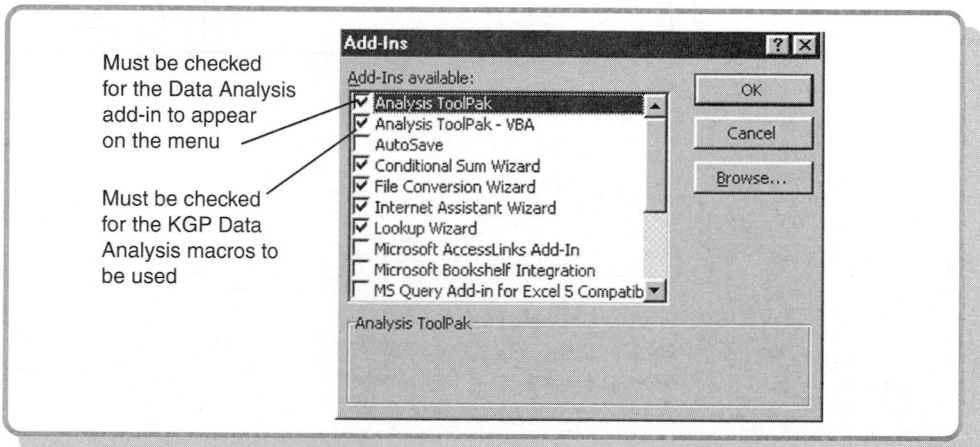

The KGP Data Analysis macros, which are saved as an ".xla" file on the CD-ROM attached to the textbook, are first opened using the **Open** userform. After this file is selected to be opened a warning will appear. As a routine matter, Microsoft Excel displays a warning message whenever a workbook that contains macros is opened. Microsoft Excel doesn't scan your floppy disk, hard disk, or network drive to find and remove macro viruses. You can decide whether to open the workbook with the macros enabled, or to disable the macros so that you can only view and edit them. A macro virus can only be harmful if it is allowed to run, so disabling the macros allows you to open the workbook safely. Your computer should scan all disks to ensure that viruses are not present. **To use the macros attached to this textbook, "Enable Macros" must be clicked.** Next, the **KGP Data Analysis** add-in will appear in the menu as illustrated below. Clicking on it will display another menu of statistical analysis options used in this textbook.

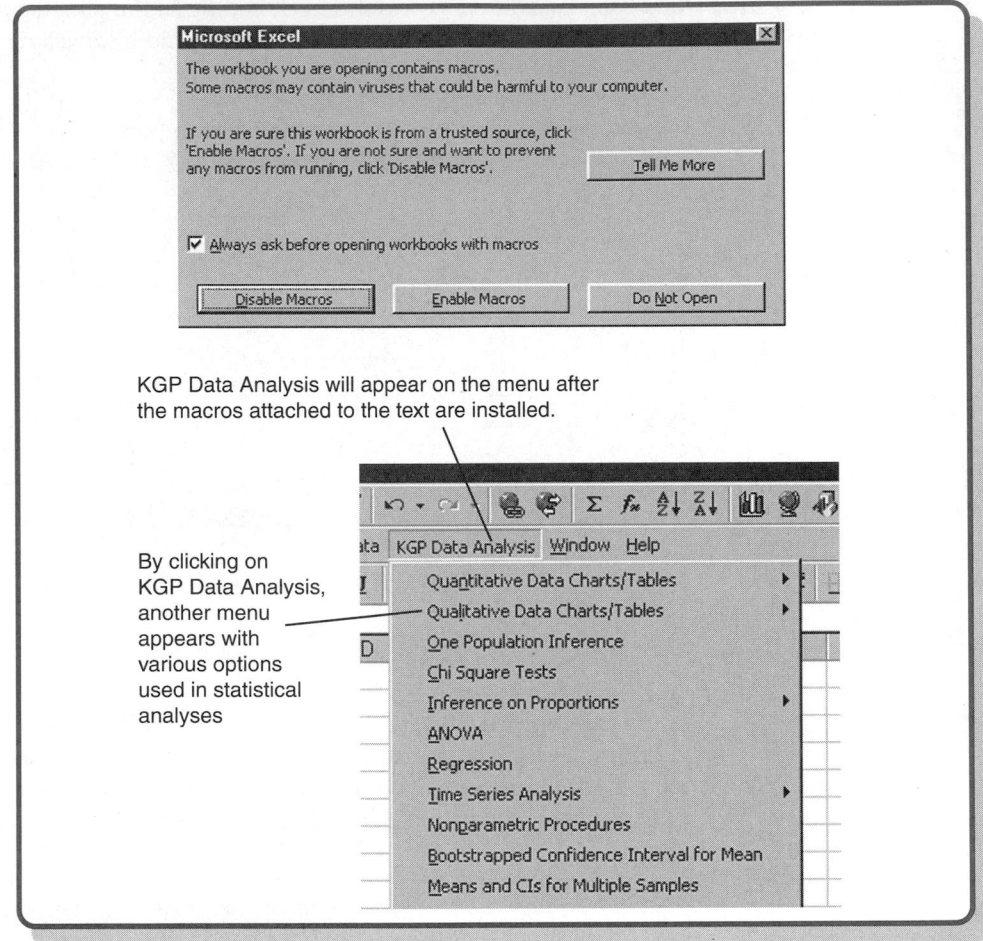

APPENDIX D   INTRODUCTION TO MINITAB

MINITAB is an easy-to-use, flexible and powerful statistical package.* It was originally designed for students and has been constantly improved over the years. Currently, it is one of the more powerful and complete statistical packages on the market.

The main MINITAB window contains two subwindows: The session window and the data window. The session window is used to display nongraphical output and can be used to enter commands. The data window is used to enter, edit, and view your data. You can position and size these windows any way you wish. Across the top of the session window is the menu bar, which allows you to open the various menus and select commands.

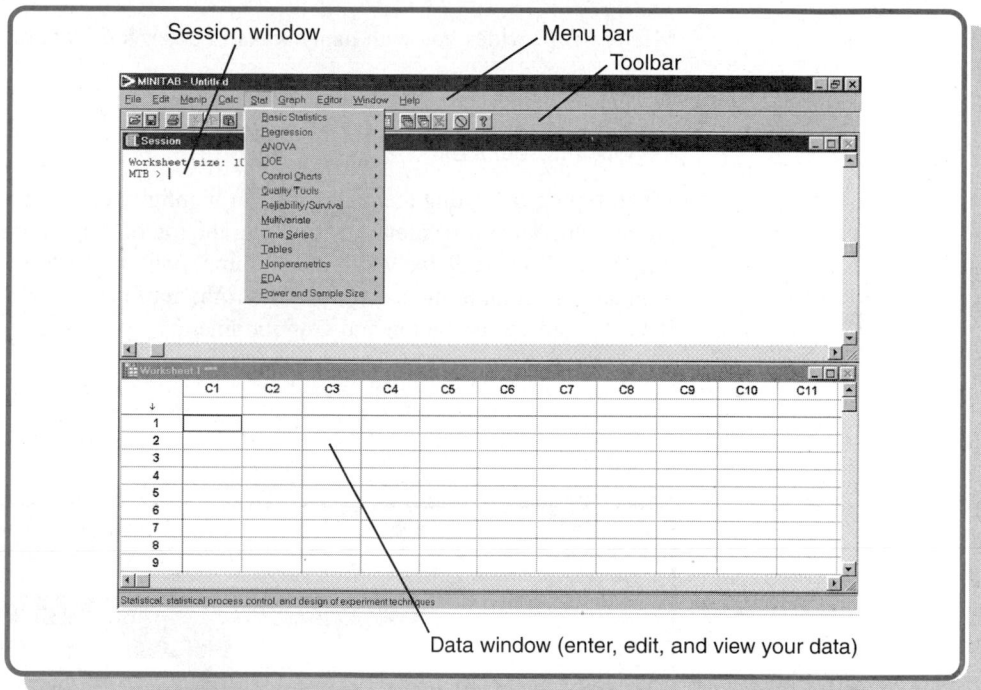

STARTING AND EXITING MINITAB

• **To start in Windows 95, Windows 98, or Windows NT 4.0**
From the Taskbar, choose **Start ➤ Programs ➤ MINITAB 12 for Windows ➤ MINITAB.**

• **To exit MINITAB**
Choose **File ➤ Exit** or click on the **Close** button (X) in the upper right corner.

ENTERING DATA INTO THE WORKSHEET

The worksheet consists of columns called C1, C2, C3, ... Most of your work will be done using columns that you can view in the data window. For example, five exam scores for Fred, Mary, and Joe are shown below. The 15 scores and the column titles (Fred, Mary, and Joe) can be typed directly into each location. To move downward in a column, you can use the down arrow key.

---

* The instructions and screen captures in this introduction use MINITAB version 12.0.

Worksheet 1 ▪▪▪	C1	C2	C3	C4
↓	Fred	Mary	Joe	
1	80	91	76	
2	77	73	85	
3	78	82	90	
4	86	94	88	
5	82	80	79	
6				
7				

MINITAB provides you with many ways to enter your data into a worksheet. You can

- Type it
- Paste it
- Open it from a file

When typing or editing the data, you can highlight an entire row by clicking on the row number and an entire column by clicking the top of the column, illustrated in the following screen. To change the width of a column, point to the top of the line dividing this column and the column immediately to the right until the cursor becomes a two-sided arrow. Press the left mouse button and drag the line.

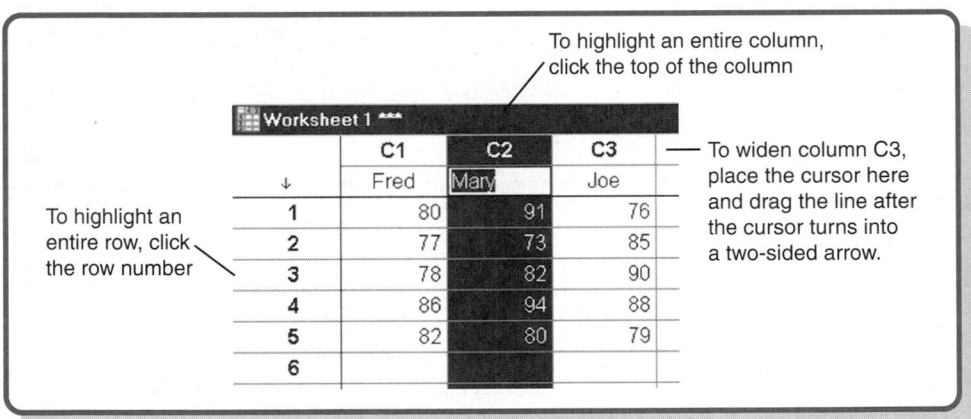

PASTING DATA

If you have copied your data from another application (such as Excel) into the clipboard, you can enter the data into the MINITAB data window by clicking on the cell that you would like to be the upper left corner of the pasted data. Choose **Edit ➤ Paste Cells** or simply hold down the **Control** key and type the letter V.

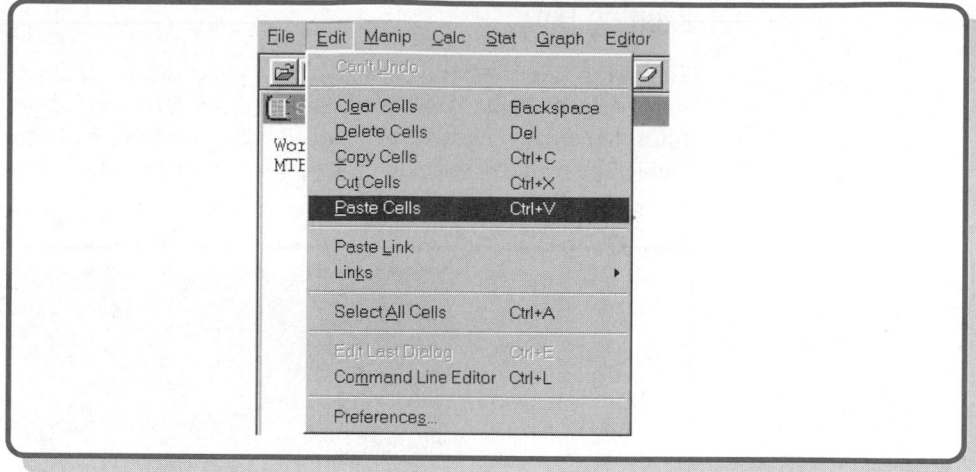

OPENING A DATA FILE

To import your data from an external file, click on **File ➤ Open Worksheet.**

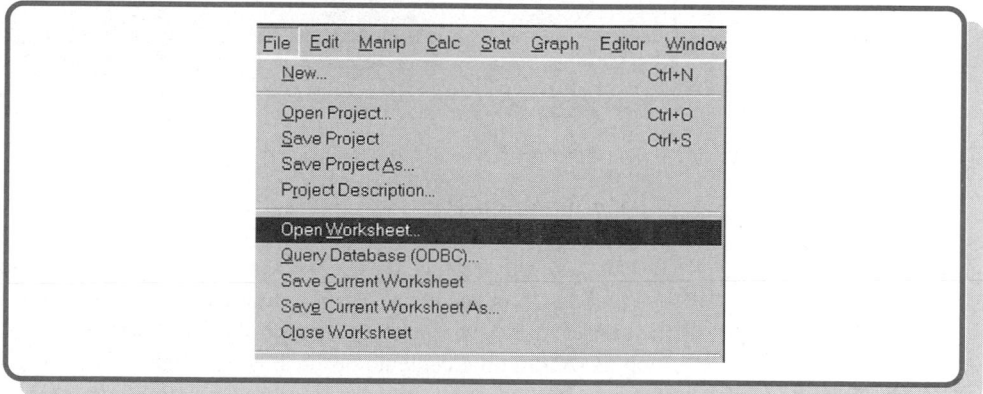

Select the file you want to open. For this illustration, we will import an Excel file named C:\TempFiles\SCORES.XLS, which contains the five exam scores (each) for Fred, Mary, and Joe. If there are no variable names in the first row, click on **Options** in the form below, and click on **None** under **Variable Names.** After opening this file, the MINITAB data window appears exactly as before.

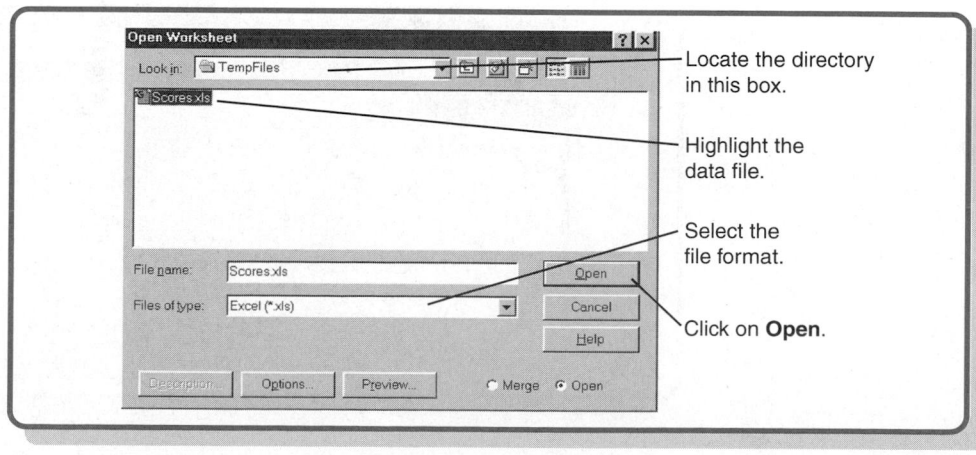

PRINTING DATA

To print the contents of the data window, select (click on) any cell in the data window and select **File ➤ Print Worksheet.** Select (or unselect) options in the following screen and fill in the data window title (optional). Click on **OK.** When the standard Windows Print dialog box appears, select the printer (if necessary) and click on **OK.**

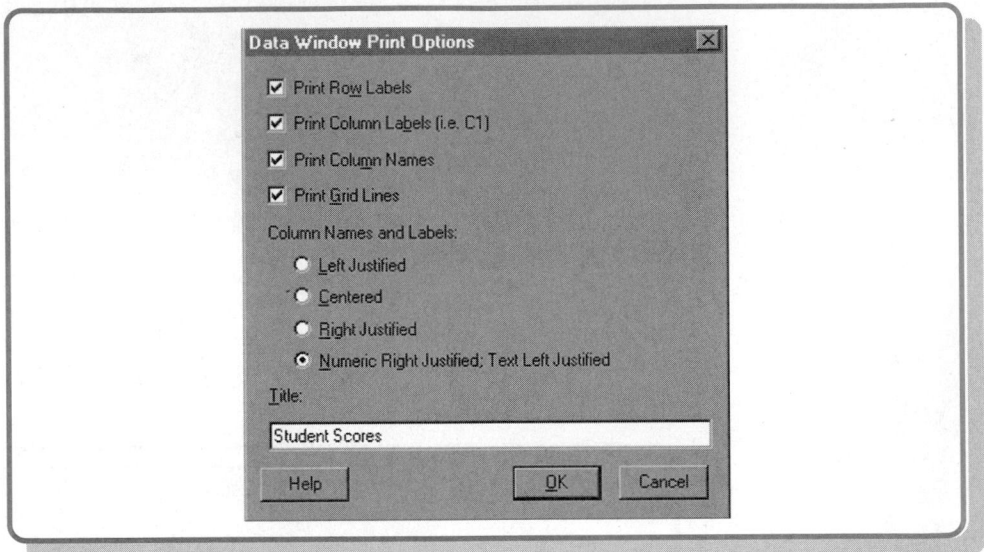

ANALYZING YOUR DATA

To carry out the various MINITAB procedures, you have a choice of clicking on the various options from the menu bar or entering a MINITAB command in the command line in the session window. You may also use the icons within the toolbar for simple operations, such as printing the contents of the session window or saving a file. To illustrate, suppose that we want to summarize (describe) the 15 exam scores, five each for Fred, Mary, and Joe.

USING THE MENU BAR

To obtain the descriptive statistics, click on **Stat ➤ Basic Statistics ➤ Display Descriptive Statistics.**

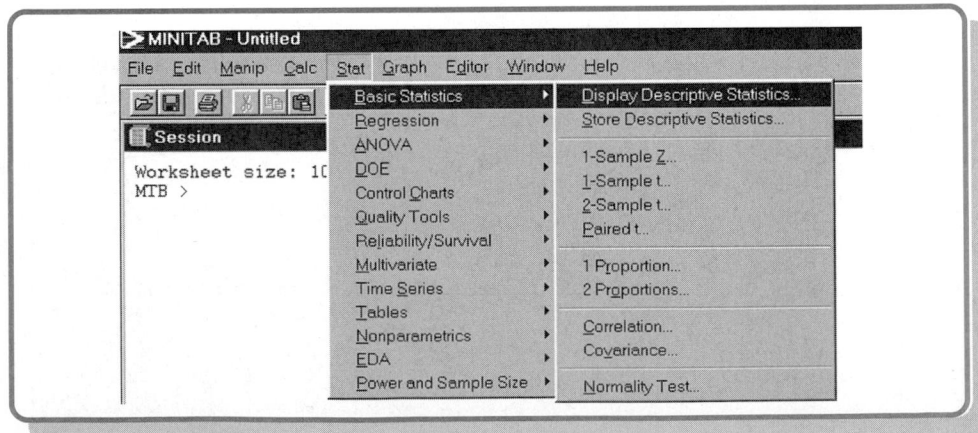

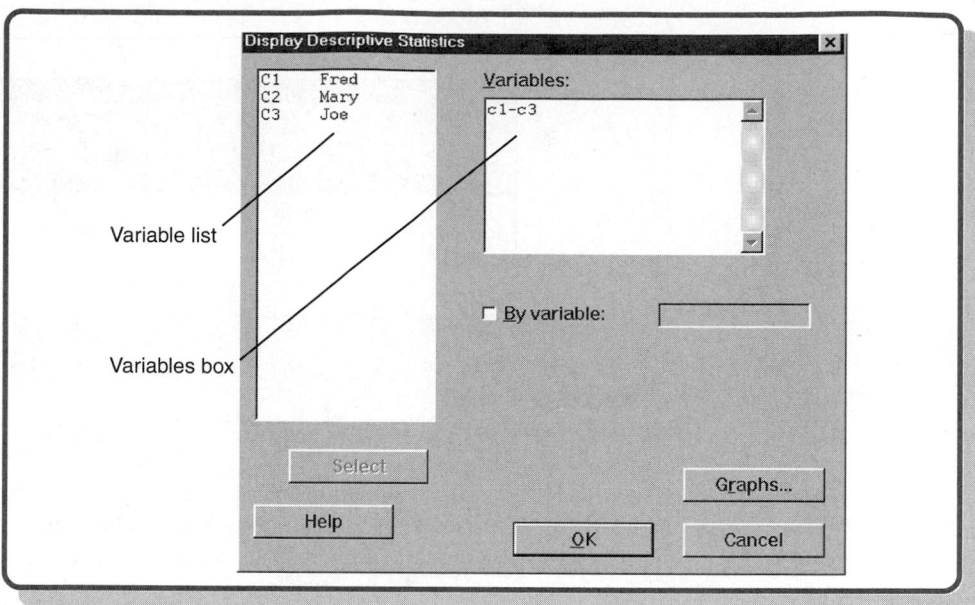

In the **Variables** box, type "C1-C3" to obtain the summary information for columns C1, C2, and C3. You can also enter a variable in the **Variables** box, by double clicking this variable (column) in the variable list. By clicking on **OK** you will obtain the following output in the session window.

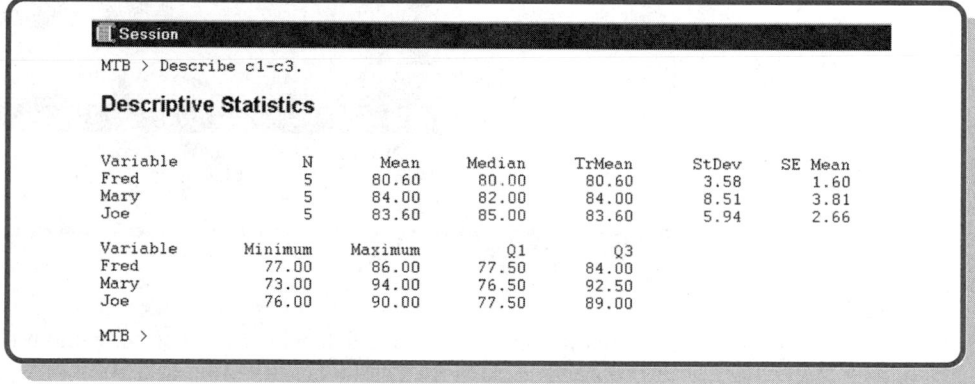

ENTERING MINITAB COMMANDS IN THE COMMAND LINE

For simple MINITAB procedures, you may elect to enter the command directly without using the menu bar. For example, you can type the command "Describe C1-C3" in this line, and you will obtain the previous output when the **Enter** key is pressed. If the command line containing "MTB > " is not visible, click on **Editor ➤ Enable Command Language.**

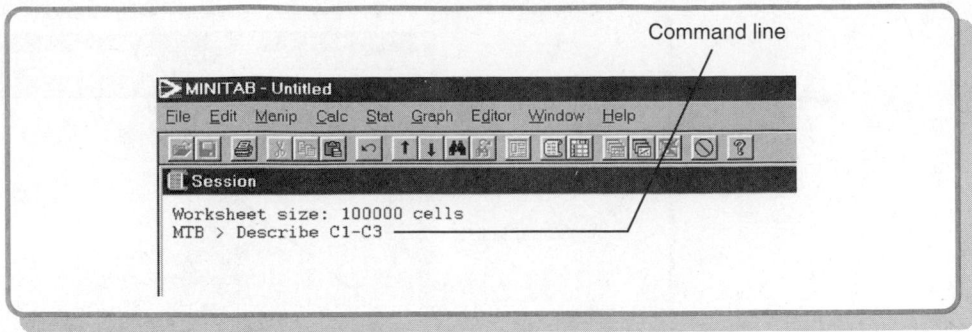

WORKING WITH TEXT FILES

If you have a text file containing columns of data that you would like to import into MINITAB, the easist way is to use the Read command in the command line. For example, suppose you have the following text file (a:scores.txt) contained on a disk in the A drive.

$$
\begin{array}{ccc}
80 & 91 & 76 \quad \leftarrow \text{File a:scores.txt} \\
77 & 73 & 85 \\
78 & 82 & 90 \\
86 & 94 & 88 \\
82 & 80 & 79
\end{array}
$$

In the MINITAB command line, type "read 'a:scores.txt' cl-c3" as shown below. The file name must be enclosed in single quotes.

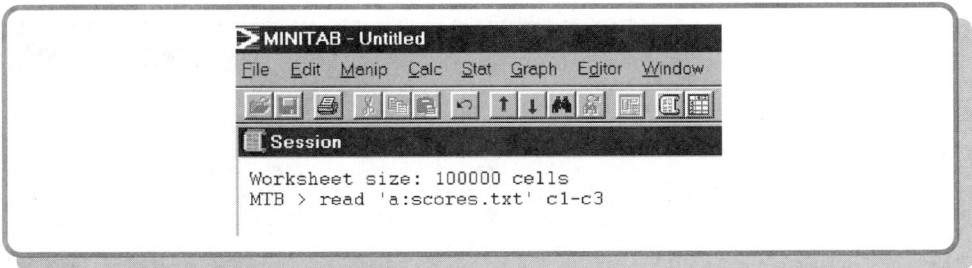

This will create the same data window as before, without the column names. To name the columns, type "Fred", "Mary", and "Joe" at the top of each column as shown in the previous data window for this illustration.

The data contained in your MINITAB data window can be stored in a text file by using the Write command. To store the 15 exam scores in a file named "a:scores.txt," type "write 'a:scores.txt' c1-c3" in the command line. The file name must be enclosed in single quotes. This will create the same text file shown previously.

SAVING AND PRINTING MINITAB GRAPHS

In Chapter 2, you are introduced to a variety of statistical graphs. MINITAB provides a mechanism for constructing these graphs, many of which contain color and are three-dimensional. One such graph (called a pie chart) is shown below and summarizes the classification (freshman, sophomore, junior, or senior) for a group of 100 students.

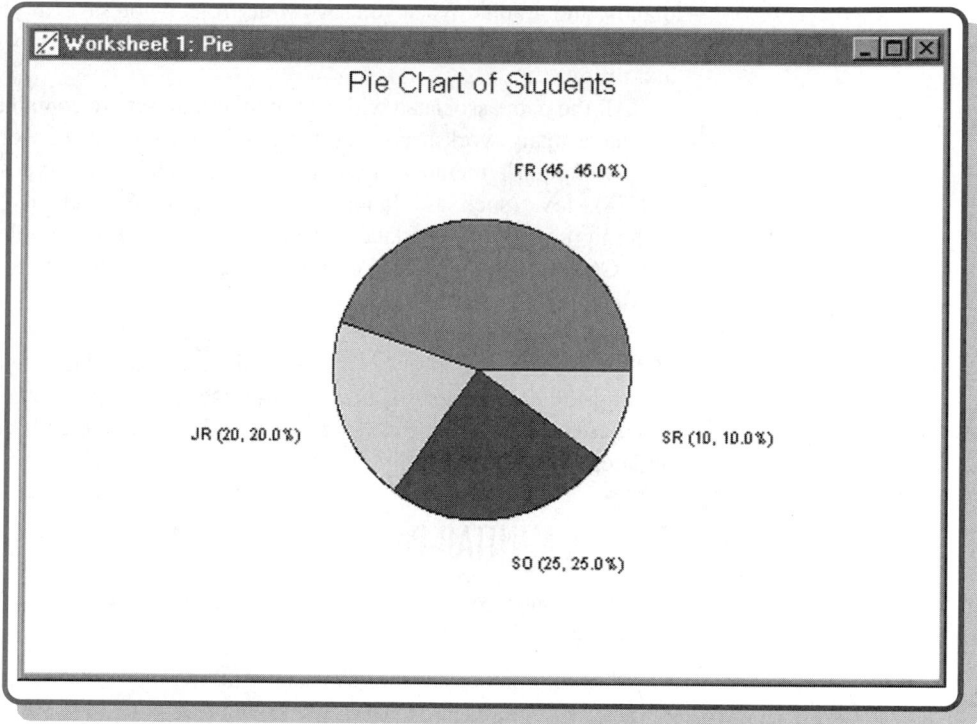

SAVING A MINITAB GRAPH

To save a MINITAB graph visible on your screen, select **File ➤ Save Graph As.** The **Save Graph As** window (below) allows you to specify the location of this saved graph as well as the desired format. The default option is to save the graph in a MINITAB Graphics Format (MGF) file. If you want to use the graph in another application, MINITAB allows for a variety of other options, including JPEG (.jpg) and bitmap (.bmp) formats. The pie chart graph is saved in file C:\temp\PieChart.mgf.

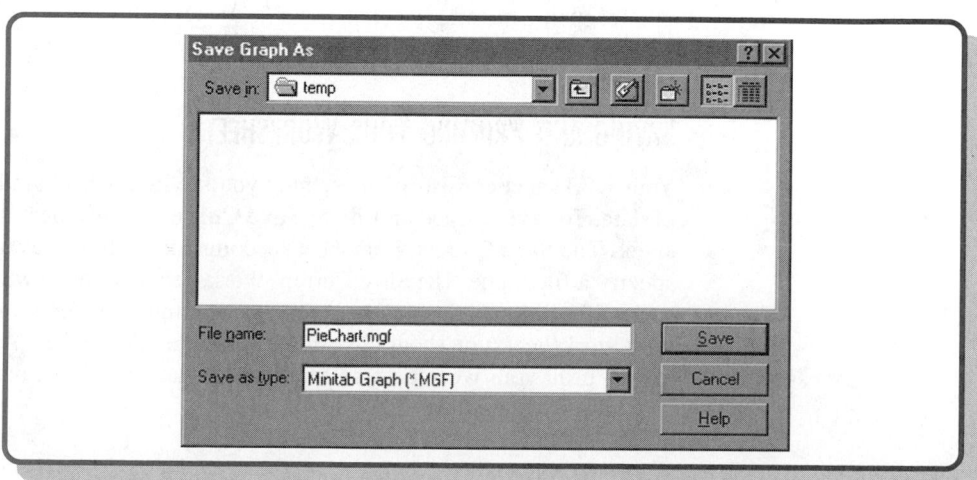

Printing a MINITAB Graph

To print a MINITAB graph, select **File ➤ Print Graph.**

All About MINITAB Projects

A MINITAB *project* contains all your work, including the data, text output from commands, and graphs. When you save your project, you save all your work at once, and when you open a project, you pick up right where you left off. Only one project can be opened at a time.

All the data associated with a particular data set are contained in *worksheets.* A project can have many worksheets, and the maximum number of worksheets is limited only by your computer's memory. A worksheet can contain three types of data: numeric (such as "15.7"), text (such as "January"), and date/time (such as "4/15/99" or "06:22:35"). Columns containing text data are labeled with "-T"; for example, "C6-T" tells you that column C6 contains text data. Columns that contain date/time data are labeled "-D", such as "C8-D."

COMMENT.   Data windows are not spreadsheets. The data window consists of rows and columns but it does not function like an Excel spreadsheet. In MINITAB, cells contain values that you type or generate with commands. However, cells do not contain formulas that update based on other cells.

Saving a MINITAB Project

When you save your MINITAB project, you save all the information about your work, including:

- The columns of data in your data window;
- The complete text in your session window;
- The description of your project if you previously clicked on **File ➤ Project Description;** and
- The description of each worksheet if you previously clicked on **File ➤ Worksheet Description.**

To save a project, choose **File ➤ Save Project.** To close a project, you must open a new project, open a saved project, or exit MINITAB.

Opening a MINITAB Project

- To open a new project, select **File ➤ New,** click **Project** and **OK.**
- To open a saved project, select **File ➤ Open Project.** Navigate to the saved project and click on **Open.**

Saving and Printing Your Worksheet

Your worksheet consists of everything you see in the data window; the columns and rows of data. To save it, click on **File ➤ Save Current Worksheet As** or **Save Current Worksheet.** The Save Current Worksheet As command will display a dialog box where you can specify a file name. The Save Current Worksheet command will save the worksheet in the same file as the file name displayed in the Minitab window title. If you have not named your worksheet, you should use the Save Current Worksheet As command.

To print your worksheet, select (click on) any cell in the data window and choose **File ➤ Print Worksheet.**

SAVING AND PRINTING YOUR SESSION

Your session consists of everything you see in the session window, such as the results of one or more MINITAB statistical procedures.

To save it, click in the session window and click on **File ➤ Save Session Window As.** Specify the file name, which will be a text file that you can print or edit with any word processor.

To print the session window, click anywhere in this window and select **File ➤ Print Session Window.** This prints everything in the window, not just what you see. To print a portion of this window, highlight the desired section (by holding down the shift key and using the down arrow) before you select **File ➤ Print Session Window** and then choose **Selection** in the Print dialog box.

WHEN EXITING MINITAB

Whenever you exit MINITAB, the program will ask if you wish to save the current project. It is not necessary to do so; MINITAB simply offers this as a protection in the event you think you might like to return to this project at a later date.

You have an option when exiting to save the session window, your worksheet, or the entire project. To save only the session window or the worksheet, click on **Save Separate Pieces.** To save the entire project, click on **Yes** in the window below.

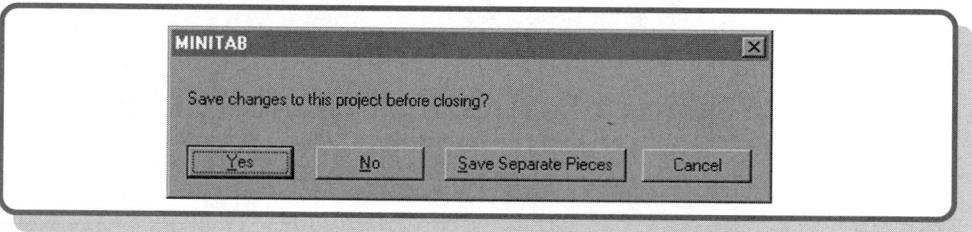

APPENDIX E   DATABASE USING HOUSEHOLD FINANCIAL VARIABLES

Variable	Description
INCOME1	Income of principal wage earner
INCOME2	Income of secondary wage earner
FAMLSIZE	Family size
OWNORENT	Own or rent (1 = own, 0 = rent)
TOTLDEBT	Total indebtedness (excluding home mortgage)
HPAYRENT	House payment or apartment/house rent
UTILITY	Average monthly utility expenditure
LOCATION	Location of residence (1 = NE sector, 2 = NW sector, 3 = SW sector, 4 = SE sector)

OBS	INCOME1	INCOME2	FAMLSIZE	OWNORENT	TOTLDEBT	HPAYRENT	UTILITY	LOCATION
84	38990	0	2	0	6467	517	170	4
85	31374	30474	2	1	11821	529	126	1
86	38261	26198	5	1	16148	1292	365	1
87	44402	0	2	0	14000	472	137	2
88	36236	19906	2	0	12131	808	212	1
89	46540	27943	5	0	17806	1389	345	1
90	43935	0	1	0	9390	459	184	2
91	31208	0	1	0	7569	429	158	1
92	51167	35540	2	1	21829	1158	285	2
93	46544	27394	5	1	18042	863	322	1
94	47872	34026	5	1	18657	1611	429	2
95	42442	14934	3	1	11884	1029	269	1
96	56144	18213	4	1	25293	1383	361	2
97	39707	0	1	0	9387	1004	231	4
98	41498	18991	2	0	12650	706	172	1
99	42080	37976	2	1	16324	813	186	3
100	41715	0	7	1	18805	449	173	1
101	43182	30686	2	1	16627	577	196	2
102	32264	24538	7	1	13825	1742	456	4
103	40757	0	3	1	11650	740	216	2
104	33405	0	4	0	3049	712	213	3
105	40467	0	4	1	9677	959	213	1
106	35922	17321	4	1	10363	994	296	2
107	47858	39787	3	1	22990	1557	386	1
108	46812	20642	3	1	15757	1351	328	2
109	40782	17549	5	0	11021	530	153	3
110	50463	0	2	1	13042	412	162	2
111	55213	0	4	1	14998	1397	349	2
112	50003	14071	2	1	12325	899	253	1
113	36590	0	4	1	16190	940	279	1
114	64553	0	2	0	8288	927	279	3
115	37727	0	6	0	14661	816	184	2
116	42400	0	2	1	19519	983	297	1
117	57121	0	2	0	14525	885	242	2
118	49123	0	3	1	18554	1439	385	2
119	46059	26636	2	1	20628	678	193	1
120	39265	35798	2	1	49397	642	188	3
121	42988	28357	6	0	21205	1122	315	2
122	45568	0	4	1	13880	713	216	4
123	33962	0	4	1	7392	990	280	1
124	54452	38577	4	1	21077	1183	308	4
125	37949	33246	5	1	17191	1344	328	3
126	39622	22258	3	1	17742	1072	300	2
127	53379	0	3	0	12139	969	261	1
128	31292	0	4	1	14193	751	223	2
129	33425	2329	2	1	16429	959	264	2
130	42964	24201	4	1	16692	1060	323	2
131	44485	33675	3	1	20759	789	239	1
132	40210	28741	3	0	9348	1045	245	2
133	47026	25096	2	0	13164	957	249	2
134	44325	0	3	0	16090	908	273	2
135	43162	21476	2	1	10988	615	221	3
136	41418	31766	3	1	11847	1130	318	1
137	68868	0	3	1	15988	1098	269	4
138	43239	0	6	1	21118	1572	432	4
139	41957	0	2	1	11504	716	161	4
140	77301	0	4	0	10355	843	209	3
141	45258	0	2	1	25971	1072	305	1
142	46992	35960	3	0	13950	773	229	2
143	41629	28568	2	0	20257	1898	517	1
144	50260	0	6	0	16187	824	232	2
145	36134	29653	4	1	14951	1012	286	1
146	45188	0	2	1	13503	704	192	2
147	31432	28726	2	1	13106	631	164	2
148	37814	20333	3	1	17391	818	237	4
149	37122	0	5	1	15213	842	249	4
150	39519	0	2	0	4592	618	146	4
151	43021	0	2	1	12383	664	162	4
152	41226	19971	2	1	11473	807	226	4
153	27796	0	2	1	17317	455	156	3
154	54939	35849	4	1	28713	1067	287	1
155	42587	28624	2	1	14506	552	177	1
156	46103	23540	4	0	18604	1017	272	2
157	35626	0	4	1	20213	875	231	2
158	31167	0	4	1	6310	835	229	4
159	41226	22823	3	1	12634	851	286	4
160	27796	19188	4	1	13694	960	231	3
161	54822	3699	2	1	20191	803	252	2
162	32397	26507	2	1	19210	1486	393	1
163	39995	28772	3	0	16133	920	257	2
164	46582	32853	4	1	19739	1350	333	2
165	64131	0	4	1	15016	1274	306	1

OBS	INCOME1	INCOME2	FAMLSIZE	OWNORENT	TOTLDEBT	HPAYRENT	UTILITY	LOCATION
1	46741	29600	4	1	19795	1238	345	1
2	37242	36414	4	1	19539	1208	310	2
3	49076	0	6	1	14045	1112	324	1
4	51633	0	3	1	12943	967	261	2
5	42980	36331	3	1	23658	1126	295	1
6	54143	34766	3	1	27532	1301	356	2
7	42082	36787	4	1	16056	1200	311	2
8	53450	0	5	1	16537	1135	331	3
9	51534	32530	5	0	20321	1026	338	1
10	50070	45961	4	1	21492	1594	434	2
11	41603	0	5	1	8416	1075	256	1
12	55092	21653	5	0	22661	1412	395	2
13	39857	33520	2	0	10616	462	145	4
14	46594	29209	2	0	20938	1346	331	1
15	36937	0	2	1	18933	560	198	3
16	45066	0	3	1	14331	1065	288	3
17	56632	33096	2	1	15726	1008	263	1
18	48521	35804	3	1	22097	1137	309	2
19	55319	0	4	1	26116	1035	278	3
20	61952	0	6	0	17548	1746	481	2
21	63899	0	7	0	21386	857	214	1
22	41989	0	4	1	10195	1615	440	2
23	46905	0	4	1	15572	828	263	3
24	55321	25350	4	0	10988	903	229	1
25	38022	27245	2	1	13923	1006	273	2
26	45210	0	2	1	19876	655	213	1
27	45549	31917	5	0	10594	1043	309	2
28	63392	0	2	1	18246	1118	300	3
29	44732	0	4	0	16904	779	243	3
30	45484	23619	2	1	13480	539	152	2
31	45864	0	5	1	13912	1167	327	1
32	42329	0	2	0	15516	1239	233	2
33	51609	0	2	1	7971	875	233	3
34	40993	0	3	0	17042	605	183	1
35	50365	21921	4	1	12071	679	209	2
36	52082	32980	3	1	21012	1724	428	4
37	49816	0	5	0	20137	652	232	4
38	33878	0	4	1	4550	748	210	3
39	38864	0	2	1	8925	627	186	2
40	41882	0	5	1	14871	748	219	2
41	41307	31803	2	1	7955	645	208	1
42	48612	0	2	1	24534	994	316	2
43	60577	19938	4	1	18182	1214	282	2
44	41876	19835	3	0	13563	916	262	1
45	39438	26465	3	0	14963	1470	343	2
46	48364	0	4	0	13759	932	243	2
47	47141	33494	3	1	21161	1257	297	2
48	50547	0	4	1	15710	1177	323	3
49	59966	36243	3	1	22408	1197	295	1
50	36922	24184	3	1	23023	1107	319	2
51	42008	22065	6	0	21844	1043	277	1
52	51204	33861	3	0	22474	1276	346	2
53	54604	0	4	0	23313	1260	322	2
54	47954	35076	4	1	14582	1073	297	2
55	36882	0	5	1	15388	1542	403	1
56	30224	0	4	1	3286	462	126	4
57	45549	20683	2	0	14764	838	272	2
58	47275	27747	2	1	22624	1018	253	1
59	38205	20723	2	1	14795	712	184	2
60	53304	0	3	1	14564	804	206	2
61	50497	22501	3	1	18806	992	276	1
62	36922	25577	6	0	16671	1306	357	1
63	42008	34443	4	1	23023	1509	369	2
64	39071	31102	3	0	21844	1204	319	2
65	41637	38132	3	0	20053	685	271	2
66	36583	31760	4	1	16547	658	206	3
67	48847	0	5	1	15857	1061	299	2
68	33384	17141	2	1	11644	837	252	2
69	44981	34534	2	0	14096	1052	323	2
70	51107	25377	2	1	20536	620	192	1
71	37980	22833	2	1	12992	1457	365	2
72	41377	31442	2	1	21749	899	279	2
73	50479	33585	4	0	27163	994	240	2
74	41870	35272	3	0	17024	1238	322	2
75	39949	0	2	1	12232	640	166	2
76	51779	30322	5	1	25185	1972	509	4
77	48300	0	2	1	13251	977	261	2
78	44405	32678	2	1	22091	868	257	1
79	50674	0	6	1	20117	1757	435	2
80	49044	0	2	1	16652	499	168	2
81	42559	23295	4	0	15304	1256	299	2
82	41905	0	3	1	13302	822	225	2
83	25802	0	5	0	4040	411	177	3

Observations 250–333

OBS	INCOME1	INCOME2	FAMLSIZE	OWNORENT	TOTLDEBT	HPAYRENT	UTILITY	LOCATION
250	51630	28155	2	1	18814	700	274	4
251	52306	33033	2	1	21040	836	252	1
252	54612	21411	3	1	21830	961	329	2
253	57479		2	0	17812	1237	143	3
254	52788	27657	2	1	17221	436	154	2
255	34021	33017	5	1	14705	649	279	4
256	42998		3	0	3256	1178	259	1
257	47490	23516	2	1	11015	259	303	3
258	51606		3	0	18331	814	291	3
259	47784	30907	3	1	10591	1058	236	2
260	35213		2	0	18209	1079	270	2
261	61211		2	0	19068	783	262	1
262	61727	32557	3	1	20127	871	259	2
263	53322	27643	3	1	23416	949	232	2
264	31711		3	0	18982	880	229	3
265	29056	23687	2	1	8896	702	291	2
266	51772	41488	2	1	16681	840	303	3
267	49236		2	0	24956	1036	167	3
268	37413	11961	4	1	8430	1051	189	1
269	33203	33202	4	1	11374	519	354	2
270	40473		2	0	21794	679	172	4
271	34514		2	0	10808	1428	243	2
272	47021	32810	2	1	15899	1172	285	2
273	59514	37023	2	1	30341	734	291	4
274	42562		2	0	12371	762	160	2
275	56698	23052	3	1	18763	557	234	2
276	38347	32771	2	1	16098	759	184	2
277	37847	29507	2	1	18704	622	248	2
278	44271	34834	3	1	19210	684	236	2
279	38653	35146	3	1	23279	946	317	3
280	39796		5	0	22664	1120	302	3
281	53599	26912	3	1	15738	1036	219	2
282	40264		3	0	11891	846	250	3
283	46603	23138	5	1	12780	782	373	4
284	45176		3	0	18270	1397	379	4
285	33237		5	0	9395	1386	177	3
286	29610	29906	3	1	6516	524	336	2
287	41215	23086	2	1	17948	768	329	2
288	37931	26952	4	1	13287	1401	267	3
289	45061	23413	4	1	16692	1207	339	4
290	47428	25656	2	1	22511	1163	202	3
291	50706	19889	3	1	22998	1180	222	2
292	44800		6	0	20138	624	279	2
293	59669		2	0	16888	701	175	1
294	25514		4	0	3286	1031	194	4
295	42162	28590	4	1	8865	588	309	4
296	37953		4	0	8280	569	378	4
297	40132		7	0	16121	1160	199	2
298	40347	22865	2	1	15808	1510	192	1
299	33300		2	0	8662	711	158	1
300	46411	27948	2	1	17432	683	254	1
301	43633		2	0	11975	511	213	4
302	48599		2	0	14077	852	355	1
303	47344		6	0	6410	768	250	3
304	36208		2	0	8963	1333	285	3
305	37715	24498	4	1	14134	702	278	2
306	46533		2	0	8274	863	425	1
307	43732		5	0	22753	1039	256	1
308	53801	22720	2	1	13107	1110	285	1
309	30385	28184	3	1	13007	1464	144	2
310	35878	32867	5	1	10391	886	321	1
311	45943	33534	2	1	16074	417	282	1
312	53425	20929	5	1	8335	1002	309	3
313	38749		4	0	9431	1312	321	1
314	39964	24390	2	1	17360	966	150	1
315	37356	23537	3	1	16264	1033	290	1
316	56767	34067	3	1	15062	405	250	2
317	58700	39840	3	1	22696	1254	162	3
318	35758		3	0	12646	1145	299	1
319	41172		3	0	16586	802	161	1
320	61209	33534	3	1	13064	1291	302	2
321	54151		2	0	11572	670	188	2
322	36318		3	0	17603	494	236	1
323	38392		3	0	5968	1096	257	1
324	44088	33899	6	1	21775	710	393	1
325	40379		5	0	18442	906	162	1
326	49557		2	0	15018	877	431	4
327	54281		3	0	14721	1679	209	2
328	34612		2	0	13079	612	259	1
329	39969	35485	2	1	8431	1805	158	1
330	37484		1	0	21364	619	182	3
331	39375		2	0	8059	972	259	3
332	48188		4	0	14921	558		2
333	47304		3	1	7837	781		3

Observations 167–249

OBS	INCOME1	INCOME2	FAMLSIZE	OWNORENT	TOTLDEBT	HPAYRENT	UTILITY	LOCATION
167	49248	0	4	1	14905	884	291	1
168	52107	46352	2	1	29255	755	211	2
169	37401	0	2	0	10256	866	237	4
170	32041	25978	3	0	12036	860	206	4
171	48947	35521	3	1	21157	1140	283	1
172	34537	27534	4	1	5417	921	243	4
173	57566	0	6	0	25377	1487	412	1
174	46022	0	6	0	18295	1735	403	4
175	46185	30531	3	1	13681	743	202	1
176	35143	32213	4	1	18630	530	160	2
177	36068	0	4	0	19619	1080	275	2
178	46548	26330	5	1	15246	913	228	2
179	37972	32843	2	1	24375	485	333	4
180	35212	0	4	0	19400	1304	221	2
181	47104	0	3	0	10687	920	419	3
182	45460	20144	6	1	10317	1636	210	3
183	26414	0	2	0	3656	867	217	3
184	38707	0	3	0	13750	578	176	4
185	44495	0	3	0	12620	820	201	1
186	48171	29902	2	1	10432	1011	163	2
187	42418	32717	2	1	9504	676	327	1
188	45304	29716	2	1	15656	482	274	1
189	41222	25231	3	1	17433	1025	314	3
190	56646	27842	2	1	25493	1060	211	1
191	57880	0	3	0	24816	1138	263	2
192	37419	31422	2	1	13735	653	238	3
193	37047	0	2	0	17070	922	304	2
194	43675	0	6	0	17010	877	207	3
195	50282	0	2	0	14460	883	376	2
196	46118	0	6	0	19251	582	202	2
197	40080	0	7	0	13894	1340	206	3
198	45259	21779	3	1	13666	772	344	3
199	51035	26857	2	1	16907	846	163	2
200	53144	19504	5	1	20556	1069	268	2
201	31916	0	2	0	15753	543	161	1
202	39937	25179	2	1	12692	1080	228	1
203	64284	30626	2	1	12026	585	215	1
204	59466	34366	2	1	24252	648	168	1
205	43652	32721	2	1	15620	874	254	4
206	41934	17596	2	1	18537	420	193	1
207	52438	36140	4	1	19209	887	214	2
208	39301	33212	2	1	10031	574	187	1
209	44861	34196	4	1	20004	751	240	3
210	42310	33429	2	1	18515	542	352	2
211	45247	0	2	0	20159	1091	260	4
212	48106	0	4	0	23655	1290	268	2
213	43725	0	4	0	8422	1022	185	1
214	51441	28590	2	1	13796	953	234	1
215	43235	0	2	0	6364	656	196	1
216	53058	0	2	0	16625	725	282	1
217	40669	30402	2	1	16051	591	151	2
218	47471	33624	5	1	22541	1025	223	4
219	35162	0	2	0	10675	597	367	3
220	40981	14154	4	1	11511	733	279	4
221	39009	0	5	0	4464	825	273	4
222	38992	16939	5	1	15560	1351	362	3
223	40974	20627	2	1	15041	830	238	4
224	49019	37554	6	1	20924	1035	155	2
225	37041	0	2	0	10451	1363	252	1
226	50138	35116	5	1	20217	973	345	4
227	38564	0	4	0	9067	642	139	2
228	38184	0	4	0	6234	518	269	1
229	67203	0	2	0	20816	840	464	4
230	36802	0	7	0	12674	1295	291	1
231	45192	34512	3	1	21000	467	386	2
232	32582	27275	3	1	13343	1143	243	4
233	48649	31271	3	1	23353	1683	301	1
234	43197	0	7	0	12001	999	344	3
235	41009	35105	2	1	22385	1553	232	3
236	34988	32653	4	1	20829	958	286	4
237	34292	17351	6	1	13382	1213	261	1
238	59379	27586	3	1	15131	1236	315	3
239	42812	30633	3	1	19527	763	296	4
240	36130	28983	4	1	15623	1238	212	1
241	45010	38401	4	1	19217	905	278	4
242	47812	0	4	0	11007	1156	175	1
243	36309	33116	2	1	7513	912	329	4
244	48210	18360	4	1	18903	830	255	1
245	46162	32023	3	1	15631	1104	262	1
246	43467	0	4	0	14548	475		2
247	50159	0	2	0	11548	1197		3
248	42285	40578	3	1	22193	905		3
249						983		3

OBS	INCOME1	INCOME2	FAMLSIZE	OWNORENT	TOTLDEBT	HPAYRENT	UTILITY	LOCATION
417	36952	27162	5	1	19048	1520	392	1
418	49441	39818	4	1	20894	1632	431	2
419	34770	15785	3	0	12883	1077	280	2
420	52500		5	0	14134	1360	371	4
421	41648		2	1	8445	655	197	1
422	56508		5	0	17717	1464	359	3
423	40635		3	0	8393	796	213	3
424	39310	28856	3	0	7684	661	195	2
425	48596	22978	2	1	15812	1350	332	3
426	39151	29987	5	0	14112	1343	303	2
427	49333		2	0	17657	631	183	3
428	26502	33517	4	0	5125	722	192	1
429	45574		2	1	24827	1136	306	3
430	46347	32510	2	0	13637	1015	232	2
431	46433		2	1	24724	929	241	3
432	44737		6	0	8918	570	191	1
433	41611	38887	2	1	22259	1521	408	2
434	54815	25475	4	0	23544	1195	327	3
435	36570	35147	2	1	18232	114	299	1
436	46965	22694	6	0	17118	924	296	2
437	44718	12746	3	1	25295	1147	364	3
438	42269	32714	4	1	16748	1003	259	2
439	42165	30733	6	0	18120	917	277	3
440	30803	27102	2	1	17672	598	149	1
441	35855	18928	6	0	12512	1304	355	2
442	46095	44892	6	1	19260	1153	302	3
443	37274	26942	2	0	15779	929	257	4
444	35240	25581	2	0	14490	817	256	2
445	44647	36804	3	1	21072	984	283	3
446	48611		8	0	11029	1557	423	1
447	48549		7	0	12772	1634	409	2
448	44579	17677	2	0	12477	564	151	3
449	39236	30043	4	1	7396	885	243	1
450	32087	32706	4	0	10641	410	166	2
451	32185		4	0	16111	1190	314	3
452	47405	32919	2	0	21554	723	223	1
453	42031	21427	2	0	9475	509	184	2
454	43718	21785	5	1	18507	606	234	3
455	56672	17368	5	0	20136	783	184	1
456	56123		2	0	23471	372	136	2
457	36390		5	1	9937	736	218	3
458	51936	22803	5	0	15499	1070	283	1
459	40550		6	0	17120	876	276	2
460	28085		6	1	7868	1204	309	3
461	43327		3	0	8572	1460	403	4
462	56357	30967	6	0	20997	1412	373	1
463	52887	26365	4	0	20351	613	153	2
464	44112	38804	2	1	21272	1548	414	3
465	36726	22241	5	0	12731	1241	315	1
466	30724	17474	2	0	16349	1360	336	2
467	40926		2	0	9719	877	234	3
468	43491	29628	2	1	22647	954	283	4
469	44661		5	0	14611	1053	303	1
470	30358	14460	3	1	10988	1067	280	2
471	38535	28490	4	0	14242	800	207	3
472	55816		2	1	13413	1077	316	1
473	46196	31166	3	0	18519	435	151	2
474	47662		3	1	13435	952	260	3
475	33982	18378	2	0	10698	670	135	1
476	30430		7	1	10350	482	159	2
477	29647		2	0	6750	1259	321	3
478	37088		4	0	18132	569	204	4
479	38495	30262	5	1	7492	1083	303	1
480	56495	24569	4	0	10138	800	289	2
481	50013	34132	6	1	25096	1075	207	3
482	42602		4	0	15775	1599	427	4
483	33025		3	1	21008	959	278	1
484	51316		1	0	5197	732	209	3
485	43962	30585	1	0	10464	503	156	4
486	34476	25915	3	1	16918	800	199	1
487	30430	30513	7	0	11901	1078	309	2
488	34457		2	1	16080	1160	345	3
489	45137		4	0	16371	1093	320	1
490	47284	20315	4	1	18132	469	143	2
491	36318		3	0	9157	1083	303	3
492	54632	30595	4	1	20526	439	142	4
493	50364		6	0	15326	1441	377	1
494	39959		4	1	8802	837	341	2
495	40755	21137	3	0	19240	906	195	3
496	34476		1	1	5197	550	253	4
497	41819		2	0	7384	775	151	2
498	51289		5	1	16505	498	190	3
499	34220	32779	3	1	19310	1168	193	1

OBS	INCOME1	INCOME2	FAMLSIZE	OWNORENT	TOTLDEBT	HPAYRENT	UTILITY	LOCATION
334	59501	29711	3	0	21627	1285	331	2
335	33468	31555	4	1	11648	1030	299	2
336	32260		2	1	9949	838	195	1
337	43949	37964	2	1	17668	695	218	2
338	45455		2	1	14648	818	241	1
339	44898	41695	2	0	17632	598	205	3
340	38763		4	1	12907	520	150	4
341	38761	36662	4	0	18549	1223	358	2
342	55234		3	1	14836	560	173	2
343	45134	28214	4	0	20103	685	212	3
344	54571	30183	3	0	24693	919	279	4
345	52837	28598	4	1	16478	1369	330	2
346	39544	24457	5	0	17820	1313	351	4
347	41257		5	1	11029	647	203	1
348	50570	19637	2	1	16761	1318	313	3
349	51795		2	0	18642	639	199	2
350	41941		2	0	5628	630	168	1
351	40859	30990	2	1	21983	811	258	2
352	39952	21363	4	0	15988	910	244	1
353	49867	27661	2	0	8570	1424	259	3
354	32975	20031	6	1	20629	549	190	2
355	43096	37372	6	0	19566	1034	250	1
356	40227	32511	3	0	19747	712	271	2
357	50148	21630	2	0	7387	961	272	3
358	38649		4	0	21974	716	158	4
359	35720	31268	1	0	14408	444	151	4
360	38151		3	0	15848	716	230	4
361	67626		5	0	9444	470	151	3
362	32690	39459	3	0	20656	850	257	4
363	45364		3	0	13591	762	196	2
364	37415	22357	3	1	21090	690	226	1
365	40695		2	0	15833	792	197	2
366	72146		4	0	15085	668	375	1
367	45418	33056	4	0	20122	1398	307	3
368	39767	23161	4	1	12971	986	264	2
369	37191	31797	3	1	11090	836	247	5
370	44354		4	0	22208	902	350	1
371	39783	24890	3	0	4744	637	203	4
372	35461		4	1	12704	743	310	2
373	31700	19092	2	0	14260	969	353	2
374	45507	31089	5	1	17974	1324	148	3
375	43502		4	1	7091	637	294	1
376	39671	31953	3	0	16045	958	259	4
377	39969	30068	5	1	14840	880	308	2
378	27339	17277	4	0	13223	1106	287	3
379	34063	31996	5	1	16213	1108	173	1
380	45681		1	0	11552	681	222	2
381	55819		4	1	14789	571	163	3
382	34319	33665	5	0	15534	719	199	2
383	36594		5	0	7578	670	331	1
384	47897	30780	2	0	24483	1222	275	3
385	48269	25045	5	0	15619	1267	344	4
386	33146		3	1	11051	763	216	4
387	36057	19398	6	1	12554	953	277	2
388	37988		2	0	15089	1827	482	4
389	33878		2	0	3804	1109	324	3
390	35745	30568	2	0	9232	857	214	4
391	36195		5	0	9609	969	152	2
392	30089	25590	3	0	10415	449	147	4
393	37973	22287	2	0	18955	1146	275	1
394	31763	27985	7	0	15445	1680	432	3
395	35740		2	1	13581	716	235	2
396	42605		2	0	11584	420	158	4
397	45828	25764	4	1	22216	800	244	3
398	42528	33362	2	1	8836	878	274	4
399	46947		3	1	24610	610	280	2
400	57932		6	1	8251	661	187	4
401	38286		4	0	7774	798	144	3
402	43316	30661	3	0	16555	918	255	2
403	48932	32535	2	0	26098	452	262	4
404	54556		2	0	5847	1406	167	3
405	41217		3	0	17521	540	377	1
406	45720		7	1	11669	988	157	4
407	43043		6	1	4519	420	267	2
408	35740	25764	2	1	11871	634	155	1
409	42605	33362	4	1	11584	800	158	1
410	42528		3	0	22216	878	244	3
411	57932	22729	2	0	24610	1027	274	3
412	42982	11276	5	0	12831	621	280	1
413	39817		3	1	20234	917	151	3
414	63279		2	0	10238	646	286	2
415	41788		1	0	14816	891	164	1
416	34220	29967	6	1	9774	862	287	3

OBS	INCOME1	INCOME2	FAMLSIZE	OWNORENT	TOTLDEBT	HPAYRENT	UTILITY	LOCATION
583	47482	0	2	0	12586	443	155	1
584	28729	25348	6	1	11420	1353	413	1
585	53294	27926	2	1	21775	892	262	1
586	42366	28342	2	1	15454	919	246	2
587	56759	0	3	1	18533	1072	314	1
588	45981	26118	2	1	19624	785	212	1
589	48596	0	4	0	7841	694	206	3
590	40382	31231	2	1	14089	1114	279	1
591	53835	0	4	1	13311	1343	296	3
592	51396	0	4	0	11503	1009	247	4
593	46365	30585	2	0	23213	769	213	1
594	46986	0	1	0	15676	748	216	4
595	51690	0	7	1	10350	1378	363	1
596	29114	0	2	1	6201	867	230	3
597	64478	26654	3	1	15581	874	221	1
598	30672	22779	2	1	14588	1468	265	3
599	47813	0	5	1	21545	1268	455	1
600	43523	0	7	0	10088	872	367	1
601	42613	0	5	1	11423	1359	193	3
602	52489	28145	2	0	21081	604	339	1
603	45996	0	4	0	12512	1446	212	1
604	51566	27737	4	1	12651	510	333	1
605	54106	20005	2	0	19452	1125	191	1
606	59294	37040	1	0	27031	897	306	1
607	32341	0	3	1	7039	449	165	1
608	47936	0	2	1	12494	739	237	2
609	37450	0	2	1	12493	1056	162	2
610	39517	0	4	0	10137	669	321	4
611	48234	0	2	0	12505	702	171	2
612	55802	0	4	0	14220	1001	212	2
613	48680	0	3	0	17146	1247	292	4
614	42046	33263	5	1	11676	1629	369	2
615	54422	0	7	0	15217	1318	430	2
616	40154	0	4	1	13391	623	336	3
617	49109	23706	2	1	19934	486	176	2
618	42901	0	2	1	18800	748	161	3
619	49035	28772	2	0	7442	973	186	2
620	34619	0	5	0	20031	677	183	3
621	42063	0	3	1	17793	1589	413	1
622	51238	0	2	1	23322	709	175	2
623	36444	37504	5	0	10682	747	186	1
624	43064	19489	2	0	19870	1389	364	1
625	45257	24988	3	1	23305	1386	349	1
626	50004	32550	5	0	12531	1066	314	3
627	52574	37014	4	1	26739	1445	374	1
628	42942	30962	4	1	21065	774	216	4
629	51107	0	3	1	14069	193	323	1
630	70047	43639	7	1	26191	1391	416	3
631	40011	0	2	0	22485	1262	346	4
632	53899	35319	3	1	19857	1179	274	2
633	54467	12141	2	1	17457	838	267	2
634	46773	0	5	1	15898	767	363	1
635	51118	24148	2	0	15247	1396	221	3
636	34895	34840	2	0	17970	990	252	2
637	38382	27535	3	0	16247	1057	297	1
638	51883	37412	4	1	16352	1132	311	3
639	52633	33368	2	1	18826	758	279	4
640	40749	39203	3	1	18104	919	247	4
641	45692	29514	5	1	16707	1369	375	4
642	35980	22069	5	1	17099	1566	404	4
643	50730	33002	3	0	19993	1047	290	2
644	43701	0	2	0	14728	1129	286	3
645	52478	0	4	0	27276	790	182	3
646	52141	34152	2	0	4506	1081	252	2
647	41539	24870	5	0	22075	726	222	4
648	30672	0	3	1	17906	1186	312	2
649	46148	0	4	0	4330	506	181	4
650	43380	0	3	0	8877	559	193	4
651	46860	18735	3	1	18821	973	286	1
652	32961	0	4	0	11042	974	246	4
653	46673	0	3	1	9331	1015	240	3
654	32490	17589	2	0	16708	860	211	4
655	34273	12682	4	1	11401	1056	245	2
656	35756	0	3	0	16098	715	233	1
657	45181	22951	2	1	17793	824	230	2
658	46269	34674	3	1	18649	770	200	4
659	44790	31478	3	1	10584	466	159	4
660	32961	0	2	0	12972	885	195	2
661	46673	0	3	0	9172	604	225	1
662	32490	28849	3	1	16974	627	165	2
663	34273	25046	2	1	14127	463	157	3
664	35756	25046	2	1	14127	463	157	3
665	35756	0	2	1	14127	463	157	3

OBS	INCOME1	INCOME2	FAMLSIZE	OWNORENT	TOTLDEBT	HPAYRENT	UTILITY	LOCATION
500	45317	0	2	1	7380	422	144	2
501	47913	18753	2	1	10122	797	253	1
502	46893	0	4	1	18236	1131	308	1
503	42450	0	2	1	14229	635	148	3
504	47293	41953	5	1	21412	1471	387	1
505	32265	28277	2	1	15405	578	145	2
506	34998	33671	3	0	20704	1060	295	2
507	45260	23285	7	1	19147	1605	439	3
508	44890	0	3	0	15100	1018	297	3
509	32271	0	3	0	6367	844	218	2
510	48690	28244	4	0	9236	463	153	3
511	50059	0	2	0	23965	888	219	2
512	43587	0	2	0	9868	654	216	1
513	46554	26556	5	0	19543	1191	329	4
514	52250	18901	5	0	16628	1415	340	2
515	42082	32148	3	1	23105	895	248	1
516	47112	0	3	0	17848	638	170	2
517	33151	26192	2	0	15320	1135	307	2
518	50771	28488	3	0	23418	866	243	1
519	41432	28764	2	0	19105	884	236	3
520	46456	38551	2	0	20123	950	248	2
521	37085	20675	2	1	13215	406	172	1
522	45167	0	4	1	10612	814	260	4
523	51118	39228	5	0	19782	1634	432	3
524	51782	29760	2	0	23280	670	163	2
525	63266	0	3	0	16862	833	230	2
526	35542	16762	6	0	15378	1583	390	1
527	34648	0	5	1	7933	503	153	1
528	35871	0	5	0	14993	1003	263	3
529	38614	26433	5	0	6506	1125	325	4
530	45457	38743	3	0	20756	1039	267	1
531	33778	33130	4	0	15430	1230	347	1
532	42328	0	2	0	10825	923	172	2
533	25879	0	3	1	8215	575	267	3
534	71958	0	3	0	20693	613	153	2
535	59823	0	2	1	22981	1056	285	4
536	54549	29551	4	1	23338	1429	374	1
537	42628	33291	7	0	14452	1233	303	3
538	60138	13795	2	1	14595	1509	422	1
539	34432	0	5	1	16608	1004	260	3
540	31042	31108	5	1	11351	871	253	3
541	36080	27607	2	0	12726	1067	319	2
542	36741	26048	2	1	21602	773	185	4
543	42811	33384	3	0	14421	1035	311	1
544	46610	19476	4	1	28860	1648	235	4
545	42478	0	4	0	19635	667	403	1
546	43276	26232	7	1	11577	569	180	4
547	35713	0	2	0	19056	552	161	1
548	33548	37641	4	0	16748	1116	340	4
549	44441	0	2	0	8023	986	229	1
550	37416	23405	2	1	16533	825	201	1
551	49376	30864	4	1	13804	797	218	1
552	38108	0	2	0	12302	1167	280	3
553	28712	27031	4	0	20963	534	160	4
554	52254	36834	3	0	19628	1160	331	2
555	48004	27404	3	0	11857	926	284	2
556	43597	25571	4	1	23598	1383	358	2
557	61722	39217	4	1	14523	1433	412	1
558	39770	31291	2	0	17160	1213	307	2
559	35913	0	4	0	12355	1015	316	3
560	40772	0	4	0	15069	1145	234	4
561	29262	26281	2	0	12167	957	307	2
562	30109	21275	4	0	2458	1336	165	2
563	58950	0	2	0	0	701	360	4
564	38882	30563	2	1	25511	558	180	4
565	48584	0	6	0	7914	1198	308	1
566	41062	0	3	1	15784	1737	442	2
567	22801	0	3	1	19112	654	200	4
568	45181	0	3	0	4849	1257	310	4
569	58554	35073	4	0	16686	1195	310	3
570	51156	0	2	0	12515	972	213	2
571	49066	20245	2	0	20858	873	236	1
572	47341	0	4	1	16978	941	249	4
573	35287	25587	4	1	18496	1281	343	2
574	40761	19260	4	1	18314	814	319	2
575	49883	0	4	0	16367	1194	337	1
576	37782	26156	1	1	8484	994	307	2
577	44170	29663	1	1	15926	1095	283	1
578	46680	0	2	0	20352	1215	338	3
579	30109	0	1	1	15926	548	161	2
580	38882	37409	5	0	20352	421	154	2
581	48584	30111	5	0	20352	1310	317	2
582	44170	0	4	1	20054	1743	422	2

OBS	INCOME1	INCOME2	FAMLSIZE	OWNORENT	TOTLDEBT	HPAYRENT	UTILITY	LOCATION
749	31528	27461	2	1	9350	1201	279	1
750	37888	25516	2	1	16247	568	177	1
751	43138		2	1	8135	800	191	4
752	52138		5	0	12066	982	254	2
753	47355		3	1	15733	1276	343	2
754	45249	16364	2	1	17965	881	224	4
755	46723		2	1	12205	1092	302	1
756	38835	19344	3	1	11557	777	238	2
757	44311	33.81	2	1	14303	759	266	2
758	42493	34497	4	1	15629	627	219	2
759	42229		2	1	12452	888	265	3
760	44632		2	1	14299	544	169	1
761	37443	18926	4	0	12505	1209	332	3
762	53191	37798	4	1	22764	826	248	2
763	37152	30623	5	0	12113	1666	453	1
764	45201		3	1	11021	1169	150	4
765	42505	18878	3	1	14069	568	332	4
766	54170	33829	3	1	20301	1034	262	2
767	39737		3	0	13843	1049	238	4
768	42516	38568	4	1	20482	1463	420	3
769	35156		4	0	8109	841	257	2
770	39980		4	1	10016	1015	289	4
771	66687	16181	4	1	20909	1566	383	3
772	47714		4	1	15603	715	229	2
773	44360	20540	2	1	10165	945	252	3
774	41563	37861	5	0	12678	1126	280	1
775	37937		2	1	20509	497	157	3
776	46202		1	1	12811	1062	281	4
777	45126		3	1	10732	454	136	4
778	54835	35859	3	0	21431	942	267	3
779	62703	19413	3	1	19645	611	158	1
780	54803	25368	5	1	12392	525	176	1
781	38762		2	1	10309	1358	344	4
782	47350		2	1	20632	1227	339	3
783	33996		3	0	16574	574	183	2
784	60996		7	1	18568	557	209	2
785	51754	30272	4	0	19471	1228	296	1
786	34679	25192	6	1	22090	1698	433	3
787	42567	33651	2	0	15340	1705	446	1
788	39013	38315	6	1	18477	1176	297	2
789	45723		1	1	16237	1201	328	1
790	35389	31756	3	1	11544	616	163	4
791	40137	23943	2	0	16548	852	240	4
792	33208	31460	3	1	14732	1078	276	4
793	51200	30796	3	1	13687	597	218	1
794	43535	24342	7	0	18213	1747	481	4
795	42491		2	0	13687	1597	403	4
796	41862		4	0	17771	754	172	2
797	42491		4	0	1723	673	182	2
798	38190		4	1	8032	995	289	1
799	61812		4	1	15021	559	189	3
800	63604	31983	4	0	11429	1068	267	4
801	38138	22896	3	0	13628	402	142	4
802	42293		2	1	18462	939	261	1
803	47671	28228	2	1	16276	947	286	2
804	46356	30663	3	1	12938	1091	252	3
805	36891		6	1	14794	791	219	1
806	51529	34610	2	1	18880	1682	422	2
807	36838	32279	3	0	8574	530	153	2
808	55033		3	1	5796	436	212	2
809	49426	35887	3	1	12635	1083	291	2
810	47141	318.1	4	1	21022	731	162	3
811	32586		2	0	17410	634	232	2
812	50246	22693	2	1	4997	787	217	2
813	39770	31787	3	1	22999	734	307	3
814	33227		4	0	13169	116	205	3
815	49687	2034	2	1	16433	732	164	3
816	33418		5	0	10226	573	330	2
817	52873	28600	4	0	12981	1345	176	2
818	30180	22251	3	0	14882	577	270	1
819	35752		4	0	10157	1000	207	3
820	48967	36763	2	1	1811	910	255	3
821	53653		4	0	16897	944	204	2
822	44017	20097	4	0	14772	741	227	2
823	62262	25650	3	1	21549	781	243	1
824	44793	29885	2	1	17931	825	259	4
825	35903		2	1	18579	719	317	2
826	36334		3	0	22132	1142	160	1
827	36077		3	0	9180	355	211	4
828	52451		2	1	11365	696	216	2
829	39208		5	1	10818	820	284	2
830			2	1	20877	1051		1
831				1	20238	560	212	

OBS	INCOME1	INCOME2	FAMLSIZE	OWNORENT	TOTLDEBT	HPAYRENT	UTILITY	LOCATION
666	50430		2	1	14939	727	218	1
667	36315	30540	2	0	19815	620	186	2
668	39879	29297	2	1	12255	838	264	1
669	46826	29975	2	1	23669	814	249	1
670	34223		2	0	9826	1284	166	2
671	47335	32098	4	1	21111	489	390	2
672	46463	17941	4	1	17912	1100	178	2
673	33723		5	1	11468	676	294	1
674	45611	28463	5	1	8840	873	207	3
675	40313		3	1	16394	774	214	3
676	38511		3	1	9667	937	187	4
677	47963		3	1	7724	625	254	4
678	39761		2	1	8580	970	161	4
679	62809		2	1	19245	888	283	4
680	31653		4	1	13179	1023	241	4
681	41014	37834	4	1	18354	963	260	1
682	38860	24890	3	1	19117	1048	310	2
683	59848	37126	3	1	23665	1198	274	4
684	33809	26577	3	1	13387	589	347	1
685	47402		5	1	12727	1827	228	2
686	49825		3	1	20210	1360	190	3
687	43881	18165	2	0	18589	1674	440	3
688	50395	19428	6	1	17242	907	348	3
689	39980	37961	3	1	16949	430	437	1
690	44353	20490	6	1	16229	935	231	4
691	46915		6	1	20409	778	189	2
692	49515	27720	3	0	8808	981	318	2
693	30688	24500	2	1	22904	1154	292	3
694	41441		4	1	13491	1456	282	2
695	41023	35883	2	1	20788	891	282	1
696	48167	24229	4	1	17974	999	485	3
697	47396	28360	3	1	17986	1211	284	1
698	40461	29834	3	1	19442	1381	264	2
699	39834	22291	2	1	9665	1012	344	2
700	42498		2	1	16823	401	277	2
701	39951	30012	3	1	13972	1132	307	1
702	37535	23321	5	1	17037	1010	330	2
703	43945		5	1	11926	762	352	2
704	38252	28986	4	1	5991	619	267	2
705	30766		2	1	12032	1339	144	1
706	60812	34445	3	1	18776	786	273	1
707	46381	25292	3	1	10933	745	236	2
708	48598	23803	2	1	12842	753	212	2
709	51817	29025	3	1	16778	585	157	2
710	35405		2	1	10963	1062	359	3
711	52256	24322	4	0	13269	942	232	3
712	44276		5	1	17169	1781	209	2
713	39530		2	1	24399	737	185	1
714	53264		3	1	14767	1007	222	4
715	41033	31099	2	0	16650	725	162	2
716	42426		2	1	19850	1455	252	1
717	62381		7	1	14284	997	464	1
718	42413	40445	2	1	17947	864	180	2
719	49467		2	1	18318	727	283	1
720	42976	16928	4	1	14587	1223	264	1
721	39079		2	1	16978	1077	402	1
722	48758	32149	3	1	12758	1395	316	3
723	65868	28129	3	1	12991	1173	236	1
724	45065	26332	5	1	16366	1280	217	3
725	41219	36818	5	1	21920	681	345	2
726	35682	20946	2	1	16335	1174	305	1
727	46891	25473	3	1	14595	1204	381	1
728	38830	25659	3	1	14977	1376	297	2
729	35440		4	1	23356	1062	387	1
730	53876	29008	2	1	23702	1804	319	2
731	47783	17328	5	1	18676	1648	210	1
732	46144	19447	4	1	12604	859	316	1
733	52129	22282	2	0	1565	1267	351	2
734	36785	31341	4	1	13767	1163	342	1
735	39313	27382	3	1	12642	640	317	2
736	54508		5	1	16366	815	434	1
737	39804	20815	3	1	14595	552	425	1
738	63346	19434	2	0	14977	1375	227	2
739	63955		4	1	23356	1074	366	3
740	54600	14062	4	1	23702	430	295	3
741	57825		3	1	18676	787	209	1
742	64527	20840	2	1	12604	640	232	1
743	38225		2	0	1565	815	199	2
744	31434	32265	4	1	13767	552	391	1
745	32811		3	0	12642	1375	273	3
746	51223		6	1	6794	1074	151	1
747	30822		4	1	9312	430		1
748	32784		2	0		787		1

OBS	INCOME1	INCOME2	FAMLSIZE	OWNORENT	TOTLDEBT	HPAYRENT	UTILITY	LOCATION
915	39401	35684	3	1	25024	910	254	1
916	44298		5		12317	959	250	4
917	35443	27302	2	1	12064	578	189	4
918	29315		5	0	7486	971	301	3
919	55779		2	0	15308	789	214	1
920	38768		2		15879	967	270	1
921	44460	24131	3		12431	906	279	2
922	49587		3		11098	915	349	1
923	53406	40393	2		16349	1291	264	4
924	51536	35386	2	1	20186	999	275	1
925	43080	24104	3	1	19757	1177	307	1
926	30616		3	0	10745	1008	278	1
927	46410		3	1	9589	932	241	2
928	41808		3	1	6808	803	195	3
929	46578		4		11761	967	272	2
930	41102		4	1	3637	1121	282	2
931	43153	25166	4	0	20084	1182	324	3
932	48924	30766	5		24518	1314	352	1
933	52265	17798	4		19085	1171	281	2
934	51211		2		13575	1214	380	3
935	38731		7		10756	435	287	2
936	48806		3		4507	720	146	2
937	42349		2		9137	1189	181	4
938	38224	33783	2		16570	917	375	4
939	36181	16924	6		14519	562	271	2
940	47051		5		15757	1046	187	3
941	37077	26012	3		10329	621	274	3
942	36135		2		12442	1358	180	1
943	42241	41812	4		23032	1018	367	2
944	41840		5		8558	1140	242	2
945	55769	29883	3		26943	1195	340	3
946	52431	18384	5		14931	732	310	3
947	45155	18406	4		22689	1034	226	1
948	41388		4		7314	1391	285	2
949	50778	23195	5		17345	1378	379	4
950	36756	16218	5		15895	605	346	2
951	36050		3		12103	809	114	3
952	47089		2		11098	1211	172	3
953	56241	32733	2		25967	966	350	3
954	51576	22866	2		20171	755	244	2
955	38122	22280	3		15196	847	232	2
956	32064		4		8330	906	211	3
957	39439	10306	2		9093	751	227	1
958	42203		2		8827	1454	218	2
959	57959	28757	4		21377	1191	364	3
960	52486		3		13037	1057	311	1
961	51631	37655	2		28794	583	288	1
962	53817		7		19728	694	193	2
963	36001	30118	4		12987	1363	178	4
964	45584	29148	4		17555	1229	370	3
965	38452		2		19707	502	300	3
966	39191		2		11172	833	167	1
967	47698	17035	4		12789	1176	216	2
968	48958	27896	2		14665	1893	267	3
969	40894		5		19306	583	316	2
970	42841		2		19317	1585	467	1
971	43886	24600	5		9954	916	155	2
972	43582	28500	2		18097	822	405	3
973	40786	25684	7		16809	1373	241	2
974	34602		4		13037	842	215	1
975	43897		4		8074	1201	333	1
976	30632	26814	2		11315	712	190	2
977	51919	31741	5		26548	1042	358	3
978	42701	25564	2		17758	1664	196	1
979	47506	26390	2		17058	1206	259	2
980	59582		4		16240	923	386	2
981	38040	29510	2		16138	894	336	3
982	63856		5		17476	780	249	3
983	44034	21663	3		16378	890	215	3
984	48678		3		19076	487	239	3
985	38056	33428	3		8324	539	262	2
986	33615		1		14307	1510	238	4
987	37980		4		15105	1205	139	3
988	60752	35153	5		16423	1090	151	4
989	49880	30716	5		12177	526	404	1
990	42924		2		13145	877	342	1
991	44380		2		15300	428	309	2
992	60192		4		16997	930	146	2
993	43867	29946	2		12090	803	154	1
994	38530		3		18462		226	1
995	42052		3		11166		119	4
996	30686		3		12557		243	2
997	30383		5		9934		254	4

OBS	INCOME1	INCOME2	FAMLSIZE	OWNORENT	TOTLDEBT	HPAYRENT	UTILITY	LOCATION
832	52382	0	5	0	12824	1240	351	1
833	61330	0	5	0	14952	787	199	3
834	41243	40240	2	1	12002	667	143	3
835	41030	0	2	0	24018	917	265	3
836	60616	0	7	0	14867	1492	418	4
837	43490	41140	2	1	7093	542	177	1
838	41444	35146	2	1	21963	684	220	4
839	35471	0	2	0	16885	744	199	3
840	43762	33119	1	1	11391	512	147	4
841	34838	0	1	0	5152	950	214	1
842	39204	23438	2	1	15875	1258	294	3
843	39391	42996	6	1	10463	1701	422	3
844	39185	0	3	0	13766	994	267	1
845	45463	0	3	0	22973	939	285	1
846	40927	30023	2	1	10887	610	194	2
847	42112	32631	2	1	17066	495	152	2
848	52389	35384	2	0	20054	1173	306	1
849	56093	36519	5	1	21012	1377	402	3
850	40557	0	2	0	19285	886	258	2
851	39580	0	2	0	12235	912	242	1
852	45663	26890	3	1	17697	488	160	1
853	39273	21169	2	1	15665	1386	420	2
854	40068	0	6	0	17392	809	245	2
855	43024	0	3	0	9662	813	231	2
856	51313	24398	2	1	7950	556	175	2
857	38005	34761	2	1	23165	919	220	4
858	37974	40403	2	1	22513	688	174	2
859	45361	22702	4	1	17664	833	321	2
860	31408	26651	4	1	11970	1314	218	2
861	44746	28949	6	1	17387	1439	383	2
862	57463	34408	3	1	23631	979	332	2
863	38751	34529	2	1	19879	958	275	3
864	35211	26870	2	0	18887	961	283	2
865	39806	0	6	0	12075	989	292	3
866	43357	19729	3	1	14538	1238	261	2
867	40178	29596	2	1	17211	1007	371	3
868	42067	20470	2	0	18483	866	233	1
869	37034	0	5	0	11564	551	233	2
870	42067	24734	2	1	9773	1296	140	3
871	31690	0	5	0	21690	1011	335	2
872	40416	0	1	0	10997	742	231	1
873	48113	0	2	0	13829	1258	188	1
874	55114	0	3	0	17609	1229	319	1
875	52022	0	2	0	7848	538	296	4
876	65414	36385	4	1	8624	659	177	3
877	36405	0	3	0	9613	757	198	2
878	37711	0	3	0	12394	1149	233	3
879	43260	0	4	0	12902	908	296	3
880	51416	25334	2	1	22330	590	182	2
881	38165	28955	4	1	16613	1216	178	1
882	30837	27470	3	1	14304	580	307	1
883	49868	0	3	0	19930	1126	436	4
884	41878	30225	4	1	10809	1059	258	3
885	35090	0	4	0	27881	1657	169	2
886	32999	0	3	0	8624	944	187	1
887	47500	17785	1	1	12394	648	325	2
888	38820	34613	4	1	22330	659	175	4
889	40888	33833	3	1	16613	661	317	3
890	47432	34349	3	1	19930	1216	248	3
891	50780	0	3	0	12685	580	275	3
892	47794	28116	2	1	13969	732	412	2
893	33251	0	2	0	18288	1085	186	1
894	61699	0	6	0	3984	1396	575	3
895	35499	29500	4	1	8266	575	161	1
896	42190	0	1	0	10299	900	299	2
897	33211	29500	4	1	20276	544	149	4
898	42706	0	4	0	11545	1093	512	3
899	39105	0	3	0	11307	834	199	4
900	46201	0	3	0	17885	1555	429	2
901	41968	25742	3	1	12097	714	210	3
902	33555	19490	1	1	9574	1498	413	4
903	57238	0	5	0	11419	716	223	3
904	34237	0	5	0	20447	1084	269	4
905	38530	23933	2	1	14830	1114	256	1
906	38290	23610	2	1	17357	1228	327	2
907	55288	21105	6	1	20148	592	151	2
908	53549	0	1	0	11545	1587	366	2
909	40993	40987	4	1	16524	512	294	4
910	43020	24743	4	1	17885	1083	199	4
911	38686	30039	2	1	12889	780	174	2
912	39628	0	7	0	15750	1696	479	1
913	51738	24641	4	1	19543	1176	343	1
914								

OBS	INCOME1	INCOME2	FAMLSIZE	OWNORENT	TOTLDEBT	HPAYRENT	UTILITY	LOCATION
1081	58358	0	1	1	19402	502	182	1
1082	65409	0	3	1	19154	821	251	1
1083	38804	30319	3	0	14042	570	178	4
1084	35855	0	6	1	17690	1490	398	4
1085	44847	0	2	0	11465	667	178	4
1086	46397	0	5	1	17198	1325	343	1
1087	40998	0	2	1	5352	960	222	3
1088	39228	0	2	1	7007	575	181	1
1089	60959	32568	2	0	14153	527	169	3
1090	48032	0	1	1	23912	735	282	1
1091	46420	0	2	1	12989	927	156	2
1092	35866	15758	2	1	12463	555	140	2
1093	47051	34802	4	1	18860	933	260	3
1094	43335	24850	4	0	7446	490	161	3
1095	42230	0	4	1	19447	1245	346	3
1096	40610	0	2	1	13595	482	179	1
1097	36804	26500	2	0	13057	570	187	2
1098	48543	0	3	0	13449	425	166	2
1099	48550	20599	5	1	15918	902	286	2
1100	42774	32388	2	0	20380	1209	327	2
1101	37873	11588	2	1	12582	412	149	2
1102	38047	0	3	1	9393	969	266	2
1103	54780	0	5	1	14994	1160	306	3
1104	71755	0	1	1	20319	1163	258	4
1105	43648	25254	4	1	15267	1127	302	3
1106	35414	26747	5	1	6886	562	200	4
1107	39735	0	4	0	19178	1331	359	3
1108	45803	24587	3	0	12590	1080	278	2
1109	37958	30377	2	1	12264	1013	275	2
1110	32357	28164	5	1	13041	578	151	2
1111	40345	19386	4	0	16358	818	345	4
1112	57670	14835	4	1	16481	1223	238	3
1113	52012	0	2	1	16616	1010	294	2
1114	38650	32671	2	0	18814	922	287	2
1115	35332	0	2	1	18776	899	264	3
1116	37062	0	4	0	7920	981	164	1
1117	41635	38094	2	1	19451	654	249	3
1118	56937	0	2	1	13493	939	215	2
1119	41309	0	2	0	12086	753	266	3
1120	31120	28488	4	1	12884	1051	199	2
1121	38667	26633	2	1	17245	595	215	1
1122	53630	0	2	1	15064	903	277	4
1123	35060	33532	2	1	16390	1003	241	1
1124	39876	17413	3	1	12663	788	242	2
1125	47401	0	2	1	11692	877	291	2
1126	47033	0	2	1	23889	1064	229	3
1127	49514	33228	2	1	11159	698	248	4
1128	39036	21211	2	1	22699	695	273	3
1129	36095	34032	3	1	11142	1215	307	2
1130	40833	16102	5	0	10568	1188	315	3
1131	49540	0	4	1	16276	802	216	2
1132	45355	20085	2	0	26929	1454	363	2
1133	55305	33100	2	1	14637	899	276	1
1134	38467	25453	2	1	19475	1111	260	2
1135	46615	33129	3	1	19301	1000	188	2
1136	42908	30455	3	1	15380	554	173	2
1137	37762	31395	7	1	23002	927	265	1
1138	82709	0	3	1	10716	2011	507	1
1139	42168	0	3	1		1221	301	3
1140								

OBS	INCOME1	INCOME2	FAMLSIZE	OWNORENT	TOTLDEBT	HPAYRENT	UTILITY	LOCATION
998	39372	29145	2	0	18349	910	228	3
999	34744	25408	2	0	16677	1209	285	2
1000	41596	24649	4	1	20092	1280	347	2
1001	39291	0	4	1	11492	1139	298	4
1002	42494	0	4	0	13533	678	187	4
1003	34539	34281	3	0	7156	998	264	4
1004	35408	26247	4	1	12987	958	256	4
1005	51166	35442	2	1	23306	832	264	1
1006	37979	31472	2	1	18921	1328	315	1
1007	37720	0	4	1	13652	714	219	3
1008	53901	0	2	1	6685	925	233	3
1009	46633	0	3	1	9221	790	199	3
1010	35887	34726	2	1	15400	783	228	1
1011	58930	27829	2	1	23593	1056	327	3
1012	37763	25852	2	1	13397	1412	407	2
1013	52199	22753	5	1	21940	1674	314	2
1014	43868	0	3	1	11990	538	153	4
1015	49313	33631	2	1	19178	1156	229	4
1016	55033	24520	2	1	22597	777	295	4
1017	36358	10409	2	1	13087	967	343	4
1018	38387	27839	4	1	15239	1257	200	3
1019	28317	0	2	1	5841	644	230	1
1020	51226	18454	3	1	22549	823	231	2
1021	45939	0	3	1	10453	836	246	2
1022	51633	25975	3	1	21257	817	348	1
1023	28077	21602	5	1	5593	1359	241	2
1024	44054	0	2	0	11855	946	164	4
1025	39671	23630	2	1	12086	420	131	2
1026	42212	0	6	1	7475	415	164	2
1027	54433	0	2	0	17790	1082	294	2
1028	30854	20835	2	1	9405	1629	140	2
1029	56384	0	6	1	22028	625	439	3
1030	46142	0	6	1	14557	1309	203	4
1031	40398	0	2	1	8986	1240	364	3
1032	49436	33329	3	1	25955	720	345	2
1033	52715	20281	2	1	19571	999	230	2
1034	36602	22250	3	1	17395	987	250	4
1035	42317	23600	3	1	14584	408	255	4
1036	40968	21458	2	0	17429	710	142	1
1037	34532	26953	4	1	16405	1047	204	3
1038	37132	22486	4	1	16325	625	259	2
1039	36597	33734	6	1	12584	1470	384	1
1040	48585	0	6	1	6755	544	154	4
1041	41115	31568	2	1	6458	969	267	4
1042	39339	0	2	0	8606	710	201	3
1043	36367	25965	3	1	18746	885	278	3
1044	31981	0	2	0	5344	629	171	4
1045	40573	0	4	1	10494	962	247	2
1046	39036	31281	2	0	39836	578	165	4
1047	37611	18409	3	1	16689	750	238	3
1048	46311	22107	7	1	18035	1092	340	4
1049	40634	0	4	1	14786	941	234	4
1050	49480	0	2	1	8046	1196	376	4
1051	54891	0	2	1	15807	725	163	2
1052	45718	23916	2	1	9826	741	195	2
1053	42840	20507	4	1	15674	1570	388	4
1054	44053	0	2	1	15449	802	225	2
1055	61582	0	3	1	20928	851	214	4
1056	47476	26318	2	0	13163	859	214	3
1057	45798	0	2	1	14906	1164	277	3
1058	51214	29933	3	1	17720	492	190	3
1059	33571	32985	2	1	19305	720	193	1
1060	36438	28686	3	1	14648	540	137	2
1061	37380	28061	2	1	17552	755	236	4
1062	41308	0	3	1	16523	810	222	4
1063	35777	0	4	1	8474	940	235	1
1064	55601	17999	4	1	19047	886	275	1
1065	41039	33992	6	1	18143	943	269	4
1066	38739	0	5	1	31000	1106	305	1
1067	52312	48200	3	1	14299	648	316	1
1068	54621	0	2	1	17697	973	205	1
1069	42400	25282	2	1	18736	1224	386	1
1070	37040	31929	3	0	20242	661	320	4
1071	56619	21180	2	1	9690	1150	211	1
1072	50444	32508	5	0	18441	429	317	1
1073	38060	0	3	1	18351	863	149	4
1074	48605	0	2	1	15221	856	260	1
1075	45380	37007	2	1	14088	600	257	1
1076	74025	0	3	1	12731	581	158	3
1077	52788	0	2	1	16186	726	149	2
1078	53550	0	3	1		742	179	1
1079	54601	0	2				219	2
1080	44449	0	3					

APPENDIX F   DATABASE USING FINANCIAL VARIABLES OF COMPANIES

The observations that comprise the database are random selections of companies listed in the Moody's Investor Service Industrial Manual. Each observation includes the following variables.

Number	Name	Description
1	BONDRATE	Bond rating as given by Moody's, where Aaa-A = 1, Baa-B = 2, Caa-C = 3
2	REGION	Region of United States where main office is located, where Northeast = 1, Southeast = 2, Southwest = 3, Northwest = 4
3	EMPLOYEE	Number of employees
4	SALES	Gross sales, in thousands of dollars
5	COSTSALE	Cost of sales, in thousands of dollars, i.e., the cost to the company to produce or manufacture the products sold
6	NETINC	Net income
7	ASSETS	Current assets
8	LIABIL	Current liabilities
9	TOTAL	Total assets or total liabilities

VARIABLES

OBS.	1	2	3	4	5	6	7	8	9
1	1	1	11600	1204236	932014	38378	355606	167371	650812
2	3	1	23000	2303731	1713703	-107331	947651	662653	1989945
3	2	1	4000	911002	692227	3116	389884	196724	511393
4	4	1	15592	9259100	6705200	310000	2617400	1424000	5282000
5	3	1	6100	1268580	991863	40723	221308	112590	407926
6	2	1	37481	3516289	3237018	-229627	20296124	1509417	4974267
7	1	1	8300	701059	460513	31215	279361	114844	469184
8	4	1	5320	413668	266110	34905	244063	76659	409064
9	1	1	51300	11113000	8332000	732000	4569000	2808000	12242000
10	1	1	141268	27148000	15129000	1538000	8960000	5636000	26733000
11	3	1	6200	1155711	857101	19088	321878	196566	401135257
12	1	1	13200	901890	613606	48844	144692	144692	685750
13	3	1	60700	4952900	3208100	408900	2432300	867200	3769000
14	3	1	34173	2094300	1407900	-10200	930800	581200	1856700
15	3	2	11082	635076	461671	25611	67696	67696	248067
16	3	1	7000	239352	119407	1798	84052	43298	114079
17	1	1	1401	100094161	200072391	20000360	60369060	181676	739445
18	3	1	7830	725241	538399	24082	271643	131605	449348
19	2	1	53000	3501000	2711000	85000	1296000	844000	2593000
20	2	1	9880	698394	368149	29531	129998	80256	377849
21	1	1	28064	3002700	2237000	152500	1101247	1138923	2685797
22	1	1	382274	62715800	51866200	3285100	18458100	15625600	37933000
23	3	1	16623	1549290	1081574	146391	455580	315248	2096345
24	3	1	750	543986	334305	9272	335606	133545	459164
25	2	2	5614	629700	722000	-25700	282933	650487	235840
26	2	1	16800	692900	425400	-12100	273500	208000	1608900
27	2	1	9174	701194	628523	39575	320402	789164	719257
28	2	1	4250	753774	496184	2931161	659121	166950	1347069
29	1	1	9400	648419	525101	4674	331613	150600	691546
30	1	4	62056	4586600	2563900	-183500	804400	762800	2086200
31	1	1	876000	102813700	88298000	294400	26768400	22848100	72593000
32	3	1	7000	514589	325545	-20426	241193	68024	290059
33	2	1	11914	2553300	1887300	-32700	611700	432600	1819700
34	2	1	18605	908800	497900	-101800	631900	266800	1265100
35	1	4	41400	3725700	2517500	-472300	1496400	1118700	4097200
36	3	4	2110	225071	109915	14296	110466	43615	155585
37	3	1	5578	1159595	773141	86112	582649	178399	819962
38	1	1	14000	2039220	1637800	85300	470600	276100	2077000
39	2	4	3650	366205	236911	7406	177766	75305	80053
40	1	2	16000	968555	431093	70476	458596	246642	1709495
41	2	4	10000	713685	566787	-1310	637237	341659	966924
42	1	3	800	154536	98537	16701	131889	30770	194958
43	1	1	265	91570	70185	-21304	71073	20676	181853
44	3	4	305	104212	80944	3126	44776	4692	46474
45	2	1	2200	54263	45068	839	18696	8216	67293
46	2	1	198038	93282	133083	8498	66041	41474	92145
47	1	1	27477	189074	73104	-10873	176558	143208	728855
48	2	4	31024	40353	45085	-182761	470600	357358	686575
49	2	4	2422	6902	4336	4336	45085	2060	8860
50	2	3	11	3601	1098	-3440	5460	1371	10270
51	3	1	1809	134189	80551	20250	117317	20874	128118
52	3	1	167	11629	8603	-3744	7149	5975	14093
53	2	3	2839	7459	6775	-1116	1546	4147	11716
54	1	2	3100	229728	188830	-7927	76659	37529	156946
55	3	4	109	2404	6056	-4245	343142	143351	541438
56	3	1	12	416	142	341	1836	614	2065
57	1	1	867	1458	1377	-7374	3001	3316	4815
58	3	4	240	23897	13277	560	9395	5393	13211
59	2	2	1086	27481	31798	-7389	13865	11574	79385
60	2	4	130	5046	3059	-20	1040	738	1576

VARIABLES

OBS.	1	2	3	4	5	6	7	8	9
61	2	3	27	2369	1459	307	1643	248	2226
62	3	1	198	784	383	-567	160	230	434
63	3	2	22000	1012451	416322	74425	561254	178721	873302
64	1	4	24	4873	2268	1509	6174	396	396
65	1	4	298	16084	12418	1217	20635	1380	6353
66	3	1	350	52684	42682	1762	34316	27731	27607
67	1	1	11	216	183	-1367	785	304	80770
68	2	4	18	1345	376	-104	8357	3139	1955
69	1	3	575	28079	18922	1148	25677	13935	8357
70	1	4	261	25244	20085	1667	7179	5842	33712
71	3	4	1222	18874	11144	-1855	985	3057	42725
72	1	3	322	29575	22577	5470	27578	7659	12894
73	1	1	17	4935	4130	-635	3529	3642	38873
74	3	1	5	18404	232245	-218346	119139	173732	4700
75	1	1	19	311813	130158	-458900	1947351	1203353	331874
76	3	1	311	11803	4961	800	4844	2661	2307941
77	3	1	520	52888	39948	1837	13548	5749	9667
78	3	1	22	3153	2118	-363	521	668	35890
79	3	2	550	25911	21515	669	8698	4014	597
80	2	3	92	339	339	-71	93	50	34817
81	2	3	292	17733	9248	72	15418	3197	186
82	3	2	278	36308	18648	793	13090	3378	22637
83	3	2	1226	50217	36964	5801	5788	5602	14586
84	2	3	36	401	401	-1386	7296	7296	88957
85	3	1	750	19266	13169	2601	3396	7251	9080
86	1	1	239	23297	21762	890	7613	5714	14160
87	3	1	175	16705	13173	710	13471	9800	17433
88	2	1	12200	240314	226140	-21103	70772	44819	18709
89	1	1	46	4703	2686	-680	2385	1180	177085
90	3	4	900	16895	7507	-5624	35503	5322	6502
91	1	1	448	65412	21440	4950	37718	12166	37860
92	1	1	460	56979	49128	-29806	34047	27093	54499
93	2	1	4100	37050	26020	-5394	45569	14330	46611
94	2	1	5	306	28	7998	101	153	68953
95	2	1	220	150118	60118	113	76174	44215	259
96	3	4	333	3055	1796	-5980	2057	802	121398
97	1	1	133	6600	7085	113	3111	9891	2648
98	3	4	28	67	1642	-1575	72341	10542	577697
99	3	3	36	26048	26048	-25478	248242	10100	2520969
100	1	1	22	2609	1610	-1144	1533	1394	1984
101	1	4	16	2534	244	901	1837	403	2079
102	1	1	12	32672	26336	-119237	58478	67334	112820
103	2	1	606	64505	42653	987	18715	9605	400027514
104	3	4	115	13575	5165	1201	6125	8836	8836
105	3	2	164	28536	21493	-400	19095	12715	23173
106	2	1	213	9193	5165	-107	7038	2108	8934
107	2	1	250	2406	1378	1061	4511	3210	16667
108	3	3	14	1199	963	137	383	277	2253
109	1	1	1470	161106	92321	18175	25897	99636	219786
110	2	1	22	53794	20000	-187850	33961	924882	235433
111	2	4	550	25406	15329	1152	15852	8167	19135
112	1	2	600	13552	10303	1079	11224	5046	13329
113	2	4	38	221	388	-2403	407	4119	948
114	2	1	667	16453	13360	3656	4333	1850	18989
115	3	4	470	33109	14368	-2711	28010	1636	34215
116	1	1	3900	1162	994	2463	1552	261	17887
117	2	3	412	47040	31478	-7941	21768	8625	26998
118	1	3	37	892	947	-309	271	274	405
119	2	2	2896	17	42	811	505	547	809
120	1	4	170	12103	10744	-1416	9990	9519	17152

OBS 181–240

OBS	1	2	3	4	5	6	7	8	9
181	2	1	37500	4332000	3913100	-152700	1183900	940300	4668900
182	2	1	21700	1791194	1160379	6304	1048104	692976	1580571
183	3	4	124196	16341000	15711000	665000	8478000	5659000	11060000
184	2	4	23333	3739970	2925870	101540	860785	547902	3533647
185	2	1	4800	919690	623817	49444	254380	115535	1600665
186	1	2	25500	1400196	808453	40138	493963	159392	658318
187	3	1	2953	216336	172221	8896	70971	35223	132180
188	2	2	46976	4378714	3173491	223225	1334792	626052	2762785
189	1	1	53731	7321000	5952000	76000	3363000	2180000	6288000
190	1	1	18300	4753700	4469100	375100	2063000	1299600	3370300
191	3	1	7074	1114242	872913	57274	436601	156671	812734
192	2	1	32200	4387623	3590044	200832	801502	730474	6025690
193	2	1	132422	22586500	18635200	1403600	5364000	5121000	14463200
194	3	2	433	35635	18045	2330	31136	14012	44947
195	3	3	52	158	309	4637	1411	937	2986
196	3	3	8207	266800	300900	-41700	228700	98900	585200
197	3	3	5100	1089020	525076	95610	417237	177057	849225
198	1	4	28030	8669000	4645000	934000	3739412	2754814	8373438
199	2	4	18400	1616267	1199454	89270	533599	325157	1145018
200	3	3	2957	885411	805473	14226	200087	94085	293559
201	1	1	2342	466320	380831	58948	256731	106031	1214177
202	3	4	42176	5911046	5150120	105285	1283476	926158	1819696
203	1	1	25100	1856300	1220400	177100	860500	486000	2360800
204	1	1	38000	4548000	3168000	219200	1283100	1469500	3650600
205	3	1	3900	294297	215147	6487	95564	48215	152350
206	1	3	273	2535000	1834000	-292000	699000	559000	3090000
207	1	1	51300	8742200	5970600	4132000	4749300	1211300	2383000
208	1	1	29100	3720400	2860100	558200	2072200	1162500	4595800
209	2	4	17500	1058702	543761	-951	587517	252545	705561
210	2	3	22000	1975221	1938202	-215742	975564	1213631	2974542
211	2	3	20600	3217700	2608900	36300	820900	635100	2721200
212	3	2	7000	634627	609940	17107	143959	91500	740485
213	3	2	638	359638	219468	70605	404602	212473	2620608
214	2	1	6965	4541296	4210826	-44957	923301	634312	2098619
215	2	1	24000	3644410	2756150	15643	1247572	1310080	2194882
216	3	1	24300	2955900	2685400	154200	1701800	503100	2932500
217	1	1	40000	4476000	1720400	660000	2339900	1170600	5163700
218	1	1	111000	25409000	16437000	1478000	5914000	4482000	17642000
219	1	1	29166	1239496	609946	167924	791584	671788	2027577
220	2	4	2600	310228	297427	15815	76635	38782	207158
221	2	1	36500	4687100	2799600	316400	1615900	975700	4461400
222	2	2	124617	15978000	8383000	1064000	5934	4319	17019
223	1	1	121000	12295700	9913000	611200	3837500	3411400	7703400
224	3	3	3300	36356	167411	28254	79085	37097	212762
225	1	1	87000	7937722	5403149	223455	1779481	1151067	3503106
226	2	1	485400	44281500	42891500	135130	2104140	1425810	6599460
227	2	1	13706	1552931	1345108	105952	753492	430290	1145647
228	2	3	67174	8577749	6603164	200445	746811	952541	3421088
229	1	1	39700	9218956	7592469	-344670	3454795	2445542	15955241
230	3	1	30350	9065819	8243368	89301	854565	742197	1797887
231	3	1	10700	3172260	2578671	58328	513939	252864	781291
232	1	1	72000	5023300	3454000	239200	2281200	1285200	5557100
233	3	1	21500	3762000	3045000	376000	1431000	1032000	4230000
234	1	1	6307	957796	717817	93217	315008	131912	834659
235	1	1	24485	2017775	1341293	370930	637626	473800	2779038
236	1	1	15110	1811937	1345108	108096	549808	197541	2060066
237	3	1	48000	5958000	3965200	17700	168400	88100	2850000
238	1	1	77100	7002900	2630100	329500	1681600	2292000	5876700
239	3	3	754	113655	269234	-184224	85803	228029	453542
240	1	1	17383	3340700	1744600	318900	729600	686400	2084200

OBS 121–180

OBS	1	2	3	4	5	6	7	8	9
121	1	4	444	19821	11676	-7423	5225	10709	17716
122	2	1	116	2720	1236	-376	1645	1579	2934
123	3	3	2050	68028	77415	4795	74395	32028	125590
124	2	4	1649	125790	86436	2402	53453	20154	72129
125	2	4	800	54662	23634	5138	28333	12705	75935
126	1	1	5065	396403	150208	54149	279364	91014	417016
127	2	2	722	110719	95927	-2228	31937	12003	106879
128	2	2	4300	616463	341375	38275	168173	88248	429618
129	3	1	68143	3923220	2342926	176260	933803	441291	1492533
130	3	1	694	31528	32910	2910	34821	5720	45944
131	3	4	19000	1625958	1095989	83222	649372	211377	928426
132	1	1	36000	3246139	1263369	450855	4214698	997955	4214698
133	2	4	28044	447755	231038	33289	131829	70662	415657
134	2	1	241	9048	529	8519	4405	2624	4405
135	2	1	83	16100	10019	1043	7792	1636	14411
136	3	1	109	14874	10818	1136	13818	3139	17877
137	2	2	23	16419	13045	900	5492	2265	19308
138	2	3	4640	532754	237877	102178	251591	237007	1310572
139	3	1	92	5429	3314	658	1663	834	6418
140	2	2	3800	192032	139229	-328	125691	68463	223898
141	1	2	1350	94570	81336	6347	40461	68463	58348
142	2	1	1200	91245	16607	2601	76845	52684	102512
143	1	3	810	83923	57542	1454	33198	12525	43078
144	2	1	183	188207	175456	-379	44878	24714	107854
145	2	4	118	40530	18645	10309	17342	13617	130776
146	2	4	150	1115406	561883	35455	501915	237036	985774
147	1	1	1227	222375	129290	16471	177608	17608	114270
148	4	1	4006	336963	183587	-18674	226914	120646	300617
149	2	3	803	62375	34255	3394	36882	12477	58566
150	2	1	31	6179	3515	1810	3896	3896	2536
151	1	1	85700	7039000	4163000	667000	3119000	1208000	5760000
152	1	1	492	64076	59623	-1555	21165	13344	55256
153	1	3	3400	930708	559949	72778	241162	230860	1981396
154	1	1	1012	56997	34530	2677	40891	7365	63105
155	2	3	1627	123325	68926	6725	73249	26255	117438
156	2	4	40	419	2120	-2742	865	354	1651
157	1	1	2464	63064	50913	667	24790	24815	44005
158	1	1	4252	169168	129118	3763	68369	19793	126061
159	1	1	1073	74947	54525	-23804	59407	23810	74767
160	1	2	11750	643831	488472	13096	228206	88742	369265
161	1	1	5400	216985	94206	12045	158011	31828	342772
162	2	1	375	39755	26113	-6156	7827	47365	60415
163	1	1	2700	423444	328995	11533	190262	78461	967444
164	2	1	215	11905	6840	867	6095	2388	16660
165	1	1	16600	1982134	1146089	4735	704536	471908	2705730
166	3	1	5400	423220	290583	-8553	209471	105311	334065
167	1	1	35700	4667200	3509600	254100	1551800	944300	6766700
168	1	1	34462	3816000	2086000	203000	1891200	1126500	3667000
169	1	1	38900	2997692	2227551	188467	1305174	712121	2080436
170	2	1	129000	14021484	10578985	144528	1638472	1312524	3590174
171	2	4	7505	800136	640518	-37608	279131	143352	521482
172	2	1	17823	995620	821493	41207	418692	198523	803310
173	1	1	2200	195010	144619	1559	98483	56593	185193
174	2	1	20000	1204246	543875	105960	769465	273284	1313414
175	1	3	3133	1132120	1034000	58900	398629	672900	8638136
176	1	1	35200	1885400	872500	158000	1046700	165300	732700
177	3	1	6000	1010300	269089	-16603	331200	103188	277828
178	3	1	4697	439727	269089	-13053	157847	117991	404158
179	3	4	2708	370882	292054	25631	257724	138025	495472
180	2	1	7947	864670	674397	25631	242637	138025	495472

VARIABLES

OBS.	1	2	3	4	5	6	7	8	9
241	3	1	4800	355377	216322	571	156951	55509	300024
242	1	3	36490	4303100	2712200	269400	1032900	804800	3676000
243	3	1	10944	1396401	1029008	77480	455659	278743	1016624
244	2	4	55500	4521002	3592465	71137	2717684	1747786	4569321
245	2	1	22950	8629988	7941301	545503	19024309	16107685	19024309
246	2	2	847	826500	881400	-20600	239600	173600	1680200
247	3	4	12714	1506200	1197110	187910	309720	210970	1886970
248	3	3	44000	6440871	4917211	225940	564050	757685	1551671
249	2	1	8600	817797	388533	59526	393187	277000	870130
250	3	3	19400	1920262	1451786	81428	913677	304393	2513343
251	2	1	5105	1430036	335530	78282	386802	234967	1404615
252	3	3	2567	399267	90210	55049	156002	80835	300351
253	1	1	68500	4752537	4421794	202344	1005376	829641	2470745
254	1	1	21000	1452010	929650	203420	786850	209750	2226150
255	1	3	151700	10376000	7533000	381000	3525000	1604000	6209000
256	1	1	9200	741586	502326	19461	423097	208670	691685
257	1	2	127400	49865000	48458000	1407000	10869000	10432000	39412000
258	1	2	51703	6879000	4341000	433000	2808000	1716000	8269000
259	3	4	15660	2110348	1985022	39411	585915	369101	969393
260	3	2	12895	1729600	1413000	75600	1206800	1124000	2904000
261	1	2	16000	972819	716833	5778	340000	172494	1656127
262	3	3	8465	374563	181201	17103	195609	74359	272127
263	3	1	4940	402357	283221	24009	164384	76143	335282
264	3	1	6000	549314	531246	-324195	477970	415135	1149950
265	2	3	307	129235	242993	-64258	45764	33121	590179
266	2	4	51000	15344143	12640306	181064	3711130	3313121	17466777
267	1	1	16300	17072610	13175600	752260	6500980	390577	1544588
268	3	4	875	811292	158898	27783	105881	105881	478464
269	3	3	2044	164991	146359	-3304	156219	24020	64589
270	2	4	220	158829	132669	-2070	56616	15924	86126
271	1	3	9600	1107564	717718	51947	466912	219168	996685
272	1	1	6257	1921223	995746	45443	851472	287827	3369278
273	1	1	14581	1290558	726975	72572	2503800	2223100	8028600
274	2	3	21800	9786000	7914000	228000	1032886	496958	1398613
275	1	1	6345	899065	644636	50228	2800000	2231000	12399000
276	3	1	2044	217296	146359	-3304	200728	108165	665042
277	3	3	1484	158829	132669	-2070	156219	120288	222451
278	2	1	27100	1611281	1413389	-59562	56616	15924	86126
279	3	2	2445	243255	198246	11036	2089903	940717	3619807
280	2	2	25600	3638900	3028500	191800	76552	40658	160699
281	2	1	12060	2067000	1346000	138000	1407100	814900	3708800
282	2	4	32641	634162	553910	47318	941000	434000	1842000
283	1	3	32641	18222000	12792000	883000	4081000	3483000	26214000
284	2	4	1134	50152	39833	5769	13004	9246	185983
285	2	2	1100	104192	61776	7225	43096	9562	87166
286	2	1	28000	1725200	1464600	82600	681100	334800	1287900
287	1	1	35724	3807634	1868402	278238	1888872	365609	3865609
288	1	1	13722	11794000	9111000	605000	4760600	365500	1126800
289	1	1	47000	2696993	2290943	-97279	604825	541357	63468
290	2	1	20900	2640450	2367800	-472000	949500	685300	264200
291	2	1	7000	1034953	1056538	9140	412333	265576	1840000
292	2	3	26600	14993000	9495000	615000	4743000	3750000	21604000
293	2	1	46500	221654	175615	23701	422872	413592	2313968
294	2	1	61000	5543000	3526000	444000	2344000	1881000	7068000
295	3	1	80185	9319800	7456900	1167100	2755600	3593800	21090900
296	3	1	34900	4835900	1515200	589500	155600	1015200	4183000
297	3	1	2266	241428	162961	22675	157228	56782	335910
298	3	1	6600	1309915	967662	71051	565527	287037	1509744
299	3	3	51095	26245000	5272000	715000	9050000	6485000	34583000
300	1	1	24149	2551469	2163448	50886	1175044	1240412	2161408

VARIABLES

OBS.	1	2	3	4	5	6	7	8	9
301	3	2	900	901875	345687	78808	787621	603680	1699314
302	2	1	1070	19246	154581	-6258	74946	30810	261306
303	2	1	15565	866629	738231	28980	823096	319922	1257428
304	3	1	20600	2233511	1776514	158268	663759	367130	1741251
305	3	1	58000	3113506	2359278	339990	1509141	982785	3117664
306	2	2	7900	648337	585573	38808	274425	108928	477078
307	3	4	43428	3811000	2870500	137600	1676500	646300	3025100
308	3	1	23000	1145122	951664	44897	264191	161937	445173
309	2	1	1010	205624	154826	8836	63095	43234	161558
310	3	2	26100	2683961	2270866	-60900	936188	699894	2002894
311	2	1	1900	335000	136600	28700	1386200	2023400	2234400
312	2	1	12500	997837	678598	125820	144028	161744	1042389
313	1	1	482000	28139000	20757000	2492000	14288000	11461000	34591000
314	1	2	39000	7223000	5783000	296000	1420000	837000	5114000
315	3	1	32100	2818300	1183800	15800	1489700	900700	2539500
316	1	2	7200	350587	103802	12515	248606	127784	336884
317	2	1	33400	3440125	3159806	78690	1305388	624229	1963670
318	2	1	600	103044	76499	-3676	222543	81461	4243400
319	1	1	47000	4366177	2622239	301734	1614694	910407	2837364
320	1	3	35000	740366	442746	97839	301188	77551	1302273
321	2	1	38162	1865700	225200	-136700	1394100	937500	4712900
322	1	1	29857	2799481	2105587	93974	1441196	711009	2355273
323	1	1	403508	34276000	16197000	4879000	27749000	12743000	57814000
324	2	1	13900	1177700	1047400	-217000	768100	337100	2427100
325	3	1	4400	5000000	3991000	305000	1628000	1332000	7848000
326	3	1	4004	401109	315456	66092	111571	59048	318045
327	3	1	1392	138158	89442	-873	111120	50195	140670
328	3	3	4000	422600	308100	-50700	271700	91900	317100
329	3	1	7200	321769	156183	22623	216282	93908	274956
330	3	1	70	2477	1038	-33224	233808	55975	240518
331	3	3	123	1911664	4219291	-1809591	1921227	3040119	12958397
332	3	3	1000	243542	175685	6236	54507	26882	86033
333	3	1	32000	1091675	788550	-59259	140683	273444	568493
334	3	1	5500	314429	209241	1610	86029	88019	234095
335	3	2	16300	919818	703576	42426	305882	120168	587945
336	3	1	4500	528483	357597	18922	158816	83884	291180
337	3	1	6333	587820	431961	20256	208205	65540	315642
338	3	1	525000	1033560	772020	36436	184877	50268	213423
339	3	1	7350	772241	603988	6695	66463	234328	172134
340	3	1	4997	975727	637382	29739	324689	266556	628924
341	3	1	6371	884726	474275	73753	466805	69973	849814
342	3	1	2100	561858	329341	32666	262230	69244	192257
343	3	1	110	553068	479267	13045	124750	1150	401892
344	3	3	1729	532	589	-8793	3614	18428	4813
345	3	1	1187	143677	73908	11968	54938	566	85079
346	3	1	1864	221	257	-4101	4889	25880	8560
347	1	1	2200	1085382	82877	3321	52080	151798	90447
348	1	3	265	1285811	1172318	15600	332149	5750	385194
349	1	1	5500	34722	31232	1137	65080	120154	96809
350	2	2	156	587492	501072	22137	125724	2219	278656
351	1	1	967	23035	5822	-3328	11648	14182	16052
352	2	2	4	30463	9047	-6460	12046	764	31476
353	1	3	75	646	600	-691	352	1411	1061
354	1	3	190	2158	5859	-5859	16526	4552	26414
355	3	3	23	8131	4394	-2915	8539	2674	15110
356	2	2	5000	5975	5675	182	3013	13379	10427
357	3	1	3917	50811	39297	1125	18468	30300	39821
358	2	1	457	200602	171578	6670000	92354	4188	186680
359	3	1	154	36605	26327	1530	15542	1239	21081
360	1	4	154	20813	12837	1967	17255	1239	22469

VARIABLES

OBS	1	2	3	4	5	6	7	8	9
361	1	2	425	24300	15172	1908	6556	5166	29941
362	1	3	75	1084	638	-1426	2510	7744	4193
363	3	1	2400	108280	21157-	390150	91781	6609	120956
364	3	2	810	124399	100770	52610	51766	8679	71806
365	2	1	265	6685	2128	-6882	4981	26313	21039
366	3	3	2485	163005	107508	7196	131685	3500	161602
367	2	2	52	4148	3727	-52270	3813	63272	7077
368	2	2	3000	45098	34644	17671	133553	9980	640576
369	3	1	742	94205	68254	2495	37188	6503	60853
370	2	2	532	35824	21794	711	23628	13743	30518
371	2	2	10336	223918	190749	4656	32504	69658	149302
372	2	3	2365	303951	183230	16951	261860	12798	406338
373	3	2	691	146800	105906	6083	95213	16544	109090
374	1	1	1545	125668	98133	5070	36267	1692	89472
375	3	1	310	36949	10999	2859	27096	6140	33580
376	3	1	910	104949	53992	7489	60545	16544	79828
377	1	3	42	5397	5749	-212	6955	4229	33930
378	3	1	320	15016	10022	700	12868	1692	20622
379	3	2	4	221258	158669	-290324	2197508	1659957	9868339
380	1	1	550	56260	48928	1257	21212	12335	29732
381	3	2	215	20758	12544	720	6796	3868	11509
382	1	3	500	11217	8750	740	5006	5345	23976
383	2	3	1434	514090	453000	-16942	303344	533582	1317613
384	1	3	976	11739	5039	1521	6137	2232	6854
385	3	3	71	1541	125	-12084	1858	2372	14980
386	3	3	33	80471	58394	746	45762	7224	130543
387	3	1	3420	31146	19581	2812	11096	15956	21197
388	2	2	480	19612	7808	1205	25497	4106	34490
389	2	1	383	119979	53942	188	21938	6812	61474
390	1	3	1700	101577	268441	6838	201938	2719	1160881
391	1	1	6	43809	35275	45975	11251	6608	20997
392	1	3	270	1235	361	1694	2704	622	5041
393	3	3	34	42004	19300	-2849	14630	8408	35739
394	3	3	845	4822	3737	58	3974	1590	31709
395	3	2	94	52166	25587	-430	26725	14264	4698000
396	2	1	104	3172000	2770000	4280	1578000	931000	1641
397	2	1	22400	181	179	-426000	29	308	16960
398	2	3	148	61805	48341	-439	14432	3750	12902
399	1	1	1000	29655	22730	1393	10538	7169	27412
400	1	3	330	46441	23126	208	24176	6444	2892
401	3	2	261	335	395	6930	2538	193	3197
402	2	3	29	156	105	-2305	2537	9472	9472
403	3	1	25	6197	3130	-1949	638	2671	72661
404	3	4	67	6603	7874	8661	63553	399	4378
405	3	4	111	1525	1227	-1415	2624	27895	53790
406	3	1	972	155327	127156	1025	42095	652187	1879122
407	1	1	886	5350638	4230063	88974	1188435	7765	38707
408	1	1	63500	27908	20104	-1206	7591	80355	405322
409	3	3	325	410345	328248	-96405	112349	72829	244062
410	3	1	176	266788	111163	23173	170198	323545	1170548
411	3	1	2664	766217	856581	-58601	609464	44749	11741
412	2	4	1800	106096	66213	2033	59861	3561	83804
413	3	2	931	23279	53636	1130	7033	16788	292196
414	3	2	460	64483	210275	10193	62627	78229	14451
415	3	1	1017	288664	1021	-8190	180494	3699	107448
416	3	1	3645	4007	61787	6520	7912	11170	53478
417	1	3	87	93285	20223	4642	41115	10452	453681
418	2	2	1100	39357	62975	-24594	34653	34427	
419	2	2	520	87180			189635		
420	2	1	800						

VARIABLES

OBS	1	2	3	4	5	6	7	8	9
421	3	1	8	17254	11630	2830	34163	34163	34163
422	3	1	127	16868	8781	2107	124992	2000	225622
423	2	3	7432	263952	213431	40952	185829	30749	567383
424	3	1	599	66549	45814	1696	20951	11396	31451
425	3	2	2100	96200	67497	3645	42137	8646	54848
426	2	1	3200	315357	227653	14320	194088	75744	308890
427	3	3	31	671	1504	-794	441	651	2294
428	3	2	308	15608	9186	1626	22632	1690	25975
429	2	1	1250	53829	39069	1466	24090	11798	35934
430	1	1	485	41446	30466	1308	22685	4738	25950
431	2	4	1522	207589	175901	850	45723	37833	76129
432	2	1	570	523146	366301	9252	135982	16960	208291
433	3	1	570	50203	33446	1510	28503	28503	32337
434	3	1	1700	251815	192014	3055	112258	83482	147866
435	3	1	3273	228599	131040	2430	80396	8937	108751
436	3	1	431	29811	13243	1983	14915	8584	23517
437	3	1	1800	115078	91191	9648	56585	20528	83110
438	3	2	1000	101944	88035	-968	31321	21094	51699
439	3	2	2794	130854	101562	1004	275867	89871	1006511
440	1	1	860	32934	23365	2151	26547	4365	42301
441	1	1	1002	50303	34223	2211	16667	4370	24353
442	1	3	4560	174224	94237	-61670	329653	222512	629256
443	2	3	690	73825	13920	-5200	52693	18913	99205
444	4	1	556	20476	-399	-650314	16269	2143	25074
445	3	2	365	327272	313430	2866	752206	157444	996267
446	2	1	1018	21710	12204	-4664	30803	12257	64906
447	2	1	2880	114057	69803	2794	98908	56933	202084
448	2	1	350	42177	14428	2785	61490	33243	120691
449	1	3	450	40126	27733	594	12128	7482	21203
450	1	2	117	117	106	480	480	920	1028
451	3	2	3307	294818	232110	19092	59755	35321	146714
452	3	2	583	47747	35752	629	16244	9566	20109
453	2	3	150	10163	7130	-1183	6475	3751	8538
454	3	1	159	2684	1076	-400	3143	904	3871
455	3	1	375	23566	16422	4740	49767	36723	241560
456	3	2	1786	11512	8653	682	9347	4853	16069
457	3	2	272	23439	17029	-3261	24301	19470	40562
458	3	3	6516	108707	110417	-800	28275	10089	47268
459	3	1	898	58707	46379	90000174	84	319	622
460	3	2	858	73	75	1745	28021	10493	28741
461	3	3	2600	36299	20880	16980	36932	22800	205267
462	3	3	2000	192599	133555	15728	127477	36953	165861
463	3	1	1177	271947	165143	8515	44162	12364	75924
464	3	1	362	142568	94404	5419	20819	5092	30498
465	3	1	6823	149519	29929	1743	29153	36943	161143
466	3	3	2641	174644	29685	18741	152852	96792	260908
467	3	3	128	1-20601	93567	861	6895	2330	9164
468	3	3	85	10241	2318	-2710	17431	4358	40014
469	2	4	27	13309	11266	2155	38279	11637	79420
470	2	3	14	747	549	159	17	6	53528
471	1	4	1400	1366381	744609	107657	279206	1241383	1128692
472	3	1	1600	32892	13668	4248	19667	4173	37126
473	2	1	5	95993	60796	5865	35578	11607	59385
474	2	4	205	314	190	-273	413	243	502
475	2	4	4303	21020	11474	-722	10265	6730	16223
476	3	1	1419	531640	323196	37818	185089	62964	311837
477	1	1	1300	195453	170739	4678	42652	25602	128265
478	2	4	208	150028	167113	-2421	32751	21898	45601
479	2	3	2	31072	6514	774	5389	3096	11682
				7703	2790	173	1043	1542	25749

VARIABLES

OBS.	1	2	3	4	5	6	7	8	9
480	1	1	724	82097	69112	1278	36433	23863	39489
481	3	4	200	1726	574	-214	425	306	665
482	3	4	1554	95637	52441	8346	73347	15104	113539
483	4	3	300	41527	40138	-156	42263	5030.	61087
484	3	1	7	663875	412882	-2035663	1189863	1068744	4737485
485	2	1	2000	68274	46906	14923	43570	20578	233376
486	3	1	77	12236	8068	213	6300	5361	28639
487	3	2	792	9654	7338	351	7163	2963	12546
488	1	2	26700	2216636	1488646	59609	1041910	549747	1793160
489	1	1	25120	2615110	1999741	226733	1079821	419683	2914319
490	1	1	15980	2169614	1453440	132764	393420	222143	1356303
491	2	2	43600	1647788	342617	103330	2278189	477067	2278189
492	3	1	6000	1960237	1893884	39079	320723	124524	205614
493	1	1	89000	4930652	4109528	174644	1235606	715694	1276230
494	1	1	13700	961077	623328	79583	597837	304262	1276230
495	2	1	22459	3173242	3073622	-19264	894956	466954	2526557
496	2	1	7800	745049	505448	33345	279903	178944	718598
497	3	1	83	34830	8395	6142	23122	5197	30465
498	3	3	45	1	1	-983	474	137	2678
499	3	1	4959	334437	151442	23406	161709	59915	369031
500	3	1	500	46391	41375	-2810	43596	9504	95791
501	3	1	500	195359	157650	-3089	28676	3489	251433
502	3	1	390	66475	48135	8590	22435	9469	60517
503	3	4	280	31399	25941	405	22706	3777	52974
504	3	3	12400	435560	359396	71164	81007	51436	115065
505	2	2	14000	666186	502736	43655	211444	145569	924533
506	3	3	3500	87205	44056	-5323	13389	14219	40057
507	3	3	190	23950	16623	167	8741	6054	12479
508	2	3	5470	460279	72009	9000	346432	251415	851426
509	1	3	1797	184296	117964	15346	132060	63273	216741
510	3	1	1601	131755	72000	7750	105599	32369	130799
511	2	1	498	53259	47236	3434	55159	15763	69364
512	2	1	1700	68274	89184	3948	36435	4632	48261
513	2	1	1486	113184	22637	6328	124629	51982	173771
514	1	2	2530	190718	171782	10118	89694	42829	122575
515	3	2	80	114319	110855	117	15001	11358	74903
516	1	3	988	473561	372511	17538	36598	35424	566769
517	3	1	1700	931934	854117	17104	105670	84356	260126
518	2	4	250	22369	50953	-27402	8276	6385	82053
519	3	3	343	16372	11749	-3639	4789	1933	10646
520	3	2	46	9249	7569	-162	3768	1451	6844
521	3	3	14	121670	75259	5529	65463	51776	119456
522	2	3	23	212886	117964	21360	104797	41371	175473
523	1	1	21800	1933055	1267918	1016571	959381	483918	1786810
524	1	1	4269	381046	305238	-46294	174763	95580	340577
525	1	1	1600	180920	91568	4073	30918	28245	96853
526	2	1	9900	757820	603568	6562	260558	121721	508098
527	1	1	1619	63225	51524	23655	40709	22813	84382
528	2	4	2150	23008	18002	-3170	15479	7212	26502
529	3	4	3300	294502	120687	-149032	442930	150405	674354
530	3	1	33747	3745400	1315200	521100	1892800	1355300	4222000
531	1	2	4730	1792632	2308025	-304800	1255525	1335022	3288484
532	3	1	1600	339190	241206	-13100	116568	62846	565746
533	3	3	6277	341382	253913	14335	162864	55853	274461
534	1	1	20500	1403472	934393	98928	481225	232787	1131988
535	1	1	16915	1784629	566049	396291	1505506	750631	2408831
536	2	1	9411	2988396	2494357	26186	530775	401302	1770232
537	1	1	4000	380501	148029	25648	110259	90442	202200
538	2	2	2300	208025	152407	-896	97055	49633	131237
539	2	1	22800	1671871	1396682	53687	604797	220378	961058

VARIABLES

OBS.	1	2	3	4	5	6	7	8	9
540	3	1	4700	267978	215548	-20861	147115	35358	188817
541	2	1	15500	2032325	1564619	35415	530459	203410	1523600
542	1	1	23645	10047000	7109000	385000	3289000	2386000	11684000
543	1	1	16000	1433940	944297	45400	659082	669418	1399176
544	1	2	27941	2920310	1623351	408085	406606	458869	2929081
545	1	2	16565	1058055	875006	2736	94212	305490	1403529
546	3	1	2325	157232	103788	5664	114883	37008	130531
547	3	1	898	780278	743890	17580	40947	66976	491889
548	2	3	857	56530	38684	1352	1352	7061	56808
549	2	1	23000	2667912	2326185	12928	1304547	848835	3027518
550	2	1	78556	6035900	4678200	217700	1748900	1351700	3909300
551	1	1	10000	961411	627078	37500	387535	166797	591908
552	1	1	7500	2045215	734983	11945	279713	105526	501707
553	2	3	17355	6343000	1340174	129934	568849	262070	2751482
554	1	1	50292	5115900	4343000	496000	2414000	1881000	7571000
555	1	1	98300	15669157	3681600	-43400	4536400	3342100	9408800
556	1	1	8982	8091000	633564	-80071	67521	236991	725649
557	2	3	193500	2291448	12373271	72727	6940346	4626477	11091787
558	1	1	18005	2723664	5225000	176000	1835000	1175000	10133000
559	2	3	20700	1880083	795614	252646	1201840	564040	2664956
560	1	1	21700	3660553	1884596	225508	686547	617053	2006068
561	1	1	2080	3102918	1652081	-99888	312085	323055	1697322
562	2	3	42100	1215064	2550072	103137	720164	388834	1197082
563	1	1	53200	235635	1052781	309484	1510068	969806	2515923
564	1	1	6400	10731000	671199	100173	219422	185113	1145227
565	1	2	2733	4008700	160217	17020	78477	42847	237405
566	1	1	117267	1858600	7771000	670800	4635300	4196400	8481800
567	1	1	30956	4822000	3595500	199700	1088200	537300	2202300
568	2	1	5500	2673	1480700	-239700	1036600	876800	3907900
569	2	1	100367	77636	2412000	465000	3973000	2206000	10608000
570	1	1	30	22285	153000	294	1175	986	2594
571	1	3	462	1606	164400	16052	13615	5424	64836
572	3	3	160	1358	20973	1920	8216	3472	73871
573	2	4	39	182344	1556	46	833	849	1399
574	2	4	135	113	1106	-1242	760	2004	3443
575	1	2	744	94031	123542	2528	65917	45053	80788
576	3	3	273	23321	331	-216	168	90	540
577	3	4	957	9484	71620	3210	37561	13321	38892
578	3	1	130	143356	14666	2633	14438	2777	24390
579	3	1	1200	17957	6592	833	3266	3443	9458
580	3	4	221	6387	118253	-2161	44006	17049	63271
581	2	1	28	208	17966	-1000	8414	2851	19651
582	2	3	2	126502	4478	-1052	4319	3809	17797
583	3	1	1400	1454	208	-420	298	7	332
584	1	4	24	86052	96362	4921	35509	18463	69321
585	2	3	1509	410	1454	-909	179	1524	5790
586	3	3	16	5679	68440	1748	26074	10488	36386
587	3	2	238	1157	296	-406	120	561	473
588	1	4	26	209787	4540	408	21652	5734	23937
589	3	1	2300	861630	844	-852	1299	302	2019
590	2	3	103	149	147536	4469	72903	26021	94204
591	1	2	10	10	632040	13220	117592	82287	205579
592	1	3	227	31290	69	-46	859	36	1641
593	1	4	976	626900	40	-30	181	12	232
594	3	4	300	1257	16445	617	10286	8663	35150
595	3	1	152	5008	613919	2906	158765	67538	164697
596	3	1	42	4887	11853	879	5326	4757	12621
597	3	2	75	1095	1095	-1341	1333	875	2008
598	3	2	889	2264	2264	486	3945	554	6204
599	2	1	486	5008	1095	300	3171	413	4700
600	1	1	75	4887	2264	300	3171	413	4700

OBS	1	2	3	4	5	6	7	8	9
601	2	1	77	2563	2467	-3929	9808	1283	14582
602	2	1	29	1092	797	-1105	2005	608	3583
603	2	4	37	32	7	-6	10	5	195
604	2	1	526	44102	17914	5222	28373	5325	33469
605	3	2	6	380	196	-533	481	239	1076
606	3	1	600	17813	11255	-1098	6653	2603	12072
607	1	1	16	767	480	-534	583	356	780
608	1	1	270	7132	5891	309	2306	1092	3882
609	3	1	123	6245	2912	-119	7596	839	10302
610	3	1	103	7027	4562	-4015	24757	1713	33118
611	3	1	30	1423	603	-822	2006	541	2563
612	3	4	8	83	32	-3	25		147
613	3	2	23	1811	928	-931	1201	1594	2956
614	1	1	1700	151828	118070	7867	49505	23838	143602
615	1	4	94	7464	4473	-72	6933	4522	7379
616	2	1	486	45974	34068	-6613	21579	18289	32689
617	3	1	2600	274198	87677	28743	132373	50890	290083
618	3	3	6438	35914	25095	5556	19060	9166	22714
619	3	1	1860	201901	187380	806	44014	24961	219695
620	2	1	149	11088	8944	-12002	13340	2646	33738
621	2	4	15	1328	508	-319	1008	125	1303
622	2	1	85	193	197	541	452	976	4294
623	2	3	68	6361	5550	-179	2480	430	27772
624	2	4	298	34520	33226	1264	15104	14662	20295
625	1	1	984	9910	4651	282	6156	969	9693
626	3	1	115	14529	7953	1515	6993	892	17743
627	2	1	684	13558	11167	-614	13734	1409	8173
628	2	4	400	6162	4028	-132	2628	1563	25794
629	3	1	350	232487	224625	588	19616	14601	94477
630	1	4	1352	109899	49385	9447	55962	15261	275663
631	1	1	432	72209	19703	-19412	89212	36717	38889
632	1	1	334	119152	98577	3899	35980	20738	6568
633	3	1	88	17800	10731	1164	6166	3834	40334
634	3	2	302	25080	22258	667	18434	10864	59886
635	3	4	473	46180	18334	5065	51680	5801	13295
636	1	4	700	54111	41395	628	8813	38506	190230
637	2	4	4400	310668	234683	12710	129085	509	3924
638	2	4	48	4177	3566	-351	2630	85753	291459
639	3	2	3347	1018431	809854	30251	133841	88	2565
640	3	3	14	80	131	-1350	119	5448	14140
641	3	1	807	44291	32986	929	11817	3391	33399
642	3	1	186	32779	20027	-3234	23329	7939	36663
643	3	1	1400	43379	22976	-1224	24671	4253	16830
644	1	1	169	22536	135037	2166	14791	26544	193278
645	2	3	2331	197659	134541	9518	144852	1098	10619
646	2	4	98	12040	6698	1120	6823	23294	92886
647	2	4	10	259	81	-8906	1761	3876	8870
648	2	1	336	16483	10225	-16920	4910	16187	68824
649	2	1	1080	125308	71221	13534	56242	29324	101651
650	3	1	2737	249570	207381	8233	70894	1045	1678
651	3	1	30	2668	2179	-644	1018	10782	29984
652	1	3	465	25872	17193	1655	11679	8547	90564
653	3	2	465	51748	22089	10367	80499	390	60
654	2	4	43	1161	515	-50	293	495	2442
655	3	1	5	510	633	-425	2126	522	1973
656	3	3	175	263	460	-99	1118	32384	154138
657	3	1	1415	149261	88902	1242	104166	1568	141
658	3	1	20	50	774	-1034	53	887	1813
659	2	1	22	678	588	-406	1483	3014	19232
660	2	3	32	2882	1435	-4359	2773		

OBS	1	2	3	4	5	6	7	8	9
661	2	4	600	78824	58592	2024	35519	10381	45688
662	2	1	124	9214	6917	93	1512	1458	3777
663	2	4	13	783	581	-375	530	239	1755
664	3	4	850	79533	58348	5243	56898	21963	72896
665	3	1	1250	4223	4135	-2398	1528	7770	5318
666	3	1	897	4253	2728	-2577	5716	735	6633
667	3	4	129	10218	8154	-1980	5833	4043	7726
668	3	1	12	480	199	-1981	325	737	869
669	3	1	63	18034	15680	-199	10495	7478	11911
670	2	3	136	212	344	-141	898	82	968
671	2	4	1570	210799	38625	30100	129729	44740	174731
672	3	4	455	76019	36623	5889	88795	22969	96689
673	3	3	11	1011	463	190	693	333	3295
674	3	3	280	10383	7143	535	3946	1090	7599
675	3	1	79	1898	1179	-1021	3250	4064	29600
676	1	4	3300	81506	27445	-2913	16705	11234	54321
677	1	1	532	172299	76492	27177	95822	19436	108801
678	2	1	955	12134	7435	198	4373	1143	6987
679	2	1	200	17146	10457	969	17561	2169	30257
680	2	1	217	12212	7642	2828	42604	3574	42995
681	2	2	2224	458377	353315	-3688	187749	74452	241939
682	2	2	400	369901	26776	-2542	19553	4070	23440
683	1	1	15	14167	230520	-244356	64393	243314	1430578
684	3	3	3787	263286	198047	14788	120620	55002	194341
685	2	3	550	35332	31575	-10489	46446	6407	124620
686	1	1	275	10021	8472	-2297	4663	1121	6147
687	2	4	112	318	19606	-19348	119853	100100	900891
688	3	1	111	994121	687580	129019	257449	100454	323540
689	1	3	1800	7935	4959	-228	5766	937	8845
690	1	1	326	10609	6332	115	2492	1066	2754
691	3	2	631	39051	34797	-7038	20808	13184	45162
692	3	4	58	4357	942	488	5818	1381	8743
693	2	2	836	22145	9557	-1044	2224	4764	6549
694	1	1	150	17545	11613	-7851	11489	3992	12859
695	2	1	181	16309	8190	-5154	14327	3212	18685
696	1	4	32	4686	1730	584	3673	2307	4422
697	1	3	68	3400	2504	-232	1661	1030	2575
698	2	4	192	10456	9424	-3935	5934	1924	17698
699	2	4	68	3818	2307	-596	1255	1610	3298
700	3	1	266	24575	15333	2771	12370	5507	22826
701	1	1	227	89528	79921	1388	26760	17033	27890
702	1	3	943	64038	60930	3815	50284	26732	62025
703	3	2	330	34685	22018	1375	9777	3641	12263
704	2	4	1100	20697	10133	1347	22572	3224	44390
705	3	4	66	6060	4426	-261	3061	1112	3640
706	3	4	900	31024	18122	7555	45022	8237	46966
707	2	3	14	549	471	9	1173	356	1316
708	1	1	118	7817	7930	-1947	6555	4699	14212
709	1	1	600	37255	23591	799	21347	9079	32545
710	2	3	8300	421612	343610	19478	194267	28031	277006
711	3	4	559	3000	1719	-1948	1593	1706	1964
712	1	3	159	10078	6671	332	3016	1939	7464
713	2	3	1501	112788	57338	3736	66001	24838	113771
714	1	1	30	720	172	-1076	1729	172	2176
715	1	1	13	976	536	-95	231	342	375
716	1	1	58	5415	3185	-294	3718	739	5165
717	1	4	660	57240	31026	715	11991	8304	15443
718	3	1	123	30965	25538	-943	14168	3911	15213
719	2	1	162	16169	13023	-4269	2990	1866	5324
720	1	2	2058	92743	67301	3778	24338	14161	57490

OBS	1	2	3	VARIABLES 4	5	6	7	8	9
721	2	3	236	32585	6822	5057	31402	4694	37598
722	3	4	360	14604	17563	-5689	4522	8049	10103
723	2	4	946	104421	75734	3463	46869	18470	67138
724	3	1	200	67828	17547	2741	13821	8288	81605
725	2	1	532	43306	36219	1457	15910	10058	34458
726	2	1	898	16593	17404	-2427	3115	4724	9693
727	3	1	146	148240	117507	-52723	162944	299776	274224
728	3	1	50	2949	1606	-227	1536	505	3282
729	1	1	696	1671	1604	-1554	1232	863	2540
730	2	1	487	197	1045	-1260	1054	1784	3046
731	2	2	281	7769	3960	-3677	2753	2492	8639
732	2	1	15	295	111	5	168	41	197
733	1	1	28	795	654	2383	907	1159	1168
734	2	4	1000	130427	94548	1150	111370	61862	132835
735	1	1	601	5878	3341	-1031	1334	1669	2129
736	3	1	895	98682	63840	5645	48793	19616	78608
737	1	3	1725	280274	237735	6249	15254	13893	72091
738	3	3	238	17938	15800	488	4365	2466	6595
739	3	1	83	9592	5870	-1102	4529	1322	6216
740	3	1	3500	1377202	1268137	1797	252644	140783	427078
741	1	1	300	45955	29465	2630	29900	7459	40771
742	2	3	665	122424	93816	507	21903	8004	29263
743	1	4	85	8716	5229	-2936	6966	1905	8169
744	1	3	433	253292	237142	-3447	76670	40007	223622
745	2	4	229	19134	16869	29	34337	15122	54067
746	2	4	105	5077	4735	-412	2550	1904	3319
747	2	4	730	7365	4485	106	13643	7524	27115
748	3	1	2443	110012	79851	613	60574	25224	77971
749	2	1	256	33642	27765	-242	7002	1322	15266
750	3	1	4061	521234	338904	40469	135397	67829	237346
751	2	2	356	55004	20153	4422	26733	17137	64178
752	1	3	181	4128	3495	-61	80	1093	2364
753	2	1	454	35649	15414	-6208	25385	6131	36225
754	3	1	688	23044	19385	-5057	11994	12019	28790
755	3	4	813	104001	65123	6792	43317	19802	50079
756	2	1	2834	160555	117299	2732	55506	39862	126685
757	3	4	300	32788	25554	1006	11522	8241	27184
758	2	2	16400	269269	220083	9055	96275	26011	229435
759	3	3	1924	27525	9107	6957	14015	6148	47214
760	3	3	4500	106990	29504	4799	14170	9795	63110
761	1	1	900	275424	183459	12797	105654	39955	229688
762	2	2	460	102983	37929	723	5966	4237	14620
763	3	4	1607	102093	39789	11488	37231	8852	75527
764	1	4	17,	18018	7305	2081	40210	2948	15456
765	1	1	262	15360	4919	560	13907	4977	6218
766	2	4	110	21417	11790	89	10982	1358	44033
767	1	1	107	4709	4898	1093	26449	16025	4103
768	1	3	1660	150648	9924	14368	75457	6676	122779
769	2	1	200	35543	26736	-927	14525	6676	16460
770	2	3	1500	9098	6179	344	2781	1205	3588
771	1	1	27	3492	1329	360	2312	1837	2467
772	1	4	4169	299524	227026	-11377	204831	50430	335307
773	1	4	50	345	230	-113	468	711	1908
774	3	3	1460	1618	676	-1734	1858	790	2175
775	3	4	579	160334	87441	11908	29301	14124	53869
776	3	1	2700	232282	126836	6838	65844	34843	131377
777	3	4	78	102691	86763	327	31252	9003	41607
778	3	1	22	53557	39610	3510	28772	12858	34556
779	2	3	1210	4132	1837	261	1391	940	9859
780	3	3	1780	174012	104187	9484	82950	18831	116994

OBS	1	2	3	VARIABLES 4	5	6	7	8	9
781	3	2	1219	507670	227848	-12980	88534	64604	499292
782	3	1	78	6063	3698	-2469	6973	1935	7971
783	3	3	416	17173	20040	-201190	1058532	87312	1095518
784	2	4	200	21447	3546	1800	15449	60002059	32205
785	1	3	299	60914	46075	1201	21032	8142	23353
786	2	1	1027	11083	7433	228	4613	1615	7022
787	3	1	3300	274510	188191	10616	118673	55572	27449
788	1	3	302	42611	37324	-2308	22882	31624	24552
789	1	1	210	14813	12454	523	8465	1667	13846
790	3	1	8	420	148	-230	550	416	843
791	2	4	311	1652	709	75	757	424	991
792	2	4	241	20412	11987	-3851	10160	6442	14775
793	2	4	127	10861	5199	1402	5620	1665	7276
794	1	2	60	320	337	-336	97	200	169
795	3	2	1298	93392	65291	215	27846	12722	70439
796	1	4	60	116201	98883	-18050	38181	8190	38181
797	3	1	321	9918	7250	439	3887	3176	9287
798	3	1	1130	9146	2209	251	3837	5632	8038
799	2	1	231	17387	13466	-1657	19517	16313	43880
800	3	1	935	68877	32684	1342	123167	67891	155527
801	2	1	2700	354927	326544	-7338	911	363	7761
802	2	1	31	1824	142	-557	5736	176	5915
803	2	1	47	3189	1442	182	21156	3988	28668
804	3	2	350	30132	1941	20002261	5879	735	3812
805	3	2	36	3041	3561	-638	8032	2883	7594
806	3	1	65	4265	12226	-2292	22376	4846	22106
807	2	1	50	15938	9770	-688	184984	26593	38048
808	3	4	312	112361	318	-9428	4538	764	6745
809	2	2	4338	14874		318	10231	67879	
810	2	1	3600	653040	461652	87542	10233	11364	723181
811	1	1	165	84822	22273	878	11862	13743	47904
812	3	2	420	77587	22657	-5255	32010	5051	45352
813	2	1	31	28292	23712	524	20004	10803	22811
814	1	3	1736	22394	16484	809	3125	23001	17543
815	2	1	400	122517	47231	3711	59902	16692	78355
816	1	2	79	84622	2791	-6484	130407	1124	36811
817	3	1	4910	4287	55593	-693	10639	36108	4952
818	1	2	1000	257547	58300	18371	9938	31078	139277
819	3	2	187	116027	8267	-21500	104609	5761	176314
820	3	1	260	12768	20979	781	5049	8103	13246
821	3	3	1556	22873	194671	-3333	4819	74799	12862
822	3	1	143	263268	6432	13244	68968	1603	126950
823	2	4	3600	4538	51944	-698	291587	2913	5339
824	3	1	4300	11710	322660	2319	9121	25754	7900
825	1	3	658	82047	21594	30	102647	155563	142260
826	2	1	1320	417628	109531	23382	17829	6623	396325
827	1	1	477	36769	78472	189	87847	23898	17240
828	2	2	1600	137245	794759	170	56583	11678	113228
829	2	3	1226	87144	119681	6680	3302	57343	34021
830	1	3	82	1036450	4972	18094	515	21516	240447
831	2	1	14	150747	805	4339	12877	1201	83348
832	1	4	280	7746	10834	-642	334053	6714	3926
833	3	3	86088	437	586649	1481	46464	99468	890
834	3	4	5642	23979	284120	1150	131946	45088	27700
835	3	3	883	810822	34524	21125	34914	18340	1106263
836	2	1	631	399006	128984	-3516	961	13917	146542
837	3	4	65	107149	493	-1081	59389	170	174447
838	3	3	615	173476	24458	-529		9991	57138
839	3	3		1137		9			1093
840	3	4		66464		4528			81353

VARIABLES

OBS.	1	2	3	4	5	6	7	8	9
841	2	1	20	591	452	-805	1553	96	1888
842	2	1	154	14207	7839	959	6169	1586	7329
843	2	1	790	67400	30175	3028	42958	18107	56259
844	2	2	170	19212	12411	858	15511	1293	18814
845	2	2	61	10211	6987	269	5208	1015	7515
846	3	4	367	18381	12683	1449	10677	6710	24200
847	3	2	470	101354	87491	1625	29422	14381	35658
848	3	2	32	1625	695	-2885	895	1779	3305
849	3	1	1888	221634	207625	833	217708	157612	293582
850	3	1	169	13428	10777	-164	10226	2645	32642
851	3	2	675	40515	12272	-3629	7804	3654	21091
852	3	4	281	21410	16277	-1775	131	195	19848
853	2	3	22	676	137	-854	15188	4667	507
854	1	1	2200	40031	10250	-1384	14568	6854	24428
855	3	4	390	20781	7527	-2487	23121	9169	20739
856	1	1	429	17452	1135	18077	167615	16593	31697
857	1	1	911	108792	33699	203	1087	770	193830
858	3	2	100	2160	1622	-335	3908	1099	1223
859	2	4	126	6343	5601	8126	35078	20338	6436
860	3	4	444	96023	25149	-12662	72201	16169	47466
861	3	1	1172	95400	58295	-926	2123	2379	114874
862	3	1	94	3466	3157	-315	705	444	4499
863	2	4	16	446	210	15730	81481	18163	1037
864	2	1	1306	129298	64412	-13600	992	3660	154741
865	2	1	33	2877	2028	-463	16731	23650	1644
866	2	1	218	169767	161097	-210	3129	2265	37355
867	3	4	324	9010	6648	96	2354	1390	4395
868	2	1	55	6275	4648	-63060	78925	87100	135226
869	2	2	4	59433	64830	6784	7361	7022	10444
870	1	1	175	76608	14387	-1079	13085	13526	34163
871	1	4	231	27025	18117	2412	28276	4271	32112
872	2	4	208	24867	10944	9487	27419	5829	59294
873	2	4	1050	75095	50935	8271	53988	8790	33063
874	2	1	2100	67000	59648	2222	18384	13117	86249
875	3	1	4300	431591	326402	6784	27875	29228	34060
876	3	1	1300	57604	76608	-1079	13085	13526	55121
877	3	1	497	95730	71424	2363	45379	19700	179
878	2	1	12	171	121	-940	135	454	38328
879	3	1	741	66257	47076	2614	27049	10154	26743
880	3	2	210	11493	6515	46	16984	6662	79294
881	1	1	1368	130718	95708	7173	62354	23223	23703
882	1	1	120	17334	12718	91	15172	7384	4442
883	3	1	22	3814	1040	1365	3556	1037	258052
884	1	1	900	136063	100237	7110	168295	53773	18291
885	2	1	225	19689	9750	1785	11321	1900	7488
886	1	1	570	14770	12390	-340	6346	4627	2584
887	3	3	41	3147	1825	994	2084	267	25201
888	3	2	1082	16981	3766	-2652	16162	2067	3009
889	3	1	52	5348	3705	-2458	1287	1160	34566
890	2	1	353	49377	30455	2957	18208	9824	14553
891	2	1	370	16277	10833	553	9495	2259	72531
892	3	1	3850	207493	142302	7485	30769	25696	1333
893	3	3	29	860	457	-708	1240	83	29531
894	2	4	373	46594	33696	1314	19772	10658	5129
895	2	1	13	1313	363	-621	7598	7598	63296
896	2	1	48	5489	3145	321	3083	682	11114
897	1	4	400	86498	34013	10943	35427	21397	186781
898	1	1	130	15731	13021	14	8667	3943	68554
899	3	1	2032	189538	93109	10789	109272	20638	
900	1	4	248	221418	200300	3012	65569	39152	

OBS.	1	2	3	4	5	6	7	8	9
901	3	1	21	769	654	411	440	925	485
902	3	4	331	21428	20457	-4477	6974	12560	27001
903	2	2	465	24734	20979	-6029	21873	2297	30733
904	2	4	722	48865	64808	-33941	32978	9658	132343
905	2	4	1050	38234	38027	18250	106297	21681	132839
906	2	4	22	1875	1090	-299	948	631	1265
907	3	3	118	5301	87	-184	126	34	200
908	3	2	311	24609	2613	235	1870	688	3355
909	1	1	91	3505	16686	-1145	8033	15642	22091
910	1	1	300	62004	1539	275	1138	471	1162
911	3	1	84	4408	46810	176	26716	13996	29167
912	1	2	660	443092	3485	-683	2517	659	3454
913	1	2	300	68148	196362	39064	255495	90074	398065
914	2	1	2917	13301	45137	4013	3634	12514	51831
915	1	2	346	184861	9077	855	2942	2942	4879
916	3	3	3579	15652	137936	2430	102137	46686	136877
917	3	2	36	349027	13592	127	6384	1590	9440
918	1	1	30	1211	245360	19434	128644	62588	236630
919	1	4	4403	1100	12	539	1772	241	2060
920	1	1	1149	291913	533	-2078	2168	394	5287
921	2	1	1601	79769	158400	32039	185824	56318	328240
922	2	2	16000	383735	35257	4710	42594	6687	57169
923	2	1	112	524358	312202	10076	99849	27219	131412
924	2	2	100	6206	188923	10947	61373	39702	212460
925	3	1	451	2303	2335	-912	6250	936	8268
926	2	2	841	2534	1566	98	906	670	2877
927	2	1	46	51869	1150	581	4079	759	4592
928	3	2	12	524	40876	-1420	38864	20535	51374
929	2	1	794	1901	447	-306	603	894	614
930	3	2	218	7189	1648	-735	701	2029	809
931	3	4	12	30237	4801	-809	4410	27056	6949
932	2	4	18	15993	26058	-1008	50618	7819	95002
933	2	1	67	42	12195	439	9008	0	22541
934	3	4	1500	741	70	-22	798	92	1800
935	3	2	2	11252	587	-125	404	3091	1226
936	3	1	1214	11530	3573	1616	9403	22175	11643
937	1	1	7	4036	77139	3367	49243	1424	63970
938	3	1	1841	125906	2867	307	1424	890	2161
939	2	1	671	166086	83917	6373	64236	29998	94970
940	3	1	78	13794	19	-423	1754	67	2195
941	1	1	22	6293	87792	13855	112561	35252	154523
942	1	1	24000	4705	7582	962	11585	4384	41176
943	3	2	115	944356	4499	11	5256	3059	6308
944	3	2	618	10211	2673	647	4992	321	5770
945	2	2	450	59323	783649	28003	205730	161708	653369
946	3	1	1200	27724	6993	405	5724	5383	8697
947	3	1	370	58717	42976	1063	27259	7459	42478
948	2	1	465	42756	24381	-723	14610	3439	22069
949	3	1	4000	236629	39992	6762	54248	28541	111511
950	3	1	4214	58717	19046	7461	12688	6910	36390
951	3	1	479	42756	191747	5033	27121	4023	40421
952	1	3	3000	77925	59209	39	135995	48588	224608
953	3	3	85	47681	20050	-2121	37198	14635	45698
954	2	1	5129	2650	5313	646	25331	9298	33065
955	3	1	130	8310	11723	472	510	3479	7925
956	2	1	6300	21363	256490	26056	5924	1190	7571
957	3	1	1561	394092	21523	-4807	11997	1907	15465
958	2	4		16736	44008	9854	140320	50767	255898
959	2	1		82526			7955	821	30971
960	2	4					73337	20477	90177

OBS.	1	2	3	4	5	6	7	8	9
					VARIABLES				
961	1	3	139	14330	5495	1101	8142	2490	12095
962	1	1	870	74444	54034	4825	26051	5991	48720
963	1	1	3	614	348	-21	166	232	277
964	1	3	2205	9031	7722	-790	4695	1450	5468
965	3	4	376	891	581	-1362	777	2373	1944
966	2	4	3000	288160	228052	17971	69631	22634	168816
967	2	1	1607	90784	75611	1972	45421	27489	50354
968	2	4	13	482	254	-389	331	445	2061
969	3	1	1138	64771	33404	-7445	65664	13412	90318
970	2	1	5672	419991	289779	24664	186911	71576	269887
971	2	1	6720	298238	216796	22190	113435	35671	173281
972	2	2	3600	423413	317117	2607	152391	77618	250427
973	1	1	207	9281	5359	-366	4627	989	6256
974	2	1	733	16016	7783	1276	11113	4265	12773
975	1	1	46	1728	904	-759	391	830	1968
976	2	1	57	4363	2930	-75	3425	1117	4214
977	1	3	1438	8086	5755	1942	4809	2362	8160
978	1	1	467	27246	13935	1425	10417	8176	15112
979	1	3	3406	237686	174743	1970	76243	44776	158461
980	2	3	1043	8510	2298	4559	2529	2324	9367
981	1	1	45	95588	52030	5581	86205	17162	128819
982	2	1	45	3901	1767	-709	2131	589	3914
983	3	1	220	53615	34352	2247	23462	9288	26704
984	3	4	180	110890	50418	5818	55283	20356	67384
985	3	1	443	84604	74095	1877	40503	5205	58203
986	3	1	1343	263164	204696	5038	86799	31182	106804
987	2	1	234	16904	6682	436	9747	2466	14303
988	3	3	313	46006	30789	4246	29793	6491	49586
989	2	1	9	306	990	-1530	184	2900	1903
990	2	1	802	70667	49443	6042	14731	6747	36304
991	2	4	4119	543041	263681	31753	135165	110798	633558
992	2	1	7531	813497	502247	86194	294387	81216	355502
993	2	3	255	24834	17293	506	13524	4590	17277
994	3	1	75	7743	5545	795	6250	2251	7122
995	2	3	4534	391700	417100	-117100	152000	88700	480200
996	1	4	3300	487685	361921	33484	99710	75445	484975
997	1	1	16	362	44	-1155	726	59	1017
998	3	3	156	1826	1028	324	1023	266	1559
999	2	1	135	27908	15965	2410	11519	3016	18394
1000	2	4	1540	194335	129150	3855	280546	32150	451404

Appendix G   Answers to Odd-Numbered Exercises

Chapter 1

1.1 The following populations are examples of populations that would be of interest to a business manager: **a.** Consumers of a certain product. **b.** Employees of a company. **c.** All electrical components manufactured by a factory. A business manager would prefer to sample from a population rather than take a census because of the cost and time involved.

1.3 Inferential statistics

1.5 a. Quantitative, ratio **b.** Qualitative, ratio **c.** Qualitative, nominal **d.** Quantitative, interval **e.** Qualitative, ratio

1.7 a. Secondary **b.** Primary **c.** Secondary **d.** Primary

1.9 a. Primary **b.** Secondary **c.** Primary. **d.** Secondary

1.11 a. To use Table A.13, do the following. (1) Start at an arbitrary position. (2) Select twenty five-digit numbers by reading either across or down the table. (3) For each five-digit number selected, place a decimal between the third and fourth digits and round to the nearest integer. If any numbers are over 500, then continue to select random numbers until twenty numbers are chosen with values between 1 and 500. **b.** Generating random numbers with Excel or MINITAB is easier, particularly if one wants to generate many random numbers.

1.13 Give five categories of income and ask the respondent to which category does he/she belong.

1.15 Some comments motivating a person to fill out the questionnaire should be included. A closing statement may thank respondents for their time.

1.17 a. This is a leading question. **b.** Ask the question about the "Nightly Business Report" after the respondent lists their favorite television programs. **c.** It is not clear whether "large" refers to population or area.

1.19 a. All citizens of the United States. **b.** Ask the general questions first and then the specific questions. **c.** The question is a leading question.

1.21 a. The firms that buy computer chips from the company. **b.** A table of random numbers can be used. Also Excel or MINITAB can be used to generate random numbers. **c.** Satisfaction by firms that buy from the company. **d.** The average of the responses can be used as the statistic to estimate the parameter in part (c).

1.23 a. Japanese companies doing business in China. **b.** Random numbers could be used to randomly select a company. **c.** A convenience sample could be taken from Japanese companies that are easy to contact. Statistical analyses require that a sample be random.

1.25 a. Represents a sample of employees at General Motors, if randomly selected from the population of all employees at General Motors. **b.** Sample **c.** Sample **d.** Population of all possible ways of choosing two cards from a deck of 52 cards. **e.** Sample

1.29 a. Working class **b.** Random numbers could be generated from a statistical software package. **c.** (1) What is

the average amount that you save on a monthly basis? (2) Do you feel that your savings are adequate for retirement purposes? (3) How much money do you plan to have at retirement? (4) How many years will it take to reach your goal of having adequate retirement funds? (5) At what age do you plan to retire? **d.** Including a ticket to a lottery drawing would be an incentive. **e.** A second mailing or a follow-up phone call reminding the participant to fill out the survey would increase the response rate.

Chapter 2

2.1 a. 1,000

b.

Lower Class Limit	Upper Class Limit
0	1000
1000	2000
2000	3000
3000	4000
4000	5000
5000	6000
6000	7000
7000	8000

c. $1200/8062 = .1488$
$1500/8062 = .1861$
$2500/8062 = .3101$
$2300/8062 = .2853$
$500/8062 = .0620$
$50/8062 = .0062$
$10/8062 = .0012$
$2/8062 = .0002$

2.3 a. $(224,000 - 111,000)/5 = 22,600$. Use a class width of 25,000.

Class Number	Class
1	110,000 and under 135,000
2	135,000 and under 160,000
3	160,000 and under 185,000
4	185,000 and under 210,000
5	210,000 and under 235,000

b. $(224,000 - 111,000)/6 = 18,833$. Use a class width of 20,000.

Class Number	Class
1	110,000 and under 130,000
2	130,000 and under 150,000
3	150,000 and under 170,000
4	170,000 and under 190,000
5	190,000 and under 210,000
6	210,000 and under 230,000

c. $(224,000 - 111,000)/12 = 9,416.7$. Use a class width of 10,000.

Class Number	Class
1	110,000 and under 120,000
2	120,000 and under 130,000
3	130,000 and under 140,000
4	140,000 and under 150,000
5	150,000 and under 160,000

Class Number	Class
6	160,000 and under 170,000
7	170,000 and under 180,000
8	180,000 and under 190,000
9	190,000 and under 200,000
10	200,000 and under 210,000
11	210,000 and under 220,000
12	220,000 and under 230,000

2.5 a. Frequency distributions are easier to examine than the raw data.

b.

Weekly Earnings	Frequency	Relative Frequency
$ 0 and under $211	1462	.2183
$211 and under $334	1295	.1934
$334 and under $493	1354	.2022
$493 and under $730	1297	.1937
$730 and higher	1288	.1924

c. .1937 + .1924 = .3861

2.7 a. CW = 3 **b.** Determine the basic "shape" of the data. **c.** Condense the 20 data items into 6 classes. Intervals are 2 and under 5, . . . , 17 and under 20.

2.9 c.

Class Number	Frequency	Cumulative Frequency	Relative Frequency	Cumulative Relative Frequency
1	15	15	.375	.375
2	10	25	.25	.625
3	8	33	.20	.825
4	5	38	.125	.95
5	2	40	.05	1.00
	40			

2.11 b. CW = .5; Number of classes = 7; Class intervals are 1 and under 1.5, . . . , 4 and under 4.5.

2.15 The most commonly quoted price is 99.

2.17 a. Class intervals are 15–24, . . . , 95–104; Cumulative relative frequencies are .03, .20, .33, .46, .56, .69, .82, .92, .99.

2.19 a.

Frequency Distribution Table		
CLASS	CLASS LIMITS	FREQUENCY
1	0 and under 6	6
2	6 and under 12	7
3	12 and under 18	5
4	18 and under 24	1
5	24 and under 30	0
6	30 and under 36	1
	TOTAL	20

2.21

Class Number	Class	Frequency	Relative Frequency
1	0 and under 10,000	9	.225
2	10,000 and under 20,000	11	.275
3	20,000 and under 30,000	9	.225
4	30,000 and under 40,000	7	.175
5	40,000 and under 50,000	3	.075
6	50,000 and under 60,000	1	.025
		40	1.00

2.23 Class intervals are 4–8, . . . , 24–28. Cumulative frequencies are 6, 12, 16, 18, 20.

2.25 b. Most of the insurance amounts are between $80,000 and $120,000. **c.** An unusually large amount of insurance would be $300,000 or more.

2.33 a. Most of the loans are being borrowed by Mexico, China, Brazil and Indonesia. **b.** Bar charts and pie charts do not order the categories and do not have a cumulative scale.

2.39 b. A histogram uses class intervals and frequencies.

2.41 c. 7.00% and under 7.25% mortgage rates are the most common.

2.43 b. 58.33% of the time 29 or more work orders come into the production workshop. 21.7% of the time 20 or more work orders are completed by the production workshop. Recommendation: increase the rate of completing orders, either by overtime or additional shift man-hours.

2.51 a. The values of 13.4 and 15.4 appear to be outliers.

2.55 a. The stem-and-leaf diagram and the histogram show similar shapes.

2.57 ARM Holdings, Broadcom, and Conecel constitute approximately 62% of the market value.

2.59 b. The V-8's have most of the gas mileages centered near 24 whereas the V-6's have most of the gas mileages centered near 22.

2.61 The first histogram shows that the number of frequent flyer miles is uniformly distributed between 10 and 30 thousand. The second histogram shows that approximately 50% of frequent flyer miles are between 18 and 22 thousand miles. If there are too few intervals, much information will be lost.

CHAPTER 3

3.1 a. 10 20 30
  Mean = 60/3 = 20
  There is no mode.
  Median = 20
  Midrange = (10 + 30)/2 = 20
b. 3 5 6 8 9
  Mean = 31/5 = 6.2
  There is no mode.
  Median = 6
  Midrange = (3 + 9)/2 = 6
c. 1 2 2 3 7 7 8 9 10 14
  Mean = 63/10 = 6.3
  Mode = 2 and 7
  Median = (7 + 7)/2 = 7
  Midrange = (1 + 14)/2 = 7.5

3.3 a. 1, 2, 7, 8, 9 **b.** 1, 3, 10, 18, 19

3.5 No, the median does not have to change by the same amount that the mean changes.

3.7 Mean = 55.77/14 = 3.98
  Median = (.5 + .68)/2 = .59
If 26.30 is omitted, the value of the mean will change more than if any other values were omitted. After omitting 26.30, the mean is 29.47/13 = 2.267. The median is .5.

3.9 a.
$$\text{Mean} = 4020.4/15 = 268.0267$$
$$\text{Median} = 168.3$$
$$\text{Midrange} = (.8 + 1400)/2 = 700.4$$
Yes, these statistics would be expected to be different especially when there is a very large value in the dataset.

b.
$$\text{Mean} = 2620.4/14 = 187.1714$$
$$\text{Median} = (70.5 + 168.3)/2 = 119.4$$
$$\text{Midrange} = 319.9$$
The value of the midrange changed the most.

3.11 c. The new mean (median) should be equal to 4.5 times the old mean (median) plus 50. **d.** The mean of the non-standardized data is 359 and the median of the non-standardized data is 365.

3.13 a. Range = 6; s^2 = 5.3; s = 2.302; CV = 52.322%.
b. Range = 12; s^2 = 13.8777; s = 3.7253; CV = 21.79%.
c. Range = 3.2; s^2 = .788; s = .888; CV = 22.09%.

3.15 a. Since the range is larger for the large carriers, one might expect this group to have more variation.
b. Standard deviation of the large group of carriers is 32.27. Standard deviation of the small group of carriers is 16.63.

3.17 $\sum (x - \overline{x})^2 = \sum x^2 - 2(\sum x)^2/n + (\sum x)^2/n = \sum x^2 - (\sum x)^2/n.$

3.19 b. Mean is 1368/7 = 195.4286. Variance is
$$\frac{276762 - (1368)^2/7}{7 - 1} = 1569.286.$$ Standard deviation is 39.614.

d. Removing the smallest and largest observations, $\overline{x}$ = 1008/5 = 201.6; $s^2 = (205912 - (1008)^2/5)/(5 - 1) = 674.8$; s = 25.977

3.21 a. Mean is 85.2, standard deviation is 47.6, coefficient of variation is 100(47.6/85.2) = 55.87, and the variance is 2266.182. **b.** The mean should change by dividing its value by 60. The standard deviation should change by dividing its value by 60. The variance should change by dividing its value by 3600. **c.** Mean is 1.42, standard deviation is .793, and the variance is .6295.

3.23 Median is 1.5, Mean is 10/10 = 1 and $s^2 = (20 - (10)^2/10)/9 = 1.111$; s = 1.054; $Sk = 3(\overline{x} - \text{Md})/s = 3(1 - 1.5)/1.054 = -1.423$

3.25 a. –2 **b.** 3 **c.** 55 **d.** 37.5

3.27 a. 73.5 **b.** 105.5 **c.** 75 = 25th percentile; 103 = 75th percentile. **d.** $\overline{x}$ = 90.6333; median = 87.5; s = 19.71781; Sk = 0.47673. **e.** The data are slightly skewed to the right.

3.29 a. 3.0496 **b.** –1.443; –.4591; .1967; .52466; 1.18049. **c.** 1

3.31 a. $\overline{x}$ = 1205; s^2 = 7,837,307; s = 2799.519; Median = 236; Sk = 1.038393. **b.** The skewness should decrease. **c.** $\overline{x}$ = 159.2857; s^2 = 8762.571; s = 93.6086; Median = 153; Sk = .20145

3.33 b. Sk = –.54168 **c.** Sk = –.677

3.35 a. 80 to 120 **b.** 100 ± 3(20)

3.37 a. $\overline{x}$ = 44.8; s = 10.5283. **b.** 44.8 ± 2(10.5283). **c.** 44.8 ± 3(10.5283). **d.** Yes.

3.39 $\overline{x}$ = 50.5; s = 9.7512; n = 30; $\overline{x} \pm s$ = 40.749 to 60.2512, 90% of the data values fall in this interval; $\overline{x} \pm 2s$ = 30.997 to

70.002, 93.33% of the data values fall in this interval; $\overline{x} \pm 3s$ = 21.246 to 79.753, 93.33% of data values fall in this interval.

3.41 $\overline{x} \pm 2s$ = 90.633 ± 2(19.71781); 96.667% of the data actually lie within this interval.

3.43 $\overline{x}$ = 12.733; s = 9.49; $\overline{x} - 2s$ = – 6.247; $\overline{x} + 2s$ = 31.713; $\overline{x} - 3s$ = –15.737; $\overline{x} + 3s$ = 41.203.

a. 14 observations lie within two standard deviations of the mean, that is 93.3% of data are within two standard deviations of the mean. 100% of the data lie within 3 standard deviations of the mean. **b.** The results in part (a) are consistent with Chebyshev's inequality.

3.45 a. The following interval contains at least 75% of the data. $\overline{x} - 2s$ to $\overline{x} + 2s$; 18335.76 – 2(2268.515) to 18335.76 + 2(2268.515); \$13,798.73 to \$22,872.79. The following interval contains at least 89% of the data. $\overline{x} - 3s$ to $\overline{x} + 3s$; 18,335.76 – 3(2268.515) to 18,335.76 + 3(2268.515); \$11,530.22 to \$25,141.31

b. 196 observations (98%) of the data lie within 2 standard deviations of the mean. The minimum number expected by Chebyshev's inequality is 150. 199 observations (99.5%) of the data lie within 2 standard deviations of the mean. The minimum number expected by Chebyshev's inequality is 178.

3.47 a. $\overline{x} \doteq 30$ **b.** $s^2 \doteq 204.0816$ **c.** $s \doteq 14.2857$

3.49 a. $\overline{x} \doteq 164.0909$ **b.** $s \doteq 38.7801$

3.51 a. $\overline{x} \doteq 19.8$ **b.** $s \doteq 5.8353$

3.55

Boxplot of C1

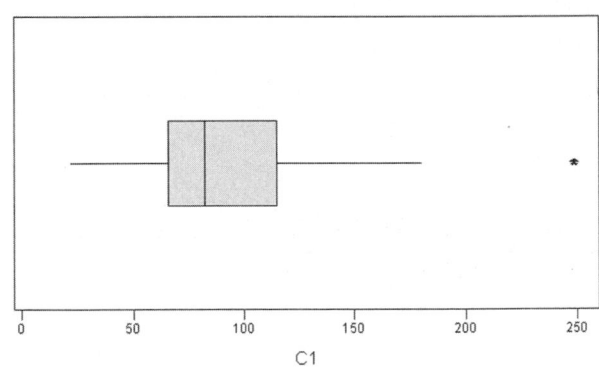

C1

3.57 b. The distribution appears to be skewed slightly to the right. There is one mild outlier.

3.61 a. $\overline{x}$ = 15.983; Median = 11.15; There is no mode. Since there is a very large value (46) in the data set, the mean will be affected. The median would be a more appropriate measure of central tendency. **b.** $Sk = 3(\overline{x} - \text{Md})/s = 3(15.989 - 11.15)/15.2472 = .9521$. The data are slightly skewed to the right. **c.** $z = (46 - 15.983)/15.2472 = 1.968$; z = .001. The first value says that Yahoo's price/sales figure is approximately 2 standard deviations from the mean.

3.63 a. 6.268 to 8.204 **b.** Interquartile range is .7. There is no change in the interquartile range when 8.0 is omitted.

3.65 a. $Q_1 = 2.7$; $Q_3 = 4.1$; IQR = 1.4; $s = 1.1757$. **b.** $Q_1 = 2.7$; $Q_3 = 3.8$; IQR = 1.1; $s = .8206$.

3.67 b. The Sharpe measure can be thought of as the reciprocal of the coefficient of variation.

3.69 a. The data are not exactly bell-shaped. However, the data appear to be almost uniformly distributed between –1.5 and 2.5. **b.** $Sk = .32$ **c.** By the empirical rule, approximately 68% of the values should fall between –1.155 to 1.655.

3.71 $45 to $105

3.73 The supervisor should accept the shipment.

3.75 a. 6054.752 to 20069.908 **b.** 25th, 50th, and 75th percentiles are 7400, 14000, and 17500.

3.77 b. The data appear to have a bell-shaped distribution. **c.** $\bar{x} = 50.2167$, $s = 15.913$, and $Sk = .04$

3.79 a.

Mean	24.872
Median	25.275
Minimum	10.21
Maximum	34.42
First Quartile	21.62
Third Quartile	28.34

b. For the case where the largest value is set to 0,

Mean	24.1836
Median	25.05
Minimum	0
Maximum	32.88
First Quartile	21.56
Third Quartile	28.34

The statistics do not change by much.

c. For the case where the four largest values are set to 0,

Mean	22.2438
Median	24.935
Minimum	0
Maximum	31.56
first Quartile	21.05
third Quartile	27.45

Note that the value of the mean has dropped by over 2 units. The mean is affected more than the median. The first and third quartiles are affected very little.

CHAPTER 4

4.1 a. $P(B) = 1.25$ cannot be a probability. **b.** The sum of the probabilities do not sum to one. **c.** The sum of the probabilities cannot be greater than one.

4.3 a. .10 **b.** .25 **c.** .60 **d.** .70

4.5 A and B are mutually exclusive.

4.7 a .2667 **b.** .5867

4.9 a. .541 **b.** .015 **c.** .5 **d.** .949 **e.** 0

4.11 a. .1565 **b.** .8435 **c.** .4445

4.13 b. .61905 **c.** Event 1 and event 2 are mutually exclusive and therefore are not independent.

4.17 b. .1 **c.** .3 **d.** .6667

4.19 a. .8 **b.** .857 **c.** .1 **d.** .333

4.21 a. .5 **b.** .8 **c.** 0 **d.** .5 **e.** 0 **f.** .2857 **g.** .375

4.23 A and B are independent.

4.25 .25

4.27 .5926

4.29 a. .54 **b.** 0.86 **c.** 0.675

4.31 .90

4.33 a. .595 **b.** .585 **c.** .3405

4.35 a.

Contingency Table							
			ATMFee				
Checkret	0	0.5	0.75	1	1.25	1.5	Grand Total
No	3	0	2	3	2	1	11
Yes	3	2	1	5	3	0	14
Grand Total	6	2	3	8	5	1	25

b. .24 **c.** .545

4.37 a. .34 **b.** .25

4.39 E_1 = drug user; B = test is positive; P(B) = .1044; $P(E_1 | B) = .9569$

4.41 .048

4.43 a. .0395 **b.** .405

4.45 a. No **b.** Yes

4.47 a. $P(A) = .5$; $P(B) = .5$; $P(C) = .5$. **b.** P(A and B) = .25; P(A and C) = .25; P(B and C) = .25. **c.** P(A and B and C) = 0. **d.** A and B, A and C, and B and C are pairwise independent. But A, B, and C are not mutually independent.

4.49 .00148

4.51 .1398

4.53 a. 45 **b.** 3,628,800 **c.** 5040

4.55 56

4.57 3003

4.59 $3^5 = 243$

4.61 20,000

4.63 16

4.65 15

4.69 .0222

4.71 0.0222

4.73 a. .12 **b.** .58 **c.** .3 **d.** 0 **e.** 0 **f.** 1 **g.** .012 **h.** .8

4.75 a. 0.091 **b.** 0.125 **c.** 0.273

4.77 a. .143 **b.** .143 **c.** .2857 **d.** 1.0

4.79 a. 0.195 **b.** .755 **c.** 0.354 **d.** No

4.83 a. 0.8 **b.** 0.2

4.85 a. .3164 **b.** .9961 **c.** .3203

4.87 a. .90 **b.** .99 **c.** .729

4.89 a. .40 **b.** .355

4.91 .8712

5

a. P(Circuit board needs to be returned to factory) $= .25$ **b.** P(Circuit board is in good working condition) $3/8 = .375$

5.3 a. 1, 2, 3, 4, 5, 6. **b.** $P(X = 0) = .33$; $P(X = 1) = .1667$; $P(X = 2) = .5$

5.5 12 outcomes, each with probability 1/12.

5.7 a. N = no refund (owes); R = refund; Possible pairs: RR, RN, NR. **b.** $X = 2$ for RR; $X = 1$ for RN; $X = 1$ for NR. **c.** $P(X = 1) = 2/3$; $P(X = 2) = 1/3$.

5.9 a. Valid **b.** Not valid **c.** Valid **d.** Not valid **e.** Not valid

5.11 Yes

5.13 Yes

5.15 c. $P(X = 3) = .456$; $P(X = 2) = .442$; $P(X = 1) = .098$; $P(X = 0) = .004$.

5.17 $P(X = x) = 1/3$ for $x = 2, 4, 6$

5.19 $P(X = 1) = 1/6$; $P(X = 2) = 2/6$; $P(X = 3) = 3/6$.

5.21 a. $\mu = 33.33$; $\sigma = 9.428$. **b.** $\mu = 17.909$; $\sigma = 7.704$.

5.23 $\mu = 3$; $\sigma^2 = 3$.

5.25 a. $\mu = -.01$; $\sigma = .9327$. **b.** $\mu = 1.99$; $\sigma = .9327$.

5.27 a. $\mu = 2.74$; $\sigma = .820$. **b.** $\mu = 1.95$; $\sigma = .7399$.

5.29 a. .177 **b.** .083 **c.** .981 **d.** .334

5.31 .3647

5.33 .506

5.35 a. .382782 **b.** .22057 **c.** mean for part (a) is 3.0, mean for part (b) is 3.7

5.37 a. .001 **b.** 3 **c.** $\sigma = 1.55$ **d.** .982

5.39 .7636

5.41 a. The mean is equal to np = 54(.65) = 35.1 (approximately 35). **b.** Binomdist (35, 54, .65, False) = .1130; Binomdist (35, 54, .65, True) = .5397. The probability of .1130 is the probability for obtaining the value of 35. The probability of .5397 is the probability for obtaining the value of 35 or less.

5.43 a. .1755 **b.** .9596 **c.** .6376

5.45 0.6353

5.47 0.9286

5.49 .33068

5.51 a. .5831 **b.** .0487

5.53 a. .9004 **b.** 2.83

5.55 a. .1992 **b.** 1.732

5.57 Only b is a property of a discrete probability distribution.

5.59 a. X can be equal to 1, 3, 4, 5, or 7. **b.** $P(X = 1) = P(X = 3) = P(X = 5) = P(X = 7) = 1/6$ and $P(X = 4) = 2/6$. **c.** $\mu = 4$ **d.** $\sigma^2 = 3.332$

5.61 This is not a likely occurrence.

5.63 .623

5.65 $\mu = 1.01$; $\sigma = 1.3304$

5.67 $P(X = 2) = 0.3739$

5.69 a. .224 **b.** 1.73

5.71 Consider this expression to be a hypergeometric with $N = 500$, $n = 10$, $k = 200$, and $x = 3$. Since n/N is less than .05, the binomial distribution (using $p = .4$) provides a good approximation.

5.73 .5

5.75 $n = 50$ $p = .53$ for X
      $n = 50$ $p = .34$ for Y

a. $P[X > 25] = .6124$
Now change P to .60
$P[X > 25] = .9022$
b. $P[Y > 25] = .0066$
Now change P to .40
$P[Y > 25] = .0573$

Chapter 6

6.3 a. .4772 **b.** .1102 **c.** .8591

6.5 a. 0.8907 **b.** 0.8907 **c.** 0.8907 **d.** 0.475 **e.** .3344

6.7 a. 1.03 **b.** 1.03 **c.** −1.76 **d.** 2.0 **e.** −2.0

6.9 $P(Z < z) = .5$ implies $z = 0$
$P(Z < z) = .97$ implies $z = 1.88$

6.11 a. .1587 **b.** 0.0228 **c.** .3830

6.13 0.0808

6.15 82.5

6.17 .0574

6.19 a. .86 **b.** .0009

6.21 a. .6563 **b.** 9.62

6.23 a. The refund damage value of $117.51 yields a probability less than .01.

6.25 The values of .0286, .0255, and .0194 for the standard deviation yield probabilities of approximately .08, .05, and .01.

6.27 b. .7019 **c.** .4639

6.29 .9612

6.31 a. .7088 **b.** .0516

6.35 a. $\mu = 62.5$; $\sigma = 4.33$; Probability is .58. **b.** 66.94

6.37 a. 0.524 **b.** 23.15 **c.** 1.819

6.39 .51

6.41 0.2997

6.43 .368

6.45 a. The uniform distribution most closely approximates the distribution of BotErr and TopErr. **b.** The approximate shape of TotalErr is normal.

6.47 a. 200 **b.** 216.8 **c.** 216.8

6.49 .6700

6.51 135.8 and 144.2

6.53 87.12

6.55 Probability is .344; $\sigma = 30$

6.57 58.89%

6.59 0.0668

6.61 .4168

6.63 a. $\mu = 1.0$; $\sigma = .289$. **b.** .3

6.65 50%

6.67 a. .344 **b.** .3707

6.69 $\sigma^2 = 43.03$

6.71 $\sigma = 12.158$

6.73 a. .3935 **b.** .8647

Chapter 7

7.1 a. .8413 **b.** .1359

7.3 a. The Central Limit Theorem tells us that the distribution of the sample mean is approximately normally distributed with a mean of 4 and a standard deviation of $1/\sqrt{50}$. **b.** If the sample size were increased to 100, the approximation of the normal distribution would be much closer for the distribution of $\overline{X}$. The mean would be 4 and the standard deviation would be $1/\sqrt{100}$.

7.5 .0022

7.7 Approximately 1

7.9 a. .9115 **b.** .8729 **c.** .8599

7.11 0.7960

7.13 0.0823

7.15 0.0038

7.17 The plot of sample means should be approximately normally distributed with a mean of 100 and a standard deviation of $20/\sqrt{10}$.

7.19 38.04 to 41.96

7.21 a. 169.183 to 180.817 **b.** 168.069 to 181.931 **c.** 165.891 to 184.109

7.25 a. 72.37 to 77.63 **b.** 73.34 to 76.66 **c.** 74.17 to 75.83

7.27 38.62 to 45.98

7.29 a. 134.67 to 159.98 **b.** 141.00 to 153.65

7.31 a. −1.325 **b.** 1.325 **c.** −1.725

7.33 a. 46.134 to 53.866 **b.** 45.32 to 54.68 **c.** 43.603 to 56.397

7.35 a. 62.24 to 73.76 **b.** 63.21 to 72.79

7.37 302.37 to 317.63

7.39 9.79 to 12.11

7.41 4.12 to 5.53

7.43 a. 68 **b.** 31 **c.** 271

7.45 16

7.47 6.1033

7.49 22

7.51 103

7.53

Confidence Level	Sample Size Required
90%	271
92%	307
94%	354
96%	422
98%	542
99%	664

7.55 Answers will vary due to the random nature of the bootstrap method.

7.57 Answers will vary due to the random nature of the bootstrap method.

7.61 Answers will vary due to the random nature of the bootstrap method.

7.63 Answers will vary due to the random nature of the bootstrap method.

7.65 14.286 to 17.628

7.67 4.47 to 5.61

7.69 2.54 to 4.25

7.71 a. 0.2266 **b.** .0329

7.73 .1994 to .2226

7.79 3.46 to 4.42

7.81 $n = 139$

7.83 9.56 to 10.792

7.85 The Central Limit Theorem says that the shape of the binomial distribution will be approximately that of a normal distribution as the number of trials become large.

Chapter 8

8.1 a. H_0: $\mu = 100$ **b.** H_a: $\mu \neq 100$ **c.** (Reject H_0, H_0 true), (Reject H_0, H_0 false), (Fail to reject H_0, H_0 true), (Fail to reject H_0, H_0 false) **d.** No, the hypothesis test procedure does not prove that the claim is right or wrong.

8.3 a. False **b.** False **c.** True **d.** False

8.5 $Z^* = 4.65$; reject H_0.

8.7 $Z^* = -3.486$; reject H_0.

8.9 Since the 95% confidence interval does not contain 2.0, reject H_0.

8.11 a. 408.615 to 451.385 **b.** $Z^* = -5.38$; reject H_0.

8.13 a. .5912 **b.** 1.0

8.15 On the average, the null hypothesis should be rejected $(.05)(100) = 5$ times.

$_0$: $\mu \geq \mu_0$; H_a: $\mu < \mu_0$. **b.** H_0: $\mu \geq 30$; H_a: $\mu < 30$.

15; H_a: $\mu \neq 15$.

. $Z^* = 2$; reject H_0. **b.** $Z^* = 0$; fail to reject H_0.

$Z^* = 1.67$; reject H_0.

3 .7642

.25 a. $Z^* = 2.34$; reject H_0.

8.27 a. reject H_0 **b.** reject H_0 **c.** fail to reject H_0

8.29 a. .0114 **b.** .0057 **c.** .0614 **d.** .0307

8.31 a. p-value $= .0524$ **b.** fail to reject H_0.

8.33 $Z^* = -1.29$; p-value $= .0985$; fail to reject H_0.

8.35 a. p-value $= .21$; fail to reject H_0.

8.37 a. $t^* = .968$; fail to reject H_0. **b.** $t^* = .968$; fail to reject H_0. **c.** $t^* = -4.6$; reject H_0. **d.** $t^* = -1.4$; fail to reject H_0.

8.39 $t^* = -1.38$; fail to reject H_0.

8.41 $t^* = 2.67$; reject H_0.

8.43 $t^* = 3.0$; $p < .005$; reject H_0.

8.45 a. p-value $= .094$

8.47 a. $\chi^{2*} < 3.94030$ or $\chi^{2*} > 18.3070$. **b.** $\chi^{2*} < 16.7908$ or $\chi^{2*} > 46.98$. **c.** $\chi^{2*} < .989265$ or $\chi^{2*} > 20.2777$. **d.** $\chi^{2*} < 57.1532$ or $\chi^{2*} > 106.629$.

8.49 a. 5.6355 to 24.237 **b.** 2.374 to 4.923 **c.** $\chi^{2*} = 4.4352$; reject H_0.

8.51 a. 1.31 to 2.48 **b.** $\chi^{2*} = 4.5$; reject H_0.

8.53 $\chi^{2*} = 21.39$; p-value $> .10$; fail to reject H_0.

8.57 Only b and d can be acceptable alternative hypotheses.

8.59 a. True **b.** True **c.** False **d.** True

8.61 a. .2274 **b.** .1279 **c.** .9830

8.63 $Z^* = -3.5$; p-value is .0004; reject H_0.

8.65 a. $Z^* = 1.95$; fail to reject H_0. **b.** $t^* = 1.95$; fail to reject H_0.

8.67 a. 14.193 to 14.807 **b.** $Z^* = 3.19$; reject H_0.

8.69 $t^* = -1.068$; fail to reject H_0.

8.71 a. $t^* = 1.72$; fail to reject H_0.

8.73 $\chi^{2*} = 14.37$; fail to reject H_0.

8.75 $\chi^{2*} = 27.22$; fail to reject H_0.

8.77 a. 5.969 to 6.885 **b.** 5.881 to 6.973 **c.** 5.709 to 7.145

8.79 a. Reject H_0.

8.81 If the mean or the standard deviation of the population were changed, the distribution of the chi-square test statistic would still be approximately the same shape.

Chapter 9

9.1 a. Independent samples; **b.** Dependent samples; **c.** Independent samples.

9.3 Dependent samples.

9.5 The sample of men and the sample of women are dependent.

9.7 The samples from the two groups are independent.

9.9 a. 1.752 to 10.248 **b.** $Z^* = -2.3235$; reject H_0.

9.11 $n_1 = 73$; $n_2 = 145$.

9.13 -4.849 to -2.951

9.15 $Z^* = 3.70$; reject H_0.

9.17 $n_1 = n_2 = 49$

9.19 $Z^* = 1.47$; p-value $= .1416$; fail to reject H_0.

9.21 $Z^* = -2.66$; reject H_0.

9.23 b. $Z^* = -1.52$; reject H_0.

9.25 a. $s_p = 1.711$ **b.** -3.132 to $-.868$ **c.** -3.3982 to $-.8018$

9.27 $t'^* = .4595$; fail to reject H_0.

9.29 $t^* = 0.4595$; fail to reject H_0.

9.31 -48.364 to -1.636

9.33 df $= 18$; $t^* = .618$; fail to reject H_0.

9.37 a. $F_{.025,19,14} \doteq F_{.025,20,14} = 2.84$; $F_{.975,19,14} \doteq 1/F_{.025,15,19} = .3816$. **b.** $F_{.90,4,14} \doteq 1/F_{.10,15,4} = .258$. **c.** $F_{.01,18,10} \doteq F_{.01,20,10} = 4.41$.

9.39 a. $F^* = 6.7618$; reject H_0. **b.** $.01 < p$-value $< .025$.

9.41 $F^* = .156$; reject H_0.

9.43 .70 to 3.91

9.45 a. $F^* = 1.37$; fail to reject H_0. **b.** The results in part (a) remain the same when 5 points are subtracted from each grade.

9.47 a. $t^* = 3.02$; reject H_0. **b.** $.005 < p$-value $< .01$

9.49 a. $t^* = 3.505$; reject H_0. **b.** 2.42 ± 1.24

9.51 $t^* = 4.46$; reject H_0.

9.53 a. Fail to reject H_0.

9.55 a. $t^* = -1.89$; fail to reject H_0. **b.** $t^* = -1.89$; fail to reject H_0.

9.57 a. $Z^* = -.197$; p-value $= .8414$. **b.** df $= 44$; $t^* = 1.59$; $.05 < p$-value $< .10$. **c.** $Z^* = 0.063$; p-value $= .4761$.

9.59 $t^* = 3.8443$; reject H_0.

9.61 $t^* = 3.79$; reject H_0.

9.63 a. 2.55 to 6.28 **b.** 1.91 to 4.71

9.65 $F^* = 2.56$; fail to reject H_0.

9.67 $t^* = 3.90$; reject H_0.

9.69 a. Yes, the p-value $= .07939$ is less than .10. **b.** $t^* = 1.159$; fail to reject H_0.

9.71 There is sufficient evidence to conclude that the variance of "with additive" is greater than the variance of "without additive." There is insufficient evidence to conclude that the mean of "with additive" is different from that of "without additive."

Chapter 10

10.1 a. .213 to .734 **b.** .315 to .769 **c.** .318 to .682 **d.** .36 to .64

10.3 a. 370 **b.** 63 **c.** 123

10.5 95% confidence interval is .465 to .903; 90% confidence interval is .502 to .884

10.7 656

10.9 8142

10.11 2019

10.13 a. .288 to .392 **b.** 381

10.15 a. $\hat{p} = .66$, estimated standard error = .0476 **c.** .5667 to .7533 **d.** Confidence interval is the same as in part (c).

10.17 a. $Z^* = -1.212$; p-value = .2262. **b.** $Z^* = -1.212$ from part (a); p-value = .1131. **c.** $Z^* = .90$; p-value = .184; fail to reject H_0.

10.19 The critical value is .502; since .50 < .502, reject H_0.

10.21 n must be greater than or equal to 167.

10.23 a. $Z^* = -2.649$; reject H_0.

10.25 $n = 363$

10.27 p-value = .121

10.29 $Z^* = .20$; fail to reject H_0.

10.31 a. −.1872 to .0372 **b.** $Z^* = -1.15$ **c.** p-value = .2502

10.35 $n_1 = 27$; $n_2 = 30$

10.37 $Z^* = -.91$; p-value = .3628; fail to reject H_0.

10.39 a. $Z^* = .795$; fail to reject H_0. **b.** $\bar{p} = .05$ **c.** $Z^* = .7947$

10.41 a. fail to reject H_0 **b.** .003 to .226

10.43 .213 to .734

10.45 757

10.47 $Z^* = 1.3488$; reject H_0

10.49 a. .23 **b.** 0.13 **c.** 42

10.53 p-value = .3557; fail to reject H_0.

10.55 $Z^* = -.512$: fail to reject H_0.

10.57 a. .0222 to .1278 **b.** $n_1 = 480$; $n_2 = 406$

10.59 a. $n_{men} = n_{women} = 1759$ **b.** $n_{men} = n_{women} = 2136$

10.61 a. $n_1 = 203$; $n_2 = 180$ **b.** $n_1 = 350$; $n_2 = 310$

10.63 We would expect $(.90)(40) = 36$ intervals to contain $p = .5$. In the graph, there are 34 intervals that contain $p = .5$.

Chapter 11

11.1 a. $s_p = 2.655$ **b.** MSE = 7.05 **c.** Yes **d.** $t^* = -2.382$; $F^* = 5.67$ **e.** Yes

f.

ANOVA

Source	df	SS	MS	F
Factor	1	40	40	5.67
Error	8	56.4	7.05	
Total	9	96.4		

g. −7.872 to −.128

11.3 a.

ANOVA

Source	df	SS	MS	F
Factor	3	252.908	84.30	22.48
Error	15	56.25	3.75	
Total	18	309.158		

b. reject H_0 **c.** 9.81 to 13.19; 18.15 to 21.85 **d.** −11.00 to −6.00 **e.** $H^* = 2.83$; fail to reject H_0 **f.** No

11.5 a.

ANOVA

Source	df	SS	MS	F
Factor	2	54.1111	27.0556	12.82
Error	15	31.6667	2.1111	
Total	17	85.7778		

b. p-value < .01 **e.** $D = 2.18$; conclude that $\mu_1 \neq \mu_3$ and $\mu_2 \neq \mu_3$.

11.7 a.

ANOVA

Source	df	SS	MS	F
Factor	2	74026.1	37013.05	8.7670
Error	21	88659.2	4221.8667	
Total	23	162685.3		

b. p-value < .01 **c.** $D = 82.2414$; conclude that $\mu_J \neq \mu_R$ and $\mu_J \neq \mu_T$.

11.9

ANOVA

Source	df	SS	MS	F
Factor	2	11.6667	5.8335	1.232
Error	27	127.8	4.7333	
Total	29	139.4667		

Fail to reject H_0.

11.11 a. $D = .275$; Active exporters are different from the other two groups at the .05 significance level. **b.** $D = .343$; Active exporters and nonexporters are different.

11.13 a.

ANOVA

Source	df	SS	MS	F
Factor	2	12	6	.715
Error	72	604	8.39	
Total	74	616		

Fail to reject H_0 **b.** No

11.15 $H^* = 4.5913$; reject H_0.

11.17 a. Closing techniques 2 and 3 appear to be significantly different. **b.** Yes, p-value is .0029. **c.** Techniques 2 and 3 differ. **e.** The ANOVA table remains the same. **f.** The sums of squares are multiplied by 100 but the value of the F statistic remains the same.

11.19 a. Completely randomized design, randomized block design, and two-way factorial design. **b.** Randomized block design. **d.** One dependent variable. **e.** 4 treatments are being considered. 24 observations are made. **f.** 24 treatments are being considered. The minimum number of total observations is 48.

11.21 b. A randomized block design can be used by letting operators be blocks and the three different machines be the levels of the factor.

11.23 a.

ANOVA

Source	df	SS	MS	F
Factor	7	70	10	4.63
Blocks	3	52.8	17.6	
Error	21	45.4	2.16	
Total	31	168.2		

The p-value $< .01$; reject H_0.

11.25 a.

ANOVA

Source	df	SS	MS	F
Factor	3	499.5	166.5	57.63
Blocks	3	183.5	61.167	21.17
Error	9	26	2.889	
Total	15	709		

b. Reject H_0 **c.** Reject H_0 **c.** $D = 3.7479$; Factor levels 3 and 4 are the only factor levels that are not significantly different.

11.27 a.

ANOVA

Source	df	SS	MS	F
Factor	2	20.333	10.167	17.931
Blocks	5	112.5	22.5	39.682
Error	10	5.667	0.567	
Total	17	138.5		

b. Reject H_0 **d.** There is a significant block effect at $\alpha = .01$.

11.31

ANOVA

Source	df	SS	MS	F
Factor	3	130	43.333	4.7273
Blocks	4	280	70	
Error	12	110	9.1667	
Total	19	520		

11.33 b.

ANOVA

Source	df	SS	MS	F
Factor	2	25.87	12.93	4.97
Blocks	9	50.80	5.64	2.17
Error	18	46.80	2.60	
Total	29	123.47		

Reject H_0 **c.** Baltimore Sun and St. Louis Post-Dispatch differ.

11.35 a.

ANOVA

Source	df	SS	MS	F
Factor	2	53,130.583	26,565.29	1.93
Blocks	7	2,745,448.000	392,206.86	28.54
Error	14	192,380.75	13,741.48	
Total	23	2,990,959.333		

Fail to reject H_0. **b.** There is a significant block effect. **c.** -218.22 to -11.78

11.37 a. $F^* = .85$; fail to reject H_0. **b.** $F^* = 2.71$; reject H_0. **c.** No

11.39 a.

ANOVA

Source	df	SS	MS	F
Keyboard Type (A)	2	242.67	121.335	68.242
Software Type (B)	2	8.22	4.11	2.312
Interaction	4	11.11	2.778	1.562
Error	18	32	1.778	
Total	26	294		

11.41

ANOVA

Source	df	SS	MS	F
CV	1	11718.06	11718.06	6.91
DT	1	19010.02	19010.02	11.22
CV×DT	1	632.52	632.52	.37
Error	396	671215.97	1694.99	
Total	399	702576.57		

Conclusion for testing CV and DT: Reject H_0
Conclusion for testing CV×DT: Fail to reject H_0

11.43 a.

ANOVA

Source	df	SS	MS	F
Exp Level	1	40.64	40.64	14.51
Speed Level	3	40.17	13.39	4.78
Interaction	3	11.67	3.89	1.39
Error	56	156.88	2.80	
Total	63	249.36		

Conclusion for Exp Level and Speed Level: Reject H_0
Conclusion for Interaction: Fail to reject H_0
b. (Experience Level 1, Speed C) differs from (Experience Level 2, Speed A), (Experience Level 2, Speed B), (Experience Level 1, Speed A), and (Experience Level 2, Speed C). (Experience Level 1, Speed D) differs from (Experience Level 2, Speed A) and (Experience Level 2, Speed B). **c.** The conclusions are the same for part (a). (Experience Level 2, Speed A) differs from (Experience Level 1, Speed C) for part (b).

11.45 a.

ANOVA

Source	df	SS	MS	F
Factor	5	.688	.1376	2.31
Error	18	1.070	.0594	
Total	23	1.758		

Fail to reject H_0. **b.** $H^* = 3.25$; fail to reject H_0.

11.47 a.

ANOVA

Source	df	SS	MS	F
Factor	2	1591	795	4.55
Error	12	2098	175	
Total	14	3689		

b. $.025 < p$-value $< .05$ **c.** 37.6 ± 12.89 **d.** 11.6 ± 25.35
e. $D = 22.30$; $\bar{x}_3 - \bar{x}_1 = 25.2 > D$.

11.49 a.

ANOVA

Source	df	SS	MS	F
Manager Level	2	780.8	390.4	5.93
Sex	1	122.7	122.7	1.86
Interaction	2	84.8	42.4	.64
Error	12	790.0	65.8	
Total	17	1778.3		

11.51

ANOVA

Source	df	SS	MS	F
Factor	3	217.9	72.63	705.1
Error	36	3.7	.103	
Total	39	221.6		

$F^* = 705.1$, p-value $< .01$, there is a difference in the four population means.

11.53

ANOVA

Source	df	SS	MS	F
Factor	2	1.9233	.9617	14.68
Blocks	7	25.5383	3.6483	55.706
Error	14	.9167	.0655	
Total	23	28.3783		

The process is significant. Blocks are significant.

11.55

ANOVA

Source	df	SS	MS	F
Factor A	1	3088	3088	6.58
Factor B	3	3400	1133.3	2.41
Interaction	3	49000	16333.3	34.79
Error	16	7512	469.5	
Total	23	63000		

11.57 $H = 2.67$; fail to reject H_0.

11.59 a. 9 **b.** 15 **c.** Increase the sample size.

11.61 a.

ANOVA

Source	df	SS	MS	F
Type	1	88.20	88.20	.43
Cost	1	88.20	88.20	.43
Interaction	1	135.20	135.20	.66
Error	16	3269.60	204.35	
Total	19	3581.20		

Fail to reject H_0 for all tests. **b.** No **c.** The value of the F statistics do not change.

11.65 a. Because the lines are not parallel there appears to be an interaction effect.

b.

ANOVA

Source	df	SS	MS	F
Experience	3	614.79	204.93	29.45
Help System	2	2.33	1.17	.17
Interaction	6	136.33	22.72	3.27
Error	12	83.50	6.96	
Total	23	836.96		

Test for interaction: Reject H_0.

CHAPTER 12

12.3 a. quality characteristic **b.** control chart **c.** process

12.7 Forty eight percent are from categories 6 and 7.

12.21 $\bar{X}$ Chart: UCL = 449.49; CL = 427.05; LCL = 404.61. R Chart: UCL = 82.23; CL = 38.90; LCL = 0.

12.23 a. UCL = 2.45; CL = 1.32; LCL = 0.18.

12.25 a. UCL = .0219; CL = .01175; LCL = .0016. **b.** Observations appear to decrease and then increase.

12.27 For Northern: UCL = 1454.2; CL = 848.47; LCL = 242.7. For Southern: UCL = 1551.123; CL = 757.633; LCL = −35.857.

12.29 For $\bar{X}$ chart: UCL = 24.84; CL = 19.71; LCL = 14.58. For R chart: UCL = 16.07; CL = 7.04; LCL = 0.

12.31 For $\bar{X}$ chart: UCL = 10.86; CL = 10.01; LCL = 9.16. For R chart: UCL = 2.14; CL = .83; LCL = 0.

12.35 UCL = .115; CL = .05; LCL = 0.

12.37 a. $\bar{p}$ = .307; UCL = .58; CL = .307; LCL = .03. **b.** No

12.39 a. c chart **b.** UCL = 13.24; CL = 5.93; LCL = 0. **c.** No, since the value for sample #11 exceeds the UCL.

12.41 For the c chart: UCL = 11.29; CL = 4.75; LCL = 0.

12.43 a. For the c chart; UCL = 13.578; CL = 6.143; LCL = 0. **b.** No, since two plotted values exceed the UCL.

12.47 Process A: $C_p = 0.78$ (inadequate); Process B: $C_p = 1.13$ (adequate); Process C: $C_p = 2.16$ (good); Process D: $C_p = 1.11$ (adequate).

12.51 a. $s' = 7.28$; $C_{pm} = 0.97$. **b.** $s' = 6.20$; $C_{pm} = 1.14$. **c.** C_{pm} converges to C_p.

12.53 a. Process A **b.** For process A, $C_{pk} = 1.08$; for process B, $C_{pk} = 1.22$. **c.** Process B, since it is more capable.

12.55 $C_{pk} = .55$; The C_{pk} index indicates that the process cannot adequately meet the process specifications since its value is less than 1.

12.63 Use C_p when the process is centered midway between the spec limits and use C_{pk} when the process is centered nearer one of the spec limits.

12.65 a. UCL = 98.50; CL = 60.55; LCL = 22.60. **b.** Patterns 1, 3, and 8 are present.

12.67 a. Scatter diagram **b.** Flowchart **c.** Control chart **d.** Pareto chart **e.** Cause-and-effect diagram

12.69 a. p chart **b.** UCL = 0.044; CL = 0.021; LCL = 0. **c.** In control.

12.71 a. c chart **b.** UCL = 6.14; CL = 1.95; LCL = 0. **c.** In control.

12.73 a. The $\bar{X}$ chart contains patterns 2, 5, and 6. **b.** The R chart gives out-of-control signals.

CHAPTER 13

13.1 $\chi^{2*} = .413$; fail to reject H_0.

13.3 $\chi^{2*} = 2.92385$; fail to reject H_0.

13.5 $\chi^{2*} = .8125$; fail to reject H_0.

13.7 $\chi^{2*} = 11.1225$; reject H_0.

13.9 $\chi^2_{.10,3} = 6.25139$; fail to reject H_0.

13.11 $\chi^{2*} = .4184$; fail to reject H_0.

13.13 $\chi^{2*} = 2.24$; fail to reject H_0.

13.15 d. $\chi^{2*} = 128.45$ (pool $X = 0,1$ and $X \geq 6$); reject H_0. **e.** $\chi^{2*} = 2.57$ (pool $X \geq 4$); fail to reject H_0.

13.17 $\chi^{2*} = 15.3383$; reject H_0.

13.19 b. No cells should be pooled. **c.** $\chi^{2*} = 1.418$. **d.** Fail to reject H_0.

13.21 a. $\chi^{2*} = 6.004$; fail to reject H_0. **b.** p-value > .10.

13.23 $\chi^{2*} = 12.087$; reject H_0.

13.25 a. $\chi^{2*} = 71.154$; reject H_0. **b.** $\chi^{2*} = .076$; fail to reject H_0.

13.27 $\chi^{2*} = 7.692$; fail to reject H_0.

13.29 a. $\chi^{2*} = 5.7733$; fail to reject H_0. **b.** Expected frequencies should be greater than or equal to 5.

13.31 $\chi^{2*} = .351$; fail to reject H_0.

13.33 $\chi^{2*} = 2.0749$; fail to reject H_0.

13.35 $\chi^{2*} = 4.6969$; fail to reject H_0.

13.37 a. $\chi^{2*} = 15.3203$; fail to reject H_0. p-value is slightly greater than .05.

13.39 $\chi^{2*} = 7.5$; reject H_0. **b.** $.005 < p$-value $< .01$.

13.41 $\chi^{2*} = 15.9$; reject H_0.

13.43 $\chi^{2*} = 52.2906$; reject H_0.

13.45 a. $\bar{x} = 28.35$; $s = 19.96$. **b.** $\chi^{2*} = 36.8822$; reject H_0. **c.** p-value $< .005$ **d.** Conclusion does not change if the significance level is .05 or .01.

13.47 $\chi^{2*} = 2.9915$; fail to reject H_0. **b.** p-value $> .10$.

13.49 $\chi^{2*} = .220$; fail to reject H_0.

13.51 b. $\chi^{2*} = 10.88$; reject H_0. **c.** $\chi^{2*} = .586$; fail to reject H_0.

Chapter 14

14.1 a. $\sum x = 24$; $\sum y = 53$; $\sum xy = 333$; $\sum x^2 = 154$; $\sum y^2 = 729$. **b.** $b_1 = 2.0258$; $b_0 = 0.876$. **c.** $r = 0.9759$.

14.3 b. $\hat{Y} = 544.008 + 3.08402X$

14.7 b. $\hat{Y} = 11.278 + .0803X$ **c.** $r = .688$

14.9 a. $b_1 = -.000775$; $b_0 = 39.065$. **b.** $SSE = 63.33$

14.11 a. .935 **c.** The correlation does not change.

14.13 a. $s = 1.4376$ **b.** 16 residuals (80%) fall within $2s$ of the mean of the residuals.

14.15 a. $\hat{Y} = -3.8889 + 5.8199X$ **b.** slope is 5.8199; intercept is -3.8889. **c.** $s^2 = 25.906$

14.17 $s = 2.6624$; all the sample residuals are within two standard deviations of the mean.

14.19 Residuals are 3312.47, 2419.06, -347.29, -1202.35, -2454.43, -670.65, and -1056.82.

14.21 a. $\hat{Y} = .7195 + .75097X$ **b.** Yes, although there is a slight left skew.

14.23 a. $t^* = 1.847$; fail to reject H_0. **b.** -1.646 to 7.646

14.25 $t^* = 27.1601$; reject H_0.

14.27 a. $t^* = 3.94$; reject H_0.

14.29 a. .117 to .297 **b.** Reject H_0

14.31 a. r^2 with Experience is .12. r^2 with TimeToSell is .66. **b.** For TimeToSell, regression model is $\hat{Y} = 265.16 + 99.27X$; $t^* = 11.9$, yes. **c.** $t^* = 11.9$, reject H_0

14.33 a. $H_0: \rho = 0$; $H_a: \rho \neq 0$ **b.** $r = -.989$ **c.** $r^2 = .978$ **d.** $t^* = -16.07$, reject H_0.

14.35 $r^2 = .97$, $t^* = 17.45$, reject H_0.

14.37 b. $t^* = -.4450$; fail to reject H_0.

14.39 $t^* = -10.88$; reject H_0.

14.41 a. .95, $t^* = 20.73$, reject H_0 **b.** $t^* = 20.73$, reject H_0 **c.** .95

14.43 a. $b_1 = 2.976$; $b_0 = -.3571$. **b.** 16.185 to 18.815 **c.** 13.555 to 21.445 **e.** Observation 8 can be considered influential.

14.45 13213 to 18716

14.47 25.45 to 36.61; Observation 4 is an outlier and an influential observation.

14.49 20782.6 to 30739.7

14.51 7.2059 to 8.4543; $s_{\hat{y}} = 0.2169$.

14.53 No. The value of $X = 15$ is probably not in the range of incomes for executives in Chicago.

14.55 a. $\hat{Y} = -1.58 + .035X$ **b.** The largest Cook's D is .25. **c.** There are no patterns, but there are three large standardized residuals and one large leverage value.

14.57 b. Observation 15 is the most influential with a Cook's D of .32. **c.** With observation 15, the r^2 is .964. Omitting observation 15, the r^2 is .975.

14.59 a. $\hat{Y} = -3.29 + 1.15X$ **b.** .934 **c.** .96 to 1.35

14.63 a. $\hat{Y} = 35.606 - .368X$ **b.** $s^2 = 90.878$

14.65 b. $b_1 = 1.1674$; $b_0 = -0.8711$; $t^* = 10.2493$; reject H_0 (i.e., a significant positive relationship exists). **c.** 0.8396 to 1.4952 **d.** $r^2 = 0.8536$ **e.** 4.032 to 10.569

14.67 a. $t^* = 19.0454$; reject H_0. **b.** 2.028 to 2.455

14.69 b. .27 **c.** $t^* = .89$, fail to reject H_0 **f.** Observation 12 would be the most influential observation with a Cook's D of .348 and a standardized residual of 2.35.

14.71 a. Total and Campbell, Total and Pet, Total and Private, and Campbell and Pet. **b.** Since the null hypothesis that the correlation between Campbell and Private is zero cannot be rejected, Campbell would not be a good predictor of Private. **c.** Campbell **d.** .7499 to 1.1201

14.73 b. The 17th observation has a Cook's D of .36. **c.** With the 17th observation, r^2 is .836. Without the 17th observation, the r^2 is .953.

Chapter 15

15.1 a. 16 **b.** 2.8

15.3 $\hat{\sigma}_e = 3.4565$

15.5 a. $\hat{Y} = 0.0090 + 1.1102X_1 + 0.13855X_2$ **b.** $SSE = 4.7289$

15.7 a. $\hat{Y} = -184.34 + .946X_1$, $s = 113.29$ **b.** $\hat{Y} = 24.32 + .493X_1 + .480X_2$, $s = 92.59$

15.9 a. $F^* = 116.25$; reject H_0. **b.** $t^* = 9.615$; reject H_0. **c.** $t^* = 19.05$; reject H_0.

15.11 a. $t^* = 3.1509$; reject H_0. **b.** $t^* = -2.205$; reject H_0.

15.13 b. 175.7

15.15

	ANOVA TABLE			
Source	df	SS	MS	F
Regression	2	1165.66	582.83	30.17
Residual	7	135.24	19.32	
Total	9	1300.90		

15.17 $F^* = 1.9994$; fail to reject H_0.

15.19 a. $F^* = 182.5$, reject H_0; $t^* = 15.25$, reject H_0 for MinutesTalked; $t^* = 15.87$, reject H_0 for MonthlyCharge

15.21 $R^2 = .896$; $R^2(\text{adj}) = .844$.

15.23 $F^* = 14.056$; reject H_0.

15.25 $F^* = 2.718$; fail to reject H_0.

15.27 For PP, $t^* = -2.16$ and for QI, $t^* = -1.414$. Since $t_{.025,241} \doteq 1.96$, PP contributes to the prediction of TT. SSR = 35.769, SSE = 206.9, $F^* = 20.83$. Since $F_{.05,2,241} \doteq 3.00$; reject H_0.

15.29 **a.** $\hat{Y} = 58.02 + 3.79X_1$, $R^2 = .0997$. **b.** $\hat{Y} = -11.62 + 4.60X_1 + 9.14X_2 + 2.53X_3$; $R^2 = .982$; partial $F = 514.7$; reject H_0.

15.31 X_1 and X_2 are highly correlated. X_4 and X_5 are highly correlated.

15.33 **a.** Yes, the overall F statistic is significant, but the individual t statistics yield a conclusion of fail to reject H_0. **b.** VIF = $1/(1 - (.9908)^2) = 54.6$. **c.** No.

15.35 **b.** R^2 using $X_1 = .951$; R^2 using $X_2 = .993$.

15.37 $F^* = 34.51$, reject H_0. **b.** No **c.** 17.7

15.39 **a.** 36 **b.** 39 **c.** 32 **d.** $F^* = 4$; reject H_0.

15.43 **a.** X_3 **b.** X_3

15.47 Assumption of equal variances for the error terms appears to have been violated.

15.49 **a.** 8.984 to 20.816 **b.** 4.895 to 24.905

15.53 **a.** $t^* = 14.8$ and $t^* = 8.5$ for AdRev and SubscriberRev, respectively. Reject H_0. **b.** 237.47 to 405.93 **c.** Observation 1 is influential. $R^2 = .977$ with observation 1 and $R^2 = .998$ without observation 1.

15.55 **a.** $\hat{Y} = 18.1 - 5X_1$ **b.** $\hat{Y} = 10.1 + 5X_1$ **c.** No, the prediction lines are not parallel.

15.57 p-value for interaction term is .0130, reject H_0. Without the interaction term, $R^2 = .9688$. With the interaction term, $R^2 = .9837$. Partial $F = 9.10$.

15.59 Since $F^* = 37.5$ and $F_{.05,3,9} = 3.86$; reject H_0.

15.61 **a.** $\hat{Y} = -1.0 + 4.8X_1 + 5.9X_2$

b.

ANOVA TABLE

Source	df	SS	MS	F
Model	2	295.3	147.65	128.4
Residual	17	19.5	1.15	
Total	19	314.8		

$R^2 = .938$ **c.** $F^* = 128.4$; reject H_0. **d.** $t^* = 9.375$; reject H_0. **e.** $t^* = 14.05$; reject H_0.

15.63 $F^* = 9.34$. Since $F_{.10,1,105} \doteq 2.75$, reject H_0. For the next variable, $F^* = 14.31$. Since $F_{.10,1,104} = 2.75$, reject H_0. For adding the last variable, $F^* = 2.31$. Since $F_{.10,1,103} = 2.75$, fail to reject H_0.

15.65 **a.** $\hat{Y} = 17357 - 1132X_1 - 33.2X_2 - 2556X_3 - 3275X_4 + 776X_5$

b.

ANOVA TABLE

Source	df	SS	MS	F
Regression	5	516005120	103201024	43.29
Error	25	59597456	2383898	
Total	30	575602432		

c. 5192 to 8437 **e.** A forward regression procedure would select the following model at the .10 significance level: $\hat{Y} = 14510 - 1581X_1 + 2841X_5$. **f.** Observation 29 appears to be an outlier since the standardized residual is equal to 3.255.

15.67 **a.** $\hat{Y} = 15.24 + 4.8676X_1 - 5.802X_2 - 2.248X_3$ **b.** $R_c^2 = .987$ **c.** $F^* = 18.1538$; reject H_0. **d.** $t^* = 22.778$; reject H_0. The outliers or influential observations are: Observation 1 (Cook's D = 1.65); Observation 7 (standardized residual = 2.269).

15.69 **a.** With first order terms, $R^2 = .690$. With interaction and square terms, $R^2 = .771$. Partial $F^* = 8.0$. Since $F_{.05,2,45} \doteq 3.23$, reject H_0. **b.** No, BothWork is a dummy variable.

15.71 **a.** $\hat{Y} = -34.91 + 15.628X_1 - 1.6553X_2$ **b.** $R^2 = .745$; $R^2(adj) = .672$. **c.** -7.96 to 1.42

15.73 **a.** The last observation which has a Cook's D of .52. **b.** Using all 40 observations, the R^2 increases from .903 to .960.

15.75 **a.** StickerPrice and OwnPickUp3 contribute to the prediction of MonthlyPay. **b.** Observation 6 is influential. **c.** R^2 decreases from .887 to .829 and all three predictors are significant.

Chapter 16

16.1 The amplitude of the seasonal effects becomes more dramatic after a long period of time.

16.5 **a.** Cyclical variation **b.** Seasonal variation **c.** Trend **d.** Irregular activity

16.7 **b.** $b_0 = -5.33$; $b_1 = 56.286$ **c.** 388.667

16.11 $\hat{y}_t = -24.418 + 6.2429t$

16.13 $b_0 = 10.60$, $b_1 = 1.384$, $\hat{y}_{18} = 35.505$

16.15 **b.** $\hat{y}_t = 92.998 + 1.567t - .153t^2$

16.19 **c.** Approximately 4 years.

16.21 **a.** $b_0 = 6.360$, $b_1 = .117$ **c.** The cycle appears to be longer than 5 years.

16.23 **a.** Cyclical components: .976, 1.01, 1.02, .996, .97, 1.02, 1.05, .99, .96, 1.01 **b.** The length of the cycle is slightly more than 3 years.

16.25 **a.** Cyclical components: .96, .99, 1.06, 1.01, .94, 1.01, 1.09, .98, .92, .99, 1.12, .99, .90, 1.01, 1.13, .99, .93 **b.** The length of the cycles are 3 years, 5 years, and 3 years.

16.27 At times 1, 2, 3, and 4, $\hat{y}_t$ is 37.5, 36, 26.5, and 35.

16.29 1st quarter: 65.4; 2nd quarter: 78.9; 3rd quarter: 87.1; 4th quarter: 84.1.

16.31 For times 37 through 48, predicted data values are: 9.9, 16.24, 12.48, 27.69, 23.98, 31.22, 54.72, 72.23, 7.14, 4.86, 4.96, 2.53.

16.33 Deseasonalized figures are 3.27, 3.25, 3.52, 3.56, 3.65, 3.57, 3.62, 3.66, 3.65, 3.57, 3.52, 3.56, 3.55, 3.78, 3.72, 3.75.

16.35 Centered moving averages are 18.5, 20.875, 22.875, 24.50. Ratio to moving average: 1.24, 1.44, .87, .61.

16.39 Seasonal indexes are .8710, .8256, .8458, .9291, 1.0276, 1.0503, 1.0730, 1.1614, 1.1411, 1.0629, 1.0452, .9670.

16.41 Seasonal indexes are 1.0913, 1.2155, .8573, .8358.

16.43 Seasonal indexes are .889, 1.081, 1.009, .965, 1.053, 1.001, .945, 1.077, 1.043, 1.000, .976, .961.

16.45 $I_t = 1.0185$

16.47 3 month moving average C_t for 1998: .9852, .9771, .9649, .9716.

16.49 Trend line through the deseasonalized data is TR(t) = 458.655 + 6.853t, TR(49) = 794.45

16.53 a. Index numbers are: 100, 116.67, 141.67, 183.33, 208.33. **b.** Index numbers are: 85.71, 100.00, 121.43, 157.14, 178.57

16.55 a. 120.6 **b.** 119.0 **c.** 118.7

16.57 a. 135.6 **b.** 136.11 **c.** 135.9

16.61 a. Laspeyres index for 1989, 115.68; for 1990, 95.4. **b.** Paasche index for 1989, 115.58; for 1990, 95.13.

16.63 a. Trend **b.** Irregular **c.** Seasonal **d.** Irregular

16.65 a. $\hat{y}_t = 32.697 + .213t$ for $t = 1, 2, 3, \ldots$ **b.** $\hat{y}_{14} = 32.697 + .213(14) = 35.68$.

16.67 a. $\hat{y}_t = 41.258 - .303t$

16.69 Use a quadratic trend to fit the data, TR(t) = 22.27 − 2.58t + .19t^2.

16.71 a. Seasonal indexes are 1.20, 1.15, 1.07, .92, .91, .95, .96, .96, .92, .93, .99, 1.05. **b.** $\hat{d}_t = 151.806 + 1.094t$ **c.** Cyclical components are 1.02, 1.01, 1.00, .99, .97, .98, .98, .99, .98, 1.00, 1.00, 1.01. **d.** June, irregular = 1.00; July, irregular = 1.00.

16.73 a. Seasonal indexes are .99, 1.02, 1.00, .98. **b.** $\hat{d}_t = 144.7426 + .8401t$. **c.** C_t: .9719, .9444, .9435, .9426. **d.** 0.9909; 1.0050.

16.75 Seasonal indexes are 1.10, 1.03, .99, .95, .94, .87, .89, .95, .98, 1.03, 1.10, 1.18.

16.77 a. Seasonal indexes are .997, .996, .992, .988, .998, 1.003, 1.011, 1.010, 1.005, 1.003, 1.000, .998 **b.** Cyclical components for 1998: 1.014, 1.013, 1.010, 1.005, 1.000, .998, .995, .994, .993, .994, .994. Irregular components for 1998: 1.000, 1.001, 1.001, 1.000, .999, 1.000, 1.002, .998, 1.000, 1.000, 1.001.

Chapter 17

17.3 For time periods 2 through 10, residuals are .9, .1, 1.5, −2.9, 5.0, −.6, −.1, −.1, 8.9. Time periods predicted poorly: 5, 6, 10

17.9 $\hat{y}_t = 44.113 + .723t$ **b.** Forecasts for the first three months of 1999: 55.688, 48.166, 89.101

17.11 $S_t(A = .1)$: 2, 2.1, 2.09, 2.381, 2.9429, 3.3486, 3.5137, 3.9623, 4.5661, 5.0095, 5.3085, 5.7777, 5.8999, 6.2099, 6.2890; $S_t(A = .3)$: 2, 2.3, 2.21, 3.047, 4.5329, 5.2730, 5.1911, 6.0338, 7.2236, 7.7566, 7.8296, 8.4807, 8.0365, 8.3255, 7.9278.

17.13 Forecast for Feb, Mar, and Apr of 1997 are 52.11, 52.39 and 52.85, respectively.

17.15 The forecasted values for 1998 and 1999 are 140.7 and 142.5, respectively.

17.17 a. The forecast for 1999 is $S_{11} + B_{11} = 134.866 + 9.644 = 144.51$.

17.19 Using all of the data, the forecast for the year 2000 is 81053. Using the data from 1989 to 1999, the forecast for the year 2000 is 81186.

17.21 a. 17.536 **b.** 17.444

17.23 Initial seasonal factors are .95, .83, 1.07, and 1.16. Least squares line is .2287 + .0109t. Forecasts for each quarter are .404, .361, .491, .538.

17.25 Forecast for the first quarter of 2000 is 313.37.

17.27 a. MAPE = .1335; MSE = 21.4. **b.** MAD = 2.125; MAPE = .1127; MSE = 6.12.

17.29 Procedure 1: MAD = 3.556; MSE = 16.556. Procedure 2: MAD = 3.333; MSE = 44.556.

17.31 a. MSE = 2,295,837 **b.** MSE = 2,713,905

17.33 MAPE = 4.894; Forecasts for the four quarters of the year 2000 are 417.134, 406.891, 462.702, and 462.320.

17.35 Predictive MSE = 7.712

17.37 a. $r_1 = 0.693$; $r_2 = 0.108$; $r_3 = -0.355$; $r_4 = -0.428$. **b.** One possible model is $\hat{y}_t = b_0 + b_1 y_{t-1} = 11.542 + 0.7105 y_{t-1}$

17.39 $r_1 = .504$; $r_2 = .024$; $r_3 = .299$; $r_4 = .489$; $r_5 = .061$; $r_6 = -.275$; $r_7 = -.070$; $r_8 = .093$; $r_9 = -.176$; $r_{10} = -.407$; $r_{11} = -.256$; $r_{12} = -.129$. The data do not appear to be stationary.

17.41 The series of second differences appears to be stationary with two period seasonal spikes.

17.43 Predictive MSE's for 1st order and 2nd order autoregressive models are 2.698 and 2.653, respectively.

17.45 $\hat{y}_t = 4.34 - .0116Q_1 - .5268Q_2 - .242Q_3 + .0295t$; $R^2 = .43$

17.47 $\hat{y}_t = .275 + .013t - .0735Q_1 - .1215Q_2 - .027Q_3$; $R^2 = .954$

17.49 $\hat{y}_t = 3.96 + 1.04t$; predictive MSE = 7.30; $\hat{y}_t = 5.122 + .996t - 3.562Q_1 - 2.341Q_2 + 3.379Q_3$; predictive MSE = .386

17.51 a. $\hat{y}_t = 108.52 + .0031X_t$ **b.** $\hat{y}_t = 74.454 + 0.252X_{t-1}$ **c.** R^2 for part (a) is 0.0 (approx.); R^2 for part (b) is .957.

17.53 $\hat{y}_t = 18.45 + 3.256t - .03125Q_1 + .0125Q_2 + 3.99Q_3$; predictive MSE = 13.197

17.55 $R^2 = .0069$ when SalesMonthly is regressed on AdvExpend. $R^2 = .100$ when SalesMonthly is regressed on AdvExpendLag.

17.57 DW = 0 implies severe positive autocorrelation. DW = 2 implies no autocorrelation is present. DW = 4 implies severe negative autocorrelation.

17.59 DW = 2.66; fail to reject H_0.

17.61 DW = 0.56; This low value of DW indicates possible positive autocorrelation.

17.63 $\hat{y}_{37} = 19.25$; $\hat{y}_{38} = 22.35$; $\hat{y}_{39} = 25.56$; $\hat{y}_{40} = 27.25$; $\hat{y}_{41} = 25.34$

17.65 a. 2313.35 **b.** 1135.78

17.67 MSE = .32

17.69 Let $Q_1 = 1$ for quarter 1, $Q_2 = 1$ for quarter 2, $Q_3 = 1$ for quarter 3. The regression equation is $\hat{y}_t = 39.275 - 16.019Q_1 - 9.613Q_2 - 4.406Q_3 + 0.79375t$

17.71 8.56

17.75 $\hat{y}_t = 28.367 + .437y_{t-1} + .147y_{t-2} + .368y_{t-3}$, predictive MSE = 31.254

17.77 a. NetProfLag4 is useful in explaining quarterly net profit. **b.** Predictive MSE = 6.508.

Chapter 18

18.1 Under state S_1, action A_1 is the best. Under state S_2, action A_1 or A_2 is the best. Under state S_3, action A_2 or A_3 is the best. Under state S_4, action A_3 is the best.

18.3

Action	States of Nature								
	5	6	7	8	9	10	11	12	13
7	−20	5	30	30	30	30	30	30	30
8	−30	−5	20	45	45	45	45	45	45
9	−40	−15	10	35	60	60	60	60	60
10	−50	−25	0	25	50	75	75	75	75
11	−60	−35	−10	15	40	65	90	90	90
12	−70	−45	−20	5	30	55	80	105	105
13	−80	−55	−30	−5	20	45	70	95	120

18.5

Action	States of Nature		
	$S_1(100)$	$S_2(125)$	$S_3(150)$
A_1	90	90	90
A_2	62.5	112.5	112.5
A_3	35	85	135

18.7 a. No, because under S_2 there is no 0. **b.** No, because there is a negative value in the table.

18.9 The minimax decision is A_2. The maximax decision is A_3.

18.11 Expected payoffs for A_1, A_2, and A_3 are 11.2, 34.0, 40.0. Expected risks for A_1, A_2, and A_3 are 220.16, 464.00, 1120.00.

18.13

Action	States of Nature		
	S_1	S_2	S_3
A_1	150	60	10
A_2	100	20	0
A_3	50	0	35
A_4	0	40	160

a. The minimax decision is A_3. **b.** The decision is A_3 based on the maximum expected payoff. **c.** Risk $(A_1) = 0$; Risk $(A_2) = 169$; Risk $(A_3) = 1642.1875$; Risk $(A_4) = 9850$.

18.15 The maximum expected payoff is A_3.

18.17 EVPI = 145

18.19 Payoff Table:

Action	States of Nature		
	1500	2000	2500
1500	750	750	750
2000	600	1000	1000
2500	450	850	1250

$110 is the maximum amount that the manager would be willing to pay for perfect information.

18.21 The maximum expected payoff decision is given by A_3; EVPI = 9,150.

18.23 EVPI = 22.75; A_1 is inadmissible.

18.25 a. A_2 is the decision based on the maximum expected payoff. **b.** A_2 is the decision based on the maximum expected utility.

18.27 The decision is A_2 or A_3 based on the maximum expected utility of the payoff.

18.29 a. The decision is A_2 based on the maximum expected utility of the payoff. **b.** The manager is a risk avoider.

18.31

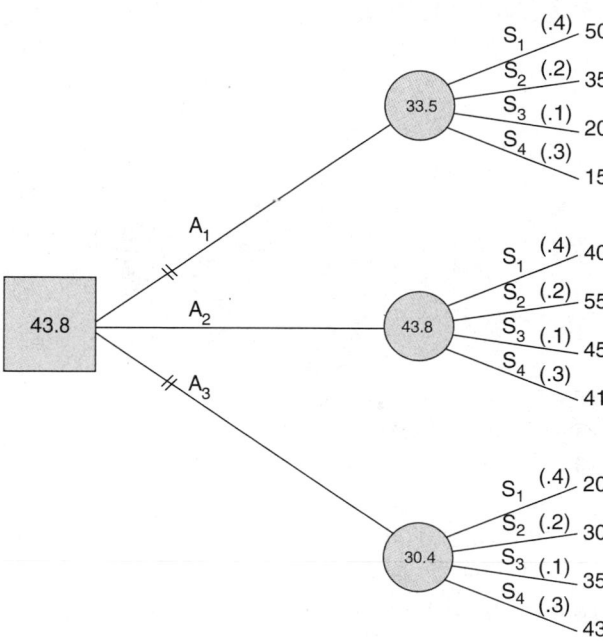

18.33

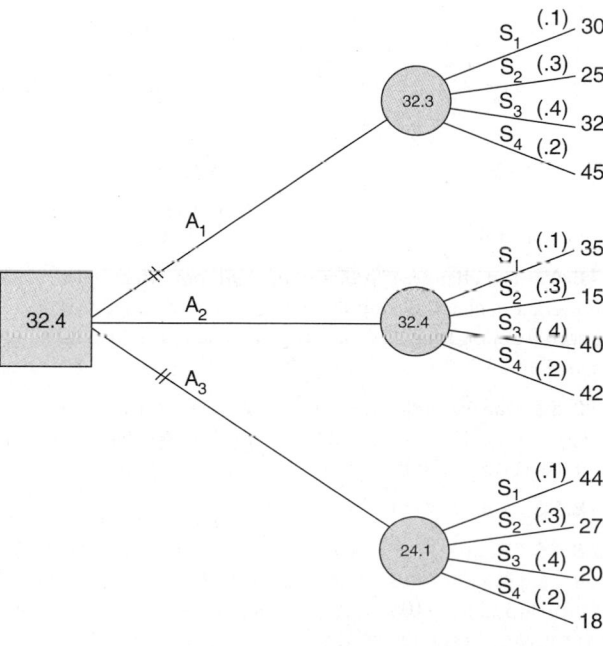

18.35

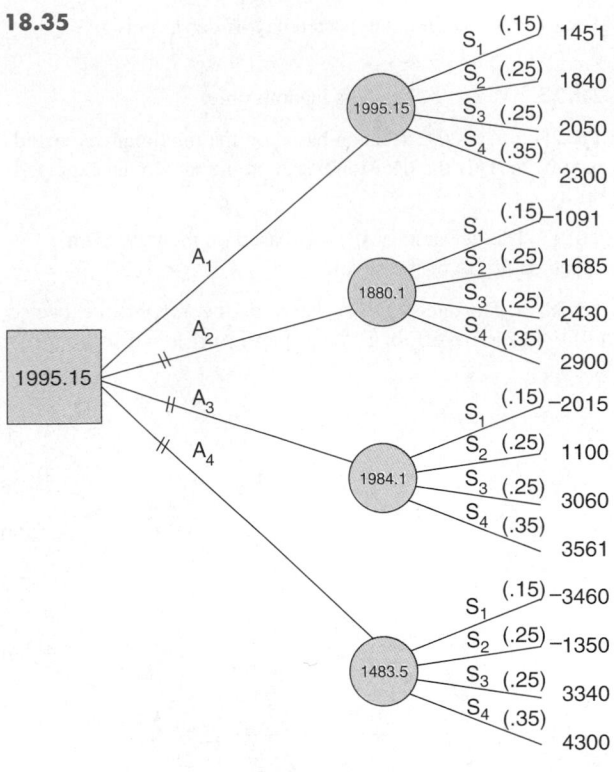

18.37 $P(A_1 | B) = .111$; $P(A_2 | B) = .111$; $P(A_3 | B) = .222$; $P(A_4 | B) = .185$; $P(A_5 | B) = .370$.

18.39 $P(\text{life}) = .0734$; $P(H | \text{life}) = .3597$.

18.41 $P(B) = .26$; $P(S_1 | B) = .2308$; $P(S_2 | B) = .2308$; $P(S_3 | B) = .4615$; $P(S_4 | B) = .0769$. Maximum expected utility of 33.23 occurs for A_2.

18.43 EVPI = 3000; yes.

18.45 a. Net expected gain of hiring the consultant is 3.428. **b.** 22.85%

18.47 a.

| | States of Nature | | | |
	S_1	S_2	S_3	S_4
A_1	0	0	10	20
A_2	4	2	0	10
A_3	4	4	0	0
A_4	6	6	14	5

b. The minimax decision is action A_3. **c.** The maximax decision is A_3.

18.49 The change of probabilities will not affect the minimax decision. Using the expected payoffs, action A_4 is the optimal action for sets 1, 2, and 4, and action A_1 is optimal for sets 3 and 5.

18.51 One example would be to let $U(x) = 0$ for $x < 0$, $U(x) = .036x$ for $0 \leq x \leq 1000$, and $U(x) = 36 + 64(.001x - 1)^2$ for $1000 < x < 2000$.

18.53 95.45%

18.55 The maximum payoff with the consultant is 1157.08. The maximum payoff without the consultant is 1105 using A_3. Since $1157.08 - 1105 = 52.08$, which is less than 350, it is not worthwhile to use the consultant's service.

18.57 a. Risk taker **b.** Risk neutral **c.** Risk avoider

18.59 .77

CHAPTER 19

19.1 a. $R = 9$; fail to reject H_0. **b.** $R = 7$; fail to reject H_0.

19.3 $Z^* = -2.56$; reject H_0.

19.5 $R = 10$; fail to reject H_0.

19.7 $R = 13$; fail to reject H_0.

19.9 $R = 12$, p-value = .00615; reject H_0.

19.11 $Z^* > 1.645$; reject H_0.

19.13 $T_+ = 50$; $T_- = 5$; reject H_0.

19.15 $Z^* = 1.09$; fail to reject H_0.

19.17 $U_1 = 52$; $U_2 = 48$; fail to reject H_0.

19.19 $Z^* = .953$; fail to reject H_0.

19.21 $U = 23.5$; fail to reject H_0.

19.25 $T_+ = 12$; $T_- = 33$; fail to reject H_0.

19.27 $T_+ = 1.5$; $T_- = 26.5$; reject H_0.

19.29 $Z^* = -2.13$; reject H_0.

19.31 $Z^* = .9769$; fail to reject H_0.

19.33 $Z^* = -6.3145$; reject H_0.

19.35 a. $Z^* = -2.0638$; p-value = .0390; reject H_0. **b.** $t^* = -1.75$; p-value = .0886; fail to reject H_0.

19.37 KW = .485; fail to reject H_0.

19.39 FR = 4.17; fail to reject H_0.

19.41 KW = 7.649; reject H_0.

19.43 KW = 6.83; reject H_0.

19.45 KW = 2.105; fail to reject H_0.

19.47 FR = 16.20; reject H_0.

19.49 FR = 2; fail to reject H_0.

19.51 p-value for the one-way ANOVA is .061; fail to reject H_0. p-value for the Kruskal-Wallis test is .0487; reject H_0.

19.53 Computed Chi-square for Friedman test is 4.02; p-value = .2593; fail to reject H_0.

19.55 $r_s = .42$; fail to reject H_0.

19.57 $r_s = .874$; reject H_0.

19.59 $r_s = -.944$; reject H_0.

19.61 $r_s = .867$; reject H_0.

19.63 $r_s = -.7249$; reject H_0.

19.65 $r_s = .964$; reject H_0.

19.67 Intercept = 2.2857 and slope = 1.4048.

19.69 Intercept = −.500 and slope = 2.80.

19.71 0 to .5

19.73 Intercept = 62, slope = −5.00.

19.75 $R = 18$; fail to reject H_0.

19.77 $r_s = .84$; reject H_0.

19.79 $U_1 = 40$, $U_2 = 24$, $U = 24$; fail to reject H_0.

19.81 $R = 4$; p-value $= .01255$; reject H_0.

19.83 $T = 27.5$; fail to reject H_0.

19.85 KW $= 13.36$; reject H_0.

19.87 a. $r_s = -.9667$; reject H_0. **b.** -1.100 **c.** -1.11

19.89 $r_s = .714$; reject H_0.

19.91 FR $= 3.2$; fail to reject H_0.

19.93 a. 6.304 **b.** 7.187

INDEX

Photo Credits

1	© PhotoDisc, Inc.
29	© PhotoDisc, Inc.
72	© PhotoDisc, Inc.
119	© PhotoDisc, Inc.
164	© PhotoDisc, Inc.
210	© PhotoDisc, Inc.
253	© PhotoDisc, Inc.
306	© PhotoDisc, Inc.
358	© Tony Stone Images/Kalzuny/Thatcher
412	© PhotoDisc, Inc.
445	© PhotoDisc, Inc.
514	© PhotoDisc, Inc.
569	© Tony Stone Images/Bob Handelman
608	© PhotoDisc, Inc.
673	© PhotoDisc, Inc.
746	© PhotoDisc, Inc.
808	© PhotoDisc, Inc.
878	© PhotoDisc, Inc.
922	© PhotoDisc, Inc.

CONTENTS OF ACCOMPANYING CD

The CD consists of six folders:

KGP Databases: Contains the two databases in Appendix E and Appendix F, saved as Excel files.

KGP Data-Cases: Contains Excel data sets for the case study (Statistics in Action) exercise at the end of each chapter.

KGP Data-Chapter Examples: Contains Excel data sets for the within-chapter examples (e.g. DATA11-6.xls).

KGP Excel-Macros: Contains the Excel add-in macros file (kgpanaly.xla) along with two accompanying help files.

KGP Data-Exercises: These are the 159 Excel data sets used in the exercises labeled **Using the Computer** (e.g. EX11-43.xls).

KGP Minitab-Macros: Contains a MINITAB macro for the Deming funnel experiment in Chapter 12.

NOTE: All Excel data files are saved as Excel 97 & 5.0/95 Workbooks. MINITAB will easily import these files when saved in this format.